Twentieth-Century Literary Criticism

Volume 7

Twentieth-Century Literary Criticism

**Excerpts from Criticism of the
Works of Novelists, Poets, Playwrights,
Short Story Writers, and Other Creative Writers
Who Lived between 1900 and 1960,
from the First Published Critical Appraisals
to Current Evaluations**

**Sharon K. Hall
Editor**

**Thomas Ligotti
James E. Person, Jr.
Dennis Poupard
Associate Editors**

**Gale Research Company
Book Tower
Detroit, Michigan 48226**

STAFF

Sharon K. Hall, *Editor*

Thomas Ligotti, James E. Person, Jr., Dennis Poupard, *Associate Editors*

Earlene M. Alber, Jane Dobija, Kathleen Gensley, Sandra Giraud, Denise B. Grove,
Marie Lazzari, Mark W. Scott, Denise R. Wiloch, *Assistant Editors*

Phyllis Carmel Mendelson, *Contributing Editor*

Carolyn Bancroft, *Production Supervisor*
Lizbeth A. Purdy, *Production Coordinator*

Robert J. Elster, Jr., *Research Coordinator*
Robert J. Hill, Carol Angela Thomas, *Research Assistants*

Linda M. Pugliese, *Manuscript Coordinator*
Donna DiNello, *Manuscript Assistant*

Cherie D. Abbey, Frank James Borovsky, Laura L. Britton, Lee Ann Ferency,
Denise B. Grove, Serita Lanette Lockard, Brenda Marshall, Marie M. Mazur,
Denise Q. Michlewicz, Gloria Anne Williams, Robyn V. Young, *Editorial Assistants*

L. Elizabeth Hardin, *Permissions Supervisor*
Filomena Sgambati, *Permissions Coordinator*
Anna Maria DiNello, Judy Kowalsky, Janice M. Mach, Mary P. McGrane,
Susan D. Nobles, Patricia A. Seefelt, *Permissions Assistants*

Copyright © 1982 by Gale Research Company

Library of Congress Catalog Card Number 76-46132

ISBN 0-8103-0181-4
ISSN 0276-8178

CONTENTS

Preface 7

Authors to Appear in Future Volumes 9

Appendix 593

Cumulative Index to Authors 609

Cumulative Index to Nationalities 613

Cumulative Index to Critics 615

L. Frank Baum 11

Hilaire Belloc 30

Andrey Bely 45

Stephen Vincent Benét 68

Ambrose Bierce 87

Bjørnstjerne Bjørnson 99

Rupert Brooke 119

Bliss Carman 132

C.P. Cavafy 151

Raymond Chandler 166

John Jay Chapman 184

Aleister Crowley 202

Arthur Conan Doyle 214

Paul Eluard 243

Miles Franklin 263

Zona Gale 276

Federico García Lorca 289

Giuseppe Giacosa 304

Jean Giraudoux 316

Ellen Glasgow 331

Laurence Housman 351

William Dean Howells 362

Joris-Karl Huysmans 402

Rose Macaulay 420

Don Marquis 433

Claude McKay 454

George Moore 472

Alfred Noyes 501

Marcel Proust 517

Marina Tsvetaeva 555

Frank Wedekind 573

PREFACE

It is impossible to overvalue the importance of literature in the intellectual, emotional, and spiritual evolution of humanity. Literature is that which both lifts us out of everyday life and helps us to better understand it. Through the fictive life of an Emma Bovary, a Lambert Strether, a Leopold Bloom, our perceptions of the human condition are enlarged, and we are enriched.

Literary criticism is a collective term for several kinds of critical writing: criticism may be normative, descriptive, textual, interpretive, appreciative, generic. It takes many forms: the traditional essay, the aphorism, the book or play review, even the parodic poem. Perhaps the single unifying feature of literary criticism lies in its purpose: to help us to better understand what we read.

The Scope of the Book

The usefulness of Gale's *Contemporary Literary Criticism (CLC),* which excerpts criticism of current creative writing, suggested an equivalent need among literature students and teachers interested in authors of the period 1900 to 1960. The great poets, novelists, short story writers, and playwrights of this period are by far the most popular writers for study in high school and college literature courses. Moreover, since contemporary critics continue to analyze the work of this period—both in its own right and in relation to today's tastes and standards—a vast amount of relevant critical material confronts the student.

Thus, *Twentieth-Century Literary Criticism (TCLC)* presents significant passages from published criticism on authors who died between 1900 and 1960. Because of the difference in time span under consideration *(CLC considers authors living from 1960 to the present),* there is no duplication between *CLC* and *TCLC.*

Each volume of *TCLC* is carefully designed to present a list of authors who represent a variety of genres and nationalities. The length of an author's section is intended to be representative of the amount of critical attention he or she has received in the English language. Articles and books that have not been translated into English are excluded. An attempt has been made to identify and include excerpts from the seminal essays on each author's work. Additionally, as space permits, especially insightful essays of a more limited scope are included. Thus *TCLC* is designed to serve as an introduction for the student of twentieth-century literature to the authors of that period and to the most significant commentators on these authors.

Each *TCLC* author section represents the scope of critical response to that author's work: some early criticism is presented to indicate initial reactions, later criticism is selected to represent any rise or fall in an author's reputation, and current retrospective analyses provide students with a modern view. Since a *TCLC* author section is intended to be a definitive overview, the editors include between 30 and 40 authors in each 600-page volume (compared to approximately 100 authors in a *CLC* volume of similar size) in order to devote more attention to each author. An author may appear more than once because of the great quantity of critical material available, or because of the resurgence of criticism generated by events such as an author's centennial or anniversary celebration, the republication of an author's works, or publication of a newly translated work or volume of letters.

The Organization of the Book

An author section consists of the following elements: author heading, biocritical introduction, principal works, excerpts of criticism (each followed by a citation), and, beginning with Volume 3, an annotated bibliography of additional reading.

- The *author heading* consists of the author's full name, followed by birth and death dates. The unbracketed portion of the name denotes the form under which the author most commonly wrote. If an author wrote consistently under a pseudonym, the pseudonym will be listed in the author heading and the real name given in parentheses on the first line of the biocritical introduction. Also located at the beginning of the biocritical introduction are any name variations under which an author wrote, including transliterated forms for authors whose languages use nonroman alphabets. Uncertainty as to a birth or death date is indicated by a question mark.

- The *biocritical introduction* contains biographical and other background information about an author that will elucidate his or her creative output. Parenthetical material following several of the biocritical introductions includes references to biographical and critical reference books published by the Gale Research Company. These include past volumes of *TCLC, Contemporary Authors,* and *Dictionary of Literary Biography*.

- The *list of principal works* is chronological by date of first publication and identifies genres. In those instances where the first publication was other than English language, the title and date of the first English-language edition are given in brackets. Unless otherwise indicated, dramas are dated by first performance, not first publication.

- *Criticism* is arranged chronologically in each author section to provide a perspective on any changes in critical evaluation over the years. In the text of each author entry, titles by the author are printed in boldface type. This allows the reader to ascertain without difficulty the works discussed. For purposes of easier identification, the critic's name and the publication date of the essay are given at the beginning of each piece of criticism. Unsigned criticism is preceded by the title of the journal in which it appeared. For an anonymous essay later attributed to a critic, the critic's name appears in brackets in the heading and in the citation.

- A complete *bibliographical citation* designed to facilitate location of the original essay or book by the interested reader accompanies each piece of criticism. An asterisk (*) at the end of a citation indicates the essay is on more than one author.

- The *annotated bibliography* appearing at the end of each author section suggests further reading on the author. In some cases it includes essays for which the editors could not obtain reprint rights. An asterisk (*) at the end of a citation indicates the essay is on more than one author.

Each volume of *TCLC* includes a cumulative index to critics. Under each critic's name is listed the author(s) on which the critic has written and the volume and page where the criticism may be found. *TCLC* also includes a cumulative index to authors with the volume number in which the author appears in boldface after his or her name.

Acknowledgments

No work of this scope can be accomplished without the cooperation of many people. The editors especially wish to thank the copyright holders of the excerpts included in this volume, the permission managers of many book and magazine publishing companies for assisting us in locating copyright holders, and the staffs of the Detroit Public Library, University of Michigan Library, and Wayne State University Library for making their resources available to us. We are also grateful to Fred S. Stein for his assistance with copyright research and to Louise Kertesz and Norma J. Merry for their editorial assistance.

Suggestions Are Welcome

Several features have been added to *TCLC* since its original publication in response to various suggestions:

- Since Volume 2—An *Appendix* which lists the sources from which material in the volume is reprinted.

- Since Volume 3—An *Annotated Bibliography* for additional reading.

- Since Volume 4—*Portraits* of the authors.

- Since Volume 6—A *Nationality Index* for easy access to authors by nationality.

If readers wish to suggest authors they would like to have covered in future volumes, or if they have other suggestions, they are cordially invited to write the editor.

AUTHORS TO APPEAR
IN FUTURE VOLUMES

Ady, Endre 1877-1919
Agate, James 1877-1947
Agustini, Delmira 1886-1914
Aldrich, Thomas Bailey 1836-1907
Annensy, Innokenty Fyodorovich 1856-1909
Anstey, Frederick 1856-1934
Arlen, Michael 1895-1956
Barea, Arturo 1897-1957
Baring, Maurice 1874-1945
Baroja, Pío 1872-1956
Barry, Philip 1896-1946
Bass, Eduard 1888-1946
Benét, William Rose 1886-1950
Benson, E(dward) F(rederic) 1867-1940
Benson, Stella 1892-1933
Beresford, J(ohn) D(avys) 1873-1947
Besant, Annie (Wood) 1847-1933
Bethell, Mary Ursula 1874-1945
Binyon, Laurence 1869-1943
Blackmore, R(ichard) D(oddridge) 1825-1900
Blasco Ibanez, Vicente 1867-1928
Bojer, Johan 1872-1959
Borowski, Tadeusz 1924-1951
Bosman, Herman Charles 1905-1951
Bottomley, Gordon 1874-1948
Bourne, George (Morris Cohen) 1842-1927
Broch, Herman 1886-1951
Bromfield, Louis 1896-1956
Buchan, John 1870-1953
Byrne, Donn (Brian Oswald Donn-Brye) 1889-1928
Caine, Hall 1853-1931
Campana, Dina 1885-1932
Campbell, (William) Wilfred 1861-1918
Cannan, Gilbert 1884-1955
Churchill, Winston 1871-1947
Corelli, Marie 1855-1924
Corvo, Baron (Frederick William Rolfe) 1860-1913
Crane, Stephen 1871-1900
Crawford, F. Marion 1854-1909
Croce, Benedetto 1866-1952
Davidson, John 1857-1909
Day, Clarence 1874-1935
Delafield, E.M. (Edme Elizabeth Monica de la Pasture) 1890-1943
DeMorgan, William 1839-1917
Doblin, Alfred 1878-1957
Douglas, Lloyd C(assel) 1877-1951
Douglas, (George) Norman 1868-1952
Dreiser, Theodore 1871-1945
Drinkwater, John 1882-1937
Duun, Olav 1876-1939

Fadeyev, Alexandr 1901-1956
Feydeau, Georges 1862-1921
Field, Michael (Katharine Harris Bradley 1846-1914 and Edith Emma Cooper 1862-1913)
Field, Rachel 1894-1942
Flecker, James Elroy 1884-1915
France, Anatole (Anatole Thibault) 1844-1924
Freeman, John 1880-1929
Freeman, Mary E. (Wilkins) 1852-1930
Gilman, Charlotte (Anna Perkins Stetson) 1860-1935
Gippius or Hippius, Zinaida (Nikolayevna) 1869-1945
Glyn, Elinor 1864-1943
Gogarty, Oliver St. John 1878-1957
Golding, Louis 1895-1958
Gorky, Maxim 1868-1936
Gosse, Edmund 1849-1928
Gould, Gerald 1885-1936
Grahame, Kenneth 1859-1932
Gray, John 1866-1934
Guiraldes, Ricardo 1886-1927
Gumilyov, Nikolay 1886-1921
Gwynne, Stephen Lucius 1864-1950
Haggard, H(enry) Rider 1856-1925
Hale, Edward Everett 1822-1909
Hall, (Marguerite) Radclyffe 1806-1943
Harris, Frank 1856-1931
Hearn, Lafcadio 1850-1904
Henley, William Ernest 1849-1903
Hergesheimer, Joseph 1880-1954
Hernandez, Miguel 1910-1942
Herrick, Robert 1868-1938
Hewlett, Maurice 1861-1923
Heym, Georg 1887-1912
Heyse, Paul (Johann Ludwig von) 1830-1914
Heyward, DuBose 1885-1940
Hichens, Robert 1864-1950
Hilton, James 1900-1954
Hofmannsthal, Hugo Von 1874-1926
Holtby, Winifred 1898-1935
Hope, Anthony 1863-1933
Howard, Robert E(rvin) 1906-1936
Hudson, Stephen 1868-1944
Hudson, W(illiam) H(enry) 1841-1922
Ivanov, Vyacheslav Ivanovich 1866-1922
Jacobs, W(illiam) W(ymark) 1863-1943
James, Will 1892-1942
Jerome, Jerome K(lapka) 1859-1927
Jones, Henry Arthur 1851-1929

Kaiser, Georg 1878-1947
Kipling, Rudyard 1865-1936
Kornbluth, Cyril M. 1923-1958
Kuzmin, Mikhail Alekseyevich 1875-1936
Lang, Andrew 1844-1912
Larbaud, Valéry 1881-1957
Lawson, Henry 1867-1922
Leverson, Ada 1862-1933
Lewisohn, Ludwig 1883-1955
Lindsay, (Nicholas) Vachel 1879-1931
London, Jack 1876-1916
Lonsdale, Frederick 1881-1954
Lowndes, Marie Belloc 1868-1947
Lucas, E(dward) V(errall) 1868-1938
Lynd, Robert 1879-1949
MacArthur, Charles 1895-1956
MacDonald, George 1824-1905
Mais, Roger 1905-1955
Mann, Heinrich 1871-1950
Manning, Frederic 1887-1935
Marinetti, Filippo Tommaso 1876-1944
Marriott, Charles 1869-1957
Martin du Gard, Roger 1881-1958
Mencken, H(enry) L(ouis) 1880-1956
Meredith, George 1828-1909
Mew, Charlotte (Mary) 1870-1928
Mistral, Frédéric 1830-1914
Mitchell, Margaret 1900-1949
Monro, Harold 1879-1932
Moore, Thomas Sturge 1870-1944
Morgan, Charles 1894-1958
Morgenstern, Christian 1871-1914
Morley, Christopher 1890-1957
Murray, (George) Gilbert 1866-1957
Nervo, Amado 1870-1919
Nietzsche, Friedrich 1844-1900
Norris, Frank 1870-1902
Olbracht, Ivan (Kemil Zeman) 1882-1952
Ortega y Gasset, José 1883-1955
Pinero, Arthur Wing 1855-1934
Pontoppidan, Henrik 1857-1943
Porter, Eleanore H(odgman) 1868-1920
Porter, Gene(va) Stratton 1886-1924

Powys, T(heodore) F(rancis) 1875-1953
Quiller-Couch, Arthur 1863-1944
Rappoport, Solomon 1863-1944
Reed, John (Silas) 1887-1920
Reid, Forrest 1876-1947
Riley, James Whitcomb 1849-1916
Rinehart, Mary Roberts 1876-1958
Roberts, Sir Charles (George Douglas) 1860-1943
Roberts, Elizabeth Madox 1886-1941
Rogers, Will(iam Penn Adair) 1879-1935
Rölvaag, O(le) E(dvart) 1876-1931
Rolland, Romain 1866-1944
Roussel, Raymond 1877-1933
Runyon, (Alfred) Damon 1884-1946
Sabatini, Rafael 1875-1950
Saltus, Edgar (Evertson) 1855-1921
Santayana, George 1863-1952
Schreiner, Olive (Emilie Albertina) 1855-1920
Seeger, Alan 1888-1916
Service, Robert 1874-1958
Seton, Ernest Thompson 1860-1946
Shiel, M(atthew) P(hipps) 1865-1947
Slater, Francis Carey 1875-1958
Sologub, Fyodor 1863-1927
Squire, J(ohn) C(ollings) 1884-1958
Sternheim, Carl 1878-1942
Stockton, Frank R. 1834-1902
Stoker, Bram 1847-1912
Supervielle, Jules 1884-1960
Swinburne, Algernon Charles 1837-1909
Symons, Arthur 1865-1945
Tabb, John Bannister 1845-1909
Tarkington, Booth 1869-1946
Teilhard de Chardin, Pierre 1881-1955
Tey, Josephine (Elizabeth Mackintosh) 1897-1952
Thomas, (Philip) Edward 1878-1917
Turner, W(alter) J(ames) R(edfern) 1889-1946
Vachell, Horace Annesley 1861-1955

Authors to Appear in Future Volumes

Valera y Alcala Galiano, Juan
1824-1905
Van Dine, S.S. (William H.
Wright) 1888-1939
Van Doren, Carl
1885-1950
Vazov, Ivan 1850-1921
Vian, Boris 1878-1959

Wallace, Edgar 1874-1932
Wallace, Lewis 1827-1905
Washington, Booker T(aliaferro)
1856-1915
Webb, Mary 1881-1927
Webster, Jean 1876-1916
Welch, Denton 1917-1948

Wells, Carolyn 1869-1942
Werfel, Franz 1890-1945
Wister, Owen 1860-1938
Witkiewicz, Stanislaw Ignacy
1885-1939
Wren, P(ercival)
C(hristopher) 1885-1941

Wylie, Elinor (Morton Hoyt)
1885-1928
Wylie, Francis Brett
1844-1954
Zamyatin, Yevgeny
Ivanovich 1884-1937
Zangwill, Israel 1864-1926

Readers are cordially invited to suggest additional authors to the editors.

L(yman) Frank Baum

1856-1919

(Also wrote under pseudonyms of Louis F. Baum, Schuyler Staunton, Floyd Akers, Laura Bancroft, John Estes Cooke, Edith Van Dyne, Captain Hugh Fitzgerald, and Suzanne Metcalf) American novelist, short story writer, dramatist, journalist, and librettist.

Baum was a prolific author who achieved lasting fame through his "Land of Oz" fantasy-adventure series. The series' first book, *The Wonderful Wizard of Oz,* is considered a classic of children's literature; its sequels, though uneven in quality, are popular favorites. "The Land of Oz" appeals to adults as well, who enjoy Baum's unsentimental and mildly satiric approach to his characters and their dilemmas. Oz so captivated the public's fancy that a succession of writers continued the series long after Baum's death. Yet for nearly thirty years critics and educators ignored Baum's achievement. They deemed his humorous, sometimes irreverent approach "unwholesome" and considered his work insignificant in comparison to children's classics like Lewis Carroll's *Alice in Wonderland.* Edward Wagenknecht, in a study published ten years after Baum's death, was the first critic to argue that such comparisons were inappropriate. He and later critics contend that "The Land of Oz" is important, for it represents "the first distinctive attempt to construct a fairyland out of American materials" and because it conveys a uniquely American concept of Utopia.

Baum traveled widely and assumed a number of professions before becoming a children's writer. As an actor he toured the eastern states in several productions, including his own drama, *The Maid of Arran.* Upon his marriage in 1882 Baum left the theater and embarked on a series of business ventures which proved unsuccessful. In connection with these enterprises he traveled thoughout the United States, and his impressions of his country's varied landscapes and lifestyles are recorded in "The Land of Oz." Baum eventually settled in Chicago, where he worked both as reporter and salesman, but his earnings did not meet the needs of his growing family. To further supplement his income, Baum, whose flair for storytelling was then admired only by friends and family, wrote *Mother Goose in Prose.* This book and its sequel, *Father Goose,* attempt to decipher the nonsense verse of nursery rhymes. Both books were well received, but their success did not prepare the author for the response to his next effort, *The Wonderful Wizard of Oz.*

Baum's intent, stated in his introduction to *The Wonderful Wizard of Oz,* was to create "a modernized fairy tale," a children's story without "the horrible and blood-curdling incidents" or the didactic themes in the tales of Hans Christian Andersen and the Brothers Grimm. Nevertheless, Baum's stories contain a number of moral lessons as well as gruesome episodes. His real achievement was in creating a fantasy land that is recognizably American in psychology and setting: the virtues of home and family are stressed, and the characters are self-reliant, forthright individuals full of optimism and the pioneer spirit. In addition, the topographical features of Oz parallel those of the United States, and the magic in Oz is generally produced by science and technology rather than by

Culver Pictures

spells and witchcraft. Moreover, Baum did not people his tales with genies, ogres, and fairies. He fashioned his characters, such as the Scarecrow, the Tin Woodman, and Jack Pumpkinhead, out of real and familiar materials. A recurring theme of the Oz books—to find happiness look no farther than your own backyard—is exemplified by the characters' search for qualities they already possess. The Cowardly Lion, for example, acts bravely throughout the journey to Oz, yet he asks the Wizard for courage; the inordinately kind and compassionate Tin Woodman requests a heart; and the Scarecrow, who manifests wit and intelligence, is seeking brains. Throughout the series, Baum emphasizes tolerant, selfless, and humble behavior. His villains and the objects of his satire are pseudo-intellectuals, the military, and figures who show greed or conceit.

The author never intended *The Wonderful Wizard of Oz* to be the first of a series. He was induced by popular demand and financial difficulties to write its sequel, *The Marvelous Land of Oz.* In such books as *Queen Zixi of Ix* and *John Dough and the Cherub* he tried to interest readers in tales of other imaginary lands, but the call for "more books about Oz" persisted, and Baum obliged. As a result, his literary reputation suffered. Most critics believe that Baum should have heeded his instincts and discontinued the series. They note that the later books, such as *The Lost Princess of Oz* and *The Magic of Oz*, appear hastily written and lack structure, style, and humor. However, commentators agree that at his best Baum was an original and innovative writer who created the most popular and imitated children's story of the century.

PRINCIPAL WORKS

The Maid of Arran [as Louis F. Baum] (drama) 1881
Mother Goose in Prose (fairy tales) 1897
By the Candelabra's Glare (poetry) 1898
Father Goose (fairy tales) 1899
The Wonderful Wizard of Oz (juvenile fiction) 1900;
    also published as *The Wizard of Oz,* 1939
American Fairy Tales (fairy tales) 1901
The Wizard of Oz (libretto) 1902
The Surprising Adventures of the Magical Monarch of Mo
    (juvenile fiction) 1903
The Marvelous Land of Oz (juvenile fiction) 1904
Queen Zixi of Ix (juvenile fiction) 1905
Daughters of Destiny [as Schuyler Staunton] (novel) 1906
John Dough and the Cherub (juvenile fiction) 1906
Ozma of Oz (juvenile fiction) 1907
Dorothy and the Wizard in Oz (juvenile fiction) 1908
The Road to Oz (juvenile fiction) 1909
The Emerald City of Oz (juvenile ficiton) 1910
Sky Island (juvenile fiction) 1912
The Patchwork Girl of Oz (juvenile fiction) 1913
Tik-Tok of Oz (juvenile fiction) 1914
The Scarecrow of Oz (juvenile fiction) 1915
Rinkitink in Oz (juvenile fiction) 1916
The Lost Princess of Oz (juvenile fiction) 1917
The Tin Woodman of Oz (juvenile fiction) 1918
The Magic of Oz (juvenile fiction) 1919
Glinda of Oz (juvenile fiction) 1920
Our Landlady (satirical sketches) 1941

THE NEW YORK TIMES SATURDAY REVIEW OF BOOKS AND ART
(essay date 1900)

It is impossible to conceive of a greater contrast than exists between the children's books of antiquity that were new publications during the sixteenth century and modern children's books of which "The Wonderful Wizard of Oz" is typical. The crudeness that was characteristic of the old-time publications that were intended for the delectation and amusement of ancestral children would now be enough to cause the modern child to yell with rage and vigor and to instantly reject the offending volume, if not to throw it out of the window. The time when anything was considered good enough for children has long since passed. . . . In "The Wonderful Wizard of Oz" the fact is clearly recognized that the young as well as their elders love novelty. They are pleased with dashes of color and something new in the place of the old, familiar, and winged fairies of Grimm and Andersen.

Neither the tales of Aesop and other fableists, nor the stories such as the "Three Bears" will ever pass entirely away, but a welcome place remains and will easily be found for such stories as "Father Goose: His Book," "The Songs of Father Goose," and now "The Wonderful Wizard of Oz," that have

all come from the hands of Baum [and his illustrator, William W. Denslow].

This last story of "The Wizard" is ingeniously woven out of commonplace material. It is of course an extravaganza, but will surely be found to appeal strongly to child readers as well as to the younger children, to whom it will be read by mothers. . . .

The drawing as well as the introduced color work vies with the texts drawn, and the result has been a book that rises far above the average children's book of today, high as is the present standard. Dorothy, the little girl, and her strangely assorted companions, whose adventures are many and whose dangers are often very great, have experiences that seem in some respects like a leaf out of one of the old English fairy tales that Andrew Lang or Joseph Jacobs has rescued for us. A difference there is, however, and Baum has done with mere words what Denslow has done with his delightful draughtsmanship. The story has humor and here and there stray bits of philosophy that will be a moving power on the child mind and will furnish fields of study and investigation for the future students and professors of psychology. Several new features and ideals of fairy life have been introduced into the "Wonderful Wizard," who turns out in the end to be only a wonderful humbug after all. A scarecrow stuffed with straw, a tin woodman, and a cowardly lion do not at first blush, promise well as moving heroes in a tale when merely mentioned, but in actual practice they take on something of the living and breathing quality that is so gloriously exemplified in the "Story of the Three Bears," that has become a classic.

The book has a bright and joyous atmosphere, and does not dwell upon killing and deeds of violence. Enough stirring adventure enters into it, however, to flavor it with zest, and it will indeed be strange if there be a normal child who will not enjoy the story.

> *"A New Book for Children," in* The New York Times
> Saturday Review of Books and Art, *September 8,*
> *1900, p. 605.*

L. FRANK BAUM (essay date 1900)

Folklore, legends, myths and fairy tales have followed childhood through the ages, for every healthy youngster has a wholesome and instinctive love for stories fantastic, marvelous and manifestly unreal. The winged fairies of Grimm and Andersen have brought more happiness to childish hearts than all other human creations.

Yet the old-time fairy tale, having served for generations, may now be classed as "historical" in the children's library; for the time has come for a series of newer "wonder tales" in which the stereotyped genie, dwarf and fairy are eliminated, together with all the horrible and blood-curdling incidents devised by their authors to point a fearsome moral to each tale. Modern education includes morality; therefore the modern child seeks only entertainment in its wonder-tales and gladly dispenses with all disagreeable incidents.

Having this thought in mind, the story of "The Wonderful Wizard of Oz" was written solely to please children of today. It aspires to being a modernized fairy tale, in which the wonderment and joy are retained and the heartaches and nightmares are left out.

> *L. Frank Baum, in his introduction to his* The Wonderful Wizard of Oz, *George M. Hill Company, 1900*

(and reprinted in his The Wizard of Oz, *Ballantine Books, 1979, p. ix).*

EDWARD WAGENKNECHT   (essay date 1929)

America is not rich in distinctive fairy lore. We have indeed, among older books, those of the great American illustrator, Howard Pyle. (p. 16)

Only, it can hardly be claimed that Pyle's fairy tales are in any definite or distinctive sense American. They happened to be written in America—that is all: the materials of which they are compounded is the fairy lore of the Old World. . . .

This is surely not the case with the writings of L. Frank Baum. Indeed it is in *The Wizard of Oz* that we meet the first distinctive attempt to construct a fairyland out of American materials. Baum's long series of Oz books represents thus an important pioneering work: they may even be considered an American utopia. (p. 17)

It is interesting to see how accidentally as it were Baum discovered the Land of Oz, and how little he realized at first just what a mine he had struck. He had written in 1897 a book called [*Mother Goose in Prose*]. This is a volume of charming stories inspired by the historic jingles, the general idea being to tell that part of the story which Mother Goose did not tell. The book is excellent in its way. . . . For our purpose, however, the point to be noted is that *Mother Goose in Prose* is English not American in its inspiration. That is to say, Mr. Baum's fancy plays about and transforms not things that he has seen but things that he has read about. . . . And the same assertion might be made about some of the later Baum books— for example, *The Life and Adventures of Santa Claus* and *Queen Zixi of Ix,* the latter certainly one of the best fairy tales in the world.

When he finished *The Wizard of Oz*, Baum at first regarded it as one of his books, no more and no less than the others. It caught on immediately and went through enormous sales the very year of its publication. This of course gratified him immensely, and the next year he came forth with *Dot and Tot in Merryland,* the story of a candy country ruled over by a doll, to me at least one of the least interesting of his books. Indeed the idea for a series of Oz books did not originate with Mr. Baum: it came from the children who after the publication of *The Wizard* deluged him with letters begging that the story might be continued. (pp. 18-20)

I have made much of the fact that these are *American* fairy tales. By this I do not mean that Mr. Baum has used no European materials. . . . [He] used very freely whatever suited his purpose from older literatures and from older cultures. Indeed had he not done this, his output could hardly have been recognized as wonder tales at all. The greatest villain in all the Oz books is the Nome King—the "G" is left out because the children cannot pronounce it!—the ruler of an underground nation of elves, as old as fairy lore itself. Again, we have Polychrome, the Rainbow's daughter, a character surely with nothing distinctively American about her. . . . (pp. 23-4)

These, however, are not the distinctively "Ozzy" characters. Suppose we look at the Scarecrow and the Tin Woodman. In *The Wizard of Oz*, Dorothy finds the Scarecrow, newly-made, with a bean pole up his back, in the middle of a corn field. She lifts him down and they go to the Emerald City together, where Dorothy plans to ask Oz to send her home to Kansas while the Scarecrow wants brains instead of straw in the painted

sack that serves him for a head. The next addition to their party is the Tin Woodman whom they find rusted in the woods and who cannot go along with them until they oil his joints so that he may walk. The Tin Woodman was once a man of flesh and blood, one Nick Chopper, in love with a pretty Munchkin girl. But a wicked witch enchanted his ax, so that as he was working in the forest he cut himself to pieces. Fortunately Nick Chopper had among his friends a very wonderful tinsmith who, as soon as any part of Nick's body had been cut off, would replace it with tin, until at last the man was wholly tin and as good as new. Only one thing was lacking: he had no longer a heart and accordingly he did not care whether he married the pretty Munchkin girl or not. The Tin Woodman therefore goes along with Dorothy and the Scarecrow to the Emerald City in the hope that the Wizard may give him a heart. Now who but an American—in a country overrun with mechanical skill—could ever have dreamed of a creature like that? (pp. 24-5)

The use of machinery in the Oz books is also characteristically American. In general, magic may be said to inhere not in persons but in things. Whoever has the magical instrument can perform magic deeds. Continually, the forces of Nature, as we know them in America, are used for purposes of conveyance. In *The Wizard of Oz*, it is a Kansas cyclone which carries Dorothy and her house over the desert and deposits them in the Land of Oz. In *Ozma of Oz*, Dorothy is shipwrecked. In *Dorothy and the Wizard of Oz*, Dorothy, in California, is swallowed by an earthquake and carried down into the center of the Earth, from whence she makes her way to Oz. (pp. 27-8)

Indeed the United States is well represented in Oz. Dorothy is from Kansas; the Shaggy Man comes from Colorado; and Betsy Bobbin's home is Oklahoma. The Wizard of Oz himself is a native of Omaha. There he was connected with Bailum and Barney's Consolidated Shows, and his magic was, all of it, pure fake. . . . It is not until later in his career when the Wizard becomes a pupil of the great sorceress, Glinda the Good, that he learns something about real magic.

Now what is the significance of all this? Not surely that American magic is any better than French magic or German magic. No. Simply that Mr. Baum has enlarged the resources of fairyland. He has not destroyed European magic: he has simply added to it. And he has done one thing more. He has taught American children to look for the element of wonder in the life around them, to realize that even smoke and machinery may be transformed into fairy lore if only we have sufficient energy and vision to penetrate to their significance and transform them to our use. (pp. 28-9)

Now this seems to me significant and important. It is not healthy—and it is not true—for children to be made to feel that romance belongs only to the past, and that everything in America today is drab, uninteresting, and business-like. . . . Thus Mr. Baum's work is primarily significant because it has pointed in the right direction: it has helped to teach us how to find wonder in contemporary American life. (p. 30)

All in all, there is much fuller command over nature in Oz than we enjoy in any country yet known. Animals can talk and mingle with human beings on terms of equality. Even flies are considerate and kindly: if one alights on you, you do not kill it: you simply request it politely to move on, and it complies with your request. Many of the inhabitants of the country, not being made of flesh and blood, do not need food, sleep, drink, or clothes. (pp. 32-3)

Best of all, there is no army in Oz. Ozma refuses to fight even when her kingdom seems in danger of invasion. "No one has the right to destroy any living creatures, however evil they may be, or to hurt them or make them unhappy. I will not fight— even to save my kingdom.'' For the safety of the world's future, the children could not well learn any more wholesome doctrine than that.

(Is it becoming clear, then, why so many of those who are well satisfied with the established order will have none of the Oz books?)

There is one element in the Oz books that the children probably do not get, and that is the element of satire. You will remember how in *The Wizard of Oz,* Dorothy, the Scarecrow, and the Tin Woodman travel to the Wizard because they want, respectively, to get home to Kansas, to receive some brains, and to be given a heart. The fourth member of the party is a Cowardly Lion, who wants courage. He is a most ferocious fighter in the jungle, but he is much concerned over the fact that whenever there is danger he is terribly afraid. . . . So he goes to Oz to ask for courage. Mr. Baum makes the whole journey a sermon on the text: ''Man does not live by bread alone but principally by catchwords.'' All through the journey, the Lion is the valiant protector of the party, and whenever any particularly difficult problem comes up, it is the Scarecrow who solves it. Once the Tin Woodman accidentally steps on a beetle and kills it. Greatly distressed over this act of clumsiness, he weeps bitter tears which run down his tin cheeks and rust the hinges of his jaw,. . . . The point is, of course, that all these creatures, except Dorothy, are already in possession of that of which they are going in search. Yet because they lack the name, the fact that they are in actual possession of the thing itself wholly eludes them.

When they arrive at the Emerald City, it is easy for the Wizard to satisfy the Scarecrow, the Lion, and the Tin Woodman. The Lion eats a dish of porridge for courage and never trembles again. A silken heart stuffed with sawdust serves the Tin Woodman a great deal better than any frail heart of flesh possibly could, and the Wizard assures him, as he puts it in his breast, that it *is* an especially kind heart. The Scarecrow's new brains are a judicious mixture of bran with needles and pins, and whenever one of these latter ingredients comes sticking through the sack covering of his head, the Scarecrow congratulates himself upon his sharpness. But Dorothy—Dorothy wants to get home to Kansas. That is a different sort of problem, and that is where the Wizard meets his downfall. (pp. 33-6)

Sometimes the satire strikes a deeper note as in the incident of the Woggle Bug having reduced all knowledge to pills, so that the students in his college do not need to spend any of their valuable time in studying but may be free to devote it all to such important thing as football and other outdoor sports. (pp. 36-7)

The Oz books are ''popular'' in character. That admits, of course, of no dispute. In distinction of style they are utterly lacking and often in imaginative distinction as well. Nobody could possibly write fifty volumes of fairy tales and keep the whole up to a high level of imaginative power. In this respect the series may be said to have declined notably as commercial considerations made it necessary to string it on indefinitely. (p. 37)

As popular literature then, and along the lines indicated in this essay, I think the Oz books deserve consideration. They are an American phenomenon. . . . And it is undeniable that literature conceived in terms of our own life and thought must have always a certain vividness for us which other, sometimes much finer, literature does not possess. (pp. 37-8)

Edward Wagenknecht, in his Utopia Americana *(copyright 1929 and 1957 by Edward Wagenknecht; reprinted by permission of the author), University of Washington Book Store, 1929, 40 p.*

JAMES THURBER   (essay date 1934)

I have been for several weeks bogged in Oz books. It had seemed to me, at first, a simple matter to go back to the two I read as a boy of ten, **''The Wizard of Oz''** and **''The Land of Oz''** . . . , and write down what Oz revisited was like to me now that my life, at forty, has begun again. I was amazed and disturbed to discover that there are now twenty-eight different books about Oz. . . . The thing is obviously a major phenomenon in the wonderful land of books. I began my research, therefore, not by rereading the two Oz books I loved as a child (and still do, I was happy to find out later) but with an inquiry into the life and nature of the man who wrote the first fourteen of the series, Mr. L. Frank Baum. . . .

Let me quote from his own foreword to the first Oz book . . . : ''**'The Wizard of Oz'** aspires to be a modernized fairy tale in which the wonderment and joy are retained, and the heartaches and nightmares left out'' [see excerpt above]. I am glad that, in spite of this high determination, Mr. Baum failed to keep them out. Children love a lot of nightmare and at least a little heartache in their books. And they get them in the Oz books. I know that I went through excruciatingly lovely nightmares and heartaches when the Scarecrow lost his straw, when the Tin Woodman was taken apart, when the Saw-Horse broke his wooden leg (it hurt for me even if it didn't for Mr. Baum). . . .

[He was forty-three] when he did **''The Wizard of Oz,''** which to him was just another (the twentieth or so) book for children. It sold better than anything he had ever written. . . . He ignored the popular demand [for more Oz books] for four years, meanwhile writing a book called **''Baum's American Fairy Tales,''** subtitled **''Stories of Astonishing Adventures of American Boys and Girls with the Fairies of Their Native Land.''** He must have been hurt by its cold reception. . . . His American fairy tales, I am sorry to tell you, are not good fairy tales. The scene of the first one is the attic of a house ''on Prairie Avenue, in Chicago.'' It never leaves there for any wondrous, faraway realm. Baum apparently never thoroughly understood that fatal flaw in his essential ambition, but he understood it a little. He did another collection of unconnected stories but this time he placed them, not in Illinois but in Mo. **''The Magical Monarch of Mo''** is not much better than the American tales; but at least one story in it, **''The Strange Adventures of the King's Head,''** is a fine, fantastic fairy tale. The others are just so-so. On went L. Frank Baum, grimly, into the short tales making up **''The Enchanted Island of Yew''**; but the girls and boys were not interested. Finally, after four years and ten thousand letters from youngsters, he wrote **''The Land of Oz.''** He was back where they wanted him. . . . The first two, **''The Wizard''** and **''The Land''** are far and away the best. Baum wrote **''The Wizard,''** I am told, simply as a tour de force to see if he could animate, and make real, creatures never alive before on sea or land. He succeeded, eminently, with the Scarecrow and the Tin Woodman and he went on to succed again in the second book with Jack Pumpkinhead, the Saw-Horse and the Woggle Bug. After that I do not think he was ever really successful. (p. 141)

I think the fatal trouble with the later books (for us aging examiners, anyway) is that they became whimsical rather than fantastic. They ramble and they preach (one is dedicated to a society in California called "The Uplifters"), they lack the quick movement, the fresh suspense, the amusing dialogue and the really funny invention of the first ones. They dawdle along like a class prophecy. None of their creatures comes to life for me. I am merely bored by the Growleywogs, the Whimsies, the Cuttenclips, the Patchwork Girl, Button-Bright, the Googly-Goo, and I am actually gagged by one Unc Nunkie. Mr. Baum himself said that he kept putting in things that children wrote and asked him to put in. He brought back the Wizard of Oz because the children pleaded and he rewrote the Scarecrow and the Woodman almost to death because the children wanted them. The children should have been told to hush up and go back to the real Wizard and the real Scarecrow and the real Woodman. (pp. 141-42)

> James Thurber, "The Wizard of Chitenango" (© 1934 The New Republic, Inc., copyright renewed © 1962 by Helen W. Thurber and Rosemary Thurber; reprinted by permission), in The New Republic, *Vol. LXXXI, No. 1045, December 12, 1934, pp. 141-42.*

FRANK BAUM   (essay date 1952)

What has made *The Wizard of Oz* so successful? There are three main factors, all of concern to today's juvenile fantasy writers.

First, the story is told clearly in simple language easily understood by the child reader. In preparing the manuscript, the author placed on the wall above his desk a quotation from the Bible to which he constantly referred: "When I was a child I spoke as a child, I understood as a child, I thought as a child." This is the first lesson every juvenile writer must learn.

Secondly, the story is properly directed to a particular age group. In no other field of writing is there such a distinct variation in the type of appeal required as in the juvenile field. (p. 19)

The Wizard of Oz was written to interest the "tender age" class but it did more than that—it also interested the adults who had to read the story to the little ones. That's one of the big secrets of writing for this early age group. To appeal to the parents the story must contain humor, often subtle, and an undercurrent of philosophy which they will recognize and chuckle over, and which will make it for them more than just a child's story.

The Wizard of Oz fantasy is woven out of commonplace material. That is the third basic reason for its success. Reality and unreality are so entwined that it is often difficult to know where one leaves off and the other begins. . . .

The opening scene [in *The Wizard of Oz*] depicts a logical situation. A little girl living on the Kansas prairie is caught in a cyclone which carries away her house while she and her little dog are inside. But in the story, the storm lands the little girl's home in a mythical country—the Land of Oz. Her problem is to get back home to Kansas.

There are blocking forces to cause trouble—the Deadly Poppy Field, the Fighting Trees, the Hammerheads, the Kalidahs and the broad river to cross with no boat or bridge available. Through it all, however, nothing happens to the leading character to make her afraid and thereby frighten the little reader. A child can carry this story into the darkness of night without fear of harm from any of the quaint characters.

The odd characters are logically explained. For example, the Scarecrow was made by a farmer to keep the crows from his field. Although he stuffed the head as well as the body, the farmer neglected to put in any brains. (p. 36)

Contrast is used throughout the book. There is the Lion who is always telling how cowardly he is, but who invariably proves to be the bravest member of the party; the Scarecrow who complains of lack of brains, yet is the one to solve every tough problem; the Tin Woodman who has no heart, yet is so kind and gentle that he cannot bear to injure the smallest ant in his path; the Wizard who is thought to be the greatest magician in the land, yet who turns out to be a fake and a humbug.

An example of whimsical humor is found when the Cowardly Lion demands he be given courage. The Wizard hands him a bowl of liquid to drink. When the Lion wants to know what it is, the Wizard explains: "If it were inside you it would be courage. You know of course that courage is always inside one so this really cannot be called courage until you have swallowed it." This sort of touch appeals to the parent who has to read aloud to the child. (pp. 36-7)

The Wizard of Oz is told chronologically so that childish minds may easily follow the sequence of events. The story leaves the reader with a feeling that it all *could* have happened just as it was told. And the end is not spoiled by the author's explanation that these marvelous adventures were a dream or a hallucination. Never attempt to explain fantasy.

In writing this book, the author refrained from the use of certain incidents and situations, either because "tender age" minds could not grasp their import or because he felt it unwise to draw attention to them. No mention is made of love or marriage; of death or sickness; of killing human beings. There is no use of such trite fairy tale devices as genie, dwarf or ogre. No blood-curdling or disagreeable incidents occur. And no attempt is made to impress a moral on the child's mind. *The Wizard of Oz* is pure entertainment. (p. 37)

> Frank Baum, "Why 'The Wizard of Oz' Keeps on Selling," in Writer's Digest, *Vol. 33, No. 1, December, 1952, pp. 19, 36-7.*

RUSSEL B. NYE   (essay date 1957)

[Baum's] strength as a storyteller for children lay in his unique ability to implement and adapt the familiar apparatus of the older tale by reworking old materials into new forms. He worked within the framework of the Grimm tradition despite his disavowal of many of its elements, constructing out of essentially traditional materials a fresh new gallery of characters and a group of delightfully varied plots. The changes he rang on the traditional fairy story, not his rejection of that tradition, account to a great extent for his effectiveness. A great part of the perennial attraction of the Oz books lies in the child's recognition of old friends in new roles and costumes.

The "horrible and bloodcurdling incident" to which Baum objected in the Grimms [see excerpt above], of course, appears nowhere in Oz. Here Baum followed out his original intentions. There are excitement and danger in his stories, but violence is absent and evil under control. The witches may enchant Dorothy; they never threaten to eat her or bake her in an oven, and the bad wizards and witches who threaten Oz are frustrated creatures whom one could never imagine victorious. The Nome King, though obviously a thorough villain, is given to temper tantrums and capricious mischief much like a spoiled child, but no more dangerous and almost as easily disciplined. (p. 2)

In his effort to create an American *genre*, Baum had least success and more or less gave up the attempt. The tremendous popularity of **The Wizard** surprised him. He had held really higher hopes for his next book, **Baum's American Fairy Tales: Stories of Astonishing Adventures of Boys and Girls with the Fairies of their Native Land**. . . . These "American" tales, laid in American locales, were lost in the instant popularity of the Oz stories, and Baum's attempt to create a native *genre* simply did not come off. Clever, inventive, with a substratum of very shrewd satire, the stories fail to measure up to the standard set by the Wizard and his crew. Nor could Baum quite keep Oz out of the book; the most effective stories in the collection are those dealing with the kingdom of Quok (another version of some of the wildly wonderful realms of the later Oz books) and with the doings of the Ryls (blood brothers of Munchkins and Gillikins).

The **American Fairy Tales** were good stories, far better than most run-of-the-mill "educational" tales for children, but in the majority of them Baum failed to observe the first rule of the wonder-tale—that it must create a never-never land in which all laws of probability may be credibly contravened or suspended. When in the first story the little girl (Dorothy by another name) replies to a puzzled, lost genie, "You are on Prairie Avenue in Chicago," the heart goes out of the story. It is only in Quok, or in Baum's zany version of the African Congo, or among the Ryls, that the book captures the fine free spirit of Oz. (p. 3)

[The Oz books became classics] not because Baum succeeded in writing a new kind of Americanized fairy story, but because he adapted the fairy tale tradition itself to twentieth-century American taste with imaginative ingenuity. There are in the Oz books a number of references to American locale, and Dorothy herself, of course, comes to Oz via a prairie twister. But beyond such casual references Oz has no real relation to the United States—it is fundamentally the out-of-time, out-of-space fairyland of tradition. Working from the midst of older materials, Baum's clever and occasionally brilliant variations on traditional themes are marks of craftsmanship and creativeness of a high order. It is not solely in their "Americanism," nor in their avoidance of the "horrible and bloodcurdling," nor in their rejection of moralism (which Baum did not wholly reject), nor in their pure entertainment value (which Baum did maintain), that the power of the Oz books lies. It stems rather from Baum's success in placing his work directly in the stream of the past, in his assimilation into Oz of the ageless universals of wonder and fantasy. What Baum did was to enlarge the resources of the European inheritance by making it possible to find the old joy of wonderment in the fresh new setting of Oz, creating a bright new fairyland in the old tradition. (p. 4)

One of Baum's major contributions to the tradition of the fantasy tale is his recognition of the inherent wonder of the machine, his perception of the magic of *things* in themselves. In the Oz books he expanded the resources of the fairy tale to include for the first time, the mechanical developments of the 20th century, when every child saw about him—in the automobile, the dynamo, the radio, the airplane, and the rest—the triumph of technology over distance, time, and gravity. No American child of Baum's time or after could remain unaware of the age of invention, or fail to feel the wonderment of what machines could do. The mechanical marvels of Oz fitted exactly the technological pattern of American life, its consciousness of machinery, its faith in the machine's seemingly unlim-

ited potential. Kipling, of course, had experimented before Baum with tales of technology, but from a much more mature and sophisticated point of view. . . . Baum, in a burst of inspiration, moved the machine into the child's world of imagination, endowed it with life and magic, and made it the ally of all the forces of good and justice and well-being in Oz.

The machines of Oz are magician's creations, with the white magic of the sorcerer clinging to them. By transforming the talking beasts of ancient folktales into talking machines, Baum grafted twentieth-century technology to the fairy tale tradition. (p. 7)

Baum was no Swift nor Twain, but he belonged in the same tradition and his wit is (on a lesser level) astonishingly subtle and ingenious. The pertinent but unexpected association of the apparently unrelated, the joy of novelty, the pleasure of recognition of the obvious in new form, . . . all the classic elements of the humor tradition appear in the Oz books.

Baum's wit, though, is geared to the child's pace. It is wit a child can understand and appreciate, since it deals with concepts within the circle of his experience and those which are applicable to his own sphere of action. Baum's skill in evoking a humorous response from a child is real and expert; he locates quickly and unerringly those areas of incongruity and absurdity that are recognizable to a child and subject to his judgment. There are witty bits in the Oz books that children may miss the first time, but if adults can be prevented from explaining the joke (this is almost a crime in Oz) they can have the wonderful pleasure of finding it the second or third time.

The humor of Oz lies in the interaction of character and situation, in the genuinely humorous creations who get into equally humorous predicaments because they are what they are. Sometimes the humor is broad and obvious—such as the Kingdom of Utensia, populated by kitchenware, whose King Kleaver often makes cutting remarks to Captain Dip of the Spoon Brigade. . . . At other times Baum's strokes are somewhat more delicate, as with Ann Soforth, the ambitious young queen who sets out to conquer the world with sixteen generals and one private, or with Diksey the jokester, who once made such a bad joke it led to war—both witty commentaries on military motivations. . . . The best illustration of all, however, is probably H. M. Woggle-Bug, T.E., a masterpiece of humorous creation. A lowly field bug with no name at all, he hid in a schoolhouse and became thoroughly educated (T. E.) by eavesdropping on the lectures of Professor Nowitall. Caught in a magic lantern lens, he was projected on the classroom screen and stepped off highly magnified (H. M.), fully qualified to be Dean of the Royal College, "the most learned and important educator in the favored land of Oz." Thus H. M. Woggle-Bug, T. E., struts his way self-importantly through various adventures, the very symbol of ostentatious erudition. All this, and much more like it, is genuine humor, touched now and then with genius. (pp. 8-10)

The First Law of Baum's Utopia of Oz, the rule that inspires its harmonious order, is Love. This theme, on which Baum played constant and subtle variations, binds all the Oz books together as a moral unit. Love in Oz is kindness, selflessness, friendliness—an inner check that makes one act decently toward human beings, animals, plants, fairies, machines, and even one's enemies. A Love Magnet hangs over the gates of the City, so magnetizing all who enter that they must love and be loved, and Princess Ozma explains her kingdom's whole reason for existence by the simple remark, "The Land of Oz is Love.'' From love comes order, harmony, discipline, happiness, plenty, and perfection. And with love there is always happiness, its inseparable companion, represented in Oz by Glinda, Ozma's close friend and the greatest of sorceresses. (pp. 10-11)

The foils to Ozma, Glinda, and Oz are Ruggedo, the Nome King, and his subjects of the Nome Kingdom. . . . The Nome King is the epitome of selfishness; his campaign against Oz is motivated solely by jealousy, conceit, tyranny, and all those qualities antithetical to love. But there is no war, for Ozma simply refuses to mobilize an army against him. . . . In the face of Ozma's faith and love, the Nome King is powerless. Beaten and frustrated, he is banished to wander homeless through the land. . . .

The theme of selflessness as the cardinal principle of love runs through all the Oz books, forming the thread that binds them together. In Baum's world of Oz Bad = Selfishness, Good = Selflessness, Love = Happiness, Hate = Evil and Unhappiness. Those who use power for selfish ends, are Bad, and are punished in proportion to their crime. (p. 11)

[During] Baum's lifetime and after, neither he nor Oz received more than casual mention in contemporary surveys of children's literature. . . .

[The reason] lies, no doubt, in the fact that Baum set his sights (by adult critical standards) fairly low, aiming at a maximum of enjoyment with a minimum of admonition. The Oz books provided only a sketchy pattern for behavior, and in comparison to Little Lord Fauntleroy, for example, gave parents very little help in their job of adjusting and civilizing the young. This lack of overt moralizing bothered the educators and the critics of Baum's time. (p. 14)

In general, modern critics of children's literature, while admitting the appeal of the Oz books, tend to class them as popular but not worth bothering about.

It is true that the Oz books do not have the depth of Howard Pyle's re-tellings of the Robin Hood and King Arthur stories, or Kipling's Jungle Books. . . . Baum's work, in the opinion of the critics, lacks literary quality. He tells his stories simply and directly, contributing little to the child's sense of language or to his awareness of its potentialities; they do not read aloud well, except with the youngest, for Baum is in no sense a stylist. There is in the Oz stories no more than a trace of fun with ideas nor any of the multi-levelled nonsense of [Edward] Lear and the logical lunacy of Lewis Carroll. And there are, however much one enjoys Baum, occasional dead spots in the action of some of the later stories.

Yet one suspects, after attempting to read Carroll or Lear to a modern American child, that Baum knew better than his critics what children enjoy and understand. The nightmarish episodes, the complex paradoxes, and the logical and mathematical implications of the *Alice* books neither fit nor satisfy the child's needs and desires, however attractive they may be to mature readers. The cloying sentimentality and obsolescent vocabulary . . . of many of the nineteenth century juvenile classics simply puzzle a modern youngster and leave him cold. The Wonderful Land of Oz, by contrast, is as real to him as his own neighborhood; the Scarecrow, the Woodman, and the Lion are old storybook acquaintances in new dress, familiar, friendly, and vividly alive. (pp. 14-15)

Baum's work does not deserve the critical neglect with which it is still treated. He wrote American tales for twentieth-century American children in an American vein, and by this he should be judged. He had his weaknesses (some of them the result of fourteen Oz books), but he had his undeniable strengths. (p. 16)

In the creation of character Baum displayed his greatest mastery. Here he need bow to no one. The Tin Woodman, the Scarecrow, and the Cowardly Lion, among others, have long since secured permanent places in the gallery of great creations, and are as well known to American children as Mother Goose. . . . Baum could enter into the child's world on the child's terms, create and preserve its delightful atmosphere, and tell his story with the genuine sincerity of a believer. . . . Baum had the child's heart, and the child's love of the strange and beautiful and good, with the ability to bring them all alive. (pp. 16-17)

Russel B. Nye, "An Appreciation," in The Wizard of Oz & Who He Was *by Martin Gardner and Russel B. Nye (copyright 1957 Michigan State University Press), Michigan State University Press, 1957, pp. 1-17.*

HENRY M. LITTLEFIELD (essay date 1964)

The Wizard of Oz is an entity unto itself. . . . But its uniqueness does not rest alone on its peculiar and transcendent popularity. (pp. 47-8)

[*The Wizard*] reflects to an astonishing degree the world of political reality which surrounded Baum in 1900. In order to understand the relationship of *The Wizard* to turn-of-the-century America, it is necessary first to know something of Baum's background. . . .

While Baum was living in South Dakota not only was the frontier a thing of the past, but the Romantic view of benign nature had disappeared as well. The stark reality of the dry, open plains and the acceptance of man's Darwinian subservience to his environment served to crush Romantic idealism. (p. 48)

Baum's stay in South Dakota also covered the period of the formation of the Populist party. . . . Western farmers had for a long time sought governmental aid in the form of economic panaceas, but to no avail. The Populist movement symbolized a desperate attempt to use the power of the ballot. In 1891 Baum moved to Chicago where he was surrounded by those dynamic elements of reform which made the city so notable during the 1890s.

In Chicago Baum certainly saw the results of the frightful depression which had closed down upon the nation in 1893. Moreover, he took part in the pivotal election of 1896, marching in "torch-light parades for William Jennings Bryan." . . . No one who marched in even a few such parades could have been unaffected by Bryan's campaign. Putting all the farmers' hopes in a basket labeled "free coinage of silver," Bryan's platform rested mainly on the issue of adding silver to the nation's gold standard. Though he lost, he did at least bring the plight of the little man into national focus.

Between 1896 and 1900, while Baum worked and wrote in Chicago, the great depression faded away and the war with Spain thrust the United States into world prominence. Bryan maintained Midwestern control over the Democratic party, and often spoke out against American policies toward Cuba and the Philippines. By 1900 it was evident that Bryan would run again, although now imperialism and not silver seemed the issue of primary concern. In order to promote greater enthusiasm, however, Bryan felt compelled once more to sound the silver leitmotif in his campaign. Bryan's second futile attempt at the presidency culminated in November 1900. (p. 49)

[The] original Oz book conceals an unsuspected depth, and it is the purpose of this study to demonstrate that Baum's immortal American fantasy encompasses more than heretofore believed. For Baum created a children's story with a symbolic allegory implicit within its story line and characterizations. The allegory always remains in a minor key, subordinated to the major theme and readily abandoned whenever it threatens to distort the appeal of the fantasy. But through it, in the form of a subtle parable, Baum delineated a Midwesterner's vibrant and ironic portrait of this country as it entered the twentieth century. (p. 50)

[The plight of the Tin Woodman shows how] Eastern witchcraft dehumanized a simple laborer so that the faster and better he worked the more quickly he became a kind of machine. Here is a Populist view of evil Eastern influences on honest labor which could hardly be more pointed.

There is one thing seriously wrong with being made of tin; when it rains rust sets in. . . . The Tin Woodman's situation has an obvious parallel in the condition of many Eastern workers after the depression of 1893. (p. 52)

Dorothy is Baum's Miss Everyman. She is one of us, level-headed and human, and she has a real problem. Young readers can understand her quandary as readily as can adults. She is good, not precious, and she thinks quite naturally about others. For all of the attractions of Oz Dorothy desires only to return to the gray plains and Aunt Em and Uncle Henry. . . . Dorothy sets out on the Yellow Brick Road wearing the Witch of the East's magic Silver Shoes. Silver shoes walking on a golden road; henceforth Dorothy becomes the innocent agent of Baum's ironic view of the Silver issue. Remember, neither Dorothy, nor the good Witch of the North, nor the Munchkins understand the power of these shoes. The allegory is abundantly clear. On the next to last page of the book Baum has Glinda, Witch of the South, tell Dorothy, "Your Silver Shoes will carry you over the desert. . . . If you had known their power you could have gone back to your Aunt Em the very first day you came to this country." Glinda explains, "All you have to do is to knock the heels together three times and command the shoes to carry you wherever you wish to go." . . . William Jennings Bryan never outlined the advantages of the silver standard any more effectively.

Not understanding the magic of the Silver Shoes, Dorothy walks the mundane—and dangerous—Yellow Brick Road. (pp. 52-3)

The Lion represents Bryan himself. In the election of 1896 Bryan lost the vote of Eastern labor, though he tried hard to gain their support. In Baum's story the Lion, on meeting the little group, "struck at the Tin Woodman with his sharp claws." But, to his surprise, "he could make no impression on the tin, although the Woodman fell over in the road and lay still." Baum here refers to the fact that in 1896 workers were often pressured into voting for McKinley and gold by their employers. Amazed, the Lion says, "he nearly blunted my claws," and he adds even more appropriately, "When they scratched against the tin it made a cold shiver run down my back." . . . The King of Beasts is not after all very cowardly, and Bryan, although a pacifist and an anti-imperialist in a time of national expansion, is not either. The magic Silver Shoes belong to Dorothy, however. Silver's potent charm, which had come to

mean so much to so many in the Midwest, could not be entrusted to a political symbol. Baum delivers Dorothy from the world of adventure and fantasy to the real world of heartbreak and desolation through the power of Silver. It represents a real force in a land of illusion, and neither the Cowardly Lion nor Bryan truly needs or understands its use. (pp. 53-4)

Those who enter the Emerald City must wear green glasses. Dorothy later discovers that the greenness of dresses and ribbons disappears on leaving, and everything becomes a bland white. Perhaps the magic of any city is thus self imposed. But the Wizard dwells here and so the Emerald City represents the national Capitol. The Wizard, a little bumbling old man, hiding behind a facade of papier mâché and noise, might be any President from Grant to McKinley. He comes straight from the fair grounds in Omaha, Nebraska, and he symbolizes the American criterion for leadership—he is able to be everything to everybody.

As each of our heroes enters the throne room to ask a favor the Wizard assumes different shapes, representing different views toward national leadership. To Dorothy, he appears as an enormous head, "bigger than the head of the biggest giant." An apt image for a naive and innocent little citizen. To the Scarecrow he appears to be a lovely, gossamer fairy, a most appropriate form for an idealistic Kansas farmer. The Woodman sees a horrible beast, as would any exploited Eastern laborer after the trouble of the 1890s. But the Cowardly Lion, like W. J. Bryan, sees a "Ball of Fire, so fierce and glowing he could scarcely bear to gaze upon it." (p. 54)

The Wizard has asked them all to kill the Witch of the West. The golden road does not go in that direction and so they must follow the sun, as have many pioneers in the past. . . .

Finding Dorothy and her friends in the West, the Witch sends forty wolves against them, then forty vicious crows and finally a great swarm of black bees. But it is through the power of a magic golden cap that she summons the flying monkeys. They capture the little girl and dispose of her companions. Baum makes these Winged Monkeys into an Oz substitute for the plains Indians. Their leader says, "Once . . . we were a free people, living happily in the great forest, flying from tree to tree, eating nuts and fruit, and doing just as we pleased without calling anybody master." "This," he explains, "was many years ago, long before Oz came out of the clouds to rule over this land." . . . But like many Indian tribes Baum's monkeys are not inherently bad; their actions depend wholly upon the bidding of others. (p. 55)

Dorothy presents a special problem to the Witch. Seeing the [mark of goodness] on Dorothy's forehead and the Silver Shoes on her feet, the Witch begins "to tremble with fear, for she knew what a powerful charm belonged to them." Then "she happened to look into the child's eyes and saw how simple the soul behind them was, and that the little girl did not know of the wonderful power the Silver Shoes gave her." . . . Here Baum again uses the Silver allegory to state the blunt homily that while goodness affords a people ultimate protection against evil, ignorance of their capabilities allows evil to impose itself upon them. The Witch assumes the proportions of a kind of western Mark Hanna or Banker Boss, who, through natural malevolence, manipulates the people and holds them prisoner by cynically taking advantage of their innate innocence.

Enslaved in the West, "Dorothy went to work meekly, with her mind made up to work as hard as she could; for she was glad the Wicked Witch had decided not to kill her." . . . Many

Western farmers have held these same grim thoughts in less mystical terms. If the Witch of the West is a diabolical force of Darwinian or Spencerian nature, then another contravening force may be counted upon to dispose of her. Dorothy destroys the evil Witch by angrily dousing her with a bucket of water. Water, that precious commodity which the drought-ridden farmers on the great plains needed so badly, and which if correctly used could create an agricultural paradise, or at least dissolve a wicked witch. Plain water brings an end to malign nature in the West.

When Dorothy and her companions return to the Emerald City they soon discover that the Wizard is really nothing more than "a little man, with a bald head and a wrinkled face." (pp. 55-6)

"It was a great mistake my ever letting you into the Throne Room," the Wizard complains. "Usually I will not see even my subjects, and so they believe I am something terrible." . . . What a wonderful lesson for youngsters of the decade when Benjamin Harrison, Grover Cleveland and William McKinley were hiding in the White House. Formerly the Wizard was a mimic, a ventriloquist and a circus balloonist. The latter trade involved going "up in a balloon on circus day, so as to draw a crowd of people together and get them to pay to see the circus." . . . Such skills are as admirably adapted to success in late-nineteenth-century politics as they are to the humbug wizardry of Baum's story. A pointed comment on Midwestern political ideals is the fact that our little Wizard comes from Omaha, Nebraska, a center of Populist agitation. (p. 56)

The Silver Shoes furnish Dorothy with a magic means of travel. But when she arrives back in Kansas she finds, "The Silver Shoes had fallen off in her flight through the air, and were lost forever in the desert" . . . Were the "her" to refer to America in 1900, Baum's statement could hardly be contradicted.

Current historiography tends to criticize the Populist movement for its "delusions, myths and foibles," Professor C. Vann Woodward observed recently. Yet *The Wonderful Wizard of Oz* has provided unknowing generations with a gentle and friendly Midwestern critique of the Populist rationale on these very same grounds. Led by naive innocence and protected by good will, the farmer, the laborer and the politician approach the mystic holder of national power to ask for personal fulfillment. Their desires, as well as the Wizard's cleverness in answering them, are all self-delusion. Each of these characters carries within him the solution to his own problem, were he only to view himself objectively. The fearsome Wizard turns out to be nothing more that a common man, capable of shrewd but mundane answers to these self-induced needs. Like any good politician he gives the people what they want. Throughout the story Baum poses a central thought; the American desire for symbols of fulfillment is illusory. Real needs lie elsewhere.

Thus the Wizard cannot help Dorothy, for of all the characters only she has a wish that is selfless, and only she has a direct connection to honest, hopeless human beings. Dorothy supplies real fulfillment when she returns to her aunt and uncle, using the Silver Shoes, and cures some of their misery and heartache. In this way Baum tells us that the Silver crusade at least brought back Dorothy's lovely spirit to the disconsolate plains farmer. Her laughter, love and good will are no small addition to that gray land, although the magic of Silver has been lost forever as a result. (p. 57)

The Wizard has become a genuine piece of American folklore because, knowing his audience, Baum never allowed the con-sistency of the allegory to take precedence over the theme of youthful entertainment. Yet once discovered, the author's allegorical intent seems clear, and it gives depth and lasting interest even to children who only sense something else beneath the surface of the story. (p. 58)

Henry M. Littlefield, "'The Wizard of Oz': Parable on Populism," in American Quarterly *(copyright 1964, Trustees of the University of Pennsylvania), Vol. xvi, No. 1, Spring, 1964, pp. 47-58.*

MARTIN GARDNER   (essay date 1973)

John Dough and the Cherub is not, in my opinion, among Baum's best fantasies, but that doesn't mean it is not worth reading. It is typical Baum, funny and exciting, packed with Ozzy characters and episodes, and with outrageous surprises on almost every page. The book has its spots of humdrum writing, and some of its ideas are hackneyed, but it is hard to imagine a young reader, even today, who would be bored by the tale. (p. 111)

Ironically, it is Chick, added to the story as an afterthought, who dominates the narrative. Is Chick a boy or a girl? Baum does not tell us. All masculine and feminine pronouns are avoided (often awkwardly, as when Chick is referred to as "it"), and at the book's close, when Chick grows up as the Head Booleywag (Prime Minister) of Hiland and Loland, we still do not know if the Booleywag is a man or woman.

Baum and his publisher exploited the mystery for all the publicity they could get. A mustard-colored contest blank, tipped in the book's early printings, offered cash prizes for the best statement of why readers thought Chick a boy or a girl. It is amusing to learn that the contest left the question unresolved. (pp. 111-12)

John Dough provides little information about Chick's background aside from the fact that Chick is the world's first incubator baby. This explains Chick's residence on the Isle of Phreex (Freaks) and probably why Baum chooses the name "Chick." (As Baum well knew—his first book was on chicken rearing—incubators were used for hatching chicken eggs long before they were used for prematurely born human babies.) Like most of Baum's child protagonists, nothing is said about Chick's father or mother. Indeed, the implication is that the Cherub *has* no parents. We do know that Chick is at least eight, blonde, blue-eyed, and curly-headed. The child is always happy, always frank, clever, "wise for one so young," creative, brave, unprejudiced, and friendly. . . .

Above all, Chick is an adventurer of the open road. The child doesn't care where it is. . . . Chick is equally unconcerned with what happens: "I'm not afraid. Anything suits me." . . .

In sum, Chick is a sandle-footed highway freak—a flower child of the counter-culture, self-sufficient, androgynous, parentless, and happily "into" oatmeal and cream instead of drugs.

Chick's companion, John Dough (an obvious pun on John Doe), is the book's principal "non-meat" personage. He is a life-size gingerbread French gentleman, with top hat and candy cane, made by Jules Grogrande (*gros* and *grande*?), a Parisian baker who has settled in an unidentified American city. The powerful Arabian elixir which brings John to life makes him wise and strong, and capable of speaking all languages, modern and classic. . . . He suffers occasionally from soggy feet, chipping, and loose glass eyes. Like the Scarecrow and Tin Woodman, he neither eats nor sleeps, though he is capable of drinking. . . .

Para Bruin, the third member of the book's unlikely trio of adventurers, is one of Baum's most lovable creations. He is made of indestructible para rubber, hollow like a rubber ball, kind and harmless . . . , and a ham vaudevillian who loves to roll up like a ball and bounce from high places to amuse the crowd. It is to his credit that he doesn't love everybody. I can still remember the satisfaction I felt as a child when Para Bruin bounced down from the sky to demolish Sport, surely one of the most unpleasant characters in all of Baum's fantasies. (p. 113)

There are scores of lesser characters in *John Dough,* both meat and meatless. Duo, the two-headed dog, anticipates the Pushmi-Pullyu of Hugh Lofting's *Dr. Doolittle* books. Sir Austin Alfred is a spoonerism on Sir Alfred Austin, poet laureate of England in 1906. Tietjamus Toips, whose symphony is harder to understand than one by Vogner (Wagner), plays on the name of Paul Tietjans, a friend of Baum who composed the music for [the 1902] *The Wizard of Oz* musical. The name is also a pun on "pajama tops." (p. 114)

The ersatz General of Phreex, whose entire body has been replaced by artificial parts, raises the same perplexing metaphysical questions about personal identity as does the Tin Woodman. Ali Dubh's Elixir of Life is similar to the Powder of Life that vivifies Jack Pumpkinhead and the Sawhorse in *The Marvelous Land of Oz.* The Beaver king's Magic Box anticipates Ozma's Magic Picture, which in turn foreshadows the television screen. (p. 115)

The humor in *John Dough* ranges from low-level word play ("I'm sure I couldn't agree with anyone who ate me," John declares; I counted more than fifteen puns on words relating to food alone) to occasional remarks of existential import. John cannot recall when he was not alive. He informs a lady who thinks he ought *not* to be alive that he cannot help it. And on another occasion he observes that "it is better to be wrong than to be nothing." (p. 117)

Hiland and Loland, where Chick, John and the rubber bear settle at last, are two rival cultures, flourishing side by side, each firmly convinced of its own superiority, each regarding its neighbors as uncouth barbarians. The wall that separates the tall, thin Highlanders from the short, fat Lolanders is no higher than the old Great Wall of China or the new Berlin Wall, or a hundred other "walls" that these material structures symbolize. Baum's vigorous plea for tolerance and understanding of alien ways is one that he would stress again in *Sky Island,* where he describes the equally irrational rivalry between the Pinks and the Blues. Need anyone be reminded that it is a moral on which the world's fate may depend? (pp. 117-18)

*Martin Gardner, " 'John Dough and the Cherub',"
in* Children's Literature: Journal of The Modern Language Association Seminar on Children's Literature and The Children's Literature Association, *Vol. 2, Francelia Butler, Editor-in-Chief (© 1973 by Francelia Butler; reprinted by permission of The Children's Literature Foundation, Box 370, Windham Center, CT 06280), Temple University Press, 1973, pp. 110-18.*

RAY BRADBURY (essay date 1973)

It is fascinating to compare memories of Dorothy and Oz and Baum with Alice and the Looking Glass and the Rabbit Hole and Lewis Carroll, who made out better with librarians and teachers.

When we think of Oz a whole mob of incredibly lovely if strange people falls across our minds.

When we think of Alice's encounters we think of mean, waspish small, carping, bad-mannered children ranting against *going* to bed, refusing to get *out* of bed, not liking the food, hating the temperature, minding the weather out of mind.

If Love is the lubricant that runs Oz to glory, Hate is the mud in which all sink to ruin inside the mirror where poor Alice is trapped. (p. xiii)

Both books, both authors, stay in our minds, for mirror-reversed reasons. We float and fly through Oz on grand winds that make us beautiful kites. We trudge and fight our way through Wonderland, amazed that we survive at all.

Wonderland, for all its fantasy, is most practically real, that world where people have conniption fits and knock you out of line on your way onto a bus.

Oz is that place, ten minutes before sleep, where we bind up our wounds, soak our feet, dream ourselves better, snooze poetry on our lips, and decide that mankind, for all it's snide and mean and dumb, must be given another chance come dawn and a hearty breakfast. . . .

Wonderland is cold gruel and arithmetic at six a.m., icy showers, long schools.

It is not surprising that Wonderland is the darling of the intellectuals.

It is similarly not surprising that dreamers and intuitionists would reject the cold mirror of Carroll and take their chances on hotfooting it over the forbidden desert which at least promises utter destruction for purely inanimate reasons (the desert, after all, is not alive and doesn't know whom it is destroying) heading for Oz. . . .

Wonderland is what we Are.

Oz is what we would hope and like to be. (p. xiv)

Oz has not fallen, has it? Even though legions of bright people with grand good taste, and thousands of librarians have fired cannonades in tandem with hosts of sociologists who fear that the mighty Wizard will pollute their children, Baum, across the years, simply reaches in his pocket and produces, Shaggy Man that he is, the Love Magnet. (p. xvi)

[In a story of mine], *The Exiles,* fine fantasists like Poe and Hawthorne, along with Dickens, and Baum, find themselves shunted off to Mars as the non-dreamers, the super-psychological technicians, the book burners of the future, advance through towns and libraries, tossing the last of the great dreams into the furnace.

At the finale of my story, a rocket arrives on Mars, bearing with it the last copies in existence of Poe and Dickens and Baum. The captain of the ship burns these books on a dead Martian sea-bottom, and Oz at long last crashes over into ruins, Tik-Tok runs to rust, the Wizard and all his dusk-time dreams are destroyed. . . .

I do not for a moment believe that day will ever come. The fight between the dreamers and the fact-finders will continue, and we will embody both in equal proportion, or risk all men singing *castratto* soprano for the literary popes.

I have not predicted futures but, as I have often hopefully pointed out, prevented them. (p. xvii)

In a world where books are machine-made for ''age groups'' and pass through dry-parchment analysts' hands before being pill-fed to kids, . . . Baum is needed. When the cities die, in their present form at least, and we head out into Eden again, which we must and will, Baum will be waiting for us. And if the road we take is not Yellow Brick why, damn it, we can imagine that it is. . . . (p. xviii)

> *Ray Bradbury, ''Because, Because, Because, Because of the Wonderful Things He Does'' (1973), in* Wonderful Wizard, Marvelous Land *by Raylyn Moore (copyright © 1974 by Raylyn Moore), Bowling Green University Popular Press, 1974, pp. xi-xviii.*

RAYLYN MOORE   (essay date 1974)

The Wizard is the best of all Oz books. Action is constant, the characters live, the plot is tightly managed, and the outcome immensely satisfactory. Above all, the allegory is sustained throughout.

Beside *The Wizard,* even *The Land of Oz* must take second place, although it too is a well conceived adventure, with allegorical overtones and a convincing set of characters. *Ozma of Oz* is less original; perhaps its best points are the introduction of two new characters (Tik-Tok and Billina) who come up in nearly every way to the standards of the earlier ones, and one of Baum's happier applications of the death-rebirth theme, in the descent to the underworld and return. In *Dorothy and the Wizard* this descent is abused by its very length and the near-horrors provided by purely evil enemies, while *The Road to Oz* errs in the other direction: it is little more than a casual excursion which ends in a party, to which Baum invites many of his characters from all his other fairy-tale books. While the quest pattern, now familiar, is preserved, there seems insufficient motivation for the sparse action here.

As if to make up for this very flaw, *The Emerald City* employs a double-quest plot; while the invaders of Oz are proceeding toward the city to destroy it, Dorothy and her party are junketing about Oz in an attempt to show Aunt Em and Uncle Henry the wonders. The stories are told in alternating chapters and suspense is sustained because the excursionists are happily oblivious to their danger until the last possible moment.

A more formal employment of the pattern appears in *The Patchwork Girl.* The reason for Ojo's long and trouble-fraught journey to the Emerald City is a valid one: he wants to save his uncle's life, and he exhibits the same sort of courage and resourcefulness shown by Dorothy in the first book. The Patchwork Girl herself is probably the last of Baum's truly successful inventions in the weird-character department. And these items may add up to making this the last of the really successful Oz books.

Probably because it was conceived first as a stage musical, *Tik-Tok* is little more than a reworking of the tailings of Baum's earlier and more successful ''strikes.'' It begins with shipwreck, as does *Ozma;* the people of Oogaboo pick everything they need from trees, as do the people of Mo (and as Dorothy picks the dinner pails in *Ozma;* McKinley's slogan in the election campaign of 1900 had been ''the full dinnerpail''). Ann Soforth's army has sixteen officers and one private, and is almost a match for Ozma's army with its twenty-seven officers and one private—but not quite. As in *Dorothy and the Wizard,*

the protagonists pick a ruler from a plant in a vegetable kingdom. And once again there is the descent to the underworld to rescue someone imprisoned there (Offenbach's *Orpheus in Hades* was very popular at the time) as there had been in *Ozma.*

The other six books trail off into various degrees of paleness. *Rinkitink* is a fairy story which has practically nothing to do with Oz (some sources say it was an earlier story pulled into the series with minor rewriting), but this is no failing in either *John Dough* or *Queen Zixi;* both are imaginative and humorous. And this is probably the root of the problem: . . . in the later books both the imagination and the humor have worn out.

Further, Oz-as-eden can now be seen to be Baum's greatest strength and greatest weakness. So long as the paradise remains in its prelapsarian state, the mother-goddess reigns unchallenged; it is only after the Fall that Eve becomes subject to her husband and the patriarchal Judeo-Christian cycle begins, with its consequent sorrows and responsibilities. And yet to remain in the Garden, never to emerge, is never to grow; it is recounting the myth (life to death) and leaving out half the story (death to rebirth). Any return to the womb is a regress to death, any attempt to exist in the static atmosphere of a state of perfect existence leads inevitably to tedium and nothingness. Where there can be no growth in any direction, there can be no freshness of change. Dorothy, because she could not grow up, could only deteriorate; Oz, always green, can never provide the cyclical miracle of the seasons. (pp. 168-71)

> *Raylyn Moore, in her* Wonderful Wizard, Marvelous Land *(copyright © 1974 by Raylyn Moore), Bowling Green University Popular Press, 1974, 213 p.*

GORE VIDAL   (essay date 1977)

Like most Americans my age (with access to books), I spent a good deal of my youth in Baum's land of Oz. I have a precise, tactile memory of the first Oz book that came into my hands. It was the original 1910 edition of *The Emerald City.* I still remember the look and the feel of those dark green covers, the evocative smell of dust and old ink. I also remember that I could not stop reading and rereading the book. But ''reading'' in not the right word. In some mysterious way, I was translating myself to Oz, a place which I was to inhabit for many years. . . . To a child-a book is a book. The writer's name is an irrelevant decoration, unlike the title which prepares one for delight. Even so, I used, idly, to wonder who or what L. Frank Baum was. Baum looked to my eye like Barnum, as in Barnum & Bailey's circus. Was it the same person? or the circus itself? . . .

Recently I was sent an academic dissertation. Certain aspects of Baum's *The Land of Oz* had reoccurred in a book of mine. Was this conscious or not? It was not. But I was intrigued. I reread *The Land of Oz.* Yes, I could see Baum's influence. I then reread *The Emerald City of Oz.* I have now reread all of L. Frank Baum's Oz books. I have also read a good deal of what has been written about him in recent years. Although Baum's books were dismissed as trash by at least two generations of librarians and literary historians, the land of Oz has managed to fascinate each new generation and, lately, Baum himself has become an OK subject if not for the literary critic for the social historian.

Even so, it is odd that Baum has received so little acknowledgement from those who owe him the most—writers. After all, those books (films, television, too, alas) first encountered in childhood do more to shape the imagination and its style than all the later calculated readings of acknowledged masters. Scientists are often more candid in their admiration (our attempts to find life elsewhere in the universe is known as Operation Ozma). Lack of proper acknowledgment perhaps explains the extent to which Baum has been ignored by literary historians, by English departments, by. . . . As I write these words, a sense of dread. Is it possible that Baum's survival is due to the fact that he is *not* taught? That he is not, officially, Literature? If so, one must be careful not to murder Oz with exegesis. . . .

The hostility of librarians to the Oz books is in itself something of a phenomenon. The books are always popular with children. But many librarians will not stock them. (p. 10)

Essentially, our educators are Puritans who want to uphold the Puritan work ethic. This is done by bringing up American children in such a way that they will take their place in society as diligent workers and unprotesting consumers. Any sort of literature that encourages a child to contemplate alternative worlds might incite him, later in life, to make changes in the iron Puritan order that has brought us, along with missiles and atomic submarines, the assembly line at Detroit where workers are systematically dehumanized.

It is significant that one of the most brutal attacks on the Oz books was made in 1957 by the director of the Detroit Library System, a Mr. Ralph Ulveling, who found the Oz books to "have a cowardly approach to life." They are also guilty of "negativism." Worst of all, "there is nothing uplifting or elevating about the Baum series." For the Librarian of Detroit courage and affirmation mean punching the clock and then doing the dull work of a machine while never questioning the system. . . .

Ray Bradbury makes his case for America's two influential imaginative writers, Baum and Edgar Rice Burroughs [see excerpt above]. . . .

[Bradbury describes Baum as] "that faintly old-maidish man who grew boys" (in a greenhouse?) "inward to their most delightful interiors, kept them home, and romanced them with wonders between their ears." Through Bradbury's rich style, a point is emerging: Inward to delightful selves. Kept them home. Romanced them. Wonders. Yes, all that is true. And hateful to professional molders of American youth. Boys should be out of the house, competing in games, building model airplanes, beating each other up so that one day they will be obedient soldiers in the endless battle for the free world. Show us a dreaming boy (or girl) at home with a book, and we will show you a potential troublemaker. . . .

Baum in his work and life (as described by those who knew him) was apolitical. . . . Only once in the fairy tales have I been able to find a direct political reference. In *Sea Fairies* there is an octopus who is deeply offended when he learns that Standard Oil is called an "octopus": "'Oh, what a disgrace! What a deep, dire, dreadful disgrace!'" But though Baum was not political in the usual sense, he had very definite ideas about the way the world should be. (p. 12)

Although it is hard to think of Baum as writing political allegories in support of Free Silver [see Henry M. Littlefield excerpt above], his inventions do reflect the world in which he grew up. When he was a year old . . . the country was swept by a Christian revival whose like we were not to see again until today's White House and the better federal prisons started to fill up with evangelical Christians. During Baum's

prepubescence the Civil War took place. In his twelfth year Susan B. Anthony started the suffragette movement; and San Francisco fell flat on its hills. In fact, all during the last days of the century, nature was on a rampage and the weather was more than usually abnormal, as the old joke goes.

In 1893, a cyclone destroyed two Kansas towns, killing thirty-one people. I take this disaster to be the one that Baum was to describe seven years later in *The Wizard of Oz.* (pp. 13-14)

Baum is sometimes regarded as a Utopian writer. But I don't think that this is accurate. Utopian writers have political ideas, and Baum seems to have had none at all. Except for a mild parody of the suffragettes, there is little to link political America with magical Oz whose miniscule countries are governed by hereditary lords. On the other hand, Baum was a social moralist who is said to have been influenced by William Morris's *News from Nowhere.* . . .

Interestingly enough, there is no reference in the Oz books to a republic of any kind. There are no parliaments or congresses. There are no elections—a most peculiar thing for an American writer to leave out. The various rulers are all feudal except in the last book of the series (*Glinda of Oz*) where Baum introduces us, surprisingly, to a Supreme Dictator. Baum was still at work on the book in March 1919 when Mussolini founded the Fascist Party. Was he, in some way, prescient? Whether or not Baum was predicting fascism, it is significant that he associates the idea of dictatorship with democracy: "'I'm the Supreme Dictator of all, and I'm elected once a year. This is a democracy, you know, where the people are allowed to vote for their rulers. A good many others would like to be Supreme Dictator, but as I made a law that I am always to count the votes myself, I am always elected.'" (p. 14)

. . . . .

I have reread the Oz books in the order in which they were written. Some things are as I remember. Others strike me as being entirely new. I was struck by the unevenness of style not only from book to book but, sometimes, from page to page. The jaggedness can be explained by the fact that the man who was writing fourteen Oz books was writing forty-eight other books at the same time. Arguably, *The Wizard of Oz* is the best of the lot. After all, the first book is the one in which Oz was invented. Yet, as a child, I preferred *The Emerald City, Rinkitink,* and *The Lost Princess* to *The Wizard.* Now I find that all of the books tend to flow together in a single narrative, with occasional bad patches.

In *The Wizard of Oz* Dorothy is about six years old. In the later books she seems to be ten or eleven. Baum locates her swiftly and efficiently in the first sentence of the series. "Dorothy lived in the midst of the great Kansas prairies, with Uncle Henry, who was a farmer, and Aunt Em, who was the farmer's wife." . . .

[With the success of the play *The Wizard of Oz,*] the idiocies of popular theater had begun to infect Baum's prose. *The Wizard of Oz* is chastely written. *The Land of Oz* is not. Baum riots in dull word play. There are endless bad puns, of the sort favored by popular comedians. There is also that true period horror: the baby-talking ingenue, a character who lasted well into our day in the menacing shapes of Fanny (Baby Snooks) Brice and the early Ginger Rogers. Dorothy, who talked plainly and to the point in *The Wizard,* talks (when she reappears in the third book) with a cuteness hard to bear. Fortunately, Baum's show-biz phase wore off and in later volumes Dorothy's speech improves.

Despite stylistic lapses, *The Land of Oz* is one of the most unusual and interesting books of the series. In fact, it is so unusual that after the Shirley Temple television adaptation of the book in 1960, PTA circles were in a state of crisis. The problem that knitted then and, I am told, knits even today many a maternal brow is Sexual Role. (p. 38)

Apparently the rightful ruler of Oz is Princess Ozma. As a baby, Ozma was changed by Mombi into the boy Tip. Now Tip must be restored to his true identity. The PTA went, as it were, into plenary session. What effect would a book like this have on a boy's sense of himself as a future man, breadwinner and father to more of same? Would he want, awful thought, to be a Girl? . . .

Essentially, Baum's human protagonists are neither male nor female but children, a separate category in his view if not in that of our latter-day sexists. Baum's use of sex changes was common to the popular theater of his day. . . .

Dorothy is a perfectly acceptable central character for a boy to read about. She asks the right questions. She is not sappy (as Ozma can sometimes be). She is straight to the point and a bit aggressive. Yet the Dorothy who returns to the series in the third book, *Ozma of Oz* . . . , is somewhat different from the original Dorothy. She is older and her conversation is full of cute contractions that must have doubled up audiences in Sioux City but were pretty hard going for at least one child forty years ago. (p. 39)

Although Baum's powers of invention seldom flagged, he had no great skill at plot-making. Solutions to problems are arrived at either through improbable coincidence or by bringing in, literally, some god (usually Glinda) from the machine to set things right. Since the narratives are swift and the conversations sprightly and the invented characters are both homely and amusing . . . , the stories never lack momentum. Yet there was always a certain danger that the narrative would flatten out into a series of predictable turns. . . .

The final Oz books are among the most interesting. After a gall bladder operation, Baum took to his bed where the last work was done. Yet Baum's imagination seems to have been more than usually inspired despite physical pain, and the darkness at hand. *Lost Princess of Oz* . . . is one of the best of the series. The beginning is splendidly straightforward. "There could be no doubt of the fact: Princess Ozma, the lovely girl ruler of the Fairyland of Oz, was lost. She had completely disappeared." . . . The villain Ugu (who had kidnapped and transformed Ozma) is a most satisfactory character. (p. 41)

Despite the Librarian of Detroit's efforts to suppress magical alternative worlds, the Oz books continue to exert their spell. "You do not educate a man by telling him what he knew not," wrote John Ruskin, "but by making him what he was not" In Ruskin's high sense, Baum was a true educator, and those who read his Oz books are often made what they were not—imaginative, tolerant, alert to wonders, life. (p. 42)

Gore Vidal, "The Wizard of the 'Wizard'" and "On Rereading the Oz Books," in New York Review of Books *(reprinted with permission from* The New York Review of Books; *copyright © 1977 Nyrev, Inc.), Vol. XXIV, Nos. 15 and 16, September 29 and October 13, 1977, pp. 10, 12-15; 38-42.*

JANET JUHNKE (essay date 1977)

The film of *The Wizard of Oz* appeals to adults because of its cerebral humor—Professor Marvel's lovably obvious fakery, the Lollipop Kids doing their twitching imitation of "tough guys," the Scarecrow's assertion that "some people without brains do an awful lot of talking," the Lion's Brooklyn accent and gag lines like "I can't sleep—I tried counting sheep but I'm afraid of them too," the Wizard's satire of educated men as he offers the Scarecrow a Doctorate of Thinkology and his satire of patriots whose courage is in their uniforms and medals, and the pun on the "horse of a different color." Many children would miss these jokes. Adults also respond favorably to the fine acting and to the film-makers' technical skills. Both children and adults love the music and songs. "Over the Rainbow," especially, appeals to all ages—to all who dream of a happier and more colorful world than their own, like Munchkinland. (pp. 172-73)

[Christopher Finch, in *Rainbow*], a life of Judy Garland, asserts that the screenplay for *The Wizard of Oz* "is one of those rare adaptations that is better than the original." However, with two such masterpieces as Baums' book and the MGM film, comparative judgments of quality are meaningless. The two versions are just different; and if the film has touched more people than the book, it is mainly because, through the medium of television, more people have been exposed to the film than to the book. From a film buff's point of view, the book may seem to contain "much superfluous material" and to be episodic and meandering" (Finch), but the same could be said of *The Odyssey, Don Quixote, Moby Dick,* and countless other narrative classics. What is good narrative prose is not necessarily good film. Film has an affinity with *drama,* where tight construction, economy of plot, and unity of character are necessary to carry the audience on through climax to conclusion in a relatively brief compass of time. Narrative prose has an affinity with *epic,* which delays the audience with various "retarding elements"—explanations, digressive speeches, stories within the story. Thus the book treats us to full histories of the lives of the Scarecrow, the Tin Man, the King of the Monkeys, and the Wizard of Oz. It marks pauses for eating and sleeping; it takes time to introduce the Kalidahs, the Winkies, and the Quadlings, and to take Dorothy through the Dainty China Country inhabited by easily broken milkmaids and shepherds and by a joker who is cracked in the head.

To be sure, the film's songs and elaborate production numbers "retard" the forward movement of the plot—but much of the book's action is telescoped into a simpler, more unified plot. The film reduces the two good witches to one. The Witch of the North, a little old woman with wrinkles, white hair, and a stiff walk, is omitted, while Glinda, the young and beautiful Witch of the South, somewhat improbably takes the roles both of sending Dorothy to Oz to find a way home *and* of telling Dorothy that the ruby slippers could have got her home anyway. She rather lamely explains why she didn't tell Dorothy the truth right away—because Dorothy wouldn't have believed her. And, of course, without the trip to Oz, there would have been no story. The Witch of the West is treated much more melodramatically in the film. The ugly green face, the marvelous cackle, the periodic threats along the way ("I'll get you, my pretty!"), the fire, the skywriting, the signs in the forest—all are absent from the book. These devices build suspense and fear—and focus the audience's emotions. The book does not use such dramatic tools.

The most striking structural difference between the book and the film, however, is in the frame for the story. In the book,

Dorothy's "farm" consists of a small one-room house alone on the prairie, neither prosperous enough for hired hands like Hunk, Zeke, and Hickory, nor near enough to other homes for Toto to bother a Miss Gulch. Those characters—and Professor Marvel—are inventions of the screen writers. The change is significant. In the book, Dorothy is simply carried away to Oz; in the film she tries first to run away from home. In the book she only wishes to escape drabness; in the film, though that drabness is wonderfully emphasized by the black-and-white photography, Dorothy also runs from the cruelty of Miss Gulch, in order to save the life of her only friend, Toto. Professor Marvel's suggestion that Aunt Em is ill adds guilt and worry to Dorothy's later desire to return home.

The reappearance of Miss Gulch, Hickory, and the others in different form in the land of Oz brings delighted recognition to the audience. But when we see them in their "proper" form at the films conclusion, the "message" of the story is quite different from that of the book. Dorothy hasn't been to Oz at all—it's all been a dream, created out of the fabric of her real life. The book offers no such "interpretation." Baum's Dorothy returns to a new house, built to replace the one the cyclone took away. She has actually been gone, and Aunt Em has missed her. When she runs up the road to the house, she says simply that she's been to Oz and that she's glad to be home again.

It is probably heretical to prefer this simple conclusion to the sentimental ending of the film, which has pleased so many viewers. But the one aspect of the film that seems cloyingly sweet is that tearful repetition: "There's no place like home. There's no place like home. . . ." (pp. 173-75)

The ending of the film is an adult ending, not a child's. Adults like to dismiss fantasy as only a dream; children know that evil witches and animate trees and talking animals are real. (p. 175)

> Janet Juhnke, "A Kansan's View," in The Classic American Novel and the Movies, edited by Gerald Peary and Roger Shatzkin (copyright © 1977 by Frederick Ungar Publishing Co., Inc.), Ungar, 1977, pp. 165-75.

ROGER SALE (essay date 1978)

[If] there is one distinctive quality about Baum's works, and about American children's literature in general, it is a sunny air of naïveté which, more often than not, does not try to hide a gloomy or obsessed concern. It is not realistic literature for the most part, but it tends to include or to accommodate the real with an ease, even an optimism, that is generally not found in European children's books. (pp. 223-24)

America is an enchanted land, and a great deal of commentary on American literature has sought to determine the terms of the spell it lies under. . . . A good deal of the best American children's literature . . . enchants by its ease, its unselfconsciousness, its naïveté. And the first to achieve this, and still the best, is Baum. (pp. 224-25)

[Until] we understand the way he loved and hated writing Oz books we will not be able to account for the careless, slapdash writing that mars and even destroys some of the Oz books, and, more important, we will not understand why, despite all that is wrong, the Oz books have rightly gained for Baum a permanent place in the minds of those who love him.

We might begin with a look at the figures who provide the easy and pleasant solutions that [are] part of the standard furniture of American children's literature. The most famous of these is the Wizard himself, but there are also the Shaggy Man and Cap'n Bill; they are all older men, dry and sexless, and they accompany Dorothy and other young heroines on their journeys to Oz. They seem types of Baum himself, and the rule about these figures is that the less one sees of them the better they appear. The humbug wizard in the first book, mild, squat, and pathetic, is rather memorable because he only appears in a few chapters, and exists mainly as the focus of others' discoveries about him. In later books he appears more frequently, mostly as Dorothy's companion on journeys, and gradually he becomes more prissy and less interesting, an adjunct to the kindly, strong magic wielded by Glinda and Ozma. Cap'n Bill has a wooden leg, but otherwise he is hard to tell from the Wizard. The Shaggy Man is occasionally better when he is embodying the shrewd restlessness of Baum himself that was responsible for getting the Wizard up in his balloon in the first place. The truth expressed by these men is that solutions are easy if you know how—how to lie to Dorothy about where the Love Magnet came from, how to catch the heads of Scoodlers as though they were baseballs, how to whistle along that portion of the Yellow Brick Road where plants will lean over and capture you if you don't. But since their effectiveness depends on their ability to do such tricks, they are good only in short bursts, and, as a result, much the best of this type is Johnny Dooit, who appears only in six pages of one book, *The Road to Oz*. . . . (pp. 227-28)

These men can for a moment or two fill up a scene as though it were all there was, as though there were no impinging past or future, and it is that which makes them impressive, more than their practical know-how. That it is the presence and not the expertise that counts is what the consistently enchanting Oz figures, Dorothy and Tip and the other children, show us. They cannot build boats in two minutes, or know when or how to whistle their way past the encircling trees. They must rely on their native sense of themselves and let that be enough. The fact that what is magical about them is their spirit and their presence and not their knowledge gives us the clue to Baum's achievement. They do not fuss, they immerse themselves in the present, which makes them children, to be sure, but it also makes them important. We are inclined to think Baum works better with girls than with boys, but Baum in fact is an almost totally sexless author and our impression is created by Dorothy alone. The other girls, Betsy Bobbin and Trot, have nothing like Dorothy's stature, and three of the boys, Tip, Inga, and Ervic, have some very fine moments. But it is nonetheless Dorothy who is most impressive, so we need to look at one of her magical journeys closely to describe what is most enchanting about Baum. (p. 229)

As one might expect, it is in the early Oz books, when there are still fresh journeys to Oz to be taken, that Baum is at his very best. After Dorothy moves to Oz permanently as part of Baum's strategy for writing no more Oz books, she loses a good deal of her sparkle and becomes like most of the other residents of the Emerald City. Baum tried with Betsy Bobbin and Trot to find substitutes for Dorothy, but his heart wasn't in such journeys any more; he knew too completely how they went and where they would end up before he started. For this reason some of his admirers wish he had been able to stop after *The Emerald City*, when he first said he wanted to be done with Oz. The later books often do, indeed, show a marked falling off in quality. *Tik-Tok* is almost entirely a reworking of old materials; *The Patchwork Girl* has Ojo, the least interesting of Baum's children, and is constantly marred by some of Baum's worst punning and horseplay; *The Scarecrow* begins well with Trot and Cap'n Bill getting to Oz but then dwindles into wooden romance; *The Tin Woodman* and *The Magic* are almost grotesquely tired; the last book, *Glinda*, had to be padded with census taking of all the old Oz characters in order to be made into one of the shortest books in the series. Furthermore, nothing in these books matches the great opening journeys in *The Land, Ozma,* and *The Road.*

This way of arguing the case, however, distorts Baum's talents and achievement even if it does isolate his very best things. Baum wrote quickly and never seems to have worried if he could sustain his interest for the length of a whole book. He seems to have known when he began a book how he wanted it to start, and perhaps where he wanted it to end, but he left the middle to be contrived as he went along. Rereading *The Wizard*, for instance, is always a strange experience for anyone who has come to know Victor Fleming's movie. Book and movie each begin wonderfully and in different ways; the movie has its spectacular cyclone and shift from brown-and-white to color, and Baum's matter-of-factness about Kansas, cyclones, and the Munchkins is winning. From then on, though, the advantages seem to belong to the movie. Baum's admirers may complain about having the whole thing be a dream, but the movie makes the dream create its own kind of sense, by emphasizing two characters, the Wizard and the Wicked Witch of the West, whom Baum uses only as part of his zoo. The second Oz book, *The Land*, and the fifth, *The Road*, are wonderful for a hundred or more pages, but then fade, while the fourth, *Dorothy and the Wizard*, and the sixth, *The Emerald City*, are among the weakest in the series. We can't, thus, imagine Baum doing wonderfully well with Oz until he lost interest because he was always capable of losing interest, of falling into slapdash writing, easy satire, or trivial zoo-keeping inventiveness. Furthermore, two of the later books, *Rinkitink* and *The Lost Princess*, though they take no journey to magic lands and therefore lack some of the moment-to-moment sparkle of some of the early books, are very good at sustaining their narrative propositions through to the end; and the last book, *Glinda*, has a fine central situation and, as we will see, one spectacular stretch.

The essence of Baum is his restless, careless ease, his indifference to the complexities of life, his eagerness to describe what enchanted him without ever exploring or understanding it. Such people often become entertainers of one sort or another, but they seldom become writers. It might be said he had a knack for writing the way some people have a knack for singing or dancing or hitting a baseball. He obviously enjoyed writing, but his view of himself as a pleaser of audiences and his indifference to any disciplining of his genius meant he often wrote a good deal he didn't want to write. He wanted above all, as we have seen, to avoid the "horrible and blood-curdling incident" he found in European fairy tales, and yet, more than once, he fell into writing such incidents almost as if without knowing he was doing so. At the time he began writing the fourth Oz book, for instance, *Dorothy and the Wizard*, he had three commercial and two artistic successes behind him. He begins by dropping Dorothy and a friend of hers into the earth—having gotten her out of Kansas by air and water, an earthquake was the next obvious step. But something about being under or inside the earth must have upset Baum in ways he did not anticipate, and so he drops Dorothy into an extremely unpleasant place, and not even dropping the Wizard in helps. The

Wizard finds himself matching wits and tricks with the Sorcerer of the Mangaboos, who are vegetable people. Since the Wizard and the Sorcerer are mostly humbug, all should be well, but Baum gets careless with his tone and mistakenly tries to make the icy Prince of the Mangaboos into an arbitrator, thereby taking the whole thing out of the Wizard's power and very far from anything in Dorothy's power. The Prince decides the tourney in favor of the Wizard, the Sorcerer tries to stop the Wizard's breath, the Wizard makes a sword out of a series of knives and slices the Sorcerer in two. Each step gets Baum inadvertently closer to uncontrollable violence, and when the Prince announces that all the strangers must be destroyed, the tone has become so grim that Baum is lost. All the responses Dorothy can make, or even that the Wizard can make in a pinch, are no longer possible, so Baum has to haul them out of this whole situation, which takes him forty uninteresting pages, and by this point the book has stumbled on for so long Baum has no interest in recovering it. So, once set wrong, Baum found it hard to do more than plunge ahead, which seldom worked well; conversely, however, once set right, he tended to be able to invent and plot with ease and grace. But his attention span, if that is the right word for it, seems to have been no longer than that of an intelligent child. As a result there is no one Oz book to which one can point as clearly the best, the one for skeptics to begin with; *Ozma of Oz* for me does more good things for the whole stretch of the book than any other, but it would be unfair to it, and to the series as a whole, to call it Baum's masterpiece. He wrote too much, too quickly, and too restlessly to have a single book as his masterpiece. He tired of many individual books before they were ended, and he tired of the series as a whole before it was ended, yet he kept on with it, and some of the characters and incidents his admirers remember best come in odd places in otherwise not very good books. (pp. 236-39)

Baum's was such a rare gift that it seems almost impertinent to ask how good he is, or how much he achieved, or to try to assess his books with great soberness. He was careless of his art and he seldom wrote as well as he could; he never thought hard about life or grasped its complexities; he could not, even at his best, convey sadness or fear or deep joy. He has always been scorned, or guardedly admired, by the traditional custodians of children's literature, so he has had to find his audience in spite of teachers and librarians, for the most part. Yet his audience is still extremely large long after he and his naïve view of life have departed. The virtues of which these many apparently crushing limitations are only the defects are virtues of the sort we believe to exist in life far more than we ever expect to see in literature, and so Baum is rightly treasured more than many who seem to have a better claim on our respect and on our imagination. (p. 243)

Roger Sale, "L. Frank Baum and Oz" (originally published in a slightly different version in The Hudson Review, *Vol. XXV, No. 4, Winter, 1972-73), in his* Fairy Tales and After: From Snow White to E. B. White *(copyright © 1978 by the President and Fellows of Harvard College; excerpted by permission), Cambridge, Mass.: Harvard University Press, 1978, pp. 223-44.*

BRIAN ATTEBERY   (essay date 1980)

[Baum created Oz] with the aid of a paradox. It is Kansas—or rather, let us say, . . . it is the United States—and it is also everything that conditions in the United States make us wish for. Oz is America made more fertile, more equitable, more companionable, and, because it is magic, more wonderful. What Dorothy finds beyond the Deadly Desert is another America with its potential fulfilled: its beasts speaking, its deserts blooming, and its people living in harmony.

If Oz is America, then Dorothy is its Christopher Columbus. . . . Dorothy is the discoverer who opens up the newest new world; later she and other children . . . chart the unknown regions remaining in Oz and the lands around it. All of the stories are based on movement. They whisk one away from known lands with a dizzying swoop, proceed over land, water, and air toward a brief action, then take off again for home. In *The Road to Oz*, indeed, there can be said to be no plot at all except the journey of Dorothy, Button Bright, Polychrome, and the Shaggy Man to Oz. The journey motif owes something to traditional fairy tale structure, . . . but it owes as much or more to an American tradition of restlessness and curiosity. Happily, the discovery of Oz undoes some of the evils that accompanied the discovery of America. The natives accept the invaders, who, in turn, leave them in possession of their lands. Profit and progress are firmly excluded, and Oz remains the sleepy paradise it began. (p. 87)

Oz is at the turning point [of America's self-image]. It could only have been invented by someone who, like Baum, personally felt the gap between American ideals and American life. In this regard it is interesting to compare the Oz books . . . with another of Baum's series, the **"Aunt Jane's Nieces"** stories. The same values are upheld in both: generosity, simplicity, individuality, and industry; but, whereas in Oz the virtues define society, in the fictional "real world" they struggle for minor victories within a system responsive only to power and prestige. Aunt Jane's nieces rely on wealthy benefactors and on a shady detective named Quintus Fogerty to help them clean up patches of corruption, but Dorothy, in Oz, can destroy a witch with a bucket of water. (pp. 87-8)

The perfections of Oz would not be so poignant if they did not so strongly suggest qualities of American life at its rare best. In this respect, I would say that the primary source of secondary belief taken advantage of by Baum is the powerful but receding faith in the American Dream, rather than any corpus of supernatural legend. That faith has not yet left us entirely (it is kept alive partly by having been realized imaginatively in Oz) so that if Kansas, for example, is proven to be a part of the fallen world, there is still a glimpse of earthly paradise farther on, in California or Alaska or on the moon. (p. 88)

That, then, is Oz, a photograph of America with its blemishes filtered out, hand-tinted with the colors of the imagination. Topographically, the four quadrants of Oz seem to represent Baum's own personal geography. The East is Baum's New York childhood, a gentle land of forest and farm, with its residents scaled down just enough to make a child comfortable. One has the impression that the land of the Munchkins is a little older, more settled, than the other regions, and there are traces there of an "old-world" heritage, analogous to the costumes and customs retained by, say, Pennsylvania Germans. Baum's own family was German. . . .

If the Munchkins live in the settled East, the Winkies are Western frontiersmen. The western quarter of Oz is roughly equivalent to South Dakota, the westernmost point of Baum's early wanderings. The Winkie country is wild. . . .

Dorothy's Kansas is evidence that [Baum] was sensitive to the problems of his rural neighbors; it is a one-sided picture of the hardships of life on the prairies. The land of the Winkies is again a reflection of pioneer life, but with an element of optimism transforming gray waste into golden plenty. Though the West of Oz seems stern and forbidding, with a malevolent nature spirit—the Witch—in command, once the witch is vanquished we see it in a new light. The Winkies, out from under the thumb of cruel necessity, prove to be friendly and helpful. (p. 89)

North and South are less clearly defined. Dorothy does not visit the northern land of the Gillikins in the first volume, and by the time Baum began to explore it, Oz had become well established in its own right and did not reflect American geography so closely. We do know that its color is purple and that it is a mountainous, timbered, largely unsettled region. It vaguely suggests northern Michigan where Baum spent vacations, or Minnesota, or the great untracked expanse of Canada. The South is primarily a region of isolated communities of eccentrics, like the people made all of china in the first book. There is no clear connection between the land of the Quadlings and the American South, with which Baum was not familiar. Its queen, Glinda, is revered as a near-goddess, suggesting the Southern worship of genteel womanhood, but then Oz itself becomes a matriarchy when Ozma comes to power. South, for Baum, more probably meant the hills of southern Illinois, Indiana, and Missouri, where he traveled selling china. . . .

The sections of Oz are unquestionably influenced by American sectionalism, though their characteristics reflect Baum's own experience rather than traditional political or economic divisions. The Munchkins do not engage in New England style manufacturing nor the Quadlings in sharecropping: neither would be in keeping with an idealized fairyland. Nevertheless, the analog is clear. But what of the center, the radiant Emerald City? What, to Baum, was the capital and heart of the country? The answer must be Chicago, the scene of his first successes. . . . His Chicago was not the jungle of Upton Sinclair's shocking exposés, nor the brawling hog-butcher of Carl Sandburg's apostrophes. It was the shining, hopeful White City, built on the shores of Lake Michigan. . . . (p. 90)

Oz is not a utopia, though it has many utopian elements. It is something more lasting, a fairyland. The difference is that Oz, like any fantasy world, allows for—rather, demands—the existence of the impossible. How does Baum integrate the impossible into a setting derived from pragmatic American experience? The best way to point out his techniques is to look at . . . [the] earmarks of fantasy: narrative structure, hero, nonhuman characters, and a coherent system of magic and significance. The fact that Baum's work, American as it is, lends itself to analysis along these lines, which were drawn originally from the British fantasy tradition, is a sign of his unprecedented entry into the mainstream of fantasy after our hundred or so years of apprenticeship.

The land of Oz is a constant throughout the series, and so may be described as if all fourteen volumes were one evolving work. But there is no overall story structure to the set; each book must be considered individually. The most important story, and the most highly structured, is that of *The Wizard of Oz*. . . .

Baum was probably unaware of most of the scholarly work being done in his time by folklorists, and in any case he lived before the important analyses of the folktale, like [Vladimir] Propp's had been made. If his story corresponds in any significant measure to the traditional structure, it indicates not a studied imitation but an intuitive grasp of the fundamental dynamics of the folktale. (p. 91)

Baum not only intuitively understood fairy tale structure, but he was also able to adjust it at will to fit his needs. The sharp break between the opening segment and the ensuing action, for example, he made serve as a crossing of the threshold into another world. By doubling and tripling certain elements he was able to take advantage of his major strengths as a writer, the portrayal of movement and the quick and comical delineation of character. The embedded plot is neatly introduced by having one character, the Wizard, take on two functional roles. The Wizard is also placed in a central position in the book, structurally and geographically, with the result that at the heart of fairyland we find Omaha-born Oz Diggs, a reminder of the opening scene of the book and a forecast of its end. Baum's skill in handling the fairy tale story line—in making it his own—surpasses, I believe, that of any of the imitators of European style fairy tales . . . , just as his grasp of American character and landscape surpasses that of all his predecessors in the native, fairies-in-America line. (p. 93)

As Baum continued to write "modernized" tales, he grew bolder in his treatment of the fairy tale structure. *The Land of Oz* has an unconventional ending: the boy hero is revealed at last to be, not a king in disguise, but a queen, transformed by witchcraft into male form. In *Ozma of Oz* and several of the later Oz books, Dorothy becomes a sort of heroine errant, performing quests not for her own sake but for other, lesser characters; the hero role is broken up, that is, into an active but unconcerned protagonist and one or more passive but needy companions. *The Scarecrow of Oz* contains a fairy tale in burlesque, the "hero" of which is the most ineffectual character in the story. Some of the books, like *Dorothy and the Wizard in Oz* and *The Road to Oz*, suppress all phases of the fairy tale morphology except the quest-journey, but they still follow the proper sequence for that segment of the full structure. In others, like *The Emerald City of Oz, Tik-Tok of Oz,* and *Glinda of Oz,* a rival story line of conquest and siege all but overpowers the individualistic fairy tale development, perhaps reflecting America's growing awareness of international strife up to and during World War I. But the underlying pattern remains constant and occasionally, as in *Rinkitink of Oz,* reappears in classic form. (pp. 94-5)

An important literary source for *The Wizard,* and probably the primary inspiration for Dorothy herself, is Lewis Carroll's *Alice in Wonderland*. When Baum set about to construct a modernized fairy tale, *Alice* was one of the few examples available to him. . . . Baum considered Alice's adventure, "rambling and incoherent as it is," to be "one of the best and perhaps the most famous of modern fairy tales." . . . [For] Baum, who was considering it as a source book, the important thing about *Alice* is not its discovery of the absurd but its development of the fairy tale hero into a distinctive, perceiving individual. (pp. 95-6)

Baum threw away offhand everything but the spirit of *Alice in Wonderland,* and in doing so produced a far worthier successor. Dorothy and Alice are two of the most likeable heroines in literature, two witty and contemporary character sketches of the sort one finds in the best domestic comedies. Carroll discovered that such a character could be removed from the social world into the world of dream, and Baum took things one step further (in terms of violations of reality) into a world of waking marvels.

Though Alice and Dorothy are both portraits of believable, modern-day children, there are important differences between them. Dorothy, unlike Alice, never wonders who she is, where she is going, or why the world has suddenly turned upside down. "My name is Dorothy," she says to the Scarecrow after only one day in the land of Oz, "and I am going to the Emerald City, to ask the great Oz to send me back to Kansas.". . . (p. 96)

Alice is English; Dorothy is aggressively, triumphantly American. As the primary link between the naturalistically portrayed Kansas of the beginning and the transmogrified America that is Oz, she must be able to make explicit the comparisons between the two, and to do so she must be accepted by the reader as a valid representative of all things American. Therefore, Dorothy is not merely a fairy tale heroine, or a believable child, she is also heir to an American conception of character, especially of its own character. And what is the essential American character? Often it is the explorer, the wanderer, who penetrates ever wilder regions of the world or the mind and comes back relatively unscathed. (pp. 96-7)

Since Dorothy is female and a Westerner, she suggests one other category of character, another peculiarly American one: the pioneer woman. There are two classes of pioneer women in the popular imagination. One is faded and bleak and particularly appealing to local color writers with a naturalistic vision. That is Aunt Em. The other is lively and attractive, drawing her strength from the earth she lives so close to. That is, of course, Dorothy, who is to some degree a forerunner of the Nebraska heroine in Willa Cather's *My Antonia*. Throughout *The Wizard,* Dorothy gives her comrades guidance and encouragement, like a little mother. . . . She does an admirable job of keeping herself and Toto provided for on an arduous journey. Nurture, comfort, and guidance: these, in mythology, are the functions of the Earth Mother. If Dorothy were allowed to mature, we might imagine her something like the grown-up Antonia, full-figured, sun-burned to earth colors, radiating order, contentment, and fertility.

She does not grow up, however. An adult heroine would . . . bring back all those troublesome questions of belief and reason that drove Poe's heroes mad. So Baum imposed on Oz an end to aging, and Dorothy, rather than maturing, began to fall into a rather gushing girlishness. That is one of the primary weaknesses of the later books, so important is Dorothy's earthiness to the fantasy. (p. 98)

What about the characters around Dorothy? Just as she is the essential tie with the familiar, they are the wonder-working helpers and adversaries who must carry us into the marvelous. How does Baum stand up on . . . [the element] of fantasy, the assortment of nonhuman characters? Excellently, for the most part. From the Good Witch at the beginning of *The Wizard* to the fascinating Yookoohoo in *Glinda of Oz,* his last book, Baum produced with seeming ease a host of vivid, unquestionably magical beings: he brought a scarecrow to life, made an engaging eccentric out of an insect, revealed a common tramp to be a wonder worker, and made witches seem like his own invention. (p. 99)

Romance writers strained to find some replacement for the countless fairies, goblins, and curious beasts of European folklore. Children's writers of the later nineteenth century either borrowed wholesale from Europe or settled for whimsy. And then there is Baum reworking old motifs with unprecedented conviction and inventing new ones seemingly out of the blue. He not only created an American fairyland where there had been none, but he also filled it with Nomes in the earth, fairies in the air, and an astounding assortment of beings in between. (p. 104)

What kind of world view does Baum express through his use of magic?

The answer is, a limited one. Baum does adopt Hawthorne's system of symbolization, so that in whatever points a character differs physically from the norm, he is also likely to illustrate a moral issue. Jack Pumpkinhead has something to say about the pumpkin-headedness of us all, and so on for each speaking creature in Oz. But Baum's introduction of characters was haphazard and frequently dictated by his impatience with the progress of the plot. Enduring characters like Jack begin, through simple accretion, to take on some philosophical complexity, but his one-shot, ad hoc creations—the Fuddles of Fuddle-cumjig are a good example, being nothing more than a literalization of the phrase ''to go all to pieces''—can hardly be said to be artistic examinations of the problems of life. Nor are they meant to be. In the often quoted phrase that became the title for the standard biography of Baum, he wrote ''to please a child.'' It is for children, not for critical adults, that he upholds such uncontroversial virtues as kindness, generosity, and self-reliance. Ambivalence and sin, with their meatier dramas, he leaves to Hawthorne.

If there is a grander scheme of philosophy in the workings of Oz, it will show up in the essential rules of magic within which Baum operates, rather than in his piecemeal inventions. The following seem to me to be the fundamental magical operations throughout the series: animation, transformation, illusion, disillusion, transportation, protection, and luck. Now these are not unusual operations; they are found throughout fairy legend and *Märchen*. But Baum has set them up in a rudimentary system, and that is an important distinction between imitation of folk forms and creative fantasy.

Animation comes in several forms in the Oz books. . . . [The] Scarecrow's unexplained awakening and Jack Pumpkinhead's birth under Mombi's cackling midwifery [are examples]. (pp. 104-05)

Things always seem to be springing to life in Oz. . . . [It] is a remarkably fertile place. But what is the end result of all this magical procreation? It is almost always to the good. By this means Oz has been provided with some of its most valuable and colorful citizens. No one could wish the Scarecrow still hanging lifeless on his stake, or Jack Pumpkinhead rotting on a compost heap. . . . The principle here seems to be that it is better to exist than not, no matter what your form or foibles. These animations are part of a general tendency toward increasing richness of life; they represent a universe slanted toward Becoming. (p. 105)

[Some] characters are created for questionable reasons or by downright wicked characters like Mombi. But in every case, things turn out for the best. It is never wrong, in Baum's view, to create, and, indeed, it is difficult to help it.

Transformation is another matter. There are many people in Oz and its environs capable of transforming objects. . . . It would seem that transformation is a neutral art, usable for either good or evil ends. But there are two quite different sorts of transformation in Oz. What Mombi and her fellow villains do is to impose a new shape on an unwilling victim, or on themselves for evil purposes. What Dorothy and her friends do is to restore victims to their original form. (pp. 105-06)

In a sense, transformation is the opposite of animation. To desire to change the people and objects around one is to deny their intrinsic importance, to wish them, as it were, unmade.

The archetype of all transformations is that fearful operation, threatened by Mombi and performed accidentally by the ambiguous Crooked Magician, petrifaction. Turning someone to stone is the ultimate denial, and of course in Oz it must eventually be undone by the affirmative act of reanimation. . . .

Illusion and disillusion form another couplet like transformation and animation. Once more, the operation that denies reality is evil, and that which restores it is good. The implication is that reality is more wonderful than any obscuring of it, in fairyland or in the real world, a belief which would not seem to lead naturally into fantasy except for the fact that, for Baum, it never hurts to add to the store of existence through imagination. Generally the same people practice illusion as indulge in transformations. But anyone with a little insight can undo an illusion, simply by ignoring it. Several times Baum has his characters pass a seeming obstacle by closing their eyes and walking through, or poking it with a pin, or making friends with what appeared to be an enemy. (p. 106)

Transportation has no particular moral value in Oz, but it does act as a sign that anything in the world is possible and within reach. Dorothy's cyclone, the enchanted road in *The Road to Oz,* Ozma's magic carpet, and so on are simply variations of the traditional seven-league boots, which carry their owner to fame and fortune. Most of the modes of transportation to and within Oz are natural objects, rather than conscious agents. They represent the unpredictability of nature, which to Baum is rarely hostile but always amazing.

Protection and luck are really two views of the same thing. Glinda's spell of invisibility over Oz, the Good Witch's protective kiss, and the Shaggy Man's love magnet are the same as Ojo the Lucky's good fortune in *The Patchwork Girl.* The only difference is that luck is a more mysterious, pervasive thing, not traceable to any knowable cause. Both operations stress, again, the benevolence of the world. It is as if there were watchful parents everywhere, some visible and some invisible. (p. 107)

[These basic principles] do not make up a very new or rigorous philosophy. It is a child's vision that Baum is presenting, and so he shies away from any more darkness or complexity than he felt a child would be prepared to deal with. Writing for children freed Baum's imagination . . . , but the boon was also a limitation. We have no proof that Baum *could* have written a more mature work of fantasy than Oz, with a more demanding and rewarding reordering of the world's laws, but he certainly could not do so as long as he conceived of fairy tales as the province primarily of children. So we have the Oz books: simple, sunny, utterly delightful, but narrow in their range of emotion and significance.

Yet the barrier had been broken, effortlessly punctured like a wall of illusion. Baum proved, without doubt, that an American writer could write fantasy from American materials, even if those materials were significantly unlike the well-developed tales and legends available to European collectors and storytellers. Other writers could build on his accomplishment, as he built on the efforts of those before him, could gradually bring into their American fairylands those questions he left out. Even with his weaknesses, he is our Grimm and our Andersen, the man who introduced Americans to their own dreams. (pp. 107-08)

Brian Attebery, ''Oz,'' in The Fantasy Tradition in American Literature: From Irving to Le Guin *(copy-*

right © 1980 by Brian Attebery), Indiana University Press, 1980, pp. 83-108.

ADDITIONAL BIBLIOGRAPHY

Baughman, Roland. ''L. Frank Baum and the 'Oz Books'.'' *Columbia Library Columns* IV, No. 3 (May 1955): 15-35.
 Surveys the author's life and work and discusses the ageless appeal of his series.

Baum, Frank Joslyn, and MacFall, Russell P. *To Please a Child: A Biography of L. Frank Baum, Royal Historian of Oz*. Chicago: Reilly & Lee Co., 1961, 284 p.
 Comprehensive but highly subjective biography. The book, coauthored by Baum's oldest son, contains a number of anecdotes and reminiscences and provides a descriptive overview of Baum's work.

Bewley, Marius. ''The Land of Oz: America's Great Good Place.'' In his *Masks and Mirrors: Essays in Criticism,* pp. 255-67. New York: Atheneum, 1970.
 Outlines the major themes and styles of the Oz books. Bewley refutes the contention that Baum's writings lack style and states that ''at his best his prose reflects themes and tensions that characterize the central tradition of American literature.''

Ford, Alla T., and Martin, Dick. *The Musical Fantasies of L. Frank Baum*. Chicago: The Wizard Press, 1958, 80 p.
 Well-illustrated survey of Baum's musical comedies.

Gardner, Martin. ''The Librarians in Oz.'' *Saturday Review* XLII, No. 15 (11 April 1959): 18-19.
 A response to librarians who charge that Baum's series is poorly written, sensational, and unwholesome.

Hearn, Michael Patrick. *The Annotated ''Wizard of Oz.''* New York: Clarkson N. Potter, 1973, 384 p.
 Critical edition of Baum's best-known work.

Sackett, S.J. ''The Utopia of Oz.'' *The Georgia Review* XIV, No. 1 (Spring 1960): 275-91.
 Studies the Oz series as an example of Utopian literature.

Schuman, Samuel. ''Out of the Fryeing Pan and into the Pyre: Comedy, Myth and *The Wizard of Oz*.'' *Journal of Popular Culture* VII, No. 2 (Fall 1973): 302-04.
 Applies Northrop Frye's interpretation of ''the mythic pattern of comedy'' to *The Wizard of Oz*. Schuman maintains that the structure of the book fits the basic outline of Frye's theory that ''comedy reproduces the pattern of the fertility rite: 'the ritual of death and revival.'''

Ulveling, Ralph A. ''Ralph Ulveling on Freedom of Information.'' *American Library Association* 51, No. 9 (October 1957): 653, 655, 721.
 Brief article in which Ulveling, director of the Detroit Public Library, refutes the charge that *The Wizard of Oz* had been banned by the library.

(Joseph) Hilaire (Pierre) Belloc

1870-1953

English poet, essayist, travel writer, biographer, critic, historian, and novelist.

At the turn of the century Belloc was considered one of England's premier men-of-letters and a most provocative essayist. His characteristically truculent stance as a proponent of Roman Catholicism and economic reform, and his equally characteristic clever humor drew either strong support or harsh attacks from his audience. But critics find common ground for admiration in his poetry. Belloc and his long-time friend and collaborator G. K. Chesterton have been lauded by W. H. Auden as the best light-verse writers of their era, with Belloc's *Cautionary Tales* considered by some his most successful work in the genre.

The son of a French father and English mother, Belloc was born in St. Cloud, France, but raised in England, studying at the best private schools. From his studies and his travels between England and France, Belloc acquired cosmopolitan interests in history, polemics, and literature, but retained anti-Semitic beliefs common to nineteenth-century France that mar some of his works. After brief service in the French military and a brilliant stint at Oxford's Balliol College, Belloc began writing for various London newspapers and magazines. His first book, *Verses and Sonnets,* appeared in 1896, followed by *The Bad Child's Book of Beasts,* which satirized moralistic light verse. His *Danton,* published three years later, was the first of several biographies on figures of the French Revolution. Critics have noted numerous inaccuracies in Belloc's many biographies and histories, but they also acknowledge his ability to vivify the past by using the techniques common to today's historical novel, such as reconstructed dialogues and fictional incidents based on informed guesswork.

Belloc's career as a Roman Catholic advocate began in 1902 with *The Path to Rome,* perhaps his most famous book, in which he recorded the thoughts and impressions inspired by a walking trip through France and Italy to Rome. In addition to its infusion of Catholic thought, the book reflects typically Bellocian elements—rich humor, an eye for natural beauty, and a meditative spirit—all of which appear in the author's other popular travel books: *Esto Perpetua, The Four Men,* and *The Cruise of the "Nona."* Belloc's Christian humanism, with its lively Rabelaisian irreverence, colored these works and much of his prose canon. Closely linked to his Catholic beliefs was Belloc's proposed economic and political program called Distributism, a system of small ownership harking back to Europe's pre-Reformation history, and fully described in the controversial 1912 essay *The Servile State.* Belloc also championed political honesty and accountability during his brief career as a Liberal in the House of Commons. He found an ally for promoting his religious and political beliefs in Chesterton. The two opposed the agnostic socialism of Fabians Bernard Shaw and H. G. Wells in a lively series of essays and debates, and founded *The New Witness,* a journal used to advance their ideas. Chesterton and Belloc also worked together on several books as illustrator and author respectively, becoming known to their public as an inseparable team. They

were jointly pilloried and immortalized in an essay by Shaw as a bombastic, ridiculous beast called the Chesterbelloc. Belloc proved, in such collections as *On Everything* and *On Nothing,* that he could write convincing and forceful essays on nearly any subject, as either controversialist or defender of the *status quo,* in a prose style marked by clarity and wit. His reputation as a polemicist reached its zenith in 1926, when he attacked Wells's *Outline of History* as simplistic and anti-Catholic in *A Companion to Mr. Well's "Outline of History."* This broadside prompted a year-long war of mutual refutation waged by Belloc and Wells in several books and essays.

As Belloc aged and his socio-political theories were brushed aside by a public more interested in Shavian and Wellsian thought, he grew increasingly bitter, and devoted much of his time to writing histories and biographies. In his last years his once lucid writing style became increasingly impenetrable. At the time of his death, Belloc had published 153 books, very few of which are read today. Constantly looking to the past—particularly to the Middle Ages—for his ideals, Belloc encountered understandable difficulty in influencing modern readers; his desire to return to the values of an authoritarian epoch, as well as his recurrent anti-Semitism both contributed to his eclipse as a major literary figure.

PRINCIPAL WORKS

The Bad Child's Book of Beasts   (verse) 1896
Verses and Sonnets   (poetry and verse) 1896
More Beasts—For Worse Children   (verse) 1897
The Modern Traveller   (verse) 1898
Danton   (biography) 1899
Lambkin's Remains   (fictional biography) 1900
Robespierre   (biography) 1901
The Path to Rome   (travel sketches) 1902
Caliban's Guide to Letters   (satirical essays) 1903
Avril   (essays) 1904
Emmanuel Burden   (novel) 1904
Esto Perpetua   (travel sketches) 1906
Cautionary Tales   (verse) 1907
On Nothing   (essays) 1908
Marie Antoinette   (biography) 1909
On Everything   (essays) 1909
The French Revolution   (history)   1911
The Four Men   (travel sketches) 1912
The Servile State   (essay) 1912
The Free Press   (essay) 1918
The Jews   (essay) 1922
The Cruise of the "Nona"   (travel sketches) 1925
A Companion to Mr. Wells's "Outline of History"
    (criticism) 1926
Many Cities   (travel sketches) 1928
New Cautionary Tales   (verse) 1930
Milton   (biography) 1935
Elizabethan Commentary   (history) 1942

THE SPECTATOR   (essay date 1898)

[*The Modern Traveller*] is in outward appearance a child's book, and doubtless it will give immense pleasure to thousands of children. In reality, however, it is an extremely spirited and happy piece of satire on the sensational explorer, the commercial empire-builder, and the cosmopolitan traveller who paints the map red. But satire, though we cannot find a better, is in truth far too heavy a word for this light, inconsequent, sly chatter in verse, where the points are doubly pointed because you never know whether they are meant or accidental. Imagine the patter and topical songs at a pantomime written by some one with a real literary instinct, and who is intellectually the descendant of Lear and Lewis Carroll, and our readers will understand the enchanting, haphazard, touch-and-go quality of our author's verse. In Lear's *Nonsense-Book* or in *Alice in Wonderland* there are a hundred shrewd hits at the follies of the time. So here we see the modern millionaire, the modern empire-builder, the "copy"-hunting traveller, and the newspaper explorer touched again and again on the hip. And yet the victim is never quite run through. The point is never quite pressed home or the moral inevitably drawn. It is an essential part of the game not to do so. It is satire,—but only by confession and avoidance. Just as the sword is going through—whoever may seem in danger of being spitted, it is turned aside with a harmless flourish in the air. The moment we get near to a real application, hey Presto! the joke has passed, and we go to something new. In truth, here is the spirit of true nonsense,— kindly and of universal application, easy and without a conscious motive, and therefore always delightful. (p. 778)

"Books: 'The Modern Traveller'," in The Spectator, Vol. 81, No. 3674, November 26, 1898, pp. 778-79.*

CECIL CHESTERTON   (essay date 1906)

[Mr. Hilaire Belloc's] detachment from modern English tendencies is very marked in his writings. It is, I believe, the true cause of that peculiar kind of paradox (at least most people would call them paradoxes) of which he appears so fond. His paradoxes are quite unlike those which other writers have made fashionable. They are not polished and ingenious inversions like the paradoxes of Oscar Wilde. Nor do they bear any resemblance to the paradoxes of Mr. Bernard Shaw or of another writer whom family circumstances forbid me to name. These writers are consciously pugnacious. They know that their propositions will startle and perplex. They arm themselves; they amplify and defend their views. Not so Mr. Belloc. He states, or more generally, implies, his paradoxes, as if he and all his readers regarded them as truisms. . . . [In] his introduction to Carlyle he speaks of France as a nation characterized by "a *military* hatred of mere force." I fancy that many modern English readers, unacquainted with Mr. Belloc's philosophy, must have read this sentence over several times in the vain endeavour to discover the misprint!

But all this only intensifies his power as a satirist. The very fact that the normal English assumptions do not strike him as normal makes it easy for him to render them suddenly grotesque. No one, whether he likes Mr. Belloc's opinions or not, can deny the sharp edge of the laughter in **"Lambkin's Remains,"** in **"Caliban's Guide to Letters,"** and in **"Mr. Burden."** The humour in these books is something personal, incommunicable, only to be defined by examples. Its chief note is a very quiet, almost secretive irony, which makes it possible to read a sentence several times before all its honey is tasted. "Jules de la Vaguère de Bissac was the first of his family to bear that ancient name, but not the least worthy." (pp. 389-91)

But it is not only his insight or his humour which makes Mr. Belloc so pre-eminently interesting a figure. It is the fact that he is one of the very few contemporary writers who has a quite definite and coherent philosophy of life. Through all his books, from serious and scholarly historical studies like **"Danton"** and **"Robespierre"** to wild carnivals of absurdity like **"Lambkin"** and **"Caliban,"** you will find that the basic point of view never varies. In **"Esto Perpetua"** he describes the threefold power that is necessary to the triumph of ideas: "First, that they are novel and attack those parts of the mind still sensitive; secondly, that they are expounded with conviction (conviction necessary to the conveyance of doctrine): and, thirdly, that they form a system and are final." All this may be claimed for Mr. Belloc's own philosophy.

What is the central message that Mr. Belloc is trying to formulate? Well, I think it may be expressed, very crudely, thus: That men in order to be tolerably happy must be continually returning to the ancient, the simple, the normally human things. He is at one with other reformers in that he finds the present condition of the civilized world intolerable and demands its overthrow. But he differs from them in this, that while they think of the world as always moving slowly forward towards a dimly discerned Utopia, he thinks of it as continually slipping back from the simplicity and sanity at which men are always aiming, and which now and again they almost achieve. (p. 392)

I think that in the main Mr. Belloc is herein saner and more in touch with facts than the more Utopian school of revolutionists. Like other men whose ideas form a system he sometimes pushes them to the point of extravagance. For example, there may be force in his contention that it is a part of man's normal desire to impress his personality upon the things around him, to "own" them as we say; yet I feel that, when he extends this proposition to include railway shares and freehold ground rents, he is himself losing his grip on realities and, to use the expression which he applies to Roberspierre, "going to the Devil by logic." (p. 393)

Closely connected with Mr. Belloc's attitude towards politics and history is his attitude towards religion. No man ever talked about his religion so much, flaunted it so defiantly, defended it so pugnaciously Yet the levity with which he treats it is startling to the reverent and discreet persons who do not believe what he believes. A friend of mine complained to me the other day of this element in **"The Path to Rome."** "I have," he said, "the deepest reverence for the Roman Catholic Church. I feel that if I found a little wayside shrine I could worship at it with the most whole-hearted sincerity. And then Belloc comes along and hangs his boots on it!" Certainly there is in **"The Path to Rome,"** and indeed in all Mr. Belloc's books, that which is calculated to startle the respectful sceptic. But it would be just because he was a sceptic that it would startle him. It was just because my friend thought of Catholicism as a beautiful illusion that the world was losing that he would have spoken of it as gently and reverently as one would speak of a dead love. And it is just because Mr. Belloc thinks the Catholic Church the eternal Home of the human spirit, the House built on a rock against which the Gates of Hell shall not prevail, that he chaffs it, as men chaff their wives and their old friends. There is nothing of the "devout layman" about him. His religious instinct is satisfied by the ancient forms of his Church. It is not, like the religious feeling of many moderns, driven back into the soul to poison the well-springs of laughter.

It is the old things that he loves; it is in celebrating them that he rises to sudden heights of poetry. Youth and feasting and comradeship and birth and death,—he feels vividly the reality of them, of the last not least vividly for all his gaiety. One does not forget the wonderful end of **"Emmanuel Burden,"**— "that primaeval Fear which has no name among living men."

Is it that fear alone which lies ahead of our civilization? Or will it after years of suffering, perhaps of slaughter and destruction, win back the youth that it has lost? Neither Mr. Belloc nor anyone else can answer that question. But this thing at least he has preached to our generation; that there is no way to the Kingdom of God but the way of an ancient simplicity. (pp. 394-95)

Cecil Chesterton, "Hilaire Belloc," in Temple Bar, *Vol. CXXXIV, No. 11, November, 1906, pp. 385-95.*

MAURICE BARING (essay date 1923)

In the year 1896, Mr. Hilaire Belloc published in London a small book of verse containing sixty-four hard pages of verse that, in a sense, was as hard as the paper on which it was printed. [*Verses and Sonnets*] was printed on cardboard, the pages are the stiffest to turn I have ever come across, and the verse had something which, at the time, appeared to be more durable than the kind of stuff which was appearing then. . . .

There is, in the early volume, a poem called **"Auvergnat"** which has lived during all that period; that is to say, it has been quoted in anthologies. . . . It also contains some sonnets, noble for gleams of vision and fitful, strong chords of expression where rhetoric suddenly melts into poetry. It also reveals an undeveloped but decided gift for epigram; and yet it seems to me that few people with this little book in their hands would have dared to prophesy great things of its writer. Or, had they prophesied, it is most likely that they would have foreseen a great prose writer and not a poet. And now, twenty-seven years later, appears a book of collected verse from an author who is known throughout the world as a writer of prose and verse, but chiefly known—to the large public, that is to say—as a writer on the War and as a writer of children's verse. This book of collected poems, to my mind at least, proves something else—I am not the least afraid of prophesying in this case, and I am quite willing to affront or confront and face the possible jeers of posterity—that Mr. Belloc has, in his collected volume, contributed to the permanent storehouse of English verse. (pp. 284-85)

[As] long as there are books, books of verse, and books of English verse—readers of various anthologies, old men and young men who read Chaucer, Shakespeare, Pope, Byron, Wordsworth, Keats, Crabbe, and any others you like to name— I am sure those same readers will read with admiration and delight a great deal of the verse Mr. Belloc has included in his latest volume.

There are, to begin with, thirty-one sonnets; and among them a few of the quite early ones of 1896. They are packed with "fundamental brain work"; they are carefully wrought; they are, if anything, over-wrought. You feel that some of them remained in the mind of the poet for years and years; that he has ruminated on them, chewed them, turned them over and over again, accepted this word and rejected that; and then once more rejected what he has accepted and reverted to what he had rejected. The result to my mind is a gallery of highly wrought works of art, if anything too highly wrought, like clothes that have been fitted and refitted until they fit too well. But, after all, that is of little consequence compared with the gleams of vision in these poems and the mastery, restraint, strength, and beauty of the expression. . . . Personally—noble as the work in these sonnets is, stern as is the stuff they are made of, and priceless their fitful gleams of vision—I do not think that it is in the sonnet that Mr. Belloc is most successful. His sonnets have sometimes the complexity of Shakespeare's without their fundamental ease and lucidity, and at moments the baldness of Wordsworth without the supreme sweep of simplicity that in Wordsworth carries you off your feet. But you notice, and I hope he will notice, that it is with Shakespeare and Wordsworth that one compares him, when talking of sonnets.

Next to the sonnets, there are the lyrical poems and ballads, one of which, **"The South Country,"** is perpetually quoted and to be found in many anthologies. In this poem the technical mastery is just as sure, complete and complex, but the elf of poetry is definitely caught in the net; for instance in these lines:

> Comes surely from our Sister the Spring
> When over the sea she flies;
> The violets suddenly bloom at her feet,
> She blesses us with surprise.

He does the same trick to my mind in a higher degree in the poem called **"Ha'nacker Mill,"** which has not only lilt, but an undefinable, vague, haunting suggestion of poetry, sadness, and doom about it. It says what it has got to say quite perfectly, but it suggests at the same time a great deal more than it says. It has magic. The same could be said of the poem which follows it in the book, **"Tarantella."** But if I were asked to quote an instance of Mr. Belloc at his very best, when his vision and his feeling are expressed at their highest pitch and are mingled, without being overladen or overcomplicated by his technical skill or by his sometimes too-active brain work, I should quote . . . from the *Dedicatory Ode*. . . . (pp. 287-89)

There are, in the book, poems which belong to four other categories. First of all, the Drinking Songs; the best of these are not in this book at all, but are to be found in a book called *The Four Men*. . . . There are, however, some good drinking songs in this book. There is this to be noted about them; they are songs that were written to be sung to definite tunes and which have been sung. It is quite wrong to call them *pastiches*. The poet probably had the tune ringing in his head to begin with, and wrote the words to suit the tune. In *The Four Men,* indeed, he gives us bars of the tunes themselves which suggested the songs.

Then there are the satirical poems. Of these one need say little, for Mr. Belloc is well known as a writer of satirical verse; but what his readers, who read and so frequently misquote these happy lines of his probably do not realise is, that his skill in this line, his cleanness and neatness of touch, his unerring rhythm (like that of W. S. Gilbert's) are quite inimitable. Even the most skilful parodists, who try to parody Mr. Belloc's light verse, even Mr. Max Beerbohm and Mr. J. C. Squire, fail; they cannot get either the requisite strength of swing, the underlying gusto, or the superficial neatness, the sharp, swift rapier play, to the same extent as their model. (pp. 290-91)

Next to the satirical verse, there is one special gift of Mr. Belloc's which I think needs pointing out, and that is his peculiar gift for writing ballades. This is a very rare gift. . . . [In] the history of literature when the ballade was first used by writers such as [François] Villon, . . . it was used to express deep and grave thoughts; its expression was intensified by the monotonous iteration of the rhymes and the stern discipline of the whole vehicle. . . . But since the death of Villon, who has written ballades of that kind? Well, Mr. Belloc has done it twice or three times in this book. Look at the last stanza of his **"Drinking Dirge."** . . . He does it again more vehemently in his **"Ballade to our Lady of Czestochowa,"** . . . and again, in his **"Ballade of Unsuccessful Men."** . . . (pp. 291-92)

Finally, there are Mr. Belloc's epigrams, in which you get the quintessence of his poetical talent. I use talent in the German sense, in the sense which Goethe used it about Byron. In this book he has not published what are, perhaps, the most successful of his satirical epigrams, but of the serious ones nothing could be better than the lines **"On a Dead Hostess"** . . . and **"The Statue."** . . . (p. 292)

I saw it stated in a review that nothing of the kind had been written as good as this since Landor. To my mind, in these epigrams Mr. Belloc succeeds in catching in his no-less-perfect net an elusive elf that escaped the classical strands of Landor's snare although he set it never so wisely. (p. 293)

Maurice Baring, "Mr. Belloc's Poems" (1923), in his Punch and Judy & Other Essays *(reprinted by permission of the Estate of the late Maurice Baring), William Heinemann, 1924, pp. 283-93.*

LEONARD WOOLF   (essay date 1925)

I have just read **"The Cruise of the 'Nona'"** . . . , of which the framework is Mr. Belloc's cruisings in his boat, the "Nona," but the substance is Mr. Belloc's reflections on life. Mr. Belloc is too good and too skilled a journalist not to be able to write still with an appearance of gusto, but the book itself leaves one with a bitter, dusty, gritty taste in the mouth.

The psychology of Mr. Belloc is an interesting study. The impression which this book leaves on one is that it is written by a man with a grievance. He is one of those Roman Catholics who is always throwing his "Christianity" in your face, and yet seems to have a profound contempt for the actual teaching of Jesus Christ. For instance, "he that is without sin among you, let him first cast a stone at her," but Mr. Belloc carries stone-throwing and uncharitableness to a pitch that is almost pathological. A man has to have been dead a very long time before Mr. Belloc has a good word for him, and even among the dead only those get a meed of praise who can be used in some way as sticks to beat Mr. Belloc's living enemies. In the whole of this book there are only, I think, two living people who get a word of praise; one of them is Mussolini, but then, as Mr. Belloc tells us, Mussolini has taken as one of his "first principles the restoration of the crucifix to the schools, and insisted upon the official world hearing Mass." On the other hand, Mr. Belloc is continually abusing, condemning, delivering judgment against other people (see Matthew vii. 1-5). Politicians, Germans, lawyers, scientists, Jews, historians, dons, capitalists, Labour leaders, writers—they are all of them corrupt, liars, swindlers, bullies, and thieves, and verily there is only one righteous man in the city, and his name is Hilaire Belloc. There is, of course, a great deal of truth in what Mr. Belloc has to say against modern political and other conditions, but he spoils his case by perpetually nagging, and still more by making it unconsciously a case of personal grievance. . . .

[One] reason why the flowers of Mr. Belloc's youthful talents withered is, I believe, to be found in his attitude towards truth. Truth is nothing to him, or perhaps his dislikes and grievances so obsess him that he now no longer realizes the meaning or possibility of objective truth. This is not very important when he is merely accusing people whom he dislikes of being humbugs and swindlers, though it becomes a little wearisome to be told that "outside the Catholic world . . . it is an approved idea that a lawyer may do his utmost to have an innocent man condemned, if only he be paid highly enough," that trade union leaders are corrupt and sell themselves to the masters, and that the motives of all men, other than Mr. Belloc and a few Catholic priests, are uniformly mean. But Mr. Belloc is himself not content to keep to this plane of personal animosity, of ascribing motives, and of a catholic uncharitableness; half his book is occupied with lectures on subjects like religion, history, and science in which—in my opinion—it is essential that the lecturer should be able to be occasionally impersonal and should have at least a glimmer of the meaning of truth. Mr. Belloc simply has not got the vestige of any such glimmer. Science, as he says, is to him "a mysterious untested authority dressed up in Print, violent in affirmation, ceaselessly contradicting itself, empty of thought." I suppose that there are people who find that kind of sentence amusing and illuminating when they read it in a weekly journal, but I cannot believe that there can be many who like it repeated, with variations of form and subject, by the same author through a book of 347 pages, and in every book which he has published for the last twenty years. But the important point is that an author who goes on writing that kind of rubbish for twenty years, even when he has the brilliant talents with which Mr. Belloc started, no longer at the end of it has any conception of the difference between what is true and what is false. Mr. Belloc, for instance has now got to the stage at which he seems to think that "it may be true" is equivalent to "it is true," provided that you want it to be true or that your great-great-grandmother, not being a Jew, Protestant, atheist, or scientist, believed it to be true.

It is extraordinary that a man like Mr. Belloc, who is always abusing other people for believing in quackery and Mumbo-Jumbo, should himself be one of the chief quacks and Mumbo-Jumboists of what he calls "this our time." Or perhaps it is not extraordinary, for there is nothing like the bitterness of domestic quarrels. But it is amusing to see him, after spending pages in sticking pins into scientists and Protestants for believing in quackery, suddenly turn round and solemnly discourse about what he calls "Catholic civilization," the most astonishing farrago of history, pseudo-history, theology, Mumbo-Jumbo, and personal prejudice that any sane man even in a dream has ever mistaken for the truth.

There are considerable portions of the book devoted to sailing and cruising, and they are much better than those which deal with Mr. Belloc's grievances, though he cannot for long forget these even on the sea. Also since the days of **"The Path to Rome"** he has developed a kind of "Wardour Street English," journalistic tricks and perversions of natural language which are apparently supposed to be impressive, but which simply set my teeth on edge. For instance, why should a man say: "There did we put out our warping ropes," and "so went I northward," instead of "we put out our warping ropes there" and "so I went northward," unless he has some false notion of "fine writing" at the back of his mind?

> *Leonard Woolf, "Mr. Belloc," in* The Nation and the Athenaeum *Vol. XXXVII, No. 7, May 16, 1925, p. 207.*

VIRGINIA WOOLF   (essay date 1925)

Where [Charles] Lamb wrote one essay and Max [Beerbohm] perhaps writes two, Mr. Belloc at a rough computation produces three hundred and sixty-five. They are very short, it is true. Yet with what dexterity the practised essayist will utilise his space—beginning as close to the top of the sheet as possible, judging precisely how far to go, when to turn, and how, without sacrificing a hair's-breadth of paper, to wheel about and alight accurately upon the last word his editor allows! As a feat of skill it is well worth watching. But the personality upon which Mr. Belloc, like Mr. Beerbohm, depends suffers in the process. It comes to us not with the natural richness of the speaking voice, but strained and thin and full of mannerisms and affectations, like the voice of a man shouting through a megaphone to a crowd on a windy day. (p. 303)

> *Virginia Woolf, "The Modern Essay," in her* The Common Reader *(copyright 1925 by Harcourt Brace Jovanovich, Inc.; copyright 1953 by Leonard Woolf; reprinted by permission of the publisher), Harcourt, 1925 (and reprinted as* The Common Reader, first and second series, *by Harcourt, 1948, pp. 293-308).**

H. G. WELLS   (essay date 1926)

I am responsible for an *Outline of History* which has had a certain vogue. . . . It is a careful summary of man's knowledge of past time. It has recently been reissued with considerable additions in an illustrated form; and Mr. Belloc has made a great attack upon it. He declares that I am violently antagonistic to the Catholic Church, an accusation I deny very earnestly, and he has produced a "Companion" to this *Outline* of mine, following up the periodical issue, part by part, in the *Universe* of London, in the *Catholic Bulletin* of St. Paul, Minnesota, in the *Southern Cross* of Cape Colony, and possibly elsewhere, in which my alleged errors are exposed and confuted.

In the enthusiasm of advertisement before the "Companion" began to appear, these newspapers announced a work that would put Mr. Belloc among the great classical Catholic apologists, but I should imagine that this was before the completed manuscript of Mr. Belloc's work had come to hand, and I will not hold Catholics at large responsible for all Mr. Belloc says and does.

It is with this *Companion to the Outline of History* that I am to deal here. It raises a great number of very interesting questions, and there is no need to discuss the validity of the charge of Heresy that is levelled against me personally. I will merely note that I am conscious of no animus against Catholicism. . . . (pp. 1-2)

In this art of controversy it is evident that great importance attaches to pose. This is plain from the very outset of Mr. Belloc's apologia. . . . He advances upon me in his Introduction with a gravity of utterance, a dignity of gesture, rare in sober, God-fearing men. There is a slow, formal compliment or so. I have, I learn, "a deservedly popular talent in fiction." I am sincere, an honest soul. My intentions are worthy. But the note changes; he declares I am a "Protestant writing for Protestants," and there is danger that my *Outline* may fall into Catholic hands. Some Catholics may even be infected with doubt. His style thickens with emotion at this thought, and he declares: "One Catholic disturbed in his faith is more important than twenty thousand or a hundred thousand or a million of the average reading public of England and America." That is why he is giving me his attention, syndicating these articles and swelling himself up so strongly against me. That is why he now proposes to exhibit and explain and expose me in the sight of all mankind. It is controversy, and everyday manners are in abeyance.

The controversial pose reveals itself further. The compliments and civilities thin out and vanish. Mr. Belloc becomes more magisterial, relatively larger, relatively graver, with every paragraph. He assumes more definitely the quality of a great scholar, of European culture and European reputation, a trained, distinguished, universally accepted historian. With what is evidently the dexterity of an expert controversialist and with an impressivness all his own, he seems to look over and under and round the man he knows, and sketches in the man he proposes to deal with, his limitations, his pitiful limitations, the characteristics, the disagreeable characteristics, that disfigure him. It is a new Wells, a most extraordinary person. I learn with amazement the particulars with which it is necessary to instruct that Catholic soul in danger before the matter of my book can be considered. I see myself in the lurid illumination of Catholic truth.

To begin with, I am "an intense patriot." This will surprise many readers. . . . I might plead that almost any chapter of the *Outline of History* could be quoted against this proposition. But Mr. Belloc is ruthless; he offers no evidence for his statement, no foothold for a counter-plea. He just says it, very clearly, very emphatically several times over, and he says it, as I realise very soon, because it is the necessary preliminary to his next still more damaging exposures.

They are that I am an Englishman "of the Home Counties and London Suburbs"—Mr. Belloc, it seems, was born all over Europe—that my culture is entirely English, that I know nothing of any language or literature or history or science but that of England. And from this his creative invention sweeps on to a description of this new Wells he is evoking to meet his controversial needs. My admiration grows. I resist an impulse to go over at once to Mr. Belloc's side. This, for example, is splendid. This new Wells, this suburban English Protestant, has written his *Outline of History* because, says Mr. Belloc, "he does not know that 'Foreigners' (as he would call them) have general histories."

That "as he would call them" is the controversial Mr. Belloc rising to his best.

Mr. Belloc, I may note in passing, does not cite any of these general histories to which he refers. It would surely make an interesting list and help the Catholic soul in danger to better reading. The American reader, at whose prejudices this stuff about my patriotism is presumably aimed, would surely welcome a competing Outline by a "foreigner." Mr. Belloc might do worse things than a little translation work.

Then the Royal College of Science shrivels at his touch to a mechanics' institute, and the new Wells, I learn, "does really believe from the bottom of his heart all that he read in the text-books of his youth." The picture of this new Wells, credulous, uncritical devourer of the text-books supplied by his suburban institute, inveterate Protestant, grows under the pen of this expert controversialist. I have next to be presented as a low-class fellow with a peculiar bias against the "Gentry of my own country," and this is accordingly done. "Gentlemen" with whom I have quarrelled are hinted at darkly—a pretty touch of fantasy. A profound and incurable illiteracy follows as a matter of course.

Mr. Belloc's courage gathers with the elaboration of his sketch. He is the type to acquiesce readily in his own statements, and one can see him persuading himself as he goes along that this really is the Wells he is up against. If so, what is there to be afraid of? If there is a twinge of doubt, he can always go back and read what he has written. The phraseology loses its earlier discretion, gets more pluckily abusive. Presently words like "ignorance" and "blunders" and "limited instruction" come spluttering from those ready nibs. Follows "childish" and "pitiable" and "antiquated nonsense." Nothing to substantiate any of it—just saying it. So Mr. Belloc goes his way along the primrose path of controversy. He takes a fresh sip or so from his all too complaisant imagination. New inspirations come. I have "copied" things from the "wrong" books. That "copied" is good! One can see that base malignant Wells fellow, in his stuffy room all hung with Union Jacks, with the "wrong," the "*Protestant*" book flattened out before him, copying, copying; his tongue following his laborious pen. Presently I read: "It is perhaps asking too much of our author to adopt a strictly scientific attitude." This, from an adept in that mixture of stale politics and gossip which passed for history in the days of Mr. Belloc's reading, to even the least of Huxley's students, is stupendous!

Still he swells and swells with self-importance and self-induced contempt for his silent and invisible antagonist. . . . The thin

film of oily politeness in the opening paragraphs is long since gone and done with, and Mr. Hilaire Belloc is fully himself again and remains himself, except for one or two returns to patronising praise and the oil squirt, for the rest of these remarkable papers. (pp. 2-5)

There is, however, one reference to the unlettered suburbanism of this ideal Wells too good to lose. I had almost let it slip by. It is an allusion to a certain publication in French. "There may be no translation," Mr. Belloc throws out superbly at the height of his form, "but Mr. Wells ought to have heard of"—the out-of-date monograph in question. "There may be no translation . . . "! How feeble sounds my protest that for all practical purposes I read French as well as I do English, and that in all probability if it came to using a German, Spanish, Portuguese, or Italian scientific work I could give Mr. Belloc points and a beating. (pp. 5-6)

His skill is undeniable; no other writer could better his unpremeditated condescension, his apparently inadvertent insults. And yet the facts beneath all this insolent posturing are quite well known and easily verifiable. I cannot imagine whom it is intended to deceive for any length of time.

Mr. Belloc is a man four years my junior, and his academic career was briefer and not more brilliant than mine. Since he came down from Oxford to the world of London thirty years ago, he has done no original historical work of any distinction. He has been a popular writer as I have been a popular writer, and he is no more if no less a scholar than I am. There has been much incidental and inconsequent brightness in his discursive career—funny verses and stories, . . . and he has done quite a number of clever revivifications of this or that historical event. That is his record. It gives him a respectable position in the republic of letters, in which also my position is respectable. No doubt he has every right and very considerable qualifications for the criticism of such a popular work as my *Outline*. But there is nothing in his career and nothing in his quality to justify this pose erudition and insolent superiority he assumes towards me, and which he has made an integral part of his attack. He has assumed it entirely in relation to this controversy. He has thrown ordinary courtesy and good manners to the winds because only in that way can he hope for a controversial advantage over me.

This disconcerting pose is part of his attack. That is why I am obliged to discuss it here. Upon many points the attack is almost pure pose; there is no tangible argument at all. It is very important to note that and bear that in mind. It has to be borne in mind when Mr. Belloc is accused of inordinate vanity or of not knowing his place in the world. . . . I realised long ago that his apparent arrogance is largely the self-protection of a fundamentally fearful man. He is a stout fellow in a funk. He is the sort of man who talks loud and fast for fear of hearing the other side. (pp. 6-7)

The necessity for a pose involving this pretence is not very difficult to understand. Long before Mr. Belloc embarked upon the present dispute he had become the slave of a tactical fiction, which reiteration had made a reality for him. . . . He has come to believe this: that there is a vast "modern European" culture of which the English-speaking world knows nothing, of which the non-Catholic world knows nothing, and with which he is familiar. It is on his side. It is always on his side. It is simply and purely Belloccian. He certainly believes it is there. It sustains his faith. It assuages the gnawing attacks of self-criticism that must come to him in the night. Throughout these papers he is constantly referring to this imaginary stuff—without ever coming to precisions. Again and again and again and again—and again and again and again, he alludes to this marvellous "European" science and literature, beyond our ken.

He does not quote it; it does not exist for him to quote; but he believes that it exists. He waves his hand impressively in the direction in which it is supposed to be. It is his stand-by, his refuge, his abiding fortress. But, in order to believe in it, it is necessary for him to believe that no other English-speaking men can even read French, and that their scepticism about it is based on some "provincial" prejudice or some hatred of Catholics, or southern people, or "Dagoes," or "foreigners," or what you will. That is why *Nature* wilfully ignores the wonderful science of this "Europe"; and why our Royal Society has no correspondence with it. But he has to imagine it is there and make his readers imagine it is there, and that there is this conspiracy of prejudice to ignore it, before he can even begin to put up any appearance of a case against such a résumé of current knowledge as the *Outline of History*. (pp. 8-9)

> H. G. Wells, "Mr. Belloc's Arts of Controversy,"
> in his Mr. Belloc Objects to "The Outline of History," Watts & Co., 1926, pp. 1-9.

V. SACKVILLE-WEST (essay date 1928)

I hope that Mr. Belloc will not take it amiss if I say that he reminds me in some degree of Mr. Cunninghame Graham. . . . Both esteem the past and the traditions of the past, far above the rush and vulgarity of the present. Both, as travellers, advocate the more leisurely methods of travel; which may seem a slight thing but is in fact indicative of their whole attitude of mind. Both have the liveliest possible sense of the uncompromising dignity and reserve that they find in Spain; again, an indication of their general temperament. Both are masters of a prose style marred only by the occasional irritating archaism. Putting all these things together, we cannot but conclude that the flower of their writings has its roots in the same kind of soil—a soil enriched by the cnturies, watered by the great streams of tradition, warmed by a southern sun and overshadowed by "that silent doom," to quote Mr. Belloc, "whereby states far nobler and greater than our own must go to sleep at last, and die in their sleep."

The many cities on which Mr. Belloc meditates [in *Many Cities*] are, naturally, all ancient cities, and most of them have a cathedral or at least a church, for his sense of history is sustained and irradiated by his passionate Catholicism. Indeed, the greater part of his book is constructed round a double, deliberate thesis: the surge of Islam, washing up to the last strongholds of Christianity, and retreating again, leaving the citadels of the True Faith triumphantly inviolate and the co-related awareness of the superimposed civilizations, the Greek and Roman pagan world, the mediaeval or Islamic, and the last "layer of Europe returning . . . our masterful stonework in the place of their weak plaster, our permanence in the place of their ephemeral though burning moods." His symbolism may be, largely, architectural; but it is with the broad deep spirit of religion and history that he is imbued.

It is for this reason that he is at his best when he writes of the cities of Spain and Northern Africa . . . for here his thesis, one might almost say his idiosyncrasy, has full scope. But it is not only in the description of cities that he excels; in his incidental sketches of landscape he enjoys an equal power of evocation. This book might well be reprinted in a more convenient form, on india-paper perhaps, to slip into the pocket, for if it is a book to read at home to stir up our *Wanderlust*, it is also a book to take with us when we follow in his footsteps. It is a book to read lying on the slope of a hill with Spain at our feet. It is easy, of course, to find fault with Mr. Belloc. It is easy to be annoyed by the small and unnecessary affectations of his style; easy, above all, to say that he dashes his head in vain as a battering-ram against the many tendencies of which he disapproves, but is powerless to correct. Not everyone, for instance, will endorse his sweeping assertion that "in this time of ours, everyting that is changed is changed for the worse." Personally speaking, I sympathize with his attitude, for I like convictions to be full-blooded, and have very little use for measured and diffident beliefs. Especially do I like enthusiastic though discriminating travellers; and on Mr. Belloc's enthusiasm and discrimination no aspersion can be cast. What he likes, he loves; and what he dislikes, he hates; and when he bestows his approval on architecture or landscape he seldom makes a mistake. (pp. 942-43)

> V. Sackville-West, "Mr. Belloc in Spain," in The Nation and the Athenaeum, Vol. XLII, No. 25, March 24, 1928, pp. 942-43.

BERNARD SHAW (essay date 1932)

[H.G. Wells] has written in this journal about Chesterton and Belloc without stopping to consider what Chesterton and Belloc is. This sounds like bad grammar; but I know what I am about. Chesterton and Belloc is a conspiracy, and a most dangerous one at that. Not a viciously intended one: quite the contrary. It is a game of make-believe of the sort which all imaginative grown-up children love to play; and, as in all such games, the first point in it is that they shall pretend to be somebody else. Chesterton is to be a roaring jovial Englishman, not taking his pleasures sadly, but piling Falstaff on Magog, and Boythorn on John Bull. Belloc's fancy is much stranger. He is to be a Frenchman, but not a Walkley Frenchman, not any of the varieties of the stage Frenchman, but a French peasant, greedy, narrow, individualistic, ready to fight like a rat in a corner of his scrap of land, and, above all, intensely and superstitiously Roman Catholic. And the two together are to impose on the simple bourgeoisie of England as the Main Forces of European Civilization. (pp. 72-3)

The Chesterbelloc denounces the Yellow Press, but only because it dislikes yellow and prefers flaming red. The characteristic vice of the Yellow Journalist is that he never says he wants a thing (usually bigger dividends) or that his employer wants it. He always says that the Empire needs it, or that Englishmen are determined to have it, and that those who object to it are public enemies, Jews, Germans, rebels, traitors, Pro-Boers, and what not. Further, he draws an imaginative picture of a person whose honor and national character consist in getting what the Yellow Journalist is after, and says to the poor foolish reader: "That is yourself, my brave fellow-countryman." Now this is precisely what the Chesterbelloc does in its bigger, more imaginative, less sordid way. . . . According to [Belloc], the Chesterbelloc is European democracy, is the Catholic Church, is the Life Force, is the very voice of the clay of which Adam was made, and which the Catholic peasant labors. To set yourself against the Chesterbelloc is not merely to be unpatriotic, like setting yourself against the Daily Mail or Express: it is to set yourself against all the forces, active and latent (especially latent) of humanity. Wells and I, contemplating the Chesterbelloc, recognize at once a very amusing pantomime elephant, the front legs being that very exceptional and unEnglish individual Hilaire Belloc, and the hind legs that extravagant freak of French nature, G. K. Chesterton. To which they both reply ''Not at all: what you see is the Zeitgeist.'' To which we reply bluntly but conclusively, ''Gammon!''

But a pantomime animal with two men in it is a mistake when the two are not very carefully paired. . . . Chesterton and Belloc are so unlike that they get frightfully into one another's way. Their vocation as philosophers requires the most complete detachment: their business as the legs of the Chesterbelloc demands the most complete synchronism. They are unlike in everything except the specific literary genius and delight in play-acting that is common to them, and that threw them into one another's arms. (pp. 73-5)

> *Bernard Shaw, "The Chesterbelloc" (originally published in another form as "Belloc and Chesterton," in* The New Age, *n.s. Vol. II, No. 16, February 15, 1908), in his* Pen Portraits and Reviews *by Bernard Shaw (reprinted by permission of The Society of Authors on behalf of the Bernard Shaw Estate), revised edition, Constable and Company Limited, 1932, pp. 71-81.*

G. K. CHESTERTON   (essay date 1936)

[The] English, of whom I am one, are romantic, and because they delight in the romance that the French are romantic, and delight in the more delirious romance that Belloc is French, they have simply been stone-blind to him when he is entirely scientific. His study of the Servile State is as strictly scientific as a military map is military. There is nothing romantic about it; nothing rollicking about it; nothing even particularly amusing about it, except the two admirable words, ''this fool,'' which occur in the calm procession of a thousand impartial words, in the chapter on The Practical Man. And even excepting that is like accusing Euclid of making a joke, when he proves a proposition with a *reductio ad absurdum*. Anyone who knows the place of reason in the modern scheme, can imagine what happened. First, before reading what Belloc wrote, the critics started to criticise what Belloc would probably write. They said he threatened us with a horrible nightmare called the Servile State. As a fact, it was his whole point that it was not a nightmare, but something that we were already almost as habituated to accepting as to accepting the daylight. (p. 306)

The thesis of the book is that the Socialist movement does not lead to Socialism. This is partly because of compromise and cowardice; but partly also because men have a dim indestructible respect for property, even in its disgusting disguise of modern monopoly. Therefore, instead of the intentional result, Socialism, we shall have the unintentional resultant: Slavery. The compromise will take the form of saying, ''We must feed the poor; we won't rob the rich; so we will tell the rich to feed the poor, handing them over to be the permanent servants of a master-class, to be maintained whether they are working or no, and in return for that complete maintenance giving a complete obedience.'' All this, or the beginnings of it, can be seen in a hundred modern changes, from such things as Insurance Acts, which divide citizens by law into two classes of masters and servants, to all sorts of proposals for preventing strikes and lock-outs by compulsory arbitration. Any law that sends a man back to his work, when he wants to leave it, is in plain fact a Fugitive Slave Law.

Now I take that one example of a scientific thesis, maintained in a purely scientific way, to show how very little the intellectual importance of Belloc's work has been understood. The reason of that misunderstanding lies in the other fact about him, which is really foreign and relatively French; the habit of separating in his own mind the scientific from the artistic; the ornamental from the useful. It is true that when a Frenchman designs a park as an ornamental park the paths are very curly indeed because they are only ornamental. When he designs a road, he makes it as straight as a ramrod, like the roads down which French soldiers used to march with all their ramrods; because a road is meant to be useful and is most short when it is straight. Belloc's little Arcadian lyric, ''When I was not much older than Cupid and bolder,'' is very like an ornamental French garden; and his book on the Servile State is very like a French military road. No man is more instinctively witty; and no man can be more intentionally dull. (pp. 307-08)

> *G. K. Chesterton, "Portrait of a Friend" (originally published in* The American Review, *Vol. VII, No. 5, October, 1936), in his* The Autobiography of G. K. Chesterton *(reprinted by permission of the Estate of G. K. Chesterton), Sheed and Ward, Inc., 1936, pp. 297-308.*

J. B. MORTON   (essay date 1948)

The driving force of a good essay, that by which it lives and moves, is the character of its author. (p. v)

Mr. Belloc's essays, whatever the subject, whatever the treatment, whatever the mood, are every one of them stamped indelibly with the mark of a man who, delighting in debate and by temperament in sympathy with the sceptic, yet has certain iron convictions on the nature of man; whence he comes, what he is, why he is here, whither he is bound. In other words his essays, like the whole body of his writings, are the work of a militant Catholic. (pp. v-vi)

But though there is this stout thread running through his essays, and connecting them with one another, there is never a shadow of monotony. . . . You meet a mind deeply interested in men and things, a mind which has digested a considerable experience of both. You find that travel and history are inseparable companions in this mind, which seeks to understand and interpret the present by a knowledge of the past. You note, as characteristics of the author, a profound respect for tradition and a distrust of the entire modern hullabaloo about progress; a hatred of prententiousness, hypocrisy, and priggishness; a contempt for muddled thinking; active enjoyment of living, and an insatiable appetite for discovery in travel, in reading, and in observation of his fellow men; an ardent love of the Roman foundation, of English landscape, of French energy.

The reader will also, I think, be aware of a recurrent theme in the essays, intimately connected with those certitudes which Mr. Belloc's religion has given him. It is the old theme of the poets, the brevity of human life; beauty fugitive, joy transient, friendship and even love doomed to perish. . . . [In his] essays, we are continually reminded that man on earth is an exile, carrying a burden. He has no true home here, but, by the grace of God, he is now and then granted some experience of beauty which is a poor foreshadowing of what he may expect hereafter. . . . But there goes with this yearning for permanence, which can find no satisfaction, a very lively enjoyment of the good things of this world; the companionship of men; drink and song and debate.

The two major excellences of Mr. Belloc's prose style are lucidity and vitality.

I hesitated for a moment in front of the word lucidity. It has been used, in connexion with Mr. Belloc, as often as the word versatility. Every critic has praised him for this quality, because, whatever one may think of his opinions, this gift of his is undeniable. . . . As A. G. Macdonell wrote of Mr. Belloc: 'You may passionately disagree with what he says, you may stubbornly disbelieve what he says, but at least you know with certainty exactly what it is that he is saying.' Mr. Belloc thinks before he writes, and, having established order in his mind, often gives an effect of pouring out what he has to say, like a good talker, with complete spontaneity. Yet, so strongly does he control the instrument of his trade that his contemptuous parentheses, his rhetorical flourishes, his unexpected apostrophes seem to fit into the pattern of the essay, instead of breaking that pattern. (pp. vi-ix)

Vitality, or unfailing energy, is as striking a mark of Mr. Belloc's style as lucidity. . . . The vitality of which I speak is energy controlled, as the movements of an athlete are controlled. Mr. Belloc's style is the style of a man of the open air, and this quality of energy is as conspicuous in his pages of weighty exposition as in his skylarking. . . . [There is] for instance, the essay called **'On Sacramental Things'**. Here is that vitality which, when it is joined with an exact use of words, gives a deceptive effect of ease, and conceals the labour of composition. Mr. Belloc's vocabulary is by no means large, but the words are carefully chosen and marshalled. By the time they have been formed into sentences and set forward, life has been breathed into them. In the lighter essays, of course, the vitality is more obvious, but in all his work there is present the poise and grace of the athlete.

Mr. Belloc's style is unmistakable. Nobody could think that any one of these essays had been written by another hand. For there are certain recurring idiosyncracies, in addition to the more important ingredients of his style, which label the work as his. He will use contrast most effectively; a swift transition from wisdom to foolery, from uproarious fun to the pensive, the tender, the melancholy. And since one thing suggests not another, but fifty others, he will digress to his heart's content. He will delight in apostrophe, which he uses with great humour, and in those 'asides', witty or bellicose, which show an alert mind. He will insist on exact definition in a piece of serious writing, and his classical sense of proportion will forbid extravagance when he is writing with imagination and vision. His impudent gambols are well known—'It was on or about a Tuesday (I speak without boasting)', and especially his habit of blessing or ridiculing his readers. Epigram he will use very sparingly, and alliteration, which can become a drug, more sparingly still. There are evidences of Mr. Belloc's mixed blood here and there. He understands fully that inarticulate love of England which he calls 'This music in their souls'. English poetry and English landscape move him intensely, and he responds vigorously to English humour at its best, that is, the humour of the old music halls. Thoroughly English is his love of adventure at sea, but that far-away landfall, that secret country of ultimate repose, is surely Hy-Brasail, seen from the western shores of Ireland. Again English is his love of beer and of singing in inns, but his love of wine, and his refusal to be bamboozled by the label on the bottle, is French. And if anyone has influenced his style it is Rabelais. When he is in tearing spirits he will take great jumbles of words and bang them about ferociously, or tell a story in a certain ludicrous

manner. He is French in the verbal precision of his more serious moods, French in his military temper, in his loathing of professional politicians, in the logical processes of his thought, in his sense of form, in his dislike of excess, and in his scorn of flaccidity.

Throughout his literary career Mr. Belloc, the best prose writer of our time, has been swimming against the tide. No contemporary author is more completely out of sympathy with what I have heard called, delightfully enough, 'the best contemporary thought'. Chesterton said that it is a good thing to suffer fools gladly, but a better thing to enjoy them tremendously. Mr. Belloc's tremendous enjoyment of the modern fool is unfailing. (pp. ix-xi)

To-day the essay as a literary form has passed out of favour. . . . But whether new essayists arise or not, Mr. Belloc will be read as long as men care for good prose. (p. xi)

> *J. B. Morton, in his introduction to* Selected Essays
> of Hilaire Belloc *by Hilaire Belloc, edited by J. B.
> Morton, Methuen & Co. Ltd., 1948, pp. v-xiii.*

RENÉE HAYNES   (essay date 1953)

[Belloc's] enormous output of work falls roughly into seven overbrimming and interleaking categories. There are the books of mockery, high spirited, genial, fierce, or bitter, expressing itself in fiction like *The Green Overcoat* and *The Mercy of Allah,* in spoof biographies such as *Lambkin's Remains,* and in the collections of comic verse, *A Moral Alphabet, Cautionary Tales, Peers,* and *More Peers,* and *The Modern Traveller.* . . . There are the [sociological] books written upon the theme summed up in *The Servile State.* . . .

There are the historical studies, mainly concerned with England and with France. . . . (p. 6)

[The] delightful *Avril; Essays on the Poetry of the French Renaissance,* [is part of] another, and too small a branch of his activity: literary criticism.

There are also the books of travel, mostly on foot or under sail.

There are the many volumes of essays, multitudinous, stimulating, irritating, reminiscent, various, as good talk.

Finally, and perhaps more lasting than all the rest, there are the poems; alive with that energy with which a formal verse structure can most fully be charged; and written to reach the heart through hearing as well as the mind's eye by the provocation of visual imagery. (p. 8)

[Among the books of mockery] Dr. Caliban's conscientious and ponderous *Guide to Letters,* with its grand financial hypocrisies and its admirable advice on the composition of Reviews, Personal Pars, Topographical Articles, Political Appeals and the rest, is perennially delightful reading, especially the chapters on Poetry and Interviewing. (pp. 9-10)

Lambkin's Remains, an equally solemn biography of an imaginary Don, is a perpetual feast to all whose palates have savoured the pomps of a minor erudition, kept conscientiously up to date; these will return to roll around their tongues Lambkin's Address to the League of Progress, Lambkin's Open Letter to Churchmen, 'Am I a Sheep or a Goat?', . . . and of course Lambkin's Newdigate Poem with its classical Second Invocation to the Muse. . . . (p. 10)

This leads to that realm of shrewd abandon (more *terre à terre* than Edward Lear's nonsense, more brutal than Lewis Carroll's) inhabited by Bad and Worse Children, Beasts, Peers, Ladies and Gentlemen, and the heroes and heroines of the *Moral Alphabet* and *Cautionary Tales*. (p. 11)

The historical justification of [Belloc's sociological] beliefs is put forward in a number of narratives and biographies. A statement of the current situation, and of alternatives for the future, is made in *The Servile State* . . . , a remarkable prophecy of economic totalitarianism. . . . [*Economics for Helen*] sets the claims of freedom and responsibility against those advantages of personal security and general stability which the Servile State may give. *An Essay on the Restoration of Property* . . . distinguishes between the Distributist and the Social Credit proposals (remarking that the ultimate end of the former is economic freedom, and of the latter increased purchasing power), advocates various means of distributing ownership in land, shops, and collective enterprises, and postulates that there will be no middle way for the future between general small ownership and general (unlabelled) industrial slavery. (p. 13)

[Belloc's] earlier historical work—among which should be counted biography as well as narrative—and indeed all the historical studies dealing with France rather than with England, are the most leisured, stimulating and agreeable. (p. 14)

In *The Eyewitness* . . . he deliberately set himself at the attempt 'to live for some moments in the past, and to see the things that had been stand and live before one'. He succeeded. The past was illuminated and there lived again in the imagination, as once they were known to perception fragmentarily, sensorily, momentarily. . . . In the other historical books this genius for knowing and presenting history in terms of individual human experience is more or less subdued to the stricter discipline of narrative. More, in the distantly focused four-volume *History of England*, and in the *Book of the Bayeux Tapestry*, with its characteristic emphasis on the Norman point of view; less, in the historical biographies, even the *Joan of Arc* written in a stylized archaic prose with Froissart's trumpets sounding round the corners of the paragraphs; least of all in the studies of the French Revolution, in which Belloc's great-grandfather fought. It breaks through and takes charge with particular vigour in the *Robespierre*, the *Marie Antoinnete*, and the *Danton*. . . . (p. 15)

This deep and vital preoccupation not so much with the material as with the incarnate is indeed a sap perpetually rising within all Belloc's serious work. It animates with especial vigour his books on travel. . . . (p. 16)

If *The Path to Rome*, marked by all the gusto of young manhood, towers above the other books of travel by land, *The Cruise of the 'Nona'*, made with the sense of growing old upon him, is incomparably the best of Belloc's writings on the sea. . . . It contains none of those cataracts of adjectives and adverbs which burst through his earlier work like volcanic geysers, linking him, oddly enough, with Charles Kingsley, who shared his passion for the style of Rabelais from which they spout up. Its currents carry the shape of thoughts conveyed with distinct animus in much of his other work, but reflected here with the profound peace of ocean, where time itself is 'more continuous; more part of the breathing of the world; less mechanical and divided'. (p. 19)

The essays are so many and various that it is almost impossible to discuss them *en bloc*. They consider with wit, ferocity,

learning, personal reminiscence, prejudice, compassion, intolerance, common sense, a wide experience of the outer world and a most noble prose style almost every aspect of individual human life; but they do not touch upon science, technics, or any sort of statistical generalization. To read them is like dining at ease with a really great conversationalist; in them the richness and depth of the written word amply replace that air of golden geniality—say the spiritual equivalent of candle-lit cigar-smoke and the lingering vibration of wine—which gives to its spoken counterpart a quality evaporated by print. (p. 20)

Belloc's prose will probably survive in part, to give enlarging joy to lovers of pre-industrial Europe and the sea. But in his poems will rest his immortality and the fulfilment of his outrageous and heartfelt pun:

> When I am dead I hope it may be said
> "His sins were scarlet but his books were read."
>
>   (p. 29)

> *Renée Haynes, in her* Hilaire Belloc *(© Profile Books Ltd. 1953), Longmans, Green & Co. Ltd., 1953, 35 p.*

BERNARD BERGONZI   (essay date 1959)

If Chesterton was at his best when writing about books, Belloc was certainly at his best away from them. One need only glance at the brief essay on Jane Austen in [his] *Selected Essays* to see how little of a critic he was, for his essential egotism prevented him from removing his attention from himself to the work in front of him for very long. But on the other hand he was very much more of an artist than Chesterton. Re-reading his poems for the first time in several years, I was agreeably surprised, for Belloc appears in them as a good minor poet who deserves at least the same reputation as that now enjoyed by Housman: his wish to be remembered primarily as a poet seems eminently reasonable. The epigrams, of course, are deservedly famous, and one wishes we had now a political satirist who could achieve the lethal compression of 'Epitaph on the Politician':

> Here richly, with ridiculous display,
> The Politician's corpse was laid away.
> While all of his acquaintance sneered and slanged
> I wept: for I had longed to see him hanged.

There are few places outside Pope where precisely this note has been struck, and struck so well. Belloc's sonnets suggest that he was one of that remarkably small company of English poets who could genuinely think and feel and write—without apparent effort—in sonnet form. The language is almost as derivative and literary as Chesterton's, but the best of Belloc's poetry does give one the traditional romantic pleasure of hearing the voice of a vigorous and authentic personality coming through the somewhat threadbare diction and conventional rhythms. To this extent, Belloc is not merely bookish. And a similar quality redeems quite a lot of his bellelettrist prose, which is written according to prescriptions not very likely to recommend it to the modern reader, for Belloc came to literary maturity when the classically-inspired canons of 'beautiful English' and the 'fine style', largely divorced from content, were still the norm. Nowadays we see prose style as much more intimately a function of content, feeling and attitude, and are readily reminded of Max Beerbohm's comment on Pater—'that sedulous ritual wherewith he laid out every sentence as in a shroud'. But the strange thing is that though Belloc wrote prose according to these somewhat external prescriptions, much of it is still good when judged by other standards. One might mention, for instance, the set-piece called **'The Relic'** in the [above-mentioned] book of essays, which conveys extremely well the intensely personal quality of Belloc's experience in a Spanish church.

In fact, Belloc's apprehension of the world seems to have needed the measured and calculated quality of his prose, or the formality of his verse, in order to be coherently conveyed at all. For despite his aggressively dogmatic and assertive manner, I feel that his inner life often existed on the edge of chaos and near-despair. The tension is certainly apparent in his writing. . . . One sees, for instance, the inner isolation and unhappiness appearing for a moment beneath the rigid mask in the conclusion of his essay, **'On Unknown People.'** . . . (pp. 130-31)

In fact, Belloc was a good deal closer to the characteristic masters of modern literature than we may at first imagine. He, too, was a *déraciné* figure with a bewildering variety of *personae*: ex-scholar of Balliol, ex-French artilleryman, Sussex farmer, Liberal politician, anti-Dreyfusard, London man of letters, sailor. All these figures in turn inspired different aspects of his writing but never gave him anything like the conviction that a genuine set of cultural roots would have done. . . . Belloc's devotion to the culture of Western Europe as a whole, and to Catholicism as the incarnation and guardian of that culture, were clearly a form of compensation for his lack of more intimate roots. This devotion . . . was not without its unfortunate side, for it could lead him into such dangerous half-truths as the pronouncement that 'the Faith is Europe, and Europe is the Faith'. Yet it is impossible not to be moved by the extent of Belloc's knowledge and love of England and France and Italy and Spain and the Catholic parts of Germany. He knew these countries and their people and buildings intimately because he had been over most of them on foot. *The Path to Rome* is as much the record of a love-affair as a travelbook. Belloc's concept of 'Western culture' was something much more personal and existential than the purely literary and eclectic kind of 'tradition' compiled by Pound or Eliot, in their rather Adam Verver-ish fashion.

But in a final judgement it is Belloc's lack of interest in a specific literary tradition, and his tendency to oppose flatly the deeper tendencies of his age rather than to interpret and explore them, which makes him remote and inaccessible to present-day criticism. And much the same is true of Chesterton. Together with their non-Christian contemporaries they lived and argued in a world that seems almost as strange and distant as the Paris of Aquinas. . . . [The] Christian humanist is as likely as the agnostic to find them fallen idols rather than living gods in the heaven of literature. But their sleeping features deserve, at the very least, a long and respectful stare, before they are finally eroded by the winds of time. (pp. 132-33)

> *Bernard Bergonzi, "Chesterton and/or Belloc" (originally published in* Critical Quarterly, *Vol. I, No. 1, Spring, 1959), in his* The Turn of a Century: Essays on Victorian and Modern English Literature *(© Bernard Bergonzi, 1973; reprinted by permission of Barnes & Noble Books, a Division of Littlefield, Adams & Co., Inc.; in Canada by permission of A D Peters & Co Limited), Barnes & Noble, 1973, pp. 124-33.**

FRANK SWINNERTON (essay date 1969)

The explanation of the failure of Belloc and Chesterton to impress younger sceptics is that both were, in a sense, defendants. They attacked the trend of modern society towards mechanization as severely as any other writers whatsoever. But they did so from the standpoint of the Catholic Church. They said that the world was in a very bad way; but they both insisted that it was once—in the Middle Ages—in a very good way. Belloc, in a really masterly short work called **"The Servile State,"** . . . established the fact that slavery is a familiar condition of European life. It is his argument that slavery was destroyed by Christianity, and that until the end of the Middle Ages it had ceased to exist in the West. He believed, and so did Chesterton, that all the ills of modern England arise from what followed the dissolution of the monasteries by King Henry the Eighth. If Henry, says Belloc, had done as he intended, and kept in his own hands—the hands of the Crown—the property taken from the clerical body, the country would have had a happy future. Henry was not strong enough to keep his appropriations; he found the rich men of his day too powerful for him, and was forced to hand over the greater part of the spoils. Hence the violent inequality of wealth and power in England out of which grew from the sixteenth century onwards the evils of Capitalism. Hence, in process of time, the inevitability of the servile state, to which all parties by one path or another have led and will lead the people of England.

It is not my business to comment upon the truth or otherwise of this theory; but there can be no question as to the clearness and power of the book in which it is outlined. And there can be no doubt, I think, that possession of such a view of history prevented Belloc and Chesterton from capturing the imagination of generations increasingly influenced by scientific and mechanical theory and practice. It is one thing to say that the world is wrong—every reformer agrees that the world is wrong;—but when, instead of proceeding to say that the world can be set right by something new, a man says that it can only be set right by a return to something old, he is thrown into a defence of the past. And the past, as Chesterton admitted, is no easy subject. "I can make the future as narrow as myself; the past is obliged to be as broad and turbulent as humanity." Both Belloc and Chesterton had to rewrite history for purposes of propaganda amid incessant interruptions both from dryasdusts and from ribalds who did not believe a word of what they said. Men who attack the present are always sure of support; men who contrast the present with the delights of an improved future society may be scorned as unpractical idealists, but they cannot be confounded by texts or refutations; men who insist that at some past time an ideal state existed may be challenged by the proven inability of that ideal state to withstand aggression, and they will certainly be floored by extracts from some old charter or pipe roll or antique letter which demolishes the whole structure they have so ingeniously erected.

That is what happened to Belloc and Chesterton. Belloc deliberately, and Chesterton with misgiving, set up a version—in Belloc's case a series of detailed versions—of what happened in England long ago. It was not accepted by Protestants, scientific historians, or sceptics. Belloc went farther. He told us in several books how the French Revolution arose, succeeded, and failed (the early chapters of his **"Danton"** give the clearest exposition of the events preceding the Revolution which I have ever read, but I do not know if they are the truest); he in one book of **"Miniatures of French History"** told us what must have happened in France at various crucial points from 599

B.C. to A.D. 1914. He traced the history of warfare in England. His mind played over the entire history of Europe, and he expressed himself as to that history with a certainty and I imagine a consistency which ought to have satisfied every reader. But he did not satisfy every reader. Every reader could relish the style in which Belloc told his story; but every reader, in spite of the charm and certainty of the narrative, felt that Belloc was a partisan, bent upon proving a case. It is nothing new in historical writing; if the case is the popular case it will be swallowed gladly; but when it conflicts with the case as presented by every Whig and Protestant historian, or with the case as overwhelmingly demonstrated by the ironist Gibbon, it is suspect from the start.

Now Belloc adored Froissart. He owed much to the gargantuan historical method of Rabelais. He believed that legends and ballads are better authorities than pipe rolls. He used his imagination in describing battles (for which he had a peculiar gift and fondness), political intrigues, and religious and economic influences as to which there are or are not written records. The results have been controversial. (pp. 75-7)

[There] are some—including myself—who believe Belloc's province to be not history, but that exceedingly personal product, the essay, of which he is complete master; and Chesterton's province not history, but poetry, or that beautiful kind of fable which he created for the exploitation of Father Brown, the priest-detective. Belloc at large, . . . writing with triumphant relish both of himself and his language (which he handles as a steersman handles a small boat at sea when the wind is freshening); Chesterton taking a common story, ingeniously twisting it, and at last leaving the earth altogether with a style that suggests the upward soaring (never the graceless flap) of a children's kite; both bringing to their art a love of life so uncommon at the present time as to ravish us with a sense of what they mean when they speak of Merrie England and "that laughter that has slept since the Middle Ages"—do they not thus establish themselve as very important figures in modern literature? (p. 78)

When Belloc wrote "The Path to Rome" he was following a recognized literary road—the writer of charm going alone upon a trip among strange people, laughing, learning, and then posing a little before the world. . . . But, miraculously, he avoided sentimentality; there was in him a certain robust and boyish courage and simplicity which, although he could chaff the reader and at times do a little bragging of one sort or another, gave "The Path to Rome" a character of its own. It remains Belloc's best long book, and the one by which most of his admirers would wish him first to be known. It is a tale of dangers run, and fears acknowledged, of hours enlivened by nonsense and accidentally good or evil meals. It is a chronicle of moods, a picture of mountains and forests and small towns, a traveller's tale, an enchanting monologue, and anything else the reader fancies. And it is the early work of a man who could already do anything he wished with his pen.

That, indeed, was one of Belloc's weaknesses—that he was always so much a master of his pen. He was too versatile for the mind of a public that prefers repetition. And furthermore it was sometimes difficult to discover at what point the serious Belloc yielded to the extravagant Belloc; for in the grand manner which he often used an able and humour-filled writer must often check himself sharply lest he guy his own grandeur. Let any reader take Belloc at his most serious, and then turn to his satirical novel, "Emmanuel Burden": it will be found that "Emmanuel Burden" contains passages, despite its satirical

character, which strongly resemble Belloc at his most serious, and barely exceed the sonorousness of his more rhetorical mood. That does not happen in so finished and consummate a work of irony as "The Mercy of Allah," of course; but "The Mercy of Allah" is extremely mature, whereas "Emmanuel Burden," being experimental, is particularly interesting to the student of Belloc as showing his mind more fitfully playing between anger and pity, and particularly informing as showing the danger to a stylist of the power to burlesque all styles, including his own.

Even so, Belloc is a more persistent and sustained writer than Chesterton, who was best in short flights. (pp. 79-80)

They had greater skill in dialectical writing than any of their contemporaries excepting only Shaw. They had the gift of writing with peculiar simplicity and beauty, and the utmost clearness. But when it comes to what they write, it must be said that Belloc was governed by his passion for propositions; and that Chesterton was governed by his passion for antithesis. Belloc said "I shall show; I shall prove; I shall establish." He would show that the French Revolution turned upon and was conditioned by its military history. He would prove that Robespierre, a weak man, did not create the Terror, but resisted it and was unwillingly driven to it by others. He would establish that the dissolution of the monasteries in England in the sixteenth century was the beginning of the industrial revolution and the Capitalist system. But he does not convince us about the French Revolution or about Robespierre or about the dissolution of the monasteries for at least three reasons. The first of these reasons is that we already hold other views (the basis for which he ignores in spite of all clamour) as to the events; the second reason is that his style being authoritative, is unfitted for persuasion; and the third reason is that despite every ingenuity he is unable in the communications he makes to fulfil the promise he has given. The third reason is the fatal reason.

Chesterton in the same way made propositions; but they were less peremptory and less serious than Belloc's. (pp. 81-2)

Now what can we do about such men? All who enjoy debate and the flexible use of thought and language must delight in their adroitness. All who can stand outside the stream of current opinion must observe how many ideas of virtue and value continually appear in their work. But when all is turmoil, as it is to-day, it is too much to expect that the occupants of a backwater will receive the proper rewards of literary genius. That is what happened to Belloc and Chesterton. They were regarded as old gentlemen doing whatever is the nautical equivalent of fiddling while Rome burns. For this reason their gifts—finally separated for ever from their views and resistances—will not be fully realized and acknowledged until at least a century has passed. How great those gifts were, in my opinion, could be stated only in terms which would seem at this time extravagant.

Frank Swinnerton, "Catholic Liberalism" (originally published in a different form in his The Georgian Scene: A Literary Panorama, *Farrar & Rinehart, 1934), in his* The Georgian Literary Scene, 1910-1935, *revised edition (© Frank Swinnerton 1969; reprinted by permission of the author),* Hutchinson, *1969, pp. 68-82.**

W. H. AUDEN   (essay date 1970)

About Belloc the artist, all readers, whatever their religious and political convictions, will agree on two points. Firstly, he is, like Swift, one of the great masters of straightforward English prose. Even when I find *what* he is saying wrongheaded or absurd, I have to admire *how* he says it, his clarity, vigor, and elegance; and whenever his subject is one to which dogmas are irrelevant, as when he is describing his experiences as a French conscript, or his adventures among savage mountains and on stormy seas, or his visits to little known cities, I am completely enchanted. Secondly, as a writer of Light Verse, he has few equals and no superiors. (His "serious" poems, like the Sonnets, seem to me *bien fait*, but without original vision, an imitation of poetry-in-general.) (p. 11)

> W. H. Auden, "Portrait with a Wart or Two" (reprinted by permission of the Literary Estate of W. H. Auden; copyright © 1970 Nyrev, Inc.), in The New York Review of Books, *Vol. XV, No. 8, November 5, 1970, pp. 11-12.*

GERTRUDE M. WHITE (essay date 1979-80)

Little is heard today of the light verse of those oddly assorted co-religionists, fellow fighters for a better world, and good friends, G. K. Chesterton and Hilaire Belloc. Indeed, their verse as a whole is out of date. . . . It is time for a fuller appreciation. For there was a time when these verses did indeed live on the lips of men and even now should not be forgotten. Whatever may be the final verdict on Chesterton and Belloc as true poets, there can be no doubt of their place on these lower slopes of Parnassus. There, they dwell secure. (pp. 1-2)

[Belloc's] light verse retains its virtue for two basic reasons: the high level of [his] technique and the individual—indeed, unique—quality of his humour.

Technique is essential to light verse, more so than to serious. . . . The effect—certainly any permanent effect—of light verse depends to a great extent on metrical skill. Even in his less successful verses, Belloc's grip on movement and meter never slips. His rhymes never seem forced, the most startling conjunctions presenting themselves seemingly as happy inspiration rather than mere ingenuity. (p. 7)

[Another] element in Belloc's mastery of technique, along with meter, movement, and rhyme: his forceful, exact, and wide-ranging vocabulary, blunt Anglo-Saxon or Latinate polysyllable, each in its fit place. . . . [It] is the pith, the force, the precision of Belloc's diction that strikes the reader of his comic verse, not the pedantry and—far from nuance or Ciceronian manner—the pellucid phraseology and crisp, direct grammar.

This technical skill and close verbal finish is not, of course, separate from substance, but is the very body of Belloc's mind, to coin a phrase. The clarity and force of that mind are apparent everywhere in his writing. Belloc's prose is always lucid, energetic, direct. But in prose he could be dry, when the occasion called for it, formidably stern, and sometimes even savage. Chesterton once spoke wistfully of the "sundering" quality of Belloc's quarrels and Belloc in turn retorted that without wounds there was no battle and no victory. But in his light verse the same mind is at play. His satire hits hard but with an almost genial ferocity, its underlying seriousness tempered by wit; his rowdy high spirits burst forth without hindrance, extravagant, absurd, rollicking and laughing not so much at their subjects as for the sheer joy of laughter. In Belloc's light verse, as seldom in his novels and essays, we sense something of that affection for his butts that distinguishes Chaucer, a playfulness

that is especially striking in the verses for children. But extravagant, absurd, or playful, Belloc's verses nearly always mirror clearly the foibles of a particular era. Edwardian England, with its class consciousness, its social and political problems, its cultural ambiance, is present in these verses, caught for all time like a fly in amber. . . . (p. 10)

[Renée Haynes, dividing Belloc's] work into seven categories, lists "books of mockery" as the first of these, the comic verse among them [see excerpt above]. It is a fair description, for Belloc's light verse is almost always mocking something or other. Even the apparently merely playful nonsense verse of the *Cautionary Tales, The Bad Child's Book of Beasts, More Beasts for Worse Children,* and *A Moral Alphabet* is part of a reaction against Victorian didacticism, a reaction which includes, for example, Harry Graham's *Ruthless Rhymes for Heartless Homes.* . . . Belloc's *Cautionary Tales* have the same casual, nonchalant brutality, but a great deal more technical polish and an ineffable mixture of mock sanctimoniousness, crisp dialogue and comment, and social satire. . . . **"Godolphin Horne Who Was Cursed With The Sin Of Pride, And Became A Boot-Black"** is a tongue-in-cheek tribute to the snobbish manners of the British aristocracy. All the *Tales* are, in fact, to some extent a mockery of the manners of their own time, while in *A Moral Alphabet* Belloc particularly enjoys himself in devising appropriate Morals to conclude the advice offered the young under each letter. Commonly, these are openly subversive of middle-class manners, customs, and institutions. . . . But the verses for children are, even more, pastiches of a kind of verse once written seriously for the instruction and edification of the young. Dear to the hearts of the Victorians, the earnest originals are now for the most part known only to scholars of the period, but something of their flavour and manner is preserved through the sea-change of imitations and parodies of which Belloc's are the best.

A Modern Traveller may . . . be a favourite in England, but is less likely to appeal to other readers. It is, for one thing, far too long-drawn-out, its length and comparative verbosity depriving it of the characteristic snap and sparkle of Belloc's briefer verses. Its satire on the hypocrisy and immorality of big business, the brutal dishonesty of Empire building and its connection with international finance rather than either philanthropy or patriotism, all the "easy speeches / That comfort cruel men," in the words of Chesterton's hymn, may be true enough in substance but is outdated in attitude and manner and sounds, for Belloc, remarkably heavy-handed. . . . Its worst effects are Belloc's unhappy attempts at what he thought of as Negro dialect.

More Peers is equally unlikely to appeal to any but a very English reader, with the striking exception of **"Lord Finchley,"** to which belongs the extraordinary distinction of inclusion in both [W. H. Auden's anthology] *The Oxford Book of Light Verse* and [Kingsley Amis's anthology] *The New Oxford Book of English Light Verse.* Its technical virtuosity still recommends it, though it may not strike quite as deep a chord in a do-it-yourself age. . . . *New Cautionary Tales* once or twice equals the boisterous high spirits of the earlier *Tales,* for the adventure of **"Sarah Byng Who Could Not Read And Was Tossed Into A Thorny Hedge By A Bull"** and **". . . John Who Lost A Fortune By Throwing Stones"** have all Belloc's youthful *joie de vivre*. But his volume as a whole does not match the former in gaiety of spirit or verbal skill and in *Ladies and Gentlemen* Belloc sounds less gay than rather perfunctory and a trifle out of temper.

There remain, aside from these, a whole variety of verses that may legitimately be called light in technique, topic, or manner. Assorted as they are, many exhibit a common trait, one which Amis in the introduction to his anthology points out as characteristic of a great deal of light verse. ". . . all light art is likely to deliver, now and then, a jolt to the gentler emotions, the more telling for its unexpectedness. . . . With light verse, this effect is obviously most likely to come near the end of the piece. At such time, I should argue, the verse ceases to be light, the poet's tone of voice begins to belong to that of high verse, and—if one imagines him reciting in public—his manner would correspondingly change." So the tripping trochaics of **"The End of the Road"** conclude with a sudden shift in meter and in mood:

> Nor ever turned my face to home
> Till I had slaked my heart at Rome.
>
> (pp. 10-13)

Belloc was a master of the epigram, with its demand for tight form and concision of thought and expression. Even more than the early verses for children these exhibit his technical skill and the range and variety of his moods. He could be complimentary, tender, and graceful, as in the many verses to Lady Juliet Duff; or amused and sardonic, as in **"On a Great Name."** . . . If Belloc's reputation as a light verse writer rested on his epigrams alone, it would still be sure. (pp. 14-15)

Anthologists, by the very nature of their task, are compelled to range widely, to sample variously, to bring many different writers together in some sort of eclectic harmony. That is their business. Neither the *Oxford Book of Light Verse* nor *The New Oxford Book of English Light Verse* can be criticised for the space they allot to authors representing the wide range of light verse in English. But how many epigrammatists are as good as Belloc? . . . Where can be found more amusing nonsense verse since Carroll and Lear than in Belloc's early books of verse? . . . Are Belloc's high spirits and Chesterton's good humour not more refreshing than some of the "low" ballads and popular verse that Auden liked and the contemporary snobbish in-group *vers de société* preferred by Amis? (p. 23)

It is enough to claim, once more and for once at some length, that Belloc and Chesterton are the most gifted light verse writers of their own times and among the most gifted of any times; and that Belloc's technical skill and high spirits and Chesterton's gift for metaphor and image, for the witty and unexpected parallelism and conjection of ideas, and his delightful but unusually sympathetic appreciation of absurdities will preserve the best of their verses from the assaults of time, for the delectation of new audiences. (p. 24)

> *Gertrude M. White, "True Words in Jest: The Light Verse of Chesterton and Belloc," in* The Chesterton Review *(© 1980 The Chesterton Review), Vol, VI, No. 1, Fall-Winter, 1979-80, pp. 1-26.*

ADDITIONAL BIBLIOGRAPHY

Adcock, A. St. John. "Hilaire Belloc." in his *Gods of Modern Grub Street: Impressions of Contemporary Authors*, pp. 13-19. New York: Frederick A. Stokes Co., 1923.
    A short biographical and critical introduction to Belloc.

Braybrooke, Patrick. "Hilaire Belloc as a Novelist." In his *Some Catholic Novelists: Their Art and Outlook*, pp. 37-71. London: Burns Oates & Washbourne, 1931.
    A discussion of *The Green Overcoat, Mr. Petre*, and *The Emerald*.

Chesterton, G. K. "Hilaire Belloc." in *G. K. as M. C.: Being a Collection of Thirty-Seven Introductions*, edited by J. P. Fonseka, pp. 96-102. London: Methuen & Co., 1929.
    Personal reminiscences and a brief assessment of Belloc's writing skill.

Hynes, Samuel. "The Chesterbelloc." In his *Edwardian Occasions: Essays on English Writing in the Early Twentieth Century*, pp. 80-90. New York: Oxford University Press, 1972.*
    Examines the effects of Belloc's aggressive, occasionally brutal personality on his work. Hynes believes that Belloc's more belligerent efforts will ever pale in comparison to his light-hearted verse and travel books.

Jago, David. "The Stoicism of Hilaire Belloc." *Renascence* XXVII, No. 2 (Winter 1975): 89-100.
    Examines Belloc's melancholia, finding him "less a writer than a failed man of action."

Jebb, Eleanor, and Jebb, Reginald. *Testimony to Hilaire Belloc*. London: Methuen & Co., 1956, 172 p.
    Essays and memoirs on Belloc's life and beliefs.

Kantra, Robert A. "Irony in Belloc." *Renascence* XVII, No. 2 (Spring 1965): 132-36.
    A brief examination of Belloc's use of irony and his philosophy of its use.

Kelly, Hugh. "Centenary of Hilaire Belloc." *Studies* LIX, No. 236 (Winter 1970): 396-403.
    A brief survey of Belloc's career.

Kilmer, Joyce. Introdution to *Verses*, by Hilaire Belloc, pp. xi-xxvii. New York: Laurence J. Gomme, 1916.
    Praises Belloc as "a poet who happens to be known chiefly for his prose." Kilmer believes that Belloc's Catholicism vivifies the poems most likely to endure.

Las Vergnas, Raymond. "Hilaire Belloc." In his *Chesterton, Belloc, Baring*, pp. 50-87. New York: Sheed & Ward, 1938.
    An excellent survey and study of Belloc's life, work, and beliefs.

Lodge, David. "The Chesterbelloc and the Jews." In his *The Novelist at the Crossroads and Other Essays in Fiction and Criticism*, pp. 146-58. Ithaca: Cornell University Press, 1971.*
    Focuses on Chesterton's and Belloc's anti-Semitism.

Lowndes, Marie Belloc. *The Young Hilaire Belloc*. New York: P. J. Kenedy & Sons, 1956, 182 p.
    A memoir of Belloc's life up to 1914, recounted by his sister.

Mandell, C. Creighton, and Shanks, Edward. *Hilaire Belloc: The Man and His Work*. London: Methuen & Co., 1916, 143 p.
    A study of Belloc's thought and work, examining separately each genre in which he wrote.

McCarthy, John P. *Hilaire Belloc: Edwardian Radical*. Indianapolis: Liberty Press, 1978, 373 p.
    Presents Belloc as a social and political radical-liberal of his day. His life and beliefs are portrayed against the background of Great Britain's foreign and domestic policies of the late nineteenth and early twentieth century.

Reilly, Joseph J. "The Art of Belloc, Biographer." In his *Dear Prue's Husband and Other People*, pp. 79-98. New York: Macmillan, 1932.
    A valuable study of Belloc's skill at biography.

Reynolds, E. E. "The Chesterbelloc." *The Critic* 37, No. 17 (March 1979): 2-3, 6.
    A short, valuable survey of Belloc's work.

Shaw, Bernard. ''How Free Is the Press?'' In his *Pen Portraits and Reviews*, pp. 35-43. London: Constable and Co., 1932.
> Reprints a 1918 review of *The Free Press,* twitting Belloc and the Chesterton brothers for their concept of coterie journalism, while agreeing with the book's basic premises.

Sheed, Wilfrid. ''Chesterbelloc.'' In his *The Morning After: Selected Essays and Reviews,* pp. 259-75. New York: Farrar, Straus & Giroux, 1971.*
> A discussion of Belloc and Chesterton, stressing their roles as promoters of Catholicism and examining their anti-Semitism.

Speaight, Robert. *The Life of Hilaire Belloc.* London: Hollis & Carter, 1957, 552 p.
> The definitive biography.

Wilhelmsen, Frederick. *Hilaire Belloc: No Alienated Man: A Study in Christian Integration.* London: Sheed and Ward, 1954, 108 p.
> A study of the various aspects of Belloc's outlook which, together, define his Christian humanism.

Andrey Bely

1880-1934

(Also transliterated as Andrei and Andrej; also Bely, Belyj, Belyi, Biely, and Beluy; pseudonym of Boris Nikolayevich Bugayev, also transliterated as Bugaev) Russian poet, novelist, short story writer, autobiographer, essayist, and critic.

Bely is recognized as the most original and influential writer of the Russian symbolist movement. A brilliant, restless, and undisciplined spirit, Bely consistently sought for spiritual meaning within the social and literary turmoil of pre-Soviet Russia. His enormous body of work, much of it autobiographical, presents a vivid impression of this quest. Bely's explorations of form and language served as a first step toward the modernist revolution of Russian verse, a call-to-arms by many young writers for more individual artistic freedom and the complete overthrow of the traditional values and social criticism of the nineteenth century. Though he was hardly a popular writer—his work was too subjective and esoteric for the general public—Bely received great attention and acclaim as the standard-bearer for those symbolists who felt that symbolism was more of a *Weltanschauung,* or world-view, than mere literary method. Bely's works are characterized by their verbal artistry, inner-rhythm, and keenly developed style.

Bely was born in Moscow. His father was one of Russia's leading mathematicians; his mother was a capricious, self-centered woman who was determined to prevent young Boris from following in the intellectual footsteps of his father. For fear of his mother's resulting tantrums, he was forced to repress any intellectual activity as a child, and he soon learned to hide behind a cloak of feigned stupidity, which he rarely shed. Fortunately, the boy was placed under the tutelage of a governess who exposed him to the world of literature and music. As he grew older, an interest in art and aesthetics eventually displaced interest in the scientific world of his father. In 1902 he published his first work, *Vtoraia simfoniia: Dramaticheskaia,* with the encouragement of Mikhail Solovyov, brother of the mystic poet-philosopher Vladimir Solovyov. The poetry of Vladimir Solovyov made a lasting impression on Bely. In his simfonii and verses Bely demonstrates his belief in the Solovyovan notion that "this world is but a shadow" of a higher, internal reality which is revealed to the poet in moments of creative ecstasy. Bely championed the ideas of symbolism until 1912, when he became absorbed in the anthroposophical doctrines of Rudolf Steiner, a quasireligious philosophy which sought the resurrection of man through love and spiritual knowledge. This attachment formed the basis of his autobiographical novel *Kotik Letaev.* During this period he also wrote *Serebrianyi golub' (The Silver Dove),* a study of a young intellectual's flirtation with, and destruction by, the mystical forces guiding a revolutionary sect in provincial Russia. *The Silver Dove* is considered prophetic of the defeat of the Russian intelligentsia who led the 1917 revolution.

As a novelist, Bely reached the pinnacle of his career with the appearance of *Peterburg (St. Petersburg)* in 1913. Many critics regard *St. Petersburg* not only as Bely's prose masterpiece, but also as the masterpiece of his generation. The novel's acoustic effects, its deliberate impression of chaos, and its rhythmical power make it one of the most arresting Russian novels of the

twentieth century. Often compared to Joyce's *Ulysses* or *Finnegans Wake, St. Petersburg* was Bely's attempt to express the depths of spiritual life and to communicate states of being beyond consciousness. Like Joyce, Bely arrived at a peculiar style comprised of neologisms, interior monologue, and a myth-like structure of plot. Essentially, *St. Petersburg* is a symbolic prophecy of the impending doom of Russia; but on another level, through its deliberate confusion of fantasy and reality and its ever-present satire, the novel illustrates Bely's conviction that life is merely an appearance, that we see only masks and reflections of truth in this world of material reality.

Throughout his life most critics belittled Bely's significance. Only the modernists and the most sophisticated readers praised his works, stressing his stylistic innovations, and his acute attention to the word as sound, as image, and as symbol. For these critics, Bely's works were a new brand of literary nominalism, a return to the primary role of literature wherein to name meant to interpret and create. Many others, however, ignored or ridiculed his efforts. They argued that his poetry was too vague and subjective, that his novels were often ponderous, and that his technical subtleties, in the end, became tiresome and irritating. It has only been in the last two decades that critics outside the Soviet Union have come to appreciate the depth of Bely's imagination and the importance of his stylistic innovations. The most famous assessment of Bely's importance was made by Vladimir Nabokov who called *St. Petersburg* one of the "greatest masterpieces of twentieth century prose."

Despite his lack of a popular literary appeal, critics in general agree that Bely is the most representative writer of the Russian symbolist movement and that, owing to his brilliance and imagination, he had a profound effect on Russian literature long after symbolism and its importance as a movement faded from the literary scene.

PRINICPAL WORKS

Vtoraia simfoniia: Dramaticheskaia (prose poem) 1902
Severnaia simfoniia: Pervia geroicheskaia (prose poem) 1903
Zoloto v lazuri (poetry) 1904
Vozvrat: Tretiia simfoniia (prose poem) 1905
Kubok metelei: Chetviortiia simfoniia (prose poem) 1908
Pepel (poetry) 1909
Serebrianyi golub' (novel) 1909
  [*The Silver Dove*, 1974]
Urna (poetry) 1909
Lug zelenyi (essays) 1910
Peterburg (novel) 1913
  [*St. Petersburg*, 1959]
Khristos voskres (poetry) 1918
Pervoe svidanie (poetry) 1921
  [*The First Encounter*, 1980]
Kotik Letaev (autobiographical novel) 1922
  [*Kotik Letaev*, 1971]
Zapiski chudaka (novel) 1922
Vospominaniya o A. A. Bloke (memoirs) 1922-23;
  published in journal *Epopeia*
Moskva (novels) 1926
Kreshchenyi kitaets (novel) 1927
Ritm, kak dialektika i "Mednyi vsadnik" Pushkina
  (criticism) 1929
Na rubezhe dvykh stoleti (memoirs) 1930
Maski (novel) 1932
Mezhdu dvukh revolyutsi (unfinished memoirs) 1934
Complete Short Stories (short stories) 1979

NIKOLAI GUMILEV (essay date 1901)

Of the whole older generation of Symbolists, Andrei Bely is the least cultured—not in the bookish culture of the academics, something of a Siamese order which is valued only because it is difficult to get, and few have it; in this culture he is strong . . .—but in the true culture of mankind, which teaches respect and self-criticism, grows into flesh and blood and puts its mark on every thought, every action of man. Somehow one cannot imagine that he was ever in the Louvre, that he read Homer. . . . And I am judging now not by *Ashes* and not by *Cup of Blizzards*, God be their judge, but by the whole creative work of Andrei Bely, which I have been following for a long time and with interest. Why with interest will be apparent from what follows.

The poet Bely quickly assimilated all the subtleties of contemporary poetic technique. Thus the barbarian immediately accepts the fact that one should not eat fish with a knife, wear colored collars in the winter or write sonnets with nineteen lines. . . . He uses free verse and alliteration and internal rhyme. But he cannot write a regular poem with clear and distinct images and without a bluster of unnecessary words. In this he is inferior even to the third-rate poets of the past. . . . And one can strongly argue against his understanding of iambic tetrameter, the meter in which almost all of *Urn* is written. Tracing the development of the iamb in Pushkin, we see that this great meter inclined more and more toward use of the fourth paeon, the one which gives verse the greatest sonority. It is incomprehensible why Andrei Bely renounces such an important means of giving life to his often wooden verses.

But what is the charm of Andrei Bely, why does one even want to think and speak of him? Because there are themes in his work, and these themes are truly profound and unusual. He has enemies—time and space, and friends—eternity, the ultimate goal. He makes these abstract concepts concrete, contrasts them to his personal "self"; they are for him real beings of his world. Combining the too airy colors of the old poets with the too heavy and harsh ones of contemporary poets, he achieves surprising effects, which prove that the world of his dreams really is magnificent. . . . (pp. 44-5)

The reader will be dissatisfied with my review. He will certainly want to know if I am praising or reproving Andrei Bely. I will not answer this question. The time for conclusions has not yet come. (p. 45)

> *Nikolai Gumilev, "Bely" (originally a speech given on May 4, 1901), in his* Nikolai Gumilev on Russian Poetry, *edited and translated by David Lapeza (© 1977 by Ardis Publishers), Ardis, 1977, pp. 44-5.*

LEON TROTSKY (essay date 1924)

The inter-revolutionary (1905-1917) literature, which is decadent in its mood and reach and over-refined in its technique, which is a literature of individualism, of symbolism and of mysticism, finds in Biely its most condensed expression, and through Biely was most loudly destroyed by [the October revolution]. (pp. 46-7)

Biely's memoirs of Blok, which are amazing in their meaningless detail and in their arbitrary mosaic of psychology, make one feel ten-fold to what an extent they are people of another epoch, of another world, of a past epoch, of an unreturnable world. This is not a question of the difference in generations, for they are people of our own generation, but of the difference in social make-up, in spiritual type, in historic roots. (p. 47)

Biely's roots are in the past. But where is the old harmony now? On the contrary, everything seems shaken up to Biely, everything is aslant, everything is thrown out of equilibrium. . . . Biely's apparent dynamics mean only a running around and a struggling on the mounds of a disappearing and disintegrating old régime. His verbal twists lead nowhere. He has no hint of ideal revolutionism. In his core he is a realistic and spiritual conservative who has lost the ground under his feet and is in despair. (p. 48)

Torn from the pivot of custom and individualism, Biely wishes to replace the whole world with himself, to build everything from himself and through himself, to discover everthing anew in himself—but his works, with all their different artistic values, invariably represent a poetic or spiritualist sublimation of the old customs. And that is why, in the final analysis, this servile preoccupation with oneself, this apotheosis of the ordinary facts of one's personal and spiritual routine, become so unbearable in our age where mass and speed are really making a new world. If one is to write with so much ritual of the meeting with Blok, how is one to write about great events which affect the destinies of nations?

In Biely's recollections of his infancy ("**Kotik Lotaev**") there are interesting moments of lucid psychology, not always artistically correct, but frequently internally convincing, yet his connecting them together with occult discussions, his make-belief profundities, his piling up of images and words, make them futile and utterly tiresome. With his knees and elbows, Biely tries to squeeze his childish soul through into the world beyond. The traces of his elbows are seen on all the pages, but the world beyond—isn't there! And, in fact, where is it to come from? (pp. 48-9)

Biely is not a maximalist, not in the very least, but an unquestioned minimalist, a chip of the old régime and of its point of view, yearning and sighing in a new environment. And it is absolutely true that he approaches everything in a roundabout way. His whole "**St. Petersburg**" is built by a roundabout method. And that is why it feels like an act of labor. Even in those places where he has attained artistic results, that is, where an image arises in the consciousness of the reader, it is paid for too dearly, so that after all these roundabout ways, after the straining and the labor, the reader does not experience aesthetic satisfaction. It is just as if you were led into a house through the chimney, and on entering you saw that there was a door, and that it was much easier to enter that way.

His rhythmic prose is terrible. His sentences do not obey the inner movement of the image, but an external meter, which at first seems only superfluous, and later begins to tire you with its obtrusiveness, and finally poisons your very existence. The premonition that a sentence will end rhythmically makes one extremely irritated, just as when one waits for the shutter to squeak again when one is sleepless. Side by side with Biely's march of the rhythm goes his fetish of the word. It is absolutely irrefutable that the human word expresses not only meaning, but has a sound value, and that without this attitude to the word there would be no mastery in poetry or in prose. We are not going to deny Biely the merits attributed to him in this field. However, the most weighty and high-sounding word cannot give more than is put into it. Biely seeks in the word, just as the Pythagoreans in numbers, a second, special and hidden meaning. And that is why he finds himself so often in a blind alley of words. (pp. 49-50)

Instead of logical and psychological analysis, he characterizes his stagnant thinking, which is essentially medieval, by the play of alliteration and by the substituting of verbal twists and acoustic ties. The more convulsively Biely holds on to words, and the more mercilessly he violates them, the harder it is for his inert opinions in a world which has overcome inertia. Biely is strongest when he describes the solid old life. His manner, even there, is tiresome, but not futile. You can see clearly that Biely himself is flesh of the flesh and bone of the bone of the old state, that he is thoroughly conservative, passive and moderate, and that his rhythm and his verbal twists are only a means of vainly struggling with his inner passivity and sobriety when torn from his life's pivot. (pp. 50-1)

Leon Trotsky, "Pre-Revolutionary Art" (1924), in his Literature and Revolution, *translated by Rose Strunsky (reprinted by permission of George Allen & Unwin (Publishers) Ltd.; originally published as* Literatura i revoliutsiia, *gosud arstvenoye izdatelstva, 1924) Allen & Unwin, 1925 (and reprinted by Russell & Russell, 1957), pp. 126-61.**

D. S. MIRSKY   (essay date 1926)

If Blok was the greatest of the symbolists, certainly the most original and influential was Bély. Unlike Blok, whose nearest affinities are in the past with the great romanticists, Bély is all turned towards the future, and, of all the symbolists, he has most in common with the futurists. The example of his prose especially revolutionized the style of Russian prose writing. Bély is a more complex figure than Blok—or even than any other symbolist; in this respect he can easily vie with the most complex and disconcerting figures in Russian literature, Gógol and Vladímir Soloviëv, both of whom had their say in his making. He is, on the one hand, the most extreme and typical expression of the symbolist mentality; no one carried farther the will to reduce the world to a system of "correspondences," and no one took these "correspondences" more concretely and more realistically; but this very concreteness of his immaterial symbols brings him back to a realism quite outside the common run of symbolist expression. His hold on the finer shades of reality—on the most expressive, significant, suggestive, and at once elusive detail—is so great and so original that it evokes the unexpected comparison with that realist of realists, Tolstóy. And yet Bély's world is an immaterial world of ideas into which this reality of ours is only projected like a whirlwind of phantasms. This immaterial world of symbols and abstractions appears as a pageant of color and fire; and in spite of the earnest intensity of his spiritual life, it strikes one rather as a metaphysical "show," splendid and amusing, but not dead earnest. The sense of tragedy is curiously absent from Bély, and in this again he is in bold contrast to Blok. His world is rather an elfland—beyond good and evil; in it Bély moves like a Puck of an Ariel—but an undisciplined and erratic Ariel. All this makes some people regard him as a seer and a prophet; others, as a sort of mystical mountebank. Whatever he is, he is strikingly different from all the symbolists by his complete lack of hieratic solemnity. Sometimes he is comic against his will, but on the whole he has not audaciously fused his comic appearance with his mysticism and utilized it with surprising originality. He is perhaps the greatest Russian humorist since Gógol, and to the general reader this is his most important and attractive aspect. But it is a humor that disconcerts at first and is very unlike anything else in the world. It took the Russian public some twenty years to learn to appreciate it, and it will hardly take the uninitiated foreigner by storm. But those who have tasted of it will always recognize it as (in the strict sense of the word) unique—one of the choicest and rarest gifts of the great gods. (pp. 463-64)

[His longer poem, *The First Meetings,*] is a charming work. Like Soloviëv's *Three Meetings*, it is a mixture of grave and gay—a mixture that is curiously inseparable in Bély. A large part of it will again seem, to the uninitiated, nothing better than verbal and phonetic play. It must be joyfully accepted as such, and as such it is most exhilarating. But the realistic part of the poem is better than that. It contains some of his best humorous painting—the portraits of the Soloviëvs and the description of a big symphony concert in Moscow about 1900 are masterpieces of verbal expressiveness, delicate realism, and delightful humor. This poem is most closely connected with his prose works, and, like them, it is all based on a very elaborate system of musical construction, with leitmotivs, "correspondences," and "cross references."

In the preface to **The Dramatic Symphony**, Bély says: "This work has three senses: a musical sense, a satirical sense, and besides, a philosophical-symbolical sense." The same may be said of all his prose, except that the second meaning is not always strictly satirical—"realistic" would be more comprehensive. The philosophical meaning is what Bély probably thinks the most important, but for the reader the first way of enjoying his prose is not to take the philosophy too seriously and not to rack his brains in trying to discover the meaning. This would be useless, especially as regards the later "anthroposophic" work, the philosophy of which cannot be understood without a prolonged initiation at Dornach. But Bély's prose loses nothing from his philosophical symbols' being taken as merely ornamental. His prose is "ornamental prose"—an expression that later became a technical term. In this ornamental prose the symbols (and sound symbols) he uses to express his metaphysics are by no means the worst ornament. "Ornamental" is not the same as "ornate" prose. It is not necessarily marked by conventionally uplifted diction, as Sir Thomas Browne's or Vyacheslár Ivánov's. On the contrary, it may be crudely realistic or even aggressively coarse (some of the younger "ornamentalists" went much farther in this respect than any naturalist ever dared to). The essential is that it keeps the reader's attention to every small detail: to the words, to their sounds, and to the rhythm. . . . It is the declaration of independence of the smaller unit. Western masters of "ornamental" prose are Rabelais, Lamb, Carlyle. The greatest Russian ornamentalist was Gógol. . . . Ornamental prose has a decided tendency to escape the control of the larger unit, to destroy the wholeness of a work. This tendency is fully developed in almost every one of Bély's followers. But in Bély's own work it is counterbalanced by the musical architecture of the whole. This musical architecture is expressed in the very name of the **Symphonies,** and it is attained by a most elaborate system of leitmotivs and "cross references," crescendos and diminuendos, and parallel developments of independent but (by their symbolism) connected themes. However, the centrifugal tendencies of the style usually have the better of the centripetal forces of musical construction, and, with the possible exception of **The Silver Dove,** Bély's **Symphonies** and novels are but imperfect wholes. The **Symphonies** (especially **The Dramatic**) contain much that is excellent, chiefly of the satirical order, but they cannot be recommended to the inexperienced beginner. (pp. 468-49)

The Silver Dove is somewhat less wildly original than his other works. It is closely modeled on the great example of Gógol. It cannot be called an imitative work, for it requires a powerful originality to learn from Gógol without failing piteously. . . . The novel is written in splendid, sustainedly beautiful prose, and this prose is the first thing that strikes the reader. . . . **The Silver Dove** is somewhat alone also in being the one of Bély's novels that has the most human interest in it, where the tragedy is infectious and not merely puckishly ornamental. . . . The novel contains much more narrative interest than most Russian novels do. The characters are vivid—like Gógol's, characterized largely by their physical features; the dialogue is alive and expressive. But what is perhaps especially wonderful is the evocations of nature, full of intense suggestiveness and pregnant poetry. The feeling of the monotonous and endless expanse of the Russian plain pervades the book. All this, together with the splendidly ornamental style, makes **The Silver Dove** one of

the works of Russian literature most full of the most various riches. (pp. 469-70)

D. S. Mirsky, "The Symbolists," in his Contemporary Russian Literature: 1881-1925 *(copyright 1926 by Alfred A. Knopf, Inc.; reprinted by permission of Alfred A. Knopf, Inc.), Knopf, 1926, G. Routledge & Sons, 1926 (and reprinted in his* A History of Russian Literature Comprising "A History of Russian Literature" and "Contemporary Russian Literature," *edited by Francis J. Whitfield, Knopf, 1955, pp. 430-84).**

YEVGENY ZAMYATIN   (essay date 1934)

What [Andrey Bely] had written was as extraordinary and fantastic as his life. This is why even his novels—not to speak of his numerous theoretical works—have always been read principally by the intellectual elite. He was above all "a writer's writer," a master, an inventor whose inventions have been used by many Russian novelists of the younger generations. None of the many recent anthologies of contemporary Russian literature which have appeared in various European languages fails to mention Andrey Bely.

But here we see again one of those paradoxes that abound in his biography, both personal and literary: the books of this master, the theoretician of an entire literary school, remain untranslated, and live only in their Russian incarnation. I am not certain, however, whether one can properly say that they are written in Russian, so unusual is Bely's syntax, so full of neologisms his diction. The language of his books is Bely's language, just as the language of *Ulysses* is not English, but Joyce's language. (pp. 241-42)

[Bely's] very first book of poems brought him into the most advanced literary circles of the time and established his close kinship with Blok, Bryusov and Merezhkovsky. . . .

[Then] Bely went on to the novel. During those years he wrote two of his best known books, **The Silver Dove** and **Petersburg.** The former introduces the reader to the weird atmosphere ruling the life of a sect known as the Flagellants and tells the story of a refined intellectual, a poet who stumbles into this milieu and is destroyed by his encounter with the dark forces of the Russian village. . . . In the latter novel, Bely shows the tsarist Petersburg as a city already doomed but still beautiful with a dying, spectral loveliness. One of the masters of this Petersburg, Senator Ableukhov, is condemned to death by the revolutionaries with whom his son, a student, is connected. This plot of the novel is built around this sharp conflict. In this book, Bely's best work, Petersburg finds its true portrayer for the first time since Gogol and Dostoyevsky.

Bely spent the prerevolutionary years . . . in restless wanderings in Africa and Europe. His meeting with the leader of the anthroposophists, Dr. Rudolph Steiner, proved decisive for Bely. But anthroposophy to him was not the quiet haven it is for many weary souls—to him it was merely a port of departure into the infinite spaces of cosmic philosophy and new artistic experiments. The most interesting of these was the novel **Kotik Letayev,** perhaps the only attempt in world literature to embody anthroposophic ideas in a work of art. A child's psyche is chosen as the screen that is to reflect these ideas—at the age when the first glimmerings of consciousness stir within the child, when the child steps out of the world of shadowy recollections of his prenatal existence, the world of four dimensions, into the solid, three-dimensional world which wounds him painfully. (pp. 243-44)

The other works of his final years—the volume of memoirs, *At the Turn of the Century,* and the two novels, *Moscow* and *Masks*—were also summations. We no longer find here the fantastic, four-dimensional world of *Kotik Letayev* and *Petersburg.* These novels are built on real, partly autobiographical, material from the life of the Moscow intelligentsia during the crucial years of change in the early twentieth century. The clearly satirical approach taken by the author was a concession to the spirit of the time, which demanded disparagement of the past. But Bely's tireless formal experimentation, this time chiefly in the lexical area, continued in these last novels as well. Until the very end, he remained the "Russian Joyce." (p. 245)

> *Yevgeny Zamyatin, "Andrey Bely" (1934), in his* A Soviet Heretic: Essays, *edited and translated by Mirra Ginsburg (reprinted by permission of The University of Chicago Press; translation © 1970 by The University of Chicago), University of Chicago Press, 1970, pp. 241-45.*

JANKO LAVRIN (essay date 1947)

The author who made a strong effort to overcome decadence in the name of a new symbolist view of life was Andrey Bely. . . . Together with the poets Alexander Blok and Vyacheslav Ivanov, Bely became one of the chief exponents of Russian symbolism. A poet, a novelist, a critic, an essayist, a first-rate authority on Russian prosody, he yet remained a brilliant experimenter whose genius failed to crystallize entirely—perhaps on account of its very wealth. Anxious to overcome his gloomy tiredness of the *fin de siècle,* he looked for an ally in his own metaphysical irony, in the philosophy of Vladimir Solovyov, and later even in the anthroposophy of Rudolf Steiner. Kant, Nietzsche, and Maeterlinck affected him also. . . . Yet the two authors who left a lasting mark on Bely's prose were Gogol and Dostoevsky. He worked out the possibilities of Gogol's ornate and musical style in so many directions that he became, together with Remizov, one of the masters of the word in modern Russian fiction, the Soviet fiction included. What brings him even closer to Gogol and Dostoevsky is his peculiar view of the world, by virtue of which he mixes—often with amusing grotesqueness—two planes of existence: the actual and the fantastic, that is, irrational. Like Gogol, he too dissociates reality, alters its proportions, and then creates a strange subjective world of his own: a blend of naturalism and apocalyptic mysticism, often seasoned with delightful puckish bouts, in which his talent for parody finds its full scope.

Bely's first novel, *The Silver Dove* . . . , was one of the most remarkable products of the symbolist period. Its prose goes back to Gogol, but Bely applies to it a conscious technical discipline and pattern. What makes this work so modern (in a morbid sense) is the subtle mixture of mystic and erotic exaltation which, on a lower level, would decidedly have led to Rasputin and Rasputinism. With care and insight, Bely discloses to the reader some of the most elusive irrational roots of a sect, to which the chief character falls a prey. In spite of its high technical standard, *The Silver Dove* is written with such unflagging verve as to be a source of delight even to people who are used to lighter fare.

More puzzling and difficult is Bely's next novel, *Petersburg.* . . . Its stammering language and deliberate confusion of reality with hallucination are reminiscent of Dostoevsky's

The Double. Worked out according to a definite ideological plan, *Petersburg* is charged with peculiar rhythm, euphony, and verbal instrumentations. Its chief character is a revolutionary intellectual in whose consciousness the Russian metropolis—or rather Dostoevsky's irrational Petersburg—looms and haunts him as a phantom of his own diseased brain. Whatever happens to him is immediately turned into a series of spooks and inner conflicts. All proportions are altered, distorted, until the hero is lost in the mazes of his own psychic chaos. This novel is too ingenious to be really enjoyable. Its very subtleties become tiresome in the end. What one admires in it is above all the tour de force of Bely's narrative technique. (pp. 164-66)

> *Janko Lavrin, "The Modernist Movement," in his* An Introduction to the Russian Novel *(Candian rights by permission of Janko Lavrin), Whittlesey House, 1947, pp. 156-70.**

OLEG A. MASLENIKOV (essay date 1952)

[Andrey Biely's] earliest literary work was essentially lyrical. It comprises his first three *Symphonies* and his first book of verse, *Gold in Azure.* . . . . The novelty and freshness of Andrey Biely's writings astonished readers who were sympathetic to modernism, and who, from the very first, recognized in Andrey Biely a radical innovator in Russian literature. His readers felt his lines vibrating with the voice of a truly "new man," who had discarded the language of his fathers, because it could not adequately convey the inner experiences of a radically changed mode of life and thought.

His first published work, the *Dramatic Symphony,* introduced a new literary genre. The *Symphony* was a lyrical tale, written in poetic prose that was heavily in debt to such diverse sources as Gogol's lyrical passages, Nietzsche's *Also sprach Zarathustra,* and the prophecies of the Revelations of St. John. It emphasized not so much the thread of narration as the rhythm and music of language, which it blended with colorful imagery, often repeated as a refrain. The *Symphony* sought to create a mood rather than tell a story, and consequently appealed to the senses more than to the intellect. The new genre was admirably suited to convey the young author's urgent, constantly repeated message that our everyday existence and our everyday world are not real, but "dreams, only dreams." This is the message that underlies Biely's imaginative writings, all of which strive to show the irreality of the our existence. In order further to stress the irreality of the physical world, Biely time and again resorts to satire in depicting scenes from life. Here he again appears as a disciple of Gogol. The apocalyptic theme present in the first three *Symphonies* harmonizes with the troubled expectancy of the mystically inclined Russian intellectuals, who at the turn of the century felt that the end of their world was imminent and that the new world would bring with it at least a new species of mankind, if not actually the millennium.

Biely's *Symphonies* were as radical a departure from Russian literary tradition as had once been Pushkin's *Ruslan and Ludmilla* or *Boris Godunov.* In many respects, Biely's work represents a transition from nineteenth-century Russian literature to a new stage. It is at once the last link in the chain that began with Pushkin, and the first link of something new. Characteristically, the writer's first book of poetry, *Gold in Azure,* broke away from the nearly century-old verse traditions of the Pushkin period.

Although in some respects Biely's poetry resembles his *Symphonies,* on the whole it is more autobiographical and personal. His *Symphonies* are prophetic visions that reveal themselves to a poet in the throes of creative ecstasy. His verses, on the other hand, record not only the poet's dreams but the flow of the moods and events of his life. Biely's poetry is as much a lyrical diary as are the verses of Alexander Blok, and his first three collections [*Gold in Azure, Ashes,* and *The Urn*] . . . record a rapturous flight toward the sun, a flight that ended in disaster, despair, and resignation.

Although in their ethereal and mystical moods his verses undeniably reflect the influence of [Afanasy Fet, Fyodor] Tyutchev, and especially Vladimir Solovyov, much in them is quite unlike anything that Russian readers had met before. *Gold in Azure* astonished the readers by its freshness and novelty.

Biely was the first modern Russian poet to break away completely from the fetters of traditional metric-tonic Russian versification. His remarkable sense of rhythm enabled him to disregard set metrical patterns and to introduce the pause as a metrical element. He applied to literary versification the rhythmic principles of the folk poetry and thus brought the written forms closer to the natural rhythm of the language. (pp. 71-3)

In his earliest verse, Biely appears as a Solovyovan prophet, whose trumpet sounds a note of apocalyptic expectancy. In foretelling the end of time and the coming millennium, he is one of the chosen few who can "foretell," who "know" that "sacred days" are at hand. . . . He senses that everything is radiantly prepared for the great day, that the air itself is "luminous to the point of pain." He rejoices as he awaits from hour to hour the advent of the millennium.

The imagery and language strike the reader by their originality. The lines are saturated with the vivid colors of a brilliant sunset, blended with the solitary melancholy of its pastel afterglow. The poet's consciousness throbs with the belief that he is one with the limitless universe. The slumbering trees, the sighing breeze, the fragments of clouds that dot the evening sky—all speak to him with the voice of eternity, which now caresses and fills him with rapture, now fills him with anticipation and then with alarm. Strange creatures populate the landscape; the fauns, giants, hunchbacks, and wizards that are resurrected from antiquity, classical mythology, and Germanic folklore, add to the "neoprimitivism" of the scenes. Typical of his mood are such phrases as "the hot sun—a ring of gold"; "eternity's streaming waterfall"; the "golden amber hour." (p. 74)

Biely seems never at a loss for words. If the Russian language lacks a word that he wants, Biely coins it, especially if it be an adjective with an exotic connotation. . . . (p. 75)

Despite the apparent optimism of [many Biely] poems, an opposite mood is also found in *Gold in Azure.* It is a mood of doubt and irony that borders on despair, hysteria, and cynicism. The poems written during 1903, especially during the month of August after his father's death, illustrate this side of Andrey Biely. (p. 76)

Up to this time the notes of melancholy and loneliness were isolated in Biely's poetry, as in **"Melancholy."** . . . For example, there are few lines such as "Wretched and poor in the wasteland I wander weeping. . . . So cold and so frightened am I" . . . ; and only occasionally did he hear the "lazily swaying rustle of oats" voice the doubts buried in his own dual nature. . . . Now, however, these *motifs* loom increasingly large and their specter soon overshadows everything else. (p. 77)

The pessimistic mood, which was distinctly shaped by the personal events in [Biely's] life, intensified as time went on. Another factor in his personal life that filled him with a feeling of futility, guilt, and remorse was his fateful and frenetic love affair with Lyubov Dmitrievna Blok, wife of Alexander Blok, whom he regarded as his "spiritual brother." . . . Sociohistorical events further heightened his growing dejection. The disastrous Russo-Japanese War . . . , the unsuccessful revolution of 1905-1906, the ensuing political reaction and the air of apathy and demoralization that subsequently enveloped much of the intelligentsia, completed the transformation of his former rapture into a mood of hysteria and despair.

Although Biely's first book of verse, *Gold in Azure,* is dominated by an apocalyptic fervor and by an impulse to reach the clean, clear azure of the sky, his second collection of poems, *Ashes* . . . depicts an abrupt descent to earth. The prophetic motifs of Vladimir Solovyov now yield to the civic despondency of [Nikolay] Nekrasov, coupled with the despairing abandon of Dostoyevsky. During the period 1904-1907, Biely completed *The Goblet of Blizzards,* his fourth and last *Symphony,* which was the shriek of a soul in agony. Biely himself termed it a "psychological document on the state of a contemporary mind." Escape became imperative. To continue along the same path would have been to agree that "nothing matters." Biely's muse consequently undergoes a transformation. No longer does he seek eternity; he is now troubled by a spectre of a new "beloved"—Russia. His vision of her is no idealization of reality. She appears to him as the land "where horror lurks under each shadow." . . . In the volume, *Ashes,* Biely cremates his early raptures and holds a wake, which in such poems as **"Joy in Russia"** amazes the reader by its rhythmic abandon and the despondency that underlies the mood. More and more, now, Biely turns to regular forms in his Nekrasovlike lament of Russia. (pp. 78-9)

Early in 1909, toward the end of this period, Biely published his third book of verse, *The Urn,* which was to symbolize the vessel in which the poet collected the "ashes of his scorched raptures." *The Urn* is as purely subjective as his previous works and clearly reflects an effort to find peace in philosophical meditation. (pp. 79-80)

Biely's purely theoretical articles of this period reflect his own disillusion with all the fond hopes of his youth. No longer does he regard symbolism as the *Weltanschauung* of the immediate future, of "tomorrow." He now sees it as an achievement only of the distant future, toward which all culture must slowly and painfully evolve. Therefore, he comes to the decision that any attempt to "define the contours of symbolism" can produce only a "temporary, working hypothesis," by means of which an all-inclusive methodological foundation of art might be gradually built. (p. 80)

The year 1908, in which Biely published his last *Symphony* and completed his two books of verse, *Ashes* and *The Urn,* terminated the lyrical period of his career. The year 1909 ended his attempts to define symbolism as a *Weltanschauung* and led him to scientific analysis of the formal elements of art.

At about the same time Biely entered upon still another stage in his literary development, by beginning his first novel [*Silver Dove*]. . . . Although in technique the novel resembles the *Symphonies,* it differs from them in that it emphasizes narrative rather than mood. While the *Silver Dove,* like the *Symphonies,* deals with the theme of doom, it differs from the *Symphonies* in that it holds no promise for the future. Its hero, Daryalski, an intellectual (who has many points in common with Biely), in seeking spiritual rebirth involuntarily turns to the Russian people but, like Biely, finds in Russia an image of chaos rather than a reflection of logos. Fatefully he is drawn into the whirlpool of the dark powers and eventually falls their prey. The *Silver Dove* reflects the influence not only of the eschatological writings of Vladimir Solovyov, but also of the tales of Gogol, and, despite its occasional lapses into the trivial, produces a powerful effect. (pp. 81-2)

In the fall of 1911, Biely began his second novel. Originally he had planned it as a sequel to the *Silver Dove,* as a second part of a trilogy *Orient and Occident.* But he became so engrossed in his plot that the book soon became an entirely independent work, and his original plan for a trilogy was abandoned. The book remained unnamed for several months, until Vyacheslav Ivanov christened it *Petersburg.* The novel again deals with an intellectual, this time with one Nikolay Apollonovich Ableukhov, whose search for truth involves him in the revolutionary movement, until one day he discovers that he is obliged to assassinate his own father, Senator Ableukhov. As important as the hero is the evil spirit that lurks in the background: Petersburg, the city of the mists. Biely's picture of the city is the crowning vision of the evil power that Pushkin, Gogol, and Dostoyevski had recorded in such works as *Bronze Horseman, Nevsky Prospect,* and *White Nights.* Some critics . . . regard *Petersburg* not only as Biely's prose masterpiece, but also as the masterpiece of his generation. The novel's planned acoustic effects, its deliberate impression of chaos, and its ponderous rhythmical majesty leave its readers at once bewildered, oppressed, and somewhat awestruck. *Petersburg* is truly the apogee of an era that stressed individualism in literature. (p. 85)

The life and works of [Andrey Biely] vividly illustrate the course of the Russian symbolist movement during the first decade of the present century. In Andrey Biely, Russian symbolism, at its greatest complexity and in its various connotations, found a striking representative. Symbolism as a state of mentality, symbolism as an art, symbolism as a way of life, are all reflected in his life and works.

Andrey Biely was a characteristic child of a generation that was lost in the wilderness of life. He typifies the intellectual who had discovered that, because of his background, he was beset with two irreconcilable desires: to *know* and to *believe.* Yet he realized that no absolute knowledge existed and also that he could not believe unquestioningly. Owing to nineteenth-century philosophical trends, to the progress of the machine age and the natural sciences, as well as to political, social, and economic conditions, Biely, like many other intellectuals, felt that the new ideas had robbed man of his immortality and dwarfed the importance of the individual. He felt that the validity of intuition had been scientifically disproved; that science had defined all that was knowable; and that no mysteries remained for men to probe or to hope for. He, like other intellectuals, rebelled against all these trends and attempted to reëstablish the importance of the individual, to reassert the validity of intuitive revelation and mystery, and to rehabilitate the value of imagination. In a word, he sought to disprove the entire system of scientific thought that found expression in positivism and materialism.

In attempting to reëstablish the importance of the individual, Biely first turned to himself. He began to regard himself, an

artist, as a superior being. In his own mind he therefore placed himself above the throng of "Philistines." He wanted to be different from them, and consequently developed his own individuality to the point of eccentricity, which he reflected in his art.

In attempting to reassert the validity of intuitive knowledge, he turned to the irrational, to the emotions. He strove to prefer intuitive apprehension to rational comprehension. He desired to restore mystery to its former place in the world. He sought a religious expression of his emotional experiences. He wanted to interpret art as a religious sacrament, as theurgy. Yet so thoroughly was he grounded in the scientific tradition of his day that he could not fully accept any notion based on an irrational interpretation of reality, despite the inner urge to do so. Therefore he found himself dangling over the void between the cliffs of belief and skepticism.

In attempting to reject the world that science had created for man, Biely turned to his imagination to find the real world. He tried to reject completely the reality of the physical, phenomenal universe; he asserted that it comprised mere shadows and echoes of the real world. Since in reëstablishing his own ego he had come to regard himself as a superior being, he now sought to accept the view that he, an artist, could in moments of inspiration glimpse a vision of the higher reality. Nevertheless, because of his scientific training, Biely could not suppress an urge to seek rational proof, irrefutable substantiation for such belief. Failing to be completely satisfied by his findings, he turned to other systems of knowledge in search of support for his urgent will to believe. (pp. 217-18)

Biely's *Weltanschauung* explains much of his art. It is the force that constantly drives him to deny the reality of the material, phenomenal, physical world; it is the power that activates his attempts to disprove and disavow what reason and science accept as fact; it is the basis for his entire artistic creation and for the individualism that underlies his work.

Biely's philosophical idealism drives him to stress the emotional and intuitive elements over the rational. He therefore stresses mood rather than narrative. He expresses himself vaguely, and frequently borders on the obscure. He seeks to transmit feelings rather than thoughts. Since he believes that music can best convey emotions, he stresses the musical element in his writing and goes so far as to attempt (in his *Symphonies*) to apply the principles of musical composition to literature. The religious trend in Biely's works is unmistakable. In following Vladimir Solovyov, Biely proclaims his teacher, together with himself and every true poet, as seer and prophet. Furthermore, since he senses subconsciously that the social structure of his day is doomed, his works possess an aspect of apocalyptic vision. Yet Biely, believing that the change will usher in the millenium, sees himself as a prophet of a new life. In rejecting science and its truth Biely proclaims the reality of the noumenal, transphysical world. Accepting the creative process of art as an infallible cognitive process, as a revelation of the absolute reality, he claims that art affords a creative artist glimpses of this reality. Consequently, he believes that artists should be leaders and teachers as well as creators, and that their duty lies in showing humanity their visions of eternity. Since a poet must, therefore, be different from the crowd, Biely attempts to make his art as individualistic as possible. His individualism also prompts him to make it subjective to the highest degree. For this reason he, like all symbolists, is largely autobiographical. (pp. 219-20)

Throughout his earliest period, Biely's personality, his faith in himself, elevated him far above the average littérateur. To others who exemplified the symbolist mentality Biely appeared as a prophet. His works of the earliest period clearly reflect vitality and faith. Art was revelation, and through it lay the road to a new culture and to a new mankind. His writings reflect a predominantly intuitive approacn and interpretation of reality.

No exact boundary can be placed to mark the end of his early, rapturous period. The change was deeply connected with the deaths of the Solovyovs and of his father in 1903. His love affair with Lyubov Blok intensified his despair. Certainly by 1906, with the Blok affair reaching its climax, and with the political events in Russia increasing Biely's hopelessness, the new mood, one of hysteria and despondency, came into full sway. All his earlier hopes for a new, beautiful life fell shattered. His faith in symbolism as a way of life dissipated into thin air. Seeking to maintain even a trace of hope for the future, he turned to philosophy.

Although chronologically Biely's philosophical studies coincided with the most despairing period of his life, they mitigated the despondency of his mood. Philosophy bred meditation, which in turn brought him to seek a *rational* justification for his beliefs. When he realized what change his mood had undergone, his despair yielded to disillusionment, his hysteria to irony. Symbolism as an intuitive revelation of truth, as a universally infallible cognitive principle was discarded. Symbolism for him had failed, and with this realization a definite period in his life came to an end. (p. 221)

Biely's own life reflects the success and failure of symbolism. He failed in his attempt to realize symbolism as a revelation of the absolute and as a way of life; nevertheless, as a symbolist artist he became a leading figure in twentieth-century Russian literature. His theoretical writings reflect his own mental outlook on reality and illustrate the philosophy typical for the "children of a lost generation," intellectuals who frantically, yet vainly, searched for an unshakable truth. . . . Few symbolist writers have influenced modern Russian literature as much as has Biely, and the most permanent achievements of symbolism have been attained largely through him. Russian literature of the twentieth century eloquently testifies that . . . Andrey Biely was the most original writer of the symbolist movement. (pp. 222-23)

> *Oleg A. Maslenikov, in his* The Frenzied Poets: Andrey Biely and the Russian Symbolists *(copyright © 1952 by the Regents of the University of California; reprinted by permission of the University of California Press), University of California Press, 1952, 234 p.**

MARC SLONIM (essay date 1953)

[Bely's importance lies] in the contribution he made to Russian prose. His *Petersburg* and his autobiographical novels [*Kotik Letayev* and *Kotik Letayev's Crime*] are specimens of Russian surrealism and also of style and pattern as presented in English by James Joyce. Independently of Joyce, however, and on a different psychological and formal level, Bely arrived at a polyphonic prose with neologisms, world-of-nebulae coinages, the interior monologue (or stream of consciousness), and a myth-like structure of plots. A clever juggler, he submitted the word, which became in his hands a sonorous and plastic instrument, to all conceivable experiments. It is dynamic and a

symbol of gesture; it emerges onomatopoetically out of word roots without regard to grammatical rules, and is thus the agent of a stylistic revolution. Bely's rhythmic prose, with its assonances and plays upon meanings, expresses the slightest and least perceptible shades of spiritual life, and at times tries to communicate states of being beyond consciousness. For instance, his *Kotik Letayev* . . . is an attempt to build up a cosmology on a system of parallels: the pre-natal impressions of a nightmare and of a symbolic world are, with the birth and growth of the child, resolved into ordinary three-dimensional manifestations that yet secrete a memory of a fourth dimension. Certain passages of his later works, such as *The Moscow Eccentric, Moscow Under the Blow,* and *Masks*. . . , are definitely 'beyond the mind's grasp,' and their spiral-like devices convey completely irrational, almost delirious experiences.

In his poetry, and even more so in his prose, Bely focused his attention on the word: as a sound, as an image and a symbol, it acquired an autonomy, became an entity in itself. Phonetical tricks, whimsical distortions of colloquial expressions, and fanciful amalgams gave rise to hints and allusions and pointed to hidden ideas. This was a new brand of literary nominalism, and to name meant to interpret and to create. It is obvious that such prose is hard to read. Bely's novels are heavyset, esoteric, often irritating and puzzling—and full to the brim with verbal brilliancy and imagination. Their inventiveness is the delight and the despair of students of philology: Bely transformed verbs into nouns, prepositions into adjectives; he blended popular speech with abstract philosophical terminology, showered neologisms, and displayed a superb defiance of grammar, syntax, and all rules of language.

The composition of Bely's novels is as involved as his style. He deliberately mixes all the planes—the real, the symbolic, and the ideological—and offers a series of separate episodes, providing a clue only at the very end of the narrative; thus there finally emerges a symphony composed of these fragmentary chords. Fantasy and reality are treated in a truly Gogolian manner; details of observation are presented as stage effects, comic and tragic incidents overlap, satire always overflows into grotesquerie. The prevalent spirit of this motley and bizarre creation is the author's conviction that life is merely an appearance, that we see only masks and reflections of truth; the task of the artist is to disclose this truth in a supreme vision that is supernatural, dim, glorious, and frightening—on the frontier of senses and reason, on the border of the sublime and the ridiculous.

Although Bely did not fully realize the style he was striving for, at least he made a break with the past and an astonishing attempt at renewing the realistic and Symbolist traditions. What he wanted to accomplish is, however, greater than what he actually did accomplish. This explains the disparity between his influence and his popularity. He served up such an overloaded fare of metaphors and experiments that it was indigestible; he piled up so many verbal tricks and linguistic eccentricities that his work became heavy, pretentious, and tiresome. And, above all, his art is so cerebral, so artificial, that its effect is merely an indirect one. Bely missed by a hair being a genius, but if, as some critics maintain, his work is on the whole a failure, it is nevertheless a magnificent failure—much more significant than many dull successes. A generation is indebted to Bely, and the historian of Russian literature will discover many traces of the impression he made during the first half of the twentieth century.

Bely augmented his creative experiments with a number of critical and philological essays that marked a period of revision and innovation in the field of literary language. His works on Symbolism, on the principles of Russian prosody, on rhythmics in poetry, all laid the foundations for a special branch of formal criticism: the analysis of rhythmical structure, of the melody and euphony of verse. (pp. 193-95)

Marc Slonim, "Blok and the Symbolists," in his Modern Russian Literature: From Chekhov to the Present *(copyright 1953 by Oxford University Press, Inc.; renewed 1981 by Tatiana Slonim; reprinted by permission of Oxford University Press, Inc.), Oxford University Press, New York, 1953 (and reprinted in his* From Chekhov to the Revolution: Russian Literature 1900-1917, *Oxford University Press, New York, 1962, pp. 184-210).**

KONSTANTIN MOCHULSKY (essay date 1955)

Andrei Bely's novel, *Petersburg,* is the most powerful and artistically expressive of all his works. It is a rendition of delirium unprecedented in literature; by means of subtle and complex literary devices, the author creates a separate world—unbelievable, fantastic, monstrous, a world of nightmare and horror, a world of distorted perspectives, of disembodied people and living corpses. And this world gazes out at us with the phosphorescent eyes of a dead man, paralyses us with horror, bewitches us with hypnotic suggestion. The most uncanny thing of all is that this world, created by a mad genius, exists in reality. In comparison with it, the fantastic dreams of Hoffman and Edgar Allen Poe, the obsessions of Gogol and Dostoevsky seem harmless and benign. In order to understand the laws of this world, the reader must abandon at the threshold his own logical preconceptions. Here common sense is abolished and causation enfeebled; here human consciousness is torn to shreds and explodes." . . . The "topography" of this world is strictly symmetrical: Petersburg with the straight lines of its prospects and the flatness of its squares, is perceived by the author as a system of "pyramids," triangles, parallelipipeds, cubes and trapezoids. This geometric space is peopled by abstract figures. They move mechanically, act like automatons, and seem to read their lines from a script. The novel is laden with events, but they do not destroy its deathly stillness. The only living thing is Petersburg. . . . (pp. 147-48)

It is difficult to speak of the psychology of Bely's characters. "Dolls," "pets," "wood-lice," faceless and clumsy monsters, mugs and silhouettes flying off into soot do not have a psychology. But in the midst of this succession of phantoms, two characters—Senator Ableukhov and his son Nikolai—preserve traces of some humanity. It is a bloodless and soulless humanity, but it is not conclusively destroyed. Here Bely touches upon reality, upon his personal experience in childhood and youth. The store of these impressions and memories seems inexhaustible for Bely as a writer. In all his novels he continually reworks the real-life material of his early years. There is something frightening, almost maniacal, in the spell of this one theme. Bely's life is not a line of ascent, but rather a closed circle. After complex worldly, ideological and literary wanderings, he always returns to the nursery of the "professorial apartment," to the close world of "family drama."

Bely's narrative prose is defined by three motifs: memories of childhood, the figure of the eccentric father, and the dual family conflict, between father and mother, and between father and son. (p. 152)

The motif of "family drama" constitutes the plot of the novel. The conflict between the father and mother is outlined: Ableukhov's wife, having abandoned her husband to run off with the singer Mindalini, returns to him after two and a half years. The conflict between the father and son unfolds as a collision of two worlds, as the symbolic image of the 1905 revolution. The image of the senator's son, Nikolai Apollonovich, the Kantian student, is a stylized portrait of the author himself in the 1905 period. At the center of the novel is an intricate "complex" of relations between the senator and his son. The "problem of the father," which weakened, almost smothered, Bely's consciousness as a child, is laid bare now as love-hate, as an unconscious desire for the death of the father. (pp. 152-53)

The son is a rebel, remotely connected with terrorists, and he despises the reactionary activities of his father. (p. 153)

The son is a potential parricide. Fate rushes along to turn his unconscious desire into reality. He agrees to take "for safe-keeping" the bomb which must blow up the senator's house. But at this point, the duality of his consciousness takes over. The thought of killing his father horrifies the son. After all, he loves him.

The relationship of the senator to his son is just as tragically dualized. He fears and hates him. . . . Not only is the son a potential parricide, but the father as well is a "comprehensible filicide." But this is only a half-truth; the complete truth is that the filicide is a most loving father. Bely loves the compatibility of incompatibles, truth in untruth, good in evil; he enjoys the tragism of opposites. One of the most powerful scenes in the novel is a conversation between father and son at the dinner table. Nikolai Apollonovich ". . . in an outburst of nervousness, rushed toward his father and began to knead his fingers. . . . Apollon Apollonovich impulsively rose before his son—jumped up, one might say". . . . A wretched conversation is wrung out between spaces of tense silence. (pp. 153-54)

In relation to Bely, Freud's doctrine about the Oedipal complex is applicable. The spiritual wound which he had received in early childhood became for him the curse of inheritance. The image of the father and love-hate toward him predetermined his tragic fate. About Ableukhov-son the author writes: "Nikolai Apollonovich became a combination of disgust, fright and lust." This is his "original sin," which he can neither exculpate nor expiate. The "hereditary triad" rules him despotically: lust toward Sofya Petrovna Likhutina, disgust toward his father and toward himself; and everlasting fright: horror before the approaching destruction (the "sardine tin" with the time mechanism must explode). He feebly tries to shift his guilt onto others ("provocateurs"), but knows very well: "the provocation was within his own self." Nikolai Apollonovich suffers from a persecution mania and a feeling of being threatened by everything. On this pathological soil, the splitting of consciousness and the dematerialization of reality takes place. The action of the novel is transformed into a heaping up of "horrors." (p. 154)

Konstantin Mochulsky, in his Andrei Bely: His Life and Works, *translated by Nora Szalavitz (translation © 1977 by Ardis Publishers; originally published as* Andrei Bely, *YMCA Press, 1955), Ardis, 1977, 230 p.*

SIDNEY MONAS (essay date 1959)

Russian symbolism was by no means only a matter of translating Baudelaire's "Correspondances" and Poe's "Raven" or of discovering that the world was thick with "forests of symbols." The symbolists prided themselves on their professional craftsmanship and their sometimes pedantic but often quite brilliant technical accomplishments in prose and verse. And yet, symbolism was as much a religious as a literary movement, and at its center was a vision of the coming apocalypse in which new Scythian hordes, new Mongol invasions, would sweep over Russia, destroying once and for all the false formal abstract imposed European culture of squares and parallelopipeds. It was a religious cult the ritual of which was expressed in obeisance to art, to the techniques of style and language, but the purpose of which was magically to usher in the apocalypse.

One of the most impressive, though by no means the greatest . . . of the symbolists was Andrey Biely. . . . He wrote two very influential novels, [*The Silver Dove* and *Petersburg*]. . . . The language in which they are composed may be properly described as "magical"—not, of course, in the dust-jacket-blurb sense, but rather because Biely attempts through language alone, brought to a perfection of sorts, a perfection of ambiguity (one can never be entirely certain that the novels were not intended as jokes) to invoke spirits, raise the dead, and usher in Nirvana. Whether the magic is to be taken seriously, or whether it is merely a parlor trick, one never quite knows. That, I suppose, is another aspect of "magical." (pp. 106-07)

[Biely is often compared] with Joyce. So many of the same influences were at work in both men (who were, after all, contemporaries), both possessed such a commanding and articulate awareness of their literary and philosophical forebears, that the comparison does not at first glance strike one as absurd. Both were stylistic innovators, both experimented with musical form in prose, both attempted to squeeze every last echo out of every word. And yet, if not absurd, the comparison is at least inappropriate. Between the symbols and the literary allusions of *Ulysses*, and even of *Finnegans Wake*, Joyce packed a detailed and sympathetic knowledge of human beings and the on-going life of the world; his work is wildly, incorrigibly affirmative. Biely strikes me as fundamentally sour, fundamentally wounded with a hurt that his "literary" excellences do not overcome. So much depends on his cleverness. There are no human beings at all in Biely's *Petersburg,* there are not even things; there is only literature. And yet, it is literature played upon with great talent, literature suffused with passion—if a somewhat sick passion—Russian literature, which almost supplies the living personality that Biely himself fails to bring to his work.

Trotsky, who was a brilliant if sometimes naive and sometimes even a vulgar critic, wrote of Biely's *Petersburg* that it was like trying to get into a house by the chimney without trying the front-door [see excerpt above]. If by "house" he meant a sense of the historical and social significance of the capital city and the events of the revolutionary year 1905, he is undoubtedly right. Trotsky was very good at entering by front-doors himself, though he sometimes took a bit of the wall down with him. But Biely was not trying to get into that house, or any house. His obsession was all with chimneys. (pp. 107-08)

Petersburg has no individual characters. No one has an integral identity. Everyone is everyone else. There are antinomies: form and content; rectilinear and circular; European and Asiatic; the spire of the Peter-Paul Fortress and St. Isaac's dome; red and green; oo-sounds and aa-sounds; reality and hallucination; cylindrical top-hats and shaggy Manchurian caps; secret police and revolutionaries; youth and old age. But these are all in dialectical interplay, change places, and turn into each other or something else with bewildering frequency. The author proposes to study "the biology of shadow," the reality of hallucinations, and the materialization of obsessions. There are masquerades, disguises, pseudonyms, explosions, and over everything the green miasmal fog of the northern marsh which dissolves all outlines and turns everything into everything else. (pp. 108-09)

In this hallucinated and hallucinative world, phantoms establish relationships—fantastic ones. The mystic, Alexander Ivanovich Doodkin (it is not his real name; he has a forged passport) and the Greek-Ukrainian-Jewish-Mongol, Lippanchenko (it is not his real name either), a man of many faces, who is both a terrorist and a police spy, a rhinoceros and sensual infant, meet each other in the context of a revolutionary conspiracy. Each tries to use the other for his own ends. The ends get lost, and the usage becomes a Svidrigailovian nightmare.

Doodkin is a prophet of the apocalypse. Brooding on the final destruction of culture, he conceives a mystic vocabulary, like that of the Cabala (or the symbolists), that will usher in the end of the world. His words, become flesh, take possession of him. In a macabre sequence, vivid, dramatic, horrifying, yet at the same time funny (it is of the essence of *Petersburg* that gripping though the scene is, it is transparently "literary," in part a parody of Pushkin and Gogol) Doodkin hears the hooves of the Bronze Horseman, who dismounts, clambers up to Doodkin's attic, sits beside him smoking a pipe, then gets up and pours himself in molten bronze down Alexander Ivanovich's throat. (p. 110)

The bomb which is intended to blow up the elder Ableukhov has as much, or as little, discreteness as any of the other phantoms that appear in *Petersburg*. Contained in a sardine tin ("neither large nor small") with a timing mechanism crudely attached, square with rounded edges, it ticks away in Nikolai's room (after he has "inadvertently" set it) behind the picture of his fickle would-be mistress, and he knows that in twenty-four hours it will go off. This clock is the basic ordering mechanism of Western civilization. By it, work is regulated, life is disciplined, and the streets of St. Petersburg arrange themselves into squares. At a given moment it will expand infinitely and turn everything around it into slush. (pp. 110-11)

The bomb does go off, but harmlessly, while no one is around. Biely actually achieves the perverse triumph of making the reader feel disappointed. There is, however, that other bomb—the symbolic bomb—which is still alive and ticking inside Nikolai. No one knows when it will explode.

There is one passage of consummate beauty in *Petersburg*. . . . Young Nikolai, appalled and fascinated at the prospect of murdering his father, recalls the lines of *Der Erl-Koenig* (with which his father used to sing him to sleep) in which the child lies dead in his father's arms. (p. 111)

In this remarkable passage we come, finally, to the real point of the novel: an evocation of the urge to begin anew. The human intellect, alienated by the pursuit of abstractions from the creative forces of nature, which by playing on the senses originally gave birth to intellect, in the heart of its most remote abstraction resumes contact with its origin. This is as close as Biely comes to affirmation. . . .

It is ironical that Biely, whose seriousness is open to question, should become posthumously an exemplar of the possible transcendance of politics through style. It is one more trick of the northern mists, perhaps. I do not know what the young Russian writers and would be writers find as they plunge through these fascinating and irritating pages, but no doubt they resume contact with that peculiar destructive, and yet creative passion—the myth of St. Petersburg. (p. 112)

Sidney Monas, "Unreal City," in Chicago Review *(reprinted by permission of* Chicago Review; *copyright © 1959 by* Chicago Review), *Vol. 13, No. 3, Fall, 1959, pp. 102-12.*

VLADIMIR NABOKOV   (essay date 1965)

Ever since the days when such formidable mediocrities as Galsworthy, Dreiser, a person called Tagore, another called Maxim Gorky, a third called Romain Rolland, used to be accepted as geniuses, I have been perplexed and amused by fabricated notions about so-called "great books". That, for instance, Mann's asinine *Death in Venice* or Pasternak's melodramatic and vilely written *Zhivago* or Faulkner's corncobby chronicles can be considered "masterpieces," or at least what journalists call "great books," is to me an absurd delusion, as when a hypnotized person makes love to a chair. *My* greatest masterpieces of twentieth century prose are, in this order: Joyce's *Ulysses;* Kafka's *Transformation;* Biely's *Petersburg;* and the first half of Proust's fairy tale *In Search of Lost Time.* (p. 57)

Vladimir Nabokov, in an interview with Robert Hughes in September, 1965, in his Strong Opinions *(copyright © 1973 by McGraw-Hill International, Inc.; with permission of McGraw Hill Book Co.), McGraw-Hill, 1973, pp. 51-61.*

PIERRE HART   (essay date 1972)

The Russian Formalist critics were among the first to recognize the particular qualities which distinguished [the Symbolists'] new orientation in fiction from that of previous generations. Yet in classifying it as a variety of ornamental prose, they underestimated the functional import of the techniques used. As I shall attempt to demonstrate in the case of Andrei Bely's autobiographical novel *Kotik Letaev,* the mode of narration was intimately related to the particular sense of reality which such authors hoped to convey. (p. 320)

Among the Symbolist writers who worked in prose, Bely was especially concerned with the portrayal of subjective experience. Even in his early *Symphonies* there was evidence that he wished to convey something of the internal crises which he had himself endured, using innovative fictional forms to achieve this purpose. While these works were centered in the realm of the adult's perceptions, the potential offered by childhood as the first stage of psychological development did not escape him. Bely recognized, however, that there were unusual difficulties inherent in such a portrayal: "How can I express through the image or gesture of ordinary reality the nightmare which stifled me in childhood? How can I create this strange nightmare for someone else with the aid of verbal combinations? Some kind of 'I' tumbled out of some other kind of 'I', the distance between the two 'I's was measured in millions of kilometers."

With these formulations of his own position as author-subject, Bely established an attitude toward the genre of childhood memoirs that was radically different from that which had prevailed during the previous half century. Numerous stories and

novellas had been published in which the child's view of the world was central. Sometimes biographical and sometimes totally fictional, works by Aksakov and Tolstoy, Dostoevsky and Chekhov all contributed to the development of the genre without exceeding certain commonly accepted limitations. . . . What generally emerged was a sort of compromise based upon reminiscence, that is, an admittedly adult narrator attempted to reconstruct the substance of his previous experience with an occasional effort being made to impart a flavor of discovery to the child's observations. While it was impossible to ignore the practical limitations imposed by his subject matter, Bely's approach was conditioned by his involvement with the new Symbolist esthetics and led to a very different type of articulation. Retaining the vocabulary of an adult, he deliberately deformed it for the purpose of conveying something of the vaguely formulated and imperfectly understood impressions of early childhood. (pp. 320-21)

The significance of style may best be understood if *Kotik Letaev* is treated as being beyond autobiography, as one of the few Russian examples of the modern psychological novel. While it is possible to identify and interpret the separate incidents as a commentary on the author's life, Bely was also attempting a statement on the cognitive process itself. Just as Proust's *A la recherche du temps perdu* has been considered an attempt to discover the nature of memory, so can Bely's novel be defined as an investigation of the evolution of human perception and intellect. In its particulars it attests to the author's intuitive grasp of developmental stages that have been confirmed more recently through the systematic clinical studies of psychologists like Jean Piaget. Beginning almost literally *ad ovum*, Bely describes a series of incidents from the boy's early childhood in Moscow at the turn of the century. It is difficult to speak of plot in *Kotik Letaev,* for it is the internal organization of individual scenes rather than an ordered progression of events which is primary. Only by juxtaposing these fragments of the boy's total experience do we arrive at a sense of the work as a whole. The primary mode of development in the novel is from lesser to greater coherency of detail within scenes. A further degree of unity is provided by the repeated viewing of objects and situations. In order to accentuate the evolution of the child's perceptual capabilities, Bely repeatedly introduces the same objective data, modified on each occasion by the increment of experience.

Two sub-chapters situated in the middle of the novel provide some indication of the overall psychological structure. Entitled "Self Cognition" and "I," they stress the distinction between various modes of being. Awareness of self is not something which evolves out of a primordial void but rather involves the substitution of a specific sense of existence for one that is less clearly articulated and characterized by the notion of universal oneness. Referred to as the "cosmos" by the adult narrator, its closest theoretical analogue would appear to be Jung's collective unconscious. As is true of the latter, there are continual archetypal protuberances into the realm of individual consciousness which, in Kotik's case, arouse fear. The process of individuation involves the accumulation of experience sufficient to suppress these fears and establish a sense of confidence in dealing with phenomena recognized as existing independently of the individual. Thus, as the narrator recounts his memories, infantile fears are increasingly counteracted by the reassuring features of a physically predictable environment. . . . (pp. 322-23)

[The] majority of Kotik's conceptions are derived from data immediately accessible to the senses. Words are therefore meaningful only to the degree that they can be coupled with particular actions or objects. . . . This emphasis upon gesture and imitation as the precursors of more abstract cognitive processes anticipates Piaget's theories on the origins of representational thought. . . . [The] child proceeds from an initial concern with the imitation of physical models which are immediately apparent to a stage in which imitation is based on mental reconstruction of the model. As an artist rather than a behavioral scientist, Bely was not totally consistent in his portrayal of such development; but in general the numerous examples of word-play which are encountered serve to indicate the child's growing capacity to think abstractly.

Early childhood, as a stage in which the organizing function of the intellect is least conspicuous, appears as a series of disconnected images in the first several chapters. Reality is confined to the single spot on which the infant's gaze is fixed, and beyond its perimeter only shadowy images of the unknown exist. While the detail of the nursery is all relatively familiar, the corridors of the apartment beyond lead to a "void.". . . [The] young child's responses are based on this extremely limited set of external referents, and indeed, there is no clear line of demarcation between the self and the object world. (pp. 323-24)

The feeling of his apprehension is further heightened by the way in which Kotik physically views individuals. In the scene with the nurse Bely has obviously tried to recreate the visual impact of an adult bending over a crib, as viewed from the child's vantage point. Rather than perceiving the nurse as a normal human figure, Kotik observes only those features which are literally thrust into his field of vision. Her evil eyes and moving mouth are the most striking traits of a face looming ever larger over him. Other adults with whom Kotik has contact are described from this same angle. Characterizations at this early point derive from a composite of visual and aural cues which undergo recombination in the boy's mind. One of the most conspicuous features associated with the doctor who attends him in infancy is the thundering noise of his large galoshes, and this sound always prepares the boy, in the manner of a leitmotif, for his visits. Of greater significance is the way Aunt Dotya's piano exercises contribute to the child's conception of her. By Kotik's own admission, she becomes "the refraction of a musical run." The very sounds of the notes that she plays . . . recall her name and elicit a vision of her.

In the case of his father there is a more sophisticated interplay between the first, physical impressions and subsequent notions related to the schoolboy's study of classical mythology. Primordial elements of thunder and fire are central to the young child's reconstructed visual image. (pp. 324-25)

In formulating this [image] Kotik commits one of several errors in construing word meaning. He equates his father's place of employment, the university, with the universe; and by means of this naive confusion he accentuates the sense of remoteness and awe inspired by the professor's appearance. On one level such semantic confusions might be treated as stylistic play on the part of the narrator, yet as the example cited appears to indicate, these errors can be logically attributed to the young child's limited verbal comprehension. The fact that they do help shape his assessment of the external world requires that we consider them highly functional elements in the novel. (p. 325)

Purely physical qualities no longer figure so prominently in the child's perception of others. In his father's case it is the alien system of his thought that provokes uneasiness. His occasional intrusions into the domestic realm of nurse, mother, and child are marked by conversation centering about the importance of the exact sciences in life. A favorite phrase, "mathematics is the harmony of the spheres," rings rather ironically, for the introduction of such phrases has a distinctly disruptive effect on the world of fantasy and fairytale to which Kotik is accustomed. It is with regard to this conflict that the boy first gives expression to his awareness of interpersonal relationships. Having outgrown a totally egocentric view of the world, he has begun to perceive a whole complex of social interactions in which he is but one of the participants. The emerging competition between mother and father becomes apparent as Kotik notes his mother's disapproving glance at the mention of mathematics. Confronted by this disparity of attitudes, the boy vacillates between the security of what is known and a growing attraction to the unfamiliar.

His first impulse is to elect the former, and in describing his mother Kotik clearly demonstrates this. Vaguely perceived during infancy, when the nurse was of more vital importance to his existence, she now assumes greater importance as he begins to judge on a less utilitarian basis. Her image is distinctly positive, being associated in the child's mind with those moments of excitement and pleasure that are important at an early stage of life. . . . (p. 327)

Familiarity inspires confidence in objects as well as persons. Moscow with its endless streets, sidewalks, walls and roofs completely encompasses the world as the boy knows it. Identity is intimately related to his sense of the total environment. . . . Predictably, then, moving to the country for the summer has a profound effect on the child; as if by magic, Moscow with all its familiar referents has "disintegrated." Lacking a coherent system for dealing with objects common to the countryside, Kotik is forced to improvise in his efforts to understand. And while his first reactions are somewhat reminiscent of those at an earlier phase of development, it is evident that all experience, however casually related, now provides a point of departure for dealing with unfamiliar phenomena. (pp. 327-28)

Two of the most basic concepts in Piaget's theory are . . . confirmed by the whole of the novel. "Assimilation" and "accommodation" form a complementary pair in the cognitive mechanism, a sort of feed-back system through which the individual strives to attain a dynamic equilibrium with his environment. Assimilation denotes the organism's tendency to incorporate information received from external sources into existing patterns of thought and behavior. As the process of assimilation continues, it results in accommodation, that is, a modification of thought or behavioral patterns that better enables the individual to cope with new changes in environment.

Kotik's ascending "the stairway of his expansion" might be construed as the artist's gloss on this clinical model, for we are witness to a continual refinement in the relationship between world and child. His efforts to convey the nature of this process required Bely to focus on words and events as meaning began to adhere to them. Far from being mere esthetic play with the stuff of fiction, *Kotik Letaev* was thus addressed to the problem underlying all of modern psychological prose—the manner of the mind's constructions. (p. 328)

Pierre Hart, "Psychological Primitivism" in Russian Literature Triquarterly *(© 1972 by Ardis Publishers), No. 4, Fall, 1972, pp. 319-30.*

SAMUEL D. CIORAN (essay date 1973)

At the turn of the century Belyj and the other young symbolists naively and romantically rushed to the banner of symbolism, for in their youthful idealism and enthusiasm, they believed that symbolism would, somehow or other, apocalyptically herald and create the new man and the new culture. There was no sophisticated or comprehensive ideology of symbolism, either as a philosophical or a literary platform, but only the incorporeal world of inner "rustlings, sounds and movements". . . . [Belyj's] cycle of four Symphonies, in particular, was the product of an intuitive symbolism which had not yet been subjected to any rigorous ideological code. Nonetheless, they represented the first attempts to realize the working hypotheses in both form and content of a literary-philosophical doctrine which, although a compromise with the current methods, would indicate what direction was to be taken. . . . (pp. 71-2)

The Symphonies, upon close examination and comparison with Belyj's later writings, prove that his work is "of a whole". In fact, the Symphonies contain all of the major themes and problems of his later and better known novels. (p. 72)

The Symphonic Cycle was written over a period of eight years . . . , but nonetheless preserves an inner unity of atmosphere, style and even theme. The introduction to *Severnaja Simfonija* carefully outlines the three basic concerns which are operative in that particular work, namely, the creation of a series of moods, satire, and finally, ideology. Typically, for Belyj, the synthesis of all three elements leads to symbolism: "Finally, the careful reader perhaps will perceive beyond the musical and satirical significance also the ideological significance which, while appearing to dominate, destroys neither the musical nor satirical meaning. The combination of all three aspects in one passage or element leads to symbolism." Nor did this "symbolic trinity" apply only to Belyj's *Northern Symphony,* for it is the general formula for all of the Symphonies. Behind this formula there exists an even more general source which provides the dramatic tension, namely, Belyj's nemesis, the crisis of the individual caught between two irreconcilable extremes and filled with the apocalyptic sense of being "on the divide". In discussing the characters of his Symphonies, Belyj summarizes their common origin in the following manner: "Clearly the author [Belyj refers to himself] is depicting on the divide of two centuries people of the divide who bear in their souls the scissors of two struggling eras: the revolutionary and catastrophic with the evolutionary and complacent." Thus, a sense of catastrophic crisis permeates the atmosphere of the symphonic cycle, cleaving the heroines and heroes between the forces of Christ and Antichrist. Consequently, the structure of all the Symphonies is based upon symbolic triads in which the various figures are hardly more than archetypal representations of apocalyptic motifs. The fable is, in each case, an allegorized apocalypse complete in itself, and the atmosphere, crisis-ridden and expectant, is likewise expressive of an eschatological frame of mind.

Belyj's *Simfonija (2-aja)* is his early masterpiece of satire, in which the mad scramblings and excesses of the Moscow mystics are depicted. . . . Belyj takes great delight in parodying the wild and diverse schemes of these apocalyptists who are attempting to bring about the real apocalypse. . . . But the real significance behind this satire becomes apparent when one realizes the extent to which this mystical mentality has so completely captivated the minds of all. Apocalyptic mysticism is not the exclusive domain of one or two crack-pots, but "every block possessed its own mystic". Madmen, bandits, intellectuals, clerks, peasants—these are but a few of those who are seized with apocalyptic premonitions and create an air of expectancy in Moscow. . . . Obviously Belyj wants to ridicule the extremes that mysticism was guilty of in its frenzied activity, the type of exaggeration which he depicted in one specialist of *The Apocalypse* who goes to Northern France in search of the apocalyptic beast, discovers it in a small child who soon dies from a stomach disorder, thus destroying Sergej Musatov's eschatological hopes. At the same time Belyj's "healthy" satire may only be a mask for a more sinister irony which is, according to Blok, the disease of his generation: "The most lively and sensitive children of our century are afflicted with a disease unknown to physical and spiritual doctors. This sickness is akin to spiritual ailments and can be called 'irony'. Its manifestations are the attacks of feverish laughter which begin with a devilishly mocking, provocative smile and end in violence and blasphemy." In other words, is Belyj not only satirizing others, but himself at the same time? The faith is a naive world of mystical and apocalyptic premonitions and hopes which the omniscient artist propagates, can also create a backlash of irony to hide the author's self-consciousness and aesthetic impudence. (pp. 72-6)

Belyj is probably closer to the apocalyptic ideas expressed in his symphonic cycle than the satire may suggest, but irony forces him to protect his own position. Nor is this irony evident only in the more obvious satire of *Simfonija (2-aja).* It runs through the other Symphonies in a series of leitmotifs which at first seem irreconcilable with the seriousness of the depiction. . . . The same ironic phrase "but it only seemed so" appears again and again, especially in *Vozvrat* and *Kubok metelej,* suggesting the irony of the impossible mystical situations and at the same time preserving the author from any literary embarrassment. . . . Yet, in spite of the fact that Belyj satirizes the Moscow mystics, the disciples of the Divine Feminine, and in general the apocalyptic expectancy of his time, all of these motifs figure most prominently not only in his later work, but in his early work as well. . . . Nor can one ignore the fact that the world which Belyj depicts in his works invariably assumes a dualistic quality, caught between reality and fantasy, an "it-only-seemed-so" world. In the Symphonies, therefore, Belyj appears to be occupying an ambiguous position: he is treating both satirically and seriously those very themes and ideas which are closest to him. The reader should not be led astray by the blatant satire of the *Second Symphony,* or the subtle irony of the other Symphonies, and made to think that the content or ideas expressed therein are in some way not the author's. (pp. 77-8)

The main characters in the symphonic cycle all share the common denominator of the search-motif. They are the Parsifalian figures who are caught between Good and Evil and are seeking some apocalyptic resolution of their dilemma. The young melancholy knight in the *Northern Symphony* is caught between the "gloomy catholic" and the holy princess. . . . Sergej Musatov in the *Second Symphony* cannot distinguish the true Christ image and that of the Antichrist. Xandrikov in *Vozvrat* is attempting to escape from the evil lecturer, Cenx (the servant of the evil serpent), and thus seeks refuge with Dr. Orlov (the personification of omniscient eternity). In *Kubok metelej* Svetlova seeks the Christ-Groom who is summoning her to eternity and resurrection, but she cannot escape the temptation of the Luciferian figure, Svetozarov.

This search is prompted by a typically apocalyptic syndrome in almost all cases: the expectation of the end, usually catastrophic, and the advent of the new age, as signified in the symphonic cycle of birth, death, resurrection and rebirth. Such a situation provided Belyj with his favourite character-crisis tension: people caught on the border of two ages. (pp. 78-9)

The structural contours of the symphonic cycle are, not surprisingly, triadic. Furthermore, it can be demonstrated that Belyj is chiefly concerned with *apocalyptic triads,* which follow naturally from his formulation of the problem. In various guises there appear in the Symphonies the oppositions of unlike qualities whether good and evil, light and darkness, or Christ and Antichrist, who do battle to determine the future course of the world. The tension which is created by the juxtaposition of these opposites is reflected in one or more central figures who are blessed with a vision of the otherworldly, but are, nonetheless, caught between the antipodal forces. For the sake of conformity these antipodal forces can be called Christ and Antichrist, for this formulation is symbolic not only of an opposition in spirit, but perhaps even more importantly, of a delusive and seductive spirit masquerading as truth. (p. 79)

If one had to designate the most significant message of the symphonic cycle, the conclusion that Belyj arrives at in each individual Symphony, it would be the theme of immortality through death in time and resurrection in eternity. This "call of eternity" . . . appears again and again in the Symphonies. . . . The call of eternity represents variously a longing to escape from this earthly realm into the otherworldly, suppressed religious-erotic desires for union between the Divine Feminine and the Christ-Groom, and the search for real being. Whatever the specific motivations, the summons from beyond nourished an intuitively mystical mood in Belyj and other symbolists.

Thus, time becomes merely a Platonic reflection of the eternity beyond, an endless flow of events which are real only inasmuch as they shadow mythically and symbolically the forces of eternity. . . . If time (as well as space) is regarded as a mirror of eternity, then it is possible to understand why Belyj in all of his Symphonies, especially *Vozvrat* and *Kubok metelej,* depicts two realms, the eternal and the temporal, and extends the myths and personal premonitions of the eternal into the temporal. (pp. 81-2)

Although time is the pale reflection of eternity and, hence, a representative of higher being, it is, nonetheless, a preparation for death which is the sphere of some Nirvana-purgatory lying between time and eternity. . . . Time is the guide through death to eternity, and it is only by dying that one is able to attain the eternal sphere. . . . When we compare the fate of the major characters in the Symphonies, it becomes quite obvious that they are resurrected into the new life only after a necessary death and sojourn in timelessness. . . . *Vozvrat* is perhaps the best example of rebirth through death. Xandrikov rows out to the middle of the lake where he answers the call of eternity by plunging into the water, thereby penetrating into the next world. . . . This particular instance of death and resurrection deserves special attention, for in *Vozvrat,* as the title implies, Belyj is propagating a doctrine of eternal return, a cyclic creation and dissolution of forms. Significantly enough, he has chosen the symbol of the lake (or sea in the child episode) to depict this repetition, for not only is the lake's glassy surface a suggestion of some Platonic reflection of the other world, but the waters themselves represent the classic creation-dissolution-creation symbol, which is traditionally associated with the figure of Aphrodite Anadiomene, the legend of the Deluge and the rites of baptism. . . . In the Symphonies Belyj is ul-

timately concerned with the cosmic issues of time, space, eternity, infinity, life, death and resurrection, all of which are also the final questions of *The Apocalypse.* His cosmic and mythic imagery embraces astrology as well as the basic elements of fire, water, earth and air, and often its implementation obscures the mutual eschatological content unless the hidden symbolism can be penetrated. (pp. 82-4)

All of the Symphonies betray an obvious orientation towards the future. The progression is from past to present with the ultimate goal in some future realm of timelessness, namely, eternity and the new millennium. This movement towards the future also signifies an eschatological direction in which the figures of this temporal realm either aspire towards or are earthly incarnations of the eternal figures. . . . These disciples of the apocalyptic future are the transitional creatures who have crossed the divide from the old into the new, from time into eternity. They are the children of the sun or the first principle of light, and therefore, of God in the universe. In Belyj's terms, they are symbolically the "white children" whom he portrays at the end of the *Pervaja Simfonija* when the last night will fall before the morning star heralds the millennium of eternal light. . . . The fact that the children are "white" and that they are "children" casts further light on Belyj's essentially apocalyptic scheme. The archetype of the child is one of the most intricate and interesting in Belyj's works. . . . Belyj projects into his child archetype that innocent, yet true knowledge which, although available only to the new-born, brings extreme vulnerability to danger. The combination of this innocence and defencelessness becomes a divine symbol of rebirth and resurrection, as in *Vozvrat.* The child is more aware of his "in-between" nature, threatened on the one hand by the forces of darkness, and protected on the other by the forces of light. (pp. 86-7)

The Symphonies reveal something more than Belyj's first attempts at symbolism and a resultant cosmic-eschatological landscape. Behind most of the Symphonies, in particular the *Second Symphony,* there lurks that sense of tragedy which is provoked by the author's physical location between the eternal vision and the temporal reality. . . . The vision of the otherworldly may bless the seer with ecstasy, but may bring madness as well. This is the curious legacy of ecstasy and despair, the proper ingredients for a metaphysical irony of which Belyj himself is a victim, in the self-parody inherent not only in the Symphonies, but in his later works as well. The visionary author becomes, in fact, quite literally the "fool-in-Christ" because of his belief in the "call of eternity" and the disparity between this and the world at large. (p. 90)

Samuel D. Cioran, in his The Apocalyptic Symbolism of Andrej Belyi *(© copyright 1973 Mouton & Co. N.V., Publishers), Mouton Publishers, The Hague, 1973, 209 p.*

JOHN ELSWORTH   (essay date 1976)

Andrei Bely is nowadays recognised in many quarters as a major novelist and a not insignificant poet. His voluminous theoretical work, however, has received rather less attention, and its status remains a matter of dispute. . . .

Bely's theoretical essays do not represent a homogeneous body of writing. They vary both in philosophical approach and style. . . . He noted himself that a number of them were written in what he called an "Argonaut" style, a lyrical, highly metaphorical style that seeks to persuade by other means than rational argument. This, though, is a feature that is not restricted to certain isolated works, but pervades very many of the essays at one point or another. it is not at all uncommon for a staid philosophical argument to break off without warning into a passage of a visionary nature. Furthermore, Bely made no attempt to work out a consistent terminology for his ideas, and created needless confusion by his use of variable synonyms and his tendency to allow a single word to assume conflicting meanings. (p. 17)

[Between 1902 and 1912 Bely] published in the periodical press over 130 separate essays (not counting short book reviews); some 80 of these were re-published in the three volumes *Symbolism, Arabesques* and *The Green Meadow,* along with a number of new works and, in the case of *Symbolism,* an extensive commentary. Yet despite this quantity of output Bely did not succeed in putting down the entire theory as he envisaged it. For one thing the periodical press demanded fresh articles far more frequently than a writer could be visited by fresh ideas, and there is in consequence a large element of repetition. Bely displays a tendency to start afresh each time he sets pen to paper, to re-formulate in new terms ideas that have been expressed before. Furthermore, the essays often bear the marks of having been written in haste; this is true even of some that were written expressly for inclusion in the collected volumes. A prime example is the most ambitious philosophical essay of all, *The Emblematics of Meaning,* a hundred pages in length, written expressly for *Symbolism,* and completed, on Bely's admission, in a week. (p. 18)

Bely's basic premise is that European civilisation is undergoing a crisis. He termed it the crisis of consciousness, and saw its expression in man's accentuated awareness of certain fundamental dualities. . . . [In *The Crisis of Consciousness and Henrik Ibsen,* Bely] enumerates five dualities: between consciousness and feeling; between contemplation and will; between the individual and society; between science and religion; and between morality and beauty. He discusses them one by one, in some cases sketching in a solution, in others merely defining the problem. (pp. 19-20)

[Of these five dualities] Bely offers solutions for three, leaving the problems of the conflicts between feeling and consciousness and between the individual and society unanswered in their present definition. Where Bely does offer a solution it may be noted that his thinking takes a triadic form: the two parts of the given duality—contemplation and will, science and religion, morality and beauty—are synthesised, Bely tells us, once the nature and the origin of the duality are fully understood.

A closer understanding of Bely's conception of the crisis of European civilization can be reached by examining his description of the attitudes adopted by those who are unsuccessful in overcoming the dualities. This description amounts to a general criticism of habits of thought prevalent at the time.

These attitudes can be divided into two groups: on the one hand, trust in abstract reasoning, in traditional morality, in the uncomplicated will to action as applied directly to empirical reality, and in the conclusions of natural science; on the other, the reliance on feeling, contemplation and beauty, resulting in the doctrine of art for art's sake and, in the absence of that coherence of experience that only religion can provide, the habit of making a fetish of the fortuitous experience. Now these composite descriptions correspond to two perennial objects of Bely's concern: the former he calls variously empiricism, positivism, or determinism, the latter decadence, indi-

vidualism or subjectivism. Decadence he saw as a reaction against positivism. This was indeed a standard interpretation of what had happened when the "older generation" of Symbolists challenged the traditions they inherited. The attitudes thought of as decadent can be abundantly illustrated from the work of that generation: the sense of the individual's isolation in a world of unique feelings, the concentration on the experience of the moment, the view of poetry as expression rather than communication, the autonomy and uselessness of art. Bely considered this reaction to have been necessary and salutary, but only of value as a transition. For in its emphasis on only one aspect of man's nature, decadence was no more capable than positivism of becoming the basis of a new organic culture. The solution to this problem is to be found in the synthesis of these opposing ideologies, the philosophy that arises from their conflict—Symbolism.

Returning to the terms of Bely's first duality in *The Crisis of Consciousness and Henrik Ibsen,* consciousness and feeling, for which no solution was offered at the time, it can now be seen that this was the general statement of the dichotomy, of which the other dualities discussed were particular aspects. Consciousness was said to be expressed in knowledge, which is the realm of science; therefore exclusive reliance on consciousness is what Bely calls positivism. Feeling is a general term to cover all that part of human experience that is not expressible in the terms of science, and exclusive reliance upon it is decadence. The duality between these two is the duality fundamental to Bely. It is variously expressed as "consciousness and life", "consciousness and experience", "feeling and reason", "intellect and feeling", but the intellectual fact to which these definitions refer is the same. It is to this central duality that Bely refers when he says that the most acute duality of all is that between the mysticism of experience and the values created by rational activities.

Bely's view of the genesis of Symbolism as a synthesis of the thesis, positivism, and the antithesis, decadence, involves the kind of foreshortening of perspective mentioned above. For a number of differing philosophical standpoints are thereby subsumed under a single rubric. The three terms: empiricism, positivism and determinism, are used interchangeably, and any philosophy correctly described by one of the three may also be included under either of the others. (pp. 24-5)

It may also be noted that there is an element of historical evolutionism in Bely's thinking. Empiricism and decadence are, on the one hand, descriptions of attitudes alive at the time of writing; on the other they refer to the dominant outlooks of succeeding periods of Russian thought. Bely's dialectical triad has a temporal dimension. He is inclined to view Symbolism as the culmination of certain historical processes. (p. 25)

It is in the light of this view of history that Bely's discussion of the conflict between the individual and society must be seen. The feature of this discussion that immediately claims attention is the fact that Bely makes no mention of the social reality in which such a conflict would normally be assumed to take place. He is concerned here, as elsewhere, with criticism of prevalent habits of thought. Two attitudes to the problem can be seen, and they fall easily into the two categories of determinism and individualism. The determinist attitude, exemplified by Marxism, subordinates the individual to what are held to be the objective facts of society. The individualist attitude, though again not explicitly described by Bely, may be taken to assert the value of the individual regardless of society. It is in the conflict between these two attitudes that Bely sees the problem, not in actual social conditions.

It is human modes of thought, for Bely, that shape the world we live in. . . . The transformation of the world within demands the transformation of man himself, and this is the ultimate task of culture. (pp. 26-7)

To sum up, Bely's fundamental conception is of a world split by the inadequacies of human thinking about it into a series of dualities. It is a view to which he adhered throughout his life; the sense of duality, the idealism and the subjectivism of this view underlie all his work. (p. 27)

The dichotomy between the form and the content of knowledge is for Bely yet another way of expressing the duality which is the fundamental characteristic of the crisis of the European consciousness as he sees it. Returning to the terms of his distinction between positivism and decadence, it may be seen that the content of knowledge, which is objective reality, is the material of positivism, and the form of knowledge, which is a subjective reaction to that reality, is the material of decadence. Just as in historical terms this duality was resolved in Symbolism, so in philosophical terms it is resolved in the symbol. . . .

Bely argues that all concepts philosophers have placed at the pinnacle of their systems . . . are reducible to the concept of value. This concept itself Bely declares to be not further reducible, and he equates it with the concept of the symbol, which thus becomes the limit of all possible formation of concepts. All philosophical systems are expressions of value: their significance is not theoretical, for theoretical significance belongs to epistemology alone, but is symbolic.

This symbolic nature is not peculiar to philosophy. All human creative activities—science, philosophy, art or religion—are ways of "symbolising human creation". This assertion makes clearer what Bely means by symbolic significance. It is particularly important that what is symbolised is "human creation". All products of human cultural activities are symbols of the act of creation, externalisations, one might say, of an internal process. This process of symbolisation is the process of the creation of values. (p. 32)

Bely thus envisages a process whereby the contents of consciousness, at first chaos, are made meaningful by the human act of creation; this act of creation is objectified, rendered communicable, by being symbolised; the symbol is then cognised and the result of the process of cognition is objective reality. (pp. 32-3)

The act of creation which the symbol represents is the process of passing objective reality through experience and thus endowing it with meaning. Bely points to the Greek derivation of the word to justify his own usage of it in the meaning of "an organic conjunction" of one thing with another. The symbol is the fusion of form and content, and the duality between form and content, in the epistemological meaning of those words, is the most concise expression of the central duality underlying the crisis of European culture.

At the same time, this definition is in effect the starting-point for Bely's discussion of the artistic symbol. . . . While art does not enjoy theoretical pride of place in Bely's philosophy, since its symbolic nature is shared by all other human creative activities, it is nonetheless to art that the greater part of his attention is devoted. Artistic creation is the way of fusing form and content with which Bely was most closely concerned, and

the interest of his epistemological theory lies mainly in its function as an introduction to his aesthetic theory.

This fusion of form and content, of experience and objective reality is present, according to Bely, in all art. For all art is symbolic, not only that which calls itself Symbolist. Classical and Romantic art differ only in the precedence they give to objective reality and inner experience. In his article *The Meaning of Art* Bely enumerates algebraically eight possible ways in which "b"—objective—and "c"—inner experience—may be combined to form "a"—the symbol. Every symbol is a unity, and the separate elements of objective reality and inner experience are "means of manifesting artistic creation", means, that is to say, of creating the symbol.

These elements, however, do not stand in an equal relationship in the symbol. In art, Bely asserts, the world of appearances . . . stands in a subordinate relationship to inner experience. This might be expressed differently by saying that what is important in the symbol is not so much the "features taken from nature" as the manner of their transformation through the experience of the artist. This is what Bely understands by style. The artist's creative experience is expressed in artistic form. (pp. 33-4)

[Bely's idea] that the form of art is also the content of art may be extracted from [his] discussion of the nature of the symbol. What is meant is that the creative action of transforming objective reality, which is what the symbol symbolises and which is given in the artistic form, it itself the content of art. Art is about that creative action, not about the phenomena used as a means to express it (content in the conventional sense). When Bely then speaks of the content of art as meaning. . . , he is referring to the meaning of such creative activity in general. The question to which this statement is properly the answer would be: what purpose does such creative activity serve at all? Bely's answer to the question of meaning is that the meaning of all art is religious.

Bely's assertion of the religious significance of art may appear at first sight to contradict his insistence that art is not to be regarded as subordinate to religion. But this contradiction vanishes if it is borne in mind that Bely regarded any dogma as "the empty shell of value". The religious significance of art does not consist, therefore, in reference to any established religious dogma, and no religious dogma may claim the allegiance of art. Indeed, in one passage Bely asserts that in religion there can be no dogmas. Art appears irreligious, in that it "seeps beyond the limits of eroded religious forms", but its religious nature lies in the fact that it "creates a different, living form which has not yet been found". The essence of religion, in Bely's view, lies in the creative activity that gives coherence to human experience. (pp. 35-6)

Bely's "creative activity" is religious because it is the way of overcoming the duality between the ego and the world. . . . Translated into the terminology of Solov'ëv, this same duality is the central metaphysical problem: the split between God and creation. The agent that performs the process of reunification is the Logos. Bely's use of this term has in common with Solov'ëv's the view of the Logos as present in the human consciousness, and while he could clearly have derived it from many another source besides Solov'ëv, there seems little purpose in his using it at all, unless it is with implicit reference to a complex of meaning such as it acquires in Solov'ëv's philosophy. If this meaning is attributed to the word "Logos" in Bely's theory then the full religious meaning of "creative activity'' becomes clear: ''creative activity'' is the manifestation of man's striving towards unity with God. (p. 38)

Bely's theory of Symbolism regards artistic form as essentially dynamic in nature, and rests upon the assumption that the good reader is guided by the form of the work back to the artist's original creative process, which he then re-enacts. This is crucial for the theurgic conception of art, for religious creation is necessarily collective and must presuppose that art is effectively communicative. But his awareness that art forms are nonetheless part and parcel of the given world leads him to demand of the artist that he should ultimately give up art and ''become his own form'', instead of creating works of art, that is to say, he must actively create his new self. (p. 40)

> *John Elsworth, ''Andrei Bely's Theory of Symbolism,'' in* Studies in Twentieth Century Russian Literature, *edited by Christopher J. Barnes (© Forum for Modern Language Studies 1975; by permission of Barnes & Noble Books, a Division of Littlefield, Adams & Co., Inc.), Barnes & Noble, 1976, pp. 17-45.*

HELEN MUCHNIC   (essay date 1978)

In the intellectually giddy, combative, brilliant period of Russian art at the turn of the century, Andrei Bely was an outstanding figure, the best representative, no doubt, of its ultra-romantic speculations and experiments. He was ''an undisciplined and erratic Ariel,'' in D. S. Mirsky's witty characterization [see excerpt above], ''a seer and prophet'' to some, ''a sort of mystical mountebank'' to others. He was a leading exponent and practitioner of Russian Symbolism, and is thought to have exercised an enormous influence on Russian literature. The scientific study of Russian prosody began with him and, in criticism, his work gave rise to the Formalist School. . . .

[In *Andrei Bely: His Life and Works,* Konstantin Mochulsky] draws a portrait of a paradoxical and complex being, a gifted man on the brink of madness, sometimes toppling over the brink [see excerpt above]. Though not sufficiently deranged to be institutionalized, he was always eccentric, suffered from delusions of persecution, and had several breakdowns. His work reflected his nature.

The beginning of Bely's life was stamped by a profoundly traumatic experience that he himself described in an autobiographical novel, *Kotik Letaev,* reconstructing, with remarkable insight and precision, a child's pitiful, amusing, helpless confusion in an unhappy world he cannot understand. . . . His father, Nikolai Vasilievich Bugaev, an eminent mathematician, . . . was eccentric, clever, and extraordinarily ugly. His mother was frivolous, coquettish, hysterical, and very beautiful. She despised her husband, opposed him in all matters; and the child was the butt of their quarrels. He loved his father for the way he taught him the Lord's Prayer and told him fascinating stories about Adam and Eve, good and evil; and his mother he adored as a fairy-tale being, all in velvet, lace, and diamonds. But this lovely mother resented the father's lessons as forcing the child to ''a premature and abnormal development.'' Her love for him, Bely wrote, was ''powerful, jealous, cruel.'' She was repelled by his resemblance to her husband. She would kiss him passionately and suddenly push him away and begin to cry, lamenting ''he's not like me, he's like his father.'' And the five-year-old boy would cry with her, feeling helpless and guilty: was it his fault that he had a bulging forehead and that his development was ''premature and abnormal''? . . .

''Reality attacked his childish consciousness,'' says Mochulsky, ''like a nightmare; the shock and fear remained with him for his entire life. Bely's literary work is an attempt to exorcise the chaos in and around himself; to save himself from destruction, to find solid ground, to find reason in the confusion of delirium. At the heart of his writing is amazement and horror at life.'' And Vladislav Khodasevich, the émigré poet and critic whose essay on Bely Mochulsky refers to more than once, writes:

> Every appearance seemed to him ambivalent, revealed itself in a dual way, in double meanings. . . . He came to love the compatibility of the incompatible, the tragedy and complexity of inward contradictions, truth in untruth, perhaps good in evil and evil in good.
>
> (p. 22)

His entire work—poetry, poetics, linguistics—reflects that ''duality'' which, says Mochulsky, ''was Bely's tragic fate.'' All his writing gives evidence of a struggle to get beyond ''the chaotic waves of life'' to some kind of absolute and stable unity, whether in a mystic apprehension of Supreme Wisdom, the creation of life through art, or the wish to discover an innate order in the origin of words. Mochulsky sums up Bely's ''mystical credo,'' his ''attempt to exorcise chaos,'' as ''Neo-Kantian idealism . . . carried to an extreme. Outside of the creative spirit the world is chaos. . . . The artist is not only a creator of words and images, but also a demiurge, creating worlds. Art becomes theurgy.''

The same is true of Bely's life. It was a battle with a repulsive world, a determination to escape from nightmarish reality into a realm of transcendent harmony. ''The boundaries between art and life,'' as Mochulsky puts it, ''almost completely disappeared. Poems were perceived as life; life created poems.'' But this confusion was not uniquely Bely's. It was characteristic of the group with whom he was associated, ''The Frenzied Poets,'' in the appropriate title which Professor Oleg Maslenikov chose for his study of them [see excerpt above]. (pp. 22-3)

A kind of spiritual attitudinizing seems to have been Bely's most astonishing trait, a habit of deceptiveness that must have made it difficult not only for others but for himself to know whether he believed what he said he believed or felt what he professed to feel. There was so much posturing in his actions, so much evasion in the ideas he propounded, so much grandiloquence in what he wrote, that even his spells of madness seem sometimes self-induced, rhapsodic inventions applauded by his friends. In his unhappy childhood, a ''diving-bell'' of pretense was a necessary protection. With the grown man, pretense became ingrained duplicity that, operating through a kind of self-hypnosis, would, on occasion, transform invented emotions into something like genuine feeling, and fanciful ideas into the semblance of sincere belief. Bely could not live without dissimulation.

Nor was there anything scientific in his attempts to ''exorcise chaos.'' He was drawn to mystic doctrines and esoteric cults: Vladimir Soloviev, the Upanishads, Schopenhauer, Nietzsche, Neo-Platonism, Neo-Kantianism, Theosophy, Anthroposophy. He wanted some quick and certain means of getting at infallible Truth, and was wholly egocentric in his philosophic speculations as well as in his poetry and in his relations with others. ''Blok sought forgetfulness in wine and passion,'' Mochulsky remarks, ''Bely in Neo-Kantian logic.'' What he wanted from philosophy was confirmation of the only reality he could accept, the reality of the ineffable.

The Symbolism of his poetry is an allegory of the ineffable. Its purpose is not to communicate meanings but, through incantatory rhythms and words used as magic, to suggest unutterable insights. Sometimes, when he happened to express himself intelligibly, he felt the need to apologize. (pp. 23-4)

If one is hard put to it to distinguish between sense and pretense in the doctrines Bely expounded, if, as Osip Mandelstam said, Bely, choking on "refined verbosity," drove words "unsparingly and unceremoniously" in "dancing prose," there is one recurrent experience in his life of which neither the reality nor the presentation can be questioned. This is the experience of nightmare. Bely was a terrified man. He felt himself in the power of hostile forces, spied upon, pursued. And for this reason, when he wrote out of the core of nightmare, his work had an integrity and strength that were lacking in his prophetic visions and his speculative lucubrations. This is notably true of *Petersburg,* which even Mandelstam exempted from his strictures. It was, he said, a work unmatched by any other Russian writer in its powerful evocation of pre-revolutionary anxiety and turmoil. (p. 24)

Petersburg, despite its potential for tragedy, is in essence comedy of an incomparable strangeness. Much of it is monstrously funny in the manner of Gogol, but by and large it provokes shudders rather than laughter, and is, in sum, a virtuoso piece of horrifying black humor. "Like many modern writers," [Robert A. Macguire and John E. Malmstad] remark, "Bely does not attempt anything resembling full psychological portraits," but just the same, his characters are "real and memorable as individuals" [see excerpt below]. They are "real," however, only because Bely has tagged them with certain recognizable peculiarities. Their distinguishing traits are external; they are figures in an intricate pattern. It was not men and women, but the pattern—of sounds, shapes, colors—that most interested Bely. . . .

[Macguire and Malmstad], in my opinion, make a virtue of what is certainly Bely's most serious deficiency, his inconclusiveness, the dubiety of a man whose mind was a tangle of philosophic odds and ends but who had no integrated philosophy of his own. He could at once extol and ridicule the speculations and emotions that absorbed him, and experience the extremities of anxiety, but he had no sense of tragedy. The world appeared to Bely as frightening chaos, as uncontrollable violence, and it was in these terms that he pictured Russia in 1905. His strength as artist lay in projecting nightmares and delirium, that is, in states of mental and spiritual disorientation; and *Petersburg,* his masterpiece, is a terrifying adumbration of some looming, imminent, but undefined disaster, horrendous and—absurd.

High claims have been advanced for *Petersburg.* Vladimir Nabokov pronounced it one of the four "greatest masterpieces of twentieth century prose" [see excerpt above]. . . . Nabokov's criterion, one should note, is style; he is writing of the greatest *prose,* not the greatest fiction, even though his four examples are all drawn from fiction. But his judgment would have been no different had he chosen to speak of novels, since style was to him of first and last importance, so much so that, on this basis, he could relegate to second place even Goethe and Stendhal, Dostoevsky and Pasternak. There are other qualities, however, by which artistic greatness may be measured: depth and range of understanding, moral vision, human sympathy,

for example. And by these measures, although one might rank Bely with Kafka, one could hardly consider either of them in a class with Joyce and Proust. (p. 25)

Helen Muchnic, "Artist of Nightmare," in The New York Review of Books *(reprinted with permission from* The New York Review of Books; *copyright © 1978 Nyrev, Inc.), Vol. XXV, No. 5, April 6, 1978, pp. 22-5.*

ROBERT A. MAGUIRE and JOHN E. MALMSTAD (essay date 1978)

At the heart of *Petersburg* lies a question that has agitated Russians for generations: the national identity. Perhaps only the Germans and the Americans, among modern western peoples, have been so obsessed with finding out who they are, and so given to questioning their own reality and authenticity. The Russian version has been shaped as much by geography as anything else. As a nation straddling Europe and Asia, Russians have sought to define a vision of themselves that would amount to more than merely a sum of "western" and "eastern" traits. This in turn has provided a context in which the great writers have explored the individual's quest for identity and meaning with an intensity and earnestness that seem quintessentially Russian. *Petersburg* represents the culmination of this tradition.

At the same time, the problem has had larger dimensions. For Russians also conceive of "west" and "east" in ways that mark the human experience generally. "West" stands for reason, order, symmetry; "east" for the irrational, the impalpable, the intuitive. At given times one may outweigh the other in society at large or in the individual consciousness; or the two may even coexist more or less harmoniously. But in the twentieth century, as Bely clearly sees, these two principles, inside Russia and out, have more often been in open conflict, with neither gaining preponderance. We have developed a characteristically "modern" terminology to express our reaction to this conflict: anxiety, apprehension, alienation, isolation. These also describe the moods that move Bely's great novel from beginning to end. (pp. vii-viii)

Petersburg paints a vivid picture of the capital of the world's largest land empire during the autumn of 1905. Russian culture was then at its most brilliant and innovative. Literature, music, theater, and ballet were beginning to win fame throughout the world. But the society from which they sprang seemed shaky. Japan had just proved victorious in a war that Russia was supposed to have won easily. Political agitation and social unrest were on the rise. Outright revolution was being preached and prepared; and from January 1905 on, the country was shaken by a series of mutinies, uprisings, assassinations, and strikes. There was a widespread feeling among those who witnessed such events that the old values were no longer adequate to the new realities, and that Russia teetered on the edge of some dreadful catastrophe. This ominous feeling, with the attendant moods of anxiety, apprehension, and disorientation, permeates Bely's *Petersburg* from the first page to the last.

Appropriately enough, conspiracy and terror are the forces that move the novel. . . . *Petersburg* is a novel of suspense. It is also a social novel, a family novel, a philsophical, political, psychological, historical novel—and even then we do not begin to exhaust the possible approaches to it. One has to go back in Russian literature at least to *Crime and Punishment* to find a work in which so many plots and subplots are as intricately and subtly interwoven, with no loose ends protruding. Yet Bely ranges much farther afield than does Dostoevsky. It is relatively easy to account for the main lines of *Crime and Punishment*, tangled though they be, whereas to do that for *Petersburg* would be to rewrite the novel: it is all but immune to paraphrase.

All these planes, levels, and dimensions come together in the characters of the novel, who are at the same time engaged in moving the story line ahead. Through the characters themselves—and not through any raisonneur-figure, or through any of those grand panoramic statements to which the nineteenth-century novelists were addicted—Bely creates a picture of Petersburg society. He focuses on the two extremes—the powerful and privileged (Apollon Apollonovich and his circle) and the poor and disaffected (Dudkin and the peasant Styopka). But he creates an impression of fullness and completeness by bringing in, if only fleetingly, representatives of other classes and groups, such as merchants and servants, and by constantly invoking the gray faceless masses of the metropolis. Through the characters he also introduces the intellectual and cultural fashions that held sway in Petersburg at the time. . . . Many of the characters also transfer universally recognizable social and psychological types into the Petersburg of 1905: Apollon Apollonovich, for one, is the quint-essential bureaucrat and the quintessential anal erotic. Even the excursions into the timeless and dimensionless realm of myth and the "cosmos" are shown as the experiences of specific characters.

Such a multiplicity of functions tends to pull the characters out of themselves. Like many modern writers, Bely does not attempt anything resembling full psychological portraits. Ultimately there are no private thoughts or private actions; all are reflexes of larger realities, which in turn are experienced by all the characters. Even something as concrete as a tic or a gesture may be shared by a number of otherwise seemingly different personages. . . . Yet it is Bely's great achievement to make these characters seem real and memorable as individuals. He endows each with certain striking physical traits which he repeats again and again by way of imprinting them on our memories. . . . Each character has his own skew of temperament, which helps determine which aspects of the vast reality of the novel he will tend to see. And Bely surrounds him with an array of objects that serve as correlatives to his outlook. Apollon Apollonovich relishes the icy symmetries of the formal rooms of his mansion, which reflect his passion for the abstractions of geometry. His son lives in three very different rooms, which suggests greater temperamental complexity: the study, with its bookshelves and its bust of Kant, mirrors his yearning for systems and his penchant for abstraction (both "western" traits); the sleeping room, which is almost entirely taken up by a huge bed, objectifies and is meant to exorcise his Oedipal obsession with the sexual "sin" of his conception; the reception room, with its oriental motifs, gratifies the "eastern" side of his character which emerges after his mother runs off with her lover. (pp. xi-xiii)

Bely's characters, then, are both general and particular, abstract and concrete, unreal and real, at one and the same time. This unity in duality is characteristic of every aspect of the novel. Consider the matter of time. The novel as a whole unfolds between September 30 and October 9, 1905. . . . Yet the chronology is constantly warped: characters and events from the literature and history of the past move into 1905; there are sudden shifts into a distant unspecified future time, and even into the timeless realm of myth. We come to see that time and timelessness are both "real" in this novel; the one does not exclude the other.

The same point can be made about the city itself. As Bely recreates it, it is as familiar to any Russian as London or Paris is to an Englishman or Frenchman. Through a careful and lavish specification of the peculiarities of climate, geography, and prominent architectural features, Bely manages to convey a sense of the actual physical presence of the city, making it so vivid and "real" that sometimes we almost think we are reading a gloss on Baedeker. (At the same time, we understand that Petersburg represents the modern city generally.) Yet it has a curiously elusive quality. (pp. xiii-xiv)

In fact, Bely readily acknowledges his debt to the version of Petersburg that has been shaped by Russian literature. Writers of the eighteenth century tended to see Petersburg as a magnificent monument to the power of human reason and will: it was a planned city, founded in 1703 and built on a trackless bog. Part I of Pushkin's "The Bronze Horseman" (1833) honors this point of view; but Part II strikes a new note that came to predominate in virtually all literary treatments of Petersburg well into the twentieth century: beneath the "western" facade lay a shadowy world of intangibilities and unrealities, alien to man's reason and apprehensible only to his unconscious being—an "eastern" world, in the Russian terminology. It was Petersburg, with its uneasy coexistence of "west" and "east," that appealed to the Russian mind as being emblematic of the larger problem of national indentity. Readers of Gogol and Dostoevsky are familiar with this double view. It characterizes Bely's novel too. He takes all the literary myths of Petersburg, which Dostoevsky called "the most fantastic and intentional city in the world," and brings them to culmination.

Each of the characters in *Petersburg* participates in the enactment and perpetuation of the myth of the city—none more vigorously and meaningfully than the Bronze Horseman. The subject of the statue, Peter the Great, was a real man and a historical figure. In his efforts to shatter and update the Russia he inherited, he was a revolutionary; yet at the same time he created the bureaucracy by which the reforms were rigidified into the self-perpetuating authority of the state. In the single-minded tyranny with which he acted, he was an "eastern" despot; but in his vision of a modern state he was "western." As the "father" of Russia, he is the ultimate symbol of the paternal authority against which the "sons" rebel in various ways. At the same time, he has a literary dimension, as the main subject of Pushkin's "The Bronze Horseman," which is constantly invoked throughout Bely's novel; the Horseman, in turn, is the most famous monument in Petersburg, and is in effect a symbol of the city. In the novel, Peter is alive and ever-present in all these manifestations—a point Bely reinforces not only by bringing the statue to life (Pushkin does that too), but also by tying Peter in with the all-pervasive theme of generational conflict and revolution, with the literary myth of the city, and with the apocalyptic destiny he sees awaiting Russia.

The Bronze Horseman is the most perceptive character in the novel. But most of the others are intelligent enough to see that they are not self-contained, that they participate whether wishing to or not, in the workings of a larger reality that exists independent of them. This reality is sometimes referred to in the novel as "abyss" or "void." Occasionally a character is vouchsafed a disturbing glimpse into it, in dreams, at the moment of death, or at times of great stress which pull him out of his routines and, in the words of [L. K. Dolgopolov] "bring him into contact with the universe [literally, 'world-structure,' *mirozdanie*] and turn him into a 'particle' of the universe too. . . .'' Such an experience is profoundly unsettling to Bely's characters, for it threatens to undo their identities as individuals. By way of resistance, they construct a world of objects with definite shapes and functions, whether the city itself, representing Peter's attempt at self-assertion and self-definition, or the more modest houses, apartments, and rooms that his heirs inhabit. All relish what they can touch and see—the visible, the finite, the specific—or what they can construct out of their own heads—systems, categories, propositions. But the narrator treats all such attempts with irony; they represent no more than a partial and provisional reality, and therefore serve only to perpetuate self-deception. (pp. xiv-xv)

What the characters fail to see is that the whole world, natural and man-made, visible and invisible, is a living entity, composed of parts which interconnect and thereby acquire their true meaning. To isolate one or more of these parts, physically or intellectually, is to diminish and damage the whole, much as the removal of an arm or a leg from the body detracts from the beauty, the efficiency, and even the health of the entire organism. But that is precisely what the characters in *Petersburg* attempt to do. Gogol was Bely's great predecessor in seeing the urge to fragment as a modern sickness. He deemed it the work of the devil. For Bely, the devil is modern urban man himself, whose obsession with the fragment is not so much an evil as a compulsion born of the fear of losing his individuality.

Language, as Bely sees it, is especially subject to the depredations of self-deception, perhaps because it is a wholly human construct. Apollon Apollonovich's habit of calling all flowers "bluebells" regardless of their variety divorces the word from living reality and turns it into an abstraction. All the other characters indulge in the same operation, to varying degrees. As a result, verbal exchanges in *Petersburg,* when not merely trivial, tend to be irrelevant and fatuous. Gestures can often be more expressive of true intentions and desires. In written form, words can be just as inadequate to deeper understanding and meaningful communication—perhaps even more so than spoken words, for they are fixed and motionless, and we tend to worship them as we worship artifacts generally. Whether spoken or written, however, language as modern man uses it is yet another of the abstractions he makes in an effort to deny the vitality, energy, and change that characterize real life. The consequences are grave, in Bely's view; for language—or, as he often calls it, "the word"—is our only means of knowing the world and ourselves. The living word, for Bely, is sound, or speech. Without it, "there is neither nature, nor the world, nor anyone cognizing them." If modern thought and modern society are in a state of crisis, as Bely believes, then that is because language, as modern man employs it, is dying. (pp. xv-xvi)

One of Bely's tasks as a literary artist is to convey a sense of the word as sound through the static medium of print. In *Petersburg,* as in several of his other works, he constantly tries to confound all our habits as visually-oriented readers for whom words are immobile, unobtrusive, and as silent as the type that encases them.

For one thing, he does violence to the accepted usages and the traditional strategies of "literary" language. He breaks his page up into small units with a profusion of dashes, dots, and new paragraphs. The result is a nervous and disjointed-looking discourse which does not flow in the majestic and seemingly effortless manner of the nineteenth-century novel. He is also addicted to catachresis: the expected word simply does not turn up in the expected place. Thus we find, to take a simple example, "thought train" . . . instead of the usual "train of thought." . . . Although there are comparatively few outright neologisms, Bely does devise unusual combinations of elements taken from standard Russian, particularly for abstract nouns, whose meaning is more or less clear, but which are not listed in any dictionary.

For another thing, he aims at creating a world of sound. Dialogue is prominent; in fact, *Petersburg* would lend itself well to adaptation for the stage or cinema. . . . From the very beginning of the novel, we are confronted with a speaking narrator, whose voice rings in our ears throughout the novel. And we quickly become aware that this narrator also strives after certain sound effects. (pp. xvi-xvii)

[Sheer] sound is so prominent as to constitute yet another level of reality with which we must reckon. From the very first page, we are conditioned to listen as well as look. We find it difficult to read rapidly or silently; our lips tend to move; and we pay closer attention than might otherwise be the case to the word itself and its components. (p. xvii)

How are we to approach a novel so complex and richly textured as *Petersburg?* (p. xviii)

Certainly we can say that Bely expects us to be more perceptive than his characters. We must resist a natural inclination to simplify, categorize, paraphrase, abstract, and fragment, that is, to treat the reality of the novel in the same way the characters do. We will not get very far if we succumb to the temptation, as some readers have done, of assuming that Bely's world is built on a system of dualities that amounts to a set of viable alternatives: east/west, animate/inanimate, revolutionary/reactionary, present/past, Christ/Satan, and so on. There are no real alternatives for Bely. Revolution and reaction are equally incompetent to deal with reality: both are constructs of the mind that end in mindless despotism; east and west are so intermingled in the Russian character that they cannot possibly be separated; there is no meaningful division between present and past, or present and future. The most useful rhetorical model for this novel is not either/or, but both/and.

Bely once remarked that "every novel is a game of hide and seek with the reader." This is particularly true of *Petersburg*. And once we realize that the game lies in the seeking itself, that there are no firm answers or final solutions, we will have begun to grasp what Bely is aiming at. Constant uncertainty, constant tension, constant change are the normal modes here. We must bend to the will of the narrator, and allow that it is highly capricious. He ironizes and he bumbles; he lyricizes and he prattles; he plays the sophisticate, he plays the fool; he identifies himself with this or that character, only to draw back and mock all the characters, the reader, and himself. At times he appears omniscient, like a typical nineteenth-century literary narrator; at times he admits to being as baffled as anyone else. Such swings of tone, manner, and posture can occur with bewildering speed, often within a single sentence. We are kept constantly off guard, never knowing what the narrator will say next, or how he will say it. (pp. xviii-xix)

The ending of the novel seems ambiguous, as do the endings in many other notable works of Russian literature. But there can be no real endings for Bely. The world of his novel is a living organism, which constantly renews itself and which makes mockery of man's efforts to cut it to his own limited horizons. As an affirmation of the life principle, it is ever-dynamic. In that sense, it stands virtually alone among the great works of the twentieth century. (p. xxi)

Robert A. Maguire and John E. Malmstad, in their introduction to Petersburg *by Andrei Bely, translated and annotated by Robert A. Maguire and John E. Malmstad (translation copyright © 1978 by Robert A. Maguire and John E. Malmstad), Indiana University Press, 1978, pp. vii-xxii.*

DIANA FESTA-McCORMICK (essay date 1979)

Andrei Bely's *Saint Petersburg* is, as the title indicates, a novel about the controversial and contradictory city of Peter the Great. It is also a symbolic prophecy of the impending doom of Russia, harassed by a recent defeat (in the Russo-Japanese War) and by an abortive revolution. A conflict of two generations is exemplified by the estrangement between father and son, at times recalling the painful struggle and pathos in Turgenev's *Fathers and Sons*. The futility of the plottings, of the endless and aimless talks by nihilists and utopians, offers a picture of the would-be revolutionaries even more ludicrous in their earnestness, and as inefficient in their powerlessness to act, as that of Dostoevski's *Demons*. The characters, fewer in number than in almost any other great work of Russian fiction, are powerfully delineated in their pathetic contradictions. The fogs in the city atmosphere, the cold, geometric beauty of the avenues and of the canals, the weight of the past and the memory of the ruthless founder, control the behavior and the dreams of the puppetlike inhabitants. Nowhere is there to be found in the large volume a carefully organized and detailed description of the scenery, of the streets and houses of the city, or even of the Neva of which one senses the constant presence. (pp. 112-13)

The initial two pages of the novel might be somewhat disconcerting for the unprepared reader, setting the tone of the narrative with insolent sarcasm that is purposely broken up by acid aphorisms. Rabelais or Swift come to mind here, rather than the more classical presentations and neatly told stories with logical sequences of events fixed in time and place. Bely refutes all the factual, descriptive sentences that, in guidebooks or geographical manuals, claim to sketch the appearance and life of a city. All logic and established patterns of the past are derided here, and Petersburg appears as a reality born of the imagination. Assertive in its pervasive reality, the city echoes the world of Gogol and Pushkin; the latter's presence is subtly evoked through the repeated allusions to the "Bronze Horseman," which delicately merge with the wavering structure and leitmotiv of the novel. The symmetry, the rectilinear avenues, the uniformity of the houses, the obedience of the servant population and of the office clerks—all conspire to make of Saint Petersburg the city of mechanized bureaucrats. The aging senator and high government official who will stand at the center of the rambling novel has himself taken on the gait and mental habits of a computer. The placidity of his unvaried existence has, however, been rudely shaken of late. (p. 113)

Nowhere is the scenery of Saint Petersburg elaborately described. Still, through vignettes, a few touches of color, repeated allusions to the greenish water of the canals, to the air saturated with moisture, to the splendor, but also to the unhealthiness of the Russian metropolis, are hauntingly recalled. The streets of the city, the author remarks early in the book, are endowed with the eerie power of transforming the passersby into shadows. One might almost believe oneself in Dickens's London on a foggy day. The canals, through which the

founder of the city had hoped to emulate his favorite harbor of Western Europe, Amsterdam, are a symbol of stagnation and of corruption. The time of the year is October, and violent gusts of autumnal wind moan along the broad, exposed perspectives. Soot rising in whirlpools from the chimney stacks lends a funereal air to the houses. [In this manner] Bely unveils the symbolic meaning of his novel, which is nothing less than an anticipation of the city's impending doom, itself a forewarning of the collapse of Russia, condemned to die so that it may be born again. (p. 115)

The structure of Bely's novel contrasts, in its apparent simplicity, with the broader expanse and symphonic construction of most of the classics of Russian fiction, from *Dead Souls* to *Doctor Zhivago*. Its casual, at times ironical tone might rather remind one of the longer stories of Chekhov. Nowhere does the narrator seem to take himself too seriously or to dissert upon the mystical significance of the catastrophe toward which is directed the attention of the reader. No claim to philosophy of history or to moralizing about the nihilists is put forward by the discreet and ironical author. The scope of the novel is, from the start, a narrow one. The working classes, the shopkeepers, the professionals of revolutionary movements are kept out of Saint Petersburg exactly as they are kept out of Proustian fiction; the only exception is that of the servants. Other novels revolving around cities, from Balzac, Hugo, and Dickens to Zola, have not resisted the lure of moralistic declamation against the monstrous destructiveness of that modern dehumanizing congeries of people. The favorite images or comparisons were those of volcanoes, blazing furnaces (or, at best, crucibles), and sewers. The symbolic masters of the cities were greedy speculators, unscrupulous politicians, Don Juans avid for sexual domination, or triumphant prostitutes like Nana.

Bely is less encyclopedic and in no way drawn to gruesome pictures of violence and vice. He is neither a social reformer nor a Savonarola vituperating against luxury. His metropolis is nowhere called a Babylon or a Nineveh, to be destroyed because of its disregard of all moral laws, or a Babel arising against some divine decree. He prefers a tone of irony to that of a solemn denouncer of monsters. His pity extends to the very characters whom he ridicules most insistently: the feeble and awkward Nikolai who plays at being an apprentice of revolutionary destruction and is embarrassed with the ludicrous sardine čan that has been palmed off upon him, and the even more pathetič father, unable to shake off his official self and to uncover what is human within him. The sections of the novel are disconnected, so as to reflect the confusion of the minds unable to grasp the significance of events. The apparent disintegration of the novel—or at least of the novel's classical structure—thus runs parallel to the mystifying quest and faltering resolve of the characters. The motif that runs all through the work, persistent, emphasized again and again through the allusions to Pushkin's famous verse tale, is always the same: the father, the son, their servants, and their friends all grope their way clumsily in the fog and under the incessantly changing skies of the Russian capital. They are but shadows in a visionary merry-go-round. A curse pursues them: the curse of their Tartar blood in the case of Apollon and his son, but also the curse of the Bronze Horseman. Peter the Great . . . had tried in vain to erect a city of harmonious and geometrical boulevards and concentric canals, reneging not only Asia but the mystical forces by which Russians are nurtured. (pp. 121-22)

Diana Festa-McCormick, "Bely's 'Saint Petersburg': A City Conjured by a Visionary Symbolist," in her The City As Catalyst: A Study of Ten Novels

*(© 1979 by Associated University Presses, Inc.),
Associated University Press, 1979, pp. 108-23.*

ALFRED CORN   (essay date 1980)

[Bely's *The First Encounter*] is one of the masterpieces of the early Soviet period; in fact, there is no long poem in Russian after this as great. . . .

The First Encounter, a record of his twentieth year (the year 1900) and the forces that shaped his aspirations as a writer, may be considered as Bely's *The Prelude.* The comparison gains force if the poem is taken in tandem with Bely's novel *Kotik Letaev. . . . Kotik Letaev,* like *The First Encounter,* is a study of the making of a poet; but it is prose fiction, and the autobiographical period covered, early childhood. (p. 461)

Divided into four parts, and with a Prologue and Epilogue, the poem is a synchronic reverie, playing freely among memories, speculations, and longings. Its non-narrative organization resembles music, with verbal and thematic motifs standing as analogues to musical themes and harmonies. . . . The Prologue is an invocation of the poetic afflatus, assimilated here to the Pentecostal descent of the Holy Spirit and the fiery gift of tongues. Part One of the poem recaptures Bely's sense of himself at age twenty, divided between scientific and mystical studies. The narrator's father is called "Dean Letaev," an indication of this poems close relationship to the novel *Kotik Letaev.* The second section of the poem introduces a nonfictional personage, Mikhail Sergeevich Solovyov, and, more hazily, the latter's older brother, Vladimir. This Solovyov is the famous philosopher and poet, one of the principal influences on the Russian Symbolists Balmont, Bryusov, and of course Bely—though Solovyov himself disdained the movement. More urgent to him was the forging of his own syncretist religion, with elements borrowed from Eastern mysticism as well as Christianity. Vladimir Solovyov found a ready, if unsolicited disciple in Bely, who was himself caught up in the project of uniting art, science, language mysticism, and syncretic religion in a new synthesis meant to dawn with the new century.

The "encounter" referred to in the poem's title, then, is a first exposure to a man and a philosophical spirit. But it is also a romantic encounter with a woman and a physical entity. That woman is given the fictional name "Nadezhda Lvovna Zarina," but is based on an actual person, Margarita Morozova. . . . The romantic encounter between Bely and this representative of the Eternal Feminine—for so she is allegorized—is the subject of the poem's third section, perhaps the most brilliant verses Bely ever wrote. The setting is the Nobleman's Assembly Hall in Moscow, the occasion, a concert of one of the Beethoven symphonies. Bely deftly captures the heated atmosphere, the throngs crowding into the hall, the chatter, the costumes, the noise of the musicians' warm-up. From a distance he sees the beautiful Nadezhda, luminous and somehow at a spiritual remove from the hurly-burly around her. She becomes for Bely an avatar of Sophia, Heavenly Wisdom incarnate. Indeed it is her *fleshly,* material reality that the poem dwells on at length. By contrast Vladimir Solovyov's characterization is largely immaterial; he exists in the poem mostly as a phantom, a spirit. This antinomy is at the heart of Bely's thought: the spirit of order on the one hand, incarnate wisdom on the other. (pp. 463-64)

In Bely's (and Solovyov's) syncretism, Christ is the Logos, and Nature (the Cosmos) is materialized wisdom. . . . Emotion and the senses belong to Cosmos-Sofia, and so the third section

of the poem fills out Bely's notion of the Eternal Feminine by presenting her at a concert of *music,* the art of sound and feeling. (The realm of the Logos is of course language, philosophy, and poetry.) The description of the concert is a long tour de force—. . . [an effort] to render, in words, musical impressions. By all accounts, Bely is more successful than any other Russian poet in this endeavor.

Part Four of the poem follows the narrator out of the concert hall and out into the streets and lanes of the winter city. There is a fleeting vision of the ghost of Vladimir Solovyov (who died in 1900); a visit to the chapel of the Blessed Virgin; and then the poem ends, concluding with a brief Epilogue, dated "Pentecost and Whitmonday, 1921." The "encounters" have taken place, and Bely's *Prelude* has been accomplished.

I suggested earlier that *The First Encounter* should be read in tandem with *Kotik Letaev,* Bely's earlier spiritual autobiography. Among the features shared by the two works . . . is the dualistic cosmology (used as an organizational principle) I have just now outlined. The sensibility of the novel's narrator is divided into "masculine" and "feminine" traits, these roughly grouped under the rubrics of "logical order" and "chaos." (p. 464)

Alfred Corn, "Russian Encounters," in The Yale Review *(© 1980 by Yale University; reprinted by permission of the editors), Vol. LXIX, No. 3, March, 1980, pp. 459-65.**

ADDITIONAL BIBLIOGRAPHY

Berberova, Nina. "A Note on Andrey Biely." *The Russian Review* 10, No. 2 (April 1951): 99-105.
    Discussion of Biely's importance as a Russian symbolist poet and novelist. The critic concludes that Biely's voice and personality most fully reflected the Russian symbolist movement.

Donchin, Georgette. "The Symbolist Aesthetics." In her *The Influence of French Symbolism on Russian Poetry,* pp. 76-119. The Hague: Mouton & Co., 1958.*
    Examination of Bely's theory of symbolism and its place in Russian literature. Donchin contrasts Bely's belief in symbolism as "a conception of life" with those other symbolists who felt that it was primarily a literary school.

Elsworth, J. D. "*The Silver Dove*: An Analysis." *Russian Literature* IV, No. 4 (October 1976): 365-93.
    Indepth analysis of Bely's *The Silver Dove.* Elsworth argues that with *The Silver Dove* Bely moved away from the formal experimentation of his earlier work and attempted to incorporate into the novel elements "belonging to the realistic tradition."

Gurian, Waldemar. "The Memoirs of Bely." *The Russian Review* 3, No. 1 (Autumn 1943): 95-103.
    Biocritical discussion of Bely's *Memoirs.* Gurian concludes that Bely will be best remembered for his *Memoirs,* in which he captured the events and important personalities during the years before and after the turn of the century.

Janecek, Gerald. "Anthroposophy in *Kotik Letaev.*" *Orbis Litterarum* XXIX, No. 3 (1974): 245-67.
    Examination of Bely's *Kotik Letaev* in light of Rudolf Steiner's writings on anthroposophy. Janecek attempts to demonstrate that Bely's novel is, "at least in part, an artistic embodiment of Steiner's precepts" set forth in his book *Theosophy.*

Janecek, Gerald, ed. *Andrey Bely: A Critical Review.* Lexington: The University Press of Kentucky, 1978, 222 p.

Volume of selected essays from the International Symposium on Andrey Bely held in 1975. The essays in this collection cover a broad spectrum of topics and approaches, from "criticism and analysis of Bely's works" to an examination of "extrinsic matters such as personal relationships and broad philosophical issues."

Mochulsky, Konstatin. *Andrei Bely: His Life and Works.* Translated by Nora Szalavitz. Ann Arbor, Mich.: Ardis Publishers, 1977, 230 p.

Unfinished biography on Bely, and the only one in Russian or English which studies all of his work in detail. Mochulsky examines Bely's literature in relation to the writer as a human being, the period in which he lived, and the people and ideas that influenced him.

Poggioli, Renato. "Symbolists and Others: Andrej Belyj." In his *The Poets of Russia: 1890-1930,* pp. 153-61. Cambridge: Harvard University Press, 1960.

Brief critical commentaries on Bely's poetry, fiction, and memoirs. Poggioli concludes that Bely, in his search for new faiths and new creeds, served the hidden historical task of the Russian symbolist movement, "which was at once to conceal and to reveal the cultural crisis of the epoch."

Reeve, F. D. "Petersburg." In his *The Russian Novel,* pp. 325-45. New York, London: McGraw-Hill Book Co., 1966.

Examination of Bely's masterpiece. Reeve analyzes *Petersburg* according to a number of different interpretations: as a satire of Russian autocracy, as an historical account of the revolutionary currents in the Russia of 1905, and as "a great game of language, written to test the limits of expressibility by the play of utmost skill."

Tsvetaeva, Marina. "A Captive Spirit." In her *Marina Tsvetaeva; A Captive Spirit: Selected Prose,* edited and translated by J. Marin King, pp. 99-159. Ann Arbor, Mich.: Ardis Publishers, 1980.

Personal reminiscences on Bely's life and career. Tsvetaeva's portrait covers two periods in Bely's life: the first, between 1903 and 1910, discusses Bely's intense friendship with Alexander Blok and his wife Liubov Dmitrievna; the second covers Bely's meeting with Asya Turgeneva and their eventual flight from Russia.

Zavalishin, Vyacheslav. "Major Prerevolutionary Writers on the Bridge between Two Cultures: The Symbolists." In his *Early Soviet Writers,* pp. 5-40. New York: Frederick A. Praeger, 1958.*

Review of Bely's work after the 1917 revolution. Zavalishin concludes that Bely's experimental style was at odds with the Soviet regime and that his literary output, with the exception of his memoirs and criticism, suffered greatly during this period.

Stephen Vincent Benét
1898-1943

American poet, short story writer, novelist, dramatist, historian, critic, librettist, and editor.

Benét holds a minor literary reputation for poetry in which he attempted to document, comprehend, and ultimately to celebrate American history. He conveyed his faith in the enduring existence of America's fundamental ideals: the virtues of the democratic system of government, the possibility of a common spirit unifying a diverse populus, and, most importantly, the value of the individual. His lengthy narrative of the Civil War, *John Brown's Body,* was acclaimed as a long-awaited American epic. For a work of poetry it gained an unusually wide readership, and Benét was awarded a Pulitzer Prize in 1929. Though criticized for a variety of faults in both style and sentiment, Benét's most important achievement still finds admirers among those who share his affection for America's past.

Benét came from a military family and as a youth read extensively in American military history as well as literature. This background prepared him for his later works on American subjects. His first work, *Five Men and Pompey,* is a series of dramatic monologues displaying the influence of Robert Browning. For the most part, however, Benét's influences were minor poems and minor poets. Critics frequently conclude that his best work is not to be found in the ambitious *John Brown's Body,* but in such lesser pieces as "The Mountain Whippoorwill" and "Mortuary Parlors," which exhibit Benét's talent for clever irony and his acute sensitivity for the macabre. With *The Ballad of William Sycamore, 1790-1880,* Benét showed both his sincerity and competence in treating American subject matter at length.

While in Paris on a Guggenheim fellowship, Benét discovered the artistic value of his native country's history, and used America's antebellum epoch as the inspiration for his most famous work. Benét described *John Brown's Body* as a "cyclorama" of shifting times, places, and viewpoints. Since its appearance critics have commented on the cinematic quality of the narrative. Benét intended its value to derive in part from an ever-changing variety of style and characters, as opposed to the unity of these elements found in the classical epic. Benét expressed dissatisfaction with this term, saying that it "suggests a portentousness and a presumption which I do not wish to claim." Nevertheless, critics have both praised and denigrated Benét's poem as a work in the epic genre. His characterizations of such historic figures as President Lincoln and General Lee have received particularly mixed criticism; some commentators dismiss the characterizations as shallow and inept, while others applaud them as insightful and faithful to their originals. Most frequently attacked in *John Brown's Body* are what Allen Tate calls its "hair-raising defects" of banal phrasing, unpoetic rhythms, and flawed diction. Benét's use of a wide range of poetic meters resulted in stylistic looseness and fragmentation, leaving his best work to be discovered in individual sections, especially the ballads, rather than the poem as a whole. A second project for an extended narrative which Benét never lived to finish is *Western Star.* He completed only the first book of what was to be a poetic chronicle of the

Culver Pictures

settlement of America's western territories. Though judged inferior to *John Brown's Body, Western Star* is a fragment that shows the author in full command of his craft.

Besides his poetic works, Benét wrote five novels, of which *Jean Huguenot* and *Spanish Bayonet* are considered the most successful, and numerous collections of short stories. Benét's novels are not as notable as his poetry and have attracted very little critical attention. His short stories, however, display many of the strengths of his best minor poems: a feeling for American folklore and legend, a skilled use of grotesque and supernatural themes, and a talent for unusual ideas and effects. His best known story, "The Devil and Daniel Webster," almost immediately entered the realm of American legendry. For these tales and for his poems on traditionally American topics, Benét has earned a position as an author who gave artistic form to a profound love and vast knowledge of his homeland.

(See also *Dictionary of Literary Biography,* Vol. 4: *American Writers in Paris, 1920-1939.*)

PRINCIPAL WORKS

Five Men and Pompey   (poetry)   1915
The Drug-Shop; or, Endymion in Edmonstoun   (poetry) 1917

Young Adventure   (poetry)   1918
Heavens and Earth   (poetry)   1920
The Beginning of Wisdom   (novel)   1921
Young People's Pride   (novel)   1922
The Ballad of William Sycamore, 1790-1880   (poetry)
   1923
Jean Huguenot   (novel)   1923
King David   (poetry)   1923
Tiger Joy   (poetry)   1925
Spanish Bayonet   (novel)   1926
John Brown's Body   (poetry)   1928
Ballads and Poems, 1915-1930   (poetry)   1931
A Book of Americans [with Rosemary Carr Benét]   (poetry)
   1933
James Shore's Daughter   (novel)   1934
Burning City   (poetry)   1936
The Devil and Daniel Webster   (short story)   1937
Thirteen O'Clock   (short stories)   1937
Johnny Pye and the Fool-Killer   (short story)   1938
Tales before Midnight   (short stories)   1939
Nightmare at Noon   (poetry)   1940
Western Star   (poetry)   1943
The Last Circle   (poetry and short stories)   1946

BABETTE DEUTSCH   (essay date 1919)

Perhaps because his subjectivity is not confined to personal experience, Stephen Vincent Benét captures [in **"Young Adventure"**] more than "a tremulous murmur from great days long dead". His is authentically a book of young adventure. He dreams with Keats in the drug-shop at Edmonton, he dines in a quick-lunch room, or paints a gorgeous, fatal, papal feast with equal ardor. There is more than a murmur of Browning in this latter poem, but it is yet a consummate thing, and full of unexpected lyrism. The courage and challenging irony of youth are the chief features of his verse. As a psychological study, no less than as vivid poetry, **"The Breaking Point"** is remarkable. So, too, is the shocking realism of **"Young Blood"**. The poet has, moreover, a pungent vocabulary and a nice sense of form. **"The Hemp"** is a splendidly dramatic ballad, and in his **"Elegy for an Enemy"** he has used the metrical scheme of [Thomas] Hood's "Bridge of Sighs" with fine effectiveness. An example of exquisite humor is the charming **"Portrait of a Baby"**. (pp. 753-54)

> Babette Deutsch, "Realists and Orators," in The
> Bookman, *New York, Vol. XLVIII, No. 6, February,*
> *1919, pp. 752-54.**

JOHN PEALE BISHOP   (essay date 1921)

[There are three young American writers] who cannot be overlooked by anyone interested in delivering the American novel from the Philistines. . . .

Francis Scott Fitzgerald is a Princetonian; Stephen Vincent Benét, Yale '19; John Dos Passos, Harvard '17. (p. 229)

The Beginning of Wisdom is a picaresque novel of a young man who successively encounters God, country and Yale. Mr. Benét treats Yale as something he remembers rather than as something lived through by his characters. He has, too, been a little too well-bred about it, for all his jibes at the pious

athletes and the impeccable parlor snakes. The only way to make literary material out of one's youthful experiences is to be shameless about one's self and ruthless with one's friends. Mr. Benét has concealed nearly everything about himself except his opinions, and what he has had to say about his friends has been said with wreaths tied with Yale blue ribbons. The unfortunate part about it is that no one at that age particularly minds being made stock of. Fitzgerald made a Princetonian figure in my image and thrust it so full of witty arrows that it resembled St. Sebastian about as much as it did me. I was undeniably flattered. Mr. Benét has visualized Yale, but he has not dramatized it. The only incident which has a present air has not to do with the college at all but with the daughter of a dilapidated dentist of New Haven. Amorously entangled, the hero marries her. A few weeks later she dies. Clearly, they order these things better at Yale. In Princeton such adventures seldom end in marriage, and when they do, the women live on forever.

Mr. Benét is a much better novelist when not retracking too closely his own footsteps, and throughout he has the courage and skill to write beautifully. He has so rare a skill with color, so unlimited an invention of metaphor, such humorous delight in the externals of things, so brave a fantasy, that he occasionally forgets that the chief business of the novelist is not to describe character but to show it in action. I am not quite sure what is intended by the beginning of wisdom—but it is certainly not the fear of the Lord. For a while, the hero seems to look toward beauty and arrogance and irony for direction in all things, but in the end he marries a girl who has been with the Y.M.C.A. in France and returns with strange ideas of "service and sanity through service." (pp. 230-31)

Fitzgerald, Benét and Dos Passos belong to the generation which suffered the actual indignities of war. In [*The Beautiful and the Damned,* **The Beginning of Wisdom,** and *Three Soldiers*] we will find an approach to the war quite other than that found in the soldier stories which three years ago begauded our magazines. (p. 231)

[Mr. Benét's experiences were] Cis-Atlantic. Book VII of his novel, written with the impudent buoyancy of the early days of the officers' training camps, includes a series of portraits—officers, men, artillery horses, and guns—and one conversation of most unsoldierlike speech on immortality. No less than the Yale section it shows Mr. Benét's tendency to treat incident visually instead of dramatically. But it also shows with what skill and humor he can evoke physical details. (p. 232)

> John Peale Bishop, "Three Brilliant Young Novelists" (*originally published in* Vanity Fair, *Vol. 16,*
> *No. 8, October, 1921), in his* The Collected Essays
> of John Peale Bishop, *edited by Edmund Wilson*
> *(copyright 1948 Charles Scribner's Sons, copyright*
> *renewed; reprinted with the permission of Charles*
> *Scribner's Sons), Charles Scribner's Sons, 1948, pp.*
> *229-33.**

STEPHEN VINCENT BENÉT   (essay date 1927)

When I first applied for a Guggenheim fellowship, I stated in the plan submitted, that what I hoped to do was to complete in the given year at least one long poem or volume of poems, with such incidental work as might naturally arise.

I had, at that time, several projects for a long poem upon an American theme. . . . But there were other projects—in particular a project for a long poem dealing with the Civil War, which I had then thought about for almost a year—and it is upon this last that I am working now.

As regards the poem itself. I have planned it in a prologue, eight books or sections, and an epilogue. The working-title I have for it at present is "The Horses of Anger," but I am not entirely satisfied with it and may change it before publication. . . .

Except for the prologue and epilogue, the action of the poem is a continuous action, beginning shortly before the John Brown raid and ending shortly after the surrender at Appomattox. But, naturally, it does not follow history in the strict sense—that is to say I have not described and do not mean to describe every battle, every fluctuation of fortune, every event. I have spent a good deal of space on various men and incidents relatively unimportant to history and dealt scantly or not at all with others of greater text-book importance. That is to say—it is a poem, an attempt at an interpretation, not a history or a recital of events. (p. 5)

The poem is schemed, I suppose, as an epic—an epic on an American theme. I do not particularly like the word—it instantly suggests a portentousness and a presumption which I do not wish to claim. The events of the time were epic, and I have tried to keep their epic quality—but to deal with them as well with enough boldness and freshness to make them real, and not a dim struggle between distant men, who had no likeness to us, but were steel-engravings in a book.

There are many characters in the poem, some real, some fictional. In every case I have endeavored to treat them as individuals and not conscious representatives of a type or a mood. The main thread of the plot is carried by six characters, two Northern, three Southern, and one from the West. Others, real or fictional, come in for a while to drop out or reappear as the poem needs them or does not need them. But I think the main thread is strong enough and clear enough to stand out against the shifting background without either dominating it unduly or being lost in its details.

In a way, the form of the book bears some resemblance to the form employed by Hardy in "The Dynasts." In a way it might be said to bear some resemblance to such books as [Mark Sullivan's] "Our Times" and [Thomas Beer's study of America in the 1890s] "The Mauve Decade," though written in neither mood. But neither comparison is particularly close. The form is a large pattern made of many shifting threads—certain threads run through and carry the strength of the verse. Some threads are real men, some people I have invented. I think I can claim that, successful or unsuccessful, it is a new form for long narrative verse—and that, if it can be classed as an epic, it is an epic told in a new way.

I have employed various metres and verse-forms in the writing and used various devices of interlude and change of pace in an attempt to keep the thing from growing monotonous. But there is a foundation or backbone of rather rough blank verse combined with a dactyllic or anapestic pentameter-form that takes the chief load and binds the whole project together. (p. 10)

[The] mere planning of such a lengthy poem as I have attempted, its difference in scheme and manner from any model that could be followed and anything I had done before, necessitated a great deal of preliminary thought and experimentation. . . .

I have, of necessity, had to do a great deal more research than I would have if I had been engaged upon a purely imaginative theme. I had, I think, at least rather better than an average layman's knowledge of the Civil War before I began—because the period had always interested me. But even so, what I had was entirely inadequate. And, without wishing to swamp my poem in unnecessary detail, I have had and will have to read hard and widely to get what I want from the books. (p. 11)

> *Stephen Vincent Benét, in his preliminary report to the Guggenheim Foundation on February 1, 1927, in "Epic on an American Theme: Stephen Vincent Benét and the Guggenheim Foundation," in* The New Colophon, *Vol. II, No. 5, January, 1949, pp. 1-12.*

ALLEN TATE   (essay date 1928)

This poem ["**John Brown's Body**"] is the most ambitious ever undertaken by an American on an American theme. . . . "**John Brown's Body**" has merit enough; it has hair-raising defects; and yet it deserves to be widely read and, within reason, praised. It is an interesting book, but it is not the kind of work that the public has been led to believe it is.

It has been called among other things an epic and it has been compared, not unfavorably, to the "Iliad." . . . The poem is not in any sense an epic; neither is it a philosophical vision of the Civil War; it is a loose, episodic narrative which unfolds a number of related themes in motion-picture flashes. In spite of some literary incompetence in the author and the lack of a controlling imagination, the story gathers suspense as it goes and often attains to power.

Many passages, particularly the lyrical commentaries scattered throughout, are so good that one suspects that the vicious writing, which is most of the poem, comes of too hasty composition. Perhaps Mr. Benét, like most Americans, is mysteriously betrayed into writing with his ear to the ground. It is not his fault; let us say it is the fault of the "system"; yet whoever may be at fault, the poem contains lines like these (which are not the worst);

> Now the scene expands, we must look at the scene as a whole.
> How are the gameboards chalked and the pieces set?

There are too many other lines quite as flat, and they are not all bad because Mr. Benét has a bad ear for verse; they are due, rather, to a lack of concentration in the grasp of the material. The transitions are often arbitrary or forced, and this blemish, which at first sight seems to be merely literary, really takes the measure of Mr. Benét's capacity as a "major poet."

For he does not see the Civil War as a whole. I do not mean that he has not visualized all the campaigns (he has done this admirably), nor that he is deficient in general ideas as to what the war was about. It is simply that his general ideas remain on the intellectual plane; they are disjointed, diffuse, uncoordinated; they never reach any sweeping significance as symbols. The symbol of John Brown becomes an incentive to some misty writing, and instead of sustaining the poem it evaporates in mixed rhetoric. Mr. Benét sees that the meaning of the war is related to the meaning of Brown; yet what is the meaning of Brown? The presentation of Brown as a *character* is interesting; but it is neither here nor there to say, symbolically, that he is a "stone" or, at the end, that the machine-age grows out of his body. It is a pretty conceit, but it is not large enough, it is not sufficiently welded to the subject matter to hold together a poem of fifteen thousand lines. Is it possible that Mr. Benét supposed the poem to be about the Civil War, rather than about his own mind? This would explain its failure of unity; for if a poet has some striking personal vision of life, it will be permanent, and it will give meaning to all the symbols of his irresistible choice. We are permitted to say that the Civil War interests Mr. Benét; it has no meaning for him. He has not been ambitious enough.

Yet Mr. Benét himself appears, in this connection, to have recognised the diffuseness of his impulse. He seems to have felt that the partial glimpses he has given us of the social backgrounds of the war were not strong enough to carry the poem along, and he has contrived a "human interest story" to take the place of a comprehensive symbol. Jack Ellyat, the Union private, is captured at Shiloh; he escapes to a cabin in the woods, where he seduces the beautiful daughter. So far, so good; but when, shortly after the war, the daughter with the baby appears at Ellyat's home-town in Connecticut, the ways of God are not sufficiently mysterious. It is a trick done for effect; the effect is bad.

Many passages in the narrative are complete poems in themselves; a bare collection of these might display Mr. Benét's true stature to better advantage than their context does. Many are distinguished poems; the **"Invocation"** is one of the best recent productions by an American.

Mr. Benét has steeped himself in the documents of the age, and many of the historical portraits are freshly done; the interpretation in some instances is highly original. The picture of Lincoln is, as usual, uncritical and unconvincing. The greatest successes are Davis and Lee. If professional historians, particularly those of the Northern tradition, will follow Mr. Benét's Davis, a distorted perspective in American history will soon be straightened out. Nowhere else has Lee been so ably presented, yet the Lee is not so good as the Davis; for, perhaps frightened by the pitfalls, Mr. Benét openly points them out, and the portrait is too argumentative. Yet these and countless minor figures—generals, statesmen, private soldiers, runaway Negroes, plantation ladies, each sharply drawn in his right character—move in an atmosphere all their own that takes us past the literary blemishes to the end. Yet is this atmosphere a quality of the poem or of our memories? Succeeding generations will decide.

Allen Tate, "The Irrepressible Conflict," in The Nation, *Vol. 127, No. 3298, September 19, 1928, p. 274.*

HENRY SEIDEL CANBY (essay date 1928)

[It] is no derogation to Stephen Benét's broad and stirring saga ["**John Brown's Body,**"] to say that time and events have made it possible. Neither he nor we could have known what a people's war meant before 1914-1918. A generation ago, before the United States became a Power and began to be described in terms less naive than Manifest Destiny, it would have been impossible to make a unity of all this confusion. We did not know enough economics, could not get the rights and wrongs in perspective, would have been content either with odes on the North and paeans on the South, or with local color sketches like Stephen Crane's "The Red Badge of Courage."

But that mid-century America is now as dead as the Past ever is. It is an Age, a Period, a Phase, still familiar but in no immediate sense Us. . . . We can see it now as we see the Revolutionary fathers, acutely and sympathetically, but as

something familiar, yet strange, that lived before our times. And this is a pre-requisite for successful studies of the Past. It must be a real Past for the imaginative artist, where he can reconstruct according to his own interests (since the Present only is alive), remaking a Crisis according to its significance for history, which means, of course, for him and for us.

And I think also that "**John Brown's Body**" owes quite as much to the wave of realism in literature that has rolled up between us and that past. It is both a tribute to the climax of realism, which was naturalism, and a sign of its passing. A romantic poem, rising to heights of eloquence, and singularly rich in passages of lyric sweetness, so that, unlike any of the American poetry of the last two decades, it moves the reader to emotional enthusiasm, it is beautiful as well as intricate, and has as much pathos as excitement, as much sentiment as intellectual analysis. And yet it is as realistic as it is romantic. (pp. 161-62)

And [Benét] has taken his zig-zag continuity, where, like pictures on a screen, or memories in the consciousness, the noble and the mean, the tragic and the funny, pass and break and are picked up again and dropped, from James Joyce and the movies, from the behaviorists and the impressionists. No, this poem could not have been written twenty years ago. . . .

Benét has as many voices as an organ. He has the art of suspense and the gift of movement which our intellectual poets definitely lack when they try to tell a story. He has a suavity of diction, when he wants it, which is dangerous in pure lyric but indispensable to a fine narrative poem. He knows how to raise the cloud no bigger than a man's hand with his opening scene on a slaver captained by a fanatic. He has the sense for drama which chooses as his protagonist, not Lincoln who carried through, but the tough-fibred individualist, John Brown, blind to immediate consequence, a stone of fate for hammering walls, Thoreau's John Brown who had the mad courage to put his conscience against reason, a man pre-doomed to failure, whose soul went marching on. He has the broad vision of the historian of the modern type, who considers vanity, greed, ignorance, the cotton in the fields, fear, things inanimate as well as animate, until history becomes as complex as life— and much too complex for a historian to strike into a unity. And yet, as the artist must, he holds to his line of significance— not slavery, not economic rivalry, not race prejudice, but the struggle of individuals caught in karma. . . .

This poem, indeed, is good history, but it is also good art. I am not inclined to be apologetic with the poet for his nationalistic theme. . . .

Indeed it is the intense nationalism of "**John Brown's Body**" that is perhaps responsible for its esthetic importance, which is not equalled, I should say, by any recent American book. For Benét is writing as Shakespeare wrote in his Histories, and Racine in his tragedies, and Vergil in the AEneid, on a great theme in which he himself has a vested interest. He cannot, and he does not, take the view of that modernistic literature from which he borrows so much in technique, that the writer should be, as a young modernist has recently said, a skilful reporter merely of phenomena whose meaning he does not pretend to understand. His poem is composed, significant, and bound together in a moral unity. . . .

For here is the inconsequentiality, the uncertainness, the mingled grossity and valor of life, the vividness of minute experience, all organized by a moral significance which in this fateful period can be shown to have given one meaning, at least, to the whole. It is the method and point of view of the great poems of the past—but this does not prove that it is wrong. His subject is a Past. On the present he does not speculate, but merely says "it is here." Perhaps only a fool expects to grasp the significance of a present, but certainly only an impressionist can write of life at all unless he tries to grasp the moral organization which makes it different from the mechanics of a coral reef.

Well, that is what **"John Brown's Body"** seems to mean for general literature. To leave these heights of criticism and come down to the valley of appreciation is grateful, for surely a year in which such a book as this is published is red-lettered for American literature.

Benét's general plan is to drive a straight road of historical narrative through the years of crisis, beside which wind the personal stories of his chief characters, some of whom are historical, others types. For his history, he has chosen a blank verse of five or six stresses, planed down almost to prose; often it is prose, and sometimes is written as such. . . . The style rises and falls with the emotions of his theme. But for his personal stories, the Georgian Wingates and Sally Dupré, Cudjo the negro butler, Ellyat the Connecticut intellectual, and the rest, there is an extraordinary variety of rhythmic movements. The versatility of his poetic style is unusual. He can do anything except the organ line in which blank verse reaches its highest powers, and perhaps for this reason the historical center of his poem is the least impressive portion, although an excellent foil for the lyric movements that surround it. Lincoln in meditation is more effective than all his accounts of Lincoln, and the silent mystery of Lee is less striking just because Lee is silent. Benét is at his best as a dramatic lyricist. Yet where most epic poets are weak, he is strong. The humorous realism of his soldiers is excellent, yet I like him best of all in those incidental narratives, touched or driven by great events yet shining with their own light of merely human interest. The negroes are the truest I know in American poetry. (p. 162)

Politically, it is a non-partisan poem, spiritually it is Northern. The fanaticism of the North as well as its commercialism he accepts as irrevocable, the romance of the South he makes as brittle as its charm and haunting melancholy are persuasive. The Connecticut Ellyat and rough boys from Illinois and Pennsylvania are much more convincing than Wingate and his Black Horse Troop, because they have psychologies while the Southerners are chiefly manners and fate. This is not true of his women. Sally Dupré, next to Melora, is his best; the Northern women are shadows. . . .

This poem is clearly a poem of the transition. In spite of the firm grip upon purpose and significance, it is too fluent for a classic taste, bursting out at corners, pouring and flashing and jumping and zigzagging through wide margins, where, when we have got on top of all the fascinating new material that realism has been gathering for us, we shall be more selective, restrained, intense. There will be more in every line and less broadcast through pages. The margins of experience will be attained by sheer skill of imaginative suggestion rather than by excessive roaming back and forth in the story. I think that this is a fair criticism of **"John Brown's Body,"** though in no sense a suggestion for revision. This poem could have been done successfully only this way now, and it is an immense credit to Benét that he has been able to recreate the rough and tumble, sweet and sour of an epoch with a modern imagination, and yet hold it all in one grand theme. If this is what comes of sending poets to Paris on a Guggenheim fellowship, let us

send them all there. But there is no such simple prescription for genius. I should say rather that this is what happens when an able poet rises to a great theme that sings in his blood. . . . (p. 163)

Henry Seidel Canby, " 'His Soul Goes Marching On'," in The Saturday Review of Literature, *Vol. V, No. 10, September 29, 1928, pp. 161-63.*

MAX EASTMAN   (essay date 1928)

Stephen Benét has the true gift of poetry, and he has a scope and energy of ambition that is rare among poets in this practical age. . . . *John Brown's Body* is the biggest thing ever attempted in poetry in America. . . . It is superior to Homer in this at least, that its action is free from the perpetual childish interference of gods. Instead of these frivolous beings hovering above the combat, Benét shows us the real people of the earth trying to live their bewildered lives of love and egotism while this bloody and roaring storm goes across them. His poetry is at times entirely compelling. . . .

Even where Benét's poetry is not so fine, it is sustained by a fine sincerity—by the poet's own heart honestly feeling all that is felt—and it is adorned with interruptions of excellent lyrical song. All these virtues compel one to judge *John Brown's Body* by the standards of great art. And as a great work of art, I think the book fails. It fails because of certain faults which are characteristic of modern America, and which have their cause.

The book is long out of all proportion to its content of intense poetry. It is prolix to the point of sloppiness. And this is but one more work of the old enemy of all art in America—the profession of journalism. . . . I merely perceive that he is swimming in the general stream of American journalism, and his book suffers from it. It lacks altogether the incisive and breathless concentration that great poetry must have. It lacks rapture and perfection. Akin to its prolixity is the layness of its rhythm. It is written for the most part in blank verse—or rather it is written partly in blank verse, partly in ordinary talk skilfully fitted into the formal pattern of blank verse. Fitting ordinary talk into this pattern without making it sound stilted or unnatural is, throughout many pages the sole occupation of the poet's skill. Benét's speech not only never does sound stilted and unnatural in this pattern, but it often sounds commonplace and undistinguished beyond belief. . . .

The absence of any point of view or passionate judgment about his subject is another thing that makes Benét's poem seem to me at least more like exalted journalism than great art. It is the fashion of contemporary famous writers to avoid saying anything with their writings, and Benét follows the fashion. Or rather he carries it a step farther. He paints on his vast canvas the most appalling thing in our history—the stern fierce god-invoking liberty ideal of the prophet, John Brown, the torrent of hatred and horror that it touched off, and how there rose up out of the blood-soaked ground nothing of what John Brown loved—not liberty, nor peace, nor excellent human relations—sky-scrapers and machines and a mechanical civilization based on "dollars and initiative". It is the real American tragedy, the tragedy of America's simple-hearted great hopes, and her complex and fantastic failure to realize them. Yet out of this supremely important act of retrospection the poet gets no wisdom. He not only has no judgment upon it, no attitude, but he explicitly advises us to have none.

Say neither . . .
It is deadly magic and accursed,
Nor 'it is blest', but simply it is here.

That is the end of his book. That is the moral of his tale. (pp. 362-63)

If Benét had written his tale with childlike simplicity and quietly stopped when it was done, I should have asked nothing more of him. . . . It is a sophisticated book an intellectual book, full of complicated, diverse and extremely up-to-date ideas. Only as a whole it lacks idea. It lacks attitude. It lacks the unity that is imparted by an intention. (p. 363)

> Max Eastman, "America Attempts an Epic," in The Bookman, *New York*, Vol. LXVIII, No. 3, November, 1928, pp. 362-63.

HARRIET MONROE   (essay date 1928)

Hats off to Stephen Vincent Benét! I have read his earlier poems—stories of King David, William Sycamore, and other adventurers, mere practice work in narrative—and I herewith joyously confess I should never have dreamed that *John Brown's Body* was in him. (p. 91)

Mr. Benét's poem is a kind of cinema epic, brilliantly flashing an hundred different aspects of American character and history on the silver screen of an unobtrusively fluent and responsive style. The scene-shiftings are sometimes jerky, not always adroit; occasionally the scenario is faulty or the camera-work slipshod, conceding a too "happy ending," for example, in at least one detail of the enormous scheme; and one is forced to admit that the poem, like most epics, falls off somewhat toward the end— *Books VII* and *VIII* do not quite keep up the gallant stride with which the poem began.

But these are minor blemishes, to be admitted but not dwelt upon when there is so much to praise. Mr. Benét has held his reins well in hand, and kept to the straight road of his subject, riding lightly and gracefully a Pegasus which has more paces than a gaited horse. Most of the narrative passages run in a loosely-syllabled variously rhymed three-time pentameter; but one never has a chance to tire of this measure, for suddenly, with a change of mood or subject in the story, the lines will trot into tetrameters, or scuffle into free verse, or, as at the opening of *Book VII*, march solemnly into four-time hexameters. And the lyrics, which happily interrupt the narrative at intervals, are beautifully set to different song-measures, from the hymn-tune of *John Brown's Prayer* to the sapphics of Sally Dupré's lament for her wounded lover. In short, the technique shows admirable variety, with fewer lapses into dullness or prosiness than one would expect in so long a poem; it is carried without strain, is usually adequate, and often brilliantly skilful.

I have said there is much to praise, and perhaps one should praise first and longest the poet's whole-hearted abandonment to his

> American muse, whose strong and diverse heart
> So many men have tried to understand,
> But only made it smaller with their art
> Because you are as various as your land.

Only a few lines may be quoted from that haughty and high-spirited *Invocation,* much as one would like to quote the whole; for there is nothing finer in the book than this key-note.

Then, after the *Prelude* in the slave-ship, and a few pages with minor characters—youth north and south—we have the bronze clangor of John Brown's magnificent prayer. . . . (pp. 91-3)

It is strange how the tough, rough figure of this pioneer crusader has taken on the glamourous proportions of a heroic myth. (p. 94)

There is nothing finer than the John Brown chapter, but some of the battle-thunders, rolling at Shiloh or Antietam or Gettysburg, strike out as heroic a tune. Throughout, the poet stands as a twentieth-century observer of all the impassioned goings to and fro; seeing the astonishing events as parts of a patterned whole, the characters as heroes or supes of a vast drama which few of them understand. He sees the whimsical, the grotesque as well as the heroic—there is icy satire, for example, in his description of the congressmen who "came out to see Bull Run." . . . (pp. 94-5)

The characterization is often marvellously vivid. Three leading actors in the drama, especially, stand out in full stature and color—Grant, Lee and Davis are like to be remembered as this poet paints them: thus they were, and are till the crack of doom. Lincoln's portrait is pretty well done, but less authoritative— for who can put into print or paint that strange and sombre figure, piteous, humorous and confoundingly wise! Some of the minor generals—Hooker, Meade, Beauregard—are vividly sketched in, and McClellan gets his dusty tag. And a few women are very much alive, mostly southern women. . . . (p. 95)

We have a whole panorama moving hardily before us on the luminous screen—soldiers, officers, civilians; aristocrats, slaves, sweethearts, lovers, killers; great and small, heroes and nobodies, they are all in the picture that moves along to the rumble of drums.

And as the picture moves, as the cinema epic swings along, the ghostly figure of John Brown reappears like a refrain. . . .

A big book. A book which reaches out over this broad America, and looks not only backward but forward. (p. 96)

> Harriet Monroe, "A Cinema Epic," in Poetry, *Vol. XXXII, No. 2, November, 1928, pp. 91-6.*

FLORENCE HAXTON BRITTEN   (essay date 1934)

So far as he has gone in "James Shore's Daughter"—and he has gone deep and fairly far—Mr. Stephen Vincent Benét has made a contribution to the fictional version of American life from, roughly, the days of the Gibson girl to the Forgotten Man, that is firm and fine—and final. Our whole story is here, on the surface or between the lines, beautifully, memorably told. . . .

"James Shore's Daughter" might have been the story of the intimate lives of two young Americans—Violet Shore and Gareth Grant; but it is so much more than that—the progress of their lives reveals so clearly the trends and changes of our times—that "James Shore's Daughter" ceases to be the mere portrait of a woman seen through the eyes of a man whose life she deeply touched, and becomes instead these two against their significant American background. . . .

This is a novel, richly peopled, as a novel should be, with living persons; and written artfully, with the narrative skill and grace of style of which Stephen Vincent Benét is so completely the master. "James Shore's Daughter" is exquisite rather than powerful; it is sound rather than sensational; and it is at all times impressive and estethically satisfying—a book that only a genuine artist could have written.

Florence Haxton Britten, "Benét's Portrait of Our Times: From the Gibson Girl to the Forgotten Man, in a Firm, Fine, Final Novel," in New York Herald Tribune Books (© I.H.T. Corporation; reprinted by permission), April 29, 1934, p. 8.

MORTON DAUWEN ZABEL (essay date 1936)

[Mr. Benét's] verse is a survival of an abundant native line; it has become a virtual guide-book of native myth and folklore, their place-names, heroes, humors, and reverences. He followed the mid-western poets of the pre-War revival in this affection; one poem in *Burning City,* a tribute to Vachel Lindsay which precedes another to Walt Whitman, reminds us of this continuity. . . . [*Burning City*] opens with a set of poems on political themes (*Litany for Dictatorships, Ode to the Austrian Socialists,* etc.), and closes with a group of *Nightmares* of the coming years—a *Blick ins Chaos* where angels in cellophane, synthetic rubber, and chromium sow the seeds of a final confusion, and the termites of Manhattan develop a taste for steel.

These are formidable subjects, but we find them approached with no fear or trembling. Mr. Benét follows in a poetic line that is never so relaxed or self-confident as in the presence of prophetic enormities that might paralyze another order of poets to the point of speechlessness. This confidence is important; it indicates his type—the romantic fabulist. It explains both the ease with which he has spun past legends out of any stuff that fell to hand—Biblical, historical, or fantastic—and the temerity that produced in *John Brown's Body* a whole textbook of dramatic and metrical varieties. Ease of this kind is as enviable as it is convenient in a poet who wants to work in the large dimensions of popular myth. There can be no undue worry about refining allegory or imagery to the point of exact meaning, no severe economy in a poem's structure, and no privacy in its references. Such verse strives to be as indulgent to the reader's attention as possible, and no generosity is greater than that exhibited by Mr. Benét's facile yarn-spinning imagination. His poem on Lindsay amounts to much more than a reproachful tribute to an ignored and neglected singer of the tribe: it shows how Mr. Benét derived, through Lindsay, from the bardic romantics who held sway in American poetry for over a century. [Kipling, John Masefield, William Morris, and Dante Gabriel Rossetti might be studied as English revivalists of ballad and epic heroics, but not necessarily, for in America this tradition, in its homeliest form, was the living authority of text-books and family anthologies all the way from [John G. Neihardt, James Whitcomb Riley, and Edwin Markham, back through John Milton Hay, Bret Harte, and Joaquin Miller], to the bearded dynasties of Longfellow and Bryant—a succession hostile to eccentric talent or refined taste, scornful of modernity or exotic influence, once the pride of the burgeoning Republic, and now chiefly a source of cheerful embarrassment to teachers and blushing incredulity to their students. Mr. Benét has aspired from his school-days to a place in this old American line. . . . Toward such bardship he has mastered a profuse stock of native lore and made himself, next to Lindsay, the most proficient balladist on native themes in the century. If the sentiment of local traditions survives for future poets, it may be largely due to his efforts. (pp. 276-79)

Why, then, with all these seductions, does one find the sympathy as rigid and skeptical as ever in reading *Burning City*? It is chiefly because the book illustrates so flatly the distinction between bard and poet. To the fluent mill of such a talent, all is grist, not merely in subject-matter, but in language as well. Mr. Benét talks about social and moral degeneration, but there is little in imagery or phrasing to suggest that its meaning has penetrated his sensibilities or intelligence. He has roughly seized upon the moment's issues and causes, run them through the familiar meters and phrases of his instincts, and produced a passable verse journalism. It would be hoping too much to expect from this journeyman attitude anything very decisive in moral judgment or memorable as poetic meaning.

The most ambitious poem in the volume is the *Ode to Walt Whitman.* Here is a full opportunity for displaying a love of American memories against a heroic theme, and the opening section is in fact a passage in Mr. Benét's most charming manner—pictures of provincial innocence moving loosely through a free verse that catches the spirit of Whitman very successfully, particularly in the image of footsteps and the approach of "Magnificent Death." The second part begins to dissipate this impressive effect by repetition and direct exposition; it betrays the absence of a central conception of Whitman as the dialogue between the poet and his interrogator descends to the most obvious contrasts between Whitman's dream of democracy and its present frustration, ending with a suspended cliché. . . . There follows a hymn-like interlude which suggests an answer to this question by hinting that heroic visions are not successful in terms of small profits and quick returns: "He grows through the earth and is part of it like the roots of new grass." The form of this passage—brief unrhymed lines of two beats—is appealing, and some of the images are delicate, but they multiply and entangle themselves to disadvantage, and as a lyric interruption it hardly strengthens the formal unity of the poem as a whole. In Part 4 the ode's resolution is completely stultified by characteristic faults: it begins with some slovenly sarcasm on the cheap way the world has with its poets, and advances into a catalogue of "the glory of America" as glimpsed by Whitman, a broad flood of visions and splendors advancing toward "the restless-hearted always, forever, Mississippi, the god." This exhibits Mr. Benét's customary deftness in producing the tones and colors of native life, but never gets beyond suggesting a check-list of his familiar references, and ends with the desultory effect of having all been heard, too many times, before. In fact, it repeats—shorn of originality or concentration—the idea of [Hart] Crane's *The River,* and invites a perilous contrast with what the theme becomes in the hand of a genuine poet.

It is this willingness to work in the loose run-of-mill material of the commonplace that besets all the more serious projects here. When one poem is entitled *Litany for Dictatorships,* it reveals its technique only too obviously: it turns out to be a long indiscriminate itemization of newspaper reports, atrocities, and horrors that finally arrives at a perfectly true and quite insignificant conclusion: "We thought we were done with these things, but we were wrong," upon which any daily editorial writer might improve. The same effect is produced in the poem on the Austrian socialists, and as for the *Nightmares,* whatever sense they convey of the impending catastrophe is cheapened as much by the juvenility of their spectres as by the reckless vulgarity of their style. These chromium-plated angels and swampy miasmas belong to thrillers by Wells or Conan Doyle, and their language should be reserved to *The New Yorker* or Paul Engle. Mr. Benét's success in echoing this last-named disciple is not the least of the discouragements his new book offers. In fact, since *Burning City* presents quite a range of styles, it may be said that the nearer it gets to suggesting a notable model, the better its items are: at the lowest level it offers such trash as *For City Spring;* its reminders of the elegiac [Archibald] MacLeish are more moving; several poems of personal accent are charming—the poem on Lindsay, *Girl Child,* and *The Lost Wife;* a brief lyric that conveys a hint of Yeats—*Memory*—is probably the finest page in the volume. (pp. 279-81)

Morton Dauwen Zabel, "The American Grain," in Poetry, *Vol. XLVIII, No. V, August, 1936, pp. 276-82.*

FRANK JONES   (essay date 1942)

"**John Brown's Body**" is no more profound in message or perceptive in the reading of history than "Gone with the Wind," and less interesting as a story. This despite the earnest interpretative intentions, the "quest of the American Muse" announced at its outset. Mr. Benét aimed high, and felt his subject as an ancestral tragedy; but tragedy must be a conflict between equally credible forces, and his presentation of the South merely exploits the commonplaces about overblown romanticism ill concealing the crime of slavery. . . . Moreover, its whole appeal of plot and character rests on figures too obviously chosen to illustrate history like pictures in a textbook. . . . [These] vague emotional reactions to the Civil War coincide with certain publicly felt demands. Still uneasy about the meaning of the conflict, folk-memory has not yet transmuted it into myth, so that imaginative evocations of it are especially welcome if they appear to facilitate shared opinions on its historical significance. With the lessening of such topical demands, the past can be poetized as story. Meanwhile only lyric poetry can universalize it permanently (Whitman's Lincoln elegy is an example), but an artistic anomaly, a subjective epic like "**John Brown's Body**," may give a convincing temporary imitation of that function. (pp. 217-18)

I think posterity will treat [Mr. Benét] much like Stevenson. Some will ignore him; the young will treasure his adventure tales, especially "**Spanish Bayonet**"; and most people will like his ballads, love poems, and prose fantasies. At his unpretentious best he is a writer of sure skill and singular charm. But his efforts as interpreter of the American scene and the world crisis will be tactfully forgotten. No matter how fertile their imagination, little of worth results when writers who do not feel *prophetically* the power of ideas attempt to express social and historical truths. They succeed only in reflecting the prevalent prejudices of a changing social structure. It is significant that although "**John Brown's Body**" hardly mentions American problems of capital and labor, in 1936 Mr. Benét suddenly intones an Ode to the Austrian Socialists. Distance and Hitler lend unforeseen enchantment. Heights of platitude, too, are reached in "**Tales of Our Time**," which regale women who read women's magazines by catering to their stuffiest notions about The Home. I like to imagine D. H. Lawrence commenting on "**The Story About the Ant-Eater**," in which a young couple who begin with ideas ("They had heard of Freud") happily end as dull as dull can be. He would probably consider it obscene. No, decidedly posterity will not approach Mr. Benét for intellectual reasons. But it was a great thing to write "**Spanish Bayonet**" in 1926 and "**O'Halloran's Luck**" in 1938, because posterity will thank its stars that someone in this grievous

century could produce entertaining stories that are not murder mysteries and can be read twice. (p. 218)

Frank Jones, "Bon Voyage, S.V.B.," in The Nation, *Vol. 155, No. 11, September 12, 1942, pp. 217-18.*

HENRY STEELE COMMAGER   (essay date 1943)

[Benét] had a passion for simple things and good things—like freedom, like democracy. Twenty years ago—it seems forever now—when it was the fashion to sneer at Main Street, to chronicle the American Tragedy, to celebrate the Waste Land, and when almost every poet worth his fare to France had fabricated his melancholy testament to futility and despair, young Benét was writing of these simple things. It is full tide now, but let us not forget what Benét wrote when the tide was at its ebb.

Let us not forget what Benét said, more insistently, more persuasively, more eloquently, than any other poet of our time. He said that there was virtue and honor and fortitude in men, and that when inspired by a worthy cause they discovered dignity and nobility, and that love of country and of freedom were such worthy causes. He recalled to us what in our pseudo-sophistication we had almost forgotten, that there were things worth dying for and worth living for, and the poet who had understood why men followed Lincoln and Lee rallied us to defend the good cause in our own day.

In "**John Brown's Body**" Benét proved . . . that the poet is the true historian of a people. . . . "**John Brown's Body**" is the best history of our Civil War that has been written, because it penetrates sympathetically and imaginatively into the minds and hearts of those who fought the war. It is this quality that, perhaps above all others, distinguishes Benét's poetry, the ability to recreate surely the thoughts and emotions of historical characters—of politicians and generals, of plain soldiers and their wives, of Yankees and Rebels, of the uncommon and the common men. It is a tribute not only to his erudition—and this was deepstruck—and to his imagination, but to the catholicity of his spirit, that he could do this. . . .

[After] "John Brown's Body," Benét turned to a larger and greater theme [in "**Western Star**"]—the Westward migration of peoples from the Old World to the New, from the Atlantic to the Pacific, the discovery of a new world, the conquest of a continent, the planting of civilization. Here was a worthy theme—one which has challenged historians and poets since William Bradford and Bishop Berkeley. Benét envisioned it not only as the story of the transplanting of people and the conquest of a continent but as the story of democracy.

He lived to finish only the first book—the first of four or five—but it is clear that this was the great theme that had captured his imagination. The new world was something more than that extension of the old that its owners and exploiters imagined; it was indeed something new, a place for new men.

Henry Steele Commager, "The Flame of Stephen Vincent Benét's Spirit: Final Poem Told of the Unconscious Shaping of Americans," in New York Herald Tribune Weekly Book Review, *June 27, 1943, p. 1.*

PAUL ENGLE   (essay date 1943)

Stephen Vincent Benét's death was a particular loss because he added to the variety of American poetry. His contribution of the historical narrative was unique, since few practised it and no other approached his success. It is important to define his effort. He was not interested in mouthing the word "America." Nor was his praise that blind rhapsody of a nation intended, by celebrating the poet's nationality, to celebrate the poet. Benét's deep regard for the U.S.A. was based not on a feeling of blood and earth, but on an honest belief in this country as remarkably permitting human freedom. He knew the misery and corruption, and you'll find them in his books. But, stronger than any other motive, you will find Benét's fascination with the effort of these states to be a place where that reckless and distorted word "liberty" actually means individual right and intellectual exemption.

Western Star is the opening book of what was to have been a long narrative of the westward movement in America, from the first landing to the end of the frontier in 1890. . . . The book's verbal intention, human attitudes, structure of event and historical sense are similar to those of *John Brown's Body*.

The basic problem in this kind of poetic narration is to locate a verse form flexible enough to admit a great multiplicity of material—known historical facts, violent action, dialogue, speculative summary—and yet right enough to retain the necessary minimum of tautness. Benét uses a fluent, loosened blank verse. . . . For the most part, it is an adequate instrument, the fundamental rhythm persisting even when it seems it will falter. To avoid monotony, the accounts of certain characters are related in rhymed couplets of four beats, but, as in the longer line, with considerable variation in the total number of syllables. There are also short sections in stanza and in a free line which depends on a lax cadence for its cohesion. (pp. 160-61)

The strength of the book—and it is the strength of everything Benét wrote—is in the warmth and vigor of the human feeling. (p. 161)

Western Star is so obviously only an introduction that a review of it can hardly be more than introductory. In a day of the concentrated line and compressed lyric, it is proper to have a fair quantity of poetry that is genial, expansive and narrative. When so much verse is allusive (rightly and richly so) it is excellent to have some whose taste in the mouth is plain, concrete, unmistakable.

Children are in this book with an exceptionally natural ease, and women bearing children with the natural pain. The flaws are of the word and not the poet, if such a distinction is possible in an art where the poet can be known only through the word. There was too ready an acceptance of the vocabulary that came too readily to the tongue. But always, beyond the verbal fault, is the small, living, warm texture of the years of men, and over all the vast conception of the westward motive. The result is a book which expands the types of our poetry. This is no small virtue. (pp. 161-62)

> *Paul Engle, "The American Search," in* Poetry, *Vol. LXIII, No. III, December, 1943, pp. 159-62.*

HENRY W. WELLS (essay date 1943)

John Brown's Body, frankly composite and typically an American product, labors under a number of embarrassments as a poem, being one-third history, one-third novel, and one-third poetry. Although a powerful work, it is in many ways admittedly imperfect, with a slightly youthful flavor. The two romantic love stories, one of a Northern couple, where wounds

and absence enforced by war supply the obstacles, and the other of a Southern couple beset with the same difficulties, hardly satisfy the standards of good novel writing. The conventional happy endings of these seem ineffectual, hurried, and dwarfed beside the graver ending of the war itself. The romance gets in the way of the history; the history intrudes on the romance; the two main narratives are wholly unrelated; and, finally, there are no really dominant symbols or ideas. The conclusion of the poem, an ode to a mechanized society, comes to an inartistic surprise, very superficially connected with the poem as a whole. Yet despite all its limitations *John Brown's Body* remains one of the most genuinely human of the long poems ever written in America and one of the most deeply marked by the typical strength and weaknesses of American poetry. To grasp its true significance in our national literature it is helpful to make comparisons with analogous foreign works of historical fiction in both prose and verse.

Such fiction is no new thing, since its origins reach back to Homer. But with the nineteenth century the rise of historical scholarship coincides with a need to give imaginative expression to the new republican and democratic theories of the state. . . . [By] far the highest English achievement in this art is reached in Thomas Hardy's *Dynasts*. This work, even more remarkable as an epic poem than as an unconventional drama or novel, affords the most illuminating contrast between the best which the Old World has to offer and *John Brown's Body,* the best in this field afforded by the New. (pp. 176-80)

For the present contrast, content becomes more important than style. Hardy's poem is much more philosophical than Benét's. And if Hardy is more inclined than Benét to enrich history with thought, he is much less disposed to dilute it with romance. The major characters in Hardy's more serious poem are almost exclusively historical persons; only unnamed and minor figures are without historical warrant. The love stories are never gratuitous. . . . Moreover, Hardy writes of characters much more accessible to popular knowledge than those chiefly celebrated by Benét. Behind the work of the Englishman stands a far larger and more illuminating literature than behind that of the American. Hardy writes of an Old World with all its cultural riches at his command. The veteran author concentrates his attention upon the chief characters who shaped public events and shows a much more thorough understanding of political and military moves and motives than Benét. His poetry hangs lovingly over the world-famous words of Pitt, Sheridan, Canning, Nelson, Wellington, and Fox. A vast wealth of political biography and a keen aptitude for the writing and understanding of such work continually buttress his own words. Although the young American gives excellent cursory pen portraits of Lincoln, Lee, Jackson, and others, these pale beside Hardy's dramatic recreations of the statesmen and generals of England and Europe. In so far as epic poetry deals primarily with war, Hardy surpasses Benét. For Hardy possesses that almost instinctive interest in military and naval tactics so common in embattled Europe, hitherto so rare in peace-loving America. (pp. 180-81)

The American poem does have its important advantages, with the unhappy circumstance that Benét, a less-seasoned artist, fails on many occasions to put his best foot foremost. The case can be summed up by observing that Hardy excels in depicting a ruling class, while Benét surpasses in depicting the people, in certain scenes of his poem the democratic masses of the North, in other scenes the representative masses of the South. . . . The true hero of Benét's poem is not the Immanent Will,

Napoleon, Nelson, or Wellington but the common man occasionally and not too happily personified in the passionate figure of John Brown. . . . His poem celebrates not individuals, as Hardy's poem does, in the manner of older political histories, but the American people as a whole, in the manner of modern sociological historians. His inexperience and awkwardness in the more delicate and poetic delineation of passion or character are compensated for by his sympathetic and imaginative grasp of his social theme. His portraits of the average soldier, whether of North or South, record his typical trials, virtues, and human limitations. This viewpoint is expressed in his emphasis upon the fading aristocracy of the South, in his love for American song and ballad, and in his genuine fondness for the underprivileged classes, the woodsmen and pioneers, the day laborers and poor farmers, and especially for the Southern Negroes. The germ of his poem, as expressed in the title, is a folk tune. It is fitting that some of the most stirring lines of *John Brown's Body* should celebrate the African race in America, their fidelity, irresponsibility, and childishness and their striking religious and musical life.

A peculiar mystical strain recurrent in Protestant America elevates Benét's own exaltation of democracy to the height of a religion. The core of his faith is expressed in a remarkable lyric passage inserted in his narrative poem. His prayer is for all sorts and conditions of men. . . . Obviously this is the mystical democracy so representative of American idealism, with its strongest expression in *Leaves of Grass*. Benét's poem is typically American in that it goes further in this direction than any modern British poem, not even excepting the great epic by the most catholic-minded Hardy. Or, if one is to find a possible British parallel, one must go backward past Milton, Shakespeare, and Spenser and even beyond Chaucer to the anonymous medieval poet who sang in *Piers Plowman* his vision of "the fair field full of folk."

Wrapped closely about the spiritual core of Benét's epic are not so much his romantic tales of love in the hearts of Ellyat and Wingate, his Unknown Soldiers from North and South, as his lines on the long-suffering Army of the Potomac and the heroic Army of Virginia. In the latter passages he writes both at his best and in his most unmistakably American idiom. His verse, significantly enough, tends to become freer and more national also, indicating the basic influence of Whitman on body and soul. When he attains full stride in these passages, one feels that he sloughs off the mortal coil of the conventional and merely derivative American romantic poet, given to celebrating the idealized South of fiction and the supposedly righteous Northern cause, and instead achieves the grave, deep voice of major poetry. The suspicion of prosaic didacticism and of the conventionally novelistic or the cinematic species of romance vanishes before a new and startling awareness of actuality. . . . (pp. 181-84)

Other poems doubtless surpass *John Brown's Body* in refinement and subtlety of imagination, as Benét himself has at times gone beyond it in his later and briefer compositions. Only by the work of Whitman and Sandburg, however, is it excelled as a literary tribute to the underlying principles of American democracy. (pp. 189-90)

Henry W. Wells, "Democratic Vista," in his The American Way of Poetry *(copyright 1943, Columbia University Press; copyright renewed © 1971 by Henry W. Wells), Columbia University Press, 1943 (and reprinted by Russell & Russell, Inc., 1964), pp. 174-90.**

CARL SANDBURG   (essay date 1943)

Like Archibald MacLeish, Muriel Rukeyser, Alfred Kreymborg, Edna Millay, Struthers Burt, Gene Fowler, Ben Hecht, and other American poets, Benét threw in with what he had. Sometimes it was good and again not so good. But because of the time element, because if you get there with too little and too late you lose the war and eat dust and ashes, Benét and those of like viewpoint let their writing for the moment go forth for the moment, hoping a little good might come of it, and keenly aware it will not do to wait, revise, wait longer, revise yet more. (pp. 258-59)

Carl Sandburg, "Poets Major and Minor," in his Home Front Memo *(copyright 1940, 1941, 1942, 1943 by Carl Sandburg; copyright renewed © 1970 by Lilian Steichen Sandburg; reprinted by permission of Harcourt Brace Jovanovich, Inc.), Harcourt, 1943, pp. 258-60.**

NORMAN ROSTEN   (essay date 1945)

The test of crisis may come to a nation or to a man, and each must meet it and be revealed. We shall not all sleep, but we shall all be changed. To Stephen Vincent Benét the test came in the shape of war. He was not found wanting, either to himself as a writer or to his country. Nor did he, as did some of his contemporaries, engage in a Hamletlike struggle with his soul. He saw the fascist idea in all its evil and murderous stature. He knew it had to be fought. His weapon was the word, and Stephen Vincent Benét rolled up his sleeves and began turning out weapons.

Here, in [*We Stand United and Other Radio Plays*], are some of them. They are modern, built to specification, made for the need and cause of our time. (p. v)

[This book] is an important addition to the published works of Stephen Vincent Benét. They are plays written with anger and passion. They are eloquent without being pompous. In these pages there is something of the spirit of *John Brown's Body,* which ringed our era with a great flame of poetry. As always, the author is a teller of tales. . . . I think this book is important because it presents the author in an entirely new medium, radio. It gives us his living words as spoken to millions of people who may never have met their great poet except for an occasional story or poem. To these new millions of listeners, his plays have brought a meaning and beauty rarely heard over the radio. To his old readers, he has proved himself equally at home on the airwaves as on the printed page. (pp. vi-vii)

As in his poetry and fiction, these radio pieces contain no tricks, deceptions, loud noises or other methods by which men seek to imitate grandeur. The grandeur is an honest man who will speak his truth—and none shall tamper with it. The greatness is the cause, and the word. He has kept faith with both. . . .

[These] are—most of them—tracts written in battle, in the hard language of battle. They are lean, without trimming. They tell us in another way what he has always told us: that as a nation we are strong, that our ancestors have given us a heritage as deep as the bone and we have fought for it and will fight again. Benét was never ashamed of his love for America, even in times when it was unfashionable to love one's country. To the cynics and unbelievers America has been merely a symbol, either great or gaudy. To Benét it has been the bread and water, the soil and air of life, a land of promise always. (p. viii)

Norman Rosten, in his foreword to We Stand United and Other Radio Scripts by Stephen Vincent Benét (reprinted by permission of Harold Ober Associates Incorporated; copyright © 1945 by Farrar & Rinehart; copyright renewed 1972 by Holt, Rinehart & Winston), Farrar & Rinehart, 1945, pp. v-ix.

ERIC BENTLEY (essay date 1953)

[In] *John Brown's Body* the issue of acting vs. reading does not arise. Here is a poem to be read, not a play to be produced. (p. 69)

In respect of Stephen Vincent Benét's poem, I can claim to have entered the theatre with that complete freedom from prejudice which total ignorance alone can confer. I have always postponed the task of tackling so long a piece of verse. If I shall now postpone it in perpetuity, it is because hardly a line I heard at the Century Theatre struck me as better than pleasant, straightforward, mildly amusing, or moderately forceful. Those whose knowledge of dramatic verse is limited to the dramas of Maxwell Anderson may find Benét sublime; any whose ears are attuned to the melody of Yeats or Eliot (to mention no greater names) will find it pedestrian. And though Benét is more successful with longer units than the line, and the cumulative effect of a page of narrative or character-revealing monologue is fairly considerable, he is excelled here by a dozen contemporary writers of prose fiction. Even so, this poetry might be accepted for what it is—if it did not pretend to be so much more. What might have been an entertainment proves an embarrassment because of the epic pretensions of form and content. Having looked back to Homer, Benét looks forward to Norman Corwin. It is not only with a Tolstoy's that his historical imagination cannot be compared. It cannot be compared with any good historical novel—say, Robert Penn Warren's *Night Rider* where some of the same problems are much more profoundly imaged. (pp. 69-70)

Eric Bentley, "On the Sublime" (originally published in The New Republic, Vol. 128, No. 9, March 2, 1953), in his What Is Theatre? Incorporating the Dramatic Event and Other Reviews: 1944-1967 (copyright 1954, © 1956, 1968 Eric Bentley; reprinted with the permission of Atheneum Publishers), Atheneum, 1968, pp. 68-71.

PARRY STROUD (essay date 1962)

Basil Davenport has pointed to the major components of Benét's romanticism: his fascination with the remote in time and place, his sense of the macabre, his sensitive awareness of landscape. To these qualities should be added Benét's concern with emotion, with states of mind, rather than with ideas. His poetry is also vivid in its imagery, richly colored like that of many romantics. In this respect he resembles the nineteenth-century English poet, designer, and craftsman whose work most shaped Benét's poetry: William Morris. Benét used the ballad form after the manner of Morris, and the octosyllabic couplets that Morris employed in some of his long narrative poems reappear in some of Benét's poems. Morris' technique of weaving song into narrative was paralleled by Benét in his two epics.

Benét's first published book of poems, however, owed more to Robert Browning than to Morris. . . . [*Five Men and Pompey*] is a series of dramatic monologues spoken by Roman leaders on the eve of Caesar's accession to imperial power.

Although the basic form derives from Browning, Benét gave his half-dozen portraits a collective significance of his own in that they trace the fall of the Roman Republic. In this way they herald Benét's *John Brown's Body,* some eleven years later, except that the American historical poem deals with the sundering and then the forging of a republic. (pp. 23-4)

The merit of *Five Men and Pompey* rests upon skillful characterization through the difficult form of the dramatic monologue, upon the successful introduction of dramatic action, and upon appropriate metrical variation of clear and vivid language. Although sometimes bombastic and melodramatic, the work reveals an auspicious talent far in advance of its author's seventeen years. (p. 24)

The two poems which followed the Roman portraits are inferior to them, particularly *The Drug-Shop; or, Endymion in Edmonstown.* Although it won its author a poetry prize at Yale, its chief importance is biographical. (p. 26)

"**The Hemp**," written a year earlier than *The Drug-Shop,* retells in ballad form an incident drawn from early Virginia history: the story of the pirate Captain Hawk, his rape of Sir Henry's daughter, and his eventual death at the hands of the vengeful father. . . . It deflects critical esteem through its violent but superficial extremes of characterization and by its costume clichés of plot and setting. Yet Benét almost brings it off; he almost contrives a first-rate literary ballad.

Benét comes so close to this achievement because of his sure control of rhythm, which is unfalteringly adjusted to the story's development; because of the power of his descriptions; and because of a certain philosophical element. This increment of meaning is expressed partly through symbolism and partly through a refrain which becomes progressively more ominous. (pp. 26-7)

Benét returned to the ballad, ultimately with better results, in subsequent volumes of poetry. . . .

In a group of ballads collected in *Tiger Joy* (the title comes from Shelley's poetic drama *Prometheus Unbound*), Benét found styles perfectly suited to very different themes: thumping rhythms and Georgia hill dialect for "**The Mountain Whippoorwill**"; swift, flailing couplets for "**King David**"; and clear, sweet pioneer music for "**The Ballad of William of William Sycamore (1790-1880).**" (p. 27)

Benét said that in ["**The Mountain Whippoorwill**"] he attempted to adapt the traditional ballad form to a contemporary American theme, to vary it as he chose, and to use colloquial speech. . . . The result was more than a minor *tour de force* since Benét not only managed to suggest through the imagery and movement of his verse the swift country bowing, but the quality of life in the hills of Georgia and Carolina. The poem is lighted with touches of pioneer tall-tale humor and old-time religion. (pp. 27-8)

Benét's "**Ballad of William Sycamore,**" often chosen by editors of anthologies to represent his lyrical Americanism, deserves the widespread admiration accorded it by common readers and by at least some professional ones. . . . The clarity and precision with which Benét sums up the life of a representative though idealized frontiersman are here precisely the qualities to be conveyed by the ballad meter, with its exact rhymes and beat. . . . Benét adroitly alternates iambics and dactyls and introduces just enough metrical variations in the short line to suggest a rippling song. (pp. 28-9)

"American Names" demonstrates the same sensitive control of meter that characterizes "William Sycamore," as well as the same command of imagery, although much of the poem's effect comes from the connotations of proper names strategically placed. The fourth stanza uses the objectionable term "blue-gum nigger," but Benét identifies him honorably as the singer of blues, the American music. A Salem tree (a majestic chestnut), a Santa Cruz rawhide quirt, and a bottle of Boston sea complete this list of American symbols. Each is recognizably American but not banal as an image: a lesser poet might have longed for Coney Island or a five-gallon Stetson. The poem's movement and meaning gather rising emphasis in the final stanza, with its succession of short, simple sentences and its assertion of a love returning home triumphant over the body's alien burial. Benét's final prayer that his heart be buried at Wounded Knee gives the poem deeper significance than it has hitherto possessed, since this South Dakota town was the scene of a tragic Indian massacre by the Seventh Cavalry in the final clash between Indians and government troops. The poet thus identifies himself inextricably with the mixture of good and bad that is his country, and his choice of burial place implies a desire for national atonement and peace.

"King David" proved Benét's ability to employ the ballad for a non-American and more sophisticated purpose, although the poem undoubtedly has American religious implications. A scathingly satiric retelling of the biblical story of David, Uriah, and Bathsheba, it points up David's smug egotism and facile repentance of his sins. Benét's edged phrasing underscores criticism of the Old Testament concept of a God who is a jealous God, a crafty God, and a too-forgiving God; and he embellishes the story as told in II Samuel so as to emphasize David's lustfulness, deviousness, and pride. The broad ironies of the story emerge through Benét's trenchant characterizations and through stinging heroic couplets with their snapping terminal iambics. (pp. 30-1)

The large majority of Benét's early poems are undistinguished by any exacting standard, ideological or aesthetic, and they particularly contrast with his handful of fine ballads. (p. 32)

Among the mass of Benét's minor poems gleam occasional diamond-like lyrics and some excellent light verse, including humorous poems and some fancies and bouquets for his lady. The "Hands" in the . . . poem of this title belong to his wife, his brother, and to Benét himself. The delicate hands of his wife and the cultivated hands of his brother are contrasted with Benét's "children of affront, / Base mechanics at the most / That have sometimes touched a ghost." The poet asks a blessing upon the first four hands but for his own hands prays for an iron stake for them to attempt to break. The powerful first lines of the last stanza invoke the blessings of "God the Son and God the Sire / And God the triple-handed fire" in a magnificent metaphorical linking of the Trinity with the human objects of the poet's invocation. Benét asks finally only a blessing for "four hands of courtesy," and his humility is the proper attitude to precede the "Amen." The short hymn-like lines, liturgically emphatic rhythm, and rich though compact imagery of this lyric combine to give it a power out of proportion to its length.

Compression also characterizes Benét's next best short lyric, "Memory," though its intensity is uneven, heightening through the second of the two eight-line stanzas, after the more open statement of the first. Its poignancy comes from its seizing of the essences of life—love, birth, age, wisdom, death—and contrasting them in terse, unrhymed lines built with mono-

syllables, six to eight per line. His love was the best part of his life, the poet says; death does not matter, for life is a ghost in the flesh that comes and goes. With an almost choking ellipsis, the poet acknowledges that though the moon burns lamp-bright it will not have *that* brightness. . . . He said her name sleeping and waking. The underlying emotion—tragic awareness of the inevitable loss of life's dearest possession—surges through the silence of what is unsaid.

A delightful cluster of gay and fanciful tributes to his sweetheart . . ., whom he later married, tributes airy and delicate as a handful of silver milkweed spores on summer wind, includes the lovely "To Rosemary." . . . (pp. 32-3)

A Book of Americans consists of fifty-odd short poems about famous and infamous figures in American history; they range from Christopher Columbus to Woodrow Wilson and include such national villains as Aaron Burr. Mrs. Benét contributed the portraits of the five women—Pocahantas, Abigail Adams, Dolly Madison, Nancy Hanks, and Clara Barton—while her husband sketched the men. . . . The result of the collaboration is a winning little book with the twin appeals of humor and insight, both historical and biographical. . . . (pp. 34-5)

That broad romantic hope of Benét's which was stirred by the American Dream contrasts strikingly with the midnight aspect of his romanticism. Sometimes, indeed, his sense of the macabre explored some frailty or sickness in the national soul, but it also had a more personal aspect. Several lyrics of medium emotional weight reveal the darker reaches of his mind, his rebelliousness, or his intermittent preoccupation with such Gothic themes as death or insanity. (p. 36)

Irony wrenched into the grotesque is the pattern of "Ghosts of a Lunatic Asylum," which attempts to heighten the terrors of insanity by describing an abandoned institution haunted by the shades of the former inmates. Benét treats the theme superficially, however, and the effect lessens rather than accentuates the horror. Considerably more powerful is "Minor Litany," which makes use of a traditional Christian liturgical form to achieve a mordant irony. In a time of confusion, "with few clear stars," either public or private, the poet supplicates on behalf of those he calls the lost, the half-lost, and the desperate—in current terminology, the mentally ill. The cumulative effect of Benét's precisely stated—or understated—dictionary of types in need of, or already under the care of, psychiatrists is almost unbearably depressing. The poet calls first upon Christ for mercy, then upon Freud, then upon Life; and a later invocation near the end of the poem implores only the mercy of drugs. The final stanzas drive home the widespread and relentless incidence of psychic traumas and climax the rising note of hopelessness—the poor in mental health ye have always with ye, so to speak—inherent in a litany without God. The ending carelessly dissipates something of the carefully built-up mood by its half-facetious phrasing, and the total meaning is circumscribed by its descriptive and unanalytical approach; yet the poem is disturbing. (pp. 36-7)

In several ways—[Benét's] general preference for traditional form, his unabashed love of his country, his somewhat ambiguous religious skepticism, his avoidance of complex symbolism and of distillations of themes remote from the commonalty of American experience—his poetry was vulnerable to attack on the critical battlegrounds of the 1920's and 1930's. (p. 37)

Morton Dauwen Zabel, editor of *Poetry* and a fine critic, in a review of Benét's *Burning City* . . . in that important magazine [see excerpt above], charged that Benét was the latest representative in a long line of American poets, going back to Longfellow and Bryant, whom Zabel labels the "bardic romantics." The whole tradition, according to Zabel, has been "hostile to eccentric talent or refined taste, scornful of modernity or exotic influence. . . ." (p. 38)

[Zabel's] insistence on Benét's lifelong ambition to become a bard in the genteel tradition is unfounded and illogical; it is difficult to reconcile Benét's admiration for Whitman—anathema to conservatives—with Zabel's charge. (p. 42)

All of [the poems in *Burning City*] are warnings of doom for America as represented by New York City. The forms of the catastrophe envisioned include destruction by natural causes, annihilation through war or through universal sterility brought on by war, and ruin of an unspecified sort brought on by collective madness, for money or some other general folly or failure. . . . The style is prevailingly conversational, with only an occasional rise to a more lyrical line; and since the symbolism is easily grasped, these poems for the most part communicate their meaning with little effort on the part of the reader. The group is full of vivid descriptive detail organized for maximum effect. (p. 43)

The mood and style of **"Notes To Be Left in a Cornerstone"** are quiet; yet they come close to creating an overwhelming sense of the tragedy in the fall of a great city. The cause of the disaster is hinted at only; Benét is unconcerned with the means of destruction. What absorbs him is the quality of life in New York, its variety and contradictions, its seasonal extremes, its ugliness and beauty. (p. 44)

In this poem Benét demonstrates a sensibility, a range of perception and feeling, and a sensitive and powerful style that go beyond the best of his ballads, dramatic monologues, and lyrics. Although these combined powers are not reflected elsewhere in *Burning City,* they are in this poem the manifestation of the much greater talent that had earlier produced *John Brown's Body.* Any critical estimate of Benét as a poet must be based primarily on this epic. (p. 45)

[A] singing quality is one of the chief beauties of *John Brown's Body.* Once or twice it overflows the narrative, but more often it sustains or enhances it. Rarely does his poetry merit the epithet "patchwork colors, fading from the first," with which Benét disparages this aspect of his work in the Invocation. Nor is it true that in place of storm-bold words he presents beggarly terms: his style when not delicately lyrical, intentionally feminine, is soldierly, direct and incisive as a saber. The spectrum of styles and the dexterity and complexity of imagery which Benét exhibits in *John Brown's Body* are not surpassed by any other modern American poet.

Benét's full realization of his poetic potential came with his choice of a great American theme; and the confluence of his talents and interests was not accidental: one called the other into life. To his task, which Allen Tate correctly gauged as "the most ambitious poem ever undertaken by an American on an American theme" [see excerpt above], Benét brought his mature judgment wrought of liberal ideals and realism, both rooted deep in the American experience. The impressive weight of scholarship behind the epic was the final factor in making the work far more than the popular success which some critics . . . have seen it to be. (p. 79)

In his first three novels [*The Beginning of Wisdom, Young People's Pride,* and *Jean Huguenot,* Benét's] energies reached naturally for problems of American youth of the 1920's; his fourth novel [*Spanish Bayonet*], though set in the Revolutionary period, has a young American as its hero; and his final novel [*James Shore's Daughter*] traces the lives of its protagonists from their childhood at the turn of the nineteenth century until their maturity during the 1930's.

Only this final work, however, is mature in conception, form, and style. (p. 81)

[*The Beginning of Wisdom*] is semiautobiographical. . . . Philosophically, the novel takes its hero to the verge of a maturity that undoubtedly resembles that of the author.

More importantly, *The Beginning of Wisdom* is shaped partly by Benét's youthful inexperience, partly by youthful daring, and partly by youthful rebellion against a prevailing literary trend. (pp. 81-2)

Throughout the novel he maintains control of his material only for short periods, and his ambition is so large and indiscriminate that the work is overstuffed. Ironically, in light of Benét's critical position, the realistic episodes are superior to the romantic ones. Benét was never to free himself wholly of his romanticism, which in certain respects stood him in good stead, but in *The Beginning of Wisdom* the vaporous imaginings of his hero are smoke in the wind. (p. 86)

[*Young People's Pride*] was written when Benét was twenty-four and intensely in love with the charming Rosemary Carr, whom he married shortly after its completion. . . . [The novel is] the product of a variety of stresses, restrictions, and interests; it is not surprising, therefore, that it is marked by confusion of form and theme.

Literary influences—or at least parallels—are also apparent in *Young People's Pride*. The arabesque style and civilized satire of James Branch Cabell are imitated to some degree, and there are resemblances to the fictional world of F. Scott Fitzgerald. The two heroes and some of the other male characters are loyal Yale men, intelligent but halfway between innocence and sophistication. They banter about, and sometimes discuss seriously, love, marriage, art, youth, money, and morality; and they desperately seek happiness. The heroes' searches take the direction of romantic love but they also aim at self-fulfillment in an art or profession. Self-discipline and conformity to adult routine are, they find, difficult after the excitements of being officers in France during the war, but they have not been wounded either psychologically or physically; unlike their compatriots of whom Hemingway wrote, they are lost only temporarily. (pp. 86-7)

[The] chief fault of *Young People's Pride* is that it contains too many themes and unresolved ideas. . . . The novel is partially redeemed by its single three-dimensional character, by its intermittent stylistic precision and liveliness, by its occasionally effective satire, and by its sporadically subtle insights into the minds of young people of the early 1920's. . . . (p. 90)

[In *Jean Huguenot*] Benét was unable to submerge his romanticism and fuse his style and themes in a common conception. Although *Jean Huguenot* is somewhat better unified than *Young People's Pride* and *The Beginning of Wisdom* and is altogether a trimmer, more carefully controlled work, it still lacks an articulated structure. . . .

Benét crowds this novel, like his others, with incidents, and the story is intermittently interesting. (p. 97)

[*Spanish Bayonet*] reveals a marked advance in his control of the form. Unified in theme and structure, limited in its objectives, consistent in the mode and quality of its style, *Spanish Bayonet* is technically a competent novel—easily Benét's best up to this time in these respects. (p. 99)

Nothing in [*James Shore's Daughter*] is badly done, most things in it are well done, and a few things are brilliantly done. The novel's moderate length demands that Benét convey the essence of a period through carefully selected details of costume, setting, and social history, and through representative characters; and, for the most part, he has done this. (p. 109)

Perhaps because of his deep-seated uneasiness with and even distaste for the short story, Benét did not experiment in its form. In his best work, however, he gave to the traditional structure an easy balance, an unobtrusive precision, and a finish that reveal nothing of his travail in its composition. (p. 114)

"**The Devil and Daniel Webster**" gave Benét national recognition unequaled in this period by any other American writer of his importance, though similar in warmth to that accorded earlier to Irving and Longfellow. (p. 116)

The story's several thematic elements and wide range of tone, from the prevailing broad Yankee humor to the notes of pathos and even nobility, are combined in a superlative tale that comes to far more than humorous fantasy: it is a classic American fable. (p. 117)

Benét did not equal this achievement in his other two Webster stories. In the sea-serpent tale, for instance, Benét creates another humorous myth but fails to weld it to a proportionate amount of national significance. And in a piece like "**The Angel was a Yankee**," he attempts to capitalize cheaply on a New England stereotype, popular religion, and the epic showmanship of P. T. Barnum. A touch of poetry in the description of the angel and occasional bits of humorous character contrast are insufficient to overcome the commonplace style and obviousness of theme. More expert is "**A Tooth for Paul Revere**," in which Benét takes liberties with the famed story to make in fresh fashion the point that the American Revolution began when the common man, through whatever homely circumstances, joined the leaders in becoming involved in political issues. (p. 119)

Not a great story, "**Jacob and the Indians**" is a good example of Benét's ability to incorporate a good deal of American history in brief compass and to give it the color of living reality.

A finer tale of the same sort, one which brought Benét the O. Henry Memorial Award for the best short story of 1940, is "**Freedom's a Hard-Bought Thing**." . . . The story acquires its impact from its thoroughgoing realism and powerfully developed moral. Once again Benét demonstrates his exceptional talent for catching the speech rhythms, the diction, and the point of view of a national or ethnic type. (pp. 120-21)

The story is virtually flawless. . . .

[In "**John Pye and the Fool-Killer**" Benét] employed folklore concerning the always lurking and invincible dispatcher of those who violate common sense—that is, everyone. (p. 122)

[In] this tale Benét varies his style to suit his substance. Although he begins by addressing the reader directly—"You don't hear much about the Fool-Killer these days"—the yarn-spinner has no identity beyond this function. He is an anonymous voice from the anonymous folk, weaving fantasy and humor and wisdom from the stuff of a people's common ex-

perience. He tells his story plainly, directly and vividly, without fuss or moralizing or metaphysical speculation. The humor he conveys dead-pan, in the tradition of Mark Twain and Artemus Ward. The humor of the first part of his story, obvious but as telling as Ward's roundly whacks American limitations and pretensions. Benét subtly accomplishes the shift into the graver part of his story with Johnny's discovery that the Fool-Killer is not the American bruiser of his imagination but the personification of Time in the guise of a familiar American figure. The theme of the story changes with Johnny's wise perception that folly is a part of all men, but *only* a part—and a humanizing one at that. His recognition of this truth is placed in the framework of the American conception of man as a creature with possibilities as well as limitations. But finally the storyteller's theme is human mortality; and quiet pathos, with a bit of transcendental hope, ends his tale.

Benét was by no means consistently successful with such material. "**William Riley and the Fates**," for example, is another fantasy attempting a humorous mixture of transcendental figures and American philosophizing, but its mode is commonplace and its meaning no deeper than that of a newsreel. "**O'Halloran's Luck**" reveals expert craftsmanship, although it relies too heavily on familiar Irish types, human and fairy, to be ranked as one of Benét's best stories. "**Doc Mellhorn and the Pearly Gates**," while commendable for its thesis that doing good works in hell is preferable to doing nothing in heaven, remains superficial in its development and suffers from the sentimental clichés which compose the chief character. "**The Minister's Books**," though it grew out of Benét's research into frontier history, has a startling thematic and stylistic resemblance to Nathaniel Hawthorne's tales of Puritan New England. Competently done, it is yet essentially imitative except in respect to Hawthorne's genius for endowing the natural and supernatural with manifold moral meaning. A quite different story with considerable imagination is "**The King of the Cats**." In it Benét ingeniously adapted an old European legend to a modern American setting for social satire, as well as pure fun. (p. 124)

In "**By the Waters of Babylon**" Benét again succeeds brilliantly in creating a narrator to develop his meaning: a noble savage made believable. . . . "**By the Waters of Babylon**" is religious not only through the primitive rites and aspirations of the narrator, but fundamentally through Benét's reverence for civilization.

Similar in conception, though less noble a tale, is "**As It was in the Beginning**." (pp. 125-26)

[The] story is weighted with associations heightened by strangeness, like a dream in which familiar elements are rearranged in new and half-mysterious yet meaningful patterns. Too explicit a declaration of the story's meaning at the outset and at the conclusion weakens the poetry of this dream of history; and the confident conclusion, implying a steady march of civilization, does not rest solidly on the chronicle's record or the historian's personal experience. Yet Benét has registered effectively through indirect means his summing up of the historic lessons of freedom.

Benét could also transmute specifically European history, ancient or modern, into a fine short story. "**The Last of the Legions**" . . . is a superb tale of the decline of the Roman Empire. (p. 127)

In "**The Bishop's Beggar**," Benét subordinated history to character and plot without reducing history to mere background and color. . . .

What saves the story from being a sentimental religious romance is the sharp realism with which Benét delineates Luigi and the bishop. (p. 131)

Benét's stories of contemporary life are collectively somewhat inferior to his tales woven from the stuffs of fantasy and history, and only one of them has the stature of "**The Bishop's Beggar.**" (p. 132)

[A] fine story which takes its flavor from the present but its theme from eternity, is "**A Death in the Country.**" One of Benét's most moving and subtle stories, it enfolds in familiar American images the common tragedy of human experience. Benét weaves in unerringly the sweetness, the formal oppressiveness, the poignancy, ugliness, pretense, and courage that mingle at a small-town funeral. (p. 134)

Like *John Brown's Body, Western Star* grew out of Benét's absorption with American history. He conceived of our history as having two major and continuing phases: the preservation of national unity and the restless mobility of our people. . . . His chief problem he envisioned as that of portraying the changing panorama of frontier life from the perspective of the frontier, rather than from that of the East. His basic method again was to interpret American history through real episodes and both real and imagined characters. (p. 144)

As the poet-historian of American democracy, Benét properly centers his narrative upon representative individuals, whether real or fictional, as their lives bear upon or shape in some degree the history of the westering frontier fanning out from England. . . . *Western Star* is thus the testament of nameless multitudes who colonized America and pushed its frontier towards the Pacific. (pp. 145-46)

Benét has seized upon a profound truth about America: that the search for her meaning and destiny must be endless. The quest must return for spiritual nourishment to the monuments, to the history brought to life momentarily, but it must forever pursue the elusive godhead of national soul. (p. 146)

In his aim of making American history meaningful through the lives of fictional characters, Benét is more uniformly successful in *Western Star* than in his earlier epic. He is, in fact, consistently successful in the difficult task of contriving men, women, and even children who are of their time, whose lives reflect in one way or another Benét's larger purposes, but who achieve individuality. (p. 147)

The historical characters are not so numerous as in Benét's first epic, nor, with the exception of John Smith, are they quite so fascinating (a fact that is not Benét's fault), but they are nonetheless incisively recorded. . . .

Benét likewise appraises groups like the Pilgrims or even the whole Indian people with insight and judicious perception. (p. 148)

While Benét thus demonstrates the same metrical resourcefulness in *Western Star* that he had evidenced in his first epic, the later work is less varied in style. It is less ambitious and exuberant. . . . (p. 149)

Another marked difference between the two epics lies in imagery and symbol. The star is the equivalent of John Brown as a unifying device, but of course it does not have any historical or myth-making function. It appears only in the Prelude and at the end of this first book of the poem, gleaming over the endless forests of the West as Dickon's sons prepare to follow it, the lure and ideal, unattainable, undefinable. Yet neither the star nor any other symbol has anything like the manifold functions of John Brown or the Phaeton clock. For this and other reasons, *Western Star* is less dense in meaning than the earlier epic.

Criticism of *Western Star* must be qualified by the consideration that it is a fragment which Benét doubtless would have polished had he lived. . . .

Western Star was a casualty of World War II in almost the same sense that its author was. Had Stephen Vincent Benét lived to follow his star to its zenith above the vanished frontier, it might have shone as a star of high magnitude. Even above today's New Frontier it forms, with its twin, an axis for a constellation unique in the broad skies of American literature. (p. 150)

Parry Stroud, in his Stephen Vincent Benét *(copyright © 1962 by Twayne Publishers, Inc.; reprinted with the permission of Twayne Publishers, a Division of G. K. Hall & Co., Boston), Twayne, 1962, 173 p.*

JOHN GRIFFITH (essay date 1973)

Allen Tate [see excerpt above], puzzling over the lack of aesthetic unity in *John Brown's Body,* once asked: "Is it possible that Mr. Benét supposed the poem to be about the Civil War, rather than about his own mind?" Actually, wrote Benét in a foreword which seems (but only seems) to answer Tate's question, "I do not think of the poem as being primarily a poem about war itself. What I was trying to do was to show certain realities, legends, ideas, landscapes, ways of living, faces of men that were ours." The point of Tate's question and Benét's answer is the same: *John Brown's Body* makes the scientific historian's assumption that the truth—reality, the past—exists, independent of any human projection, waiting to be caught. Benét's **Invocation** describes his poem as an effort to reconstruct that past—

> To build again that blue, American roof
> Over a half-forgotten battle tune
> And call unsurely, from a haunted ground,
> Armies of shadows, and the shadow ground.
>
> (pp. 4-5)

His attention is always outward, toward the past he is seeking to capture, rather than inward, toward what Tate seeks in the poem but fails to find, "some striking personal vision of life" which might give internal meaning to the poem's events and people. (p. 5)

A few critical attempts have been made to establish an imaginative unity in the poem. But no one has gotten around the patent fact that its strongest unifying feature is its conventional chronology of the war's battles and campaigns. As Benét said, "Except for the prologue and epilogue, the action of the poem is a continuous action, beginning shortly before the John Brown raid and ending shortly after the surrender at Appomatox." Each of the eight books treats prominently one or more military events: Book I, Harper's Ferry; Book II, the firing on Fort Sumter and the Battle of Bull Run; Book III, Shiloh; Book IV, the campaigns of the East and the West, Fair Oaks, Fredericksburg, and other battles; Book V, Antietam and the hard winter of 1862; Book VI, the Wilderness Campaign, Grant and Sherman at Vicksburg; Book VII, Gettysburg; Book VIII, Sherman's march to the sea and the surrender at Appomatox. Included in this chronology are numerous other public events—

the hanging of John Brown, the election of Lincoln, the formation of the Confederate cabinet, the appointment and dismissal of various generals, the death of Jackson, the death of Lincoln.

Metaphorically one might picture the poem as a kind of insulated cable. At its core, advancing along a chronological line, is the war itself, the essential historical Civil War. The cable's outer surface is the ideal discipline of historiography, cultivated with the best modern scholarly tools—detachment, sobriety, open-mindedness, exhaustive research. It is only between this core and this outer surface that the poet exercises his license; his fancy is never allowed to drift too far from the "ascertainable facts" of his source books. (pp. 5-6)

The fabric which encases the military chronology consists of a number of roughly graduated viewpoints from which the war is seen. Closest to the center are Benét's anonymous or near-anonymous historical figures, who see war only as personal experience, immediate and without much abstract meaning. . . . Benét's fictitious figures, presented at their most unreflective and immediate in a kind of *style indirect libre,* produce more highly-wrought rhetoric but no broader sense of understanding. . . . One remove from this are characters [such as Lincoln], fictional and historical, who try to formulate some larger meaning for the war—some, at least, personal moral lesson. . . . One more step away from the experiential core is the poet, writing in a summary way of the actors' attitudes and feelings. . . . And then, at the outer layer of this texture of viewpoints, is the poet-historian in his study with his maps and battle-plans and his surveys of social history that give the large, disinterested perspective of the twentieth century. (pp. 6-7)

My elaborate image of the poem as a core of historical events layered about with individual impressions at various distances implies, I think, something of the poem's essentially unplanned quality, even in the presence of such care and meticulous research. Benét depends on a rough historical calculus, assuming that if he assembles all the standard themes and viewpoints surrounding the war itself, then a significant configuration will inevitably form—the shape of "the golden prey" he sets after in his Invocation. It is a calculus which, Benét assumes, operates independent of his own imagination—the shape of history will automatically appear if the right facts and opinions and first-hand impressions are brought in.

Principles of selection are, of course, necessary, lest the poem reach to infinity. Like most of the historians who were his contemporaries, Benét doesn't seem to have done much conscious thinking about how one selects facts on which to focus. Generally his view of the Civil War accords with that which Thomas B. Pressly calls "the nationalist school," which he says "was characterized primarily by its spirit of nationalism and sectional reconciliation." In this view, the Civil War had no major villain; Lincoln and Lee were both to be admired. "This so-called 'cult of Lincoln and Lee,'" says Pressly, "reflected the widespread agreement among historians that supporters of the Union, typified in Lincoln, and supporters of the Confederacy, typified in Lee, had acted in the main from honorable and justifiable motives." What caused the war, in this view, was not some*one* but some*thing*—as Pressly says, "inanimate forces were the primary cause of the conflict between North and South rather than the actions of evil individuals." Benét agrees. . . . (pp. 7-8)

As far as one can judge by its effect on his narrative technique, the most pervasive implicit thesis in Benét's interpretation is that the war resulted from what Pressly calls "deep-seated, fundamental, irreconcilable differences" between the country's sections. Following, whether consciously or not, Frederick Jackson Turner's image of the United States as a group of culturally discrete sections dynamically juxtaposed, Benét pictures the Civil War as primarily a conflict between the bourgeois Puritan temper of New England and the romantic-aristocratic Southern temper, embodied in the characters and customs surrounding Wingate Hall. . . . With the Wingate plantation—granted by England's Charles II to "our well-beloved John Wingate"—as the symbolic center, Benét presents an integrated series of Southern characters—Clay Wingate, the scion; Mary Lou Wingate, his mother, who "gathered the reins of the whole plantation" . . . ; Cudjo and Aunt Bess, the loyal slaves, and Spade, the runaway; the coquette Lucy and the slightly wild, barely respectable Sally Dupré; and all the young gallants who attend the soirées at Wingate Hall and ride in the Wingates' Black Horse Troop. (p. 8)

As for the other geographical sections, their representatives are more lightly sketched. But they, no less than Wingate and Ellyat, are clearly products of what Morton Zabel [see excerpt above] has called Benét's love of "the large dimensions of popular myth." They are quintessentially conventional, drawn according to social and geographical types, depending on the most standard themes and images. John Vilas is a romantic individualist, set to hunting "the wilderness stone" as he avoids being caught up in the war. Benét said that he was meant to represent "the Border States and the growing West." Luke Breckinridge of the Tennessee mountains is ignorant, superstitious, a hard-eyed feuder and a keen shot with his long rifle. Jake Diefer of Pennsylvania is a sturdy German peasant who goes to war and loses an arm and stolidly comes back to his plow again. Sophy is the lower-class Southern white, "scared chambermaid in Pollet's hotel," who would "like to smell sweet . . . like a lady" . . . ; Shippy, "the little man with sharp rat-eyes," is her counterpart from the North, a base-spirited peddler who carries spy-reports in his boots and dies whining. Bailey is Ellyat's fiercely provincial, ignorant, tough-talking Midwestern compatriot from Illinois.

There is a sense in which Benét's very epistemological assumptions require him to use such stereotypes. If, as his Invocation implies, the essential American past is to be found in an amalgamation or juxtaposition of a finite number of recognizable viewpoints—the "hundred visions" from which he proposes to make one—then those viewpoints must exist, and in finite number. The farther Benét might move toward imagining his characters as individuals, each with his own peculiarities, the more he fragments his quest for the historical truth—the more he strays away from those "harmonious wholes" which he and A. B. Hart and the other scientific historians believed in. To picture Clay Wingate as a Southern aristocrat who reads Byron and gambles and polishes his boots and his honor is a way of pointing the reader's attention outward, toward the historical "reality." Typical or stereotyped regional representatives are, perhaps, one kind of comprehensive historic fact to be discerned in the welter of particular instances.

This conception of significant truth as something to be caught rather than created has a crucial effect on the poem's schematic structure, or lack of it. Benét has made little apparent effort to establish a total meaning or pattern within the poem itself—a significant relationship between images, say, or between themes or even characters. Henry Seidel Canby [see excerpt above] has claimed to have found a moral unity in the poem, based on the fundamental theme of "the struggle of individuals caught in Karma." But this is surely the laxest kind of pattern. Consider the particular "karmas" of the central figures: for Ellyat, a going away from home, a meeting with a lovely gypsy girl, a separation and a miraculous reunion; for Wingate, the bittersweet loss of the prettily romantic world of which Lucy Weatherby is queen, and the gaining of the more real, mysterious and sensuous love of Sally Dupré. For Diefer, dogged duty, resulting in the loss of an arm. For Spade, the break for freedom, the disillusionment by Northern cruelty, and the final subdued triumph of finding a job on Diefer's farm. For Lucy, a chivalric lark that goes sour. For Cudjo and Mary Lou Wingate the tragic destruction of the old aristocracy. For Lincoln, the running down of the quarry, God's intention; for Grant, professional success after a career of failure; for Lee, a Stoic lesson in defeat; for John Brown, martyrdom. To find the significance of these fates we look not to structural bonds and contrasts between them, but outward, to the historical reality they refer to.

The same centrifugal motion is visible in the poem's prominent rhetorical devices. They owe their impact, characteristically, to a tension between the poem and something outside it, rather than between parts of the poem itself. Benét relies, that is to say, on his audience's general familiarity with the central issues of the war, its leading heroes and the names of its great battlefields. His poetic trademark is the mild ironic spark he strikes between that general myth of the Civil War and his own wry, rather tight-lipped understatements about it. Lincoln, Lee, Grant, the ante-bellum South, Puritanical New England, the great American war—all have a popular romantic aura which Benét evokes in hundreds of allusions, most of them pointedly clipped and restrained. (pp. 9-11)

Paul Engle has said of Benét's historical verse that "always there is the conviction that the act of history means little unless it ends in a human image, and the act of expressing poetry means little unless it works through mortal object, through used, known, touched, feared, accustomed detail." The converse of this is also true, perhaps truer: that for Benét the human image, the mortal object has little meaning—an uncertain place in the mind's universe—unless it is rather solidly attached to standard historical landmarks. *John Brown's Body*'s most prestigious defenders have been historians, for most of its governing assumptions are rooted in historiography: strict regard for documented fact, chronological structure emphasizing great public events, attention to the geographical sections of the country, and so on. Benét's whole narrative technique is, in its own way, intended to be transparent, so historical reality can shine through. His manner is easy, relaxed, discursive, structurally uncomplicated, bearing little relation to the new poetics of Pound and Eliot and Williams or even Whitman. Above all, it is confident and unselfconscious, and it does what it was intended to do: convey with considerable reportorial felicity the solid, respectable history in which the poem's meaning is grounded. (p. 11)

> John Griffith, *"Narrative Technique and the Meaning of History in Benét and MacLeish," in* The Journal of Narrative Technique *(copyright © 1973 by* The Journal of Narrative Technique*), Vol. 3, No. 1, January, 1973, pp. 3-19.**

WILLIAM J. HARRIS   (essay date 1976)

I would not be very troubled about Benét's literary misfortunes if he had only written *John Brown's Body* and **"The Devil and**

Daniel Webster," his most famous works. . . . Yet he has written a few short stories that should not be forgotten—**"Johnny Pye and the Fool-Killer"** and **"A Death in the Country,"** in particular—and written an important and successful epic poem, *Western Star.*

John Brown's Body, the poem for which he is famous, is a cartoon of the Civil War. . . . In this poem Benét's imagination sinks to the level of a best-selling novelist like Frank Yerby or Irving Wallace. There is not one living three-dimensional character in the whole book. That part of his imagination that could write hack and conventional stories has won out over the more serious part. Yet it is a poem of a humane man who could see goodness in both the North and the South but could not imagine a living universe. It is not Benét's heart that fails in this work but his imagination.

"The Devil and Daniel Webster" is not a product of a "cheap" imagination but it is too fragile a vehicle to handle its profound message about the brotherhood of man whether he be damned or saved. Benét's imagination becomes profounder in both prose and poetry as the poet grows older. *Western Star,* his last poem, published posthumously and unfinished, is a serious epic which presents a humane and peopled history of America's first years.

Even though *Western Star* is different from our standard modern epic poem—*The Cantos, Paterson, The Waste Land*—it should be accepted into the canon of modern literature. In fact, the canon—our conception of literature—should be expanded. The roots of the modern epic can be found in Whitman's *Leaves of Grass.* . . . For our time, *The Waste Land* is the prime example of the modern epic: it is difficult, obscure, rich in world mythology, fragmented, plotless; it lacks characterization and it is despairing. Whitman's roots have been somewhat twisted and mutated by the twentieth century: the epic has darkened.

Western Star has characters we grow to know and even care about; it is easy to read; it is not esoteric in any way; it has a plot and its history is either familiar or Benét gives the reader any background information he might need. And it is a poem of praise, praise of the ordinary people who established this country. But Benét's praise is different from Sandburg's, our other champion of the common folk. He does not praise the people, the mob, an abstraction. . . . Rather, Benét praises concrete individuals from all classes who were involved in the early history of America. . . . The people come through in *Western Star.*

More than plot or obscurity, what most separates *Western Star* from the modern epic is that it is not a poem of despair but of praise. . . . I am not trying to say that *The Waste Land* is false—that this has been a great century and this is the best of all possible worlds. *The Waste Land* is a great and influential poem which has documented a great spiritual crisis of our civilization: the death of God, the destruction of traditional values for many sensitive individuals. . . . Benét is an artist who does not really care much about the existence of God but does care about the conditions of man on this earth; he is a humanist. . . . In fact, Benét's world is not religious but historical and political. (pp. 172-75)

By the end of *Western Star* we care deeply about the people in the poem. . . . Benét, the reasonable and compassionate man, moves from a cartoon civil war to a real world which deserves his reasonableness and compassion.

In *Western Star* we get to know the Puritans as people. (pp. 175-76)

Benét's interest in religion is not salvation (like Eliot's) but freedom. There is the same concern about freedom and sanity in *John Brown's Body* as in *Western Star;* it is only more humanly realized in the later poem. (p. 176)

"**The Devil and Daniel Webster**" contains Benét's vision as completely as any of his works: damned or not men are brothers and there is the possibility of decency in every man. It is the liberal vision of man. I believe the message but though Daniel Webster may be able to melt the hearts of the jury from hell Benét does not manage to melt my heart with his tale. The telling of the story is too cute. In the first two paragraphs of "**The Devil and Daniel Webster**" we can see its almost arty folksiness. . . . (p. 177)

It's too self-consciously an American folk tale. . . . [It's] too preciously colorful; the paragraphs are too contrived with their opening and closing lines, shouting this is a gen-u-ine American Tall Story.

"**Johnny Pye and the Fool-Killer**" says all men are fools because they must die. . . . Johnny Pye spends his life trying to escape the Fool-Killer, a supernatural agent of death. . . . Eventually he discovers that all men are fools and there is no way to escape death. In fact, in his early nineties he welcomes the Fool-Killer.

"**Johnny Pye and the Fool-Killer**" has a resonance that "**The Devil and Daniel Webster**" does not. The Fool-Killer is authentic. I gather from reading "**A Death in the Country**," one of Benét's best stories, that the Fool-Killer is a "real" boogieman from his childhood. Grown-ups told their children that they better watch out for the Fool-Killer. Benét has taken this childhood boogieman and has transformed him into an excellent personification of death. There is nothing arch about him. As LeRoi Jones says: "The most powerful way to deal with an image is to make sure it goes deeper than literature. That it is actually 'out there.'" The Fool-Killer is more "out there" than "**Daniel Webster**." Yet by the time of *Western Star* Benét is able to make history "out there," to make history as living as his personal experience.

Allen Tate, in *The Nation* [see excerpt above], said of *John Brown's Body* shortly after its first appearance that "it has hair-raising defects" and I agree with Mr. Tate. Earlier I spoke of what a poor story *John Brown's Body* told and as a poem it is almost as bad. There are good individual sections, like the "**Invocation**," but there is much flat language in it. But to dismiss *John Brown's Body* should not mean the dismissal of Benét. I do not find very many hair-raising defects in *Western Star* and "**Johnny Pye and the Fool-Killer**": they are moving and effective works. Not only are the characters better drawn in *Western Star* than in *John Brown's Body* but the poetry is better. Even though *Western Star* is generally simple and direct it is effective because it is suited to its subject matter. (pp. 177-78)

[*Western Star*] is not great poetry—the language does not excite. . . . However, it is workmanlike verse that is good for telling a story and presenting characters. This is the style of most of the poem but at times the poetry does become more lyrical. (pp. 178-79)

Western Star generally avoids the weaker lines that Tate so deplored in *John Brown's Body*. (p. 179)

I cannot truly say how highly Benét should be ranked in comparison with other modern American writers—it has been an incredibly rich century for literature—but I think Benét has written at least a very good poem and a few stories that deserve to survive. His work is an excellent expression of the liberal imagination. *The Waste Land* must make room for *Western Star*. The world of the religious and the spiritual must make room for the world of the political and social. The Anglo-Catholic church is one solution for modern man's problems but another is the community of man, Benét's answer. We are all brothers faced with the Fool-Killer and we have the potential if not of an "earthly paradise" at least of a workable democracy. But we need new Daniel Websters in order to find this democratic decency in our hearts. (pp. 179-80)

> *William J. Harris, "Stephen Vincent Benét's 'Hair-Raising Defects'?" in* A Question of Quality: Popularity and Value in Modern Creative Writing, *edited by Louis Filler (copyright © 1976 Bowling Green University Popular Press), Bowling Green University Popular Press, 1976, pp. 172-80.*

ADDITIONAL BIBLIOGRAPHY

Allen, Hervey. "Of Book Reviewing: 'John Brown's Body'." In *A Preface to Literature*, edited by Edward Wagenknecht, pp. 353-55. New York: Henry Holt and Co., 1954.
> Praises *John Brown's Body* for liveliness, dramatic effect, and characterization.

Benét, Laura. *When William Rose, Stephen Vincent and I Were Young*. New York: Dodd, Mead & Co., 1976, 111 p.
> Benét's early family life as remembered by his older sister.

Benét, Stephen Vincent. "Stephen Vincent Benét." In *Portraits and Self-Portraits*, edited by Georges Schreiber, pp. 13-16. Boston: Houghton Mifflin Co., 1936.
> Autobiographical sketch.

Benét, William Rose. "My Brother Steve: A Poet Who Has Never Cared Much about an Ivory Tower." *The Saturday Review of Literature* XXVI, No. 13 (27 March 1943): 5-7.
> Biographical sketch.

Canby, Henry Seidel. "Stephen Vincent Benét." *The Saturday Review of Literature* XXVI, No. 13 (27 March 1943): 14.
> Estimates that Benét's significance will grow since he wrote his epic, *John Brown's Body*, at a time when poetry was becoming too cerebral and because he supplied a poetic basis for America's mounting nationalism.

Fenton, Charles A, *Stephen Vincent Benét: The Life and Times of an American Man of Letters: 1898-1943*. New Haven: Yale University Press, 1958, 436 p.
> Sympathetic biography that offers background to the critical reception of Benét's works.

Fenton, Charles A. "The Writer as Correspondent: The Letters of Stephen Vincent Benét." *The Virginia Quarterly Review* 36, No. 3 (Summer 1960): 430-41.
> Examines Benét's habits of correspondence.

Fitts, Dudley. "Shorter Notices: 'John Brown's Body'." *Hound and Horn* II, No. 1 (Septmeber 1928): 85-6.
> Observes faults in *John Brown's Body*, but concludes that the poem is no "mean feat."

Jackson, Frederick H. "Stephen Vincent Benét and American History." *The Historian* XVI, No. 2 (Autumn 1954): 67-75.

Finds that although "Benet is not one of the great poets of world literature . . . [he] is without peer in his poetical representation of the American past."

LaFarge, Christopher. "The Narrative Poetry of Stephen Vincent Be- nét." *The Saturday Review of Literature* XXVII, No. 32 (5 August 1944): 106, 108.
    Hails clarity as the primary virtue of Benét's poetry.

O'Neill, Eugene. "S. V. Benét." *The Saturday Review of Literature* XXXII, No. 32 (6 August 1949): 34-5.
    Analysis of *John Brown's Body* as a failed epic.

Untermeyer, Louis. "Stephen Vincent Benét." In his *American Poetry Since 1900*, pp. 242-46. New York: Holt, Rinehart & Winston, 1923.
    General appraisal stressing the bizarre and macabre in Benét's early poetry.

Walsh, Thomas F. "The 'Noon Wine' Devils." *The Georgia Review* XXII, No. 1 (Spring 1968): 90-6.*
    Examination of Katherine Anne Porter's short story "Noon Wine" against the Faustian pattern in Benét's "The Devil and Daniel Webster."

Wiggins, Eugene. "Benét's 'Mountain Whippoorwill': Folklore atop Folklore." *Tennessee Folklore Society Bulletin* XLI, No. 3 (September 1975): 99-112.
    Benét's "Mountain Whippoorwill" examined in relation to doc- uments about mountain fiddling.

Wiley, Paul L. "The Phaeton Symbol in *John Brown's Body*." *Amer- ican Literature* XVII, No. 3 (November 1945): 231-42.
    Evolution from youth to maturity of Jack Ellyat, the Connecticut boy who joins the Union Army, in *John Brown's Body*.

Ambrose (Gwinett) Bierce

1842-1914?

(Also wrote under pseudonyms of Dod Grile and William Herman) American short story writer, novelist, journalist, poet, essayist, and critic.

Bierce's literary reputation is based primarily on his short stories of the Civil War and of the supernatural, which make up a relatively small part of his total output. Often compared to the tales of Edgar Allan Poe, these stories share the same attraction for death in its more bizarre forms, featuring depictions of mental deterioration, uncanny manifestations, and expressing the horror of existence in a meaningless universe. Like Poe, Bierce professed to be mainly concerned with the artistry of his work, yet critics find him more intent on conveying his misanthropy and pessimism. In his lifetime Bierce was famous as a California journalist dedicated to the truth as he understood it, which was little comfort to those whose reputations were harmed by his attacks. For his sardonic wit and damning observations on the personalities and events of the day, he became known as "the wickedest man in San Francisco."

Bierce was born in Meigs County, Ohio. His parents were farmers and he was the tenth of thirteen children, all of whom were given names beginning with "A" at their father's insistence. The family moved to Indiana, where Bierce went to high school, later attending the Kentucky Military Institute. At the outbreak of the Civil War, he enlisted in the army. In such units as the Ninth Indiana Infantry Regiment and Buell's Army of the Ohio, Bierce fought bravely and extensively in numerous military engagements, including the battles of Shiloh and Chickamauga and in Sherman's March to the Sea. After the war Bierce traveled with a military expedition to San Francisco, where he left the army and prepared himself for a literary career.

Bierce's early poetry and prose appeared in the *Californian*. In 1868 he became the editor of *The News Letter*, for which he wrote his famous "Town Crier" column. Bierce became something of a noted figure in California literary society, forming friendships with Mark Twain, Bret Harte, and Joaquin Miller. In 1872 Bierce and his wife moved to England, where during a three-year stay he wrote for *Fun* and *Figaro* magazines and acquired the nickname "Bitter Bierce." His first three books of sketches, *The Fiend's Delight, Nuggets and Dust Panned out in California,* and *Cobwebs from an Empty Skull,* were published during this period. When the English climate aggravated Bierce's asthma, he returned to San Francisco. In 1887 he began writing for William Randolph Hearst's *San Francisco Examiner,* continuing the "Prattler" column he had done for *The Argonaut* and *The Wasp.* This provided him with a regular outlet for his essays, epigrams, and short stories.

Bierce's major fiction was collected in *Tales of Soldiers and Civilians* and *Can Such Things Be?* Many of his stories draw upon his experiences in the Civil War, earning him a reputation as a realistic author of war fiction. However, Bierce was not striving for realism, as critics have pointed out and as he himself admitted, for his narratives often fail to supply sufficient verisimilitude. His most striking fictional effects depend on an adept manipulation of the reader viewpoint: a bloody battlefield seen through the eyes of a deaf child in "Chickamauga," the deceptive escape dreamed by a man about to be hanged in "An Occurrence at Owl Creek Bridge," and the shifting perspectives of "The Death of Halpin Frayser." The classic Biercian narrative also includes a marked use of black humor, particularly in the ironic and hideous deaths his protagonists often suffer. The brutal satire Bierce employed in his journalism appears as plain brutality in his fiction, and critics have both condemned and praised his imagination, along with Poe's, as among the most vicious and morbid in American literature. Bierce's bare, economical style of supernatural horror is usually distinguished from the verbally lavish tales of Poe, and few critics rank Bierce as the equal of his predecessor.

Along with his tales of terror, Bierce's most acclaimed work is *The Devil's Dictionary,* a lexicon of its author's wit and animosity. His definition GHOST—"the outward and visible sign of an inward fear"—clarifies his fundamentally psychological approach to the supernatural. In *The Devil's Dictionary* he vented much of his contempt for politics, religion, society, and conventional human values. A committed opponent of hypocrisy, prejudice, and corruption, Bierce acquired the public persona of an admired but often hated genius, a man of contradition and mystery. In 1914 he informed some of his correspondents that he intended to enter Mexico and join Pancho Villa's forces as an observer during that country's civil war. He was never heard from again, and the circumstances of his death are uncertain.

(See also *TCLC*, Vol. 1.)

PRINCIPAL WORKS

Nuggets and Dust Panned Out in California [as Dod Grile] (sketches) 1872
The Fiend's Delight [as Dod Grile] (sketches) 1873
Cobwebs from an Empty Skull [as Dod Grile] (sketches) 1874
The Dance of Death [with Thomas A. Harcourt under the joint pseudonym of William Herman] (satire) 1877
Tales of Soldiers and Civilians (short stories) 1891; published in England as *In the Midst of Life*, 1892
Black Beetles in Amber (poetry) 1892
The Monk and the Hangman's Daughter [translator; with Gustav Adolph Danzinger] (novel) 1892
Can Such Things Be? (short stories) 1893
Fantastic Fables (satire) 1899
Shapes of Clay (poetry) 1903
The Cynic's Word Book (satire) 1906; also published as *The Devil's Dictionary*, 1911
The Shadow on the Dial, and Other Essays (essays) 1909
Write It Right (essay) 1909
The Collected Works of Ambrose Bierce. 12 vols. (short stories, sketches, poetry, essays, homilies, and satire) 1912

GERTRUDE FRANKLIN ATHERTON (essay date 1891)

[Ambrose Bierce] has the best brutal imagination of any man in the English-speaking race; his sonnets are exquisitely dainty and tender; his fables are the wittiest that have been written in America. Poe never wrote anything more weirdly awful than *Chicamauga, The Coup De Grace, My Favorite Murder,* and *The Watcher by the Dead.* The reserve and the cynical brutality of these stories produce an impression never attained by the most riotous imagination. In point of art I have no hesitation in saying that Bierce overlooks Poe. In the latter's work one can pick out each stone from each structure as one reads, analyzing its shape and ingredients. But Bierce's art of construction is so subtle and his power so dominant that the minds of his readers are his until they lay down the work. It is claimed by his friends that no such English has been written since Swift, and I certainly recall no one who writes with more classic severity. (p. 271)

> Gertrude Franklin Atherton, *"The Literary Development of California,"* in The Cosmopolitan, *Vol. X, No. 3, January, 1891, pp. 269-78.*

THE ATHENAEUM (essay date 1892)

Mr. Bierce's collection of American tales of horror [*In the Midst of Life*] is occasionally marred by extravagance of style, and some of the more terrible descriptions of solitary suffering are too long drawn out. His themes are chosen for the most part from the Civil War, and it is characteristic of the nature of that struggle that the pride of soldiership nowhere appears in these descriptions. We read of nothing but the minutest details of bodily and mental pain: of tragedies like '**A Horseman in the Sky,**' where a skirmisher shoots his father (of the opposite faction), who has bound him to "do his duty" in the war; like '**Coulter's Notch,**' where an artillerist plays upon his own house, held by the enemy, and slaughters unwittingly his wife and child; like the frightful story of panic, '**A Tough Tussle,**' when a man in an agonizing state of nervous tension takes the corpse of an enemy for an assailant, and is slain himself while engaged in his ghastly onslaught. . . . It will be seen the writer can give a vivid description. Perhaps the most gruesome of all the military stories is that of the lost child at Chickamauga, who slept through the battle, and, guided by the wounded crawling to the river, found its home burnt, its mother slain, and was struck deaf and dumb with the shock. In this the details are given with the sort of power one sees in a Russian battle-piece, and will repel more readers than they attract. Incidentally one can realize something of the visible experiences of that most strange, Titanic, and unorthodox of wars, with its ambitious strategy and confused manoeuvring, and its incessant embarrassment owing to the vastness and complexity of natural obstacles. We should consider this part of the book extremely unsuitable for young readers, to whom it is surely more wholesome to present the nobler side of war. Of the civilian stories, '**A Holy Terror**' and '**The Middle Toe of the Right Foot**' quite correspond to the promise of their titles, and are calculated to be read with most result after a heavy supper, though '**A Watcher by the Dead**' and '**The Man and the Snake**' may also affect the nerves. In '**Haita the Shepherd**' and '**An Heiress from Redhorse**' the author endeavours, most inadequately, to reassure his readers. Is "Sepoy," by the way, established American for British India?

> *"Novels of the Week: 'In the Midst of Life',"* in The Athenaeum, *Vol. 99, No. 3356, February 20, 1892, p. 241.*

GEORGE STERLING (essay date 1922)

Bierce is of the immortals. That fact, known, I think, to him, and seeming then more and more evident to some of his admirers, has become plainly apparent to anyone who can appraise the matter with eyes that see beyond the flimsy artifices that bulk so large and so briefly in the literary arena. Bierce was a sculptor who wrought in hardest crystal. (p. xxxiv)

The tales [in *Tales of Soldiers and Civilians*] are told with a calmness and reserve that make most of Poe's seem somewhat boyish and melodramatic by comparison. The greatest of them seems to me to be *An Occurrence at Owl Creek Bridge,* though I am perennially charmed by the weird beauty of *An Inhabitant of Carcosa,* a tale of unique and unforgettable quality. (pp. xxxiv-xxxv)

Personally, I have always regarded Poe's *Fall of the House of Usher* as our greatest tale; close to that come, in my opinion, at least a dozen of Bierce's stories, whether of the soldier or civilian. He has himself stated in *Prattle:* "I am not a poet." And yet he wrote poetry, on occasion, of a high order, his *Invocation* being one of the noblest poems in the tongue. Some of his satirical verse seems to me as terrible in its withering invective as any that has been written by classic satirists, not excepting Juvenal and Swift. Like the victims of their merciless pens, his, too, will be forgiven and forgotten. Today no one knows, nor cares, whether or not those long-dead offenders gave just offense. The grave has closed over accuser and accused, and the only thing that matters is that a great mind was permitted to function. One may smile or sigh over the satire, but one must also realize that even the satirist had his own weaknesses, and could have been as savagely attacked by a mentality as keen as his own. Men as a whole will never greatly care for satire, each recognizing, true enough, glimpses of himself in the invective, but sensing as well its fundamental bias and cruelty. However, Bierce thought best of himself as a satirist. (p. xlii)

[The] white flame of Art that he tended for nearly half a century was never permitted to grow faint nor smoky, and it burned to the last with a pure brilliance. (p. xlvi)

> *George Sterling, ''A Memoir of Ambrose Bierce,''*
> *in* The Letters of Ambrose Bierce *by Ambrose Bierce,*
> *The Book Club of California, 1922 (and reprinted*
> *by Gordian Press, 1967), pp. xxxiii-xlvii.*

SAMUEL LOVEMAN (essay date 1922)

In Bierce, the evocation of horror becomes for the first time, not so much the prescription or perversion of Poe and Maupassant, but an atmosphere definite and uncannily precise. Words, so simple that one would be prone to ascribe them to the limitations of a literary hack, take on an unholy horror, a new and unguessed transformation. In Poe one finds it a *tour de force,* in Maupassant a nervous engagement of the flagellated climax. To Bierce, simply and sincerely, diabolism held in its tormented depth, a legitimate and reliant means to the end. Yet a tacit confirmation with nature is in every instance insisted upon.

In **''The Death of Halpin Frayser'',** flowers, verdure and the boughs and leaves of trees are magnificently placed as an opposing foil to unnatural malignity. Not the accustomed golden world, but a world pervaded with the mystery of blue and the breathless recalcitrance of dreams, is Bierce's. Yet curiously, inhumanity is not altogether absent. Think of the episode of the deaf and dumb derelict at Chickamauga and the altogether lovable little Jo—Dickens done to life but with how much more consummate artistry. (p. 4)

> *Samuel Loveman, ''A Note,'' in* Twenty-One Letters
> of Ambrose Bierce *by Ambrose Bierce, edited by*
> *Samuel Loveman, George Kirk, 1922, pp. 3-5.*

VINCENT STARRETT (essay date 1923)

It seems likely that the enduring fame of the most remarkable man, in many ways, of his day, chiefly will be founded upon his stories of war—the blinding flashes of revelation and interpretation that make up the group under the laconic legend, **''Soldiers,''** in his greatest book, *In the Midst of Life.* In these are War, stripped of pageantry and glamor, stark in naked realism, terrible in grewsome fascination, yet of a sinister beauty. Specifically, it is the American Civil War that furnishes his characters and his texts, the great internecine conflict throughout which he gallantly fought; but it is War of which he writes, the hideous Thing.

Perhaps it is the attraction of repulsion that, again and again, leads one to these tales—although there is a record of a man who, having read them once, would not repeat the experiment—but it is that only in part. There is more than mere terror

in them; there is religion and poetry, and much of the traditional beauty of battle. Their author was both soldier and poet, and in the war stories of Ambrose Bierce, the horror and ugliness, the lure and loveliness of war are so blended that there seems no distinct line of demarcation; the dividing line is not a point or sign, but a penumbra. Over the whole broods an occult significance that transcends experience.

Outstanding, even in so collectively remarkable a group, are three stories, **''A Horseman in the Sky,'' ''A Son of the Gods,''** and **''Chickamauga.''** (pp. 48-9)

''A Horseman in the Sky'' is one of the most effective of his astonishing vignettes, and is given first place in the volume. It has one objection, an objection that applies to all terror, horror, and mystery tales; once read, the secret is out, and rereading cannot recapture the first *story* thrill. (pp. 51-2)

There is less of this *story* in **''A Son of the Gods,''** but as a shining glimpse of the tragic beauty of battle it is, I believe, unique; possibly it is Bierce's finest achievement in the art of *writing.* (p. 52)

In his more genuinely *horrible* vein, **''Chickamauga''** is unrivaled; a grotesquely shocking account of a deaf-mute child who, wandering from home, encounters in the woods a host of wounded soldiers hideously crawling from the battlefield, and thinks they are playing a game. Rebuffed by the jawless man, upon whose back he tries to ride, the child ultimately returns to his home, to find it burned and his mother slain and horribly mutilated by a shell. There is nothing occult in this story, but with others of its *genre,* it probes the very depths of material horror. (p. 54)

The tales of civilians, which make up the second half of Bierce's greatest book, are of a piece with his war stories. Probably nothing more weirdly awful has been conceived than such tales as **''A Watcher by the Dead,'' ''The Man and the Snake,''** and **''The Boarded Window,''** unless it be Stevenson's ''The Body Snatcher.'' The volume entitled *Can Such Things Be?* contains several similar stories, although, as a whole, it is apocryphal. In **''The Mocking Bird''** we find again the *motif* of **''A Horseman in the Sky;''** in **''The Death of Halpin Frayser''** there is a haunting detail and a grewsome imagery that suggest Poe, and in **''My Favorite Murder,''** one of the best tales Bierce ever wrote, there is a satirical whimsicality and a cynical brutality that make the tale an authentic masterpiece of *something*—perhaps humor! (pp. 55-6)

Bierce the satirist is seen in nearly all of his stories, but in *Fantastic Fables,* and *The Devil's Dictionary* we have satire bereft of romantic association, the keenest satire since Swift, glittering, bitter, venomous, but thoroughly honest. His thrusts are at and through the heart of sham. (p. 56)

The solemn absurdities of the law were Bierce's frequent target; thus, in his *Devil's Dictionary,* the definition of the phrase ''court fool'' is, laconically, ''the plaintiff.'' His biting wit is nowhere better evidenced than in this mocking lexicon. Bacchus, he conceives to be ''a convenient deity invented by the ancients as an excuse for getting drunk;'' and a Prelate is ''a church officer having a superior degree of holiness and a fat preferment. One of Heaven's aristocracy. A gentleman of God.'' More humorously, a Garter is ''an elastic band intended to keep a woman from coming out of her stockings and desolating the country.''

In the same key are his collected epigrams, in which we learn that ''woman would be more charming if one could fall into her arms without falling into her hands.''

With all forms of literary expreession, Bierce experimented successfully; but in verse his percentage of permanent contributions is smaller than in any other department. His output, while enormous, was for the most part ephemeral, and the wisdom of collecting even the least of his jingles may well be called into question. At least half of the hundreds of verses contained in the two volumes of his collected works given over to poetry, might have been left for collectors to discover and resurrect; and some delightful volumes of *juvenilia* and *ana* thus might have been posthumously achieved for him by the collecting fraternity. (pp. 57-8)

Happily, in the ocean of newspaper jingles and rhymed quips there is much excellent poetry. Kipling, by some, is asserted to have derived his "Recessional" from Bierce's **"Invocation,"** a noble and stately poem; and in **"The Passing Show,** "Finis Aeternitatis," and some of the sonnets we have poetry of a high order. Maugre, we have much excellent satire in many of his journalistic rhymes. Like Swift and Butler, and Pope and Byron, Bierce gibbeted a great many nobodies; but, as he himself remarked, "satire, like other arts, is its own excuse, and is not dependent for its interest on the personality of those who supply the occasion for it." If many of Bierce's **Black Beetles in Amber** seem flat, many too are as virile and keen as when they were written; and if he flayed men alive, just as certainly he raised the moral tone of the community he dominated in a manner the value of which is perhaps measureless.

The best example of poetry, however, left us by Bierce, *me judice,* is that great prose poem, **The Monk and the Hangman's Daughter**. . . . Saturated with the color and spirit of the mediaeval days it depicts, it is as authentic a classic as *Aucassin and Nicolette;* and its *denouement* is as terrible as it is beautiful. The strange story of Ambrosius the monk, and the outcast girl Benedicta, "the hangman's daughter," is one of the masterpieces of literature.

Ambrose Bierce was a great writer and a great man. He was a great master of English; but it is difficult to place him. He is possibly the most versatile genius in American letters. He is the equal of Stevenson in weird, shadowy effect, and in expression he is Stevenson's superior. Those who compare his work with that of Stephen Crane (in his war stories) have not read him understandingly. Crane was a fine and original genius, but he was, and is, the pupil where Bierce is Master. Bierce's "style" is simpler and less spasmodic than Crane's, and Bierce brought to his labor a first-hand knowledge of war, and an imagination even more terrible than that which gave us *The Red Badge of Courage*. The horrors of both men sometimes transcend artistic effect; but their works are enduring peace tracts.

It has been said that Bierce's stories are "formula," and in a measure it is true; but the formula is that of a master chemist, and it is inimitable. He set the pace for the throng of satirical fabulists who have since written; and his essays, of which nothing has been said, are powerful, of immense range, and of impeccable diction. His influence on the writers of his time, while unacknowledged, is wide. Rarely did he attempt anything sustained; his work is composed of keen, darting fragments. His only novel is a redaction. But who shall complain, when his fragments are so perfect? (pp. 58-61)

Vincent Starrett, "Ambrose Bierce," in his Buried Caesars: Essays in Literary Appreciation *(reprinted through permission of Michael Murphy, Literary Executor, Vincent Starrett), Covici-McGee Co., 1923, pp. 33-72.*

H. P. LOVECRAFT   (essay date 1927)

Bierce's work is in general somewhat uneven. Many of the stories are obviously mechanical, and marred by a jaunty and commonplacely artificial style derived from journalistic models; but the grim malevolence stalking through all of them is unmistakable, and several stand out as permanent mountain-peaks of American weird writing. (p. 385)

Bierce seldom realises the atmospheric possibilities of his themes as vividly as Poe; and much of his work contains a certain touch of naiveté, prosaic angularity, or early-American provincialism which contrasts somewhat with the efforts of later horror-masters. Nevertheless the genuineness and artistry of his dark intimations are always unmistakable, so that his greatness is in no danger of eclipse. (p. 387)

H. P. Lovecraft, "Supernatural Horror in Literature" (1927), in his Dagon and Other Macabre Tales, *edited by August Derleth (copyright 1965 by August Derleth; reprinted by permission of Arkham House Publishers, Inc.), Arkham House, 1965, pp. 347-413.**

H. L. MENCKEN   (essay date 1927)

Bierce, I believe, was the first writer of fiction ever to treat war realistically. He antedated even Zola. It is common to say that he came out of the Civil War with a deep and abiding loathing of slaughter—that he wrote his war stories in disillusion, and as a sort of pacifist. But this is certainly not believed by any one who knew him, as I did in his last years. What he got out of his services in the field was not a sentimental horror of it, but a cynical delight in it. It appeared to him as a sort of magnificent *reductio ad absurdum* of all romance. The world viewed war as something heroic, glorious, idealistic. Very well, he would show how sordid and filthy it was—how stupid, savage and degrading. But to say this is not to say that he disapproved it. On the contrary, he vastly enjoyed the chance its discussion gave him to set forth dramatically what he was always talking about and gloating over: the infinite imbecility of man. There was nothing of the milk of human kindness in old Ambrose; he did not get the nickname of Bitter Bierce for nothing. What delighted him most in this life was the spectacle of human cowardice and folly. He put man, intellectually, somewhere between the sheep and horned cattle, and as a hero somewhere below the rats. His war stories, even when they deal with the heroic, do not depict soldiers as heroes; they depict them as bewildered fools, doing things without sense, submitting to torture and outrage without resistance, dying at last like hogs in Chicago, the former literary capital of the United States. . . . Man to him, was the most stupid and ignoble of animals. But at the same time the most amusing. (pp. 260-61)

H. L. Mencken, "Ambrose Bierce," in his Prejudices, sixth series *(copyright 1927 by Alfred A. Knopf, Inc., renewed 1955 by H. L. Mencken; reprinted by permission of Alfred A. Knopf, Inc.), Octagon Books, 1927 (and reprinted by Alfred A. Knopf, Inc., 1977, pp. 259-65).*

GEORGE STERLING (essay date 1928)

"I am not a poet," Ambrose Bierce said more than once, with word of mouth and pen. In so saying, he meant to convey his knowledge that his satiric verse was not poetry; and yet he must have known that when he chose, as he infrequently did, to dip that pen in a diviner fluid, he could produce poems of no low order of merit. (p. ix)

Bierce's supreme poetic achievement is . . . the great poem . . . **"An Invocation."** And strange to say, that poem was one of occasion, written deliberately, to be read at a Fourth of July celebration in San Francisco!

Written deliberately, perhaps; for it is not easy to forget the theory of inspiration when one reads these majestic stanzas, strangely prophetic as well as nobly poetic. The poem ends on the note of hope, but well nigh drowning that note is the diapason of a dread that becomes yearly more justified, as one sees those hollows, worn by the feet of thieves, cut deeper and deeper into the foundations of the republic, sees too, how Mammon sits yearly more malignly entrenched among the sheaves, chuckling as the reapers mourn.

Like Kipling's famous "Recessional," **"An Invocation"** ends with an acknowledgment of a divine Power and an appeal to its mercy. That, in the case of Bierce, was less sincere than artistic. "God," he once wrote, "is to be used as a poetic property. It is necessary in poetry, as in life, to create Him, if He do not exist." And yet that cry,

> God of my country and my race,

rings with as apparent an assurance as any voice from the heart of Longfellow or Whittier, neither of whom came within leagues of anything so tremendous in its scope as this poem. Is one to believe, then, that the poetry of insincerity outranks the verse of conviction?

Bierce was often accused of misanthropy and lack of patriotism, and indeed he buffeted his fellows with immense gusto, and wrote that he did love his country,

> But 'tis infested of my countrymen!

Yet in a conversation with me he disclaimed both charges, saying that he loved his country and his fellowmen. One is constrained to accept that assertion, however much the evidence to the contrary in his work. And in **"An Invocation"** we have indeed literary proof that his heart went out to the land he fought so bravely to hold united. But he saw it saved, if saved it was to be, not by a vague and capricious Providence, but by the faith and devotion of its people. (pp. xii-xv)

George Sterling, in his introduction to An Invocation *by Ambrose Bierce, J. H. Nash, 1928, pp. ix-xvi.*

ARTHUR M. MILLER (essay date 1932)

In the last decade of the nineteenth century, when the short stories of Ambrose Bierce first appeared in book form, there developed the beginning of that body of critical opinion which yet persistently links the Bierce narratives of death and horror with the terror tales of Edgar Allan Poe. (p. 130)

Did Bierce adopt Poe's principles, as has been suggested, and, if so, where may the points of direct contact be found? Were there definite borrowings of story materials, incidents, or ideas? If so, what and where? (p. 133)

As regards bare plot mechanics, **"Beyond the Wall"** by Bierce has several points in common with "The Fall of the House of Usher."

"Beyond the Wall" opens, as does "Usher," with the visit of a man to the house of a boyhood friend whom he has not seen in many years. Careful attention is given to the description of the dwelling, an "ugly" one, situated in a desolate place. Its grounds were "destitute of either flowers or grass," but had three or four trees "writhing and moaning in the torment of the tempest." Altogether it was a "dismal environment," and one which made him shudder. Thus the beginning of the story seeks to establish a situation almost identical with the one in "The Fall of the House of Usher." Several of the words, such as "gloom," "shudder," and melancholy," are used also by Poe.

Continuing, there is a likeness in the description of the boyhood friend. He belongs to an ancient and illustrious family, and is scholarly and addicted to "the study of all manner of occult subjects"; he is prematurely aged and changed beyond the expectations of the visitor. According to Poe, he had a "ghastly pallor of the skin" and a "miraculous lustre of the eye." Bierce has it that his complexion was "dead-white," and that his eyes "glowed with a fire that was almost uncanny." In both stories he receives the visitor with more than ordinary hospitality, then proceeds to tell about the sad condition which he is in.

"Beyond the Wall" is a much slighter work than "The Fall of the House of Usher." Its incisive, unencumbered style provides a contrast to the thick embroidery and atmosphere wrought by Poe. Yet it seems that this difference is merely one of degree, and that Bierce must have begun with "Usher" in mind.

The plots just compared each typify a different kind of influence: (1) a studied use of Poe material, combined with a theme taken elsewhere, resulting in a powerful story being constructed; (2) a short incident closely following the plan of a Poe tale, imbedded in a longer narrative not otherwise Poe-esque; and (3) a romantic "echo," on general lines, at the beginning of a story.

The next group of comparisons deals with device.

An instance of both authors employing the same instrument to produce horror occurs in the use of a cat on the head of a corpse.

Poe's tale, "The Black Cat," tells of a man who, through perverseness, needlessly persecuted his former pet, a cat, and thereafter is beset with one misfortune after another. Finally, while he is aiming a blow at the feline offender, his wife interferes, and he buries the ax in her brain. He conceals her body behind a wall in the cellar. When the police come to investigate her disappearance, the mewing of the cat directs them to the hidden corpse. The cat, stained with carnage, is found perching on the head of the dead wife. In Bierce's **"John Mortonson's Funeral,"** the friends of the deceased are gathered about the coffin. The culmination of the scene comes when the distraught widow seeks to gaze upon the face of the dead through a glass plate in the casket. She falls back in a faint. Others look and do likewise. In the turmoil the glass is broken and a cat with a crimson muzzle crawls out.

In Poe's tale the cat serves both as a foil for the chief character's perverseness and as an appropriate symbol of terrible consequences incurred by him. Bierce waives all ethical considerations. He writes his story for the gruesome activities of the cat alone. In **"Granny Magone,"** another of his tales, a cat plays the key rôle. The cat eludes watchers by the body of a dead woman, and leaps upon its head. The hand of the dead, however, rises and hurls away the intruder. In this case, also, the cat on the head of the corpse is the realistic feature which makes the episode a sensational one. It colors the unnatural phenomenon.

Both Poe and Bierce employed perspective illusion as a device to evoke terror. Poe's story, "The Sphinx," is an exposé of the experiences of a man who sits before an open window and, seeing a tiny insect suspended on a spider's thread near at hand, mistakes it for a great monster on a distant hill. The story exploits the unnerving effect which the "inexplicable incident" had upon the man; he considered the vision "either as an omen of my death, or, worse, as the forerunner of an attack of mania."

When describing to the coroner's jury how he felt when he first saw the "unfamiliar and unaccountable phenomenon" of wild oats being pressed down as by an invisible force, the witness in **"The Damned Thing"** by Bierce recalled a strange experience which he had formerly had:

> . . .—that once in looking carelessly out of an open window I momentarily mistook a small tree close at hand for one of a group of larger trees at a little distance away. . . . It was a mere falsification of the law of aërial perspective, but it startled, almost terrified me. We so rely upon the orderly operation of familiar natural laws that any seeming suspension of them is noted as a menace to our safety, as warning of unthinkable calamity.

Perhaps this phenomenon has been employed more than a few times in literature. Still, it is sufficiently rare as a mere terror device to attract notice.

The field of supernatural phenomena is wide, yet even here it is possible to collate similarities.

Take, for example, the trick of making live persons invisible. The narrator in "MS. Found in a Bottle" by Poe is precipitated onto a mysterious ship on which his presence is not noticed, even though he mingles openly with the crew. Barr Lassiter, in Bierce's **"Three and One Are One,"** returns to his home to visit his parents and sister after being away in the war for two years. Everything is the same, but he cannot make himself visible to them. (pp. 142-45)

The foregoing examples of Bierce's use of device are, in the aggregate, highly significant. Their very close likeness to Poe materials, together with the fact of their frequency, discredits any explanation as to their accidental nature. Taken as a whole, they point towards the conclusion that Bierce did not hesitate to appropriate devices from Poe's stories to use in his own. (p. 146)

Bierce's estimate of Poe as a writer was extremely high, and . . . he accepted Poe's dicta on the novel almost verbatim, as he did, also, the pronouncements concerning the brief tale and the length of the poem. On other fundamental points of literary theory, such as realism, probability, and the use of coincidence, Bierce kept in close agreement; while in practice he incorporated plot fragments, devices, and ideas, once used by Poe, into his own writings on such a scale as to indicate that the works of the earlier writer must have served him well for source material and starting ideas.

It is true, however, that Bierce usually changed what he borrowed. He combined different themes with great effect, so that everything which left his hand exhibited characteristic Biercean qualities. It would seem that he placed the utmost importance on the style of a written piece and that, in his view, originality consisted in giving freshness and wit to any, perhaps an old, idea. More efficacious than any of these explanations, however, may be the suggestion that Bierce's literary standards were affected by the exigencies and necessities of newspaper work.

In any event, the influence of Poe on him is seen to be far-reaching. Having accepted Poe as the leading arbiter and expert in the field of the short story, he wrote after his leadership, and tired to excel him. Nor did he seem ever to question the entire adequacy of the other's story method. To Bierce there was only one "right" kind of fiction form, and Poe had invented it. (pp. 149-50)

> *Arthur M. Miller, "The Influence of Edgar Allan Poe on Ambrose Bierce," in* American Literature, *Vol. IV, No. 2, May, 1932, pp. 130-50.*

JAMES MILTON HIGHSMITH (essay date 1970)

The various satiric forms which Bierce explored in his journalism have not been appreciated as have his successful short stories, such as **"An Occurrence at Owl Creek Bridge,"** **"Chickamauga,"** and his other psychological and macabre productions that consciously opposed the smiling aspects of life presented by Miss Nancy Howells, as he called William Dean Howells. . . .

An examination of Bierce's forms of burlesque in *The Devil's Dictionary* offers a more reliable evaluation of his achievement than does his content. He never developed a system of thought, and he was capable of changing his attitudes with great facility from idealism to cynicism, from philanthropy to misanthropy. With time, furthermore, he ceased to hope that the world would take cognizance of his ideas, although he occasionally suggested ironical remedies for the American failure to perceive the genius of his satire. . . . Bierce, nevertheless, did not appear to be composing his burlesque for moral effects. Neither did he seem to have principally in mind the other usual reasons for creating satire—for the sake of fun alone; or for a means of criticizing contemporary romantic fiction in behalf of realism, as Walter Blair claims for the literary comedians; or as a means of learning literary craftsmanship by imitating acknowledged models, as Franklin Rogers states for Twain. Rather, Bierce's definitions suggest that he was interested in exploring the nature of the forms themselves and making them more functional in terms of the material at hand.

Bierce turned his attentions more and more toward form, with equal amounts of contumely for the public and courage for experimentation. Besides, for the modern writer with a conservative predisposition, form was the only avenue of creativity left. As Bierce expressed it, "Nothing new is to be learned in any of the great arts—the ancients looted the whole field. . . . originality strikes and dazzles only when displayed within the limiting lines of form." We are even reminded of Oscar Wilde's aestheticism by Bierce's claim, "In literature, as in all art, manner is everything and matter nothing; I mean that matter, however important, has nothing to do with the *art* of literature; that is a thing apart."

To develop and explore satiric forms, Bierce applied his experiences in journalism as well as his own cherished ideal of a witty and polished style. Writing for newspapers in London and in America trained him in succinctness and in arranging material for maximum clarity and effectiveness. Certainly such a background was congruent with his own preference for neoclassical wit and polish in style. Wit, he explained over and over in his essays, should replace humor in satire, for it has the distinct and incisive shape of a poniard and is not sentimental and amorphous: "Humor is tolerant, tender; its ridicule caresses. Wit stabs, begs pardon—and turns the weapon in the wound." He also viewed polish as prerequisite for literature, because the power of expression "is not a gift, but a gift and an accomplishment. It comes not altogether by nature, but is achieved by hard, technical study."

Because of his interest in the aesthetic nature of form, it is not surprising to find in his burlesque something other than a mere imitation of a vogue that had been in the air for at least half a century. The definitions in *The Devil's Dictionary* suggest, in fact, that our diabolical lexicographer may have aimed at refining satiric forms for American humor. Certainly we can see an effort to sharpen and differentiate the various forms of burlesque—mock-heroic, parody, Hudibrastic, and travesty. Many of the entries are, of course, the happy results of mixtures and are not pure examples of any single form.

Bierce's manipulation of burlesque indicates a passing familiarity with the historial development of traditional forms as well as an interest in adjusting them to his own personality and values. Although he was not the scholar of literature that he liked to imagine, he had been exposed to the European heritage of burlesque before initiating his own burlesque definitions. (pp. 116-17)

Since to some extent Bierce was writing within a historical tradition, it might not be amiss to approach his burlesque with the formal terms ordinarily applied to earlier achievements in burlesque.

What Bierce achieved with the four forms of burlesque (mock-heroic, parody, Hudibrastic, and travesty) can be clearly ascertained by comparing examples of them with his definitions that do not employ such forms, as the long and amorphous essay defining INADMISSABLE, or even the quatrain defining DEAD:

> Done with the work of breathing; done
> With all the world; the mad race run
> Through to the end; the golden goal
> Attained and found to be a hole!

Here there is no imitation of high (or even low) matter or manner, no satiric incongruity between content and form. There is merely unabated, metrical cynicism, and the final effect of the definition is unimpressive.

But when we come to his entries that show a manipulation of burlesque forms, what a different result! Here, we feel, is a satirist who, with great aplomb, has created definitions distinctively his own.

Bierce enjoyed all four forms of burlesque. As might be expected, he was especially effective with high burlesque, since its emphasis on style was congenial to his ideas of wit and polish. To create mock-heroic definitions, he did not draw on the epic machinery of Homer or Vergil. *His* culture came to a focus in the panegyric, the polemic, the evangelical harangue, and even the epitaph. Such forms, as bombastic as epics some-

times are, were for Bierce deplorable modern attempts to fashion forms that would emulate the serious and significant achievements of the ancients. But in effect, such attempts merely acknowledge the general diminution of the grand in modern times.

The devil would indeed be pleased with the mock-heroic definition of ABDOMEN, which treats this organ in the incongruously high manner of a panegyric:

> The temple of the god Stomach, in whose worship, with sacrificial rights [*sic*], all true men engage. From women this ancient faith commands but a stammering assent. They sometimes minister at the altar in a half-hearted and ineffective way, but true reverence for the one deity that men really adore they know not. . . .

By his ironical sublimation of a purely physical matter, our lexicographer reminds us of how arbitrarily we elevate and define our values and beliefs, which are often in reality not so sublime after all. By the definition's implications, actual gluttony is contrasted with pretended sacrosancity, but the cynicism implied does not disturb us, because of our pleasure with the exaggerated and ironical laudation of the "rights." (pp. 117-18)

Other definitions that might be thought of as mock-heroic satirize the general style of the polemic while never imitating a specific model as would parody. In such definitions as FLY-SPECK, K, and ZENITH, Bierce condemned the whole tribe of scholars by imitating their serious, elaborate, and monotonous style. Apparently, he considered scholarly polemics to be deplorably recognizable by classifications (such as of the forms of burlesque), analogies, digressions, Latinate terms (e.g., *Musca Maledicta* for house-fly in FLY-SPECK), acknowledgments to sources and to etymologies and to other scholars and their hypotheses, and, above all, a pedantic objectivity. The point of the satire is usually the contrast between the form of the polemic and its inconsequential or ridiculous subject matter. (pp. 118-19)

Besides his mock-heroic treatments of panegyrics, polemics, and evangelical harangues, we may include even his ironical epitaphs as exemplifying those definitions whose high and serious forms offer satiric contrast with low content. In such definitions as EPITAPH, PIE, and CEMETERY, we find a variety of rhyme and meter for what Bierce's civilization has often considered a noble form of expression. . . .

Bierce, like other San Franciscans, was especially prolific with parodies, which also capitalize on the effect of a contrast of a grand style with a trivial content. But these forms are less general than those of the mock-heroic. Not a genre but a *particular* author's work or work's style is imitated in a parody, and the reader is expected to recognize satiric adumbrations of the original. As David Worcester explains it, "we do not find a parody printed side by side with its original. It is the reader's part to supply knowledge of the model. He must hold up the model, and the author will furnish him with a distorted reflection of it." . . . Like the parodies by other San Franciscans, those by Bierce often indicate an awareness of English or European models. But he never seemed to consider his parodies a matter of apprenticeship to the styles of the masters, as perhaps Twain and Bret Harte came to view their burlesques of novels. When Bierce created a parody, it had the air of being a true historical judgment or even an act of justice on a so-called masterpiece, though under the guise of irony. Fortunately, this self-seriousness does not impede the *esprit* of *The Devil's Dictionary,* which is itself a parody of Webster's dictionary and reflects a rather general interest in words and word-making at this point of American literary culture. (p. 120)

In Bierce's definiton of FEMALE he employed a Hudibrastic doggerel of unremitting iambic tetrameter that whisks us, not along a narrative line, but through little dramatic vignettes, the general treatment of which adds little credit to the idea of femininity. And at the same time the rhyming couplets outrageously juxtapose objects and ideas that are normally unassociated with each other but which might be paradoxically related, such as snails and males, advice and dice, strife and wife. . . . (p. 122)

An implied similarity between a degrading or jocular treatment and a subject inherently noble is characteristic of travesty, though here the subject is more particular (specific authors, people, books) and not as general as *females* or *human wisdom*. In his satiric thrusts Bierce was not above deflating names revered in the history of Western culture. . . . (p. 124)

For the subjects of his travesties, Bierce did not rest with particular figures of myth and cultural history. He was apt at zeroing in on his own renowned contemporaries, whom he loved to depict in unbecoming and inconsistent postures. Choosing one's contemporaries may limit the effectiveness of a travesty, of course, if their significance becomes obscured with time. But Bierce's subjects usually had the prestige (whether actual or self-imagined) that made them fit targets for satiric assault. (p. 125)

Whether he was treating a high subject ignominiously or a low subject grandly, Bierce was aware of the importance of form, its wit and polish. . . . If he was diabolical, it was in the sense of Blake's devil, who did not rest with the establishment and its dictates. Bitterness and cynicism are certainly present, but with what diabolical pleasure we other devils enjoy the style! Perhaps it is time, then, to recognize, the *The Devil's Dictionary*'s experimentation with the forms of burlesque, a contribution to American Letters. As Bierce claimed in his definition of Dictionary, *his* lexicon is a most useful work. (p. 126)

> *James Milton Highsmith, "The Forms of Burlesque in 'The Devil's Dictionary'," in* Satire Newsletter, *Vol. VII, No. 2, Spring, 1970, pp. 115-27.*

ROBERT C. McLEAN   (essay date 1974)

["**The Death of Halpin Frayser**"] is most frequently viewed as a traditional Gothic tale, expressing a sense of the occult and the supernatural. The epigraph (purportedly written by a sage named Hali) suggests the possibility that zombies walk the earth, and it reinforces the impression that Halpin Frayser is brutally and senselessly garroted by an agent from another world. Yet in his flat, matter-of-fact prose, Bierce unobtrusively presents an intelligible pattern of clues to suggest that the murder of the titular hero is coldly calculated and executed by his father. In short, Bierce provides the basis for a rational, psychological explanation of events without destroying the supernatural quality of the story. "**Halpin Frayser**" is therefore in the mainstream of the distinctly American or ambiguous Gothic, a mode practiced by Charles Brockden Brown, Poe, Hawthorne, and James. Just as these writers present apparently supernatural events at the same time that they provide other evidence to explain them rationally, so does Bierce exploit strange and terrifying occurrences and Gothic decor—mysti-

fying fog, ruined buildings, decayed gravemarkers, and soulless corpses—to invoke an aura of the spectral while concurrently providing documentation for an alternative, rational reading.

Although critics of "**Halpin Frayser**" recognize its complexity, they deny the intentionally ambiguous quality of the tale. Consequently they ignore any realistic solution for the apparently supernatural horrors that occur. (pp. 394-95)

Although Bierce's tale certainly explores the Oedipal guilt of Halpin Frayser and demonstrates contempt for the limited human abilities to reason, its major interest lies in its fair but limited human abilities to reason, its major interest lies in its fair but practiced deception upon the reader concerning the baffling circumstances surrounding the violent deaths of Halpin Frayser and his mother, Catherine Frayser/Larue. Bierce has been so successful in his deception that critics have failed to perceive properly the relationships among the characters or to identify correctly those guilty of murder.

The complexity of the tone and structure of "**Halpin Frayser**" exacts strict attention from the reader. It requires him to observe carefully shifts in points of view and to distinguish between fact and inference, the rational and the irrational. Moreover, though he must decipher the last, fourth section of the story before coming to terms with the other three, he must retain a large number of facts from those early sections in order to comprehend what is documented in section 4. Sections 1 and 3 explore Halpin Frayser's consciousness just before his strangulation upon a grave later revealed to be his murdered mother's. Because these two portions reflect the subjective impressions of a disordered brain in deep sleep and nightmare, the reader gains a vivid portrait of Halpin Frayser's fears and anxieties, but nothing that he can rely upon as objective fact. Section 2 is presented as a flashback and provides all the information given concerning Frayser's life before he left Tennessee for California and was "shanghaied" to an island in the Pacific for six years. Here Bierce employs a conventional omniscient narrator, but one who raises rather than explains questions about family tensions. Section 4 reports the discovery of Halpin Frayser's body by Holker, a deputy sheriff from Napa, and Jaralson, a detective from San Francisco, in the course of their supposed attempt to locate and capture an insane murderer. The evidence, clearly objective, is presented for the most part in dialogue between the two sleuths. Since the details are accurate, the reader is faced with the burden of interpreting the significance of what is described or recorded and making it coherent with the evidence presented in the other three sections. (pp. 395-96)

Although Bierce's description of the murder [in section 4], distilled through the consciousness of the distraught victim, invites a psychological interpretation, there is clear evidence that the strangler is a human being with palpable physical strength. Seeing what appears to be an "apparition . . . regarding him with the mindless malevolence of a wild brute," Halpin Frayser is "spellbound." But he realizes that "such fancies are in dreams" and he "regain[s] his identity almost as if by a leap forward into his body, and the straining automaton had a directing will as alert and fierce as that of its hideous antagonist." . . . The description of the body viewed by the officers of the law testifies that Frayser's brutal murder is not committed by a phantom of the mind:

> All about were evidences of a furious struggle; small sprouts of poison oak were bent and de-

nuded of leaf and bark; dead and rotting leaves had been pushed into heaps and ridges on both sides of the legs by the action of other feet than theirs; alongside the hips were unmistakable impressions of human knees.

(p. 397)

A logical explanation exists, one that relies not on supernatural events, incredible coincidence, or psychological specters, but on information drawn from all four sections of the story: Halpin Frayser is followed to California by his mother, and the two live together for a time in incestuous union under the pseudonym of Larue; ultimately, in guilt and revulsion, he slays her. Jaralson, in reality Halpin Frayser's father and the living husband of Katy Larue, first stalks then strangles his son in vengeance. He brings Holker to view the body in order to provide himself with an alibi and to direct the blame toward the supposedly unapprehended slayer of Katy Larue. (pp. 397-98)

Perhaps the "awakening word"—"Catherine Larue"—which calls Halpin Frayser from his "dreamless sleep" is uttered by the father-killer to arouse his son's guilt before throttling him. In any event, Halpin Frayser repeats the name, which triggers a nightmare involving sex, sin, and death. It is a name he "had not in memory," but it is also one he "*Hardly had in mind*" . . .—in other words, a name he represses from consciousness but cannot eradicate from the recesses of his mind. The dream he falls into is a powerful representation of a sinner's inadvertent revelation of guilt, fear of punishment, and futile protestation of innocence. (pp. 399-400)

Halpin Frayser's guilt is associated in his terrifying dream with the creation of poetry and therefore with his incestuous relationship with his mother. He is impelled to fabricate the writing of verse, which symbolically calls up the revered work of his great-grandfather Bayne and—climactically—the image of his murdered mother: "he found himself staring into the sharply drawn face and blank, dead eyes of his own mother, standing white and silent in the garments of the grave!" . . . Awakened by the presence of an avenging father, Halpin Frayser, still in thrall to the fear of his mother's eternal vengeance, sees his punishment as fated but to be resisted. But all defiance is futile, "wasted in a void." Just as he dies, there comes "a sharp, far cry signing all to silence." . . . (pp. 400-01)

Jaralson's complicated involvement must be established by careful inference. Ostensibly he has sought the killer, like Holker, for a five-hundred-dollar reward. But, though Jaralson tries to conceal his real motive of revenge, he inadvertently reveals his culpability. In recalling the name of the man who murdered his wife, Holker mentions that the victim was a widow and evokes from Jaralson an indication of guilt. "She had come to California to look up some relatives," Holker recalls; "there are persons who will do that sometimes. But you know all that." Jaralson's brief, enigmatic reply—"Naturally" . . .— testifies to his maniacal delight in having avenged his son's dishonor to family and reputation and suggests that Holker, his acquaintance of several years, knows that Jaralson too has come to California "to look up some relatives." As though relishing his dual role as enforcer of public and family law, Jaralson tacitly agrees that he wants Holker's aid in bringing to justice "one of the corpses in the graveyard." . . . And he must have in mind family lore that his wife's grandfather was a mad poet who "had revisited the glimpses of the moon" . . . when he tells Holker that "not another soul knows that [the killer of Catherine Larue] is this side of the Mountains of the Moon." . . . (p. 401)

Holker finds Halpin Frayser's signed pocketbook, and Jaralson again almost overreaches himself as he identifies the poem in it as being "like Bayne." . . . For "it was observable that . . . . [a] Frayser who was not the proud possessor of a sumptuous copy of the ancestral 'poetic works' (printed at the family expense, and long ago withdrawn from an inhospitable market) was a rare Frayser indeed. . . ." . . . Though Jaralson is "something of a scholar in his way," his recognition of the poem as sounding "like Bayne" and his arrogant admission of owning—as only a Frayser would—"the collected works" . . . , along with corroborative evidence, clearly identify him as a Frayser and the logical candidate for the murderer of Halpin Frayser.

At the close of the tale, Holker, reading the name on the fallen headboard, almost puts the facts together; he recalls that the murdered Catherine Larue once bore the same surname as the slain Halpin Frayser, thus all but connecting the victims-victimizers as at once Fraysers and Larues. The implications of Holker's near miss reverberate throughout the tale, bestowing ironic dimension to Holker's earlier guess that Jaralson's purpose is to "arrest one of the corpses in the graveyard" . . . , to Jaralson's assessment of the crime as "the work of a maniac" . . . , and to his current comment, "There is some rascally mystery here, . . . I hate anything of that kind." . . . Then, growing out of silence and dying away into it as the story ends, comes Bierce's "low deliberate laugh" . . . , disdaining mankind for its gullibility as well as its barbarity. (p. 402)

Robert C. McLean, "The Deaths in Ambrose Bierce's 'Halpin Frayser'," in Papers on Language and Literature *(copyright © 1974 by the Board of Trustees, Southern Illinois University at Edwardsville), Vol. 10, No. 4, Fall, 1974, pp. 394-402.*

PHILIP M. RUBENS   (essay date 1978)

Though there have been many attempts to place Ambrose Bierce's work into a variety of categories, one of the most persistent aspects of scholarship and criticism is its uniform insistence that he is somehow a gothic writer. . . .

In fact, it is possible to find many of the traditional gothic devices throughout his works that have a distinctive Biercian quality. [To] accomplish such an end, it will be necessary to isolate and describe those elements of Bierce's work that have a distinctive gothic quality. These elements include narrative technique, supernatural agents, setting and characterization, and the curse. . . .

Through his narrative style, Bierce extends the protagonist's quandary into the reader's mind. This style, like that of many other gothic works, at first seems loose and sprawling; in fact, it typically involves narratives within narratives. However, Bierce's abrupt transitions, discursive presentation of events, and reliance on psychological time typify three important methods he utilizes to achieve his objective of direct reader involvement. Bierce views the use of these techniques in terms of the "parted clew." . . . By offering evidence from several viewpoints and by altering time, he creates a conundrum saturated with clues the receptive reader can employ to unravel the *outré* events of the tale. In "**An Occurrence at Owl Creek Bridge,**" for instance, Bierce alters the times sequence from present to past to future to present to establish the confused nature of the protagonist's mind. He also uses Henri Bergson's ideas of durée to establish the psychic quality of this experience. That is certain aspects of the phenomenal world force the protagonist into an interior world where he attempts to create a temporary order. This is evident in his observations on the physical environment immediately before his hanging and the relation of such observations to the hallucinations he has in the seconds before death.

The inability to separate the idealistic dreams of life from its harsh reality creates an impassable barrier for Bierce and prompts his interest in the world of dreams and imagination as a gothic medium. This concept allows him to produce landscapes where spectres do, in fact, exist: a fictional locale generated by repressed fears and guilts struggling into consciousness. It is the active nature of Bierce's ghosts that represents a marked departure from his predecessors. Most gothic spirits are characterized as pallid and helpless; they generally appear only to foretell a catastrophe, harass a guilty conscience, or request burial. Unlike Bierce's spectres, they are usually not so much characters as props and contribute little more to the gothic atmosphere than their general surroundings. In Bierce's tales, however, the ghost can often become the principal agent of retribution and actively, violently, and cruelly wreaks vengeance by physical means; such spectres strangle, shoot, and occasionally frighten their victims to death. His definition of ghosts as the "outward and visible sign of an inward fear" . . . aptly summarizes his interest in these phenomena. (p. 29)

Although Bierce's characters are trapped in a gothic world of horror and terror, their reactions are based upon the exaggeration of normal emotions. This response heightens the protagonists' sensibilities and makes them almost preternaturally observant. In keeping with the silence of the Biercian setting, these figures remain remarkably inarticulate; they expire without a whimper to forces elicited from their own subconscious, and their very silence comments on man's inability to understand such powers. Whether inextricably trapped in a collapsed building or bound by duty to face a dead man, the Biercian protagonist vacillates between hope and despair. Unable to comprehend his situation, he begins to examine his own emotions and abdicates to cowardice, fear, and finally death. Facing an unusual crisis and possessing an inordinate attitude toward courage, pride, or reason, he dies an ignoble death at the hands of his own imagination. In short, Bierce's characterization depends on the creation of solitary figures whose eminently rational nature forces them to ignore even the remotest possibility of a supernatural realm. . . .

Heredity is an extremely important as well as vexing topic for Bierce. He assiduously studied theories about heredity and wrote his own evaluations with great frequency. From such statements, it can be gathered that Bierce sees heredity in terms of a controlling influence; in fact, he writes of it as though it is deterministic or even worse, a manifestation of what one might call the gothic curse. For Bierce one thing is certain: the sins of the fathers *are* visited on their children. . . . From the storehouse of heredity, perhaps a collective unconscious would work just as well; Bierce's characters receive intimations of a hidden past that contains the possibility of the genuinely active supernatural in men's daily affairs. Yet, these characters cannot comprehend the import of such suggestions, or they simply and violently assert their incredulity about such phenomena. The complexity of Bierce's protagonist's response is always based on reason, but that intellectual basis continually is undercut by the emotional and imaginative. Bierce's characters refuse to admit that hereditary influences can have any effect on their lives; this stance forces them to undergo the rigors of a numinous experience. (p. 30)

The unique qualities of the Biercian gothic, then, are found first in his narrative technique. By the use of parted clues, by employing multiple narratives, and by the manipulation of time, Bierce attempts to actively and emotionally involve the reader in the terror his characters experience. His use of dreams and ghosts demonstrates both his preference for the "realm of the unreal" and an interest in a deeper psychology. Setting, regardless of its spatial nature, becomes a means of isolating man in order to expose him to supernatural intervention—real or imagined. Finally, Bierce's treatment of character is unique in that it clearly demonstrates his concern for the role of the past—psychological or phenomenal—on the lives of men. His ultimate concern—the fulfillment of his obligation as a writer by informing all men that the past with its repressed fears and guilts, waits patiently to assail their reason and emotion—demonstrates an abiding interest in the psychological aspects of human nature, the proper domain of the Biercian gothic. (pp. 30-1)

> *Philip M. Rubens, "The Gothic Foundations of Ambrose Bierce's Fiction," in* Nyctalops *(copyright © 1978 by Harry O. Morris, Jr. and Edward P. Berglund; reprinted by permission of Philip M. Rubens), Vol. 2, No. 7, 1978, pp. 29-31.*

DONALD SIDNEY-FRYER (essay date 1979)

When we consider that [Bierce's] published verse must total somewhere around eight hundred pieces in all, and that this total represents around one fifth or one sixth of his over-all literary output (as assembled in his *Collected Works*), we have ample assurance that Bierce must have placed some value on his verse, whatever he may have said or written to the contrary. Today much of it seems little more than competent versifying, generally light in character and (more often than not) of a satirical nature, attacking the fads, foibles, and personalities of Bierce's day. His best poems lie embedded in a mass of typically Biercean satire in verse mainly apropos of persons who were once celebrities of the West Coast but who are now nonentities except to the specialist in Californian history and literature. Read infrequently and at the rate of a few pieces at a time, this satirical verse is apt and amusing; but read in a large quantity, it rapidly becomes tiresome, if not downright unbearable.

But a modicum remains of real poetry, compact, imaginative, and powerful; or—quite unexpectedly—tender with a tenderness not usually associated with one who has on occasion been called "The Devil's Lexicographer." (p. 10)

[On] the basis of his best poems Bierce clearly merits the attention of the discriminating lover and student of poetry.

In the tradition of Edgar Allan Poe, the American and now largely underground school of "pure poetry" has been peculiarly associated with Bierce, directly or indirectly. In form and in language he was a traditionalist, a purist of the most rigid kind; in this we may perhaps see something of an all-pervading life-attitude that he gained from his military experience during the Civil War. In his critical theories he was above all else a proponent of *la poésie pure*. And much of his taste and preference in verse may be gauged from the fact that he considered Coleridge's "Kubla Khan" the most nearly perfect poem in the English language. (p. 11)

It would be pleasant but scarcely accurate to claim for his best poetry a spectacular originality. While a good proportion of his output in verse—considered as poetry—may seem "negligible'' and even ''trivial'' as some critics have maintained, yet his best is neither, and well rewards sympathetic attention. At this best Bierce as a poet is, beneath a seemingly conventional exterior, very much his own man. (pp. 18-19)

Usually personal, Bierce's ''sentimental'' poems, evidently written during the apogée of late Victorian times, are singularly unsentimental, and refreshingly simple and direct statements of emotion. His love sonnets in particular may come as a surprise to the reader acquainted primarily with Bierce's pungent satire or with his unforgettable supernatural stories. His best serious poetry is largely to be found in *Shapes of Clay*. Apart from a handful of pieces, *Black Beetles in Amber* contains only satirical or humorous verse. The weary reader discovers the few serious poems in the latter collection almost with a sense of relief. However, even his satirical pieces considered collectively, too often like so many peas in a pod both in language and in substance, do not appear unfavorably against the background of late Victorian and of Edwardian poetry, but rather as agreeably nasty cast-iron thorns in the Victorian rose-garden. (p. 19)

''Invocation'' remains one of the best things of its kind, and far more than a mere *pièce d'occasion,* a mere piece of facile chauvinism made to order. Although not quite a hundred years have now passed since ''Invocation'' was first proclaimed, most of Bierce's thoughts on the good and evil possibilities inherent in liberty still hold true. The reader will note that the God that Bierce posits in his apostrophe (see particularly quatrains 10 through 25) is not the compassionate deity presented in the New Testament.

Moreover, the reader should not construe from these references to a conventional divinity (as well as from those in other poems) that Bierce was in any sense a strict religionist. Although highly moral—even puritanical—in his own lifestyle, he was of course very much of a freethinker. As he once wittily remarked in a letter to poet-pupil George Sterling, God ranked in the sphere of poetic reference as one of the most useful items (or ''properties'') from the poet's given repertoire of tropes. If God had not already existed as a reality, or merely as a figure of speech, then the poets would have been obliged to have invented Him out of sheer necessity.

Many critics have considered ''Invocation'' to be Bierce's greatest poem; actually it is not; such an honor should probably go to the tercet ''Creation,'' that little masterpiece of boldness and compression. Nonetheless, ''Invocation'' does contain a number of magnificent and nominally great passages. (p. 20)

In the twenty-two tercets of ''Basilica,'' Bierce relates and develops a comparatively simple story in terms of highly colored and often macabre imagery in the manner of Keats, Coleridge, or Poe. The poet or narrator is walking along the seashore and sees in the midst of some rocks what appears to be a radiant gem but which resolves itself into a weirdly shining cockatrice when the poet essays to grasp it. Thus, Nature or Life leads us ever onward with her external shows of beauty but when we try to plumb the mystery of loveliness we find only evil and corruption. The imagery is notable for its lurid imaginativeness: ''The groaning sea, wind-smitten white'' / ''ocean's leprous agony'' / ''A glinting gem with lustrous sheen'' / ''An opal chalice brimming gold'' / ''dim with amber-tined air'' / ''Gem-tinct with gleams of prismic ice.'' The fulsome description of the basilisk is not without a certain effectiveness. . . . (pp. 22-3)

This type of vividly colored imagery descends in part from Poe and in part from the English Romantics and, before them and

singularly influencing them, from Edmund Spenser and the concentrated, brilliantly hued, and highly symbolic imagery of ''The Faerie Queene''; and it anticipates the characteristic, Late Romantic imagery of both [George] Sterling and [Clark] Ashton Smith. Not only is Bierce's imagery in **''Basilica''** concentrated but the poem itself is a concentration of such imagery developed on the foundation of a simple narrative. Since he considered imagery to be the heart, the soul, the essence of poetry—to him the imagery *was* the poetry—then in theory a poem successfully constructed along these lines would be the most poetic possible, that is, the most imaginative. (pp. 23-4)

In vision, in theory, and nominally in accomplishment, Bierce had prepared the way for both later poets through his essays and through his best poems.

As among his best and briefest poems we should consider the excellent and highly imaginative titles Bierce chose for his two volumes: *Shapes of Clay* and *Black Beetles in Amber*. Indeed, much of the best of his invention and mordant wit is to be found in his titles. For example, an early prose collection has the vivid and poetic title *Cobwebs from an Empty Skull*. For another example, **''To Dog,''** constructed on the analogy of ''To Man'' (Bierce apparently detested dogkind as much as he did mankind). For yet a further example, **''Oneiromancy''** which, in terms of the love poem it entitles, signifies not only divination through dreams but also ''O Near Romance, See.''

Exclusive perhaps of the two early pieces which are nonetheless effective, the poems in this selection reveal Bierce as an adroit and facile versifier. He is a master of the run-over line. His handling of rime, metre, consonance, assonance, etc., is assured and often ingenious. He is able to make his poetic statement move through difficult and demanding traditional forms with singular ease. He sometimes achieves some of his best effects—effects of power or of grim humor—simply through his punctuation: **''Creation''** in particular furnishes a good example of this. Although his diction may seem somewhat old-fashioned today, and perhaps over-all somewhat conventional, it also possesses here and there subtle little touches of originality. He has a good ear for colloquial speech, and he has a good eye for the unexpected and homely detail, as well as a good instinct for the unexpected and homely resolution, usually presented at the end of a given poem in sharp contrast to what has preceded it. In many of his pieces both satirical and personal, he has anticipated the modern poetic temper at once ironical and colloquial. Although **''Invocation''** shows him as a master of the grand manner and the solemn ''tense'' or tone (a manner and a tone with which much of present-day taste appears to have little sympathy), in most of his poems he simply uses his own conversational style, anticipating the same in contemporary modes of poetic expression. Perhaps not in terms of versification, but at least in terms of ''a vision of doom,'' Bierce is quite a modern poet. (pp. 25-6)

While there is less of the sardonic and often grimly playful sense of imagination in his verse over-all than what we find in his best and most characteristic prose fictions; yet many, if not most, of Bierce's best poems are unusually fantastic and macabre. Even those poems not overtly macabre Bierce seems to have written in the Valley of the Shadow of Death. The grim presence of Death stalks through most of his personal poems, even his love sonnets and other pieces. Bierce's verse at its best is austere, even angular, with an almost provincial sparseness; rather like a corpse whose bones have been clean-picked by some thoughtful scavenger. As always, there is something harsh and unyielding, and even cold, about Bierce and his best work; a quality well-summarized by the contemporary science-fiction author Fritz Leiber in his phrase "Bierce, the Man with the Phallus of Ice."

For all of Bierce's own personal preference for a rich Spenserian or Shakespearian imagery in the poems of other poets—for the overflowing purple and gold of *The Arabian Nights*—the reader will find little such in Bierce's own poetic works. Instead, he will discover something different, an unique savor not found quite anywhere else. While we must agree with H. P. Lovecraft, speaking of Bierce in the monumental essay *Supernatural Horror in Literature,* that "the bulk of his artistic reputation must rest upon his grim and savage short stories," his best verse clearly deserves more attention and appreciation than what it has received to date. (p. 28)

> *Donald Sidney-Fryer, "A Visionary of Doom" (1979), in* A Vision of Doom: Poems by Ambrose Bierce, *edited by Donald Sidney-Fryer (copyright © 1980 by Donald Sidney-Fryer), Donald M. Grant, 1980, pp. 9-32.*

DAVID PUNTER (essay date 1980)

It has been pointed out that of the sixty-eight short stories Bierce wrote, only two are not to do with death, and the kinds of death which form focal points of action run the gamut of violence and terror. On the strength of these stories he was hailed, somewhat prematurely, as the new Poe, but although Poe was clearly a pronounced influence, there are vital differences of emphasis and tone. Chiefly, what Bierce has in common with Poe is an economy. In his role as literary critic he consistently sneered at the novel, claiming it to be a temporary eccentricity of literary history, incapable of the intensity and compression which were the virtues of the short story, and as a writer his greatest skill lies in paring his story down to the bare and grisly bones, an 'un-fleshing' to reveal the skull beneath the skin. Yet even there, where economy and brevity in Poe are generally supplemented by a momentary but intense involvement with the psychological state of the protagonist, Bierce gives his reader almost nothing to compensate for the absence of developed character. As a writer his stance is brutal: this, he implicitly says, is what occurred, in all its nastiness. It carries no particular significance, and even if it had, the realisation would have come too late for the protagonist. (pp. 268-69)

The very fact of Bierce's refusal of 'character' intensifies the tragic moment by universalising the experience. It seems, in fact, to be the case that Bierce's style produces a situation in which, since so many of the accustomed markers of realism are missing anyway, there is no difference in texture between dream and reality; since life is itself spread so thinly, only the moment of death can give us confrontation with the significant. (p. 271)

In a style of military precision Bierce metes out to his readers Old Testament prophecies and warnings of doom, a doom which is nonetheless unavoidable because it is laid down in advance. It is partly this tone of peremptory and irritable warning which causes the 'familiar fascistic ring' of which Edmund Wilson speaks, and it is also partly Bierce's assumption of an aristocratic role in relation to his audience. His literary and cultural tastes looked back to the English eighteenth century, which he saw as a time of order and stability which nevertheless permitted a controlled benevolence based on an awareness of social and intellectual distinction; he saw this as the best that could be achieved to palliate the terror of mortality. His combination of Puritan and military morality is responsible for the form of his more complex stories, in which deliberate difficulties are set in the path of understanding: **'The Suitable Surroundings'** is virtually narrated backwards; **'The Night-Doings at "Deadman's"'** announces its mockery of the reader in its subtitle, 'A Story That is Untrue'. Life for Bierce was a 'sickness unto death', but this perception permitted of no defiant grandeur, merely a stoical mixture of acceptance and resentment, a knowledge that the shock of realising truth would kill, but that this does not matter, because such realisation can in any case only come at the very point of predestined death. (pp. 274-75)

> *David Punter, "Later American Gothic: Ambrose Bierce, Robert W. Chambers, H. P. Lovecraft," in his* The Literature of Terror: A History of Gothic Fictions from 1765 to the Present Day *(© 1980 Longman Group Limited), Longman, 1980, pp. 268-90.**

ADDITIONAL BIBLIOGRAPHY

Cooper, Frederick Taber. "Ambrose Bierce." In his *Some American Story Tellers,* pp. 331-53. New York: Henry Holt and Co., 1911.
  Praises Bierce's technique in the short stories while deprecating his choice of subject as having "too much the flavor of the hospital and the morgue."

De Castro, Adolphe [pseudonym of Gustav Adolph Danziger]. *Portrait of Ambrose Bierce.* New York, London: The Century Co., 1929, 351 p.
  Among the less reliable biographies. The author was Bierce's "collaborator" on *The Monk and the Hangman's Daughter.*

Fatout, Paul. *Ambrose Bierce: The Devil's Lexicographer.* Norman: University of Oklahoma Press, 1951, 349 p.
  Comprehensive biography.

Grenander, M.E. *Ambrose Bierce.* New York: Twayne Publishers, 1971, 193 p.
  Bio-critical study that employs primary sources for biographical information to avoid the misinformation of previous biographies.

McWilliams, Carey. *Ambrose Bierce: A Biography.* New York: Albert & Charles Boni, 1929, 358 p.
  Early biography with a chapter devoted to criticism of the short stories.

Monaghan, Frank. "Ambrose Bierce and the Authorship of *The Monk and the Hangman's Daughter.*" *American Literature* II, No. 4 (January 1931): 337-49.
  Examines the question of authorship of this book, comparing Bierce's version to the original by Richard Voss and finding Bierce's little more than a literal translation.

O'Connor, Richard. *Ambrose Bierce: A Biography.* Boston, Toronto: Little, Brown and Co., 1967, 333 p.
  Popular biography that perpetuates some misinformation concerning Bierce's personal life and literary career.

Roth, Russell. "Ambrose Bierce's 'Detestable Creature'." *Western American Literature* 9, No. 3 (November 1974): 169-76.
  Biographical reading of "Killed at Resaca."

Snell, George. "Poe Redivivus." *Arizona Quarterly* 1, No. 2 (1945): 49-57.
  Comparative study of Bierce and Lafcadio Hearn as minor writers in the tradition of Poe.

Bjørnstjerne (Martinius) Bjørnson

1832-1910

Norwegian dramatist, novelist, novella writer, poet, journalist, and editor.

Bjørnson was the leading literary and political voice of late nineteenth-century Norway and the first Scandinavian to receive the Nobel Prize in literature. Intensely patriotic and unfailingly optimistic, Bjørnson, to the Norwegians, embodied the spirit of the country itself. He realized international acclaim through his novellas *Synnöve Solbakken, Arne,* and *En glad gut (A Happy Boy)*, which depict the assimilation of the peasantry into modern society. Later, in his social dramas, Bjørnson wrestled with a series of controversial moral problems that faced the upper and middle classes. These plays, particularly *En fallit (The Bankrupt)* and *Redaktören (The Editor)*, introduced social realism to the Scandinavian stage and influenced Ibsen's work. Though didactic and superficial in their approach, Bjørnson's efforts were nevertheless crucial to the development of modern drama.

Bjørnson spent most of his childhood in the Romsdal district of western Norway, a picturesque, pastoral environment that inspired the romantic style and settings of his early work. He began his writing career as a journalist and theater critic. With the success of his drama *Mellem slagene*, Bjørnson succeeded Ibsen as director of the national theater in Bergen. While in Bergen, he campaigned vigorously for an end to Norway's cultural and political dependence on Denmark and Sweden. His efforts were instrumental in bringing about Norway's complete independence in 1905, and his lyric poem *Ja, vi elsker dette landet* became the national anthem.

Critics usually divide Bjørnson's work into two phases. The first consists of romantic epic dramas, such as *Halte Hulda* and *Sigurd Slembe,* and impressionistic "peasant tales," such as *Synnöve Solbakken* and *Arne*. In these works Bjørnson writes in a terse, rugged prose style reminiscent of the sagas. His themes and Viking-like characters are also borrowed from old Norse literature. The protagonists in his peasant tales, as well as those in his epics, are social misfits, crude and often animalistic in temperament. To survive and prosper they, like their counterparts in the sagas, must learn the ways of Christianity and civilization. Bjørnson's purpose was to reconstruct the heroic past of his country, to inspire pride in Norway's history and achievements. Critics have praised the lyric quality, the narrative power, and the psychologically complex characterizations of these early dramas and novellas, which are considered Norwegian classics.

With his social dramas, or problem plays, Bjørnson (acting on critic Georg Brandes's advice that drama should debate the moral issues of the day) embarked on the second phase of his career. These works reflect the author's growing concern for, yet ultimate faith in, the good of humanity. *The Bankrupt* attacks modern business ethics and was the forerunner of Ibsen's *Pillars of Society*. *The Editor* criticizes the unscrupulous use of power by the press. *Leonarda* and *En hanske (A Gauntlet)* focus on the then-controversial subjects of divorce and the sexual double standard. Though Bjørnson's realistic and socially relevant plays preceded Ibsen's, they lack the skillful

characterization and dramatic depth evident in the latter's work. Bjørnson's dramas, the critics contend, concentrate solely on a problem and its solution; his characters are little more than mouthpieces for the author's sermons on morality and religious tolerance. Moreover, he overlooked those aspects of society and human nature that were not in keeping with his optimistic view of life and weakened the impact of his problem plays by the use of happy, sentimental endings. However, in *Over aevne, I (Beyond Our Power, I)*, considered his best drama, Bjørnson transcended these prescriptive and superficial tendencies. *Beyond Our Power, I* tackles the problem of religious fanaticism, detailing the effects of one man's zealous belief in the supernatural. Unlike his earlier efforts, *Beyond Our Power, I* ends tragically and offers no clear-cut or simple resolution. Critics find it the most dramatically intense and theatrically effective of Bjørnson's plays.

Though innovative and controversial in their time, Bjørnson's social dramas now seem dated and trite, and Bjørnson's reputation, once equal to that of Ibsen's, has declined considerably. Critics maintain that Bjørnson's early novellas and epic dramas are of more lasting importance and appeal than later works. Today he is chiefly remembered as a patriot and as a precursor of modern realism.

PRINCIPAL WORKS

Thrond (novella) 1856
Mellem slagene (drama) 1857
Synnöve Solbakken (novella) 1857
  [*Synnöve Solbakken*, 1881]
Arne (novella) 1858
  [*Arne*, 1861]
*Halte Hulda (drama) 1858
En glad gut (novella) 1860
  [*The Happy Boy*, 1870]
Sigurd Slembe (drama) 1863
  [*Sigurd Slembe*, 1888]
Maria Stuart i Skotland (drama) 1867
  [*Mary Stuart in Scotland* published in journal
  Scandinavia, 1883-84]
Arnljot Gelline (poetry) 1870
  [*Arnljot Gelline*, 1917]
Digte og sange (poetry and songs) 1870
  [*Poems and Songs*, 1915]
En fallit (drama) 1875
  [*The Bankrupt* published in *Three Dramas by Bjørnson*,
  1914]
Redaktören (drama) 1875
  [*The Editor* published in *Three Dramas by Bjørnson*,
  1914]
Kongen (poetry) 1877
Leonarda (drama) 1879
  [*Leonarda*, 1911]
En hanske (drama) 1883
  [*A Gauntlet*, 1890; also published as *A Glove* in journal
  Poet Lore, 1892]
Det flager i byen og på havnen (novel) 1884
  [*The Heritage of the Kurts*, 1892]
Over aevne, I (drama) 1886
  [*Pastor Sang*, 1893; also published as *Beyond Our Power,
  I* in journal *Poet Lore*, 1905]
På Guds veje (novel) 1889
  [*In God's Way*, 1889]
Paul Lange og Tora Parsberg (drama) 1901
  [*Paul Lange and Tora Parsberg*, 1899]
*Hjertets og Aandens Skønhed (drama) 1957

*These are dates of first publication rather than first performance.

HJALMAR HJORTH BOYESEN (essay date 1873)

Bjørnson is a Norseman to the core, and even if he had never attained the high rank he now holds as a poet and dramatist, his journalistic and political character would have stamped him as a typical Norseman. (p. 112)

His first drama, *Valborg,* was accepted by the directors of the stage, and procured for its author a free ticket to all theatrical representations; and through the opportunity he thus gained of acquainting himself with the requirements of the drama, he was soon convinced of the immaturity of his production, and of his own accord withdrew it, without awaiting the verdict of the public. His continued visits to the theatre soon enabled him to see the unworthy condition of the national stage of the capital; and with more patriotic zeal than critical judgement,

in a series of newspaper articles, he boldly attacked the Danish rule as anti-national in its origin and tendencies. (p. 114)

[*Synnöve Solbakken*] attracted general attention, both as being the first successful effort to introduce the primitive life of the Norse peasantry into the world of fiction, and because it revealed a great and rich poetic soul, of a cast altogether grand and strikingly original. There was, moreover, a certain nervous strength in the narrative; which, whatever might be said of its provincialisms and occasional obscurity of expression, seemed to indicate an immense reserve power; and the artless simplicity of the style betokened the author's perfect confidence in the intelligence of his readers,—a feature which never fails to bring its own reward with a sincere and enlightened public. (p. 115)

[In *Arne, Halte Hulda (Limping Hulda),* and *Mellem Slagene (Between the Battles),* Björnson] followed Shakespeare's example in violating sacred Aristotelean unities of time and place, and he even limits the number of acts in one case to three, and in another to two. The untraditional shape of Björnson's dramas gave little trouble to Scandinavian critics, and did not subject them to the harsh treatment which probably they would have met with at the hands of the French and German members of that powerful brotherhood. (pp. 115-16)

[After] the publication of the grand drama **"King Sverre"** and the wonderful trilogy **"Sigurd Slembe,"** the subjects of which were taken from Snorre Sturlason's "Sagas of the Kings of Norway," the national drama was no longer a mere vague ideal or an imaginary promise of the future, but a grand and powerful reality, which even the most reluctant of critics were forced to recognize. . . . [Björnson's] dramas have been the chief attraction of the theatres all over the Scandinavian kingdoms. . . . In the drama **"Mary Stuart in Scotland"** he has for the first time chosen a foreign subject for his treatment, and has perhaps "Norsified" it more than the kinship of Norsemen and Scotch Highlanders would naturally justify. . . . *De Nygifte (After the Wedding)* is a short dramatic sketch full of truth and pathos, dealing with social life at the present day. The last work we have seen from Bjonson's pen is the epic poem *Arnljot Gelline.* . . , describing the life, conversion, and death of a Norse warrior of the old Viking breed. Like Tegnér's *Frithof Saga* . . . , it is written in cantos of different form and metre, and is characterized by a certain rude and honest strength, which, we suppose, would be more readily appreciated by the original Norsemen than by those who know the spirit of the Sagas only from cursory extracts and translations. The poet is here liable to criticism for the liberties he takes with his verse, often breaking off in the middle of a stanza, and introducing his rhymes, as it seems, very much at random; moreover his fondness for compressed vigor often makes his poetic similes extremely obscure. (pp. 116-18)

Björnson's works comprise almost all the more important branches of literary art; but . . . it is more especially his dramas whose influence has made itself so widely felt among his own nation. . . . [*Halte Hulda,*] although belonging to an early period of the author's life, is marked with all the characteristics of his style, and moreover possesses the advantage of being intelligible even to those who have never had a peep into the mysteries of the old Sagas. The action is laid in the thirteenth century,—when the political power of Norway was in steady decline; when the *Asa* faith had long been supplanted by a nominal Christianity; while the old pagan customs, and the old notions of revenge, manliness, and honor still held [a] powerful . . . sway over the minds of the Norsemen. . . . The time, then, nearly coincides with that of *Njal's Saga;* with which, indeed, *Halte Hulda* has many traits in common,—of course with due allowance for the natural differences between a drama and an historical tale.

A dramatic as well as a tragical situation always involves a conflict; it is the individual asserting his freedom as opposed to some greater power beyond and above him. In the ancient Greek dramas, this Destiny is an external and arbitrary power, which the hero only recognizes because he is forced to do so, while his moral nature may silently rebel against it. But how infinitely more powerful or how much more *tragic* does not the situation become where this limiting power, this Destiny—or perhaps *Necessity* is the better word—is no longer an interference from without, but is found in man's own moral consciousness. This circumstance Bjornson has fully appreciated; it is the corner-stone in this as in many of his other dramas. Aslak, the father of the murdered Gudljek, is old, and shrinks from the duty of vengeance, which his own conscience enforces. He knows that Eyolf Finson, the slayer of his son, is the greatest warrior in the king's body-guard, and that death is certain if he attacks him. Therefore when his sister, Halgerda, throws the red cloak of the avenger about his shoulders, he says, "O Jesus Lord, methinks that there thou laid'st my shroud upon me."

But the old pagan idea, which still clings to him, declares him a villain if he flees from the terrible duty. And he struggles, strikes, and is slain. (pp. 118-19)

The *dramatis personae* [in *Halte Hulda*] are few, and the complications of the plot not hard to unravel. It is characteristic of the author that he never depends upon complexity of intrigue for effect; he never shrinks from great psychological problems, but scorns to resort to mere ingenious intricacies. Hulda, the heroine, is the widow of Gudljek Aslakson, who has been slain only a few days ago by the king's warrior, Eyolf Finson. There is a mystery about her, a strange, fatal charm. . . . (pp. 120-21)

In the characters of Halgerda and Thordis, we note the author's fine sense of the picturesque, and his skill in truly dramatic characterization. What could more powerfully relieve the revengeful gloom of the former's mind than the fresh, half-shrinking happiness of a young maid's new-born love? It is not a mere rude contrast, such as every mechanical scribbler could readily have invented, nor an often-repeated antithesis, which wearies more than it delights, but a vigorous and truthful delineation of two typical characters, which although old as the world, gain a fresh charm in the peculiar coloring of the old Norse Sagas, and in their relation to that age which the Sagas depict. (pp. 122-23)

It has been remarked, and not without justice, that Eyolf, with his wavering and apparent duplicity, can hardly enlist our fullest sympathy as a hero. But it is this very wavering, this vagueness of purpose, which in the drama is made a mainspring of action, which involves him in such hopeless complications, and in the end draws the inevitable doom down upon his head. . . . (p. 137)

Hulda's character is indeed grand in its conception, and its development is forcibly marked in the progressive action of the drama. In its general aspect, as a nature of grand possibilities, hitherto cramped and subdued, but suddenly by the vivifying spark of love waked to a consciousness of its own power, it is not altogether a novelty to the world of fiction; but in her peculiar relation to the age and the society in which she is placed, that is, in her peculiar Norse aspect, Hulda is

without a predecessor. And the same may be said of almost every character which Björnson's art has brought into being. . . . Björnson saw in the rugged Norwegian peasant the true type of the national greatness, and pressing his ear close to the nation's heart he heard the throbs of its hidden emotions. And when he raised his voice and sang every Norseman felt as if the voice were his own, as if the words had welled forth from his own inmost soul. Therefore in Björnstjerne Björnson has Norway found her national poet. (pp. 137-38)

Hjalmar Hjorth Boyesen, "Bjornstjerne Bjornson As a Dramatist," in The North American Review, *Vol. CXVI, No. 238, January, 1873, pp. 109-38.*

KRISTOFER JANSON (essay date 1881)

As Björnson's **"Synnöve Solbakken"** and **"A Happy Boy"** are considered the author's most pleasing stories, so **"Arne"** is thought to be the profoundest in sentiment. In it the reader will find many richly-colored pictures of the various phases of Norse peasant life; will find the Norse mountaineer depicted in his sin and shame, as well as in his sincerity and honesty. In Arne's father, Björnson has portrayed a genial but uneducated man who, heart-broken by a false step in his youth, takes to drinking and makes a wreck of his life. . . . The scenes from Arne's childhood, which lie at the bottom of all the sadness in his character, are painted with an awful realism. Arne's mother is a mild but faint-hearted and shallow-minded woman, who, anxious lest she may lose her only child, conceals letters which are sent to him and which she fears may induce him to leave her. . . . (pp. 140-41)

The character of Arne is singularly characteristic of the Norse people. He is one of the large number of peasant boys who wander about among the lofty mountains, full of unrealized purposes, dreaming, and longing to see other lands, but lacking the energy to take the first difficult step. . . . He grows more and more sad and silent, and has only one comfort, which consists in allowing all his longing and sorrow and bitterness to burst forth in poems. . . . Some of these poems of Arne's have become favorite songs in Norway, especially the one entitled **"Over the Lofty Mountains,"** one of the most beautiful and profoundly significant of Björnson's lyrics.

Finally, Arne gets acquainted with Eli Böen, the daughter of the same woman whom Arne's father had once dishonored. By Eli, Arne is taught that happiness does not consist in seeking adventures in foreign lands, but in the building up of a quiet home life, in love and peace, and in adding his mite to the progress and weal of his native country; and by his marriage with her, old sins and old enmities are expiated. These chief figures of the story Björnson has surrounded with many other interesting characters. . . . At the same time, the author gives most fascinating pictures of Norwegian scenery, in which the grand nature of Norway lies sparkling like drops of dew. (p. 141)

Kristofer Janson, "A Norse Prose Idyl," in The Dial, *Vol. 2, November, 1881, pp. 140-41.*

GEORG BRANDES (essay date 1886)

In his noble qualities and in his faults, in his genius and in his weak points, [Björnson] as thoroughly bears the stamp of Norway as Voltaire bore that of France. . . . None of his contemporaries so fully represent this people's love of home and of freedom, its self-consciousness, rectitude, and fresh energy. Indeed, just now he also exemplifies, on a large scale, the people's tendency to self-criticism, not that scourging criticism which chastises with scorpions, . . . but that sharp, bold expression of opinion begotten of love. He never calls attention to an evil in whose improvement and cure he does not believe, or to a vice which he despairs of seeing outrooted. For he has implicit faith in the good in humanity, and possesses entire the invincible optimism of a large, genial, sanguine nature. (p. 309)

"Mellem Slagene" (Between the Battles), an earnest little play in one act, that treats of an episode from the Norwegian civil war of the early Middle Ages, and whose terse, rugged prose style, which formed the sharpest contrast to the sonorous, verbose iambics of the Danish dramas of the Oehlenschläger school, inaugurated a new form of the Northern style. . . . How far Björnson and the entire later poetic literature have progressed on the path thus broken, can be best observed by witnessing to-day a theatrical performance of this little drama, which on its first appearance repelled, because of the supposed wildness of its materials and the harshness of their treatment, and which now actually seems to us quite idyllic and by far too sentimental.

Meanwhile, his mission to write novels of peasant life became even clearer to Björnson, and after publishing anonymously a few shorter stories, by way of experiment, he gave the public . . . his **"Synnöve Solbakken."** This literary début was a victory, and the reception of the little volume in Denmark, whose verdict is usually the decisive one for the poetic creations of Norway, especially tended to make it a decided triumph. The fresh originality, the novelty of the materials, and the manner in which they were handled, does not sufficiently explain this success. It was the result of the remarkable harmony of the book, with all that was desired and demanded of a poetic work by a portion of the reading world of the day. The national liberal party of that time . . . absolutely determined the literary taste; it demanded something of a primeval Northern, vigorously national, ancient Scandinavian character, and at the same time,—an element which seemed curiously at variance with this,—Christian ethics, combined with an innocent idyllic tone, a poetry which banished Titanic defiance and modern passion with equal severity from its sphere. . . . Björnson's stories of peasant life, without considering their great and true merits, almost seemed like the fulfilment of the party programme. (pp. 313-14)

Björnson belongs to those fortunate beings who are not compelled to seek a form, because they possess one of their own. His earliest novel is a thoroughly ripe fruit. In his first venture he is classic. . . . Indeed, his development has been of such a nature that even at the outset, with his original comparative narrowness or poverty of ideas, he grasped the highest artistic perfection of form, and eventually imparted to his works an ever richer ideal life and an ever increasing knowledge of the human heart. In thus enlarging their scope, however, he has never marred their poetic worth, but he has frequently somewhat sacrificed their plastic and classic equilibrium.

Nevertheless, it must not be thought that Björnson's first works were hailed with the unanimous applause which people now often profess to believe they received. . . . His first novels and dramas formed too strong a contrast with all that the public had been accustomed to admire to be received without opposition, and many people of literary culture who had been in hearty sympathy with the previously prevailing poesy, could not but feel their aesthetic creed to be violated by them. . . . I recollect distinctly how strange and novel **"Synnöve Solbak-**

ken" and **"Arne"** seemed to me on their first appearance. (pp. 315-16)

The excellencies [in Björnson's peasant tales] were specifically poetic; the tenderest sentiment was cast in the hardest form; the most refined, versatile observation was united with a lyric ardor which permeated the whole and burst into a freer course in numerous fugitive child, folk, and love songs. A vein of fundamental romance hovered over the narrative. The new order of novel admitted of being preluded without any disharmony by a nursery story, as in **"Arne,"** in which plants conversed and vied with one another in their efforts. Notwithstanding the dry realism of certain of the characters, it was so idyllic that little detached stories, in which woodland sprites played a rôle, became wedded to the universally prevailing tone without causing any breach with the spirit of the general action. Björnson was a good observer and had amassed a store of little traits from which he constructed his tales. . . . And yet sagas, folk-songs, and folk-tales were the currents through whose intermingling his art-form became crystallized. He did not give it isolated grandeur, but kept himself through it in rapport with the popular mind.

"Synnöve Solbakken" was the plastic harmony within the limitation of Norwegian life, and the hero Thorbjörn was the type of the vigorous, stubborn youth, whose nature could only ripen to maturity through calming, soothing influences. **"Arne,"** on the other hand, represented the lyric, yearning tendency of the people, that impulse of the viking blood which has been transformed into desire for travel, and the hero the type of the tenderhearted, dreamy youth who needed to be steeled in order to become a man. (pp. 319-20)

If the two larger stories **"Synnöve"** and **"Arne"** formed such perfect complements of each other, the third story **"En glad Gut" (A Happy Boy)** was like a refreshing breeze bringing deliverance from the brooding melancholy that oppresses the Norwegian mind, and sweeping it away in the name of a healthy temperament. This production contained the joyous message of unsophisticated vital powers and love of life; it was like a fresh song, bubbling over with laughter and purifying the atmosphere. (p. 321)

[A] keen sense of nature is common to all Björnson's Norse characters of the olden time. He has imparted to them his own modern feelings. The little epic poem, **"Arnljot Gelline"** (consisting of fifteen brief cantos), in particular, is unsurpassed for the beauty of its descriptions of nature. The song, **"During the Springtime Inundation,"** describing the plunge which the mountain streams, swollen by the water from the melting snow, make into the valleys below, and the anxious huddling together in the mountain caves of the terrified wild beasts, paints in indelible colors an annual episode of Norwegian nature, transplanted some eight hundred years into the past, and which is consequently rendered wilder and more forcible than at the present day. The canto **"Arnljot's Yearning for the Ocean,"** in whose rhythm we feel the monotonous ebb and flow of the sea, is one of the most beautiful of all the poems that have ever portrayed the poetry of the sea. Byron had depicted the unruliness, the inexorableness, the fury of the ocean; Björnson paints the deep melancholy, the phlegmatic coldness, the ransoming freshness of the surging billows. (p. 325)

[Björnson's] experiences as a stage-manager have served him in very good stead as a play-writer; nevertheless, he has never attained technical perfection in this capacity. His dramas contain far more poetry than skilful manipulation. . . . His vigorous and wildly passionate youthful drama, ["**Halte Hulda**"], gains little or nothing by being put on the stage. Two of the plays of his first period, however, have met with a complete stage success, ["**Maria Stuart in Scotland**" and "**De Nygifte**" (**The Newly Married Couple**)]. . . .

"**Maria Stuart**" is a rich and powerful work, full of dramatic life, almost too violently intense. All the details of the plot are admirably linked together,—Rizzio's murder, Darnley's death, and Bothwell's elopement with Maria; the finale alone is weak, or more correctly speaking, the drama has no finale. It is my belief that the poet succeeded so well simply because on Scottish soil he still felt himself encompassed by the atmosphere of Norway. These Scots of his are of Norse origin. . . . In this Norwegian-Scottish world, the poet feels perfectly at home, and the characters, created by him without any breach with local coloring, have traits very nearly akin to the forms from the Norse Middle Ages that he was so well accustomed to portray. The most marked of the main characters are the Puritan John Knox, the gloomy yet pleasure-loving, wildly energetic Bothwell, and the weak, boyishly revengeful and unworthily humble Darnley; Bothwell a genuine Renaissance personality, Darnley almost too modern. Maria Stuart herself is not so successfully drawn; the traits of her character are too effeminately indistinct. She is conceived as a being, the mysterious foundation of whose nature is revealed in two opposite poles,— that of absolute feminine weakness, and that of absolute feminine strength. . . . She is, however, by virtue of Northern idealism, by virtue of the innate modesty of the poet who is a priest's son, entirely too lacking in the sensuous element, moreover, too passive to be the heroine of a drama. . . . She is enveloped in a cloud of adjectives designating her character, hurled at her in masses by the other characters in the drama. "**Maria Stuart**" owes its origin to a period in the progress of Björnson's development, when he had a tendency, perhaps owing to Kierkegaard's influence, to describe his characters psychologically, instead of allowing their natures to unfold of themselves without any commentary. All the personages in these dramas are psychologists; they study one another, explain one another's temperaments, and experiment with one another. . . . While all the characters thus think like psychologists, they all speak like poets, and this Shakespearean splendor of diction, so true to life because the people of the Renaissance period, being poetic throughout in their feelings, used a flowery, highly figurative language, enhances the charm with which the profound originality of the main characters invests the drama.

The little drama, "**The Newly Married Couple**" treats of a very simple yet universal human relation, the severing of the ties that bind a young wife to the parental home. . . . (pp. 327-29)

Its execution suffers under a twofold defect. The fact is, the tone of this drama, as well as of "**Maria Stuart**," is weakened, in the first place, by excessive Northern modesty, and in the second place, by the psychological caprice of the author. . . . The manner in which love and passion are treated throughout this drama is peculiar to that period in the spiritual life of Björnson, and of Norwegian-Danish literature in general. Northern people took very little interest at that time in the tender passion for itself alone; the emotions were studied and portrayed in their relation to morality and religion. (pp. 329-31)

[Eminence] was early reached by Björnson. When but thirty-one years of age he had written all the best works of his first period, and they were even then viewed by the public as a completed whole. No one could overlook his magnificent endowments; it produced rather a painful effect, however, that no development of them could be detected. His creative power for a long time remained centered in one and the same point; but his views of life did not expand; they remained childish and narrow. Sometimes he could actually be trivial. . . . He kept himself, for the most part, at a distressing distance from the life and the ideas of his contemporaries. Or rather, if he did represent the ideas of his contemporaries, it was involuntarily; they were brought forward in the theatrical costumes of the ancient Norsemen or of the Scottish Middle Ages. In "**Sigurd Slembe**," Helga and Frakark discuss in the year 1127 the relation between the immortality of the individual and that of the race in phrases which remind us too strongly of the year 1862; and the same chieftains, whose minds are filled with almost modern political reflections, who use such expressions as vocation and fundamental law, . . . have the imprisoned Sigurd, from motives of revenge, broken limb by limb on the wheel. . . . People that express themselves in terms indicative of so much culture do not break their enemies on the wheel; they scourge them with their tongues.

To this lack of unity in passion and thought was added the unhappy necessity of the poet to so group and combine his principal dramatic forms that the mantle of the orthodox church faith should be draped about them at the moment when the curtain falls. In "**Maria Stuart**" the form of John Knox is not subject to the dramatic irony that governs the other personages. Björnson does not reserve to himself a poetic supremacy over him: for Knox is destined to step forth from the theatrical framework at the conclusion of the play, with the pathos of the poet on his lips, and, as the representative of the people, receive the political inheritance of Maria. The vigorous combats in "**Sigurd**," as well as the passionate emotions in "**Maria Stuart**," find their outlet in a hymn. . . . Gradually it began to appear as though the once so rich vein of the poet was well nigh drained. His later stories ("**The Railroad and the Churchyard**" and "**A Problem of Life**") bore no comparison to his earlier ones. . . . The last cantos of "**Arnljot Gelline**," which were written several years later than the rest, are decidedly inferior to those composed in the first glow of inspiration. Evidently no new ideas germinated in Björnson's mind. (pp. 334-35)

[However], after his fortieth year new and rich streams had welled up in the innermost depths of his being. Suddenly it became apparent that his productiveness had soared upward into a new state of activity. The modern world lay open before his eyes. He had gained, as he once wrote to me "eyes that saw and ears that heard." The ideas of the century had, unconsciously to himself, worked their way into his receptive spirit and secretly fructified it. During these years he had read, with ravenous eagerness, books in all languages and of every variety, works on the natural sciences, critical, philosophical, and historical works, romances, foreign periodicals, and newspapers by the quantities. A profound impression was made upon him by the calm grandeur and the sublime free thought of Stuart Mill; Darwin's powerful hypotheses widened his intellectual horizon; the philological critique of a Steinthal, or a Max Müller, taught him to review religions, the literary critique of a Taine taught him to view literatures with new eyes. The young Danish school contributed not a little, as he has himself publicly declared, toward tearing him away from old things. The significance of the eighteenth, the problems of the nineteenth century unfolded before him. (p. 337)

The first extensive work with which Björnson made his appearance before the public, after a silence of several years, was the drama **"En Fallit" (The Bankrupt),** that met with such unwonted success in Germany as well as at home. It was a leap into modern life. The poetic hand which had wielded the battle-swords of the Sigurds did not esteem itself too good to count the cash of Tjaelde or to sum up his debts. Björnson was the first Scandinavian poet who entered with serious earnestness into the tragic-comedy of money, and the victory that crowned his effort was a brilliant one. Simultaneously with **"The Bankrupt"** he issued the play called **"Redaktören" (The Editor),** a scathing satire on the condition of the press in Norway. Then followed in rapid succession the great dramatic poem **"Kongen" (The King),** the novels **"Magnhild"** and **"Captain Mansana,"** the dramas **"Det ny System" (The New System),** and **"Leonarda."** (p. 338)

[No one] who looks farther than failures in details can be obtuse enough not to detect the fountain of new and individual poesy which streams through all of Björnson's works of the second period, or second youth, as it might be called. An ardent love of truth has imprinted its seal on these books; a manly firmness of character proclaims itself in them. What a wealth of new thoughts in all provinces of state and society, marriage and home! What an energetic demand for veracity toward one's self and toward others! Finally, what benignity, what sympathy with people of opposite lines of thought. (p. 339)

The opponents of Björnson's new departure now maintain that, as long as he kept outside of the circle of burning questions and living ideas, he was great and good as a poet, but declare that he has retrograded since he embarked on the sea of modern problems and thought; that, at all events, he no longer produces artistically finished works. . . . It is true that Björnson, in his second period has not yet attained the lucidity and harmony of style that characterized his first efforts; but it is neither just nor wise to declare for this reason that he has retrograded. (p. 340)

The exposé in **"The Bankrupt"** is one of the best the literature of any land can produce, and the diction in **"The Editor,"** especially in the first act, is the most excellent that Björnson has attained. (p. 341)

In **"The Bankrupt"** the demands of truth in the humble walks of life are urged. The poet holds up, within the plain, commonplace life of the people, the ideal of truth as a simple matter of rectitude. His poetic eye, however, sees that rectitude is not so simple as it appears. Nothing is so reprehensible for the merchant as to risk the money of others, and yet, to a certain degree, it is impossible for him to avoid it. The moral problem revolves about the delicate boundary lines between where it is allowable and where not allowable to risk it. **"The Editor"** demands truth in the higher domains, where it is, a bounden duty to keep it in sight, and yet dangerous to carry it into execution. While in the mercantile world there is danger of disappointing and ruining others through self deception, in the journalistic world the temptation is to keep silence concerning the truth, or to deny it. And this, too, cannot be altogether avoided; for it is out of the question for the politician to acknowledge everything he knows. (pp. 341-42)

The unusual vigor of the play, however, is dependent on the fact that, in addition to the great breadth of its horizon, it is individual and characteristic to a degree that has never been surpassed by Björnson.

"The King" deals with political questions, as **"The Bankrupt"** and **"The Editor"** with social ones. Here the problem is psychological. The poet himself fights with the king of the drama his inner flight, and lets his attempts to reconcile the requirements of his nature with those of his position [stand]. Is the problem satisfactorily solved? Is not the unhappy result in too high a degree caused by the king's wretched past and his weak character? The worth of the play does not depend on the answer, but on the depths to which it penetrates, on the fresh charm which hovers about its love scenes, and on the rich, sparkling wit of its dialogues. In **"Magnhild"** and **"Leonarda,"** a new modern problem is dealt with that had germed in the poet's own soul,—the relation between morality as a virtue and as an institution, as a law of the heart, and as a law of society. The doctrine proclaimed in **"Magnhild"** is imparted in the modest form of a question: Are there not immoral marriages, which it is our highest duty to dissolve?

"Magnhild" is a work that, in its search for reality, denotes a turning-point in Björnson's novel-writing. In its characterizations it displays a delicacy and a power the author had not previously attained. The public had scarcely credited him with the ability to portray figures like the young musician Tande, the beautiful Mrs. Bang and her husband. And Magnhild's relation to this group is quite as exquisitely delineated and as correctly conceived. Nevertheless, it is very apparent that the author is moving in a sphere which is still somewhat an unfamiliar one to him, that of social high life. (p. 343)

The novel suffers from a double defect. In the first place there is a decided lack of clearness in the characterization of one of the main personages, Skarlie. He is meant to impress the reader as a sort of monster, and yet the reader feels continually obliged to sympathize with him in his relations with his reserved, ideal wife. In the most guarded manner conceivable, it is indicated that Skarlie is a highly depraved person, and yet this monster of sensuality, in his dealings with his own wife, . . . displays a moonshine-like ideal of a Platonic relation between husband and wife, . . . and is content with the modest satisfaction of clothing and feeding her. The second deficiency strikes deeper into the philosophy of the novel. There is a good deal of old mysticism in the handling of the doctrine concerning the "destiny" of men and women, about which the story revolves, and (as is always the case with both Björnson and Ibsen) the mysticism is strangely interwoven with rationalism. Björnson seems to wish to have it firmly established as the sum of the story that there is another way to happiness and beneficient activity for woman than a relation to the man whom she loves, but the idea is not clearly expressed.

"Leonarda," although not conspicuous for its dramatic merits, belongs to the most thoroughly and richly poetic of the author's works. Outside of the Scandinavian North, a drama of this kind cannot be fully appreciated; perhaps the powerful, intellectual influence it has exercised can scarcely be comprehended. When placed upon the boards in Christiania it made its marked sensation, because it rang like a word of deliverance into Norwegian affairs. The message of **"Leonarda"** is that of moral and religious tolerance, from which the author himself, in his early days, was so far removed. In this drama, with wonderful display of intellectual superiority, Björnson brought forward a whole series of generations of Norwegian society, showing the faults and virtues of each generation, and allowing the great-grandmother, who . . . represents the culture of the eighteenth century, . . . to utter the solemn amen of the play. Her concluding words read as follows:—

> The time of deep emotions has, indeed, come
> back again.

With "Leonarda," however, not only the time of deep emotions but that of hardy thoughts had returned. . . . (pp. 344-45)

Henrik Ibsen is a judge, stern as one of the judges of Israel of old; Björnson is a prophet, the delightful herald of a better age. . . . Björnson's is a conciliatory mind; he wages warfare without bitterness. His poetry sparkles with the sunshine of April, while that of Ibsen, with its deep earnestness, seems to lurk in dark shadows. Ibsen loves the idea,—that logical, and psychological consistency which drives Brand out of the church, and Nora out of the marriage relation. Ibsen's love of ideas corresponds with Björnson's love of humanity. (p. 345)

> *Georg Brandes, in his essay from his* Eminent Authors of the Nineteenth Century, *translated by Rasmus B. Anderson (reprinted by permission of Harper & Row, Publishers, Inc.), Thomas Y. Crowell Co., Inc., 1886 (and reprinted as "Björnstjerne Björnson," in his* Creative Spirits of the Nineteenth Century, *translated by Rasmus B. Anderson, Thomas Y. Crowell Co., Inc., 1923, pp. 306-48).*

[W. D. HOWELLS]   (essay date 1891)

People who like a strong novel, with intense yet real feeling in it, and the suggestion of earnest thinking, cannot do better than turn to [*In God's Way*]. . . . Norway is a little country and America is a big one, but the spiritual conditions are much the same; the type of pharisaism is the protestant type in both, and the questions involved fit either civilization. (p. 482)

We must leave the reader to follow the story through the evolution of its entirely human characters, and the passages of a drama which has moments of breathless interest; but we can assure him he will not be trifled with or defrauded by any trick of the trade in any part of the action. We ask him to note how probably, and yet how unexpectedly, the different men and women grow out of the children whose life is first presented to us. That is a very great thing, and very uncommon; it is only Tolstoï, that other giant of the North, who has known how to do it as well; and certainly even Tolstoï has not known better how to indicate the compensation of error and virtue in the same person. Any one who loves truth must feel a thrill of delight in the variety of the conceptions in this book, and of more than delight, of fervent gratitude. . . . Björnson never fails of reality in the high level his imagination keeps. (p. 483)

> [*W. D. Howells,*] *"Editor's Study," in* Harper's Monthly Magazine, *Vol. LXXXII, No. 489, February, 1891, pp. 478-83.**

EDMUND GOSSE   (essay date 1894)

[Now that the body of Björnson's] work is mature, and that he himself has passed into the sixties, we can more plainly than before observe a general tendency running through the web and woof of his multifarious writings, and we acknowledge in Björnson . . . a consistent manner, a persistent intention, which lend to his work the character of wholeness which it once seemed to lack. (p. vii)

Many of his apparent inconsistencies are explained when we recognise in the author of *Sigurd Slembe* and of *In God's Way* the Janus-glance that looks directly backwards and directly forwards at the same moment. Björnson is a passionate admirer of the ancient glories of his country . . . ; in this direction, he is all for individual heroism, for the antique virtues, for the

local and historical prestige of Norway. On this side of his character, he is an aristocrat. But there is another side on which he throws himself with no less animation into the problems of the future, is ready to try all spirits, to risk all political and social experiments, to accept with cheerfulness every form of revolution. Here he is no less definitely and obtrusively a democrat. The danger that waylays criticism in endeavouring to do justice to the qualities of this stimulating writer is that of confounding the action of this double strain with mere feebleness of purpose. The two ideals are really less incompatible than they at first appear. (pp. viii-ix)

Björnson has explained that his early literary ambitions were divided between observing the peasant in the light of the saga and creating the saga in the light of the peasant. We may take the former of these first, although the two strains ran side by side throughout the labours of some twenty years. The earliest published story of Björnson which we possess is, I believe, a little sketch called *Thrond,* which has unduly escaped the notice of the critics. . . . It has this peculiarity, that we find in it, so far as the outer form is concerned, no immaturity or crudity. *Thrond* is composed, with absolute firmness of touch, in the style invented by Björnson for his pastoral stories, and it is no better and no worse, in this respect, than the more ambitious novels which succeeded it. It might be taken as a model in miniature of the class of *bonde-novellen.*

To realise how original such a piece of writing as *Thrond* must have seemed to attentive readers, we need to know how unparalleled it was in Scandinavian literature. These stories, and the earliest tragedies of Ibsen, made their appearance in a society which had successfully starved the romantic parts of literature, and in which nothing fresh or brilliant was even looked for. In the much more cultivated and literary neighbour-country, Denmark, to whose population the Norwegian poets had to look for their main audience, letters were far from being in so abject a state. Yet here the ideal was one of delicacy and polish, rather than of native freshness. (pp. xii-xiii)

[*Thrond*] is written in curt, unadorned sentences, almost in monosyllables, and with a simplicity of manner which is the product, not of artlessness (for modern artlessness is florid and voluble) but of the most careful art. The tale is one of the purest Norwegian isolation. (p. xviii)

The allegory [in *Thrond*] is translucent. It is one to which, in different shapes, Björnson often recurs. The poet is one who, in the solitudes of life, surrounded by no favourable influences but those of nature, yearns with a passionate longing to make music for mankind. . . . But, always, when he has his first opportunity, it is to meet with disappointment and disenchantment that he has come so far. . . . But, in spite of disillusion, there is no possibility of return for him to the old conventions and respectabilities. He has to stay in the harsh world, and learn to master the instrument that has befooled him, before he can betake himself again to the country of his childhood.

Of realism, as we now conceive it, there was little in such a story as *Thrond.* But of reality there was a great deal. Here, for the first time, the imaginative quality in the character of the peasant was truly and consistently depicted. *Thrond,* too, was but a sketch; it was quickly followed by pictures conceived in the same style, but executed with greater elaboration. . . . [In *Synnöve Solbakken, Arne, A Happy Boy, The Fisher Maiden,* and *The Wedding March*] a Björnson can be studied who was for a long time the only one recognised through Europe, and who even yet is the best known, the author of pastoral prose-sagas of modern life which have not been surpassed for naïveté, freshness and sprightly delicacy. (pp. xix-xxi)

[Any prejudice] which the somewhat exotic diction of these peasant-novels may have caused at first, has long ago ceased to exist. They brought with them the ineffable freshness of the remote Norwegian landscape. . . . And with all this, in sequestered and scattered villages, whose soul, as Björnson says, is the church-spire, they suggested the hard Calvinism of the North, the austere biblical protestantism, externally so cold, holding underneath its crusts such burning possibilities of passion. With all this, a mode of artistic procedure far more minute and realistic than we were then accustomed to, Björnson was unconsciously working in the same direction as the great Russians were. (pp. xxiv-xxv)

In Björnson's peasant-novels, the freshness and the verisimilitude of the conversations is above praise. (p. xxv)

It will probably be conceded that the earliest of these stories are the best. Even *A Happy Boy,* entertaining as it is, strikes a moralising note in its hortatory optimism which is not so pure a delight as the development of the savage beauty of Thorbjörn's character in *Synnöve Solbakken,* or of the dreamer and enthusiast in *Arne.* These two stories seem to me to be almost perfect; they have an enchanting lyrical quality, without bitterness or passion, which I look for elsewhere in vain in the prose literature of the second half of the century. *The Fisher Maiden* is not so simple or direct. Interesting as it is, as a study of the processes by which a young woman of genius arrives at a command of her own resources, it is injured, as a simple peasant-story, by the incursion of foreign elements, by an excess of theological subtlety, by a modernity, in fact, which disturbs the harmony of the parts. Finally, *The Wedding-March* is a trifle; it is one of Edvard Grieg's *Norse Dances* translated into words. It recurs to the old manner which Björnson had invented twenty-five years before, and it repeats it with agility, but nothing is added, while certainly something is lost of freshness and sincerity. It is by *Arne* and by *Synnöve Solbakken,* two little masterpieces of the purest water, that the Björnson of the *bonde-novellen* lives and will continue to live.

While, however, Björnson was observing the peasant in the light of the saga, in his prose-stories, he was busily engaged all the time in creating the saga in the light of the peasant, in what he called his national dramas or *folkestykker.* (pp. xxv-xxvii)

The elements of several of Björnson's favourite theories may be perceived in the working out of *Between the Battles,* a dramatic sketch which lacks coherence, but is full of life, of freshness, of an audacious method in the treatment of history.

Of the form of *Between the Battles* something must be said. As in the story called *Thrond,* Björnson created, at the first attempt, a kind of tale hitherto unattempted, a kind, too, which he would not succeed in modifying as he proceeded, so in this earliest and somewhat crude theatrical sketch, he struck forth a new species of dramatic form, of which he was destined to make repeated and indeed constant use. *Between the Battles,* although a contribution to heroic drama, was written in prose, and that of a kind distinctly novel in character, terse, direct and personal. There was a total absence of the rhetoric hitherto deemed requisite for tragedy, and absence of the *cliches* of tragic poetry. In all this, Björnson was a serious innovator. (pp. xxix-xxx)

[*Sigurd Slembe*] is one of his most emphatic successes. In all the various repertory of Björnson, there is perhaps no single work in which so high a level of technical excellence is aimed at, and at the same time so harmonious and dignified a result obtained. (p. xxxi)

This marvellous poem is, what none of Björnson's other essays in the same direction succeed in being, a complete saga in dramatic form. The peculiar simplicity and strenuous passion of the old semi-historical chronicles of Iceland are here preserved to the full, and there is added to them a modern complexity in the evolution of character. (p. xxxii)

In all the saga-plays of Björnson a type constantly reappears, in which it is not difficult to perceive the poet's portrait of his own shadow thrown huge and vague upon the mists of history. He is Sverre, the man with the devil in him cast out as a disturber of Norway, yet consumed with a love of his country; he is Sigurd the Bastard, his patristic birthright denied, his claim to serve his people repudiated, his warmest ambitions foiled; he is Sigurd Jorsalfar, sick and mad until he learns the lesson that moral health is only found in the modest pursuance of civic duties. These plays were the expression of a stormy egotism, which contained nothing ignoble or small, but much which was disturbing and experimental. Hence, with the one exception of *Sigurd Slembe,* which is a very noble piece of sustained writing, the saga-dramas are curious and interesting, rather than satisfactory. They might be pages out of Hamlet's commonplace book, scenes hastily scrawled to test the capacity of his players. Björnson's ambition in writing them was to found with them a national Norwegian drama, but on the stage their theatrical limitations become instantly obvious. . . . When it is considered that Björnson, for a great part of the time in which these essays at folk-drama were being made, was manager and director of a theatre, it is strange that he never contrived to bring his own poetry and the stage into practical interrelation. (pp. xxxv-xxxvi)

[Performances of Björnson's first social drama, *The Editor,*] led to disturbances and to an angry public controversy. From the first, justice was not done to *The Editor,* and it has never been appreciated. It was an attack on the egotism and passion of the press, and, as a matter of course, the journalists could not endure it. That Björnson should dare to attack this privileged class—the sacred priesthood of the close of the nineteenth century—was a vivid proof of his courage or at least of his temerity. But he was promptly punished for his audacity.

Yet, to an unprejudiced reader, *The Editor* seems an extremely interesting and original work, faulty, indeed, in its daring realism, but full of cleverness and verve. It is a sort of allegory, too, in which the author, half-unconsciously, gives himself the rôle of hero, and we see, with curiosity and amusement, what Björnson thought in 1874 of himself and the figure he cut in Norway. (p. l)

Preposterous as it is in many ways—and especially in its close, where Harald breaks a blood-vessel and dies on reading an unparalleled article in the newspaper, and the Editor happens, as a passer-by, to be called in to carry his dead body to the bed—this play is full of vitality and a sort of mysterious vivacity. . . . The second act is of a real theatrical ingenuity; the action passes in a street of the city, in dense fog, and figures pass, strange and typical figures, laden with fate and intrigue. The conversations throughout are more sparkling than any which Björnson had written up to that date. It was a very remarkable experiment in dramatic composition, and one which was to lead its author and the literature of his country far.

If Björnson succeeded in ruffling the temper of his countrymen with *The Editor,* he immediately reconquered their suffrages with his extremely popular drama, *A Bankruptcy*. The action of this piece is very simple. Tjælde is the head of a respectable Norwegian family, all the different members of which are presented to us in an interesting and sympathetic manner. (pp. l-lii)

A Bankruptcy has been one of the most popular of all Björnson's writings, but it cannot be considered one of the most important. It owes its popularity to a certain concession made in it to the Teutonic family instinct, to the love of the homely, the comfortable and the domestic. Tjælde's business affairs lack breadth of public interest, and the field of his operations has nothing national about it. No great public calamity fills the background with its shadow, and consequently the imagination is not deeply moved. The blow will fall on the group of indolent, good-natured, unoccupied persons who are introduced to us in the first act, and our interest in it is bounded by our interest in them. That, indeed, is considerable, for the poet has defined them so clearly and so genially, with a humour so serene and a satire so unconscious of poison, that we share their anxieties as though they were personal friends. The second act of *A Bankruptcy* deserves higher praise than the rest of the play; it is admirably conceived and executed with a positive profusion of wit and vivacity. (pp. liii-liv)

But I cannot give *A Bankruptcy* so high a place as has been claimed for it by many critics of weight. The realism of the detail, which dazzled its earliest admirers, has become in the course of twenty years a matter of no extraordinary moment. In the light of Gerhard Hauptmann and Henri Becque it no longer seems effulgent. The drama is a very good, practical family drama of the Teutonic sort, but it is not a great imaginative masterpiece. (pp. liv-lv)

We now approach a period in Björnson's literary life where it is difficult and even dangerous for criticism to follow him. During the last ten years his appearances have been few, and with a single exception they have been confined to fiction. (pp. lxviii-lxix)

[**"Flags Are Flying in Town and Port"** and **"In God's Way"**] are the works by which Björnson is best known to the present generation of Englishmen. They possess elements which have proved excessively attractive to certain sections of our public; indeed, in the case of *In God's Way*, a novel, which was by no means successful in its own country at its original publication, has enjoyed an aftermath of popularity in Scandinavia, founded on reflected warmth from its English admirers. It cannot but be admitted that these are interesting books, original and pleasing in their evolution, well executed in detail and full of valuable and exact observation of human life. In each, the growth of character is chronicled with so agreeable a fidelity to nature, that the attention is riveted until the narrative is—not completed, for Björnson never completes—but relinquished. In these two novels, moreover, Björnson returns, in measure, to the poetical elements of his youth. He is now capable again, as for instance in the episode of Ragni's symbolical walk in the woodlands, in *In God's Way,* of passages of a pure idealism. The character of Ragni, throughout, in relation to scenery and physical phenomena, is sustained at a high imaginative level. If we judged by these two books alone, we should conceive that Björnson had lost his worst provincial faults, had gained firmness and consistency of treatment, and was on his road to successes greater than any that he had yet dreamed of. (pp. lxix-lxx)

Björnson is practially the best living instance of what M. Edouard Rod calls "intuitivism" in imaginative literature. He does not argue or generalise; he forms, without reasoning, a perception of character, and he puts this perception on paper, with agitation, with a certain precipitancy of the sensitive consciousness, convinced that disturbance will destroy for ever the fugitive idea. Hence the occasional incongruity of his forms; hence the almost constant inability to tie up the ends of a story, to conduct it to a harmonious and graceful close. The intuition ceases, and with it the tale must cease. The author is actuated by no series of principles, is attended by no array of collected phenomena, but is a free lance dependent entirely on the dash and impetus of his immediate apprehension. If this distinction be seized and accepted, it is seen to place a chasm, not merely between the Naturalists and Björnson, but between him and such writers as Tolstoi and Dostoieffsky.

If this be true, and I believe that in no other way can the oddities of Björnson's attitude towards life and literature be explained, it leads us to a certain regret that he should not have resigned himself more frankly than he has done to his singular gift of instinctive appreciation. With such flashing insight, with so little need to lean upon experimental knowledge, he should have been pre-eminently an artist. But his whole effort seems to have been to quench the artist in himself, and to urge into activity a prophet, a hieratic personage, whom he conceived to be devoted to sacred uses and the renovation of mankind. . . . He is not content to contemplate or to create; he must be pulling down and digging up. For him, the pessimistic attitude of Ibsen—so cold, so dignified, so self-restrained—presumes an intolerable bondage. . . . [Björnson] longs to act, to correct, to ameliorate social conditions. All this at once animated and weakens his literary production. Ceaseless revolt is not a favourable attitude for poetical composition, nor is mere temerity in itself an illumination, and Björnson would . . . be a more charming writer, if he had gradually allowed the turbulent vehemence of his youth to evaporate, instead of carefully generating and feeding it. (pp. lxxii-lxxiv)

> *Edmund Gosse, "A Study of the Writings of Björnstjerne Björnson," in* The Novels of Björnstjerne Björnson: Synnove Solbakken, Vol. I *by Björnstjerne Björnson, edited by Edmund Gosse, translated by Julie Sutter, Macmillan and Co., 1894 (and reprinted by William Heinemann, 1909), pp. v-lxxvi.*

WILLIAM LYON PHELPS   (essay date 1910)

Of all forms of literature, pastoral tales, whether in verse or in prose, have been commonly the most artificial and the most insipid; but [in *Synnöve Solbakken*] was the breath of life. I can recommend nothing better for the soul weary of the closeness of modern naturalism than a course of reading in the early work of Björnson.

He followed this initial success with three other beautiful prose lyrics—*Arne, A Happy Boy,* and *The Fisher Maiden*. These stories exhibit the same qualities so strikingly displayed in *Synnöve Solbakken*. In all this artistic production Björnson is an impressionist, reproducing with absolute fidelity what he saw, both in the world of matter and of spirit. We may rely faithfully on the correctness of these pictures, whether they portray natural scenery, country customs, or peasant character. . . . Björnson says, "The church is in the foreground of Norwegian peasant life." And indeed everything seems to centre around God's acre, and the spire of the meeting-house points in the same direction as the stories themselves. Many beautiful passages affect us like noble music; our eyes are filled with happy tears.

In view of the strong and ardent personality of the author, it is curious that these early romances should be so truly objective. One feels his personality in a general way . . . ; but the young writer separates himself entirely from the course of the story; he nowhere interferes. The characters apparently develop without his assistance, as the events take place without any manipulation. As a work of objective art, *Synnöve Solbakken* approaches flawless perfection—forward. The persons are intensely Norwegian, but there their similarity ends. Each is individualised. The simplicity of the story is so remarkable that to some superficial and unobservant readers it has seemed childish. (pp. 85-7)

The novels in Björnson's second period are so totally unlike those we have just been considering that if all his work had been published anonymously, no one would have ventured to say that the same man had written *A Happy Boy* and *In God's Way*. (p. 88)

Now Björnson feels [responsibility for the universe] with all the strength of his nature, and however admirable it may be as a moral quality, it has vitiated his artistic career. As he renounced Christianity for agnosticism, so he renounced romance for realism. The novels written since 1875 are not only unlike his early pastoral romances in literary style; they are totally different productions in tone, in spirit, and in intention. (p. 90)

In addition to many short sketches, his later period includes three realistic novels. These are: [*The Heritage of the Kurts*], . . . a study in heredity; *In God's Way*, loudly proclaimed as his masterpiece, and *Mary*. . . . In these three novels the author has stepped out of the rôle of artist and become a kind of professor of pedagogy, his specialty being the education of women. In [*The Heritage of the Kurts*] the principal part of the story is taken up with a girls' school, which gives the novelist an opportunity to include a confused study of heredity, and to air all sorts of educational theory. The chief one appears to be that in the curriculum for young girls the "major" should be physiology. Hygiene, which so many bewildered persons are accepting just now in lieu of the Gospel, plays a heavy part in Björnson's later work. . . . [The book] is, frankly speaking, an intolerable bore. The hero, Rendalen, . . . is the mouthpiece of the new opinions of the author; a convenient if clumsy device, for whenever Björnson wishes to expound his views on education, hygiene, or religion, he simply makes Rendalen deliver a lecture. Didactic novels are in general a poor substitute either for learning or for fiction, but they are doubly bad when the author is confused in his ideas of science and in his notions of art. One general "lesson" emerges from the jargon of this book—that men should suffer for immorality as severely as women, a doctrine neither new nor practicable. The difficulty is that with Björnson, as with some others who shout this edict, the equalising of the punishment takes the form of leaving the men as they are, and issuing a general pardon to the women. (pp. 90-2)

It is pleasant to take up the volume *In God's Way*, for, however disappointing it may be to those who know the young Björnson, it is vastly superior to [*The Heritage of the Kurts*]. It is what is called to-day a "strong" novel, and has naturally evoked the widest variation of comment. By many it has been greeted with enthusiastic admiration and by many with outspoken disgust. Psychologically, it is indeed powerful. The characters are interesting, and they develop in a way that may or may not be God's, but resemble His in being mysterious. One cannot foresee in the early chapters what is going to happen to the

dramatis personae, nor what is to be our final attitude toward any of them. . . . Not one of these characters remains the same; each one develops, and develops as he might in actual life. Björnson does not approach his men and women from an easy chair, in the descriptive manner; once created, we feel that they would grow without his aid.

For all this particular triumph of art, *In God's Way* is plainly a didactic novel, with the author preaching from beginning to end. The "fighting" quality in the novelist gets the better of his literary genius. We have a story in the extreme realistic style, marked by occasional scenes of great beauty and force; but the exposition of doctrine is somewhat vague and confused, and the construction of the whole work decidedly inartistic. Two general points, however, are made clear: First, that one may walk in God's way without believing in God. . . . This is a modern view, and perhaps a natural reaction from the strictness of Björnson's childhood training. Second, that virtue is a matter entirely of the heart, bearing no relation whatever to the statute-book. . . . Björnson has taken an extraordinary instance to prove his thesis, a thesis that perhaps needs no emphasis, for human nature is only too well disposed to make its moral creed coincide with its bodily instincts.

The same theme—mental as opposed to physical female chastity—is the leading idea of *Mary*. . . . This work of his old age shows not the slightest trace of decay. It is an interesting and powerful analysis of a girl's heart, written in short, vigorous sentences. . . . Her theory of conduct (which exemplifies that of Björnson) is that a woman is the sovereign mistress of her own body, and can do what she pleases. There is nothing immoral in a woman's free gift of herself to her lover, provided she does it out of her royal bounty, and not as a weak yielding to masculine pursuit. (pp. 93-5)

In comparing the three late with the four early novels, the most striking change is instantly apparent to anyone who reads *Synnöve Solbakken* and then opens *In God's Way*. It is the sudden and depressing change of air, from the mountains to the sick-room. The abundance of medical detail in the later novel is almost nauseating and would be wholly so were it not absurd. (p. 96)

As a destructive force Ibsen was stronger than Björnson, because he was ruthless. But one had the courage of despair, while the other has the courage of hope. Björnson does not believe in Fate and is not afraid of it. He loves and believes in humanity. His gloomiest books end with a vision. There is always a rift in the clouds. (p. 97)

William Lyon Phelps, "Björnstjerne Björnson," in his Essays on Modern Novelists *(reprinted with permission of Macmillan Publishing Co., Inc.; copyright 1910 by Macmillan Publishing Co., Inc.; renewed 1938 by William Lyon Phelps), Macmillan, 1910 (and reprinted by Macmillan Publishing Co., Inc., 1924), pp. 82-98.*

LAFCADIO HEARN   (essay date 1915)

[Björnstjerne Björnson was] destined to revive the ancient saga literature in modern times, and so make a new literature unlike anything that had been before it. (p. 76)

[The wonder of "*Synnöve Solbakken*"] was not in the story, not in the plot; it was in the astonishing method of the telling. The book reads as if it had been written by a saga man of the ninth or tenth century; the life described is indeed modern, but the art of telling it is an art a thousand years old, which scholars imagined could never be revived again. Björnson revived it; and by so doing he has affected almost every literature in Europe. Perhaps he has especially affected some of the great French realists; at all events, he gave everybody interested in literature something new to think about. But this first novel was only the beginning of a surprising series of productions,—poetical, romantic, historical and political. . . . But his chief merit is that he is the father and founder of a new literature, which we may call modern Norse. (p. 77)

Moreover, you will find in the work of this man the most perfect pictures possible to make of the society and the character of a people. . . . [This] life he portrayed in a way that has no parallel in European literature with the possible exception of the Russian work done by Turgueniev and others. He has also given us studies of Norwegian character among the middle class, among the clergymen, and among the highly cultivated university people. . . . But these studies are interesting only to the degree that they show the real Norse character, such as the peasant best exemplifies, in spite of modern education. It is a very stern, strong and terrible character; but it is also both lovable and admirable. Brutal at moments, it is the most formidable temperament that we can imagine; but in steadfastness and affection and depth of emotional power, it is very grand. . . . [**"Synnöve Solbakken"**] is a very simple story of peasant life. It describes the lives of a boy and girl in the country up to the time of their marriage to each other, and it treats especially of the inner life of these two—their thoughts, their troubles, their affections. There is nothing unusual about it except the truth of the delineation. (pp. 78-9)

> *Lafcadio Hearn, "Studies of Extraordinary Prose: Björnson," in his* Interpretations of Literature, Vol. II *(copyright, 1915 by Mitchell McDonald; copyright renewed © 1942 by Kazuo Koizumi), Dodd, Mead and Company, 1915 (and reprinted by Dodd, Mead, 1926), pp. 71-82.*

WILLIAM MORTON PAYNE (essay date 1917)

The biographer of Björnson, Christian Collin, characterizes both Björnson and Ibsen as men of "two-story minds," and suggests that herein lies the secret of their power and charm. The foundation-story, in both cases, is built of material quarried from the historical and legendary past of Norway, its sagas, its folk-lore, and its mythology and in this rich treasure-house of imagery and fundamental motive both poets found the poetical inspiration of their earlier work. Then the ferment of modern thought became active in their minds, and they built their superstructure out of the materials—political or social, intellectual or moral—provided by contemporary life, discussing or envisaging the problems of the modern world in the light of the creative imagination that had come to maturity during their preoccupation with the deep-rooted ideas that were their racial inheritance. Certainly, the outstanding fact in the career of both poets is the transformation in form, if not in spirit, that came over their work at the age of forty or thereabouts. (p. vii)

If, on the other hand, we ask how the two poets are differentiated, it seems fair to say that Björnson's lower story has deeper foundations, and is more solidly built, than Ibsen's, and that his superstructure does not exhibit so absolute an abandonment of the material previously used. Ibsen's earlier recourse to saga and legend was rather the expression of the romantic temperament than the result of a racial mandate. . . .

The latter half of his life found him a romanticist turned realist, and that is all. Now Björnson was also a romanticist turned realist, but his romanticism was of the type which only a Norseman could exhibit, and the realist that he afterwards became never wholly lost those racial traits that made him throughout his career preëminently the voice of his people. . . . He could never be quite the cosmopolitan that Ibsen became, because, however wide-spreading his tree in its foliage, its roots were firmly planted in his native soil. . . . However sophisticated his work became, it never wholly lost the elements of *naïveté* and raciness that marked the earlier manifestations of his genius. (pp. vii-viii)

Arnljot Gelline and the saga-trilogy of *Sigurd Slembe* constitute Björnson's highest achievement in his reconstruction of the heroic past of Norway. The two works are closely akin. Each of them has a protagonist whose presentation is a miracle of creative power—a figure taken from the saga-literature, and endowed with a warmth and richness of life that the original barely suggests, a life which the poet infused with his own personality. . . . Björnson raised these two legendary figures into the light of day, looked into his own heart for inspiration, and made them the mouthpiece of all that was deepest in him of human sympathy, of devotion to country, and of religious aspiration. It is not often in literature that one can see the creative process so clearly at work as when one compares the scanty and episodical materials furnished by the *Heimskringla* with the warm and vital portraiture of the heroes of these two masterpieces. (pp. viii-ix)

[*Arnljot Gelline*] had occupied him, off and on, for more than ten years, the *Sturm und Drang* period of his early manhood. It had done him the service of the Aristotelian *katharsis*. (p. xi)

In the matters of orthography and vocabulary, the poem exhibited many innovations, although it by no means went to the lengths advocated by the *maalstraever*, or champions of a distinctively national form of speech. It was written, as most Norwegian works were and still are, in the literary language of Denmark. . . . The poem offers a great variety of rhythms, each of the fifteen Songs having its own characteristic form of verse. Only three of them—the first, the fourth, and the seventh—are rhymed throughout. . . . The rest of the poem is in what it is now the fashion to call *vers libre*, irregular and rugged, the lines having stresses varying from one to five. The general movement of the verse is trochaic, with the latitude and flexibility offered by a liberal use of dactyls. Alliteration is frequently employed, but not systematically. Careful observation will disclose the fact that the rhythms, however lawless they may seem at times, give us forms that are rigorously subordinated to definite conceptions, fitted, as only a true poet can fit them, to the dramatic and emotional requirements of the respective Songs. (pp. xii-xiii)

> *William Morton Payne, in his introduction to* Arnljot Gelline *by Björnstjerne Björnson, translated by William Morton Payne, The American Scandinavian Foundation, 1917, pp. vii-xiv.*

HAROLD LARSON (essay date 1944)

Among the poets of the world it would be hard, indeed, to find a more vigorous and manly figure than Björnstjerne Björnson. When Norwegians cherish his memory today they pay tribute quite as much to his vibrant personality as to his writings or to his achievements. For more than fifty years he was the storm center of Norwegian life, never sparing himself when there was a cause he could serve. (p. 16)

[It was] patriotism which motivated his career as the national poet of modern Norway. His literary debut was made in 1854 with a review of *A New Year's Book,* an anthology to which the leading Norwegian poets had contributed. With the audacity of youth Björnson swept aside the older celebrities on the Norwegian literary scene and announced the coming of a new generation of poets who should follow the cheerful and lifelike national poetry of Henrik Wergeland. A scant two years later, in 1856, Björnson himself was ready to lead this new generation of poets. Nor in the ensuing years did he restrict his literary production to a single field. Stories, dramas, novels, poems and songs flowed from his pen in a steady stream. Thus Björnson gave to his native land the nucleus of the modern and truly Norwegian literature that emerged in the course of the nineteenth century. . . .

The first published poem (1851) which bears Björnson's name is a tribute in verse to his boyhood home in Romsdal. He himself, however, traced his determination to become a poet to the eventful year 1856. Fresh from the conflict over the Danish influence in the Christiania Theater, Björnson has described how, joyfully, he attended an inspiring Scandinavian student gathering in Sweden in June, 1856. There according to his own account he was overwhelmed by memories of the past and by the sight of the garments, weapons, and tombs of the Swedish kings. More than ever before he was impressed by the work of P. A. Munch in revealing the history of Norway. The thought came to him that the Norwegians also had celebrated ancestors and that from the sagas of their kings could be created a historical gallery in which a poet would find interesting studies. (p. 31)

Beginning with his very first literary works Björnson used the device of having his characters reveal their hidden feelings in poem and song. Only rarely do his stanzas appear alone. In general they fall into the pattern of a drama or a story and almost always they deal not with nature but with the character, the deeds, and the fate of man. Because they are occasional, Björnson's poems and songs account for but a small portion of his entire literary production. Yet they have become so much a part of Norwegian life, so national in fact that one can safely say that no Norwegian of today could reach maturity without having made their acquaintance in one form or another. Björnson's own collection of his *Poems and Songs* . . . ran into approximately 100,000 copies. Aside from his national anthem, *Ja, vi elsker dette landet (Yes, we love this land),* which occupies a special position of its own, his lines have been printed and reprinted in numerous books, readers, anthologies, pamphlets, and newspapers in his native land. No other Norwegian poet has appealed so strongly to Norwegian composers as has Björnson. As a result his words, set to music, have resounded from one end of the country to the other. Familiar to all Norwegians are such exquisitely tender bits of verse as "Synnöve's Song" in *Synnöve Solbakken,* and the inspiring lines of the poems, "Love Thy Neighbor" and "Lift Thy Head," which appear in *A Happy Boy.* Characteristic of Björnson himself is his poem "I Choose April." That month appealed to him precisely because it was stormy. But the basic subject of Björnson's verse was "patriotism in the broadest sense." Compact, abrupt, suggestive, dramatic, his poems and songs are primarily expressions of the patriot paying tribute to the Norway he loved. That no doubt is why to this day they are treasured by the Norwegian nation.

Björnson's poems and songs were only a small though highly significant portion of his entire contribution toward a modern Norwegian literature. (pp. 31-2)

Collin says Björnson's first patriotic song was *Over de höje Fjelde (Over the lofty Mountains),* which describes one of the chief motivating forces in the entire history of the Norwegian people, the inner impulse to expansion and the adventurous longing for the great and the distant. This song, originally appearing in *Arne,* dates from that sojourn in Bergen (1857-59), which saw the flowering of his nationalism. But his first national song written for the public was *Der ligger et land (There lies a land),* composed for that memorable May 17 [national holiday] in Bergen in 1859. Early in the summer of that same year at Hop near Bergen he wrote the original version of *Ja, vi elsker dette landet (Yes, we love this land),* which later in modified form has become Norway's national anthem.

The two patriotic songs mentioned above were revised considerably by the author in 1863, and the changes then made are significant. *There lies a land* originally began with the banal line, "We Norsemen shall sing for Norway a song," for which was substituted the picturesque and sonorous opening verse depicting the land of eternal snow, whose mighty spirit watches like a mother over her children. Still more noteworthy are the alterations in *Yes, we love this land.* Omitted was the one stanza, intended for Charles XV, which glorified the Union with Sweden, and an entirely new closing stanza was added, wherein the initial lines of the first stanza, "Yes, we love this land . . .", are repeated although the thought no longer is directed toward father and mother and the dreams of sagas of the past but is turned instead toward the future of the land, with the promise that if need be, "We shall take the field in its defense." No translation can do full justice to the original, but since it has become the national anthem a brief characterization of its contents will not be amiss. First the poet conjures up the vision of his beloved native land towering ruggedly above the waters. Next follows an array of historic figures—Harold Fairhair, who united the country; Olaf the Saint; King Sverre, who defied Rome; and Tordenskjold, the naval hero. Past is linked to present, not in the spirit of glorification but rather of humble pride: "we were not many but we sufficed . . . sooner would we burn the land than let it fall." Hard times we endured "but in our worst need, blue-eyed freedom to us was born." But "thanks be to God, protector of the land, we won our right." Then comes the closing stanza—"Yes, we love this land," etc.—which as Francis Bull rightly claims, gives the song its strength, its harmonious unity, "where present and past meet and the future is built on the groundwork of the past." With the inclusion of this stanza, says Bull, the song for the first time became the rallying national anthem.

But the national anthem was not complete until a melody had been composed for it by the gifted young Richard Nordraach (1842-66). Originally intended to accompany Björnson's celebrated *Answer from Norway,* directed at a speaker in the Swedish *Riksdag* who had ridiculed the Norwegian flag, the basic melody was later incorporated by Nordraach in the now familiar musical accompaniment of *Yes, we love this land.* Singing it was once likened by Björnson to looking upward to a mountain, and it owed its strength, he believed, to its timeliness and to its intensely Norwegian character. (pp. 73-5)

Harold Larson, in his Bjornstjerne Bjornson: A Study in Norwegian Nationalism, *King's Crown Press, 1944, 172 p.*

ALRIK GUSTAFSON (essay date 1947)

It is as a lyric poet and as a teller of peasant tales that [Björnson] is most apt to live for future generations of Norwegians; but in the drama he has also written a few plays of permanent importance, certain of his plays being in their day of crucial significance in the development of the modern Scandinavian drama. To Björnson, for instance, must be given the credit for writing . . . the first "social-reform play" that really succeeded in the theatre (*A Bankruptcy*), a play which apparently encouraged Ibsen to continue with a type of drama with which he had experimented only halfheartedly before. (p. 45)

[His] dramatic trilogy *Sigurd the Bastard* found numerous admirers, among them Hans Christian Andersen in Denmark, and Ibsen. . . . (pp. 45-6)

Though *Sigurd the Bastard* is entirely too lengthy to succeed as a popular acting drama, it has on occasion been staged. It has frequently been compared with Ibsen's *Pretenders,* particularly because of certain similiarities in characterization and in the ultimate fates of the central characters in the two dramas. Sigurd, like Earl Skule in Ibsen's drama, is a pretender to the throne, and one who strives to attain his ends even though his claim to the throne is at best questionable. Like Earl Skule, Sigurd also fails in his efforts, and his death clears the way for a just determination of who shall finally occupy the throne. Ibsen's *The Pretenders* reveals, however, a much more profound understanding of psychological motivations, though *Sigurd the Bastard* reflects a finer sense of general historical perspective. In certain individual scenes also Björnson's drama has great power, particularly in the second part of the trilogy. Both Shakespeare and Schiller had left obvious imprints on *Sigurd the Bastard,* and when Björnson wrote his next play, *Mary Stuart of Scotland* . . . , he tried his hand, not unsuccessfully, with an historical character whom Schiller also had handled. This play about Mary Stuart is, next to *Sigurd the Bastard,* Björnson's best historical drama; but it has nevertheless numerous rather glaring defects, the closing act being on the whole unsatisfactory, and the characters being too much concerned with "explaining themselves" in rather tiresome rounds of dialogue. The characters in themselves are interesting enough, however, especially the sensitive and will-less but deeply loyal Darnley, and Knox, the man whom even the Queen comes to admire despite her distaste for all that his forbidding Puritan idealism stands for. (p. 46)

Though none of [Björnson's problem plays] is of permanent importance, each originates in a vital idea, and each served in its day to "put problems into debate" in the same manner as Ibsen's social-reform plays. Two of them, *The Bankruptcy* and *The Editor,* antedated by some years Ibsen's plays in the same genre. (p. 47)

[*A Bankruptcy*] immediately enjoyed a phenomenal success in the theatres of all three of the Scandinavian countries as well as in Germany. Its clearly delineated characters and lively dialogue, together with its happy ending, made it very acceptable theatrical fare for the general run of audience which could scarcely distinguish its dramatic inadequacies. Both *The Editor* and *A Bankruptcy,* however, served a vital purpose in breaking down the historical tradition in the Scandinavian drama of the day and in pointing a way toward new dramatic themes. "They were the signal rockets," wrote Strindberg in the 1880's, "which rose toward the heavens and broke out into salvos whose echoes we have not yet forgotten." Both Ibsen and Strindberg were to go much farther than did Björnson in the creation of a new modern drama, but it remains an historical fact that Björnson provided the original impetus toward these new forms when . . . he published *A Bankruptcy* and *The Editor.*

Perhaps the two most interesting of Björnson's early group of social-reform plays are *The King* and *Leonarda,* both because they deal somewhat more boldly than was usual in Björnson with what at the time were really delicate problems, and because in each of these plays the central character is conceived with a depth and understanding not always characteristic of Björnson. Spontaneity of dialogue and rapid sweep of dramatic movement are more apt to be the qualities found in Björnson's dramas than psychological profundities. But in the sensitive, solitary character of the King and in the nobly passionate struggle of Leonarda to find a place for herself in life, Björnson has succeeded in creating figures not unworthy of his countryman Ibsen. Both of these characters are conceived as victims of social conditions, though in the case of Leonarda some elements in society seems at the end of the play to be prepared to make what restitution they can for the wrongs they have perpetrated in the name of truth and morality.

In *Leonarda* it is noteworthy that a churchman is the personage who at the end of the drama admits that society and the Church have been unfair in judging Leonarda as they did. Björnson's satire on the Established Church as the instrument of a narrow dogmatic morality is thus somewhat unexpectedly tempered at the end of the play. In *Beyond Human Power I,* Björnson writes a purely religious play, and one which in the scope of its thought, the depth of its feeling, and the noble pathos of its tragedy ranks as one of the very few really great Scandinavian plays on a religious theme. *Beyond Human Power I,* is not concerned primarily with religious practices or religious dogmas as they may find expresion in any particular society or community; it is concerned rather with a much more profound and universal aspect of religious experience and practice—the tendency on the part of certain religions, particularly perhaps Protestant Christianity, to stress the supernatural to the point where human life is frequently distorted and ideal values are destroyed. . . . Björnson wishes in this play to illustrate that an idealism which postulates that which is impossible of attainment leads inevitably to evil rather than to good. *Beyond Human Power I* rises above its thesis, however, developing with a dramatic power and a sustained poetic feeling that Björnson attains in none of his other dramas. In construction it is firm, balanced, thoroughly classical both in line and in form. Though its moods shift from moment to moment in the cxourse of its rapidly developing action, over the whole rests a serenity, a quiet self-contained majesty such as is found only in the greatest works of classical art. (pp. 48-9)

If in *Beyond Human Power I* Björnson had created a work of great and timeless art, raised far above the concerns of immediate contemporary "problems," in another play, *A Gauntlet,* . . . he descends again into the hurly-burly of the marketplace, mounts the rostrum, and proceeds to preach—this time more vehemently than ever before in his plays. *A Gauntlet* is nothing more nor less than a sermon, in thinly disguised dramatic form. (p. 49)

Unimportant as *A Gauntlet* is from a purely dramatic point of view, its subject may be said to provide a kind of general point of departure for most of Björnson's later plays. Though the play might on first reading seem to be concerned exclusively with a question of private morality, it is clear from Björnson's statements at the time that he was primarily concerned with a larger question, the preservation of the family as the basic unit in the development of the nation and the race. And it is therefore that Bjørnson comes more and more in his later plays to focus on problems concerned more or less directly with love and marriage and life within the home. In *Love and Geography* . . . he writes an ingratiating but pointed comedy on the relation between a man and his wife and child. [In *Laboremus* and *At Storhove*] . . . he contributes a couple of dramatic studies in the fatal effect which the completely emancipated woman can exercise on marriage relationships. And in [*Dayland* and *When the Vineyards Are in Blossom*] . . . he deals with the subject of the proper adjustment between parents and children. In only two of the plays that Bjørnson composed between the middle of the 1880's and his death in 1910 can it be said that the family is not at the focus of his attention. These plays are *Beyond Human Power II*, dealing with the relationship between labor and capital, and *Paul Lange and Tora Parsberg*, concerned primarily with a political problem.

Beyond Human Power II, is a reasonably successful play, though one tends to be critical toward it because its title invites comparison with Bjørnson's great play, *Beyond Human Power I*. . . . In its general construction and the pointing of its central idea, *Beyond Human Power II* is certainly a satisfying play, but its handling of character tends to be schematic and abstract. In *Paul Lange and Tora Parsberg*, however, Bjørnson is occupied much more profoundly with character than with ideas and dramatic patterns; and he succeeds in giving us a wholly convincing picture of the way in which politics distorts fine individual values and finally destroys them altogether. Paul Lange has much in common with Ibsen's Johannes Rosmer, though unlike Rosmer he has had a political career when we meet him in the drama. Like Rosmer he is sensitive, idealistic, but with a strain of weakness in his character. It is this weakness that causes him to hesitate at a moment of crisis in his political career, with the result that an insensitive public, including some of his best friends and former political associates, misunderstand his motives and accuse him of disloyalty to his earlier political program. This leads to his suicide—a victim of political badgering of the most unfeeling and vicious kind. . . . Bjørnson had not infrequently in earlier plays been concerned with political problems, most markedly in *The Editor* and *The King;* but only in *Paul Lange and Tora Parsberg* has he managed to write a political play of first importance. The chief reason for his success in this instance is perhaps that he has come to see more deeply than before the personal problem in politics, and the relation of his personal problem to the whole question of human progress. (pp. 49-51)

> *Alrik Gustafson, "The Scandinavian Countries" (reprinted by permission of the Literary Estate of Alrik Gustafson), in* A History of Modern Drama, *edited by Barrett H. Clark and George Freedley, Appleton-Century-Crofts, 1947, pp. 1-75.**

HARALD BEYER   (essay date 1952)

During the years from 1856 to 1872 Bjørnson carried on his curious "crop rotation," which meant that he worked alternately at country tales and saga dramas. The purpose was to show the kinship between the peasant of today and the heroes of the saga. He found some of the same qualities in both—restrained strength, emotional reserve, desire for adventure, inability to speak out. The saga dramas were to strengthen the national backbone of the people, so that they could assert themselves against their brother nation. The rural tales were a link in the social and political conflict of the times. They were not merely intended to oppose skeptical opinions concerning the peasant, but also to give the latter self-confidence and the courage to take his proper part in the building of the country.

There was also a personal message in his writing. He felt in his own character the conflict between, on the one hand, savagery, force, unscrupulousness, vengefulness, vanity, and on the other, the humanitarian impulse to live for others, to seek harmony and a social, ethical, and religious subordination of self. He wished to strengthen the forces for good. . . . (p. 190)

The theme of all his writing in this period is the idea that every talented individual must pass through a school of suffering. All his heroes are robust fellows who have to overcome some weakness of character to be useful in life. Thorbjørn in *Synnøve Solbakken* has a hard struggle to overcome the savagery in his own nature. But he wins out through persistence and with the help of Synnøve's love. In the same way Arne has to overcome his desire to emigrate and his dreamy romanticism. Øivind in *A Happy Boy* . . . is hampered by his ambition and his self-love. The same fundamental idea occurs in the masterful short story "The Father."

All the country tales end happily. The church holds a high position in them; in Bjørnson's words, "the church in a Norwegian valley stands in a high place." Religion is to teach people to turn from self-love to neighborly love. But the saga dramas usually end tragically. Here Christianity and culture combine in order to tame the viking spirit and create a social attitude, force the viking nature under the laws of love and life. But the savagery is too powerful, and the hero is destroyed. The young, vital Sigurd Slembe has more than enough abilities, and the world is open to him, but he fails to win the throne of Norway because he cannot conquer himself.

Bjørnson did not want his rural folk to be "Sunday peasants" like those in [Adolf] Tidemand's paintings. We sometimes feel that they are idealized, while his own times accused them of coarseness. Actually, they are neither. They do not tell us a great deal about the daily problems of the farmer, but then they were not intended to be primarily pictures of folk life. They are studies of character. As such they certainly do not lack realistic details; we need only think of Nils the Tailor's tragedy in *Arne* or the story of Aslak in *Synnøve Solbakken*.

The most important literary impulses for the writing of *Synnøve Solbakken* were [Peter Christen] Asbjørnsen's folk tales, the sagas, and Hans Christian Andersen's fairy tales. But the style was felt as something entirely new. The whole rhythm and tempo was a break with the more circumstantial style of an earlier generation of writers. There was a more Norwegian choice of words, short, vigorous sentences, bold images, and usually something unspoken to be read between the lines. If we read the stories without prejudice, we can still feel the freshness of the style. It is a masterful story, fully worthy of inclusion in world literature. *Arne* is more uneven, but has splendid passages like the opening chapter about "clothing the mountain." It gives a kind of perspective on Norwegian history, and its anti-emigration theme ties up with his play *Valborg*. . . . *A Happy Boy* is the most cheerful in tone and lyrical in form. It may seem almost too idyllic today, but it is genuinely poetic and has considerable historical interest. It gives us valuable glimpses of Ole Vig's work for popular education and Gisle Johnson's revivalism, as well as the activities of the first agricultural schools. (pp. 190-92)

The saga dramas were more uneven. *Between the Battles* was a fine beginning. *Lame Hulda* was weaker, reminiscent of

[Adam] Oehlenschläger with its iambic pentameter and its theme of the conflict between paganism and Christianity. The play *King Sverre* . . . was a complete failure and was badly received by the critics, to Bjørnson's great distress. But he recovered and wrote the best of his saga plays, the trilogy *Sigurd Slembe* (p. 192)

Harald Beyer, "The Young Bjørnson," in his *A History of Norwegian Literature,* edited and translated by Einar Huagen (copyright 1956 by the American-Scandinavian Foundation: originally published as Norsk Litteraturhistorie, *1952),* New York University Press, 1956, pp. 185-95.

JAMES WALTER McFARLANE (essay date 1960)

[In *Synnøve Solbakken, Arne,* and *A Happy Boy*] the basic pattern is identical: the tracing of a career from childhood through suffering and tearful experience to wedding bells. Bjørnson himself confessed to writing the final pages of *Synnøve Solbakken* with tears in his eyes; and any statistical count of the vocabulary of these stories would surely give the verb 'to weep' a high rating. Tears of sorrow, tears of joy, manly tears, red eyes, sniffs and choking sobs are never long absent. . . . Yet it would be false to interpret this as a sign of cheap sentimentality; the insistence on tears is unexpectedly a corollary of one of the real merits of Bjørnson's narrative: the depth of feeling communicated by the very reticence of his characters. There is in many of the situations a genuine and, as it were, 'built-in' pathos, and the characters are at the mercy of strong emotion which they do not fully comprehend, and which is defined by the nature of the dilemma and not by any analysis or verbal formulation; even in some situations not far short of the melodramatic, there is a terse understatement in the conversational exchanges that is wholly in keeping with the nature of the characters and their experience and which holds the narrative taut. (pp. 77-8)

This taciturnity is, however, compensated for by the often logically improbable but aesthetically well-conceived introduction of passages of pure lyric poetry. . . . Without the relief of this formal eloquence, these stories would have little more than the strong and urgent simplicity of a vintage Western where, against a background of wild but essentially unhostile nature, the men are tight-lipped, the women weep, and drink is a ubiquitous evil. The element that one sadly misses in these stories is some kind of good-humoured irony. . . . One feels indeed that, had it not been that the author loved his characters too well, these stories might easily have had tragic instead of happy endings; the seeds of tragedy are often there in the characters, and the logic of the action often seems to point in that direction; but Bjørnson's artistic detachment was overwhelmed by his affection for those he was writing of. The only surprising thing is that some contemporary criticism should have thought these works too 'raw'; modern opinion thinks rather the reverse. (pp. 78-9)

[In his early] dramas, the motives determining the actions of the characters are elemental and undifferentiated, the situations *allgemein menschlich.* In the case of the women, love rules all; in the case of the men, power; these are the categorical imperatives, these the daemonic powers deep in their nature that they are powerless to disobey. Inga, in *Between the Battles,* abandons husband, home and family to follow her lover; Hulda clings to her husband's murderer in defiance of society's laws; they and their sisters in these dramas are prey to the overwhelming passion that breaks down all reserves, drowns any

voice of conscience, defeats all convention; this is their all or nothing in a society that offers no other avenue of self-fulfillment, and makes of their love a desperate thing. The men of these dramas are heroic, but in a Viking rather than a Greek sense; physical strength is as much a part of the complete man as moral fearlessness; they are impelled by motives of ambition, of personal power, as often as not into mortal conflict with their nearest kin; and it is part of the masculine principle in these works that the men can find only momentary satisfaction in the happiness of a life *à deux.* Inevitably then the dramatic conflicts—the one tending towards jealousy, and the other towards revenge—are so to speak coupled in series rather than in parallel: woman seeks fulfilment in man, and man among men. . . . Any problems, any misgivings they may severally have are nevertheless of the same order—how far they may go and what means they may employ to achieve their ends—but they terminate at different points.

One acknowledges, however, two exceptions to these generalizations: in *Mary Queen of Scots* the traditional roles of man and woman are reversed, with the ruthless and ambitious Mary displaying the more obviously masculine characteristics, and the weak Darnley representing the forces of eroticism and jealousy; and in *Sigurd Slembe* Bjørnson has created in the figure of Harald Jarl a character of subtle modernity, a man who, though humiliated and banished by his half-brother, finds any thought of revenge or of the re-acquisition of power wholly distasteful. (pp. 80-1)

[The changes initiated by *A Bankrupt* and *The Editor*] were extensive, whilst nevertheless leaving the fundamentals of his dramatic art largely untouched. . . . Love and power are still the forces that move his men and women, but there has been a kind of institutionalizing at work: raw passion is replaced by concern for the decencies of matrimony, the naked will to power becomes a reactionary intrigue to preserve it; instinct gives way to expediency, the urgent fearlessness of kings and nobles has become the defensive ruthlessness of ship-owners and company directors, editors and industrialists. The rhetorical gestures are still there; but instead of the arms flung wide as though to embrace and welcome, the finger is pointed in accusation.

Following the pointed finger, one contemplates a series of representative figures whose careers enact their author's optimistic faith in the power of common decency. Consul Tjælde in *A Bankrupt,* the title figure of *The Editor,* as well as Riis, the director-general of *The New System* . . . , all represent the *status quo;* all of them fight a rearguard action, showing much resourcefulness and little integrity, when their positions of power and authority are in jeopardy. But in as much as these three plays tell of the victory of a simple, and largely unarticulated, community good over a private, though socially engendered, evil, they are theatrical rather than dramatic. There is a demonstration of how such modern concentrations of authority tend to corrupt; and there is also an invitation (clear in *A Bankrupt,* less explicit in the other two plays) to see something morally cleansing in being stripped of these modern and unnatural garments of power. Certain institutions of modern society that these figures represent, certain attitudes of mind that they personify, are thus indicted, but the offence is merely sordid; what we have is an accusation, a documenting of the social crime, whereupon justice is done, and seen to be done; but there is no serious clash of personalities, no real thrust in the conflict of ideas, for there is in these plays none of equal stature to oppose or, as it were, cross-examine the delinquents. (pp. 81-2)

After the late 1870s, Bjørnson's work entered a kind of vigorous middle-age, with all the merits and demerits that this implies. His style shows all the confidence of the mature artist, yet with all the old élan unimpaired, so that this last period of his authorship contains much of what is undoubtedly his best work; but it is set in its habits and . . . all the works that follow fall conveniently under two headings: those like the dramas [*Leonarda, A Gauntlet, Geography and Love, Laboremus, Daglannet* and *When the New Wine Blooms*] . . . , which along with the narrative works [*Dust* and *The Heritage of the Kurts*] . . . , deal with private and largely individual problems . . . ; and on the other hand, those like the dramas *Beyond Human Might* and *Paul Lange and Tora Parsberg* and the novel *In God's Way* . . . which treat of the individual's relations with some supra-personal authority. (p. 84)

For Bjørnson's women, the way towards greater independence leads via their discovery of the beastliness of men. *Leonarda* is a highly contrived drama on the theme of women and divorce, in which the men either drink, or deceive their wives, or spread nasty rumours, or marry where there is no longer any love; as a drama, it tends to lose its way in a maze of emotional entanglements, and sacrifices too much to the one supremely theatrical moment when Leonarda triumphs over the bishop. . . . In time, however, the women in Bjørnson's plays take their revenge: Karen Tygesen in *Geography and Love* brings her egotistical scholar husband to heel by absenting herself from the household for a few days . . . ; in *Daglannet* there is a similar wifely victory over an overbearing husband; whilst in *When the New Wine Blooms,* Bjørnson varies the situation by exploiting the same device he had used in *Mary Queen of Scots;* he invests the wife with what had been traditionally the husband's authority, sends her out into the great world of commerce as a career woman, and allows the husband to revenge himself by running off to Australia. (pp. 84-5)

In general, however, the women in these works commend themselves as representatives of their sex rather than as unique or idiosyncratic individuals; they can be counted on to demand an end to their degradation by a society dominated by the male, to seek for educational opportunities and the right to enter the professions, to insist on such sexual restraint from men as is by convention expected from women, and to claim an equal voice not merely in domestic but also in public affairs.

Can it be wholly by chance that Bjørnson was infinitely more successful with that other group of works, of which *Beyond Our Power* is unquestionably the most brilliant? . . . What began as yet another theatre-launched denunciation, ended as a beautifully poised, almost laconic piece in two acts, taut, concentrated, and with a richness of implication that accounts in great measure for its uniqueness in Bjørnson's published work. Elsewhere it is generally only too clear whose side Bjørnson is on, and we are never left in any doubt as to where our sympathies are meant to lie; but here is a play impious in design yet sustained by a great piety, where sceptic and believer appear equally vulnerable, where fanaticism is not without sublimity, where reasonableness seems faintly comic, and where irony never loses its dignity. . . . *Beyond Our Power* reflects Bjørnson's newly-won conviction that decency and morality count for more than any officially Christian faith, and that a belief in the miraculous is unhealthy and remote from life as we know it. (pp. 86-7)

The geometry of the novel *In God's Way* is from one point of view quite intricate: the quadrilateral of a man's relationship to his wife, to his sister and to her husband, with a criss-cross

of diagonal loyalties and attractions, of passions and friendship and family. . . . The personal relationships in the novel are of subsidiary importance in comparison with the fact that the two men, parson and doctor, represent two conflicting philosophies, from the clash of which comes a strong plea for tolerance. In construction, this novel is shapelier than *The Heritage of the Kurts* and reveals a certain readiness on Bjørnson's part to reject material that might have halted the onward movement of the narrative; so that there is (as Hamsun said in his review of it) nothing merely routine in it. But any more positive approval of it would have to be hedged round high with reservations. The most impressive proof of Bjørnson's artistic vitality is provided by the drama [*Paul Lange and Tora Parsberg*]. . . . (p. 87)

Bjørnson is perhaps at his most characteristically Bjørnsonian in his lyric poetry. . . . [His poems'] peculiar power lies in the directness and forcefulness of their altruism, in the simple and moving enunciation of the homelier emotions; they are moreover supremely singable, and this, along with their strongly patriotic appeal, took them deep into the national consciousness.

And no doubt it is here that one can see some reason for Bjørnson's comparative lack of appeal to an English-speaking public so ready to acclaim his contemporary, Henrik Ibsen: namely that this public is made up of detached bystanders who have never been compounded into a responsive audience; belonging to a different national tradition, it is insulated against his spell. In his works he reached on occasion heights of sublimity unapproached by any other Norwegian writing in his century, Ibsen not excluded; but taken all together, the whole corpus of his writing is too often and too deeply riven by serious flaws of taste, of artistry, of structural design—flaws for which the fervour of his enthusiasms and the vigour of his denunciations do not wholly compensate. Great though his stature may be as a figure in world literature, to Norway he meant infinitely more as a noble and generous and eloquent spokesman; and an outsider's view of his works sees them more as permanent reminders of brilliance than as living proofs of it. (pp. 87-9)

*James Walter McFarlane, "Bjørnstjerne Bjørnson,"
in his* Ibsen and the Temper of Norwegian Literature
(© Oxford University Press 1960; reprinted by permission of Oxford University Press), Oxford University Press, London, 1960, pp. 73-89.

HARALD NORENG (essay date 1965)

The classical picture of Bjørnson has its origins not only in Bjørnson's own personality but in the wish of a whole age to see in him, and no other, the great writer and national leader. But in the last generation a new and greatly revised picture of Bjørnson has slowly taken shape. The scholars and artists mentioned above had all met Bjørnson in person and received indelible impressions of his powerful humanity and the contemporary glory surrounding his art. A new generation of scholars has experienced Bjørnson, both the man and the artist, at a distance, and they have not in the long run succeeded in subscribing to the official and traditional idolism of Bjørnson.

The revaluation of Bjørnson that is taking place can, it is true, be traced far back into the nineteenth century. As early as 1869 Henrik Ibsen had drawn in the figure of Stensgaard in "De unges forbund" a none-too-flattering portrait of an ambitious politician and windbag in many ways reminiscent of the young Bjørnson. We also find strongly critical portraits of Bjørnson in "Fra Kristiania-Bohêmen" by Hans Jaeger . . . , and in "Kong Midas" by Gunnar Heiberg . . . , in which the main character, the tactless and megalomaniac moralist, the editor Johannes Ramseth, is an incarnation of the Bjørnson traits which Gunnar Heiberg most disliked.

But the new picture of Bjørnson that is taking shape has as its most important foundation the intensive work in collecting and publishing new Bjørnson material which has been pursued since the writer's death, and which cannot yet be considered wholly completed. (pp. 8-9)

Thanks to the newly presented material, which is constantly being increased by new discoveries of letters, Bjørnstjerne Bjørnson the man gradually emerges with somewhat different features from his traditional and official image. Bjørnson's character must have been full of violent contradictions. In many of the letters to his own children and his wife, or to close friends, he reveals a human compassion and love that can be quite captivating. . . . But in violent contrast to the gentle and amiable sides to his nature there were primitive urges and a lust for power which could produce shocking results. (p. 10)

In traditional character-sketches of Bjørnson, the writer's unique helpfulness and generosity towards colleagues like Ibsen and Lie, Kielland and Hamsun, Strindberg and many others is rightly emphasized. The letters, however, also support the belief that all that was noble in Bjørnson's mind had a dark reverse that expressed itself in the form of cocksureness, pettiness and indiscretion. (p. 11)

But Bjørnson's stature is not diminished by the results of the new research. We see better than before the strength in his talents, and the scope of his contributions is greater than we could have expected. But the man is less homogeneous than many earlier biographers of Bjørnson had thought. The great Bjørnson scholars of an older generation had their intellectual roots in the nineteenth century's optimism and bright faith in man. Our own century . . . has difficulty in holding to this faith. The new picture of Bjørnson has sharper contours than the old, and deeper shadows. But in return it may be more accurate and more genuine.

At the same time the assessment of Bjørnson as a writer has undergone basic changes. In the scholarly tradition of the nineteenth century Bjørnson stood as the sane and supreme writer, successor to Wergeland and his match as a poet, on equal terms with Ibsen—indeed, sometimes his superior as a dramatist. . . . It was long considered a matter of course that Bjørnson should be the only writer of the "great four" in nineteenth-century Norway to be honoured with the Nobel Prize. But fifty years after his death Bjørnson, the novelist, is not much read among the younger generation, and while Ibsen's plays have had ever greater success on the stages both of Norway and abroad, Bjørnson's have steadily declined. (p. 12)

[More] recent research has tried to show that, at its best, Bjørnson's art is not balanced and idyllic, but reflects violent contradictions in the writer's mind. In 1934 John Nome . . . published a prize thesis on "Bjørnsons dikterproblem. Studier omkring 'Over aevne'—ideen". Nome asserts . . . that the "beyond human power" idea has its origin in Bjørnson's own uncompromising personality. He was early forced to fight his own aspiration to all that lay outside or beyond normal human attainments. Bjørnson's longing for classical moderation and harmony . . . was grounded in deep personal necessity. (pp. 12-13)

Bjørnson wrote for the constricted stage of the middle classes, the peep-show theatre, as it is known. An investigation of the dramatic action in each of the plays shows that Bjørnson has a tendency to reconcile contrasts and create harmonious solutions, which are often weakened by moralizing or sentimentality. Bjørnson's characters are always ready to grapple with the moral and social problems typical of middle-class society in the nineteenth century. . . . [Four] of Bjørnson's modern plays have tragic form, viz. ["**Kongen,**" "**Over aevne I,**" "**Over aevne II,**" and "**Paul Lange og Tora Parsberg**"]. . . . Whether Bjørnson has succeeded in endowing the main characters in all these plays with true tragic dimensions is a matter for debate. In "**Over aevne I**" he has succeeded in creating a work of literature which leaves an impression of deep tragedy. The strength of this play lies not only in the characterization, but even more in the peculiar poetic atmosphere with which Bjørnson has surrounded the action, both with the help of stage symbols and a delicate poetic language. In "**Over aevne I**" the contrast between the writer's conscious denial of the miracle and his unconscious longing for it has created the fruitful dramatic tension. (pp. 13-14)

Another expression of the revaluation of Bjørnson's writing can be seen in the fact that Bjørnson's larger epic works, especially the stories and the ponderous novels from the period after 1875 have not tempted scholars to a systematic investigation, as has been the case with the short stories and novels of, for example, Jonas Lie, Alexander Kielland and Amalie Skram. The short and medium-length peasant tales from Bjørnson's earliest literary period have not only better withstood the pressures of time, but even shine with a warmer glow than before. Our generation can easily see that the bright and optimistic characterization appears against a background of shocking and ungovernable passions. (p. 14)

Many individual problems await solution in the years to come. There is a need for comprehensive studies of Bjørnson's poetry, his multifarious epic works, renewed investigations of his best plays and of his letters, articles and speeches. Different aspects of his varied public activity also invite historical investigation. But in the not-too-distant future the time should be ripe for a large systematic work on Bjørnson which must be based not only on the good Bjørnson research of the past, but also on the specialized investigations that have appeared since and on the new assessment that has taken place. (p. 15)

Harald Noreng, "Bjørnson Research: A Survey," in Scandinavica *(copyright © 1965 by the editor of* Scandinavica; *reprinted with permission), Vol. 4, No. 1, May, 1965, pp. 1-15.*

BRIAN W. DOWNS (essay date 1966)

During their lifetime Ibsen and Bjørnson were looked on at home and abroad as the Castor and Pollux of Norwegian literature. There was much argument about which of the two was the greater, and there still is. The argument is bedevilled by the fact that literary merit alone is not at issue. When, in the early years of the century, the Swedish Academy awarded the first Nobel Prizes for Literature, they gave one to Bjørnson, but never to Ibsen. Their terms of reference enjoined them to take 'idealistic tendency' into account, and herein Ibsen was found wanting, many thinking, as some perhaps do today, that he represented an anarchic, pessimistic principle.

Factors such as these bulk especially large in the appraisal of Bjørnson. . . . Posterity, on the whole, has come down on the side of Ibsen . . . , as in another sense it has come down on his side when it has been concerned to weigh literary merit alone. Ibsen remains a great power in the whole Republic of Letters. The same cannot be said of Bjørnson. (pp. 17-18)

[Nevertheless] Bjørnson's work almost always commands attention. In part, though only in part, this springs from the fact that he was a pioneer. Through his peasant-tales he was the first to win recognition for the new Norwegian literature abroad. The renascence of European drama in the latter part of the nineteenth century was due, it is usually accepted, mainly to the example of the two great Norwegian practitioners, Ibsen and him. Though by nearly five years the junior, he found himself the more quickly and in several respects acted as the pacemaker. (p. 18)

He came to historical drama by way of two somewhat trifling costume plays—[*Between the Battles (Mellem Slagene),* and *Limping Hulda (Halte Hulda)*] . . .—dramas of intrigue that happen to be set in bygone times, of which the theatrical idol of the day, Eugène Scribe, was the acknowledged master. The genuinely historical series began in 1861, by which time Bjørnson had turned his back on Scribe and put himself at the feet of Oehlenschläger, Schiller, Kleist and Shakespeare, exemplars of the earlier romantic theatre. It comprises, strictly speaking, only two items, [*Sigurd the Bad (Sigurd Slembe)* and *King Sverre (Kong Sverre)*]. . . . (p. 21)

Sigurd the Bad is the tragedy of an obscure twelfth-century pretender to the Norwegian throne. It calls once more Schiller and Shakespeare to mind, the former by its division into three parts, like *Wallenstein,* the latter not merely by the general features which also characterized [*Mary Stuart in Scotland (Maria Stuart i Skotland)*] but more essentially by its theme. In Sigurd, Bjørnson presented another and a greater Macbeth, the heroic figure of a barbarous age, . . . but also *in esse* and *in posse* a wise, magnanimous statesman, conscious of his abilities and convinced of the legitimacy of his claim to royal station, whom the intrigues and perfidy of a degenerate court drive to armed revolt, fratricide, massacre and treason. The execution is worthy of the theme, whether judged for psychology or theatrical power. The majestic poetry of *Macbeth* is not equalled, but otherwise Bjørnson may here challenge comparison with the English master. (p. 22)

A different Bjørnson is put on the stage in [*Paul Lange and Tora Parsberg (Paul Lange og Tora Parsberg)*]. . . . [The] play is one of his masterpieces. The integration of the public and private action is even closer than in [*The King (Kongen)*], notably in the splendid second act, in a political drawing-room, when the long-sustained, mounting excitement and indignation at Paul Lange's last speech in Parliament is quelled by the coming of the hostess Tora Parsberg with the request to hand her in to dinner. Bjørnson never handled a crowded scene better, never made debate, whether in a crowd or—as in the quiet Acts I and III—between two persons, more effective in dramatic terms. Though he presented himself in Arne Kraft, it is remarkable that Bjørnson never came near to turning his play into either a self-justification or a lecture on politics. A 'fable' from real life is treated with complete artistic integrity.

For all its equally fine embodiment in a dramatic action, *Beyond Our Powers* . . . has, from the title onwards, *tendens* as a prime ingredient. Written with the same emotional involvement as *Paul Lange and Tora Parsberg,* it comes from the author's pen at the culmination of his long and agonizing religious wrestling. . . . Theme and story are magnificently invested: first

and foremost through the character of the central figure, a sincere, humble clergyman, free of all cant and self-deception, and at the same time a devoted, understanding husband and father, killed by the realization of limits to his powers just when for a brief moment he believes that they have bent Heaven to his purposes. Then there is the twofold setting: on the one hand, the poor country parsonage isolated amid threatening forces of nature, and, on the other hand, a vast concourse of folk (tactfully kept out of sight, but not out of hearing), attracted both by the 'miracles' that have been performed and the miracle that is expected, including a party of clergymen, reverently and on occasion humorously treated, who discuss miracles from various standpoints. And lastly there are the strong, but legitimate theatrical effects—organ-music, hallelujahs, church-bells and the like—with the fatal collapse of Pastor Sang and his wife at the acme of their hopes. (pp. 35-6)

(From the first, Bjørnson planned to complement the negative aspect of his theme with a more positive counterpart. That was ultimately attempted in *Beyond Our Powers,* **Part II** . . . , and far from successfully. . . . Lacking all the human interest that makes the strength of Part I, it is no more than a melodrama about an industrial dispute—done much better by Galsworthy in *Strife*—interesting only because its schematic personages and arguments adumbrate some of the methods and ideas of the later Expressionist dramatists).

Among Bjørnson's plays, then, three are outstanding: *Sigurd the Bad, Beyond Our Powers* (**Part I**) and *Paul Lange and Tora Parsberg,* all on weighty themes pursued with immense power to a tragic end. At their centre stand in clear lineaments memorable personages, affording first-rate acting opportunities. They move amid a large, fluid and animated company of well-marked, credible minor figures who contribute to what is perhaps these plays' greatest strength, the convincing solidity of their social setting. The scenario is carefully and economically constructed to keep the focus steadily on the main theme and to preserve dramatic tension throughout.

The remainder of Bjørnson's plays fall a good deal below the standard of his great three, save for these workmanlike qualities, which, admirable as they are, towards the end of his career often constitute their principal recommendation. It is commonly said that Bjørnson's work is deficient in psychological penetration; and it is certainly true that it was never his aim, nor was it his unconscious achievement, to explore any of the characters he projected to the deeps that Ibsen plumbed. (pp. 36-7)

[Turning to the writing of novels], Bjørnson took much longer to find a manner suited to his new utilitarian ideal than that he had so quickly evolved for his plays. So disappointing were [*Magnhild* and *Captain Mansana (Kaptejn Mansana)*] . . . that Georg Brandes recommended him to take lessons in the contemporary French school of fiction. He complied, but with small profit. The bases of their Naturalism were abhorrent to him. . . . It was not until he had been given congenial native examples of a middle-of-the-road realism by [Jonas Lie and Alexander Kielland] . . . that he was able to work out the synthesis of truth-to-life, *tendens* and imaginative appeal to which he aspired.

Lie and Kielland were novelists in the English tradition, in the same broad sense as Bjørnson the dramatist was in the [Emile] Augier tradition; and Bjørnson, who had followed up his course in French with one on English literature, is equally to be ranged in it. Superficially, this shows in Bjørnson's two most substantial novels, of which the earlier, *The Flags are out in Town and Harbour (Det flager i Byen og paa Havnen),* appeared . . . with its somewhat rambling construction, the relatively large number of persons whose interlocking fortunes are related in some detail, the boisterousness of its humour and its lapse into theatricality.

The propaganda in the book is also of English inspiration. Bjørnson, whose reading of books in English in the years just before the publication of *The Flags are Out* was by no means confined to fiction, had been deeply impressed by Herbert Spencer's *Education,* and . . . his novel is a tractate on that subject. It is a somewhat confused one, since it is the education of the *male* in sexual ethics that the author of *A Gauntlet* had at heart, while it is now a *girls'* school, teaching Hygiene in its 'advanced' syllabus and encouraging free discussion among its pupils, round which he built his story. (pp. 37-8)

Nevertheless, Bjørnson was happily inspired in his setting. . . . His Nora, Tora, Tinka and Milla, who form the headmistress's 'general staff', are all admirably done; they give *The Flags are Out* a freshness and gaiety that cover over its unevennesses and doctrinal anomalies and make it the most generally liked of Bjørnson's novels. With the predominance of the feminine element a story likely to win the habitual novel-reader lay to hand. One of the girls had to 'get into trouble'. Over-sexed and impetuous Tora (who acts like a complete little fool throughout) is gotten with child by a wealthy and licentious naval lieutenant, who thereupon proposes to make a match with rich, vain Milla—and Milla, though fully aware of her friend's predicament (in outline at least), is quite amenable, being as unaffected by her education on the best Bjørnsonian principles as Tora. The upshot is a scene in the grand tradition of melodrama; the unmarried mother flings herself and her babe before the altar at the fashionable wedding for which all the flags are out in town and harbour. The intimation, to wind up with, that the future of his odd school is assured through the betrothal of the headmaster to the steadiest of his girls comes as an anti-climax of an equally bizarre character.

The wedding-scene, however, Bjørnson having thrown all *tendens* to the winds, carries everything off, its sinister kernel completely overlaid by its pulsating life and a good deal of deliberate fun that has no trace of cynicism about it. . . . (pp. 38-9)

[*On God's Paths (Paa Guds Veje)*] contains a bravura piece, comparable with this, the description of a provincial ball—hot, stuffy, a little dowdy and surrounded by a fringe of animality, but full to bursting with the energy and joy of the participants—not altogether integrated with the rest. It too, like *The Flags are Out,* has a loose kind of prologue, making a gap of perhaps twenty years between the first chapters and the others. But since it rounds out three of the principal characters by showing them as children, it fits into the general scheme more smoothly; and in structure and the fuller realization both of its theme and of the personages through whom it is worked out *On God's Paths* surpasses its predecessor. It should indeed be ranked among the outstanding examples of typically Victorian fiction. (pp. 39-40)

Brian W. Downs, "Bjørnson," in his Modern Norwegian Literature: 1860-1918 *(© Cambridge University Press 1966), Cambridge at the University Press, 1966, pp. 17-42.*

HENNING K. SEHMSDORF (essay date 1973)

Bjørnson's major peasant stories can be classified as stories of initiation where the difficult passage from childhood to adulthood leads through "the usual three stages, separation, isolation, aggregation, to a renewed communion with society on a higher and more informed plane of living." This statement applies fully to [*Synnøve Solbakken* and *En Glad Gut*] . . . , but only with certain reservations to *Arne.* . . . To put it briefly, the initiation of Arne Kampen into the established order of the adult community is complicated by overwhelming personal problems: one could say that psychologically he is arrested at the second stage, the stage of isolation. Arne makes an external adjustment to society, he is married with a show of communal harmony, but internally he remains separated by deep-seated anxiety and guilt feelings. (p. 310)

The instinctual bond that enslaved his parents and engendered their hate and suffering, fills Arne with deep distrust toward sexuality as well as toward any strong human attachment. Moreover, at the moment he raised his hand against [his father] Nils to defend his mother, Arne felt his father's brutality well up and erupt in himself; thereafter he is afraid of the monster in his own heart. Anxiety and guilt fuse into a nameless fear of people, of life and of the God who now seems a mockery of the just and loving creator he had been taught to believe in. Thus, during the years when the adolescent normally prepares for adult participation in the community, Arne's mind is fixed on escape. (p. 311)

While other young people in the village naturally seek each other out, Arne separates himself from the others in order to find refuge in the solitude of the forest where he spends his days herding sheep. But the forest, too, soon becomes a mirror of the fears welling up from within and twisting his perception of the world. His poem **"I bygden er det uro"** makes the anguished statement that wild nature gives no reprieve from the terror he feels inside of himself. (pp. 312-13)

[Another] poem expresses a contrasting feeling. Although Arne's verses speak of fear and distrust, he is hardly conscious of the extent to which he has become incapable of grasping and accepting life. But a sudden wave of self-recognition washes over him when he hears a lyric sung by a man who lives on their farm, withdrawn like Arne into secret despair. **"Ingerid Sletten,"** a beautiful song patterned after the traditional *folkevise,* tells the haunting story of a girl who lost her chance of a meaningful life because she was afraid to reach out for it. . . . Arne responds with a burst of compassion to this song, but also with sudden panic. (p. 313)

This moment of self recognition motivates Arne, for the first time, to break out of his isolation and to find his way back to the community. But this search forces him into a self confrontation so painful that it pushes him to the limits of his sanity. The gradual movement toward this crisis is externalized by three stories of murder and punishment. Two of them are told by guests at a wedding which Arne and his mother attend, and as he listens it seems that they are about himself and that he is being accused of murder. . . . These two stories mirror Arne's own state of mind and thus trigger a spontaneous reaction. . . .

The story that he tells is a fantastic vision which lays bare his innermost fears. Just as in the poem **"I bygden er det uro,"** we hear in Arne's story about a boy who dreams that he has killed his father. He meets a troll who puts a spell on him so that he forgets his guilt. (p. 314)

In traditional ballads and legends the troll is described as an external demonic reality, an uncanny force capable of luring human beings into its power and making them forget their humanity. Similarly, in Arne's story, the troll spell takes away the boy's ability to suffer guilt and compassion for others. (p. 315)

[Finally, having] learned that the loss of self is more frightening than guilt, the boy accepts his guilt, in other words he redis- covers his conscience. His tears dispel his dream; he awakens and is, once more, a human being.

This story, boiling up from Arne's unconscious, gives ex- pression to the gist of his conflict. His struggle to understand whether he is gulty of murdering his father, the desire to escape from conflicts, fear and isolation, and the perception that there is no escape, are fused together to a vision that poses an ir- reducible paradox: either to accept a horrible guilt and the resulting fear of self and of life, or to be swallowed up by that void which is madness. (pp. 315-16)

Arne's next poem, **"Det var slik en vakker solskinnsdag,"** shows a remarkably new tone. It again juxtaposes his search for peace and serenity with the hopelessness of this search. It expresses the gulf of feelings still separating mother and son. But while previously these themes had been treated with despair and even cynicism, his present song is ironic, self-mocking, in mood. It shows that Arne has entered a period of transition.

Soon thereafter Arne sees Eli Bøen for the first time. He is strongly drawn to her, but his feelings are deeply ambivalent. To his mother erotic love had meant an enslavement from which she was freed only through the death of Nils, and this rela- tionship left a deep scar on Arne's mind. Therefore, after meet- ing Eli, he writes a poem in which passion is seen as hopelessly tragic. (p. 316)

The gradual change in his response to Eli is made clear by the poem **"Over de hoje fjelle."** . . . But the poem implies, too, that Arne's choice is not free of ambivalence. To be bound to the valley means that the "eagle" will never fly beyond the "walls of ice and terror"; never will he raise himself above a reality that is "oppressively and devouringly narrow." In the final stanza, however, the conflict between the urge to flee and the desire to remain, is poetically resolved by being transmuted into an infinite longing which transcends this life. . . . (pp. 318-19)

But the reconciliation remains poetic and transcendent. On the concrete, psychological level his conflicts continue largely un- resolved and recede into the background of the story. Instead the action of the last half of *Arne* is dominated by the unrav- elling of certain subordinate motifs: Margit's comical intrigues to prevent Arne's emigration to America; the hesitant courtship of Arne and Eli; and the reconciliation between the two fam- ilies. These motifs are carried to a happy resolution implying a world view that is essentially free of the insecurity and am- bivalence experienced by Arne, a view that is predicated on the power of love and God's ability to heal all wounds and solve all problems. Here certain patterns found in the majority of Bjørnson's peasant stories come to the surface. Themati- cally, the last part of *Arne* focuses on the depiction of a hero struggling with communal and moral problems, and of a her- oine who symbolizes the ideal goal for which the hero strives. As in *Synnøve Solbakken,* the achievement of this goal is brought

about through a physical crisis liberating the persons involved from their characteristic taciturnity. (pp. 319-20)

Why Bjørnson left Arne's inner conflicts essentially unre- solved, while enforcing a solution on the surface, is a matter of speculation. But we have reason to believe that he was not really aware of this incongruity until after he had re-read *Arne* in the fall of 1859. In a letter to Clemens Petersen, Bjørnson laments that his "untamed passions" had tricked him and that he could hardly believe that he was the author of this "ugly" book. Per Amdam has interpreted this confession as a reflection of unresolved erotic conflicts and guilt feelings which Bjørnson was struggling with at the time. He points out that Bjørnson immediately started to revise the book and primarily toned down the motifs of murder and sexual passion. This supports the hypothesis that throughout *Arne* we can detect a sustained effort to "cover up" the real problems by an apparently har- monious transformation of the hero. (p. 321)

It is debatable whether [Björnson's] changes actually root out the contradictions and ambiguities in the characterization of Arne and provide a better motivation for the happy end of the story. But it is clear that the revised version of *Arne* is not a profounder, more significant work. On the contrary, the ex- plicit shift to a moralistic interpretation of love and religious growth narrows the vision of the ambiguities of life achieved in the original form of the story. The version of 1872 has a clearer and less controversial message: but this gain is paid for by a loss of depth. Regrettably, this is the version usually reprinted in new editions of Bjørnson's *Arne.* (p. 323)

Henning K. Sehmsdorf, "The Self in Isolation: A New Reading of Bjørnson's 'Arne'," in Scandinavian Studies, *Vol. 45, No. 4, Autumn, 1973, pp. 310-23.*

ADDITIONAL BIBLIOGRAPHY

Björkman, Edwin. "Björnstjerne Björnson: Poet, Politician, Prophet." In his *Voices of Tomorrow: Critical Studies of the New Spirit in Literature*, pp. 121-38. New York: Mitchell Kennerly, 1913.
    Details Bjørnson's political and literary careers. Through anec- dotes and examples, Björkman describes the author's popularity among his people.

Gassner, John. "The Scandinavian Succession and Strindberg." In his *Masters of the Modern Drama*, rev. ed., pp. 384-96. New York: Dover Publications, 1954.*
    Discusses the impact of Ibsen, Strindberg, and Bjørnson on mod- ern theater. Gassner observes that Bjørnson's enthusiasm and per- suasiveness coupled with Ibsen's depth and intensity assured the success of dramatic realism.

Koht, Halvdan, and Skard, Sigmund. "The Warmth of Bjørnstjerne Bjørnson." In their *The Voice of Norway*, pp. 235-59. New York: Columbia University Press, 1944.
    Studies Bjørnson's changing religious, political, and social be- liefs; the controversies Bjørnson generated in Norway; and his influence on nationalism.

Larson, Harold. *Björstjerne Björnson: A Study in Norwegian Nation- alism.* New York: King's Crown Press, 1945, 172 p.
    Traces the roots of Bjørnson's nationalistic sense and explains his role in the creation and definition of modern Norwegian literature.

Payne, William Morton. *Björnstjerne Björnson: 1832-1910.* Chicago: A. C. McClurg & Co., 1910, 98 p.
    Tribute to the author containing a survey of his work and bio- graphical information.

Rupert (Chawner) Brooke

1887-1915

English poet, critic, dramatist, essayist, and journalist.

One of the Georgian movement's primary organizers and contributors, Brooke is better known today for his war poetry and for his mystique as the embodiment of idealized youth. Of the war sonnets from *1914, and Other Poems,* Brooke's "The Soldier," celebrating a life gladly given in England's service, is world-renowned: hailed for its noble sentiments by many, and scorned for its naiveté by others. Aside from the "1914" cycle, Brooke's lesser known works, such as "A Channel Crossing," "The Fish," and "The Great Lover," reveal an evolving poetic style, of which the war poems mark a regression.

After showing promising poetic talent as a teenager, Brooke's career began at King's College, Cambridge in 1906, where he established himself with the Cambridge Review as a poet inclined to the decadents, and as a perceptive critic of modern literature and art. Extraordinarily handsome and charming, Brooke easily drew an admiring circle of literary friends, both at King's and later at his Grantchester home. Notable among his friends were Henry James, Walter de la Mare, Virginia Woolf, and Edward Marsh, his patron, who encouraged Brooke in the publication of *Poems* in 1911. This collection of self-consciously decadent poems along with moving metaphysical verse evidences a shift in the poet's interests from *fin-de-siècle* writers to John Donne and Robert Browning, and even its detractors saw it as a herald of significant talent. In 1912, following an emotional breakdown, Brooke spent several months recovering in Berlin, where he experimented with Georgian realism, writing verse concerning daily life and using common speech patterns. Later in the year, he joined John Drinkwater, Wilfrid Gibson, and Harold Monro in planning the Georgian movement's first volume, *Georgian Poetry: 1911-1912,* to which he contributed "The Old Vicarage, Grantchester," one of his best known poems. Brooke then embarked on a year-long trip to North America and the South Pacific in 1913, recording his experiences and impressions in a series of articles and letters published in the *Westminster Gazette* and in his *Letters from America.*

World War I was the greatest influence on the poetry for which Brooke is remembered today. Commissioned an officer in the Royal Naval Division, he never saw the horror of battle, and his famed "1914" sonnets demonstrate a romantic, crusading vision typical of the English civilian spirit during the war's early stages. Brooke rose to national attention when "The Soldier" was read aloud in St. Paul's Cathedral on Easter Sunday, 1915. Shortly afterward, while preparing for the assault on Gallipoli, Turkey, the poet died of blood poisoning aboard ship in the Aegean.

The idolatrous praise heaped upon Brooke following his death attracted a tremendous readership to his poetry. Most of Brooke's work is light, witty, and occasionally sentimental—the last-named quality serving to fuel his tragic "young Apollo" image, against which critics have been forced to struggle ever since the poet's death. Soon after World War I, critical attention turned against Brooke; his poetry was rejected as the

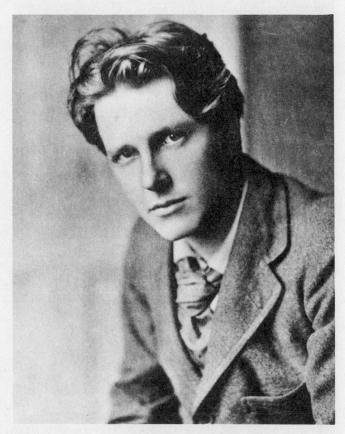

Culver Pictures

musings of a pampered darling. Several verse fragments, found among Brooke's personal effects and since published, vindicate his reputation somewhat, demonstrating a maturer attitude toward life and conflict than does his earlier work. Today, with the recognition of Brooke's foreshortened artistic development, he remains a fixed though minor figure in English literature.

(See also *TCLC,* Vol. 2.)

PRINCIPAL WORKS

Poems   (poetry)   1911
The Collected Poems of Rupert Brooke   (poetry)   1915
Lithuania   (drama)   1915
1914, and Other Poems   (poetry)   1915
John Webster and the Elizabethan Drama   (essay)   1916
Letters from America   (travel essays)   1916
The Poetical Works of Rupert Brooke   (poetry)   1946
The Prose of Rupert Brooke   (essays and criticism)   1956

THE NATION (essay date 1912)

There is no mistaking the formal skill in Mr. Rupert Brooke's "**Poems.**" It is the more evident as Mr. Brooke is fond of setting it to work on unpromising tasks, which demand an athletic vigor of activity—on the sensations of sea-sickness, for instance, or on the aspect and odour of two slumbering Germans in a third-class compartment of an Italian night-train. Whether such poems are successful or not is a question whose answer must hang on what one means by poetic success. The skill itself is, unquestionably, extraordinarily efficient; but does it effect a mere insolent display of acrobatics, or a triumphant transformation of the commonplace into the unique? It seems that Mr. Brooke has been profoundly influenced by a poet who, for sheer skill, has hardly an equal in our literature—John Donne; and Donne, as might be expected, has taught him to be not only remarkably skilful, but to be insolently skilful also. Unfortunately, however, Mr. Brooke allows this learning to dominate his verse. Nearly every one of these poems has, more or less, the air of the poetical exercise; but nearly every one has also the air, not of having been conceived as an exercise, but only of turning out so in the execution. When it came to the actual composition of the poem, the skill of words and metre, that should have been the servant, was allowed to become the master; and, as usually happens in such cases, the servant proved an insolent master. But we must not be led astray by a metaphor. What we have called the insolence in Mr. Brooke's poetry, is a quality that we would very gladly find more frequently than we do in contemporary verse. It is the sign of an energetic and original talent somewhat too determined to be sure of itself. That may mean, perhaps, that it is not really sure of itself; but, at any rate, it is ready to attempt new and surprising things. It is not content to do the familiar old things with a difference; it will not let itself follow the line of least resistance. Mr. Brooke's talent, in fact, is pugnacious; and that is what a poetic talent should begin by being. We judge him instinctively with reference to the larger, finer work which this present volume seems, if there is any logic in psychology, to promise with tolerable certainty—the work he will do when the mere skill which is so notable in it shall be content to exchange mastery for service. His passions of love and jealousy will then seem something more than the themes of poetical exercises; we may even be able to believe in his sea-sickness, and in his disgust with sleeping Germans. Already his "**Poems**" give some fulfilment of this promise. In two or three, the skill is genuinely subordinate to the creative power which lies behind all skill—the power which can seize on a commonplace moment of existence, and fashion it into something unique and glorified. "**Dining-room Tea**" is a poem that shows what we may expect of Mr. Brooke. The question here is not at all whether, in the skill which can deal exquisitely with such common matter, there be not something insolent, but very much whether in the imagination urging the skill there be not something magnificent. (pp. 515-16)

> "*Three Poets,*" *in* The Nation, *Vol. XI, No. 14, July 6, 1912, pp. 514-16.**

HENRY JAMES (essay date 1915)

[I greet the "**1914**" sonnets] gladly, and am right consentingly struck with their happy force and truth: they seem to me to have *come*, in a fine high beauty and sincerity (though not in every line with an equal *degree* of those—which indeed is a rare case anywhere;) and this evening, alone by my lamp, I have been reading them over and over to myself aloud, as if fondly to test and truly to try them; almost in fact as if to reach the far-off author, in whatever unimaginable conditions, by some miraculous, some telepathic intimation that I am in quavering communion with him. Well, they have borne the test with almost all the firm perfection, or straight inevitability, that one must find in a sonnet, and beside their poetic strength they draw a wondrous weight from his having had the *right* to produce them, as it were, and their rising out of such rare realities of experience. . . . In order of felicity I think Sonnet I comes first, save for a small matter that (perhaps superfluously) troubles me and that I will presently speak of. I place next III, with its splendid first line; and then V ("In that rich earth a richer dust concealed!") and then II. I don't speak of No. IV—I think it the least fortunate (in spite of "Touched flowers and furs, and cheeks!") But the four happy ones are very noble and sound and round, to my sense, and I take off my hat to them, and to their author, in the most marked manner. There are many things one likes, simply, and then there are things one likes to like (or at least that I do;) and these are of that order. My reserve on No. I bears on the last line—to the extent, I mean, of not feeling happy about that *but* before the last word. It may be fatuous, but I am wondering if this line mightn't have acquitted itself better as: "And the worst friend and foe is only death." There is an "only" in the preceding line, but the repetition is—or would be—to me not only not objectionable, but would have positive merit. My only other wince is over the "given" and "heaven" rhyme at the end of V; it has been so inordinately vulgarized that I don't think it good enough company for the rest of the sonnet, which without it I think I would have put second in order instead of the III. The kind of idea it embodies is one that always so fetches *this* poor old Anglo-maniac. But that is all. . . . (pp. 462-63)

> *Henry James, in his letter to Edward Marsh on March 28, 1915, in his* The Letters of Henry James, Vol. II, *edited by Percy Lubbock (copyright 1920 Charles Scribner's Sons; copyright renewed 1948 William James and Margaret James Porter; reprinted with permission of Charles Scribner's Sons), Charles Scribner's Sons, 1920, pp. 462-64.*

CHARLES HAMILTON SORLEY (essay date 1915)

I saw Rupert Brooke's death in *The Morning Post*. *The Morning Post*, which has always hitherto disapproved of him, is now loud in his praises because he has conformed to their stupid axiom of literary criticism that the only stuff of poetry is violent physical experience, by dying on active service. I think Brooke's earlier poems—especially notably *The Fish* and *Grantchester*, which you can find in *Georgian Poetry*—are his best. That last sonnet-sequence of his, . . . which has been so praised, I find (with the exception of that beginning 'These hearts were woven of human joys and cares, Washed marvellously with sorrow' which is not about himself) overpraised. He is far too obsessed with his own sacrifice, regarding the going to war of himself (and others) as a highly intense, remarkable and sacrificial exploit, whereas it is merely the conduct demanded of him (and others) by the turn of circumstances, where noncompliance with this demand would have made life intolerable. It was not that 'they' gave up anything of that list he gives in one sonnet: but that the essence of these things had been endangered by circumstances over which he had no control, and he must fight to recapture them. He has clothed his attitude in fine words: but he has taken the sentimental attitude. . . . (pp. 97-8)

Charles Hamilton Sorley, in his letter to Janetta Sorley on April 28, 1915, in his The Poems and Selected Letters of Charles Hamilton Sorley, *edited by Hilda D. Spear, Blackness Press, 1978, pp. 97-8.*

HENRY JAMES (essay date 1915)

[Rupert's] place is now very high and very safe—even though one walks round and round it with the aching soreness of having to take the monument for the man. . . . He has something, at any rate, one feels in [*1914, and Other Poems*], that puts him singularly apart even in his eminence—the fact that, member of the true high company as he is and poet of the strong wings (for he seems to me extraordinarily strong,) he has *charm* in a way of a kind that belong to none of the others, who have their beauty and abundance, their distinction and force and grace, whatever it may be, but haven't that particular thing as he has it and as he was going to keep on having it, since it was of his very nature—by which I mean that of his genius. The point is that I think he would still have had it even if he had grown bigger and bigger, and stronger and stronger (for this is what he *would* have done,) and thereby been almost alone in this idiosyncrasy. Even of Keats I don't feel myself saying that he had charm—it's all lost in the degree of beauty, which somehow allows it no chance. But in Rupert (not that I match them!) there is the beauty, so great, and then the charm, different and playing beside it and savouring of the very quality of the man. What it comes to, I suppose, is that he touches me most when he is whimsical and personal, even at the poetic pitch, or in the poetic purity, as he perpetually is. And he penetrates me most when he is most hauntingly (or hauntedly) English—he draws such a real magic from his conscious reference to it. He is extraordinarily so even in the War sonnets—not that that isn't highly natural too; and the reading of these higher things over now, which one had first read while he was still there to be exquisitely at stake in them, so to speak, is a sort of refinement both of admiration and of anguish. The present gives them such sincerity—as if they had wanted it! I adore the ironic and familiar things, the most intimately English—the **"Chilterns"** and the **"Great Lover"** . . . and the **"Funeral of Youth,"** awfully charming; and of course **"Grantchester,"** which is booked for immortality. I revel in **"Grantchester,"**—and how it would have made one love him if one hadn't known him. As it is it wrings the heart! And yet after all what do they do, all of them together, but again express how life had been wonderful and crowded and fortunate and exquisite for him?—with his sensibilities all so exposed, really exposed, and yet never taking the least real harm. (p. 473)

Henry James, in his letter to Edward Marsh on June 6, 1915, in his The Letters of Henry James, Vol. II, *edited by Percy Lubbock (copyright 1920 Charles Scribner's Sons; copyright renewed 1948 William James and Margaret James Porter; reprinted with the permission of Charles Scribner's Sons), Charles Scribner's Sons, 1920, pp. 472-74.*

JOHN DRINKWATER (essay date 1916)

The development of Rupert Brooke's poetic power was, it seems to me, unlike that of most poets. The early verse of men who afterwards prove their authenticity generally shows a great emotional force with little intellectual power of arrangement, and a weakly imitative craftsmanship. . . . But in Rupert Brooke's beginnings there is none of this. The volume of *Poems*

. . . , which contains work written as early as 1905, when he was eighteen, shows an art curiously personal, skilful, deliberate. It shows, too, an intellectual deftness altogether unexpected in so young a poet, and it shows finally, not always but often, an indifference to the normal material upon which poets good and bad are apt to work from the outset, and in the shaping of which ultimately comes all poetry that is memorable. Nearly every page is interesting on account of its art and intellectual deftness, qualities that we should not expect to be marked. But there are many pages where we do not get the real glow of poetry, and this because the content, it seems to me, often fails to satisfy the demands of poetry. It is true enough to say that it does not matter what subject the poet may contemplate, but there is an implied provision that the subject shall be one that grips his emotions, one, that is to say, that he perceives poetically. It so happens that this capacity in subject-matter for stirring the emotion to poetic intensity is nearly always coincident with a sympathy with the common experience of the world. A poet may write in praise of his mistress as freshly to-day as if none had written before him, but, although we say that he may choose what theme he will, we could not respond to him if he told us in his song that, while he loved his lady and her beauty and his wooing was in all ways prosperous, the thing that he most desired was never to see her again. We should at once know that the attitude was a piece of cold intellectuality, that it was against poetry in substance.

In Rupert Brooke's earliest work there is a strain of this intellectual coldness. . . . The most common note that we find in his first book in illustration of my meaning is the presence at love's moment of the knowledge that women grow old and beauty fades. The reflection is true in fact, but is not poetically true, and so, in its present shape, it is false. That is to say, we know that, although women do grow old, the lover in the delight of his mistress does not realise this, and that the assertion that he does is not emotional passion of conviction but intellectual deliberation. Rupert Brooke goes one step further into danger; not only does he assert that the lover feels something that we know he does not feel, but—it is perhaps an equitable penalty for the first false step—he makes the realisation of a fact that we know is not realised in the circumstances, a source of revulsion, when we know that if the lover felt at all about his mistress's old age it would certainly be with peace and surety. (pp. 180-84)

We find, then, in a great many pages of this first book, an instrument that on so young lips is efficient and enchanting against almost all example, yet playing a tune that does not come wholly from the heart. Never, I think, has technique reached so great a perfection without corresponding authenticity of impulse. Only half a dozen times in the book do we get such phrases as "rife with magic and movement," or "whirling, blinding moil," and even in the poems where most we feel the lack of emotional truth, there is a beauty of words that made the book full of the most exciting promise. Already, too, there was in certain poems assurance against the danger that this intellectual constraint might degenerate into virtuosity. In the song beginning:

"Oh! Love!" they said, "is King of kings,"

the intellectual mood, even in the love traffic in which it has been most shy, is adjusting itself finely to the clear and common impulses of mankind, while in *Dust, The Fish, The Hill, The Jolly Company, Ambarvalia, Dining-Room Tea,* and the lovely opening sonnet . . . there is a movement, a perfect visualisation of image and a clarity of individual thought, that mark him as being of the great tradition, and endowed with the spontaneity that fellowship in that tradition implies.

In the volume published after his death, Rupert Brooke seems to me to have passed into full and rich communion with the great normal life of the world. There are three poems: *All suddenly the Wind comes soft, The way that Lovers use is this,* and *Mary and Gabriel,* that are just a little formal perhaps, by no means valueless, but touched with some literary memory at a moment when the poetic faculty was not as alert as usual. There are two poems: *There's Wisdom in Women,* and *Love,* where the old detached and ironic mood that was once unreal returns not quite happily, and another, *The Chilterns,* in which it has been transmuted into a gracious and acceptable humour. Also there is a sonnet, *Unfortunate,* in which there is a reminiscence of the old mood, but it is now treated very reverently and with superb psychological insight. For the rest we have thrilling and adventurous beauty from beginning to end. There is no more tender landscape in English poetry than *Grantchester,* suffused as it is with a mood that never changes and yet passes between the wittiest laughter and the profoundest emotion with perfect naturalness. The subject-matter throughout the book no longer forces us to dissent or question. It has become wholly merged in the corporate art, and we accept it unhesitatingly as we accept the content of all splendid work. As in all really fine achievement in poetry, there is in his choice of form a glad acceptance and development of the traditions that have been slowly evolved through generations, and a perfect subjection of those forms to his own personality, until a sonnet becomes as definitely his own as if he had invented the external structure. We find, too, that the early constraint, even though it led to a touch of falsity at the time, has not been without its uses. The common emotions of the world he has, after jealous waiting, truly discovered and won for himself, unstaled of the world's usage. His passion is extraordinarily clean, burning among all simple things, clear, untroubled, ecstatic. Except in the two of three pages of which I have spoken, we find everywhere an almost fierce renunciation of anything that would not stir the plain knitters in the sun, with an unwearying determination to translate all this common simple life into the most exact and stirring beauty. It is true that in one or two cases, notably *Heaven,* the image that he creates of this simplicity of passion is such as not to relate itself easily at first glance to the clear normal thought that is nevertheless its basis if for a moment we consider its significance. When the poet elects to make brief intellectual holiday, so long as he does so in the terms of his own personality, we should do nothing but make holiday gladly with him. And we may well do so at intervals in a book that moves in the high consciousness of rare but natural poetic achievement, alert with the freshness and daring of splendid youth, grave in that profoundest knowledge which is imagination; a book that, will surely pass to vigorous immortality. (pp. 184-88)

> *John Drinkwater, in his* Rupert Brooke *(reprinted by permission of the Literary Estate of John Drinkwater),* Chiswick Press, *1916 (and reprinted as "Rupert Brooke," in his* Prose Papers, *Elkin Mathews, 1918, pp. 174-92).*

WILLIAM LYON PHELPS (essay date 1918)

Rupert Brooke lived to be nearly twenty-eight years old, a short life to show ability in most of the ways of the world, but long enough to test the quality of a poet, not merely in promise,

but in performance. There is no doubt that he had the indefinable but unmistakable touch of genius. Only a portion of his slender production is of high rank, but it is enough to preserve his name. His *Letters,* which have been underestimated, prove that he had mental as well as poetical powers. Had he lived to middle age, it seems certain that his poetry would have been tightly packed with thought. He had an alert and inquisitive mind.

Many have seemed to think that the frequent allusions to death in his poetry are vaguely prophetic. They are, of course—with the exception of the war-poems—nothing of the kind, being merely symptomatic of youth. They form the most conventional side of his work. His cynicism toward the love of the sexes was a youthful affectation, strengthened by his reading. He was deeply read in the seventeenth-century poets, who delighted in imagining themselves passing from one woman to another—swearing "by love's sweetest part, variety." At all events, these poems, of which there are comparatively many, exhibit his least attractive side. (p. 127)

He was perhaps, too young to understand two great truths— that real love can exist in the midst of wild passion, and that the best part of it can and often does survive the early flames. Such poems as *Menelaus and Helen, Jealousy,* and others, profess a profound knowledge of life that is really a profound ignorance.

His pictures of nature, while often beautiful, lack the penetrative quality seen so constantly in Wordsworth and Browning; these greater poets saw nature not only with their eyes, but with their minds. Their representations glow with enduring beauty, but they leave in the spectator something even greater than beauty, something that is food for reflection and imagination, the source of quick-coming fancies. Compare the picture of the pines in Brooke's poem *Pine-Trees and the Sky: Evening,* with Browning's treatment of an identical theme in *Paracelsus,* remembering that Browning's lines were written when he was twenty-two years old. Brooke writes,

> Then from the sad west turning wearily,
>   I saw the pines against the white north sky,
> Very beautiful, and still, and bending over
>   Their sharp black heads against a quiet sky.

Browning writes,

> The herded pines commune, and have deep thoughts,
> A secret they assemble to discuss,
> When the sun drops behind their trunks which glare
> Like grates of hell.

Both in painting and in imagination the second passage is instantly seen to be superior.

The war sonnets of 1914 receive so much additional poignancy by the death of the author that it is difficult, and perhaps undesirable, to judge them as objective works of art. They are essentially noble and sincere, speaking from the depths of high-hearted self-sacrifice. He poured out his young life freely and generously, knowing what it meant to say good-bye to his fancy. There is always something eternally sublime—something that we rightly call divine—in the spendthrift giving of one's life-blood for a great cause. And Rupert Brooke was intensely aware of the value of what he unhesitatingly gave.

The two "fish" poems exhibit a playful, charming side to Brooke's imagination; but if I could have only one of his pieces, I should assuredly choose *Grantchester.* Nostalgia is the mother of much fine poetry; but seldom has the expression of it been mingled more exquisitely with humour and longing. (pp. 128-29)

William Lyon Phelps, "Brooke, Flecker, De La Mare, and Others" (originally published in a different form as "The Advance of English Poetry in the Twentieth Century," in The Bookman, New York, Vol. XLVI, No. 6, February, 1918), in his The Advance of English Poetry in the Twentieth Century, *Dodd, Mead and Company, 1918 (and reprinted by Dodd, Mead and Company, 1925), pp. 124-56.**

F. L. LUCAS (essay date 1927)

[John Webster's] youngest critic—Rupert Brooke will always remain that—is still, I think, his best. *John Webster and the Elizabethan Drama* is indeed a very youthful book: that is why it is so good. Its author had not time to amass the mountainous erudition which goes with much modern study of the Elizabethans: but another quality, rarer in commentators and even more essential here, he did possess—he was alive to the fingertips. And accordingly he not only did his share in clearing up the facts of Webster's work: he seems to me to have done more than anyone else to place that work, without exaggerating its faults or ignoring them, in its just position among the lasting possessions of English literature. From the exclamations of Lamb and the roarings of Swinburne on the one hand, as from the outcries of Kingsley and Archer and Shaw on the other, it is to him that one learns to come back in search of sanity. (pp. vii-viii)

F. L. Lucas, "Preface" (1927), in The Complete Works of John Webster, Vol. I *by John Webster, edited by F. L. Lucas (reprinted by permission of the Executors of the late F. L. Lucas), Chatto & Windus, 1928, viii-xiii.*

FRANCES CORNFORD (essay date 1947)

[*The Poetical Work of Rupert Brooke*] contains thirty-eight new poems, all of them early ones. . . . These early pieces show little more than adolescent, poetic emotion, and the determination of a most serious and scholarly apprentice to master the full orchestration of the English language. A very little of his early work is quite enough to show how gifted he was from the beginning, and how much skill he had learnt from Belloc, Housman, Dowson and the 'decadent' poets of the nineties. But these were, on the whole, dangerous influences—he was far too apt to absorb not only their skill but their mannerisms.

'If,' said a young friend recently, reading an anthology of modern verse by the fire, 'I come across the word *lunar* again this evening, I shall scream.' How far more screamable though, and damaging to Brooke's reputation for sincerity, not to say humour, are his red mournful roses, flesh more fair than pale lilies, his ultimate sad breaths, grey-eyed lute-players, and all the rest of it. . . . The only addition which seems to me worth while is the odd, entertaining, Henry Jamesian *Colloquials*. . . .

Humorous is indeed a keyword. Brooke mocked at the things— people, places and ideas alike—that he loved most tenderly, and loved the things he laughed at. At any given moment in a poem it is often impossible to discern which he is doing most. This is, I think, a very English state of mind; perhaps because we are often half-ashamed of our own sensibility and afraid it

will incapacitate us. To many people (I imagine most French people) it is both an incomprehensible and a tiresome one. I can well understand this point of view, but can only add that if it is yours then Rupert Brooke is not for you; for in this mood of his there was nothing assumed, it was part of his being. He was not one of those poets, who, in a single line can lift us straight into another region, even though he knew all about that region, and could have analysed it, perhaps, better than any of them. Yet in their most juvenile Juvenilia, would surely be found some early jewel, coming to them 'full-formed like Venus rising from the sea' to make the whole worth preserving. However musical and moving Brooke's poetry later became he does not, in my experience at least, belong to their rare company. He was from the first a deliberate, intellectual and accomplished writer. (p. 17)

Brooke was an 'introvert', and though psychological terms are distasteful, this one does conveniently cover those like himself (and Plato) to whom the inner world is finally the real world. When in *The Great Lover* he makes his ecstatic defiant list of the outward things he has loved, it seems, quite apart from the introductory fanfare, which is deliberately grandiloquent, to have a faintly forced ring. He is disguising himself as the complete extrovert he isn't. An almost religious emphasis on the importance of direct sense-perception was beginning to be in the air (a necessary reaction from Victorian idealism) and he was always sensitive to what was coming and what mattered in contemporary atmosphere. . . . Even in an early sonnet where the Lady Venus stands in a flowered dell and the gold waves, regrettably, still purl amidst the green above her, come the sudden lines:

> Life one eternal instant rose
> Clear out of time,

foreshadowing the far more moving and individual *Diningroom Tea*, with the arrested amber stream of its teapot; nor can too frequent quotation wither or stale the end of the War Sonnet, *The Dead*, and its simile of the eternalizing frost, Perhaps all writers, poets and scholars alike, are possessed by a few basic ideas which they return to again and again through life, urged each time to shape them more truly. The inevitable tragicness of love was, I believe, another such theme for Rupert Brooke. He would have echoed Aragon's *Il n'y a pas d'amour heureux;* and naturally knit with this was the inevitable loneliness of every human being. . . . Already in 1908 he shows himself 'pitying well' even the stars for their solitude, discovering that they were not after all a Jolly Company (still an Edwardian phrase). . . . Even the lightest of the love-songs have some touch of 'that old dust of misery'; in others the jauntiness appears forced, the pain authentic. . . . Certainly it is clear from the love-poems that, in company surely with most poets down the ages, he loved different women in different ways, and each for her uniqueness. . . .

Through the most moving of the love-poems we seem to get glimpses of one quite frequent but agonizing human situation, though universalized as in all genuine poetry. The poet turns, it seems, to one very young woman as to a mother; and when she behaves like any other young woman, capriciously, perhaps faithlessly, his whole world disintergrates. He flays her, and he flays himself, who could not ever again love her simply as a young woman:

> It was great wrong you did me and for gain
> Of that poor moment's kindliness and ease
> And sleepy mother-comfort. . . .

But it is a shame to quote **Retrospect** in fragments, nor will I let myself maltreat the most satisfying sonnet he ever wrote, **The Busy Heart;** with its sustained music of reconciliation to life. (p. 18)

Frances Cornford, "Rupert Brooke," in Time & Tide, *Vol. 28, No. 1, January 4, 1947, pp. 17-18, 20.*

CHRISTOPHER HASSALL   (essay date 1956)

[Brooke's] earliest published poems were written in 1903 when he was sixteen. Until April 1909 (when he composed the sonnet **'Oh death shall find me'** and **The Voice**) he wrote nothing of much value except, perhaps, **Seaside** . . . , and yet this period, when he was at first luxuriating in, and then trying to throw off, the influence of the 'nineties, constitutes a third of his whole output. Nothing much more of note was done until a year later when he wrote **Dust** and **Dining-room Tea.** The latter deserves rather special notice. One imagines a young man who has been reading Donne's **The Ecstasy** in a room upstairs (the poem records an actual experience he had among his friends at Limpsfield) being summoned by a decorous bell to join the family for a meal. He goes down to the dining-room with one of the great love poems of the world still murmuring in the back of his head, enters the Edwardian social scene (one visualizes it like the second act of a play by Pinero) and walks straight into an imaginative experience which makes a deep impression upon him. . . . It may seem invidious to speak of such a masterpiece in the same breath with Brooke's lightweight poem, but he was clearly aiming at nothing more profound than what he precisely and, for the first time, with delicate artistry accomplished. It was a distinct stage in his development. There is no evidence, of course, for what he was actually reading during that week-end. . . . His copy [of Donne's poetry] is underscored in pencil at the lines 'All day the same our postures were, And we said nothing all the day.' In Brooke's case, this time in a social setting, in circumstances far less intense, and only for a moment, the indoor light seemed to be falling 'on stiller flesh, and body breathless'. This is not to suggest that the one poem is derived from the other. The discovery of a master has often led the young poet, not so much to the writing of pastiche, as to the discovery of *himself.* An instant of revelation while reading a poem is enough to show at once a new aspect of life and a way of communicating it. Although it was not Donne whom Brooke resembled when his individual character was fully apparent, as we shall see, he never quite abandoned the master who had rescued him from the late-Victorian 'decadence'. In the second and best of his war sonnets . . . there is a direct and conscious quotation from *The Anniversarie* on which the whole poem, again one of his most successful, is built as a variation.

After **Dining-room Tea** another year elapsed before we notice a change. This time (in **Thoughts on the Shape of the Human Body,** for instance) it is hardly to be wondered at that there should be signs of Jacobean rhetoric, since much of the past year had been spent among the texts of the old dramatists. Then in 1912 . . . came **The Old Vicarage, Grantchester,** another lightweight poem, again successful, but this time on a more expansive scale and at last, most splendidly, a masterpiece of his own.

The difference between the new manner and the old can best be measured by comparing two poems in the same metre and almost identical in theme, **The Fish** (March 1911) and **Heaven** (December 1913), both good poems, but the latter in an altogether superior category. **The Fish** will only be read because it is by the author of **Heaven.** This applies to almost all his poetry before 1912—which is more than three-quarters of the whole. (pp. xxxviii-xl)

After that short burst in the spring of 1912, practically nothing more that is worthwhile was written until he was at Mataiea in the Pacific a year and a half later. Probably the first to come were the fine sonnets, **Clouds** and **Psychical Research.** He had been constantly badgered by Marsh to write more verse now that he was free of the *Westminster* letters. 'You have achieved your instrument,' Marsh wrote to him in Tahiti, 'and I expect a time will come when you will want to play on it again. . . . By the way, when I made my impertinent remark about your running Love to death, or whatever I said, I didn't mean love as a subject, but Love with a capital L as an abstraction, it seemed to be becoming a mannerism of style.' Such was the gentle hint from London, but already, determined to oblige his friend by avoiding abstractions at least for once, Brooke had written **The Great Lover,** almost in a spirit of defiance, a poem which is little more than a list of concrete images, and a curiously successful list it is, in that the items are so managed as to add up to a unit of poetry. **Retrospect** and **Tiare Tahiti** also came of this same Tahiti vintage. By comparison, the five war sonnets of December in the same year, which suddenly made his reputation, are slightly retrogressive. The heroic theme which circumstances had thrust upon him could not have been treated in the serio-comic manner which had become peculiarly his.

Since May 1912, having learned what he could from Donne, he had brought to his verse something of his own nature, a quality light-in-hand and, so to speak, playful, which brought him into the neighbourhood of Marvell. And there, with Marvell, helped a little to shine rather than overshadowed by his poetical ancestor, he belongs. Although the last lines of the **Psychical Research** sonnet are a close parallel of a passage in Marvell's *Dialogue between Soul and Body,* I suspect that this was a coincidence. Granted the discovery of Donne, I think it was in Brooke's nature to develop in this direction. The intellectual parlour-game he played with the Platonic Ideas in **Tiare Tahiti,** for instance, would have been just to the taste of Marvell complaining 'by the tide of Humber'. And as to 'tone of voice', if a young player in a literary guessing game were to be confronted with 'Annihilating all that's made To a green thought in a green shade' and were to guess 'Brooke' he would lose a mark, and perhaps the game, but he would be no fool.

Within less than three months of finishing the war sonnets (January 1915) he was entering on a new stage of progress, or so I believe, although there are only a few fragments to go by. . . . [Knowing] that a hazardous campaign was imminent, he had begun, I suspect, to anticipate not his own death so much as the loss of his friends. His theme was love of country, in a far broader sense than was implied in the war sonnets ('In Avons of the heart her rivers run'), and sacrificial death. Only one short poem in blank verse (itself a new departure for him) and a few disconnected sentences exist to hint at this, but any scrupulous follower of his development, who pays Brooke the compliment of taking him a little more seriously than at first glance he may seem to warrant, will detect these beginnings of a change. . . . One can only judge a man by what he has actually done to his satisfaction, and so, in considering Brooke, one must go back to what might have been called his early Marvell period (1912-1914) in order to assess his contribution to poetry. It is distinctive and delightful, but a little more of life and another poem might have made it look by comparison rather small. (pp. xli-xliv)

The quality peculiar to Brooke is a combination of wit and emotional feeling, not alternating, as in Byron, but inextricably at one, so that the conception of the poem, as well as each of its details, is a witticism. The quality is of course what we have come to know as 'metaphysical'. In *Tiare Tahiti* or *The Old Vicarage* the gravity makes fun of itself, the levity takes itself seriously. Is he sincere? one asks. Does he *really* want so much to go back to Grantchester? Does he *honestly* want to know what there is for tea? Or is the whole thing just a decorative verbal gesture? And while we are wondering, the poem has quietly come and gone, not wanting to stay for question, like the ghost in *Hamlet*. It was a delicate, slight thing, with a life and a will of its own, and saw no good reason why it should hang about while we made these plodding, cerebral enquiries. What we did manage to catch was an undertone of simple, carefully measured music. (pp. li-lii)

Perhaps it would be easier for Brooke if he were not *quite* so engaging. One feels the Georgian self-consciousness in the presence of an audience, and that the poem was posted when the ink was hardly dry and forthwith delivered on a salver in the drawing-room, or is it the dining-room where, contrary to usual custom, tea is laid? At any rate it is a world of gracious living, too recent in time to be regarded objectively as 'historical', too remote—almost incredibly remote—in spirit to be thoroughly understood. It is in fact (as are the poems) 'old-fashioned'. The grace, the amplitude, the air of sumptuous living, the rooted hopefulness, all are gone. And Brooke realized their transience. There is a passage in one of his letters in which he seems almost to see himself and his world with our latter-day eyes and to be anticipating our slightly critical (and perhaps envious) remarks about his conscious charm, so proper to an age of gracious literary manners, his unaustere view of things, his radiant . . . optimism. (pp. lii-liii)

> With such superb work to do, and with the wild
> adventure of it all, and with the other minutes
> (too many of them) given to the enchantment
> of being even for a moment alive in a world of
> real matter (not that imitation gilt stuff one gets
> in Heaven) and actual people—I have no time
> now to be a pessimist.

It is that gone world of 'real matter' which he evokes in his prose writings, more in the manner of the telling, than in what he tells. It may remind those who have too readily accepted the symbolic Soldier figure as the beginning and end of the matter that Brooke was a man-about-town in a time of peace, Cambridge scholar-poet and traveller about a globe where men had the wits, and the world still had the time, for leisurely and lighthearted discussions on the Beautiful and the Good. (pp. liii-liv)

> *Christopher Hassall, in his introduction to* The Prose of Rupert Brooke *by Rupert Brooke, edited by Christopher Hassall, Sidgwick and Jackson, 1956, pp. ix-liv.*

A. C. WARD (essay date 1956)

Rupert Brooke had at first been attracted by the artifices of the eighteen-nineties group of writers, but he quickly reacted against their vitiated hot-house atmosphere, and wallowed in ugliness

in order to demonstrate his distaste for 'pretty' poetry. He wrote sonnets on seasickness and other unsavoury subjects; and, as a protest against the exclusively romantic view of classical heroes, affirmed in the *Menelaus and Helen* sonnets that 'the perfect knight' and 'the perfect queen' afterwards degenerated into disgusting senility. He quickly passed out of that phase, however. Sitting at a Berlin café in 1912 he thought of the 'incredibly lovely superb world', and wrote his poem about one of the loveliest places he knew, *The Old Vicarage, Grantchester*. Though he himself referred to this poem as 'hurried stuff', it was found as cool and refreshing as the May fields (of which he speaks) to 'the bare feet that run to bathe'. His love of Nature was neither mystical nor metaphysical. He saw and touched and enjoyed; that was enough. . . . (pp. 172-73)

In *The Great Lover* he wrote of the hundred and one everyday things that gave him joy—plates and cups, dust, wet roofs, wood-smoke, 'the cool kindliness of sheets . . . and the rough male kiss of blankets'. He invested this domestic catalogue with significance and beauty, and turned the commonplace into the strangely new.

Though the five sonnets entitled *1914* were enthusiastically received at their first appearance, their poetic qualities probably did not undergo close scrutiny. When wartime emotions had been forgotten, it became fashionable to decry Rupert Brooke, and to challenge those who admired him. On the evidence of the *Collected Poems* it would be rash to describe him as a great poet; yet the *1914* sonnets hint at a growing 'high seriousness' which might have matched his sense of melody with a measure of sustaining thought. Because of its prophetic interest, *The Soldier* became the one poem inseparably linked with Rupert Brooke's name. It is, for all time, his epitaph—beautiful and tranquil; but its broken, staccato movement (awkward for the sonnet form) places it, as poetry, below the first and third sonnets of the *1914* group (*Peace* and *The Dead*) ('Blow out, you bugles, over the rich Dead!').

It is natural, though unprofitable, to speculate as to what might have been Rupert Brooke's place in English poetry if he lived on. The marks of greatness in his poems are few, but such marks there are. He saw the world with a clear eye and recorded what he saw with directness and clarity. (p. 173)

> *A. C. Ward, "Poetry," in his* Twentieth-Century Literature: 1901-1950, *third edition, Methuen and Co. Ltd, 1956, pp. 143-201.**

T.N.S. LENNAM (essay date 1957)

In the Spring of 1914 [Rupert Brooke] was in Tahiti and stayed at Mataiea, a place some distance from Papeete the principal town. He has described Mataiea as "the most ideal place in the world to live and work in" and it was here, probably around February—March, that he recommenced writing verse. Of the three poems which are the product of this period—"**Retrospect**," "**Tiare Tahiti**" and "**The Great Lover**"—the last named alone has achieved popularity. (p. 402)

[In these poems] powerful nostalgia seems to provide Brooke with the necessary tension fruitful to his creative imagination.

"**The Great Lover**" is certainly a product of this mood. Its catalogue of loved objects is a nostalgic evocation of the sight, sound, smell, touch of the familiar and everyday as recollected from the poet's temporal and spatial isolation among the strange and exotic. The fact that the things brought to mind are for the most part either domestic minutia or the sensorily commonplace increases rather than diminishes the vitality of the poem and its nostalgic undertone. This section a list of sensory experiences—"these I have loved"—forms the main body of the poem. It is preceded by a twenty-five line introduction and followed by a somewhat shorter tail-piece.

The opening eleven lines of the introduction are a fairly clear if conventional statement of the Lover's predicament and his intention to list and praise what he has loved. It concludes with a question:

Shall I not crown them with immortal praise
Whom I have loved, who have given me, dared with me
High Secrets, and in darkness knelt to see
The inenarrable godhead of delight?

Now what exactly does Brooke mean here? The choice of relative pronoun is, to say the least, enigmatic, in so far as the catalogue is impersonal throughout. How does one reconcile "strong crusts of friendly bread" for instance or "the good smell of old clothes" with the giving and daring of "high secrets" or to the sight of "the godhead of delight" which he (and they) kneel to see "in darkness?" As it stands the question has no clear relation direct or symbolic with the body of the poem, and thus divorced of contextual significance, simply appears as high-sounding romantic claptrap.

The dichotomy between the introductory matter and central section is further extended in the lines that follow. Here we have three statements:

Love is a flame: we have beaconed the world's might.

A City: and we have built it, these and I.

An Emperor: we have taught the world to die.

It must be supposed that "we" is a unity of Lover and loved. On that supposition the first two statements, if extravagances, are at least acceptable conceits. The third cannot so justify itself. The disparate images of this statement have not been successfully yoked into a metaphysical unity—and the whole, like its preceding figures, have no relation to the rest of the poem. The remaining six lines of this section degenerate into a series of abstractions remote from any recognizable significance. At best they are rhetoric. In Yeats' words, "the will is trying to do the work of the imagination."

Brooke has failed to make clear the relationship of the parts to the whole. The result (or cause?) of this failure is that several passages achieve an audible effectiveness at the expense of sense. This breakdown does not merely confuse but obstructs the logic of the poem. A detailed analysis is not intended here. **"The Great Lover,"** one must assume, finds its way into the popular anthologies (and more regrettably, School Texts) upon merits which have nothing to do with lucidity. It is in fact a triumph of sound over sense.

Mention of the sound of the poem brings us to the main proposition. Even a cursory reading of the poem leaves a distinct and persisting aural impression. Here and there words chime like faint though familiar bells. An analysis of the verbal content throws an interesting light upon Brooke's poetic talent and raises the question of the nature and extent of his indebtedness to Keats' "Ode To a Nightingale."

A first impression of this similarity arises from isolated word-echoes. The multiplicity of which, as they accumulate, suggest

a lingering Keatsian undertone throughout the poem. Words such as: "pain,' "cheat," "darkness," "benison," "foam," "despair," "immortal," "Emperor," "faery," and line endings "blown" and "known," "death" and "breath." These individual tonal similarities emerge more clearly and forcibly into recognizable patterns as the phrasal parallels, both singly and in suggestive clusters, . . . attract both eye and ear. . . . Perhaps the strongest link with Keats is Brooke's use of the word "high." It is one of Keats' favourite epithets, recurring in poem after poem, sometimes abstract, vague, romantic, at other times concrete enough. . . . One is accustomed to accept "high" as a familiar word in Keats' "romance" terminology. It is interesting to note that Brooke uses this adjective no less than four times in **"The Great Lover":** "dared with me high secrets," "for the high cause of Love's Magnificence," "break the high bond we made," and finally "sleep; and high places." An intriguing and slightly ironic comment upon these parallels is to be found in a letter written by Brooke in mid-December 1913. Therein, and talking of Samoa, he wrote: . . .

It is sheer beauty, so pure that it's difficult to breathe in it like living in a Keats world, only its less syrupy—Endymion without sugar.

Nevertheless Brooke did breathe in it—and deeply; nor has he been able to avoid the syrup. There are parts of **"The Great Lover"** which are undeniably melliferous. (pp. 402-05)

T.N.S. Lennam, "A Nightingale amongst the China," in The Dalhousie Review, Vol. 36, No. 4, Winter, 1957, pp. 402-05.

THE TIMES LITERARY SUPPLEMENT (essay date 1957)

It is important that a writer should be remembered for his true qualities rather than be exalted or attacked as a symbol of something he never set out to stand for. Rupert Brooke's legend was brewing even before his death in the classical isles; living today, he would be rising seventy, and the uncharacteristic 1914 sonnets would have dropped back into place. Just as "England expects—" was not the entire Nelson, so it is certain—and [*The Prose of Rupert Brooke*] does more than his collected poems to prove it—that an English corner of a foreign field was not the whole of Brooke. . . .

[Brooke's] is a vigorous, full-toned, challenging voice. . . . The melody is always there, and Brooke meant that it should be. None of that rhythmical prose comes in unconsciously. The term "aesthetic emotion" had been permissible in the Cambridge of 1910; but how much, Brooke asked, was the verbal beauty, and how much the horror, responsible for the audience's reaction to a tense scene in *Macbeth?* His own American travel sketches, written for the *Westminster Gazette,* bring us the question in an easier form. Much of his information about types and towns and habits seems as stale to us now as it did at the time to his friend, the expatriate Henry James. There remain the vividness of his descriptions and the apparently effortless beauty of his writing. While ringing with melodic overtones from his poetry it yet avoids the slushiness of "poetic prose," as dexterously as a poem like **"Grantchester"** keeps clear of whimsy. These word pictures of Canada, where "the air is unbreathed, the earth untrodden," may not be what the modern would express, but they have their magic. . . .

As a critic of literature, with all the downright positivity of youth, Brooke could be strikingly sound at times, at others merely impressionistic. . . . "Beware of the dead." he writes in ["**Democracy and the Arts**"] arguing that all art has an appeal for its contemporaries that dies away and prevents its immortality. It is a shaky argument; Brooke's own passion for the Elizabethans was beyond any admiration he felt for his fellow artists.

On Elizabethan drama, represented here by extracts from the Webster book, he thunders gorgeously. His prose is grandiloquent, his metaphor searing. Who, having met with it years ago, can forget the figure of Webster as "the last of Earth gazing out over a sea of saccharine"? But the shouting and the exultation may break off on a note of flat banality, and the lurid colouring of his portraits cover a deficiency of bony structure. Himself intoxicated by the tragedians' prose, he uses words like a painter who slams on pigments with a palette knife. And indeed the pictorial side of drama meant so much for him that he found the text of a great play quite inadequate, alone, to convey its force. This view, repeated in discussing Craig's and Poel's productions of Shakespearian "raw material," suggests that his future in the theatre would have been as producer rather than playwright. There was room for refinement of the critical faculties; but the things that matter for a writer in his twenties with a career ahead of him are vitality, appreciation, strength of opinion, eloquence of diction, and an impassioned love of creative art and life. Rupert Brooke had all; with a gift of fun that made him so much saner than the legend.

"The Prose Voice of Rupert Brooke," in The Times Literary Supplement (© *Times Newspapers Ltd. (London) 1957; reproduced from* The Times Literary Supplement *by permission), No. 2864, January 18, 1957, p. 36.*

BERNARD BERGONZI (essay date 1965)

[Of] all the myths which dominated the English consciousness during the Great War the greatest, and the most enduring, is that which enshrines the name and memory of Rupert Brooke: in which three separate elements—Brooke's personality, his death, and his poetry (or some of it)—are fused into a single image. Brooke was the first of the 'war poets'; a quintessential young Englishman; one of the fairest of the nation's sons; a ritual sacrifice offered as evidence of the justice of the cause for which England fought. His sonnet, '**The Soldier**', is among the most famous short poems in the language. If the Tolstoyan theory of art had any validity it would be one of the greatest— as, indeed, it is considered to be by the numerous readers for whom the excellence of poetry lies in the acceptability of its sentiments rather than in the quality of its language. (p. 36)

To extricate Brooke's poetry from the personal legend in which it played a merely contributory role is not at all easy, but the critic and literary historian must make the attempt. In the first place, the poetry can best be understood by placing it in its proper context in the Georgian movement. . . . [No] matter how remote and old-fashioned the Georgians may seem now, at the time they regarded themselves, and were regarded, as somewhat revolutionary. Their comparative bluntness of language, and liking for 'ordinary', unpretentious subjects, was not to everyone's taste; and Brooke found himself in a good deal of trouble over one of his early poems, '**A Channel Passage**', which deals with love and sea-sickness in a self-consciously brutal fashion. . . . (pp. 37-8)

In one of Brooke's most famous poems, '**The Old Vicarage, Grantchester**', we have a lucid instance of the Georgian con-

centration on rural England; this poem was written in Berlin, and Christopher Hassall observes that Brooke originally intended to call it 'The Sentimental Exile', and suggests that the public might in that case have read it less solemnly. This is possibly true, and such a reading may have been closer to Brooke's intention; the fact remains that the whole poem displays a kind of switchback irregularity of tone, alternatively satirizing the Cambridge landscape (and by implication the poet) and idealizing it. Such uncertainty is a perhaps inevitable concomitant of Georgian Little Englandism: it is difficult for the retreat to a rural fastness, no matter how delectable, to be entirely whole-hearted. At the same time as he wrote '**The Old Vicarage**' Brooke was concerned about the possible advent of a European war.

What we think of as the characteristic 'war poetry' of 1914-18 was, in fact, a continuation of the Georgian movement by poets who, volunteering in defence of the England they had written about so lovingly, found themselves thrust into the melting pot which Forster had envisaged at the conclusion of *Howards End*. . . . In a prose piece [Brooke] indicates the state of mind of innumerable young men like himself at the start of the war: '**An Unusual Young Man**', published in the *New Statesman* on 29th August 1914, supposedly describes the state of mind of a friend on the outbreak of war, though this figure is clearly a vehicle for Brooke's own opinions. He thinks about Germany, a country he knows and likes, and is incredulous at the idea of an armed conflict between England and Germany. . . . Brooke continues the essay with a rhapsodic description of the Southern English landscape in a passage recalling the similar descriptions in *Howards End*. This passage has been subjected to a withering analysis by Cyril Connolly in *Enemies of Promise;* Connolly describes it in this way: "'England had declared war," he says to himself, "what had Rupert Brooke better feel about it?" His equipment is not equal to the strain and his language betrays the fact . . . ' As a critical judgment this is undoubtedly penetrating. And yet it is not the most interesting thing that one can say about this piece of writing: Brooke was having to fake up an emotional attitude precisely because the experience of England being involved in a major war was so alien and ungraspable. There was, too, a curious interplay between the literary cult of rural England fostered by the Georgians, and the degree of patriotism that it is traditionally proper to feel when one's country goes to war: Brooke's feelings are very literary indeed in their mode of expression, but are not thereby prevented from being genuine. As Connolly says, Brooke's equipment was unequal to the strain: but so was that of every other writer in those days. (pp. 40-1)

[Brooke's "**1914**" sonnets] are not very amenable to critical discussion. They are works of very great mythic power, since they formed a unique focus for what the English felt, or wanted to feel, in 1914-15: they crystallize the powerful archetype of Brooke, the young Apollo, in his sacrificial role of the hero-as-victim. Considered, too, as historical documents, they are of interest as an index to the popular state of mind in the early months of the war. But considered more narrowly and exactly as poems, their inadequacy is very patent. Such a judgment needs qualification. It is, for instance, a commonplace to compare Brooke's sonnets with the work of later war poets, notably Wilfred Owen. This seems to me to prove very little, except, in a purely descriptive way, that poets' attitudes changed profoundly as they learned more about the war. Beyond this one might as well attempt to compare the year 1914 and the year 1918. A more useful comparison is with Brooke's own earlier poetry, and with contemporary works that express a broadly similar state of mind. Brooke's poetic gifts were never robust, and he was very far from being the most talented of the Georgian group, but at his best he had a certain saving irony and detachment of mind, which, very naturally, were absent from the 1914 sonnets. At the same time, the negative aspects of his poetry, a dangerous facility of language and feeling, are embarrassingly in evidence. To compare like with like, the sonnets seem to me inferior to Kipling's 'For All We Have and Are' and to Julian Grenfell's 'Into Battle', both products of the opening phase of the war.

One very pressing difficulty in reading these sonnets is that elements that can be called representative, expressing currents of popular feeling, are closely interwoven with others which are purely personal to Brooke himself. Thus, to take the octet of the first sonnet, **'Peace'**:

Now, God be thanked Who has matched us with His hour,
   And caught our youth, and wakened us from sleeping,
With hand made sure, clear eye, and sharpened power,
   To turn, as swimmers into cleanness leaping,
Glad from a world grown old and cold and weary,
   Leave the sick hearts that honour could not move,
And half-men, and their dirty songs and dreary,
   And all the little emptiness of love!

I do not think I am alone in finding these lines disagreeably lax in movement, and excessively facile in much of their detail; in a phrase like 'old and cold and weary' the words seem to be thrusting ahead of the sense. Yet there can be no doubt that they expressed quite closely a dominant state of mind . . . : a turning aside from the stalely familiar, and an eager acceptance of new and unknown experience. . . . Brooke was also expressing certain wholly personal preoccupations, whose nature is apparent from Hassall's biography. Professor D. J. Enright, in a sharp comment on these poems [see excerpt below], has asked, referring to the line 'the little emptiness of love', 'whose love?' On the level of intention, at least, the love in question seems to be Brooke's long and gruelling affair with 'Ka'.

This self-regarding element is very much in evidence in the poems, cutting across their apparent glad transcendence of the merely personal; the result can be called theatrical, and it is this, rather than Brooke's blank ignorance of things that no one else at that time knew much about either, that makes the sonnets hard to accept as poems. In the most famous of them, **'The Soldier'**, Brooke uses the Georgian concentration on rural England as a focus for a meditation on his own possible death. He identifies his own body and the soil of England in an almost mystical fashion. . . . The oratorical tone . . . seems to be part of the poem's essential intention: not for nothing has it become a set-piece for recitation at school prize-giving days and similar public occasions. Yet though the poem aims at oratorical impersonality, it is also an insistently self-regarding performance. There is an unresolved conflict between a subjective lyric impulse, not at all sure of its language, and the assumed decorum of patriotic utterance. As Mr. Enright has observed: 'The reiteration of ''England'' and ''English'' is all very well; but an odd uncertainty as to whether the poet is praising England or himself—''a richer dust''—remains despite that reiteration.' (pp. 41-4)

> Bernard Bergonzi, *''Poets I: Brooke, Grenfell, Sorley,'' in his* Heroes' Twilight: A Study of the Literature of the Great War *(© 1965 by Bernard Bergonzi; reprinted by permission of A. D. Peters &*

Co. Ltd), Constable and Company Ltd., 1965, pp. 32-59.*

MICHAEL HASTINGS   (essay date 1967)

[We see Brooke] as a strange literary critic. No doubt of it: he was very knowledgeable about the metric art of poetry, but he couldn't understand the soft foot in Ezra Pound's early poems, or indeed even the use of the extended line in free-verse. . . . The puritanical classical compound in Brooke comes through in his statement 'the foot is immensely important in English', and his root-deep feeling that metre plus rhyme equals poetry. This is a very *derrière-garde* maxim for a man whose contemporary writers were Hulme and Eliot. But he also firmly believed Donne's work, which Coleridge described as intellectual pokers turned into love knots, to be great poetry, because of the very combination of brain, soul and heart. It just might be that brain, soul and heart had never combined in Brooke, so when faced with the younger Pound's work, he wouldn't allow the American the freedom to write rather than to write poetry with a capital P. (pp. 213-14)

The mystery about Brooke is that as an artist he was in two minds. He wanted to write as if the 'heart's a wonder', but something held him back. It can be seen not only in his criticism of Pound, but also in his remark to Frances Cornford where he chided her for poetry which he called 'heart-cries'.

At the same time he imagined a world of art and knowledge and letters as something timeless, as if the guru was in his blood-stream, as if through Bhakti Yoga he was trying to sing pure delight:

'Here, in this world we move in, everything is useful. All things are becoming, and influencing and changing, and beyond improved. We are full of reforms and renovations, are we not? I beseech you to remember the Kingdom of Art. There nothing is useful nothing changes. All things are taken out of the flux for ever. They are themselves. They intensely are. You shall meet the lover there and the perfect evening and all the faces that did so ludicrously, so pitiably change. *There* is *no* alteration, no growing old or going away. There is no decay.' (p. 214)

[One of Brooke's publications] which I find interesting, and that because I am a playwright, is a one-act play called **Lithuania**. Set in a forest in some mythical European country, the play describes in rather nicely cadenced sparse dialogue how a young man, who comes to stay the night with a couple and their daughter, is murdered for money he has on him. Unfortunately, the victim slain by the Daughter is the couple's lost son: the girl murderer is the victim's sister. This may be reminiscent of Macbeth, but it is no more so than a dozen other similar stories. . . .

The quality of the lines is akin to some of [John] Masefield's first stage efforts, where the very bare acting dialogue, with no fat at all, has been obviously put together by a poet with a good ear for emphasis and for clear distribution of meanings in the speeches. One is made aware, at least, that Brooke had a natural flair for voices from a stage, and for movement, even if he didn't have too good an idea of people's high emotions and tragic moral problems. . . .

I'm not sure how much one ought to explore this very minor melodramatic piece, although I do see in it the real glimmerings of theatrical writing. (p. 222)

Michael Hastings, in his The Handsomest Young Man in England: Rupert Brooke *(© Design Yearbook Limited 1967; reprinted by permission of Jonathan Clowes Limited, Literary Agents), Michael Joseph, 1967, 235 p.*

D. J. ENRIGHT   (essay date 1973)

There is little compulsion behind Brooke's peace-time poetry: apart from some pleasant light verse, it is only accomplished, self-consciously graceful, and vaguely portentous within the bounds of good manners, except when setting out to be bad-mannered and turning into schoolboy cynicism. It is his war poems we are concerned with, however: the sequence of sonnets entitled *1914.*

Sonnet I, *Peace,* propounds the idea that war is clean and cleansing, like a jolly good swim. A grand change, in fact, from 'all the little emptiness of love' (whose love?) and from 'half-men, and their dirty songs' (who are they? Was one obliged to listen to their songs?). The only thing that can suffer in war is the body. (Enough, one might think—and later writers showed how wrong Brooke was, at that.)

Sonnet II, *Safety,* testifies in a cloud of witness to the safeness of war. War may even lead to death, which is the safest of all shelters against the dangers of life. (These dangers are not specified: they may be the 'dirty songs' of the preceding poem.)

Sonnet III, *The Dead,* is a conventional trumpet-piece, free from the utter irrationality of the first two sonnets, though later poets were not so sure about the grand abstractions of the sestet: 'Honour has come back, as a king, to earth . . .'.

Sonnet IV, *The Dead,* has none of the petulant anti-life feeling of I and II; indeed, the octave concerns the past life of the dead, rather affectedly described but not perverse. The sestet describes water which has frosted over, and seems to have nothing to do with the octave.

Sonnet V, *The Soldier* (amusingly summed up in a student's comment in the Asian library copy before me as 'frank and unashamed peace of patriotism'), . . . is certainly Brook's most celebrated poem and probably still more widely read than Owen's *Strange Meeting*. . . . In its simple-minded flamboyant way, it seems successful enough, a pleasant period piece, 'frank and unashamed'. But a second reading suggests that a little shame could well have leavened the frankness. The reiteration of 'England' and 'English' is all very well; but an odd uncertainty as to whether the poet is praising England or himself—'a richer dust'—remains despite that reiteration. Moreover, the 'mysticism' of the sestet, whereby the treasures enumerated in the octave are to be given back ('somewhere', to somebody), is hardly more convincing, though obviously better educated, than the pathetic desiderations found in the 'In Memoriam' column of any local newspaper.

In short, Brooke's war poetry is typically pre-War poetry. (pp. 163-64)

> *D. J. Enright, "The Literature of the First World War," in* The Modern Age: Volume 7 of the Pelican Guide to English Literature, *edited by Boris Ford (copyright © Penguin Books, 1961, 1963, 1964, 1973; reprinted by permission of Penguin Books Ltd), third edition, Penguin Books, 1973, pp. 162-77.**

JOHN LEHMANN   (essay date 1980)

On 22 May 1913 Rupert left on his travels to America and further west. (p. 81)

Just before he left, Naomi Royde Smith, still literary editor of the *Westminster Gazette,* to which he had contributed so often over so many years, persuaded the editor-in-chief, J. A. Spender, to commission a series of articles from him about his travels. . . .

The thirteen articles he wrote duly appeared in the *Westminster,* and were republished after his death [as *Letters From America*] . . . , with two other articles he sent to the *New Statesman.* (p. 82)

The *Westminster* articles reveal a new side to Rupert's talents, as an accomplished travel-writer. They are written with a restrained and graceful skill; the general tone is sophisticated and urbane, with a continual undertone of irony and humour. His descriptions of people he met, and above all places he visited, are witty and imaginative; and some of the bravura pieces, for instance the pictures of Niagara Falls and of Lake Louise, are fresh and poetic and exact. They undoubtedly strengthen the view of some of his contemporaries that his eventual literary career would have been even more as a prose writer than as a poet. (pp. 83-4)

It was the war sonnets that changed him into the almost sacred, supreme poet-figure of his generation, the mellifluous mouthpiece of the sentiments that had before been half incoherently felt by all those English people who were struggling to make sense of the war into which they had so suddenly been plunged, and who clung to the hope that the trials and sufferings, still only mistily revealed, that lay before them could be considered as part of a crusade of right against wrong, as a testing ground of courage and belief in their own country and its cause.

At the same time it is possible that with a subsequent generation who saw the noble sentiments as glib idealism and unrealistic day-dreaming, his name might not have fallen into the disrepute that has lasted until today; a generation whose fathers and elder brothers had lived through the senseless horrors of the Flanders trenches, and who found in the poetry of Siegfried Sassoon, Wilfred Owen and Isaac Rosenberg the true response to modern warfare at its most futile and morally degrading. No thoughtful and sensitive young man could imaginably have gone into the fighting of the Second World War with the lines of Brooke's sonnets *The Dead* and *Peace* echoing in his mind to inspire his vision and steel his purpose. If, however, those sonnets had not been written, such young men might still have delighted in the lyrical freshness of *Tiare Tahiti,* the light-hearted nostalgia of *Grantchester,* and the debunking wit and technical skill of his remodelled fish poem, *Heaven;* and a number of others where the sentiment is not forced and the language keeps rhetoric under a more caustic intellectual control. That he had seen how important such discipline was is shown by his wholehearted admiration for the poetry of John Donne. (pp. 132-33)

The chief weakness of [Brooke's] poetry—and it is a weakness markedly in contrast to the mastery in this particular sphere shown by Donne and by his almost equally admired Webster—was a preference for vague grandiloquence and high-sounding generalities in preference to the concrete word and the freshly illuminating image, the poetical cliché instead of the original imaginative discovery. It may be partly due to a lingering fondness for the affected romanticism of the nineties he had felt in his youthful phase; it continued to slip into his more mature poetry all too often when his mind was not working at top pressure.

Phrases such as 'in wise majestic melancholy train', 'some low sweet alley between wind and wind', 'dark scents whisper', 'the grey tumult of these after-years', 'song's nobility and wisdom holy', 'the heart of bravery swift and clean', which have a fine exalted ring but when examined mean nothing precise at all, from time to time pad out his verses throughout his adult career and not merely his beginnings when he was searching for a style; in fact they become his style as soon as he forgets his wit and light-heartedness and abandons those realistic touches that so shocked the critics of his first book. With what relief, then, one comes across the precise and vivid images with which in *The Great Lover* he enumerates the concrete things that evoke his love in recollection: 'wet roofs, beneath the lamplight', 'the rough male kiss of blankets', 'the good smell of old clothes', 'brown horse-chestnuts, glossy new'; though even in this attractive and original, though imperfect, poem he cannot resist the glib poetical rhetoric of phrases such as 'the inenarrable godhead of delight' and 'out on the wind of Time, shining and streaming'.

The weakness of the war sonnets lies not merely in their even more fulsome use of such insubstantial rhetoric, but in the fundamental shallowness and inadequacy of the sentiments expressed in relation to the grimness of the challenge which faced the young men on the German as well as the British side. (pp. 134-35)

The vague high-sounding generalities appear so profusely in the sonnets that it would be tedious to list them all. Worst of all, perhaps, in this respect is the second sonnet, *Safety*. The poet, addressing his beloved, enumerates the phenomena, 'all things undying', which make them feel 'safe.' . . . (p. 135)

Every image in these lines is obvious and of the most general kind, and contributes nothing concrete to the idea, or makes any imaginative discovery that can be called in any way original: it is little more than a lulling incantation of clichés. The same process is almost disastrously at work in the fourth sonnet, called *The Dead*. . . . [One] can only register astonishment that Brooke, who could be so precise when he liked, can crowd so many nouns denoting vaguely emotive general concepts, 'unbroken glory', 'gathered radiance', 'shining peace' into two lines.

The two most quoted and probably most popular sonnets—certainly most popular at the time—are the first, *Peace,* and the fifth, *The Soldier.* The first, *Peace,* is the sonnet that most successors of a younger generation, and probably most soldiers who saw more of the war than Rupert ever saw, have jibbed at as shallowy sentimental and unrealistic. What soldier, who had experienced the meaningless horror and foulness of the Western Front stalemate in 1916 and 1917, could think of it as a place to greet 'as swimmers into cleanness leaping' or as a welcome relief 'from a world grown old and cold and weary'? (p. 136)

What is peculiarly disturbing about *Peace* is that it gives sudden and violent expression to Rupert's always latent puritanism. The soldiers are awakened 'from sleeping' and are leaping 'into cleanness' in getting away from their everyday pursuits (though *The Dead* seems to express an entirely opposite point of view); fighting redeems a world 'grown old and cold and weary' even though it involves killing and destruction and waste; the whole of Rupert's past life is characterized as

The sick hearts that honour could not move,
And half-men, and their dirty songs and dreary,
And all the little emptiness of love.

Who are these 'half-men' and 'sick hearts' unmoved by honour? What poet was singing 'dirty songs and dreary'? . . . [Was] he thinking again, obsessively, of the emotional shocks he endured at Lulworth in the New Year of 1912, with Lytton Strachey and other denizens of Bloomsbury as the 'sick hearts' and 'half-men' who wounded him so mysteriously? And if so, why did they now become symbols of all that had made up civilian existence before the war, as if civilized peaceful living itself was only worth throwing away *in toto*?

The Soldier is as eloquent and skilful a piece of verse-making as anything Rupert ever produced, with its repeated plangent harping on the word 'England' and all the historic and patriotic overtones it evoked. The movement of the argument and the tone are both flawless, and one can easily see how in the anxious, emotional mood of the early months of the war it could bring tears to any sensitive eye. And yet, looked at dispassionately today, it is difficult not to feel that it is riddled with sentimentality and narcissistic fantasy, whatever he may have meant in imagining himself 'a pulse in the eternal mind' purified of all unworthy thought and feeling. Even at the time, while the guns were still thundering, there were not a few, and among them his intellectual peers, who questioned his attitudinizing. (pp. 136-37)

E. J. Dent, who knew him so well, . . . thought that the sonnets, 'beautiful as they are in technique and expression, represent him only in a phase that could only have been temporary'. . . . Perhaps, if [Brooke] had survived into 1917 and 1918, he would have dismissed the legend himself more ruthlessly than anyone else. Perhaps only he could have done it— and been disbelieved. (pp. 168-69)

> *John Lehmann, in his* Rupert Brooke: His Life and His Legend *(© 1980 by John Lehmann; reprinted by permission of David Higham Associates Limited, as agents for the author; in Canada by Weidenfeld & Nicolson), Weidenfeld & Nicolson, 1980, 178 p.*

ADDITIONAL BIBLIOGRAPHY

Cunliffe, J.W. "Masefield and the New Georgian Poets." In his *English Literature in the Twentieth Century*, pp. 292-329. New York: The Macmillan Co., 1935.*
    Praises *1914, and Other Poems* for its power to fire the patriotic spirit of its readers.

Eagle, Solomon [pseudonym of J. C. Squire]. "Rupert Brooke in Retrospect." In his *Books in General, second series*, pp. 256-61. New York: Alfred A. Knopf, 1920.
    Finds Brooke to be a budding genius, prevented by death from becoming a new Keats.

Hynes, Samuel. "Rupert Brook." In his *Edwardian Occasions: Essays on English Writing in the Early Twentieth Century*, pp. 144-52. New York: Oxford University Press, pp. 144-52.
    Blasts Brooks's poetry, finding it to be little more than the efforts of a dilettante.

Mais, S.P.B. "Rupert Brooke." In his *From Shakespeare to O. Henry: Studies in Literature*, rev. ed., pp. 258-81. London: Grant Richards, 1923.
    Emphasizes the influence of John Donne.

Morley, Christopher. ''Rupert Brooke.'' In his *Essays*, pp. 56-69. Garden City, N.Y.: Doubleday, Doran & Co., 1928.
  Praises Brooke's work for capturing the vital spirit of England's youth.

Nesbitt, Cathleen. ''Cathleen Nesbitt Talks to Michael Elliot about Rupert Brooke.'' *The Listener* 87, No. 2234 (20 January 1972): 83-5.
  Recollections of Brooke by the woman he loved.

Weygandt, Cornelius. ''The Last Romantics.'' In his *The Time of Yeats: English Poetry of To-day against an American Background*, pp. 363-85. New York: Russell & Russell, 1969.*
  A survey of Brooke's canon, acknowledging the difficulties posed to the critic by the poet's all-pervading ''young Apollo'' myth.

Woodberry, George Edward. ''Rupert Brooke.'' In his *Studies of a Litterateur*, pp. 319-28. 1921. Reprint. Freeport, N.Y.: Books for Libraries Press, 1968.
  A glowing tribute to Brooke and his work.

(William) Bliss Carman

1861-1929

(Also wrote under pseudonym of Louis Norman) Canadian poet, essayist, and editor.

In his lifetime Carman was considered Canada's leading poet, the Canadian Parliament honoring him as the nation's poet laureate in 1928. His early collections especially gained admirers for their lyrical, moody depictions of nature and for a free-spirited bohemianism found particularly in the popular *Songs from Vagabondia*. Carman's poetic world revolves primarily around the beauty of things seen, the mystery of things unseen, and the music of language. Themes derived largely from the romantics and Victorians typify his work, and in the twentieth century his popularity steadily declined. The author of what are still regarded as some of the finest and most nearly perfect poems in Canadian literature, he is now portrayed in literary histories as a minor poet with a vivid sense of atmosphere.

Carman, born in Fredericton, New Brunswick, was descended from American Loyalists who fled to Canada from New England during the Revolution. He was educated at Fredericton Academy and later attended the University of New Brunswick, the universities of Oxford, Edinburgh, and Harvard. For a time he studied law and civil engineering, but devoted himself solely to literature after his stay at Harvard. There he profited from contact with a brilliant generation of teachers and students, including Josiah Royce, William James, Bernard Berenson, and George Santayana. He also met Richard Hovey, with whom he composed the three collections of vagabond lyrics. Carman moved to New York in 1890, and for the next twenty years he worked for various American publications as editor and writer, while still returning frequently to Canada. In 1897 he met Mary Perry King, a proponent of the doctrine of unitrinianism, whose followers embraced a struggle for harmony of the mind, body, and soul. Always receptive to philosophical influences, Carman integrated this doctrine with the generally transcendentalist world view he maintained throughout his life.

Carman's first collection, *Low Tide on Grand Pré*, established what would become his most enduring artistic persona, that of a poet of delicate moods and mysterious landscapes. "Meditative," "melancholy," "haunted" are common epithets applied to these poems. Carman stated that he wanted to convey a unity of tone in assembling the pieces in this collection. However, after a number of Carman's books had appeared, critics labeled this unity as monotony, though Odell Shepard has argued for the poet's range and variety. In *Behind the Arras*, Carman's predominately sad and somber voice strikes a note of deeper pessimism, while further developing a strain of visionary mysticism displaying the influence of Poe. Despite his frequently grave tone, Carman in recent decades has been criticized for his optimism. Commentators trace his hopefulness to the influence of Emerson's transcendentalist philosophy and the vague assurance Carman maintained that unseen powers are working for the good of the human spirit. In such essay collections as *The Kinship of Nature* and *The Friendship of Art* he outlines his optimistic and inspirational outlook.

In his elegiac poems to Shelley, Keats, and others Carman acknowledges some of his strongest influences, and critics point out many more, including Wordsworth, Whitman, Rossetti, Tennyson, Arnold, and Browning. The poems in the vagabond series are found by some critics to be the least derivative, though others view the boisterous bohemian tone as essentially affected. Carman's later poetry collections, such as *April Airs* and *Later Poems*, offer little artistic development and add nothing to his reputation. While he wrote in a number of traditional poetic forms, with ambitious attempts at lengthy narrative poems, Carman is chiefly remembered today as a lyric poet who, not often but conspicuously, excelled at conveying a personal, highly contemplative appreciation for the beauty and mystery he perceived in nature.

PRINCIPAL WORKS

Flower of the Rose [as Louis Norman]   (poetry)   1892
Low Tide on Grand Pré   (poetry)   1893
Songs from Vagabondia [with Richard Hovey]   (poetry)   1894
Behind the Arras   (poetry)   1895
A Seamark   (poetry)   1895

More Songs from Vagabondia [with Richard Hovey]
   (poetry) 1896
Ballads of Lost Haven (poetry) 1897
By the Aurelian Wall, and Other Elegies (poetry) 1898
Last Songs from Vagabondia [with Richard Hovey]
   (poetry) 1901
Ballads and Lyrics (poetry) 1902
From the Book of Myths (poetry) 1902
From the Green Book of the Bards (poetry) 1903
The Friendship of Art (essays) 1904
The Kinship of Nature (essays) 1904
Sappho (poetry) 1904
Songs from a Northern Garden (poetry) 1904
Songs of the Sea Children (poetry) 1904
From the Book of Valentines (poetry) 1905
The Poetry of Life (essays) 1905
The Making of Personality [with Mary Perry King]
   (essays) 1908
The Rough Rider, and Other Poems (poetry) 1909
Echoes from Vagabondia (poetry) 1912
April Airs (poetry) 1916
Later Poems (poetry) 1921
Wild Garden (poetry) 1929

*These works were published as *The Pipes of Pan* in 1906.

WILLIAM SHARP (essay date 1894)

All who follow closely the drift of contemporary poetry must have had their curiosity piqued again and again within recent years by the fugitive verse of Mr. Bliss Carman. . . .

Prof. [Charles] Roberts and Mr. Carman are admittedly the finest poetic voices heard as yet in the Dominion, and it would be difficult to select work surpassing theirs from the mass of verse of high quality produced by the younger American writers. Certainly there is none of a more exquisite lyrical note than that of Mr. Carman. In this peculiar grace he has but one rival among his compatriots, if the living can be said to have a rival in the dead—Isabella Valancey Crawford, who died young some years ago, but not before she had given warrant of rare powers. . . .

[It] seems to me regrettable that [Mr. Carman] has refrained from publishing [in *Low Tide on Grand Pré*] some of his most beautiful and, certainly, most mature work. For not only has he excluded several of those noteworthy ballads of which he has given some of us a foretaste, the Arnold threnody, and other verse of an exceptional quality; but he has even omitted certain ballads and lyrics, already published, which would surely have interfered in no way with the homogeneity of the present volume. In Mr. Lighthall's Anthology [of Canadian Verse], for instance, there is the **"Wraith of the Red Swan,"** with its firm delicate touch and haunting cadences. . . . (p. 7)

[The] author has a prefatory note, wherein he sets forth that the poems that follow have been collected with reference to their similarity of tone, and that all are variations on a single theme, more or less aptly suggested by the title, *Low Tide on Grand Pré*. It seemed better, adds Mr. Carman, to bring together between the same covers only those pieces of work which happened to be in the same key, than to publish a larger book of more uncertain aim. Here, of course, we have sufficient

explanation of the author's reticence; though I still think these Grand Pré lyrics might have formed, so to say, a section rather than an independent whole. (pp. 7-8)

Grand Pré is the part of Acadia in Nova Scotia which Longfellow has made familiar in "Evangeline." . . . The real poetic Acadia exists, perhaps, only in the mind. . . . But those who would know it in the spirit will discern it . . . clearly in the lyrics of Charles Roberts and Bliss Carman. . . .

It is difficult to distinguish the charm which haunts these Acadian lyrics. There is in them a delicate air that reaches us, . . . a serene calm, . . . a sense of melancholy and regret, ever wrought by an instinct with nature. . . . All are dominated by an overmastering sense of beauty, and permeated with a love of nature for which there is no epithet so apt as the much misused and hackneyed word "intense." If ever there was a child of nature, it is the author of **"The End of the Trail,"** **"The Vagabonds,"** **"Pulvis et Umbra,"** and other poems in a lovely slow-music that is all his own. . . . Here and there in this book, and particularly in **"The Vagabonds,"** there is proof of kinship with Omar Khayyam. . . . And with the New World singer as with the old Persian poet, there is the same acceptance of the common doom. . . . Occasionally the singer forgets his craft, but only once disastrously, as in the unforgivable final quatrain of **"Seven Things."** He must be on his guard, too, against repetition of favourite effects and words; and at "auroral," "leaguer," "lyric" as an epithet, "dream," and "bugling" he should for a time look askance, despite their beauty. (p. 8)

> William Sharp, " 'Low Tide on Grand Pré'," in The Academy, No. 1131, January 6, 1894, pp. 7-8.

FRANCIS THOMPSON (essay date 1894)

[The] authors of the small joint volume called *Songs from Vagabondia* have an unmistakable right to the name of poet. These little snatches have the spirit of a gipsy Omar Khayyám. They have always careless verve, and often careless felicity; they are masculine and rough, as roving songs should be; sometimes also unfinished, as no songs should be. For finish is not polish, though it is frequently confounded with polish; and a thing as rough as Esau's hand may have had the last touch which an understanding art exacts. But here, certainly, is the poet's soul; and how sick we all are of pratings about the poet's art! . . . You have the whole spirit of the book in such an unforgettable little lyric as **"In the House of Idiedaily."** . . . And throughout the book, in addition to the more omnipresent qualities we have before noted, start up touches of a higher mood; as when, for example, in the admirable **"Joys of the Road,"** lilting, vagrant, irreflective, as a road-song should be, we are suddenly startled by such a Wordsworthian subtlety of expression as this:

> The outward eye, the quiet will,
> And the striding heart from hill to hill.

Wordsworth has taught us the divinity of the "inward eye"; but it was left, appropriately, for this roaming singer to discern, that the outward eye is in its season a gift of the gods, seldom truly possessed but by the child and the poet. (pp. 292-93)

[**"The War-Song of Gamelbar"** shows] how fierily these authors can handle the old martial ballad. The names have a pleasant ring of the old country, pleasant for kindred's sake in the mouth of an American. . . . Good is here, but no less good remains behind; for which we refer the reader to the delightful little volume itself, which comes as a welcome interlude amidst the highly-wrought introspective poetry of the day. (pp. 294-95)

> *Francis Thompson, "Americana: 'A Partnership in Song'" (originally published as "A Partnership in Song," in* Merry England, *December, 1894), in his* Literary Criticisms, *edited by Rev. Terrence L. Connolly, S. J., E. P. Dutton & Company, Inc., 1948. pp. 292-95.*

HELEN A. CLARKE (essay date 1896)

Not lately has a more alluring volume of poems appeared than Bliss Carman's **'Behind the Arras.'** Here are both fancy and thought mingled in an art that at its best attains exquisite expression. The poem that christens the book presents on the whole the happiest combination of the poet's qualities. The rhythm chosen, of long and short lines rhyming together, reflects most effectively the illusive yet fascinating suggestiveness of the symbolism. Any icy monotony that might result from such studied irregularity is melted in the warm, easy flow of the language and the inevitableness of the rhymes. (p. 95)

After reading this poem one feels as if emerging from some mystic realm, where, by means of etherealized symbols, the mind has caught glimpses of the vanishing-points of thought, yet it is all so simply, even reticently done. And the drift of it? Mayhap the climbing of the spirit to ever higher regions of beauty through the growth of will and love! More mysterious, if possible, is the **'Moon Dial,'** whose dread records of the world's supreme passions none have ever seen and lived to tell the meaning thereof.

In some of the poems one must admit that there are what seem to be echoes from certain master-spirits of the age. **'The Cruise of the Galleon'** and **'The Song before Sailing'** recall Whitman's favorite figure for eternity,—the seas of God,—wherein the soul sets sail in its eidolon yacht upon its journey into eternity. But where Whitman gains his effect of inconceivable vastness by large sweeps of the imagination that leave a certain vagueness, Bliss Carman gains his effect by setting up a more specialized relationship between the seen and the unseen, and thereby succeeds in presenting to the mind a startlingly definite image of the unimaginable. (p. 96)

One must be reminded, too, of Browning's 'Abt Vogler,' in reading **'Beyond the Gamut.'** Both poems essay the solution of the problem of good and evil by means of the symbolism and analogies offered by music, and in both it is the musician himself who speaks. However, Abt Vogler at his organ bases his analogies entirely upon music's laws of artistic construction; while Bliss Carman's musician, with his beloved Amati on his arm, seeks analogies in the physical or scientific aspects of musical laws, where he finds material for some beautiful and uncommon imagery. Whether Bliss Carman's musician had read Rowbotham's really poetic history of music we cannot say; but he has hit upon the same analogy used by that author between the idea of the music of the spheres and a scientifically observed fact, and given it the final poetic setting. . . . (p. 97)

[So] from various special inter-relations of music with sense and thought, he works up to the consideration of good and evil, harmonizing them as a musician does his dissonances and his concords, very much as his elder brother Abt Vogler does.

But here again, though there are these self-evident similarities to Browning's great poem, Bliss Carman's is lifted beyond the plane of mere imitation because it is pervaded by the peculiar aroma of his own individual genius. He amplifies the thought into a complete expression of what we take to be his own philosophy, briefly stated,—the development of the soul by means of the senses, the final annihilation of evil, and the perfect fruition of love. The blossoming of thought without any loss of picturesqueness in these last poems of Bliss Carman's is an indication that in him we have one of the few latter-day poets with possibilities of development,—one who can transmute, if he will, the enormously complex material of modern knowledge and thought into the lovely creations of art. (pp. 97-8)

> *Helen A. Clarke, "Recent American Verse: 'Behind the Arras, a Book of the Unseen'," in* Poet Lore, *Vol. 8, No. 2, February, 1896, pp. 95-8.*

GREENOUGH WHITE (essay date 1899)

[Charles G.D. Roberts and Bliss Carman] are rural poets condemned to live in cities. . . . They long for the country and the forest—not so much for Nature in her more majestic aspects of mountain and ocean, as for the woods, streams, and winds of Canada. . . . The ground tone of both poets (as the Germans would express it) is elegiac; it is grave but not sad—not to say pessimistic; and it is by no means irreligious, but, in the case of the first mentioned, decidedly religious. Their verse is exceedingly easy and fluent; they are fond of the measure known in hymnody as "common metre," with only one rhyme in a quatrain. . . . It really seems, considering the fact that they have no Orphic message to deliver as best they can, as if they might pay a little more attention to poetic art—to the harmonies of rhyme and metre. To conclude these resemblances with one little point: they both show fondness for the unusual word "plangent." (p. 49)

If Mr. Roberts is the more thoughtful of the two, graver, deeper, and clearer, Mr. Carman appears to us to have more of the poetical temperament, to be more imaginatively suggestive. His is a roving genius; favorite terms with him are *quest* and *trail;* his book [**"By the Aurelian Wall and Other Elegies"**] ends with the words "the endless trail." (p. 50)

There is a strange beauty about certain of [his] wordings—a visionary quality that wakes the imagination, suggestions vague or vivid, faint impressions, as of something seen or heard in dreams. This is what we value most in Mr. Carman; but in his desire to produce these impressions, to be freshly and vividly descriptive, he experiments too frequently and daringly with novel terms of speech. (p. 51)

His subjects are elegiac, being threnodies for dead men, mostly poets. We have a dactylic experiment on Phillips Brooks, which is a marvel of harsh sound, and strikes one as devoid of genuine inspiration—as written to order; a dirge for Henry George; and verses in memory of Lovelace, Blake, Keats, Shelley, Stephenson, and Verlaine. Indeed, by his elegiac strain, the critical vein that crops out here and there in his poems, and his passion for nature, Mr. Carman reminds us of Arnold, or, better, of Arnold's shadow, Mr. William Watson. It is here that we place him in contemporary poetry. . . . "There is no other way to redeem the world," he avers, "than the way of the rebels and saints." He betrays a sympathy for those who dare to make desire a duty. . . . (pp. 51-2)

He lacks Mr. Watson's incisiveness, but, for compensation, is free from his melancholy pessimism. . . . The influence of the gentle spirit of Longfellow is apparent. . . .

Finally, the landscape that lingers upon the mental retina after finishing his poems is not unlike Mr. Roberts': a large red sun sinking behind wooded hills, a twittering bird note in the still air, a meditative evening calm. (p. 52)

> *Greenough White, "A Pair of Canadian Poets," in The Sewanee Review, Vol. VII, No. 1, January, 1899, pp. 48-52.**

WILLIAM ARCHER   (essay date 1902)

A fascinating and somewhat baffling talent is that of Mr. Bliss Carman. His weird and fantastic imagination is enlisted in the service of a far-reaching philosophy which purports to gather the whole universe into its embrace; but the precise nature of that philosophy I cannot for the life of me discover. A half-stoical, half-rollicking Bohemianism is one of its prevailing notes; yet every now and then it passes over, without the slightest modulation, into a sort of grim and cynical pessimism; while in a number of poems one is tempted to call it sheer rigmarole, a long-drawn pageant of symbols which symbolise nothing. I feel that here I am on dangerous ground. It is quite possible that there may arise—if it has not already arisen—a sect of Carmanites who, by brooding on the enigmas of *Behind the Arras,* may hatch out a religion from the germs of thought which are scattered through its pages in reckless profusion. Militant sects have been founded ere now on less cryptic, and certainly less thoughtful, scriptures. I myself, were I casting about for a religion, should be tempted to shut myself up for six weeks or so in a lonely tower, with no literature in my portmanteau but *Behind the Arras* and *Low Tide on Grand Pré.* One might easily find much duller and less melodious sacred books. But as I feel no pressing need for a new revelation, I am bound to say, at the risk of figuring as an incredible dullard in the eyes of a Carmanite posterity, that I prefer the Bohemian and humorist in Mr. Carman to the metaphysician and moralist, and am more grateful to him for one whiff of downright Nova-Scotia brine, than for all his researches in the stifling caverns of symbolism.

Let me not be understood, however, to bracket together *Low Tide on Grand Pré* and *Behind the Arras.* When he wrote *Low Tide on Grand Pré* Mr. Carman was not consciously and deliberately a symbolist. This "Book of Lyrics," as he calls it, is genuinely lyrical in intention and in tone; but one respectful and indeed admiring reader must confess his inability, in most cases, to make out what the lyrics are about. Not that they are obscure; on the contrary, taken stanza by stanza, they seem as clear as daylight; but when you have read a lyric through, there is nothing for you to take hold of; nothing to bite on the mind. Even a pure lyric should tell its story, or at least suggest its situation; whereas Mr. Carman rhymes on and on, with grace, feeling and distinction, to leave us wondering at the end of a poem why it was ever begun. In saying this I probably do him injustice. I lack some key, whether of personal knowledge or local association, that should unlock for me the mystery of these Acadian lyrics. (pp. 66-7)

Mr. Carman uses the English language with such force, freedom and distinction, that one is positively puzzled to know why so few poems in this book give permanent and substantial pleasure. . . . [Two] poems at the end of the book, *Marian*

Drury and *Golden Rowan,* point the way to Mr. Carman's *Ballads of Lost Haven,* an important contribution to the sea poetry of the language.

Not many poets, even in our island speech, have had a keener or more intimate feeling for the sea than breathes in this little book of Mr. Carman's. . . . The ballad [entitled *The Yule Guest*] is perhaps a little too long, but it is beautiful throughout. A similar criticism applies to *The Marring of Malyn* and *The Kelpie Riders.* Mr. Carman lacks the gift of compression, and does not excel as a narrator. He is at his best in poems that hover on the border-line between the ballad and the mere fantasy, such as *The Nancy's Pride* and *The Master of the Isles,* and in pure lyrics like *The Ships of St. John.* But though uneven in their inspiration, these poems, one and all, bring home to us with a peculiar and searching power the mystery and terror of a stormy northern seaboard.

Perhaps I ought not to write of *Behind the Arras,* for all I can say of it is, in effect, that this sort of unconditioned symbolism has for me personally little or no message. The symbols seem, as it were, to be always shifting their plane, and my mind wearies in the effort to keep, from stanza to stanza, at the right perspective. Mr. Carman's thought is certainly "undulant and diverse" to a degree. Imagine a procession in which the figures do not move steadily past the eye at a constant distance, but are for ever making huge leaps to the right and left of their line of route, now springing forward till you see the whites of their menacing eyes, and anon whisking away till they almost vanish on the far horizon! . . . The meaning of many of the poems, such as *The Moondial, The Face in the Stream, The Lodger* and *Beyond the Gamut,* entirely eludes me. In others the intention is visible enough, but in a flickering, inconsequent and finally wearisome fashion. The poem which gives the book its title, *Behind the Arras,* is one of the more perspicuous, and certainly not the least powerful. Compression is what it seems chiefly to lack. The fantasy is overwrought in its sixty stanzas. If the whole were as strong as some of its parts it would be a masterpiece. (pp. 69-73)

It is refreshing to turn from *Behind the Arras* to the two series of *Songs from Vagabondia,* which Mr. Carman has published in fellowship with Mr. Richard Hovey. The poems are unsigned, but I am able, from private information, to set apart the contributions of the two poets. I should have been puzzled to do so from internal evidence, so cleverly has each caught the other's strain of humour. This word I use advisedly, for the note of the booklets is a freakish, devil-may-care whimsicality. Tavern staves and jingles alternate with society verses, rollicking Irish ballads, and death's-head fantasies. But there is literary power everywhere; and here and there true poetry, in the narrower sense of the word, breaks through. Among Mr. Carman's contributions there is none more truly inspired, I think, than [*Daisies*]. (p. 75)

[In] *By the Aurelian Wall, and other Poems: A Book of Elegies,* there is still a good deal of that insubstantiality, I had almost said inconsequence, of thought which baffles one in *Low Tide on Grand Pré.* The name-poem, an elegy on Keats, presents a definite, but not, I think, a very consistent or luminous image, while *The White Gull,* written for the centenary of the birth of Shelley, seems to me to say very little in a great many words. (pp. 77-8)

There is beautiful work in *The Country of Hur,* written for the centenary of Blake's *Songs of Innocence;* but the most successful poems in the book, to my mind, are those inspired by

American subjects, the elegies on Phillips Brooks, John Eliot Bowen, and Henry George. In *Ilicet,* an elegy on a suicide, Mr. Carman has again invented a beautiful measure, but has left his thought too patently under the control of his intricate rhyme-scheme. . . . The verses on Verlaine are clear in idea, but not specially inspired; and the remainder of the book is given up to poems commemorating friendships and comradeships in the love of wild nature, which contain many beautiful details, but no single number that seems to me quite masterly and satisfying.

Of Mr. Carman's remarkable gifts there can be no doubt whatever. His fluency is sometimes a little out of proportion to the substance of his thought. He is apt, now and then, to dilute his ideas to the point of extreme tenuity, or to whip them up into a shimmering but elusive froth. Of his mysticism, as aforesaid, I desire to speak with all caution, for no doubt I lack the temperamental clue to it; but there are a good many poems of no specially mystical cast, in which the words seem to me simply to drown and disintegrate the thought. He is always a poet, however; his vision is intense, his imagination potent, his diction strong and free; and when he achieves compression and clarity, the result is poetry of a very high order. (pp. 78-9)

> *William Archer, "Bliss Carman," in his* Poets of the Younger Generation, *John Lane, 1902 (and reprinted by Scholarly Press, 1969?), pp. 66-82.*

C.G.D. ROBERTS (essay date 1904)

Perhaps the most perilous and the most alluring venture in the whole field of poetry is that which Mr. Carman has undertaken in attempting to give us in English verse those lost poems of Sappho of which fragments have survived. The task is obviously not one of translation or of paraphrasing, but of imaginative and, at the same time, interpretive construction. It is as if a sculptor of to-day were to set himself, with reverence, and trained craftsmanship, and studious familiarity with the spirit, technique, and atmosphere of his subject, to restore some statues of Polyclitus or Praxiteles of which he had but a broken arm, a foot, a knee, a finger upon which to build. Mr. Carman's method, apparently, has been to imagine each lost lyric as discovered, and then to translate it; for the indefinable flavour of the translation is maintained throughout, though accompanied by the fluidity and freedom of purely original work. (pp. xiv-xv)

> *C.G.D. Roberts, in his introduction to* Sappho: One Hundred Lyrics *by Bliss Carman, L. C. Page and Company, 1904 (and reprinted by Chatto & Windus, 1930, pp. ix-xv).*

THE NEW YORK TIMES SATURDAY REVIEW (essay date 1908)

Bliss Carman, in his charming book, **"The Making of a Personality,"** . . . points the way to an elysium peopled with good women and men in every way sound and attractive. His prescriptions are based on what he calls a "triunistic or unitrinian philosophy," the essence of which is a personal culture in which physical, mental, and moral development are co-ordinated.

Of course, the elysium is only theoretically attainable. Few of us will go in for the improvement of our bodies, minds, and souls to the extent requisite for the full realization of the ideals with which Mr. Carman tempts us. Many of us will yearn for the perfection of personality we are urged to acquire, but to the most of us the price is staggering and prohibitive. We are asked to give up things we prize, to do things that bore us, to work strenuously and unceasingly, inwardly and outwardly, in order to accomplish our uplifting.

Even in the matter of dress reform demands are made at which many of us balk. For example, Mr. Carman wants unstayed women, and certainly that is a very large order. Still further removed from unanimity would be the acceptance by our women of Mr. Carman's ideas as to footgear. Women of these days are not inclined to listen approvingly to the man who purchases broad-toed, heelless shoes, modeled as closely as may be to the Indian moccasin. "If," says Mr. Carman, "I were a fairy and asked to bestow a gift on the man and woman of the twentieth century, I would give them each a pair of model shoes."

Only a limited number of us will undertake to renovate ourselves thoroughly and make new beings of ourselves, proceeding in accordance with Mr. Carman's philosophy. But there is not a word to be said against the philosophy. It is a beautiful philosophy, most delightfully set forth, and whoever looks into it will feel impelled to do some of the things he is invited to do. Probably that is quite as much as Mr. Carman expects or even hopes for.

> *"Bliss Carman's Ideas," in* The New York Times Saturday Review *(© 1908 by The New York Times Company; reprinted by permission), June 20, 1908, p. 356.*

R. H. HATHAWAY (essay date 1921)

Canada has full right to be proud of her poets, a small body though they are; but not only does Mr. Carman stand high and clear above them all—his place (and time cannot but confirm and justify the assertion) is among those men whose poetry is the shining glory of that great English literature which is our common heritage. (p. vii)

[You] cannot fully know or estimate his work by one book, or two books, or even half a dozen; you must possess or be familiar with every one of the score and more volumes which contain his output of poetry before you can realise how great and how many-sided is his genius.

It is a common remark on the part of those who respond readily to the vigorous work of Kipling, or Masefield, even our own Service, that Bliss Carman's poetry has no relation to or concern with ordinary, everyday life. . . . I grant that you will find little or nothing in it all to remind you of the grim realities and vexing social problems of this modern existence of ours; but to say or to suggest that these things do not exist for Mr. Carman is to say or to suggest something which is the reverse of true. The truth is, he is aware of them as only one with the sensitive organism of a poet can be; but he does not feel that he has a call or mission to remedy them, and still less to sing of them. He therefore leaves the immediate problems of the day to those who choose, or are led, to occupy themselves therewith, and turns resolutely away to dwell upon those things which for him possess infinitely greater importance. (p. viii)

Well, the things which concern him above all, I would answer, are first, and naturally, the beauty and wonder of this world of ours, and next the mystery of the earthly pilgrimage of the human soul out of eternity and back into it again. (p. ix)

This is manifest most in certain of his earlier books, for in these he turns and returns to the greatest of all the problems of man almost constantly, probing, with consummate and almost unrivalled use of the art of expression, for the secret which surely, he clearly feels, lies hidden somewhere, to be discovered if one could but pierce deeply enough. . . . He comes but little nearer success in this than do most of the rest of men, of course; but the magical and ever-fresh beauty of his expression, the haunting melody of his lines, the variety of his images and figures and the depth and range of his thought, put his searchings and ponderings in a class by themselves. (pp. ix-x)

"Pillared dust and fleeing shadow." Where in all our English literature will one find the life history of man summed up more briefly and, at the same time, more beautifully, than in that wonderful line? (p. xi)

Mr. Carman has had three distinct periods, and . . . the poems in [*Later Poems*] are of his third period. The first period may be said to be represented by the *Low Tide* and *Behind the Arras* volumes, while the second is displayed in the three volumes of *Songs from Vagabondia,* which he published in association with his friend Richard Hovey. Bliss Carman was from the first too original and individual a poet to be directly influenced by anyone else; but there can be no doubt that his friendship with Hovey helped to turn him from over-preoccupation with mysteries which, for all their greatness, are not for man to solve, to an intenser realisation of the beauty and loveliness of the world about him and of the joys of human fellowship. (p. xv)

Some of the finest of Mr. Carman's work is contained in his elegiac or memorial poems, in which he commemorates Keats, Shelley, William Blake, Lincoln, Stevenson, and other men for whom he has a kindred feeling, and also friends whom he has loved and lost. (p. xvi)

No summary of Mr. Carman's work, however cursory, would be worthy of the name if it omitted mention of his ventures in the realm of Greek myth. *From the Book of Myths* is made up of work of that sort, every poem in it being full of the beauty of phrase and melody of which Mr. Carman alone has the secret. . . . And beauty, after all is said, is the first and last thing with Mr. Carman. (p. xviii)

Kindred to *From the Book of Myths,* but much more important, is *Sappho: One Hundred Lyrics,* one of the most successful of the numerous attempts which have been made to recapture the poems by that high priestess of song which remain to us only in fragments. Mr. Carman, as Charles G.D. Roberts points out in an introduction to the volume [see excerpt above], has made no attempt here at translation or paraphrasing; his venture has been "the most perilous and most alluring in the whole field of poetry"—that of imaginative and, at the same time, interpretive construction. . . . [*Sappho: One Hundred Lyrics*] is literally a storehouse of lyric beauty.

I must not fail here to speak of *From the Book of Valentines,* which contains some lovely things, notably **"At the Great Release."** This is not only one of the finest of all Mr. Carman's poems, but it is also one of the finest poems of our time. It is a love poem, and no one possessing any real feeling for poetry can read it without experiencing that strange thrill of the spirit which only the highest form of poetry can communicate.

"Morning and Evening," "In an Iris Meadow," and "A Letter from Lesbos" must be also mentioned. (pp. xviii-xix)

Mention must be now made of *Songs of the Sea Children,* which can be described only as a collection of the sweetest and tenderest love lyrics written in our time. (p. xix)

Memories of his childhood and youthful years down by the sea are still fresh in Mr. Carman's mind, and inspire him again and again in his writing. **"A Remembrance,"** at the beginning of [*Later Poems*], may be pointed to as a striking instance of this, but proof positive is the volume, *Songs from a Northern Garden,* for it could have been written only by a Canadian, born and bred, one whose heart and soul thrill to the thought of Canada. (p. xx)

But Mr. Carman is not only a Canadian, he is also a Briton; and evidence of this is his *Ode on the Coronation,* written on the occasion of the crowning of King Edward VII in 1902. . . . [It] expresses more truly and more movingly the deep feeling of love and reverence which the very thought of England evokes in every son of hers. . . . (pp. xx-xxi)

I must say at once that, while I yield to no one in admiration for *Low Tide* and the other books of that period, or for the work of the second period, as represented by the *Songs from Vagabondia* volumes, I have no hesitation in declaring that I regard the poet's work of the past few years with even higher admiration. It may not possess the force and vigor of the work which preceded it; but anything seemingly missing in that respect is more than made up for me by increased beauty and clarity of expression. The mysticism—verging, or more than verging, at times on symbolism—which marked his earlier poems, and which hung, as it were, as a veil between them and the reader, has gone, and the poet's thought or theme now lies clearly before us as in a mirror. (pp. xxi-xxii)

Later Poems, I dare affirm, must and will be regarded as the fine flower and crowning achievement of the genius and art of Bliss Carman. (p. xxii)

R. H. Hathaway, "Bliss Carman: An Appreciation" (1921), in Later Poems *by Bliss Carman, Small, Maynard & Company Publishers, 1922, pp. vii-xxii.*

ODELL SHEPARD (essay date 1923)

Low Tide on Grand Pré, although it appeared when its author was thirty-two years of age, is in every good sense a young man's book. . . . It contains half a dozen pieces of pure verbal witchery which were made for no conceivable reason in the world except for love of beautiful sound. Aimless and fragile as thistledrift they are, but magical, and lovely forever. English words have, seldom been more cunningly woven together to make a web of haunting beauty than in the poem *Why.* . . . There are several much better poems than this in *Low Tide on Grand Pré,* but this, with its atmosphere of mystery and distance, its vague thoughts of love and vague melancholy, may be said to indicate with some accuracy the tone of the volume. . . . Already, then, in this carefully winnowed and delicately harmonized collection, it was made evident that America had a new poet who could both sing and say, who combined a finished craftsmanship with unmistakable power.

The Vagabondia books are still too well known to stand in need of extended comment. The writer has heard Mr. Edwin Arlington Robinson say that these three little books first gave American readers of the nineties reason to suspect that we might after all have a contemporary American poetry, and it has become almost a commonplace for critics and historians of our recent "poetical renaissance" to date from them. (pp. 34-6)

Most of the poems in them were written light-heartedly, many of them were written carelessly as mere whiffs of song. Some of them, nevertheless, are very interesting technically and as evidence of growth in ease and mastery on the part of Bliss Carman. . . . Unquestionably the best of them all, a poem never surpassed in its kind, is *A Vagabond Song*. . . . *Behind the Arras* is a volume of poems even more intensely unified than *Low Tide on Grand Pré*, but here the key is that of brooding rather than of vague and shifting dream. Atmosphere it has as certainly as the earlier book, although of a very different sort. The simple love of beauty tinged with melancholy seen in *Low Tide* and the frank hilarity of the *Songs from Vagabondia* give place here to a questioning, a hesitation, a doubt, as though the poet's faith had been put to severe trial. In the title poem, gnarled and powerful in stanzaic structure as it is in thought, the poet looks more directly into the shadow than anywhere else, perhaps, in all his work. In the powerful and repellant *Red Wolf*, he tells us what he sees there. These are deeply impressive poems, and they do not stand alone. *Behind the Arras* is one of the three most remarkable books Mr. Carman has published. . . .

In his next book of importance, *Ballads of Lost Haven*, Mr. Carman employed a form which he had used before, to be sure, in such spirited narrative songs as *Lal of Kilrudden* and *Buie Anajohn*, but never in poems of considerable length. . . . [His] interest in the ballad has been long and deep. Few of his poems conform at all closely, it is true, to the generally accepted definitions of the ballad. To him, apparently, almost any long narrative poem dealing with legendary and supernatural events may be called a ballad without too great a violence to the word. The abrupt transition, elimination of superfluous explanation, and "incremental repetition" of the traditional form are found in some of his ballads but not in all, and he has seldom attempted such archaic diction as Coleridge used in *The Ancient Mariner*. The chief defects of the ballads, considered as such, are seen in the absence of really dramatic elements and in the weakness of the narrative. Most of them, such as the *Kelpie Riders*, merely build up a romantic atmosphere or present, like *The Yule Guest*, an interesting situation, with little development. When there is some action, as in *The King of Ys* and *Master of the Scud*, it is not always clearly presented.

Not more than half of the poems in this volume are ballads even in name. All of them, however, deal with the sea in one way or another. As the London *Nation* said of it at the time of its appearance, this book "is one hundred pages of salt sea without a trace of Kipling, and yet having a sea-flavor as unmistakable as his, and with a finer touch—with less of repetition, less of mere technicality, and a more varied human interest." One should add that Mr. Carman makes no attempt in this book or elsewhere to write of the sea as a sailor might do, but that he sees and hears it always as a landsman. He regards the sea, in fact, not exactly as a lover of it but somewhat in the way of the ancient Greeks, as mysterious, unfriendly, even hostile, and in several poems of this book he treats it as a symbol of death. Out of the *Ballads of Lost Haven*, however, comes one of the burliest and most manly of all our songs of the sea, *The Gravedigger*. . . . (pp. 37-41)

By the Aurelian Wall is a book entirely composed of elegies and memorabilia. The title poem, of course, is addressed to the memory of John Keats. *The White Gull* was written for the

centennial of Shelley's birth, and William Blake is celebrated in *The Country of Har*. Raphael, Paul Verlaine, Andrew Straton, and Henry George swell the strangely assorted company. Probably the best and certainly the best known of the poems in this book is *A Seamark*, a threnody for Robert Louis Stevenson. For clarity of outline, passages of exceptional beauty, and sustained dignity of tone, this poem takes high rank in its author's work. (p. 42)

A Winter Holiday is the record in verse of a trip to the Bahaman Islands and of a short stay in White Nassau—a book of travel sketches. One poem, *Flying Fish,* stands vividly forth in this little book, a gleaming marvel of dexterous craftsmanship in words. . . . (p. 47)

In the first of the five books which were brought together under the general title *Pipes of Pan* the poet turns definitely to the ancient classics for subject matter and for models of form. In *The Book of Myths,* also, the didactic bent of his work in the second period is for the first time clearly evident. One is made to feel for the first time in this book, moreover, a certain lack of coherence, a tendency to over-word the thought. Several of the poems are clearly too long. The first poem, for example, although it has no narrative element, extends to nearly five-hundred lines. Mr. Carman has shown in scores of poems, particularly in the *Songs of the Sea Children,* unusual powers of compression, but those powers are not evident in *The Book of Myths.* Here he seems to depend for his effects rather upon accumulation of details than upon selection. He believes, and no doubt rightly, that a main service of rhythm, rhyme, and meter in poetry is to charm and lull our work-a-day moods into sleep, "to elude the too vigilant reason and so gain instant access to the spirit." (pp. 49-50)

There is no serious objection to be taken to this theory, but its author would readily admit that it may be carried too far. One observes that the tendency to sing on on on, as though the poet had been too completely mesmerized by the cadence of his own lines, is observable only in the rhymed poems, and chiefly in those written in the octosyllabic line. In rhymeless stanzas, where the form is largely determined by thought rather than by sound, Mr. Carman's work is always succinct, close-knit, beautifully proportioned. *The Lost Dryad,* an unrhymed but stanzaic poem in the book under discussion, is an admirable example of what may be called thought architecture, and the *Dead Faun,* the finest poem in the volume, is not a line too long or too short. (p. 50)

[*The Green Book of the Bards*] is composed entirely of nature poems, many of which are pure songs of delight in the bounty of Earth, but others show the increasing grip upon the poet's mind of certain metaphysical ideas. The five poems entitled *Among the Aspens* are certainly the best things in the book, conveying as they do at one and the same time a feeling of closest intimacy with nature and a sense of her unapproachable mystery.

Songs of the Sea Children, a strangely entitled sheaf of one hundred and twenty love songs, is by all odds the most beautiful and perhaps also the most impressive of all Bliss Carman's books. The faults of didacticism and of sprawl which are to be seen elsewhere in the work of this second period find no entrance here. Every poem in the book is pure and flawless and unalloyed song, exclusively lyrical. This book alone would ensure the lasting fame of the man who wrote it. He is known to-day only as a nature poet, and yet the *Songs of the Sea*

Children, his best book, is centered entirely about the theme of love. (p. 51)

Songs From a Northern Garden, which appeared one year after *Songs of the Sea Children,* is so different from that book that it would hardly seem to have come from the same pen. Most of the poems in this collection are inordinately long, and thought takes the place of song in most of them. The best poem of the thirteen is *Above the Gaspereau,* strangely but effectively rhymed and in long looping lines, a memorandum of the poet's brooding during an Acadian summer on the patient processes of nature.

The Book of Valentines is more various in contents than most of the poet's other volumes. . . . [It contains] one great poem in blank verse, the summit of Bliss Carman's poetical achievement, *At the Great Release.* Nature, love, and religion are brought together and fused in the powerful focus of this poem. Splendor of imagery, nobility of diction, perfection of form, tenderness and passion thrilling from end to end, assure every worthy reader that these thirty-five lines can never be forgotten. (pp. 53-5)

The one hundred lyrics of *Sappho* may be regarded as in some ways a continuation of the *Songs of the Sea Children,* for they are all love songs, and all very brief. . . . Neither translations nor paraphrases—although in many lines they follow the original closely—they are an attempt to complete and fill out the Sapphic fragments in the spirit of the originals. . . . The hundred lyrics taken together make a less brilliant effect, certainly, than do the *Songs of the Sea Children,* but one feels little hesitation in saying that *Sappho* follows immediately after that volume among the three best books of poems that Mr. Carman has given to the world. (pp. 55-6)

The Rough Rider, like the *Book of Valentines,* is less a unit in tone and subject matter than the other volumes. . . .

Daughters of Dawn and *Earth Deities* stand by themselves as designed primarily for public reading. They are, so to speak, dance librettos, poems to be acted, little masques. (p. 56)

If little is said in this place about the four prose books—*Kinship of Nature, Friendship of Art, Poetry of Life,* and *Making of Personality*—that should not be interpreted to mean that they are thought to be of little importance. (p. 57)

The four prose books were written, as one would expect, in Mr. Carman's second period, the period of rationalizing, or clear and abstract thinking. One is not surprised, therefore, to find that the style in which they are written is remarkable first of all for its pellucid clarity. . . . It is the prose of thought rather than of feeling, and there is evidence of "fundamental brain-work" on every page. (pp. 58-9)

Later volumes of verse such as *Echoes From Vagabondia* and *April Airs,* since they contain no important departures from the styles and materials with which we have already dealt, need not detain us from a consideration of the kinds of poetry to be found in the poet's books. Mr. Carman himself classifies all his poetry under two heads: poetry of love and poetry of religion. This is made more intelligible by his explanation that nearly all his nature poetry is religious in its intention and ultimate meaning. If we adopt this broad classification we see at once that there are several subsidiary kinds. There is a great difference, for example, between the treatment of love, deeply earnest and thrilling and passionate in some of the *Songs of the Sea Children* and the delicate badinage with which the same

theme is treated in the *Book of Pierrot.* The range of the poems of religion, nearly all of which seem at first to be nature poems, is still wider. It is hard to find a place in either group for the memorabilia of *By the Aurelian Wall,* for poems of pure phantasy and verbal magic like *Marian Drury,* for the studies in the occult of *Behind the Arras,* for pieces of grotesque humor such as *The Hearse-Horse,* or for the numerous and important ballads. One may at least say with assurance, however, that the dominating moods are those of love and religion. Of these, the second is by much the more important, the theme of love being treated almost as frequently in a religious aspect as is the theme of nature.

We arrive, then, at something like unity. Religion, in a certain unusual but none the less real sense of the word, is the central and pervading theme of Mr. Carman's poetry. In what sense he himself understands the word may be seen in the following statement: "As we think of the long list of poets whose names still survive, whose words are still alive in our ears, we shall find them dividing themselves mainly into two groups,—the religious poets and the dramatic,—those who were inspired by the moral temper of their time and those who devoted themselves to the entertainment of their fellows. . . ." If this classification is correct, then it is clear that Mr. Carman must be a religious poet, since there is extraordinarily little of the dramatic in his work. (pp. 60-1)

He is religious in much the same way that Shelley, the alleged and self-styled atheist, was so. . . . In such things as *Easter Eve, On Ponus Ridge, Above the Gaspereau,* and *Resurgam,* the religious and transcendental trend of all his thought is revealed and the deeper meaning of even the glancing momentaneous lyrics is clearly shown. (pp. 61-2)

Besides this faith and aspiration growing out of the very materials for despair, one may characterize as Christian the free and extensive use of symbols in Bliss Carman's poetry of Nature. (p. 63)

He might agree with Arnold that "the strongest part of our religion to-day is its unconscious poetry," but he would rather say that the strongest part of our poetry is its unconscious religion.

Although he uses nature, like all other Christian poets, as a symbol of spirit, Bliss Carman sees the natural object vividly and clearly, like a Greek, as it really is. (pp. 65-6)

He has tried to make his poetry a clear mirror of his mind in a time when most poets have taken perverse delight in offering the world only shattered bits of brilliant but meaningless glass.

After having spoken of the unity of Mr. Carman's work one must go on as nearly as possible in the same breath to point out also its variety—that true variety as distinguished from mere miscellaneity which is secured only under the control of some single governing principle. (p. 67)

The variety of Mr. Carman's work is almost as likely to escape notice as its unity. The early and enduring popularity of the Vagabondia series has given many readers their only idea of what he can do. (p. 68)

Some part of the blame for our failure to realize the range of Bliss Carman's work must be borne, however, by the poet himself. In the prefatory note to the first edition of his first volume he wrote: "The poems in this volume have been collected with reference to their similarity of tone." . . . Much has been gained by it for the unity of individual volumes, but much has been lost also for the poet's reputation, since the only way of discovering the extraordinary scope and range of his work has been that of reading all, or very nearly all, his books. (pp. 69-70)

Not only has this method of publication retarded the poet's reputation; it has rendered some of the individual volumes monotonous in effect. . . . [The reader] finds the constant succession of the same sort of stimuli ultimately equivalent to no stimuli whatever, and concludes that this poet has little to say.

A selected edition of Mr. Carman's poems, arranged with an eye to contrast and variety, is for these reasons much to be desired. Such a book would do for his work much the same sort of service that Matthew Arnold's anthology did for that of Wordsworth. It would present him in a new light, as a poet of very extraordinary range, and as one who has done memorable work in each of the many kinds of poetry he has written. His work has much to gain and nothing to lose from the lightening necessary to almost any poetic cargo which is to make a long journey across the years. (pp. 70-1)

In a comparison of Bliss Carman's poetry with that of his three chief masters—Arnold, Browning, Emerson—one sees that the stream of emotion has washed his poetry, after all remarkably free from the dross of didacticism. He has much the same things to say that they said, and he has learned his manner and technic in no small degree from them, but his poetry contains less alloy of doctrine than theirs, his singing is more purely song. (p. 118)

He has a thrilling way, too, of leading his reader through a poem on a comparatively commonplace theme, and then, in the final stanzas, filling and firing the imagination with sudden gleams and hints of larger significance which come like a burst of sun at the end of a lowering day. (p. 119)

The thought of the longer poems is obviously moving in the direction of prose, and one would have had a sense of incompletion if actual prose had not been reached. One finds in the prose books the same materials that glow in the kaleidoscope of his poetry, but uncolored. (p. 123)

His philosophy, for which he has invented the name "unitrinianism," teaches as its main tenet the parity and unity of body, mind, and spirit. Defect or excess in any one of these leads to a corresponding failure in the life. (pp. 123-24)

In its metaphysical aspects Bliss Carman's philosophy is scarcely distinguishable from Transcendentalism, although he interprets that hazy doctrine even more liberally than most of its earlier exponents.

Bliss Carman is so little a metaphysician, however, and so much a philosopher in the better sense that one feels it almost a waste of time to discuss the larger outlines of his thought. He believes that a man's philosophy should affect his life in some way, that his thought should cleave down to his daily conduct, and that the supreme test of his thought is found in his actual living. For the day by day guidance of conduct, Transcendentalism gives place to his unitrinian belief, and to this he applies only the pragmatic test. In developing and defending this doctrine he has used no dialectic whatever, but only a very uncommon sense, scarcely to be distinguished from intuition, and all that he claims for it is that it "works," that it really makes the lives of men and women more gracious, more satisfying, more serviceable and joyous. Such a turn

against its Transcendental masters is characteristic of a mind which, for all its interest in vague and misty modes of thought and feeling, still loves precision and clear outlines. Not for nothing does he say that the Kingdom of Poetry is bordered on the north by mathematics. The supreme position held by the Reason in Emerson's thought he gives to Intuition, asserting that this latter is a higher faculty but feeling that it needs the constant check and control of the lower. (pp. 131-32)

The supreme test of right living, and therefore of the beliefs which govern living, he knows, is simply the test of happiness. (p. 132)

Believing so profoundly as he does that life's meaning is to be found only in the development of balanced, rounded, perfected individuals, his sympathies are naturally with the aristocratic point of view, since this consummate development of the individual is an aristocratic ideal. (p. 135)

[An] uneasy mood of solipsism has been known to many a poet, for in its very nature it is related closely to the sense of solitude and concentration upon the inner life in which the poet's work is done, but it has never been more vigorously phrased than in *Behind the Arras*. For the most part, Bliss Carman's thought is healthily objective, but here it is inward bound. In this book there is a tinge of pessimism, a suggestion of weariness, not to be found elsewhere in his work, which produce in *The Red Wolf* one of the least pleasant and least forgettable things that have come from his pen—a poem which gives us a glimpse of the savageries lying asleep in man's brain and blood, of the dark red gulfs of animalism over which we sustain our lives. . . . (pp. 141-42)

Behind the Arras modulates through various minor keys into a final triumphant major. The poet passes out of solipsism into a more congenial idealism, or, in the terms of his metaphor, he comes to see that the tapestry is not of his weaving but of God's. Thus he escapes from the prison of self into the breathing sun-lit world again, with a new and more grateful sense of its beauty. (pp. 144-45)

He retains from the experience recorded in *Behind the Arras* a poignant sense of the pathos of life, caught as it is in the meshes of destiny, but there is nowhere else any suggestion of weariness or of fear. From that experience he may have derived also his feeling that over-subtle intellectual analysis is dangerous to that grateful acceptance of life which is his normal attitude. In his later work he rests more heavily upon intuition. He depends, of course, not upon argument at all but solely upon intuition in all that he says and implies concerning what lies on the other side of death. . . . In his moments of intensest living Bliss Carman finds it impossible to doubt that life must endure. (pp. 146-47)

Although the mood of vagabondage was long ago outgrown, the theme has pervaded Bliss Carman's work from his earliest writing down to the present. . . . With [Hugo] De Vries and [Henri] Bergson and G. B. Shaw, he believes that the controlling factor in the evolutionary process has been this tireless upward reach and yearning, and not a mere blind chance.

The metaphors of roving and vagabondage are as significant with relation to Bliss Carman's art and technic as they are with relation to his thought. One sees in the length, in the leisurely and circuitous movement of many of his poems, that he finds it "more blessed to have travelled than to have arrived." (pp. 154-55)

The rambling of many of Bliss Carman's poems is partly due, no doubt, to his habitual use of a very facile measure—the octosyllabic line arranged in alternately rhymed quatrains. The stringent discipline of the sonnet, one feels, would have been beneficial. The eight-syllable line has a specious look of compactness, but its use really leads to "padding," and is hostile to the virtues of severe simplicity and brevity. The best work of Bliss Carman has been done in the longer line. On the other hand, although he needs more space in the single line, his best poems are short. Perhaps this is no more than to say that he is essentially a lyric poet. (pp. 155-56)

[Carman's] is a style full-bodied, muscular, masculine, coming just short of Tennysonian amplitude. Its defect is a certain tropical luxuriance through which the edge of thought is not always keen enough to cut—but then, to balance this, what masterpieces of rejection and self-denial in the purer lyrics, what ascetic subtleties of suggestion! (p. 164)

In this matter of style the comparison with Emerson is again helpful. Like that of his remote kinsman, the style of Bliss Carman has two phases. It can be either lowly or exalted, familiar or restrained. At one extreme it is sometimes almost as colloquial—except for the absence of dialect—as that of James Whitcomb Riley; at the other it shows affinities with the grand manner of Matthew Arnold. By joining these two extremes he has fashioned an idiom as easily recognizable and strongly-marked as that of Swinburne or that of Poe, although it is less easily parodied than either. In the best of his work perfect dignity and utter simplicity are fused together into a style of high distinction. (p. 165)

> *Odell Shepard, in his* Bliss Carman *(copyright 1923 by McClelland and Stewart, Limited; reprinted by permission of The Canadian Publishers, McClelland and Stewart Limited, Toronto), McClelland and Stewart, 1923, 184 p.*

JAMES CAPPON (essay date 1930)

Among the early poems of Carman **"Pulvis et Umbra"** is a striking example both of Poe's influence on his imagination at this time and of the way in which he makes what he borrows his own by additions and transformations. The poem is an original sort of fantasia on Poe's "Raven." The poet floats away through time and space into those twilight chambers of fancy that Poe loves, and drapes them, much as Poe did, in sombre hues of gloom and mystery. The night-moth as a visitor to the lonely study has not quite the sombre significance of the raven with his refrain of "Nevermore," but Carman is able to give a *locale,* a cottage near the sea, a fine bodeful colour of mystery and doom. . . . One can see there that the gentle accents and mild phrase of Longfellow are haunting his ear, but in the series of questions which he puts to his little guest, the gleam of Poe's phantasy is evident. . . . (pp. 12-13)

Carman's ideal of poetry at this time is still vaguely aesthetic, many of his early poems are pure phantasies in Poe's manner. The mysterious background, the vaguely outlined situation, the tone of sadness which Poe recommends as the highest note of poetry (a tone quite discarded in Carman's later poetry and indeed professionally disowned), even Poe's specific suggestion that the loss of a beautiful woman bewailed by her lover is the most effective of poetic subjects, and that there should be a "circumscription of space" to a chamber or garden made sacred by memories of some lost Lenore, all these as well as some other minor suggestions are faithfully followed in Car-

man's Gwendolen poems, and other lyrics of that type, eventually collected and published in his first volume *Lost Tide on Grand Pré.* They read as if they might have been written to try out Poe's theories. . . . But among these early lyrics there is one in which Carman has raised this vague emotionality into classical clearness and firmness of structure. In **"Low Tide on Grand Pré"** the situation and the emotions are definite enough to suggest that some fibre of reality is stirring in its reminiscences. There is still the shadow of a lost Lenore in it, but its pensive melancholy is without weirdness or mystery. . . . **"Low Tide on Grand Pré"** is too slight an effort to be called a masterpiece—that much abused word in America and in book-cover testimonials everywhere—but it is an unforgetable addition to the stock of fine Canadian lyrics. And for once the poet has been careful not to destroy the plastic perfection of his poem by dilation or too much vagrancy of fancy. (pp. 14-18)

Such poems as I have been speaking of may be taken as representing Carman's early leanings towards the aesthetic schools of poetry and an almost purely aesthetic exercise of his imaginative faculty. But even in them we see that his imagination is haunted by a sense of mystical super-realities which earlier Poes and Gautiers had only played with as artists. In some of the poems of this period there is already a systematic symbolism which seeks to make a moral synthesis of life. (p. 21)

[In 1893, Carman] made his formal appearance as such before the public in a small volume of lyrics. It took its title from the opening poem which was on the whole the most perfect thing he had done yet, *Low Tide on Grand Pré.* (p. 24)

[The] chief interest of the volume for readers who like the mystical element in Carman's poetry may lie neither in its love idylls nor in its nature poetry, but in poems like **"Wayfaring"** and **"On the Trail"** in which his transcendental vision is concentrated on the interpretation of human effort and aspiration. (p. 29)

The essential character of Carman's poetic gift shows itself clearly enough in this early volume. In his later work there are new notes of course, and the vague romanticism and visionary elevation of his first songs become a closer reflection of his real experience. But the form of vision which gives him wings does not change. It is always a transcendental exaltation of experience, often a little mystical yet always trying to maintain itself on a foundation of rational thought. The great question for him was to find a supreme expression for this transcendental form of vision, an embodiment of it significant enough perhaps to stand as a new poetic interpretation of life. (p. 36)

In 1895 Carman published *Behind the Arras: A Book of the Unseen.* The two principal poems in the volume, **"Behind the Arras"** and **"Beyond the Gamut"** are a metaphysic in verse almost systematically complete in its way and genially illustrated by poetic allegory and metaphor. (p. 42)

"Behind the Arras", the title poem, begins with a genially conceived allegory of the soul in its house of life, as the habitant of a visible but circumscribed world into which intimations of a great invisible reality penetrate with impressive power but are of uncertain significance. (p. 43)

Of course an allegory of this comprehensive kind is not likely to go far without getting into some logical trouble. He can find no other way of representing the actual movements of life than by supposing them to be figured on the arras, "woven to the life". The arras in this way represents the psychological isolation of the ego over against the world-curtain of appearances. And the allegory begins to wear thin as the poem goes on to describe the experiences of the soul in a world of reality and the way in which scenes change there under winds of the spirit that come none knows whence. . . . And now the poet begins to speculate on the character of the Power that works behind this metaphysical curtain. . . . What heavenly music, for example, this "veiled mysteriarch" plays on the old Aeolian harp that swings in the house! That last is an ingenious tribute to Aeolic song and all that descends from it, but is also extended by Carman in his easy way to include the gentle breath and blossoming of spring. It is in this value of the Cosmos for the aesthetic sense that the poet finds reassurance as to the benevolent character of the inscrutable Power. Such music must be, he reasons, "the sacrament of love". . . . That is the turning point in the logical movement of the poem. In the existence of this rhythm, this music of the universe, the poet finds a sufficient warrant for faith and glad acquiescence in life—The reality behind the arras must be an infinitely wise and benevolent one. (pp. 44-7)

"**Behind the Arras**" is Carman's greatest effort in this philosophical species of poetry. The allegory is brilliantly sustained in its first movement, but it soon encounters difficulties in the wide expansion Carman has given it and tends as an allegory to fade away into a freer movement of thought. One could conceive the first part modelled into a fine artistic whole by itself. He has fine intuitions and a touch full of tact in idealistic philosophy, with something also of the mystic in him that is always tempting him to cross the border. But the mystical element in his poetry is not independently developed; it is only the penumbra of his transcendental philosophy, not the idiosyncratic vision of a Blake or Swedenborg, not the rigid abstractness of the Oriental mystic for whom phenomena are but the deceptive veil of the Infinite, nor even that of the modern psychological poet who finds his new conceptions of reality in the obscure sub-conscious cistern from which consciousness emerges. Carman is the pure transcendentalist for whom the Eternal and its manifestations have equal yet distinct reality, and he is a poet with a passion for the clear sensuous image. Hence the symbolical allegory is his favourite form. (pp. 48-9)

The monologue of reasoned or philosophical discourse in particular is highly congenial to his imaginative faculty and the qualities of his style. . . . And he is very much at home too in those brilliant casual descriptive bits and piquant asides with which Browning enlivens a philosophical theme. In "**Beyond the Gamut**" Carman gives us a monologue in this more lively dramatic style. It develops further with special illustrations from the art of music the idea of the divine rhythm in the universe. . . . Carman goes on to develop the idea that the soul's capacity for fulness of life hereafter depends on its cultivation of that capacity here on earth. . . . [One] feels that Carman's idealizing fancy is too little under the control of reason.

In accounting for the existence of evil or discord in the divine harmony of the world, he takes the safer line of giving us an eclectic variety of solutions from different systems of thought. . . . I shall not follow Carman's philosophical discourse further. Its substance has already been given, namely, that evil and deformity in the world are negligible in its general harmony, and in any case fated to disappear in a new life of the soul in the Absolute or in some advanced form of existence. (pp. 49-52)

[The range of notes in *Songs from Vagabondia* is] fairly wide. They are not merely, as *The New York Times* in a very favourable notice wrote of them, "merry pipings" with "not a line that was made in the sweat of the brow". (p. 69)

Under that quiet, impassive exterior, as the younger Roberts describes it, there was considerable spiritual versatility. [Carman] has very happy veins of light irony and gay satire, and these find a natural place in the Vagabondia volumes, as part of the spiritual Bohemian's gaiety and his scoffing exposure of the world's moral fanfaronade. Little pieces like "**The Unsainting of the Kavin**" and "**A More Ancient Mariner**" have a sparkling wit and an artistic completeness which did more perhaps to bring him into favour with the American public than his elevated poetry. . . . He can be, too, in "**The Sceptics**", piquantly mordant, though in that piece and in "**Philistia**" he comes rather near the shirt-sleeves style of the "colyumist". The "**Hearse-Horse**" and "**The Night-Washers**" are brief but striking essays in a grim Macaberesque vein of humour rather rare in him. "**The Gravedigger**", too, in another collection shows a command not much exercised of the weird and grotesque in art. (pp. 76-7)

[In the centenary poem for Shelley, "**The White Gull**"] Carman sought his highest elegiac note. (p. 87)

The shadow of something "ineffectual" in Shelley's fight, or of something sombre in the grandeur of the Shelleyan universe casts a poetic gloom at times on the poem, with its central idea of a somnolent humanity that is difficult to lead to the light. But the vision is quite in harmony with the genius of Shelley and the spirit of his poetry, with its images of mortality and the desolations of Time, and of the never ending Promethean struggle. Carman's poem brings into strong poetic relief this view of Shelley as a great "soldier in the war of liberation of humanity", . . . yet as a sort of leader of a forlorn hope sent out to an august doom by the Fates. It is brilliantly imaged, with a passionate depth of imagination that carries well its soaring symbolism and opulence of epithet. (pp. 89-90)

When [Carman's] transcendental vision of life began to emerge out of the vague aestheticism of his early Grand Pré poems into the clear philosophical outline it has in *Behind the Arras,* it went on expanding itself into the vast survey of things we have in *The Pipes of Pan,* with a variety of illustration drawn from many fields of life and thought, often from exotic regions where his tact and touch were imperfect. His interpretation of life becomes in this way a comprehensive but rather inconsistent and confused expression of all the idealism floating loosely in the over-saturated consciousness of the age. (p. 100)

There are five volumes of the *Pipes of Pan* published at various intervals from 1902 to 1905. A general view of their contents indicates Carman's comprehensive design of illustrating the evolution of human culture in its aesthetic and religious aspects, and the collective title alone would suggest that the whole process was to be regarded from a high philosophic point of view as the world-music of nature. But the scheme is too vast for Carman to give it a clear logical development or any unity of artistic treatment. The symbolism of the Pan poems in the first volume has little or no harmonic continuation in the variety of tones and treatment in the other volumes. Carman's great lyrical variety leaves no room for that epical wholeness of tone and vision which would give interior harmony and artistic relief to the design. The fundamental idea itself of Pan's music as a world-process reveals itself fitfully and obscurely at times in a medley which contains everything from pantheistic hymns and cosmic idealizations of Pan and Ishtar, love lyrics and spring songs, fragments of Indian and Norse legend, to prayers to the Overlord and pious marvels from French Canadian history. Of course there are good things in the collection, light-winged stanzas in Carman's best manner which future anthologers are not likely to overlook in their search for the gems of the Canadian lyric, but there are no poems in it great and distinctive enough to have made even the well disposed Canadian public realize the great design. One would not have minded some laxity and even inconsequence in such a series, if there had been something strong and genial enough to fix the design unforgettably. (pp. 125-26)

Carman's prose essays look as if they were partly intended to supplement and explain the idealistic vision of life in his poetry. They are mostly written in the lighter style of the aesthetic essay of the Victorian period, often a half-playful ingenious rather than a systematic treatment of the subject, with lively touches of paradox and extravagance at times yet always with a serious groundwork of aesthetic and transcendental theory. For the essays do reinforce his poetry in this way—whether poetry should need that is another question—setting its ideals and principles in a clear light, defending its uncompromising optimism, its conservative literary and moral standards and explaining its mystical strains of thought, sometimes qualifying them or reducing them to bring them nearer the ordinary or normal conception of life. They certainly complete the idea of the poet's personality, for those who are willing to read through four fairly large collections of essays. . . . Quite a number of his essays in the first two volumes [*The Kinship of Nature* and *The Friendship of Art*] are just prose versions of his spring song, and he repeats in prose as callously as he does in verse. They show little of that precision of observation or analysis which you find in [American naturalist John] Burroughs or [John] Ruskin. . . . The phrasing is poetically eloquent, effulgent, often exquisite; we admire the luxurious workmanship but we do not lose ourselves in it as we do when Burroughs is describing for us the shy approach of April. . . . And we do not lose ourselves in it because Carman does not lose himself in it, but is so busy with his flowers of expression that he hardly lets the facts speak. (pp. 184-87)

In his more critical essays, when he is discussing theories and standards of art and literature, his tone is somewhat different, serious, even didactically moral and in general highly conservative and orthodox. (p. 188)

But if Carman's essays are not a great contribution to critical thought, his pages are bright with the same poetic fancy and transcendental vision that you find in his poems. Carman's prose style is always pleasing. It moves with alertness and grace; its refined simplicity and transcendental piquancy are of Emersonian quality but without the austerity of that sage, for Carman is often sentimentally effusive and indulges in light veins of extravagance. There is an old-fashioned charm about his essays; they have the sweet breath of a more romantic and polished generation, elegancies of tone, sentimental loiterings and lingerings by the way, not often found now in the harder realism or the caricaturing humour or paradox of the modern genius. Where the theme suits his transcendental form of thought, it gets brilliant expression from him. (p. 196)

[In] 1909 a new period of poetic productivity began with *The Rough Riders*, [*Echoes from Vagabondia,* and *April Airs*]. . . . (p. 199)

The mystical light was fading into that of common day and in most of the later poems his style is no longer so strongly oriented by it: the phrase is less mystically abstract. Even in his nature poetry, a more normal form of sentiment takes the place of transcendental reverie oftener than it used to do, or at any rate brings it nearer to our ordinary sense of nature. . . . The cosmic idealism which used to give a mystical colour to his poem is often now hardly more than familiar poetic hyperbole or personification. . . . For these quieter moods with their more subdued lyrical exaltation, Carman is naturally readier than he was to use blank verse as a vehicle, the quiet reflective type of blank verse he has in "**A Mountain Gateway**", smooth in movement and regular in accents, or the slightly more cadenced verse of "**Pan in the Catskills**". Both poems express the same spiritual experience with a slight variation in the surroundings. . . . There is something of the old exaltation in its thought, the poet refuses to believe in death and pain, but the atmosphere is not so mystically loaded. Even Pan is no longer the world deity of the earlier volume but is shrinking back into something nearer his native form of the Arcadian god symbolizing a wild music of nature. . . . As the mystical exaltation subsides in his later poetry he naturally seeks some new forms of expression for his lyrical ecstasy and optimistic vision of life. New reflective tones also emerge; with the wisdom of years he seeks to enter into more tranquil possession of himself and of what fate has given him with a corresponding resignation as to what it seems to have denied him. In some modest audits he makes now of his life and work, you can feel that his pulse is beating less feverishly. "**Apologia**" is an apology in the old Vagabondia tone for the Bohemian truancy of the poet's life . . . willing to loiter and let the world be. (pp. 199-205)

The old cosmic idealism still animates his poetry at times but mostly in casual lines or reduced to the ordinary philosophic naturalism which would learn its lesson from nature. . . .

What perhaps distinguishes most his later poetry is a new type of composition in pieces like "**On the Plaza**", "**A Painter's Holiday**", "**The Man with the Tortoise**", and "**Mirage**", in which his treatment of his subject is less purely lyrical in tone and style and seeks to present more of the ordinary movement of life, and in a more familiar realistic way. (p. 212)

In "**On the Plaza**", which appears in his volume of *Later Poems*, there is the sober art of his later period; the composition is well kept together, without loose excursiveness. (p. 215)

In "**A Painter's Holiday**" and "**Mirage**" the poet uses the dramatic monologue to penetrate into the inner world of the artist's creative life and suggest the depth of aesthetic feeling from which the ideal vision comes, the moment of illumination, of enchanted experience. (p. 217)

The poems I have been considering represent a serious effort of Carman to use a form of composition less dependent on lyrical exaltation than his usual style and more capable of presenting the concrete aspect of life with epical fullness and objectivity of vision. But even in them the lyrical hyperbole takes command of his style to the detriment of the critical and reflective faculty; the quality of his observation is damaged by it, made secondary and subservient to its call and kept working in old romantic grooves. That may seem to be an unsympathetic judgment, but a critical estimate of Carman has to show why he with his genuine lyrical gift, great descriptive power and lively imagination leaves only a clouded and ambiguous impression of genius in his higher efforts. From the beginning he has been accustomed to express the imaginative reach of his thought in symbolical phrases which carry him beyond the world of definable experience to a world of vague confines and mystic horizons. It is a style which raises conceptions from a measurable place in the world of realities to some immeasureable power of suggestion in a world without logical limits. He moves habitually and best in an atmosphere of mystical reverie or unconfined exaltation where the reality is only a stepping stone into regions of phantasy, a fragment in the whole; and he can give that fragment well. (pp. 221-22)

In his later poems Carman's mystical fancy dying down or discouraged by its native form often finds shelter in the pious legends or occultism of the Middle Ages, especially those saintly tales which still linger in the borderland of Christian faith. (pp. 223-24)

Carman's latest volumes cannot call for much notice except as illustrating some new interests that were entering his life. (p. 227)

> *James Cappon, in his* Bliss Carman and the Literary Currents and Influences of His Time, *The Ryerson Press, 1930, 340 p.*

L. A. MacKAY   (essay date 1933)

The most important part of his training [Carman] got at Harvard; the chief influences on his thought and manner are American: Poe, whose influence he partly outgrew—luckily, for I agree with your young Mr. Huxley that Poe is a very vulgar poet—and Emerson, who does no man very much harm, and Thoreau, and Whitman. You even get more Longfellow than Shelley, for example. He preferred to live in the States, and even to be buried in the States. Most of his nature poetry is quite as much at home in New England as in Nova Scotia, and he has virtually no influence on our best poets since his time. . . .

[It] seems to me that the thing that matters is the quality of his poetry. . . .

I shouldn't call him a Longfellow. Longfellow has a precision, a certainty, in his verse, that Carman lacks. He knew what word would express his idea, a thing that Carman seems never to have known clearly. (p. 182)

You can see the same thing, too, in the management of the longer poems. Longfellow has an economical drive, an organizing grasp that makes Carman seem vague and pottering by comparison. . . . I can never count formlessness as one of the genuine constituents of art. (pp. 182-83)

Carman, you see, was a professional poet—a very bad thing to be. Dramatic poetry, of course, may be excepted; but a professional lyric poet is like a professional fisherman. He is bound to haul in and expose for sale all sorts of catch. . . . Unless he has an independent income, he should earn his living some other way, out of respect for the dignity of the poetic impulse. It's much too wayward and occasional, and too fine, to be milked regularly. . . .

I don't say he's exactly cheap, but he's certainly much too smooth and fluent. . . . And the repetition is frightful. He never seems to know when he has said a thing, and keeps on attempting to do it over again in other words, not always very different. . . .

Facile, spontaneous, and impressionable, but very diluted. He takes fire like dry grass, spreads as loosely, burns out as rapidly. He said a number of good things, but as you say, hardly seems to have been aware of it. The fact is, he was never a real master of language; he let it run away with him. He was much too prone to regard stock poetic diction as the equivalent of poetry. . . . Now [Archibald] Lampman, for example, though not a great poet either, is what I should call an accurate and definite poet, and in so far, superior. . . .

[Think of Andrew] Marvell anywhere, for that matter. Think of the solidity, the sharp actuality, the sudden and surprising illumination. . . . Well, then, look at this, **'The Master of the Scud'**, or any of this sea stuff, and compare it with the [E. J.] Pratt which I see lined up on the shelf at your elbow.

I grant your point. Carman's is the literary sea, Pratt's the Atlantic Ocean. But remember, the sea is as hard to get into words as into paint, and not many, even of the best of them, have the knack. And since I see you're into the *Songs of the Sea Children* now, I'll save you the trouble of observing that in emotional actuality and economy of phrase they are no match for a number of things of your young friend Dorothy Livesay. . . .

I think his lyrics of the open road and all that, are a bit mawkish and posturing. And when he gets familiar and colloquial it's just callow and slipshod.

I know; a sort of false heartiness, foreign to an essentially gentle nature. . . .

And he can't handle a general idea, or a dramatic situation, half as vividly, or concisely, or livingly, as [A. M.] Klein. . . .

And I think I see the name of Marjorie Pickthall trembling on the edge of your lips, too. You're still harping on your old delusion that Carman is a Canadian poet, and must be judged as such. Why, in heaven's name, when you don't want him any more than he wanted us? . . .

I should put it this way: at times, at his best, to the very end of his work, he retains what I think is his genuinely personal note; a sort of shy, awkward, half-inarticulate adolescence, its quick fresh exuberance, the smooth-skinned, soft-fleshed delicacy, and the graceful charm, of one of Donatello's youths.

It is the great mass of inferior work that hurts his reputation. Some day, someone will make the right, judicious selection, and Carman will be rediscovered in his true place, as one of the most agreeable, if one of the slightest, of the American minor poets. (p. 183)

> *L. A. MacKay, "Bliss Carman," in* The Canadian Forum, *Vol. 13, No. 149, February, 1933, pp. 182-83.*

E. K. BROWN   (essay date 1944)

The note of **"Low Tide on Grand Pré,"** which Carman sought to maintain throughout the entire volume to which it gave a name, is indeed a unique note, and not only in Canadian poetry. No one else has ever written quite in [this] manner. . . . In its quiet delight in nature, its idyllic imagery and dreamy music, its perfect relaxation and unbroken gentleness of tone, this is all of a piece, and the piece is perfect. (p. 54)

Of all Carman's merits the beauty of his music is the most remarkable: his first collection is one of the most musical volumes of verse in the entire century. Again and again the ear is excited by such magical phrases as **"Golden Rowan of Menalowan"** or **"The Trail Among the Ardise Hills."** Sometimes, more often in the work of his youth, entire poems have a musical perfection. . . . In his other musical vein, a familiar, rather shrill vein, he is seldom altogether happy. None of his poems is better known than one that illustrates this vein and Carman's failure with it, the **"Spring Song"** in *Songs from Vagabondia*. . . . The word for [its] movement and manner is jaunty; and it is scarcely possible to be poetic and jaunty. The jaunty manner is an impure manner. It will be more evident perhaps that this is so if we pause on another aspect of Carman's jauntiness, his jauntiness in diction. "Neuter" is jaunty, and so is "oaf"; these are words that can be used in serious verse (as distinguished from light-hearted satire such as Burns could write so masterly) only when the intention is bitter. Pope could have used them, or Browning, but in their hands the terms could have had a searing force. Carman uses them playfully, just as he uses his jaunty poetic manner playfully. The worst about them is not merely that they are unpoetic—which is arguable endlessly—but that they are cloying.

This word brings us to the central weakness of Carman. His poetry as a whole is cloying. The truth of this complaint has occurred even to so worshipping an admirer as Odell Shepard [see excerpt above]. Mr. Shepard regrets Carman's notion of each of his volumes as a perfect unity. . . . Mr. Shepard pleads that the tone of one collection differs enormously from that of another, and that in consequence if Carman is read as a whole he will satisfy us of the variety of his poetry and appear as "a poet of very extraordinary range and as one who has done memorable work in each of the many kinds of poetry he has written." This claim cannot, I think, be wholly accepted. What is true is that Carman is reasonably versatile in his choice of subjects, no more so, however, than Roberts, and much less so than Mr. Shepard's praise would suggest; but it is also true that in turning from one of his nature lyrics to one of his elegies and then to one of his dreamy meditations, what strikes one is not the change in subject but the sameness in manner. He is always trying to cast almost exactly the same spell; and before long we become uneasy and the spell ceases to take effect. The monotony that Mr. Shepard admits as a trait in the several collections is a trait of the work as a whole.

It is worth inquiring into the causes of this monotony. In the first place Carman lacks the mastery of pictorial detail that marks all his chief Canadian contemporaries. In his poetry it is seldom that a scene is clearly and sharply drawn, all his autumns are the one hazy autumn, all his sunrises the one golden sunrise. More fatal still is his incapacity for restraint: what would have been charming and, to use Mr. Shepard's word, memorable, loses its effectiveness because, instead of being said firmly and finally, it is played with through stanza upon stanza until the reader has only two feelings, that the music is charming but soporific, and that there is no reason why it should ever cease. The thought is almost always exceedingly tenuous: a vague transcendentalism similar to Roberts's. It is true that out of transcendentalism great poetry can come; but only when transcendentalism is very strongly felt by the poet. If the idea that all is one, and the idea that nature corresponds with spirit, and the idea that man is an element in the world soul strike the poet with a shock of immense surprise, making him feel that his eyes have been suddenly unsealed, then great poetry may emerge. But Carman takes transcendentalism lightly; to him it is all so obvious. And from transcendentalism taken lightly no poetry can come, except an occasional verse or at most a brief lyric. And it is Carman's briefest lyrics that in the main make his best work. (pp. 54-7)

E. K. Brown, "The Development of Poetry in Canada," in his On Canadian Poetry *(reprinted by permission of McGraw-Hill Ryerson Limited and Mrs. E. K. Brown), revised edition, Ryerson Press, 1944 (and reprinted by The Tecumseh Press, 1973), pp. 28-87.**

PELHAM EDGAR   (essay date 1948)

Within a somewhat restricted range, Bliss Carman has made an exquisite if not powerful contribution to Canadian poetry. He has little dramatic or narrative force, and is out of tune with contemporary tendencies in thought and action. Our age has chosen to voice itself through a literature that is predominantly realistic and pessimistic. Carman's temperament compelled him in the direction of romance and a rarely failing optimism. His nature gave him no scope for stormy despair or rebellious protest. He had a mild distaste for commercialism and science, but since no compulsion rested upon him to shape his life in their direction, he serenely passed them by. Yet it would be a grave error to conclude that his life was controlled by merely negative evasions. Poetry such as his is not written without passion, and Carman was swayed by loyalties from which he never swerved. One cannot serve abstractions; and when we say that one of his prime devotions was to the principle of beauty it means that he was in love with its concrete manifestations as he saw them on this rolling earth. His love was almost a childlike surrender to the message of sea and earth and sky, for to most of us it seems that the revelations of beauty they yield are not an effective makeweight to the problems that life presents. It is only fair to Carman, when assessing the primitive simplicity of his poetry, to realize that his surface contacts with transcendental philosophy had given him intellectual justification for his beliefs. (p. 45)

With all deductions made, Carman's poetry has enduring value. Grant other poets their greater profundity and wider range, make what concessions you will to the extremists who urge his failure to march with his age, there will always remain the magic of his phrase and the charming waywardness of his fancy to keep his poetry vital. Some of his lyrics will last while the language endures. (p. 48)

Pelham Edgar, "Bliss Carman," in Leading Canadian Poets, *edited by W. P. Percival (copyright © McGraw-Hill Ryerson Limited, 1948; reprinted by permission of the Literary Estate of W. P. Percival), Ryerson Press, 1948, pp. 45-50.*

DESMOND PACEY   (essay date 1950)

An interesting study could be made of the curve of Bliss Carman's reputation. At the height of his fame, in the first two decades of this century, he enjoyed a status higher than that ever accorded another Canadian poet. . . .

Today, of course, all that is changed. Carman's name is seldom heard outside of Canada, and even here he is either given grudging and defensive praise or contemptuously dismissed as the facile and vulgar exponent of a cheap and shallow romanticism. To what extent is this critical revolution justified, and to what extent is it mere fashion and prejudice? . . .

The first task of the critic in approaching the poetry of Bliss Carman is to perform a surgical operation. He must cut away the mass of inferior work and hold up for analysis the areas of healthy tissue. (p. 2)

[There are] certain large masses of material that can be excised in their entirety. Some of them make acceptable light verse; but almost all of them are negligible by any strict standard of poetic value. In spite of Charles Roberts' assertion that Richard Hovey was 'a broadening and emancipating influence' who 'had the effect of liberating those robuster elements in Carman's character', the poems written under Hovey's influence seem to me to present us with the embarrassing spectacle of an effeminate man flexing his flabby muscles and pounding his skinny chest in public. They represent the Canadian counterpart of the English counter-decadent, blood-and-guts school of poetry which included W. E. Henley, R. L. Stevenson, Rudyard Kipling, and Sir Henry Newbolt. The school professed to sound the call for freedom from the artificial life of cities, drawing-rooms, and boudoirs, but it was itself a highly artificial movement—as witness the fact that almost all its members were confirmed invalids. Their work, and that of Carman in their manner, was in reality a shallow and factitious attempt to escape the pressures of late nineteenth century disillusionment. At any rate, it is difficult to find anything from this category with which to buttress Carman's sagging reputation. . . .

We can also leave out of account most of Carman's poetry of passion—or what passes with him for passion. The poems in which he attempts to give expression to the raptures of sexual love are in the perfervid manner of Swinburne. . . . (p. 3)

It would be with less certitude and more regret that the surgeon-critic would excise the mass of Carman's philosophical verse. The doubt and the regret would arise from the presence in the long, ambitious, and essentially hollow philosophical poems such as **"Beyond the Gamut"** or **"Behind the Arras"** of isolated lines and images which are effective and arresting. But the excision must be made, for Carman had little power of original thought. (p. 4)

Carman's social and political ideas are even less acute and original than his ethical and metaphysical ones. . . . But such 'topical' verse is rare in Carman. For the most part he seems to move in a social vacuum, unaware of the problems of his time. He has almost none of the social consciousness which marks [Archibald] Lampman's later poetry.

There is a final group of poems whose value is almost negligible: the narratives. The contemporary vogue of the ballad led Carman to attempt a form for which he was singularly unsuited. Simplicity, directness, economy, a sense of character and dramatic situation—these are the qualities demanded by the ballad form, and Carman had none of them. All that he had that was useful was a strong sense of rhythm, and this sometimes, as in **"Arnold, Master of the Scud"**, almost carries him successfully through. (pp. 4-5)

After all this cutting, what is left? The poems—a mere handful when compared with his total output—in which Carman is content to create a mood, an atmosphere, by exploiting the music of words and the symbolic qualities of the New Brunswick landscape. (p. 5)

Carman's poems of mood and atmosphere may be divided into two groups. The first and less wholly satisfying group includes the poems in which he celebrates the coming of spring. Here the mood is ecstatic and rapturous, the atmosphere colourful and bright. . . . [We] can observe the difference between Carman's approach to landscape and that of Roberts and Lampman. He has little of their regional particularism: he isn't concerned with the processes of New Brunswick agriculture, as Roberts was, nor with the precise details of the flora and fauna of his region in the Lampman manner. He paints with a broader brush, making his effects by bright splashes of colour and by isolating for special attention only those details which are symbolic and suggestive. (pp. 5-7)

Good as some of these spring poems are—and it must be admitted that they are good in parts rather than as wholes—they are surpassed by Carman's poems in an elegiac mood of hopeless longing and charged regret. On the best of these melancholy poems—**"Low Tide at Grand Pré"**, **"A Northern Vigil"**, **"The Eavesdropper"**, **"Marian Drury"**, and **"The White Gull"**—his reputation must finally rest. Here is displayed at its purest his peculiar gift: the capacity to create an effect of haunting melancholy and mysterious sadness by the use of slow, involved, troubled verbal melodies and symbols of loneliness, desolation and pain drawn from the scenery and climate of his native environment.

"Low Tide on Grand Pré" has been so frequently anthologized that it has become difficult for us to look at it freshly. In my opinion it is, in spite of one weak stanza, the most nearly perfect single poem to come out of Canada. It will withstand any amount of critical scrutiny. Here Carman found, in the desolate mud flats left by the retreating Fundy tides, the perfect symbol for his mood. . . . He plays with the fancy that the wandering river is searching for the girl he has lost, and this leads naturally into the central sequence of the poem, in which he recreates the climactic day of their courtship. . . . (pp. 7-8)

[The] magnificent tenth and final stanza effectively bursts this bubble of romantic illusion. Time is inexorable; night must fall. This last stanza completes the pattern of the whole poem: the 'unelusive glories' fall no longer; night has replaced twilight; the tide has come and overwhelmed the land with water and the poet with grief. . . . We have here a supreme example of the blending of the particular and the universal: a natural phenomenon peculiar to the Fundy coast has been used to illuminate a truth of human experience.

A comparable but not quite equal success is achieved in **"A Northern Vigil"**. Here Carman has found the objective correlative for his mood of hopeless longing in the intense cold of a Canadian winter night. . . . The central section describes his lonely night-long vigil; and the poem ends with the coming of dawn. . . . But this poem, though it contains some of Carman's finest stanzas, has not the sustained power of **"Low Tide on Grand Pré"**.

I have not the space to more than glance at the other poems which, though they are not as fully satisfying as these two, are worthy to be set beside them as constituting the enduring part of Carman's work. **"The Eavesdropper"** contains the perfect stanza:

> Outside, a yellow maple tree,
> Shifting upon the silvery blue
> With tiny multitudinous sound,
> Rustled to let the sunlight through.

"Marian Drury" employs again the symbolism of the marshes and the tide. **"The White Gull"**, Carman's elegy on Shelley, though rather too diffuse, also exhibits his power of finding symbol and suggestion in the natural landscape. . . . (pp. 9-10)

The huge reputation which Carman enjoyed at the first of this century was undoubtedly an inflated one. It resulted in part from the fact that his best work was done when there was a dearth of great poetry on both sides of the Atlantic. . . . But on the other hand Carman is a better poet than our recent neglect of him would suggest. Faults he has in abundance: he is vague in thought and sometimes even in description; he can be guilty of astonishing carelessness of technique; his bohemianism is a pose; he is often boisterous to the point of vulgarity; his eroticism is forced and silly; he is ignorant of the real issues of social and political life; he has the fatal gift of facility; his rhythms and themes incline to monotony; the great mass of his work lacks depth, originality, and distinction. But he has gifts which we should not overlook, and which go far towards compensating for his deficiencies. He is a master of mood and music. At his best, he achieves a melodic beauty equalled by no other Canadian poet, and he knew better than any other how to employ the distinctive features of his native environment to effect a compelling atmosphere. If there are any 'masters' of Canadian poetry, Carman is of their company. (p. 10)

> *Desmond Pacey, "Bliss Carman: A Reappraisal,"*
> *in* Northern Review, *Vol. 3, No. 3, February-March,*
> *1950, pp. 2-10.*

NORTHROP FRYE   (essay date 1955)

[The] lyric poet, after he has run his gamut of impressions, must die young, develop a more intellectualized attitude, or start repeating himself. Carman's meeting of this challenge was only partly successful, and it has long been a commonplace that he badly needs a skilful and sympathetic selection. This is provided in *The Selected Poems of Bliss Carman,* edited by Lorne Pierce. . . . (p. 34)

Carman should, of course, have edited himself. I have heard the late Pelham Edgar turn a poem of Carman's into a thing of unalloyed delight by leaving out a couple of bad lines, but what a public reader can do an editor cannot do. What the selection brings out is that Carman's conscious mind and his poetic instinct were disastrously at odds. The first stage in the development of a romantic poet's mind is normally a sense of the unity of that mind throughout its variety of impressions: this in turn is likely to be projected as some form of pantheism, which has its advantages if properly developed, as Wordsworth shows, but the disadvantage of adding vagueness to monotony if it is not. Carman's conscious mind stuck at a broken-down and corny version of Emersonian over-soulfulness: his editor, with a touch of distaste, speaks of "his elaborate theory of Unitrinianism—spirit-leading; mental guidance, physical fulfilment—the full revelation of the doctrine of Personal Harmonizing." I don't know what all this means, but it sounds in more than one sense too awful for words, and I note that most of the poetic results are omitted from this selection. On the other hand, Carman's poetic sense told him, as it told Isabella Crawford before him and Pratt after him, that the most obvious development of a romantic landscape poet is towards the mythological, towards making his emotional impressions into a *dramatis personae* of forces at once human and natural. Carman's formative influences were late Victorian, and he follows Swinburne, Morris and Rossetti in enamelling nature with primary colours and peopling it with the pagan gods of the turning year, "Our Lady of the Rain," the dying gods Adonis and Attis, nymphs and fauns. And while his conscious mind called for songs of the open road and getting in tune with the infinite, his real poetic imagination became increasingly

brooding, lonely and haunted. . . . This is the kind of thing we remember from Carman, and we are grateful to Dr. Pierce for confining himself to the memorable work, ignoring the pseudo-Carman, with his stentorian hymns to the Great Beyond like **"Lord of my heart's elation,"** which are usually what get into anthologies. (pp. 34-5)

> *Northrop Frye, "Letters in Canada, 1954: Poetry,"*
> *in* University of Toronto Quarterly *(reprinted by permission of University of Toronto Press), Vol. XXIV,*
> *No. 3, April, 1955 (and reprinted in his* The Bush
> Garden: Essays on the Canadian Imagination, *Anansi, 1971, pp. 1-127).**

DONALD STEPHENS   (essay date 1961)

Carman wrote some fine regional poetry, and his knowledge of the maritime scene is authentic and clear. But does regionalism make a good poet? Because a poet is remarkably Canadian, and captures the Canadian mood, does this make him great? . . . Regionalism does not make a poet great, though to listen to some Maritime scholars, one would certainly think so. What about the poetry, then?

The most remarkable thing about Carman's poetry—if not remarkable, at least it is the most noticeable—is that it is so highly imitative. (pp. 38-9)

The most obvious pattern in Carman's poetry is one that is essentially Romantic in character and tone. From the publication of [*Low Tide on Grand Pré*, through the *Songs of the Sea Children* and *April Airs,* and in the *Later Poems*], there is the always present Romantic tone. Carman, like his Canadian contemporaries, was much attracted to the beauty and magic of the songs of Wordsworth, Coleridge, Byron, Shelley, and Keats. He sang of Nature as Wordsworth did, with the same attitude of child-like fascination. From the Lyrical Ballads he learned that simple diction was the best method to describe Nature. It was easy to imitate Wordsworth; there was the similar environment. Carman was a young man with wild nature all about him, and one whose memories were deeply rooted in New Brunswick's wind-swept marshes and rocky coast-lines when the nature poetry of Wordsworth with its lyrical magic took possession of his verse.

Carman's haunting lyricism is best when he writes about Nature. . . . Like Wordsworth, Carman revelled in the physical beauty of external Nature; he worshipped the vivid loveliness of a budding tree, a blooming flower, and the restless inimitable sea. He attempted, as Wordsworth did, to liken man to Nature and its phenomena. . . . Here is Wordsworth's contemplation and music, mingled with his plaintive wistfulness. Carman adopted the Wordsworthian philosophy that Nature was good. Both poets believed in the essential goodness of man and Nature; and Carman saw God in Nature. . . . But Carman cannot be called . . . a true Wordsworthian Canadian poet, for he was too conscious of symbols in his Nature poetry. He saw himself as a part of Nature and considered that he, too, was growing like a plant. . . . Wordsworth used the flower as a symbol of Nature, but his Nature poetry was a summation of philosophy rather than true symbolism. Carman used Nature, its growth and decay, as an inherent symbol, and he related his myth of man to Nature and the seasons.

As did Coleridge and Shelley, Carman expressed his ideas in terms of physical sensations. He modelled his first ballads after Coleridge's "Rime of the Ancient Mariner"; the suggestive and pictorial metaphors are not always concrete and are often illuminated mystically as are Coleridge's. Many of his poems, and especially **"The White Gull"**, suggest Shelley; there is the use of similes in great profusion and the restless spirit of Shelley. . . . (pp. 39-41)

But where Carman occasionally uses the fervid tones of Shelley, he sings most frequently in the autumn calms of Keats. The Keatsian love of beauty is manifest in all his work; every object to Carman was a 'thing of beauty', and what was sordid he disregarded. By the use of exquisite diction, he tried to attain Keat's supremely natural utterance in order to create a poem that would be individual, spontaneous, and poignantly musical. He never attained the rapture, the joy, and the exuberance which Keats created, but at times he almost succeeded. With his classical training, Carman could equal Keats in subject matter, but the Keatsian atmosphere was unattainable. The influence of Keats is strongest when Carman uses metaphor and personification to give an excessively Romantic character to his verse. . . . (p. 41)

Possibly, too, the undercurrent of melancholy in Carman's verse owes much to Keats. This note was originally heard in his first volume, *Low Tide on Grand Pré* . . . , and was to occur in most of his verse. He sang sad songs of absent women, of unrest, the futility of striving, and the Arcadian gardens where one would find love and dreams. (pp. 41-2)

Keatsian metaphors seem to come naturally to Carman. . . . The images are specific; flowers, for example, are never merely flowers, nor trees mere trees; they are always definite species (a marigold, a daisy, a scarlet maple, a silver birch). The Keatsian qualities—those of predominant colours, love of beauty, the poignant melancholy—are obvious influences upon Carman's poetry. (p. 42)

Woven into the pattern of Carman's poetry is one of the marked characteristics of the Victorian age—moral purpose. Carman was brought up in an environment which accepted the Victorian values, a society which demanded that any creative work should justify its own existence by having a definite moral significance. Carman was deeply aware of Tennyson, Browning, Arnold, Carlyle, and Ruskin—men who were definite teachers of society with faith in their message and a conscious purpose to uplift and instruct. But Carman did not have Tennyson's capacity for working out the flaws in his poems, either because he did not recognize them or because he was too impatient to make a satisfactory change. He did, at times, attain the Tennysonian quality of rhythm and musical cadence. . . . If Tennyson was an inspiration to Carman's method of description and atmosphere, he was also the source for didacticism and moralism. Carman saw, as Tennyson had seen, that perfect man was a result of a reign of order. (pp. 42-3)

Though the Victorian age is generally characterized as practical and materialistic, nearly all the writers, and especially the great poets, attacked materialism and exalted a purely idealistic concept of life. Carman saw Tennyson and Browning as exemplar poets fundamentally, since love, truth, brotherhood, and justice were emphasized by them as the chief ends of life. He agreed with their ideas, and their poetry had a rapid and far-reaching effect on his own verse.

One aspect of Carman's poetry which is practically ignored by his critics is his love poetry. Here, the influence of Rossetti is seen most strongly. His metaphors have the Rossetti qualities of picture and suggestion, and are often magically illumi-

nated. . . . He followed Rossetti's extensive use of colour words to create mood. Though Rossetti's words are usually applied to physical descriptions or room furnishings, Carman applies the medieval colour words to external Nature. He follows Rossetti in an over-indulgence in detailed descriptions. But often his many pictures are too heavy for his verse. (pp. 44-5)

Carman's poetry is only occasionally Pre-Raphaelite, and when it is, it is more a blending of Keats, Rossetti, and Carman's own distinctive application of the influences. From the Pre-Raphaelite Brotherhood, Carman assimilated a musical quality ("noons of poppy, noons of poppy"), a richness of colour ("Gold are the green trees overhead, and gold the leaf-green grass"), and a reaffirmation of the Keatsian love of beauty. The Pre-Raphaelites strengthened Carman's interest in the first Romantics and so, from the "last Romantics", Carman created a poetry which is for the most part Romantic in style, thought, and tone.

Bliss Carman bridged the era between the last of the great Victorians, and the new writers who evolved the complexities of Twentieth Century poetry. During this period no great major poet appeared on the literary scene. . . . (pp. 45-6)

Despite this, Canadian poetry flourished. The well-known Canadian poets—Carman, Roberts, Lampman, Duncan Campbell Scott—wrote at this time. None of them were innovators; most of them were imitators. Carman is typical of them in that his poetry is a restatement of certain Nineteenth Century poetic values. These poets were greatly influenced by the writers in England, and tried to make Canadian poetry in the British tradition. Some poetry of imitation reaches beyond the teacher, but the verse of these poets does not. Rather, it is poetry which is reminiscent of English poetry, that vaguely refers to the Canadian scene, and poetry that is never completely successful. It is characteristic of Canadian writers to forget that to write in the English language is to compete with the best writers in Britain and the United States. (p. 46)

The whole tone of Bliss Carman's poetry is that of the Romantic Movement. His poetry is the manifestation of all the basic assumptions of Romanticism. He had the Romantic's faith in the creative imagination and the potentialities of the individual; the preoccupation with the particular rather than the general; an interest in the past; and a feeling of close companionship with Nature and God. Since his was an emotional rather than an intellectual personality, Carman found reflections of his own attitudes and moods chiefly in the poetry of the Romantics and the Victorians, concerned as they both were with subjectivity. When Carman is influenced by the Victorians, the Romantic elements of their work appear in his poetry. Carman brought nothing new to poetry as poetry—though it was new to Canadian poetry—and sought only to bring together his own favourite expressions in poetry which seemed to suit his limited view of life.

Carman's whole attitude to poetry was that of the devotee rather than a true creator. He worshipped at the shrine of poetry, but was unable to penetrate to the inner circle; his was a minor inspiration because of the narrow range of subject matter and mood. Had Carman been a truly original poet—in so far as any poet can be original—he would have shown a development toward a greater assurance of style and a deeper emotional and intellectual content. However, between the early Carman and the late Carman the differences are of minor tones and that, for a time, one idea is predominant over others. For a while one may believe that there is a development, but always he returns to something which he had pursued before. (pp. 47-8)

In the Maritimes, the people worship at this shrine of Carman, as Carman himself worshipped at the shrine of poetry. Perhaps the lack of real knowledge about his work indicates that Carman contributed nothing to world poetry, but because he was at least a poet in a world of few poets there should be the bronze bust, the plaque, and the grave-tree. . . .

The myth persists. Should it persist? Everything that Carman said had been said before; it was only the monotonous effect which was characteristically Carman. He used the same styles and themes as had the Victorians and Romantics, but in Carman the original intensity was lost. There is about his work a pervading monotony of tone, a lack of strength, and a slightness of content. His diction and his ideas lack the vigour of a Shelley or a Browning. He was a poet who had very little to say; yet, there is a characteristic quality to his work, a tone showing a delicacy of expression, a haunting melancholy, and a musical lyricism. Within his own artistic limits he displayed a consistency of expression; he was always able to capture the melody of a mood, the tone of an atmosphere, the colour of a setting. And even though his themes are limited, he was able to give a spontaneous quality to his verse. But all this does not make him a great poet; neither does it put him into the category that critics often do, that of a "minor but good" poet, an excuse which the myth surrounding his name seems to demand. It is the quantity rather than the quality of his verse which gives him a place in a study of Canadian poetry. He brought to Canadians an awareness of poetry and poets, and also the knowledge that when good poetry is wanted, it is found in other places rather than Canada. (p. 48)

Donald Stephens, "A Maritime Myth" (reprinted by permission of the author), in Canadian Literature, *No. 9, Summer, 1961, pp. 38-48.*

D. G. JONES   (essay date 1970)

Carman, it is true, in poems such as the early and well known **"Low Tide on Grand Pré,"** exhibits a nostalgic regret and disillusionment reminiscent of Roberts. Both his occasional melancholy and the frequent jubilant celebration of the joys of the open road owe a good deal to the conventions of the period. The gusto with which he sings of the vagabond life is frequently forced. His delight in nature and his optimistic conception of man's relationship to her can be superficial in expression or intolerably vague. He wrote too much and often too glibly. Ultimately, however, Carman's outlook rests upon a vision of nature as realistic as any we can find in Roberts.

Carman's poetry does not exhibit the violence or the variety of life that we find in Roberts' animal stories; nevertheless, Carman was aware of the darkness as well as the light, of the lethal as well as the vital implications of all life, love, or action. And he accepted them both without the reservations that troubled Roberts. For this reason, it would seem, he escaped the sort of paralysis that overtook Roberts, going blithely if naïvely on his way. Carman's image of the individual life, of his own life, is characteristically modest, delicate, even fragile. It is the image of the snowflake in **"The Great Return,"** of the moth in **"Pulvis et Umbra,"** of the wind-flower in the poem of the same name. (pp. 94-5)

The hands of chance and change do not dismay Carman, do not take him by surprise, as they did Roberts. He is prepared to accept the mortal and ephemeral nature of all things and still affirm the glory and value of the individual life. His conception of nature was not so much childish as childlike. More than any other Canadian writer he had the kind of faith in the goodness or justice of life that is implied in Christ's parable of the lilies of the field, which neither toil nor spin and yet are clothed in a glory greater than Solomon's. (p. 95)

Carman is the only poet of his immediate generation who could fairly be called a love poet—a distinction which seems ordinary enough within the context of the whole history of lyric poetry, but a significant one within the context of his own generation and in the perspective of our present discussion. Unlike Roberts, Carman continued to give his heart up straightaway unto love. However it might hurt him, his initial impulse was not to defend himself from the world, to order and control it, but to love it. Thus, though his writing was marred by a lack of critical insight and by much that was conventional in thought and expression, throughout his career he was able to write poems in which we glimpse an authentic sense of the joy and poignancy of being alive—of what it means to love a woman or the world. (pp. 95-6)

D. G. Jones, "The Problem of Job," in his Butterfly on Rock: A Study of Themes and Images in Canadian Literature *(© University of Toronto Press 1970), University of Toronto Press, 1970 (and reprinted by University of Toronto Press, 1976, pp. 83-110).**

D.M.R. BENTLEY   (essay date 1979)

Of all the Confederation poets, Carman drew most extensively on the myth of Pan, making the goat-god a symbol of "the mystical confluence of Earth and Spirit in nature and man." . . . [A] major theme of Carman's work from the nineties onwards was the "kinship among all that exists." It is hardly surprising, therefore, that in the early years of the present century, Pan, traditionally symbolizing the fusion of the earthly and the divine, the physical and the spiritual, became, not only Carman's "favourite deity," but also an "up-to-date figure in [his] cosmology."

In the title poem of *The Pipes of Pan* series, Carman, like Lampman in **"The Song of Pan,"** rehearses the myth of Pan's pursuit of Syrinx and his construction of his pipe from "a swaying river reed." He then proceeds to assert, in stanza after stanza, that Pan's spirit, an omnipresent and omniscient power in history, in man, and in nature, can still be apprehended in "Mountain brook," "orchard bird," and, indeed, in all the voice of creation. Carman's exhaustive, and exhausting, catalogue of these various voices includes, amongst others, frogs (of course), crickets, cicadas, owls, cattle, horses, sheep, wolves, eagles, and even mink and moose—all of whose "bubbling notes once ran / Thrilling through the pipes of Pan." In short, **"The Pipes of Pan"** makes it abundantly clear that, for Carman, Pan is a "world deity," an ever-present force both in the world of nature and in the affairs of man. Following a poem on **"Marsyas,"** whom Carman, like Roberts, perceived as a cognate of Pan, the first volume of *The Pipes of Pan* continues with related poems such as **"Syrinx," "The Magic Flute," "A Shepherd in Lesbos," "The Lost Dryad," "The Dead Faun,"** and **"A Young Pan's Prayer,"** this last of which is less a treatment of the Arcadian god than an expression of Carman's own poetic and spiritual aspirations. . . . Suffice it to say that, for a time, Pan stood at the very centre of Carman's conception of the essential unity of creation and was for him a figure whose eternal pipes, when heard by the young Pan-poet, could restore to him the elemental power of nature.

James Cappon [see excerpt above] is right in observing that the Pan of Carman's later poetry is no longer the "world deity" of **The Pipes of Pan** but, rather, is a more muted and less omnipresent god who symbolizes merely "a wild music of nature." Nevertheless, whether his pipes are heard in the song of Catskill thrushes, as in **"Pan in the Catskills,"** or in the music of a hurdy-gurdy man, as in **"The Urban Pan,"** the goat-god is still very much alive in the less vigorous but often technically more accomplished poetry of Carman's last period. . . . The nostalgia evoked by the pipes of Pan in these later poems is a nostalgia for a lost, pastoral ideal located in an Arcadian world whose memory enables the poet to transcend for a moment "the noise of truck and van" and to participate in "the springtime of the world." It is tempting to see the vanished, halcyon past for which Carman laments in **"The Urban Pan"** as the pastoral past, not merely of Acadia, but of America too; for by 1906 when this poem was first published in the May 5 issue of the *Saturday Evening Post* urban life was, increasingly, more of a reality for more people than were the pastoral haunts of the typical Confederation Pan. (pp. 68-9)

> *D.M.R. Bentley, "Pan and the Confederation Poets" (reprinted by permission of the author), in* Canadian Literature, *No. 81, Summer, 1979, pp. 59-71.**

ADDITIONAL BIBLIOGRAPHY

Daniells, Roy. "Crawford, Carman, and D. C. Scott." In *Literary History of Canada: Canadian Literature in English,* edited by Carl F. Klinck, pp. 406-21. Toronto: University of Toronto Press, 1965.*
Highlights Carman as nature poet.

Gundy, H. Pearson. "Flourishes and Cadences: Letters of Bliss Carman and Louise Imogen Guiney." *The Dalhousie Review* 55, No. 2 (Summer 1975): 205-26.*

Publishes the correspondence of the two poets, supplying background information on their relationship.

Marshall, Tom. "Mountaineers and Swimmers: Roberts and Carman Revisited." In his *Harsh and Lovely Land :The Major Canadian Poets and the Making of a Canadian Tradition,* pp. 9-16. Vancouver: University of British Columbia Press, 1979.*
Briefly examines Bliss Carman as a major Canadian poet contributing to the "making of a 'distinguished and distinguishable' poetic tradition in English."

Pacey, Desmond. "Bliss Carman." In his *Ten Canadian Poets: A Group of Biographical and Critical Essays,* pp. 59-113. Toronto: The Ryerson Press, 1958.
Concerned with Carman's poetic philosophy and his personality as exemplified in his poems.

Pierce, Lorne. Introduction to *The Selected Poems of Bliss Carman,* by Bliss Carman, edited by Lorne Pierce, pp. 17-30. New York: Dodd, Mead & Co., 1954.
Biocritical overview.

Roberts, C.G.D. "Bliss Carman." *The Dalhousie Review* IX, No. 4 (January 1930): 409-17.
Remembrance of Carman as a youth by his cousin and fellow poet.

Roberts, C.G.D. "More Reminiscences of Bliss Carman." *The Dalhousie Review* X, No. 1 (April 1930): 1-9.
Conclusion of reminiscence, concerned primarily with Carman's university years.

Rogers, A. Robert. "American Recognition of Bliss Carman and Sir Charles G. D. Roberts." *Humanities Association of Canada* XXII, No. 2 (Spring 1971): 19-25.*
Account of Carman's reception among American critics.

Ross, Malcolm Mackenzie. "A Symbolic Approach to Carman." *The Canadian Bookman* XIV, No. 11 (December 1932): 140-44.
Examines Pan as a symbol in Carman's poetry.

Stephens, Donald. *Bliss Carman.* New York: Twayne Publishers, 1966, 144 p.
Introductory study divided into four main chapters examining Carman's life, his works, his literary influences, and his lasting importance.

C(onstantine) P(eter) Cavafy
1863-1933

(Also transliterated as Constantin and Konstantinos; also Patrou and Petrou; also Cavafis, Kavafis, Kavifis, Kabaphē, and Kabaphēs) Greek poet and essayist.

Cavafy has written what many regard as the most important modern poetry in the Greek language, while also achieving the universality necessary to have an artistic impact on world literature. Most of his poems are set in the outland regions under Roman conquest during the declining years of the empire. They feature both historic characters, such as Nero and Julius Caesar, and fictional ones, often Greek poets and artisans who commemorate some recurring theme in Cavafy's ancient world. Among these themes are the vanity of wordly triumph, the transient nature of human life, and the tragedy of a precarious existence relieved only by transcendent moments of romantic passion. Cavafy called himself "an historical poet," but his thematic concerns are nonetheless modern as well as being extremely personal.

Cavafy was born in Alexandria, Egypt, to a Greek family which for a time ran a successful import-export business. As a child he lived in England, and his earliest poetic efforts were in English. After the bankruptcy of the family business, his mother took him to Constantinople, where they lived for three years and where Cavafy probably had his first homosexual encounters. In 1885 he returned to Alexandria, living the remainder of his life there as a clerk of the Egyptian Ministry of Public Works. For most of his life Cavafy lived a pained and isolated existence which was intensified by his homosexual nature. He wrote poems constantly, most of which he destroyed, though he had a small number of them privately printed for a select group of readers.

Copyright © 1972 by Princeton University Press

Cavafy's early poems exhibit the influence of the symbolist and decadent movements in late nineteenth-century European literature. They often express the melancholy typical of *fin de siècle* poetry, and Cavafy later repudiated their self-consciously poetic quality for a spare, prosaic style which he developed to perfection in his mature poems. Often called a poet of old age, Cavafy denied his poetry displays of linguistic virtuosity, emphasizing instead his experience and perceptions stated with the greatest possible plainness. Though he drew upon the entire history of the Greek language, from its most elevated to its most vulgar forms, he did so not as much to create verbal complexity as to provide a simple reworking of a few tragic themes. Foremost among these themes is that of human mortality and the sense of beauty, frustration, and loss which derives from it. Consciously avoiding a dependence on metaphor and imagery, Cavafy effects much of his impact with pure narrative or straightforward comment.

In his poetry Cavafy was inspired by parallels between the modern age and that of the Hellenistic and Greco-Roman periods. George Seferis, among others, points out that in a Cavafy poem the past illuminates and illustrates the present, as well as documents the state of the poet's mind and spirit. Throughout the poetry the hedonism of Rome comes to represent the pitfalls as well as the glorious moments of sensual indulgence, just as the new religion of Christianity represents an austere but satisfying alternative to the ultimate futility of a life based on eroticism. These opposing themes frequently arise in Cavafy's love poems, in which he portrays homosexual relationships without guilt or sentimentality and often expresses a universal sentiment of the genre: that of longing for pleasures untasted. Cavafy's most important poems, however, take politics and history as their ostensible subjects in order to impart a personal vision. In "Waiting for the Barbarians" for example, Cavafy documents the ironically enthusiastic response with which a civilized culture greeted insurgent barbarism; in "Ithaka" he conveys that the journey to one's destination is more important than the arrival; in "The City" he warns that to leave one's city amounts to an unsuccessful escape from oneself. With W. H. Auden, critics often find Cavafy's value to reside in his particular tone of voice, which conveys a pagan sensitivity to physical pleasure and a painful sense of tragic futility. Unquestionably a champion of personal courage, Cavafy has been recognized in Greece and the wider literary community as one of the great poets of the twentieth century.

(See also *TCLC*, Vol. 2.)

PRINCIPAL WORKS

Poiēmata (poetry) 1933

The Complete Poems of Cavafy   (poetry)   1948
Poems   (poetry)   1951
Anekdota peza keimena   (prose)   1963
Hapanta   (poetry)   1963
Peri ekklēsias kai theatrou   (prose)   1963
Peza   (prose)   1963
Fourteen Poems   (poetry)   1966
Poiēmata 1896-1933   (poetry)   1966
"Ars Poetica"   (essay)   1968; published in journal *The Charioteer*
Autographa poiēmata (1896-1910)   (poetry)   1968
K. P. Kabaphē anekdota poiēmata 1882-1923   (poetry) 1968
Passions and Ancient Days   (poetry)   1971
Selected Poems   (poetry)   1972
Kavaphika   (poetry)   1974
Collected Poems   (poetry)   1975

ROBERT LIDDELL   (essay date 1948)

[Cavafy's] work, printed in a piecemeal fashion, and circulated in an eccentric way, has a unity—a unity which it is important to examine, for Cavafy is one of the 'Four Great Dead Poets' of Modern Greece. A critic of Cavafy must try to find what Henry James called 'the Figure in the Carpet'.

Monsieur [Samuel] Baud-Bovy, in his recent book on Greek poetry, professes to have found the figure in Cavafy's carpet. He tells us—what is only too well known—that Cavafy was sexually abnormal, and he makes everything hang upon that fact. (p. 188)

Sexual abnormality coloured Cavafy's carpet, there is not a doubt of it—but it did not form the pattern, which is more complicated and interesting than Monsieur Baud-Bovy would have us believe. Another phrase of Henry James's will help to define it: 'The Sense of the Past', and some words of George Seferis: 'Cavafy little by little obtained a historical sense of himself, and of the world in which he lived.' (pp. 188-89)

He is the heir of Ancient Alexandria—a different place from ancient Athens, indeed. (p. 189)

Yet Cavafy does not merely write as if he had been born in A.D. 400, instead of 1863. He has come into an older world, and later into the history of Hellenism. He does not only draw on Alexandria for inspiration, but on all the Greek world—ancient, medieval and modern. But he looks at it from an amused sceptical Alexandrine point-of-view. Moreover, he has read the Symbolists, and has assimilated such modern themes as *Tædium Vitæ*. This has inspired several of his early poems, notably *The City*. (p. 190)

From the Symbolists Cavafy also learned how to tell a story, and Browning may have been another influence here—though, happily, Cavafy never wants to point a moral. This story-telling, and this kinship with the Symbolists, will often remind an English reader of the early Eliot. . . . With ironic nostalgia he recreates his own past, and the varied past of his race. . . .

He comments on Greek themes from an elderly, disillusioned point of view. For him the Gods of Olympus are at best stupid and ineffective, at worst malicious. But on the whole the ancient world was too bright and young and heroic for this cyn-

ical, middle-aged poet. Moreover, he was Hellenic, not a Hellene; and as an Alexandrian he felt more kinship with the other outposts of the Greek world, than with Athens herself. . . .

From the sub-Greek world he chooses the kind of theme fitted to his poetry. There must be a picture, a story, or a character, clear enough to be conveyed in his terse, epigrammatic lines—he will convey it with acidity, but not wholly without pity. It is likely to be a story of defeat. Such a poem is *Waiting for the Barbarians*. Byzantium, or whatever Greek beleaguered city is here intended, is revealed as only waiting to give herself up. . . . (p. 191)

Cavafy's pessimism or defeatism is not to be called a philosophy: he was not a philosopher, he was an historian. If he had any philosophy, it was the most elementary philosophy of history: he knew that people do not learn by their mistakes, or by those of others, and that the eminent frequently come to a bad end. He did not whimper over his share of the human burden, like [A. E.] Housman—he was too brave, and too well-bred. He did not chuckle over the misfortunes of other people, like Hardy—he did not really very much care about what happened to other people. Of the places of the past that inspired his poems, Troy and Thermopylae are destined to fall—so is Alexandria. . . . (p. 193)

In Cavafy's panorama of the past we are not to expect to see heroes. . . . (p. 194)

In Cavafy's picture of the ancient world people change easily to the religion or the politics of the victor. (p. 195)

Two judgements of Mr. [T. S.] Eliot's about two other twentieth-century writers probably express better than any other words one could find the nature and unity of Cavafy's work. Of James Joyce's use of myth, he has written: 'It is simply a way of controlling, of ordering, of giving a shape and a significance to the immense panorama of futility and anarchy which is contemporary history.' And in introducing the poems of Ezra Pound he wrote: 'When he deals with antiquities, he extracts the essentially living; when he deals with contemporaries, he notes only the accidental. But this does not mean that he is antiquarian or parasitical on literature. Any scholar can see Arnaut Daniel or Guido Cavalcanti as literary figures; only Pound can see them as living beings. Time, in such connexions, does not matter; it is irrelevant whether what you see, really see, as a human being, is Arnaut Daniel or your greengrocer. It is merely a question of the means suited to the particular poet, and we are more concerned with the end than the means.'' (p. 196)

Perhaps of all Eliot characters, Cavafy is most like Tiresias, the seer of *The Waste Land*, in whom all the men and women of the poem meet. . . . In this little, old, sexually abnormal Alexandrian poet, looking without fear, and without very much compassion, on the futility and anarchy which is contemporary history, Hecuba, Cratesiclea, Anna Comnena, Pompey, Antony and John Cantacuzene melt into each other, and are not wholly distinct from the equivocal characters that haunt the dark, hot streets of Alexandria in our own century. His historical and his modern poems form part of the same synthesis.

And the sense of the past permeates his modern erotic poetry. He writes as an elderly man, with poignant nostalgia for youth. . . . His poems are set in his own past (real or imagined) which is itself a period of Greek history like any other. Some of them (not necessarily autobiographical) bear such titles as: **'In his twenty-fifth year'**, or **'Days of 1896'**, or of 1901, 1908,

1909, 1910 and 1911. For all their passionate intensity, few are in the present tense. Moreover, he is almost pedantically accurate in telling us how much their heroes earn at their work, at cards, or trictrac, or prostitution. (pp. 196-97)

And the mood is like that of ancient poetry. If at times one is reminded of Walt Whitman, it is rather to Tibullus and the Greek Anthology that one must look for counterparts to the lovers in his poems. (p. 197)

It must be said frankly that all Cavafy's love-poetry is homosexual. Some naïf readers have mistaken the character of some of the poems. Greek is an inflected language, and can get on without saying 'he' or 'she' all the time. Cavafy would no doubt have rejoiced at the resulting ambiguity in so far as it made his poetry more universal—it would certainly have revolted him to become the object of a special cult. Moreover, many of his poems are as universal in their appeal as any love-poetry of any sort. On the other hand he would have scorned to conceal by any subterfuge what form of the universal passion of love it was that inspired his poetry.

Though he was by nature extremely timid, and had more than his share of the Oriental anxiety about 'what people say', and though in some ways he was almost as tortuous an intriguer as Pope, yet, like Pope, he was essentially a brave and nobel character. He risked family troubles, social ostracism, and even the danger of enforced exile from his beloved city, for the sake of his uniquely honest work—and he lived to be not only tolerated but honoured there.

In his work 'the love that dares not speak its name' does not vaunt itself, is not puffed up, does not behave itself unseemly—neither is it wry and tortured, a misery to itself, and an embarrassment to others, as in *A Shropshire Lad*. Cavafy does not take the disguise Proust took; nor yet does he offer the defence that Proust offered when he spoke out—that all love is a sickness or perversion, and homosexual love only another variety. When people tried to interest him in Proust, he did indeed read the death of the grandmother with rapture—but the famous exordium to *Sodome et Gomorrhe* left him cold. He said it was pre-war and out of date.

Without exhibitionism, and without apology, Cavafy did his readers the honour to assume that their experience would not be too limited for them to understand his form of love, and that they would be too well-read to be shocked at its expression—how little ancient love-poetry is about heterosexual love! He was fully aware of the official disapprobation of religion and society—he had felt it—but that was another thing. He wrote about the themes ancient Greek and Latin poets wrote about, and wished to be read naturally, as they are read.

He is probably at his best in those poems where he is at the same time a love-poet, and a poet of the Alexandrine past, in the exquisite poems on dead boys of the Hellenistic age. In this age he was, for other reasons, imaginatively most at home—and he could now write of love as freely as Callimachus or Theocritus. (pp. 198-99)

Robert Liddell, "Studies in Genius: Cavafy," in Horizon, Vol. XVIII, No. 105, September, 1948, pp. 187-202.

REX WARNER (essay date 1949)

[Cavafy's] world is the world which most English schoolmasters would describe as 'decadent'. It is a world without any of the obvious epic, lyric or tragic grandeurs. Yet it is a world that existed and exists. It can be examined minutely and dispassionately. And to this examination Cavafy brings a peculiar point of view together with a singular integrity.

His point of view is, in a way, the inversion of the heroic. He loves to insist not on some great completed accomplishment or successful quest, but on the importance of first steps or of incidents by the way. In the end the effect is often one of heroism, but it is of the quiet heroism of the individual rather than of the heroism of cause or state or professional strong man. (p. 1)

There is more here than stoicism, more than the dutiful acceptance of experience. There is the conscious, almost the sensual pride in saying 'yes' rather than saying 'no.' There is the curious paradox of defeat and failure being turned not into victory and success but into something almost or quite as respectable.

[In "Ithaca'] what is emphasised is the immense value of individual experience rather than the strained pursuit of an ideal or the heights and depths of cataclysmic events. Angry Poseidon, the savages and the Cyclops do not really exist or, if they do, they exist only in your own mind. Ithaca itself is only the excuse for a long journey. You must be in no hurry to arrive there. . . . And in the end, when you arrive at the poor and rocky island, you will have every reason to be satisfied. (p. 3)

["Waiting for the Barbarians"] is a fine ironical picture of Emperor, consuls and praetors, all in their best clothes, waiting to receive and to impress a barbarian army that never arrives. The people are excited and curious. Something strange and unexpected is on its way. But when, at nightfall, news comes that the barbarians have either disappeared or been annihilated, there is an increase of sudden gravity as the people return hurriedly to their houses. . . . Again it is a world that might be called 'decadent'—the world where a rich and civilised people await with keen curiosity the invasion of a barbarian army, not, it seems, concerned to repel the invaders by force, but interested in the situation, not unduly alarmed, and reasonably convinced that the foreigners will be impressed by red togas, bracelets, jewels and 'precious walking-sticks'. It is a scene very different from what could be imagined of Marathon or of Salamis, yet Cavafy's art is such that we are not out of sympathy with the crowd of sightseers either in their curiosity or in its disappointment. These studies of the unheroic have something of their own which, while it is not heroism, is a kind of dignity. It is the dignity and pathos of the real life which persists under whatever changes of government.

So, in the poem "Alexandrian Kings" which describes a magnificent military parade at which the children of Cleopatra are invested with the most high sounding titles, Cavafy re-creates an atmosphere which seems more real, more, in a sense, historical than that of Plutarch or of a professional historian. He makes no mention of Julius Caesar or of Antony. Cleopatra is only referred to incidentally. What he sees are the gay crowds coming to the spectacle, the royal children, particularly Caesarion. . . . (p. 4)

The picture of a youth standing in a pink dress at a splendid parade moves Cavafy's imagination more than does the love of Antony and Cleopatra or the successes of Octavius. It is perhaps an unusual point of view, but it is a view of reality. (p. 5)

There is another poem, written in 1926, and called **"In a Township of Asia Minor"**, where the great names of Antony and Octavius are treated most characteristically. The battle of Actium has been commemorated in poetry of the very highest order. There is the Ode of Horace. There is Shakespeare. . . . Cavafy is interested in a different kind of truth from that which inspires Horace or Shakespeare. He takes the point of view of a small town whose inhabitants have expected Antony to win and have composed already a flattering address to him. In fact it is a matter of complete indifference to these humble people which of the great emperors wins the decisive battle. They therefore make a simple alteration in their address. . . . There is much more than cynicism in such a poem. It expresses an intelligible and a respectable truth, different indeed from the truth of Shakespeare, but still true.

Many poems of Cavafy could be cited as evidence for his invariable refusal to take up anything that could be called a conventional point of view. (pp. 5-6)

What was it that gave Cavafy the power to produce poetry of such integrity, of such individual insight? He is aided certainly by his discovery of what amounts to a personal mythology. Imaginary or real characters from the Hellenistic court of Asia, Macedonia or Egypt somehow provide him . . . with symbols that have the same appropriateness to his own genius as were to Yeats the mythologies of ancient Ireland or to T. S. Eliot, in "The Waste Land", the stories concerning the Holy Grail. So to Cavafy the secondary characters of ancient or Byzantine history—Galba, Caesarion, Orophernes—the imagined life of Antioch or Alexandria, where creeds and races were mixed, but where life was lived, provide the exactly appropriate symbols for the expression of a modern and unique outlook on the world. It is the outlook of a mind that is disillusioned, but never, in spite of appearances, cynical; of a meticulous critic, who loves the material exposed to the critical faculties. Yet it is poetry, not criticism, that we read and admire in Cavafy. Together with and underneath the controlled attitude, the steady point of view, we find the sudden flash of insight, the vigorous assertion of emotion. If we are to take the poet's own word for it, love affairs of a disreputable character were a source of immense inspiration. . . [The] sources of his inspiration are not confined to his studies of ancient history. The fastidious moral and aesthetic sense of T. S. Eliot will reject or only use for purposes of denigration the "one-night cheap hotels". Cavafy is equally fastidious, but in a very different way. In such places he finds the life that exists even without Antony and Octavius, the valued experiences that give value to an Ithaca which otherwise is of little account. . . . Cavafy in general finds his "entire beauty" in what to many would seem to be unlikely places. What matters is that he found it, finding also at the same time a kind of truth, which has a peculiar relevance for the modern world. He is aware of all kinds of complexity, but not for that reason tempted into hysteria, exaggeration or over-emphasis. His quiet style and his choice of subject exactly represent his genius which accepts life without extravagant illusions. Yet in this particular act of acceptance he has somehow transformed what was there before. He has not only taken and described but created and discovered a world. (pp. 7-9)

Rex Warner, "Introduction" (1949), in Poems by C. P. Cavafy, *translated by John Mavrogordato (translation © John Mavrogordato 1951; reprinted by permission of the Estate of Rex Warner and The Hogarth Press Ltd), Hogarth Press, 1951 (and reprinted by Chatto & Windus Ltd., 1971), pp. 1-9.*

E. M. FORSTER (essay date 1951)

[All of Cavafy's] poems are short. They are learned, sensuous, ironic, civilised, sensitive, witty. Where's their centre? Courage enters, though not in an ordinary nor a reputable form. Cavafy appreciates cowardice also, and likes the little men who can't be consistent or maintain their ideals, and can't know what is happening and have to dodge. (pp. 246-47)

Courage and cowardice are equally interesting to his amoral mind, because he sees in both of them opportunities for sensation. What he envies is the power to snatch sensation, to triumph over the moment even if remorse ensues. Perhaps that physical snatching is courage; it is certainly the seed of exquisite memories and it is possibly the foundations of art. The amours of youth, even when disreputable, are delightful, thinks Cavafy, but the point of them is not that: the point is that they create the future, and may give to an ageing man in a Rue Lepsius perceptions he would never have known. (p. 247)

The attitude recalls Proust's, but the temperament differs. Cavafy is never embittered, never the invalid. He is thankful to have lived, and 'young men even now are repeating his verses. His visions pass before their lively eyes, and even now they are moved by his revelation of beauty.' He has something of the antique faith in fame. He is not a super-sensitive Frenchman. He is not English. He is not even British. Alexandria's his home. (pp. 247-48)

His material as a poet, then, begins with his own experiences and sensations: his interest in courage and cowardice and bodily pleasure, and so on. He begins from within. But he never makes a cult of himself or of what he feels. All the time he is being beckoned to and being called to by history, particularly by the history of his own race. History, too, is full of courage, cowardice, lust, and is to that extent domestic. But it is something more. It is an external inspiration. And he found in the expanses and recesses of the past. . . . something that transcended his local life and freshened and strengthened his art. (p. 248)

The warmth of the past enthralls him even more than its blunders, and he can give the sense of human flesh and blood continuing through centuries that are supposed to be unsatisfactory. . . . Sometimes the supernatural appears, and not always ominously: as in **'One of their Gods,'** it may enrich voluptuousness. . . . The idea that the Divine should descend to misbehave, so shocking to the Christian, comes naturally enough to a paganising Greek. . . . (p. 249)

His attitude to the past did not commend him to some of his contemporaries, nor is it popular to-day. He was a loyal Greek, but Greece for him was not territorial. It was rather the influence that has flowed from his race this way and that through the ages, and that (since Alexander the Great) has never disdained to mix with barbarism, has indeed desired to mix; the influence that made Byzantium a secular achievement. Racial purity bored him, so did political idealism. . . . The civilisation he respected was a bastardy in which the Greek strain prevailed, and into which, age after age, outsiders would push, to modify and be modified. (p. 249-50)

[His] words make one think—words of a very wise, very civilised man, words of a poet who has caught hold of something that cannot be taken away from him by bankruptcy, or even by death. (p. 250)

E. M. Forster, "The Complete Poems of C. P. Cavafy" (originally published in The Listener, Vol.

XLVI, No. 1166, July 5, 1951), in his Two Cheers for Democracy, *Edward Arnold & Co., pp. 246-50.*

KIMON FRIAR   (essay date 1953)

It is true that the homosexuality of Kavafis gives a certain tone and coloring to all his work. Only about a fourth of his erotic poems rank among his greatest work, yet they are integrally important because they are, to my knowledge, the only poems which depict the lusts, guilts, anxieties, and nostalgic satisfactions of an illicit love without sentimentality.

But it is in his contemplative and historical poems that Kavafis attains his true stature. *Waiting for the Barbarians* is deeply moving to those who understand the secret temptation in the hearts of free men to cast off their responsibilities and yield themselves to directing power. The poem tells of the Senators, the Praetors, the Consuls, and the Emperor decked out in their finery, abjectly preparing to hand over their civilization to what they consider to be the invincible Barbarians. But a report comes from the frontier that "There are no Barbarians any more," and the poem concludes: "And now what will become of us without Barbarians?—Those people were some sort of a solution." In *Ithaka* we are told that it is not the arrival, but the journey of adventures and experiences that matters: the grapple with the Laestrygones, the Cyclopes, and angry Poseidon, or with the Phoenician trading station, the perfumes and jewels: "Ithaka has given you your lovely journey. / Without Ithaka you would not have set out. / Ithaka has no more to give you now." Kavafis often said that if he were not a poet he would have been a historian. Most of his poems, even the erotic and contemplative ones, are set not in Classic times, but in Hellenistic, Greco-Roman, or Byzantine ages. His interest lies not in world-shaking events but in human frailties attending upon them. His heroes often show courage and character, but more often frailty, egotism, opportunism, which Kavafis depicts with sympathy and understanding. The poems are neither emotional nor lyrical, but dramatic, narrative, objective, realistic, a recounting of facts and episodes with subtlety and irony in a tone of voice which is dry, precise, deliberately prosaic, and, above all, ironic. They belong to the tradition of Greek epigrams of the fourth century B.C. and afterwards, to those of Simonides, Callimachus, Appolonious of Rhodes, to the polished verse of Alexandrine and Byzantine intellectuals. Although his language and syntax is based on the demotic tongue of the educated modern Greek, it is heavily weighted with words and turns of expression or grammar borrowed from the entire tradition of the Greek language since classical times: from Hellenistic, Medieval, Byzantine, Alexandrine, and Church Greek. This is, of course, impossible to reproduce in translation, as impossible almost as the diction of Hopkins, but what does remain is the dry line or situation evocative of great irony. (pp. 19-20)

Kimon Friar, "One of the Great," in The New Republic *(reprinted by permission of* The New Republic; © *1953 The New Republic, Inc.), Vol. 128, No. 4, January 26, 1953, pp. 19-20.*

FRANCIS GOLFFING   (essay date 1955)

The exquisite craftsman who fashions his own life as though it were a poem appears as the constant protagonist of so much contemporary verse, and most signally of the verse of Cavafy. The spheres of action and contemplation, most rigorously distinguished in the past, are now readily collapsed into one: to remember imaginatively is to *act* . . . to act, that is, as well as circumstances permit. All procedure, henceforth, are prudent procedures; and all action described as moral is seen to be no more than procedure. Such overt action as is still maintained has one function only: to lead up to retirement, to the Voltairean cultivation of one's backyard; it is recommended to the seeker as adding relish to his final retreat. Thus we are brought round once more to the hedonistic bias, that bias which Cavafy has expressed so movingly in his poem, **"Ithaka"**:

> Setting out on the voyage to Ithaka
> You must pray that the way be long,
> Full of adventures and experiences . . .

and so on, until the arch of the poem closes ominously:

> Ithaka has given you your lovely journey,
> Without Ithaka you would not have set out.
> Ithaka has no more to give you now.

> Poor though you find it, Ithaka has not cheated you . . .

Yes, it has; for expecting to find a small derelict polity, Ulysses has only found a hole fit to die in.

The reader need not be told how utterly different this attitude is from the one expressed in Tennyson's *Ulysses*. But it might be worth pointing out that in "Alexandrian" poetry the dramatic character (whether mythological or otherwise) becomes not only more disabused and meaner but more complicated as well. Tennyson's Ulysses still speaks regally, in his own voice; the hero of Cavafy's poem is admonished, through the mouth of the poet, not to mind his eventual return to the drab island which, after all, has served its purpose as a jumping-off place. The fact that Cavafy's hero stands as fully for himself as Tennyson's did for the earlier poet does not obliterate the difference but, on the contrary, makes it all the more striking. For the voice, half hectoring half cajoling, which in the later poem addresses the hero's own conscience carries no suggestion of either triumph or resignation: behind the accents of evening glow and tranquil remembrance we are made to sense, as everywhere in this poet's lines, the murk of quiet desperation. (pp. 76-7)

Francis Golffing, "The Alexandrian Mind: Notes toward a Definition," in Partisan Review *(copyright* © *1955 by Partisan Review, Inc.), Vol. XXII, No. 1, Winter, 1955, pp. 76-7.*

PHILIP SHERRARD   (essay date 1956)

The last decades of the nineteenth century, during which the Alexandrian poet Constantine Cavafis grew to maturity, were, as far as certain literary circles are concerned, decades of a peculiar temper. It was then that æstheticism came into fashion, and decadence. There was, in these circles, a craving for sensation, a fastidious search for exotic refinement, a cultivation of art as something removed as far as possible from the common affairs of men, and from nature. (p. 83)

Art was thought to be a kind of sensation, evoked by and having for its end the expression and re-evocation of sensations. The love of art was equated with a love of fine sensations and works of art came to be looked upon as little more than a superior and sophisticated form of aphrodisiac.

Cavafis' early poems, those, let us say, which he wrote before 1901, in the main reflect at second-hand this fashionable romantic exoticism and decadence of the late nineteenth-century literary world. Behind them one can discern the compound but etiolated shadow of Gautier, of Henri Murger, of Baudelaire, Wilde and Pater, affected, æsthetic, feminine, haunted by the sense of corruption, by the canker in the rose, and reverent before the studied artificiality of Art. . . . There is the scornful indifference to nature. . . . The sensitive soul is above the pollution of the crowd, he does not allow himself to be soiled by the common and vulgar world. . . . With this studied, self-satisfied superiority and aloofness there is also the refined melancholy of the dandy and of the sophist, of the aesthete for whom the sensation of the passing moment is the only things of value which life has to offer and who is overcome by the oppressive sadness of things. . . . (pp. 84-5)

The trouble with [Cavafy's early poems] . . . is that they are too vague, generalised, and mushy to be convincing. They convey an amorphous sentimentality rather than any sincere and precisely realised experience. In the absence of anything significant to express, the poet is indulging in a vapid romanticism of a fashionable type, and so it is not surprising that really nothing is communicated to us, that we are not given any insight which adds to or alters the way we look at things.

Nevertheless, it is the note of refined melancholy that dominates even the best of Cavafis' early poems, those in which some slight intimation of real quality begins to sound. It is not the melancholy of Keats. . . . It is not the melancholy that follows in the wake of joy tasted, but the melancholy that comes from thinking on joys which never have and never will be tasted, which are doomed to remain for ever unrealised—it is this melancholy that Cavafis feels. . . . There is an echo of [Thomas Gray's "Elegy in a Country Churchyard"] here. . . . But for Cavafis the regret is not so much for those whom history has destroyed wantonly, without any apparent rhyme or reason, before they have had time to develop, or even for those who because of circumstance have been wasted. He laments rather those moments of pleasure which have been lost through weakness and indecision, through fear of the consequences or because it seemed there would be another opportunity. . . . (p. 85-6)

In another early poem, **"The City,"** the theme of failure and of frustration is enlarged and at the same time made more direct. . . . [The] poet now seems to carry on an internal dialogue with himself. One part of himself tempts him to flee from this town where his life has been ruined, by holding out before him the romantic possibility of finding somewhere else to live where he can begin over again and perhaps after all make a success of things. . . . The other part of himself knows that there is nowhere he can go, that he himself is the city from which his romanticism tempts him to flee: he himself is the condition that he describes, and from himself there is no escape, nowhere to flee to. . . . And in another one of these early poems, Cavafis seems to imply that there comes a moment in life when you, inhabitant of this city which is so to speak your shadow, have the power to choose, to accept it or to reject it; if you accept it, if you make the refusal to go some other way, you will be for ever crippled; yet you will not repent, you will have been true to what you are, you will have had the courage to live a life which, however appalling, it was your destiny to live, even if only to reveal the full horror of its degradation. . . . [It] seems that the borrowed aestheticism of the early poems is giving place to a more positive attitude; the poet is beginning to integrate himself with a world and with a pattern which he was at first only imitating. What began as an affectation is becoming a personal destiny, is becoming

the poet's own life. He has chosen and reconciled himself to his City, his aesthetic City, as it was his lot that he should. His task now as a poet is to explore in all its aspects that City which, at the price of immolation, he has chosen; which, having chosen, he has become. . . . It is to make a myth of that City which is his own condition. It was to the creation of this myth that the greater part of Cavafis' mature poetry was devoted.

[Part of the weakness of those early poems] is due to the fact that Cavafis has written them without possessing any real background, without having integrated himself with and made his own a landscape with wider terms of reference than that provided by the rootless "fin de siècle" aestheticism whose moods and attitudes he was borrowing. (pp. 87-90)

It is when there is no such common framework to society that the poet's task is more difficult. Traditional values, traditional terms of reference break down, the poet no longer shares any immediate and recognised means of communication with the people, and, forced back upon himself, his poetry tends to become increasingly private and "esoteric." The kind of poetry written during periods of dissolution tends to be what is called romantic poetry; tends, that is, to be the expression of individual emotion rather than expression controlled by the discipline of consciously held values and purposes. (pp. 90-1)

Cavafis began to write in a period when the process of dissolution was well under way, when all those tendencies latent in social break-down and which at first seem full of energy and excitement, have run their course and are exhausted and when new and perhaps unwelcome syntheses begin to appear on the horizon. . . . Thus isolated on the one hand from a community, and on the other unable to find in life any purpose which transcends his own inidividuality, the poet tends to find value only in the immediate gratification of the senses, in the stimulation of aesthetic beauty, in pursuits which concern the life of sensation only. (p. 91)

It was in such a situation as this I have described that Cavafis found himself. . . . (p. 92)

Quite how Cavafis lighted on that landscape through which his vision could be given coherence it is impossible to say. . . . In Cavafis' case, it may have been that in the modern Alexandria in which he lived there were enough visible remains of, and associations with, an older Alexandria towards which his mind was turning to stimulate his curiosity and to suggest that act of recreation which his poetry was more and more to become. . . . At all events, behind the dull, constricting provinciality of present-day Alexandria, with whose *bourgeois* sense of values and moral philistinism Cavafis had slight sympathy, he began to discern the lineaments of an Alexandria which promised to be far more congenial to his temperament and one through whose figures he might express himself with greater assurance and freedom.

The Alexandria which Cavafis began to see as his City was the great hellenistic Alexandria, the capital of the Ptolemies, whose ground-plan had been traced out by Alexander himself between Lake Mareotis and the Mediterranean Sea. Under the protection and patronage of its rulers, the Ptolemies, chief city of a flourishing kingdom and a rich terrain, standing at a vital point between East and West and master thus of all the commerce of Europe with the East, Alexandria quickly became the most splendid and wealthy city of the known world. . . . It was a curious, chequered world, knit only perhaps by the common Greek language. (pp. 92-3)

[The] re-creation of a certain period of the past by the poet—and this may be an imaginary past as well as an historical past—provides a point of view from which the present may be looked at, its actions mirrored; it provides an image in which the present may see itself. In either case, it is the present that matters. As soon as the poet loses his sense of the present, of actual experience, and uses what should be his means of expression as an end in itself, he stops being a poet and becomes something else. . . . To have a sense of the past is above all to have a sense of living human beings and of human life. To make history live in the way here implied one must first of all have actual experience. And Cavafis, because he had this sense of the present, of an actual human condition, is able in his poetry to make the past live. (pp. 94-5)

We are now in a position to see what kind of myth Cavafis was to create out of his Alexandrian hellenistic past. We have already seen that his early poetry reflected at second hand the prevailing aestheticism of the late nineteenth century, with its refined hedonism, its value of the pleasure of the moment, its dislike of dogma and orthodoxy, its search for the exotic and the abnormal, its feminine feeling for beauty, its hostility towards the unknown and the supernatural, its fear of death and its worship of Art as the only thing deserving the respect of civilised man. But Cavafis until now had not been able to integrate this aestheticism with any background of his own. It had been but an attitude, a daring pose in the face of the strait-laced mercantile society in which he moved. With his discovery of the old Alexandria, however, a new perspective was added to his poetry. The past belonged and was accessible to everyone. . . . We must now consider this view of life as it is presented to us through Cavafis' myth of the City of Alexandria and of the world of which it was the centre.

The first thing about this hellenistic world whose features Cavafis is to examine is of course its whole-hearted dedication to the life of sensation, its downright hedonism. I have already indicated how it is that in a period of dissolution when all values are discredited and life emptied of all metaphysical content, all that is left is the immediate gratification of the senses, and . . . Cavafis recounts in bored, ironic, blasé accents the attitude of one superficially disillusioned with every ideal and "higher purpose" and consequently having nothing left to value but such gratification and indulgence, for which, indeed and fortunately, he is admirably equipped. (pp. 95-6)

At the centre of this Cult of Pleasure and Art of Alexandria is the worship of the beauty of the male body. Aestheticism, no doubt because it stimulates the sentimental and passive side of man's nature, that feminine side which "senses" things and reacts to them, seems generally speaking to go hand in hand with homosexuality. . . . The worship of the male body where Cavafis' world was concerned was rather on account of the pleasure it could give, for the pleasing associations and sensations it evoked, than for any purpose connected with the State or with any quasi-religious ideal. And, according to one of Cavafis' characters, there is "an erotic tension" . . . , "an especial voluptuousness" . . . in a homosexual relationship which the normal relationship does not contain. Cavafis' erotic poems generally describe incidents in the lives of such lovers. . . . Sometimes he describes some psychological aspect of this love [as in **"A Young Poet, in his 24th Year"**]. . . . Or on another occasion he speaks of the pleasure of some association to which the sight of a handsome body gives rise. . . . And in another poem [**"One of Their Gods"**] he describes such a figure of ideal beauty passing through the streets of one of those "pleasure-loving, absolutely aesthetic" hellenistic cities, this time Seleukeia, on his way to some enjoyment. (pp. 98-100)

Here then is the first part of Cavafis' myth, this picture of a pleasure-delighting, beauty-haunted world of wit and sophistication, proud of its fine aesthetic sense and artistic skill, supercillious towards and sceptic of high-sounding ideals and other worldly faiths, tolerant, lazy, refined, bored, and capable only of reverence before the æsthetic perfection and sensual possibilities of the male body. But this is by no means the whole story. If the voice of the cultivated hedonist in a sentimental mood or a mood of self-esteem was the only one which Cavafis possessed, he would not be the significant poet he is. But so far the myth as been only partially inked in. The aesthetic world, being a world divorced from any principle, is a world of disorder, uncertainty, and despair. It is a doomed world. It is subject to attacks, against which it is powerless, both from without and within. From without, it is subject first of all to attack from any temporal power possessed with the sense of an historical mission or simply possessed with the desire for domination and conquest. Such a power Cavafis indicated when he speaks of the Romans. Rome, as an efficient State and military machine, and as a type of all efficient State and military machines, is hostile to practically all the values of that cultivated aesthetic humanism of which Cavafis' hellenistic world is the portrait. From the historical point of view, Rome's great military power overthrew those small kingdoms upon whose existence the superficial poise of hellenistic life depended, and such a life, lacking any true stability, must always be in dread of such temporal calamities. (pp. 101-02)

But the Romans in Cavafis' myth do more than merely reveal the instability of a life based on no deep foundations. . . . [The] overshadowing might of the Romans throws into relief the vanity, irresponsibility, and inner decay of the aesthetic state. . . . [The poems **"The Battle of Magnesia,"** **"Of Demetrius Soter [162-150 B.C.],"** and **"To Antiochus of Epiphanes"**] imply as much as anything else that the corruption and decadence of this state invites its own overthrow, that the Romans are simply the unconscious instruments in the execution of a sentence which those who live the superficial, self-indulgent life of the senses call down on themselves. . . . If sometimes Cavafis' poems seem to extol the life of aesthetic humanism, they more often reveal with astonishing and dreadful clarity the hollowness and inner rot of those who do in fact live it. . . . Cavafis is perhaps at his best when he is revealing the deceit, insecurity, mistrust and frightful corruption which lie beneath the surface of the aesthetic life and which are the price it pays for those moments of pleasure and fugitive beauty which it sometimes, but rarely, achieves. Few men have charted this world of decay so vividly.

Yet from the point of view of the aesthetic humanist that temporal power which Cavafis indicates when he speaks of the Romans is not only an impersonal instrument of self-induced punishment or virile aggression. It is more than that. The Romans in Cavafis' myth are also efficient organisers, image of State interference and discipline, or jurisprudence and prudery, and as such enemies of the cultivated laxity and laissez-faire of the tolerant sentimentalist. . . . (pp. 103, 106-07)

The second power which challenges the delicate balance of the aesthetic life is that of a dogmatic militant and moralising Church. In Cavafis' myth of the hellenistic world this power is of course represented by the Christian Church, which scorned and attacked the pleasures of the flesh, the refined sensuality, the naturalistic art with its sentimental idealisation of the human body, which burnt temples and broke idols, and which sought for justification of earthly life in a world beyond the tomb. The aesthetic humanist is of course quite incapable of any deep understanding of the religious life and in consequence the demands which that life makes on the individual appear to him to be merely so many obstacles between him and his pleasure, while those who are obedient to such demands are fit only to be mocked. . . . Having, as I said, no religious capacity of his own, the aesthete substitutes a vacuous and sentimental worship of "gods" who correspond to no reality but allow him to indulge in a certain wistfulness and romantic fancy. . . . (pp. 108-09)

But Cavafis' aesthete, himself without any faith but living in a world where such a faith exists, even, through fear, pretending indeed that "he too was a Christian," cannot but be aware of the consolation and reward such a faith can give. (p. 111)

But if a dogmatic militant church with whose creeds the aesthete has little sympathy is bad enough, far worse is the reformer and proselytiser who seeks to make an official State religion out of what in fact amounts to a parody of a way of life whose great attraction is a freedom from compulsion and a tolerance bred in an atmosphere of enlightened *laisser-faire* and sophisticated indifference. Any State-sponsored religion amounts of course to a negation of that cultivated delicate artificiality which is the aesthete's substitute for religion, but to institutionalise this artificiality so that what is a purely private allegiance becomes a public duty; to solidify the frail creation of the aesthete's distilled sensibility into a world of prescribed rite and blue-print morality: this is the final insult. There is little so irritating and offensive as the spectacle of someone of whom one does not approve making a public parade of, and advocating for general practical consumption, a vulgarised version of one's own particular sympathies, especially if part of the charm of these sympathies depends upon them being the possession of but a few of the more exclusive and select members of society. Yet this, in Cavafis' myth of the hellenistic world, is precisely what Julian the Apostate does. He is one of these reformers and proselytisers, and as such is the continual butt of scorn and mockery for both heathen and Christian alike. In the eyes of the aesthetic pagans he is a ridiculous interfering and pedantic prig, and in the eyes of the Christians an uncouth and bombastic sinner. Cavafis wrote five poems of which Julian is the direct subject, and in only one, **"Julian at Nicodemia,"** does he receive even slight sympathy. (pp. 114-15)

The most absolute and irresistible enemy of the aesthetic state, the one against which it is most defenceless, and the root of its *malaise* and despair is, however, the awareness of mortality, death, and of the terrible transience of all to which its affections are attached. It is here that we reach the real pathos of the aesthetic condition and it is not hard to understand why. (p. 117)

There are many poems of Cavafis which illustrate in ironic terms the vanity of the purely human state, its defencelessness before fate and death. There is the somewhat didactic **"Theodotos."** According to Plutarch, Theodotos persuaded the Egyptians to kill Pompey when he landed, and Cavafis uses this alleged incident to point his moral. . . . Or there is the picture of the hedonist Nero, self-deceived by the ambiguous reply of the Delphic Oracle into thinking that he has many years yet of indulgence left before him. (pp. 117-18)

But the aesthetic way pursued with logic to its end contains a more bitter irony. For by a sort of infernal movement within this way itself, the greater the degree to which one refines one's sensitivity, the more aware one becomes of the terrible impermanence and fleeting nature of all that upon which one's sensitivity depends for its sustenance; the keener grow one's love of sensuous beauty divorced from any comprehension of the roots of that beauty, the more one becomes aware of its fragility and of one's powerlessness to enjoy it except in a most partial and temporary way, in such a way, in fact, that makes one's very attachment the cause of an acute and growing distress. For this distress must become greater as with age the capacity to enjoy the world of pleasure dwindles, as the approaching shadow of death threatens to annihilate even that which one can still enjoy. Begotten thus more and more by Despair upon Impossibility, the aesthete's love can find outlet only in a sort of parody, a profane and perverted parody, of that act of recollection which for the religious life is a way to spiritual realisation. . . . In fact, the very purpose of the aesthete's art is not to remind us of a supersensual world, of which, as we said, he has no notion, but is rather to assist in this process by which the artist seeks to deal with the dread problem of time's and his passing. . . . For the aesthete, tortured by the endless dance of time and death that sweeps all that he values into oblivion, art seems the only way by which he can relieve his suffering. In his poetry, this idiotic chasing of moment after moment, this time, is frozen into a spatial form from whose contemplation is generated a sort of timeless untroubled mirth. For that is the only solution left to this tired, rapacious, over-refined man who is the generic hero of Cavafis' myth, homo Europaeus, as we might call him, of our late aesthetic humanist period. (pp. 119, 121-22)

Philip Sherrard, "Constantine Cavafis," in his The Marble Threshing Floor: Studies in Modern Greek Poetry *(reprinted by permission of the author and Denise Harvey & Company), Vallentine, Mitchell, 1956 (and reprinted by Denise Harvey & Company, 1981), pp. 83-124.*

RENATO POGGIOLI (essay date 1959)

Like most of Cavafis' poetry, which includes a string of highly personal lyrics, [**'Waiting for the Barbarians'**] is a historical tableau: one of the many that found their inspiration in the late, forgotten ages of classical antiquity . . . The model that suggested such compositions was perhaps Hérédia's *Trophées.* Yet Cavafis was far from being an imitative artist: he replaced the decorative indifference of that Parnassian craftsman with a lucid and ironic vision, and with a passionate austerity of diction and form. He treated history not as an archaeological pageant but as a dramatic parable illustrating the facts of life and the ways of man.

This is particularly true of **'Waiting for the Barbarians,'** which could be defined as a little tragicomedy, unfolded in a single scene. Its locale might be either Rome or Byzantium, or any one of the many temporary capitals of the Empires of the East and of the West. As for the time of the action, we may place it anywhere we wish in that long series of centuries historians designate as those of the 'great migrations' or of the 'barbaric invasions,' according to whether they complain or rejoice in their outcome, which might be viewed as the dawn of the modern age or the collapse of the ancient world.

The scene unfolds in dialogue form, as a succession of questions and answers by anonymous speakers, lost in the crowd filling the *forum* or *agora*, not for consulation or deliberation, but merely to wait there for an event of which most of them have neither knowledge nor understanding. The first question suggests with great immediacy the collective mood, which is a mixed one, made of hesitant expectation and of impatient curiosity. As for the first answer, it is a direct and simple acknowledgment of the impending happening everybody is consciously or unconsciously waiting for:

> —What are we expecting, gathered in the square?
> —On this day the barbarians will arrive.

All questions that follow stem not from the questioners' inner reflections but from their external observation; and this prevents the reader from deciding immediately whether the emotion ruling the crowd is fear or hope. The crowd is not an unruly mob, but a throng of curious onlookers; all they do is wonder aloud about what is now happening before their eyes, which a few of them, those providing the answers, seem to apprehend better than the others. The unusual civic activities and ceremonies they are witnessing are *per se* neither good nor bad omens; yet, representing a break in the routine of city life, they must portend an exceptional event.

The multitude cannot for instance fail to observe that the Senate is in session yet transacts no business; that the Emperor sits outdoors on his throne, rather than in his palace; that the supreme magistrates, who are wont to greet foreign guests on the stairs of their official residences, are now on the open road, as to welcome visitors worthy of extraordinary honors; that despite so many signs of solemnity and festivity, there are no rhetors to deliver the orations required by public celebration or official occasion. Many ask the 'why' of all this; some give replies that either repeat the initial statement, which thus becomes the poem's insistent and compelling refrain; others offer elaborate explanations, often in the form of rhetorical questions. The gist of it all is that things are being done or left undone in order to please the barbarians, or at least not to displease them. . . . (pp. 139-40)

Yet, since the expected visitation fails to occur, the emotional state of the crowd gradually changes, and at the fall of evening their passive excitement turns into confusion and worry. The poem's splendid anticlimax compels the reader to recognize that the early mood of the multitude had been festive and hopeful, while the present one is made of uneasiness and doubt. This means that the whole citizenry, not merely the populace, desperately wanted the barbarians to come, and on that very day; and that what everybody is now suspecting, with a feeling of disappointment and loss, is that they will come neither tomorrow nor ever. In brief, the crowd fears the very thing for which normally it should fondly wish and hope. That thing would be, and is, the absolute certitude that the barbarians have disappeared forever into a mysterious nowhere. . . . (p. 141)

The poem closes with a final question, which is far from being rhetorical, like all questions we ask in anguish and despair. The only answer such questions elicit is man's confession of his impotence: and the poem ends with the acknowledgment of the utter powerlessness of a decadent society in the presence, and even in the absence, of the iron law of historical necessity:

> —What will happen to us with no barbarians?
> Those people, after all, were a solution.

By ending on this note of cynic pessimism, Cavafis' poem proves *ad abundantiam* the paradoxical truth that the decadent mind can find peace only by submitting itself to the most inexorable of all the enemies of civilization, to the annihilating upsurge of the barbaric spirit. The problem of decadence is to be seen in its inability to resolve its own dialectic, in its eagerness to see its own Gordian knot brutally cut by the barbarian sword. The very notion of decadence, at least in its modern version, is practically inconceivable without this psychological compulsion, on the part either of the individual or of the group, to become the passive accomplice and the willing victim of barbarism. (pp. 141-42)

'Waiting for the Barbarians' is a dramatic dialogue, commenting on an action, or a lack of action, that is watched rather than lived. It is the contrast between what the characters see and what we know that turns the dialogue itself into a tragicomedy. But the dialogue itself is pure comedy, and comedy of manners at that. Manners are but the mirror of morals: thus Cavafis' poem belongs to high comedy, which is marked by the high seriousness, or the objectivity, of its social and psychological outlook. This is why the speakers of Cavafis' poem are not. . . 'poets and sages,' the aristocrats of decadence, its 'happy few,' but rather its 'men in the street.' The poet does not speak for them; he merely lets them speak, listening to their chatter, which is all they have to say. The total effect is that of a satirical parable, full of moral insight. **'Waiting for the Barbarians'** portrays decadence as a way of life without issue, as a fatuous automatic suicide of the will. It is in a negative, and, ultimately, non-tragic sense that such a life finds the solution of its inner crisis—that is, by ignoring it. Strictly speaking, the decadent society that Cavafis represents needs no help from inside or outside to go to its doom. Without internal or external violence (the barbarians may, after all, never come) it will finally crumble, and vanish forever into dust. (p. 148)

In a sense, the real subject of Cavafis' poem is decadence's disappointment at being ignored and neglected, at being left alone to live, or rather to die, by its own wits. It is this theme, temper, or mood that makes of **'Waiting for the Barbarians'** not only the tragicomedy of decadence, but its mock tragedy as well. What renders its ending really unhappy is that there is neither release nor relief, or more simply, that there is no ending at all. (pp. 149-50)

> *Renato Poggioli, "Qualis Artifex Pereo! or Barbarism and Decadence," in* Harvard Library Bulletin *(copyright 1959 by the President and Fellows of Harvard College), Vol. XIII, No. 1, Winter, 1959, pp. 139-50.**

GEORGE SEFERIS (essay date 1966)

[With] Cavafy something very extraordinary happens. In the poems of his youth and even certain poems of his middle age he quite often appears ordinary and lacking in any great distinction. But in the poems of his old age he gives the impression that he is constantly discovering things that are new and very valuable. He is "a poet of old age." . . . So far as my own knowledge of literature goes, I know of no other poetry so isolated as his. . . . There is, I mean, no close affinity which affects his work organically. The only thing I observe here is that Cavafy has certainly breathed the atmosphere of contemporary European poetry as it was when he was between twenty and thirty-five years of age. That is, the atmosphere of the school of Symbolism from which have sprung the most important and the most dissimilar figures in prewar poetry. But he does not show the influence of any one specific writer. . . . (pp. 121-22)

Cavafy is, I think, the most "difficult" poet of contemporary Greece, and we shall understand him more easily if we read him with the feeling of the continuous presence of his work as a whole. (p. 125)

Let us use it to try to discover, even in a limited way, what Cavafy feels about time. (p. 127)

The first date given to us by the poem ["**These Who Fought for the Achaean League**"] is that of the year when the Achaeans fell at Leucopetra, fighting the "everywhere victorious" Romans, who now abolish all traces of Greek independence. The year is 146 B.C. In Cavafy's poetry this date has a firm connection with two other previous events which he mentions elsewhere and which were disastrous for Hellenism. One of these events is the battle of Magnesia (190 B.C.), in which the Seleucid Antiochus the Great was utterly defeated by Scipio; and the other is the battle of Pydna (168 B.C.), in which Aemilius Paulus defeated the Macedonians and made an end of their power forever. This historical moment, about fifty years in length, is in the mind of the anonymous Achaean when he envisages the beautiful dead "as something holy which you approach in adoration," and when he whispers: "If Diaios and Critolaus were at fault, you are blameless."

The last generals of the Achaean League, Diaios and Critolaus, were undoubtedly at fault. . . .

The tree was rotten and had to be felled. The whole period is sick. . . . (p. 128)

It is this atmosphere which is emotionally identified by the poet with the atmosphere of 1922, just before "the destruction of the race." . . .

How does Cavafy bring these two periods together? He does it by introducing a connecting link, a third intermediary date, the seventh year (the last but one) of Ptolemy VIII, Lathyrus, 109 B.C. This also was a troubled period. . . . This is the "present time" of the poet as he writes his epigram ["Written in Alexandria by an Achaen/In the seventh year of Ptolemy Lathyrus"]; and the writer of the epigram, in this seventh year of any Ptolemy Lathyrus, is Cavafy, is the nameless Achaean, is both of them together. (p. 130)

All I ask my reader to remember is this: that by alluding, almost imperceptibly, to the fault of Diaios and Critolaus and then to the seventh year of Ptolemy Lathyrus, Cavafy is able to identify the past with the present in a simultaneous moment. . . . Diaios, Critolaus, Philip, Demetrius, Ptolemy Lathyrus, the Achaean, are inside us, and inside us now; each of them could be you and I and everybody who has some consciousness of the evil and of the calamity. (p. 131)

To put it more simply—there is a feeling of temporal identification; past and present are united and with them, perhaps, the future as well. . . . (p. 132)

[This way of using time, is already underlined by T.S.] Eliot in the observations which he makes on James Joyce's *Ulysses*. "In using the myth, in manipulating a continuous parallel between contemporaneity and antiquity, Mr. Joyce is pursuing a method which others must pursue after him. . . . It is simply a way of controlling, of ordering, of giving a shape and a significance to the immense panorama of futility and anarchy which is contemporary history. It is a method already adumbrated by Mr. Yeats, and of the need for which I believe Mr. Yeats to have been the first contemporary to be conscious."

I think that I can legitimately maintain that this method is not only adumbrated, but is systematically employed by Cavafy long before the appearance of *Ulysses* and Joyce, and long before Yeats also.

"I am a historical poet," Cavafy said towards the end of his life. "I could never write a novel or a play; but I hear inside me a hundred and twenty-five voices telling me that I could write history."

Like most fragments of ordinary conversation, this phrase has no very precise meaning. However, I think that "historical poet" does not mean a poet who is also a historian. If the word "poet" has any meaning at all, it must mean a man who has this kind of feeling for history, this historical perception, which we have been examining. . . . (pp. 136-37)

His mind hears the beloved voices in his thought. His "art of poetry" amounts to: "Attempts to numb the pain, in Imagination and Word." (p. 139)

But, one may ask, if Cavafy is incorporating his sensibility in his poetry, why is he so arid? (p. 141)

[Cavafy] seems to reject altogether the unframed expression of emotion. He goes even further; he not only insists on the agility of his characters, the lapidary quality of his events, and the clarity of his historical perceptions which form his own "objective correlative," but he also seems to erase, to neutralize, all other kinds of emotive expression either by the robustness of the language or by the use of other poetic modes, imageries, comparisons or transpositions. . . . [This is one] reason why Cavafy has been called graceless and prosaic.

Very often in Cavafy's work, while the language itself is neutral and unemotional, the movement of the persons and the succession of the events involved is so closely packed, so airtight, one might almost say, that one has the impression that his poems breathe emotion through a vacuum. This vacuum created by Cavafy is the element which differentiates his phrases from the mere prosaicness which his critics have fancied that they saw in his work. (pp. 145-46)

Cavafy has told us: "Seldom, if ever, do I make use of emphasis." When we do encounter it, it should certainly mean something. It did not come there by chance or through a kind of lyrical transport. (p. 148)

So Cavafy's poems often give us the impression that somebody who is not exactly there, but who nevertheless exists, will very soon wake up and then everything will be overturned.

What comes after this I do not know. From this point everyone must proceed in his own way. If poetry were not deeply rooted in our bodies and in our world, it would be a short-lived thing. To stop short at this point, it would have had to be a short-lived thing. We do not know the end of poetry. (pp. 149-50)

[Let] us look back at that phrase of Cavafy's: "I am a historical poet." I said that this could only mean that he is a poet with a certain kind of feeling for history. On this point Eliot has some very definite ideas. Let us consider some of the most characteristic of these.

For Eliot "the historical sense involves a perception, not only of the pastness of the past, but of its presence"; and it "compels a man to write not merely with his own generation in his bones, but with the feeling that the whole of the literature of Europe from Homer and within it the whole of the literature of his own country has a simultaneous existence and composes a simultaneous order.'' So far from being an indolent absorption in the tepid waters of old ways and manners, it is ''what makes a writer most acutely conscious of his place in time, of his own contemporaneity.''

I do not know what Cavafy's views were about his own contemporary world nor about the value of man in general. But when I look at his work I can not help observing that his poetic conscience behaves as if it were in agreement with these views which have just been expressed; his historical sense not only makes him eminently contemporary, but also provides him with just the same method. The permanent element that is endlessly stressed by Cavafy—so much so that it becomes a kind of basic code in his poems—is deception, derision. The panorama unfolded by his poems is a world of dupes and swindlers. Ever since his early years (when in a poem later suppressed he wrote, ''O wretched lyre, victim of every kind of deceit''), ever since his first poems (in one of which he shows Apollo deceiving Thetis like a common scoundrel), up to the very last verse he wrote ('' . . . let him babble./ The important thing is that he nearly burst with rage''), his whole work presents a web of trickeries, traps, ruses, machinations, fears, suspicions, faulty reckonings, mistaken expectations, vain efforts. His gods mock, deride and jeer, his characters are deceitful and at the same time mere playthings in the hands of the gods, of time, of fate, of luck, ''a bone thrown to puppies, a crust of bread in a fishpond, an ant's hardships and drudgery, scurrying of mice, puppets moved by strings.''

There is no saving faith, only a faith in art, and this serves as a king of narcotic elixir in the general betrayal, where we find spun round in the dreadful vortex the noble resignation of a few elderly ladies and a bitter devotion to the great race and tradition of the Greeks. Everything is ''in part . . . in part.''

Cavafy's world exists in the twilight zones, in the borderlands of those places, individuals and epochs which he so painstakingly identifies. It is an area marked by blending, amalgamation, transition, alteration, exceptions; the cities that glow and flicker—Antioch, Alexandria, Sidon, Seleucia, Osroene, Commagene; a hermaphroditic world where even the language spoken is an alloy. And his much publicized eroticism either takes on the behavior of a condemned person, growing old in prison, who, with a fierce insistence, tattoos erotic scenes upon his skin, or else it is diluted among a multitude of dead people and their epitaphs. The tomb of Eurion, the tomb of the Grammarian Lysias, the tomb of Iases, the tomb of Ignatius, the tomb of Lanes; Leucios, Ammones, Myres, Marylos—and so many others. There are so many dead and they are so much alive that we are unable to distinguish them from the men we saw a minute ago, as we were walking in the street, standing at the door of the café, sitting by a casino table, or working in an ironsmith's shop. His ''vain, vain love,'' his barren love is unable to leave anything behind except a mortuary statue, typically beautiful, a cinnamon-brown suit, frayed and discolored, tragically alive, as though fallen from time's saddlebags. This is Cavafy's panorama. All these things together make up the experience of his sensibility—uniform, contemporary, simultaneous, expressed by his historical sense. If I did not think of him in this way, I should not be able to understand him at all. . . . (pp. 150-53)

So much for the historical sense of the old poet of Alexandria. One must own that though he has employed it among innumerable forms and though he has entrusted to death the key, he transmits to us the taste of a kind of horror. (p. 153)

Cavafy is not burdened by the absence of a tradition. On the contrary, what he feels is the dead weight of a tradition which is thousands of years old and which he has done nothing to acquire, since he ''carries in him'' this ''glorious'' literate tradition of the Greeks. He is the solitary of an extreme period of Hellenism, the period of the twentieth century. We may compare him with Synesius in the fifth century A.D., bishop of Ptolemais, admirer of Homer, friend of Hypatia, who was baptized on the same day as he was made bishop; or with the archbishop Michael Choniates in the twelfth century, lamenting over the ancient glories of Athens. So in this boundless country surrounded by ''great and high walls'' he goes forward, treading with his sensitive feet upon ''faces of the dead.'' And the whole question is whether the graves will suck him down or whether he will be able to bring to life with his own blood even so much as a single dry twig in this dead garden—a thing that, for a thousand years before him, no one has yet done in this tradition.

This duality, or division, in Cavafy is something innate. He does not come across it as he grows; he started with it and from it. He does not try to repress it; instead he looks for a way of bringing it together as he gradually develops, ''almost imperceptibly,'' in accordance with his own way, his inner nature, his particular sincerity. . . . And the symbols of his ''waste land'' may be found without going back to forgotten myths; they are inside him; they are himself. For in the ultimate analysis of his poetry only two symbols are left: the dead Adonis who is not restored to life—the sterile Adonis, and Proteus, old, exhausted and sick—the ''Fisher-King,'' who can no longer take on different shapes, and who asks from the magicians of the East herbs and distilled potions to dull the pain of his wound. (pp. 156-57)

The job of a poet is not to solve philosophical or social problems; it is to offer us poetic catharsis by means of his passions and his thoughts, which are concerned both with his inner self and with the world outside him, as is becoming to a living man with his share in this world. Cavafy, as I see him, lying stranded, as he is, in the net of the dead god, gives us this poetical catharsis out of his spiritual heritage, out of his foreknowledge of the world, out of his buried secret, and out of the logic of his personality. However, from his ''waste land,'' as from that of Eliot, there is no exit. The problem remains, and to solve it one would have to change many things in the life of the world we live in. But that is another matter.

This ecumenical problem, in its various forms and its various reactions, goes very deep and marks very deeply the living literature of our times. It is also expressed, as I have attempted to show, by the poetry of Cavafy, Cavafy the grammarian, if we look at him, ''with a searching soul,'' that is to say a soul which cannot but be part of the world we live in. (p. 159)

[Outside] his poems Cavafy does not exist. As it seems to me, one of two things will happen: either we shall continue to write scholastic gossip about his private life, fastening upon the bons mots of provincial witticisms; and then, of course, we shall reap what we have sown; or else, starting from his basic characteristic, his unity, we shall listen to what is actually said by his work, this work in which, drop by drop, he spent his own self, with all his senses. And after having done this, we might attempt to place him and to feel him within the framework of the Greek tradition, the whole tradition, indivisible as it is. (pp. 160-61)

George Seferis, ''Cavafy and Eliot—A Comparison,'' in his On the Greek Style: Selected Essays in

Poetry and Hellenism, *translated by Rex Warner and Th. D. Frangopoulos (translation © Rex Warner 1966; reprinted by permission of Little, Brown and Company in association with the Atlantic Monthly Press), Atlantic-Little Brown, 1966, pp. 119-62.*

A. DECAVALLES (essay date 1968)

Far from being a precocious genius, Cavafy went through long years of trial and experimentation. The few extant remnants of his early verse do not reveal him the poet that he was to be, but around 1903, when he was forty years old, he had already found his way, had already mastered the secrets of the art that was to be characteristically his own for the next thirty years. . . . The word is also especially revealing of the time, circumstance and spirit in which **"Ars"** [in *K. P. Kavafes: Anekdota peza Keimena (C. P. Cavafy: Unpublished Prose Pieces)*] was written. In 1903, as if ready now to launch himself, with clear beliefs, objectives, prospectives and mastered media, upon his future development, he seems, for an instant, to turn a scrutinizing eye back upon the already covered distance, the written poems, to see whether they would fit into the concept of unity that he wanted his work to achieve.

Such a scrutiny would require set standards, set objectives, a theory of poetry. But behind the theorist—who, in the second part is identified, in respect to action, with the philosopher and the poet—there is the practitioner. In these few pages, the poet himself draws the limits of his ground, of his realm, stating the outcome of his experience with his craft, informing us of his poetic creed and the nature that he wished his poetry to have.

The poet, in this respect, should not be the philosopher. "Even when he works the most philosophically" he should remain the artist. He may be aware, as much as the philosopher is, of the multiple and often self-negating and contradictory aspects of things, of the dualities in life. He may be aware of the "highest philosophy" that is "the absolute worthlessness of effort and the inherent contradiction in every human utterance." (p. 70)

Cavafy never aspired to pose as a critic, nor does the document we present have the ambition to present him as one. After all, it is only an unfinished manuscript in his archives. His art was his strength and his limitation. One should not fail to notice, however, the extent to which its few statements, made in 1903 or even earlier, contain clearly the essence of what was to be the poetic theory of the second half of our century, T. S. Eliot's anti-romantic approach to art, the emphasis on objectivity, on self-effacement, on dramatic presentation, on the art of indirection, of the unsaid, of "hints and guesses," on the function of art to raise the individual experience, no matter how truthful, how faithful to reality, to the level of universality.

The second part, a vindication of the poet's claim upon the "high endeavor," as compared with and contrasted to that of the man of action, the hero, states Cavafy's conviction that art does not stand apart from life. His artistic creed stands in strong opposition to the *fin de siècle* fashionable principle of "art for art's sake." His affinities are with Browning rather than Wilde.

The theorist, the philosopher, the poet, do not live in ivory towers. They supply the ideas that the hero materializes. . . . The poet is the chess player, whereas the hero is the pawn in his chess game, Cavafy indicated in one of his poems of 1903 which has not survived. The great events in history, the great cultural movements of humankind, the great revolutions had their origin in the mind and word of the theorist, the philosopher and the poet. Almost a century before, Shelley had called the poets "the unacknowledged legislators of the world." (p. 71)

A. Decavalles, "The Poetics of Cavafy," in The Charioteer *(copyright © 1968 by Parnassas), No. 10, 1968, pp. 69-71.*

ANTHONY BURGESS (essay date 1971)

Cavafy's poems [in **"Passions and Ancient Days"**] are naked, arhetorical, disdainful of such traditional "poetic" properties as the illustrative image (which usually draws attention to nothing but itself) and a diction evocative more of literature than of life. . . . Cavafy's personages, historical or mythical, seem to derive from a living current that bypasses books. This is true even of the poem—**"O Basileus Klaudios"**—that is a wry and politically sophisticated commentary on Shakespeare's own "Hamlet." We are aware of an unassailable poetic complex of heroism and noble agony somewhere far in the background, but we are immediately concerned with the stripped actualities of a political situation: one of the strengths of the poem lies in its tension between two approaches to the subject-matter. Similarly, the figures of Julian the Apostate and Simeon Stylites ("so great a saint, so wonderful a man"—Cavafy's own note in his copy of Gibbon) are seen from an angle that diminishes, even ridicules. The richness of Cavafy is a richness derived from a simultaneous multiplicity of approach; it does not flash out from imposed embroidery.

The erotic poems are not what today's world would call erotic. In the "whorish photograph" ("porniken aute photographia") which is "secretly sold (the policeman mustn't see) around the corner," the poet views, simultaneously with the vulgarity and degradation, "the figure shaped for and dedicated to Hellenic love." If this calls up a *fin-de-siècle* flavor of a maudlin unfrocked classics master in a brothel, we have to counter with the precise meaning of "Hellenic" as Cavafy uses it. Hellenism means more than sentimental velleities; it means the only way of life worth following, strengthened rather than impaired by racial bastardy and the corruptions of exile. In the poem **"Return from Greece"** the speaker despises the "minor kings" who hide Arabia under "their showy hellenified exteriors." . . . (pp. 7, 42-3)

[In Edmund Keeley's and George Savidis's translations the] plain literal English has its own powerful resonances; literary as well as linguistic skill is at work. And yet the voice is Cavafy's, and his only. (p. 43)

Anthony Burgess, "From 75 That Lay on the Bench," in The New York Times Book Review *(© 1971 by The New York Times Company; reprinted by permission), April 18, 1971, pp. 7, 42-3.*

JAMES MERRILL (essay date 1975)

Cavafy is that rare poet whose essential quality comes through even in translation. One sees why Auden thought so. By limiting his subject to human deeds and desires, and his mode to statement, Cavafy makes the rest of us seem to be reading ourselves laboriously backward in a cipher of likenesses and generalizations. He writes without metaphor. Of the natural world we see nothing. The Nile?—an agreeable site for a villa. Flowers?—appropriate to grave or banquet table. Not for Cavafy to presume upon his kinship with sunset and octopus. Having once and for all given the lie to the nonhuman picturesque in eight appalling lines (**"Morning Sea"**), he is free to travel light and fast and far. His reader looks through brilliantly focused vignettes to the tonic ironies beyond.

What ironies? Well, take **"The Mirror in the Front Hall."** The handsome delivery boy gets that far and no further into the house, whose rich privacies would in any case be lost on him. Nor is Cavafy about to pretend interest in anything so conventional, so conjectural, as one more young man's inner life. Is there to be no "understanding," then, beyond that which brings him and his boys together in some anonymous room with its bed and its ceiling fixture? Ignorance is bliss, he might answer—or would he? for it is not ignorance so much as a willed narrowing of frame; and it is not bliss but something drier and longer-lasting, that radiates its own accumulated knowledge. Always, in Cavafy, what one poem withholds, another explains. This coldness of his comes through elsewhere as reticence imposed by an encounter with a god. . . . Indeed, one way to sidestep any real perception of others is to make gods of them. But the ironic wind blows back and forth. The gods appeared to characters in Homer, disguised as a mortal friend or stranger. Put in terms acceptable nowadays, that was a stylized handling of those moments familiar to us all, when the stranger's idle word or the friend's sudden presence happens to strike deeply into our spirits. Moments at the opposite pole from indifference; though on that single pole Cavafy's world revolves.

The unity of divine and human, or past and present, is as real to him as their disparity. Between the poor, unlettered, present-day young men and the well-to-do, educated ones in his historical poems ("Myris . . . reciting verses / with his perfect feeling for Greek rhythm") there is an unbroken bond of type and disposition: what Gongora called "centuries of beauty in a few years of age." This bond is at the marrow of Cavafy's feeling. It reflects his situation as a Greek, the dynamics of his language—indeed the whole legacy of Hellenism—and incidentally distinguishes him from, say, that German baron who spent his adult life in Taormina photographing urchins draped in sheets and wreathed in artificial roses. (pp. 12, 14)

So, in Cavafy, the Greek—or Hellenized—character shines forth: scheming, deluded, gifted, noble, weak. The language survives the reversals of faith and empire, and sharpens the dull wits of the barbarian. The glory dwindles and persists. The overtly historical poems illustrate this great theme in a manner which certain Plutarchian moments in Shakespeare—Casca's deadpan account of a crown refused—read like early attempts to get right. Cavafy himself draws on Plutarch, Herodotus, Gibbon, and a host of "Byzantine historians" whom he praised for writing "a kind of history that had never been written before. They wrote history dramatically." So did he.

Unexpected strands interconnect these historical pieces. A Syrian **"Craftsman of Wine Bowls,"** at work fifteen years after Antiochus the Great's defeat at Magnesia in 190 BC, is overheard while decorating a silver bowl with the remembered figure of a friend killed in that battle. **"The Battle of Magnesia"** itself reminds Philip of Macedonia of his own defeat by the Romans; with scant pity to waste on Antiochus, he calls for roses, music, lights. . . .

Thus, fixed to earth at . . . several points (I have omitted a few), the tent of an entire lost world can be felt to swell and ripple in the air above them. It is not Cavafy's concern to occupy—by spelling out every connection, or cramming with detail—this historical, no, this emotional space. He does some-

thing more skillful yet by suggesting it, by manipulating it. (p. 14)

[Most readers will not] know the fuller context of the historical pieces. But we know what happens in history, to ideas and nations. And we know what happens when a loved one is struck down in youth, or disfigured by age, or leaves us for somebody else, or for Australia. To Cavafy's moments of truth are appended consequences so implicit in the nature of things as hardly having to be uttered. . . .

A reader without Greek will finally, or first of all, respond to the earmark of nearly every Cavafy poem. Like all experienced raconteurs he knows how to repeat himself. Key words—often whole lines—get said over, reiteration serving, since no detail's value can be assured until it "comes to rest in this poetry," to woo it back, fix it more lastingly in the mind. The over-all brevity and compression lend relief to these touches, by turns poignant, wry, haunted. Cavafy's economies are lavish. (p. 15)

[The] mature Cavafy writes a subtle, flexible Greek whose elements—classic, purist, regional, demotic—come together, as Kimon Friar observes, in "an artifice suited to and made integral by his temperament." A comparison to the shifts of manner in a Pound canto would be to the point if, in Cavafy, the unity of temperament weren't everything. . . .

Singlehanded in our century, Cavafy showed the Greek poets who followed him what could be done with their language. In that quarter, he has had the greatest conceivable influence. Yet these later men, with their often superior lyric or epic gifts, their reverence for Earth, their virtuoso talent for metaphor, next to him strike me as loud and provincial (Kazantzakis) or curiously featureless (Seferis and Elytis), through overlong immersion in the new international waters of Eliot, Perse, the surrealists. They have, of course, claimed huge territories for Greek letters; but how gladly, having surveyed those shifting contours, one re-enters the relative security of Cavafy's shabby flat with its view of the street and of the ages. (p. 16)

James Merrill, "Marvelous Poet," in The New York Review of Books *(reprinted by permission of the author), Vol. XXII, No. 12, July 17, 1975, pp. 12-17.*

WILLIS BARNSTONE   (essay date 1977)

When Cavafy uses the Homeric myth, as in the poem **"Ithaka,"** we see the spirit of the young Cavafy. . . . [The] poem is clearly a parable. It tells the reader how to make his life—how Cavafy, identifying with Odysseus, can recall adventure and sensual experience. He uses legend, rather than history, but a legend so deeply part of the Greek mind that the two categories merge. To the Greek, Odysseus and Alexander are hardly of opposing categories of imagination and history. Rather, they lean on each other for completeness as Noah and Moses do in the Bible. For cultural purposes, for the Greek self-image, as it were, history and legend complete and reinforce each other, and each new archeological find—from the labyrinth at Knossos to the bull-horn mountains overlooking Delphi and Nestor's Palace—points to the interdependence of history and myth. (pp. 63-4)

When Odysseus reaches the island of Ithaka, the island is poor. Yet it has not cheated him. With his experience, with his wisdom, he knows what Ithaka means. It is his past. The island gave Odysseus a memory and the voyage to Phoenician markets, Egyptian cities, sensual perfumes and fine things, summer mornings on the wild seas. As for the dangers, the Laistry-gonians, Cyclops, wild Poseidon will not harm him if his spirit is elevated, if he himself does not create these dangers in his soul. For Cavafy the poem is unusually optimistic. Odysseus is near the end of his life. He has been rewarded both with the eventful voyage itself and the knowledge and memory of the voyage. In other poems—the majority—the past looms as both rich and painful; for while Cavafy obscures distinctions of past and present by going back in time—in his room, alone, drunk with a memory of that past—there is in the return an implicit act of desperation. For the need to relive an earlier experience suggests that the present is less rich than it should be, that future time is nothing—in effect, that the thread of hope, which requires a notion of futurity, is missing. Loss haunts him. The excellent poem **"The Afternoon Sun"** speaks of the room of love as now an office for agents, tradesmen, and companies. (pp. 65-6)

Joy and despair pervade the poems: joy and ecstasy identified with a recollection of a sensual love experience in the past; despair tinging everything as historical figures are revealed as victims of their own weakness, futilely driven to acting out their roles. Despair is most decisively apparent when the action is focused on a recognition of a present with future impossi-bilities, with a future blackened by unredeemed death. In the famous poem **"Waiting for the Barbarians"** . . . , the theme of despair or hopelessness is considered with allegorical humor. The barbarians are coming. We will change our lives, we will prepare, we will practice our speeches and put on our best robes. But then word comes that the barbarians are not coming, that indeed there are no more barbarians. We can do nothing now, he writes. They were some kind of solution. Elsewhere Cavafy looks for light and then turns away. He is distressed by the impotence and weakness of age and what further light may reveal to him. Even in an early poem like **"The Win-dows,"** a note of pessimism, remarkably like a Kafkian par-able, is already there. . . . (p. 66)

I have indicated that in Cavafy, myth and history come to-gether. And this is central to Cavafy's historical preoccupation. (p. 67)

[In **"The God Abandons Antony"**] is the evocation of a great figure, Antony. Yet in keeping with the practice of . . . Cavafy to seek man's frailty, the humanity that makes a historical personage credible, Antony is depicted as one who now must no longer fool himself with empty hopes. His courage . . . lies in listening to the music of Alexandria, in acknowledging the Alexandria he is losing, in accepting stoically the death which will confirm the reality of earlier failure. (pp. 69-70)

Cavafy lives to the end exploiting personal and historical mem-ory of real and imaginary events; he lessens the despair of the voyage because of his involvement in the fictions he creates, in short, through his poems, which he would not publish during his life. (p. 72)

Willis Barnstone, "Real and Imaginary History in Borges and Cavafy," in Comparative Literature *(© copyright 1977 by University of Oregon; reprinted by permission of* Comparative Literature*), Vol. XXIX, No. 1, Winter, 1977, pp. 54-73.**

GEORGE ECONOMOU   (essay date 1981)

[**"Craftsman of Wine Bowls"**] distinctly illustrates the com-bination of the personal and political, the private and public, spheres that so often intersect in some of Cavafy's most com-plex and memorable poems. Here the artist, working on com-mission by a great family, has the power nonetheless to insin-uate his individual celebration of his love as he experiences simultaneously the eroding effects of time upon his memory of that love. The poem dramatizes a moment of artistic assertion undercut by the recognition of the difficulty of successfully fulfilling its goals. The poem is one of many in the Cavafy canon that express something he stated more generally in prose in an essay he wrote in English:

> I have said above that the poet always remains
> an artist. As an artist he should avoid—without
> denying—the seemingly highest—seemingly,
> for it is not quite proved that it is the highest—
> philosophy of the absolute worthlessness of ef-
> fort and of the inherent contradiction in every
> human utterance.

That the artisan dates his loss by the battle that marks the onset of Roman dominance in the Hellenized East, provides an ironic historical context that is perhaps more meaningful to the reader than to the speaker of the poem. Relative chronological prox-imity to the battle provides the speaker with his poignancy, chronological distance provides the reader with his ironic per-spective. The final Cavafian twist (if it can be called that) proposes that by extension the poet himself as well as his reader, just like the craftsman-persona, are participants in their own immediate situations which are subject to partially under-stood historical forces and are full of passion and loss. Pathetic, often tragic, these situations are intermittently dignified by art's attempt to record their sincerity and intensity.

As is true of many Cavafy poems, **"Craftsman of Wine Bowls"** can be read as part of a set of poems linked by an historical event. . . . [It is] part of a constellation of poems formed on the basis of their individual dealing with the aftermath of the battle of Magnesia (190 B.C.). This important trait of Cavafy's historical poems is enhanced by the fact that quite a few of them have a share in more than one set, which emphasizes their quality of being self-contained, finished fragments of a greater whole, serviceable pieces carefully cut out of the seam-less garment of history. Yet **"Craftsman"** can be as reward-ingly studied in the context of its belonging to a large group of poems that are connected through thematic affinity. A good number of Cavafy's poems deal specifically with the problems of the artist and poet, most notably the problem of the effects of time upon the artist's ability to memorialize in his work a person or experience, invariably recalled for their erotic sig-nificance, that he cares for profoundly. In fact, eros, memory, and art, whether interacting in an historically based monologue or in one of the "autobiographical" poems, are among the major topical forces in Cavafy's total work. It is not surprising that the best criticism of that work . . . warns against a too rigid classification of his poetic corpus; for it is through the successful integration of his perception of the meanings of eros, memory, and art that Cavafy achieved the vision that he so convincingly expressed through so many personae in so many times and places. (p. 31)

George Economou, "Eros, Memory, and Art" (copyright © 1981 by World Poetry, Inc.; reprinted by permission of George Economou), in The Amer-ican Poetry Review, *Vol. 10, No. 4, July-August, 1981, pp. 30-1.**

ADDITIONAL BIBLIOGRAPHY

Durrell, Lawrence. "C. P. Cavafy: A Real Heart-Transplant into English." *The New York Times Book Review* (21 January 1973): 2-3.
> Accolade for Cavafy's current translators and editors and some reasons for his slow recognition.

Enright, D. J. "Tales of Alexandria." *New Statesman* 62, No. 1589 (25 August 1961): 244-45.
> Compares John Mavrogordato's English translation of Cavafy in 1951 to Rae Dalven's in 1948.

Golffing, Francis. "The Alexandrian Mind: Notes toward a Definition." *Partisan Review* XXII, No. 1 (Winter 1955): 73-82.
> Facets of recurrent Alexandrianism defined, Cavafy representing a recent incarnation.

Klingopulos, G. D. "E. M. Forster's Sense of History: And Cavafy." *Essays in Criticism* VIII, No. 2 (April 1958): 156-65.*
> Credits Cavafy with broadening Forster's historical perspective.

Liddell, Robert. *Cavafy: A Critical Biography*. London: Gerald Duckworth & Co., 1974, 222 p.
> Details the life and works.

Plomer, William. "C. P. Cavafy." In his *Electric Delights*, pp. 151-54. Boston: David R. Godine, 1978.
> Summary of elements in the poetry; for example, Cavafy's "sense of continuity" and "erotic intensity."

Smith, William Jay. "Poet of the City." In his *The Streaks of the Tulip: Selected Criticism*, pp. 330-36. New York: Delacorte Press, 1954.
> Brief discussion of Cavafy's style and themes.

Raymond Chandler

1888-1959

American novelist, short story writer, essayist, screenwriter, poet, and critic.

Along with Dashiell Hammett, Chandler elevated the genre known as the hard-boiled detective story into an American art form. His novels describe luridly realistic action in a sophisticated literary style uncommon to pulp mystery fiction. Chandler wanted to treat genuine mysteries which do not lend themselves to the solutions of deductive reasoning, and added an element of fantasy to his work in order to suggest, as he put it, "the country behind the hill." At the same time, his detective hero Philip Marlowe operates in a world of banal corruption and commercialized living. For many readers Chandler's books represent the essence of southern California: the superficialities of Hollywood, crime and vice glossed over with wealth, the cult of glamor, and a certain enduring mystery which eludes precise definition.

Chandler was born in Chicago. When he was seven years old, his parents divorced and he was taken by his mother to live in England. He grew up in a suburb outside London and attended Dulwich College, acquiring a thorough classical education and taking a particular interest in languages. Among those he studied were Latin, French, German, Armenian, and Hungarian. After graduation he traveled in France and Germany, returning to England to work as a civil servant. During this time he also wrote poetry, reviews, and essays for *The Academy* and the *Westminster Gazette;* much of this work displayed the aesthetic concerns and romantic themes of his later detective fiction. In 1912 Chandler abandoned his literary career, left England, and came to the United States. During the First World War he joined the Canadian Army, still feeling himself a British subject, and fought at the front lines in France. His next return to the United States was permanent. He moved to California, married Pearl Cecily Hurlburt ("Cissie"), a woman eighteen years his senior, and worked for the Dabney Oil Syndicate. It wasn't until Chandler was middle-aged, and had lost his job as a chief executive with the oil firm, that he again began writing.

Chandler's initial efforts in fiction were short stories written for pulp detective magazines like *Black Mask*. In the beginning he had little experience with mystery stories, either as reader or writer. He studied the form, familiarizing himself with the narrative devices of such successful authors in the genre as Erle Stanley Gardner, creator of Perry Mason. Ultimately, Chandler brought to the detective story a verbal expertise and highly original talent for characterization and description, but the demands of the market and the short story form limited the full use of his powers. In his novel-length fiction Chandler was allowed to expand his stylistic traits. Much of the material from the short stories was "cannibalized" for the longer works; characters, scenes, and descriptions, as critical analyses have shown, were often vastly improved.

Chandler's first novel, *The Big Sleep,* introduces the detective and narrator Philip Marlowe. Though Marlowe had prototypes in the hard-boiled sleuths of the short stories, he now appears as a protagonist of unmistakeable originality while

also bearing an ironic resemblance to the stereotypical private eye. As many critics have recognized, Marlowe's flinty persona—his cynical outlook, bitter wit, and outlaw self-image—is a thin disguise for the frustrated ideals and sentimentalism of one of the most romantic characters in American literature. He is often likened to the knights of medieval romance. *Farewell, My Lovely,* Chandler's second and some say his best novel, established him as a major detective writer. The identifying characteristics of his work are now apparent, primarily his use of a central mystery revealed by a story's characters rather than the plot complications of traditional whodunits. The next two novels, *The High Window* and *The Lady in the Lake,* are generally considered lesser productions. In *The Little Sister* Chandler makes use of his experiences, mostly unpleasant, as a Hollywood screenwriter. Critics have noted, and Chandler himself admitted, that this novel contains the most intense cynicism of any Marlowe adventure.

Chandler's last major work, *The Long Goodbye,* was an occasion for the author to extend the possibilities of the mystery genre, developing its capacity for social and psychological analysis and expanding the role of the detective. Marlowe's attitude toward women in most of the novels has often been labeled misogynistic; commentators sometimes psychoanalyze him as an immature, ideal-seeking romantic at best, and possibly a woman-hating homosexual. However, in *The Long Goodbye* Marlowe is seen by some critics as making a leap toward the reconciliation of romance and reality. As well as exposing a beautiful and psychopathic blonde as the murderer, as in other novels, Marlowe also meets the woman who becomes his wife in the unfinished *Poodle Springs Story*.

Throughout his career Chandler attempted to remove his writings from the formulaic suspense of detective fiction, to the extent that he is often considered an excellent novelist but a rather lame mystery writer. The foregoing estimate of Chandler's literary value is perhaps best expressed by W. H. Auden, himself a devotee of mysteries, who maintained that Chandler's books should be evaluated "as works of art."

(See also *TCLC*, Vol. 1.)

PRINCIPAL WORKS

The Big Sleep (novel) 1939
Farewell, My Lovely (novel) 1940
The High Window (novel) 1943
The Lady in the Lake (novel) 1944
The Little Sister (novel) 1949
The Simple Art of Murder (essay and short stories) 1950
The Long Goodbye (novel) 1954
Raymond Chandler Speaking (letters, short story, and unfinished novel) 1962
Killer in the Rain (short stories) 1964
Chandler before Marlowe (poetry, essays, and criticism) 1973
The Notebooks of Raymond Chandler, and English Summer (notebooks and short story) 1976
Selected Letters of Raymond Chandler (letters) 1981

WILL CUPPY (essay date 1939)

[*The Big Sleep*] should stir up a lot of valuable discussion. It can boast of an admirable hard-boiled manner, it contains several characters who will scare you with their extraordinary brands of wickedness, and the nightmare atmosphere is the real thing in spots. In our opinion, though, Mr. Chandler has almost spoiled it with a top-heavy cargo of lurid underworld incident, and he should therefore be stood in a corner and lectured upon the nature and suitable use of his talents. . . . Phil Marlowe is a slick sleuth in the Hammett tradition. It's a much better than average tough item; we're only saying that it might have been better with less high-pressure plot—but, then, it would have been another story. Moreover, Mr. Chandler deserves a medal for his handling of some wicked scenes; we shudder to think what some of our bad young bafflers would have done with them.

> *Will Cuppy, "Mystery and Adventure: 'The Big Sleep'," in* New York Herald Tribune Books, *February 5, 1939, p. 12.*

RAYMOND CHANDLER (essay date 1939)

The Big Sleep is very unequally written. There are scenes that are all right, but there are other scenes still much too pulpy. Insofar as I am able I want to develop the objective method—

but slowly—to the point where I can carry an audience over into a genuine dramatic, even melodramatic, novel, written in a very vivid and pungent style, but not slangy or overly vernacular. I realize that this must be done cautiously and little by little, but I think it can be done. To acquire delicacy without losing power, that's the problem. (pp. 209-10)

> *Raymond Chandler, in his letter to Alfred A. Knopf on February 19, 1939, in his* Raymond Chandler Speaking, *edited by Dorothy Gardiner and Kathrine Sorley Walker (copyright © 1962 by the Helga Greene Literary Agency; reprinted by permission of Houghton Mifflin Company),* Four Square Books, *1962 (and reprinted by Houghton Mifflin Company, 1977), pp. 207-10.*

ISAAC ANDERSON (essay date 1940)

["**Farewell, My Lovely**"] is a tough one: superlatively tough, alcoholic, and, for all its wisecracks, ugly rather than humorous. Like many "swift-moving" tales, it is sometimes confusing in its rapid succession of incidents which may or may not have an integral connection with the plot. And the actual mystery is not important. It isn't so difficult to guess what had become of the beautiful cabaret singer Velma. The identity of the unpleasing Lindsay Marriott's slayer has no pressing interest. The murder casually committed by that elemental giant Moose Malloy is only an episode to start the story going. No, the appeal of "**Farewell, My Lovely**" is in its toughness, which is extremely well done.

Jessie Florian may know something or nothing about Velma, but Philip Marlowe's questioning of that gin-soaked old woman makes as sordid a bit as you're likely to be looking for. Beautiful Mrs. Grayle has a real place in the story, but it's the sense of evil all about her that gives you goose-flesh. And Amthor the "psychic consultant" and Sonderberg the "dope doctor" are lesser figures in a novel in which no detail is left undescribed.

But the story's ever-present theme is police corruption, seen in a murky variety. And several kinds of dreadfulness are handled with a grisly skill.

> *Isaac Anderson, "New Mystery Stories," in* The New York Times Book Review *(© 1940 by The New York Times Company; reprinted by permission), November 17, 1940, p. 29.**

RAYMOND CHANDLER (essay date 1945)

All I wanted to do when I began writing was to play with a fascinating new language, to see what it would do as a means of expression which might remain on the level of unintellectual thinking and yet acquire the power to say things which are usually only said with a literary air. I didn't really care what kind of story I wrote; I wrote melodrama because when I looked around me it was the only kind of writing I saw that was relatively honest and yet was not trying to put over somebody's party line. So now there are guys talking about prose and other guys telling me I have a social conscience. P. Marlowe has as much social conscience as a horse. He has a personal conscience, which is an entirely different matter.

There are people who think I dwell on the ugly side of life. God help them! If they had any idea how little I have told them about it! P. Marlowe doesn't give a damn who is President; neither do I, because I know he will be a politician. There was even a bird who informed me I could write a good proletarian novel; in my limited world there is no such animal, and if there were, I am the last mind in the world to like it, being by tradition and long study a complete snob. P. Marlowe and I do not despise the upper classes because they take baths and have money; we despise them because they are phoney. (pp. 214-15)

Raymond Chandler, in his letter to Dale Warren on January 7, 1945, in his Raymond Chandler Speaking, *edited by Dorothy Gardiner and Kathrine Sorley Walker (copyright © 1962 by the Helga Greene Literary Agency; reprinted by permission of Houghton Mifflin Company),* Four Square Books, 1962 (and reprinted by Houghton Mifflin Company, 1977), pp. 214-15.*

W. H. AUDEN (essay date 1948)

Mr. Raymond Chandler has written that he intends to take the body out of the vicarage garden and give murder back to those who are good at it. If he wishes to write detective stories, *i.e.*, stories where the reader's principal interest is to learn who did it, he could not be more mistaken; for in a society of professional criminals, the only possible motives for desiring to identify the murderer are blackmail or revenge, which both apply to individuals, not to the group as a whole, and can equally well inspire murder. Actually, whatever he may say, I think Mr. Chandler is interested in writing, not detective stories, but serious studies of a criminal milieu, the Great Wrong Place, and his powerful but extremely depressing books should be read and judged, not as escape literature, but as works of art. (p. 408)

W. H. Auden, "The Guilty Vicarage: Notes on the Detective Story, by an Addict," in Harper's *(copyright © 1948; copyright renewed © 1976 by Monroe K. Spears and William Meredith as executors to the Estate of W. H. Auden; reprinted by permission), Vol. 196, No. 1176, May, 1948, pp. 406-12.**

RAYMOND CHANDLER (essay date 1949)

I believe *Farewell, My Lovely* would be called the best of my books, *The High Window* the worst, but I have known people who would pick any of them as against the others. In some ways my last, [*The Little Sister*], is the best. But I'll never again equal *The Big Sleep* for pace nor *Farewell, My Lovely* for plot complication. I probably don't want to; the time comes when you have to choose between pace and depth of focus, between action and character, menace and wit. I now choose the second in each case.

Raymond Chandler, in an extract from his letter to Alex Barris on April 16, 1949, in his Raymond Chandler Speaking, *edited by Dorothy Gardiner and Kathrine Sorley Walker (copyright ©1962 by the Helga Greene Literary Agency; reprinted by permission of Houghton Mifflin Company),* Four Square Books, 1962 (and reprinted by Houghton Mifflin Company, 1977), p. 222.*

R. W. LID (essay date 1969)

Chandler was an extraordinary cultural historian, and, while time and circumstance have somewhat lessened the immediacy of his Los Angeles of the '30s and '40s, they have not rendered it obsolete. (p. 153)

It was Chandler's seriousness which set him, like Dashiell Hammett, apart from the *Black Mask* school of hard-boiled writers out of which they emerged. The extraordinary colloquial quality of Chandler's prose was an aspect of this seriousness: it made available the expression of his vision. Chandler's sun-bleached landscape, for all the Hollywood glitter, is in part a fallen paradise, a Garden of Eden after the serpent has done his work.

As Chandler so often reminds us, his demiparadise is a land of drifters, grafters, and minor hoodlums; of lone women on the make or on the downhill; of sad drunks and mean drunks, and just drunks: people with better days behind them. In this world cops, as often as not, are crooked, politicians corrupt, and businessmen walk the narrow line between legitimate and illegitimate enterprise. "There ain't no clean way to make a hundred million bucks," says Bernie Ohls, a tough and honest cop, to Philip Marlowe, Chandler's private detective, in *The Long Goodbye*. Some 60 pages later, in the same novel, Chandler's private detective says to Ohls: "We're a big rough rich wild people and crime is the price we pay for it, and organized crime is the price we pay for organization. We'll have it with us a long time. Organized crime is just the dirty side of the sharp dollar." In both instances the voice speaking is the thinly disguised voice of the author. It is almost as if Chandler, making his own goodbye in his last serious novel, wanted to state directly what the plots of his earlier novels had failed fully to convey. For it was part of Chandler's originality that he saw the American psyche as criminally obsessed with the dollar, and, perhaps without being fully aware of it, society itself as criminal. In the end Chandler's romantic sensibility recoiled from the vision of evil which his art insisted upon.

Something of the same sense of a lost paradise which haunts the last page of *The Great Gatsby* pervades Chandler's Pacific Eden. I have in mind Nick Carraway's evocation of "the fresh, green breast of the new world" and his vision of its trees, which "had once pandered in whispers to the last and greatest of all human dreams." Chandler similarly poses through the juxtaposition of landscape and people the imaginative possibilities of the American continent, and also suggests some reasons for the failure to realize them. But unlike Fitzgerald in *Gatsby*, Chandler in his fiction was mainly concerned with the aftermath of the dream, the fallen state of the world after the dream has not merely become tawdry and tarnished but exists only as a debased passion. (pp. 154-55)

Chandler was a master at portraying the schizoid aspects of American culture and the ways in which the base and ideal and their manifestations are so closely intertwined as to be inseparable, if not indistinguishable. The lives of his characters reveal this split in motive and intention and conduct, just as the patterns of his novels reveal the cohesiveness of American life which underlies and makes a whole of this self-perpetuating opposition.

Marlowe crosses and crisscrosses the landscape of greater Los Angeles, which provides almost infinite variety of background, moving from terrain to terrain, locale to locale, setting to setting. Chandler bears down so heavily on landscape in his novels that physical property almost takes on a value and meaning of its own; one is reminded of the motion pictures and the way in which the camera invests physical props with significance by panning back and forth over them, by lingering with them.

But, while the vastly different places Chandler's Marlowe visits, and the people he encounters, are seemingly held together by a thread of meaning solely of Marlowe's making, a pattern gradually emerges, a meaningful arrangement and sequence of events: and behind this pattern lies, broadly speaking, the pattern of American society as Chandler sees it: mobile, fluid, a reticulated crisscrossing of people through time and circumstance. One begins to see why, in Chandler's fiction, the world of Los Angeles' Bunker Hill, with its decayed buildings and decaying people, is just a stone's throw away from the deep lawns and private driveways and stately mansions of Santa Monica; why, in other words, all segments of society are inextricably linked in Chandler's sun-filled but nightmarish landscape. (pp. 156-57)

[In] general, it could be fairly said that Chandler extended the form by making available to writers who came after him a more complex understanding of the fabric of society and a more serious and sensitive view of its dynamics. This is no small achievement in itself.

Along with Hammett, Chandler gave the detective story back its inherent realism. But he also added a personal dimension to the form—and here Marlowe played a less traditional role than the one . . . in which his function was to search out and make visible the links between people and events and reveal the developing pattern of significance.

Chandler once said that "Marlowe just grew out of the pulps. He was no one person." . . . Marlowe seems to have made possible . . . the emergence of a highly personal voice, one that seemed to speak directly to readers everywhere in the authentic rhythms of American speech. Precisely how Marlowe made these developments possible for his British-educated author is a somewhat complex matter, as is the whole question of Chandler's relationship with his narrator-hero and its meaning for his art. (pp. 158-59)

[While] Chandler's wasn't a native American voice, Philip Marlowe's invented voice is. (p. 160)

Chandler's alien voice can be heard quite clearly in the volume *Raymond Chandler Speaking,* particularly in his letters to his English publisher, Hamish Hamilton, and to Charles W. Morton, an editor for the *Atlantic Monthly.* (p. 161)

It is hard at times to estimate the sincerity of the Chandler of the letters, for one thing because, without being a poseur, he is obviously posing to a certain extent. This Chandler is bent on justifying his career and propagating his reputation. And underneath, much of the time, he is feeling sorry for himself. He unjustly arraigns other writers. He makes mock modest comparisons between his achievements and those of others, denying that he is in their class as a writer but implying all the while that he is every bit their equal or better. He is seemingly humble while really prideful, his ironic sense of self dominating his feelings: "What greater prestige can a man like me (not too greatly gifted, but very understanding) have than to have taken a cheap, shoddy, and utterly lost kind of writing, and have made of it something that intellectuals claw each other about?" He is also neglecting Hammett, whose earlier achievement might be described in precisely the same terms.

He will knock the intellectuals, while being one himself. He harbors petty grievances. He sees himself in most situations as wronged. He is contentious. He indulges himself by answering letters from readers in which he argues in detail the personal habits of Marlowe, momentarily turning him into a real person. There is a certain self-laceration here, because he knows the reader is interested in Marlowe, not Chandler. And all the while, it strikes one, Chandler is strangely disaffected with Marlowe; or perhaps he is merely aware that in Marlowe he created a man more admirable than himself, forgetful that without Raymond Chandler there would be no Marlowe. In any case, he envisions Cary Grant as the movie actor who could best portray Marlowe as he conceives of him—a transplanted Englishman with inherently nice manners. One can't help but feel that Marlowe would be amused by this identification; but, I think, he would also find it revealing of his author, and in keeping with his character.

The Raymond Chandler of these letters, which were written mainly during his sixties, is a man under considerable personal and psychological stress. He is preoccupied with himself in ways that are somewhat touching, and also pathetic. He shows a certain helplessness. He suffers mild paranoia. And he reveals, without intending to, something of the transformation of character, the rearrangement of personal experience, which went on in the creation of his fiction, as well as the role Marlowe played in this transmutation.

Essentially Marlowe released in Chandler a vein of self-criticism and self-knowledge. He tapped the secret resources, the reserves of his author's personality, those hidden forces which drove him to fiction, and made them available to the fiction writer as they weren't to the letter writer. All of Chandler's hostile emotions, his aggressive tendencies, his anti-social feelings, his loneliness, his self-pity, which he never fully mastered, were transformed in fictional creations which not only bore a striking resemblance to the real world but revealed memorable truths about that world.

Marlowe gave Chandler someone to talk to, as well as speak through, so that the speaking voice we hear in Chandler's fiction is not an alien voice but that of a man purified in the fire of the human inferno. (pp. 162-63)

Over the years readers of Chandler's novels, as well as commentators on his art, have been struck by the heavy vein of gratuitous emotion in the Marlowe of *The Long Goodbye,* Chandler's last novel of importance. . . . (p. 170)

The Long Goodbye turns out to be a profoundly autobiographical novel in which the author on an imaginative level explores his own past and those aspects of his personality which continued to engage him. Ultimately the emotion that Marlowe expends in *The Long Goodbye* is for his author and the butt-end of his days.

In retrospect, even the minor figure of the writer in *The Long Goodbye* bears a broad resemblance to Raymond Chandler. Roger Wade is the author of a dozen best-selling historical novels; Chandler was the author of a half-dozen highly successful detective novels. Also, Chandler wanted to be a historical novelist but was talked out of it by his publisher. Wade drinks excessively, he has trouble finishing the book he is working on. He thinks little of himself and his talent. "You're looking at a small time operator in a small time business. . . . All writers are punks and I am one of the punkest." In discussing with Marlowe the possible reasons for Wade's drinking, his wife offers the suggestion that perhaps she's the cause. "Men fall out of love with their wives." Marlowe replies: "I'd say it's more likely he has fallen out of love with the kind of stuff he writes." In terms of the plot of *The Long Goodbye,* both Mrs. Wade and Marlowe are partly right. (pp. 171-72)

It would of course be a dubious procedure to read Roger Wade's statements in *The Long Goodbye* as having a point-by-point application to Chandler personally, though it seems likely that on some level Chandler was working out the ambivalence he felt toward his own achievement as a writer in ways impossible to relate in his correspondence. In *The Long Goodbye* Roger Wade's wife and his publisher want to hire Marlowe to guard him from drinking and doing himself bodily harm so he can finish the book he is working on. Marlowe wants to refuse but never fully does so. He rescues Wade from the ranch of a doctor in Sepulveda Canyon who is drying him out, and he intervenes on other occasions. It is almost as if Marlowe were Roger Wade's guardian angel, and also as if, on another level, a part of Raymond Chandler were keeping watch over another. Not surprisingly, in terms of events in the novel Wade's compulsive drinking is only in a limited way connected with his writing: all the talk about writing is in point of fact irrelevant—except that it vitally concerns Raymond Chandler.

In the end Marlowe cannot save Roger Wade from suicide, or, rather, from being murdered, for his wife kills him and makes it appear a suicide; but this event occurs only when the plot of Chandler's long novel demands his death—when, in effect, Chandler's new alter ego has said all that he wants him to say. By then, the essential parallel between Chandler's doubles has been directly sounded. At one point in the novel, the writer says to the detective: "You know something, Marlowe? I could get to like you. You're a bit of a bastard—like me." When, much later in the novel, Marlowe informs Wade's publisher, Harold Spencer, of his death, the words he uses echo this conversation: "Roger Wade is dead, Spencer. He was a bit of a bastard and maybe a genius too. That's over my head. He was an egotistical drunk and hated his own guts." Where in all this maze of romantically conceived self-criticism Raymond Chandler really stood is perhaps impossible to tell, and ultimately it is unimportant, for it is clear that Chandler was harder on himself than anyone else ever was—or will be. (pp. 172-73)

> *R. W. Lid, "Philip Marlowe Speaking," in* The Kenyon Review *(copyright 1969 by Kenyon College), Vol. XXXI, No. 2, Spring, 1969, pp. 153-78.*

FREDRIC JAMESON   (essay date 1970)

Chandler thought of himself primarily as a stylist, and it was his distance from the American language that gave him the chance to use it as he did. In that respect his situation was not unlike that of Nabokov: the writer of an adopted language is already a kind of stylist by force of circumstance. . . . The detective story, as a form without ideological content without any overt political or social or philosophical point, permits . . . pure stylistic experimentation. (p. 625)

[A] case can be made for Chandler as a painter of American life: not as a builder of those large-scale models of the American experience which great literature offers, but rather in fragmentary pictures of setting and place, fragmentary perceptions which are by some formal paradox somehow inaccessible to serious literature. (p. 626)

The last great period of American literature, which ran more or less from one world war to the other, explored and defined America in a geographical mode, as a sum of separate localisms, as an additive unity, at its outside limit an ideal sum. But since the War, the organic differences from region to region have been increasingly obliterated by standardization; and the organic social unity of each region has been increasingly fragmented and abstracted by the new closed lives of the individual family units, by the breakdown of cities and the dehumanization of transportation and of the media which lead from one monad to another. (p. 628)

Chandler lies somewhere between these two literary situations. His whole background, his way of thinking and of seeing things, derives from the period between the wars. But by an accident of place, his social content anticipates the realities of the fifties and sixties. For Los Angeles is already a kind of microcosm and forecast of the country as a whole: a new centerless city, in which the various classes have lost touch with each other because each is isolated in his own geographical compartment. If the symbol of social coherence and comprehensibility was furnished by the nineteenth-century Parisian apartment house (dramatized in Zola's *Pot-Bouille*) with its shop on the ground floor, its wealthy inhabitants on the second and third, petty bourgeoisie further up, and workers' rooms on top along with the maids and servants, then Los Angeles is the opposite, a spreading out horizontally, a flowing apart of the elements of the social structure. (p. 629)

The action of Chandler's books takes place inside the microcosm, in the darkness of a local world without the benefit of the federal Constitution, as in a world without God. The literary shock is dependent on the habit of the political double standard in the mind of the reader: it is only because we are used to thinking of the nation as a whole in terms of justice that we are struck by these images of people caught in the power of a local county authority as absolutely as though they were in a foreign country. The local power apparatus is beyond appeal, in this other face of federalism; the rule of naked force and money is complete and undisguised by any embellishments of theory. In an eery optical illusion, the jungle reappears in the suburbs.

In this sense the honesty of the detective can be understood as an organ of perception, a membrane which, irritated, serves to indicate in its sensitivity the nature of the world around it. For if the detective is dishonest, his job boils down to the technical problem of how to succeed on a given assignment. If he is honest, he is able to feel the resistance of things, to permit an intellectual vision of what he goes through on the level of action. And Chandler's sentimentalism, which attaches to occasional honest characters in the earlier books, but which is perhaps strongest in *The Long Goodbye,* is the reverse and complement of this vision, a momentary relief from it, a compensation for it: where everything is seen in a single light, there is not much possibility for subtlety or variety of feelings to develop, there is available only the ground tonality and its opposite. (pp. 632-33)

Raymond Chandler's novels have not one form, but two, an objective form and a subjective one, the rigid external structure of the detective story on the one hand, and a more personal distinctive rhythm of events on the other, arranged, as is the case with any novelist of originality, according to some ideal molecular chain in the brain cells, as personal in their encephalographic pattern as a fingerprint, peopled with recurrent phantoms, obsessive character types, actors in some forgotten psychic drama through whom the social world continues to be interpreted. Yet the two kinds of form do not conflict with each other; on the contrary the second seems to have been generated out of the first by the latter's own internal contradictions. Indeed, it results from a kind of formula on Chandler's part:

It often seems to this particular writer that the only reasonably honest and effective way of fooling the reader that remains is to make the reader exercise his mind about the wrong problem, to make him, as it were, solve a mystery (since he is almost sure to solve something) which will land him in a bypath because it is only tangential to the central problem.

For the detective story is not only a purely intellectual mode of knowing events, it is also a puzzle in which the faculties of analysis and reasoning are to be exercised, and Chandler here simply generalizes a technique of outwitting the reader. Instead of the innovation that will only work once (the most famous is of course that of Agatha Christie in *The Murder of Roger Ackroyd,* where as is well known the murderer turns out to be the narrator himself), he invents a principle for the construction of the plot itself. (p. 644)

[As] has already been made apparent in Chandler's description of his own plot construction, this trail of bloodshed is a false scent, designed to draw the reader's attention to guilt in the wrong places. The diversion is not dishonest, inasmuch as the guilt uncovered along the way is also real enough; the latter is simply not that with which the book is directly involved. Hence the episodic nature of the diversionary plot: the characters are drawn in heightened, sharp fashion because we will never see them again. Their entire essence must be revealed in a single brief meeting. Yet these meetings take place on a different plane of reality from that of the main plot of the book. It is not only that the intellectual function of our mind is busy weighing and selecting them (are they related in some way to the search or are they not?) in a set of operations which it does not have to perform on the materials of the main plot (the client and his or her household, the person sought and his or her connections). The very violence and crimes themselves are here apprehended on a different mode: since they are tangential and secondary for us, we learn of them in a manner not so much realistic (novelistic) as legendary, much as we would hear about occasional violence in the newspaper or over the radio. Our interest in them is purely anecdotal, and is already a kind of distance from them. Whether we know it yet or not therefore, these characters of the secondary plot exist for us in a different dimension, like glimpses through a window, noises from the back of a store, unfinished stories, unrelated activities going on in the society around us simultaneously with our own.

The climax of the book must therefore involve a return to its beginning, to the initial plot and characters. Obviously the person searched for must be found. But in a perhaps less obvious way, the guilty party must turn out to be in one way or another a member of the family, the client or a member of his entourage. Chandler's novels are all variations on this pattern, almost mathematically predictable combinations and permutations of these basic possibilities: the missing person is dead and the client did it, or the missing person is guilty and the body found was that of somebody else, or both the client and a member of her entourage are guilty and the missing person is not really missing at all, and so forth. (pp. 646-47)

The final element in Chandler's characteristic form is that the underlying crime is always old, lying half-forgotten in the pasts of the characters before the book begins. This is the principal reason why the reader's attention is diverted from it: he assumes it to be part of the dimension of the present, of the events going on before him in the immediacy of his narrated universe.

Instead, it is buried in that world's past, in time, among the dead evoked in the memorable closing page of *The Big Sleep*.

And suddenly the purely intellectual effect of Chandler's construction formula is metamorphized into a result of unmistakable aesthetic intensity. From the point of view of abstract curiosity we might expect the reader to have a reaction not altogether unmixed: satisfaction at the solution of the puzzle, irritation at having been misled through so much extraneous material which had no real bearing on it. And on the aesthetic level the irritation remains, but transfigured.

For now, at the end, all the events of the book are seen in a new and depressing light: all that energy and activity wasted to find somebody who had in reality been dead for so long, for whom the time of the present was little more than a process of slow physical dissolution. And suddenly, at the thought of that dissolution, and of the mindless lack of identity of the missing person so long called by name, the very appearance of life itself, of time in the present, of the bustling activity of the outside world, is stripped away and we feel in its place the presence of graves beneath the bright sunlight; the present fades to little more than a dusty, once lived moment which will quickly take its place in the back years of an old newspaper file. And our formal distraction at last serves its fundamental purpose: by diverting us with the ritual detective story aim of the detection of the criminal, and of his transformation into the Other, it is able to bring us up short, without warning, against the reality of death itself, stale death, reaching out to remind the living of its own mouldering resting place. (pp. 649-50)

Fredric Jameson, "On Raymond Chandler" (copyright, 1970, by Fredric Jameson), in The Southern Review, *Vol. VI, No. 3, Summer, 1970, pp. 624-50.*

JACQUES BARZUN (essay date 1973)

As an essayist, Chandler is known to the general public solely as the author of **"The Simple Art of Murder."** This sentimental piece glorifying the tough American tale and its hero has been much reprinted because it expresses a number of emotions that continue to haunt the insecure American mind: hostility to things English, resentment against both convention and corruption, and self-pity over the common lot, mixed with the illusion of self-reliance in the effort to down surrounding evils.

One of the interesting results of going back to Chandler's early essays and verse is to find the germs of these attitudes in a young writer who was not reared in America and who harbored them many years before the disillusionment of the Great Depression. But before one looks at these early records of feeling and opinion, it is only right to bear in mind one critical fact: whereas the "philosophy" of Philip Marlowe, the Galahad-detective, deserves only a smile when inspected in essay form, it is dramatically right for a hero in his situation, private and professional; and as such it is a splendid source of motive power in the great tales of Chandler's maturity.

Nor should the reader conclude that Chandler was nothing more than a story-teller. In the letters and other writings of his novelistic period that have been published and anthologized, he shows himself a better and sterner mind than in his war-horse essay on fictional murder. He is never an exact critic, but he often manages some detachment from his sense of wrong, and what he says suggests that he has read and reflected on literature at large, and not merely English and American detective fiction. (pp. ix-x)

About Chandler's verses there is little to say except that they are without merit of any kind. The most searching detection does not discover one line capable of sticking in the memory, even when the author lifts whole phrases from Blake or Wordsworth. Only three pieces (one of them quite late and presumably inspired by the death of his wife) show any knowledge of contemporary diction and technique. What strikes us in the reading is the recurrent theme of being weighed down by some unnamed tyranny and the equally frequent defiance of it by the heroic ego. The poet calls upon Art or Thought or some other underdog entity to make war upon the resistless conspiracy of material interests. The verse, in short, contains in essence the root idea of all the later tales.

Now it is true that the primacy of art and beauty was a favorite theme of the Symbolist period in which Chandler came of age. But when he began to publish, the Nineties had *established* the superiority of art over commerce and politics and there was no reason, except in Chandler's inner self, for feeling put upon. That (as Marlowe might say) is the fishy bit that provides us with a clue.

Turn next to the essays, and observe that the first three, all in the last months of 1911, sound the note of angry dissent: **"The Literary Fop," "The Genteel Artist,"** and **"The Remarkable Hero"** exhibit as many aspects of resentment tinged with envy, the target being the esthete. A literature of refinement is hateful to the young Chandler, and it is he who in connection with it raises the spectre of "the barricades." His later assumption that whatever is elegant is both sissyfied and corrupt underlies these short but effective diatribes, even though literature, not life, is their ostensible object.

For the positive side, we need only refer to "Realism and Fairyland," in which "life's refuse" (= realism) is embraced and equated with what is truly human, besides being representative of "a large class of people." Populism, realism, and moral egalitarianism are declared the premises of true art. By moral egalitarianism I mean the proposition that "We are all realists at times, just as we are all sensualists at times, all liars at times, and all cowards at times." This would be hard to prove, especially as to realism and sensuality, but as a political philosophy for novels of crime and corruption, it is perfect. (pp. x-xi)

[Two] other small points are relevant and corroborative. One is the care and compression of the young man's prose. Chandler at 23 is in command of his means and enjoys putting things just so—even when he derides "the Phrasemaker." The other point is his insistence on one or two ideas, whether in verse or prose. That is unusual in so young a writer. The obsessive character of his thought, which gives the novels much of their power, is right here, full force, in these youthful pages. . . . (p. xii)

Jacques Barzun, "The Young Raymond Chandler," in Chandler Before Marlowe: Raymond Chandler's Early Prose and Poetry, 1908-1912, *edited by Matthew J. Bruccoli (copyright © 1973 by the University of South Carolina Press), University of South Carolina Press, 1973, pp. ix-xii.*

FRANK MacSHANE (essay date 1976)

Some readers, knowing a little about Chandler's own nature, have imagined that he created in Marlowe an idealized concept of himself, making up for his own deficiencies. Such a procedure might have appealed to a young writer bent on self-expression, but Chandler was fifty when he began *The Big Sleep* and no longer a child. He had the far more difficult problem of investing a type of person he probably never even met with attributes that would make him bearable as a narrator yet realistic as a character. (p. 70)

In his early fiction in particular, Chandler thought of Marlowe as a catalyst, a means of bringing to the foreground the other characters who are the real substances of his fiction. This was an act of compromise, as writing so often is; but it was an original and important one, for in effect it was an attempt to give real substance to a popular form of literature. If fantasy and reality are blended in Chandler's work, another pair of opposites were equally necessary. "There must be idealism," he wrote, "but there must also be contempt." The balancing act this attitude requires affects Marlowe as narrator. Although he is a creature of fantasy, he also serves as a guide for the reader. Marlowe is like Vergil in Dante's *Divine Comedy:* he says what the reader might say about the world of Los Angeles were he to encounter it himself. The reader cannot sensibly associate himself with Marlowe as a character in the novel, but he readily accepts his voice. Because it is casual, witty, and forthright, he naturally likes to identify himself with it. This is one of the reasons for Chandler's popularity as a writer.

Chandler's longer fiction also enlarges his focus. Where in his shorter fiction he limited his range to those immediately involved in the criminal world, in *The Big Sleep* he points his finger at those who are responsible for the corruption of society or who live off it, often unaware that they are parasites. . . . In *The Big Sleep* Chandler is more overt in his social commentary than he is in his later novels; it's as though, at the outset, he thought he ought to make it clear where he stood, not quite trusting the story to make the point for him. (p. 71)

The Big Sleep is a comedy—a comedy of human futility. Chandler was not interested in making social statements: he was just eager to write an extended story and have the jokes come off. He succeeded because he wrote the book quickly and because its serious side is expressed obliquely. The energy of the narrative and the wit of the dialogue are what the reader remembers. Cities and society in decay are notably capable of giving off this energy—their corruption is vivid and picturesque—whereas it's far more difficult to write about honest and high-minded people. (p. 72)

Farewell, My Lovely is an improvement [over *The Big Sleep*] because the focus of the story is more clear. In *The Big Sleep* Chandler's indignation is generalized in a dislike for the rich, but here he concentrates on Bay City, an independent part of Los Angeles, in which the extent of corruption in California life is more vividly demonstrated. "Sure, it's a nice town," says Marlowe. "It's probably no crookeder than Los Angeles. But you can only buy a piece of a big city. You can buy a town this size all complete, with the original box and tissue paper." . . . For Chandler, Bay City was a symbol of hypocrisy: he hated the pretense of uprightness in a place virtually owned by a few people with money. "This Grayle packs a lot of dough in his pants," says Marlowe of the millionaire in the novel. "And law is where you buy it in this town." (p. 90)

This, then, is the setting for Chandler's comedy. The novel is laid out like a play and the plot proceeds through a series of dramatic scenes between characters. The story is based on the old chestnut of disguised identity, but Chandler gets away with it by using another traditional dramatic device, the love triangle, in which Marlowe is played off against the glamorous Velma Valento (alias Mrs. Grayle) and the plainer but more honest Anne Riordan. Like much of Chandler's fiction, *Farewell, My Lovely* resembles a Restoration comedy in which the plot is not so important as the picture of life portrayed through its characters and the humor produced by the jokes and situations. Marlowe also plays a role that is more customary in dramatic comedy than in fiction. He is attracted by both women in a superficial way. He leaves Anne Riordan's house, knowing that hers "would be a nice room to wear slippers in." Later, he claims that Mrs. Grayle is his type and says, "I like smooth shiny girls, hard-boiled and loaded with sin." But he always goes home to his own apartment, where there is a "homey smell, a smell of dust and tobacco smoke, the smell of a world where men live, and keep on living."

The conventions of the detective story, as used by Chandler, are very similar to those of comic drama; and in *Farewell, My Lovely,* as in most of his novels, Marlowe is like the clown in *Pagliacci* standing before the curtain to introduce the characters of his *commedia*. In this particular novel Chandler provides as wide a range of lesser characters as in *The Big Sleep,* but they are more representative. General Sternwood and his psychotic daughter Carmen, not to mention the pornographer Geiger, are all rather special types. The characters of *Farewell, My Lovely* may have ordinary biographies, but Chandler makes them all vivid and memorable and often very funny. Moose Malloy, the giant jailbird who opens the book; Jessie Florian, the alcoholic widow of a tavern keeper; the anonymous Negro manager of the Hotel Sans Souci ("Trouble, brother, is something we is just fresh out of")—all these are believable as people and are related directly to the life of Los Angeles. They are a cross-section of the city, many of them proof of the failed dream of California, Chamber of Commerce assurances to the contrary. (pp. 91-2)

The High Window has a curious tone, for it wobbles between burlesque and an expression of anger against ruthless behavior. . . .

The burlesque element of the book is oddly mixed with the central theme: the misuse of power and the control of one person by another. Also a favorite subject with Hawthorne and James, this theme is revealed mainly through Mrs. Murdock's control over her weak son and her complaisant and neurotic secretary, Merle Davis. (p. 97)

Chandler's hatred of ruthless bullies is so great that at times *The High Window* sounds almost like a tract. There are plenty of wisecracks and funny scenes to balance the seriousness; but rarely in other books does Chandler generalize as he does, for example, in a conversation between Marlowe and two Los Angeles policemen about a case in which a rich man's son and his secretary were found dead. A coverup for the case was arranged so that the secretary was blamed for the murder of the rich boy, Cassidy. "Did you ever stop to think," says Marlowe, "That Cassidy's secretary might have had a mother or a sister or a sweetheart—or all three? That they had their pride and their faith and their love for a kid who was made out to be a drunken paranoiac because his boss's father had a hundred million dollars?". . .

Chandler's anger at a world in which innocent people are made to suffer by the unscrupulous rich is expressed mainly in the story of Merle Davis, the timid secretary who has been brainwashed into believing that she pushed Mrs. Murdock's first husband out of a window because he made a pass at her. (p. 98)

The seriousness of Chandler's theme shows how ambitious he was for the detective story. It may also explain why he thought he had to exaggerate the jokes and the characters in order to make the book palatable. *The High Window* has thematic unity and a pace that suggests fresh work. But it is also odd, a curious mixture of elements that seem somewhat uncomfortable together. (p. 99)

[*The Lady in the Lake*] lacks the sparkle of the early books, although it is better than *The High Window*. The fault probably lies in its extraordinarily long period of gestation: it's hard to maintain a feeling of spontaneity over four years. Also, the war influenced the book. Chandler has sometimes been accused of ignoring social conditions in his books, writing escapist fiction that takes no account of the realities of the Depression and the war. It is true that he did not write social realism or politically committed fiction, but as should now be evident his novels embrace the political and social realities of Southern California. *The Lady in the Lake* also brings in the war. In **"No Crime in the Mountains"** there is an absurd intrusion of a Japanese spy and of a Nazi who cries "Heil Hitler!" before he quite unjustifiably shoots himself instead of the narrator. But in the novel, Chandler's war references are less hysterical and therefore more realistic. (pp. 101-02)

But there is also a secondary or subconscious influence on the book. When Marlowe calls on his client for the first time, everything is gray—the client's suit, the dull silver walls of the reception room, and even Adrienne Fromsett, the main girl in the story: "She wore a steel-grey business suit and under the jacket a dark blue shirt and a man's tie of lighter shade. The edges of the folded handkerchief in the breast pocket looked sharp enought to slice bread. She wore a linked bracelet and no other jewelry." *The Lady in the Lake* is a somber book because it concentrates on those who are caught up in the system of Southern California instead of those who direct it. They are the foot soldiers of society rather than the picturesque eccentrics of *The High Window* to whom the system belongs. The richest man in *The Lady in the Lake,* Derace Kingsley, is only the head of a cosmetics company. "I have a good job here," he explains when he hires Marlowe, "but a job is all it is." The novel is about all the middlemen who are forced to conform to the style and habits of a materialistic world. Everybody is under some sort of tension, even the country cop who is up for reelection and whose political slogan is "Keep Jim Patton Constable. He Is Too Old To Go To Work." As in the army, circumstances control people: no one, except Marlowe, is a free agent, and he is one only because he is not involved in the central story. What Chandler shows us is a society of men and women trying somehow to keep their lives together, but always under pressure and therefore susceptible to violence. They are monkeys in the same zoo, and for that reason *The Lady in the Lake* is less comic than Chandler's other novels; there is no romance in the book either, no blondes for Marlowe to play with.

This novel, then, is like a morality play, a portrait of society in trouble. The police, who are entrusted with maintaining order, are attacked more vigorously than in any other Chandler book. Once again, Bay City is the setting for much of the action, along with the mountains above San Bernardino. Chandler does not attack all police, but he shows how one corrupt cop can poison an entire police force. During the course of his investigations Marlowe is threatened by the police, beaten up, arrested, and blackjacked, as well as forced to drink whiskey in order to appear drunk. He is jailed, knocked out, drenched with gin, and framed for murder—all under the orders of a single police officer, Lieutenant Degarmo, who not surprisingly also turns out to be the murderer. He gets away with what he does because nobody else cares enough to stand in his way. Some of Degarmo's fellow officers in Bay City know the truth about him and other corrupt policemen, but as one of them says, "To hell with them, I'll be in the army in two weeks." (pp. 102-03)

[Chandler] invested *The Little Sister* with an extra dose of characterization, wit, and description.

The result is an overripe book. It contains many familiar Chandler features, but there is no organic development beyond what he had written before. The "little sister," Orfamay Quest, is an extension of Merle Davis, the terrified secretary in *The High Window.* But, unlike Merle, Orfamay is a part of a family that includes a confidence trickster who tries to blackmail his other sister, a rising movie star, who in turn is a friend of a prostitute and a racketeer. These relationships give Chandler an opportunity to write about the interlocking levels of Hollywood society, although *The Little Sister* is in no sense a real Hollywood novel. (pp. 149-50)

The Little Sister shows the results of Chandler's dispiriting years in Hollywood, but most of the scenes that deal with the movies are just decorative. There is a scene in an agent's office where the waiting room is filled with out-of-work actors. It is funny in the way it shows everyone's pretentions, but it is also a sad revelation of the empty lives involved. (p. 150)

The main trouble with these scenes is that they have little to do with the story. They are included because Chandler is trying to expand Marlowe's consciousness, but they don't come across as a necessary part of the novel. The seams show. Chandler also uses descriptive passages to establish Marlowe's mental state. One chapter opens with Marlowe driving along Sunset Boulevard and commenting on the hot rods driving in and out of the traffic and the "sleazy hamburger joints that look like palaces under the colors." Gradually Marlowe becomes depressed by the restless emptiness of everything, the lack of human communication, the indifference and the ugliness. Years later Chandler wrote that the scene was "an attempt to find out whether purely through the tone of the description I could render a state of mind." Much of the passage is objective, but some of it is mannered: "California, the department store state. The most of everything and the best of nothing." (p. 151)

Although it is cast in the form of a detective novel in which Marlowe eventually reveals the murderer of two of the characters, *The Long Goodbye* is really about the nature of friendship, its uses and abuses, and about the qualities of love. (pp. 199-200)

From the beginning of the book it is obvious that Chandler intended *The Long Goodbye* to be his major effort as a novelist. It has an expansiveness his other books lack. It is not as crisp and fast-paced as *Farewell, My Lovely,* but here Chandler wanted to do something different. He enriches *The Long Goodbye* with comments of all sorts about the society in which Marlowe lives. These are made far more relevant to the story itself than they were in *The Little Sister.* Early in the book Marlowe is questioned by the police and then put in jail under suspicion of being an "accessory" to the crime. This curious booking has no legal status, and the Los Angeles police have to release their suspects after the third day so as not to violate habeas corpus. It is nevertheless unpleasant, and Chandler uses the occasion to describe what it's like to be in jail, the imperson-

ality, the boredom. Also, when a lawyer is sent to make plans for Marlowe's release, an arrangement he rejects, the two men discuss a number of illegal police maneuvers. These comments on society are a natural part of the story and are not obtrusive. There is only one extraneous chapter, and that is one in which Chandler describes a typical day in Marlowe's life. The phone calls and visitors have nothing to do with the central plot, but the writing is amusing enough to let Chandler get away with it. Sometimes the interjections don't quite come off, as when Chandler includes a long commentary on blondes. Here he seems to be trying to fill in all the interstices, to make this novel the definitive Chandler. (p. 205)

Judgment of *The Long Goodbye* depends on the standards that are being applied. Certainly Marlowe does not attain the degree of understanding and liberation achieved by the great heroes of European fiction. But he is not unlike the heroes and heroines of Hemingway, Faulkner, Steinbeck, and Dreiser. These fictional men and women are divided individuals who are trying to come to terms with their surroundings. In order to give themselves some stability, they evolve patterns of behavior that permit them to cope. Their lives may be tragic, spoiled by the very codes they live by or fail to live by, but they have little option to do otherwise. Chandler seems to have had a clear idea of the effect of his nationality on Marlowe, for he wrote in his notebook: "To me Marlowe is the American mind; a heavy portion of rugged realism, a dash of good hard vulgarity, a strong overtone of strident wit, an equally strong undertone of pure sentimentalism, an ocean of slang, and an utterly unexpected range of sensitivity."

In the company of the writers mentioned above and with such a character, *The Long Goodbye* has stature. Chandler engages Marlowe in new experiences and reveals sides of him that were formerly hidden. He has a friendship with Terry Lennox and a brief affair with Linda Loring. At the end there is just a blank, a void that has to be filled with something, even a code of behavior that sounds sentimental; but that is the nature of America as Chandler saw it. (p. 207)

Frank MacShane, in his The Life of Raymond Chandler *(copyright © 1976 by Frank MacShane; reprinted by permission of the publisher, E. P. Dutton, Inc.), Dutton, 1976, 306 p.*

STEPHEN PENDO (essay date 1976)

[From analyses of several screen adaptations of Raymond Chandler's novels], two general patterns emerge. One deals with the process of transforming a detective novel into a film; the other reflects the differences in a literary hero and the screen image of him. (p. 198)

[A] central trend runs through all the Marlowe films, and this pattern appears applicable to other film adaptations of books as well. In the case of each Marlowe film, the screenwriter passed through three basic steps: simplifying the plot, intensifying the characters, and finding filmic equivalents of key passages in Chandler's writing.

Simplification of the plot collectively resulted in several basic changes. Elimination of minor incidents not pertinent to the major thread of the story was accomplished. The major portions of the plot were condensed and shortened to better fit the filmmaker's time limitations. Paradoxically, this "simplification" did not always make the story easier to understand. In *The Big Sleep,* for example, the storyline was simplified and shortened at the expense of some necessary explanations concerning the action found in the novel. The complete elimination of these pieces of information did not make the screen version of the novel any easier to understand. In general, however, these condensations and shortenings resulted in less complex plots than in the novels.

The film intensification of certain characters also helped to shorten and tighten the story. Many minor characters in the six novels were dropped, and only a few new ones were added to the Marlowe films. Moose Malloy in *Murder, My Sweet,* a composite of the book characters of Malloy and Second Planting, and Linda Wade in [Stirling] Silliphant's *Long Goodbye* script, a fusion of the novel's Linda Loring and Eileen Wade, illustrate how aspects of several characters were sometimes combined into one, much in the same way Chandler combined his short story characters when he included them in a novel. Ann Grayle in *Murder, My Sweet,* who was a member of the family and therefore had a personal interest in the case, is an example of how screen character changes resulted in a tightening of relationships. In addition, a character's importance was sometimes increased or diminished. All these character changes served to make the films more unified than the novels.

Visual equivalents of some of Chandler's passages were harder to accomplish than plot or character changes. Most filmmakers used standard photographic methods to accomplish their aims, but others embellished on ordinary cinematic techniques. Robert Montgomery, for example, tried to capture the Chandler spirit by total use of the subjective camera [in *The Lady in the Lake*]. On the other hand, the makers of *Murder, My Sweet* mixed a few subjective shots with narration. And the creators of *Farewell, My Lovely* combined narration with a recreation of the actual Los Angeles Chandler wrote about. However it was done, each group of filmmakers tried to capture the Chandler spirit the author had conveyed so well in his descriptive passages. (pp. 198-99)

Throughout the Marlowe pictures, as well as the unproduced version of *The Long Goodbye,* Marlowe is more personally involved with violence than his novel counterpart. Chandler's Marlowe is a relatively nonviolent person. He moves within a violent world, but rarely is he the perpetrator of violence or its victim. In the first five Marlowe pictures, however, our hero suffers far more beatings than in the original sources. In this case we see a traditional Hollywood attitude toward the filmic tough guy image: the hero can take physical punishment without serious injury. In the Silliphant script and the final movie version of *The Long Goodbye* and in the film *Farewell, My Lovely,* Marlowe is not subject to these extra beatings. But the detective metes out violence in incidents not in the novels. In Silliphant's *Long Goodbye* script (never shot), Marlowe kills Chick Agostino in self defense; in the filmed version, the hero murders Terry Lennox. And in *Farewell, My Lovely,* Marlowe shoots and and kills Mrs. Grayle as well as a couple of thugs. These incidents run contrary to the Chandler originals, for his Marlowe never killed anyone after *The Big Sleep.*

Another principal difference between the book and screen versions of the Marlowe character concerns sex. The filmic Marlowe on the whole takes far more interest in women than Chandler's original hero, and each of the first five Marlowe pictures has a romantic encounter. *The Brasher Doubloon* and *Marlowe* are, in fact, heavily laced with sex. George Montgomery goes to the Murdock mansion because he likes Merle's voice and stays on the case because of her. James Garner, in the sexiest Marlowe film, has a steady girl friend who spends the night in his apartment, the closest we ever come to seeing Marlowe in bed with a woman. Interestingly, the films, *The Long Goodbye* and *Farewell, My Lovely,* as well as Silliphant's *Long Goodbye* script, do not hold true to this pattern. The absence of any romantic adventures for Marlowe in *The Long Goodbye* is in this case contrary to Chandler, for that is the only novel under discussion in which the detective does engage in sex. *Farewell, My Lovely,* however, does remain faithful to its source by not giving Marlowe a girl friend. The last two Marlowe pictures, then, show a break in the romantic aspect of Marlowe's character established in the first five films.

The filmic Marlowe has distinct traits and it is now appropriate to summarize the movie version of the hero. This character is relatively poor, kept that way by his moral code which does not allow him to accept unearned money. This code, of course, also compels the detective to seek the truth and see justice done no matter what the personal risk. The filmic sleuth rebounds quickly from physical injury and sometimes commits violent acts. Although he operates alone, he frequently carries on a romantic relationship. Generally, the film Marlowe operates without harassment from the police and is far ahead of them in finding the truth. The emergent image, then, is that of a violent, sexually successful, self-assured individual. (pp. 199-200)

More than any other actor, Bogart captures the true spirit of Marlowe and, as Stirling Silliphant suggested, if Bogart were still alive people would be flocking to Marlowe pictures starring the actor. Everything about Bogart's performance is superb: the fast-paced way he delivers his lines, coupled with his skill at verbal fencing, expertly conveys Chandler's crackling dialogue; the way Bogart moves his hands—for instance, tugging at his ear—adds interesting bits of business to the picture; the actor's "lived in" face and rumpled appearance make him seem the perfect visual equivalent of Chandler's detective; and Bogart's ability to seem tough just by his presence, rather than by his actions, all combined to make Humphrey Bogart the best of the screen Marlowes. (p. 202)

Murder, My Sweet and *The Big Sleep* are, without doubt, the two best Marlowe films. Both effectively capture the Chandler spirit and both present excellent screen personifications of the author's hero. To choose one above the other is a difficult, and perhaps not entirely necessary, task at best. But I believe *The Big Sleep* stands out as the most effective Marlowe picture. (pp. 202-03)

Stephen Pendo, in his conclusion to his Raymond Chandler on Screen: His Novels into Film *(copyright © 1976 by Stephen Pendo), The Scarecrow Press, Inc., 1976, pp. 198-206.*

JULIAN SYMONS (essay date 1978)

Chandler remained by temperament a romantic aesthete. His feebly literary early essays and poems are full of either/ors like science and poetry, romance and realism. Are we to be saved 'by the science or by the poetry of life'? That, he said, 'is the typical question of the age', and he came down on the side of poetry as opposed to science and of romance against realism. Or rather, of realism seen romantically, so that 'any man who has walked down a commonplace city street at twilight, just as the lamps are lit' would see that a true view of it must be idealistic, for it would 'exalt the sordid to a vision of magic, and create pure beauty out of plaster and vile dust'. The phrases echo Chesterton, and also look forward to the famous peroration of **'The Simple Art of Murder'** which runs: 'Down these mean streets a man must go . . .'. It was Chandler's strength, and his weakness, that he brought this basically sentimental aestheticism to the crime stories, so that they had increasingly to be about a romantic hero whose activities gave the novels at least 'a quality of redemption' so that he could think of them as art. That was the weakness. The strength lay in the fact that by treating seriously everything he did Chandler achieved even in his early stories for the pulps more than his fellow practitioners. (pp. 22-3)

Chandler was not a prolific writer. He wrote in all twenty stories for the pulps, at the rate of two, three or four a year. It is true that almost all of them were much longer than the usual story, and that they might almost be called short novels, but even so the output was small. (pp. 24-5)

About the pulp stories considered as stories there is little to say except that they are not very good. 'Everybody imitates in the beginning,' as Chandler said himself, and the writer he imitated most was [Dashiell] Hammett. The young blond gunman in **'Blackmailers Don't Shoot'** is obviously derived from Wilmer in [Hammett's] *The Maltese Falcon,* the sadistic thug in **'Pick-Up on Noon Street'** is based on Jeff in [Hammett's] *The Glass Key,* and there are other echoes. Standard scenes and characters appear in most of the stories. There will be at least one night club scene, a variety of villains will appear in every story, and some of them will be gangsters or gamblers who own the night clubs. The hard men who hit the detective over the head will be exceptionally stupid, and the gangsters will be only a little smarter beneath their thin veneer of sophistication. The police will be tough, cynical, and occasionally corrupt. There will be a lot of shooting, with an Elizabethan litter of corpses piled up by the end. At the heart of the trouble there will be a girl, and she is almost never to be trusted, although she may have 'the sort of skin an old rake dreams of' (Rhonda Farr in **'Blackmailers Don't Shoot'**) or hair that is 'like a bush fire at night' (Beulah in **'Try the Girl'**) or even hair that 'seemed to gather all the light there was and make a soft halo around her coldly beautiful face' (Belle Marr in **'Spanish Blood'**). The women in the short stories are not as deadly as they become in the novels, but they are dangerous enough.

These standard properties are used in a standard way. The detective himself is not much more than a man whose head is harder and whose gun is faster than his rivals'. This is true of Marlowe, who appeared first in 1934, as much as of Mallory or Carmady [in the early short stories]. But the basic defect of the stories is that the length to which they were written did not fit Chandler's talent. The weakness of his plotting is more apparent in the stories than in the novels. The demand of the pulps, he said later, was for constant action, and if you stopped to think you were lost. 'When in doubt, have a man come through a door with a gun in his hand.' The novels gave more space for the development of situations and the creation of an environment. One of Chandler's great merits was his capacity to fix a scene memorably. He sometimes did this in a phrase, but he could do it even better in a paragraph or a page. The stories did not give him time to create anything of this kind. Everything that did not carry forward the action was excised by editors.

If we read the stories today it is for occasional flashes of observation that got by the blue pencil, and for the use of language. Chandler's ear for the rhythms of speech was good from the beginning, but it developed with astonishing speed. The stories written in the later 1930s, like **'Killer in the Rain'**,

'The Curtain', 'Try the Girl' and **'Mandarin's Jade'** are often as well written as the novels, where the early tales are full of clichés. **'Smart-Aleck Kill'** . . . has eyes that get small and tight, eyes with hot lights in them, eyes that show sharp lights of pain. There are cold smiles playing around the corners of mouths, and mirthless laughter. But within a very few years these have almost all disappeared, and we recognize the sharp cleverness of the novels when we are told that the garage of a modernistic new house is 'as easy to drive into as an olive bottle' or that a smart car in a dingy neighbourhood 'sticks out like spats at an Iowa picnic'.

It was these later and better stories that Chandler cannibalized, to use his own word, to make three of the novels. This was an extraordinary process. Other writers have incorporated early material in a later work, but nobody else has done it in quite this way. Most writers who adapt their earlier work take from it a particular theme or character and jettison the rest. Chandler, however, carved out great chunks of the stories, expanded them, and fitted them into an enlarged plot. Where gaps existed, like spaces in a jigsaw, he made pieces to fit them. It meant, as Philip Durham has said, adapting, fusing and adding characters, blending themes from different stories, combining plots. Much of his first novel, *The Big Sleep,* was taken from two stories, **'Killer in the Rain'** and **'The Curtain',** plus fragments from two other stories. About a quarter of the book was new material, but the passages from the two principal stories used were much enlarged. There could be no better proof of the limitation Chandler felt in being forced to work within the pulp magazine formula. (pp. 25-7)

The pulp magazines had shaped him, but once he had learned the trade they were a restriction. The novels enabled him to burst the bonds and to express the essential Raymond Chandler: a romantic aesthete and a self-conscious artist, an introvert with the power of catching the form, the tone, the rhythm, of American speech supremely well on paper. In its kind Chandler's mature dialogue is perfect. One cannot see how it could be better done. The stories are not much in themselves, but without them perhaps we should never have had the novels. (p. 29)

Julian Symons, "An Aesthete Discovers the Pulps," in The World of Raymond Chandler, *edited by Miriam Gross (reprinted by permission of A & W Publishers, Inc.; copyright © 1977 by Weidenfeld and Nicolson), A & W Publishers, 1978, pp. 19-30.*

JACQUES BARZUN   (essay date 1978)

Raymond Chandler undertook to 'raise' the detective genre into the circle of respectable reading matter—as if the best minds had not already discovered the pleasures of crime fiction taken on its own merits. The justification for this self-conscious and self-righteous effort to elevate a genre was the syllogism that literature deals with reality, that the sign of reality is horror and squalor, and hence that a tale impregnated with these flavours would—other things equal—be literature.

We may be grateful that from these fallacies so much good work has come. But there is no warrant for the commonly held belief that the tough detective tale yields greater truth than the gentler classical form and marks a forward step toward 'the real novel'. The 'soft' genteel story, in which the corpse is found in a library by the butler, may be a period piece, but is in itself neither truer nor falser than the story set in the back alleys of Glasgow or Los Angeles. Butlers may be an anachronism, but so are bootleggers—and private libraries are still more numerous than private eyes. Nor is habitual vulgarity of speech 'more real' than civil talk among educated people.

On these points the literary mind has been influenced and—as it seems to me—perverted, by Raymond Chandler's famous essay. His definition of **'The Simple Art of Murder'** was taken as the burial service read over the corpse of the classical tale, and his words were reprinted over and over again. (p. 160)

But Chandler started from an untenable premise in his first sentence: 'Fiction in any form has always tended to be realistic.' And he never bothered to analyse what he meant by realism. So he never saw the other side of the coin, which shows, not that the classical mode is more real than Chandler admits, but that realness is irrelevant.

This must be so, since the tough mode, including Chandler's own admirable work, is open to the same objections as the other. Consider the tough formula: a private detective, usually low in funds and repute, undertakes single-handed and often without fee the vindication of some unfortunate person—a man or woman with no other friends. The attempt pits the hero against a ruthless crime syndicate or against the whole corrupt government of the town, or both. During his search for evidence, he is threatened, slugged, drugged, shot at, kidnapped, tortured, but never downed for very long. In many of the variants of the genre, he drinks quantities of whiskey neat and proves equally ready for fighting and fornication. None of this affects his work; he is guaranteed indestructible. Others' bullets pass him by; his own—especially in the final scene of carnage—always find their mark. And despite the gruelling physical pace, he finds the time and the wit, without the aid of discussion or note-taking, to figure out the discrepancies that reveal the culprit and his motive.

Now if in comparing the tender and the tough conventions one is looking for 'real life' in the verifiable sense, one must conclude that although the first kind of story will not bear sceptical examination, the second is—as Shakespeare says apropos of two liars—'an even more wonderful song than the other'. Nor is this all that Raymond Chandler's essay brings to mind. The tender school aims at producing a denouement having the force of necessity, as in Greek tragedy. All the facts (clues, words, motives) must converge to give the mystery one solution and one only. That by itself is a good reason for making the crime occur in a law-abiding circle, where the habits of the *dramatis personae* are by hypothesis regular and reasonable. In such a setting the violence of murder is the more striking, and stronger also the desire to manacle the offender. Murder among thugs and drug addicts is hardly unexpected, and the feeling that in this milieu anything can happen does not increase but rather lessens the interest. Hence the artistic need for the tough writer to involve some innocent, whose ways *are* peaceable, and to put steadily in peril the detective-defender of that lump of virtue. In short, in murder à la Chandler, murder is not enough to keep us going—and neither is detection, since it is never a feature of the foreground.

Chandler as artist is so aware of these lacks that he reinforces the damsel-in-distress motive with what is nothing less than a political motive. He makes it clear in his essay that the hero of the new and improved genre is fighting society. Except for the favoured victim, he alone is pure in heart, a C-green incorruptible. The rich are all crooked or 'phonies', and cowards in the end. Since the police, the mayor, the whole Establishment are soon shown as a conspiracy to pervert justice and kill

off troublemakers, we naturally share the detective's smothered indignation and are powerfully driven, like him, to see the right vindicated.

The tough story was born in the Thirties and shows the Marxist colouring of its birth years. It follows that in Chandler's essay the critique of the classical formula seems to spring not solely from a mistaken demand for realism, but also from a hostility to the solvent way of life. That the well-to-do could be honest, 'genuine', and lovable apparently was not 'realistic' either. (pp. 161-62)

Who's the sentimental tale-spinner now? After thirty years it makes no difference to our enjoyment of the great sagas by Chandler, Ross Macdonald, and others that the eternal Robin Hood should have got mixed up with Marx's angry young men and Tennyson's Galahad, and wound up in self-contradiction. What was and remains comic is that Chandler should have chosen for his California hero the name Philip Marlowe, which from first name to final *e* connotes Englishness, Elegance, and Establishment. (p. 162)

Jacques Barzun, "The Illusion of the Real" (reprinted by permission of A & W Publishers, Inc.; copyright © Jacques Barzun and Wendell Hertig Taylor, 1971), in The World of Raymond Chandler, *edited by Miriam Gross, A & W Publishers, 1978, pp. 159-64.*

PETER J. RABINOWITZ   (essay date 1980)

Critics from W. H. Auden to S. S. Van Dine have long delighted in tabulating the laws which govern the classic detective story. But most of them view the genre—and criticism of it—as a diversion, and consequently treat the rules like those for any other game. . . . [If] we do a little pruning, if we take off some excess foliage to look for the *essential* rules which show up explicitly or implicitly on every list, then we begin to see that their ramifications extend beyond game playing.

The genre, in fact, hinges on three primary conventions; most of the other rules that critics and authors have enunciated are trivial or else are elaborations or consequences of these three. First of all, as S. S. Van Dine puts it, "There must be but one culprit." Second, the detective must always triumph by restoring order in the end; as Van Dine archly notes, "The detective novel must have a detective in it; and a detective is not a detective unless he detects." Finally, the crime must turn out to be the result of some idiosyncratic aberration, succeeding temporarily only because it operates under a veil of falsehood; the criminal, therefore, can always be uncovered through simple rational procedures—which Van Dine calls "logical deductions." (p. 226)

Now these three rules are *not* "purely literary." As soon as we examine the kind of imaginative universe which such rules generate, we can begin to see social underpinnings. . . .

[Agatha] Christie's novels always open with the same conflict: the peaceful, natural social order (often a small country village) is threatened by disruption through a murder or series of murders that seems bizarre and inexplicable. But this specter of social disruption is always laid to rest in the same way. According to the first rule of the genre, the threat always turns out to come from an individual rather than from a social failing; the restoration of order guaranteed by the second rule thus never requires a serious alteration—or even examination—of society. Furthermore, according to the third rule, evil can operate only as long as "the truth" remains concealed. This, of course, simplifies the detective's task of restoration, for once the deviant individual is unmasked, he or she is powerless to operate further. (p. 227)

Raymond Chandler's vision can be crystallized in a phrase Marlowe twice uses to describe Carmen [Sternwood's] sinister, moronic giggles "rats behind the wainscoting." The apparent respectability of the world masks a fundamental core of horror: corruption, perversity, death. Marlowe's world is not one where it is lost, as in Hammett's. In Chandler's world, innocence simply does not exist.

Given that Chandler did not share the political vision [of optimism and stability] implied in the classical detective story, one might well ask why he chose to revamp the genre rather than to write in another genre, such as that of *The Day of the Locust, To Have and Have Not, U.S.A.* One reason may have been the reciprocal relationship between convention and attitude. That the conventions of a genre are morally or politically unsound is reason enough to challenge them on their home ground. Jane Austen began her string of realistic novels with the upside-down gothic of *Northanger Abbey.* (p. 231)

Although *The Big Sleep* is not a traditional parody, it does, as I have said, topple all the fundamental conventions of the genre. Most obvious is Chandler's violation of our first rule. In a Christie novel, a string of crimes always has a single source. But here, the number of criminals seems endless; as Harry Jones remarks, "We're all grifters. So we sell each other out for a nickel." . . . Geiger, Brody, Taylor, Lundgren, Canino, Carmen, and Mars: that's enough to populate an entire decade of Christie productions. Guilt is thus impossible to localize in Chandler's urban jungle—and we shall see later on why this is so important. (pp. 231-32)

More startling still is Chandler's violation of the second rule: the detective fails to bring the most vicious of these criminals to justice. To be sure, the novel opens with the promise of his success, for against the grim background of California degeneracy, the virtues of Philip Marlowe stand out in bold relief. With his vigorous intelligence and unusual (although not superhuman) physical stamina, with his honesty, integrity, justice, and even chastity, he is—as Chandler himself often stressed—a modern knight. Marlowe first appears in *The Big Sleep* and the knighthood theme is announced in the second paragraph, which foreshadows Marlowe's later "rescue" of the nude Carmen: "There was a broad stained-glass panel showing a knight in dark armor rescuing a lady who was tied to a tree and didn't have any clothes on but some very long and convenient hair. . . ." (p. 232)

But while few readers miss the promises held out by the imagery of Marlowe's knighthood, a curious number have failed to realize that they are never fulfilled. . . . *The Big Sleep* does not depict the triumph of justice and fair play; to the contrary, it traces Marlowe's descent from moderately optimistic knighthood to a despairing recognition of his own impotence. For in contrast to the similar virtues of [Agatha Christie's Hercule] Poirot, Marlowe's virtues are powerless against the vastly superior forces of evil. He may be able to perform a few good acts, such as protecting General Sternwood from heartbreak and avenging Harry Jones's death. But this is a far cry from the administration of justice, which Marlowe comes to realize is no longer possible for an individual in our urban society.

In order to understand how Marlowe fails, we must first understand the plot—no mean feat. Specifically, we must rec-

ognize the central villain. Actually, this is more of a problem than might appear. As we have noted, Chandler's world is infected with far more widespread guilt than Christie's; and certainly, many of the evildoers are punished, even overpunished. Geiger, Brody, and Owen Taylor are just as dead for their crimes as the far more vicious Canino is for his; Carol Lundgren is in jail; and Carmen, the kind of traditional "aberrant individual" that Christie would have made the villain (which may explain why so many readers falsely see her as such) is about to be institutionalized. Don't we have enough retribution for a dozen novels?

Chandler's world is more vicious than Christie's, and it is not surprising that his novels end in more bloodshed. But this should not fool us. Chandler, in order to stress the theme of widespread evil, may have given us a large number of criminals; but in order to stress the note of despair, he has made one of them stand out above the rest and has left him quite untouched at the end. This is not a trivial point; it is this structural twist which keeps the plot from resolution and which consequently provides much of its political force. Since so many readers and critics, however, have misread the novel's denouement, it may be necessary to demonstrate that Eddie Mars and not Carmen is, in fact, the closest thing to a central villain in the novel; that Chandler has purposefully structured his novel to make him the evil counterpart to Marlowe's virtue (in effect, he plays the dragon to Marlowe's knight); and that by leaving him unpunished, Chandler puts the capstone on the theme of failure he builds throughout the entire novel. (pp. 232-33)

Chandler saw Mars as a primary thread linking the disparate plots, and made whatever alterations were necessary to point up his function as Marlowe's antagonist. As a final touch, he gave hero and villain. . .names to emphasize their respective roles—another sign of his extreme care in writing. The theme of the individual's weakness in the face of evil is doubly reinforced by Marlowe's name, which is surely *not* the "coincidence" [Frank] MacShane claims it is [see excerpt above]. First, while *The Big Sleep* is not modeled on [Conrad's] *Heart of Darkness* in the same way that Robbe-Grillet's *Les Gommes* is modeled on *Oedipus,* British-educated Chandler must have had Conrad in mind when he finally chose the name of his detective, for the general drift of the two novels is strikingly parallel. Both tell of idealists whose adventures seem destined to bring them in contact with some kind of truth, but who in fact find only a hollowness and a horror. Significantly, both these lovers of truth learn that the only way to deal with the horror they have exposed is to bury it once again with a lie, a lie that leaves the hero perhaps wiser, but also more bitter; and a lie that leaves the evil fundamentally untouched.

In addition, the name harks back to E. C. Bentley's famous detective novel, *Trent's Last Case.* This is a classic, but one that breaks several traditions of the genre: most important, there are two people who act as "detectives," both of whom come up with "solutions," neither of which is correct, as we learn only when the real killer confesses. The names of these two flawed detectives? Philip Trent and Marlowe!

Similarly, as the central force behind the novel's violence, Mars is of course well-named after the god of war; likewise, his position as Marlowe's antagonist is emphasized by having their names begin in the same way. He "mars" everything decent around him. Given all this, it is a delightful coincidence—if coincidence it be—that Kurtz, Marlowe's antagonist in *Heart of Darkness,* is associated too with the planet Mars. (p. 235)

Both the multiplicity of the evildoers and Marlowe's failure to restore order are echoed in Chandler's disruption of the third rule of the genre: for the evil in the world of the novel comes less from the quirks of deviant individuals like Carmen than from society itself. Chandler emphasizes this point by his grim portrayal of the environment of his tale: Christie's genteel countryside has been replaced by the dirty sump where the "horrible decayed" . . . body of Regan lies. Chandler himself would argue that his portrayal was more "realistic" than Christie's, but as I have suggested, behind that claim lies a particular view of reality: only if you start with a socially critical attitude toward crime are you likely to view Chandler as more "realistic." And it is to encourage that attitude that he draws the picture he does.

Chandler's disruption of the three basic conventions of the genre, then, correlates with a vision of the world far less comforting than Christie's. Evil cannot be uprooted by logic alone: there is simply too much of it; it is too well organized and too well protected by "legitimate" institutions. It is hard, sometimes impossible, to capture the wrongdoers—and even if you can, society is such that it will continue to spawn them. (p. 238)

[The conventions of the detective novel] serve a formal aesthetic function, but they also serve political ends through their reciprocal relationship with social attitudes. The structure of Christie's novels reflects a passive form of conservatism and encourages us to believe that the problems of violence and social disruption can be eliminated without changing the structure of society. Hers is a soothing voice which holds out promises of harmonious resolution if only we will sit still and let the experts take charge. Chandler's reversal of those conventions reverses the effect. His emphasis on the social origins of crime, and his consequent refusal to resolve his plot in traditional fashion, challenges those conservative assumptions. Instead of calming us, Chandler purposely irritates us, disrupts our peace; at the end of *The Big Sleep* we feel dissatisfied. Chandler forces us to disapprove of the world we live in and demands that we reexamine our political outlook.

Does this make Chandler a "political" writer? Many critics have insisted that he is not, because he does not offer any solutions. As Wilson Pollock puts it, "although some of his works might seem to reveal a political consciousness, it wasn't there. . . .He merely believed that society was corrupt, that the only god was the fast and easy buck, and that there was not very much anyone could do about it." In a sense, this is true. Although Marlowe's continuing battle against corruption offers a model of behavior which is not as passive as Pollock implies, it certainly is possible to read Chandler's novels as essays in mere negativity, cynical suggestions that things are so bad that there is no point in trying to change them.

But Marlowe as a model of behavior—indeed, the whole question of "solutions"—is really beside the point. Chandler is a political writer, not because he promotes a particular political line, but because his novels challenge, in a dynamic and forceful way, the hidden political assumptions of other novels which have been widely read and extremely influential. Such an intellectual challenge may or may not be more important than a political program but it probably has to precede one, and in many ways, it is the most valuable and important work that a writer can do. (pp. 241-42)

> Peter J. Rabinowitz, "Rats Behind the Wainscoting: Politics, Convention, and Chandler's 'The Big Sleep'," *in* Texas Studies in Literature and Language *(copyright © 1980 by the University of Texas Press), Vol. 22, No. 2, Summer, 1980, pp. 224-45.*

JERRY SPEIR   (essay date 1981)

Philip Marlowe crackles to life on a cloudy October morning in the first paragraph of *The Big Sleep*. . . . ''I was wearing my powder-blue suit, with dark blue shirt, tie and display handkerchief, black brogues, black wool socks with dark blue clocks on them. I was neat, clean, shaved and sober, and I didn't care who knew it. I was everything the well-dressed private detective ought to be. I was calling on four million dollars.'' Already he exhibits the wry self-mockery which occupies us throughout the novels. The tone is self-assured, even cocky, but it also maintains the ironic detachment of a man conscious of his own pose. By the end of the novel, however, these high spirits will have changed dramatically. And it is precisely in such alterations of Marlowe's mood and in the revelations which precipitate them that Chandler imbeds the meaning of his stories. (p. 19)

Critics have often complained that Chandler was overly concerned with sentimentalism and the tropes of the chivalric romance; the kind of elements on which this glass panel focuses. But even a cursory look at Chandler's overt references to the romance and knight-errantry within the novel, as here, indicates a decided touch of irony in his treatment of the subject. Indeed, *The Big Sleep* might be read as a chronicle of the *failure* of romance. In the midst of one of his confrontations with Carmen, for example, Marlowe turns to his chess board for distraction. He makes a move with a knight, then retracts it and comments, "the move with the knight was wrong. I put it back where I had moved it from. Knights had no meaning in this game. It wasn't a game for knights." (p. 30)

[*Farewell, My Lovely*] continues to elaborate many of the basic themes established in *The Big Sleep.* It seeks simple, straightforward explanations for the plot's sinister actions but must settle, finally, for conjecture on the multiplicity of possible motivations behind its characters' deeds. Sentimentalism and the quest of the romantic knight are again mocked, and Marlowe, again, undergoes an experience of recognition which embodies the book's essential message. The controlling notion which is new to this plot involves what appears at first to be some sort of general conspiracy aimed at Marlowe's elimination. (p. 32)

Farewell, My Lovely is a book which raises many questions about the relationships between people and the forces of good and evil at loose in the world. In characteristic Chandler fashion, several of these are never really answered, but those that are and those about which answers are hinted outline for us the motivations which propel this plot and, by extension, which propel society. (p. 40)

[The] major irony pervading this book evolves from the fact that love is at its root. Moose loved Velma, and his unrelenting search for her generated this legacy of death. As Marlowe says, "That's what makes it funny, tragic-funny." As in *The Big Sleep,* evil and death have again been spawned by an essentially pure, if naive, motive. And, again, the notion of the romantic quest is thoroughly mocked. Velma is here transformed (mostly by money) into a "grail," the object of the knight's traditional quest. But Moose Malloy, a bumbling knight at best, finds that his search for the lovely, if not holy, Mrs. "Grayle" only leads to death—at her hands.

Moreover, at the end of the book, Chandler offers a comment on sentimentality, a quality associated with romanticism and of which he is often accused. Trying to explain Velma's suicide, Marlowe argues that it was perhaps a generous gesture, an effort to spare her aging husband the embarrassment of a trial, to protect "an old man who had loved not wisely, but too well." (pp. 42-3)

[As Chandler was putting the final touches on *The High Window*], he wrote his publisher:

> I'm afraid the book is not going to be any good to you. No action, no likeable characters, no nothing. . . .

But a weakness even closer to its surface lies in the fact that *The High Window* is two stories that are insufficiently woven together. One story involves an older woman (Mrs. Elizabeth Bright Murdock), her young, neurotic secretary (Merle Davis), and a blackmail scheme which stems from the questionable circumstances surrounding the death of Mrs. Murdock's first husband eight years in the past. The second story concerns the theft and counterfeiting of an antique gold coin, the Brashear Doubloon, the original of which has disappeared from Mrs. Murdock's collection. (p. 44)

The doubloon story occupies by far the greater portion of the book and of Marlowe's time. But finally the motive behind the doubloon counterfeiting is revealed to be strictly a desire for quick profit. Simple greed—a powerful part of the human psyche to be sure—is just not as engrossing as the subtler shades of trust, mistrust, love, power, and mental derangement that Chandler handled so skillfully in the first two novels. While the plot does explore such motivations to a degree, its power is diminished by the secondary status given to the more intriguing relationship between Mrs. Murdock and Miss Davis. Moreover, Chandler's efforts to link these plots are unconvincing. Even though the man behind the counterfeiting, Vannier, is also Mrs. Murdock's blackmailer, we rarely encounter him, and the crucial bridge between the two stories is never adequately realized.

But neither is *The High Window* a complete failure. To consider it so would be to fall into the trap of reading Chandler strictly for plot, an approach against which he cautioned many times.

What success the novel achieves is precisely in its examination of its two central female characters. (pp. 44-5)

[In its simplest form, *The Lady in the Lake*] tells the story of a vain, greedy, jealous woman who kills three people in a misguided attempt to free herself of personal entanglements. She is then herself killed by her former husband, who meets his own ignominious death at the hands of a young soldier. Significantly, World War II, a major distraction for Chandler (and the world) at the time, is here insinuated into his fiction. The story is sustained by one of the oldest tricks in the genre, mistaken identity, but the cleverness with which it is managed leaves the reader aghast at his own willingness to be duped. Perhaps the most engaging thing about the book is that Chandler is able to maintain this illusion, and even to mock what he is doing, without the reader being the wiser until the very end. (p. 51)

[The book draws] a portrait of evil finding its way even into society's remotest, most idyllic hideaways. Evil has escaped the city and reveals itself as a product of individual avarice and passion capable of carrying on quite well outside the modern urban wilderness.

But, beyond its general thematic stance, the novel also offers us insight into Chandler's approach to his craft. Although he despised the demands placed on him by the genre for neatly dovetailed plots, the evidence of *The Lady in the Lake* suggests that he was here attempting to demonstrate both that he could write such a plot and that he could parody the very exercise simultaneously. The plot is a fairly simple one, complicated by the old trick of mistaken identity. But it is sustained and rendered unique by the things about which Chandler truly cared— the language itself and the distinctive tone and narrative style which is Philip Marlowe. (pp. 56-7)

[Critics have berated the misanthropic aspects of *The Little Sister*] and Chandler himself asserted that "it's the only book of mine I have actively disliked. It was written in a bad mood and I think that comes through."

Indeed, there are aspects of the novel which suggest a genuine absence of human values; seven people meet their deaths here while blackmail, greed, and envy divide friendships and families alike. But there are also elements of the novel which mark Chandler's further development as a writer. Its plot resolution exhibits a more sophisticated ambiguity as Marlowe achieves new insight into his own inescapable connection with this debased society. And, as an emblem of degradation, the movie industry provides extensive material here for the first time in the novels. (p. 57)

The book portrays gangsters against gangsters, friends against friends, and family against family—all for the greater glory of the almighty dollar and the power associated with it. But what is at the core of this human disaster? At least a part of the answer is Hollywood.

While we may agree with Frank MacShane [see excerpt above] that *The Little Sister* is not "a real Hollywood novel," in the sense that it does not attempt a complete portrait of that phenomenon, clearly Chandler is concerned here with the effects of Hollywood and the Hollywood mentality on individuals and, by extension, on society. (p. 58)

It is not a pretty story. A large and powerful industry based on illusion transforms the youth from America's heartland into conniving, sadistic automatons, and the family, which we expect to resist such impulses, only aggravates this lust for power. The conflicting forces stirred up by this bizarre plot allow for no simple resolution. Indeed, the ending that Chandler finally did contrive marks a perceptible change in his handling of the mystery novel and in Marlowe's comprehension of his peculiar fictional world. (pp. 59-60)

It is not "a proper mystery" in the sense that it refuses to establish simple cause-effect relationships and pin the guilt, finally, on a single character. This disregard for the genre's demand for straightforward puzzles is, of course, not new with *The Little Sister,* but this novel does leave a great deal more "hanging in the air" than any of its predecessors. And its ambiguity takes its toll on Marlowe. Near the end of the book, he muses: "Sometimes when I'm low I try to reason it out. But it gets too complicated. The whole damn case was that way."

The illusoriness of Hollywood and of human action seem to have converged. Marlowe has watched the whole drama unfold and still it makes no sense. (p. 60)

The outlook is decidedly pessimistic. But beyond its black foreboding, *The Little Sister* is also a considerably better work of fiction than is generally credited. In its complications of family, organized crime, and Hollywood, it achieves a panorama of the modern condition which is new for Chandler. And in its discovery of ways to demonstrate Marlowe's connection with the human weaknesses on which the story turns, it provides new insight into his central character. It is a fitting prelude to Chandler's next and, in many ways, most ambitious novel, *The Long Goodbye*. (p. 63)

[*The Long Goodbye*] is Chandler's most personal novel and his most ambitious. It is at once his most autobiographical work and his boldest attempt to exceed the confines of the detective mystery. (p. 65)

The organization of this novel is of considerable interest as well since Chandler here succeeds in expanding the story well beyond its central mystery plot. His selection of characters, locales, and situations gives him abundant opportunity for digressions on a wide variety of topics—and the asides frequently grow into small essays. Roger Wade, the writer, delivers several of these sermonettes on such diverse subjects as Freud, drunks, prayer, money, homosexuals, and the writer's dependence on similes. Harlan Potter, a wealthy entrepreneur, discourses ironically on Man, democracy, newspapers and consumerism. Inclusion of the publisher's agent, Howard Spencer, provides a forum for discussing the publishing business in general and historical romances in particular. And Marlowe himself delivers a number of these brief essays on subjects ranging from jails, blonds, and public relations to nursing homes, lawyers, and TV commercials. Chandler has been criticized for interrupting his plot with these apparently extraneous, often splenetic interludes. Such criticism, however, demonstrates rather traditional expectations of detective mysteries and totally neglects the larger story which Chandler has here set himself to tell.

On its most straightforward level, *The Long Goodbye* is a story of friendship established and friendship betrayed. But on a grander scale that story is only the microcosm of a more general social deterioration. (pp. 65-6)

This book is perpetually asking the question "Why?" Frequently the query involves Marlowe's own introspection: Why does he stick with being a private investigator? Why does he take certain actions and not others while he is on a case? The concern so pervades the novel that at one point it even provides the author an occasion for self-parody: an extended joke about California's weather and the smog ends, "Once in a while a whole day would be clear, nobody quite knew why." Though the remark calls our attention to the absurdity of pushing one's quest for causes too hard, it also recalls the cosmic mystery still evident in the play of sunlight in the bushes at the end of *The Big Sleep*. Concern for causes, of course, is a basic convention of the genre. But one of Chandler's recurrent themes is the practical, human limits of such concerns, and nowhere is he more explicit about that theme than in *The Long Goodbye*. (pp. 68-9)

Terry Lennox is the real focus of the book. Marlowe's final assessment of him is that he has only private standards, with no sense of a general ethic. Lennox himself admits to living his life as an act, that "an act is all there is," but . . . our judgment of him is mitigated by our recognition of the horrifying past which he has survived. Even Marlowe will not judge him because he recognizes the limits of his own ability to comprehend another man's pain, a pain articulated by Lennox only in the vague phrases, "I got badly hurt and it wasn't any fun with those Nazi doctors. It did something to me."

In the midst of all this, is Philip Marlowe who describes himself only as "a romantic. . . . I hear voices crying in the night and I go see what's the matter." But the line is delivered with some ironic reflection, and, by the end of the novel, we and Marlowe have sufficient reason to question the practicality of such an approach to a fallen world. The world, in fact, shows ample signs of having changed in such a way as to make romantic heroes obsolete. War on a new scale has shattered at least one man's sense of any ethic beyond the personal, and Lennox's experiences and the coincidences surrounding them plant the seeds of destruction in several other lives. Chandler has clearly accomplished his announced purpose of making Marlowe look "in the end either sentimental or plain foolish" for trying to be an honest man in the face of "this strange corrupt world we live in." (pp. 75-6)

The Long Goodbye is clearly Chandler's last great effort to push the mystery novel out of its stereotyped niche. Unlike any of its predecessors, it takes on the whole modern society as its subject. It concentrates its examination of the effects of that society on three specific individuals: Terry Lennox is a casualty of the mass insanity of modern war; Roger Wade is a product of the great entertainment (read: escape) industry and the modern perversion of art; Marlowe is the spirit of another age striving desperately to maintain a sense of decency. And all three, of course, are projections of different aspects of the character of Raymond Chandler. The book turns both outward toward the world and inward toward the self. It recognizes human weakness. It ends on a puzzled note of quiet reflection. And it does so with the conviction that the world's problems are finally the problems of individual human beings. Terry Lennox may well have the war and a tyrannical father-in-law to blame for much of his plight, but he surrenders rather easily when he discovers that "the brass ring . . . wasn't gold." Roger Wade may well blame his hysterical wife and a modern longing for artistic pabulum for his unhappy career, but he must also recognize his own contributions to both. And Marlowe is himself left to wonder what it is he wants, exactly, and what it is that he expects of other people. He is unsure, finally, and his uncertainty underscores the book's ambiguity. Either the world is dominated by forces truly beyond individual control or individuals have merely acquiesced to those unprincipled elements of a society whose only measures of value are power and money. Neither alternative is pleasant. The plight of the individual in the modern world is the essence of Marlowe's dilemma at the end of *The Long Goodbye;* we are uncertain of what we want and, by extension, of who we are. (pp. 77-8)

[*Playback*] has been called "undistinguished," "a forgettable work," and "a sad hoked-up job." While it lacks much of the plot and character complication which mark the earlier books, it still displays the characteristic Chandlerian wit and provides certain insights into the author and his attitude toward his work in his later years. . . .

Unusual aspects of the book include Marlowe's increased sexual interest in the two primary female characters, a genuinely sympathetic treatment of big-city police, inclusion of some quite lengthy scenes which have little or nothing to do with the plot line, and, rather astonishingly for a Chandler novel, an apparent disinterest in the final fate of characters: the two principle female characters each simply "disappear" from the story without a real resolution. (p. 78)

Part of Chandler's striving was to deal somewhat more realistically with male-female struggles than previous books had allowed him. Toward that end, Marlowe and Helen Vermilyea establish a rendezvous for the evening and the two finally wind up in bed together. Each, however, is restrained from a genuine commitment by memories of past loves. Marlowe does not want to make love to her in his own apartment because "I had a dream here once, a year and a half ago. There's still a shred of it left. I'd like it to stay in charge." Helen's memory is of her former husband, a jet pilot killed in a plane crash. . . . Such statements and actions manifest an extreme idea of love as one pure encounter never to be equalled, always invoking an impossible standard from the past—an idea which has difficulty coexisting with the vagaries and ambiguities of day-to-day existence.

Marlowe himself suffers from a similar problem which finds its clearest expression in the book's final chapter. Characteristically, he has returned home from a case despondent over his relative ineffectiveness in the face of a world which refuses to conform to his stylized notions of decorum. He goes so far as to deny himself a drink, saying "Alcohol was no cure for this. Nothing was any cure but the hard inner heart that asked for nothing from anyone." His instinct counsels withdrawal and a hardening of the spirit against the cold, insensitive world.

But, shortly, that attitude undergoes a radical transformation. The telephone rings and Linda Loring, Marlowe's dream from a year and a half ago (in *The Long Goodbye*), is on the other end. She is calling from Paris and asking Marlowe to marry her. After a brief lover's argument over who is to pay for whose plane ticket—Marlowe insists on paying—Marlowe is a changed man. His romantic reverie ends: "The air was full of music."

In *The Poodle Springs Story*, the novel he was working on at his death, Chandler has Marlowe married to Linda Loring. The inevitable conflicts growing out of their totally different economic and social backgrounds were to provide a major subplot for the book. In the fragment of the story which survives, Marlowe is looking for office space in Poodle Springs (a parody of Palm Springs) and discovers that he is preceded everywhere by gossip about his wife's wealth. Chandler intended their relationship to be "a running fight interspersed with amorous interludes," but in *Playback,* Linda's appearance serves a considerably more harmonious function.

Her phone call in the last chapter, which has no connection at all to the plot line, is virtually a *deus ex machina* resolution which culminates a long series of reflections on the past, or playbacks, that structure the novel. . . . Linda Loring surfaces from Marlowe's past to rescue him, at least momentarily, from the depths of depression and to underscore the role of fate and chance in a world not nearly so ordered as Marlowe's dated sensibilities might desire. (pp. 80-1)

Chandler is no more complex or incomprehensible than his age, and *Playback* is no less than the last pitch from the heart of an articulate witness of a dying order and a dawning confusion. (p. 83)

Chandler's novels, of course, followed his noteworthy career as a writer of short stories for popular "pulp" magazines. A survey of those stories gives evidence of considerable experimentation in subject matter, style, point of view, and detective types which contributed to the novels' later success. Some of the stories were "cannibalized," as Chandler put it, into the novels, and a close look at that process allows us the unusual opportunity of observing the writer at work, transforming his own earlier, simpler material into the broader vision of the

later books. But even the stories that weren't cannibalized have much to teach us about Chandler's development as a writer, and it seems appropriate here to look back at those stories for the deeper appreciation they may give us of the novels and the novelist. (p. 85)

The greater restrictions of the short story were responsible, especially in his early stories, for limiting Chandler's subject matter as well as his style. His first story, **"Blackmailers Don't Shoot"** . . . , explores a theme common to many of Chandler's early efforts. Its fury arises from the internal struggle of rival racketeers and its social comment from the close connection between the rackets and the "authorities"—police, lawyers, and politicians. **"Blackmailers Don't Shoot"** is, in fact, one of Chandler's better early stories. It complicates the organized crime story with a young movie starlet, Rhonda Farr, who, in her attempt to adapt to the wickedness of the town and profession in which she finds herself, contrives a public relations stunt which backfires. The initial captivation of the story derives from the rather curious circumstance that the detective, Mallory, appears to be one of the blackmailers. But Mallory's act proves to be only part of a game which he is playing for his employer, a minor rackets figure named Landrey. The object of the game is, evidently, to revive the lost romance between Landrey and Rhonda Farr, the starlet. Finally, as is typical of Chandler even in this very first story, the facts of the matter are decidedly unclear. We are left with the police explanations, which are self-satisfying and internally consistent, but which we, and Mallory, know to be false.

In its obscuring of the truth, indeed in its suggestion that the truth is hopelessly elusive, the story establishes a pattern evident throughout the Chandler canon. Mallory here, as Marlowe frequently does in the novels, constructs several alternative possibilities for why things happened the way they did. None of them are totally satisfying. And yet we sense in this story motivations basic to human nature and not overly complex. Mallory speaks of Landrey's motives in these simple, if oblique, lines: "He crossed everybody up and then he crossed himself. He played too many parts and got his lines mixed. He was gun-drunk. When he got a rod in his hand he had to shoot somebody. Somebody shot back." It is a tale of cunning, self-deception, and a random violence directed only at "somebody" in a mysterious world where that "somebody" can shoot back.

The story is decidedly Chandlerian—in its refusal to offer a simple resolution, in its choice of subject matter and suggestion of a general corruption, and in its flashes of descriptive power and brilliant dialogue. But, given the stylistic excellence which the novels have led us to expect, there are also lapses here which startle the ear. Two such shortcomings occur on the story's first page. In the opening description of Mallory, we read: "His hair was crisp and black, ever so faintly touched with grey, as by an almost diffident hand." The word *diffident* calls undue attention to itself as rather exaggerated for the context. And our first look at the starlet begins: "Rhonda Farr was very beautiful." It is the kind of flat abstraction which we do not expect of Chandler and which rarely recurs after this first effort. (pp. 91-2)

[His next two stories, **"Smart Aleck Kill"** and **"Finger Man"**], are very similar to **"Blackmailers Don't Shoot"** in their subject. Both chronicle a series of struggles within the rackets organizations and highlight the involvement of an important political figure in those organizations. But because they lack some of the complications of **"Blackmailers"**—the confused and confusing starlet, the bizarre love interest as catalyst—these are rather slight stories by comparison.

[But Chandler's fourth story, **"Killer in the Rain,"**] marks a new direction in which organized crime is no longer the central motif. The first story to be "cannibalized" (for *The Big Sleep*), it concerns Carmen and the smut-lending business of a man named Steiner (cf. Geiger). The story ends with a shootout at Joe Marty's apartment which is similar to, but more violent than, the scene at Joe Brody's in the novel. But, though the story shares many features of the novel, its most curious twist is in the handling of the father. Carmen's father here is a "former Pittsburgh steelworker, truck guard, all-round muscle stiff" who wandered to California and blundered into a fortune when oil was discovered on his property. A curious touch is added to the story when he confesses, "Carmen—she's not my kid at all. I just picked her up in Smoky, a little baby in the street. She didn't have nobody. I guess maybe I steal her, huh?" And the strange quality of the tale is compounded when he asserts further that he is now in love with her and wants to marry her. His concern is that she has developed an interest in this Steiner character, and he wants help in ending it.

Though there is still an element of organized crime lurking in the shadows, the story focuses on this bizarre romance which leaves the detective, in anticipation of Marlowe, wondering "why I had taken the trouble" and feeling "tired and old and not much use to anybody." Curiously, the detective is never given a name in this story; he is just an anonymous first-person narrator.

Throughout his career as a short-story writer, Chandler was obviously searching for the ideal detective and the ideal narrative stance. His next story, **"Nevada Gas"** . . . , attempts to bridge the gap between first- and third-person narration. It opens with a powerful scene of vindictiveness which a first-person detective narrator could not describe—simply because he could not have been on the scene. But once the detective, Johnny DeRuse, enters the story, he is followed very closely—in the manner of a first-person narration. Chandler was here striving to fuse the objectivity of the third-person point of view with the subjectivity of the first person. The dichotomy was one which he toyed with throughout his early career. First-person narration, of course, limits an author to the perceptions and experiences of his narrator. Third-person narration, on the other hand, denies the author the immediacy of his detective's sensibilities and reactions. The objectivity of the third person obviously appealed to Chandler early; six of his first nine stories are written from that point of view. But then a string of first-person stories reversed that pattern, and eleven of his last thirteen detective stories have first-person narrators. Chandler's final resolution of this subjective-objective problem in the novels, of course, was to create a first-person narrator, Marlowe, with a very objective narrative style. His very "objectivity," then, provides a veil for what are obviously very intense subjective responses to the events of the novels, and Chandler is able to achieve some of the virtues of both points of view. (pp. 92-3)

As a group, the stories display for us the mind of a technician in the midst of honing his craft. The crisp declarative style, plain descriptions, terse characterizations, sardonic wit, and ominous mood can all be seen here in their formative stages. But it is only in the novels that all those elements so characteristic of Chandler achieve their maturity. The difference is partly a matter of space—space to allow for dramatic and character development and to get away from the requisite, slavish devotion to plot. And it is partly a matter of the creation of the voice of Marlowe who, though he may appear in the stories in prototype, is only realized completely in the longer works. The novels, unlike the short stories, consistently make their impression upon the reader through the sympathy they evoke for this endearing, nobly motivated detective. (p. 104)

> *Jerry Speir, in his* Raymond Chandler *(copyright ©️ 1981 by Frederick Ungar Publishing Co., Inc.), Ungar, 1981, 166 p.*

ADDITIONAL BIBLIOGRAPHY

Cawelti, John G. "Hammett, Chandler, and Spillane." In his *Adventure, Mystery, and Romance*, pp. 162-91. Chicago, London: The University of Chicago Press, 1976.*

> Compares Hammett's objective style with Chandler's figurative one, and Hammett's pessimism to Chandler's idealism.

Conrad, Peter. "The Private Dick As Dandy." *The Times Literary Supplement*, No. 3956 (20 January 1978): 60.

> Discusses Chandler as romantic aesthete.

Durham, Philip. *Down These Mean Streets a Man Must Go: Raymond Chandler's Knight*. Chapel Hill: The University of North Carolina Press, 1963, 173 p.

> Biocritical study.

Fleming, Ian. "Raymond Chandler." *The London Magazine* 6, No. 12 (December 1959): 43-54.

> Recollections of Chandler, as well as letters Chandler exchanged with Fleming, creator of James Bond.

Schopen, Bernard A. "From Puzzles to People: The Development of the American Detective Novel." *Studies in American Fiction* 7, No. 2 (Autumn 1979): 175-89.

> Includes a consideration of Chandler's influence on the detective novel, which he liberated from "the rigidly naturalistic world in which it had been born."

Shatzkin, Roger. "Who Cares Who Killed Owen Taylor?" In *The Modern American Novel and the Movies*, edited by Gerald Peary and Roger Shatzkin, pp. 80-94. New York: Frederick Ungar Publishing Co., 1978.

> Study of the adaptation of *The Big Sleep* into Howard Hawks's 1946 film.

Sington, Derrick. "Raymond Chandler on Crime and Punishment." *The Twentieth Century* 165, No. 987 (May 1959): 502-04.

> Chandler's opinions on penal reform and his opposition to capital punishment.

Smith, David. "The Private Eye of Raymond Chandler." *Journal of American Studies* 14, No. 3 (December 1980): 423-41.

> Philip Marlowe contrasted with his milieu of urban corruption.

John Jay Chapman

1862-1933

American critic, essayist, dramatist, poet, and translator.

Though he wrote in a variety of genres, Chapman is best remembered for his literary and social criticism. His essays on Emerson and on Greek literature inspired Edmund Wilson to call him "the best writer on literature of his generation," and some critics have characterized him as a neglected genius. In a long and varied career Chapman wrote on topics as diverse as modern political reform and ancient Greek tragedy. He produced translations of Dante and Sophocles as well as plays for children. Some critics blame his diversity for his failure to capture a wide audience in any one genre. Others see this diversity as symptomatic of a potentially great mind lacking focus.

An active concern for social change was conspicuous in Chapman's family background. He was descended from abolitionists Eleanor Jay and Maria Weston Chapman, and his maternal grandfather was Chief Justice John Jay. A lawyer active in New York politics, Chapman joined the City Reform Club and the Good Government Club. He also began publishing *The Political Nursery*, a periodic political review. Chapman exercised an intense zeal in his political, religious, and moral beliefs, often suffering periods of extreme physical and emotional stress. On one occasion, after what he took to be an offense against the woman he loved, Chapman violently beat a man. After his outburst, he deliberately burned his hand, which was subsequently amputated. Repeated personal tragedies eventually affected Chapman's incisive but unstable intellect and in his later years he devoted himself to increasingly incoherent causes, becoming convinced that America had to sacrifice its young men in war to atone for its sins; that the Roman Catholic church was trying to take over America; and that a Judaic world government was in fact forming.

Chapman's early works are critical essays, the most notable of which are his studies of Ralph Waldo Emerson, who had a profound effect on Chapman's own writing style. These essays are both an appreciation of Emerson and an extension of Emerson's philosophy of humanism and individualism. The studies of both Emerson and William Lloyd Garrison have their basis more in Chapman's personal view of the men than in his research on them. Though longer than essays, they lack the objectivity, proportion, and chronology of biographies.

Chapman is most appropriately classified as a cultural critic. His eclectic writings espouse an aristocratic appreciation of individualism: that is, a person first has to be a fully realised member of society before becoming an individual. Chapman's two books about American politics, *Causes and Consequences* and *Practical Agitation*, were favorably received. In the first work he diagnoses the causes and consequences of the corrupt alliance of business and government; then in *Practical Agitation* he prescribes a means of political reform. Today these two volumes are ranked with his Emerson studies as his best works. Chapman's writing style is vigorous and straightforward. Chapman formulates novel ideas in words that have the force of often-repeated sayings. He is admirable for this clarity of expression and for his thoughtful urbanity. Perhaps his great-

Culver Pictures

est fault was his tendency to sum up his topics in neat formulas—often unsuccessfully applied to his biographical subjects—whose scope was often greater than a clever epigram could encompass.

Chapman's detractors do not attack his form, but his ideas. Recent critics, notably Alfred Kazin, tend to see Chapman as something of a dilettante, content to be thought the radical "wild man" of his group of upper-class New England clubmen. They point out that Chapman did not produce one work of real scholarship or lasting value. Admirers of Chapman see him as a man out of step with his age: a translator of the classics when nobody was reading them, a political writer whose talents matured while a political class of educated readers was disappearing. Edmund Wilson wrote that "perhaps no writer of his generation had dealt at once so realistically and with so much clairvoyance with the modern American world."

PRINCIPAL WORKS

The Two Philosophers (satiric verse) 1892
Causes and Consequences (essays) 1898
Emerson, and Other Essays (essays) 1898

Practical Agitation   (essays)   1900
Four Plays for Children   (drama)   1908
Learning and Other Essays   (essays)   1910
The Treason and Death of Benedict Arnold   (drama)   1910
William Lloyd Garrison   (biographical essays)   1913
Greek Genius and Other Essays   (essays)   1915
Memories and Milestones   (essays)   1915
Notes on Religion   (essays)   1915
Songs and Poems   (poetry)   1919
A Glance toward Shakespeare   (essays)   1922
Letters and Religion   (essays)   1924
Dante [translator]   (poetry)   1927
Lucian, Plato and Greek Morals   (essays)   1931
New Horizons in American Life   (essays)   1932

THE DIAL   (essay date 1897)

Two recent numbers of "The Atlantic Monthly" have included in their contents an essay well calculated to startle the readers, especially the older readers, of that conservative magazine. The essay in question ["Emerson Sixty Years After"] is from the pen of a new writer [John Jay Chapman], and is nothing less than a frank revaluation of the work of Emerson. Discarding as far as possible, all traditional judgments, the attempt is made to estimate, from the broader because more cosmopolitan standpoint of these latter days, and in the light of a fuller knowledge than was in the possession of an earlier generation, the value of Emerson's contribution to American thought and American literature. Some of the conclusions reached by the critic are so far at variance with those that have long been seemingly crystallized in the histories of our literature that one rubs his eyes at the iconoclastic utterances, and wonders if anything is sacred to these daring young men who so busily engaged in bringing us new lamps to exchange for our old ones. It is not that the essay betrays animus, or is in any offensive sense an attack upon a great and cherished reputation, but rather that its writer has set about a *de novo* exposition, and has freed himself from the trammels of the conventional phrase and the conventional attitude. (p. 137)

> *"The Revaluation of Literature," in* The Dial, *Vol. XXII, No. 257, March 1, 1897, pp. 137-39.**

HENRY JAMES   (essay date 1898)

[While] we watch all the developments of American literature with hope, we fix our eyes with especial interest on the attempt in the direction of criticism which from time to time reach us across the Atlantic. This it is which leads us to speak at some length of the really rather notable essays of Mr. John Jay Chapman [*Emerson, and Other Essays*]. Merely as a writer, Mr. Chapman does not attract us very much. We acknowledge in him many merits. He is vigorous, incisive, terse. He makes quite clear to himself what he means to say, and says it straight. And the total effect is, in ours ears at least, a little *staccato*, a little smart, even a little flashy. . . . Mr. Chapman is so anxious to put off the frippery of conventional literary diction, that he assumes with undue readiness the frippery of slang. . . . He is singularly free from that trick of gravely repeating commonplaces which seems inherent in the method of some even of the most eminent critics. He does not take up a subject

unless he has something really to add, to elucidate. And, therefore, even where you disagree with him most, it is at least not waste of time to hear what he has to say. He may not be final, for all his attitude of finality; but certainly he will be suggestive, stimulating. Besides seeing for himself, Mr. Chapman has the determination, so characteristic of what is best in the distinctively modern attitude to things, to see precisely, to see the object as it is. Consequently his criticism is often, in appearance, destructive rather than constructive. Before you can get at what a thing is in literature, you have to blow away and dispel so many popular phantasies of what it is not. . . . [To] ruthlessly analyse and destroy such falsely idealised portraits, to get rid of all the sentimentality and fluff of popular criticism, is one of Mr. Chapman's favourite exercises.

You find him so occupied in two of the best essays in the book, those on Walt Whitman and Robert Louis Stevenson. . . .

Mr. Chapman would set up a new image [of Whitman], based on deeper insight and finer analysis. Whitman is of cosmic rather than local import, a type, but in no way a distinctively American type. He is one of the tramps of nature; one of those for whom civilisation is a fetter and organisation a drudgery, and a life in the open air, by the roadside, the only tolerable existence. . . .

Mr. Chapman [would] explain the truth and beauty of Whitman's work as an expression of "the physical joy of mere living," side by side with its falseness and tawdriness as an expression of the manner of man's life in the human relationships, in multitudes and in cities.

Mr. Chapman's essay on Stevenson takes a line of deliberate, though by no means unqualified, depreciation. Stevenson's popularity has run, he tells us, "at times into hero-worship and at times into drawing-room fatuity." And then he goes on to show that Stevenson was not great, because he never wrote at first hand. He was always repeating with infinite versatility and grace the manner of some other man who had attracted him. He was "the most extraordinary mimic that has ever appeared in literature." Remorselessly Mr. Chapman tracks this clue through the tale of Stevenson's volumes, finding the root of the whole matter in the excessive self-consciousness of the writer's method, his fixed intention to be an artist. (p. 163)

Mr. Chapman is debatable. He trails many a coat. But he cannot be neglected. He compels either the revision of your conceptions, under the influence of his, or the confirmation of them, in conflict with his. And surely the power to do this is of the essence of that dynamic force in which the potency of veritable criticism it consists.

The Whitman and the Stevenson are, we think, the most successful papers in the book. There is good stuff in the long essay on Emerson and the shorter study of Browning, but Emerson and Browning do not lend themselves to Mr. Chapman's method quite so well as the lesser men. Mr. Chapman is rather fond of summing his subjects up in formulas, and it is characteristic of the big natures, who touch life at many points and are never consistent, that they elude formulas. Certain soul-sides, therefore, of Emerson and Browning, their common interest, for instance, in the individual human personality, Mr. Chapman brings out crisply and well; others remain unplumbed. On the other hand the two essays devoted to literature of an earlier period than that with which Mr. Chapman chiefly occupies himself—*A Study of Romeo* and *Michael Angelo's Sonnets*—

have something which is lacking in his work elsewhere, a note of reverence. . . .

We shall hope to come across Mr. Chapman again. Few living critics go so straight to the heart of their problem, or waste so little time in writing "about it and about." (p. 164)

Henry James, "Transatlantic Criticism," in The Academy, No. 1371, August 13, 1898, pp. 163-64.

EDWARD E. HALE, JR.   (essay date 1898)

Certainly we have in [*Emerson, and Other Essays,* by John Jay Chapman] more serious work than usually appears in such collections,—serious, not thereby dull and tedious, but worth considering. . . .

[The essay on Robert Browning] seems to me admirable. It takes rather a simple but a perfectly maintainable view, and keeps it before the reader clearly and well. It is a view which will open Browning up to a good many people. To Browningites it may not bring much,—not even pleasure. But not everybody has read Browning yet; there are a good many who are only now beginning the experience. Mr. Chapman says that the great mass of Browning will in future be rediscovered by "belated sufferers from the philosophy of the nineteenth century." . . . Mr. Chapman's essay ought to put them in the right way; and this is proof of its excellence in another direction, a direction in which Mr. Chapman was probably aiming. . . . Mr. Chapman's idea was to show what had actually been the relation of Browning to the middle of the nineteenth century. He is a critic who studies the fact with disinterestedness, not a diffuser of popular culture. Still, if Mr. Chapman has arranged the standpoint so that approachers of Browning see everything in right perspective, it is probable that he has clearly in mind the way the thing really was to contemporaries. So I admire the essay on Browning, although it does not say much of one element in Browning's work with interests some people,—namely, the "literary side." Mr. Chapman considers the philosophical and historical aspects [of Browning's work], and also the diction and metre; and as these are the things which are of interest to most people, he does well. I have an interest in the fact that we have in Browning, as in any author, life, emotion, passion, taking literary forms, and in these circumstances attending metamorphoses. But these things do not occupy Mr. Chapman's attention very much. I imagine he thinks them rather trivial.

The essay on Stevenson, like that on Browning, is an explanation of the nature of the man and of his "relation to his time," or, practically, what he really has in him that is worth while. Here I cannot feel that Mr. Chapman repeats his success. It seems to me that he offers a facile explanation born rather from his own mind than from any especial knowledge of Stevenson's work. He thinks that Stevenson was devoted to Art, that he thought that the way to write with art was to write as other great men had written, that he therefore imitated all sorts of people, that the things written in this way looked so much like real literary things that people who did not know any better were quite taken in by them. He thinks that Americans were well pleased with Stevenson's stories and things, and were fascinated to see that what they liked had the characteristics which reminded them of standard authors, and therefore seemed literary. Hence America urged Stevenson to write twenty thousand dollars' worth a year, and praised him to the skies. This

process Mr. Chapman sums up under the genial epigram, "It is Chicago making culture hum." (p. 128)

As to the matter of style, I cannot say enough just here to present all the difficulties that I seem to see in Mr. Chapman's work. I must content myself with noting that I think he does not at all understand the attitude of a writer to what he writes, nor the attitude of Stevenson to what he wrote; and also I cannot feel that he has any particular acquaintance with the way Stevenson did write. I mean he does not seem to have read his books carefully with a view to style—a matter which is of slight interest to him.

If I am right here, it is necessary that Mr. Chapman should be wrong; and he does not get on better by misrepresenting various things, through negligence or what not. It would be uninteresting to go over minor errors, but of course a number of confident assertions of things that are not so, even if they be not important, does much to weaken one's confidence in the foundation of a critic's views. . . .

[In] this essay he has seized, distorted, and exaggerated a detail, and not mentioned the main point at all. He has not shown any especial reason why people who really know what is good should find in Stevenson anything worth while. The things that I have said about these two essays might also be said of the essays on [Ralph Waldo] Emerson and [Walt] Whitman. That on Emerson is as good as the Browning essay, or even better, and in the same way, with the addition that Emerson really was primarily a social force as Mr. Chapman considers him, whereas Browning was primarily a poet. The essay on Whitman, however, is as wrong as the essay on Stevenson, and in just the same way, too; it does not mention the main point, but devotes itself to exaggeration of minor matters. . . .

[The Whitman and Stevenson] essays are really a little behind the times: as controversial documents they are good; as critical judgments, failures. (p. 129)

[The] most important thing to note about Mr. Chapman as a critic [is that he] is too apt to be irritated at current popular opinion and feeling, contemptuous of it, unsympathetic, uncomprehending. He is quite willing to utter the truth, and to have people take it or leave it. But as for any real human interest in the people he is writing for, he has not a cent's worth. He cannot think of the American literary public with interest, or even with equanimity; he cannot speak of it without cold sarcasm. (pp. 129-30)

Mr. Chapman's way is probably not a good way to influence America; nor for himself, in the long run at least, is the result likely be good. In the first place, with his lack of feeling for his countrymen he will probably fail ever to say much that is important to them; and in the second, with his own disposition he will often be irritated by harmless fallacies or fancies into ebullitions which will send him a long distance from the right road. . . .

Mr. Chapman, as everyone is aware by this time, has enough power to carry a good deal of weight. As has been often enough said, he is delicate, keen, strong, clever, and full of courage. The disposition which I have noted may render a good deal of his work of slight effect; on the other hand, he may find out how to use it to good purpose, to make it telling. Certainly for the time being, it makes essays rather more amusing to people who do not get vexed at them. (p. 130)

Edward E. Hale, Jr., "Chips from a Critic's Shoulder," in The Dial, Vol. XXV, No. 293, September 1, 1898, pp. 128-30.

CHARLES HALL GRANDGENT (essay date 1927)

Must the *traduttore* [translator] always be a *traditore* [traitor]? No longer can one respond with a confident yes, after reading John Jay Chapman's little *Dante*. . . Yet here is a test as hard as test can be: a genius as difficult as he is beautiful, and as remote as he is difficult. To translate him, however, a real poet has arisen, and the result is very far from justifying a verdict of treason. . . . [It is] an unpretentious booklet, just a rendering of a dozen or so of Mr. Chapman's favorite passages, equipped with the least bit of coyly disguised exegesis.

At the beginning and the end of the volume are some general observations on Dante, considered as a poet for to-day. . . .

[Here] we find, as we found in the same author's backward look at Shakespeare, a good dose of novelty infused with quite as much truth as resides in the many-times-said. . . . Mr. Chapman stresses Dante's reverence for the poet's mission, his high seriousness, the constantly personal character of his writings, his intensity, his loneliness,—the "solitary egoist", Mr. Chapman calls him.

But the translation's the thing. Let it be said at once that there are no prosy spots. Even terrifying lists of proper names need have no terrors for readers of Mr. Chapman. Is it Dante? Occasionally: as often, perhaps, as any poet can hope. Is it near-Dante; does it convey to the twentieth century something of the tingle which the original sent down the marrow of the fourteenth? Pretty consistently. . . . [The] few divagations are due, not to sterility, but to a Dantesque fecundity. (p. 157)

Charles Hall Grandgent, "Chapman's Dante," in The Forum, Vol. LXXVIII, No. 1, July, 1927, pp. 157-58.

EDMUND WILSON (essay date 1929)

Almost everybody has at least heard of John Jay Chapman's **"Emerson,"** and almost everybody is conscious of Chapman as an original and powerful personality; but, on the whole, he is little read by the present generation, who have no idea of his real importance. (p. 28)

"Emerson and Other Essays" was published in 1898: it had a considerable success, and it remains one of the most brilliant volumes of literary criticism ever written by an American. Three of the essays dealt with writers—Whitman, Browning and Robert Louis Stevenson—who were still great contemporary reputations and dealt with them with such boldness and insight as is always difficult to bring to bear on contemporary reputations, and such as must have been, at that period, particularly rare. In spite of all the debunking of Stevenson, for example, which has been attempted in our own day, there has certainly never been any more searching diagnosis of the causes of Stevenson's second-rateness than Chapman's of 1898. There were also essays on the Fourth Canto of the "Inferno," on Michael Angelo's sonnets and the character of Romeo; and the long study of Emerson. This book, like the volumes which have followed it, revealed Chapman as a literary critic of unique gifts among the critics of his generation. . . . [Chapman] writes as a man of the literary world who has read widely for his own pleasure, and—what is even more important—as one who has

not only loved poetry, but written it. It is certainly not Mr. Chapman's verse and plays which are the most valuable part of his work. We find in his blank-verse dramas, for all their antiquated tone and convention, the same psychological truth, the same penetrating sense of reality, which never seem to fail Chapman; and he has written a few really fine lyrics, especially when inspired by Hudson River landscapes. But he is a much greater essayist than poet—or rather, the true poet is in the essays, which put him not with [Irving] Babbitt and [Paul Elmer] More, but with Thoreau and with Emerson himself.

In the same year, Chapman published another book equally important in a different field. **"Causes and Consequences"** deals with the debasement of American politics and government by business interests. . . . The first thing that strikes us about this book, and its companion, **"Practical Agitation"** . . . , is the same sort of thing that strikes us about Chapman's comments on Stevenson—that in their day they must have sounded revolutionary: this was before Roosevelt and the Progressive party, before Wilson and the New Freedom. Chapman was among the first battalion of political reformers and his influence upon political thought was at this time considerable. . . . Chapman's books mark the turning of the tide in the open discussion of the relations between American public life and business: I suppose that nothing so deep-going and outspoken had yet appeared at that time; and, in spite of the fact that many of Chapman's opinions have since become commonplaces, in spite of all the radical and liberal writing of the quarter-century between us and them, it is improbable that we have had anything better: these books have still the power to thrill us and rouse us. They still remain one of the profoundest, one of the frankest and one of the most uncompromising examinations of the realities of modern America which any American has written. (pp. 28-9)

Chapman has never been surpassed even by [H. L.] Mencken in his hard-hitting criticism of the mediocrity and timidity of American intellectual life. . . .

Chapman's practical agitation is of a peculiar and unexpected kind. As a result of his experience as a reformer, Chapman has ceased to believe in the possibility of organized political reform under the American conditions of the time. One of the most amusing and searching passages of **"Practical Agitation"** describes the absorption and the complete neutralization of a reform movement by the forces which it has set out to correct. The commercial solidarity of society has rendered organized reform impossible. One might expect such a man to turn Socialist, but Chapman is to follow a different course, which is to make him one of the most original and most interesting Americans of his time. He states his position in regard to Socialism as follows:

> The function of Socialism is clear. It is a religious reaction going on in an age which thinks in terms of money. We are very nearly at the end of it, because we are very nearly at the end of the age. Some people believe they hate the wealth of the millionaire. They denounce corporations and trusts, as if these things hurt them. They strike at the symbol. What they really hate is the irresponsible rapacity which these things typify, and which nothing but moral forces will correct. In so far as people seek the cure in property-laws they are victims of the plague. The cure will come entirely from the other side; for as soon as the millionaires begin to exert

and enjoy the enormous power for good which
they possess, everybody will be glad they have
the money.

Chapman is an individualist and a moralist. (p. 29)

Chapman's practical agitation [was] a protest of the individual.
And any adequate account of his career should include a record
of his public acts. It should tell, for example, how at the time
of the writing of his political books, he ran and wrote most of
the contents of a political weekly, in which he attacked the
pseudo-reform of Roosevelt and Seth Low; as well as how, at
a later time, he hired a hall in Coatesville, Pennsylvania, where
a Negro had recently been burned alive, to hold a meeting of
protest—or rather of confession of common guilt—in connection with this event. . . . [But] it is as a prophet and a sage
rather than as an agitator that Chapman is to find his destiny.
The solitary figure of Emerson is always to loom in the background of his mind. Emerson has been one of the great influences on his thought. . . .

Chapman [became] a true carrier-on of the intellectual tradition
of Emerson. But there is a very important difference between
Chapman's situation and Emerson's. Emerson was a New Eng-
lander, who, though a rebel against the society in which he
lived, found at least in that society an audience able to read
and appreciate him. But Chapman came at a later day, when
the intellectual appetite of America was less eager and the
literary taste less sound. (p. 30)

[Chapman] illustrates more clearly and picturesquely than perhaps any other contemporary American the peculiar position
in America of the man of high moral and intellectual standard
who is unable to compromise with American life. Chapman is
too violent, too fastidious and too honest to become either a
popular writer or a successful politician. . . . To his solitary
position he probably partly owes the unique freshness and independence of his point of view. It is not only his criticism of
America which is original, but also his criticism of the world
in general. Nine times out of ten he takes our breath away by
going straight to the root of the matter, by breaking through
all the conventions and pretensions with which the subject has
been surrounded—as in his essay on Euripides, for example,
he manages to approach Greek tragedy from a point of view
independent of either German or British classical criticism (he
says that the absorption of Greek literature by the scholarship
of the English universities has been "part of the history of
British expansion in the nineteenth century"). "He just looks
at things," says William James in one of his letters, "and tells
the truth about them—a strange thing even to *try* to do, and
he doesn't always succeed." He doesn't always succeed because his very position of independence, his very enforced
intellectual isolation, tends to make him a little of a crank. . . .

[In] asserting the importance of the individual in a democratic
world, in maintaining the point of view of the humanist in a
world preoccupied with trade, Chapman has, in the long run,
paid the penalty of being almost forgotten by that world. For
twenty people who have read his **"Emerson,"** there is probably
hardly one who has read his later volumes of essays. Yet
"Greek Genius," for example, . . . which contains essays on
Euripides, Shakespeare, Balzac, and the problems of expatriate
Americans, is as vigorous and brilliant as his early literary
criticism, and in **"Letters and Religion,"** . . . the "style all
splinters" of which William James wrote at the time of **"Practical Agitation,"** has become an instrument of perfect felicity,
limpidity, precision and point. (p. 31)

His later books are, in fact, in some ways superior to his earlier
ones, and we follow them with eagerness and in suspense as
to where the thought of such a man will lead him. Obviously
a man who might well have occupied a position of importance
and power, he has been obliged to forgo power. He is thrown
back and in upon himself, but it does not happen with him, as
with many Americans who find themselves in the same situation, either that his energies are diverted from the field which
he has originally chosen, or that with time he consents to accept
compromises. His final phase is already indicated at the end
of his book about William Lloyd Garrison. . . .

[He] has become preoccupied with religion, and his position
on this subject is an interesting one. . . . Chapman has ended
up with the most extreme Protestant point of view imaginable.
This point of view is set forth in **"Notes on Religion"** . . .
and **"Letters and Religion."** . . . Every man is to interpret the
Scriptures for himself. We are to depend not upon any Church
but upon the religious instinct of the individual. (p. 32)

[Chapman] should be studied more carefully and at full
length. . . . We should have a collected edition of Chapman.
Perhaps no writer of his generation has dealt at once so realistically and with so much clairvoyance with the modern American world, and has in consequence so much to say to the
younger generation. If his books were reprinted and read, we
should recognize that we possess in John Jay Chapman—by
reason of the intensity of the spirit, the brilliance of the literary
gift and the continuity of the thought which they embody—an
American classic. (p. 33)

> Edmund Wilson, *"John Jay Chapman," in* The New
> Republic, *Vol. LIX, No. 755, May 22, 1929, pp. 28-
> 33.*

LUCIEN PRICE (essay date 1932)

From the first [Mr. Chapman] struck me as among the few
who could give lucid ideas about our land and time and who
had taken the trouble to try to understand them. So long as
one is willing to scrape along, living from hand to mouth in
an attempt to comprehend what life is about in these United
States in the early decades of the twentieth century, he can get
plenty of snacks and hand-outs, but when the deeper searchings
begin, "What *is* vital here? What *is* significant? What sort of
brute *is* the American? *Is* there a meaning in it all? What leading
traits have we?" it is disconcerting to find how little help there
is in the imposing reputations. . . . That [Mr. Chapman's]
voice should have remained so comparatively little heeded all
these years is a devastating commentary on the estate of American culture. His pages, it is true, have their faults, and I am
going to speak of them, but before I do, let me say that for
writing like his, one must generally go to England, and to the
England of Oxford and Cambridge at that. Had he been an
Englishman his talent would have been in request from university to Parliament. England has made brilliant use of talents
not nearly as distinguished, and I seldom think of Mr. Chapman
(whom I have never seen) without the words, "Of whom his
age was not worthy."

He writes a kind of Greek English. It has the rightfully rich
colour of English and the stripped muscularity of Greek. As
you read along you realize that the intellectual pace is fast, the
shooting straight, and the marksmanship deadly. These virtues
may explain his lack of the popularity which he deserves, for
Americans are not accustomed to being told their faults in

accents disconcertingly precise, they are not accustomed to having the conceit knocked out of them, and unless they belong to a peculiar type, grateful to anyone who can do this for them, they do not thank the man who does it. Also, Mr. Chapman is a master of irony, which Americans do not understand and intensely resent. Now the question is not so much whether he is right or wrong, just or unjust; so much greater is the value of the sincere and intelligent friend who is not afraid to speak out. Ten years ago when I first read his *Life of William Lloyd Garrison,* it seemed to me final as a pronouncement in that class of subject matter. This impression, although it has since been qualified, survived re-re-readings, and any American citizen who finds himself a minority man in a chaotic and none too tolerant democracy may derive no little solace from that volume. Mr. Chapman was, of course, of all persons the one best qualified to write it. He was nourished in the abolitionist tradition and is himself a crusader by instinct. . . . I wonder if this has not been just the trouble. He has been a crusader without a cause. There were causes enough and he espoused them, but never *the* cause, the girl he could have given his whole heart to. (pp. 841-43)

The virtues of the born crusader are not those which ingratiate a guest at the symposium. St. Paul may have shone on the Aeropagus; it is not so certain that his talents would have had an equal success in the Academe or even the Lyceum. For all his Hellenic culture, Mr. Chapman remains a Hebraist at heart and an Old Testament prophet is not the person to write a book about Plato. . . . The book may be excellently written, as Mr. Chapman's *Lucian, Plato and Greek Morals* is, but the author is speaking from the wrong shore of the Aegean. Nor is this a personal matter. The main intellectual tradition of America, stemming as it does chiefly from Puritan New England, is Hebraist by way of the Protestant Reformation and the English Bible, excepting of course the scientists who politely keep their mouths shut and saw wood, leaving the preachers to preach. Mr. Chapman has come well toward the end of this frieze of Old Testament prophets of the New England Hebraist line and their stature is not diminished in him. He has deserved much better of his fellow countrymen than he has ever received. Or ever will receive? No. My belief is that some decades hence, when the contemporary furor for university education shall have raised the index of average taste and intelligence in our American citizenry to some point within grasp of Mr. Chapman's earnest and beautiful and true and moving pages, they will be read with delight and profit, and astonishment that a man having so little public recognition could have mustered the heart and will to write so well throughout a lifetime. (p. 843)

Lucien Price, "Book Reviews: 'New Horizons in American Life'," in The New England Quarterly, *Vol. V, No. 4, October, 1932, pp. 841-43.*

OWEN WISTER　(essay date 1934)

Jack Chapman: he comes more readily to the mind so than as John Jay Chapman. Throughout his days he was not John Jay but Jack, even to many who had never seen him. . . . Undoubtedly an imp lived in him, almost inextricable from the rest of him; peeping out with a wink or a mischievous chuckle in his talk, his conduct, his writing, even upon his deathbed—and sometimes prancing at large. His thoughts were sudden; they took him by surprise just as if someone else had spoken them, and they delighted him just as much. But the laughter was merely one sign of the man, like his style; and who shall explain personality? (p. 524)

Judicious he seldom was, and counted on others to supply this useful commodity for him. He would read aloud some paper in first draft, and listen to comments with a watchful eye, accepting correction well aimed with instant agreement and complete humility, scrawling rapid notes on the margin.

So was he accustomed—but more in youth than later—to thump some doctrine down till the china danced—and then to ponder and respect adequate dissent from it. Arrogance and modesty, ruthlessness and sweetness—such contradiction lay in him deep; but the sweetness was the deeper, and, long before the end of his life, prevailed. And at no time, not even when his assertions were pouring out most truculently, was he a talker who listened only to himself. Clever people there are who while you take your turn in conversation sit watching you with an eye of forbearance, and resume with an air as if you had taken a liberty which they would pass over. Jack Chapman played fair, generous to your thoughts, generous with his. Agree with him or disagree—and both might easily happen in the same five minutes—either was a luxury. Whichever way, your very best wits were set tingling. Any of your shortcomings were likely to bring out the imp, who could tease skillfully. The solemnity of pedants was a favorite mark. (p. 526)

He did not come as a bolt from the blue. The contending elements in him, the contradictions—passion, reason; fierceness, sweetness; arrogance, modesty; defiance of conventions, orthodox propriety—all these that inhabited him and chased each other in and out without ever affecting the depths of his spiritual essence are direct inheritance, easily to be traced. Only the perpetual mystery of genius remains. Others have had more; but, by the turn of his, he was an apparition in American Letters, in his own way as much out of the established picture as Poe, or as Byron in England. He clashed with Conformity, shocked the respectable, jolted the timid, ripped the standardized pattern to rags. Repentance came to him in later days for some of his excesses in attacking such persons as President Eliot or Professor Norton. Some of his shafts were truly aimed and struck home, but were cruel; and he fitted his own words about the abolitionists: 'The antislavery people were not always refined. . . . Garrison's rampant and impersonal egotism was good politics, but bad taste.' You may call Chapman a belated abolitionist, and not be far out of the way. But when the imp vanished and became crusader, then this soldier of God against Mammon could so tower as to make one think of Lincoln. (pp. 526-27)

Owen Wister, "John Jay Chapman," in The Atlantic Monthly, *Vol. 153, No. 5, May, 1934, pp. 525-39.*

M. A. DeWOLFE HOWE　(essay date 1937)

Chapman's nervous and emotional forces were never of that stability which affords insurance against excess. Indeed there were periods, in his teens, in his twenties, and as he was passing out of his thirties, when the instability went to formidable lengths. These were periods from which he emerged, tried as by fire, and sensitized to pity and other promptings of the heart as few can be who have not suffered deeply in spirit as well as in the body. Without these experiences, without his freedom from many of the responsibilities to which most men are subject, it is impossible to say what he would have done with his remarkable powers of thought and expression. For the biographer this freedom of Chapman's has the virtue of imparting a corresponding freedom: there is no need—as there might be in dealing with an active participant in politics, education, or what not—to justify his opinions or their expression. There was an impish quality in him, something the joy he ascribed to an older critic suspected of liking to excite interest by his sallies: 'After one of them he would chuckle like a naughty gamin who has thrown a stone cleverly and knocked off an old gentleman's hat.' Chapman spoke truthfully of his more serious writings, however, when he wrote: 'I am saying things which will some day be thought of, rather than trying to get the attention of anyone.' Yet there were spirits, an alert minority, from whom he always got attention.

One thing seems certain—that for all the diversity, or, as it was sometimes thought, the perversity, of his manifestations, for all the contradictions between what was best and what was worst in them, a single unifying thread ran through the fabric of his life, the thread of deep, continuous concern for the spiritual realities of human existence, the ultimate truth underlying the relation between the temporal seen and the eternal unseen. The very subjects of his most characteristic writings in the field of literature—the Greek dramatists, the Bible, Dante, Shakespeare, Emerson—suggest this commerce with what is most important and best, the stuff that matters with your true aristophile, as I like to call one so catholic and yet so keenly eclectic. The trivial, minor figures and topics of his time were alien to him, except as figures and topics for the fun of which his great gift of humor made him capable. Centering his attention, then, upon the more enduring things, it was but natural that the most enduring of all, the concept of union between God and the soul of man, the unceasing search for it, should have run through all his thought. The term 'religions' for this habit of thinking, the term 'mystic' for this type of thinker, have as mere words so many connotations and such varieties of meaning in various minds that the definition of anybody as a religious mystic exposes itself to challenge. Yet no other single term can suggest so accurately the essential quality that made a unit of this intense and vehement creature, or indicate more truly the midmost point to which his swinging pendulum would always return. The personal knowledge of him on which this belief is based finds confirmation from a study of his life and thought as recorded in published and voluminous unpublished writings.

Of what does the record consist? In the first place there are some twenty-five books, generally of slender proportions—critical essays (relating chiefly to literature and politics), biography, translations, plays, and poems. The most substantial single work was his **'William Lloyd Garrison,'** not so much a biography as an extended essay on agitation and reform. Most of his writing appeared first in periodicals, with the result that the books in which the articles are assembled produce frequently a fragmentary effect, increased by the fact that the separate articles often lack the advantage of a definite element of structure. They prevailed in many instances through the brilliancy of single pages, through a rare rightness in imagery, humor, insight, and vehemence, working together for effectiveness of verbal expression. (pp. 2-4)

> *M. A. DeWolfe Howe, in his prelude to* John Jay Chapman and His Letters *by John Jay Chapman, edited by M. A. DeWolfe Howe (copyright 1937 by M. A. DeWolfe Howe; copyright renewed © 1965 by Quincy Howe, Helen Howe Allen and Mark DeWolfe Howe; reprinted by permission of Houghton Mifflin Company), Houghton Mifflin, 1937, pp. 1-9.*

EDMUND WILSON (essay date 1948)

[At] the present time hardly one reader in a million has heard of even the name of John Jay Chapman. His later books have had no circulation, and most of his earlier ones are out of print. How, then, is it possible to attach . . . importance to a writer who has been persistently ignored by the historians of American literature and who has been read by almost nobody, even during these last twenty years when so much rummaging has been going on in the attic of our literary history? How has it been possible thus for a writer who was at one time a conspicuous figure and who is still valued so highly by a few readers, to become completely invisible to the general reading public even while he was still living and writing? (pp. 133-34)

[Perhaps our most vivid impression as we read about Chapman]—especially through the first half of his life—is that we have encountered a personality who does not belong in his time and place and who by contrast makes us aware of the commonness, the provinciality and the timidity of most of his contemporaries. (p. 134)

[In March 1897 Chapman began publishing a review called the *Political Nursery*.] This review, which he carried on through January 1901, is one of the best written things of the kind which has ever been published anywhere. Chapman wrote most of it himself, and he dealt with philosophical and literary, as well as with political, subjects. Here he began the characteristic practice which William James described when he wrote of him: 'He just looks at things and tells the truth about them—a strange thing even to *try* to do, and he doesn't always succeed.' But he did succeed pretty often, and he is at his best during this early period. (p. 138)

In 1898, he published a volume of literary papers called **Emerson and Other Essays.** In this collection and in the *Political Nursery,* he wrote a commentary on authors then popular—Stevenson, Kipling, Browning, etc.—of which in our day the acumen seems startling. I cannot remember any other American critic of that period—except, in his more specialized field and his more circumlocutionary way, Henry James—who had anything like the same sureness of judgement, the same freedom from current prejudices and sentimentalities. Chapman was then, as, it seems to me, he was to remain, much our best writer on literature of his generation—who made the [Irving] Babbitts and the [Paul Elner] Mores and the [W.C.] Brownells, for all the more formidable rigor of their systems and the bulkier mass of their work, look like colonial schoolmasters. (pp. 140-41)

But the long study of Emerson had a special importance. It was something other than a mere essay on Emerson. It was rather an extension of Emerson, a re-creation of Emerson for a new generation, for it was really an expression—the first full expression—of Chapman's own point of view. And what Chapman got out of Emerson was something entirely different from the gentle and eupeptic personality—though that was a part of the real Emerson, too—of Van Wyck Brooks's . . . portrayals. What Chapman got out of Emerson was a sort of beneficent Nietzscheanism, as electrical as Nietzsche's but less rhetorical. It had seemed to him at college, Chapman wrote, 'as if Emerson were a younger brother of Shakespeare. . . . I was intoxicated with Emerson. He let loose something within me which made me in my own eyes as good as anyone else.' It was Emerson who had first made it possible for him to say to himself: 'After all, it is just as well that there should be *one* person like *me* in the world.' John Jay Chapman was thus a continuator of the individualist tradition of Emerson, which is also the tradition of Thoreau. (Chapman speaks of Thoreau less often, though it seems to me that he is in some ways even more closely akin to him.) (pp. 141-42)

And he was to take the Thoreauvian intransigence into society instead of into solitude. John Jay Chapman's attitude toward politics is to develop with a curious logic, which is set forth in two other remarkable books: *Causes and Consequences . . .* and *Practical Agitation. . . . Causes and Consequences* is one of the most powerful tracts ever written on the debasement of our politics and government by unscrupulous business interests. It begins with a pungent fable about the gradual but complete domination of a small American town by a railroad which passes through it. This, says Chapman, when he has told his story, is the whole history of America since the Civil War. And he shows the results of this process in the general cultural life with a force which was not later surpassed by [H.L.] Mencken or Van Wyck Brooks. . . . (pp. 142-43)

The diagnosis of *Causes and Consequences* is followed by a program of action in *Practical Agitation;* but Chapman's practical agitation is of a special and unexpected kind. As a result of his experience as a reformer, he has ceased to believe in the possibility of organized political reform under the American conditions of the time. One of the most amusing and searching passages of *Practical Agitation* describes the rapid absorption and the complete neutralization of a reform movement by the forces it has set out to correct. The commercial solidarity of society has rendered such crusading futile. (pp. 143-44)

The young John Jay Chapman had plunged into the thick of the conflicts of his time. *Emerson* and *Causes and Consequences* had been talked about and read, had had their influence. In both his political and his literary writing, he had dealt with matters of current interest. But . . . [after a breakdown in 1900] he seems to have withdrawn from contemporary life, and tends to confine himself to history and the classics. He seems almost to be talking to himself, he seems hardly to expect or hope for an audience; and so people cease to listen to him. The second half of Chapman's career must inevitably be surprising and depressing, though not entirely disappointing to one who has been stirred by the first. . . . [But] it is the proof of the authenticity of his genius that, throughout this long period when he is turned toward the past, when, as a rule, he emerges into the present to raise only trivial or unreal issues, he keeps his power not merely to charm but also sometimes to stimulate. (p. 149)

Let us see how he occupies himself. He begins by writing little plays for children—then, later, tries longer plays. *The Treason and Death of Benedict Arnold . . .* is perhaps the best of these and has a certain personal interest—with its Coriolanian picture of a man of touchy pride and strong self-will driving through a perverse course of action, which will bring him, among his enemies, honor but no comfort and which will separate him forever from the cause for which he has fought. . . . (p. 151)

[On the whole,] Chapman is unable to transmit to his characters his own power of self-dramatization. He shrank from and had little comprehension of the new dramatic forms of Ibsen and Shaw, as he shrank from the world they reflected. The companion of Shakespeare and Aeschylus, he followed their methods as a matter of course, with results which are not hopelessly academic only because he could not help getting some reality into everything that he wrote. His plays were mostly in verse; and his verse—he also made some translations from the Greeks and published a certain amount of miscellaneous poetry—is usually only effective when it approximates to the qualities of his prose. There are a few exceptions to this, such as his fine translations from Dante; but the poet that there undoubtedly was in Chapman—perhaps some Puritan heritage had its blight-

ing effect here—found expression chiefly in preaching. As a moralist, John Jay Chapman is a highly successful artist; and it is mainly as a moralist now that he will continue to hold our attention.

With his illness, there emerges a new point of view—really a sort of rarefication of his earlier one. It was before the days of psychoanalysis, and he had been helped through his breakdown by 'faith healers.' In a peculiar and personal way, he now becomes religious. (p. 152)

To one who, like the present writer, is fundamentally unsympathetic with all modern manifestations of religion, the books of John Jay Chapman on this subject—*Notes on Religion . . .* and *Letters and Religion . . .*—seem genuine and impressive in a way that most other such recent writings do not. There have been lately in fashion among literary people two main ways of being religious: one historical, philosophical and ritualistic—the convert turns to the Catholic Church; the other through a substitute pseudo-religion, like that proposed by H. G. Wells. But in the flashes of revelation that were intermittently noted by Chapman, we seem to touch a live spiritual experience as we do not often do with these writers. It is, of course, intensely Protestant: it is Emersonianism again. We are not to look for direction to any established church; each is to trust his own instinct and to interpret the Scriptures for himself. . . . (p. 153)

Yet the instincts of individuals are to unite in communion the whole of mankind. With the capacity for deep humility and the sympathy with American life which saved his sense of superiority from snobbery, he was able to interest himself in philanthropies and popular churches. . . .

The later Chapman is a lesser Tolstoy, fighting out on his estate on the Hudson the same kind of long war with his conscience which Tolstoy fought at Yasnaya Polyana. And we feel about him somewhat as the contemporaries of Tolstoy seem to have felt about him: that, whatever his inconsistencies and his crusadings for mistaken causes, his spirit and example were a force of incalculable value. (p. 154)

Besides these religious *pensées,* Chapman publishes during this period several volumes of essays, literary, historical and social, and some memoirs of New York and Boston. He perfects himself now as a writer: in these books, the 'style all splinters,' of which William James wrote at the time of *Practical Agitation,* is hammered out into an instrument of perfect felicity, economy, limpidity, precision and point. Some of his most beautiful prose is in his very latest writings. And he can still take our breath away by laying hold of the root of some subject, by thrusting through, with a brusque direct gesture, all the familiar conventions and pretensions with which it has been enclosed.

In his relation to the literary classics, he was that almost unprecedented phenomenon, a highly intelligent and well-educated American who paid almost no attention to European criticism and scholarship. Well as he knew Europe, he was never afflicted with the nostalgia for it which seized so many of the cultivated Americans of his time. In his opinions on European culture, he was as naturally and uncompromisingly American as Walt Whitman or Mark Twain. The accepted apparatus of learning he either quarreled with or disregarded—characterizing, for example, the taking-over of Greek literature by the mandarins of the English universities as an incident in the expansion of the British Empire.

To Chapman, the great writers of the past were neither a pantheon nor a vested interest. He approached them open-mindedly and boldly, very much as he did living persons who he thought might entertain or instruct him. Not that he judged them by contemporary standards; but he would go straight to them across the ages in the role of an independent traveler, who was willing to pay his toll to the people that kept the roads but wished to linger with them as little as possible. He sometimes committed blunders: he got the relationships mixed up in the *Antigone*, and he never grasped the simple enough principles which govern, in the *Divine Comedy*, the assignment of the souls to the different worlds—complaining that Dante's arrangement involved a good deal of injustice. 'You know,' he says in a letter, 'I've never known the literature of the subjects I wrote on. I never knew the Emerson literature—except Emerson himself.' But Chapman has at least always got there and had a good look at the man; and he can always tell you about him something that you have not heard before. To me, Chapman's flashlighting and spotlighting in his studies of the Greeks, Dante, Shakespeare and Goethe . . . are among the few real recent contributions to the knowledge of these familiar subjects. He cannot help bumping into aspects which, though they bulk very large in these authors, have so often been ignored or evaded that many people have never noticed they were there. He saw the basic barbarity of Greek tragedy, which he denounced Gilbert Murray for sentimentalizing; he saw the importance of the pederasty of Plato: Diotima, he writes, is 'an odious creature, being a man in disguise'; he saw, through all the Dante commentaries, how impossible it is to interpret Dante in terms of medieval theology. (pp. 156-57)

What a pity, one is moved to exclaim, that John Jay Chapman remained a dilettante! Yet 'dilettante' is not the proper word for one who worked at his writing so diligently and so seriously. And his literary essays, after all, are only a part of his general commentary, which possesses a sort of center of its own, independent of the various subjects treated.

Aside from this purely literary activity, he carried on a certain amount of agitation, sporadically and in behalf of a strange diversity of causes. His rejection of economics, his failure, when he had recognized political corruption as a mere by-product of the industrial-commercial system, to study the mechanics and the history of that system, had left him without bearings in the political world. (p. 158)

> *Edmund Wilson, "John Jay Chapman" (originally published in a different form in* The Atlantic Monthly, *Vol. 160, No. 5, November, 1937), in his* The Triple Thinkers: Twelve Essays on Literary Subjects *(reprinted by permission of Farrar, Straus and Giroux, Inc.; copyright 1938, 1948 by Edmund Wilson; copyright renewed © 1956, 1971 by Edmund Wilson, and 1976 by Elena Wilson, Executrix of the Estate of Edmund Wilson), revised edition, Oxford University Press, New York, 1948 (and reprinted by Noonday, 1976), pp. 133-64.*

STUART GERRY BROWN (essay date 1952)

In 1929, when John Jay Chapman was sixty-seven years old, Edmund Wilson, writing in *The New Republic*, referred to him as an American "classic" and called for a collected edition of his writings [see excerpt above]. The same critic, writing in *The Atlantic Monthly* in 1937, less than four years after Chapman's death, guessed that there were scarcely more than a hundred Americans who ever looked into his books and not many more who could remember his name [see 1948 revised version of this essay excerpted above]. In the ensuing decade . . . , Chapman's name and work have moved smoothly and unnoticed into oblivion. (p. 147)

The current of public approval submerges far more writers than it buoys up; and the plain reader ought to be glad that this is so. Otherwise he would be even more nearly choked with printed matter than he is. And on the whole the public taste is right. Not many really good writers fail to survive even in the short run, and none is ever permanently lost. But there are some, like Herman Melville, who become so waterlogged that they require years of drying out and repairing before they win general admiration. (pp. 147-48)

In these days there is a need . . . for a revival of the writings of men like John Jay Chapman. In a public sense, indeed, the need is far greater. Our art and literature will progress in proportion as our society remains alive and progressive. But our condition is dangerously unhealthy. In an age of revolution we are too easily content to parrot the old shibboleths about free enterprise, the law of supply and demand, and sound business principles. . . . Chapman is a good signpost. He points to Emerson; and Emerson points to the inherent strength and benign power of the human spirit, when it will make the great effort to put away selfishness and personal concern. And our need in America is above all a need for unselfishness. That is always the human need, but it is peculiarly and especially the American need now. Individual, personal, heroic unselfishness was the center of Emerson's gospel; and Emerson, for all his faults, was the wisest of our seers and poets. John Jay Chapman, better perhaps than any other American, understood and believed in Emerson's teachings and made applications of them to the problems of his life and time. For this reason, if there were no other, we should do well to look into his life and writings. In Chapman there is inspiration because there was faith in the potency of unselfish behavior. But the rewards of reading Chapman are not moral only. The curious reader will find humor, and charm, and wit, and urbanity, all those qualities of personality which have so often been the product of the humanities and which are now so sorely lacking in our education. The loss of these things has contributed greatly to that impoverishment of the American spirit, which, in turn, has emphasized our growing isolation from the rest of the world. One of Chapman's chief virtues was that he refused to accept these artificial and false divisions. For him there was no ultimate distinction between private morality and politics, between politics and religion, between religion and art; all were either humane and of the spirit, or they were false and treacherous. (pp. 148-49)

John Jay received through [his father's] side of his family the inheritance of the authentic American reforming spirit. Though he was a late product of the great tradition, the fervent spirit of uplift (as he himself liked to call it) was never more active than in him. His friend Owen Wister aptly spoke of him as a "belated abolitionist." It was the zeal for reform which dominated the first phase of his career, both in his life and in his writing. . . . But in the second phase, from his middle years to the end, though his life was sedentary and contemplative and his zeal was quieted, the old fire of dissatisfaction with things as they are continued to inform his writing and from time to time drove him into momentary bursts of action of the sort which he himself called "practical agitation." (p. 150)

Almost all of [Chapman's] writing deals in one way or another with the problem of discipline and freedom, from his early study of Emerson to his final book, *Lucian, Plato, and Greek Morals.* (p. 155)

[Early in his career] Chapman's best energies were going into his [law practice] and into a developing interest in the politics of New York City. Ultimately the law, politics, and literature were to be brought together into the focus of his first (and most important) three books, which came close upon each other from 1898 to 1900. Meanwhile the young moralist and critic was trying in all earnestness to practice the teachings of Emerson, who had already become the steady inspiration of his life.

By this time he was deeply committed to the reform movement in New York politics. . . . His experience in practical political work broadened and deepened his vision. . . . [Chapman concluded that political reform was not enough.] There must be reform, too, in religion, in literature, in the fine arts. Agitation, however laudable the end in view, and however broad, was not enough. Someone was needed who should pierce and probe, without fear, until the cause of the disease itself was discovered. It would require all, or most, of the people to effect the cure; but an individual like himself might show how it was to be done. After all, had not Emerson long before told us that in the individual is the source of all truth, and all social health?

It was such meditations as these which led him to take up Emerson with a fresh earnestness of purpose and which found expression in the title essay on his first book, *Emerson and Other Essays,* and the two more generalized volumes which followed, *Causes and Consequences* and *Practical Agitation.* . . . [The essay on Emerson] is at once primary and central among Chapman's writings, and deserves to be reviewed at length, both for its importance as an expression of Chapman's life and thought and for its own intrinsic merit. The piece has usually been neglected by students of Emerson and is little known to the general public, yet it is among the best things we have on Emerson, and one of the soundest and liveliest critical and appreciative essays yet written in the United States. (pp. 156-58)

[The pieces in *Emerson and Other Essays*], and all the early essays and lectures, many of which were delivered before groups of young people, have a single theme—the dignity and creativity of the individual human spirit as antidote to the stultifying pressures of society and convention. In most accounts of Emerson this phase of his work culminates in the great essay on "Self-Reliance," but as Chapman reads him it is the lecture on "The Conservative" which sums up the others and carries the greatest force. "Hardly," he says, "can such a brilliant statement be found elsewhere in literature." . . . He is not content to make a fresh estimate of a revered American writer. He is making use of him as a sharp-edged weapon in his own reform campaigns. In a year or two he will be striking the same blows with his own fists, boldly assuming the character of Emerson for his own generation. But for the moment he is playing the rôle of evangelist; and the gospel is moral courage. Emerson's works are all "one single attack on the vice of the age, moral cowardice." (pp. 161-62)

Chapman does not allow his political application of [Emerson's ideas] to interfere with his literary judgment, and as he approaches the midpoint of his essay he turns directly to literary considerations. In passages such as these, Chapman shows not only first-rate perception of the characteristic qualities of Emerson's style but inadvertently gives a good account of his own style and value as a man of letters. . . . (p. 163)

If Chapman's analysis has at this point a weakness worth noting it lies in his account of Emerson's failure in the logical construction of his lectures and essays. Chapman sees well enough how much of this is to be attributed to his manner of platform delivery and his habit of piecing together his essays from his journals. But he does not fully see that there is a kind of literary logic in Emerson which transcends formal articulation of parts into wholes. . . . If Chapman was too seriously intent upon Emerson's meaning fully to grasp this subtlety of his art, it is easy to forgive him. For no one has read his works with clearer insight into their moral and practical implications, nor interpreted his character with more persuasive understanding and conviction. (pp. 163-64)

Seldom in American literature has anyone written with such vigor and conviction about a classic author. The reasons are clear enough. Chapman was trying, with Emerson's help, to understand the problems of social stagnation and corruption in the reform of which he was engrossed. At the same time Emerson served him well as a source of inspiration in his struggle to maintain moral courage in the face of deadly social pressures. For him Emerson was not merely a writer, but a prophet and a seer whose wisdom could be applied in ordinary life. He was like a father, whose faults could be seen in clear perspective, but whose genius was a living force. Chapman's own gift of style enabled him to illuminate Emerson's. His passionate nature, held under a kind of tense moderation only by great effort of will, led him to write of Emerson almost as though he were speaking of his own hopes and convictions. Chapman, at the age of thirty-five, was himself burning with the fire kindled by "The American Scholar." And it is the measure and quality of his masterly essay that he seems never to have thought of Emerson as a revered sage among the honored dead, but rather as a contemporary who was already living. (p. 171)

It was during [the late 1890's] that he wrote his powerful books on politics and morality—*Causes and Consequences* and *Practical Agitation.* . . .

The chief enemy of public morality, and hence of honest politics, Chapman thinks, is money—money as an end in itself. "Misgovernment in the United States is an incident in the history of commerce," is the opening sentence of *Causes and Consequences.* Yet he is certain that man is also an unselfish animal. The solution to be found, not in movements and organizations, but in the remaking of the individual human character. Men will reform themselves if they are told the truth. (p. 173)

In his third book, *Practical Agitation,* Chapman records the lessons of his career as a reformer. . . . [For Chapman the] reform of society logically begins with private life. Public agitation for better government is effective only as a large-scale expression of private discontents. . . . Having cleared your own motives on the score of truth and sincerity, proceed to tell the truth as you see it, for always it is the truth which hurts.

Immediately the objection is raised that such behavior is Quixotic if not merely boorish. But Chapman was not afraid of such charges. He was indeed often Quixotic and sometimes boorish. Any man who is really sincere will sometimes offend, and sometimes his individualism will seem futile. But there is no sanctity in good manners when they result in ignoring real evils. And the individual, unaided, can do much. (pp. 176-78)

[The] great value of Chapman for our time lies not so much in his particular teachings as in his being a spokesman for the individualistic tradition, his carrying on of the faith and vitality of Emerson. (p. 180)

Stuart Gerry Brown, "John Jay Chapman and the Emersonian Gospel," in The New England Quarterly, Vol. XXV, No. 2, June, 1952, pp. 147-80.

ALFRED KAZIN   (essay date 1957)

Chapman's great quality was always a gift for stirring up again the embers of our old faith. In a culture like ours, which possesses so few traditions in common that it must emphasize certain spiritual episodes in its past, a figure like Chapman, who on every side of him, up to his very name, incarnates continuity, serves with peculiar emotional force to remind us of the heroic period in our history, to revitalize the symbolic theme of our experience. And Chapman himself, like so many American literary critics, was himself so nostalgic, so imprisoned in memory by the epoch to which he thought he belonged, that he did his best work in magnificent essays on Garrison and Emerson. . . . (pp. 64-5)

[Each of these essays] has a peculiar emotional vibrancy which reveals Chapman's passion and relief at being able to live again in his rightful period. In each, Chapman assumes the greatness of his subject as a matter of course, and though Garrison and Emerson are very different, Chapman manages to make the reader feel that they are part of the same movement of greatness in the American mind.

In reading these essays, one has the sense of being recharged and uplifted—not by mere partisanship of old causes, such as professional liberals give us when they invoke the past as a slogan, but through imaginative reinvolvement. Chapman prefaces the second edition of his book on Garrison by telling us of a historian who, while the Civil War was in progress, actually felt no interest in it, but who in 1895 became so absorbed and excited in writing a biography of Lincoln that "he lived it over again and could not sleep at night." Chapman had that gift of imaginative participation to an astonishing degree. But what is most astonishing about it—and peculiarly the mark of a critic rather than of a historian—is that he was excited by old ideas, fought them over again, saw them at work in his own life, wrote about them with a vehemence that makes the reader of these two extraordinary essays believe that Chapman wrote about Garrison and Emerson because he felt that he was engaged in exactly the same struggle.

But he was not. And it is this lack of actual historical sense, despite his strong identification of himself with the past, that makes Chapman so passionate and yet so baffling a figure. Chapman is "religious," a visionary, in the sense that he sees his own ideals as permanent and classic features of thought, cannot admit that the ideal may be present under another name, sees Emerson and Garrison struggling for the light against the commercial interests that, of course, particularly oppressed Chapman's own generation in the years between the Civil War and the First World War. Although Chapman's material is history, always history, he has actually little historical detachment, and this is why he excitedly relived Garrison's life instead of writing *about* him. Equally, the essay on Emerson, though magnificent in its moral exaltation, is really a portrait of the superior individual in the Industrial Age threatened by the mob; it does not come to grips with the first—and decisive—phase of Emerson's thought, his attempt to convert the religion of his fathers into a personal ritual. "If a soul be taken and crushed by democracy till it utter a cry, that cry will be Emerson." That cry was uttered by John Jay Chapman, not by Ralph Waldo Emerson. Emerson never cried out at all—at least not in public (and not very much, we may be sure, in private). Chapman *always* cried out. His tragedy, as everyone who has studied his career knows, is the tragedy of a man born out of his time (or who thought that he was, which can be the same thing), a man dominated by historical wistfulness and forced to posturings in his immediate circle, a man who kept fighting for causes that had long since been won because he was not able to define to himself the causes—partly personal, mostly circumstantial—that oppressed him in his own lifetime.

The proof of this is Chapman's telltale reliance on "passion" for its own sake, on "religion" as a self-conscious gesture, on vehement outbursts against "America" and the "modern" rather than against the comfortable clubmen among whom he lived and whom he always enjoyed, in his own complacent way, far more than he could admit. The causes that Chapman gave himself to in his own time were always incidental or incoherent. Exactly like Theodore Roosevelt (his one-time crony in civic reform movements) in his unconscious snobbery, his hectoring of the American people—he, too, hysterically insisted from 1914 on that America had to sacrifice its young men in the war. . . . (pp. 65-6)

Chapman was always the would-be saint, the spoiled priest of his preparatory school set, calling attention to himself as "religious" and "fiery" when he plainly felt peculiar and inert. Chapman's letters . . . show a man who more and more was content to be the "wild man" of his clubby, chummy, smug little group. His utter hysteria about the First World War, like his later hysteria about Jews and Catholics, shows a man whose eye is not really on the ball, who devotes himself to causes but who is not really absorbed by any subject, who is constantly posing, "shocking" his little group, flitting from enthusiasm to enthusiasm.

In part this is the tragedy of a certain lack of *profession*. Admittedly, he was no more of an amateur than Emerson was, or than many American critics have been. They have all been commentators at large. But it is not his little plays and poems, his selective little translations of Dante, his presumption in writing a book on Lucian, that make him so irritatingly the pretentious country squire, the intellectual Boy Scout or T. R. of the period; it is his self-consciousness.

From Emerson to Mencken, we have always had a great tradition of the critic as iconoclast and reformer. But even Mencken, with his personal smugness, makes you feel that when he is lambasting the boobisie, he is really writing about *them*, not saving himself from them. And just as Emerson had this gift for raising his discourse above himself, so one feels about Chapman that he is always a little too conscious of being "mad Jack Chapman," the *enfant terrible* of his circle, the only man in it who *thought* it required great courage to speak out against President Eliot.

It is typical of Chapman's essential incoherency and complacency that when, in his old age, a friend urged him to "save" the Episcopal Church, he answered "there must be some things for which I do not agitate."

But, typically enough, it was middle-class Jews in Atlantic City that offended him, not the Sacco-Vanzetti case; it was Al Smith daring to run for the Presidency, not the smugness of Herbert Hoover, or the horrors of mass slaughter in the First

World War. And the Chapman who hobnobbed with Nicolas Murray Butler at Fred Vanderbilt's party was the same man who could attack Whitman as a "tramp" and applaud [George] Santayana only when the latter attacked German philosophy in the First World War; who was proud of being considered "mad" and "bad," but was simply the pet bulldog of his clan and, even more egregiously than [Bernard] Shaw, the pet entertainer of the group he was always pretending to defy, no danger to anybody. It was Chapman, ironically enough, who said of certain writers and painters of the Nineties that they were . . .

> . . . O my! all amateur. Neither John Sargent nor Whistler nor Henry James had the attitude of workaday artists toward their work. They were each doing a stunt. . . . And all these people gas and talk and attitudinize. As for Shaw, he's the caricature of a caricature—the monkey of the show.

But if these things are true of Sargent and Whistler and Henry James, what—O my!—should be said of John Jay Chapman, who never did a book that was a solid contribution to the subject, and who spent so much of his life evading any test of strength with his gifted contemporaries?

The truth is that John Jay Chapman is significant not for what he wrote but for what he was. He is the symbol of an ordeal—the ordeal of the gifted and sensitive individual, almost crushed by an inimical setting, who no longer has a *subject* to turn to. Despite the many books that Chapman wrote, his life gives out an unmistakable suggestion of idleness and personal embarrassment. He knew how he wanted to live, not what he wanted to live for. When he writes that "All life is nothing but passion," he is of no interest. When he relives Garrison's life and flames out again, he is significant and moving because, in writing about Garrison, he dramatizes the plight of the individual conscience in his own time.

But unlike Garrison and Emerson, who actively disturbed the peace, who determined the history of this country, Chapman's importance is symbolic, circumstantial. What he wrote matters far less than what he represents in our modern history and the fact that he knew this himself explains not only his suffering, but—what I have not even touched on here—his extraordinary intelligence. In the last analysis, Chapman's bond with other great historical actors of this period—Roosevelt, William James, Shaw—is not his gift of "passion," but of intelligence. No one can read his work . . . without realizing how much more Chapman could have given us, if he had not had to spend so much of his energy in saving himself. (pp. 67-9)

> *Alfred Kazin, "A Leftover Transcendentalist: John Jay Chapman" (1957), in his* Contemporaries *(copyright © 1924, 1946, 1952, 1955, ©, 1956, 1957, 1958, 1959, 1960, 1961, 1962 by Alfred Kazin; reprinted by permission of the author), Little, Brown and Company, 1962, pp. 64-9.*

JACQUES BARZUN (essay date 1957)

[All of Chapman's work] is an image of him and it contains things which tell us why he was at once a superior critic of his America and quite incomprehensible to it. (p. viii)

[The] tag of "belated Abolitionist" which Chapman's friend Owen Wister tried to fasten on him [is inadequate (see excerpt above)]. There was nothing belated about Chapman, and his fanaticism is not abolitionist but creative. . . . [Chapman] wrought no fictions . . . ; he created because he worked to bring into existence in the culture of his time something which no one before had conceived—a new American type which, while remaining native and natural, would differ in thought and feeling from the American, common or distinguished, of the post Civil War period. (p. ix)

[Chapman's] soberest, wisest thoughts reached little farther than the circle of friends who found him "fascinating."

No one using that word then or now seems to be aware that it implies the immobility and imminent end of a weak creature in the grip of a strong and strange one. But the fact remains that he who fascinates is bound to destroy, not create. And this suggests the way in which the lack of a suitable environment eliminates genius—by surrounding him, not with calculated antagonism and directed force, but with weakness and passivity. It was this kind of environment, conformist by commercial tradition, that Chapman found smothering American culture and thwarting the country's possible destiny.

Chapman is obviously a forerunner, with Mencken and the writers of *The Smart Set,* of the critical activity which gave its character to the twenties. But though Chapman lived until 1933 he did not take part in the great postwar change or clearly grasp its significance. To him "the war" and "the postwar mood" always meant the events and attitudes of his formative years, the brassy, resonant, hollow years from 1861 to 1914. The second aftermath of blood held nothing for him. The First World War had wounded him in his attachment to European civilization, had deprived him of a much-loved son, and had left the death side of him uppermost. In the twenties his balked energies burst forth spasmodically in utterances of the most deplorable sort against racial and religious groups, contradictory explosions of anger which he soon forgot, but which revealed in him the accumulation of guilt, the frenzy of impotence seeking a scapegoat for its failure to achieve cultural regeneration.

[It] is as by a kind of capricious flame that his genius gave life to the most miscellaneous of miscellaneous writings—two books on political reform, essays on Greek genius, on Emerson, Whitman, Balzac, Shakespeare; sketches of his contemporaries; translations and moral and religious speculations; a life of William Lloyd Garrison; and numerous attempts at original plays—for adults and for children—on such native themes as Benedict Arnold and John Brown. Much of Chapman's best work was published in periodicals and later gathered into volumes now very scarce; but much else remains, unknown even to scholarship, in the Houghton Library at Harvard. (p. xi)

[Chapman possessed] two characteristics uniquely his—his humor and his style. To this day, and perhaps for all time, the fact that his work gives no earnest of solemnity will stand in the way of his acceptance by some readers: it is so hard, apparently, to believe words that one can readily make out, and so unneccesary to be grateful for thoughts that are given us fully, quickly, and agreeably. Some remnant of savage fear tells us that profundity has no business with the easy and the agreeable, so that in our atavistic moments we do not trust the man who writes as if improvising and who flouts professionalism. (pp. xi-xii)

It is easy to see why Chapman was not taken up by the professionals—whether academic pundits or established critics. And in their understandable resentment against a man who breaks up their game and says that literature is an elemental fact rather than a genteel livelihood, they did not bother to find out what he was after. . . .

[Chapman] made cultural criticism his sole vocation and he suffered the penalty. For it is obvious that the Republic has no use for critics of his sort. Partisan objectors, yes, since they satisfy party feelings. But a Socrates, no. Not only does such a man annoy, without furnishing a reasonable ulterior motive, but he is usually hard to interpret. What, for example, is Chapman's book on Garrison? How do we classify it? Longer than an essay, it is not a biography, for it pays no heed to proportion or chronology; and though based on much reading and reflection, it does not exhibit that sashaying among monographs which we readily take as a guaranty of soundness.

American historians now treasure Chapman's *Garrison,* which is hard to come by, but its author made not the slightest attempt to have his readers either like it or approve it. Pretense of any kind was foreign to him, and he felt no shame in writing to his wife, about his projected *John Brown,* "You know I've never known the literature of the subjects I wrote on. I never knew the Emerson literature—except Emerson himself." (p. xiii)

[We] may expect Chapman's fame to increase slowly. Present-day readers who might want to like him because he is very much what they profess to admire—an individualist, a dissenter, an enemy to business mores as to all "other-directed" behavior—will have a hard time swallowing his aristocratic levity and Romantic passion. They will be alienated by his violence, not seeing that in being upset by what they rightly call aberrations, their judgment of the man is unbalanced in just the degree to which aberration upsets the balance in him. Having the gift of passion, Chapman necessarily erred more than once in his expression of it, especially in private life. (p. xiv)

[In 1885] Chapman joined the City Reform Club, founded by Theodore Roosevelt, and gave up a dozen years to maneuvering, addressing crowds, pamphleteering, and quarreling with T. R. The happy result for us is the pair of descriptive and philosophical volumes, *Practical Agitation* and *Causes and Consequences.*

Wishing to remain honest rather than to gain power, Chapman gave up practical agitation and turned to cultural criticism which, when genuine, is always marked . . . by politics. But by the time that Chapman had matured his talent a properly political class of educated readers was disappearing. The application of cultural criticism from Tocqueville to Whitman had been too spasmodic, political power had been too freqently dispersed among successive new classes, to produce a continuing audience for such writings as Chapman's. These writings were "curious," "fascinating," even "amusing," but they could not affect minds that were either indifferent to or scornful of politics.

His thought was too sinewy, too concentrated, and too simple all at once. The cultural critic has to have an audience that knows what to make of his utterances—or else he must exhort them to do this or that in detail, which is not his business and spoils his art. (pp. xv-xvi)

Having recognized the futility of shouting at men who refuse power because they are either frightened of it or more interested in money, Chapman [turned to education]. . . . Chapman's intent was not in fact to reform education, but to make it work—

for the first time on this continent—in the hope of giving it a national utility.

The first step was to break the popular association of intellect with programs and institutions, the bad habit of looking upon learning as properly quarantined in the schools. To this end Chapman worked in a manner that knew no limits of occasion or seemliness. From the epistolary rockets he discharged at the headmasters of his boys' schools to the vivid expositions of the intangible in *Learning and Other Essays,* he kept his eye on what might be in place of what was. (p. xviii)

Under the mask of frivolous anecdote lies Chapman's thesis that intellect can be a social force. Chapman was one of the first critics of false specialization through the elective system, and one of the first advocates of general education. As things stood he saw no meaningful relation between the university and the *literacy* of the country it was supposedly serving. On the one hand were the few boys who are born with an insatiable desire for true culture, and on the other, the rest who "come up to college with broken sets of rudimentary reminiscence, and without knowing what they want or how to get it." Neither group received anything but mechanical attention; it was a travesty of learning (as it still is) to "set a man to making original researches in anthropology and Hindu metaphysics when he has had no experience of life and only a classroom knowledge of books."

We should linger on that last phrase lest it be confused with the vulgar contrast of book knowledge with experience: Chapman refers to "a classroom knowledge *of books*" and calls for an experienced knowledge of books. (p. xix)

In this view the contents of books are a necessity, not for relaxation (neurotic idea!), not for the cultivation of the genteel virtues, and even less for the acquiring of "valuable information," but for the extension of the sense of life, and especially the sense of the scale of life. In the superb piece on Balzac, Chapman shows how it happens that in the writings of the masters art and life are continuous, and consequently how a piece of art becomes, for the fit reader, a piece of life added to his personal stock. (pp. xix-xx)

To Chapman, art of this sort was a secret, a mystery. "We cannot hope to know what it is." Perhaps he should have had an inkling, for his own work partakes of this art, in essence and in expression. His thought finds images without poeticizing and leaps logical chasms surefootedly. Occasionally choppy for fear of academicism ("gamboge and style, with its however's and moreover's and semi-colons"), he seldom deviates from *his* style, which is that of perfect informality and vehement lucidity. (p. xx)

> *Jacques Barzun, "Introduction" (reprinted by permission of Farrar, Straus and Giroux, Inc.; copyright © 1957 by Jacques Barzun), in* The Selected Writings of John Jay Chapman *by John Jay Chapman, edited by Jacques Barzun, Farrar, Straus and Cudahy, 1957, pp. v-xxi.*

RICHARD B. HOVEY   (essay date 1959)

Although the reviewers [of *Causes and Consequences* and *Practical Agitation*] were generally favorable to Chapman, his thought and style puzzled them. Too much taken up by Chapman's application of idealism to politics, they failed to appreciate the force of his analysis of the American state of mind. Two of his American critics boggled over Chapman's irony. (p. 115)

There are several reasons why such readers missed much of what was in Chapman. In what he had to say he was ahead of his times. Besides, his was a genuinely new style for an American writer. His wit in itself might be an obstacle in a nation that by the nineties had produced a fair share of humorists but whose wits from Franklin to Dr. Holmes could be counted on the fingers of one hand. He used a shock techique, akin to the paradoxical manner of [Bernard] Shaw and to Emerson's deliberate use of overstatement. Dr. Barzun has pointed to Chapman's affinity with Samuel Butler: "both used violent exaggeration to blast through the hard cake of customary thought; and both believed acidulated humor a good medium for serious criticism." Since it has become an American prejudice that a man's sincerity is to be doubted if he speaks of serious things in a playful manner, here may be another obstacle to appreciating Chapman. Of course his subtlety, irony, quickness, and erudition might confuse the meagerly educated reader. And for the academic reader Chapman may seem undisciplined in the conventions of thought. Besides, we could condemn these two books for the very fact that in them Chapman has expressed himself in the language of successful art. A rich, swift, and complex imagination has in them achieved a picture of a crucial phase of America's story; and nowadays we have come to suspect that brilliancy and vivacity can never get at realities half as well as can plodding ponderosities—and the jargon of scientism. To be sure, Chapman has his limitations. He pushed to extremes a doctrine of individual responsibility that in itself cannot cope with all the actualities in a world dominated by corporatism and pressure groups. Grant also that he gives little heed to economics, which he too readily reduces to a branch of ethics merely. Of course Chapman did not tell the absolute truth—nor all of the truth: no man can. Of course he failed to solve the conflict between action and thought: no man has. It was ideas he cared about in the first place. It is the ideas he gained from his actual experience that are precious to us. His career becomes intelligible when we see him not as a political radical who retired when the fight exhausted him, but as a man of letters whose long experience in reform work was an essential education for his true calling: critic of the American mind. (pp. 116-17)

Though by temperament he was a poet, what was poetic in him Chapman expressed in his prose. He had developed a prose style unique and his own—in its rhythms, its tone, its diction and imagery. The fire and wit and drama of that prose come from his deepest impulses and work in perfect harmony with his conscious intellect. The man in his fullness is everywhere in Chapman's prose, and his style is an original contribution to our literature.

In contrast, Chapman's voice in his poetry is often so muffled and disguised that one can scarcely recognize it. Another man— a considerable number of other versemakers—could have written [Chapman's] poems. In them is a voice of the past, of the Victorian romantic tradition. In his verse, Chapman's wit is dulled; his images are mostly those tried and made safe by the centuries; and too often his diction is artificial, sometimes curiously Old World, occasionally antiquated. (p. 240)

> *Richard B. Hovey, in his* John Jay Chapman—An American Mind *(copyright © 1959 Columbia University Press; reprinted by permission of the publisher), Columbia University Press, 1959, 391 p.*

SHERMAN PAUL   (essay date 1960)

In 1928 John Jay Chapman published a translation of *Philoctetes*. Like his other translations from the *Iliad* and *The Divine Comedy* and of *Antigone* and *Medea*, its freshness and fidelity won the reluctant approval of scholars; for like all of his invasions into literature, whether into Plato, Shakespeare, Balzac, Goethe, or Emerson, it was issued under the banner of an "amateur" who used every occasion to assault "the campfollowers and sumpter mules of learning. . . ." He only claimed the translation was the pastime of an elderly gentleman with time on his hands.

But Chapman had more than time on his hands. He was not simply refurbishing his Greek, not even, as one always suspects, finding another way, however polite or remote, of relieving himself in attack. Nor was his profound concern for revitalizing the humanities at the bottom of this work. He had no literary preoccupations. . . . Everything he wrote was struck from the rock of his life. With him the essay became again what it had been for Emerson and Thoreau and would become for Randolph Bourne, the robust and challenging expression of man-thinking. Even his lesser work, his traditional poems and plays, especially his plays for children, reveal the man for whom time had created insupportable burdens. . . .

[The] fairy tale trappings of his plays for children disguised his self-analysis. "To tell thy guilt dissolves it," one character says; he wrote to confess and to assuage himself, to ask forgiveness. (p. 255)

Obviously, these plays were not meant for children. But the children's play was congenial to Chapman's imagination. Pitting good against evil, it permitted him to express his sense of evil and his conspiratorial mentality. His evil characters work by means of *Realpolitik,* his good characters by means of love. His moralism is strong because his view of morality is weak. His work is composed of simples, of "two hierarchies of power." He sees it as a child sees it.

The sense of conspiracy still oppresses Chapman in *Philoctetes*. He identifies himself with Philoctetes because he, too, believed that he had been abandoned by others because of his illness; he, too, had a "nameless, blasting wound" and had become (especially in the 1920's) "a maniac in hate." He can understand the pain that makes Philoctetes desire to cut off his foot, for in his youth he had himself been driven to destroy an offending hand. (p. 256)

Chapman's words are bolts of character. What he said of Emerson can be said of him: "Open his works at hazard. You hear a man talking." His voice is still one of the most engaging in American letters. Essayists are out of fashion and memorialists are rare; Chapman's literary achievement is in the essay and memoir. This must be acknowledged. But this is not so much in question as his stature. (p. 257)

[The] fame Chapman gains by association, he loses by comparison; and none of Chapman's critics has taken the risk of comparing him. . . . [Is he] a critic whose reputation can no longer be deferred because we stand in need of his qualities? Does he belong in another order, that suggested by Austin Warren when he said that Chapman was "a saint writing about saints, himself not the least of them"? Or is he after all . . . only a minor representative figure? And one wonders most just what it is (since it is not his skill as an essayist) that we have overlooked, and what arouses the sympathy of his recent champions. (p. 258)

Emerson and [William Lloyd] Garrison were Chapman's heroes of conscience. During much of his life he pitted them against each other as he wavered between the efficacy of saying and the efficacy of doing. Courageous men both, they needed each other; they were the "head" and the "heart" Chapman hoped but failed to unite in himself. . . .

Chapman's criticism of Emerson was severe not simply because the seer lost power by not acting, but because Emerson had become profoundly a part of himself. No one ever gave himself over so entirely to Emerson as Chapman did. . . . Though he later repudiated the "Emerson madness"—the fanaticism and self-will Emerson had released—he never repudiated the individual moral heroism that had made it acceptable. (p. 259)

[All the] paradoxes that one finds in Chapman are the detritus of social change. They are common enough in "stranded" intellectuals who after a lifetime's devotion to American culture may feel, as Edmund Wilson does now, that "I don't want any more to be bothered with the kind of contemporary conflicts that I used to go out to explore. . . . When, for example, I look through *Life* magazine, I feel that I do not belong to the country depicted there, that I do not even live in that country." (p. 262)

Sherman Paul, "The Identities of John Jay Chapman," in Journal of English and Germanic Philology *(reprinted by permission of the author), Vol. LIX, No. 2, 1960, pp. 255-62.*

MELVIN H. BERNSTEIN (essay date 1964)

In his remarks on American, English, French, Greek, Italian, and German literature (and the language and art of biblical writing), [Chapman's] intention as critic of intellect and character in America is persistently and consistently revealed. Why Chapman did not concentrate exclusively on the writing of literary criticism, for which his expert intuition was an incalculable, natural asset, is a minor mystery. The solution probably lies in the fact that he had a horror of specialization because it warped the judgment. Particularism was an intellectual vice. He wanted to put together a critical method which was a synthesis of different methods, including the literary. Besides, he dabbled; but he dabbled seriously, for he loved the literature he criticized. He was, perhaps, victimized also by his facility in various genres, by his suspicion of the narrowly preoccupied literary person, and by his overriding desire to be a historian of manners and morals in a unified sense. (pp. 83-4)

He saw himself as an iconoclast, a window-breaker. (p. 84)

Chapman's interest in and knowledge of the techniques and history of literature were utilized appreciatively in all his literary estimates, but he concentrated his critical energies on the "doctrine" of the man under scrutiny, the ideas which made the writer doctrinal to man's best hopes for man. Sometimes these ideas revealed in a flash a nation; other times, only a sign of good or bad times ahead. (p. 97)

In Chapman's view, the practice of literary criticism was a very dubious enterprise. Obviously, when a writer exhibited himself preciously in a work, or when his baneful ideas were hardly worth the art, his work was bad for readers. A critic was useful when he pointed out these faults. But when critics, translators, or academic scholars deflected the right understanding of Greek literature (or Shakespeare), it was a worse situation. They were doing positive evil not only to the works themselves but to generations of schoolboys who studied their perverse pronouncements. Chapman's scepticism of the value of literary criticism appears to beg the question of Chapman's own criticism. If, to Chapman, criticism was in the first place impotent to explain art, then both he and the critics were in a root-and-branch sense quite dispensable. But critics criticized; they could not be ignored. Making the best of a bad situation, it was important, therefore, to Chapman to diminish the dissemination of positively bad criticism. The historical criticism of the nineteenth century was a case in point.

English scholarship on Greek literature was dominated in the late nineteenth century by two Englishmen, Benjamin Jowett (died 1893) and Gilbert Murray (alive and famous when Chapman argued against his influence). English cultural imperialists, they Victorianized the Greeks. Murray especially, supported by the sickly estheticism of Pater and Swinburne, had translated sturdy Greek literature into a "limp Grecism." Citing hemistich and strophe of Murray's translations, Chapman showed how Murray had Anglicized, moralized, sentimentalized—in short, perverted—the Greek genius. For Murray to introduce modern theological ideas into Greek texts and to splash a sentimentalized Christian God all over their pages were unconscionable errors. "The reader becomes so concerned about Mr. Murray's religious obsessions that he forgets the Greek altogether. . . ." Chapman insisted that the Greek genius was different from the English genius. Arnold's sweetness and light and Murray's sweetness and pathos better explained the sorry condition of intellectual England than they defined the intrinsic attributes of Greek civilization. (pp. 98-9)

To rescue not only Greek literature but also Shakespeare from the pedants with the burglar tools and blackjacks was another of Chapman's lifelong, self-imposed, happy tasks. . . . Chapman slipped through the dense underwater growth of Shakespeare criticism with the skill and touch of an electric eel. He was blithely secure in his possession—never fixed, always imaginatively liberating—of Shakespeare. (pp. 99-100)

Chapman coaxed readers away from the steadily proliferating Shakespeare criticism and back to the texts, away from the second-hand experiences of the critics to the first-hand subjective, psychological, literary and magical experience of the reader himself. (p. 100)

To Chapman, Shakespeare's plays were only comprehensible if one imagined how vibrant manners and customs were in Elizabethan days. "We in America, with our formal manners, our bloodless complexions, our perpetual decorum and self-suppression, are about as much in sympathy with the real element of Shakespeare's plays as a Baptist parson is with a fox hunt." . . . Reading Shakespeare did not lead back to the aridities of historical scholarship but forward into an understanding of current American life. He was to be read only for the pleasure that permits contact with his large, impersonal mind—with "its fondness for the dramatic beauties of the old religion"—but he was to influence us in myriad ways. "He is by far the most popular poet in the world," Chapman wrote in *Greek Genius*, "and teaches metaphysics to millions who do not know they are learning, but find in him merely a fellow-being who loves and understands them." (pp. 100-01)

Chapman insisted he was rescuing Shakespeare the artist from the landslide of accumulated criticism that had almost buried him. (p. 101)

The reader who does not approach Chapman with the acceptance of his religiousness does injustice to himself and to Chapman who candidly asked to be read in this fashion. This fact illuminates the relationship Chapman established with Emerson, and it also distinctly marks the difference between the two men.

It is critically insufficient to call Chapman a reborn Emerson. He was Emerson with a difference. The two men criticized the same things. The two men were sharply intuitive, richly associative, and sympathetically ethical in their demands for the perfection of the individual and, by extension, of society. But—and it is a crucial but—where Emerson had edited the familiar God from his essays, his poems, and his Transcendentalism, Chapman the redactor of the American past had written God back into the documents, the history, the dreams and the nightmares, and the promises of American life. Chapman's American scholar was different from Emerson's. Chapman's scholar was urged to study not nature capitalized but God. (p. 124)

The critical American reading public of Chapman's lifetime . . . could and did balk at treating the world's new problems by recourse to the old solution. . . . Hardly does the reader get involved in an intellectual journey exploring a set of facts with Chapman than he is switched to the Celestial Railroad. True, it was an independently owned, privately run, customer-sharing-the-profits-run railroad; but it was, just the same, an express to heaven. The mood of Chapman's audience was to adopt other (in Chapman's view, misleading) approaches—strikes, unions, science, social science, or psychology. The American temper of Chapman's readers had a strong touch of Huck Finn's skepticism of having been "there" before.

In addition, Chapman's refusal (like Emerson's) to join and work with organizations, and Chapman's mysticism (like Emerson's) alienated the organization-mindedness and the preference of pragmatism and expediency of twentieth-century American thinking. When Chapman pleaded for Emerson's nineteenth-century self-reliant man to be reborn in the twentieth century as the big individual, his readers read but could not believe in his rebirth. The Goliaths of big war, big business, big wealth, big corruption, big unions, big poverty, big malnutrition, big unemployment, big armies, big science, big technology, and big bombs—all these overmatched, plainly and tragically, the Davidic individual. Yet Chapman's optimism was for David, who was, let us note, also an artist, a singer of Psalms to the Lord God. The American public in the twentieth century accelerates in everything including its secularization of values. It reads Chapman (if it reads him at all) understanding that he stood for nothing it stands for, and reads him understanding that he stood for something long ago abandoned—the old American dream abandoned for an empirical, un-utopian modernism.

With these reasons in mind, we can understand why the acute, sensitive, and sensible Alfred Kazin—richly aware of both the high seas and the deep currents running in American life—recently and erroneously bestowed on Chapman the epithet of our times. With distaste associated with the adjective, Kazin called Chapman "a leftover Transcendentalist" [see excerpt above]. Each age writes its own books, rewrites history, composes its obituaries, shapes its dreams, draws up its menu, and, understandably, disdains leftovers. When Owen Wister called Chapman "a belated Abolitionist" [see excerpt above] and when Kazin calls Chapman "a leftover Transcendentalist," we have offered to us two major views of the American past that qualify our present. The abolitionist intent of Chapman—to

eliminate the masks of intellectual and social habits of slavery, political timidity, and the happy family adjustment to things as they are—is the more accurate definition of Chapman's concern with American life. (pp. 125-26)

It is tempting to pin Chapman's achievement to a phrase, but his variety defeats the attempt. Little influences sometimes too easily deflected, but not for long, the force he gathered and spent upon the world. The torque of the times he lived in twisted him, too. Some critics would hold his diffuseness against him and label it quixotism. To be himself, he could not have been anything but an anti-specialist. If he was a Don Quixote, Chapman gives us back Yeats's image of a world without zest in which "The best lack all conviction, while the worst / Are full of passionate intensity"—and so in the end we esteem him for renewing our faltering humanity.

Chapman reminds American readers of what they have been and might be. In him and his family, history itself is caught up and held. His writings reveal the heritage of major ideas that tumble in almost disorderly haste through the brief and intense course of American history—despite the attempts of a Max Lerner, Van Wyck Brooks, Wilson, or Kazin to get them to march in ranks and series. (p. 128)

Melvin H. Bernstein, in his John Jay Chapman *(copyright © 1964 by Twayne Publishers, Inc.; reprinted with the permission of Twayne Publishers, a Division of G. K. Hall & Co., Boston), Twayne, 1964, 144 p.*

LARZER ZIFF (essay date 1966)

In the nineties John Jay Chapman made his life an experiment. . . . Chapman greatly resembled the nonconforming Henry David Thoreau, who embarrassed even his friends by his determined habit of placing himself athwart his society. Just as Thoreau insistently traced the progress of the tax dollar to where it paid to return a fugitive to slavery or to arm a gun against Mexico, so Chapman traced the normal activities of a business firm to the ultimate purchase of an alderman or silencing of an editor. Just as Thoreau was considered impractical in the extreme, because to insist on moral connections to the extent that he did was to advocate a passive revolution, so Chapman was considered impractical in the extreme, because his similar insistence might paralyze political processes. Thoreau responded with his theory of civil disobedience, proclaiming the moral superiority of the single conscience, and Chapman responded with his theory of practical agitation, urging each man to disengage himself from the corrupt alliance of business and politics by asking questions to which proper names were attached. A man need not attack the Pennsylvania Railroad, but any citizen, learning that the alderman's nephew held a position in the town freight yards, must question it loudly and not accept it as the way of the world. Just as Thoreau said a few honest men in jail would counterbalance all the dishonest men out of it, so Chapman believed that a few honest men loudly and persistently raising questions about what they noted in their communities could counter the corruption of the many dishonest men in power. "Misgovernment in the United States," he affirmed, "is an incident in the history of commerce," and with brilliant originality he made the connection clear. (pp. 244-45)

[Chapman saw] an American destiny, not one of imperialism, but one of practical independence, related to the individualism of Emerson and Thoreau. He demanded that his age bring forth its individuals and that its literature escape the pumice stone of conformity.

Chapman, by sponsoring his own publications, did escape the pumice stone, and his writings in the nineties—not the least of which were his brilliant letters—charm through the force of their singular sanity. His judgments ring clear in a remarkably virile way, whether he is discussing public policy or accounting for such a cultural phenomenon as the Browning rage. . . . (pp. 246-47)

John Jay Chapman did not withdraw from the storm of events as did some members of his class, for instance F. Marion Crawford, nor did he play the game as did others, for instance Theodore Roosevelt. In consequence, when Henry Adams in 1900 saw him and Elizabeth Chanler, whom he had married after the death of his first wife, he reported that the Chapmans "I find to be the most ordinary conventional, simple-minded of cranks, about as near our time as they are to the twelfth century." Chapman's reform rhetoric, not Crawford's romancing, was what was old-fashioned in the eyes of the pessimistic little historian. The man who, like Thoreau, threw his moral force against the drift of society was an anachronism in 1900. Within a month of Adams' having seen him, in the spring of 1900, John Jay Chapman, thirty-eight years old, collapsed from a massive nervous ailment which paralyzed him, and his wife removed him to her childhood home, Rokeby. There the man who had been run over by society lay in a darkened room, all sounds about him hushed, and when he arose two years later, although he occasionally practiced on an old target or two, he was changed, and he turned his marvelous style more and more to the service of those who, like his brother-in-law William Astor Chanler, saw the Jews as the greatest threat to the triumph of civilization. Now commercialism in itself became for him a sufficient object of contempt, and his talent for tracing consequences was exercised chiefly on behalf of privilege, though from time to time there was a flash of the old reformer. In the main, however, John Jay Chapman was a different man. The old Jack Chapman had not played the game in the nineties and he had gone under as a result of the experiment he had conducted in that decade. (pp. 248-49)

Larzer Ziff, "Being Old-Fashioned: F. Marion Crawford and John Jay Chapman," in his The American 1890s: Life and Times of a Lost Generation *(copyright © 1966 by Larzer Ziff; reprinted by permission of Viking Penguin Inc.), Viking Penguin, 1966, pp. 229-49.**

RICHARD B. HOVEY (essay date 1970)

[Chapman] has, by and large, been omitted from literary histories, ignored by critics and scholars, and excluded from anthologies and textbooks. He is still not rightly and comprehensively known, even by those who should be his readers.

Granted, when we try to assess his achievement, we face certain problems. Since he cannot be pigeon-holed, the tidily academic mind tends to dismiss him. His unusual style—the wit, irony, acidulous humor, the speed and concision of his thought, his deliberate use of hyperbole—all this puts an extra demand on the reader's attention and can be a trial for the literal-minded. Besides, in some few of his causes, Chapman's blunders and his occasional sensationalism have obscured his real value. After we subtract every possible debit, however, Chapman is still simply too big to be any longer ignored. In what he has

to say about the woes of our world, much of his work has astonishing relevance.

Chapman is best described as a critic of culture. Primarily an essayist, his subject is the American mind, or, if you will, the state of mind, the condition of the house of intellect, in this country. His focus is on four expressions of that mind: politics, literature, religion, and education. Always his essays are distinguished by those qualities which marked the man: a powerful individuality, tremendous passion and moral seriousness, intellect which cut to the core of an issue, and the rare gift of wit and high humor. (p. 451)

Chapman can be blamed that throughout his life he was uninterested in the moderns; nonetheless, our avant-garde critics, and especially the academics, could learn from the immediacy and directness of Chapman's approach to the classics.

Engagé but disinterested, he deals only with subjects he becomes involved in; he writes not as a student or reader but as one for whom literature is an experience. He is too wise to worry about the "definitive," is too sophisticated to have faith in system-making or methodologies, is amused at pedantry and the scholarly training which makes men "unimaginative and suspicious," and knows that the user counts for more than the tool. Chapman is aware that criticism is an art, not a technique to be acquired by willed effort. He dares to specify for the critic the *"knack of a loose and dreamy attention."* As to sensibility, Chapman would, so to speak, think with the heart and feel with the head. His great gift is to cut through sham and stereotyped response and come to the heart of the matter, to get on speaking terms with the great spirits of the past. His defense of the classic tradition is simple; "the humanities make people capable of life"; they are "an aid to spiritual power and happiness." (p. 452)

But should anybody read Chapman today? Yes—if he responds to the crusading zeal of Ralph Nader, those against-the-grain books of Norman Mailer, the persistent truth-telling of I. F. Stone, or the gallantry of the lady who gave us *Silent Spring*. So long as we care about values like these, we are still not too far from the spirit of John Jay Chapman. (p. 453)

Richard B. Hovey, "Book Reviews: 'The Collected Works of John Jay Chapman'," in The Modern Language Journal, *Vol. LIV, No. 6, October, 1970, pp. 451-53.*

ADDITIONAL BIBLIOGRAPHY

Barzun, Jacques. "Against the Grain: John Jay Chapman." *The Atlantic Monthly* 79, No. 2 (February 1947): 120-24.
Discusses Chapman as a literary critic, and compares him favorably to such masters of American literature as Poe, Hawthorne, and Melville.

Dobkowski, Michael N. "The End of Confidence: The Patrician Anti-Semitism of John Jay Chapman and William Astor Chanler." *The Markham Review* 7 (Fall 1977): 14-17.*
An analysis of the anti-Semitic tendency within the "patrician" class of old and established American families in the early 1900s.

Santayana, George. "The Alleged Catholic Danger." In his *George Santayana's America: Essays on Literature and Culture,* edited by James Ballowe, pp. 150-55. Chicago: University of Illinois Press, 1967.

Contemporary account of the anti-Catholic sentiment in the early 1900s, with comment on Chapman's anti-Catholicism.

Sherman, Stuart. ''Essays of John Jay Chapman.'' In *Shaping Men and Women: Essays on Literature and Life,* edited by Jacob Zeitlin, pp. 51-8. Magnolia, Mass.: Peter Smith, 1932.
Extensive review of *Learning and Other Essays*. The critic cites ''the sheer moral idealism'' underlying Chapman's style, ''touched with irony and subdued humor.''

Stocking, David. ''John Jay Chapman and Political Reform.'' *American Quarterly* II, No. 1 (Spring 1950): 62-70.
Discusses Chapman's political writings and activities. Stocking relates Chapman's interpretation of Emerson's philosophy as justification of his own individualistic course in political reform.

''An American Moralist.'' *The Times Literary Supplement*, No. 1489 (14 August 1930): 645-46.
Contemporary overview of Chapman's political as well as literary criticism, praising his ''perspicacity and directness.''

Aleister Crowley

1875-1947

(Born Edward Alexander Crowley; also wrote under pseudonyms of Frater Perdurabo, Count Vladimir Svareff, George Archibald Bishop, St. E. A. of M. and S., a gentleman of the University of Cambridge, Abhavananda, H. D. Carr, Master Therion, and Rev. C. Verey) English occult writer, poet, novelist, short story writer, dramatist, essayist, critic, and translator.

Crowley's reputation as a leading occult figure in the twentieth century overshadows his literary accomplishments. He was a master of esoteric knowledge and his most important contributions are in the field of mysticism and ritual magic. His iconoclastic views and behavior—primarily his routine blasphemies and liberal indulgence in drugs, sex, and satanism—earned him the title of "The Wickedest Man in the World" in the English press. Most literary critics have either ignored or dismissed his prolific output of poetry, fiction, and drama. Many of his commentators outside occult circles consider him important only as a cultural symbol foreshadowing modern trends in drug experimentation, occultism, and bizarre sexuality. However, his writings are those of an exceptional personality who continues to have a wide spiritual influence, and at least one critic has ranked this master of magic with the masters of poetic art.

Born in Leamington, Warwickshire, Crowley was raised by intensely religious parents who belonged to a strict Protestant sect known as the Plymouth Brethren. As a child Crowley piously followed the rigid theological tenets that he later attacked as monstrous absurdities. After his father died, Crowley lost all vestiges of conventional religiosity and devoted himself to violating traditional moral codes. His autobiography describes this youthful conversion as a complete mystery and offers no explanation for it. Eventually he viewed his devout mother as a "religious bigot," and she referred to him as "The Beast." In adulthood he would welcome the role as the Beast of *Revelations,* the Antichrist, whose number is 666. The young Crowley pursued assorted vices, traveled widely, and became an adept mountain climber. He attended Trinity College, Cambridge, where he studied literature and wrote poetry.

In 1899 Crowley was introduced to Samuel Liddell Mathers. Mathers was the head of the Hermetic Order of the Golden Dawn, an occultist society whose membership included W. B. Yeats and Arthur Machen. Crowley was initiated into the order, acquired the magical name of Perdurabo ("I will endure to the end"), and worked his way into the society's inner circle of the Red Rose and Golden Cross. While traveling in Cairo, Crowley experienced a revelation in which *Aiswass,* his Holy Guardian Angel and one of the Secret Chiefs of the universe, informed him that a new era of humanity had begun. Crowley transcribed his *Book of the Law* under the inspiration of this superhuman entity, this work yielding the dictum "Do What Thou Wilt Shall Be the Whole of the Law." This was to be the motto for a new age. On the basis of his new found knowledge, Crowley attempted to assume leadership of the Golden Dawn, provoking the opposition of Mathers and Yeats, the latter referring to Crowley as "a quite unspeakable per-

son." He eventually organized some of his followers into a small colony inhabiting an abbey outside the village of Cefalu in northern Sicily. Crowley founded this community to implement the doctrine of *thelema* ("will") outlined in his *Book of the Law,* a doctrine that demanded the practice of sex magic and the use of narcotics. At the time of his death, Crowley's daily intake of heroin had far surpassed dosages fatal to a normal addict.

Most of Crowley's writing has received little important comment, though on the dedication page to *The Stratagem and Other Stories* he claims that Joseph Conrad "applauded the first story." At one time the author-magus even offered a cash prize for the best critical essay on his work. His novels, *Diary of a Drug Fiend* and *Moonchild,* are usually regarded as fictionalized autobiography. Crowley's real autobiography, *The Confessions of Aleister Crowley,* is considered to be by far his most entertaining and enlightening prose work. As a poet Crowley has inspired some extreme critical positions. C. R. Cammell places him in the company of Marlowe, Shelley, and Gerard Manley Hopkins; more often he is condemned as a smut-peddler. The fact that one of the early collections of poetry, *White Stains,* was published by Victorian pornographer Leonard Smithers apparently supports these critical condemnations. But *White Stains*, as John Symonds has indicated, is a demonstration of Crowley's "tongue-in-cheek facility." Here, as in much of his work, Crowley's ironic attitude toward his blatantly immoral subject matter is frequently misjudged, so that he is taken either more or less seriously than he should be.

In his autobiography Crowley expresses the serious aspect of his art when he defines his conception of poetry as "a series of words so arranged that the combination of meaning, rhythm, and rime produces the definitely magical effect of exalting the soul to divine ecstasy." The drama *Rites of Eleusis* demonstrates the interdependence of art and mystical experience in Crowley's work, each heightening the effect of the other. This central purpose, despite Crowley's eccentricities, places his writings in a tradition of mystical literature, where they have a distinction as extreme examples of the conjunction between the sacred and the profane.

PRINCIPAL WORKS

Aceldama, a Place to Bury Strangers In   (poetry) 1898
Jephthah (poetry) 1898
Jezebel (poetry) 1898
The Mother's Tragedy (poetry) 1898
Songs of the Spirit (poetry) 1898
The Tale of Archais (poetry) 1898
White Stains (poetry) 1898
The Soul of Osiris (poetry) 1901
Alice: An Adultery (poetry) 1903
The Argonauts (poetry) 1904
Snowdrops from a Curate's Garden, 1881 A.D.   (poetry) 1904
The Sword of Song (poetry) 1904
Rosa Mundi (poetry) 1905
The Works of Aleister Crowley. 3 vols.   (poetry and prose) 1905-07
Gargoyles (poetry) 1906
Konx Om Pax (essays) 1907
Clouds without Water (poetry) 1909
The Rites of Eleusis (drama) 1910
The Book of Lies (occult treatise) 1913
The Diary of a Drug Fiend (novel) 1922
Magick in Theory and Practice (occult treatise) 1929
Moonchild (novel) 1929
The Stratagem and Other Stories (short stories) 1929
The Book of the Law (occult treatise) 1938
The Confessions of Aleister Crowley (autobiography) 1969

THE ACADEMY   (essay date 1901)

[Mr. Crowley] shows a promise, in certain qualities, above any recent poets we have seen. Mr. Crowley, in his *Soul of Osiris,* has what hardly any of them have—a forceful, if narrow, inspiration, both in respect of imagination and emotional power. It is forceful rather than forcible, influent rather than affluent; not broad and opulent, but straight and intense. It is a geyser rather than an ample and irresistible river. For he is, alas! often tense instead of intense, and always more or less troubled by violence; but it is, on the whole, not the violence of weakness, but of somewhat anarchic strength. There is no necessity that

this Nazarene should be shorn, but he would be the better for having his hair combed. For (dropping all metaphor), apart from his violences, Mr. Crowley has defective technique. Strange as it appears in one with such evident force and glow, it would seem as if "the sweet trouble" of the poet were too often a burden of spirit to him and the bands of rhyme too strong for him. Those flowery shackles clearly cut into the flesh of his expression in more than one place. Thus—

> A mystic mortal and a maid,
> Filled with all things to fill the same,

shows an awkwardness of diction which can only be explained by the supposition that he found it uneasy to fill up the rhyme to "name" and "flame." Another instance of poor technique follows directly after:

> To overflow the shores of God,
> Mingling our proper period.

Few will discern at first sight that the sense of the last line is—"Confusing our natural limits." The obscurity is caused by the ungrammatical use of "mingling" with a singular noun. We do, indeed, say "he has mixed the idea," or, "he has mixed the whole business." But these are sufficiently loose colloquialisms, and should have no place in literature. Moreover, in the second case, "business" is regarded as a collective noun. "Period" here is not. We might point also, had we space, to cases of grammatical ambiguity, which would be easily neglected in an easy poem, but in abstruse poetry (like Mr. Crowley's) are swiftly resented by the strained attention. And the reader does well to be angry. A broken round in the ladder makes small odds when we are mounting the garden wall: it is quite another thing in the rope ladder whereby we are scaling a precipice. The harder the theme the more severely should a poet close up every rivet in the expression. But from this same poem ("**Asmodel**") may be quoted stanzas showing Mr. Crowley at his best. (pp. 508-09)

But the poem, like all the poems, must be read entire to appreciate it. It will be obvious . . . that they are mystical and therefore difficult. Strength and emotional intensity are what distinguish Mr. Crowley from a score of others with far greater gift of technique. They are what excuse—and cause—much that needs excuse. They are what should bring him to a prominent place among later poets, when he has learned to possess instead of being possessed by them, and to master technique, instead of suffering his inspiration violently to break open the gates of speech. (p. 509)

"Minor Verse: 'The Soul of Osiris'," in The Academy, *No. 1519, June 15, 1901, pp. 508-09.*

G. K. CHESTERTON   (essay date 1901)

To the side of a mind concerned with idle merriment there is certainly something a little funny in Mr. Crowley's passionate deities who bear such names as Mout, and Nuit, and Ra, and Shu, and Hormakhu [in his collection of poems *The Soul of Osiris*]. They do not seem to the English mind to lend themselves to pious exhilaration. Mr. Crowley says in the same poem:

> The burden is too hard to bear;
> I took too adamant a cross;
> This sackcloth rends my soul to wear
> My self-denial is as dross.
> O, Shu, that holdest up the sky,
> Hold up thy servant, lest he die!

We have all possible respect for Mr. Crowley's religious symbols and we do not object to his calling upon Shu at any hour of the night. Only it would be unreasonable of him to complain if his religious exercises were generally mistaken for an effort to drive away cats.

Moreover, the poets of Mr. Crowley's school have, among all their merits, some genuine intellectual dangers from this tendency to import religious, this free-trade in Gods. That all creeds are significant and all Gods divine we willingly agree. But this is rather a reason for being content with our own than for attempting to steal other people's. The affectation in many modern mystics of adopting an Oriental civilisation and mode of thought must cause much harmless merriment among actual Orientals. The notion that a turban and a few vows will make an Englishman a Hindu is quite of a par with the idea that a black hat and an Oxford degree will make a Hindu an Englishman. We wonder whether our Buddhistic philosophers have ever read a florid letter in Baboo English. We suspect that the said type of document, is in reality exceedingly like the philosophic essays written by Englishmen about the splendours of Eastern thought. Sometimes European mystics deserve something worse than mere laughter at the hands of Orientals. (p. 44)

That our world-worn men of art should believe for a moment that moral salvation is possible and supremely important is an unmixed benefit. . . . If Mr. Crowley and the new mystics think for one moment that an Egyptian desert is more mystic than an English meadow, that a palm tree is more poetic than a Sussex beech, that a broken temple of Osiris is more supernatural than a Baptist Chapel in Brixton, then they are sectarians. . . . But Mr. Crowley is a strong and genuine poet, and we have little doubt that he will work up from his appreciation of the Temple of Osiris to that loftier and wider work of the human imagination, the appreciation of the Brixton Chapel. (p. 45)

> *G. K. Chesterton, in an essay in* Daily News, *London, June 18, 1901 (and reprinted in* The Legend of Aleister Crowley: Being a Study of the Documentary Evidence Relating to a Campaign of Personal Vilification Unparalleled in Literary History *by P. R. Stephensen, second edition, Llewellyn Publications, 1970, pp. 44-5).*

THE NATION   (essay date 1901)

[Aleister Crowley calls **'The Soul of Osiris'**] with its four books "a History"—the history, evidently, of a very modern spirit as it has passed from the rule of the bodily senses and [Charles] Baudelaire to the most exalted moods of mysticism. "Man's approach to God is regulated by the strictest laws, and follows a true mathematical curve"—these words from Mr. Thorold Rogers's Introduction to the 'Dialogue of St. Catherine' might well serve as a motto for **"The Soul of Osiris'**; and the rationale of the transformation might be summed up in these other words of Mr. Rogers's:

> The desire for ecstasy is at the very root and heart of our nature. . . . Human life is informed at every stage by this desire for ecstasy, of self-escape into something higher. Mysticism alone affords to those favored beings who are competent in brain and will for its ardors a true and lasting realization of this desire. Neither the sensual nor the sentimental life can do so, for nature or society constantly throws us

by illnesses or laws on the hither or farther side of its perfect realization. . . .

The depth and volume and the passionate intensity of the feeling in many of these poems are unmistakable, as are also the frequent richness and visionary splendor of the imagery and the aptness and transfiguring power of the rhythms. But equally clear is the fact that the usual faults of the mystical imagination are already hurting the poet's work. We all know what happened to the transcendently beautiful lyrical genius of [William] Blake. Aleister Crowley should keep a copy of the 'Prophetic Books' next the whipcord scourge in his anchorite's cell. Already the world that he bodies forth in his verse is too often merely a clotted mass of wilful emotional symbols. . . .

No one who reads such poems as these, and in addition the strangely visionary **"Nameless Quest,"** the sonnet to Allan Macgregor, and **"The Rosicrucian,"** can doubt that this poet is authentic and will reveal to the world much new beauty. Unless his eye be dizzied and his brain distraught by the raptures of Mysticism. . . .

> *"Recent Verse: 'The Soul of Osiris',"* in The Nation, *Vol. 73, No. 1886, August 22, 1901, p. 153.*

THE ATHENAEUM   (essay date 1901)

Mr. Aleister Crowley is a kind of middle-class [Algernon Charles] Swinburne at second hand, without the scholarship, without the splendid phrase, without the ardour of beauty. He has a certain rhythmical fluency, and in that statement all his literary merits are summed up. If the reader can form a conception of a wind-bag foaming at the mouth, he will get some notion of *The Mother's Tragedy, and Other Poems*. . . . Even this mixed metaphor will not convey to him the morbid unpleasantness of Mr. Cowley's taste in subjects. **'The Mother's Tragedy'** is a drama of incest, crudely and violently treated. Some of the shorter poems are worse.

> *"Recent Verse: 'The Mother's Tragedy, and Other Poems',"* in The Athenaeum, *No. 3853, August 31, 1901, p. 282.*

G. K. CHESTERTON   (essay date 1904)

Mr. Aleister Crowley has always been, in my opinion, a good poet; his **"Soul of Osiris,"** written during an Egyptian mood, was better poetry than this Browningesque rhapsody in a Buddhist mood [**"The Sword of Song"**]; but this also, though very affected, is very interesting. But the main fact about it is that it is the expression of a man who has really found Buddhism more satisfactory than Christianity.

Mr. Crowley begins his poem, I believe, with an earnest intention to explain the beauty of the Buddhist philosophy; he knows a great deal about it; he believes in it. But as he went on writing, one thing became stronger and stronger in his soul—the living hatred of Christianity. . . . Mr. Crowley has got something into his soul stronger even than the beautiful passion of the man who believes in Buddhism; he has the passion of the man who does not believe in Christianity. He adds one more testimony to the endless series of testimonies to the fascination and vitality of the faith. . . . A casual carpenter wanders about a string of villages, and suddenly a horde of rich men and sceptics and Sadducees and respectable persons rushed at him and nailed him up like vermin; then people saw that he was a god. He had proved that he was not a common man, for he was murdered. And ever since his creed has proved that it is not a common hypothesis, for it is hated. (pp. 50-1)

> *G. K. Chesterton, in an essay in* Daily News, *London, September, 1904, (and reprinted in* The Legend of Aleister Crowley: Being a Study of the Documentary Evidence Relating to a Campaign of Personal Vilification Unparalleled in Literary History *by P. R. Stephensen, second edition, Llewellyn Publications, 1970, pp. 50-1).*

ALEISTER CROWLEY (essay date 1904)

[Aleister Crowley replied to G. K. Chesterton's 1904 review of **"The Sword of Song"** (see excerpt above) as follows:]

Our Author's main argument for the Christian religion is that it is hated. To bring me as a witness to this colossal enthymeme he has the sublime courage to state that my **"Sword of Song"** begins with an effort to expound Buddhism, but that my hatred of Christianity overcame me as I went on, and that I end up literally raving. My book is possibly difficult in many ways, but only Mr. Chesterton would have tried to understand it by reading it backward.

It is surely an ascertainable fact that, while the first 29 pages are almost exclusively occupied with an attack on Christianity as bitter and violent as I can make it, the remaining 161 are composed of (*a*) an attack on materialism; (*b*) an essay in metaphysics opposing Advaitism; (*c*) an attempt to demonstrate the close analogy between the canonical Buddhist doctrine and that of modern Agnostics. None of these deal with Christianity at all, save for a chance and casual word. I look forward with pleasure to a new History of England, in which it will be pointed out how the warlike enthusiasm aroused by the Tibetan expedition led to the disastrous plunge into the Boer War; disastrous because the separation of the Transvaal which resulted therefrom left us so weak that we fell an easy prey to William the Conqueror. . . .

But to the enthymeme itself. A word is enough to expose it. Other things have been hated before and since Christ lived,— if he lived. Slavery was hated. Does Our Logician argue therefore the vitality of slavery? Does the fact that a cobra is alive prove it to be innocuous?. . .

With the reported murder of Jesus of Nazareth I am not concerned. Surely Our Fid. Def. will find little support in his claim on behalf of death. We all die. The two thieves were "nailed up like vermin" on either side of Christ by precisely the same people; are they also Gods? To found a religion on the fact of death, murder though it were, is hardly more than African fetichism. Does death prove more than life? Will Mr. Chesterton never be happy until he is hanged?. . . !

But he knows as well as I do that there are thousands in this country who would gladly see him writhing in eternal torture,— that physiological impossibility—for his word "a casual carpenter," albeit he wrote it in reverence. That is the kind of Christian I would hang. . . . (pp. 51-2)

> *Aleister Crowley, in an extract from "A Child of Ephraim," in* Mr. Crowley and the Creeds and the Creed of Mr. Chesterton *by G. K. Chesterton, 1904 (and reprinted in* The Legend of Aleister Crowley: Being a Study of the Documentary Evidence Relating to a Campaign of Personal Vilification Unparalleled in Literary History *by P. R. Stephensen, second edition, Llewellyn Publications, 1970, pp. 51-2).*

THE TIMES LITERARY SUPPLEMENT (essay date 1922)

[In **The Diary of a Drug Fiend**] Mr. Crowley has not the literary fascination of a [Thomas] De Quincey or the power and stark realism of [an Émile] Zola. His most conspicuous gift is an effervescent imagination, an exuberant diction; and in the rhapsodies, despairs, and regeneration of Sir Peter and Lady Pendragon, ardent devotees of cocaine and "heroin," retailed in a "Paradiso" (by Sir Peter), an "Inferno" (by his wife), and a "Purgatorio" (by Sir Peter), we certainly do not reach, though he avers it to be a "true story," any impression of a real human experience. They roam about Paris and Europe, palpitating at first with "internal ecstasy and the intoxicating sense that the whole world admired and envied us." They "had sprung in one leap to be conterminous with the Universe" and so on; then they sank into abysmal miseries with a rare lapse into "boundless bliss" but drifting "down the dark and sluggish river of inertia towards the stagnant, stinking morass of insanity"; and through the horrors of despair they reach at last the Abbey of Thelema, where diminution of doses and dissertations on life and its meanings, control of the will, and the 'credo' of a Gnostic and Catholic Church of Light, Life, Love and Liberty give them mastery of the will and of degenerating emotion; and the belief that there is nothing in nature, even drugs, which cannot be used for our benefit. The book teems both with an immense fertility of incidents and idea; and with an amazingly rich crop of rhetoric. It is impossible to say that at any moment in the career of Peter and his wife do we seem to be in touch with reality. It is all a phantasmagoria of ecstasies, despairs, and above all verbiage.

> *"New Books and Reprints: 'The Diary of a Drug Fiend'," in* The Times Literary Supplement, *No. 1087, November 16, 1922, p. 749.*

CHARLES RICHARD CAMMELL (essay date 1951)

It is to be noted (and this is in his favour) that the quality of Crowley's verses is always in ratio with the quality of his themes. His finest poetry (as poetry) is always that which treats of loftiest or loveliest matter. His worst lines are those conceived of rotten ideas. When he is really shocking his verses are quite contemptible. He could, though, in a manly old-time rollicking mood, throw off stout racy stanzas like

> The World for a whore!
> The Sky for a harlot!
> All life—at your door—
> For a woman of scarlet!
>
> (p. 16)

Crowley loved children, and could write of them thus profoundly:

> For, mark you! babes are ware of wiser things,
> And hold more arcane matters in their mild
> Cabochon eyes than men are ware of yet.
> Therefore have poets, lest they should forget,
> Likened the little sages unto kings.

These lovely verses are from Crowley's poem on Auguste Rodin's statue *La Jeune Mère*, a gem from his **"Chaplet of Verse"** on Rodin's sculptures, which he called also **Rodin in Rime**. . . . The poems are among the very best that he ever wrote, and form a really wonderful commentary on Rodin's works. They are noble poems, chaste, dignified and impassioned, like Rodin's genius. (p. 30)

To compare Crowley's poetry with Ernest Dowson's or Alfred Douglas's or A. E. Housman's were as absurd as to compare [John] Milton's with [Thomas] Gray's or [William] Cowper's, Tintoretto's art with the art of Cosway or Constable, or Wagner's music with Chopin's or Mr. Mark Lubbock's.

Yet Crowley challenged Lord Alfred Douglas on his own ground—and even Dante Gabriel Rossetti. In fact no large body of English sonnets since Rossetti's *House of Life,* except Douglas's, and the profound, passionate sonnets of Adrian Bury . . . can be compared with Crowley's two marvellous sequences of love-sonnets, *Alice: an Adultery* and *Clouds without Water,* the first in the Italian, the second in the Shakespearean form—a series terrible in its tragic intensity. These poems were the direct fruits of experience, and in them glows every fiery hue of passion's opal.

"The woman (Crowley tells us of 'Alice') was herself entirely worthless from the point of view of the poet . . . but it is just such women as Alice who inspire masterpieces, for they do not interefere with one's work." He knew that the sonnets were a "sincere and shame-free expression of every facet" of his mind. . . . (p. 65)

For Crowley, volcanic in his fiery violence, barbaric in his jewelled raiment, as he is in those tremendous fantastic flights with which we chiefly associate his genius, could, when he chose, write verses as exquisite, and verses as simply natural as anything the masters of the exquisite or the masters of the natural in verse, alike the old poets and new, ever composed. (p. 66)

When the mood moved him, the bard of exotic orient-pearled rhapsodies, could improvise lyrics so sweetly musical, so naturally wild and artless, that the melodies run in the hearer's head like the airs of mediterranean love-songs, the rhymes of which are enriched by the emphasis of a guitar. Such a song is *La Gitana* [in the collection *Konx Om Pax*], which the poet, I believe, loved best of all his lyrics. . . . He was an artist great enough to leave untouched in its absolute naturalness this wild flower of spontaneous emotion. (pp. 67-8)

[Crowley, like Swinburne, has] been stupidly censured by the unknowing in matters of poetry for delighting in the use of alliteration. (p. 69)

Alliteration with a poet, writing under inspiration, is altogether unconscious: it is part of the music with which he is inspired.

Imagery, metaphor and music are the essentials of poetry, whatever may be the thought which they envelop and adorn. In all these essentials Crowley's poetry is eminent. He employed every measure, and in his hand every measure is melodious. His images and ideas are of almost infinite variety—now majestic, now fanciful, now crazy, now uncannily sure and memorable. As for metaphor: if we except [James] Macpherson's reconstruction of *Ossian,* which contains more original and beautiful metaphors than any other work in the English language, Crowley's poetry contains similes as striking and various as any poet's. He is in this essential of fine poetry the rival of such acknowledged masters of metaphor as [Edmund Spenser and Christopher Marlowe, as Richard Crashaw and Drummond of Hawthornden, as Abraham Cowley, Milton and Percy Bysshe Shelley]. (pp. 71-2)

In Crowley's poetry the originality of the thought, language and movement is as striking as the power. Not that he was altogether uninfluenced. Of every poet, be he ever so great, the forbears may be traced; "for (said [John] Dryden) we have

our lineal descents and clans, as well as other families." Thus the impression on Crowley's mind of Robert Browning, and on his style of Swinburne, must not be ignored; though truly he resembles Swinburne in nothing but the passionate music which informed them both. Their ears were attuned to the same melodies, and each delighted in the beauty of words, of phrases and metrical *tours de force.*

All this is true of Crowley's poetry, but there is a reverse to every coin, however pure may be the gold from which it is cast. Of Crowley's poetry it must be said that its very qualities tend to exhaust the reader. Splendour succeeds splendour; the sumptuosity is barbaric; like the palace of an eastern king, all is bejewelled gold. Not all; for there are, beyond the magnificent apartments, sequestered courts where fountains play softly their peaceful tunes; but these quiet places are not many in the vast edifice of his creation.

Exaggeration was a prominent feature in the poet's personality. It distorts his opinions and often the facts of his experience as related by himself; and although it exalts his Pindaric flights, it destroys that peace of mind which is the boon granted by the greatest masterpieces of literature; whether poetry or prose. (pp. 74-5)

His poetic achievement, his excess of daring, whether in mountain exploits, desert travels or magical conjurations, his passions and debauches, his hatred and his love, were all immense. In poetry he is in this the peer of Marlowe; and as with Marlowe, it is wonder, excitement, exaltation, that his poetry awakens, rather than those deeper, tenderer emotions, that calm of stilled storms, that peace of windless woods, with which the poets we love the most soothe our sorrows and refresh our weariness. (pp. 75-6)

Rosa Mundi was written in a tent on a shooting expedition in Ceylon. That it is "a magificent poem", one of the great love lyrics in the language, is admitted by all connoisseurs of poetry not stupidly prejudiced against its author. "As a cold fact (says Crowley) its only rival is *Epipsychidion.*" He is close to the truth: apart from Shelley's rhapsody, only Spenser's *Epithalamion,* and in its very different way, *The Blessed Damosel* of Rossetti, can be compared with it for beauty. Crowley was speaking of "love lyrics", so [Alexander] Pope's quite incomparable love poem, *Eloisa to Abelard,* which is an Epistle, lies beyond the range of comparison. (p. 82)

Crowley had some talent for drama, and wrote one remarkable tragedy, *Mortadello, or The Angel of Venice,* a *tour de force* of rhymed Alexandrine verse, after the manner of the French tragic poets. His heroine, the "Angel of Venice", is, however, a far more fiendish personage than [John] Webster's *White Devil.* (p. 133)

Of all Crowley's activities, of all the facets of his genius, his poetry only possesses permanent value; for his scholarship was misapplied. Nothing can exceed the splendour of imagery, the witchery of music, in his highest lyric flights. With awe and pathos, too, they are deeply charged.

They have the qualities of Eastern, rather than of Western poetry: the luxuriance and ambiguity. Were they more consistently endowed with a greater lucidity and purity, and with the reverence for holy things which sanctifies the highest poetry, they might claim that exalted rank. (pp. 203-04)

Charles Richard Cammell, in his Aleister Crowley: The Man, the Mage, the Poet *(copyright © 1962 by*

University Books, Inc.), Richards Press, 1951 (and reprinted by University Books, 1962), 229 p.

W. SOMERSET MAUGHAM   (essay date 1956)

[Crowley was a voluminous writer of verse.] He had a gift for rhyming, and his verse is not entirely without merit. He had been greatly influenced by Swinburne and Robert Browning. He was grossly, but not unintelligently, imitative. As you flip through the pages you may well read a stanza which, if you came across it in a volume of Swinburne's, you would accept without question as the work of the master. *"It's rather hard, isn't it, Sir, to make sense of it?"* If you were shown this line and asked what poet had written it, I think you would be inclined to say, Robert Browning. You would be wrong. It was written by Aleister Crowley. (p. viii)

[Though Aleister Crowley served] as the model for Oliver Haddo [in *The Magician*], it is by no means a portrait of him. I made my character more striking in appearance, more sinister and more ruthless than Crowley ever was. I gave him magical powers that Crowley, though he claimed them, certainly never possessed. Crowley, however, recognised himself in the creature of my invention, for such it was, and wrote a full-page review of the novel in *Vanity Fair,* which he signed 'Oliver Haddo'. I did not read it, and wish now that I had. I daresay it was a pretty piece of vituperation, but probably, like his poems, intolerably verbose. (p. x)

> *W. Somerset Maugham, "A Fragment of Autobiography," in his* The Magician *(reprinted by permission of the Trustees of the Estate of the late W. Somerset Maugham), revised edition, William Heinemann Ltd, 1956, pp. v-xi.*

D. J. ENRIGHT   (essay date 1969)

[*The Confessions of Aleister Crowley*] is unlikely to establish him as anything more than another English Eccentric, *fin de siècle* variety, graded unsuitable for promotion by the British Council. It will not raise his stock in the literary world; as for the arcane world, it is hard to judge, for on the showing of Crowley's confessions this world is as disorderly, mean and shabby as the literary one. (p. 212)

[William Butler] Yeats, Crowley informs us, was conscious of 'his incomparable inferiority' to Crowley as a poet. . . . The trouble with Yeats's work was that 'it seemed to me to lack virility'. Crowley's own verse, except when facetious or polemical, is Dowson with a generous dash of sherbet, but it cannot be said to lack virility if for Crowley's 'cuddle' and 'kissable' we substitute, as the context of the quotations invites us to do, the four-letter word and its formations.

Crowley is by no means a figure of fun, and much of this book (though far from all its thousand pages) is extremely readable. (pp. 212-13)

He speaks pungently against the Victorian age and the sentimental view of it which later generations have taken: 'A sovereign of suet, a parliament of putty, an aristocracy of alabaster, an intelligentisia of india-rubber, a proletariat of pulp . . .'.

This last quotation demonstrates Crowley's favourite literary device, and crude though it is, it works quite effectively when he is being indignant or contemptuous. Also when he is characteristically assigning women to their proper place: 'The caresses of no Calypso could chain me in her courts, the cup of no Circe corrupt my chastity, the song of no Siren seduce me to suicide. . . .' (Or, more plainly, 'A man who is strong enough to use women as slaves and playthings is all right'.) Elsewhere the alliterative obsession causes trivialities to assume monstrous proportions—'we hired a hopeless headman, who sub-hired sleepy and sinister servants, and dismissed all these damnable details from our minds'—or else procures a comic effect where none is intented—'I have always had this peculiar passion for putting myself in poisonous perils'—which is characteristic of the striving of the decadents (and alas of [Joseph] Conrad in *Heart of Darkness*) to express the inexpressibly depraved. (p. 214)

But the sheer arrogance which makes Crowley's confessions initially so readable begins to pall. (p. 216)

As the book goes on, and Crowley becomes increasingly involved in the occult, so it grows increasingly repellent. There are oases, as when he describes Fifth Avenue as 'a sort of ditch lined with diamonds and over-rouged stenographers, all at price totally disproportionate to the value of the article', but though the breezy style persists, it is a breeze in a hothouse. While Crowley continues with little self-pity to represent himself as a genius misunderstood, he displays his closest associates as unequivocally squalid or foolish, as weaklings, drunkards, drug addicts, swindlers, pimps, perverts. . . .

Juding from this book, Crowley was a person of astonishing energy and pertinacity, and of remarkable courage, unable to break away from the twin bonds of Plymouthism and Aestheticism; at the best a lesser [Oscar] Wilde, amazing the bourgeoisie at excessive length; at the worst a sinister-shabby megalomaniac, a Nietzsche of the spiritualists. Perhaps the world is fortunate in that he felt nothing but contempt for secular politics. (pp. 216-17)

> *D. J. Enright, "A Sound Magician Is a Mighty God: The Confessions of Aleister Crowley" (1969), in his* Man Is an Onion: Reviews and Essays *(reprinted by permission of The Open Court Publishing Company, LaSalle, Illinois; © 1972 by D. J. Enright), Open Court, 1972, pp. 212-17.*

JULIAN MITCHELL   (essay date 1970)

Aleister Crowley wasn't superman, he was an absurd bore of a peculiarly English kind, the man who lives for being a "gentleman"—which no real gentleman, naturally, ever does. He is the apotheosis of the amateur. His prose is all pomp and circumstance, just as his verse is all Swinburne. His vehement boasting rings in the ear like a beggar's whine. He is a snob, and like all snobs, suffers from terrible social insecurity. What it all springs from is never explained, though it's easy to guess that Plymouth Brethren and two public schools had a lot to do with it. Despising the public schools, he is a typical obsessed product. He needs no instruction in anything; he is a gentleman; he knows how to teach himself.

As a result, he knows nothing worth knowing. It is all conceit and how to spell Abracadabra and Magick. It is twaddle.

When I was a schoolboy the more lurid Sunday papers used to carry frequent articles about Crowley and the nameless orgies that went on at his "abbey" at Cefalu. No orgy is nameless these days, of course, and California beats Cefalu any day for black magic and murder; but perhaps Crowley's name still carries some weight.

["The Confessions of Aliester Crowley"] should settle his reputation once and for all. It is a sharp stake through the heart of the Beast 666.

Julian Mitchell, "He Knew How to Spell Abracadabra and Magick," in The New York Times Book Review (© 1970 by The New York Times Company; reprinted by permission,), February 22, 1970, p. 8.

ALEISTER CROWLEY   (essay date 1970)

[In] *Aceldama,* my first published poem of any importance, I attained, at a bound, the summit of my Parnassus. In a sense, I have never written anything better. It is absolutely characteristic. Its technical excellence is remarkable and it is the pure expression of my unconscious self. I had no corresponding mental concepts at the time. It enounces a philosophy which subsequent developments have not appreciably modified. I remember my own attitude to it. It seemed to me a wilfully extravagant eccentricity. I had no idea that it was the pure water of the Dircean spring.

A certain amount of conscious aspiration is, however, evident in *Songs of the Spirit.* This book is a collection of lyrics which reveal an ill-defined longing for spiritual attainment. The background is vividly coloured by observation and experience. The atmosphere of the old streets of Amsterdam, of the colleges of Cambridge and of the mountains, lakes, forests, and rivers, among which I wandered solitary, is evident in every stanza. The influence of my reading is almost negligible. The 'wish-phantasm' of the book is principally that of a wise and holy man living in a lonely tower, master of the secrets of nature. I had little consicous aspiration to that ideal. In practice, I was living for pleasure.

Another book of the transition period was *Green Alps.* This was never published. . . . The collection was marked by a tendency to earthly passions; and its title shows that I already regarded human love as an idea to be transcended. *Green Alps* are pleasant pastures, but I was bound for the peaks.

My essential spirituality is made manifest by yet another publication, which stands as a testimony of my praeterhuman innocence. The book is called *White Stains* and is commonly quoted by my admirers as evidence of my addiction to every kind of unmentionable vice. Asses! It is, indeed, technically, an obscene book, and yet the fact that I wrote it proves the purity of my heart and mind in the most extraordinary fashion.

The facts are as follows: In the course of my reading I had come across von Krafft-Ebing's *Psychopathia Sexualis.* The professor tries to prove that sexual aberrations are the result of disease. I did not agree. I thought that I was able to understand the psychology involved; I thought that the acts were merely magical affirmations of perfectly intelligible points of view. I said to myself that I must confute the professor. I could only do this by employing the one form at my disposal: the artistic form. I therefore invented a poet who went wrong, who began with normal and innocent enthusiasms, and gradually developed various vices. He ends by being stricken with disease and madness, culminating in murder. In his poems he describes his downfall, always explaining the psychology of each act.

The conclusions of the book might therefore be approved in any Sunday School, and its metaphysics is orthodox from the point of view of the theologian. I wrote the book in absolute seriousness and all innocence. It never occurred to me that a demonstration of the terrible results of misguided passion might be mistaken for pornography. Indeed, now that I do understand that vile minds think it a vile book, I recognize with grim satisfaction that *Psychopathia Sexualis* itself has attained its enormous popularity because people love to gloat over such things. Its scientific form has not protected it from abuse, any more than the artistic form of my own reply to it. But von Krafft-Ebing has not been blackguarded as I have. The average man cannot believe that an artist may be as serious and highminded an observer of life as the professed man of science. (pp. 126-27)

[In my last year at Cambridge] I longed for perfect purity of life, for mastery of the secret forces of nature, and for a career of devoted labour on behalf of 'the Creation which groaneth and travaileth'.

My poetry at this time is charged to the highest point with these aspirations. I may mention the dedication to *Songs of the Spirit,* 'The Quest', 'The Alchemist', 'The Philosopher's Progress', 'A Spring Snowstorm in Wastdale', 'Succubus', 'Nightfall', 'The Storm', 'Wheat and Wine', 'Vespers', 'Astrology' and 'Daedalus'. In 'The Farewell of Paracelsus to Aprile', 'The Initiation', 'Isaiah' and 'Power', I have expressed my ideas about the ordeals which might be expected on the Path. All [these] poems were published in 1898. In later volumes, *Mysteries Lyrical and Dramatic, The Fatal Force, The Temple of the Holy Ghost* and *Tannhäuser,* these ideas are carried further in the light of my practical experience of the Path.

It may seem strange that, despite the yearning after sanctification, which is the keynote of these works, I never lost sight of what seems on the surface the incompatible idea of justification by sin. 'Jezebel' and the other poems in that volume prove this point. It is as if my unconscious were aware that every act is a sacrament and that the most repulsive rituals might be in some ways the most effective. The only adequate way of overcoming evil was to utilize it fully as a means of grace. Religion was for me a passionate reality of the most positive kind. Virtue is etymologically manhood. Virility, creative conception and enthusiastic execution were the means of attainment. There could be no merit in abstention from vice. Vice indeed is *vitium,* a flaw or defect. (pp. 135-36)

[In *The Temple of the Holy Ghost*], the reader may trace the progress of my soul's development. A few of the poems in this book are comparatively normal. One can see the extent of my debt to various predecessors, especially Baudelaire. But while there is a certain delight in dalliance with demoniac Delilahs, there is a steady advance towards the utmost spiritual purity. In 'The Athanor', the invocation of the Holy Guardian Angel reveals my true aspirations; while in 'The Mountain Christ', 'The Rosicrucian' and others, it is evident that my ambition was not to become superior to the rest of mankind except in order that I might redeem them. (pp. 183-84)

While at Akyab [in Burma] I wrote *Ahab,* which, with a few other poems, was published as a companion to *Jezebel.* I had also, at odd times, continued *Orpheus* and *The Argonauts.* The latter play is really five separate plays of the Greek pattern. The effect of my journey is very manifest. I had entirely neglected the obvious astronomical symbolism of the Golden Fleece, and had introduced a number of Hindu ideas, both about Magick and about philosophy. To illustrate the voyage, I included lyrics descriptive of actual observations of Vera Cruz, Waikiki Beach, Hong Kong and other places which had excited me.

The best thing in Book III of *Orpheus,* which occupied this period, is, perhaps, the invocation to Hecate, which I recited at Akyab with full magical intention. The goddess appeared in the form of Bhavani. The fact made more concrete my perception of the essential identity of all religions. Sinai and Olympus, Mount Kailasha and Mount Meru differed from each other as do the Dent Blanche, Monte Silvio and the Steinbockhorn. It is the same mountain seen from different sides and named by different people. It encouraged me to continue my studies in the Cabbala, which claims to reduce all possible ideas to combinations of comparatively few originals, the ten numbers, in fact; these ten numbers themselves being of course interrelated.

From the beginning I had wanted to use my poetical gift to write magical invocations. Hymns to various gods and goddesses may be found scattered through my works; but in Book III of *Orpheus,* Persephone is invoked directly by commemorating her adventures. I developed this much further in Book IV of *Orpheus.* The idea was put into my mind by Euripides, whose *Bacchae* I had been reading at odd times. . . . When I had first read it, for academic purposes, I had entirely failed to realize that the play was an invocation of Dionysus. I now began to see that by commemorating the story of the god one might identify oneself with him, and thus constitute a subtler, stronger and more complete invocation of him than by any direct address. I might even go so far as to say that the form of the latter implies the consciousness of duality and therefore tends to inhibit identification.

My predilection is due to the fact that I am primarily a lyric poet. My deepest natural tendency is to exalt my soul by what I may call straightforward intoxication. Thus Shelley and Swinburne come more natural to me than Aeschylus and Shakespeare, who intoxicate the reader by transporting him to their wonderland. (pp. 277-78)

[It] may be that history will yet say that *Clouds without Water,* a story told in quatorzains, as [*Alice: An Adultery*] in sonnets, is my supreme lyrical masterpiece.

At least I have not died without the joy of knowing that no less a lover of literature than the world-famous Shakespearian lecturer, Dr. Louis Umfraville Wilkinson, has dared to confess publicly that *Clouds without Water* is 'the most tremendous and the most real love poem since Shakespeare's sonnets' in the famous essay 'A Plea for Better Morals'. (p. 359)

My entire previous life was but a preparation for [*The Book of the Law*]. . . . (p. 413)

[The following is] the claim of *The Book of the Law* in respect of religion. The importance of religion to humanity is paramount. The reason is that all men perceive more or less the 'First Noble Truth'—that everything is sorrow; and religion claims to console them by an authoritative denial of this truth or by promising compensations in other states of existence. This claim implies the possibility of knowledge derived from sources other than the unaided investigation of nature through the senses and the intellect. It postulates, therefore, the existence of one or more praeter-human intelligences, able and willing to communicate, through the medium of certain chosen men, to mankind a truth or truths which could not otherwise be known. Religion is justified in demanding faith, since the evidence of the senses and the mind cannot confirm its statements. The evidence from prophecy and miracle is valid only in so far as it goes to the credit of the man through whom the communication is made. It establishes that he is in possession of knowledge and power different, not only in degree but in kind, from those enjoyed by the rest of mankind.

The history of mankind teems with religious teachers. These may be divided into three classes.

1. Such men as Moses and Mohammed state simply that they have received a direct communication from God. They buttress their authority by divers methods, chiefly threats and promises guaranteed by thaumaturgy; they resent the criticism of reason.

2. Such men as Blake and Boehme claimed to have entered into direct communication with discarnate intelligence which may be considered as personal, creative, omnipotent, unique, identical with themselves or otherwise. Its authority depends on 'the interior certainty' of the seer.

3. Such teachers as Lao-Tzu, the Buddha and the highest Gnanayogis announce that they have attained to superior wisdom, understanding, knowledge and power, but make no pretence of imposing their views on mankind. (pp. 415-16)

The Book of the Law claims to comply with the conditions necessary to satisfy all three types of inquirer.

Firstly, it claims to be a document not only verbally, but literally inspired. *Change not as much as the style of a letter; for behold! thou, O prophet, shalt not behold all these mysteries hidden therein . . . This book shall be translated into all tongues: but always with the original in the writing of the Beast; for in the chance shape of the letters and their position to one another: in these are mysteries that no Beast shall divine. Let him not seek to try: but one cometh after him, whence I say not, who shall discover the Key of it all.*

The author claims to be a messenger of the Lord of the Universe and therefore to speak with absolute authority.

Secondly, it claims to be the statement of transcendental truth, and to have overcome the difficulty of expressing such truth in human language by what really amounts to the invention of a new method of communicating thought, not merely a new language, but a new type of language; a literal and numerical cipher involving the Greek and Hebrew Cabbalas, the highest mathematics etc. It also claims to be the utterance of an illuminated mind co-extensive with the ultimate ideas of which the universe is composed.

Thirdly, it claims to offer a method by which men may arrive independently at the direct consciousness of the truth of the contents of the Book; enter into communication directly on their own initiative and responsibility with the type of intelligence which informs it, and solve all their personal religious problems.

Generally, *The Book of the Law* claims to answer all possible religious problems. One is struck by the fact that so many of them are stated and settled separately in so short a space. (pp. 416-17)

The emancipation of mankind from all limitations whatever is one of the main precepts of the Book.

Bind nothing! Let there be no difference made among you between any one thing & any other thing; for thereby there cometh hurt. (p. 419)

There is no need to develop the ethics of . . . [*The Book of the Law*] in detail, for everything springs with absolute logic from the singular principle, 'Do what thou wilt shall be the whole of the Law.' Or, to put it another way, 'There is no law beyond Do what thou wilt.' And, 'Thou hast no right but to do thy will.' This formula itself springs ineluctably from the conception of the individual outlined in the preceding section.

'The word of Sin is Restriction.' 'It is a lie, this folly against self.' The theory is that every man and every woman has each definite attributes whose tendency, considered in due relation to environment, indicate a proper course of action in each case. To pursue this course of action is to do one's true will. 'Do that and no other shall say nay.' (p. 422)

[During the spring of 1912] I could point to one solid achievement on the large scale, as I must consider it, although it is composed of more or less disconnected elements. I refer to *The Book of Lies.* In this there are ninety-three chapters: we count as a chapter the two pages filled respectively with a note of interrogation and a mark of exclamation. The other chapters contain sometimes a single word, more frequently from half a dozen to twenty phrases, occasionally anything up to a dozen paragraphs. The subject of each chapter is determined more or less definitely by the Cabbalistic import of its number. Thus, Chapter 25 gives a revised ritual of the Pentagram; 72 is a rondel with the refrain 'Shemhamphorash', the Divine name of 72 letters; 77 Laylah, whose name adds to that number; and 80, the number of the letter Pé, referred to Mars, a panegyric upon war.

Sometimes the text is serious and straightforward, sometimes its obscure oracles demand deep knowledge of the Cabbala for interpretation; others contain obscure allusions, play upon words, secrets expressed in cryptogram, double or triple meanings which must be combined in order to appreciate the full flavour; others again are subtly ironical or cynical. At first sight the book is a jumble of nonsense intended to insult the reader. It requires infinite study, sympathy, intuition and initiation. Given these, I do not hesitate to claim that in none other of my writings have I given so profound and comprehensive an exposition of my philosophy on every plane. I deal with the inmost impulses of the soul and through the whole course of consciousness down to the reactions of the most superficial states of mind. (p. 750)

Liber Aleph, The Book of Wisdom or Folly, which is beyond question a consummate masterpiece in its particular sphere in literature. It has always been my custom to practise with a rapier very thoroughly before fighting a duel. If occasionally these friendly bouts have resulted in a few deaths—the more the merrier!

Liber Aleph, The Book of Wisdom or Folly was intended to express the heart of my doctrine in the most deep and delicate dimensions. (p. 914)

Liber Aleph is the most tense and intense book that I have ever composed. (p. 915)

> *Aleister Crowley, in his* The Confessions of Aleister Crowley: An Autohagiography, *edited by John Symonds and Kenneth Grant (reprinted by permission of Hill and Wang, a division of Farrar, Straus and Giroux, Inc.; in Canada by Routledge & Kegan Paul Ltd; copyright © 1969 by John Symonds and Kenneth Grant), Hill & Wang, 1970 (and reprinted by Bantam Books, 1971, 1058 p.).*

P. R. STEPHENSEN   (essay date 1970)

"Promethean Grandeur" had been Crowley's cardinal sin against his Age. We "seek it vainly elsewhere," not only in the pages of the Cambridge anthology, but amongst all the joblot of poets of that collapsed Edwardian age. The other poets, without exception, were shirking their responsibilities as Makers. Alone, amongst a crowd obsessed with minutiae, Aleister Crowley was attempting, and it does not even matter if he failed, to formulate a poetic consciousness of the human Universal. Poetry was petering out into triviality, indeed the whole Nation was petering out spiritually; and Crowley had the courage to tackle his poet's job of re-integration. He will yet be honoured for this courage, even if his achievement be condemned. He belonged to no schools or coteries; he was romantic and wild and boisterous when all others were becoming so "refined" that they almost vanished in transparency. No one could suggest seriously that poets like Dowson, and [Thomas] Middleton, and Yeats, will ever be placed in the great succession of English poets who worked cosmically—the major poets who worked widely on the whole human canvas! Shakespeare, and Blake, and Milton, and Shelley, and Swinburne with all their faults; even Browning. After Swinburne and Browning, is there one poet, to our day, who has worked on that Grand Plan of poetry which shirks nothing human?

In *scope,* in cosmic self-definition, in the Grand Manner unashamed—only Aleister Crowley!

For all his perverseness, for all his rocketing violence, for all his downright folly, he is full of meat and blood where his contemporaries are most stuffed with straw—in the vitals.

I leave the discussion at present with this dogmatic statement, dogmatic because I cannot prove it, and cannot expect readers to believe it, until the day, which may never come in our lifetime, when his COMPLETE WORKS are available to students possessed of some time-perspective of this Age. (pp. 100-01)

> *P. R. Stephensen, in his* The Legend of Aleister Crowley: Being a Study of the Documentary Evidence Relating to a Campaign of Personal Vilification Unparalleled in Literary History *(copyright © 1970 by Llewellyn Publications), second edition, Llewellyn, 1970, 157 p.*

THE TIMES LITERARY SUPPLEMENT   (essay date 1973)

[Edward Alexander Crowley was a] bad man, bad mage and bad poet.

White Stains was one of seven verse volumes he ejaculated in 1898, the seminal year of his majority.

Even by Victorian standards, *White Stains* was not pornographic. It was sick, dirty, or, more precisely, "ostrobogulous", which according to Victor Neuburg, Crowley's neophyte Frater Omnia Vincam, meant etymologically full of (Latin, *ulus*) rich (Greek, *ostro*) dirt (schoolboy, *bog*). Even after he became Ipsissimus, Crowley was full of rich schoolboy dirt.

Lord Longford and Mrs Whitehouse would find it difficult to wade through the purple blasphemies of *White Stains* to their necrophiliac end without switching on television for some more invigorating lasciviency. Seldom has a book so resolutely shocking been so unreadable. Swinburne had blazed the trail. Crowley plodded behind in dirty plimsolls. . . .

Magick is the sort of book of which C. R. Cammell would have disapproved but which Charlie Manson and the murderers of Sharon Tate, awaiting the electric chair to which they will probably never go, would consider, as does the blurbwriter, Crowley's masterpiece.

[*Magick*] is a dangerous and nonsensical book, the more so because it has in certain passages, as in the study of meditation, much that is wise. . . .

After this warning, it seems absurd to point out the nonsense, such as the esoteric explanation of Little Bo Peep:

> "Bo" is the root meaning Light, from which spring such words as Bo-tree, Bodhisattva, and Buddha.
>
> And "Peep" is Apep, the serpent Apophis. . . .

The line dividing Crowley's jokes from his magick is so faint that it is hard to know whether he is consciously or unconsciously funny.

> *"Full of Rich Dirt,"* in The Times Literary Supplement (© *Times Newspapers Ltd. (London) 1973; reproduced from* The Times Literary Supplement *by permission), No. 3725, July 27, 1973, p. 871.*

JOHN SYMONDS   (essay date 1973)

Crowley's best known, and perhaps best, verse is that which was written under the influence of his magical or mystical ideas—three of his poems are printed in the *Oxford Book of English Mystical Verse*—or when he was seized by the spirit of Pan, the god of lust.

He could also be masterly at composing songs which have a kind of music-hall zest about them:

> Did you feel
> Through the silence and the softness all the tension of
>   the steel?
> For your hair was full of roses, and my flesh was full
>   of thorns
> And the midnight came upon us worth a million crazy
>   morns.
>
>   (pp. xi-xii)

White Stains belongs to the type of light erotic verse in which Crowley always showed a certain tongue-in-cheek facility. The subject-matter as well as the titles of *La Juive, Volupteé* and *Necrophilia,* apart from the poems in French (a language which Crowley did not know well), reflect of course *Les Fleurs du Mal.* But Crowley could no more transplant the satanism of Baudelaire to England than Swinburne had done, for he entirely lacked Baudelaire's consciousness of sin and redemption. A few years later, however, through his Holy Guardian Angel or *alter ego,* Aiwass, Crowley did succeed in planting satanism in English soil as an occult movement, and in becoming the inspired leader of the movement, 'the demon Crowley'. Crowley identified Aiwass, who dictated to him in Cairo in 1904 *The Book of the Law,* with Set, the brother of Osiris (the evil principle closely connected with the devil). To judge from the utterances in *The Book of the Law,* Aiwass was totally devoid of moral feeling. The poetry, and especially the ideas or message of *The Book* are not without their interest, and in these times of chaos, they raise this seemingly absurd but in truth disturbing pamphlet to the level of another pamphlet which had dire consequences for mankind, *The Communist Manifesto,* 1848. Already the twenty-two-year-old author of *White Stains* had adopted the attitude which was to remain with him his whole life, that of being every man's evil shadow:

> Another prophet shall arise, and bring fresh
> fever from the skies; another woman shall awake
> the lust & worship of the Snake; another
> soul of God and beast shall mingle in the
> globéd priest; another sacrifice shall stain the
> tomb; another king shall reign.
>
>   *The Book of the Law*

Nothing less than a 'new aeon' is adumbrated, not solely the rise of Lenin and of Hitler, both of whom certainly poured fever from the skies. Nostradamus also foretold a new aeon (it was to begin in 1792), the rise of Hitler and a return to paganism. Crowley saw greater horrors, even the total destruction of civilization as we know it.

'Another woman shall awake . . .'. In man's imagination, the Virgin can be displaced by the Terrible Mother who will certainly awaken lust and the worship of the snake, a mystery which is slumbering in the depths of man's being. Whether Aiwass's alarming predictions will come true or not depends upon the strength of man's faith in the Higher Values. In these times of chaos, the threat needs to be taken seriously.

Crowley, who lived through the night, not the day, did not of course add his name to *White Stains,* but he acknowledged authorship of the work in his *Confessions*. . . . It was not his first lubricious book: he had, he says, paid [pornography publisher Leonard] Smithers to print his *Green Alps,* which would have been issued had not the printers' works been destroyed by fire. 'The collection was marked by a tendency to earthly passion,' wrote Crowley of *Green Alps* [see excerpt above], 'and its title shows that I already regarded human love as an idea to be transcended. *Green Alps* are pleasant pastures, but I was bound for the peaks'.

The 'peaks' are *White Stains,* a work to reveal—as Crowley wrote—his essential spirituality, his praeterhuman innocence, and prove the purity of his heart and mind 'in the most extraordinary fashion'. In accordance with this innocence, *White Stains* was ascribed by its anonymous 'editor' to George Archibald Bishop. Tom Bond Bishop was Crowley's pious Plymouth Brother uncle who had stood *in loco parentis* to him on his father's death and of whom Crowley wrote, in his first attempt at autobiography, that 'no more cruel fanatic, no meaner villain, ever walked this earth'. When the mother of the unfortunate poet of *White Stains* is described as the Scarlet Woman of the Apocalypse, and her son as Antichrist, the vague features of George Archibald Bishop shift to the unmistakable face of Aleister Crowley, the Beast 666 and the real author of the work. (pp. xii-xv)

> *John Symonds, in his introduction to* White Stains *by Aleister Crowley, edited by John Symonds (© John Symonds 1973), Duckworth, 1973, pp. vii-xv.*

J. F. BROWN   (essay date 1978)

The theatrical urge in Crowley becomes apparent from whatever direction he is viewed. His early interest in the occult and its secret systems of knowledge was quickly focused on ritual magic. His poetry was soon elaborated into dense mystery plays. He even dramatized the personality conflicts between himself and others—William Butler Yeats, for one—by engaging them in "magical combat."

The *Rites of Eleusis* occurred in Aleister Crowley's life at a point midway between a series of visions he had in North Africa in 1909, which revealed to him his true nature as a Magus, and his involvement with a secret society called the O.T.O. in 1912, from whom he learned the rudiments of the sex-magic that obsessed him for years. He was 35 years old at the time of the performances. The persecution by the press, which was to last until he died in 1947, had not yet begun. He saw himself as the prophet of a new religion—Crowleyanity—and the *Rites* were to be his first great evangelization.

The individual rites that make up the seven *Rites of Eleusis* can be viewed as acts or scenes in a single drama which, as it moves from one plane of consciousness to the next, presents the play's central idea in a manner appropriate to that plane. The main point of interest in Crowley's production was the technique he used to transport his audience to those planes and to induce in them—through a bizarre marriage of kabbalistic ritual and performing arts—specific ecstasies. (p. 5)

The title Crowley chose for his series of dramas refers to the Eleusinian Mysteries of pre-Hellenic Greece and to the Sacred Drama of Eleusis in which these cosmological and psychic mysteries received theatrical expression. The ancient drama is a blending of two myths—the story of Dionysus and the legend of the abduction of Persephone, daughter of Demeter, by Pluto. Crowley's *Rites* made occasional reference to these myths, but the action of the *Rites* has almost nothing in common with the story told by the Sacred Drama. Rather, Crowley put together bits and pieces from any number of knowledge systems and directed all of it toward a single end—the exaltation of anarchic lust, personified in the god Pan. Each *Rite* served to dramatize the single idea that the gods are dead, and therefore every person should do whatever pleases him. (The fact that he left Pan still living does not seem to have bothered Crowley.)

The plot of the *Rites of Eleusis* is difficult to summarize, not because of its narrative complexity but rather because of its abundance of contradictions and its purposeful obscurity. Briefly, however, it can be said to begin with Man attempting to solve the Riddle of Existence. Frustrated by his inability to find an answer, he turns to the gods. Saturn (extreme old age) answers with the single word "Despair." Jupiter (dignity and wisdom) turns out to be impotent. And so it goes through the next five, each proving to be wanting in one way or another. Finally at the end of the seventh rite, Pan ("the spirit of the Infinite All") appears and tears away the veil (of illusion) to reveal the hope of humanity, the Crowned Child of the Future (i.e., the man who needs no gods and whose only law is "Do what you will.").

The sequence of events within each rite varies somewhat, but generally begins with a so-called "Banishing Ritual" by the temple attendants, moves through passages of cryptic dialog regarding the omens of sacrifices ("The black lamb has no heart"), presents the discovery of a traitor, false priest, or demon within the temple and his ritual murder, enacts the evocation of the particular god, and ends with either a suicide or a transformation.

In his *Confessions,* Crowley admonishes himself for diminishing the importance of the dramatic elements. He says that, as it turned out, "the dialog and action were little more than a setting for the soloists," meaning himself, Neuburg, and Waddell. It seems probable that members of the audience knew little of what was going on (the room was almost always in near-total darkness) and, had they known, would not have understood it. In his masterwork, *Magick in Theory and Practise,* Crowley makes it a point to warn those who wish to engage

in dramatic ritual to be sure that the participant-spectators "all be initiates of the same mysteries, bound by the same oaths, and filled with the same aspirations."

Through the use of dramatic ritual, Crowley felt he could restore to the drama "its historical importance as a means of arousing the highest religious enthusiasm." (pp. 8-11)

In attempting to give his *Rites* a dramatic structure, Crowley the playwright came into conflict with Crowley the magician. His purpose, stated over and over again, was to produce religious ecstasies in the audience, to initiate them, as it were, into the mysteries of Crowleyanity. It is here that this model, the Sacred Drama of Eleusis, becomes important. Crowley felt his drama also must have a myth, to serve as the vehicle of initiation. He thought he could create one, perhaps comparable to that of Dionysus and the abduction of Persephone. What he came up with appeared as nothing so much as a group of secret society initiates dressed in magical robes knocking persistently on heaven's door and being told to go away. (p. 12)

In his explanatory article in *The Bystander,* Crowley recounted how he set about constructing the *Rites of Eleusis.*

> Let us put ourselves in the position of the dramatist. Working on tradition . . . we find Saturn as a black, melancholy God, the devourer of his children. Ideas of Night, Death, Black hellebore, Lead, Cypress, Tombs, Deadly Nightshade. All these things have a necessary connection with Saturn. . . .The first condition of this rite is, then, to make the temple a kind of symbolic representation of the sphere of Saturn. So the representative of Saturn wears the Black Robe. The time is declared to be midnight. If the brethren are fed, it is "on the corpses of their children". . . . If they drink, it is "Poppyheads infused with blood"—symbols of sleep and death. . . . It is then the primitive darkness of humanity that is represented in this ritual.

One of Crowley's main reasons for choosing the deities associated with the days of the week for his drama was that the kabbalistic correspondences of color, form, idea, aroma, etc., for them were already so well worked out. It is this system of correspondences—set forth in the esoteric Hebraic tradition of secret knowledge and used in the rituals of occult societies such as the Golden Dawn—that determined such features of the drama's staging as the colors of costumes and lights, the props employed, the perfumes used, the sacred names intoned, and the placement of the performers in the acting space.

In a number of ways, Crowley's ceremonial stage is reminiscent of the performances of Symbolist works at the Théâtre d'Art in Paris twenty years earlier . . . Crowley was evidently aware of the Symbolist style of staging. He once remarked, regarding the production of the *Rite of Saturn:* "Nothing of Maeterlinck's ever produced so overpowering an oppression as this invocation of the dark spirit of Time." The kabbalistic correspondences are based on a numerical system of relationships that—like Symbolist poetics—propose a series of metaphysical links between various aspects of human life and universal principles. Although the further correspondence suggested by Symbolist poetics—that between the percepts of different senses—is not stated as such in the kabbalistic system, it is implied as a concomitant phenomenon of rising on the planes of consciousness. Whether Crowley sought to induce synesthesia in his audience is impossible to say. In his *Confessions,* however, he recorded numerous occasions on which he himself experienced it.

Other elements in the productions derived from the tradition of ceremonial magic—and also utilized in Symbolist staging—were the use of successive layers of veils between the action and the audience, and the semiobscurity—sometimes total darkness—within which the drama was performed. Both of these elements were also used to accentuate action, the veils being lifted or ripped and the room being flooded with light at significant points in the ritual. (pp. 12-13)

Crowley used a number of Swinburne's poems in the *Rites of Eleusis.* It is significant that the ones he chose (''Atalanta,'' ''Illicit,'' ''The Garden of Proserpine'') are among the best illustrations of Swinburne's belief in the state of trance as a special poetic concept and in the power of verse to induce in the reader a visionary state that opens the mind to the realms of symbolist mystery. One of the ways in which this is achieved is through hypnotic rhythms, as in the opening lines of ''The Garden of Proserpine. . . .'' Crowley hoped to apply the methods of Swinburne's sleep-trance poetics to the traditional ritualistic oaths and formulaic speeches of ceremonial magic. ''There is no more potent means than Art of calling forth true Gods to visible appearance,'' he wrote in his instructional manual of *Magick.* (pp. 14-16)

Crowley's own poetry in the *Rites* is an obvious attempt to create a hypnoidal state in the listener through the techniques identified by Edward Snyder in his study of ''spellweaving'' poems published in 1930. Among the characteristics of such poems he lists: an unusually perfect pattern of sound; freedom from abrupt changes in content; vagueness of imagery; use of frequent repetition; and the presentation of suggestive problems that have no solution and easily fatigue the mind. All of these characteristics occur in Crowley's poetry, and are supplemented by the insertion of magical phrases and lengthy litanies. It is interesting to note that Crowley placed great importance on ''focusing the attention'' of the audience on the lyrics by throwing the room into almost complete darkness save for the flickering of a flame. Focusing the attention is the intial step of any technique of hypnotic induction.

Unfortunately, Crowley had neither the poetic discipline nor the sensibilities of Swinburne. His poetry seems more capable of inducing sleep than trance. . . . If, indeed, altered states of consciousness cause a shift in esthetic perception, and such a shift occurred in the listener during the *Rites,* perhaps Crowley's poetry can be fairly evaluated only under such circumstances. (p. 16)

In the *Rites of Eleusis,* Aleister Crowley attempted to induce in an audience altered mind states through an esthetic assault on the senses. He used rhythmic music, repetitive prayers, and hypnotic poetry to lull the mind through the sense of hearing. He used light, veiled action, and flickering flames to fatigue the sense of sight. He used incense and perfumes to overload the sense of smell. He used possession dance to enact in physical space the kinesthetic potential of the audience's passive trance. He used psychoactive drugs to alter body chemistry and shift consciousness. Any alteration of normal consciousness has associated dangers, which can be identified in the terms of religions, psychologies, physiologies, or—as in Crowley's case—through the codified knowledge system of an occult

philosophy. In such a system, as in many others less esoteric, the dangers are seen as deriving from contact in the altered mind state with forces more powerful than oneself. Ritual performs a protective function for the individual in his contact with such forces. Crowley, familiar with the phenomenology of xenophrenic states (he used the term ''unsanity'') had an instinctive awareness of this function, and set his techniques of ecstasy induction into the ritual framework of a ceremonial magic based on the kabbala.

The *Rites of Eleusis* represent an approach toward a theatre of altered consciousness whose audience and actors alike ''rise on the astral planes'' toward ecstasies induced through shifting esthetic perceptions. Perhaps the failure of Crowley's experiment lies in the fact that he had a visionary sense of the potentialities of human consciousness combined with the esthetic sensibilities of a bad 19th-century romantic poet. Despite its failure, however, Crowley's basic concept remains a fascinating one, possibly now made feasible through the clinical and artistic researches into human consciousness of the past ten years. (p. 26)

> *J. F. Brown, ''Aleister Crowley's 'Rites of Eleusis','' in* The Drama Review *(© 1978 by* The Drama Review; *reprinted by permission; all rights reserved), No. 2, 1978, pp. 3-26.*

ADDITIONAL BIBLIOGRAPHY

Burnett-Rae, Alan. *Aleister Crowley: A Memoir of 666.* London: Victim Press, 1971, 20 p.
  Recollections of Crowley circa 1934 by his former landlord; includes four poems by Crowley: ''Hymn to Terminus,'' ''The Lizard,'' ''Cradle Song,'' and ''Inside Information.''

Dennis, Nigel. ''Marks of a Buddha.'' *New York Review of Books* XIV, No. 5 (12 March 1970): 3-4, 6.
  Favorable review of *The Confessions.*

Ellmann, Richard. ''Black Magic against the White: Aleister Crowley Versus W.B. Yeats.'' *Partisan Review* XV, No. 9 (September 1948): 1049-51.
  Account of the Crowley-Yeats struggle for leadership of the *Golden Dawn.*

Praz, Mario. ''Byzantium.'' In his *The Romantic Agony,* pp. 287-411. New York: Meridian Books, 1956.*
  In an extended footnote, disparages Crowley's ''slavish imitation of Swinburne'' and his decadent ''effusions'' on themes of masochism and hermaphroditism.

Regardie, Israel. *The Eye of the Triangle: An Interpretation of Aleister Crowley.* St. Paul, Minn.: Llewellyn Publications, 1970, 517 p.
  Defense of Crowley against what Regardie considers the ''totally contemptuous attitude'' of the Symonds biography.

Roberts, Susan. *The Magician of the Golden Dawn: The Story of Aleister Crowley.* Chicago: Contemporary Books, 1978, 337 p.
  Biography written in a narrative style.

Symonds, John. *The Great Beast: The Life of Aleister Crowley.* New York: Rider, 1951, 316 p.
  Most complete biography.

Wilson, Robert Anton. *Masks of the Illuminati.* New York: Pocket Books, 1981, 294 p.
  Novel featuring a portrait of Crowley as the comic hoaxer who wrote *Clouds without Water. Masks of the Illuminati* itself is written in the Crowleyan manner of erudition and irony.

(Sir) Arthur Conan Doyle

1859-1930

English short story writer, novelist, essayist, historian, and poet.

Though "there was far more in Doyle's literary life than the invention of his fascinating and volatile detective," as Ivor Brown has noted, it is as the creator of Sherlock Holmes that Doyle is remembered. His extensively researched historical romances, popular in their time, have not endured. Likewise, his adventure stories, and some early science fiction in the manner of Wells and Verne, are largely overshadowed by the exploits of Sherlock Holmes, the world's first consulting detective and one of the most famous literary creations of all time.

Doyle was born into genteel poverty in Edinburgh and educated at the strict Jesuit schools of Hodder and Stonyhurst. There he thrived on the harsh regimen and especially enjoyed the emphasis on sport. Despite his early religious orthodoxy, as a young doctor he left the church and refused the aid of wealthy relatives who demanded that he accept the family faith. Doyle took his medical degree in 1881; he served as surgeon on a whaling ship in the Arctic and on a passenger vessel in the tropics before establishing a medical practice which was never successful, and which he abandoned after his first few sales as a writer. At the age of forty he volunteered for the military during the Boer War, and, when turned down, gave his services to a field hospital. For this, and for his explication of Britain's part in the war in his work *The War in South Africa*, he was knighted in 1902. In later years Doyle involved himself in politics and stood twice for Parliament, but was defeated both times.

During his years as a student Doyle sold a few short stories, none of which attracted much notice. After setting up his medical practice, Doyle produced the detective novel *A Study in Scarlet*, basing his character Sherlock Holmes on Edgar Allan Poe's Dupin and Emile Gaboriau's Lecoq. The inspiration for his detective's amazing powers of deduction was a medical school instructor, Dr. Joseph Bell. Although Holmes was not the first, he remains the best known fictional detective. In conveying a stylized view of life in Victorian England, Doyle utilized crisp narrative and an instinctive eye for detail. England's old order was fast disappearing, but in the Holmes saga it endures forever. The character of Holmes, in Watson's words "cold, precise, but admirably balanced," served to uphold traditional mores, entering into a case, as Bonnie Menes has noted, "not when a law, but when a norm, has been broken." The Holmes adventures were very popular with the British and American reading public, but Doyle grew bored with his creation and weary of the endlessly contrived plots. He also wanted to devote more time to what he considered his important work, the writing of historical romances. He began, half jokingly, to demand huge sums of money for the Holmes stories, and was surprised to find publishers anxious to pay.

Doyle eventually did kill Holmes in the course of an adventure, but public outcry and repeated editorial requests led to his resuscitation ten years later. During the decade-long hiatus, Doyle had some success with two volumes of stories about the

swashbuckling Brigadier Gerard, a gallant Napoleonic soldier, whose unperturbable self-confidence contains a trace of Holmes. Also successful were the boxing adventures *Rodney Stone* and "The Croxley Master," boys' stories that reflect, as do all of Doyle's writings, the author's strongly ingrained sense of decency and fair play. He also created a dashing scientist-explorer, Professor Challenger, whose first adventure, *The Lost World*, formed the basis for the film *King Kong*.

Of the historical novels, *Micah Clarke* and *The White Company* were the first and best, possibly because they were written before the early Holmes stories became greatly popular and Doyle was still able to consider historical fiction his primary work. Doyle devoted years of research to the background of *Micah Clarke*, and adopted the style of Walter Scott and Thomas Macaulay. The result was "less a historical novel than a statement in fictional form," Pierre Nordon has noted, with "the charm of a chronicle." Of *The White Company* Doyle himself wrote: "I was young and full of the first joy of life and action and I think I got some of it into my pages."

Despite Doyle's preference for his historical fiction, it is Holmes who has consistently captured the public imagination. A large literature, amounting to a cult, has grown up around this character, often to the exclusion of his creator. Dozens of Sherlock Holmes clubs meet all over the world, taking their names from the sixty Holmes "cases." Much time and scholarship is devoted to the study of the canon, or conan, as Sherlockians call it. While this "bastardized academism," in Clive James's phrase, is inexplicable to some, it makes perfect sense to those who feel, as does Vincent Starrett, that the stories "are not great at all—only Sherlock Holmes is *great*." There is no doubt, however, that Doyle vitalized and popularized the detective story, creating in Holmes a character who, according to Colin Wilson, "was more than a fictional character; he was a response to a deep-rooted psychological need of the late Victorians, a need for reassurance, for belief in the efficacy of reason and for man's power to overcome the chaos produced by this new disease of alienation. The need is as strong today as it was in 1890, which no doubt explains why Holmes is still so very much alive."

PRINCIPAL WORKS

A Study in Scarlet (novel) 1888
Micah Clarke (novel) 1889
The Captain of the Pole-Star (short stories) 1890
The Sign of Four (novel) 1890
The White Company (novel) 1891
The Adventures of Sherlock Holmes (short stories) 1892
Mysteries and Adventures (short stories) 1893
The Refugees (novel) 1893
The Memoirs of Sherlock Holmes (short stories) 1894
Round the Red Lamp (short stories and essays) 1894
The Stark Munro Letters (short stories) 1895
The Exploits of Brigadier Gerard (short stories) 1896
Rodney Stone (novel) 1896
Songs of Action (poetry) 1898
The Tragedy of the Korosko (novel) 1898
The Great Boer War (nonfiction) 1900
The Hound of the Baskervilles (novel) 1902
The War in South Africa (history) 1902
The Adventures of Gerard (short stories) 1903
The Return of Sherlock Holmes (short stories) 1905
Sir Nigel (short stories) 1906
The Croxley Master (short stories) 1907
Songs of the Road (poetry) 1911
The Lost World (novel) 1912
The Poison Belt (novel) 1913
The Valley of Fear (novel) 1916
The British Campaign in France and Flanders. 6 vols.
    (history) 1916-19
His Last Bow (short stories) 1917
The New Revelation (essays) 1918
The Wanderings of a Spiritualist (essays) 1921
The History of Spiritualism. 2 vols. (nonfiction) 1926
The Case-Book of Sherlock Holmes (short stories) 1927
The Maracot Deep (short stories) 1929
The Edge of the Unknown (essays) 1930

THE ATHENAEUM   (essay date 1890)

A detective story is usually lively reading, but we cannot pretend to think that **'The Sign of Four'** is up to the level of the writer's best work. It is a curious medley, and full of horrors; and surely those who play at hide and seek with the fatal treasure are a strange company. The wooden-legged convict and his fiendish misshapen little mate, the ghastly twins, the genial prizefighters, the detectives wise and foolish, and the gentle girl whose lover tells the tale, twist in and out together in a mazy dance, culminating in that mad and terrible rush down the river which ends the mystery and the treasure. Dr. Doyle's admirers will read the little volume through eagerly enough, but they will hardly care to take it up again.

> *"Novels of the Week: 'The Sign of Four',"* in The Athenaeum, *No. 3293, December 6, 1890, p. 773.*

THE SPECTATOR   (essay date 1891)

The *White Company* is a stirring tale of the reign of Edward III., setting forth how a monastery-bred lad of twenty, with decidedly monkish proclivities, was transformed, in the short space of a year, into a bold knight and lover, and convinced of the superiority of an active life over a contemplative one. . . . The many deeds of derring-do described are told with so much spirit, that one does not care to inquire very closely into their probability; and perhaps the best of any is the account of the gallant last stand made by the White Company in the Spanish *barranca*, where 370 men are pitted against 6,000. . . . The Black Prince, Du Guesclin, and other historical personages are introduced into the story; "quoth" is habitually substituted for "said;" curious expletives, such as "by my ten fingerbones" and "by my hilt," occur continually; and the characters have a way of expressing themselves in queerly turned speech, which at all events serves the purpose of making it impossible for the reader to forget that the story does not refer to the present period, though whether the phraseology is distinctive of Edward III.'s reign, or any other either, we cannot take upon ourselves to say. There is not a vestige of a plot; but that deficiency will probably be no serious drawback in the eyes of boys, who are the class of readers to whom the book seems especially likely to commend itself, as being full of action, bristling with adventure, and not hampered by any squeamish regard for life or mawkish love-making. Older people, more critical and disposed to compare historical novels with the masterpieces of Scott and Dumas *père*, will find it fall short of that standard, and will miss (amongst other things) those touches of a living human nature common to all ages alike, with which the two above-mentioned great writers knew how to endow their *dramatis personae*, and without which fictious individuals are apt to resemble wooden dolls moved by mechanism, and not particularly distinguishable from one another save by the costumes they wear. (pp. 680-81)

> *"Three Novels,"* in The Spectator, *Vol. 67, No. 3307, November 14, 1891, pp. 680-81.**

THE ATHENAEUM   (essay date 1892)

For those to whom the good, honest, breathless detective story is dear Dr. Doyle's book [**"The Adventures of Sherlock Holmes"**] will prove a veritable godsend. Of its kind it is excellent; there is little literary pretension about it, and there is hardly any waste of time about subtle character-drawing; but incident succeeds incident with the most businesslike rapidity, and the unexpected always occurs with appropriate regularity. Of the dozen stories of which the book is made up there is not one which does not contain a thorough-paced mystery, apparently insoluble; but the solution is always satisfactorily wormed out by that marvellous amateur detective, Sherlock Holmes.

The adventures are all vastly improbable; but no matter; that has never detracted from an orthodox detective story. For genuine horror Dr. Doyle has a lively turn; in **'The Speckled Band'** and **'The Engineer's Thumb'** (mark the subtle suggestions of terror in the titles) the reader is worked up to such a pitch of nervous excitement that he is ready for almost anything; the first of these is worthy of Wilkie Collins. The chief defect of the book is the attempt to infuse vitality into Sherlock Holmes. It would have been better to leave him more of a detective-machine; as it is, one gets rather wearied of his swaggering assurance, of his nights of silent thought, and of his habit of mystifying inoffensive strangers by describing to them all their little weaknesses. Still, much may be forgiven him for his wonderful 'cuteness and for his hardly veiled contempt of our official detective police—a trait which is said to tell with the British public. The English is not always irreproachable: "If you will keep the two corner seats I *shall* get the tickets," for example, is bad.

> *"Novels of the Week :'The Adventures of Sherlock Holmes',"* in The Athenaeum, *No. 3393, November 5, 1892, p. 626.*

WILLIAM MORTON PAYNE   (essay date 1892)

When Dr. Doyle published **"The Sign of Four"** and **"A Study in Scarlet,"** he projected a new figure into literature. Since then he has told us, from time to time, of still other doings of his observant and analytical hero, until the name of Sherlock Holmes has come to stand for a distinct sort of literary sensation. He is a subtler detective than [Émile] Gaboriau ever imagined, he is omniscient upon all subjects that relate to his profession, and his creator has provided him with experiences so varied that we can only wonder at the fertility of invention displayed. **"The Adventures of Sherlock Holmes,"** now published, deals with a dozen episodes—most of them unfamiliar to us—in the career of this acute tracer of criminals and disentangler of intricate complications. Some of them we have already seen in the magazines, but most appear to be new. **"A Scandal in Bohemia"** tells how Sherlock Holmes was for once outwitted, and, to make the matter still more humiliating, by a woman. **"The Five Orange Pips"** is a thrilling story of the Ku Klux Klan. **"The Red-Headed League"** is a striking illustration of the author's originality. Although there is a certain monotony in the mechanism of these tales, there is none in their succession of incident, which is simply bewildering in its variety. Dr. Doyle has signed work of far greater permanent value than any to be found in this volume, but he is responsible for nothing more absorbing of the immediate interest.

> *William Morton Payne, "Recent English and Canadian Fiction: 'The Adventures of Sherlock Holmes'," in* The Dial, *Vol. XIII, No. 154, November 16, 1892, p. 311.*

ARTHUR BARTLETT MAURICE   (essay date 1900)

In looking over the work of Dr. Doyle during the past three or four years, one realises with the keenest sort of regret the unfortunate mistake he made in putting an end to Sherlock Holmes. The originality, the dramatic attractiveness of this character, were so striking that it is only now in looking back through the tales of *The Adventures* and *The Memoirs,* that we appreciate how utterly inferior they were in construction and dialogue. Since he wrote *The Study in Scarlet* Dr. Doyle has been learning much about craftsmanship. Sherlock Holmes in

the author's hands to-day might not be any more striking and vivid a creation, but he would assuredly stand out from a better setting. We should probably have considerably less of his friend and alleged historian, the very tiresome bore, Watson. The latter was always quite incorrigible in his expression of polite astonishment. When after Holmes, for the three hundredth time, had deduced alimony, a bad digestion and a West End scandal from an inspection of a visiting-card or an old hat band, Watson broke into his conventional volley of superlatives, the whole matter became just a little wearisome. For a time after Dr. Doyle's first success and popularity there were strong indications of a general fizzling out of his originality. Upon one occasion he practically rewrote, with new characters and a few minor changes, a story which he had told a few years before. In the case to which we refer the second story was called **"The Illness of Signor Lambert"**; the first was included in the volume which bore the title *Round the Red Lamp.* There were many such indications of waning strength. But of late he seems to be coming up again; one might sum it up by saying that he is getting his second wind. Much of his very recent work [such as **"The Croxley Master"** and *Rodney Stone*] is marked with all his early fire spontaneity, and yet there are many of these later tales which we lay down with disappointment simply because we feel how much better they would have been woven about the strange gifts, the personality, the omnipotence and omniscience of Sherlock Holmes. A notable story of this kind was **"The Story of the Lost Special,"** which appeared in the columns of an English magazine about two years ago, but which, to the best of the recollection of the present writer, has not yet been brought out in book form. It was simply the story of a train—locomotive, tender and two passenger-coaches—which, running in broad daylight through one of the most thickly populated districts of England, disappears without leaving the slightest clue of importance as to its fate. One could not readily conceive more startling and daring a plot, yet when the mystery is ultimately cleared away the whole thing seems possible enough, and had the explanation been brought about, as it should and might easily have been, by Sherlock Holmes and the science of deduction, the story would have taken rank with the very best that have come from Dr. Doyle's ingenious pen. (pp. 224-25)

Of **"The Croxley Master"** one need only say that it strengthens the conviction which came from reading *Rodney Stone*—that Dr. Doyle is to-day absolutely unrivalled as a chronicler of the romance of the ring. Perhaps it was because he had already been accepted as a mere literary amuser that the critics and the reading public in general have so understimated it as a book of real and lasting value. They have looked at the story, they have found it a good one, but what they have not seen and realised is that it is a powerful picture of the England of that day. There are a thousand romances and histories from which we may reconstruct the period. We may follow the Napoleonic Eagles from capital to capital. We may see Pitt and Fox and Byron and Tom Moore and poor old George the Third and his son, the inventor of a shoebuckle, the First Gentlemen of Europe. But none the less real are the rough men who gathered about in black thousands when Jack Harrison and Crab Wilson faced each other in the ring on Crawley Downs. (pp. 225)

> *Arthur Bartlett Maurice, "The Romance of the Ring," in* The Bookman, *New York, Vol. XI, No. 3, May, 1900, pp. 223-25.*

THE ATHENAEUM   (essay date 1904)

Sir A. Conan Doyle would appear to be deserting letters for affairs, so that it is difficult at present to judge of his true quality as a writer of fiction. Evidently he began with a more romantic feeling and a finer sense of the adventurous than he went on with. His fire seems to have decreased; he gives the impression of becoming more deliberate and less imaginative, and of attaining philosophy inconsistent with true artistry. It looks as if in his maturer years this ready writer were precipitating in the average British way. He always had an element of deliberation, such as one dissociates at once from inspiration and the "daemonic" force of art. Yet what an admirable piece of work was **'The White Company,'** which suffered no whit because it was descended from [Charles Reade's] 'The Cloister and the Hearth' and [Walter Scott's] 'Quentin Durward'! **'Micah Clarke,'** too, stands high among historical novels. . . . **'Rodney Stone'** is not a tale, but a cinematograph of the Regency period. It is vivid, wonderfully well studied, and understanding to a fault; but it falls short of fiction. The same hole may be picked in **'The Stark Monro Letters,'** which, for all that, contain some of the best material that the author has put together. It strikes one as odd and unfortunate that, with the author's power of visualizing a scene, he should have been, on the whole, so little successful in visualizing a character. He has invented some, no doubt, and several of these are in **'Micah Clarke.'** He has also hit upon an excellent type in Brigadier Gerard. But he shows no gallery of portraits; they lack life, but are set generally in a moving landscape. It is some kink in the imagination. The work that has made this author popular is the series of tales, admirable in their way, associated with Sherlock Holmes, a character, as is now generally known, imitated from Poe. Sherlock Holmes has so seized the popular ear that he almost alone of the abundance of men and women provided by living authors supplies a familiar reference used everywhere, an ineffaceable part of the English language. Such impression of a figure on the public is an achievement of the rarest (it is only equalled, as far as we recall at the moment, by the case of Jekyll and Hyde), but in this case it is an achievement which has little to do with letters.

"The Novels of Sir A. Conan Doyle," in The Athenaeum, *No. 3976, January 9, 1904, p. 40.*

MAX BEERBOHM (essay date 1905)

Evidently, I am growing old. Sherlock Holmes is dead, and to young readers it may be that he is not even a dear memory. But I was at an impressionable age when he burst upon the world; and so he became a part of my life, and will never, I suppose, be utterly dislodged. I cannot pass through Baker Street, even now, without thinking of him. Long ago I had decided exactly which were the two windows of the sitting-room where Watson spent his wondering hours; and, only the other day, I had a rather heated dispute with a coaeval who had also long since "placed" that sitting-room—"placed" it, if you please, on the side of the street opposite to that where it really was (need I say that I mean the right-hand side as one goes towards Regent's Park?). My sentiment for Sherlock Holmes was never one of reverence unalloyed. Indeed, one of the secrets of his hold on me was that he so often amused me. I would have bartered a dozen of his subtlest deductions for that great moment when he said (presumably on the eve of his creator's departure for a lecturing tour in America) "It is always a joy to me to meet an American, for I am one of those who believe that the folly of a monarch and the blundering of a minister in far gone years will not prevent our children from being some day citizens of the same world-wide country under a flag which shall be a quartering of the Union Jack with the

Stars and Stripes.'' I learned that speech by heart, years ago; and, to this day, I generally try it on any American to whom I am introduced—sometimes with most surprising results. Sir Arthur (then mere Mr.) Conan Doyle's own attitude towards life, and his own extraordinary versions of the familiar things around us—what would Sherlock have been without these assets? (p. 374)

Max Beerbohm, "At the St. James' Theatre" (originally published in The Saturday Review, London *Vol. 99, No. 2584, May 6, 1905), in his* Around Theatres *(reprinted by permission of Mrs. Eva Reichmann), revised edition, Rupert Hart-Davis, 1953, pp. 373-76).*

G. K. CHESTERTON (essay date 1907)

The return of Sherlock Holmes to the *Strand Magazine* some years after his death, put a finishing touch to the almost heroic popularity of a figure whose reality was like the universally admitted reality of some old hero of medieval fable. Just as Arthur and Barbarossa were to return again, men felt that this preposterous detective must return again. He had emerged out of the unreality of literature into the glowing reality of legend, and in proof of this he has inherited the most widespread and pathetic of the characteristics of legendary heroes; that characteristic which makes men incredulous of their death. A slight and fantastic figure in a fugitive and ironical type of romance, he may seem too insignificant a subject for such a description. Nevertheless the fact remains that Mr. Conan Doyle's hero is probably the only literary creation since the creations of Dickens which has really passed into the life and language of the people, and become a being like John Bull on Father Christmas. It is remarkable to notice that although we possess many writers whose popularity is attested by enormous sales and general discussion, there is hardly one of them except Conan Doyle in this instance whose characters are familiar to everyone as types and symbols, as Pecksniff was the type of hypocrisy or Bumble of officialism. Rudyard Kipling, for example, is undoubtedly a popular writer. But if we were to go up to any man in the street and say that a particular problem would have puzzled Strickland he would receive it with a very different expression of countenance to that which he would wear if we said that it would puzzle Sherlock Holmes. Mr. Kipling's stories give inexhaustible intellectual delight, but the personality which we remember is the personality of the story, not the personality of the character. We remember the action, but forget the actors. In no other current creation except Sherlock Holmes does the character succeed, so to speak, in breaking out of the book as a chicken breaks out of the egg. (pp. 168-69)

The fact that Sherlock Holmes alone has succeeded in familiarising himself at once with the cultured and the uncultured and turned his name into almost as descriptive a word as Dr. Guillotin or Captain Boycott, involves certain conclusions, which are for the most part worthy and reassuring. The phenomenon corrects finally, for example, much of the foolish and foppish talk about the public preferring books because they are bad. The stories of Sherlock Holmes are very good stories; they are perfectly graceful and conscientious works of art. The thread of irony which runs through all the solemn impossibilities of the narrative gives it the position of a really brilliant addition to the great literature of nonsense. The notion of the greatness of an intellect, proved by its occupation with small things instead of with great, is an original departure; it constitutes a kind of wild poetry of the commonplace. The intellectual clues and cruces upon which the development of each story turns are perhaps incredible as fact, but they are thoroughly solid and important as logic; they are such problems as a great lawyer might extract from two bottles of champagne; they are full of the very revelry of reason. The figure of Conan Doyle's detective is, in its own wild and trifling way, good literature.

Now, there are in London more than nine hundred and ninety-nine detective stories and fictitious detectives, nearly all of which are bad literature, or rather not literature at all. If, as the saying goes, the public likes books because they are bad, it would not be the fact that the one fictitious detective who is familiar to the whole public is the one fictitious detective who is a work of art. The fact of the matter is that ordinary men prefer certain kinds of work, good or bad, to certain other kinds of work, good or bad, which they have a perfect and obvious right to do. . . . But, preferring a certain thing, they prefer it good if they can get it. (pp. 169-70)

All English people have read the stories about Sherlock Holmes. Work like this is so good of its kind that it is difficult to endure patiently the talk of people who are occupied only in pointing out that it is not work of some other kind. The specific quality of a story of this sort is strictly what may be called wit; it is obliged to have some definite invention, construction and point, like a joke in the comic papers. Such work is inexpressibly superior to most mediocre serious work. There has to be something in it; it cannot be an entire imposture. A man can pretend to be wise; a man cannot pretend to be witty. His jokes may be much worse in your opinion than they are in his opinion; but after all they must be jokes; they cannot be entirely shapeless mysteries, like many modern works of philosophy.

Many men can make an epic who could not make an epigram. What is true of the comic anecdote is true also of that extended anecdote, the sensational story with a point to it. All real philosophy is apocalyptic, and if a man can give us revelations of heaven it is certainly better than giving us horrible revelations of high life. But I would rather have the man who devotes a short story to saying that he can solve the problem of a murder in Margate than the man who devotes a whole book to saying that he cannot solve the problem of things in general.

Sir Arthur Conan Doyle certainly weakened his excellent series of stories by being occasionally serious; especially he weakened it by introducing a sort of sneer at Edgar Allan Poe's Dupin, with whom he sustained no comparison. Sherlock Holmes's bright notions were like bright Cockney flowers grown in very shallow soil in a suburban garden; Dupin's were flowers growing on a vast, dark tree of thought. Hence Dupin, when he quits the subject of crime, talks in the tongue of permanent culture of the relations of imagination to analysis or of the relations of the supernatural to law. But the greatest error of the Sherlock Holmes conception remains to be remarked: I mean the error which represented the detective as indifferent to philosophy and poetry, and which seemed to imply that philosophy and poetry would not be good for a detective. Here he is at once eclipsed by the bolder and more brilliant brain of Poe, who carefully states that Dupin not only admired and trusted poetry, but was himself a poet. Sherlock Holmes would have been a better detective if he had been a philosopher, if he had been a poet, nay, if he had been a lover. It is remarkable to notice (I assume that you are as intimate with Dr. Watson's narratives as you should be)—it is remarkable to notice that the very same story in which the biographer describes Holmes's inaccessibility to love and such emotions, and how necessary

it was to the clear balance of his logic, is the very same story in which Holmes is beaten by a woman because he does not know whether a certain man is her fiancé or her lawyer. If he had been in love he might have known well enough.

The only real danger is that Conan Doyle, by spreading the notion that practical logic must be unpoetical, may have encouraged the notion, too common already, that imagination must be absent-minded. It is a false and dangerous doctrine that the poet must be absent-minded. The purely imaginative man could never be absent-minded. He would perceive the significance of things near to him as clearly as he perceived the significance of things far off. (pp. 171-72)

The real moral of the popularity of the adventures of Sherlock Holmes lies in the existence of a great artistic neglect. There are a large number of perfectly legitimate forms of art which are almost entirely neglected by good artists—the detective story, the farce, the book of boyish adventure, the melodrama, the music-hall song. The real curse of these things is not that they are too much regarded, but that they are not regarded enough; that they are despised even by those who write them. Conan Doyle triumphed and triumphed deservedly, because he took his art seriously, because he lavished a hundred little touches of real knowledge and genuine picturesqueness on the police novelette. He substituted for the customary keen eyes and turned-up collar of the conventional detective a number of traits, external and pictorial, indeed, but honestly appropriate to the logical genius, traits such as an immeasurable love of music and an egotism which was abstract and, therefore, almost unselfish. Above all, he surrounded his detective with a genuine atmosphere of the poetry of London. He called up before the imagination a new and visionary city in which every cellar and alley hid as many weapons as the rocks and heather-bushes of Roderick Dhu. By this artistic seriousness he raised one at least of the popular forms of art to the level which it ought to occupy.

He wrote the best work in a popular form, and he found that because it was the best it was also the most popular. Men needed stories, and had been content to take bad ones; and they were right, for a story in itself is a marvellous and excellent thing, and a bad story is better than no story, just as half a loaf is better than no bread. But when a detective story was written by a man who refused to despise his art, who carried all their dreams to fulfilment, they preferred him to the bungling and irresponsible authors who had catered for them before. (pp. 173-74)

G. K. Chesterton, "Sherlock Holmes" (originally published as two essays in Daily News, *1901 and 1907), in his* A Handful of Authors: Essays on Books & Writers, *edited by Dorothy Collins (reprinted by permission of the Estate of G. K. Chesterton), Sheed and Ward, Inc., 1953, pp. 168-74.*

T. S. ELIOT (essay date 1929)

It is a great convenience to the critic to be able to compare what he is writing about with something else. But I cannot think of anything to which to compare Sherlock Holmes. He does not seem to be descended from either Sergeant Cuff or Monsieur Dupin. His relationship to Lecoq is quite superficial. He has had, on the other hand, a numerous progeny. So has Professor Moriarty. Only Mycroft Holmes, that colossal genius, has, so far as I know, no descendants. In Arsene Lupin, even in Raffles, we distinguish the features of the Robin Hood type. But Holmes was always reticent about his family: in fact he has no family to be reticent about. Another, and perhaps the greatest of the Sherlock Holmes mysteries is this: that when we talk of him we invariably fall into the fancy of his existence. Collins, after all, is more real to his readers than Cuff; Poe is more real than Dupin; but Sir A. Conan Doyle, the eminent spiritualist of whom we read in Sunday papers, the author of a number of exciting stories which we read years ago and have forgotten, what has he to do with Holmes? The only analogies are such as make the case more puzzling. We can think of Sam Weller without thinking of Dickens, or of Falstaff or Hamlet without thinking of Shakespeare: yet we do not compare Conan Doyle with Dickens or Shakespeare. Even Holmes's reality is a reality of its own kind. Never is he impeccable. He employs the most incredible disguises. (pp. 553-54)

It is of course, the dramatic ability, rather than the pure detective ability, that does it. But it is a dramatic ability applied with great cunning and concentration; it is not spilt about. The content of the story may be poor; but the form is nearly always perfect. We are so well worked up by the dramatic preparation that we accept the conclusion—even when, as in *The Red-Headed League,* it is perfectly obvious from the beginning. . . . Also, it must be remarked that the author (for we must mention Sir Arthur now and then) shows wisdom or instinct in keeping the sentimental interest down. Several times he trips. . . . But on the whole Sir Arthur kept the sentiment in its place; and it is superfluous sentiment that dates a detective story. (pp. 554-55)

[Every writer of detective fiction] owes something to Holmes. And every critic of The Novel who has a theory about the reality of characters in fiction, would do well to consider Holmes. There is no rich humanity, no deep and cunning psychology and knowledge of the human heart about him; he is obviously a formula. He has not the reality of any great character of Dickens or Thackeray or George Eliot or Meredith or Hardy; or Jane Austen or the Brontes or Virginia Woolf or James Joyce: yet, as I suggested, he is just as real to us as Falstaff or the Wellers. He is not even a very good detective. But I am not sure that Sir Arthur Conan Doyle is not one of the great dramatic writers of his age. (p. 556)

> *T.S. Eliot, "Books of the Quarter: 'The Complete Sherlock Holmes Short Stories'" (reprinted by permission of Mrs. Valerie Eliot and Faber & Faber Ltd.), in* The Criterion, *Vol. VIII, No. XXXII, April, 1929, pp. 553-56.*

DOROTHY L. SAYERS   (essay date 1929)

Conan Doyle took up the Poe [detective story] formula and galvanised it into life and popularity. He cut out the elaborate psychological introductions, or restated them in crisp dialogue. He brought into prominence what Poe had only lightly touched upon—the deduction of staggering conclusions from trifling indications in the Dumas-Cooper-Gaboriau manner. He was sparkling, surprising, and short. It was the triumph of the epigram.

A comparison of the Sherlock Holmes tales with the Dupin tales shows clearly how much Doyle owed to Poe, and, at the same time, how greatly he modified Poe's style and formula. Read, for instance, the opening pages of *The Murders in the Rue Morgue,* which introduce Dupin, and compare them with the first chapter of *A Study in Scarlet.* (p. 28)

See how the sturdy independence of Watson adds salt and savour to the eccentricities of Holmes, and how flavourless beside it is the hero-worshipping self-abnegation of Dupin's friend. See, too, how the concrete details of daily life in Baker Street lift the story out of the fantastic and give it a solid reality. The Baker Street menáge has just that touch of humorous commonplace which appeals to British readers. (pp. 29-30)

Compare, also, the conversational styles of Holmes and Dupin, and the reasons for Holmes's popularity become clearer than ever. Holmes has enriched English literature with more than one memorable aphorism and turn of speech. (p. 30)

So, with Sherlock Holmes, the ball—the original nucleus deposited by Edgar Allan Poe nearly forty years earlier—was at last set rolling. As it went, it swelled into a vast mass—it set off others—it became a spate—a torrent—an avalanche of mystery fiction. (p. 31)

> *Dorothy L. Sayers, "Introduction" (reprinted by permission of David Higham Associates Limited, as literary agents for the Estate of Dorothy L. Sayers), in* The Omnibus of Crime, *edited by Dorothy L. Sayers, Payson and Clarke Ltd., 1929, pp. 9-47.**

CHRISTOPHER MORLEY   (essay date 1933)

The whole Sherlock Holmes saga is a triumphant illustration of art's supremacy over life. Perhaps no fiction character ever created has become so charmingly real to his readers. It is not that we take our blessed Sherlock too seriously. . . . But Holmes is pure anesthesia. We read the stories again and again; perhaps most of all for the little introductory interiors which give a glimpse of 221B Baker Street. (pp. 71-2)

The character of Holmes, Doyle has told us, was at any rate partly suggested by his student memories of Dr. Joseph Bell of the Edinburgh Infirmary, whose diagnostic intuitions used to startle his patients and pupils. But there was abundant evidence that the invention of the scientific detective conformed to a fundamental logic in Doyle's own temper. . . . [One example] was his ingenuity in transmitting news of the war in cipher to British prisoners in Germany. This he did by sending books in which he had put needle-pricks under various printed letters so as to spell out the desired messages; but beginning with the third chapter, believing that the German censor would examine the earlier chapters more carefully. Of his humor there is a pleasant income tax story. In his first year of independent medical practice his earnings were. £154, and when the income tax paper arrived he filled it up to show that he was not liable. The authorities returned the form with the words *Most Unsatisfactory* scrawled across it. He returned it again with the subscription *I entirely agree.* As many readers must have guessed, *Round the Red Lamp* and *The Stark Munro Letters* were very literally drawn from his own experiences in medicine.

"Art in the blood is liable to take the strangest forms," Sherlock Holmes once remarked. Undoubtedly Doyle was thinking also of his own inheritance (both artistic and Irish) and certainly he himself, though he looked so solidly Watsonian, gave his friends many surprises in the mutations of his vigorous career. One of the quaintest of these must have been his collaboration with [Sir. J. M.] Barrie in an operetta. Of the final spiritualist phase only those who have made careful study of those problems can profitably speak. But there was no stage of the life, from the poor student doing without lunch to buy books to the famous author enduring painful hostility for his psychic faith, which did not reflect the courage, the chivalry, the sagacity we would have expected from the creator of Holmes. Certainly it was characteristic of that student of mysteries to attack the greatest one we know.

Those of us who in earliest boyhood gave our hearts to Conan Doyle, and have had from him so many hours of good refreshment, find our affection unshakable. What other man led a fuller and heartier and more masculine life? Doctor, whaler, athlete, writer, speculator, dramatist, historian, war correspondent, spiritualist, he was always also the infracaninophile—the helper of the under dog. Generous personality, his virtues had always something of the fresh vigor of the amateur, keen, open-minded, flexible, imaginative. If, as Doyle utterly believed, the spirits of the dead persist and can communicate, there is none that could have more wholesome news to impart to us than that brave and energetic lover of life.

A blessing, then, on those ophthalmic citizens who did not go to that office at 2 Devonshire Place, near Harley Street, where in 1891 Dr. A. Conan Doyle set up consulting rooms as an eye specialist. It was there, waiting for the patients who never came, that he began to see the possibilities in Sherlock Holmes. No wonder that Dr. Watson too sometimes rather neglected his practice. (pp. 78-80)

> Christopher Morley, "In Memoriam Sherlock Holmes," in his Internal Revenue (copyright, 1926, 1927, 1928, 1929, 1930, 1931, 1932, 1933 by Christopher Morley; copyright renewed © 1960 by Helen F. Morley; reprinted by permission of Harper and Row Publishers, Inc.), Doran & Company, Inc., 1933, pp. 70-80.

VINCENT STARRETT   (essay date 1940)

There were characters in English fiction before Holmes who stepped out of their pages and became the living familiars of their admirers. There was Mr. Pickwick, for example; and fat Jack Falstaff. Still, it may be doubted whether any other "household word" had ever quite so authentic an existence as the indestructible detective. Literally thousands of persons who have never read the stories by Sir Arthur Conan Doyle are familiar with the name and fame of his detective. If you are in any doubt about this, just ask the first bus conductor or billposter that you meet. The plain fact is that Sherlock Holmes is still a more commanding figure in the world than most of the warriors and statesmen in whose present existence we are invited to believe. I may have said something of this sort before; but it is the sort of thing I like to say and that, in my opinion, can not be said too often.

The plain fact also is this: he is more real than his literary progenitor. For what, as Mr. T. S. Eliot once asked, "has that eminent spiritualist, of whom we read in the Sunday papers, to do with Sherlock Holmes?" Nothing, of course. It was not Arthur Conan Doyle, the eminent spiritualist, who begat immortal Sherlock; it was Dr. A. Conan Doyle of Bush Villa, Southsea, an impoverished young Iro-Scot, recently graduated from Edinburgh University. In begetting him, Dr. Doyle—in the Frankenstein tradition—gave birth to a monster that, in the end, threatened to devour his creator. But a monster who, perhaps more than any ectoplasmic emanation since Pickwick, has been gathered in the world's embrace.

Conan Doyle's attitude toward his gigantic child—an attitude in which toleration, resentment, bitterness, and resignation alternated—illustrates one of the tragedies of his long and successful life. Tragedy in the Jamesian sense, that is—the au-

thor's lifelong struggle to kill off a character who was making him much money, in order to devote himself to what he took to be more important work. For in the beginning the doctor planned no such career for the detective as Holmes has had. [A Study in Scarlet, The Sign of Four, The Adventures of Sherlock Holmes, and The Memoirs of Sherlock Holmes] . . . served their purpose, as far as Doyle was concerned, when they paid his bills. And they were really all he had to say about Sherlock Holmes. He was frankly tired of the fellow as early as 1894. Old inhabitants will remember with what appalling finality he killed the detective off in the last story of the *Memoirs*.

Yet five volumes were to follow. Public horror and indignation harassed him until, in 1902, he yielded to supplication and gave the world *The Hound of the Baskervilles*. Another surrender, in 1905, brought us *The Return of Sherlock Holmes* and the glad tidings (for the *Hound* had been a memory, not a new adventure) that the detective was not dead at all. He never *had* been dead! There are still living in the world many citizens who remember the ecstasy of that moment. Holmes had retired, however, to his bee farm in Sussex, and Conan Doyle again had reached an end to such ephemeral matters as these melodramatic chronicles of crime and detection. But *The Valley of Fear* appeared in 1917, and *His Last Bow* (it wasn't) just two years later. In *The Case-Book of Sherlock Holmes* there was an indubitable end, however; and three years later Conan Doyle was dead.

It is an odd story and perhaps it is a fable for writing men and women. One senses its resemblance to von Chamisso's fable of *Peter Schlemyl or The Shadowless Man*. Peter Schlemyl's shadow, in the old allegory, became independent of its master, waxed wealthy, and eventually hired him as a silent, obsequious attendant. The shadow had discovered that its own lack of a shadow caused inconvenient comments. It is certain that Conan Doyle feared some such loss of personal identity; at very least he felt that other and better work than his Holmes tales were suffering an unjust obscurity. Many times he confessed that he had come "almost to hate poor Sherlock"; but, as suggested, his most drastic effort to rid himself of the detective—by causing him to disappear over the Reichenbach Fall—was not regarded by the public as justifiable homicide. The uproar was prodigious. "You beast!" "You brute!" his readers cried at him; and Holmes reappeared. There was money in him, of course; and better money than ever, we may be certain, after the resurrection. But there is no doubt that several times over the long years of the detective's career his creator would cheerfully have shown him the door.

It was Conan Doyle's idea that he was an historical novelist; and so he was—one of the best the world has known. By such tales as *The White Company, Micah Clarke, The Refugees, Uncle Bernac,* and *Rodney Stone*, he takes rank with the greatest writers in that field. *The White Company* already is a classic, and probably it is immortal. Loving Holmes, one yet understands his creator's emotion. But would *The White Company* and *Micah Clarke* rank higher in the world's esteem if Sherlock Holmes had never lived in Baker Street? It seems only silly to believe so. They will last—along with Sherlock—and, if anything, will be helped by the detective, whose fame will constantly draw new readers to everything that carries the signature of Arthur Conan Doyle. It is a little surprising perhaps that Doyle, himself, was not able to realize this. Certainly the tales of Sherlock Holmes are not the author's greatest performances. They are not great at all—only Sherlock Holmes is *great*. But, after reading the nine volumes that comprise the Holmes saga, there will always be readers who will turn to those other titles on the long list, where they will make the acquaintance of some very attractive gentlemen of fortune.

But to the end Sir Arthur resented his most popular creation. ''I do not wish to be ungrateful to Holmes, who has been a good friend in many ways,'' he wrote in his autobiography; and thereafter he went on to criticize the detective rather sharply. ''My most notorious character,'' he called him, with wry humor. Sir Arthur's own favorite among his stories was *Sir Nigel,* which again reveals how notably a writer may be mistaken about his own work; for the novel, although good, is not a patch on *The White Company,* a masterpiece. (pp. 198-202)

> Vincent Starrett, ''From Poe to Poirot,'' in his Books Alive: A Profane Chronicle of Literary Endeavor and Literary Misdemeanor (reprinted by permission of Michael Murphy, Literary Executor for the Estate of Vincent Starrett), Random House, 1940, pp. 184-210.*

HESKETH PEARSON   (essay date 1943)

Though he expended more energy in sport than most men give to work, Doyle produced more work than those of his contemporaries who had neither time nor inclination for sport. He could write under any sort of condition. Sometimes he went to his study before the rest of the household was awake and wrote hard until breakfast-time. Sometimes he sat down immediately after a game of golf and worked until his brain gave out. He could detach himself completely from his surroundings and knock off a story while a crowd of people were talking and laughing in the same room, suddenly interjecting a remark which showed that he had followed the conversation while his pen had never ceased moving. Occasionally he slaved away as if his life depended on it. When he heard of the Congo atrocities he got all the first-hand accounts available and shut himself up in his study for a week, not once taking his slippers off to go out until he had written his pamphlet [*The Crime of the Congo*]. Thus, in spite of his physical activities, his output was considerable, and in the first decade of the century the public were treated to more Holmes stories, more Gerard stories, more short stories about sport, warfare, and adventure, a volume of talk about his favourite books, *Through the Magic Door,* and another long historical novel, *Sir Nigel,* which describes the early life of Loring, hero of *The White Company.* If anything the later book is the better of the two, yet it never became so popular, much to the disappointment of the author, who did not perceive the cause. In the intervening fifteen years the public had vicariously enjoyed its bath of blood. [Horatio] Kitchener had obliged it with the battle of Omdurman, which had manured the desert with dervishes, the Matabeles had provided much food for powder, and the Boers had been even more accommodating. The age no longer panted for deeds of chivalry, and the idealistic pre-Quixote note of *Sir Nigel* found no echo in a country that had just concluded a series of campaigns for dividends.

But there was no falling off in the demand for Doyle's short stories, which whetted the popular appetite for sport, mystery, thrills and horror. He could not help giving the man in the street what he wanted because he himself was the man in the street; indeed so exactly did he represent the normal man that one might call him Everyman in the street. But the normal man is not the healthy innocent our newspapers would like us to think him. He is a mixture of strange desires, domestic sen-

timent, cruelty, kindness, and morbidity; and Doyle expressed his less pleasant characteristics as unerringly as his more presentable ones. The story in which the leper woman infects Captain Sharkey; the episode of the jealous Turk who persuades his wife's lover, an eminent surgeon, to remove her lower lip while she lies drugged, her features hidden by a yashmak; the torturing of the Marquise de Brinvilliers; these and a dozen other yarns display Doyle as the medium for what was barbarous in the ordinary man. 'I have myself, in my complex nature, a hunger after all which is bizarre and fantastic,' says the teller of one of these tales. Doyle was simple enough to think himself complex merely because he was not all of one pattern. Sir Max Pemberton tells us that Doyle's 'bias towards the horrific' was apparent in his conversation as well as in his stories. . . . (pp. 150-52)

Doyle, in macabre vein, was a disciple of Poe. He was brimful of fancy and restricted in imagination. But he was too normal to get Poe's effects, and when he tried to outdo Poe in horror he overdid it, giving the reader a physical shock instead of a spiritual shudder. He had an adolescent ambition to make the reader's flesh creep, and editors sometimes found it necessary to make him tone down his work for publication. One of his tales, **'The Curse of Eve',** is a description of an *accouchement* which, after a crisis, ends with the mother and child doing well and the father in a state of rapture. But Francis Gribble told me that he heard Doyle read it at the Authors' Club before it appeared in Jerome's paper *The Idler,* and that in the original version the wife died and the bereaved father tried to kill the baby, shouting at it, 'You little beast, you've murdered your mother!' Doyle saw life melodramatically, like Dickens, his characters being as theatrical as those of Dickens, though much less various.

Such sense of reality as Doyle possessed only functioned when he described scenes of action. Here Scott was his master in the longer romances, while his short tales (other than those about Holmes and Gerard) have something in common with the stories of Maupassant. Of course Maupassant, being French, was obsessed with sex, while Doyle, being more English than an Englishman, was obsessed with sport. . . . (p. 153)

Not wholly unaware of the fact that there is no recommendation like self-dispraise, Doyle sometimes affected a humble attitude in estimating his fictional achievements: 'If we writers of stories have not great brains ourselves, we can at least provide something which will rest or distract the brains of others who work at more serious tasks than our own.' Yet he was far from indifferent to criticism, kept press-cuttings about his books, and once begged Lacon Watson to review his poems for *The Bookman.* This was a ticklish job, because the writing of poetry was not among Doyle's many gifts. He could write verse, of a sort, but not once throughout a volume of it is a deep emotion distilled by the imagination into perfect expression. His most successful effort combines his love of sport and Puritanism, the conflict between the two providing him with one of those excellent strokes of comedy which give vitality to all his best work. **'Bendy's Sermon'** tells how Bendigo, the famous Nottingham prize-fighter, takes to religion and preaches at revivalist meetings all over the country. On one such occasion a crowd of fellow-bruisers turn up and interrupt his prayers with ironical comments. He prays hard for strength to endure the mockery, but at last he gives in . . . He leaps from the pulpit and proceeds to knock hell out of the sceptics. . . . (pp. 154-55)

Doyle's personal tastes are reflected in everything he wrote and one has only to read his books in order to understand why he was liked by nearly everyone who met him. He could discuss religion or sport or literature or war or torture or politics or science or murder with equal zest because he was equally interested in all of them. (p. 155)

> *Hesketh Pearson, in his* Conan Doyle: His Life and Art *(reprinted by permission of the Executors of the Estate of the late Hesketh Pearson), second edition, Methuen & Co., Ltd., 1943, 193 p.*

EDMUND WILSON (essay date 1945)

I will now confess [that] . . . I have myself become addicted, in spells, to reading myself to sleep with Sherlock Holmes, which I had gone back to, not having looked at it since childhood, in order to see how it compared with Conan Doyle's latest imitators. I propose, however, to justify my pleasure in rereading Sherlock Holmes on grounds entirely different from those on which the consumers of the current product ordinarily defend their taste. My contention is that Sherlock Holmes *is* literature on a humble but not ignoble level, whereas the mystery writers most in vogue now are not. The old stories are literature, not because of the conjuring tricks and the puzzles, not because of the lively melodrama, which they have in common with many other detective stories, but by virtue of imagination and style. These are fairy-tales, as Conan Doyle intimated in his preface to his last collection, and they are among the most amusing of fairy-tales and not among the least distinguished.

The Sherlock Holmes stories, almost as much as the Alice books or as Edward Lear's nonsense, were the casual products of a life the main purpose of which was something else, but creations that in some sense got detached from their author and flew away and had a life of their own. Conan Doyle, it seems, worked conscientiously to document his historical romances, which he considered his serious work, but he regarded Holmes and Watson as the paper dolls of rather ridiculous and undignified potboilers, and he paid so little attention to what he wrote about them that the stories are full of inconsistencies, which Doyle never bothered to correct. He forgot Watson's Christian name and later on gave him a new one; he shifted the location of his wound; he began by making an ignorance of literature an essential trait of Holmes's personality and then had him talk about Petrarch and Meredith; and he even, on one occasion, changed the season abruptly from July to September. (It is an odd evidence of Holmes's vitality that some of his admirers should have gone to the trouble of attempting to account for these discrepancies, as if Watson and Holmes had been real men, and that they should actually have published their conjectures in a volume called *Profile by Gaslight*.). Doyle had become so impatient with his hero by the end of the second series in the *Strand Magazine* that he got rid of him by killing him off, totally without preparation, in a manner that was little short of frivolous. But Sherlock Holmes was like a genie let out of a bottle; there was no way of getting him back and, once at large, he was always available to minister to his master's wants. Doyle eventually brought Holmes back to life and wrote five more volumes about him. For perhaps the only time in his life, he had hit upon a genuine spell.

Whence had he mustered this spell and what elements had been mixed to make it? Well, there was Poe, of course, and there was also unquestionably R. L. Stevenson's *New Arabian Nights. The Adventure of the Hansom Cab* and *The Adventure of the Superfluous Mansion* must have suggested both the Sherlock Holmes titles and the formula of taking people to unexpected places and having them witness mysterious happenings. But Doyle, though much less "literary" than Stevenson, somehow got solider results, which depended on quite different qualities from Stevenson's suave Oriental tone and the limpid iridescence of his fantasy. For one thing, Stevenson was weak on character, whereas Doyle had produced two real personalities. And, for another, Conan Doyle had created his own vein of fantasy, which was vivider, if rather less fine, than Stevenson's. You see the force of his imagination exemplified in a curious way in some of those stories in which the dénouement is inadequate or disappointing. (pp. 267-69)

[Doyle exploits] a device quite remote from the suave story-spinning of Stevenson: he is working in the familiar tradition—in which the English art of fiction has excelled since the days of *Robinson Crusoe*—of the commonplace and common-sense narrative which arouses excitement and wonder. He can make us feel the presence of the "sinister"—to use one of his favorite words—even in a situation which does not include any fantastic ingredient. Take the story of *The Naval Treaty*, which follows *The Greek Interpreter* in Doyle's carefully varied program. A young man in the Foreign Office has been entrusted with an important document, which he has been copying at night in his office. He is alone and there is no entrance to the room save by a corridor that leads to the street. No one except the Foreign Minister knows that he has the treaty. At last he rings for the doorman to bring him some coffee, but an unknown woman answers the bell, large and coarse-faced and wearing an apron. She says that she is the doorman's wife and promises to send the coffee, but some time passes and the coffee does not come, and he goes downstairs to see what is the matter. He finds the doorman asleep, but the man is immediately awakened by a bell that rings loudly overhead.

> 'I was boiling the kettle when I fell asleep, sir.' He looked at me and then up at the still quivering bell with an ever-growing astonishment upon his face.
>
> 'If you was here, sir, then who rang the bell?' he asked.
>
> 'The bell!' I cried. 'What bell is it?'
>
> 'It's the bell of the room you were working in.'

Both these incidents, so soberly told, the appearance of the woman and the ringing of the bell, give us shocks that reverberate. Of course there is no one upstairs in the room and the naval treaty has been taken.

The stories have also both form and style of a kind very much superior to what one finds in our padded novels, though sometimes, it seems to me, the requirements of length for short stories in the *Strand Magazine* compelled Doyle somewhat to skimp his endings. There is wit, not mere tricks, in the "deductions" of Holmes and wit in the dialogue, and not only in the interchanges between Watson and Holmes but even in some of the stagy lines which Doyle's very sure sense of point save from being merely absurd. (pp. 269-71)

The writing, of course, is full of clichés, but these clichés are dealt out with a ring which gives them a kind of value, while the author makes speed and saves space so effectively that we are rarely in danger of getting bogged down in anything boring. And the clichés of situation and character are somehow made to function, too, for the success of the general effect. This effect owes its real originality not only to the queer collocations of elements, such as those I have mentioned above, but also to the admirable settings: the somber overcarpeted interiors or the musty empty houses of London, the remote old or new country places, always with shrubbery along the drives; and the characters—the choleric big-game hunters and the high-spirited noble ladies—have been imbued with the atmosphere of the settings and charged with an energy sufficient—like the fierce puppets of a Punch-and-Judy show—to make an impression in their simple roles.

But over the whole epic there hangs an air of irresponsible comedy, like that of some father's rigmarole for children, like that of, say, Albert Bigelow Paine in his stories about the Coon, the Possum and the Old Black Crow who all lived together in a Hollow Tree. The story-teller can make anything happen that will entertain his nightly audience and that will admit some kind of break at bedtime. The invention of Professor Moriarty, that scentific master-mind of crime who was to checkmate the great scientific detective, is simply an improvisation to bring to an end an overlong story, and the duel in which each is straining to outthink and outtrick the other is exhilarating because totally impossible. I do not share the prejudice of some Holmes experts against the two latest series of stories. Inferior though these often are in plot, Doyle amuses himself here in a way which makes them extremely funny. I am delighted by *The Adventure of the Dying Detective,* in which Holmes feigns a tropical disease and refuses to let Watson treat him: "Facts are facts, Watson, and after all, you are only a general practitioner with very limited experience and mediocre qualifications. It is painful to have to say these things, but you leave me no choice." "I was bitterly hurt," says Watson. And it was a capital idea to have Watson himself sometimes undertake the inquiry and bungle it, or conversely, in other cases, to have Holmes tell the stories instead of Watson, in an attempt to divest them of the fortuitous glamor which he insists that his friend has added. (pp. 271-72)

[And it all takes place in that] atmosphere of "cozy peril," to quote a phrase from, I think, Mr. Morley, who . . . has written so well on this subject. They will, of course, get safely back to Baker Street, after their vigils and raids and arrests, to discuss the case comfortably in their rooms and have their landlady bring them breakfast the next morning. Law and Order have not tottered a moment; the British police are well in control: they are the stoutest, most faithful fellows in the world if they can only be properly directed by Intellect in the form of a romantic personality possessed by the scientific spirit. All the loose ends of every episode are tidily picked up and tucked in, and even Holmes, though once addicted to cocaine, has been reformed by the excellent Watson. In this world, one can count on the client to arrive at the very moment when his case has just been explained, and Holmes and Watson always find it possible to get anywhere they want to go without a moment's delay or confusion. (pp. 272-73)

Edmund Wilson, "'Mr. Holmes, They Were the Footprints of a Gigantic Hound!'" (originally published in The New Yorker, Vol. XXI, No. 1, February 17, 1945), in his Classics and Commercials: A Literary Chronicle of the Forties (reprinted with the permission of Farrar, Straus and Giroux, Inc.; copyright 1950 by Edmund Wilson; copyright renewed © 1978 by Elena Wilson), The Noonday Press, 1950, pp. 266-74.

S. C. ROBERTS   (essay date 1953)

[The] personalities of Holmes and Watson took such universal hold upon the hearts and imaginations of readers and have retained that hold so tenaciously over a period of sixty years that their lives, their habits, and their characteristics have become an object of greater interest than the adventures which they shared.

'The truth is', wrote Johnson in a highly disputable passage in the Preface to his edition of Shakespeare, 'that the spectators are always in their senses, and know, from the first act to the last, that the stage is only a stage and that the players are only players.'

Of the drama of Sherlock Holmes the very reverse is the truth. The spectators are not always in their senses and they refuse to treat Holmes and Watson as 'only players'. Conan Doyle, in spite of his own waning interest, created not puppets but characters whom his readers have insisted on regarding as flesh and blood rather than as dramatis personae. Never were two characters more desperately in search of an author than were Holmes and Watson in the years succeeding the tragedy of the Reichenbach Falls; and when *The Empty House,* the story that heralded 'The Return', appeared . . . , the scenes at railway bookstalls resembled the struggles in a bargain-basement. One critic remarked that, although Holmes was not killed when he fell over the cliff, he was never quite the same man afterwards. But for the common reader it was not the quality of the later stories that mattered; what mattered was Holmes's restoration to life, to detective activity, and to Baker Street. For Holmes returned to a familiar scene and a beloved companion: 'It was indeed like old times when, at that hour, I found myself seated beside him in a hansom, my revolver in my pocket and the thrill of adventure in my heart.' This was what Watson felt, and the renewal of the old-time thrill was communicated to a multitude of readers. The Baker Street *mise en scène* is indeed one of Conan Doyle's master-strokes. In some way not easy to define, No. 221B has become a focal point of the metropolitan civilization of the 'nineties—the November fogs, the hansoms, the commissionaires, the gasogene, the frock-coats, the Wigmore Street post office. . . . Many of the adventures contain fantastic elements and conjure up scenes of distant devilry and romance; but Holmes and Watson always have their feet upon the ground. They travel on well-known railways, they frequent a well-known Turkish bath establishment, they read the *Daily Telegraph,* they are in touch with all classes of society. If they are dealing with members of the middle class (doctors, solicitors, schoolmasters, engineers, tradesmen) they are treading on ground familiar to the great mass of readers; if, on the other hand, they are dealing either with Cabinet Ministers and political dukes or with the crooks and loafers of London's underworld, they give the same readers the thrill that comes with an introduction either to the highest, or to the lowest, strata of society. But, in any event, the reader feels that he is encountering real people, people who do not demand of him any wide exercise of imagination.

In recent years, of course, the public has become familiar with detective stories of vastly more intricate plot, stories of greater complexity and finer ingenuity. Surveying the Sherlock Holmes adventures, the conscientious critic of today would probably give high marks to *Silver Blaze,* for example, or to *The Speckled Band,* but might well think poorly of some of the later stories. (pp. 105-07)

[But] it is needless to argue about the faults, or the occasional absurdities, of the Sherlock Holmes stories. From the beginning, a magic seal was set upon them; they were the reminiscences of John H. Watson, M.D., and Watson had the quality which is now regarded as the highest virtue in a broadcaster—he could make his audience feel that he was telling the story from the fireside: '"My dear fellow", said Sherlock Holmes, as we sat on either side of the fire in his lodgings at Baker Street, "life is infinitely stranger than anything which the mind of man could invent. . . ."'; or '"Holmes", said I, as I stood one morning in our bow-window looking down the street, "here is a madman coming along. . . ."'; or '"I am afraid, Watson, that I shall have to go", said Holmes, as we sat down to our breakfast together one morning. "Go! Where to?" "To Dartmoor—to King's Pyland". . . .'

It is this direct, personal introduction that makes the whole scene friendly, intimate, enticing; and at once the reader is agog to hear the details of the latest mystery.

'Come, Watson, come,' cried Holmes, breaking unconsciously on one occasion into a poetical invocation:

> The game is afoot. Not a word!
> Into your clothes and come!

In ten minutes Watson was not only in his clothes, but in a cab, rattling through the streets to Charing Cross Station. There will never be wanting a crowd to follow that cab. (pp. 107-08)

> *S. C. Roberts, in his* Holmes & Watson: A Miscellany *(reprinted by permission of Oxford University Press), Oxford University Press, London, 1953, 137 p.*

SAM MOSKOWITZ (essay date 1963)

Professor George Edward Challenger, a fictional character created by Arthur Conan Doyle, has frequently been referred to as "The Sherlock Holmes of Science Fiction." To literary critics and researchers alike, he presents unshakable evidence that outstanding characterization is possible within the fabric of the true science fiction story. Professor Challenger appeared first in *The Lost World*, a novel serialized by *Strand* in England in 1912, and continued to figure prominently in Doyle's literary output until the publication of *The Maracot Deep*, a collection of stories issued in 1929. (p. 157)

The time Doyle spent on Sherlock Holmes added immeasurably to the development of the detective story and the reading pleasure of the world. . . .

Though his best science fiction was written long after the fame of Sherlock Holmes had made his name a household word throughout the world, for a brief time in his early years science fiction competed with the historical novel, the detective story, the adventure thriller, and the weird tale as the vehicle which Doyle hoped to ride to substantial literary recognition. (p. 158)

[Doyle's] first important science fiction story was . . . , *The Doings of Raffles Haw*. The subject matter was derived from Poe's *Von Kempelen and His Discovery* and dealt with the experiences of a man who discovers a method of converting baser metals into gold.

This story remains today one of the finest ever written on the theme. Usually, in such tales, the method by which the transmutation process is accomplished serves merely as a backdrop for the story. Doyle, possibly because of his excellent scientific education, convincingly describes the laboratory, machinery,

methods, and theory by which such transmutation is made possible.

That Doyle's plots and character types were not to any marked degree original has been pointed out many times by discerning critics. Ordinarily an imitator would have to play second fiddle to the man he copies, but Doyle was never an imitator in a commonplace way. *The Doings of Raffles Haw* reveals, as do the Sherlock Holmes and other stories, an almost uncanny ability to make characters come alive from the printed page. (pp. 160-61)

[Until 1894 Doyle experimented] with tales that roughly were recognizable as science fiction, but he was to drop this tack for another eighteen years, conceding by default to the young H. G. Wells, who was to become pre-eminent as a writer of scientific romances during the same period.

The reasons were obvious. Sherlock Holmes had by now achieved a fabulous world-renown, although Doyle tried to kill him off in 1893. The public began to buy Doyle's historical work, *The White Company, The Refugees,* and *Micah Clarke,* in great quantities, despite the less-than-enthusiastic reviews of the critics. The year 1894 also saw the creation of another Doyle character which the public took to their hearts, Brigadier Gerard. With all these successes contributing to his prominence at the same time, Doyle could well afford to let the science fiction slide. (p. 164)

[When] *The Terror of Blue John Gap*, a short science fiction story, appeared in *The Strand Magazine* for September 1910, it was little more than a happenstance. But it signified that in science fiction, as in other fields, he had matured as a writer.

This little-known story shares with *The Horror of the Heights* the distinction of being Doyle's finest short science fiction. It deals with a bearlike creature, as large as an elephant, which is a nightly marauder in northwest Derbyshire. The creature is stalked to its lair by Dr. James Hardcastle, but outwits and overcomes him. Dr. Hardcastle is fortunate to escape with his life. The writing is excellent and the theory as to the creature's origin postulates the existence of giant caverns inside the earth, where bizarre conditions have given rise to plants and animals that ought never to see the light of day.

While the theoretical concept stems from Verne's *A Journey to the Center of the Earth,* we begin to find Doyle adding a new dimension to an old idea, and plotting and writing in a manner distinctly his own.

There seemed to be no special reason why Doyle should have returned to the serious writing of science fiction, as he did in 1912. . . . Perhaps it was the example of H. G. Wells, a friend and correspondent, who had established his reputation in the world of the scientific romance. Whatever the reason, he wrote to Greenhough Smith, editor of *The Strand,* regarding *The Lost World*:

> I think it will make the very best serial (bar special S. Holmes values) that I have ever done, especially when it has its trimming of faked photos, maps, and plans. My ambition is to do for the boys' book what Sherlock Holmes did for the detective tale. I don't suppose I could bring off two such coups. And yet I hope it may.

A goal had been set. A. Conan Doyle was determined to build for himself a reputation in science fiction as great as the one that caused him to be canonized by detective story lovers. When *The Lost World* appeared it seemed that it was almost within his ability to accomplish that feat. Though the basic idea, like that of *The Terror of Blue John Gap,* was unabashedly inspired by Verne's *A Journey to the Center of the Earth*, the superior elements of characterization, humor, and pace that Doyle added to the idea set it distinctly apart.

The main character, George Edward Challenger, if not the finest drawn character in all science fiction, is at least on a par with Verne's Captain Nemo, Burroughs' John Carter, and Stanley G. Weinbaum's alien entities. The dumpy, barrel-chested, black-bearded, bad-tempered, intolerant, egotistical, driving, but truly brilliant Professor Challenger, despite his faults, or possibly because of them, bubbles into believability from the black type of the printed page.

We enjoy reading about him, even when his exploits and accomplishments fail to involve fantastic events. As we get to know him better we find that he is a man of sincerity, possessing true loyalty for his friends and acquaintances, a redeeming sense of humor, and a wealth of tender affection toward his tiny, fragile wife. The people who surround him— E. D. Malone, the young, athletic Irish reporter; Lord John Roxton, the adventurer; and Professor Summerlee—are all cut from fine literary cloth. (pp. 164-66)

Superb characterization, coupled with fine humor and good science, lifted *The Lost World* above the level of the average adventure story. As a result, the novel was an instant success and new editions began to multiply. . . .

[*The Poison Belt*] has always been overshadowed by the fame of *The Lost World*, but it is outstanding in its own right. For this story, Doyle borrowed again from Edgar Allan Poe, enlarging on the idea presented in *The Conversation of Eiros and Charmion:* the atmosphere of the earth is "poisoned" by a change resulting from conditions in outer space. In this novel, Challenger, foreseeing catastrophe, gathers his wife and the three companions of his previous adventure in an airtight room in his home. There, sustained by containers of oxygen, they watch the entire world come to a catastrophic stop. The penetrating British humor stands up even across the gulf of the years. As they prepare for the hour of doom, Challenger turns to his manservant, and says, quite calmly, "I'm expecting the end of the world today, Austin."

　　"Yes, sir," the servant replies. "What time, sir?"

Doyle strikes a telling blow at the theory of the survival of the fittest when he permits the only person in all London apparently still alive to be an asthmatic old woman, who thought she was having an attack when the character of the atmosphere began to change and fed herself oxygen out of a container she kept at her bedside for emergencies. (p. 167)

The Lost World and *The Poison Belt* provided evidence that Doyle had it in him to be one of the greatest science fiction writers of all time. Certainly it is known that he loved Professor Challenger above all of his literary creations. It is reported that he used to assume Challenger disguises solely to startle his friends. He regarded Challenger as the science fiction version of Sherlock Holmes, unraveling scientific mysteries with the same skill his detective fiction counterpart used to solve crimes against society. (p. 168)

[*The Horror of the Heights*] may be the source from which flying saucer enthusiasts have derived the imaginative concept that alien and incredible life forms dwell in the upper atmosphere of the earth. The concept, for the year 1913, was a novel one and Doyle's handling of the theme was skillful indeed.

His ability as a very logical type of prognosticator was dramatically demonstrated when in *Danger!* . . . he detailed in fictional form how Britain could be brought to her knees by submarines. The story recommended tunnels under the Channel and also made mention of airplanes with engine silencers as valuable war weapons. *Danger!* caused quite a stir and some people later accused Doyle of giving Germany the formula for submarine warfare.

The fantastic masterpieces of H. G. Wells were getting fewer and farther between. A great romancer of the scientific tale had arisen in America: Edgar Rice Burroughs, whose Tarzan was to challenge Sherlock Holmes for world-wide popularity. Years later, Burroughs' famous novel, *The Land That Time Forgot*, owing a debt to *The Lost World* in the development of its unique evolutionary theory, was to reveal that Doyle could lend as well as borrow. But now, this was the man Doyle had to surpass to emerge as top man in the field.

Then a strange thing happened. A. Conan Doyle, who had been an agnostic since his youth, found religion. But it was not the religion of the orthodox. Years earlier his first wife had died and he had married Jane Leckie, a woman whom he loved very dearly. Friends and relatives of Doyle's were killed during World War I, but the hardest blow was when his wife's brother, Malcolm Leckie, joined the list. He believed that he had received at a séance a very personal message from Leckie, an emotional experience which caused him to write: "It is absolute lunacy, or it is a revolution in religious thought—a revolution which gives us an immense consolation when those who are dear to us pass behind the veil."

The writing of science fiction was now forgotten. Sherlock Holmes became only an infrequent, irksome task. Doyle threw himself wholeheartedly into the cause of spiritualism. Books with titles like *The New Revelation, The Vital Message, Wanderings of a Spiritualist* poured from his pen. When no one would publish them, he paid the cost himself. He traveled widely, preaching the new religion and devoting his energies to defending its adherents. In a ten-year period he spent well over a million dollars for the cause. This took such curious turns as *The Comming of the Fairies* . . . in which, in photos and text, Doyle lent his name to championing the physical existence of the "little people."

It is questionable if Doyle would have returned to science fiction again had it not been for Hollywood. *The Lost World*, made into a motion picture and distributed in 1925, starred such prominent screen personalities as Wallace Beery, Lewis Stone, and Bessie Love. The prehistoric monsters, recreated for the screen, were masterfully done, and the public took the film to their hearts.

The year the film was released Doyle fans were electrified to learn that *The Strand* would feature a new Professor Challenger novel, the longest one yet, *The Land of the Mist*. They might have been justifiably uneasy had they known that the prepublication title of the novel had been *The Psychic Adventures of Edward Malone*.

As it was, dismay was widespread when reading revealed that Challenger, now somewhat older and a widower, receives a message from his departed wife from the spirit world . . . and is converted to spiritualism. The characterization is as splendid as ever and the novel has some poignant moments, even though the body of the story is episodic and tarnished by preachments.

[The appearance of *The Maracot Deep*] indicated a renewal of Doyle's interest in the writing of science fiction. A new scientific hero, Professor Maracot, was created and Atlantis rediscovered. There are elements of good storytelling, but the scientific premise of the tale again is marred by the introduction of spiritualism. (pp. 168-70)

Two other Professor Challenger stories were to follow and these were collected into a book with *The Maracot Deep* . . . less than a year before Doyle's death. The shorter one, *The Disintegration Machine,* deals with a man who invents a device for dissolving solids into atoms and threatens to sell it to a foreign power. Professor Challenger disposes of the problem by dissolving the inventor with his own machine. The story is as weak as it sounds.

The other, a novelette, *When the World Screamed,* is something else again. In it, Professor Challenger drills a deep tunnel into the bowels of the earth and causes all the live volcanoes on the planet to erupt simultaneously and an earthshaking scream of pain to issue forth when a giant drill pierces a soft, membranous substance eight miles beneath the surface, thereby proving that our planet is one gigantic living creature covered by a hardened crust.

Though the tale barely escapes being facetious, the strong originality and adroit handling of its concept make it the best of the later Challenger stories. It seemed to indicate that Doyle was recapturing his old ability as a master craftsman in the genre. . . .

[But Doyle's] last creative achievements in the field were destined to be stopped by his death, which occurred on July 7, 1930. (pp. 170-71)

> *Sam Moskowitz, "Arthur Conan Doyle: A Study in Science Fiction," in his* Explorers of the Infinite: Shapers of Science Fiction *(copyright © 1963, 1959, 1958, 1957 by Sam Moskowitz; reprinted by permission of the author), World Publishing Co., 1963, pp. 157-71.*

PIERRE NORDON   (essay date 1964)

Anchored as he was to a respectable but old-fashioned literary tradition, Conan Doyle did not feel any need for a change in the school of historical novel writing founded by Walter Scott. This is only another aspect of his neo-Conservatism, and his later development made his inability to adapt himself to his age even more obvious. His contribution to Scott's tradition was not a matter of kind but of degree: he himself preferred to show originality as a disciple than to be an innovator. Nor is there any essential division between the ideology and aesthetics of Conan Doyle's historical novels and those of the Holmes stories, in spite of differences of genres and values. In the historical novels we again find the aesthetics of the theatre, and action that is essentially episodic and cinematic, so to speak. We also find the same angle of incidence, the same cross-section through the different social classes existing at a given period in the history of the country, the same careful identification of the characters and their respective categories, the same apologia for the solidarity between the different members of society. (p. 287)

While with his left hand he somewhat casually created the immortal Sherlock Holmes, his right hand was lovingly engaged on work more in keeping with his sincerest literary ambitions. 'I wish Macaulay had written a historical novel,' he was to write later on. *Micah Clarke* raised a preliminary echo of this nostalgic reflection. Without losing his own identity, Conan Doyle virtually modelled himself on the brilliant historian of the English Revolution, even adopting Macaulay's view of the events in his history. This was the longest of all the historical novels. . . . [As] one of his letters show, he devoted two years to a study of the subject. . . .

The character who gives his name to the novel is both hero and narrator; but in the interests of historical truth Conan Doyle has explained in a long sub-title written in archaic style that the book is less an historical novel than a statement in fictional form. . . .(p. 288)

In spite of this precaution many readers compared it to *Lorna Doone,* which was still very popular and was also set against a background of Monmouth's rebellion. But whereas in Blackmore's novel the historic setting is a mere pretext for a romantic plot, the reverse is true of *Micah Clarke,* which consists of episodes, some based on tradition, others invented by Conan Doyle, strung together on the thread of the historical narrative. It has the charm of a chronicle rather than a novel. (p. 289)

In spite of the density of the historical narration and the realism conveyed by its colour and contrast—Conan Doyle here shows himself an excellent pupil of Defoe's—some of the episodes, particularly in the fourth part of *Micah Clarke,* have a 'cloak and dagger' flavour. The necessity for this part is not very clear, for it is in fact a long digression. The most memorable scene of this huge canvas is without doubt the battle of Sedgemoor. Conan Doyle has here made good use of detailed topographical and military exactness and truly remarkable descriptive virtuosity. His instinctive eye for picturesque detail, and his gift for dialogue, give the narrator's story all possible realism, without sacrificing the vision of the whole which enables us to grasp the movements of armies and the different stages of the conflict. His incidents are always vivid and have an air of complete authenticity. Against the background of this sometimes exact and sometimes romantic page of national history, Conan Doyle has created several characters in whom the artistic purpose of the novel is realised and justified. 'To me it always seems,' he writes in his preface, 'that the actual condition of a country at any time, a true sight of it with its beauties and its brutalities, its life as it really was, its wayside hazards, and its odd possibilities are of greater interest than the small aims and petty love story of any single human being. The lists, the woodlands, and the outlaws are more to me than Rebecca and Rowena.' (p. 292)

[Conan Doyle] seized the chance offered by the theme of his first novel to attempt a dialogue with himself about the religious doubts which still attacked him. As the son of an independent puritan father and a conformist mother, Micah Clarke finds himself at the crossroads. While respecting his father's religious convictions, he himself chooses the least dogmatic religion possible—latitudinarianism: 'I was no keen religious zealot. Papistry, Church, Dissent, I believed that there was good in all of them, but that not one was worth the spilling of human blood.'

If *Micah Clarke* can be said to contain a message, it is that since religious dissension is merely a form of civil unrest and an excuse for unleashing cruel passions, the reader of 1885 is entitled to be complaisant about the progress made since 1685. As for Conan Doyle, he adhered more closely and completely than his ancestors had done to his belief in progress, and found justification in it for his religious faith: Micah Clarke, like Conan Doyle, separates faith from morality and rejects the one in order to defend the other more effectively. (pp. 295-96)

The division of the narrative into two parts prejudices the unity of Micah Clarke's character. We easily accept the frank, courageous village lad given us in the first chapter, and we are equally ready to accept him as narrator, since the energy and liveliness of his style fits in with this image. But he becomes much less convincing when he takes the tone of a professional historian. Some pages smack too much of a historical synopsis, while in others the prophetic tones of the author emerge too clearly from the text.

Thus, in spite of the undeniable power of some scenes, the varied action, and the skill with which the young novelist has made use of his characters to carry out his purpose and bring alive in all its picturesque detail the spirit and conditions of a past age, this work does not perhaps possess the necessary homogeneity to make it a truly great historical novel. It would have been better to prune away certain scenes. . . , and to modify others. Conan Doyle was aware of this, and considered making cuts, but seems never to have made up his mind to it. . . .

There is no need to study this book very long, however, to realise how much maturity and facility its author had already achieved, and his manner is entirely suitable to an historical novel of more than four hundred pages. (p. 296)

Micah Clarke is a fresco, whose detail is less important than the whole composition; its unity is not built up of chapter and sentence, but of episode and paragraph. This somewhat monumental treatment—and we shall see that it was not altogether in accord with Conan Doyle's genius—allows of great flexibility and subtlety in the narrative, and the use of a great variety of rhythms and tones. In his few, very restrained descriptions, Conan Doyle gives rein spontaneously and in the simplest manner to rhythmic, colourful prose. . . .

The dialogue naturally plays an essential part, by allowing the characters to display themselves in the liveliest way and consistently with the images that are impressed on the reader's memory. Conan Doyle was always careful that his conversational style should be true to life, and even in his earliest books he avoided the error of which Goldsmith accused Dr. Johnson, of 'making his little fishes talk like whales'. The dialogue has an almost descriptive effect when someone like Sir Gervas, Joseph Clarke or Decimus Saxon is speaking, whereas a character like Solomon Sprent achieves deliberately comic effects by exaggeration. (p. 297)

In *The White Company* Conan Doyle returned to the Middle Ages, a period which appealed both to his heart and his imagination. (p. 298)

This new venture gave him greater latitude as a writer; the problem of historical accuracy was less stringent than in *Micah Clarke,* where the historical events were strictly determined and most readers better informed about them. Here, on the contrary, there was no need for the narrative to be chronologically exact. But Conan Doyle did not take advantage of this to superimpose a romantic plot in the style of Walter Scott on historical foundations. He was probably thinking of this sort of plot when he said that a plot in an historical novel was an

insult. The relationship between young Alleyne Edricson and the beautiful Maude, daughter of Sir Nigel Loring, hardly deserves the name: it is merely a necessary concession to romance and nothing could be simpler nor more restrained. As for the purely historical part of the narrative, although it contains an arbitrary number of scenes and episodes, it is free from those digressions which sometimes slow down the movement of *Micah Clarke*. In a more harmonious composition, great care has been given to creating a picture of the manners and daily life of the fourteenth century, yet there is less didactic emphasis. (p. 300)

It is clear that Conan Doyle wanted to give the reader as vast and faithful a retrospect of the medieval world as possible. He has succeeded perfectly, not by presenting us with a historian's chronicle of events, but by making us witnesses of warm, living reality. And although much thought and careful documentation has evidently gone to the creation of the characters, although they are essentially mere types, Conan Doyle's creative imagination has succeeded in bringing them convincingly to life. Nor has he sacrificed their individuality to that of the usual historical personages.

It is left to the latter to show us the world of chivalry from within, coloured by the refraction of their different personalities. The Black Prince, Duguesclin, Chandos and Pedro of Castille none of them occupy the front of the stage, and seem—as they probably were—the natural emanation of the communities that produced them. And we see, circulating among them, a cheerful crowd of students and soldiers of fortune, artisans, brigands, monks, peasants, colporteurs, innkeepers, sailors, pilgrims, sellers of indulgences or holy relics. Conan Doyle views this fourteenth-century world from the same angle he has used elsewhere. It is also the viewpoint of Scott and Charles Reade. And his curiosity about the past has a seriousness and a verdant freshness that takes us straight back to Chaucer. Conan Doyle has seen with the eyes of a fourteenth-century poet, and it is not irrelevant that Chaucer's description of Sir Topaz putting on his armour was found among his notes for the book. (p. 302)

The direct, concise, vivacious style of this novel has much in common with the spirit of the medieval story-teller. Among the lesser characters, Sir Oliver Buttesthorn, the greedy knight, is an entirely characteristic creation, amusing and full of delicious good humour. The four chief characters are also touched by humour, particularly Sir Nigel and his family. The feelings of Sir Nigel, his wife and daughter for one another are suggested with that lightness of touch that arouses an imperceptible but irresistible movement of gaiety in the reader. (p. 303)

Conan Doyle was to try in vain, later on, to recapture the practical inspiration which runs through this novel, in his three volumes of rhymed verse: [*Songs of Action, Songs of the Road,* and *The Guards Came Through*]. . . . Anecdotes, ballads, odes, comic verse or doggerel, their unpretentiousness charmingly excuses their insignificance. But if they mark the lowest level of Conan Doyle's inspiration, they also stress the diversity of his ambitions and literary activities.

None of his other works vibrates with so much seriousness and enthusiasm as *The White Company.* Of all his literary achievements it must remain the most memorable. In 1921, the journalist Herbert Ashley asked him which of his books he had most enjoyed writing. It was *The White Company,* Conan Doyle told him: 'I was young and full of the first joy of life and action and I think I got some of it into my pages.' In his other novels he may have sought after a more complicated dramatic design or a less traditional theme. But its personal significance makes *The White Company* the most attractive of them all. This is because the writer's ego appears there in its most permanent aspect, dissociated from biographical contingencies. The magic, the fervent idealism and tenderness which envelop the characters, reveal for us, as nowhere else, the face of the knightly author with his visor raised. (pp. 309-10)

> *Pierre Nordon, in his* Conan Doyle, *translated by Frances Partridge (translation © John Murray 1966; originally published as* Sir Arthur Conan Doyle: L'homme et l'oeuvre, *Librairie Marcel Didier, 1964), John Murray, 1966, 370 p.*

CHRISTOPHER ISHERWOOD   (essay date 1966)

Since I was ten years old, the adventures of Sherlock Holmes have been my favourite escape-reading; again and again I have turned to them in times of sadness, boredom and ill-health and never found myself disappointed. . . . Today—seventy years after the first of the Holmes novels was published—the name of Holmes is still a household word, even among those who have never read anything that Conan Doyle wrote about him and have caught only a few distorted glimpses of him in some television serial or newspaper cartoon. Perhaps he will survive to bury Doyle's books and turn into a purely legendary figure whose creator has been forgotten.

In my opinion, Holmes is one of the truly great comic characters in our literature; but it is doubtful if Doyle himself would have agreed with this statement or even if he would have taken it as a compliment. Admittedly, Holmes was not conceived in comedy, like Falstaff and Micawber; he can only be considered comic in retrospect, if at all—like Captain Ahab. His comic quality seems to me to be this: he is the classic caricature of the Amateur Detective, in whose person the whole art of detection is made ridiculous. I don't believe that Doyle consciously intended this ridicule—and yet it is what makes Holmes lovable and immortal. (p. 88)

[Holmes] has the sanction of his own peculiar kind of madness. Like Captain Ahab, he is possessed by the insanity of the chase. Holmes's Moby Dick is Dr Moriarty, the arch-criminal; and Doyle's instinct was sound when he made Moriarty turn to bay and kill Holmes, just as the White Whale killed Ahab. I find Holmes's subsequent resurrection both embarrasing and unnecessary—for Doyle could easily have predated his later stories about Holmes, just as he did pre-date *The Valley of Fear* in order that Moriarty could reappear in it.

To get properly acquainted with Holmes, one should begin at the beginning—with *A Study in Scarlet*. Dr Watson, back from the Afghan War, is looking for someone with whom he can share the expenses of furnished rooms. He consults a colleague, who recommends Sherlock Holmes—though with reservations. . . . (pp. 88-9)

[This is] the beginning of a wonderfully sustained sequence, in which [Watson] vainly tries to discover what Holmes's profession is and gets repeatedly bewildered by the variety of Holmes's tastes and the extraordinary gaps in his knowledge. . . . Finally the mystery is solved—long, long after every reader has guessed the solution; this being of the essence of the comedy—Holmes is a private detective. (pp. 89-90)

In his Sherlock Holmes stories, Doyle became one of the great exponents of the romance of London at the turn of the century—

city of Night, pea-soup fogs, gaslight, hansom-cabs and opera-hats. Robert Louis Stevenson was before him in this field, with his *New Arabian Nights*. G. K. Chesterton was his successor. Hollywood took over the London they had created, slightly modernized it and put it again and again upon the screen. When, at last, it became outmoded (since, nowadays, most films about London are actually made there) a leading English newspaper lamented the fact, saying: 'We have lost a city that we had learned to know almost as well as our own.' (p. 90)

> *Christopher Isherwood, "'The Speckled Band' by Arthur Conan Doyle," in his* Exhumations: Stories, Articles, Verses *(reprinted by permission of Candida Donadio & Assoc. Inc.; copyright © 1966 by Christopher Isherwood),* Methuen & Co. Ltd., 1966, pp. 88-90.

TREVOR H. HALL   (essay date 1969)

Mr. Guy Warrack [in *Sherlock Holmes and Music*] has said that Sherlock Holmes was "clearly schizophrenic". This opinion was based on the evidence of Watson's description of his friend listening to Sarasate's violin one afternoon at St. James's Hall during the case of Jabez Wilson, the pawnbroker, and his half-pay assistant John Clay, the "murderer, thief, smasher and forger" of Eton and Oxford. Mr. Warrack attached significance to Holmes's "gently smiling face and his languid dreamy eyes" as he "sat in the stalls wrapped in the most perfect happiness, gently waving his long thin fingers in time to the music", and to the contrasting relentless, practical astuteness when in action of the foremost consulting detective and criminal agent in the world.

The point is an interesting one, but I feel that the assertion that Holmes was suffering from schizophrenia is going rather far. One dictionary definition of this condition is "dementia praecox, or kindred form of insanity, marked by introversion and loss of connexion between thoughts, feelings and actions", which makes Mr. Warrack's suggestion a startling one in regard to the mental state of the best and the wisest man Watson had ever known. It is true that [in *The Reigate Squires*] the "smart, keen-faced" young Inspector Forrester of the Surrey County Police thought initially that Holmes had been "behaving very queerly" and "that there was madness in this method", an opinion that seems to have been at least partially shared by Colonel Ross of King's Pyland [in *Silver Blaze*]. Both these gentlemen, however, withdrew their criticisms unreservedly and could not praise Holmes's work too highly when the facts became available. "My dear sir, you have done wonders", exclaimed Colonel Ross with enthusiasm after the denouement of *Silver Blaze*, whilst in the corresponding circumstances Inspector Forrester was reduced to staring about himself in bewilderment. Mr. Warrack's suggestion, moreover, is effectively countered by the professional opinion of Dr. Watson, who described his friend's mind as "cold, precise, but admirably balanced", adding that Holmes was "the most perfect reasoning and observing machine that the world has seen". This assessment cannot be reconciled with schizophrenia by any stretch of imagination.

On the other hand, as I have said in an earlier essay, there can be little doubt that the tragic events of Holmes's youth had produced symptoms of manic-depression, which seem to have been severe in the early years of his professional career, for Watson commented upon them repeatedly. He wrote, as part of his earliest impression of Holmes:

Nothing could exceed his energy when the working fit was on him; but now and again a reaction would seize him, and for days on end he would lie upon the sofa in the sitting-room, hardly uttering a word or moving a muscle from morning to night.

There was evidently a slight improvement in the depressive phases of Holmes's condition when Watson recorded the Hurlstone case, for by that time Holmes could at least muster sufficient energy to rise from the sofa:

> The outbursts of passionate energy . . . were followed by reactions of lethargy, during which he would lie about with his violin and his books, hardly moving, save from the sofa to the table.

Be that as it may, the evidence for Holmes's symptoms is overwhelming. He could, on occasions, be "bright, eager, and in excellent spirits, a mood which in his case alternated with fits of the blackest depression". Watson said of him, indeed, with the authority of a medical man and an intimate friend:

> In his singular character the dual nature alternately asserted itself, and his extreme exactness and astuteness represented, as I have often thought, the reaction against the poetic and contemplative mood which occasionally predominated in him. The swing of his nature took him from extreme languor to devouring energy.

With the facts of the matter assembled, it is hard to avoid the conclusion that the unkind suggestion that Holmes was schizophrenic was simply part and parcel of the iconoclasm that similarly caused Mr. Warrack to suggest that Holmes never wrote his famous monograph on the Polyphonic Motets of Lassus in 1895, and that it "was at best only projected, at the worst a complete myth". (pp. 86-8)

Faced with Watson's positive statement (twice) [in *The Bruce-Partington Plans*] that Holmes was indeed responsible for this most remarkable piece of original research, Mr. Warrack had also perforce to deal with Watson's equally positive observation that Holmes's privately printed monograph had been acclaimed by experts as the final, authoritative word on the subject. Here, I fancy, we have the melancholy proof that Mr. Warrack's determination to denigrate Holmes's musical erudition was such that he was willing to go beyond the bounds of even speculative criticism:

> Who were the experts who proclaimed the problematical monograph on de Lassus 'to be the last word on the subject'? . . . The experts were, in fact, just as genuine as the monograph itself.

Mr. Warrack did not offer any evidence in support of this assertion, and ignored all the evidence against the inherently improbable suggestion that Holmes, the logician who had insisted to Watson that "all things should be seen exactly as they are, and to under-estimate oneself is as much a departure from truth as to exaggerate one's own powers", could be capable of such falsehood. The preparation of the monograph, for example, was only a single incident (admittedly an important one) in Holmes's patient pursuit of the larger "subject which he had recently made his hobby—the music of the Middle Ages". It can scarcely be supposed that Watson, Holmes's daily companion, could be pointlessly bamboozled by his friend into believing that Holmes enjoyed such a hobby if it were not true.

Watson's remark that Holmes "had undertaken" to prepare the monograph, moreover, suggests that he had been invited to do so. The fact that Holmes had "lost himself" in the work, and immediately "returned refreshed" to his labours after the intervention of the Cadogan West affair (which he obviously regarded as of much less importance) would lead us to believe that he had a strong motive for finishing the monograph without delay to please his postulated patron. Before quoting the passage in the text that strongly suggests who that patron might have been, it is useful to recall that Queen Victoria was deeply interested in music. . . . From girlhood she applied herself to the study of music "with persistence and delight" and she was "distinguished by much musical taste and accomplishment". (pp. 88-90)

Two facts are clear. First, after a lifetime of diligent study the Queen would only need to seek instruction in regard to a musical subject upon which printed sources were incomplete and original research was needed. Secondly, she would invite an acknowledged expert to undertake the work for her. We know that Holmes was devoted to the Queen, for we recall his fervently patriotic "V. R." in bullet-pocks [in *The Musgrave Ritual*], and would be delighted to please her however intricate the task might be. With this established, the significance of the text and the juxtaposition of the all-important sentences become clear for the first time, and we know at last why Holmes was summoned to Windsor:

> He returned refreshed to his monograph upon the Polyphonic Motets of Lassus, which has since been printed for private circulation, and is said by experts to be the last word upon the subject. Some weeks afterwards I learned incidentally that my friend spent a day at Windsor, whence he returned with a remarkably fine emerald tie-pin. When I asked him if he had bought it, he answered that it was a present from a certain gracious lady in whose interests he had been fortunate enough to carry out a small commission.

I feel strongly that Mr. Warrack's citing of Holmes's lethargy and visible eccentricities whilst listening to Sarasate is an ill-chosen example of his odd behaviour (if it was odd behaviour) on occasions. Mr. Warrack knows better than any of us how deeply devoted Holmes was to music. Its effect upon him, like its effect upon Queen Victoria, was understandably more marked than upon lesser enthusiasts. (pp. 90-1)

> *Trevor H. Hall, in his* Sherlock Holmes: Ten Literary Studies *(copyright © 1969 by Trevor H. Hall), Duckworth, 1969, 157 p.*

KENNETH REXROTH   (essay date 1973)

The average literate person if asked to respond with the name of a fictional character to the figures 1885-1905 without pausing for the thought, would almost be sure to answer, "Sherlock Holmes!" From George Meredith to George Gissing, from Samuel Butler to H. G. Wells, the late Victorian Age has been elaborately documented. Above all other periods, it has been most fertile in historical and critical social documents disguised as fiction. Some of these novels are great works of art too, beautifully constructed and with new and profound insights into the human mind, and written in differing but superlative prose. Yet the time lives for us most clearly in our literary memories in a collection of tales, often poorly constructed, hastily written for money, the best ones wildly improbable, peopled with stereotypes, devoid of any insights into human character, profound or otherwise, and regarded by their author, at least so he claimed, as a burden in the writing.

Are these charges true? If so, how can "Sherlock Holmes" be a classic? Are the Greek Romances, like Heliodorus' *Ethiopian History,* classics? Did Walter Scott write classics? Did the elder Dumas? If the *consensus orbis terrarum,* that which is held by all, at all times, everywhere, is the test of faith in literature as in religion, a considerable number of the great works of entertainment, originally commercial fiction, will find their way to places not far below the lofty regions occupied by Sophocles or Dante or Shakespeare. There are probably twice or three times as many devotees of the cult of Sherlock Holmes, from the Argentine to Japan, as there are of William Blake and D. H. Lawrence put together, and Blake and Lawrence are very great writers indeed, however much their admirers may tend to band into cults. (pp. 116-17)

An undertone of mockery, sometimes subtle, sometimes not so subtle, usually benign, sometimes malicious, runs through all the sixty adventures of Sherlock Holmes and gives them their peculiar style. Holmes himself is as wild a caricature as Dicken's Mr. Micawber. Yet like Mr. Micawber, we are convinced of his reality, precisely because he is an ironic caricature, like so many of the people we have known in real life, who are more outrageous than any character of fiction. Landladies, page boys, countesses in distress, August Personages in trouble, adventurers home from the seven seas, gentry, merchants, clerks, and not least the Archetypal Old India Army Man, Dr. Watson, all are seen slightly askew, distorted by irony and garbed in stereotype like an immense cast of the *commedia dell'arte* of the glory of empire.

This does not mean that Conan Doyle was another Samuel Butler or H. G. Wells, and that "Sherlock Holmes" is an anti-Victorian onslaught like [Butler's] *The Way of All Flesh* or [Wells's] *Tono Bungay.* Quite the contrary. Conan Doyle would not have been so successful if he had not believed almost all of the myths of Victorianism. A Sherlock Holmes who was an admirer of Kier Hardy, founder of the Labour Party, or of Oscar Wilde, would be an embarrassing absurdity. The official Sherlock Holmes societies, like the Baker Street Irregulars, amuse themselves at their dinners by reading papers proving just such possibilities with elaborate parade of scholarship, that Holmes was the Stuart Pretender, or a defrocked Anglo-Catholic priest, or the head of an anarchist conspiracy, or that Dr. Watson was Jack the Ripper, or a woman in man's clothing, or that the entire Sherlockian corpus is a cryptic exposition of Marxism. The secret of the fascination of the world of Sherlock Holmes is its terrifying normality . . . and that, alas, we have never been able to get back to.

Yet it was a more normal world than ours and its glories were real, if a little sooty. . . . [The] adventures of Sherlock Holmes form a great comic epic of Victorianism. Conan Doyle, himself an Irishman and an outsider, catches and transmits the intense individualism and the universal consent, and instinctively emphasizes the source of this vast unstable, dynamic balance—empire.

India, China, the South Seas, the Far West, his characters come home from the ends of the earth to blackmail and murder each other, while heavily veiled noblewomen and frightened governesses and ladies of the proletariat and absconding brokers and hoodwinked royalty drive up through the rain and fog under the gas lamps to the rooms at Baker Street seeking salvation. Holmes is Justice, neurotic, capricious, but humane. The erring escape the vengeance of their own misdeeds, the evil go to dooms they have prepared for themselves. If Sherlock Holmes' adventures truly reflect life between 1885 and 1905, it was haunted by a dangerous insecurity. But so in fact it was. And the symbolic detective is natural law finding out and healing that insecurity—solving the mysteries and absolving the anxiety. The eccentric Holmes, a total personal exceptionalist, is the exception that both proves and suspends The Rule.

The plots are by no manner of means models of the ratiocinative detective story. Even Poe does better. Conan Doyle's favorite stories, **"The Speckled Band"** and **"The Hound of the Baskervilles,"** are not merely implausible, they are impossible, and the Sherlockian societies have had immense fun correcting or accounting for their errors with much heavy scholarship. R. Austin Freeman's Dr. Thorndike tales are infinitely more logical expositions of criminal induction—which Holmes and Watson persist in calling "deduction." But not until [Georges] Simenon's Maigret comes on the scene will Law, not police law, but natural law, treat the foolish and evil with such humanity.

There are no better records of the profoundly normal oddity of Victorian England and early twentieth-century France, nor more human ones, than the detective tales of Conan Doyle and Simenon. And they are possessions like unto pearls of great price, for alas, we will never be as odd again. (pp. 117-19)

> *Kenneth Rexroth, "Sherlock Holmes," in his* The Elastic Retort: Essays in Literature and Ideas *(copyright © 1973 by Kenneth Rexroth; reprinted by permission of the author), The Continuum Publishing Company, 1973, pp. 116-19.*

SAMUEL ROSENBERG   (essay date 1974)

The "Conan Doyle Syndrome" was discovered serendipitously during my search among the Sherlockian adventures for booktitle clues like *The Origin of Tree Worship,* which might allude to Friedrich Nietzsche and Dionysus. My procedure was a simple one: When a book was mentioned, I read the book, something about its author in various reference works, and then wrote a brief gloss of the story and scene in which the book was mentioned.

Soon, after I had repeated this process with the books mentioned in fourteen stories, a very strange phenomenon began to loom up out of the pages of *The Complete Sherlock Holmes.* My accumulated notes had revealed that in almost every story I'd synopsized, the *printed or written work in any form*— books, book titles, magazines or newspaper articles, advertisement, signs, diaries, manuscripts, letters, words scribbled on scraps of paper, words written on the wall (even in blood) or in the floor dust of a murder chamber, or even expressions read in a person's face—was always accompanied by an allusion to some form of forbidden sexual expression, either heterosexual or homosexual, or both. This allusion was usually associated in turn with images of draconian punishment in the form of the murder of individuals or of masses of people in Sodom and Gomorrah, Khartoum, Jericho or Milan, or in the English and the American Civil Wars.

Astonished by the discovery of this rigid and repetitive constellation of images secretly revolving about one another within so many of Doyle's "simple detective stories," I continued my study of these exciting obsessive idea and image clusters, and I found that they usually appeared in an obligatory or climactic scene in tandem with other obsessive elements, all of which were irrelevant to the stories in which Doyle had implanted them!

It was now obvious that this observed pattern was far from random. It was a syndrome of compulsively linked images, ideas, persons, and actions which functioned like any other medical or philosophical syndrome: If any single element of the pattern appeared, I could now accurately predict that every other element in the constellation would, like "Mary's little lamb," be sure to follow.

Yes, Conan Doyle thought in "syndromic" terms: in *A Study in Scarlet*, he has his great explainer Holmes, while defining his philosophy of crime detection, speak of the "logician" who could:

> From a drop of water . . . infer the possibility
> of an Atlantic or a Niagara without ever having
> seen or heard of one or the other. So all life is
> a great chain, the nature of which is known
> whenever we are shown a single link of it.
>
> (pp. 67-8)

This "sin-drome," so called because of its central theme of illicit love or sexuality linked to a set of unique Doylean images and ideas, is expressed with the following elements:

(A) After using his superlative reasoning and detective powers to penetrate the mystery brought to him, Sherlock Holmes generally anticipates the criminal's plan of action and goes to the scene of the intended crime. In other instances he sets a trap for the suspected malefactor.

(B) There, with Watson and sometimes others as well, he conducts a vigil at night or in a dark room for the

(C) arrival of the unknown person (or one known only to Holmes) or of a dangerous criminal or murderer.

(D) Before or after, sometimes before *and* after, the arrival of the expected "man of violence" one or more printed or written word references will be made (books, words written on paper, walls, etc.), usually by the all-revealing Sherlock Holmes, which evoke the already mentioned heterosexual or deviant sexuality, which is then linked to some form of drastic punishment and the private and legal murder of individuals and of masses of people.

(E) When the expected "unknown violent man" does finally appear after the long night vigil, another uniquely Doylean surprise will occur: There is a sudden reversal, switching or confusion of the sexes. Instead of a man, a woman will appear, or a man dressed as a woman. Or he will prove to be effeminate or weak. Conversely, a suspected woman will appear as a man, or disguised as a man (Irene Adler in *A Scandal in Bohemia*). In one story (*The Yellow Face*) a "hideous man" who is seen in a second-story window turns out to be a pretty little black girl who has been wearing a mask!

Sometimes the confusion or switching of the sexes is expressed by Doyle in verbal terms: by the verbal manipulation of names or by means of allusions to literary works in which transvestism plays a very important part.

(F) A hand-to-hand combat will follow the arrival of the awaited villain or criminal. Alone or with the help of Watson and others Sherlock Holmes will overpower him (usually) and turn him over to Scotland Yard for arrest and punishment. In the few

stories where the "unknown person" who appears in the "syndromic" dark room proves to be a woman, there is no hand-to-hand combat or wrestling match, and she usually goes unpunished. (Again, Irene Adler in *A Scandal in Bohemia*.)

(G) Perhaps the most important element of the *Doyle Syndrome* and allegory: In every story Sherlock Holmes is the unquestioning, incorruptible guardian of the Victorian criminal and moral codes. As such his unvarying role is that of the detector, preventer, judge, and punisher of every larcenous or immoral act, especially those that are sexually deviant.

With very few exceptions (*His Last Bow* is one) Conan Doyle stages his syndrome and allegory in a curious architectural setting: the "second story" of a residence or in a "two-storied house." The significance of this unique arena of action? I have verified and now believe that any description in a Sherlock Holmes story of a house as "two-storied" means that Doyle has consciously or unconsciously created a theater of allegory in which an actual house with two floors or stories is also a house with *two stories to tell*, or a house with *stories on two levels of meaning*.

We find this remarkable stage-setting first and most importantly in the fact that Sherlock Holmes's residence and office is on the second floor of the mythical house on Baker Street. (pp. 69-70)

Even the famous house number "221B" may be read as an allegorical clue. Taken literally it reads and means: "two-twenty-one." Or, if regarded as a play on words, it can be read as the number of a mythical house with two stories to tell since "221" can be interpreted as "two-to-one," or two meanings in one place.

Similarly the letter "B," or "bis": *The Oxford Unabridged Dictionary* defines "bis" as the French word meaning twice, encore, or repetition. We see, therefore, that every troubled or mystified client who arrives at the mythical house numbered "221B" climbs to the second story, where he/she sets in motion a Doylean story (mystery or allegory) with several layers of meaning for Sherlock Holmes and the reader to unravel.

The next stage of Conan Doyle's unique use of this architectural place symbolism occurs whenever Sherlock leaves his study to inspect the scene of the reported crimes or place of eventual showdown with the suspected criminal or villain.

This second theater of allegory is frequently described by Dr. Watson (Dr. Doyle, of course) as a "two-storied house." I have found these symbolic settings in many stories including *The Sign of Four, The Man with the Twisted Lip, The Yellow Face, The Adventure of the Empty House*, and *The Red-Headed League*. (p. 71)

One superb example of the syndrome in action: In *His Last Bow*, we recall, the German master spy Von Bork is given a handbook of bee culture instead of the volume of British naval secrets he had been promised by the disguised Sherlock Holmes, who is acting as a double agent. (The alias used by Holmes is Altamont, a Doyle family name: another fact identifying Sherlock Holmes as one alter ego of Doyle.)

Like every other book mentioned by either Watson or Holmes, this bee book, written by Dionysus-Holmes himself and bearing the subtitle, *With Some Observations upon the Segregation of the Queen*, fulfills Doyle's strange need to associate sexual intercourse with mutilation and murder with a book-title. After a queen bee is fertilized by the drone, she kills him [by tearing out his sexual organs]. . . . (pp. 72-3)

Also, the required syndromic metaphor of the murder of great masses of men tied "irrelevantly" to the homicidal sexual act (of bees) is conveyed by the fact that the book Von Bork *thought* he was getting contained top military secrets he would have used to kill many thousands of British sailors, soldiers and civilians. (p. 73)

> *Samuel Rosenberg, in his* Naked Is the Best Disguise: The Death & Resurrection of Sherlock Holmes *(copyright ©1974 by Samuel Rosenberg; reprinted by permission of Samuel Rosenberg),* The Bobbs-Merrill Company, Inc., *1974, 203 p.*

CLIVE JAMES   (essay date 1975)

Sir Arthur Conan Doyle wrote little about Sherlock Holmes compared with what has been written by other people since. Sherlock has always been popular, on a scale never less than worldwide, but the subsidiary literature which has steadily heaped up around him can't be accounted for merely by referring to his universal appeal. Sherlockology—the adepts call it that, with typical whimsy—is a sort of cult, which has lately become a craze. (p. 15)

The most foolish book of the bunch . . . is *Naked Is the Best Disguise*, by Samuel Rosenberg (see excerpt above), which has been welcomed in the United States with reviews I find inexplicable. Mr. Rosenberg's thesis, briefly, is that Moriarty is Nietzsche and that Doyle is acting out a psychodrama in which Sherlock is his superego suppressing his polymorphous perversity. Even if it had been reached by a convincing show of reasoning, this conclusion would still be far-fetched: fetched, in fact, from halfway across the galaxy. But it has been reached by no kind of reasoning except casuistry. Mr. Rosenberg argues in one place that if a Sherlock Holmes adventure is set in a house with two storeys, that means there are two *stories*—i.e., two levels of meaning. His arguing is of the same standard in every other place. (pp. 17-18)

It would be overpraising the book to call it negligible. . . .

Though *Naked Is the Best Disguise* considers itself to be high scholarship, it reveals itself instantly as Sherlockology by worrying over the importance of minor detail in stories whose major action their author could scarcely be bothered to keep believable. The chronology of the Holmes saga is indefinitely debatable because Doyle didn't care about establishing it. Early on, Sherlock was ignorant of the arts and didn't know the earth went around the sun: later, he quoted poetry in several languages and had wide scientific knowledge. Sherlock was a minor occupation for Doyle and he was either content to leave such inconsistencies as they were or else he plain forgot about them. Mysteries arising from them are consequently unresolvable, which is doubtless their attraction. . . .

Sherlockology is bastardized academism, but academism is one of the forces which Doyle instinctively set out to fight, and Sherlock, his Sunday punch, is not yet drained of strength. Sherlock was the first example of the art [Friedrich] Dürrenmatt later dreamed of—the art which would weigh nothing in the scales of respectability. Doyle knew that Sherlock was cheap. What he didn't guess before it was too late to change his mind was that the cheapness would last. The only coherence in the Holmes saga is a coherence of intensity. The language is disproportionate and therefore vivid. "He was, I take it, the most perfect reasoning and observing machine that the world has seen." The images are unshaded and therefore flagrant. "I took a step forward: in an instant his strange headgear began to move, and there reared itself from among his hair the squat diamond-shaped head and puffed neck of a loathsome serpent."

But Sherlock's world was all fragments, and no real world could or can be inferred from it. In *The Valley of Fear* the Scourers work mischief to no conceivable political purpose. Moriarty machinates to no ascertainable end. The Sherlockologists would like to believe that this abstract universe is concrete, and that large questions of good and evil are being worked out. But the concreteness is only in the detail; beyond the detail there is nothing; and the large questions must always lack answers.

Doyle asked and tried to answer the large questions elsewhere, in the spiritualist faith which occupied his full mental effort. Eventually his seriousness went out of date, while his frivolity established itself as an institution. But since his mind at play could scarcely have played so well if it had not been so earnest a mind, there is no joke. (p. 18)

> *Clive James, "Sherlockology," in* The New York Review of Books *(reprinted with permission from* The New York Review of Books; *copyright © 1975 Nyrev, Inc.), Vol. 22, No. 2, February 20, 1975, pp. 15-18.*

ELIZABETH LONGFORD   (essay date 1976)

The gusto and innocence of a golden age permeate the 'Napoleonic' stories of Conan Doyle. This collection [*Adventures of Gerard*] comes to us like Wordsworth's vision of childhood, 'trailing clouds of glory'. Adventures are thrilling, even gory, without in any way suggesting horror and violence as we know them today. Sex is imperious and delightful—how should it be otherwise in the life of a gallant Frenchman?—but it requires only the flash of a woman's eye or the flutter of her long black lashes to tell Gerard that she loves him; no need even to kiss more than her hand. (p. 7)

Perhaps my impression of this gusto and innocence comes partly from the time at which I first discovered the *Adventures*. World War I had not long ended and I was in the midst of a glorious spring holiday from school. The dell in the garden was full of blue anemones in flower. It was hot enough to lie on the grass and read. As a schoolgirl, I was more absorbed by the horses which Brigadier Gerard rode than by the women he loved. (pp. 7-8)

On re-reading the *Adventures of Gerard* I was surprised and enchanted to find how well the animation, pace, suspense, characterization and humour had worn. (p. 8)

[In the first of these adventures,] Gerard gave his ear for his lady-love. As far as I know, this is the only physical sacrifice which he made for the ladies. That he never found it necessary to give his life for love or even his right arm, but only an ear, is somehow characteristic of the special flavour which enhances Gerard's adventures. (p. 9)

Cynical would be too heavy a word for something so lighthearted. One might say that his adventures are never quite straightforward. There is always a twist, an undertone or overtone, which make a confidential appeal to the adult reader, so to speak, while youth at the same time is most generously served.

In the second story we move to the Peninsular War, with the siege of Saragossa (1808-9). It has a deservedly authentic ring despite Gerard's invented dénouement. For Conan Doyle had studied the sources with care. In his own Preface he named the various French military memoirs from which he had gained 'an understanding of the Napoleonic soldier', notably *Les Cahiers du Capitaine Coignet* and *Les Mémoires du Sergeant Bourgoyne*. Not only did these genuine warriors beget the imaginary Brigadier Gerard, but also André Maurois' fictional Colonel Bramble and Docteur O'Grady of World War I. Nor did Conan Doyle confine his studies to French memoirists. It is clear that he was well versed in the recollections which had been published by the beginning of this century of British Peninsular soldiers such as Captain Johnny Kincaid, Private Wheeler, Rifleman Harris, General Cavalier Mercer, and of course Wellington's Despatches.

The story of **'How He Captured Saragossa'** brings out the dashing Gerard in all his gay true colours—a Frenchman for whom *'la gloire'* is the be-all and end-all of a soldier's life. (pp. 9-10)

Gerard's naïve boastfulness, which is soon to become so familiar and endearing a feature of his make-up, is introduced by Conan Doyle with a skilful whiff of criticism. Thus any inclination which the reader might have to object to such self-conceit is pre-empted. . . .

'Romance nicely mixed with a right flavouring of Baron Munchhausen', has been suggested as the hall-mark of the Brigadier Gerard stories. True so far as it goes, this description perhaps fails to stress adequately the pleasant bursts of irony and rollicking humour. The third and fifth stories in this series, **'How The Brigadier Slew The Fox'** and **'How He Triumphed In England'**, are examples of Conan Doyle at his boisterous best. (p. 10)

There is much to enjoy in Gerard's adventures both among the guerrillas of the Peninsula (1810) and the Russians around Minsk during the French retreat from Moscow (1812). Conan Doyle has not hesitated to show a fictional guerrilla leader (the Smiler) as a monster of cruelty. Undoubtedly this is how the guerrillas appeared to the French; to Wellington's army they were noble patriots. It is interesting to find Gerard employing in this story a method of transport which had actually but inadvertently been used by one of Wellington's soldiers in Portugal. But if I gave the game away at this stage Gerard would be sadly disappointed in my English sportsmanship.

''Gamesmanship' rather than sportsmanship is the word that seems to sum up Gerard's debonair yet cunning attitude to life. The word has come too late for him to use, but the idea is implicit in all his exploits. It is there above all during that last long day of his life as an active soldier, a double-barrelled saga of Waterloo.

Part I opens with a typically Gerard-esque explanation of France's failure at that supreme test. (p. 11)

[Part II] gives a marvellously vivid picture of the French defeat and retreat. Sprinkled with thoughts and impressions which many Frenchmen must have experienced, it should be read by anyone who wants to *feel* the Battle of Waterloo from the French angle. (p. 12)

Brigadier Gerard may not command the immensely wide public of Sherlock Holmes. This would no doubt deeply wound our French friend's pride. But let him rest assured of one thing. His re-birth in a new edition of the *Adventures* is a truly happy event. No one, young or old, can fail to be hilariously alive in Etienne Gerard's company. (pp. 12-13)

Elizabeth Longford, ''Introduction'' (© Elizabeth Longford 1976), in Adventures of Gerard *by Sir Arthur Conan Doyle, Jonathan Cape, 1976 (and reprinted by Pan Books, 1977, pp. 7-13).*

COLIN WILSON (essay date 1976)

What is it about Holmes that fills his admirers with such an appetite to go on reading about him?

A partial answer, the beginning of an answer, emerges from the account of Doyle's literary struggles. I cannot think of any other writer of the nineteenth century, with the possible exception of Balzac, with such a passion for the factual detail. . . . In a story, a certain amount of fact is like grit in chicken food—it makes it more digestible and nutritious. . . . Doyle instantly perceived the value of the method, and proceeded to employ it (with the confidence of a duck taking to water) in *A Study in Scarlet.* When Watson meets Holmes in the laboratory at Bart's (about 1881), Holmes has just discovered an infallible test for bloodstains. Such a test was not actually discovered until 1900 by Paul Uhlenhuth, and first used to convict a murderer in Germany in 1904. Like other men of genius, Doyle had the power to tune in to the spirit of the age; and at the time when he conceived Holmes, crime detection was finally achieving the status of an exact science. In the mid-1880s, Scotland Yard was brooding on whether to adopt the Bertillon system of fingerprinting as a basic method of criminal identification. As a doctor, Doyle had the necessary background for pursuing the science of medical jurisprudence. He might have applied his talents as a police surgeon or pathologist; instead, he wrote stories. But, as one reads those first two chapters of *A Study in Scarlet,* one senses that Doyle had struck a rich vein, and could easily spend the next hundred pages discussing crime, medicine, detection, the science of deduction.

The reader catches his enthusiasm. A critic once said of Balzac that no other novelist produces such an illusion of reality, of talking about the real world. This is one of the secrets of the fascination of the Holmes stories. On this level of criminal investigation and medical jurisprudence, they have the ring of authenticity. This is why readers want to go on playing the game, and reading books about Holmes and his cases. . . . I believe it may also explain why the various Holmes pastiches by Adrian Conan Doyle, John Dickson Carr, August Derleth, et al. have never caught on. They imitate the style and the mannerisms but fail to throw in the handful of grit, the illusion of fact; you know they are inventions.

All this may help to explain the popularity of the Holmes biographies, in which the writer tries to sort out Watson's muddled dates; but it hardly begins to explain the fascination of the character of the Great Detective. This is an altogether more complex matter. But you can see the essence of the trick in the passage about the ex-Commissionnaire. Watson, vaguely irritated by Holmes's air of intellectual superiority, points to a man on the other side of the street and wonders what he is looking for: ''You mean the retired sergeant of Marines?'' says Holmes. A few minutes later the man delivers a letter to them.

> Here was an opportunity of taking the conceit
> out of him. He little thought of this when he
> made that random shot.

"May I ask, my lad," I said, in the blandest voice, "what your trade might be?"

"Commissionnaire, sir," he said gruffly. "Uniform away for repairs."

"And you were?" I asked, with a slightly malicious glance at my companion.

"A sergeant, sir, Royal Marine Light Infantry, sir. . . ."

And there you have it; Holmes the cool and infallible; Holmes the superman who is never wrong.

Doyle knew that this was what his readers wanted: the satisfaction of an "infallibility fantasy." With the story teller's instinct, he uses the same situation again and again, knowing that his readers will never tire of it, as children never tire of seeing the clown walk into the custard pie. To increase the effect, Watson plays the stooge to an extent that is slightly unbelievable. When a man is really telling a story against himself, he does it with a self-deprecating grin, and tries to soften the effect: "Naturally, I assumed this was mere brag and bounce." Watson tells such stories as if he were his own worst enemy. In the opening chapter of the *The Sign of Four*, the whole scene is repeated with embellishments. He begins by "raising his eyebrows" when Holmes describes himself as the only unofficial consulting detective (although Holmes has told him as much in *A Study of Scarlet*), gets irritable when Holmes criticizes the earlier case history, and then becomes angry when Holmes tells him the story of his alcoholic brother from the marks in his watch case. The reaction is overdone. A real man would say: "But that is remarkable, Holmes. Are you *sure* you knew nothing about my brother beforehand?" Watson limps "impatiently about the room with considerable bitterness in his heart," and snorts: "This is unworthy of you, Holmes," accusing him of chicanery. And so, when Holmes explains how he made the deduction, the impact is doubled.

For most readers these opening sections—in which Holmes demonstrates the science of deduction—are the best part of the story. Of course, we enjoy it as Holmes and Watson rattle off in a cab to catch the 2:15 from Waterloo; but we have to admit that there is an air of sameness about the cases—the attractive girls in distress, the bullying villains who bend pokers (which Holmes immediately straightens again), the sinister figure from the past who comes back to take revenge. (I have never worked out how many of the stories depend on this device, but it must be at least a quarter.) But in the opening pages of the stories, Doyle is at his most inventive, and his most realistic. These are the pages that make us want go on reading about Holmes's life and background. Why? Because we like to be assured that Holmes is a real person; that is an important part of the pleasure. That basic *effect*—the hero once more proving himself infallible—is the effect of the fairy tale. Children love to identify themselves with heroes who possess all kinds of interesting devices for overcoming danger—magic hats that make you invisible when you turn them around, tinder boxes that grant your wishes. They love to identify with brave but perfectly ordinary little tailors who pose as conquerors and somehow manage to get away with it. As we get older, the fairy tales fail to satisfy, because we now know that the world is more difficult and demanding than that. Realistic novelists like Flaubert, Balzac, Stendhal make a virtue of this, and tell us stories of weak heroes who are finally defeated. But we don't

really like their tales of defeat, for there is something in us that hungers for triumph and conquest. So if a writer is kind enough to tell us an apparently realistic story in which the hero triumphs like the brave little tailor, our gratitude is immense. Like children, we read and reread the fantasy, blissfully identifying, and reveling in the details that assure us that all this is real. (pp. 314-17)

But in order to grasp the full significance of Holmes, I believe we have to see him in an altogether broader perspective. At the risk of seeming too abstract and metaphysical, let me try to explain what I mean.

The novel as we know it came into existence in the year 1740, with Samuel Richardson's *Pamela*. There had been novels before this, but they tended to be either fairy tales or picaresque "true narrations." What Richardson did was to create a highly elaborate daydream about a servant girl who resists all her master's attempts to seduce her, and ends by marrying him. I doubt whether many readers had ever identified with Don Quixote or Gil Blas; but every male could identify with the lustful Mr. B, and every female with the virtuous Pamela. *Pamela* was a magic carpet to another world—a world of the imagination; at the same time, the sheer mass of its physical and psychological detail convinced the reader of its reality.

Within a decade of the publication of *Pamela*, England had become "a nation of readers." . . . (pp. 317-18)

The trouble is that after that splendid start, the novel began to find itself in difficulties. Serious novelists like Balzac and Flaubert continued to pursue the line of realism developed by Richardson. But they no longer had the old universal appeal of Richardson and Scott, because they were no longer satisfying the wish-fulfillment fantasy. Everybody agreed that Balzac was a greater novelist than Dumas; but for every one who admired *Père Goriot* or *Lost Illusions*, a hundred read *The Three Musketeers* and *The Count of Monte Cristo* (surely one of the great wish-fulfillment fantasies of all time). Even Dickens made the same discovery; *Hard Times* and *Bleak House* are greater novels than *Pickwick Papers* and *Nicholas Nickleby*, but they were never half so popular; they are too "real," and they lack the element of the wish-fulfillment fantasy.

And so, in the second half of the nineteenth century, literature split into two camps: realists and fantasists. On the one hand you had the Dickens of *Bleak House*, Ibsen and his disciples, Gissing, Zola, Dostoevsky; on the other, Dumas, Stevenson, Haggard, Marie Corelli, and dozens of now-forgotten writers of romances and historical dramas.

From the beginning, Conan Doyle recognized himself as a member of the second group. One critic thought that **"J. Habakuk Jephson's Statement"** was by Stevenson. Doyle regarded his Holmes stories as entertainments, not to be taken too seriously; he felt that his finest work was to be found in **Micah Clark, The White Company,** and other historical novels. But even if, like Winston Churchill, you happen to be an admirer of the historical novels, you cannot help noticing that they are basically escapist fantasies, in which the modern Londoner turns back nostalgically to the days of chivalry, when Robin Hood lurked in the green-wood and crusaders rode around on white chargers. (pp. 318-19)

Holmes, on the other hand, has his feet planted firmly on the hard pavements of nineteenth-century London. He is a connoisseur of "every horror perpetrated in the century." He is a scientist, and often speaks the dry, abstract language of science. And while this great tide of Victorian London swirls around him, with its crime and violence and misery, he holds aloof in his room in Baker Street, surveying it all with the eye of a philosopher. Most emphatically, he possesses what T. S. Eliot called "a sense of his own age."

It is rather interesting to watch the way that his character develops. The famous list at the beginning of *A Study in Scarlet* emphasizes his ignorance of many subjects, including literature, philosophy, astronomy, and politics. He tells Watson that he doesn't know whether the earth goes around the sun or vice versa, and now that Watson has told him, will forget it as quickly as possible. Yet in *The Sign of Four* he recommends Watson to read "one of the most remarkable [books] ever penned," Winwood Reade's *Martyrdom of Man*, a work of historical philosophy. And later in this novel he discourses on miracle plays, medieval pottery, Stradivarius violins, the Buddhism of Ceylon, and the warships of the future, "handling each as though he had made a special study of it." In other stories we learn that he is the author of a monograph on the motets of Lassus, loves the opera, knows something of painting ("my grandmother, who was the sister of Vernet, the French artist . . . ") and is a connoisseur of food and wine. ("I have oysters and a brace of grouse, with something a little choice in white wines"—the latter possibly a Montrachet, which makes its appearance in **"The Veiled Lodger."**) Doyle's original idea was to make Holmes a rather limited character, like Fleming's James Bond; but he found himself unable to stick to this resolution, and Holmes emerges finally as a kind of "universal man," with an encyclopedic knowledge on every subject, as well as remarkable physical powers. (The prize fighter in *The Sign of Four* assures him that he could have aimed high if he had chosen to become a professional boxer.)

Holmes's character develops in another significant way. In the early work he is definitely an esthete; he says things "querulously" and "languidly," his cheeks burn with unhealthy red spots, he injects himself with morphine and cocaine and lies around for days on the settee "with a dreamy, vacant expression in his eyes." His power of imaginative projection is highly developed; in **"The Beryl Coronet"** he tells Watson that, while his mind has been in Devonshire, his body has, "I regret to observe, consumed in my absence two large pots of coffee and an incredible amount of tobacco." Huysmans's novel *A Rebours* appeared in 1884, two years before Doyle conceived Sherlock Holmes; its hero, Des Esseintes, also lives a kind of monastic existence in his luxurious rooms, attempting to live a life of the mind and the senses, and behaving as if the outside world could be ignored. (pp. 319-20)

In Sherlock Holmes, Doyle created his own esthetic hero [in the manner of Huysman's Des Esseintes and Wilde's Dorian Gray]. With his dressing gown, violin, and hypodermic syringe, Holmes is a second cousin of Des Esseintes. When Watson protests, in the name of common sense, against the use of cocaine, Holmes replies, "I cannot live without brainwork. What else is there to live for? Stand at the window here. Was ever such a dreary, dismal, unprofitable world?" . . . But, unlike Des Esseintes, Holmes has good reasons for going out into the fog. Crime fascinates him, as it did Baudelaire and Dostoevsky. ("Everything in the world exudes crime," said Baudelaire.) But he derives his greatest delight from pitting his wits against criminals. He has not turned his back on the world outside; on the contrary, he regards himself as a last court of appeal.

Quite unconsciously, certainly unaware of what he was doing, Conan Doyle had solved the problem that had tormented and frustrated the novelist since Richardson. He had created a romantic hero, a man whose life is entirely the life of the mind ("I cannot live without brainwork"), yet succeeded in steering him out of the cul-de-sac of despair and defeat that destroyed so many of the best minds of the *fin de siècle* period. Morever, it was quite logical, without any element of contrivance. (pp. 322-23)

Holmes was more than a fictional character; he was a response to a deep-rooted psychological need of the late Victorians, a need for reassurance, for belief in the efficacy of reason and for man's power to overcome the chaos produced by this new disease of alienation.

The need is as strong today as it was in 1890, which no doubt explains why Holmes is still so very much alive. (p. 328)

Our ancestors spent most of their lives dealing with physical problems; they fought, they loved, and they worked, and reality endowed them with a certain strength. Modern man finds himself in an immensely confusing world that offers no opportunity for the heroic virtues. If he wants to achieve eminence, he needs highly complex disciplines of the mind and emotions, and a great deal of luck. The trouble is that, just as the sound of the trumpet causes the sinews to stiffen, so lack of challenge induces boredom, ineptitude, and a general draining of self-confidence. We can fight this with the imagination. Now, more than at any other time in history, man needs "the strength to dream.". . . [Daydreams] are tension-inducers, and they are an important part of his resistance to the general softening effect of civilization. (p. 329)

The Holmes stories belong among those works that we know to be full of romantic absurdities, like *The Prisoner of Zenda*, yet which still move us because they are so beautifully done.

Holmes is magnificent because he seems to be, in a sense, larger than his creator. From all we know about him, Doyle seems to have been more like Watson than Holmes. . . .

Still, it must be admitted that, in the final sense, there is a dimension lacking in Holmes. And this is because there was something lacking in Doyle himself. He knew it himself. And his artistic instinct was sound when he decided to kill Holmes at the Reichenbach Falls. For Holmes is doomed to remain static; his superb qualities of character and intellect can never develop. Crime is, after all, a relatively trivial subject in itself. (p. 330)

It is true that Holmes was never quite the same man after he fell over the Reichenbach Falls (although some of the stories are very fine indeed); to engage Doyle's real creative interest, he should have developed. For example, Doyle was always deeply concerned with the problem of life after death; he even dared to convert Professor Challenger into a believer in *The Land of Mist*. Yet because he had created Holmes as a skeptic, a "thinking machine," he was unable to introduce this concern into the stories and novels. This might seem to be good sense, for we cannot imagine Holmes attending a séance—at least, not as a believer. (pp. 330-31)

I suggest this as only one of the possible directions in which Holmes could have been developed. But the truth is that if Holmes had been a real human being, he would have developed in other ways. After the Reichenbach episode, Doyle set out to develop him into a universal man, but his imagination failed him. He was too much absorbed in his make-believe world of history—which was not remotely like the reality of the Middle Ages—to attempt to make Holmes a real man in a real modern world. A man with so much interest in crime would have developed an interest in the sociological causes of crime, in the psychology of crime, in the causes of modern man's alienation. Doyle himself investigated a strange case of an animal-disemboweler—the Great Wyrely mystery—but only because an innocent man was accused; he obviously dismissed this sadistic Ripper as an unpleasant madman, without asking himself what could have motivated such a man. The real Holmes would have *wanted* to know. He would also have wanted to know what turns a mathematical genius into a Napoleon of crime. His literary works would not have ended with a monograph on beekeeping or the Chaldean roots of the Cornish language; he would have devoted his retirement to an enormous work on the part played by the sociology of crime in the decline of the West.

In short, Doyle failed to think his creation through to its logical conclusion, thereby demonstrating that he was not the intellectual equal of Sherlock Holmes. But then, perhaps that is just as well. (p. 331)

[Doyle] never made the mistake of trying to think things through to their conclusion. In *The Sign of Four,* Holmes quotes the German romantic, Richter, and comments: "He makes one curious but profound remark. It is that the chief proof of man's real greatness lies in the perception of his own smallness. It argues, you see, a power of comparison and appreciation which is in itself a proof of nobility." This is a view you might expect of Holmes in his early esthetic period. Yet in spite of his belief in the powers of the intellect, Holmes only becomes more pessimistic with the passage of years. His last appearance is in **"The Retired Colourman,"** in which we find him telling Watson: "Is not all life pathetic and futile? Is not his story a microcosm of the whole? We reach. We grasp. And what is left in our hands at the end? A shadow. Or worse than a shadow—misery." This kind of sentiment reassures the reader, like Shakespeare's speeches on the futility of human existence. It convinces him that, even if Holmes *is* an intellectual superman, the superiority is only skin-deep; basically, he is as helpless and defeated as the rest of us. Unlike Shaw, Doyle was a master of protective coloring. The result is that, while Shaw's reputation has suffered a steep decline since his death, Doyle—and Holmes—is as popular as ever. Human beings love to admire a superman; but they greatly prefer a flawed superman. (pp. 332-33)

Colin Wilson, "The Flawed Superman" (© 1976, Colin Wilson; used with permission of the publisher; The Bobbs-Merrill Company, Inc.), in Beyond Baker Street: A Sherlockian Anthology, *edited by Michael Harrison, Bobbs-Merrill, 1976, pp. 311-34.*

RONALD PEARSALL (essay date 1977)

The first vehicle for Sherlock Holmes was to be entitled *A Tangled Skein,* but eventually this title was discarded and *A Study in Scarlet* substituted. When it was completed, Doyle sent it to [James] Payn, editor of the *Cornhill,* for serialization. Payn told him that it was both too long and too short for his magazine. . . . (p. 28)

It is surprising that Payn did not recognize the potential of *A Study in Scarlet.* Admittedly it was not stylish, but, as Somerset Maugham commented in his notebook for 1941, that really does not matter.

Doyle's style hardly altered for forty years. He sat down and wrote, unworried by the hesitations and concern for literary

propriety that make 'artistic' novelists of his time (such as George Moore) almost unreadable. He was never brainwashed by 'fine writing', whereas people like Payn, old literary hands who had been through the machine, were. (p. 28-9)

A Study in Scarlet may not be the best of Doyle's books, though some would claim it to be, considering what came later, it is perhaps his most important. Structurally it is a mess, with a centre section that is melodrama of the most off-putting kind. The basic plot is taken from Robert Louis Stevenson's *The Dynamiter* . . . and although the partial setting in America may have been responsible for the strong American interest, it was an America that only existed in Doyle's imagination. But it did not matter, for the novel bubbles with life from the time the sturdy Dr Watson seeks out his possible flat-mate. (p. 30)

The clumsy structure, the almost criminal carelessness, the offhand quality of some of the writing [*A Study in Scarlet* and *The Sign of Four*] were unimportant. Doyle had done more than find a formula—he had popped a needle into the vein of the public, introducing an antibiotic against the ills of the *fin de siècle*. He gave the reading public an archetype, a hero figure who was absolutely new and unique, far removed from the hearties and vainglorious oafs with which he had peopled his 'serious' novels. It is now traditional to regard Sherlock Holmes as a real person, Dr Watson as his Boswell, and Doyle as a somewhat tiresome in-between, part stenographer, part literary agent. Holmes made Doyle uneasy; he had created a monster who was more real than himself, though this was not immediately apparent. . . .

The contradictions and confusions contained in the Sherlock Holmes saga have been the cause of much scholarly amusement on the part of the Sherlockians. Though *A Study in Scarlet* and *The Sign of Four* were written in quick succession, it seems remarkable that a young author setting out on a career should not at least have reread his manuscripts and ironed out any discrepancies. One of the most careless errors concerns Dr Watson's celebrated wound. In *A Study in Scarlet* he is 'struck on the shoulder by a jezail bullet, which shattered the bone'. In his first meeting with Watson, Holmes observes that Watson's left arm has been injured, and 'he holds it in a stiff and unnatural manner'. In *The Sign of Four* Watson refers to his wounded leg, through which he has had the self-same jezail bullet (a jezail is a long and heavy Afghan musket). 'Though it did not prevent me from walking, it ached wearily at every change of the weather.' Subsequent stories locate the wound in the leg, though Holmes speaks of a 'damaged *tendo Achilles*'. By the time of *The Hound of the Baskervilles,* the wound causes no more trouble. Watson is a fair runner, and 'reckoned fleet of foot'. (p. 34)

Strongly characterized as were Holmes and Watson, subsidiary characters are not so consistent, as if Doyle could not remember what they looked like, as if they were mere props. One of the most permanent of these minor personalities is Inspector Lestrade, present in thirteen of Holmes's cases. Introduced in *A Study in Scarlet* as a 'little sallow, ratfaced, dark-eyed fellow', he is transformed in *The Hound of the Baskervilles* into a 'small wiry bulldog of a man'. He also has, like many of Doyle's characters, a limp, provided so that Holmes can spot his footprints amidst a host of others. Although the physical requirements for a Victorian policeman were not too rigorous, there was little scope for a small man with a limp.

There can be few writers of stature who have been so casual about their characters (even to Mrs. Watson calling her husband

'James' when everyone knows his name is John), and if Doyle had had a clear picture in his mind of Lestrade when he invented him, what caused such an astonishing lapse? If he wanted, for the purpose of the plot, a detective with the qualities of a wiry bulldog it would have been more logical, and no disadvantage to the story-line, to bring in a policeman with a different name.

Only in retrospect were such contradictions noticed, for at the time it was believed that *A Study in Scarlet* and *The Sign of Four* were routine productions of no great consequence. The class of reader who bought such books would be looking for an easy read. Not for them puzzlement that a doctor should be so ignorant of poisons that he would let Holmes speculate that the pills that killed the villain of *A Study in Scarlet* contained 'South American arrow poison', presumably curare, which is harmless taken internally. (p. 35)

But, as Somerset Maugham said about style, consistency did not matter. Doyle did not write for learned snail-watchers who would build a hide about each contradiction, and chatter to each other over their latest findings. There may be some uncertainty about Holmes's habits, but there is a commendable zest and certainty in building up the picture of the individual himself. Doyle did not baldly state that Holmes was a man apart, but demonstrated it. (p. 36)

Doyle may have slipped up in detail, but never with the spirit of place. Although his knowledge of London in 1886 was no more than that of the occasional visitor, his accuracy in drawing the decaying inner suburbs showed that he had taken in the essence of such places, perhaps bolstered by his knowledge of the London equivalents in Portsmouth and, above all, Birmingham. Number 3, Lauriston Gardens, was the archetypal seedy setting. It 'wore an ill-omened and minatory look. It was one of four which stood back some little way from the street, two being occupied and two empty. The latter looked out with three tiers of vacant melancholy windows, which were blank and dreary, save that here and there a "To Let" card had developed like a cataract upon the bleared panes.'

The description, terse and unsensational, is as explicit as a Victorian wood engraving, and throughout the first section [of *A Study in Scarlet*] there is no hint of overwriting, no forced purple passages, the customary defects of first novels. . . . Certainly his apprenticeship in short stories helped him to keep his matter trimmed to the bone, and his models encouraged brevity—Bret Harte and Stevenson.

There is not much detecting in *A Study in Scarlet*. Holmes deduces that Watson is a military man who has seen service in Afghanistan, that a visitor is an ex-sergeant of the Royal Marines and that a cab and not a carriage was at the scene of the crime, but one of the minor feats is more impressive because it occurs in passing. On the wall of the murder house the word RACHE is scrawled in red. The police jump to the conclusion that this was destined to be RACHEL, the writer being interrupted in his work. Holmes believes that it is *Rache*, German for revenge, a blind 'to put the police upon a wrong track'. 'The A, if you noticed, was printed somewhat after the German fashion. Now, a real German invariably prints in the Latin character, so that we may safely say that it was not written by one, but by a clumsy imitator who overdid his part.'

This was to become the kind of classic clue for detective-story writers of the following generation, but at the time it seemed very novel, ingenious without exceeding the bounds of probability. Verisimilitude in detail helped the reader to overlook some of the wilder flights of fancy. (pp. 36-7)

The ability of a person to disguise himself or herself at will was one of the conventions taken over from earlier writers and dramatists, such as Shakespeare, and Doyle frequently made use of it for a plot twist or variation. In his last Sherlock Holmes novel, *The Valley of Fear,* the whole story turns on disguise. But in real life disguise is not so easy, and in particular the quick changes often demanded are impossible to carry out. Convincing make-up is not, as Doyle seemed to think, removed in a trice by a few deft movements with the wrist and a splash of water.

Throughout the gestation and production of the early work, Doyle did not conceal his preference for [his] historical novels. But he had a sneaking suspicion that there was a lot of mileage in Sherlock Holmes. (p. 38)

> *Ronald Pearsall, in his* Conan Doyle: A Biographical Solution *(copyright © 1977 by Ronald Pearsall; reprinted by permission of A D Peters & Co Ltd, as agents for the author; in Canada by George Weidenfeld & Nicholson Ltd.), Weidenfeld and Nicholson, 1977, 208 p.*

E. F. BLEILER   (essay date 1979)

Today we think of Doyle primarily as the foremost writer of detective stories since Poe, but he was also preëminent in historical fiction, science fiction, adventure and sports stories, topical stories, historical works and journalism. In his own opinion, with which I concur, his best work was the fascinating novel of events in the 13th-century Europe of the Black Prince, *The White Company*.

Doyle also moved much in public life and had opinions, often worth listening to, on many contemporary matters, including military science, in which he was a generation ahead of his day. A staunch supporter of the Establishment in most things, he received a knighthood for his work as an apologist for the British side in the Boer War. In World War I he was semi-official chronicler of the British Army. A remarkably generous man, sincerely moved by abuses of power, he also devoted much time to correcting two judicial injustices, the famous Slater and Edalji cases.

In later life, around 1915-6, Doyle became converted to Spiritualism, and most of his activity thereafter was concerned with missionary work. He travelled and lectured, wrote pamphlets and books, and considered himself bound to defend every aspect of his creed against all comers. (p. vi)

Doyle wrote only fourteen supernatural short stories and four supernatural novels, three of which are short. This is not a large production, especially when one compares it with his writings in other areas. He wrote some sixty stories about Sherlock Holmes and sixteen about Brigadier Gerard of the Napoleonic Army, while his literary corpus comes to more than four hundred works, not counting individual poems and minor journalism

Yet these few stories reflect his inner personality and interests, just as his sport stories reflect his bouncing athleticism. While his earlier supernatural stories were journalistic, they did not fall into the easy path of the conventional Victorian ghost story, but introduced ideas that he had picked up during his serious reading. His later stories, on the other hand, were often frankly propaganda for the Spiritualist cause. (pp. vi-vii)

Most of the stories in [*The Best Supernatural Tales of Arthur Conan Doyle*] originated in ideas that can be traced without too much difficulty either in Doyle's life or in the cultural atmosphere of the day. The earlier stories show an apt journalistic versatility that was able to seize on concepts that were already fairly familiar and channel them into new stories.

["**The American's Tale**"], Doyle's second published story, is probably based on the wonderful man-eating plant of Madagascar. This was a traveller's tale familiar to Victorian readers and often retold in popular articles about natural wonders, true or otherwise. (p. ix)

More personal to Doyle is the pellucid horror of "**The Captain of the *Polestar***" . . . , with the darkless brilliance of endless day and the horrors of night. It obviously draws on Doyle's experiences in the whaler *Hope*, even to the personalities of the Scottish crew members, who are recorded in Doyle's papers. As for the ghost that pursues and lures, is there perhaps an echo of *Frankenstein*? (p. x)

["**J. Habakuk Jephson's Statement**,"] is in a class by itself as a fantasy of history. Like Arthur Machen's "Angels of Mons" or [Wilhem] Meinhold's *Amber Witch*, it is one of the few pieces of fiction that have been taken seriously as fact and have been hotly refuted or defended by persons who should have known better.

This story, which appeared anonymously, was based on the historical incident of the *Mary Celeste*, one of the great mysteries of the sea. (p. xi)

While most of Doyle's readers probably had enough sense to recognize that Mr. J. Habakuk Jephson was a Yankee of literature and that his adventures on board the *Marie Celeste* (Doyle's spelling) were unlikely, Mr. Solly Flood, Her Majesty's Advocate-General and Proctor at Gibraltar, who had handled the salvage of the *Mary Celeste*, sent public telegrams denouncing the story as untrue. He followed this with an official report to the Admiralty proclaiming Jephson to be a hoaxer. Needless to say, the press, when details emerged, was delighted, as was Dr. Doyle.

Less likely to be taken for current events are Doyle's two Egyptological stories . . . ["**The Ring of Thoth**" and "**Lot No. 249**"]. Both good thrillers, they show the intense interest in ancient Egypt that arose during the last part of the 19th century after the findings of the Egypt Exploration Society. (pp. xi-xii)

Arthur Conan Doyle, it must be admitted, was not the towering figure in supernatural fiction that he was in the detective story or the historical novel. No one places his name with those of his contemporaries Bram Stoker, M. R. James, Algernon Blackwood, Arthur Machen or Ambrose Bierce. His was not a new vision, as was theirs; his was merely respectable accomplishment.

This is not to say that his supernatural stories are not worth reading. Doyle was one of the finest storytellers in modern English literature, and the dynamism of his better work often appeared in his lesser writings. If his weak area is idea, the zest and vitality with which his stories are told, the clear and forceful expression outweigh deficiencies. The situation in "**The Great Keinplatz Experiment**" is farcical, yet the reader is likely to remember Professor von Baumgarten, while the strange, immortal Egyptian of "**The Ring of Thoth**" may haunt the memory corridors of our mind-museums long after Doyle's "better" stories are forgotten. (pp. xiii-xiv)

> *E. F. Bleiler, in his introduction to* The Best Supernatural Tales of Arthur Conan Doyle *by Arthur Conan Doyle, edited by E. F. Bleiler (copyright © 1979 by E. F. Bleiler), Dover Publications, Inc., 1979, pp. v-xvi.*

JULIAN SYMONS (essay date 1979)

Conan Doyle's output as an imaginative writer, distinct from factual histories and pamphlets, falls into three groups: the Sherlock Holmes and other mystery stories, the historical and sporting novels and short stories, and what we would now call the science fiction. There are also a few books that do not fit into any of these categories, and a number of plays. (p. 83)

The first three collections of short stories [about Holmes], *The Adventures, The Memoirs* and *The Return*, are much superior to the last volumes, *His Last Bow* and *The Case-Book*. The first two belong to the eighteen nineties, and the stories in *The Return* had been completed by 1904. *His Last Bow* appeared in 1917, and *The Case-Book* ten years later. There are good stories in these last volumes, along with some weak ones, but the enthusiastic delight in his own creations that marked the early books is missing. The old master is going through the motions, and doing so with skill, but no longer with pleasure. In part no doubt this comes from the fact that the later stories deal with a time long past. "**His Last Bow**", which was set in August 1914 just at the beginning of the War, was actually written in 1917, and this was the nearest thing to a contemporary setting in the later stories. The tales written in the nineteen twenties deal with a Victorian or Edwardian England that was by now only a memory to their creator.

Some of the other mystery stories written at intervals over the years make lively reading, and in two cases carry a faint echo of Sherlock Holmes. Both "**The Last Special**" and "**The Man with the Watches**" are railway mysteries, the first of them being particularly ingenious, and both contain references to the theories of "an amateur reasoner of some celebrity" in one story, and "a well-known criminal investigator" in the other. These theories get near to the truth of the puzzle in the stories, although they do not uncover it.

The four Sherlock Holmes novels all have their partisans, particularly *The Hound of the Baskervilles* . . . , but not many people would place them on the same level as the short stories. Conan Doyle's genius was expressed in the short detective tale, not the novel. Both [*A Study in Scarlet* and *The Valley of Fear*] . . . give up detection part of the way through, to deal with life in an American Mormon community and in a miners' settlement. One reason for this was that Conan Doyle liked writing adventure stories, but he had also run out of detective steam. *The Hound* does not err in this way, but we know the villain's identity two-thirds of the way through the book, something that is displeasing to most modern detective story readers. Conan Doyle lacked the skill in spacing out clues and red herrings throughout a novel which became a commonplace of detective stories in the nineteen twenties. The Sherlock Holmes novels were, from the point of view of plotting, enlarged short stories. (pp. 83, 85-6)

It was upon [the historical novels], in particular *The White Company* . . . and *Sir Nigel* . . . that Conan Doyle placed his chief hopes of being remembered as a writer. He thought, as he said later, that they "would live and would illuminate our national traditions". He was disappointed by critics' reaction to *The White Company* even though it was praised, because they treated it "too much as if it were a mere book of adventure . . . whereas I have striven to draw the exact types of character of the folk then living and have spent much work and pains over it, which seems so far to be quite unappreciated by the critics''. *Sir Nigel* seemed to him his high-water mark in literature, and again he was disappointed that the novel received no particular critical recognition.

These books, upon which he spent so many pains, are of all his imaginative writings the least congenial to modern taste. We value his ''mere tales of adventure'' more highly than he did, because they are so well told. The books he took more seriously, on the other hand, seem to most readers now rhetorical and wooden in much of the writing, and to take an idealistic view of the past that we cannot share. *Micah Clarke* . . . is an agreeable although conventional historical novel about Monmouth's rebellion, but in *The White Company* Conan Doyle attempted more and achieved less. The picture of fourteenth century life, with its insistence on patriotism and the importance of team spirit seems to be viewing the Middle Ages in Victorian terms, the author's passionate support of the ruling order in society would be disagreeable if it did not seem a little absurd, and most of the characterization is as stiff as the writing. There are fine scenes in the book, like the account of the siege of Villefranche and the discussion of the importance of the English archers in the campaign, but they are produced by the writer of adventure stories. The idea of a company of knight-errants moved by the mediaeval conception of chivalry even as they fight seems to us today simply to ignore the realities of history. The same criticism applies to the high romanticism of *Sir Nigel*, which shows us characters already met in *The White Company* at an earlier period in their lives. Conan Doyle took great trouble to get right the details about armour and archery, but the people drawing the bow and inside the suit of armour are not human beings as we know them. (pp. 86, 89)

One or two of the less-regarded historical novels are more interesting, partly because their author tried less hard with them. *Uncle Bernac* . . . has found few admirers, and Conan Doyle himself always felt that there was something wrong with it, but the book has a marvellous opening. Young Louis de Laval, who has escaped to England during the French Revolution, is asked by his Uncle Bernac to return. He does so, ignoring the words ''Don't come'' written above the letter's seal, and is plunged into a series of misadventures which are brilliantly maintained without complete explanation for a full fifty pages. The book falls away, but the portrayal of Uncle Bernac is a good deal more interesting than anything in the two novels Conan Doyle valued so highly. The picture of Napoleon in the final chapter is done in a distinctly starry-eyed manner, alien from the rest of the book. There were times when Conan Doyle tended to identify heroes with dictators.

Most of the other historical novels need little comment because they are inferior versions of those already discussed. *Rodney Stone* . . . , however, is something different. Conan Doyle's love of sport and games shows comparatively seldom in his writing. He wrote very little about cricket or football, almost nothing about billiards, fishing or golf. But he did write a novel and some good short stories about boxing, and both *Rodney Stone* and the long short story **''The Croxley Master''** display his narrative and descriptive powers at their peak.

Conan Doyle said that he thought nobody but a fighting man could fully appreciate some of the detail in *Rodney Stone,* and the book gives scope to his feelings that the old bare-knuckle fighting of the prize ring was ''an excellent thing from a national point of view''. Its success depended upon people who

like himself loved what he called the chivalry of sport, and he noted that the standards of British boxing had been corrupted during the nineteenth century by ''the villainous mobs'' who were concerned only with making money by betting. *Rodney Stone* is set in the chivalric time and it views the great fighters of the early nineteenth century, like Gentleman Jackson, Mendoza and Jim Belcher, with the awe-struck eyes of a boy—a boy, however, who knows what he is writing about in a technical sense, and is able to create the visual background of the period with great skill. **''The Croxley Master''** is just as good on a smaller scale. The picture of the Master, who might have been one of the great fighters of his time but for an accident which broke his thigh and left one leg shorter than the other, ungainly as a crab in advance or retreat but able to pivot on his bad leg with extraordinary speed, is brilliantly done. The success of these stories emphasizes again that his mastery as a writer was mostly in rendering the external surface of things, whether it was a boxing match or the investigation of a crime.

This exultant acceptance of physical exertion and struggle is to be found, together with a typical love of extrovert characters, in *The Exploits of Brigadier Gerard* . . . and *The Adventures* that followed. . . . The Brigadier is an officer in Napoleon's army, a swaggering vain braggart who is also brave, imaginative and resourceful. He is based fairly closely on the Baron de Marbot, whose memoirs show him to have been a real life Gerard so far as boastfulness went, and whose dash and skill were acknowledged even by those who most disliked him. Conan Doyle did not think very much of the Gerard stories. They sprang from his absorption for three years in things Napoleonic, an absorption responsible for *Uncle Bernac* and also for what the author deprecatingly called his little book of soldier stories. (pp. 89, 91-3)

[The Gerard stories] have the life and verve that is missing in *The White Company* and *Sir Nigel*. Perhaps it is an exaggeration to say, as one critic does, that he never wrote anything else as good as these tales, but they do show what he could achieve in the way of characterization. Gerard . . . was the kind of character he could perfectly understand. All Gerard's qualities show upon the surface. From his boastfulness and courage, his unquenchable self-satisfaction and its frequent humiliation, his disastrous mistakes and adroit recoveries from them, there is built a comic character who is still not absurd. It would be too much to call Gerard one of the great comic characters of literature, but on his own level he is unmatchable. (p. 93)

Most of the stories are anecdotes . . . , but they are marvellously well told, with a humour and good humour that carries a reader along. Brigadier Gerard is, after Holmes and Watson, Conan Doyle's most successful literary creation. (p. 94)

[Science fiction was a] development that came late in Conan Doyle's writing career, and is represented by three novels, [*The Lost World, The Poison Belt* and *The Maracot Deep*] . . . , as well as some short stories. The first, and much the best, of these novels is about a journey to Amazonia, where Professor Challenger claims to have traced some prehistoric animals still living on a great plateau. The irascible Challenger, a figure based on the professor of anatomy at Edinburgh, takes a party of adventurous spirits to look for this lost world. Their adventures are marked by that speculative ingenuity which was one of Conan Doyle's most engaging marks as man and writer, and by an imaginative quality that came into play most fully when he was dealing with scenes outside everyday life. The description of the Amazonian forest obviously owes something to the author's travels, yet it has a kind of spectral quality that removes it from literal reality.

Challenger is also the central figure in *The Poison Belt,* which starts from the not unusual science fiction premise that by some means (in this case the earth moves into a poison belt) human life comes to an end. Challenger gathers together wife and friends in an air-tight shelter, and hopes to survive. Most modern stories would be concerned with what happened to them after the extinction of civilised life, but Conan Doyle was too optimistic a man to consider seriously the end of life as we know it. It turns out that the poison belt through which the earth passed has induced unconsciousness, not death. Everybody wakes up, and life goes on as before. It is a feeble, unsatisfying ending. In *The Maracot Deep* the people of Atlantis are discovered by submarine explorers to have survived the flooding of the city. Wireless, television and nuclear energy are introduced into a story containing many inventive effects, unhappily largely dissipated by the introduction of such unlikely creatures as a giant caterpillar armed with a death ray.

The two books that conspicuously fail to fit into any category of Conan Doyle fiction are *The Stark Munro Letters* . . . and *A Duet, with an Occasional Chorus.* . . . The first of these is a fairly direct autobiographical narrative, put in the form of sixteen letters from the young doctor of the title to a friend in America. . . . The book is far from a perfect novel, but it is infused throughout with Conan Doyle's energetic temperament and over it all broods the spirit of Dr. Budd, the badhat whose reckless daring fascinated Conan Doyle to the end of his life.

The book is important to anybody interested in understanding the author's character, and so is *A Duet,* a story which shows a flippancy and lightness unique in Conan Doyle's work. . . . The book's lightness of tone is not successful, yet the author was not altogether wrong when he wrote to [his mother]: "My inmost soul tells me that it is not a failure." *A Duet* is a gesture, never repeated, in the direction of a novel of social manners, and as an experiment it is certainly not without interest.

That is the sum of Conan Doyle's activities as a literary man, with the exception of his plays and poems. The published texts of his plays make it clear that he was not a natural dramatist, and the collected poems show that he was a competent maker of verses rather than a poet. Anybody who wants to approach him as a man of letters should read the Sherlock Holmes stories, the major historical novels, the Brigadier Gerard tales, one of the science fiction novels, and a selection of the short stories. Only the scholar will want to go further. Conan Doyle was a skilful writer, with a real gift for narrative, but in the end he was a fine craftsman rather than an artist. (pp. 94, 98, 100)

> *Julian Symons, in his* Portrait of an Artist: Conan Doyle (© *Julian Symons 1979; reprinted by permission of Andre Deutsch*), Whizzard Press, 1979, 138 p.

BONNIE MENES (essay date 1980-81)

Sherlock Holmes is the defender of social norms; he enters a case not when a law, but when a norm, has been broken. In story after story this is so. Two people who love each other are kept from marriage. This is not illegal; it isn't even immoral. Wages should be commensurate with work; an exorbitant wage is caused for investigation. There should be no secrets between a husband and wife, yet one spouse in a marriage is acting mysteriously. Two people are scheduled to marry, but one fails to show up at the altar. No public crime has been committed, no private transgression even, but an unspoken social rule has been broken. A man, defender of home and family, is missing and thus unable to defend his home and family. Social fabric is torn. Holmes, in each instance, is called in.

Sherlock Holmes is no mere defender of the law. Like many another modern detective in literature, Holmes often finds himself an unwitting accomplice in a man's death, or the advocate of deliberate deception or disruption of one kind or another. The London in which Conan Doyle sets Holmes down is a complex place, so complex that Holmes himself, for his own good reasons, must sometimes actually break the law. But he rarely enters a case only because a law has been broken, a crime committed. More often he enters before any crime has taken place, before the murder, before the blackmail. Or perhaps there is no clear crime at all; it is only that someone or something is missing. (p. 101)

Strange business, unhappy coincidences, suspicious circumstances—these are what propel Sherlock Holmes into action. What is illegal is not necessarily, for him, what is of interest. "We have in this case one singular incident coming close to the heels of another singular incident," Holmes explains in **"The Adventure of the Norwood Builder,"** "[and] the police are making the mistake of concentrating their attention upon the second, because it happens to be the one which is actually criminal. But it is evident to me that the logical way to approach the case is to begin by trying to throw some light upon the first incident—the curious will, so suddenly made, and to so unexpected an heir."

More important, once on a case Holmes does not invariably enforce the law. Sometimes he turns lawbreakers over to the authorities, but sometimes not. What is more, Holmes is quick to reprimand his own clients, to berate them when he does not approve of their behavior, even to refuse a client's gratefully outstretched hand. Holmes is often referred to as "a specialist in crime"; yet his is a special kind of specialty—it is in logic, not law. He is not a policeman and as far as possible from prosecutorial. Justice is always served, but the Baker Street logician never brings men to justice. (pp. 101-02)

Sherlock Holmes does not represent positive law, because he does not always agree with the law and because he himself frequently goes beyond the law. Holmes hangs out no shingle but dwells in shadow and, often, deceit. He keeps secrets, which is one of the reasons his clients seek him out. . . .

If Holmes is not public defender, neither is he a private eye, a sleuth checking up on cheating wives. Morality is private and, as such, Holmes deems it none of his business. He takes a scientific view of his cases. He leaves it for others to unravel the morality behind their courses of action. He does not fight evil; he investigates problems. The universe is too much a puzzle to him to impose his own moral views on it. As he remarks in **"The Adventure of the Cardboard Box"**:

> "What is the meaning of it, Watson?" said Holmes, solemnly, as he laid down the paper. "What object is served by this circle of misery and violence and fear? It must tend to some end, or else our universe is ruled by chance, which is unthinkable. But what end? There is the great standing perennial problem to which human reason is as far from an answer as ever."

Neither goodness nor justice but social order is Sherlock Holmes's desire. The idea of law, of life bounded by order and regularity, lies beneath all positive law, moral sanctions, social norms. Positive law and rules of morality are kinds of norms, and Holmes does uphold them on occasion. But for the most part his actions are in the social realm. You will not find the rules that guide him in the statutes or prayer books; the kind of order he upholds is unwritten. While it is neither legally nor morally right to murder, Holmes does not, in **"The Adventure of Charles Augustus Milverton,"** mourn a mudered man:

> "Well, I am afraid I can't help you, Lestrade," said Holmes. "The fact is that I knew this fellow Milverton, that I considered him one of the most dangerous men in London, and that I think there are certain crimes which the law cannot touch, and which, therefore, to some extent, justify private revenge. No, it's no use arguing. I have made up my mind. My sympathies are with the criminals rather than with the victims. . . ."

At the end of each case in a Sherlock Holmes story, disorder is redressed, not necessarily in legal or moral terms, but socially a balance of sorts has been restored. (p. 102)

In some of Holmes's unsolved cases, a social balance is not restored, seemingly because he—or, more precisely, Conan Doyle—does not consider the broken norm a valid one at the outset. In **"A Scandal in Bohemia"** Holmes is outwitted by an actress who has the means to backmail the kind of Bohemia. Scandal is of course a social phenomenon, and one might have expected all parties to join together to uphold the prestige and reputation of royalty. But Holmes has little respect for royalty, and his lack of respect is reflected in the fact that the case goes unsolved. **"The Yellow Face"** has to do with a woman conspiring to keep her mulatto child, offspring of her former marriage to an American black. Holmes implicitly approves of her keeping the child and thus does not succeed in solving the case, and hence in restoring the normative order. Inevitably Holmes shows a blind spot in cases that entail norms which he feels should be changed or are in fact changing. As the defender of social norms, he fails or loses interest when the norms he is asked to defend are in his view indefensible.

The social realm, distinct from law and distinct from morals, has a powerful attraction for Sherlock Holmes. Everywhere he upholds the family relationship, and in many instances he upholds property relations. He is busied with thoughts of class and social structure, isolation, and the significance of the urban landscape (to use a bit of contemporary jargon). (pp. 102-03)

On closer investigation, facing social problems often turns out to be Sherlock Holmes's chief role. Especially does Holmes become interested when a social problem entails one norm in conflict with another. In the regular and repeated clashing of norms in the Sherlock Holmes stories, Conan Doyle conveys how increasingly complex life has become. A man wants to be an upstanding citizen and devoted father, but he also wants to earn enough money to live well; so he disappears and lives in deceit in **"The Man with the Twisted Lip."** In another story, **"A Case of Identity,"** a young woman wants to marry and yet to obey her rigid stepfather, and cannot do both. In these two cases—and one could adduce others—we are presented not with a contest between good and evil but one between conflicting demands.

Behind so many of these conflicting demands in the Sherlock Holmes stories is the question of conflicting identities. The problem that arises time and again is that of competing loyalties, due to competing identities in an increasingly complex world. . . . The title **"A Case of Identity"** could just as well be used for several other Sherlock Holmes stories. Disguises and deceptions are part of nearly every story; past identities clash with present identities, native with foreign. (pp. 103-04)

These conflicts, wrought by different identities, are in large part responsible for the flavor and feel of Victorian England in the Sherlock Holmes stories, their appealing complexity and their charm. The modern detective, unlike Holmes, has at his service social security numbers, license plate numbers, finger prints on file. The modern detective's problem is usually to locate the criminal instead of discerning under what guise he committed the crime—a problem of whereabouts not whoabouts. At the same time, the criminal in modern detective fiction presents no such problem in identity because he has no single secure identity. He may be a cardsharp or murderer by night, an insurance agent or poet by day. One thing that separates Sherlock Holmes from Lieutenant Columbo, manner aside, is Holmes's dated concern with conflicting loyalties, as expressed by conflicting identities. (p. 104)

> *Bonnie Menes, "Sherlock Holmes and Sociology," in* The American Scholar *(copyright © 1981 by the United Chapters of Phi Beta Kappa; reprinted by permission of the publishers), Vol. 50, No. 1, Winter, 1980-81, pp. 101-05.*

ADDITIONAL BIBLIOGRAPHY

Baring-Gould, William S. *Sherlock Holmes: A Biography of the World's First Consulting Detective*. London: R. Hart-Davis, 1962, 284 p.
    Illustrated biography of Holmes by a prominent Holmes scholar.

Carr, John Dickson. *The Life of Sir Arthur Conan Doyle*. New York: Harper & Brothers, 1949, 304 p.
    Extensive biography of Doyle.

De Waal, Ronald Burt. *The World Bibliography of Sherlock Holmes and Dr. Watson: A Classified and Annotated List of Materials Relating to their Adventures*. Boston: New York Graphic Society, 1974, 526 p.
    Inclusive bibliography of essays and books on Holmes and Watson.

Gillis, James M. "Conan Doyle." In his *False Prophets*, pp. 64-84. New York: The Macmillan Co., 1934.
    Skeptical assessment of Doyle's qualifications as an investigator of psychical phenomena. Gillis gives examples of Doyle's credulity when faced with apparently blatantly faked psychic experiences.

Hardwick, Michael, and Hardwick, Mollie. *The Sherlock Holmes Companion*. London: John Murray, 1962, 232 p.
    Reference guide, including a list of the most significant characters in the Holmes adventures, plot synopses, and brief biographical sketches of Holmes, Watson, and Doyle.

Hardwick, Michael, and Hardwick, Mollie. *The Man Who Was Sherlock Holmes*. New York: Doubleday & Co., 1964, 92 p.
    Biography of Doyle, concentrating on the popularity of Holmes.

Harrison, Michael. *In the Footsteps of Sherlock Holmes*. Rev. ed. Newton Abbot, England: David & Charles, 1971, 292 p.
    Retrospective survey of facts of everyday life in late nineteenth-century England related to the "life" of Holmes.

Keating, H.R.F. *Sherlock Holmes: The Man and His World*. New York: Charles Scribner's Sons, 1979, 160 p.
    Profusely illustrated volume relating the character of Holmes to his country and to his era.

Nicholas, Constance. "The Murders of Doyle and Eliot." *Modern Language Notes* LXX, No. 4 (April 1955): 269-71.

Demonstrates the extent to which T. S. Eliot borrowed from Doyle's "The Musgrave Ritual" in writing *Murder in the Cathedral*.

Ousby, Ian. "Arthur Conan Doyle." In his *Bloodhounds of Heaven: The Detective in English Fiction from Godwin to Doyle,* pp. 139-75. Cambridge: Harvard University Press, 1976.

Analysis of the character of Holmes, "the perfect hero for his age," in relation to aspects of Doyle's life and personality.

Preston, Priscilla. "A Note on T. S. Eliot and Sherlock Holmes." *The Modern Language Review* LIV, No. 3 (July 1959): 397-99.

Shows many instances of Eliot's appropriation of characteristics of figures from the Holmes stories, which Eliot applied to some of his own characters.

Ritunnano, Jeanne. "Mark Twain vs. Arthur Conan Doyle on Detective Fiction." *Mark Twain Journal* XVI, No. 1 (Winter 1971-72): 10-14.

Traces the direct relationship between Doyle's *A Study in Scarlet* and Twain's later "A Double-Barrelled Detective Story."

Sayers, Dorothy L. *Unpopular Opinions.* New York: Harcourt, Brace and Company, 1947, 236 p.*

Discussion of such aspects of Holmes's and Watson's "private lives" as Holmes's college and Watson's marital history.

Starrett, Vincent. *The Private Life of Sherlock Holmes.* Rev. ed. Chicago: The University of Chicago Press, 1960, 155 p.

A collection of essays dealing both with the facts of Doyle's life and the "facts" of Holmes's life.

Stout, Rex; Davis, Elmer; Barcun, Jacques; and Van Doren, Mark. "A. Conan Doyle: 'The Adventures of Sherlock Holmes'," In *The New Invitation to Learning,* edited by Mark Van Doren, pp. 236-51. New York: Random House, 1942.

Involving conversation about *The Adventures of Sherlock Holmes.* The participants discuss the characters of Holmes and Watson more than the writer Doyle.

Paul Eluard

1895-1952

(Pseudonym of Eugène Grindel; also wrote under pseudonyms of Jean du Hault and Maurice Hervent) French poet and essayist.

After the First World War, Eluard, along with André Breton, founded the surrealist movement in France. Though he formally abandoned the movement in 1938, Eluard never ceased utilizing the methods he developed as a surrealist. Most critics recognize Eluard for the purity, the lyricism, and the highly visual content of his poetry. Recurring themes of love, female guidance, fraternity, and universal harmony established Eluard as an optimistic voice in a time when France was filled with despair and alienation. Eluard spent his life working for peace, justice, and the end of human suffering, and his poetry is a unique record of a man's attempt to break down the barriers of human solitude.

Eluard was born of working-class parents in an industrial suburb of Paris. At the age of sixteen, due to a serious illness, he was forced to leave his family home for a Swiss sanatorium. While there he read much poetry, including the works of Rimbaud, Lautréamont, and Vildrac. Shortly after his return to Paris, he enlisted in the army and during World War I fought in the trenches along the front. There he was gassed and, as a result, suffered gangrene of the bronchi. His early contact with human misery inspired him to write *Le devoir et l'inquiétude* and *Poèmes pour la paix* after the war. In Paris Eluard met other young writers, namely Breton, Louis Aragon, Philippe Soupault, and Tristan Tzara, who were then active in the Dadaist movement. From the anarchy of Dada they invented surrealism, an elaborate discipline formed as a response to the limited logic and reasoning of the literary status quo, which the young artists held responsible for the ineptitude of language and the stagnation of society as a whole. During his long association with surrealism, Eluard published an enormous volume of work, including *Répétitions*, *La vie immédiate*, and *Capitale de la douleur (Capital of Pain)*, which many critics consider one of his greatest achievements. Before the German occupation of France, Eluard confirmed his affiliation with the Communist party, which led to his break with surrealism. During the occupation, Eluard engaged in underground activities and wrote his "poems of Resistance," many of which had an uplifting effect on French morale. Immediately after the war Eluard published *Poésie ininterrompue*, also considered one of his best works and the one in which he most completely expressed the themes central to his thought.

Imagery plays an important role in Eluard's writing. Within the poetic image, according to Eluard, everything finds an echo and a resemblance, everything is comparable to everything else. The strength of Eluard's poetry, and its unlimited potential for expansion, is due to this cult of the image, along with the free association of metaphors and the play of dualities, such as "It's the moon that is at the center of the earth / It's greenery that covers the sky." According to this method, Eluard expressed the themes and subjects he cared for most: the liberating power of love, the universal woman, and the unity of all people. These can be found throughout his works, but they are most successfully conveyed in the collections *Capitale de*

la douleur and *Poésie ininterrompue*. Eluard felt that love was the only force capable of breaking through the barriers of language and reason. His poetry repeatedly suggests that man, in his love for woman, can experience the deepest meanings of life. In this respect, woman becomes a kind of mirror—a metaphor used often by Eluard—in which the motions of the universe are reflected.

Critical opinion of Eluard has remained quite constant; he is considered the most representative poet of surrealist theory and technique. Much of the critical acclaim for Eluard's work has focused on the strength of his lyrics, the economy of his language, the vivid texture of his poetry, and his skilled use of the image in accordance with surrealist methods. Some critics argue that Eluard's association with surrealism hindered his poetry, that a simple and sensitive talent such as his was forced to take on the protective design of an established literary movement in order to be accepted in an age filled with cynicism and doubt. Overall, Eluard is appreciated for his ability to mix natural talent with elaborate discipline in order to give his poetry new force and meaning. His increasing consciousness of a poetry involved in human affairs and his desire to communicate with a larger public elevated Eluard in his

lifetime to a stature many of his surrealist contemporaries never attained.

PRINCIPAL WORKS

Le devoir et l'inquiétude   (poetry)   1917
Poèmes pour la paix   (poetry)   1918
Les nécessités et les conséquences des rêves   (poetry)   1921
Les malheurs des immortels [with Max Ernst]   (poetry)   1922
   [*Misfortunes of the Immortals*, 1943]
Répétitions   (poetry)   1922
Mourir de ne pas mourir   (poetry)   1924
Capitale de la douleur   (poetry)   1926
   [*Capital of Pain*, 1973]
L'amour la poésie   (poetry)   1929
L'immaculée conception [with André Breton]   (poetry)   1930
A toute épreuve   (poetry)   1930
La vie immédiate   (poetry)   1932
La rose publique   (poetry)   1934
Facile   (poetry)   1935
L'evidence poétique   (essay)   1936
   [*Poetic Evidence*, 1936]
Les yeux fertiles   (poetry)   1936
Cours naturel   (poetry)   1938
Chanson complète   (poetry)   1939
Donner à voir   (poetry)   1939
Le livre ouvert 1938-1940. 2 vols.   (poetry)   1940-42
Poésie et vérité   (poetry)   1942
   [*Poetry and Truth*, 1942]
Au rendez-vous allemand   (poetry)   1944
Le lit, la table   (poetry)   1944
Le dur désir de durer   (poetry)   1946
   [*Le dur desir de durer*, 1950]
Poésie ininterrompue   (poetry)   1946
Poèmes politiques   (poetry)   1948
Premiers poèmes, 1913-1921   (poetry)   1948
Une leçon de morale   (poetry)   1949
Selected Writings of Paul Eluard   (poetry)   1951; also
   published as *Uninterrupted Poetry*, 1975
Le phénix   (poetry)   1952
Les sentiers et les routes de la poésie   (poetry)   1952
Oeuvres complètes. 2 vols.   (poetry and essays)   1968
Last Love Poems of Paul Eluard   (poetry)   1980

LOUISE BOGAN (essay date 1939)

Paul Eluard, one of the original members of the Dada "school," moved into Surrealism, under the leadership of André Breton, when "the Dada anarchy" was outlawed. He has held closely to the tenets of Surrealism through all their hardening and stiffening, in spite of the fact that his gifts seem perfectly opposed to all that Surrealism once stood for, and all it stands for now. The reasons for his alliance with Dada would be somewhat difficult to determine. It was natural, certainly, that a talent like Eluard's—simple and sensitive, quite unclouded by the fumes of the macabre, and undisturbed by the sardonic horseplay and involved cynicism of his sturdier contemporaries—should be forced, during the twenties, to take on some

kind of protective coloring, make some defensive alliance, in order to exist. Such a talent was of the exact kind to move his contemporaries to parody. Eluard's complete complaisance to Surrealist doctrine before and after Surrealism's alliance with "the revolution," permitted him to go on writing; but his passivity has lapsed, at times, into a kind of masochism, vitiating his work and making his "thinking" ridiculous. . . . Eluard has obeyed, it is true, without once changing his fundamental poetic nature. He stands today in the peculiar position of a poet who has remained a depository of one kind of poetic expression . . . , while paying more than lip-service to doctrines [Surrealist and Communist] in every way inimical to the development of that expression. (pp. 112-13)

It is a limitation in Eluard that he is aiming at one kind of poetry and producing another. Loose form and the continually changed image must have beneath them—or rather, must rise from the very existence of—a ground-swell energy, wildness and ferocity in the poet. When the poetic gift is sensitive, and its projection mild, on the other hand, it is form alone which gives edge to its nuances. Eluard is far closer . . . to the German poet's nostalgia and "suffering" than to the French poet's sublimity and lucidity. (p. 120)

Emotion, when it rises above pathos, immediately takes on complexity. Eluard, well below the complex level, and attempting to work with the automatic and hallucinatory, at the end is left with his vocabulary (simple, exquisitely chosen), his syntax (also of the simplest), and his one emotional effect: "an amorous and dolorous obsession of an infinitely pathetic character."

Eluard is incapable of the poem of revolt. When he feels that such a poem is required of him, he writes . . . undistinguished and adolescent lines. . . . (pp. 120-21)

The kindest of Eluard's critics have warned him against the traditional French affectation into which his writing can so easily be led. He shows this tendency in his comparisons, which are likely to compare something of emotional weight to something pretty or abstract, or charmingly strange. Or delicate attributes are given to creatures and objects of a certain natural energy and strength. . . . And it is possible, in Eluard, as in any poet, to detect the faked phrase, put in to make things harder, or to render matters, to the casual glance at least, more profound. All the manifestoes in the world cannot infuse import into "agile incest," or "fishes of anguish." This sort of thing, if persisted in, becomes *mignardise et confiserie* [prettiness and confectionery].

Eluard's virtues are apparent, and his influence, if not strong, might be importantly pervasive. His basic naturalness, existing uniquely among his contemporaries, preserves in French literature (at a time when such a delicate ingredient might be entirely lost) a *pathétique* equally as valuable as the sublimity, wit, irony, malice, and corrosive rhetorical splendors with which that literature has always been so well supplied. . . . That Eluard's gifts should have been forced, by the fashion or neurosis of his period, to disguise themselves as "unconscious" (so that their true imaginative flights will not lie open to scorn), and be reduced to the level of a word game, is peculiar enough. That they should have been twisted into the use of propaganda, and made to function under manifestoes, literary and otherwise, will certainly amuse future critics and diagnosticians of his era. (pp. 121-22)

Louise Bogan, "Paul Eluard" (1939), in her A Poet's Alphabet: Reflections on the Literary Art and Vo-

*cation, edited by Robert Phelps and Ruth Limmer
(copyright © 1970 by Ruth Limmer as Trustee; reprinted by permission of Ruth Limmer, literary executor, Estate of Louise Bogan), McGraw-Hill Book
Company, 1970, pp. 112-22.*

CAROL SEELEY (essay date 1949)

It is a surprise to come on the lucid, tender poetry of Paul
Eluard's latest book, and to remember that he was the major
Surrealist poet of the twenties and thirties. Or perhaps, looking
at it the other way, it is not his *"Poésie ininterrompue"* that
is surprising—for the book is well named, the sequence of his
work unbroken: he has always written sympathetic poetry. But,
looking back on Eluard's work, it is odd to find him so much
a part of the Surrealist movement. . . .

Eluard was deeply involved in the psychic changes of the time.
Where reason had failed, perhaps exploration into other levels
of experience would give the answer. Art had always made
great use of the subconscious: Surrealism seemed to provide a
direct road. Eluard wrote, "Forgetfulness plays a constant role
in dreams", and this became the heart of Surrealism. (p. 29)

Eluard's own work lay carefully within the Surrealist idiom.
He made practical jokes to upset the tradition reverencing
bourgeoisie. From his "proverbs" I quote: "I came I sat I
departed", and "One good mistress deserves another". These
are on a par with fitting the Mona Lisa with a mustache. He
wrote without logic. This is not new to poetry, since emotional
logic has always been important, but Surrealism carried the
principle to its furthest consequences, underlining the effect of
the new relationship, the unexpected, the surprise. The new
freedom was often powerful. . . . (p. 30)

Eluard rarely experimented with the extremes of nonsense. He
was always interested in recording a specific impression: a
state of mind, the elements of emotion, ways of being—always
observations from experience. [In a poem to Jean Arp,] it is
the glimpsed reality from which the artist Arp worked, a reality
understood through dreams. Speed, extreme smallness, the
search, which are part of this poem, are common thematic
material of dreams, which everyone has experienced and which
have been dealt with at length by the psychologists. The Surrealists generally considered the dream as the more valid experience in itself. Eluard works the other way; he uses the
dream to interpret and to unmask the world of appearances.

The painted Surreal landscape has become familiar to us in
these years: the ruins, classical architecture, the desert, human
forms in trees, the clarity of atmosphere, the odd juxtaposition
of the beautiful nude. Eluard's poetry too has an unmistakable
quality. . . . [In a poem to René Magritte the] theme is of
things mysteriously hidden, missing. . . . Eluard is content to
point out the mystery, as he believes Magritte was. The Surrealists are not seekers: they do not look for an answer, because
they do not believe there is one. They only state the riddle,
the unknown.

This mystery is one of Eluard's two major themes. Ultimately
it is the mystery of death. He has made clear how close we
are to death in *"Le Plus Jeune"*, where it is part of the natural
world and of the child's world, though scarcely thought of;
part of the adult world, it is unbearable. We have found no
logic that can include it. . . . [Death is] a great black stone
which we carry on our shoulders. It is a powerful image.
Darkness and fear are hand in hand. The symbol of blindness
is frequent with Eluard: not seeing, we do not understand.

Dumb and deaf, we do not communicate, but live each of us
alone in a world where the things of time simply pass away.

All this is a well-known part of Surrealism. But there is the
other side of Eluard's expression that is outside of what all the
others have in common, their love of the macabre, their violence and desperation, their self-consciousness and complexity.
These are qualities which we have come to identify with the
movement. Yet Eluard, who did much of the drafting of the
definitions of Surrealism, is free of them all. He is a lyricist.

Lyricism is perhaps an anachronism in this age of disenchantment. Certainly it is an oddity in the midst of Surrealism, which
greets the tender emotion with derision and finds the flight of
the imagination naif. It is as if Eluard were *faute de mieux* [for
want of something better] Surrealist, as if, in a less neurotic
age, he might have been a traditionally romantic poet. He is
incapable of violence; his poetry is unclouded by the macabre.
He has modified Surrealist shock into surprise, and this gives
his poetry a power it might otherwise not have.

Love is the second of his two major themes. His spontaneity
and directness of feeling gives peculiar success to his love
poetry. He writes freely, in a tone as natural as conversation,
tender and musical. . . . Eluard's preoccupation with the mystery, even with death, does not lead to desperation—as most
Surrealism does—because he *believes* in love. And just as his
images of that mystery are all of darkness, blindness and hidden
things—the image of love are of light. (pp. 31-3)

A remarkable quality of [Eluard's] style is its purity. Eluard
has no interest in the grotesque; the texture of his poetry is
luminous, calm and simple. The diction is straightforward and
with wonderfully pure taste. His images are less curiosities (as
Surrealist images tend to be) than symbols. As far back as the
little poem to Ap, he had begun striping his imagery down to
a personal essential. The bird became a favorite symbol, evoking the magic of flight, the swiftness, the bright air. In this
one poem the whole phenomenon of flight, wings, speed, wind,
space, are all named. Eluard uses a vocabulary refined to an
extreme point, abstracted from the multiple detail of experience. Like the bird, other words are found over and over in
his poetry, severely selected till the total effect is irridescent.

His images show how Eluard has been affected by close association with the painters. The stairs, the perspective, the
insistence on light, the enormous clarity of all his poetry must
come from a preoccupation with visual symbols. He has written
poems to many modern artists who are his friends. . . . [He]
has been closer to Picasso than to any of them, and yet there
would seem to be little in common between the two. Picasso
is not interested in the tender emotions, perhaps he is not
interested in the heart at all. His work is of violence and cruelty,
of exuberance and richness from which Eluard is remote.

But Picasso is the great expressionist, and this is the important
element which he and Eluard share. Their art is the expression
of emotion; it has to do with man; its moods are those of
humanity. This is not new in art, but it is striking in comparison
with the intellectual experiments of Surrealism . . . Eluard was
never concerned with psychic experience for its own sake. He
is interested in emotions: love and friendship, relations between
people, and relations between the individual and the world,
are the basis of most of his poems. . . . His care is for the
individual.

Picasso on the universal scale and Eluard on the scale of the
personal life, share 'a fragile key to reality': it is the point of

communication between man and the world he lives in, the world of appearance and the world of reality.

During the occupation of France, Eluard wrote much poetry for the clandestine press. His name was linked with [Louis] Aragon's as the hero-poets. Their subject was death by violence, new heroisms and new degradations, revenge and anguish and hope. This poetry seems not Eluard's at all, forced out in the crude form of ordinary communication. It was a time for action. Only occasionally in his *"Rendez-Vous Allemand"* is there some of the old imagery. . . . Now, later, that life has resumed its more monotonous and less heroic track, most of [*"Rendez-Vous Allemand"*] turns out to be hardly poetry at all in the sense of Eluard's high conception.

Whether it was actually the effect of the occupation, an enormous shock to every Frenchman, or the experience of this other kind of writing—Eluard's [*"Poésie ininterrompue"*] was different. He barely mentioned the war years directly: once he underlined the hope that we had come from the horrors with hands and eyes open again. But the emotion was more sober than in his earlier work, and had some of the formality and directness that come after suffering. "Uninterrupted" it was; much of the technique was still part of Surrealism, though only fully Surrealist in isolated spots. . . . He had inevitably the bifocal sense of time and he made use of the dream and the brilliant images that stand alone on the Surreal desert. He still used many of the symbols we have become familiar with, the mirror that is the confusing other side of reality, the wings of love, the blindness of our pathetic mortality. But they seem to have greater force behind them. . . . Surrealism has become for him a means rather than an end, and in this way it does enrich the individual experience and make more understandable the lives we lead.

It is interesting to come on two poems in this small volume called, *"Le Travail du Poète"* and then *"Le Travail du Peintre"*, the latter dedicated to Picasso of course. The first is a very personal poem in which Eluard speaks of the things he has loved, of his work, of love, of his present state of mind. It is the first time he has spoken in terms of morality, and he understands well how this lies within each person. . . . It is a good poem, but, in spite of its unpretentiousness, it is like most self-portraits: one naturally chooses the sober face as one turns to the mirror; one is too precise.

The poem to Picasso is more exciting, and oddly enough more revealing of the ways of creation. Eluard represents the creative act as a spear thrown into open space: the image is not particularly unusual (he admits himself it is a bit conventional, though who could reproach him?)—but it shows again the spontaneous pleasure he takes in the free completion of the other's work. . . . He speaks of the hard quality of Picasso's art which is so different from his own, and has still had so great an influence on his life. . . . Eluard himself is approaching this point, where art is the sole means of communication. Art as "expression" is an old romantic notion that has no significance in this earnest time. There is no way to speak more simply than through art, and the important thing is for others to understand the artist's image of that other reality. . . . (pp. 34-7)

He is still pre-occupied with light, that is timeless, past our sense of time and space; and with darkness that is the symbol of our mortality. *"Poésie ininterrompue,"* the title poem, is, I believe, the finest that Eluard has written, and surely one of the most moving of our time. Eluard is an older man now: his work has greater weight and greater severity. He has come to some conclusion with all the varieties of emotion he had discovered. His object is a new one, seeking to state certain relationships which will add up to a greater whole. It is again a question of realities. He pushes to its logical answer the questions brought up by Surrealism; he goes beyond Surrealism (posing the question) into the fields of cause and effect, which are the elements of tragedy.

In this one poem there is a wide variety of tone and texture and the whole moves together with the naturalness that is Eluard's accomplishment. It is hard to quote from, for much of the beauty and sensitivity and intelligence comes from the entire composition, the balance of forms, the large movement and its smaller echoes and repetitions. (p. 37)

Eluard's well-known early text comes to mind: "Everything can be compared to everything, everything has its reason, its echo, its resemblance, its opposition and its becoming everywhere and this becoming in infinite." This might be the theme of *"Poésie ininterrompue"*. It combines a dozen subjects—crowds and solitude, innocence and experience, the seasons, age, and love, and death. Yet all the elements of this poem we have seen before in his poetry. Retrospectively we can see in the past the cause of what has occurred in the present.

There are two themes, a dark and a bright element, whose opposition and uniting make the pattern. Love is the bright theme of the poem and the great affirmative movement and the final answer to the tragedy of life. (pp. 37-8)

Starting as it does from nowhere (a line of dots follows the title), it seems like a waterfall that finally has its way with you. It is a bold way of forcing the quality of the present, the being non-past and non-future, the immediacy of a complex moment—which love, of all things, gives most completely. (p. 38)

Eluard's poetry reflects the difficult time we live in, a time of greater insecurity even than the Surrealists guessed. We live lives of opulence and comfort, but perilously . . . To the individual is left only the responsibility of his own personal life: "Nothing reduces us To sleep without dreams To endure the shadow". The greatness of man is exactly his belief in himself and in the things which he has named good, and his care for the future. The image of reality, which Eluard writes of, seems to answer closely the individual pattern: it is made up of small despairs and inconsequential happiness, and a pathetic wonder at our own mortality, and sudden sweeps of excitement in which, forgetting ourselves, we become greater than ourselves . . . The truth is a contradiction: love and fugitive time—a personal sorrow which none escapes. (p. 41)

Carol Seeley, "Note on the Poetry of Paul Eluard," in The Western Review, *Vol. 14, No. 1, Autumn, 1949, pp. 29-41.*

WALLACE FOWLIE (essay date 1950)

Love, even when it is treated negatively as a force *in absentia*, is the essential theme of all poetry and all literature. . . . Love is at the same time, paradoxically, our surest way of escaping from the world and our profoundest way of knowing the world. Paul Eluard is perhaps the most eminent among the surrealists, as D. H. Lawrence is perhaps the most eminent modern writer outside the ranks of the surrealists, who have maintained an extraordinary and lofty awareness of this truth. They both knew that behind the multiple hyperboles and absurdities of love, behind the delirious profusions of love, it is the one force in man capable of breaking through the iron gates of language and reason: the two obstacles to love which have been inherited from man's age-old fear of love and its falsely named debilitating power.

I thought for a long time that Eluard's particular conception of love was comparable to the system of chivalric love, to something quite similar to courtly love of the early romances of the troubadours . . . , where man lives in an idolatrous submission to his lady. There are moments in his poetry when this comparison might justifiably be made. But on the whole, I now see his conception of love possessing a somewhat different emphasis. Woman is quite often absent from his poetry, but his love for her has made practically impossible the kind of solitude which is so characteristic of previous poets. The experience of love has finally dominated the experience of solitude, or has made out of the literal experience of solitariness another kind of possession. The eternal presentness of love is the new experience which Eluard explores in his verse.

It would almost seem that his volume of 1926, *Capitale de la Douleur,* is a new approach to the doctrine of love, a new erotology, one in which love is reconsidered as the great cosmic drama for man and in which the particular rôle of woman is accorded a new pre-eminence.

Eluard's thought plays with the reality of love as if it were the poet's magnet. He moves toward it and then moves away. Although his amorous ecstasy is always severe and illuminated, one feels that love itself is an experience which has taken place at a great distance from the earth and beyond the limits of time, in some dark abyss. Love is the experience greater than man himself which he records and reproduces. It is older than he and more rigorously solitary than he is. It is also that experience in the midst of which man is unable to rest or establish himself with respect to space and time. Love is so perfectly composed of desire and despair that it is always in motion. Man is unable to fix himself within any part of it. He lives and grows and changes in love. And poetry is his metaphysical book on love, his guide book perhaps, the *summa* of all his questions and answers. Love is the supreme experience where the flesh and the spirit cease contradicting one another, and this is the exact phrasing which Breton used in defining surrealism in his first manifesto. After all the poems on the obsession of purity, *Capitale de la Douleur* comes as a book on the obsession of love in which man is portrayed as being both tragically and spiritually dependent on love. (pp. 145-47)

[The poem *Première du Monde* contains in its images] the secret of woman, of the first woman, and the secret place she holds in the universe. (p. 147)

Eluard surpasses in such a poem as *Première du Monde* the glorification of the solitary male genius. In his poetry man is no longer looking at himself for he has begun to contemplate the mysteries and has quite rightfully begun with the mystery of woman. . . . [Eluard feels] the magic of all the objects of his desire, the all-encompassing realm of magic which woman represents and creates. (pp. 148-49)

In such a poem, it is quite possible to see what surrealist inspiration, largely under the influence of Rimbaud, whose methodology in *Les Illuminations* is here appropriated, has been successful in creating. What once was epic drama and historical recital, is now cerebral and psychic. The drama of love is played in the mind. It is lyricism of one moment, a flash of time, that is never over, that is anonymous and universal and hence mythical. The mind appears before itself, filled with the image of woman so resplendent in her nudity that she is all degrees of light: angelic and demonic, carnal and spiritual, unique and universal.

The final poem of the volume, *Capitale de la Douleur,* is appropriately placed at the end because it summarizes the work and the theme, and appropriately entitled: *Celle de toujours, toute* ("She of all time, all"). The poem is the apothesis of song, the opening out of meaning and deliverance in which we may see more clearly than anywhere else in the book the relationship between man and woman. . . . [Now] the poet tells us that woman is not the femaleness of his body . . . and that explains why he has to abandon her. He has never boasted of accomplishing absolute union with woman. As the fog through which he has moved doesn't know whether he passed or not, so woman, in her eternal and all-encompassing principle, is unaware of the passing or the accident of man in her life. (pp. 150-51)

The ending of the poem, the final eight lines, is the definition of the poet. He is the singer, the one who sings the joy of singing about woman, whether she is present or absent. This would seem to be the key to the new erotology of Eluard. Woman, by her very existence, suppresses the concept of absence. . . . She is everything that he is, but in a higher degree, and this is set forth in the final line where woman's purity is sung of as being purer than man's. (p. 152)

On a very superficial level, on a narrow psychoanalytic level, the particular relationship which man bears to woman, as shown in this poem, might be defined as masochistic. But the meaning seems to me go much deeper than that. Man is attached to woman, as he is attached to all the mysteries through which his life unfolds. He is attached to woman because he is man and dependent upon her for the event of his life. Eluard's is not the worship of the chivalric poets. They had nothing of the deep sense of tranquility which is the principal character of Eluard's love. The particular suffering of love, generated by the coming together of the Christian concept, the *Agapé,* with the Pagan concept, *Eros,* which became the drama of love in the Western world from the story of Tristan to the novel of Proust, is not completely absent from the poetry of Eluard, but it is strongly counteracted by a worship of the mystery of love, by a tranquility in the presence of love which seems far more primitive than either Christian or Ancient. . . . Something of the tranquil worshipfulness of woman as a mystery, which Eluard may have first seen in the paintings of Picasso, as well as those of Gauguin, has been carried over into his verse, where there is an abundant song of woman without the harrassing agony of sexuality. Love is not for Eluard, as it is for Tristan, the experience and the desire for death; it is rather the sense and meaning and ambiency of life. (p. 153)

*Wallace Fowlie, "Eluard: The Doctrine on Love,"
in his* Age of Surrealism *(reprinted by permission of
the author), The Swallow Press, 1950 (and reprinted
by Indiana University Press, 1960, pp. 138-56).*

LEROY J. BENOIT (essay date 1951)

Eluard's first two noteworthy collections [*Mourir de ne pas mourir* and *Capitale de la douleur*] . . . , gathered together his most significant poems and immediately marked him as the brilliant leader of the younger poets. . . . Eluard's wider purpose would nevertheless point towards a series of persistent efforts to liberate the human mind from the melancolia and spleen of Baudelaire, and to counterbalance within this sphere the destructive influences of nihilistic and dadaistic poetry. (p. 217)

[*L'Amour la poésie,* dedicated to his wife, Gala,] stands out now as a work encompassing something more than the love of *one* man for *one* woman. Gala is not portrayed as a living and corporeal individual of flesh, but rather as an impersonal and ethereal universal creature, symbolizing all womanhood and the sufferings that she brings to man. We now know that Baudelaire's concept of woman as expressed in *Les Paradis artificiels* had a strong fascination for Eluard. . . . Indeed Baudelaire's erotology or interpretation of love of woman as an amplification of man's sensory perceptivity in all domains gains great momentum in Eluard's poetry, finally to become the central theme even today. . . . [For Eluard,] woman glimpses the meanings of the Universe with vision that sharply contrasts with that of her partner, man; her omniscience surpasses in time and space the restricted mental and intuitive comprehension of the male. Her horizons, says Eluard, are universal, while those of man are sadly inhibited and often limited to purely sensual delights, which he terms "l'éveil au désir." Man then seeks his own satisfaction; woman seeks identification with the Infinite. Man must find the moral truths in the "deux miroirs" which are her eyes. Moreover, this impersonal and universal quality of woman now becomes sublimated into an idyll of time and space. . . . Despite occasional reference to poetic banalities (such as *yeux, noeuds, pièges, baisers dans les yeux*) Eluard uses more sensual images of love to make vivid the transition from the carnal to the sublime. . . . (pp. 219-20)

Even though Eluard had not completely divorced himself at this juncture in his career from melancolia, the shift is nevertheless more and more pronounced. One may still discover poems where he speaks of [darkness and sorrow]. . . . But more often there come optimistic messages. . . . (p. 220)

[In *L'Amour la poésie*] optimism and hope show themselves more persistently in Eluardian verse and will remain henceforth as a guiding pattern for his work. He directs his energies towards the social harmony sought by Romains and Claudel. The preoccupation with despair of his predecessors, such as Lautréamont, Tzara, and Apollinaire, now leaves him completely. Indeed, one may assert that for Paul Eluard the mission of poetry is to enfold all men and seek to translate their eternal altruism and common brotherhood. . . . Eluard conceives of his art as the framework for inspired messages directed to society for guidance. . . . Thus, in surrealist imagery, Paul Eluard defends unanimism as valid, but he retains his privilege of externalizing poetic association far beyond the things which are always materially tangible. . . . (pp. 221-22)

Eluard's most surrealist collection of poetry is *La Rose publique.* Here the reader meets a long series of love stanzas in which happiness and confidence, although restrained and serious in tone, stand as an overt break with themes of his earlier works. To the carelessness and even temporary violence of his first poems, there now succeed anxiety, gentleness, concern, and pity. He makes secret confessions to his readers, and often they assume the shape of resolutions that never materialized. . . .

From 1936 to 1942 Eluard's work gained great richness and measure from social and economic circumstances beyond his immediate personal preoccupation. This next phase marks a strong philosophic conversion towards Communism for the poet. . . . The later sequence of events in Spain moved Eluard's

poetry toward a wider social pattern; poets, he asserted, must descend from their ivory towers. . . . Poetry, then, must help men to liberate themselves from social injustice and unite them in a common cause for freedom; it must inspire all men with a divine spark. . . . (p. 222)

[*Le Livre ouvert*] contains Eluard's prophetic pre-war poems of which a portion composed later and written under the German occupation is entitled "**Au Rendez-vous allemand.**" In this volume he decries the selfishness and the heedlessness of a nation unprepared for the catastrophe which was to strike. . . . Indeed, he says, no man is alone, and no one bears his suffering in silence; rather does man's plight become the mutual burden of all. (p. 224)

Amidst the pessimism that was rampant in France during the occupation years, Paul Eluard persisted in his messages of fortitude and courage. He visualized the desires of human beings as simple and modest and based upon a measure of justice for all. . . . [The] theme of solitude and its debilitating effect upon the human mind is reflected with more insistence in the post-war period. For Eluard it represents the greatest and most profound curse that can be visited upon us all, and one against which all our energies must be directed. (pp. 225-26)

Paul Eluard has indeed grown since the termination of the war. As one of the most optimistic poets of western Europe today, he is convinced that the second global conflict of our century, instead of creating moral and intellectual disillusionment in the world, has on the contrary dispelled from the hearts of his countrymen the spectre of solitude and cowardice. The war and its winning have proved his faith in justice and have renewed man's faith in his neighbor. This theme is vividly portrayed in his collection, *Poésie ininterrompue* . . . , in which he reaffirms the mission of the poet. . . . (p. 226)

Where the casual reader may have entertained reservations respecting certain anomalies in Eluardian verse, especially the curious fluctuations between hope and sadness in *Capitale de la douleur,* this new collection, *Poésie ininterrompue,* stands out as the valid solution reached through experience and mature reflection. It is the most harmonious of Eluard's works. The tone and style are infinitely more varied than the earlier volumes, and it integrates his introspections and his ruminations upon the moral lessons of life. Eluard now seems to be master of his course, navigating with a clear set of guiding markers towards a definitive, yet uninterrupted, philosophy, as the title indicates. Eluard's purpose is to elicit comparisons between the eternal problems of life and then postulate answers to them: if the universe appears on the surface full of bright and sordid contrasts—society and solitude, youth and old age, the search for love and flight from death—these paradoxes are in truth only the manifestation of the interresemblance and interplay of *all* within the universe. All these elements, asserts the poet, continuously form mergings and tangencies, dynamic attractions and repulsions, and constitute in this way the great mirror of life. Eluard tells us that the key to life's riddle will be found, at least in part, in love and self-sacrifice. Resuming his belief in the predominance of female guidance, this collection stresses feminism through an erratic yet spontaneous enumeration in adjective form of all the virtues and vices common to woman. Eluard places woman at the center, at the focal point of all creative art. . . .

Man's inspiration and altruistic drives come, says Eluard, from great emotional stimuli which give meaning to his otherwise meaningless existence. With a great love to live by, he reflects like a mirror this love upon others, for he wants every man to know his sublime happiness. . . . (p. 227)

Indeed, it would be extremely difficult to find among contemporary French poets one who voices a more optimistic philosophy. Baudelaire's aphorism respecting life as "le miroir de notre désespoir" [the mirror of our despair] no longer holds in the reëvaluation of the twentieth-century world. Eluard's poetry, on the contrary, offers meaningful vistas to guide our hopes. (p. 229)

> *Leroy J. Benoit, "Poetic Themes of Paul Eluard,"* in Modern Language Quarterly, *Vol. 12, No. 2, June, 1951, pp. 216-29.*

LOUIS PARROT (essay date 1951)

In his notes published at the end of *Au Rendez-vous Allemand* which reprints several of his best-known poems, Paul Eluard gives us further clarification of the circumstances in which most of them were written. Thus, the poems and the commentaries that enrich them are doubly precious to us. They explain each other reciprocally. The commentaries keep alive in us the memory of the times which saw these poems' birth, and links us to them by a thousand visible bonds. The poems inform us, better than any long chronicle, of the mental state of French intellectuals during the four occupation years. And if these short passages, written with a moving simplicity, were not as perfect as the best prose pages of Paul Eluard, they would still have the irreplaceable value of fixing for us the oft-disputed relationship between a poetic work and the times which inspired it. How many poems has Eluard taken from some banal episode, some small fact which would have furnished others with only poor substance for a newspaper article. They are still the same words, the same events of our day; but the poet has given them their true significance; he makes them live, regroups them according to an order to which he has submitted himself, without knowing the laws of it too well. Thanks to him, the history of these past years, marked by so many incidents, happy and sad, hours of defeat or hope, passes in its entirety in a few verses which will preserve for us its image faithfully inscribed in a poetic memory that forgets nothing. (pp. xxi-xxii)

"The pallid pre-war, the grey war of oppression with its eternal wonders"—later, during the winter of 1940-41 when he "remained, because of the cold, a month without opening the shutters." to the epoch when "notices, threats, lists of hostages spread over the walls of Paris, striking fear in some and shame in all" inspired some of Eluard's most celebrated poems. In them he sings the misery of a country which will not despair and which finds in its suffering the very reason for its revolt. He evokes Paris, Paris which sings no longer in the streets, her unresigned people, the faces of the innocent being led to death, the struggle carried on by so many heroes who had nothing left but the desire to wipe out the despicable invader. All who have met Paul Eluard in the streets of this city where he has always lived have understood the esteem in which he holds this people who "tolerate no injustice." (pp. xxii-xxiii)

Some of his poems—*Les Armes de la Douleur* in particular—are only poetic transcriptions of the sorrowful miscellany that the German newspaper in Paris and Vichy published each day in their chronicle of terrorism. Inspired by the events themselves, these admirable poems of circumstance were to make a redoubtable propaganda weapon in the hands of our partisans. They were published everywhere in France, multigraphed, re-produced in tracts circulating from one maquis to another. Eluard's poetic activity, which from that time on was to mix with his patriotic activity, multiplied. (p. xxiii)

We remember the welcome given *Poésie et Vérite* 1942 by all free men. In *Une Seule Pensée* (I was born to know you—to name you) he exalted our own confiscated liberty and from Geneva to Algiers, from New York to Moscow, all the world's magazines reproduced these passionate stanzas. (p. xxiv)

> *Louis Parrot, "The Poet and the War," in* Selected Writings *by Paul Eluard, edited and translated by Lloyd Alexander (all rights reserved; reprinted by permission of New Directions Publishing Corporation), New Directions, 1951, pp. xxi-xxvi.*

LOUIS ARAGON (essay date 1951)

Poetry is language, and for this reason nothing is so necessary for a poet than first to make the trial of language; no one was more deeply convinced of this than Eluard in the period following the first war. In a degree, the very fact of approaching, on the morrow of this last war, what painters call "la grande composition" [his *Poésie Ininterrompue*] can only be taken as a sign of resolved difficulty, as the passage to a new stage of this poetic thought which has never yielded to facility or self-satisfaction. (pp. xxvii-xxviii)

[In] modern poetry there is this novelty, to which no one can make us return in the name of eternal Platonism; it is that man is no longer thought of without woman, nor woman, without man, and that the high expression of love in these times is no longer an *idea* of love, or the unilateral expression of desire, no longer the lover but the couple; and the poetry of Eluard is fully lighted with this novelty. . . . (p. xxix)

[A] quotation reveals to me, in the envisaged couple, the perspective of entire humanity. It is the love-language of man and woman, with its oppositions, its contradictory play, but the profound will of the poem breaks out almost immediately. Which is the resolution of these contradictions in the love of all men, of the man. . . . (pp. xxx-xxxi)

Here too is one of the universal characteristics of modern love, which is the object of the new poetry . . . : that the love of man and woman in the couple finds its harmony precisely when the man and woman rise simultaneously to the same conception of the world, where their adventure widens and the love of human becoming identifies itself. (p. xxxi)

And it is from this newly found certitude that we mark the starting point of what is at once resolution and crowning point of the poem. . . .

It is a poem in distiches, at first heptasyllabic, which rises from the depths of all sorts of nights, from the depths of misery, massacres, shabbiness, insignificance, luxury, pessimism . . . interrupting itself like a spoken phrase . . . which repeats itself in vain, which is not a refrain but a march, and the double beating of the couplets draws us through this lightless world. . . . (p. xxxii)

[Throughout] this poem we go up by degrees which I shall not make you follow toward this moral of Eluard's poetry ("I was born to know you—To name you—Liberty") which of course can appear only with the characteristics of another year when we truly believed the moral born from earth. . . .

Here the poem becomes a canticle and ends in the fulfillment of the couple in which it takes its origin and sap. . . . (p. xxxiv)

Poésie Ininterrompue is not only this poem, it is a book—and not a chance composition, an anthology. The five other poems which complete this great initial work may be separated by their subject matter, but they are animated by the same spirit, they are moments of the same quest, in which denunciation of the world as it is, of the black world, is reached by a call from a different world, by negation of the original pessimism. . . . (pp. xxxiv-xxxv)

> Louis Aragon, "Uninterrupted Poetry," in Selected Writings *by Paul Eluard, edited and translated by Lloyd Alexander (all rights reserved; reprinted by permission of New Directions Publishing Corporation), New Directions, 1951, pp. xxvii-xxxvi.*

JOSEPH CHIARI   (essay date 1952)

Eluard, even in his earliest poetry, which is at times so Surrealist that it can only be apprehended as scintillations from the night of the poems and not as a complete living experience, is on the whole successful. His earliest poetry shows already the marks of outstanding talent.

Consider for instance the little poem **"Vache"**. This poem is full of fantasy. It comes perilously close to a play on words, yet it escapes that pitfall and remains like the graceful caprice of some nymph or impish gnome of the woods. The same could be said about **"Poisson"** or about most of the poems of **"Les Animaux et leurs Hommes"** which show the same whimsicality, humour and skilful juggling with words verging on the pun and yet avoiding it.

The volumes which followed—**"Capitale de la Douleur"**, **"La Pyramide Humaine"**, **"L'Amour la Poésie"**, and **"A Toute Epreuve"**—contain good poetry although at that time Eluard was writing under strong Surrealist influences. Sometimes one prefers his prose; a rich prose packed with images, carefully integrated, but shot through every now and then with a kind of poetry in which there is a theme. (p. 126)

"La Rose Publique" marks the apex of Eluard's Surrealist tendencies and can be regarded as a turning-point in his poetry. . . . The poems in this volume are also autobiographical; most of the incidents described, most of the images, have a relation to the poet's life. (p. 127)

After having surveyed his past life, he takes his bearings and sets off with the mind of a poet who knows what he wants and who has a guiding star. To be true, that guiding star existed before; it shines in poems such as **"L'Amour la Poésie"**, **"Capitale de la Douleur"** and others, but he had neither reached the plenitude of his poetic power, nor the full maturity of his personality. Already, before **"La Rose Publique"**, love was the most important of Eluard's poetic themes but his love, though all-embracing, was somehow uncertain; it could not abolish the future and his poetry, still in its early developments profoundly surrealist, made use of dreams and hallucinations and exploited to the point of abstruseness the advantages of discontinuity and surprise. It was at times like a mysterious world strewn with beautiful images, colours and sounds, but difficult to penetrate.

With **"Facile"** and **"Les Yeux Fertiles"** a new chapter begins. Eluard still retains his convictions about the value of the subconscious as a source of great poetry; but as his life has now a steady centre round which everything revolves, so his poetry will show more and more traces of that harmony which is due to the application of the laws of numbers; the poetic experience, being really the very essence of the poet's life, reflects the same obedience to the laws of harmony. The past is now abolished, faded away in the night, the future is completely veiled by the present and exists only in the present. Nothing exists except the moment lived, ever renewed, and Eluard walks on earth with love renewing every second of his life. The whole being, spiritual and physical, is fused into the moment lived, the moment which continuously solders past and future into a whole. From these poems onwards, Eluard's poetry begins to show a great concentration and purity. (p. 130)

"Les Yeux Fertiles" bears the mark of Eluard's ever-growing concern with some of the problems of daily life. Those were the years when the first rumblings, which were going to shake the world from 1940 to 1945, were heard in Spain and in China. Eluard, like many artists and intellectuals of his time, was deeply perturbed by the signs of the coming storm, and it was at this time that he wrote "the moment has come when all the poets have the right and the duty to maintain that they are closely merged into the daily life of other men". The poet, more aware that the average human being of the subterranean stirrings of mankind, must be the "consciousness" of his fellow-beings, the beacon which rallies them and points to them the way. Eluard's poetry echoes more and more intensely the general preoccupations of mankind. (p. 131)

On the whole, this volume of poems states the theme, which together with the theme of love, forms the foundation of Eluard's poetry—the conception of the poet or the artist as the very consciousness of life. Eluard has written poetry which reaches beyond time towards the eternity which it makes; but he has also written poetry, and some of it most important poetry, which is not only in time but where the purity of the poet's heart reflects the age in which he lives. The other volumes **"Cours Naturel"**, **"Donner à Voir"**, **"Chanson Complète"** which followed **"Les Yeux Fertiles"** emphasize that preoccupation of Eluard with the problems of his time and with the sufferings of his fellow beings. (pp. 132-33)

For Eluard the poet is the seer who can look into the future. He has a strong sense of duty and finds himself opposed to those who believe in art for art's sake or the refuge in the ivory tower. He believes that his duty is to warn men and to inspire them to struggle along the road which leads to greater happiness. The past, "Paradise Lost", the misty millennium of the Golden Age, holds no appeal for Eluard. What counts for him is the present and the future towards which he constantly reaches in order to transform it into a happy present. Eluard does not linger by the groves of the past. To live for him is to live in the present. . . . Eluard continued to write poems in the Surrealist tradition which show a remarkable feeling for all the subtleties of music and a very fertile imagination. Although they lack organic unity they are held together by a unity of tone. (pp. 133-34)

"Vivre", which begins the volume **"Le Livre Ouvert"**, succeeds in conveying an intense experience, an experience which in itself suggests a conception of life—and this conception is now transmuted into poetic terms. Life for Eluard is continuous, integral, and cosmic. . . . The individual separated from his background does not exist. He exists only as a part of the whole in relation to the beings and things which surround him, and although his consciousness seeks to define itself by finding out the line of demarcation which separates it from the ambient world, consciousness is ever invaded by its surroundings and exists in relation to them. . . . Life is love, the rest is nothingness. . . . One is strongly impressed by the fact that life for Eluard takes place only in the present, and is a continuous emergence from nothingness which surrounds it, literally eats up the moment lived and gapes at the vacuum ahead on the road which the self must tread. Life is thus always in the making but, in contrast with Valéry's absolute scepticism, Eluard believes in perfectibility. He believes in the value of human exertions to reach the good, and above all he believes in the value of the poet's exertions to bring to an end the iniquities and injustices of life. (pp. 135-36)

Eluard's consciousness of the problems of his time, his profound preoccupation with human suffering, are genuine and express his personality. . . . Few men have been more moved than Eluard by the suffering which he saw during the war. . . . But Eluard is a poet, a real poet and so in the end what matters is not so much the value of his feelings and their value as poetic material as the poetry itself. There is no doubt that Eluard has written a *poésie engagée,* a poetry which deals with problems of his time, but he has done so as a poet who transmutes into poetry every subject that he touches. He has succeeded because poetry is the crowning activity of his life; his political beliefs, his social preoccupations, his love, the love inspired by women and by his fellow-beings, fuse the moment into perenniality, and this timelessness only happens in the poem, which is the end of the journey through life and the physical world, culminating in the ideal world, which is the poem. (pp. 137-38)

[For Eluard,] the journey to knowledge is made by the ways of love through the loved woman and its end is the supreme ideal embodied in the poem. . . . [Eluard shows the] absolute love for the woman and for the world whose principle she is. Love is . . . the means of union with the world and the *sine qua non* of Existence, of eternal Existence, for love is the source of [his] constant rebirth out of the night of nothingness, out of the night of Time. (p. 138)

Throughout Eluard's poetry we find expressed, or rather suggested, the conviction that love creates Eternity, and that Time is abolished in moments of love. . . . He can make full use of an unfettered imagination bordering on fancy, and yet the tenseness of the feelings expressed is such as to make the poem rise to the heights of a pure lyrical meditation. The poet's imagination, however rich and nimble, remains within the given theme, which is sublime love. . . . [Eluard believes] that the poet can combine the world of ideas and the world of the senses into the transcendental form of the poem, and that this presents a world of innocence and magic, a world which brings Time back to its source. (p. 140)

[With] the exception of a few poems at the end, **"Le Lit La Table"** is entirely devoted to the world of which Eluard is a supreme voice, the world of love. . . . Eluard continues in his own way the building of that miraculous cosmos based on one single word and all its complications, love. (pp. 140-41)

The idea of the dawn has a striking importance in the poetry of Eluard. His poetry is never, or hardly ever, a poetry of assertion or even of concrete presences and palpable objects; his poetry is a poetry of transparences, of absences, emerging like islands from the tenuous liquid words which surround them and leave room for their emergence. We seem to be constantly on the verge of a mysterious world which only the divine grace of love can reveal to us; a unique dawn where we can remain for ever as "youth unconscious of evil". But it is a fragile world always threatened by night, the night of death, the night which the poet will transcend in the act of dying, and so pass into the Eternity of his love which becomes the poem. Eluard

is one of those who believe that it is that Eternity which brushes the shores of the subconscious where all great poetry has its source. . . . Eluard realizes that nothing living, reason included, can be bullied, without provoking a resistance. Reason must be coaxed into quietness and silence. That can only be done by recognizing its existence, and by gradually diminishing the logic of language, but not beyond the point where Reason will attempt to discover the lost thread and resume its favourite game of putting together the jig-saw puzzle and finding its way to the heart of the maze. In other words, Reason must always retain a very slight, very unobtrusive control over the workings of the imagination. And that is what happens with Eluard, whose poetry shines with all the colours of a vivid imagination and is at the same time luminous, practically without obscurity, and is both universal and impersonal. It is a poetry which remains extremely remote from the personal poetry of the Romantics—here Eluard is as remote as Valéry—yet every poem belongs to a world which nobody but Eluard could have built. We cannot fail to recognize its origins.

But we must not forget that, with the desire to create a pure impersonal poetry, Eluard was deeply moved by the events and troubles of the world in which he lived. The last poems of **"Le Lit La Table"** show once more his awareness of human suffering. . . . Above all there is **"Le Rendez-vous Allemand"**, Eluard's war poems, poems in which not only did he completely depart from his former rather impersonal poetry but in which he took the trouble to describe some of the events which gave birth to the poems. Yet these poems, which are amongst the most moving to be written during the war, transcend the event which inspired them. Poems like **"Sept Poémes d'Amour en Guerre"**, **"Critique de la Poésie"**, **"Les Armes de la Douleur"**, or **"Enterrar Y Callar"**, **"Pensez"**, are poems of extreme tension which have gained from their localization in time and space the pathos which makes them unforgettable. Here we can see how the myth rises from the event through the medium of poetry. (pp. 141-43)

The last poem of Eluard is **"Poésie Ininterrompue"** which is a Surrealist poem, but it is a Surrealism personal to Eluard. Here we have probably the best example of that power to suggest the absent object. The words shape the object and the hollow it must fill. They are words which at times have no weight and seem to efface themselves from the page; they simply give a flame which lights up the next word and then disappears and the trail of fire lights up the form of the living thing which is the poem and which becomes part of our experience. The beginning of the poem is composed of an amazing series of adjectives without substantives, a process which consists in surrounding the thing without ever naming it, using the words as Mallarmé used them sometimes, not in order to name the thing but in order to destroy the real object which they represent, so that all that remains is the hollow which contained the object and the object itself becomes more real by its absence than by its presence. Eluard applies this method with consummate success in **"Poésie Ininterrompue"**. (p. 144)

"Poésie Ininterrompue" is a succession of autobiographical soliloquies by the poet and the loved woman. Their meditations are so entangled that the whole poem appears to be a kind of day dream in which consciousness yet plays a tenuous part since the poem has a philosophical drift. The drift is at times difficult to follow and in spite of impressively successful passages, these are too disconnected. There are not only many successive themes, but the poem raises a number of conceptual problems, and therefore the lack of a single pattern makes the reader too anxious to find the missing links. It excites the reason and inhibits the state of expectation and perfect receptivity which is necessary before the poetic experience can be born. The philosophy is that which we are accustomed to find in Eluard's poetry. The central symbol is the loved woman . . . and through the woman Eluard reaches once more the beliefs which are his and which are fairly close to the main tenets of existentialist philosophy. . . . Once more we find the idea of perfect love reducing Time to the eternal present. . . . The love of words in **"Poésie Ininterrompue"** manifests itself in a pure verbalism which in a few instances seems to be the only link between the consecutive meditations. Yet the poem has enough passages of moving beauty to be given an important place in the poetry of Eluard.

Our emotions radiate upon the cosmos in which we live, and this in turn lives in us and with us. The poet echoes the interplay of these sounds; he is the central vision, source and reflection, the clearest expression of the self. The universal self speaks through him, and he then becomes man, sole witness to the existence of God and the cosmos. Thus the poet can be subjective and impersonal in the highest degree, and this is the case with Eluard whose poetry is for everybody, and by everybody, for the poet is the voice of all those silent ones who feel dimly but cannot speak. (pp. 144-46)

For Eluard, the mediator, the source of Life and Eternity, the shield which shelters him from Time, is the woman, complement of man and the womb of life. The greater part of Eluard's poetry is a dialogue between him and the loved woman, or a meditation on the woman who is love. In that very human and yet transcendental love—for it embraces the earth, life itself, and becomes the source of eternity—there is no mention of Divinity. The "I and Thou" dialogue is between man and woman in Time, combining into "the one" which transcends Time. Life begins with the loved one. . . . The woman is the mirror; in her, in her face, in her eyes, the poet sees himself and the world reflected, and through her he shares in the sufferings of men and in the infinite life of the universe. . . . The symbols of night, light, the sun, the mirror, continuously recur in Eluard's poetry. It is a poetry essentially humane, ethereal, anthropomorphic; a poetry in which the here and now are at the source of the transcendental experience which is the poem. . . . It is a poetry without metaphysical anxieties. The idea of sin does not exist; night is not the night of Baudelaire, nor the night of Hugo. It is the night which the sun-love dispels. The *Angst* of Kierkegaard, the "Creux toujours futur" of Valéry or of the existentialists are unknown to Eluard. His poetry is the poetry of the moment, the point around which everything centres. His poetic images follow the pattern of his life; they do not unfold along a kind of imaginary line; on the contrary, they revolve round a central point which continually creates them and to which they consistently return. . . . [Eluard's poetry seeks] to convey the timeless experience born from Love. Without Love, the self continuously endeavouring to reach the absolute through absolute knowledge, would devour itself and compel the death of the self by the suicide of the body. (pp. 146-48)

Eluard's latest poetry seems to me to confirm two aspects of his poetic genius—the purely lyrical and the social, or, rather, the human aspect of his poetry. Eluard has succeeded in integrating in his poetry his social and political views. He has succeeded where so many poets of our time who tried to do the same thing have failed, because his love of his fellow-beings is not sectarian. . . . (pp. 149-50)

In short, if Eluard succeeds where others failed, it is because he loves men as persons and not as groups or historical concepts, and because he speaks about them as a man who is profoundly and sincerely moved by the suffering which he has experienced and not as the mouthpiece of the historical forces which he expresses. These remarks point to what is Eluard's most distinctive and greatest gift—the gift of lyricism, a gift which seems to me to be the most remarkable of our time. Few poets have ever succeeded in expressing as poignantly, as movingly, as he has done, the hollowness and yet the harrowing presence of absence. . . .

Few poets have succeeded in conveying as movingly and as penetratingly as Eluard the experience of love, half-dead, half-living, decaying under the earth and yet burning with life through the senses, the eyes and the hands of the one who has remained behind. . . . (p. 150)

Those last poems of Eluard bring to mind the poetry of Donne, and Donne's name shines with a light which, if it does not illumine vast oceans and continents, has for the human heart a glow more moving and more lasting than many more far-reaching rays. (p. 151)

> *Joseph Chiari, "Paul Eluard," in his* Contemporary French Poetry, *Philosophical Library, Inc., 1952, pp. 125-51.*

HENRI PEYRE (essay date 1960)

Éluard, like the other Surrealists, was fundamentally an optimist: he was confident that ways could be found or devised to alter man's fate and to accomplish the "miracle" of a loving couple challenging the misery of the world. But like all men, he knew moments of dejection, and the title of his early . . . volume *Capitale de la douleur* evokes the images of a metropolis of sorrow. *"A peine défigurée"* (**"Scarcely Disfigured"**) alludes to the slight alteration made upon a fair face by the intrusion of sorrow. Sorrow was rejected, but it returns, and one is wiser to welcome it as the faithful companion of love. (p. 106)

Love had been derided by Mallarmé and Valéry as a fit subject for poetry; there are few, if any, heroines in Sartre and Camus. Éluard, however (along with Giraudoux, who sang the praises of *jeunes filles* in many a page of prose), celebrates an almost Petrarchan cult of woman. His verse makes frequent allusion to the hair, eyelid, lips, and breasts of women; and kisses are exchanged—but with a strange chastity. Éluard seems to have found most satisfying "the harmonies of absence," as he calls them, for they make dreaming easier and desire more imaginative. In such love poetry there is no possessiveness in the man, no coquettish cruelty in the woman. All is stylized; both seem to have become actors of some cosmic drama through which liberating forces will be unleashed into our captive world. Even during World War II, when Éluard was hunted down as one of the most courageous writers of the Resistance and when he witnessed untold suffering among his countrymen, he remained, like Aragon, the devotee of the love of woman as the first step toward the love of other men and the love of freedom. . . .

[For Éluard] images are the soul of poetry; but Éluard's images do not aim at surprising and they are seldom elaborately rare. They spring in the poet's mind as he walks among other men and feels a new secret bond between them and himself. . . . Alone he heaps up treasures of sensations, of exploration of his deeper self. He penetrates to the heart of symbolic forests (those of sleep, illuminated by the glowing rocket of dream), his head crowned by the luminous night that he has pierced: the night of dark truths. (p. 107)

Éluard abhorred all that was ornamental and rhetorical in poetry; he wished to be understood even by the workmen of Saint Denis, among whom he had been born. By simple language and evocative imagery, [his] love-songs carry an energy that is immediately conveyed to the reader. (p. 108)

> Henri Peyre, "Paul Eluard," in The Poem Itself: 45 Modern Poets in a New Presentation: The French, German, Spanish, Portuguese, Italian Poems, Each Rendered Literally in an Interpretative Discussion, *edited by Stanley Burnshaw (copyright © 1960 by Stanley Burnshaw; reprinted by permission of Holt, Rinehart and Winston, Publishers), Holt, Rinehart & Winston, 1960 (and reprinted by Schocken Books, 1967), pp. 104-09.*

J. H. MATTHEWS (essay date 1969)

[Eluard's *Les Nécessités de la Vie et les Conséquences des Rêves*] marks the first important stage in his evolution as a poet. *Les Nécessités de la Vie* shows him moving from the negative attitude of Dada toward the positive program soon to be called surrealism. (p. 102)

The important questions raised by Eluard's poems concern the poetic treatment of the familiar phenomena of the world we know, the manner in which these phenomena are to be communicated. It becomes self-evident that these questions are of central importance in Eluard's case, as soon as we attempt to understand how and why he wrote lines like "The earth is blue like an orange" (*L'Amour la Poésie*). . . . The shock administered to rational preconception by verses of this kind is proof that the answers we require are to be sought in an attitude before the surreal, in which response to the real is only incidental.

It is not a question of elevating one Eluard at the expense of another, of declaring it is better to regard Eluard as a surrealist than as a poet of the Resistance, or as a Communist. It is quite simply a matter of accepting the fact that the lyrical quality his admirers agree in considering the great distinction of Eluard's poems first found impetus during the period when their author looked to surrealism for the controlling principles of life and art. (pp. 102-03)

[The] special characteristic of his contribution to surrealism is the apparent ease with which he reduced the surrealist message to emotions directly communicable, in a form stripped of the linguistic sophistication which some find to be the stumbling block of surrealist poetry. Eluard is to many readers the most accessible of the surrealists, the surrealist poet who gains their confidence with least delay, and perhaps most lastingly. No surrealist, in any case, persuades us more quickly that poetry is an act of cooperation between writer and public, an act requiring generosity on the part of the former as much as it demands faith of the latter.

Eluard's attitude in this matter sets him apart from most of his fellow surrealists. . . . Eluard gives no sign of being aware of any obstacle between himself and his readers. He seems to feel no need to create obstacles, and to have no reason to believe he must overthrow any in order to communicate freely. (p. 103)

Eluard's enslavement to visual impressions is voluntary, gladly accepted, because the freshness his glance has acquired eliminates the supposed difference between the visible and the invisible. (p. 104)

Sight, to Eluard the supreme sense, confirms revelation, and the consequences (needing no sanction from reason) are dramatically impervious to rational protest. The imagery characteristic of Eluard's poetry mingles references to the familiar world, yet uses them in a manner which severs their connections with that world. . . . The result is frequently hallucinatory, as the poet allows us to share what he sees. (p. 105)

The external world ceases to exist as immutable reality, to become merely a source of impressions, from which subjectivity creates poetic objectivity. . . .

The poet's strength is in poetic imagination, a subjective force bringing together elements borrowed from the reasonable world in a manner defiant of reason's authority. His emphasis upon the visible indicates that Eluard is not concerned with mere postulation, and that he refuses to equate the imaginary with the fanciful. (p. 106)

[Eluard alludes to] hallucination, to resemblances and to subjectivity, in order to remind us that, for him, the surreal is the result of the interaction of these elements, while "reality" plays a subsidiary role. In other words, he is defining his own ambition, when praising Picasso in *Donner à Voir* for reestablishing contact between the object and the man who looks at it. . . . Eluard's poetry bears testimony that the world exists insofar as it echoes his own existence. (pp. 106-07)

From the first, Eluard repudiated the hypothesis that the search for the surreal can be begun only after the real has been excluded. Setting out to uncover the surreal potential of the universe about him, he never once doubted that it lay within his power to make readers aware of the proximity of the surreal. . . .

Dismissing reason and intelligence as tools of doubtful poetic utility, Eluard announces in *Donner à Voir,* "I do not invent the words. But I invent objects, beings, events and my senses are capable of perceiving them." It becomes impossible for him to doubt the reality of subjective impression. . . . To him, imagination is no more evasion than it is fancy. It is the creative act from which poetic reality grows. . . .

The desires Eluard shares with us have set aside the claim of time and space, evidencing no respect for natural laws. Hence one of the most arresting features of his complex simplicity is the ease with which such laws are shown to be no longer relevant. . . .

Perspective is just one of the characteristics lending stability to the old world which Eluard disregards in his poetry. Not that dismissal of the habitual relationship of the real is an aim in itself. To Eluard this is merely incidental; it can be accepted without comment or explanation, taken for granted in the wider vision of transformation. Here the menace presented to everyday reality by an Eluard poem makes itself felt more insistently. (p. 107)

Of course, Eluard does not address himself to readers content to accept the world as it is, denying that the earth can be blue as an orange. . . .

Eluard's verse demonstrates he will go to any lengths to avoid the sad consequences of acceptance. . . . Throwing himself headlong in the direction of newborn images, Eluard is held back by no mental reservations, as excitement draws him onward. (p. 108)

Words do not lie, because verbal simplicity is in Eluard's writing a kind of trap, designed to ensnare the wary, not the unwary. His glance penetrates, while appearing to go no further than the surface of things; and the word arrangements transmitting his vision attain the status of *poems,* as he uses the word in his essay "Physique de la Poésie" from *Donner à Voir:*

> Poems always have big white margins, big margins of silence in which ardent memory is consumed to create anew a delirium with no past. Their principal quality is not to evoke, but to inspire. . . .

Evocation takes second place to inspiration under the influence of verbal magic. . . . The concrete world of commonplace reality feeds poetic imagination, so that the poet's voice can present its testimony.

Eluard's verse never displays the verbal violence of Aragon's surrealist poems. Their mood is notably different from Péret's. However, their author's firm refusal to accept commonplace reality warns us not to be deceived by the softness of his tongue. . . . [In] his best poetry, reason is inverted by an approach to language specifically surrealist in nature. Eluard's surrealism reveals a universe released from questionable stability and subjected to imaginative rearrangement. . . . As used by Eluard, the simple word *comme* ("like") functions like a trip wire: by the time we realize it has served its purpose, it is too late for us to retreat; reality has been booby-trapped, and the bridges cut behind us. We can no longer return to familiar ground. *Comme* announces poetic prescience, in opposition to general acceptance. It marks the triumph of imagination, not imagination's compromise with reason.

In this way, Eluard discovers the infinite possibility of the real, illuminated by the internal light of desire. . . . In verbalization, the poem fixes desire, showing the dependence of the external world upon desire, without which it would lack meaning. Meanwhile the interdependence of desire and its object guarantees faith in an infinite that compensates for the finitude of human life. (pp. 109-10)

The object of his desires, the focal point of his poetic effort is woman. . . . Woman is the mirror in which the world is reflected in new perspective. . . . [As] so often in Eluard's surrealist verse, the experience of love, the emotions it engenders, the vision it releases make possible the poetic domination of the material world. (p. 110)

This is poetry which makes the promise that nothing will be lost to man by the intervention of love, the major liberating force in human life. . . . Meanwhile Eluard calls upon nature to image his love, finding in the excitement of his emotion bold imagery which is the token of a new view of things. . . .

Nature becomes the mirror of love, while woman assumes the supreme role surrealism reserves for her, that of mediatrix. Love now orchestrates the universe. Nothing has the right to resist the influence of the object of the poet's desire. (p. 111)

As one would expect, the effects of the sovereignty of love, everywhere visible in Eluard's poetry, impress us most often in visual images. . . . [Through his poetry] we are made to see the poetic projection of desire, not the dreams of fancy. Eluard's distinction between poems and dreams calls for emphasis once more, especially since in many of the finest of his poems, love functions as a catalyst upon poetic sensibility. The poem becomes the precipitate of desire. . . . (p. 112)

Love does not offer temporary escape, so much as it reveals a side of the real which has been hidden by the habits convention inculcates. . . . Frustration is absent and can never cast its shadow upon the poet's lyricism. When Eluard writes in *La Vie immédiate* "Love is man unfinished," he is presenting an optimistic view of perpetual self-creation, as in his image of the stone revolving about the rings it has made in water.

A world re-created through poetic image simply provides an accompaniment to the song of man engaged in self-exploration. The elements here brought together in mysterious relationship are reality transformed and the presence of woman. . . . [The] mystery linking woman and the material world is the mystery of man, and the fascination exercised by woman is an image of mystery, reflected in the mirror of a world seen anew. (pp. 112-13)

In the elusive fascination of the female image, Eluard seeks an understanding of the consciousness of mankind upon the basis surrealism considers to be the only valid one. He uses the poetic means surrealism regards as best suited to freeing the writer from limitations reason otherwise imposes upon perception, when rational thought threatens the free play of poetic intuition. The presence of woman and the poetic images released in Eluard's sensibility by contact with her, "Through mental rust / And walls of insomnia," are of supreme importance. They promise man success in his battle with the oppressive forces which would confine his gaze to the material universe. . . . The idea of *transparence,* of the penetration of surfaces, of passing the frontiers of the real, and of reaching the free realm of the surreal—this is the source of the joy which Eluard's surrealist verse captures, and which only those readers for whom the earth can be blue as an orange will understand and share. (p. 113)

J. H. Matthews, "Paul Eluard (1895-1952)," in his Surrealist Poetry in France *(copyright © 1969 by Syracuse University Press), Syracuse University Press, 1969, pp. 102-13.*

HERBERT S. GERSHMAN (essay date 1970)

[Eluard] is a poet of substance as well as of sentiment, an innovator without being raucous, a revolutionary unafraid to defend certain traditional values. As with all the other major surrealists, Eluard began his literary career before Dada or surrealism had been heard from: this is of some importance as there are still those who remain firmly convinced that the designation "surrealist" automatically invalidates any attempt to view the work so marked in a literary frame—unless it suits their critical purposes. Eluard's war poems of 1916-17 are as engagés as those, far more effective, that were to elevate him to popular acclaim almost thirty years later: if he voices all the stereotypes, he manages to keep them free from the grime of reality. The end of World War I and his encounter with the future surrealists Breton, Soupault, and Aragon encouraged him to expand his subject matter and to vary his style. If friendship makes the surrealist, and Breton's actions often suggested this, then Eluard was one, although there is little indication he practiced the delving techniques that were presumably an integral part of surrealist writing and living. . . . What sets Eluard apart from his immediate contemporaries is his delicate touch: style and typography interested him less than meaning, and meaning less than sentiment. In a sense he is the last of the great lyric poets: love and the despair that inevitably accompanies a driving passion, friendship and the limited tranquillity it brings in its wake, fleeting beauty, everpresent death, poetry—these are his constant themes. Like all fine poets he is clearly in love with words: thick words, thin words, words in all their variety; words applied tenderly, on rare occasions fiercely; words used to extract everything possible from physical reality—semantically, visually, allusively, and with simple directness. (pp. 59-60)

Though Eluard regularly avoided the verbal provocation of his more surrealist colleagues, he joined them in their search for effective images (those that say the most with the least) and striking rhythms. And some of his finds are among the most impressive French verse has to offer. . . . To what extent is this poet who refused to be bound by the recipes of automatic writing and its concomitant hermeticism a surrealist? The question is quite legitimate, given our mania for classifying. The only satisfactory answer that comes to mind is that surrealism is less a point than a line, less a carefully spelled-out program than a spectrum of tendencies. Eluard and Aragon represented the literary or traditional extreme, Péret surrealist purity. (p. 60)

Eluard was one of the few poets of this century . . . whose work was relatively well received by both conservative critics and those who pioneered on the literary frontiers. The former saw in his verse a familiar symbolist mystery, voluptuous surprises, and the recurrent theme of solitude and sorrow, a sorrow which only love could banish. . . . Scratchy dissatisfaction with the society of his day led Eluard into the Communist camp. There he succeeded in accomplishing what critics of the art-for-art's-sake persuasion had long claimed impossible: writing circumstantial verse of high quality. . . . Eluard was less a politician than a sensitive and superb craftsman who had no use for poverty, injustice, or bloodshed: to confront the same emotions day after day, with ever-heightened sensibility, is a pastime which will keep one fully occupied. This is not indulgence, nor is it conspiracy, it is art. And in art it is always the example that survives. Only the reader, not the poet, can profit from the triumphs and the failures which are mirrored in the lines of this rare poet. Surrealist or no, he succeeded in striking age-old chords and in identifying a range of problems neglected by less talented or less perceptive authors. (p. 61)

> *Herbert S. Gershman, "The Complete Eluard," in* Books Abroad *(copyright 1970 by the University of Oklahoma Press), Vol. 44, No. 1, Winter, 1970, pp. 59-61.*

MARY ANN CAWS (essay date 1970)

Eluard is so naturally a poet that he states his theories of art more convincingly in his poems themselves than in any of his prose writings. His notion of the image as a "perfect contact" and as a "confluent point," of the poet as the double of the beings he observes and whose truth he guarantees, and as the person uniquely responsible for the spiritual and actual inventory of the real . . .—these form an integral part of his verse. They *are* poetry as much as they are reflections upon it, in the same way as the reflection of love implies a parallel identification. All Eluard's theories are mingled in a relationship which endlessly mirrors the aim of poetry or of art, an aim of multiplicity, expansion, and endless communication. It is hard not to see this refusal to stand outside his own poems, this quiet integration of theory and poetry, as a further example of his basic modesty and understatement, the necessary and oddly

touching opposite (or double) of his requirement that poetry have the volume of a shout of joy, and the irreversible force of a wave. . . .

[In *Cours naturel*] a title that indicates a certain acceptance of things as they are, Eluard meditates at length on the language which is the point of contact between the order of man and the order of the world, on its value and on the realm of poetic creation which is as unlimited as the realm of vision. All words are marvelous by their nature, all are *equivalent:* for Eluard, the poet's task is also to make equivalents of all possible questions, their answers and their echoes. Poetry is a principle of balance ("ma limite et mon infini") and a realm of potential rearrangement over which it is man's privilege to reign. . . . (p. 145)

[Along] with the consciousness of multiplicity runs a parallel consciousness of immediacy; the contact between the object and the person who sees it is reestablished so that the poet is in no way separate from his world. He has the power to create a special universe outside himself and contrary to all usual perception, which is, however, a universe that closely resembles him ("Tonight I shall build an exceptional night / Mine") and reflects his vision like a perfect mirror, multiplying his image and giving him the sense of community with his fellowmen. The most perfect example of this ideal (and perhaps also real) community and its poetic vision of liberation is expressed in the often-quoted and majestic poem **"Sans âge,"** also from *Cours naturel*. Entirely constructed about the themes of creation, fraternity, childlike innocence and freshness, and around the parallel images of purity and light, joy, warmth, and language, **"Sans âge"** can be read either as a poem about surrealism or about Communist fraternity, or about the fraternity of poets, or better still as an example of the similarity between all three. . . . (p. 146)

All the elements of [**"Sans âge"**] are equal to each other. . . . When the divisiveness of space is overcome, size and categories have no function. The occasional startling image . . . is swallowed up in the simple progression of the whole poem as it moves from consciousness of self to freedom and fraternity. The innocent revolution against habit and outgrown language and toward the positive integration of the natural with the human . . . are exactly in accordance with Eluard's ideal of art, which requires that the elements and man be set at liberty and renewed in clarity. (pp. 150-51)

It is clear that a poetry "sans âge" [free from time] can, in this context, no longer be the whispered and intimate communication of a merely personal sentiment. To reflect these universal similarities and to make moral or active statements, only a poetry of deliberate outward expansion is appropriate. . . . The poet must create a language larger than himself, which will precede him and extend his horizons; in fact Eluard often identifies language with the path itself. (pp. 151-52)

[*Pouvoir tout dire*] contains a summation of Eluard's fully developed poetic theory with its wholehearted faith in reality, community, and regeneration. . . . As all the actions of yesterday are wiped out by the *presence* of poetry, so all the distances of solitude and strangeness are effaced, and no one will ever again have to speak "une langue étrangère." But the faith in poetry is accompanied this time by a genuine modesty. All the limits outside the poet have been erased, and still the poet senses an interior limit he will never overcome. . . . (pp. 152-53)

Of all the surrealist and ex-surrealist poets, Eluard is unquestionably the clearest in his poetry and in his vision. For that reason he has been able to give, as he says himself, a perfect form to his joy and his poetic understanding. His poems are more elemental than subtle and more lyric than profound, which is as appropriate for a poet of the people as it is for a ''frère voyant'' in the community of artist and poet visionaries. (pp. 153-54)

[In *Les Nécessités* de la vie] there is a remarkable prose poem, dedicated to Tzara, which summarizes in its brevity a strange and pathetic movement from the Dada ideals of activity, purity, and dynamic ''order'' through a sobering contact with reality—the initial optimism of the voyage (''aller et retour'') is canceled out by images of a long passageway lined with dirty children and empty bags, and by the reddened eyes of the traveler—toward the final unhealthy images of fatigue and despair. . . . (p. 155)

[The] striking alternation of despair and contentment will always be characteristic of Eluard's vision and of the poetry which it determines: ''Je voulus chanter l'ombre'' / (I wanted to sing the shadow); ''Et pourtant j'ai su chanter le soleil'' / (And yet I have been able to sing the sun). (p. 156)

In the long poem **''Univers—solitude''** found in [*A toute épreuve*], the despair is at its extreme point; the accustomed transparency of the poet's connection with the world is interrupted, and all the exterior light which usually accompanies it has been exhausted. There is no vitality, and no communication. . . . (p. 158)

[Later, in *La Rose publique*,] the poet is once more subject to the same overwhelming despair and emptiness. The calm garden where he used to work alone with the sun burning his hands now becomes ''an island without animals,'' disconnected from reality, inhabited only by an endless consciousness of the unreliability of individual judgment and of one's essential uselessness to others. . . .

And yet Eluard claims, in another poem from the same collection, that even the man ''filled with emptiness'' must continue to ''seek the earth,'' even though the journey is to be ''A travers des rouilles mentales'' . . . / (Across mental blights). (p. 159)

Eluard's alternations from one side of the contrary perceptions to the other are full of nuance, and they extend to all the facets of his poetry and his theory, complicating the simple surface.

For Eluard, as for all the surrealist poets, poetry is a clear but marvelous extension of vision and of comprehension, and an enlargement or crescendo of ''reality.'' The deliberate expansion of poetic consciousness depends on a continuous series of contradictions, on the possibility of shifting from extreme to extreme, while the poet participates in all the movement and in all the *being* of which he can be aware, reflecting and *repeating* the world and refusing any interior limits. . . . He is the double of the elements surrounding him, and their being enlarges his own. . . . Not only is the individual consciousness identified with the consciousness of all those around him, but now he is able to move high and low, near and far, to feel himself vague and precise, ''immense et plus petit''; in all directions, he is able to extend his apprehensions beyond the normal state in which such oppositions would be impossible. . . . Of course, in the poems of war and of grief, it is just this *expansion* which is suddenly forbidden. Cracked or immobile mirrors replace those Eluard usually associates with motion (''miroirs mouvants'') and the passionate identification with the multitude and the exalted consciousness of multiplicity

yield to a desperate solitude. . . . This is a poetry of reduction and absence, whose exact opposite is the expansive poetry of surrealist vision. Eluard's most despairing poems are haunted by the spectacle of walls closing in to shut off liberty and light, and with them, the sense of man's individual significance. He forgets and is forgotten by all, as his image, once unique . . . , fades away, and light succumbs to death. . . . [Eluard] is always preoccupied by his own image and its preservation, both in his own mind and in the sight of others. This explains his fascination with mirrors and eyes, and his dread of walls and shadows which contradict light and are the absolute denial of reflection and of potential multiplicity. (pp. 160-62)

Eluard's love poems present exactly the opposite vision; in its striking innocence and essential purity, surrealist love is the human equivalent of the image, miraculous in its unfailing capability of restoring the poet to a perfect world of immediacy and presence. As the whole calendar of days is seen emerging from a single dawn, so a single kiss is infinitely reproduced with the ''faith of eternal youth'' by the woman, whose endless complexities and contradictions it reveals. . . . All Eluard's love poems to Gala, to Nusch, and to Dominique are infused with this sense of purity and presence. For the poet, the woman loved has a power sufficient to overcome all consciousness of distance, spatial (''l'absence'') or temporal (''l'oubli''); she offers him a ''perpetual childhood'' of immediacy and fulfills all his ''desires of light.'' His reliance on the individual woman is mirrored in his poetry. (pp. 162-63)

The many forms of oppositions which the surrealist poet unceasingly perceives within himself and in his relationships toward the exterior world are intensified and made concrete in his relations with woman. First of all, the woman celebrated in surrealist poetry is not simply an individual who is pictured in detail, but is at once herself and all women (''une pour toutes''). (p. 164)

As the unique woman is simultaneously many women, she reflects the image of the poet himself as a multitude of individuals, each participating entirely in the multiple and single truth to which she bears witness. Her eyes not only mirror his multiple reflection, but they give birth to an infinite series of reflections. . . . (p. 166)

But just as constant as the renewal of vision is the alternation of hope and despair, appropriate to the two elements of the relationship of love: each of the partners is the double for the other, in a constant clarity of reflection, and yet that reflection itself has its own double, which denies it: ''Je ne suis plus le miroir.'' Sentiments are not simple, they are at least dual. (p. 167)

Eluard is in some senses a simple poet, and certainly he is a poet of a simple, luminous love in all its purity and its order. . . . But more significantly, he is a surrealist poet, faithful until the end of his life to the play of dualities which give to surrealism its genuine profundity and its unlimited potentiality of expansion. In the volume of Eluard's last love poems, there are brief, and therefore often overlooked, references to the essential alternation scattered among his famous images of pure radiance. The *vision* is not simple; it includes both the opaque and the transparent, the fresh and the aging. . . . Eluard takes as much pride in his experiences of the ''ravines'' as in those of the summits; the profundity of his feeling and of his expression comes exactly from the awareness of contraries. . . . (pp. 168-69)

Deprived of the darker images, the range of [Eluard's] perspective would be far more limited, incapable of the tension stretching between extremes on which its peculiar strength depends. The consciousness of possible height is magnified (or multiplied) by the other consciousness, its double in this typically surrealist vision of love. (p. 169)

> *Mary Ann Caws, "Paul Eluard," in her* The Poetry of Dada and Surrealism: Aragon, Breton, Tzara, Eluard & Desnos *(copyright © 1970 by Princeton University Press; reprinted by permission of Princeton University Press), Princeton University Press, 1970, pp. 136-69.*

ANNA BALAKIAN (essay date 1970)

When just prior to World War II Aragon and Eluard broke up with André Breton they obviously ceased to be "surrealists" in the limited sense of the word; but were they able to shed so lightly and so abruptly the surrealist state of mind which had served as the original motivation for their writing? (pp. 213-14)

What Eluard wrote during the trying years [of occupied France] could . . . fall into two groups: the directly circumstantial verse representing the basic local color of events and his subtler interpretations of the disaster. In *Vérité et Poésie* and *Au Rendezvous Allemand,* the militant tone of anger and indignation sometimes overpowers the surrealist manner. *Le Livre Ouvert* . . . includes fewer of the heavily documented pieces. But whether Eluard was describing the defeat of Paris or the less obvious consequences of the disaster, he generally retained his basic surrealist tendency to disregard arbitrary divisions between the concrete and abstract worlds. Even the essentially circumstantial poem "Liberté," whose timeless and simplicity of language gave it a fame beyond its literary merit, was brought into the surrealist orbit of perception by the breaking down of the abstract concept into series of images whose common denominator consists of the subconscious associations they hold with his notion of liberty. Except when indignation makes him lose his identity as an artist, his word-images of good and evil, life and death, poverty and fear, or even the undefinable word "misère" are vivid metaphors representing distortions of perspective, undulations or splurges of color, a sudden brilliance, a striking detail. (pp. 219-20)

Eluard had been an expert at materializing the invisible. Obsessed more than ever by the presence of death, which he has considered the greatest challenge to the human imagination, he succeeded in representing its earthly presence in other than negative terms. He coordinated the subjective and objective hollows which the dead created in the material world when with reluctance they departed. By strategic use of the incomplete image he vivified the missing: absence of hearts, absence of towns, emptiness of prison cells.

The dominant characteristic of Eluard in his earliest surrealist poetry was the love theme. In his later period, love remained for him, as well as for Aragon and Breton, an expression of the innermost recesses of human personality. A spontaneous physical and spiritual relationship with the loved one makes her the intermediary between the creative sensibility of the poet and the sensations to be conjured from the earth. In her are reflected the beauties of the material world and the impressions of the poet. Love makes the senses keener and the imagintion more acute, delivers the poet better than anything else from the notions of time and space; love is at the same time the center and the circumference of his universe. . . . (pp. 220-21)

[It is in *Poésie Ininterrompue*] that Eluard gave his most complete expression of his parallel loves for his wife and for humanity, and the ultimate relationship of these feelings with the universe. With the surrealist's belief that this world is all, and that there is enough here if only we develop sufficient elasticity of insight, he proceeded from the narrow perception of the blind of eye and of heart to the apocalypse of the visionary. He draws upon multiple perspectives as he and his loved one rise step by step, widening the scope of their senses and exploring their powers of divination. First the range of sight is limited: walls, trees, rain; along with the physical barriers there is an isolationist aspect to the love enclosing the two in a world of elemental needs. And this relationship has in the background the stolid contradictions in universal man: his slow-moving barbarism, his stagnation, confusion of instincts, his blindness, and on the other hand his flashes of insight. . . . [He] proceeds to a closer contact with the disorder of the world. The pace quickens, movement sets in, words like *new, open, light, awake, dawn, laughter* precipitate a succession of images with which love repossesses the world. His vision fluctuates between darkness and light, between reminiscences and foresight. Exterior calamities and the miracles of love struggle to mold to their respective dimensions from the human habitat. Moral conviction of right and wrong results from his gradual cognizance of the real world, which he then molds into the dream. But these are not phantom dreams; they are the quintessence of sensuous experiences of the most unrestrained contact with the light and warmth of the world. The earthly dreams have love as their center. . . . (pp. 221-22)

There is no juvenile cry of revolt or weary pessimism [in *Poésie Ininterrompue*] but a virile struggle against the physical forces of evil with weapons that have no superhuman qualities. It is a step by step rejection of the past, a gradual enrichment of existence, an entrance into a four-dimensional world of freedom in which the words *infinite* and *immortal* are the treasured possessions of those who have learned to hope and be faithful to life on earth. . . . (pp. 222-23)

Though motivated by special circumstances, [the] postwar works of Aragon and Eluard give clear evidence of the aesthetic continuity of surrealism: the survival of the cult of the image and the resulting *rapprochement* of the subject and the object; a mystical approach to temporal events; free association of metaphors with a disregard for logical sequence; and a composite expression of physical and spiritual love. Their *post*-surrealism was an evolution rather than a change: increasing consciousness of the social message of the poet; and with this feeling there arose an increasing wish to communicate with a larger public; this objective brought about a modification of their use of language. (pp. 224-25)

> *Anna Balakian, "The Post-Surrealism of Aragon and Eluard," in her* Surrealism: The Road to the Absolute *(copyright © 1959, 1970 by Anna Balakian; reprinted by permission of the author), revised edition, E. P. Dutton & Co., Inc., 1970, pp. 213-30.**

ROBERT NUGENT (essay date 1974)

The poetic achievement of Paul Eluard is complex and diverse. Underlying this diversity runs a theme which unifies the various concerns of his verse into a coherent picture of the poet's universe. This theme is that of the poet's loneliness in particular, and of man's loneliness in general. (p. vii)

Perhaps the most immediate reality for a poet lies in his relationship to his age; in Eluard's case this relationship found expression in the Surrealist revolution in literature and art. This revolution called for a review of a poet's role in society and—at the same time—for new responses in dealing with experience, in choice of subjects, in means of poetic expression. . . . Through a Surrealist aesthetic, he deepened two traditions of nineteenth-century poetry. Eluard continues the Romantic portrayal of the artist-poet, divorced from society by reason of his uniqueness and poetic sensibility; and that of the poet-seer who could give direction to society. For Eluard, these two portraits were intensified through his solitude, made more intense by way of a Surrealist search for originality. The second tradition, that of the artist-priest, from Baudelaire and the Symbolists on, gave rise—in Eluard's poetry—to a personal anguish, through a Surrealist experimentation which called for a total renewal of art.

To describe adequately and properly a seizure of reality, in these terms of poetic sensibility defined in relationship to his age, a poet must deal in images. . . . "Images think for me" is an often quoted statement by Eluard. It implies both an awareness of the poet's individual poetization of the world and an absolute existence of imagery which does not depend on the individual poet. (pp. vii-viii)

Once a poet, and especially a primarily visual poet such as Eluard, discovers how he sees the world and how he pictures the world, he must define for himself content and meaning. These have to do with basic emotions, help him to face solitude and to solve the problem of personal uniqueness. Eluard found that this varied spectrum of experience, especially that of love, could best be given a profound and moving expression through poetry. On the basis of these feelings, he could then proceed to form ideas or ideals of the world, and from this formalism work towards a theory of poetry and of the specific intent of words. . . .

Eluard's world, moreover, is made up of not only an outside world together with an inner world of love for one individual, of ideas, of aesthetic preoccupations, but also of people. For Eluard the facts of experience were varied: Other than love, there was poverty, war, politics, the struggle for freedom; these latter were also the conditions of society. (p. viii)

Underlying the diversity of Eluard's poetic output can be found a theme which unifies this diversity into a coherent picture of the poet's universe. This theme is that of the poet's solitude in particular, and man's solitude in general. It has thus been my main purpose to discover how this loneliness appears in the poet's experience. For Eluard this vision is urgent and he succeeds in imparting to the reader the urgency of his vision. (p. ix)

Robert Nugent, in his Paul Eluard *(copyright ©1974 by Twayne Publishers, Inc.; reprinted with the permission of Twayne Publishers, a Division of G. K. Hall & Co., Boston), Twayne, 1974, 153 p.*

MALCOLM BOWIE (essay date 1977)

Certain general characteristics of Paul Eluard's verse have found their place in the mythology of modern literary culture. The Eluard myth (I shall refer to it as 'Eluard' for the sake of brevity), compounded of much that the poet was and a good deal else that he was not, is so convincingly neat as an imaginative construction that it is often cherished for itself and checked only half-heartedly against the poems actually written. 'Eluard' was invented because the century made him necessary: in an age when anxiety and neurotic distraction were a dominant emotional mode, he represented joy and tranquillity; amid the oppressive clamour of mass society, his voice sounded a note of intimacy and delicate restraint; in an atmosphere of energetic verbal experiment, he was the complete possessor and master of a language; and above all he was an inveterate lyricist, surviving by some unaccountable grace of history into an era of political barbarism and world war. The imagery of 'Eluard' is appropriate to the qualities of sensibility that he is held to epitomise: wings, light, flowers, stars, water, mirrors, the female body in its particulars and its broad outlines. In the world these objects inhabit, energy is transferred in accordance with a restricted set of dynamic principles: diffusion, diffraction, reflection, immersion, interpenetration. The single most appealing and most praised feature of 'Eluard' is that the activities of the poetic mind flawlessly reflect, and are reflected in, the physical processes of the world outside it. That discontinuity between self and world, which for generations of Romantic artists had been a source both of pain and of pride, and a spur to the creative power, has at last given way to willing and versatile collaboration. (p. 149)

Eluard's poems of erotic celebration are his best known. But he also wrote many poems which explore moods of doubt and anxiety; many which take suffering, war, bereavement, cruelty and social injustice as their themes; many which were inspired by political passion and have outspokenly political aims; many which are the product of a finely developed 'negative capability' and show the creative intelligence at grips with an insinuating sense of futility. . . . (pp. 149-50)

Eluard's poetry is richly appealing to the senses. Sense-impressions appear on the surface of many works as an insistent, baffling Brownian motion. Although large, informing patterns of imagery may emerge early in our reading of a poem, our attention is often distracted from these by a jostle of short-lived micro-sensations. The newcomer to Eluard, finding the texture of the poem so alive and so mobile, may have difficulty in deciding where to apply his imaginative effort, or how best to bring the whole thing into focus. What is strange, however, is that the objects which prompt the reader to this abundant sensory activity are often of the barest and most everyday. Eluard's chosen objects are without feature or detail; their surfaces have no roughness or variegation to engage the eye. What is more, he seldom seeks to explore their inner grain, or the minutiae of organic process. (p. 150)

[In an Eluard poem each] thing is enlivened and particularised by its contact with the others and becomes a blank universal when considered alone. Many of these relationships are minutely but firmly subversive and require us to revise the average, practical-minded expectations of order and consequence with which we confront the world. The syntax of the poem provides conditions of exact equivalence for realms of experience that, in the interests of clear thinking and purposeful behaving, it is our custom to keep distinct and to think of hierarchically: the poet's affection is such that no useful distinction remains between natural and man-made, intimate and impersonal, physical and mental, spoken and tacit. (p. 151)

Eluard expects of his reader that he will enjoy thinking laterally, that he will rapidly adopt and discard alternative frames of reference as a poem proceeds and be prepared to seek unusual connections between usual things.

On occasion he relies heavily on the speculative prowess of his reader. The following is an extreme instance, but is in one important way typical of Eluard's method:

> Les oiseaux parfument les bois
> Les rochers leurs grands lacs nocturnes.
>
> [Birds perfume the woods
> Rocks their great nocturnal lakes.]

The reader of this poem may be content to leave the objects it names hovering in a mildly countrified mental cloud—in which case the poem is trivial. Or he may try to determine the exact relations between those objects—in which case he has an embarrassing wealth of possible patterns, none having conspicuously more imaginative authority than the rest. . . . The poem is a teeming manifold of potential relationships. It is fascinating in its huge preponderance of implication over statement—but otherwise scarcely at all. None of the objects has sufficient presence or physical individuality to make relation-seeking into anything more than a faintly amusing intellectual pastime. But we can observe here in miniature a process that takes place in many of Eluard's strongest and most original poems. The lines name physical objects and a single physical action, but their ambiguous syntax gives them a large abstract component. The Eluard landscape does not stay still: we not only see things differently, but we see different things, as fresh syntactic relationships are discovered. The object seen at once in several contexts soon becomes a theoretical, a mentally construed, point of intersection between a variety of possible scenarios. We are invited to look away from the physical object in order to discover what and where it is. The whole process of reading these unstable texts is an oscillatory one: perceived things produce abstract ideas, and those ideas in turn re-generate the very things we departed from. (pp. 152-53)

Syntax of this shifting, multi-dimensional kind is only one cause among many of the constant ferment which takes place within an Eluard text. In my remarks on ['**Première du monde**'] I shall describe several further causes, but I shall also be asking whether—and if so, how—the poet keeps the inner multitude of relationships under control, and so prevents his work from inducing in the reader that state of mental panic which William Empson called 'madhouse and the whole thing there'. . . . The poem traces a simple contour of sexual arousal and fulfilment. But it would be quite inappropriate to say that '**Première du monde**' is 'about' sex, if by this we meant that its diverse nature imagery is present simply to illustrate the modes and rhythms of sexual desire. For the large ontological theme announced in the title is forcibly restated and developed. The phases of sexual self-discovery are timed to coincide with those of a primordial coming-into-being. The poem depicts the emergence of a discrete self within the spawning of phenomena: a sudden, threatened, intermittent awareness of an independent 'me' glimmers within the created order. But this birth is no one-way, progressive movement. Throughout the poem clear contrasts are made between openness and closure, liberation and repression, energy and inertia. The striving of the emergent self towards freedom and autonomy is checked and contested by a backward-looking impulse towards prenatal selflessness. This inner drama now echoes, now is echoed by, the unceasing cosmological drama which surrounds it.

Two important features of Eluard's imagery in this poem belong within familiar and fertile metaphorical traditions. Countless poets have described the female body in geographical or topographical terms, or tinged their landscapes with erotic suggestion. . . . Moreover the interpenetration of woman and landscape in '**Première du monde**' is part of an embracing, pantheistic view of creation at large which also has its distinguished poetic antecedents. . . . But simply to recognise the images as traditional and the theme as archetypal is not to discover the clue to a coherent reading of the text. For Eluard does not work the theme out as a developing story or argument, and does not appoint each image to a fixed place within an overall scheme. In the absence of such a scheme, we have an unusually free choice in deciding how long and how intensely any one impression should flourish before we pass on to the next. The images are loosely organised in accordance with an underlying emotional rhythm: we move from pain and anguish at the start, through various intermediate stages of puzzlement and yearning, towards a tranquil half-resolution in the last line. Although the sleeping woman appears at the end as a dissolver of contradictions, the instance of her power that is specified here . . . refers only obliquely to the crucial inner divisions of self that have gone before. Many Eluard poems end in this way—on a line which, while bringing certain of the main issues to a clearly marked close, leaves us with a strong residue of paradox, and a sense that reflection upon the remaining issues could be extended indefinitely within and beyond the printed limits of the poem.

The underlying emotional pattern is not strong enough to impose any permanent shape upon the volatile word-by-word substance of the text. The fluid and unpredictable exchanges which take place between its local details give the text a remarkable recalcitrance when we seek to tighten our rational grip upon it. . . . Vivid 'cosmic' images and equally vivid images of imprisonment and oppression occur at irregular intervals throughout. Although each set of images tends, by the mutual attraction of its components, to become a self-contained system, the links between the sets are casual and unsystematic. The two may appear to tug against each other, or suddenly to merge. . . . The syntax of the poem, being for the most part composed of the simplest propositional, imperative or interrogative forms, has little power to resist the cross-currents of association that sweep back and forth in the text. Further connections are suggested by Eluard's delicately interwoven transformations of sound. . . . Some of thse links reinforce, and some minutely deflect, the general semantic thrust of the sentences in which they occur.

There is, therefore, a constant tension between the general discursive frames we construct in order to make the detail of the text intelligible and the capacity of the text to produce surplus meanings which none of our frames applied singly can house. The difficulties and discomforts involved in this process should not be exaggerated. For some tension of this sort is inherent in the act of reading: we need a large conjectural sense of any text in order to know how to read its particulars, and we need to keep consulting those particulars in order to know which conjectures are possible and worth pursuing. What is different about poems like '**Première du monde**' is that they are constructed in such a way that the moment of perfect fit between large sense and particulars is indefinitely deferred. For Eluard this imperfection is a guarantee of creativity. (pp. 153-57)

The reader who is accustomed to the robustness and precision of Baudelaire's images, or the piercing brilliance of Rimbaud's, or the bountiful, agglomerative energy of image-makers such as Hugo, Verhaeren or Péguy, may find the sensuous fabric of Eluard's verse thin and insubstantial. But if we take

Eluard on his own terms, we can see that the recreation in words of an immediate, abrasive contact with the sensible world was not among his aims. He gives us in each poem a series of potential impressions. The fluctuating and often incompatible structures around which the text is built compel us to think and feel in the transitional realm *between* images and turn us into the inventors rather than the simple receivers of sensation. If the reader withholds his inventive power he is likely to be disappointed, and to find his imagination rewarded with no more than a pleasant, quickly forgotten ripple-and-flutter. (p. 157)

The intuition that, in Walt Whitman's words, 'a vast similitude interlocks all', provides Eluard with one of his most absorbing themes. . . . It is remarkable that an idea declared as often as this, and having in certain of its versions an unwieldy absoluteness about it, should not become a nostrum, a comforting doctrinal appurtenance, but should remain available to the poet as a spur to further innovating thought.

The idea reached its highest point of development and of usefulness as a structural device in the long poem *Poésie ininterrompue*. . . . In this work the discovery of sameness appears not only as the essential creative impetus within the life of the mind, but as an essential tendency of the 'world-process' as a whole. *Poésie ininterrompue* is Eluard's most ambitious attempt to represent the sensation of perfect continuity and an endless, abundant overspilling of vital energy. It begins and ends with suspension points, presenting itself as no more than a sample excised from a larger, unstoppable process. Eluard was outstandingly resourceful in adapting the tone and diction of his short lyrical poems to the new demands which this project made. (pp. 159-60)

The general plan of Eluard's [*Poésie ininterrompue*] is extremely simple. The opening section contains a vision of sameness. This is followed by an extended section in which the notion of sameness is reiterated, challenged by difference and discrepancy, and amplified to include these challengers within itself. The poem ends . . . with a restatement of its dominant idea, but now seen as unconditional, unlimited in scope and invulnerable to contradiction. It is difficult to imagine less promising dramatic material than this totalising and equalising vision of human experience. Yet Eluard creates and maintains dramatic intensity in his poem, by presenting sameness in sharply differentiated versions. (pp. 160-61)

Poésie ininterrompue is a brilliant poem. In it Eluard works out his largest and boldest poetic design and successfully incorporates within that design a host of clearly focused and clearly related particulars. There is no separation between the sensible and intelligible worlds: seeing, feeling, imagining and abstract thinking flow along together in ever-changing alliances. Conceptual pattern-making emerges in *Poésie ininterrompue* not as a means of retreat from the uncertainties and perils of sensory awareness, but as an enhancement of that awareness, and as a potent expression of animal vitality. Eluard seeks to re-activate the grand emotional commonplaces and to harness those underlying rhythms of the human organism from which sensations, feelings and ideas derive their peculiar shapes. This enterprise is a dangerous one and offers much scope for loose, sub-philosophical rant. Eluard has avoided the danger by attending closely to the minute and the strange in human experience, and by restoring to commonplaces their share of dramatic surprise. (pp. 164-65)

Eluard's imagination endows the world with a new teeming energy and an exhilarating plurality of forms. Familiar distinctions and definitions are set aside, and objects are freed from their everyday settings. But for his thought to be thought at all the poet must seek for new distinctions within his unstable, recreated world. And this difficult quest is permanently threatened by the seductive and terrifying equation: anything = anything else.

My main objection to the Eluard I sketched at the beginning is that the myth misrepresents the texture of Eluard's verse and understates by far the imaginative and intellectual excitement which it can provoke in the reader. To be 'Eluardian', within the terms of the myth, is to be uncommonly alert to minor nervous tremors, skilled in the expression of elementary emotion, fluently continuous in utterance—and little else. This will not do, as I hope I have shown. Eluard's verse has, to be sure, an exceptional fluidity of texture; there are few radical breaks within any one poem, and no monumental finalities; every idea, image and emotion is subject to transformation. But this constant self-adjustment of the text does not produce a smooth-moving pavement on which the reader is unthinkingly transported. . . . Eluard's text derives its mobility not from the mutual confirmation of image by image, but from a complex play of internal tensions, which is sustained by a sequence of paradoxes, anomalies and imaginative side-steppings. By placing discrete materials side by side and by setting up and then rapidly replacing his explanatory frameworks, the poet constantly calls upon the collaborative intelligence of his reader. The paradoxicalness and crowded multiplicity of the text make considerable demands upon our patience and ingenuity. But we are rewarded for our pains by a wonderfully strong and delicate imaginative pattern. (p. 166)

Malcolm Bowie, "Paul Eluard," in Sensibility and Creation: Studies in Twentieth-Century French Poetry, *edited by Roger Cardinal (© 1977 by Roger Cardinal; by permission of Barnes & Noble Books, a Division of Littlefield, Adams & Co., Inc), Barnes & Noble, 1977, pp. 149-67.*

MARILYN KALLET   (essay date 1980)

The love which illumines the verses of Eluard's late poetry takes different forms as the poet is confronted by sudden personal tragedy in 1946 and must find his way back to the living through language. The music of each book differs. There are poems in *The Firm Desire to Endure* that seem to play jigs ("**To Marc Chagall**"); songs that sound more solemn, wedding hymns ("**Order and Disorder of Love**"); other poems sing the blues ("**Here**"). In *Time Overflows* there are poems of grief that have barely crossed the border into speech but, once uttered, present not merely a personal voice, but a human voice as rich with sorrow and as disciplined in its expression as ancient tragic verse.

In *Memorable Body* there is sensual music, and *The Phoenix* offers us a fervent, "lively air" of reawakened love. Eluard was fifty-six at the time of the composition of *The Phoenix* . . . ; he brings all of his experience and technical skill to bear to make the poems flow easily toward the reader. Having found love again at this time in his life, the poet conveys to us a sense of steadiness and affirmation at the heart of the marvelous.

Together the four books tell a personal and mythic story: of Eluard's love for his wife Nusch and for a life graced by their love; of shock and grief over his wife's sudden death; of purgatory, the life of the senses renewed through friendship and sensual love; of the rebirth of the couple and community through a new marriage to Dominique. The pattern is Orphic, expressing a drama of descent from bliss into extreme suffering, then reemergence into strength and oneness. But the pattern is not arbitrary—for Eluard had a will and a passion for renewal. While he did not seek grief and solitude, he was determined to begin again with "new and pure eyes" after each confrontation with the depths of the abyss.

The important books of *Last Love Poems* . . . were selected from among other works written by Eluard in the late 1940s and early 1950s. The surrealist poets, among whom Eluard was a moving force in the nineteen-twenties and thirties, delighted in seeing the surprises, unexpected meanings, and hidden poetry that juxtapositions could create. The four books juxtaposed against one another as we find them dramatize a plot and a marvelous poetic continuity that underlies Eluard's late work. (pp. xvi-xvii)

[The mood of *The Firm Desire to Endure*] is predominantly one of joy and innocence, for the poet takes renewed delight in seeing Paris and the world around him that has been freed from Nazi occupation. In these poems Eluard luxuriates in the bonds that he shares with his wife Nusch, whose love has provided a source and symbol of cohesiveness against the destructiveness of war. Eluard rejoices as well with tenderness for the French people, his community, which has survived the disaster. The poems are more than a sigh of relief, they are songs and celebrations of relief; yet all the while the verses retain a memory of the war's shattering power. Like Blake's *Songs of Innocence* the poems of *The Firm Desire to Endure* contain traces and omens of a world of experience and destruction. There are still "waves of walls and the absent air of children" to remind us of the misery caused by the Second World War. Though Eluard's songs are apparently simple, they are never foolish in their joyfulness. The "firm desire to endure" is also a difficult desire to endure: it is hard to sustain hope in a time when so much has been devastated.

The first poem in this series of love poems is to Marc Chagall. It is fitting that the book opens with a song that transmits the poet's love of seeing. What we see is renewal: fresh, bright colors of gold, green, red, and blue tint this poem, and set the tone for this book of inner brightness and renewed hope. In the way of the best surrealist collaborations, Eluard wrote the poem in a style imitative of Chagall's lyricism and playfulness in painting (while knowing that the poem would be illustrated by Chagall in the first edition). Animals come dancing in on the first line; man is not far behind, and he, too, is a dancer with his woman. The buoyancy of the poem defies gravity and sets the stage for gestures of ascent and return that are reenacted throughout Eluard's poetry. Eluard wanted his poems to be heard, sung, painted, danced, to be enjoyed to the utmost by his readers.

The most striking of the books, perhaps one of the most beautiful and sad works in French poetry, is *Time Overflows*. . . . These poems require all of Eluard's mastery and control to express his overwhelming grief after Nusch's death. Here is an honest language, stripped of any verbal or emotional pretenses. (pp. xvii-xviii)

In *Time Overflows* Eluard expresses a state of stasis, dismemberment, as he is severed from his wife and from himself: "My eyes tore themselves from your eyes / They lose their confidence they lose their light." Eluard finds himself in an "extended desert" where time and space no longer promise growth,

but threaten him with a terrible emptiness. The poet is never sentimental in these poems of grief; he states his feelings directly, as facts: "I was so close to you that I am cold near others."

Yet the last poem in the book is one of hope, for "the firm desire to endure" pushes the poet toward life again, toward life-giving sources. By temperament Eluard could not tolerate solitude; in his sorrow he turned all the more to a vision of intimacy and community for solace. . . . (p. xviii)

The poems in *Memorable Body* . . . sing of the return of the poet's senses; the language has to it an atmosphere of lubricity, evoking the "sleek and humid spectacle" of the lover's body. Time, which had tortured Eluard in his grief, again holds the possibility of pleasure. . . . However, *Memorable Body* is also a book of conflict, for the memory of Nusch keeps calling the poet away from life. (pp. xviii-xix)

The poems of *The Phoenix* . . . are a tribute to Dominique, and to love's power to restore a man's life. Images of the community return with the return of personal love and commitment; the networks of communication that make the world a habitable place are re-created for Eluard. . . .

Yet one might find traces in *The Phoenix* of Eluard's premonition of his death. There is a tone of urgency in **"Seascape"** as Eluard sings, "Outside the boats are in low tide / Everything must be said in a few words." In these lines Eluard sums up his sense of responsibility to his craft. The poet knows that he speaks to and for many, and that he must do so with the greatest economy. . . .

The accessibility of Eluard's late poetry is a sign of his respect for the reader. His poems do not turn in and round upon themselves in glorification of their own form, but make a fraternal gesture toward the reader. The purpose of the love poems is to communicate, to share feeling and the joys of perception through music. Eluard frequently uses the word *nu*, or *naked*, in his poetry—like the lover's body the poet's language "simplifies itself" in its bareness. The banishment of excesses and eccentricities of style helps the poet to reach a wide audience.

Eluard usually relies on a basic vocabulary, one in common usage. We are not distracted by the words of Eluard's poetry and therefore through their combinations words are free to deliver up the poems' incantatory power. (p. xix)

Even in the incantations the poet's statements are direct, spoken with the rhythm of speech or song, conveyed in the syntax of the ordinary sentence. The refrain, such as that used in **"I Love You,"** is one of the basic devices of poetry, and as such is not only incantatory but is a sign of a common experience: the refrain repeats and rehearses the poet's feelings so that the reader understands and participates in the story, in a progression of emotion toward joy. (pp. xix-xx)

Though Eluard never sought to distort language in his poetry, his early dadaist and surrealist works are by their nature experimental and therefore less direct than later poems such as *Last Love Poems*. These love poems represent the summation of a career; they are the result of a poetic evolution that took place over thirty years. Historical circumstances as well as constant experimentation with the craft of poetry helped to reinforce in Eluard a commitment to poetry that would be less hermetic than surrealist poetry. (p. xx)

Eluard did not give up his love of the marvelous in the late poems, as we can see from the most surrealistic poem in *Last*

Love Poems. **"I Still Live,"** with its "blue globules of a discolored world," its dreamlike imagery, or from the "rainbowed" surfaces of **"To Marc Chagall."** But the poems, the "human trellis between us," always return to earth, to the people who live within them. The last love poems have content, not just imagery; they tell of love and of a will to keep living.

More than a quarter of a century after Eluard's death, we can now see that he was not only a surrealist innovator but also a great poet, whose life impressed upon him the need to communicate with his society. Eluard is a love poet, a poet of dreams and of the inner life responsive to the external world. His passion to create poetry that includes people and can be shared, a language "of one and two, of everyone," that keeps extending itself, is a kind of Whitmanesque devotion to language that joins people and sings their lives. It is not with Breton, but with [Pablo] Neruda that we should compare Eluard, in terms of his stature as a poet and of his impact on his audience. Neruda admired Eluard greatly for his "passionate lucidity." Eluard's poetry, like Neruda's, became a public language and a public good. The inner action of Eluard's poetry, the "firm desire to endure," reminds us to listen for "language charged with hope even when it is desperate" among our best contemporary poets. (p. xxiii)

> *Marilyn Kallet, "Introduction" (reprinted by permission of Louisiana State University Press; copyright © 1980 by Marilyn Kallet), in* Last Love Poems of Paul Eluard *by Paul Eluard, translated by Marilyn Kallet, Louisiana State University Press, 1980, pp. xv-xxiii.*

ADDITIONAL BIBLIOGRAPHY

Carmody, Francis J. "Eluard's Rupture with Surrealism." *PMLA* LXXVI, No. 4 (September 1961): 436-46.

Discussion of the history and events surrounding Eluard's break with surrealism and André Breton in 1938. Carmody considers the possible reasons for Eluard's rupture with surrealism and how the break affected the poet in the following years.

Hubert, Renée Riese. "Ernst and Eluard: A Model of Surrealist Collaboration." *Kentucky Romance Quarterly* XXI, No. 1 (1974): 113-21.

Critical discussion of the collaboration between Eluard and surrealist painter Max Ernst on the volume *Répétitions*. Hubert discusses the effect, in *Répétitions*, of merging the visual and literary arts.

Roy, Claude. "Paul Eluard." In *Selected Writings of Paul Eluard*, by Paul Eluard, translated by Lloyd Alexander, pp. vii-xx. Norfolk, Conn.: New Directions, 1951.

Brief biography which attempts to capture the essence of Paul Eluard by discussing his life and his writing.

Showalter, English, Jr. "Biographical Aspects of Eluard's Poetry." *PMLA* LXXVIII, No. 3 (June 1963): 280-86.

Examination of three major crises in Eluard's career—his disappearance from Paris in 1924; the breakup of his first marriage in 1930; and his rupture with Breton and the surrealists in 1938—as revealed in Eluard's poetry of the time.

Wake, C. H. "Eluard: 'L'Extase'." In *The Art of Criticism: Essays in French Literary Analysis*, edited by Peter H. Nurse, pp. 287-99. Edinburgh: Edinburgh University Press, 1969.

A critical analysis of Eluard's poem "L'extase" in his collection entitled *Le temps deborde*.

Whiting, Charles G. "Eluard's Poems for Gala." *French Review* XLI, No. 2 (December 1967): 505-17.

Critical discussion of Eluard's relationship with his first wife, Gala, and its influence on his poetry from early 1914 through 1936, seven years after their separation. Whiting contends Eluard's poetry was affected by the flagrant contradictions between his idealized vision of woman and the actual turmoil surrounding his marriage with Gala.

Whiting, Charles G. "Verlainian Reflections in Eluard's Poetry." *Romantic Review* LXI (1970): 182-86.

Discussion of the possible influence of Verlaine on the early poetry of Eluard.

York, R. A. "Eluard's Game of Construction." *Orbis Litterarum* 32, No. 1 (1977): 83-96.

Critical study of Eluard's poetic technique, particularly his structuring of images in *Capitale de la douleur*.

(Stella Maria Sarah) Miles Franklin

1879-1954

(Also wrote under pseudonym of Brent of Bin Bin) Australian novelist, biographer, critic, and autobiographer.

Franklin made a sudden appearance on the literary scene with her first novel, *My Brilliant Career*, written when she was sixteen. Though the work contains the flaws of structure and composition that might be expected from such a young author, it also displays vigor, budding talent, a pervasive feminism, and the strong nationalism that was developing in Australia. A. G. Stephens, editor of the Sydney *Bulletin*, praised *My Brilliant Career* as "the very first Australian novel to be published . . . that might not have been written by a stranger or a sojourner."

Franklin was born on her grandmother's cattle station in southern New South Wales and grew up in the Australian outback. She later recounted her youth in *Childhood at Brindabella*, an idealized autobiography. *My Brilliant Career*, when it first appeared, proved an embarrassment to Franklin's family and friends, who, along with most contemporary critics, assumed the poverty, drunkenness, and melodramatic episodes portrayed in the novel were more autobiographical than fictional. In fact, while her heroine's attitudes were Franklin's, the details of her heroine's life were not. Upset by the misinterpretation, Franklin wrote a satiric sequel, *My Career Goes Bung*, which was not published for forty-five years. Franklin eventually suppressed her first book, making provisions for its publication ten years after her death. She referred to the novel in her volume of literary criticism, *Laughter, Not for a Cage*, as a "girl's story . . . conceived and tossed off on impulse in a matter of weeks." She withdrew the work from print because of "the stupid literalness with which it was taken to be her own autobiography," which "startled and disillusioned then constrained her." After *My Brilliant Career* was published, Franklin worked briefly in Sydney as a freelance journalist before traveling to the United States. She worked in Chicago for the National Women's Trade Union League, and wrote the novel *Some Everyday Folk and Dawn*, in which she attempted unsuccessfully to write about the United States with the same informal intimacy that had characterized her Australian stories. At the start of World War I Franklin moved to London, becoming active in social work, and did not return to Australia until 1933. It was in her later life that she established the Miles Franklin Award, a prize of five hundred pounds awarded annually to the best novel illuminating a phase of Australian life.

In 1930 *Up the Country* appeared under the pseudonym "Brent of Bin Bin." Since at that time Franklin had published only her first two books, she was not thought of as the possible author. But as more of her works appeared, along with five more novels by "Brent of Bin Bin," critics began to note the similarities of style, vocabulary, characterization, theme, and setting in both Franklin's and "Brent's" works. Events in the Bin Bin books, which corresponded to events in Franklin's own life, seemed to support the argument of her authorship. Franklin never publicly claimed authorship of the Bin Bin books, but friends have said that in her last years she privately admitted having written them. Most critics today believe that

Courtesy Australian Information Service

she did so, although some cite her steadfast public denial as proof of alternate authorship. Some critics have conjectured that she possibly wrote them in collaboration with another author, or that she worked almost directly from existing records. The novels signed by "Brent of Bin Bin" share with those signed by Miles Franklin pride and joy in Australian nationalism, dissatisfaction with the status of women, and great admiration for the pioneer, the squatter, the farmer, and the swagman, who explored, homesteaded, and opened up the new continent.

Aside from *My Brilliant Career*, Franklin's most significant work is *All That Swagger*, a saga spanning well over a hundred years in the lives of a family of European immigrants in Australia. The chief figure in the chronicle is Danny Delacey, called Franklin's most skillful male characterization. Delacey was based, as was the hero of the earlier *Old Blastus of Bandicoot*, on Franklin's grandfather; in fact, most of Franklin's plots and characters were drawn from her life and family history. It is when she attempted to write about non-Australian places and people that her writing was weakest. *All That Swagger*, and the "Brent of Bin Bin" novel series, helped to popularize the saga form in English writing.

Franklin is not recognized for style and technique; she never fully mastered either. Rather, it is for her vivid portrayal of a unique period in the history of Australia that she is remembered. She recreated Australia's pastoral age from the point of view of those who, as Franklin's biographer Marjorie Barnard phrased it, brought about "the peaceful conquest of a continent."

PRINCIPAL WORKS

My Brilliant Career (novel) 1901
Some Everyday Folk and Dawn (novel) 1909
Up the Country [as Brent of Bin Bin] (novel) 1928
Ten Creeks Run [as Brent of Bin Bin] (novel) 1930
Back to Bool Bool [as Brent of Bin Bin] (novel) 1931
Old Blastus of Bandicoot (novel) 1931
All That Swagger (novel) 1936
Pioneers on Parade [with Dymphna Cusack] (novel) 1939
Joseph Furphy [with Kate Baker] (biography) 1944
My Career Goes Bung (novel) 1946
Prelude to Waking [as Brent of Bin Bin] (novel) 1950
Cockatoos [as Brent of Bin Bin] (novel) 1954
Gentlemen at Gyang Gyang [as Brent of Bin Bin] (novel) 1956
Laughter, Not for a Cage (criticism) 1956
Childhood at Brindabella (autobiography) 1963

HENRY LAWSON (essay date 1901)

A few months before I left Australia I got a letter from the bush signed "Miles Franklin," saying that the writer had written a novel, but knew nothing of editors and publishers, and asking me to read and advise. Something about the letter, which was written in a strong original hand, attracted me, so I sent for the MS., and one dull afternoon I started to read it. I hadn't read three pages when I saw what you will no doubt see at once—that the story had been written by a girl. And as I went on I saw that the work was Australian—born of the bush. I don't know about the girlishly emotional parts of the book—I leave that to girl readers to judge; but the descriptions of bush life and scenery came startlingly, painfully real to me, and I know that, as far as they are concerned, the book is true to Australia—the truest I ever read.

I wrote to Miles Franklin, and she confessed that she was a girl. I saw her before leaving Sydney. She is just a little bush girl, barely twenty-one yet, and has scarcely ever been out of the bush in her life. She has lived her book, and I feel proud of it for the sake of the country I came from, where people toil and bake and suffer and are kind; where every second sunburnt bushman is a sympathetic humorist, with the sadness of the bush deep in his eyes and a brave grin for the worst of times, and where every third bushman is a poet, with a big heart that keeps his pockets empty.

Henry Lawson, in his preface to My Brilliant Career *by Miles Franklin, William Blackwood & Sons, 1901 (and reprinted by Washington Square Press, 1981, p. v).*

HAVELOCK ELLIS (essay date 1903)

[*My Brilliant Career* is what] we may reasonably expect from a new country; the novel of the young and ambitious woman who dreams of the large world beyond the loneliness and pettiness of her own narrow life. . . . It is a vivid and sincere book, certainly the true reflection of a passionate young nature, impatient of the inevitable limitations of the life around her. Such a book has psychological interest, the interest that belongs to the confessions of a Marie Basghkirtseff of the bush; but something more than emotion is needed to make fine literature; and here we miss any genuine instinct of art or any mature power of thought, and are left at the end with only a painful sense of crudity. Miles Franklin is ardently devoted to Australia, but to a remote ideal Australia, and in the eagerness of her own embittered and egoistical mood she tramples under foot the things that really make Australia.

Havelock Ellis, in his excerpt (originally published in "Fiction in the Australian Bush," in Weekly Critical Review, *September 17, 1903), in* Miles Franklin *by Ray Mathew, Lansdowne Press, 1963, p. 8.*

ARTHUR ASHWORTH (essay date 1951)

When all six books, [*Prelude to Waking, Up the Country, Ten Creeks Run, Cockatoos, Gentlemen at Gyang Gyang,* and *Back to Bool Bool*], are available an estimate of the full importance of Brent of Bin Bin in our literature may be attempted. But for the present an interim report can be made.

The final estimate will be even more interesting if the conjectures of many critics as to the identity of the fabulous Brent are correct. At the moment, however, nothing can be added to these surmises, based on the provocative clues contained in prefaces and dedications, and on other clues internal and external. The identity of Brent of Bin Bin is to be revealed after the six novels have been finally published. It seems only fair that an anonymity so carefully preserved for twenty-five years should be maintained until the works have all appeared.

Apart from *Prelude to Waking,* the Brent novels develop the themes and follow the fortunes of the pioneer families of Bool Bool and their descendants. The as yet unpublished novels *Cockatoos* and *Gentlemen at Gyang Gyang* are referred to in footnotes in *Back to Bool Bool* in explanation of past incidents touched on there. Thus the last five novels have this unity, and, as far as one can tell, form a sequence. The people of the last novel, *Back to Bool Bool,* are referred to in the last paragraph of the first novel, *Up to Country,* and the "homecoming festival" foreshadowed there forms the conclusion to the last book. It is the completion of a plan, the scope of which covers some eighty years from approximately 1850 to 1930, and which traces the lives of a great number of people, bringing the latest generation back to the scene of the first for a "grand corroboree of remembrance". Thus we have what must be Australia's greatest chronicle novel, written in five solid volumes. (pp. 196-97)

It is surprising to find *Prelude to Waking* cropping up at this time as the first [episode in the saga of the pioneer families of Bool Bool]. It is a difficult, ill-wrought and uneasy book, a period piece already though it is set in the early twenties and the London of that time. It is perhaps a prelude to the waking of the author to the rich sources and materials discussed in the preface to *Up the Country*. In its play of ideas it is closest to *Back to Bool Bool*. . . . Like that novel, it comments extensively on the state of things then, as they concerned the world at large and Australia and England in particular.

But it seems safe to take *Prelude to Waking* as being written before the five Bool Bool novels. The difference in grasp of technique and handling of situation and character between it and the later novels is remarkable, even though the same mind left its distinctive mark on all of them. The adolescent fooling in the writing and the verbal pyrotechnics, the exuberant use of exclamation marks and pointed underlinings, the tortuous and cunning intricacies of style, the extravagant names given the people—especially the women—the bizarre words employed on occasions, the odd characters from romantic fiction and the films: all these things are less apparent in the later books. In them is indicated a growing confidence and sense of craftsmanship.

The mannerisms of style and expression in *Prelude to Waking* must cause any reader to pause. There seems to be no need for such exuberant and embarrassing foolery as is contained in the style of writing of the first few pages, and it has the further disadvantage in that few reviewers of the book appear to have survived them. Until the explanations are made, the flash-backs completed and the situation clarified so that the plot can begin to unwind, it is difficult to distinguish the wood from the trees. What Brent has to say is generally worth hearing, but these perverse difficulties force a reader to the task of over-hearing rather than hearing.

Yet *Prelude to Waking* grows in force as all the Brent books do. It has many aspects: part treatise, part romantic love story, part a penetrating and realistic analysis of relations between the sexes, and part an exact picture of the life of the time when it was written. It foreshadows most of the themes that are typical of the Brent books: the views on what England and Australia can learn from each other, the position of women in the community, the war of the sexes and a complex anti-male attitude. Of these, in the words of Brent, "more anon". (pp. 197-98)

This difficult, subtle and curious novel is a strange introduction to Brent of Bin Bin. But with the decision to embark upon the long chronicle of Bool Bool and its people, the writer moved into a setting fixed in certainty by long association and early memory, and into a period given validity and colour by legend and reminiscence. (p. 198)

[The Bool Bool books] follow the general pattern of *Up the Country* in construction, opening with a significant event, in this case the marriage of Rachel Mazere, which will bring a great number of people together. When they are assembled the "possuming" process begins in a series of flash-backs, setting them in place as members of the community and establishing their relationships to each other. Then the plot moves forward from point to point, the focus of interest moving swiftly from one to another, weaving together in a complex pattern a number of lives and motives.

In effect, what the technique reduces itself to is a very clever understatement of an almost epic theme. It is achieved by a rigid attention to the affair immediately in the focus of attention, and only in the big crowded scenes—race-meetings, balls, weddings and funerals—is a glimpse of the larger pattern allowed. At the end of the book the intention of the writer becomes plain. The reader has been forced to live through the day to day commonplaces, trials, decisions, family tragedies, of a great number of people, without it being insisted that these are the human threads which are woven into the cloth of history.

But suddenly the cloth is produced and the significance of all its threads becomes plain.

More than this, as far as one can tell without the evidence of the two still unpublished works, the effect of the novels is also cumulative. The last one, *Back to Bool Bool,* brings the descendants of the original people back to the original place for the final crowd scene. The full pattern is circular in its return to the starting point, in its re-enacting of the vanished and the storied past, in the weird tragedy at the Fish Hole where the legendary Emily Mazere was drowned on the day before her wedding. Thus the present can be evaluated in the light of the now fabulous past. But also the patterns of conduct of the present follow the old tracings; history is duplicated in a more profound way than the sentimental pageantry of Back to Bool Bool Week. The full import of the irony is revealed suddenly and unexpectedly in the deliberately contrived disaster of the last few pages; the living actors are caught in the same web as those of the past, and move towards the same frustrations or partial fulfilments.

The glamour of the past, lying upon the events and the eras of the early novels in the series, lends an air of romance to the books. It is a shock to discover that the technique of the writer can achieve this by the same method of keeping each single incident in the complex maze on a plane of present reality. The great flood of the Yarrabongo, and the drowning of Emily in the Fish Hole are two key events in *Up the Country*. They are done in graphic manner in a mood of straight realism. But later, in the reminiscences of other characters in other books, in the minds of the aged who were young then, they acquire the colour of romance. Eventually they become legendary, part of the high romance of the rich and glowing past. The art of the chronicler allows the reader to have it both ways.

These novels are invaluable as chronicles which depict the squatting era in New South Wales with an intimacy and penetration which bespeak first hand information, if not experience. (pp. 199-200)

But the Bool Bool novels are not only chronicle novels. They investigate with some skill the private struggle. The clash of temperaments within families and the relations between the sexes are the two main aspects of this. From one aspect they are all love stories, repeating in a variety of forms the Brent version of the war of the sexes. And this is a most fascinating war, because one is beguiled into romance and sentiment, then shocked by the writer insisting upon realism at a point where a really romantic writer would consider it a most impossible intrusion. Romantic happiness is reserved for the lesser characters, and a tragic frustration, allied with fortitude, is the lot of the chief personages. "Amour" is analysed with a clinical objectivity, due tribute being paid to its glamour, its power to "roll the universe into a ball and toss it towards the overwhelming question", and also to the astonishing lack of permanence in an emotion which is so convincing because it seems eternal. Merlin Giltinane, the first Brent woman, is one with Freda Healy, the last, in being capable of love and its pangs but incapable of consummation. Freda's analysis of herself on this question in *Back to Bool Bool* is one of the most subtle and penetrating studies of a woman's mind one is likely to read anywhere. But Merlin and she, along with others of this fascinating and perverse type of woman created by Brent, are doomed to "fortitude", so that they move towards a state of mind which no disaster can upset.

Alongside these are set a gallery of women who seek their consummation in romantic marriage, deliberate contrasts to the woman who eschews sentiment completely in the sex relationship, even though she can suffer greatly through being in love. The third group is a bitter one, of the unloved and unlovable woman.

The men characters are convincing enough, but are not as intimately analysed. They are done from the outside, particularly men like old Mr Mazere of Three Rivers. Only the sensitive and artistic men like Dick Mazere reveal their minds to any depth. Men are shown also mostly in their relations with women, and here the interactions of characters are extremely well portrayed. But scenes of men in relationship with men and among men are not handled.

Over the novels the spirit of peace broods with a compelling charm. "The rivers lean on the mountains and the mountains lean on the sky." The setting is created with a lyric fervour that springs from a delicate and loving perception. Its presence grows and pervades, becoming stronger as the associations of time passing are bound up with it, and the roots of people are established in localities. The backdrop is always present in memory or in picture as the rivers of the Monaro come down to the Murrumbidgee.

The books, of course, make few concessions to the reader. This is part of an attitude which makes it more difficult for one without the necessary background to appreciate the final quality of the achievement. For those who have never lived "up country", or are unacquainted with its literature, certain things are withholden. They are never explained, and a great deal is taken for granted. We are, naturally, in better case than the reviewer of *Ten Creeks Run* in the *Times Literary Supplement* in 1931 who wrote: "A rattling good book which even the hideous Australian place-names cannot disfigure." The names at least are not hideous to us now. Neither should the idiom be—in turn dry, sardonic, exuberant, sentimental, crude; or the style—casual, wilful, deceptively haphazard. The writer, like Furphy, had to find a new way of conveying the flavour of a life which had not been completely captured before. The Jindyworobaks, in a different medium, strove for the same thing. These books are determinedly Australian, though not offensively so, and they offer the same sort of independent challenge that Ben Jonson did in his prologue to the Masque *Hymenaei:*

> And I do heartily forgive their ignorance
> Whom it chanceth not to please.

(pp. 200-02)

Arthur Ashworth, "Brent of Bin Bin," in Southerly, *Vol. 12, No. 4, 1951, pp. 196-202.*

MILES FRANKLIN   (essay date 1954)

The first part of this century in our writings was a prolongation of the eighties and nineties. . . .

Two first novels were hailed for their Australianism: *My Brilliant Career,* by Miles Franklin and *Such is Life,* by Tom Collins (Joseph Furphy). The first was adolescently vehement, defiant in realism but winning attention from the critics here and abroad, as well as ardent readers of all ages and both sexes in every quarter of the Commonwealth, though it was refused publication here. (p. 118)

My Brilliant Career and *Such is Life* were widely different. There was a corresponding difference between their authors, one a girl, the other, as he said when introducing himself to her, a mature philosopher. The girl's story was conceived and tossed off on impulse in a matter of weeks, spontaneously out of inexperience and consuming longings and discontents, and half humourously, as its author has stated in print, to show how impossible the Australian scene was for novel-making. Inadvertently the opposite was demonstrated to an extent which enabled [A. G. Stephens, editor of the Sydney *Bulletin*] on occasion to cite *My Brilliant Career* when estimating the realism of more mature efforts. Furphy's novel, he said, "embalms accurate representations of our characters and customs, life and scenery, which in so skilled and methodical a form occur in no other book I know". He said further that its author was a "humorous priestly rationalist", that the book contained all the wit and wisdom gathered in his lifetime—". . . it is his one book—it is himself".

A man writing, not a writing man: a girl and a man writing: one dashing off an impatient animadversion, the other composing a serious treatise to which readers could listen or not, though the author was patiently and humorously confident that in the long run they would. Furphy was experienced in Australian life, had libraries of literary and miscellaneous knowledge in his memory, and was over forty before he could sit down to write: he was sixty when his novel got into print. A novel of sixteen and one of sixty, yet there was such kinship between the authors that Furphy's extravagant hopes for his young contemporary, his belief in her "genius", embarrassed her, while he became an object of reverent affection to her both as man and writer. The two novels are urgent in attitudes that were ripening throughout the continent and focused by the *Bulletin.* Miles Franklin was outside the *Bulletin*'s circle, and is the only writer of comparable ability whose name is not in the weekly's seventieth anniversary roll call. Her early novel nevertheless burns with the nationalism rampant at the time. After a number of editions, the author firmly withdrew it because the stupid literalness with which it was taken to be her own autobiography startled and disillusioned then constrained her. It has long been out of print and therefore of no further concern herein. (pp. 118-19)

[Into the second century] the Australian writer found himself with a usable past and began to exploit it with the zest of a parvenu discovering he has a family tree. . . . Two vigorous writers who began to recall old days as a pair by contrast are Brent of Bin Bin and Brian Penton. Brent deals with the cool country in the south-east of New South Wales, Penton with a warmer climate in the south of Queensland. (pp. 173-74)

P. R. Stephensen refers to the "vast jollity" of Brent of Bin Bin, C. H. Grattan to his "great chronicle". Mr Penton imbibed the current excitants: Brent succumbed to tenderness. *Up the Country,* the unpretentious title of the first story of three, is as ductile geographically as *Such is Life* is philosophically. It suggests indulgence of unashamed reminiscence by a returning native. This mood continued through *Ten Creeks Run* and remained in uneasy streaks in *Back to Bool Bool.* Brent dotes on his people and is incapable of sustaining villainy in any of them. He showed, however, when the softening haze of the past melted in the hard light of the present, a political and sociological awareness of much that was disturbing, though the infatuation and tenderness remained. He abrogated sophistry and was indifferent to possible neglect. . . . (p. 180)

The characters and their lives are treated as seriously and minutely as those in successful European novels of the date, and with horses remarkable as personalities. . . .

Such an intricate presentation of a portion of Australian life on its own terms without concessions to the current compulsions may have been a waste of zest and talent. (p. 181)

> *Miles Franklin, "The New Century" and "Reappearance of the Australian Novel in Force" (1954), in her* Laughter, Not for a Cage: Notes on Australian Writing, with Biographical Emphasis on the Struggles, Functions, and Achievements of the Novel in Three Half-Centuries *(reprinted with the permission of Angus & Robertson (UK) Ltd Publishers), Angus & Robertson, 1956, pp. 118-38, 167-86.**

BEATRICE DAVIS   (essay date 1955)

[Miles Franklin] was great in character and in talent, great in her devotion to Australia, great in constant affirmation of the Australian outlook that was her creed.

The circumstances of her life are essential to an understanding of the person—the *personage,* indeed—that was Miles Franklin. They show the outback origins from which her love of the Australian landscape sprang, the influence of the writers of the nineties on the young girl she was then, the youthful revolt and almost morbid sensitivity that made her forsake her Australia for nearly thirty years, the immense nostalgia (dating from her self-banishment) that gave her writing and her conversation such intensity of Australian vision. . . . Memories of the Monaro and of the Murrumbidgee, and of the country near Goulburn to which her father moved in the nineties, form the background, crystallized and magnified, for most of Miles Franklin's novels—and for those of Brent of Bin Bin.

As well as being in love with the Australian countryside and seeing her family and other pioneering families as part of an Australian pageant and tradition, Miles Franklin was a critic of the social order of her day, and particularly of the dullness and "tame hennishness" (as she termed it) of women's lives. *My Brilliant Career,* written when she was seventeen and published in 1901, is ebullient in lyricism and passionate in protest; and, being autobiographical in form, it caused some stir among family friends as well as among critics. While being acclaimed by A. G. Stephens as "the first Australian novelist", Miles Franklin, with the kindly connivance of her parents, disappeared—to spend twelve months in Sydney and Melbourne as a domestic servant, from which experience she hoped to gain material for a further novel. . . . Then, in 1905, she left Australia and did not return (except to visit her parents briefly in 1923-4 and in 1930) until 1933.

Miles Franklin's time abroad appears to have been devoted mainly to causes that stirred her sympathies. In America she worked with Alice Henry for the National Women's Trade Union League which published the magazine *Life and Labor,* seeking better conditions for women in industrial life. In London, during World War I, she joined the Scottish Women's Hospital and served in the Balkans. After the war she was associated with the Housing Ministry in London. Of all these activities her friends had only the most fragmentary accounts, bereft of her personal experiences or feelings. And during this long period she published only three novels: [*Some Everyday Folk—and Dawn, Old Blastus of Bandicoot* and *Bring the Monkey*]. . . . (pp. 83-4)

Brent of Bin Bin, however, had appeared with [*Up the Country, Ten Creeks Run,* and *Back to Bool Bool*]. . . . Brent was warmly appreciated as the creator of a saga of pastoral pioneers; but it was not until *All That Swagger* was published . . . that Miles

Franklin was thought to compare with "Brent" in status. For all their gaiety and verve, her subsequent novels, [*Pioneers on Parade* and *My Career Goes Bung*] . . . did not add to her literary reputation; and her finely sympathetic study of Joseph Furphy (with Kate Baker) had naturally a limited public. Why, then, should she have abstained from crowning her achievement by claiming the Brent authorship or the part of it that was obviously hers? A love of mystery, a conviction that women authors were not taken as seriously as men, a belief in the sales value of anonymity, the fact that the work was perhaps not entirely hers? . . . The three further Brent novels, [*Prelude to Waking, Cockatoos* and *Gentlemen of Gyang Gyang*] . . . all bear the Franklin imprint in style and outlook—and there is great sadness and defeat behind their crusading spirit and limpid Australianism. (p. 84)

To those who were her friends, Miles Franklin is perhaps more vital as a person than as a writer. But the author of *All That Swagger* and possibly of the Brent of Bin Bin chronicles is a being of vastly greater importance to Australia as it is and as it may be. (p. 85)

> *Beatrice Davis, "Tributes to Miles Franklin: A True Australian," in* Southerly, *Vol. 16, No. 2, 1955, pp. 83-5.*

JOHN K. EWERS   (essay date 1959)

[Australian writer Joseph] Furphy is significant and important because he stands at the beginning of the century, holding open the door for other writers to saunter through. And saunter is what they did. . . .

With him at this time—actually preceding him by two years in the date of publication—was Miles Franklin whose *My Brilliant Career,* written while she was still in her teens, was published in 1901. Henry Lawson in a Preface says, "the book is true to Australia—the truest I ever read". Joseph Furphy, too, was quick to recognize its merits and a friendship sprang up between these two—the elderly, wise philosopher and this young girl startled by the lionizing that accompanied the instant success of her first book. Distance soon separated them for Furphy removed to Western Australia and Miss Franklin went overseas. But the mutual respect they held for each other's work continued. These two had much in common. Both had a clear vision of reality and both scorned humbug and pretence. These qualities inform every page of *My Brilliant Career* and are no less strong in the sequel, *My Career Goes Bung,* which, although written in the embarrassment of the enthusiasm evoked by the former book, was not published until 1946. The books should be read together for a clear picture of the extraordinary mind of this young girl who was to grow into one of the most far-sighted of Australian writers and further enrich the Australian novel in a later generation. (pp. 55-6)

Without a doubt, the most important new writer of the post-war decade was "Brent of Bin Bin" whose [*Up the Country* was followed by *Ten Creeks Run* and *Back to Bool Bool*]. . . . The first two deal with the fortunes of a group of pastoralist pioneers in southern New South Wales up to the 'nineties. They are full of colour and recapture the atmosphere of the period without being in any way concerned with matters extraneous to the immediate surroundings of the characters. The lives of the early squatters are, we feel, complete in themselves, cut off from the growing metropolis of Sydney. The Riverina is their world and they accept it as such. Not that they are unaware of the larger world outside, but it is a place to be explored and ransacked when opportunity occurs rather than the cause of an exile's nostalgia. These books are a contrast to the attitudes of the people in [Henry Kingsley's] *Geoffry Hamlyn,* but not too violent a contrast. It is the younger generation of the Mazeres and Malones who go off to take Europe by storm, and it is these young adventurers, some of them brilliantly successful overseas, who return in *Back to Bool Bool* to mingle once again with the sights and sounds that are part of their natural inheritance. *Back to Bool Bool,* it was explained at the time, was really the fourth of the series. The third volume was withheld because, in the words of the author, "through too much footle about past days to the neglect of unprejudiced illumination of present realities, Australian fiction is in danger of foundering in infant senility."

At the time of its publication, *Back to Bool Bool* sounded a strongly topical note. It was full of exciting hints of the burgeoning of cultural activity that characterized the 1930's. Contemporary social problems had been, for some reason, avoided by most Australian writers, but *Back to Bool Bool* was right in step with the times.

Since then the "Brent of Bin Bin" books have been republished in Australia, including three of the hitherto missing volumes, [*Prelude to Waking, Cockatoos* and *Gentlemen at Gyang Gyang*]. . . . The republication of *Back to Bool Bool* . . . completed the series.

Who is "Brent of Bin Bin"? This question was, of course, asked when first his books began to appear. Early speculation attributed authorship to Miles Franklin who strenuously denied it during her lifetime. Apart from stylistic and other similarities of all the books to the writings of Miles Franklin, there is ample evidence in *Cockatoos* to challenge her denials of authorship. The story of Ignez Milford is so close to that of Miss Franklin's own girlhood that one cannot avoid the conclusion that she was very largely, if not wholly, responsible for these books. (pp. 66-8)

[Miles Franklin] had been so long absent from the Australian literary scene that her reappearance in 1932 was almost like the emergence of a new writer. The novel which reintroduced her to the Australian reading public bore the extraordinary title of *Old Blastus of Bandicoot.* Not quite as fearsome as it sounds, it was an interesting if not outstanding reconstruction of life in the Canberra district before it became Federal Capital territory. Her next novel, *Bring the Monkey,* . . . was a mildly amusing mystery story but added nothing to her literary reputation.

Then in 1936, her *All That Swagger* won the S. H. Prior Memorial Prize for that year. This is an historical novel that rivals *Landtakers* for vigour of action and clarity of characterization. The period is well realized and her central character, Danny Delacy, is one of the finest in Australian fiction. The book abounds in the wit and humour of the mature Miles Franklin. Written from a strongly feminine point of view, it spares no pains to chide male shortcomings yet, at the same time, does so with understanding and tolerance. In 1938 she shared the S. H. Prior Prize for that year with Kate Baker for a biography, *Joseph Furphy, the Legend of a Man and His Book.* Revised and in part rewritten, it was published in 1944. The collaboration creaks somewhat and as a biography the book lacks unity, but it is an invaluable source of information concerning the literary career of one of Australia's finest writers. In 1939, Miles Franklin collaborated with Dymphna Cusack to produce a clever satire, *Pioneers on Parade,* which contains some bril-

liant shafts at smug Australians anxious to overlook their convict ancestry.

A children's book, *Sydney Royal* . . . , was followed by *Laughter, Not For A Cage,* published posthumously in 1956. This lively, if unconventional survey of Australian writing (mainly its prose writing) reveals Miles Franklin in a new role, but nothing she has written expresses more clearly her personal vision and the brilliantly original mind through which it was fashioned. To these later works must be added the companion pieces of her youth, *My Brilliant Career* and *My Career Goes Bung,* . . . and that rarely seen volume, *Some Everyday Folk And Dawn,* published while she was abroad in 1909. There are, too, the "Brent of Bin Bin" books of which it now seems safe to say she was the literary executant, even if in the early stages of their writing a real person, "Brent of Bin Bin" himself, prompted her pen. (pp. 107-08)

John K. Ewers, in his Creative Writing in Australia: A Selective Survey, *revised edition, Georgian House, 1959, 203 p.**

CECIL HADGRAFT (essay date 1960)

In 1901 appeared what A. G. Stephens termed "the very first Australian novel to be published", by which he meant that it caught an Australian outlook in Australian idiom. This was *My Brilliant Career,* written by Miles Franklin. . . . It is the autobiography of Sybylla Penelope Melvyn, a young Australian girl living in north-western Victoria, a Cinderella without a prince. The book is perfectly Australian—in setting, in circumstances, in vocabulary. (p. 163)

This total and willing if unconscious acceptance of milieu and language as source and means indicates that the writer feels at home. It is a remarkable first book for a young woman. But it is foolish to praise it for what it is not. It is unlikely, for instance, that she should possess mastery. The book contains the artless outpourings of a youthful spirit dissatisfied with its material and spiritual lot. She wants companionship of kindred souls, the experience of art, and the love of her ideal man— though she cannot explain what this is to consist in. Odd, contrary, perverse, she seems doomed to find herself a misfit, and at the end of the book no solution is in sight. The youthful *cri du coeur* has been compared to the diary of Marie Bashkirtseff; but it is of slighter material. Inevitably, it lacks depth. And it lacks sophistication of manner. The expression is immature, the devices of language not fully assimilated. . . .

There is the queerest mixture of the spontaneous and the affected in this book. Its liveliness, its verve, and its oddness of theme will preserve it. It is likely to be read for many years as a picture of an unusual Australian girl, with something of the pathetic priggishness of intellectual aspiration. But its literary value is not equal to its human interest. (p. 164)

[In] *My Career Goes Bung,* Sybylla becomes famous or notorious in the district as the author of an unorthodox book, and then goes to Sydney on exhibit as a sort of infant prodigy.

The style, lively in the former novel, now becomes more colloquial, and develops in the process a chirpiness, a cockiness, that is not an improvement. The satiric note is more acid, possibly because the objects of it, "Society" and "birth" and the like, are more open to attack. They invite attack, true, but they allow the author to grow corners, to start to carry a chip on the shoulder. She underlines her dislike by the use of capital letters—SOCIETY—a device that relies on printing instead of on skill.

Once again we can say the novel is remarkable for a young woman. It is sincere, but the personality that grimaces through the pages begins to take on the quality of oddness. It becomes after a time a trifle wearing. The literary champion of women's rights has begun to displace the literary woman. (pp. 164-65)

In 1936 *All That Swagger* won the S. H. Prior Memorial Prize. A long novel, it covers a century from 1833, the date when Danny Delacy left Ireland with his bride and came to N.S.W. to settle and prosper near the Murrumbidgee. A saga novel like this, tracing the fortunes of a family and district over such a period of time, perhaps inevitably overloads itself with historical detail. Some of the earlier pages read like potted colonial history. We learn about land laws, land grants, emigration, the price of horses, of furniture, and of food, the manner of living, cattle duffing, and the background activities that can often read like the product of research. (p. 165)

An enormous amount is packed into the short sentences and short paragraphs at the start of the novel. Incidents crowd thick—exploration, settlement, aborigines, horses—each incident tersely related; and then we are hurried on. As the tale continues the family bulks larger—their internal and outside relations, their traits and speech, marriages, hates and loves. The novel has been frequently claimed—and acclaimed—as Miles Franklin's best work. But many will prefer her first fresh and breathless effusion.

The middle section of the novel is best: here she deals with persons. The last section is sociological and economic, as the first was historical. The danger in dealing with large conceptions, with visions of a national future, with idealistic panoramas, is the collapse into the bathetic on the one side or an inflation into the pretentious on the other. (pp. 165-66)

Her work has been overpraised. . . . She is not a major novelist; she survives as a personality and will be remembered for her first gauche and artless and vital book.

If, as seems probable, Miles Franklin also wrote, or helped to write, or revised the books of Brent of Bin Bin, then she was prolific enough. There are six books under this author's name: [*Up the Country, Ten Creeks Run, Back to Bool Bool, Prelude to Waking, Cockatoos,* and *Gentlemen of Gyang Gyang*]. . . . The first three and the fifth belong to a group. The first covers a period in the relations of certain families from the forties to the sixties of last century, the second continues to the nineties, the third deals with the twenties of this century, and the fifth partly fills in the gap between the last two. *Prelude to Waking* is set in England.

The best of the volumes is *Up the Country,* the first and the freshest. It is prefaced by a rather defensive Author's Note: "I don't care what folks who are artists in literature rather than in life, or who substitute sophistication for wisdom, think or don't think about it." It is a wholesome and in the main a cheerful book, smelling of the open air, a little like Henry Kingsley without his snobbishness.

It is, as its subtitle says, a novel of the squattocracy. It is not about pioneers in the usual sense, for when we meet the families in it—Mazeres, Pooles, Stantons, Labosseers, and the rest—they are already occupants of considerable holdings. The book deals with their inter-relations, mostly by marriage. So that it is partly a social picture. It draws on the customary material, and the list is exhaustive—floods and rivers in flood and cross-

ings and even a death by drowning, gold fields, cattle duffing, herding, overlanding, bush races, bushrangers on a local limited scale—so that a reader wonders what is going to be left for the volumes that are to follow. The picture is thus a full one. The note is one of plenty. . . . It is a little idealised and heroicised. An adult reader reaching the middle of the book does not put it down; indeed he reads with a surface interest; but he finds it difficult to feel emotion that engages him very deeply in the lives and adventures of the characters.

The novels that follow are in general inferior to *Up the Country*. . . . The setting becomes more urbanised and ends up in Sydney suburbs, so that the interest shifts from outdoor incidents to characters often indoors. Dialogue becomes chit-chat. Sometimes this is illuminating, a light thrown on the fondness for scandalmongering so characteristic of small Australian communities; and mostly it falls into a pattern—people do something, others talk about it and them.

The heroic note in the early novels becomes a sermon or a satire in the later ones. (pp. 166-68)

One point of interest in a later work, *Cockatoos*, is the figure of Ignez, a young girl of considerable gifts, pianist, singer, and author of a novel that portrays the life and characters of Oswald's Ridges near Goulburn, the country community where she lives. The figure is markedly like that of Sybylla in Miles Franklin's *My Brilliant Career*.

Some of the attention aroused by the Brent novels is almost certainly due to the mystery of their authorship. The reputation they have enjoyed in some circles seems higher than is warranted by their qualities of style and characterisation. Their setting gives them greater claims to permanence. It is possible that they suffer under the disadvantage of being so many and so long. Had only the first appeared it would hold a greater interest. (p. 168)

Cecil Hadgraft, "The New Century: First Harvest of Fiction," in his Australian Literature: A Critical Account to 1955 *(© Cecil Hadgraft 1960), Heinemann, 1960, pp. 145-68.**

RAY MATHEW (essay date 1963)

Miles Franklin was one of the "established" names when my generation was growing up, but her reputation seemed one of the least meaningful and easiest to destroy. So few of her books were in print, and even those which were published as new belonged so obviously to the nineties' period of aggressive proclamation and nostalgic Australianism, which both liberates and embarrasses the writer of today, that they seemed easy to dismiss as specimens of literary history. Those critics who noticed her novels seemed bedazzled by memories of her age at the time of writing, of the historical importance of their first appearance, of her piously-stated chronicle intentions, or of the brilliance with which her personality displayed itself in life. (p. 5)

[What matters] to Miles Franklin is the family facts—about her own life, about her parents' lives and their parents' lives, and these facts are the basis of *All that Swagger* . . . , which was her most acclaimed work. Openly chronicle in form, recording the history of a particular family and its connections in a particular district, it begins in 1815 with Waterloo stunning Europe and Danny Delacey asking his "brave" Johanna to come with him to Australia.

Their story of land-clearing and child-bearing, family marriages and continuation ("the productivity of seed . . . against the ephemerality of the separate life span") is an attempt to image Australia—the place—and the pioneering that deserved that place with all its manners, its hopes, its swagger; to give its 1930 characters, *and* its author, a justification and a style; to "set the fashion in all that swagger".

Justification, style, swagger—there is, after all, nothing else: "death—time—just a brush or two—and all that swagger, where is it?" Even the swagger survives only in the "archives of imagination", in the words of some "old song". This is Miles Franklin expressing her own childless despair (as Brent of Bin Bin does) and justifying her urgent, pious chronicling.

This chronicling is not (and she knows it) what a novel (or even an anti-novel) should be. . . . For all its simplification of emotion and motivation, its crowding of incident relevant to its chronicle aim (they "lacked leisure and the arena . . . to develop picturesque flourish in manners and to pursue *amour* as a fine art"), the book forms a whole only in the sense that Danny gives it a beginning and an end, and Danny is never given (because of "the dignity of reality"?) a single moment, which might give his life meaning and unity. . . . (pp. 15-16)

Danny does, however, exist; one recognizes him as one does no one else in the book; the others are acceptable as fiction-faces or history-acts but Danny is greeted by the reader and he and his ways stay in the mind like memory.

If the book lives, it will be for him—and because of his creator's embarrassing sincerity. She crams her paragraphs with the history of agriculture, dissertations on the horse, theories about society, seignorials and sex. And, for all the bad grammar, the imprecision of language, the coyness of sentiment, the guide-book boredom and the dishonesty of emotion, one feels one ought to be interested and—surprisingly—if one perseveres, one is. It is though the eighties, the nineties, and the early part of this century which are most alive—as reportage and as art. When the author abandons her "scrapbook" source and writes of what she remembers and cares about, the book has a feminine bite and an admirable display of artistic impatience when it is difficult to know just how seriously she takes herself (or how completely she deceives herself). "It was a pleasant and distinguished occasion for all concerned"—is this naive or ironic, a lazy writing or a cleverly contrived display of the Australian habit of reneguing praise? It is certainly a left-over from the snubbing tactics of *My Brilliant Career,* but is here a distrust of emotion so great that it can lead to bathos. And, again, even precise observation of contemporary life reads unconvincingly; it becomes clear that nothing since 1900, her adolescence, is real to her or can be accepted by her as reality. (pp. 16-17)

> *Ray Mathew, in his* Miles Franklin, *Lansdowne Press, 1963, 37 p.*

MARJORIE BARNARD (essay date 1967)

In 1928 the publishing house of Blackwood, in Edinburgh, brought out a novel called *Up the Country, a Tale of the Early Australian Squattocracy* by Brent of Bin Bin. Who, everyone began to ask, is Brent of Bin Bin? No one had ever heard of him. His only address was the British Museum. . . .

As it would be most convenient to settle this matter now, I must go ahead of the story for proof. Evidence of authorship is internal, external and supporting. The internal evidence includes style, vocabulary, background, subject matter, general attitudes; and one of the Brent books, *Cockatoos,* is so close a reproduction of Miles's own history and known feelings as to be conclusive. There is a strong similarity of style between such books as *All That Swagger* by Miles Franklin and *Up the Country* by Brent of Bin Bin. (p. 94)

[In] page after page, volume after volume, the similarity mounts up. . . . The likeness and the cadences are there.

Miles had a very individual vocabulary using a lot of strange words and phrases. Some of them were old-fashioned, traditional to the bush and rarely if ever heard today. Others she invented. They run through both series of books. Here are some examples from Miles's acknowledged work: *combobulated, chrysalism, drivellage, feraboraceous, squashation, dumpedees, comflummixed, tormentatious, opuscule.* Other examples are from the Brent series: *temerarious exodists, circumioluated pioneeristically, impavidly, stultiloquence, flutterbudgets, obanbrant, mulierosity, ramfeezled, hornstooggled.* Then there are common to both those bush sayings—*good iron wingey, bottle of smoke, raised under a hen, to jump off his pannikin, bogey, poking borak.*

The shared backgrounds of the two series supply more evidence. Two areas in Australia were part of Miles's youth and left an indelible impression on her mind and heart. One was the high Monaro country of Brindabella, stronghold of the squattocracy and where horses and cattle were bred, the other was the area round Stillwater, Thornford, called the Goulburn district. Here on poorer less mountainous land small farmers made a hard living.

In her acknowledged novels Miles uses the Monaro as background in what is probably the most important of her books, *All That Swagger,* and the Goulburn district in *My Brilliant Career, My Career Goes Bung* (with excursions to Sydney) and *Old Blastus of Bandicoot.* Of two unimportant books *Some Everyday Folk and Dawn* is placed in Penrith and *Bring the Monkey* in England.

Of the Brent series *Up the Country, Ten Creeks Run, Gentlemen at Gyang Gyang* and *Back to Bool Bool* are set in the Monaro, the last named with part of the action in Sydney. *Cockatoos* is located in the Goulburn district with backward glances at the Monaro. The action in *Prelude to Waking,* a minor work, takes place in London with a few nostalgic dollops of Australian scenery thrown in. All this can hardly be coincidence.

To pick up one point amongst many the same rivers haunt both series. (pp. 95-6)

Both series are inhabited by the same sort of people—squatters, small farmers, bush characters in great variety. There is the same type of humor in incident and characterization, the same idealistic love of the Australian earth. There is the same diffuseness in treatment, the discursive, disorganized construction; similar lapses into stiff dialogue and obscure sentences; the same lift into poignant clarity in moments of tragedy, whether it be Brent's description of the drowning of Emily Mazere or Franklin's picture of the utter loneliness of Johanna with her home burned and her child dying. The imprint of Miles is on them all.

It is clear to the perceptive reader that Brent is a woman, not a man. Her effort to write in the first person as Nigel Barraclough in *Prelude to Waking* is lamentable. The prevailing feminism is identical with Miles's brand of the same article; heroes and heroines all have the Milesian touch.

Names and events link the Brent books to the Franklin books. Incidents like Miles's mother's journey through the snow [while pregnant with Miles] occur both in *Up the Country* as Charlotte's journey, and in *All That Swagger* as Della's journey. In *My Brilliant Career* we hear of family properties called Bin Bin East and Bin Bin West. Miles calls the Monaro town of Tumut Gool Gool. Brent calls it Bool Bool. And so it goes on.

The Brent book *Cockatoos* is as nearly autobiographical to Miles as her acknowledged book *All That Swagger* is to her Irish grandfather. As the Brent series progresses the cover of anonymity grows thinner and thinner. As for external evidence there is some of that too. Miles was annoyed when people asked her point-blank if she were Brent of Bin Bin but her canons of truthfulness did not allow her to deny it categorically. The handful of friends who were admittedly in the secret have never denied Miles's authorship outright either. (pp. 96-7)

Those who wrote to Brent at his table in the British Museum received answers. At least two reliable witnesses corresponded with both Miles and Brent and they declare the letters from Brent were written on Miles's typewriter, a machine with various faults and tricks, and that both used the same type of flimsy paper.

An alternative to sole authorship is that Miles collaborated with someone else in at least three of the Brent of Bin Bin books. That is possible but no satisfactory person has ever been put forward as the collaborator. Mary Fullerton was the most likely. They were in touch at the time the books were written; Mary was an Australian writer of the bush school. Personally I do not think that there was a collaboration nor, if I am wrong about this, do Mary Fullerton's other novels suggest that she had anything to do with it. No, Miles wrote them all.

As early as *My Career Goes Bung* Miles was thinking of assuming a pen name. . . . [After critics interpreted *My Brilliant Career* literally, Miles] suffered acutely from the displeasure of her relations and the feeling of shame that this gave her. The wound was deep, the scar remained till the end of her life. Now after years of silence the compulsion to write was on her again and she planned a series of books set in the Monaro of her childhood and loaded with characters some of which may well be taken from life either directly or in composite form. She shrank from putting her name to such a chronicle. Even when she was seventy, and all the people she remembered in her childhood were dead, she could not bring herself in *Childhood at Brindabella* even to give place names correctly, much less to any of the people who thronged her pages. (pp. 97-8)

There was nothing to suggest why she chose the pen name of Brent of Bin Bin. It had to be a man's name. It was a man's world and she was convinced that to pose as a man gave her a chance of success that would be automatically denied to a woman. "Bin Bin" was already in her mind. It may have been a code name for some place she knew. "Brent" has an American flavor and she may have picked it up there. The whole name suggests a squatter. It is quite usual to add the name of his property to a man's name; thus Miles herself writes of Mazere of Three Rivers. It always sounds like an aristocracy in the making, as one says Lord Montgomery of Alamein. That would appeal to Miles's romantic streak without offending her egalitarianism since it was ordinary practice. Finally, Miles is reported to have said that a mystery was a good advertisement and helped sales.

Brent of Bin Bin published three books in quick succession. They were: [*Up the Country, Ten Creeks Run,* and *Back to Bool*

Bool]. . . . They represent the first, second and fourth parts of a saga. The missing books were *Cockatoos,* which was not published until 1954, the year of Miles's death, and *Gentlemen at Gyang Gyang,* published posthumously in 1956. They were deliberately held out of sequence because Miles felt her readers wanted to rest from the bush and the past. *Up the Country* covers the period 1830 to the end of the 1860's; *Ten Creeks Run,* 1870-1895; *Cockatoos,* 1899-1906; *Gentlemen at Gyang Gyang,* 1926; *Back to Bool Bool,* 1927-1928.

It is a pity that Miles broke the flow of this great chronicle. She probably had reasons other than the one she divulged. *Cockatoos* does stand apart from the other books. It was written much earlier and later adapted to fit into the chronicle. *Gentlemen at Gyang Gyang* is also an old book brought up to date and in time it is almost a twin with *Back to Bool Bool.* I have thought it best to treat the books in chronological order—not necessarily the order in which they were written.

The five books of the saga form a whole as well as remain separate entities. Together they make a vast sprawling chronicle of life in the Monaro over nearly a century. It is, as the subtitle of *Up the Country* says, a tale of the squattocracy. When the saga begins, the first labor of pioneering is over, the station properties have taken shape, squattocracy is at its peak. Life is still hard and demanding; men must have courage and women must have more courage but a society has come into being. It is complete, touched with a bloom of idealism and memory. It has an appearance of timeless permanence but like dawn it cannot last and the chronicle traces the gradual destruction of the golden age. (pp. 98-9)

There is no plot in the ordinary sense. The narrative winds and loops and circles about a thousand natural obstacles. (p. 100)

The organic discursiveness of the writing was . . . intentional. Miles modelled her style on her material; she gave it an authentic bush flavor by following the meanderings of a yarn. (pp. 101-02)

But there is more to it than that. There is a dimly seen circular pattern. Event and memory repeat themselves. Fine threads of memory turn the circle into a cobweb. The death of beautiful Emily Mazere by drowning on the eve of her wedding echoes through the series: "as beautiful as Emily Mazere" the old hands say, Emily, the drowned forever enshrined in legend. The tragedy happens near the beginning of the trilogy, which ends in another drowning at the Mungee hole, but this time—in reverse—it is the fiance of Laleen Mazere, who is the image of the lost Emily, who drowns. (p. 102)

Up the Country is often acclaimed as the best of the series. It is the richest and most complex. . . . There are so many events and incidents that there is not room in the book, long as it is, to develop any of them fully. Sometimes in a page or even in a line you have enough, if reasonably expanded, to furnish a whole novel. Miles found plenty of time for descriptions and for talk, the endless yarning and chattering of a vast miscellany of minor characters. The yarning and chattering forms a chorus reflecting on characters and happenings and throwing light on them from several angles at once. The descriptions are magnificent. For many people they are the best part of the book because they bring to life again a world that has gone forever.

There is . . . the picture of a bush home, the homestead at Three Rivers, exact in every detail, and written with the clarity you always find in Miles's work when she conjures up a picture, perfectly remembered. It is not only that she tells you the plan of the house, the materials of which it is built and the use of every room but she conveys its orderliness, the near luxury even, that by good management and constant care has been created out of the simplest materials. Then there is the scene in the kitchen where the baking is in progress for Rachel's wedding. It is fully realized and lovingly detailed; you can see it and smell it. (pp. 102-03)

Many more words are expended on the descriptions than on events. When she comes to a crisis in her narrative all Miles's garrulity disappears. What has to be said is said simply and plainly and from this comes the sense of bareness.

It is not possible to summarize the story. It is, as someone has said, "like the billabongs of an inland river." It moves from episode to episode without much structure to support it, held in a farflung net of personalities. It is as if this first book were a sort of quarry from which the blocks used in the following volumes are taken; it sets the tone for the whole, introduces the characters and provides the bouquet.

The action moves in loops. There are two main movements: the first comprises floods—Rachel's wedding—Mrs. Mazere's brave crossing of the river to help a neighbor; and in the second movement, Emily's coming-of-age ball—Bush rangers—Emily's drowning. The wedding gets everyone onto the stage and the ball sorts them all out. From it springs most of the action in the rest of the book, the loves, the engagements, the heartbreaks. So little is drama considered that at one point Mrs. Mazere is left in a frail boat on the swirling, flooded river in imminent danger of her life, while the author breaks off to give a lengthy account of pioneering experiences. (p. 104)

The book ended with the death of old Mazere. Instead of "The End" Miles wrote "Interval." (p. 105)

If *Up the Country* was the richest, sunniest and most pleasing, *Ten Creeks Run* is the best constructed of the series. The narrative with its two main plots and one leading sub-plot is clear. It has to do with two marriages of May and December and the sub-plot is about a horse lost and found again. The setting is the same as in *Up the Country* and the characters are the same with a few new ones, like Ronald Dice, added and the Milfords brought closer into the picture. (They will be wanted later.) The action moves to Ten Creeks Run, the property of Jack Stanton, otherwise known as Skinny-Guts, or S P over J from his brand. From this it can be seen that he is not one of Miles's best-loved characters.

A great many characters mill about between the covers and each adds something to the narrative, a comment, a sidelong glance, a touch of humour. (pp. 105-06)

The book begins, as usual, with a social occasion, a horse muster; this brings everyone, human and equine, into the picture. The heroine Milly Stanton . . . is still a little girl not yet in her teens. Bert Pool is still the hero and Milly's adopted uncle. (p. 106)

[This book] is, I think, in many ways the best that Miles wrote and only by quotation can I give you the true flavor of it or show you its quality of innocent romance. It is old-fashioned, even prim, but it has a spirit of gentleness and goodness, of something everlastingly valuable preserved with love. (p. 110)

Cockatoos fits into the series at this point. Its first draft was written before Miles left Australia for America. Its original title was *The Outside Track*. When, in bush parlance, someone takes the outside track it means that he or she travels alone.

For Miles it came to mean a hard and lonely journey through life. Why she changed the title I do not know; it is more attractive than *Cockatoos* and fits the subject very well. Possibly she thought that *Cockatoos* fitted better into the series as it focused attention on the whole group of characters instead of, as *The Outside Track* did, on one. Neither do I know how she went about adapting it into the Brent chronicle. Did she, for instance, introduce characters in the earlier books, the Milfords and others, in order to include them in *Cockatoos*? I think it more likely that she changed the names and some of the circumstances in *The Outside Track* and renamed it.

If *Cockatoos* does not quite reach the high standard of *Ten Creeks Run* in its genre, it is still one of the most sympathetic of Miles's novels. It is largely autobiographical and I dare Miles to contradict me. The scene is no longer the Monaro but Oswald's Ridges in the Goulburn district, poor country cut up into small dairy and other farms. The Mazeres and the Healeys had moved there from Bool Bool very much as the Franklins left Brindabella for Stillwater. . . . (pp. 110-11)

When Miles wrote of the Monaro she was a romantic, when she wrote of Oswald's Ridges or 'Possum Gully she was a realist. (p. 111)

[*Cockatoos*] is also very much in the tone of *My Brilliant Career*, Miles's own rebellious reaction to life in 'Possum Gully, alias Stillwater. (p. 112)

In the Monaro, idealized by memory, no drought ever came. Oswald's Ridges also is country Miles remembered from youth. It takes on the color of her frustration and rebellion just as the Monaro is drawn from pictures of happiness and affluence. The drought scenes are reminiscent of *My Career Goes Bung* but better done. . . .

The book is well supplied with heroines. Sylvia is in the glamorous tradition, and Freda Healey, "a little girl in kip boots splashed with whitewash and an apron of sacking over her frock," is being groomed as the heroine of another book. The real heroine is Ignez Milford. Her name, we are told, is pronounced Ee-nith. (p. 113)

She wanted to study music, piano and singing, as Miles did. . . . Like Miles her talent was ruined by bad teaching and the complete incomprehension of its worth of all around her. (pp. 113-14)

Cockatoos has much in common with *My Brilliant Career* and *My Career Goes Bung* but is more mature. There is the scenery, the drought, the spirited and rebellious young girl who writes a book and is horrified by the shock of seeing it in print. There are the visits to Sydney, the satire on society, the machinations of the sophisticated man about town. In *My Brilliant Career* Sybylla has to go to the pub to bring her drunken father home. In *Cockatoos* Ignez must do the same service for Larry, but here our sympathy is enlisted for the sensitive badgered man who takes refuge in drink when he can no longer bear the conditions of his life. Ignez, however, is a more lovable character than Sybylla. Sensitive, spontaneously affectionate, always willing to help, she has little in common with the spirited egotistical girl whose career went bung. *Cockatoos* is dedicated to Sybylla "Salutations to Sybylla Melvyn the legendary and temerarious."

The book is circular in construction. This was a favorite device with Miles; apparently she found it satisfying. The action is securely tied in. (p. 117)

With *Gentlemen at Gyang Gyang; a Tale of the Jumbuck Pads on the Summer Runs* Miles has moved out of the past into the present. It is set in 1926 or there about. But the scene is still laid in the Monaro; the summer runs are the mountain pastures to which sheep, the Jumbucks, and cattle are taken in summer for the superior feed that they offer. Gyang Gyang is the name of a bird, and in this book the summer run leased by Sylvester Labosseer, son of Rachel and Simon, is named after it.

Miles is never really happy writing of the present day, or that is my impression. Nineteen twenty-six was the present for her although it is fast becoming our past. As she moved into the present she felt more and more impelled to take a satirical view of life and happenings. This will become clearer in the last book of the series, *Back to Bool Bool.* In *Gentlemen at Gyang Gyang* she puts a brake on time. Amongst the immemorial mountains time stands still. Everything, or nearly everything, is the same as it used to be in the golden age of the squatters. Men do not have a chance to grow soft. Miles may be said to have retreated to the mountains to make her last stand for idealism.

This is not one of her important books. There is something makeshift about it, something unreal and manufactured. Compared to *Up the Country* it runs very thin indeed. It is not well written, apart from some highly quotable descriptive passages. The dialogue is stiff, the tale is novelettish. (pp. 118-19)

This book may well have been an early one which Miles adapted for her Brent of Bin Bin series. If so, she did not do as good a job as she did in *Cockatoos.* She did not have the same personal stake in *Gentlemen at Gyang Gyang.* The main reason for disappointment is that the characters are not sympathetic. They lack warmth and reality. Bernice is not a typical Franklin heroine; Miles does not love her. Even if she is as "old-fashioned as Eve" she lacks the embattled purity of the genuine heroine. There is nothing of Miles herself in her. She is little more than a peg on which the story is hung and to which Miles hitches some of her favorite hobby-horses. [The hero,] Peter Poole, for all his excellent "press" and Miles's adulation, does not come alive. He is quite impossibly noble and the reader is apt to tire of him. The minor characters, Beardy Tom, the Dude, Mona, Doll and the rest are better done and certainly talk more naturally.

The value of the book is in its background and its Australian rhythms of life. The mountains are pure, untouched. It is a landscape of hope. Here was the new beginning and the men who inhabited the country . . . took on its virtues. (p. 120)

There is genuine bush lore here but there is not enough of it to save the book from its pervading triteness.

In *Gentlemen at Gyang Gyang* war was declared between the bush and the city. . . .

This is the theme, or one of the themes, of *Back to Bool Bool.* The worst has happened and the cavalry has been unhorsed; the remnant of the Mazeres has left the bush and gone to live in the suburbs among the "bally imbeciles." *Back to Bool Bool* is set in Sydney but with (about two-thirds of the way through the book) a pilgrimage of all the characters back to Bool Bool and their origins. The Mazeres have come via Oswald's Ridges to the suburbs. As I have already pointed out, Miles grows progressively tarter and less idealistic the further she gets from the High Monaro. The sub-title and dedications by their obscurity should warn readers that in this book she is a long way

from the sweet romance of *Up the Country* and *Ten Creeks Run.* (p. 121)

In moments of high tragedy, as the drowning of Emily Mazere, or tender romance as those describing the love of Bert and Milly, Miles's prose has a pure and simple line. When she descends from these heights and writes satirically it becomes coy and encumbered. The *enfant terrible* in Miles comes to the surface.

The dedication of *Back to Bool Bool* is intentionally provocative and is intended to throw some more darkness on the authorship of the Brent of Bin Bin books. (p. 122)

The period covered is 1928-1929 or right up to the moment of writing. Miles who was sentimental about the past was caustic about her present. For example take *My Brilliant Career, My Career Goes Bung,* the political parts of *Some Everyday Folk and Dawn,* and, to some extent, *Cockatoos,* though here her attitude softens to disappointment and youthful frustration.

To return to the contents of the book, the story it tells is a large and sprawling one. The "exodists" of *Cockatoos* come home again and with them several other expatriates not described in detail before. . . . (p. 123)

The action in *Back to Bool Bool,* as in most of Miles's novels, moves in jerks from one occasion to another. There is the family reunion with a great deal of trivial talk faithfully reported, and much food (Miles, abstemious herself, had little sympathy with heavy eating); Madam Austra's concert; Bernice's studio party; the opening of a memorial park; and so on. These occasions bring all the characters together. Two-thirds of the way through the book the mass-return to Bool Bool acts as a catalyst. They all go back to their pioneer origins and the beauty and reality of the bush purges the artificiality of the city. (p. 128)

In this, the last book of her saga, Miles shows all her faces; she is in turn the idealist, the sad disillusioned onlooker, the satirist, the romantic, the little girl who never missed anything, the *enfant terrible,* the campaigner, and Miles. The book suffers from having too much of everything. There is certainly too much soap-box oratory. By the time she wrote *Back to Bool Bool* Miles was no longer an active feminist. There was no need to be. Women in Australia at least had full civil rights, the vote, the right to work and to exercise their talents in the professions. The unions had recognized them as workers and the law protected them. The large families of the Victorian era with the consequent strain on the mother were almost a thing of the past. Her cry here is fewer people and a better life. . . . (p. 129)

Perhaps if you could only read one book by Miles Franklin *Back to Bool Bool* would be the best to choose. It is characteristic in so many ways. All her virtues and all her faults are there, but you would not be bored. (p. 130)

Marjorie Barnard, "Brent of Bin Bin Steps out of the British Museum," in her Miles Franklin *(copyright © 1967 by Twayne Publishers, Inc.; reprinted with the permission of Twayne Publishers, a Division of G. K. Hall & Co., Boston), Twayne, 1967, pp. 94-130.*

HARRY HESELTINE (essay date 1976)

The task of advancing Australian fiction along its necessary path fell . . . chiefly to the writers of saga, picaresque, and documentary. And among these central writers of the tradition, clearly a number must be accorded positions of special importance. As one who gave the saga its characteristic shape and qualities, Miles Franklin occupies a place of honour—as much by virtue of the persistence of her efforts as by the merit of her individual works. She had started writing well before 1920—*My Brilliant Career* was published in 1901; *My Career Goes Bung,* though written at much the same time, was not published until much later. . . . She ushered in her post-war career with the whimsical *Old Blastus of Bandicoot* . . . , but it was not until 1936 that *All that Swagger,* the cornerstone of her achievement, appeared. The novel spans something like a hundred years, from the 1830s to the 1930s, and moves from Ireland to the Murrumbidgee and Monaro districts of New South Wales. The plot is centred in the character of Danny Delacy, who brings his young bride to the new colony, where he becomes a successful, if eccentric, squatter and, in the fullness of time, dies surrounded by prosperity and several generations of the dynasty he has founded.

Into its hundred year span, *All that Swagger* packs a great wealth of incident, of the strenuously physical and exciting nature made so readily available by the circumstances of pioneering. The mass of events, however, is given very little shape beyond arrangement in chronological order. Neither does the style do much to bring the book's material under control. In some random historical summaries which are interjected into the Delacy narrative, indeed, it breaks down into fairly clumsy reportage. For most of the book it is adequate to the demands of a simple characterization and the flow of an unsophisticated plot. Only when Franklin turns her attention to the natural beauty of the region that she loved is her language charged with some lyric emotion.

In effect, much of the appeal of *All that Swagger* resides in its unabashed romanticism. In a sense, it is simply another version of the success story: the poor Irish migrant makes good in a new land. But there is a more particular, and more significant kind of romanticism in the book—a kind indicated by the title itself. This is the saga of Australia on horseback, a nostalgic tribute to the gaiety and swagger that accompanied lives spent largely in the saddle. The values of *All that Swagger* might with some justice be described as chivalric. To be sure, it is a chivalry modified by the physical conditions of the Australian land and the social pressures of Australian democracy, but it is still there: the *élan* of the mounted man, the thrill of the cross-country gallop, even the high standards of public morality. More than chivalric, the book is patriarchal. That grand old leader, Fearless Danny, is most memorable when in the company of his faithful retainers, the aboriginal Doogooluk and the Chinese Wong Foo. Throughout, he carries something of the air of the benevolent despot. It is certainly Delacy who assures the continuing vitality of the book. He is created simple, but created fresh and alive. With his Irish verve and wit, he epitomizes that blend of dash and democracy which Miles Franklin saw as the special mark of the nineteenth-century mounted bushman. After Danny's death, the life fades rapidly from the whole book, which not even the romance between Clare Margaret and Darcy can revive. It sinks to rest with an unconvincing attempt to transfer the swagger of the horseman to the aeroplane pilot, the rider of the skies and new man of the twentieth century.

If, as there can be little doubt, Miles Franklin was Brent of Bin Bin, her place at the centre of the saga tradition is made doubly sure. In a series of five novels, Brent of Bin Bin chronicled the histories of some half dozen families who settled in the same general area as is treated in *All that Swagger.* The Brent books also display the same regional love of place as occurs in Franklin's prose. In general structure they are very similar to *All that Swagger,* recounting a profusion of events with little more order than arrangement in chronological sequence. Their enormous proliferation of characters accords them at least one virtue not present in *All that Swagger,* the sense of the warp and weave of the social fabric of an Australian pastoral community. The limits of observation are so widely extended in time and space that the division of the chronicle into five separate books becomes almost a literary necessity as much as a publishing convenience. (pp. 203-05)

*Harry Heseltine, "Australian Fiction Since 1920,"
in* The Literature of Australia, *edited by Geoffrey
Dutton (reprinted by permission of Penguin Books
Australia Limited), revised edition, Penguin Books
Australia, 1976, pp. 196-247.*

EILEEN KENNEDY   (essay date 1981)

My Brilliant Career—told in the first person—is the story of the late-adolescent, Sybylla, living in the outback in the 1890s, a time of political and social unrest in Australia. She is rescued from the alcoholic incompetence of her father and the unguarded hostility of her mother, the poverty and ugliness of their mean farm, by a sojourn with her affluent, kindly, practical, and refined grandmother. Fiercely independent, Sybylla is a highly intelligent hoyden, an examiner of spiritual and humane values. Brave, embittered, convinced that she is so plain no man will ever love her, she views life as a quest for her freedom as a woman; and her search is played out against a burning love for the landscape lit by garish, gorgeous sunsets; cluttered with drudges, beggars, farmers and sheep-herders; torn between Victorian façades and the open-handed, crude goodness of a pioneering people. The major event in her quest for liberation is her relationship with Harold Beecham, initially the very prosperous, imperturbable, sought-after young bachelor who owns an extensive estate near her grandmother's.

Of course, there are flaws in the novel: some of the plot devices seem out of *Jane Eyre;* and stylistically, Miles Franklin oscillates between some clean honest writing of the Australian landscape and character and a stilted pompous diction. But Franklin's portrayal of the strong, complicated heroine makes these criticisms trifling.

What is probably the most original insight in the novel—and what the film did not grasp, nor does Sybylla, who is so obviously the author's voice—is that the heroine is sado-masochistic. Neither Sybylla, nor Franklin, nor Callil, in the introduction [see excerpt below], appears to realize the meaning of the powerful destructive currents in the girl's actions, in her swift alternations of sexual mood—but the careful reader does. And part of the force of this novel lies in the tension between the narrator's point of view and the reader's assessment of it.

Eileen Kennedy, "'My Brilliant Career'," in Best
Sellers *(copyright © 1981 Helen Dwight Reid Educational Foundation), Vol. 40, No. 11, February,
1981, p. 389.*

ADDITIONAL BIBLIOGRAPHY

Dale, Marguerite. "An Appreciation of Stella Franklin." *Southerly* 16, No. 2 (1955): 86-7.

Personal reminiscence of Dale's acquaintance with Franklin in London in 1922.

Duncan, Roy. "Miles Franklin—An Unpublished Teenage Novel." *Australian Literary Studies* 8, No. 1 (May 1977): 91-3.
Discussion of the plot of an unpublished novel of Franklin's, called *Within a Footstep of the Goal*, which seems to predate *My Brilliant Career*.

Green, H. M. "The Novel. Novels of the Countryside Continued: 'Brent of Bin Bin'; Miles Franklin; Mrs Gunn; Others." In his *A History of Australian Literature, Pure and Applied, Vol. 1: 1789-1923*, pp. 634-47. Sydney: Angus and Robertson, 1961.*
Brief overview of both "Brent's" and Franklin's works. Green compares Franklin and "Brent" but mentions a letter he received from Franklin denying that she was "Brent."

Henry, Alice. "Stella Miles Franklin—Australian Novelist." *Memoirs of Alice Henry*, edited by Nettie Palmer, p. 89. Melbourne: 1944.
Personal reminiscence by the founder of the National Women's Trade Union League with whom Franklin worked while she was in the United States.

Hooper, F. Earle. "Stella Miles Franklin: A Memory." *Southerly* 16, No. 2 (1955): 85-6.
Recounting of Hooper's first meeting with Franklin "at one of Miss Rose Scott's famous Friday soirées," shortly after the publication of *My Brilliant Career*.

Hope, A. D. "Review of Miles Franklin's 'Joseph Furphy'." In *Australian Nationalists: Modern Critical Essays*, edited by Chris Wallace-Crabbe, pp. 108-13. Melbourne: Oxford University Press, 1971.
Review of the biography *Joseph Furphy*, which Franklin co-authored with Kate Baker.

Lindsay, Norman. "Thumbnail Profiles: Miles Franklin." In his *Bohemians of the Bulletin*, pp. 143-45. London: Angus and Robertson, 1965.
Brief account of an early meeting with Franklin in the offices of the Sydney *Bulletin*. Lindsay saw Franklin as "a symbol of the free feminine, seeking self-expression in the Word."

McInherny, Frances. "Miles Franklin and the Female Tradition." *Australian Literary Studies* 9, No. 3 (May 1980): 275-85.
Compares Franklin's novel to the fiction of the Brontës, Barbara Baynton, and other women writers.

Rose, Phyllis. "Her So-So Career." *The New York Times Book Review* (4 January 1981): 8, 21.
Reveals the circumstances surrounding the writing and publication of *My Brilliant Career*. Rose offers some criticism of the novel and a brief account of Franklin's life.

Sutherland, Bruce. "Stella Miles Franklin's American Years." *Meanjin Quarterly* XXIV, No. 4 (December 1965): 439-54.
Brief biography of Franklin, concentrating on her work with the National Women's Trade Union League in Chicago, and also her journalistic work for *The Union Labor Advocate* and *Life and Labor*.

Zona Gale

1874-1938

American novelist, short story writer, dramatist, essayist, poet, biographer, and autobiographer.

Now largely forgotten, Gale was recognized during the 1920s as a leader in the American "revolt from the village," a movement fueled by the popularity of her *Miss Lulu Bett*. Originally a novel chronicling a woman's escape from small-town dullness and drudgery, *Miss Lulu Bett* was dramatized by Gale, who subsequently won the 1921 Pulitzer Prize in drama.

Raised in Portage, Wisconsin, Gale was an only child whose parents deeply influenced her life and work. Her father introduced her to the writings of Plato, Emerson, Darwin, and Swedenborg, impressing upon her a belief in philosophic idealism. Her mother, a possessive, highly devout woman, shaped Gale's perception of divinity as an all-pervading feminine lifeforce. Gale's mysticism, which grew stronger with the years, was a blend of theosophy and transcendental pantheism, summed up and simplified in her motto: "Life is something more than that which we believe it to be." This was a recurring motif in her work.

Gale began her writing career working as a reporter in Milwaukee and then in New York City. She published her first novel, the flowery *Romance Island*, in 1906. Pressure from her mother to come home from New York to the idyllic life of Portage inspired Gale to write the first stories of Friendship Village—a town modelled on her home town—before she returned to Wisconsin in 1911. *Friendship Village, Friendship Village Love Stories*, and several other volumes present Gale's philosophy of love and community in stories filled with the sentiment, wholesomeness, and folksiness that marked her as a defender of the nineteenth-century village mythos. The success of her books provided her with the money and influence to actively support the various causes that drew her loyalty. Gale spoke and wrote on behalf of women's suffrage, trade unions, world peace, and the liberal Progressive Party of Wisconsin. During World War I, her pacifist activities led her Portage neighbors to suspect her of German sympathies, and they expressed pleasure when she was placed under federal surveillance. Hurt by this betrayal, Gale slowly came to see the Midwestern village as a mixture of good and bad elements—although not entirely as the suffocating, spiritual hell insisted upon by her literary contemporaries. Her disillusionment was voiced in *Birth, Peace in Friendship Village, Miss Lulu Bett*, and *Faint Perfume*, novels stripped of Gale's former romanticism and excess verbiage, and imbued with impressionistic realism. For several years in the early 1920s she was considered comparable to Sinclair Lewis in exposing middleclass dullness and provincialism. Receiving the Pulitzer Prize for *Miss Lulu Bett* in 1921 climaxed Gale's career.

Gale's mother greatly influenced her daughter's spiritual life, maintaining a hold that was intensified by her death in 1923, when Gale turned away from realism to explore her growing mysticism. Beginning with *Preface to a Life*, her books became increasingly burdened with spiritual matters which outweighed her story lines, causing her decline in popular and critical favor. Gale spent her last years writing and speaking for her favorite causes.

Culver Pictures

Today Gale's stature is measured by the influence she exerted in promoting human rights and by *Miss Lulu Bett*, which *The Nation* hailed as belonging "among the very earliest of plays which broke away from theatrical convention to establish upon the stage a new American literature."

(See also *Dictionary of Literary Biography*, Vol. 9: *American Novels, 1910-1945*.)

PRINCIPAL WORKS

Romance Island   (novel)   1906
The Loves of Pelleas and Etarre   (short stories)   1907
Friendship Village   (short stories)   1908
Friendship Village Love Stories   (short stories)   1909
When I Was a Little Girl   (short stories)   1913
Birth   (novel)   1918
Peace in Friendship Village   (short stories)   1919
Miss Lulu Bett   (novel)   1920
Miss Lulu Bett   (drama)   1920
Faint Perfume   (novel)   1923
Preface to a Life   (novel)   1926
Yellow Gentians and Blue   (short stories)   1927

Borgia (novel) 1929
Frank Miller of Mission Inn (biography) 1938
Magna (novel) 1939
The Unfinished Autobiography (unfinished autobiography) 1940; published in *Still Small Voice: The Biography of Zona Gale*

*This work is an adaptation of the novel *Miss Lulu Bett*.

AMY C. RICH (essay date 1906)

Romance Island is well named. Those who have enjoyed Miss Gale's quaint and thoroughly delightful stories of Pelleas and Etarre which have appeared in *The Outlook* and other magazines during the past year, will, I fear, be disappointed in the present volume, which is [a] wildly improbable . . . tale of mystery and adventure. . . . The story is thrillingly exciting from cover to cover and there is a delightful love romance running through it which terminates most happily. Those readers who do not demand the element of probability, or even of possibility, in their novels, will enjoy *Romance Island*.

> Amy C. Rich, "Books of the Day: 'Romance Island'," in The Arena, Vol. 36, No. 205, December, 1906, p. 688.

FREDERIC TABER COOPER (essay date 1909)

Of Miss Zona Gale we need have no serious misgivings. Whatever she may write, we can rest assured it will always have the same delightful repose of style and deliberate restraint of substance. Charming as *The Loves of Pelleas and Etarre* was found to be, the delicate interest of her new volume, *Friendship Village,* not only needs no apologetic endorsement, but in spite of its outward wide divergence reveals itself to the discriminating few as essentially a work in the same key, a story of the same elusive quality. It would be vain to attempt to epitomise the theme of *Friendship Village*. It is enough to say that there is in it a great deal of Mrs. Gaskell's *Cranford*, of Jane Austen's *Pride and Prejudice*. But there is a great deal more of Zona Gale than of any of the predecessors to whom she is indebted. We may not have personally met Mis' Postmaster Sykes or Mrs. Ricker-and-Kitton or Mis' Holcomb-that-was-Mame-Bliss, or any of the other grotesque and unforgettable figures that wend their curious way through *Friendship Village*. And yet, we all have known some such environment either in life or in our dreams. We all have lived to some extent in such an environment of kindly feeling, according to our several deserts. And the true test of the rare quality of *Friendship Village* is the unmistakable call that it has upon all of us for something that we individually have known and felt.

> Frederic Taber Cooper, "Some Recent Novels: 'Friendship Village'," in The Bookman, New York, Vol. XXVIII, No. 5, January, 1909, p. 476.

THE NATION (essay date 1918)

["**Birth**" is an American novel] of serious purpose and responsible workmanship. . . . Miss Gale places her little drama in the customary village setting, with its comic accessories and quaint "character" parts. But in essentials it is a drama that in other terms and with another accent might be played in any other time or place. . . . This is the story of a human personality of intrinsic worth compounded from the most unlikely materials, and to all appearances, in the most haphazard fashion. . . . We find here what we have found before in Miss Gale's work—a marked unevenness in characterization. . . . Miss Arrowsmith, whom we are called upon to admire with all her faults, at no time succeeds in rising above feebleness and futility. The women at Mrs. Arrowsmith's luncheon-party, who are understood to be traveled and superficially cultivated at least, talk like vulgar schoolgirls "playing society." Mis' Hellie Copper, and her cronies, and poor silly Barbara, and the child and cub and stumbling youth Jeffrey, are people we know. But it is in Marshall Pitt that the book presents a figure memorable and almost unique, a hero who is a helpless ass, a touching nuisance, a stray mongrel fated to sniff always at the heels of life, with no reward but the inner rewards of love and humility. (pp. 809-10)

> "Two Novels of Source," in The Nation, Vol. 107, No. 2791, December 28, 1918, pp. 809-10.*

CONSTANCE MAYFIELD ROURKE (essay date 1920)

Certain significant phases of the American novel and tale are plainly reflected in the work of Zona Gale. The typical Friendship Village story is also a typical American story. Calliope Marsh, who is made to do most of the telling, is an own sister of those many dealers in maxims who have adorned our literature. Uplift is her purpose; she wants improvement. But her tone is the familiar tone of content with our American life. The stories which she often quite unnaturally sets forth [in **"Peace in Friendship Village"**] are full of a factitious optimism, with an occasional dash of native wit, and a general air of provincial blessedness overspreading all. Calliope always finds the sweet and wholesome and good. **"Rose Pink"** is the title of one of her stories, and for the most part this popular color wraps the flimsy manufactured episodes like masses of tissue paper and yards of ribbon. Still, in the last of the volumes of Friendship Village, there are a few tales which lead away from contentment. The note of uplift remains but it is less assured. Certain considerations as to immigrants, naturalized foreigners, idle women who are losing the solace of the Red Cross, are advanced with the sharp note of satire. Certain juxtaposition of event and character are pungent. The change in Calliope Marsh may be taken as significant. In **"Rose Pink"** she is a dainty little lady, an unbelievable Dresden figure. In the later stories she appears, at least by implication, as a plain, downright village woman, a capable executive, given to rocking chairs and a wrapper in her leisure moments.

But even after this hint of change one is wholly unprepared for **"Miss Lulu Bett."** This last story of Zona Gale's teaches no lesson and holds no brief. It is written almost bitterly. Drastic and severe, it presses home every advantage in situation after situation, driving past a surface satire to the last ironic possibility open to the unflinching observer. Its situations—or its one closely knit situation—are thoroughly American. But contentment has fled. Dwight Herbert Deacon, his wife Ina, Di his older daughter, the child Monona, doddering old Mrs. Bett, are ruthlessly drawn; and at every turn they are made to betray the looseness of fibre, the tedious facility of thought and speech and action, the basic conventionalism, which characterize much of our native provincial life. Yet the book is something more than drastic. It has its narrowly limned beauty, and this, too, is native. In Lulu Bett herself, the obscure drudge in the Deacon home and the center of the story, Miss Gale has created a character which she would be right in saying is completely American; and it is not simply that Lulu, like the Deacons and like her mother, belongs to the States by every accent. She has something of that sure and delicate innocence of spirit, village old maid that she is, which Henry James was so fond of portraying in young women of quite different character and surroundings and which he somehow contrived to present as a growth from our soil. This luminous central quality Miss Gale shows without a trace of sentimentality or even of sentiment; she reveals it almost without tangible means. Nor is the tortured pathos of Lulu, as she is caught in the mesh of the Deacon family, ever directly commented upon; and Lulu's slow, spasmodic climb to self-assurance, her fronting of the magnified situation in which she finds herself, are drawn simply with clarity.

It would be interesting to know the road by which Miss Gale travelled out of Friendship Village into the greater world in which this last story lives; but this is her own affair. Whatever its antecedents, the book stands as a signal accomplishment in American letters, and it may also be a portent. If a single storyteller can pass from the empty slipshod formalism which has marked so much American narrative into something deep-cutting like **"Miss Lulu Bett,"** there may be a chance that our narrative art will emerge into a firmer growth. . . . In **"Miss Lulu Bett"** not a verbal stroke is missed, yet there is no mechanized precision. Its style is close, astringent, and it remains unobtrusively American. (pp. 315-16)

> *Constance Mayfield Rourke, "Transitions," in* The New Republic, *Vol. XXIII, No. 297, August 11, 1920, pp. 315-16.*

ALEXANDER WOOLLCOTT   (essay date 1920)

[In the play called **"Miss Lulu Bett,"**] there are a good many sources of genuine pleasure for those who are both familiar with and fond of the book. What impression it would make on that *tabula rasa* which must be counted upon as the average playgoer's mind, it is not possible to say with any assurance. One can only guess, and the guess would be that the stray visitor to the Belmont [Theater] would find there a rather dull and flabby play, one somewhat sleazily put together by a playwright who has but slight sense of dramatic values and no instinct at all for the idiom of theatre.

Of that curious distillation of the pettiness and exasperation of life which she was able to put into the finest veins of her book, not much is carried unspoilt as tonic for the play. There are drops of it in some of the characterization, particularly in the rôle of the grandmother as written by Zona Gale. . . .

[The company] does handsomely by a play that is not, by a good deal, as worth their while as it might have been.

> *Alexander Woollcott, "Zona Gale's Play," in* The New York Times *(© 1920 by The New York Times Company; reprinted by permission), December 28, 1920, p. 9.*

ZONA GALE   (essay date 1921)

Miss Lulu Bett, as a play, has an ending which is technically known as "happy". As a book, it has an ending which the stage would have termed unhappy. In the book, Lulu's first marriage proves invalid and she marries another man. In the play such a consummation was impossible. Lulu could not

marry two men in the space of an evening, no matter how vehemently the programme announced that time had elapsed. . . . So *Miss Lulu Bett,* the play, takes on by simple means the ending which life does actually compass over and over again. The first husband proves the real and only husband—the "happy" ending. . . . But—if a play is to present life—it must not always end an episode unhappily, because life does not always do so. It is true that the ironic, the satiric, the tragic, the casual, must close many and many a volume, must constitute many and many a curtain. But not all.

> *Zona Gale, in her excerpt from "'Miss Lulu Bett'," in* The New York Tribune *(© I.H.T. Corporation; reprinted by permission), January 21, 1921 (and reprinted in* Still Small Voice: The Biography of Zona Gale *by August Derleth, D. Appleton-Century Company, 1940, p. 146).*

LUDWIG LEWISOHN   (essay date 1921)

At the end of the first performance of **"Miss Lulu Bett"** . . . it was difficult not to be persuaded that here was the most genuine achievement of the American stage since Eugene O'Neill's "Beyond the Horizon." One saw at once that Miss Zona Gale had not mechanically dramatized her novel, but had turned her original fable into a play and had given it in its new form a weightier and severer ending. The dramatic action which she had built up was, save for a single debatable use of accident, the most inevitable that we recall in the work of any American playwright. Almost immediately pressure was brought to bear upon the author and the producer of the play from two different sources. Because Miss Gale had hitherto been known as a novelist, and because her play dispensed with the flashy artifices of the theater, the critics, who are wedded to a rigid and mechanical theory of technique and divorced from any fellowship with that creative imagination which builds its fit form anew every time it is exercised, promptly declared **"Miss Lulu Bett"** to be undramatic. . . . The public, persuaded and abetted by such criticism, agreed to find the play dull and in the second week of its career a new third act was substituted for the original one. In this new act the unnecessary spouse of Ninian Deacon obligingly dies and Lulu achieves respectable wifehood interrupted only by such quite safe vicissitudes as excite but do not trouble the all too tender heart. Her act of liberation is thus stultified and with it the significance and strength of the dramatic action sacrificed at one blow.

What still remains, especially for those who have the self-mastery to leave at the end of the second act, are Miss Gale's people and the moral atmosphere she has created. The second element is the rarer and the more notable. What differentiates Hervieu from Bernstein, Hauptmann from Lindau, Galsworthy from Jones, is, above all things, the feeling that the dense and peculiar moral atmosphere of life must be brought upon the stage if any interpretative illusion of reality is to be created. The conventions of the theater may let the drama flare up for an hour; they cannot make it live. Now it is not too much to say that no other American dramatist has succeeded in so fully and richly transferring to the stage the exact moral atmosphere of a class, a section, and a period, as Miss Gale. That Deacon family group on its front porch is magnificent and memorable. The preaching and blustering and nagging of Dwight, the prattling and posturing of his wife, the cold and weary resistance of Lulu, the crafty little rebellions of the child Monona, the sentimentalized scorn and detachment of Diana—these things that project the strain and tug and essential hollowness and maladjustment of the lives involved, mark an enormous advance in the American drama. . . .

Ludwig Lewisohn, "Native Plays," in The Nation, Vol. 112, No. 2900, February 2, 1921, p. 189.*

CARL VAN DOREN (essay date 1922)

[Before *Main Street* Sinclair Lewis] had been forced by the neglect of his more serious work to earn a living with the smarter set among American novelists, writing bright, colloquial, amusing chatter for popular magazines. If it seems a notable achievement for a temper like Mr. [Edgar Lee] Masters's to have helped pave the way to popularity for Mr. Lewis, it seems yet more notable to have performed a similar service for Zona Gale, who for someting like a decade before *Spoon River Anthology* had had a comfortable standing among the sweeter set. She was the inventor of Friendship Village, one of the sweetest of all the villages from Miss Mitford and Mrs. Gaskell down. Friendship lay ostensibly in the Middle West, but it actually stood—if one may be pardoned an appropriate metaphor—upon the confectionery shelf of the fiction shop, preserved in a thick syrup and set up where a tender light could strike across it at all hours. In story after story Miss Gale varied the same device: that of showing how childlike children are, how sisterly are sisters, how brotherly are brothers, how motherly are mothers, how fatherly are fathers, how grandmotherly and grandfatherly are grandmothers and grandfathers, and how loverly are all true lovers of whatever age, sex, color, or condition. But beneath the human kindness which had permitted Miss Gale to fall into this technique lay the sinews of a very subtle intelligence; and she needed only the encouragement of a changing public taste to be able to escape from her sugary preoccupations. Though the action of *Miss Lulu Brett* takes place in a different village, called Warbleton, it might as well have been in Friendship—in Friendship seen during a mood when its creator had grown weary of the eternal saccharine. Now and then, she realized, some spirit even in Friendship must come to hate all those idyllic posturings; now and then in some narrow bosom there must flash up the fires of youth and revolution. It is so with Lulu Bett, dim drudge in the house of her silly sister and of her sister's pompous husband: a breath of life catches at her and she follows it on a pitiful adventure which is all she has enough vitality to achieve but which is nevertheless real and vivid in a waste of dulness.

Here was an occasion to arraign Warbleton as Mr. Lewis was then arraigning Gopher Prairie; Miss Gale, instead of heaping up a multitude of indictments, categorized and docketed, followed the path of indirection which—by a paradoxical axiom of art—is a shorter cut than the highway of exposition or anathema. Her story is as spare as the virgin frame of Lulu Bett; her style is staccato in its lucid brevity, like Lulu's infrequent speeches; her eloquence is not that of a torrent of words and images but that of comic or ironic or tragic meaning packed in a syllable, a gesture, a dumb silence. Miss Gale riddles the tedious affectations of the Deacon household almost without a word of comment; none the less she exhibits them under a withering light. The daughter, she says, "was as primitive as pollen"—and biology rushes in to explain Di's blind philanderings. "In the conversations of Dwight and Ina," it is said of the husband and wife, "you saw the historical home forming in clots in the fluid wash of the community"—and anthropology holds the candle. Grandma Bett is, for the moment, the symbol of decrepit age, as Lulu is the symbol of bullied spinsterhood. Yet in the midst of applications so universal the

American village is not forgotten, little as it is alluded to. If the Friendships are sweet and dainty, so are they—whether called Warbleton or something less satiric—dull and petty, and they fashion their Deacons no less than their Pelleases and Ettares. Thus hinting, Miss Gale, in her clear, flutelike way, joins the chorus in which others play upon noisier instruments. (pp. 164-66)

Carl Van Doren, "New Style," in his Contemporary American Novelists: 1900-1920 (reprinted by permission of the Estate of Carl Van Doren; © 1922 by Macmillan Publishing Co., Inc.; copyright renewed © 1949 by Carl Van Doren), Macmillan, 1922, pp. 132-76.*

THE BOOKMAN New York (essay date 1923)

Until she wrote **"Miss Lulu Bett"**, Zona Gale had always been too verbose. . . . Her stories of that strange place, Friendship Village, and of those too-good-to-be-true old people, Pelleas and Etarre, are weighted down with words that do little to lead the characters along. She repeats herself many times in these tales—I suppose the editors have besieged her so often, and the pay offered has been so enormous, that she couldn't resist just one more manuscript. This of course led to another—and another. She certainly got all there was to be got out of an astonishingly thin vein. There never was a town like Friendship Village either in the middle west, which Miss Gale pretends, and ought, to know, or in the far east. Many of the characters talk as no American smalltowner could dream of talking. It is always Miss Gale projecting herself upon the canvas; and though she is strong on quotation marks, she is light on verisimilitude—sometimes. And the mush those old people of hers have uttered! Thank heaven she killed them off long ago, and got down to brass tacks in **"Birth"**.

Here she found herself; here she was on firm soil. The people leap from the printed page, talk like human beings, are revealed in all their littleness, and in all their bigness. The poor little man who is the protagonist is a creation. Lulu Bett fades into nothingness beside him. From that hot day in the village street when we first see him, he grows in our affections, he becomes part of Burage, and part of us. The story moves to its inevitable climax with all the starkness and beauty and majesty of a Greek tragedy. I venture to say it is one of the few outstanding novels of American life; yet how many people have read it? (pp. 170-71)

Some of the critics spoke of its bulk; and when Miss Gale came to write her next novel, she made up her mind that she would follow the advice of men like Wilson Follett and hew, compress, condense until for sheer economy of words her story would be faultless. Wouldn't **"Lulu"** have been better, had it been embellished a bit more? Didn't Miss Gale go too far in the process of whittling? I shall always think so. There are chapters that seem to me more like a rough outline than the completed product. I prefer the richness of **"Birth"**, with its piercing comments on life, and its constant humor, forever leavening the underlying tragedy. (p. 171)

She took the Pulitzer award for the play of **"Miss Lulu Bett"**, though I think better judgment would have been shown if the novel from which the dramatization was made had captured this prize. As a play, **"Miss Lulu Bett"** is full of technical faults. When it was suggested that a trained dramatist be called in to do the stage version, Miss Gale believed she was quite as capable of doing the job as anyone. I don't think she was.

Her mind runs to character analysis rather than to dramatic situations. In **"Birth"** there is scarcely a scene which by the wildest stretch of the imagination could be called exciting. Miss Gale doesn't understand such necessary things of the stage as "curtains", and the elopement scene, so powerful in the novel, missed fire completely in the play. She simply did not know how to get the situation before the audience in a logical way, and, like the amateur she was in a new field, she bungled, slipped—and finally fell down.

There are moments when I could figuratively shake her. In **"Birth"** she repeats a phrase like "over-shoulder" until one cries out with impatience. But she is fond of these little mannerisms, which annoy her readers—if she but knew it—and add nothing to her reputation as a stylist. She is so clever that she should know better. But here her stubbornness steps in once more. She will eliminate whole passages, if necessary, but she won't cut out a word that happens to please her—and pleases, unfortunately, no one else. . . .

It is good that she seems to have overcome her early sentimentality—her gravest danger as an artist. . . . Is she of the calibre that will press forward now, or will she slip back into an easy and comfortable popular vein? It will be interesting to watch her development from this crossroad. (p. 172)

> *"The Literary Spotlight," in* The Bookman, *New York, Vol. LVII, No. 2, April, 1923, pp. 168-72.*

WILLIAM LYON PHELPS   (essay date 1923)

I have been reading Zona Gale's *Faint Perfume,* with the accent on the second syllable. The case of Zona Gale is extremely interesting. . . . She began her career by writing a few sentimental novels, which, except in intermittent flashes, gave no hint of the true flame in her soul. Then, without any preliminary flourishes, in the year 1919 she produced a novel significantly called *Birth,* which signalised her own. There is no suspicion of sentimentality; the story is written with austere dignity, and she might honestly have placed the motto on the title-page which Guy de Maupassant put on his first and best novel— *l'humble vérité.* Fine as *Birth* is, it attracted little attention; but in its composition Zona Gale had attained mastery; for in the next year, 1920, she produced *Miss Lulu Bett,* which is remarkable in many ways, but chiefly in this: in a short book she accomplished perfectly what most of her contemporaries failed to do in five times the space. The outline of *Miss Lulu Bett* is like a Greek statue, in its economy, severity, and restrained beauty. The life and career of the unfortunate Lulu are completely set before the reader, not by the multiplication of details, but by what is emphasised and by what is omitted. Such a novel is interesting in content, and beautiful to contemplate. Three years later, with the same method—the method of selection and omission—she repeats her success. *Faint Perfume* is the best American novel I have thus far read in 1923. I smell only one danger; in her extreme care not to print a single sentence until it has been hammered, carved, and filed she may possibly fall into the pit which Henry James eventually reached. It would be sad if she should lose the capacity of saying a simple thing in a simple way.

But *Faint Perfume* would be an honour to any living writer; with so many novels loosely constructed and slovenly written, *Faint Perfume* looks as if it had been made not by a pen, but by a chisel. (pp. 199-200)

William Lyon Phelps, "The Gale Brings a 'Faint Perfume' from Wisconsin" (originally published as "As I Like It: 'Faint Perfume'," in Scribner's Magazine, *Vol. LXXIV, No. 1, July, 1923), in his* As I Like It *(copyright 1922, 1923 by Charles Scribner's Sons; copyright renewed 1951 by Celeste P. Osgood and Dryden L. Phelps; reprinted with the permission of Charles Scribner's Sons), Charles Scribner's Sons, 1923, pp. 199-200.*

JOSEPH WOOD KRUTCH   (essay date 1929)

There is no contemporary author whose evolution is more interesting than that of Zona Gale. From the days when she began to compose somewhat sentimental stories in the manner of the local colorists down to the present when she is writing psychological novels in a manner very distinctly her own, the course of her development has been continuous and self-directed. There were those who saw in **"Miss Lulu Bett"** the irresistible influence of a fashion in realism, and who hailed it as a sign that Miss Gale had been persuaded to climb on the literary band-wagon; but the aloofness of her spirit ought to be in itself sufficient to guarantee that nothing of the kind had happened, even if it were not for the fact that since the publication of the book her work has departed farther and farther from conformity to modish patterns. The truth seems to be that if she crossed the stream at that point it was only by accident, and the fact that she has continued to live in the relative isolation of a Wisconsin village is the outward sign of a preoccupation with self-development too complete to permit any dalliance with literary fashion. She discovered naturalism for herself and then abandoned it in favor of the far more personal method which achieves very absorbing results in **"Borgia."** She has her "early," her "middle," and her "late" manners, but they are stages in the development of a highly individual talent.

This latest novel is concerned with telling the strange story of a girl who seemed to bring calamity to all whom she touched. . . .

This heroine is not "right" with the world. Her will is not good despite the fact that she is not grossly or even consciously malignant. Willing evil she is the occasion of it, not because she plans or knows, but because the spiritual universe works in ways we do not understand and responds to evil suggestions which we do not have to express in plans of our own. Love and hate take short cuts through it. They are forces in and by themselves.

Now for this species of mysticism in itself I have scanty intellectual respect, for its smells unpleasantly of New Thought and the Yogi of California. But for the art with which Miss Gale has used it, for the skill with which she has evoked an atmosphere at once apparently realistic and yet charged with a sense of the ominously mysterious, I have a very high admiration. An effect like that which she creates cannot be pursued directly; it cannot be achieved through direct description or direct narration. It must be hinted between the lines, enmeshed in a network of words which seem to be concerned with something else. And Miss Gale has succeeded amazingly in doing what she set out to do. Her story is absorbing and strangely disconcerting. Her book is one of those rare ones which cast a genuine spell.

The story is laid in the Middle West of today and the manners described are the manners of ordinary upper-class people, but the author has the true mystic's gift for looking so intently at the familiar that it begins to seem strange. One knows these people very well, yet at the same time it seems that one has never really been aware of them before. There is no elaborate background, no lengthy disquisition, and yet everything necessary is somehow presented. Here, in a word, is a very individual vision plus a very accomplished technique. Miss Gale's isolation has not doubt encouraged a great deal of self-communion, but she has never forgotten that her business is ultimately to communicate; and what we get, therefore, is a manner as crisp, as deft, and as definite as the mood is tenuous and intangible.

> *Joseph Wood Krutch, "Zona Gale's New Manner,"*
> *in* The Nation, *Vol. 129, No. 3362, December 11,*
> *1929, p. 725.*

HAMLIN GARLAND   (essay date 1932)

Zona Gale had been my neighbor in Wisconsin and I had followed her progress with sincere interest. I had read her Friendship Village stories with delight, although they were, at times, unduly sentimental; and I had followed her as (in her novel **"Birth"**) she swung toward the starkly realistic method, and now, in the first week of January, 1921, I was called upon to judge her play, **"Miss Lulu Bett,"** which was being played at the Belmont Theater, for I was serving as one of the advisory committee for the Pulitzer Prize award. I would have seen the play in any case, for Miss Gale was in the city and had invited my wife and daughters to the performance.

I found it most amusing with many exquisite touches of characterization, but I came away with a sense of disappointment. It didn't quite carry all the way through. In trying for success, the dramatist—or the manager—had fumbled about for a "happy ending." . . . [The] most original character in the play was "Granma," a testy old woman whose defective hearing left her outside the family conversation. She carried on her own lines of thought, however, and her occasional interruptive remarks were curiously and amusingly out of key.

[Garland here quotes from his diary:] "She is one of the most original characters in our present-day drama . . . , Lulu, the household drudge, was equally original in conception. In fact this whole family is of a sort never before seen in our theater. This play is Zona Gale at her best—skillfully concise, caustic, yet never cruel, an admirable report of a commonplace Wisconsin family moving in the deep rut of a small-town routine. It is well worth considering as a claimant for the Pulitzer Prize."

William Allen White was in the audience, plump and smiling. "I am delighted with the play," he said, and during one of the intermissions we all met the author and her manager. . . . I said to her, "Your novel is well advertised and while this play may not prove a money success, it is a good start. It is amazingly unconventional in phrasing and characterization." (pp. 329-30)

> *Hamlin Garland, "'A Daughter of the Middle Bor-*
> *der'," in his* My Friendly Contemporaries: A Lit-
> *erary Log (Canadian rights by permission of the Lit-*
> *erary Estate of Hamlin Garland), The Macmillan*
> *Company, pp. 329-42.**

IMA HONAKER HERRON   (essay date 1939)

Beginning her career as a chronicler of the Middle Western town . . . , Zona Gale eventually joined the hostile camp of village critics and, equipped with new materials, began in convincing fashion the exposure of small town intellectual aridity. An examination of her first village studies but heightens, through contrast, the tone of her later critical attitude.

Following the negligible work of **Romance Island** . . . and **The Loves of Pelleas and Etarre** . . . , Miss Gale in 1908 first gained attention from critics with **Friendship Village**, a series of sentimental sketches in which she expressed an idealistic village creed. The intimate associations of little home towns provided motivation not only for **Friendship Village** but likewise for [**Friendship Village Love Stories, Neighborhood Stories, Peace in Friendship Village**], and other stories. The keynote to Miss Gale's earlier attitude appears in her delight in community fellowship. This simple basic emotion, she says in **Friendship Village Love Stories**, is the foundation for her joy in village life. In Friendship Village folk adventured together, "knowing the details of one another's lives, striving a little but companioning far more than striving, kindling to one another's interests instead of practising the faint morality of mere civility." In all of the Friendship series revelations are made of neighborhood intimacies, church affairs, and civic matters. All the young people "keeping company" in the village are discussed in informal colloquies over back fences, at the front gate, and at church socials. Miggy and Peter and other young couples are gossiped about with the usual freedom of the small town by Mis' Toplady, good-hearted Calliope March, Mis' Sykes, and other interested elders of the village sisterhood. In short, what one of her villagers termed the "togetherness" of small town life made a strong appeal to Miss Gale, who herself was reared in the little town of Portage.

Restricted in theme to the commonplaces of narrow lives, all the Friendship stories, nevertheless, are happily optimistic in tone. The busy men and women of the town find time to enjoy the neighborliness of a limited environment. The village women, especially, are always ready to meet any emergency. . . . Little is said of the village fathers, but one may suppose that they, too, were both competent and Samaritan-minded. Otherwise, they could not have lived in Friendship, the sweetest of villages, one, says Carl Van Doren [see excerpt above], that should stand "upon the confectionery shelf of the fiction shop, preserved in thick syrup. . . ." . . . While Friendship Village, with no definite location upon the printed map of the world, may once have been praised as worthy of abiding permanently in the memories of countless readers, "who in the enjoyment of its chronicles have been able temporarily to forget the latitude and longitude of their own personal cares and sorrows," it is really no haven for the modern escapist. The eternal saccharine might prove too strong.

Even Miss Gale herself wearied of her own idyllic creed, as her later and more mordant village ctiticism shows. The influence of *Spoon River Anthology* marks her complete change of style in **Birth** . . . , a novel of a small Wisconsin town. Realistic description, natural characterization, and logical plot indicate a pronounced deepening of Miss Gale's understanding of village manners. Here she has such an assemblage of types that her *dramatis personae* resemble a living picture of the eighties. The portrait of Marshall Pitt—a timid little man pitied by his son and neighbors—gives promise of what Miss Gale later was to do in **Miss Lula Bett**. The heroine's desertion of her husband and native town in the hope of finding beauty and pleasure in the city foreshadows *Main Street*. For the first time in her recording of inhibited lives Miss Gale, like many of her Western contemporaries, declared in this novel her revolt fron the village.

In 1920 appeared the novel, *Miss Lula Bett,* Zona Gale's most artistic and masterly interpretation of the village type. A brief, yet definite and realistic, portrayal of uninspired American family life, *Miss Lulu Bett,* like *Birth,* is another study of inhibition. The plot, terse and dramatic in every respect, moves toward the triumphant revolt of a village drudge, who unexpectedly rebels against her menial position in the household of her silly married sister. . . . A trivial story of trivial people, *Miss Lulu Bett* is also a sympathetic study of a kind-hearted, yet pathetic, village woman.

Terseness of style marks both the depictions of Warbleton, a dull and petty place, and of the commonplace Deacon family. By daring to write genuinely dull dialogue, Miss Gale not only departs from the traditional artificial conversation in American drama, but ridicules, almost without a word of comment, the affectation of this ordinary household. Typical American family conversation serves as the medium for presenting George Herbert Deacon, "the high priest of this elaborate banality," and Monona, "the first normal stage child." Miss Gale's adherence to uninspiring reality violates the traditional rules of the drama. Above all, she creates ordinary, dull people. Mrs. Bett is an old woman who is not sweet and Monona is a child who is not cute. Dwight and Ina Deacon are dull, middle-class villagers, while Lulu is, in the words of Van Doren, "the symbol of bullied spinsterhood." The same uninspired dialogue throughout but intensifies a stultifying atmosphere of monotony and domestic routine.

While more emphasis is placed upon the Deacon household and the pathos of Lulu's position, the picture of Warbleton is not dimmed. The Chautauqua Circle, the popularity of croquet, and a picnic furnish details indicating that "if the Friendships are sweet and dainty, so are they—whether called Warbleton or something less satiric—dull and petty, and they fashion their Deacons no less than their Pelleases and Etarres."

Miss Gale's abandonment of the Friendship formula is further evidenced in the literary maturity and undeniable artistry distinguishing her later fiction. *Preface to a Life* . . . illustrates both the development of her fictional powers and her further change in attitude toward small town life. The revolt indicated in *Birth* and *Miss Lulu Bett* reaches a new stage in this story of Bernard Mead, a small town businessman. In sketching Bernard's experiences from his young manhood to his fifty-second birthday Miss Gale pictures life in the little town of Pauquette, near Chicago, during the era of 1900 and later. Like *Main Street,* this is a story of attempted escape from the village virus. (pp. 345-48)

[This novel, with later stories, such as *Yellow Gentians and Blue,*] contains acid sketches of small town characters far different from those of the friendly folk of Friendship Village. Unsavory gossip, hypocrisy, and other kindred marks of repressed lives fill these records sufficiently to place Miss Gale in the newer school emerging during the years following *Spoon River Anthology.* She, too, looked at the village from a new viewpoint, but never with the complete cynicism or utter futility of some of her contemporaries. As the conclusion of *Preface to a Life* suggests, she leaves a little bit of hope in her diagnosis of small town cases. (p. 349)

Ima Honaker Herron, "Crusaders and Skeptics," in her The Small Town in American Literature *(reprinted by permission of the Publisher), Duke University Press, 1939, pp. 334-428.*

AUGUST DERLETH   (essay date 1940)

[While Zona Gale was writing her early stories] about Friendship Village and about Pelleas and Etarre, she wrote her first published novel. This was in 1905, and in October of the following year the Bobbs-Merrill Company published *Romance Island.* The story was a slight one: of a retreat on a fancied island—a trivial light romance, overwritten in part, almost frothy. She treated her subject matter in a highly romantic manner; this was the strength of her former devotion to Romance and Beauty, doubtless. The germ for the novel came to Zona on . . . [a] trip to Portage, when she learned . . . of a friend who had spent several years practising medicine in India, and her interest in Yogi; the mysticism of Yogi appealed to her, and, curiously, she made a return to mysticism later in her work. The book tells enough of Zona to be of interest. The Olivia of the story who takes pity on mad old Malakh is clearly Zona. She betrays her interest in astronomy. She gives the first evidence of something which she never conquered, unquestionably a hangover from the years of her dedication to Romance and Beauty: the use of odd names for her women; Medora and Elissa occur here. Already in this book she affirms her stand against capital punishment, a stand to which she held firm. . . . (p. 71)

[*The Loves of Pelleas and Etarre* was] filled with loosely connected stories about the various love affairs in which her two protagonists, both in their seventies, had a hand. In this book she brought to life Nichola from her first unpublished novel, she created an Avis in the tradition of the unusual names she loved. The sweetness and light, the thick, syrupy sentimentality which reached its height in the Friendship Village stories, were obvious here. For the first time she set down a credo about love—not just romantic love, but love for humanity, for all humanity. (p. 74)

Well-liked as had been her stories about Pelleas and Etarre, they did not nearly meet with the public favor given to the Friendship Village narratives which were appearing in one magazine after another. . . . Their popularity brought them into book form soon enough; within a year after *The Loves of Pelleas and Etarre, Friendship Village* appeared. (pp. 91-2)

Thus was the period of sweetness and light definitely launched in her work; intimations of it were already present in *The Loves of Pelleas and Etarre,* but, while that book was wrought of sheer fancy and romance, the *Friendship Village* stories had something more in their tenuous but real umbilical cord to reality. The fault lay no longer in the accusation that such people as those about whom Zona wrote didn't exist, for they did, but that such people alone do not make up any village. The book thus marked an advance over her earlier books. If it was possible for William Allen White to say more than a decade later of Sinclair Lewis's *Main Street,* that it was only one side of the street, then it was equally possible to say of Zona's *Friendship Village* that it, too, was but one side of a street, with a composite of the two giving us the village as it was in reality. Her village was presented through the eyes of Calliope Marsh, a middle-aged spinster, who told scores of stories about the innate kindness in all people, creating very real and all too human characters who had faults enough, who might be mean and petty and gentle sinners, but who could repent in tears through the beneficence of "loving and helping"; in all the Friendship Village books there was no evil and no sin. (pp. 92-3)

[Zona Gale] followed *Friendship Village* with *Friendship Village Love Stories,* with *Mothers to Men,* the story of an adopted boy, typical of those other Friendship Village stories even in its tears, which are usually tears never of bitterness, not of sorrow, but of joy at the innate goodness of people; with *Neighbourhood Stories,* and *Peace in Friendship Village.*

The series was broken by four books.

Christmas, with one root in Dickens' *Christmas Carol,* and one in Zona's *Neighbours,* the first and best of the Friendship Village plays, is distinguished for a fine characterization, that of Mary Chavah, and the indication that Zona is surer here in her dealing more maturely with a more important problem. The story is a homily, a tale of how a village was caught on the one hand with the necessity of doing without Christmas celebration and on the other with Mary Chavah, who professed not to believe in Christmas at all: a story on the Christmas spirit, primarily—"self-giving, joy-giving, a vast, dim upflickering of humanity of what this thing really is that it seeks to observe . . . the rudiments of divine perception, of self-perception, of social perception."

When I Was a Little Girl deserves extended comment; despite the long fairy tales put into the text of this autobiographical book, *When I Was a Little Girl* has a reality none of Zona Gale's previous novels had. (pp. 96-7)

Portions of this book, deriving as they did from Zona Gale's actual living, represent the best writing she had done up to this time. This could not be untrue; the fidelity of her portrayal of childhood grew out of her own experience; it was, moreover, closely allied to that magic dream world in which she had lived as a child, and which in this book she wove into the texture of her own story. (pp. 98-9)

The third of the books which broke into the Friendship Village group was *Heart's Kindred,* which has a curious place in her work and belongs to a new development within herself. (p. 99)

[It] remains today as evidence that no author can consciously sit down and successfully write art designed to be propaganda. *Heart's Kindred* was candidly a tract against war, sententiously dedicated *To Those Who Obey the Sixth Commandment.* (p. 108)

The fourth novel [which interrupted the Friendship Village books] was a best-seller: *A Daughter of the Morning,* . . . a short-length novel ostensibly told by a young girl in typical midwestern village dialect. Zona's prejudices again came clear, for her Mr. Bingy, a drunkard, was horribly exaggerated, a beast who never existed. The book also had its ax to grind, and was likewise in a way propaganda, this time far more successfully done. Her thesis was set forth unmistakably: better working conditions for women, and, by inference, for all who work. The women in this book came through so credibly that the assumption that Zona must have known their prototypes is inescapable; but the men are only sketched into the text as something necessary but not vital, if such a distinction could be made. (p. 111)

It was still a decade before *Miss Lulu Bett* when Zona came back [from New York] to live in Portage, and already then she was at work on a long book [*Birth*], a book she called her first novel, her first real novel, a book which occupied more of her time than any other. . . . (p. 118)

If Zona Gale wrote anything at all that has the mark of greatness upon it, that book is *Birth.* . . . The book *Birth* remains her longest, her best, her truest portrait of village life, her most careful work; this stark, realistic story of Marshall Pitt, an insignificant little man who strove to do his best in his small

life but could not sell himself, is a village tragedy of the first water, a human tragedy that is as universal as earth itself. From cover to cover, her characterizations in this book are sharp and true, her examination of village life mature, her outlook balanced; nothing of Friendship Village was permitted in Burage, the Portage of *Birth.* Her Mr. Pitt—humble to a fault, pathetically inarticulate with his longing to rise in the eyes of his fellow-men, demanding sympathy in his utter humanity—is a character who will stand beside any character of Dreiser's, of Masters's, of Anderson's or Lewis's or Cather's. The tragedy is unrelieved; no one believed in Pitt's innate fineness, his selfish, thoughtless wife deserted him, his son was ashamed of him, unable to recognize his father's unselfishness; but it is not a drab story, it is not bitter, it is not ironic. (pp. 120-21)

With the publication of *Miss Lulu Bett,* it was apparent beyond further doubt that Zona Gale had chosen the direction manifested unmistakably in *Birth,* for this brief, pointed novel, this remarkably excellent characterization was devoid of all sentimentality and even of sentiment, was possessed of a singular directness, a drastic, almost bitter theme, in which Zona Gale had utilized to best advantage every situation to press home the irony and inherent tragedy in her simple little story of Lulu Bett. (pp. 140-41)

[When *Faint Perfume,*] very similar in effect to *Miss Lulu Bett,* was submitted to Glenn Frank for *The Century,* he accepted it without hesitation, seeing in it another fine family story with the same homely, direct truth which distinguished the earlier short novel so consistently rejected by every magazine editor to whom it was submitted. The difference in her prose style was by this time marked; there were no longer the leisurely introductory pages; there was not even an introductory paragraph. . . . The story, like that of *Lulu Bett,* flowed smoothly; it was a delight to read, a story to pick up and read again. . . . This story of a young woman who is a writer, who has been in New York, who comes back to Prospect for reorientation bears certain skeletal similarities to autobiography. But it is not subjective; it is objective autobiography. (pp. 151-52)

[Zona's growing mysticism] led her to incorporate something of what she felt in her new novel. This book *Preface to a Life,* was published in 1926, a book with again many fine and true descriptions of life in a typical midwestern village, this time Pauquette (an historical Indian name with a Fort Winnebago background, and, like Friendship Village, Burage, Prospect, Kaytown, again Portage), the story of Bernard Mead, who finds love and honor in opposition, tries compromise, and becomes maladjusted to the point of insanity before finding himself again. The mystic note is not only strong, but often turgid, with the result that the book, promising to be one of her best, ultimately does not quite come off. (p. 193)

[A short story collection,] *Yellow Gentians and Blue,* was published in 1927, its short, poignant tales divided into two sections, appropriately headed by a quotation from Noah Webster: "The yellow gentian, which has a very bitter taste," and another from *The New Botany:* "Flowers, pushing through from some inner plane of being, and with such energy that they are visible to man. Especially the blue gentian." The stories were, as suggested, bitter and sweet; they were far more distinguished than anything in her Friendship Village books. . . . Her stories were told concisely, concretely, ably; her points were made with equal clarity, whether they were tragic or essentially pleasant. The tales in the volume included the psychic story, *The*

Voice. Most popular of the tales in this book was unquestionably *The Biography of Blade*. . . . (pp. 197-98)

[*Portage, Wisconsin, and Other Essays*] contained some of the best work salvaged from many published essays and lectures delivered in the course of the decade past. She wrote about Portage, about her mother and her father with deep affection, fine, precise essays which, too, deserve to rank with her best work. (p. 199)

She had two books under the Appleton-Century imprint in 1933. The first of these was a short novel, one of her best, a book in which at last she abandoned any subterfuge and called her town Portage, and one in which for the first time the Wisconsin River came to life as a part of her setting. This was *Papa La Fleur,* whose fine, human story is written with rich understanding and sympathy, so much indeed, that it would seem a great part of her late father went into the creation of the aged Frenchman, though the story of the conflict of generations could not have stemmed from him. The tragedy in the story is simply change, the change in life which is inevitably the signature of age and death, the widening chasm between Papa Le Fleur and his daughters, Linnie and Dorothy. About all her descriptions in this short novel there is a quality of mysticism so strong as to be almost a wide-eyed wonder, as if she were now indeed seeing something more behind the surface. And yet this mystic quality took nothing from the clarity of her vision. . . . She expanded the concise limning of her characters only slightly from her manner in *Miss Lulu Bett* and *Faint Perfume,* with, if anything, an increase in the effect she strove to achieve. (pp. 227-28)

The second book published in 1933 failed to approach her best work. This was *Old-Fashioned Tales,* which contained stories published largely in the so-called "slick" magazines. The title possibly derived from the fact that the stories, most of them, were blatantly concerned with love and marriage, a fact which very probably grew from her own happy marriage. There are, however, some interesting and speculative details about the book. After a lull in her use of quaint nomenclature, she returned to her former pleasure with a vengeance in *Old-Fashioned Tales,* for in this single volume are over a dozen—Foxhall, Letta, Marah, Larch, Bethna, Lucilla, Camilla, Marda, Laird, Boro, Agna, Mavis, Delphine, Madrona. While most of the stories in the book are very slight, it is evident that Zona still caught the little *moments* which always stood out in her work, and at least four of the stories rank with her best work: . . . *Lights Out, Mallard's Vacation, Larch Barden,* and *A Winter's Tale.* There is, too, a change now and then to city settings. (p. 229)

In form and manner, [*Light Woman*] is very similar to *Miss Lulu Bett* and *Faint Perfume,* though unequal in performance. The novel, with its story of Mitty, whose appearance justifiably disrupted the Belden family, was in great part an elaboration of one of her favorite themes: that good people bring out the best in those less good by the example of their living alone. Despite the fact that for the first time Zona deserted the midwestern setting to stage her book in upstate New York, the people and familiar earth were very much of the Portage country. Her Mitty was a light-headed, hoydenish woman, a type seldom done by her before. (pp. 256-57)

If even the best of her work is not great in the long view, yet it remains the tangible strength of Zona Gale's certain, unwavering, still small voice. If she is not in the inexorable rolling away of years a great author, nothing can detract from her stature as a woman who was supremely great. (p. 267)

August Derleth, in his Still Small Voice: The Biography of Zona Gale *(copyright, 1940, by August Derleth; copyright renewed © 1967 by August Derleth), D. Appleton-Century Company, 1940, 319 p.*

HAROLD P. SIMONSON (essay date 1962)

"There is no contemporary author whose evolution is more interesting than that of Zona Gale," wrote Joseph Wood Krutch after Alfred Knopf published *Borgia* in 1929 [see excerpt above]. Behind her now were novels ranging from syrup to vinegar to ambrosia, and criticism surveying the whole. Probably the key statement in all her critical theories came in the essay **"Beauty and the Commonplace,"** in which she wrote: "The fiction of the future will realize angels in the commonplace." After such a prophecy, one would naturally await Zona Gale's next fictional work and expect therein to find a few angels. What the reader came to was *Borgia* . . . ; what he found in it was Marfa Manchester, who, in truth, was a little lower than the angels. Nevertheless she was a strange woman and certainly not another Lulu Bett or Leda Perrin.

Krutch was certain he found something in the novel that "smells unpleasantly of New Thought and the Yogi of California." In this discovery he was correct. Enamoured more of her esoteric theories than of art, Miss Gale disastrously chose to expound metaphysics rather than to create convincing situations of metaphysical import. Making her intentions so ruinously explicit grew from her longing "to have people understand this book." . . . [The] book fails to match conception with performance and therefore falls short of art. Nevertheless, it underscores once again her intrepid concern with the invisible world and her identity in it.

The problem she poses concerns the nature of evil. Though hardly of the magnitude of a whale hunt, the action centers upon Marfa, who is morbidly bewildered because she suspects she herself is an agent of evil. Everything she touches turns to disaster. (pp. 119-20)

By weaving all this evil mystery into commonplace happenings, Zona Gale intended something terribly esoteric. Echoing Marshall Pitt's puzzlement in *Birth,* Marfa wonders what to make of a world wherein even a chance word brings death and misery. Incredulous that such things could ever have happened to a Saint Francis, she thinks that perhaps something is wrong not with the universe but with her. . . . Haunting Marfa are Max Gavin's words: "If you want the truth, you're probably all out of key." He said she needed to get her body "polarized to draw the good and not the ill." Marfa resolves, therefore, to re-make herself "so certain things'll follow me instead of the devilish ones."

Confused, like a primitive rising from Middle West ooze (Zona Gale's image), the twenty-three-year-old Marfa exclaims, "My God, *I'm* real." This is her turning point. Max was right: she has been an "inharmonious person." Now she confronts her real identity, not an evil Borgia but someone perhaps as perfect as "tree and star." With the mystic's gift, she sees beauty like a meteor-flash; suddenly she becomes "an island of being in a sea of non-being." And as long as she can continue to subdue flesh to spirit, she will be "right" with the world. (p. 120)

One finds little in this fiction to satisfy an intellectual appetite. . . . Zona Gale's attempts to describe the spiritually awakened individual rarely match her skill in depicting persons who are still spiritually asleep. Her metaphysical intentions smother her execution; her theories kill artistic performance.

As if to suggest that after mystical illumination one must again return to the light of common day, Zona Gale left her readers on the pinnacle of *Borgia* but for a moment before plunging them into the oppressive everyday actualities in *Bridal Pond*. . . . In a similiar way she earlier had followed *Preface to a Life* with *Yellow Gentians and Blue*. In her new book Marfa Manchester's dizzy ecstacies are nowhere to be found. Instead *Bridal Pond* contains realistic slices of life, thirteen short tales in a minor key. Only seldom do mystical strains show through. When they do, as in **"Jailbird"** and **"Springtime,"** the enfolding gloom appears only darker. In the majority of these stories Zona Gale journeys into the depthless realms of the mind to find not beauty but guilt, frustration, and madness.

The stories provide an excellent cross-section of her literary forte: the provocative and nimbly told short story. Reaching as far back as 1909 for her *Atlantic Monthly* piece, **"The Cobweb,"** she carefully chose for this book her best uncollected short fiction. The result assuredly shows her as an adroit stylist whose eye and ear deftly catch the Portage moment.

Weakest among these stories are **"The Cobweb"** and **"White Bread"**; they are better than most of the small-town chronicles written during her Friendship Village period but still too thickly coated with cake icing. Other stories in the collection achieve a quivering intensity. Her tight style restrains poignant sympathies for the oppressed and inarticulate, for the sadly limited people who hope to no avail, who toil and die. (p. 121)

The story **"Bridal Pond,"** from which the book takes its title, is Zona Gale's most successful effort to explore the regions of insanity. Jens Jevins, the richest farmer in the county, confesses before the court to the murder of his wife Agna. (p. 122)

In this allegory of death-in-life, Jens [is] awakened to the perception that for thirty-seven years of marriage he and Agna have been dead to a higher plane of existence and that his own lethargy killed her. . . . The story is dramatically unified and the language is unobtrusive and at times extraordinarily evocative ("The court-room was held as a ball of glass, in which black figures hang in arrested motion"). It leaves the reader with the tantalizing thought that Zona Gale's fiction, given more range and control, could have brought her into the front ranks of American literature. (p. 123)

To the last, Zona Gale believed that universal love was an art man would master. . . .

Undoubtedly this lofty idealism, in the abstract, would have constituted large parts of the autobiography she wished to write but never completed. Before illness forced her to discontinue it after the first chapter, she arranged for the publication of *Magna* . . . which in December to February of 1932-1933 had appeared serially in *Harper's Magazine*. Love was its theme, the same kind of idealistic love . . . [Rabindranath] Tagore platonically professed. (p. 134)

The novelette is in fact a study in the "levels" of love: from Earl Pethner to Bolo Marks who respectively murder and marry their lovers. Earl's love for Helga is madness; Alec's love for Magna is physical ecstacy—or rather it is potentially so, as much as a midnight kiss in a Zona Gale novel can arouse. But in Bolo's love for Magna there is neither madness nor emotional storm but rather "the warmth and peace of the sun." This was love as spiritual union. If a still higher love exists, clues come from old Lydia who intermittently appears in the story to announce that her husband, Jute, who for twenty years has been in his grave, "is coming home to-night." This is love death cannot touch.

Again in *Magna* Zona Gale characteristically fastens weighty ideas to thin straws. One's reluctance in assenting to these ideas is due to suspicion that the world of mind and spirit is too complex to be audaciously summarized, for instance, by old Lydia. By not complicating her ideas, Zona Gale hopes that a spoken line or image will carry the burden of their complexity. Poetry succeeds in this compression. Something electric, a fine frenzy, can be compounded from imagination and the precise statement. In such a way Zona Gale intended her slender novel to envelop realms of abstractions about love. However, she did not completely avoid the danger of having this compression lead only to cracked wisdom.

As a delicate portrayal of Magna's first love and then of her tranquil acquiescence to more mature love requiring neither moonlight nor music to sustain it, this novel is as sophisticated as anything Zona Gale wrote. A similar polish gives works like *Miss Lulu Bett, Faint Perfume,* parts of *Birth,* and certain stories in *Bridal Pond* their verisimilitude. But Zona Gale expected more from *Magna* and from such novels as *Preface to a Life* and *Borgia*. Her predilection for ideas about the intangible in *Magna* too often befogged the clean, hard lines of her realism. Thinking her delicate and often successful art insufficient to stand by itself, she hung huge, evanescent conceptualizations upon it, as if she hoped to fortify already good wine with wood spirit. (pp. 134-35)

One is safe in saying that few persons in recent years have read many Zona Gale novels. (p. 136)

To someone rediscovering them or to the person coming to them for his first time, their effect strangely echoes Walt Whitman's prophecy that who touches *Leaves of Grass* "touches a man." From these Wisconsin books more than a novelist, a reformer, or a Portage citizen emerges; for whoever comes to them comes to Zona Gale, the woman. Though anyone reading her work might find it vulnerable to criticism in matters of technique and subject matter, Zona Gale's solid core, her private character, remains unscathed. (pp. 136-37)

At first glance her world of Portage is too remote today for serious concern, for all about are the more urgent issues of world revolutions, rockets to outer space, genocidal weapons, and Johnny's chance for college. . . . If further evidence is needed to show her distance from today's reader, the fact that she died believing Neville Chamberlain had averted war with Hitler should suffice.

Zona Gale's case, however, is not so simply closed. Underneath her social criticism and domestic satire was the conviction that people have dignity which no individual, business, or government has the right to exploit. In her early Friendship Village stories this dignity lacked the sinew necessary to save it from sentimentality. In attempting to depict the inherent value in simple people, she was overly naïve. But she widened her dimensions of observation to show these people heroically fighting to stave off doubts about their own human value. Suddenly the reader confronts the contemporaneity of her theme; it is of the little man in a world he never made. (p. 137)

More to the point in a critical assessment is to judge the artistic expression of her ideas. Regardless of an artist's illusions, she is still responsible for unifying them with the reality of experience and then transforming them into some form of expression in which, in Eliot's terms, the dancer and the dance become one. All parts must unite into a single organism, yet each part should manifest its own complexity. Artistic success rests upon this paradox of integration and tension. In the case of Zona Gale, several parts of her fiction, when considered separately, show remarkable merit. Her conception, faithful observation, and language point to artistic achievement of a potentially high order. But her failure to sustain artistically the complexities of both illusion and reality leaves her considerably short of first-rate success. Needless to say, her failing is a common one. It comes not because the artist is unable to resolve his own ambivalences (Zona Gale's wavering between the mundane and the spiritual persisted to her death) but because the artist lacks the imagination to create a world in which these ambivalences powerfully interact. (pp. 138-39)

[In] her own way, Zona Gale will be remembered as a village laureate whose stories range from the saccharine to the bitter, from the idyllic to the mordantly critical. Her assemblage of village people—the spiritually awakened, the drudge, the deranged, the pathetic, the inarticulate, the kind-hearted—will continue to preserve for remembrance the American small town which, in national literature, has unfolded so much of national drama. (p. 139)

> *Harold P. Simonson, in his* Zona Gale *(copyright © 1962 by Twayne Publishers, Inc.; reprinted with the permission of Twayne Publishers, a Division of G. K. Hall & Co., Boston), Twayne, 1962, 157 p.*

ANTHONY CHANNELL HILFER   (essay date 1969)

A new [literary] generation emerging in the teens and twenties found that the prevailing forms no longer answered, and they began to discover new nexuses of identity under the tutelage of Brooks, Mencken, and other rebels against the genteel tradition. . . . [Zona Gale was not] directly influenced by either Brooks or Mencken, but in 1918 and 1920, she wrote novels that were variants on, respectively, the buried life theme and the anticonformity theme. Miss Gale's changing idea of the village serves as an index to the increasingly irresistible pressures of rejection that built up in the teens and were released in the twenties. (pp. 132-33)

[*Birth*] shows a view of the small town very near to the buried life tradition. The description of Barbara Ellsworth generalizes a village type that can be characterized mostly in terms of what environment has failed to provide. . . . Having no mind of her own, Barbara's judgments are the mere reflex of the town's. Her God is "popularity," the idol of the young and spiritually immature.

Barbara marries Marshall Pitt who is even more radically deprived. Pitt comes from those vague lower depths of American life which by comparison make even village life seem rich in forms and manners. Because of Pitt's awkwardness and ignorance of social mores, Barbara loses her "popularity," the climax being her anguished reaction to being left out of a picnic. So far the story could almost occur in Friendship Village, except that no magical agency sets things right in the end, with Barbara discovering Pitt's true worth, Pitt's character becoming stronger in the worm-turned pattern, or some other sentimental resolution. Instead, Barbara runs off with a flashy circus man who abandons her when he finds she is married and has a baby. (pp. 133-34)

The ignorance and stupidity of Miss Gale's characters offer nice comic possibilities; but Miss Gale plays for pathos, and it is here the book goes wrong, showing Miss Gale's inability to fully overcome the sentimental idealism of her earlier fiction. She tries to mitigate the harshness of her novel with vague idealistic undertones, hinting that there is a larger design behind the apparent chaos. Miss Gale's idealism is soft and its vagueness is suspect: either she does not know what she is talking about or she knows it is too nonsensical to be openly treated. Miss Gale cannot throw off the genteel tradition; she is dogged by an idealism and a watered-down optimism that she can give no proper warranty for in her novel, thus having to resort to rhetoric in attempts to show that her characters' lives are not so empty of meaning as they quite evidently are.

The "idealism" shows in Miss Gale's assurances that Marshall Pitt, a nullity if there ever was one, is in truth a great soul. Pitt's virtue is unselfishness. Here Miss Gale's Victorianism shows like a slightly tattered slip. The virtuous character in Dickens is the one who never, never thinks of himself at all. Self, Self, Self is the enemy. Miss Gale's hero, like many of Dickens' abnegators, is unselfed rather than unselfish. One simply cannot create a character in such negative terms and then expect to generate much pathos.

The effectively pathetic character must have a convincing drive for life, a touch of the demonic perhaps, a soft flame the snuffing of which expresses the brutishness and waste of life. A mere loser, a void of potentiality, arouses a pity closely akin to disgust, like one's pity for a masochist. Such characters after all, deserve their troubles in a natural if not an ethical way: they are *suited* to their misfortunes. Thus, Miss Gale's pathos goes soft and rotten beside the successful naturalistic pathos of Masters and Anderson. . . . (pp. 134-35)

[*Miss Lulu Bett*] is a slimmer book, and one more in tune with the twenties ethic of anticonformity and self-fulfillment. . . . Lulu rebels against a life of thankless and meaningless service and strikes out for her own happiness, a bit sorry, but not too much, at having to leave Dwight in a lurch. *Miss Lulu Bett,* then, is an opposite of *Friendship Village;* Miss Lulu breaks away from her family, shows no need of the community, rejects service to others as a "sell." As in the *Friendship Village* stories, however, the novel ends happily with the old formula of a marriage. The happy ending is not unrealistic and is called for by the minor comic tone of the novel. It is a pleasantly satisfying use of the worm turns convention. Still, the use of this convention shows a final scruple of optimism in Miss Gale that reveals her as something of a fellow traveler rather than a full-scale village rebel. Caught in a transitional period, Miss Gale never was altogether in phase with the emerging spirit, though dragged along without overmuch reluctance by the new current. The force of the current is shown by the reversals in patterns of feelings we find in Miss Gale's novels. (pp. 135-36)

> *Anthony Channell Hilfer, "Brooks, Mencken, and the New Zona Gale," in his* The Revolt from the Village: 1915-1930 *(copyright © 1969 by The University of North Carolina Press), University of North Carolina Press, 1969, pp. 111-36.**

JUNE SOCHEN   (essay date 1973)

The feminist writers of every generation are the literary spokeswomen and propagandists for the feminist cause. They give public expression to the ideas of the visionaries as well as the pragmatists in the movement. In 1920, the Pulitzer Prize for drama was given to Zona Gale, the author of *Miss Lulu Bett.* When it came out as a novel in the early part of the year, it was an immediate best-seller, with *Main Street* its only rival. (p. 123)

Her early published works were modest, realistic stories about small towns. *Miss Lulu Bett,* however, had a depth of characterization and poignancy that her earlier work lacked. Further, it displayed in dramatic, literary terms one of the major dilemmas faced by American women. It is in this respect that the book is germane; it portrayed quite effectively what happens to a woman who does not marry—how she is treated and how she sees herself. . . . A spinster, the outcast of American society, she performed all the domestic chores of her sister's household but always remained dutifully in the background. Her brother-in-law, Mr. Deacon, a pompous dentist and justice of the peace, continually reminded her of her dependency status. The plot thickened when Ninian, Deacon's brother, came to visit. (p. 124)

Lulu married Ninian and left town with him, only to return shortly thereafter without him, having discovered that he had been married before and did not know whether his first wife was living or dead. Eventually, Lulu married another man and left her sister's home forever. But the focus of the play, its power and success, rested upon its effective characterization of a woman coming into selfhood, an inhibited thirty-four-year-old woman named Lulu, who had had no identity before a man courted her. *Miss Lulu Bett* shows implicitly how impossible the status of an unmarried grown woman is in our society. She owned nothing, had no sense of self, was a nonperson. Only when a man paid attention to her, when she married, did she reach fulfillment. Ironically, the happy ending of the story dramatized the narrow vision of our society regarding women. The only hope for happiness for women, Zona Gale seemed to be saying, was marriage.

And yet in "real" life, Zona Gale knew about feminism and the urge to freedom that women were experiencing in greater numbers in the early 1900's. . . . She believed in woman's natural right to determine her own future and did not accept as gospel the traditional view of only one future for all women. One of her women characters in *A Daughter of the Morning* questions whether motherhood is the destiny of all women. . . . Another heroine was a writer. In fact, independent women were generally featured in all Zona Gale's writing. (pp. 125-26)

Although she continued to write [during the twenties], her stories dealt with popular themes of love and the problems of romance. Her heroines were no longer feminist but either strong-willed girls who learned how to lead their men around or selfish divorcees who ignored their parents' wishes; they displayed no doubts about the role women were to play in the modern world. (p. 126)

June Sochen, "The Hope Deferred, 1920-1940," in her Movers and Shakers: American Women Thinkers and Activists, 1900-1970 *(copyright © 1973 by June Sochen; reprinted by permission of Times Books, a division of Quadrangle/The New York Times Book Co., Inc.), Quadrangle, 1973, pp. 97-170.**

PARK DIXON GOIST   (essay date 1977)

Zona Gale's Friendship Village tales—eighty-three stories in all appeared between 1908 and 1919. They are romantic sketches in praise of the simple community fellowship of the small town. The village is presented as a "middle door to experience," a familiar environment which mediates between old and new, blending past and future in an understandable present. In Friendship anything new is subsumed to the eternal needs of the tried and true. The telephone is an example. After carefully but impersonally giving Central the number of the party being called, a caller is as likely as not to be told by the Friendship operator: "Well, I just saw Miss Holcomb go 'cross the street. I'll call you, if you want, when she comes back." Then Gale makes sure her readers understand the point by remarking: "The telephone is modern enough. But in our use of it is there not a flavor as of an Elder Time, to be caught by Them of Many Years from Now?" . . . As the town has a definite place, it also has a temporal geography—it is an historical middle landscape, tempering the rough edges of the future by insisting on the importance of traditional forms.

Calliope Marsh is the main figure in Friendship. Shrewd and sixty, Calliope is the moving spirit behind much that takes place in the village. She is *in* the town and most thoroughly *of* the town. But it was not always so. Calliope tells the narrator of the sketches that at twenty, just after her fiancé had run away with another woman, "I was lonesome, an' I hated Friendship an' I wanted to get away—to go to the City to take music, or to go anywhere else." . . . She feels estranged from the town. (pp. 18-19)

Her early feelings of alienation from the townspeople of Friendship anticipate by a decade or more the frustrations of other thwarted small town midwesterners in the fiction of Sherwood Anderson and Sinclair Lewis. But Calliope is not defeated by the town, nor does she escape to the city as George Willard does in *Winesburg, Ohio.* . . . When offered the chance to leave Friendship, Calliope says yes, she wants to, "But wantin' to mustn't be enough to make you do things." The town experience has taught her that one does not live for oneself alone. God had made her "to help in some great, big hid plan or other of His. An' quick as I knew that an' begun wantin' to help, He begun showin' me when to." She has become one with the town—"I've grown to Friendship, an' here I know what's what." . . . Her urge for individual expression has found an outlet in the greater service of community helping.

The sense of belonging to the community was an inherent virtue of the small town for John Harkless and Calliope Marsh, as for so many of their real and fictional contemporaries. As she expressed it in *Friendship Village Love Stories* . . . , for Zona Gale the sense of community existed essentially in the "fellowship" of the town. . . . (pp. 19-20)

As for Booth Tarkington, so for Zona Gale community meant people interacting ("adventuring," "companioning") and sharing one another's lives and interests. In the terms of later sociologists, community meant solidarity. It also meant achieving individual significance amidst the good people of the town. Calliope Marsh finding herself, her place, her role as a helper in the town, for example. And it meant doing all these things right in Friendship, a specific and well-defined place. Thus, for Gale, Tarkington, and many of their contemporaries community was made up of the same characteristics which recent sociologists have located as essential. But contrary to some contemporary thought, they insisted on the importance of place as a basic element of community. For them community existed in small town America; for them the small town meant community. (p. 20)

Park Dixon Goist, "The Town As Ideal Community: Booth Tarkington and Zona Gale," in his From Main Street to State Street: Town, City, and Community in America (copyright 1977 by Kennikat Press Corp.; reprinted by permission of Kennikat Press Corp.), Kennikat, 1977, pp. 13-20.*

ADDITIONAL BIBLIOGRAPHY

Collins, Joseph. "Gallantry and Our Women Writers." In his *Taking the Literary Pulse: Psychological Studies of Life and Letters*, pp. 118-29. New York: George H. Doran Co., 1924.*

A colorful review of *Faint Perfume*, noting character types carried over from *Miss Lulu Bett*.

Forman, Henry James. "Zona Gale: A Touch of Greatness." *Wisconsin Magazine of History* XLVI, No. 1 (Autumn 1962): 32-7.
A biographical and critical essay praising Gale's "nobility of mind" as her greatest personal and literary strength.

Overton, Grant. "Zona Gale." In his *The Women Who Make Our Novels*, pp. 143-56. Rev. ed. New York: Dodd, Mead & Co., 1928.
A survey of Gale's work through *Yellow Gentians and Blue*.

Federico García Lorca

1898-1936

Spanish poet, dramatist, critic, and essayist.

García Lorca is considered Spain's most important twentieth-century poet. All the main streams of Spanish culture converge in his work. He combined a knowledge of Spanish and classical literature with folk and gypsy ballads to create an idiom at once traditional, modern, and personal. One of his ambitions was to revivify language by drawing new and startling images from his Andalusian environment. His verse—harshly realistic yet lyrical, often violent and primitive—attests to the beauty and excitement of life lived close to a natural order. His drama, like his poetry, runs a wide gamut, from puppet plays and farces to tragedies patterned after the Greek classics. A number of García Lorca's plays represent the most successful counterparts in modern literature of Spain's classic and romantic drama.

Born in rural Andalusia near the city of Granada, García Lorca grew to be an exceptionally attractive man of intense vitality and personal charm. After attending school in Almeria, he studied literature and law in Granada. There he published his first work, *Impresiones y paisajes,* a lyrical interpretation in prose of the austere, melancholy countryside surrounding Castile. In 1919 he moved to Madrid and lived for several years at the Residencia de Estudiantes, a flourishing center for writers, critics, and scholars of cultural liberalism. During the 1920s García Lorca devoted himself almost entirely to poetry. During this time he suffered an emotional crisis, stemming from the conviction that he could not maintain his immense popularity and literary status while living in Spain, and in 1929 he went to New York. After his initial contact with America, García Lorca wrote *Poeta en Nueva York (Poet in New York),* which illustrated his horror at a mechanized civilization. Returning to Spain, he concentrated on drama and wrote what many consider his best plays, *Bodas de sangre (Blood Wedding)* and *Yerma.* During this period he founded and codirected "La Barraca," a traveling experimental theater under federal sponsorship. Shortly after the outbreak of the Spanish civil war, when he was at the height of his powers, García Lorca was abducted from a friend's home and murdered, apparently by Franco nationalists.

With the publication of *Romancero gitano (Gypsy Ballads),* García Lorca struck his most authentic note, that of re-creating the popular and primitive spirit of his native Andalusia. *Gypsy Ballads* best displays the poet's unique genius—his bold imagination and his completely reliable sense of the popular consciousness. Its themes of life and death, fantasy and reality, fulfillment and sterility, vital female and inadequate male are all strictly Andalusian in their presentation, yet universal in their significance. *Gypsy Ballads* was the culmination of García Lorca's talent, a new style based on a concentrated density of expression and an extraordinary imaginative power drawing its images from both the modern and the traditional background of the Spanish environment. García Lorca's poetic genius is also apparent in his plays, especially the three tragedies, *Blood Wedding, Yerma,* and *La casa de Bernarda Alba (Bernarda Alba).* These works portray characters caught in the throes of elemental passions, individuals dominated by a

premonition of fate in which dream and reality intermingle. Largely expressionistic in form, they remain masterpieces of naked dramatic art. At times, the intensity of their passion and their poetic force approach that of Greek tragedy.

García Lorca's work has won the unanimous admiration of a worldwide public as well as the interest of numerous critics. Certainly his immense popularity is due in large part to his dynamic life and tragic death. In recent years, however, critics have begun to take a more sober view of his art. In general, García Lorca is considered most intense when dealing with the major themes of his philosophy: death, barrenness, and the triumph of cruel, primitive forces over contemporary life. On the other hand, he is judged least dynamic in his surrealist efforts, such as *Poet in New York,* wherein he abandoned these themes for an abstract view of the world. Though he is still placed among the great contemporary dramatists, critics have faulted a number of his plays for a lack of dramatic intensity and psychological weight, resulting in a drama in which his characters lack true-to-life motivation. Despite these shortcomings, few have questioned the genius that adapted the folktale to a relevant position in modern literature. García Lorca's work represents an authentic poetic expression of universal passions and human suffering, and it stands as the perfect embodiment of the Spanish character.

(See also *TCLC*, Vol. 1.)

PRINCIPAL WORKS

Impresiones y paisajes   (sketches)   1918
El maleficio de la mariposa   (drama)   1920
  [*The Spell of the Butterfly*, 1957]
Libro de poemas   (poetry)   1921
Canciones   (poetry)   1927
Mariana Pineda   (drama)   1927
Romancero gitano   (poetry)   1928
  [*Gypsy Ballads*, 1953]
La zapatera prodigiosa   (drama)   1930
  [*The Shoemaker's Prodigious Wife* published in *From Lorca's Theatre*, 1941]
Poema del cante jondo   (poetry)   1931
El amor de Don Perlimplín con Belisa en su jardín (drama)   1933
  [*The Love of Don Perlimplín* published in *From Lorca's Theatre*, 1941]
Bodas de sangre   (drama)   1933
  [*Blood Wedding*, 1939]
Yerma   (drama)   1934
  [*Yerma* published in *From Lorca's Theatre*, 1941]
Doña Rosita la soltera   (drama)   1935
  [*Dona Rosita the Spinster*, 1941]
Llanto por Ignacio Sánchez Mejías   (poetry)   1935
  [*Lament for the Death of a Bullfighter* published in *Lament for the Death of a Bullfighter, and Other Poems*, 1937]
Poems   (poetry)   1939
Poeta en Neuva York   (poetry)   1940
  [*Poet in New York*, 1940]
Selected Poems of Federico García Lorca   (poetry)   1943
Así que pasen cinco años   (drama)   1945
  [*When Five Years Pass*, 1941]
La casa de Bernarda Alba   (drama)   1945
  [*Bernarda Alba* published in *III Tragedies: Blood Wedding, Yerma, Bernarda Alba*, 1947]
Lorca   (poetry and drama)   1960
The Cricket Sings   (poetry)   1980
Deep Song and Other Prose   (lectures, poetry, and essays)   1980

STARK YOUNG   (essay date 1935)

"Bitter Oleander" ["Blood Wedding"] is by a genuine poet, and the piece itself is said to have made some dramatic history in Spain. In the story of Señor Lorca's play the bride runs away with a former lover, now married; there is a stabbing and the mother of the bridegroom is left without any of her men. There are dances and songs, a wedding and so on. . . .

Racially the play is hopelessly far from us. A country like ours, where the chief part of a wedding is the conference between mothers-in-law, the trousseau, the presents and the going-away gown, can scarcely be expected to feel naturally in terms of wedding songs, grave and passionate motivations, rich in im-

provisations and earthborn devotions. No amount of dance lessons, chantings and drill can remove this portion of "Bitter Oleander" into what is convincing. The whole of it at best is an importation that is against the beat of this country.

"Bitter Oleander," in its poetry and in its method, suggests now and again [Gabriele] D'Annunzio's "Daughter of Jorio," one of the most hopelessly inexportable fine dramas of our time. For the seventh century B.C., for Sappho's era, in the Grecian isles, there are many motifs and movements and lyricisms in "Bitter Oleander" that would have been easy. Mr. Lorca's bold and poetic mind expects a flowering toward the splendor and rigor and gravity of the heart. Fundamentally the difficulty of this play for our theatre is that we cannot sufficiently take it for granted, with all its full choric passion, its glowing simplicity and its basis in a Latin tongue, whose deceiving simplicity mocks translation.

        Stark Young, "Spanish Plays," in The New Republic, *Vol. 82, No. 1056, February 27, 1935, p. 35.**

WILLIAM CARLOS WILLIAMS   (essay date 1939)

There are two great traditional schools of Spanish poetry, one leaning heavily upon world literature and another stemming exclusively from Iberian sources.

Lorca was child of the latter, so much so that he is often, as if slightly to disparage him, spoken of as a popular poet. Popular he was as no poet in Spain has been since the time of Lope de Vega. He belonged to the people and when they were attacked he was attacked by the same forces. But he was also champion of a school. (p. 219)

There has always seemed to be a doubt in the minds of Spaniards that their native meters were subtle enough, flexible enough to bear modern stresses. But Lorca, aided by the light of twentieth-century thought, discovered in the old forms the very essence of today. Reality, immediacy; by the vividness of the image invoking the mind to start awake. This peculiarly modern mechanic Lorca found ready to his hand. He took up the old tradition, and in a more congenial age worked with it, as the others had not been able to do, until he forced it—without borrowing—to carry on as it had come to him, intact through the ages, warm, unencumbered by draperies of imitative derivation—the world again under our eyes.

The peculiar pleasure of his assonances in many of the poems in [*Llanto por Ignacio Sánchez Mejias*] retains the singing quality of Spanish poetry and at the same time the touch of that monotony which is in all primitive song—so well modernized here: In the first of the *romances* which make up the book's latter half, *La Casada Infiel*, the play is on the letter o; in *Preciosa Y El Aire* upon e; in *Romance de la Guardia Civil Española* upon a; etc., etc. This is straight from *El Cid;* but not the scintillating juxtapositions of words and images in the three *Romances Históricos* (at the very end), where the same blurring of the illogical, as of refracted light, suggests that other reality—the upward sweep into the sun and the air which characterized the aspirations of St. Teresa, of El Greco and the [Luis de] Góngora whom none understood or wished to understand in his day. . . . (p. 226)

The first stanza of Lorca's greatest poem, the lament, has for every second line the refrain: *A las cinco de la tarde*—"at five in the afternoon."

That refrain, *A las cinco de la tarde,* fascinated Lorca. It gives the essence of his verse. It is precise, it is today, it is fatal. It gives the hour, still in broad daylight though toward the close of the day. But besides that it is song. Without reading Lorca aloud the real essence of the old and the new Spanish poetry cannot be understood. But the stress on the first syllable of the ''cin*co''* is the pure sound of a barbaric music, the heartbeat of a man's song, *A las* cin*co de la tarde.* What is that? It is any time at all, no time, and at the same time eternity. Every minute is eternity—and too late. *A las* cin*co de la tarde.* There is the beat of a fist on the guitar that cannot escape from its sorrow, the recurring sense of finality translated to music. The fatality of Spain, the immediacy of its life and of its song. *A las* cin*co de la tarde,* Mejías was killed! was killed on a bull's horns. *A las* cin*co de la tarde,* he met his end.

This is the brutal fact, the mystical fact. Why precisely *a las* cin*co de la tarde?* The mystery of any moment is emphasized. The spirit of Góngora, the obscure sound of the words is there. (p. 227)

Two years after the event the Spaniard takes a man killed in action—a bullfighter killed in Mexico—for his theme. No matter what the action, he was a man and he was killed: the same ethical detachment and the same freedom from ethical prejudice which characterized *El Cid* and the *Book of Good Love.* The same power also to make poetry of the here and the now. The same realism, the same mounting of the real, nothing more real than a bullfighter, mounting as he is, not as one might wish him to be, directly up, up into the light which poetry accepts and recasts. That is Lorca. (pp. 227-28)

In reading Lorca the whole of Spanish history must be borne in mind, Saint Teresa with her bodiless thrust of soul, the steadfastness, the chastity—*but* also the reality of the Spaniard. Spanish poetry says [Salvador de] Madariaga, is both above and below the plane of thought. It is superficial to talk of Lorca as a sensualist. He is a realist of the senses and of his body but he is far from the common picture of a sensualist. The cold and elevated plateau which has bred the chastity of the *copla* . . . enters into all of Lorca's work. Read carefully, the icy chastity of Spanish thought comes through the reality of the event from which the man does not flinch—nor does he flinch before the consequence. He will give the body, yes, but the soul never! The two realities, the earth and the soul, between these two the Spaniard swings, firm in his own.

These are the influences that made Lorca. The old forms were bred of and made for song. The man spent his life singing. That is the forgotten greatness of poetry, that it was made to be sung—but it has been divorced from the spoken language by the pedants.

Lorca honored Spain, as one honors a check, the instinctive rightness of the Spanish people, the people themselves who have preserved their basic attitude toward life in the traditional poetic forms. He has shown that these modes, this old taste, are susceptible of all the delicate shadings—without losing the touch of reality—which at times in their history have been denied them. In such ''obscurities'' of the words as in the final *romances* in his book, the historical pieces addressed to the saints, he has shown how the modern completes the old modes of *The Cid* and *The Book of Good Love.* He has carried to success the battles which Juan de Mena began and Góngora continued. (pp. 228-29)

William Carlos Williams, ''*Federico García Lorca*'' (*originally published in* The Kenyon Review, *Vol. I, No. 2, Spring, 1939*), in his Selected Essays of William Carlos Williams (*copyright 1954 by William Carlos Williams; reprinted by permission of New Directions Publishing Corporation*), Random House, Inc., 1954, pp. 219-30).

ANGEL del RIO   (essay date 1941)

As is so often the case in Spanish literature, Lorca's dramatic work is inseparable from his poetry and is a natural emanation from it. We have many examples of this: Gil Vicente, Lope de Vega, the Duke of Rivas, Zorrilla; in modern times, Villaespesa, Marquina, Valle-Inclán, Unamuno, and the Machado brothers. In European Romanticism we frequently find the phenomenon of lyrical poetry being turned into dramatic poetry. In this respect, as in so many others, Lorca can be placed within the framework of the Romantic attitude. But let us understand Romanticism not as a school of a certain period, but as a manner of feeling and artistic expression.

Lyricism and Romanticism seem to be fused from the start of his career. His first play, *El maleficio de la mariposa (The Spell of the Butterfly)* was written at the same time as his Symbolistic early verse and was animated by the same inspiration as his poems about insects and animals.

Leaving aside the dramatic intensity of his poetry, especially that of the *Gypsy Ballads,* his dramatic work developed side by side with his poetic work, both oscillating between the two magnetic poles of his inspiration and his style, the poles of the select and the popular, the capricious and the tragic, the stylized grace whose art was close to the art of the miniature painter, and the anguished passion within a whirlwind of sensuality. (p. 140)

[Several] years after the premature *Spell of the Butterfly,* Lorca really began his dramatic career with *Mariana Pineda.* Conceived in the popular vein, the work suggests a childhood ballad: ''Oh, what a sad day in Granada.'' It follows a technique similar to that of many of his first poems and songs. We see here the attempt, probably intuitive, to fuse elements of the classical and Romantic theater and to do so with a modern flair. From the classical tradition he takes the essential spirit, the dramatization of a popular ballad in whose verses the drama is suggested. On the other hand, from the Romantic era he takes the historic theme, the feeling of background, and above all the character of the heroine, an angel sacrificed on the altar of love. Judged on its own merit, the work lacks true dramatic dimensions. It is a static picture. Only in one or two dialogues between Pedrosa or Fernando and Mariana can we catch a glimpse of the clash of wills without which there can be no drama. As for the intimate conflict of the heroine, Marianita, it is barely sketched. From the very beginning she seems predestined to her end; she is the embodiment of sacrifice: neither the hope of saving herself, nor the certainty of Don Pedro's love for her can change her tone of resignation. . . . She is revealed to us not through action nor in intimate dramatic soliloquies but in lyrical fugues, as in the beautiful ballad that begins with the lines, ''With what an effort / the light leaves Granada!'' In the rest of the play the same thing happens. The best moments are due to the presence of lyrical elements, either directly, separated from the action, as in the ballads describing the bullfight in Ronda and the arrest of Torrijos, or as a lyrical motif in contrast to the dramatic action. The latter we find in the ballad of Clavela and the children or the song in the garden, ''Beside the water.'' In many scenes there is a pathetic, almost musical atmosphere. On the whole we detect throughout the play the lack of maturity of an author who is experimenting with a new technique. Even his verse has a naïve and occasionally clumsy cadence. Though doubtless inferior to the poetry of these years, in which Lorca had already written many of his *Gypsy Ballads, Mariana Pineda* is not without interest. In more than one way we can catch a glimpse in it of the great merit which the best dramatic work of Lorca was to exhibit. There is a clear feeling for the tragic and a faultless good taste: aesthetic dignity saves the most dangerously poor passages, those on the border of immature and trite melodrama, like the scene of the conspirators, the seduction attempt on the part of Pedrosa, and the chorus of novices. Above all, there is a conscious effort of innovation in his intention to synthesize in the theater the plastic, lyrical, dramatic, and musical arts into a superior unity. For this reason Lorca took great pains to "tune up" each scene within a stylized atmosphere of colors, lights, allusions, and constant musical interludes and backgrounds, until at the end of the play a sort of operatic and symbolic apotheosis is achieved. (pp. 140-42)

Far better constructed, although of less emotional intensity, are the works which followed *Mariana Pineda*. We find in them again the same qualities—expertness, self-confidence, stylization—as in his *Book of Songs*, but here enriched by a well-defined and conscious ironic grace.

Three farces in prose, written between 1929 and 1931, make up this phase of his work and constitute at the same time a group by themselves within his theatrical writings. The first is *Amor de Don Perlimplín con Belisa en su jardin (The Love of Don Perlimplín for Belisa, in His Garden)*. . . . Then came *La zapatera prodigiosa (The Shoemaker's Prodigious Wife)*, . . . and finally the delightful *Retablillo de Don Cristóbal (In the Frame of Don Cristóbal)*. (pp. 142-43)

They have in common the same stylized popular background and a similar theatrical technique which results from the combination of elements taken from the courtly comedies at the end of the seventeenth and the beginning of the eighteenth centuries, from the Italian stage, from the puppet theater, and from the modern ballet. Each one, depending on which element predominates, has its particular character.

The Love of Don Perlimplín is the most cultivated of the group in technique and the most lyrical in spirit. Although not distinguished by the careful technique or the lively movement of *The Shoemaker's Prodigious Wife*, it is nevertheless superior in its poetic qualities. Always within the framework of irony, we can detect passages of beautiful lyricism, as in Perlimplín's lament: "Love, love, wounded love," and in Belisa's song: "Along the banks of the river." In the third scene—Perlimplín's suicide—buffoonery is raised to an atmosphere of delicate melancholy. The playfulness of the farce becomes impregnated by a pathetic aura, diffused in soft tones like the sonatas of Scarlatti, which were used by Lorca as melodic interludes, or like the poetic theater of Musset, which Lorca had read with great interest. We find ourselves at the limit of pantomime where an intentional dehumanization of characters takes place, and nevertheless we perceive in the comic profile of Don Perlimplín his sentimental anguish, caused by a love which is at the same time pure and grotesque.

The Shoemaker's Prodigious Wife is a stylization of pure folk charm, the most complete and successful work of this group. Directly inspired by folklore, the shoemaker and his wife, the chorus of neighbors, the dialogue and the action are conceived with a picaresque, old Spanish flavor, which reminds us of certain short plays of the Golden Age. The popular ballad of the shoemaker preserves the common and clumsy flavor of the ballads commonly recited by blind men, refined through touches of the best poetic quality. The play is an exercise in wit: the few dramatic scenes are expressed in a knowing gradation through the contradictory feelings of the shoemaker's wife toward her husband. Throughout she is bad-tempered and tender, piquant and impudent. The farce is resolved in the triumph of love, when the shoemaker and the shoemaker's wife are reunited. Even within the framework of comedy Lorca places a trace of bittersweetness, when after the reconciliation of the couple the work closes with the half serious, half ironic lamentations and insults of the shoemaker's wife: "How unfortunate I am with this man that God has given me!" We should take notice of this ending, basically a happy one, because it is the only time that it occurs in Lorca's dramatic works, which are primarily concerned with frustrated love. As in his other plays, the music—song, rhythm, background—has an essential role, producing an effect of unreality and giving the play the subtlety, grace, and movement of a ballet.

In the Frame of Don Cristóbal, like *Los títeres de Cachiporra (Cachiporra's Puppets)*, comes from the period of the first youthful experiments and was inspired directly by the puppet theater. It is not much more than a game, a folk Andalusian *divertissement;* it is important only as an example of Lorca's versatility, that constant search for a better integration of the arts which characterizes his theatrical writings as much as his poetry. It also reveals the piquant background of malicious country wit which was part of his mental makeup and added spice to his conversation. *In the Fame of Don Cristóbal*, full of naïve fantasy, is a magnificent example of "naughtiness" and spontaneity.

These short unpretentious plays illustrate typical aspects of Lorca's artistic personality; his more profound self we find in his treatment of anguish and tragedy, but even here we shall continue to find a counterweight of light and joyfulness, of pleasure generated by wit and innocent irony.

Asi que pasen cinco años (If Five Years Pass) and some scenes from the drama *El público (The Public)* . . . belong to the period in which he was interested in Surrealism. This work comes a little after or at the same time as his poems about New York City. (pp. 143-44)

The fragments that we know from *El público* do not give us an accurate idea of the total work. It seems to have been inspired by the problem of reality and poetic "super-reality" on the stage and in real life. Besides, we can detect in several episodes a vein of perverse and abnormal sensuality corresponding to the preoccupations which must have tormented him during those years. The characters are beings of fantasy and beings taken from real life, without any distinction between them. All act and speak with the same incoherent automatism. The play is full of bloody and violent images mixed with humor. (pp. 144-45)

If Five Years Pass ("a legend about time in three acts and five scenes") is of greater interest than *El público*. Here the theme is a combination of two typically Lorcan preoccupations: the passing of time and the frustrations of love. The central characters, the young man and the fiancée, are new versions of Marfisa and Don Perlimplín and the waiting for a wedding which never takes place is almost a foretaste of *Doña Rosita la soltera (Doña Rosita the Spinster)*. The technique and the atmosphere are, however, completely Surrealistic. It is an atmosphere of dreams, with masks, mannequins, clowns, or real people like the rugby player or the card players dehumanized in the manner of the characters of Gómez de la Serna, to whose influence his work is largely indebted. Lorca manages to sustain an unreal atmosphere suspended somewhere between humor and drama and with an undercurrent of mysterious sensuality. As in the best of his plays, the lyric elements are ever present. . . . The dialogue, whether in prose or in verse, almost always shows a growing mastery of the theatrical technique which the poet was slowly acquiring through his various experiments. Lorca never confined himself to a definite type of poetry or of drama nor to the inflexible formula of any fixed school. Thus, having learned all he could from it, he soon abandoned Surrealism and returned for inspiration to the feelings and themes of Spanish reality where his art finally found its focal point. (pp. 145-46)

If his tragedies represent a balance between lyricism and drama, *Doña Rosita* is the fusion of poetry and comedy, with subtle historical overtones.

The author describes the work as "a poem of Granada in 1900 divided into various 'gardens' with scenes of singing and dancing." Like *Mariana Pineda,* to which it bears a strong resemblance in technique and mood, it deals with the evocation of a period. But the shading of the poetic, plastic and emotional elements of the play is better achieved. The direct romanticism of the earlier work now becomes soft irony. The intense drama of love becomes diluted and is dissolved into lyrical fragrances. The somewhat artificial pathos of *Mariana Pineda* is replaced by a sweet melancholy, a pure and intense emotion. Doña Rosita, a woman (the most important characters in Lorca's plays are always women), is not a heroine but rather a symbol of womanhood in the Spanish provinces at the end of the century. Thus we have a lack of real dramatic intensity. In order to become a deep psychological play it would have had to delve into the individual soul of the characters. This is precisely one of the main shortcomings in all of Lorca's plays, including his tragedies, where passion never quite acquires full psychological embodiment and always remains skin deep, with no motivation other than a kind of tragic destiny before which the characters submit with hardly a struggle. What happens in *Doña Rosita* is that the poet turns this limitation into his main creative force. The drama of resigned love incarnated in Doña Rosita, the endless waiting for the sweetheart who will not return, is consciously subordinated to a more impersonal anguish: what moves the spectator is neither the passion nor the suffering of the protagonist but the bodiless presence of time itself hovering over the stage and the life of every character. Lorca is a master of creating a lyrical atmosphere, and in this play he succeeds completely. The evocation of those quiet years from 1890 to 1910 in which Spanish life seemed to be at a standstill as if it had lost all its vital springs gives us a perfect picture of both reality and trite pathos, touching in its irony. All the sentimental mood of the play, all its lyrical quality find their maximum expression in the "language of flowers," a symbol of existence without desires and without ambitions, and a symbol at the same time of the slow withering of Doña Rosita. (pp. 146-47)

Some critics have mentioned the influence of Chekhov. There seems to be a definite similarity between both writers. The end of the play, when the mother, governess, and Rosita leave the house, taking with them all their memories, while the wind softly moves the curtains and the stage is engulfed by the weight of loneliness, cannot but remind us of the almost identical end

of *The Cherry Orchard.* Other points of coincidence with Chekhov, whose works Lorca doubtlessly knew, could be found. There is the fact that both turn to nature when looking for a symbol of action and a lyrical background. The atmosphere in *Doña Rosita* reminds us in many ways of the melancholic atmosphere in *Three Sisters.* But the parallels seem to end there. There can be no similarity between Lorca's characters, as simple as shadows, and the characters created by the Russian playwright, who are at the brink of desperation, and struggle tragically while looking for a justification of their existence. Chekhov's lyricism is the result of a delving into the deepest layers of human feelings and human anguish; in Lorca lyricism is a poetic fact alien to every intellectual and psychological motivation.

Neither in *Doña Rosita* nor in his dramas can Lorca's art be characterized by its intellectual strength. Its essence is rather an instinctive intuitive penetration and an extraordinary gift for poetical expression. (pp. 147-48)

[In *Blood Wedding*] Lorca for the first time finds the right expression for the passionate intensity vibrating in the inner recesses of his best poetry: a peasant tragedy. At times the dehumanized, stylized art of his songs and stage artifices make us forget the frantic trembling of life and nature which the voice of this dark and passionate poet brought to us from the time of his earliest creations. This constantly present trembling of life can be found in the dramatic quality of his lyrical poetry as well as in his tragedies, where it comes to be felt with all its violence, subordinating the lyrical content to the dramatic tone in a perfect fusion which Lorca had to achieve if he wished to express fully his most complete self.

"I was," the Fiancée says, "a burnt woman, full of sores outside and within. And your son was a drop of water from whom I expected children, earth, health." Here is the essential element of tragedy: beings who are scorched by a deep passion against which it is futile to struggle. The situation is a simple one and an old one: the rivalry within a family, and the rivalry of two men for a woman who struggles between the attraction of a fiancé, who offers her peace of mind, and the more powerful attraction of her lover. (pp. 148-49)

Blood Wedding is a work of the highest artistic rank. In it we can detect the breath of classical influence, a touch of Mediterranean tragedy and even a certain Shakespearian quality. . . . [It] is impossible to doubt the exceptional value of this play. The unity of its poetic elements, the moving clarity of its drama, and the breath of folk life that animates it make it the most complete and beautiful masterpiece of Lorca's theater and place it well above the mediocre productions of today's Spanish dramatic literature.

Yerma, written two years later, is similar in its main idea and its technique to *Blood Wedding.* In many ways it is a more finished product. The subject is a more ambitious one. Lorca had been elaborating it for many years. It deals with a love frustrated because of man's powerlessness to respond to woman's passion. The subject appears in some of Lorca's earliest poems and reappears later as an obsession in *Mariana Pineda,* in some of the *Gypsy Ballads,* in *Don Perlimplín,* in *If Five Years Pass,* in *Doña Rosita.* Sometimes he deals with spiritual love, sometimes with sensuous lubricity. In *Yerma* the situation develops within the framework of frustrated motherhood, and the passion becomes intimate and spiritualized. The play's structure follows an order in which dramatic elements predominate. The lyrical elements—songs, washerwomen's chorus—

are less important. The tragic conflict acquires greater density because within a primary climate of passion surrounding the characters there is a more complex hierarchy of forces. As in *Blood Wedding,* there is a suggestion of pagan forces struggling in Yerma's soul against her moral sense of duty, until she is incapable of giving in to either of the two forces and decides to kill her husband.

In spite of all this and perhaps because of its ambitious scope, Yerma does not quite reach the artistic level of *Blood Wedding.* It does not have the same artistic unity; the dramatic motivation is less clear. In *Blood Wedding* everything is concrete and basic, earthy, within a folk poetic atmosphere. In *Yerma* at bottom every element strains toward abstraction. We would well suspect that [Miguel de] Unamuno's presence hovered around Lorca's subconscious while he was writing *Yerma.* The very character of the heroine reminds us of Unamuno's literary creations. . . . Doubtlessly Lorca wanted to go beyond Unamuno's disembodied approach to tragedy; he wanted to add to it life, blood, individuality. He managed to do so up to a point, but in order to give to Yerma's intimate anguish all its pathos and its universal meaning he needed instruments for abstract reasoning and at the same time for subtle psychological penetration. These Unamuno possessed abundantly but Lorca lacked, being an intuitive spontaneous artist. Lorca's domain extended from direct speech to symbols, from folk elements to stylization. That is why the reading of *Yerma* is somewhat disappointing. We do not find in it the lyrical pathos or the burning dialogue of *Blood Wedding.* Perhaps on stage the effect would be more positive. Lorca's theater is in great measure a spectacular theater and words lose a great part of their meaning when read outside a total atmosphere that was posited at the very moment the work was written. Lorca was a past master in the rendering of dramatic elements in terms of visual details, rhythm, and lyrical symbols. (pp. 151-53)

> Angel del Rio, in an essay in his Federico García Lorca: Vida y obra *(reprinted by permission of the Literary Estate of Angel del Rio), Hispanic Institute, 1941 (translated by Gloria Bradley and reprinted as "Lorca's Theater," in* Lorca: A Collection of Critical Essays, *edited by Manuel Duran, Prentice-Hall, Inc., 1962, pp. 140-54).*

JOHN GASSNER   (essay date 1954)

Painter, musician, actor, and stage director, as well as playwright, Lorca was obviously . . . inclined toward the theatrical mode of expression. . . . Had Lorca elected to play at dramatics as a sophisticated game, he could have carried if off with rare ingenuity, and he would have added true poetic sensibility to the performance. Had he chosen, instead, the Copeau-influenced moderate "pure in heart and pure in wisdom" kind of theatrical playwriting we find in [André] Obey at his best, it is probable that Lorca would have succeeded, too. In fact, he revealed all of the above-described qualities supremely in *The Love of Don Perlimplín for Belisa in His Garden.*

To the student of "pure" theatre nothing would be more rewarding than a close study of this play of changing moods and identities as a man of fifty, married to a voluptuous girl, invents a lover for her and kills himself for her, in order to teach her the meaning of love. (p. 224)

The décor and the costuming are fantastically theatrical in every respect. Among the theatricalist details provided by Lorca are an extravagantly large bed, five balconies to the bedroom with

five ladders hung to the ground, a man's hat beneath each of them!, and Don Perlimplín seated in bed with decorated gilded horns fully sprouted from his forehead. The quick unrealistic shifts of scene and the action, which is entirely histrionic as the husband impersonates the invented, entirely non-existent lover, are especially theatrical. In Lorca's play, all elements are a single essence, so that it is impossible in *Don Perlimplín* to make any distinction between a play-text and theatre, whereas in the usual realistic play, regardless of the relevance of its so-called ideas, the pattern is the clumsy one of separate "content" or word-action and largely supplementary stage business for the actor. (pp. 224-25)

In his major plays *Blood Wedding, Yerma,* and *The House of Bernarda Alba,* Lorca retained all the theatrical afflatus I have lamely tried to suggest in the above-made references to *Don Perlimplín.* The fact that it has not been possible to capture that afflatus in New York productions accounts, in part, for the failure of these later plays to get their due credit from audiences and reviewers. Lorca is simultaneously poet and theatrician in his use of a lullaby in the first scene and of a lament in the last of *Blood Wedding.* He is no less effective in the almost Dionysian clothes-washing scene set on the bank of a mountain stream, in the second act of *Yerma.* He is also a formalist, especially in the forest scene of *Blood Wedding* (Act III, Scene I), in which, drawing upon the classic tradition of Spanish theatre, he uses Death and the Moon as allegorical figures to prefigure a fatal duel. Properly played, that scene is true magic, and it can also constrict the heart with unease and tragic pity.

Yet Lorca is so much more than a theatrician in his mature work that he could never be confused with a coterie writer. He is, on the one hand, local and rooted in a people's way of living and feeling that supersedes literary notion-refining and vacuous theatre-mongering. And, on the other hand, he became something more than a mere writer of substantial folk plays; he became a tragedian. We have evidence, moreover, that he was consciously moving away from lyrical drama toward poetic realism in his drama of family pride and frustration *The House of Bernarda Alba.* He was moving, without losing "poetry" or "theatre," toward cosmopolitan analytical drama and social drama when a Falangist firing squad executed him in 1936. (pp. 225-26)

> John Gassner, "The Rebuilders: Federico García Lorca," in his The Theatre in Our Times: A Survey *of the Men, Materials and Movements in the Modern Theatre (copyright © 1954 by John Gassner; used by permission of Crown Publishers, Inc.), Crown, 1954, pp. 224-26.**

GUSTAVO CORREA   (essay date 1962)

Yerma has an appropriately symbolic title, since its central theme is that of frustrated motherhood. The word "yermo" means in Spanish "uninhabited, deserted, uncultivated, not productive," and is applied principally to sterile land. It may also be used as a noun meaning "uncultivated grounds"—*yermos.* In Lorca's tragedy Yerma is the protagonist—a tragic figure precisely because she is *yerma.* She carries within herself the tragic mark. She struggles desperately against her fate, but in vain; she finds her womb dried up—dried up like the arid deserts, and dried up like the cursed fig tree of the Bible: because it bore no fruit it received the curse of Christ. . . .

At the end of the tragedy she considers herself to be the final instrument of her own desolation. Her struggle through the years to overcome her fate has been in vain. It has been more powerful than she, and her dried-up womb will remain so forever, thanks to her own criminal hands. (p. 96)

Yerma is essentially Spanish. The very theme of maternity is especially so. The Spanish woman possesses what we might call an exclusivist or exaggerated idea of maternity. The cradlesong is her obsession from childhood on. She not only wants to have a child, but several, lots of them. She knows that only in this way can she accomplish her mission in the world. To be childless constitutes a kind of ostracism which has no remedy. Not only is it a private tragedy, but social too—that is, imposed from without by society, as evidenced by the remarks of the laundresses, who consider childless Yerma a most unfortunate woman. The structure of Spanish society, with all the powerful force of tradition, has imposed upon its women a duty, a mission; before all else she is to be a mother. Her place is static and predetermined: "The sheep in the fold and women at home," says Yerma's husband. Matrimony is the Spanish woman's occupation, and her only horizon the walls of her house. (p. 98)

In order to understand the meaning of *Yerma,* then, it is necessary to bear in mind that we are dealing with a society in which this problem of maternity is alive with all the force of a private destiny which has received a social investiture. Very possibly *Yerma* would not even be a tragedy outside Spain—which perhaps partially explains the fact that people of other countries have misunderstood it.

Yerma is also essentially Spanish because of the problem of honor. If its only problem were that of maternity at any cost, Yerma could easily have sought the love of a man other than Juan. But this is impossible precisely because society has assigned her fixed and immutable relations with men. Illicit love is out of the question. (p. 99)

Yerma appears to be a strong link in this chain of Spanish tradition: it is an honor play, to a certain extent, and would have no *raison d'être* unless the traditional codes of honor were still alive in the Spanish provinces. Here, rather than in the city, tragedies arise out of honor. Yerma's husband must be assured that people are not talking about him and his wife. He brings two sisters to his home to watch Yerma; he doesn't like her to leave the house. . . .

Later Juan would like to take revenge on Yerma by divulging her supposed shame, but he doesn't, since it would redound to his own dishonor. . . . (p. 101)

Rumors begin; the family honor is in danger. People grow silent at Juan's approach; they have doubts about Yerma's honor. . . .

A curious fact: *Yerma* contains a fusion of . . . [two concepts of honor]—reputation and private virtue. Yerma will not surrender to her desire because she is an heroic woman, of real quality, "of the caste *(casta)*"—above temptation and others' opinions. She maintains her purity and accepts the tragedy of her frustrated maternity. (p. 102)

For Yerma, a woman of intrinsic quality—*casta*—the code of honor is inexorable, and it is just as impossible to break its laws as it is to break those of Nature: "Do you think I could know another man?" she declares. "Where would that leave my honor? Water cannot turn back, nor does the full moon rise at noonday."

Yerma's moral greatness rises above the conventional arrangements of her society, and though she could be impure in order to avenge herself of her husband and of the gossipers, though she could be impure in order to resolve the great tragedy of her life, she chooses renunciation.

The triumph of honor, however, does not prevent her final revenge in a moment of delirious obsession, and so with her own hands she strangles the one who some day might have been able to give her a child.

The two concepts of honor, then, are principal elements in *Yerma.* Frustrated maternity could not be understood as tragic apart from the code of honor.

It should be added that this is a tragedy among country people, and that the two concepts of honor are as valid for them as for the nobility. In our opinion Lope de Vega was the first great standard-bearer for the honor of the lower classes, and *Yerma* is one more triumph for this democratic spirit which has prevailed in Spain for centuries. (pp. 102-03)

Yerma and *Blood Wedding* are twins. They are rural tragedies; the characters are both specific—local—and cosmic. The cosmos becomes manifest in the elemental, dark, and primitive forces which shape man's destiny. Honor, of course, with its apparatus of external conventions influences the direction of events. But the tragedy arises with the conflict between the direction taken by events and the one taken by personal inclination.

"Inclination" means in *Yerma,* as in *Blood Wedding,* the inclination of the blood—biological life force. In *Yerma* this means maternity. To frustrate it is to poison the blood and consequently to provoke tragedy. Yerma, it will be remembered, calls the curse "a puddle of poison on the wheat heads." Poisoned blood in *Yerma* is like corrupted blood in *Blood Wedding.* To follow the inclination of the blood in *Yerma* is to accomplish the greatest mission, to reproduce oneself as does all Nature. And all Nature is a great invitation to Yerma to realize her mission as mother, but she must hang her head in defeat and consume herself in a hopeless waiting. . . . (p. 103)

Man's position in the cosmos is not so clearly dramatized in *Yerma* as in *Blood Wedding.* In *Yerma* the act of conception acquires a lyrical sublimation; the purely physiological is abandoned and conception becomes something enchanted, and act of magic—something that happens between singing participants. (p. 105)

The rural setting of *Blood Wedding* and *Yerma* is not, of course, exclusively Lorca's possession. Other Spanish dramatists have used it; Jacinto Benavente has given us some of the most important rural plays, particularly *La Malquerida.* Faithful to the call of the blood and of the earth, it has points in common with the rural plays of Lorca, especially *Blood Wedding.* An elemental, primitive level—the dark force of basic passions—furnishes the dramatic motivation, although in *La Malquerida* the cosmic element is lacking.

It would be interesting to study how the rural play has crystallized elsewhere, especially among the Romance languages. Italy affords modern examples of the rural play in the classical tradition, a noteworthy specimen being Gabriele d'Annunzio's *Jorio's Daughter,* a country tragedy in three acts. This play is like a ritual ceremony. The elemental forces apparent there resemble very closely the motivations underlying the dramatic development of *Blood Wedding* and *Yerma;* but in Lorca the life forces are oriented toward the cosmic and the biological, while in the D'Annunzio play they have a meaning which is manifestly traditional and historical. The ritual element gives it a solemnity, a sacred tone. *Yerma,* certainly, achieves something of a ritualistic feeling with the pilgrimage of the sterile women to the miraculous hermitage and the final dance in which symbolic chants are intoned to the mystery of conception. But this ritualistic atmosphere is sporadic and never completely saturates the action. In *Jorio's Daughter,* however, ritual has a major importance. Italy, a land of eternal Renaissance where the flame of Greco-Latin tradition was never extinguished, interprets the rural themes within a sacred and ritual atmosphere similar to that with which the ancients invested their tragedies. Spain, on the other hand, faithful to its own cultural tradition, interprets through Lorca the rural drama according to the dictates of the Spanish theatre. (pp. 105-06)

> Gustavo Correa, "Honor, Blood, and Poetry in 'Yerma'" (copyright © 1962 by Gustavo Correa), in The Tulane Drama Review, Vol. 7, No. 2, Winter, 1962, pp. 96-110.

ALLAN LEWIS (essay date 1971)

[All three plays in Lorca's rural trilogy,] *Blood Wedding, Yerma,* and *The House of Bernarda Alba,* are aspects of a central theme: the conflict between the law of honor and the law of the passions. They are intense lyrical dramas of sex in which woman, who should be fruitful, remains unfulfilled. The worship of virginity to preserve the right of inheritance, the code of moral conduct to insure the continuity of life, is in violent opposition to the natural flow of the emotions, but the code is preserved. The rotting past weighs down the living, and the women are left alone among the dead, or go mad with frustration, "dried up forever." Out of the tragedy of women is implicit the story of Spain herself. (pp. 248-49)

In *The House of Bernarda Alba,* the last of the trilogy, there are only women, from the old crazed grandmother to the young and sensuous Adela. Bernarda Alba, proud of her blood, holds her five daughters locked within the house after the death of her second husband, to mourn for eight years. She looks down upon the villagers as beneath her family, none of the men worthy of marrying her daughters. She is the upholder of the past, the morality of the clan. Face in the eyes of the world and honor of the name are above any concession to the starved emotional life of the women. The daughters writhe in revolt, terrified by the mother but secretly longing for release. (pp. 256-57)

Bernarda Alba is the most realistic of the three tragedies and therefore the most comprehensible. Its form is the developed situation of the well-made play, and the characters are more psychologically realized. The images center around the house, doors, windows, walls that hold out the world beyond and keep the women cloistered from life. The theme is the same in all three plays—darkness and love, sex and frustration, passion and death. Women bear the tragedy, for they are the bearers of life, and are left alone to mourn in silent suffering the renewal of their fate and the emptiness of their bodies. The cycle repeats, for Lorca's plays are a tribal theatre of primitive power, ancient in form but shaped by a sophisticated modern mind. (pp. 257-58)

> Allan Lewis, "The Folklore Theatre—García Lorca," in his The Contemporary Theatre: The Significant Playwrights of Our Time (copyright © 1971 by Allan Lewis; used by permission of Crown Publishers, Inc.), revised edition, Crown, 1971, pp. 242-58.

VIRGINIA HIGGINBOTHAM (essay date 1976)

[Lorca's comic spirit is] apparent in his lyric poetry; his poems are full of dialogues and characters conceived in dramatic form. Occasionally, situations in which there are no active characters are handled in a theatrical or visually dramatic manner. Many of the brief dialogues and personages that appear in his lyric works are humorous, indicating Lorca's natural proclivity for creating comic characters and scenes. Thus, while Lorca's verse is, for the most part, not amusing, it reveals the diversity of his comic spirit. From reading Lorca's poems it also becomes apparent that he began to conceive of comic characters and situations from the beginning of his career.

In his first book, *Libro de poemas,* Lorca began learning his craft by writing fables. Though he did not cultivate the genre assiduously, he resorted repeatedly to the animal metaphor, amused by the implied resemblance, both physical and behavioral, between animals and humans. (p. 2)

The fables of *Libro de poemas* are the poetic exercises of a young poet amusing himself by mocking the characters of the adult world—the teachers and the elderly—whom he confronted as a child. . . . For Lorca, laughter—whether simple or complex, disarming or desperate—was an instinctive reaction to life. This is apparent in *Libro de poemas,* in which the poet expresses his sense of loss as his childhood and religious faith recede into the past. Unlike the fables, many poems in this early book are not amusing but present life as a grim joke. (p. 3)

Satirical commentary from the mouths of animals and mockery of the experiences and beliefs of childhood do not, at first glance, seem particularly menacing. It is important, however, to keep in mind that such satirical laughter conceals wounds that never entirely disappear from Lorca's psyche. The antiauthoritarian poems of *Libro de poemas* are amusing in their puerile challenge of the powers that restrain youth. This apparently harmless humor is repeated later in *Mariana Pineda,* in which two nuns, as ingenuous yet as perceptive as children, question the authorities' claim that the frail Mariana is a political threat. In the later plays, Lorca's protest against authority grows more aggressive and overt.

Just as caricature and *humour noir* express the young poet's disillusionment and dissatisfaction with authority, the fear of death is also concealed behind a variety of comic disguises. As in all Lorca's works, death haunts *Libro de poemas.* (pp. 5-6)

The ominous humor of *Libro de poemas* expresses the adolescent's abrasive first contact with and defense against the realities of the adult world. In this early book, childhood has not entirely faded from Lorca's mind, yet his delight in the toys and fables of his past is fraught with apprehension and visions of death. Turning increasingly to the avant-garde, Lorca began to write freer, less serious verse; the frivolity of *Canciones,* his first avant-garde book, contrasts sharply with the somber *Libro de poemas.* The poet appears to have regained his sense of merriment and is at play with the words and images of his craft. Much of the verbal frolic of *Canciones* is devoted to the cultivation of images, one of the foremost concerns of avant-garde poets during the 1920's. Yet the book is not merely a Gongoristic exercise in image making, for Lorca is no longer concerned with aesthetic beauty. Humor is of central importance in *Canciones*. Breaking away from traditional forms, such as ballads and fables, Lorca now turns to children's songs and nursery rhymes. These verses add spontaneity and zest to the incongruous humor and delight in nonsense that characterize his outlook on life. (pp. 6-7)

Canciones is a collection of ironic, sarcastic, and frivolous verses in which Lorca learned to manipulate striking imagery and new techniques of poetic expression. The jovial exuberance of the book results from a new literary iconoclasm which Lorca found, not in the highly distilled technique of [Stéphane] Mallarmé, but in the humorous aesthetics of Gómez de la Serna's *greguerías*. Lorca was not solely dedicated to "dignifying" the purely metaphorical element of poetry but instead sought a poetic idiom capable of expressing the witty and capricious, yet sardonic and macabre, thoughts inherent in his attitude toward life. Thus, it is mischief rather than dignity that best characterizes the poems of *Canciones*.

In his best-known book of poems, *Romancero gitano,* Lorca's imagination is drawn away from the child's realm of fables and fantasy toward the equally exotic world of gypsies. Lorca knew how to make this strange (for many Spaniards as well as the non-Spanish) subculture his own. By use of comic techniques that make alien behavior seem familiar, Lorca rendered the gypsy kingdom accessible to all. Like the poor everywhere, the gypsy society is a marginal one, lacking sufficient power and prestige to ensure immunity against brutal attacks from outside antagonists, such as the police. In *"Romance de la guardia civil española"* Lorca again resorts to caricature, satirizing the civil guard as repulsive and menacing creatures who lurk about at night. . . . In terms equivalent to those used by the black people of the South to satirize white Klan members, Lorca portrays the civil guards as comic grotesques whose minds are as deformed as their bodies. They take advantage of their position of authority to terrorize the gypsies. Discovering a fiesta in the gypsy quarter, complete with carousing, lights, and banners, the guards move in and sack the area. The gypsies, surprised by the onslaught, become the helpless victims of the brutal guards. The defensive humor of caricature is the gypsy's only means of expressing his protest and hatred of oppression by the civil guards. (pp. 9-10)

Of the eighteen poems in *Romancero,* half are comic or ironic. In most of these the play between naïve amusement and deep pessimism creates a tense situation, the outcome of which is made to seem surprising: an eccentric British consul appears just in time to save Preciosa from certain disaster; an innocent gypsy boy falls victim to an enchanting figure who dances about in an outlandish dress; without explanation, the virile don Pedro becomes a corpse, playing with frogs underground; the manly saints of Christendom seem ridiculous when dressed like dolls by superstitious gypsies. J.-L. Schonberg describes this book as a "guignolade," a puppet show; for, despite its dark themes of murder and martyrdom, *Romancero* conveys the mock-serious tone of an amusing charade. (p. 14)

Lorca cannot, of course, be considered a comic poet; yet many of his poems are ironic and whimsical, and one of his books, *Canciones,* is almost entirely composed of literary antics. Only two of Lorca's major lyric works do not express his sense of humor or comic absurdity in some way. One that naturally does not is the elegy on the death of Ignacio Sánchez Mejías. Lorca had no need to dramatize the unmitigated grief of this poem with irony or to conceal death's palpable presence behind a comic guise. *Poeta en Nueva York* is the other of Lorca's major

lyric works that does not express his comic spirit. . . . Both in a personal as well as in a literary sense, Lorca's experience in New York was a *saison en enfer* [season in hell] during which the poet, temporarily lacking the customary reserve of inner strength and poise that allowed him to deride hopelessness and horror, lost his ability to laugh at monsters. The grotesque images of *Poeta en Nueva York* show none of Lorca's previous delight in horror that he expresses, for example, in the prose *Narraciones*. Although, in the poems of New York, technological man seems to be more brutal than the primitive blacks of Harlem, this irony is conveyed only by visions of slaughter. The poet protests injustice and cruelty; he can, however, no longer relish the ridiculous image of his enemies that he had previously created with the grotesque caricatures of the civil guards and in the religious satire of his early poems and prose. The extreme desolation of *Poeta en Nueva York,* unbroken by any vestige of humor, is clearly the result of a collapse of the poet's psychological defenses. (p. 17)

Virginia Higginbotham, in her The Comic Spirit of Federico García Lorca *(copyright © 1976 by Virginia Higginbotham), University of Texas Press, 1976, 181 p.*

BETTY JEAN CRAIGE   (essay date 1977)

[*Poet in New York*] was indeed a startling departure from the poetry of Lorca's *Libro de poemas* and *Romancero gitano,* and because of its surface resemblance to some [André] Breton's and [Paul] Eluard's surrealist poetry, *Poet in New York* was generally categorized as surrealist. Consequently it received only minor critical attention as a serious work of symbolic expression which was influenced by surrealism, certainly, but was finally illuminated by "the clearest consciousness." Yet when the poems are analyzed structurally (as well as imagistically and thematically), they reveal not a new technique of poetic creation adopted by the poet, but rather a sudden, radical estrangement of the poet from his universe. Lorca has gone from the state of participation in nature and in his community manifested in the rhythmical, frequently dramatic poetry of imagery drawn from the natural world of southern Spain (in *Romancero gitano*) to a state of extreme alienation now expressed in the dissonant subjective poetry of violent imagery drawn from the technological world of New York. Thus *Poet in New York* is the symbolization of Lorca's experience of depression and isolation in a foreign reality he apprehends as a hostile chaos. This is therefore the account of his psychic journey from alienation and disorientation toward reintegration into the natural world.

Poet in New York, however, transcends the poet's private vision of modern civilization: it becomes modern man's recognition of the spiritual "waste land" in which he discovers himself alone, empty, without roots, and without a god. Locked in the cell of his subjectivity, he no longer belongs to the world and no longer moves in time to the rhythms of the cosmos. For now he is "conscious," and his vision separates him from the world and his gods; now he is "fallen." (pp. 1-2)

Federico García Lorca's expression of the twentieth-century reality he beholds in New York City is profoundly subjective, for the poetry is born of his private anguish of alienation. Yet it is by this profound subjectivism that *Poet in New York* is finally a universal, "objective" vision of modern civilization, for the poet whose cry issues from the primordial depths of experience is the voice of mankind—in this case modern man separated from nature and abandoned by his gods—giving words to the pain of his time. Thus the vision is somehow familiar to us, as are the visions of Eliot's *The Waste Land* and "The Hollow Men," of Yeats's "The Second Coming," and of Pound's "Hugh Selwyn Mauberley." These poets all see "a botched civilization," an "unreal city," a world where "the light is buried by chains and noises in the impudent threat of knowledge without roots." Rootless knowledge—this is the meaning of the fall into consciousness. (p. 4)

Poet in New York is a poetry of anguish and outrage, a poetry of the solitary individual isolated within a chaotic, hostile universe with which he has no communication. The apparently surrealistic imagery expresses a very different world from the Andalucía of *Libro de poemas* yet the poetry reveals an attitude toward the world that is not, finally, radically different from that of Lorca's early twenties. The poet who longed to touch the stars, elegized Juana la Loca, knew the taste of death within his bones, and yearned for his innocence forever gone is the same poet who raises his cry against the modern, dehumanized civilization of New York. But now the personal meaning of the myth of the fall into consciousness has become social, and consciousness has attained concrete reality on a societal level. The poet's voice becomes the cry of the blood against the myriad office buildings, the river drunk on oil, and the suits of clothing empty of humanity, all of which represent the results of the development of man's intellect. And in the midst of all the noise the poet's desire for a moment of stillness and fulfillment (not to be had) and his nostalgia for childhood grow ever stronger, as Eden grows more remote. So as Lorca formerly identified with the tree that could not bear fruit because of its self-consciousness and therefore could not participate fully in nature, by the end of *Poet in New York* he identifies with nature, with the blood and human vitality of natural violence, and fights the sterile "waste land" of the "sleepless city." He takes the side of the Negroes of Harlem and their great desperate king, for they still have red blood racing furiously through their veins, and they will rebel. In his anguish he experiences all the pain of consciousness, and, rendered passive by the impact of this metallic world upon his suffering sensibility, he can only name the objects of his nightmare vision. (p. 10)

Lorca's New York poetry can be seen as a two-staged process in which he first defines his world by naming it (in surrealistic imagery of illogical language) and then reacts against it, imposing the demands upon reality which he has always imposed. The "pattern beneath the phenomena" which the poet discloses in his poetry comes from the poet's own mind. Consequently, we can speak of the fall into consciousness as the underlying myth not only of *Poet in New York*, but also perhaps of all of Lorca's poetry. For this myth is the symbolization in time of the knowledge of absence, which dominates the whole of his work. (pp. 14-15)

In *Poet in New York* a revolution seems to have occurred in the poet's relation to "external reality." The incantatory rhythm of the *Romancero gitano* is gone, although it returns in the last poem of the volume, **"Son de negros en Cuba"** (**"Sound of blacks in Cuba"** . . .), written after Lorca had left New York City and gone to Cuba. In its place is a verse of irregular rhythm and rhyme whose sound is frequently harsh. By the very dissonance of the New York poetry the reader is kept at a distance from the world described and is not seduced into participating vicariously in the action of the poet's world by a lowered level of consciousness. The reader remains fully con-

scious, shocked by the poet's images, and therefore as fully alienated from that hostile reality as the poet. Just as the poet is frustrated in his attempt to make order out of that chaos, so is the reader, who receives the unconnected, dissimilar images in the same way that the poet as perceived the chaos. With the disappearance of rhythm and discursive language, which would express logical relationships in time, temporal depth disappears. The reader now apprehends the whole series of images on the same flat plane and faces them uncomprehendingly.

Nor can the reader retain the illusion that he is a disinterested observer of the world presented in this poetry. Since the poet is no longer narrating action outside himself, but rather is expressing the impact of the world upon his consciousness, his poetry will necessarily be in first person or from the first person point of view. The reader then identifies with the voice of the poetry and perceives the world through the poet's eyes. Instead of imitating the rhythms of nature, the reader imitates the alienation of the poet from nature.

Poet in New York, then, does represent a revolution in Lorca's relationship with the natural world. The mystical longing for a moment of harmony with the universe which brings into being his early poetry is indirectly the motivating force of his New York poetry, as the theme of the Fall, ever present on a personal level in *Libro de poemas,* becomes the social and metaphysical theme of *Poet in New York,* where the word threatens the blood with extinction. And Lorca, in his initial confrontation with the city, experiences loss of identity and impotence against the universe from which he is radically alienated; he can only name the elements of his vision. . . . But finally he does recover his identity. As Lorca finds his voice, as he prophesies the collapse of the cerebral world which has made human beings bloodless, his poetry becomes more discursive, simpler. For when he knows again that he belongs with the forces of nature, then his verse reflects this recovered balance and unfolds in time, "because we want´to be fulfilled the will of the Earth / that gives its fruits for all." (pp. 30-1)

> *Betty Jean Craige, in her* Lorca's "Poet in New York": The Fall into Consciousness *(copyright ©* *1977 by The University Press of Kentucky), University Press of Kentucky, 1977, 96 p.*

EDWARD F. STANTON   (essay date 1978)

Music formed an intimate part of García Lorca's life and work. His charisma as an individual and a poet was perhaps due above all to a basic musical feeling, attested to by those who knew him. Lorca carried the songs of his land in the blood, as if by a millennial inheritance. . . . From his native soil Lorca imbibed the musical grace and sense of tragedy that give his work its unmistakable accent. Yet he was not a regional poet. He considered himself to be first a brother of all men, then a Spaniard, finally an Andalusian and Granadine. He may have been the most Spanish of writers; he is the only modern poet of his country with a worldwide reputation. His poetry sounds a unique melody, but one that counterpoints the anguish of our century. What in other artists is the product of historical circumstances, or the spirit of the times, in Lorca is an attachment to the earth and its ancient voices. The most profound of these voices make up the music known as *cante jondo* [or flamenco, the traditional music of Lorca's native Andalusia].

Lorca rarely tried to imitate the poetry of this music. There are echoes of traditional songs in his early plays, and especially in his Andalusian verse—*Poema del cante jondo, Romancero gitano, Llanto por Ignacio Sanchez Mejfas,* and *Diván del Tamarit.* In these works, as well as in his major tragedies and the *Poeta en Nueva York,* the indirect resonances of *cante jondo* are more subtle and elusive, yet far more important: a geographic and temporal precision, a kind of visceral suffering, an atmosphere of extremes, an oscillation between plenitude and death, and finally, a dramatic attitude, ecstatic tone, and graphic imagery whose closest model would probably be the *saeta.* (p. 115)

None of the typical elements of *cante jondo* is missing from his verse: song, dance, guitar, *pena,* Andalusia, gypsy. Stylized and transfigured to the plane of poetry, they serve as stepping stones to a highly original creation. . . . Lorca absorbed the traditional songs of Andalusia so thoroughly that they merged with his own inspiration, giving birth to a new and superior world of poetry.

Like the Hispano-Arabic lyricists and the popular poet, Lorca found the raw material for his art in the world around him, rather than in an inner realm of thought and feeling. Thus his verse abounds with local and temporal elements. Concrete things and the sensations they provoke expand into a world of cosmic dimensions—scent, light, and emotion turned to a music full of distance and memory. The tangible allusions to Andalusian objects, people, and songs become part of a new whole, unlimited in time or space. Lorca might conceivably have taken a different road, constructing a private world of image and revery in the recesses of his being. This was the way of Juan Ramón Jiménez. But the poet of the *Llanto* chose another path, at once easier and more arduous. He reached the domain of beauty and myth through a transcendent vision of a specific reality. In this sense he remained faithful to *duende* and the spirit of the land.

Thus Lorca, like the anonymous poets of *cante jondo,* drew his inspiration from a concrete reality. His art could be called more physical than spiritual; in it the will prevails over reason in a premoral and subintellectual world. The categories of time, space, substance, and form are sometimes operative, but they are frequently suspended too. As in ancient myth, objective events and subjective states bear a peculiar relation to one another. Lorca and the *cantaor* observe the cosmos in a way comparable to that of primitive man: the coincidence of events becomes more important than their sequence according to the law of causality. Natural phenomena, such as the appearance of the moon, may influence human destiny—usually in a negative manner. Life flowers in images, light, and fables yet it is constantly imperiled by mysterious forces.

We find in Lorca and *cante jondo* a return to the elementary which is one of the marks of a world in revolt against itself. Extremism, violence, and blood betray a tendency to rebellion which has its origins in the darkest places of the mind. The ultimate consequences of Lorca's creation, if extended to the real world, would be no less than revolutionary in both a political and a psychological sense. The poet stands on the side of instinct, freedom, and the oppressed members of society, whether they be children, women, blacks, or gypsies. The forces that brought about his death were appropriately those of reaction, yet Lorca, like the *cantaor,* never attempted to transpose his art onto a political, social, or philosophic plane. *Duende* represents an end in itself and offers no solutions in a world fatally marked by suffering.

For Lorca, his native land came to signify a region saved from the worst abstraction and materialism, where an ancient culture had firm roots, where communal art forms like bullfighting and *cante jondo* could flourish, and where the brave man still commanded respect. In his work, almost unique in modern poetry, a world remains of which man is the sole master. The characters of his plays, the anonymous figures of his poetry, the gypsies and Sánchez Mejías confront death, fate, and injustice with a clear dignity. In a contest in which they are conquered from the outset, they refuse to accept defeat. Bravery, duty, love, and risk are the tributes man pays to his honor in this unequal campaign. It is a matter of being faithful to the rule of battle. This thought may suffice to sustain a mind such as Seneca's. It has supported whole cultures, in particular the Andalusian. If Lorca comes to be recognized as something more than an exotic magician of the word, his message must reside in this deep sense of human suffering and dignity: fruit of a racial inheritance and a personal intuition.

In the poet's work and in *cante jondo,* the subject matter and related emotions tend to fall into a characteristic pattern of meaning. Though happiness and optimism are not entirely absent, this basic pattern discloses what could be called a tragic vision. As described by Northrop Frye, the archetype of the tragic plot or myth in literature might illuminate Lorca's poetry in relation to *cante jondo.* In general, the human world of the tragic myth is represented as a tyranny or anarchy, symbolized by the isolated hero. The animal world is seen in terms of wild rather than domesticated creatures—beasts, birds of prey, serpents. The vegetable world appears as a forest or wilderness. Finally, the mineral world condenses in stones and ruins.

We do not have to stretch our imagination to realize the significance of such a pattern for our subject. Of course the scheme is highly oversimplified. Only the specific context of each work will yield the meaning of its images and symbols. The lyrical climate of the Andalusian song, in its most basic forms, portrays a wasteland peopled by solitary men. In the *Poema del cante jondo,* lonely, anonymous gypsies plod to their unhappy end amid an equally sterile landscape. In the *Romancero gitano,* man also finds himself in a hostile atmosphere; the gypsies embody the human lot. In both *cante jondo* and the works of Lorca, the injustice of society is understood a priori; the rich and the powerful govern without compassion or appeal. The individual has nothing to guide him but his own instincts; the result is an anarchy of opposing wills. There is little more than fleeting contact between men, virtually no feeling of community. (pp. 116-18)

Both *cante jondo* and Lorca's poetry revolve around the declining phase of the natural, organic, and human cycles, suggested by images of twilight and darkness, autumn and winter, decay and death. This is the scenario for tragedy and elegy in literature—for myths of fall, the dying god, violent death, and sacrifice. The *Llanto,* with the solitary hero's quest for life against the dark powers embodied by the bull, acted out upon a symbolic landscape, may be one of the most consistent and profound expressions of the tragic myth in modern poetry.

Thus myth and the tragic vision are the unifying forces between Lorca's work and *cante jondo.* In the traditional Andalusian song, anguish and suffering may manifest themselves through the words of the poetry, but chiefly through the suggestions of the music. The tragic sense in Lorca also transcends the verse, since it derives from a feeling too vast, complex, and indefinable to be contained in words alone. (pp. 118-19)

In Lorca and *cante jondo* we sense a strife between the artist and his inspiration or *duende.* The singer's emotion is so overbearing that it breaks the limits of form. In the poet, feeling may be more controlled, but the impulse is the same. In both, the taste of mortality, the overflow of pathos, and the dwelling on pain are out of proportion to their possible causes. Death lurks in the shadows, then swallows man in a climate of mysterious signs and premonitions. The odds are weighed against human life; a benevolent providence does not watch over men. The good are not rewarded, crime goes unpunished. In this terrifying universe, there is no quarter from the hounds of destiny, no margin for compromise. (p. 119)

> *Edward F. Stanton, in his* The Tragic Myth: Lorca and "Cante Jondo" *(copyright © 1978 by The University Press of Kentucky), The University Press of Kentucky, 1978, 139 p.*

GWYNNE EDWARDS   (essay date 1980)

In many ways *Blood Wedding* seems to mark a new point of departure for Lorca in relation to his earlier plays. The experiments with the techniques of puppet theatre and farce and the bold incursions into the realm of surrealism become here the representation of a world that is more immediately recognizable, more 'real' in the sense that its settings are Spanish houses and villages and its characters people with whose passions, for all their power, we can identify. It is, indeed, a play which reflects to a large extent, through the medium of a simple, direct and powerful plot, the reality of the narrow and crushing forces of honour and tradition that, heightened in rural areas, were nevertheless characteristic of Spanish society in general. One source of the play, was, indeed, a real incident described in a Granada newspaper years before the composition of the play. (p. 126)

If a real event provided an outline for the action of the play, its poetic elements have their roots in other, more important sources, notably in Lorca's own poetry and drama and in the poetic drama of Spain's Golden Age with which he was so familiar. In his *Poem of Deep Song (Poema del Cante Jondo)*, . . . the themes of fate and death are already presented in a powerfully dramatic form, and two poems in particular ['Dialogue of the Bitter One' and 'Song of the Mother of the Bitter One'] anticipate scenes in *Blood Wedding*. . . . The general situation, particular words and phrases and the emotional impact of the incident [in 'Song of the Mother of the Bitter One'] reveal that an episode of *Blood Wedding* already had an antecedent in poems written seven years earlier. Similarly, in many of the poems in *Gipsy Ballads* the themes of love and death, passion and destruction, and the motifs of the horse and the moon, are prominent and their treatment highly dramatic. The sensuality of 'The Unfaithful Married Woman' *(La casada infiel)*, the dead girl illuminated by moonlight in 'Somnambulistic Ballad' *(Romance sonámbulo)*, the lament in 'The Death of Antonito el Camborio' *(Muerte de Antoñito el Camborio)*, anticipate elements of *Blood Wedding*. (pp. 127-29)

When we turn from Lorca's poetry to his earlier plays, it is clear that many of the themes of *Blood Wedding* have an antecedent there. The theme of passion was expressed to some extent in the figure of Curianito in *The Butterfly's Evil Spell*, in the heroine of *Mariana Pineda*, and in the passionate Belisa of *The Love of Don Perlimplín*. But it is in *When Five Years Have Passed* that the theme is stated with greatest power, in the figure of the Secretary who longs for the Young Man, the Bride who sees in the Rugby Player the ideal of virility, and the Rugby Player himself who embraces her passionately,

breathing smoke in her face, 'like a dragon'. Here, more than anywhere, are the earlier versions of the Bride and Leonardo of *Blood Wedding*.

The theme of frustration, so often connected with the theme of love in Lorca's writings, is, logically enough, reflected in the same characters. Thus, Curianito, Mariana Pineda, and the Secretary of the plays mentioned above are victims of love's frustration. In *The Public* Juliet expresses the theme too, but of the plays which preceded *Blood Wedding* it is clearly *When Five Years Have Passed* which develops this typical Lorca theme with the greatest consistency. The Secretary, the Mannequin, the Young Girl all have a dream of love's fulfilment which is never realized, while the Young Man, the Friend, the Second Friend, and others with them, see their hopes and ambitions ruthlessly destroyed.

Another variation on the theme of love, its frustration by death, is central to the whole of Lorca's drama. Curianito and Mariana Pineda die at the end of the plays in question, Juliet in *The Public* voices the theme of love overtaken by death, and at the end of the play the Director is confronted by death, the end of everything, in the form of the Juggler. Here, indeed, is an antecedent of the figure of Death in the final Act of *Blood Wedding,* but it is again *When Five Years Have Passed* which best anticipates this play, for in the terrible figures of Harlequin and the Clown and the three Cardplayers who pay the Young Man the fateful visit, the doom-laden final Act of *Blood Wedding* has a clear precedent.

As far as the influence of the theatre of Spain's Golden Age is concerned, *Blood Wedding* bears the particular imprint of Lope de Vega, and it is interesting to note in this connection that Lope's *The Sheep Well (Fuenteovejuna)* and *The Knight from Olmedo (El caballero de Olmedo)* were in the repertory of *La Barraca* and were directed by Lorca himself. . . . In writing the first scene of his own third Act Lorca may well have been reminded of Lope's play, of the ominous atmosphere of the wood and of the song of the peasant that seems to be echoed in his own woodcutters. In any case there can be no doubt that the songs and dances that announce and celebrate the wedding in Act II, as well as the atmosphere of rural life that impregnates the play, belong to a tradition of Spanish drama of which Lope, above all, had been the greatest exponent. In *Peribáñez* the flavour of country life and, in particular, the songs and dances that accompany the wedding of Casilda and Peribáñez are highly reminiscent of similar elements in Lorca's play. It seems clear enough that the influence of Lope, in general if not in particular, was very strong. It is worth noting, too, that in *Blood Wedding,* to a greater extent than in the plays that followed it, Lorca, like Lope in so many of his plays, has no clear-cut protagonist but a number of important characters amongst whom the focus of attention is fairly evenly divided. (pp. 129-31)

A general influence that must also be mentioned is that of Greek tragedy. Some critics have, to a considerable degree, seen in the various elements of the play a clear Aristotelian pattern. To this extent it meets the requirement that, to awaken the tragic emotions of pity and terror, the characters who suffer should be close to each other. Secondly, the catastrophe that overtakes the Mother and the Bride may, in Aristotle's terms, be attributed to their 'error', the Mother's residing in her persistent hatred of the Félix family which, in effect, makes her drive her one remaining son to an attempted vengeance that brings about his death, the Bride's in her marrying a man she does not love. Thirdly, inasmuch as the Mother brings about the opposite of what she seeks there is the 'reversal of intention' of Greek tragedy, and in her understanding of the Bride's contribution to the death of her son the Greek 'recognition'. The ultimate anguish and solitude of the Mother and the Bride, more than the deaths of the two men, awaken pity and terror. In the figures of the Moon, Death, the girls who, like the Fates, unwind and cut the thread of life, we have the equivalent of the Greek *Deus ex Machina*, the supernatural forces that intervene in human lives. And, finally, in the dirge-like pronouncements of the Woodcutters, the song of the three girls, and the final lamentations of the Mother, the Bride, Leonardo's wife, and the Neighbours, there are clear echoes of the Greek Chorus. One might say, as a general conclusion, that Lorca, like any educated dramatist, was familiar with the character of Greek tragic drama and that its influence is evident in *Blood Wedding,* but it would be as wrong to overstate that influence as to underestimate the expression in the play of the concern with fate, with passion, with sorrow and death that is peculiarly Andalusian.

The title of the play contains a striking element of paradox that captures the essence of the contrary and contrasting movements of its action. The wedding is suggestive of everything creative and harmonious, of man and woman, of families joined together in love, joy and celebration, and of their continuity in and through their children. Blood, on the other hand, evokes the opposite of all these things: violence, death, destruction, men and women, individually or collectively, set against each other, and the bitter grief and anguish that are the outcome of such conflict. The paradoxical nature of the title suggests, indeed, the paradox of life itself which is precisely a composite of things perpetually in opposition to each other. But in the order of the words in Spanish—*Wedding of Blood*—there is too a logical, deliberate progression from one set of implications to another that, embodied in the principal characters and actions of the play, anticipates its movement from harmony to chaos, from hope and aspiration to despair. Furthermore, the words of the title evoke an attraction of men and women to each other that is purely instinctive and irrational, a marriage of the blood and of natural passion in contrast to all that is traditional and arranged. It anticipates, indeed, the power of instinct that in this play is a permanent link between mankind and the natural world of which he is a part, and which is reflected in all the major characters. The title of the play is, then, a pointer to its predominant direction and to the impulses that lead in that direction. And it catches too, in its unexpectedness, the disquieting, ominous, almost inevitable note of doom that, inherent in the play from its beginning, progressively descends upon it. (pp. 132-33)

[The first three scenes of the play illustrate] the clash between the demands of passion, which seeks to satisfy itself, and society, in the interests of which men must subordinate their instincts. The clash is, moreover, progressively one-sided in its outcome. [In Scene One] the Mother attempts to dominate her feelings, accepting the Neighbour's advice that her son's happiness is more important. In Scene Two Leonardo, though tormented by his passion for the Bride, seeks to assert instead his duty towards his wife and child. In Scene Three the Bride strives to conform to her father's wishes for her marriage to the Bridegroom: 'I'm happy I've said "yes" because I wanted to.' . . . All of them seek to deny their natures in the interests of a greater good, but of the three only the Mother is in any way successful, her fears yielding to resigned acceptance. Leonardo and the Bride confirm, in contrast, the unmitigating rule of passion and personify the clash between the individual

and society that in Lorca's rural tragedies is its outcome. The Act is a movement towards individual and collective harmony, but it is also, disturbingly, a movement away from it. The Father and the Mother, for all their good intentions, cannot in the end contend with the passions that, disrupting already the lives of Leonardo and the Bride, will soon disrupt the lives of others, and the social striving of the Act becomes the spectacle of individuals divided within themselves and from each other. There exists for the Bride only the dark, chaotic world of her longing for Leonardo, its growing, suffocating hold upon her caught and expressed in the descent of night as the Act concludes.

The sense of isolation and enclosure dominates the beginning of the second Act. . . . We are presented here, as elsewhere in Lorca's rural plays, with a vision of men and women set in a hostile world and subjected to Nature's unrelenting domination. And if there are suggestions of a different world—the land from which the Bride's mother came, the fertile vineyards of the Bridegroom—it is the harsh, oppressive landscape of the beginning of this second Act that becomes the focal image, the central, dominating landscape of the play. The other, more comfortable areas of experience are left progressively behind. The Bridegroom's journey takes him into the burning, destructive heat of 'the wastelands' and the Mother and Leonardo are, metaphorically, his companions. There is conveyed to us quickly and intensely both the particular and the more general sense of human beings beset by forces that are alien and irresistible. (pp. 137-39)

In one direction the movement of this play is positive, caught and reflected in the efforts of men and women to shape their lands and families into ordered, harmonious patterns, and to resist and overcome the inner forces that threaten to disrupt their lives. But finally, for all his forward-looking and constructive striving, it is the individual and collective tragedy of men and women that they cannot deny the reality of those powerful and often anarchic elements that are contained within their being. (p. 147)

The initial setting for the final Act is the humid forest in which Leonardo and the Bride seek to conceal themselves from their pursuers. Hemmed-in and encircled by the trees and the darkness of night, the lovers are surrounded too by their pursuers. But the physical imprisonment of the fleeing couple is merely the consequence of the way in which they are progressively hounded by their natures, ruled by a passion that cannot be denied. . . . The setting of the great wood is the evocative symbol, both of enclosure and of the forces that in the rural tragedies work as much through men as Nature, and it is appropriate that Leonardo and the Bride, Nature's children, should be cocooned within this womb-like place. And what is true of them is true now of the Bridegroom too, for he is equally the instrument of instinct, pursuing the lovers blindly, drawn to their hiding-place by some mysterious power. (pp. 147-48)

The sense of human beings worked upon is immeasurably heightened in this scene by its prevailing mood and atmosphere. From the outset the two violins create an insistent, inescapable melancholy, and the woodcutters intone their persistent, dirge-like chorus into which the audience is increasingly drawn. But the aura of doomed inevitability that descends upon the scene is suggested most effectively by the intervention in the affairs of men and women of the superhuman agencies represented here in the figures of the Moon and Death. The forces that in Acts I and II are said to intervene in our affairs but whose influence seems merely part of the belief of men and women, suggested but unproven, are seen now to be a reality, a controlling power in the lives of human beings. The Moon's words are full of menace. This figure with a white, inhuman face illuminates the world of human beings with a terrible, merciless and icy light from which no one and nothing can escape. And the Moon has, as its co-conspirator, Death, in the form of an old beggar woman, her features, like those of the moon, lacking a distinguishable human form. . . . They are formidable and frightening adversaries who accentuate the smallness and insignificance of their human victims, for it is they who between them control the action, arrange the scenario and mark the spot where human beings are about to meet their end. (pp. 148-49)

The initial impact of the play's final scene is one of starkness and simplicity, of timelessness and monumentality. The room with its white walls, its white floor, and its total lack of shadow and perspective, is simultaneously the world, the cell that in a multiplicity of forms is the sphere of our birth, our living and our dying. Within the room the female figures, darkly dressed and unwinding the thread of red wool, are starkly symbolic. On the one hand they are village girls engaged in the simple, traditional art of knitting, but throughout the scene, as elsewhere in this and other plays, there is another, symbolic level of meaning whereby the girls become the Fates who unwind the thread of life and control the destinies of human beings. Their initial song has, in one sense, a popular character, for it is one of those songs that throughout the ages has accompanied the tasks of ordinary people, but there are, too, deeper implications that are all to do with life and death. . . . (pp. 151-52)

The deaths of Leonardo and the Bridegroom evoke in this final scene the tragic sense of loss, of waste. The three girls, First Girl, Second Girl, and Little Girl, assume the role of the Chorus, setting in motion the elegiac lament that grows in its intensity as the action draws to its conclusion. . . . The grieving relatives express their sense of loss in terms of the beauty of Nature withered and turned to dust. (p. 153)

Our awareness of the helplessness of human beings, together with our recognition of the pitiful destruction of their beauty and of all the point and purpose of their lives, dominates the ending of the play. If Leonardo and the Bride are powerless to control their passion for each other, the Mother, the Bridegroom, the Father and the Wife are equally helpless both to alter the course of events and to escape their grief, fear and despair. On this account we pity them intensely. The lamentation for youth and beauty uselessly destroyed underlines that pity. . . . The lament which concludes the play, involving the Wife, the Mother and the Bride, is a common one, for they grieve the same event, echo each other in their utterances, and they are, of course, in close proximity to each other on the stage. But in the last resort they are isolated from each other, their individual anguish as unshareable as it is incommunicable. There is also a common bond between them to the extent that the fate of the one is or becomes the fate of another. The Bride and the Wife, inasmuch as they have lost their husbands by the play's conclusion, are what the Mother was at its commencement. And the Wife's child, together with her unborn baby, parallel the Bridegroom in the sense that they have no father. But again the common nature of their fate heightens our awareness of their common isolation, and the final curtain falls on the spectacle of women weeping, a communal and collective weeping—The NEIGHBOURS, *kneeling on the floor, sob.*—that is a composite of individual and solitary anguish—the essence of the tragic suffering presented to us in the bleak and pessimistic vision of this play. (pp. 155-56)

Gwynne Edwards, in his Lorca: The Theatre Beneath the Sand *(© 1980 Gwynne Edwards), Marion Boyars, 1980, 310 p.*

HELENE J.F. de AQUILAR   (essay date 1981)

[A] dizzying but not entirely *satisfactory* language pervades [García Lorca's *Deep Song and Other Prose*]. Of the thirteen essays in this collection six, in fact, are closer to *verónicas* than to prose; the words glitter and swirl like a bullfighter's cape and their impact on the reader resembles the impact in the ring when, to quote Lorca himself, "The embroidered jackets . . . become too brilliant, the sweating bull ran about . . . wearing fleeting vines of silver." ("Sun and Shade.") If one really regarded these lines as prose, one would very likely end with a headache. It is their obvious poetry that redeems them, and the wild elation of their barely disguised meter. (p. 254)

[The] excitability of Christopher Maurer's English [translation is] exactly suited to García Lorca, whose own temperament was at once so unpredictable, unopposable, and mercurial that it reminded his friends of the weather. . . . Lorcan weather predictions in *Deep Song and Other Prose* are mainly for sudden squalls and gale warnings over exquisitely rippling, sunny seas. Even the more scholarly and subdued essays—the ones closest to prose, those of less obstreperous metaphoric billows—tend intermittently to crest in sudden, menacing swells, darker and deeper than the preceding sentences might have led one to expect. . . . Images of a motionless, pictorial purity ("cheekbone and distance") shrouded in soft language and "mist" yield to the savage razor slash, reminding us that Lorca was for quite a while a committed surrealist of the pro-*Chien Andalou* faction.

"On Lullabies" is a good example of Lorca's better, though still not his best, essays. In it he reveals formidable, albeit jerky musical insights. A gifted composer, an excellent improvisor, and a reputable musicologist at a moment of intense and nationalistic musical fervor in Spain, Lorca was a friend of [Felipe] Pedrell and of [Manuel] De Falla as well as a passionate—sometimes too passionate—defender of the folk tradition. But this very passion leads him astray, as it so often does everyone. The orgiastic allusions which conclude "On Lullabies" leave the reader breathless and quivering: otherwise, however, not much wiser. It is rather as though, having ignored the gale warnings, one had plunged into the deceptively beckoning sparkle of the waves and been caught in one of the squalls. . . . These seizures of infused imagination, often degenerating into blatant untruthfulness (Lorca, of course, oblivious to the lapse) repeatedly and abruptly foreclose on the poet's impressively well-reasoned, educational observations. He thinks, alas, in metaphor.

By far the most enlightening—as distinct from bedazzling—selection in Maurer's anthology is the famous lecture called "The Poetic Image of Don Luis de Góngora." Its twenty-six pages make it also the most sustained piece. Now Góngora and Quevedo are the two glories of the Spanish Baroque; the former, however, while *openly* regarded as incomprehensible is *furtively* regarded as unbearable by many, many readers. Thus Lorca's achievement is considerable: he makes these snarling, skeptical, and resentful readers change their minds. Here as nowhere else Lorca's prose is under absolute restraint, his mind resolved on discipline: in deference, no doubt, to the only artist in the history of Spain whose metaphors eclipse, both in brilliance and in apparent obscurity, his own. . . . This stable, non-volatile prose, a concession to uninterruptedly "logical" discourse, represents a prolonged self-denial which nothing and nobody save the seventeenth-century idol could have wrested from his twentieth-century worshipper. (pp. 255-57)

Helene J.F. de Aquilar, "Warring with Time," in Parnassus: Poetry in Review *(copyright © Poetry in Review Foundation), Vol. 9, No. 1, Spring-Summer, 1981, pp. 253-68.**

ADDITIONAL BIBLIOGRAPHY

Adams, Mildred. *García Lorca: Playwright and Poet*. New York: George Braziller, 1977, 204 p.
> Biocritical study. Adams concludes that García Lorca can be understood only through an objective study of his life and, in particular, by analyzing the effect his visits to North and South America had on his work and philosophy.

Allen, Rupert C. *The Symbolic World of Federico García Lorca*. Albuquerque: University of New Mexico Press, 1972, 205 p.
> Attempts an analysis of the function of different types of symbolism in García Lorca's work, including mythic, esthetic, and psychological uses of symbolism.

Barrick, Mac E. "'Los antiguos sabian muchas cosas': Superstition in *La casa de Bernarda Alba*." *Hispanic Review* 48, No. 4 (Autumn 1980): 469-77.
> Discussion of the role that superstition plays in the development of García Lorca's last play.

Cabrera, Vicente. "Poetic Structure in Lorca's 'La casa de Bernarda Alba'." *Hispania* 61, No. 3 (September 1978): 466-70.
> Structural analysis of *Bernarda Alba*. Cabrera attempts an analysis of García Lorca's final play to prove that everything within the work is "symbolically meaningful or has a strict poetic function."

Carrier, Warren. "Meaning in the Poetry of Lorca." *Accent* X, No. 3 (Spring 1950): 159-70.
> Focuses on García Lorca's technique and his use of metaphors in *Gypsy Ballads*.

Colecchia, Francesca, ed. *García Lorca: A Selectively Annotated Bibliography of Criticism*. New York, London: Garland Publishing, 1979, 313 p.
> Divided into sections on the author's life, general criticism of his work, and criticism of individual dramas and poetry collections, as well as such specific subjects as surrealism.

Crow, John A. *Federico García Lorca*. Los Angeles: University of California Press, 1945, 116 p.
> Biography with critical commentary on García Lorca's poetry and drama. Crow, a fellow-student and friend of García Lorca while both were attending Columbia University in New York, attempts to reconstruct the writer's life through personal memoirs and an examination of his work.

Duran, Manuel, ed. *Lorca: A Collection of Critical Essays*. Englewood Cliffs, N.J.: Prentice-Hall, 1962, 181 p.
> Includes essays by such critics as William Carlos Williams, J. B. Trend, Roy Campbell, Edwin Honig, and Louis Parrot.

Fletcher, John Gould. "Lorca in English." *Poetry* LVI, No. VI (September 1940): 343-47.
> Review of the translations of three of García Lorca's works: *Poems of F. Garcia Lorca, The Poet in New York and Other Poems*, and *Blood Wedding*.

Ilie, Paul. "The Aseptic Garden," "The Georgics of Technology," and "Biocultural Prehistory." In his *The Surrealist Mode in Spanish Literature*, pp. 57-79, 80-91, and 92-104. Ann Arbor: The University of Michigan Press, 1968.
> Critical analysis of Lorca's surrealist poetry. Ilie examines the poet's surrealist verse, in particular his three odes, paying close attention to the central images.

Morris, C. B. "The Game of Poetry: Guillen, Lorca, Alberti, Salinas." In his *A Generation of Spanish Poets: 1920-1936*, pp. 82-118. London: Cambridge University Press, 1969.*
> Focuses on the playful and humorous elements in García Lorca's major poetic works.

Giuseppe Giacosa

1847-1906

Italian dramatist, librettist, short story writer, and essayist.

Giacosa was the leading popular dramatist in late nineteenth-century Italy. Along with other Italian realists of his time, especially Gabriele D'Annunzio and Giovanni Verga, Giacosa introduced the concerns of Zola's naturalism and Ibsen's realism to the Italian theater. Giacosa differed from his countrymen D'Annunzio and Verga, however, in two important respects. First, he did not establish new trends in the Italian theater: his dramas reflected rather than created literary styles. Second, Giacosa's plays have rarely been as popular in other countries as they have been in Italy. His international reputation rests primarily on the libretti he wrote with Luigi Illica for three operas of Giacomo Puccini: *La bohème (The Bohemians)*, *Tosca*, and *Madama Butterfly (Madame Butterfly)*.

Giacosa was born and raised in the mountainous Piedmont region of northern Italy, and the hills, valleys, streams, and ruined castles of his native area serve as the setting of many of his short stories and his early medieval plays. Trained as a lawyer, Giacosa's initial, inefficacious courtroom appearance coincided with the success of his first one-act play, *Una partita a scacchi (The Wager)*, and he decided to devote himself to the theater.

Giacosa's work can be divided into three periods. His earliest plays were romantic melodramas based on medieval legends, which he interpreted in Martellian verse, a fourteen-syllable rhymed form. Notable among these are *Il trionfo d'amore (The Triumph of Love)* and *The Wager*, which remain popular with amateur theater groups in Italy. Giacosa next produced a number of historical dramas, still in verse and medieval in concept, but evincing a transition from light romanticism to the social themes that were finding expression in the works of Zola, Ibsen, and Tolstoy. The best of these was *Il Conte Rosso*, based on the life of Count Amadeus VII of Savoy. Giacosa's last plays are generally regarded as his best. With his first realistic drama, *Tristi amori (Unhappy Love)*, Giacosa abandoned his usual rhyme scheme for a prose style. Called "an Italian *Madame Bovary*," *Unhappy Love* broke sharply with the customary plot line of Italian drama. Though employing the venerable "triangle" theme, Giacosa eschewed the usual murder of the unfaithful wife by her husband; instead they agree to stay together to raise their daughter. This ending, initially regarded as too weak, is seen by some modern critics as more realistic than the time-honored murder. In the Ibsenesque *Il diritti dell'anima (Sacred Ground)*, Giacosa varied the "triangle" theme in yet another way. The wife is unfaithful in thought only, and the man she loves is dead when the play opens. Some critics believe that it was in this play only that Giacosa escaped what they saw as his "besetting sin" of avoiding the logical, but too tragic, ending. *Come le foglie (As the Leaves)*, has been considered the definitive Italian verist drama of the late 1800s, as Giacosa here created high drama out of events in the lives of ordinary people. The last play Giacosa wrote, *In piú forte (The Stronger)*, was again somewhat unique to Italian theater for its absence of a love interest. The conflict is between two types of conscience, one embodied in a father who justifies his unscrupulous business dealings by the good

he does for his family; and the other in his son, who cannot accept his father's double standard of morality.

Giacosa returned briefly in his career to the romanticism of his early efforts with *La Dame de Challant*, another interpretation of a medieval legend, written as a vehicle for Sarah Bernhardt. When Bernhardt brought the play in repertory to the United States, Giacosa accompanied her, later writing of his experiences in a volume of essays, *Impressioni d'America*. He also wrote a volume of short stories, *Novelle e paesi valdostani*, and one of archaeological studies and historical sketches, *Il castelli valdostani e canavesani*, both drawing on his native Piedmont.

It was relatively late in his career that Giacosa collaborated with Luigi Illica on the libretti of Puccini's three most popular operas: *The Bohemians*, *Tosca*, and *Madame Butterfly*. These operas have been so successful, and have remained so popular, that despite his considerable achievements in other genres, and an oeuvre containing at least one of every type of drama in vogue in Italy during his career, it is as a librettist that Giacosa is remembered today.

PRINCIPAL WORKS

Una partita a scacchi   (drama)   1871
   [*The Wager*, 1914]
Il trionfo d'amore   (drama)   1872
   [*The Triumph of Love*, 1887]
Il marito amante della moglie   (drama)   1877
Il fratello d'armi   (drama)   1878
Il Conte Rosso   (drama)   1880
Luisa   (drama)   1880
Novelle e paesi valdostani   (short stories)   1886
Tristi amori   (drama)   1889
   [*Unhappy Love*, 1916]
La Dame de Challant   (drama)   1890
Il diritti dell'anima   (drama)   1894
   [*Sacred Ground* published in *The Stronger; Like Falling
      Leaves; Sacred Ground: Three Plays*, 1913]
La bohème [with Luigi Illica]   (libretto)   1896
   [*The Bohemians*, 1905]
Il castelli valdostani e canavesani   (historical essays)   1898
Impressioni d'America   (travel essays)   1898
Tosca [with Luigi Illica]   (libretto)   1899
   [*Tosca*, 1900]
Come le foglie   (drama)   1900
   [*As the Leaves*, 1908; also published as *Like Falling
      Leaves* in *The Stronger; Like Falling Leaves; Sacred
      Ground: Three Plays*, 1913]
Madama Butterfly [with Luigi Illica]   (libretto)   1904
   [*Madame Butterfly*, 1954]
Il piú forte   (drama)   1905
   [*The Stronger* published in *The Stronger; Like Falling
      Leaves; Sacred Ground: Three Plays*, 1913]

THE CRITIC   (essay date 1891)

'La Dame de Challant,' the new play by Giacosa . . . is founded
upon an Italian story of the sixteenth century, and is by no
means a bad piece of its class, notwithstanding the morbid and
extravagant character of its motive. It is entitled fairly to the
description of romantic melodrama, being full of action and
color, and moving in an atmosphere of intrigue and passion.
The personages are drawn vigorously and are grouped with a
keen sense of theatrical effect, while the incidents in which
they figure are sufficiently logical in their sequence, after the
reasonableness of the premises in which they are supposed to
originate has been granted.

> "'*La Dame de Challant*'," *in* The Critic (©The Critic
> 1891), *Vol. XVI, No. 415, December 12, 1891, p.
> 338.*

SOFIA De FORNARO   (essay date 1902)

[Giuseppe Giacosa] early began his literary career with fables
in verse on mediaeval subjects, among which "**La Partita a
Scacchi**" and the "**Trionfo d' Amore**" had great success with
women and young people. But this was rose-water romanticism, and these plays have now disappeared from the dramatic
stage, to remain favorites with amateur actors. His genius,
however, ripened quickly in strong and vigorous works in the
historical field, as "**Il Conte Rosso**" and "**La Dame de Challant**," and in delineations of modern life, producing in this
latter field the masterpiece of the Italian stage, in the severe,
simple, and pathetic drama, "**Tristi Amori**." Besides being a

profound psychologist, a distinguished poet, and a brilliant
dramatist, he has also won high place among novelists by his
"**Novelle Valdostane**." (p. 101)

> *Sofia De Fornaro, "Italian Writers of To-day," in*
> The Critic, *Vol. XLI, No. 2, August, 1902, pp. 99-
> 107.**

L. D. VENTURA   (essay date 1902)

Giuseppe Giacosa, a Piedmontese writer, is not only known
in Italy, but is widely read in France and in Germany. A scholar
and a man of rare common sense, he excels in portraying
nature. A witness of my assertion is his famous book, "**Novelle
e Poeti Valdostani**." Besides this, Giacosa is a happy contributor to the Italian stage. "**Il Conte Rosso**," "**La Partita a
Schacchi**," "**Il Trionfo d' Amore**," "**Il Fratello d' Armi**,"
"**Rienzi**," "**Luisa**," "**Cleopatra**," "**Contessa di Challand**,"
especially written for the sole use of Sarah Bernhardt, are
dramas of rare beauty, constantly before the Italian audiences.
(p. 297)

> *L. D. Ventura, "Modern Italian Literature," in*
> Overland Monthly, *n.s. Vol. 40, September, 1902,
> pp. 292-300.**

THE ATHENAEUM   (essay date 1906)

[With the death of Giacosa] Italy loses one of her foremost
dramatists. His earliest works, the '**Partita a Scacchi**' . . . and
the '**Trionfo d' Amore**,' are delicate and legendary in character,
and composed in *versi martelliani*. More strictly historical and
more ambitious, but still mediaeval in spirit and old-fashioned
in conception and execution, are the '**Fratello d' Armi**,' the
'**Conte Rosso**,' and '**Luisa**.' Had Giacosa written nothing besides these plays (and certain libretti), it is safe to assert that
he would have had admirers and been regarded as a sound
craftsman; but he would have played no part in the great movement that has revolutionized the contemporary drama of Europe. It is on the two masterpieces of his latest manner, the
'**Tristi Amori**' and '**Come le Foglie**,' that Giacosa's fame will
rest. The former deals with the worn theme of adultery, but
the treatment is fresh; and while sentimentality finds no place,
the outlook is tolerant, and the knowledge of men and women
profound. In '**Come le Foglie**' a typical modern Italian family
is dissected with relentless truth, with power and sincerity. The
philosophy is harsh, yet the tenderness of the writer's heart,
here as always, underlies the conception and its development. . . . The dialogue and general workmanship of these
pieces are on the whole admirable, in spite of a tendency to
artificiality in the intrigue. '**Come le Foglie**' is perhaps too local
for non-Italian audiences; but the '**Tristi Amori**' is universal
in its appeal. . . .

> *H. O., "Giuseppe Giacosa," in* The Athenaeum,
> *No. 4115, September 8, 1906, p. 283.*

ADDISON McLEOD   (essay date 1912)

Next in importance after [Gabriele] D'Annunzio as a popular
figure, and far ahead of him as a real student of life, comes
Giuseppe Giacosa. He is one from whom the average Italian
playwright would learn much if he would consent to study as
well as to praise. For Giacosa, while he was not much above
several, though a little above all his contemporaries in the
delineation of character, gained his pre-eminence by his knowl-

edge of how a play should live and move. I have read plays of his, which, though commonplace in their themes, gave, nevertheless, the impression of being eminently actable. Giacosa's work was unequal, and he has left none of those brilliant light comedy pieces which we have from others. But three of his pieces have an outstanding reputation and will probably outlive the vicissitudes of the day.

These are 'Tristi Amori' (Sad Loves), 'Come le Foglie' (As the Leaves), and 'Il Più Forte' (The Strongest). The last I have not seen acted, and it is a play to which the action of the stage means everything. The other two are most striking, certainly; and [are among] . . . the most telling prose plays on the modern Italian stage. (pp. 68-9)

[In one of the English reviews, the reviewer has] opined that 'Come le Foglie' was too purely and intimately Italian to arouse the sympathies of an English audience. From that opinion I beg respectfully to dissent. In the first place, since the review in question was printed, the play has been translated into French and acted in Paris with great success; and I do not think that the Parisians are in a better—if, indeed, they are in an equally good—position for understanding the inner life of an Italian family. In the second place, I do not know whether the reviewer in question had seen the play acted or had only read it. To me it is one of the most deceptive I have ever come across. Read it, and you will say to yourself 'Absorbing, but it is not drama'; see it acted, and you will say 'Splendid, but it cannot be literature:' the fact being that its qualities on either side are so high, and so well balanced, that the one towards you conceals the other; you are so entirely satisfied with what is nearest to you, that you cannot believe that there is anything else.

I am inclined, then, to believe that 'Come le Foglie' is Giacosa's greatest play: his most profound and original; his most worthy to be remembered. It is particularly Italian, true; and without universality there can be no real greatness. But some men have a way of gaining this by a sort of direct attack, by themes which are, in their nature, of world-wide application: such were Shakespeare and Molière. Others make the windows of particularity frame for us broad stretches of the open world: such was Jane Austen; such also, Giacosa. He looked out of the window of the commonplace. He burrowed down, down into the trivial, the every-day that lay about him. And from these recesses, as a man at the bottom of a well can see the stars of heaven, he gained for himself and perpetuated for us, a vision of things beyond: of things which, though simple in themselves, and proceeding from simple hearts and hands, are transcendental in their pathos, noble in their impulse, profound in their truth.

All this is revealed to us in 'Come le Foglie'; but the play reveals a good deal more. It may seem fantastic to compare such a play as this with the awful tragedy of 'Macbeth.' . . . Yet the plays, while in their themes they are as the poles asunder, have at least this much in common: namely, the remorseless persistency with which the inevitable comes on. As by Shakespeare, so in his humbler way by Giacosa, the end is never lost to view. Touch after touch, word after word, event after event—trivial, almost imperceptible, by itself—build up a misery that debases many lives and wellnigh leads to a poor girl's suicide. (pp. 69-71)

At the risk of giving an exaggerated impression of the play, I will add that, if Giacosa has approached Shakespeare in its construction, so he has Molière in the goodness of the things said. Like, after all, does not mean equal. Even an Italian

would laugh if it were suggested that Giacosa was a rival for either of these giants: but that need not prevent us from illustrating, by reference to them, things which otherwise might be but imperfectly grasped by the reader. (p. 71)

Addison McLeod, "Italian Plays and Playwrights," in his Plays and Players in Modern Italy; Being a Study of the Italian Stage as Affected by the Political and Social Life, Manners and Character of To-day, *Smith, Elder & Co., 1912 (and reprinted by Kennikat Press Corp., 1970), pp. 33-174.*

STANLEY ASTREDO SMITH (essay date 1913)

[*Game of Chess*] consists of but one act, preceded by a prologue. It is written in the fourteen-syllable verse called "Martelliano," the Italian verse corresponding to the French Alexandrine. It takes us back to feudal life in the Valley of Aosta in the fourteenth century, and presents a variation of a widespread literary motif, the winning of a lady by the performance of a difficult task. (p. 7)

[The] plot of the play is far from impressing one, and, indeed, this work cannot stand upon its merits as a piece of dramatic literature. It contains no motivation, and no analysis of character or of passions; the characters speak and act as the author's fancy dictates. Furthermore, the picture of medieval life which it presents to us is exceedingly shadowy and indefinite. The piece is chiefly valuable as an exquisite bit of lyricism; from the beginning to the end we have poetry charming both in substance and in form. The author tells us in his prologue that the work is a product of a daydream suggested by the reading of a medieval legend, and this gives us the atmosphere of the entire poem. It is an atmosphere, not of excitement, as the stake of the game of chess would naturally suggest, but of dreaminess. We sympathize heartily with our gallant though arrogant hero, as with our beautiful heroine, and we never seriously imagine that they are going to be unhappy. We feel all the time as though we were being lulled to sleep by beautiful music.

Many critics have condemned this little play in the harshest possible terms, but from the very start the *Game of Chess* has charmed Italian audiences and readers, and to-day, after forty years, it is as popular as ever. (pp. 7-8)

The *Triumph of Love* is, like the *Game of Chess*, extremely romantic. Its principal motifs are favorite ones in romantic literature. Its setting, the wild and picturesque Valley of Aosta, is romantic. It is full of romantic situations, and lastly, its main characters are romantic dreamers ever longing for a life different from the one they are leading. But this play is more than a beautiful lyric poem cast in dramatic form, for it contains some motivation and some analysis of character and passion. The change in the heroine's attitude toward the hero is well worked out. The picture of medieval life given by this play is no more real than that found in the *Game of Chess,* but the characters, in spite of their romantic traits, are human. Though inferior to the former work in lyrical beauty, it still marks a step forward in the author's career as far as dramatic art is concerned. (pp. 8-9)

[*The Brothers at Arms* is] in many respects the most typically romantic of all his plays. Again we are taken back to the Piedmont of the Middle Ages (this time to the Valley of Soana and to the thirteenth century), and again we have a play in Martelliano verse, but this time it is no "dramatic legend"; we have a drama in four acts. It is a story of exaggerated ideals and excessive passions, and ends very logically in a tragedy. (p. 9)

Moreover, the author makes use in this play of some of the "horror" elements common in certain early romantic literature: prophecies of mad women, dark and terrible dungeons, hidden passages the secret of which long has been lost, and which, suddenly rediscovered, give entrance to the enemy, etc. But the passions and characters, such as they are, show in general a good analysis, and the end of Valfrido and Ugone, given the exaggerated ideal upon which the main action hinges, is logical. Moreover, the play has its full share of beautiful lyrical passages, and it gives us a much more vivid and clear-cut picture of medieval life than either the *Game of Chess* or *The Triumph of Love*. It is certainly a greater play than either of these two.

In *The Red Count*, written three years after the *Brothers at Arms*, Giacosa has produced a truly great play—the greatest of the plays of the type we are considering. We still have romantic characters and romantic scenes, and the piece is constructed on romantic lines, but we find few of the romantic exaggerations that characterize the plays already discussed. We have human misfortunes touchingly and vividly pictured, human passions truly and keenly analyzed. We have strict unity of action, too, for all turns upon the struggle of a noble-minded though vacillating son with his strong-minded and unscrupulous mother, a struggle in which the son is constantly deterred from action by filial respect and by the desire to preserve at all costs the honor of his family name, and in which he very naturally succumbs. The setting here, too, is medieval. . . . The verse is no longer the dreamy, romantic Martelliano, but the nervous, decisive, unrhymed hendecasyllable. (pp. 10-11)

Giacosa gives us a vivid picture of the political life of Savoy and Piedmont at the end of the fourteenth century, with its tragic, comic, and pathetic shades, and in this frame he sets a drama of human passions which will appeal to readers of all ages, and this he does without introducing the love motif into the main action. The play is much more realistic than any of those thus far considered. (p. 13)

[When] Giacosa started to write, the battle for Italian independence was won; the patriotic motive was no longer the most compelling. On the other hand, the Romantic School, as such, had been dead for thirty years, and the morbidness of that school would naturally not appeal to our author, however romantic he might be in other respects. The world looked beautiful and the future bright to the young Italians of the early seventies. A great and noble work had been accomplished, and they felt they might give free play to their romantic imagination and pretty fancies for a while before turning to the more serious problems that their new status had created.

This is what Giacosa did. Like a true romanticist, he turned to the Middle Ages, that period which has so allured poets and scholars from the days of Herder down to the present time, and like a true Italian, he turned to that corner of Italy which was his very own, for the affections of every Italian are divided between his country and his native province. Giacosa turned to the mountains of upper Piedmont, those rugged, snow-capped mountains among which he had been born and to which he later returned to die, those mountains which had long been the heritage of that hardy race of counts, dukes, and kings which had made Italian unity a possibility. Nearly all his plays which have a historical setting take us to his native Valley of Aosta or into that vicinity. (pp. 16-17)

[As Giacosa] showed himself from the start free from some of the most serious defects of the romantic drama, so was he to take a stand characterized by his usual moderation with reference to the modern society drama. As early as March, 1875, in an interlude written in honor of [Carlo] Goldoni, we find him railing at the excesses of both the romantic drama and the thesis play. To these he opposes the sane, healthy tradition of the great Venetian, in whose plays, as he expresses it, social problems are not solved, and the stage is not converted into a hospital for diseases of the soul. Years afterward, near the very end of his life, Giacosa reaffirmed this judgment in an article which he wrote on the art of Goldoni. The modern drama, he says, is full of dark threats, or, at best, derisive and spasmodic laughter. If we want true, unadulterated mirth, we must turn back to Goldoni: "He alone still calls back to our lips that most pure and choice flower of the soul—the smile." (p. 18)

With a few lapses, Giacosa's work has always been characterized by good humor and good sense, and these qualities, though certainly innate in him, were doubtless confirmed and strengthened by his study of the father of modern Italian comedy.

In addition to his plays which we have classed as historical and romantic, and to his society dramas, Giacosa's works comprise another type of play—the light comedy. . . . Two of them, *The Husband in Love with His Wife* and *Late Repentance*, bear unmistakable general resemblances to Goldoni's work. (p. 19)

[The romanticism of *The Husband in Love with His Wife*] is of the whimsical type found in certain plays of [Alfred de] Musset. Taken in chronological order, this would be the third of Giacosa's important plays, and as such, marks a decided improvement over *The Game of Chess* and *The Triumph of Love*, as far as psychological analysis is concerned. Count Ottavio is really in a serious quandary for a while, and the doubts and hesitations arising from his anomalous situation are exceedingly well brought out. (p. 20)

[*The Husband in Love with His Wife*] deserves to rank with his best romantic work or with his social plays. . . .

[His first successful social play, the *Luisa*,] a drama in three acts, is still in Martelliano verse, and was written in the late seventies. In this play, the heroine, Luisa, commits suicide in order to save her lover, Count Andrea, from the vengeance of her husband, Count Gino, who is a reprobate of the worst type. Any brief analysis would do the play great injustice for it might convey the idea that it is a vulgar drama of illicit love. It is nothing of the sort. The fatal network of circumstances is so woven about our hero and heroine that their fault is perfectly logical, and their innate nobility of soul is made to stand out through the entire play in their actions and their speeches. There is little moralizing, and what there is goes straight to the point. The characters are very well drawn, especially those of Count Gino and of Enrico, the frivolous though good-hearted friend of Luisa and Andrea. (p. 21)

In *Unconditional Surrender,* the next important play in this series, we have a four-act comedy, which furnishes a severe criticism on the frivolous, artificial, and unhealthy life of a certain class of high society. (p. 23)

[The plot of *Unconditional Surrender*] is an unnatural one, a purely literary invention, but most people who have read or seen the play will agree that the invention is not an unhappy one. . . . Events move on rapidly and logically, and the dialogue, like that of all Giacosa's plays, is natural and spirited. The picture of the special class of society with which the play deals is vivid and complete. The comedy and social satire are excellent, as is also the characterization. . . . The play is a good, clean comedy, which combines the serious and comic elements very skillfully and is in no wise lacking in dramatic interest. (pp. 23-4)

[*Hapless Love*] is regarded by some as his best social drama, and, indeed, as the best play he ever wrote. We should say that it is worthy of sharing this honor with *As the Leaves,* written twelve years later.

It is, as the title suggests, a story of illicit love. The action takes place in a small provincial city. We have, as is usual in such cases, the classic trio of the husband, the wife, and the lover. The theme is only too common, but Giacosa has succeeded in giving us in this little three-act play what it would probably be no exaggeration to call the sanest treatment of this theme to be found in modern dramatic literature.

The piece is classic in its simplicity of plot and structure. (p. 24)

This is the most closely knit of all Giacosa's plays. Everything in it moves rapidly and logically and converges upon one central point. The whole action takes place within one room and within a single day. We have the climax of a bourgeois drama absolutely true to life and full of human interest. No artificial means are used to stimulate this interest; no exaggerations are employed to elicit sympathy for the hero and heroine. They are unhappy, they sin, and they pay the penalty. The husband, too, has erred, and he, too, pays his score. As for the dénouement, some might object that it is illogical. If Ibsen had written the play, Emma and Fabrizio would doubtless have run away together, leaving poor little Gemma on her father's hands; but, given our characters, the outcome which we have is the logical one. It is characteristic of Giacosa, too, that the play ends with a ray of hope. (pp. 25-6)

It has been said that in Giacosa's work we find examples of every type of drama which has had any vogue in Italy during the last fifty years. It is true that he has reacted to many and varied literary influences. Perhaps no other type of play was more foreign to his genius than the Ibsenian, and yet he has left us a play of that type.

The *Rights of the Soul,* a one-act play dating from 1894, treats a problem somewhat similar to the one found in the *Doll's House*. (p. 26)

In spite of his previous achievements, Giacosa was ever reaching out towards something higher, and however successful he might prove in handling themes like those of the last two plays discussed, he was not naturally in sympathy with such themes. . . . [In] his best historical play, *The Red Count,* the love motif is scarcely present in the main action. He now proceeded to write two society plays, unfortunately the last he was to produce, in which this motif is a distinctly subordinate one. Indeed, in the second of these two plays, *The Stronger,* it is practically wanting. In *As the Leaves,* the love of Massimo and Nennele certainly adds interest and freshness to the play, besides furnishing a happy dénouement, but the main problem involved is the fate of a family of the upper bourgeoisie, which lives beyond its means, because of the frivolity of the wife and son, and the weakness and inattention of the hard-working and well-meaning father. (p. 27)

As the Leaves is a great modern play—modern in both substance and structure. While it lacks the classic unity of *Hapless Love,* it makes up for this in its wider, healthier, and more varied interest. (pp. 27-8)

In *The Stronger,* Giacosa's last play, we have treated a problem of the same general character as that found in *As the Leaves.* This time it is the moral struggle between a man who, though a devoted husband and father, is unscrupulous in his business dealings, and his inexperienced son—who has been brought up to different ideals, thanks to his father's unremitting toil. (p. 28)

[The characters] are not as clear-cut and logical as they might be, but here again our author shows his restraint and his humanity. (p. 29)

The Stronger is still a great play, though not as great as *Hapless Love* or *As the Leaves,* and those who claimed on its first appearance that the piece did not seem to be from the pen of Giacosa forgot their author for the moment, for it does show some of his most admirable characteristics.

If now we cast a glance back over Giacosa's work; if we consider the different types of plays he wrote at different periods of his life, and then remember that these general classes are susceptible of almost unlimited subdivision; if we then recall that he wrote in collaboration the librettos for Puccini's three best operas, that he was a very successful lecturer, the director of a magazine, the author of excellent short stories, and of works embodying serious historical study, we shall realize how difficult a general estimate of his works must be. (p. 30)

Some broad generalizations, however, we can make. We have already described Giacosa's romantic plays as healthy and normal, and this characterization holds for his other work. He grew with the world he lived in, but he assimilated the best that the past had to offer, and he never abrogated his own ideals. He did not write for the especial purpose of proving one thesis; his ideas on literary standards underwent a natural evolution; but his human standards remained ever the same. His work may lack unity of purpose, but it certainly possesses unity of spirit. To the careful student, the man's character as it was manifested in his private and public life stands out clearly throughout his work: a sympathetic and generous spirit, a noble mind, capable of high flights of imagination, but always held within natural bounds by innate good humor and common sense. (pp. 30-1)

                    Stanley Astredo Smith, "Giuseppe Giacosa," in The
                    Drama, *Vol. 10, May, 1913, pp. 5-31.*

LANDER MacCLINTOCK (essay date 1920)

The work of Giuseppe Giacosa links together in a very interesting way the old and the new manners in Italian drama. He began as a writer of verse plays, of delicate trifles . . . ; later he became a Verist . . . and finally a Realist. . . . Now while is it true that three changes of manner within an artistic lifetime are a bit confusing and create an atmosphere of fragmentariness, it is also true in Giacosa's case that it enhances his value and his interest to the literary historian; for he reflects to a nicety the varying dramatic taste of his time. His changes from *A Game of Chess* to *Surrender at Discretion,* that is to say from romanticism to realism, from realism to verism, as in *Sad Loves,* from verism to idealistic realism, as in *As the Leaves* and *The Stronger,* reflect with precision the evolution of public taste and the fluctuations in the world of art of the twenty-five years from 1880 to 1905. It might be well to point out just here that in connection with this aspect of Giacosa's history one could put a finger on his weakest spot; the very thing that insured his popularity was an indication of his fundamental lack of originality: he was a follower, never a pioneer. He interpreted his age, yes, but well after the epoch-making cat had jumped. His mind was sensitive to the intangible prophecies of fashion, clear in observation, keen in analysis. Perhaps these qualities preclude genuine creativeness or philosophical speculation. (pp. 35-6)

Others had been before him in the writing of medieval legends, but none of them has equaled in charm *A Game of Chess* or *The Red Count;* the Verist movement was well under way when *Sad Loves* appeared, yet that play is acknowledged as a type; the excitement about Verism had waned when he produced *As the Leaves,* which may be called the masterpiece of idealistic realism in Italy. (p. 36)

Although Giacosa wrote in many forms—essays, criticism, stories, books of travel, such as *I Castelli Valdostani e Canovesi,* showing fine appreciation and sound knowledge of archaeology—still his real passion was for the stage, and to the drama he devoted his best efforts.

A discussion of Giacosa's dramatic work falls rather naturally into two parts, since this division represents a genuine cleavage in his performance. One part concerns itself with the lyrical plays and the historical plays, which are for the most part in verse; the other concerns itself with the comedies and the dramas of contemporary life. (pp. 37-8)

[*A Game of Chess (Una Partita a scacchi)*] can scarcely be called a play in a technical sense but is rather what the French call a *saynète,* a delightful idyl . . . placed in a medieval setting. It is filled with the spirit of youth, the love of adventure, romantic love, expressed in gay and fluent verse. The simplicity and purity, the gentle melancholy, while still the tradition of the drama in verse, had nevertheless a something different about them that was like a breath of pure fresh air. . . . Giacosa offered no manipulated historical truth, but frankly ventured forth into the realm of the imagination. The situations and characters are false to life but true to art. Because of its disingenuousness and youthful vitality the little piece took Italy by storm. (p. 38)

[The plot of *A Game of Chess*] is a variation on an old theme,—the hero winning the heroine by the performance of a difficult task. The prologue is delightful, setting the tone of the play, telling of the inception and conception of the scene. . . . Giacosa's verse is agile, swift, pliable, remarkably well suited to the ideas and feelings to be expressed. (pp. 38-9)

A Game of Chess is, as may be gathered, merely a dainty trifle, but after the violent passions of the Neo-Romantics, it was welcomed with an appreciation and relief that amounted to a furor. It still remains the most popular of plays for amateurs in Italy.

The Triumph of Love (Il Trionfo d'Amore, leggenda drammatica in due atti) . . . is in the same tone and concerns itself with a very similar situation. (pp. 39-40)

These two plays may be classed together as romantic idyls of the Middle Ages, delicate in fancy, dainty, owing little to reality. Nothing could be less lifelike than this papier-mâché and Sèvres china Middle Ages, false to nature and false to psychology. But Giacosa was making no attempt at anything

so serious as truth. His ideal was that which he attributes to Goldoni in his verse, **"Prolog for a monument to Goldoni."**

"Thus from the multiform aspects of the idea there grew up with renewed vigor an art which was alive, rich, varied as life itself. We were ingenuous, I admit, and it used to be said that the theatre was to amuse. Social problems were not solved there, nor were theatres changed into hospitals for diseases of the mind. It may seem exaggeration, but now and then there were good people on the stage."

This was his ideal in 1877,—to amuse; in later life it became just what he repudiates in this gently ironic passage,—social criticism.

Meanwhile, however, he felt that the field of the Middle Ages was not yet exhausted. He produced several historical plays in the next fifteen years, **The Red Count, The Brothers-in-Arms, The Lady of Challant,** all historical plays dealing with the Renaissance and the Middle Ages.

The first of these, **The Brothers-in-Arms (Il fratello d'armi)** . . . , is considered a very good play of the bombastic, pseudo-medieval type. A change in Giacosa's manner is immediately evident. He has left the idyl and is writing plays in the narrower sense, conflicts of character, tense situations, complicated intrigue. He has abandoned altogether his dreamy and enchanting tone for one of more violence, but no more reality. (pp. 40-1)

While he was occupied with these verse plays, Giacosa had written other plays which are collected in the volume *Commedie e scene,* and one melodrama in three acts, in verse. *The Husband in Love with His Wife (Il Marito amante della moglie)* . . . in its good-humored artificiality and its impossible plot . . . is cleverly done.

The Red Count (Il Conte Rosso) . . . has created a great diversity of critical opinion in the Peninsula. [Benedetto] Croce, for example, while he admits its importance in Giacosa's development, does not think much of it as a play; D'Oliva, on the other hand, exalts it into a national tragedy; and the public has always enjoyed it. Croce says *The Red Count* marks Giacosa's transition from Romanticism to realism and it is easy to identify in it elements of both. . . . The plot does not center in a love interest but turns rather on the ambition of a prince to rule liberally and justly, to suppress his unruly barons, and to elevate the people. The play contains interesting and striking pictures of Piedmontese life in the sixteenth century, apparently studied with care; the speech and thought correspond to the atmosphere and have a consistent tone of actuality. . . . (pp. 42-3)

It must be conceded, then, that Croce's point is well taken, that this play is the turning-point in Giacosa's career as a dramatist; not that this is the first play in which may be found pictures of life in its actuality, nor the last in which fantastic and unreal elements appear. But it is the play in which it becomes evident that Giacosa is consciously and conscientiously trying to square his material by the measures and standards of fact.

One more historical drama remains to be examined,—*The Lady of Challant.* . . . It is not, from any point of view, one of Giacosa's happiest ventures. He wrote it for Sarah Bernhardt, who brought it to America in 1891. . . . (p. 43)

The play is powerful and well constructed; Giacosa abuses, to be sure, the well-worn tricks of the stage that every practical playwright knows. Bianca as the fallen woman redeemed by love, Don Pedro, the chivalrous dupe and idealist, are *vieux jeux,* but in the hands of Sarah Bernhardt the play was galvanized into an astounding vitality, and just missed by a hair's-breadth being a convincing bit of art.

These historical plays are not the only products of the years from 1880-1889. During this same period Giacosa wrote both verse tragedies and prose plays of contemporary life. It need hardly be pointed out that in this latter type Giacosa found his congenial and distinctive vehicle; here he felt at home; here he produced his best work, and knew that it was his best. (p. 44)

[*Mountain Torrents (Aquazzoni in montagna)*] is a rollicking play with a suggestion of Eugène Labiche in it; *The Late Repentance (La tardi ravveduta)* . . . , the story of a marchioness who, having been an actress, returns to the stage, repenting late, but not too late, that she had ever left her proper sphere. [*The Thread (Il Filo,* scena Filisofico-morale per marionette), *The Cat's Claw (La zampa del gatto),* and *The Siren (La sirena)*] . . . , all of this period, are comedies. Probably the best known of Giacosa's plays of this very fruitful ten years are [*Surrender at Discretion (Resa a discrezione)* and *Luisa*]. . . . The latter is a modern problem play in verse—a mongrel type in any case, and Giacosa's attempt to combine the uncongenial elements is not a success. It is the only play of Giacosa's which has suicide as a finale. . . . Giacosa has been criticized for cutting the Gordian knot of his situation with the dulled and commonplace blade of suicide. His defense is, "It happens in real life that people take their own lives, so why not in a play?"—lame enough and totally unconvincing unless the psychology of the situation absolutely dictates suicide. Although the effectiveness of *Luisa* is much hurt by the alien medium of verse, the play nevertheless laid the foundation of Giacosa's reputation as a social critic, and ushers in a long series of successful dramas of this type.

Surrender at Discretion is of quite different caliber and nature, being a true comedy of manners, a scathing but accomplished attack on the uselessness and corruption of Italian high society. . . . It is at once evident that Giacosa has taken a great step. No longer are the characters invented or imaginary; they are studied from life, and set in everyday situations. (pp. 45-6)

Surrender at Discretion savors strongly of Gallic influence. It is in some respects a conventional situation with conventionalized characters, but there are good scenes which are quite freshly inspired, and there is about all an economy of means and material that is most acceptable and promising.

This play is the first of Giacosa's which exhibits that aspect of this work which is most emphasized by his critics,—his prepossession with moral situations and problems. . . . Like Ibsen, his far greater contemporary, Giacosa cut to cure; but he was no profound thinker, only a good-natured, sensible man who having passed through life's vicissitudes with his eyes open, is willing to give good sound bourgeois advice about human relations. The guiding stars in his moral firmament are personal integrity, honesty, directness and charity, a sense of justice tempered by humanity and sympathy. Giacosa dreamed of a new moral world where these virtues functioned. But it was his own *bonhommie* that betrayed him and deranged his scheme. Of course this quality endeared him as nothing else could have done to his public, who wanted and needed this ready and comfortable faith, but it came near to undoing him

as a dramatic artist. His desire to supply each play with a happy ending, a conclusive curtain, a dénouement acceptable to a bourgeois audience, led him many times into lapses from dramatic logic and from entire intellectual honesty.

These illogical and manipulated conclusions are not, however, due wholly to Giacosa's complaisance; they grow out of that optimistic philosophy which will not admit an insoluble problem. It is because of this that he more than once falls into the trap that caught even Molière in *Le Misanthrope* and *Tartuffe,* where, rather than not offer a solution of his complication, he solves it by means of what may be called a ratiocinative *deus ex machina,* quite external to the nature of the complex. So in *Surrender at Discretion,* for example, the only logical ending would have been tragic . . . ; also in *Sad Loves* the dénouement is accidental, not organic; and the same thing must be said of *As the Leaves.*

No doubt this illogicality and obscurantism seemed to Giacosa and to his pleased audiences only a necessary part of "holding up the banner of the ideal", perhaps even an essential procedure in vindicating a beneficent order of the universe. Giacosa undoubtedly felt that the society of his age and nation needed lessons in the simple virtues of honesty and purity. It is quite consistent to say that he presented these plays first of all to please and amuse; but as a by-product and collateral effect he aimed to cure his age of certain dangerous social maladies. (pp. 47-9)

[Giacosa] felt that there was need of upholding the rights and claims of society against the individual, rather than asserting the rights of the individual as against society which has been the theme of most contemporary dramatists of other countries. (p. 49)

The first night of the initial run of *Sad Loves* may be said to be the most significant date in the history of contemporary drama in Italy, for it definitely signalized the triumph of the naturalistic school. Of course, there had been naturalistic, even Verist plays offered before. . . . [But *Sad Loves*] established in the Italian theatre the principle of the scrupulous presentation of life on the stage.

It could not be otherwise than that Giacosa should have been deeply influenced by the theories and the work of the great French naturalists. He was peculiarly sensitive to literary influence,—and even if he were not, he could not have escaped the teachings of such masters as Zola, Flaubert, the De Goncourt brothers, naturalists, Alphonse Daudet and De Maupassant, realists, but especially perhaps of Henri Becque. . . . [Giacosa, in *Sad Loves,*] chose a bourgeois *milieu,* utterly commonplace; his persons are merely men and women of the middle class, no better, no worse than the rest of us; nothing "happens" in the entire course of the play. Of course Giacosa, with the peculiar bent we have discussed above, was not content to let it rest at that, he gave it a moral, a didactic bearing. And those critics who condemned him as being a mere photographer were either unjust, or were blind to the characteristic turn that Giacosa gave to the play. Yet in spite of the moralizing, Giacosa did not sacrifice the verity of his picture; his first critics, not prepared to appreciate this, did say: "But this is not art, this is photography." In spite of much severe disapproval, in spite even of a few unappreciative hisses, *Sad Loves* triumphed and with it the Verist school in the Italian theatre. (pp. 50-1)

With consummate art Giacosa brings out all the banality, the sordidness of adultery, its mean pettinesses and lies, its deceptions and utter commonplaceness. (p. 51)

Giacosa, though he followed the Becque formula in *Sad Loves,* which he somewhat ironically called a "comedy," was too human and kindly to achieve that impersonality, the impassibility of Flaubert, which was Becque's greatest artistic asset. . . . In all the characters [there is a] clear consciousness of ethical issues. Giacosa solved the problem as best he could, retaining the integrity of the family, justifying the husband, packing off the lover, disposing of everybody in a bourgeois and highly moral manner. That the dénouement is not the logical and inevitable conclusion of the play is a grave fault. This Giacosa undoubtedly knew. He compromised with his own dénouement. . . . [But] in spite of his weakness *Sad Loves* remains the best of Italian Verist dramas. (pp. 53-4)

[*Rights of the Soul (Diritti dell' anima),*] Giacosa's next play, is an Ibsenite study in feminine psychology,—Ibsenite by actual imitation rather than merely by tendency, for Giacosa was under the direct sway of the great Norwegian and intended to translate his idiom into Italian by means of *Rights of the Soul.* It is the most purely intellectual of his plays, a geometrical problem, a ratiocinative exercise. There is a touch of the Scandinavian frost in the cold analysis of a woman's soul. It may have been because of its purely abstract nature, perhaps because of conscious effort on Giacosa's part, that *Rights of the Soul* escapes his besetting fault and drives home its conclusion clear to the head, not for a moment evading the question at issue.

Like *Sad Loves, Rights of the Soul* is concerned with a question of adultery, foregone in the former play, contemplated in the latter, a matter of intellectual unfaithfulness. (p. 54)

It is difficult to account for the hostile tone of the criticism that this one-act play of Giacosa's has evoked. One feels that it must be due to the fact that he did not supply it with the conventional pleasant ending; the situation is interesting and pathetic; the emotional reactions of the two persons are psychologically sound; the dénouement natural and satisfying in the premises. Two faults it has: the dramatist is too obviously present; we are reminded that the play is a *tour de force,* and that its author is constantly in the background manipulating his figures to his own ends,—that, therefore, in this game the dice are loaded. In the second place the play is too short for the complete presentation of the material; Giacosa cannot compress into one act all he wanted to say, all that needed to be said. To this brevity and concentration has been sacrificed clarity and verisimilitude. (pp. 55-6)

[The success of *As the Leaves (Come le foglie)*] was the crowning achievement of Giacosa's long career and designated him for the time the first prose dramatist of Italy. Scarcely ever, perhaps indeed never, in the history of the Italian theatre had there been so immediate and so striking a success; certainly the unanimity of admiration has never been equaled. Public and critics both joined in enthusiastic approbation of the man upon whom the mantle of Goldoni had fallen, who could write an honest, clean, wholesome piece of work which could, as the theatre should, *"corriger les moeurs en riant"* ["correct the mores while laughing"]. With this play Giacosa had delivered a bold and telling stroke in his great social campaign. It is the protest of bourgeois good sense against the excesses of the super-refined. (p. 56)

As the Leaves is excellently managed from a technical point of view. The characters are well defined and distinguished; the dialogue is crisp, witty, pungent; there is an upward curve of interest and suspense until the dénouement; it gives also a remarkable illusion of life and living. It may safely be called the best of Giacosa's plays. (p. 58)

[In *As the Leaves* and *The Stronger*] amorous passion takes a decidedly secondary place, while adultery is entirely absent from both. His timely innovation was welcomed with enthusiasm. The old themes were pretty threadbare, and consequently the study of the fallen fortunes of a family in *As the Leaves,* of a question of probity in *The Stronger* had the charm of freshness and the prestige of importance.

Cesare Nalli of *The Stronger (Il Più forte)* . . . is a great financier of the family of Le Sage's "Turcaret" and Balzac's "Mercadet", who has amassed a huge fortune by means which, if not illegal, are certainly not nicely honorable. A wolf and a devourer in the business world, he is at home the tenderest of husbands, the kindest of fathers. . . . By an accident Silvio discovers his father's crookedness. . . . The scene in which the father and son have an explanation is the capital one of the play and brings out Giacosa's thesis,—Which is the Stronger? To any one with a knowledge of Giacosa the answer is obvious; right must triumph. (pp. 58-9)

The Stronger, particularly the character of Cesare Nalli, has been frequently compared with its French prototype *Les Affaires sont les affaires* of Octave Mirbeau, much to the disadvantage of *The Stronger.* Giacosa's financier has not the consistent hardness, the logical sternness of Mirbeau's Isadore Sechart, nor does Giacosa push the play—his old fault—through to its logical conclusion. . . . [It] is the secondary characters who, by an interesting paradox, stand out. Indeed, in Giacosa's plays this fact can scarcely be called paradoxical, for the minor and secondary personages in all the important plays are the ones depicted with the firmest strokes. As a matter of fact, Giacosa's grasp on character was not so notable as his mastery of situation and his clear-sightedness in moral issues.

Giacosa also took an interest in what we may call a neglected if not deserted branch of art allied to drama,—the operatic libretto. He longed to renew the fallen art of the librettist and wrote, together with Luigi Illica, books for the following music of Giacomo Puccini: *La Bohème, La Tosca,* and *Madame Butterfly.* They are assuredly not very successful as literature. They inevitably suffer from being obliged to adapt themselves to music to which after all they are external, but at least they are better than most other librettos. (pp. 59-60)

In turn neo-romantic, semi-realistic, veristic, genuinely realistic, with an Ibsenite interlude, [Giacosa] followed closely the intellectual and dramatic fashions of his artistic lifetime. His changes of manner, however, must not be charged to superficial versatility or to indifference. There is none of that copious fertility which merely follows the mode; his plays are the product of slow and painstaking elaboration. Rather is his work the product of his intimate and varied contact with the life of his time, the response of his sensitive soul to the changing psychic and social atmosphere of the last quarter of the nineteenth century. It was late in life when in the realistic bourgeois comedy he finally found himself; he seemed to grow more modern as he grew older. His first romanticism, however, was quite as truthful and sincere a manifestation of his artistic personality as was the verism of the last remarkable plays.

In each of the dramatic genres he essayed Giacosa has left a work, in some more than one, of genuine significance even when not absolutely vital and enduring. His gift to the Italian stage was a body of new themes, a corpus of new subject-matter; he renovated the drama with his fresh and clean ideas and clear style. (pp. 60-1)

Lander MacClintock, "Giuseppe Giacosa," in his The Contemporary Drama of Italy *(copyright © 1920* by Little, Brown and Company; copyright renewed 1947 © by Lander MacClintock; reprinted by permission of the Literary Estate of Lander MacClintock), Little, Brown, 1920, pp. 35-61.

STANLEY ASTREDO SMITH (essay date 1920)

No other Italian dramatist of the second half of the nineteenth century responded to so many influences as did the author of *Tristi amori,* and in no other is the response at the same time so sympathetic and so original. Romanticism and realism, history and pure fancy, rollicking comedy and poignant tragedy, golden dreams and unerring psychological analysis—all this we find in his plays; but they are pervaded by a genial understanding and by a spirit of mental and moral rectitude that give them a strong inner unity. (p. 1)

[*Tristi amori*] is, in many respects, Giacosa's masterpiece. It is certainly the most closely knit and the best balanced of all his plays. In it he has achieved the all but impossible task of giving a sane, wholesome, and, at the same time, intensely dramatic treatment to the well-worn, or ill-worn, "triangle" theme. Furthermore, he has accomplished this with a remarkable simplicity. The setting of the play could scarcely be more commonplace, and certainly no plot could be freer from obtrusive complications and technical devices. The situations are logically and naturally motivated, and the words and acts of the participants in the drama are fully justified by situation and by character. Nothing is in the remotest degree sensational or rhetorical. The piece is characterized by the strictest economy in dramatic construction.

It is of interest to note that the play embodies a strict observance of the classic rule of the unities. All three acts take place within a single room in a period not exceeding nine or ten hours. Some critics have quibbled as to the unity of action, asking whether the main subject of the drama is the "hapless love" of Fabrizio and Emma or the domestic infelicity of Giulio. As a matter of fact, the husband, wife, and lover all occupy the center of the stage, and the subject is the triple tragedy to which their relations give rise. We cannot separate the fate of any one of them from the fate of the other two.

The materials that Giacosa has used are, of course, not new, but the skill and the restraint with which he has used them give the play an indisputable claim to originality. . . . That Giacosa may unconsciously have used motifs and incidents that must have been familiar to him through his reading is, of course, quite probable, but that is all that we can affirm with safety.

Plainly discernible, however, is the influence of the age to which the play belongs. When *Tristi amori* was produced, naturalism had established itself both in French and Italian literature. (pp. 6-7)

The main elements of the naturalistic formula as applied to the drama are, of course, familiar. It reduces a play to the proportions of a mere *tranche de vie* ["slice of life"] or to a series of *tranches de vie;* it insists upon an absolutely objective representation of reality, unobscured by moral or sentimental preoccupation; it dispenses with all rhetoric and with all artificiality.

Tristi amori complies with these requirements. Some critics have argued that it betrays a certain moral preoccupation on the part of the author in that he has insisted on providing a partially satisfactory future for the Scarli family. It is interesting to recall in this connection that the dénouement caused the

failure of the play on the occasion of its first presentation in Rome, and that even at Turin, where it was presented several months later with great success, the critics noted that the ending left many unconvinced. But the terrible [final words of the husband] . . . , and the continued torment they suggest, are at once utterly tragic and, in the premises, utterly inevitable.

From the generality of modern dramatic treatments of the "triangle," *Tristi amori* differs in that its important characters, thoroughly human and thoroughly interesting, possess no claim to distinction as heroes, rogues, victims, egotists, or singular products of a corrupt civilization, and in that its moral atmosphere is healthy without being clouded by didactic preoccupation. It reveals to us an outlook upon life that is not characterized by the anti-social individualism of the romanticists, nor by the blatant defense of society found in so many "thesis plays," nor by the sterile cynicism common to most naturalistic dramas. It is this cynical attitude of the naturalists, coupled with their mania for pursuing the singular and the local, that has led them so often to choose as the objects of their study portions of humanity in which the evil so far outmasses the good that the good serves only to make the evil stand out in a more glaring light. Their art is no more objective, in the broadest sense of the word, than is the art which is inspired by an excessive idealism. True objectivity implies the power to view things in a serene and unbiased manner, the power "to see life steadily and to see it whole." This, in *Tristi amori,* Giacosa has achieved. The play leaves upon us an impression of infinite sadness, but it does not revolt us. As the curtain falls, we feel that the world is peopled exclusively by monsters, cads, and fools. We have witnessed the sin and the suffering of human beings, and we have suffered with them.

If true classic art be distinguished by a grasp of those traits that are most permanent and universal in human life, and by insistence upon the fundamental principle that human nature is partly good and partly bad, then we have a right to say that *Tristi amori,* while fulfilling the main requirements of the artistic formula of the naturalists, is animated by a classic spirit. (pp. 7-9)

Stanley Astredo Smith, in his introduction to Tristi amori *by Giuseppe Giacoso, edited by Rudolph Altrocchi and Benjamin Mather Woodbridge (reprinted by permission of The University of Chicago Press; copyright 1920 by The University of Chicago), University of Chicago Press, 1920, pp. 1-13.*

FRANK W. CHANDLER (essay date 1931)

The recent Italian drama grew out of a movement toward realism following the romantic impulse which entered Italy from France. (p. 529)

The new realists recognized that the drama must possess a popular appeal, that it must be useful and moral. They determined to make art a faithful transcription of life, something as certain and logical as science. . . . But the Italians never achieved a drama of social issues at all comparable to the French or the English. . . . There was no special pleading in Italian drama for feminism, socialism, or industrial reform.

Giuseppe Giacosa is the first important realist among the modern Italian playwrights. . . . [He] studied law, practiced journalism, wrote fiction, books of travel, and critical articles, but was most successful as a dramatist. In his more than thirty works for the stage he shows the progress of a sane and healthy artist from romanticism to a chastened realism. His first plays, in verse, hark back for their subject matter to medieval times, beginning with the still popular *A Game of Chess* and including *The Triumph of Love, Brothers in Arms,* and, best of all, *The Red Count. A Game of Chess* might have come from the pen of Alfred de Musset, with its jaunty page who plays chess with the duke's daughter, agreeing to lose his head if he cannot win from her, and to marry her if he can. . . . A contest in wit for the hand of another lady is the basis of *The Triumph of Love. Brothers in Arms* and *The Red Count* show conflicts in character against an historical background. The plots of both are complicated, and the language is rhetorical rather than idyllic. (pp. 529-30)

Giacosa cultivated comedy, also, meeting with most success in *The Husband in Love with his Wife* and *Late Repentance.* But he was more and more attracted to the social drama, and after various experiments in this field, he won applause with his *Luisa* and *Unconditional Surrender,* pieces still flavored with romance. The first is a problem play in verse, exalting love as a redeeming influence, a wife laying down her life in order to save her lover from her husband. The second is a comedy of manners which follows a favorite pattern with Giacosa, for it shows a coquette who, after endeavoring to wreck the career of a noble youth, falls in love with her victim and repents.

It was in *Unhappy Love,* however, that Giacosa rose to the full height of his powers, varying the triangular plot with refreshing sobriety, preserving the unities, and avoiding theatrical claptrap. . . . Here is realism at its best, with nothing forced, and an ending, however moral, not too happy.

Giacosa's historical drama, *The Lady of Challant,* written to afford Sarah Bernhardt an opportunity for displaying her powers in the rendering of passion, derives from a story by Bandello, and turns upon the redemption through love of a fallen woman. It was in the playwright's older manner. He returned, however, to the modern world, seeking especially to emulate Ibsen in *Rights of the Soul.* Like *A Doll's House,* the play unfolds with subtlety the relations of a married pair, and pleads for the woman's right to freedom of spirit. (pp. 530-31)

The later work of Giacosa, who died in 1906, includes librettos for Puccini's operas *La Bohème, Tosca,* and *Madame Butterfly,* written in collaboration with Luigi Illica, and two plays that stress character and minimize the love interest so usual upon the Italian stage. Both are family studies. (p. 532)

The best-known play of Giacosa, *As the Leaves,* considers again bourgeois business, and faintly echoes [Björnstjerne] Björnson's *A Bankruptcy.* It presents the condition of an upper-middle-class group unexpectedly exposed to the winds of adversity and fluttering to earth like the leaves of Autumn. . . . "Sweet are the uses of adversity" might have been the motto of this play. Be content with poverty and work, for it is only through these that you can develop character. Giacosa fails to establish our belief that money will inevitably ruin its possessors. (pp. 532-33)

It is the merit of Giacosa to have conveyed the sense of life in his plays, creating flesh-and-blood characters who talk simply and effectively and illustrate moral themes. He nowhere assails social institutions, unless it be by implication the institution of marriage when it would destroy the individual soul. Rather, he is intent in his serious plays upon showing the need of restraint, self-sacrifice, and industry. (p. 533)

Frank W. Chandler, "Italian Verists: Giacosa, Verga, Rovetta, Praga, Bracco," in his Modern Continental Playwrights *(copyright, © 1931, by Harper & Row, Publishers, Inc.; copyright renewed © 1958 by Adele Walton Chandler; reprinted by permission of the publisher), Harper & Brothers, 1931, pp. 529-46.**

VINCENT LUCIANI (essay date 1961)

Giacosa's lasting contribution . . . is the one he has made to the Naturalistic theatre with his two classics, [*Tristi amori* and *Come le foglie*]. . . . The first mentioned set the pattern for the triangle play in Italy, just as Becque's *La Parisienne* . . . had set it in France. It deals with the discovery of an illicit relation that causes untold grief to those involved. Giulio Scarli, a successful lawyer and good husband, loves but neglects his wife Emma, who is attracted to his assistant Fabrizio and becomes his mistress. When her adultery is discovered, her maternal instinct prevents her running off with her lover. Giulio allows her to stay for his child's sake, but he will never forgive. The play is pervaded by an atmosphere of tragic sadness that raises it high above the usual drama of adultery. The three main protagonists are serious, innately honest individuals that seem persecuted by a dire fate. The milieu is skilfully depicted, and the minor characters, Ranetti and Fabrizio's father Ettore, are well portrayed.

Come le foglie represents a rich family reduced to poverty. The father, Giovanni Rosani, had been too busy amassing a fortune to fortify his children against the cruel struggles of life. So they, utterly weak-willed, fall like leaves before the autumn wind. The son Tommy, unable to shed the vices of luxurious living, marries a wealthy Russian adventuress to free himself from his gambling debts. Giulia, the frivolous, selfish second wife of Giovanni, is about to heed the call of illicit romance. The daughter Nennele, aghast at what is happening, is on the verge of suicide, but is saved by the thought of her poor industrious father and the strength of her cousin Massimo, a self-made man who loves her.

In these two plays Giacosa proves himself to be a fine observer of contemporary society and a creator of some unforgettable characters, such as Tommy, Giulia, and Count Ettore. He makes effective use of dialogue and displays a sense of humor and a broad human compassion which relieve his pessimism. A defender of bourgeois morality, he has not the heart to follow his situations to their bitter conclusion: e.g., the utter destruction of Giulio's family or the suicide of Nennele. Some critics have considered this a defect in Giacosa's art, and they may be right, but only in part. Giulio's lack of action is perhaps inconsistent with his character, but Nennele's suicide is surely not inevitable. (pp. 2-3)

Vincent Luciani, "Giuseppe Giacosa and Verism," in Come le foglie *by Giuseppe Giacosa, edited by Vincent Luciani (copyright 1961 by S. F. Vanni), S. F. Vanni, 1961, pp. 1-3.*

MOSCO CARNER (essay date 1974)

[There were] two literary members of the 'holy trinity' . . . which was to produce the trio of Puccini's most popular operas: Giacosa and Illica. Of the two, Giacosa was by far the more outstanding personality and the greater artist. To the world at large the name of Giuseppe Giacosa . . . is today known merely as that of one of Puccini's chief librettists; yet in his time Giacosa stood in the front rank of those Italian writers and playwrights whose works form the transition from the romanticism of a [Giosuè] Carducci and [Giovanni] Pascoli to the French-influenced realism in the last two decades of the nineteenth century. Giacosa was a gifted poet and essayist and the author of finely observed short stories; but, above all, he was a dramatist with a subtle psychological insight, with thirty-two tragedies and comedies to his name, of which [*Tristi Amori* and *La Dame de Challant*] . . . won him international acclaim.

Giacosa had first come into contact with [Puccini] in 1889, when he had been preparing for him the abortive 'Russian' libretto, and then again in connection with *Manon Lescaut;* but with *La Bohème* this collaboration was to become a close and lasting one. That [Puccini's publisher Giulio] Ricordi should have been most anxious to enlist the co-operation of so eminent a writer as Giacosa for his favourite composer seems to argue the growing importance that was being attached in Italy to the literary quality of an opera 'book.' . . . (p. 77)

In their work for Puccini there existed a kind of division of labour between Giacosa and Illica. While Illica would draw up the scenario and develop the plot in detail, Giacosa's assignment was to cast the prose text into verse, elaborate the lyrical situations, introduce a more balanced order into the succession of scenes and, generally, lend the libretto literary polish and refinement. Whereas Illica contended that in the last analysis a libretto was merely a canvas to be filled in, expanded or contracted by the composer, according to his requirements, Giacosa maintained that 'it was one thing to sketch out scenes more or less fully, but another to condense the subject into a few verses and, at the same time, try to throw the essential elements into relief and attend to the shaping of the scene and verse. Such detailed and intricate work needs time and patience and much toil.' . . . Giacosa would and could not be hurried. Unlike Illica, he was a slow and painstakingly conscientious worker attempting to reconcile the practical and less subtle exigencies of a libretto with the demands for literary quality. This was for him a hard task because he naturally inclined to approach it from the angle of the poet and playwright and was loth to consider a libretto as primarily a means to an end. In Giacosa there was a permanent conflict between his artistic integrity and his self-criticism on the one hand, and the wishes of publisher and composer on the other. . . . By the time the *Bohème* libretto was completed, his irritation with Puccini's perpetual demands for alterations had reached such a pitch that he wrote to Ricordi (25 June 1895): 'I swear to you that I shall never be caught again writing another libretto.' Doubtless the fact that he was an acclaimed writer in his own right was apt to make Giacosa feel easily hurt in his professional pride when having to submit to someone else's wishes. . . . Giacosa's susceptibility to imagined slights was such that it sometimes prompted him to make unreasonable demands himself. . . . But at heart good-natured, accommodating and generous, he was unable after such outbursts of indignation to harbour resentment for long and in the end always yielded to the combined entreaties of composer and publisher to return to the fold. And oddly enough, though he kept complaining that the writing of libretti was for him a most uncongenial occupation interfering with his true vocation as poet and playwright . . . on at least two occasions he volunteered to write one. . . . There cannot be the least doubt that what tender lyrical poetry and verbal felicities there are in the text of *La Bohème, Tosca* and *Butterfly,* flowed in from Giacosa's pen. The element in which Puccini must have felt a particularly close affinity with Giacosa was the latter's insight into the female psyche, his *feminismo,* which characterized the treatment of his heroines in his plays and stories. (Is it not

significant that out of Puccini's twelve operas, seven should be named after the heroine?) (pp. 77-9)

If there was a serious difficulty [in producing the libretto of *Tosca*], it lay in Giacosa's profound dislike of the play, which struck him as being devoid of any lyrical and poetic situations and therefore hard to versify. He was convinced of its absolute unsuitability for an opera and declared that while *Le Bohème* was all poetry and no plot, *Tosca* was all plot and no poetry, with puppets instead of real characters in it. (p. 102)

[The] adaptation of *Madam Butterfly* proceeded with remarkable smoothness: like Sardou's *Tosca,* [David] Belasco's play was a clever piece of stage-craft and needed, in the main, only extension into three acts. For meanwhile the composer had dropped his original idea of 'two quite long acts', insisting now and for a considerable time to come on a full-length opera in three acts. It was his sudden decision, subsequently, to revert again to the plan of a two-act structure that created the only really serious difficulty in the gestation of the libretto. (p. 130)

Whether he was wise in his decision remains an open question: the two-act structure of the opera was, no doubt, a contributory factor in the fiasco that attended the première; but seen in retrospect, I am persuaded that Puccini's instinct was right in thus dividing the work. . . .

At first, however, Puccini did not have it all his way and the strongest opposition to his plan of telescoping the second and third acts into a single act was put up by Giacosa, who refused point-blank to have anything to do with it. (p. 131)

In the end, however, the good-natured Giacosa yielded and did Puccini's bidding. (p. 133)

Mosco Carner, in his Puccini: A Critical Biography *(© Mosco Carner, 1958, 1974; Holmes & Meier Publishers, Inc., New York, reprinted by permission; in Canada by Duckworth & Company, Ltd.), second edition, Duckworth, 1974 (and reprinted by Holmes & Meier, 1977), 520 p.**

DOMINIC MANGANIELLO (essay date 1977)

Much of the criticism dealing with [James Joyce's] *Exiles* has centered on the influence exerted on Joyce by Ibsen. This tendency, though understandable in view of Joyce's manifest devotion to the Norwegian playwright, has diverted attention from other relevant areas of enquiry. In Trieste Joyce profited by the exposure to Italian culture, and he interested himself particularly in the native drama. The Italian theatre appealed to Joyce's penchant for raising relatively unknown names from obscurity. The themes of the plays also proved congenial to him, as he assimilated and transformed them to suit his art. Joyce himself indicated the undercurrent of Italian drama in his preliminary notes to *Exiles;* namely, Giacosa's *Tristi amori* and [Marco] Praga's *La Crisi.* (p. 227)

As early as 1901 Joyce described Giacosa along with Sudermann and Björnson in "The Day of the Rabblement" as "earnest dramatists of the second rank" who, at any rate, "can write very much better plays than the Irish Literary Theatre has staged." And as late as 1939 Joyce, in a letter to Livia Svevo, alluded to *Come le foglie* . . . , considered by some critics to be Giacosa's masterpiece. (p. 228)

In its presentation of the perennial "triangle," *Tristi amori* stands out from the great mass of similar plays because of the treatment of the husband. To this simple, kindhearted, sympathetic country lawyer everything even remotely connected with his wife is of necessity perfection. This admiration for Emma gives to his discovery of the truth a special poignancy. Some critics have argued that Giacosa is too didactic by having the wife and the disillusioned husband agree to remain together for the welfare of the child. Joyce avoids this pitfall in *Exiles* by not making Archie a stepping-stone towards reconciliation, but also by leaving the very nature of the reunion in doubt. Giulio does not resort to violent action in vindication of his wife's adultery, just as Richard or Bloom do not rely on physical retaliation. More importantly, Giulio's implicit offer of liberty to his wife strikes a "modern" note which Joyce detected and transformed into Richard's express invitation to Bertha.

If the fact that Joyce used *Tristi amori* as a model for the "triangle" theme in *Exiles* is not evident except through the preliminary notes, this does not hold true for *Ulysses*. Molly states at one point that "I wont forget the wife of Scarli in a hurry supposed to be a fast play about adultery" and remembers that someone in the gallery hissed Emma during the performance. *The Wife of Scarli* . . . has been identified as an English version by G. A. Greene of Giacosa's play. That Joyce used Emma as a prototype for Molly is borne out by Molly's claim that "its all his own fault if I am an adulteress as the thing in the gallery said." This is a reference to Giulio's indirect admission of his own guilt in his final speech where he proposes to give his daughter a rich dowry so that she may be free to marry a man of leisure and not one like himself who, in being so busy at earning a living, neglects his wife. Moreover, Molly echoes the reconciliation scene of *Tristi amori* when she says, "Why cant we remain friends over it instead of quarrelling." (p. 229)

> *Dominic Manganiello, "The Italian Sources for 'Exiles': Giacosa, Praga, Oriani and Joyce," in* Myth and Reality in Irish Literature, *edited by Joseph Ronsley (copyright ©1977 by Joseph Ronsley), Wilfrid Laurier University Press, 1977, pp. 227-37.**

REBECCA KNAUST (essay date 1978)

[The reception the first-night audience gave Giacomo Puccini's *La Boheme*] was a far cry from that given his *Manon Lescaut*. While that opera had delighted everyone when it opened on the same stage just three years before, the present offering, *La Boheme,* was so unstructured, so light and simple, so uncomfortably realistic, no one knew quite how to greet it. (p. 5)

The libretto was drawn from French writer Henry Murger's semiautobiographical novel, *Scenes de la Vie de Boheme,* and the five-act play, *La Vie de Boheme,* written by Murger in collaboration with Theodore Barriere and produced in Paris in 1849. The librettists Puccini chose to work with, Giuseppe Giacosa and Luigi Illica, early declared their determination to preserve as much of the flavor and atmosphere of the acclaimed and popular works as they could. Murger had conceived *Scenes* first as a collection of sketches celebrating Left Bank living. . . . [It] was the uniquely warm, natural and conversational style he adopted that brought the noisy, sooty carnival of Bohemia and its scruffy denizens to life. It was this naturalness the librettists hoped to capture in their version.

This was not a simple goal, however. While Murger had peopled his stories with a host of colorful eccentrics, Puccini's team of writers, inhibited by the strictures of the operatic form, was forced to edit out all but the essential personalities and vignettes. Nor was it any easier to derive a cohesive opera plot from such a segmented format. Somehow, though, a libretto that satisfied the demands of the composer as well as those of his poets was eventually settled on. . . .

[The initial, unenthusiastic critical reaction to *La Boheme*] is not really such a puzzle. In retrospect, of course, it is easy to say they were foolish, even blind, to insist it was a terrible piece, a failure, but not all of them bore Puccini ill will. Certainly *La Boheme*'s dramatic content is unremarkable. There is nothing extraordinary about the way things develop in the story. And the work is without the usual theatrical distractions. There are no intensely charged confrontations to be found among its acts, no wildly violent outbursts, no dazzling special effects. Instead, what happens on stage is at all times very believable, very convincing, and the opera's air of ordinariness, its complete lack of pretention, was not too welcome at first. . . . (p. 6)

[Puccini] had learned it was to his advantage as a composer to expect more of a contribution from his librettists. . . . [*La Boheme*] is commendable above all for its understatement, and its unity, tight construction, skillful transitions and imaginative, well-colored orchestration reveal a musician of considerable ability, one capable of making great strides in a short period of time. . . . [The] same pair of writers, Giacosa and Illica, were to work with Puccini on his other hugely successful operas, *Tosca* and *Madame Butterfly.* (p. 8)

> *Rebecca Knaust, in her introduction to her* The Complete Guide to "La boheme" *(copyright © 1978 by McAfee Books, a division of McAfee Music Corp., copyright assigned 1980 by Belwin-Mills Publishing Corp.; used with permission; all rights reserved), McAfee Books, 1978, pp. 5-8.*

ADDITIONAL BIBLIOGRAPHY

Ashbrook, William. "The Big Three: *La boheme, Tosca, Madama Butterfly.*" In his *The Operas of Puccini,* pp. 48-124. New York: Oxford University Press, 1968.*
    Discusses Puccini's most famous operas, and Giacosa's contributions to those operas.

Carner, Mosco. *Madame Butterfly: A Guide to the Opera.* London: Breslich & Foss, 1979.*
    Traces the various sources Giacosa, Illica, and Puccini drew upon for their version of the "Butterfly" story.

Kennard, Joseph Spencer. "Some Contemporary Italian Dramatists." In his *The Italian Theatre from the Close of the Seventeenth Century,* pp. 286-313. New York: Benjamin Blom, 1932.*
    An account of Giacosa's most important works, including extensive plot analysis and some criticism.

Lawton, Ben. "Giuseppe Giacosa, 1847-1906, and Giacomo Puccini, 1858-1924." In his *Abroad in America: Visitors to the New Nation, 1776-1914,* edited by Marc Pachter, pp. 247-59. Reading, Mass.: Wesley Publishing Co., 1976.*
    Recounts Giacosa's reactions to his trip to America in 1898.

(Hippolyte) Jean Giraudoux

1882-1944

(Also wrote under pseudonyms of Andouard, Jean Cordelier, Maurice Cordelier, and J.-E. Manière) French dramatist, novelist, short story writer, scriptwriter, and essayist.

Giraudoux is recognized primarily for his highly stylized dramas centering around the elemental themes of love, death, and war. His plays are distinguished as dramatizations of ideas, rather than as character studies. His characters, in fact, are often abstractions of universal themes, individuals absorbed in intellectual dialogue and elegant language. Because of his facile use of language, Giraudoux acquired a reputation early in his career as a precious, cultivated impressionist. But behind the playful mastery of his diction, his plays and novels—especially his final works—reveal a cynicism based on his observation of human apathy as well as an idealism founded on his desire for an incorruptible world.

Giraudoux was born in the provincial region of Limousin. A gifted and brilliant student, he majored in Germanic studies at the École Normale Superieure in Paris, traveling to Germany when his studies were completed. The radical dichotomy between Germanic and Gallic influences was to concern Giraudoux throughout his life and to figure prominently in much of his work. Giraudoux served in the military during World War I and became absorbed with the problem of a postwar reconciliation between France and Germany. This concern formed the subject of *Siegfried et le Limousin (My Friend from Limousin)*, a novel which made him immediately popular. Giraudoux adapted the novel for the stage when he was in his midforties; this marked the beginning of his dramatic career and his important association with Louis Jouvet. As actor/manager, Jouvet brought out a new Giraudoux play almost every year during the 1930s. At the time of the dramatist's death, one year before the end of World War II, Giraudoux was among the most popular playwrights in Europe.

Behind his ornamental, impressionistic, and essentially poetic works, Giraudoux was a man preoccupied with ethics and philosophy—a Platonist at heart. His surface techniques conceal a number of serious themes: the spiritual relationships between two countries, as seen in *My Friend from Limousin;* the inevitability of war and revolution, portrayed in *La guerre de Troie n'aura pas lieu (Tiger at the Gates)* and *Electre (Electra);* the relationships between a mortal and a god, in *Amphitryon 38;* and the corruption of modern society, in *La folle de Chaillot (The Madwoman of Chaillot)*. Giraudoux's work demonstrates a passionate concern for the human condition, a concern free from a rigid ideological and philosophic framework. Two major motifs consistently appear in his plays and novels: the encounter between the mundane and the supernatural, and the image of a pure, ethereal woman counterpoised against the coarseness and banality of everyday existence. This second element is the essential ingredient to Giraudoux's idealistic and optimistic literature of the 1920s and 1930s. For him, woman was a natural, instinctive creature endowed with subtle and delicate sensibility; she was, above all, the only one who could discover the poetic possibilities in ordinary existence. Giraudoux's vision demanded that the only true goal of humanity be the absolute or the ideal, and his female protagonists, such as Electra, Lia in *Sodome et Gomorrhe,* and Lucile in *Pour Lucrèce (Duel of Angels)*, personify this vision.

Critical opinion of Giraudoux's work is varied. Many early critics felt that his art was artificial, precious, and insignificant, arguing that he was at his best when dealing with comedy or light subjects. Others criticized his characters as vague, inchoate creations oscillating between the realms of allegory, symbol, and reality. Some questioned his commitment to art and to the concerns he voiced in his work. Though a few of these sentiments are still voiced today, most critics now accept Giraudoux as a serious writer whose ornamental and precious language was well-suited to his peculiar brand of literature. In general, most agree that Giraudoux was a superb craftsman in both fiction and drama, and that his popularity is not limited to his "middlebrow" appeal, but also arises from his treatment of such serious themes as love, death, war, and humanity's relationship to the universe.

Despite the debate over his work, Giraudoux remains an important writer because of his completely individual and arresting vision of the world, a vision that grew more somber and pessimistic toward the end of his life.

(See also *TCLC*, Vol. 2.)

PRINCIPAL WORKS

Provinciales (short stories) 1909
L'école des indifférents (short stories) 1911
Le retour d'Alsace (memoirs) 1916
Lectures pour une ombre (essays) 1917
  [*Campaigns and Intervals*, 1918]
Amica America (essays) 1918
Simon le pathétique (novel) 1918
Adorable Clio (essays) 1920
Suzanne et le Pacifique (novel) 1921
  [*Suzanne and the Pacific*, 1923]
Siegfried et le Limousin (novel) 1922
  [*My Friend from Limousin*, 1923]
Juliette au pays des hommes (novel) 1924
Bella (novel) 1926
  [*Bella*, 1927]
Eglantine (novel) 1927
Siegfried (drama) 1928
  [*Siegfried*, 1930]
Amphitryon 38 (drama) 1929
  [*Amphitryon 38*, 1938]
Les adventures de Jérôme Bardini (novel) 1930
Judith (drama) 1932
  [*Judith* published in *The Modern Theatre*, 1955]
Intermezzo (drama) 1933
  [*The Enchanted*, 1950; also published as *Intermezzo*, 1967]
Combat avec l'ange (novel) 1934
La guerre de Troie n'aura pas lieu (drama) 1935
  [*Tiger at the Gates*, 1955]
Electre (drama) 1937
  [*Electra* published in *From the Modern Repertoire, second series*, 1952]
Choix des élues (novel) 1939
Ondine (drama) 1939
  [*Ondine*, 1949]
Sodome et Gomorrhe (drama) 1943
La folle de Chaillot (drama) 1945
  [*The Madwoman of Chaillot*, 1949]
Pour Lucrèce (drama) 1953
  [*Duel of Angels*, 1958]

ANDRÉ GIDE (essay date 1917)

We are reading aloud . . . *Le Retour d'Alsace* by Giraudoux, of which the first pages delight us. Yet one cannot but be embarrassed, eventually, to see those pathetic events painted with the brush of a miniaturist. But, he could reply, so long as we remained ignorant of the events in Alsace, what we were living had nothing pathetic about it and was just as I have depicted it. —Of course, and that is just the most pathetic aspect of the affair; but one feels it despite Giraudoux. I confess that right up to the very end I hoped for some more virile pages, which might have put all that prettiness in its proper place.

> *André Gide, in a journal entry in 1917, in his* The Journals of André Gide: 1914-1927, *Vol. II, edited and translated by Justin O'Brien (copyright 1948, copyright renewed © 1975, by Alfred A. Knopf, Inc.;*

reprinted by permission of Alfred A. Knopf, Inc.), Knopf, 1948, Secker & Warburg, 1948, p. 194.

THE NORTH AMERICAN REVIEW (essay date 1918)

Perhaps no more sincere, more exact, more unconventional or more various record of war impressions was ever written than that which Jean Giraudoux has given us in his book *Campaigns and Intervals*. The effect of many passages of this record is so simple and so strong as to remind us of the work of Stephen Crane. But *Campaigns and Intervals* is not, of course, as is *The Red Badge of Courage*, a one-idea-ed book: it is not a study merely of one chain of events or of one emotion. It is both more delicate and more versatile than Crane's masterpiece; and the fact that it records real instead of imaginary occurrences, increases both one's estimation of its value and one's admiration for the art with which it is executed. (pp. 607-08)

Sometimes, too, the author mingles psychology with spectacular bits of description and with humorous observation in a manner that produces an astonishingly complete and convincing picture of the reality. . . .

A certain steadiness, a certain "lucidity of soul" is manifest through the whole book. Without attempting in the least to disengage the ethical or spiritual elements from the human spectacle, M. Giraudoux enables us to perceive the nobility of human nature as represented in the French civilian turned soldier: he lets us see that this soldier, strangely and sometimes absurdly affected as he is by the terrors and the incongruities of the war, has a soul. (p. 608)

> *"New Books Reviewed: 'Campaigns and Intervals'," in* The North American Review *(reprinted by permission from* The North American Review; *copyright © 1918 by the University of Northern Iowa), Vol. 207, 749, April, 1918, pp. 607-08.*

LOUIS KRONENBERGER (essay date 1927)

The publication of **"Bella"** by Jean Giraudoux confirms the impression conveyed by his **"Suzanne of the Pacific"** and his **"My Friend from Limousin"**—that he . . . has claims to distinction, and that those who enjoy contact with a subtle and civilized mind should give him their attention.

Some readers are likely to be scared away from **"Bella"** because it is a key novel, a novel in which under thin disguises two great contemporary French statesmen are counterpoised. M. Giraudoux's American publishers state that these portraits are commonly supposed to represent [Pierre] Berthelot and [Raymond] Poincaré. But the factual element behind these figures, if it is what has most attracted French readers (**"Bella"** caused a sensation in France), is what will least interest most Americans. When a novel offers such fine portraiture, such brilliant knowledge of manners, such wit and irony as **"Bella"** does, it is scarcely necessary, it is scarcely pertinent, that we conjoin the fiction with the fact; our gossiping instinct yields to our capacity for intellectual enjoyments, our curiosity for facts to the satisfactions of art, our interest in personal satire to an interest in literary satire. Removed from France to America, the only thing (beyond its style) which **"Bella"** loses is its popular appeal. In France, no doubt, **"Bella"** was primarily regarded as a roman à clef; in America we shall regard it primarily as a work of art.

On the other hand, no one can read this novel without being aware that in both subject-matter and method it is decidedly French, that M. Giraudoux the artist and M. Giraudoux the satirist and M. Giraudoux the contemporary historian has derived from the France of the past, and now turns his mind upon the France of the present. No one can mistake the fact that his contrast between the Dubardeaus and the Rebendarts is a contrast, as he says himself, between "the two different types of honor, courage and generosity in the French character." And no one can help being interested in the significance of this contrast. Who Dubardeau is in real life, or who Rebendart, is not sociologically or artistically important compared with what they stand for in contemporary French civilization. . . .

[The] portraits are brilliant. In their selectiveness, their wit, their penetration, their seizing upon the eccentricities of those they describe to make them memorable, they remind one of, say, a character sketch by Lytton Strachey. Satirized and intellectualized as they are, these people yet are human, people we recognize, understand and cannot forget. Into these portraits M. Giraudoux has poured many talents, his talent for characterization, for wit, satire, analysis, for understanding France and the French. He has fused them into something richly amusing. They vary from the exuberant comedy of the amazing brothers d'Orgalesse to the tender satire on Bella's father, Fontranges; from the vigorous portraiture of the Dubardeaus to the subtle portraiture of the Rebendarts. . . .

One of the incidental delights of the book, for Americans as well as for the French, is the world of high politics and high society in which it is laid—a world full of references to Wilson, the Prince of Wales, Edward VII, Viviani, Pershing, Anatole France. "Our friends," says the narrator of his childhood, "were little Hugos, little Claude Bernards, little Renans and little Gobineaus."

Bella's sudden death is the one slightly inexplicable event in a book more distinguished, as all good books are, for its recognitions than for its surprises. But this event is more than justified by the fine last chapter to which it gives rise, in which Bella's father comes so touchingly to life and becomes conscious of his own undeveloped soul. This wise and charming record of a new experience perfects the characterization of Fontranges and places it beside those of the Dubardeaus and the Rebendarts. It concludes a book which is relatively short and yet packed with riches, a book whose sophistication is so authentic that it takes a minor but worthy place in the long line of books founded in the Gallic tradition. It is not a profound book and it is not a great one—but it is just about everything else.

> Louis Kronenberger, "French Manners and Politics in a New Satirical Novel," in The New York Times Book Review (©1927 by The New York Times Company; reprinted by permission), June 12, 1927, p. 11.

JEAN-PAUL SARTRE   (essay date 1940)

Everything we know about M. Giraudoux leads us to believe he is "normal", in the most popular as well as in the highest sense of the word. In addition, his critical studies have enabled us to appreciate the subtle delicacy of his intelligence. Nevertheless, immediately upon opening one of his novels, we feel as though we were entering the private universe of one of those waking dreamers known medically as "schizophrenics", who are characterized, as we know, by the inability to adjust to reality.

M. Giraudoux assumes and artfully elaborates all the main characteristics of these patients, their rigidity, their attempts to deny the reality of change and to refuse to recognize the present, their geometrical mentality, their fondness for symmetry, generalizations, symbols and magical communication across time and space. These qualities constitute the charm of his books. I have often been intrigued by the contrast between the man and his work. Could it be that M. Giraudoux has been amusing himself by playing the schizophrenic? (p. 42)

[*Choix des Elues*] seemed to me a valuable book because it provided an answer to this question. It is certainly not M. Giraudoux's best work. But just because many of his charming devices have developed, in this book, into mechanical tricks, I found it easier to grasp the turn of this curious mind. I realized, first of all, that I had been diverted from the true interpretation of his works by a prejudice which I no doubt shared with many of his readers. Until now, I had always tried to *translate* his books. By this I mean that I proceeded on the assumption that M. Giraudoux had accumulated a great many observations, had extracted a certain wisdom from them, and then, out of a fondness for a certain preciosity, had used a code language to express this experience and wisdom. These attempts at decoding had never been very fruitful. M. Giraudoux's depth is real, but it is valid for his world, not for ours.

And so this time I did not want to translate. . . . I took it all at face value, with the aim of acquiring a deeper understanding, not of men, but of M. Giraudoux. (pp. 42-3)

I was not wrong. In the America of Edmée, Claudie and Pierre, rest and order come first. They are the goal of change and its only justification. These clear little states of rest struck me from the very beginning of the book. The book is composed of rests. A jar of pickles is not the fortuitous aspect assumed by a dance of atoms; it is a state of rest, a form closed in upon itself. (p. 43)

These ends, these limits assigned to the evolution of matter, we shall call, in medieval fashion, "substantial forms". M. Giraudoux's mind is such that the first thing he perceives is the species in the individual, and thought in matter: "A truth which was Edmée's face", he writes. That is how things are in his universe; first come truths, first come ideas and meanings that choose their own signs. "Jacques, like an *artless little boy,* with his reticence in joy and sorrow alike, had immediately turned his head aside." This little Jacques is not, to begin with, an accident, a cluster of proliferating cells; he is the embodiment of a truth. The occasion, the hour, the blue of the sky are such that a certain Jacques is meant to represent the truth common to artless little boys in a certain part of America. But this "substantial form" is independent of its embodiments, and many other little boys in many other places look away in order not to see their mothers' tears. We might say, as the schoolmen did, that in this case matter is the individualizing element. Hence this curious fondness of M. Giraudoux for universal judgments: "All the clocks in the town were ringing ten . . . All the roosters . . . All the villages in France . . ." This is not a matter of schizophrenia. These generalizations, which are tiresome in the evolving world where they would be merely an inventory of chance encounters, correspond here to those exhaustive reviews of all the children meant to embody the "artless little boy" and of the the nickel and enamel cylinders supposed to embody the "clock".

These lists generally end with the mention of an exceptional case, an oddity. ''They lunched on the bank . . . feeding the birds with their crumbs, except for one bird, a suspicious fellow who had come to look at them and not to eat, and who flew away during the dessert to deliver a report somewhere.'' This is what we might term the playfulness of M. Giraudoux. He uses it skilfully; the general survey with the poetic or charming or comic exception is one of his most familiar devices. But this disrespect toward the established order can have significance only in relation to that order. In the work of M. Giraudoux, as in the proverb, the exception exists only in order to prove the rule.

It would be a mistake, however, to regard M. Giraudoux as a Platonist. His forms are not in the heaven of ideas, but among us, inseparable from the matter whose movements they govern. They are stamped on our skin like seals in glass. Nor are they to be confused with simple concepts. A concept contains barely more than a handful of the traits common to all the individuals of a given group. Actually, M. Giraudoux's forms contain no more, but the features that compose them are all perfect. They are norms and canons rather than general ideas. There can be no doubt but that Jacques applies spontaneously, and without even thinking about them, all the rules which enable him to make of himself the perfection of the artless little boy.

The very gesture which created Pierre has made him the most perfect realization of the scientist-husband. . . . ''The annoying thing about Pierre was that by dint of wanting to represent humanity, he had actually managed to do so. Each of his gestures, each of his words, was only the valid sample of human language and movement.'' So it is with all of M. Giraudoux's creatures. His books are samplings. Socrates, when questioned by Parmenides, hesitated to admit that there might be an Idea of filth, an Idea of the louse. But M. Giraudoux would not hesitate. The lice with which he is concerned are admirable in that each one represents the perfection of the louse—and each to the same degree, though in different ways.

That is why these substantial forms deserve to be called archetypes, a name which the author himself occasionally employs, rather than concepts. (pp. 43-5)

The world of *Choix des Elues* is a botanical atlas in which all the species are carefully classified, in which the periwinkle is blue because it is a periwinkle and the oleanders are pink because they are oleanders. Its only causality is that of the archetype. Determinism, that is, the causative action of the preceding state, is completely foreign to this world. But you will never find an *event* in it either, if by event you mean the irruption of a new phenomenon whose very novelty exceeds all expectation and upsets the conceptual order. There is almost no change, except that of matter as it is acted upon by form. And the action of this form is of two kinds. It can act by *virtue*, like the fire of the Schoolmen which burned because of phlogiston. In this case, it takes root in matter and fashions and directs it at will. The movement is merely the temporal development of the archetype. That is why most of the gestures made in *Choix des Elues* are the gestures of madmen. The characters and objects merely realize their substantial forms in stricter fashion, the former by their acts and the latter by their changes. (pp. 45-6)

Thus, the various changes in this universe, which we must reluctantly call events, are always symbols of the forms that produce them. But the form may also operate through elective affinity, whence the title: *Choix des Elues (Choice of the Elect)*.

There is not one of M. Giraudoux's creatures who is not one of the ''elect''. A form, lurking in the future, lies in wait for its substance; it has elected it; it draws it unto itself. And that is the second kind of change: a brief transition from one form to another, an evolution narrowly defined by its original and final terms. . . . About this evolution itself there is nothing to say, and M. Giraudoux speaks of it as little as possible. Nevertheless, the subject of *Choix des Elues* is an evolution, the evolution of Edmée, the chosen one. But M. Giraudoux presents only its stages. Each of his chapters is a ''stasis'': Edmée at her birthday dinner, Edmée at night, a description of Claudie, Edmée at Frank's, sitting quietly with the weight of a light head on her lap; Edmée in the park, ''outside time'', Edmée at the Leeds', and so on.

The transitions take place behind the scenes, like the murders in Corneille. Now we understand that air of schizophrenia in M. Giraudoux's world which struck us earlier. It is a world without any present indicative. The noisy and unshapely present of surprises and catastrophes has shrunk and faded; it goes by quickly and tactfully, excusing itself as it passes. There are, to be sure, a few scenes and gestures here and there that are ''performed'', a few adventures that ''happen''. But these are all more than half generalized away, for they are primarily descriptions of the symbols of certain archetypes.

While reading, we constantly lose our footing, we glide, without realizing it, from present individuality into timeless forms. Not for a moment do we ever *feel* the weight of the head resting on Edmée's lap, nor do we see this head in its frivolous and charming individuality, bathed in the light of an American springtime. But that is unimportant, since we are concerned only with determining whether it is in the nature of a scientist's head to weigh more than the wild head of an artist. The reason is that there are two presents in M. Giraudoux's work: the ignominious present of the event, which you hide as best you can, like a family taint—and the present of the archetypes, which is eternity.

These constant limitations of the developmental process naturally accentuate the discontinuous character of time. Since change is a lesser state which exists only in order to bring about a state of rest, time is no more than a succession of little jolts, a film that has been stopped. Here is how Claudie thinks about her past:

> There had been a series of a hundred, a thousand little girls, who had succeeded each other day after day in order to result in today's Claudie. . . . She assembled the photographs of this multitude of Claudies, Claudettes, Claudines, Clo-Clos—there had been a Clo-Clo, the farm-girl for six months—not as photographs of herself, but as a collection of family portraits.
>
> (pp. 46-7)

This explains M. Giraudoux's partiality for first beginnings. ''For the first time . . .'', ''it was the first time . . .''. Perhaps no other phrase occurs more frequently in his works, and never so frequently, perhaps, as in *Choix des Elues*. . . . The reason is that in M. Giraudoux's world, forces do not involve progression. . . . [Changes] are instantaneous because they obey the famous principle of ''All or Nothing''. When the necessary conditions have been fulfilled, the form suddenly appears and embeds itself in matter. But should it lack one element, one only, the tiniest one—nothing happens.

Thus, as we read, we are led from one beginning to another, through an awakening world. If there is any atmosphere common to *Simon le Pathétique, Eglantine* and *Jerome Bardini,* it is that of morning. Throughout these books, despite ageing and the dying of the day and even massacres, the sun always rises. *Electre* ends in catastrophe and at dawn. But may I venture to say that while reading *Choix des Elues,* I no longer had the impression of those enchanted dawns that Jerome and Bella chose for their meetings? I felt as though I had been condemned to an eternal morning.

The endings, like the beginnings, are absolute. Once the balance has been destroyed, the form goes away just as it came, discreetly and entirely. "Edmée was there in the light of early morning, without a wrinkle or blur on her face, and the long night which had just passed seemed even to have been subtracted from her age." Traces, wrinkles and blemishes will do for our world, but the world of M. Giraudoux is the world of regained virginities. His people share a metaphysical chastity. They make love, of course. But neither love nor maternity leaves any mark on them. The nudity of his women is certainly a nudity that is "most definitely nudity". . . . Like the film stars that Jean Prévost called "glove-skinned women", their bodies are as thoroughly scoured as Dutch kitchens, and their gleaming flesh has the freshness of a tiled floor.

This orderly house is, however, subject to the laws of magic, or rather of alchemy, for in it we find strange transmutations—in the medieval sense of the transmutation of metals—strange, remote influences. (pp. 47-9)

[In] order to exorcise the devils who have assumed Claudie's shape, it is enough to treat them *as if* they were Claudie. What does . . . this mean? M. Giraudoux himself explains it to us:

> With Claudie, *everything that resembled Claudie* in this low world approved of her . . . Her peace with little Claudie meant peace with everything that was not part of the everyday world, with the mineral and vegetable, with all that was great and enduring.

This is what characterises all enchantment and spells, namely, that there is an action that makes for resemblance. We must understand that in the work of M. Giraudoux resemblance is not something perceived by the mind; it is *realized*. The "like" which he uses so frequently is never intended to clarify; it reveals a substantial analogy between acts and between things. But this need not surprise us, since his universe is a Natural History.

For him, objects somehow resemble each other when they somehow share the same form. Edmée, of course, seeks peace with Claudie alone. But Claudie is precisely that which is "not part of the everyday world". Making peace with Claudie means adapting herself more closely to the form she currently embodies, to the form of "what is great", of "what endures". Thus, by drawing closer, through love of Claudie, to the perishable embodiment of an eternal archetype, Edmée thereby finds herself mysteriously in tune with all the embodiments of that archetype, with the desert, the mountains and the virgin forest. But this is *logical,* if you consider that Edmée has come to terms, once and for all, with a universal form. Magic is merely an appearance; it arises from the fact that this form is refracted through innumerable particles of matter. Whence the profound analogies M. Giraudoux likes to reveal between the most varied kinds of objects.

The presence of forms divides the universe into an infinite number of infinite regions, and in each of these regions any object, if properly examined, will inform us about all the others. In each of these regions, loving, hating or insulting any one object means loving, hating or insulting all the others. Analogies, correspondences and symbolisms, those are what constitute the marvellous for M. Giraudoux. But as with medieval magic, all this is nothing more than a strict application of the logic of the concept.

And so we are given a ready-made world, not one which makes itself. It is the world of Linnaeus and not of Lamarck, of Cuvier and not of Geoffroy Saint-Hilaire. Let us ask ourselves what place M. Giraudoux has reserved in it for Man. We can guess that it is cut to size. If we bear in mind that its magic is only an appearance, that it is due only to hyperlogicality, we shall realize that this world is, to its very core, accessible to reason. M. Giraudoux has banished every possible element of surprise or bewilderment, including evolution, development, disorder and novelty. Man, surrounded by ready-made thoughts, the reason of trees and stones, of the moon and water, has only to enumerate and contemplate. (pp. 49-50)

A philosophy of the concept, scholastic problems (which is the individualizing element, matter or form?), a shame-faced evolution defined as the transition from potential to act, a white magic which is simply the superficial appearance of a rigorous logicality, an ethics of balance, happiness and the golden mean—these are the elements revealed by a candid examination of *Choix des Elues.* We are a long way from the waking dreamers. But there is an even stranger surprise in store for us. For it is impossible for the reader not to recognize, from these few characteristic traits, the philosophy of Aristotle.

Was not Aristotle primarily a logician—both a logician of the concept and a magician of logic? Is it not in Aristotle that we find this tidy, finite, classified world, a world rational to the core? Was it not he who regarded knowledge as contemplation and classification? Indeed, for him, as for M. Giraudoux, man's freedom lies less in the contingency of his evolution than in the exact realization of his essence. Both of them accept first beginnings, natural places, discontinuity and the principle of "all or nothing". M. Giraudoux has written the novel of Natural History, and Aristotle its philosophy. However, Aristotle's philosophy was the only one capable of crowning the science of his time. He wanted to systematize the accumulated treasures of observation. Now, we know that observation, by its very nature, ends in classification, and classification, likewise by its very nature, is inspired by the concept. But we are at a loss to undertsand M. Giraudoux. (pp. 53-4)

Where does [Aristotle's] ghost come from? How could a contemporary writer have chosen, in all simplicity, to illustrate by fictional creations the views of a Greek philosopher who died three centuries before our era? I admit I don't know. (p. 54)

Jean-Paul Sartre, "M. Jean Giradoux et la philosophie d'Aristote: A propos de Choix des elues" (© Editions Gallimard 1947), in Nouvelle revue française, *Vol. 54, No. 318, March, 1940) (and reprinted as "Jean Giradoux and the Philosophy of Aristotle," in his* Literary and Philosophical Essays, *translated by Annette Michelson, Rider and Company, 1955, pp. 42-55).*

JEAN ANOUILH (essay date 1959)

Oh the exits from *Siegfried.* . . . Dear Giraudoux, who will tell you now, since I never dared or wished to tell you, what strange encounters of despair and the harshest joy, of pride and the tenderest humility, took place in this young man who stumbled down from the upper gallery of the *Comédie des Champs-Elysées?* (p. 3)

Dear Giraudoux, I didn't tell you something else, it was the evening of *Siegfried* that I understood. As a consequence, I was to enter into a long night from which I have not yet completely emerged, from which, perhaps, I shall never emerge, but it is because of those spring evenings in 1928 when I, the only spectator, wept, even at the amusing dialogue, that I have been able to move somewhat out of myself.

Then came *Amphitryon, Intermezzo,* both farther from me; then, irritated with the man who produced them and intransigent as innocence is wont to be, I no longer saw your plays performed. I would read them, overwhelmed, without opera *décor,* without glitter, without excess of magic tricks, without that imposing air of gala which your *premières* always managed to take on somewhat too lavishly. I would talk about them with Pitoëff—my other master, but with whom I was on familiar terms—who regretted so much your admirable *Elèctre* and then, finally, I experienced that tender despair a last time with *Ondine.*

When Jouvet—detested (I was his secretary) and then suddenly pardoned for so much just nobleness of spirit—lay down in his black armor upon that long grey stone, a despair rent me which I shall never forget.

It was not only too beautiful, it not only made ridiculous everything I had wanted to do, it was tender, solemn, and definitive like a farewell. I had a very certain feeling about it: the farewell of Hans to Ondine took on the meaning of another farewell which wrenched my heart. It was the time of the phony war and we dreamt about lives in danger. I believed, naively, that this mysterious farewell concerned me. (pp. 4-5)

> *Jean Anouilh, "To Jean Giraudoux" (copyright, © 1959 by Jean Anouilh; reprinted by permission of Michael Imison Playwrights Limited, 150 West 47th Street, New York, NY 10036), in* The Tulane Drama Review, *Vol. III, No. 4, May, 1959, pp. 3-5.*

FRANÇOIS MAURIAC   (essay date 1961)

To the best of my knowledge, no one has ever pointed out what a raging passion inflames Giraudoux's plays. It is the same passion that fired those charming and terrible faces painted by [Quentin de] La Tour, which, as I realized with delight every time we met, Giraudoux's own face resembled.

The author of *Electra* envelops his mockery in a cloud that recalls the devices dear to the tribe of the Encyclopedists. But our friend need not bother to mollify his most devout and Christian majesty the king nor the Jesuits nor even the indulgent M. de Malesherbes. The beautiful, many-hued cloud draped about his audacities is not designed as a protection. It is a condensation of poetry that enchants and delights its author until he forgets the passion that animates him.

What passion is this? The gods annoy him. The gods . . . but is this the point? With the single possible exception of his *Judith,* Giraudoux has never written anything for the theater more powerful than this play, which was a semi-flop on the stage. In it he was measuring himself against his true adversary, and he did not name him Jupiter but called him by his real name. He danced his terrible dance around the God of Abraham, Isaac, and Jacob—the gentle, consoling God to whom the Psalmist appealed on such an un-Giraudoux-like note: "My

sacrifice, O God, is a contrite spirit; a contrite and humbled heart, O God, thou wilt not despise."

All the graceful slaps that Giraudoux lavishes elsewhere on Jupiter, are they not actually aimed at Him whom he just once (and without meanness or hate, needless to say) attacked head-on? Giraudoux's work is conceived in the spirit of the eighteenth century battling with the Angel, but in him this spirit is purified and decanted. What progress! Our latter-day Voltaire would be incapable of thinking, much less writing, "Let us crush this infamy!" We no longer find the smile hideous but charming, this smile of Jean Giraudoux.

No party in France can exploit his rich resources for their own purposes. Giraudoux is the single flower of what our pious instructors used to call the "godless" school. In its fifty-year-long search for a morality, this group has been counting on Sorbonne professors and school inspectors to discover one. Why doesn't it turn instead to this graduate of the lycée of Châteauroux who amuses himself in the playground by shooting beribboned arrows at heaven? Must I tip them off to the fact that the work—the plays especially—of Giraudoux contain a magnificent little catechism for humanists?

It is a small, earthly catechism, naturally, and one which through time and use would find itself utterly demolished. The cutting edge of Giraudoux's mind collides with a hard stone against which Greek thought before him blunted itself, the stone that we call original sin; he puts his trust in Nature and does not know that she is flawed. All the same, the little Giraudoux catechism would be a miracle. Even when pulverized by the other, its débris would be precious and useful to the sons of men. (pp. 126-28)

> *François Mauriac, "Jean Giraudoux," in his* Second Thoughts: Reflections on Literature and on Life, *translated by Adrienne Foulke (reprinted by permission of Georges Borchardt, Inc.; translation copyright © 1961 by The World Publishing Company),* World Publishing Co., *1961, pp. 125-28.*

JUDITH S. CALVIN   (essay date 1962)

Although it is doubtful that Bernard Shaw and Jean Giraudoux ever met, and there is no evidence to prove that either was familiar with the other's work, traces of Shavian thought permeate the dramatic works of Giraudoux. Both men, incidentally, were in some way connected with politics, wrote novels before entering the dramatic field, and wrote their first plays when they were no longer young men. . . .

If we take several of Shaw's most oft-used concepts and apply them to Giraudoux's plays and compare certain characters and similar ideas, the similarities between Shaw and Giraudoux are strikingly illustrated. Since the confines of this article do not permit a thorough analysis and study of all the works of these two prolific authors, only the most obviously analogous ideas are examined here. The most evident areas of comparison are to be found in *Saint Joan* . . . and *Ondine* . . . , the ideal woman theme; Father Keegan and Countess Aurelia, the hypersane lunatics; and in the historical plays. Traces of Shaw's concept of the Life Force and original morality are seen in several of Giraudoux's plays, though most predominantly in *Judith* . . . and *The Enchanted.* . . . (p. 21)

Giraudoux's most recurrent themes (much like those of Shaw) are war, the nature of woman, the place of death in the human scheme of things, the proper relation of man to God, love, marriage, and, above all, destiny. Destiny or fate plays a major role in a number of Giraudoux's plays, especially *Tiger at the Gates, Judith, Electra* and *The Enchanted*. Giraudoux's attitude toward style (which is too broad a topic to be treated here) is one essential common bond between him and Shaw. "If Giraudoux insists repeatedly on style as the first attribute of the writer, he is in no wise minimizing his function. It is by his use of language that the poet [and especially the dramatic poet] communicates his revelations, by his metaphors that he conveys his intuitions of the intimate structure of the world." Kenneth Tynan, in a review of *Ondine* at the Bristol Old Vic in 1955, reflected: "As a prose architect he [Giraudoux] easily eclipsed Shaw in the art, now forgotten but once obligatory, of providing long speeches for crucial moments." Whether we agree with Mr. Tynan or not, it should be pointed out that this is one of the very few comments by any author in which the names of Shaw and Giraudoux have been linked.

Another of the rare references to similarities between these two authors is found in Maurice Valency's introduction to the *Mermaid Dramabook* collection of Giraudoux's plays, in which Valency points out that Giraudoux's dramas are often "mounted firmly on the solid structure of the *pièce bien faite*. Shaw did not scruple to borrow clichés of Adelphi melodrama for purposes of his theatre of ideas. In somewhat the same way, Giraudoux borrowed the stereotypes of the thesis play for his own poetic purposes."... However, Giraudoux's plays differ from the thesis plays of [Eugène] Brieux and others. His dramas "avoid the particular reality of historical or contemporary events, substituting a quasi-real world, but only in order to clarify issues of contemporary urgency." Such plays as *Tiger at the Gates, The Enchanted,* and *The Madwoman of Chaillot* will last much longer, retain their "topical pertinency" more completely (since they are not topically dated), and adapt more readily to changing social and political atmospheres than *Maternity, Damaged Goods,* or any of Brieux's other plays which Shaw admired. (pp. 21-2)

Shaw and Giraudoux use the didactic form of drama "to propagate new secular philosophies." Yet both were aware of the fact that forced, obvious didacticism would be more of a hindrance than an aid in fulfilling this desire. Consequently, we have plays which are extremely frothy on the surface.... (p. 24)

Similarly to Shaw [according to *The Times Literary Supplement*], Giraudoux "is not happy with the conventional dramatic plot in which the fuse is carefully lit in the first act and the explosion occurs in the last. No dramatist, of course, can do without suspense completely, but in Giraudoux's world the tension is always wholly intellectual. All his plays find their form in the bringing together of opposites, moral, mental, and on one occasion [*Siegfried*], national."... This idea of antithesis closely parallels Shaw's use of disillusionment and conversion. When the antithetical elements of Giraudoux's world meet, some sort of conversion must take place on the part of one or both of the poles....

Giraudoux enumerated these antithetical elements in *Visitations:* "'that the living must live, that the living must die,... that there is happiness, that catastrophes are legion, that life is a reality, that life is a dream, that man lives by peace, that man lives by blood...'" We see this most frequently in his "continuing search for harmonization of the real with the idea." ... In *Tiger at the Gates,* the struggle of Hector and the other characters in favor of peace are defeated by those who want war; in *Ondine,* Giraudoux illustrates the fact that *Ondine,* and

her ideal conception of humanity, is incapable of existing in our world. In many of Giraudoux's plays the use of disillusionment and conversion is apparent. Though Giraudoux's idea of antithesis does not always take the same form as Shaw's theory of disillusionment and conversion, the similarities are unmistakable. In the plays of both authors are to be found sets of characters with conflicting opinions and beliefs; therefore, part of the action of their plays results from the interaction and reaction of diametrically opposite personages.

The clearest Shavian traces in actual dramatic works are found in Giraudoux's treatment of the Saint Joan figure. (p. 25)

Joan is an ideal. As [Eric] Bentley has pointed out, she "unites the down-to-earth personality of the Lady Cicely's, the vitality of the Lina's and carries as far as Shaw can take it, the spirituality of the girl heroines. . . .

Ondine is also an ideal. She is [according to Frederick Lumley] "Giraudoux's achievement of the feminine ideal; he shows through Ondine, a woman who is more than a woman, the impossibility for men to understand perfection.". . .

Joan is the illustration of an individual against an organization and the consequent treatment of such an outsider by society. Man is afraid of the Joans because they threaten the routines of society; therefore, society must do away with them. Ondine is also an individual, though a supernatural one (Giraudoux's counterpart to Shaw's saint), against the established order. She represents love as perfect as man can imagine it. When Hans rejects this love, he goes against nature and is doomed. Ondine, because she represents total love, makes life for those around her, namely Hans, unbearable. Therefore, she is a threat to society and cannot remain.

The Old One knows that Ondine cannot survive in the human world because she is a spirit (or saint) and warns her of her danger, which warning she ignores, just as Joan pays no heed to those who warn her of her pending doom should she continue to ascribe her deeds to the voices of St. Margaret and St. Catherine. Ondine is too ideal for the world, just as Joan is. (p. 26)

Another parallel between Shaw and Giraudoux was noted by Mary Douglas Dirks in [an] article about *Judith:* "Judith has been given to us as a kind of fleshly Saint Joan in her battle for truth. She has killed for love and not for God, and she is willing to face the consequences—in all likelihood, torture and death at the hands of her countrymen." . . . However, the parallel between Judith and Joan is not so clear or so conclusive as that between Joan and Ondine. To the inhabitants of Bethulia, Judith is the symbol of the pure young girl, but she is not nearly so pure as people think she is. True, Judith looks upon herself as God's choice to save Bethulia, but she also believes that it was originally her idea and that God was depriving her of her just desserts because she waited too long to claim the idea as her own. She is not so interested in serving God as in projecting her own fame, quite unlike Joan who does God's will because she has to and who takes no credit for initiating the plan. At the close of the play, Judith claims she has killed Holofernes for love, but an archangel sent by God informs her that she has merely been an instrument of God's will—she killed Holofernes for God's wrath, not her love. The archangel tells Judith that she must tell the people this and refute what she has previously stated. As a result, Judith recants and accepts the divinity robes bestowed on her by the rabbis. However, this recantation is quite ignoble when compared to that of Joan.

Although Judith is not completely pure in that she gave herself to Holofernes because of love, she does [in Joseph Chiari's analysis] "represent . . . perfect purity and pride and love. She also has a past embedded in heredity and environment. She too [like Joan] is inescapably one of the chosen people. And being singled out by God [as Joan is], here as in Greek tragedy, means something very like damnation." Giraudoux continually points out that perfection is not possible for man, cannot be accepted in man's world, and must be eliminated. "When the pure do not die but compromise and live on [and this the only way in which they can be accepted by Society], as is the case with Judith, then, and only then, we have according to Giraudoux tragedy."

A similarity almost as obvious as that which exists between *Ondine* and *Saint Joan* is seen in the respective plays of these two profuse writers that deal with "lunatics," namely *The Madwoman of Chaillot* and *John Bull's Other Island*. In both of these works, important characters, Countess Aurelia and Father Keegan, appear at first glance to be somewhat demented . . . ; however, upon closer examination, we see that in reality they are the only truly sane people in the plays. Giraudoux and Shaw continually attempted to blend the ideal with the real in search of something closer to plausible perfection (Giraudoux tending more toward fantasy and idealism perhaps than Shaw). Slightly mad as these two characters appear (and in the case of *The Madwoman* we find a whole chorus of apparently mad people as a background supporting Aurelia who therefore seems more normal—certainly more intelligent and intuitive by comparison), they both serve as the vehicles of expression for their creators, and it is through them that some of the most poignant comments appear—comments concerned with political themes of graft, corruption, and waste.

It is interesting to note that both the Irishman and the Frenchman use as a framework for these political theories a preeminently comic style. Again we find Giraudoux turning more to the realm of fantasy and allegory, yet both plays are witty, amusing, and at times extremely lighthearted, almost, but not quite, bordering on sentimentality. (pp. 27-8)

Throughout Giraudoux's plays we see his desire and his continual search for a better world, a world free from the evils such as those he shows in *The Madwoman* and *Judith*. Shaw, too, has these ideals; we see his dream of a better world in the dream of Father Keegan who claims that "Every dream is a prophecy; every jest is an earnest in the womb of Time." (p. 29)

Keegan is a Shavian saint possessing saintly short range impracticality and long-range sureness of vision. Aurelia, too, has this sureness of vision; however, she, because she exists in a framework of unreality, is given the powers to comprehend *and* act. She tells Gabrielle and Constance that ". . . The world has gone out of its mind. Unless we do something, humanity is doomed." When the last of the evil people have descended into the Parisian sewers, she remarks: "They've evaporated, Irma. They are wicked. Wickedness evaporates," and as the curtain lowers, "The world is saved. And you see how simple it all was? Nothing is ever so wrong in this world that a sensible woman can't set it right in the course of an afternoon.". . .

Both Shaw and Giraudoux occasionally turned to the past or to ancient myths and legends for the genesis of their plays. As in his first play, *Widower's Houses*, in which he used an old Germanic myth, Shaw used myths and legends in several of his plays including *Pygmalion, Androcles and the Lion,* and

Saint Joan, since comment on present day situations can often be more easily and more effectively made by choosing subject matter from the past. . . . In his historical plays, Shaw's heroes are taken off their pedestals and given life. Their weaknesses as well as their virtues are held up to the reader's view. By removing his heroes from their high seats, he makes them real to us. . . . (p. 30)

These traits can be found in Giraudoux as well, especially in *Tiger at the Gates,* his most universal play. The topical pertinency of this play could hardly have eluded anyone when it was first presented in 1935. World War I was over and World War II was about to begin. Just as in the opening of the play, Andromache says: "Hector . . . promised me this war would be the last." Cassandra answers: "It is the last. The next is still ahead of him." (A statement Shaw might easily have made.) Today we are in the same position as the audiences of 1935, though hopefully not so close to another war. The play is also universal because the Trojan War, somewhat prehistoric and mythological as it is, presents the challenges of all wars. Hector strives heroically to prevent war with the Greeks, but his efforts are in vain. Destiny, the tiger, is greater than the individual; man's wills and reason are governed by his unrelenting force. (pp. 30-1)

Giraudoux's concept of destiny allows that man cannot change what is going to happen, but he can do his utmost to try to live as he should, doing what he has to do to the best of his ability. Destiny for Giraudoux is the Life Force for Shaw. There is no free will in Shaw's world. Man does what he has to do, not what he wants to do, because of the Life Force. However, in Shaw's universe, destiny is more controllable than in Giraudoux's. In "Don Juan in Hell," Shaw states that the people who are going to improve the world are those who learn navigation in order to steer instead of drift. Man must learn to steer himself in order to fulfill his own destiny. (p. 32)

The meaning of life for Giraudoux has been pointed out by Le Sage and others: "Man living according to his nature exploiting the area assigned to him in the universe need not lament his lot. . . ." Man's salvation comes from finding his place in the universal order and by living in accordance with his preordained nature. This is, in essence, Shaw's man of original morality in the grip of the Life Force. Man attempts to fulfill his destiny, being forced onward by a power mightier than himself. The Shavian hero has a "freedom of faith in his own real conscience. Whether he is right or wrong is nothing to me [Shaw] as a dramatist: he must follow his star, right or wrong, if he is to be a hero.". . .

In *Judith,* Holofernes can be described as a man of original morality according to the Shavian meaning of this phrase. He, like Shaw's heroes, has a "freedom of faith in his own real conscience" and is not bound by conventional ethics. A. C. Ward might have been talking about Holofernes (or Giraudoux) when he remarked in his biography of Shaw that "he [Shaw] had the same stubborn belief [as Joan of Arc] in the right of individual judgment based on the voice of conscience.". . . (p. 34)

The statement "Life does not cease to be funny when death occurs, as it does not cease to be serious when people laugh," included by Shaw in the program notes of a revival of *The Doctor's Dilemma,* very aptly applies to Giraudoux's dramaturgy. Whether or not these two men were cognizant of each other's works, there are definite parallels in their dramatic theories and in certain of their ideas concerning life, death, war, and destiny. . . . Whether or not Giraudoux was directly influenced by Shaw, the essence of Shaw is to be found in much of Giraudoux's drama and dramatic philosophy. (p. 35)

Judith S. Calvin, "The GBSsence of Giraudoux," in The Shaw Review *(copyright 1962 by The Shaw Society of America, Inc., and The Pennsylvania State University Press), Vol. V, No. 1, January, 1962, pp. 21-35.*

JOHN H. REILLY   (essay date 1978)

[During the time Giraudoux worked for the newspaper *Le Matin*], he was involved with the publication of the short stories that made up his first major work, *Provinciales*. . . . Although the stories in this collection were written about the same time as those of [*Les Contes d'un matin*] *Short Stories for a Morning,* the style is clearly different, suggesting that he was very much aware of the publics for which he wrote and that he aimed his material accordingly. *Provinciales* is made up of short stories of greater substance. . . . (pp. 28-9)

In *Provinciales,* he drew upon his early boyhood years in the Limousin region. In effect, right at the beginning of his writing career, he utilized the two major sources of so much of his work, Germany and France. The short stories of *Provinciales* are rooted in French life at the turn of the century, and the characters are types Giraudoux must have known during his childhood—the middle-aged spinsters, the civil servants, the young girls. At first glance, the basic outlines of the stories do not suggest anything terribly unusual. . . . "**The Small Duke**" relates how a young, friendless boy named Jean finds a companion in another young boy, called *le petit duc*. This boy becomes the idol of Jean's lonely life, until one day Jean, because he is the son of a tax collector, denounces a smuggler. *Le petit duc* disapproves of Jean's action and turns away from him. In ["**The Pharmacist's Wife**"] a wealthy matron tries to interest a road surveyor in her two eligible daughters. In so doing, she plays a trick on him to take him away from the pharmacist's wife of whom he is enamored.

Each one of these stories could be the subject of a work by Alphonse Daudet, whom Giraudoux had admired at one time. However, instead of merely providing a sentimental, nostalgic look at his childhood, the author places his writing in a broader, more universal context. As René Marill Albérès comments, *Provinciales* establishes what is to be the essential law of the esthetics of Giraudoux: "Place the most minuscule, even the most banal of human life in a cosmic context, see man only in relation to the universe." Giraudoux takes the everyday happenings from his boyhood and gives them a sense of the cosmos; the small moments of the day are placed in a larger setting, linked to the world surrounding them. His characters are closely related to the seasons, to the sun, and references from the animal and natural worlds are frequent.

In almost everything that he wrote, Giraudoux's main preoccupation was the search for something surpassing man's everyday existence. Even the reality of his beloved Limousin area was sometimes marked by a drabness in his mind. He constantly tried to provide a sense of poetry to man's arid existence, to effectuate a cosmic relationship for man and to establish a connection with nature. Moreover, in these first stories, we can also see the beginning of the structural pattern that would predominate in most of his works: the search for the ideal transcending reality, the failure to sustain the moment of the ideal, followed by the somewhat reluctant and stoical return

to reality to seek out the poetry to be found therein. In "**The Small Duke**," Jean's friendship with the new boy becomes a marvelous period in his otherwise lonely existence; but this friendship does not last and he must return to his previous solitary way of life. In "**The Pharmacist's Wife**," the road surveyor finds the title character so enticing that his life is enriched immeasurably. However, because of the trick played upon him, he loses her, probably forever. (pp. 29-30)

Provinciales is the first attempt by the author to transcend reality. Later efforts will be more powerfully written, and the writer's basic theme will be clearer. Yet much of the essence of Giraudoux can be found in this early work.

In 1911, Giraudoux published his second work, *L'Ecole des indifférents (The School for the Indifferent),* composed of three short stories that had previously appeared in various journals. The three stories ("**Jacques l'égoïste**," "**Don Manuel le paresseux**," and "**Bernard, le faible Bernard**"), while separate in their plot lines, are unified in that each of the main characters is apparently meant to represent an aspect of Giraudoux as he saw himself at an earlier period in his life. Like many authors when they first begin writing, Giraudoux turned to his own life and drew directly from his own feelings, often describing himself in a rather unflattering light. (pp. 30-1)

In all three cases, the central characters are people who have withdrawn from the responsibilities of life—they have removed themselves in one form or another from its realities, having accepted a detachment that has resulted in indifference. (p. 32)

In this respect, *The School for the Indifferent* is not very appealing; the characters are unattractive and seem shallow, scarcely worthy of our attention. Yet the stories retain our interest for other reasons. They provide us with a candid accounting of the personality of the writer at an early period in his life and help us to understand his feelings about reality. The superior attitude displayed by his characters at this point is the forerunner of an important trait found in the protagonists of later works. As he continued writing, the author developed the concept of the *élus,* the chosen ones—those people who are superior because they have the ability to see beyond the everyday reality, to perceive the relationship of man and the universe. As a result, the unsympathetic, somewhat arrogant characters of the early works change into the exciting, more profound *élus* of later novels and plays. Finally, Giraudoux's style compensates for many other weaknesses. The author had an unusual ability to take an ordinary situation and, through an unusual comparison or metaphor, to present an original and fresh description. . . . Even in his less effective works, Giraudoux's inventive mind and his touch with language turned his writing into an imaginative experience. (pp. 32-3)

[*Simon le pathétique (Simon the Sensitive)*] had an unusual composition. The author began the main part of the work as early as 1911, and a section of it appeared in the newspaper *L'Opinion* in 1914. Everything was interrupted during the war, but the writer picked it up again and continued working, publishing a new version in 1918. . . . Basically, *Simon the Sensitive* is divided into two parts: Simon's days as a student and his first adventures in the world, followed by the section dealing with his love for Anne. There is little doubt that Simon is very much like his creator. Although the character is fictionalized, the personality is similar to that which we associate with Giraudoux, and Simon's reactions to life help us to understand the young Giraudoux. (p. 37)

Although *Simon the Sensitive* is the first complete novel that Giraudoux wrote, one stylistic trait is immediately clear: the writer was not interested in creating three dimensional characters. The protagonists in his works are there to reflect the ideas of the author, and little attention is paid to psychological development. As the various versions of the novel took shape . . . , Giraudoux took whole scenes and speeches from Gabrielle and Hélène and gave them to the constantly expanding role of Anne, who originally was a minor figure. It did not matter to him that the personalities of Gabrielle and Hélène might have been different and that the speeches would not be suitable to the character of Anne. Basically, Giraudoux's protagonists are there to serve his purposes. If we can speak of any character development at all, it is only in the direction of the preconceived "essences" set up by the author and toward which each person must head. (p. 39)

With *Suzanne et le Pacifique (Suzanne and the Pacific)* . . . , Giraudoux found clearly and definitively the theme and structure that he would use in most of his future writings: the flight from humanity, the search for a different reality, the discovery of the ideal; followed by disappointment, and the return to, and acceptance of, humanity. This theme expressed Giraudoux's own deeply felt need for the imaginative world, away from reality, and represented his attempt to find a balance between his desired ideal and the reality in which he had to live. In this work, for the first time the writer utilizes the young girl, the *jeune fille,* as his main character, probably because he saw her adolescent state as an appropriate period in life for revery. It is also probable that Giraudoux felt that he should no longer present his ideas through a semi-autobiographical hero, as he had done in *Simon the Sensitive,* for his writing now touched upon his emotions as an adult, not safely removed in the world of childhood as his earlier works had been. The discreet and reserved novelist undoubtedly did not want to disclose too much of himself. (pp. 44-5)

Suzanne and the Pacific is a typically fanciful Giraudoux tale, accompanied by digressions and stylistic devices. Whimsical, amusingly inventive, it is more deeply felt than it may seem at first. Although the writer regarded reality with detachment, he was profoundly aware of its imperfections and felt a strong need to escape. Suzanne is, of course, the symbol of this need. By the device of the shipwreck, Giraudoux places her as a stranger in a new environment, a situation frequently repeated in his works. Having been thrust out of the normal pattern of her existence, she creates a new life for herself within the open framework of nature. But it soon becomes apparent to Suzanne—and to Giraudoux—that such an attempt is not satisfactory. She is alone, isolated, lost. She begins to feel deceived and almost smothered by nature. At times, especially during her visit to the second island, nature becomes an enemy, actively hostile, trying to humiliate her. In effect, though, nature is simply preparing her for what is to take place—her return to the real world. Even though Giraudoux sees links between the two realms, he is also aware of a radical separation between the two and understands that man cannot live only in the ideal. (p. 46)

Laurent LeSage suggests that the tale represents a passage of the protagonist from adolescence to maturity, and this is very likely the case. For the moment, Giraudoux accepts reality as part of the process of maturity. But this compromise is tenuous and filled with some deception. Later, the fragile agreement will come apart.

Having once established the theme that would be the basis of his writings, Giraudoux now turned to the two sources that most represented this theme in his own inner being: France

and Germany. . . . France and Germany symbolized very deep-rooted sides of Giraudoux's personality, and it was natural that he should use the two countries as bases for his writing. *Siegfried et le Limousin (My Friend from Limousin)* . . . represents the most ambitious work undertaken by the novelist up to that point. The search for a French-German entente indicates Giraudoux's need to find an equilibrium in his soul, an accommodation within his own being. (pp. 46-7)

In the novel, a French soldier, Jacques Forestier, has been wounded and is picked up by the Germans. Suffering from amnesia, he cannot remember his identity. Because his uniform has been ripped away, the Germans have no way of identifying him, but they assume that he must be a fellow countryman. They retrain him, and he is given a new name, Siegfried von Kleist. (pp. 47-8)

[There is one character in the novel] who offers a possible fusion of the French and German qualities. Zelten, a German living in Paris, is first presented as a romantic, mysterious, poetic figure of Old Germany. He incarnates the Germany of the imagination. . . . At the same time, he loves France and hopes to establish a government in Germany in which the first law will involve a French-German agreement. When he does try to set up such a government, he fails, and this failure also results in Siegfried's downfall. Zelten may represent Giraudoux's hopes that a union of the two sides can be achieved, but his defeat, along with Siegfried's return to France, indicates a pessimistic attitude on the part of the author in this matter.

My Friend from Limousin contains so much of Giraudoux that it enthusiastically brims over with ideas, information, and opinions. The novel is extremely important in the author's works precisely because it is so deeply felt on his part. (pp. 49-50)

Giraudoux's next work, *Juliette au pays des hommes (Juliette in the Land of Men),* . . . is related in theme to the earlier novel, *Suzanne and the Pacific.* Once again, the central character is a young girl seeking adventure in the world, eventually realizing that she must accept a limited but still poetic reality in her everyday life. Once more, the young girl represents the adolescent stage where life has infinite possibilities, but she finds that the ideal of her dream world is not to be found, and her flight from reality comes to an end. (p. 51)

Since *Juliette in the Land of Men* is so similar to *Suzanne and the Pacific,* it does not offer anything new to Giraudoux's work. As with all his novels, however, it does allow him to display his delightful style with its many digressions and its unexpected associations on a series of bizarre and unusual characters. In addition, the author does include one highly interesting section that is quite extraneous to the action but that provides a fascinating glimpse into his conception of his art. [In Chapter Six, the narrator lets Juliette] read an essay he has been working on called "Prayer on the Eiffel Tower." (p. 52)

In these very few pages placed in the middle of *Juliette,* Giraudoux has offered us an accurate and incisive portrait of himself as an artist, he has given us his *art poétique.* (p. 53)

[*Bella*] is the story of a dispute between two important political families: the Dubardeaus (Berthelot) and the Rebendarts (Poincaré). The novel is recounted in the first person by Philippe Dubardeau (the Giraudoux character), son of René, one of the members of the Dubardeau family. The account relates the differences between two types of people, both from the French upper classes. The Dubardeaus are sensitive, cultured, free spirits, and like many of Giraudoux's main characters, they have found a certain peace in their existence by following the natural rhythms of life. (pp. 54-5)

In sharp contrast, the Rebendart group has a narrow vision. It lacks the wide contact or appreciation of the world seen in the Dubardeaus. The men are all lawyers, and within their profession, they deal with criminal cases, which results in their deep distrust of humanity. At the same time, they have unlimited respect for the law and see themselves as totally honest. (p. 55)

In the midst of these two conflicting families, Giraudoux sets up a romantic entanglement. Bella, the widow of the son of the minister of justice in the Rebendart family, falls in love with Philippe Dubardeau, a love that must be concealed because of the families' feud. . . . [She] attempts to reconcile the two families. Dubardeau is willing to forget the past, but Rebendart refuses, and following this, Bella collapses and dies.

Interestingly enough, the novel does not end with the death of Bella. At this particular point, Giraudoux adds another chapter, picking up the character of the Baron de Fontranges, Bella's father, introduced earlier in the novel. The author recounts Fontranges' sadness at the death of his daughter in a lyrical and tender manner. Ending the work with Fontranges may have developed from Giraudoux's interest in the theme of the generations and their relationship in view of his own situation as a parent. However, it is more likely that the author became involved with the character of Fontranges and assigned a greater importance to him than originally planned. Moreover, he continued to use Fontranges as a major figure in later works such as *Eglantine* and *Aventures de Jérôme Bardini.*

René Marill Albérès has noted that *Bella* seems to break the cycle in Giraudoux's novels in which the theme usually is a conflict between the cosmos and the real. While it is true that the novel was written for a very specific purpose growing out of Giraudoux's life, the vindication of Berthelot, *Bella* nevertheless fits into the normal pattern of Giraudoux's writings, and we can see how the work still reflects the conflict of the real and the ideal. The Rebendarts symbolize the side of the novelist attached to his past, to the values of provincial life, to order and logic. The author purposely distorts and exaggerates this side in his presentation, making the family seem reactionary and narrow-minded, because he wants to make his point about Poincaré. Nevertheless, the basic attachment to clarity and reason expressed by the Rebendarts was definitely an important part of Giraudoux and his life. The Dubardeaus, on the other hand, typify the pleasures of life and the freedom of spirit that the author sought for Juliette and for Suzanne. And, once more, a girl, Bella, attempts to bring the two sides together. This time, though, all efforts at unity fail, and Bella's death is the overt sign of this failure. Indeed, the choice of death as an end to the situation is somewhat unusual in Giraudoux's writing, suggesting a stronger disappointment than usual with reality. Such an ending also prefigures the somber and pessimistic tones of the later works. (pp. 56-7)

[In] *Combat avec l'ange (Struggle with the Angel),* the author once again deals with a moment of crisis and a feeling of dislocation with reality. . . . (p. 88)

The most astonishing aspect of the novel is the central character, Malena, who has a definite psychological disturbance and pathological obsession. She is so different from the previous Giraudoux heroines, the *jeunes filles,* that it seems likely that the novelist was drawing upon recent experiences in his own life, on perhaps in his family, for his subject matter. The problems in his marriage were beginning to trouble him greatly,

and the difficulties of the male-female relationship now appeared with increasing frequency in his writings. Malena and Jacques had at first seemed like the perfect couple. However, when she becomes aware of his idealized image of her and of her own romanticized vision of him, she realizes reality's inadequacy. Man in his everyday existence can never live up to the ideal that he can create in his mind. But, rather than accepting this situation and doing what she can with it, Malena becomes obsessed with the idea of the perfect couple, trying to put Jacques and Gladys together, while at the same time suffering terrible attacks of jealousy, an indication of Giraudoux's increasingly pessimistic attitude regarding the possibility of happiness for the couple.

Along with the story of Malena, Giraudoux included an alternating plot line in the novel, and the two narratives together make a very curious combination. This second story allows him to deal with the diplomatic milieu, a subject that he had presented in *Bella,* and to treat another theme of growing interest, the question of war and peace. In describing the diplomatic world, which he knew so well, the novelist was able once again to satirize its bureaucratic foibles. He was also able to present a serious picture of Europe in the early 1930s, when the Western European countries were struggling with the possibility of war and the very real threat of financial disorder. (pp. 89-90)

This rather awkward merger of the two stories gives some indication of the weakness of the work. Giraudoux's loosely structured novels usually are successful because the writer's fanciful imagination has room in which to develop. However, at times, as in *Struggle with the Angel,* his imagination is too extravagant, destroying much of the reader's participation in the work. Nevertheless, the novel is of interest in the progression of Giraudoux's writings for it reveals that the author was finding reality increasingly difficult and that his world was in crisis. (p. 90)

The last novel that Giraudoux wrote was also his most somber. *Choix des élues (The Chosen Ones)* . . . reflects the writer's darker view of life. Once again, departure is the main theme, and this time it represents an almost unbearable need to escape everyday reality. Whereas Suzanne or Isabelle [in *Intermezzo*] had their moment of the ideal as part of their adolescence, returning to a reality that they were generally willing to accept, Edmée, the mature protagonist of *The Chosen Ones,* returns to an infinitely more complicated and difficult existence.

Undoubtedly, Giraudoux's personal life had much to do with the tone of the novel. His marriage had disintegrated, and it is known that the author had his own method of flight, either through trips around the world as required by his diplomatic career or simply by leaving his family for weeks on end. Moreover, later, in the last months of his life, he moved out of the family apartment entirely and into a hotel. Edmée's abandonment of family in the novel may possibly indicate many of Giraudoux's own wishes. A second theme in the work, but one almost as important, involves Claudie, Edmée's daughter, and the changes in her personality and in her relationship with her mother during Claudie's childhood and adolescence. Such a topic may have as its source Giraudoux's dealings with his own son, Jean-Pierre. (p. 112)

This final summation of Giraudoux's ideas in novelistic form is rich and complex. In spite of the fact that the writer had used the theme of departure so many times previously, he was still able to make it fresh and compelling, probably because it always represented such a deep part of his inner being. What had started as the reactions of a young man to the world around him had become the perceptive, troubled observations of a man in his middle years. Edmée and Claudie, the "chosen ones," superior to humanity, have nothing but sadness awaiting them. In spite of their attempts, they cannot escape reality. Giraudoux felt this same burden and expressed it in his writings. The charm—and harmony—found in *Amphitryon 38* or *Intermezzo* now tended to disappear. Although the author would continue to write works of sparkling wit and whimsy, the remaining publications would also be filled with greater irony and deeper pessimism. (p. 115)

> *John H. Reilly, in his* Jean Giraudoux *(copyright ©1978 by Twayne Publishers, Inc.; reprinted with the permission of Twayne Publishers, a Division of G. K. Hall & Co., Boston), Twayne, 1978, 167 p.*

MAURICE VALENCY (essay date 1980)

[The novel *Siegfried et le limousin*] is obviously autobiography in the same sense as *L'École des indifférents* and *Simon le pathétique*. It suggests through a series of imaginary situations the inner conflicts of a mind troubled by opposing viewpoints and impulses, which on the social and national plane are seen to correspond with world-views and national concepts that culminate periodically in violence. These correspondences naturally involve some element of allegory; but the rambling nature of the anecdote makes it unnecessary to treat the detail with the solemnity of a realistic portrayal. The events of the narrative, and the characters involved in them, are intended to serve mainly as symbols, and have therefore no more solidity than is required to prefigure a fantasy. The attention in this tale is concentrated on the psychic predicament of the hero, and on its reflection in the mind of Jean, the narrator—that is to say, in the mind of Jean Giraudoux, the author. What happens there is the essence of the story, and that is best developed lyrically, as a kind of revery, a poem. It was in this manner that *Siegfried et le limousin* was conceived.

In 1928 a play, however, was thought to require a more substantial outline.

In the first version of his dramatic adaptation, entitled *Siegfried von Kleist*, Giraudoux replaced Jean with Robineau, a genial professor of philology. Robineau, like all good philologists of the period, had studied at Bonn with Diez and Foerster, and was therefore in a better position than most to explain the Germans to the French. Zelten became a romantic, an energetic frequenter of the Montparnasse cafés. In the play he is a professed revolutionist, and Siegfried is a thorn in his flesh. He has therefore brought Robineau and Geneviève to Germany to unmask Siegfried as the former French journalist Jacques Forestier.

In this manner Giraudoux tightened the plot by introducing a villain. There was still lacking the indispensable love-interest. This was provided by Geneviève Prat. Her equivocal, and largely aimless, role in the novel was normalized in the play. Here she is no longer Zelten's divorced and disconsolate wife. She is now Forestier's bereaved fiancée, the girl he was going to marry, who has piously preserved his image in her heart, and is therefore able to reconstruct him as the man he once was. In this manner the normal triangular design of French domestic drama was superposed on the novel, so that in a climactic scene French Geneviève and German Eva are able

to struggle, both as women and as national representatives, for the soul of the ambiguous hero whom they both love.

In this form the symbolism of *Siegfried* comes even closer to allegory than it did in the novel. (pp. 224-25)

Siegfried is a good example of the application of Symbolist principles in a period when successful drama was still primarily realistic. In plays like *Pelléas et Mélisande*, [Maurice] Maeterlinck had attempted to give universality to a realistic situation by withdrawing his characters as far as possible from actuality. But Siegfried is not in any sense a fairy tale. It is set in the city of Gotha in Thuringia, in an architectural milieu which is in part medieval, in part baroque, and in part modern, and its date is precisely specified. It takes place in the week of January 12, 1921, and makes use of historical characters with impressive names—Ludendorff, Rathenau, and Hindenburg. But apart from these realistic touches everything is fanciful. (p. 226)

In the appendices to *Siegfried,* which Giraudoux continued to write after the production of the play, we are told that "the author, who has never understood dramatic architecture save as the articulate sister of musical architecture, could not forego the opportunity to write a funeral march." The musical structure he had in mind was less that of a symphony than of a suite, for, in addition to his *marche funèbre,* he added two "fugues," a divertissement, and a *lamento*. These are, in fact, scenes that were cut in the stage version and that he was reluctant to relinquish. Thus, even in its final version, *Siegfried* remains unfinished and chaotic. It represents a compromise between the freedom of prose narrative and the exigencies of the stage; but in spite of all the restriction to which the novel was subjected, the play preserves the effect of revery and at least to some degree evades the control of the ordering principle. Thus what was at one time considered bad craftsmanship was by 1928 elevated to the dignity of an artistic principle. Giraudoux was not ready at this time, or in fact at any time, to define artistic probity as "a minimum of rational interference." That was Beckett's phrase. But *Siegfried,* without being an especially radical departure, indicated the direction in which the drama of the future might be expected to develop. Its success was, in a sense, prophetic. (p. 227)

Amphitryon 38 is a bedroom farce. But a bedroom farce on a cosmic scale necessarily has serious overtones. It was indeed the first of the plays in which Giraudoux exhibited his lifelong preoccupation with the theme of love and marriage. Marriage, as he saw it, had both metaphysical and psychological aspects, and its tensions reflected on the level of the individual the plight of humanity in general, uncomfortably situated between earth and heaven, torn between its need for security and its longing for adventure, its need for order and its craving for freedom. (p. 229)

Giraudoux's first play has precise scene descriptions and stage directions. There is little of this in *Amphitryon 38*. With few exceptions the mise en scène is left to the imagination. (p. 232)

The opening scene is comic, learned, erotic, and excessively arch. Taken together, this string of adjectives may well serve to characterize Giraudoux's style in this play. The characterization is marvellously light and deft. Jupiter is properly majestic; but for the moment he is at a loss, for Alcmena's chastity is celebrated throughout the universe. Mercury however knows what is to be done. He advises his master to whip up a little war with the neighbors in order to get Amphitryon out of the way, and then to take on his guise and thereby his wife. The scene that follows is, from a technical viewpoint, outrageous.

Amphitryon's servant Sosia is to read a proclamation to the sleeping city. He orders the City Trumpeter to sound a call. . . . The trumpet sounds. The proclamation follows, and it is long. It is scarcely ended when a huge warrior appears. He orders the Trumpeter to sound another note. He is about to proclaim war.

The scene of the Trumpeter is entirely characteristic of Giraudoux's dramatic style. It is a decorative interlude, barely functional. In the economy of the play, it cannot be justified. But one would not willingly dispense with it. It gives the action the lyrical quality of a poem. Similar things might be said of Giraudoux's dialogue. His speeches are ample, musical, and artfully composed with clausulae and parallelisms that recall the copious style of the Roman orator. (pp. 232-33)

Amphitryon 38, however, is not essentially dramatic. It is a sequence of tableaux hung on a narrative armature which hardly amounts to a plot, and it depends more on the wit of the presentation than on the ordering of events which, from the time of Aristotle, has been said to be the soul of a dramatic composition. (p. 233)

In spite of the humor of the situation and the delightfully erotic atmosphere in which it develops, *Amphitryon 38* may be taken seriously. The parallel between the holy nuptials of the pagan god and those of the God of the New Testament is made with great delicacy, but it can hardly be missed. The ceremonies attendant on the relatively immaculate conception of the Greek messiah are thoroughly looked into, and when Alcmena ventures to give Jupiter some practical hints on how a friendly god would run the cosmic establishment it is to be hoped, evidently, that her advice may be borne in mind by future divinities.

Amphitryon 38 approaches, perhaps for the first time in the contemporary theatre, the special sort of Gallic wit that one associates with La Fontaine. Its humor is not the humor of Molière; still less does it resemble the desperate clowning of [Georges] Labiche or [Eugène] Feydeau. . . . Giraudoux's wit is warmer and probes more deeply. Like Voltaire, Giraudoux was an accomplished rhetorician. He spoke with the tongues of men and of angels; but he had charity. And, unlike Voltaire, Giraudoux was a Symbolist, and therefore had intimate dealings with the infinite. Consequently his sense of the comic was at once Olympian and earthy, and while his wit is sharp, his humor is warm. (p. 235)

Some years after the première Giraudoux told an interviewer that *Intermezzo* was suggested by a sixteenth-century painting depicting a troupe of *comici dell'arte.* Save for the traditional name of Isabelle, there is not much in *Intermezzo* that recalls the scenario of a *commedia dell'arte;* but there are several scenes which might by some stretch of the imagination be called *lazzi*—the scene of the Mangebois sisters, the examination of the little girls, the astronomy lesson, the exorcism perhaps. These are interpolated episodes which justify themselves principally as "numbers," and they are delightful; but they are divertissements not strictly germane to the plot. They are, of course, in no sense professional improvisations. They are independent comic routines strung together on the narrative thread in a manner far removed from the strict economy of well-made plays. They are intermezzi. The title of the play bears out this idea. It refers to the interlude in the life of a woman, the passage from girlhood to womanhood, a period of special interest to the author.

Intermezzo is a ghost story. It reflects the intense interest in spiritism and the occult that characterized the Symbolist move-

ment of the 1880's, and was still influential in the first decades of the twentieth century. Giraudoux's works are full of supernatural manifestations. It is true that he treats the spirits with less than complete solemnity. Here, as elsewhere, he forbears to commit himself: he was the least *engagé* of the writers of his time. Nevertheless his world is populated with angels, spooks, dryads, and nymphs, and the nature he shows us is sentient and vibrant with life. (pp. 243-44)

In addition to developing the question of the supernatural, *Intermezzo* touches closely upon the *querelle des femmes,* the age-long controversy as to the merits of the feminine half of the western world. . . . In *Intermezzo* women are expressly associated with the world of the spirit. The Inspector is not only a materialist, but a staunch anti-feminist. The Supervisor of Weights and Measures is the local champion of women. He is also, in a curious fashion, a realist who transcends somehow into the world of the ideal.

The triangular plot of *Intermezzo* recapitulates the design of *Amphitryon 38.* The heroine, Isabelle, is required to choose, like Alcmena, between two loves, an earthly and a heavenly love. In this case, the heavenly lover is not a god. He is not even a spirit. He becomes a spirit only toward the end of the play. Isabelle is not a queen, like Alcmena. She is a young schoolteacher. The Supervisor of Weights and Measures is no Amphitryon. Nevertheless he serves very well to exemplify the solid Philistine virtues of a good middle-class husband, and also to display the modest fancy which constitutes the poetry of everyday life. The Supervisor is totally excluded from the world of the elect, the transcendental sphere. Marriage is the chief bulwark of humanity against the encroachments of the spirit. (pp. 244-45)

Intermezzo marks a high point in Giraudoux's career as a dramatist, perhaps the highest. It was not his most successful play. But it is one of his masterpieces. From the standpoint of construction both *Siegfried* and *Judith* are open to criticism, and one may find fault, if one wishes, with *Amphitryon 38. Intermezzo* is beautifully articulated. The main plot concerns the conflict of Isabelle and the government Inspector. The sub-plot develops the rivalry of the Supervisor and the Ghost. The resolution of the sub-plot results in the solution of the primary conflict. The pattern is classic. (pp. 246-47)

[*Intermezzo*'s] spontaneity is at the other pole from what we think of as Surrealist spontaneity. It was not by accident that [Francis] Poulenc wrote the incidental music of *Intermezzo* for the harpsichord. *Intermezzo* is a piece in the style of Haydn. (p. 247)

Giraudoux brought to [*Ondine*] all the poetic virtuosity he had developed in his earlier plays and also all his dramatic experience. In some sense it sums up his former work. There is no difficulty in identifying *Ondine* thematically with *Siegfried, Amphitryon 38, Judith,* and *Intermezzo,* all of them variations on a favorite theme. Essentially this involves the contrast of two worlds—the world of matter and the world of the spirit, the real and the ideal—and the predicament of the soul that is torn between its need for the one and its love of the other. In *Ondine* this conflict is given its clearest and most poignant development. The story of Hans and Ondine is no ordinary love story. It transcends its characters. What is described is the tragic love of the two worlds, eternally yearning to be united and eternally frustrated by their very nature. (p. 277)

The symbolism of *Ondine* is not abstruse. It leads directly to the heart of the problem, which is the problem of marriage.

Ondine belongs to the infinite; but Bertha is skilful with the needle; she can discuss the financial situation; she remembers appointments. Hans's problem is the problem of husbands. Sworn to monogamy, men invariably marry two women, neither of whom exists. They marry Ondine with Bertha in mind. They marry Bertha, thinking of Ondine. The women are in a similar case, lost between Hans and Bertram. In these circumstances constancy is not possible. Where there is love, there is heartbreak. And when there is love no longer, for Giraudoux it is the end of the world. (p. 279)

[In] *Ondine,* Giraudoux takes sides on the issue of primitivism, the return to nature and the naive, to the instinctual life which underlies the veneer of culture. (pp. 279-80)

Like *Electre* and *Intermezzo, Ondine* is a revery, a further example of the sort of *divagation poétique* which Giraudoux considered all his plays to be. It would be inept to apply realistic standards to a play of this sort, and in fact it defies logic. *Ondine* is a poem, not a thesis play; and very likely any attempt to extract a thesis from it would be a discourtesy to the author. The problem it suggests is a first-rate subject for meditation. There is no effort on the author's part to suggest a solution. Among the ondines, we are told, marriage presents no problems. It is otherwise in the world of men: there the problem of marriage is, seemingly, insoluble; and Hans very wisely dispels it by dying while he can. (pp. 280-81)

Far from being a poetic divagation in the manner of *Electre* or *Ondine, The Apollo of Bellac* is a perfect constructed one-act play, a marvel of dramatic workmanship. In form it resembles a fable, and is thus somewhat closer to allegory than to symbolism; but thematically it might serve as a manual for Symbolist playwrights. It is a first-rate example of Giraudoux's mature style, an enchanting blend of fancy and wisdom. (p. 282)

In *The Apollo of Bellac* Giraudoux proposes a simple solution to the problem of the sexes which seems so complex in *Ondine* and *Intermezzo*. It is essentially a matter of mutual admiration. "This young woman," the President tells his wife, "tells me I am beautiful. It is because she is beautiful. You keep telling me I am ugly. I have always suspected it: you are hideous." Apart from the question of utility, these ideas raise the question of reality and representation in the Schopenhauerian sense. To Agnès the President seems beautiful: he responds by becoming beautiful. In his wife's eyes he is ugly. He obliges her in similar fashion: the uglier she thinks he is, the uglier he becomes. In this world, it is implied, truth is a matter of opinion; but The Man of Bellac is aware of the Absolute. There exists somewhere the ideal beauty by which all earthly beauties are measured, and from which all human ideas of beauty are derived: there is Apollo, whose features The Man of Bellac can evoke, but whom Agnès cannot bring herself to contemplate. There is also the practical question of marriage. (p. 285)

Finally, there is the question of the author. In *The Apollo of Bellac* he supervises everything. In scenes in which he does not speak, he hides behind the statue of Archimedes, and pokes his head out periodically, with grimaces of encouragement or disapproval. Toward the end he assumes the mantle of the *raisonneur,* and at the last, like the Ghost in *Intermezzo,* he kisses the heroine before she is launched into the world of weights and measures. The author is completely identified with The Man of Bellac, and, like the puppeteer of the Japanese Bunraku, he is at the same time visible and invisible, so that without being in the least intrusive, he makes us conscious at every moment of his presence. (pp. 285-86)

La Folle de Chaillot is an up-to-date version of a miracle play, of the type of the Miracles de Notre Dame, a medieval genre, in which through the intervention of the Blessed Virgin, the faithful are miraculously saved from impending disaster. It was not unusual for such plays to be set in taverns or other resorts where thieves convened, for in the middle ages God's messengers frequented all levels of society. *La Folle de Chaillot* begins in a tavern and ends in a cellar adjoining a sewer. (p. 294)

La Folle de Chaillot makes a novel effect, but it is constructed along quite conventional lines. There are two plots. The main plot concerns the efforts of a group of unscrupulous promoters to convert Paris into an oil field. The subplot involves the love of a young man called Pierre for a lovable girl called Irma, who is the dishwasher at the Café Chez Francis, avenue Montaigne. This love-story, itself quite rudimentary, is doubled by the tragic love of the Madwoman, the Countess Aurélie, for one Adolphe Bertaut. . . . (p. 295)

In *La Folle de Chaillot* Giraudoux rang still another change on the theme of the *élues*. The Madwoman is one of the elect, and she is singled out for a heroic mission: she is to save the world. In the case of Judith, similarly chosen, the outcome is bitterly ironical, though it is successful. Isabelle's mission is forever frustrated. Electra restores justice at the expense of everything else. *La Folle de Chaillot* seems more optimistic. The Madwoman acts. The world is saved. There are no unpleasant side-effects. The solution is direct, uncomplicated, and delightfully simple. The evil of the world is flushed down the drain, and at once a new era dawns. There is no irony in this outcome. Only madness. (pp. 295-96)

Maurice Valency, "Giraudoux," in his The End of the World: An Introduction to Contemporary Drama *(copyright ©1980 by Oxford University Press, Inc.; reprinted by permission), Oxford University Press, New York, 1980, pp. 206-309.*

ADDITIONAL BIBLIOGRAPHY

Chiari, Joseph. "Jean Giraudoux." In his *The Contemporary French Theatre: The Flight from Naturalism,* pp. 113-40. London: Rockliff Publishing, 1958.
    Survey of major plays.

Dobbs, Bryan Griffith. "*Electre:* Significant Structures." *L'Esprit Createur* IX, No. 2 (Summer 1969): 104-17.
    Discusses Giraudoux's concept of the theater. Dobbs argues that Giraudoux's theater is based on the "post-Ibsen tradition of inductive didacticism" and reveals a parareligious or cathartic quality similar to Mallarme's. He attempts to demonstrate this point through an analysis of *Electre.*

Falk, Eugene H. "Theme and Motif in *La Guerre de Troie n'aura pas lieu.*" *The Tulane Drama Review* III, No. 4 (May 1959): 17-30.
    Indepth analysis of Giraudoux's *Tiger at the Gates.* Falk presents a scene-by-scene account of the play focusing on Giraudoux's vision of the tragedy inherent in human life.

Ganz, Arthur. "Jean Giraudoux: Human and Suprahuman." In his *Realms of the Self: Variations on a Theme in Modern Drama,* pp. 86-104. New York, London: New York University Press, 1980.
    Studies a number of Giraudoux's plays paying close attention to the playwright's quest for the ideal while remaining ambiguously attached to the real world. Ganz concludes that in Giraudoux's work "a supramortal world summons his heroes to forsake the

human one'' while the author himself retains an allegiance to the limits of reality.

Giraudoux, Jean. ''Discourse on the Theatre'' and ''The Eternal Law of the Dramatist.'' In *The Creative Vision: Modern European Writers on Their Art,* edited by Haskell M. Block and Herman Salinger, pp. 135-41 and pp. 142-44. New York: Grove Press, 1960.

> Essays by the playwright himself. In the first essay Giraudoux discusses the important role of the theater in the history of human affairs; in the second he posits two rules which consistently govern the work of the dramatist: the independence of the play once it has succeeded and the unique role of the playwright as spokesman for humanity.

Guicharnaud, Jacques. ''Theatre as Proposition: Jean Giraudoux.'' In his *Modern French Theatre: From Giraudoux to Genet,* pp. 17-43. New Haven, London: Yale University Press, 1967.

> Indepth study of the different aspects of Giraudoux's dramatic works. Guicharnaud concludes that Giraudoux's universe ''is created more through the fixed elements of his theatrical vision than through the choice and evolution of certain themes and ideas, so often catalogued and analyzed.''

Hooker, Ward. ''Giraudoux's Last Play.'' *Hudson Review* XII, No. 4 (Winter 1959-60): 604-11.

> Analysis of Giraudoux's final work, *Duel of Angels.* Hooker attempts to demonstrate that *Duel of Angels* is the most satisfying of Giraudoux's tragedies and that Lucile is the most fully realized of his dramatic heroines.

Inskip, Donald. *Jean Giraudoux: The Making of a Dramatist.* New York, London: Oxford University Press, 1958, 194 p.

> Biocritical account of Giraudoux's life and work. Inskip states that the purpose of his book is to ''place this highly individual and significant dramatist in a somewhat fuller context than has yet been attempted, and in particular to describe in greater detail his actual work and life in the theatre with his friend and interpreter Louis Jouvet.''

LeSage, Laurence. ''Forgotten Stories of Jean Giraudoux.'' *The French Review* XXIV, No. 2 (December 1950): 97-104.

> Discusses a number of stories written by Giraudoux early in his career. LeSage argues that these obscure first stories reveal a ''forgotten or unknown side of Giraudoux, a literary direction which he followed for a few years at the outset of his career and then abandoned.''

LeSage, Laurence. *Metaphor in the Nondramatic Works of Jean Giraudoux.* Studies in Literature and Philology, no. 6. Eugene, Oreg.: The University of Oregon Press, 1952, 75 p.

> Investigation of one important aspect of Giraudoux's work. LeSage isolates and analyzes Giraudoux's metaphors for the purpose of contributing to ''a fuller understanding of twentieth-century French 'imagism'.''

Lewis, Roy. ''Giraudoux's Dark Night of the Soul: A Study of *Les adventures de Jerome Bardini.*'' *French Studies* XXVIII, No. 4 (October 1974): 421-34.

> Analysis of Giraudoux's novel *Les adventures de Jerome Bardini.* Lewis states that ''it is as a chapter in its author's spiritual autobiography that we propose to examine the novel.''

Raymond, Agnes G. *Jean Giraudoux: The Theatre of Victory and Defeat.* Amherst: The University of Massachusetts Press, 1966, 196 p.

> Biocritical study of Giraudoux's ''Siegfried'' pieces and his drama during the German occupation of France. Raymond analyzes these works in their historical, biographical, and sociopolitical contexts in an attempt to reveal how they reflect the poet's vision of reality.

Ellen (Anderson Gholson) Glasgow

1874-1945

American novelist, poet, short story writer, essayist, and autobiographer.

Glasgow was one of America's foremost regional writers, and her work is often credited as being the first of the powerful new southern literature which dominated the American literary scene during the early twentieth century. Glasgow began her career at a time when most southern fictions were romanticized portraits of the ideals and institutions lost after the Civil War. She rebelled against this unrealistic tradition, depicting the South's social and moral code as restrictive and false, and satirizing its idealization of the past.

Born in Richmond, Virginia, to a wealthy family, Glasgow was privately tutored and received much of her education from the classics in her father's large library. She grew up reading Plato, Hume, Fielding, Austin, Tolstoy, and Hardy, whose philosophy of fate and social determinism had a profound effect on much of her work. At eighteen she secretly wrote and destroyed her first novel, for in her family's eyes it would not have been proper for a young woman to write fiction. Her first published novel, *The Descendant,* was written after her mother's death and appeared anonymously. She did not, however, successfully come to terms with her subject and style until she wrote *The Voice of the People* three years later. Here, in a somewhat romantic manner, Glasgow determined to write the truth about the South and its people. In 1913 she received recognition for *Virginia,* an historical novel laden with irony. But she did not gain wide critical acclaim until after World War I and the publication of *Barren Ground.* This work is considered by many critics as Glasgow's greatest achievement and the one novel in which she most poignantly expressed the feminist struggle for freedom and individuality in a hostile environment. Often compared to Glasgow herself, Dorinda Oakley is the author's concept of the model woman who refuses to feel guilt or repentance over an illegitimate child; instead she utilizes her talents and reaps success from the "barren" land.

Like no other writer of her time, Glasgow attempted to relate the American South to the rest of the world. Her fiction is an account of the old plantation civilization invaded by industrialization and a rising middle class; of a society dying under outmoded manners, opinions, and methods; and of a woman's place in such an environment. Her novels modulate in range and tone from the comic to the tragic, the two opposing realms bridged by her ironic sense of the disparities in human existence. In her best works, *Barren Ground* and *Vein of Iron,* Glasgow created fiction of epic and, occasionally, tragic depth and fullness. These novels are notable for their lifelike characters, controlled language, and the infusion of what Glasgow called "blood and irony," a phrase she coined for the realistic, critical focus of her narration. Glasgow's art can be divided into three stages. Her early stories, such as *The Descendant* and *The Battle-Ground,* belong to the very school she later satirized. Nevertheless, one may see in these "sword-and-cape" romances the young author's first attacks on the romanticized traditions of the South. Glasgow's work matured in the years following World War I. This was perhaps her greatest period,

including such novels as *Barren Ground* and her "comedies of manners"—*The Romantic Comedians, They Stooped to Folly,* and *The Sheltered Life*—wherein Glasgow criticized the social manners of Virginian men and women with penetrating satire. Among her repertoire, these works are unsurpassed in their brilliant style and in their mostly sympathetic, though sometimes malicious, representation of character. In her third stage, which includes such works as *Vein of Iron* and *In This Our Life,* for which she won a Pulitzer Prize, Glasgow became more conservative. Whereas in her early work she empathized with the doubts of the aged and the protests of the young, her advice now was to simply endure the hardships that life offered. Glasgow was most efficient in presenting the struggle of human life through the development of her heroines, such as Dorinda Oakley in *Barren Ground* and Gabriella Carr in *The Sheltered Life.* These women were the survivors of a dying aristocracy, existing solely by their stoicism and self-reliance, though often at the expense of their own humanness.

Early in Glasgow's career, critical opinion of her work varied according to its origin: in the South she was severely criticized for her negative portrayals; in the North she was lauded as the South's first realist and as a master of satire. With the passage of time, Glasgow's realism was interpreted as something more akin to idealization; her plots were often felt to be unreal, and the uncommon success of her heroines led many critics to believe that she refused to accept the world as it was. Though many have praised her for her knowledge of Virginia social life and manners, her ability to interpret the complexities of southern history, and her insight into the intricacies of human nature, other critics have attacked Glasgow for her inability to use symbol, her failure to pay closer attention to the structure and form of her novels, and the lack of psychological depth of many of her characters. Her work has also been criticized for its lack of tragedy. Glasgow rebuked this claim, saying that her major theme was the conflict of individuals with human nature, and that "tragedy lies not in defeat but in surrender."

Despite her lack of wide popularity, Glasgow remains an important figure in American literature. She was, as Henry Seidel Canby has said, "a major historian of our times, who, almost singlehandedly, rescued southern fiction from the glamorous sentimentality of the Lost Cause."

(See also *TCLC*, Vol. 2, and *Dictionary of Literary Biography*, Vol. 9: *American Novelists, 1910-1945*.)

PRINCIPAL WORKS

The Descendant (novel) 1897
Phases of an Inferior Planet (novel) 1898
The Voice of the People (novel) 1900
The Battle-Ground (novel) 1902
The Freeman, and Other Poems (poetry) 1902
The Deliverance (novel) 1904
The Wheel of Life (novel) 1906
The Ancient Law (novel) 1908
The Romance of a Plain Man (novel) 1909
The Miller of Old Church (novel) 1911
Virginia (novel) 1913
Life and Gabriella (novel) 1916
The Builders (novel) 1919
One Man in His Time (novel) 1922
The Shadowy Third, and Other Stories (short stories) 1923
Barren Ground (novel) 1925
The Romantic Comedians (novel) 1926
They Stooped to Folly (novel) 1929
The Sheltered Life (novel) 1932
Vein of Iron (novel) 1935
In This Our Life (novel) 1941
A Certain Measure (essays) 1943
The Woman Within (autobiography) 1954
Letters of Ellen Glasgow (letters) 1958
The Collected Stories (short stories) 1963
Beyond Defeat (novel) 1966

WILLIAM MORTON PAYNE (essay date 1897)

The anonymous author of "**The Descendant**" is unduly oppressed with the doctrine of heredity. His thesis seems to be that the invidious bar of birth lies athwart the best intentions and the most resolute character, shaping the life in spite of itself. This thesis is worked out in the character of a man whose childhood has been hopelessly embittered by the slurs cast upon it on account of illegitimacy, who leaves his country home for the city, who throws his whole energy into journalism of a radically socialistic and destructive type, who wins only to scorn the love of the woman who might have saved him, and whose maturer realization of the folly of his course results only in a fit of passion that makes him a murderer and lands him in a felon's cell. The book is undeniably strong, and rises to the height of genuine passion in its climacteric scenes; but it is crude in the working-out of many of its episodes, and is rather suggestive of future possibilities than the earnest of achieved mastery. (pp. 310-11)

> William Morton Payne, "Recent Fiction: 'The Descendant'," in The Dial, Vol. 22, No. 262, May 16, 1897, pp. 310-11.

FREDERIC TABER COOPER (essay date 1911)

In glancing backward over the twelve or fifteen years during which Miss Ellen Glasgow has been practising her careful, deliberate, finely conceived art, and patiently striving, not without an occasional blunder, toward her present mastery of technique, one feels that, all things considered, she has not yet had in full measure the generous, widespread and serious recognition to which she is entitled. Some of her volumes, to be sure, have enjoyed an encouraging popularity; and in many quarters she has had cordial critical appreciation. And yet, at best, it seems distinctly disproportioned to a talent which stands in the forefront of American women novelists, outranking on the one side Mrs. [Gertrude] Atherton, as far as it outranks Mrs. [Edith] Wharton on the other,—a talent which sees life, if not more deeply than the author of *The House of Mirth*, at least through a far wider angle; a talent which replaces the riotous unrestraint of the author of *Ancestors* with that greater strength of logical purpose and symmetry of form. (p. 90)

Miss Glasgow's creed in fiction is obviously that of the realists,—although her adherence to it is not so rigid as to preclude her from an occasional excursion into romanticism. Her novels are not only realistic but, like the novels of Frank Norris, Robert Herrick and David Graham Phillips, they are, in the best sense of the term, Zolaesque; that is to say, they have an epic sweep and comprehension, an epic sense of the surge of life and the clash of multitudinous interests. (p. 91)

[It] is curious that the first woman among our modern writers to achieve this type of novel should have happened to be a Southern woman. Because, since Miss Glasgow happens by birth and education to have a knowledge of Virginian scenes and people beyond that of other parts of the world, she has simply been obeying the most elementary principle of good technique when she chooses for her setting the region that she knows best; while such a volume as *The Wheel of Life*, in which the scene is laid in New York, is to be classed, in spite of much that is good, among the number of the author's blunders. One feels in this New York story as though Miss Glasgow were slightly out of her element, as though she lacked sympathy even for the best of the characters in it, and frankly disapproved of the others. It is even more difficult for a woman than for a man to attain the attitude of strict impersonality which is demanded by the highest rules of modern construction—and herein, one feels, lies one of Miss Glasgow's failings. She could not, if she would, help showing us how her heart goes out to certain favorite characters, young and old, white and black alike—nor would we have it otherwise, because in her affection for these people, whom she understands so profoundly, lies the secret of the abiding charm which they in turn possess for us.

Human stories, strong, tender, high-minded, her volumes undeniably are. But what one remembers about them, even after the specific story has faded from the mind, is their atmosphere of old-fashioned Southern courtesy and hospitality, of gentle breeding and steadfast adherence to traditional standards of honor. She has dealt with special skill with the anomalous and transitory conditions of society that followed the close of the war—the breaking down of old barriers; the fruitless resistance of conservatism to the new tendencies of social equality; the frequent pathetic struggles to keep up a brave show in spite of fallen fortunes; the proud dignity that accepts poverty and hardship and manual labor with unbroken spirit. Such books as *The Battle-Ground, The Deliverance, The Voice of the People,* are in the best sense of the term novels of manners, which will be read by later generations with a curious interest because they will preserve a record of social conditions that are changing and passing away, more slowly yet quite as relentlessly as the dissolving vapors of a summer sunset. (pp. 92-4)

[*The Romance of a Plain Man*] was easily Miss Glasgow's most thoughtful, most mature and altogether biggest novel. It is a peculiarly American novel, since it symbolizes with a subtlety that is essentially feminine and a force that is almost virile the practical limitations of the doctrine that all men are born free and equal. It was quite natural that, in reading it, one should say: In this book Miss Glasgow has come to full maturity; she may give us many other volumes worthy of a place beside it, but surely nothing better or stronger! But in *The Miller of Old Church* she has climbed to a still higher level, because never before has she succeeded in being at once so pre-eminently local and so universal in her appeal. Old Church deserves to become one of those historic landmarks in fiction, with a physiognomy and an individuality as unmistakable as George Eliot's St. Oggs, and Thomas Hardy's Wessex. Yet the underlying problem, while presenting a certain surface newness, is in reality not peculiar to Old Church, or to Virginia, or to the New South, but is as old as civilization itself. It is new to this extent only: that the specific conditions which determine its episodes are of recent origin, forming a definite stage in the slow transition in Southern social and economic life that began with the reconstruction period and is not yet ended. But in its essence Miss Glasgow's theme is nothing more nor less than that of the universal and inevitable struggle of the lower classes to rise, and the jealousy of caste that would hold them back if it could—and it is precisely the universality of the theme, studied under vividly local conditions, that gives to the book a large degree of its vitality and strength. The central human story of *The Miller of Old Church* has to do with the complex fortunes of Molly Merryweather, the illegitimate daughter of Janet Merryweather and Jonathan Gay, both of whom have been dead many years before the opening of the story. (pp. 104-05)

In the broadest sense this book is not so much the history of Molly Merryweather as it is the story of the New South. The various factors that tend either to hasten or retard development are personified one by one in the several characters of this little local drama. In Angela, for instance, we have the incarnate spirit of the old-time Southern aristocracy, with its pride and its traditions,—sorely stricken since the war; moribund, yet still clinging to life with the amazing tenacity of chronic invalidism. In the older Jonathan, we have the bygone type of the reckless, devil-may-care, hot-blooded Southerner, who at

any cost would maintain his family standards and traditions; and in the younger Jonathan and Abel Revercomb we have respectively the new dignity of labor and the new and broader tolerance of gentle breeding. And lastly, if we read Miss Glasgow's purpose rightly, we have in Molly Merryweather herself the future solution of the social problem. In her origin and in her character, Molly represents a mixture of two natures, a compromise between the upper class and the lower, combining the better qualities of each; furthermore, she typifies a social intermingling which, a generation earlier, was not to be thought of, but which to-day, owing to changed conditions, has come more and more to be tolerated. In other words the stigma of the girl's illegitimacy stands as a symbol of the social ostracism of the poorer whites, even for many years after the war; and her belated recognition by her father's people, in consequence of his posthumous acknowledgment of her, symbolizes the reluctance with which the social barriers begin to yield. And even Molly's marriage has its deeper, hidden significance: even had Jonathan lived, she would not have married him, the representative of an effete social code; she would inevitably have taken the man whom she did take, the sturdy Miller of Old Church,—because the younger society of the New South is destined more and more to recruit itself from the vigorous ranks of the rising democracy. Such at least is what Miss Glasgow seems to have set herself to say,—and in this it is not easy for the reader to misunderstand her; for she has said it with a courage, a clearness and a strength of conviction that make it easily her best book, her wisest book, the book that amply justifies the most sanguine prophecies of those who have had an abiding faith in her. (pp. 109-11)

Frederic Taber Cooper, "Ellen Glasgow" (originally published in a different form in The Bookman, *New York, Vol. 29, No. 6, August, 1909), in his* Some American Story Tellers *(copyright 1911 by Holt, Rinehart, and Winston; reprinted by permission of Holt, Rinehart and Winston, Publishers), Holt, Rinehart and Winston, 1911 (and reprinted by* Books for Library Press, *1968; distributed by Arno Press, Inc., pp. 90-111).*

H. L. MENCKEN (essay date 1929)

[As] recently as twenty years ago it was hard to imagine a Southerner (not obviously insane) poking fun at the South, but now, under the tutelage of Miss Ellen Glasgow and James Branch Cabell, they are all doing it, and some of the imbecilities that they expose, it must be confessed, are really most amusing. In **"They Stooped to Folly"** Miss Glasgow herself shows how neatly and effectively the thing may be done. Her theme is nothing less than the Southern attitude toward fornication—certainly a ticklish enough subject, even today; in the old days the barest mention of it would have covered the James river with blue flames. The action swirls around the bewildered soul of Mr. Virginius Curle Littlepage, a human bridge between the old Virginia and the new. Brought up during the Civil War *Katzenjammer,* with the Victorian domestic ethic in full blast about him, he saw his Aunt Agatha, for a trivial slip, exiled to the third floor back, and there doomed to drag out her years in sombre atonement. The next generation, his own, took a bold step toward antinomianism. The voluptuous Amy Paget, caught in indiscretion, was incarcerated in no such hoosegow. To the contrary, she went to Paris, acquired there the whitewash of a husband, buried him in Père Lachaise, and then came back to flaunt her sins and tempt poor Virginius himself. It is not Amy, however, who gives him the most painful cause to think, but his young stenographer, Milly Burden. She represents the new generation, wholly emancipated and completely appalling. She neither falls on the field, like Aunt Agatha, or runs away, like Amy. Instead, she stands her ground, admits everything shamelessly, and defies anyone to do anything about it.

The fable, in its essence, is not Virginian; it might be laid in any State of this imperial realm, North, East, West or South. But Miss Glasgow is no mere story-teller. Her merit lies precisely in her skill at giving her tale a local investiture and a local significance. Her Virginius Littlepage is not simply an American staggered by a more or less familiar situation; he is a Virginian utterly demoralized and undone by a situation that, in the Virginia now dying so stertorously, remains unimaginable to a man of the right instincts. What makes the comedy is his effort to dispose of it in the traditional Southern manner—by encasing it in humane assumptions, by refusing to regard its more inconvenient facts, by waving it away with gallant and poetic gestures. The device used to work magnificently, but no more. We are in a new world. The Aunt Agathas of today, even in Virginia, refuse to climb the obliterating third-floor stair. They remain in the drawing-room, discussing the business as if it were a public question. Worse, they get a great deal of plausibility in what they say: it becomes increasingly difficult to think of effective answers to them. Thus poor Virginius swoons out of the picture, shocked and gasping. The human race, in its reproductive aspect, has become unintelligible to him. He has begun to distrust all women. He has even begun to fear for himself.

Miss Glasgow writes very skillfully. She knows how to manage situations and she has an eye for the trivialities which differentiate one man or woman from another. Her humor is not robust, but it is sly and never-failing. If she has a salient defect, it is that she sometimes yields a bit too easily to the lure of pretty phrases. Her dialogue could be a great deal more realistic than it is; only too often her characters simply make speeches to one another. They are usually amusing speeches, but that fact doesn't dispose of their stiffness. Rather too much of the story, it seems to me, is devoted to Milly and her Greenwichy rebellion. It is too typical of the age to need so much exposition. I'd like to have heard more about the discreet peccadilloes of Mrs. Dalrymple, *née* Paget, and a great deal more about the disaster of Aunt Agatha. In Aunt Agatha, indeed, there is plainly a whole book. It would be instructive to find out precisely how she got into her forlorn third-floor back, and what went on in her head during her long years of expiation there. That story would be worth the telling. (pp. 251-52)

> H. L. Mencken, "Two Southern Novels," in American Mercury *(used by permission of The Enoch Pratt Free Library of Baltimore in accordance with the terms of the will of H. L. Mencken), Vol. XVIII, No. 70, October, 1929, pp. 251-53.*

RANDALL JARRELL   (essay date 1935)

A group of Scotch emigrants settled in Pennsylvania, then went south to Virginia; their minister was John Fincastle, called by his Presbyterian congregation the "Scholar Pioneer." . . . When Miss Glasgow's [*Vein of Iron*] begins, in 1901, he is living in the Fincastles' old house, in a small Virginia town, Ironside. With him live Grandmother Fincastle, his wife, Mary Evelyn, his sister, Meggie, and his ten-year-old daughter, Ada. *Vein of Iron* is the story of this family.

If Miss Glasgow had been writing fifty or a hundred years ago, she would have given directly the history of Ironside and the Fincastles; today, she chooses to inform the reader obliquely. "Toward Life," the first part of the book, tells the story of one day in the child Ada's life. Different chapters are narrated from the points of view of Ada, Grandmother Fincastle, John Fincastle, Mary Evelyn, and Meggie Fincastle. The characters occupy themselves little with action or perception; their concern is recollection. They repeat with unvarying delight, the histories of their families, the names of their mothers, the events of their childhood—things familiar to them, no doubt, but things which the reader has to learn. If one were to begin a novel by making the hero almost drown, so that all his life might "flash before his eyes," the readers would feel that he had chosen a somewhat arbitrary mechanism of information; the reminiscences of Miss Glasgow's characters are almost as extensive, and they have not the excuse of being about to drown. Miss Glasgow selects for their reveries that form of presentation halfway between the modern novelist's version of James' stream of consciousness, and an earlier convention of the reporting of thought: that is, some of the character's thoughts are given in direct quotation, and some are told about indirectly, and, further to vary the texture of the mass, momentary sensory details are constantly thrown in. To handle this method satisfactorily, the writer must have sensibility of almost exaggerated delicacy so far as stylistic effects are concerned. Generally, the method handles the writer.

Telling a story from several points of view has its disadvantages and difficulties. For one thing, the characters' turns of thought, their styles of rumination, must be differentiated; in this, it seems, Miss Glasgow usually fails. What differences of content or elevation there are, are obscured by a certain regularity and heaviness of style. In the novel the little girl differs from the adults mainly in that she thinks in shorter sentences; one reviewer cites this as a notable example of Miss Glasgow's artistry.

Vein of Iron is, in short, what Ada did and what her father thought. (pp. 397-98)

Miss Glasgow's attitude toward our time is uncompromising. Burke once said, you can't indict a whole people; such a thought would never enter Miss Glasgow's head. It would be difficult to exaggerate her dislike for the superficial qualities of our age. . . .

There is a troubling flavor of the tabloids about most of Miss Glasgow's judgments. Short skirts and rouge have for her the fascination of obscenity. What she says is very familiar, and very obviously said; she has given us her dislike pure, not bothering to make it over into art. (p. 399)

Possibly the last great German idealist, according to Miss Glasgow, said that the American people might some day realize that John Fincastle was their greatest thinker; writing about a great philosopher has its difficulties and its rewards. The smallest feather of so rare a bird should engage the reader. We are charmed to know that Kant liked "any music, just so it's loud and military," not because of the opinion but because it was the great Immanuel Kant who held it. But for this interest to attach to John Fincastle, we must feel that he *is* a great philosopher. To convince us, Miss Glasgow would have to be either a great philosopher or a great writer: that is, either give the philosophy itself, or else make a character whose acts and sayings are so entirely consistent and point so certainly in one direction, that they force us to believe in him unreservedly, and to feel that it is merely because it would take too long, and because we might not be able to understand it, that we are not given the philosophy as well as the philosopher.

Miss Glasgow is of course not interested in the first of these alternatives; the most definite thing she says about Fincastle's great book is that it was a "reconciliation between the will and the intellect." (p. 400)

Miss Glasgow has not the professional's attitude toward philosophy, and so fails to give it to John Fincastle. (Quoting Miss Glasgow: "Philosophy is not a reform but a consolation . . . it is still what it has always been, the only infallible antidote to life." The function of philosophy is to—console! One assures Miss Glasgow that this is *not* what philosophy "has always been.") Philosophy for her is essentially ethics; she is decidedly what James called "tender-minded." If Miss Glasgow were aroused in the middle of the night by a burglar, who clapped a pistol to her head and demanded, "Name me a philosopher!" you can be certain it would not be Hume. John Fincastle occasionally says things worthy of himself; but his thoughts in general, his judgments about the "Dying Age," are not so much those dramatically proper to the character of a great philosopher as those that Miss Glasgow happens to have herself. His sayings too often make up in sententiousness for what they lack in logical acuteness. The reader believes in him as a religious thinker, a noble and sympathetic character—not, however, as a great philosopher.

Miss Glasgow's style may be called commonplace; she is fond of the most obvious and familiar rhetorical devices, and these are most evident in important scenes, scenes in which she depicts some irresistible emotion, some mystical rapture. In general, her style is a good, average, useful style, but when one compares it with a first-rate one, both its inadequacies and ornaments become obvious. This style is at its best in occasional very slight, very sensitive, discriminations, especially in similes designed to convey the effect of sense perceptions. Some of these are unusually successful: "The syllables were as empty as old wasps' nests . . . The row of sandstone slabs, as yellow as old teeth . . ."

Miss Glasgow is generally better in handling unpleasant scenes than in handling pleasant ones. In fact, it is surprising to see how much she depends upon shock as an aesthetic device; Miss Glasgow, in a review, once spoke with energetic despair of the methods and effects we associate with such Southern writers as Faulkner and Caldwell. Miss Glasgow is at times not so far removed from them as she might think.

One feels about *Vein of Iron* that it was intended to be a great book; the plan of the whole novel is very impressive; and yet the texture and details are too often commonplace, the words of the characters too often have the value of something overheard in the street or over the telephone—no more. Miss Glasgow has seen to the spirit, and let the letter take care of itself. Then too, Miss Glasgow comes to her work hardened, full of prejudice and presupposition.

Still, Miss Glasgow's book has considerable power. We readily believe in the characters as real people, in the story as something that really happened. . . . (pp. 400-01)

> *Randall Jarrell, "Ten Books," in* The Southern Review, *Vol. I, No. 2, October, 1935, pp. 397-401.**

JOSEPH WOOD KRUTCH (essay date 1943)

The most obvious way to classify [novelists] is to make a division into the good and the bad; but this is not the only way,

and it is not always or for all purposes the most significant way. Another very useful classification which may cut across the obvious one is made if we separate those who have from those who have not practiced their craft under the control of the assumption that novel writing is a unique art, with aims as well as methods peculiar to it. . . . The former write novels to accomplish something which they feel would not be accomplished at all if novels were not written. It is not a question of art for art's sake—whatever that may mean. The novels may be written not for art's sake but in order, to take a phrase from [Ellen Glasgow's **"A Certain Measure"**], "to increase our understanding of life and heighten our consciousness." But the novelist, on this assumption, has a unique way of doing both these things.

Obviously one of Ellen Glasgow's claims to distinction is that she belongs to the rather small company of Americans who have persistently written novels on this assumption. The subtitle of the present volume—"An Interpretation of Prose Fiction"—is somewhat misleading. Actually it is not a treatise on the art of prose fiction but a collection of individual prefaces for an edition of her own novels. But because she has consistently been a certain kind of novelist these prefaces almost inevitably do become a defense of that general conception of the novelist's art to which she has been steadfastly loyal. For that reason also they give a meaning to her career.

Leave out of account the controlling faith, take what the merely hard-boiled would declare "the facts in the case," and that career might become the occasion for obvious irony. Here is a woman who began as a rebel against the genteel tradition and who ends, as rebels so often do, protesting against the rebelliousness of a new generation. (pp. 442-44)

Now if she were actually saying no more than that while one bastard is necessary, too many of them—literal or figurative—are shocking, she would merely be furnishing an example to support the often-advanced proposition that all generations are alike in that each is convinced its elders did not go far enough and its younger contemporaries are going too far. But Miss Glasgow is interesting because she makes a good case for her contention that the essential difference is not merely a matter of far enough and too far. . . . [She contends] that "the republic of letters" has "surrendered unconditionally to the amateur"—and by the amateur she means the novelist who may seek sensation on the one hand or earnestly propagate some moral or political doctrine on the other, who may even empty, with what he hopes is scientific objectivity, his notebooks into his novels, but who is not, in her sense, a novelist at all because he is not a writer who feels that novel writing is the result of a unique activity in the course of which reality as the individual sees it is recreated in a form from which his own deepest feeling toward it and judgment of it will emerge.

A review offers no opportunity to debate the validity of judgments implied or of aesthetic principles laid down. It does, however, permit the statement that Miss Glasgow's pages afford admirable occasion for such debate, as well as an admirable account of her own attitudes toward life and art. A large part of her work has been concerned with people living with a dying tradition, one which, in the novelist's opinion, both should and inevitably must die. Yet there is nothing in which she has believed more firmly than in the necessity of a tradition to a good life. Speaking of one of her novels she says: "My major theme is the conflict of human beings with human nature, of civilization with biology. In this constant warfare tragedy lies not in defeat but in surrender." Perhaps the fact that it was her fate to develop in a society where the only definable tradition was one already doomed to death is in part responsible for the evolution of her own dominant mood, which she describes thus: "Although a kind of cheerful pessimism, lightly turning into ironic amusement, has hardened to fortitude, both my sympathy and my resentment are still as easily aroused as they ever were in the past. I have never lost the old irrational sense that, by some sinister fate, I had become in part responsible for the evils of a world which, like the Shropshire Lad, I had never made." (p. 444)

Joseph Wood Krutch, "A Novelist's Faith," in The Nation, *Vol. 157, No. 16, November 16, 1943, pp. 442, 444.*

ELLEN GLASGOW (essay date 1943)

In *Vein of Iron* I had tried to isolate and observe the living pulse of endurance, of that deep instinct for survival which has enabled man to outlast not only catastrophe, but even happiness, even hope. The external world had changed while I was writing, and the habits and the watchwords, if not the nature, of human beings were changing as rapidly. There was still more to be said in defense of fortitude, and there were other angles of vision. Although *In This Our Life* follows the general theme of *Vein of Iron,* the later book is in no sense a sequel. One of my generous critics has compared these novels to two movements of a symphony which might be entitled *Modern Times*. (p. 248)

[The] central figure in this novel is larger than any individual character, for it embraces the interior life of a community. If I seem to labour this point, it is because, to my astonishment, the meaning has eluded a number of casual readers. I had innocently imagined that the silhouette of roofs and spires on the dust-jacket would convey at least the bare idea that my outlook would be more diffused than individual; and there is always a shock in the discovery that, in print, one must be brutally obvious if one wishes not to be misconstrued.

The problem I had set myself was an analysis in fiction of the modern temper; and the modern temper, as it pressed round me, in a single community, appeared confused, vacillating, uncertain, and distracted from permanent values. We are living in an age of disenchantment which, illogically, resents disenchantment in literature. For I was dealing less with a declining social order than with a dissolving moment in time, with one of those perpetually returning epochs, which fall between an age that is slipping out and an age that is hastening in. Already, the potential tragedy of Europe could be felt by minds sensitive to vibrations. Yet on this isthmus of time, or narrow neck of eternity, while hostile forces thundered in the air, on the earth, or within our hearts, the few isolated free peoples, violent but unarmed, threatened with empty hands as they grasped frantically at the running shadow of happiness.

The scene, then, in this book is the intrinsic life of a community, as portrayed through the group consciousness. My major theme is the conflict of human beings with human nature, of civilization with biology. In this constant warfare tragedy lies, not in defeat, but in surrender. Time is presented always as flow, not as duration, and the stream of life should appear to move as the tide moves, ebbing and flowing, spreading out, or stealing in rivulets through separate minds, murmuring away and whispering back in subtle variations, like the sound of a recurring phrase in music, or the familiar repetition of winds and falling waves. For I was groping after that elusive signif-

icance of the profound within the simple. Thus I felt rather than thought that the fugitive illuminations must come through personalities long intimate with the scene and with the kind of life lived there in the past, as well as in the immediate present with which I was concerned. At least one well-intentioned friend has called *In This Our Life* "rambling," as if he were using the sharpened point of offense, when, by his criticism, he was, in reality, describing just that splintered light which I had attempted to shed on my narrative. In idea, if not in effect, I followed this wandering flow of thought and emotion, whether it was revealed on the surface, in conscious reflections and in eddying shallows and broken images, or whether, as impulse and sensation, a wave stirred and broke in the darkened reaches of the unconscious mind. Always the background and movement are those of the inner world. Though light and shadows fall directly, they fall inward, and external objects are perceived through that reflected light which is identity. (pp. 249-51)

Asa Timberlake mirrors the tragedy of a social system which lives, grows, and prospers by material standards alone. That Asa should be regarded as my idea of a failure by so many, if by no means the greater number, of readers proves the truth of Mr. Van Wyck Brooks's assertion that as a nation, or at least as a nation of writers, we are in danger of forgetting that character is an end in itself. (p. 253)

If Asa was the pivotal figure in this revolving group consciousness, Roy was the first character to push into my mind. As she appeared, she was saying over and over: "I want something to hold by. I want something good!" Hers is that special aspect of youth—yesterday, today, and tomorrow—with which I have always felt most sympathetic: that youth of the adventurous heart, of the everlasting search for perfection, of the brave impulse to hazard everything upon the first, or upon the last, chance of happiness. Roy was a part of life, with its softness and its hardness, with its strength and its weakness. She was not ever on the outside, waiting for something to happen. That final incident, with the stranger in the strange house, was actually the beginning of the book. As I went on, and as the pattern developed, I saw that this scene, important as it was to my meaning, might seem to have in the book's organic structure no part. I knew that more than one reader would find that meeting but casual. Yet in the end, I retained the complete episode, because of the illumination it shed on the major theme. I needed it for certain symbolic implications which could not, otherwise, be brought out in the narrative. In a narrow field, and in a small society, I was trying to reflect the disorders of a world without moorings, and driven by unconscious fears toward the verge of catastrophe. The significance of the lost Englishman, in part, was that he embodied a modern malady, an individual fear of life which was seeking to lose itself in a collective fear of death. "It is a psychological truth about war," observes a critic, who appeared to perceive my intention, "that is not to be confused with political or military truth." (pp. 255-56)

Because I was interested, above all, in the souls of these people, I may confess to annoyance whenever the careless reader appears to regard the soulless little pleasure-seeker, Stanley, as the core of this book. From the first page to the last, she is treated objectively, and this may be the reason that, to readers who do not look below the printed page, she has seemed especially vivid. For me, she remains always a part of the background, not vital in herself, but with clinging tendrils which reached out for support to the more real figures. She is not evil; she is insufficient. She is not hard; she is, on the contrary, so soft in fibre that she is ruled or swayed by sensation. She embodies the perverse life of unreason, the logical result of that modern materialism which destroys its own happiness. It was her father who said of her: "I sometimes think she has no real existence apart from her effect upon other people." That was the way I meant to depict her. (p. 259)

As with all my other work, readers have liked or disliked, very positively, *In This Our Life;* but few have remained merely untouched and indifferent. This is the case, I think, with all strongly individual personalities, whether in life or in letters. Temperament has more than reason to do with critical judgment. As Thoreau has said, in a phrase which Stevenson calls the noblest and most useful passage he remembers to have read in any modern author, "It takes two to speak truth—one to speak it and one to hear it." And, in another sense, is this not the way in which any living book must be read—any book, indeed, that contains the essence, or the extension, of a distinct identity? We find, in a certain measure, what we have to give, if not what we seek, both in the external world about us and in the more solitary life of the mind. (p. 264)

> Ellen Glasgow, "'In This Our Life'," in her A Certain Measure: An Interpretation of Prose Fiction (copyright 1943 by Ellen Glasgow; renewed 1971 by First and Merchants National Bank of Richmond; reprinted by permission of Harcourt Brace Jovanovich, Inc.), Harcourt, 1943, pp. 246-64.

[VIRGINIUS DABNEY]   (essay date 1945)

The greatest woman Virginia has produced is dead. . . . Ellen Glasgow was one of this country's supreme artists, and as a person she was endowed with qualities which were rare in any age. . . .

[Beginning with her first novel, *The Descendant,*] Miss Glasgow displayed not only high literary craftsmanship, but an intellectual integrity and an inquiring spirit which few men or women of her generation could match. She was from the outset in revolt against the sentimental and romantic traditions which had been woven about the Old South. Her pen was a javelin with which to pierce the false fronts erected below the Potomac under the chivalric tradition. In her novel, *Virginia,* for example, she declared that the heroine's education was "founded on the simple theory that the less a girl knew about life, the better prepared she would be to contend with it," and was designed "to paralyze her reasoning faculties so completely that all danger of mental 'unsettling' or even movement was eliminated." (p. 209)

[She] resolved to take literary cognizance of the fact that there were Southerners and Virginians who did not fall into the conventional patterns so often depicted in the novels of the period. She actually drew some of her heroes from among the "poor whites," an element which had been shown theretofore in the role of mere hangers-on or flunkeys to the aristocracy.

With these basic concepts permeating all her work, Miss Glasgow produced 20 novels, a book of poems, and a volume of critical essays. . . . At times she wrote in the serious mood of *Barren Ground* or *Vein of Iron,* and at others she was brilliantly epigrammatic, as in the *Romantic Comedians* and *They Stooped to Folly,* but her work was always distinguished. Toward the close it had the ripeness which marks the mature artist, and the style took on an even finer texture and surface. (pp. 209-10)

Her sympathetic nature and her concern for humanity was implicit in all her writing. (p. 210)

As her great spirit passes on, we know of no more inspiring words with which to describe her role in the upbuilding of Virginia and the nation, than those she herself used in another connection when addressing the Richmond Woman's Club about a quarter of a century ago: "Because I am a Virginian in every drop of my blood and pulse of my heart I may speak the truth as I understand it. No Virginian can love and revere the past more than I do. To me Virginia's past is like a hall hung with rare and wonderful tapestries, or perhaps it would be truer to say it is like a cathedral illumined by the gold and wine color of stained glass windows. It is a place to which we should go for inspiration and worship; it is a place from which we should come with renewed strength and courage; but it is not a place in which we should live and brood until we become like those ancient people whose 'strength was to sit still.' (pp. 210-11)

"If Lee had clung to tradition, to crumbling theories of right, would he have left the old army and the old standards and have passed into the new army to fight under the new flag? He spoke the language of the future, he marched onward—not backward.

"A future worthy of Virginia's history is to be gained, not by copying the past, but by lighting again and again our fresh torches by the flame of the old. . . ." (p. 211)

> [Virginius Dabney,] "A Great Virginian Passes" (originally published in Richmond Times-Dispatch, November 22, 1945), in The de Graffenried Family Scrap Book by Thomas P. de Graffenried, The University of Virginia Press, 1945, pp. 209-11.

JAMES BRANCH CABELL   (essay date 1947)

Now that Ellen Glasgow is dead, I need to quote from the first article which I typed concerning the remarkable Commonwealth of Virginia, as far back as in the spring of 1925; and which began roundabout by remarking, in the *Nation,* that of all the novels published by Ellen Glasgow, prior to and including 1925, *Barren Ground* was, to my finding, her masterpiece.—For I still think *Barren Ground* to have been the most important of my dead friend's novels.

I record this statement (so did I continue in 1925) after a lengthy appraisal of the book's many forerunners. And in considering this list, I am surprised by two phenomena. One of them is the startling approach to completeness, presented by these books as a whole, of Ellen Glasgow's portrayal of social and economic Virginia since the War Between the States. The other is the startling announcement, upon the dust wrapper of *Barren Ground,* that "with *Barren Ground* realism at last crosses the Potomac."

Nobody disputes that upon dust wrappers wild statements appear to be as frequent as cardinal virtues in a cemetery. Yet this particular statement, when it is advanced, or at any rate countenanced, by the firm which now for some twenty-five years has been issuing Ellen Glasgow's novels, arouses a troubling suspicion that her publishers may have been regarding her books, all the while, as being pleasant, slight tales of the only sort which, prior to the appearance of *Barren Ground* (still to quote from this dust wrapper), had yet been written about the State of Virginia—"as a land of colonels, of old mansions, and of delicate romance." (pp. 231-32)

[No] matter what her publishers may assert, I reflect, here in these books by Ellen Glasgow is an almost wholly realistic and but very slightly expurgated depicting of our present-day Virginia, along with some seventy-five years of Virginia's past. Here is a vast panorama of—upon the whole—six decades of well-mannered futility. (p. 232)

So far as go the colonels and the old mansions, it seems plain that for the deciduous aristocracy of that commonwealth which most often and most resonantly figures in oratory as a mother and as a cornerstone and as a guiding star and as a cradle, Ellen Glasgow, in the double-edged phrase, has not any use—except only as bijouterie. The virtues, the highbred vices and the graces of the unhorsed Virginian Cavalier have survived, not without pathos, their heyday; and they serve her turn. So, because of their ornamental qualities, she cherishes and she at need extols these matters, with the perturbing and cool amiability of a past mistress in the art of parenthetic malice. And the one element of approved romance to be found in Ellen Glasgow's books about our latter-day life in Virginia is so far from being outmoded that it remains always, after a fashion which I hope to indicate, quite actually the *dernier cri.*

In *Barren Ground* we have a renewed but a more obvious hint as to what I take to have been its writer's philosophy, throughout very many books, in regard to the better-thought-of constituents of romance. This novel is the story of Dorinda Oakley, born in Virginia of the tenant farmer class, and getting, somehow, through an existence in which the traditionary ardors and anguishes of human life do not ever ascend to their advertised poignancy. (pp. 233-34)

[You] will find that a great many of Ellen Glasgow's protagonists attain to very much [the same jaded state of mind as Dorinda Oakley] before reaching the end of the particular novel of Virginian life in which each one of them figures. The experiences which, by every known rule of romantic Southern tradition, ought to have mattered most poignantly have, in reality, "meant nothing."

—Not that Ellen Glasgow, any more than does life, permits her Virginians to remain in this state of mind. (pp. 235-36)

[Time] upon time, does Ellen Glasgow, after having evinced no parsimony in supplying her Virginians with trials and defeats and irrevocable losses, yet almost always manage to end, somehow, upon [a] brave note of recording her people's renovated belief in a future during which everything will turn out quite splendidly. (p. 237)

Just so does the Dorinda Pedlar of *Barren Ground*. . . . [She decides] that the best of her life is still to come; and the book leaves her in a placid state of anticipation.

—For Ellen Glasgow comprehends the bi-pedal fauna of her chosen hunting ground far too well to boggle over the event that almost all mortal beings, toward fifty, do glimpse the truth as to their personal experience with romance—or to omit the more significant fact that, after having done so, they, with extreme haste and good sense, resort to narcotics in the form of fine fairy stories concerning tomorrow. Ellen Glasgow knows that after all imaginable trials and defeats and losses, life does, illogically and relentlessly, yet again fill up the battered human machine with fresh optimism, very much as when, at more palpable filling stations, fresh gasoline is pumped into an automobile; and the machine is thus kept going. (pp. 237-38)

Barren Ground was brought out in the spring of 1925. Then alone did it occur to anyone of any least importance, so far as I know, to appraise seriously the work of Ellen Glasgow by any aesthetic canons. (p. 240)

The belatedness of this recognition . . . seems extraordinary. Yet I think, too, there is to be found in the earlier work of Ellen Glasgow the influence of certain modes, then current, each one of which made directly for the timely and popular appeal of the book at the date of its publication, and each of which, as literary fashions shifted, had tended to hide the book's merit as a work of art. (pp. 240-41)

[These] earlier stories about the State of Virginia were written at a time when novels in dialect were prevailingly popular. Moreover, these books were written at a time when all American novels ended happily, as a polite matter of course.

These things are trivial. These things are, in every case, extraneous to the main matter of the book wherein they occur. Yet it was just these things, I believe, which for so long a season had combined to make many of those earlier books by Ellen Glasgow appear, to the casual eye, somewhat stolid- and wholesome-looking, a good while after stolidity and wholesomeness had been expunged from the list of possible literary virtues.

Today we declare that Ellen Glasgow was never stolid, and that "wholesome" is precisely the last adjective which any patriotic Southron would ever hurl at her. Today we recognize that in these superficial matters Ellen Glasgow conformed to the mode of her day very much as she then wore her beautiful bronze hair à la Pompadour. My point is merely that it was this wise-seeming conformity, I think, which delayed the recognition of Ellen Glasgow's importance. (pp. 241-42)

[You] have in the work of Ellen Glasgow something very like a complete social chronicle of the Piedmont section of the State of Virginia since the War Between the States, as this chronicle has been put together by a witty and observant woman, a poet in grain, who was not at any moment in her writing quite devoid of malice, nor of an all-understanding lyric tenderness either; and who was not ever, through any tiniest half-moment, deficient in craftsmanship. You have likewise that which, to my first finding, seemed a complete natural history of the Virginian gentlewoman throughout the last half-century, with all the attendant features of her lair and of her general habitat most accurately rendered. But reflection shows the matter to be a great deal more pregnant than I thought at outset; for the main theme of Ellen Glasgow, the theme which in her writing figures always, if not exactly as a Frankenstein's monster, at least as a sort of ideational King Charles's head, I now take to be The Tragedy of Everywoman, As It Was Lately Enacted in the Commonwealth of Virginia.

You will note that almost always, after finishing any book by Ellen Glasgow, what remains in memory is the depiction of one or another woman whose life was controlled and trammeled and distorted, if not actually wrecked, by the amenities and the higher ideals of our Virginian civilization. The odd part of this is that it so often seems a result which the authoress did not foreplan, and more often than otherwise, an outcome which by no system of logic follows, of necessity, from the "story" of the book. It is merely that, from the first, Ellen Glasgow has depicted all gentlewomen—and in some sort, every one of her feminine characters—as being the victims of Virginia's not utterly unadvertised Southern chivalry. That is a conviction to which the faith of Ellen Glasgow has been given with a wholeheartedness such as no other belief has ever awakened in her nature; and it follows that whensoever she touches upon this conviction, her fervor ignites. (pp. 242-44)

I think of all [the luckless women in her novels] and of yet other women whose histories have been recounted by Ellen

Glasgow. And everywhere I find the problem: What is a woman to do before the top-lofty notions which are entertained by the romantic Virginian male as concerns women? Is it best to conform to these notions, at the cost of a cankering dishonestness and of a futile pottering over ever-present small household tasks? or to ignore these notions, at the cost of a chilled and futile spinsterhood not over-patiently endured by the casual charity of your nearer and less sympathetic relatives? or to rebel against these notions by letting ''human nature behave like human nature,'' at the cost of acute discomfort and of ostracism and, in the end, of futility?

Such is the problem which in its every solution involves futility. Such is the problem which Ellen Glasgow tacitly declares to have been, in the Commonwealth of Virginia, throughout the last fifty-odd years, The Tragedy of Everywoman—for all that Ellen Glasgow has found it a tragedy of the mixed Jacobean school, in which the comic scenes are as plentiful as the sad ones; and it is the former which she touches up with the larger gusto. (pp. 246-47)

> *James Branch Cabell, ''Miss Glasgow of Virginia,'' in his* Let Me Lie: Being in the Main an Ethnological Account of the Remarkable Commonwealth of Virginia and the Making of Its History *(copyright © 1947 by James Branch Cabell; copyright renewed © 1974 by Margaret Freeman Cabell; reprinted by permission of Margaret Freeman Cabell), Farrar, Straus & Giroux, 1947, pp. 229-68.*

BLAIR ROUSE (essay date 1962)

[*The Descendant*, Ellen Glasgow's first novel], shows her concern with material she treated more effectively later. An apprentice novel, it evinces in tone and in substance insights that promised successful writing. Though readers in 1897 could not have realized this, the book clearly expresses the author's anguish of soul and her rebellion. (p. 45)

The novel contains many unassimilated ideas drawn from Ellen Glasgow's reading in the biological and social sciences and in philosophy: the emphasis upon the significance of heredity and environment, the deterministic view of biological and social problems, and the pessimistic tone. These ideas, to have been effective in the novel, should have been depicted through action and character development. Instead, the novelist relied too much upon description, narration, and philosophical commentary. Although much of this comment is pertinent, witty, and epigrammatic, it is not an effective substitute for dramatic projection of character. (p. 46)

Ellen Glasgow was rebelling intellectually and emotionally against the unrealistic, sentimental fiction with which she had been surfeited, but she had not learned how to give adequate aesthetic expression to her rebellion. In this novel she often slipped, therefore, into unmeaning rhetoric, purple passages, and melodramatic posturing. She relied on the repetition of phrases or descriptive characteristics without always making clear their importance. (p. 47)

In spite of shortcomings, *The Descendant* was a commendable first novel. It possessed a vitality which made it readable, and the people in it live as they had lived for the author. Though we may not always understand them completely, we are aware of them as human beings. (pp. 47-8)

In *Phases of an Inferior Planet* Ellen Glasgow wrote of rebellion against convention and personal difficulties. She again brought her central characters from Virginia to New York. In this novel, however, Virginia is one of the places heard about but never seen, and the Southern backgrounds of the characters count for nothing.

Ellen Glasgow is less convincing as a novelist and as an intellectual rebel in *Phases of an Inferior Planet* than in *The Descendant*. Marianna's musical involvement is asserted, not shown. She represents art, as Algarcife represents science and a new philosophy; both stand for a revolt against convention in morals and beliefs. Despite her attempts to dramatize rebellion, the effect is theatrical and melodramatic. Marianna is at first the ingenue and later the lady of the camellias. Algarcife is more a Byronic figure than the central character in a drama of intellectual and spiritual revolt. His intellectual brilliance is not clearly demonstrated, and his power over his parishioners derives from histrionics rather than spiritual force, from a spell-binding personality rather than from a soul. Ellen Glasgow makes it clear that Algarcife has become a priest as his way of repaying Father Speares. He is, then, a hypocrite and a liar. Yet the author does not take this into account in her characterization. The last half of the book is much too contrived. (pp. 48-9)

Ellen Glasgow in her first books sought expression for confused feelings and thoughts born of a frustrated childhood and youth and of wide but poorly organized reading. She believed herself in revolt, but she was uncertain of the nature of her rebellion. In *The Voice of the People* . . . , she turned from New York, which she knew slightly, to Virginia and to the characters which belonged to the country of her mind. She determined to celebrate both the new and the old but to look forward to an arriving, living culture rather than back upon a departed South. With this novel she began her Virginia social history in the form of fiction. (p. 50)

In *The Voice of the People* Ellen Glasgow portrayed the complicated social relationships of planter aristocracy, poor-white farmers, village lower middle class, and Negroes in a pattern woven by the traditional and the new in Virginia society, when men from the ''lower orders'' were entering politics. She knew that caste was a reality in the lives of most Americans, especially Virginians. Although earlier Southern literature assumed that the population was composed of aristocrats and Negroes, she knew that the small farmers and the small town merchants and artisans contributed importantly to Virginia life. She desired to write truthfully of the life lived around her, and she recognized that truthful portrayal must include the lives of all classes. (p. 51)

Ellen Glasgow notably improved her style in *The Voice of the People*. Her descriptions are lively and evocative; her narration carries the reader with it. Now and then appear touches of the epigrammatic observation and the ironic thrust characteristic of her best work. Only now and then, however, as in the ironic lines which etch the figure of Mrs. Webb, does Ellen Glasgow touch character and scene with the note of satire. She is at her best when she records the speech of the uneducated village and country white people and the plantation Negroes.

The Voice of the People marked Ellen Glasgow's advance from apprentice writer to professional novelist. Her personal elements are still evident, but her emotional and intellectual stress is no longer so obvious. (p. 53)

[*The Deliverance*] was superior to anything Ellen Glasgow had written before, and it compares well with much of her later fiction. It covers a period following the bitterest events of the

Reconstruction, when the social structure of Virginia had been disrupted violently by the war and its aftermath, and the ladies and gentlemen of the aristocracy were exhausted not only economically but often spiritually. (p. 56)

Ellen Glasgow showed improvement in her craft in *The Deliverance*. Structural relations of character, scene, and action are more effectively developed; there is more awareness of fictional techniques. The author uses Carraway to control point of view and occasionally as a "chorus" voice through whom she comments on people and action or suggests the direction of thought. Now and then some of the common folk or the Negroes function in the same way.

The essay about *The Deliverance* in *A Certain Measure* is notable for Ellen Glasgow's observation that "in this novel, as in *Barren Ground*, [she had] tried to depict that land as a living personality, and to portray its characteristics in the central figures." (p. 61)

The Romance of a Plain Man and *The Miller of Old Church* may be read as companion studies of the changing status of Virginia common folk and aristocrats in the urban and rural areas of the Commonwealth. As a result of Ellen Glasgow's clearer view of her Virginia neighbors and their ways, these novels come to grips with the personalities of Virginia people without having less universal pertinence. (p. 64)

The Romance of a Plain Man is heroic romance although the scene is post-bellum Richmond rather than Camelot, the armored steeds are locomotives, the weapons are stocks and bonds, and the lists the stock exchange, the bank, and the coal mine. Read thus, the novel carries a flavor and a meaning which is not evident if it is considered a straightforward, realistic narrative. . . . [We might] be tempted to call this novel a mock heroic work in prose except for the fact that Ellen Glasgow did not mock, nor do her form and her style represent a mock imitation. There is satire, indeed, but not that of the mock epic. (pp. 65-6)

The structure of this novel shows marked improvement over that of preceding books. Character, action, and atmosphere are pertinently related. (p. 68)

[In *The Miller of Old Church*] are present plebeian emergence, aristocratic decadence, and the complexities of a rural society in transition. *The Romance of a Plain Man* focuses attention upon the economic and social ascent of a plain man in the commercial and social world of Richmond, but *The Miller of Old Church* is concerned not only with economic and political change for the small farmer but with its relation to the changing status of the rural aristocrat at the close of the century. Both *The Miller of Old Church* and *The Deliverance* present, therefore, conflicts between plebeian and aristocrat. In both books the common folk attempt to improve themselves economically and socially, while the aristocrats appear in a decadent situation. (p. 69)

With a divided emphasis, the structure of *The Miller of Old Church* is much looser than that of *The Romance of a Plain Man*. The reader's attention is directed from common folk to aristocrat and back again; but Molly Merryweather, with her heritage from both classes, weaves the pattern of forces which compose the action. The characters of *The Miller of Old Church* may remind us of the people, suggest some of the English peasants in *Under the Greenwood Tree* or *The Mayor of Casterbridge;* the aristocrats sometimes suggest the ladies and gentlemen in *Tess of the D'Urbervilles.* (p. 70)

The Miller of Old Church is a realistic analysis of social transition in post-bellum Virginia and of romantic involvements in the lives of the rural community. Ellen Glasgow was always concerned with the interesting relationships of romance and with the actualities of simple lives. As with Hardy in his novels of rural life, she never wearied of examining the intricacies in the lives of seemingly complacent, quiet communities. Even in its romantic, highly idealistic involvements, *The Miller of Old Church* reveals ironic contrasts in the lives of these people. Although given to exhibiting the ironic bitterness "under the greenwood tree" and in the fields and along the streams, Ellen Glasgow did not lose sight of the presence of romantic idealism among her Virginians. She castigated the false romance, the evils of self-pity and the "evasive idealism" while she stressed the presence of beauty and goodness in commonplace lives. The reality of the romantic and the irony of everyday existence more and more invited her feeling and wit.

Ellen Glasgow saw *The Miller of Old Church* as paralleling *The Deliverance*. She thought *The Miller* was the last of her books written in her earlier manner—a somewhat confusing notion until we realize that she is thinking that the novels which followed it reveal a different tone and style—and not necessarily different subjects. (p. 75)

[To *Barren Ground*] Ellen Glasgow brought most of what she had learned in a rich but tormented existence. She believed that, in her fortitude and her ironic view of humanity, she possessed the means of defending herself against the onslaughts of circumstance. Out of her own sorrow, anger, resentment, despair, rationalization, and hope for something better, she created the pattern of Dorinda Oakley's life. Out of her love of beauty and her faith in the fortitude which she believed sustained her, Ellen Glasgow drew the sources of Dorinda's survival, if not her triumph. (p. 86)

The central theme of *Barren Ground* is as old as Greek epic and drama, older perhaps than recorded literature: Character is Fate. Although Ellen Glasgow did not discard her evolutionary faith nor her interest in heredity and environment, she showed throughout the novel that she believed that human lives are, ultimately, "determined" by the factors which comprise the character of each individual. (p. 90)

Barren Ground is superior in design and construction to Ellen Glasgow's earlier novels. By centering her narrative upon Dorinda, she maintained a tightness of structure and an inevitable movement of action interrupted in only one important respect. The interlude in New York when Dorinda conveniently suffers a miscarriage is out of harmony with the rest of the novel, for New York serves as a means for getting around a structural difficulty. Less obtrusive defects are those portions of the narrative in which characters are removed who might interfere with concentration upon Dorinda. Of this sort are the deaths of Mr. and Mrs. Oakley; the hurrying of Rufus to the city and out of the story; and even the demise of Nathan, although this event has justification in the irony inherent in Nathan and his life. Although she took pride in her powers of imagination, invention was not Ellen Glasgow's strength as a novelist; and this lack is evident even in one of her finest novels.

Especially noteworthy in *Barren Ground* is Ellen Glasgow's use of symbolic imagery. The three parts of the book are subsumed under the symbols of broomsedge, pine, and life-everlasting: broomsedge has associations with betrayal of the land and of Dorinda and with an enveloping, smothering tradition; pine, its connotations of strength, beauty, and a sustaining belief in growth and hope of achievement; and life-everlasting, its meanings of beauty in a world of material achievement and of life achieved in spite of hardship and disappointment. (p. 92)

Ellen Glasgow developed for this novel a style which is neither gloomily depressing nor disconcerting as a too lovely or epigrammatic diction would be. The narrative, interspersed with its dramatic scenes, moves with dignity and has apparent inevitability. Although there is much that is somber, the grey light is frequently brightened by the color that is always present. We may come away from *Barren Ground* with the impression of darkness lit up with ever-recurring light and color—a symbol of the nature of human life which the novelist endeavored to suggest. Although Ellen Glasgow's use of language continued to follow traditional lines, she experimented with a tentative stream-of-consciousness effect useful in bringing out meanings where the usual narrative or dialogue forms would not serve. She later carried this experimentation in style much farther in the novels after *Barren Ground*.

Barren Ground possesses both epic and tragic qualities. It has the heroic movement and character development associated with epic literature; scenes, people, and actions are somehow larger than in ordinary life. Yet Ellen Glasgow did not carry this epic suggestiveness beyond the limits of the realities in the lives of her people. She escaped the somewhat blurred, even distorted effect often noticeable in the writings of Elizabeth Madox Roberts, such as *The Time of Man*, where the activities of ordinary folk take on an almost supernatural quality. (pp. 93-4)

Three novels published after *Barren Ground* represent Ellen Glasgow's commitment to an ironic view in her interpretation of Southern manners and morals. [*The Romantic Comedians, They Stooped to Folly,* and *The Sheltered Life*] are concerned with related aspects of the code of polite action. Southern, and even more specifically Virginian, these novels extend far beyond geographical and chronological boundaries to encompass timeless, limitless meanings. (p. 97)

In the novels which compose her triptych of manners, Ellen Glasgow explored the meaning for her Virginians of a change in moral attitudes. In these novels she showed plainly that she could neither accept nor wholly reject the code of behavior which had governed polite society or, indeed, all of society in Virginia since colonial times. (p. 98)

The Romantic Comedians is that jewel in fiction: the serious interpretation of life which is a joy for the reader. Our delight in the play of Ellen Glasgow's wit or in her malicious yet never ill-tempered thrusts at the foibles of her ladies and gentlemen may prevent us from perceiving the artistry of the book and the keen wisdom of its pages. Throughout this novel, Ellen Glasgow subjects human struggles to the clarifying, cleansing effects of the silver laughter of comedy; and the focus of the comic vision eliminates the confused and blurred views of sentimentality or "evasive idealism." Always, as in serious comedy, our laughter is very close to the tears of tragedy; we see people and their actions as participants in the follies of the comic genre; but we see, too, that a very slight shift of emphasis may reveal a tragic mask upon the actors. In *The Sheltered Life* the manner and the tone are frequently comic, but the ultimate emphasis is tragic. In *The Romantic Comedians* and in *They Stooped to Folly* the emphasis is comic, but there are tragic overtones. (pp. 99-100)

[*They Stooped to Folly*] is subtitled "A Comedy of Morals." Ostensibly its central theme is the idea of the "ruined woman,"

of what her "ruin" consisted, and of the ironic contrasts involved in changing attitudes toward her. The morals of this comedy, however, extend beyond the relatively simple problem of the violation of a sexual code. Essentially, this book is about a topic that is so often the subject of platitude that it might seem hopelessly outworn: what men and women live by is not simply what they *think* they live by; it is something which exists in the inner depths of their being and motivates all their actions. (p. 102)

[*The Sheltered life*] is Ellen Glasgow's finest novel, for in this tragedy of manners she combined most effectively all the elements of her material and art. In it character, action, and atmosphere interact to reveal not only the tragedy in lives shaped by the code of polite behavior and by the pretenses of a cult of Beauty but also the evil lurking in assumptions of innocence. She cast over these people a magic portrayal, a brilliance of life, and a beauty which makes superb the irony in the charm of their outward lives and their darker implications. (p. 108)

In the style of the book she exhibited a sense of taste and an understanding of the demands of her subject and material which were close to perfection. Tone, timing, and deftness of touch are also combined to convey precisely the mood—and the meaning in it—requisite for each passage of narrative, dialogue, and commentary. Symbolic elements, such as the pervading neighborhood smell, function in an usually ironic counterpoint against the lives of the Archibalds and the Birdsongs. Throughout the novel, in the language, in what the language states, and in what is left unsaid, the current of irony carries with it clarity of idea and feeling, illuminates scene and character, and underlines the tragic meaning. (p. 114)

[*Vein of Iron* and *In This Our Life*] are not a sequence, nor do they form parts of a trilogy or tetralogy with *Barren Ground* and *The Sheltered Life*. Both *Vein of Iron* and *In This Our Life* are, however, closely related not only to each other but to these earlier novels in material, tone, themes, and characters. All four emphasize growth and decay in a changing social order; a transition in social and moral values or an actual loss of values; and the role of manners in an increasingly unmannered, amoral barbarism calling itself civilization. In these novels, as in her other fiction, Ellen Glasgow explored an ultimate question: what can be the role of fortitude for men and women who live, as Thoreau believed, "lives of quiet desperation." (p. 115)

The style of *Vein of Iron* is excellently suited to its purposes; but it does not exhibit the brilliantly epigrammatic qualities, the irony of wit and commentary, of the three previous novels of manners. Instead, the style is fitted to the people of the book and the movement of their lives; it is rich in evocative imagery, and it moves with steady, solid yet never heavy rhythms suggestive of the strength, force, and tempered steel of the Fincastle character. The style of *Vein of Iron* is successful also in its power to suggest clearly the characters as wholly rounded individuals, each vivid in his own idiosyncrasies yet never a caricature; these men and women are alive. Setting is created in the imagination of the reader in light and form, shadow and line; and the very atmosphere of Shut-In Valley and Ironside with the mountains isolating the people who live in their shadows, or Queenborough and Mulberry Street with all their human associations become alive. Language which can evoke this awareness is effective; and it is such language that creates *Vein of Iron*.

[*In This Our Life*] is remarkable for beauty and clarity of style and for force in narration and character portrayal. Miss Glasgow suspected that this might be her last novel; she tried to make it as fine a book as she had ever written. (pp. 121-22)

Because Ellen Glasgow wished to present the "interior life of a community," she so designed her novel that the "outlook would be more diffused than individual. . . ." She thought of her problem as "an analysis in fiction of the modern temper . . . a dissolving moment in time . . . one of those perpetually returning epochs, which fall between an age that is slipping out and an age that is hastening in." She thought that she interpreted in her novel "the intrinsic life of a community, as portrayed through the group consciousness. . . ."; that her theme was revealed as "the conflict of human beings with human nature, of civilization with biology." (pp. 122-23)

Both *In This Our Life* and *The Sheltered Life* treat the evils of sham, of happiness-hunters, and of dangerous selfishness masquerading as innocence. The earlier novel, however, moved with a lightness of touch illuminated by a style and tone very different from the ironic thrusts and the stylistic brilliance of *In This Our Life*. In *The Sheltered Life* and in the two preceding comedies of manners, as well as in *Vein of Iron*, Ellen Glasgow interpreted human lives with a mockery, sometime stinging, often cutting, yet rarely mortal in its thrusts; but for *In This Our Life* she used a sharper, crueler pen. Her ironic view darkens to a bitterly sardonic tone, but her bitterness she in part modified with a pity for all tormented mortals conveyed through Asa Timberlake. (p. 124)

Although it may be thought that *In This Our Life* is an unpleasant book, it is not. It is a very serious book, but it is neither despairing nor morbid. The excellence of the writing, as well as the strength of Asa and Roy, offsets the dark evil of other features of the novel. Though the tone of the book is sombre, it is frequently illuminated by flashes of light. To achieve these affects, the method of narration is well chosen. Usually analytical, cool, ironic, clear, and objective, this approach and this cool attitude are constrasted with warmth of feeling such as is found in the sections revealing Asa or the Negro family.

Readers surprised by *The Woman Within,* should have read *In This Our Life* more carefully. Ellen Glasgow's troubled vision of life in her late years is evident in this last novel, but it is not finally a despairing conclusion to which she brings herself and her characters Asa and Roy. Into this book Ellen Glasgow poured her pity, her malice, her hatred of sham, her longing for the strength she lacked, her hatred of cruelty, her search for values, and her yearning, with Roy Timberlake, for something good to hold by. (p. 129)

> *Blair Rouse, in his* Ellen Glasgow *(copyright © 1962 by Twayne Publishers, Inc.; reprinted with the permission of Twayne Publishers, a Division of G. K. Hall & Co., Boston), Twayne, 1962, 160 p.*

RICHARD K. MEEKER   (essay date 1963)

On November 22, 1897, after publishing her first novel, *The Descendant,* Ellen Glasgow wrote to Walter Hines Page, then an editor on the *Atlantic Monthly,* "As regards my work I shall follow your advice in full. I shall write no more short stories and I shall not divide my power or risk my future reputation. I will become a great novelist or none at all." Literary history has already recorded and applauded the eighteen novels which she wrote thereafter; however, history has failed to notice how often Miss Glasgow broke that promise to Page. As a matter of fact, she published eleven short stories by 1925 and left another one in manuscript. . . . A partial collection, *The Shadowy Third and Other Stories* . . . has been out of print for over twenty years. It is time to consider whether such neglect of Ellen Glasgow's short stories is justified. (p. 3)

Every review of *The Shadowy Third* was favorable, and every reviewer pointed out the prepondernace of the supernatural in the stories. Ellen Glasgow obviously arranged them to emphasize this effect. The Shadowy Third is the spirit of a dead child who is visible only to sensitive persons; scientifically minded people never see the spirit. Two other stories have spirit characters. In **"The Past"** Vanderbridge's first wife returns to haunt him and his second wife. In **"Whispering Leaves"** Mammy Rhody returns to protect little Pell from harm. These three spirits are all seen by objective narrators with a reputation for reliability. A fourth story, **"Dare's Gift,"** contains a house haunted by the spirit of treachery, which corrupts every inhabitant. These, the first four stories in the book, are plainly intended to dominate it. (p. 8)

Miss Glasgow was working in a familiar literary tradition. Although she might have been reluctant to admit it, she was exploring the same psychological vein that Rudyard Kipling and Henry James had explored a decade before. Kipling in "They" and James in such stories as "The Turn of the Screw," "The Jolly Corner," and "The Beast in the Jungle" were fascinated by the power that ideas, especially fears, have over men's minds. As their stories show, a fear or a wish can be so strong that the object takes on a concrete existence. However, their symbolic ghosts are visible only to the afflicted characters; Miss Glasgow's ghosts are more "real" than that. . . . They take us nearer to modern ghost stories, like Kafka's, where the ghost becomes human and the dream completely displaces reality. For Kipling, James, and Glasgow, ghosts could have either good or bad influences; modern ghosts, supported by Freud and Jung, are consistently frightening because they represent the unconscious levels of the mind.

The first four stories in *The Shadowy Third* have another feature in common: the influence of Edgar Allan Poe. . . . This kinship is worth exploring. We might begin by noticing the parallel in plot between Poe's "Ligeia" and Glasgow's **"The Past."** In both stories the first wife tries to destroy the second by supernatural means. The Glasgow approach differs in that the first Mrs. Vanderbridge, who appears in her own body, retires in defeat when the second Mrs. Vanderbridge proves her own moral superiority. However, Poe might well have preferred the first wife.

Whereas "Ligeia" is similar only in plot, "The Fall of the House of Usher" must be admitted as a deep and pervasive influence on all four ghost stories in the Glasgow collection. First, observe that three of the four stories—**"Dare's Gift,"** **"Whispering Leaves,"** and **"Jordan's End"**—are set in symbolic country houses that supply the titles for their stories. All four houses exert a definite moral influence over their inhabitants. The treachery of Sir Roderick Dare in Bacon's Rebellion causes the betrayal of a Union soldier by his Confederate sweetheart and the deception of a corporation lawyer by his wife. Successive acts of treachery have corrupted the very walls of the house. Dr. Lakeby makes this point clear: "Did you ever stop to wonder about the thoughts that must have gathered within walls like these?—to wonder about the impressions that must have lodged in the bricks, in the crevices, in the timber and the masonry? Have you ever stopped to think that these multiplied impressions might create a current of thought—a mental atmosphere—an inscrutable power of suggestion?'' This is identical with Roderick Usher's theory of the ''sentience of vegetable things.'' (pp. 11-12)

The prize demonstration of the House-of-Usher influence is reserved for the last story in *The Shadowy Third* collection, ''Jordan's End.'' Even the title bears the same dual symbolism as the Poe story. Jordan's End is simultaneously the name of the crumbling old Virginia plantation and the epitome of the decaying family that inhabits it. (p. 13)

[The narrator] recognizes that both the house and its inhabitants once had charm, even distinction. Although the eaves are now falling away, the shutters sagging, the windows broken, and the boards rotting, the house was once of an impressive Georgian design with beautiful details. ''A fine old place once, but repulsive now in its abject decay, like some young blood of former days who has grown senile,'' the doctor muses. Similarly, the Jordan family was once the proudest in the county until the Civil War. ''Jest run to seed,'' Father Peterkin, the old Negro says. Intermarriage is a partial explanation.

But Miss Glasgow uses the House-of-Usher theme to make a point that Poe was unable to make about the South because he was too close to it. The degeneration which the house always symbolizes is brought about by the refusal of the inhabitants to trust more than their senses. The families that go to seed are those that refuse to believe in the intangible. They love material comfort more than beauty; they love tradition more than progress. **''Dare's Gift''** and **''Whispering Leaves,''** Ellen Glasgow's most ambitious stories, show both the necessity and the difficulty of believing in the intangible. The ghosts are only objective correlatives for this idea. We need not believe in them so long as we believe in what they stand for. (pp. 13-14)

All four of the ghost stories in *The Shadowy Third* collection have another feature in common: the use of a first-person narrator. Again, the influence of Poe is possible. (p. 14)

Only one story in *The Shadowy Third*, **''The Difference,''** is narrated from Ellen Glasgow's favorite point of view, the central intelligence. However, James would have found little to praise in her use of it. For example, the viewpoint in **''The Difference''** shifts abruptly from Margaret Fleming to her opponent Rose Morrison so that we can see how Margaret looked to Rose. Four out of the five uncollected stories are also handled from the central intelligence viewpoint, but there is no hint yet of Miss Glasgow's concentrated use of it in *Barren Ground,* or of the multiple viewpoint which she was to use so brilliantly in *They Stooped to Folly, Vein of Iron,* and *The Sheltered Life.*

All five of the uncollected stories and **''The Difference''** from *The Shadowy Third* have as their theme that limitless subject— the relationship between men and women. Although Ellen Glasgow's ''social history'' of the South appears to have been her main concern, the real focus in all her fiction seems to be the struggle of women for respect in a world dominated by men. Her short stories dramatize a complete cycle of relationships, from the first apprehensive encounter to the last bitter rejection. To a Darwinian, love is apparently a struggle for dominance. Miss Glasgow's women hope that love is something better than that, but they are usually disappointed. Her typical plot sequence runs: girl meets boy; girl is taken advantage of by boy; then girl learns to get along without boys, or, girl gets back at boy. (pp. 15-16)

Four stories constitute a ''marriage group,'' and three of them preach a similar moral: in marriage the woman gives up ev-

erything, while the man gains himself a servant. Three husbands are depicted as selfish brutes, ranging from Stanley Kenton in **''Romance and Sally Byrd,''** a philanderer who deceives an innocent kindergarten teacher, to George Fleming, who includes both golf and adultery among his favorite recreations in **''The Difference,''** to Dr. John Estbridge in **''The Professional Instinct,''** who self-righteously decides to abandon his domineering wife. (p. 17)

''The Difference'' and **''Romance and Sally Byrd''** present the double standard in marriage that irked Miss Glasgow so much. The patient wives endure their husbands' unfaithfulness as if there were no hope for a fairer relationship. . . .

In **''The Professional Instinct''** Miss Glasgow ironically presents the same theme . . . from the point of view of the selfish husband. Dr. Estbridge, a psychoanalyst, is prepared to elope with Judith Campbell, a philosophy professor and author of *Marriage and Individuality,* but when he hears at the last minute of a chance at the chair in psychology at the state university, he leaves Judith waiting at the station. Judith, incidentally, has given up a chance at a college presidency in order to elope with Estbridge. The story fairly bristles with such obvious irony. . . .

''Thinking Makes It So'' catches Miss Glasgow in a rare sentimental mood about marriage. Here she describes a romance by correspondence between two middle-aged lovers who have been bruised and worn by life. They still have their dreams, however, and thinking makes them so. . . . It is unquestionably the weakest of the Glasgow stories, made up of leftovers from *Life and Gabriella.* Its only interest is biographical.

A more successful attempt to take a comic view of romance is **''The Artless Age,''** which describes a teenage courtship, or rather, two of them. This story is a symbol-hunter's paradise, because the Old-Fashioned Girl, Mary Louise Littleton, and the Modern Girl, Geraldine Plummer, are competing for the affection of the American Boy, Richard Askew. (p. 18)

Here and in two novels, *The Romantic Comedians* . . . and *They Stooped to Folly* . . . , Miss Glasgow managed to take a comic view of the world in the 1920's, but her heart was not really in it. At any rate, in **''The Artless Age,''** her analysis of love has come full circle. In twenty-five years Lucy Smith has been replaced by Geraldine Plummer.

Two more stories focus on an abstract moral problem—what we now call mercy killing, or euthanasia. Two persons with no reason for living are put out of their misery with the assistance of their fellow men. Is this a crime? There are subtleties in each case which complicate the moral decision. In **''A Point in Morals''** an alienist is asked for a package of opium by a passenger on a train, who has botched his life and wants to commit suicide. The alienist, finally convinced by the young man's story that he has no reason for living and many reasons for dying, leaves the fatal package on the seat when he gets off the train.

Because she has effaced herself completely from the story by means of a dramatic framework, Miss Glasgow makes evaluation of the doctor's act very difficult. The story begins as a dialogue among the five characters around a dinner table on a ship: a journalist, a lawyer, an Englishman, a girl in black, and the doctor. The discussion turns to whether the saving of a human life might become positively immoral. At this point the alienist begins his story, into which he inserts the unhappy man's biography, making a story-within-a-story-within-a-story.

The reaction of the audience gives us no clue as to an official interpretation. Each of the characters is ridiculed at some point. Perhaps Miss Glasgow had no stand here but merely wanted to embarrass all these sophisticated observers with a moral problem beyond the reach of science. If we assume that she disliked this alienist as much as those in the other stories, then the doctor must be labeled a monster. We should recall, however, that this is an early story, written before Miss Glasgow had rejected science in favor of philosophy.

An answer may be easier after we consider a parallel situation in the previously discussed "Jordan's End." Alan Jordan, incurably insane, dies mysteriously after an overdose of the opiate that the doctor-narrator has prescribed. The doctor knows that Jordan's wife must be to blame, but he cannot bring himself to question her. Jordan's death solves many problems and will cause none, so long as everyone remains silent. The doctor and Mrs. Jordan are described so sympathetically that one is tempted to condone this mercy killing. Taken together, the two stories reflect Ellen Glasgow's early realization that the most serious human problems lie beyond the reach of science. This theme, too, links her with Poe and with the agrarian branch of the Southern literary tradition. (pp. 19-20)

Ellen Glasgow's best stories are those which owe nothing to her novels. They are independent moral and philosophical analyses of the nature of reality and of man's relationship with his fellow man. "A Point in Morals," "The Difference," and "Jordan's End" are not so daring today as they once were, but they are the products of a bold mind, and "Jordan's End," at least, escapes being a period piece. The device of making ideas visible in the four "ghost" stories is psychologically sound, if not artistically successful. . . .

[Her] twelve short stories prove that, contrary to what Miss Glasgow believed about herself, her literary talents were not confined to large-scale evolutionary studies. This prejudice she acquired from her early models. She was fundamentally a moralist rather than a historian. Her epigrams reveal a dazzling talent for condensation. Her inclination toward irony and paradox shows up particularly well in a small space. In short, she had all the equipment of a great short story writer, except a respect for the form. (p. 23)

> Richard K. Meeker, in his introduction to The Collected Stories of Ellen Glasgow, edited by Richard K. Meeker (reprinted by permission of Louisiana State University Press; copyright 1963 by Louisiana State University Press), Louisiana State University Press, 1963, pp. 3-23.

TONETTE L. BOND (essay date 1979)

The story of Dorinda Oakley [in Barren Ground] is the record of her redemption through the reordering of her physical and mental environments to accord with the pastoral ideal, a primary mode of the creative imagination. Since Virgil, the pastoral landscape has represented an ideal terrain, a poetic metaphor for a state of mind in which the visionary's longings for a lost harmony, simplicity, stability, and beauty are fulfilled in a setting remote from the complexities and corruptive influences of civilization. Eden, Arcadia, and the Golden Age are ideal pastoral landscapes which visionary artists have ever used to project the colors of imagination upon their worlds, to remake their worlds to accord with the mind's most ancient longings. (p. 565)

The old vision of a lost Arcadian South harbored by Dorinda's ancestors is part of Dorinda's imaginative inheritance. Ellen Glasgow's central thematic concern in Barren Ground is to show Dorinda's coming to terms with her psychological and social heritage. In telling us Dorinda's story, Glasgow shows that the ancient pastoral dream of a humanized nature is still potent in its power to reconcile the mind to life in the fallen world. Dorinda has internalized her forebears' vision of a lost Southern Arcadia and to the task of giving reality and permanence to that dream she dedicates her full creative powers. (p. 566)

Glasgow sends Dorinda, her artist-heroine, on a heroic quest for essential meaning, a search which is fulfilled when Dorinda succeeds through pastoral vision in remaking her world to harmonize with that "more vivid world of the imagination."

In choosing her heroine from the descendants of Calvinist farmers in rural Piedmont Virginia, Glasgow enlists character and setting in the service of a poetic vision of a renewed South, for Dorinda incarnates the imagination and creative energy which Glasgow prescribed for the salvation of the South itself. In A Certain Measure, Glasgow offered her diagnosis of the cause of the decay of the old South after the Civil War:

> Though it [the old South] gave its life for a cause, it was wanting in the subjective vision which, together with creative impulse, remoulds a tragic destiny in the serene temper of art. . . .

By endowing her heroine with the "subjective vision" and the "creative impulse" to "remould" her fallen world, Glasgow can use the story of Dorinda's self-redemption through pastoral vision as a means of prophesying a new South built upon the permanent values of the mind made universal in art. At least since Virgil wrote his Fourth Eclogue, pastoral has been the literary prophet's mode for envisaging a new order of spiritual vitality and social harmony. Glasgow needed the strategies found in pastoral tradition in order to give artistic expression to her humanistic remedy to a society demoralized by the values of a commercial technology.

A part of Dorinda's psychological heritage is her mother's unfulfilled dream of missionary glory in a fallen tropical Eden. Mrs. Oakley's frustrated dream is internalized by Dorinda as an unremitting quest for meaning in life. Dorinda is repeatedly visited by an "old baffling sense of a secret meaning in the universe, of a reality beneath the actuality, of a deep profounder than the deeps of experience." However skeptically she may at times regard such fugitive visitations, they testify to the imaginative sensitivity and vitality that beome the source of her victory over circumstances. On one level, Barren Ground can be read as a chronicle of Dorinda's discovery of meaning through pastoral vision. (pp. 567-68)

The story of Dorinda is a record of her triumph over her hereditary circumstances in Pedlar's Mill, circumstances which defeated first her parents and then Jason and Geneva Greylock. The pattern followed is first Dorinda's betrayal by and then triumph over the emotions which led her to a delusory love of Jason and, finally, Dorinda's psychological renewal which she achieves through imposing pastoral values upon her internal and external environments. Glasgow uses the pastoral garden that Dorinda creates out of the chaos of Old Farm as an objectification of the internal, psychological harmony which in middle age Dorinda finally constructs for herself out of the ruins of her affair with Jason.

In her youth, Dorinda found in her love for Jason a vitalizing principle around which to order and structure her life. By nature sensual and imaginative, Dorinda constructed for herself a psychological paradise in which her physical desires and emotional needs were satisfied in her affair with Jason. Her fate results from an interplay between the forces within her own nature and those operating in her environment. (pp. 568-69)

Glasgow shows that the forces working upon and within Dorinda are predatory. Compelled by the internal dynamics of sexual desire working in conjunction with an imaginative perception of the possibilities inherent in human life, an intuition unsuppressed by the poverty of her environment, Dorinda falls victim to self-delusion. (p. 569)

In her quest for meaning and beauty in life, Dorinda is betrayed by the imperatives of biology into a delusory love of Jason Greylock, a man too emasculated by heredity and environment to struggle against a sorry fate. All along, though, Glasgow gives Dorinda prescience that her emotional Arcadia is a delusion. . . . Though Glasgow keeps before the reader Dorinda's tendency to idealize reality, she also shows Dorinda's resisting a full surrender to an easy idealism. (p. 570)

After the collapse of her false dream of love, Dorinda consciously rejects her societal role as wife and her biological role as mother in service to the ancient dream of converting Old Farm into a pastoral paradise. To reclaim Old Farm, Dorinda must salvage it from the fiery broomsedge, associated throughout the novel with the wilderness of uncontrolled human passion, depleted land, and the weakness of Jason's character. Though Dorinda succeeds in creating pastoral order and harmony among the ruins of Old Farm, she does so by repressing all sexual passion and starving her natural sympathy and emotional warmth. She enters a celibate marriage with Nathan Pedlar in order to gain a strong partner to help her achieve permanence for her ideal. Nathan, who holds substantial mortgages on Five Oaks, is also the means of Dorinda's gaining the Greylock farm. Dorinda's desire to own Five Oaks is motivated by more than just a desire to avenge herself on Jason Greylock. She wishes to redeem the house and farm from the neglect and squalor into which it has slumped and to restore it to its "underlying character of honesty and thrift" . . . , agrarian virtues which undergird Dorinda's ethical code. (p. 571)

Glasgow is too emotionally and artistically honest, too much the realist, not to show Dorinda's sufferings and doubts as she struggles under the pressures of her emotional and physical needs and desires in the emotional vacuum she has created for herself. After Jason's burial, Glasgow brings Dorinda to a hard confrontation with the emotional void at the center of her life. (p. 572)

But the "vein of iron" inherited from her Calvinist forebears provides her with the resolution to do more with her energies than waste them in futile perseverance as did her father, or to use her dreams to escape "things as they are," as did her mother. . . . Glasgow invests her heroine with the artistic vision and the stamina to remake her world in the image of the mind's most ancient dream of perfection, the pastoral paradise. Dorinda's imagination and creative energy enable her to transcend the limitations of heredity and environment which defeated her parents and the Greylocks. In her youth, she sought fulfillment in the dream of love; she placed upon love the artistic burden of ordering experience, of giving it meaning, direction, of absorbing her creative energies and fulfilling her innate need to impose her own order upon life, to transform

Pedlar's Mill according to her own vision. . . . When she awakens to the truth of Jason's character and to the delusory nature of love itself, she in essence weds herself to the solid permanence of the land and from the imaginative union creates a garden out of the broomsedge wastes of her hereditary fields. The reclaimed Old Farm and Five Oaks are the creations of her poetic vision of possibility and form a living tribute to her artistic energies. Through rigorous self-sacrifice and discipline in the service of her creative vision, she transforms the farms into the idyllic setting of her youthful dream and in the process establishes upon a harsh reality a vision taking the shape of her ancestors' dream of an Arcadian South. She has spun out of her own viscera the meaning which she has sought throughout her life: her search for the "permanent design beneath the fragile tissue of experience" . . . is fulfilled when she creates out of the barren chaos of Old Farm a pastoral garden which accords with her ancestral vision of potential order and harmony. (pp. 572-73)

Tonette L. Bond, "Pastoral Transformations in 'Barren Ground'," in The Mississippi Quarterly *(copyright 1979 Mississippi State University), Vol. XXXII, No. 4, Fall, 1979, pp. 565-76.*

JULIUS ROWAN RAPER   (essay date 1980)

Life and Gabriella grew out of [Glasgow's] years in New York. In this novel and in the ghost stories of 1916, a solution began to emerge to the central problem—how, in fiction, to handle large powers and emotions that seem to come from outside the characters and take authority over their lives. To put it simply, Glasgow began to locate the source of such invisible powers no longer in the transcendental world, but in the human psyche. Like Miss Effie in **"Whispering Leaves,"** her later characters see ghosts or experience cosmic powers or accept the peace of absolutes, not because such forces come from without to take over their lives, but because such forces mirror their fears or complement their needs. Her own pursuit of authority had taught her that ghosts, powers, and absolutes are simply the misunderstood yet essential phantasies people, in life and in fiction, create to satisfy their needs and to confess their fears. Between 1913 and 1923, she learned that even though *fantasies* are fanciful illusions, *phantasies*, in the root sense of their Greek name, are images that "show forth" the otherwise hidden motions of the soul. (p. 12)

Glasgow was able to develop a more intensely psychological novel after 1916 because she began to use phantasies as an essential test of the reality within which her protagonists find themselves, and these phantasies generally emerge as projections upon other characters who possess an inordinate fascination or antipathy for the protagonist. Asa Timberlake expresses the concept beautifully when he tells Roy that, although she seems to be holding to him, she is in fact drawing upon her "own inner strength." . . . The novels that use phantasies in a positive manner are at base novels of personality development, whereas *The Sheltered Life* takes a tragic turn because it is a novel about the way one culture distorts emotional growth by controlling the dream life of its members. In other words, *The Sheltered Life* places the essentially comic thrust of growth within a tragic order. To appreciate this deviation, we first need to consider the recurring pattern.

With the apparent exception of *The Sheltered Life*, all nine novels [written after 1916] describe patterns of emotional evolution or at least attempts to grow. This is the conclusion we reach by keeping our eyes on the phantasies that the protagonist of each projects on other characters. The chief differences lie between the patterns followed by female characters and those followed by males.

Gabriella Carr establishes the basic structure of feminine evolution when she rejects the static security promised by Arthur Peyton to pursue the romantic difference of George Fowler, then grows disillusioned, and pragmatically courts Judge Crowborough for his money and advice until in Ben O'Hara she finds romance and masculine authority combined with a number of other abstract virtues, including democracy and cleanliness. The abstractions that conclude the novel suggest a collection of essential phantasies which Gabriella has embodied imperfectly in O'Hara but which nonetheless point the way to future growth. In *The Builders,* Caroline Meade sees David Blackburn initially as a figure of wealth and mystery; but later he too turns into a man of abstract authority like Ben O'Hara, a sort of ideal father to guide Caroline past the hole in reality. In *One Man in His Time,* Corinna Page finds herself in a phase much like Gabriella's growth when she reached out to a man of democratic energy; to Corinna, Gideon Vetch speaks with the voice of collective mankind. The most complexly rounded female character that Glasgow ever created, Dorinda Oakley of *Barren Ground,* reveals all of Gabriella's drives, plus several that give Dorinda her added depth. Upon Jason she initially projects her need for romance, sex, and a new life. Nathan becomes her image of authority and success. But Nathan also, inasmuch as he allows Dorinda to use him as a handyman, becomes an object, along with Jason, through which she works out her hatred for men. In John Abner she finds a recipient for her advice and her stored-up pity. In addition to her men, the earth mirrors her unused fertility and unacknowledged desire for revenge.

In *The Romantic Comedians,* Annabel Upchurch grows first by seeking freedom in wealth and later by turning, like Edmonia Bredalbane, from the slavery of wealth and age to the healthy freedom of youth. In *They Stooped to Folly,* Victoria's development fails on two occasions: first, when she settles for Virginius rather than the Lochinvar of her wildest dreams and, second, when she rejects the wild freedom she sees in Milly Burden for the fear that governs her role as southern lady. She longs to grow, but she attempts nothing. If we omit *The Sheltered Life* and move to *Vein of Iron,* we find that Ada Fincastle originally seeks in Ralph romance, freedom, and an even more ecstatic joy than that Dorinda sought in Jason. But she comes to regard Ralph as the mirror of her sexual freedom and settles in time for the simpler phantasies of a normal family life, solidarity with friends in adversity, and an opportunity to start life again in the home of her fathers. Finally, Roy Timberlake of the last two novels begins with romantic illusions, passes through disillusionment with men, moves to pity for individuals and collectives, then in an act of rebellious freedom attempts to sacrifice herself for something larger than herself, and ends holding to the strength and goodness she projects upon her father. The recurring situations in these novels make Glasgow's answer to Freud's famous query, "But what do women want?" quite clear: in their youth they want romance with a handsome man and sexual freedom; in maturity they want authority, a fatherly man to mirror their own strength and to support their wisdom. At all times they want strength to live and freedom to grow.

Because these novels usually center around women, the pattern of growth found in the males appears far simpler. Since the men are generally weaker than the women, their development often seems distorted. Gabriella's first love interest, Arthur Peyton, reveals the basic male distortion when he seeks in Gabriella an ideal wife to substitute for his ideal mother. He thus looks back to Harry Treadwell, the mother-trapped son of Virginia Treadwell in *Virginia,* and forward to a number of characters who impose a static feminine ideal upon the women they know. Gabriella's second lover, George Fowler, marries her as a substitute for his mother and sister, less because she is an ideal than because he needs a woman to mother him in his selfish hedonism. Compared to Peyton and Fowler, Gabriella's final interest, Ben O'Hara, seems an embodiment of simple health. He sees in her an expression of feminine fortitude and, at the same time, a woman to protect as one might a daughter. In *The Builders,* David Blackburn grows from his wife Angelica, the sick ideal he protects, to Caroline Meade, a strong daughter-disciple he can steer toward the light. In *One Man in His Time,* Stephen Culpeper turns his back on Margaret Blair, the old-fashioned ideal of the perfect lady, and seeks health in the youth, beauty, and wild freedom of Patty Vetch. Jason Greylock, Dorinda Oakley's incubus, has long before resigned himself to failure. At first he seems to regard Dorinda as a disciple; but instead he takes the path of many Glasgow males in using Dorinda, like Geneva Ellgood, as a comfort for his body and a mirror of his remaining male vanity. Both the male body and vanity are made to seem aspects of the fatality in which Jason has been nurtured; he ends as Dorinda's helpless dependent.

For all his humorous excess, Judge Gamaliel Honeywell of *The Romantic Comedians* probably remains the most complexly rounded of Glasgow's male characters. He moves from the static beauty of Amanda Lightfoot to Cordelia Honeywell, the ideal wife and mother, before returning, with help from the pragmatism of Bella Upchurch, to the youthful energy of his daughter-wife, Annabel Upchurch. He evolves despite keeping only one ear open to the comic advice of his realistic sister, Edmonia. In the end he discovers that all his women wear the masks of his mother, whom he passionately loved. With far more timidity than Honeywell, Virginius Littlepage in *They Stooped to Folly* pulls against his safe mooring beside the ideal Victoria and nudges the sister ship of his vanity and sexual desire (Amy Dalrymple) at the same time that he reaches out to protect the daughterly beauty of Milly Burden; ultimately he returns to the safety of Victoria.

Skipping once more over *The Sheltered Life,* we find that Ralph McBride of *Vein of Iron* has been so thoroughly trapped by his mother that he experiences freedom only in the sort of perverse rebellion that proves self-destructive. He follows his instincts, including vanity and sexual desire, to abuse the conscience he received from his mother. Unfortunately, the strength and goodness of Ada Fincastle cause him to associate her with his conscience, while beauties like Janet Rowan and Minna Bergen continue to mirror his ego and sexual needs. Ada's father, John Fincastle, spends his life in pursuit—first of a divine father, then of a transcendental absolute that leads him to the void. The moment he dies, he discovers that what he wanted all the time was his stern mother to come take him out of the world of idiots; and in that moment he achieves the consummation of every puritan's deepest desire—to die. In the final two novels, Asa Timberlake emerges as perhaps the psychologically strongest of all Glasgow's male characters. He has grown from early dominance by a loved mother, through a freedom of perverse rebellion against his mother, and through a long life supporting Lavinia, the sick ideal of his rebellion.

He has earned the right to live with Kate Oliver, a strong erect woman who personifies the benevolent and feminine aspects of Hunter's Fare. At the same time, despite his debilitating love for Stanley, he has given Roy a model of strength and integrity as well as a good father's support, a support gentle enough to force upon her the growth that is freedom. From all these examples, we may conclude that what Glasgow's men want generally costs women a good deal. At their worst, men seek comfort for their bodies and a mirror for their egos; at their best, they want a good earthy woman like Kate to hold to and a daughter like Roy to guide. Otherwise, Glasgow's men seek the static ideal of beauty and motherly chastity. And this proves perhaps the most pernicious need of all, for it denies the women in whom they invest their ideal the freedom to grow.

With this summary of the basic female and male patterns of development in the novels, we stand ready to reconsider *The Sheltered Life*. We can now appreciate the pressure that exists between the need of Jenny Blair, George, and Eva to grow and the antithetical need of General Archbald for women to embody his ideal of a good that is beyond the truth of this world. Archbald's need may be a key to his fulfillment as a moral idealist, but it nonetheless has tragic consequences in the lives of Eva, George, and Jenny Blair. As the mind of the past, Archbald bears more responsibility than anyone else in the book for creating the social ideal that perverted Eva's natural growth by making her play her static role, the belle of Queenborough. Because Eva allows Archbald's ideal to put an end to her natural self, the reader understands why George finds himself longing for the energy, vivacity, and sexuality of younger women like Memoria, Delia Barron, and Jenny Blair. Again it is tragic that George's desire should pervert Jenny Blair's elemental needs—to be alive, to experience her peculiarities of self, and to discover a protecting father—tragic that he should so twist her phantasies that she dreams the banal dreams of the flirt. Although the flirt plays a socially acceptable part, she can only metamorphose into the belle or the mistress, and neither of these represents growth. All Jenny Blair's growth Archbald finally turns backward toward childish irresponsibility when he restores the shelter of innocence after she has caused Eva to shoot George.

The great pressure created by this profound need for growth in the other characters works against Archbald's absolute order, a shelter without visible walls, to generate the tension essential for tragedy. *The Sheltered Life* thus contrasts significantly with *They Stooped to Folly*, in which Virginius' timid rebellion against the unwitting matriarchy of Victoria—an order he has willed into being—can only generate the feeble tension of satire. In *They Stooped to Folly*, Glasgow avoided increasing the pressure by keeping the young people, who have a strong need to grow, shadowy and at a distance. But in *The Sheltered Life*, she brought the two most forceful currents of her life into the most effective configuration possible. Earlier, in *The Builders*, she had identified the conservative spirit with realism: it sees "things as they are" and stresses race, tradition, philosophy, and age; it is, in short, the vision of the late nineteenth century. In the same book she equated the progressive spirit of the early twentieth century with romance: it sees things "as they ought to be" and stresses the individual, adventure, experience, and youth. In *The Sheltered Life*, she embodied the conservative order in Archbald and the progressive drive in Jenny Blair and then forced them to collide. The approach (if not the result) was much like the tension Herman Melville achieved when he confronted the democratic individualism of his youth with the

limits of his Calvinistic ancestors; or Nathaniel Hawthorne, when he checked the romantic individualism of Hester with the Calvinistic fatalism of Dimmesdale; or Eugene O'Neill, when he crossed the Freudian drives of Christine Mannon with the puritan disgust of Ezra Mannon (*Mourning Becomes Electra*); or, for that matter, Shakespeare, when he blocked Iago's Renaissance defense of self and Edmund's appeal to nature with the medieval world order. Both the pressure for change and the unyielding order must be embodied convincingly if tragedy is to result. In Glasgow's early novels, the spirit of determinism proved too strong to permit a tragic force to develop. In *The Romantic Comedians,* the spirit of comedy is too insidious and the narrator too Olympian to yield either pity or terror—only delight. In *Barren Ground* and *Vein of Iron,* the heroines prove too resilient to confront their tragedy squarely. In Glasgow's last two novels, although the lives are tragic or at least pathetic, the stress falls upon the consolation of philosophy. But in *The Sheltered Life,* everything is right for tragedy. And there remains a good deal to be said for the pure forms, comedy and tragedy. The dramatic objectivity of tragedy enables the male part of the reader both to pity the bind of Archbald living in a world that does not match his ideals and to feel terror at the way he sacrifices his women to fulfill himself. At the same time, the female part of the reader pities the sacrificial women and feels terror both at the way Jenny Blair pursues her vain, romantic goals and at the way Eva takes her revenge.

Thus, although *The Sheltered Life* tests our case for essential phantasies, it is less a refutation of the argument than a challenge to refine distinctions between phantasies and illusions, between psychological growth through imagination and the malignity of evasive idealism. In the year after Glasgow published *The Sheltered Life,* another acute student of dreams, Nathaniel West, working independently, wrote as follows in *Miss Lonelyhearts* . . . : "Men have always fought their misery with dreams. Although dreams were once powerful, they have been made puerile by the movies, radio and newspapers. Among many betrayals, this one is the worst." . . . There is then a difference, for West and for Glasgow, between essential phantasies, on the one hand, that arise spontaneously from the shadow side of the mind to guide individuals in their growth, and dreams, on the other, that have been perverted and rendered useless by the mass mind. For West, the media render our dreams puerile. For Glasgow, it is the mass mind in any form, but especially the group mind working through tradition, that perverts essential phantasies of individuals into a culture's static ideals or into an outsider's banal dreams of despair. Because the chief tradition of her region was that strange cult of the lady that southern males willed into being, her strongest theme is the male perversion of female growth phantasies into the lifeless evasive idealism of an Eva Birdsong or into the revengeful rage of a Dorinda Oakley. All her life Glasgow fought against her culture to dream a better dream so she would not be caught either, like Eva, in the static role of lady or, like Dorinda, in the sterile illusion of revenge. Her fiction was, it seems, the essential phantasy that grew, almost a volunteer, in the garden of her mind—essential, because as long as the phantasy continued to thrive, she was free to unfold. And it grew until the end—although less strongly after *The Sheltered Life*. In this sense, her life and her approach to fiction were one. (pp. 193-201)

Julius Rowan Raper, in his From the Sunken Garden: The Fiction of Ellen Glasgow, 1916-1945 *(reprinted by permission of Louisiana State University Press;*

copyright ©1980 by Louisiana State University Press),
Louisiana State University Press, 1980, 220 p.

C. HUGH HOLMAN   (essay date 1980)

[Allen] Tate defines the primary change from the writing of
the nineteenth-century South to that of the Southern Renascence
as being "a shift from rhetoric to dialectic," a change from
the writer as "the old Southern *rhetor* . . . who was eloquent
before the audience but silent in himself" to the writer who
carries on an argument within himself with the result that "the
Southern dramatic dialectic . . . is resolved . . . in action."
The Romance of a Plain Man, although Glasgow's only first-
person novel, presents such a dialectical struggle within its
narrator-protagonist, and more important—and usually ignored
by its critics—a dialectical view by Glasgow herself of the
struggle which the action of the novel embodies, a view different from that of the narrator-protagonist. (p. 154)

The Romance of a Plain Man is the story of Ben Starr, a very
poor Richmond boy who by persistent effort and intelligence
rises from grocery delivery boy to tobacco factory worker to
investor and banker and finally is offered the presidency of the
South Midland and Atlantic Railroad, the major railway system
of the South. In one sense, this story, laid between 1875 and
1908, is the account of an Horatio Alger hero's rising to greatness through the ranks in the impoverished South immediately
after the Reconstruction period. It is this aspect of the novel
upon which most critics have centered their attention, and they
have tended to see the parallel—but in no way conflicting—
story of Starr's worship of, love for, and marriage to Sally
Mickelborough over the opposition of her family and the society of Richmond as simply one aspect of the poor boy's rise
to fame and fortune. This second story, however, is the dialectical center of the novel, and, however accurate the broad
historical outline of events in the building of a New South
through the banking and railroad interests may be—and Stanly
Godbold, himself an historian, declares it to be accurate—
Glasgow's most significant historical attitudes are expressed
through Ben Starr's relation to Sally Mickelborough, her maiden
aunts the Misses Bland, and the aristocratic society of Richmond to which she belongs. (pp. 155-56)

Glasgow says that *The Romance of a Plain Man* "parallels *The
Voice of the People* in my social history of Virginia. Both
volumes deal with the rise of the working man in the South,
but the point of view is dissimilar and the theme is approached
from opposite directions. In *The Voice of the People*—the story
of the rise of a poor farm boy to the governorship of the State
of Virginia—"I was writing objectively, of the 'poor-white'
farmer in politics, and in *The Romance of a Plain Man,* I was
treating, subjectively, the progress and decline of a modern
industrialism." The parallel between the objective telling of
Nicholas Burr's story in *The Voice of the People* and the subjective telling of Ben Starr's story is important, for it is in that
subjective story, the story of the inner emotional life and the
choices made within that emotional life that the key to the
meaning, the method, and the value of *The Romance of a Plain
Man* truly lies. Equally important is her statement that she, in
tracing the rise of the working man, is tracing "the progress
and decline of modern industrialism," for its decline is a significant element in *The Romance of a Plain Man.*

Ellen Glasgow has been severely criticized for giving the novel
an ending that is viewed as sentimental. Edward Wagenknecht,
usually an admirer of Glasgow's work, for example, says that

The Romance of a Plain Man has "a sentimental and evasive
ending, with Ben quite unconvincingly relinquishing the goal
of all his striving to devote himself, at long last, exclusively
to her [Sally]." The criticism is unjust. The choice that Ben
Starr makes is actually, in terms of the movement of history,
between the Old South and the New, and the time is the first
decade of the twentieth century. . . . If the Sally Mickelborough story in *The Romance of a Plain Man* is, as I believe it
is, a fable of history, a retelling in miniature of the rise of the
middle class, it is also a retelling of the way in which that
middle class was torn between the ideals and forms of an
aristocratic society which it admires but cannot understand and
the demands of a new and vigorous world which it must follow
if that world is to come fully and healthily into being. . . .
Ben Starr's choice is that of heart over head, that of the wistful
poor boy still lost in the dream of the "enchanted garden,"
but as a parable of history it is tragic. That Ellen Glasgow
should encompass that grave and finally grim choice in a gentle
and appealing love story in which the attractive and pleasant
heroine is in a sense the embodiment of the darker side of the
choice which the post-Reconstruction South face is, I think,
the problem which has led the critics examining the book to
fail to appreciate the skill with which it is constructed.

I think what Glasgow is doing here is what she did in a number
of her fictional social histories, and it is what Faulkner was
also to do in his long legend of Yoknapatawpha County—that
is, to present historical movements not through a record of
large historical events, but rather through their representation
in smaller units, a synecdochal process by which Ben Starr
becomes not only himself, a unique individual rising from the
lowest levels of the middle class to positions of power, but
also a representative form of a large historical movement. Sally
Mickelborough represents much that is strong, good, appealing, and delightful about the aristocratic Old South. To Ben
Starr, she is the embodiment, the virtual avatar of the "'something else'" that distinguished her class, of "this humour, this
lightness, and above all this gallantry, which was so much a
part of the older civilization." Glasgow said of her in *A Certain
Measure* that she was "a mingling of all those characteristics
we used to think of as especially Virginian," and Sally and
her friends from the higher classes of Richmond society represent the whole class of which they are a part. The story of
her life—that is, of her surrender to the forces of innovation
and energy which the post-Civil War world demanded—represented the momentary fascination of that aristocracy with the
energy and power of the New South. General Bolingbroke
represented the way in which some members of that aristocracy
had maintained their position while working vigorously with
the new middle class and even aiding it as he aided Ben Starr.
Yet Sally comes to see, as Glasgow herself said on one occasion, that "progress more fatal than poverty, destroyed the
lingering charm of the old culture." I believe that it was her
awareness that she had caught large historical movements in
private and personal stories that led Ellen Glasgow to say,
when she reread *The Romance of a Plain Man* thirty years later,
that it was "an authentic rendering of unwritten history."

The historian Henry Steele Commager has said, "It was the
revolution of opinion that Miss Glasgow traced—especially
feminine opinion . . . the society of . . . [Virginia] was never
so dependent on money as that of the northern cities, [thus] it
was not so vulnerable to the assaults of new wealth." Indeed
in *The Romance of a Plain Man* the embodiment of attitude
and opinion is essentially feminine. The clearest expression of
the attitude of Richmond aristocracy is that of Miss Mitty and

Miss Matoaca Bland, Sally Mickelborough's aunts, total embodiments of the aristocratic traditions of a world that is already past. Miss Mitty will not tolerate Ben Starr, for his father was a working man, and who someone's father is is for Miss Mitty more important than character or accomplishment. Miss Matoaca, an active woman suffragist, a feminist pamphleteer, who dies in a march for women's rights, has turned to this active statement of conscience in the world as a result of the frustrations of a society which has maintained a double standard of sexual purity for its men and women. (pp. 157-59)

Historically-minded writers are likely to be fascinated with and emotionally wedded to a past which inevitably is leaving, while they applaud the new world being born, and in their work to follow a familiar course from revolution to reaction, from espousing the new to lamenting the passage of the old. *The Romance of a Plain Man* stands in the middle of this process for Ellen Glasgow, and it embodies in as nearly perfect a balance, I believe, as she ever achieved, the middle course which heroes of historical novels have taken from [Sir Walter] Scott to Allen Tate.

One of the primary glories and difficulties of *The Romance of a Plain Man* is its choice of the first-person narrative point of view and the use to which Miss Glasgow puts that choice. She acknowledged that the use of a male narrator in the novel presented "almost insurmountable disadvantages," but she said, "My intention was to write a romance of the ordinary, and to treat, with a faintly satirical flavour, a series of adventures in the democratic society of our time." She chose, therefore, to tell the story "from within, and to combine the participant and the narrator." This narrative point of view was associated, she believed, with "heroic enterprises," and its choice established a tone of gallantry for a novel which was to be a "romance of the ordinary." (pp. 160-61)

Even the title established this basic irony. *Romance* is used in the medieval sense of a narrative of the deeds of a swashbuckling aristocratic hero, but *Plain Man* is Ellen Glasgow's term for one of the plain people, as opposed to good families. Actually the young Ben Starr is more than once referred to as "poor white trash." Both the title and the basic attitudes and problems of emotional allegiance for the authors are similar in *The Romance of a Plain Man* and *A Connecticut Yankee in King Arthur's Court*. Glasgow depended on the discrepancy in using a point of view associated with heroic enterprises to recount a romance of the ordinary, confident that, as she expressed it, it would "lend a sharper edge and occasionally ironic tone to this realistic romance of an average man of good will." It is lost on the critic who fails to see the irony implicit in the point of view.

Even those of us not of a phenomenologist persuasion tend to classify writers by the common characteristics of their collective works, and we have long ago classified Ellen Glasgow as primarily a verbal ironist and praised her for a felicitous, witty, but overly self-conscious style. When, as in *The Romance of a Plain Man,* her irony is not in the direct verbal constructs of her style but in the relationship of that style to her subject matter, when it is structural, a function of the narrative point of view rather than the literal written words, we tend to miss it, as we do in *The Romance of a Plain Man,* and therefore to feel that the book has a peculiar flatness and lack of wit.

Ben Starr is made into what Wayne Booth calls an unreliable narrator, yet he is in a sense a naive narrator, since both Glasgow and the reader understand him and his situation better than he does. This kind of dramatic irony is peculiarly present in the case of one of the most mechanical characters in the book, Ben's sister Jessy, whose eyes are so firmly fixed upon the material things of this life, upon money, advancement, clothes, the outward symbols of success, that she becomes both a little ridiculous and a little repulsive. Ben dislikes Jessy's materialism intensely without ever realizing that he is himself caught in exactly the same materialism and that, though in his case the complications are enormously greater, he consistently makes in regard to his beloved Sally the same kinds of choices that he thoroughly condemns in his sister.

The point of view has been criticized because there is very little detail, very little historical fact, and very little technical information about business and industry in a story told by a man who was deeply caught up through much of the time of action of the book in these very things. McDowell says, "Such a tale is sentimental when, as here, business success and failure are only vaguely related to economic milieu, and when the drive for financial power is an insistently mentioned fact rather than an imaginatively recreated reality. . . . Miss Glasgow's failure, however, to discuss the disturbingly close alliance between the railroad interests and the Democratic political machine in Virginia in the early twentieth century detracts from the verisimilitude and significance of the novel." Yet it can be argued with equal force that the book is not about business at all but that business, industry, and politics are subsidiary to the fundamental choice which Ben Starr must make between two irreconcilable attitudes toward life and history. Indeed, while the inclusion of a larger amount of material on the technical aspects of business, industry, and politics might satisfy those who want to see the book as grounded firmly in the specific events of history, it could be done only at the cost to the book of its primary synecdochal value as a record of a choice which the New South made. . . . William Dean Howells' *The Rise of Silas Lapham,* although one of its major moral decisions hinges upon the business dealings of Lapham, tells us remarkably little about business, business techniques, and almost nothing about the paint industry on which Lapham's fortune rests. Blair Rouse is only partly correct when he argued in Glasgow's defense that she was interested not in the details of business but in "the *effect* of the business struggle on individuals." Indeed I think she is not truly interested even in this effect but rather in the opportunity of choice which successful business endeavors force upon the protagonist.

Among those books which have been cited as examples of stories that somehow parallel *The Romance of a Plain Man* and might have been in Glasgow's mind—and they include the Horatio Alger books and Dickens' *Great Expectations*—should be added Henry James's *The American,* a book remarkably similar from a plot standpoint, though not in its ultimate meaning. Both the James novel and *The Romance of a Plain Man* have self-made protagonists who rise through unusual intelligence and industry to great business leadership in the period after the Civil War. Both these protagonists are ignorant of aristocratic values and traditional methods but are deeply enamoured of them. Both feel that in a sense money and financial success are keys to the acquisition of these cultural values. Both are rejected by families who disapprove of the union of their young women with these crass nouveau riche protagonists. Both ultimately fail in maintaining both the aristocratic dream and the financial success. Here the difference between the two novels becomes most pronounced, for Christopher Newman renounces the right to revenge, gives up the dreams of European culture, and goes back home, whereas Ben Starr makes exactly the opposite choice and renounces the raw energy which has given him his strength and power and embraces the life pattern of his aristocratic wife.

Viewed in this ultimate sense *The Romance of a Plain Man* is a skillfully contrived and effective narrative in which the self-made man, through the dreams of rewards and glories which are in a sense forbidden to him and which he thinks he can get only through energy and money, steadily and completely entraps himself in an emotional and psychological situation fraught with tragic possibilities. At the end of the story the answer Ben Starr gives to the dilemma that confronts him is indeed a tragic answer, for the self-entrapment has been so complete that there is no way out that is not either individually or historically destructive. To have embodied this kind of statement about the history of her region in a novel that is on the surface the love story of a self-made man is no small accomplishment. In writing *The Romance of a Plain Man*, Ellen Glasgow embodied in her characters and the action of her novel no simple rhetorical assertion but a dialectical examination of the complex issues of a moment of significant historical choice. The resulting book deserves from us a kind of attention different from that which we have been giving it. (pp. 161-63)

> C. Hugh Holman, "The Tragedy of Self-Entrapment: Ellen Glasgow's 'The Romance of a Plain Man'," in Toward a New American Literary History: Essays in Honor of Arlin Turner, edited by Louis J. Budd, Edwin H. Cady, and Carl L. Anderson (reprinted by permission of the Publisher; copyright © 1980, by Duke University Press, Durham, North Carolina), Duke University Press, 1980, pp. 154-63.

ADDITIONAL BIBLIOGRAPHY

Brooks, Van Wyck. "South of the James." In his *The Confident Years: 1885-1915*, pp. 337-52. New York: E. P. Dutton & Co., 1952.*
  Brief critical remarks on Glasgow's major novels. Brooks considers Glasgow the first southern novelist to challenge the idealism and sentimentalism of southern literature, and the first to portray the conflict between the South's agrarian past and its rising industrialization.

Ekman, Barbro. *The End of a Legend: Ellen Glasgow's History of Southern Women*. Stockholm: Almqvist & Wiksell International, 1979, 171 p.
  History of the southern woman from the Civil War up to the Second World War as seen in the novels of Ellen Glasgow. Ekman divides Glasgow's female characters into a number of sub-groups, such as "The Southern Belle," "The Womanly Woman," and "The Liberated Woman," and discusses each in an attempt to determine which, if any, are realistically portrayed, and which are romanticized.

Fishwick, Marshall W. "Cabell and Glasgow: Tradition in Search of Meaning." *Shenandoah* VIII, No. 3 (Summer 1957): 24-35.*
  Discussion of the "modern novel" as demonstrated in the works by James Branch Cabell and Ellen Glasgow. By examining a number of their works, the critic shows how Cabell and Glasgow develop characters in a "common-place world."

Godbold, E. Stanly, Jr. *Ellen Glasgow and the Woman Within*. Baton Rouge: Louisiana State University Press, 1972, 322 p.
  Biography and examination of Glasgow's work. Godbold emphasizes only those aspects of Glasgow's novels "that touch directly upon her own life and are thus a part of her biography."

Mann, Dorothea Lawrance. *Ellen Glasgow*. Garden City, N.Y.: Doubleday, Doran & Co., 1928, 46 p.
  Brief biography with critical essays on Glasgow's work by Carl Van Vechten, Joseph Collins, and James Branch Cabell.

Myer, Elizabeth Gallup. *The Social Situation of Women in the Novels of Ellen Glasgow*, Hicksville, N.Y.: Exposition Press, 1978, 80 p.
  Examination of Glasgow's female characters and their social situation in the South. Myer praises Glasgow for her attempt to portray women as individuals and her assistance in the "emancipation of woman from bondage to the Victorian ideal."

Overton, Grant. "Ellen Glasgow." In his *The Women Who Make Our Novels*, pp. 157-66. New York: Dodd, Mead & Co., 1928.
  Discussion of Glasgow's life and work. Overton concludes that Glasgow is an important novelist not because of the points most critics refer to—"her breach with Southern literary tradition, her education of women, her choosing to write about the farmer class"—but because she "evidently contributes to our knowledge of human nature."

Sherman, Stuart. "Ellen Glasgow: The Fighting Edge of Romance." In his *Critical Woodcuts*, pp. 73-82. New York, London: Charles Scribner's Sons, 1926.
  Discussion of Glasgow's style and her place in the contemporary literary world. Sherman argues that it is absurd to consider Glasgow as "essentially a writer for the South," when in fact "she treats provincial life from a national point of view."

Tuttleton, James W. "Hardy and Ellen Glasgow: *Barren Ground*." *The Mississippi Quarterly* XXXII, No. 4 (Fall 1979): 577-90.*
  Discussion of the similarities between Glasgow's *Barren Ground* and Thomas Hardy's novels of Wessex County. The critic argues that "in *Barren Ground*, Ellen Glasgow, like Hardy, aspired to write a philosophical novel."

Wagner, Linda W. "*Barren Ground*'s Vein of Iron: Dorinda Oakley and Some Concepts of Heroine in 1925." In her *American Modern: Essays in Fiction and Poetry*, pp. 56-66. Port Washington, N.Y., London: Kennikat Press, 1980.*
  Study of Dorinda Oakley in relation to a number of other heroines portrayed in works published in 1925. Wagner views Dorinda Oakley as "one in a gallery of literary portraits of peculiarly American women," such as Daisy Buchanan, Ellen Thatcher, and Lady Brett Ashley.

Laurence Housman

1865-1959

English poet, novelist, dramatist, short story writer, critic, and autobiographer.

Housman is probably best known as "England's most censored playwright" because of a ban, which was eventually lifted, on a number of his plays some dealing with Biblical characters and some with members of the British royal family. Though he began his literary career as a writer of fairy tales and as a poet, Housman later turned to drama as the medium for expressing his views on religion and life in Victorian England. Housman invented the play-cycle, short biographical pieces designed to develop a single character, commonly a political or religious figure. The most popular of his historical pieces, *Victoria Regina*, was a critical success, and it clearly showed Housman's ability for delineating character and dramatizing social events. These sketches also demonstrate the author's capacity for biting humor and gentle cynicism. His religious cycles, such as the *Little Plays of St. Francis*, are often simple and romantic, noteworthy in their themes and presentation, but lacking the character development which was the hallmark of his historical dramas.

Born at Bromsgrove, Worcestershire, England, Housman was the sixth child in a family of seven, and the younger brother of the poet A.E. Housman. The young Housmans were encouraged by their stepmother to take an interest in literature and the arts. At the age of eighteen Housman went to London to study art, but six years later he turned to writing, beginning with fairy tales, legends, and poems, all of which he illustrated himself. His first popular success came by accident when he published anonymously *An Englishman's Love Letters*. Not recognized as the fiction it was, the work created a sensation and brought Housman unexpected wealth. Despite his accomplishments as a prose writer, Housman eventually made drama the mainstay of his literary efforts. At the insistence of Harley Granville-Barker he wrote his first play, *Bethlehem*, but the work was banned by the Censor's Office for depicting the character of Jesus on stage. Thus began a series of confrontations which resulted in the eventual censorship of some thirty plays. Undaunted, Housman continued to write drama throughout his life. Much of his later work, such as the *Little Plays of St. Francis* and *Victoria Regina*, express his concern over the religious questions and historical events of his day.

Housman called the *Little Plays of St. Francis* his "best work," and the one most likely to live after him. The play-cycle is indeed an excellent representation of Housman's literary career. Through his portrayal of the life of St. Francis, Housman was able to attack the ineffectiveness of organized Christianity and to proclaim the idea that humanity's inherent goodness might overcome sin through a direct and simple approach to God. The concept of innocence meeting and defeating evil, the attempt to emulate Christ, and the need for humility before the throne of God, are all important themes represented in the *Little Plays*. In his so-called "royal" plays, such as *Victoria Regina*, Housman presented the monarchy as a unique and isolated entity in British life. He had hoped to capture the essential drama in the lives of such prominent figures as Queen Victoria by contrasting their often unpleasant private existence

S&G from Pictorial Parade

with their social and historical significance. While many of the "royal" plays fail because of Housman's inability to dramatize these differences, others, such as *Victoria Regina*, are considered great achievements in the art of character delineation.

Housman has been both praised and severely criticized for his works in every literary genre. As a poet he was lauded for his mystic vision and the technical beauty of his verse; at the same time he was attacked for his archaic diction and his themes of self-abasement. As a dramatist he was commended for his strong characterizations and scope of imagination, but he was also criticized for an undramatic quality in many of his plays and a tendency to lapse into discussions and lectures. Though his popularity has diminished considerably, Housman represents an important aspect of British literature: besides inventing the play-cycle, he helped bring about a revival of religious drama to the English stage, and his treatment of subjects banned from the British theater helped pave the way for future playwrights such as T. S. Eliot and Christopher Fry.

(See also *Dictionary of Literary Biography*, Vol. 10: *Modern British Dramatists, 1900-1945*.)

PRINCIPAL WORKS

A Farm in Fairyland (fairy tales) 1894
All-Fellows (folklore) 1896
Green Arras (poetry) 1896
The Field of Clover (fairy tales) 1898
Spikenard (poetry) 1898
Rue (poetry) 1899
An Englishwoman's Love Letters (fictional letters) 1900
Bethlehem (drama) 1902
Prunella [with Harley Granville-Barker] (drama) 1904
The Cloak of Friendship (fairy tales) 1905
Mendicant Rhymes (poetry) 1906
Pains and Penalties (drama) 1911
Nazareth (drama) 1916†
*Angels and Ministers (drama) 1921†
Possession: A Peep-Show in Paradise (drama) 1921†
Dethronements (drama) 1922†
**Little Plays of St. Francis (dramas) 1922
A Doorway in Fairyland (fairy tales) 1923
**Followers of St. Francis (dramas) 1923†
**The Comments of Juniper (dramas) 1926†
*Palace Plays (dramas) 1931
*The Queen's Progress: Palace Plays, second series
   (dramas) 1932
What O'Clock Tales (fairy tales) 1932
Ye Fearful Saints! (drama) 1932†
*Victoria and Albert: Palace Plays, third series (dramas)
   1933†
The Unexpected Years (autobiography) 1936
The Collected Poems of Laurence Housman (poetry)
   1937
Palace Scenes: More Plays of Queen Victoria (dramas)
   1937†
My Brother, A.E. Housman (reminiscences and poetry)
   1938
***Palestine Plays (dramas) 1942†
***Samuel, the King-Maker (drama) 1944†
The Family Honour (drama) 1950†

*These works, along with others, were published as *Victoria Regina* in 1934.

**These works, along with others, were published as *Little Plays of St. Francis* in 1935.

***These works were published as *Old Testament Plays* in 1950.

†These are the dates of first publication rather than first performance.

WILLIAM ARCHER (essay date 1899)

The distinction of Mr. Laurence Housman's workmanship, the nimbleness of his fancy, and the sombre strength of his imagination, must be patent to all readers of *Green Arras* and *Spikenard*. No one is more authentically a poet than he; yet the forms of thought which almost exclusively preoccupy him are to me so foreign, and, to be quite frank, so uninteresting, that I must own myself incapable of doing full justice even to his purely literary merits. He envisages the world from a point of view at which I cannot place myself, even in momentary make-believe. I lack all clue, in my own experience, to the processes of his mind. Consequently, I can but apologise in advance for

the inadequate and perhaps utterly mistaken appreciation of his talent which is all I can offer. In the preface to his *All Fellows*, a book of prose legends "with insets of verse," Mr. Housman says, "Unfortunately there are to be found, to sit in judgment, minds of a literal persuasion, that take from the artist his own soul, to set it in the image that he has made." In what I have to say I may fall into this error. But a single attitude of mind is so consistently maintained throughout Mr. Housman's verse, that it is impossible to conceive it a mere artistic pose.

On the contrary, it seems to me that sincerity is what distinguishes Mr. Housman from most of his school. His kinship with Rossetti, for example, is unmistakable; but what to Rossetti was mythology and decoration, is to Mr. Housman religion and tragic fact. His Catholicism is not like that of some other poets, a mere refuge from pantheism, a robe deliberately woven to clothe and confine an invisible, elusive deity. At the root of his thinking lies, I take it, a genuine Conviction of Sin. It is his instinct to prostrate and abase himself before the rulers of the universe, and to blame himself, not them, for whatever in himself he finds amiss. . . . It is his part rather to kiss the rod, and wreathe it in garlands of flowers; to groan in the fetters of flesh, while damascening their links. Life is to him a prison-house, and it does not occur to him to question the moral authority of the warrant that consigned him to it. The senses are tempters lurking in the darkness. He has not even the consolations of evangelical religion, the faith in another life and in personal salvation. He seems rather to conceive deity as the spirit of nothingness; to regard existence in itself as sin, and more especially the sense of beauty in existence; and to yearn for annihilation as the highest grace to which mankind, guilty of having been born, can possibly aspire. This spirit seems to me to inspire, not only his poems, but the designs which illustrate them: everywhere there is passionate depth of conception and great beauty of line; but everywhere there is a sense of oppression, of contortion, of grey gloom even in the sunshine, which not seldom results in a general effect of ugliness. (pp. 196-97)

In *Green Arras* there are touches, never of gladness, never even of stoicism, but of sheer pulsing humanity, that come upon us with a sense of refreshment in the incense-laden atmosphere of Mr. Housman's temple of art. (p. 199)

There is not a poem in the book which has not individuality and strength. . . . Everywhere, as it seems to me, Mr. Housman's work is essentially poetic, but robust or exhilarating it certainly is not. "Morbid" is a word one shrinks from using, but in this context it is inevitable. (p. 200)

"A Book of Devotional Love Poems"—so Mr. Housman himself describes *Spikenard*. It is a sequence of ecstatic lyrics, each suggested by or associated with some feast of the church, and all wearing, and wearing with power and grace, a seventeenth-century form. The book leaves on my mind a sense of manufacture, of deliberate archaism in thought no less than in form, which is probably due to a lack, on my part, of imaginative sympathy. Of the merits of its craftsmanship there can be no doubt. Mr. Housman always writes with distinction, sometimes with real beauty, and generally with as much perspicuity as can be demanded of a poet who dwells exclusively on matters which, by hypothesis, transcend human reason. (pp. 200-01)

William Archer, "Laurence Housman" (1899), in his Poets of the Younger Generation, *John Lane, 1902 (and reprinted by Scholarly Press, 1969), pp. 196-205.*

MAX BEERBOHM   (essay date 1907)

["**Prunella**," by Mr. Laurence Housman and Mr. Granville Barker,] is one of the most "important" of modern English plays; for it is the most spontaneously poetic. It owes nothing to the tradition of poetic drama. It is a perfectly natural product of the time we live in. It comes not of a laudable determination to handle grand passions in the grand manner, but of an impulse to express something that was in the hearts of the authors—a wistful and melancholy little something, belonging to a time in which people, for all their outward strenuousness, are so frail, and so sick at heart. The something that the authors had to express was rather an emotion than an idea. There is nothing modern in the idea that youth wanes, and passion fades, and pleasure palls, and after the spring comes the autumn. What is modern is the sense that after all it doesn't much matter, alas, and can't, alas, be taken quite seriously. That is the sense which pervades "**Prunella**." We feel that in the character of Pierrot the authors have dramatised themselves, and us. . . . However, it is not for its significance that "**Prunella**" is most highly to be valued, but rather for the mere story of it. The play is a succession of deliciously well invented scenes; and I know not which of these is the best. . . . [The] way in which Pierrot is converted from himself, and the play ends, seems to me the one fault in the play's scheme. It is a pretty notion that Pierrot should really love Prunella, and should prove his love by daring to touch her after she has told him that she is a phantom, and that if he touches her he too will die. But it is not a notion in key with the rest of the play. It is a dodge for securing a happy ending at the expense of truth to Pierrot's character. Either Prunella ought to be actually a phantom, and Pierrot to consent to touch her simply because he has lost even the melancholy joy that he once had in life, and because he is rather inquisitive of death; or Prunella ought to die in Pierrot's arms, and he to take a certain pleasure in the completeness of the romance, and in the arrangements for a prettily sombre funeral. There is for "**Prunella**" no possibility of a happy ending that shall be logical and congruous. The ending made by Mr. Laurence Housman and Mr. Granville Barker is not really a happy one; for we are sure that Pierrot, in his heart, was rather disappointed when, after touching Prunella, he found himself alive with a living girl in his arms. However, the play is in itself too exquisite a thing to be utterly marred for us by a wrong conclusion. (pp. 466-67)

> *Max Beerbohm, "A Revival of 'Prunella'" (originally published in* The Saturday Review, *London, Vol. 103, No. 2689, May 11, 1907), in his* Around Theatres *(reprinted by permission of Mrs. Eva Reichmann), revised edition, Rupert Hart-Davis, 1953, pp. 466-69.*

HAROLD WILLIAMS   (essay date 1914)

[Mr. Laurence Housman] is an illustrator, a poet, a novelist, a critic, a dramatist. To most readers he is known as the author of *An Englishwoman's Love Letters* . . . , one of the poorest and least characteristic of his writings. . . . As a poet he is to be counted with the inner circle of the mystics, for he often writes in hieroglyphs of no meaning to the exoteric mind. He has written five volumes of verse, haunted with a mystic consciousness and a spirit of morbid self-abasement before the thrones, dominations and powers of this universe, verse which places him at the opposite pole to his brother [A. E. Housman]. The severe simplicity, the clear-eyed stoicism give place to cryptic involvements and a tangled spirituality. In wistfulness

and melancholy the minds of the brothers meet, but while one faces life's complexities "abashless," the younger brother is diffident and abashed to find himself alive. The note of morbid spiritual wistfulness makes the poems of [*Green Arras, Rue,* and *Spikenard*] . . . almost unreadable save to the mind rightly attuned. The atmosphere of these poems is that of Mediaeval Catholicism, with its renunciation of the passions and its desire for virgin purity. *Spikenard* is a series of mystical rhapsodies following the cycle of the ecclesiastical year: *Rue* is the simplest and most intelligible of these volumes. Of the technical beauty of the verse there can be no question, though Mr. Laurence Housman does not rival his brother in mastery of the simplest forms. (pp. 104-05)

[In *Mendicant Rhymes*] we escape to a healthier and more human atmosphere, emerging from the ecstasies of the hermit's cell and the meditations of the cloister to the open air, the inn and the battle-field. And when in occasional poems he reverts to doctrinal mysticism it is with new power, especially in the opening stanza of the impressive '**Deus Noster Ignis Consumens.**' . . . The emotional strength of writing like this raises the poem far above the morbid, obscure and tenebrous mysticism of the earlier volumes: it is like escaping from a cave of shadowy unrealities to a bright and clear sky. But as a draughtsman and as a poet Mr. Laurence Housman is the direct descendant of the Pre-Raphaelites; and the greater part of his verse writing is almost unintelligibly mystical. This is, nevertheless, far from being his only mood. In prose he can be realistic, and even effectively satirical. (pp. 105-06)

> *Harold Williams, "The Passage of the Centuries" (1914), in his* Modern English Writers: Being a Study of Imaginative Literature, 1890-1914, *Sidgwick & Jackson, Limited, 1918, pp. 55-139.**

CHARLES LEWIS HIND   (essay date 1921)

Laurence Housman is more a man of the world [than his brother, the poet A. E. Housman]. He is keener in getting wrongs righted than in the accuracy of Latin texts; in the equalisation of the franchise than emendations of Juvenal. His interests are many—playwriting, fiction, art, craftsmanship, poetry, woodcuts, fairy tales. He has published many books, and I suppose that the most popular, the most successful was "**An Englishwoman's Love Letters**," issued anonymously in 1900. This sensitive and sentimental book led the critics a pretty dance. For weeks guesses at the authorship were made in the literary journals, and all sorts of people had to deny that they had written "**An Englishwoman's Love Letters**." Then one day a student of modern belles lettres brought into the *Academy* office an article proving, through citations from other books by Laurence Housman, that he was the author of the confessions of this love-hipped Englishwoman. That ended the quest, Laurence now acknowledges the authorship of this pretty book. He did not conceal that he was the author of "**Rue**."

Very many people in England and America are grateful to him for that delightful play "**Prunella, or Love in a Dutch Garden.**" I cherish a moving memory of his "**Bethlehem: A Nativity Play**," and I have just read his "**King John of Jingalo.**" About this I feel, as I feel about other of his books, and about his poetry and illustrations. It is on the threshold of being a fine book but it does not quite succeed in being one. As to "**The Sheepfold**" a curious experiment in biography, it would have been better if fiercely pruned to half the length. It is in him, I believe, to write a great book.

Meanwhile he has done a service to letters by reminding a busy world of A. E. and incidentally of himself.

Laurence has strong views about American Freedom, and American Poetry, and is fearless and polite in expressing them. (pp. 155-56)

Charles Lewis Hind, "The Housmans," in his Authors and I, *John Lane Company, 1921, pp. 152-56.**

A. EMIL DAVIES   (essay date 1922)

Even more ingenious than Mr. Laurence Housman's little plays are his apologies for them. [*Possession: A Peep-Show in Paradise*], for instance, was originally intended to be bound up with *Angels and Ministers,* but it was separated as a concession to the Victorian taste for keeping politics and religion apart. . . . Mr. Housman's explanation [for this] may be thought logical if you are willing to forget that some of the best Victorians stirred up their politics and religion as thoroughly as anybody could desire, while others, like Mr. Shaw, are still vigorously at work on the task. The name of Mr. Shaw must be brought into the argument because—protest as the author may—he is one of the spiritual fathers of *Possession.* This "peep-show in Paradise," exhibiting a comfortable Victorian family engaged, after death, in getting precisely the Heaven it wants and deserves, is a work of original and delightful irony. The italicised commentary running through it in the guise of stage directions, and purporting to explain the mental processes of the characters, is a piece of hackneyed and tiresome cleverness. Nobody but Mr. Shaw can be so familiar with his puppets, or so knowing about them; and nobody should attempt a style that is inimitable. Journalists are constantly attempting it with poor results; for dramatists it is fatal.

If, however, everything that Mr. Housman tries to tell us directly about his Victorian family be mentally blue-pencilled out, what he tells us indirectly remains to form an entertaining play. We should like to see it performed; and the fact that the personages are continually popping into and out of sight, disappearing from the neighbourhood of coal-scuttles or emerging from the face of mirrors, only adds zest to this desire. It may be that the author regards it as a hopelessly unpractical work from the theatrical point of view; but if so, he may be assured that he is wrong. It is a technically sound and perfectly workable one-act play, which would gain in force by being lifted out of its present wordy setting, and would demand of a producer no more than average imagination and some familiarity with modern lighting methods. Of course, if the play is produced, Mr. Housman cannot have all the visible Victorian detail—the horsehair-and-antimacassar detail—that he would like. . . . We offer this suggestion, not only in the pleasurable hope of seeing *Possession* performed, but also because published and unacted plays, thought to be unactable, sometimes derive prestige from what is at best an immunity.

A. Emil Davies, "Reviews: 'Possession: A Peep-Show in Paradise'," in New Statesman (© 1922 The Statesman Publishing Co. Ltd.), *Vol. XVIII, No. 458, January 21, 1922, p. 454.*

THE TIMES LITERARY SUPPLEMENT   (essay date 1922)

In a spirited preface which he contributes to [the **"Little Plays of St. Francis"**], Mr. Granville Barker discusses at length the inevitable clash that has been established by the conditions of modern life between drama as an art and the theatre as a paying concern, and frankly places Mr. Housman's **"Little Plays"** on the side of the poor and of the angels [see excerpt below]. Considering what their theme is, that is just as it should be. . . .

Nevertheless, the problem of religious drama is an interesting one, and we can hardly discuss these plays of Mr. Housman's without fringing upon it. The prevalence of a kind of criticism called aesthetic has blinded many to a fact it might have been expected to bring into prominence—the fact that effect in art is conditioned by the nature of the theme. A corollary to this is that the basis of religious art is religious faith. The greatness of Giotto's "Life of Christ" at Padua, or of the music of Bach's Mass, rests on the simple and devoted belief which both had in the truth of the Gospel story. Moreover, these works were composed for a generation of men to whom the story was equally acceptable and familiar; and here we have a further condition of religious art. Its theme must be not only believed but known. The religious emotions of St. Francis and his followers are an extremely rebellious subject-matter, unless we can presume an audience to whom the Franciscan legend is a second Bible. That was Mr. Housman's initial difficulty; he knew that no such audience was to be found in England. Where knowledge of the saintly life is presupposed the artist can devote himself to the exhibition of its religious sublimity; when the life itself has to be constructed the religious element can only be gradually disengaged. In the one case we are convinced of certain verities before the play begins, in the other it is for the artist, as he proceeds, to convince us of them; and then, since his vehicle is a play, he has first to engage our dramatic sympathy, to inolve and extricate his characters, to provide surprises and reversals of fortune; for we are to be gradually lifted to the religious attitude, and must first be approached on the purely human level.

Mr. Housman has tackled this part of his problem with the greatest ingenuity and good will. It is, of course, a drawback to his plays, in their relation to the theatre, that there are so many of them; though each is in a manner independent, they imply one another and are a developing series; and what audience could sit through a series of eighteen acts? On the other hand, how was the religious exaltation of St. Francis to be expressed in its peculiar *débonnaireté*, except against a large background of the life out of which it grew? The glamour and intensity, the indifference and squalor, of the Middle Ages must be before us in violent contrast before we can appreciate the genius of "The Poverello" or understand its appeal.

His dramatic incident is better than his diction. This is, in the blank verse, excessively Shakespearian, as any three lines quoted at random will show. . . . Surely, too, it is a mistake to introduce the emotional style of poetry into stage directions. . . . Artifices of this kind, which never reach an audience, impair the dramatic illusion even when we read the play, forcing us to stop and ask ourselves whom they are intended to impress. The lyrical element in Mr. Housman's work, which is abundant—for was not Francis himself a poet?—is also decidedly a weakness. . . . The words are more ingenious than convincing, and their reliance on the virtues of rhyme and alliteration is scarcely in tune with the thought they convey or the occasion on which they are uttered. It was, undoubtedly, an error to attempt the presentment on the stage of S. Francis in ecstasy, above all, in that culminating ecstasy in which he received the stigmata; nor do we understand how the instrumental accompaniment and the scenic apparatus for producing effects of thunder and lightning and moonlight and golden showers could be provided under the simple conditions of the rural stage. All through the plays there is, in fact, too little consideration of economy of mechanism.

"Franciscan Drama," in The Times Literary Supplement *(© Times Newspapers Ltd. (London) 1922; reproduced from* The Times Literary Supplement *by permission), No. 1062, May 25, 1922, p. 334.*

MARIANNE MOORE (essay date 1923)

[In *Moonshine and Clover* and *A Doorway in Fairyland*], the outstanding impression is that of moral sensibility; a heightened sense of the appropriateness of outward beauty to inward—as in the case of Mr Housman's novel, *The Sheepfold.* But whereas the austerity and calm but torrential force in *The Sheepfold* make it unique, there is variableness in the symmetry and in the power of the telling of these later stories. The fairy-tale, like the question, bespeaks faith in the outcome of what is not yet evolved; and in their prime quality of illusory credibility, Mr Housman's tales command belief. One reads eagerly until the end has been reached, infinitesimally disaffected by an occasional flaw. Although usually in the fairy-tale, good triumphs over evil and virtue is synonymous with beauty, an appearance of moral insouciance is essential; and in a number of these stories, one sees perhaps too plainly, the wish to bless. Also, evolving from an affection for the child mind and perhaps from a wish not to labour the matter, we have from time to time a kind of diminutive conversation as of an adult in the nursery, which is death to the illusion of make-believe. (p. 293)

In these two books there is a disparity in favour of *Moonshine and Clover,* there being perhaps but one story in a *Doorway in Fairyland,* "The Ratcatcher's Daughter," which may surely be depended upon to remain in the mind. (p. 294)

One must not monopolize; one need not avenge oneself; in improving the morals of the world, one should begin by improving one's own; these are the mordant pro-occupations about which Mr Housman's fancy plays. (p. 295)

Marianne Moore, "Gentle Sorcery," in The Dial *(copyright, 1923, by The Dial Publishing Company, Inc.), Vol. 75, No. 3, September, 1923, (and reprinted by Kraus Reprint Corporation, 1923), pp. 293-95.*

H. GRANVILLE-BARKER (essay date 1926)

There is an art of the theatre and there is a theatrical industry, and it is absurd to expect that the interests of the two can be continuously identical; it is difficult, rather, to see why nowadays they should ever coincide. . . .

The sophisticated in such matters, then, will not expect even the most enterprising London manager to pounce upon this sequence of plays setting forth the life of St. Francis of Assisi. . . . (p. vii)

Mr. Housman himself—as experienced in the industry as he is practised in the art—probably does not envisage any such immediate fate for these plays. But we must not conclude because of this, and because they make their first bow to the public from the printed book, that they are therefore undramatic, merely literary, more fitted for the study than the stage—because they have not been fitted to the Procrustean bed of the commercial theatre. And, while a theatrical generation ago some critics might have thought to couch praise in such terms,

to-day (alas for the theatre!) it is equally foolish to use them as blame. (p. viii)

Now it cannot fail to strike one how perfectly—whether by accident or design—Mr. Housman has provided in this sequence of plays for the needs and ambitions of [amateur] players. The multiple unit is a most useful economic form. You may pass from your single play to your section and later accumulate resources to capture the whole work without any waste labour. More importantly, here is religious drama; and—if one may beg a question which each reader may claim to answer for himself—drama that is religious not in name only.

It is surely a very salient sign both of our new drama's vitality and of the fact we have alleged that its life is now truly a part of the people's life, when it turns—and quite simply and normally turns—to religion for a topic. For a topic, in that here we have living religion, not dead. The dress may be twelfth century, but if the faith were not alive and the thought immediate, neither would pass the dramatic test to which Mr. Housman has boldly put them. But let half a dozen actors, thinking more of their art than of themselves, and for the time being more of St. Francis than of either—let them give such life as is in them to any one of these plays, and . . . they will find without fail that the life of the play's art and the intenser life of its purpose will give increase tenfold. For—passing the test—that is drama's achievement and reward. (pp. xiv-xv)

H. Granville-Barker, in his preface to Little Plays of St. Francis: A Dramatic Cycle from the Life and Legend of St. Francis of Assisi *by Laurence Housman, revised edition, Sidgwick & Jackson Ltd., 1926, pp. vii-xv.*

RAMSDEN BALMFORTH (essay date 1928)

[An] artistic treatment of the problem of the after-life by means of the drama is given by Mr. Laurence Housman in his little play *Possession: A Peep-Show in Paradise.* The scene is fixed in what Mr. Housman calls "The Everlasting Habitations," and the play describes a middle-class Victorian household as it survives in the shadowy realm of the Elysian fields. The characters are two maiden ladies, Julia and Martha Robinson; a third sister, married, Laura James; their mother, Susan Robinson; their father, Thomas Robinson; William James, the husband of Laura; and Hannah, the family servant. The household in this land of Shades is just a replica of the earthly home which these gentle and ungentle spirits have so recently left. But the chief characterisitic of the play is the delicate irony with which the dramatist depicts the spiritual atmosphere—supposed by most of them to be heaven—in which his characters live. The cultured gentleness, slightly tinged with patronage and snobbery, of Miss Julia; the acid, fault-finding disposition of Laura (Mrs. James); the dog-like loyalty and fidelity of the old servant, Hannah; the depressed and subdued sister, Martha; the gentle and lovable but self-willed mother; the weak and shifty Mr. James, who has deserted his wife after enduring her as long as he could; the dandified father who, like Don Juan, prefers the liveliness of hell to the tedium of heaven. All these are drawn with a delicacy which is none the less fine and effective because it is mingled with both irony and gentle charity. But the ethical principle underlying the little drama is that which is the foundation of Mark Twain's fine spiritual romance, *Captain Stormfield's Visit to Heaven.* Everyone gets what he desires—a harp, a halo, a pair of wings—and soon finds that the satisfaction of such desires palls. (pp. 135-36)

[The play suggests that] the highest of possessions is self-possession. But how if the self we possess is a poor, attenuated, little, shallow self, which is cursed with an incurable blindness? Here, we are back at the old problem of determinism, and I am afraid that Mr. Housman does not help us to solve it. For if we do but continue in the next life the self we have developed here, with all its shortcomings and blindness, who is responsible for that narrowing and encircling rim which determines the quality of the self? Surely there must be some way out—perhaps through the purification of the spirit by sorrow and suffering—to greater light. Mr. Housman, I say, does not help us to answer these questions, but he does bring before us . . . the psychological law which lies at the back of religion and spiritual evolution. The play ends in futile and miserable little quarrel between the sisters about the "possession" of a silver tea-pot which Laura is anxious to get hold of. . . . (pp. 136-37)

It is the atmosphere which the characters create by their various temperaments which tells upon the audience and the reader, and in the creation of this atmosphere Mr. Laurence Housman is an artist. (p. 137)

> Ramsden Balmforth, "The Problem-Play in Relation to Ethical and Religious Problems," in his The Problem-Play and Its Influence on Modern Thought and Life, George Allen & Unwin Ltd, 1928, pp. 77-140.*

THE TIMES LITERARY SUPPLEMENT　(essay date 1932)

Mr. Laurence Housman works tirelessly at his hard task—to make a popular religious drama—and seems to have a fine ingenuity ever at hand. His purpose [in the **"Little Plays of St. Francis"**] is pre-eminently religious, yet it is of a sort that has dramatic affinities. His purpose is hardly, in theatre or village hall, to reassert the achievement within church walls of the greater liturgies; it is not, though his persons are under vows, an invitation to the cloisters; nor is it to give lessons on conduct, as in the moralities. He carries a lamp of simple faith and arranges on his stage a transparency through which it may shine; or, to speak differently, draws a pure violin note across the silence after an orchestra ceases. Thus, for example, he has a market-place rampant and then suddenly stills it with a sanctified argument, so that the fluid assembly is given a memorable rigidity—which is vision—and seems stayed to be apprehended in a gentle and affectionate pity. Those who carry the lamp of faith, to do the shining, are St. Francis and the delightful simpleton, Brother Juniper, the latter chosen because "out of the faithfulness of a fool's service comes at last strange wisdom, or something at least that brings wisdom to others," and because "the gay and serene character of Francis needed its foil." They play a pretty game of faith one with another, and the deep trust of Juniper in the little Father, even in face of teasing, brings a tear to the eye of the saint.

Where the plays seem weak, considered in the light of the theatre, is that the special religious mood is applied to a world too narrow and conventionalized. The idea of holiness is well; the idea of the earth on which it operates is not so well. Beggars, simple women, stupid merchants, the folk of these Italian assemblies are too easy a paper for the candle of vision to burn through. Our sympathy, not greatly seduced by this slender worldliness, is already from the outset too much in favour of simple faith; and the conflict between good and evil does not reach the height of the greatest drama. These pieces, therefore, stand as evocations of spiritual feeling by an arrangement, often ingenious, of events; they aim at presenting one emotion rather than the serious combat between two.

The note they strike is naive. This poverty and obedience, this entire submissiveness are far from the present temper of the Western world. The audience must consent to a landscape wherein it is natural to speak of "Sister Ram, Brother Ox, Sister Fear, Sister Death." But the very childishness wins its own victories. It is said that such plays (and one may indeed believe it) can illuminate a village hall or small theatre, more especially when performed by sincere, though unskilled, amateurs; they certainly are, as Mr. Granville-Barker's preface [see excerpt above] claims, the vital contrary of "the new mechanical drama of the movie and talkie." Mr. Granville-Barker adds:—"Only those who have tried—and failed!—know how hard it is in any art to achieve a simplicity which is not mere emptiness." Mr. Housman avoids this, and avoids that other danger in things naive—mere silliness—by adroitness in humour. He will even venture near satire, as in **"The Makers of Miracles,"** which turns a laugh against pompous devotion. He delights indeed to show the pure Franciscan flame brightening through a thickening atmosphere of formality, such pieces being set within the cloisters. Several of the plays relate incidents that happened after the death of Francis; and in these Mr. Housman most effectively suggests a feeling of the saint's lingering—and wonder-working—presence.

> "'Little Plays of St. Francis'," in The Times Literary Supplement (© Times Newspapers Ltd. (London) 1932; reproduced from The Times Literary Supplement by permission), No. 1567, February 11, 1932, p. 91.

THE TIMES LITERARY SUPPLEMENT　(essay date 1932)

[In *The Queen's Progress: Nine Palace Plays,* a series of short dramas] extending from the first Privy Council in 1837 to the Diamond Jubilee sixty years later, Mr. Housman indicates the development of Queen Victoria's character. The sketches are extremely slight. In none is any attempt made to search deeply into policy or to penetrate far below the surface of the royal mind: it being a part of the dramatist's chosen method not to impose opinion on his audience or to confuse them with controversy, but rather to introduce them on various occasions into castle or palace and allow them, with humour but with convenient discretion, to eavesdrop.

The first piece, *Poor Mamma!* shows the Queen in contact with her uncles and the Duchess of Kent immediately after her accession, and suggests the rapidity with which she broke free from restrictive influences. . . . [*Woman Proposes* and *Leading Strings*] . . . bring Prince Albert on the scene, first as a young foreigner to whom Victoria offers her hand, afterwards as a man determined to become something more than his wife's plaything and to win for himself a share in the work of her life. These two incidents are prettily told; and if they suggest neither the fieriness of the girl's passion nor the streak of personal rashness that was conspicuous in her during the early years of her reign, these omissions are inevitable in a portrait so lightly drawn, and there are compensations for them—the humour and firmness of the outline. *The Intruder* . . . tells of the encounter, in one of the drawing-rooms late at night, between a harmless madman, who has broken into the palace, and the Prince, who has come down to see that the candles have been put out and the furniture covered in accordance with his orders. From this and the following sketch, which introduces King Edward as a youth, Martin Tupper and Disraeli, the conscientious stiffness of the Prince Consort clearly emerges. Mr. Housman's interpretation of him is unsparing, but neither cruel nor insolent; indeed, it is admirably balanced and gives distinction to the book.

The Queen's objection that in Benjamin Constant's painting of her the face was not red nor the ribbon of the garter blue enough, is related with ingenious shrewdness; there is an amusing battle between two determined ladies when audience is granted to a Canon's wife known as the "She-bear of Windsor"; Mr. Gladstone hands in his resignation (March, 1894) and Mrs. Gladstone is affectionately kissed by the Queen; and on June 20, 1897, the great lady, *Happy and Glorious,* is wheeled out on to the balcony to receive the cheers of the crowd. Not all of the pieces have substance enough to hold the stage in detachment from their fellows, but they make collectively a volume of lively entertainment that is not in the essentials of character either unjust or untrue. The dialogue—particularly that in which Disraeli and his Royal mistress discuss at delicious cross-purposes the merit of Martin Tupper—is clear and flowing; the intertwining of etiquette with personal feeling is neatly done; and, though we see the Queen from without, rather than from within, the peculiar quality of her greatness—her power to exclude from consideration those aspects of a problem that might have confused her judgment—does steadily appear.

> *"The Queen's Progress: Nine Palace Plays," in* The Times Literary Supplement *(© Times Newspapers Ltd. (London) 1932; reproduced from* The Times Literary Supplement *by permission), No. 1599, September 22, 1932, p. 654.*

QUEEN'S QUARTERLY   (essay date 1932)

The present generation has much reason to be grateful to its biographers. In older days the great figures of the past were only to be met in full canonicals, and making their acquaintance was a serious business. Under Mr. Housman's guidance we come to intimacy by a process that is easy and wholly pleasant. Easy for us, but not so easy for him, for his is an art that conceals a deal of artfulness. (p. 745)

[*The Queen's Progress, Nine Palace Plays*] fill out the Victorian scene which Mr. Housman began to sketch in *Angels and Ministers* and in *Palace Plays.* Like Lytton Strachey he has succumbed to the majestic simplicity of Queen Victoria. Fortunately in his surrender he too retains the comic spirit, which enables men to see what is ridiculous in those they love without loving them less. And in the end all ridicule fades from his portrait of "the great, wonderful, little, old Lady", who is the central figure in each of these sketches.

Anyone who has read Mr. Housman's earlier dramatic dialogues will greet this further instalment with enthusiasm. Nor will he be disappointed. There is less laughter in them, the fun is more restrained, the Personage has mastered him. But his smile is as delicate and keen as ever.

Mr. Housman will deserve even better of his generation if he publishes all the Victorian sketches in one volume—and then adds some more. In that long life there are plenty of other incidents worthy of his illuminating pen. (pp. 745-46)

> *"Book Reviews: 'The Queen's Progress, Nine Palace Plays'," in* Queen's Quarterly, *Vol. XXXIX, November, 1932, pp. 745-46.*

RICHARD CHURCH   (essay date 1933)

[In *Victoria and Albert,* the final series of *Palace Plays,*] Mr. Housman gives us 13 dramatic vignettes of incidents in Queen Victoria's life from the time of her marriage in 1840 to the year of Jubilee in 1897. His most serious purpose is to show the gradual ascendency of the Prince Consort in his capacity as Lutheran husband and more-than-English statesman. Mr. Housman does not make him a pleasant person. We see an august figure ruthlessly determined upon the establishment and maintenance of his own dignity: a man who was kind upon principle, with parsonic views of philanthropy enlarged to the terms and conditions of his unusual position. . . . So far as one sees him in these sketches, his political purpose seems to have been solely to increase the prerogative of the Crown, and especially to make the Foreign Office part of the domestic machinery of Buckingham Palace. We are not shown the reason for his policy, but are led to suspect that it was merely the instinctive one of a German husband engaged in keeping his wife in her place and at the same time increasing her prestige in the world beyond the domestic hearth. He was succeeding in this Old Testamentish aim, but unfortunately caught cold and died.

Mr. Housman gives us the death scene, and the Queen appears there as a very small-minded and self-centred person. In fact, on thinking over the plays after closing the book, one realizes that the Queen is nothing more than a parochial snob with the political sagacity of a country squire's "lady" or a clergyman's wife in the happy days when those positions gave ample scope for petty tyranny. . . . These 13 vignettes of the Queen might surely have shown other aspects of her character, and thus might have enabled us to understand why she so signally commanded the century as to give her name to it, and why she domineered so powerfully even over such egotistic giants as Palmerston and Gladstone. Rank alone could not give her this ascendancy, for she rode and survived the great wave of Republicanism that swept Europe during her reign.

> *Richard Church, "Mr. Housman's Queen Victoria," in* The Spectator *(© 1933 by* The Spectator; *reprinted by permission of* The Spectator), *Vol. 151, No. 5490, September 15, 1933, p. 349.*

THE TIMES LITERARY SUPPLEMENT   (essay date 1934)

The ordinary reader thinks he knows a good deal about the Victorian Age, an assumption which must hamper to a certain extent the flight of Mr. Housman's imagination [in **"Victoria Regina"**]. . . .

But Mr. Housman, in spite of the inconvenient nearness of the Victorian Age, seems to have all the freedom he requires. Indeed he sometimes seems too much at his ease. **"Victoria Regina"** contains the plays which have appeared in **"Angels and Ministers," "Palace Plays," "The Queen's Progress"** and **"Victoria and Albert,"** and to these one new play has been added. In most of these plays the reader's credulity is well sustained and very well rewarded; but occasionally the dramatist contents himself with an effect which is too easy, and the illusion fails. When the Queen consults the Dean of Windsor on a religious difficulty, a difficulty occasioned by the story of Jonah and the Whale: when she expresses her pity for Mrs. Gladstone's misfortune in being the wife of Mr. Gladstone: when, at the end of the best known and perhaps the best of the plays, Lord Beaconsfield "falters into poetry" as he takes his leave of the Queen: on these and on some other occasions

Mr. Housman insists too much on the effect he has contrived, an insistence which will make the unskilful laugh and the judicious grieve. His new play, *Aims and Objects,* is without this overemphasis. It is dated 1849 and is ingenious and effective, both in itself and in its relation to the other plays. In the earlier ones we have been shown the Queen as she was in the first years of her marriage, behaving to her husband as a dutiful wife on the one hand and an imperious Queen on the other, and combining these two attitudes with perfect ease and assurance. In these plays we were shown the Prince pleading for more power and the Queen refusing it. Now, in 1849, Mr. Housman shows us the position reversed; the Prince has all the power he once pleaded for, and it is now the Queen who complains that he is not allowed to have more.

> *"Unreliable History," in* The Times Literary Supplement *(© Times Newspapers Ltd. (London) 1934; reproduced from* The Times Literary Supplement *by permission), No. 1717, December 27, 1934, p. 918.**

THE TIMES LITERARY SUPPLEMENT   (essay date 1937)

Rumour, which so rapidly acquires the authority of fact even when spread only by word of mouth, has surely gained a new and dangerous ally in Mr. Housman. For his plays about Queen Victoria, with their quietly convincing detail and studied moderation, have an authenticity which belongs to art but brilliantly imitates that of history. The muse of comedy has put on the decorous trappings of Clio, and may play an alarming role in this disguise. No doubt Mr. Housman is conscientious about the truth; his preface [to **"Palace Scenes: More Plays of Queen Victoria"**], in which he explains that his twelve new plays are designed to fill in certain gaps to make the whole series complete, also gives his view of the part that Queen Victoria played in her century. . . .

It is a reasonable view and one which is fairly expressed in the plays, and there is also Mr. Housman's assurance that each of them contains "a germ of history"; but he must also have his conscience as an artist, and it is his art to add to the germ of fact and to give to all the additions the authenticity of an eye-witness's account. In the last of the new plays, which takes place after the Queen's death and shows two Royal ladies destroying certain passages in her diaries, it is hinted that some of the details in the play may have come from the diaries. This is to suggest, whether seriously or not, a yet more baffling mixture of truth and fiction than one had imagined, but this new perplexity is scarcely needed to add to the bewilderment of pedantic historians. They had better not read the plays at all if they do not wish to be confused between documented facts and rumour, true or false, which gains new strength from Mr. Housman's power of giving an unemphatic solidity to all his characters and situations.

It is, of course, Mr. Housman's fault if one begins to make irrelevant inquiries about the truth of his plays. Their truth has nothing to do with their merits, but it is their merit that, slight and often gentle as they are, they appear to be fragments from a continuous and authentic chronicle. And several of the new plays suggest that the chronicle is complete and minute enough to include the smallest details. . . . [Most] of these plays belong to the small gossip of history. Like real gossip, they stick in the mind, making the background of history and illuminating lay figures. And when the background is so substantial, the illumination so bright, it is really disappointing to have to wonder how much is exact.

> *"More Palace Plays," in* The Times Literary Supplement *(© Times Newspapers Ltd. (London) 1937; reproduced from* The Times Literary Supplement *by permission), No. 1833, March 20, 1937, p. 211.*

AGNES REPPLIER   (essay date 1940)

The Housman who has a Christian (and a very great saint's) name has been so brilliantly versatile that there is hardly a field of letters which he has left untried and unadorned. The overwhelming success of *Victoria* (on and off the stage) has lifted him as high as ambition can reasonably expect to climb. It leaves us speechless with admiration for the author's understanding of a life which he has never been compelled to share. Dullness is not confined to courts. It is as universal as death. It gives lectures, it preaches sermons, it dines out, it sings comic operas. But it has never been so unerringly drawn as in Mr. Housman's two volumes on the Queen. The treadmill is riotously gay as compared to one of Victoria's dinners. Yet there is nothing accentuated in their soberness. . . .

Now to have made dullness entertaining is surely the triumph of a great artist. . . . [The] conversation at Mr. Housman's court dinners is possessed of a perfect and complete nothingness. It is this nothingness which, in the author's hands, makes them supreme. . . .

One very distinct impression gleaned from these dramas and sketches is that Victoria was a disagreeable woman. She did not want to be disagreeable. She tried to be otherwise. But nature, represented by ancestors, was too much for her; and it is on the whole easier for a queen than for a subject to be untrammeled. Her control must come from within, whereas most of us are firmly controlled from without. (p. 47)

Laurence Housman takes the world of London lightly. It has been in a caressing mood, and he has submitted to, rather than courted, its caresses. Perhaps he recalls from time to time the short-lived enthusiasms of his own life; but we all expect to be remembered a little longer than we remember others. Perhaps he really knows how flawlessly he has done the work he assigned himself. Victoria's reign was a gold mine from which he extracted the pure metal. (p. 49)

> Agnes Repplier, *"The Brothers Housman," in* The Atlantic Monthly, *Vol. 165, No. 1, January, 1940, pp. 46-50.**

GERALD WEALES   (essay date 1962)

Laurence Housman's work reaches across the history of [the religious drama movement] from his initiatory *Bethlehem* . . . to his collection *Old Testament Plays.* . . . For a man so involved with the growth of religious drama in England, Housman's relationship to Christianity has been a markedly ambivalent one. (p. 122)

For Housman, as the plays so often give evidence, the church not only fails to stimulate, it actively hampers faith, and yet, for all his distrust of and distance for the church, he was attracted to it all his life. . . . Perhaps his willingness to work with groups such as the Religious Drama Society is an expression of the need for community that he is unable to find in the church itself. Certainly, at least half of his work as a religious propagandist—which he is in and out of his plays— is aimed at the reform of the institution; the other half argues for faith in man and the doctrine of love and warns the believer to beware of organization.

Some of the attitudes that were to mark Housman's later work are already apparent in *Bethlehem*. In his Nativity, which describes, in verse and song, the angels bringing the news to the shepherds, the wise men following the star and the adoration, the emphasis throughout is on love. In many ways . . . *Bethlehem* is more conventionally Christian in emphasis than the later plays, yet its impact is not that of a simple celebration of the incarnation. (pp. 123-24)

Housman's Nativity play suffers from the kind of poetic effects—archaic language, reversed syntax—that are typical of his nondramatic poetry and of most of the dramatic poetry of the early part of the century. The other chief defect of the play—one that Housman shares with most of the writers of modern Nativities—is the false simplicity of the shepherds. The excessively folksy and supposedly comic shepherds with the rich country dialect are the heritage that the Nativity maker of today has received from his medieval predecessor. . . . (p. 124)

Between *Bethlehem* and *St. Martin's Pageant* . . . , Housman wrote a few short plays on religious subjects, *Nazareth* . . . shows Jesus as a child in his father's carpenter shop, but the emphasis is on the Passion to come. *The Lord of the Harvest* . . . , a muddled attack on greed, is an odd mixture of religion, politics, and economics. In *The Unknown Star* . . . , a Nativity which Housman wrote with H. M. Paull, a reluctant Jupiter is forced to abdicate in favor of the new god who has just been born. (pp. 124-25)

Set in Amiens in 350, [*St. Martin's Pageant*] shows St. Martin sharing his cloak with a beggar to whom the cloak brings not only warmth, but vision. What the beggar sees is a procession of figures from the dead Caesar, who represents the passing of Rome, to modern Quakers working in prisons. Each of the characters in some way represents the idea of fellowship (St. Martin's cloak is the cloak of fellowship) working in society. . . .

One of the scenes in *St. Martin's Pageant* shows St. Francis with St. Clare, reciting the Canticle of the Sun. It is not surprising that St. Francis should appear in Housman's pageant, for the author's long-time preoccupation with the saint had by this time already resulted in the first of the *Little Plays of St. Francis*. (p. 125)

The reason for Housman's attraction to St. Francis is obvious. The saint, as the playwright understands him, represents a religious point of view that the author accepts as his own. . . . In the essay **"Prophets, Ancient and Modern"** he says, "St. Francis of Assisi had the extraordinary notion . . . that man is more inclined to do good than to do evil. . . ." The idea of man's inherent goodness might be for St. Francis the overcoming of sinfulness through a direct and simple approach to God, the attempt to emulate Christ, but the attitude of the [*Little Plays of St. Francis*]—for all the talk of sin that fills them—is actually an emphasis on goodness that does away with the idea of original sin. For Francis is a symbol of man's potential perfectability through love and brotherhood. . . . The idea of innocence meeting and defeating evil, violence, and power appeals to Housman in Francis and even more in Brother Juniper. Francis also represents for Housman simple faith contrasted to the worldly and complicated machinery of faith (or power) represented by the church. Housman's own doubt about many of the tenets of Christianity does not keep him from

giving St. Francis his full quota of doctrinal faith, his visions, his stigmata, but the emphasis in the mystical scenes is a little distant, almost clinical, as though the playwright sees, but does not understand; Housman seems happier, more warmly drawn to his characters when Francis or Juniper come up against prejudice or pretension.

The First Series of the *Little Plays of St. Francis* has a thematic organization that is no longer apparent in the 1935 edition, the three-volume collection that covers not only the First Series but all the St. Francis plays that Housman added later. The early collection consists of eighteen short plays, divided—six each—under three headings—The Foregoing, The Following, The Finding. Each of the main parts has its own subject and its own tone. In the plays that make up The Foregoing, Francesco (the name Francis is not used until he becomes a priest) is shown as a typical Renaissance young man—drinking, reveling, gambling (no wenching, however)—who is attracted strangely to poverty and disease, but is not quite aware of the nature of his own attraction. The plays are dressed, verbally at least, in a literary courtliness that suggests other and older plays; *The Revellers* and *The Bride Feast,* for instance, strongly echo *Romeo and Juliet.* The hints of what is to come for Francis are strewn through all six of the plays. (pp. 126-27)

The second group of plays, The Following, shows Francis at his strongest, his most certain and most joyful. The emphasis is on his personal following, their devotion to him and to God. In *The Builders,* in which Francis and his followers are actually and symbolically rebuilding the church of St. Damian's, Juniper is introduced. He is portrayed from the beginning as a solidly stupid man who is accidentally wise, genuinely good, and continuously funny, although the amusing things that he does and says are often more apparent to Francis and the brothers than they are likely to be to an audience. Some of the plays in this section—*Brother Sun* and *Brother Wolf*—deal with legendary stories of St. Francis. . . . (pp. 127-28)

In The Finding, the third group of the *Little Plays,* Housman deals a little angrily with the institutionalization of Francis. In many of these plays, the saint is a forlorn figure, no longer at home in the movement that he founded; Juniper is even more out of place. (p. 128)

After the First Series of *Little Plays,* Housman began to add to the group, filling in corners of the St. Francis story that he had not touched originally. (p. 129)

The writing of the *Little Plays of St. Francis* . . . covers a period of almost twenty years. The First Series is best, both as a unit and individually. Housman's fascination with Francis's slow attraction to poverty and his finally forcing himself to touch the diseased and the corrupt is apparent in the early plays, but there is no indication that Housman approves, only that he observes. In fact, in *The Lepers* and *Our Lady of Poverty,* the physical manifestations of Francis's love are decidedly unpleasant. Housman admires Francis's view of human goodness, but he does not mask him by seeing him simply as the man who preached to the birds. In the later plays, when Housman adds the melodramatically cruel father, the story of Francesco becoming Francis is somewhat obscured. The addition of the many Juniper plays changes the focus of the center group, those that deal with Francis at his best, and in a sense change the original impulse that produced the series. . . . Often the plays in the series become undramatic—as in *The Seraphic Visions;* often they are too patently discussions or lectures. Still, the plays as a group convey an impression of St. Francis, which while it may be historically inaccurate, is fascinating both in itself and in relationship to the beliefs for which Housman speaks. (pp. 130-31)

Housman wrote a series of biblical plays during the forties, all of which illustrate his distaste for the harshness of the Old Testament God and of the patriarchal figures. In *Abraham and Isaac* . . . , neither Sarah nor Isaac understand Abraham and his God; they are aware only that he is suffering from a command that he thinks his God has given. The logic that Abraham uses to grasp God's will is a little suspect; since the one thing that he would not do for God is kill Isaac, then the sacrifice of Isaac becomes God's command. In reducing the conflict between Abraham and God to an internal one, Housman is able to make the point that his play intends—that the will of God lies in the hearts of men—but he also unfortunately weakens the character of Abraham by turning him into a somewhat silly and superstitious old man. (pp. 131-32)

[In *Jacob's Ladder*], Housman again gives a personal interpretation of a biblical character and, as with Abraham, his Jacob loses some of his biblical charm. . . . In Housman's hands, the fun goes out of [Jacob's] deceits; Jacob becomes primarily a self-deceiver. The two Voices that give a running commentary on Jacob's character emphasize the self-deception and remind Jacob and the audience that he must come to recognize himself as he is before he can realize the promise of his vision of the ladder. (p. 132)

[In *The Burden of Nineveh*], Housman retells the story of the chastening of Jonah, but in his version, the whale is frankly an invention. "Is it not strange, Shemmel," says Jonah, "that to make men believe the truth, we prophets have to tell lies." The emphasis of the play, like that in the Bible, is on the mercy of God and his prophet's distaste for it; it is through Shemmel—Housman's amusing addition to the Bible story—that God rebukes Jonah. (pp. 132-33)

[In *Samuel the Kingmaker*], Samuel is shown as a political figure, striving to hold onto his power, using his God as an excuse for his actions. "My play is written to demonstrate that on these occasions Samuel's God was Samuel himself," Housman says of Samuel's moments of prophecy. The play is filled with speeches in which Samuel equates his desires with God's will. . . . It is the Witch of Endor, whom Housman uses, as he says, "to run Samuel down to earth (where he properly belongs)," who defines the two gods of the play, Samuel's and hers, which is to say Samuel's and Housman's. . . . In the end, Samuel dies alone, deserted by his sons and his followers. In a final scene, the Witch of Endor comforts Saul, making him see that he is suffering at the hands of his own fear, not from any punishment of Samuel's God.

Housman's last biblical plays sum up most of his ideas on religion. In them, he speaks for a distant, a noninterfering God, one that is a Law or the voice within man himself. He speaks against violence and fear in the name of God and for love and understanding. If he returns too insistently to these ideas, if he labors too heavily against the Old Testament patriarchs as they are and against the miracles and wonders that are so much a part of their stories, he does so from humanitarian motives. Many of these last plays suffer from this insistence. They are, however, Housman's best work in religious drama. In them, he manages to overcome many of the faults—the sentimentality, the archaism, the cuteness even—that marks much of his earlier work, including the *Little Plays of St. Francis*. Housman's conception of the Old Testament characters is certainly

not the heroic one that those figures might be given, but they are all seen sharply as individuals and they all have vitality by virtue of the contexts in which Housman places them. (pp. 133-35)

Gerald Weales, "Laurence Housman and John Masefield," in his Religion in Modern English Drama (copyright © 1961 by Gerald Weales), University of Pennsylvania Press, 1962, pp. 122-41.*

HELEN BEVINGTON (essay date 1974)

Twelve of Laurence Housman's stories, long out of print, have been . . . [collected under] the title **"The Rat-Catcher's Daughter."** While they show he was hardly cut out to be the third Brother Grimm or pass as a late-Victorian Hans Christian Andersen, he does have a wide acquaintance with fairies. One can trust his report. . . . [Housman's] tales have a look of gold about them. His fairies, like the rest of their cheeky kind, are a meddlesome lot, given to prying into human affairs and making a temporary mess of things. Then they choose to rectify matters, they bestow favors like rubies, such as making one invisible, casting spells, changing a white doe or peahen into a white maiden, changing leaves to gold. Their ruthless talent for mischief inevitably leads to the marriage of the maiden to whoever claims her as his own (generally considered a happy solution in fairy tales), and all is forgiven.

The delightful title story, **"The Rat-Catcher's Daughter,"** may not reflect Housman's social conscience as a man who became a feminist, pacifist, socialist, Quaker and staunch defender of Queen Victoria. But it does reveal his lifelong objection to greed. The old rat-catcher is properly paid off for plotting to become the richest man in the world and (an afterthought) marry his beautiful daughter to the king's son. Any rogue mean enough to catch rats may be relied on to catch a gnome in a trap and drive a hard bargain. Accordingly, the rat-catcher acquires sacks of gold, while his daughter Jasomé disappears with the gnome into the heart of the earth. There for three years the gold dust settles on her hands and hair, over her skin, into her mind, till she is turned into a golden girl. . . .

A charming tale it is, with an unexpected twist acceptable to young and old. Instead of a laughing golden girl, what does the prince find out but one marred in her beauty, lying in a pool of her own tears, shedding great golden tears from grieving golden eyes. Though he is ready to die for love of her, no man can kiss a girl with stiff gold lips or marry a solid lump of gold.

Obliging and prompt, the gnome sets everything right by scrubbing away at the sad maiden till she is flesh again, pink and shining and clean, presentable as a wife. As for the greedy rat-catcher, deprived of his illgotten hoard, he has the last grumbling word: ungrateful daughters are like ungrateful gnomes—how sharper than a serpent's tooth to have a thankless child.

Helen Bevington, "Tales with a Look of Gold," in The New York Times Book Review (© 1974 by The New York Times Company; reprinted by permission), May 5, 1974, p. 17.*

ELLIN GREENE (essay date 1974)

[To Laurence Housman], drama was the best possible medium for portraying human nature in its infinite variety: "The good and the bad, the wise and the foolish, the noble and the ridiculous.'' He invented the play-cycle, chapters of dramatic biography with one character as the main subject.

Laurence Housman has the distinction of being England's most censored playwright. His plays were censored because they portrayed royalty and religious personages, sometimes in an unfavorable light. *Victoria Regina,* the play by which Housman is probably best known to an American audience, suffered this fate. . . . Housman considered this play and his play-cycle of the life of St. Francis, *Little Plays of St. Francis,* his best works.

Housman wrote with tremendous charm. It would be hard to excel the sheer verbal beauty of his fairy tales. The writing is lyrical. The tales have a bittersweet quality—romantic, but never saccharine; poignant, relieved by touches of humor. The individual stories are hauntingly beautiful, but it is only on reading several of them one after another that the reader feels the impact of Housman's style and philosophy. The humanist strikes out against vanity, greed, and thoughtless cruelty in such tales as **"The Rat-Catcher's Daughter"** and **"Gammelyn, the Dressmaker."** (pp. 166-67)

> *Ellin Greene, "Afterword" (copyright © 1974 by Ellin Greene; reprinted with the permission of Atheneum Publishers, New York), in* The Rat-Catcher's Daughter *by Laurence Housman, edited by Ellin Greene, Atheneum, 1974, pp. 164-69.*

ADDITIONAL BIBLIOGRAPHY

Blunden, Edmund. ''Fallen Englishmen.'' In his *Votive Tablets: Studies Chiefly Appreciative of English Authors and Books,* pp. 363-67. New York, London: Harper and Brothers, 1932.
> Brief review of *War Letters of Fallen Englishmen*, actual correspondence of World War I soldiers edited by Housman. Blunden praises these letter-writers for their ''heroic imagination'' and commends Housman for his sensitive selection.

Brown, John Mason. ''From England and Ireland: Helen Hayes and *Victoria Regina*.'' In his *Two on the Aisle: Ten Years of the American Theatre in Performance,* pp. 116-20. New York: W. W. Norton & Co., 1938.
> Critical review of Housman's *Victoria Regina* as performed for the first time on the American stage with Helen Hayes in the title role. Brown praises the overall quality of the play but criticizes certain of its qualities, such as the dialogue, the time span, and number of scenes, which do not adapt well to the stage.

Chesson, W. H. ''Dramatised Ruminations.'' *The Bookman,* London LXIV, No. 383 (August 1923): 237-38.
> Discussion of Housman's *Dethronements*. Chesson questions the believability of the playwright's three main political characters —Parnell, Chamberlain, and Woodrow Wilson—as presented in each of the three playlets within the volume.

Fairchild, Hoxie Neale. ''Nothing Very New.'' In his *Religious Trends in English Poetry: 1880-1929, Gods of a Changing Poetry, Vol. V,* pp. 195-221. New York: Columbia University Press, 1962.*
> Discussion of the religious themes and symbolism in Housman's early poetry.

William Dean Howells

1837-1920

American novelist, critic, essayist, travel writer, short story writer, autobiographer, dramatist, poet, and biographer.

Howells was the chief progenitor of American realism and the most influential American literary critic during the late nineteenth century. He was the author of nearly three dozen novels, few of which are read today. Despite his eclipse, he stands as one of the major literary figures of the nineteenth century: he successfully weaned American literature away from the sentimental romanticism of its infancy, earning the popular sobriquet "the Dean of American Letters."

During his youth in Ohio, Howells developed an interest in literature while working in his father's print shop. He later served on the staff of various newspapers in Jefferson and Columbus. Although his first book, *Poems of Two Friends*, received favorable reviews, it was with his second, an 1860 campaign biography of Lincoln, that Howells attracted national attention. *Lives and Speeches of Abraham Lincoln* earned Howells a government appointment to the U.S. consulate in Venice, where he lived during the American Civil War. Howells's impressions of Europe provided him with material for several travel books as well as his first novels.

Howells's long career as a novelist is divided into three overlapping phases. During the earliest, his work paralleled that of Henry James: beginning with *A Foregone Conclusion* in 1875 and ending in 1886 with *Indian Summer*, Howells wrote novels of manners, portraying young, strong-willed American women encountering European culture. The influence of Nathaniel Hawthorne and Ivan Turgenev—both favorites of Howells—is apparent in the work of this period, each *nouvelle* featuring a small group of characters, intensely examined. Gradually Howells turned to writing novels that focused on social problems. Most of these present a provincial character who is defeated by the corrupt city in his attempts to succeed. This middle phase, including *The Undiscovered Country* and *The Minister's Charge; or, The Apprenticeship of Lemuel Barker*, contains Howells's best-known work, *The Rise of Silas Lapham*, and what he considered his "strongest" novel, *A Modern Instance*.

Howells's social concerns intensified in his third stage of development. His "economic novels" were the product of his growing awareness of the hardships inflicted upon the poor and working class by the Gilded Age's *laissez-faire* capitalist system. The popular but unjust persecution of four anarchists convicted of the 1886 bombing of Haymarket Square in Chicago was a major factor in Howells's transition to writing economic novels. As a nationally recognized literary figure, he risked his reputation in pleading for the lives of the Haymarket anarchists. After this incident Howells followed Leo Tolstoy's example and promoted Christian socialism as a just alternative to economic inequalities and injustices. During his third period, Howells also extensively explored Tolstoy's theory of complicity: the doctrine that each person bears responsibility for the spiritual and physical well-being of all other persons. Included among the economic novels are *The World of Chance*, the utopian *A Traveler from Altruria*, and *A Hazard*

Culver Pictures

of New Fortunes, which depicts a group of diverse characters working to establish a magazine in New York. Howells considered *A Hazard of New Fortunes* his "most vital" novel and critics generally agree that it marked the peak of his achievement as a novelist.

Rebelling against the popular romantic fiction of his day, Howells sought through realism, a theory central to his fiction and criticism, to disperse "the conventional acceptations by which men live on easy terms with themselves" that they might "examine the grounds of their social and moral opinions." To accomplish this, according to Howells, the writer must strive to record impressions of everyday life, in detail, endowing characters with true-to-life motives and avoiding authorial comment in the narrative. Howells expounded realism from the "Editor's Study" and "Editor's Easy Chair," monthly columns written during his long tenure as editor of *Harper's Magazine*. *Criticism and Fiction*, a patchwork of essays from the "Editor's Study," is often considered Howells's manifesto of realism, although, as René Wellek has noted, the book is actually "only a skirmish in a long campaign for his doctrines."

Throughout his professional life, Howells worked as a literary critic and magazine editor, his essays appearing in many major periodicals. As editor of *The Atlantic Monthly*, Howells introduced new features and changes of style which gained the magazine a national readership. He provided a forum for Henry James's short fiction in *The Atlantic*, and, as James's editor and literary agent, played an instrumental role in guiding the younger writer's career. Howells was also the first critic to recognize the satire that underlay much of Mark Twain's work. Twain and Howells were best friends, each offering criticism of the other's works-in-progress. (The popular theory that Howells channeled Twain's work into genteel respectability has been greatly discounted by Twain scholars, notably, Bernard DeVoto.) In addition to his discussions of Twain, Howells perceptively reviewed three generations of international literature, urging Americans to read Zola, Shaw, Ibsen, Emily Dickinson, and other important authors.

During his last years, Howells fell into critical disfavor; as he was supplanted by other, more bitter realists and naturalists, his work was viewed as prissy, tea-party fare. In a 1915 letter, Howells wrote: "I am comparatively a dead cult with my statues cut down and the grass growing over them in the pale moonlight." His novels were ignored after his death, and have never regained popularity, although critics have since regained respect for his work. *The Rise of Silas Lapham* in particular, according to Edwin H. Cady, "has endured with great vitality the decades of ignorant and often malicious anti-Howells prejudice, and it may be expected to prosper further in readers' attention now that prejudice has begun to subside." Although many of his works are rarely read today, Howells's influence on modern American literature cannot be discounted, for he laid the groundwork for modern literature and helped shape several decades of American fiction.

PRINCIPAL WORKS

Lives and Speeches of Abraham Lincoln   (biography)   1860
Poems of Two Friends [with John J. Piatt]   (poetry)   1860
Venetian Life   (travel sketches)   1866
Their Wedding Journey   (novel)   1872
A Foregone Conclusion   (novel)   1875
The Lady of the "Aroostook"   (novel)   1879
The Undiscovered Country   (novel)   1880
Doctor Breen's Practice   (novel)   1881
A Modern Instance   (novel)   1882
The Rise of Silas Lapham   (novel)   1885
The Garroters   (drama)   1886
Indian Summer   (novel)   1886
The Minister's Charge; or, The Apprenticeship of Lemuel Barker   (novel)   1887
Annie Kilburn   (novel)   1889
A Hazard of New Fortunes   (novel)   1890
Criticism and Fiction   (criticism)   1891
The World of Chance   (novel)   1893
A Traveler from Altruria   (novel)   1894
Stops of Various Quills   (poetry)   1895
The Landlord at Lion's Head   (novel)   1897
The Kentons   (novel)   1902
The Son of Royal Langbrith   (novel)   1904
My Mark Twain   (criticism and memoir)   1910
The Leatherwood God   (novel)   1916
Mrs. Farrell   (novel)   1921
The Complete Plays of W. D. Howells   (dramas)   1960

[JAMES RUSSELL LOWELL]   (essay date 1860)

The two Friends [of *Poems of Two Friends*] are Messrs. John J. Piatt and W. D. Howells. The readers of the "Atlantic" have already had a taste of the quality of both, and, we hope, will often have the same pleasure again. The volume is a very agreeable one, with little of the crudeness so generally characteristic of first ventures,—not more than enough to augur richer maturity hereafter. Dead-ripeness in a first book is a fatal symptom, sure sign that the writer is doomed forever to that pale limbo of faultlessness from which there is no escape upwards or downwards.

We can scarce find it in our hearts to make any distinctions in so happy a partnership; but while we see something more than promise in both writers, we have a feeling that Mr. Piatt shows greater originality in the choice of subjects, and Mr. Howells more instinctive felicity of phrase in the treatment of them. Both of them seem to us to have escaped remarkably from the prevailing conventionalisms of verse, and to write in metre because they have a genuine call thereto. We are pleased with a thorough Western flavor in some of the poems, especially in such pieces as "The Pioneer Chimney" and **"The Movers."** We welcome cordially a volume in which we recognize a fresh and authentic power, and expect confidently of the writers a yet higher achievement ere long. The poems give more than glimpses of a faculty not so common that the world can afford to do without it.

> [*James Russell Lowell*,] "*Reviews and Literary Notices: 'Poems of Two Friends'*," *in* The Atlantic Monthly, *Vol. V, No. XXX, April 1860 (and reprinted as "Review of Criticism: James Russell Lowell," in* Critics on William Dean Howells, *edited by Paul A. Eschholz, University of Miami Press, 1975, p. 13).*

HENRY ADAMS   (essay date 1872)

An interesting question presents itself to the cautious critic who reads . . . [*Their Wedding Journey*], and who does not care to commit himself and his reputation for sound judgment irretrievably to the strength of such a gossamer-like web: it is whether the book will live. Why should it not live? If extreme and almost photographic truth to nature, and remarkable delicacy and lightness of touch, can give permanent life to a story, why should this one not be read with curiosity and enjoyment a hundred or two hundred years hence? Our descendants will find nowhere so faithful and so pleasing a picture of our American existence, and no writer is likely to rival Mr. Howells in this idealization of the commonplace. The vein which Mr. Howells has struck is hardly a deep one. His dexterity in following it, and in drawing out its slightest resources, seems at times almost marvellous, a perpetual succession of feats of sleight-of-hand, all the more remarkable because the critical reader alone will understand how difficult such feats are, and how much tact and wit is needed to escape a mortifying failure. Mr. Howells has a delicacy of touch which does not belong to man. One can scarcely resist the impression that he has had feminine aid and counsel, and that the traitor to her sex has taken delight in revealing the secret of her own attractions, so far at least as she knows it; for Mr. Howells, like the rest of mankind, after all his care and study, can only acknowledge his masculine incompetence to comprehend the female character. The book is essentially a lovers' book. It deserves to be among the first of the gifts which follow or precede the marriage offer. It has, we believe, had a marked success in this way, as a sort of lovers' Murray or Appleton; and if it can throw over the average bridal couple some reflection of its own refinement and taste, it will prove itself a valuable assistant to American civilization.

Henry Adams, "Critical Notices: 'Their Wedding Journey'," in The North American Review, Vol. CXIV, No. 235, April, 1872 (and reprinted as "Review of Criticism: Henry Adams," in Critics on William Dean Howells, edited by Paul A. Eschholz, University of Miami Press, 1975, p. 14).

HENRY BLAKE FULLER (essay date 1885)

The literary gossip of the last ten years, whether of tongue or type, has perhaps employed no phrase with more assiduity or gusto than that of "Howells and James." The language, in its printed form, at least, has even been enriched with a doubly hyphenated adjective which seems to express more fully and exactly than any less modern phrase a certain sort of hero and heroine, a certain sort of plot, and a certain set of ideas with regard to the methods and ends of fiction. Such being the case, one may well justify himself in the intimation that this particular expression has perhaps been a trifle overworked, and allow himself the suggestion that so well worn a collocation of words now give way to the related but dissimilar one of "Howells or James?" Substituting, then, for the complacent period the restless mark of interrogation, let us now consider points of difference instead of points of similarity,—asking ourselves which of these two representative writers is to be pronounced most instrumental in the shaping of American fiction, and which of them will ultimately come to be recognized as most firmly and completely a factor in an historical American literature. Mr. Howells, it is true, generously conceded, a year or so ago, the first place to Mr. James. But the vigorous and dextrous opening of [The Rise of Silas Lapham] clearly indicates that his hand has lost none of its mastery, and his prompt and authoritative welcome lately extended to certain newcomers in the ranks of Realism unmistakably shows that he does not consider his own position that of a subordinate; so he will perhaps tolerate the hint that to him and not to his friend is entrusted the direction of our contemporary novel-writing, and that he, rather than any one else, may be allowed by the opinion of another generation, the place of undisputed chief. It is worthwhile, on this point, to note the attitude of each toward life and society in general, and toward American life and society in particular.

We may say, in general, and for the purpose of a direct comparison, that Howells is a realist, and James an idealist. Few, perhaps, who have in mind Mr. James' first and most famous "international" effort will regard the creator of Daisy Miller—least of all, the perpetrator of Daisy Miller's little brother—as an idealizer. But a man has a right to ask that we judge him by his highest and best, by the nature of that whose representation is to him most congenial and self-satisfying. If, then, Mr. James' most finished and elaborate portraits of persons are marked with exceptional attributes of wit, polish, beauty, culture, wealth, intellect,—and if his most careful and ambitious portraits of places (the phrase is his own) result, after his own peculiar process of selection, rejection, and combination, in a whole of unblemished picturesqueness and unbroken harmony, his claim to the title of idealist seems placed beyond dispute. That he deals, ultimately, in realities, is true enough; but a realism made up of select actualities is pretty apt to come out idealistically in the end.

Now we, in these days of democracy, take a very frank and undisguised interest in ourselves; we are a good deal concerned with our own day and generation—in our art as well as elsewhere. . . . We are not ashamed to confess that at the present time we take but a limited interest in, for example, an Achilles or a Beatrice, while we vehemently discuss, *con amore,* the character of a Bartley Hubbard [of "A Modern Instance"] or the doings of a Lydia Blood [of "The Lady of the Aroostook"]. . . . Realism seems coincident with modern democracy, and the advance of the one will doubtless be accompanied by the spread of the other. Realism as Mr. Howells himself has lately said, is but a phase of humanity; and the writer who is most thoroughly permeated with the realistic spirit may confidently expect the widest hearing and the securest place.

Again: Mr. Howells' attitude toward life is sympathetic; Mr. James' is rather the reverse. James has, of course, his own peculiar sympathies and predilections, but they are of a very exclusive and circumscribed character. He regards life as a superficies; Howells looks at it as a substance. James makes a survey of it; Howells gives us a cross-section of it. The one is satisfied with the cultivation of the mere top-dressing; the other has a healthy liking for the honest clay and gravel of the great middle stratum. James has, of course, his due liking for virtue, truth, justice, and the rest, but he does not always appear to appreciate them at their full value when unlinked with fortunate circumstances and the culture of a refined society. Howells, on the other hand, can interest himself sympathetically in all the qualities—not the good, merely; but the doubtful and the bad as well—which may present themselves to him in his actual contact with society in any of its forms. He himself declares that the study of human life, if close, is sure to be kindly. And a hearty sympathy with the general life of the community has never met with a readier recognition and response than it meets with today.

The present attitude of these two authors, respectively, with regard to our own particular life and society, assuredly need not be made matter for formal exposition. But it is interesting to note that within the last few years the attitude of the one has materially changed, while that of the other has become, if anything, more statuesquely immovable. The time is not far back when both Howells and James were stationed at the far end of that transatlantic bridge which it is the chief boast and distinction of the latter to have constructed between the Old World and the New. Howells, with a clear perception of the direction in which the cat—to use the common phrase—was about to jump, crossed over a few years back (pausing in the middle for the **"Foregone Conclusion"** and the **"Lady of the Aroostook"**) and has steadfastly remained with us ever since. James, with a perception less clear, or from preferences not easily to be overcome, has held to the same remote standpoint that he occupied when his striking figure was first discerned by the modern novel-reader. . . . That each is now permanently established on his own ground, and fully fixed as to his own point of view, the fall announcements of the publishers made yet more sure. Mr. Howells, in the **"Rise of Silas Lapham"** will still farther extend the field of sympathetic realism which he first entered in the **"Modern Instance."** Mr. James, in the "Princess Casamassima" . . . will bring to a still higher degree of perfection his own particular little garden of exotic culture which has already blossomed with "Roderick Hudson" and the "Portrait of a Lady."

A common complaint against the novels of both Howells and James—how easily the phrase runs off!—has been that most of them have been unduly taken up with various small and insignificant questions of social manners and usages that ruffle the mere surface of society without by any means stirring its depths. But there are now indications that the depths are to be stirred, after all. The stratification of our society has undeniably begun, and symptoms of the movement are coming to appear in print. Now the novel in our day has become the great universal medium. New theories in philosophy, new ideas in art, new phases in religion, politics, and what not, now hasten to enclose themselves within the covers of a "fiction." And if all these, why not sociology, as well? May we not reasonably look for the formulation of American society in the pages of the *Atlantic* or the *Century*? And such a process—to whom would we most willingly entrust it, to Howells or to James? Who would do it most kindly, most sympathetically—he who deals with the normal earning of money at home, or he who prefers to deal with the exceptional and privileged spending of money abroad? He who lives amongst us and knows us intimately and treats us all with the fullest measure of good will; or he who alienates himself from us, knows us, in general, none too perfectly, and doesn't feel sure but that we are a big mistake, after all? With the strong intimation that Mr. Howells has just given of his design to bring order out of our social chaos, I am glad to remember that he is an "Ohio man," and it was toward Ohio, let us recollect, that Mr. Matthew Arnold directed his gaze when searching for the "average American."

Mr. James, no doubt, would be glad to like us, if he could; perhaps he has been conscientiously endeavored to do so. But an undue insistence upon agreeable externals has worked to prevent his becoming acquainted with us as we really are. He leaves us in no doubt that he prefers, for instance, weather-stained stucco to freshly-painted clapboarding; and a pair of sabots strikes in him a responsive chord that a pair of plain cowhide boots quite fails to affect. The boots and the clapboarding repel him; so he stays over there with his sabots and his stucco. Mr. Howells' organs of aesthetic digestion are much more healthy and vigorous. He approaches boldly all the various externals of American life—grotesque though they be, and ugly, and irritating, and distressing—which so often cause us to quail before the gaze of our European censors, and subdues them instead of letting them subdue him. He can print the word "buggy" without the help of quotation marks, and writes "guess" with an unconscious freedom that Mr. James has never attained. (pp. 160-64)

> *Henry Blake Fuller, " 'Howells or James?'—An Essay by Henry Blake Fuller" (1885), edited by Darrel Abel, in* Modern Fiction Studies *(© 1957 by Purdue Research Foundation, West Lafayette, Indiana 47907, U.S.A.), Vol. 3, No. 2, Summer, 1957, pp. 159-64.*

HENRY JAMES (essay date 1886)

As the existence of a man of letters (so far as the public is concerned with it) may be said to begin with his first appearance in literature, that of Mr. Howells . . . dates properly from the publication of his delightful volume on *Venetian Life*—than which he has produced nothing since of a literary quality more pure—which he put forth in 1865, after his return from the consular post in the city of St. Mark which he had filled for four years. He had, indeed, before going to live in Venice, and during the autumn of 1860, published, in conjunction with his friend Mr. Piatt, a so-called "campaign" biography of Abraham Lincoln; but as this composition, which I have never seen, emanated probably more from a good Republican than

from a suitor of the Muse, I mention it simply for the sake of exactitude, adding, however, that I have never heard of the Muse having taken it ill. . . . [It] may be considered that the happiest thing that could have been invented on Mr. Howells's behalf was his residence in Venice at the most sensitive and responsive period of life; for Venice, bewritten and bepainted as she has ever been, does nothing to you unless to persuade you that you also can paint, that you also can write. . . . [Mr. Howells's] papers on Venice prove it, equally with the artistic whimsical chapters of the Italian Journeys, made up in 1867 from his notes and memories (the latter as tender as most glances shot eastward in working hours across the Atlantic) of the holidays and excursions which carried him occasionally away from his consulate.

The mingled freshness and irony of these things gave them an originality which has not been superseded, to my knowledge, by any impressions of European life from an American standpoint. . . . He wrote poetry at Venice, as he had done of old in Ohio, and his poems were subsequently collected into two thin volumes, the fruit, evidently, of a rigorous selection. They have left more traces in the mind of many persons who read and enjoyed them than they appear to have done in the author's own. It is not nowadays as a cultivator of rhythmic periods that Mr. Howells most willingly presents himself. Everything in the evolution, as we must all learn to call it today, of a talent of this order is interesting, but one of the things that are most so is the separation that has taken place, in Mr. Howells's case, between its early and its later manner. There is nothing in *Silas Lapham*, or in *Doctor Breen's Practice*, or in *A Modern Instance*, or in *The Undiscovered Country*, to suggest that its author had at one time either wooed the lyric Muse or surrendered himself to those Italian initiations without which we of other countries remain always, after all, more or less barbarians. It is often a good, as it is sometimes an evil, that one cannot disestablish one's past, and Mr. Howells cannot help having rhymed and romanced in deluded hours, nor would he, no doubt, if he could. The repudiation of the weakness which leads to such aberrations is more apparent than real, and the spirit which made him care a little for the poor factitious Old World and the superstition of "form" is only latent in pages which express a marked preference for the novelties of civilization and a perceptible mistrust of the purist. I hasten to add that Mr. Howells has had moments of reappreciation of Italy in later years, and has even taken the trouble to write a book (the magnificent volume on *Tuscan Cities*) to show it. Moreover, the exquisite tale *A Foregone Conclusion,* and many touches in the recent novel of *Indian Summer* (both this and the *Cities* the fruit of a second visit to Italy), sound the note of a charming inconsistency.

On his return from Venice he settled in the vicinity of Boston, and began to edit the *Atlantic Monthly*. . . . (pp. 41-3)

He was still under the shadow of his editorship when, in the intervals of his letter-writing and reviewing, he made his first cautious attempts in the walk of fiction. I say cautious, for in looking back nothing is more clear than that he had determined to advance only step by step. In his first story, *Their Wedding Journey,* there are only two persons, and in his next, *A Chance Acquaintance,* which contains one of his very happiest studies of a girl's character, the number is not lavishly increased. In *A Foregone Conclusion,* where the girl again is admirable, as well as the young Italian priest, also a kind of maidenly figure, the actors are but four. Today Mr. Howells doesn't count, and confers life with a generous and unerring hand. If the profusion of forms in which it presents itself to him is remarkable, this is perhaps partly because he had the good fortune of not approaching the novel until he had lived considerably, until his inclination for it had ripened. . . . The feeling of life is strong in all his tales, and any one of them has this rare (always rarer) and indispensable sign of a happy origin, that it is an impression at first hand. Mr. Howells is literary, on certain sides exquisitely so, though with a singular and not unamiable perversity he sometimes endeavors not to be; but his vision of the human scene is never a literary reminiscence, a reflection of books and pictures, of tradition and fashion and hearsay. I know of no English novelist of our hour whose work is so exclusively a matter of painting what he sees and who is so sure of what he sees. People are always wanting a writer of Mr. Howells's temperament to see certain things that he doesn't (that he doesn't sometimes even want to), but I must content myself with congratulating the author of *A Modern Instance* and *Silas Lapham* on the admirable quality of his vision. The American life which he for the most part depicts is certainly neither very rich nor very fair, but it is tremendously positive, and as his manner of presenting it is as little as possible conventional, the reader can have no doubt about it. This is an immense luxury; the ingenuous character of the witness (I can give it no higher praise) deepens the value of the report.

Mr. Howells has gone from one success to another, has taken possession of the field, and has become copious without detriment to his freshness. I need not enumerate his works in their order, for, both in America and in England (where it is a marked feature of the growing curiosity felt about American life that they are constantly referred to for information and verification), they have long been in everybody's hands. Quietly and steadily they have become better and better; one may like some of them more than others, but it is noticeable that from effort to effort the author has constantly enlarged his scope. His work is of a kind of which it is good that there should be much today—work of observation, of patient and definite notation. Neither in theory nor in practice is Mr. Howells a romancer; but the romancers can spare him; there will always be plenty of people to do their work. He has definite and downright convictions on the subject of the work that calls out to be done in opposition to theirs, and this fact is a source of much of the interest that he excites.

It is a singular circumstance that to know what one wishes to do should be, in the field of art, a rare distinction; but it is incontestable that, as one looks about in our English and American fiction, one does not perceive any very striking examples of a vivifying faith. There is no discussion of the great question of how best to write, no exchange of ideas, no vivacity nor variety of experiment. A vivifying faith Mr. Howells may distinctly be said to possess, and he conceals it so little as to afford every facility to those people who are anxious to prove that it is the wrong one. He is animated by a love of the common, the immediate, the familiar and vulgar elements of life, and holds that in proportion as we move into the rare and strange we become vague and arbitrary; that truth of representation, in a word, can be achieved only so long as it is in our power to test and measure it. He thinks scarcely anything too paltry to be interesting, that the small and the vulgar have been terribly neglected, and would rather see an exact account of a sentiment or a character he stumbles against every day than a brilliant evocation of a passion or a type he has never seen and does not even particularly believe in. He adores the real, the natural, the colloquial, the moderate, the optimistic, the domestic, and the democratic; looking askance at exceptions and perversities and superiorities, at surprising and incongruous phenomena in general. One must have seen a great deal before one concludes; the world is very large, and life is a mixture of many things; she by no means eschews the strange, and often risks combinations and effects that make one rub one's eyes. Nevertheless, Mr. Howell's standpoint is an excellent one for seeing a large part of the truth, and even if it were less advantageous, there would be a great deal to admire in the firmness with which he has planted himself. He hates a "story," and (this private feat is not impossible) has probably made up his mind very definitely as to what the pestilent thing consists of. In this respect he is more logical than Mr Émile Zola, who partakes of the same aversion, but has greater lapses as well as greater audacities. Mr. Howells hates an artificial fable and a *dénouement* that is pressed into the service; he likes things to occur as they occur in life, where the manner of a great many of them is not to occur at all. (He has observed that heroic emotion and brilliant opportunity are not particularly interwoven with our days, and indeed, in the way of omission, he *has* often practiced in his pages a very considerable boldness. It has not, however, made what we find there any less interesting and less human.)

The picture of American life on Mr. Howells's canvas is not of a dazzling brightness, and many readers have probably wondered why it is that (among a sensitive people) he has so successfully escaped the imputation of a want of patriotism. The manners he describes—the desolation of the whole social prospect in *A Modern Instance* is perhaps the strongest expression of those influences—are eminently of a nature to discourage the intending visitor, and yet the westward pilgrim continues to arrive, in spite of the Bartley Hubbards and the Laphams, and the terrible practices at the country hotel in *Doctor Breen,* and at the Boston boarding-house in *A Woman's Reason.* This tolerance of depressing revelations is explained partly, no doubt, by the fact that Mr. Howells's truthfulness imposes itself—the representation is so vivid that the reader accepts it as he accepts, in his own affairs, the mystery of fate—and partly by a very different consideration, which is simply that if many of his characters are disagreeable, almost all of them are extraordinarily good, and with a goodness which is a ground for national complacency. If American life is on the whole, as I make no doubt whatever, more innocent than that of any other country, nowhere is the fact more patent than in Mr. Howells's novels, which exhibit so constant a study of the actual and so small a perception of evil. His women, in particular, are of the best—except, indeed, in the sense of being the best to live with. Purity of life, fineness of conscience, benevolence of motive, decency of speech, good nature, kindness, charity, tolerance (though indeed, there is little but each other's manners for the people to tolerate), govern all the scene; the only immoralities are aberrations of thought, like that of Silas Lapham, or excesses of beer, like that of Bartley Hubbard. In the gallery of Mr. Howells's portraits there are none more living than the admirable, humorous images of those two ineffectual sinners. Lapham, in particular, is magnificent, understood down to the ground, inside and out—a creation which does Mr. Howells the highest honor. I do not say that the figure of his wife is as good as his own, only because I wish to say that it is as good as that of the minister's wife in the history of *Lemuel Barker,* which is unfolding itself from month to month at the moment I write. These two ladies are exhaustive renderings of the type of virtue that worries. But everything in *Silas Lapham* is superior—nothing more so than the whole picture of casual female youth and contemporaneous "engaging'' one's self, in the daughters of the proprietor of the mineral paint.

This production had struck me as the author's high-water mark, until I opened the monthly sheets of *Lemuel Barker,* in which the art of imparting a palpitating interest to common things and unheroic lives is pursued (or is destined, apparently, to be pursued) to an even higher point. The four (or is it eight?) repeated ''good-mornings'' between the liberated Lemuel and the shop-girl who has crudely been the cause of his being locked up by the police all night are a poem, an idyl, a trait of genius, and a compendium of American good nature. The whole episode is inimitable, and I know fellow novelists of Mr. Howells's who would have given their eyes to produce that interchange of salutations, which only an American reader, I think, can understand. Indeed, the only limitation, in general, to his extreme truthfulness is, I will not say his constant sense of the comedy of life, for that is irresistible, but the verbal drollery of many of his people. It is extreme and perpetual, but I fear the reader will find it a venial sin. Theodore Colville, in *Indian Summer,* is so irrepressibly and happily facetious as to make one wonder whether the author is not prompting him a little, and whether he could be quite so amusing without help from outside. This criticism, however, is the only one I find it urgent to make, and Mr. Howells doubtless will not suffer from my saying that, being a humorist himself, he is strong in the representation of humorists. There are other reflections that I might indulge in if I had more space. I should like, for instance, to allude in passing, for purposes of respectful remonstrance, to a phrase that he suffered the other day to fall from his pen (in a periodical, but not in a novel), to the effect that the style of a work of fiction is a thing that matters less and less all the while. Why less and less? It seems to me as great a mistake to say so as it would be to say that it matters more and more. It is difficult to see how it can matter either less or more. The style of a novel is a part of the execution of a work of art; the execution of a work of art is part of its very essence, and that, it seems to me, must have mattered in all ages in exactly the same degree, and be destined always to do so. I can conceive of no state of civilization in which it shall not be deemed important, though of course there are states in which executants are clumsy. I should also venture to express a certain regret that Mr. Howells (whose style, in practice, after all, as I have intimated, treats itself to felicities which his theory perhaps would condemn) should appear increasingly to hold composition too cheap—by which I mean, should neglect the effect that comes from alternation, distribution, relief. He has an increasing tendency to tell his story altogether in conversations, so that a critical reader sometimes wishes, not that the dialogue might be suppressed (it is too good for that), but that it might be distributed, interspaced with narrative and pictorial matter. The author forgets sometimes to paint, to evoke the conditions and appearances, to build in the subject. He is doubtless afraid of doing these things in excess, having seen in other hands what disastrous effects that error may have; but all the same I cannot help thinking that the divinest thing in a valid novel is the compendious, descriptive, pictorial touch, *à la Daudet.* (pp. 44-50)

> Henry James, *"William Dean Howells," in* Harper's Weekly, *Vol. XXX, No. 1539, June 19, 1886 (and reprinted in* Howells: A Century of Criticism, *edited by Kenneth E. Eble, Southern Methodist University Press, 1962, pp. 41-50).*

AMBROSE BIERCE   (essay date 1892)

The master of [the detestable realistic] school of literature is Mr. Howells. Absolutely destitute of that supreme and sufficient literary endowment, imagination, he does not what he would but what he can; takes notes with his eyes and ears, and writes them up as does any other reporter.

He can tell nothing that he has not seen or heard, and in his personal progress through rectangular streets and between trim hedges of Phillistia, with lettered old maids of his acquaintance courtseying from doorways, he has seen and heard nothing worth telling.

Yet, tell it he must, and, having told, defend.

For years this diligent insufferable has been conducting a department of criticism in *Harper's Magazine* with the sole purpose of expounding at the expense of his employers thought, theories, and principles which are the offspring of his own limitations.

> Ambrose Bierce, *"Sharp Criticism of Mr. Howells," in* The New York Times, *May 23, 1892, p. 5.*

BERNARD SHAW   (essay date 1895)

I have discovered, quite by accident, an amusing farcical comedy [**"The Garroters"**]. Somebody told me that there was a farce by Mr. W. D. Howells at the Avenue Theatre. I looked in the daily paper, but could find no mention of the name of Mr. Howells. However, it was evidently quite possible that the management had never heard of Mr. Howells, just as they had apparently never heard of me. So I went, and duly found the name "Howels" on the programme. The little piece showed, as might have been expected, that with three weeks practice the American novelist could write the heads off the poor bunglers to whom our managers generally appeal when they want a small bit of work to amuse the people who come at eight. But no doubt it is pleasanter to be a novelist, to have an intelligent circle of readers comfortably seated by their firesides or swinging sunnily in hammocks in their gardens, to be pleasantly diffuse, to play with your work, to be independent of time and space, than to conform to the stern conditions of the stage and fight with stupidity before and behind the curtain. (pp. 265-66)

> Bernard Shaw, *"Told You So" (originally published in* The Saturday Review, London, *Vol. 80, No. 2093, December 7, 1895), in his* Dramatic Opinions and Essays, with an Apology, *Vol. 1, Brentano's, 1907, pp. 258-66.*

HARRY THURSTON PECK   (essay date 1896)

Mr. Howells is so universally admitted to hold the primacy among living American men of letters as to make his appearance in a new field of effort an event of peculiar interest. That he should turn to poetry [in *Stops of Various Quills*] is particularly certain to excite both curiosity and comment, for in many ways his theory of art is one that finds its most natural exemplification in prose, eschewing as it does the ideal and holding fast to the obvious and the actual. These productions of his, therefore, conceived in poetical form, have an unexpectedness about them that will inevitably lead to their being read with a sensation not unmingled with surprise.

The first and strongest impression that one gets from the perusal of this volume is an impression of intense sadness. A profound melancholy pervades every one of the short poems that are here collected. There is scarcely a line that sounds the note of carelessness and joy; and when the major chord is struck, it only gives additional intensity to the minor that invariably succeeds. This melancholy, this pervasive sadness, one cannot quite call pessimism, for it does not spring from a pessimistic spirit. True pessimism is seldom dissociated from cynicism, and is by no means inconsistent with a tone of gaiety. The standpoint of the real pessimist is that which is indicated in the famous saying, "There's nothing good and there's nothing true, and it doesn't signify." Mr. Howells, too, holds apparently that there is nothing good and nothing true, but to him it signifies very much indeed. It wrings his heart and afflicts his whole being with a sense of pain and of disappointment. The lines in which his feeling finds expression describe the mind of one who has hoped much and met nothing but disillusion; of one whose nerves are overstrained, whose spirit is sickened, and whose very soul is sorrowful and despairing. Life is one great failure—a mystery whose veil is quite impenetrable, and which, if one could penetrate it, would doubtless show us only forms more fearful and anguish still more intense.

This mental attitude is one that the readers of Mr. Howells's later novels have come to recognise to some extent; it finds voice in the social discontent of *A Hazard of New Fortunes* and *The World of Chance;* and even in the half-humorous pages of *A Traveller from Altruria* this undercurrent of melancholy is perceptible; yet nowhere before is the impression so powerfully conveyed as in these scattered poems; for here there is no byplay, no mitigating humour, nothing to distract the attention of the reader from the dominant motive; and the very brevity and concentration of the thought drive its full meaning home to the consciousness. (p. 525)

[In one poem] Mr. Howells gives his whole view of life—a hurried, meaningless rout, amid which man is a bewildered guest, one who was not asked to come, who has never seen his host or had from him a word of welcome; but who, as he stands gazing on the foolish scene about him, hears from time to time a ghastly shriek as some one is hurried away to be seen no more. Each page bears witness to a like emotion, an emotion almost of disgust at the cross-purposes and senseless folly of all that men see and hope and do. The *Weltschmerz,* the *taedium vitae,* casts a grey light over every line.

It is all very strong writing. As literature it ranks very high. Does it rank equally high as poetry? Let those who can claim to speak with some degree of authority give an answer to this question. For our part, we do not think that these impressions of life gain much from the metrical form in which they appear. Without it, published as short prose impressions, like some of Mr. Hamlin Garland's, they would, we think, be equally effective; for their excellence from a literary point of view depends wholly upon their possession of the qualities that are peculiarly conspicuous in all of Mr. Howells's work. A marvellously keen eye for detail, a strong grasp upon the characteristic features of what he wishes us to see, an unerring instinct in language, and an exquisite sense of word-values—all these are present in his verse, but yet no more so than in his prose. (p. 526)

Nor is the structure of the verse wholly satisfactory, for it is too often at variance with the requirements of rhythmical consistency. One is tempted to attribute the frequency of this sca-

zonic movement to technical inexperience; but Mr. Howells is too thoroughly an artist to make this explanation tenable. It is likely that he purposely admits irregularities, as a musician admits dissonances, to heighten the effect of what is regular and metrically normal in the adjacent lines. Tennyson did this frequently, far too frequently, in fact, in his later verse, just as some of the Latin poets broke the inevitable monotony of their hexameters by playing tricks with the caesura. But Mr. Howells should have remembered that while this is allowable and even commendable in long stretches of verse, it is a positive defect in a poem of only a dozen or twenty lines, in reading which the ear does not have time to tire or to demand variety, but is far better pleased with perfection of melody and regularity of cadence. (pp. 526-27)

Harry Thurston Peck, "Mr. Howells As a Poet," in The Bookman, *New York, Vol. II, No. 6, February, 1896, pp. 525-27.*

WILLIAM DEAN HOWELLS (essay date 1903)

It was kind of you to include [Henry] James's early letters to yourself among those Miss Grace is sending me, and I won't pretend I have read them with less interest because of certain allusions to me in them. In a way I think their criticism very just; I have often thought my intellectual raiment was more than my intellectual body, and that I might finally be convicted, not of having nothing *on,* but of that worse nakedness of having nothing *in.* He speaks of me with my style, and such mean application as I was making of it, as seeming to him like a poor man with a diamond which he does not know what to do with; and mostly I suppose I *have* cut rather inferior window glass with it. But I am not sorry for having wrought in common, crude material so much; that is the right American stuff; and perhaps hereafter, when my din is done, if any one is curious to know what that noise was, it will be found to have proceeded from a small insect which was scraping about on the surface of our life and trying to get into its meaning for the sake of the other insects larger or smaller. That is, such has been my unconscious work; consciously, I was always, as I still am, trying to fashion a piece of literature out of the life next at hand. (pp. 172-73)

William Dean Howells, in his letter to Charles Eliot Norton on April 26, 1903, in his Life in Letters of William Dean Howells, Vol. II, *edited by Mildred Howells (copyright © 1928 by Doubleday, Doran & Company, Inc.; copyright renewed © 1955 by Mildred Howells; reprinted by permission of the Literary Estate of William Dean Howells), Doubleday, 1928, pp. 172-73.*

MARK TWAIN (essay date 1906)

Is it true that the sun of a man's mentality touches noon at forty and then begins to wane toward setting? . . . I can point him to a case which proves his rule. Proves it by being an exception to it. To this place I nominate Mr. Howells.

I read his *Venetian Life* about forty years ago. I compare it with his paper on Machiavelli in a late number of *Harper,* and I cannot find that his English has suffered any impairment. For forty years his English has been to me a continual delight and astonishment. In the sustained exhibition of certain great qualities—clearness, compression, verbal exactness, and unforced and seemingly unconscious felicity of phrasing—he is, in my belief, without his peer in the English-writing world. *Sustained.* I intrench myself behind that protecting word. There are others who exhibit those great qualities as greatly as does he, but only by intervaled distributions of rich moonlight, with stretches of veiled and dimmer landscape between; whereas Howells's moon sails cloudless skies all night and all the nights.

In the matter of verbal exactness Mr. Howells has no superior, I suppose. He seems to be almost always able to find that elusive and shifty grain of gold, the *right word*. . . . There is a plenty of acceptable literature which deals largely in approximations, but it may be likened to a fine landscape seen through the rain; the right word would dismiss the rain, then you would see it better. It doesn't rain when Howells is at work.

And where does he get the easy and effortless flow of his speech? and its cadenced and undulating rhythm? and its architectural felicities of construction, its graces of expression, its pemmican quality of compression, and all that? Born to him, no doubt. All in shining good order in the beginning, all extraordinary; and all just as shining, just as extraordinary to-day, after forty years of diligent wear and tear and use. He passed his fortieth year long and long ago; but I think his English of to-day—his perfect English, I wish to say—can throw down the glove before his English of that antique time and not be afraid.

I will go back to the paper on Machiavelli now, and ask the reader to examine [nearly any] passage from it. . . . (pp. 228-30)

You see how easy and flowing it is; how unvexed by ruggednesses, clumsinesses, broken meters; how simple and—so far as you or I can make out—unstudied; how clear, how limpid, how understandable, how unconfused by cross-currents, eddies, undertows; how seemingly unadorned, yet is all adornment, like the lily-of-the-valley; and how compressed, how compact, without a complacency-signal hung out anywhere to call attention to it. (p. 231)

When I go back from Howells old to Howells young I find him arranging and clustering English words well, but not any better than now. He is not more felicitous in concreting abstractions now than he was in translating, then, the visions of the eyes of flesh into words that reproduced their forms and colors. . . . (p. 233)

Mr. Howells's pictures [of Venice in *Venetian Life*] are not mere stiff, hard, accurate photographs; they are photographs with feeling in them, and sentiment, photographs taken in a dream, one might say.

As concerns his humor, I will not try to say anything, yet I would try, if I had the words that might approximately reach up to its high place. I do not think any one else can play with humorous fancies so gracefully and delicately and deliciously as he does, nor has so many to play with, nor can come so near making them look as if they were doing the playing themselves and he was not aware that they were at it. For they are unobtrusive, and quiet in their ways, and well conducted. His is a humor which flows softly all around about and over and through the mesh of the page, pervasive, refreshing, healthgiving, and makes no more show and no more noise than does the circulation of the blood.

There is another thing which is contentingly noticeable in Mr. Howells's books. That is his "stage direction"—those artifices which authors employ to throw a kind of human naturalness around a scene and a conversation, and help the reader to see the one and get at meanings in the other which might not be perceived if intrusted unexplained to the bare words of the talk. Some authors overdo the stage directions, they elaborate them quite beyond necessity; they spend so much time and take up so much room in telling us how a person said a thing and how he looked and acted when he said it that we get tired and vexed and wish he hadn't said it at all. (pp. 235-36)

But I am friendly to Mr. Howells's stage directions; more friendly to them than to any one else's, I think. They are done with a competent and discriminating art, and are faithful to the requirements of a stage direction's proper and lawful office, which is to inform. Sometimes they convey a scene and its conditions so well that I believe I could see the scene and get the spirit and meaning of the accompanying dialogue if some one would read merely the stage directions to me and leave out the talk. (p. 237)

Mr. Howells has done much work, and the spirit of it is as beautiful as the make of it. I have held him in admiration and affection so many years that I know by the number of those years that he is old now; but his heart isn't, nor his pen; and years do not count. Let him have plenty of them: there is profit in them for us. (p. 239)

Mark Twain, "William Dean Howells," in Harper's Monthly Magazine, *Vol. CXIII, No. DCLXXIV, July, 1906 (and reprinted in his* What Is Man? and Other Essays, *Harper & Brothers Publishers, 1917, pp. 228-39).*

H. L. MENCKEN   (essay date 1917)

Americans, obsessed by the problem of conduct, usually judge their authors, not as artists, but as citizens, Christians, men. Edgar Allan Poe, I daresay, will never live down the fact that he was a periodical drunkard, and died in an alcoholic ward. . . . As for William Dean Howells, he gains rather than loses by this confusion of values, for . . . he is almost the national ideal: an urbane and highly respectable old gentleman, a sitter on committees, an intimate of professors and the prophets of movements, a worthy vouched for by both the *Atlantic Monthly* and Alexander Harvey, a placid conformist. The result is his general acceptance as a member of the literary peerage, and of the rank of earl at least. For twenty years past his successive books have not been criticized, nor even adequately reviewed; they have been merely fawned over; the lady critics of the newspapers would no more question them than they would question Lincoln's Gettysburg speech, or Paul Elmer More, or their own virginity. The dean of American letters in point of years, and in point of published quantity, and in point of public prominence and influence, he has been gradually enveloped in a web of superstitious reverence, and it grates harshly to hear his actual achievement discussed in cold blood.

Nevertheless, all this merited respect for an industrious and inoffensive man is bound, soon or late, to yield to a critical examination of the artist within, and that examination, I fear, will have its bitter moments for those who naïvely accept the Howells legend. It will show, without doubt, a first-rate journeyman, a contriver of pretty things, a clever stylist—but it will also show a long row of uninspired and hollow books, with no more ideas in them than so many volumes of the *Ladies' Home Journal,* and no more deep and contagious feeling than so many reports of autopsies, and no more glow and gusto than so many tables of bond prices. The profound dread and agony of life, the surge of passion and aspiration, the grand crash and glitter of things, the tragedy that runs eternally under the surface—all this the critic of the future will seek in vain in Dr. Howells' elegant and shallow volumes. And seeking it in vain, he will probably dismiss all of them together with fewer words than he gives to "Huckleberry Finn." . . .

Already, indeed, the Howells legend tends to become a mere legend, and empty of all genuine significance. Who actually reads the Howells novels? Who even remembers their names? **"The Minister's Charge," "An Imperative Duty," "The Un-expected Guests," "Out of the Question," "No Love Lost"**—these titles are already as meaningless as a roll of Sumerian kings. Perhaps **"The Rise of Silas Lapham"** survives—but go read it if you would tumble downstairs. The truth about Howells is that he really has nothing to say, for all the charm he gets into saying it. His psychology is superficial, amateurish, often nonsensical; his irony is scarcely more than a polite facetious-ness; his characters simply refuse to live. No figure even re-motely comparable to Norris' McTeague or Dreiser's Frank Cowperwood is to be encountered in his novels. He is quite unequal to any such evocation of the race-spirit, of the essential conflict of forces among us, of the peculiar drift and color of American life. The world he moves in is suburban, caged, flabby. He could no more have written the last chapters of "Lord Jim" than he could have written the Book of Mark.

The vacuity of his method is well revealed by one of the books of his old age, **"The Leatherwood God."** Its composition, we are told, spread over many years; its genesis was in the days of his full maturity. An examination of it shows nothing but a suave piling up of words, a vast accumulation of nothings. The central character, one Dylks, is a backwoods evangelist who acquires a belief in his own buncombe, and ends by an-nouncing that he is God. The job before the author was ob-viously that of tracing the psychological steps whereby this mountebank proceeds to that conclusion; the fact, indeed, is recognized in the canned review, which says that the book is "a study of American religious psychology." But an inspection of the text shows that no such study is really in it. Dr. Howells does not *show* how Dylks came to believe himself God; he merely *says* that he did so. The whole discussion of the process, indeed, is confined to two pages—172 and 173—and is quite infantile in its inadequacy. Nor do we get anything approaching a revealing look into the heads of the other converts—the sal-eratus-sodden, hell-crazy, half-witted Methodists and Baptists of a remote Ohio settlement of seventy or eighty years ago. All we have is the casual statement that they are converted, and begin to offer Dylks their howls of devotion. And when, in the end, they go back to their original bosh, dethroning Dylks overnight and restoring the gaseous vertebrate of Calvin and Wesley—when this contrary process is recorded, it is ac-companied by no more illumination. In brief, the story is not a "study" at all, whether psychological or otherwise, but sim-ply an anecdote, and without either point or interest. Its virtues are all negative ones: it is short, it keeps on the track, it deals with a religious maniac and yet contrives to offer no offense to other religious maniacs. But on the positive side it merely skims the skin.

So in all of the other Howells novels that I know. Somehow, he seems blissfully ignorant that life is a serious business, and full of mystery; it is a sort of college town *Weltanschauung* that one finds in him; he is an Agnes Repplier in pantaloons. In one of the later stores, **"New Leaf Mills,"** he makes a

faltering gesture of recognition. Here, so to speak, one gets at least a sniff of the universal mystery; Howells seems about to grow profound at last. But the sniff is only a sniff. The tragedy, at the end, peters out. Compare the story to E. W. Howe's "The Story of a Country Town," which Howells himself has intelligently praised, and you will get some measure of his own failure. . . . Such a book leaves scars; one is not quite the same after reading it. But it would be difficult to point to a Howells book that produces any such effect. If he actually tries, like Conrad, "to make you hear, to make you feel—before all, to make you *see*," then he fails almost completely. One often suspects, indeed, that he doesn't really feel or see himself. . . .

As a critic he belongs to a higher level, if only because of his eager curiosity, his gusto in novelty. His praise of Howe I have mentioned. He dealt valiant licks for other débutantes: Frank Norris, Edith Wharton and William Vaughn Moody among them. He brought forward the Russians diligently and persua-sively, albeit they left no mark upon his own manner. In his ingratiating way, back in the seventies and eighties, he made war upon the prevailing sentimentalities. But his history as a critic is full of errors and omissions. One finds him loosing a fanfare for W. B. Trites, the Philadelphia Zola, and praising Frank A. Munsey—and one finds him leaving the discovery of all the Shaws, George Moores, Dreisers, Synges, Gal-sworthys, Phillipses and George Ades to the Pollards, Meltzers and Hunekers. Busy in the sideshows, he didn't see the ele-phants go by. . . . Here temperamental defects handicapped him. Turn to his **"My Mark Twain"** and you will see what I mean. The Mark that is exhibited in this book is a Mark whose Himalayan outlines are discerned but hazily through a pink fog of Howells. There is a moral note in the tale—an obvious effort to palliate, to touch up, to excuse. The poor fellow, of course, was charming, and there was talent in him, but what a weakness he had for thinking aloud—and such shocking thoughts! What oaths in his speech! What awful cigars he smoked! How bar-barous his contempt for the strict sonata form! It seems in-credible, indeed, that two men so unlike should have found common denominators for a friendship lasting forty-four years. The one derived from Rabelais, Chaucer, the Elizabethans and Benvenuto—buccaneers of the literary high seas, loud laugh-ers, law-breakers, giants of a lordlier day; the other came down from Jane Austen, Washington Irving and Hannah More. The one wrote English as Michelangelo hacked marble, broadly, brutally, magnificently; the other was a maker of pretty waxen groups. The one was utterly unconscious of the way he achieved his staggering effects; the other was the most toilsome, fastid-ious and self-conscious of craftsmen. . . .

What remains of Howells is his style. He invented a new harmony of "the old, old words." He destroyed the stately periods of the Poe tradition, and erected upon the ruins a com-plex and savory carelessness, full of naïvetés that were so-phisticated to the last degree. He loosened the tightness of English, and let a blast of Elizabethan air into it. He achieved, for all his triviality, for all his narrowness of vision, a pungent and admirable style. . . .

H. L. Mencken, "The Dean" (originally published in The Smart Set, *Vol. LII, No. 2, June, 1917; copy-right 1919 by Alfred A. Knopf, Inc., renewed 1947 by H. L. Mencken; reprinted by permission of the publisher), in his* A Mencken Chrestomathy, *edited by H. L. Mencken, Knopf, 1949.*

WILLIAM LYON PHELPS (essay date 1924)

The literary career of Mr. Howells covered exactly sixty years, his first book appearing in 1860. . . . Despite the enormous quantity of his production, his composition shows no evidence of haste. He seemed to write evenly and tranquilly, with a style accurately fitted to the subject. (p. 156)

It is as a novelist that Howells will be remembered. He set up a department-store of literature, where the visitor could buy anything from a song to a sermon; but much of the stock remains on the shelves. I have never met anybody who could quote a line of his poetry; and his essays in literary criticism are perishable freight. His criticism is valuable for the revelation of his own temperament, for its shrewd observations on life in general, for its delicate humour; but he never had the truly critical mind. He seemed to me to betray this fact—quite unconsciously, of course—in one of the conversations it was my privilege to have with him. "I am tempted to make a resolution never to write another word of literary criticism. When I write any critical judgment, it seems to me to be wholly, definitely true; I cannot for the life of me see how anybody else can hold a different opinion. Then some days or months later, I experience a disagreeable shock; for I discover that some other person contradicts everything I have said." He spoke these words with no trace of humour, no mock dismay; they were uttered seriously, with charming candour. I confess I was amazed. No matter how strong one's convictions may be or how tenaciously held, it seems to me that the first requisite of criticism should be the ability to understand how a person of at least equal intelligence and probity should support precisely opposite opinions with equal ardour. (pp. 160-61)

Mr. Howells's belief in realism amounted almost to a religion. He felt that art, like human intercourse, should be founded on literal truth. To him all romanticists were liars. (p. 161)

Mr. Howells simply showed the door to romanticists; whereas a realistic work, although it violated his habit of reserve, was greeted with enthusiasm. His public reception of *Jude the Obscure* was almost obstreperous in its heartiness; yet I believe he would have died rather than have written such a book.

Although the novels of Mr. Howells are for the most part rigorously objective, one cannot fail to obtain through them some notion of their author's temperament and character. (p. 163)

For many years he was looked up to as the first of our living writers of fiction, and he had more effect on the tone, quality, and tendencies of American novels than any other person. From the earliest story of Mary Wilkins to the latest tale by Zona Gale, Mr. Howells is somewhere in evidence. His two great rivals, Mark Twain and Henry James, could not possibly throw the breadth of literary influence extended by him; for Mark Twain had the uniqueness that sometimes, though not always, accompanies genius, and Henry James, unfortunately for the world, has never been read except by a few. His influence is deep rather than wide; it is seen in individuals.

Many rebellions were organised against the domination of Mr. Howells; but they sputtered out. One reason for their futility was the fact that those who tried to break the chains of what they called his tyranny were themselves conspicuously feeble; for, quarrel with his reticences and his superficialities as we may, from the very start he possessed the secret of style. He seems always to have known how to write—a fundamental thing in literary art, though contemporary poets and novelists may not all think so.

Even his chronicles of very small beer—*Annie Kilburn* for example—are exquisitely done. It is easy apparently for his adverse critics to make the mistake of identifying his creations with himself—of supposing, because he deliberately chose to write of commonplace characters and trivial incidents, that therefore he himself was trivial and commonplace. But it was quite otherwise. His hatred of melodrama and sentimentality made him select those aspects of life which are samples, where people of average intelligence, average character, average income, pass through average experiences. He was a skilful player without any trumps. What would some of our successful shockers do with the cards he drew from the pack?

He chose to portray real life as he knew it by observation and experience. He was a Realist by instinct and by training. . . . [The] two things in the world he hated most were falsehood and affectation. The word *Snob* made him see red. (pp. 165-67)

It was, I think, merely his love of truth that made him write stories where every page could be verified, and made him unsympathetic to books of romance. He was right in despising many of the pseudo-historical romances with which America was flooded during the last decade of the last century; he lumped all these together as "romantic rot," and I have seen him laugh till the tears came while quoting specimens of their anachronistic oaths and bogus jargon. (pp. 167-68)

Although he was twenty-three when his volume of poems was published, his first novel did not appear until he had reached the age of thirty-four. During the intervening eleven years he was storing observations and impressions of Italy and Europe, and by constant practice had obtained a command of the art of writing English prose, proved in four separate publications, dealing with foreign travel and suburban sketches at home. His first novel and the two that shortly followed it were satisfying evidence that a new master of the art of fiction had appeared in America. These three books, *Their Wedding Journey, A Chance Acquaintance, A Foregone Conclusion,* exhibit a variety of qualities that unite in a general effect of charm. Real characters, steadily if slowly advancing narrative, brilliant dialogue, salted with genuine humour—these are the invariable features of Mr. Howells's early stories. (pp. 170-71)

I cannot help thinking that . . . [early] journalistic work on [an] Ohio newspaper affected [Mr. Howells's] art in no small degree. It made him observant rather than introspective, a chronicler rather than an analyser of life. He never lost zest for minute observation; nothing characteristically human seemed dull or unimportant. His eye was microscopic, and when he turned it on what some call commonplace events or commonplace people, they swarmed with exciting activities, as any tiny bit of life does under a microscope. "We had no idea it was so interesting!"

The novels of his first decade—the 'seventies—reached a climax in *The Lady of the Aroostook*. . . . I remember the delight with which I read this new book. To those who have forgotten it I can still heartily recommend taking the voyage to Europe with Lydia, and seeing Italy with her clear, virginal vision. The contrast between her rural home in New England and her Italian environment makes for a pure type of high comedy. Mr. Howells is one of that small minority who can see fellow countrymen and women travelling about Europe, without hating them. I do not know why it should be so; but men of all nations who have been "abroad" seem to find their fellow citizens in foreign scenes unendurable. (pp. 172-73)

Unquestionably, the best part of his career was the decade between 1880 and 1890, for, although he was to write steadily for thirty years after the close of this period, he never, with one exception, came near the heights again. As has happened so frequently with other creative artists, he produced in rapid succession works that constitute his surest claim on the future. He was in the vein, and must have known it. In a short space of time, he published *A Modern Instance, The Rise of Silas Lapham, Indian Summer,* and *A Hazard of New Fortunes*—books too familiar to need any particular comment here, except to remark that the first two of the quartette are perhaps the most purely American of all his productions; *Indian Summer* reveals the charm of the city of Florence so poignantly that it makes one homesick for the Arno; *A Hazard of New Fortunes* exhibits that dawning interest in sociological problems, which, together with the influence of Tolstoi, was to affect his work not wholly beneficially for the rest of his life. Although *The Rise of Silas Lapham* is almost universally regarded as his masterpiece, I think it inferior to *A Modern Instance*—the most tragic, the most powerful, the most deep-rooted of all his novels.

In 1890 appeared a delightful bit of autobiography, called *A Boy's Town*. . . . Then for thirty years came a steady succession of novels, plays, works of criticism, autobiographical writings, none of which is without value, but all—with one exception—making no real addition to his fame. (pp. 174-75)

The exception is the novel called *The Kentons*. . . . As I am afraid that this book is not nearly so widely read as it deserves to be, and as I am certain that nine out of ten readers will share my enthusiasm for it, I wish to say emphatically that it is one of the finest works of fiction Mr. Howells ever composed; it reveals all the qualities that made his reputation in the 'eighties, mellowed and sweetened by age. . . . Every character in this story is a triumph of creation; they are so real that they leave the reader in a glow of enthusiastic recognition. (pp. 175-76)

> *William Lyon Phelps, "Howells," in his* Howells, James, Bryant and Other Essays *(reprinted by permission of the Literary Estate of William Lyon Phelps), The Macmillan Company, 1924, pp. 156-80.*

OSCAR W. FIRKINS (essay date 1924)

The style of Mr. Howells may be roughly sketched in three periods. (p. 311)

[The first, exemplified by the style of **"Their Wedding Journey,"**] has a gleaming, a lustrous, clearness; the freshness of youth exhales in its always unshackled, though never unguided, motion; it maintains a high decorum never stiffening into propriety. Its serene and high art is evident chiefly in the flawless sculpture of the sentences in which clause answers to clause with the sureness of brow to nose or arm to trunk in statue of the Phidian era.

Even at this period, when the style is robing itself in beauty and magic, the delicacy is not absolute. Here is a slight asperity: "They hailed the first car that passed, and got into it." It would have been easy to avoid the prickles in the last phrase by saying "and mounted the steps"; perhaps Mr. Howells preferred an obvious defect to a facile correction. Whether the fault be voluntary or not, it remains true that the sentences are not uniformly or meticulously patterned; and that distinction is not evenly distributed like a stucco. (p. 312)

[The mid-period is also marked by] admirable writing. If the youthful coloring is a little dimmed, the youthful figure is intact. The contours are firmer, not less fine; the main difference is the rise of a new element into parity with form, an element which an Elizabethan would have curtly called wit and a modern Frenchman, I suppose, might still call *esprit,* but for the denotement of which the modern "wit" is too narrow and the English "spirit" too ambiguous. Let us make shift with the word "point," meaning by that a stimulation which may appear in half a dozen forms, of which humor, simile, contrast, parallelism, allusion, may be offered as examples. Styles of this type are wont to be a little noisy and strutting; the crackle accompanies the flash. In Mr. Howells, as in Mrs. Wharton and in Anatole France, the flash is noiseless. Imagine a feat performed with the ease and quietness of a gesture, and you have a perfect image of this medial phase of the style of Mr. Howells. By a curious paradox, taste, measure, and tranquillity are the saliencies in this author's work; the brilliancy seems an afterthought or adjunct.

To be just, however, to the range of Mr. Howells's manner, I must quote [the following] passage, which I select from **"The Minister's Charge."** . . . (p. 313)

> At last the wagon came to a place that he saw was a market. There were no buyers yet, but men were flitting round under the long arcades of the market-houses, with lanterns under their arms, among boxes and barrels of melons, apples, potatoes, onions, beans, carrots, and other vegetables, which the country carts as they arrived continually unloaded. The smell of peaches and cantaloupes filled the air, and made Lemuel giddy as he stood and looked at the abundance. The men were not saying much; now and then one of them priced something, the owner pretended to figure on it, and then they fell into a playful scuffle, but all silently. A black cat lay luxuriously asleep on the canvas top of a barrel of melons, and the man who priced the melons asked if the owner would throw the cat in. There was a butcher's cart laden with carcasses of sheep, and one of the men asked the butcher if he called that stuff mutton. "No: imitation," said the butcher. They all seemed to be very goodnatured. Lemuel thought he would ask for an apple, but he could not.

This reveals progress on another line. The object is here clearly to throw up or relieve the fact; point is shut out, and style is, so to speak, in hiding. Nevertheless, the exercise of choice in the matter is patent to a receptive ear, and form or contour in the sentences is screened rather than slighted. The black-cat sentence is an outstanding exemplar of perfect finish in absolute simplicity. Elegant and subtle writer as Mr. Howells was, we must never forget that his hold on realities was powerful, and that this power was predestined to mark his style.

There is another point in Mr. Howells's narrative which has attracted the elect in the measure in which it has repelled the untutored. To him, as to most disciplined minds, the time-order in its nudity or crudity is a little wearisome, and he allays its harshness by the constant introduction of relations of contrast or resemblance or causation. To effect this end, he sometimes obscures, sometimes very slightly inverts or displaces, the order of particulars in time. This substitution of finer for cruder relations is an inspiration and refreshment to the trained mind; but the untrained mind, for which the bare time-order is imperative and sacrosanct, rejects brusquely this encroachment on its rights. A sentence or two may exemplify the point.

> The mill property had been a long time abandoned before Libby's father bought it, and put it in a repair which he did not hasten to extend to the village. This had remained in a sort of picturesque neglect, which harmonized with the scenery of the wild little valley in which it nestled.

Now the facts in their plain order are simply these: Libby's father bought a mill property in a village in a wild little valley, repaired the property, and neglected the village. But Mr. Howells wishes to suggest two subtler relations, the contrast between property and village, and the resemblance between village and valley; and, to attain this end, he has postponed the normally antecedent fact about the wildness of the valley to a point where its affinities would be seasonable. (pp. 313-15)

[The reader] will perceive that, while clearness and vigor still persist, the form of [his later] style has disintegrated.

If the reader will tolerate a classification that does no justice to the delicacy and diversity of the phenomena, we may tabulate the three periods as follows:

In the first period, we have form with incipient point; in the second, form and point both eminent; in the third, point with decadent form. . . .

[In] his increasing acquaintance with life and Tolstoi—two powers that were almost bi-cameral in the constitution of his universe—he came more and more to depreciate style in the traditional sense, and to advocate an uncompromising and undeviating directness and honesty of expression. There are philosophers in our day, called the new realists, who believe that the thought of an object in the human mind may be hardly more than an extension or spur of the object itself. Mr. Howells believed that by absolute straightforwardness and disinterestedness on a writer's part an object might be virtually lifted, transported as it were, from the field of reality to the reader's mind. The writer's function corresponds to that of the central operator in the telephone office, who has merely to establish a circuit and to avoid interference.

There was a time in Mr. Howells's career when it seemed as if the effect of these ideas upon his own practice was to be the advent of a new, sound, and forcible method. . . . ["**The Kentons**"] seems to me to illustrate the possibility of a felicitous compromise between his earlier ideal and his later theory. It pleases me rather less than his second manner, but I think it almost unrivalled in its suppression of what I may call the author's *brokerage,* in the sense it conveys that the thought is shaped by its own life and moved by its own energy. It is not the *author's* manner, but the *thought's*. (p. 316)

For a parallel in the essay form to this narrative method in which the story becomes in a sort in the novelist, the studious reader may turn to the first paper in "**Literature and Life**." But Mr. Howells did not pursue this manner with consistency. He fell into other ways; he neglected form; he declined in impact; he sometimes, I fear, became a prey to that carelessness which lies in wait to betray the preacher of spontaneity. The later group of travels exhibit the dissolution of form and the thinning-out of substance; they rely on feeling and point, and the charm of the feeling and the point is evinced in the fact

that the books do not pine, and sometimes actually thrive, on this limited and insecure nourishment.

In these later travels Mr. Howells has a pretty habit of figuring his younger self in quaint proximity and dramatic contrast with the older self who handles the pen. I cannot help wondering what that younger self who wrote "**Venetian Life**" would have said to the author of this sentence in "**Roman Holidays**": "I recall a brother in a cutaway coat, and a daughter in a tieback, embraced in their grief and turning their faces away from their mother toward the spectator; and doubtless there were others whom to describe in their dress would render as grotesque." (p. 317)

This is mere laxity, the line of least resistance. Now in Mr. Howells the line of least resistance is not simplicity, as it might be in a cruder man, but a formless complexity; when he is heedless, he becomes involved. He falls into what I have called the snowball sentence, the loosely accumulative aggregate, which, in the uncertainty of its route, appears to invite suggestions from any idea or object or phrase upon which it stumbles in the meanderings of its course. (p. 318)

Let it be clearly understood that here the theory of intellectual decay is quite untenable. The vigor of the thought is intact, the scintillations have not paled; the faculty of style is still dominant in sentences of Phidian profile, or even in whole papers like "**The Counsel of Literary Age.**" The loss, then, is voluntary. Whether the trouble-saving impulse has affected that volition I do not know. The wish to spare one's self is a dissembling motive, and may have cloaked itself in the form of a homage to truth, especially in a case where that homage was very strong and undoubtedly sincere. In other points one searches in vain for an abatement of watchfulness or energy.

A modest parallel may be drawn between the fortunes of the two elements of art and style in Mr. Howells. At their meridian both were exquisite, but to some extent both suffered—the art more continuously and lightly, the style more gravely and more narrowly—from realism or the kindred cult of spontaneity. I think the circumstance unfortunate. The passion for form is ineradicable, and the fewer the depredations that the pursuit of truth can make on things which the race cherishes so earnestly as art and style, the better not only for art and style, but for the pursuit of truth likewise. The greater part of Mr. Howells's work seems to lend salutary and vigorous support to the idea that the differences between realism and art, between sincerity and style, are not irrepressible conflicts but adjustable and curable misunderstandings; I am sorry that another part should lend a semblance of color to the adverse conclusion. It pains me to see him throw his style overboard; I cannot willingly see him "scatter all his spices on the stream, enrobe the roaring waters with his silks." (p. 319)

Style is a perishable commodity, and the high-bred, high-strung styles seem especially subject to reactions of distrust or recoils of satiety on the part of their versatile practitioners. Such men feel sometimes, no doubt, that mastery in these lines is another name for thraldom; they dread to be subject, or abject, to style. In this matter the analogy between Mr. Howells and Mr. James is interestingly close. In the work of both men the impression of literature is transcendent; both had what Lowell would have called *costly* styles; in both, the composition was distinguished by a delicate exactness of contour and a fine, not to say proud, reserve of tone. In the later life of both, this perfection of form and fineness of reserve underwent a marked disintegration, though both processes were carried to burlesque excess by Mr.

James, who apparently lost his head and "broke the good meeting with most admired disorder." (pp. 319-20)

One further observation must be made. The style of Mr. Howells, in its ripe and unflawed excellence, is no trick, no separable accomplishment, no masterpiece of naked virtuosity. The style has a preëxistence in the psychology, is in essence the ingress of that psychology into language. The peculiarity of the writing might be defined as a rare ease and quietness in the setting forth of delicately intricate relations. But this trait merely images, merely registers, the lasting condition of its author's mind. The impartial and almost universal curiosity of Mr. Howells made it natural that, in his perception of one object, he should become vividly conscious of all its kinsfolk and neighbors; and his eye for relation enabled him to traverse instantly and readily the manifold threads of connection which fastened it to the surrounding world. Since he was adept in all the leanings or inflections of a thing, his options in expression were numerous, and, in this spaciousness of choice, it was easy for him to solve the recurrent problem of style, to discover the doubly apt phrase which at once fills up the measure of the thought and integrates the contours of the sentence. I transcribe a few lines: "It was not a question of Dryfoos's physical presence: that was rather effective than otherwise, and carried a suggestion of moneyed indifference to convention in the grey business suit of provincial cut, and the low wide-brimmed hat of flexible black felt." Now the average novelist's spontaneous perceptions would stop short at the grey suit and the felt hat and their unmistakable relation to Mr. Dryfoos, and the lack of alternatives would force him into a directness of expression which would no doubt further his prospects with the average man. But a man who, without search, could relate that suit and hat to a moneyed indifference to convention could have related them without trouble to a half a dozen other things, and, among these various approaches to the thought, some one approach will probably signalize itself by the fitness of the correlative phrase to dignify and harmonize the sentence. This is artifice only in the sense that, being the final choice among several routes, it has not the inevitableness which belongs to the choiceless acceptance of one. It has its basis, its complement, in a state of mind, the state of mind of a man who sees each object as the point of intersection for many highways, and who utilizes this variety of approach and departure to indulge his predilection for rhythm and symmetry in the fashion of his English. (pp. 320-21)

> *Oscar W. Firkins, in his* William Dean Howells: A Study *(copyright © 1924 by the President and Fellows of Harvard College; copyright renewed © 1952 by Frances Firkins and Orra Estelle Firkins; excerpted by permission), Cambridge, Mass.: Harvard University Press, 1924, 356 p.*

SINCLAIR LEWIS (essay date 1930)

With a wealth of creative talent in America, our criticism has most of it been a chill and insignificant activity pursued by jealous spinsters, ex-baseball-reporters, and acid professors. Our Erasmuses have been village schoolmistresses. How should there be any standards when there has been no one capable of setting them up? (p. 14)

It was with the emergence of William Dean Howells that we first began to have something like a [national literary] standards, and a very bad standard it was.

Mr. Howells was one of the gentlest, sweetest, and most honest of men, but he had the code of a pious old maid whose greatest delight was to have tea at the vicarage. He abhorred not only profanity and obscenity but all of what H. G. Wells has called "the jolly coarseness of life." In his fantastic vision of life, which he innocently conceived to be realistic, farmers and seamen and factory-hands might exist, but the farmer must never be covered with muck, the seaman must never roll out bawdy chanteys, the factory-hand must be thankful to his good employer, and all of them must long for the opportunity to visit Florence and smile gently at the quaintness of the beggars.

So strongly did Howells feel this genteel, this New Humanistic philosophy that he was able vastly to influence his contemporaries, down even to 1914 and the turmoil of the Great War.

He was actually able to tame Mark Twain, perhaps the greatest of our writers, and to put that fiery old savage into an intellectual frock coat and top hat. His influence is not altogether gone today. (pp. 14-15)

> *Sinclair Lewis, "The American Fear in Literature" (originally his Nobel Prize address, 1930), in his* The Man from Main Street: Selected Essays and Other Writings, 1904-1950, *edited by Harry E. Maule and Melville H. Cane (copyright © 1953 by the Estate of Sinclair Lewis; reprinted by permission of Random House, Inc.), Random House, 1953, pp. 3-17.**

LUDWIG LEWISOHN (essay date 1932)

[The] age of Howells and James, the years roughly from 1970 to the turn of the century, was the age of gentility. Both novelists had, more or less, to render the society in which they lived. And that society was the most ill-mannered that has probably ever existed. It was so disgustingly "pure" because it was so violently sex-conscious. It was so afraid of vulgarity because it was so immitigably vulgar. I may adduce, without delay, two characteristic and amusing instances. The new house that Howells' Silas Lapham was building on the Back Bay had not progressed much beyond the shell. Lapham and his daughters climb about the new structure on ladders. Young Tom Corey comes to join them and Lapham expounds the rising structure. "This is my girls' room," he said. "It seemed terribly intimate"; Howells adds, "Irene blushed deeply and turned her head away." These people evidently couldn't even think of a young woman's future room without an immediate image of sexual activity. The taboo was so strong because the thing tabooed filled their inner vision. (p. 238)

Of the quality of this situation and of the blight thrown by it upon manners and society, upon life and letters Howells seems to have been wholly unaware. James . . . was not. But Howells yielded without so much as an inner protest to Boston and this pusillanimity of his is the worm that may hollow out the otherwise extraordinarily fine structure of his best work. There is in his treatment of the major human emotions a shocking and contemptible moderation; there is in his attitude to marriage, above all, an unbearable stuffiness and creeping prose which, being so obviously characteristic of his age, makes one wonder that the Feminist revolt in America was not even more violent and acute. The superstition prevails among the unthinking that Howells and the genteel age took a high view of marriage. The contrary is true. The view taken of marriage was revolting to every generous instinct; it relegated married people, however young, to a situation that smelled of ill-aired clothes-presses and kitchen soap; . . . it consented drily to the elimination between people once safely married of gallantry, delight, even of courtesy and delicacy; it shoved them into the limbo of nothing but cooking-stoves and diapers with a quiet but relentless sadism. In so early a work as **"A Chance Acquaintance"** Howells writes: "Of his wife's wardrobe he had the ignorance of a good husband, who, as soon as the pang of paying for her dresses is past, forgets whatever she has." In this unsmiling sentence is the genteel age's view of the most important of human relations. It threw, to be sure, a sop to the sex it still called fair. "If my wife," says the young journalist in **"The Rise of Silas Lapham,"** "wasn't good enough to keep both of us straight, I don't know what would become of me." This moral influence of women was a sincere part of the period's creed; on the same page of **"Silas Lapham"** Howells observes that "of the vast majority of married Americans, a few underrate their wives, but the rest think them supernal in intelligence and capability." There is no mention of charm or of any amenity. Wives, poor things, had to be contented with capability. The result was that they, as a natural compensation, drove their capability hard and the total image of married life to be derived from the delineations of Howells is that of men grossly henpecked by women who were stripped on principle of any of the attractions that alone can make female tyranny endurable. A rational man may happily endure the exactions of a delightful woman. But the women of the genteel age stood in evil odor if they did not cease being delightful—the exclusive right of the *jeune fille*—the moment they left the minister's house. We find, then, that with but one or two exceptions the married people of Howells are elderly in attitude if not in fact, and that this elderliness is accepted as the characteristic virtue of the married state. Thus bride and groom in **"A Modern Instance"** are described as briefly parting "with an embrace that would have fortified older married people for a year's separation" and in so late a work as **"The Kentons"** Mr. Kenton is described as in that state of "subjection to his wife's judgment which befalls and doubtless becomes a man after many years of marriage." But this was not all. Even of those superlatively innocent relations which in his stories lead to marriage Howells' opinion was low. "The whole business of love and love-making and marrying is painted by the novelists in a monstrous disproportion to the other relations of life. Love is very sweet, very pretty. . . ." Thus speaks the otherwise neither foolish nor unmanly clergyman in **"The Rise of Silas Lapham."** And this view Howells shared or honestly thought he shared, declaring in **"Criticism and Fiction"** that grief, avarice, pity, ambition, hate, envy, devotion, friendship have all a greater part in life "than the passion of love." On his principle that the sovereign virtue of art was truth to reality, he was forced of course, in view of the inhibitions of his time and his personal practice, to take precisely this attitude. It is needless to insist on the crushing handicap imposed upon himself at the outset by a creative artist who regards as trivial the instinct which, as psychology has demonstrated and the great artists have always known, is implicated not only with our biological functioning but in infinite ramifications with our higher nerve-centers and is thus a central element of every human activity from the humblest to the most exalted. That Howells, with this handicap, comes off upon the whole as respectably as he does, is a very high tribute to his native gifts. (pp. 239-41)

Ludwig Lewisohn, "The Rise of the Novel," in his Expression in America *(copyright © 1932 by Harper & Brothers; copyright renewed © 1955 by Louise Lewisohn; reprinted by permission of the grandchildren of Ludwig Lewisohn), Harper & Brothers, Publishers, 1932, pp. 233-72.**

GRANVILLE HICKS   (essay date 1935)

[If, during the Gilded Age,] politics had little attraction as a literary theme, industry attracted even fewer authors. Despite the romantic rapidity with which the great financiers and industrialists had risen to wealth and power, despite the extent to which their achievements shaped the ambitions of millions of Americans, the sixties and seventies slipped by, and no novelist had chosen to make a serious study of that amazing national phenomenon, the multimillionaire. Not until 1885 was there an author courageous enough to make the attempt, and even he shrank from the implications of his task. It is useless to criticize William Dean Howells for not making *The Rise of Silas Lapham* a different sort of book; he was limited by his experience, his interests, and the literary standards of his day. And yet, when one considers his desire to treat realistically the representative phenomena of his own civilization, and when one remembers how constantly present to his mind the exploits of the moneymasters must have been, his book is only less astonishing, as a revelation of the confusions and blindnesses of an obviously intelligent man, than Henry Adams' *Democracy.*

Silas Lapham, as everyone will remember, had made his fortune by exploiting a paint mine that his father had discovered before the war. (p. 74)

The chief problem that occupies Lapham at the outset of the story is the establishment of social relations that will make his daughters happy, and the author's major interest seems to be in showing the situation that arises from the impact of a person of humble origins and slight education upon a polished, complacent, and firmly rooted society. Many of the great money barons did, of course, seek social rank, but they seem to have met no such obstacles as Howells throws in the way of the well-meaning Lapham. (p. 76)

The climax of the story, one recalls, comes with Lapham's great decision: twice he is tempted to sacrifice personal integrity in order to keep his fortune, once when he has the opportunity to sell a worthless mill, again when an alliance with his principal rivals is possible if he conceals his financial status. Both times he is firm, and he ends with honor, if in poverty. Such a dilemma, so far as one can see, never disturbed for a moment even the more restrained generals of industry. The climactic decisions of their lives related to concrete problems of manufacture, transportation, and finance. (pp. 76-7)

It is ironic, but by no means surprising, that the first novel of post-war industry should have as its central character a business man who, in methods, outlook, and ideals, belonged to the generation before the war. Although in the early years of the industrial revolution the Laphams had flourished, creating small fortunes by the relatively honest conduct of a single enterprise, they could play but an inconsiderable part in the new era of amalgamation and large-scale exploitation. Lapham belonged to the past, and so, as a matter of fact, did the grandeurs of the Boston society that he viewed with awe. Equally remote, though that was less apparent at the time, was the romantic dilemma of the Lapham girls and Tom Corey, which Howells placed, in the construction of the novel, on the same level as Lapham's great decision. Yet *The Rise of Silas Lapham* was considered too bold and too searching by many of its readers, and Howells almost boastingly counted the cost of his "frankness about our civilization." (pp. 77-8)

[*The Rise of Silas Lapham*] is a fair sample of its author's work. Whatever else may be said of William Dean Howells, he was the one writer of the period who was convinced that "every inch of this America is interesting," and who acted on that conviction. Regardless of his limitations, it is only fair to observe that he wrote about more aspects and more important aspects of life in the United States than either his contemporaries or his predecessors. Cooper had written of Indians and sailors; Hawthorne had been at home only in a world of his own imagining; Melville had explored the Pacific. Howells refused to be so limited: he wrote of East and West, of villages and metropolises; he wrote of farmers and business men, journalists and doctors, Bohemian artists and Back Bay aristocrats.

In the novels of rural life in New England Howells shows himself almost as shrewd as the best of the regionalists and far less likely to deal with the purely idyllic. As a study of the New England character nothing could be better than the last chapter of *The Lady of the Aroostook*. Both *Annie Kilburn* and *A Traveler from Altruria* portray the trouble-breeding impact of summer visitors on the life of a small village. The effect of the city on the kind of character the country has formed is the theme of *A Modern Instance* and *The Minister's Charge*. Two of Howells' most impressive characters are village radicals and eccentrics—Squire Gaylord in *A Modern Instance* and Ralph Putney in *Annie Kilburn* and *The Quality of Mercy*.

In the city, especially Boston, Howells is even more at home. As one reads his books, noting the recurrence of certain characters in novel after novel, one appreciates his understanding of the kind of society that city produced in the days of its decline. There are played-out aristocrats such as Corey and Bellingham, substantial men of affairs such as Hilary and Halleck, eccentric and impractical reformers such as Miss Vane, . . . and unscrupulous reporters such as Hubbard and Pinney. Howells sees their virtues and limitations, the Bostonian bias in their way of thinking, their relation to the compact society of which they are part, and in the novels and parts of novels that deal with Boston he is not far from creating a convincing world.

New York, as Howells quickly realized, was not so easy to master as Boston, but he made a brave effort "to use some of its vast, gay, shapeless life" in his fiction. *The World of Chance* and *The Coast of Bohemia* limit themselves to the lives of publishers and artists, but *A Hazard of New Fortunes* aims at nothing less than a portrayal of the city's magnificent variety. Howells' choice of Basil March, one of his favorite Bostonians, as central character, is wise: nothing in the book is better than the chapters in which the Marches simply wander about the city, noting its buildings and its people. But these stanch Bostonians, it is made quite clear, are not the only persons who have been attracted to the metropolis, and we find in the novel the middle-western millionaire Dryfooses, the upstate Leightons, and the almost professionally southern Colonel Woodburn and his wife and daughter. The characters happen to be linked together by their common interest in a magazine, *Every Other Week,* but they are representative of thousands of New Englanders, Westerners, and Southerners, caught in the whirlpool of commercialism, and the various attitudes they take towards the spirit of business enterprise are representative attitudes: Fulkerson is its prophet; Conrad Dryfoos is its victim; March tries to be its detached critic; Lindau, immigrant and socialist, is its bitter enemy; Colonel Woodburn is a survivor of the

system it has destroyed. No other American novel of the nineteenth century, except possibly *The Gilded Age,* can be compared in its scope with *A Hazard of New Fortunes.*

Howells knew what he was doing. When, in 1879, Henry James pointed out that America had "no sovereign, no court, no aristocracy, no church, no clergy . . . no country gentlemen, no palaces, no castles nor manors," and patiently asked what was left that the novelist could deal with, Howells replied, "We have the whole of human life remaining, and a social structure presenting the only fresh and novel opportunities left to fiction." These are words there should have been someone to say, someone who voiced not a youthful nationalism but a serious esthetic conviction. And, as his career was to show, Howells had a right to say those words if anyone did. He devoted his life to showing that America was rich in materials for the artist, not merely picturesque fragments out of the colorful past of the frontier, but great movements, dramatic characters, vivid situations.

Yet it is impossible to maintain that Howells made the most out of these materials, that he did for America what Tolstoy did for Russia or Zola for France. Whenever one reads a novel by Howells, one feels, as has already been observed in connection with *The Rise of Silas Lapham,* that he has not quite forced his way through to the center of the situation he has chosen to deal with. One feels, so to speak, that he is either asking the wrong questions or giving the wrong answers. In *The Quality of Mercy,* for example, he is asking whether a defaulter should repent, not why a business man is false to the trust that has been placed in him. In *Annie Kilburn* he wonders how the rich can help the poor, not how rich and poor happen to be in their relative stations. On the other hand, *Dr. Breen's Practice,* raising the question of women in medicine, confuses the answer by ending the book on a sentimental note. Similarly, *A Modern Instance,* which is concerned with divorce, fails to state the problem in its most representative terms, and, by turning Bartley Hubbard from a likable poseur to a contemptible rascal, distracts attention from the major issue.

Silas Lapham, one is further forced to admit, is also representative of Howells' work in that, though the material is typically American, the emphasis falls on elements of experience that do not quite correspond to the major movements in the life of the nation. In *A Hazard of New Fortunes* the reader, feeling that something important is being neglected, becomes impatient with the amount of attention devoted to the progress of the magazine, the home life of the Woodburns, and the various love stories. In *Annie Kilburn* there is far too much about amateur theatricals and far too little about the conflict between Gerrish and Peck. And there are the many novels, such as *April Hopes, The Coast of Bohemia, The Story of a Play,* and *The Vacation of the Kelwyns,* that, though good enough in their way, never once suggest a valid reason for Howells' having chosen to write them. There is something ironic in his making so little use of the wealth of resources of which he boasted to Henry James. Indeed, much of the time, instead of exploiting those resources, he was content to pose the kind of problem that James was posing, to much better effect of course, in terms of the established society and traditional culture of Europe. (pp. 85-8)

It is, moreover, clear that Howells had not sufficiently mastered the civilization of which he was part to be able to deal incisively even with minor issues. In *A Hazard of New Fortunes* the characters are confronted with the commercial spirit, but, whether they go with it, are broken by it, or seek to remain aloof from it, they do not understand it. Neither did Howells, and it is no wonder that, as he said, the novel "seemed to flounder along on a way of its own." Emerson, Melville, and Whitman have been called seers; that is the last thing one would think of calling matter-of-fact, easy-going William Dean Howells.

In his aims Howells was the kind of novelist America needed, and our literature would in many respects be poorer if he had not lived; but it is his aims that are important. For them we can be grateful, and we cannot too harshly condemn the failure of his actual achievement since we can so easily explain it. On the one hand, his experience was limited to a degree that was fatal to his ambitions as a novelist of contemporary America, limited by the kind of life he led and also by a certain deliberate unwillingness to look about him. On the other hand, he was a product of his age and subject to the confusions of that age. For Howells to have done what he really wanted to do he would have had to transcend personal, moral, and intellectual limitations of a sort that, as a matter of fact, no one in the years of his prime could transcend. (pp. 88-9)

Yet we must not put too much of the responsibility for his faults on his seclusion and blindness; the nature of his approach to his material was also to blame. Howells called himself a realist, and within the rather narrow limits that have been indicated it was as a realist that he wrote. But the kind of realism that he believed in was inadequate for the task he had set himself, and behind that failure of method was a failure of understanding.

The type of novel Howells wrote is implicit in his two volumes about Italy, his first published work except for the Lincoln biography and the book of poems he wrote with J. J. Piatt. The success of *Venetian Life* and *Italian Journeys,* in which he presented the fruit of his observations during his four years in Venice, led him to wonder if the same method could not be applied to material nearer home, and he wrote *Suburban Sketches,* which differs from the earlier books only in the fact that it is based on observations made in Cambridge. It was a short step thence to *Their Wedding Journey,* with sketches of a railroad station, a hot day in New York, a trip on the Hudson River, and the scenery at Niagara Falls, and with a thread of narrative on which the sketches hang. The same formula served for *A Chance Acquaintance, The Lady of the Aroostook,* and *A Fearful Responsibility*. Not until he wrote *Dr. Breen's Practice* was Howells ready to dispense with his descriptions of travel and to unite his characters in a dramatic situation. The brief sketch had developed into something like the novel, and the novel itself, in the form of *A Modern Instance,* was just around the corner.

Gradually Howells had developed a definite and almost unique type of novel. He had no theory at first, but in time the theory was formulated, and expressed in *Criticism and Fiction*. He scorned, of course, the improbable incidents of the romantic novel; he repudiated as well the grotesqueries and exaggerations of Dickens and the commentaries of Thackeray. Of his contemporaries he chiefly admired the Russians, for they knew how "to forbear the excess of analysis, to withhold the weakly recurring descriptive and caressing epithets, to let the characters suffice for themselves." But he made no attempt to reproduce the intensity of Dostoyevsky or the sweep of Tolstoy. He preferred a more modest, more placid kind of fiction, and it is by no means strange that, among English novelists, Jane Austen won his heartiest admiration. American conditions, he believed, invited "the artist to the study and appreciation of the common, and to the portrayal in every art of those finer and higher aspects which unite rather than sever humanity." "The talent that is robust enough," he wrote, "to front the every-day world and catch the charm of its work-worn, care-worn, brave, kindly face need not fear the encounter."

To front the every-day world was precisely what, all his life, Howells tried to do. From the Negro maid and the horse-car conductor in *Surburban Sketches* to Parthenope Brook and Alvin Kite in *The Vacation of the Kelwyns,* his characters are ordinary, if not always completely representative, Americans, faced with ordinary situations. They meet and marry, or they meet and separate. They write plays or preach sermons or manufacture paint. Howells was afraid of neither coincidence nor anticlimax. If a man and woman met and nothing came of their meeting, that was only what one could expect of life. If it was the merest accident that brought success to a struggling author, that was the sort of thing that happened in a world of chance. (pp. 93-4)

Such a conception of the novel was not likely, it is clear, to summon forth all Howells' powers; though it encouraged the growth of observation, it discouraged the exercise of the will and the imagination. . . . The realist, Howells said in *Criticism and Fiction,* "finds nothing insignificant; all tells for destiny and character; nothing that God has made is contemptible. He cannot look upon human life and declare this thing or that thing unworthy of notice any more than the scientist can declare a fact of the material world beneath the dignity of his inquiry. He feels in every nerve the equality of things and the unity of men; his soul is exalted, not by vain shows and shadows and ideals, but by realities in which alone the truth lives." But truth, neither for the artist nor for the scientist, is merely a matter of observation. Just as the scientist must seek relationships, must find the bearing of one fact upon another in order to comprehend either, so the artist must perceive, in his examination of this event and that event, some hidden pattern.

Nevertheless, this theory of Howells' was, though he did not recognize it as such, a necessary compromise between the demands of literary integrity and the difficulties of his era. It was essential that he should cling to the importance of the isolated observation, since he could perceive no all-embracing pattern. His work had to be more or less dull, more or less trivial, more or less confused, if it was to be honest. Had he been aware of a fundamental unity in American life, had an adequate social philosophy helped him to see the significance of what he described, had he possessed what we sometimes call vision, observation would have fallen into its properly subordinate place. As it was, fidelity to fact was his one great virtue and within limits he made the most of it. (pp. 95-6)

His social views are fully recorded in two books that take their place with the scores of Utopian novels written in the decade before and the decade after 1900. *A Traveler from Altruria* is primarily a criticism of the organization of society in America, written from the point of view of a member of a perfect society. In *Through the Eye of the Needle* the Altrurian returns to his native land, taking with him an American wife, whose letters to a friend describe the customs of that pleasant country. Altruria, we learn, after passing through a competitive stage, abolished private property and substituted social equality. Each citizen is required to work three hours a day, which is sufficient to provide all with the necessities of life. The remainder of the day is the citizen's, to spend as he likes, and it is in this period of voluntary labor that the nation's many works of art are produced. The needs of the people are slight: food—a purely vegetarian diet prevails; shelter—the climate has been changed so that this is an inconsiderable problem; clothing—there is a graceful but unpretentious national costume. They are very religious, and there is a devout sense of the brotherhood of man.

Pretty as all this is, it has, one can see, very little to do with the realities of the American problem. Howells was, in the first place, concerned with ends rather than means, and, except for his insistence on the peacefulness of the change, he paid little attention to the methods by which such a society might be created. In the second place, he carefully eliminated the whole question of industrialism by assuming that the Altrurians were for the most part able to dispense with machinery and by neglecting to tell how such machinery as they had was made and operated. In the third place, he assumed that social stability depends on a spiritual attitude, to which objectors are converted, rather than on any concrete program of production and distribution.

There is only one point at which Howells was able to relate the life of Altruria to his own American experience: he repeatedly calls attention to the fact that there are no domestic servants in Altruria. This emphasis reminds one of the extent to which he discusses the relations between servants and masters in his novels. Suddenly one realizes why this question so constantly concerns him: it is one social problem that actually touched his own life. And there is Howells—a kindly man, disturbed by the humiliations of butlers and maids, grieved by such sufferings as he might see on the street, depressed by obvious cases of the miscarriage of justice. It was all very unpleasant, but what could he do? . . . He could not, after these long years of isolation, lead a political party or throw in his lot with the labor movement. He could not even—and this is the tragedy—free himself enough from the habits and prejudices of his upbringing and his manner of life to see the problem clearly.

Howells' socialism was at best the vague reaction of a well-intentioned, sensitive man to the contemporary spectacle of misery and greed. . . . We owe a dozen of his best books to the fact that, as he wrote Stedman in 1888, the economic phases of American life had become increasingly important to him. But that interest did not lead to an understanding of economic forces. That is why Howells could not strike to the center of American life; that is why the issues in his books are never clear; that is why the persons and events he describes always seem to be not quite perfectly realized. That is why *The Rise of Silas Lapham* is not truly a novel of American industrialism, why *A Hazard of New Fortunes* fails to give a satisfying picture of New York in the eighties, why *A Traveler from Altruria* is only one more Utopian novel. That is, in short, the principal explanation of Howells' inability to make us feel that here is a master.

Limited by his way of living and his views on morality, confused in his thinking and condemned by that confusion to work with superficial phenomena, Howells was grievously handicapped in his attempt to make an enduring record of the life of his country and his time. Yet he tried, and it is to his credit that he tried so persistently. On certain important questions he saw the truth and held to it. He saw that the primary concern of American authors must be American life, and he practiced what he preached. He saw that the basis of fiction must be honest observation and a passion for truth. He had no fear of the commonplace, and it required merely courageous unconventionality to make his type of realism a useful instrument for the recording, if not for the interpreting, of the American

scene. He was not too narrow-minded to praise Zola, and he did much to popularize Turgenev, Dostoyevsky, and Tolstoy in the United States. . . . Wrong as he was on many issues, weak as he was at many points, he was, through the seventies, eighties and nineties, a force that impelled American literature, however hesitatingly, however feebly, in what history has shown to be the right direction. (pp. 97-9)

Granville Hicks, "The Battlefield: William Dean Howells," in his The Great Tradition: An Interpretation of American Literature since the Civil War *(copyright © 1933, 1935 by Macmillan Publishing Co., Inc.; originally published in 1933 by The Macmillan Company, New York; new material in the revised edition copyright © 1969 by Granville Hicks; reprinted by permission of Russell & Volkening, Inc., as agent for the author), revised edition, Macmillan, 1935, Quadrangle Books, 1969, pp. 84-99.*

ALFRED KAZIN   (essay date 1942)

[Early] in December of 1891, William Dean Howells surprised his friends and himself by taking over the editorship of the failing *Cosmopolitan* in New York. . . . Six months later Howells suddenly resigned. The experience had proved an unhappy one. It was the climax to a series of publishing ventures and experiments through which he had passed ever since he had left the *Atlantic Monthly* in 1881 and taken the literary center of the country with him, as people said, from Boston to New York. (pp. 3-4)

A great change had come over Howells. The eighteen-eighties, difficult enough years for Americans learning to live in the tumultuous new world of industrial capitalism, had come upon Howells as a series of personal and social disasters. The genial, sunny, conventional writer who had always taken such delight in the cheerful and commonplace life of the American middle class now found himself rootless in spirit at the height of his career. . . . Now, despite his winning sweetness and famous patience, the capacity for good in himself which had always encouraged him to see good everywhere, his tender conscience and instinctive sympathy for humanity pricked him into an uncomfortably sharp awareness of the gigantic new forces remaking American life. (pp. 5-6)

[In] his social novels of the eighties and nineties—*A Hazard of New Fortunes, Annie Kilburn, The World of Chance, The Quality of Mercy, A Traveler from Altruria, Through the Eye of the Needle*—Howells was delineating the new America of industrial capitalism with a felicity, a precision of intention, and a power of emotional suggestion that some of his more robust disciples could not match. He too had staked his career on realism, and if his countrymen looking upon him in his disturbed middle age had but known it, Howells had fought for realism all the more bravely, since the objects of its interest required a new education. He had come to realism on the strength of the very morality that was to constrict his application of it, since it was a morality founded on a simple belief in a simple justice. He had been drawn to it slowly and reluctantly, shedding his lifelong prejudices and his characteristic disposition to please, alienating many of his old friends; but he had come to it because his conscience and his tender regard for humanity were the very springs of his talent. He had experienced the transformation of American life after the Civil War almost as a personal disaster, and his novels now became the record of that experience.

It was entirely in keeping with the quality of Howells's mind and the very nature of his career that these autumnal novels should not be his best. He was not even to hold to this rebellious mood very long, yet how painful it was for his sunny optimistic nature to acclimate itself to a proletariat and class struggles, to street-car strikes and discussions of Socialism, the pompous banker faces and even more pompous banker prejudices that now entered his novels! For some of these works he reached back into the novels he had written in his forties, for with his feeling for the vast cousinship of American village life Howells liked to use a few favorite characters in novel after novel. He had always thought of American middle-class folk as one family, and forgotten uncles and cousins and aunts and happy young couples grown middle-aged and tired now gathered in his books as at a funeral—the funeral of the romantic and facile promise of the American dream. Yet many of his characters were startling figures. The acquiescent *Atlantic* editor whose social views up to Haymarket had been those of his good friend John Hay, his good friend Lowell, his good friend and coeditor Aldrich, the Wall Street poet-financier Edmund Stedman—the very best gentility of the Gilded Age—now introduced German Marxists and Tolstoyan Communists, speculative intellectuals and hungry radicals who argued out the imperfections of the human race amidst the clamor of New York elevated trains. And with them appeared oil millionaires and hard-fisted village entrepreneurs, workingmen on strike and scabs, commercial-minded unscrupulous journalists, and idealistic young men who thought it degrading to participate in business and finance. The archetypal Silas Lapham, a good fellow despite his crudity, now belonged to another order; the humorous, placid old merchants who had personified the values of another day now yielded to speculators and defaulters and the vulgar new rich. . . . And on the piazza of summer hotels, that favorite mise en scène where Howells had once delighted to have young couples meet romantically, he now staged the most devastating scenes of his Utopian satire, *A Traveler from Altruria.*

Howells in these years called himself a Socialist, but he had no social program to espouse, no will toward Socialism; even in his most unhappy moments he could speak with wonted facility of a vague new beneficence that would somehow take care of everything in the end. The characters in these late novels did not revolt against the established order; *they testified against it.* One idealist went mad, a few fled, others compromised—as Howells himself later compromised; but their personal determination to understand the new forces in economic and social life never transcended the dictum of old David Hughes in *The World of Chance:* "The way to have the golden age is to elect it by Australian ballot." Indeed, they rarely spoke of the golden age; and with the exception of Peck, the tragic minister in *Annie Kilburn* who renounced the church to work among the laborers in the cotton mills, they did not even act upon their convictions. They were witnesses to spiritual disorder, observers of social change; their function was to act as a Greek chorus and to furnish the spare but haunting commentary that gave these novels their purpose and texture.

What interested Howells at this period was the education of men of goodwill—the slow and painful growth of a few sensitive minds in the face of materialism and inequality. He went on spinning plots with his gentle, even skill, pulling people together mechanically, staging dinner parties and symposia for no better purpose than to have people talk; but within this fog of discursive amiability and New England twang, people lived "in an age of seeming preparation for indefinite war." It was the element of conscious sensibility that gave these novels their spare, incisive drama. Unlike most of his fellow realists, who described the ravages of the new industrial-technological order in terms of mere victimization—usually their own—Howells presented his stories as parables and quiet homilies. He brooded over his characters as his characters brooded over society, and to the same purpose; for like Tolstoy, he considered it his function to mediate between moral men and immoral society. Each character in these novels now had his representative place in that society, each his characteristic criticism or apology; when they talked together, they represented a whole society in meditation. This stratification of character became so necessary to Howells that in 1894 he even rejected formal realism to write his first Utopia, *A Traveler from Altruria,* a morality play in which Banker Bullion, Novelist Twelvemough, the Altrurian Mr. Homos, the Society Woman, the Professor, the Minister, the Worker, vie with each other in dialectic. The professor mumbles heartless platitudes on "the law of supply and demand," the minister asks naïvely why there are no workers in his congregation, the socialite reminisces on her trivial pleasures, and the Utopian—who acts as a catalyst—asks his half-sorrowful, half-mocking questions.

Like his friend Henry James, Howells now felt a need of a foreground observer, a central intelligence in all these novels. His observers, significantly enough, were usually natives who had returned from a long journey abroad, or had been away in more primitive regions, and who now returned to learn that a new world had destroyed or absorbed the one they had known. Like the heroine of *Annie Kilburn,* who returned from a long sojourn in Rome to discover that Hatboro', Massachusetts, was not the pleasant sleepy New England village she had left, they were dismayed and frightened. (pp. 38-41)

So in *The World of Chance* old David Hughes returns from a Utopian community with his almost maniacally sensitive son-in-law, Anselm Denton, to try desperately to struggle against the commercialism around them. In revolt against a materialism to which no sensitive conscience can appeal, Denton destroys a new tool he has invented because it may lose a few workers their jobs, and hopes to expiate the sins of his greed-laden generation by committing suicide. A ridiculous and pathetic figure? Even Howells may have thought so, but he understood Denton. For the values of an earlier day, the values of Brook Farm, Emerson, and Thoreau, could still press themselves upon the Christian mind with new pertinence against a world that had passed them by. Surely someone had to say to the whole capitalist-financial order what Thoreau had said to the imperialists of the Mexican War: *Non serviam? . . .*

Even the obligations of traditional morality, Howells now felt, no longer possessed their sanctioned force in such a society. Capitalism was a world of chance whose motive power was the rule of the jungle. In an unsuccessful but curiously haunting novel of this period, *The Quality of Mercy,* Howells wrote a devastating indictment of hypocritical morality. Northwick, a commonplace but inordinately greedy businessman of little education, embezzles his company's funds and runs off to Canada. The village is thrown into feverish excitement, but the son of the industrialist whom Northwich has defrauded sneers at Gerrish and the vigilante spirit he has aroused. "I don't know that [justice] isn't any more repulsive than the apparatus of commerce, or business, as we call it," says Matt Hilary. "Some dirt seems to get on everybody's bread by the time he's earned it, or his money even when he's made it in large sums as our class do." (p. 42)

With bitter irony Howells went on to point out that Northwick's real victims, the workers in his mills, had no feeling against him—they were "too tired." The town bourgeoisie, led by the ineffable Gerrish, had refused to suspect Northwick until the facts were made public, and then characteristically sought to evict his daughters from their home. Howells's great moment in this novel, however, came when he portrayed Northwick in flight. Here was the characteristic product of a whole society and its traditional devotion to business; yet when Northwick lay sick and alone in his Quebec refuge, his only occupation was to watch over the money he had stolen. Music, books, conversation, even the obvious attractions of a new land, meant nothing to him; he had, like the businessman Henry Fuller described in *The Cliff-Dwellers*, "never lived for anything but business . . . never eaten and drunk for anything but business . . . never built for anything but business . . . never dreamed for anything but business . . . wrote about nothing but business," and his reward was bleak sterility in exile. It was an amazing presagement of one of the great episodes in American realism: the flight and decline of Hurstwood in Dreiser's *Sister Carrie*.

Howells arrived at the full expression of his social views only in his Utopias. (p. 43)

In the thirteen years of life that remained to him after the publication of *Through the Eye of the Needle* [Howells] mellowed into what was, for him, a normal acquiescence. As the rebellions and desperations of the farmers were channeled into the middle-class reform spirit of the Progressive period and the imperialist complacency after the Spanish-American War, Howells, so long the faithful reporter of his countrymen, went with them. The realistic movement had got beyond him, and his ingrained prudishness came to the fore again. (p. 44)

He had never enjoyed the "crucial" novel, the anxiety and the polemics that had attended the campaign for realism. In a generation of realists each of whom was in some fashion a realist *malgré lui*, he was a monumental example of the antiquated nineteenth-century conscience upon whom a new order of society had placed an intolerable burden. He had certainly never meant by realism what his young friends Frank Norris and Stephen Crane had, within the short space of their lives, already shown it to mean. . . . [At] most realism had been for Howells only a method of inquiry and an acknowledgment of the spiritual realities that bound men—particularly Americans—together. . . . He had in his own person—reluctantly, yet with deep and unconscious ardor—united the world of Emerson and the world of Zola; he had riveted his education into the language. Who, indeed, had done as much as he to unify the traditions of American literature? He was more than an Elder Statesman of letters; he had been the greatest single force in the literature of his epoch. Had he read it, he would have enjoyed John Macy's quip, "for years Howells was the Dean of American letters, and there was no one else on the faculty." It was true. He was one of the solitary—if minor—architects of the American imagination. (p. 46)

Alfred Kazin, *"The Opening Struggle for Realism,"* in his On Native Grounds: An Interpretation of Modern American Prose Literature *(copyright 1942, 1970 by Alfred Kazin; reprinted by permission of Harcourt Brace Jovanovich, Inc.), Reynal & Hitchcock, 1942, pp. 3-50.*

LOUIS J. BUDD (essay date 1952)

Much of the modern disappointment with William Dean Howells' work grows from a failure to understand his aims. This misunderstanding arises partly because his literary rationale was far from being as systematic and uncompromising as has often been assumed; close study of the entire body of his critical essays and reviews shows that he did not reject all fiction which departed from a circumstantial fidelity to life. In essence, Howells felt that authenticity concerning human character was the touchstone of great art and that problems of method were secondary. Although he condemned most non-realistic fiction as untrue and therefore finally vicious morally, he was willing to allow imaginative play in that writing which did no harm or which, better still, aimed at faithfulness to the inner verity of existence. Howells, like Hawthorne and many other eighteenth- and nineteenth-century writers, distinguished between the realistic novel and the prose "romance," and he of course generally preferred to write the realistic novel. But, instead of being "unsympathetic to books of romance" or harboring a "suspicion of all romantic tendencies including his own," he also accepted the romance as an estimable genre of fiction.

The self-educated Howells, lacking formal training, did not always employ terms with academic precision, and he never struggled long and reflectively to codify his esthetic principles. Nevertheless, he did separate the prose romance from the novel at an early stage in his career. In 1873 he wrote of Victor Cherbuliez' *La Revanche de Joseph Noirel*, "The book is a romance, not a novel, and it would not be right to judge it by the strict rules of probability applicable to the novel . . . ". Very shortly before his own triumph as a practicing realist with *A Modern Instance*, Howells chided Henry James: "No one better than Mr. James knows the radical difference between a romance and a novel, but he speaks now of Hawthorne's novels, and now of his romances, throughout, as if the terms were convertible; whereas the romance and the novel are as distinct as the poem and the novel." This dichotomy, with its allowance to the romance of an inner liberty above realistic detail so long as artistic congruity was achieved, was never abandoned by Howells, and although traditionally seen as the first native realist, he often praised the prose romance and even on occasion adopted its technique in his own creative works. (pp. 32-3)

Howells showed a somewhat divided approval of writing which departed from constant attention to the real and the commonplace. At times he thought of non-realistic fiction such as the "fantastic romance—the romance that descends from Frankenstein" as merely one of the "graceful things that amuse the passing hour." Or he somewhat apologetically declared: "I will not altogether refuse the pleasure offered me by the poetic romancer or the historical romancer because I find my pleasure chiefly in Tolstoy and Valdés and Thomas Hardy and Tourguenief at his best." As Howells restated his position, "What I object to is the romantic thing which asks to be accepted with all its fantasticality on the ground of reality; that seems to me hopelessly bad." In other words, while Howells spurned as morally confusing most unrealistic fiction like the historical tales of F. Marion Crawford, he could enjoy the avowedly light historical romance or the casual "psychological romance" which dealt superficially with the perennial subject of love and marriage. Finally, he also granted that even the fantastic romance could at times "convey a valuable truth"; Robert Louis Stevenson's *The Strange Case of Dr. Jekyll and Mr. Hyde*, for example, performed a valuable service by showing vividly that "if we indulge the evil in us it outruns the good."

Much more important, however, was Howells' admiration for that prose fiction which, without claiming to capture the fidelity to everyday experience which he valued, attempted to distill and analyze inner human experience, to study with poetic liberty and insight the mental drama, and to allegorize the laws of man's psychological or moral make-up. As a result, he was able to admire Henry James's tale, "A Passionate Pilgrim," a serio-comic and improbable account of an American's ill-fated idealization of his British ancestry. James was praised for achieving the "finer air of the romance" in "A Passionate Pilgrim," and the critic contended that "you gladly accede to all the romantic conditions, for the sake of otherwise unattainable effects." (pp. 33-4)

Howells' unflagging admiration of the prose romance can be best exemplified and also partially explained by his deep and lasting respect for the art of Hawthorne. . . . It is reasonably probable that Hawthorne's own usage of the word "romance," as in the preface to *The House of Seven Gables,* formed the main source upon which Howells patterned his own terminology, for Howells many times echoed Hawthorne's dictum which assigned to the novel "minute fidelity . . . to the probable and ordinary course of man's experience" while allowing for the romance "circumstances of the writer's own choosing or creation" for the purpose of exposing the "truth of the human heart."

Through Howells' comments about Hawthorne, the realist's attitude toward the serious prose romance which dealt with character types or allegorized the moral order emerges most clearly. . . . In brief, Howells granted that the inmost human truth—the goal of his own minute realism—could be found through other ways also. Accordingly, he could write, "I always liked Hawthorne because he seemed to me to be true, and to wish always to be so"; he felt that the "characters of Hawthorne speak and act for themselves, and from an authentic individuality," and therefore "Hawthorne's creations are *persons,* rounded, whole"; in *The Scarlet Letter* he sensed "strong truth beating with equal pulse from the core of the central reality." Although Howells himself aimed at capturing the outward air of the commonplace, the new elements in his working creed should not be allowed to obscure his wide tastes and the undogmatic nature of his conception of fictional realism. In the final summation, he valued the inner ethical verity of fiction more than surface method, and he ultimately defined realism in moral rather than technical terms.

Howells' ideal of fiction lay closer to Henry James's psychological realism than is adequately remembered. Hawthorne helped to teach Howells that the best subject for fiction was the subsurface drama, and helped to reinforce his disinclination toward the prominent use of adventurous incident, such as the awkward and uncharacteristic shipwreck and castaway episodes of *A Woman's Reason.* (pp. 36-7)

Of the multitude of forces whch impelled Howells toward literary realism Hawthorne made a specific and influential one, and Howells stands forth as a writer who combined the ethical seriousness of such differing nineteenth-century novelists as Hawthorne and Eliot with a forward-looking attention to greater dramatic impact for the truth of the human heart through realistic atmosphere and detail. All great fiction is, of course, serious in intention and somewhat dramatic in presentation, but, insofar as the two concepts can be genuinely separated, one can perceive that he mediated between the nineteenth-century emphasis upon meaning or content and the twentieth-century emphasis upon form or technique. (p. 38)

To be correct, Howells' acceptance of the romance must not obscure his criticism of romantic fiction for the "specious

mixture of good and bad" which served to "confound the conscience by the spectacle of noble rascality or virtuous rascality." Too, he castigated the new flood of historical romances at the turn of the twentieth century which struck the popular fancy only "to flatter it with the false dreams of splendor in the past . . . to corrupt it to an ignominious discontent with patience and humility, and everyday duty, and peace." Believing as he did that fiction was an influential guide for morality, Howells regarded as harmful the adventurous or Graustarkian romance which carelessly glossed over ethical considerations or even gilded questionable conduct with the trappings of daring or glamor, as some irresponsible historical novels have done and continue to do today. So concerned was he with artistic fidelity and moral honesty that he feared that even the most serious prose romance might be vitiated by shutting itself off from the minute observation and portrayal of the caprices, vacillations, and mutabilities of actual life, tending to allegorize its characters beyond the realm of individuality and credibility. (p. 41)

When we see that [Howells] opposed solely that fiction which misstated the sum of human experience and that he valued imaginative writing which, without striving to reproduce realistic detail, truly reflected humanity, we see that his realism aimed at fidelity to inner character and emotional conflict; he fully accepted that vein of romanticism which studied the nature and destiny of the individual. His was not basically a critical or pessimistic realism which hoped to cross-section all life, the unsmiling and weeping aspects included, and we can better understand why the socialistic Howells, who wished to belittle capitalistic society, did not create a true precursor of *The Jungle* or *The Grapes of Wrath* but instead, after an attempt at using a wider canvas in *A Hazard of New Fortunes,* could turn for further protest to his two utopian romances. (p. 42)

Louis J. Budd, "W. D. Howells' Defense of the Romance," in PMLA, 67, *Vol. LXVII, No. 2, March, 1952, pp. 32-42.*

EDWIN H. CADY   (essay date 1956)

In the light of the eighty years of literary and cultural history since, it requires an act of the historical imagination to see why [*The Rise of Silas Lapham*] should have stirred up so much fuss in its time. In larger scale than any of Howells' previous novels, with the same intense moral and cultural penetration as *A Modern Instance* and with much of the technical virtuosity of *Indian Summer,* it is an excellent and important work of fiction. . . . [But its] fine evocation of time and place has ceased to have relevance except as social history; and, as is usual with Howells, it takes the mature effort of a good reader to grasp the depths of the novel.

On the surface of *The Rise of Silas Lapham* things seem rather tame. The main plot concerns an up-country farm boy come to Boston as an incipient millionaire from his devoted exploitation of a paint mine on the ancestral farm. In the struggle between his conscience and the immoral requirements of competitive success in the business world of the Gilded Age (the novel's time is 1874), Silas at first succumbs to the strong romanticism of the Business Mind and devours a partner. Ultimately, however, he is able to fight and suffer triumphantly against a series of temptations to save his wealth and business by still shoddier practices. In restoring his conscience he loses his million—and this is the (moral) rise of Silas Lapham, Horatio Alger upside down.

The subplot, yet another variation on the conventional-unconventional conflict, shows Howell's lover's quarrel with Boston-Under-the-Scalpel again. The energetic son of an otherwise decadent Brahmin-Proper Boston family, Tom Corey, comes to work for Lapham. This introduces him to Penelope and Irene Lapham, Silas' daughters, and he falls in love with Penelope. This, in turn, introduces the families, bringing the New Man, the Business Man and his wife, into polite conflict with the Bostonians, and giving new dimensions to the familiar conflict. . . . Since Irene is blonde and pretty and Penelope dark and bookish, the Laphams make the unBostonian assumption that Tom has come courting the blonde rather than the brain, and this provides Howells with another go at a romanticism he had already hammered in *Indian Summer*—the sentimental feminine quixotism of self-sacrifice.

The Rise of Silas Lapham was a big and a controversial book because it spoke directly to the condition of its time. In creating the first important literary projection of the American business man, his mind and his morality, Howells provided symbols of the greatest importance for minds seeking to grasp the new culture. His picture challenged the comfortable optimisms of the Gospel of Wealth and of Social Darwinism—which made it the more important. While unsettling readers with its challenge to the new, however, the book also made its contribution to the advance of the newness. Its author was openly out to demolish what he regarded as the false emotions and outworn clichés of the obsolescent and irrelevant romanticistic past. (pp. 230-32)

[Nothing] about Howells seems to have stirred up quite as much dust in his own time as his effort to shatter the "chivalric" fiction of woman's helpless nobility and set women free to become simple, equal participants in modern culture. (p. 232)

[In *The Rise of Silas Lapham* he] studied the marriages of the Laphams and of the Coreys carefully, drawing out in each case the strengths and weaknesses of the wives to show what contribution they made to Silas' fall and rise. Even more carefully he worked over the courtship to reveal the tangle of love, egotism, feminine logic, and quixotism which contributed so much unnecessary agony to it. (p. 233)

[He] hoped for the emergence of a modern ideal of marriage which would forever displace the ancient notion of Patient Griselda—who nobly triumphed over every evil and spite from her husband by an unutterably sweet and passionately passive endurance. His new ideal would be "that of a sort of Impatient Grizzle, who achieves through a fine, rebellious self-sacrifice all the best results of the old Patient one's subjection. It is the wife who has her will only the better to walk in the husband's way."

The key word, the dangerous word, there was "self-sacrifice." Howells became permanently concerned about that state of "emotional anarchy" in America, as one of his keenest contemporary appreciators put it, in which "an emotion is so sacred a thing that not only no outsider but not even its possessor may presume to undertake its regulation," leaving us thus "a society without an emotional code." From Swedenborg by way of his father, Howells believed that the sacrifice of self to moral right and the good of others was essential. All good came from self-abnegation, all evil from selfishness. But the clarity of his moral vision perceived that, in a state of emotional anarchy, a sentimental quixotism of self-sacrifice was a peculiarly insidious and destructive form of egotism. The roots of this kind of self-abnegation were subjective emotional de-bauchery and ego-loving pride. Evidently, he thought American women susceptible to that vice, for he portrayed them suffering in its toils and threatening to destroy the lives of others with it repeatedly, and established the Rev. Mr. Sewell in *The Rise of Silas Lapham* apparently mostly for the purpose of preaching against it.

Thus Howells' mind was becoming thoroughly and seriously, not merely literarily, antiromantic. And the freshest part of *The Rise of Silas Lapham,* the criticism of business, showed the effect of that change. Seeking to grasp the psychological meaning of the emergence of the business mind, Howells concluded that it was founded on a new kind of romanticism. "Money," says Bromfield Corey, ". . . is the romance, the poetry of our age. It's the thing that chiefly strikes the imagination." Nothing is clearer about Silas Lapham than the fact that only his business has romance in life for him. Mrs. Lapham charges him bitterly with having made his paint his god, but she, as usual, has only half understood him. His paint business and his success are much realer to Silas than God. Only when he is living and talking paint does Silas truly come alive. There his treasure is and his heart also, and he is even more deeply in need of a cleansing shower of cool, moral realism than the most quixotic of women.

The Rise of Silas Lapham is the testament of a realist who wishes his reader to see directly the moral confusion into which the new times have fallen. He also insists that the reader see critically how false, feeble, or irrelevant are the moral resources of the past, especially when those resources are obsoletely romantic. In doing this he is renewing and extending the insights of *A Modern Instance*. And much as Marcia Gaylord was a kind of Maine Medea, Silas is a businessman Faust. Wealth, and more meaningfully the pride of power in life which comes from money success in the Gilded Age, have poured in on him. By trampling under his partner Rogers, Silas has elevated himself at the opening of the book to a position of sinful pride. Then the question becomes: what shall it profit a man to gain the whole world and lose his own soul? But with it goes the question: what kind of world—American world—was it through which Silas moved to his victory-in-defeat? The moral-spiritual rise of Silas Lapham was a worldly descent from arrogance to doubt to struggle and at last to repentance. (pp. 234-35)

Lapham is not really either a comedy or a tragedy—insofar as analogies from the techniques of the drama are useful in understanding it—but a mixed form, what play analysts of Howells' time called a *drame,* a free mingling of the comic and tragic. In one sense *Lapham* is a comedy in that there are striking and sometimes very funny satiric and ironic scenes and moments throughout it. In a different sense it is "comic" like Dante's *Divina Commedia*. It ends well: as Christian faith has always insisted the cosmic drama and the drama of human history will end—in victory for God and goodness; or as the drama of any individual life may end—in the hard-won triumph of grace and conscience over sin. . . . But in other ways *Lapham* is tragic. Like Christianity, it intimates that man's love of his prideful ego, its immunities and power, its aggressiveness and treachery, must lead to destruction. Either it will harry him into disaster, or it must be self-suppressed and humiliated. Even more, Howells' theoretical, Swedenborgian "knowledge" of the self-damnation—the worldliness—of the world became acutely real as it was dramatized in the texture of his novel. Who would have supposed the worlds of Boston—all of them and therefore the contemporary world everywhere—were so undone?

In his book, Silas Lapham moves through a series of morality plays, meeting persons clothed in the realistic texture of commonplace life, all of whom tend to corrupt rather than save him, in all of whom moral deficiencies and cultural inadequacies are organically united. In himself there is Colonel Sellers' irresponsible business romanticism united with what John Woolman called "the spirit of fierceness," the arrogant economic individualism which says: you shall serve and suffer; I shall take, exult, and perhaps enjoy. . . . Stronger and fiercer as well as luckier than many, Silas was able to crowd out his rather vague partner, Rogers, and then to know in the face of the predatory Railroad later on what it was like to be under the wheel.

The Lapham daughters and, for much of the time, Mrs. Lapham are so caught in the meshes of female quixotism on the one hand and social competition on the other that they simply obscure Silas' vision and confuse his mind even more. That aside, however, there are two other large movements in this rich book which profoundly reveal the deficiencies of Silas' world. One of these centers on Mrs. Lapham, the other on Bromfield Corey and his family. Taken together in their major implications, these constitute a sweeping criticism of the New England of Howells' day—and therefore of the civilized world.

At first blush Mrs. Lapham might be taken as the moral *raisonneur* of the novel, Howells' spokeswoman. She sees and condemns Silas' treachery to Rogers; she understands and condemns his motives and emotions. She represents the stern Puritan tradition of the Vermont countryside from which the Laphams have come. For a long time she is Silas' conscience, unsparing, caustic, pessimistic. But the country culture from which her Puritan hang-over comes Howells had long seen to be riddled with dry rot. All the Lapham boys had gone West, Silas only returning to the farm for a few years before the War and his exodus to the city. The vitality of cultural relevance is gone from Persis Lapham's morality (no longer rooted in religion) as surely as it was gone from Marcia Gaylord's Equity, Maine, or from the old farms going back to brush in *Private Theatricals*. Consequently, Persis cannot avoid becoming trapped in the sins of conspicuous consumption and yearning to help Silas and her daughters compete with the Coreys. She cannot avoid giving in to the code of respectability and so forcing Silas to be secretive in helping the wife and daughter of his old comrade-at-arms and so betraying both herself and him in flying into a fury of misguided wifely outrage when a malicious note intimates that Silas is really keeping Zerilla as a mistress rather than a typist. Consequently she falters and fails Silas completely when the crisis of his struggle for righteousness comes. In that crisis he is left entirely alone, deserted by the dry-rotted culture of his past as by the wife who embodies it.

The least well-digested part of *Lapham*, indeed, is Howells' vision of slum Boston, given briefly and more or less incidentally in glimpses of Zerilla (Millon) Dewey and her plight. Obviously, Howells' concern for "the other half" was deepening. Silas' refusal to deny help to Zerilla for the sake of respectability and his insistence on taking personal responsibility for keeping her from being lost in the morass of Boston slum life make him morally superior to his wife as well as to the frivolous Lady Bountiful humanitarianism of Clara Kingsbury and her ilk. But it is also clear that Howells himself, though troubled, was not yet ready to come to grips with that problem.

He understood much better how to handle Bromfield Corey, the perfect blend of Brahmin and Proper Boston, who had made a failure of being a painter and a great success of "gentlemaning as a profession." One could take the four houses in *Lapham*—the Vermont farmhouse where Silas begins and ends, the Lapham's vulgar Nankeen Square house, their fine but doomed, architect-built, Beacon Street house, and Bromfield Corey's home—as the organizing centers for an understanding of the esthetic-cultural (as on the whole distinct from the moral-cultural) core of the book. Corey is a gentleman *par excellence*. He is utterly cultivated and all but utterly civilized. He knows how to appreciate the best in Silas, and he has, at least potentially, the resources to teach Silas how to enjoy his wealth through beauty. Corey has the generosity and even the imagination to see where he, his family, and his son really stand in modern society and therefore the magnanimity to encourage Tom to go into business with Silas, even to marry Penelope Lapham if he really wants to. He sees that it is good for Tom, since he honestly can, to throw himself into the mainstream of modern life and restore the living relationship to it which Bromfield's "India Merchant" father had enjoyed and dilettante Bromfield lost. He knows, but cannot himself overcome, his own "sterile elegance."

Bromfield Corey can rise above the snobbish hostility which makes Penelope say, as she drives away with Tom on the way to live in Mexico after her marriage: "I don't think I shall feel strange amongst the Mexicans now." But his condemnation and that of his class is that they can offer Silas no help in his moral warfare. Their elegance is better than his vulgarity, but they and their culture also leave him isolated in his struggle with good and evil.

At the crucial moment in the novel, Silas can still save himself and his wealth if he will connive at a deal cooked up by his old partner Rogers. . . . In two quick, deliberately underwritten scenes of great emotional power and moral implication, Howells then achieves the climax of his novel. (pp. 235-38)

The Jacob image, so natural to Persis Lapham's Puritan heritage, functions very richly as a symbol in [the climactic scene of Silas' "rise"]. Jacob, a far from attractive man, became the father of his people after wrestling all night with an angel and refusing to let him go "except thou bless me." Whereupon the angel both blessed him and crippled him for life. The popular clichés—all too popular in the best-selling fiction of Howells' day—demanded that chimes of blessing resound in this world and the next at a deed of moral heroism. Silas' deed is stumbling, not dramatically clean-cut, and it is heroic mainly in the consequences he has to bear. No heavenly music warms his lacerated spirit. He is crippled, and in worldly terms his blessing seems negative. He relinquishes the material gain, the loot, of his sin. He rises—but only out of the pit—up to the heights of humiliation, left there to work out the rest of his salvation with the blessing of the clarified vision his victory has won him. This is the way an agnostic moralist and literary realist will have us see the world. He has not written a novel against business, but against a world in the bonds of selfishness. The modern world had left behind such anomalies as feudal classes and slavery, but Howells wished to make it see that it had reclothed the spirit of fierceness in the business mind and in the gospel of wealth. *The Rise of Silas Lapham* remains important to us as one of its age's supremely suggestive aids to the historical imagination in its vivid presentation of the life of a lost era. As drama of the moral imagination, however, it is relevant now, at least as meaningful to an American of the second half of the twentieth century as to one of the nineteenth.

It is fruitless to argue that *Lapham* is or is not the best of Howells' novels. That the question is arguable is high tribute to the excellence of the comparable works, for this one is unchallengeably major. It has endured with great vitality the decades of ignorant and often malicious anti-Howells prejudice, and it may be expected to prosper further in readers' attention now that prejudice has begun to subside. (pp. 239-40)

> Edwin H. Cady, in his The Road to Realism: The Early Years 1837-1885 of William Dean Howells (© 1956 Syracuse University Press), Syracuse University Press, 1956, 283 p.

RICHARD FOSTER   (essay date 1959)

Howells was a realist not merely in the notions he had about his obligations and techniques as a novelist, but in the fullness of his portrait of a time and a place. It is this accomplishment—his panoramic delineation of life in provincial America at the close of the last century—that puts him into relation with Trollope and Hardy. But there is a still larger world in Howells' fiction, the sort of world that is never entirely contained or completed, that diminishes and changes and develops even as the artist perceives it: it is the world of the "human condition" at any juncture of time, the sort of world that was the substance of Balzac's Human Comedy and that is the substance of one of the great sagas of our time, Faulkner's cultural tragedy of the American South in transition. But a Howells novel, with its flavor of urbanity and gentility, must seem somehow too simple and domestic a thing for such comparisons. For it was the nineteenth-century novel of manners, to be sure, that supplied Howells, as it supplied his friend Henry James, with his principal dramatic strategies. Yet Howells adapted such traditional devices as the "social occasion" and the journey to his very special needs as a modern: teas, balls, musicales and dinners, ships, trains, hotels and boarding houses—he saw how aptly these lent themselves to dramatic experiments in cultural collision. It was in such domestic and local situations, in those scenes familiar to older fiction where people are at leisure to eat and drink, to talk and ruminate and recreate themselves, that Howells focused the dissonances of the larger world in those of smaller and dramatically more accessible ones. And through them, from chapter to chapter and novel to novel, Howells was able to accumulate his larger panorama: a world of present cultural formlessness ironically juxtaposed with a background of felt organic traditions out of the past. Howells' novels are remarkable, then, in that they discovered so early and so fully, in such ordinary events seen from an ordinary perspective of middle-class decency, what is perhaps the great informing myth of our century—that complex phenomenon that has since been variously described as the "revolt of the masses," the "decline of the West," the "dissociation" of modern sensibility, the "breakdown of tradition."

Tradition meant to Howells the perpetuation of a homogeneous society within which the individual can act intelligently and morally as a social being. It is significant that his characters are everywhere plagued by uncertainty and indecision. Taking action is either difficult or impossible for them, and the result, often, is that the ultimate issue of a Howells novel is no more than someone's hesitant formulation of a moral judgment. The reason that Howells' characters have so much difficulty acting and deciding is that in their world they no longer have clear and publicly recognized traditions to guide and sanction their actions. But the motives that animated these traditions—which

we may group roughly as religious, political, and communal in kind—hover everywhere in the novels as mute interpreters of the action at hand.

When the hero of *A Hazard of New Fortunes* passes through New York's Mott Street, he notices a Roman Catholic church that has about it, amid the tangled life of the neighborhood's many races and nationalities, a queer sense of "missionary quality": "It seemed to have come to them there, and he fancied in the statued saint that looked down from its façade something not so much tolerant as tolerated, something propitiatory, almost deprecatory." This is a pictorial statement of Howells' conviction that the Church of Rome, a universal religious structure that formed the past, has declined in the present to a form relatively without a force, to a symbol without meaning. (pp. 55-7)

But as an American Howells was more interested in the corresponding decay of institutional Protestantism, a decay measured often in the novels by the presence of "spiritualism" and various kinds of fanaticism and superstition. It is not a misrepresentation of Howells' insights to interpret *A Modern Instance,* one of his three or four finest novels, as the typical tragedy, told in terms of the collapse of Marcia and Bartley Hubbard's marriage, of the general dissolution of New England's spiritual traditions. (p. 57)

[Howells goes] to some trouble to surround the smallness of their destiny with larger causal implications. Squire Gaylord, Marcia's father, is himself presented as the embodiment of the old Puritan spirit of justice disinherited from its God. In his grand moment of triumph over Bartley, the runaway husband, at the end of the novel, he is described by Howells in the imagery of savage animality; and when he is "struck down" we understand that he is justice without religion, which soon turns into the sin of vengeance. The club-footed Ben Halleck, Marcia's unrequited lover, is his opposite; he is charity, but charity crippled—charity without the informing sanction of religion. This is why Ben is such a hopeless romantic, why he cannot act decisively in relation to Marcia, why in the end he can only flee to the old fundamentalistic faith where, though unable to accept its spirit, he can come to rest in the letter of its Law. The novel expands, then, as so many Howells novels do, from the dead center of a domestic problem to an implicit analysis of the spiritual debilities of a whole culture. It deserves more than *Main Street* to be thought of as, in its own way, America's *Madame Bovary*.

Howells recognized a second unifying tradition lost to the present in the cultivated and responsible aristocracy of means which guided the American republic through the first five or six decades of its life. Even in his earliest novel, *Their Wedding Journey,* Howells observed a Southern and a Northern representative of this tradition in its decadence: the Southerner, a victim of cataclysm, is disinherited from his graceful way of life, impoverished by the results of the War, and impotently bitter toward the North; the Northerner, diseased by the slow rot of the new commercial spirit, now represents nothing more than "a social set, an alien club-life, a tradition of dining." In the noisily modern New York of *A Hazard of New Fortunes,* there is an aging and displaced Southern gentleman who insists that Scott and Addison are "the only authors fit to form the minds of gentlemen," and who proclaims a universal benevolent slavery to be the only solution to present-day labor problems. Bromfield Corey, his Northern counterpart and Howells' most memorable gentleman, is less naïve. And because of that he is more decadent in his inability to take moral action. In

The Rise of Silas Lapham and elsewhere he is nevertheless a touching and appealing type of the gentleman without a societal function; in a world of commerce and competition he is inevitably doomed to the role of moral aesthete in a state of recumbency. (pp. 58-9)

A third and final tradition that Howells pictured in its decline is less easily defined, though I think it may have assumed in his awareness the largest importance of all. It is essentially a communal tradition, a "way of life" centering in the family and maintained from generation to generation in the middle-class life of the old provincial towns and the agrarian life of "good stock" on the soil. It is founded on the ideals of practical self-sufficiency and total moral integrity, and it assumes the continuity of father and son. There are many examples in Howells' novels, with Silas Lapham the most celebrated one, of the unhappy consequences of separation from this tradition. But perhaps the most vividly and fully realized instance of this breakdown, a breakdown that is partly willed and partly the fault of history, occurs in the portrait of the Dryfoos family in *A Hazard of New Fortunes*.

Almost without knowing how or why, Dryfoos has become a man of wealth. He has deserted the land and the certain values of his Midwestern provincial culture for New York City, which has no laws but those of force and survival, no way of life more profound than the civilized niceties of the "good society" he cannot understand. Because he has lost touch with his past, Dryfoos has also lost touch with his conscience; and for Howells this means that he is morally crippled, that he can act only chaotically. The symbolic function of the paternity theme is again important. Dryfoos' children are foreign to him: Christine has become savage and rebellious because of the formlessness of their new life, and Conrad is a stranger to his father because Dryfoos has dwindled to a moral inferior of his own son. Conrad's insistence on maintaining his own moral integrity in the face of his father's moral confusion finally so baffles and enrages Dryfoos that he cruelly strikes Conrad, a gesture of recognition of the difference between his son's moral health and his own. Conrad is cut by his sister Christine's ring, which his father is wearing. The ring—which is associated with Europe, with the rebellious Christine, and with the decadent aesthete who seems on the verge of becoming her lover—is a final symbol of the breakup of Dryfoos' tradition and of those alien influences which make him finally the vicarious murderer of his own Christlike son.

But Dryfoos, like Silas Lapham, is at bottom too naïve to be an evil man; we will have to await a later generation of American fiction before the real titans are upon us. Dryfoos and his family are simply transitional human beings lost between two worlds. Dryfoos' answer to his wife's yearning to "go home" is the pathetic cry of the homeless and the lost: "If I was to give all I'm worth this minute, we couldn't go back to the farm, any more than them girls in there can go back and be little children." . . . It is Dryfoos' personal tragedy, as it is Silas Lapham's in *The Rise* and Northwick's in *The Quality of Mercy*, that he is self-doomed to be the victim as well as the demon of his new world.

We normally think of politics as the most comprehensive public expression of the condition of a society as a whole. But Howells' novels are almost notoriously barren of contemporary political issues. There is only one instance of the kind, and that hardly developed at all—in *Their Silver Wedding Journey*, when the "king of New York" is observed in a box at a German opera, a brief and inconclusive discussion of Tammany ensues,

and the matter is dropped. But the absence of direct political and social investigations in Howells' novels is not, as some of the last generation of critics would have it, a symptom of genteel squeamishness. For in more than one novel Howells made skillful and forthright use of the institutions of journalism, which he knew from the inside out, as a sharp if indirect reflection of what a society that has come under the rule of "business principles" is like as a whole. He knew that our newspapers and magazines are the daily report of the state of our societal soul. (pp. 60-2)

He saw in the direction that modern journalism was taking a clear indication of the kind of society that could result as the principles of success and profit more and more became the institutional replacement of traditional values. (p. 63)

> Richard Foster, "The Contemporaneity of Howells," in The New England Quarterly (copyright 1959 by The New England Quarterly), Vol. XXXII, No. 1, March, 1959, pp. 54-78.

DONALD PIZER   (essay date 1960)

The main plot of *The Rise of Silas Lapham* concerns Silas's financial fall and moral rise. It revolves around his business affairs and social aspirations, and it concludes with his decision to sacrifice wealth and position rather than engage in business duplicity. The subplot centers on the triangle of Tom Corey and Irene and Penelope Lapham. Tom is mistakenly believed by all to be in love with Irene. The dilemma caused by his revelation that he loves Penelope is resolved when Irene is informed of the error. Irene then withdraws, leaving Tom and Penelope free to marry.

The dilemma or conflict within the subplot is solved by the use of an "economy of pain" formula. Despite Penelope's willingness to sacrifice herself, Irene must be told of Corey's true sentiments, and Penelope and Corey must be encouraged to fulfil their love. In this way Irene suffers but Penelope and Tom are spared the pain of thwarted love. One rather than three suffers lasting pain. Of the three characters who determine the resolution of the subplot, Lapham realizes instinctively the correct course of action, Mrs. Lapham is helpless and hesitant—this despite her moralizing throughout the novel—and the clergyman Sewell articulates the principle involved and confirms Lapham's choice.

The problem which Silas must solve in the main plot parallels that in the subplot. The three groups who will be affected by his decision are he and his family (Lapham is a participant now as well as an arbiter), Rogers and his family, and the English agents who wish to purchase Lapham's depreciated mill. The crucial point is that the Englishmen are more than mere scoundrels and more than the agents for an "association of rich and charitable people", they also represent society at large. This fact is somewhat obscured in the context of the financial trickery involved in the sale, since the agents are willing to be cheated. But Howells indicated the social implications of the sale when he immediately compared it to the defrauding of municipal governments. In both instances wealth and anonymity encourage dishonesty, and in both instances dishonesty undermines that which is necessary for the maintenance of the common good—effective city governments on the one hand, fair play and honest dealings in business affairs on the other. Lapham's refusal to sell therefore ultimately contributes to the well-being of society as a whole.

The thematic similarity in the two plots is that both involve a principle of morality which requires that the individual determine correct action by reference to the common good rather than to an individual need. Within the subplot this principle requires Lapham to choose on the basis of an "economy of pain" formula in which the fewest suffer. Within the main plot it requires him to weigh his own and Rogers's personal needs against the greater need of all men for decency and honesty. His "rise" is posited exactly in these terms, for at one point in the events leading up to his rejection of the Englishmen's offer he reflects quizzically that "It was certainly ridiculous for a man who had once so selfishly consulted his own interests to be stickling now about the rights of others."

The method used to achieve moral insight is also similar in both plots. What is required is the ability to project oneself out of the immediate problem in which the personal, emotionally compelling need or desire is seen out of proportion to the need of the larger unit. In the subplot Mrs. Lapham finds this difficult, and Sewell asks her, "'What do you think some one else ought to do in your place?'" In the main plot it is no doubt Silas's realization of the honesty that he would ask of other men in a similar situation which aids him in making the same demand of himself. Lastly, as in the subplot, Silas is capable of moral insight, Mrs. Lapham again falters, and Sewell (at the end of the novel) attempts explanations.

One of the functions of the subplot is therefore to "double" the moral theme of the novel, to intensify and clarify it by introducing it within a narrower, more transparent dilemma. The subplot also plays other important roles. Dominating the center of the novel, it is solved before the full exposition of Lapham's business crisis. It occurs, in other words, between Howells's early remark that Lapham "could not rise" to unselfishness in his dealings with Rogers and Lapham's own words at the close which indicate a concern for the "rights of others." The subplot thus contributes to the "education" of Lapham in the correct solution of moral problems. His moral rise is the product of more than a conscience troubled by his earlier treatment of Rogers. It is also the result of his ready absorption of the "economy of pain" formula as a moral guide in the subplot, a formula which he later translates into its exact corollary, the greatest happiness for the greatest number, when he is faced in the main plot with the more difficult problem of the ethical relationship of the individual to society. To sum up, the subplot of *The Rise of Silas Lapham* serves the functions of doubling the statement of the novel's theme, of foreshadowing the moral principle governing the main plot, and of introducing Lapham to the correct solution of moral problems.

It is possible, at this point, to suggest that the ethical core of the novel can be described as utilitarianism (as interpreted by John Stuart Mill), since both plots dramatize a moral principle in which the correct action is that which results in the greatest happiness for the greatest number. I do not wish to intimate that Howells consciously employed the ethical ideas of Mill. Rather, I believe that the similarity between Mill's utilitarianism and the ethical principles of *The Rise of Silas Lapham* is probably the result of parallel attempts to introduce the ethical teachings of Christ within social contexts and yet avoid supernatural sanctions. Howells's emerging Christian socialism in the late 1880's is well known. . . . (pp. 322-25)

That Howells was conscious of the applicability of the Golden Rule to the theme of *The Rise of Silas Lapham* is clear, I believe, from his ironic use of it in connection with Rogers.

When Rogers senses that Lapham may reject the Englishmen's offer, his appeal to Lapham is based on the premise that

> In our dealings with each other we should be guided by the Golden Rule, as I was saying to Mrs. Lapham before you came in. I told her that if I knew myself, I should in your place consider the circumstances of a man in mine, who had honourably endeavoured to discharge his obligations to me, and had patiently borne my undeserved suspicions. I should consider that man's family, I told Mrs. Lapham.

But Lapham's answer is the response of a man who is aware of the sophistry of a narrow use of the Golden Rule and who recognizes the necessity for the consideration of a wider range of obligation than individual need. "'Did you tell her,'" he asks Rogers, "'that if I went in with you and those fellows, I should be robbing the people who trusted them?'"

There is a twofold advantage in viewing the main and subplots of *The Rise of Silas Lapham* as controlled by a similar conception of moral behavior. First, the novel takes on a thematic unity and structural symmetry. It is within a single moral system, for example, that the apparent conflict between the attack on self-sacrifice in the subplot and Lapham's self-sacrifice in the main plot is reconciled. Penelope's self-sacrifice would diminish the sum total of happiness of those affected by her action, and therefore is wrong; Silas's self-sacrifice increases the happiness of mankind collectively, and therefore is right. Secondly, the theme of the novel anticipates Howells's acceptance of Tolstoy's ethical ideals within the next few years and helps explain his response to those ideals once he encountered them. For in the two plots of *The Rise of Silas Lapham* Howells had already begun working out a belief that man must rise above himself and view life, as, he later explained, Tolstoy had taught him to view life, "not as a chase of a forever impossible personal happiness, but as a field for endeavor toward the happiness of the whole human family." The conviction that man's primary commitment is to mankind was to be one of the themes which Howells emphasized in the series of novels from [*Annie Kilburn* to *A Traveler from Altruria*]. In *The Rise of Silas Lapham* that theme appears in a less obvious social context (Howells had to strain for the connection between the English agents and society) and—more importantly—as an obligation which the average individual can grasp and fulfil. His novels during the years following . . . were to examine the theme of man's duty to his fellow men more intensively but less hopefully. (pp. 325-27)

Donald Pizer, "The Ethical Unity of 'The Rise of Silas Lapham'," in American Literature *(reprinted by permission of the Publisher; copyright © 1960, Duke University Press, Durham, North Carolina), Vol. XXXII, No. 3, November, 1960, pp. 322-27.*

WALTER J. MESERVE (essay date 1960)

As he wrote in his autobiography, W. D. Howells could scarcely remember when he was not interested in the theater. Plays had always fascinated him—reading them or seeing them performed. . . . But it was not until 1874, when he was thirty-seven, that he made his first contribution to the theater.

Later to an old man writing of his youth, the years seemed to have gone remarkably fast. But he had accomplished a great deal: he had become one of the outstanding novelists of his century, and he had long been considered America's foremost critic. Advocating a truthful treatment of material, he championed and wrote works characterized by attention to everyday experiences seen in a perspective not easily mastered by a generation whose view of art was falsified by sentimentality. And partially satisfying the ambition of his youth, he had become a playwright of some reputation. It is true that his successes in the theater were few and that he had definite limitations as a dramatist; yet, as a part of his artistic contribution and in relation to the rest of American drama, his plays become significant in the rise of realism in the United States and in the development of American social comedy. . . . [The] average person enjoyed these amusing little plays; but they held little attraction for theater managers, and since Howells' death they have slipped further and further away from critics and managers as well as audiences.

One could list many reasons why Howells' plays were not more widely accepted in the theater. But perhaps most important, he wrote mainly one-act plays, and as Augustin Daly told Howells in a letter (January 11, 1893, Harvard Library), ". . . one act pieces bring no profit & very little lasting reputation to authors, actors or managers." (pp. xv-xvi)

One of the reasons why Howells was not more successful on the stage—his choice of scene, characters, and action—is the same reason why many of his plays are pleasant reading today. He wrote mainly of a Boston Back Bay aristocracy, a society which also formed a meaningful background for his ideas. There were the Robertses and the Campbells and Mr. and Mrs. Fountain (*The Night Before Christmas* and *The Impossible*), all members in good standing of this society. Other characters indicated their comparable social level by their manners and actions: they had summer residences (*A Previous Engagement, An Indian Giver*); they took trips abroad (*Parting Friends*); they gave afternoon receptions (*Bride Roses*); or they showed a particular sense of propriety (*Self-Sacrifice: A Farce Tragedy*). Against this social background Howells sometimes placed people from lower social levels, such as the Irishman McIlheny in *The Albany Depot,* the Main girl in *The Smoking Car,* the tramps in *Out of the Question,* and the fellow passengers of *The Sleeping Car.* Another group of common but thoroughly respectable people hovered socially just below the Robertses and the Campbells. One sees them in *The Parlor Car* and *The Register* and perhaps at their worst in *Room Forty-Five.* Of all Howells' published plays there are only two—*A True Hero: Melodrama* and *Saved, An Emotional Drama*—that seem to utilize no particular social background, although even in these two satires on melodrama the general moral sense of Howells' society pervades.

Against this well-established social background Howells frequently gave his audience farce action with scarcely a serious thought in plays such as *The Sleeping Car, The Elevator,* and *The Smoking Car.* Because of this social atmosphere, however, more than a third of his published plays contain in both idea and execution some of the characteristics of social comedy. One often-repeated social-comedy theme is the ever-present struggle between man and woman. In these plays the initiating situations vary, but the result is always the same: The woman wins. With the exception of Willis Campbell and Dr. Lawton of the Roberts-Campbell plays, Howells' men generally lack those qualities which would make them even capable contenders in this universal struggle; and sometimes even Campbell and Lawton find themselves totally inadequate in coping with woman and her logic (*The Unexpected Guests*). *The Mouse*

Trap and *A Likely Story* clearly show that there is no question concerning the superiority of women. In plays that do not feature the Robertses and the Campbells, Howells, in a kind of habitual behavior, treats this conflict between the sexes in a plot involving an engagement which is either being made for the first time or being remade after some confusion. No less than seven plays—*The Register, An Indian Giver, A Previous Engagement, Her Opinion of His Story, The Parlor Car, Parting Friends, Self-Sacrifice: A Farce Tragedy*—have remarkably similar plots. In each instance the women are, in various degrees, charming and shrewd but always intelligent in knowing how to control men. These women may hate each other—and Howells seems to feel that women traditionally and instinctively dislike each other—but they understand men, at least Howells' men, and have few problems with them. The men, on the other hand, try to seem completely understanding when actually they understand nothing. Usually they are marked by a single-minded persistence which does not always do credit to their intelligence and by a blind devotion which romantic women admire. (pp. xvi-xvii)

Through characters, social background, a concern for truth and realism, and some repeated themes, Howells' plays manifest a certain similarity, but it would be inaccurate to suggest anything like a unifying thematic structure running through his work. In most of his plays his major objective was obviously enjoyment—good fun; and while he attained this generally by poking fun at aspects of society, his method was chiefly farce. Techniques of humor in Howells' plays, therefore, assume some importance. Actually he shows no great originality, but his variety is interesting. The situation, of course, is an obvious technique: two doctors arrive simultaneously at a house and must be kept apart; a man knocks down a friend and takes his watch under the impression that he is recovering his own watch from a thief; a man cannot find his dress suit; a woman is afraid of a mouse. . . . As one would expect in a farce, there is much physical humor, most noticeable in such plays as *Room Forty-Five* and *Evening Dress*. . . . Other techniques include understatement, overstatement, inconsistent behavior, minstrel-show humor, puns and other plays on words, gross exaggeration and even lies, gross stupidity, humor built around foreign character traits, and so on. Wit, too, has a prominent place in these plays. Howells wrote brilliant conversations, far more witty and clever than anything being written in American drama of his time. The dialogue of *Five O'clock Tea* is perhaps the most frequently quoted example, but the fast repartee in *A Letter of Introduction* is worthy of note, as well as the conversation in *The Garroters* and *The Unexpected Guests*. In such instances the dialogue raises the play above the limitations of farce and creates social comedy—a witty portrayal of a fashionable society.

Enhancing the wit of the plays and adding to the characteristics of social comedy is Howells' use of satire—essentially a means for producing enjoyment but frequently having serious implications. With a certain mischievousness, Howells satirized particularly the Boston woman of fashion. No doubt he admired the ladies and enjoyed their company, but one feels that he would not have appreciated them half so much if they had been as logical and consistent as men think they would like them to be. Plays such as *A Letter of Introduction,* probably his most successful satire, indicate the great pleasure he took in pointing out the ridiculous attitudes and foibles of society and the socially-acceptable person. In this play he manages to ridicule Englishmen, New Yorkers, American language and culture, critics, American artists, Boston snobbery, and the cultivated

Bostonian family. Two of his plays are satiric in theme: *A True Hero: Melodrama* satirizes the traditional melodramatic hero, and *Saved, An Emotional Drama* satirizes the entire range of melodramatic techniques. More significant, however, are the two plays featuring Mr. and Mrs. Fountain, *The Night Before Christmas* and *The Impossible*. They not only contain bitter ironies concerning society and man—in contrast perhaps to the pathetic irony in *Bride Roses*—but also question meaning in society and ponder man's serious inadequacies.

Complementary to Howells' concern for social comedy is his interest in realism—his attention to details in dialogue and his numerous references to contemporary events and real persons; when new inventions appeared, such as the elevator, the phonograph, the telephone, the air brake, the Miller platform for railroad cars, and the motorcar, he frequently employed them in a farce. . . . Language, too, was important in Howells' realism, and his actors' speeches are filled with commonplace phrases and the overused expressions of average conversation. . . . In general, Howells' respect for minutiae of fact is considerable. For example, the Robertses and the Campbells had a train to catch in *The Albany Depot,* and the Boston-and-Albany train schedule of that time indicates that they took the right one. There was a difference in Howells' day between the operation of the steam elevator and the hydraulic elevator, and Howells makes central use of this difference in *The Elevator*. As in his fiction, then, Howells' use of realistic detail was a much-studied aspect of his art.

More important than these details in Howells' art, however, are the truthfulness and the moral value that accompanied his concern for reality. . . . There can be no question that a realistic but humorous view of life was Howells' main objective, although he was not consistently successful in achieving his goal. But his secondary purpose was to bring to his audience a greater understanding of life. Consequently, in a number of his plays, Howells directly posed a problem of real life in which truthfulness became either a central or an important contributory issue. *A True Hero: Melodrama,* for example, attempts to suggest a way in which man may equate truth and reality in life. Here truth is much more than a romantic, idealized concept; it is the function of Dr. Tolboy in this play to show the young hero that if twisted values and naïveté prompt one to lie in the name of truth, it will be morally impossible for him to be true to himself. (pp. xvii-xix)

A large number of other plays make less extensive, but no less pointed, use of questions of truth and morality. In *The Albany Depot,* Willis Campbell tries to explain that one must sometimes give the truth a "slight twist in the right direction," resulting in the ideal truth than the real truth, but Howells is quick to show that the ideal truth is never adequate and that, as in this play, one is soon left with only the "bare truth." (p. xix)

Perhaps more widely than in his other literary works, Howells' plays present a personal philosophy and an attitude toward social life. He was a man who liked to laugh, and he made fun an objective of his dramas. He was a man who held a thoughtful literary creed, and his best plays, sketches though they may be, suggest his basic critical theories. He was a man not always happy with the life that he saw around him, and in his plays, as well as in his fiction, he commented on human society as he saw it—superficial, proper, ridiculous, or truthful. Much of the time in his dramas he was playful, but he was also capable of great seriousness. There are, for example, few places in his writings where he talks about death and the

mystery of what lies beyond with more beauty and feeling than in *The Mother and the Father*. (p. xix)

Although it is difficult to generalize about Howells' development as a dramatist, his humorous and serious plays divide quite clearly into two periods of his life. It is a fact, for example, that the twelve Roberts-Campbell comedies—all but two written in the 1880's—are his most humorous and stageworthy plays. After *A Masterpiece of Diplomacy* in 1893, Howells returned to his Robertses and Campbells only in *The Smoking Car,* a most inadequate play. . . . The Robertses and the Campbells served him mainly as vehicles for fun and satire, and with them he reached his highest point as a dramatist in the theater. When life became more complicated, personally and philosophically, he abandoned these characters as such (although in essence the character types remained with him) and tried to express his ideas in another framework. The drama always remained a challenge to his creativity and an outlet for his realistic creed, but the late plays are much less consciously an attempt to appeal to the requirements of the stage and reflect more fully Howells' mature thought. (pp. xix-xx)

> *Walter J. Meserve, in his introduction to* The Complete Plays of W. D. Howells *by W. D. Howells; William M. Gibson and George Arms, General Editors (reprinted by permission of New York University Press; copyright ©1960 by New York University and the heirs of William Dean Howells), New York University Press, 1960, pp. xv-xxxiii.*

RENÉ WELLEK (essay date 1965)

The theory of realism was imported from Europe very late, though the practice of close observation and realistic techniques in local-color fiction, Western humor, and even the sentimental novel was widespread long before. Americans could also draw on the solid English tradition of the novel of manners. Poe, Hawthorne, and Melville, who today seem the greatest writers of the age, were romantic and symbolistic artists who either escaped their society or transmuted its problems in a manner very different from what proponents of literature as a "mirror of society" require. . . . But the advent of the French theory of realism was hardly slowed by the lessons of these masters. The long resistance against French realism was rather due to moral and religious objections: to the "lubricity" of French fiction and its pessimistic, irreligious implications.

William Dean Howells succeeded in formulating a theory of realism for the America of his time precisely because he emphasized the difference of his views from those of the French and drew support instead from the masters of realism in Russia, Italy, and Spain. His little book of rather random reflections, *Criticism and Fiction* . . . is usually considered the manifesto of American realism, but it was actually only a skirmish in a long campaign for his doctrines. (pp. 206-07)

Howells' theory of the novel crystallized in the early years of his editorship of the *Atlantic Monthly* (1866-81), when he became acquainted with the French, the German peasant novelist Berthold Auerbach, and Turgenev. At that time Howells' main theoretical concern was the principle of noninterference by the author, of complete objectivity of presentation. In 1869 he praised one of Auerbach's stories for "telling itself." "One does not think of the author till the end." He describes his own ideal when he tells us that Turgenev is "the most self-forgetful of the story-telling tribe, and he is no more enamored of the creations than of himself; he pets none of them; he upbraids none; you like them or hate them for what they are; it does not seem to be his affair." Turgenev "leaves all comment to the reader"; he cares for character and minimizes plot; he uses "the play method"—that is, he dramatizes and does not comment and explain. Henry James realizes this ideal in America: "artistic impartiality" is his "characteristic quality" and, as with Turgenev, "it is the character, not the fate of his people which occupies him." (pp. 207-08)

[*Criticism and Fiction*] hardly says anything new. Literature and art are "the expression of life," and "are to be judged by fidelity" to it. What is needed in criticism is not reference to other artists or the tradition of art, but an appeal to life: comparison with the things that the readers have known. Negatively this means a condemnation of romanticism, or rather of romantic devices; positively, an emphasis on probability of motive, a rejection of catastrophes and accidents. Fiction should minimize plot and center on character. It should reflect life as it is, in the United States, and hence it should not be so tragic and gloomy as Dostoevsky's novels. In a well-known passage—often quoted outside its context of the contrast with Dostoevsky's criminals and revolutionaries—Howells asserts his optimistic, democratic faith in human nature and America. "Our novelists, therefore, concern themselves with the more smiling aspects of life, which are the more American, and seek the universal in the individual rather than the social interests. It is worthwhile, even at the risk of being called commonplace, to be true to our well-to-do actualities." These actualities include a cleaner and saner view of the relation between the sexes than prevails in the French novel. Howells admits that "there is vicious love beneath the surface of our society" but insists that it is not characteristic. In the novel sex should be minimized. Passion is not only sexual passion: "the passion of grief, the passion of avarice, the passion of pity, the passion of ambition, the passion of hate, the passion of envy, the passion of devotion, the passion of friendship; and all these have a greater part in the drama of life than the passion of love, and infinitely greater than the passion of guilty love." Finally, this basically optimistic, democratic, decent art of the American novel must serve the good of humanity, must make men "kinder and better." Tolstoy has become Howells' "final consciousness." "The supreme art in literature had its highest effect in making me set art forever below humanity." Compared to the early reviews of Turgenev and Henry James, Howells has lost interest in technical prescriptions for the novel. Tolstoy seems to him the only writer who has "no manner" at all, whose fictions "seem the very truth always," whose "frank and simple kindliness is what style is in the merely literary author." Howells criticizes Tolstoy only when he deviates from this straightforward recording: when he becomes parabolical, as in his late peasant tales, or "descends to exegesis," as in *The Kreutzer Sonata* and applies to all marriages "the lesson of one evil marriage." In general, Howells feels that Tolstoy's art is so simple, so unassuming, so "real" that it ceases to be "literature in the artistic sense at all" and becomes life itself.

Howells' scattered later writings clarify and elaborate his point of view but hardly modify it. A lecture, **"Novel-Writing and Novel-Reading,"** . . . expounds the creed again. "Truth is the prime test of a novel," and truth means life and is the guarantee of beauty. Howells defends its going into the "dark places of the soul, the filthy and squalid places of society, high and low." "Let all the hidden things be brought into the sun, and let every day be the day of judgment. If the sermon cannot any longer serve this end, let the novel do it." But he recognizes that direct instruction will not achieve this end. "If it is a work of art, it promptly takes itself out of the order of polemics or of ethics and primarily consents to be nothing if not aesthetical. Its story is the thing that tells, first of all." What matters is "the effect of life," which Howells seems to think of as triumph of deception. Theoretically he knows that art is not life but the art of the novelist is something like a *trompe d'oeil,* an optical illusion. "The effect is like that in those cycloramas where up to a certain point there is real ground and real grass, and then carried indivisibly on to the canvas the best that the painter can do to imitate real ground and real grass. . . . If we are very skilful and very patient we can hide the joint." With a different figure Howells says the same when he says that "the business of the novelist" is "arranging a perspective for you with everything in its proper relation and proportion to everything else." But he adds immediately, it is also the novelist's function "to help you to be kinder to your fellows, juster to yourself, truer to all." The type distinctions sketched in Howells' lecture make this ideal of illusionism with a didactic purpose much more concrete. There are "truthful" and "untruthful" novelists. Jane Austen, George Eliot, Anthony Trollope, Thomas Hardy; Flaubert, Maupassant, the Goncourts, Daudet and Zola, Turgenev and Tolstoy are all "truthful." Thackeray, Dickens, Bulwer, Reade, Dumas, and "measurably" Dostoevsky are "untruthful." There are three types of novels in descending order of greatness: the novel, the romance, and the "romanticistic" novel, a different classification, which allows for Hawthorne as a writer of romance. *Pride and Prejudice, Middlemarch, Anna Karenina, Fathers and Sons* belong to the first class; the novels of Dickens and Hugo, to the third and lowest. Another threefold classification Howells introduces in the lecture has the same value criterion: the autobiographical form is the most narrow, the most difficult as to keeping of illusion: it includes *Gil Blas, Barry Lyndon* (Thackeray's best book in Howells' estimate), *Henry Esmond, The Blithedale Romance,* and *David Copperfield.* There is, secondly, the biographical novel with one central figure, of which Howells gives only one example: Henry James' *Roderick Hudson;* and there is, thirdly, the "historical" novel, by which Howells means the novel told as if the material were real history, by a universal intelligence, the omniscient author. It is by far the highest form, though it is "almost shapeless, as it is with the greatest difficulty, with serious limitations of its effects, that you can give it symmetry. Left to itself, it is sprawling, splay-footed, gangling, proportionless and inchoate; but if it is true to life which it can give no authority for seeming to know, it is full of beauty and symmetry." An unreal solution is propounded: its trust in the ultimate artistic success of deception, formlessness, literal truth, seems constantly withdrawn by a realization that art is not life, that the artist has to choose and arrange, has his technique and point of view. (pp. 208-11)

There are many inconsistencies in Howells' later criticism: fits of mawkish prudishness are followed by generous praise for Zola as "one of the greatest and most heroic of French citizens." His books, "though often indecent, are never immoral, but always most terribly, most pitilessly moral." Grossly exaggerated praise for trivial women short-story writers alternates with severe censure of the greatest masters. Howells' critical standards are relaxed, uncertain, and wavering, because basically, in spite of his enormous output, he did not care for criticism as analysis and judgment. (pp. 211-12)

René Wellek, "American Criticism," in his A History of Modern Criticism: 1750-1950, the Later Nineteenth Century *(copyright © 1965 by Yale University), Yale University Press, 1965, pp. 191-212.**

WILLIAM McMURRAY (essay date 1967)

[*A Hazard of New Fortunes,*] called by Howells the "largest canvas" he had yet allowed himself, explores the American social and economic scene as it appeared in the New York of the later nineteenth century. Yet, the novel is not mere fictionalized sociology. . . . [If] the novel's title points to the overt theme of the story, it points also to the larger theme of the risk of living in a world where fortune is always uncertain in the complicity of experience.

The novel is divided into five parts. In the first three we meet the characters, have views of New York, and watch the interweaving of the lives of the characters whose fortunes are involved with the launching of the new magazine *Every Other Week*. The people associated with the magazine form a microcosm of the greater world. Basil March, the magazine's literary editor and the novel's central character, is a Westerner, as are Fulkerson, the magazine's genial director, and Jacob Dryfoos, a "natural-gas" millionaire who is the magazine's "Angel." Its art editor, Angus Beaton, the son of a tombstone cutter and "Scotch Seceder," is from Syracuse, New York. Colonel Woodburn, a contributor, is from Charlottesburg, Virginia. In Berthold Lindau, the old German socialist who translates European literature for the magazine *Every Other Week* takes on an international flavor. (pp. 67-8)

The conflict of the novel, as George Arms has observed, appears in part three when March, anticipating his first meeting with Dryfoos, experiences a "disagreeable feeling of being owned and of being about to be inspected by his proprietor." . . . This incipient conflict erupts in part four when March refuses to submit to Dryfoos' dictatorial command that Lindau be fired from *Every Other Week*. In part five of the novel the conflict expands outward to society in the New York street car strike, and it reaches its climax in the riot in which Conrad Dryfoos is shot and killed.

To comprehend the scope and nature of the conflict in Howells' novel, however, it must be viewed in contexts other than the economic one, and to do this task we need to look at the history of some of the characters. Howells' story suggests, for example, that perhaps there is some kind of necessity or determinism which runs through things. At the beginning of the novel, when he is urging March to come on to New York as literary editor of *Every Other Week,* Fulkerson reminds March that he has never liked the insurance business—"'it's killing you. You ain't an insurance man by nature. You're a natural-born literary man, and you've been going against the grain. Now, I offer you a chance to go *with* the grain'." . . . The implication is that March, somehow, is meant to be a literary man. . . . What the character of this determinism is, Howells' novel does not finally say. Perhaps it is a naturalistic determinism, as . . . ["grain" suggests]. Or, as Dryfoos, speaking out of some residue of an earlier Calvinism, suggests, perhaps the determinism is a divine predestination. Through March and Conrad, Howells lets us see that one's vocation, one's calling, may not be viewed merely in terms of social or economic circumstance, though that circumstance, too, can not be ignored.

However, it may also be that chance operates in things. . . . When, in chapter two, March sounds his wife about Fulkerson's "scheme" for the new magazine, she asks her husband: "'But what have you got to do with it?'" March's reply not only suggests the operation of chance in things, it includes the idea of a possible inevitability in his fortune.

> It seems that Fulkerson had had his eye on me ever since we met that night on the Quebec boat. I opened up pretty freely to him, as you do to a man you never expect to see again, and when I found he was in that newspaper syndicate business I told him about my early literary ambitions. . . .

Moreover, it turns out, according to Fulkerson, that the idea for the magazine came originally from March himself when the two men met, apparently by chance, years ago. Anticipating March's moral stand against the capitalist Dryfoos later in the story, we do well to take note here of the [cooperative financial base of the magazine] March envisioned to Fulkerson at their first meeting. . . . Thus, March's antipathy for Dryfoos before meeting him has roots in March's past. Determinism and chance seem to have cooperated in the making of March's fortune, as they seem to have in the making of the fortune of *Every Other Week*. . . . When, from the vantage point of the end of Howells' novel, we look back to the beginning and hear March tell his wife—Fulkerson "'says he owes it all to me; that I invented the idea—the germ—the microbe'," . . . the rich irony of the novel's complicity strikes us forcefully.

In addition to a possible determinism and chance as operative in things, there is also individual volition. Our sense of Jacob Dryfoos in the novel is of a man of strong will. He would rule, both in his private and public affairs, with a sure hand. One of Howells' favorite images for the man of will is that of the horse driver (cf. Silas Lapham), and it appears at least three times in the novel in connection with Dryfoos. . . . Jacob Dryfoos' role as the man of will and as the patriarch has rich implication in the novel. Early in it, for example, Fulkerson, telling March how Dryfoos left his Indiana farm and got into the natural-gas business, half jokingly remarks that Mrs. Dryfoos backed her husband all the way. "'She thought whatever he said and did was just as right as if it had been thundered down from Sinai'." . . . But our sense of Jacob Dryfoos as a man of righteous will comes most forcefully from his lording it over his obedient and gentle son; and when, in the climactic scene between the two, Jacob strikes his son, wounding him "in his temple" with Christine Dryfoos' intaglio ring, and Conrad, in "grieving wonder," exclaims, "'Father!'" the implications of significance are fertile indeed. As Everett Carter has suggested, the episode carries with it strong overtones of the Biblical Hebraic and Christian myths. (pp. 68-72)

His son's death is a crushing blow to Dryfoos, and it breaks his fierce pride and his will. Our last view of him as he prepares to embark for Europe with his family is of a man "wearied and bewildered" by what he has come to. Before Dryfoos leaves New York, he sells *Every Other Week*, "the thing," he calls it, after the manner of Fulkerson—sells "the thing" to Fulkerson and March, and March is thrilled by the "wonderful good-fortune as seemed about falling to him." . . . At the last, then, March does have his magazine, the magazine which, we recall, was his idea in the first place. In another way, too, Howells at the last humorously points the organic symmetry of his story in which diverse fortunes yet are one. Married now to Miss Woodburn, Fulkerson goes with her "down the St. Lawrence to Quebec over the line of travel that the Marches had taken on their wedding journey. He had the pleasure of going from Montreal to Quebec on the same boat on which he first met March.'' . . . (pp. 73-4)

Free will, chance, necessity: all seem at work in what the novel shows as the complicity of experience. Experience itself is neutral, however, and it takes on significant form only as the characters themselves give it form out of their needs, their beliefs, and their acts. Angus Beaton in the novel, by turns a painter, a writer, a sculptor; a man who in doing whatever he likes finally does nothing he likes . . . , illustrates the way experience is formless until the individual gives it form. In its neutrality, Howells' complicity of experience resembles what William James called "pure experience." That is, pure experience is the flux of things as yet unformed. In James's words, it is "a *that* which is not yet any definite *what*, tho' ready to be all sorts of whats." In the complicity of Howells' novel there is no hard and fast line between circumstance and character, between private and public experience. In the broadest sense, the conflicts in the novel stem from different and opposing claims to know what form experience ought to take to realize justice, both for the individual and for society. If the novel does not resolve the problems it raises, its complicity nonetheless reveals a willingness to let all things grow together, and where there are conflicts of interest, to conserve as many interests as possible in accordance with something like the "economy of pain" formula announced by Sewell in *The Rise of Silas Lapham*. Thus, we may say that, in a real sense, complicity in Howells' novel is an aesthetic form of the novelist's socialism.

Toward the last, March, speculating on the meaning of the death of Conrad Dryfoos, says to his wife: "'I don't know what it all means, Isabel, though I believe it means good'." . . . March's statement is a measure of his education in the novel, for his distinction between knowledge and belief is central to Howells' realism. In the novel it is in the characters' enactment of their beliefs that they shape their reality, and in that shaping is the pragmatic hazarding of their fortunes. March's affirmation that it all "means good," is not a superficial optimism. Rather, it is an affirmation of faith in the goodness of life in the awareness of the limits of human knowledge. What Howells' novel finally asks of us, as George Arms has said, "is awareness, an awareness not merely of society but of ourselves in society." (pp. 74-5)

> William McMurray, in his The Literary Realism of William Dean Howells (*copyright © 1967 by Southern Illinois University Press; reprinted by permission of Southern Illinois University Press), Southern Illinois University Press, 1967, 147 p.*

WILLIAM M. GIBSON   (essay date 1967)

[Howells's] first ambition was to become a lyric and narrative poet like Longfellow, sustaining himself by literary journalism until poetry would support him. But the popular failure of [*Poems of Two Friends* and of *No Love Lost, a Romance of Travel*] became the "turning point" of Howells's life, as he later explained, especially in the light of the high critical success of *Venetian Life*. . . . In this new kind of travel book, the first of many, Howells had contrasted the high art and the deep past of Venice with people and incidents in the shabby-picturesque present. The point of view is distinctly American, the tone is ironic in the manner of Heine, the style is finished. His "fatal gift of observation" already apparent, the young exconsul and *Atlantic* editor turned to fiction.

From **"The Independent Candidate, a Story of Today"** (1854-55, never collected) to *The Leatherwood God* . . . Howells wrote thirty-five novels—and more than forty tales and sketches. Apart from the juvenile **"Candidate"** story, **Suburban Sketches** . . . is Howells's first tentative venture into fiction. With an eye educated by the Italian experience, Howells drew Irish and Italian and Negro figures in the Cambridge background, and expanded his scenes from the serving girl at home and doorstep acquaintance, through horsecar vignettes, to Boston and Nahant. . . . The public response was favorable, and Howells took a long step toward the novel in his next book. (pp. 16-17)

The biographical elements in *Their Wedding Journey* . . . are apparent in Howells's letters of the time and in the manuscript. Howells framed his narrative on his summer's travel with his wife, in 1870, from Boston to New York and Albany, Buffalo, Montreal, and Quebec. . . . Within this framework, nonetheless, *Their Wedding Journey* is fiction. Rapidly limned characters encountered along the route come to life as Basil and Isabel March, delayed honeymooners, talk with them and react to them. The Marches, in fact, provide such action as there is by humorous persiflage and frequent clashes of opinion and occasional quarreling. They also lend depth to the travelogue by recalling Francis Parkman's interpretations of the French-Canadian past, and by comparing Canadian to European sights. Howells provided a rationale for his story thus: "As in literature the true artist will shun the use even of real events if they are of an improbable character, so the sincere observer of man will not desire to look upon his heroic or occasional phases, but will seek him in his habitual moods of vacancy and tiresomeness." . . . *Their Wedding Journey*, which Henry Adams called "a pleasing and faithful picture of American existence" [see excerpt above], thus exemplifies Howells's early, anti-romantic, Emersonian theory of realism, a tradition that led to Eugene O'Neill's *The Emperor Jones*.

The Saguenay-Quebec travel scene again forms the background for *A Chance Acquaintance* . . .—"There's nothing like having railroads and steamboats transact your plot for you," said Howells to a friend in 1871. But Kitty Ellison, who had appeared briefly in *Their Wedding Journey*, is a real creation. She is a girl from the West, . . . with natural good manners and taste. She finds the Canadian scene and character as rich and strange as Miles Arbuton of Boston thinks them dull, especially by comparison with European counterparts. Howells probably found his idea for the clash of such differing temperaments in Jane Austen, but his characterization is original—and so is his conclusion. Kitty in the end rejects Arbuton's suit, wholly in accord with Howells and James's shared determination, at this time, to avoid the "everlasting young man and young woman" as a subject for serious fiction. Howells's satire, moreover, on one kind of Boston manners—the stiffness, coldness, and extreme self-regard of Arbuton—is pointed and amusing. . . . [James] wrote his friend [that] he delighted in a figure "so real and complete, so true and charming." It is no wonder, for Kitty is the older sister of James's Daisy Miller, the first fictional portrait of "the American girl" who would make for Howells and James a linked reputation.

Howells's first "true novel," *A Foregone Conclusion* . . . , was also his first international novel. He was now prepared to venture beyond Canadian-American or native East-West contrasts, and by juxtaposing characters of the New World in the Old, to dramatize a tragic *donnée*. "The hero is a Venetian priest in love with an American girl," he wrote James. "There's richness!'' . . . *The Tragedy of Don Ippolito*, as Howells first titled the novel, gains its depth from four fully imagined characters, a tragic action that develops from their relationships, and a highly functional setting. (pp. 17-20)

Howells's development as a novelist cannot always be neatly periodized. After completing a major work, he frequently lapsed into an earlier accustomed manner before venturing further—or continued to satisfy the taste of his public for psychologized tales of courtship. So, although it comes after [*A Modern Instance* and *The Rise of Silas Lapham*] . . . , both works of more scope, *Indian Summer* . . . may be said to culminate Howells's first period of small-scale novels of manners, and is probably the best of them. Two interim works preceding *Indian Summer* are "Private Theatricals" . . . and *The Lady of the Aroostook*. . . . The first is a brilliant comic account of Belle Farrell's destroying the friendship of two young men who both become her suitors. A master of feminine psychology, Howells surpassed himself in delineating Mrs. Farrell, a New England Hedda Gabler before Ibsen. Like De Forest's Mrs. LaRue, she is beautiful and clever and irresponsible and yet somehow sympathetic, because she is driven by passions she does not fully understand. The second is a once very popular but much slighter work. (pp. 21-2)

Indian Summer, Howells told Mark Twain, "is all a variation on the one theme" of January and May, of youth and age. The variations are amusing and complex. Effie Bowen, whom De Forest considered "the most perfectly painted child in fiction," appears to be twelve. Her mother, Lina Bowen, is a charming widow of thirty-eight. Imogene Graham, their guest in Italy, twenty, a happier Florida Vervain, is counterpointed against mother and daughter. And the forty-one-year-old Colville, involving himself with all three, creates discords among them and multiplies the bemuddlement and the humor before final harmony is attained. Two memorable "confidants" help to spin the plot and clarify the theme. Elderly, curious Mrs. Amsden is always one stage behind in tracing the changes within the triangle and thus maintains the comic note. The Reverend Mr. Waters, aged seventy, who has cheerfully left Haddam East Village for Florence, forever, considers Mrs. Bowen and Colville young and provides Howells perspective.

The narrative method of *Indian Summer* is dramatic. The mood is nostalgia for lost youthful love and the Italian past, in the manner of Turgenev, well tempered by irony and wit. The characters . . . are Americans in Italy, of all ages. The action is single, culminating in Colville's marriage to Mrs. Bowen, after his engagement to the girl, Imogene, breaks of its own sentimental weight. But Howells's transforming into fictional life his leading ideas—that longing for youth when youth is past results only in the waste of human energy and devotion, and that the notion of self-sacrifice may prove a pure mischief—is achieved only by close attention to motive and characterization. When Imogene strikes youthful attitudes, or confides her delusions to her astonishing diary, or teeters happily at the edge of a mismarriage, she errs foolishly and openly. Mrs. Bowen's faults are more subtly, though quite as clearly, indicated. The older woman's repressed jealousy and her wish to conform to European codes of behavior lead her to bewilder Colville and to torture Imogene and herself. Colville, though he often acts like a proto-Prufrock, is a paragon of common sense compared to the women of the novel. As for the carriage accident that reveals Colville's love for Mrs. Bowen, or Effie's appeal at the last moment to prevent Colville's leaving, these are acceptable *coups de théâtre*, because Colville now rec-

ognizes Imogene's immaturity, and Imogene has weighed Colville's social ineptitudes and found him wanting. The tone is high comedy. Only the dullest reader would expect disaster in *Indian Summer*. (pp. 22-4)

[In Howells's first period] he began by adapting his formula of travel and observation to fiction, with the sanction of the picaresque novel and perhaps of Heine's *Pictures of Travel*. The methods of Hawthorne and Turgenev and maturing concepts of motive and character led to the comedies of manners and courtship—with the Howellsian difference. Toward the end of the period Howells considered himself a "built-in novelist" because he was competent to begin serializing a work before he had finished it. Yet, despite increasing intensity in plot, the early books are alike in their depending on intersectional and international clash and contrast and on dramatic encounter between "two persons only, or three or four at the most."

In the second period, 1880-86, Howells turned to the American scene and to certain large problems of contemporary life. His characters increased in number and variety; his novels grew longer, from six to eight or ten magazine installments. He found justification first in Zola and then in Tolstoi for his matter and his motives. Most strikingly, he had come to the decision to excise those humorous or reflective comments on which he had heretofore leaned heavily in order to win approval for a character or an action—asides which formed for many readers a signature of his style and manner. Thus, the manner of Goldsmith or Thackeray or Heine is much diminished in *A Foregone Conclusion*, and by the time of *Indian Summer*, it has either vanished or become an element of the speech of Colville, a created character.

The second period opens with *The Undiscovered Country* . . . , "a serious work" Howells called it, which ventures into an area that he would explore again and again: the channels into which the will to believe was flowing in contemporary America, as religious convictions decayed and religious sanctions weakened. In this novel Howells sets the delusions of spiritualism in New England against Shaker belief and practice. . . . Apart from its intrinsic interest and its treatment of the father-daughter relation, the novel forms an interesting link between Hawthorne's *Blithedale Romance* and James's *The Bostonians*. (pp. 25-6)

[*Dr. Breen's Practice*] also explores the growing feminist mood of the decade, but the author's stance is at least as masculine and satirical as it is sympathetic. Though Dr. Grace Breen, a homeopathist fresh from medical school, is first humbled by and then humbles the allopathist Dr. Mulbridge, her marriage to the man she loves cannot alter her bottom nature. She is a belated Puritan, a devotee of New England "dutiolatry." . . .

[*A Modern Instance*] is a very different story. It was born in Howells's mind as "The New Medea" when he conceived an Indiana divorce case as a commonplace example of the dire ancient conflict in Euripides' drama. (p. 26)

Despite the weakened dramatic tension in the last chapters, Howells achieved his "strongest" work, as he himself believed, in *A Modern Instance*. It is a moving representation of moral ignorance and moral decay, unmatched until Dreiser imagined Hurstwood and Fitzgerald created Dr. Diver. (p. 28)

[*The Rise of Silas Lapham*] opens dramatically with an interview between Bartley Hubbard [of *A Modern Instance*], still a struggling reporter, and the newly rich paint-king of Boston, on the perennially fascinating subject of how he had made his million. The novel has always been popular, partly because it presents Lapham's financial and social failure as "consciously and deliberately chosen" when he has to decide whether he shall cheat and stay on top in business, or tell the truth and fail irrecoverably. Lapham's true rise is therefore moral, and all the more dramatic in the context of the elastic business codes of the Gilded Age and his own business failure. (pp. 28-9)

[In] terms of style, the novel deserves its reputation. Bromfield Corey's wit and Penelope's tartness gain from contrast with Colonel Lapham's boastful speech, in the idioms and rhythms of his New England vernacular. Howells's narrative prose is equally functional, concrete, and clear. This was the style that both James and Twain, themselves stylists, found so distinctive and took so much pleasure in.

The serious motive and the large impression of occupations and professions that Howells sought in the fiction of his second period gave way to profound concern with social and economic questions in the third period, the decade from 1887 to 1894. (p. 30)

Most of his novels in the period have been characterized as "economic" novels, and it is true that they share certain characteristics of the *tendenzromansk* or propaganda novel, a form Howells scorned. Ideologically they culminate in *A Traveler from Altruria* . . . , a Utopian romance that brings together Howells's ideas in defense of liberty, equality, and fraternity in that altruistic "other land" which America only partially shadowed forth. But "novels of complicity" is a more accurate tag than "economic" novels, because complicity is the dominant concept in them; and a "panoramic theory of fiction"— Howells's own phrase as Van Wyck Brooks later reported it— is equally useful since it fits these works concerned with the lives of many rather than few characters. These definitions, however, apply only to the main stream in the third period; they will not account for . . . [*April Hopes* or *The Shadow of a Dream*]—both substantial novels and each different in form and motive.

In *The Minister's Charge or The Apprenticeship of Lemuel Barker* . . . Howells first fully stated his doctrine of complicity, combining it with that major motif of the nineteenth-century novel, the provincial in the city. The minister, Sewell, has unintentionally encouraged Lemuel to come to Boston from his home in the country by politely dishonest praise of the boy's poems. . . . "The Country Boy in Boston"—this was Howells's first title for the novel—fails and returns to the country; and thus Howells stands the American drama of the self-made man on its head. The work is suffused with other and subtler ironies that delighted Mark Twain, for example, which make up for the blurred double focus on Sewell and Barker. To suggest only two: Sewell preaches complicity but is unable to conceive of Barker's torment when he falls in love with the gentle Jessie Carver while he is still pledged to Statira. . . . The society girl Sibyl Vane treats Barker as her inferior with cutting arrogance, even as she finds time to bestow "a jacqueminot rosebud on a Chinaman dying of cancer" in a charity hospital.

The naked issue of charity versus justice becomes, in fact, the central issue of *Annie Kilburn* . . . , though Howells keeps his actors in this Tolstoian novel thoroughly limited and human. (pp. 31-3)

Between March 1889 and October 1891, Howells published in serial form three extraordinary books: [*A Hazard of New Fortunes, The Shadow of a Dream,* and *An Imperative Day*]. . . . The third is an intensely imagined study of miscegenation. The second, taking its title from *The Scarlet Letter,* explores the morbid psychology of jealous delusion; it is an experimental novel rendered from three points of view, anticipating rather than following James. The first is very simply Howells's biggest novel. It sets forth panoramically, as *Manhattan Transfer* would later, the struggles of fifteen major characters and a host of minor figures to establish a national magazine in New York City and to enter into its "vast, gay, shapeless life." (pp. 33-4)

A Hazard of New Fortunes envisions the city as a magnet and a microcosm. In social terms it contrasts Margaret Vance, the sensitive girl of old New York society, with the Dryfoos daughters, Christine and Mela, whose one aim is to break into society under the guidance of the well-paid Mrs. Mandel. The elegant but unsure Beaton wavers in the middle, courting independent Alma Leighton and flirtatious Christine. At the bottom are Lindau and a prostitute pursued by the police, slum-dwellers, the one by choice and the other by necessity. In political-economic terms, the novel presents Dryfoos as the coldest of newly rich entrepreneur-speculators, with Fulkerson as his prophet, in contrast to Conrad Dryfoos, the son, who turns from his father and his father's life to passive resistance and Christian socialism. Similarly, Colonel Woodburn, whose private integrity matches his admiration for the feudal institutions of the prewar South, is set against Lindau, a German revolutionary who has lost his forearm fighting slavery in the Civil War. Still another kind of contrast appears in the characters' attitudes toward art: Beaton's great talent, Alma Leighton's aspirations, the barbarous taste of the Dryfoos family. In moral worth as well, Howells sets his characters in a kind of hierarchy, as George Arms has argued, from lowest to highest: Beaton, Dryfoos, Fulkerson, March, Woodburn, Lindau, and Conrad Dryfoos. (p. 34)

[The] novel singularly combines the wit of Jane Austen and the elaborate irony of Thorstein Veblen, before Veblen. It is a broad, vital comedy, as provocative in its implications as it is entertaining in its fable, in which Howells artfully and unobtrusively colored the public dream of success with private awareness of complicity.

Following the period of novels of complicity, which ended in the romance *A Traveler from Altruria,* Howells reverted to smaller canvases in his fiction, now persuaded that the great social questions must be represented from within rather than from without. Characteristic and perhaps best of the novels between 1894 and 1908 is *The Landlord at Lion's Head*. . . . Here Howells's idea was to bring a true New England rustic type into conflict with Cambridge and Harvard society, and his bottom motive was to realize "that anti-Puritan quality which was always vexing the heart of Puritanism." . . . More nearly naturalistic than any other story by Howells, it is as Delmar Cooke judged it "a master novel."

Finally, *The Leatherwood God* . . . represents a late, fine flowering of Howells's talent and his one punitive tragedy. It recreates the rise of an actual Ohio backwoodsman of the 1840's, who deluded others and even himself momentarily into believing that he was God. (pp. 35-7)

William M. Gibson, in his William D. Howells
(American Writers Pamphlet No. 63; © *1967, Uni-*

versity of Minnesota), University of Minnesota Press, Minneapolis, 1967, 48 p.

JAMES L. DEAN (essay date 1970)

W. H. Auden admirably suggests some of the problems and possibilities of travel writing in his prefatory essay to Henry James' *The American Scene:* "of all possible subjects, travel is the most difficult for an artist, as it is the easiest for a journalist. For the latter, the interesting event is the new, the extraordinary, the comic, the shocking, and all that the peripatetic journalist requires is a flair for being on the spot where and when such events happen—the rest is merely passive typewriter thumping; meaning, relation, importance, are not his quarry. The artist, on the other hand, is deprived of his most treasured liberty, the freedom to invent; successfully to extract importance from historical personal events without ever departing from them, free only to select and never to modify or to add, calls for imagination of a very high order."

W. D. Howells' travel literature, at its best, demonstrates this kind of imagination. (p. 1)

Howells encountered problems of technique from the beginning of his career. His experience as an author and a reviewer of travel books for the *Atlantic Monthly* led him toward several worthwhile conclusions about the limitations and artistic possibilities of the genre. Of those conclusions he reached, the following are significant: The narrator must be both vital and consistent. The angle of vision counts for much more than new material. By effective use of humor and irony, the artist can counter the sterilities of conventional treatment, where style, feeling, choice of picturesque detail, jokes, and rhapsodies about art drearily conform to expectation. He can not easily resolve the moral, philosophical, and aesthetic problems posed by Europe's long history and wealth of art. He must confront them, however, and devise techniques to handle them. . . . I would like to examine some aspects of the confrontation of American and European values, since this confrontation notably influences the technical resources the artist brings to bear on the issues.

American writers frequently have expressed ambivalent attitudes about the Old and New Worlds. Cushing Strout rightly maintains in *The American Image of the Old World* that an acute necessity for reconciling this ambivalence existed in all major American writers of the nineteenth century, from Cooper to James; all were fascinated by the American-European conflict which, Strout suggests, had mythic proportions and multiple implications: "The dream of a primitive innocent New World was thus brought into contact with the facts of a complex sophisticated society, and the encounter, unsettling to American poise, fostered the ambiguity which was to mark serious American literature in the nineteenth century."

American travel literature, as much as its fiction, displays this ambiguity. Howells' reviews indicate that he found it in the accounts of others, and his readers easily perceive it in his own work. Like many Americans when first in Europe, he had strong convictions of the moral superiority of American life, yet his years in Venice as American consul made him increasingly sensitive to the values of European culture. . . . Howells achieved a more balanced perspective in later years, but his early uneasiness led him to engage in romantic posturing, sweeping cultural indictments, and self-conscious demonstrations of literary style and poetic feeling. In an 1867 review

Howells ironically enough castigates W. Pembroke Fetridge, author of *Harper's Handbook,* for committing sins quite similar to some Howells himself committed a few years before. (pp. 2-3)

If nothing else, the "personal flavor and feeling so unusually strong" which Fetridge imparts to his volume causes Howells seriously to consider the problem of the function of the narrator in a travel account. A travel book with an oppressive personal cast has affinities with confessional literature—though, to be sure, the traveler's confession is unconscious. Yet a book must reveal the character of the writer to some extent; Howells "likes to find a man as well as an author in a book." A vivid and forcible narrator is an asset, particularly if the narrator does not indiscriminately take duties upon himself which more properly belong to the philosopher, the poet, the historian, and the comic.

Howells learned that consistency in point of view is instrumental in creating unity of effect. He also recognized the difficulty the narrator has in being always an active consciousness and unifying center—especially since the material of travel appears fragmentary and lacks apparent significance. Only a few writers, Howells finds, are aware of the necessity of creating a consistent, yet flexible narrative viewpoint. He sees advantages in a restricted point of view and a narrow range of facts, for within these limitations a good writer can move with enough imaginative freedom to create "a whole world of character, of experience, of feeling." Howells' ideal narrator is one who can suggest complexity and significance as well as record surface phenomena, preserve a balance between himself and the facts observed, and advance general conclusions based on his observations. Such tasks demand great technical facility as well as "imagination of a very high order."

Howells recognizes that poetic vision can render a truth which exists beyond the facts, statistics, and generalizations based on them. A writer's angle of vision signifies more than what is seen: the writer who attempts to be definitive sees less than he should because he considers the ends more than the means. Howells also inclines to see poetic vision as superior to scientific vision; observation and recording of facts without insight into their implications strike him as futile. Ideally, Howells suggests, an unscientific travel account can reveal "something of the grace and freedom and keen mental insight which we require in a work of fiction."

Because he desires freshness of vision, he often bridles at the tiresome repetition of well-known facts, emotions, scenes, and conditions. No more satisfactory are accounts which are primarily subjective in nature. The writer must see significance beyond the merely personal. Howells' reaction against sentimentality stems from his belief in the necessity of clear vision. The sentimental is pernicious because it distorts reality: The traveler sees through a colored glass. And when one can not see, he can always resort to the conventions of sentiment— substitute an expected feeling for a truly felt one (or lack of a felt one) or paste a feeling over a fact. Sentiment, when overused, becomes a kind of emotional editorializing.

Howells finds the traveler who sees only conventionally as distressing as the one who misses Europe altogether, as Fetridge appears to have done. Because he came to recognize the dangers to the writer of seeing only what conventions have taught one to see, Howells suggests the need for constant examination of beliefs in light of new experiences and contrasting viewpoints. The conventional takes many forms; at its most damning it suggests that a writer has principally seen only what he has read. If an innocent on tour, he more often than not find himself tied to his guidebook; if more experienced, he usually finds a formula which satisfies him, and hopefully, his readers. In either case he misses the sense of personal discovery, the excitement of mental or emotional adventure. (pp. 3-5)

Humor—and many manifestations appear in American travel books written during Howells' lifetime—often serves as a conventional device of the writer. (p. 5)

Alexis de Tocqueville finds little evidence of humor in Americans, but more perceptively remarks: "among democratic nations the existence of man is more complex; the same mind will almost always embrace several objects at once, and these objects are frequently wholly foreign to each other. As it can not know them all well, the mind is readily satisfied with imperfect notions of each." Tocqueville could not know what Howells discovers; entertaining "imperfect notions" simultaneously does not necessarily imply superficiality, for the "imperfectness" may be counterbalanced by the complexity of the perspective which entertains them. American humor, because it can reflect this complexity, may fill the gap between multiple foreign objects, or arbitrate between them. A flexible, complex narrator who is very much aware of how he sees, if not certain of the significance of what he sees, can provide some stability in a mental environment characterized by flux.

Howells realizes that because humor is Janus-faced, it can effectively criticize at the same time it induces laughter. If judiciously employed, it can reveal much about national shortcomings. But more significantly, Howells maintains that humor in the travel book must be an integral part of a larger intention—it should reflect the writer's vision of reality more than his desire to amuse.

Howells' irony, as much as his humor, functions critically as part of a larger invention. As a device in travel literature irony has several obvious advantages over didactic statement. As a double-edged device it affords the writer two ways of seeing something, neither of which need be definitive; it is, in a sense, a device of the open end, and thus particularly suited to the "realist." Irony accords the writer greater flexibility—he may be ironic both about himself and about what he observes. Finally, it provides a means for balancing between contingency and irresolution on one hand and fixed notions and stated values on the other.

Irony and humor can not, of course, be considered apart from style, and Howells often concerns himself with matters of style. He has stylistic standards he would like to see observed by more travel writers. He advocates simplicity and naturalness (not easily come by), grace (which suggests a distrust of rigid rhetorical patterning), sincerity, vigor, and economy. Howells also prefers a colloquial style to one characterized by finish and wit, for the former better depicts the commonplace realities encountered during travel. Moreover, it serves as an antidote to excessive poetic enthusiasm, artificiality, and imitative qualities. (pp. 6-7)

Howells' travels are outwardly uneventful, inwardly eventful. Howells proves himself an uncommonly good writer of travel literature, for it is his unique talent to find new adventure in old places, to discover the extraordinary in the ordinary, and to impart to the common and incidental the luster of art. Those things Auden asks of travel writing—meaning, relation, and importance—are certainly evident in Howells' books of travel. Howells does more than practice the craft of travel writing; he demonstrates that he knows much about the theory underlying his practice. By considering such matters as vision, role of the narrator, function of irony and humor, appropriate style, and use of art and history in a travel account, he convincingly shows his awareness of the necessities of his craft and the value of travel literature as a means of revelation and discovery. (pp. 8-9)

> *James L. Dean, in his* Howells' Travels Toward Art *(© 1970 by the University of New Mexico Press), University of New Mexico Press, 1970, 145 p.*

GEORGE PERKINS (essay date 1974)

William Dean Howells displayed more consciousness of the evils of the Gilded Age than he is frequently given credit for, indicating it in his persistent distrust of the city and its ways. Much of the importance of *The Rise of Silas Lapham, The Minister's Charge,* and *A Hazard of New Fortunes* lies in the implied rejection of the city which each embodies, and this theme is clearly foreshadowed in *A Modern Instance* . . . , the novel in which Howells makes his first significant use of the city environment. (p. 427)

[*A Modern Instance*] concerns a marriage and a divorce, and the divorce occurs between two country people who have come to the city. (p. 428)

To represent *A Modern Instance* as devoted chiefly to divorce problems is to misrepresent its scope. In it Howells dealt not simply with the evils of divorce, not simply with the question of remarriage, but more generally with human desires and responsibilities not only in the marriage relationship, but in the social and economic relationships of a young couple making their way in the city. It is not the divorce which is important: it is the background for the divorce. Although Howells provided no clues as to what would have resulted had Bartley and Marcia remained in the country, he did insist on Barley's large capacity for good, and he clearly indicated the rôle of city pressures in bringing about his moral disintegration.

"Success," as Bartley and Marcia understand it, is a concept vital to an understanding of *A Modern Instance*. The city makes demands unheard of in the country, and many of the problems of the novel arise from the attempts of the Hubbards to meet those demands. Howells defines the goals in social and economic terms, and does not always separate the two. Bartley and Marcia need money for their immediate physical needs, but they also need it to live well socially. (pp. 428-29)

Bartley achieves his greatest economic success from his contact with the Boston newspaper world. . . . The editor who buys his second piece invites him to join the men at the newspaper club that evening. Since Bartley had intended to celebrate the sale of the article by taking Marcia to dinner at the Parker House, he indicates the high place of economic success in his scale of values by immediately accepting the editor's invitation. Marcia, too, reveals her worship of the same gods by her prompt response, "I hope you accepted!" (p. 429)

In the world of journalism in *A Modern Instance* Howells creates a society dominated by a moral laxity which he typifies in the publisher Witherby. Clarifying his conception of that condition by his portrayal of Ricker, editor of the *Chronicle-Abstract* and a thoroughly respectable man, he makes clear that

Witherby embodies the newer American business trends. He endows Bartley with a nature which causes him to aim high, but always to take the easiest road, and he covers the terrain of journalism with easy roads. Bartley wants to succeed as a husband, and he wants to prosper economically. No man to worry about the unpredictable future, he concerns himself with the need of a steady income in the immediate present. He allows his long-standing legal ambitions to diminish rapidly as he becomes more successful in journalism: he clearly envisions the rewards of the one field, while the rewards of the other remain beyond his view. Marcia constantly reminds him of his former desire to study law, but he constantly reminds her of their present need of an income—he does not desire to resolve the conflicting demands by hurting her, and if he seems impatient with her vocational ambitions for him, he also provides her with a better than average income. Both of them measure success largely in terms of income, but both live from day to day in expectation of the time when Bartley will have his ''basis,'' the salaried position which will remove from him the pressures of free-lancing.

Howells provides the chance for the basis at a critical moment, and thus clarifies the circumstantial nature of Bartley's downfall. He has taken Bartley to a point where his continuing success in journalism appears doubtful. . . . As a result, he determines to seek a place in Atherton's law office. The moment is important: when one considers Bartley's character (his potential for good) and the character of the legal profession as portrayed in Howells (almost always admirable, and preferable to journalism) one has little doubt that Bartley's entrance into the law office may result in his moral salvation. Howells presents him with a choice for good or evil, but arranges matters in such a way that Bartley cannot know the nature of the choice, or even that he has one. On his way to Atherton's office, Bartley stops in to see Witherby, who offers him a position on the *Events* at three times the salary he had hoped to receive from Atherton. Neither Bartley nor Marcia look further than the salary. . . . In this fashion Bartley makes the choice which leads to his moral disintegration, but few people, given the same choice, would behave differently. Bartley does not destroy himself. He succumbs to a destruction that comes from without, through the pressure of social circumstances which offers him little or no moral support.

Had Bartley attached himself permanently to another newspaper he might have found it possible to maintain his integrity, but on the *Events* he comes into contact with too much that is corrupt. Howells characterizes Witherby as in almost every way a small and contemptible man. . . . In going to work for him Bartley encounters a force which can have only a corrupting influence.

Howells fails to present dramatically the corruption which ensues from Bartley's association with Witherby, but he soon externalizes this corruption as seen through the eyes of Ricker:

> as he looked at Bartley's back he had his misgivings; it struck him as the back of a degenerate man, and that increasing bulk seemed not to represent an increase of wholesome substance, but a corky, buoyant tissue, materially responsive to some sort of moral dryrot. . . .

Here Howells has somewhat obscured his intent. Bartley has not done anything very wrong, yet the author brands him as degenerate. Granted that he later causes him to live up to this branding, he has already brought him to an unregenerate point

without allowing the reader to watch his descent. In the circumstances one can only applaud the nineteenth-century critic who commented: ''We vaguely feel, somehow, that Bartley would have prospered, with his unscrupulous views about journalism, if he had not got fat, and that then he would not have left his wife.'' Seeing only the effects of Bartley's degeneration, one may miss the immediate significance of the conditions which have brought it about: Bartley has got into the wrong company. (pp. 430-32)

Howells includes another element of confusion when he follows Bartley's moral descent by an economic one. Bartley possesses all the qualities for continuing success, as Howells defines it in the novel. Yet the end comes quickly and unbelievably: out of a job, bound for Chicago (but thinking of returning), he has Halleck's $1,200 stolen from him. He can not go back, and whether or not Howells intended a conscious irony in his insistence that ''nothing remained for him but the ruin he had chosen'' . . . , the fact remains that Bartley has not ''chosen'' at all. At the most he has acquiesced in following the paths which most clearly lead to economic success. The reader may accept his moral downfall, without seeing why that downfall should affect Bartley's economic status.

Howells parallels the Hubbards' economic contacts with Boston by their relationship to Boston society, but he does not make their main problem one of social acceptance. Originating as country people, they remain too unsophisticated to realize that they never move in the best society. They accept the kindnesses of the Hallecks and the friendly interest of Atherton and Clara Kingsbury without asking for more. Howells raises a question not of acceptance, but of support—what support has the city of Boston to offer a marriage which hovers continually on the brink of disaster? Answer: none. Howells had not yet developed his theory of complicity, but he had already developed ideas of man's responsibility to his fellow-man, and in *A Modern Instance* he strongly suggests that some of that responsibility applies to the relationship between Boston and the Hubbards. Since others can influence the Hubbards so easily, they ought to be able to influence them to good effect as well as to bad.

Boston society does not provide good influences. Although Howells obviously intends to characterize all of the people whom the Hubbards meet on the social level in Boston as good people, he provides them with a real deficiency—the lack of any dynamic quality which will transmit their goodness or make it worthy of emulation. (pp. 432-34)

Howells presents his most important criticism of Boston, perhaps, in his portrait of Atherton, but he does not make it completely lucid. Atherton dominates the last few pages and speaks the last words in the novel. He communicates some of its most weighty sentiments; in the following passage, he seems to speak for Howells as well as for himself:

> The natural man is a wild beast, and his natural goodness is the amiability of a beast basking in the sun when his stomach is full. The Hubbards were full of natural goodness, I dare say, when they didn't happen to cross each other's wishes. No, it's the implanted goodness that saves—the seed of righteousness treasured from generation to generation, and carefully watched and tended by disciplined fathers and mothers in the hearts where they have dropped it. The

flower of this implanted goodness is what we call civilization. . . .

If Howells means this statement as his own, he provides in it one of his most forthright defenses of patrician Boston against the influences which were so rapidly changing it. But if the reader attempts to consider it as a major theme of the novel, he finds the effort unrewarding because of the lack of support elsewhere, and he cannot value it as he otherwise might because of its position in the unsatisfactory last few chapters of the book.

Had Howells done better in this section the reader might know better what he meant. He seems, however, to intend a development of the idea of "complicity," to which he later gives a name in *The Minister's Charge* and which dominates the still later *Annie Kilburn* and *The Quality of Mercy*. At the same time he seems to intend a relation between complicity and a stable society. In a later phase of the same conversation, Atherton makes the connection explicit:

> You know how I hate anything that sins against order, and this whole thing is disorderly. It's intolerable, as you say. But we must bear our share of it. We're all bound together. No one sins or suffers to himself in a civilized state. . . . It's strange that it should be so hard to realize a thing that every experience of life teaches. We keep on thinking of offences against the common good as if they were abstractions!
>
> (pp. 434-35)

Because Howells tends in these statements towards a type of social comment which he made much more important in his later novels (and which he generally omitted from his earlier ones) he forces the reader to give this section of the novel more attention than it otherwise merits. But considering the quotations only in their application to the function of Atherton in *A Modern Instance*, one sees clearly that he serves as a spokesman for a sanity based on a knowledge of the mores of the old Boston and a recognition of the demands of the new. He treads the middle ground between the debased semisophistication of Bartley Hubbard and the tortured, unsuccessful asceticism of Ben Halleck. And he, practical man that he is, the one man in the novel who might be expected to have all the answers, finally can do no better regarding the solution of the problem with which the novel ends than to confess: "Ah! I don't know! I don't know!" . . . Howells must have intended the irony which is implicit in the situation: Atherton can recognize his share in the suffering of people like the Hubbards while at the same time he remains totally unable to afford them any help. In characterizing him, Howells provides one of his best examples of urbane practicality tempered by sensitivity and humanitarianism, but he makes him finally ineffectual.

In Atherton's failure Howells symbolizes the failure of the best of Boston society. The "implanted goodness" of an ordered civilization perhaps resulted in the salvation of an earlier Boston, but in Atherton's time it has become inoperative against the disorders of the Gilded Age. Howells recognizes the worth of the society which Atherton represents, but he does not fail to see some of its shortcomings. If first Halleck and then Atherton can torture themselves over the moral problems involved in the question of remarriage, how can one expect Bartley and Marcia to cope with the difficulties of a marriage which they have already made, and made badly? The Hubbards have brought the problem with them from the country, but had they remained in the country they might have proved able to cope with it. In the city they find it aggravated by the degeneration of Bartley's character, a degeneration which occurs under conditions and as a result of pressures which they would not have encountered at home.

If Howells inserted a social message into *A Modern Instance* it was a message not about the evils of divorce, but about the laxness of a society which encourages rather than retards the development of a character such as Bartley's. Bartley possesses the qualifications for financial and social success in such a society; the arbitrary failure which Howells assigns him clouds but does not obscure the point. Because Howells interested himself more in Bartley and Marcia than in the society which surrounded them, he failed to create a novel which rises clearly to an indictment of Boston business and social mores. Perhaps at this time he would have said he did not see the necessity for such an indictment—nevertheless he made it implicit in the characters and situation which he created.

Howells displays his uncertainties in *A Modern Instance* most clearly in his treatment of Bartley. He fails to make Bartley's economic descent a necessary and logical consequence of his moral descent, and in his zeal to punish him he fails to stress the elements of chance which bring about the final just retribution. He seems almost to believe that he has made Bartley's failure not only just, but inevitable. Yet in such a belief, if he held it, he contradicts much of the general implication of the book. In the city, as he depicts it here and in later works, he provides very little connection between a man's morals and either his economic or his social success, and what connection he does provide is inverse: Silas Lapham's moral rise necessitates the end of his economic and social ambitions. (pp. 436-38)

Despite the confusion of *A Modern Instance,* it represents a major step toward the greater clarity of *The Rise of Silas Lapham, The Minister's Charge,* and *A Hazard of New Fortunes*. Howells provided the foundation here for the total rejection of the values of the city which he implied in those later novels. (p. 438)

> George Perkins, "'A Modern Instance': Howells' Transition to Artistic Maturity," in The New England Quarterly (copyright 1974 by The New England Quarterly), Vol. XLVII, No. 3, September, 1974, pp. 427-39.

SCOTT A. DENNIS   (essay date 1980)

In 1893, W. D. Howells published a curious and remarkably revealing novel, *The World of Chance,* which describes the adventures of a young, naive, romantic novelist who comes to New York to seek his literary fortune. For much of the novel, Howells leaves us to wander through the quagmire of half-formed thoughts and feelings of this adolescent, ambitious, and often foolish young author who has the absurd name of Percy Bysshe Shelley Ray and who has written an absurdly bathetic Hawthornian romance called *A Modern Romeo*. Howells also presents us with an odd assortment of Utopians whom he, almost gleefully, kills off with diphtheria, scarlet fever, and prussic acid. Along the way, he provides us with an attempted murder and a suicide characteristic of the rankest melodrama. Eventually, in a stridently deterministic non-scheme of things, Ray's bathetic novel improbably succeeds.

What are we to make of such a sensationalistic plot when it comes from the pen of America's leading spokesman for realism? One response is to decry the plot as an artistic failure. The novel might be described as a crudely effected collage of material that Howells worked up from sources readily at hand: thinly disguised autobiography, reiteration of characters and themes from the recently published *A Hazard of New Fortunes* . . . , and an author's-eye view of the publishing trade. . . . Are we to assume, however, that an author of Howells' literary sophistication unwittingly allowed these bizarre occurrences in his novel? A more thoughtful response to the novel suggests that the sensationalism is purposeful and yields some important insights into Howells' feelings about his life and work circa 1893. *The World of Chance* presents a cynical view of life in general and literary success in particular, and it does so with a large irony that often approaches self-parody.

The character of Percy Ray alone suffices to establish the element of self-parody. In creating him, Howells drew heavily upon his own experience as a young, Midwestern journalist coming to New York to make his literary fortune. . . . [Howells] invests Ray with his own youthful, priggish disgust at "Bohemianism." . . . Significantly, *The World of Chance* begins precisely where Howells' autobiographical memoir of his Ohio days, *Years of My Youth* . . . , ends—at the point where, tired and satiated with small talk, the young author parts with his friend and co-editor late at night in a train depot.

Howells sharpens the self-censure implied by his identification with the priggish young novelist by using Ray to parody his own fiction. (pp. 279-80)

[Howells'] use of autobiographical material provides him with a protagonist and a literary framework for a novel, which, in turn, becomes an occasion for self-mockery. Often touted himself for his rise from obscurity to the heights of the literary establishment, Howells, in his portrait of Percy Ray, created his ultimate parody of the writer as a Horatio Alger character.

The best evidence of Howells' ironic and self-mocking characterization of Ray lies in the young writer's literary tastes or, more precisely, his "literosity." Ray's passions are Thackeray and Hawthorne, two of Howells' early favorites; but, as Howells tells us in *My Literary Passions* (begun the same year that the novel was published), his love of Thackeray was a mistake of youth, when he was "on a very high aesthetic horse." Thackeray's appeal, Howells tells us, lies in his snobbery, his facile satire of society, his sentimentality and "easy pathos," and his self-conscious use of literary allusion. . . . Thackeray, in short, is an author whom one outgrows. . . . That Ray remains enamored of Thackeray and imitates his snobbery, sentimentality, and aestheticism, suggests, in the context of Howells' own aesthetic history, his youthful immaturity and his blindness to economic and social reality.

Hawthorne, Ray's other literary passion, plays a far more complicated part in *The World of Chance* than Thackeray. (pp. 282-83)

The interplay of autobiographical and fictional elements among Hawthorne, Howells, and Percy Ray grows more and more elaborate . . . until it becomes clear that Howells intended to create a complex play within a play. For, in addition to Ray's speculations about Brook Farm and the Hawthornian elements in his novel, the plot of *The World of Chance* itself takes on overtones of *The Blithedale Romance*. It presents, after all, a community of Utopians (albeit displaced and disillusioned ones)

visited by a young author who detachedly observes them. Their number includes a zealous social reformer who bears curious sway over two very different women, one passive, spiritual, and silent, the other voluble, gay, and down to earth. The Hughes family with the fanatical Ansel Denton and his hold on the Hughes sisters, Peace and Jenny, bears close resemblance to the Blithedale family of Hollingsworth, Priscilla, and Zenobia. (p. 284)

With the echoes of Hawthornian character and plot in *The World of Chance*, Howells also reactivates certain Hawthornian themes. Kane, with his cynical fondness for a turn of phrase, for the aphorism, for *Hard Sayings* (the name of his book), uses a language that petrifies experience and isolates him from life. Percy Bysshe Shelley Ray's love of romantic and literary effect (implied by his full name), and his corresponding disgust for tawdry reality, isolate him from life also. While mentally rewriting his novel still another time, Ray witnesses the arrest of a shoplifter: "The intrusion of such a brutal fact of life into the tragic atmosphere of his revery made the young poet a little sick, but the young journalist [in him] avidly seized upon it." . . . Ray is a parasitic—or worse, an indifferent—voyeur.

Both Ray and Kane commit, in their ways, the old Hawthornian sins of egotism and detachment. . . . [Howells] clearly means to rebuke the aesthete in Ray and, in the final analysis, to deplore the cynical dilletantism of Kane; but he is just as harsh with the self-sacrifice of Ansel Denton, whose fanatical devotion to the well-being of fellow workers becomes a form of insanity, and with Hughes, the communitarian, whom Ray finds to be "rather too much of the Hollingsworth type." . . . As Hawthorne makes the point at the end of *The Blithedale Romance* that Hollingsworth has "too much purpose" and Coverdale too little, it is also clear in Howells' novel that Hughes and Denton have sacrificed too much to their hopelessly idealistic schemes and that Ray and Kane, with their literary affectations, have sacrificed too little. (pp. 284-85)

In *The World of Chance*, Howells writes not an imitation but a contemporary version of *The Blithedale Romance*. Like Hawthorne, whose "concern with the Socialist Community is merely to establish a theatre," he allegorizes social and moral problems by presenting various character types and bringing them together in an unlikely setting. Howells is, in effect, suggesting that if Hawthorne's Brook Farmers were transplanted into the chance world of the 1890s, they would be a group of failed communitarians in an urban slum.

Howells strives for the truth, Ray the effect. Ray spends a great deal of time concocting endings that will appeal to the public taste. Before he knows who Peace is, he fantasizes her in various relationships with a husband and a lover; some of the resulting denouements are "powerful," some "popular," and one is "at once powerful and popular" . . . ; but none of them, at any rate, has any resemblance to the realistic turn of events in which Ray and Peace quietly decide that they must go their separate ways and not marry. Further, Ray never understands Peace, the only character in the novel who does recognize the truth of the human heart. Ray's fiction runs directly counter to Howells' dictum: "The novel ends well that ends faithfully." (p. 286)

Howells satirizes Ray's brand of romanticism and the critics who promote it when he has the reviewer who launches *A Modern Romeo* describe Ray as a prophet, "a Moses, who, if we followed him, would lead us up from the flesh-pots of Realism toward the promised land of the Ideal." . . . Nor were the graphic depictions of scarlet fever, the El-rattled tenement, or the prussic-acid suicide in *The World of Chance* designed to soothe critics of "photographic" realism. Howells intended to demonstrate that realism could better reveal human character and motivation than neoromanticism. The naked light bulb was preferable to the romantic nimbus that failed to illuminate Percy Ray's mind. As Howells had argued to Henry James in defense of Hawthorne, American writers did not need the castle, the ivy, the ruins, or the other paraphernalia of the romance because they had left to them the full range of human experience.

Yet we must remember that Ray recalls a part of Howells, not only his own youthful romanticism but his mature interest in the new genre of psychological romance and in psychic phenomena. Howells called both his Hawthornesque *The Shadow of a Dream* . . . and his allegorical *A Traveler from Altruria* . . . "romances"; and he would write several stories on mental telepathy, a topic that Brandreth suggests to Percy Ray. Perhaps the search for himself in the long ago time of midcentury Ohio that Howells began in the 1890s was partly a romantic inclination. Howells clearly had no tolerance for neoromanticism—for the histrionic, the sentimental—but he recognized these tendencies in his own imagination and indicted them in the character of Percy Ray.

In this game of the play within the play, one must finally consider the implications of the Hawthornian themes for the playwright, for Howells himself. One implication is that Howells saw himself as a Coverdale. The novel raises the issue of the artist-as-voyeur: can a writer eschew the ethical value of a scene for its aesthetic value without compromising his humanity? "The aesthetic temperament," Howells tells us, "is as often the slave as the master of its reveries." . . . Ray's tendency to weave romantic fantasies about people he meets is one that Howells had to fight in himself. . . . Secondly, as Hawthorne dramatized his own inability to commit himself emotionally and practically to Brook Farm in *The Blithedale Romance,* so Howells depicts his own misgivings about his involvement with the sordid realities of social reform. Plagued with doubts about the effect of his temperament on his work and about his artistic duty, Howells once again declared a kinship with Hawthorne by presenting these doubts against the backdrop of *The Blithedale Romance.*

Howells dramatizes his self-doubts in *The World of Chance* by assigning, perhaps unconsciously, the conflicting parts of his own personality to the novel's various characters. Thus the conversations of Ray the romantic, Kane the litterateur, Brandreth the businessman, Chapley the Tolstoian, and Hughes the reformer constitute an internal dialogue. . . . In its contrast between the naive young romantic from the country and a writer working on his opus in an urban slum, *The World of Chance* serves, like Melville's *Pierre,* to dramatize the struggle within the artist to determine the best form for his art.

Ultimately, the clash of viewpoints in *The World of Chance* leaves the novel without a moral focus. If Kane seems wise and sophisticated and Ray selfish and fatuous at the beginning, by the end of the novel Kane's failure to get involved with the Hugheses' problems makes clear the hollowness of his *Hard Sayings.* David Hughes's call for brotherhood is taken so literally by Denton that he drinks prussic-acid in order to offer himself as a sacrifice for the atonement of the guilty; and, though Hughes voices many of Howells' beliefs, he dies a failed Utopian with his book unpublished. Hughes's challenges of Ray, moreover, are themselves challenged by Kane and undercut by the public acceptance of Ray's book. Mr. Chapley

cannot succeed in his Tolstoian withdrawal from materialism; but Brandreth, by his own admission, is little more than a gambler. Despite the variety of alternatives—romanticism, aestheticism, commercialism, withdrawal, reformism—the novel offers no viable philosophy. This is not the usual case of questioning the efficacy of a moral protagonist, as in *The Rise of Silas Lapham* or *The Minister's Charge,* nor is it the moral pluralism of *A Hazard of New Fortunes.* Rather, with its successive undercutting of each character's viewpoint, the novel seems morally nihilistic. Unlike *Silas Lapham* or *A Hazard,* where moral rises are possible even if material success or social reform is not, *The World of Chance* is remarkable for presenting a world where individual actions are irrelevant and futile.

Mrs. Denton and the witty, worldly Kane prove to be the novel's most engaging characters largely because they provide a refreshing contrast to Hughes's polemicism and Ray's stuffiness, because they are immune, that is, to the attempts of others in the novel to take themselves too seriously. Their attitude is Howells' own. The moral vacuum of *The World of Chance* comes as much from the sense of aloofness that informs the novel as from a deliberate attempt to offset antithetical characters. . . . Howells could not, finally, take his own characters seriously.

This disengagement from the novel signifies a creative impasse. To a point, Howells consciously parodied his own youthful aestheticism and romanticism with his sometimes lighthearted, sometimes sardonic treatment of Ray. The employment of Hawthorne is also clearly deliberate—a means of contrasting the value of the honest romance with the "effectism" of Percy Ray and a means of introducing moral themes that Howells held in high regard. Ultimately, however, Howells abdicated conscious control of the novel because he could not integrate the self-parodic subplot of the development of the artist with the subplot of the social and economic misfortunes of the Hugheses. Ray, Howells' youthful persona, remains incapable of understanding his success, his love, or the social forces around him. Yet Howells never liberates us from the confused ramblings of Ray's mind at the end of the novel because the ironic treatment of Ray had become less a narrative strategy than an unconscious dramatization of self-doubt. The tone of *The World of Chance* suggests, finally, the discouragement of an author who had been over this economic ground before, who was experiencing the clash between the artist and the social reformer and growing more fatalistic about it, and who now sensed that no ideological prescription was going to cure society's ills—certainly no artistic scheme. Artistic efficacy had become a vital question for Howells in the face of a world he perceived as deterministic. (pp. 287-91)

The novel's conclusion is an appropriately pessimistic shrug of the shoulders. Returning to Midland on a train, Percy Ray spends a restless night pondering the reasons for the success of his book and the failure of his relationship with Peace. After a series of puerile fantasies and speculations, he concludes that events occur in "the operation of a law so large that we caught a glimpse of its vast orbit once or twice in a lifetime"; . . . but this concept of "Providence" proves to be just another facile indulgence of Ray's romantic imagination. Ray realizes that he may have gotten the notion of the larger law from Kane, whose *Hard Sayings* sacrifices truth to neatness. Howells further deflates such musing by having Percy fall asleep while dreaming of his first love at the novel's end: "Then it was not he, and not she. It was nothing." (p. 291)

The last sentence of the novel, "It was nothing," carries multifold meanings. First, it deliberately echoes—and parodies—Ray's explanation at the end of the penultimate paragraph: "It was Providence." Secondly, it resonates back into the novel itself, rendering judgment on the significance of Ray's story and suggesting that, as a self-contained work of art, the narrative is something of a grim joke, filled with ultimately meaningless philosophical puzzles. The novel ends, after all, precisely where it begins, on a night train with the drowsy speculations of a romantic novelist; and this novelist's extraordinary experiences have left his character unchanged and his questions unanswered. Finally, the phrase "It was nothing" seems to dismiss Howells' own efforts, not only in *The World of Chance* but in the whole New York arena. Like Ray's train, one thread of Howells' imagination was moving away from New York, away from the harsh, urban socioeconomic realities, and pulsing back toward the Midland and toward his past. (p. 292)

Another facet of Howells' imagination, however, was dramatically opposed to this nostalgic retreat. His immediate answer to the dilemma posed in creating *The World of Chance* was to dramatize the existing conflict between art and morality in his Utopian satire, *A Traveler from Altruria*. . . . The character most skeptical of the Altrurian visitor's Utopian ideas is the narrator, Mr. Twelvemough, a writer of romances such as *Glove and Gauntlet* and *Airs and Graces* that deal only with young love. Twelvemough is, essentially, Percy Ray grown more self-satisfied, complacent and supercilious with age. In effect, Howells makes him a personification of fatuity and thus renders his strongest indictment of the popular taste in American letters. With its interactions among Utopians, workers, businessmen, polite society, and a fatuous writer/narrator, *A Traveler from Altruria* contains the same basic ingredients as *The World of Chance*. Yet the satiric vehicle of the Altrurian outsider gave Howells the sure-handed narrative control missing from the earlier work. The faltering stride of *The World of Chance* appears to have been a necessary preliminary to the sharply focused irony of the Utopian satires.

The World of Chance reveals a Howells in transition, a Howells revaluating his art and his career. The last of the economic novels, it stridently amplifies the characters and themes in *A Hazard of New Fortunes* even while it presages new directions in Howells' work. The novel's murky mixture of autobiography and satire was destined to settle out into the literary memoirs and social satire that constituted—with the exception of *The Landlord at Lion's Head* . . .—Howells' most lucid and powerful work of the next decade. (p. 293)

> Scott A. Dennis, "The World of Chance: Howells' Hawthornian Self-Parody," in American Literature *(reprinted by permission of the Publisher; copyright © 1980, Duke University Press, Durham, North Carolina), Vol. LII, No. 2, May, 1980, pp. 279-93.*

ADDITIONAL BIBLIOGRAPHY

Bennett, George N. *William Dean Howells: The Development of a Novelist.* Norman: University of Oklahoma Press, 1959, 220 p.
   A valuable biocritical work.

Bennett, George N. *The Realism of William Dean Howells: 1889-1920.* Nashville: Vanderbilt University Press, 1973, 254 p.
   Elucidates each of Howells's novels written from 1889 until his death.

Brooks, Van Wyck. *Howells: His Life and World.* New York: E. P. Dutton & Co., 1959, 296 p.
   An excellent biography.

Budd, Louis J. "William Dean Howells' Debt to Tolstoy." *The American Slavic and East European Review* IX, No. 4 (December 1950): 292-301.
   Outlines the Christian ideals which Howells learned from Tolstoy.

Cady, Edwin H., and Frazier, David L., eds. *The War of the Critics over William Dean Howells.* Evanston, Ill.: Row, Peterson and Co., 1962, 244 p.
   A festschrift of criticism on Howells, including essays by Henry Van Dyke, Owen Wister, Ernest Boyd, and many others.

Carrington, George C., Jr. *The Immense Complex Drama: The World and the Art of the Howells Novel.* Columbus: Ohio State University Press, 1966, 245 p.
   An excellent examination of the relationships of form, subject, theme, and technique in Howells's novels.

Carter, Everett. Introduction to *A Hazard of New Fortunes,* by W. D. Howells, pp. xi-xxix. Bloomington, London: Indiana University Press, 1976.
   Ties the ideas of *A Hazard of New Fortunes* to various crises facing Howells at the time of writing.

Clemens, Samuel L., and Howells, William D. *Mark Twain-Howells Letters: The Correspondence of Samuel L. Clemens and William D. Howells 1872-1910.* 2 vols. Edited by Henry Nash Smith and William M. Gibson. Cambridge: The Belknap Press of Harvard University Press, 1960.
   Letters chronicling the authors' long friendship.

Cooke, Delmar Gross. *William Dean Howells: A Critical Study.* New York: E. P. Dutton & Co., 1923, 279 p.
   An able examination of Howells's work by genre.

Cumpiano, Marion W. "Howells' Bridge: A Study of the Artistry of *Indian Summer.*" *Modern Fiction Studies* XVI, No. 3 (Autumn 1970): 363-82.
   A close reading of *Indian Summer.*

Eble, Kenneth E., ed. *Howells: A Century of Criticism,* Dallas: Southern Methodist University Press, 1962, 247 p.
   A collection of critical essays by Henry James, C. Hartley Grattan, Edwin H. Cady, and many others.

Eschholz, Paul A., ed. *Critics on William Dean Howells.* Coral Gables: University of Miami Press, 1975, 128 p.
   Collected criticism on Howells.

Garland, Hamlin. "Howells." In *American Writers On American Literature by Thirty-Seven Contemporary Writers,* edited by John Macy, pp. 285-97. London: Horace Liveright, 1931.
   A defense of Howells's character drawing. Garland cites Howells's interest in the average person as the reason for his frequent depictions of unpleasant characters.

Hough, Robert L. *The Quiet Rebel: William Dean Howells As Social Commentator.* Lincoln: University of Nebraska Press, 1959, 137 p.
   A study of Howells's role in promoting such liberal causes as women's suffrage and labor reform, emphasizing his faith in his writings as agents of change.

Kirk, Clara M., and Kirk, Rudolph. *William Dean Howells.* New York: Twayne Publishers, 1962, 223 p.
   A useful biographical and critical study.

Reeves, John K. "The Limited Realism of Howells' *Their Wedding Journey.*" PMLA 77, No. 5 (December 1962): 617-28.
   Finds, from examination of the author's manuscript, that Howells softened some potentially offensive passages of *Their Wedding Journey.*

Tarkington, Booth. Introduction to *The Rise of Silas Lapham*, by William Dean Howells, pp. xiii-xxi. Boston: Houghton Mifflin Co., 1937.
    Praises Howells as one of America's literary giants, who, with Twain and James, stood as nineteenth-century America's answer to England's Meredith and Conrad.

Trilling, Lionel. "William Dean Howells and the Roots of Modern Taste." In his *The Opposing Self: Nine Essays in Criticism*, pp. 76-103. New York: The Viking Press, 1955.
    An essay examining the causes of Howells's unpopularity with twentieth-century readers.

Vanderbilt, Kermit. *The Achievement of William Dean Howells: A Reinterpretation*. Princeton: Princeton University Press, 1968, 226 p.
    Interprets four Howells novels in light of concurrent biographical events.

Van Nostrand, Albert D. "Fiction's Flagging Man of Commerce." *The English Journal* XLVIII, No. 1 (January 1959): 1-11.
    Contrasts *The Rise of Silas Lapham* with John Marquand's *Point of No Return* as novels concerned with American businessmen.

Wagenknecht, Edward. *William Dean Howells: The Friendly Eye*. New York: Oxford University Press, 1969, 340 p.
    A psychological interpretation of Howells's life and work.

Joris-Karl Huysmans

1848-1907

(Born Charles-Marie-Georges Huysmans) French novelist, critic, essayist, short story writer, and hagiographer.

Although Huysmans began his career as a strict naturalist and ended it as one of the most important Catholic novelists of the nineteenth century, his most influential work is *À rebours (Against the Grain)*, which became a manifesto of the decadent movement in European literature. A catalogue of the exquisite and bizarre tastes of its protagonist, Duke Jean Floressas des Esseintes, this book not only served to define an already existing artistic trend but also encouraged and gave direction to its progress. A proliferation of literature exploring perversity and the cult of sensation followed, reaching a high point in such *fin de siècle* figures as Oscar Wilde and Aubrey Beardsley. Huysmans's later study of satanism in *Là-bas (Down There)* contributed to his reputation as an analyst of moral decay. These works, however, are equally significant as Huysmans's reaction against his naturalist beginnings and as stylistic experiments pointing toward later developments in modern fiction.

Huysmans was born in Paris, the only child of a French mother and Dutch father. His childhood was upset by the death of his father and the remarriage of his mother in the following year. Huysmans resented his mother for what he felt was a premature second marriage. After earning his degree under private tutorship, he studied law at the University of Paris and went to work as a civil servant in the Ministry of the Interior, where he remained for the next thirty-two years. Huysmans's first book, *Le drageoir à épices (A Dish of Spices)*, was reasonably well received. Patterned after the prose poems of Aloysius Bertrand and Charles Baudelaire, this collection shows Huysmans's early fondness for elaborate style and exotic subjects. These characteristic traits are later revived in *Against the Grain*.

Huysmans's early novels are notable for their acute observations conveyed with a stylistic precision and originality which he practiced throughout his career. His first novel, *Marthe*, was inspired by the works of Edmond de Goncourt, following the popular realist trend of minute psychological portraiture. Like Huysmans's other early novels, *Marthe* is devoted to the faithful rendering of the banality and desperation of daily life. In the foreword to this book the author states: "I write what I see, what I feel, and what I have lived through, the best I can, and that is all there is to it." This credo of the naturalist writer also pervades *Les soeurs vatard*, which Huysmans dedicated to Émile Zola. The short story "Sac au dos" ("Knapsack"), based on Huysmans's military experience during the Franco-Prussian War, was published by Zola in his anthology of naturalist fiction, *Les soirées de Médan*. Gustave Flaubert's *L'éducation sentimentale* influenced Huysmans's depiction of romantic discontents in his next work, *En ménage (Living Together)*. With *A vau-l'eau (Downstream)* Huysmans introduced the kind of hypersensitive, tortured protagonist that critics have frequently identified as being patterned after the author himself. He also began moving away from the rigid objectivity of naturalism, which he described as "suffocating," in favor of a more subjective and literary style.

Against the Grain was Huysmans's experiment in a new form, a work dubbed by Remy de Gourmont as "the consecration of a new literature" and by Arthur Symons as "a breviary of the decadence." Rather than describing the outward conflicts common to naturalism, *Against the Grain* portrays the inward struggle of a spiritual crisis. The neurotic hero of the book is known as the prototype of the decadent connoisseur of new sensations, celebrating the superiority of imagination to reality. Des Esseintes's exotic tastes in literature, art, romance, and decor defined him as a new character type, one whose successors appear in such works of European decadence as Oscar Wilde's *Picture of Dorian Gray* and George Moore's *Confessions of a Young Man*. Some critics, however, have read *Against the Grain* as a parody of the decadent sensibility, intended to ridicule not glorify. But the likeness des Esseintes bears to his author, particularly in his desperate religious conflict, is submitted as evidence of Huysmans's seriousness.

The concern with religious questions again appears in *Down There*, which introduces Durtal, Huysmans's fictional alter ego who returns in the later Catholic novels. The novel opens with a dialogue on the inadequacy of naturalism to portray the inner mysteries of the mind and soul with the same detailed analysis as is given to the outer world of human society. Durtal, while working on a biography of the murderer and convert Gilles de Rais, seeks a new "spiritual naturalism." The study of satanism eventually leads Durtal to the Catholic religion and the arduous process of conversion depicted in *En route, La cathédrale (The Cathedral)*, and *L'oblat (The Oblate)*. These works—while sometimes criticized for their erudite digressions on art, architecture, and ecclesiastical history—are considered among Huysmans's best. In them the author details the progress of his own conversion to Catholicism. While not questioning his sincerity, a number of critics have pointed out that Huysmans's Catholicism displays many of the characteristics of his decadence, taking the form of a world-rejecting aestheticism rather than conventional Christian virtue. The equivocal nature of Huysmans's conversion, however, is of less importance to his stature as a writer than his certain achievements in artistic form and his contribution to an important movement in literature.

PRINCIPAL WORKS

Le drageoir à épices (prose poems) 1874
  [*A Dish of Spices* published in *Downstream (A vau-l'eau),
    and Other Works*, 1927]
Marthe (novel) 1876
  [*Marthe* published in *Downstream (A vau-l'eau), and
    Other Works*, 1927]
Les soeurs vatard (novel) 1879
Croquis parisiens (prose poems) 1880
  [*Parisian Sketches*, 1962]
"Sac au dos" (short story) 1880
  ["*Sac au dos*" published in *Short Story Classics*, 1907;
    also published as "Knapsack" in *Great French Short
    Stories*, 1928]
En ménage (novel) 1881
  [*Living Together*, 1969]
A vau-l'eau (novel) 1882
  [*Downstream* published in *Downstream (A vau-l'eau), and
    Other Works*, 1927]
L'art moderne (art criticism) 1883
À rebours (novel) 1884
  [*Against the Grain*, 1922]
En rade (novel) 1887
Certains (art criticism) 1889
Là-bas (novel) 1891
  [*Down There*, 1924]
En route (novel) 1895
  [*En Route*, 1896]
La cathédrale (novel) 1898
  [*The Cathedral*, 1898]
De tout (essays) 1902
L'oblat (novel) 1903
  [*The Oblate*, 1924]
Les foules de Lourdes (nonfiction) 1906
  [*Crowds of Lourdes*, 1925]

PAUL BOURGET (essay date 1880)

M. Huysmans' prose is certainly the most Byzantine product of our epoch. Extremely elaborate, full of rare words, sometimes crude to brutality, sometimes refined to enervation, this prose is akin to that of Baudelaire and the brothers Goncourt, but preserves a very original note which secures for its author a place apart. M. Huysmans, who is a passionate admirer of Dickens, often employs the method of the great novelist in depicting the smallest details of miserable objects. (p. 81)

> *Paul Bourget, "Paris Letter," in* The Academy, *No. 430, July 31, 1880, pp. 79-81.**

ÉMILE ZOLA (essay date 1893)

Nothing could be more simple than ["**Soeurs Vatard**"]. It is not even a complicated plot, for a complicated plot necessitates a drama. There are two sisters, *Céline* and *Desirée*, two sewing girls, who live with a dropsical mother and a lazy, philosophical father. *Céline* leads a fast life. *Desirée*, who is keeping herself for a husband, enters into an honorable love affair with a young workman, whom she leaves in the end; then she marries another, and that is all—this is the book. This bareness of plot is characteristic. Our contemporaneous novel becomes more simple every day from its hatred of complicated and false plots. One page of human life and you have enough to excite interest, to stir up deep and lasting emotions. The slightest human fact takes stronger possession of you than any other of no matter what imaginary combination. We shall end by giving simple studies without adventures or climax, the analysis of a year of existence, the story of a passion, the biography of a character, notes taken from life and logically classified.

Behold the power of human data. M. Huysmans has cast aside all arrangements of scenes. No straining of the imagination, but scenes in the workman's world, Parisian sights bound together by the most ordinary story in the world. Well, the work is full of intense life; it clutches you and impassions you; it raises the most vexing questions; it has the heat of battle and victory. Whence comes this flame that darts from it, then? From the truth of the pictures and the personality of the style, and nothing else. Modern art is here exemplified.

In the first place, let us look at the surroundings. These surroundings, these sewing girls' workshops, which M. Huysmans paints with a frightful intensity, have a terrible odor. Doubtless many people would say they were exaggerated. Dare to enter a sewing woman's workroom. Question, inquire, and you will see that M. Huysmans has still remained outside of the truth, because it is impossible to print certain things. All this workingman's atmosphere, this corner of misery and ignorance, of tranquil degradation and naturally tainted air, has been treated in the "**Soeurs Vatard**" with a scrupulous exactitude and rare firmness of touch.

Then come the characters. They are marvelous portraits in resemblance and in tone. You may be certain that they were taken from nature.

Here is *Père Vatard*, who has only two mortifications—his wife's disease and the conduct of his daughter *Céline*. Her first fault filled him with emotion. I quote: "He had a moment of sadness, but he consoled himself quickly. Desirée was old enough to care for him, and to take her mother's place; and as to Céline, the best thing for him to do was to close his eyes on her conduct. He had acted a father's part, moreover; he had reproached her, in court of assizes terms, for the impropriety of her manners; but she had become angry, had thrown the house into a topsy-turvy condition, threatening to overturn everything if she were annoyed again. Vatard then adopted an air of great indulgence; besides, his daughter's terrible gabble amused him in the evening." This is complete. This is the father of our faubourgs, such as most commonly the promiscuous mingling that springs from poverty and the degradation of his surroundings, make him. We do not wish to understand that the moral sense is merely relative, and distorts and changes itself according to its conditions. What is an abomination in the middle class is but a sad necessity with the people.

And this *Céline*, is she strongly encamped in her reality? She is but one of a thousand. It is not the question of an exception, but of a majority. Go and see for yourself instead of protesting.

Desirée is of a rarer type. But she exists, and she will console pure souls a little. Not that at bottom she follows any conception of virtue, for she really only follows her instinct. She is an apathetic girl, who is not drawn toward man, and whom her sister's example restrains. She dreams of marriage. Nothing could be more admirable than her idyl with *Auguste,* an idyl of the outdoor boulevard life, of dining in a saloon, strolling in the vague night of the long avenues, of good-by kisses given behind the walls of some unfinished building. No impurity of any kind. He did not wish to marry, but he is captivated, and they held long conversations on the future, filled with touching nonsense, the eternal duet which the idealists have put in the clouds and the naturalists place on the sidewalks. This homeless love is just so much the more the tender that it is lived, and that you jostle it on each boulevard of our faubourgs.

I reach the climax, one of the most deeply touching passages that I have read for a long time. Little by little the two lovers have become cold. *Desirée,* detained by her mother's illness, has missed several rendezvous, and when she meets *Auguste* again they are both embarrassed. The young man already thinks of marrying elsewhere. The young girl, now that her father has given his consent to her marriage, listens to her sister, who speaks of another man. And it is *Céline* who brings matters to a climax in provoking an explanation and a last adieu. The scene takes place at the doors of a *café* on the corner of the Quay de la Tournelle and the Boulevard Saint Germain. I know nothing so piercing, stirring the human heart as it does to its depths. All our loves, all our joys dreamed of and lost, all our hopes ceaselessly killed and ceaselessly being born again, are they not there in these two simple creatures, who are leaving each other after having loved, who are going far away from one another to live a life apart which they had sworn to live together? They talk for the last time sweetly, softly, they give each other details on their respective marriages, they thee and thou each other again, and all at once memories are awakened; they recall what they did on such and such a day, at such and such an hour; tears spring to their eyes; perhaps they would have come together again had not *Céline* hastened to separate them. It is ended; they are now two strangers.

I would like to quote this episode entirely to make my readers feel the thrill which passed through me as I read it. What misery and infirmity are ours! How everything falls from our fingers and is broken! These two young creatures disclose the depth of our frailty and our nothingness.

The only criticism which I shall make on M. Huysmans is an abuse of rare words which at moments takes away from his best analyses their living air. These words cover the first part of the book especially. I also prefer the second part, which is more simple and more human. M. Huysmans has a style that is marvelous in its color and in throwing objects into relief. He inserts into beings and things an admirable intensity of life. This is really his principal quality. I hope they will not style him a photographer, although his pictures are very exact. The

people who have made the innocent discovery that naturalism is nothing more than photography will understand this time, perhaps, that, though priding ourselves upon absolute reality, we mean to breathe life into our productions. (pp. 245-50)

Émile Zola, "Three Débuts: J. K. Huysmans," in his The Experimental Novel and Other Essays, *translated by Belle M. Sherman, Cassell Publishing Company, 1893, pp. 245-50.*

HAVELOCK ELLIS (essay date 1898)

[Huysmans] possessed no native genius for the novel. But with a very sound instinct he set himself, almost at the outset of his career, to describe intimately and faithfully the crudest things of life, the things most remote from his own esoteric tastes but at that time counted peculiarly "real." There could be no better discipline for an idealist. Step by step he has left the region of vulgar actualities to attain his proper sphere, but the marvellous and slowly won power of expressing the spiritually impalpable in concrete imagery is the fruit of that laborious apprenticeship. . . . Essentially Huysmans is less a novelist than a poet, with an instinct to use not verse but prose as his medium. Thus he early fell under the influence of Baudelaire's prose-poems. His small and slight first volume, *Le Drageoir à Epices,* bears witness to this influence, while yet revealing a personality clearly distinct from Baudelaire's. This personality is already wholly revealed in the quaint audacity of the little prose-poem entitled **"L'Extase."** Here, at the very outset of Huysmans' career, we catch an unconscious echo of mediaeval asceticism, the voice, it might be, of Odo of Cluny, who nearly a thousand years before had shrunk with horror from embracing a "sack of dung;" "quomodo ipsum stercoris saccum amplecti desideramus!" **"L'Extase"** describes how the lover lies in the wood clasping the hand of the beloved and bathed in a rapture of blissful emotion; "suddenly she rose, disengaged her hand, disappeared in the bushes, and I heard as it were the rustling of rain on the leaves;" at once the delicious dream fled and the lover awakes to the reality of commonplace human things. That is a parable of the high-strung idealism, having only contempt for whatever breaks in on its ideal, which has ever been the mark of Huysmans. His sensitive ear is alive to the gentlest ripple of nature, and it jars on him; it becomes the deafening Niagara of "the incessant deluge of human foolishness;" all his art is the research for a Heaven where the voice of Nature shall no more be heard. Baudelaire was also such a hyperaesthetic idealist, but the human tenderness which vibrates beneath the surface of Baudelaire's work has been the last quality to make itself more than casually felt in Huysmans. It is the defect which vitiated his early work in the novel, when he was still oscillating between the prose-poem and the novel, clearly conscious that while the first suited him best only in the second could mastery be won. His early novels are sometimes portentously dull, with a lack of interest, or even attempt to interest, which itself almost makes them interesting, as frank ugliness is. They are realistic with a veracious and courageously abject realism, never, like Zola's, carefully calculated for its pictorial effectiveness, but dealing simply with the trivialest and sordidest human miseries. His first novel *Marthe*— which inaugurated the long series of novels devoted to state-regulated prostitution in those slaughter-houses of love, as Huysmans later described them, where Desire is slain at a single stroke,—sufficiently repulsive on the whole, is not without flashes of insight which reveal the future artist, and to some readers indeed make it more interesting than *La Fille Elisa,* which the Goncourts published shortly afterwards. . . . This first novel remains the least personal of Huysmans' books; in his next novel, *Les Soeurs Vatard*—a study of Parisian workgirls and their lovers—a more characteristic vision of the world begins to be revealed, and from that time forward there is a continuous though irregular development both in intellectual grip and artistic mastery. **"Sac au Dos,"** which appeared in the [anthology of naturalist stories] *Soirées de Medan,* represents a notable stage in this development, for here, as he has since acknowledged, Huysmans' hero is himself. It is the story of a young student who serves during the great war in the Garde Mobile of the Seine, and is invalided with dysentery before reaching the front. There is no story, no striking impression to record—nothing to compare with Guy de Maupassant's incomparably more brilliant "Boule-de-Suif," also dealing with the fringe of war, which appears in the same volume—no opportunity for literary display, nothing but a record of individual feelings with which the writer seems satisfied because they are interesting to himself. It is, in fact, the germ of that method which Huysmans has since carried to so brilliant a climax in *En Route.* All the glamour of war and the enthusiasm of patriotism are here—long before Zola wrote his *Débâcle*—reduced to their simplest terms in the miseries of the individual soldier whose chief aspiration it becomes at last to return to a home where the necessities of nature may be satisfied in comfort and peace. (pp. 163-67)

The best of Huysmans' early novels is undoubtedly *En Ménage.* It is the intimate history of a young literary man who, having married a wife whom he shortly afterwards finds unfaithful, leaves her, returns to his bachelor life, and in the end becomes reconciled to her. This picture of a studious man who goes away with his books to fight over again the petty battles of bachelorhood with the *bonne* and the *concierge* and his own cravings for womanly love and companionship, reveals clearly for the first time Huysmans' power of analysing states of mind that are at once simple and subtle. Perhaps no writer surprises us more by his revealing insight into the commonplace experiences which all a novelist's traditions lead him to idealise or ignore. As a whole, however, *En Ménage* is scarcely yet a master's work, a little laboured, with labour which cannot yet achieve splendour of effect. Nor can a much slighter story, *A Vau l'Eau,* which appeared a little later, be said to mark a further stage in development, though it is a characteristic study, this sordid history of Folantin, the poor, lame, discontented, middle-aged clerk. Cheated and bullied on every side, falling a prey to the vulgar woman of the street who boisterously takes possession of him in the climax of the story, all the time feeling poignantly the whole absurdity of the situation, there is yet one spot where hope seems possible. He has no religious faith; "and yet," he reflects, "yet mysticism alone could heal the wound that tortures me." Thus Folantin, though like André in *En Ménage* he resigns themselves to the inevitable stupidity of life, yet stretches out his hands towards the Durtal of [*En Route*].

In all these novels we feel that Huysmans has not attained to full self-expression. Intellectual mastery, indeed, he is attaining, but scarcely yet the expression of his own personal ideals. The poet in Huysmans, the painter enamoured of beauty and seeking it in unfamiliar places, has little scope in these detailed pictures of sordid or commonplace life. At this early period it is still in prose-poems, especially in *Croquis Parisiens,* that this craving finds satisfaction. Des Esseintes, the hero of *A Rebours,* who on so many matters is Huysmans' mouthpiece, of all forms of literature preferred the prose-poem when, in the hands of an alchemist of genius, it reveals a novel concentrated into a few pages or a few lines, the concrete juice, the essential oil of art. It was "a communion of thought between a magical writer and an ideal reader, a spiritual collaboration among a dozen superior persons scattered throughout the world, a delectation offered to the finest wits, and to them alone accessible." Huysmans took up this form where Baudelaire and Mallarmé had left it, and sought to carry it yet furhter. In that he was scarcely successful. The excess of tension in the tortured language with which he elaborates his effects too often holds him back from the goal of perfection. We must yet value in *Croquis Parisiens* its highly wrought and individual effects of rhythm and colour and form. In France, at all events, Huysmans is held to inaugurate the poetic treatment of modern things—a characteristic already traceable in *Les Soeurs Vatard*—and this book deals with the aesthetic aspects of latter-day Paris, with the things that are "ugly and superb, outrageous and yet exquisite," as a type of which he selects the Folies-Bergère, at that time the most characteristic of Parisian music-halls, and he was thus the first to discuss the aesthetic value of the variety stage which has been made cheaper since. For the most part, however, these *Croquis* are of the simplest and most commonplace things—the forlorn Bièvre district, the poor man's *café,* the roast-chestnut seller—extracting the beauty or pathos or strangeness of all these things. (pp. 168-71)

[*A Rebours*] must ever remain the central work in which [Huysmans] has most powerfully concentrated his whole vision of life. It sums up the progress he had already made, foretells the progress he was afterwards to make, in a style that is always individual, always masterly in its individuality. Technically, it may be said that the power of *A Rebours* lies in the fact that here for the first time Huysmans has succeeded in uniting the two lines of his literary development: the austere analysis in the novels of commonplace things mostly alien to the writer, and the freer elaboration in the prose-poems of his own more intimate personal impressions. In their union the two streams attain a new power and a more intimately personal note. Des Esseintes, the hero of this book, may possibly have been at a few points suggested by a much less interesting real personage in contemporary Paris, the Comte de Montesquiou-Fezensac, but in the main he was certainly created by Huysmans' own brain, as the representative of his author's hyperaesthetic experience of the world and the mouthpiece of his most personal judgments. (p. 172)

For some years after the appearance of *A Rebours* Huysmans produced nothing of any magnitude. *En Rade,* his next novel, the experience of a Parisian married couple who, under the stress of temporary pecuniary difficulties, go into the country to stay at an uncle's farm, dwells in the memory chiefly by virtue of two vividly naturalistic episodes, the birth of a calf and the death of a cat. More interesting, more intimately personal, are the two volumes of art criticism, *L'Art Moderne* and *Certains,* which Huysmans published at about this period. Degas, Rops, Raffaelli, Odilon Redon are among the artists of very various temperament whom Huysmans either discovered, or at all events first appreciated in their full significance, and when he writes of them it is not alone critical insight which he reveals, but his own personal vision of the world.

To Huysmans the world has ever been above all a vision; it was no accident that the art that appeals most purely to the eyes is that of which he has been the finest critic. One is tempted, indeed, to suggest that this aptitude is the outcome of heredity, of long generations devoted to laborious watch-fulness of the desire of the eye in the external world, not indeed by actual accumulation of acquired qualities, but by the passing on of a nervous organism long found so apt for this task. He has ever been intensely preoccupied with the effort to express those visible aspects of things which the arts of design were made to express, which the art of speech can perhaps never express. The tortured elaboration of his style is chiefly due to this perpetual effort to squeeze tones and colours out of this foreign medium. The painter's brain holds only a pen and cannot rest until it has wrung from it a brush's work. But not only is the sense of vision marked in Huysmans. We are conscious of a general hyperaesthesia, an intense alertness to the inrush of sensations, which we might well term morbid if it were not so completely intellectualised and controlled. Hearing, indeed, appears to be less acutely sensitive than sight, the poet is subordinated to the painter, though that sense still makes itself felt, and the heavy multicoloured paragraphs often fall at the close into a melancholy and poignant rhythm laden with sighs. It is the sense of smell which Huysmans' work would lead us to regard as most highly developed after that of sight. The serious way in which Des Esseintes treats perfumes is characteristic, and one of the most curious and elaborate of the *Croquis Parisiens* is "Le Gousset," in which the capacities of language are strained to define and differentiate the odours of feminine arm-pits. (pp. 187-89)

The two volumes of essays on art incidentally serve to throw considerable light on Huysmans' conception of life. For special illustration we may take his attitude towards women, whom in his novels he usually treats, from a rather conventionally sexual point of view, as a fact in man's life rather than as a subject for independent analysis. In these essays we may trace the development of his own personal point of view, and in comparing the earlier with the later volume we find a change which is significant of the general evolution of Huysmans' attitude towards life. He is at once the ultra-modern child of a refined civilisation and the victim of nostalgia for an ascetic mediaevalism; his originality lies in the fact that in him these two tendencies are not opposed but harmonious, although the second has only of late reached full development. In a notable passage in *En Rade*, Jacques, the hero, confesses that he can see nothing really great or beautiful in a harvest field, with its anodyne toil, as compared with a workshop or a steamboat, "the horrible magnificence of machines, that one beauty which the modern world has been able to create." It is so that Huysmans views women also; he is as indifferent to the feminine ideals of classic art as to its literary ideals. (pp. 190-91)

Certains was immediatley followed by *Là-bas*. . . . Huysmans reaches, by firm precision and triumphant audacity, the highest point he has attained in the analysis of the secrets of passion. But though full of excellent matter, the book loses in impressiveness from the multiplicity of these insufficiently compacted elements of interest.

While not among his finest achievements, however, it serves to mark the definite attainment of a new stage in both the spirit and the method of his work. . . . [In] his previous novels his own native impulse was always a little unduly oppressed by the naturalistic formulas of Goncourt and Zola. The methods of these great masters had laid a burden on his work, and although the work developed benath, and because of, that burden, a sense of laborious pain and obscurity too often resulted. Henceforth this disappears. Huysmans retains his own complexity of style, but he has won a certain measure of simplicity

and lucidity. It was a natural development, no doubt furthered also by the position which Huysmans had now won in the world of letters. *A Rebours,* which he had written for his own pleasure, had found an echo in thousands of readers, and the consciousness of an audience inspired a certain clarity of speech. From this time we miss the insults directed at the *bêtise* of humanity. These characteristics clearly mark Huysmans' next and perhaps greatest book, in which the writer who had conquered all the secrets of decadent art now sets his face towards the ideals of classic art.

In *En Route,* indeed, these new qualities of simplicity, lucidity, humanity, and intensity of interest attain so high a degree that the book has reached a vast number of readers who could not realise the marvellous liberation from slavery to its material which the slow elaboration of art has here reached. In *A Rebours* Huysmans succeeded in taking up the prose-poem into his novel form, while at the same time certainly sacrificing something of the fine analysis of familiar things which he had developed in *En Ménage.* In *En Route* he takes the novel from the point he had reached in *A Rebours,* incorporates into it that power of analysis which has now reached incomparable simplicity and acuity, and thus wields the whole of the artistic means which he has acquired during a quarter of a century to one end, the presentation of a spiritual state which has become of absorbing personal interest to himself. (pp. 193-97)

En Route is the first of a trilogy, and the names of the succeeding volumes, *La Cathédrale* and *L'Oblat,* sufficiently indicate the end of the path on which Durtal, if not indeed his creator, has started. But however that may prove, whatever Huysmans' own final stage may be, there can be little doubt that he is the greatest master of style, and within his own limits the subtlest thinker and the acutest psychologist who in France to-day uses the medium of the novel. Only Zola can be compared with him, and between them there can be no kind of rivalry. Zola, with his immense and exuberant temperament, his sanity and width of view, his robust and plebeian art, has his own place on the high-road of modern literature. Huysmans, an intellectual and aesthetic aristocrat, has followed with unflinching sincerity the by-path along which his own more highstrung and exceptional temperament has led him, and his place, if seemingly a smaller one, is at least as sure; wherever men occupy themselves with the literature of the late nineteenth century they will certainly sometimes talk about Zola, sometimes read Huysmans. Zola's cyclopean architecture can only be seen as a whole when we have completed the weary task of investigating it in detail; in Huysmans we seek the expressiveness of the page, the sentence, the word. Strange as it may seem to some, it is the so-called realist who has given us the more idealised rendering of life; the concentrated vision of the idealist in his own smaller sphere has revealed not alone mysteries of the soul, but even the exterior secrets of life. True it is that Huysmans has passed by with serene indifference, or else with contempt, the things which through the ages we have slowly learnt to count beautiful. But on the other hand, he has helped to enlarge the sphere of our delight by a new vision of beauty where before to our eyes there was no beauty, exercising the proper function of the artist who ever chooses the base and despised things of the world, even the things that are not, to put to nought the things that are. Therein the decadent has his justification. And while we may accept the pioneer's new vision of beauty, we are not called upon to reject those old familiar visions for which he has no eyes, only because his gaze must be fixed upon that unfamiliar height towards which he is leading the men who come after. (pp. 203-05)

Havelock Ellis, "Huysmans," in his Affirmations, *Walter Scott Limited, 1898 and (reprinted by Houghton Mifflin Company, second edition, 1922, pp. 158-211).*

HARRY THURSTON PECK   (essay date 1898)

What is the psychological secret of the mysterious connection that exists between religious desire in man and the desire that is sensuous and even sensual? (p. 135)

The subject is, perhaps, a little dangerous, and one need not here pursue it any further; yet it is quite irresistibly suggested by a volume which now lies before me, entitled *En Route,* and which one may without exaggeration think not only the greatest novel of the day, but one of the most important, because it is one of the most characteristic books of our quarter of the century. Until its author, M. Huysmans, wrote it, his name suggested to the readers of French literature nothing more than naturalistic fiction of the rankest and most brutal type—fiction that surpassed the most typical work of Zola in the frankness of its physiology and the shamelessness of its indecency. With *À Rebours,* . . . this Flemish Frenchman reached a sort of morbid climax both in subject and in treatment, and because of this Herr [Max Nordau in his *Degeneration*] chose him out as embodying the quintessence of moral and literary degeneracy. Yet it seemed to many at the time of its appearance that in *À Rebours* there was to be detected a new and striking note, an indication of new currents of tendency, a drift away from merely physical analysis, a reaching out towards something which, if not ethically higher, was at any rate more subtle and more psychologically interesting. The later works of M. Huysmans have made it plain that this assumption was a true one; and since *Là Bas* has been succeeded by this latest work, the true significance of the change is very clear. Taking these three novels together, one may rightly view them as embodying a single purpose—a purpose of which perhaps and probably the writer was himself not always fully conscious, but which, as his task proceeded, fully seized upon his intellect and was, no doubt, developed with the simultaneous development of his own experience.

For it is permissible to think that in setting before us the evolution of a true degenerate, M. Huysmans has been writing a spiritual and intellectual autobiography. . . . It seems, indeed, impossible that the strange things set forth in *À Rebours* could have been imagined by a person whose own life had been free from any such experience, or that the intensity of feeling that marks the strongest chapters of *En Route* could be merely the *tour de force* of a clever writer. We shall not, therefore, be far wrong if we assume that we have now before us the record of a searching self-analysis, however much the superficial incidents of the story be altered from the actual facts. This must be borne in mind, for the books, that form a sort of series, refer ostensibly to different persons; yet it is, in reality, but one single experience that M. Huysmans is relating. For whether the protagonist be spoken of as Des Esseintes in *À Rebours* or as Durtal in *En Route,* the change of name implies no change in personality, nor in the conditions of the psychological and moral problem that is presented for our contemplation.

The story itself is the narrative of a man who has deliberately cultivated sensation to the point where it has touched the very extreme of enervation, and who in this persistent quest has exhausted the possibilities of physical pleasure, until at last the morbid and the abnormal have reached the narrow line that marks the verge of sanity. This phase is set before us in *À Rebours,* perhaps the strangest effort of perverse imagination that literature can show. . . . On the face of it there seems to be nothing in the tale but what is morbid and delirious, and to a healthy mind both hideous and revolting. Yet, as has been already said, one can here detect a subtle note that is not found in *Marthe* or *Soeurs Vatard.* The cult of the purely physical has ceased to satisfy, and there is a vaguely outlined longing for something intangible which the flesh alone cannot allay.

In *Là Bas,* the second novel of the series, this longing has taken a more definite form. We see a quite distinctly formulated interest in the spiritual, or at least the supernatural. Mere animalism retires into the background of the mental picture, though it still exists as a discordant and disturbing element. The degenerate hero of the book has turned his mind towards the phenomena of the religious sentiment as a sphere neglected heretofore, and perhaps quite capable of affording new sensations. Yet, as before in other things he utterly reversed all normal notions, so in this new quest his impulses are inspired by perversity. . . . Yet one feels in laying down the book that the end is not yet; that Durtal is still groping in the darkness, and that the very violence and outrageousness of his impulses may lead him at last into a reaction against the physical and moral disease that vexes him.

In *En Route* we observe a striking contrast at the very outset. Durtal is presented to us as already weaned, in spirit at least, from the life that he has led so long. He is shown as one who has accepted in the fullest sense the faith of the Catholic Church. (pp. 136-44)

En Route is interesting in many ways. It is unique among the other books of Huysmans in style no less than in spirit. Here he has wholly put aside the studied bareness and hardness of expression that characterize his earlier method, and the descriptive passages glow with color and abound in strange felicities of expression. His enthusiasm for the purely mediaeval fairly carries him away, and I think has led him into indefensible extremes. . . . His enthusiasm leads him also into long and rather tedious digressions upon the history of the mediaeval saints, whose lives he insists upon detailing with remorseless elaboration, so that the effect produced is thoroughly inartistic from a literary point of view, and gives the impression of one who has crammed up a subject and is unwilling to lose any portion of his material.

Interesting also is the psychological side of the book, with its implied thesis that faith, like all other emotions, is contagious; and with its illustration of the thought with which I commenced this paper, that the sensual nature under certain influences can become the most profoundly spiritual and religious. (pp. 150-52)

Harry Thurston Peck, "The Evolution of a Mystic," in his The Personal Equation, *Harper & Brothers, 1898, pp. 135-56.*

VIRGINIA M. CRAWFORD   (essay date 1899)

In the history of a human soul there are times of stress and times of lull; there are days of fiery combat followed by long months of seeming inertia and spiritual torpor. It was of the former that M. Huysmans wrote in *En Route,* perhaps the most extraordinary book of recent years. In *La Cathédrale* he has led his pilgrim Durtal by slow and deliberate steps through the intermediate stage that divides his repentance at La Trappe from his entrance into the Benedictine monastery of Solesmes. It is a period of introspection and orientation, of patient self-communing and silent longing, a period that must come to every soul if the work of conversion and illumination is to be a permanent one. Its interest is purely subjective; there is no action, no incident, hardly any characterisation. It belongs to M. Huysmans alone to create a novel from such a lack of external circumstance. I doubt whether any other living writer would have ventured on so apparently thankless a task. Of necessity the dramatic element which played so large a part in *En Route* is entirely absent from its sequel. The great fight between faith and unfaith is over; and as far as the outside world is concerned, the curtain might well have been rung down on the victor. But to Huysmans as to Maeterlinck, and indeed to all whose gaze would penetrate beneath life's surface, the real tragedy of our existence only begins there where external adventures and dangers cease, and the silent hidden life of the dreamer and the mystic possesses a charm and a value denied to that of the man of action.

For my own part, I am filled with a sense of gratitude towards M. Huysmans for having given us *La Cathédrale*. It is full of beautiful writing, of wonderful descriptive pages, of delicate appreciations, of spiritual insight into Christian symbolism. (pp. 78-9)

No writer can equal M. Huysmans in sheer descriptive power. Flaubert produced an incomparable effect by his deliberate detailed pictures, his unrivalled skill in the choice of an appropriate adjective. Zola merely sees the obvious and superficial, and enumerates his points like the items in a catalogue. But Huysmans seizes at once the spiritual and the material; he identifies himself with his subject, he breathes its atmosphere, and not a detail of the physical features escapes him. (pp. 81-2)

Many will be tempted to read *La Cathédrale* solely for the sake of the beautiful descriptive passages which abound in its pages. And from that point of view alone the book is infinitely worth reading. And yet the descriptions of Chartres are subsidiary in intention to the description of Durtal's state of soul, and the great moral purpose of the book is of higher import than its aesthetic qualities. In its spiritual aspect, if not in all its material details, *La Cathédrale* is a chapter in an autobiography as truthful and as penetrating as any of the great confessions which remain for all time among the most fascinating and instructive of human documents. No one in discussing, let us say, the *Confessions of St. Augustine*, would restrict himself solely to the literary aspect of the work, and to do so in the case of Huysmans would be not less ineffectual. *Là Bas, En Route*, and *La Cathédrale* form the veracious history of a soul's conversion from materialism of the grossest kind to faith of a high spiritual order. And the story has been told by one of the greatest literary artists of the day. (pp. 85-6)

> *Virginia M. Crawford, "J. K. Huysmans," in her* Studies in Foreign Literature, *Duckworth and Co., 1899 (and reprinted by Kennikat Press, 1970), pp. 78-105.*

ARNOLD BENNETT   (essay date 1902)

Huysmans is one of the most distinguished and adept of living artificers in words. He is capable of succeeding in feats which might have baffled even [Robert Louis] Stevenson. To watch him describe anything, no matter what, is a pleasure; to the expert it is a treat. His power of observation is cultivated to an extraordinary degree, and it is accompanied with absolute fidelity by the expressive power. In other words, what he sees he can make his readers see. Yet it appears to us that the most interesting thing about Huysmans is Huysmans, and not his work. It is not too much to say that the phenomena of his religious experiences have amazed, while they have fascinated, intellectual Europe. There was something highly piquant in the fact that the man who wrote *A Vau l'Eau* in his youth should in his maturity write *La Cathédrale* and that nightmare of literary asceticism, *Sainte Lydwine de Schiedam*. But there was something more than piquant, there was something unconvincing and incredible, in the statement that a man with a type of mind—brilliant, cynical, curious, truth-seeking and careless of the results of that search—such as Huysmans originally had and as all his work proves it still to be—that such a man had accepted the rule and sovereignty of the Roman Catholic Church. Huysmans' is a first-class intelligence, an intelligence incapable of fear, of opportunism, of delusion. No one who has read *À Vau l'Eau,* that pitiless and bitter sketch, is likely to deny that the writer of it was necessarily a man of singular moral courage. And one has the right to ask, without giving offence: What first drove that man to the sackcloth mood of repentance? It is not, of course, about the route that we demand information, but about the original impulse. Was it fear, remorse? It could not have been. But might it not have been curiosity, that restless and unappeasable curiosity which marks all his career? It is difficult to imply that we wish to imply with a due regard for the punctilio of criticism. Nevertheless we shall permit ourselves to say that, abating no particle of our admiration for Huysmans, we doubt the entire reality of his religious experiences. We do not doubt his conviction of his own sincerity, but we venture to suspect that he may have deceived himself and the world too. These things have happened before. People have ignored a church, "embraced" it, and lived to ignore it again. We have said that Huysmans' intelligence is incapable of delusion. But we would add, trying not to split hairs or to reach the meaningless, that it is perhaps not incapable of amusing itself. While incapable of delusion in the ordinary sense it might be capable of erecting one vast and splendid delusion, of arranging a factitious spectacle of emotions for its own diversion—as the Shah goes to the Empire. The capacity of the human mind to deceive itself is illimitable; and the greater the mind, the greater, in a fine way, that capacity. . . .

[A book like *De Tout*] decidedly increases the difficulties of comprehending the strange case of M. Huysmans. Here we have a collection of twenty-four miscellaneous essays, on such extremely diverse subjects as saints, monks, frequenters of cafés, barbers, Bruges, sleeping-cars, railway station refreshment rooms, and the "Vierge noire" of Paris. They first appeared, these essays, in such places as the *Echo de Paris,* where one remembers to have read the fleshly masterpieces of de Maupassant, the frank lubricity of the late Armand Silvestre, and the weird memoirs of Edmond de Goncourt. They are the expression of a mind apparently irreligious to its foundation, *railleur,* enquiring, destructive. . . .

As a literary performance the book is simply beautiful from beginning to end. No one has written better about Bruges than M. Huysmans does here. And certainly no one has shown a more penetrating insight into the true inwardness of cafés than he shows in the essay *Les Habitues de Café.* You would think that the painter of Chartres Cathedral could never have left the inner boulevards. (p. 251)

Arnold Bennett, "A Psycholgoical Enigma," *in* The Academy and Literature, *Vol. LXIII, No. 1584, September 13, 1902, pp. 251-52.*

J. K. HUYSMANS (essay date 1903)

[Nothing] is more disenchanting, more painful than to examine one's phrases again after an interval of years. They have been in bottle, so to speak, and form a deposit at the bottom of the book; and, most times, volumes are not like wines which improve with age; once clarified in the fulness of time, the chapters grow flat and their bouquet evaporates.

Such is the impression certain bottles stacked in the "**Against the Grain**" bin made upon me when I had to uncork them. (p. xxxiii)

At the date when "**Against the Grain**" was published, in 1884 that is to say, the state of things therefore was this: Naturalism was getting more and more out of breath by dint of turning the mill for ever in the same round. The stock of observations that each writer had stored up by self-scrutiny or study of his neighbours was getting exhausted. (p. xxxv)

I was striving in vain to escape from a *cul-de-sac* in which I was suffocating, but I had no settled plan, and "**Against the Grain**," which, by letting in fresh air, let me get away from a literature that had no door of escape, is a purely unpremeditated work, imagined without any preconceived ideas, without definite intentions for the future, without any predetermined plan whatever. (p. xxxvi)

[Today] as I skim, after more lengthy and more trustworthy investigations, the pages of "**Against the Grain**," that deal with Catholicism and religious art, I note that that miniature panorama I then sketched on leaves of block-books, is accurate. What I depicted then was succinct, wanting elaboration, but it was veracious. I have confined myself subsequently to enlarging and developing my outline drawings.

I might quite well sign my name at the present moment to the pages of "**Against the Grain**" relating to the Church, for they appear in very deed to have been written by a Catholic. (p. xxxvii)

[All] the romances I have written since "**Against the Grain**" are contained in embryo in that book. The successive chapters are nothing more nor less than the priming of the volumes that followed.

The chapter on the Latin Literature of the Decadence I have, if not developed, at any rate probed deeper into, when treating of the Liturgy in *En Route* and *L'Oblat*. (p. xxxviii)

The chapter on precious stones I have recapitulated in *La Cathédrale,* in the second case treating the matter from the point of view of the symbolism of gems. I have there given life to the dead stones of "**Against the Grain**." Of course I do not deny that a fine emerald may be admired for the flashes that sparkle in the fire of its green depths, but, if we are ignorant of the idiom of symbols, is it not an unknown being, a stranger, a foreigner with whom no talk can be had and who has no word to say himself, because we do not understand his language? But he is surely something more and better than that. (p. xxxix)

The chapter in "**Against the Grain**" is therefore only superficial, a flush-bezel setting, so to speak. It is not what it should be, a display ranging beyond the mere material stones, it is made up of caskets of jewels more or less well described, more or less artistically arranged in a show-case—but that is all, and that is not enough. (pp. xxxix-xl)

As for the terrible Chapter VI, the number of which corresponds, without any preconceived purpose on my part, to the Commandment it offends against, as also for some portions of Chapter IX that may be classed with it, I should obviously not write them in the same vein again. They should at least have been accounted for, in a more studious spirit, by that diabolic perversity of the will which affects, especially in matters of sensual aberration, the exhausted brains of sick folk. It would seem, in fact, that nervous invalids expose fissures in the soul's envelope whereby the Spirit of Evil effects an entrance. But this is a riddle that remains unsolved; the word hysteria explains nothing; it may suffice to define a material condition, to mark invincible disturbances of the senses, it does not account for the spiritual consequences attached to the phenomena and, more particularly, the sins of dissimulation and falsehood that are almost always engrafted on them. What are the details and attendant circumstances of this malady of sinfulness, in what degree is the responsibility diminished of the individual whose soul is attacked by a sort of demoniac possession that takes root in the disorganization of his unhappy body? None can tell: on this point Medicine talks mere folly, Theology holds her peace.

In default of a solution which manifestly he could not supply, Des Esseintes [the protagonist] should have viewed the question from the point of view of sinfulness and expressed at any rate some regret. He refrained from abusing himself, and he did wrong; but then, though educated by the Jesuits, whose panegyrist he is,—and a more ardent one than Durtal [the protagonist of *En Route*],—he had grown subsequently so recalcitrant to the Divine constraints, so obstinately resolved to wallow in the mire of his carnal appetites!

In any case, these chapters seem to be mark-stakes unconsciously planted to indicate the road *Là-Bas* was to follow. It is noteworthy moreover that Des Esseintes' library contained a certain number of old books of magic and that the ideas expressed in Chapter VII of "**Against the Grain**" on sacrilege are the hooks on which to hang a subsequent volume treating the subject more thoroughly.

As for this book *Là-Bas,* which frightened so many people, neither should I write it, if I had to do the thing again, in the same manner, now I am become a Catholic once more. There is no doubt indeed that the wicked and sensual side therein developed is reprehensible; but at the same time I declare I have glazed over things, I have said nothing of the worst; the documents it embodies are in comparison with those I have omitted, but which I have among my papers, very insipid sweetmeats, very tasteless tit-bits.

I believe, nevertheless, that in spite of its cerebral aberrations and its abdominal follies, the work, by mere virtue of the subject it laid bare, has done good service. It has recalled attention to the wiles of the Evil One, who had succeeded in getting men to deny his existence; it has been the starting-point of all the studies, revived of late years, on the never-changing procedure of Satanism; it has helped, by exposing them, to put an end to the odious practices of sorcery; it has taken sides, in fact, and fought a very strenuous fight for the Church against the Devil.

To come back to "**Against the Grain**," of which this book is only a succedaneum, I may repeat in connexion with the flower chapter what I have already stated with regard to precious stones.

"Against the Grain" considers them only from the point of view of shapes or colours, in no wise from that of the significations they disclose; Des Esseintes chose only rare orchids, strange blossoms, but without a tongue. It is fair to add that he would have found it hard to give speech in the book to a flora attacked by aphasia, a dumb flora, for the symbolic language of plants died with the Middle Ages, and the vegetable creoles cherished by Des Esseintes were unknown to the allegorists of those days.

The counterpart of this flower study I have written since in *La Cathédrale,* when dealing with that liturgical horticulture which has suggested such quaint pages in the works of St. Hildegard, St. Meliton and St. Eucher. (pp. xl-xlii)

[I do not anticipate] that I shall ever come to appreciate the modern religious authors scourged in **"Against the Grain."** . . . Their juleps strike me as insipid; Des Esseintes has passed his taste for spices on to Durtal, and I think they would come to a good understanding together, both of them, at the present moment, to prepare, in lieu of these emulsions, an essence savoury with the stimulating condiment of art. (p. xliii)

To conclude the list, if ever chapter can be considered the starting-point of other books, it is surely the one on plain-chant which I afterwards amplified in all my publications, in *En Route* and above all in *L'Oblat*.

As result of this brief review of each of the special articles exhibited in the show-cases of **"Against the Grain"** the conclusion is forced upon us,—the book was priming for my Catholic propaganda, which is implicit in it in its entirety, though in embryo.

Indeed the misunderstanding and stupidity of sundry pedants and agitated members of the priesthood strike me, yet once again, as unfathomable. Year after year they clamoured for the destruction of the book, the copyright of which, by-the-bye, I do not own, without ever realizing that the mystic volumes that came after it are incomprehensible without being as it is, I reiterate the statement, the root from which they all sprang. Besides this, how it is possible to appreciate the work of an author in its entirety, if it is not taken from its first beginnings and followed up step by step; above all, how is it possible to realize the progress of God's Grace in a soul, if the traces of its passage are neglected, if the first tokens left by its presence are effaced?

One thing at any rate is certain, that **"Against the Grain"** marked a definite rupture with its predecessors, with *Les Soeurs Vatard, En Ménage, A vau-l'eau,* that with it I entered on a path the goal of which I did not so much as suspect. (p. xliv)

> *J. K. Huysmans, "Preface: Written Twenty Years After the Novel" (1903), in his* Against the Grain (A Rebours), *translated by John Howard, Three Sirens Press, 1931 (and reprinted by Dover Publications, Inc., 1969), pp. xxxiii-xlix.*

ARTHUR SYMONS   (essay date 1908)

To the student of psychology few more interesting cases could be presented than the development of Huysmans. From the first he has been a man "for whom the visible world existed," indeed, but as the scene of a slow martyrdom. The world has always appeared to him to be a profoundly uncomfortable, unpleasant, and ridiculous place; and it has been a necessity of his temperament to examine it minutely, with all the patience of disgust, and a necessity of his method to record it with an almost ecstatic hatred. In his first book, *Le Drageoir à Epices,* published at the age of twenty-six, we find him seeking his colour by preference in a drunkard's cheek or a carcase outside a butcher's shop. *Marthe* . . . anticipates [Jules Goncourt's] *La Fille Elisa* and [Emile Zola's] *Nana,* but it has a crude brutality of observation in which there is hardly a touch of pity. *Les Soeurs Vatard* is a frame without a picture, but in *En Menage* the dreary tedium of existence is chronicled in all its insignificance with a kind of weary and aching hate. "We, too," is its conclusion, "by leave of the everlasting stupidity of things, may, like our fellow-citizens, live stupid and respected." The fantastic unreality, the exquisite artificiality of *A Rebours,* the breviary of the decadence, is the first sign of that possible escape which Huysmans has always foreseen in the direction of art, but which he is still unable to make into more than an artificial paradise, in which beauty turns to a cruel hallucination and imprisons the soul still more fatally. The end is a cry of hopeless hope, in which Huysmans did not understand the meaning till later: "Lord, have pity of the Christian who doubts, of the sceptic who would fain believe, of the convict of life who sets sail alone by night, under a firmament lighted only by the consoling watch-lights of the old hope."

In *Là-Bas* we are in yet another stage of this strange pilgrim's progress. The disgust which once manifested itself in the merely external revolt against the ugliness of streets, the imbecility of faces, has become more and more internalised, and the attraction of what is perverse in the unusual beauty of art has led, by some obscure route, to the perilous halfway house of a corrupt mysticism. The book, with its monstrous pictures of the Black Mass and of the spiritual abominations of Satanism, is one step further in the direction of the supernatural; and this, too, has its desperate, unlooked-for conclusion: "Christian glory is a laughing-stock to our age; it contaminates the supernatural and casts out the world to come." In *Là-Bas* we go down into the deepest gulf; *En Route* sets us one stage along a new way, and at this turning-point begins the later Huysmans. (pp. 138-40)

At once the novel showed itself capable of competing, on their own ground, with poetry, with the great "confessions," with philosophy. *En Route* is perhaps the first novel which does not set out with the aim of amusing its readers. It offers you no more entertainment than *Paradise Lost* or the *Confessions* of St. Augustine, and it is possible to consider it on the same level. The novel, which, after having chronicled the adventures of the Vanity Fairs of this world, has set itself with admirable success to analyse the amorous and ambitious and money-making intelligence of the conscious and practical self, sets itself at last to the final achievement: the revelation of the subconscious self, no longer the intelligence, but the soul. Here, then, purged of the distraction of incident, liberated from the bondage of a too realistic conversation, in which the aim had been to convey the very gesture of breathing life, internalised to a complete liberty, in which, just because it is so absolutely free, art is able to accept, without limiting itself, the expressive medium of a convention, we have in the novel, a new form, which may be at once a confession and a decoration, the soul and a pattern.

This story of a conversion is a new thing in modern French; it is a confession, a self-ascultation of the soul; a kind of thinking aloud. It fixes, in precise words, all the uncertainties, the contradictions, the absurd unreasonableness and not less absurd logic, which distract man's brain in the passing over him of sensation and circumstance. And all this thinking is concentrated on one end, is concerned with the working out, in his own singular way, of one man's salvation. There is a certain dry hard casuistry, a subtlety and closeness almost ecclesiastical, in the investigation of an obscure and yet definite region, whose intellectual passions are as varied and as tumultuous as those of the heart. Every step is taken deliberately, is weighed, approved, condemned, viewed from this side and from that, and at the same time one feels behind all this reasoning an impulsion urging a soul onward against its will. (pp. 141-43)

In *La Cathédrale* we are still occupied with this sensitive, lethargic, persevering soul, but with that soul in one of its longest halts by the way, as it undergoes the slow, permeating influence of *"la Cathédrale mystique par excellence,"* the cathedral of Chartres. (p. 144)

[In *La Cathédrale* Huysmans carries] further the principle which he had perceived in *En Route,* showing, as he does, how inert matter, the art of stones, the growth of plants, the unconscious life of beasts, may be brought under the same law of the soul, may obtain, through symbol, a spiritual existence. He is thus but extending the domain of the soul while he may seem to be limiting or ignoring it; and Durtal may well stand aside for a moment, in at least the energy of contemplation, while he sees, with a new understanding, the very sight of his eyes, the very stuff of his thoughts, taking life before him, a life of the same substance as his own. What is Symbolism if not an establishing of the links which hold the world together, the affirmation of an eternal, minute, intricate, almost invisible life, which runs through the whole universe? Every age has its own symbols; but a symbol once perfectly expressed, that symbol remains, as Gothic architecture remains the very soul of the Middle Ages. To get at that truth which is all but the deepest meaning of beauty, to find that symbol which is its most adequate expression, is in itself a kind of creation; and that is what Huysmans does for us in *La Cathédrale.* (pp. 145-46)

From this time forward, until his death, Huysmans is seen purging himself of his realism, coming closer and closer to that spiritual Naturalism which he had invented, an art made out of an apprehension of the inner meaning of those things which he still saw with the old tenacity of vision. Nothing is changed in him and yet all is changed. The disgust of the world deepens through *L'Oblat,* which is the last stage but one in the pilgrimage which begins with *En Route.* It seeks an escape in poring, with a dreadful diligence, over a saint's recorded miracles, in the life of *Sainte Lydwine de Schiedam,* which is mediaeval in its precise acceptance of every horrible detail of the story. *Les Foules de Lourdes* has the same minute attentiveness to horror, but with a new pity in it, and a way of giving thanks to the Virgin, which is in Huysmans yet another escape from his disgust of the world. But it is in the great chapter on Satan as the creator of ugliness that his work seems to end where it had begun, in the service of art, now come from a great way off to join itself with the service of God. And the whole soul of Huysmans characterises itself in the turn of a single phrase there: that "art is the only clean thing on earth, except holiness." (pp. 151-52)

> *Arthur Symons, "The Later Huysmans," in his* The Symbolist Movement in Literature, *E. P. Dutton and Company, 1908, pp. 136-52.*

JAMES HUNEKER   (essay date 1909)

Joris-Karl Huysmans has been called mystic, naturalist, critic, aristocrat of the intellect; he was all these, a mandarin of letters and a pessimist besides—no matter what other qualities persist throughout his work, pessimism is never absent; his firmament is clotted with black stars. He had a mediaeval monk's contempt for existence, contempt for the mangy flock of mediocrity; yet his genius drove him to describe its crass ugliness in phrases of incomparable and enamelled prose. It is something of a paradox that this man of picturesque piety should have lived to be the accredited interpreter, the distiller of its quintessence, of that elusive quality, "modernity." The "intensest vision of the modern world," as Havelock Ellis puts it, Huysmans unites to the endowment of a painter the power of a rare psychologist, superimposed upon a lycanthropic nature. A collective title for his books might be borrowed from Zola: My Hatreds. He hated life and its eternal *bêtise*. His theme, with variations, is a strangling Ennui. With those devoted sons of Mother Church, Charles Baudelaire, Barbey D'Aurevilly, Villiers de l'Isle Adam, and Paul Verlaine, eccentric sons whose actions so often dismayed their fellow worshippers of less genius, Huysmans has been affiliated. He was not a poet or, indeed, a man of overwhelming imagination. But he had the verbal imagination. He did not possess the novelist's talent. His was not the flamboyant genius of Barbey, nor had he the fantastic invention of Villiers. He seems closer to Baudelaire, rather by reason of his ironic, critical temperament than because of his creative gifts. Baudelaire's oriflamme, embroidered with preciously devised letters of gold, reads: Spleen and Ideal; upon the emblematic banner of Huysmans this motto is Spleen. His work at times seems like a prolongation in prose of Baudelaire's. And by reason of his exacerbated temper he became the most personal writer of his generation. He belonged to no school, and avoided, after his beginnings, all literary groups.

He is recording-secretary of the petty miseries and ironies of the life about him. Over ugliness he becomes almost lyric. "The world is a forest of differences." His pen, when he depicts an attack of dyspepsia or neuralgia, or the nervous distaste of a hypochondriac for meeting people, is like the triple sting of a hornet. He is the prose singer of neurasthenia, a Hamlet doubting his digestion, a Schopenhauer of the cook-shops. (pp. 167-69)

His method is not the recital of events, but the description of a situation; a scene, not a narration, but large tableaux. Action there is little; he is more static than dynamic. His characters . . . suffer from paralysis of the will, from hyperaesthesia. The soul in its primordial darkness interests him, and he describes it with the same penetrating prose as he does the carcass of an animal. He is a luminous mystic who speaks in terms of extravagant naturalism. A physiologist of the soul, at times his soul dwelt in a boulevard. His violent, vivid style so excellent in setting forth coloured sensations is equally admirable in the construction of metaphors which make concrete the abstract. There is the element of the grotesque, of the old, ribald Fleming, in Huysmans, though without a trace of hearty Flemish humour. He once said that the memory of the inventor of cardplaying ought to be blessed, the game kept closed the mouths of imbeciles. Nor is the pepper of sophistry absent. He sculptures his ideas. He is both morose and fulgurating. He squanders his emotions with polychromatic resignation unlike a Saint Augustine or a Newman; yet we are not deeply moved by his soul-experiences. It is not vibrating sincerity that we miss. . . . Lucid as is his manner, clairvoyant as the exposition of his soul at the feet of God, there is, nevertheless, an absence of unction, of tenderness, which repels. Sympathy and tenderness are *bourgeois* virtues for Huysmans. (pp. 172-73)

He was not a normal man. He loathed the inevitable discords of life with a startling intensity. The venomous salt of his wit he sprinkles over the raw turpitude of men and women. Woman for him was not of the planetary sex, but either a stupid or a vicious creature; sometimes both. Impassible as he was, he could be shocked into a species of sub-acid eloquence if the theme were the inutility of mankind. No Hebraic prophet ever launched such poignant phrases of disgust and horror at the world and its works. (p. 174)

As a critic of painting Huysmans revealed himself the possessor of a temperament that was positively ferocious in the presence of an unsympathetic canvas. His vocabulary and peculiar gift of invective were then exercised with astounding verbal if not critical results. Singularly narrow in his judgments for a man of his general culture, his intensity of vision concentrated itself upon a few painters and etchers; during the latter part of his life only religious art interested him, as had the exotic and monstrous in earlier years. And even in the former sphere he restricted his admiration, rather say idolatry, to a few men; he sought for character, an ascetic type of character, the lean and meagre Saviours and saints of the Flemish primitives arousing in him a fire almost fanatical. (pp. 178-79)

[*L'Art Moderne*] deals with the official salons of 1879, 1880-81 and the exposition of the Independents, 1880-81. The appendix, 1882, contains thumbnail sketches of Caillebotte, . . . Gauguin, Mlle. Morisot, Guillaumin, Renoir, Pissaro, Sisley, Claude Monet, "the marine painter *par excellence*"; Manet, Roll, Redon, all men then fighting the stream of popular and academic disfavour. Since Charles Baudelaire's Salons, no volume on the current Paris exhibitions has appeared of such solid knowledge and literary power as Huysmans's. Admitting his marked prejudices, his numerous dogmatic utterances, there is nevertheless an attractive artistic quality backed up by the writer's stubborn convictions that persuade where the more liberal and brilliant Théophile Gautier never does. "Théo," who said that if he pitched his sentences in the air they always fell on their feet, like a cat, leaned heavily on his verbal magic. But even in that particular he is no match for Huysmans, who, boasting the blood of Fleming painters, sculptors, and architects, uses his pen as an artist his brush. (pp. 180-81)

In his description of the Independent exposition (1880) to which Degas, Mary Cassatt and Berthe Morisot, Forain, and others sent canvases, Huysmans drifts into literary criticism; he saw analogies between the paintings of the realists, impressionists, and the modern men of fiction, Flaubert, Goncourt, Zola. "Have not," he asks, "the Goncourts fixed in a style deliberate and personal, the most ephemeral of sensations, the most fugacious of *nuances*?" So, too, have Manet, Monet, Pissaro, Raffaelli. (pp. 182-83)

Scattered through his novels—if one may dare to ascribe this title to such an amorphous form—there are eloquent and burning pages devoted to various painters, but not with the amplitude and cool science displayed in his studies of Degas, Moreau, Rops, The Monster in Art—a monstrous subject masterfully handled—and Whistler. He literally discovered Degas, and in future books on rhetoric surely Huysmans's descriptions of Degas's old workwomen sponging their creased backs cannot be excluded without doing violence to the expressive powers of the French language. His eye mirrored the most minute

details—in that he was Dutch-Flemish; the same merciless scrutiny is pursued in the life of the soul—he was Flemish and Spanish: Ruysbroeck and St. John of the Cross, mystics both, with an amazing sense of the realistic.

Without a spacious imagination, Huysmans was a man of the subtlest sensibilities. There is a wealth of critical divination in his studies of Moreau and Whistler. Twenty or thirty years ago it was not so easy to range these two enigmas. Huysmans did so, and, in company with Degas and Rops, placed them so definitely that critics have paraphrased his ideas ever since. (pp. 183-84)

A Rebours is the history of a decadent soul in search of an earthly paradise. His palace of art is near Paris, and in it the Duc des Esseintes assembles all that is rare, perverse, beautiful, morbid, and crazy in modern art and literature. *A Rebours* is in reality a very precious work of criticism by a distinguished critical temperament, written in a prose jewelled and shining, sharp as a Damascene dagger. (p. 185)

Joris-Karl Huysmans should have been a painter; his indubitable gift for form and colour were by some trick of nature or circumstance transposed to literature. So he brought to the criticism of pictures an eye abnormal in its keenness, and to this was superadded an abnormal power of expression. (p. 188)

[As to the quality of *Three Primitives*] there can be no mistake. It is masterly, revealing the various Huysmanses we admire: the mystic, the realist, the penetrating critic of art, and the magnificent tamer of language. Hallucinated by his phrases, you see cathedrals arise from the mist and swim so close to you that you discern every detail before the vision vanishes; or some cruel and bloody canvas of the semi-demoniacal Grünewald, on which a hideous Christ is crucified, surrounded by scowling faces. The swiftness in executing the verbal portrait allows you no time to wonder over the method; the evocation is complete, and afterward you realise the magic of Huysmans. (p. 189)

Huysmans was not a man possessing what are so vaguely denominated "general ideas." He was never interested in the chess-play of metaphysics, politics, or science. He was a specialist, one who had ransacked libraries for curious details, despoiled perfumers' catalogues for their odourous vocables, pored over technical dictionaries for odd-coloured words, and studied cookbooks for savoury terms. His gamut of sensations began at the violet ray. He was a perverse aristocrat who descended to the gutter there to analyse the various stratifications of filth; when he returned to his ivory cell, he had discovered, not humanity, but an anodyne, the love of God. Thenceforth, he was interested in one thing—the saving of the soul of Joris-Karl Huysmans, and being a marvellous verbal artist, his recital of the event startled us, fascinated us. (p. 205)

James Huneker, "The Pessimists' Progress: J.-K. Huysmans," in his Egoists, a Book of Supermen: Stendhal, Baudelaire, Flaubert, Anatole France, Huysmans, Barres, Nietzsche, Blake, Ibsen, Stirner, and Ernest Hello *(copyright 1909 Charles Scribner's Sons; copyright renewed 1937 by Josephine Huneker; reprinted with the permission of Charles Scribner's Sons), Charles Scribner's Sons, 1909 (and reprinted by Charles Scribner's Sons, 1920), pp. 167-206.*

REMY de GOURMONT (essay date 1921)

[When the unexpected *A Rebours* appeared] it was not a point of departure, but the consecration of a new literature. No longer was it so much a question of forcing a brutal externality to enter the domains of Art by representation, as of drawing from this very representation motives for dreams and interior revaluations. *En Rade* further developed this system whose fruitfulness is limitless,—while the naturalistic method proved itself still more sterile than even its enemies had dared hope,—a system of strictest logic and of such marvelous suppleness that it permits, without forfeiting anything to likelihood, to intercalate in exact scenes of rustic life, pages like "Esther" or like the *"voyage sélenién."*

The architecture of *Là-Bas* is based on an analogous plan, but the license profitably finds itself restrained by the unity of subject, which remains absolute beneath its multiple faces: the Christ of Gunewald, in his extreme mystic violence, his startling and consoling hideousness, is not a fugue without line, nor are the demoniac forest of Tiffauges, the cruel Black Mass, or any of the "fragments" displaced or inharmonious; nevertheless, before the freedom of the novel, they had been criticized, not in themselves, but as not rigorously necessary to the advance of the book. Fortunately the novel is finally free, and to say more, the novel, as still conceived by Zola or Bourget, to us appears a conception as superannuated as the epic poem or the tragedy. (pp. 195-97)

[Huysmans] no longer writes novels, he makes books, and he plans them according to an original arrangement; I believe that is one of the reasons why some persons still take issue with his literature and find it immoral. This last point is easy to explain by a single word: for the non-artist, art is always immoral. As soon as one wishes, for example, to translate sexual relations into a new language, he is immoral because he discloses, fatally, acts which, treated by ordinary procedures, would remain unperceived, lost in the mist of common things. Thus it is that an artist, not at all erotic, can be accused of stupid outrages by the foolish or the mischievous, before the public. It, nevertheless, does not seem that the facts of love or rather of aberration related in *Là-Bas* at all entice the simplicity of virginal ignorance. The book rather gives disgust or horror of sensuality in that it does not invite to foolish experiences or even to permissible unions. Will not immorality, if we behold it from a particular and peculiarly religious point of view, consist, on the contrary, in the insistence upon the exquisiteness of carnal love and the vaunting of the delights of legitimate copulation? (pp. 197-99)

Huysmans one day found himself converted to mysticism, and wrote *En Route,* that book which is like a statue of stone that suddenly begins to weep. It is a mysticism a little raucous and hard, but like his phrases, his epithets, Huysmans is hard. Mysticism first came to him through the eyes rather than through the soul. He observed religious facts with the fear of being their dupe and the hope that they would be absurd; he was caught in the very meshes of the *credo-quia-absurdum,*—happy victim of his curiosity.

Now, fatigued at having watched men's hypocritical faces, he watches the stones, preparing a supreme book on "The Cathedral." There, if it is a question of feeling and understanding, is it especially a question of sight? He will see as no other person has seen, for no one other person has seen, no one ever was gifted with a glance so sharp, so boring, so frank and so skilled in insinuating himself into the very wrinkles of faces, rose-windows and masks.

Huysmans is an eye. (pp. 200-01)

Remy de Gourmont, "Huysmans," in his The Book of Masks, *translated by Jack Lewis, J. W. Luce and Company, 1921 (and reprinted by Books for Libraries Press, 1967; distributed by Arno Press, Inc.), pp. 195-204.*

GEORGE ROSS RIDGE   (essay date 1961)

The decadent is the scion of the romantic dandy. As a matter of fact, this is almost his exclusive lineage directly from romanticism. He shares little with other types of the romantic hero. The decadent, for example, is not a romantic seeker, i.e., a man engaged on desperate pursuits of lost horizons. Idealistic quests are too juvenile to fit into decadent philosophy. Nor is the decadent really a man of fate, someone emprisoned in a social and cosmic context, destroying either himself and/or others as he writhes in anguish. As far as fatality is concerned, the decadent is like the dandy: he refuses to be embroiled in human relationships, and he lacks the man of fate's capacity for social and cosmic feeling. (pp. 48-9)

There is in the French decadence an archetypal hero who incarnates all these traits. It is Duke Jean des Esseintes in Huysmans' *A Rebours*. . . . He towers above all other heroes of the decadence. As Barbey d'Aurevilly said and as Huysmans himself sensed, this novel, if such it may be called, carried the idea of decadence to the point of no return. After it there was nothing new to add, the subject was at its philosophical end, and later work would necessarily be a valedictory. *A Rebours* is the central work of decadent literature. Its hero—a metaphysical hero—typifies the decadent soul.

Against the Grain—the very title summates the cult of artificiality which is not only basic to decadent aesthetics but is also fundamental in the decadent order of things. The decadent hero is immediately characterized as unnatural, i.e., the man of antinature. Though this fact is obvious, it must not be glossed over. Just as decadent style and predilections in art and literature are twisted and involuted, so too (for deeper reasons) the blood of the decadent is tainted. Or as Spengler would say, his cosmic beat is discordant with the rhythms of nature. The image is one which decadent writers would approve.

The story is instructive. Jean des Esseintes is an effete young man, independently wealthy, who has devoted his life to the pursuit of pleasure. He has no other interest. Yet his sensual experiences leave him the bitter dregs of satiety and ennui. He remains unsatisfied. In a desperate attempt to key up his failing senses, he retires to a country house at Fontenay. He fits it out like a monastery, served only by two faithful domestics, and enters his aesthetic paradise. He withdraws from society, however, not to retire from luxury but to find again the sensual pleasures dulled by his excesses in Paris. They alone make his life bearable. Des Esseintes interprets life always in sensual terms. He is an organism with acute antennae responding to subtle stimuli. Beyond this he has neither aim or *raison d'être*. Once pleasure inures his senses, he is faced with an enigma: He must either find new avenues to excitement, or he withers upon the vine. Thus Fontenay is at once his pleasure house and his last resort. (pp. 49-50)

There are several aspects to the decadent, as evidenced by Des Esseintes. First, he is a cerebral hero. Emprisoned in his abulia, he cannot act in even mundane matters. Second, he has a strong aesthetic penchant, characterized by *l'art pour l'art*. He turns to painting and literature for the sensations they afford. Third, the decadent is a cosmopolitan, often a traveler who has encountered the unusual and the exotic. But even when like Des Esseintes he has traveled little, he is still a man of the world.

He is at his ease in society and can frequent the great salons. He typifies the cosmopolitan's relativism, for he has neither regional ties nor the personal beliefs engendered in space by time. He is not a man of the blood and the soil but one of the city. Fourth, the decadent is a kind of pervert. Certainly his tastes and inclinations are perverse in comparison with the norm. Des Esseintes typically enjoys his perversions. In his cult of artificiality he cultivates perversity in order to heighten excitement to its greatest pitch. Unlike the pathological hero in romanticism, however, the decadent is content with his perversities, and he usually maintains some control over himself: he deliberately chooses the paths of perversion, whereas the romantic's pathology is forced upon him by conflict from within or without.

Fifth, an extension of the four types mentioned, the decadent is a metaphysical hero. As a passive hero who has passed beyond activity, he is disenchanted with life. Thus he tends to become a negation of life, an imp of the perverse, as he strives to titillate his sleeping senses. His artistic sensitivity is much darker than the dandy's. He is *faisandé*, gamy, whereas the dandy retains a cold intellectual posture before life. Furthermore, the decadent reveals a metaphysical attraction to death which the dandy rarely displays. The dandy is willing, sometimes eager, to destroy others, but he does not often turn his destructive energy in upon himself. The decadent does. He has a deathwish working against the forces of creation and life in himself and in nature. He develops the cult of artificiality, then, to its completion: the purposeful violation of nature and natural process. (pp. 54-5)

The decadent as metaphysical hero, like Des Esseintes, has a worldview in which art subsumes the ideas of nature and life. A part of life, one aspect, becomes greater than the whole. The idea of totality is reformulated. This is essentially the theory of *l'art pour l'art,* which of course does not refer to a weak decadent fondling sunflowers in a blue vase. By epitomizing the anti-natural, art replaces nature and occupies the former role of life as totality. Form, structure, style are corollaries of this social and cosmic view of art, which gives rise to a new psychology. (pp. 55-6)

Art is a magic realm where it is transmuted into nature, reality. It is a metaphysical message. The decadent turns to art, as Schopenhauer recommends, as a kind of mysticism. Like Des Esseintes he converts his sensual energy into a type of intellectual and aesthetic chastity. Schopenhauer is not by chance the favorite philosopher of Des Esseintes: the connection between pessimism and decadent art is unseverable. (p. 58)

The decadent is what he is because of his peculiar place in space and time, and the decadent is always aware of the theatrical role he plays. He is the creature of nerves and heredity, of society and the cosmos. He knows it all too well. His consciousness of space and time, unidealistically perceived through his acute sense-impressions, makes him a metaphysical hero. He is a pragmatist, even a positivist, who sometimes becomes a nihilist. His sophistication, like that of Des Esseintes, ultimately becomes inertia, a fatal indolence. He suffers from a moral and physical abulia that is overwhelming in face of his crumbling world. Destiny moves. He must move with it. The metaphysical hero can resist destiny, or nature, only by becoming anti-nature, by desperately grasping for something permanent—a happy moment dimly perceived—in the swirling onrush of time. And this he does. (p. 66)

George Ross Ridge, "The Decadent: A Metaphysical Hero," in his The Hero in French Decadent Literature *(copyright © 1961 by University of Georgia Press; reprinted by permission of the author), University of Georgia Press, 1961, pp. 48-66.**

JOHN D. ERICKSON (essay date 1970)

[*Là-bas*] is about search, and no other character in it quests in greater frenzy than the hero, Durtal. Huysmans uses a particular image to convey the sense of his character torn by the conflict between bodily and spiritual needs. Durtal is suspended between the pure mechanism of sensation and the pure void of spirit. (pp. 418-19)

Durtal suffers from this limbo he inhabits, from this state in which he rejects the base materialism of his fellow men, but has not yet succeeded in replacing it with the spiritual ideal he longs for. He suffers from a vertigo of the soul. His condition does not appear to offer improvement, and in this sense the novel consists in an enduring crisis that refuses to unravel— the Chantelouve episode is over, the life of Gilles de Rais is past history, but the story of Durtal bids fair to continue forever. Durtal appears immobilized at the end of the novel, despite his furious activity, despite his desperate quest for a solution to the enigma contained in the character of the person whose history he has undertaken to write, Gilles de Rais, and in the character of the woman he has undertaken to know, Mme Chantelouve. Durtal's life, such as we see it here, resembles an unresolved search. Indeed, it *is* an unresolved search.

A complex metaphor underlies Durtal's search in *Là-bas,* and provides the novel with the basis for its elaborate development. The life of Durtal on a metaphoric level is nothing other than the search of the medieval alchemist for the elusive philosopher's stone. The love Mme Chantelouve inspires in him, like the fascination which he feels for Gilles de Rais, evolves on an analogy with the obsession of the alchemist for his Stone. The alchemist of former times sought restlessly to decipher the enigma of the ancients, lost to them for several centuries. Durtal faces enigmas just as obdurate—the first of these lies in the character of Gilles de Rais (or Retz) who became a Marshal of France at the age of twenty-five, who was a retainer of Charles VII, who served as the guarantor of Jeanne d'Arc and rode with her entourage against the English at Rouen. After Gilles de Rais' service with the king, he retired to his domains, where, following a period of incredible extravagance, he tried to recoup his fortunes by the practice of necromancy and black magic. Durtal is fascianted by the bizarre mixture of goodness represented in his character and in his relations with the Maid of Orléans and the proclivity to evil found in his alleged torture and murder of several hundred children.

How is it that a personality like that of Gilles de Rais could have existed? How can a woman like Mme Chantelouve incorporate two natures (her spiritual side and her carnal side) so antithetical? Durtal relentlessly pursues a formula. The medieval alchemists entertained the notion of a Golden Age—the time of the ancients when the formula for the discovery of gold was known—and Durtal equally looks back upon an age of gold. For it is the Medieval Age that holds the secret formula sought by Durtal, the age when the gold of the spirit was known, when the formula existed to find in the dross of the body the most precious metal of all—faith, goodness. . . . [We] can easily discern, on a temporal level, the antipodes of the novel: the present as against the Middle Ages which, for Carhaix, as well as for des Hermies, Durtal and Gévingey, represent the Golden Age, the time when there existed a profound unity between man's soul and body, between the spiritual and carnal. That unity, which Huysmans calls "spiritual naturalism," was known to the fifteenth century, with its platonic notion of the individual as a reflection of the Divine, and of all things of this world as incarnating the idea of a divine counterpart.

The Middle Ages offer a way to the "là-bas" of love, of human compassion. We recall the primitive artists described in *Là-bas,* who depicted the Christ of the poor, the very human Christ of Saint Justin, Saint Basil, Saint Cyril, of Tertullian, the Christ beset by doubt, who suffered very real fleshly agony. These artists presented matter, the flesh, transfigured by the spirit, just as in Huysmans' life of Gilles de Rais the great and horror-inspiring criminal will become transfigured by faith, by a humility greater than his criminality, or again, just as the parents of Rais' victims are transfigured by such sublime spirit that they weep out of pity for the monster who has violated and massacred their children.

The Middle Ages for Huysmans allowed of such a conjunction of spirit and flesh. It was the time when the safe conduct of a little peasant girl who was destined to become the savioress of France might be assured by a Gilles de Rais. Such a remarkable event might appear ironic in the extreme to us, but it is a paradox understood without difficulty by a man of the Middle Ages, or by a Huysmans, for the Saint and the great criminal after the fashion of Gilles de Rais are not without relationship. . . [The] unity of the Middle Ages is reflected not only in what we today think of as religious subjects; rather, it is a unity found in the interrelation of all the sciences, religion, and mysticism. . . . In contrast, in Huysmans' time, things signify nothing but themselves. The philosopher's stone for Huysmans stands in contrast to the positivist spirit of the modern age. The secrets of the ancients are lost to us.

It is those lost secrets that Durtal seeks. His brute manner is Gilles de Rais and Mme Chantelouve. His progress, if he were able to understand and accept the unity which they exemplify, would not be the material progress of his age, but spiritual progress, the capacity to undergo a transformation of faith and to believe. But for Durtal all effort leads in the end only to failure. (pp. 419-21)

[*Là-bas*] is the story of Durtal, the eternal alchemist, who rejects the way to evil but who cannot find the way to good. He suffers from the satiation of the material present and from the insatiability of his thirst for the ideal future he cannot attain. All that is necessary is a leap, but Durtal stands too deep in the mire of his time. (p. 425)

> *John D. Erickson, "Huysmans' 'Là-Bas': A Metaphor of Search," in* The French Review *(copyright 1970 by the American Association of Teachers of French), Vol. XLIII, No. 3, February, 1970, pp. 418-25.*

ANTHONY WINNER   (essay date 1974)

Much late nineteenth-century fiction occurs in twilight, is marked by exhaustion, entropy, the failure of illusion or vision, the disappearance of God. . . . No one fiction so succinctly or self-consciously evokes this paralyzing depression as Huysmans' early short novel. **"Down Stream"** (**"A Vau-l'eau"**) . . . , once described by James Gibbons Huneker as the "Iliad of indigestion," depicts with loathing the failure of actuality to provide any reward, meaning, or *raison d'être*. The plenitude of Balzacian materialism, the belief in the organizing possi-

bilities of the "seen," the moral and dramatic values of character, the germinal energy that quickens so much naturalistic fiction—all are eroded to a defeated weariness. The Paris in which the protagonist, the middle-aged clerk Folantin, lives is no longer the treasure trove of stories, sketches, and mysteries mined by Balzac and others but an "interminable barracks," a "sinister Chicago." "M. Folantin suffered, in this new Paris, an impression of uneasiness and anguish." . . . Folantin is an exhausted survivor not merely of the rich Paris that once was but also of a vision of the meaning to be found in real things, a vision now elapsed.

In place of what is gone there is a diffuse, etiolated version of that "lust for metaphysics" which Irving Howe finds characteristic of the late nineteenth and early twentieth century. Yet the lust is here little more than an irritating remnant of vision, serves only to trouble the misery of earthbound existence. When Folantin's cousin, his last relative, dies in her convent, he momentarily envies "her calm and silent life" and regrets "the faith he had lost." "But why," he asks, "is this consoling religion only made for the poor in spirit?" In any case, the deprivations of the cloistered life are a futile sacrifice. "Good heavens! it was paying dearly for the improbable happiness of a future life, he thought. The convent appeared to him a house of detention, a place of desolation and of terror."

He must cleave to the patterns of his daily round, which are valid because and, desolatingly, only because they exist. He disdains the facile escapes of popular imaginative or adventure literature; "he cared only for the things of real life; and so, his library was limited, in all, to half a hundred volumes. . . ." Like his creator, Folantin is a realist *malgré lui*. The technique employed to reproduce this existence among real things is appropriately representational, at times even documentary, but the meaning once envisioned by realism has evaporated, leaving glumness, a pervasive feeling of loss, and anxiety: the hope, disenchanted almost at its inception, that there must be or have been something better somewhere, something more to life than its realities—a plea to be repeated down to our own time by hosts of naturalistic protagonists. (pp. 39-41)

The year-long slice of Folantin's melancholia bears essentially the same message as the sophomorically romantic prose poem **"Ecstasy"** collected in Huysmans' first volume, **"A Dish of Spices"** (**"Le Drageoir à épices"** . . .). . . . No less stereotypically romantic than the "expressive" and exclamatory style is the theme of the deflating enslavement by which mundane fact traduces the infinite. Yet the theme remains dominant even in the maturity of **"Down Stream"**: ignobility and vulgarity, still defined by the loss of a delicious dream, are the mean burden of Folantin's experience. Huysmans' presentation recalls the realism which is Flaubert's calculated aesthetic response to the futility of romantic dreaming. But here disenchantment strikes even at the possibility of dreaming. Emma Bovary could at least entertain, however sentimentally, the effulgence of the inifinite, the ideal. For Folantin this highest good has become simply the "impossible." Seeking the absolute amid the reduced circumstances of the actual, his dreams can aspire no higher than the reasonable contentment of a decent meal. And not even tempered well-being comes his way. His expectations are blocked, thwarted not by any exalting nemesis, not by the machinations of a society with which he is at war, but by the indifference of a reality governed by what Schopenhauer calls "Will." At the conclusion, Folantin reflects that Schopenhauer "was right. 'The life of man oscillates, like a pendulum, between sorrow and boredom. . . .'"

Folantin's accumulated miseries are revealed as a triumph of Will as most French pessimists of the period understood the concept: in A. G. Lehmann's paraphrase, a "metaphysical entity . . . blind, impersonal, and totally indifferent to all man's efforts towards happiness, goodness, or truth. . . . The Will itself has no aims; it drives forward incessantly, leaving in its train misery, disaster, and the defeat of human aspiration." Cast adrift from purpose and fulfillment, reaching not even a dead-end, Folantin's experience conveys more bleakly than any other of its epoch the engulfment of the simplest human efforts at a meaningfully organized existence by universal indifference. (pp. 41-2)

In **"Down Stream,"** antedating Durtal's cogitations [in the later novels] by nine years, Huysmans creates an art that stands its ground. But this is as much as it can do; there is no possibility of what Durtal calls "spiritual naturalism." Folantin's story is distinguished from other monotonous studies of mediocre beings by its self-conscious awareness of its own sterility. Though the good taste, in its several meanings, with which Folantin is endowed hints at some prior initiation into true value, at the rudiments of a soul, his experience is bounded by what Thorwald terms the "sentimental and sensuous reactions" of disillusion; his viewpoint is essentially that of a documentary veracity capable only of inverting materialism into disgusted disenchantment. Realism functions as a safeguard against romantic claptrap: a negative rôle acted out by Folantin. (pp. 47-8)

Real things no longer satisfy even the senses. But there is no alternative to realities; their impetus carries all before it, bears all down stream: *à vau-l'eau,* an expression connoting drift, abandonment, floundering, disorder. In Folantin the appetite for life fails, purpose and energy are dissipated into the irritated stasis which A. E. Carter sees as the characteristic distinguishing decadent from romantic melancholia. No longer is there the flattering disjunction between rich desire or imagining and a used-up world which Chateaubriand defined as the *vague des passions.* Folantin's balked comfort is without the dignity of philosophy, the meaning of socio-economic injustice, the pathetic victimization of determinism. The reality principle of a spent energy, he has not the "courage to abandon" his district, the site of his office, his birthplace, and his few, now futile, memories of better days. Des Esseintes, two years later in **"A Rebours,"** will be able to decorate his rooms to represent the pleasures of movement without its irritations: will have, for a time at least, the resources to imagine defenses against an unendurable reality. Folantin's imagination has been rendered impotent; he stays put, knowing only that the slightest venture invites an increase of suffering or ennui. Not only is he deprived of the large appetite that marks the heirs of Lazaro and Sancho, he is equally set off from the descendants of Don Quixote, who rebel against the material for the sake of a dream or ideal. (pp. 48-9)

Anthony Winner, "The Indigestible Reality: J.-K. Huysmans' 'Down Stream'," in The Virginia Quarterly Review *(copyright, 1974, by* The Virginia Quarterly Review, The University of Virginia), *Vol. 50, No. 1, Winter, 1974, pp. 39-50.*

G. A. CEVASCO (essay date 1975)

The belief that J.-K. Huysmans meant his *A Rebours* to be read as satire or parody is frequently heard. Possibly this opinion is echoed about most by English readers of the novel; for, as the most recent translator of *A Rebours* into English has written:

"There are . . . critics who maintain that Des Esseintes was intended to be a caricature of such aesthetes as Montesquiou, just as Amarinth in Robert Hichen's novel *The Green Carnation* was meant as a satire on Wilde." (p. 278)

For the average reader who chances upon *A Rebours,* any interpretation may be grist to the mill. Even the devotee of French letters can be excused if he assumes that Huysmans' decadent masterpiece is mainly satire or parody. There is no reason, however, for the serious student of Romance literature to repeat such interpretations; indeed, it may be incumbent upon him to explain that *A Rebours* is neither satire, nor parody, nor caricature.

The provocative but erroneous view that *A Rebours* is essentially satire and parody first found full expression almost fifty years ago when an American scholar [F. L. Van Roosbroeck; see excerpt above] developed an elaborate theory on the subject. His speculations made an interesting article, one that seemed worthy of publication because it purportedly presented a key to "the proper understanding" of a singular novel. Contrary to other previous interpretations of *A Rebours,* this imaginative critic wrote: "I believe it to be neither an autobiography nor the truthful photograph of a living 'decadent,' but mainly a caricature. . . . All through the book runs, like a red thread, a constant vein of parody. . . ." (pp. 278-79)

While it could be reasonably argued that there are certain parodic levels of meaning in *A Rebours,* they are not aimed at Decadence. Indeed, any parodic element would have ironies of its own and hardly could serve as a key to "a proper understanding"; nor would any combination of parodic elements—"red threads," as they were labelled—weave a meaningful pattern of interpretation. (p. 279)

If the novel is labelled "a satirical study," it is reasonable to ask: what is being satirized? Is it Decadence? Is it the world of the *haute noblesse?* Is it the personage of the real Comte Robert de Montesquiou, one of the prototypes of the hero of the novel? Is it the wildly eccentric life of the fictional Duc Jean Floressas des Esseintes? (pp. 279-80)

A Rebours did more than reflect decadent tastes: it helped create them. As Mario Praz put it, Huysmans' remarkable achievement is "the pivot upon which the whole psychology of the Decadent Movement turns; in it all the phenomena of this state of mind are illustrated down to the minutest detail." And, if *A Rebours* were essentially a caricature, why and how did it become in England, in the memorable phrase of Arthur Symons [see excerpt above], "the breviary of the Decadence?"

Despite unfounded opinions that the novel is not autobiographical, it is, essentially, just that. Obviously, this is not to suggest that *A Rebours* is Huysmans' personal confession. It is not a record of what he did, but of what he would have done if he had had the means, what he would have done if fortune had made him a Comte about Paris instead of a clerk in the Ministry of the Interior. What is more than coincidental is that though Huysmans lacked Des Esseintes' wealth and title, he shared his hero's ultra-sensibility, his monomania, and his detestation of all that was common and vulgar. Both are thirty years old, without parents, indifferent students but excellent Latinists, jaded by experience but fascinated by art and literature, and possessed of a curious interest in theology. Spiritually, character and creator are one in their quest for some key to life's meaning, their intense search for happiness. (p. 281)

G. A. Cevasco, "Satirical and Parodical Interpretations of J.-K. Huysmans' 'A Rebours'," in Romance Notes, *Vol. XVI, No. 2, Winter, 1975, pp. 278-82.*

EDITH HARTNETT   (essay date 1977)

From *A rebours* onward [Huysmans] never relinquished the aesthetic Decadent view of art and life. His style is a blend of the universal idiom of terror and his unique sense of the Flemish grotesque, to which he liked to think he had ancestral as well as artistic ties. His Decadence, arising as it did in a disordered post-industrial world, caused him to recast medieval beliefs, or rather the artifacts produced by those beliefs, into a modern cult. There is no real change from one book to the next; Huysmans simply shifts his attention from one art form to another, demonstrating the Decadent's incapacity to separate the artistic and the spiritual. Except for a minor medieval doctrine that helps him harmonize sexual and spiritual conflicts, there is no self-questioning or moral renewal. (pp. 368-69)

[Husymans] never wholly disengaged himself from Des Esseintes. The Church, for Huysmans, was its art; his exclusive emphasis on the thingness of the Church amounted to its profanation.

The emphasis upon art is an extension of the Decadent style. It is Naturalistic, except that it lavishes excessive attention on details at the expense of the whole and, most important, chooses as its subject an artifact rather than society. Indeed Huysmans continued to the end of his days to have a great deal in common with Zola: his passion for documentation, his indifference to plot, his love of walking through squalid sections of Paris, his attraction to disease, even the fact that both men spent most of their lives in rooms that had once been monks' cells. But Huysmans . . . trained his Naturalist's eye on a very different object. He wanted a stable authoritarian order and he sought a pre-revolutionary model. This occurred at a time when the social implications of his misanthropy, his racism, his disgust for the world could only be corporatist. Catholic corporatism is institutionalized nostalgia; Huysmans saw in the Church a social organization that one does not question because it supplies the answers to life's vexing problems. He seems not to have taken into account the fact that medieval guilds and monasteries were social and religious entities consistent with a universal Catholic society, all of which was hierarchically arranged so that class conflict was unimaginable. Further, they were devoted to some form of austere religious exercise. They were not mere safe havens and refuges from social disorder.

Two Catholic doctrines appealed especially to Huysmans: the doctrine of Mystical Substitution and the law of Solidarity in Good. The second persuaded him that his ideal hierarchical "guild" of artists and of art devotees had to be exclusively Catholic. The first helped him to explain in orthodox Catholic terms his lifelong fascination with suffering; it was deliberately undertaken as an artifact because *in itself* it was meritorious, so the beholder could transform his sadistic satisfaction into a religious *frisson.* Moreover, it disposed of the problem of the sufferings of the innocent, which so distressed Zola. The sufferings were not a social injustice; they were a sign of election, of a special sanctity. To a doctor who wrote that no Catholic physician who believed in Mystical Substitution could treat a patient, since he might be thwarting Providence by curing an expiatory victim, Huysmans replied that no one could be cured except by the will of God. He also believed that illnesses could at times be diabolical in origin. He affirmed that Mystical Substitution, although the doctrine was not preached because

of its severity, "still remains the essence of Catholic belief, the lesson taught us by Calvary, the purest mystical theology."

It is not without a certain aesthetic fitness that this man, whose nervous irritability was such that he could not bear a badly played piano or an inferior cigarette, should have died an agonizing death. God, the divine Decadent, arranged matters so that in 1907 Huysmans died atrociously, of a disease that caused the lower half of his face to putrefy and fall away in chunks. His eyes became so horribly infected that his lids had to be sewn shut. This voyeuristic Catholic "in his piety . . . believed that these eyes, through which he had received so much pleasure, were taken from him by way of enforcing penitence." His death was a perfect *objet d'art.* Like Saint Vincent, he lay still and prayed; he bore his ordeal with patience and stoicism; he refused morphia and all comfort except the solicitude of his friends. He kept his sense of humor; the grotesque element in his plight did not escape him. He kept his sense of style, leaving instructions that he be buried in his Benedictine habit and composing the invitation to his funeral so that it was in impeccable taste. It is not easy to decide whether, like a true Decadent, he orchestrated his own death and funeral, or whether his long immersion in Catholic art had helped him "to throw a little light, however uncertain, upon the dark and terrifying mystery of suffering." (pp. 375-76)

Edith Hartnett, "J. K. Huysmans: A Study in Decadence," in The American Scholar *(copyright © 1977 by the United Chapters of Phi Beta Kappa; reprinted by permission of the author), Vol. 46, No. 3, Summer, 1977, pp. 367-76.*

JOSEPH HALPERN   (essay date 1978)

What makes *A Rebours* a novel rather than a short story is that digressive quality of the text which subverts narrative logic and delays the consummation of an ending for 200 pages, for fourteen of the book's sixteen chapters. The linear development of narrative sequence is held at bay by a discourse that is not essentially narrative but rather encyclopedic and descriptive, engendered by the house at Fontenay, which occupies a self-sufficient and self-replicating space not subordinate to narrative sequence, and to which des Esseintes retreats. The House serves as the impetus for the continuation of the story and the extension of the text. Yet when des Esseintes disappears into the house, so does narrative development. By choosing this retreat, des Esseintes is, in fact, choosing death in the form of isolation, enclosure, and artifice; he is also choosing stasis. . .—the house is like a womb which sustains the life of character and discourse. The inventory of the possessions of the house (paintings, jewels, books, etc.) is the stuff of the book . . . ; for fourteen chapters we have a sense of entropic degeneration: des Esseintes's health spirals up and down without any real change. Such a digression, because it is analytical, additive, and categorizing, substantially thwarts the narrative sequence. The House is a trope of embellishment and embroidery, a device which allows for critical expansion (des Esseintes as the exegete of the texts of flowers and fluids), social discussion and philosophical contemplation. The discourse takes the place of the hero here, procreating text against time and the impotence of determined narrative. . . . [The] point of death, interrupted coitus, repeats itself in a series of ritual deaths throughout the novel. In the dream of the Woman who is Flower (and Death), des Esseintes almost touches the dream image and when she seizes him, he feels himself dying and wakes. Stasis (masking entropy) and dynamism (energy) are the axes of the text: death and life, house and narrative, digression and progression, diversion and syllogism, paradigm and syntagm. (pp. 94-5)

A Rebours, according to Huysmans, is written against Zola, against the "moribund" naturalist form. . . . To deliver this "coup terrible," Huysmans chooses to operate by parody, which kills and revives in one stroke. On the one hand, he bases *A Rebours* on the model of heredity and degeneration which governs Zola's novels. On the other hand, he destroys the aesthetic pose and "dysenergy" of Decadence through caricature. Des Esseintes's aggressiveness is manifest. . . . But what should also be clear is that the energy that both drives him toward death and constantly revives him is built into his character from the very beginning in the *Notice.* . . . [The] emblematic Decadent weakening of the will attendant upon a moribund society awaiting the barbarian rape, does not afflict des Esseintes. In him it is only the flesh that is weak, only the senses that "fall into lethargy." . . . A number of the chapters in *A Rebours* close with some sort of fall—either the physical act of falling back into a chair or, on another level, the relapse of an illness or the "falling back" to reality—and Huysmans's energy to resume the narrative runs parallel to des Esseintes's capacity for self-creation and self-definition. (pp. 97-8)

Des Esseintes creates a world for himself through negation—but not passively. His flight from reality comprises a need, a rage, a furious desire intensely concentrated. . . . [It] ought in principle to admit neither extension nor succession, delay nor mediation. But immediacy and satiety are death . . . and des Esseintes never quite dies. The house at Fontenay represents the mediation and displacement of desire; his body, locus of desire and sexual revenge, crime and punishment, leads him to the point of death and holds him there. . . . As in all dreams, he wakes without dying: sadomasochistic sexuality punishes his parents in his own body, but not to the point of self-extinction.

A Rebours, in truth, is written against itself;/at every moment character and text undo themselves. . . . To commit sacrilege, one has first to accept the sacred; to debunk nature, one has first to glorify it; to correct the novels of Zola, Huysmans swallows them. Toward the aesthetics of the "roman concentré en quelques phrases". . . , Huysmans contributes a text full of the "longueurs analytiques" and the "superfétations descriptives" that des Esseintes despises. Inevitably, such a work becomes a parody of itself. The relationship between Huysmans and his main character is a complex one, and the degree to which they share common aesthetic principles or to which Huysmans condemns des Esseintes would only be determinable if the irony of Huysmans's style were exactly measurable. But, as in all pastiche, the fundamental ambivalence of the style precludes precise decoding. (p. 99)

Stylistic parody enables Huysmans to elaborate each individual sentence and, thereby, to lengthen the novel. Because the decadent use of language itself is offered as the subject matter of the text, Huysmans's style is marked by the open-endedness of the prose sentence and the interminable regression of parodic repetition. It does not take much of a critical bias to see that the question of language is central to *A Rebours.* There is little need to have recourse to Schopenhauer, Ribot, Egger, or any other nineteenth-century subjectivist theorist to understand that style, for a writer of this period, is in itself an organization of reality, and that the use of language, the systematic distortion of syntactic norms, the panoply of "deliquescent" rhetorical devices in *A Rebours* is as much a part of the inventory of the

house at Fontenay as the books des Esseintes catalogues. Death is impatient and life is patient, according to Freud in *Beyond the Pleasure Principle;* the *roman concentré* is unravelled in *A Rebours* by the patiently extended "joke" of the style, by the punch line that is always deferred.

If des Esseintes never quite dies, then neither does he go mad, despite the doctor's predictions. Madness does not really lie within the possibilities of this discourse: *A Rebours* is never a text monstrously out of control. It does come to an end in a mere 250 pages, after all—its encyclopedism is a restrained tendency, subject to logical rules of development. The detailing of the interior of the house gradually builds, according to classical rules of composition, toward the discussion of the modern library. Huysmans lists the works of the decadent Latin writers and then proceeds chronologically to the works of his contemporaries . . . ; when he comes to Mallarmé . . . the force of digression begins to sputter out. The return to Paris may not constitute a coherent development of the algebra of the *Notice,* but it does provide an adequate container (departure/return) for the Fontenay episode.

Without analyzing Huysmans's style in detail, since that has been done so thoroughly elsewhere, it is evident that the constant *retouches* of *écriture artiste,* the attempt to shape the French sentence into forms of greater expressiveness, do not give birth to unbridled proliferation but rather attest to an attempt to further control language—as it is not controlled in some of the Latin farrago texts des Esseintes so admires. . . . And this kind of dualism permeates the whole of *A Rebours.* The novel admits both the multiplicity of ambivalence and the limitations of precision—definition, comprehensibility, exhaustibility. Diversion is not infinite extension, paradox is not nonsense. At Fontenay, des Esseintes's world is a controlled world—controlled to the point of obsession. Only one thing escapes control—his body. And it is his body, acting out the contradictory imperatives of desire, that determines the action; it sends him to Fontenay and it brings him back. (pp. 101-02)

Joseph Halpern, "Decadent Narrative: 'A Rebours'," in Stanford French Review, *Vol. II, No. 1, Spring, 1978, pp. 91-102.*

ADDITIONAL BIBLIOGRAPHY

Baldick, Robert. *The Life of J.-K. Huysmans.* Oxford: Clarendon Press, 1955. 425 p.
    Definitive biography.

Brandreth, Henry R. T. *Huysmans.* London: Bowes & Bowes, 1963, 127 p.
    Introductory critical study.

Brombert, Victor. "Huysmans: The Prison House of Decadence." In his *The Romantic Prison: The French Tradition,* pp. 149-223. Princeton: Princeton University Press, 1978.
    Study of the theme of isolation in Huysmans's works and the symbolic connection between "images of enclosure and reveries of impotence and eroticism."

Brookner, Anita. "Huysmans." In her *The Genius of the Future: Studies in French Art Criticism,* pp. 147-67. London, New York: Phaidon, 1971.
    Finds Huysmans's art criticism increasingly concerned with theme and meaning rather than strictly artistic qualities.

Cevasco, George A. "Huysmans: Fifty Years After." *Renascence* IX, No. 3 (Spring 1957): 115-19.

Defense of Huysmans during a period of neglect, with an overview of his works and their critical reception.

Cevasco, G[eorge] A. *J.-K. Huysmans: A Reference Guide*. Boston: G. K. Hall & Co., 1980, 155 p.
Annotated bibliography of criticism in English.

Frost, Mary D. "J. K. Huysmans." In her *Contemporary French Novelists*, pp. 351-73. New York, Boston: Thomas Y. Crowell & Co., 1899.
Sees Huysmans's conversion, along with that of his literary alter-ego Durtal, as more aesthetic than Christian.

Highet, Gilbert. "The Decadent." In his *Talents and Geniuses: The Pleasures of Appreciation*, pp. 92-9. New York: Oxford University Press, 1957.
Portrays Huysmans as a supersensitive artist of ugliness and a "mystic of suffering."

Krutch, Joseph Wood. "Making Good." *The Nation* 119, No. 3099 (26 November 1924): 575-76.*
Finds *The Oblate* "the least interesting of the tetralogy of which *Là-Bas* is the first volume."

Laver, James. *The First Decadent: Being the Strange Life of J. K. Huysmans*. London: Faber & Faber, 1954, 283 p.
Popular biography discussing the novels by way of plot outlines.

Lavrin, Janko. "Huysmans and Strindberg." In his *Studies in European Literature*, pp. 118-30. London: Constable & Co., 1929.
Connects the two writers as representatives in European literature of the "curious transition from naturalism to extreme mystic symbolism."

Nordau, Max. "Decadents and Aesthetes." In his *Degeneration*, pp. 296-337. New York: Howard Fertig, 1968.
First published in English in 1895, the classic diatribe against late nineteenth-century art, calling Huysmans "the classical type of the hysterical mind without originality."

Ridge, George Ross. *Joris-Karl Huysmans*. New York: Twayne Publishers, 1968, 123 p.
Critical study examining Huysmans in turn as naturalist, decadent, and spiritual writer.

Shenton, C. G. "'A vau-l'eau': A Naturalist *Sotie*." *The Modern Language Review* 72, No. 2 (April 1977): 300-09.
Reads *A vau-l'eau* as a comic novel which derives its humor "from the farcical application of the naturalist-realist manner."

Taylor, John. "Joris-Karl Huysmans as Impressionist in Prose." *Papers on Language & Literature* VIII, supp. (Fall 1972): 67-78.
Demonstrates the influence of the French impressionist school of painting, particularly its emphasis on subjective experience, on Huysmans's prose style.

Turnell, Martin. "Romantics and Decadents." *The Spectator*, No. 6567 (7 May 1954): 559-60.
Classifies Huysmans as a minor writer whose novels are "not creative" but "simply an account of his own spiritual ordeal cast in the form of fiction."

Van Roosbroeck, G. L. "Huysmans the Sphinx: The Riddle of 'À Rebours'." In his *The Legend of the Decadents*, pp. 40-70. New York: Institut des Études Françaises, Columbia University, 1927.
Reads *Against the Grain* as a satire on the decadent movement.

(Dame Emile) Rose Macaulay
1881-1958

English novelist, essayist, poet, critic, and biographer.

Macaulay is best known for her final novel, *The Towers of Trebizond*, and for her satirical novels of the 1920s, including *Potterism* and *Told by an Idiot*. In the satires Macaulay voiced her generation's contempt for the commercialism and superficiality of post-World War I society. Of greater significance, however, is the *Towers of Trebizond*, Macaulay's fictionalized account of her own travels through Turkey. Ostensibly, the book is an entertaining composite of autobiography, travel diary, and comic novel. On a deeper level, it is a poignant statement of religious faith.

Macaulay was born into a family of eminent clerics and scholars. Her genteel ancestry and upbringing are evidenced in much of her work; in all her novels the heroines—successful, independent, well educated—are thinly disguised self-portraits. Admired for her intelligence and wit, Macaulay appeared regularly on the BBC program "Brains Trust" and frequently contributed to England's leading newspapers and periodicals. Shortly before her death, she was named a Dame Commander of the British Empire.

Macaulay's first novels, such as *Abbots Verney*, *The Furnace*, and *Views and Vagabonds*, assert the values of conventional lifestyles and virtuous behavior. The author's first widely popular novel, *Potterism*, appeared after World War I, and focuses on the phenomenon of yellow journalism, ridiculing the profit motive of the press as well as the unthinking gullibility of the public. Because the narrator's derisive and nihilistic point of view mirrored the trend of contemporary thought, "potterism" became the byword for all that was hypocritical, superficial, and vulgar in society. Macaulay's canon, spanning forty years, reflects a spiritual quest toward reconciliation and reaffirmation of her Anglican faith. Her search was fulfilled and illuminated in *The Towers of Trebizond*. The principal character, Laurie, is considered Macaulay's most fully realized and emotionally honest self-portrait.

Generally, critics have styled Macaulay a witty, entertaining, but minor novelist whose satires appeal to the intellect rather than the emotions. They note that such works as *Told by an Idiot*, *Dangerous Ages*, and *Crewe Train* are topical comedies in which characters raise and debate issues which afford the author opportunities for satire. As a result, her characters are social "types" rather than flesh and blood individuals. Critics also find her frequent pose of cynicism and indifference excessively mannered and caustic. However, in *The Towers of Trebizond* Macaulay transcends the limitations of the topical comedy; the novel is free of the affected style that mars her earlier efforts and provides a humorous, rational view of humanity.

Though her satirical novels have been praised as timely and effective social commentary, *The Towers of Trebizond* is regarded as Macauley's masterpiece: the novel in which her true vision, personality, and talent emerged.

PRINCIPAL WORKS

Abbots Verney (novel) 1906
The Furnace (novel) 1907

The Lee Shore (novel) 1912
Views and Vagabonds (novel) 1912
The Two Blind Countries (poetry) 1914
What Not (novel) 1918
Potterism (novel) 1920
Dangerous Ages (novel) 1921
Told by an Idiot (novel) 1923
A Casual Commentary (essays) 1925
Crewe Train (novel) 1926
They Were Defeated (novel) 1932
Milton (biography) 1934
The Writings of E.M. Forster (criticism) 1938
The Towers of Trebizond (novel) 1956
Letters to a Sister (letters and unfinished novel) 1964

THE ATHENAEUM (essay date 1907)

The merit of this able novel ["**Abbots Verney**,"] lies chiefly in the striking illustration it affords of that "manly and self-respecting reserve'' which is supposed to dignify the family relations of Englishmen, and which in effect is doubtless responsible for much of the misunderstanding and discomfort of our national domestic life. We hope that it is not often carried to such an extent as between the grandfather and grandson in this book. The consequent waste of happiness, affection, and money is from the Philistine reviewer's point of view even more irritating than deplorable; yet it is impossible not to feel some degree of sympathy for both the persons concerned, especially the younger, who is natural and attractive beyond the general measure of heroes in fiction. His ''struggle for existence'' during the hot season in Rome is an original and convincing piece of description, though the purposelessness of it all rather detracts from the artistic effect. The heroine is frankly something of a bore, and carries to excess, to say the least, her principle of tactful nonintervention.

> *''New Novels: 'Abbots Verney','' in* The Athenaeum, *No. 4134, January 19, 1907, p. 70.*

KATHERINE TYNAN   (essay date 1916)

[Rose Macaulay] lavishes all her art on the failure, the beloved vagabond who loses the world and saves his own soul: the poor in heart for whom is the kingdom of heaven. . . .

All of Miss Macaulay's heroes and heroines whom I know and love—Benjie in **''Views and Vagabonds,''** Peter in **''The Lee Shore,''** Eddy in **''The Making of a Bigot,''** and Alix in **''Non-Combatants,''** go out as failures from one point of view or another: prosperity is possibly the thing in human life which Miss Macaulay most abhors.

She has a rich and fruitful theory of life, or perhaps one should say, philosophy of life. She has an abundant and humane humour. She has an exquisite capacity for depicting natural beauty. . . . She creates a great number of characters and makes one realise each one. . . .

Her names are not fortunate. **''Views and Vagabonds,''** suggests a volume of essays. You open it and you are absorbed into a new Sentimental Journey, clean and innocent. . . . (p. 37)

The story dates itself. It belongs to a period *antebellum* when the leisured played at many things, and the strenuous found queer outlets for their energy. . . . It is dated, but it is not dowdy as dated books are apt to be—in the first place because it is pure literature, in the second place because it deals with the eternal young, who when the grass has grown over the battlefields will again be breaking the energy in them against shams and shames, as Benjie Bunter did. A charm of the book is its suggestion of the University atmosphere, with its young theorists riding forth like the immortal Don to tilt against windmills.

Benjie leaves the house of his aristocratic parents to become a working blacksmith. In pursuance of his theories he marries a working woman, a real working woman, with a soft and faithful heart, but no other alleviations: and there Rose Macaulay shows the artistry that is in her, for she has no base temptation to make Louie possible because of rare virtues or adaptabilities. . . . The attitude of Lady Lettice, Benjie's supposed mother, of Mr. Bunter, the Conservative Member of Parliament, and all their friends, towards Louie, is rendered with exquisite humour. It is, in fact, pure comedy. . . . [Miss Macaulay's characters] really live and move. Then there come in the real persons of the Sentimental Journey, those beloved vagabonds, the Crevequers, against whom and their pernicious

and very Southern idea of happiness for themselves and the whole world Benjie wages war. . . . The Crevequers are something not to be forgotten with their soft stutter, their animals, their wasteful inconsiderate giving to the just and the unjust. They shall long abide with us as Peter in **''The Lee Shore''** abides, going away from house and comforts and respectability and all the things decent folk care for into the evening gloam with the stars over them, and a cart or a ditch for all of concrete home. . . . Miss Macaulay adores the irresponsibles, the God's Fools of the world. (pp. 37-8)

I can find no better word than distinction for her views of life and character. Not only distinguished, but distinctive. Her most minor characters stand out startlingly real and remain with us as living people. (p. 38)

> *Katherine Tynan, ''The Bookman Gallery: Rose Macaulay,'' in* The Bookman, *London, Vol. LI, No. 302, November, 1916, pp. 37-8.*

KATHERINE MANSFIELD   (essay date 1919)

[**'What Not'** is] Miss Rose Macaulay's brilliant little comedy. . . . One does not dream of questioning the large freedoms enjoyed by the heroine, Miss Kitty Grammont; one can only admire her excellent control of them. Dare we hope that this fascinating creature is the forerunner of the business woman, the ''political'' woman, the woman whose business it is to help govern the country? Miss Macaulay presents us to her when she is attached to the Ministry of Brains. . . . The wonderful system of classification with which we have become so familiar serves this time a twofold purpose: it not only registers the mental category of every man and woman in England, it also tells him or her whom to marry and whom not to marry. Miss Grammont, whose brains were of the highest order, was classified ''A;'' but the Minister of Brains, for all his brilliant powers, was uncertificated for matrimonial purposes because of mental deficiency in his family. He was ''A'' (Deficiency), and thereby hangs the tale. . . . [They] find their official co-partnership inadequate, and as though these obstacles were nothing more than convenient stiles to lean across, like any simple two, they fall in love. Realizing ''it will come out as certainly as flowers in spring or the Clyde engineers next week,'' they marry. And it does come out. The dreadful truth wrecks the Ministry of Brains and ruins their careers, but leaves them ''laughing ruefully.''

This is the bare theme from which Miss Macaulay composes her ingenious and delightful variations. Although one feels her fertility of invention is so great that nothing would be easier for her than to obtain an ''easy effect,'' it is their chief excellence that each one is as unexpected as the last. It is only in the enjoyment of Miss Macaulay's nice sense of humour, matched with her fine, sensitive style, that one realizes how rarely the two qualities are found together. (pp. 9-10)

> *Katherine Mansfield, ''Two Novels of Worth'' (originally published in* The Athenaeum, *No. 4641, April 11, 1919), in her* Novels and Novelists, *edited by J. Middleton Murry (copyright 1930, copyright renewed © 1958, by Alfred A. Knopf, Inc.; reprinted by permission of The Society of Authors as the literary representatives of the Estate of Katherine Mansfield), Knopf, 1930, pp. 7-10.**

R. BRIMLEY JOHNSON   (essay date 1920)

With Miss Macaulay at her best one is captured, irresistibly, by sheer delight in good workmanship: art, which does not, as it happens, at all depend on the special characteristics which we associate with quite modern fiction. The distinction, in fact, touches the heart of things: because, in her work, one is as much, if not more, interested in individual characters, as in thought or manner. Under the spell of her art we forget artifice. (p. 65)

Much the same may be said about her management of dialogue; which has distinguished courage.

Conducting a spirited discussion upon Women's Suffrage, for example, she introduces the disputants with stark, and surprising simplicity: "Mr. Robinson said. Benje said. Louie said. Jerry said. Cecil said. Mr. Robinson said. Louie said."

Here is a daring repudiation of the rules against repetition, of which the dramatic value is obvious. We feel at once how one after the other drops in his contribution to the controversy: the quick response, the ready tongue, the appreciation of each other's point of view. Talk reported in this manner becomes revelation of character.

Miss Macaulay, in fact, sees her people dramatically; she visualises their personality: producing its full significance in a graphic word-picture. There is no blurring nor hesitation, no fumbling after the sub-conscious. It is not, of course, that she depends only on surface values, or paints from the outside. She has plenty of penetration and much subtlety; but her mind is made up: she writes as a spectator, not identifying herself with the creatures of her imagination, trusting rather to insight than instinct. Her understanding, indeed, is as truly a question of deliberate art as the crisp narrative interpretation.

Curiously enough, her first novel, **"Abbot's Verney,"** approaches more nearly than any of her later work to the singularities of the new method. It is more sub-conscious and enquiring: the whole story is seen through the hero. The characters are much given to egotism. In Verney, indeed, the absorption in self has been forced upon him by cruel circumstances. Between an impossible father . . . , and a grandfather, rendered suspicious by pride and love, he has simply no chance for normal development. Being, however, essentially a "white man"—of the type that builds empires: he wins through in the end. Dramatic and vivid in all its side issues, admirably finished as are all the persons of the tale, it is a one-man, one-idea'd book: despite even the wonderful Rosamund, with her true heroism in friendship. Here are profound psychological problems: an individual (with whom Miss Macaulay goes near to identifying herself) struggling to *be* himself—which is the modern Idealism—against most severe odds. But it remains more drama than revelation: modern enough in setting, but a familiar type. (pp. 67-8)

[Tragedy] pervades the most powerful of Miss Macaulay's novels—**"The Valley Captives"**; . . . [a] dramatic picture of the understanding between a brother and sister, misunderstood of others. Fate (here embodied in a weak father) has literally imprisoned the two with his brutal and over-bearing step-children. . . . None of the group has any absorbing business in life; and existence for them becomes concentrated upon Hate in a cage. Though the sister has more character, and far greater courage, she—too—is dragged into the conflict through her devoted loyalty: and the end is—inevitable—melodrama: but melodrama that is *not* false to Truth. These are all real people, for whom we are moved to intense pity.

In her second tragedy, **"The Secret River,"** Miss Macaulay is not convincing. Curiously enough the half-magic subtlety, which she handles with rare skill as an episode or a character-trait—has not enough hold of her to sustain a complete story. Michael is neither a real man nor true mystic. He fails miserably as a lover: nor can he read rightly the tale of the reeds—so that the cool, dim waters closed about his body and covered him wholly.

"Views and Vagabonds," on the other hand, brings us back—with a fresh, wholesome wind blowing, to the full vigor of Miss Macaulay's sprightly genius. Pleasantly flavoured with that youthful alert dogmatism which permits universal tolerance and incites to endless curiosity, characterising all undergraduates; it further demonstrates her fine sympathy with the ideals of unconventionality. (pp. 70-1)

In her two stories directly inspired by the war, Miss Macaulay covers very interesting ground. **"Non-Combatants"** takes a high rank among the attempts . . . to produce the home-atmosphere of the disturbed period. It touches . . . the pacifist conscience; it covers a great variety of temperaments—rudely awakened to new personal problems, and for the most part—furious at the appalling waste. (p. 73)

Here we find just that bewilderment that was our actual inheritance through those fateful years: the sense that everything was the same and yet nothing was the same; the terrible feeling that we had to go on, day after day, doing little things apparently so pitifully trivial: which were yet—by some mysterious law of our nature—the things that must be done. . . . **"What Not"** scarcely maintains the same level. Here—as in the **"Secret River"**—Miss Macaulay builds a whole story on *one* of her special gifts: her skill in light irony; and it will not bear the load. This rather whimsical satire . . . misses fire. . . .

[In **"Potterism,"**] Miss Macaulay has carried on what one may call her record of contemporary impressions beyond the Armistice. . . . (p. 74)

Superficially, that is in its local colour, this story completes **"Non-Combatants"** as a record we have all been thinking and saying about the great war, and, here again, no serious generalisations and no profound philosophy are attempted.

It is true that the principal characters are all engaged with varying degrees of intensity, in a crusade against "Potterism." . . . The Potter Press, run parallel with the Northcliffe, by Mr. Potter, Senior, is the embodiment of imperial and capitalist cant. . . . (p. 75)

I am disposed to think that Miss Macaulay means these things seriously: that she actually hates Potterism:

"Oh Lord, we are all Potterish," says Gideon, "every profiteer, every sentimentalist, every muddler. . . . You find it everywhere, the taint; you can't get away from it. Except by keeping quiet and learning and wanting truth more than anything else."

That, as we have seen everywhere, is the inspiration of the new novelists: to "want truth"; they are all up against Mr. Potter.

And yet, Miss Macaulay has exercised, in its finest perfection, all her compact geniality in narration, all her laughing humour, to keep us upon the surface of things. She seems always intent upon showing us how amusing these serious young people are; without giving us a chance to pause and wonder what their poor minds are worrying about.

There is, moreover, a really remarkable result of her extraordinarily capable manner of telling a story. The actual plot is pure tragedy. (pp. 76-7)

But it is quite impossible for me to feel miserable about [her characters'] misfortunes. (p. 77)

As a whole, however, Miss Macaulay carries one with her triumphantly through the wildest of Youth's enthusiasms. . . . For the most part, we find ourselves in the delightful company of College friends who "always know what you mean"; who all wish "to be the sort of person who ignores foolish laws"; dismissing the more conventional as "too old to know better." (pp. 78-9)

> *R. Brimley Johnson, "Rose Macaulay," in his* Some Contemporary Novelists (Women), *Leonard Parsons, 1920 (and reprinted by Books for Libraries Press, 1967; distributed by Arno Press, Inc.), pp. 63-79.*

J. W. KRUTCH   (essay date 1924)

Miss Macaulay means the title of her brilliantly executed satire [*Told by an Idiot*] to be taken seriously, but it is with difficulty that she achieves gloom. Through her pages, liberally sprinkled with exploding bombs of wit, she leads one character who bridges the three generations described, who watches with bitter detachment the flux of enthusiasms and absurdities which constitute life, and who ends with Macbeth's words upon her lips. But though one has laughed often the tears do not come, for obviously Miss Macaulay is one of those born satirists who find too much fun in exhibiting human follies ever to regret that man is not more wise. To read the book is to know that, for her, gibing is a sufficient end in itself and that even if God made the world for no other purpose than to make satire possible (and this theory fits the facts as well as any other) she has no real cause for repining. Disillusioned she is, but bitter she only tries to be. . . . [Speaking] of freedom she remarks: "There's one thing about it; each generation of people begins by thinking they've got it for the first time in history, and ends by being sure the generation younger than themselves have too much of it. It can't really always have been increasing at the rate people suppose, or there would be more of it by now." However tragically true these things are, for the person who can state them so jauntily and so wittily, the joy of the phrase more than compensates for the sadness of the fact. What Miss Macaulay gives us is moderately good fiction, competent social history, and superlative wit, but, as for the tragedy, it has about as much chance of coming off as "Hamlet" would have if it were staged in the midst of one of Mr. Pain's most elaborate exhibitions of the pyrotechnic art.

"In the year 1879, Mrs. Garden came briskly into the drawing room from Mr. Garden's study and said in her crisp, even voice to her six children, 'Well, my dears, I have to tell you something. Poor papa has lost his faith again.'" So she begins, and so she continues, sweeping with unfailing wit and gusto through the [Victorian years]. . . . She touches off with burlesque or epigram every familiar type from the painfully liberal-minded clergyman to the latest flapper philosopher, every "movement" from Ruskin to Freud. Whoever wishes to know what the typical contemporary sophisticate thinks of himself and his grandfather will find it here, for **"Told by an Idiot"** is the History of Our Own Times as seen by that "younger generation" which is just now growing old, and it is a magnificently witty summing up.

Yet in spite of Miss Macaulay's dominant thesis, which is that all times are changing times, all women new women, and every year the end of an epoch, I venture the opinion that her book could not have been written except at the end of a definite literary period. Satire as easy, pointed, and unerring is not achieved on unfamiliar themes and is possible only when the object of attack is definitely recognized by all, and when we can perfect our weapons with a full knowledge of the victim's weak spots. Victorianism is dead—so dead that only an exhibition of skill as superlative as Miss Macaulay's can interest us in seeing it killed again, and if literature is not to become definitely stereotyped some new approach must be found. Perhaps there are choices other than the choice here offered between black despair and satire for satire's sake; perhaps, indeed, Victorian seriousness will come back, though not in the way our conservative friends would hope. Consider, for example, poor papa, in whom "broadmindedness amounted to a disease" and who had "believed much and often." He and his fellows fought battles against terrible monsters of superstitition and tradition, losing their livelihoods and their peace of mind in the struggle, and if today the monsters they faced seem but unreal chimeras that is only because they did their job so well. (pp. 288-89)

> *J. W. Krutch, "Taking Stock," in* The Nation *(copyright 1924 The Nation,* Vol. 118, No. 3062, March 12, 1924, *pp. 288-89.**

ALFRED KAZIN   (essay date 1935)

The paramount characteristic of Milton is his dislocation from his age, that astounding separation from the normal currents of sevententh-century English literary culture which makes any analysis of him impossible save in terms of a unique logic and another age. "He was the least English, and the most alien, of the English poets. One approaches him dubiously. . . rather in fascinated surprise than in love, for her seems a phoenix, that self-begotten bird from afar, of brilliant plumage and that self-begotten bird from afar, of brilliant plumage and strange cries." Rose Macaulay gets the matter straight here, although she seems unsure of it later, and weakens a very charming little biography [*Milton*]. . . .

[Milton] went through life searching for the moral ideal in experience; he did not find it and changed his values to quantitative ones, and in "Samson Agonistes" he had his ideal hero only because Samson possessed all the external characteristics he wanted so badly and couldn't have. Miss Macaulay gets this side of Milton very well, but she is too staid in her characterization. For an exceedingly clever woman she takes Milton too heavily. (p. 230)

> *Alfred Kazin, "Counsellor of Perfection," in* The New Republic, *Vol. LXXXIII, No. 1074, July 3, 1935, pp. 230-31.*

MARGARET LAWRENCE   (essay date 1936)

Rose Macaulay is bored. Her writing is emancipatedly spinsterish. The whole human enterprise reads to her like a tale *told by an idiot*. She does not even give it the dignity of insanity. It is all sheer idiocy. It is neither touching nor amusing. It is just silly. She looks the scene over, and is aware of no brooding presence in fate. Only a crazy unpatterned hit-or-miss conglomeration of events into which human beings are drawn because there is nothing else for them to do. (p. 203)

Told by an Idiot is the key book in the case of Rose Macaulay. That is, it gives the key-note to her performance.

There is a key book in the case of every author, past and present, male and female. For there is one initial drive into writing in the personal history of every writer. It lies, as cannot be said too often, in self-portraiture. (pp. 205-06)

[Rose Macaulay] has remained precisely with the pattern set in *Told by an Idiot*. She wrote books before this; she has written books since. But all of them have struck the same creative sound.

It is a sound of definite sharpness. It is the definite sharpness of an observing, skeptical, practical woman, than which there is no more devastating sharpness. (pp. 206-07)

Her technique is the consummation of the go-getters' technique in writing. Without waste of either energy or emotion she opens her story and presents the histories of her people. It is the narration of a sequence of events in all cases under her delineation proceeding from an initial stupidity. Upon this sequence she has trained her powers of observation. Enough detail is given to indicate the characterization without causing the least hesitation in the narrative outline. Like all the go-getters she covers an amazing space in s short time. (p. 207)

[The go-getter] selects what she intends to see. In such a light she is subjective; but in no other. Having surrendered to subjectivity in her subconscious selection of what she intends to see, she leaves it and becomes in all others matters exactly objective.

Edna Ferber chose to see the heroics of femininity. She saw it and set it down for all the world as if it were a passing story . . . picked up on the way. . . . Rose Macaulay chose to see the copy-cat tendencies of history as particularized in modern women with a consequent inevitable boredom to the observing watcher. She set it down judiciously as a casual fact while she turned out a story or so of the illusions people call events in their lives. (pp. 208-09)

> *Margaret Lawrence, "Go-Getters," in her* The School of Femininity: A Book for and about Women as They Are Interpreted through Feminine Writers of Yesterday and Today *(reprinted by permission of JCA Literary Agency, Inc.), Frederick A. Stokes Company, 1936 (and reprinted by Kennikat Press, 1966), pp. 183-209.*

ELIZABETH BOWEN   (essay date 1938)

[It was high time that Mr. E. M. Forster's] work should be related into a body and its importance considered as a *whole*. A study of him was wanted, and had to be undertaken by someone whose range was wide, who could appreciate his range. Miss Rose Macaulay's study, *The Writings of E. M. Forster,* has been looked forward to, and now fulfils its promise. This is an outstanding piece of critical work. To begin with, Miss Macaulay has succeeded in writing both for those already familiar with Mr. Forster's writings and for those who still hardly know them at all. For the first, what she says will have the fascinating aspect of a discussion; to the second it will be at once invitation and guide. The structure of her book—which might be a difficult problem—is excellent: here is an intellectual portrait, with its background, and a comprehensive study of all Mr. Forster's work, with a simultaneous running analysis. His writings are considered from two points of view—as pure art and as the exposition of his feeling for life.

The analysis of the novels is brilliantly done: it cannot have been easy, in a few pages, to give the outline, the character,

and above all the import of each. Besides this, there is an examination of the critical writings, the essays, the work on the novel, the prefaces, the biography and the guide book. Perhaps not enough is said about the short stories, whose technical interest is immense. In some of her most valuable chapters Miss Macaulay suggests the passing of time in those spaces between the too rare appearances of the books. Mr. Forster's intervals of silence have been a perplexity, as well as a deprivation. Silences, in a man from whom we have exorbitant expectations, take on a sort of positive character. Miss Macaulay has sketched something into the silences, described travel, touched in preoccupations. The greatest achievement of her book is that she has strung the works—from the longest novel down to the shortest essay—on what seems to be a line of personal continuity, so that the appearance of each, in its time, appears inevitable. Sympathy, admiration and unobtrusive perception have made her achievement possible. Her own style, pointed and lucid, and covering ground in a few and well-chosen words, her avoidance of constricting generalizations, and the smiling detachment with which criticisms are levelled, not only give *The Writings of E. M. Forster* a distinction worthy of its subject, but make it an important addition to the body of Miss Macaulay's work. (pp. 125-26)

> *Elizabeth Bowen, "Various" (originally published in* The New Statesman & Nation, *n.s. Vol. XV, No. 371, April 2, 1938), in her* Collected Impressions *(reproduced by permission of Curtis Brown Ltd, London, as literary executors for the Estate of Elizabeth Bowen), Alfred A. Knopf, 1950, pp. 116-59.**

WILLIAM C. FRIERSON   (essay date 1942)

As someone remarked in the postwar years, Rose Macaulay was looked upon as a highbrow by the flappers and as a lowbrow by the intellectuals. As a matter of fact, she stood squarely between. For the flappr there was absolute clarity, an easy style, a good story, a lively presentation of family situations, and a mild flavor of pessimism pervading the conversations of a recognizable upper crust. For the highbrow there was a broad sanity and a tendency to *épater le bourgeois*, witty observations, a sympathy with pagan values, and the realistic portrayal of a lost generation of doubting and diffident young people who were discovering a world in which there was no meaning, no order, no sense.

The tone of Rose Macaulay's work is sprightly and belies the author's pessimism. But the pessimism gradually obtrudes as the reader discoveries that the characters which are presented sympathetically acknowledge no values, no obligations, and the pressure of no lasting affection. Caprice and obsession but prey upon the spirit as it travels through the void. Successive books intensify the impression of nihilism even while the author with humane amusement deftly sketches the color and variety of a life that is no whit dulled by its hopelessness. (pp. 255-56)

She has written too much and too rapidly, but her dexterity is remarkable and the "unredeemed levity" of her castigation of cranks and poses has become increasingly evident with the passage of years. (p. 258)

> *William C. Frierson, "The Post War Novel, 1919-1929: Sophisticates and Others," in his* The English Novel in Transition: 1885-1940 *(copyright 1942 by the University of Oklahoma Press; copyright renewed © 1969 by Mrs. William C. Frierson), University of Oklahoma Press, 1942, pp. 237-78.**

W. R. IRWIN (essay date 1956)

At first thought it may seem whimsical to compare Rose Macaulay's *Told by an Idiot* . . . and Victoria Sackville-West's *The Edwardians*. . . . The former is an exemplary narrative, basically satiric and retaining much of the exhibitory quality of formal satire; the latter a combination of ordinary romance of caste and a kind of *Bildungsroman*. What have they in common beyond the semi-oblivion which seems the final resting-place of many worthy and interesting modern novels? The answer, I believe, is that both center on a theme of inexhaustible importance: the interaction of permanence and change in the lives of people and of societies. And in coming through sensibility rather than systematic speculation to a problem which properly belongs to philosophy the two authors are only marching with that apparently limitless expansion of empire which is one of the major characteristics of modern fiction.

The two novels have a common setting in time and place. The action of *The Edwardians* begins in 1905 and ends in 1910, with the coronation of George V; that of *Told by an Idiot* opens on the eve of the crucial decade of the 1880's and, following its characters through three generations, comes to a close in 1923. *The Edwardians* is, however, lengthened by the overbrooding of the past, especially as embodied in the ducal seat Chevron, and the adumbration of an ominous future.

Within the period which she chronicles Miss Macaulay sees much apparent change, much real sameness. Her thesis is suggested, though not comprehended, by the epigraph from *Fermé la nuit,* by Paul Morand: "L'histoire, comme une idiote, mécaniquement se répète." Miss Macaulay says in effect; "What a vast difference there seems to be between late Victorian and early Georgian—almost two worlds, unable to communicate. But do not be deceived. The changes, such as they are, come in order, each growing from a previous one; 1923 is the grandchild of 1879, greatly altered of face, but in character of the same family." Miss Macaulay conducts her demonstration by following the varied and presumably typical history of the versatile Gardens. (p. 63)

As with the Gardens, so with the public events of the nation. . . . Change succeeds change, but the most obvious ones are superficial, and the progress often pridefully cited is mainly an illusion. Miss Macaulay does not deny progress. Rather, she implies, it comes not straightforwardly and triumphantly, but from slow, always shifting modifications of the old by the new. The results can scarcely be assessed at all—much less assessed optimistically—except from a vantage point of perspective. It is impossible, of course, that real change by otherwise, for its determinant, the human spirit, is characteristically stubborn, for all that one generation may rebel against the superficial attitudes of its predecessor. One cannot make any simple generalization about it. . . .

In *Told by an Idiot* permanence and change, far from conflicting, are forces which interact bewilderingly to form the illusions by which most men live. Not so in *The Edwardians.* Here the conflict of permanence, as manifested in tradition, and change is real, for individuals and for society. (p. 64)

Plainly, in *Told by an Idiot* the thesis—or better the material through which the thesis is demonstrated—and the form are far from smoothly integrated. The thesis is, of course, familiar: history repeats itself, not in any rhythmic cycles during which nations rise and fall and time sweeps all before it, but almost statically, from one generation to the next, so that significant change is imperceptible to its contemporaries. The inference is plain also: the excitement which accompanies superficial change is unwarranted, signifies nothing. Miss Macaulay chose to objectify these opinions in the history of a family sufficiently cohesive to be microcosmic, sufficiently expansive to come into contact with the major movements of a span of time. The scheme works well enough in the early stages of the novel, but as the Gardens multiply and extend themselves, their implication in contemporary life becomes too complex for her narrative plan. It is not long before the strain of the novelist's divided attention shows itself. Miss Macaulay evidently wished to continue presenting the Gardens—or some of them—as created characters and not merely as straightforward embodiments of the history of their own times. In *Potterism* . . . and *Dangerous Ages* . . . , both novels dominated by thesis and rich in references to contemporary events, she had succeeded in keeping harmony between evolving characters and their public milieu. *Told by an Idiot,* however, is more ambitious in its coverage. The family ramifies and diversifies, as families do; Miss Macaulay was obviously no more content with oversimplifications of current history than are the "unsentimental precisians of thought" to whom she dedicated *Potterism*. She avoided the leisurely methods of Galsworthy and, not at all experimental, attempted nothing like the techniques by which Dos Passos in *U.S.A.* achieved his amazing range and even more amazing economy. As a result the unity of Miss Macaulay's novel is deeply impaired. More and more the fortunes and misfortunes of individual Gardens are presented in brief, formulary chapters; more and more contemporary history is rehearsed by means of catalogues of direct allusions, rich in connotation to the informed reader, and of satirical generalizations. (pp. 65-6)

Throughout it became increasingly difficult for Miss Macaulay to keep up her attempted fusion of the Gardens and their milieu. Actually, this disjuncture is primarily the result of an inherent difficulty in the formula for historical fiction first fully exploited by Scott—to introduce as central and influential actors in some recorded crisis one or two fictive persons, often lovers, whose private fortunes, of much concern to the reader, are involved in the results of that crisis. Miss Macaulay made her problem even more intractable by creating a large family, without any occupational or dynastic unification; by refusing Scott's cheerful, dramatic over-simplifications and manipulations of historical fact; and finally by compressing all into the limits of a novel of ordinary length. The wonder is that her book does not founder in mid-passage.

For several reasons *The Edwardians* is formally neater and requires less discussion. The actors and the social milieu are highly homogeneous, as befits a work which has some of the characteristics of comedy of manners in fiction. Miss Sackville-West made no attempt to explore the complexities of contemporary history. . . . *The Edwardians* enables the reader to create a self-sufficient illusion.

The most important reason, however, for the integration of theme and form in *The Edwardians* is that tradition and change are represented as forces necessarily in conflict, whereas in *Told by an Idiot* their interaction is confusing and the results ambiguous. . . . Actually the paradoxical interplay of permanence and change which Miss Macaulay assumed is conceptually more defensible than the notion of inimical time, but it cannot compete with the poignancy to be derived from skilfully presented mutability, whereby change begets decay and decay begets death, which remorselessly gathers into its insatiable darkness all that was lovely and gallant and bright. It is much to Miss Sackville-West's credit that her exploitation of this kind of melancholy is restrained. Even so, her adherence to a conventional romantic assumption enabled her to achieve a unity of theme and form which Miss Macaulay denied herself from the outset.

Miss Macaulay is one of her own "unsentimental precisians of thoughts," and, though far more compassionate than critics like Stuart Sherman pretend, disposed to satire. Necessarily she is more committed to reality, as she sees it, than to the "vision of reality" which W. B. Yeats, orthodoxly enough, thought the essence of art. For Miss Sackville-West the vision is dominant and this fundamental difference between the two writers is manifested in their different representations of the same theme. (pp. 66-7)

> W. R. Irwin, "Permanence and Change in 'The Edwardians' and 'Told by an Idiot'," in Modern Fiction Studies (©1956 by Purdue Research Foundation, West Lafayette, Indiana 47907, U.S.A.), Vol. II, No. 2, May, 1956, pp. 63-7.*

FRANK SWINNERTON   (essay date 1967)

One of the skeins in English life which non-English people, including the other British, find hardest to unravel is that apparently tangled but in fact intricately woven phenomenon known as the class structure. . . . For all their unity in times of danger, the English are first of all individualistic and then set-forming. (p. 591)

I always felt that [Rose Macaulay's first] book, *Abbots Verney,* owed much to a contemporary novelist, Mrs. Humphry Ward, who, as granddaughter to Arnold of Rugby, was preoccupied with class, conscience, and social criticism. Mrs. Ward's *Robert Elsmere,* in particular, was at the end of the nineteenth century reverenced by the serious-minded; and Rose was serious-minded. She was also inexperienced. Therefore, she could not emulate Mrs. Ward's air of authority. She did the next best thing.

This was, to deal solely with the types known to her; the educated, aesthetic, traveled, and talkative young men and women of temperament who "had been born and bred in a nursery which sharpened wits, and attached to learning a weight which seems to many societies extravagantly disproportionate." One young person . . . spoke for Rose herself when she said "You see, it always rather riles me . . . to see people behaving in what strikes me as—well, as a foolish manner of behaving, you know." Rose was already the mentor, wise, shrewd, but unemotional; and *Abbots Verney,* a young book, had great accomplishment and a cool sense of rightness. (p. 595)

Rose Macaulay certainly had no expectation that the world of her childhood was likely to change. Her second novel, dedicated to brothers and sisters as "the other citizens of Santa Caterina, Varazze," with the promise of reunion "in the spacious days of leisure that age shall bring," carried matters no farther than *Abbots Verney.* The scene this time was Naples; the characters were Bohemian or non-Bohemian, but chiefly very young and given to painting or writing; and . . . there was a young woman, . . . Prudence Varley, who betrayed "a certain detachment, lack of human interest." (p. 596)

Prudence Varley and Warren Venables, both attracted to a pair of young vagabonds, refuse to sentimentalize them; and in the end cast them to the winds of chance. They have themselves, however, brought about an awakening in the vagabonds, who,

after glimpsing the superiority of educated virtue, have lost ease of conscience. There may be a hint of *Roderick Hudson* in *The Furnace;* but Rose was less of an artist than Henry James, and more of a moralist; hence the mutual disclosures and a little sententiousness. . . . [She] was an exponent of sincerity and good behavior. (p. 597)

The Making of a Bigot established once and for all the special type of comic, caustic novel which came to be associated with the name Rose Macaulay. The book was an exercise in ridicule. It showed a merciless eye for the unpardonable in prejudice and the exploitation of sentimentalists, and real compassion for the gullibility of educated youngsters. Many of these youngsters had been . . . undergraduates at Cambridge; for Cambridge, she said in another novel, *Non-Combatants and Others,* shone with "intelligence, culture, traditionalism, civilization, some intellectualism, even some imagination," which made it susceptible to ideas, ideals, and fashions in contemporary thought. Outside Cambridge was the coarser world, which Rose never really explored; in the twilight region inhabited by good-workers and dogmatists little could be found but confusion. . . .

The Making of a Bigot was produced before the outbreak of war in 1914; and that war caused a break not only in the progress of civilization (in which, until then, liberals had believed) but in the happy life she led with people of her own or similar background. . . . (p. 600)

She continued to write; but the effort was great and the performance lacked spontaneity. She was no longer amused by sillinesses. At last she found a job in the War Office and (I know nothing of the facts at first hand) fell in love with a married man. This was a cardinal happening in her life, enriching it with emotion, but also underling the general futility in human affairs. Too many of her serious-minded young graduates had been killed; too much was apparent to her in London of intrigue, folly, and unscrupulousness. In reaction from these, she formed a resolve to "wear cap and bells, to dance through life to a barrel organ, to defeat a foolish universe with its own weapons."

What Not, the novel from which these words are taken, mirrors something of her wartime experience. It indicates a pessimistic belief that the finest spirits and the noblest ideals are doomed to defeat in a world given over to selfishness and chicane. This was a postwar mood, aptly named by the title of C. E. Montague's book of reminiscences, *Disenchantment;* and Rose was one of the disenchanted. Her intellect was not powerful, and not highly original; but it was acute and sensitive, and she allowed it to pass very critically from what she had noted at the War Office to an imaginary Ministry of the immediate future. The result was one of the first anti-Utopian novels of the period, and a picture of bureaucracy at work. (p. 601)

Rose now gathered new strength for a discussion of the popular press to which she gave the ironic name of Potterism. *Potterism* was a most striking novel of this satirical class. Experience of journalism, supplemented by new observation of the ways in which common thought was manufactured, not alone by officialism but by newspaper proprietors in the Harmsworth tradition, gave her portrayal of a press magnate's family, the junior members of which progress from bogus moral hostility to their father's newspapers to calculated self-advancement even more disgusting than his, a new quality of scathingness. The book was a success in both England and the United States. Although she wrote better novels afterward, it is by *Potterism* that she is still, perhaps, most generally remembered; and it is significant that the noblest person in the book is a Jew who deliberately sacrifices his life for an idea. No other sacrifices are made. (pp. 601-02)

Potterism expressed most of (Rose's) intolerances, doing this with tremendous élan. The book was subtitled "a tragi-farcical tract"; and I think there can be no doubt that under its pungent destructiveness it was a work of despair. It contained more feeling than any of its forerunners.

A very curious little jeu d'esprit followed shortly afterward. This was called *Mystery at Geneva,* and it made fun of the diplomats gathered in that city after the war in connection with the League of Nations. The author protested that she knew nothing of the League's proceedings; and indeed they supplied only a background to the recital of a long-cherished obsession. This was that Rose should really have been a boy. The hero of *Mystery at Geneva* was a naïve as Eddy, in *The Making of a Bigot.* The difference between them lay in the fact that, although disguised her own foolish purposes, he was really a young woman. The deceit, of course, was immediately exposed by a former employer who had dismissed this young woman for incompetence; and the book's intrigue, of scheming and kidnapping, is equally farcical.

Much more interesting was Rose's own favorite, *Orphan Island,* which she enjoyed writing, and in which she revealed one of those leaps into maturity which occur in most novelists of genuine talent. Like many others of her generation, she had been fascinated in childhood by *Robinson Crusoe, The Swiss Family Robinson,* and, in particular, R. M. Ballantyne's *The Coral Island,* which told how three boys were cast ashore in the South Seas from the wreck of a sailing ship. (pp. 602-03)

Reliving childhood, she imagined a Victorian spinster, in charge of a large party of emigrating orphans, being wrecked as Ralph, Jack, and Peterkin had been, together with a tippling and free-moraled Irish doctor. Then, skipping forty years, she invented a modern family from Cambridge, a professor and his three children, learning by chance of the spinster's charges and resolving to find their haven.

Having found it, they discover that the spinster, who had been forcibly married by the Irish doctor and made to bear children who were not orphans, is an aged widow and despotic ruler. Her descendants are all aristocrats; the offspring of the original orphans are definitely "no class." Although one member of the professor's family ruminates that in England class seems to depend on "what their people are, and what schools they went to, and all that," it is clear that on the island the distinction is that of birth. This is immutable.

That was as far as Rose could go. Like the Admirable Crichton, in Barrie's play, who saw that circumststances may alter cases and invert classes, she believed that some sort of class structure was a law of nature. (pp. 603-04)

[*Orphan Island*] was the most spirited and confidently ironic novel [Rose] had written. Its immediate successors were less noteworthy, *Crewe Train,* for example, being a return to the world of second-rate literary gossips and rivals. It contains her only bitter sketch, of a mischief-making woman novelist, together with another self-portrait of a dreamy child who cannot adjust herself to conventional society. The child was to make two further appearances (three if one counts Ellen, in *And No Man's Wit*); the bitterness never recurred; the three finest novels

she wrote were still to come. These were *And No Man's Wit, They Were Defeated,* and *The Towers of Trebizond.*

All three books were rich, the one in historical re-creation, the others in learning and humor, and, in the case of *The Towers of Trebizond,* a revelation of the woman behind 50 years of novel-writing. Dealing, as it did, with ideas and events which, although significant and, at the time, important to lovers of freedom, were pushed aside by the still more crucial struggle of the second World War, *And No Man's Wit* "date" more than its successors. (pp. 604-05)

[The] major theme is one of debate on the problems of Spain and its people as they carry despair to thinking minds. The book's true value as a vivid echo of the '30s and a philosophical arraignment of eternal bigotries will therefore be better appreciated in a wider historical perspective. Of its nobility there is already no question.

They Were Defeated illuminates comparable follies of the past, when England had its own Civil War and fratricidal savageries, its witch hunts and doctrinal extravagance. It can be read, if one wishes, as a companion-piece to *And No Man's Wit,* although I think it more profound. *The Towers of Trebizond* carries us farther abroad geographically, and still deeper into the author's personal character. All the reading she had done, from that of poetry as a child to that of seventeenth-century history and literature during her years at Somerville [College] and that of archaeology and theology ever since, proved to be of superlative value. More important still, while she consciously deployed it, she did this exultantly in *The Towers of Trebizond* and very beautifully in *They Were Defeated.* She was as assured as Walter Scott in writing of a past time, using an approximation to Scott's method of indulging the characters in conversation (with, of course, her own lyrical gift to poeticize the atmosphere) and showing no fear of solecism or anachronism. The result is very fine. . . . (pp. 605-06)

They Were Defeated can appeal only to those who know something of seventeenth-century politics and who have a feeling for poetry. Its readers have therefore been fewer than the quality of the book deserves. It will continue to be read for its sensitiveness and its beautiful pictures of Cambridge and the West Country; but it is the work of a poet and scholar, and as such may tire readers as Julian, its heroine, tired her sophisticated lover. *The Towers of Trebizond* is a different matter. It will be read with admiring enjoyment for many years to come. It is, as to one part, a record of travel on the shores of the Black Sea, to which the narrator, Laurie (another boy's name, it will be noted), has been taken by a crusading aunt in company with a very High Church priest. As to another part, it is an excursion into ancient history and a deliciously comic portrayal of aunt, priest, Turks, and a cynical camel who is denounced as neurotic by a Turkish woman psychologist. But finally it is personal to Rose herself. She laughs her way through the absurdities of the journey as she might have done in gay letters home; for the style she adopted in this book allowed of all sorts of quipping and merry nonsense. She ridicules her own romantic adoration of old cities and ancient landmarks. She sports with variations of religious practice. And at the very kernel of the book is Rose's own heart, open to be understood by readers who say, with the dwarf in the fairy tale, "Something human is dearer to me than all the wealth of all the world," and to those other readers who appreciate candor in whatever form it is expressed. (pp. 606-07)

[Rose] was a brave, kind, honest woman who wrote much that was amusing, much that was beautiful, and one classic book,

The Towers of Trebizond, in which all these influences, and all her virtues, were given a chance to demonstrate what they had done to form a character admirable in its simplicity. (p. 608)

Frank Swinnerton, "Rose Macaulay," in The Kenyon Review (copyright 1967 by Kenyon College), Vol. XXIX, No. 5, November, 1967, pp. 591-608.

WILLIAM J. LOCKWOOD (essay date 1967)

Rose Macaulay is a minor novelist not because of the eccentric nature of her materials, but because of the fact that she is limited in her ability to handle them. The range of her vision is confined to the upper middle-class, Anglican-Cambridge stratum of society, even though she tries to work beyond that range. Also, she is limited in her ability to deal with the disturbing, personal repercussions of the world she represents. Indeed, it almost seems that she knew she was going beyond herself in her choice of materials, and in trying to face up to the job, developed a no-nonsense, oversimplified and often, therefore, artificial manner of representation.

But admitting these limitations, and they are severe in too much of her writing, she *has* won a distinct identity in modern British literary history; we recognize a voice that is uniquely Rose Macaulay.

One first notices that voice in *The Lee Shore.* . . . Not a great novel in itself, it is worth reading for two reasons. First, we can see in it elements that recur in the novels, certain images and themes defining the pattern that eventually emerges from her writings. Secondly, this novel is worth reading because in it we find a novelist without the defenses of sophistication that she later finds in the satiric novels, a writer solemn and almost naked in her earnestness. And it is out of this vulnerable, inner self that, much later, following the long drought in her creativity between 1934 and 1955, renewal comes in *The Towers of Trebizond.*

The title, *The Lee Shore,* suggests its hero's abandonment of the world and his drift toward a place of refuge from it. At the same time, this image reflects the poetic quality of this novel, one that becomes dominant at the end and ultimately defines the hero's quest for and achievement of personal salvation.

The hero's salvation is awarded by default. It follows from loss, from the failure of human relationships. One aspect of a complex set of human relationships depicted in this novel is the triangle that forms when Dennis, the older half-brother of the unlucky hero, Peter Margierson, marries. . . . The story that follows is one of painful estrangement. (pp. 136-37)

The crisis of the novel coincides with the breaking away from human relationships and the subsequent drift to the "lee shore," the out-of-the-way Italian coastal town Peter and his son ultimately find. (p. 137)

One of the chief pleasures of this novel is Rose Macaulay's lee shore landscapes. (p. 139)

This vision of sea, flowers, and fruit recurs throughout [her] writings. . . . Rose Macaulay's real kinship is with a world beyond human relationships.

Unfortunately, however, the transcendent, lyrical beauty of the novel's end does not undo the author's failure to fill in this complexly designed, at times impressively poetic, novel with real flesh and blood. She asserts suffering but does not convey

it as a living reality. For example, her handling of what is, structurally, the crucial Lucy-Peter scene in the novel is completely inadequate. The whole situation seems absurdly artificial. . . . A related weakness in this novel . . . is Miss Macaulay's handling of the lower classes. Her representation of the "Have-nots" is mannered, sentimental, and faintly condescending (though not meant to be so). At times her naïveté is embarrassing, as when, for example, she talks very seriously about Lucy's true identification with all the "down-below" people. . . . It is of interest, too, to note that most of her down-below people, both in *The Lee Shore* and *Views and Vagabonds* are not the English poor but exotic types—mainly Italians or gypsies, more often than not somehow connected with the bohemian life.

In *Views and Vagabonds* . . . we find another suffering antihero in Benjie. Even more principle-conscious than Peter, Benjie renounces his middle-class identity . . . and embraces socialism. (pp. 139-40)

By way of contrast with Benjie, Miss Macaulay offers in the Crevequers a vision of selfish, pagan joyfulness. An Italian gypsy family and the vagabonds of the novel's title, they sponge without conscience in times of need, and share without restraint or discrimination in time of prosperity. . . . They offer gaiety in despair, a reassertion of the need to enjoy the simple pleasures of life as they come. The resolution is similar to that of *The Lee Shore,* but it seems more contrived because of the obviously conceptual nature of the opposed views. The author seems to be trying too hard to write an E. M. Forsterian novel.

Views and Vagabonds looks forward to *Potterism* and the novels of the twenties. There are more ideas here—Fabianism and free love for example—that represent the drift of the times. Moreover, the cynical figures of Anne Vickery and Hugh Bunter, and the representation of the absurdly committed Cecil, point to a new interest in detachment. The attractive, mocking personality of Anne Vickery in this novel . . . suggests the cool tone and ironic point of view that Miss Macaulay is on her way to discovering.

[In *Potterism* a] new hardheaded breed of clear-thinking, non-sentimental young people displace the vulnerable and suffering idealists of the earlier novels. A far wiser lot, they are committed to nothing more than seeing things *as they are.* (pp. 141-42)

Side by side in this novel, Miss Macaulay presents a satiric attack on the Potters of the world and, in the Gideon story, a vision of futility. Essentially they are of the same stuff for the one is ultimately ineffective and the latter simply leads R. M. [the narrator] back to a deepened sense of the necessity of noncommitment in an absurd universe. (p. 145)

The cynical, noncommitted position suggested here affords Rose Macaulay a discriminating yet inclusive point of view. The fine balance she strikes between the two in *Potterism* accounts for the consistency of tone and the overall success of this novel. . . . The strong suicidal note which runs through Rose Macaulay's next novel, *Dangerous Ages,* is a manifestation of loss of proportion, the great danger besetting the cynic's precise but brittle technique. Likewise, in this period of her writing, all manifestations of sentimentality are suspect. But there is a point beyond which such an attitude becomes limiting; and it must be admitted that one of Rose Macaulay's major limitations as a novelist is her distrust of natural feeling. . . . One wonders, what with all the aborted love relationship in her novels due to the accidental death of the lover involved, whether her attack on sentimentality is not defensive, a reaction to the expression of natural human feeling—especially between the sexes and in particular of a sexual nature—which basically frightens her. The recurrent motif (almost a preoccupation) concerning the relative freedom of women, specifically their freedom from motherhood, may, apart from the fact that it was an issue of the times, be related to this fear. (pp. 145-46)

Of the three novels in this major phase of Rose Macaulay's career *Dangerous Ages* is least good. It is structurally deficient; no very coherent reflection of human experience is achieved by the time one comes to the closing pages. But there are some unfused elements, very good in themselves, that anticipate her impressive *Told by an Idiot*.

One of these elements, the recurrent image of seaweed, passively drifting with the tide and being tossed about in the waves, looks both backward and forward. It recalls the poetic quality of *The Lee Shore*, while at the same time, in that crucial scene wherein a group of persons are very nearly swept out to sea and drowned, it is a darker, more despairing image. No promise of a lee shore comes out of this visualization. The poetry is derived from danger, a brush with death, and this is the kind of concentration and intensity one feels in viewing the smashup of civilization at the end of *Told by an Idiot*.

In *Dangerous Ages* the sea does have a peace-giving power, of course. If nothing else it can, in making one aware of the vanity of life, reinforce one's resistance to worldliness. Thus Nan, the middle-aged woman entering her forties, who may I suppose be regarded as the novel's heroine, finds comfort in the sound of the sea. . . . In the same way, Imogen in *Told by an Idiot* is to find an anodyne in the routine of war office work, a numbing of the pain of having lost, in the war, first her lover and then her brother.

The deepening of Rose Macaulay's cynicism in this crucial period of the twenties is evident. It manifests itself in the loss of the poetic, seascape image in *Told by an Idiot* and in the consequent shift toward a dry, almost purely intellectual plane. And it may be plotted in the change of setting in these three novels: from Soho and Picadilly Circus in *Potterism* to Nan's retreat to an out-of-the-way seacoast town in *Dangerous Ages* to Rome Garden's drawing room in *Told by an Idiot*.

The scenes set at Polperro, the seacoast town in *Dangerous Ages,* mark the turning point in this stage of Rose Macaulay's career. Nan's cycling down twisting roads on the edge of ocean precipices is thrilling, but this impatience of hers of "vehement living" is suicidal. (pp. 146-48)

[*Told by an Idiot*] offers the reader one of the author's most attractive heroines in Rome Garden. Her vision of the world is taken from that moment in *Macbeth* that supplies both Rose Macaulay and William Faulkner a title: "Life's but a walking shadow . . . it is a tale / Told by an idiot, full of sound and fury, / Signifying nothing." Admitting this vision of nonsignificance, Rose Macaulay is nevertheless able to identify with Rome Garden's enjoyment of "the cheering spectacle of human absurdity." Beautiful and cynical, Rome Garden is an eighteenth-century figure, akin to Voltaire—cleareyed, mocking, and gay.

The point of view implicit in a splendid scene in *Dangerous Ages* is taken up in this novel and sustained. In that scene Miss Macaulay renders the reluctant visit of Mrs. Hilary with Rosalind, a langorously beautiful and morally relaxed young woman

whom her son plans to marry. . . . The pleasure to be derived from this scene is in the writer's control of the comic situation, an awareness of the incongruity of manners she perceives in this Victorian mother's embarrassed visit with this distinctly modern, and for her, incomprehensible woman. Seeing Mrs. Hilary's emotional fuss over the welfare of her son as a lost cause, or at any rate an unnecessary one in an altered world, Miss Macaulay adopts a point of view which resembles Rome Garden's in *Told by an Idiot* wherein Rome is described as a "slight, pale, delicate young woman, with ironic green eyes and mocking lips a little compressed at the corners." (p. 148)

A shift in tone, from the gaiety of the circus spectacle to the grotesque fantasy of a world going to pieces, may be observed as one nears the end of this tale. With its approach and the coming of World War I the tempo of the novel becomes desperate in its ironic juxtapositions of Imogen's fantasies about life on a fruit-laden Pacific isle and the coming cataclysm. The fact that Rose Macaulay skips over the years 1914-18 and describes them only in retrospect may be held against her. Whether she does this out of a sense of her own limitations as a writer or out of her inability to face up to some of the more disturbing realities of the twentieth-century world is difficult to say with assurance—most probably, both. Perhaps it is unkind to find a correspondence between her avoidance of the war in this novel (as in all her novels) and her failure in handling love relationships. But once again the love relationship between Rome Garden and her lover, Mr. Jayne, is aborted by his violent, accidental death. It is in harmony with the dark, cataclysmic vision she presents in this novel, but there is, fundamentally, a certain fear of the animal-man, whether at love or at war.

One final aspect of *Told by an Idiot* needs to be discussed, and that concerns the author's technique. The success of the novels in this period owes much to the fact that Rose Macaulay finds a voice suited to her, one of coolness and detachment that gives her writing a consistency of tone and of point of view. The technique that suits this purpose is chiefly one of juxtaposition whose effect is ironic, humorous, mocking. As a means toward seeing things objectively, as they are, this is an impressive form and works consistently well in *Potterism*. But to fix on the shattered pieces of life and to ignore the life principle is to court despair. Moreover, there is the danger of method becoming mannerism, a way of seeing that becomes constrictive, and ultimately fixed and sterile. (pp. 150-51)

After *Told by an Idiot* Rose Macaulay veers away from serious treatments of her subject. She attempts to revive the humor of *Potterism* and turn it into comedy. Her most nearly successful attempt is *Orphan Island* . . . , a satiric, utopian novel. . . . Social and religious absurdities of Victorian England are represented and laughed about. But Miss Macaulay's talents have rather dried up and her dependence upon old materials is obvious. There is little imagination in the working out of this interesting idea.

But there is even less in the other seven novels she writes in this period, most of them also using Potterite themes and techniques. Thus Denham, in *Crewe Train* . . . , a reworking of Imogen in *Told by an Idiot,* is a creature of animal spirit who goes to London but refuses to be civilized. Aside from the idea itself, which has possibilities, there is little of interest in this static and poorly structured novel. There is an increase of missionaries (chiefly eccentric Anglican ones) but her treatment of them is dry and unless one enjoys Church jokes they are a pretty dull lot. (pp. 151-52)

Wit combined with fantasy or with narrative romps characterize [*Keeping Up Appearances, Staying with Relations* and *Going Abroad*]. Of these *Going Abroad* is most interesting because of the presence of certain elements she later uses in *The Towers of Trebizond*. . . . The descriptions of the Basque landscape . . . are quite good in themselves; they foreshadow those of the more strange and more beautiful shores of the Black Sea in *The Towers of Trebizond*.

In *The Towers of Trebizond* . . . Rose Macaulay discovers a new voice. It is not the cool, detached voice of an agreeable *persona* as in the novels of the twenties, but is the personal voice of her own, hitherto submerged, personality. It is heard in the amusing scenes and episodes that abound in the novel. (p. 152)

[Her] style is more gentle, less affected, and funnier. Also, the lyrical, first person narration gives a warmth and a consistency of tone and point of view, qualities lacking in many of her earlier novels.

The real magic of this novel is the ease and naturalness with which it appears to have been constructed. Once the central unifying image was conceived and understood, the design and the words seem simply to have followed it through. Trebizond, cite of the splendid, ancient Byzantine city on the shores of the Pontine, comes to be identified with the heroine Laurie's frustrating, lifelong quest for some lost core of meaningfulness. (p. 153)

In the Trebizond symbol Rose Macaulay has achieved a strong and beautiful resolution of the conflicting tendencies in her real and in her fictional personality. She has struck a note of concord and mellowness in her lifelong love-hate relationship with the modern world, neither reacting against it nor submitting to it, but treating it with generous humor. (p. 155)

> William J. Lockwood, "Rose Macaulay," *in* Minor British Novelists, *edited by Charles Alva Hoyt (copyright © 1967 by Southern Illinois University Press; reprinted by permission of Southern Illinois University Press), Southern Illinois University Press, 1967, pp. 135-56.*

ALICE R. BENSEN (essay date 1969)

As a tract, *Potterism* expounds, in its essay elements, the theory that the power of a sensational press is made possible by the attitudes of the encircling public—their refusal or inability to think, their preference for conventionality and emotionalism as against precise thinking and a disciplined search for facts. As a satire, it frequently simplifies the Potters to types and even to figures of farce. As a "novel," it probes deeply into human susceptibility to deep fears and neurotic greediness; it also presents the consciousness of three persons—Anti-Potterites—who are capable of experiencing tragedy. (pp. 68-9)

The Potter twins, Jane and Johnny, have intelligent, disciplined minds; but, swayed by the instinct to "grab" and vitiated by spiritual laziness, they are eventually drawn in by the vortex of the press. Ancillary to this Potter solar system is Mrs. Potter (Lady Pinkerton), its moon, who under the pen name of Leila Yorke, swings the tides of feminine emotionalism by her untiring production of novels. . . . Claire Potter, the older daughter, has the mindless, hysterical nature that her mother's novels encourage. Although functioning in the structure of the book mainly as types, the Potters are shown frequently enough at

close range to add vividness to the work by their individual traits.

In opposition to the Potter way of life, the author has set three persons, all representative of "positions": Juke, a spiritually perceptive young clergyman; Gideon, the "hero" of the opposition—a precise-thinking and sensitive young Jew; and Katherine, a young woman scientist of great delicacy of feeling, who services almost as the spirit of reason. The plot deals with the gradual subversion of most of the "Anti-Potterites" by the insidious lures of Potterism. (p. 69)

In an attack on the abuses of journalism, there is an appropriateness in using a form of fiction that itself includes journalistic elements—passages that are, in effect, essays or short articles. Some of the critics, although praising the book, raised questions about its tone or its form. (pp. 69-70)

[A *Times Literary Supplement*] reviewer found "no good reason" for the device of dividing the narration between "R. M.," who "tells" the first and last parts, and Gideon, Leila Yorke, Katherine, and Juke, who "tell" the other four. Undoubtedly, there is some awkwardness in the management of the six parts. The author certainly does not "tell" her own two sections—the style is impersonal and extremely crisp; and the three Anti-Potterite accounts seem intended for no particular reader or audience. Perhaps the formula of "bearing witness" in a trial is intended. But of first importance to this novel is the sense of individual human beings pitting themselves against the juggernaut of Potterism; and the efforts of Gideon, Katherine, and Juke—as well as the pity of their inevitable failure—gain greatly by their individual testimonials. As for Leila Yorke's part, this could not possibly have been presented in any other way with equal effect; and it is one of the wittiest sequences that Rose Macaulay ever wrote.

Despite the notion in some quarters that the "novel of ideas" is a misconceived form, since it must be devoid of drama, *Potterism* is highly dramatic. It contains the usual sources of drama in overall plot and in scene, although directly presented "scenes" do not make up as large a proportion of the book as they do in a typical "illusionist" novel. Primarily, the work is dramatized through the author's ironic style. The brilliance of her irony carries on a combat with the sentimentality and the unimaginativeness of the forces she attacks.

The opening paragraph indicates at once the importance of style in this novel: "Johnny and Jane Potter, being twins, went through Oxford together. Johnny came up from Rugby and Jane from Roedean. Johnny was at Balliol and Jane at Somerville." The wooden simplicity signals the roles of Johnny and Jane as types, and it also prepares for the discovery in them of a certain stolidity, which, despite their intelligence, causes them to fail more and more obviously to meet the imaginative standards of Arthur and Katherine. (pp. 70-1)

The second paragraph indicates that actualities will be used; there is a journalistic bit of offhand book-reviewing: actual novels are referred to; and there are passing references to contemporary novelists. The book progresses with discussions of relevant topics between characters, with short essays, and with dramatized passages. When World War I breaks out, the author is able to compare reactions by having each of the young people speak for his "position." During the war, conversations between Jane and the author's *raisonneur*, Katherine, bring out the irony of the fact that Jane (and those she stands for), despite her intellectual Anti-Potterism, cannot resist profiting quite Potterishly from the chaotic situation. (p. 71)

Part II is presented by Gideon, who is used by the author very economically. . . . [Gideon's] courage in the war and the loss of his foot make him initially sympathetic to even those readers who would tend to be antagonistic to his views. (p. 72)

Part III is narrated by Lady Pinkerton, under her pen name, Leila Yorke; and the author's satire in this section reaches pure farce. . . . Part III is, in fact, a book review in the form of parody. Written in the style of sentimentalists, it presents their self-deception. . . . (p. 73)

Part IV is presented by Katherine, a young woman described by Gideon as one "whose brains, by nature and training, grip and hold.". . . Her quiet, precise thought "places" the confused emotionalism of Leila Yorke. (p. 74)

The journalist-novelist has produced a tightly constructed work. The unity is achieved largely by the use of irony. From the start, the language indicates an exterior view of the Potter clan, a conception of these characters as types; for only occasionally are they viewed so closely as to affect us as individuals. Hobart, who must die, is kept so distant that his death presents no risk to the tone. The three other Anti-Potterite characters are also kept close to their "positions." Two tragic events involving them . . . are caused by elements of life identified with Potterism and so become subordinate to the main movement of the plot, which demonstrates that Potterism can be successfully opposed only by individuals who, as in a tragedy, pay for their freedom with their lives or with a major renunciation. But, as in comedy, Potterism can ironically discomfit itself through its overweening self-assurance.

The varying of the distancing of the characters, from the distance of satire to the close-up of a "natural" view or of an interior monologue, is facilitated by the linguistic flexibility, which, from the opening page, allows the author to move between ironic farce and controlled awareness of tragedy. This changing is aided also by the use of the voices of four other speakers besides the author. The discussion of the actualities of the 1914-1920 period, such an important element in the book, is limited to those topics related to the theme, Potterism. Perhaps the greatest temptation to an author in a work of this sort is to stray to tangent topics, or to engage in discussions at a length or with a weight disproportionate to the "novel" elements. This temptation the author has almost entirely avoided. (pp. 76-7)

The Towers of Trebizond is an extraordinary work. . . . In spite of the almost universal delight in the book, the critics by no means agreed as to its main theme or mood. The book is indeed a teaser for criticism, for any unimaginative application of criteria of genres would condemn it to be judged very faulty. (pp. 154-55)

The author was distressed that some readers missed the "gravity" completely and saw the book as merely a satire on the Church and its clergy. She wrote her sister that she had meant the book "to be about the struggle of good and evil, its eternal importance, and the power of the Christian Church over the soul, to torment and convert.". . .

The external action is a picaresque sequence of incidents that ramble toward a tragic climax. The chief character is Laurie, an unmarried person under forty, who is adulterously in love with Vere; but which lover is of which sex is not made explicit until the last pages—after the death of Vere. . . . The ambiguity, real at first, becomes a game of virtuosity later when the reader has rightly guessed that, although Laurie is very

adequately human, Laurie is not masculine enough to be a man. (p. 156)

[The narrative] is a mosaic of which the pieces (colored variously with satire, restrained lyricism, symbolism, intellectual musing)—scattered and continually reappearing—are travel description and comment, speculation on many aspects of religion and on the potentialities of human nature, and confession. Glinting out from these are tangential ideas and much sheer fun.

What holds these elements together? If the action is loose, it continually affords occasions for one or another—or several—of the themes; and these themes are symbolically related. But the most important continuum is one of the aspects of the confession: the voice of the first-person narrator. Actually, it is a double voice—perhaps not intended to be so as a formal element, but, since the writer was not primarily a formalist, permitted for the sake of the richness that results. The moral frame of the book is Laurie's fictional confession and, doubling it, the confessional testimony of the writer. . . . The narration is done ostensibly by Laurie, but a voice is frequently heard through hers—that of the experienced elderly woman who looks back at her own Laurie aspect and at her life as a whole. A rich voice, it is not limited to the expression of moral probings but conveys the witty, teasing, erudite thoughts of the author of the whole sequence of Macaulay writings.

Laurie is akin to those varied non-conforming girls and young women [in Macaulay's early novels]; but she is unmistakably different from any one of them—older and more experienced, better read (although much less erudite than her creator), of adequate worldly know-how, somewhat weary with a mid-century defeatism; but she is graced, at the same time, with a certain childlike acceptance. . . . (pp. 157-58)

[Macaulay's] style is surely intended to demonstrate that Laurie's refusal of the meaningful life offered in religion has reduced her to a state where values are becoming hopelessly confused.

In this far from simple novel, this style also skeptically questions these values. "From time to time," Laurie says, "I knew what I had lost. But nearly all the time, God was a bad second. . . .". . . . Laurie feels her estrangement from the Church of her ancestors as a tragedy, but she cannot return to it without impoverishing her life of good things of this world which, as a human being as well as (and if) an immortal soul, she must greatly cherish. As believer, she finds the right choice too hard; as skeptic, she finds the right choice uncertain. The human condition as tragedy is basic to the book and, in the last pages, is acutely presented; but the human condition as comedy is more extensively explored. (p. 158)

As in any work of sophisticated wit, there are some pages that amount to semi-private jokes between the author and one or another limited group of readers—travelogue readers, Anglicans, London Anglicans, or readers of certain Sunday papers. In no instance, however, need the reader be a member of any special "in"-group to perceive what the general point is; there is nothing "snob" involved; and a certain degree of exciting urgency in regard to the general matters discussed is engendered by these links with actuality. In this category may be listed tangential bits that old Macaulay hands are intended to recognize; the skill with which the author brings them in amounts to a game.

Because of her age when writing this book and because of uncertain health, Rose Macaulay realized that it might well be her last one. . . . Into this type of book, where the action takes place at the level of thought, she could pack even more of her current ideas than into a work of more traditional form. Newspapers and governments come in for satire, especially in connection with aunt Dot's and Father Hugh's Russian interlude. Although this adventure is the least integrated part of the plot, it was highly topical in the mid-1950's when two British physicists had just deserted to Russia and when all countries were jittery from spy-scares and were tightening their visa restrictions. (pp. 162-63)

The central conflict in the book is treated in a manner much more lyric than dramatic; Laurie feels nostalgia for the City of God, but she is not depicted as struggling against her love. The self-regarding, or purely "religious," aspect of her sin is frequently presented; but its effect on Vere's wife, the ethical aspect, is given only brief mention and then after Vere's death. Perhaps this relative unconcern is indicative of the decay of Laurie's conscience. But aside from her relation with Vere, Laurie's sinfulness is mild enough; at most, she is rather indolent and purposeless. . . .

Sinfulness, as an element in the book, is dispersed among all the central characters, and it ranges from the spiritual pride of aunt Dot and Father Hugh through the declinations of those jealous, untruthful, and selfish young men Charles and David, to David's outright plagiarism. David's appropriation of Charles' writings after Charles' death indicates a laxity toward which Laurie may be sliding; the "blackmail" that she practices on this erring young man is presented, however, in a comic ambiance and she is fulfilling the social code of not tattling. The scene in which she lets David see how much she knows is the funniest of all the dramatized scenes in the book; the comic style is tantamount to a pardon for her complicity.

Of the non-dramatized passages, the first page, which is packed with wit, and the introductory pages on the mystical affinity between Anglican clergymen and angling are among many that are as entertaining as any that Rose Macaulay had ever written. (p. 164)

> *Alice R. Bensen, in her* Rose Macaulay *(copyright © 1969 by Twayne Publishers, Inc.; reprinted with the permission of Twayne Publishers, a Division of G. K. Hall & Co., Boston), Twayne, 1969, 184 p.*

THOMAS M. DISCH (essay date 1980)

The Towers of Trebizond begins with one of the great opening lines of the English novel ("'Take my camel, dear,' said my aunt Dot, as she climbed down from this animal on her return from High Mass."), and the first chapter closes with a succinct confession of the narrator's (and author's) faith: "I agree with those who have said that travel is the chief end of life." For readers who share that faith, this book, first published in 1956, must be accounted one of the most pleasurable novels of the century and one of the best travel books of all time. Not since Kinglake's *Eothen* in 1844 has anyone 'done' Turkey and the Middle East with quite the same inspired sense of when to

snap a picture and when not, of showing what is typical without becoming a bore.

An ideal travel book, like an ideal traveler, must be free to wander and associate freely. To this end Rose Macaulay developed a "rather goofy, rambling prose style" (her own description), which reads like a postcard correspondence between Hemingway and Gertrude Stein. . . .

To know Turkey inside out and to write of it divertingly is still something less than writing a novel. There is a plot to *The Towers of Trebizond,* but so slight that I found, rereading it after a 12-year interval, that I'd remembered scarcely a twist of it. There are also characters, too, more memorable than the plot, but all in the Micawber mold, created at a stroke and never varying from their original oddity. Its chief novelistic merit is its central, ever-more elaborated vision of heaven (and/or the Anglican Church) as a city, like Trebizond, that the mortal tourist hungers for and travels toward but never reaches. For all her casual airs, the narrator knows what ruin the centuries have brought to her citadel. Indeed, the novelist in her relishes the very hopelessness of her hope, since there is nothing so productive of vigorous art as an irresolvable dilemma. In her last years, by her own account, Rose Macaulay was able to return to the communion of her own church. In this, her last novel, she resisted the temptation to resolve the conflict on the C-major chord of Faith.

Not that she lacked faith herself, but that she could remember too well what it was like, as an unbeliever, to have to sit still in church and how the mind will wander off; and suddenly, at the most hushed and solemn moment, one is giggling. The satirist in her, who wrote a whole string of brilliant pasquinades in the '20s and '30s (many as deserving of republication as *Towers*), can't resist pointing out the absurdity of the missionary impulse and the cross-cultural comedies it necessarily creates. . . .

> *Thomas M. Disch, "Take My Camel, Dear," in* Book World—The Washington Post *(© 1980, The Washington Post), October 26, 1980, p. 10.*

ADDITIONAL BIBLIOGRAPHY

Benson, Alice R. "The Skeptical Balance: A Study of Rose Macaulay's *Going Abroad*." *Papers of the Michigan Academy of Science, Arts, and Letters* XLVIII (1963): 675-83.
> Discusses the novel *Going Abroad* as both a comedy of manners and a serious examination of modern morality.

Benson, Alice R. "The Ironic Aesthete and the Sponsoring of Causes: A Rhetorical Quandry in Novelistic Technique." *English Literature in Transition* 9, No. 1 (1966): 39-43.
> A study of *Views and Vagabonds.* Benson contends that in this novel Macaulay failed to reconcile her theme of respect for individual lifestyles, no matter how unconventional, with her belief in the importance of traditional values.

Smith, Constance Babington. *Rose Macaulay.* London: Collin, 1972, 254 p.
> A biography of Macaulay, including a somewhat lengthy appendix of reminiscences by her friends and professional acquaintances.

Don(ald Robert Perry) Marquis

1878-1937

American humorist, essayist, poet, dramatist, novelist, and short story writer.

Marquis was one of the most widely read humorists in the United States from 1912 to 1925, the years during which he produced a daily newspaper column. Though Marquis also wrote novels, poetry, light verse, short stories, and dramas, especially after giving up newspaper work, it was through his column, and in particular through the character of Archy the cockroach, that Marquis was best known. For he has been chiefly remembered, as he feared he would be, "as the creator of a goddamned cockroach."

The son of a country doctor, Marquis drew on memories of his native Walnut, Illinois, to create Hazelton, the setting of his unfinished, semiautobiographical novel *Sons of the Puritans*. This novel reflects a tension, somewhat evident in all of Marquis's work, between his strictly religious upbringing and his personal beliefs; it also expresses the cynicism that deepened throughout a life of numerous tragedies. After a year at Knox College in Galesburg, Illinois, Marquis worked on Philadelphia and Atlanta newspapers and on the newly formed *Uncle Remus's Magazine* with Joel Chandler Harris. During his two years on Harris's magazine, Marquis learned two storytelling devices—the frame and the dramatic monologue—which he later employed in his columns. A year after Harris's death Marquis left *Uncle Remus's Magazine* and went to New York. Several years of newspaper experience on different papers culminated in the fulfillment of Marquis's ambition—his own column. For ten years with the *New York Evening Sun* and another three with the *New York Tribune* he created in his column vivid characters typical of the American scene in the early 1900s.

It was in the "Sun Dial," his column with the *New York Evening Sun*, on March 29, 1916, that Marquis described how he arrived at his office earlier than usual "and discovered a gigantic cockroach jumping upon the keys" of his typewriter. This was the origin of Archy, the lowly cockroach with the transmigrated soul of a *vers libre* bard. At first just a way to fill up a column quickly (Archy's short, unpunctuated sentences took up much space) Archy became Marquis's most popular creation and his favorite means of oblique commentary on public affairs. Marquis introduced a cast of other characters who, like Archy, were typical city-dwellers: Mehitabel, the corybantic alley cat, whose motto was *"toujours gai"*; Freddy the Rat, the archetypal critic—he ate what he didn't like; Warty Bliggens, the egocentric toad who believed himself the center of the universe; and an equally fascinating crew of human characters, including Clem Hawley, the "Old Soak," who spoke against Prohibition, and Hermione, the emancipated "advanced thinker." Christopher Morley wrote that while Marquis was producing his column, "most of us didn't consult the leading editorials to know what to think. The almost universal reflex, in New York at any rate, was let's see what Don says about it."

Ironically, the nature of the daily column, which gave Marquis the avenue for some of his best and most creative writing, also imposed limitations, mostly of time, on his work in other genres. Marquis later said that he wished he had devoted some of his years as a columnist to more serious work as an author. He worked ten years on a drama based on the passion of Christ, *The Dark Hours*, which he considered his most important dramatic work. Though the play itself was favorably reviewed, it was inadequately produced and directed by Marquis's second wife, and its performance was a critical failure.

Marquis's popularity declined after his death. Though his novels, short stories, and poems were well received, the daily presence of his column led critics to think of him as a columnist who only incidentally wrote in other genres. Marquis remains, however, one of the few American writers to have created, in Archy the cockroach, a lasting comic character.

PRINCIPAL WORKS

Danny's Own Story   (novel)   1912
Dreams and Dust   (poetry)   1915
The Cruise of the Jasper B.   (novel)   1916
Hermione and Her Little Group of Serious Thinkers
   (humorous essays)   1916

Prefaces (humorous essays) 1919
Carter and Other People (short stories) 1921
Noah an' Jonah an' Cap'n John Smith (verse) 1921
The Old Soak, and Hail and Farewell (humorous essays)
    1921
The Old Soak (drama) 1922
Poems and Portraits (poetry) 1922
The Revolt of the Oyster (short stories) 1922
*Sonnets to a Red-Haired Lady (by a Gentleman with a Blue
    Beard) and Famous Love Affairs* (verse) 1922
*The Old Soak's History of the World, with Occasional
    Glances at Baycliff, L.I., and Paris, France*
    (humorous essays) 1924
The Almost Perfect State (essays) 1927
*Archy and Mehitabel (humorous essays and verse) 1927
Love Sonnets of a Cave Man and Other Verses (poetry and
    verse) 1928
When the Turtle Sings and Other Unusual Tales (short
    stories) 1928
A Variety of People (short stories) 1929
The Dark Hours (drama) 1932
*Archy's Life of Mehitabel (humorous essays and verse)
    1933
Chapters for the Orthodox (short stories) 1934
*Archy Does His Part (humorous essays and verse) 1935
Sons of the Puritans (unfinished novel) 1939

*These works were published as *The Lives and Times of Archy and
  Mehitabel* in 1940.

THE NEW YORK TIMES (essay date 1912)

Possibly if **"Danny's Own Story"** . . . were told in a somewhat
modified dialect it would read more easily and perhaps more
satisfactorily, but even as it is, it is a lively autobiography,
with a number of unusual situations offered, all interesting,
and several of them very droll indeed. . . .

There is much of broad humor in the story, not only in language, but in situation, and with it is much that is stirring and
almost tragic making it of absorbing interest throughout—not
as a literary production, but as a readable tale.

> *"Western Tales and Biblical," in* The New York
> Times *(© 1912 by The New York Times Company;
> reprinted by permission), February 18, 1912, p. 82.**

JOYCE KILMER (essay date 1915)

The [*New York*] *Evening Sun*, a paper notorious for its flirta-
tions with the muses, now rejoices in possessing upon its staff
two full-fledged poets. The full fledging was accomplished by
the publication of Mr. Don Marquis's *Dreams and Dust,* and
Mr. Dana Burnet's *Poems.* Mr. Marquis has exhibited in his
famous Sun Dial column his power to turn deft and amusing
rhymes on topics of the day; in the book now under consideration he has included only his more serious poems. It cannot
be doubted that these poems were written, all of them, in
response to an actual poetic urge, rather than merely for the
sake of writing; if there ever were such a thing as inspiration,
it is evident in **"The Tavern of Despair"** and **"Silvia."** When
some discerning anthologist brings together a collection of poems
about New York, he must give the place of honour to Mr.

Marquis's **"From the Bridge,"** which is the most vivid reflection of the City ever caught by a verbal mirror. (pp. 460-
61)

> *Joyce Kilmer, "This Autumn's Poetry," in* The
> Bookman, *New York, Vol. XLII, December, 1915,
> pp. 457-62.**

H. W. BOYNTON (essay date 1916)

[*The Cruise of the Jasper B*. is a story] with a good deal of
humour. The adventures of Cleggett have a delightfully Stocktonian flavour. After long service as a drudge in a newspaper
office, Cleggett suddenly comes into a legacy of a half-million.
He is not yet past his youth, and the world is all before him.
He buys an old hulk which has long been stuck in the mud of
a Long Island cove. His plan is to fit her out and sail whither
he will in quest of adventure. But there turns out to be a proper
mystery about the *Jasper B*. which presently involves Cleggett
and his crew and various others in sufficiently thrilling adventures before they have had a chance to try their seamanship,
and their luck at happenings, away from Long Island muck.
The thing is done, I say, with a quaint yet unforced extravagance. . . .

> *H. W. Boynton, "Some Stories of the Month," in*
> The Bookman, *New York, Vol. XLIII, No. 6, August,
> 1916, pp. 618-23.**

CHRISTOPHER MORLEY (essay date 1918)

[Don Marquis] stands out as one of the most penetrating satirists
and resonant scoffers at folderol that this continent nourishes.
He is far more than a colyumist: he is a poet—a kind of Mer-
edithian Prometheus chained to the roar and clank of a Hoe
press. He is a novelist of Stocktonian gifts, although unfortunately for us he writes the first half of a novel easier than
the second. And I think that in his secret heart and at the bottom
of the old haircloth round-top trunk he is a dramatist.

He good-naturedly deprecates that people praise "Archy the
Vers Libre Cockroach" and clamour for more; while "Hermione," a careful and cutting satire on the follies of pseudo-
kultur near the Dewey Arch, elicits only "a mild, mild smile."
(pp. 22-3)

Don Marquis recognizes as well as any one the value of the
slapstick as a mirth-provoking instrument. (All hail to the slapstick! it was well known at the Mermaid Tavern, we'll warrant.)
But he prefers the rapier. Probably his Savage Portraits, splendidly truculent and slashing sonnets, are among the finest pieces
he has done.

The most honourable feature of Marquis's writing, the "small
thing to look for but the big thing to find," is its quality of
fine workmanship. The swamis and prophets of piffle, the
Bhandranaths and Fothergill Finches whom he detests, can only
create in an atmosphere specially warmed, purged and rose-
watered for their moods. Marquis has emerged from the underworld of newspaper print just by his heroic ability to transform the commonest things into tools for his craft. Much of
his best and subtlest work has been clacked out on a typewriter
standing on an upturned packing box. . . . Newspaper men are
a hardy race. Who but a man inured to the squalour of a
newspaper office would dream of a cockroach as a hero? Archy
was born in the old *Sun* building, now demolished, once known
as Vermin Castle.

"Publishing a volume of verse," Don has plaintively observed, "is like dropping a rose-petal down the Grand Canyon and waiting to hear the echo." . . . But little by little his potent, yeasty verses, fashioned from the roaring loom of everyday, are winning their way into circulation. Any reader who went to *Dreams and Dust* . . . expecting to find light and waggish laughter, was on a blind quest. In that book speaks the hungry and visionary soul of this man, quick to see beauty and grace in common things, quick to question the answerless face of life. . . . (pp. 24-5)

Marquis is more than the arbiter of dainty elegances in rhyme: he sings and celebrates a robust world where men struggle upward from the slime and discontent leaps from star to star. The evolutionary theme is a favourite with him. . . . (p. 27)

[Don's] dry battery has generated in the past few years [in his column, Sun Dial, in the New York *Evening Sun*] a dozen features with real voltage—the Savage Portraits, Hermione, Archy the Vers Libre Cockroach, the Aptronymic Scouts, French Without a Struggle, Suggestions to Popular Song Writers, Our Own Wall Mottoes, and the sequence of Prefaces (to an Almanac, a Mileage Book, The Plays of Euripides, a Diary, a Book of Fishhooks, etc.). Some of Marquis's most admirable and delicious fooling has been poured into these Prefaces: I hope that he will put them between book-covers. (pp. 28-9)

But Don Marquis's mind has two yolks (to use one of his favourite denunciations). In addition to these comic or satiric shadows, the gnomon of his Sun Dial may be relied on every now and then to register a clear-cut notation of the national mind and heart. (p. 30)

Greatly as we cherish the Sun Dial, we are jealous of it for sapping all its author's time and calories. No writer in America has greater or more meaty, stalwart gifts. (pp. 31-2)

He is a versatile cove. Philosopher, satirist, burlesquer, poet, critic, and novelist. Perhaps the three critics in this country whose praise is best worth having, and least easy to win, would be Marquis, [Simeon] Strunsky, and O. W. Firkins. And I think that the three leading poets male in this country to-day are Marquis, William Rose Benét, and (perhaps) Vachel Lindsay. (p. 33)

Hermione and her little group of "Serious Thinkers" have attained the dignity of book publication, and now stand on the shelf beside **"Danny's Own Story"** and **"The Cruise of the Jasper B."** This satire on the azure-pedalled coteries of Washington Square has perhaps received more publicity than any other of Marquis's writings, but of all Don's drolleries I reserve my chief affection for Archy. The cockroach, endowed by some freak of transmigration with the shining soul of a vers libre poet, is a thoroughly Marquisian whimsy. . . . I love Archy because there seems to me something thoroughly racial and native and American about him. Can you imagine him, for instance, in *Punch*? His author has never told us which one of the vers libre poets it is whose soul has emigrated into Archy, but I feel sure it is not Ezra Pound or any of the expatriated eccentrics who lisp in odd numbers in the King's Road, Chelsea. Could it be Amy Lowell? (pp. 33-4)

[Using] the word ephemeral in its strict sense, Don Marquis is unquestionably the cleverest of our ephemeral philosophers. This nation suffers a good deal from lack of humour in high places. . . . But Don has just chuckled and gone on refusing to answer letters or fill out Mr. Purinton's blasphemous efficiency charts or join the Poetry Society or attend community

masques. And somehow all these things seem to melt away, and you look round the map and see Don Marquis taking up all the scenery. . . . He has such an œcumenical kind of humour. It's just as true in Brooklyn as it is in the Bronx.

He is at his best when he takes up some philosophic dilemma, or some quaint abstraction (viz., Certainty, Predestination, Idleness, Uxoricide, Prohibition, Compromise, or Cornutation) and sets the idea spinning. Beginning slowly, carelessly, in a deceptive, offhand manner, he lets the toy revolve as it will. Gradually the rotation accelerates; faster and faster he twirls the thought (sometimes losing a few spectators whose centripetal powers are not stanch enough) until, chuckling, he holds up the flashing, shimmering conceit, whirling at top speed and ejaculating sparks. What is so beautiful as a rapidly revolving idea? Marquis's mind is like a gyroscope: the faster it spins, the steadier it is. There are laws of dynamics in colyums just as anywhere else. (pp. 36-7)

I would fail utterly in this rambling anatomy if I did not insist that Don Marquis regards his column not merely as a soapslide but rather as a cudgelling ground for sham and hypocrisy. He has something of the quick Stevensonian instinct for the moral issue, and the Devil not infrequently winces about the time the noon edition of the *Evening Sun* comes from the press. There is no man quicker to bonnet a fallacy or drop the acid just where it will disinfect. (pp. 40-1)

> *Christopher Morley, "Don Marquis," in his* Shandygaff: A Number of Most Agreeable Inquirendoes upon Life and Letters, Interspersed with Short Stories and Skitts, the Whole Most Diverting to the Reader *(copyright, 1918, 1946 by Christopher Morley; reprinted by permission of Harper & Row, Publishers, Inc.), Doubleday, Page and Company, 1918 (and reprinted by Scholarly Press, Inc., 1971), pp. 22-42.*

RICHARD Le GALLIENNE (essay date 1922)

Don Marquis is a great comfort. We naturally "drop the 'Mr.'" in his case, as we drop it with our familiar friends, being as he is, a household word. To some it may be hard to realize that the inventor of "Archy the Cockroach," "Hermione" and "The Old Soak" is also the writer of the remarkable poems in his new volume **"Poems and Portraits."** We are so unaccustomed nowadays to "complete" men in any sphere of activity, least of all in the sphere of literature, that the combination of humorist, journalist and poet is hard to credit. The phenomenon was not always so rare, as the names of Tom Hood, Théophile Gautier, H. C. Bunner, Eugene Field and Andrew Lang bear witness. Thackeray may be added to this company, and now, far from least, Don Marquis. Don Marquis is a human being, a fellow-man. It looks almost as though he may be the last of his clan. He is not ashamed of being versatile, of doing many things well. He is not afraid that his "art" as a poet may suffer less "highbrow," even "Philistine" faculties which contribute to make him, in Bacon's phrase, "a full man." It is for this very reason that his poetry has such deep roots, is so forceful and poignant, with the beauty and bloom of it perhaps as its greatest surprise. The heart of the true humorist, as distinct from the quaint verbal juggler with dialect or slang, has always been a deep well. He has been the man who has laughed lest he should weep, the clown of the seven-times broken heart. Don Marquis gives us a vivid expression of this old truth in **"The Jesters."** . . .

This jester, in the form of savage satirist, has a section all to himself in this volume, a section entitled "Savage Portraits." "Savage" indeed they are, but not too savage for their subjects. Such merciless truth of portraiture has been lacking in English for many a day. It makes one understand the pleasure Samuel Pepys took in attending executions. . . .

It is no flattery to say that such satire as ["**Phyllida**" and "**The Spinks**"] is masterly. If Don Marquis could do nothing else, he need do no more. But how strange it is in turn from this second section of his volume to the first, to the "Poems," fenced off from the rest. In what a different world we are! And the only correspondence between the two sections is that in both cases a powerful pen is at work, in the one case dipped in gall, in the other dipped in the warm blood of our common humanity, in tears, in April, in the woodland, in moonlight, and particularly in the world of ghostly remembrance. I know no poems so genuinely, so thrillingly haunted as these poems of Don Marquis, with, so to speak, cosmic as well as personal hauntings. With deep beauty, and sometimes almost with intolerable heartaches, Don Marquis makes us realize what a lovely, haunted world it is we live in. . . .

I cannot but repeat how strangely haunted these verses are, haunted by all sorts of ghosts, the ghosts of heredity as in "**Heir and Serf,**" a most vivid statement of the modern and so ancient scientific conception. . . .

But most remarkable, creepily vivid, and shudderingly sympathetic, are the poems directly concerned with that "animula, vagula, blandula" that flutters lingeringly on the threshold of the life it knew, the "ghosts" of "**Those That Come Back.**" . . .

The poem "**A Ghost Speaks**" makes one feel that Don Marquis has been down with Odysseus where the many ghosts flocked together from every side about the bloodfilled trench, "and pale fear gat hold on me." . . .

No such vital volume of verse has been published for a long time. There is not a dead spot in it. Every poem is animated by striking thought and deep feeling, expressed in terms of beauty, strength and wit. It is a book you want to share with some one right away, and when you get reading it aloud to a friend, dipping about here and there for this and that good thing, you end by reading it all—for there is nothing in it but good things—and, for once, your friend makes no frantic efforts to escape, but enjoys your enthusiastic buttonholing. . . .

Wherever one turns one finds Don Marquis's head and heart in their right places. They never fail us. One feels this particularly in his poems of the war, with his noble praise of France and his comradely appreciation of "**The Laughter of the English,**" that "golden nonsense of the heart," with which he himself is so humanly gifted.

Richard Le Gallienne, "Don Marquis, 'Last of His Clan'," in The New York Times Book Review (© 1922 by The New York Times Company; reprinted by permission), March 26, 1922, p. 9.

CARL VAN DOREN (essay date 1923)

What distinguishes Mr. Marquis from his rivals among the columnists is a racy substance in him which makes him able to create character as no one of the others can. He has more point than Mr. [Christopher] Morley; he has a more burly energy than Mr. [Franklin P.] Adams; but he lives for his public primarily in the careers of those preposterous, fascinating personages who wander on and off his daily stage. That they are in outline the broadest kind of caricature does not seem to matter. Archy the cockroach, Mehitabel the cat, Hermione the platitudinarian, Fothergil Finch the minor poet, Prudence Hecklebury the incomparable prude, Captain Fitzurse the swaggerer, Al the bartender, the Old Soak who in dry days lifts his thirsty voice with incredible ingenuity of protest—they all have their absurd outlines filled in with comically real human elements. Mr. Marquis has the gift of using a vernacular technic with classical materials. Once he has hit upon a given character, he continues to exploit it almost as if he were a cartoonist, with a set figure to show off day by day in slightly new adventures. . . . [Readers] might be surprised to learn at how many points Archy and Mehitabel suggest the beast fables of medieval France and how often Captain Fitzurse suggests the braggart soldier of Latin comedy. There is of course no imitation to be hinted at. The likenesses come from the fact that Mr. Marquis fixes his eyes upon the aspects of the comic scene which in every age attract shrewd satirists. And he is more than a mere satirist, winging folly in his own person. He is so much of a dramatist that he must invent stalking-horses behind which to shoot and must make the creatures look so much alive that they seem at any moment about to gallop off on their own affairs.

Having in him the substantial quality needed by a creator of characters, Mr. Marquis seems something more, also, than a mere town wit. He suffers less than most of the New York columnists when put to the test of being read at a distance from New York, possibly because he has spent a larger part of his life outside metropolitan circles. He knows provincial humors and turns of speech. Without being in any respect a small town philosopher, he has a knack at understanding and reproducing the processes of thought and the shades of feeling which belong to villages rather than to cities. In this sense he smacks of the American soil as it exists in the interior districts which cosmopolitan humorists find chiefly laughable. If his methods suggest the cartoonist of the comic strip, so do they suggest the older tradition of native humor as it descends from Jack Downing and David Crockett to Artemus Ward and Mark Twain. He is robust, hilarious, given to vast exaggeration, capable of vituperative outbursts. Even when he appears simply wrongheaded, as in his sentimental praise of booziness, he conducts his arguments with such random vitality that they are funny. The same vitality marks his verse, which ranges from graceful lyricism to a mad mélange of topsy-turvy burlesque. In verse as in prose he moves with a rush that carries him frequently through his whole column with a single item, which he may find it necessary to continue to another day. It is significant, however, that he loses something when he turns to the conventional forms of literature: his stories are not particularly distinguished, and the successful play which he built around the Old Soak has little besides its leading character to recommend it. Mr. Marquis is thus proof that, no matter how many elements may enter into the art of the columnist, it is a special art, requiring certain special gifts no one of which in the case of any individual columnist can by him be safely dispensed with. (pp. 313-14)

Carl Van Doren, "Day In and Day Out; Adams, Morley, Marquis, and Broun: Manhattan Wits" (reprinted by permission of the Estate of Carl Van Doren), in The Century, Vol. 107, No. 2, December, 1923, pp. 309-15.*

STUART SHERMAN (essay date 1925)

[Don Marquis] is a poet of very nearly the rarest sort—a dramatic poet. He has published a drama of poignant beauty and memorable reality on the betrayal, trial and crucifixion of Jesus, **"The Dark Hours."** Whether any other poet in America could have approached his achievement on this theme, I do not know. No one has. He has accomplished what I had thought was impossible: He has thoroughly dramatized the chief narrative of the New Testament, developing with marked originality several of the principal characters, notably Judas, and freely inventing incidents and speeches for subordinate figures, yet—to my sense, which is reasonably sensitive—without striking a note which is not in harmony with the tone and atmosphere of the Gospels. In the case of the central figure, he attempts no interpretation that deviates a hair's breadth from the Christian tradition. The character and personality of the Son of Man, the Son of God, are left quite inviolate; and this makes the more marvelous the congruity of his own developments. His feeling about the delicate ethical and artistic questions involved in handling this material he discusses with admirable taste and insight.

I have almost nothing strictly parallel to compare with the effect of **"The Dark Hours"** except a Passion Play which I saw a few years ago solemnly presented in a canyon of southern California, with the Crucifixion dim on the hilltop above it. With its elaborate reproduction of Palestinian dwellings, costumes and scenery, it was pictorially correct, like the colored illustrations in a modern Bible, of which it constantly reminded me, and the lines were gravely and eloquently recited, yet somehow it seemed remote and it left me cold—as cold as a colored picture in a Bible.

"The Dark Hours," on the other hand, even silently read, is of a seizing and transporting reality. Its tremendous dramatic stress is intensely felt. It puts one there—in ancient not modern Palestine. . . . I believe this to be a great tragedy, greatly conceived and written with austere sincerity. When it is adequately produced, as I hope it may be, it should affect us as the tragedies of Æschylus and Sophocles affected the Greeks—religiously.

Socrates argued all night on one occasion to prove that the type of mind best adapted for tragedy is also the type of mind best adapted for comedy. If you reflect just a little about **"The Dark Hours"** you recover from your first surprise at the thought of its coming out of a mind which had just produced **"The Old Soak's History of the World."** . . . [The] Crucifixion, the execution of Socrates—all such incidents in history may be conceived of as tragic and stupendous jokes. In order fully to appreciate them one must be endowed with a comic poet's comprehension of the immensity of human folly, which is the prime source of all tragedy. To put the matter in more familiar terms, no one can adequately know how dreadful the World War was who does not at the same time adequately know how absurd it was, how ridiculous, what an inexhaustible subject for the laughter of gods and men. In Don Marquis the tragicomic spirit is very strong. He respects gods because he knows fools so well, so intimately. . . . (pp. 214-17)

The book with which he seems to be most familiar is the Bible. Next to that, I should say the most obvious influences traceable in his prose and poetical styles and in the form of his humor are Mark Twain's "Huckleberry Finn" and "Tom Sawyer," the various yarns of Frank Stockton, O. Henry, perhaps H. C. Bunner, the poems of Swinburne, Kipling and Arnold, and an extensive study of prosody.

His first published book, **"Danny's Own Story,"** . . . , is a picturesque narrative with an earthy Mid-Western flavor, Illinoisian, and much in the vein of Huck Finn, whose domain lies in the same rich humor belt, to the south. (p. 217)

In 1915 Don Marquis made the first collection of his serious poems, under the title **"Dreams and Dust."** In 1916 he uttered a farcical Stocktonian yarn, **"The Cruise of the Jasper B.,"** which relates the adventures of a romantic journalist attempting to sail his schooner, scow or canal boat—it isn't quite clear which—from her moorings *on* a brick pier *in* Long Island. In the same year appeared **"Hermione and Her Little Group of Serious Thinkers,"** asking themselves at bedtime many heart-searching questions. In 1919 a volume of **"Prefaces"**—thirty-two of them, introducing A Check Book, A Cook Book, The Works of Billy Sunday, etc. In 1921 appeared the first records of **"The Old Soak"**; also a notable collection of short stories, **"Carter and Other People,"** and a volume of humorous verse, **"Noah an' Jonah an' Cap'n John Smith."** Next year, 1922, a second collection of serious verse, **"Poems and Portraits,"** in which Don Marquis takes the war seriously, and adds thirty-three satires with teeth. In 1922, **"The Revolt of the Oyster,"** containing some capital stories of dogs and boys and the ripe tale of **"The Saddest Man"**; also **"Sonnets to a Red-Haired Lady."** In 1924, **"The Old Soak's History of the World,"** **"The Dark Hours,"** and, with Christopher Morley, **"Pandora Lifts the Lid."**

There are some things among these fourteen volumes of a sort which I never read except in the line of duty. With me, a very little Stocktonian extravaganza goes a long way. So does a very little of the ordinary run of humorous verse. Practically all the rest goes very well, including the satires in "Savage Portraits," which are as neat and sharp as those of the Roman masters. But I enjoy Don Marquis most when he is enjoying himself most, and that is obviously when his imagination is at work and he is creating something, if it is only a prolific cat, a loquacious cockroach, or a special kind of thoroughbred dog: "*Any* dog can be full of just *one* kind of thoroughbred blood. That's nothing! But Spot here has got more different kinds of thoroughbred blood in him than any dog you ever saw." I admire the creative energy with which Don Marquis steers his elderly inebriate through his barroom reminiscences; I prefer the Old Soak's gorgeous, glowing historical style in his account of Ancient History to that of Gibbon, Wells or Van Loon, and I admire immensely the masterly poetizing stroke in the invention of "that damn little athyiss, Hennery Withers." That is Shakespearean—no less.

But previous to **"The Dark Hours"** I suspect the most memorable writing that Don Marquis has done is in eight or ten short stories: **"Old Man Murtrie," "Never Say Die," "McDermott," "Looney, the Mutt"** and **"The Locked Box"**—in **"Carter and Other People"**; and **"The Saddest Man"** and the dog and boy stories in **"The Revolt of the Oyster."** In reading this group of stories I have no compunctious feeling that I am enjoying humor by the sacrifice of a poet; for in the wider sense of the word these stories *are* poetry. Several of them are, I think, the kind of poetry in which Don Marquis expresses himself most adequately, that is, tragi-comic poetry. (pp. 218-20)

[There is in **"Dreams and Dust"**] little indication of historical passions, little indication of locality, no very particular or specific attachment to "Nature," and no significant love-interest. The dominant note is an almost Arnoldian concern about God and the soul and their relations in a world which has lost faith in supernatural guidance.

Whenever he turns from polishing a rondeau or a triolet, which he does very nicely, to grappling with a theme, he is idealistic and religious. He sounds the silver trumpet to "paladins, paladins, youth, noble-hearted." He scornfully bids farewell to the "lost leader." He sees that man has "at his noblest an air of something more than man." He is the receiver of mystical intimations. He speculates on the mystery of the Self. Disillusioned, he yet sees man as the god-seeker, the god-maker, and he respects man's aspiration, in the face of "the hissing hate of fools, thorns, and the ingrate's scoff." . . . (pp. 220-21)

> *Stuart Sherman, "Don Marquis, What Is He?" in* New York Herald Tribune Books *(© I.H.T. Corporation; reprinted by permission), February 8, 1925 (and reprinted as "Don Marquis, Poet," in his* Critical Woodcuts, *Charles Scribner's Sons, 1926, pp. 209-21).*

DON MARQUIS (essay date 1928)

So many people used to say to me, when I ran a column in a New York newspaper, "I don't see how you fellows can keep it up every day!" and otherwise express their curiosity concerning the columnist's job, that I am forced to the conclusion that there must be a good deal of public interest in the matter. I have been out of the game for more than three years, and I can look back upon the thirteen years when I was chained to a column—like the well-known Prisoner of Chillon—almost as if that overwhelmed and struggling journalistic captive had been someone else. . . .

I remember that while I was at it I always told people it was easy. . . . For the fact is, that while it ruined me, I loved it. It sapped my vitality, made corns and bunions on my brain, wrecked my life, and I adored doing it. During the three years since I have quit it I have had four or five terrible struggles not to go back to it. I am apt to walk into any newspaper office in America at any hour of the day or night and hand in half a dozen columns if I don't watch myself, and give them away for nothing but the pleasure of seeing them in type. I loathe, hate, abhor and dread the column-writing game; I think of it as the most poisonously destructive vice to which any writer may become addicted, and the hardest work to which any human being might contract himself; and at the same time I love it and adore it and yearn for it and have to fight against it. (p. 6)

. . . . .

When I first got the signed column I had so long been struggling for I was ready for it. As I saw it coming nearer, I had written and saved up for it some of the best general stuff I could do; and the day I got it, I began slamming into it the stuff I had saved. The Sun Dial . . . caught on with the town almost from the first week. Before it had been running two months I began to get kindly letters about it from generous professional workers in New York with whom I was not personally acquainted—I remember, offhand, William Winter, the veteran dramatic editor of the Tribune; Robert Underwood Johnson, the editor of the Century; that versatile all-around genius, James Huneker; Bob Davis, the editor of Munsey's, and many others—men whose work and opinions I had admired and respected. (p. 59)

A column must have plenty of white space, a challenging make-up, constant variation in typographical style; not only must it catch the eye but it must have points and corners and barbs that prick and stimulate the vision, a surface and a texture that intrigue and cling to and pull at the sight. Franklin P. Adams, of the New York World, is the master hand at this sort of thing. Heywood Broun, now on the New York Telegram, usually neglects it. I used to have spells when I was very careful about it, like Adams; then I would get bored with the trouble and neglect it, like Broun. But it should never be neglected. It advertises to people that here is quick and easy reading, and people like easy reading. They will even take a difficult thought if you wrap it up in easy reading for them.

I tried to get as much variety in the stuff itself as there was in its typographical presentation. So, besides the verse, paragraphs, sketches, fables and occasional serious expressions of opinion, I began to create characters through whom I might comment upon or satirize current phases of existence, or whom I might develop for the sheer pleasure of creation. A few of these characters became rather popular: Hermione, the Modern Young Woman, and her little group of serious thinkers; Captain Fitzurse, a would-be duelist at ninety-two, and an extravagant liar; Aunt Prudence Hecklebury, the ancient and indubitably virgin reformer; Fothergil Finch, the boy bard, and his nut friends; Archy, the literary cockroach; Mehitabel the Cat, a member of the oldest profession on earth; and Mr. Clem Hawley, the Old Soak, with his friends Al the Bartender, Jake Smith the Bootlegger, and so forth. The Old Soak was, for me, the luckiest find; I have got two or three books of prose and verse out of him, a dozen short stories, a play and a moving picture, and I discover even yet a certain public unwillingness to allow him to lapse into his ultimate alcoholic coma. Incidentally, he all but ruined my reputation. For a period of six years, after Lipton's closed, I never drank a drop; during that period the Old Soak was going strong in song and story, and it used to come back to me from every side that I was an old soak myself. (p. 60)

From the Sun I went to the Tribune, but before I did so I took a six weeks' vacation and wrote as much good stuff as I could, so as to start in on the Tribune with a smash. They syndicated my stuff to twenty papers throughout the country, eight or ten being papers of the first importance. For two years and a half, on the Tribune, I did better stuff than I'd ever done before.

Then I struck a spell where I couldn't go on. I told the editor and proprietors. They were very liberal; they offered me as long a rest as, and any assistance, I wanted. I was nervously ill; it became an obsession with me that I must quit or die. I got to seeing that column as a grave, twenty-three inches long, into which I buried a part of myself every day—a part that I tore, raw and bleeding, from my brain. It became a nightmare. Finally Mr. Ogden Reid, the proprietor of the Tribune, seeing that I really couldn't go on, and was not just being stubborn about it, very kindly canceled my contract, which still had three years to run, and I went away from there.

Within two months I wanted to do a column again, and was able to, and I've had to fight against the craving ever since. But it grows less with time—and never will I yield, so help me! I shall be firm till the end comes and I go away from here forever. (p. 62)

> *Don Marquis, "Confessions of a Reformed Columnist," in* The Saturday Evening Post *(reprinted with permission from* The Saturday Evening Post © *1928),*

Vol. 201, Nos. 25 and 26, December 22 and December 29, 1928, pp. 6-7, 53; 59-62.

CHRISTOPHER MORLEY (essay date 1939)

My thesis is that [Don Marquis] is our closest spiritual descendant of Mark Twain (the Old Soak would say descended off of Mark Twain). I suggest the idea to anyone who desiderates a rewarding study in literary ramification. I attempt here only to give something of the psychic background for such an essay. (p. xiv)

[The] subtle psychological observation that the things that actually happen to us are often wretchedly unrepresentative of our true selves is one to which Marquis often recurs. But I want to make plain that I think the twelve years of column writing in New York, theoretically the worst possible vehicle for a finely imaginative talent, were in fact magnificent. There, with increasing power, his essential originality came through. (p. xix)

In the recurrent hodiernity of the Sun Dial, from 1913 to 1922 in the New York *Evening Sun,* six days a week, bedeviled by a million interruptions and beclamored by all the agreeable rattles, the social riveters who gang round a man trying to work, Marquis created something utterly his own. It was as racy of our day as Addison and Steele's *Spectator* of theirs. I have said before, the American press has much to apologize for—more all the time with its increasing elements of what Lewis Carroll called Uglification, Distraction, and Derision—but much can also be forgiven when you think of the newspapers, the *Sun* and the New York *Tribune,* that saw Don's quality and gave him free hand.

From the files of the column came his book of prefaces; then that notable series of philosophic ruminations called **The Almost Perfect State;** the volumes of verse; the soliloquies of the Old Soak; and the adventures of archy and mehitabel. These things were born in the rough and tumble of a newspaper office; I remember that in the early days of the Sun Dial, when the paper moved from Park Row to Nassau Street, Don's typewriter desk got lost in the skirmish; so for some years he rattled out his daily stint with his machine perched on an upended packing case. This box had stenciled on it the statement 1 GROSS TOM CAT, which meant Tomato Catsup, but became by legend the first suggestion of mehitabel.

In a daily column, necessarily a great deal of matter is of ephemeral reference. A proportion of Marquis's most brilliant work in those years was oblique comment on public affairs. In those days, when anything happened, I give you my word, most of us didn't consult the leading editorials to know what to think. The almost universal reflex, in New York at any rate, was Let's see what Don says about it. I'm not saying that I always agreed, then or now, with Don's notions; but every so often he would turn on some particular fog of hooey and cut it with a blade that would divide floating silk. With a magic that seemed like that of Alice going through the mirror, suddenly we saw the whole furniture of affairs from the other side. For instance, when President Wilson brusquely dismissed his Secretary of State, Mr. Lansing, and Marquis burlesqued it by dismissing archy. There had been no such commentator on public affairs since Mr. Dooley; they don't come often. But it is only too characteristic of the Solemn Skullworkers that because many of Marquis's pungent comments on the human comedy were put in the form of soliloquies by the Old Soak

or by archy the roach they could not recognize their high coefficient of seriousness.

archy the roach began as a "dee-vice" of scoff against the vers libre poets who were pallidly conspicuous some thirty years ago. But that idea was soon forgotten. mehitabel the corybantic cat, with her doctrine of *toujours gai,* came on the scene to provide lyric spasms; archy became less the clown and more the skeptic. The roach and the cat, by their humble station in life and the lowliness of their associates, provided an admirable vantage for merciless joshing of everything biggity. (pp. xx-xxii)

The laughter in **Chapters for the Orthodox** is sometimes cerebral, sometimes violently of the midriff, but those who will take pains to explore under the superficial shock will find it always the laughter of a friend.

In short, the book is devout to the point of scandal. . . . Marquis once remarked that he had a great idea: he was going "to dramatize some of Bernard Shaw's plays." What he did in **Chapters for the Orthodox** had something of the same double-edged riposte: by taking ticklishly beautiful things with simple seriousness he explodes (in shattering laughter) the towering falsehoods of our genteel imposture. And then humorously rebuilds them, knowing well that by make-believe we live. (p. xxv)

[You] will find in Marquis and Mark Twain temperamental affinity. You will observe it in their fundamental comedian's instinct to turn suddenly, without warning, from the beautiful to the grotesque, or vice versa. You will find it in a rich vein of anger and disgust, turning on the genteel and cruel hypocrisies with the fury of a child or an archangel. You will find it in a kindly and respectful charity to the underdog: they are both infracaninophiles. You will find it in their passionate interest in religion and philosophy—with which is joined a blandly mischievous delight in shocking those for whom shocking is good. You will find it in their habitual employment of a devastating Anglo-Saxonism of speech and epithet. And finally you'll observe that both had a keen (and somewhat ham) dramatic sense, which Marquis expressed in plays and Mark Twain in his superlative performances on the lecture platform.

But there is one quality in Don that Mark never had—or at any rate it was only latent in Mark. Don is a poet, and a poet of high technical dexterity. He remarked once that publishing a volume of verse was like dropping a rose petal down the Grand Canyon and waiting for the echo. One reason why the echo has been little audible is that he has puzzled the critics by writing verse of so many different kinds. His gamut has run from lyrics of the most serious and tender mood to the genial fooling of **Noah an' Jonah an' Cap'n John Smith** or the farcical **Famous Love Affairs** or the sardonic ferocity of the Savage Sonnets. (p. xxvi)

Don Marquis was, regardless of mediocre work done under pressure, a deeply mercurial intuitive artist and passionately concerned with the ardors and problems of art. A human being so largely and kindly planned moves always in widening rings of irony. It was tragic to realize that he, who uttered so many genial shouts in praise of idleness, was actually broken by overwork. He was, if I ever saw one, a victim of the constantly tightening strain and pressure of our present way of living. There was, in the last two years (after a cerebral stroke), nothing left of him but the look in his eyes, and it was grim to speculate how much he realized of what had happened. I cannot help thinking that he had a very special message to younger artists, a message which was implicit in many of his seemingly jocular paragraphs. It was this: energy is not endless, better hoard it for your own work. Be intangible and hard to catch; be secret and proud and inwardly unconformable. Say yes and don't mean it; pretend to agree; dodge every kind of organization, and evade, elude, recede. Be about your own affairs, as you would also forbear from others at theirs, and thereby show your respect for the holiest ghost we know, the creative imagination. I read him wrong unless I see that cry in many a passage. Read, and perhaps be startled by, the angry trio of sonnets called *A Gentleman of Fifty Soliloquizes* (which he wrote several years before reaching that age). (pp. xxvii-xxviii)

Of this man, more than of any I have known, the great seventeenth-century words apply—words three centuries old and still the most expressive of masculine love and fellowship. I change only the name—*O rare Don Marquis*. (p. xxx)

> *Christopher Morley, in his introduction to his* Letters of Askance *(copyright, 1939, by Christopher Morley; reprinted by permission of Harper & Row, Publishers, Inc.), J. B. Lippincott Company, 1939 (and reprinted in* The Best of Don Marquis *by Don Marquis, Doubleday & Company, Inc., 1946, xiii-xxx).*

BERNARD DeVOTO (essay date 1950)

[Don Marquis's *Prefaces*] is a collection of prefaces, none of them longer than one newspaper column, to unwritten books. The last page is a "Preface to a Book of Prefaces," which says that this book is not precisely what the author intended it to be and that as a matter of fact his books never are. The next one, he is determined, is going to be a Volume with a Moral Purpose, "but it may turn out to be a Volume with a Moral Porpoise. Things of that sort happen to us." . . . (p. 66)

[E. B. White remarked] that when he edited an anthology of humor which had about a dozen classifications in it, Don seemed to fit them all. Mr. White ends by deciding that at bottom he was a poet. Yes, for you need a dozen classifications for his poetry, but again no, for you need a dozen more for his prose. (p. 67)

Here I was going to support my point by some quotations from *The Old Soak* but I find it has disappeared from my shelves. Don's books have a way of doing that. . . . Well, we have got to make room somewhere for *The Old Soak* and, as Mr. White remembers, there is *The Almost Perfect State.*

It is the damnedest book, but which of Don's books isn't? You learn from it that the soul comes just down to the midriff. You run into superbly angry outcries against man's nature and man's fate, usually with topspin and usually in the vernacular he had forged and burnished from the current slang. At least fifteen different ways of establishing the Almost Perfect State are explored in detail, but there are going to be no reformers in it for it is better to behead a man than to reform him, and the inhabitants are going to be equally divided between radicals and conservatives who will never work at either trade. . . . Dialogues so exquisite and cockeyed that partial quotation would spoil them are scattered through the text, and so are bits of Don's verse, played on every instrument from a violin to a kazoo. At intervals the way is cleared for another instalment of his theory of history, that the decadence of peoples and the fall of nations can always be traced to baked beans. So the book carries an appendix which begins, "If you *will* eat beans, here is the way to prepare them." . . . (pp. 67-8)

A year or so ago I tossed an allusion to Hermione into a review of a silly book; at least one scarred veteran of her era was soothed by it, for he wrote and told me so. Mr. White, though I gather he doesn't think these days any less preposterous, says that that dewy age was "pleasantly preposterous." It was at that, but Hermione is with us still, and Fothergil Finch, and her whole Group. Their stuff is in a different key from the original one; but only the key ever changes, the melody is the same forever and one of Don's agents even turned it up in king tut ank amen s time. Hermione still thinks that the Bhagavad Gita is simply *wonderful* and she thinks Tagore is too, though he is using an alias now. It still comes back to her "again and again how Primitive I am in some ways"; and "What would modern thought be without Subtlety?" (p. 69)

But Mr. White is right: it is the poet we come back to in the end. . . . Throughout the *Sun Dial,* throughout the books, you keep coming on verse that delights you and frequently holds you breathless while you watch a jagged and vertiginous imagination shoot through the air like a skyrocket, giving off odd-shaped and slightly drunken stars of gold. . . . But a clear, disturbing music comes through the oddest contexts; and maybe you had better look up those contexts, and some crystalline images, and the last four sonnets [of *Sonnets to a Red-Haired Lady*], before you decide what classification Don Marquis fits. I'd be willing to waive taxonomy, if some scholar would turn up fifty unpublished ones, or even two.

There are other sonnet sequences but this one is the best. Let's admit that some of Don's verse is tolerably bad; I could never like, for instance, the variations on brains, eyeballs, poached eggs, and pickled onions as interchangeable parts. But you can never be sure. The most innocent-appearing start may presently pull the rug out from under your feet as **"The Country Barber Shop,"** or as **"God and Magog"** may bump you dizzily to the edge of mania. Or a trite line suddenly breaks in a curve and gives you a glimpse of something dreadful or insane or damned, or a glimpse of beauty from the murky fire-opal that was Don's mind.

But Archy and Mehitabel have everything. All of them that has survived newsprint is in the book Mr. White has introduced, *the lives and times of archy and mehitabel*. . . . There has never been anything like Archy and Mehitabel and there never will be. Don Marquis got all his rich and strange talent into a cockroach who had the literary urge because his soul was that of a *vers libre* poet, and a cat on her ninth life who had been Cleopatra and many other adventurous, unlucky dames but who was always a lady in spite of hell. Only fantasy was wide or versatile enough to contain him; his mind kept escaping through cracks in the sane, commonplace world out into dimensions that were loops and whorls and mazes of the unpredictable. And he would not stay put. (pp. 69-71)

Simply, [Don Marquis] was wonderful to read in those "pleasantly preposterous" days and reads better now. I have difficulty in remembering the names and books of a good many writers of that time who got the right certificates with red wax seal and dangling ribbons, and my inability is pretty widespread. But no one who ever read Don Marquis has forgotten him. . . . (p. 72)

Let us avoid offense by calling it literature, which is a uniform substance that reacts dependably to standard tests, whereas Don Marquis is always slipping through your fingers. But the shelf his books stand on is not crowded. There is a small bulk of writing, winnowed out from the massive and rewarding, that people insist on reading for its own sake, regardless. They have always held it more precious than rubies and if it isn't literature, then literature be damned. (p. 73)

Bernard DeVoto, "Almost Toujours Gai" (originally published in Harper's, *Vol. 200, No. 1198, March 1950), in his* The Easy Chair *(copyright 1945, 1946, 1947, 1948, 1949, 1950, 1951, 1952, 1953, 1954, 1955, by Bernard DeVoto; reprinted by permission of Houghton Mifflin Company), Houghton Mifflin, 1955, pp. 65-73.*

E. B. WHITE   (essay date 1950)

Among books of humor by American authors, there are only a handful that rest solidly on the shelf. [*The Lives and Times of Archy and Mehitabel*], hammered out at such awful cost by the bug hurling himself at the keys, is one of those books. It is funny, it is wise, it is tender, and it is tough. The sales do not astound me; only the author astounds me, for I know (or think I do) at what cost Don Marquis produced these gaudy and irreverent tales. He was the sort of poet who does not create easily; he was left unsatisfied and gloomy by what he produced; day and night he felt the juices squeezed out of him by the merciless demands of daily newspaper work; he was never quite certified by intellectuals and serious critics of belles lettres. He ended in an exhausted condition—his money gone, his strength gone. Describing the coming of Archy in the Sun Dial column of the New York *Sun* one afternoon in 1916, he wrote: "After about an hour of this frightfully difficult literary labor he fell to the floor exhausted, and we saw him creep feebly into a nest of the poems which are always there in profusion." In that sentence Don Marquis was writing his own obituary notice. After about a lifetime of frightfully difficult literary labor keeping newspapers supplied with copy, he fell exhausted. (p. xvii)

The device of having a cockroach leave messages in his typewriter in the *Sun* office was a lucky accident and a happy solution for an acute problem. Marquis did not have the patience to adjust himself easily and comfortably to the rigors of daily columning, and he did not go about it in the steady, conscientious way that (for example) his contemporary Franklin P. Adams did. Consequently Marquis was always hard up for stuff to fill his space. . . . Marquis, cramped by single-column width, produced his column largely without outside assistance. He never assembled a hard-hitting bunch of contributors and never tried to. He was impatient of hard work and humdrum restrictions, yet expression was the need of his soul. (It is significant that the first words Archy left in his machine were "expression is the need of my soul".)

The creation of Archy, whose communications were in free verse, was part inspiration, part desperation. It enabled Marquis to use short (sometimes very, very short) lines, which fill space rapidly, and at the same time it allowed his spirit to soar while viewing things from the under side, insect fashion. Even Archy's physical limitations (his inability to operate the shift key) relieved Marquis of the toilsome business of capital letters, apostrophes, and quotation marks, those small irritations that slow up all men who are hoping their spirit will soar in time to catch the edition. Typographically, the *vers libre* did away with the turned or runover line that every single-column practitioner suffers from.

Archy has endeared himself in a special way to thousands of poets and creators and newspaper slaves, and there are reasons for this beyond the sheer merit of his literary output. The details of his creative life make him blood brother to writing men. He cast himself with all his force upon a key, head downward. So do we all. And when he was through his labors, he fell to the floor, spent. He was vain (so are we all), hungry, saw things from the under side, and was continually bringing up the matter of whether he should be paid for his work. He was bold, disrespectful, possessed of the revolutionary spirit (he organized the Worms Turnverein), was never subservient to the boss yet always trying to wheedle food out of him, always getting right to the heart of the matter. And he was contemptuous of those persons who were absorbed in the mere technical details of his writing. "The question is whether the suff is literature or not." That question dogged his boss, it dogs us all. This book—and the fact that it sells steadily and keeps going into new editions—supplies the answer.

In one sense Archy and his racy pal Mehitabel are timeless. In another sense, they belong rather intimately to an era—an era in American letters when this century was in its teens and its early twenties, an era before the newspaper column had degenerated. (pp. xviii-xix)

The days of the Sun Dial were, as one gazes back on them, pleasantly preposterous times and Marquis was made for them, or they for him. *Vers libre* was in vogue, and tons of souped-up prose and other dribble poured from young free-verse artists who were suddenly experiencing a gorgeous release in the disorderly high-sounding tangle of non-metrical lines. Spiritualism had captured people's fancy also. Sir Arthur Conan Doyle was in close touch with the hereafter, and received frequent communications from the other side. Ectoplasm swirled around all our heads in those days. (It was great stuff, Archy pointed out, to mend broken furniture with.) Souls, at this period, were being transmigrated in Pythagorean fashion. It was the time of "swat the fly," dancing the shimmy, and speakeasies. Marquis imbibed freely of this carnival air, and it all turned up, somehow, in Archy's report. Thanks to Archy, Marquis was able to write rapidly and almost (but not quite) carelessly. In the very act of spoofing free verse, he was enjoying some of its obvious advantages. And he could always let the chips fall where they might, since the burden of responsibility for his sentiments, prejudices, and opinions was neatly shifted to the roach and the cat. It was quite in character for them to write either beautifully or sourly, and Marquis turned it on and off the way an orchestra plays first hot, then sweet.

Archy and Mehitabel, between the two of them, performed the inestimable service of enabling their boss to be profound without sounding self-important, or even self-conscious. Between them, they were capable of taking any theme the boss threw them, and handling it. . . . It seems to me [illustrator George] Herriman deserves much credit for giving the right form and mien to these willful animals. They possess (as he drew them) the great soul. It would be hard to take Mehitabel if she were either more catlike, or less. She is cat, yet not cat; and Archy's lineaments are unmistakably those of poet and pest.

Marquis moved easily from one form of composition to another. In this book you will find prose in the guise of bad *vers libre*, poetry that is truly free verse, and rhymed verse. Whatever fiddle he plucked, he always produced a song. (pp. xx-xxii)

Marquis was by temperament a city dweller, and both his little friends were of the city: the cockroach, most common of city bugs; the cat, most indigenous of city mammals. Both, too, were tavern habitués, as was their boss. Here were perfect transmigrations of an American soul, this dissolute feline who was a dancer and always the lady, *toujours gai*, and this troubled insect who was a poet—both seeking expression, both vainly trying to reconcile art and life, both finding always that one gets in the way of the other. Their employer, in one of his more sober moods, once put the whole matter in a couple of lines.

> My heart has followed all my days
> Something I cannot name . . .

Such is the lot of poets. Such was Marquis's lot. Such, probably, is the lot even of bad poets. But bad poets can't phrase it so simply. (pp. xxiii-xxiv)

> *E. B. White, "Introduction" (copyright © 1950 by Doubleday & Company, Inc.; reprinted by permission of the publisher), in* The Lives and Times of Archy & Mehitabel *by Don Marquis, Doubleday & Company, Inc., 1950, pp. xvii-xxiv.*

HAMLIN L. HILL (essay date 1961)

Carl Van Doren suggested that Marquis "smacks of the American soil. . . . If his methods suggest the cartoonist of the comic strip, so do they suggest the older tradition of native humor as it descends from Jack Downing and David Crockett to Artemus Ward and Mark Twain. He is robust, hilarious, given to vast exaggeration; capable of vituperative outburst" [see excerpt above]. These qualities in Marquis's humor, particularly in the Archy and Mehitabel stories, are largely absent from other contemporary humorists because they are derived from sources not utilized by [Robert Benchley, James Thurber, or S. J. Perelman], for example. Marquis used the techniques and methods of native American humor, especially as he learned them from Joel Chandler Harris; and an examination of this indebtedness not only adds an important link in the continuity of that type of humor, but it also explains in part the neglect Marquis has suffered and the decline into which his reputation has fallen. (p. 78)

The very fact that Marquis was writing humor for a newspaper column joins him with some of the most important figures in native American humor. . . . Marquis long afterwards confessed that "when I was a kid . . . I read, every day, Eugene Field's column in a Chicago paper; and later George Ade's sketches, and I decided I wanted to do something like that." In 1907, he got his chance, as a columnist for *Uncle Remus's Magazine*, which Harris edited from 1907 until the summer of 1908. Marquis [was] always grateful for the opportunity to write for Harris. . . . In that column, "A Glance in Passing," Marquis was, as Harris had originally been, "a commentator on current events rather than a . . . story-teller." In one issue . . . , for example, he commented on the defeat of Georgia's governor Hoke Smith, on spiritualism, and on the danger of July Fourth celebrations; the next month he devoted paragraphs to presidential candidate Taft, to socialism, prohibition, and the Georgia penal system. (pp. 78-9)

Marquis was familiar with the aspects of native American humor which the Uncle Remus stories embodied; Harris printed a number of the stories in the magazine, those that were later collected into *Uncle Remus and the Little Boy*. . . . And Marquis was not merely in contact with Harris and his Uncle Remus material, but he was also sensitive to the qualities which made the Uncle Remus tales certain of fame, as he pointed out in a perceptive tribute on the occasion of the elder humorist's death: "This sense of the basic kinship of all things which exist is very familiar in all his writings, it is the quality which makes his 'creeturs' half human, sympathetic, understandable characters, instead of merely caricatures of animals or stories about animals."

After Harris's death in the summer of 1908, Marquis was asked to accept a reduction both in salary and in column space; so he decided to leave his job, and the column for August, 1908, was his last regular contribution to *Uncle Remus's Magazine*. But when he left, he took with him an intimate knowledge of Harris's techniques and literary devices, a knowledge that would be put to use on almost every page of *the lives and times of archy and mehitabel*.

Marquis's basic and most apparent similarity to Harris is of course in the technique of humanization of animals. Within the Uncle Remus stories there is a community of animals, which, as Harris felicitously put it, are "just enough human to be humorous." . . . Marquis's animals are human too, literally: Archy and Freddy the Rat are transmigrated *vers libre* poets, Mehitabel claims she was Cleopatra, and one of Mehitabel's beaux was François Villon. Archy's world is populated, in addition, by countless humanized insects, spiders, lady bugs, dogs, and Mehitabel's other boy friends.

Not only are both Uncle Remus's and Archy's worlds inhabited by humanized animals, but each has a somewhat bloodthirsty moral code. (pp. 81-2)

Harris utilized in the Uncle Remus fables two structural techniques, the frame and the dramatic monologue. Actually, they worked something like a double framework. In the first frame, the style was normal and the scene was set for the Uncle Remus story. Harris himself was narrating. The second framework was Uncle Remus's dramatic monologue, his introductory remarks to the story. And finally there was the fable itself. Except that the first frame was not always included, the formula was an introductory frame in normal diction and grammar, a frame in the form of a dramatic monologue by the story-teller, and the story. It was an ideal device for characterization, contrast, and humorous incongruities.

This is exactly the formula which Marquis employed in the Archy stories. Frequently, as in the Uncle Remus tales, the first frame was missing; but the device was utilized in twenty-seven of the stories in *the lives and times of archy and mehitabel*. In this frame, Marquis himself intrudes into the story, comments on Archy, explains the roach's whereabouts, and even questions or converses with Archy. In the second frame Archy, like Uncle Remus, reveals his "ways of thinking, of looking at things." . . . Just as Harris did, Marquis used the "dramatic monologue as a principal means of character revelation, though brief descriptions . . . interpolated throughout the stories add to the graphic presentation."

Another similarity between Uncle Remus and Archy is the predilection for proverbial sayings. Throughout *the lives and times of archy and mehitabel* there are sections devoted to short epigrammatic sayings, many of which are in the tradition of Uncle Remus's "Plantation Proverbs." Archy's maxims are from his own world and environment; they comment on the servant problem, prohibition, monkey glands, Einstein, unemployment, and governmental bureaucracy. They rely on the animal world, using ants, bees, fleas, and roaches for their analogies. In the same manner, Uncle Remus's proverbs utilize possums, moles, hogs, bees, mules, dogs, chickens, jay-birds, coons, and black-snakes. . . . Marquis uses in these proverbs a homespun, provincial quality which has antecedents more in the native tradition of Harris than, say, Twain's *Pudd'nhead Wilson's Calendar* or Josh Billings' *Sayings*. (pp. 83-5)

Marquis also employed other devices in *the lives and times of archy and mehitabel* which, though not relating specifically to Harris, were in the peculiar tradition of native American humor, and which were not in common use by other contemporary humorists. In employing the epistolary form, the humorous letter, Marquis was using a device that had worked for Down East humorists like Seba Smith and Charles A. Davis in Downing letters and James Russell Lowell in the *Biglow Papers,* for Southwest humorists such as William Tappan Thompson in the Major Jones series, and for literary comedians like David Ross Locke in the Petroleum Vesuvius Nasby papers. Political and social satire, euphemism, exaggeration, understatement, and some of the elements of the tall tale all enter into the patterns of Marquis's humor. (pp. 85-6)

But Marquis's humor was nevertheless in some respects difficult for the average reader, the one to whom native humor had been primarily aimed for over a century. In spite of its native qualities, the orthographic high-jinks in the Archy stories presented obstacles to that audience that was applauding the other twentieth-century vestige of native American humor, Will Rogers. Even so, the elements of native humor in *the lives and times of archy and mehitabel* so coalesced that those two characters belong, possibly, at the end of the gallery of humorous characters which began with Major Jack Downing and proceeded through Simon Suggs, Sut Lovingood, Artemus Ward, Josh Billings, and Uncle Remus. And the creation of a lasting humorous character is an accomplishment of which few contemporary humorists can boast. (p. 86)

> *Hamlin L. Hill, "Archy and Uncle Remus: Don Marquis's Debt to Joel Chandler Harris," in* The Georgia Review *(copyright, 1961, by the University of Georgia), Vol. XV, No. 1, Spring, 1961, pp. 78-87.*

EDWARD ANTHONY (essay date 1962)

Greenwich Village was very much in the news in those days. Marquis decided to see for himself. He had written that one of the wonderful things about New York was that everything was so neatly departmentalized—there was a cloak-and-suit area, a jewelry district, a big fish market, a neighborhood devoted to the fur business, etc., etc.—and if you wanted to look over the latest thing in pseudo-culture you could go to Greenwich Village. (p. 169)

[After a few] trips to Greenwich Village Marquis launched a eries in "The Sun Dial" that was destined for fame—**"Hermione and Her Little Group of Serious Thinkers."**

The Hermione series had none of the angry overtones of [his introductory poem about the Village] and therefore had more bite. Marquis returned to the device that enabled him to achieve his most felicitous effects: kidding. Occasionally the spoofing was rough-and-tumble but in the main it was good-natured, doing its deadliest work when the writing was blandest. Which is another way of saying that Marquis, in satirizing current fads and fancies, was at his best as a deadpan comic.

Pseudo-intellectuals, Marquis thought and wrote, were Old Stuff. There was nothing new about charlatanry in the arts; but never had he seen it so lavishly practiced. And never had he known it to be so accessible. It was as great a convenience,

he told friends, as an established red-light district. If you were in the mood for a cultural bordello you knew just where to go. Here in the New Bohemia the seven lively arts daily grew livelier if not lovelier. (p. 171)

Marquis's timing was good. He created Hermione at the psychological moment. She was a much-needed antidote; and soon she was being widely quoted. New Yorkers who had suffered through endless stretches of the "futile Piffledom" Marquis described in his opening blast hailed her and joyfully used her pet phrases as a device for kidding the phony in every field.

It wasn't long before Appleton and Company . . . asked for a book. It was published in 1917 and gratefully received by most of the reviewers. The title was the same as the one Marquis used in his column except that it was split into title and subtitle, as follows:

Hermione
And Her Little Group of Serious Thinkers

It was made up of sixty of the Hermione pieces that Marquis had published in the *Sun*, each one making its own particular point. Here are some typical chapter heads:

> Vibrations
> The Swami Brandranath
> Aren't the Russians Wonderful?
> Soul Mates
> Literature
> Mama Is So Mid-Victorian
> Beautiful Thoughts
> Will the Best People Receive the Superman
>   Socially?
> The Parasite Woman Must Go!
> Fothergil Finch Tells of His Revolt against
>   Organized Society
> On Being Other-Worldly
> Psychic Power
> The Little Group Gives a Pagan Masque
> The Bourgeois Element
> The Japanese Are Wonderful, If You Get
>   What I Mean

In the book-publishing world, whose editors, readers, and sundry other workers had suffered through so much of the New Literature, Hermione's pet expression, "if you get what I mean," became a shibboleth.

Hermione is still an impressive book. Flip it open almost anywhere and you come up with a reasonably good lampoon, though, of course, some of the things Marquis satirized have long since been laughed out of court. (pp. 172-73)

> *Edward Anthony, in his* O Rare Don Marquis: A Biography *(copyright © 1962 by Edward Anthony; reprinted by permission of Doubleday & Company, Inc.),* Doubleday, 1962, 670 p.

NORRIS W. YATES (essay date 1964)

One of the ironies of Marquis' career is that he sometimes worried about being remembered mainly for creating a cockroach. The irony is compounded by the casualness with which he created Archy the roach and his companion, Mehitabel the cat. . . . Archy and Mehitabel appeared intermittently in "The Sun Dial." At first Marquis was merely using this humorous free verse as an easy way of filling his insatiable column with short lines when he was hard up for other material. The pegs on which the first Archy poems were hung were free verse and reincarnation. During the poetic renaissance of 1912-1920, *vers libre,* including the "Imagism" of Amy Lowell and translations from the work of Rabindranath Tagore—two poets whose writing Marquis particularly detested—attracted much attention. Reincarnation too was in the public eye. John Kendrick Bangs, George Ade, and Wallace Irwin were among the humorists who had already made game of spiritualism, transmigration, and other ventures into the occult. Marquis' prose introduction to the first Archy poem contains a dig at Madam Blavatsky the theosophist, and it may well be that her particular version of transmigration (borrowed largely from Pythagoras) supplied the egg from which Archy was hatched in the humorist's mind. (pp. 197-98)

In "The Coming of Archy," the columnist described how he arrived at the office earlier than usual one morning and found a roach jumping up and down on the keys. He couldn't work the capital shift key and had great difficulty operating the carriage mechanism. On reading what the bug had written, the columnist found,

> expression is the need of my soul
> i was once a vers libre bard
> but i died and my soul went into the body of a cockroach

These early themes of free verse and reincarnation were never entirely neglected, but Archy and his feline friend soon were commenting on many other matters and playing several other roles. Through these two waifs Marquis could express provocative and even iconoclastic views without giving offense to the Dagwoods who chuckled over their newspapers on subway or streetcar. Who would mind what an alley-cat and a "poor little cockroach" had to say? Moreover, consistency did not bother Marquis much, and he freely changed the roles of his characters to fit his mood of the day. Archy most commonly vacillates among three separate though occasionally merging roles: the wise fool, the solid citizen, and the trickster-outcast. As the fool he is versifier, hobohemian, philosopher, and vessel of conceit. As middle-class citizen he waxes cautious in judgment, conventional in morals, and middlebrow in taste. As social outcast he is cynical, and the values he emphasizes are the naturalistic ones of bare survival.

Occasionally he plays a fourth role, that of a columnist very like the author himself. E. B. White lists several ways in which Archy's behavior resembled that of his creator, but Marquis usually tried to hind behind a mask of self-mockery in whatever role he chose for Archy at the moment. Marquis could thereby offer certain values to be considered seriously and yet, at the same time, make fun of them as mere prejudices or passing moods:

> please forgive
> the profundity of these
> meditations
> whenever i have nothing
> particular to say
> i find myself always
> always plunging into cosmic
> philosophy
> or something

The note of self-burlesque here is relatively moderate; on occasion Marquis could mock at himself as bitterly as [Ring] Lardner. Cosmic philosophy was actually one of Don Marquis' main interests, but through the roach he often pretended to apologize for his indulgence.

As bohemian poet-fool, Archy is a well of self-pity and envy. In him stirs the defense-mechanism of incompetents of all kinds:

> gods i am pent in a cockroach
> i with the soul of a dante
> am mate and companion of fleas
> i with the gift of a homer
> must smile when a mouse calls me pal
>
> (pp. 199-200)

As foolish poet and philosopher, Archy is flattered when the author seeks his opinions on astronomy, archaeology, evolution, life, death, prophets, politics, literature, and many other complex topics. In delivering his views, he sometimes dodges from role to role within the same column. (p. 200)

Marquis often uses the "numbskull" technique of having a character speak ineptly in favor of that which the author wishes to satirize. By having Archy declare his intent "to see if i cannot reform insects in general" as a "missionary extraordinary" to "the little struggling brothers" in his phylum, Marquis hits at overzealous missionaries spreading the American brand of "civilization" in primitive lands. Through the same technique Marquis jabs at reformers in general, pontifical radio commentators (whom Archy impersonates as "the Cosmic Cockroach"), Senator Bilbo, technocracy, popular-science writers, and literary fads. Mehitabel too is a numbskull, in a different way. Through her crude assertions that she is refined, "still a lady in spite of h dash double l," Marquis satirizes all bumptious pretenders to social elevation. Further, because of these claims to refinement, the author's broader target, hypocrisy in general, is hit every time Mehitabel sings on a fencetop, allows herself to be gracefully seduced by a tom, scoops an eye out of that tom when the romance is over, or abandons her kittens to be drowned.

The actors' strike of 1919, and other labor troubles, gave Marquis a chance to portray both Archy and his boss as rogues and fools who speak in favor of that which the author is really against. Archy becomes a militant striker and his boss an arrogant, double-talking employer. (pp. 201-02)

When contrasted by the author with Mehitabel, Archy sometimes appears as a sober moralist. Concerning the cat's motto, "toujours gai," Archy muses,

> boss sometimes i think
> that our friend mehitabel
> is a trifle too gay

After Mehitabel has told him of how Percy the tomcat doublecrossed her, Archy moralizes, "i think / that mehitabel s unsheltered life sometimes / makes her a little sad." . . . As John Q. Citizen, Archy is always sensible enough, but not as penetrating as Mencken's sound thinker. Marquis is essentially on Archy's side, but rarely without mocking overtones. Archy in this role is a little pompous and is inclined to oversimplify problems. (pp. 202-03)

Not all of Marquis appears in Archy the wise fool or Archy the custodian of middle-class norms. Something of Marquis the dreamer, cynic, and questioner of norms, appears in the trickster who scuttles through many of the poems. The trickster-hero and outcast has many incarnations in world folklore, including Reynard the Fox of the medieval beast-epics, Anansé the spider of West African folktales, Br'er Rabbit in the stories of Uncle Remus, and Raven and Coyote in American Indian folk narrative. The trickster is weak physically and must live by his wits in an environment dominated by his enemies. He cannot afford to obey their rules and he is therefore a social outcast. As such, Archy knows "what family skeletons" hang in the closets of "the lordly ones." . . . [Marquis frequently used] Archy's outcast role to suggest that all men are in the same relation to nature (meaning, for Marquis, the cosmos) as the roach is to the hostile "society" of humans and other animals in which he skips precariously about. Men and insects are alike in being forced to obey universal natural law. The trickster is in part a means by which Marquis gave guarded expression to his skeptical naturalism, and this attitude, or rather group of attitudes, needs to be defined.

As outcast, Archy ponders four of the tenets held in common by most of the writers loosely termed naturalistic, from Émile Zola to Norman Mailer. First, nature is a perpetual struggle for survival. Archy demonstrates this in his own foot-to-mouth existence; he even has to scurry into the typewriter to avoid being eaten by Mehitabel. Second, nature is utterly indifferent to man. (pp. 205-06)

Third, man himself is merely an insignificant and inferior part of nature and shows it in his purblindness, irrationality, and pride. . . . Fourth, as a segment of nature, man is not free; his fate is predetermined by chance, heredity, and environment. Far from being "the captain of my / soul the master of my fate," Archy cannot even commit suicide—being only a roach, he is too light to kill himself by falling or by hanging. His plight is an allegory of man's unfreedom.

To make the hard lot of man bearable, Marquis through Archy suggests several possible attitudes. One is a somber hedonism. . . . Mehitabel's hedonism is more frenetic, but it too expresses one of Marquis' moods:

> i know that i am bound
> for a journey down the sound
> in the midst of a refuse mound
> but wotthehell wotthehell
> oh i should worry and fret
> death and i will coquette
> there s a dance in the old dame yet
> toujours gai toujours gai
>
> (pp. 207-08)

Archy had other attitudes toward nature and toward man as part of nature. After hearing "an elderly mother spider" bewail the use of fly swatters "what kills off all the flies," because "unless we eats we dies," he signs off with "yours for less justice / and more charity." In addition to having, in certain moods, compassion for all beings, Archy occasionally feels almost reconciled to nature's indifference. . . . He can even sing of the harmony and beauty to be found in nature along with the brutality. Man, he feels, has retained the brutality but lost the harmony and beauty. . . . Because he has lost his connection with the rest of nature, man has ruined his natural environment, the American "paradise / of timberland and stream," through "greed / and money lust," and "it won't be long / till earth is barren as the moon / and sapless as a mumbled bone." (pp. 208-09)

Despite the increasing bitterness of Marquis' writings after the middle twenties, a reverence for nature and an insistence on man's need to feel a harmonious identity with it recur in his work from first to last. . . . Marquis published *The Almost Perfect State,* a collection of pieces from his column that treated further of man's need to live in harmony with his nonhuman surroundings. (pp. 209-10)

The agrarianism of *The Almost Perfect State* shows how very American was Marquis' kind of naturalism. He may have been, temperamentally, a city-dweller, but in his longing for a simple agrarian society purged of commercialism and prudery, he exemplified a major literary tradition that included, despite their differences, Thoreau, John Burroughs, Mark Twain, Robert Frost, William Faulkner, E. B. White, and perhaps Will Cuppy, who called Marquis' utopia "probably the only one fit to live in." Like many city-dwellers, Marquis may have yearned also, at times, for the small town and green fields of his boyhood, in spite of the bitter memories that often crowded into his mind. . . . [A] pessimistic strain predominated in *The Almost Perfect State,* as it did elsewhere in Marquis' work and in the naturalistic writers of his time generally. Man *was* hopelessly separated from nature, and Marquis had no idea how to remedy the situation. He made clear that in *The Almost Perfect State* he was just getting his kicks through utopian speculation. (pp. 210-11)

In their hedonism, Archy and Mehitabel are both wise fools, but Mehitabel can play one role denied to Archy, that of the frowsier sort of flapper. As such, she is an instrument for satirizing the more lurid goings-on of unconventional womanhood, including famous actresses and movie stars, during the restless war years and the decade that followed. The ancient excuse for promiscuity—I was pure, but a villain ruined me—takes on new flavor in her mouth. . . . The rationale that true romance needs absolute freedom also is satirized through Mehitabel. She proclaims herself never "an adventuress" but "always free footed / archy never tied down to / a job or housework"—a follower of the "life romantic." After acquiring seven kittens in Hollywood by an unknown father, she neglects them and talks about her responsibilities to her career and how her art comes before motherhood—"an artist like me shouldn't really have offspring." The transparency of her excuses and the fact that she is only a cat after all, render her personification of the flapper as inoffensive as it is exaggerated and oversimplified.

A separate book could be written on women in twentieth-century American humor, especially the New Woman of the Progressive iconology. Next to the Archy poems, Marquis' liveliest work is the monologues collected as *Hermione and Her Little Group of Serious Thinkers*. . . . Hermione resembles those daughters and wives . . . [who have been] given money and leisure to waste. Her main interest is occultism in all its current phases—psychical research, New Thought, Cosmic Consciousness, "vibrations"—but she also falls for other fads that were in the news from about 1912 to 1916. . . . [In] rapid succession she and her Little Group take up spiritualism, eugenics, genetics, the superman, woman suffrage, welfare work, prison reform, and—with the help of the *vers libre* bard Fothergil Finch, "Poet of Revolt"—the more esoteric phases of the fine arts, including cubist painting, Gertrude Stein, and Sergei Diaghilev. She is an unconscious hypocrite in that she believes herself one of the "Leaders of Modern Thought" but is unaware of the unoriginality of her ideas and the irrelevance and triviality of her motivations. (pp. 211-13)

Behind the portrait of Hermione lie standards of sincerity, moderation, and common sense, all misapplied or absent in this girl. Politically, Marquis was at that time a Taft Republican, or rather merely an anti-Wilsonian, but the exaggerated and harmless nature of his version of the New Woman made it possible for both conservatives and liberals to be amused. Morally, Marquis has no grave criticism of Hermione except her pretentiousness. She is respectable but pretends to be daring; Mehitabel is disreputable but pretends to be a "lady." From his citadel of masculine common sense, Marquis satirized both types of erring female.

Largely in protest against prohibition, Marquis created a crackerbarrel philosopher in his column and put twenty-two of the sketches about him into *The Old Soak*. . . . The "Old Soak" also yarned and capered through a successful play of that title, [through a second book of sketches, *The Old Soak's History of the World,* and in magazine stories later included in *When the Turtles Sing* and *A Variety of People*]. . . . (pp. 213-14)

Clem Hawley, the Old Soak, lives out in Baycliff, Long Island, ostensibly a suburb of New York City but actually given a rural flavor that makes it indistinguishable from "Hazelton," Illinois, in [the semiautobiographical] *Sons of the Puritans*. In Marquis' fiction all the small towns are essentially the Walnut, Illinois, of his boyhood, as all of Mark Twain's fictional towns were Hannibal, Missouri. Clem's main activity is procuring enough bootleg liquor to keep himself moderately soused, though not sodden. Except for his interest in hootch, he is a bit like Will Rogers, who showed an appreciation of Marquis that was heartily returned. . . . (p. 214)

In his illiteracy and in his devotion to drink, he is the wise fool. In his tales and aphorisms he appears as the rustic oracle. In his economic stability and family difficulties, he is the solid citizen, and one sees again how traits associated with these three roles may be blended in a single character.

Even the use of several different comic masks gave incomplete expression to the contradictions in Marquis' personality. One of these contradictions was between the conventional lyricist and the humorous writer of free verse. "My heart has followed all my days / Something I cannot name," he wrote in *Dreams and Dust* . . ., his first book of serious verse. . . . In several books of poems, Marquis wrote lyrics in the sonnet form and in other traditional poetic molds. The more interesting of these poems were satirical, like some of the [*Sonnets to a Red-Haired Lady* and *Love Sonnets of a Cave Man*]. . . . The serious ones tended to be sentimental.

A related contradiction existed between Marquis' naturalism and his religious leanings. Most of his significant humor expresses his naturalistic, skeptical bent, and that side of Marquis has consequently received the most emphasis in this discussion. But Christopher Morley, a close friend, called him a "divinity student," and he even tried Christian Science for a short while. In his writing, Don's religious interest manifested itself in a number of short stories (notably those in *Chapters for the Orthodox*) and in *The Dark Hours,* a play about the Crucifixion into which Marquis put years of work—and which failed at the box office, though some reviewers were impressed by the printed version. This contradiction is only partially resolved in his early poem, **"The God-Maker, Man,"** where he avers that ". . . the gods are not / Unless we pray to them." . . . (pp. 214-15)

A third contradiction, related to the discrepancy between the serious lyricist and the comic free-versifier, is that between the romantic rebel and the plodding bourgeois. Marquis romanticized, or sentimentalized, the young, eager girl in revolt, in Ruby Tucker of *When the Turtles Sing* . . . and Sally Cass in *Off the Arm* . . . ; he even approved of Ruby's "a-takin' chances" that included leaving a worthless husband and uniting in joyous adultery with "a travellin' piano tuner." Likewise Marquis often endorsed the attempts of males to live their lives

in defiance of convention, like the free-loving patriarch Jason Tucker and the bohemian novelist Hugh Cass, and like those old loafers Noah and Jonah and Cap'n John Smith, who spend their time "strummin' golden harps, narreratin' myth." The adventures of some of these men and women are told by the Old Soak, and when Marquis is wearing the Old Soak's mask of wise fool, he is willing to live and let live, but the reckless Mehitabel gets severe treatment from Mr. Marquis when he speaks through Archy as solid citizen.

However, by casting Archy also in the role of trickster-outcast and by making the Old Soak a substantial citizen who rebels only against a few specific laws, Marquis could exploit if not resolve his inconsistent attitudes. He could be skeptic as well as dreamer, philosopher as well as vagabond, rebel as well as Rotarian—and above all, a somber humorist with a crooked smile. (p. 216)

> *Norris W. Yates, "The Many Masks of Don Marquis," in his* The American Humorist: Conscience of the Twentieth Century *(© 1964 by Iowa State University Press, Ames, Iowa 50010; reprinted by permission), Iowa State University Press, 1964, pp. 195-216.*

LOUIS HASLEY   (essay date 1971)

Don Marquis produced a score and a half of bewilderingly various novels, short stories, poems, satire, paragraphs, and dramas. Now in the fourth decade after his death, he is remembered almost solely for a trilogy in verse about a cockroach and a cat (but, oh, how joyfully remembered!), besides scattered pieces of satire and short fiction. Though the trilogy, *the lives and times of archy & mehitabel,* has become a classic in the literature of American humor, its outstanding prestige has, I believe, contributed to the unjust neglect of a substantial amount of Marquis's other writing.

In particular, I would have readers aware of the high enjoyment to be found in two of his sonnet sequences, along with random unrelated poems; in twenty or twenty-five outstanding short stories; in some excellent satire, as in *Hermione and Her Little Group of Serious Thinkers;* in a reverent and worthy drama of the Passion of Christ, *The Dark Hours;* and in a superb though unfinished novel, *Sons of the Puritans*. These, with *the lives and times of archy & mehitabel,* are the blessings and they are worth counting. (pp. 59-60)

Marquis's career may be taken as the paradigm of that of the journalist-litterateur, at least in our time and country. He feeds on the rich experiences and racy conditions of his daily journalistic rounds. The pressures of multitudinous events, the attraction of outpouring knowledge, the demands for a high standard of living, the opportunities for self-indulgence, the prevailing rivalry within and between classes, the caprice of fashion in art and manners, the attrition of the spirit in commercialism, the political and economic corruption, the kaleidoscope of change, the imminence or presence of war—all tend to breed a nervous restlessness that allows only a precarious, fingertip hold on reality and prevents sustained artistic achievement. (pp. 60-1)

[Marquis] wrote almost obsessively in prose and verse against Prohibition. Evolution was a frequent theme, as was the great American preoccupation with loss of innocence. He wrote a good deal of oblique commentary on public affairs. Though not so pervasively as in Thurber, there is an unmistakable strain of misogyny in his work. And he never ceased to speculate about theology. To the very end, as the Anthony biography well shows, mirth and disillusion, belief and skepticism, battled for possession of his mind.

Like Lardner, Marquis gained his extensive apprenticeship through his newspaper columns: the miscellaneous writing of verse, fictional sketches, and satire. Nevertheless his first book was a full-length novel, *Danny's Own Story.* . . . It was followed four years later, after his first book of poetry, by a second novel, *The Cruise of the Jasper B. Danny* is a land-based, episodic, picaresque, hidden-identity story that reads well but is under the heavy influence of *Huckleberry Finn* in theme, incidents, characters, and the psychology of adolescence. The second novel, *The Cruise of the Jasper B.,* is a wholly different, stylized performance, burlesquing the cloak-and-dagger detective story with as many preposterous clichés of situation and rhetoric as the nimble imagination of Marquis could marshal. It has much less to recommend it than the somewhat appealing odyssey of the waif in the earlier novel, *Danny's Own Story.*

Though Marquis's first of six collections of short stories did not appear till 1921, he had, years before, begun to establish his competence in this genre. An excellent one-volume selection of outstanding stories from the six volumes could readily be made. At least four stories were included in the distinguished annual O'Brien and O. Henry collections and fifteen or twenty more of equal distinction should be rescued from neglect.

In his overall work but also within the genre of the short story Marquis demonstrates an astonishing versatility. In the best single collection, *A Variety of People* . . . , the stories touch randomly in time from 1500 B.C. to the present. Singly, the temper of the stories is equally diverse, being stamped with realism, idealism, romanticism, melodrama, tragedy, or the grotesque. There are stories set in a rural environment, stories set in Manhattan, psychological stories, humorous stories, stories of burglary, a portrait of an old actor, a circus story, a Georgia hillbilly story. . . . Amidst Marquis's fine craftsmanship about the only deficiency discernible to the sensitive reader is the occasional lack of the intense assimilation of the author or narrator into several of these stories that would conceal the presence of the shaping imagination.

We may distinguish by subject three prominent kinds of stories scattered through the six volumes: the religious stories, the dog-boy stories, and the Irish O'Meara stories.

The theologically oriented stories are found principally in *Chapters for the Orthodox.* Whereas Eliot has declared that the world can't stand too much reality, Marquis declares it "can't stand too much spirituality." He scorns both those who are too righteous and those who feel that the Church and Christianity must placate the Devil in order to exist at all. For all their fanciful situations and characters, the polemic is arrestingly dramatized. (pp. 62-4)

What I have called the dog-boy stories must take high place in the Tom Sawyer tradition. Warm in the yeasty excitement of Midwestern boyhood adventure and humor, they are the best of the stories in the volume entitled *The Revolt of the Oyster.* Most of them are told by a mongrel dog, Spot, who owns a boy, Freckles. (p. 64)

In a wildly fanciful vein are the humorous Irish stories about "The O'Meara." Anxious to show his ancestors in a favorable light to his two doubting sons, Timothy O'Meara spins glistening stories of heroism and variegated prowess about several remote ancestors who he claims had the same name as his own. . . .

If these stories can re-establish Marquis as a gifted writer of both serious and humorous short fiction, it is nevertheless true that his most impressive work of fiction is a wholly serious novel, *Sons of the Puritans.* Its time span straddles the end of the last century and the beginning of this. Its setting, the small town of Hazelton, Illinois, provides a stifling, provincial religious atmosphere that constitutes a late but memorable chapter in the Revolt from the Village. Over-zealous churchgoers are counterpoised to Doctor Stuart and his daughter Barbara, who represent sympathetically the free-thinking element. (p. 65)

The novel, published posthumously in 1939, is unfortunately incomplete. Yet it is a sound, solid, interesting, and varied block of life. The notes Marquis left for its completion are not unlike an epilogue in an older novel. Implicit in the completed portion and expressed in the notes is once again an example of Marquis's lifelong balancing act on the wire between skepticism and belief. . . . Ultimately here, and probably in his final thought, Marquis seems to believe that God is the creation of each individual according to his need.

Marquis's ventures into playwrighting were a disappointment to him, for he says, "I was born stage-struck. . . . The stage to me is still the most glamorous thing in human life." His one success, which ran for a healthy 426 performances, was *The Old Soak,* produced in 1922 when sentimental nostalgia for the comradeship afforded by the Prohibition-banished old-time saloon gave it a special appeal. The character of Clem Hawley, the Old Soak, still retains a minor place in literature as not actually a drunkard but one whose devotion to alcoholic fellowship and endearing generosity of spirit superseded the practical concerns of work and family support. A second play, *The Dark Hours,* a work to which Marquis gave his sincerest efforts, deals with the Passion and death of Christ. It never achieved adequate production. As a reading experience it follows faithfully the orthodox Biblical presentation as to Christ's public life and death, while supplying some contextual circumstances and special insight into the mind of Judas. The play carries the urgency and import of its great theme with sympathetic reverence. The several other plays which Marquis wrote betray, as Simeon Strunsky pointed out in the New York *Times,* a lack of vigor for present-day dramaturgy. (p. 66)

It is in poetry that Marquis most fully realized his talent. From the derivative, immature first volume, *Dreams and Dust* . . . , to the three volumes of *the lives and times of archy & mehitabel* . . . , Marquis gradually sensitized his poetic skill and creative judgment till he carved out a work of humorous, satiric genius.

As with the short fiction, there is need of a "selected" volume to be culled out of Marquis's six volumes of "non-Archy" poems. A great proportion of these poems are in metrical verse. Of them, a small number are serious, delicate, but immaturely romantic lyrical effusions that can gracefully be passed by. Some other serious poems that are in conventional meters afford high pleasure, notably the group of thirty-four sonnets, "Savage Portraits," found in the best of these six volumes, *Poems and Portraits.* . . . These portraits are indeed savage, even though the satire is not without the wit of invective and colorful epithet. Among the portraits are those of Tood, "Pun-Hawker, Smirker, Smut-Wit, Wags' Review"; Froggles, the name dropper, who "knew celebrities"; Pink, who "might have been twice nothing, were he twins"; Polter, "a dribbling conduit through which slander flows"; and Klung, "unspecked of life,'' whose only fault was to have no fault at all. Of course other random serious poems deserve reprinting, such as **"The Heart of the Swamp,"** telling of a sinister murderous tryst between lovers; **"The Fellowship of Caiaphas,"** ironically contrasting Caiaphas's friends with the companions of Jesus; and **"A Princess of Egypt,"** pregnant with the somber Ozymandian perplexities of time and death and future life.

At its best, Marquis's metrical prowess (though it often lapsed through haste) was prodigious. He was a master of the intricate twenty-eight-line French ballade (three eight-line stanzas, a four-line stanza, or envoi, the whole limited to two rime sounds and the same refrain line at the end of each stanza). The meters employed in the many humorous poems are ingeniously varied. (pp. 68-9)

In the scores of Marquis's humorous metrical poems it is only too infrequently that he reaches that final plateau of precision, shape, imagery, pace, and surprise that brings off the poem triumphantly. While it is true that his capacity for self-criticism was erratic, one must conclude that through time pressures or through negligence he was often too easily satisfied. How one wishes that he could have spent the same amount of time on half the number of humorous poems that he wrote. The yield of fully satisfying poems would surely have been greatly increased.

Among the metrical humorous and satirical poems, few readers would want to miss the thirty-six sonnets, "stinging cocktails of song" in Christopher Morley's phrase, found in *Sonnets to a Red-Haired Lady and Famous Love Affairs*. . . . In them the language burlesques the romantic sonnet sequence by daringly intermixing romantic clichés with mocking slangy irreverence. (p. 69)

Though there are a number of excellent metrical poems in the three Archy volumes [*archy and mehitabel, archy's life of mehitabel, archy does his part*] . . . , the entire body of Archy poems is usually thought of as free verse. (pp. 69-70)

In his reincarnation Archy sees life now from the underside, a new vista for him equivalent to that of "the little man." Archy quickly makes the acquaintance of a free-living female cat, Mehitabel. Through Archy's former humanity and his low-pitched philosophizing, Marquis has set up a novel and forceful strategy for humor and satire. . . . The use of lower case typography, the absence of punctuation, and the occasional comic grammar are kin to the devices employed by the Literary Comedians of the post-Civil War era. Some of the separate Archy episodes use the box-within-a-box (framework) narration, so prevalent in old literature. Though Archy writes mostly in understatement, snippets of the frontier "brag" appear now and then. . . . The use of Archy as a mouthpiece is also akin to nineteenth-century pseudonymous humorous commentary (Artemus Ward, Josh Billings, etc.) that allows Marquis to be dissociated from a reader's adverse reactions to ideas put forth playfully or seriously.

A great canvas of life both as of the twenties and as of *sub specie aeternitatis* is unfolded in this masterpiece. Its humor is rich, warm, kind, and penetrating. It has social and political commentary. It does serious philosophical and theological probing. It examines evil and corruption and social injustice. . . . When an announcer asks, "Do you think the time is ripe for launching a third national political party in America?" Archy replies, "it is more than ripe it is rotten." As to Marxism, he asserts, "i always liked harpo and groucho but i could never see karl." (pp. 69-71)

When one looks back in summary over Marquis's life and writings, one sees, in almost everything important that he wrote, a profound and unflagging concern for the spirit. He tried—unsuccessfully, he felt—to be a Christian. (pp. 71-2)

In respect to temperament displayed in both his life and his work, he is much akin to Mark Twain. In self-education, conscience, Puritanism, saltiness of personality, philosophical and eschatological concerns, the untimely deaths of wives and children, comic invention, satire against hypocrisy and philistinism, didacticism—their similarities are legion, though no one will contend that the very real achievement of Marquis, substantial and memorable though it is, rivals that of Twain.

It is interesting that Marquis, as a writer of works cherished now for half a century, made no contributions to strictly literary technique, though there is originality in his manner of fleshing out old structures such as the sonnet form in "Savage Portraits" and in the *Sonnets to a Red-Haired Lady*. Several of his stories show modernity in their employment of psychological modes, though by far most follow long established conventions of the public, more external, type of fiction.

Of course the most distinctive manifestation of his many-sided genius is in his two incomparable creations, the philosophical cockroach, Archy, expressing the views, ruminations, and frustrations of the little man, and the indomitable Mehitabel, with her compulsive zest for the life corybantic. The poems in that trilogy, taken as outline, recapitulate the manners, conscience, and public questions of the two decades from 1915 to 1935. (pp. 72-3)

Louis Hasley, "Don Marquis: Ambivalent Humorist," in Prairie Schooner (reprinted from Prairie Schooner by permission of University of Nebraska Press; © 1971 by University of Nebraska Press), Vol. XLV, No. 1, Spring, 1971, pp. 59-73.

EDWARD A. MARTIN   (essay date 1975)

In Archy, Don Marquis created a mock-heroic image for the years from roughly 1910 to the mid-thirties. Although he died in 1937, his verse still appears in anthologies; two Archy books are in print; and a Marquis legend lingers in the minds of those who knew him or knew about him. A romantic whose closest archetype was probably Byron, he wanted, sometimes desperately, to succeed as a writer of heroic and lyric verse and prose. But he wrote best, and most successfully, when the ironic, satiric, or satanic mood was upon him. Like many satirists he could be both congenial and uncongenial, both smiling and savage. Like all satirists he had discovered the grave absurdity of his world, and he wrote about it in such a way that a concerned hostility could be expressed rather than repressed. His talent and his era combined to make him memorable as a satirist, even while he sought compulsively to transcend such a role. (p. 623)

Like the young Mencken, Marquis wanted first to be a poet; unlike Mencken he did not reject poetic yearnings as the folly of youth, but continued all his life to write and publish serious as well as satiric verse. Both were journalists; Marquis in fact made his reputation almost entirely as a newspaper columnist.

They were alike, too, in their curious mixture of Rabelaisian liberality and Puritan fastidiousness. Marquis may never have read and been directly influenced by Nietzsche, but he was in his Nietzschean individualism like Mencken, who had interpreted and often misinterpreted Nietzsche for his countrymen.

Both Mencken and Marquis sensed and hated the hypocrisy and repression of individuality that they found in humanitarian movements, especially in organized religions; both ridiculed the middle-class values that had been part of their upbringing. (p. 625)

Marquis shared the creative compulsions of many other Americans especially from the 1890s down to our own time. He must have been frustrated by the knowledge that younger men such as Hemingway and Fitzgerald had already conspicuously achieved by 1928 what he still hoped to achieve. Yet he had accomplished what he himself could never fully appreciate: the creation in Archy, the cockroach, of an enduring, ambivalent image of the poet as both myth-maker and myth-destroyer, as revealer of the absurdities of his time; as a figure of the light-weight defying gravity and precariously surviving in a dark urban world overrun by predators. While a cosmopolitan Archy shares Mencken's attitude of horror and mock hostility toward provincial life, there is also the oblique expression in his ridicule of a nostalgia for an insect Arden where snakes and birds don't eat bugs, a pastoral world where the penalty of Adam, and of Satan, is not felt. (p. 626)

The Archy and Mehitabel fables celebrate irrationality, which is a way of expressing hostility toward man and society. They reveal man's inadequacy before the terrors of both the known and unknown universes. They emphasize the foolishness of man's claim to superiority as a form of life. The fables are primarily vehicles for satire, and satire serves at least two purposes. There is specific topical satire, as in Archy's debunking of prohibition, free verse, and theories of evolution, or as in Mehitabel's eulogies on the bohemian life. The purpose implied by such writing would seem to be the reformation of a culture, as in a great tradition of puritan satire, beginning with [John] Bunyan, [Daniel] Defoe, and even [Jonathan] Swift. But there is also paradoxically more general, unspecified satire of the structure and values of that same culture. Marquis seeks, and asks his readers to share, relief and release from the demands made by his world for coherence, logic, progress, and allegiance, through his glorifying what is impulsive, anarchic, illogical, and disaffected. His best writing is generated out of the tension between his impulses toward puritanical reformation on the one hand and toward anarchic dissolution on the other. (pp. 635-36)

Archy has a dual nature, and he thereby reflects his creator's sense of the role of the artist. As an insect Archy is an upsetting nuisance; he threatens frequently to become an unsavory pest by drowning himself in mince pies, stews, and soups. As a poet he is both an articulate rational creature and, like his master, driven by an inner romantic intensity: "expression is the need of my soul." Archy "was once a vers libre bard." When he died, his "soul went into the body of a cockroach." As a result of this transmigration he finds that he has "a new outlook upon life," for he sees "things from the under side." (p. 636)

Most of the early verses by Archy as bard of the animal and insect worlds concentrate on ridicule of artistic affectation. In one of the fables Archy overhears an argument between a spider and a fly. The fly argues that he should not be eaten, for he serves "a great purpose / in the world." He says he is a "vessel of righteousness" because he spreads diseases that kill people who have led wicked lives. The spider offers a higher argument. He says he serves "the gods of beauty" by creating "gossamer webs" that "float in the sun / like filaments of sng." . . . There is an oblique satiric purpose in the poem:

the creative imagination is seen as part of a world dominated by predatory instincts.

The world of Archy is struck through with the comic and the satiric; it is also a place of violence, terror, and sudden death. Archy is always in danger of annihilation. He is pursued by mice, and even by his friend Mehitabel, when she is moved by hunger or playfulness. On one occasion he is stepped upon, but his soul enters the body of another cockroach. (pp. 637-38)

During the 1930s much of Archy's commentary was topical and aphoristic. The depression, and recovery schemes, proved a rich source of comic material. But the tone was very different from that in the wilder fables of the first fifteen years. Archy became simply a mouthpiece who spoke gentle irreverences in the manner of Will Rogers. (p. 640)

It was a time for reconstruction, not for debunking. Satire, it seemed, could entertain, but not radically criticize. Marquis made some unsuccessful attempts to introduce other animal and insect characters: there were Pete the Pup, Henry, another cockroach, and Lady Bug. None of them was the equal of Archy or of Mehitabel. The most notable character was Warty Bliggens, the toad who believed that the universe had been created for his pleasure and benefit. But he too was an early creation, and appeared only once. Archy, who in a sense as the biographer of Mehitabel was also her creator, remains the most enduring figure in the Archy and Mehitabel saga.

An undercurrent of hostility and disaffection formed the mainstream of Archy's character. As an insect and commentator on humanity, he was, of course, superior and hostile in his attitudes toward human hypocrisies and ideals. Most of all he hated false optimism, which was epitomized for him in the vapid chirping of crickets. . . . He is both artist and predator. As artist expression is the need of his soul; with passionate intensity he creates order and form. As predator he is a nuisance and a pest who nibbles constantly at order and form in what is imagined as a total attrition and descent back into anarchy, a return to hell. Marquis similarly conceived of a dual role for himself as artist: a role as both poet and satirist, as both myth-maker and myth-destroyer. He was never comfortable with knowledge of this division in himself, yet the artist in him created a memorable image for one of the tensions of American life in the twentieth century. (pp. 640-41)

He had a deep and frustrating sense of failure, a sense that he was not one of the elect, that he was the victim of something as pervasive as original sin. One of his responses was to glorify that awareness of damnation, and this is part of what produced Archy and Mehitabel. The images of Archy's world arise out of a tension between Marquis's sense of a need for purification set against his impulses toward anarchic destruction. Marquis, like many of his contemporaries, felt that the values of middle-class culture no longer made sense. His response was to create a fabulous world where hostility, violence, and the predatory instinct were the ordinary ingredients of existence, and thus were brought within a kind of tenuous artistic control. Marquis believed that mere anarchy was loosed upon the world. So he created and set loose an Archy of his own. He wanted to counteract the mereness, the absurdity of existence as he viewed it, through an ironic glorification of irrationality and of anarchy itself. (p. 642)

Edward A. Martin, "A Puritan's Satanic Flight: Don Marquis, Archy, and Anarchy," in The Sewanee Review *(reprinted by permission of the editor; © 1975* by The University of the South), Vol. LXXXIII, No. 4, Fall, 1975, pp. 623-42.

DAN JAFFE (essay date 1975)

I like to reread the poems of don marquis when the world seems too much with me, which is almost always directly after the 10 p.m. news. And although I am hardly profound then, having been pretty thoroughly worked over, I keep getting clear intimations that don marquis, or should I say archy, not only cheers me up but also has a lot to say. This has been the judgment made for more than 50 years by American readers despite the fact that courses in American literature, influential textbooks, and intellectual historians generally ignore don marquis and his friends. That's more than I'm willing to do for the following reasons:

Archy the cockroach has his own voice, fashioned out of the total language; he captures the American idiom but remains distinctly himself.

Archy is a compassionate realist. He faces the hardness of the world and still cares about the hurts of others.

Archy plays the game of poetry, making strengths out of limitations. Archy writes in lower case because he can't operate the capital lever. But his lower case turns, in addition to other things, into symbolic, class commentary.

Archy presents us with a wide range of concerns, locales, characters, and feelings.

Archy loves disguises. Only disguised could an American *epic* so full of cynicism, criticism of the culture, reminders of our pretentiousness and silliness not only be published in the commercial press but become widely successful.

Archy can dance to other people's music, mimic other people's gestures. Often his allusions, stylistic and referential, have ironic bite. How we love his satire and parody.

At times he even gets metaphysical.

Archy is the only cockroach I know who is a hero. (pp. 427-28)

> Dan Jaffe, "'Archy Jumps over the Moon'," in The Twenties: Fiction, Poetry, Drama, *edited by Warren French (© copyright 1975 by Warren French), Everett/Edwards, Inc., 1975, pp. 427-38.*

LYNN LEE (essay date 1981)

During his lifetime, Marquis created several characters who rivaled Archy and Mehitabel in popularity; the most popular was Clem Hawley, The Old Soak. He is the hero of two books, two plays, and several short stories. Clem came from "The Sun Dial," where so much of Marquis's best humor originated. He grew out of Prohibition, the great "moral experiment" of the early twentieth century, about which Marquis had very definite feelings, all negative. "He wrote almost obsessively in prose and verse against prohibition."

The Old Soak is not an alcoholic; he is ". . . one whose devotion to alcoholic fellowship and endearing generosity of spirit superseded the practical concerns of work and family support." Clem Hawley is much closer to the comic strip characters, Jiggs or Major Hoople, or to the character played by W. C. Fields in some of his films than he is to the drunkard of nineteenth-century melodrama. Ironically, the popularity of The

Old Soak gave Marquis a reputation for being a drunk himself, a title he deserved only on infrequent occasions.

In *The Old Soak* . . . , Marquis assembled twenty-two of his many columns about Clem Hawley. (pp. 50-1)

Because it is a collection of columns, *The Old Soak* has a loose framework. In a sense, Marquis borrows the frame, a standard device with nineteenth-century humorists, in which the author sets a meeting between the author and a humorous character and, after a brief introduction, lets the storyteller tell the story in his own style and language. In the opening chapter of *The Old Soak*, Clem visits Marquis; after warning of the dangers of home brew, he announces he is writing "A kind of gol-dinged autobiography of what me and Old King Booze done before he went into the grave and took one of my feet with him." (p. 51)

Throughout *The Old Soak*, Marquis uses the clichés common to domestic humor. (p. 52)

[*The Old Soak's History of the World*], like *The Old Soak,* was a collection of newspaper columns. The two books are quite similar. In the second, Clem Hawley moves from discussing the old-time bar room to giving his very individualistic treatment of the Bible, ancient history, the French Revolution, and foreign culture in general, in addition to throwing in anecdotes about Baycliff, Long Island. This is certainly not an original approach for a work of humor, as it had previously been used by Mark Twain, Artemus Ward, Bill Nye, and others.

As in *The Old Soak,* Clem takes a moral stance: "You mustn't go too fur with it whatever it is." (pp. 53-4)

On the whole, the burlesque of the Bible and ancient history is not much more profound than a television skit. After one grasps Clem's basic philosophy of life, it is easy to forecast his opinion of a particular individual or event. If anything, the humor is old-fashioned for the 1920s, almost succeeding on the level of nostalgia. (p. 55)

In both Old Soak books, particularly the last, Marquis indulges in one of his vices—using the same material, slightly altered, more than once. *The Old Soak's History of the World* has condensed versions of three previously published short stories narrated by Clem, while, in the same book, Clem relates a tall tale, found in both *Danny's Own Story* and *Sons of the Puritans,* describing how he fell down a well while drunk and was forced to remain in the well while the Reverend Mr. Hoskins preached an inspired revival service over him, until Clem agreed to sign the pledge for three months. (p. 56)

Finally, Marquis's most profitable use of Clem Hawley was in *The Old Soak,* which ran for 423 performances on Broadway in 1922-1923, by far the longest run for any of his plays. It is an oldfashioned melodrama involving Clem Hawley, his family and friends. In his highly favorable review of *The Old Soak,* Alexander Woollcott dismissed the plot as unimportant, placing his emphasis on "the rich and abundant and delightful overlay of humor and whimsicality that makes the plot . . . a mere prop for a genuine and hearty entertainment . . . 'The Old Soak' is gorgeously entertaining . . . an authentic popular success." (pp. 56-7)

Since the plot and characters are largely lifted from melodrama and other popular literature, what gives *The Old Soak* whatever distinctiveness it has? Chiefly, the character of Clem Hawley who is not much changed from the other works bearing his name. He is a lovable human being who likes to drink with his friends; he is not mean or nasty. Although much of the play is taken from Clem's earlier appearances in print, one of the most popular and most successful devices in the play is not in the other Hawley books. This is the introduction of Pete the Parrot, who is used to test the quality of Al's home brew. (pp. 57-8)

Clem is given more dignity and heroic qualities in the play than he possesses in the books. Yet, this is not inconsistent with his role as a cracker barrel philosopherhero who stands behind such values as family, home, and Bible. (p. 58)

The Old Soak does not have the comic appeal he offered in the 1920s. However, as a commonsense cracker-barrel "wise fool," he is in the direct line of native American humor, representing a conservative, humane view of human nature. Like other American sages, Clem Hawley knows that people are not basically very good, but he also knows that they must be loved as they are if life is to have any meaning. . . .

Besides The Old Soak, one of the earliest humorous characters created by Marquis in "The Sun Dial" was Hermione, the wealthy dilettante. In 1916, he published *Hermione and Her Little Group of Serious Thinkers* (hereafter called *Hermione*), drawn from the column. The character of Hermione grew out of Marquis's intense dislike of pretension. (p. 59)

[The] tone of *Hermione* is not a bitter one. . . . Marquis allows Hermione and her group to speak for themselves without showing his own distaste very much. (p. 60)

Like *The Old Soak, Hermione* is a collection of columns, almost all of them monologues by Hermione. Once one gets past the introductory poem, the book is not organized in any particular order. Hermione is pathetically shallow and self-centered. Yet, Marquis does not treat her savagely, in the grand manner of classic satire. He is aiming at those who pretend to be intellectuals, who pretend to be artists, who pretend to be concerned, but who flit from fad to fad without ever going beneath the surface where they might actually have to do something or produce a real work of art. (p. 61)

Undoubtedly, Marquis uses Hermione to support his suspicion of the American tendency to praise something because it is new or exotic and to deal with this new fad superficially.

The fad that Marquis disliked as strongly as any was the one with which Hermione became most closely involved—vers libre. In the years immediately before World War I, vers libre was an emotional issue, with the Imagists—Amy Lowell, Ezra Pound, and their supporters—hurling charges and countercharges at one another. In *Archy and Mehitabel,* Marquis makes his dislike of vers libre quite clear. In *Hermione,* largely through the character of Fothergil Finch, Marquis attacks the image of the vers libre bard; to Marquis, saying someone is a vers libre bard is simply another way of saying one is a fake.

Fothergil Finch (the name in itself is comic as is "Hermione") is Hermione's ideal artist; he has spiritual, not physical, virility. (p. 63)

Fothergil Finch combines the shallowness, pretentiousness, posturing, and the false virility and strength Marquis associated with Greenwich Village and, on a broader level, bad art in general. (p. 65)

If Marquis were alive today, he would certainly find Hermione alive and well everywhere, possibly a little more worldly, but still in the grip of each new fad. (p. 66)

With his great love of and exposure to the theater, why wasn't Marquis more successful as a playwright? He wrote six plays, four of which were produced on Broadway. Yet, only two of them, *The Old Soak* and *Everything's Jake,* had runs of any length and *The Old Soak* was his only real financial success as a dramatist; it was also his first Broadway production. In *The Old Soak,* Marquis does demonstrate a knowledge of popular stage techniques. However, this was, in many ways, an old-fashioned play, drawing a good deal of its effectiveness from nostalgia. . . . [*The Old Soak* and *Everything's Jake*] were basically comedies, lacking much depth.

Marquis's four other plays were commercially unsuccessful. *The Dark Hours* ran for eight performances; *Out of the Sea* had only a few performances; *Master of the Revels* was never produced on Broadway. The failure of the first two plays has been commonly blamed on inadequate direction, while *Master of the Revels* was never brought to New York, on the advice of Brooks Atkinson. Marquis's sixth play, *The Skinners,* was a comedy satirizing ". . . a then current craze which Marquis had used as a target in his columning days; the wholesale quest for dukedoms—or what have you—by title-smitten wealthy Americans." . . . Unfortunately, *The Skinners* was given only one performance and never reached Broadway.

If Don Marquis had been asked what his greatest artistic disappointment had been, he almost certainly would have named the failure of *The Dark Hours,* his play dealing with the passion and crucifixion of Christ. When the Broadway production failed in 1932 through a combination of poor direction, an uneven cast, and, certainly, a far from perfect script, it nearly destroyed Marquis financially and, I believe, so demoralized him that he could never regain his earlier form as a writer.

Marquis had begun *The Dark Hours* with his first wife's enthusiastic support. Although published in 1924, after Reina's death, the play was dedicated to her. Reviews of the published play were good, with particular praise for Marquis's not allowing Christ to appear on stage and for his ability to make high drama from a very familiar story. *The Dark Hours* was certainly responsible, in part, for Marquis's being taken more seriously by critics who had dismissed him as a mere humorist.

When one reads *The Dark Hours,* he would be going against Marquis's own views to look for a radically revised or modernized version of these events. Marquis believed he was sharing a tradition, not attempting an original interpretation. He presents five scenes, each coming directly from the biblical account. (pp. 106-07)

Marquis felt strongly that *The Dark Hours* could succeed only if Christ spoke but did not appear on stage. At first, he felt that the taboo on Christ's appearance was purely religious. Later, he realized it also came from dramatic values realized by many people and cultures. Anyone who has seen any of the Hollywood versions on the life of Christ, where Jesus is portrayed by an actor, would certainly agree with this view. Marquis did not, however, place the same restrictions on the other characters in the play. He admits to elaborating on the biblical Judas, Peter, John, Pilate, and Mary Magdalene. . . .

From the beginning of the play to the end, there is a sense of a few men playing out a predetermined drama in the midst of a mob that can be easily swayed by either side. In the first scene, while Caiaphas, the High Priest, and Annas, his father-in-law, are plotting Christ's downfall, believing he must be destroyed or he will bring about a conflict with Rome that will obliterate Jerusalem, the crowds of people in Jerusalem for the

Passover pass by the house chanting hymns of praise to Jehovah while also showing great respect for Christ. Marquis uses the people like a chorus, allowing individual voices to speak out, but always giving the impression of a unified and brutal mob, a mob so brutal that at the moment when Pilate is appealing to Caiaphas to let Christ go, it murders two or three people who attempt to speak for Christ.

The character of Judas is given a partly original interpretation in the first scene. Judas is portrayed as a man who both loves and hates Christ. (p. 108)

Judas considers himself bewitched, with angels and demons fighting to control his spirit. As traditionally accepted, Judas also admits that he believed he was to be the chamberlain when Christ became King of the Jews. Now, he realizes this is not to be. Yet, the overwhelming reason for his betrayal is that ". . . we were born to be each one the other's bane. And we have felt that . . from the first." Whether one accepts this interpretation of Judas or not, it does work dramatically, making Judas a rather sympathetic character.

The other disciples are treated quite conventionally. . . . Similarly, the characters of Caiaphas, Annas, and the other priests are presented as one finds them in the Gospels.

Marquis uses several devices to sustain dramatic tension. One, mentioned previously, is the character of Judas. Another, also previously noted, is the use of the crowd as a chorus. They support Christ at first—then they turn on him. We even get the impression that their pressure intimidates Pilate so that he gives Christ to the mob. The trial before the Sanhedrin builds up to the climactic moment when Christ admits to being the Son of God. Marquis has citizens, servants, and some disciples form another chorus of sorts outside the courtroom. They comment on the trial and debate whether or not Christ did perform miracles.

The witnesses are dramatically effective. One testifies to Lazarus being raised from the dead while Peter and John, outside the courtroom, debate rescuing Christ; John insists that death means nothing to Christ. The most interesting witness is the Gadarean swineherd whose two thousand hogs were destroyed when Christ took devils from a possessed man and put them into the hogs. The swineherd is upset because he has lost his job and is now a beggar because of what he considers to be witchcraft. (Marquis was so fond of the swineherd that he made use of him again in *Chapters for the Orthodox.*) The general atmosphere at the trial is one of doubt and uncertainty, even among the disciples. When Christ admits to being the Son of God, Caiaphas tears his clothing, the mob becomes enraged, and Christ's doom is certain.

While Marquis does show proper respect toward the Passion story, this is not what gives the play whatever dramatic impact it has. His attempt to show how the events affected those who were present makes the play work as well as it does. Possibly this "sympathetic reverence" is why the last two scenes are weaker than the earlier part of the play. The scene with Pilate is almost totally conventional. Marquis manages to have Pilate say "What is truth?" and to have him wash his hands; to have him find Jesus innocent, but to have him give in to the mob. The only real dramatic power of this scene comes from the mob's attacks on anyone who attempts to defend Christ and its growing impatience and anger, finally unnerving Pilate to the point of giving in.

The final scene at Golgotha is, again, quite conventional, with the centurions casting lots for Christ's robe and Christ uttering the seven last words. Although the dialogue is conventional, Marquis does use lighting rather well in this scene, darkening the stage completely for the eclipse and then bringing in a very bright light at the moment of death and triumph. The play concludes with the centurion announcing, "Truly, this was the Son of God!" The mob, including Caiaphas and Annas, flees in terror.

There can be no doubt of Marquis's sincerity, his desire to present the Passion story as recorded. Unfortunately, when *The Dark Hours* was finally produced on Broadway in 1932, his most important point was ignored. His second wife, Marjorie Vonnegut, a highly respected actress, directed the play. For some reason, never clearly explained, she chose to represent Christ on stage. The only reason she ever gave for this was that she thought her husband was trying to be too subtle. She felt he might lose his audience if the play were produced without Christ being on stage. The play ran for only eight performances. . . . (pp. 109-10)

It would be a disservice to Don Marquis to insist on his being a great American writer. Undoubtedly, *Archy and Mehitabel* will survive; however, very few of Marquis's nonhumorous poems, stories, novels, and plays have stood the test of time; possibly none of them deserves to. The simple fact is that Marquis was very uneven. At best, he could leave pages that are as fresh as the day Archy or The Old Soak "wrote" them. . . .

I do believe that without his ventures into nonhumorous writing, Marquis would not have been so successful as a humorist. . . . [The] same themes turn up in both his humorous and nonhumorous work: the question of reincarnation, human vanity, man's belief, the value of the artist, individualism, the need for love, the need for freedom, man's cruelty to man. While these are not at all original with Marquis, he does use them very well in his best work. (p. 141)

Like Twain, he produced a great deal of inferior work and a small amount of very good work.

Whether Marquis is a minor major humorist or a major minor humorist or, as I believe, a major American humorist is unimportant. He will never, I suspect, be put on a level with Thurber, Perelman, Benchley, or E. B. White, although, at his best, he was certainly their equal. (p. 145)

> *Lynn Lee, in his* Don Marquis *(copyright © 1981 by Twayne Publishers, Inc.; reprinted with the permission of Twayne Publishers, a Division of G. K. Hall & Co., Boston), Twayne, 1981, 164 p.*

ADDITIONAL BIBLIOGRAPHY

Allen, Everett S. "Donald Robert Perry Marquis." In his *Famous American Humorous Poets*, pp. 61-70. New York: Dodd, Mead & Co., 1968.
    Anecdotal account of Marquis's life and career.

Anthony, Edward. "Don Marquis Revisited." *Columbia Library Columns* XII, No. 2 (February 1963): 3-12.
    Biographical notes and some quotes from Marquis's autobiographical writing.

"Don Marquis." In *The Literary Spotlight*, edited by John Farrar, pp. 277-86. New York: George H. Doran Co., 1924.
    An informal biographical sketch.

Kirby, Rollin. "Don Marquis: Delayed Elizabethan." *American Mercury* LXIV, No. 279 (March 1947): 337-40.

    Brief overview of Marquis's life and career as a columnist on *The New York Sun*.

Middleton, George. "Hollywood: The Stage and Screen Face It Out." In his *These Things Are Mine: The Autobiography of a Journeyman Playwright*, pp. 347-99. New York: The Macmillan Co., 1947.

    Personal reminiscence of Marquis's brief stay in Hollywood and his unsuccessful attempts at screenwriting.

Morley, Christopher. "Archy—from Abdera." *The Saturday Review of Literature* XVI, No. 3 (15 May 1937): 10-11.

    Appreciation of Marquis's humorous columns, in particular those featuring Archy and Mehitabel.

Claude McKay

1889-1948

(Born Festus Claudius McKay; also wrote under pseudonym of Eli Edwards) American poet, novelist, short story writer, journalist, essayist, and autobiographer.

McKay was the first prominent writer of the Harlem Renaissance. More than any other black writer of his time, he managed to convert anger and social protest into poems of lasting value. The publication of his most popular poem, "If We Must Die," in 1919 is considered by some to be a major impetus behind the growing civil rights movement during the decade after the war. The poem was at once a shout of defiance and a proclamation of the unbreakable spirit and courage of the oppressed black American. McKay was a vital, catalytic voice during the 1920s, a period when blacks fought to reclaim their cultural heritage. In all his works, he searched among the common folk for a distinctive black identity, and for a means of preserving the African spirit and creativity in an alien world.

McKay was born in the hills of Jamaica, the son of poor peasant farmers, and educated by his older brother and an English squire named Walter Jekyll. The Englishman, a specialist in Jamaican folklore, taught McKay how to use the native dialect in his first poems. The result of these efforts were two collections, *Songs of Jamaica* and *Constab Ballads*, published in England in 1912. In that same year McKay came to America to study agriculture. He attended Tuskegee Institute and Kansas State College until 1914, when he decided to quit his studies and move to New York, determined to be a writer. McKay's Jamaican background did not prepare him for the overt racism he was to encounter in America, and his first collection published in the United States, *Harlem Shadows*, shows the author's anger and concern over the treatment of blacks in American society. After the appearance of *Harlem Shadows*, he left America for twelve years, traveling to Russia, Germany, France, Spain, and Morocco. During his absence he wrote and published all of his fiction: *Home to Harlem* (the first best-selling novel by a black author), *Banjo, Gingertown*, and *Banana Bottom*. The last three were almost wholly neglected by the reading public. McKay returned to a depressed America in 1934 and to a vanishing market for "black renaissance" literature. These circumstances, coupled with his eclipsed reputation, discouraged him from producing any further significant work.

McKay reached his zenith as a poet with the publication of *Harlem Shadows*. As with all of his verse, the poems in this collection are based on conventional forms— the sonnet and traditional rhymed and metered verse. Though his poetry often lapsed into an outdated Victorian structure and tone, these shortcomings were balanced by the importance of his themes and the vigor and passion with which he developed them. McKay expressed the vitality and spontaneity of the common folk; against this vitality he opposed a restrictive and inhumane materialistic society. He attempted these same themes in his novels and stories, with less critical success. *Banana Bottom* is the only work in which McKay was able to dramatically express his ideal of existence for the black living in the white man's world. The novel's heroine, Bita Plant, takes only what is necessary from her English upbringing and chooses a life

rooted in her Jamaican past. In essence, she manages to merge instinct and intellect. Unfortunately, McKay was unable to resolve this dualism as convincingly in his other works.

Critical opinion of McKay's work has never been as high as it was during his brief period of fame in the 1920s, and even then McKay was frequently attacked by many black critics, such as W.E.B. DuBois, for his presentation of "low-life" blacks in his novels. In the years since, McKay has been criticized for not developing a sustained style in both his poetry and fiction. His poetic forms were thought to be too conventional and too limiting for the density of his themes; his prose was considered formless, unpolished, and spoiled by a shallow exoticism that obscured its basic seriousness. However, in recent years he has been praised for the intensity and ardor of his poetry and for his ability to convert social protest into art. McKay's novels have also received greater praise, if only because they were an attempt by the author to express new visions of life for black Americans.

Despite the critical debate over McKay's work, it is generally agreed that he was an essential, driving force behind the renaissance of black literature during the 1920s. His work helped crystalize a growing belief among black writers that their cultural heritage was worthy of a place in American literature.

(See also *Dictionary of Literary Biography,* **Vol. 4:** *American Writers in Paris, 1920-1939.*)

PRINCIPAL WORKS

Constab Ballads   (poetry)   1912
Songs of Jamaica   (poetry)   1912
Spring in New Hampshire and Other Poems   (poetry) 1920
Harlem Shadows   (poetry)   1922
Home to Harlem   (novel)   1928
Banjo   (novel)   1929
Gingertown   (short stories)   1932
Banana Bottom   (novel)   1933
A Long Way from Home   (autobiography)   1937
Harlem: Negro Metropolis   (historical essay)   1940
Selected Poems of Claude McKay   (poetry)   1953

WILLIAM STANLEY BRAITHWAITE   (essay date 1919)

The most significant accomplishment among . . . recent poems are two sonnets signed by "Eli Edwards" which appeared in *The Seven Arts* for last October. "Eli Edwards," I understand, is the pseudonym of Claude MacKay, who lives in New York City, choosing to conceal his identity as a poet from the associates among whom he works for his daily bread. His story as it is . . . is full of alluring interest, and may one day be vividly featured as a topic of historic literary importance. For he may well be the keystone of the new movement in racial poetic achievement. (p. 277)

[In **"The Harlem Dancer,"** there is, indeed, a] genuine vision that evokes from the confusing details of experience and brings into the picture the image in all its completeness of outline and its gradation of color, and rendered with that precise surety of form possessed by the resourceful artist. The power in this poet is, I think, his ability to reproduce a hectic scene of reality with all the solid accessories, as in **"The Harlem Dancer,"** and yet make it float as it were upon a background of illusion through which comes piercing the glowing sense of a spiritual mystery. Note the exalted close of Mr. Edward's riotous picture of the dancer when . . . he translates the significance of the intoxicated figure with its sensuous contagion into something ultimate behind the "falsely-smiling face," where "herself"— be it the innocent memory of childhood, perhaps of some pursuing dream of a brief happiness in love, or a far-away country home which her corybantic earnings secures in peace and comfort for the aged days of her parents—is inviolably wrapped in the innocence and beauty of her dreams. This sonnet differs in both visionary and artistic power from anything so far produced by the poets of the race. The visual quality here possessed is extraordinary; not only does Mr. Edwards evoke his images with a clear and decisive imagination, but he throws at the same time upon the object the rich and warm colors of his emotional sympathies. (p. 278)

William Stanley Braithwaite, "Some Contemporary Poets of the Negro Race," in The Crisis, *Vol. 17, No. 6, April, 1919, pp. 275-80.**

BURTON RASCOE   (essay date 1928)

"Home to Harlem" is a book to invoke pity and terror, which is the function of tragedy, and to that extent—that very great extent—it is beautiful. It is hard to convey to the reader the impression this novel leaves upon the mind, just as it is hard to convey the impression that a blues-song leaves upon the mind. One reads, one hears and the heart is touched.

Out of his individual pain, Claude McKay, the poet, has fashioned his lyrics; and out of his impersonal sorrow he has written a fine novel. **"Home to Harlem"** is a story involving the lives led by the lost generation of colored folk in the teeming Negro metropolis north of One Hundred and Tenth Street, New York. It is a story not of the successful Negroes who have done well in the trades and professions and have built themselves homes, sent their children to school, and engaged in civil and social pursuits of a sober and respectable nature: it is the story of the serving class—longshoremen and roustabouts, house-maids and Pullman porters, waiters and wash-room attendants, cooks and scullery maids, "dime-snatchers", and all those who compensate for defeat in life in a white man's world by a savage intensity among themselves at night. . . .

"Home to Harlem" is not a novel in the conventional sense. The only conflict in the mind of Jake, the hero, is as to whether he will keep on working at whatever insecure, underpaid drudgery he can find to do on the docks, in the stoke-hole of a steamer and in dining-cars or turn his handsome body and good looks into the shameful asset of a "sweet-man", kept in luxury on the earnings of a woman. The only conflict of wills engaged in by the hero is when he takes a girl away from his former buddy, and anger and hate flare into being, with drawn gun and open razor. When the book closes and he is going away to Chicago with the girl to start life anew, he is the same wondering, indecisive being he was in the beginning, who "preferred the white folks' hatred to their friendly contempt" and found a sinister satisfaction in the fact that the white man is too effete to know the sensual pleasures of the blacks. (p. 183)

The language of **"Home to Harlem",** whether Mr. McKay is setting forth dialogue in a perfect transcription of Negro slang and dialect or is telling his story in the Negro idiom, is a constant joy. . . .

Mr. McKay is not at all solicitous toward his reader. He makes no case, he pleads no cause, he asks no extenuation, and he doesn't explain his idiomatic phrases. There is no glossary at the end of the book as there was to Carl Van Vechten's "Nigger Heaven"; and the unsophisticated happily will read whole pages of this novel depicting the utmost moral degradation without ever knowing what it is about. And this is just as well. (p. 184)

Burton Rascoe, "The Seamy Side," in The Bookman, *New York, Vol. LXVII, No. 2, April, 1928, pp. 183-85.**

W.E.B. D[U BOIS]   (essay date 1928)

[Cluade McKay's **"Home to Harlem"**] for the most part nauseates me, and after the dirtier parts of its filth I feel distinctly like taking a bath. This does not mean that the book is wholly bad. McKay is too great a poet to make any complete failure in writing. There are bits of **"Home to Harlem",** beautiful and fascinating: the continued changes upon the theme of the beauty of colored skins; the portrayal of the fascination of their new yearnings for each other which Negroes are developing. The chief character, Jake, has something appealing, and the glimpses of the Haitian, Ray, have all the materials of a great piece of fiction.

But it looks as though, despite this, McKay has set out to cater for that prurient demand on the part of white folk for a portrayal in Negroes of that utter licentiousness which conventional civilization holds white folk back from enjoying—if enjoyment it can be called. That which a certain decadent section of the white American world, centered particularly in New York, longs for with fierce and unrestrained passions, it wants to see written out in black and white, and saddled on black Harlem. This demand, as voiced by a number of New York publishers, McKay has certainly satisfied, and added much for good measure. He has used every art and emphasis to paint drunkenness, fighting, lascivious sexual promiscuity and utter absence of restraint in as bold and as bright colors as he can.

If this had been done in the course of a well-conceived plot or with any artistic unity, it might have been understood if not excused. But "Home to Harlem" is padded. Whole chapters here and there are inserted with no connection to the main plot, except that they are on the same dirty subject. As a picture of Harlem life or of Negro life anywhere, it is, of course, nonsense. Untrue, not so much as on account of its facts, but on account of its emphasis and glaring colors. I am sorry that the author of "Harlem Shadows" stooped to this. I sincerely hope that he will some day rise above it and give us in fiction the strong, well-knit as well as beautiful theme, that it seems to me he might do.

> W.E.B. D[u Bois], "The Browsing Reader: 'Home to Harlem'," in The Crisis, Vol. 35, No. 6, June, 1928. p. 202.

WALLACE THURMAN (essay date 1928)

McKay's first volume [Songs of Jamaica] was published while he was still in Jamaica, a compilation of folk-verse done in the native dialect. The Institute of Arts and Science of Jamaica gave him a medal in recognition of this first book. It is in many ways remarkable, and in it the poet gives us a more substantial portrait and delves far deeper into the soul of the Jamaican than [Paul Laurence] Dunbar was ever able to in the soul of the southern Negro in America.

McKay's latter poetry is often marred by bombast. He is such an intense person that one can often hear the furnace-like fire within him roaring in his poems. He seems to have more emotional depth and spiritual fire than any of his forerunners or contemporaries. It might be added that he also seems to have considerably more mental depth too. His love poems are not as musical or as haunting as Mr. [Countee] Cullen's, but neither are they as stereotyped. His sonnet to a Harlem dancer may not be as deft or as free from sentiment as "Midnight Nan" by Langston Hughes, but it is far more mature and moving. All of which leads us to say that a study of Claude McKay's and of the other better Negro poetry convinces us that he, more than the rest, has really had something to say. It is his tragedy that his message was too alive and too big for the form he chose. His poems are for the most part either stilted, choked, or over-zealous. He could never shape the flames from the fire that blazed within him. But he is the only Negro poet who ever wrote revolutionary or protest poetry. (p. 559)

> Wallace Thurman, "Negro Poets and Their Poetry," in The Bookman, New York, Vol. LXVII, No. 5, July, 1928, pp. 555-61.*

JOHN CHAMBERLAIN (essay date 1930)

The work of McKay in prose is always poetic, for McKay brings his Jamaica world of color to everything he writes. There is a racial rhythm out of Langston Hughes in his first novel, Home to Harlem, a book that is saved from the rut of naturalism by the undertone of brooding provided by an intellectual Negro who is probably one aspect of McKay himself. Banjo, McKay's second novel, shows both advance and retrogression—advance because it is substantially richer, retrogression because the material is spread so profusely that it tends to clog the movement. McKay's defects as a novelist lie in his deficiencies as a dramatist; he has not yet seized on a problem that must spend itself in time with serious effects upon the involved characters. (p. 606)

It is interesting to see what different critics do with the poetry of Claude McKay. Mr. [Countee] Cullen thinks the poems collected in Harlem Shadows show McKay as "most exercised, rebellious, and vituperative to a degree that clouds his lyricism in many instances". Yet has rebellion clouded Mr. McKay's perfectly wrought sonnets, with their powerful sestets that end in stinging couplets? It is Alain Locke's opinion that to the "extent that the radical challenge is capable of pure poetry, Claude McKay has realized it". . . . It is quite true that McKay is a propagandist, and bitter to an extent that occasionally betrays him into bombast, but it must seem that his reputation as a revolutionist serves to obscure to interested critics the positive virtues of his masculine resonance, his often tropic color, his solidity and his bite. When he is at his best his rebellion is in perfect leash; and his convictions are such that he has something discernible to say, whether you agree with it or not.

A test of McKay may be made by reading the best Negro anthology, that of Cullen's called Caroling Dusk in which there is a relatively dreary stretch between the names of James Weldon Johnson and McKay. . . . The names tend to merge into a caricature of all that one has cast aside as insipid in poetry. But the miasma is dispelled the moment that one launches into McKay's "Flame-Heart" and "Desolate", the first a poem of rich lines and often gorgeous coloring, and the second a passionate variation on the theme of self-disgust. To go on with the anthology and read the poems of Arna Bontemps, Jonathan Henderson Brooks, Blanche Taylor Dickinson, Clarissa Scott Delany and Gwendolyn B. Bennett, is only to accentuate the suspicion that McKay has a gift beyond that of most of his racial contemporaries. (pp. 610-11)

> John Chamberlain, "The Negro as Writer," in The Bookman, New York, Vol. LXX, No. 6, February, 1930, pp. 603-11.*

JAMES WELDON JOHNSON (essay date 1931)

McKay belongs to the post-war group and was its most powerful voice. He was preëminently the poet of rebellion. More effectively than any other poet of that period he voiced the feelings and reactions the Negro in America was then experiencing. Incongruous as it may seem, he chose as the form of these poems of protest, challenge, and defiance the English sonnet; and no poetry in American literature sounds a more portentous note than these sonnet-tragedies. (pp. 166-67)

The terrifying summer of 1919, when race riots occurred in quick succession in a dozen cities in different sections of the country, brought from him the most widely known of these sonnets, ["**If We Must Die**"], a cry of defiant desperation, beginning with the lines:

> If we must die—let it not be like hogs
> Hunted and penned in an inglorious spot,

and closing with:

> Like men we'll face the murderous, cowardly pack,
> Pressed to the wall, dying, but fighting back!

This is masculine poetry, strong and direct, the sort of poetry that stirs the pulse, that quickens to action. Reading McKay's poetry of protest and rebellion, it is difficult to imagine him dreaming of his native Jamaica and singing as he does in "**Flame Heart**" or creating poetic beauty in the absolute as he does in "**The Harlem Dancer**," "**Spring in New Hampshire**," and many another of his poems. Of the major Negro poets he, above all, is the poet of passion. That passion found in his poems of rebellion, transmuted, is felt in his love lyrics. (p. 167)

> *James Weldon Johnson, "Claude McKay" (copyright 1922, 1931 by Harcourt Brace Jovanovich, Inc.; copyright 1950 by Grace Johnson; copyright 1959 by Mrs. Grace Nail Johnson; reprinted by permission of the publisher), in* The Book of American Negro Poetry, *edited by James Weldon Johnson, revised edition, Harcourt, 1931, p. 165-80. [The excerpt of Claude McKay's poetry used here was originally published in his* Selected Poems of Claude McKay *(copyright 1981; reprinted with the permission of Twayne Publishers, a Division of G. K. Hall & Co., Boston), Twayne, 1953].*

BENJAMIN BRAWLEY   (essay date 1937)

Most vigorous of Negro poets in the years immediately after the World War was Claude McKay. . . . His daring sonnet, "**The Harlem Dancer**," attracted attention, and in the course of the war the militant poem, "**If We Must Die**," was much quoted. (pp. 241-42)

To turn from the poems of Claude McKay to the novels he has written is to be aware of something very close to a tragedy. For years he had been writing exquisite or dynamic verse, and the favor of the public, judged at least by commercial standards, was but luke-warm. Now there was a change of tone and emphasis. It is impossible for him to write incompetently; on everything he puts the stamp of virility. After the success of Mr. Van Vechten's *Nigger Heaven*, however, he and some other authors seemed to realize that it was not the poem or story of fine touch that the public desired, but metal of a baser hue; and he decided to give what was wanted. The result was a novel, *Home to Harlem,* that sold thousands of copies but that with its emphasis on certain degraded aspects of life hardly did justice to the gifts of the writer. Jake Brown, on his first night home from France, meets in a cabaret the little girl Felice, and the book is largely concerned with his search until he finds her again. There is not much of a story, but the realism is stark, the color vivid, and there is an impressionistic view of the crowds in the Harlem streets. Importance attaches to Ray, a character of superior intellect who might be taken for the novelist himself. He overlooks the scene and makes shrewd comment, reappearing in *Banjo,* a longer but more formless work dealing with a group of adventurers left in the wake of the war. This book is not without its deeper notes; the didactic strain in fact may even seem to be overdone. (pp. 244-45)

Gingertown is a collection of twelve stories, six of which are set in Harlem and the others in the West Indies. The author shows that he is best when he is on his native heath, but all of the stories are marked by robustness, though again and again the characters are wanton or gross. *Banana Bottom* goes back to Jamaica and in telling of the career of Bita Plant gives a fine satire on the ways of benevolent folk. An exceptional character is Squire Gensir, an Englishman interested in studying folk-ways but without any semblance of patronage. This book like the others has elements of strength, but one can not help thinking what Mr. McKay might do if he would take a little vacation from slums and water-fronts, see life somewhat more as a whole, and conceive the really great novel of which he is undoubtedly capable. (p. 246)

> *Benjamin Brawley, "The New Realists," in his* The Negro Genius: A New Appraisal of the Achievement of the American Negro in Literature and the Fine Arts *(copyright 1937 by Dodd, Mead & Co., Inc.; copyright renewed © 1965 by Thaddeus Gaylord), Dodd, Mead, 1937 (and reprinted by Biblo and Tannen, 1966), pp. 231-68.*

ROBERT A. SMITH   (essay date 1948)

Claude McKay fits into a pattern of thought which had its genesis directly after World War I. He did not agree with the theory of passive resistance, or of complacent nonchalance, as did some Negro writers. His strongest attribute was the extreme dislike for prevailing standards of racial discrimination; hence he lost no opportunity, when writing, to attack the *status quo*. . . .

Previously, most poets had written for the love of the art; now they decided, for the most part, to use their poetry as *media* for attacking race prejudice in all of its ramifications. Negroes had no swords, so the poets took up pens for them. Foremost in this movement was Claude McKay, whose vituperation was the extreme. (p. 270)

[*Harlem Shadows* is McKay's] best known collection of poems. This book spoke the passionate language of a persecuted race, and its author did not make the least attempt to disguise his feelings. He did not attempt to please his white readers; his voice is a direct blast at them for their policy of discrimination. Many of the poems are saturated with protest. . . . One can easily find here the philosophy of a race expressed in the few lines of a poem. This is not the poetry of submission or acquiescence; this is not the voice of a gradualist. . . . It is one of scorching flame, a voice conscious of persecution, that dares to strike back with vehemence. (pp. 271-72)

McKay was simply defiant in his protest poetry. So much so was he, that in many instances this characteristic completely obscures his lyricism.

In the title poem, "**Harlem Shadows**," one finds various shades of this protest, yet there is also some semblance of beautiful lyricism. There are some good interpretations of life in Harlem. . . . The poem is mediocre, but reveals the author's bitterness toward the conditions which produce the Negro prostitutes of Harlem. I question the poet's choice of such as a title poem for his book. Certainly this is a sordid aspect of the race to thrust forward. In addition, it is not the best poem in the collection. The greatest justification that can be found for it is that it is realistic, and accurately describes a phase of existing life.

One must admit that the author's most powerful dudgeon lay in this protest poetry. Whether he wrote an epigram, a sonnet, or a longer poem, his thought is sustained. He expressed the deepest resentment, but even when doing so his feelings were lucid. He did not stumble as he attempted to express himself. This dynamic force within his poetry caused him to be constantly read and re-read by his admirers and critics. They realized that here was a man of deepest emotions, as well as one who was a skilled craftsman.

In the sonnet, McKay had found a verse form peculiarly adaptable to his taste and ability. His talent was diversified, but this form with its rise and fall seemed quite the thing for the thought which he wished to convey to his readers. (pp. 272-73)

Occasionally, however, one sees another side of McKay. When he puts down his rancor, his lyricism is entirely clear. He paints pictures that are beautiful; especially is this true when he describes scenes of his native islands. One sees in the poet a sort of nostalgia for home, for relatives, and for the scenes of childhood days, long past. It is in this idyllic mood that McKay appears in an entirely different light. . . . Their mood is one of quietness also. Others in this group show McKay's range and facility. There is sheer delight in reading them, and the collection would be richer with more of the same tone. . . .

McKay took upon himself a tremendous task when he chose to be the leading spokesman of an oppressed race. The question always arises as to whether a poet loses any or all of his effectiveness when he takes upon his shoulders the problem of fighting. Does one's lyrical ability become clouded by his propaganda or bombast? is another question. This, it seems, may or may not be true. In the case of McKay, what he has had to say, for the most part has been important. Literary history is full of humanitarians who attacked conditions that were unsavory. Some were successful in their attacks; others were not. Although he was frequently concerned with the race problem, his style is basically lucid. One feels disinclined to believe that the medium which he chose was too small, or too large for his message. He has been heard. (p. 273)

Robert A. Smith, "Claude McKay: An Essay in Criticism," in PHYLON: The Atlanta University Review of Race and Culture, *9 (copyright, 1948, copyright renewed © 1976, by Atlanta University; reprinted by permission of* PHYLON), *Vol. IX, No. 3, Third Quarter (September, 1948), pp. 270-73.*

ROBERT BONE   (essay date 1958)

McKay's first novel, *Home to Harlem* . . . , was an immediate popular success. Like many novels of the 1920's, it opens with a farewell to arms. Jake, the central character, goes AWOL from the white folks' war and comes "home to Harlem." He picks up a "tantalizing brown" for $50, but she returns his money as a gift, after leaving him during the night. The plot, which is little more than a device, concerns his attempt to find her again. The narrative structure is loose and vagrant, tracing Jake's movements from cabaret to "rent party," from poolroom to gin mill, from the docks to the dining car. McKay depends upon atmosphere to carry the book. The style is appropriately impressionistic, full of hyphenated adjectives aimed at vivid impressions of Harlem life.

The beginnings of a dramatic structure may be seen, however, in the characters of Jake and Ray. Jake represents pure instinct. Physical well-being—whether from good food, good liquor, or a good woman—is his prime value. Work when you feel like it. Loaf when the mood strikes you. Take life easy. Joy is the key word in understanding Jake; lust is a sign of repression. . . . Through Jake, McKay strikes at the heart of the Protestant ethic. Jake's very existence is an act of affirmation, an injunction to enjoy life!

Ray is a young Haitian, consumed with a desire to write, whom Jake befriends on his railroad run. Ray embodies the dilemma of the inhibited, overcivilized intellectual. A misfit in the white man's civilization, he refuses to be penned in. . . . Yet he is unable, like Jake, to entrust himself wholly to instinct. For Ray, "Thought is suffering"—the opposite of joy. He is depressed by the state of contemporary society. . . . His is that profound disgust which modern life sometimes evokes in men of artistic sensibilities.

Through a faulty denouement, the symbolic import of Jake and Ray is imperfectly conveyed. Ray, disgusted with all that is sordid and ugly in the lives of the dining-car waiters, ships out on a freighter bound for Europe. Jake, in the closing pages of the novel, finds his lost Felice, whose name signifies joy. By contrasting Jake's happiness with Ray's restless wandering, McKay attempts to convey the superiority of instinct over reason. But at bottom, Jake and Ray represent different ways of rebelling against Western civilization. Jake rebels instinctively, while Ray's rebellion occurs on an intellectual plane. Both characters acquire a broader significance only through their negative relationship to contemporary society. McKay's failure to develop this relationship is the failure of the novel.

Jake is the typical McKay protagonist—the primitive Negro, untouched by the decay of Occidental civilization. The validity of this symbol, however, depends upon McKay's view of contemporary life. Since the author cannot take this view for granted, he introduces himself into the novel as Ray, in order to expound it. But Ray hardly helps matters; in *Home to Harlem* he does little more than state his prejudices. As a result, the novel is left without a suitable antagonist. Jake and Ray are vivid enough, but what they would deny is not always clear. The novel, unable to develop its primary conflict, bogs down in the secondary contrast between Jake and Ray.

In *Banjo* . . . , the sequel of *Home to Harlem,* McKay comes closer to realizing his central theme. He is moving slowly toward the finished form which he finally achieves in *Banana Bottom.* The setting of *Banjo* has shifted from Harlem to the waterfront at Marseilles, but the main symbols are the same. Jake's role is played by Banjo, an irrepressible, joy-loving vagabond, while Ray is present once more to act as interpreter. (pp. 68-9)

Ray editorializes freely throughout [*Banjo*], and from his lengthy discourses we can reconstruct McKay's indictment of European civilization. To begin with, Western society harbors against the colored man a not-so-blind prejudice. . . . Commercialism is the canker which is destroying the soul of the West. Hypocrisy is its handmaiden—a pious pose of patriotism, Christianity, and sexual purity which cloaks colonialism, economic rapacity, and bawdiness. An unwholesome attitude toward sex is warping the personality of "civilized" man. . . . Finally, a sterile trend toward standardization and conformity threatens to destroy the rich cultural diversity exemplified by such minorities as the Jews, the Irish, and the American Negro.

In dramatizing his indictment of Western civilization, McKay relies too heavily on Ray's rhetoric, but he also gropes toward a fictional presentation. The American steamship company named the Dollar Line, the brutality of the French police toward the beach boys, and a pornographic film of the "Blue Cinema" variety, help him to make his point. The French chauffeur, who intends to buy a suburban lot from his proceeds as a pimp, is a symbol of bourgeois respectability founded on sordid commercialism. The setting of the novel is likewise symbolic. Marseilles is the chief port of Mediterranean commerce and the crossroads of Europe and Africa. Its waterfront district provides a worm's-eye view of European civilization. But these scattered symbols can never replace successful characterization. Even in *Banjo,* McKay's antagonist remains an abstraction.

The protagonist of the novel, however, succeeds as both character and symbol. Convincing as a person, Banjo takes on additional depth, until in the end he comes to stand for a way of life. McKay expects us to see beyond the Ditch [the Marseilles waterfront section] to the positive values which Banjo embodies. A careless attitude toward money is central to these values. . . . He plays jazz for fun, not for the commercial motives of the white musicians. He knows how to laugh, how to love, how to enjoy life in the carefree manner of the vagabond. Above all, he is a folk artist—a symbol of the Negro's inventiveness and creativity. His nickname and his instrument link him to the world of jazz, with all its connotations of impudence, freedom from restraint, spontaneous improvisation, and defiance of everything drab and respectable.

In seeking values to oppose to those of bourgeois society, McKay falls back upon a separate Negro culture. Banjo's devotion to "nigger music," the beach boys' gift of language . . . , and Ray's more sophisticated interest in African folk tales and primitive African sculpture are obvious manifestations of McKay's Negro nationalism. It follows from McKay's position that he must resist assimilation into the dominant culture. In all of his novels he bitterly attacks the mulatto middle class for its "imitativeness." The lower-class Negro's stubborn resistance to assimilation is the true theme of *Banjo*. . . . (pp. 70-1)

McKay poses the central conflict in these terms: black vagabond vs. white civilization. At this point, however, the novel breaks down. Although the author intends a decisive rejection of "civilization" in favor of "Banjo," he cannot dramatize it successfully through the character of Ray. At the end of the novel Ray joins Banjo in the vagabond life. But Ray, who is more the child of modern civilization than he would care to admit, can never be a Banjo. His intellect is too great a barrier. For Ray no decisive choice is possible, but only a more or less unsatisfactory compromise. . . . The novel thus slips out of a clear-cut dualism into a fuzzy dialectical structure—*thesis,* white civilization; *antithesis,* Banjo; *synthesis,* Ray.

Banana Bottom . . . represents the culmination of McKay's search for a form. Cultural dualism is his central theme, and for its most successful expression he turns to his native Jamaica. Here the folk culture is more developed, and the clash between "native" and European values sharper. McKay has dispensed with Ray and achieved a proper distance between himself and his novel. The Craigs, a white missionary couple, are his first successful personification of Anglo-Saxon civilization. In Bita, their protégé, McKay has at last found his protagonist. Jake and Banjo, while they embodied McKay's values, were static characters. Ray, being an intellectual, was limited in his powers of renunciation. But Bita is a peasant girl, educated by white missionaries. Caught between two cultures, she is yet free to return to the folk. (pp. 71-2)

McKay uses sex as the chief means of dramatizing his theme. He understands that the major conflicts in a woman's life will be sexual, and that Bita's struggle with the Craigs will naturally assume this form. Bita rebels against her guardians by forming an attachment to a fun-loving, irresponsible scamp named Hopping Dick. In order to prevent her from backsliding, the Craigs try to arrange a marriage with a respectable young divinity student. Much to their consternation, the prospective bridegroom puts himself out of the running by defiling himself with a goat. Encouraged by her moral victory, Bita goes her own way, and the novel reaches a climax when she participates in an atavistic dance ritual. Since Hopping Dick is not a marrying man, Bita eventually settles down with Jubban, a sturdy black peasant, whose child she conceives during their engagement. . . .

[*Banana Bottom*] moves at the leisurely pace of the life which it portrays. Its tone is tranquil, in contrast to the tumultuous quality of McKay's earlier novels. Ray's tirades are gone, along with the hyphenated adjectives which McKay formerly employed to present a panorama of urban life. He strives instead for a simplicity of style suited to his pastoral setting. Much of the novel is devoted to exotic descriptions of Jamaican peasant life. Partly ornamental, these scenes are also functional in revealing the beauty of the life which Bita embraces. (p. 73)

Banana Bottom is McKay's romantic escape from the machine age, and his symbolic link with the Expressionists. Like Gauguin, the founder of French Expressionism who sought inspiration in the South Seas, McKay found artistic fulfillment in his novel of West Indian peasant life. If McKay's spiritual journey carried him "a long way from home," in the end he returned to his native island. (pp. 74-5)

Robert Bone, "The Harlem School," in his The Negro Novel in America (© 1958 by Yale University Press), Yale University Press, 1958, pp. 65-94.*

JEAN WAGNER (essay date 1962)

The two collections [of poetry] published in Jamaica in 1912 constitute a diptych of McKay's experience in his native island. The first, *Songs of Jamaica,* is a sort of highly colored epitome of the years of childhood and young manhood spent in the mountains, where he listened to Nature's great voice and shared the life of the black peasantry. Often in direct opposition to these first poems are those of *Constab Ballads,* which reveal the disillusionment and pessimism the poet felt when plunged into the life of [Kingston]. These first two volumes are already marked by a sharpness of vision, an inborn realism, and a freshness which provide a pleasing contrast with the conventionality which, at this same time, prevails among the black poets of the United States.

Not the least original aspect of these seventy-eight poems is the rough but picturesque Jamaican dialect in which most of them are written, and of which they constitute the earliest poetic use. . . . Here everything is entirely and authentically Negro. It all comes directly from the people and is rooted in the soil, alike the phonology, often flavored with a delightful exoticism, and the rather summary morphology; the typically fantastic placing of the tonic accent and the somewhat rudimentary syntax, seldom in accord with the Queen's English; and, finally, the often unexpectedly roughhewn words and images, which originate in the hard-working folk's immediate contact with a soil reluctant to part with its riches. (pp. 204-05)

Every bit as much as their language, it is the poetic quality of these works that links them genuinely to the people for whom they were written. It was no mere rhetorical flourish when McKay entitled his first collection *Songs of Jamaica*. For six poems, he adds in an appendix melodies which he composed. The songs and ballads he did not set to music are so rhythmical that a musical accompaniment could easily be provided. (p. 205)

How close the bond of sympathy was between McKay and the people is manifested also by the realism with which he characterizes the black Jamaican peasant. . . . McKay's portraits at once transcend the limits which . . . inevitably weighed on American Negro dialect and forced it to sound only the registers of humor and pathos. In any case, there is no humor to be found here, nor will it play any part in the later work. These peasants are not . . . ignorant, lazy, thieving clowns . . . , stereotypes designed to amuse the members of a superior race. . . . Unlike the character portraits usually associated with American Negro dialect, these portraits are the actual incarnation of a whole people's racial pride.

McKay's characterization of the Jamaican peasant is substantially that of the peasant anywhere in the world: deeply attached to his plot of land, over which he labors with an atavistic skill; and unsparing of himself, yet seemingly condemned to unalleviated poverty, since there is always someone to snatch the fruits of his labor. He owes his pride to the sense of work well done, and has no feeling of inferiority vis-à-vis the whites whom, when the occasion arises, he will address in the bluntest terms. (p. 206)

All in all, health, vigor, and self-assurance make up the impression left by this portrait of the black Jamaican peasant, whose age-old practical virtues and wisdom have not been sapped by his material poverty. Thus the optimism that McKay discovers in this rural milieu is derived, in the first place, from extant moral values. But there are racial reasons also. For it is highly significant that all these country folks are blacks, excluding the mulattoes whom McKay implicitly rejects as all too eager to see in their white ancestry a justification for disdaining the blacks. Finally, the real values that constitute the superiority of the black peasant reside in his closeness to the soil of Jamaica. One can scarcely overstress the importance of this element in McKay's trinitarian symbolism, which associates the good with the black race and the soil. . . .

[McKay's] roots in the soil of his native island are amazingly deep and lasting. These roots make him one with the soil. Through them he draws in his nourishment; the island's enchanting scenes call forth his earliest verses, and no one will ever rival him in praise for the mildness of its climate, the vividness of its colors, the luxuriance of its vegetation, or the coolness of its streams. (p. 211)

Like [the English Romantics], McKay felt constantly drawn to nature and sensed the need to become totally merged in it. The emotion it aroused in him transcended by far the exclusively aesthetic plane. For Nature is an ever renewed source of strength, and instinctively he returned to commune with it. (p. 213)

The earth is the whole man. [McKay] had already proclaimed this before he had turned twenty, and he realized it all the more clearly after he had left it and experienced enormous disillusionment in contact with the city, whose inhabitants he looked on as rootless, in the most concrete sense of the word. . . .

He attributed to his native soil, the nurturer, all the strength of his character and his poetic vigor. . . .

Between the black man and the earth there is a total identification. When, vexed by the city, he returns to his mountains, he will see in this return not only a reunion with the earth, but with his people also. . . . (p. 214)

Thus the racial values he associates with the soil also help to tinge his feeling for nature, and in his mind he conceives nature and the city as mutually exclusive forces. (pp. 214-15)

Hatred of the city is one of the principal motifs in McKay's Jamaican poems, and the American poems will offer variations on the same theme. In [Paul Laurence] Dunbar's work one could already note some aversion toward urban civilization, but this was only sporadic, and the motivation behind it was entirely different. . . .

But with McKay the theme is not merely more amply treated; it acquires in the racial context a symbolic importance not found in Dunbar. The city, presented as the antithesis of the land, is consequently the enemy of the black man also. (p. 215)

[In McKay's *Constab Ballads,* the] city symbolizes an evil that is multiple. In part it finds expression in the traditional ways but also, and especially, it adopts other forms that are significant in the racial context. (p. 217)

The vehemence of [a] protest against oppression . . . and the boundless despair [in many of the poems in *Constab Ballads*], are in violent contrast with the cold objectivity of the social critique voiced in the rural poems of *Songs of Jamaica*. It heralds what will be McKay's stance in his American poems. . . . Thus it serves to make entirely plain the changes that city residence brought about in McKay. (p. 218)

[McKay's] American poems give vent to his racial pride with a forcefulness he had never exhibited before. This outburst is so authentic, and so much in keeping with his own fiery, passionate temperament, that little influence need be attributed to the stimulus he could have found elsewhere. . . . Furthermore, as he faced the onslaught of white insolence, his pride grew in militancy without losing any of its nobility. . . .

As this pride is strengthened and tested by adversity, he raises racial consciousness to the aesthetic plane. One would almost be tempted to affirm that the poet is inaugurating a hedonism of color, when one beholds how with a supremely refined sensuality he savors the heady joy of his blackness, gaining awareness of it amidst a community that tortures him, but to which he feels superior in every fiber of his being. . . . (p. 223)

No one ever expressed with such a wealth of nuances the opposing eddies that swirl in a mind in search of equilibrium amid stupidly hostile surroundings. This attempt at introspective insight clearly demonstrates how racial pride can act as a redemptive force. (p. 224)

To no lesser degree than the intoxication of being black, Claude McKay learned in America how intoxicating it is to hate. . . . Hatred has acquired quite a power of transfiguration. It becomes the favored theme of the poet's song, for it alone can make his surroundings bearable. (pp. 224-25)

It was once declared that hatred is not a poetic emotion. If this act of exclusion were to be acquiesced in, it would oblige us to find no poetic merit whatever in Claude McKay's most striking poems since he, among all black poets, is *par excellence* the poet of hate. This, when situated in its racial context, has a very special characteristic. . . . [It] is the actual prerequisite for his survival, since it transmutes into a paradise the base inferno of the white world. It is a sort of antidote secreted throughout his being and which prevents the White City from emptying him of his substance—were it not for this fostering flood of hatred, which constantly provides him with fresh energies, he would be reduced by the city to the level of a skeleton, of a sea creature's abandoned shell. Hatred is the compensatory factor that assures the equilibrium of his personality, allowing him to adapt himself adequately to his environment. (pp. 225-26)

[With the publication of **"If We Must Die,"** McKay became] the incarnation of the new spirit and the spokesman for a whole people at last resolved to witness no longer, in resignation and submissiveness, the massacre of its own brothers at the hands of the enraged white mob, but to return blow for blow and, if necessary, to die. (p. 229)

The welcome accorded [**"If We Must Die"**] is . . . due, in part, to its being one of those poems in which McKay's poetic gift reaches beyond the circumstances of the day to attain the universal. Along with the will to resistance of black Americans that it expresses, it voices also the will of oppressed peoples of every age who, whatever their race and wherever their region, are fighting with their backs against the wall to win their freedom. (p. 230)

McKay appears to have expressed all the complexity of his real feelings about America in the sonnet entitled **"America"**. . . .

What is predominant here, and basic also, is his love for America, whose strength acts on the poet like a stimulant. The other half of the picture, the hatred that America has for blacks, does not obliterate the poet's love for it. McKay's hatred does not mean a rejection of America; it is a reproach directed against the country's inability to reconcile discriminatory practices with egalitarian democratic doctrines. In the last analysis, what he hates is not America, but evil. (p. 231)

We know that the essential evil is the division between man and man, the white man's hatred and contempt for his fellow man, and the exploitation of black by white. In the "civilized hell" of America, evil adopts the most varied guises. But a natural defense reaction leads McKay to note those in particular which deny the black man's humanity. The metaphors often depict America as a kind of vampire seeking to deprive the victim of his substance and to leave him a mere shell or skeleton. America becomes, for instance, a tiger, his striped coat representing the stripes of the American flag, who seizes his prey by the throat and nourishes himself on the blood. (pp. 231-32)

[In other poems], whites are depicted as birds darkening the sky with their wings, then swooping down on their victims to gorge themselves on the hearts. . . .

Blood and heart quite assuredly have a symbolic value in these poems, which denounce the depersonalization of the black man and his exploitation by society's rulers, who glut themselves on his financial and artistic substance. But this carnage also requires a more literal interpretation, so that the poems may be understood as a condemnation of lynching, like the sonnet **"The Lynching,"** where McKay speaks more openly. (p. 232)

Though McKay may justifiably be called the poet of hatred and rebellion, his real personality would be seriously misrepresented if one were to treat him as an out-and-out rebel. . . . To adopt this point of view is to overlook the remarkable self-mastery that McKay could summon up, and to neglect the personal purification and, when all is considered, the moral elevation that McKay believed he could derive from his hate.

It is, indeed, admirable that in his case hatred and rebellion did not become, as they might have, a vehicle lurching onward without reins or brakes. Even when he revels in his hate, he does not wallow in it, and in the midst of the hurricane he retains his control. . . .

However passionate his rebellious flights of rhetoric, they are always lucid and dominated by an unflagging will to self-transcendence. . . .

He simply does not look on hatred as an end in itself. It is but a stage on the path that ends in the divine charity, for which its purifying action prepares the way. Understood thus, McKay's hatred is a holy anger the manifestation of which occurs only in entire clarity of mind. . . . Ultimately, what sets a limit to hatred is the spiritual. Such is the message of the sonnet **"To the White Fiends,"** in which God compels hatred to stop on the brink of murder, directing it to a higher goal. . . . (p. 235)

Thus, far from being a "way of life," McKay's hatred undergoes a sublimation that induces it to consume itself. In its place comes a tranquillity that is not indifference, but a deepening and internalization of racial feeling. . . .

In McKay's work, the feeling for nature occupies almost as important a place as racial feeling. One could, indeed compose a Jamaican flora by citing not only his poems, but also the novel **Banana Bottom** and some of the short stories included in **Gingertown**. His nature poems are all the more admirable for sounding a truer note. . . . [McKay brings to nature] the understanding and sympathy of a person who grew up in it and whose rare sensitivity brought him to an authentic integration with it. In **Harlem Shadows,** the nature poems make up nearly one-third of the volume. The languorous sweetness of their lyricism is like a cool breeze from the Isles, introducing a note of most welcome tranquillity into the militant fierceness of the poems of rebellion. (p. 236)

In the freshness of this panorama of idyllic life in the tropics, we find all that is antithetical to the ugliness and gloom of Western civilization, which is symbolized by the city. . . . Around this polarity more than one poem in **Harlem Shadows** is constructed. . . . (p. 238)

It can be seen that McKay's feeling for nature has no autonomous existence. Since it is linked with the racial symbolism of the earth and remains closely subordinated to it, seen from this point of view it most often amounts to the enunciation of a sense of belonging.

Its expressive value, because of this role, falls together with that of the African theme as treated by many poets of the Negro Renaissance. For them, Africa is the land still unpolluted by the inhuman machine outlook of the white man, hungry to enslave his fellow men. But for them—those who are unable to identify with America, the land that treats them inhumanely—Africa is the substitute land where they can seek their roots; Africa is the mother with whom, in the place of stepmotherly America which has rejected them, they try to form an *a posteriori* bond of relationship.

McKay is totally unconcerned with these substitute values. . . . He has no need to go all the way to Africa to find the palm trees to which he can compare the black girls. Jamaica is his Africa, and its exoticism is a genuine exoticism, not a dream escape to some substitute fatherland the need for which springs from a feeling of frustration.

It is not surprising, therefore, that he keeps the African theme within much more modest limits than the other Renaissance poets, whose feeling of unqualified admiration for Africa he does not share. The whole body of his work contains scarcely more than half a dozen poems devoted to Africa, and not one of them can be considered an apologia. (pp. 238-39)

In "Outcast," it is again the sense of being captive in the white man's empire that occupies the poet's mind, rather than any feeling of solidarity with Africa. Nevertheless, this second factor emerges with greater clarity here than in any other poem by McKay. But he is less intent on affirming his link with Africa than in regretting that the elements forming this link have been lost or forgotten. . . . He must be taken to express his kinship with the blacks of the United States, whose spokesman he has become, and to state the truth, as suggested by the poem's title, that he himself has been rejected by the white American majority. These two ingredients are more obvious than any putative avowal of genuine solidarity with Africa. (p. 242)

In no single instance does McKay play the part of an apologist for Africa. He might even be blamed, if not for failing to foresee, at least for not having hoped for and more boldly desired an African renewal. . . . [The] firmness of his attachment to Jamaica, as much as his intellectual probity and his clearsightedness, precluded his seeking an unrealistic solution for his own problems by evading them in favor of participation in solving others' problems, even if these others should be Africans.

Thus if McKay is a forerunner of the Negro Renaissance, this is not due to his vision of Africa. The genuine quality of his Jamaican exoticism had immunized him against the heady African mirage, and his ability to stand resolute against its seductions attests, in the last resort, the cohesiveness and equilibrium of his personality. . . .

McKay has left us only a few poems dealing with Harlem. . . . [*Harlem Shadows*] has but two poems on the theme, the title poem and "The Harlem Dancer." (p. 243)

Yet, though for these reasons he can scarcely be called the poet of Harlem, at least he has the merit of being the first to introduce Harlem into Negro poetry. . . . Earlier than Langston Hughes, it is Claude McKay who provided the first annotations on the frivolous night life that . . . would enable Harlem to prosper. These poems might also be said to constitute the first poetic documents on the reactions of the black man borne to the urban centers by the tide of the Great Migration. There is nothing astonishing in the fact that McKay, as a shrewd observer of every aspect of city life, paid particularly close attention to this phenomenon.

"Harlem Shadows" is a poem in a minor key on the prostitutes that urban civilization, with its lack of humanity, had thrown onto the Harlem sidewalks. The poem is reminiscent of those that McKay, in the 1912 volumes, had devoted to the moral debacle of two country girls as a result of their going to live in Kingston. But "Harlem Shadows" is an innovation in the sense that McKay attributes a primordial importance to the prostitutes' color (blackening them further by referring to them as shadows) and makes their downfall symbolic of the whole race's. In each case, the blame is implicitly allotted to racial oppression. This biased suggestion deviates significantly from

McKay's usually realistic, objective manner, and one would have expected him to treat these prostitutes as victims of the city rather than as slaves of the master race. This deference to racial propaganda spoils the end of the poem, which otherwise would have been very much to the point. . . . (p. 244)

"The Harlem Dancer" plunges us into the atmosphere of one of the countless night spots that sprang up in Harlem after World War I. This sonnet raises the problem of another sort of prostitution, that of Negro art to popular (mainly white) demands. White people appear in the sonnet as drunken spectators who gobble up with their eyes the form of a naked black dancer. Between the young whites, in search of venal pleasures, and the nobility of the black beauty, the comparison is to the advantage of the latter. She appears before us in all the pride of a tall palm tree swaying majestically in the wind, yet she is an uprooted palm tree, torn from a kindlier country where she has left her soul. Her natural grace and beauty contrast with the artificial setting into which she has been transplanted, and her forced smile cannot hide her longing for her native land. Underneath the exoticism of detail, we once again come upon a thesis greatly favored by McKay and the Negro Renaissance, maintaining that the white world, more often than was generally believed, was a setting unfit to receive all that blacks have to offer it. (pp. 244-45)

Poets have often been attracted by the theme of black dancers. [Paul Laurence] Dunbar, it will be recalled, has left us entertaining portrayals of evenings spent dancing the quadrille with, in his day, the added savor of forbidden fruit. Jazz, in its turn, will soon find its true poet in Langston Hughes. Thus it need not surprise us that McKay also should have chosen to see in the liberation of the dance, as in the spontaneity and the subtle rhythms of the dancers, an especially revealing manifestation of the "immortal spirit" of his race, since here one could note the urge to expand, to express oneself, to free oneself, instincts that in daily life had to be kept in check at every instant.

But whereas Dunbar and Hughes let themselves be swept away by the vortex of the dance, McKay remained the detached observer, though sensing the emotion that radiated from the dancers to him. His view is an external one; a space remains between him and the crowd of dancers and allows him no identification with them. He, unlike Dunbar and Hughes, is not one of the dancers he describes. . . . It can be sensed that McKay experiences a measure of despair vis-à-vis the tragedy of this superficial response of a whole race to the oppression and contempt by which it is victimized.

This is . . . another manifestation of McKay's reserved attitude when confronted by the folk temperament, with which he never felt entirely at ease. Other elements that lead us to the same conclusion are the total absence of humor throughout his poetry and his preference for such classical poetic forms as the sonnet. Spirituals, blues, and jazz . . . have no place in McKay's poetic work. . . . [McKay] must have had a background awareness that the popular forms and outlook could become, as has in reality often occurred, an excuse for avoiding personal reflection, and so would have been only another sort of escapism for the poet. Thus, while he defends Negro art against the deformations that whites inflicted on it, he defended it no less vigorously against those Negroes who were tempted to ask of it something that it could not provide: a soul. . . . [In] Harlem he could now see to what a degree . . . culture was emptied of substance the moment it lost contact with the soil, which alone could give it life, and was transported to the city, which in McKay's eyes had ever been a corrupting influence. In a word, he judged Negro popular culture, as he had encountered it in America, to be incapable of fulfilling his need for an authentic spiritual life. (pp. 246-47)

[McKay], with his nonconformist temperament, was repelled by the idea of adhering to traditions that took the place of individual reflection. His religious poetry is the expression of an inner growth, and his discovery of God the result of his individual search for truth. From a more general vantage-point, his poetic opus may be considered as the account of a vast attempt at a synthesis between the antagonistic elements of the black world and the Western world warring within him. There can be no denying that McKay, like every black exiled in a white milieu, was for a long time a divided man, so that it is possible to speak of his cultural dualism. But he never acquiesced in being torn apart by this dichotomy. His whole being urged him to find unity. The critique to which he subjected the antinomies deprived them, little by little, of their contingencies and laid bare their authentic values. In Jamaica, he affirmed the primacy of the soil and contrasted it with the inanity of the dream, cherished by the mulattoes, of a heightened social status. He rejected the mirage of Africa as a source of racial pride, looking on it as merely pathetic. He shunned the nationalism of a [Marcus] Garvey, whom he regarded as a charlatan, and while he defended Negro folklore against whites, who would have denatured it, he nevertheless could not find spiritual sustenance in it. On the other hand, it was his natural instinct to evaluate the possibilities of spiritual advancement offered by Western, Christian culture, but there too he perceived the corroding evil that sowed hatred between men. In his dialogue with the West, conducted through the medium of his hatred, this emotion was slowly filtered of its dross as he came to grasp the necessity of raising himself above it. Unless the individual is engaged in a ceaseless effort to transcend himself, no victory over hatred will ever be possible. Neither rationalism nor Communism could provide the higher principle capable of reconciling the conflicting theses of his cultural eclecticism. At long last he discovered this principle within himself, and at the same time he discovered God. Thus his spiritual itinerary is an account of the internalization of his racial feeling. (pp. 248-49)

Be that as it may, the poet's critique of what we shall call the official faith soon led him to become his own spiritual advisor. This imbues him with a taste for that upward movement of the soul that a victory over his passions represents, and it accustoms him to view progress as a continual upgrading of the individual through self-transcendence, which alone makes existence worthwhile "in an empty world." These are the qualities of soul that McKay brings to the spiritual enrichment of black poetry, as his voice blends in with those of the American black poets. (p. 251)

Jean Wagner, "Claude McKay," in his Black Poets of the United States: From Paul Laurence Dunbar to Langston Hughes, *translated by Kenneth Douglas (copyright 1973 by The Board of Trustees of the University of Illinois; reprinted by permission of the author; originally published as* Les poètes nègres des Etats-Unis, *Librairie Istra, Paris, 1962), University of Illinois Press, 1973, pp. 197-257.*

ARTHUR D. DRAYTON (essay date 1967)

[Claude McKay] is known best and often only for his race-conscious verse, sometimes only by his much-quoted sonnet [*If We Must Die*]. . . .

[The] charge of racial hatred [in McKay's poetry] is difficult to support; and unless we are to argue a complete change in McKay between this later protest verse and his earlier dialect poems, it is a strange assertion. For, quite apart from the evidence of the protest verse itself, it assumes a new dimension if one is familiar with McKay's two publications of dialect poems before he left Jamaica to take up residence in the United States.

But it is not surprising that McKay should have won recognition through his verse written around the theme of Negro suffering in the States. For this has the virility one might expect of a Caribbean poet shocked by what he discovers in America. Coming from quite a different kind of experience of Negro degradation in Jamaica, McKay was fired by what he saw in the States and helped to give to American Negro poetry a distinctly different voice. (p. 76)

[McKay's] early years in America coincided with crucial years for the Negro cause, and the virility of his verse was in keeping with the prevailing atmosphere. But, looked at closely, this virility reveals itself as based on something more than mere bitterness; it includes and depends on a certain resilience— perhaps stubborn humanity would be better—on the part of the poet. And this in turn is to be traced to McKay's capacity to react to Negro suffering, not just as a Negro, but as a human being; to react to human suffering as such. (pp. 76-7)

[McKay, in his poetry,] is moved by what he sees as a noble duty devolving on the Negro to save not just himself but the human race; to restore, if necessary through the Negro's very sacrifice, the dignity of man. It is a sentiment, in brief, informed by a sense of responsibility to mankind. . . . This, then, is one way in which he escapes the blight of racial hatred which would have been fatal to his humanist concern.

Sometimes, too, there is a certain poignancy as he attempts to reconcile his reaction as a Negro with his larger reaction as a human being. To see his verse in terms of mere racialism is to miss this quality. . . . (pp. 77-8)

[The] human pity was there from the beginning and evident in his early dialect verse. Its source lies in the poet's tender, gentle spirit. And both in his early and later verse it saves him from racial extremism. (p. 78)

An undercurrent of protest is always [present in McKay's early work], but it is social protest—though in the context of Jamaica in the first two decades of the century this inevitably meant protest on behalf of the black man. To write about those who suffered was to write about the black man, and the fact that they were black must have quickened McKay's interest in them. However, one does not get the impression that his protest emanates primarily from a sense of race, but rather from his shocked sense of fair play, ultimately and instinctively from that very characteristic trait of McKay's to which reference has already been made, his tender, gentle spirit that was appalled at human suffering. (pp. 78-9)

[McKay's] first volume, *Songs of Jamaica,* does not deal with [his experiences on the Jamaican Police Force] but was written to relieve his feelings while in the Force. Here then was a situation that might have produced one of two elements or both, anger and sentimentality. Of the latter there is very little; and nowhere in this volume is there any anger in McKay's voice, although over and over again he is reprimanding those responsible for social injustices to his people. No doubt McKay, writing to relieve his feelings, must have sought for redeeming features in the dark picture. So that while his gentle nature led him to pity his people's suffering and to protest against this, his need for relief must have compelled him to celebrate their cheerfulness and other such qualities. That is to say, what emerges from this volume is not only his keen sense of suffering, and his people's suffering, but also his deep knowledge of what sustains them and makes them interesting and vital as human beings, their cheerfulness and good humour in spite of dispiriting conditions. (p. 79)

The technique which is used [in *Songs of Jamaica*] is to make the suffering of his people the starting point, often by critising those responsible for it or oblivious of it, and then without inconsistency to proceed to sing of the cheerfulness and glory of the victims. This conflict between suffering and cheerfulness is there, both in the people forming the subject of the poems and in the poems themselves, even in poems where he is not explicitly criticising anyone; in the latter it is always resolved in the unstated authority of the poet to sing of both, having shared in both. (pp. 81-2)

[Both] early and late McKay evinces a sensitive identification with his people, whose suffering is his suffering, whose joys are his joys. He is proud of his race, and is hurt by the wrongs they suffer. And yet in his early work there is no strident racial protest. . . . What we have here is primarily not a racial poet but someone whose human pity finds ample scope in the social and economic inferiority of his people. When he takes up residence in the United States amid the welter of human suffering, he will quite rightly be concerned first of all with the victims of it, the Negroes; but this will not prevent him from seeing other implications, terrible and far-reaching, for those who are guilty of the evil, for mankind as a whole, and not least for himself as a poet and as a human being. (p. 82)

McKay wrote his first volume of verse to relieve his feelings, to avoid self-pity; and in doing so he celebrated precisely those qualities on which people must fall back if they are to avoid it. In his second volume of Jamaican poems, *Constab Ballads,* he faces his personal dilemma more squarely; nor does the question of self-pity arise, since he recognises that his dilemma does not exist in isolation. . . .

[These] ballads represent a wide variety of moods, and as the poet catalogues the different kinds of suffering which it is the lot of the policeman to encounter, it is as though he is recording his disappointed hopes for mankind. It is, in a word, his human pity which directs him from his personal dilemma to a more universal one. (p. 83)

[If] McKay were simply a racial poet it would have been a short step, in [the] new conditions [of his life in America], from his Jamaican verse to bitter race-conscious work. Instead, however, we find for a long time a sober reaction to his new and disturbing environment. However much this new environment was dominated by the race question, it is clear that McKay . . . was determined that the dignity of the poet's calling was not to be sullied. He refused to allow the quality of his reaction as poet to be warped; and equally he refused to allow his ambitions and status as a human being to be destroyed. All this affected his poetry, and explains the apparent ambivalence in his love-hate relationship with America. (p. 84)

[McKay] sees not only the violence done to his own people, but the violence which the whites inflict on themselves as well. This, then, is McKay refusing to be stampeded into hysterical protest, served well by his breadth of vision which his capacity

for human pity had strengthened. He can still be touched by misery pure and simple. . . .

It is not that McKay is not reacting to Negro suffering. It is rather that he is meeting America's challenge as man and poet. He meets the challenge which America's hate sets for his humanity, and in his resistance he flings back his challenge to the forces of hate in America. As poet and man he must discipline himself, and this gives to his pain a dignity through which his verse sometimes transcends racial protest and becomes human protest. (p. 85)

[At] a time of hatred [McKay] does not lose his sense of balance nor his breadth of vision. Fully sensitive to the Negro plight, sharing in it and bitter about it . . . he nevertheless contrives to maintain his equilibrium while protesting vehemently. It is sometimes a protest on behalf of humanity, for he is a poet. But he was also a black man in the United States, and it is more often a protest on behalf of his people, and for this he reserves a language that is often bitter and violent. But he never loses his temper; his poetry does not become undisciplined because of anger; he can achieve his effect through the dignity of his pain, through the controlled power of an image. . . . He does not seek to hide his bitterness. But having preserved his vision as poet and his status as a human being, he can transcend bitterness. In seeing, as he does, the significance of the Negro for mankind as a whole, he is at once protesting as a Negro and uttering a cry for the race of mankind as a member of that race. His human pity was the foundation that made all this possible. (pp. 87-8)

Arthur D. Drayton, "Claude McKay's Human Pity: A Note on His Protest Poetry," in Introduction to African Literature: An Anthology of Critical Writing from "Black Orpheus," *edited by Ulli Beier (© Ulli Beier and Mbari, 1967), Longmans, 1967 (and reprinted by Northwestern University Press, 1970), pp. 76-88.*

KENNETH RAMCHAND   (essay date 1970)

Home to Harlem and *Banjo* had ended with the departures of exiles. *Banana Bottom* begins with the return of a native. The characters of the first two novels extracted a living on the edges of society, the characters of the third are rooted in a landscape. The violent debates of the earlier works, in which there is only a thin line between author and character are now succeeded by the controlled idyllic tone of a distanced narrator. The central character is not a figure of *malaise* like Ray of the preceding novels, nor does McKay find it necessary to externalize *malaise* in the form of a complementary but separated pair such as Jake and Ray or Banjo and Ray. The polarized pair of heroes of the first two novels are replaced by a single heroine. Bita Plant, the daughter of a Jamaican peasant, is brought up by the Reverend Malcolm Craig and his wife Priscilla. After seven years abroad at an English University and on the Continent, Bita returns to her native land. *Banana Bottom* tells the story of how she gradually strips away what is irrelevant in her English upbringing, and how she marries Jubban the strong silent drayman in her father's employ. To put it in this way is to make it clear at once that McKay's theme is still cultural dualism. The differences between *Banana Bottom* and the other novels are differences in art. Bita Plant is the first achieved West Indian heroine and *Banana Bottom* is the first classic of West Indian prose.

The action of the novel alternates between the village of Banana Bottom where Bita spends her early years, and the adjoining town of Jubilee where she is groomed by the Craigs; and McKay makes unobtrusive use of the nominal difference between the two in order to symbolize Bita's final liberation and embrace of the folk. . . . From [the] opening moments of the novel, McKay steadily builds up a sense of a way of life. Its constitutive elements are tea-meeting, picnic, market, harvest festival, pimento picking, house-parties and ballad-making. Its people range themselves across an ordered spectrum of swiftly and vividly drawn individuals. . . . (pp. 259-60)

The main action takes place against a background buzzing with life and implication. But it is more than this. Bita belongs to a sustaining community. . . . It is because Bita belongs, and because the community is realized as having spontaneous values of its own that we can credit her fictional process. The incident with Crazy Bow which leads to Bita's adoption by the Craigs illustrates how McKay enriches the background life of the community by drawing out one of the background characters to perform a specific significant function and then letting him slip back into his independent life again. The incident also illustrates how McKay at last integrates music (a recurrent vitalizing element in the other novels) into the action and meaning of the novel without signs of straining. (pp. 260-61)

To be noted here is that McKay has dispensed with the hyphenated words, the impressionistic dots, and the ancestral transports of dancers and players which characterized music passages in the earlier novels. . . . Because the community has replaced a vague ancestral land, like that evoked in *Banjo,* and because each character in it has a specific past to which to refer, McKay's rendering of the moving power of . . . music needs no authorial insistence. (pp. 261-62)

Relating Crazy Bow to the earlier novels we might note that he combines vagabondage with music. . . . Crazy Bow represents the same kind of protest against civilization as the guitar-playing Banjo, but McKay's well-proportioned world does not admit of that protest being over-insistent nor of the protesting character being central. The value that Crazy Bow represents is a real one which the society must assimilate. But it does not set itself up as the only value. Where Matthew Arnold fails, McKay triumphs sweetly. (p. 262)

The Crazy Bow incident establishes Bita's natural connection with the Banana Bottom world. Her transference to Jubilee and tutelage under the Craigs is an artificial thing. When Bita returns after her seven years abroad she is still herself. The character who is a returned native presents McKay with a plausible medium for the nostalgia expressed in his poems and in the earlier novels. (p. 264)

The clash between Bita and Mrs. Craig is successfully dramatized as a particular one between two incompatible people. From [a] sound beginning it develops into a confrontation between two ways of life. Instead of the rhetoric of an authorial voice, we move into the consciousness of a character seeking a *modus vivendi.* . . . (pp. 266-67)

McKay's presentation of Herald Newton Day is enhanced by the new sense of characterization and human relationships that we see in *Banana Bottom,* and by the newly discovered comic resources. Because Day poses a threat to the heroine we can enjoy his deflation. . . . McKay lets Day's own pompous language do the work, and he allows Bita and Gensir to patronize him. . . . Since Day is the willing protégé of the Craigs, McKay can satirize him plausibly as a Negro who gets a white man's education and learns to despise his own people. . . . Herald Newton Day is the same type as the Martiniquan attacked by Ray in the novel *Banjo,* but it is only within the regulating structure of *Banana Bottom* and with McKay's sense of Day as an individual in the fictional world that the satiric effect can be achieved without signs of authorial straining. But the art of *Banana Bottom* is not free from impurities: it seems to be an indication of a loss of control in the novelist as well that, by the most violent irony [Herald Newton defiles himself with a goat]. . . . The plot demands that Herald Newton should be removed from the scene but one cannot help feeling that the author is indulging a spiteful impulse. (pp. 268-70)

Bita's conflicts with Mrs. Craig and her antagonism to Herald Newton Day are associated with her alienation from the town of Jubilee, and with her increasing preference for the village of *Banana Bottom* where she had spent her early childhood. (p. 270)

Bita's increasing sense of her rootedness in the Banana Bottom community is reflected in her deliberate flouting of Mrs. Craig's wishes. A climax of a kind is reached when with Herald Newton long banished, the two women clash over Hopping Dick's coming to the mission to escort Bita to a dance. . . . Moving from this particular show of antagonism between the two characters, and with the weight of similar demonstrations in earlier episodes behind him, McKay enters the consciousness of Bita. . . . The passage is a crucial one in the sense that the doctrine it contains plays a part in the conception of the novel, but it is also crucial in terms of Bita's growing self-awareness. (p. 271)

McKay's heroine . . . is involved in a process of self-assertion. By the end of the novel, Bita has married Jubban . . . and the land has prospered under his hand. . . . In the world of *Banana Bottom,* life is going on. The recurrent McKay experience of *malaise,* of being born 'out of time', lies behind *Banana Bottom.* But the achievement of the artist in this work is the creation of a world that disperses *malaise.* . . . Art reveals possibilities. . . . In *Banana Bottom,* Claude McKay imagined a community to which it is possible to belong. (pp. 272-73)

Kenneth Ramchand, "The Road to 'Banana Bottom'," in his The West Indian Novel and Its Background *(© 1970 by Kenneth Ramchand; by permission of Barnes & Noble Books, a Division of Littlefield, Adams & Co., Inc.), Barnes & Noble, 1970, pp. 239-73.*

NATHAN IRVIN HUGGINS (essay date 1971)

McKay's [*Home to Harlem*] is far more evocative than [Carl Van Vechten's *Nigger Heaven*]. The fact that *Home to Harlem* was written from the "inside" is apparent from its confusion. Van Vechten's novel described life that the author had observed as a chosen part of his experience. McKay, on the other hand, wrote about his own context and his own frustration; he could not detach himself through an act of mind or will. He tried to be light and amoral with Jake, yet he was burdened by the heavy seriousness of Ray, whose mind would not let him escape the large issues of race and civilization. He wanted to emphasize that the simple primitive values were life-sustaining and humane, yet he was compelled to describe the violent, self-destructive, and life-destroying acts that gambling, prostitution, and narcotics occasion. . . . These ambiguities are not merely described, they are deep within McKay—his own ambivalence.

Jake is not the "noble savage" traditional in American literature. Most notably, he is completely and enthusiastically urban; there is not the slightest whimsy about his living by rural or country values. While his morality is simple and direct, his values are strictly personal and have no universal application. Jake does not despise and cannot hate; he is ashamed and sick on the two occasions when he is moved to violence. Like Natty Bumpo in James Fenimore Cooper's novels, Jake's life is a criticism of conventional morality and order. But unlike Cooper's "noble savage," Jake is unconscious of the disparity; he is indifferent to the larger society. Nor is he bigger than life, as is characteristic of the folk hero: McKay would have liked to have drawn Jake equal to life. Jake is a child-man, having the simplicity and innocence of Mark Twain's Nigger Jim, and the childlike openness and spontaneity of E. E. Cummings' Jean Le Nègre.

Jake's personal code permits him a rather wide moral swath. Cocaine, alcohol, and sex are all part of living. He does not care about the other men who have been in his women's lives. He refuses the many offers to be a "sweet man" or a pimp, but he sympathizes with a pimp and defends him as one who "also loved." His venereal disease discomfits him, but only because of the pain and the proscription of food, drink, and sex that it demands. He just does not want to hurt anybody, that is his singular moral judgment.

In many ways *Home to Harlem* amplifies themes that are in *Nigger Heaven*, treating them more authentically and forcefully. The lurid and sensational character of the book doubtless contributed to its commercial success. The reader could find here the apotheosis of the savage. Yet, beneath the surface lurked notions that were more ominous and critical. Ray, as McKay's voice, attacks with genuine bitterness the United States, white men's civilization, and European domination of dark people. The focus of the novel is elsewhere—on Jake's search for Felice—but there is a foreshadowing of a radical, racial primitivism (that rejects white men) which would dominate McKay's next novel, *Banjo*. . . . Notably, too, *Home to Harlem* totally lacks any accepted basis of order. . . . Overtly as well as covertly, McKay, through Ray, attacks progress, achievement, and success as measured by the alien white world—the human-consuming machine of the European-American culture. Van Vechten, like Cooper, is moved to find a respectable, proper, and moral lady to be the official heroine of his novel—it is a fault in *Nigger Heaven*. Agatha, Ray's nice girl friend, however, promises him only the life of the "hog." She is not intended to be a paragon. Actually, none of McKay's women are fully drawn. They are mere instruments for male behavior. Thus, he skirts the problem of an amoral heroine. Without a stable sense of moral order, *Home to Harlem* has none of the appeal to decadence that is apparent in *Nigger Heaven*. Van Vechten had to assume a morality in order to invert it. McKay's novel accepts no moral order; thus it does not experiment with it. Ironically, despite its disparagement of white values and commerce, the novel became a best seller precisely because it pandered to commercial tastes by conforming to the sensationalism demanded by the white vogue in black primitivism.

McKay's life was marked by a deep skepticism, and he at one time or another assumed many of the attitudes of the late Victorians. . . . But, altogether, it made a difference that he was black and hardly a real part of that tradition that the late Victorians found in disarray. McKay seemed to believe that the man nearest to nature and his instincts did not have to worry about purpose or games. But the paradox was, as Ray made

clear, when one knew enough to understand that, it was already too late. (pp. 124-27)

Nathan Irvin Huggins, "Heart of Darkness," in his Harlem Renaissance (copyright © 1971 by Oxford University Press, Inc.; reprinted by permission), Oxford University Press, New York, 1971, pp. 84-136.*

RICHARD K. BARKSDALE   (essay date 1972)

Traditionally, there have been two rather disparaging views of Claude McKay's *Home to Harlem*. . . . The first point of view is that it is not a well-made novel; proponents of this view charge that its plot lacks unity and is pock-marked by episodicity; there is no character development and far too much "atmosphere"—too many lyrical arpeggios to the intoxicating, soul-swaying beauty of the Black Experience. These critics usually conclude that a good poet like McKay would inevitably produce a poorly made work of fiction, for it is written that good poets do not good novelists make. A second disparaging point of view is that *Home to Harlem* is full of a repugnant realism. It exposes the seamy underside of Black community life where pimps, whores, gamblers, and slicksters congregate and where real, true-to-life bedbugs bite. Critics representing this group share the reaction of W.E.B. Du Bois who, after reading *Home to Harlem*, felt unclean and in need of a bath. Certainly, there is much in the novel which would have given offense to the sensitivities of a Black bourgeoisie which in the Harlem of the late 1920's was interested in leading the Black community to the best kind of accommodation to, and respect from, a racist America. To these leaders *Home to Harlem*'s Black settings reeked of a racial hedonism and exoticism scarcely compatible with accepted notions of racial progress. In their view a carefree hedonist like Jake, with his boundless and roaming sexual appetite, fitted the white man's racial and social stereotyped view of the Black male and could do little to enhance the Black man's image within the large community. (pp. 338-39)

Fortunately, the passage of time has helped to erode or modify these hostile critical judgments of McKay's first novel. . . . [Critics] have come to believe that the racial settings of *Home to Harlem* are positive and racially affirming rather than negative and racially demeaning; these settings, they believe, recapture the *elan* of the Black Experience in all of its color and rich emotional variety. The novel's episodicity of plot, it is also argued, is the common mark of a picaresque novel like *Home to Harlem*. Indeed, in this interpretation Jake becomes a flawed hero but a very likeable one—a sort of Black Tom Jones, good-hearted and virile and ensnared only by an occasionally unhappy sexual liaison. Like his white English counterpart of two centuries past, his motives are always good and unsullied. He does not customarily strike or beat women; he carefully avoids physical confrontations with his quarrelsome friends; in many instances, he is a peacemaker with an instinct for rational withdrawal from overly complex situations. . . . So Jake may be a carefree hedonist, but he is also something of a paragon among men—a man of proper instincts moving in a society in which so many men are governed by improper instincts.

The fact that Jake is so sharply differentiated from his associates in moral outlook and in his almost completely self-sufficient individualism suggests another interpretation of *Home to Harlem* that goes far beyond the conclusion that the novel is no more than a naturalistic *exposé* of Black urban ghetto life of the late 1920's. Such an interpretation posits that the novel is actually a study in symbolic conflict—a symbolic conflict that occurs on two levels. On the first level the conflict is between order and disorder, order being symbolized by Jake and disorder by the characters and settings which furnish the background for the action in the novel. In such an interpretation, Jake becomes a wise primitive who has been blessed with an intuitive sense of order. . . . Apparently, he is rarely, if ever, troubled or insecure or overwhelmed or incapacitated by doubt, fear, or uncertainty. In this sense he is different from Zeddy, Congo Rose, Billy Biasse, and Ray who either become disconcerted by the disorder surrounding them or deeply involved in that disorder. This is not to say that Jake is an outsider or a neutralist or an observer who stands apart. Like [Ralph] Ellison's much more intellectualized hero of a later date, Jake participates in the seething disorders that swirl around him, but unlike Ellison's hero he always carefully extricates himself in time to remain his own man. He does not have to suffer the happy accident of falling out of the world of time and space into a hole of self-discovery. (pp. 339-40)

The symbolic conflict between disorder and order in *Home to Harlem* is reinforced by another level of symbolic conflict—a conflict between the rational and the animalistic. The novel is filled with animal imagery to describe disorderly and violent situations or people. (p. 343)

Inevitably, an interpretation of *Home to Harlem* stressing symbolic conflict between order and disorder, reinforced by a conflict between the rational and the animalistic, implies that the novel is more than just an *exposé* of the "joy belt" of Harlem. McKay meant to provide more than a guided tour through the bars, buffet flats, speakeasies, gambling joints, and whorehouses of the sprawling Black city. The implication is that Harlem represents disorder as much as Brest or London and that Jake, the wise primitive and man of order, finds the place to which he has returned not "Gawd's own country," but a snare and a delusion. So one may justifiably hypothecate that the title of the novel is ironic, for in a world in which men are everywhere disorderly and animalistic, a man like Jake can never truly find a "home." . . . As the novel ends, Jake is on his way to Chicago to find another "home" with Felice, whose name means "happiness." One may assume that there he finds the ordered kind of pleasure he is seeking, but in *Banjo,* McKay's second novel, Jake explains to Ray that he has been happy but he is ready to move on to some other city. So it is and will be for all men who, like Jake, want to escape the "mud-hole" of human disorder. They will keep moving on in a fruitless quest and never truly find a "home"—not even in Harlem. (pp. 343-44)

> *Richard K. Barksdale, "Symbolism and Irony in McKay's 'Home to Harlem',"* in CLA Journal *(copyright, 1972 by the College Language Association), Vol. XV, No. 3, March, 1972, pp. 338-44.*

GEORGE E. KENT (essay date 1972)

For McKay, himself, soul was the assertion of a naturalness of being to be maintained in the face of the most complex patterns of Western culture. Abosrbing what was inescapable in Western culture and what must be mastered in order to live in the "modern" world, he attempted to develop from within. That is, he wished to draw into himself strands of Western culture that agreed with his own rhythms, but not to be shook by its devitalizing vibrations. . . .

As to the masses of Blacks, McKay felt in them a warmth, an assertion of spirit in the face of pain, a bounce and spontaneity of feelings and emotions, and a striving for the fruits of life based upon deep and persistent responses to the rhythms of their universe. He tried to insist, despite threatening evidence to the contrary, that the ordinary Black possessed an instinctive healthiness and innocence which would secure him from the waves of corruption that pounded into his cage in Western culture.

What McKay brought to the Harlem Renaissance then was the attempt to project a positive *niggerhood*—a voice that could celebrate or defy with apparent simple directness. (p. 36)

In 1919, his voice smashed through a sound barrier in America, with the appearance of the explosive and famous sonnet **"If We Must Die."** . . . It gained a black audience, whose deep emotions and post-World War I spirit of defiance were at the heart of its explosive lines, and it was reprinted in black newspapers and magazines. Paradoxically, the poem bore a form validated by centuries of European culture, the Shakesperian sonnet. *Harlem Shadows,* . . . the book of poems that clearly pointed to the incipient Renaissance, also exploited traditional forms, and reflected an author who could render the illusion of being completely present in his emotions, whether raging or tender. Thus the most radical sounding voice of the Renaissance is projected from the most traditional forms. . . .

McKay's Jamaican background provided him with a source of sensibility that gave him certain advantages over American born black writers. On the other hand, the circumstances of American born black writers provided a peculiarly intimate knowledge of oppression amidst the massive presence of whites and a variety of survival devices developed through historical tradition. (p. 37)

McKay's development of sensibility under less embattled conditions than those confronting American born black writers made certain rejections and perceptions easier. The furor over whether a black man was to be a black poet or just "a poet" which seemed to consume much psychic energy from many American black writers gave him no trouble. It seemed to him that to refuse to be a black writer if one was black was to reject one's identity. It was a false issue, simply silly, since nonblack writers used their own racial identity as an asset. (p. 39)

[A] romantic stance of the individual nourishing himself on the poetry of existence intrudes upon McKay's very serious moments and attenuates their quality. It seems to make for a kind of romantic egoism that produces solitariness where kinship with larger issues and people is required, and a startling myopia. The result is divisive tensions: rhythms of a natural black style, romantic rebellion, bohemian estheticism, egoism, and a sharp realistic social vision, uneasily commingling. (p. 41)

[McKay's] sonnets are usually credited with representing his highest point of achievement in poetry. In general, they are best when they do not evoke the specific name of one of the masters of romantic tradition, or make obvious a standard romantic posture—standard dangers in working a well-tilled tradition.

This "best" group of sonnets involves a deep souled speaker, who powerfully opposes his inner togetherness to terrible hatred and oppression. Even the speaker in **"If We Must Die,"** the poem that seemed to be an address to the masses of Blacks and whose rage is a response to the violent riots and lynchings of post-World War I, proceeds from this highly developed personality. (p. 42)

In **"If We Must Die,"** the powerful voice of a high-spirited and cultivated black man merges with the rage of his people, and, through its realistic imagery . . . and contemporary relevance replaces the tone of European tradition inherent in the sonnet form. In other fine sonnets, McKay is able to make us feel first the note of the black soul, although the echo of European tradition may not be entirely suppressed. The emotion derives primarily from the black speaker of the poem, secondarily from the plight of his people. (p. 43)

Some sonnets contain interesting statements, even when they are somewhat marred by defects. In general, the romantic rebel of 19th Century Romantic tradition hovers nearby some of the best sonnets and threatens to break through the black face. (p. 44)

It should be seen, however, that in the best of his sonnets, McKay's expression of a powerful, defiant, and embattled black soul, reveals the hand of a master. (p. 45)

The best of McKay's poems that are not written in sonnet form are distinguished and lifted by a flowing music. Traditional in form and replete with the attitudes and ceremonies of 19th Century Romanticism, they, nonetheless, establish the poet's more than legal rights to the ground that he tills. Although it is not virgin soil, it is also not barren, and yields poems of frank manly sentiment made worthy of repeated readings by the stoic and together soul from whom their drama and music derive. (pp. 45-6)

What McKay frequently needs is the single imposing image or the suggestive phrase that will make the poem an extraordinary experience for the mind. In many poems, the images are without the sharply etched visual outlines that would deepen meaning and distinguish them from their use by other poets. Other flaws: the lame last line, excessive labeling of feelings and emotions, over-simple oppositions of the virtues of the country and the evils of the city. In sum—the poetic concepts, trappings, and ceremonies of 19th Century Romantic tradition, frequently bring a brilliant flight to a sudden and premature end.

But the poet's story emerges, nonetheless, from the body of the poetry. It is the story of a soul whose flight from the village into the machine cultural centers of the West creates a sense of permanent loss. It is conscious now of the disinheritance of all black people, wherever the West has entered with its ''wonders,'' and it can only keep itself together by a sense of its inner rhythms, its occasional glimpses of a warmer world behind, its fleeting loves and fellow-feeling, and its capacity for hatred. (p. 46)

> *George E. Kent, ''The Soulful Way of Claude McKay,'' in his* Blackness and the Adventure of Western Culture *(copyright © 1972 by George E. Kent), Third World Press, 1972, pp. 36-52.*

HELEN PYNE-TIMOTHY (essay date 1975)

The literary works of Claude McKay . . . provide interesting insights into the varied ways in which an early black writer viewed the black female. As poet, novelist and essayist McKay discussed with great sensitivity, facets of the personality of the black woman which seemed to him to represent both her strengths and her weaknesses. His viewpoint is simply that of the black male artist. But in his world the black woman plays an important, even vital role: that of sustaining the needs of the black man and of defining the future of the race. Yet his apprehension of her meaning does not lead him to present her in idealistic or exaggerated terms. His work attempts to relate the ideal to the reality which is the life of every black man or woman in modern Western civilization. Accordingly McKay's black woman emerges as a multi-faceted creature, as fascinating in her complexity as in her diversity.

All of McKay's work reiterates the thesis that the black man stands in a peculiarly unhappy position in the Western World. Cut off from his roots, socially, economically and spiritually deprived, he must depend on the black woman for support. The support which he gains from her may be economic. But McKay seems to value more highly the important psychological forms of support which (he seems to suggest) only the black woman can give. (p. 152)

In a poem such as **"A Memory of June"** he records the importance which a sensitive black man can attach to even a brief one-night liaison which, because of the peculiar warmth and sensitivity of his partner meant much more than he could have expected. (p. 153)

In fact, moments which are similar to that recorded in **"A Memory of June"** occur more frequently in McKay's poetry than those which reflect the permanent and ideal partnership. . . . The black woman cannot achieve permanence in isolation: in other words, she shares the rootlessness of her male counterpart, and suffers from his inability to provide her with a decent living and a home. The view of her lack of proper integration into the normal social fabric is especially meaningful to McKay in the setting which is Harlem. Here is a community which is essentially restless, lonely and rootless. Here all members suffer real poverty, hardship, lack of employment or employment in the most menial jobs. Life may be somewhat easier for some of the women. But for the majority the struggle for survival is only relatively less fierce than it is for the men. Yet McKay seems to appreciate that here many black men must depend on the ability of the black woman to give of herself, both physically and spiritually at that moment when the black man needs her most. Even in these passing relationships then, the black woman must fulfill this vital role, must give sustenance even when the man to whom she relates may be a stranger.

Indeed, in much of McKay's work he underlines the almost mystic view which he seems to hold of the physical side of the black woman. He views her body with admiration and passion; and seems to suggest that even in her physical self she provides a kind of renewal for the troubled and lost black male. This viewpoint is made explicit in both *Home to Harlem* and *Banjo*. (pp. 153-54)

[The] problem of prostitution among black women is one which McKay treats with a great deal of sensitivity. Many of the black women of whom he treats, are in fact engaged in this profession. McKay regarded this type of black woman as a commonplace; and felt that he ought to render her significance within his work. He recognised that the frequency of the necessity for the black woman to involve herself in this type of life lay in the economic situation of the race. In order to live the black woman, whether in America or in Europe, must often find herself on the streets. Yet McKay notes that the shackles of prostitution need not rob the black woman of that spontaneity and warmth which he particularly values. These two assessments of the problem of prostitution form important bases in his total conception of the role of the black woman. (pp. 154-55)

[In] spite of the obvious sincerity which lay beneath the sorrow of the understanding of the reasons for prostitution among black women, McKay does not moralise about their position. Indeed the majority of the black women who appear in his works are either prostitutes or women who are in the business of procuring. In fact, . . . he anticipated that the black intelligentsia would be offended that in his prose works at least, his black women would not be "good virgins." But it appears that McKay realised that the question of virginity was simply irrelevant to the functions which he perceived that the black woman must serve in relation to the black man. The black woman, because of her sex could survive in economic terms by practising this profession. The level of existence at which the black race clearly dwelt in the Harlem of 1914-1922, bare survival was something of a miracle. Through the living which the black woman was able to make she could support her man, keep him alive. (pp. 155-56)

[From] McKay's point of view, the ready availability of sincere sexual responses, as well as material help from the "fallen women" of Harlem is one of the few resuscitating events in the normal life of the disfranchised black man. He suggests that the black woman is able to maintain her generosity towards the black male even in the most adverse circumstances. (p. 156)

It is not only through the rewards of prostitution, however, that the black woman has managed to materially support the black man. In the Harlem setting the black woman, again because of her sex, proved to be far more acceptable to American white society than her male counterpart. In McKay's time the black woman could usually find employment. . . . Indeed the relationship in which the woman is the breadwinner, while the man remains idle is the most common male-female association in McKay's work. The men understand that this position has to be assumed because of stark necessity. The women also understand the reasons for this necessity; yet it does not seem to affect their sense of the value of male companionship. Women like Congo Rose are sincerely willing to help out their men from their slender earnings.

Thus far it is clear that McKay values the black woman most highly for her contributions to the survival of the black man. If this were his total view of her, however, he might well be accused of betraying a lack of genuine understanding of the needs of the black woman. In other words he could be seen as adopting the stance of male dominance in which the woman's role as contributor to the survival of the race may only be achieved through the male. But fortunately McKay recognises that the black woman also has her peculiar problems; that just as her sex may be of benefit, it may also be a disadvantage. Often the women in McKay's works find themselves exploited, preyed upon, even betrayed by the very black men whom they have attempted to help. Often, too, their romantic notions and their finer feelings are brutally stamped on. They too, must learn the mechanisms of survival in an essentially hostile environment. McKay records the devices by which black women attempt to make their lives bearable. In these portrayals McKay is not motivated merely by empathetic understanding. As an artist he is also concerned with the validity of his presentation. . . . The reality is that life was no less harsh for the black woman than for the man. Her methods of survival had to be as varied and as diverse and would depend on her individual

responses to given situations. Nevertheless certain major patterns for survival may be identified in McKay's work.

In *Home to Harlem* many of the women do manage the business of survival rather well. There are those like Congo Rose, the cabaret dancer, full of colour, vibrancy and movement, generous to her men, willing to lend support from her slender earnings to the man who will stay with her. Yet she is constantly being deserted. Her generosity and attractiveness, her physical poise cannot guarantee happiness for her. Possibly in reaction to the unloveliness of her existence she has become "hard and insensitive." She is not . . . capable of responses which are warm or instinctive. The plane on which she exists demands that sexuality must be completely physical and love can only be properly expressed through violence and brutality. Apparently Congo Rose has managed to match the violence of her environment by responding to masochism.

Congo Rose appears to have understood a notion which troubled McKay. It is the overriding recognition that in the civilized world, the primitive and instinctive humanity which is the natural adjunct of sexuality has been lost. He felt that viciousness and savagery have replaced humanity where this basic need of human beings is constantly exploited to become part of the system of money and power. But he seems to feel that in this primeval battleground of the sexes, women, black as well as whites, have a far greater potential capacity for wringing "the basest thrill and the most complete advantage" out of the situation. Men are really the victims. Women like Congo Rose, therefore, having succumbed to the cruelty and made it their code may survive, but in the final analysis they seek to brutalise the men with whom they became involved. (pp. 156-58)

[The] ideal coupling situation which McKay envisages is very clearly expressed in *Banana Bottom*. All of his ideals concerning the manner in which the black woman, and through her the race, could possibly survive are carefully presented in this book, his last fictional statement. Bita, the Jamaican peasant girl is subjected, at an early age to an illegal though instinctive, sexual experience. . . . Bita is apparently saved from the possible consequences of her early sexual encounter by adoption into the white community, training in white religions and moral norms and even more important, the exposure to a white expatriate education. But she soon realises that while these benefits have been useful, while they enabled her to develop into a mature, well-poised individual, capable of escaping the trap of a grindingly harsh life, they must be thoroughly evaluated in terms of their contribution to her total identity as a black woman. For McKay Bita is the ideal black woman; proud, intelligent, yet realistic, she understands that her racial identity and her integration into the black community are the cornerstones of her psyche, and the foundation of her happiness. Her education and training must serve to aid her understanding of these facts. They must also serve to make her aware that, as a black woman, her instincts, her recognition of the correctness of the need for fulfillment of her physical desires, must be preserved. In this understanding, Bita is strongly contrasted with Mrs. Craig, her white adopted mother, who despised physical responses, valuing only the life of the mind and spirit. Bita merges with and marries Jubban, an uneducated black peasant. Yet their union represents fulfillment because Jubban is in perfect harmony with himself and his environment, truly natural, spontaneous, gentle and instinctive. Their child has a primeval vigour; he is the ideal result of the combination of Western European values and education, and African spontaneity and instinctiveness. Bita and Jubban, together, will nurture a powerful hope for the future, while the Craigs contrastively may only conceive a defective child.

McKay had always suggested that the black man seemed incapable of placing a proper value on the possession of Western education. In his hands a white education merely contributed to the destruction of his identity and to his exclusion from the mass of his people. In Bita he suggests that the black woman is far more capable of holding such an education in its true perspective; and of using it for personal satisfaction and development, while retaining a deep-rooted understanding of the meaning of being black. It is all a part of her realism and her more developed ability to survive. (pp. 160-61)

For Claude McKay then the black woman is her best self when like Bita, she demonstrates a near-perfect understanding of her environment and recognises that her personality may fully flower when she develops both her intellectual capacities and achieves physical union with the black man. He also perceives that the black man, deprived as he is in Western society, must depend heavily on her help in obtaining material necessities, when he is out of work. Even more important she must provide psychological help and support when he is lost, lonely or bewildered. In addition she must herself survive, must devise a method for her own existence. He recognises that her problems are many; often her means for survival are minimal, and she easily becomes the victim of the socio-economic and racial situations. Such women, in becoming victimised, lose their warmth and the spontaneity, with which they have been endowed by their African heritage. . . . [This] loss prevents them from ever achieving satisfying relationships with the black man. Their inability to survive militates against their happiness; they cannot offer to the black man the resources he himself needs. McKay views their loneliness and confusion with compassion and understanding. Those who survive and those who are victims are equally relevant to his perceptions of the black woman. (p. 164)

> *Helen Pyne-Timothy, "Perceptions of the Black Woman in the Work of Claude McKay," in* CLA Journal *(copyright, 1975 by the College Language Association), Vol. XIX, No. 2, December, 1975, pp. 152-64.*

JAMES R. GILES (essay date 1976)

McKay's autobiography, *A Long Way From Home* . . . and his sociological study, *Harlem: Negro Metropolis* . . . , are initially disappointing books. There is, however, much more value to the autobiography than to the study of Harlem. The key to both the disappointment and the merit of *A Long Way From Home* lies in the fact that it is not the usual kind of autobiography. If one approaches it expecting an intimate portrayal of Claude McKay, he will be disappointed; if he seeks in it an account of McKay's struggle to reconcile his views of art with his concepts of self, blackness, and the proletariat, he will find it valuable. *Harlem: Negro Metropolis* is more difficult to accept on any basis; for, while it contains some valuable insights into the major forces operative within the American and the world black communities, its last half is so full of passages of intensely vitriolic anger and despair aimed at the black intellectual establishment and at the Communist party that the entire book seems tinged with paranoia. This is not to say that there was no validity to McKay's bitterness toward black intellectuals and the Communist Party: it is simply to recognize that McKay's desperate need to attack these targets again and again overshadows the ostensible subject of the dis-

cussion. The book's supposed purpose of giving an objective account of the social and historical development of the New York black community is sidetracked; and the tone of the last half of the book is so overtly and desperately hostile that any artistic merit or sociological objectivity is destroyed.

In contrast to *Harlem, A Long Way From Home* ends on a hopeful, pacific note with one of McKay's most aesthetically satisfying discussions of black pride. In fact, the entire autobiography is written with such extreme restraint and control that the restraint becomes the book's main problem. (p. 124)

Still, there is a level on which the autobiography is a disappointment. . . . One apparent theme of *A Long Way From Home* is McKay's refusal to be dominated by anyone. Ironically, however, one feels upon finishing the book that he has portrayed Frank Harris, Max Eastman, Charlie Chaplin, Edna St. Vincent Millay, Isadora Duncan, and numerous other famous and nonfamous personalities more clearly than he has Claude McKay. It would seem impossible for a man who is writing his autobiography to proclaim repeatedly his sense of independence and still fail to provide a complete and satisfactory view of himself as a personality. Nevertheless, that is precisely what happens in *A Long Way From Home.*

The irony of McKay's failure to depict himself adequately in his autobiography is compounded by the fact that . . . his fiction often tends to become too overtly autobiographical. Frequently, he does not maintain an adequate distance between himself and his materials in his fiction, but he keeps too distant in his autobiography. This distance is especially disappointing if one approaches *A Long Way From Home* expecting an autobiography comparable to Richard Wright's *Black Boy*. . . . One feels certain that McKay felt as intensely and responded as deeply as Wright to the unique drama of his life; but, with the exception of a few major events, one does not get a sense of this intense personal response in *A Long Way From Home.*

McKay's reluctance to deal with the complexities of his own personal life does not prevent him from being convincing in his assertions of independence, but he does not assert his total independence from any and all larger groups. . . . Early in *A Long Way From Home,* McKay states that no artist can have a true sense of self unless that self is rooted in a nation or in a race. Thus, the Jamaican's sense of the uniqueness of Claude McKay and his feeling of belonging to the black race are inextricably linked. He does repeatedly, and convincingly, stress his independence from individuals and groups which attempt to control his individuality. These individuals and groups are predominantly white, either in actuality or in point of view. That Claude McKay could be the unique individualist and a black artist, just as Byron could be Byron and a distinctly English poet, is the book's final message. . . . His final loyalty in the autobiography is to himself and to his blackness.

For all these reasons, the way to read *A Long Way From Home* is not as an autobiography but as literary theory accompanied by a view of the significant people, places, and events of a period. While McKay is persuasive in his assertion of his pride in self and in blackness, that self remains largely hidden behind a peculiar kind of restraint. Once again, it is the people McKay knew, including some potential destroyers of his individuality, who come the most alive in this book. (pp. 125-26)

McKay "comes home" at the end of his autobiography, and his "home" is black consciousness that rests firmly in faith in the Negro masses. Moreover, his idea of his use of his art in the search for black identity and power is a statement of the basic purpose behind his novels and much of his poetry. The autobiography completes, therefore, the period of McKay's greatest achievement—in the years 1919 to 1937, he produced the work that made him one of the most prophetic black writers of his time. Reading *A Long Way From Home* in this light enables one to accept it as a meaningful statement of artistic principle and to understand its apparent failure as autobiography. If one is not allowed an intimate perception of McKay the man, he does find an account of the essential beliefs of McKay the black artist. Moreover, he is shown all the people, places, and ideologies that threatened to draw McKay away from black consciousness; the fact that these false gods often eclipse McKay in the narration demonstrates their strength and thereby makes their rejection all the more meaningful. (pp. 142-43)

Despite the significance of *A Long Way From Home* as an account of McKay's development as a black artist and as his last aesthetically satisfying statement of black pride, and despite the moments of prophetic insight in *Harlem: Negro Metropolis,* one wishes that McKay had published fiction after *Banana Bottom.* However, as the letters to Eastman reveal, he was deeply discouraged by the failure of his Jamaican novel. . . . Moreover, the reception of *Banana Bottom* had caused him to doubt its worth and significance. Probably a desire to produce something which the temper of the times could accept led him to autobiography and sociology. Always a highly romantic novelist, his personal suffering had made him a bitter, vindictive man; and the result is highly slanted and unsatisfactory sociology. Only in the autobiography in which he can look back to happier times does he approach the convincing power of his best fiction, and even there he strangely keeps himself hidden from his reader. Perhaps the experiences of being neglected by old friends and former readers, of working for a dollar a day in a welfare camp, and of being remembered, if at all, as an outdated symbol of a dead past made him reluctant in his autobiography to open himself more than necessary to any additional hurt. If so, one understands. (pp. 150-51)

> *James R. Giles, in his* Claude McKay *(copyright © 1976 by Twayne Publishers, Inc.; reprinted with the permission of Twayne Publishers, a Division of G. K. Hall & Co., Boston), Twayne, 1976, 170 p.*

ADDITIONAL BIBLIOGRAPHY

Barton, Rebecca Chalmers. "Claude McKay: *A Long Way from Home.*" In her *Witnesses for Freedom: Negro Americans in Autobiography,* pp. 135-46. New York, London: Harper & Brothers Publishers, 1948.

   Discussion of McKay's autobiography, *A Long Way from Home.* Barton supports the impressionistic style of *A Long Way from Home,* arguing that McKay did not want to produce a "chronological record" but, instead, hoped to capture "the stuff of which one person is made, the raw materials of his creativeness."

Bronz, Stephen H. "Claude McKay." In his *Roots of Negro Consciousness, The 1920's: Three Harlem Renaissance Authors,* pp. 66-89. New York: Libra Publishers, 1964.

   Discussion of the major events in McKay's life and an analysis of their effect on his work. Bronz traces McKay's poetry, fiction, and prose within the context of his life: his Jamaican heritage; his immigration to the United States; his reaction to American racism; his expatriate years in Russia, Europe, and Northern Africa; and his eventual return to America as a forgotten writer.

Collier, Eugenia W. "The Four-Way Dilemma of Claude McKay." *C.L.A. Journal* XV, No. 3 (March 1972): 345-53.

   Analysis of McKay's poetry with respect to four distinct crises he faced as a black writer. Collier suggests that McKay's poetry was affected by a series of dilemmas peculiar to the black man in white America.

Cooper, Wayne F. "Claude McKay and the New Negro of the 1920's." *Phylon* XVI, No. 1 (1964): 297-306.

   Discussion of McKay during the decade of the Negro Renaissance. Cooper concludes that McKay will be best remembered for his poetry, wherein he expressed "the New Negro's determination to protect his human dignity, his cultural worth, and his right to a decent life."

Cooper, Wayne F. Introduction to *The Passion of Claude McKay: Selected Poetry and Prose, 1912-1948,* by Claude McKay, edited by Wayne F. Cooper, pp. 1-41. New York: Schocken Books, 1973.

   Biographical discussion and thematic survey of McKay's works. Cooper stresses McKay's preoccupation with the black man's search for a viable identity in the modern world.

Fullinwider, S. P. "The Renaissance in Literature." In his *The Mind and Mood of Black America: 20th Century Thought,* pp. 123-71. Homewood, Ill.: The Dorsey Press, 1969.*

   Brief examination of McKay's Harlem fiction. Fullinwider argues that McKay's fiction was "false" in that it appealed to the white apologists rather than black Americans.

Gloster, Hugh M. "Fiction of the Negro Renascence: The Van Vechten Vogue." In his *Negro Voices in American Fiction,* pp. 157-72. Chapel Hill: The University of North Carolina Press, 1948.*

   Discussion of McKay's three novels, *Home to Harlem, Banjo,* and *Gingertown.* Gloster concludes that McKay, in his fiction, capitalized on the sex, exaggeration, and libertinism first utilized by Carl Van Vechten in his novel *Nigger Heaven.*

Lang, Phyllis Martin. "Claude McKay: Evidence of a Magic Pilgrimage." *C.L.A. Journal* XVI, No. 4 (June 1973): 475-84.

   A biographical account of McKay's eight-month trip to Russia during 1922 and 1923. Lang attempts to measure McKay's immense popularity in Russia and suggests that only in that country was he truly recognized as a great writer and spokesman for the working class.

McLeod, Marian B. "Claude McKay's Russian Interpretation: *The Negroes in America.*" *C.L.A. Journal* XXIII, No. 3 (March 1980): 336-51.

   Critical analysis of McKay's essay *The Negroes in America,* written and published during his trip to Russia. McLeod suggests that McKay's obscure Russian essay provides new light on his political and literary philosophy. The critic also questions much of the content in both McKay's autobiography and his historical study, *Harlem: Negro Metropolis.*

Priebe, Richard. "The Search for Community in the Novels of Claude McKay." *Studies in Black Literature* 3, No. 2 (Summer 1972): 22-30.

   Analysis of McKay's three novels. Priebe examines the dominant theme of a search for community in each of McKay's novels.

Singh, Amritjit. "Race and Sex." In his *The Novels of the Harlem Renaissance: Twelve Black Writers 1923-1933,* pp. 41-69. University Park: The Pennsylvania State University Press, 1976.*

   Critical discussion of McKay's three novels. Singh argues that McKay is a more significant novelist than given credit because he searched for new, positive definitions of black life and helped define the black experience in the West in terms of the Negro's African roots.

George (Augustus) Moore

1852-1933

Irish novelist, autobiographer, novella and short story writer, critic, essayist, dramatist, poet, biographer, and editor.

Moore is commonly credited with importing the themes and techniques of French naturalism into English literature. His most acclaimed novel, *Esther Waters*, was notorious in its time for depicting human weakness and degradation with the kind of detailed objectivity made popular in France by the novels of Émile Zola. At the same time, Moore professed to be less interested in the human aspect of his works than he was in their artistic purity. In his critical writings he advocated the aesthetic doctrine of pure form, and in his fiction attempted to give precedence to artistic design over statements about the world or the lives of his characters. Nevertheless, Moore excelled at characterization, and with accuracy and insight realistically portrayed the life of his native Ireland.

Moore was born at Moore Hall, County Mayo, Ireland, to a family of the landed gentry. At the age of twenty-one he moved to Paris to study painting and painters, meeting Degas, Manet, Pissarro, and others. He also made the acquaintance of many prominent French writers, and his inclinations toward painting, never very devoted or promising, were channeled into literature. His first efforts were the poetry collections *Flowers of Passion* and *Pagan Poems*, self-consciously decadent verse displaying no more than a shallow familiarity with Baudelaire and the current theories of symbolism in French literature. Moore's first prose work, the autobiographical *Confessions of a Young Man*, recounts his Paris years with more regard for colorful anecdote than accuracy, while providing readers with an ironic portrait of the author's complex personality.

During this time, Moore met Zola and was impressed with his naturalist approach to fiction. The novels *A Modern Lover* and *A Mummer's Wife* were Moore's first attempts in the new mode. Though stylistically crude, these works served to introduce forbidden subjects into the overly genteel fiction of the day. Moore's unsentimental attitude toward sex and lower-class existence appears in its most polished and compelling form in *Esther Waters*. The story of a servant girl and her illegitimate son, *Esther Waters* displays what would become Moore's novelistic strong points: realistic background, stylistic expertise, and objective analysis of a central character while maintaining genuine sympathy. *Evelyn Innes* and its sequel, *Sister Teresa*, are further triumphs of this kind.

In his autobiographical trilogy, *Hail and Farewell*, Moore records his return to Ireland and his association with such Irish Literary Renaissance figures as W. B. Yeats, J. M. Synge, and Edward Martyn. With Yeats and Martyn, Moore collaborated on several plays which were produced at the Abbey Theater. Personal and artistic differences with these and other authors soured Moore's decade-long homecoming, and in *Hail and Farewell* he renounces his Irish heritage and harshly assesses most of his former associates. Moore's fiction of this period includes the short story collection *The Untilled Field* and the novel *The Lake*, sensitive psychological studies of Irish

characters as well as exercises in the melodic prose style of Moore's late novels.

Moore's final creative period began with *The Brook Kerith*. Based on the premise that Christ did not die on the cross, this novel aroused both religious and artistic controversy. Moore's ambitions with this work, as with his retelling of a medieval romantic legend in *Héloïse and Abélard*, were chiefly stylistic. He wanted to develop his story as if it were a piece of music, following a seamless melody which binds the novel's various parts into a musical unity. The result has received uneven critical reaction, some viewing it as a masterpiece of prose and others calling it a tiresome labor of pure style. Moore's lifelong preoccupation with artistic purity is articulated in his introduction to *An Anthology of Pure Poetry*. Moore offers the poems in this anthology as examples of his credo that the highest art makes no attempt to communicate ideas or human feelings, but operates in an aesthetic dimension outside life. Whatever their ultimate judgement of Moore as an artist, critics acknowledge that if he did not own to the ambition, he certainly possessed the ability to render the life he saw and experienced with tangible feeling and often deep perceptiveness.

Moore broke artistic ground in championing naturalism in England before it became a popular movement. A writer who

472

picked up many influences, he in turn influenced others. For example, James Joyce's *Portrait of the Artist as a Young Man* in its themes and structure owes much to Moore's *Confessions of a Young Man*. Moore's career and works set a precedent and provided a model worth emulating for many English language writers in the first half of the twentieth century.

(See also *Dictionary of Literary Biography,* Vol. 10: *Modern British Dramatists, 1900-1945*.)

PRINCIPAL WORKS

Flowers of Passion   (poetry)   1878
Pagan Poems   (poetry)   1881
A Modern Lover   (novel)   1883
Literature at Nurse   (essay)   1885
A Mummer's Wife   (novel)   1885
A Drama in Muslin   (novel)   1886
A Mere Accident   (novel)   1887
Confessions of a Young Man   (autobiography)   1888
Impressions and Opinions   (criticism)   1891
Esther Waters   (novel)   1894
Celibates   (novellas)   1895
Evelyn Innes   (novel)   1898
The Bending of the Bough   (drama)   1900
Sister Teresa   (novel)   1901
Diarmuid and Grania [with William Butler Yeats]   (drama)
   1902
The Untilled Field   (short stories)   1903
The Lake   (novel)   1905
Memoirs of My Dead Life   (autobiographical essays)   1906
Hail and Farewell: Ave   (autobiography)   1911
Hail and Farewell: Salve   (autobiography)   1912
Hail and Farewell: Vale   (autobiography)   1914
The Brook Kerith   (novel)   1916
A Story-Teller's Holiday   (short stories)   1918
Avowals   (dialogues and essays)   1919
Héloïse and Abélard   (novel)   1921
An Anthology of Pure Poetry [editor]   (poetry)   1924
Conversations in Ebury Street   (criticism)   1924
A Communication to My Friends   (letter)   1933
George Moore in Transition   (letters)   1968

THE SPECTATOR   (essay date 1883)

What Tito Melema was in the grand life of Romola [in George Eliot's *Romola*], Mr. George Moore's very cleverly drawn "modern lover" is, in the several lives of three women who love him, trust him, and sacrifice themselves to him, each in her different way and according to the opportunities afforded them by his various needs at the time. Of the refined and poetical tone and atmosphere of the book that gave us an unrivalled picture of moral good-for-nothingness in old Florentine days, there is no trace in this essentially modern story; they are replaced by plain prose, and realism which, while it is not coarse, and, unlike the tone of the "naturalistic" writers (for whom we suspect Mr. Moore of an admiration much to be deplored), does not offend, takes the gilt off the gingerbread of sentiment, and ignores romance in a more thorough style than we are accustomed to, except in the utterances of professed cynics. The author of *A Modern Lover* is not a cynic; he not only recognises, but he respects goodness, purity, and disin-

terestedness, and although the story he tells is all about the woeful waste of those feelings upon a person absolutely unworthy of them, he is quite alive to the pity of it, and gives his readers the notion that he really would have liked to make Lewis Seymour a better fellow, if he could. He cannot, however, for *A Modern Lover* is not a bit of a built-up story; it has a very uncommon note of spontaneity; it tells itself, and its faults are the defects of its qualities of moderation and sincerity. The book has more power than the story; the characters have more interest than the incidents; the first volume is the best as a conception and a composition, but the third is superior to it as a picture of society: it gives a clever evolution of character without exaggeration, and a view of modern life which, while it is tinged with pessimism, is not scornful or bitter, but on the whole tolerant and good-humoured. . . .

[Mr. Moore's is] not an ideal novel; it is a study from life, and lifelike,—more's the pity! It is faulty, but always interesting; it has both pathos and humour, and it is pervaded by a frank, revealing spirit that tells of observation of men and things, intelligent, not malicious, and commonsensical. The world and its way neither take in this writer, nor do they disgust him; he sees the poetry of things, but he knows that it is the prose of them that lasts; he is just as much "up to" the jargons of humanity as ever was the thunderous philosopher of Chelsea; but he does not thunder,—he listens, smiles, and makes a note of them. Art jargon, the affectations of criticism, and the huggermugger of Art Societies have not been better exemplified than by his Mr. Harding, Mr. Thompson, and other members of Seymour's social world. All this portion of the book is characterised by judgment; it is not overdone, it is not offensively personal, it is amusing and true. The author's style leaves much to be desired. He passes from English into French [abruptly] . . . with the incoherence of a man who is accustomed to think in either language indifferently; and he has not looked after the printers' errors in his French. His sentences are occasionally, let us say, haphazard; not exactly ungrammatical, but wanting in accuracy. The literary method is defective, but the work is one which will make its mark,—the best sort of mark for an author, for it means that its readers will look with expectation for its successor.

"Books: 'A Modern Lover'," in The Spectator, *Vol. 56, No. 2877, August 18, 1883, p. 1069.*

WILLIAM WALLACE   (essay date 1887)

A Mere Accident is the best written, and, on the whole, the least realistic of Mr. George Moore's novels. There is, of course, a good deal of morbid sensuality in it. The hero, John Norton, who is composed, in about equal parts of fool, priest, and prig, talks sad nonsense. . . . He dreams asceticism, and bores his visitors with monasticism, but he can give them brandy and soda, and, if need be, absinthe; while on the walls of his rooms are French pictures, and on his shelves are French novels. Of course, also, *A Mere Accident* ends tragically; the heroine, poor innocent Kitty Hare, having been outraged by a tramp, goes mad and throws herself out of window. But there is in it none of the man-millinery, and comparatively little either of the gorgeousness or the suggestiveness which spoiled *A Drama in Muslin. A Mere Accident* also shows that, if Mr. Moore were so minded, he could draw healthy, virtuous people and their simple surroundings with more than ordinary ability. Probably he will take to this line of fiction when he has finished his studies of the skin-diseases of humanity.

William Wallace, "New Novels: 'A Mere Accident'," in The Academy, Vol. XXXII, No. 794, July 23, 1887, p. 51.

ARTHUR SYMONS   (essay date 1891)

Mr. George Moore has been described, with impressive inaccuracy, as the English Zola. At what was practically the outset of his career he gained a certain notoriety, which did him, artistically, both good and harm. . . . It did him good, by calling public attention to an unknown name; it did him harm, by attaching to that name a certain stigma. . . . Mr. Moore, it is true, had been guilty of certain audacities; he had not written precisely for the young person; it was evident that he had lived in France and studied French masterpieces. So, for those who believed in the Continental rather than the Modern British canons of art, his coming was welcomed as the coming of a deliverer. Unfortunately Mr. Moore has delivered nobody, not even himself. He has written one book which to my mind is a masterpiece, *A Mummer's Wife,* and another book which is amazingly clever, *The Confessions of a Young Man,* with four or five other novels which are—well—*manqués,* in spite of their ability, their independence, their unquestionable merits of various kinds. . . .

Mr. George Moore's literary career has been singularly interesting; his character as a writer is very curious. A man who respects his art, who is devoted to literature, who has a French eye for form, he seems condemned to produce work which is always spotted with imperfection. All his life he has been seeking a style, and he has not yet found one. At times he drops into style as if by accident, and then he drops style as if by design. He has a passionate delight in the beauty of good prose; he has an ear for the magic of phrases; his words catch at times a troubled, expressive charm; yet he has never attained ease in writing, and he is capable of astounding incorrectnesses—the incorrectness of a man who knows better, who is not careless, and yet who cannot help himself. The impression produced by his best work is that of large, forthright power, and also of measure, design, the capacity for construction. *A Mummer's Wife* is admirably put together, admirably planned and shaped; the whole composition of the book is masterly. The style may drag, but not the action; the construction of a sentence may be uncertain, but not the construction of a character. The actor and his wife are really living people; we see them in their surroundings, and we see every detail of those surroundings. What is most wonderful, perhaps, is the atmosphere. Mr. Moore, when he turned from painting to literature, preserved the essential quality of the painter. He might have painted his impressions badly in oils; in words he paints them well.

Mr. Moore's new book, a collection of essays, has the appropriate name, *Impressions and Opinions.* The essays are concerned with literature, with the drama, and with pictures. . . . So interesting, so suggestive, so valuable a volume of critical essays has not appeared since Mr. Pater's *Appreciations.* In saying this I had no intention of comparing Mr. Pater and Mr. Moore, who certainly are, in all obvious qualities, extremely unlike. But they have, after all, when one thinks of it, something in common. Alone among English men of letters who write criticism, they have a complete emancipation from English prejudices in art; they alone can be trusted for an unbiased opinion as to the words of, let us say, Goncourt, Flaubert, Mérimée. . . . Mr. Moore, like Mr. Pater, and like no one else whom I can think of, has an absolute devotion to art as

art; he is rightly incapable of taking anything into consideration but the one question—is this good or is it bad art? With all those questions that haunt the ordinary English brain he is totally unacquainted—those dragging considerations of tendency, of advisability, of convention. He receives impressions, he forms opinions, and he states his opinions, he indicates his impressions, frankly, simply, without conceiving the need of reservations, without feeling impelled to insist on limitations. So he has written an essay on Balzac, which does really drive home on us the intense and universal power of the man; he has written an essay on Turgueneff, which only a fellow-craftsman could have written; he has been the first to introduce to English readers the greatest living French poet—Paul Verlaine. In his consideration of the drama of to-day Mr. Moore has had the courage to say the truth at all costs—not without exaggeration, at times, but at all events fearlessly and with emphasis. Mr. Moore's views of dramatic art seem to me, as a rule, unimpeachably sound; and it is refreshing to read so much sober good sense on a question which has been more hotly discussed, and to less purpose, than anything public or private outside Ireland. In the section devoted to art, Mr. Moore gives us impressions and opinions which are specially valuable on account of his intimate technical knowledge of the subject. He at least answers to Mr. Whistler's requirement: he is a critic of pictures who has actually painted pictures himself. (p. 274)

The value of Mr. Moore's book is that it is the work of an artist who understands art, and who is entirely honest, absolutely unaffected, in his noting down of exactly how he has been impressed by this or that novel, drama, or picture. Understanding criticism, as he says, "more as the story of the critic's own soul than as an exact science," he tells us, in the most straightforward and convincing way, just what his own sensation has been, not in the least caring to arrive at any sort of abstract critical truth—as if that were possible!—not in the least caring if he seems in one place to contradict what he has said in another. . . .

Reading over what I have just transcribed, I am half tempted to go back and alter what I said at the beginning about a writer who can write so well. But no, let it stand: what I said was perfectly true. Yet the author of *A Mummer's Wife,* of *The Confessions of a Young Man,* of *Impressions and Opinions,* has more narrowly escaped being a great writer than even he himself, perhaps, is aware. (p. 275)

Arthur Symons, "Literature: 'Impressions and Opinions'," in The Academy, Vol. XXXIX, No. 985, March 21, 1891, pp. 274-75.

ARTHUR QUILLER-COUCH   (essay date 1894)

[Mr. George Moore] has steadily laboured to make himself a fine artist, and his training has led him through many strange places. I should guess that among living novelists few have started with so scant an equipment. As far as one can tell, he had, to begin with, neither a fertile invention nor a subtle dramatic instinct, nor an accurate ear for language. A week ago I should have said this very confidently: after reading *Esther Waters* I say it less confidently, but believe it to be true, nevertheless. Mr. Moore has written novels that are full of faults. These faults have been exposed mercilessly, for Mr. Moore has made many enemies. But he has always possessed an artistic conscience and an immense courage. He answered his critics briskly enough at the time, but an onlooker of common sagacity could perceive that the really convincing answer was held in reserve—that, as they say in America, Mr. Moore "allowed" he was going to write a big novel one of these days, and meanwhile we had better hold our judgment upon Mr. Moore's capacity open to revision.

What, then, is to be said of *Esther Waters,* this volume of a modest 377 pages, upon which Mr. Moore has been at work for at least two years?

Well, in the first place, I say, without hesitation, that *Esther Waters* is the most important novel published in England during these two years. We have been suffering from the Amateur during that period, and no doubt (though it seems hard) every nation has the Amateur it deserves. To find a book to compare with *Esther Waters* we must go back to December, 1891, and to Mr. Hardy's *Tess of the D'Urbervilles.* It happens that a certain similarity in the motives of these two stories makes comparison easy. Each starts with the seduction of a young girl; and each is mainly concerned with her subsequent adventures. From the beginning the advantage of probability is with the younger novelist. Mr. Moore's William Latch is a thoroughly natural figure, and remains a natural figure to the end of the book; an uneducated man and full of failings, but a man always, and therefore to be forgiven by the reader only a little less readily than Esther herself forgives him. Mr. Hardy's Alec D'Urberville is a grotesque and violent lay figure, a wholly incredible cad. Mr. Hardy, by killing Tess's child, takes away the one means by which his heroine could have been led to return D'Urberville without any loss of the reader's sympathy. Mr. Moore allows Esther's child to live, and thus has at hand the material for one of the most beautiful stories of maternal love ever imagined by a writer. I dislike extravagance of speech, and would run my pen through these words could I remember, in any novel I have read, a more heroic story than this of Esther Waters, a poor maid-of-all-work, without money, friends, or character, fighting for her child against the world, and in the end dragging victory out of the struggle. In spite of the Æschylean gloom in which Mr. Hardy wraps the story of Tess, I contend that Esther's fight is, from end to end, the more heroic.

Also Esther's story seems to me informed with a saner philosophy of life. There is gloom in her story; and many of the circumstances are sordid enough; but throughout I see the recognition that man and woman can at least improve and dignify their lot in this world. (pp. 195-97)

The story of Tess, in which attention is so urgently directed to the hand of Destiny, is not felt to be inevitable, but freakish. The story of Esther Waters in which a poor servant-girl is allowed to grapple with her destiny and, after a fashion, to defeat it, is felt (or has been felt by one reader, at any rate) to be absolutely inevitable. To reconcile us to the black flag above Wintoncester prison as the appointed end of Tess's career, a curse at least as deep as that of Pelops should have been laid on the D'Urberville family. Tess's curse does not lie by nature on all women; nor on all Dorset women; nor on all Dorset women who have illegitimate children; for a very few even of these are hanged. We feel that we are not concerned with a type, but with an individual case deliberately chosen by the author; and no amount of talk about the "President of the Immortals" and his "Sport" can persuade us to the contrary. With Esther Waters on the other hand, we feel we are assisting in the combat of a human life against its natural destiny; we perceive that the woman has a chance of winning; we are happy when she wins; and we are the better for helping her with our sympathy in the struggle. That is why, using the

word in the Aristotelean sense, I maintain that *Esther Waters* is a more "philosophical" work than *Tess.* (pp. 198-99)

> *Arthur Quiller-Couch, "Mr. George Moore" (1894), in his* Adventures in Criticism *(copyright under the Berne Convention; reprinted with the permission of Charles Scribner's Sons), Charles Scribner's Sons, 1896 (reprinted by G. P. Putnam's Sons, 1925, pp. 195-200).*

GILBERT K. CHESTERTON (essay date 1905)

Mr. George Moore began his literary career by writing his personal confessions; nor is there any harm in this if he had not continued them for the remainder of his life. He is a man of genuinely forcible mind and of great command over a kind of rhetorical and fugitive conviction which excites and pleases. He is in a perpetual state of temporary honesty. He has admired all the most admirable modern eccentrics until they could stand it no longer. Everything he writes, it is to be fully admitted, has a genuine mental power. His account of his reason for leaving the Roman Catholic Church is possibly the most admirable tribute to that communion which has been written of late years. . . . Mr. Moore hates Catholicism because it breaks up the house of looking-glasses in which he lives. Mr. Moore does not dislike so much being asked to believe in the spiritual existence of miracles or sacraments, but he does fundamentally dislike being asked to believe in the actual existence of other people. Like his master Pater and all the aesthetes, his real quarrel with life is that it is not a dream that can be moulded by the dreamer. It is not the dogma of the reality of the other world that troubles him, but the dogma of the reality of this world. (pp. 128-29)

Mr. Moore's egoism is not merely a moral weakness, it is a very constant and influential aesthetic weakness as well. We should really be much more interested in Mr. Moore if he were not quite so interested in himself. We feel as if we were being shown through a gallery of really fine pictures, into each of which, by some useless and discordant convention, the artist had represented the same figure in the same attitude. "The Grand Canal with a distant view of Mr. Moore," "Effect of Mr. Moore through a Scotch Mist," "Mr. Moore by Firelight," "Ruins of Mr. Moore by Moonlight," and so on, seems to be the endless series. He would no doubt reply that in such a book as [**"Confessions of a Young Man"**] he intended to reveal himself. But the answer is that in such a book as this he does not succeed. (pp. 131-32)

In reading [Mr. Moore's **"Confessions"**] we do not feel the presence of a clean-cut personality like that of Thackeray and Matthew Arnold. We only read a number of quite clever and largely conflicting opinions which might be uttered by any clever person, but which we are called upon to admire specifically, because they are uttered by Mr. Moore. He is the only thread that connects Catholicism and Protestantism, realism and mysticism—he or rather his name. He is profoundly absorbed even in views he no longer holds, and he expects us to be. And he intrudes the capital "I" even where it need not be intruded—even where it weakens the force of a plain statement. Where another man would say, "It is a fine day," Mr. Moore says, "Seen through my temperament, the day appeared fine." Where another man would say, "Milton has obviously a fine style," Mr. Moore would say, "As a stylist Milton had always impressed me." The Nemesis of this self-centred spirit is that of being totally ineffectual. Mr. Moore has started many interesting crusades, but he has abandoned them before his disciples could begin. Even when he is on the side of the truth he is as fickle as the children of falsehood. . . . His weakness of introspection and selfishness in all their glory cannot prevent him fighting; but they will always prevent him winning. (pp. 132-34)

Gilbert K. Chesterton, "The Moods of Mr. George Moore," in his Heretics, *John Lane Company, 1905, pp. 128-34.*

CORNELIUS WEYGANDT   (essay date 1913)

[George Moore's short stories and novels], more than any writing of his, reveal his inherent dramatic power. By dramatic power I mean not his power of situation and evolution of dramatic technique, but his power to change his point of view with the character he is creating. A sensual exquisite himself whose predominant thought is of woman, and of woman from a standpoint closely akin to an epicure's toward an ideal meal, Mr. Moore can identify himself with people in whom there is none of himself but the essential humanity common to mankind. Most wonderful of many wonderful realizations of viewpoint so different from what is his personally is his realization of the attitude of Father MacTurnan, an old priest, celibate by nature, who put aside his books, as ministering to the pride of the intellect, and sat, night after night, with them by his side in the study, but always unopened, while he was knitting socks for the poor of his parish. Better known, of course, than this character of Father MacTurnan is that of Father Gogarty in **"The Lake,"** but for all his sympathetic elaboration of this bemused and distraught cleric the character is never wholly opposed to that of Mr. Moore himself as is the character of Father MacTurnan.

It is this power of Mr. Moore that makes him the great novelist that he is, this power of identifying himself with the personality and this looking out on life from the viewpoint of Esther Waters or Lewis Seymour, or Edward Dempsey or Rose Leicester, of Kate Lennox or Mr. Innes. . . . The English novel has been famously deficient in story-telling ability since Scott's day, and Mr. Moore is no exception to the rule. As, however, the emphasis of all his stories is on character, his deficiency in narrative power matters hardly at all.

Mr. Moore is, then, Ireland's greatest novelist because he has in greatest measure—in full measure—this greatest gift of the Gael, the gift of dramatic impersonation of all manner of men in all their changing moods. (pp. 99-101)

Almost any novelist, sooner or later in his career, dabbles in drama. . . . **"The Strike at Arlingford"** [Mr. Moore's first play] has its excellences: its plot is logically unfolded; it is believable; it is true to human nature; it has moments of intensity. Had Mr. Moore power of dialogue it might have been a fine play, for the characterization is what one would expect from so conscientious a depicter of life as Mr. Moore, and the problem, a man's choice between his love and his duty, one that has never failed to appeal to men. (pp. 103-04)

"Esther Waters" the play was like **"Esther Waters"** the novel, solely the work of Mr. Moore. The critics seem agreed that it was long drawn out and undramatic, but that it was well written and well acted. I suppose that the preoccupation with **"Esther Waters"** that this dramatization reveals is because **"Esther Waters"** was written in that period of his life when Mr. Moore was most himself. After ten years in London he had escaped considerably from the French influence of his young manhood,

and his genius had not been warped out of its true plane, as he would doubtless now say, by Irish mists. Mr. Moore must have felt that there was something not wholly himself in much of **"The Untilled Field"** and in much of **"The Lake,"** that the minds of Mr. Yeats and Mr. [George] Russell had in a way dominated his mind, and that not even the hardly tolerated Mr. Martyn had been without influence upon him. (p. 112)

It is not, I think, particularly difficult for one who understands the old-fashioned camp-meeting "getting of religion" to understand this "Celtic episode." Mr. Moore got Celtomania; a sort of "spiritual consumption," he calls his possession in one place, as a certain other type of sinner "got religion" in the old shouting days. That is, Mr. Moore wrought himself up partly in the spirit of Synge's Playboy, and was wrought up to some degree willy-nilly until he could write his speech of February, 1900, on **"Literature and the Irish Language,"** and, finally, a little later, could return happily to the country that until then he could endure only now and again.

But as a matter of fact the motive that led Mr. Moore back to Ireland matters not at all to literature. What beauty of writing that return led to matters a great deal. Had he not returned to Ireland, we should not have had a good deal that adds to the joy we win from satiric laughter, we should not have had **"Hail and Farewell"**; had he not returned we should not have had a book that adds to the treasure of beautiful feeling and beautiful writing there is in English literature, a treasure that there is no chance of ever having too large; we should not have had **"The Lake,"** which is Ireland, West Ireland, Catholic Ireland, a land under gray skies that the priests its masters would, too many of them, make a land of gray lives. (p. 113)

Cornelius Weygandt, "Mr. Edward Martyn and Mr. George Moore," in his Irish Plays and Playwrights (copyright 1913 by Cornelius Weygandt and copyright renewed 1941 by Cornelius Weygandt; reprinted by permission of Houghton Mifflin Company), Houghton Mifflin, 1913 (and reprinted by Kennikat Press, 1966), pp. 72-113.*

KATHERINE MANSFIELD   (essay date 1920)

We have no other writer who is so fond of talking of his art [as Mr. George Moore]. So endless in his patience, so sustained his enthusiasm, we have the feeling that he cannot refrain from confiding in the stupid public, simply because he cannot keep silent. And yet—there is the strange fact. While we are engaged in reading Mr. George Moore's novels he is 'there,' but once they are put back on the shelves he has softly and silently vanished away until he is heard of again.

The publication of a new edition of **'Esther Waters'** provides an opportunity for seeking to understand this curious small problem. It is generally agreed that this novel is the best he has written, and the author himself has expressed his delight in it—'the book that among all other books I should have cared most to write, and to have written it so much better than I ever dreamed it could be written.' **'Esther Waters'** is, on the face of it, a model novel. Having read it carefully and slowly—we defy anyone to race along or skip—from cover to cover, we are left feeling that there is not a page, paragraph, sentence, word, that is not right, the only possible page, paragraph, sentence, word. The more we look into it, the more minute our examination, the deeper grows our amazement at the amount of sheer labour that has gone to its execution. (p. 243)

And yet we would say without hesitation that **'Esther Waters'** is not a great novel, and never could be a great novel, because it has not, from first to last, the faintest stirring of the breath of life. It is as dry as the remainder biscuit after a voyage. In a word it has no emotion. Here is a world of objects accurately recorded, here are states of mind set down, and here, above all, is that good Esther whose faith in her Lord is never shaken, whose love for her child is never over-powered—and who cares? (pp. 244-45)

What it comes to is that we believe that emotion is essential to a work of art; it is that which makes a work of art a unity. Without emotion writing is dead; it becomes a record instead of a revelation, for the sense of revelation comes from that emotional reaction which the artist felt and was impelled to communicate. To contemplate the object, to let it make its own impression—which is Mr. Moore's way in **'Esther Waters'**—is not enough. There must be an initial emotion felt by the writer, and all that he sees is saturated in that emotional quality. It alone can give incidence and sequence, character and background, a close and intimate unity. Let the reader turn to the scene where Sarah gets drunk because her horse has lost. It is a fearful scene, and so closely described that we might be at her elbow. But now Sarah speaks, now Esther, now William, and all is as cold and toneless as if it were being read out of that detective's notebook again. It is supremely good evidence; nothing is added, nothing is taken away, but we forget it as soon as it is read for we have been given nothing to remember. Fact succeeds fact, and with the reflection that Esther and her husband 'fell asleep, happy in each other's love, seeming to find new bonds of union in pity for their friend's misfortune,' the scene closes. Is that all? No wonder we forget Mr. George Moore. To praise such work as highly as he does is to insult his readers' intelligence. (pp. 245-46)

> Katherine Mansfield, "'Esther Waters' Revisited" (originally published in The Athenaeum, August 6, 1920), in her Novels and Novelists, edited by J. Middleton Murry (copyright 1930, copyright renewed © 1958, by Alfred A. Knopf, Inc.; reprinted by permission of The Society of Authors as the literary representative of the Estate of Katherine Mansfield), Knopf, 1930, pp. 242-46.

JOHN FREEMAN (essay date 1922)

Controversy has played a far from insignificant part in the life of George Moore, and the publication of *A Modern Lover* gave him an admirable opening for his pugnacity. The beginnings of the campaign are recorded in *Literature at Nurse, or Circulating Morals,* a pamphlet issued in 1885, in which he asserts rather than explains the position of the artist. . . . Moore's pamphlet cites at length the harmless passage which gained the book's [*A Modern Lover*] refusal as an immoral publication. . . . He [then] took three novels which had not been refused by the libraries, summarized their plots, and quoted a questionable scene from each, crying, 'Look on this picture, and on this!' The method is elementary but effective. . . . (p. 90)

Literature at Nurse is merely the earliest of those challenges to the stupid which George Moore has always rejoiced in uttering. Whatever dignity he presents to our view—and it is almost solely the dignity of an artist's achievement—he has never cared to assume that of suffering fools gladly; perhaps because it is an attitude which the fool himself can so easily feign. (p. 91)

The year 1887 saw the publication of a curious, chaotic book, *Parnell and His Island,* a study in a forsaken mode of political-social interests, with the familiar Balzacian interventions and interludes. (p. 125)

The scenes of the book, [Moore] says, have been chosen because they seemed typical and picturesque aspects of a primitive country and barbarous people. Unconcerned with this or that interest, indifferent to this or that opinion, his desire was to produce a series of pictures to touch the fancy of the reader as a Japanese ivory or fan, combinations of hue and colour calculated to awake in him fictitious feelings of pity, curiosity and nostalgia of the unknown. But have these scenes been 'chosen' at all? I call the book chaotic, and a slight glance will show that it is made up in part of the material used in other books. Cut out of it certain considerable passages to be found in *A Drama in Muslin,* and you cut out much of the best of the book. There is the fashionable dressmaker, for instance, the ear for all confidences and intimacies in both books; there is an almost precise repetition of that oddly effective scene in the novel, in which the Barton tenants insist upon a reduction of their rents by twenty-five per cent; but in *Parnell and His Island* the spectator is the poet who, intensely wearied, strives to amuse himself by recalling a sonnet of Mallarmé's. . . . These returns and renewals illustrate once again his frugal habit; for Moore's is not a royal and prodigal gift, and for all his supreme interest in the story and ease in telling a story, there is no careless largesse anywhere, but rather the anxious concentration which a growing accomplishment has taught him both to increase and to disguise. (pp. 125-26)

Parnell and His Island is an essay in literature, and its real value is that of the marking on a wall by which a towering small child's height is taken on successive birthdays. As politics it need not be read, much less censured, and as literature it can be remembered for the simplest uses of history and portraiture. (p. 127)

Hail and Farewell is remarkable in its devotion to an antipathy. It was not published until some time after Moore's sojourn in Ireland was over, and to few men is it given to nurse either their admiration or their contempt with such perfect success as he achieves. Admiration cools, gods are dethroned or diminished in glory, and the contempt which we feel one year fades to indifference the next; but Moore's admiration of A. E. and his manifest affection for Edward Martyn do not perceptibly dwindle, nor does time rob him of his contempt for others. Men are sometimes ashamed of an overweighted dislike; but Moore has avowed his desire not to conceal or be ashamed of anything, no, not even of the touch of inhumanity which gives a final salience to his amazing inventions. (p. 150)

There can be no question of George Moore's devouring zeal for art, when it involves this general sacrifice of friends and acquaintances. His eye is acute, his tongue merciless, his judgment cynical, and having discovered his power (for it was not always apparent to himself) he proceeds to a malicious employment; yet not because of deliberate malice, but because he cannot abstain from the sharpest exercise of this newly-found gift. He can admire his victims, but they are his victims none the less, and he admires nothing so much as his own ingenuity when he looks again and again at the palpitating shapes that once were theirs. . . . Never have the privileges of friendship and the accidents of acquaintance been more richly misused; the fretful porcupine has no more painful quill than that of the author of *Hail and Farewell*. Small consolation is it to the fantastically twitching corpses that Moore has displayed his own character with at least equal clearness, and breathed a morose or amused *Non dolet.* . . . He will say things in his own name, as of himself, and he will say things of others, which most men would shrink from saying out of mere prudence or generosity; and it is the same impersonal wantonness that impels him, the same fear of being ashamed or seeming ashamed of any thought or imagination which comes into his head. *Hail and Farewell* is romantic biography as well as romantic autobiography, and when all is said, in praise and in excuse, it remains equally admirable and inexcusable. But time will diminish the offence without dulling the beauty, and the trilogy will assuredly remain a delight long after most of the victims of it are forgotten. (pp. 164-65)

Among the [*Memoirs of My Dead Life*] one might expect to find what is in fact found, some clear echoes of earlier voices. . . . (pp. 171-72)

[Moore] is at times deliberately renewing fading memories, anxious to revive his dead life and in reviving to give it the shape that pleases him now. He cannot look upon Paris without emotion, for he thinks it made him, and now he exists in two countries and is furnished with two sets of thoughts and emotions, especially the pleasure of a literature which is his without being wholly his. He calls himself the youngest of the naturalists, the eldest of the symbolists; a decayed terminology, truly, in the ears of 1921. He speaks, in the chapter on 'Spent Love,' of women as the legitimate subject of a man's thoughts, saying that women are forgotten when men think about art, though only for a little while; but the writing of these *Memoirs* itself proves, with the support of so much besides, that this is untrue. Again, he remarks that the passing of things is always a moving subject for meditation, but the taking of a pen would destroy the pleasure of meditation. He would give much for another memory, but memory may not be beckoned.

As token, or instead of another memory, you are offered a long episode, **'The Lovers of Orelay.'** It is a curiously artificial piece, a garrulous simulation, into which wantonness creeps like a cold, crystal trickling of water. . . . It is his crystalline coldness that robs our author's offence of offence, and makes the wantonness of this episode a purely intellectual adventure. There still remains the wonder why a writer of George Moore's genius should care to waste himself in these dubious excursions. . . . (pp. 172-73)

> John Freeman, *in his* A Portrait of George Moore in a Study of His Work, *T. Werner Laurie, Ltd., 1922 (reprinted by Scholarly Press, Inc., 1971), 283 p.*

EDMUND GOSSE   (essay date 1923)

Mr. George Moore is one of the best living writers of English prose, and I think he is the most conscientious. He is never satisfied with the choice of his language and the structure of his sentences, and he longs, more passionately than any one else, to achieve the impossible perfection. So few writers indulge any such longing, or, indeed, have ever dreamed that perfection in prose can exist as an ideal, that Mr. Moore's vagaries with regard to revision ought to be treated tenderly, even respectfully. He, at least, is an artist through and through, and posterity will bring him his reward. (p. 327)

When a man is so profoundly and continuously occupied with the various problems of style as Mr. Moore manifestly is, to remark that it is not worth while for him to take so much trouble is an impertinence. His natural reply is that he does

not write to arrest our indolent attention with a tale, but to add to the literature of the country another durable ornament. That being the case, he is haunted by the fear lest, as it has been given to the public, it may contain "disgraceful"—by which he means awkward and inharmonious—pages, and he re-reads it with that suspicion. His taste, trained to an extreme delicacy, prevails upon him to conceive that this fear is indeed well founded.

Given this scruple of the disinterested artist, and it is difficult to see how Mr. Moore can be expected to resist the impulse to re-write. His variations of his early text are inevitable; the only alternative would be for him to moon around in silence nursing an afflicted conscience. (p. 328)

Against the practice of re-writing books already accepted by the public there is a great deal to be said. In the first place, it is a falsification of history. Everybody has reviled Pope for altering and heightening the style of his own correspondence when he gave it to the booksellers to publish, but if he chose to regard a letter as a piece of literary art, how does he differ from Mr. George Moore tinkering *The Lake* or *Evelyn Innes*? In each case the next text does not represent the mood of the old time, and must therefore be in discord with it and with the new time as well.

When Mr. Moore published *A Mummer's Wife*—that is to say, thirty-seven years ago—he did not write so correctly as he does now; indeed (to be brutally frank), he often wrote very indifferently. But it is of the greatest interest to observe the growth of Mr. Moore as a writer; the imperfections of *A Mummer's Wife* add a peculiar lustre to the beauty of *The Brook Kerith*. Yet when the author, to satisfy the craving for uniform perfection, "re-writes" in the language of 1920 what he composed in 1880, we lose all indication of development, and the gain is far less than would be the composition, in the hours so fantastically spent, of a new work of art, in spirit as well as form, appropriate to the author's maturity.

Another objection is that, however generously the new wine is poured into the old bottle, there is always some old wine left in the bottle, and this produces a mixture of dubious gusto. These "revised" and "re-written" chapters invariably present a confusion of styles, an irregularity of tone. The appended pages do not complete the design of the author, which ought to proceed, if he must be consistent, until nothing of the old is left. (pp. 328-29)

> Edmund Gosse, "Second Thoughts," *in his* More Books on the Table, *Charles Scribner's Sons, 1923, pp. 325-33.**

PADRAIC COLUM   (essay date 1926)

Anything that draws us to a re-perusal of George Moore's **"Hail and Farewell"** is to our betterment: it is a work that is vastly entertaining; it is in a species to itself; it reveals to us, moreover, possibilities in writing: it is one of the few works of our time of which the reading forms a real experience for a writer. In short, it is a masterpiece. . . .

It was George Moore's good angel that sent him back to Ireland in the early nineteen hundreds. He got a succession of books out of his return, the chief of them all being **"Hail and Farewell"**, a book to put beside his other masterpiece, **"Esther Waters"**. At the moment neither London nor Paris could have given him any more: he had fully exploited the naturalistic novel in **"Esther Waters"** and **"A Mummer's Wife"**; he could have gone on elaborating his **"Confessions"** (he did), but only at the risk of becoming garrulous. His return to Ireland gave him a chance of exercising the two faculties he had developed and of exercising them in a new way and on new material—the faculty for detached observation which he had been trained in through the writing of the naturalistic novel, and the faculty for self portraiture which he had developed in his memoir writing. His return, as I have said, permitted his using these two faculties in a new way and on new material. It did more than this: it restored to him a style that, although not hitherto used by him, was native to him—the vocal sentence which Irish people take to naturally. . . . (p. 555)

"Hail and Farewell" is speech written down and it is an Irishman's speech. Later on, in **"The Brook Kerith"** and in **"Heloise and Abelard"** he overdoes this speech, and, by keeping it on one tone, he makes his writing monotonous. But in **"Hail and Farewell"** it helps to give the effect of a flowing narrative. Yes, it was fortunate for George Moore that he returned to Ireland, and it was fortunate that he returned just at the time he did. In the space between the downfall of Parnell and the rise of the Irish Volunteers the intellectuals had the whole stage in Ireland—I use the word "intellectuals" in its best sense—and they had formed a coterie in which everybody knew everybody else's foibles and oddities but which, at the same time, was made homogeneous by an enthusiasm and by the sense of possessing an unacknowledged national leadership. George Moore could not deal with men of action, but he could deal with men of ideas, and especially with men such as these men were, all with a touch of fantasy in their personalities or ideas. . . .

[It was George Moore's] theory that given a good model and the ability to copy the model, anyone who was a writer at all could get down a work of literature. Poets, as he has often told them, do not use their eyes to advantage. "Your best poems have come to you through your eyes", he told Yeats. George Moore knows how to use his eyes—there is no doubting that; he saw certain things as clearly and as firmly as any man ever saw them before; his training as a painter, no doubt, helped him to this accomplishment. And with the eyes there went a pair of ears that were just as good. He saw and he heard. His aural and his visual memory were clear. His recall of what has been said to him or said in his hearing is astonishing: the characteristic words, the shape of the sentence, the tone of the voice, to one who has known the speaker, come clear out of George Moore's pages.

But if **"Hail and Farewell"** were simply a record, a report, no matter how unmatchable, it would not have the entertainment, the refreshment, that it has for us. The record, the report, are there, but the work lives as a piece of storytelling. The story is about George Moore. And the author has been able to project a consistent character in the George Moore of the book—a candid, detached, whimsical, sensible, credulous, and penetrating person. And, oddly enough, an engaging person—that is, if we are not too deeply involved in what he confesses of other people's faults and foibles. (p. 556)

This is the place, I think, to set down what, to my mind, is the weakness of **"Hail and Farewell"** as a piece of storytelling. There is a breakdown in the narrative, and the breakdown is made evident in the new edition which divides the story into two equal parts. Part One tells the story of George Moore's coming to Ireland. Part Two tells the story of his leaving Ireland and his return to England. But Part Two is not so entertaining as Part One; it seems to be diffuse and disjointed. And the

reason, as it seems to me, that this is so, is because the issue on which his return depends is not a human issue, but purely a mental one.

It comes over George Moore suddenly that Catholics have produced no literature since the hardening of dogma brought about by the Catholic Reaction. But Ireland is a Catholic country. Therefore Ireland can produce no literature. As a protest against that state of affairs George Moore decides to rise up and leave the country. This is the theme of the second volume, and I submit that it is not enough to carry a narrative of nearly five hundred pages. I am not now discussing whether the author of **"Hail and Farewell"** is right or wrong in his judgment about the production of literature in modern Catholic countries; he makes the production or nonproduction of literature in Catholic countries a theme for a long narrative, and this theme, to my mind, is not good enough because it is not human enough.

The first part of the narrative goes with a human theme—memories evoked by references to one's native country, the influences of such a pair as Edward Martyn and W. B. Yeats, curiosity, the momentary dedication to a cause—the theme is so human, so immediate, that episodes like the journey to Bayreuth, really external to it, are drawn into the narrative. In the second part there is not current enough, and so the external episodes remain external, and we get the effect of a narrative disjointed to some extent, and somewhat diffuse.

But if as a story **"Hail and Farewell"** breaks down in the second part, there is no break in the first; there is nothing in that five hundred—or nearly five hundred—pages but entertaining and subtilely humorous narrative. And the second part, apart from the pages of theological argument, is full of delightful episodes. One turns again and again to pages in both volumes that are delightful for their humor, wonderful for their insight, or that have claim to be thought upon because of the quality that is in their writing. (p. 558)

Padraic Colum, "Dublin in Literature," in The Bookman, *New York, Vol. LXIII, No. 1, March, 1926, pp. 555-61.**

HERBERT READ (essay date 1926)

Definitions of poetry are extremely rare; it is not a subject about which many people have felt it necessary or desirable to be dogmatic. The critics have been content with descriptive classifications, the true poets with their practice, and the plain man with his enjoyment. Therefore, we should honour Mr. George Moore's *Anthology of Pure Poetry* with a criticism more pertinacious than the casual reviews that appeared at the time of its publication. For Mr. Moore is an imaginative artist who should possess a direct intelligence of art, and is, moreover, at least by pretension, an objective artist from whom we might expect a detached and logical statement of his views. There is no doubt that his Anthology is a work of criticism; it is one of the few that have such a rational justification. And Mr. Moore has done his work well: the Anthology is consistent with its avowed aim and makes a very formidable pretence of infallibility. It is, what Mr. Moore intended it to be, "a real advancement in the study of poetry". (p. 59)

What, for example, does [Mr. Moore] mean by "pure" poetry, if not poetry which attains *absolute* beauty, for it is beauty, we are told, not subject to change. (p. 61)

I have never thought of Mr. Moore as particularly classical in his attitude towards life or in his art; he writes, it is true, possibly the best intimate style of his generation. For the rest he is as romantic and as subjective as anyone possibly could be. He is a typical Rousseauist, exploiting his sensations for the benefit (or to the detriment?) of his art. He never rises above these sensations, to transmute them into universal terms. He is for this reason incapable of any of the major forms of art, and has had to confine himself to the romantic exercises of a novelist and raconteur. He may pride himself that *Esther Waters,* for example, is a tolerably objective performance, but it may be doubted whether it is more than a pastiche in the manner of Flaubert. It has no inner conviction of necessity, like *Madame Bovary,* no intelligent significance, like *L'Education Sentimentale.* It is difficult, in fact, to know what Mr. Moore means by objectivity. He seems to imagine that the objective faculty is solely concerned with "things", and by "things" he means the material objects of everyday life. And presumably subjectivity is correspondingly only concerned with images or ideas. But subjectivity is rather an attitude that when completely developed includes the whole of the sensible universe. It is the total orientation of an individual's sensibilities, and all things in his mind, whether thoughts or things, are set in one direction. Equally objectivity involves all aspects of experience, and an idea can be as impersonal to its beholder as any material thing. It is only to be remembered that the completely objective man, equally with the completely subjective man, is a fiction of our milder mythologies. (pp. 62-3)

If Mr. Moore had wanted to use a psychological phrase, he might with more exactness have resorted to terms which would rasp as uncouth neologisms on his ear—I mean the terms *extraversion* and *introversion.* For these imply not, like objectivity and subjectivity, the mind and a state or existence external to it, but merely conditions of the mind itself.

But he might then have discovered that for his purpose there was no need to press the distinction. For personalities may be extravert or introvert, and are both by turns and together; and in this respect poets—true poets, poets such as Mr. Moore has honoured in his Anthology—are no different from the rest of us. (p. 65)

> Herbert Read, "Pure Poetry," in his Reason and Romanticism: Essays in Literary Criticism, *Faber and Gwyer, 1926 (and reprinted by Russell & Russell, 1963), pp. 59-66.**

FRANK SWINNERTON (essay date 1934)

"The sly smile, the malice, the vanity": one sees them all in Moore's more personal writings, *Confessions of a Young Man, Memoirs of My Dead Life, Hail and Farewell, Avowals, Conversations in Ebury Street.* At first, until the attention is caught, they may seem the outstanding characteristics of his work; but no writing as limpid as his could escape insipidity if it were not that every sentence has been overseen by a mind both keen and clear. (pp. 176-77)

Moore was candid when he wished to be candid; and . . . in his printed discussions it is always he who chooses the ground, just as it was always Socrates, another deceptively simple casuist, who chose the ground upon which he could discomfit other spirits more generous in assertion. Moore's criticisms of Thomas Hardy, to take one instance, are based upon isolated passages or single poems, and they take no heed of Hardy's work as a whole or of Hardy's character as a writer. It is true that Hardy's poetic preoccupations are often with death and

decay. It is true that Hardy's prose style is occasionally clotted. One could catalogue other faults. But if preoccupations and faults and single paragraphs were to settle a writer's calibre, some of Moore's own shortcomings could be made to damn him for ever. (p. 177)

The truth is that there is a coldness in all of Moore's writing, and he was never more cold than he was in that tale of love *Evelyn Innes.* His realistic novels set down a series of facts which one accepts or rejects according to one's own experience; and I am far from rating them as positively high as some other commentators would do. They seem to me to have a woodenness, an unleavened literalness, which takes no heed of surrounding colour and movement. They have no humour. Not only has the author no passion, but his dramatis personæ kiss without conviction —one seducer enchants his love by dilating upon the qualities of Balzac as a writer, and, having had his offer of horses refused, is more successful with a set of the *Comédie Humaine.* By comparison with books written since in the same order, they are one-syllabled and one-toned. But when they are read in relation to the history of the novel, as pioneer works in a stage of fictive literature which otherwise was largely sentimental or decorative, they are outstanding. While other writers of the eighties and early nineties were being "just literary," or witty at the expense of others (few can be witty, of course, at their own expense; but still fewer make the attempt), or romantic, or ingenious, Moore and [George] Gissing alone, or almost alone, were trying in the published novel to tell the world something about life at first hand. And in Moore's case it was quite extraordinary how the choice of detail and the continuous succession of plain incidents produced both an effect of nature and a progressive interest. Where Gissing showed his personal grievance and rebelliousness, Moore recorded. He was detached. He did not explain or expound (as Gissing did), but refrained from all personal comment, leaving to his characters any reflections which had properly to be made upon such situations as seemed inevitably to arise in the course of the tale. To me these books miss a thousand shades; but that is their strength, for they are as firm as engravings. No wonder they impressed themselves, and still impress themselves, upon candid minds as very striking reproductions of reality. There is no question that they gave rise, toward the end of the nineties, to a new school of naturalistic writers, Edwin Pugh, Arthur Morrison, Somerset Maugham, and others. We know that a reading of *A Mummer's Wife* drew Arnold Bennett towards that re-creation of life in the Five Towns upon which his lasting fame depends. Merely to record the facts is to establish Moore's importance as an influence upon his age. (pp. 177-78)

It is interesting to recall that when Moore was writing his early novels, they were the cause of fierce combats with the libraries and the moral censors of their day, when in reality no more rigidly moral novels have ever been composed; and that whenever he wrote of Ireland he was the centre of noise and argument inseparable from all discussion of Irish affairs; and that as he took up the life of Christ similar discord marred the acceptance of his work and averted its neglect. Like other Irishmen, he enjoyed exasperating his fellows; and in the future, when passions are concentrated upon more contemporary matters, he may lose some of the benefits of exasperation and fall into oblivion. . . . What will survive is the personality of Moore.

Not a creative personality; a critical, discomfiting personality, malicious, relentless, much-considering, cold, and with no capacity for self-sacrifice. Not without sympathy, for otherwise he could not have written novels such as *Esther Waters* and *A Mummer's Wife*, but as shrewd as he was vain, as teasing as he was unhumorous. (pp. 179-80)

Our judgment of Moore is imperfect if we neglect two qualities in him, his observant quietness and his scrupulousness. Though his perceptions are tinged with cruelty, they are untinged with sentiment; they are referred always to his sense of truth, and what he sees he expresses with a fidelity as fine as it is beautiful. What he sees. . . . It was not a generous mind, but though full of treacheries to friendship it was unwavering in strict loyalty to itself. I say, not a pleasant person, but a deeply interesting mind and one of immeasurable value in its time and place. (p. 181)

Frank Swinnerton, "Black and White: George Moore, Arnold Bennett, John Galsworthy, Somerset Maugham," in his The Georgian Scene: A Literary Panorama *(copyright 1934, © 1962 by Frank Swinnerton; reprinted by permission of Holt, Rinehart and Winston, Publishers), Farrar & Rinehart, 1934, pp. 169-208.**

CHARLES MORGAN (essay date 1935)

[The stories of *The Untilled Field* are beautiful,] rich in natural humour, free of the false emphasis that too often reduces a short story to a trick; they have the air, which was to be the mark of all that was best in Moore's later work, of being governed by the people themselves, not by the writer. They are not his puppets; they do not obey him or illustrate any moral of his; and their adventures are being told, for the first time in English, with that ordered simplicity, that idealization of the rhythms of the speaking voice, which was the prose instrument that Moore invented and perfected. We see him here exchanging the literary approach to narrative for that of a *raconteur*, and from this book onwards may follow the development of his peculiar method. *The Lake,* which was continually re-written and continually simplified, is an almost flawless instance of the application of that method to a longer and more complex narrative than any contained in *The Untilled Field,* and already modifications have begun to appear in it. A *raconteur* would have begun at the beginning of the priest's tale, but Moore, desiring to preserve in the lake itself a strict unity of scene, was driven, after many experiments, to use for opening an elaborate retrospect, a task of infinite difficulty to him, who, being no comfortable grammarian, shrank from the troubles of the English pluperfect. The difficulty was brilliantly overcome. The story reads "like milk". It has indeed a seeming ease, and is governed by a rule against divagation, which make of it the pleasantest of all introductions to Moore's work. (pp. 25-6)

[It] is worth recording that Moore's especial pride was in his power to invent anecdote. He was aware that his later narrative method was made perilous by its smoothness; at the same time he was determined that this smoothness must at all costs be preserved, for, if it were not, his whole purpose would be defeated, . . . and an element of fashion would appear in his prose. To be fashionable was what Moore did not desire, for to be fashionable to-day is to be unfashionable to-morrow, and his aim was to write a prose independent of every colloquialism, every trick of phrase, every contemporary allusion that might make it obscure or tedious in the future. He carried this quest of an absolute prose so far that he rejected where he could, and sought occasion to reject, the use of the second person plural, feeling that this use of verb and pronoun was rubbed, and that "thou" and "thee" and "thine" had the double merit of freshness to-day and of an unshakable establishment in the Bible. But he knew that this smoothness laid a weight on narrative; after many pages the reader might turn from it, seeking stronger contrast, richer variety, more abundant vigour than was to be found in these intertwining cadences, unless by anecdote he was led on from page to page. . . . Moore desired above all else to evolve a new method of storytelling. He used to say that he had introduced "the aesthetic novel" into England. This is true, but the phrase was not fortunately chosen; it expresses only a part of the truth and, at the same time, obscures it, for to many minds the word "aesthetic" suggests the beauty of contrivance, not that perfect marriage of form with purpose which was Moore's understanding of it. He saw round him, and might still see if he were alive, the English novel struggling beneath a burden of literary convention. The uses of dialogue, the means employed to pass from dialogue to narrative and back again, the methods of communicating retrospect, had all stiffened. (pp. 45-7)

Consider first his treatment of dialogue and the means he discovered to preserve at once an impression of natural speech and the continuity of a prose that would have been broken by photographic naturalism. Abélard has been likening the whiteness of Héloïse to the whiteness of summer:

> But my summer is not yet come, Abélard, she said; I am but the month of April. Call me not the month of March, for this is a cold month, and I am not cold. A fair month indeed, he answered, is the month of April, one not to be despised, though the month of May is a better month, and the month of June is—Well, June is a month for the Gods. But thy June, Héloïse, is many months distant, and waiting for it shall be my joy. Wilt grow tired of waiting? she asked. Tired of waiting? How little thou knowest yet about love. A true love never tires or wanes, Héloïse, but is with us always, like our blood, like our breath.

In this passage there are seven sentences. Each sentence, without exception, hands on a key-word to be repeated in its successor, precisely as each stanza of *terza rima* hands on a rhyme. The first sentence lays an emphasis on "month". The second repeats it twice, and produces an internal echo by a double use of the word "cold". The third sentence has the word "month" no less than six times, and another internal echo on the word "June". The fourth sentence repeats "June", and introduces a new word, "waiting", with a final muffled echo of "month". The fifth sentence repeats "waiting"; the sixth echoes it interrogatively, and strikes the new word "love", to which the last sentence instantly replies. By this means was Moore's dialogue bound together, his repetitions and his vowel-sounds linking his prose as rhyme links a sonnet. The significance of his prose escapes us unless we observe that the purpose of such elaboration was not decorative but structural. He was not making pleasant sounds because they pleased his ear; he was binding dialogue, as an architect binds into unity the component parts of his design. (pp. 51-3)

Charles Morgan, in his Epitaph on George Moore *(© 1935 by Charles Morgan; copyright renewed © 1963 by Hilda Vaughan Morgan; reprinted by permission of the Literary Estate of Charles Morgan), The Macmillan Company, 1935, 56 p.*

W. B. YEATS (essay date 1935-36)

George Moore had a ceaseless preoccupation with painting and the theatre, within certain limits a technical understanding of both; whatever idea possessed him, courage and explosive power; but sacrificed all that seemed to other men good breeding, honour, friendship, in pursuit of what he considered the root facts of life. (pp. 402-03)

His *Modern Painting* has colloquial animation and surprise that might have grown into a roundness and ripeness of speech that is a part of style had not ambition made him in later life prefer sentences a Dublin critic has compared to ribbons of toothpaste squeezed out of a tube. When the Irish Theatre was founded, he had published *A Mummer's Wife*, which had made a considerable sensation, for it was the first realistic novel in the language, the first novel where every incident was there not because the author thought it beautiful, exciting or amusing, but because certain people who were neither beautiful, exciting, nor amusing must have acted in that way: the root facts of life, as they are known to the greatest number of people, that and nothing else. Balzac would have added his wisdom. Moore had but his blind ambition. *Esther Waters* should have been a greater novel, for the scene is more varied. Esther is tempted to steal a half-crown; Balzac might have made her steal it and keep our sympathy, but Moore must create a personification of motherly goodness, almost an abstraction. (p. 406)

Because Moore thought all drama should be about possible people set in their appropriate surroundings, because he was fundamentally a realist . . . he required many dull, numb words. But he put them in more often than not because he had no feeling for words in themselves, none for their historical associations. He insisted for days upon calling the Fianna 'soldiers'. In *A Story-teller's Holiday* he makes a young man in the thirteenth century go to the 'salons' of 'the fashionable ladies' in Paris, in his last story men and women of the Homeric age read books. . . . He would have been a master of construction, but that his practice as a novelist made him long for descriptions and reminiscences. If *Diarmuid and Grania* failed in performance, and I am not sure that it did, it failed because the second act, instead of moving swiftly from incident to incident, was reminiscent and descriptive; almost a new first act. I had written enough poetical drama to know this and to point it out to Moore. (p. 436)

I no longer underrate him, I know that he had written, or was about to write, five great novels. But *A Mummer's Wife, Esther Waters, Sister Teresa* (everything is there of the convent, a priest said to me, except the religious life), *Muslin, The Lake*, gained nothing from their style. (p. 437)

Style was his growing obsession, he would point out all the errors of some silly experiment of mine, then copy it. It was from some such experiment that he learnt those long, flaccid, structureless sentences, 'and, and and, and and'; there is one of twenty-eight lines in *Muslin*. Sometimes he rebelled: 'Yeats, I have a deep distrust of any man who has a style', but it was generally I who tried to stop the obsession. 'Moore, if you ever get a style', I would say, 'it will ruin you. It is coloured glass and you need a plate-glass window.' When he formed his own circle he found no escape; the difficulties of modern Irish literature, from the loose, romantic, legendary stories of Standish O'Grady to James Joyce and Synge, had been in the formation of a style. He heard those difficulties discussed. All his life he had learnt from conversation, not from books. His nature, bitter, violent, discordant, did not fit him to write the sentences men murmur again and again for years. Charm and

rhythm had been denied him. Improvement makes straight roads; he pumice-stoned every surface because will had to do the work for nature. I said once: 'You work so hard that, like the Lancelot of Tennyson, you will almost see the Grail'. But now, his finished work before me, I am convinced that he was denied even that 'almost'. (p. 438)

W. B. Yeats, "Dramatis Personae" (originally published as "Dramatis Personae: 1896-1902," in London Mercury, Vol. XXXIII, Nos. 193, 194 and 195, November, December, 1935 and January, 1936), in his Autobiographies *(reprinted with permission of Macmillan Publishing Co., Inc.; in Canada by M. B. Yeats, Anne Yeats; copyright 1916, 1935 by Macmillan Publishing Co., Inc., renewed 1944, 1963 by Bertha Georgie Yeats), Macmillan & Co Ltd, 1955, pp. 383-458.*

SEÁN O'FAOLÁIN (essay date 1936)

We have in Moore as in Pater a dichotomy . . . between the man interested in life (*The Mummer's Wife; Esther Waters; Ave, Salve, Vale*) and the man interested in Art *à la* Wilde, "—rhythmical sequence of events described in etc."

The lack of "heart" in Moore is surely patent? And he might well be proud of *Esther Waters* because she squeezed out of him all the heart he had to give: more proud of the *Ave* trilogy [*Hail and Farewell*], especially the first and third books, because he there balanced finely, perfectly even, his wit and his affections, so that Edward [Martyn], who is one of the fine bits of portraiture in English literature, and whom as a man I do believe he loved in his own cold way, is that rare, rare thing in fiction, a kindly and rounded satire.

I have been re-reading a good deal of Moore, especially his essays, and here and there in *Ave*, and *Esther Waters*, and *The Lake* that I used to think was his best book in days when I thought he was a novelist, but I find more of him in *Confessions of a Young Man* than in any of these. "The seed of everything I have written," he said, "will be found herein," and he is right. Not merely the seed, in the sense of what influenced him—Shelley, the flood-tide of 1830, Gautier, Balzac, Zola, Flaubert, Goncourt, and Pater (". . . the book to which I owe the last temple of my soul, [Walter Pater's] *Marius the Epicurean*") but George Moore himself in his fullest imitation of personality. . . . [There] is Moore the emerging stylist: there is above all Moore the novelist, with his own ideas as to what the novel should be. (p. 335)

Even *Esther Waters* is in *The Confessions of a Young Man*, in the Emma of that book (on Moore's admission)—not, in honesty, the excellence of the naturalism of the novel, but its "give-away." For it shows, what I have said already, that Moore really was not interested in life but in himself—the true characteristic of the Parnassian—not in Emma but in his own "Art." (p. 336)

Moore was not a realist novelist—even in this his best novel—because, like all Romantics of his date, he was interested only in himself. These "novelists" as Susan Mitchell said, do not merely steal the jam—they smear themselves all over with it.

That is not to say he was not a romantic novelist; and very much of his time, but with more impassivity and less sensibility, equal delicacy, equal morbidity, none of the plenitude of the great French writers he admired, and not an iota of their sense of the "majesty of mystery." Never does he vibrate, because the emotional instrument he employed was too soft:

there is not a trace of the sound of the cymbal in Moore. Monotonous, and even wearying, his flute pipes on and on, often crooning "contralto"—a favourite word of his—into a rich moody turn that is the nearest he ever comes to the Orpheus note of the poetry he so loved. . . . There is no passion in all his work from beginning to end, content with what he called a "ray of eroticism," and what was natural was distasteful to him unless he could smoothe it into some graceful shape.

In truth, Moore was, as a novelist, the serious-minded and persevering dilettante: and his true métier, in which he produced work of great talent, work that is beyond criticism, was that of satirist, wit and essayist. He did his best work, essays aside, between 1900 and 1914, with, later, one lovely elaborate pastiche in *Héloise and Abelard.* All else is well-nigh unreadable. As for his style, it was an excellent style when he had good things to say. It became as he had less and less to say, more and more like a bit of chocolate that a child has sucked clean of its inscription. . . . (p. 337)

Seán O'Faoláin, "Pater and Moore" (reprinted by permission of the author), in The London Mercury, *Vol. XXXIV, No. 202, August, 1936, pp. 330-38.**

OSCAR CARGILL   (essay date 1941)

The merits of *Esther Waters* are great: it may bluntly be said that the author has more nearly achieved verisimilitude in this one book than has Hardy in all his novels. And curiously, this is one of the most English books ever written: where else is there a better study of the betting fraternity, of the whole serving class, of the British "pub" than here? In the decay of British genius it took an Irishman to do it, but that has in no way affected the authenticity or accuracy of the work. The characterization of Esther herself is the prime achievement of the novel, yet the minor people are sharply limned and live beyond the story's duration. Stack and Journeyman who have different systems for the horses, Mrs. Spires who "cares" for the unwanted children of serving girls until they conveniently expire, Sarah who steals her mistress' silver for a lover who deserts her, Fred Parsons who becomes a captain in the Salvation Army after Esther chooses William Latch in his stead— all these may be seen in any East End tavern. Without challenging credulity, Moore has given Esther an amazingly rich experience in order to reveal the great variety of ways in which the serving girl is victimized by those who employ her. As wet nurse, she is expected to allow her own child to die in order that the infant of higher birth may be properly suckled; she must, when receiving a mere pittance as housemaid, resist the temptation to pick up the small coin which has been deliberately "planted" merely to test her; and her duty is to report the foolish attentions of a son to her mistress though it means the forfeiture of her job. Esther displays a fine fortitude in the most trying situations, yet all that her pluck does for her is to land her precisely where she was at the beginning of the story, back at Barfields as a servant. Moore succeeds in convincing us, however, that without her strength of character Esther would have been forced down and down into prostitution and early death. She is the exception which really does prove the rule, and the thesis that the odds are against human beings, like herself, creatures of the lower class, is as well illustrated here as in any novel. Yet determinism is a generally conceded fact at the instinct level of intelligence, and what, after all, Moore has illustrated best is the blind nobility of maternal sacrifice in Esther Waters. It is a flawless character study. (pp. 79-80)

Oscar Cargill, "The Naturalists," in his Intellectual America: Ideas on the March *(reprinted with permission of Macmillan Publishing Co., Inc.; © 1941 by Macmillan Publishing Co., Inc.; copyright renewed © 1969 by Oscar Cargill), Macmillan, 1941, pp. 48-175.**

VIRGINIA WOOLF   (essay date 1942)

Perhaps it is not accident only, but a vague recollection of dipping and dallying in *Esther Waters, Evelyn Innes, The Lake,* which makes us take down in its new and stately form *Hail and Farewell* . . .—the two large volumes which George Moore has written openly and directly about himself. For all his novels are written, covertly and obliquely, about himself, so at least memory would persuade us, and it may help us to understand them if we steep ourselves in the pure waters which are elsewhere tinged with fictitious flavours. But are not all novels about the writer's self, we might ask? It is only as he sees people that we can see them; his fortunes colour and his oddities shape his vision until what we see is not the thing itself, but the thing seen and the seer inextricably mixed. There are degrees, however. The great novelist feels, sees, believes with such intensity of conviction that he hurls his belief outside himself and it flies off and lives an independent life of its own, becomes Natasha, Pierre, Levin, and is no longer Tolstoy. When, however, Mr. Moore creates a Natasha she may be charming, foolish, lovely, but her beauty, her folly, her charm are not hers, but Mr. Moore's. All her qualities refer to him. In other words, Mr. Moore is completely lacking in dramatic power. On the face of it, *Esther Waters* has all the appearance of a great novel; it has sincerity, shapeliness, style; it has surpassing seriousness and integrity; but because Mr. Moore has not the strength to project Esther from himself its virtues collapse and fall about it like a tent with a broken pole. There it lies, this novel without a heroine, and what remains of it is George Moore himself, a ruin of lovely language and some exquisite descriptions of the Sussex downs. For the novelist who has no dramatic power, no fire of conviction within, leans upon nature for support; she lifts him up and enhances his mood without destroying it.

But the defects of a novelist may well be the glories of his brother the autobiographer, and we find, to our delight, that the very qualities which weaken Mr. Moore's novels are the making of his memoirs. This complex character, at once diffident and self-assertive, this sportsman who goes out shooting in ladies' high-heeled boots, this amateur jockey who loves literature beyond the apple of his eye, this amorist who is so innocent, this sensualist who is so ascetic, this complex and uneasy character, in short, with its lack of starch and pomp and humbug, its pliability and malice and shrewdness and incompetence, is made of too many incompatible elements to concentrate into the diamond of a great artist, and is better occupied in exploring its own vagaries than in explaining those of other people. For one thing, Mr. Moore is without that robust belief in himself which leads men to prophesy and create. Nobody was ever more diffident. . . . But with the timidity of the mouse he has also its gigantic boldness. This meek grey innocent creature runs right over the lion's paws. There is nothing that Mr. Moore will not say; by his own confession he ought to be excluded from every drawing-room in South Kensington. If his friends forgive him it is only because to Mr. Moore all things are forgiven. (pp. 156-58)

Virginia Woolf, "George Moore," in her The Death of the Moth and Other Essays *(copyright 1942 by*

Harcourt, Brace Jovanovich, Inc.; renewed 1970 by
Marjorie T. Parsons, Exectrix; reprinted by permission of the publisher; in Canada by the Author's
Literary Estate and The Hogarth Press Ltd), Harcourt, 1942, pp. 156-61.

WILLIAM C. FRIERSON   (essay date 1942)

[Two] major influences transformed the English novel: natu-
ralism, which changed the current of English thought and expression; and "spiritualistic naturalism" as it appeared in [Joris-
Karl] Huysmans' writings and was later to affect England through
[Romain Rolland's] *Jean Christophe*. George Moore was the
English pioneer who first adopted both of these modes of narration and explored the possibilities of each. Under naturalism
and the "experimental novel" we may loosely classify [*A
Modern Lover, A Mummer's Wife, A Drama in Muslin, Vain
Fortunes, Esther Waters,* and "**Mildred Lawson,**" from *Celibates*]. . . . Under "spiritualistic naturalism," or naturalism
of the spirit, we may put [*A Mere Accident, Mike Fletcher,
Evelyn Innes, Sister Teresa,* and *The Lake*]. . . . Books like
[*The Brook Kerith* and *Héloïse and Abélard*] . . . are properly
historical novels, the first with a naturalistic bent, the second
containing many reminders of Huysmans. (p. 61)

A Modern Lover is a story of a young artist, only moderately
talented, who rises to fame and fortune through the influence
of women. Compared with Maupassant's subsequent creation,
Bel-Ami, Moore's lover is rather colorless and passive. Still
he is a naturalistic "central character" rather than a hero and
he possesses a sufficient quantity of nonheroic qualities. He is
an amoral artist who lives only for his art, his emotions, and
his success. Moreover, the chief feminine character is a woman
of quality, who, to the immense surprise of English readers,
tells lies with the greatest ease and facility. Liaisons are quite
discreetly handled, and all that the reader sees are handclasps
and two furtive kisses. Yet the remarkable fact is that as early
as 1883 a liaison does take place in an English novel between
two fairly nice and eminently respectable people, and the participants suffer no harm. As regards narrative techniques, there
are regrettable coincidences in the novel but in the main the
trend of the story is logical and sound. (p. 63)

A Mummer's Wife is an excellent piece of work, of far more
distinction than the dull *Esther Waters* that later caught the
public's attention. (p. 65)

Like Zola, George Moore can give us the atmosphere and
feeling of a human enterprise. The world of traveling entertainers in *A Mummer's Wife* becomes a separate and distinct
world of its own with its own laws and customs. The novel is
the happy result of note-taking, for to prepare himself for writing this book Moore spent several weeks traveling with a group
of actors. The world of artists was well enough handled in *A
Modern Lover,* but it is nowhere comparable to the world of
the Opera-Bouffé company. A certain genius is further shown
in the portrayal of Dick Lennox, director of the company. He
is a dynamic character, virile, devoid of scruples, but humanly
likable. He marries Kate eventually but feels no particular
responsibility for her. George Moore has no especial talent for
creating vital characters. Dick Lennox is, like Mike Fletcher,
one of the exceptions.

A Drama in Muslin is a different kind of writing. Moore was
determined to become popular and to force the circulating libraries to use his books. So he would write something in the
vein of Jane Austen, and he would arrange for serial publication

in a newspaper. The husband-hunt in a Dublin castle atmosphere was the theme he now selected. Documentation would
be a simple matter since, as an Irish landlord and a bachelor,
he had an entree; and his naturalistic interests might be centered
upon the analysis of varied universal types of young womanhood. Moreover, in the structure of the novel which he envisaged there would be opportunity for social criticism directed
against the uncultivated aristocracy; against the effect of the
Catholic religion upon the rich, who accepted it as a form, and
the poor, who groveled under its mysteries; against social displays; and against the ugliness of an ill-planned social order.

Like the novels of Jane Austen, *A Drama in Muslin* is not
altogether a satire. Moore is fairly well pleased with his bevy
of young ladies, and he permits them a considerable amount
of lively, casual chatter as well as some love-making. But . . .
the destiny of each young lady is carefully linked with her
physical equipment. . . . (pp. 67-8)

What may we finally say of *A Drama in Muslin*? On the whole
it is somewhat important. It is probably the first "impersonal"
social study that appeared in English fiction. And all of its
material is native. In this regard it contrasts with *A Modern
Lover* and *A Mummer's Wife,* which, with certain exceptions,
show continental characters in an English setting. But *A Drama
in Muslin* is a native naturalistic study in a lighter mode.

Spring Days and *Vain Fortunes* we may consider as distinctly
minor works. *Spring Days* concerns itself with the loves of the
son and three daughters of a rich distiller. The distiller is much
preoccupied with seeing that the marriages of his children do
not result in draining his private fortune. As Moore describes
his effort, he intended to write "the tale of a city merchant
who is worried about his daughters—a sort of comic King
Lear." He also intended to "recreate Jane Austen's method"
and to write a book suitable for serial publication in *The Evening News.* The novel taxes the reader's credulity and it exposes
Moore's weakness as a writer of love stories. As the story
progresses, attention is centered on a romantic and ineffectual
artist, Frank, who loves one of the distiller's daughters, Maggie. But Frank is a vain creature who poses with pistols and
daggers when Maggie will not have him, and he even attempts
suicide. Later, after the two are engaged, Frank is easily offended, and a sentimental, protective love for a barmaid overpowers him. He is about to get reconciled to the distiller's
daughter when the yearning for the barmaid becomes too strong
to resist.

Spring Days was badly received. A writer for *The Academy*
declared it was the worst novel ever written. (pp. 70-1)

Vain Fortunes is about a struggling dramatist whose adopted
daughter is in love with him. Wedded to his work, he is hardly
conscious of the girl's love, only knowing that she is jealous
of his interest in his work. He inherits a fortune and marries
his housekeeper, who is his critic. The adopted daughter commits suicide.

Here are an inherited fortune and a suicide—not the best material for a naturalistic study. It was a hasty work, written in
the winter of 1890-91 and destined for serial publication in the
Lady's Pictorial. We recognize the Strindberg theme. The novel
is earnest but mild. The significance of the novel is that it
begins a new phase. The evenness of tone and the psychological
preoccupation of *Vain Fortunes* is continued in an intensified
form in "**Mildred Lawson,**" the half-novel which appeared in
Celibates. Moore had now discarded Zola and the more typical
naturalists. In this work he is little concerned with milieu and

determinism; he is bent upon a psychological portrayal of a subclassification of the human species. (p. 71)

"Mildred Lawson" is a careful and expert piece of work. It has the distinctive quality of being well molded. . . .

Esther Waters, the life history of a servant girl, is about as dull and unpleasant a book as was ever written. The fact that Esther has an illegitimate baby and later marries a tuberculous man who runs a "pub" gives little significance to a monotonous life of drudgery. . . .

Esther is a heroine, and, like Tess, a "pure woman." The novel is a story of a struggle against heavy odds. (p. 73)

A Mere Accident, which portrays a religious obsession, was the fourth book George Moore published, coming immediately after *A Mummer's Wife.* It owes something to Huysmans and begins the second phase of Moore's writings. Nevertheless the religious theme which Moore here attempts was dropped with the publication of this book and not resumed for fourteen years. It is true that in *Mike Fletcher* and in *Evelyn Innes* we have much of Huysmans' dislike of humanity and his disgust with vulgarity. But religious preoccupation as a central theme was abandoned for fourteen years.

That George Moore abandoned the theme is not surprising. Perhaps more surprising is the fact that he ever attempted it, and that he attempted it for a second time after the lapse of fourteen years.

Matters of literary influence often surprise the scholar. Knowing Moore's propensity to assimilate, one would carelessly assume that Maupassant's *Bel-Ami* provided inspiration for *A Modern Lover.* But Moore's work preceded that of Maupassant by two years, and we must assume that Maupassant was the borrower. In *A Mere Accident* one notices that Moore gives us lyrical and despairing passages on human grossnesses and a search for spiritual tranquillity in following the observances of the Catholic Church. But though the lyrical and despairing passages may well be reflections of Huysmans—and George Moore all but tells us this in the *Confessions*—Huysmans' *En route* was published nine years after *A Mere Accident*! (pp. 74-5)

John Norton, the young squire in [*A Mere Accident*], has a temperamental aversion to life which came from neither satiety nor any physical weakness. (p. 75)

John Norton's revulsion and his sickness of soul is not alone responsible for his determination to separate himself from the world and lead an ascetic life. He has a tangible fear of the fires of Hell. But no separation from life is possible in the country home of his mother, with whom he lives. So he betakes himself to a university and arranges his room like that of a monastery. He makes friends with Jesuits, comes more and more under their influence, and begins plans for converting the country home into a monastery. While carrying out these plans he falls under the influence of a young girl. His interest in her destroys his ascetic leanings.

The story so far might well fit into what Huysmans called "spiritualistic naturalism," but Moore introduces a complication. Returning home one day, the young girl is attacked by a tramp, who rapes her. Hating the sight of men, she goes to her room and refuses to leave it. When Norton, much agitated, calls to inquire about her, she sends word that she is willing to see him. On his appearance, however, she jumps out of a window and is killed. John Norton decides to give up his former

plans. He goes into the world of men, resolving to make the world his monastery, whatever that may mean.

A Mere Accident was soundly panned by the critics, and justly. Moore himself soon lost confidence in the novel. It is connected neither with social interpretation nor with a true "soul crisis." The story is here mentioned in some detail in order to emphasize the difference between naturalism and the dramatic portrayal of soul-sickness, which is the main concern in the books of Moore's second period.

Is a "sprirualistic naturalist" a naturalist? He is probably not, yet he has strong naturalistic propensities. (pp. 76-7)

[Though *Mike Fletcher*] is "spiritual naturalism," the religious preoccupation is not present. Instead the author allows himself a liberty of expression second only to the *Confessions* in describing Mike Fletcher's states of soul—feelings of love and yearning and satiety and despair. And, in his best mode, he employs a poetic prose of color and variety. Furthermore, Mike is a character whom George Moore likes. He is virile and lovable; he is hearty and without any particular moral sense; he is sensual and possessed of delicate sensibilities. (p. 79)

We like in *Mike Fletcher* the monologues which continue from page to page, the echoes of Schopenhauer, and the grave and sombre tonal quality of the last quarter of the book. But externals are treated casually. Mike's satiety might have been more convincing if his search for sensations had been revealed more openly.

A novel of this type properly concerns itself very little with milieu; nevertheless George Moore gives us a good picture of the turbulent nineties. . . . (pp. 80-1)

We constantly regret the restraints under which Geroge Moore wrote. *Mike Fletcher* might have been a great novel. But the sensualities of the sensual Mike are virtually omitted and a character which Moore created with fervor does not live his full life on Moore's pages. (p. 81)

[The] continuity between *Mike Fletcher* and the *Evelyn Innes—Sister Teresa* story is not broken. Both are spiritual biographies and both are discreet handlings of unconventional relationships. Perhaps Moore felt that he had gone far enough in making Evelyn the mistress of the man who developed her into a great singer, and that he need not go into detail about the love situation. What makes it worse is that George Moore in the preface calls his book a love story, "the only prose love story in the English language." He explains that a love story is one in which love is the only theme. As for love, we do not see that Evelyn or any other woman would have been spontaneously attracted to the austere and philosophic Sir Owen. Neither the author nor Sir Owen nor Evelyn ever unbends.

Evelyn Innes and *Sister Teresa* are, as Moore explains, really the halves of a single volume. Evelyn has the background, intelligence, looks, and talent to make her a great singer. Sir Owen sees this; sees also that she has every quality for a highly civilized mistress. We appreciate the highly civilized nature of Sir Owen. We appreciate his highly civilized intent to develop every quality of Evelyn and to develop not merely the voice but the woman. We are convinced of the successive stages by which Evelyn rose to fame. But as to the love affair, we are merely willing to admit that it is the most highly civilized one in the English language and let it go at that. *Sister Teresa* also fails us somewhat. It is not that the atmosphere of the nunnery lacks anything. It is not that Evelyn lacks devotion. It is merely that successful opera singers in England do not enter convents.

Altogether the religious phase of Evelyn's life is more convincing than her love affair. George Moore can make us feel a convent atmosphere—perhaps because the windows of his study overlooked the cloisters of a nunnery. He can make us feel devotion. And he gives up some sense of the cold wind that blows between the worlds. Evelyn feels its permeating influence. . . . (p. 82)

There are various endings to the different editions. In perhaps the best one, Evelyn is only moderately successful in her attempts at expiation. The consolations of religious contemplation are perhaps not as great as those of human service. So she departs.

The historical novels, *The Brook Kerith* and *Héloïse and Abélard,* are properly outside the limits of this study of transitional influences. And yet I cannot forbear mentioning that Moore the Naturalist is everywhere present in *The Brook Kerith.* Jesus, a former carpenter, joins the monastic order of Essenes and absorbs their teachings. He hates insincerity and hypocrisy sufficiently to stage a revolt against the Pharisees. Lifted up in pride he feels himself the Son of God. He is saved from death by an admirer, the rich Joseph of Arimathea, who procures the yet-living Jesus from a corruptible Centurian and has him nursed back to health. Afterwards Jesus becomes a shepherd again, humbly regretful of the pride which had lifted him to claim kinship with God. And yet Moore credits Jesus with his miracles.

As to *The Lake,* it is the "spiritualistic naturalism" of a post-Huysmans George Moore. We recall that the *Confessions* were very strongly pagan. (p. 83)

The Lake is pure pantheism. Father Gogarty virtually drives from the village an unmarried expectant mother. Later she writes to him and brings him a vision of far places and the joys of human life. He rediscovers nature and the influence of trees and flowers and forest. He finds that "he and the trees were one, for there is but one life, one mother, one elemental substance out of which all has come." Life, he decides, "is oriented like a temple, there are in every existence days when life streams down the nave, striking the forehead of God." Chastity is an evil because "woman is life." Father Gogarty leaves the church and George Moore, having finally expressed a vision which we may really call his own, retired to the realms of literary criticism and historical romance.

As we have seen, George Moore reflected his generous enthusiasms by imitating widely, but his place in English literary history is that of an innovator. His early naturalistic novels were read with mild interest even before the controversy over naturalism was well under way. By the time that naturalism was winning wide popular acceptance in England George Moore had become disgusted with it. His spiritual biographies—*A Mere Accident, Confessions of a Young Man, Mike Fletcher, Evelyn Innes, Sister Teresa,* and *The Lake*—were influential in shifting English interest from social to personal problems. They helped bring about the vogue of the life-novel in the years 1910-17. The paganism of the *Confessions* gave him prophetic standing in the war-conscious years of the twenties. And if, as H. G. Wells forsees, the novel is to give place to biography and autobiography, George Moore will be abreast of the new tendencies with his trilogy, *Hail and Farewell,* which includes [*Ave, Salve,* and *Vale*]. . . . (p. 84)

William C. Frierson, "George Moore: Naturalist," in his *The English Novel in Transition, 1885-1940* (copyright 1942 by The University of Oklahoma Press; copyright reassigned 1965 to Mrs. William C. Frierson), University of Oklahoma Press, 1942 (and reprinted by Cooper Square Publishers, Inc., 1965), pp. 60-84.

SONJA NEJDEFORS-FRISK   (essay date 1952)

[In] *A Modern Lover, A Mummer's Wife, A Drama in Muslin, Esther Waters,* Moore followed Zola more or less closely. It is true that only *A Mummer's Wife* can be described as purely naturalistic, but the other three abound in naturalistic ideas. The milieus described, of the fashionable artistic world, of the Irish upper classes, of a theatrical company, of race-courses, were not new to Moore. He had seen them with his own eyes, and studied life there with the intention of writing about it. The particulars seem to be authentic and they are never so numerous as to tire the reader. Moore includes merely those necessary to make us understand the development of character.

The principal ideas of the naturalistic school are thus all to be found in these particular novels of Moore's output. He began, a little hesitatingly, in *A Modern Lover,* to show where the influence of milieu could bring a weak character. This identical idea is stressed more strongly in *A Mummer's Wife,* where all the stages from a normal being to a helpless decadent creature are analysed. The degrading influence of race-courses on weak characters is the theme of *Esther Waters,* though the persons involved in the catastrophe are the secondary characters of the novel. The importance of hereditary qualities appears very clearly in all these works, but not quite to such an extent as in *A Drama in Muslin.* In all these novels but the last one, the instinctive life of man is dwelt upon, and taken together they exhibit quite a large collection of persons of weak character. Examples of animal behaviour are most numerous in *A Mummer's Wife,* but they are also to be found in the other novels. Nauseous scenes for which the naturalistic school was taken to task so severely, are only to be found in *A Mummer's Wife.* (p. 130)

Naturalistic tendencies are incidentally obvious in Moore's other works, but they must be regarded as reminiscences only of the period treated.

George Moore had no followers in England. *A Mummer's Wife* is the only English novel that can be called purely naturalistic. But the example he had set, meant a great deal to English fiction. He directed attention to many new subjects, and various social problems could now be discussed more freely. He opened people's eyes to the fact that much of value could be found in contemporary fiction outside England. He fought for literary tolerance, and, as is shown by the later development of English fiction, he had not done so in vain. (p. 131)

Sonya Nejdefors-Frisk, in her *George Moore's Naturalistic Prose* (excerpted by permission), Cambridge, Mass.: Harvard University Press, 1952, 135 p.

MALCOLM BROWN   (essay date 1955)

The preface to *Martin Luther* relates that Moore met Bernard Lopez in December, 1875, at about the time he made up his mind to abandon painting. He confessed to Lopez that his thoughts were turning to poetry, and he asked that incredibly experienced man of letters to explain how one proceeded in that direction. Lopez replied:

. . . choose subjects that would astonish the British public by their originality—for instance, if instead of inditing a sonnet to my mistress's eyebrows I were to tell the passion of a toad for a rose. Not that, of course not that, but poems on violent subjects. "A young man's love for a beautiful corpse," I interjected.

In keeping with his lifelong habit of precipitate action, Moore apparently resolved instantly to make thought and action one, for upon opening *Flowers of Passion,* his first surviving work, one finds on the very first page the title, **"Ode to a Dead Body."** . . . The corpse appears and reappears through the volume, and, while composing a later sonnet on the subject, the neophyte poet had kept his copy of *Les Fleurs du Mal* open on his writing desk. . . . [Most] of the verse is English in derivation, consisting in a close imitation of all the decadent hints Moore could discover in nineteenth-century English poetry. His long dramatic poem **"Annie"** is an imitation of Tennyson's "Maud." A dramatic monologue **"Bernice"** seems to have borrowed its title from Poe's story, "Berenice," and its manner from Browning's "Porphyria's Lover," which it parodies with delicate malice just sufficient for the destruction of his model. (pp. 66-7)

Flowers of Passion contains clear echoes of Rossetti, especially in two sonnets, **"Summer"** and **"Summer on the Coast of Normandy,"** in which the poet lolls in the meadow where "the tedded grass breathed fragrance of crushed thyme" and the "linnets from the flowerful closes gave / Forth sweetly songs in sad uncadenced rhyme," giving way to sensations that achieved, in the last line, a Rossetti-like trance "hushing the pain of every memory." Anticipating Oscar Wilde, the volume includes two poems exploiting the epicene, **"Hendecasyllables"** and **"A Sapphic Dream."** *Mademoiselle de Maupin* had authorized this subject, and Moore continued to play with it, though apparently merely out of a sense of duty to art. . . . Finally, the volume contains a sonnet on Moore's abandonment of painting, a prosy exercise but interesting for stating doubt that he could write better than he could paint. . . . (p. 68).

[*Martin Luther*] was published with a long preface consisting of eighteen letters exchanged between the two collaborators [Moore and Lopez] on the subjects of censorship, literature, painting, play construction, art history, religious history, and the connections between religion and art. (p. 69)

The letters exhibit a pattern of critical discourse which Moore's later essays on literature and painting adopted as their permanent form. The sweeping denunciation, the savage exposure of artistic cant, the unbounded range of reference, the freshly perceived detail, and the vertiginous transition—all appear first in the letters of Lopez but are quickly taken over by the pupil, who had chosen for the first victim of the method the English drama. He was eventually to proceed through all the genres of English and other literatures in the same manner. . . . (pp. 70-1)

Pagan Poems is the longest and most interesting work in Moore's opening literary phase. It echoes the themes of the earlier published volumes and repeats some of the poems that had appeared in the first collection of verse. But in its general scope it moves slightly ahead, enlivened mildly by the appearance of new ideas. Meanwhile it carries the old commitments to their ultimate statement, closing with an impasse Moore's first efforts to master the literary art.

The new poetic imitations, though seemingly solemn in intent, continue suspiciously to skirt the comic. A longer poem, called **"The Temptation,"** plagiarizes Poe and shows Moore in the act of going overboard for a new idea, Baudelaire's ambivalence. It achieves one of the more remarkable statements in literature of the ancient theme of *la femme fatale.* . . . (p. 75)

A three-hundred-line poem, **"Ode to a Beggar Girl,"** marks the acquisition of another new idea. In the opening lines Moore sees a beggar girl wandering through the streets of Paris. . . . At first he sees her sorrow as romantically charming, but on further thought the "dreams of fancy" give way to cold reality. . . . (p. 76)

[Moore] held a lifelong opinion that English novelists were constitutionally unable to conclude their tales; his own solution for the problem of ending a novel was to bring it back, according to the principle of eternal recurrence, to the point from which it had started, a solution he was to employ with perfect tact, fifteen years after the **"Ode to a Beggar Girl,"** in the much imitated closing chapters of *Esther Waters.*

Pagan Poems occasionally shows Moore beginning to ponder themes which could not be contained in the borrowed vessels of Swinburne and Poe and which would shortly rescue him from the mistakes of his false start. One long poem, **"La Maîtresse Maternelle,"** despite lines like *"Et dans une douce indolence / La lune dort comme une fleur,"* still manages to state without utter nonsense the germ of his first realistic novel, *A Modern Lover.* Another, **"A Modern Poem,"** deals with the theme of the decay of the "big house" and the attendant marriage-mart haggling, the subject of his third novel, *A Drama in Muslin.* Another, **"A Parisian Idyll,"** was rewritten a generation later to make his famous scandalous short story, **"The Lovers of Orelay."**

Sometimes the volume experimented with "shameless" confessions in anticipation of *Confessions of a Young Man* and *Hail and Farewell.* One sonnet, for example, asserted that notoriety was worthwhile in a world where other values had disappeared. . . . (pp. 78-9)

Occasionally there appears in the volume, as there always would in even his most perverse work, a trace of genuine individuality and freshness of outlook. (p. 79)

Still, *Pagan Poems* mainly reveals a poverty of poetic talent. The volume was clearly the work of a writer virtually deaf to poetic rhythms; and Moore's later gift for weaving mellifluously cadenced prose demonstrates, like the combination of poetic genius with musical obtuseness in Yeats, that these special talents are not interchangeable among the genres and the related arts. The volume also showed Moore still seriously troubled with the lack of an assured direction. The theories of Théophile Gautier had not transposed well into art, and Moore's first work shows an alternation of overanxious and half-hearted allegiance. The poems frequently suggest Moorisms; in several, the self-mocking note cannot be missed. The poem **"Sappho,"** for example, in describing the epicene setting and the "essences, pomatums, pins, and depilatories" appropriate to Lesbos, places in their midst a marble cupid "blowing from his nostrils two jets of water, one hot, the other cold." And yet Moore's "sincerity" in holding Gautier's views cannot be denied. The intermingling of pious acceptance and uncontrollable mockery of the same object, while it did not make poetry, did produce an interesting mishmash. Moore's contemporaries, however, were not interested. London took note of

Pagan Poems only to invent a new name for the author, "Pagan" Moore. . . . (p. 80)

Moore's criticism showed a marked bias toward formalism, a tribute to his masters, Gautier, Flaubert, and Whistler. (p. 204)

[Formalism] came naturally to Moore because of his role in the history of the English novel. As a rebel against the middle-class myth which formed the substance of the Victorian novel, he was necessarily driven to abandon its form as well. The teleological cosmology and the teleological plot machinery of his predecessors were inseverable. He could hardly use the forms that George Eliot had developed for her parables illustrating the moral balance of the universe to project a view of the human predicament such as he had stated in *A Mummer's Wife:* "Our lives run in grooves; we get into one and we follow it out to the end." Working without the security of an established English tradition, he was forced to devise his own form out of recollections of the French novelists and the fruits of his own painful experiments, piecing them together as best he could as he went along. It was not possible for him to avoid an absorbing concern with the technical problems of narrative form.

The critical principles that arose out of this special interest were the common dogmas identified with *l'art pour l'art.* He defined the novel as "a rhythmical sequence of events described with rhythmical sequence of phrase," an epigram that might sound flippant if one did not remember how many years of travail lay behind the simple little phrase, "a rhythmical sequence of events," and what an absolute break from the Dickens-Thackeray tradition it marked. (pp. 205-06)

Similarly, the ideal of artistic "purity" absorbed Moore throughout his life. As early as *Confessions of a Young Man* he had become infatuated with a curious distinction between "ideas" and "things" and had concluded that literature would be pure if it could avoid ideas and deal only in things. If only Shakespeare "could be freed from his ideas," he said, "what a poet we should have." . . . In 1924 he published a little collection of verse called *An Anthology of Pure Poetry,* introduced by an essay composed in the melodic line, an extended Moorism consisting of an inimitably personal argument on behalf of impersonal art.

The overt purpose of *An Anthology of Pure Poetry* was to exalt the "pure" poem—for example, Gautier's "La Tulipe"—over an "impure" poem like Shelley's "Hellas," which had fed on "duty, liberty and fraternity," ideas that no longer interest mankind after the age of thirty. All this is of course trivial as theory, merely Gautier's witty "the visible world is visible" made turgid. His insight did have a certain significance, however. The verses in his anthology consist mostly of isolated transfiguring images—flashes, bells, bleats, blowing horns, and the like—separated from any context that might indicate what sort of transfiguration the poet had been minded of, a distillation of the "pure," neat spirits of poetry. His fixation on these images shows him to have been groping, like many of his more philosophically gifted contemporaries, toward the distinction between "existence" and "essence," or between "presentational" and "discursive" statement, to use the vocabulary that became popular some time after his death. Unknowingly Moore was marching *dans le mouvement.* His anthology is a fitting exhibit of the age that produced the more precisely verbalized theories of the imagists and that led in the era of the cold war to the revival of Hopkins and Emily Dickinson as the ultimate poets of "thisness."

Moore's theories of "pure" narrative were similar, though somewhat less muddied. Pure narration did nothing but narrate, and required the unbroken thread, the suspended cadence, the incessant transition that had been brought to perfection in his old age in the melodic line of the last novels. (pp. 206-07)

His critical sensitivity was sharpest in observing the consecutiveness and development of a narrative, in watching "the music of sequence," moving rhythmically toward some destination. He found it in its "purest" form in *Oedipus Rex* and occasionally even in English novels, in *The Mill on the Floss,* for example, which he understood to possess "rhythm and inevitability, two words for the same thing." But failures were far more common than successes in his opinion, and his critical writing is filled with castigations of novels which either petered out in an aimless and fatuous ending, in the manner of *Robinson Crusoe,* or else were caught in the monotonous turning of the wheel and repeated themes over and over again without progression. (pp. 207-08)

The nihilism implicit in these ferocious standards is clear. It should be said of Moore, however, that he applied the rules to himself as mercilessly as to any other writer. The harshness of his own self-discipline is now legendary. (p. 211)

[In the end, Moore's] soul remained divided against itself, committed to incompatibles. Yet he was fundamentally an honest man, infinitely less limited than he might have been; and he sensed, even if he could never bring himself to say so directly, that his aesthetic masters, despite their command of paradox, had missed the most important paradox of all their experience: that too much sensitivity, as well as too little, may anaesthetize; that in the name of art one may either exalt or destroy art; that hatred of philistinism may transform a writer into a perfect likeness of the philistine, moving through the cultural heritage like a hooligan, like the philistine himself, finding the literary tradition only so much tiresome absurdity, seemingly demolishing it all, though not really—for only a very suggestive reader would throw his *Tess of the D'Urbervilles* or his *Vanity Fair* into the trash basket merely on George Moore's advice. One need not condescend: for its purpose, Moore's critical manner could hardly be improved upon. It is owing to George Moore as much as to any artist of his time that the formlessness, the sentimentality, the tendentiousness, the evangelical piety, the compulsive dishonesty that were once all but universal in English fiction have today disappeared from the serious novels written in our language. (p. 216)

Malcolm Brown, in his George Moore: A Reconsideration *(© 1955 by the University of Washington Press), University of Washington Press, 1955, 235 p.*

ROBERT GRAVES   (essay date 1956)

It is in wartime that books about Jesus have most appeal, and *The Brook Kerith* first appeared forty years ago during the Battle of the Somme, when Christ was being invoked alike by the Germans and the Allies for victory in a new sort of total war. This paradox made most of us English soldiers serving in the purgatorial trenches lose all respect for organized Pauline religion, though still feeling a sympathetic reverence for Jesus as our fellow-sufferer. . . . Moore's story—at the end of which Paul dramatically disowns the real Jesus (who has escaped alive from the Cross) and goes off to preach the transcendent Jesus Christ of his own epileptic imagining among the Italians and Spaniards—made good cynical sense to us.

Moore regarded Jesus as a superman, an ex-shepherd of immense compassion, untrammelled by dogma or prejudice, and with miraculous curative powers, whom the wicked Pharisees persuaded the Romans to crucify, but whom a rich young Jew, Joseph of Arimathea, a protégé of Pilate's, rescued and took to a place of safety. This Jesus, who afterwards confessed to presumption in having made Messianic claims, was cast in a sympathetic mould; but, personally, I could not like the book. Moore had cultivated a brilliant prose style, based on French models, and seemed more interested in the irrelevant ambition of writing a literary masterpiece than in getting at the factual truth about the Gospel story, which to me mattered enormously at that time; and still does.

His thesis, that Jesus survived the Cross, was not new—I had seen it much more plausibly argued in Samuel Butler's *Fair Haven.* . . . So the novelty of *The Brook Kerith* did not impress me, and I found it difficult to read; because he had omitted all quotation marks, and made every paragraph immensely long. (pp. 123-24)

Moore shows no understanding whatsoever of the Pharisees, Sadducees, Essenes and Herodians, and there is a familiar smoky atmosphere warming the book, parts of which read like a fine, gentle old tale of saints, Fenian heroes, and *piasts*, told by some travelling *sgéalai* over a peat fire in County Antrim. . . . (p. 126)

I wish I were less afflicted by my critical conscience, and could enjoy the colourful scenes he depicts: such as the cockfight at Tiberias, organized by Herod Antipas, in which Joseph of Arimathea gets mixed up. They still say in Ireland: 'That bangs Banagher, and Banagher bangs cockfighting, and cockfighting bangs the devil!' But Moore had been too busy polishing his style to take time off for cockfighting or historical research, so that he fell down on the technical details of this bloody and (to me) tedious sport, and could not even get the breeds right. If Herod Antipas, a very rich man, sent his servants out for the best cocks in the Eastern Mediterranean, they must have brought him Delian, Tanagran, or Alexandrian birds, not the breeds invented by Moore: Cappadocian and Bithynian.

I wish I were even detached enough to laugh at his utter nonsense, such as Jesus's pet lamb, christened 'Caesar', which he reared with a feeding-bottle—by the way, I once knew a little boy living in New Hope, Pennsylvania, who called his tame snapping-turtle 'Fluff'. Or at the sentence: 'Many [followers of Jesus], afraid lest the agents of the Pharisees should discover them, left Jerusalem for Galilee on the Friday evening'—study it carefully, Sunday School children, and see how many factual errors you can detect!

No, it's no good. Forty years have passed, and I still fidget in Moore's company. Nevertheless, and notwithstanding, how can I fail to give the ignorant old rascal credit for the three bold and accurate guesses on which he based the book? That Paul wilfully misrepresented Jesus; that Jesus survived the Cross; and that he then considered himself to have offended God by 'forcing the hour'—these seem to me logically inescapable conclusions. (pp. 127-28)

> *Robert Graves, " 'Don't Fidget, Young Man!' " (reprinted by permission of Robert Graves) in* The New Republic, *Vol. 135, No. 16, October 15, 1956 (and reprinted in his* 5 Pens in Hand, *Doubleday & Company, Inc., 1958, pp. 123-28).*

HELMUT E. GERBER   (essay date 1967)

George Moore at one time or another thought of himself as an Irishman, a Frenchman, and an Englishman, but he was not and could not be any of these in any binding way. At one time or another, he claimed Gautier, Pater, Shelley, Zola, Baudelaire, Balzac, Turgenev, Flaubert, and many other artists, as his masters, and, yet, none of these was or could be his master unconditionally. Although Balzac might seem to be the one exception, it is not one Balzac to whom Moore paid homage throughout his career; rather, it is many Balzacs, each in his turn, to whom he bowed. Moore was briefly a practicing painter, briefly a poet, a music critic, an art critic, a playwright, a short story writer, a novelist, a polemicist, and a memoirist. In one sense, however, he was not, with a specialist's devotion, any of these. Moore was an artist. As an artist whose sole enduring obsession was with a concept of art that allowed no other allegiances, he could not enter into any demanding contract with any nation, religion, class, or person. He took what he needed from any nation that in some way could serve his artistic purposes, as he took such materials as would serve his own art at the moment from his various masters, from Catholicism and Protestantism, from the various arts with which he flirted at one time or another, from the various genres of each art, and from the people he came to know.

None of Moore's temporary allegiances and none of his many artistic activities were wasted; all contributed to a constantly evolving, often self-contradictory, complex, never systematized philosophy of art. Perhaps it was finally no philosophy at all but rather a bag of impressions and opinions or a series of avowals. All through his work, however, one clear motif is sounded again and again: that art is autonomous and that the perfection of form is virtue. While such a summary statement has a simple and familiar ring to it, Moore's way of discovering and rediscovering and his way of stating this motif are far from simple and not at all so familiar as it may seem. (p. 281)

In Moore's work the central credo of his entire artistic career is first crudely announced in [*Flowers of Passion* and *Pagan Poems*]. . . . Except in a few modern instances, these two collections have been consistently maligned; their purpose, their place in Moore's career, and their various indebtednesses have been misrepresented by over-simplification or by taking at face value Moore's own comments on them, chiefly in *Confessions of a Young Man.* . . . Mostly they have been ignored. . . . As his poetry was early and more conclusively written off as the product of Baudelaire's litter, so many of his early novels were dismissed as the product of one wallowing in Zola's sty. For the first ten to fifteen years of his writing career, Moore did little to discourage this kind of notoriety. He was intent on being noticed, on gaining a reputation for himself at very nearly any price, and, more important perhaps, he was intent on freeing the artist of pressures and requirements he considered peripheral to the artist's primary concern. For both purposes allusions to French writers of the time were particularly serviceable. Thus, until the publication of *Esther Waters* . . . , Moore liberally sprinkled favorable references to French writers throughout most of his non-fiction and, in his own imaginative writings at least, allowed the public and the critics to think that he was mainly a follower of the French schools of Baudelaire, Gautier, and Zola in poetry, in aesthetics, and in prose fiction.

The title of his first book of poems obviously demands that the reader associate it with Baudelaire's *Fleurs du mal*. Similarly, his early novels [*A Modern Lovers, A Mummer's Wife, A Drama in Muslin, A Mere Accident, Spring Days*, and *Mike*

Fletcher], . . . many with the designation "A Realistic Novel," were intended to call up the names of Zola, the Goncourts, Huysmans or Flaubert. And much of what Moore had to say, perhaps more the way he chose to say it, in *Confessions of a Young Man* . . . was understood by many critics and by much of the English public to be mimicking what they thought the French writers were saying. On Moore's part, the choice of subjects in his poems and novels, the frank and detailed depiction of certain scenes, and the rather flamboyant language of *Confessions of a Young Man* were part of a calculated strategy of *épater le bourgeois*. . . . (pp. 281-82)

His early critics and, with few exceptions even critics since then, have not read Moore very attentively. At least, they seem to have remembered only every other phrase—the noisy ones—culled from *Confessions*. . . . The critics and the reading public fixed upon the vivid image of Amico Moorini, the flamboyant polemicist, the amoralist, if not immoralist, the sensualist; and they have ignored George Moore, the austere, fanatically dedicated, and often painfully self-critical artist. For this distorted or at least partial view of himself as artist and critic he was as much as responsible as his readers.

Most of his writing from the early poems to *Esther Waters* is admittedly ambiguous and illustrates a division of purpose, or, if not a division of purpose, then at least two mutually exclusive purposes: to get attention and to insist on the autonomy, the integrity, of art. To get attention, he used his art impurely, and to insist on the autonomy, the purity, of art, he also used his art impurely. The first two volumes of poems and the first half-dozen novels are both an attempt to illustrate pure art in practice and to write manifestoes in defense of the purity of art. The poems and the early novels are in a sense negative moralities. They exist not solely as things in themselves but also for the purpose of making a point. To make his campaign on behalf of the integrity of art and the freedom of the artist the more effective, he chose French masters and French models partly because of genuine admiration but also because they could best serve him as proven and as the most potent weapons. He could just as well have chosen other masters and other models. He did not need Baudelaire to write the poetry he wrote, as, I believe, he did not need Zola or the Goncourts to write the novels he wrote. In fact, in *Confessions,* in some of his prefaces, in reviews, and in many articles, he provides ample evidence that there were other masters and other models, that in fact there was an English tradition for much of what he was espousing. Again, Moore's early critics chose to emphasize the evidence for his Frenchness and to overlook that for his Englishness.

In *Confessions of a Young Man* Moore introduces his description of *Flowers of Passion,* which he calls "Roses of Midnight," in this passage, with references not to French poets but to Poe, Swinburne, and Rossetti. . . . Moore's roses were not so much borrowed directly from Baudelaire as they were from the French poet once removed through Swinburne. (pp. 282-83)

While Moore's tendency during the first fifteen years of his writing career to trumpet forth outrageous overstatements and to insist rather noisily on his Francophilism jars with his espousal of a non-polemical art, the reader must recognize that much of this sound and fury is on the surface. Beneath the often too gaudy surface and in conjunction with the offending French "masters," there are quieter tones and less controversial "masters" which modify the whole work and give increasing evidence of an individual and independent voice. Gau-

tier has his counterpart in Pater, Baudelaire has his in Swinburne and Rossetti; others have their counterparts in Shelley and Keats, even in Tennyson; and Zola, Huysmans, and Flaubert are modified by Samuel Richardson, whose *Clarissa* Moore much admired, and Dickens, toward whose work Moore was capable of showing considerable respect. (p. 285)

As Moore's double voice, the voice of the polemicist and self-advertiser and the voice of the artist, is evident in his early poems, so it is evident also in the early novels. This may be illustrated briefly by the fact that in *A Mere Accident* Moore intrudes the rape scene with an eye to the shock effect it will have, but in his revision of the novel as "**John Norton**" in *Celibates* the scene is implied and followed by three chapters which give the psychological effect on Kitty of the attack. In the revised version Moore is interested in his character, in his art, not in spanking the critics and the public. Even in *A Mummer's Wife,* which he tried to make as much a Zolaesque sensation as possible, Moore has created scenes and portrayed subtleties of character in Kate Ede and Dick Lenox which have little to do with an assault on the lending libraries or the morality of the villa. Later still, in writing the stories of *The Untilled Field* . . . , Moore set out, as on many earlier occasions, in his polemical vein to teach the Irish about literature and the repressive influence of Catholicism. The stories were to serve as a textbook for use in Gaelic schools. Prior to the publication of the volume, his letters are riddled with references to "excessive Catholicism" and to the didactic intentions of the volume. As he wrote and revised, however, the stories absorbed Moore as stories, the priests were, as he said in one of his letters, humanized. The stories that appeared in Unwin's first English edition were clearly more the work of the artist than the polemicist.

What is most important in Moore's work between 1878 and about 1894 is not the somewhat pungent and often inartistic surface, nor the gallery of specific masters he puffs rather loudly, but the aesthetic position toward which he was urging English poets and prose writers and for the acceptance of which he in large measure helped to prepare the way. Whether as polemicist or as practitioner, Moore played a significant role in preparing the way for T. S. Eliot, John Crowe Ransom, and, in general, the position that has become associated with the label *New Criticism*. The poems of *Flowers of Passion* and *Pagan Poems* were Moore's earliest expression of an aesthetic he was to restate many times in many different ways throughout his career. His 1885 attack on the lending libraries, *Literature at Nurse, or Circulating Morals,* although specifically concerned with the moral stranglehold of the circulating libraries on the novel, is another early expression of one aspect of Moore's aesthetic. His literary essays in *Impressions and Opinions* . . . and his art criticism in *Modern Painting* . . . ; his artistic practice in parts of such novels as *A Modern Lover, A Drama in Muslin, A Mummer's Wife,* and even *Esther Waters;* and the reminiscences in such books as *Confessions of a Young Man,* are volleys fired in the battle for artistic freedom, for pure poetry and pure criticism in the broadest sense. Somewhat ironically, it was not until he wrote his preface to and directed the compilation of *Pure Poetry: An Anthology* . . . , after much of the propagandizing had disappeared from his own fiction, after he had, in effect, said "the public and the critics be damned," after, in fact, the battle had virtually been won, that Moore was ready to employ the word *thesis* rather than *confession, impression, opinion,* or *avowal.* Yet, although Moore had been saying much the same thing for some forty-five years, this little anthology has had more serious attention from professional critics and aestheticians than a great deal of the more important, the more original, and the better work that preceded it. The Preface to *Pure Poetry* should be read with the background of forty-five years of persistent crying-up of the same ideas in mind. In *Pure Poetry* Moore was at least able to segregate his statement of a thesis and its illustration by selecting poems of other poets as evidence. (p. 286)

[Moore] cast the Preface to *Pure Poetry* into the form of a dialogue between himself, John Freeman, and Walter de la Mare. Allowing himself the luxury of talk in such company, Moore slipped into his characteristic tendency to overstate a position or to undermine the seriousness of his intention with seeming casualness of manner. . . . (p. 287)

From *Flowers of Passion* to *Pure Poetry* may seem a devious road, but it is a road carefully marked by a sequence of related milestones: *Flowers of Passion, Pagan Poems, Literature at Nurse, Confessions of a Young Man, Impressions and Opinions, Modern Painting, Evelyn Innes, Sister Teresa, Avowals, Pure Poetry*. The course so traveled links Pater, Gautier, Baudelaire, Coleridge, Shelley, Swinburne, and many other writers with post-1920 practices in poetry and with modern criticism. (pp. 289-90)

> Helmut E. Gerber, "George Moore: From Pure Poetry to Pure Criticism," in The Journal of Aesthetics and Art Criticism (copyright © 1967 by The American Society for Aesthetics), Vol. XXV, No. 3, Spring, 1967, pp. 281-91.

BRENDAN KENNELLY (essay date 1968)

In his introduction to *Celibate Lives,* George Moore has an imaginary conversation in which, with a characteristically light touch, he reveals something of his attitude to the short story. When his imaginary protagonist asks Moore if he is for or against adventures, he replies that he does not deal in adventures "but in soul cries". Here, Moore gets to the very core of what has preoccupied Irish short story writers ever since his time—the problem of man's loneliness. . . . It is not unfair to say that George Moore gave Irish short story writers that theme of human loneliness which has so fascinated their imagination. It is in every story of *Dubliners,* and that remarkable collection ends with a lyrical affirmation of the fact that man is essentially alone. . . . Frank O'Connor, Seán O'Faoláin, Liam O'Flaherty, Mary Lavin, and Benedict Kiely continually and skilfully explore the dark pit of loneliness. The same preoccupation is evident in the work of more recent writers such as Edna O'Brien, James Plunkett, and John McGahern. . . . [It] was Moore who first pointed out to modern Irish writers and the fact that the best short stories consist of brief but profound and luminous insights into the lives of those who haunt the fringes of society, drab figures who live anonymously and suffer quietly. (pp. 144-45)

Celibate Lives would have been more accurately entitled *Lonely Lives* because in this collection of stories one is struck not so much by the celibacy of any of the characters, but by the loneliness that is their typical condition. The five stories in the volume have for titles the proper names of the main characters concerned, and Moore subjects each of these people to a penetrating and sustained scrutiny. The opening story, **"Wilfrid Holmes"**, concerns a typically casual outcast, the "fool" of the Holmes family, the one who refuses to work, and therefore mars the respectability which his relatives esteem so much. Wilfrid is a childlike figure who, in his timid and harmless

way, plays at being scholar, musician, composer, and journalist, living all the time on a small allowance from his aunt. The crisis in his life comes when the allowance fails to arrive, and he experiences that moment of bitter self-awareness, of implacable self confrontation, which so many of Joyce's characters also experience in *Dubliners*. Wilfrid sees himself for the outcast he is. He understands that he cannot understand, and that he cannot be understood. (pp. 145-46)

In both Moore and Joyce, one of the chief effects of a fully realised loneliness is the brutal moment of self-knowledge that is merciless and complete. Though Moore's story ends on a comparatively happy note, we have seen Wilfrid Holmes stripped bare as a tree in winter down to his essential timidity and mediocrity a black sheep without talent or resource, a devoted nonentity, a pariah committed to a life of quiet absurdity. (p. 146)

An important aspect of Moore's genius is that he continually sees loneliness as an integral part of ordinary life. (p. 147)

All the main characters in *Celibate Lives* opt out of the bustle of daily life in one way or another, and Moore, in a subtle but adamant way, repeats that sexual inadequacy is one of the truest sources of loneliness. Moore makes this point, not in an overt or brutal manner as certain modern novelists do, but through gradual implication, thereby creating a profound and far-reaching sense of the human complexity of the problem. In the final story, **"Sarah Gwynn"**, we meet a young woman who retires to a convent to spend her life in prayer for the prostitute who helped her when she was in dire need. Again, Moore is here treating a theme which would have been a disaster in the hands of a less sophisticated writer. . . . (p. 151)

Moore's insight into the mind of the self-effacing and distant Sarah is extremely penetrating. When Sarah takes up the narrative, going into a long monologue about her own life, we see deeply into a person whose hardship is equalled only by her courage. Moore had a gift fairly rare among short story writers and novelists—he could create totally authentic female characters. *Esther Waters* is his finest achievement in this respect, but Sarah Gwynn is also a triumphant creation. Moore puts in her mouth a completely appropriate language. (p. 152)

"Sarah Gwynn" is a moving conclusion to a moving book. Her calm, resolute withdrawal from life follows a pattern typical also of the other main characters. *Celibate Lives* proves that loneliness always has its origin in the heart but can lead practically anywhere; **"Sarah Gwynn"** shows that it can sometimes lead to a kind of peace.

Whatever loneliness and deprivation are in *The Untilled Field* are attributed by Moore to the stultifying influence of the Roman Catholic Church in Ireland. Irish writers from Moore to Edna O'Brien have noted this and have very scrupulously and insistently pointed it out. Behind Irish puritanism and repression stretches a long, dark history of methodical English tyranny and futile Irish protest that helps to account for the emotional and moral climate of *The Untilled Field*. This collection of short stories is essentially a scrutiny of spiritual inertia just as *Dubliners* is an exposition of various kinds of paralysis. In the penultimate story, **"The Wild Goose"**, Moore very succinctly describes how, in Ireland, inspiration degenerated into stagnation and passionte Christianity became pious inhibition. (pp. 152-53)

The lamentable change in Christianity from an inspired love of creation to a resolute distrust of life is the central theme of

The Untilled Field. Other pathetic features follow from this: the atmosphere of unrelieved poverty and squalor; the frustration of all ideals; the suppression of individual thinking; the hysterical fear of sex as the supreme evil of which man is capable; the confusion of servility with obedience, furtive inhibition with virtuous self-denial, caution with wisdom; the fear of full expression and hence the distrust of the artist—all these things are examined by Moore with considerable skill and subtlety. Co-existing with this theme of stagnation is the theme of escape—especially to America, the land of promise where it seems possible to fulfil these aspirations so tragically stifled in Ireland. In **"Home Sickness"**, Moore not only points out how unquestioned clerical authority throttles all genuine vitality, but also effectively contrasts Irish sluggishness with American competence. (pp. 153-54)

If Moore had insisted that every Irish priest was despotic and narrow-minded, his stories would have degenerated into sledge-hammer polemic. But he is careful to set one priest's generosity against another's meanness, one's tolerance against another's inhumanity. In **"Patchwork"**, there is a calm but effective contrast between an old priest's warmth and a young one's repressive pettiness. Moore is here examining a national dilemma from within, and fairly presenting both sides of the story. The only trouble is, one feels, that the views of the young priest will prevail. (p. 155)

Consistently, throughout *The Untilled Field,* there is this balance between tyranny and tolerance, brutality and benevolence. One of Moore's most sympathetically-drawn characters is old Father Mac Turnan who, fearing for the future of Catholicism, writes a letter to the Pope in which he requests that the law of priestly celibacy be abolished. In this way, he calculates that all the priests of Ireland could become the fathers of thousands of Catholics, thereby ensuring the stability of that religion. Moore creates a strong picture of the old priest's naïveté and simple goodness and, during an interview with his Bishop concerning the letter to Rome, we are made aware of Mac Turnan's essential, customary loneliness, hidden under his concern for his poor parishioners. (p. 156)

[In] the last story of the book, **"Fugitives"**, John Rodney, a young sculptor, is hired by a priest, Father McCabe, to do a Mother and Child for McCabe's new church. Rodney gets McCabe's cousin, Lucy Delaney, to pose in the nude for him; McCabe discovers this and, after Rodney's sculpture is destroyed by Lucy's two young brothers, Rodney decides to leave Ireland for good. There is no place for the artist in a society where creative originality is frowned on, and sensuousness is equated with sin. . . . (p. 158)

"Fugitives" ends with an ironic exposition of the priestly faith in bad art and bad taste, since bad statues are "further removed from perilous nature". By making the political idealist and the creative artist victims of those shoddy values, Moore reveals the shady weaknesses and implacable mediocrity of Ireland as he knew it. There have been many changes in Irish society (and many for the better) since Moore's day, but *The Untilled Field* is still a monument in the history of the Irish short story. Its influence on Joyce, O'Connor, and O'Faoláin is, I would say, profound. *Dubliners* is, in many ways, like a more sophisticated and more cleverly-organised version of *The Untilled Field.* The two themes of paralysis and escape are common to both books, although Moore is more optimistic insofar as in his stories the characters' desire for escape is frequently realised whereas in *Dubliners* it is usually thwarted. Moore was not being immodest when he claimed that "*The Untilled Field* was

a landmark in Anglo-Irish literature, a new departure", although we may disagree with his opinion of the extent of its influence on Synge. In *The Untilled Field,* Moore began to examine a certain sickness at the very heart of Irish society which Joyce later examined at far greater depth. Moore's young sculptor, John Rodney, is remarkably like Joyce's Stephen Daedelus in his deliberate choice of exile, but he lacks Stephen's lofty ambition to forge in the smithy of his soul "the uncreated conscience of my race". Joyce regarded *Dubliners* as "a chapter in the moral history" of Ireland and the Irish people. In this, he was quite right, but *Dubliners* is the second chapter of that moral history. *The Untilled Field* is the first.

One of the more regrettable aspects of Moore's career as a short-story writer is that he did not continue in the realistic vein of *The Untilled Field.* The stories in that collection are neatly chiselled, and their critical comments on life in general and Irish life in particular are made in a cleancut, incisive manner which makes a strong and enduring impact on the reader's mind. One would have expected Moore, therefore, to continue in this manner, but instead, he turned his back on the contemporary scene and returned in *A Story-Teller's Holiday* to the colourful primitive world of early Ireland. Even the title indicates a new slackness in Moore and, although *A Story-Teller's Holiday* contains some very fine stories, the collection as a whole lacks the urgency and passion of *The Untilled Field.* It may be that Moore was reacting against the puritanism which he examined so penetratingly in *The Untilled Field* because the first volume of *A Story-Teller's Holiday* . . . deals almost completely, either in comic or tragic terms, with the theme of temptation. Early Irish Christianity was infinitely less inhibited, and far more expressive, than the modern version, and Moore must have taken great delight in portraying piety enlivened by abandon and in showing how devotion is animated by a vigorous sex-life. As well as that, *A Story-Teller's Holiday* enabled Moore to explore the nature of the *form* of the short story, and this he does with obvious relish and delight in his own experimentation. . . . [*A Story-Teller's Holiday* is] an attempt to show the differences between primitive and sophisticated story-telling. To do this, Moore introduces Alec Trusselby, the *shanachie* or traditional story-teller from Westport, who, at his best, narrates with something approaching the crude, colourful energy that one finds in Old Irish epics such as *Táin Bó Cúailgne.* Alec is the superbly articulate primitive, the Connemara Homer delighting in outrageous events, flamboyant characters and extravagant language spiced with vivid image and metaphor. He is a born story-teller, nothing else seems to matter to him, and he successfully communicates his own profound delight in the world evoked by his primitive imagination. He is, in short, Moore's "original self" against which Moore puts his "acquired self", the educated, sophisticated writer who tells stories in a crisp, modern idiom which, if it lacks the expansive energy of Trusselby's language, has yet an urbane precision and telling restraint that make it a completely appropriate vehicle for the sophisticated story-teller. Much of the delight of *A Story-Teller's Holiday* springs from the balance which Moore creates between the primitive and the sophisticated. The opening of the book is marred by dull gossip, slack reminiscence, a conscious "artiness", and ponderous philosophising, but when he actually gets down to dealing with the theme of temptation from both the primitive and sophisticated points of view, we find ourselves, as if by magic, in a vanished Ireland where the tragedy and the comedy of temptation are revealed in a rich, lively language. Moore's monks and nuns form a panorama of bawdy innocents who might have been created by an Irish Boccaccio. Their thoughts aspire to heaven, but they are very much of the earth. . . . Moore, equipped with a dynamic sense of mischief, [had] ample scope for exploring the humorous potential of a world in which monks went to bed with nuns to measure the nuns' power of attraction against their own power of resistance, and by so doing, to discover precisely the nature of the evils and the imperfections of this world, and consequently to aspire more ardently to the perfection of the next.

The second volume of *A Story-Teller's Holiday* deals mainly with the love-story of Ulick and Soracha, the bastard nobleman and the beautiful nun who ran away together and, after many adventures, finally came to grief. Moore here sustains the method of story-telling he used in the first volume, and both Moore and Trusselby tell different parts of the story, so that when the reader is beginning to feel that Moore's sophisticated method and idiom are wearing thin, he is jolted into a new awareness by the sudden advent of Trusselby's primitive energy. At odd moments throughout the tale, Moore halts the narrative to discuss it with Trusselby, so that we never lose sight of the fact that Moore is consciously experimenting with the form of the story.

The love-story itself is skilfully and movingly told, but the most impressive thing in it is the fate of Ulick's old harper, Tadhg O'Dorachy, who, after Ulick and Soracha are dead, lives on, marries a young woman and, after a life completely devoid of love-making, dies watching his wife in her nakedness. Significantly this part of the story is told by the Westport shanachie, Trusselby: it is Moore's final act of faith in the primitive. (pp. 159-62)

Yet, despite its many merits, *A Story-Teller's Holiday* is a retrograde step for Moore. It has very little of the formal compactness and concentration of *The Untilled Field;* there are long patches of loose, slack writing, with the result that we occasionally tend to lose interest in the narrative. The lack of contemporary interest is another defect, and while his treatment of the theme of temptation and calculated resistance is extremely amusing, it tends to become rather repetitive. One must conclude that Moore should have continued to cast his cold eye on contemporary Ireland rather than exploring the monkish and nunnish pranks of a much earlier time.

Nevertheless, Moore's importance as a short-story writer is considerable. He has had a deep influence on the Irish short story and, in fact, consciously intended to do this. He considered *The Untilled Field,* he said, as "a book written in the beginning out of no desire of self-expression, but in the hope of furnishing the young Irish of the future with models". . . . Moore had a thematic and formal influence on Joyce. Just as Moore in *The Untilled Field* chose to depict the inhibitions and frustrations of rural Ireland, so Joyce in *Dubliners* chose to describe Catholic Ireland, particularly Catholic Dublin, in all its pious mediocrity, claustrophobic middle-class respectability, garrulous sentimentality, and superstitious religiosity. Though Moore's world is, for the most part, rural, and Joyce's is urban, there are distinct similarities between them. (p. 163)

On the whole, Irish prose is more distinguished for its short stories than for its novels (despite *Ulysses, Finnegans Wake, At-Swim-Two-Birds,* and *Thy Tears Might Cease*). A very distinct Irish short story tradition exists, and today that tradition is being extended by writers such as Brian Friel, Benedict Kiely, Patrick Boyle, John Montague, John McGahern, James Plunkett, Edna O'Brien, and others. It is not at all certain that these writers have read Moore's stories, but it must be conceded

that Moore is a foundation stone of that tradition. (pp. 164-65)

Brendan Kennelly, "George Moore's Lonely Voices: A Study of His Short Stories" (© Oliver and Boyd Ltd. 1968; reprinted by permission of the author), in George Moore's Mind and Art, edited by Graham Owens, Oliver and Boyd, 1968 (reprinted by Barnes & Noble, Inc., 1970), pp. 144-66.

CHARLES BURKHART (essay date 1969)

[Moore's short stories] like most of his work, have been neglected since his death in 1933; and what critical references there have been to them, no matter how favorable, are no more than cursory, nor do his stories appear in anthologies. But there are signs of a Moore revival. . . . What may very well be reassessed as among Moore's best work, and even, one wishes to claim, as among the best of their genre, are Moore's short stories.

These stories are seldom of the usual modern type, which is often called "single incident," and in which each item of character or dialogue or setting contributes to a unique event of psychological peripateia. . . . But unfashionable in this as in every matter of literary craft, Moore preferred the ancient form of the tale to the single incident. In the tale, rather than the one event, there are events harmoniously interdependent, and they fit together in such a way that the tale has a shape—often a more difficult shape to determine than the easy outline, the steady rise and quick fall, of the single incident story. Moore prided himself on his ability to shape his narrative, one event growing smoothly and firmly into the next through the medium of his celebrated "melodic line." . . . The stories in *A Story-Teller's Holiday* and *Celibate Lives* are generally tales; the stories in *The Untilled Field* are either tales ("**The Wild Goose,**" for example—a story that, in the person of an Irish-American journalist and politician, symbolizes the restless wandering of the Irish, their "wild goose" nature) or they are single incident or they fall somewhere between the two ("**The Window**" has a central, unifying event, Biddy M'Hale's giving the new church a stained-glass window; but in its variety of sub-incident and mood, from the priest's testy impatience to Biddy's religious ecstasy, and in its leisurely pace and amplitude, more nearly resembles the tale). Still, Moore did not write to formula, and his short stories, like the rest of his work, show ceaseless experimentation and inventiveness, rigid classification being as pointless here as it generally is.

Another unusual aspect of Moore's short stories is that the borderline between fact and fiction in his work is all but impossible to trace. Is "**The Lovers of Orelay,**" his once-famous account of a middle-aged love tryst in *Memoirs of My Dead Life,* more autobiography or imagination? No writer has more skillfully blended truth with fantasy, more calculatedly traded in print on his own privacies. (pp. 165-66)

Moore's theory of fiction, as one pieces it together from his letters from his critical writings, and from his actual practice, helps to explain why his short stories tend to take the form of tales and why in every book he wrote there are elements of autobiography. Though he passed through many stages, and experimented with realism, naturalism, symbolism, to mention only three modes, his deepest beliefs seem to be consistent. He may have changed his mind about Flaubert, once his idol, but he never altered his opinion, for example, that the source of art is in folk. . . . The narrator he created for *A Story-Teller's*

Holiday is Alec Trusselby, fern-gatherer and *shanachie* (storyteller). . . . (p. 167)

Moore's best stories are laid in Ireland. Just as he recognized in the old Irish story-tellers, the *shanachies,* his own kin, so in subject and treatment his best inspiration was his most Irish. . . . Moore's success in capturing the Irish idiom is part of the same craft that led him to choose ancient Irish tales as his subjects in *A Story-Teller's Holiday.*

We hear the *shanachie's* voice; and, like children or primitive peoples, we are close to the springs of narrative. Moore's preference for the first person creates the same intimacy with his readers that exists between story-teller and listener. Literature must be personal in every way; it must be filtered through the teller's personality and colored with his temperament. . . . [Like] Flaubert and Joyce, Moore believed that the artist should be objective; he should neither approve nor disapprove; his entire concern should be with presentation. He was even more sharply divorced from the English traditions of fiction by his frequently stated dislike of "psychology." The flow of the narrative line must not be suspended by static interior exploration or monologue. (Any paragraph of Moore's late works will show how artfully he dips in and out of his characters' minds without ever losing sight of the immediate and external.) . . . Moore avoided passion and violence, agreeing with Turgenev that they were not sufficiently representative of life. Nor did he approve of humor. . . . (pp. 168-69)

[*The Untilled Field*] became a study of the Irish temperament, especially as it manifested itself in the relationship between priest and peasant. Since Moore was not yet the notorious anticleric he was to become later, we find studies of both sympathetic and unsympathetic priests. He did not despise the peasant, as Yeats came to despise him, nor did he glorify the peasant's eccentricities and idiom, as Synge was doing; he never forgot his own, and Turgenev's, criterion of objectivity. So that whether he is describing the suppression and exile of an ardent and sensual girl, Kate Kavanagh, by a powerful priest ("The Wedding Feast") or the pathetic attempts of Father McTurnan to succor his starving parishioners by building "A Play-House in the Waste," he takes no sides. But the stories are not cold; one feels, as in Joyce's stories, the human sympathies beneath the composed objectivity of the method. . . .

In terms of Moore's own development as a writer, *The Untilled Field* was, as he himself called it, "a frontier book, between the new and the old style." (p. 170)

The Untilled Field is also important in the history of the short story. According to H. E. Bates, the modern short story, including *Dubliners,* derives from Moore. Moore broke away from the tradition of exaggerated anecdote, in which Irish eccentricities were paraded for alternate effects of humor and pathos; instead his stories are shaped from "natural common clay," with "fresh exquisite realism." (pp. 170-71)

It is in *A Story-Teller's Holiday* that Moore fuses the theory and art of the short story. Moore called it his "joyous book," and these medieval tales are indeed much more humorous than the earlier stories. . . . The tales are told by Alec Trusselby and by Moore himself, the Anglo-Irish of Alec (Moore had considerable assistance with the idiom from James Stephens and others) contrasting with the more literary English of Moore. They are "ear stories," not "eye stories," as Moore himself remarks, and confirm Moore's belief in his role as shanachie and in the power and intimacy of the oral as opposed to the written. (pp. 172-73)

In his old age Moore turned to subjects from remote times and places, as in his novels *The Brook Kerith* and *Aphrodite in Aulis* and *Héloïse and Abélard.* His belief that modern civilization was a wasteland and that both the English literary tradition and the English language were worn out or exhausted led him to seek out in the past what was permanent and simple; and in his tales of Ireland when it was covered with forests and overrun by Normans or Scots, he sought to turn the clock back. Scholars have quarreled with some of his medieval details, but the atmosphere of *A Story-Teller's Holiday* is like what we know of the medieval age from books of hours or carvings or the cathedrals that remain. (p. 173)

Nowhere is Moore's artistry more evident than in the framework to these medieval tales. . . . By a careful progression from the temporal and immediate to what abides, in nature and in the relations between man and woman, Moore moves into the past and takes us with him. The epilogue of the book, which concerns Moore Hall, his ancestral home, is equally artful, for here he examines his own roots just as he has examined the roots of Irish history and legend in the tales he and Alec have told.

Though he left Moore Hall and Ireland for Paris and London, he returned, both in spirit and in fact. Many of his later books, like *A Story-Teller's Holiday,* have Ireland for their setting, and it was on the shores of Lough Carra that Moore wished to be buried. *A Story-Teller's Holiday* was also a return, a return to the ancient form of the tale for his narratives. Unique as his Irish tales are, they perfectly satisfy the final dictates of his unique aesthetic; and to those whose taste they please they flow as continuously and melodiously as Ana Liffey herself. (p. 174)

Charles Burkhart, "The Short Stories of George Moore," in Studies in Short Fiction *(copyright 1969 by Newberry College), Vol. 6, No. 2, Winter, 1969, pp. 165-74.*

I. A. RICHARDS   (essay date 1970)

As a physicist studies his particles and their interrelationships not immediately but through what may seem devious indications, or as we catch at our own thoughts and feelings through words they play with and hide behind, so what [*The Brook Kerith*] is primarily concerned for is advanced through differing minds whose idiosyncrasies are in the utmost degree realized, displayed, allowed for. Joseph, Dan, Peter and his fellow fishers, Nicodemus, Esora, Matthias, Hazael, Jesus, and Paul are as different as people can be. Yet they are all, to a compelling degree, living *and* comprehensible. And this is certainly a condition of our being able through them to grasp a little of the mystery within which they with other living minds, play their parts. (pp. 212-13)

Now that the dust cloud has settled it is easier to think about what Moore was here doing. He was writing a novel about the religious quest. (He had written on a related theme earlier in his *Evelyn Innes* and *Sister Teresa.*) He was not taking part in any doctrinal or historical discussions, not saying his or anyone else's say about the "historicity" of Jesus or about the role of a belief in the Resurrection in a Christian life. The demands of his novel required him to keep it clear from all such concerns; entanglement with them was indeed the most to be feared. . . .

Questions of biblical exegesis had above all to be avoided. In taking the greatest and most familiar religious figure as his hero he was exposing his work to endless interferences from the preconceptions and imaginative routines of his readers. How insulate it? How not affront? How in fact prevent confrontations? We can study his problem concretely by noting how he deals with the little actually said in the Gospels about Joseph of Arimathea. (p. 213)

[Moore] so leads the reader into Joseph's mind (or Joseph into the reader's) and so builds up the strain that by the time Mary and Martha are telling him how they "found the stone rolled away and a young man in white garments in the sepulchre" we are listening to them with him and alive with his apprehensions. Jesus is unconscious, precariously hidden in the gardener's empty cottage and at any moment a house-to-house search may begin. It is characteristic that Joseph should fall to "wondering at the answers he would make to Pilate, and at the duplicity of these, for he had never suspected himself of cunning. But circumstances make the man, he said, and before Jesus passes out of my keeping I shall have learnt to speak even as he did in double meanings, as Pilate did—as indeed all men do."

Few come nearer to their own thoughts than Moore's chief characters. It may be the roominess and richness of their awarenesses of their own thinking that allows the book to retell such a story with impunity. In the end it is the book's resourcefulness and honesty with itself that protects it as a critique of religious passion and reflection. (p. 214)

> *I. A. Richards, "Jesus' Other Life," in* The New York Review of Books *(reprinted with permission from* The New York Review of Books; *copyright © 1970 Nyrev, Inc.), Vol. XV, No. 10, December 3, 1970 (and reprinted in his* Complimentarities; Uncollected Essays, *edited by John Paul Russo, Harvard University Press, 1976, pp. 209-14).*

GRANVILLE HICKS   (essay date 1971)

Esther Waters strikes the reader as a "modern" novel, as nothing of Gissing's does. The plot is simple and unforced, and there are no Victorian sermons or conversations with the reader. The method is rigorously objective, and yet there is neither real nor pretended indifference to the fact of the characters. It is unfair, perhaps, to compare it with *Tess of the D'Urbervilles,* for Hardy was writing high tragedy, but, if the comparison is made, *Esther Waters* seems the more nearly perfect achievement. If it never moves the reader as *Tess* does, it never irritates with incredibilities or irrelevances. It is realism in the best British tradition, but it is realism purged—thanks to Moore's discipline in the French school—of faults that had beset that tradition for a hundred years.

To one who has read Moore's books, both before and especially after *Esther Waters*, the novel seems miraculous. If, comparing it with other novels of the nineties, one is impressed by the absence of both squeamishness and moralizing, one is amazed, comparing it with Moore's other books, by the freedom from snobbishness and pose. Hardy would have felt called upon to defend Esther. Gissing would have attacked her and her William as vulgar, and would have denounced Barfield's wastrel habits. Moore accepts them all. And yet, for all its beautiful lucidity, the book is never cold. Moore, in defiance of all his theories, boasted that the novel, by its depiction of the evils of baby-farming, "had actually alleviated more material suffering than any novel of its generation." True or not, the boast suggests that more feeling for humanity went into *Esther Waters*

than found its way into anything Moore wrote thereafter. (pp. 146-47)

> *Granville Hicks, "The Miracle of 'Esther Waters'" (reprinted by permission of Russell & Volkening, Inc.; as agents for the author), in* The Man of Wax: Critical Essays on George Moore, *edited by Douglas A. Hughes, New York University Press, 1971, pp. 141-50.*

WAYNE SHUMAKER   (essay date 1971)

Hail and Farewell differs from the run-of-the-mill autobiography in two important ways. First, a vividly sensed meaning preceded the search for compositional methods; and because the meaning served as a reference frame for the determination of material limits and structural techniques it came to inform every page and paragraph of the finished narrative. The ordinary autobiography lacks such a meaning. The typical impulse to the writing of personal lives seems to be not a sudden, compelling insight into experience but a complacent recognition of public interest in some activity with which the writer has been brought into first-hand contact. . . . Secondly, in *Hail and Farewell* the ratiocinative meaning is supported by an identical perceptual meaning. The complex perception which arises from a perusal of the work is exactly equivalent to the rational proposition that it was Moore's desire to render persuasive. The thesis is twice proved: logically, by means of argument, and to the senses, by making accessible the feelings which implied the logical statement. And this second achievement is more rare even than the first. Almost never, in autobiography, are historical moments represented as happening *now*. What is usually presented is not the experience itself but a hurried summary or the strained substitute for experience which remains in a rational paraphrase.

Moore's autobiographical techniques, which approximate the techniques of the novel, are not within the reach of every autobiographer. Possibly it is well that they are not. There are values, certainly, in the methods which in this context it has been necessary to disparage—values arising partly but not wholly from the fidelity of a dull life record to a dully sensed life. Nevertheless one may record one's admiration for the artistic integrity of *Hail and Farewell* and suggest that if so much could be made of Moore's not intrinsically extraordinary experiences, the use of equally appropriate techniques by other autobiographers would do much to redeem a literary genre which, in the gross, cannot be said to have earned the name of an art form. (pp. 262-63)

> *Wayne Shumaker, "The Autobiographer As Artist: George Moore's 'Hail and Farewell'" (reprinted by permission of The Regents of the University of California), in* The Man of Wax: Critical Essays on George Moore, *edited by Douglas A. Hughes, New York University Press, 1971, pp. 233-66.*

SUSAN DICK   (essay date 1972)

[*Confessions of a Young Man,* George Moore's] first autobiography, like all of his early works, is highly eclectic. During this period, Moore was adopting ideas, styles, and opinions without concern for the consistency of one with another; yet at the same time, he seemed instinctively drawn toward those artistic forms and themes which would in the future prove most germane to himself and his contemporaries: the paganism and aestheticism of Gautier, the decadence and cynicism of Baudelaire, the elitism of the symbolists, the precision and concreteness of Parnassian verse, and the uninhibited choice of subject matter enjoyed by the Impressionists and naturalists. Arthur Symons, W. B. Yeats, and other writers who followed Moore in looking to French literature for invigoration would find more subtle qualities to praise. If Moore was most affected by the daring themes, decadent mood, and uncompromising public stance of the French avant-garde, it was because these qualities were what most distinguished them from the English. The impatience and scepticism Moore displays in *Confessions* toward nuances of experimentation in language and form is only partly satirical exaggeration; it also reflects his eagerness to overthrow the stale literary establishment as quickly as possible.

This emphasis on the unorthodox gives *Confessions* its particularly exuberant and rebellious tone. In its display of intellectual attitudes, although not in its playful tone, it echoes Huysmans' novel *A Rebours*. . . . Moore reread *A Rebours* in 1886 and told Theodore Duret that it was "very good, very good." Huysmans' hero, Des Esseintes, expresses contempt for the bourgeois, love of the artificial and arcane; he admires the poetry of Baudelaire, Verlaine, and Mallarmé and the opera of Wagner. To complete his decadent tastes, he endorses a Schopenhauerian outlook on life. All of these themes have a place in the intricate fabric of *Confessions* and recreate for English audiences the aura of decadence which was to transform their artistic world in the 1890s.

Thus when Moore returned to London in 1879, he was filled with both revolutionary artistic theories and a naive confidence in his role as chief importer of French aesthetic tastes into England. In reading the section of *Confessions* which deals with this effort (the last five chapters) it is important to keep in mind the mixture of fact and fiction which makes up the book. At this point in the narrative, the margin between the two becomes increasingly blurred. Ostensibly, *Confessions* ends with the young hero struggling to write his first novel—which would date the ending as 1882, for *A Modern Lover* appeared in 1883. (pp. 3-5)

[Each] of the novels which preceded *Confessions* had a double identity. From the outset of his career, Moore was a serious writer and his experiments with fictional forms were genuine attempts to find his voice as a novelist. At the same time, Moore was never forgetful of his public or of the kind of fiction which would be most likely to upset the middle class, or villa, conventions. If these early novels were not wholly successful works of art—and Moore soon agreed that they were not—their failure can be blamed on the dual role they were expected to play. The artist who confronts an age inimical to experimentation, one which threatens his development as an artist, can either use his art to fight that age and thus, as Moore did, create works with definite flaws, or he can choose, as the aesthetes of the nineties would, to scorn his age in the belief that art has ultimately the power to alter life. During this period, Moore was convinced that the artist was to a large extent determined by his age. (pp. 12-13)

Confessions and his early novels had played an important part in the defeat of Victorianism. Moore would now turn his attention to quieter themes: the spiritual life and music, Irish, Biblical, and classical themes. But he would never forget the formative years of his career or abandon the book which had chronicled them.

Moore later called *Confessions* the genesis of everything he had written after it. The reader can easily see justification for this claim. Moore contributed to a number of literary genres: autobiography, criticism, the novel and short story, drama, and least significantly, poetry. Each of these is present in some guise in the narrative of *Confessions*. Autobiography most interests us here since *Confessions* was the first but by no means the last of Moore's autobiographical works.

In five other autobiographies, plus one unfinished autobiographical fragment, he recorded and refashioned segments of his past life. The first to be written after *Confessions* was *Memoirs of My Dead Life* . . . which is composed of chapters loosely related to one another by the continuity of the narrator. Speaking in the first person, Moore muses about his past and remembers many of the women in his life, especially the younger ones. The amount of truth in the episodes he recounts is questionable, and his whimsical, sometimes humorous, manner suggests that his narrative is more fiction than fact. He tells, for example, of a young woman who comes from Texas to ask him to sire a child for her. Her noble aim is to give a writer to Texas, and Moore obliges her with a mixture of wonder and aplomb.

Memoirs is an autobiography of a personality, not of facts. Every anecdote adds to the configuration of the narrator's character, and it becomes the real subject of the book. Moore's narrator, although apparently simply the author, is as much a refracted image of Moore as is the hero of *Confessions*. In his earlier autobiography, he is the exuberant prodigal; in *Memoirs*, he is the urbane lover. Both images had firm roots in Moore's personality and both were self-portraits he sought to emulate in his own life. The latter, the urbane lover, was to many of his friends an affectation. His companions were often embarrassed by his outspoken tales, but they were seldom convinced. Moore's love affairs, like his early life in Paris, became staple legends in his repertoire. (pp. 17-18)

[His next autobiographical work, *Avowals*,] like *Confessions* (and unlike *Memoirs*), is a mixture of literary criticism and autobiographical references. Its form is not that of a novel, but a combination of dialogue, in the manner of Landor's *Imaginary Conversations*, and monologue, the musing voice heard in *Memoirs*. The emphasis is on critical rather than autobiographical commentary, and when Moore cites his past, it is to support some opinion. His memories seem to be clustered together in constellations rather than preserved in a sequential form, and the freedom with which he ranges over the different segments of his past, connecting reminiscences with no regard for chronological accuracy, creates a timeless narrative. The only point of reference is the narrator, and the exfoliation of his personality dominates, as it does in *Memoirs* and *Confessions,* the mood of the book.

The narrator of *Avowals,* perhaps because his subject is mainly his opinions rather than his actions, seems to be less a created persona and more a clear reflection of the author. The reader feels a similar identity of author and narrator in Moore's next autobiography, *Hail and Farewell*. This long trilogy [*Ave, Salve, Vale*] . . . grew out of his memories of his eleven years in Dublin (1900-11) and his participation in the Irish Renaissance. As in *Memoirs* and *Avowals*, the past resurrected in *Hail and Farewell* is made up of constellations or atoms of memories. Based in the present, Moore's mind moves into the past, like Proust's, by focusing on complete and isolated segments of time. While the structure of his memories is similar, his method of remembrance differs from Proust's, for his memories are not triggered by sensation, but spun on a purely mental thread of suggestion. The opening of *Ave* establishes the method of narration used throughout the three books. He begins in the present and talks with Edward Martyn about the revival of the Irish language in Ireland. Leaving Martyn, Moore walks back to his rooms in the Temple, and as he walks, his thoughts roam from the discussion he has just had to the Irish writers who have remained in Ireland, to the idea of nationality in art, to his own self-exile from Ireland, and to a conversation he once had with [Edouard] Dujardin which, as he recounts it, expands his present attraction to and rejection of Ireland. This skillful weaving of past and present, of the general and the particular, is never digressive, for Moore maintains a firm control over the direction of his thoughts. He creates a sense of timelessness, ranging from the present to the mythic past, while retaining simultaneously a clear sense of the setting of his narrative in a definite time and place.

Hail and Farewell possesses the characteristic mingling of fact and fancy found in *Confessions, Memoirs,* and *Avowals.* Like *Confessions, Hail and Farewell* has a narrative line which is formed by Moore's discovering a pattern in his past. He emphasizes, as he does in *Confessions,* certain actions and opinions and suppresses others. He recalls not only his eleven years in Dublin, but also his early life in Mayo, London, and Paris, and he recounts again, and in greater detail, many of the events found in *Confessions.* In weaving these memories into his narrative, Moore recasts them to suit his present theme, for besides being a chronicle of his part in the Irish Renaissance, *Hail and Farewell* is an autobiography aimed at self-discovery. Throughout his narrative, Moore confesses to flaws in his character and moral lapses in a manner similar to that in Rousseau's *Confessions* or Gide's later *Si le grain ne meurt.* Unlike his *Confessions,* in which candour is joined with bravado, his candid self-revelations are earnest here, and like Rousseau and Gide, he anatomizes his past self to seek in it hints of his present self.

Among the works written after *Hail and Farewell* are two in which Moore again returned to his past for his subject. *A Story-Teller's Holiday* . . . is a rambling reminiscence which is composed of several stories (some told by Moore and some by "Alex Trusselby," an old fern gatherer), memories of his childhood and Paris in the 1870s, thoughts about Protestantism and Catholicism, and other reflections which occur to him as he returns to Ireland on holiday. His memories of Paris and the Nouvelle Athènes are juxtaposed to memories of Moore Hall. Although he feels an aversion toward his home, he acknowledges that it made his Paris life possible. *A Story-Teller's Holiday* is a celebration of the past rather than a chronicle of it, and like *Memoirs of My Dead Life,* an expression of the emotional texture of Moore's personality.

In contrast to this emphasis on mood, *Conversations in Ebury Street* . . . is, like *Avowals,* a collection of Moore's opinions on literature. He again mixes dialogue and monologue to present in an informal manner his critical judgments on subjects ranging from Baudelaire to Roger Fry. As *Confessions* was the first to show, Moore's life and his literary opinions were always inextricably joined, and he refers in this book to his early life in Paris when he speaks of Balzac and Zola.

After these two mixtures of reminiscence, fiction, and criticism, Moore returned in his final work to "pure" autobiography. In *A Communication to My Friends,* which he was writing at the time of his death in 1933, he recreated the period of his life which had been the subject of his first autobiography. His reason for writing this book, he explained, was to describe "how literature hailed me." He obviously felt that *Confessions,*

which had dramatized the same summons, was an inadequate account of his early career, and even cited it as "one of the hardships" he encountered in writing this later version. These declarations give *A Communication* the semblance of a factual account, but Moore was actually mingling fiction and fact as he had in all his earlier autobiographies. His memory may very well have been clouded by age (he was eighty) and confused by the earlier interpretations he had given his past, but his obvious desire to tell a good story was also a source of distortion.

Although *A Communication* is unreliable as history, it is an invaluable reflection of Moore's mature opinions on aspects of his personality. His comment that "a mate and the writing of books are incompatible," for example, while simplifying the question of why he never married, also expresses his life-long obsession with art.

Few writers have been so assiduous as Moore in the exercise of autobiography. Many artists have put as much of themselves into their work—Yeats and Joyce are two good examples—but few have chosen to display their past as directly as Moore did. He reflected upon the function of memory at the end of *A Story-Teller's Holiday:* "It is the past that explains everything, I say to myself. It is in our sense of the past that we find our humanity, and there are no moments in our life so dear to us as when we lean over the taffrail and watch the waters we have passed through. The past tells us whence we have come and what we are." One is reminded of Proust's exhaustive search into his past and of his final discovery that time is incarnate and holds the clue to what men are. For Moore the process of revision was very like the process of remembrance. Returning to past works with the hope of bringing them closer to perfection was not unlike returning to memories in order to find their durable significance. In revising *Confessions,* Moore was involved in both worlds, his work and his life. Thus the revised versions instruct us on his changing conceptions of himself both as a writer and as a man. (pp. 18-22)

Susan Dick, "Introduction" (© 1972 McGill-Queen's University Press), Confessions of a Young Man *by George Moore, edited by Susan Dick (©1972 McGill-Queen's University Press), McGill-Queen's University Press, 1972, pp. 1-22.*

JANET EGLESON DUNLEAVY   (essay date 1973)

Pattern and rhythm sometimes reminiscent of French idiom characterize the prose of Moore's last novels. . . . [In the prose of *The Brook Kerith, Heloise and Abelard, Ulick and Soracha,* and *Aphrodite in Aulis,*] the unhurried, rhythmic effect is achieved through repetition and assonance and through the natural cadences of cultured English speech sprinkled with archaisms, especially those constructions in which the inflection rises slightly at the end of a clause. The narrative is composed of sensuous lines that wind in and out and around characters and events in a rhythmic pattern that stops but does not end. Sounds and words are repeated within each passage to provide rhythm. The style is consciously artistic, a combination of techniques drawn from Moore's experiences as artist and art critic, from the musical devices he learned from Dujardin, and from the prose of Pater.

As Moore repeats sounds and words in a passage to give it rhythm, so does he create events that recur and people that reappear, in the larger narrative, to establish pattern. It is the story that appeals to curiosity and the plot to intelligence, according to Forster, but it is pattern that appeals to the aesthetic sense. Pattern, of course, had been a major concern of Moore's in his early work, but it had been applied artificially. The pattern of Moore's later novels is organic, related to rhythm in sentence and paragraph, serving the author's synergistic vision. It is constructed in part from the recurrent use of characteristic symbols: the nest of rooks, or other birds; the lake, stream, or other body of water. (pp. 137-39)

Sentences in *The Brook Kerith, Heloise and Abelard, Ulick and Soracha,* and *Aphrodite in Aulis* wind back on themselves, then spiral out again in new clauses; characters weave in and out of the narrative; the rooks rise from the nest in ever-widening circles; in the smooth water of the bay, which meets the curve of the beach, the soft, sinuous roll of the hills is reflected. Everywhere the serpentine line is evident, recalling the contrast of curve and angle in *A Mummer's Wife* and the aesthetic theories of harmonious line that had been established by such artists of the past as Hogarth, Delacroix, and Ingres, and that had been adopted by later painters in both England and France. Each of the later novels ends, not with a conclusion, but with an unfinished curve, left to fall and rise again in the pattern that had been established. In *The Brook Kerith,* Paul is left at the end of a day in which he has expounded on the kingdom of God and the birth, death, and resurrection of Jesus; another day, clearly, will follow: "He spoke from morning to evening," writes Moore in the penultimate paragraph. The last paragraph is composed of one line only: "The rest of the story is unknown." But the suggestion is clear: there was more. Similarly in *Heloise and Abelard* the lovers are left riding toward Troyes. The rest of their story, Moore says, is a matter of record: so there was more. Rhesos and Earine, at the end of *Aphrodite in Aulis,* hasten to Aulis: "Already the company may be wondering at our absence," says Earine, "and I am looking forward to seeing the sculptor of Aphrodite and the builder of her temple stand side by side to receive the homage that is their due." Under the greenwood, by the Bay of Aulis, they have just conceived a child. So, once again, there was more.

As Moore's last novels indicate, style, not story, was his chief concern during the final years of his life. Friends have reported that he revised endlessly, often beating out the rhythm of his long, winding sentences with his hand as he tested passages he had recently committed to paper. His goal was to recreate the flowing, musical, incantatory prose of the oral storyteller, and often he would struggle for days to find the exact word—one that would provide the tonal quality he desired as well as the meaning he wished to communicate.

For such prose Moore needed appropriate characters. The modern, urbane, witty men and women drawn from Dublin life whom he set in verbal opposition to himself and others in *Hail and Farewell* would not do. The style he wished to develop was ancient, noble, dignified: his characters must be, too. (pp. 140-41)

History and legend provided Moore with the new subjects he needed for his new style. Thus *The Brook Kerith* was based on accounts of the life of the historical Jesus, with Joseph of Arimathea as the character in focus; *A Story-Teller's Holiday,* an exchange of playful, irreverent stories between an Anglo-Irish George Moore and a Mayo fern gatherer, was woven out of Mayo legend and practices associated with Irish monastic discipline; *Heloise and Abelard,* Moore's much praised novel of the middle ages, was based on the letters of the famous lovers; *The Pastoral Loves of Daphnis and Chloe* was a trans-

lation of a story by Longus, for the most part from the French of Jacques Amyot; *Perronik the Fool* was a retelling of an old Breton legend; *Ulick and Soracha* was suggested by incidents from the history of the Bruce invasion that involved Carra Castle; and *Aphrodite in Aulis* was a blending of themes, thoughts, characters, events, and places out of history and old mythologies artfully worked into a story set in fifth-century Greece. (pp. 141-42)

Janet Egleson Dunleavy, in her George Moore: The Artist's Vision, the Storyteller's Art *(© 1973 by Associated University Presses, Inc.), Bucknell University Press, 1973, 156 p.*

ANTHONY FARROW (essay date 1978)

Moore gave a clear idea of his view of the magnitude as well as the kind of his achievement in his claim that *Paradise Lost* and *Héloise and Abelard* comprise two of the only three epics in the English language (the third, he thought, is *The Brook Kerith*). Frustrated readers, who may find nothing in common between *Paradise Lost* and *Héloise and Abelard* except a concern with one great sin, perhaps ought to console themselves with the thought that many of Moore's major achievements fit only uneasily into traditional genres, and that this is especially true of the later works, which resemble nothing so much as other late works by George Moore.

While it would not be true at all to say that *Héloise and Abelard* is a translation (a task Moore was to undertake with *The Pastoral Loves of Daphnis and Chloe*), it is incontestable that on commencing this work the novelist was confronted with an existing masterpiece, or rather two masterpieces, Abelard's *Historia Calamitatum* and the collection of letters that makes up the correspondence of the separated lovers. Much actual material in the same words is introduced from the sources into the novel; and in the roughest terms it is possible to say that, in part, there is an act of collaboration taking place between Moore and the original versions comparable with the relationship between the traditional storyteller and his sources. One reason Moore may have been willing to give himself to such a collaboration is that, in the medieval original, a great deal that is characteristic of George Moore already existed. Abelard in his espousal, and Héloise in her practice, of the theory of intentionalism, are "Protestants" in Moore's sense, testing their actions by their own motives rather than by external authority. Héloise's famous comment that though she is guilty, she is also innocent is a statement of such a curious psychological complexion that it allies her with Moore's complicated heroines Grania, Evelyn Innes, and Soracha (once again Moore is apter in his delineation of his heroine in this novel than of the hero). Abelard, too, seems to have his avatars among previous Moore heroes, for the view taken in *Historia Calamitatum* that his liaison is a sort of temptation, leading him away from his mission, is precisely that adopted by Jasper Dean, from *The Bending of the Bough,* John Reid, from *The Strike at Arlingford,* and Diarmuid, from *Diarmuid and Grania* when they begin to fall in love. Again, Abelard's attempt to sublimate Héloise's now unattainable love for him after his castration into a symbolic love of Christ as bridegroom does fit into a traditional religious iconography; but it is an iconography keenly explored by Moore in all his works about the religious life, particularly *Sister Teresa* and *A Story-Teller's Holiday.* (pp. 151-52)

The choice for Héloise (and for many of Moore's heroes) is between a more or less ordered Apollonian atmosphere where all is predictable and personal experiences count for very little, and a Dionysian life of new encounters, which of its nature is inevitably disorderly in some sense or other. In the Nietzschean coloring given to this sort of decision, Moore is possibly betraying his reading of the German philosopher (whom he certainly did know, for there are specific citations in *Memoirs of My Dead Life* and *Evelyn Innes*), but he is just as likely extrapolating from his own life choices, since the poems and autobiographies betray the same fascination with the root alternatives of human experience as that developed in *Héloise and Abelard*.

On first hearing Abelard lecture in public Héloise betrays the peculiar fusion of passion and intellectual acuity which so distinguishes her sensibility: overcome with the relentless progress of his reasoning, she throws herself at his feet and kisses his hand. Yet in her admiration of his philosophical ability she is attracted by that aspect least susceptible to humane considerations, since Abelard is described as a pitiless logician "who cares for nothing but his art." (p. 155)

Abelard, beneath his official, philosophical role, has another self, keenly emotional and active, threatening at any moment to upset his chosen task in life. In this, of course, he is not unlike Héloise, and one needs to balance Héloise's remark to Abelard, "there is a philosopher and a poet in thee, and both seeking for rivalry," with the later observation by Abelard's sister Denise, that he has found his own image and likeness in meeting Héloise. (p. 156)

[When Héloise becomes pregnant] Abelard returns to Paris, while Héloise remains in Brittany for her confinement; it is in Paris that Abelard discovers that his affair has been regarded by his students as a betrayal of philosophy: "For a thousand years the world has waited, since Plato and Aristotle, and now you would throw God's gift aside for a girl's face. . . . Jesus had no wife, Paul had none, nor had Buddha, but Socrates had, and we know the trouble and ridicule that she brought upon him. . . ." Thirty years and longer spent in writing stories and novels about celibates lie behind these lines, and one would think that no mind but Moore's could have conceived them, were it not for some very similar ideas expressed by Abelard in the *Historia Calamitatum*. At all events the students are to have their wishes fulfilled in a decisive way, since Fulbert [Héloise's uncle], incensed at what he sees as an abandonment of Héloise, hires cutthroats who castrate Abelard, thus removing all impediments to a career in philosophy.

This is the point at which Moore originally intended to end the story, but in fact the conclusion is more than two hundred pages away, for the rest of the account is spent in relating the experiences of Héloise, now retired to a convent so as not to interfere with the vocation of her husband and wholly ignorant of the mishap which renders their relationship no more than symbolic. Two hundred pages in the course of which nothing of any weighty consequence happens is variously a *tour de force* or narrative blunder, depending on one's point of view, but at all times the pace of *Héloise and Abelard* is leisurely, breaking off on occasion for meditations contained in sentences fully two pages long or a page devoted to the resemblance between swallows in their evening flight and bats. But a peculiar virtue of this slowly flowing style is its comprehensiveness, for it is able to embrace all the countless anecdotes of luckless lovers, abducted daughters, and wounded men and animals which clearly and abundantly reflect the main course of the story as it ripples by. And into this is woven the historical material which amplifies, not bloats the text, since the deluded

Crusaders who, for an idea, ruthlessly kill entire families of men, women, and children, occupy a contrapuntal relationship with those who, for the sake of philosophy or other fixed notions, bring Abelard and Héloise to their sad end. (pp. 157-58)

Anthony Farrow, in his George Moore *(copyright ©1978 by Twayne Publishers, Inc.; reprinted with the permission of Twayne Publishers, a Division of G. K. Hall & Co., Boston), Twayne, 1978, 169 p.*

WAYNE E. HALL   (essay date 1980)

Esther Waters describes what happens to a person who attempts to succeed, in the way that would make her happiest, within a society that precludes success and streaks of luck. (p. 84)

In exploring the theme of defeat in the world of action and society, Moore took up problems that grew out of his own roles as both a novelist of insecure financial and aesthetic means and the landlord of a large estate in late nineteenth-century Ireland. The novel's depictions of the emotions and consequences of failure draw much of their immediacy of feeling from his anxieties about his status within the circles of artistic talent and landed power. Moore Hall faced the same economic pressures threatening thousands of large Irish estates at that time: how to control its own fortunes during the major social transition increasingly eroding the wealth, power, and privileges of the landed gentry. (pp. 84-5)

Along with his Irish material in *Parnell and His Island* and *A Drama in Muslin,* the novel *Esther Waters* falls directly between the homecomings. In its concern with the theme of failure, the work points towards both the plight of the Big House and the mystique of the lost cause cultivated by the Renaissance writers. The kind of ambivalence that turned Moore's attitude towards the artistic movement into deflating irony also marked his view of his own class, his alternate repudiation of and then identification with the gentry. In the fictional world of *Esther Waters,* which emerges as a further attempt to answer his own personal Irish question, Moore sought to resolve the uneasy union of aesthete and landlord, to balance his desire to escape from his point of origin against his need to return to it.

Esther Waters is his best-conceived treatment of the experience and emotions of failure, and one of the best nineteenth-century novels by any Irish writer. In this work action becomes irrelevant, success only a transitory illusion, society an unbeatable opponent in a series of wagers destined to come up losers. Unlike the other characters in the novel, however, Esther manages to free herself from a reliance on external supports and from the irrational and desperate hopes for a reversal of fate. Finally outside of the constricting pressures that Moore felt surrounding him, she gains an enviable position through her return to and complete acceptance of simple and fundamental beginnings. And insofar as Esther represents Moore's concept of an idealized self, the novel offers one more form of the autobiography that continually occupied him during his career. (p. 100)

[Moore structures *Esther Waters* around] the opposition of desire and instinct, the external world and the internal self, sense and spirit, complexity and simplicity. One way, the way of the attractions of the world, raises people's hopes and lures them into an active involvement with life. The other, instinctive and religious, seeks through a withdrawal from the world to find contentment in an inner-directed state of mind and a simpler range of human needs. In the course of Moore's novel Esther alternates between these two poles and finally reconciles them into a stable synthesis. . . . By at last coming to rely on her inner nature, by wanting only a simple existence and no more, she brings desire and instinct into balance. There, Moore would have it, does she win salvation. (p. 104)

The final stage in Esther's life does not carry enough conviction, does not ring true enough with what has come before, to carry the universality with which Moore would burden it. Insofar as Esther's solution negates experience, it becomes unacceptable outside her own life, even in a world that irresistibly contaminates action and turns it to failure and ruin. Her happiness on returning to Woodview is too much a negative happiness, the relief one feels when the pain and suffering finally stop. (p. 110)

All of Moore's characters share in the common experience of failure and defeat. Esther's particular response to her disasters may not be as uniquely ideal as Moore claims. Her retreat into peace, silence, and simplicity may rather be very human weakness, an understandable exhaustion with the world, an acceptable desire just to withdraw from it all.

If we as readers cannot take Esther's final stage as a response to emulate, Moore himself had even greater difficulties. Esther is about thirty-eight when her story closes. At that age, Moore was beginning to turn over in his mind the ideas for the novel **Esther Waters,** a book that would bring a solid measure of success to a career that would last four more decades. His next major heroine, Evelyn Innes, would retire from the world because of too much commercial and artistic success, not because of too little. (p. 111)

Moore projected onto the whole of society the limited experience of his own landed class. The social transition that meant ruin to the Irish gentry meant economic advancement for the tenants and cottiers who could at last purchase their holdings under a more favorable land policy. If a pattern of defeat and failure indeed characterized the status of the gentry, however, it could also warn off those who would materially profit even more from social change. Such attempts to win external success, the novel cautions, can only bring disappointment. There had been a time in Ireland, as Moore recalled in **Parnell and His Island,** when his class lived in security and elegance. The politicans, the demands for land reform, the agrarian agitation, and the weak and compromising landlords changed all of that. Esther represented a return to the simplicity of an earlier age, a time before the balances in Ireland began to shift. The undeniable loss of that age contributed to Moore's depiction of her within a general environment of defeat and ruin. Yet he also hoped to find that a spiritual return to simple beginnings need not end in ruin, that individual human character might still succeed where history had gone frighteningly wrong. Esther's heroic self-sufficiency seemed to offer Moore an answer to his personal and class anxieties, an internal peace beyond the need for social gains. Not finally able to follow her example of material poverty, he still sought to retreat from the world into the artificial monastery of his work. If success did not lie within society, he would seek it through the ideal constructs of art, led on by the hope of salvation within the self. (pp. 111-12)

Wayne E. Hall, "'Esther Waters': An Irish Story," in Irish Renaissance Annual I *(© 1980 by Associated University Presses, Inc.; reprinted by permission), Vol. I, No. 1, April, 1980 (and reprinted in a slightly different form as "George Moore," in his* Shadowy Heroes: Irish Literature of the 1890s, Syracuse University Press, 1980, pp. 83-112).*

ADDITIONAL BIBLIOGRAPHY

Burkhart, Charles. "The Short Stories of George Moore." *Studies in Short Fiction* VI, No. 2 (Winter (1969): 165-74.
    Finds that Moore did not write in conventional forms but experimented constantly with the short story.

Cunard, Nancy. *GM: Memories of George Moore.* London: Rupert-Hart Davis, 1956, 206 p.
    Recollections and impressions of George Moore by a young friend and admirer.

Ferguson, Walter D. *The Influence of Flaubert on George Moore.* Philadelphia: University of Pennsylvania Press, 1934, 108 p.
    Extensive analysis of Flaubert's subjects, characters, and themes in Moore's fiction.

Henn, Thomas Rice. "George Moore." In his *Last Essays: Mainly on Anglo-Irish Literature,* pp. 173-89. New York: Barnes & Noble, 1976.
    Biographical essay which describes the bickering among Yeats, Moore, and Martyn, the early Abbey Theatre "triumvirate."

Hone, Joseph. *The Life of George Moore.* New York: The Macmillan Co., 1936, 515 p.
    Definitive biography, including many extracts from Moore's letters. The book concludes with a biocritical essay by Desmond Shawe-Taylor.

Hough, Graham. "George Moore and the Nineties" and "George Moore and the Novel." In his *Image and Experience: Studies in a Literary Revolution,* pp. 179-210. London: Gerald Duckworth & Co., 1960.
    Describes Moore's development from aestheticism to naturalism.

Howarth, Herbert. "George Augustus Moore." In his *The Irish Writers, 1880-1940,* pp. 32-82. New York: Hill and Wang, 1958.
    Sees in Moore's various works acts of rebellion against society, family, and religion.

Jeffares, Norman A. *George Moore.* London: Longmans, Green & Co., 1965, 43 p.
    Introductory survey of Moore's prose, plays, autobiographies, and essays.

Sherman, Stuart P. "The Aesthetic Naturalism of George Moore." In his *On Contemporary Literature,* pp. 120-68. New York: Henry Holt and Co., 1917.
    Traces Moore's development from aestheticism to naturalism to symbolism.

Temple, Ruth Zabriskie. "George Moore." In her *The Critic's Alchemy: A Study of the Introduction of French Symbolism into England,* pp. 231-66. New York: Twayne Publishers, 1953.
    Discusses Moore's role in bringing the themes and theories of French symbolism into English literature in the late nineteenth century.

Wolfe, Humbert. *George Moore.* London: Thornton Butterworth, 1933, 135 p.
    Asserts that Moore adapted his literary persona to accommodate his varied reading audiences.

Alfred Noyes

1880-1958

English poet, critic, essayist, short story writer, novelist, biographer, autobiographer, and dramatist.

Noyes was a minor poet carrying on the long tradition of English poetry, a follower of Wordsworth and Tennyson. Though his subjects were for the most part standard—everyday life, England's past, the English countryside, the sea—his use of language and rhythm was fresh. A prolific writer popular with the reading public, Noyes was never recognized as an important poet by most critics, and his traditional style led to his eventual neglect after World War I and the rise of modernism.

After a youth spent by the sea and an Oxford education, Noyes moved to London. George Meredith encouraged him to write poetry and the popularity that Noyes won so early in his career made it possible for him to support himself by writing. The poet's first work, *The Loom of Years*, demonstrated his strong command of language and meter. Its cheery lyrics, fanciful tales, and dance-like rhythms met with immediate success. Two slightly later works, *The Flower of Old Japan* and *The Forest of Wild Thyme*, echo the romantic, balladic quality that marks Noyes's most popular verse.

In "The Highwayman," the poet's frequently anthologized piece, he intensifies a dramatic, romantic story line with driving rhythms. In mood and pacing "The Highwayman" presages *Tales of the Mermaid Tavern*. The latter is a narrative hodgepodge of blank verse and songs projecting the poetic persona back to the famed Elizabethan pub to share in the badinage of Marlowe, Shakespeare, and Jonson. Critics view *Tales of the Mermaid Tavern* as a well-researched historical piece, although some find it lacking in psychological subtlety.

The poet's most ambitious works, *Drake* and *The Torch-Bearers*, received mixed critical response. *Drake*, Noyes's serialized sea epic, highlights the exploits and adventures of the famed English navigator. *Drake*'s grandeur, scope, and strong nationalist overtones drew praise from some critics while others objected to the epic's ornate and archaic diction and to the predictability of its plot. *The Torch-Bearers*, a trilogy devoted to scientific advancements in astronomy, biology, and modern discoveries and inventions, is judged a notable but uneven and unsatisfying work. Most critics consider the poet's attempt to reconcile science and religion a task better suited to prose than to verse. Critics prefer the "singing" melodic line of the lyrics to the stately blank verse of the epics.

Temperamentally and stylistically wed to the poetry of an earlier era, Noyes rejected the innovations of twentieth century literature. As a distinguished advocate of traditional English literature, he chose traditional subjects and experimented within the confines of traditional prosody. His midlife conversion to Roman Catholicism reinforced his conservatism. In such late prose works as his *Some Aspects of Modern Poetry*—a virulent attack upon modernism and a staunch defense of Tennyson and other maligned literary giants—and in his biography of Voltaire, he affirms his commitment to and defense of traditional literary and religious ideals. Noyes thus successfully

Courtesy of Princeton Photographs Division, Library of Congress

resisted what he considered to be the caprices of modernism, and has consequently suffered the neglect of modern readers.

PRINCIPAL WORKS

The Loom of Years   (poetry)   1902
The Flower of Old Japan   (poetry)   1903
The Forest of Wild Thyme   (poetry)   1905
Drake   (poetry)   1906-08
Tales of the Mermaid Tavern   (poetry)   1913
*Watchers of the Sky   (poetry)   1922
Some Aspects of Modern Poetry   (criticism)   1924
*The Book of Earth   (poetry)   1925
*The Last Voyage   (poetry)   1930
Voltaire   (biography)   1936
Collected Poems   (poetry)   1950
Two Worlds for Memory   (autobiography)   1953
A Letter to Lucian, and Other Poems   (poetry)   1956

*These works were published as *The Torch-Bearers* in 1930.

THE BOOKMAN London   (essay date 1906)

In the case of a poet extreme accuracy of dates is of no special importance. I will, therefore, content myself with saying that it was perhaps a little more than three years ago that I first met Alfred Noyes in poetry, and, shortly afterwards, in person. I had received for purposes of review a heavy pile of books of verse, and had laboured over them with, I trust, a sufficiently conscientious view of my duties. I thought I had completed my task, and was about to despatch the copy when my eyes fell on a little volume bound in white vellum that had hitherto escaped my notice. With a sigh of weariness, I took it and opened it. It was **"The Loom of Years,"** by Alfred Noyes. As I turned the pages weariness gave way to interest, and interest soon rose to enthusiasm. Here at last was the real thing: music, colour, and sparkle were in these poems. Here was no mere poetaster's trick of fixing words together in a Chinese puzzle of rhyme. This singer had imagination and delight to fuse his thoughts. Technical dexterity he had in abundance, but the dexterity was his servant and not his master. His outlook was broad, his sympathies were fresh; he had a fine gift of unfettered expression, and he had a high respect for the great traditions of English poetry. (p. 199)

Since **"The Loom of Years"** four books of poetry have come from Mr. Noyes's busy pen. First was **"The Flower of Old Japan,"** a child's dream vision told in beautiful verse. There were dashes in this of the Robert Browning who wrote "The Pied Piper of Hamelin"; there was a fine flavour of the Coleridge of "Christabel," but chiefly there was Mr. Noyes himself. The story, as a reviewer said at the time, "goes from peaceful delight without a break into regions of dreadful forewarning, and emerges into magic palaces of bloom and colour and song." This was followed by **"Poems,"** a fine sturdy volume published by the Blackwoods, and containing manifold proofs both of Mr. Noyes's genius and of his amazing versatility. **"Apes and Ivory,"** for instance, recalls **"The Flower of Old Japan."** **"Sherwood"** is a delightful poem of brake and woodland; **"A Song of England"** and **"The Phantom Fleet"** strike a noble note of patriotism; and **"The Barrel Organ"** is a dream of lilacs and violets and Kew Gardens all mixed up together in a beautiful confusion. . . . Next came **"The Forest of Wild Thyme,"** to my mind the most beautiful thing Mr. Noyes has yet done. It is a continuation of **"The Flower of Old Japan,"** and is formed on the same general plan, but there is in it a special note of tenderness and pity which gives it a beauty of its own. Nothing is overstrained: there is no gush of mere sentimentalism, but a true feeling for childhood and mystery and the deep things of life.

Last comes **"Drake, an English Epic."** This is as yet incomplete. Three books of it have appeared in three successive numbers of *Blackwood's Magazine,* and they have since been republished in book form. This is an enterprise of great courage on the part of Mr. Noyes. Hitherto he has been satisfied with smaller ventures. Now he is launched on the great sea of poetry. The subject is a magnificent one, and Mr. Noyes has so far treated it in a fashion which must make all lovers of adventure and poetry hope for the speedy and fortunate fulfilment of his task.

Here I must end this brief notice of one of the most interesting personalities in the literature of to-day. In the natural course of things Mr. Noyes has many years of poetic achievement still before him. His career will be watched with profound interest by all those who have at heart the re-establishment of the great traditions of English song. (p. 200)

"The Bookman Gallery: Alfred Noyes," in The Bookman, *London, Vol. XXX, No. 180, September, 1906, pp. 199-200.*

THE ATHENAEUM   (essay date 1913)

Mr. Alfred Noyes writes with a sustained, yet not quite convincing zest. In the present work [**"Tales of the Mermaid Tavern"**] he fables to us that, having become in dream a potboy at the Mermaid Tavern in its great days (perhaps the finest thing in the book is the introductory description of his ride through London, and of the vision which culminated in this dream), he was witness of the convivialities, confidences, plots, tragedies, and embroilments of which Greene, Marlowe, Shakespeare, Jonson, and Raleigh were the heroes. Of these he gives us an onlooker's account. His poem takes the form of a narrative in somewhat irregular and conversational blank verse, broken at intervals by lyrical interludes or by songs, the latter given, it may be, by worthies who leap on to the table to sing them, and refresh themselves with sack between the rounds. The tumultuous energy of the whole performance suspends criticism when we come freshly to it. We submit readily to the buffetings of an impulsive muse, and, carried along on a swift stream of words, hardly stay to sound the depth of the current which is bearing us. The play of rhythm is, indeed, various and cunningly handled. The blank verse has an easy ruggedness which contrasts well with the all but intoxicating lilt of the ballads, elegies, and other lyrical set pieces. Perhaps it is not till we set down the book that feelings of dissatisfaction begin to stir our minds. (p. 691)

[The] procession song for the funeral of Mary, Queen of Scots, is one of the most carefully wrought of Mr. Noyes's intermezzi, and it has passages of great beauty. But even here he has allowed a subtle and inventive ear to impose upon a too easily contented imagination.

The same fault is discernible in another of his more ambitious lyrics—that in which Ben Jonson sings a dirge for his departed comrades. . . . The variations and recurrences, Kit for Marlowe, Robin for Greene, are perhaps intended to call up the companionable atmosphere of the mermaid. The effect they actually produce is, we think, that of a rather chilly contrivance; they even suggest that feeling has been sacrificed for the sake of a tune. The rollicking measures in which Mr. Noyes more frequently indulges carry the same fault to excess. The result is that his volume as a whole, in spite of its many passages of vivid insight and firm craftsmanship, cannot be accepted as faithfully mirroring the spirit of Elizabethan times. The impression we get of Mr. Noyes's Elizabethans is that they are over-aware of the vivacity, dignity, and daring of themselves and their set, are so studiously engaged in clapping one another upon the back that they have no leisure to be collected, and to see things in their natural colours and proportions. (p. 692)

"Literature: 'Tales of the Mermaid Tavern'," in The Athenaeum, *No. 4470, June 28, 1913, pp. 691-92.*

WILLIAM LYON PHELPS   (essay date 1918)

[Mr. Noyes] is prolific. Although still a young man, he has a long list of books to his credit; and it is rather surprising that in such a profusion of literary experiments, the general level should be so high. He writes blank verse, octosyllabics, terzarima, sonnets, and is particularly fond of long rolling lines that have in them the music of the sea. His ideas require no enlargement of the orchestra, and he generally avoids by-paths, or unbeaten tracks, content to go lustily singing along the highway. Perhaps it shows more courage to compete with standard poets in standard measures, than to elude dangerous comparisons by making or adopting a new fashion. Mr. Noyes openly challenges the masters on their own field and with their own weapons. Yet he shows nothing of the schoolmasterish contempt for the "new" poetry so characteristic of Mr. [William] Watson. He actually admires Blake, who was in spirit a twentieth century poet, and he has written a fine poem *On the Death of Francis Thompson,* though he has nothing of Thompson in him except religious faith.

In the time-worn but useful classification of verse makers under the labels *Vates* and *Poeta,* Alfred Noyes belongs clearly to the latter group. He is not without ideas, but he is primarily an artist, a singer. He is one of the most melodious of modern writers, with a witchery in words that at its best is irresistible. He has an extraordinary command of the resources of language and rhythm. Were this all he possessed, he would be nothing but a graceful musician. But he has the imagination of the inspired poet, giving him creative power to reveal anew the majesty of the untamed sea, and the mystery of the stars. With this clairvoyance—essential in poetry—he has a hearty, charming, uncondescending sympathy with "common" people, common flowers, common music. One of his most original and most captivating poems is *The Tramp Transfigured, an Episode in the Life of a Corn-flower Millionaire.* This contains a character worthy of Dickens, a faery touch of fantasy, a rippling, singing melody, with delightful audacities of rime. (pp. 57-9)

His masterpiece, *The Barrel Organ,* has something of Kipling's rollicking music, with less noise and more refinement. Out of the mechanical grinding of the hand organ, with the accompaniment of city omnibuses, we get the very breath of spring in almost intolerable sweetness. This poem affects the head, the heart, and the feet. I defy any man or woman to read it without surrendering to the magic of the lilacs, the magic of old memories, the magic of the poet. Nor has any one ever read this poem without going immediately back to the first line, and reading it all over again, so susceptible are we to the romantic pleasure of melancholy. (pp. 59-60)

Alfred Noyes understands the heart of the child; as is proved by his *Flower of Old Japan,* and *Forest of Wild Thyme,* a kind of singing Alice-in-Wonderland. These are the veritable stuff of dreams—wholly apart from the law of causation—one vision fading into another. It is our fault, and not that of the poet, that Mr. Noyes had to explain them: "It is no new wisdom to regard these things through the eyes of little children; and I know—however insignificant they may be to others—these two tales contain as deep and true things as I, personally, have the power to express. I hope, therefore, that I may be pardoned, in these hurried days, for pointing out that the two poems are not to be taken merely as fairy-tales, but as an attempt to follow the careless and happy feet of children back into the kingdom of those dreams which, as we said above, are the sole reality worth living and dying for; those beautiful dreams, or those fantastic jests—if any care to call them so—for which mankind has endured so many triumphant martyrdoms that even amidst the rush and roar of modern materialism they cannot be quite forgotten." (p. 60)

Nearly all English poetry smells of the sea; the waves rule Britannia. Alfred Noyes loves the ocean, and loves the old sea-dogs of Devonshire. He is not a literary poet. . . . He has the blessed gift of admiration, and his poems on Swinburne,

Meredith, and other masters show a high reverence; but they are without subtlety, and lack the discriminating phrase. He is, however, deeply read in Elizabethan verse and prose, as his *Tales of the Mermaid Tavern,* one of his longest, most painstaking, and least successful works, proves; and of all the Elizabethan men of action, Drake is his hero. (p. 61)

[Mr. Noyes called *Drake*] an English Epic. It is not really an epic—it is a historical romance in verse, as *Aurora Leigh* is a novel. It is interesting from beginning to end, more interesting as narrative than as poetry. It is big rather than great, rhetorical rather than literary, declamatory rather than passionate. And while many descriptive passages are fine, the pictures of the terrible storm near Cape Horn are surely less vivid than those in *Dauber.* Had Mr. Noyes written *Drake* without the songs, and written nothing else, I should not feel certain that he was a poet; I should regard him as an extremely fluent versifier, with remarkable skill in telling a rattling good story. But the *Songs,* especially the one beginning, "Now the purple night is past," could have been written only by a poet. In *Forty Singing Seamen* there is displayed an imagination quite superior to anything in *Drake;* and I would not trade *The Admiral's Ghost* for the whole "epic." (pp. 61-2)

Alfred Noyes is "among the English poets." His position is secure. But because he has never identified himself with the "new" poetry—either in choice of material or in free verse and polyphonic prose—it would be a mistake to suppose that he is afraid to make metrical experiments. The fact of the matter is, that after he had mastered the technique of conventional rime and rhythm, as shown in many of his lyrical pieces, he began playing new tunes on the old instrument. In *The Tramp Transfigured,* to which I find myself always returning in a consideration of his work, because it displays some of the highest qualities of pure poetry, there are new metrical effects. The same is true of the Prelude to the *Forest of Wild Thyme,* and of *The Burial of a Queen;* there are new metres used in *Rank and File* and in *Mount Ida.* The poem *Astrid,* included in the volume *The Lord of Misrule* . . . , is an experiment in *initial* rhymes. (p. 63)

The English national poetry of Mr. Noyes worthily expresses the spirit of the British people, and indeed of the Anglo-Saxon race. We are no lovers of war; military ambition or the glory of conquest is not sufficient motive to call either Great Britain or America to arms; but if the gun-drunken Germans really believed that the English and Americans would not fight to save the world from an unspeakable despotism, they made the mistake of their lives. . . . Alfred Noyes made a correct diagnosis and a correct prophecy in 1911, when he published *The Sword of England.* (p. 64)

I think none the worse of the mental force exhibited in the poetry of Alfred Noyes because he is an optimist. It is a common error to suppose that cheerfulness is a sign of a superficial mind, and melancholy the mark of deep thinking. Pessimism in itself is no proof of intellectual greatness. Every honest man must report the world as he sees it, both in its external manifestations and in the equally salient fact of human emotion. Mr. Noyes has always loved life, and rejoiced in it; he loves the beauty of the world and believes that history proves progress. In an unashamed testimony to the happiness of living he is simply telling truths of his own experience.

Alfred Noyes proves, as Browning proved, that it is possible to be an inspired poet and in every other respect to remain normal. He is healthy-minded, without a trace of affectation or decadence. He follows the Tennysonian tradition in seeing that "Beauty, Good, and Knowledge are three sisters." He is religious. A clear-headed, pure-hearted Englishman is Alfred Noyes. (pp. 64-5)

> *William Lyon Phelps, "Phillips, Watson, Noyes, Housman" (originally published in a different form as "The Advancement of English Poetry in the Twentieth Century," in* The Bookman, *New York, Vol. XLVI, No. 3, November, 1917), in his* The Advance of English Poetry in the Twentieth Century *(copyright, 1917, 1918 by Dodd, Mead and Company, Inc.), Dodd, Mead and Company, 1918 (and reprinted by Dodd, Mead, 1925, pp. 35-70).*

THE SATURDAY REVIEW London   (essay date 1922)

To praise **'The Torch-Bearers'** of Mr. Noyes (we are as yet given only one of its three intended sections) will indicate a keen modernity of outlook. But whatever its vicissitudes, **'The Torch-Bearers'** will remain the last and the best—if it abides by its present promise—of the Edwardian poems. It does not oscillate, like much Georgian poetry, between violent extremes; nor, like Georgian poetry of an opposite school, does it drone contentedly along one drab level. Its general conception is spacious and its detail beautifully executed. It is eminently readable, so that those to whom the readability of a poem is a phenomenon gravely to be suspected, will betake themselves in all haste to the incoherent utterances of more dynamic writers.

In its general technical quality, **'The Torch-Bearers'** belongs to that complacent age which extends from the death of Lord Tennyson to that shocking moment which gave birth to 'The Everlasting Mercy.' Its blank verse is never padded out and is always melodious. It seems likely that much of this poem was written during the war, and if the accusation is made against Mr. Noyes that the large suave movement of his poem is not quickened and distorted by the agony of those times, he might well quote the example of Jane Austen at a similar epoch, or Condorcet writing so evenly under the shadow of the guillotine. In theme no less than in manner is Mr. Noyes eminently Edwardian, a foster-child of the Laureate. The conception came to him, characteristically, on the night he was "privileged to spend on the Sierra Madre Mountains, when the first trial was made of the new 100-inch telescope." **'The Torch-Bearers'** of this first volume are the **'Watchers of the Skies'**—Copernicus, Tycho Brahe, Kepler, Galileo, Newton, William and Sir John Herschel. Mr. Noyes has told their stories with great ease and fluency. He has found not only that their lives were, in some cases, connected by links of real event, as if deliberately by some genius of Unity, but that their recorded association with poets and poetry assisted him considerably to bind their histories into a whole. Tycho Brahe and Kepler, for instance, wrote a large number of poems, whilst the visits of Sir Henry Wotton to Kepler and of Milton to Galileo were of obvious value in the hands of so eager a craftsman.

If Mr. Noyes never attains a formidable height of poetry, it is impossible not to admire his ease and ingenuity. It is these very qualities, however, which make his incidental lyrics so flaccid, and which account for Mr. Noyes's present lapse from the reverence of our strenuous age. And when at the end of this volume the planets and the sun lyrically commune together, it is as if Faustine and Dolores and the anaemic ladies of Swinburne's poetic acquaintance arose to lament in harmony

around the grave of the dead poet, in melancholy and impeccable quatrains. (p. 421)

> *"The Last of the Edwardians," in* The Saturday Review, *London, Vol. 133, No. 3469, April 22, 1922, pp. 420-21.*

RICHARD Le GALLIENNE   (essay date 1922)

Alfred Noyes is far from being Rudyard Kipling, and I only mention them together because their success in selling their books makes them alike the target of those who have failed in that desirable end. . . . It is to be feared that, in Mr. Noyes's case, his popularity is to be regarded as something in his disfavor as a poet, however much it may be to his credit as an astute business man, who has, very properly, made the most commercially of his talents. . . .

It may come of this box-office fame, or it may have been natural to him, that [Mr. Noyes] has for some time been attempting ambitious themes, which, one regrets to say, are so very much bigger than himself. . . . He writes words, as the phrase is, with no little skill and gusto, to the old familiar ballad tunes. Occasionally in his first and best volume he struck a more personal lyric note, with real singing charm, and sometimes an intenser thrill. . . . But that volume gave a promise which no succeeding volume by Mr. Noyes has kept. . . .

[In] "**Watchers of the Sky**," which is but the first part of a "trilogy" entitled "**The Torch-Bearers**," Mr. Noyes regards himself summoned to celebrate in song the achievements of the great astronomers, to sing the epic of scientific discovery. He seems to be under the impression that the idea has occurred to no other poet before him. . . . In reading the "Prologue" one had already felt certain misgivings as to Mr. Noyes's power to cope with his high argument, as one noted what little use he made of the humbler poetic possibilities ready to his hand in his account of his journey to that observatory on the Sierra Madre Mountains. Here at least was the opportunity for some fine descriptive writing. One must be pardoned for thinking of Tennyson's powers in that direction. Though Tennyson might have failed with Copernicus or Galileo—and it is unlikely that he would have failed—it is easy to imagine what pictures he would have drawn of that august approach. . . .

When Mr. Noyes finally settles down to tell the stories of his various astronomers, from Copernicus to William and Sir John Herschel, one simply wonders—why? It is hard to see what gain there is either to poetry or science in such uninspired restatement, in the most denatured blank verse that has been written since Lewis Morris, of such glorious matters as Mr. Noyes has had the temerity to make his province. Such "poetry" as Mr. Noyes has achieved is confined to a lyric or two. And, as for "science," the "poetical" verbiage employed merely darkens the radiant theme. Here is no such interpretative grasp of the imagination such as could alone justify Mr. Noyes's doubtless well-meant endeavor. It is questionable whether good blank verse would be properly employed on such a theme. But Mr. Noyes's blank verse!—well, the rest is silence. . . .

I am bound to say that the articles in the Encyclopaedia Britannica on astronomy and astronomers thrill me with a deeper sense of the poetry of their theme than all Mr. Noyes's iambic decasyllables. . . .

Mr. Noyes seems to retain the old-fashioned idea that to make a great poem you have only to take a great subject and pour over it a kind of poetic sauce. He seems to possess an inexhaustible supply of such poetic sauce, and he has poured it over every subject, every great theme. . . . (p. 9)

Richard Le Gallienne, "Alfred Noyes among the Star Gazers," in The New York Times Book Review *(© 1922 by The New York Times Company; reprinted by permission), May 28, 1922, pp. 9, 25.*

THE TIMES LITERARY SUPPLEMENT   (essay date 1924)

In Mr. Noyes's book of collected essays on poetry ["**Some Aspects of Modern Poetry**"] there is a good deal of negative criticism: that is, of attacks on literature that he does not like. Some modern literature and criticism worry him, like insults to a friend, and he is apt to worry them, like a terrier. In separate papers these flouts and snaps might seem each a point neatly scored: repeated in a book of collected essays (and such a book must always ask indulgence for the repetitions in it), they suggest a lack of patience, a state of irritability foreign to good criticism. And this failing is not altogether absent from his considered judgments of the literature at which he snaps. He shows a lack of hopefulness and of wide vision. He believes that the present revolution in art and letters is different from all that preceded it. . . .

Many of the essays in this book are constructive criticism. They include papers on Shelley, on Tennyson, on Wordsworth, and on Swinburne's tragedies; and the core of the whole matter lies in the long essay on Tennyson. Mr. Noyes is not one to make half-claims. That Tennyson was a master of onomatopoeic verse, of vowel-sounds, of metres, and of rhythms is a plain fact which to deny is only to show oneself word-blind or cowardly conventional. Mr. Noyes claims much more for him than that. His examination of Tennyson's technical methods and his exposition of details in it make the best study of the subject that we know; but he does not leave us with the idea that to imitate the cooing of doves or the noise of waves upon a cliff or of armour clanging on rock is the last purpose of poetry. This technical skill is the means, the only means as Mr. Noyes sees the matter, of expressing subtle thoughts, high thoughts, difficult thoughts. Tennyson can tell the story of geology or of evolution in a few lines, not because he is a man of science, but because he is a poet, a master of words which are the doors to thought. And from the intellectual we pass to the spiritual. Mr. Noyes is, we think, a little hard on science. He does not realize how far in recent years science has turned from its downward path toward the particular, upward toward becoming what Shelley called it, the sister of poetry. But that does not affect his argument. . . .

We welcome the paper on Shelley all the more because it defends his poetry, not against the rebels of the present day, but against those very Victorians who chiefly damned it with faint praise. Mr. Noyes, of course, in speaking well of Shelley or of Wordsworth, lays himself open to the charge of being a "conventional," who will side with any revolution that has won the day; and the stress that he lays on Shelley as "the poet of light" (might he not equally well be named "the poet of water"?) smacks a little of the trick of seeing only one thing at a time which our critic blames in others. But here, better than in the bold plea for Emerson and the easily disputable judgment on Henley, we have the complement of the paper on Tennyson, and the constructive criticism which, like poetry itself, is a channel for the universal and eternal truth and beauty.

"Mr. Noyes's Essays," in The Times Literary Supplement, *No. 1185, October 2, 1924, p. 608.*

WILLIAM ROSE BENÉT   (essay date 1925)

Mr. Noyes revivifies legend. His "**Orpheus and Eurydice**" seems to me one of the finest lyrical achievements of our time. In fact, the man is a far better poet than the critics of the day will allow. And for this he is, himself, chiefly to blame. He has written too much, his reach has frequently exceeded his grasp, and he has become absorbed in delivering a "message." Consequently a great many of his poems have degenerated into propaganda for his own particular vision of Christianity. He takes the pulpit. In "**Some Aspects of Modern Poetry**" he takes the pulpit again. He is going to save the age from its critical chaos, its lack of standards, its Bolshevism in the arts.

Mr. Noyes is dogmatic. He cannot understand why in our modern books we cry at one moment that we are agnostics, quite firmly assume the world to be meaningless, and then, in the next breath are thrilled, perhaps, by the sight of a sunset. But I do not see why that should so puzzle a human being among human beings. It seems to me that the last thing human beings are is logical and consistent. Agnosticism is simply a frank recognition of human inconsistency. Atheism appears to me to be a foolish dogmatism, but so does Mr. Noyes's insistence that all who do not believe in a God, or an Infinite Power, or a Great Idea, behind the universe are trivial if not wicked. . . .

There is to me something extremely depressing in Mr. Noyes's "**Some Aspects**," not because he praises certain masters of another era, but because he seems to be so utterly unaware of anything of real moment that is being done in our own time.

Mr. Noyes is enraged by our time, especially by the poetry of our time. Of the only modern American poet he cites, Carl Sandburg, he displays as galling an ignorance as the ignorance of the versifying mayflies that disgust him so when they ridicule Tennyson. He displays an utter ignorance of the merits of James Joyce, whose "Ulysses" he roundly denounces in good set terms. He declares indeed, inferentially, Mr. Joyce's "A Portrait of the Artist as a Young Man" is "contemptible in every respect" and the praise of Joyce a "national disgrace." Nowhere does he mention names or titles, but those are the names and the titles. . . .

Elsewhere in his volume of critical essays, which are only mildly critical save when the terms "radical," "free verse," "Bolshevism," act as a red rag to Mr. Noyes's suddenly congested gaze and he is off on a rampage—elsewhere in this volume the poet has some shrewd true things to say upon the merits of the poetry of Emerson, Tennyson, Longfellow, Alice Meynell, Henley, Stevenson, and Austin Dobson—upon Shakespeare, Wordsworth, Shelley and Swinburne. He is chiefly concerned with a counterattack upon modern critics who would belittle the achievement of these poets, especially of Tennyson and Longfellow.

In speaking of Stevenson, Mr. Noyes endeavors to prove that the verses in a "Child's Garden" bear a significance and present a symbolism which, it seems to me, were certainly not in the mind of the author at the time of their composition. He also underestimates Henley's "odes, anthemes, and voluntaries," while adequately praising his powers of portraiture. Tennyson keeps recurring in almost every essay, until even the mind that, at the outset, found itself quite in sympathy with the defense of a master "out of fashion" begins to weary of Tennyson's perfections. Longfellow is greater in the ballads of King Olaf and in Scanderbeg than in anything Mr. Noyes quotes. But in his slighter essays on "**Some Cambridge Poets**" and on **"James Thomson"** this grand marshal of the heroic past suddenly becomes less oracular and more curiously pleasant, and his paper on **"The Spirit of Touchstone"** expounds a valid and interesting theory.

We wish the violent pulpiteering were absent from this volume, for Mr. Noyes knows great verse when he sees it, and can explain its merits. He takes much too seriously the lunatic fringe of contemporary poetic experimentation, and, as we have said, seems entirely blind to a certain solid amount of contemporary accomplishment. He frequently construes personal irritation as righteous wrath. . . .

Mr. Noyes is a reckonable poet. He will continue to waste his energies in mere religiosity, will continue to exercise his Messiah complex. He will leave to this generation a handful of poetry eventually to be recognized as genuine, original and refreshing. The rest is silence.

William Rose Benét, "What Kind of a Noyes—?" in The Saturday Review of Literature, Vol. I, No. 26, January 24, 1925, p. 476.

OLIVER LODGE (essay date 1925)

Mr. Noyes's method, in [**"The Book of Earth"**] as in his previous volume [**"Watchers of the Sky"**], is to throw himself back in time, so as sympathetically to represent the feelings and gradual glimmerings of the past, as if he were a sympathetic and privileged spectator; picking out, as before, certain typical individuals, and displaying what he conceives to be their thoughts and hopes, and the way in which their discoveries might have appealed to them at the time; utilizing for this purpose any recorded fragments of conversation or speech or writing, and amplifying these fragments by sympathetic and dramatic interpretation. . . .

[He takes] as his typical representatives Pythagoras, Aristotle, Leonardo, Linnaius, Lamarck, Goethe, and Darwin, introducing incidently many others, such as Pascal, Buffon, Cuvier, Lyell and other less known names. . . .

This volume, which deals with the study of the earth, its natural features, its fossils, its living creatures, and the problems and possibilities underlying them all, opens with a vision of the Grand Canyon in Colorado as one of the most impressive of terrestrial scenes—the relics of whose time-expunged and distorted and superposed strata speak of extravagant antiquity. Then it goes back to early human efforts of knowledge, as sympathetically seen by one who in imagination can revisit and gain glimpses of the past. So onwards, through a variety of imaginative incidents, and the dangerous turmoil of a people's revolution. The volume concludes, curiously but impressively, with the comparatively modern conflict between science and theology, as dramatized by the well known episode of the verbal controversy between Huxley and Bishop Wilberforce at a British Association Meeting in Oxford. The methods of controversy are here well exemplified: the triumph of Huxley as he stands for the honor of science, as opposed to the frivolous dependence on documents dating from times of comparative ignorance, and as denouncing the obscurantism so constantly associated with professional dependence on tradition,—this is brought out on the one hand, and then it is shown how this triumphant certainty of opposition to falseness and prejudice is nevertheless combined with humility and doubt, when confronted, not with the ravings of men but with the eternal grandeur of nature herself.

Oliver Lodge, "Pioneers of Science," in The Saturday Review of Literature, Vol. II, No. 1, August 1, 1925, p. 5.

PERCY A. HUTCHISON (essay date 1925)

It is by a curious coincidence that Mr. Alfred Noyes's **"The Book of Earth"**—which is Book 2 of the trilogy, **"The Torch Bearers,"** and has for its theme the evolutionary interpretation of creation—should have made its appearance so shortly after the trial in Dayton focused public attention upon the question of evolution. Not since "Paradise Lost" has there been so serious an attempt as Mr. Noyes's to interpret through the medium of poetic verse the history of man and man's relation to God. It is, therefore, with "Paradise Lost" that **"The Book of Earth"** challenges comparison.

Yet at the very outset it must be admitted that the wide gulf which separates the two poems places certain difficulties in the way. In "Paradise Lost" Milton took the compressed biblical account of creation and expanded it. The room thus provided for the range of the poet's powers of pictorial imagination were all but limitless. Mr. Noyes, by reason of the fact that he deals directly with events and more with intellectual origins, largely cuts himself off from such opportunities. . . . His achievement, consequently, must be judged more upon its intellectual worth than upon the color and the breath and the animation of the painted scene. Whether Mr. Noyes was wise in the method of approach chosen—whether, indeed, he did not willfully blind himself to the tremendous poetic possibilities which opened before him the moment he elected to treat poetically the theme of evolution—is a question which may be postponed for the moment. Before attempting to say what Mr. Noyes might have done, it is first necessary to see just what it is that he has done. (p. 12)

Even in the structure of the blank verse is this challenge made, for if Mr. Noyes's line is not so sonorous as Milton's it is more flexible, and in its thrust and parry more delicately adjusted to a scientific interpretation of creation than would have been the Miltonic line. In other words, Mr. Noyes's verse is adequate to his theme; and his theme is an exalted one.

On the other hand, this theme, despite its loftiness, when the effect has passed away, leaves the reader cold, as he is not left cold when the effect of "Paradise Lost" has passed away. But this is not to condemn Noyes any more than it is to elevate Milton. The cause goes deeper. In the biblical account man is the central figure; in the scientific account man falls from his heights. He is but a part of a creation which is vastly larger and more important than himself. The human element—and because the human element the most truly profound poetic element—is absent from **"The Book of Earth"** just in proportion as it is present and all-pervading in "Paradise Lost." Evolution, because of the subordination of the human element, can never make good its hold on man's imagination. When Arnold said "the strongest part of our religion today is its unconscious poetry" he spoke not merely for today but for all days.

We cannot but feel, to come back to our beginning, that Mr. Noyes would have done better to have avoided his philosophers and his scientists and followed in colorful verse the pageant of evolutionary processes. But this he did not elect to do; and it will remain a theme for some later poet to undertake. Nevertheless, the net result would not have been different. Man would still be subordinate. **"The Book of Earth"** will not live as ''Paradise Lost'' has lived because of the lacking human factor. But because of its epic sweep, its dramatic power, most of all because of the loftiness of the design—Mr. Noyes's epic may not be neglected. It is a modern attempt in the ''grand manner'' of Dante and Milton. It is not entirely the poet's fault if failure was from the outset inherent in whatever might be his measure of success. (p. 23)

> Percy A. Hutchison, '''The Book of Earth','' in The New York Times Book Review (© 1925 by The New York Times Company; reprinted by permission), August 30, 1925, pp. 12, 23.

EDWARD DAVISON   (essay date 1928)

Mr. Alfred Noyes has generally been associated, at least in name, with Mr. Rudyard Kipling and Sir Henry Newbolt in the so-called ''imperialistic'' school of modern English poetry, and thus, although he is not yet fifty, it is very easy to think of him as one of the older poets. (p. 199)

Mr. Noyes had not discovered any particular idiom of his own with which to match Mr. Kipling's individual voice; but his choice of poetic material was generally acceptable, pleasant, appealing, full of crude movement, good stories, whispers of fairyland, coarse music and romantic colours. He wrote ''poetic'' poetry; he was not afraid of rhetoric. (p. 200)

''Drake'' with its pseudo-epical quality and patriotic appeal sealed his temporary fame and Mr. Noyes was everywhere praised prematurely as a great poet. Then, with the outbreak of war and the sudden flux of ''new'' poetry, his reputation suffered a gradual decline. His earlier work was not vital enough to last in the memory. . . . Mr. Noyes was never so much of a jingoist as Mr. Kipling, but in the pre-war years he allowed his verse to be over-influenced by topicalities, just as he tended to write poetry according to the popular conception of what poetry should be instead of according to the purer conception which is held in his various critical essays on the work of other poets. (pp. 201-02)

In most of [Mr. Noyes's] earlier work there was too much rhetoric in the composition of the poetry. His ballads and many of his lyrics were padded with fustian verse between their higher passages. . . . Mr. Noyes has never been able to modify his very genuine enthusiasm for big (not necessarily long) words. He loves a plangent line, a ringing phrase. . . . Mr. Noyes frequently strains too far to be noble.

It is not until his later work that he succeeds in combining the elements of poetry and rhetoric. His earlier poems are crowded with gratuitous roses, moons, galleons, and all the paraphernalia of the ready-made romantic manner. He drags in the picturesque word, the bright-coloured symbol without always stopping to consider its fitness. A facile, though not really subtle metrist, he has usually been clever enough to dress such weaknesses in some kind of infectious rhythm.

Like many another English poet whose work reveals progressive improvement, Mr. Noyes appears to be known in America chiefly by this less satisfactory early work. . . . [His] more recent writings do not appear to be very well known by comparison with such volumes as *The Flower of Old Japan, Lord of Misrule,* and *The Forty Singing Seamen.* That this should be so is an unhappy irony in view of the fact that only during the past six years has he really achieved a poetry which compels high admiration. It is early as yet to attempt any valid criticism of *The Torch Bearers,* the ambitious trilogy, epic in its character

and proportions, of which the first two books only have been published. . . . In the first book, ''**Watchers of the Sky,**'' Mr. Noyes is concerned with the history of astronomy; in the second, ''**The Book of Earth,**'' he follows the discoveries of such men as Pythagoras, Aristotle, Leonardo, and Goethe in their struggles to solve the profound mysteries surrounding the origin and nature of man. This very ambitious poem springs directly from the author's genuine sense of wonder. I say genuine because the verse in which his ideas are conveyed rings true from the outset. Here is all the difference between his old and new work. This recent poem, which might so easily have toppled into dullness, is actually his most exciting work. Many of its best passages are executed in something akin to the grand manner. (pp. 202-06)

In his earlier work the language usually exceeded the ideas. If Mr. Noyes finds his final balance in the forthcoming and final book of *The Torch Bearers* we may expect a really important contribution to the poetry of this decade, something far superior to anything he has yet written.

Nevertheless the balance of his achievement is still quantitatively on the wrong side. . . . For a time the barrel organ has changed into something more nearly resembling a real organ. It is impossible not to grant some real justification to the poets and critics in England who have refused to concede high honours to Mr. Noyes's verse when we consider it as a whole. To put the matter in a colloquial nutshell, he has failed in the dangerous attempt to eat his cake and have it too. He has not been able to create an audience of poetry-lovers out of an audience of verse-likers. He will not easily win the confidence of those who recognized the comparative coarseness of his previous work. On the other hand, very few of the people who admired ''**The Barrel Organ**'' (Come down to Kew in lilactime) will be likely to appreciate *The Torch Bearers,* for it belongs to an altogether different class of literature. . . . The difference between these poems by Mr. Noyes is between two planes of writing, the one poetry, the other, ordinary picturesque verse, making a bid for the praise of the multitude. Mr. Noyes has not really deserved to be treated as an important poet until quite recently. In general his verse may be divided into one of the two categories suggested above. They have little to do with his subject-matter as such, or even with his mood. (pp. 208-09)

Mr. Noyes has never lacked facility in making verses. Facility may almost be said to have been his curse. Even at its best his verse is rather too uneconomical to rank with the very finest contemporary work. He multiplies words to gain effects that other living poets would achieve in half the space and with half the apparent energy . . . It may be remarked as a slight but significant instance that he has always relied to a suspicious degree upon the extraneous aid of punctuation to emphasize his meaning and metre. . . . For the art of Mr. Noyes is seldom so skilful as to be able to dispense with these extraneous aids. They indicate better than anything else the shortcomings of his artistry. The first-class poet only uses such devices as a means to emphasize something already carefully emphasized in his words, and even then, with scrupulous economy. In most instances they will be superfluous. In the poetry of Mr. Noyes they are seldom superfluous . . . . (pp. 212-13)

He works best on a large canvas. . . . His effects at their best are the bold and generous kind apparent in ''**Drake**'' and *The Torch Bearers.* He cannot command those delicate subtleties of sense and sound that mark so much of what is typical in the work of his best contemporaries. But it would be a great mistake to let this lack obscure his characteristic, and sometimes peculiar, virtues. . . . The truth is that underneath all his noisy optimism, melodrama and rhetoric (discounting for the moment those earlier jingles wherein he made a bid for immediate popularity) there exists a mind of large and generous quality, ever ready in sympathy, sensitive to the eternal struggle between man and his problems. When he touches upon the eternal verities—increasing age, death, love in its nobler aspect, the shackles often fall away and he becomes wholly free of the larger world of poetry. (pp. 214-15)

Perhaps the greatest merit of Mr. Noyes's work—and it cannot be too highly praised today—is its simplicity and straightforwardness. If anything he dots too many I's and crosses too many T's. He means just what he says and no more. Occasionally, unfortunately, he perhaps means even less than he appears to say. His verse, even when it deals, as in *The Torch Bearers*, with the very quality and range of the human intellect, can never be called intellectual. The reader cannot plunge through depth after depth of parallel meaning. . . . In the strictest sense of the word Mr. Noyes is a simple poet—"elementary," or "obvious" might be better words if we could divorce them from certain uncomplimentary connotations. He is to be compared with Longfellow rather than with Wordsworth in this matter of simplicity. One does not return to his earlier poetry with the knowledge that each new reading will increase one's sense of its significance. Its values are face-values; its music, plain song, seldom harmonic. Only in the longer, later, more ambitious work is there a hint of a fuller purpose. In *The Torch Bearers* Mr. Noyes set out to conquer new latitudes of poetry. It will be interesting to see what treasure he ultimately brings home. (pp. 216-17)

> Edward Davison, "Alfred Noyes" (originally published in a slightly different form in The English Journal, *Vol. XV, No. 4, April, 1926), in his* Some Modern Poets and Other Critical Essays *(copyright 1928 by Harper & Brothers; copyright renewed © 1955 by Edward Davison, reprinted by permission of Harper & Row, Publishers, Inc.), Harper & Row, 1928, pp. 197-218.*

WALLACE B. NICHOLS (essay date 1929)

Coming to the work of Mr. Alfred Noyes after a certain interval, it has been interesting to try to assess the permanence of the earlier impressions. . . . I thought then, and I still think, that Mr. Noyes has three gifts in prominence: the power of narration, the instinct for colour and tone in verse, and the quality of spontaneity.

Few poets whose verse is as consciously wrought as his—by which I mean verse which has real craftsmanship—are as free from academic "patterning" or verbal preciosity. Mr. Noyes's technique is always fullbodied, but it is not niggling; it is fluid and limpid. He may be upon occasion—often the right occasion—rhetorical, but he is never turgid. His blank verse, though it may derive to some extent from the Tennysonian method, especially in the habit of ending a statement by a full line rather than by the Miltonic half-line or quarter-line, is original and personal in its tone values, but perhaps less original in movement, in sentence-sweep. He can vary its pauses well and learnedly; but occasionally I feel that he should be more on guard against a certain mannerism. . . .

Turning to colour and tone in verse, Mr. Noyes's instinct needs no criticism. . . . The Prologue to "The Torchbearers" and "Earth and Her Birds," to mention no other examples, are

proofs of a delicate receptiveness to word-values that few of his contemporaries possess, though one or two may have a greater mastery of atmospheric suggestion. . . .

But when we turn to the power of narrative in Mr. Noyes we are at once on less challengeable ground. I doubt if any living poet has power of narrative in the grand manner to the same extent as the author of **"Tales of the Mermaid Tavern"** and **"The Torchbearers."** . . . Mr. Noyes is obviously nearer to the Chaucers and the narrative masters than to the Shelleys and the more lyrical singers. He seems to me to be in the direct line from Chaucer, and I question if "The Canterbury Tales" has had a more varied authentic successor than **"Tales of the Mermaid Tavern."**

But Mr. Noyes is a lyric poet also. . . . [In] the lyrical form he is not always so successful, for he is apt to be diffuse, to continue rather longer than he should. . . . A lyric is twice lyrical when it is brief. Mr. Noyes here sins among a vast company.

Perhaps the least happy of his poems are his sonnets. None of the examples in the sonnet form in ["**Ballads and Poems"**] seem to me to have the real sonnet touch. They are not constricted enough, nor is their music sufficiently organ-toned or swelling to the climax. Again, there is a curious lack of the dramatic sense. The last lines of Mr. Noyes's sonnets are nearly always weaker than the first.

But, these few strictures made, there is a wealth of beauty and music in the work of Mr. Noyes that is of a rare quality. He is almost alone in the present time in having the feeling for large design. He is no "idle singer," but fills his verse with a noble seriousness that looks back to the larger tradition. He is, above all, a narrative poet. (p. 226)

Mr. Noyes, because he belongs to no coterie and believes that to be traditional is still to be vital, has had many foolish stones cast at him by those who consider that Art cannot be Art unless it is dressed in the latest ephemeral fashion, and perhaps a little outrageously. . . . Mr. Noyes, when all the stones have been cast, remains a poet in lineal descent, a poet of a wider range than have the majority of his contemporaries, though I would not claim for him a subtler reach nor a more magnetic intensity. But in one province of the Muse he has no present-day compeer. The narrative poet of **"Drake," "Tales of the Mermaid Tavern"** and **"The Torchbearers"** stands alone for vivid and equable achievement. (p. 227)

> Wallace B. Nichols, "Alfred Noyes," in The Bookman, *London, Vol. LXXV, No. 448, January, 1929, pp. 226-27.*

WALTER JERROLD (essay date 1930)

In the case of the work of Alfred Noyes it seems to me best to consider it in broad divisions of diversity, rather than as a succession of volumes chronologically displayed, even though such divisions must of necessity have boundaries that no commission of experts could definitely determine. Presenting the poet's work chronologically might illustrate his development as a singer, show the constancy of certain qualities in his work, the growth of what might be termed the sense of poetic responsibility, an increasing command of his great medium—most notably perhaps in the use of blank verse which, compared with the earlier essays, acquired a great ease and certain floridity in *Drake,* and perhaps something of a simpler dignity in his lately completed trilogy—*The Torch-Bearers.* (pp. 25-6)

The completion of the remarkable trilogy in which Alfred Noyes has set forth the story of scientific discovery makes it appropriate to start an attempted appreciation of his work generally with a particular examination of the "**Torch-Bearers**"—a great essay in objective poetry in which the poet may be said to give fine expression to the best thought of his time no less surely than Tennyson suggested the half-wistful hesitancy between faith and doubt of his period in *In Memoriam.* . . . [It] may well be that this brave undertaking is the work which will stand as Noyes's most distinctive achievement. It *was* a brave undertaking, for to the non-scientific reader the suggestion that a work deals with Science is more likely to act as a repellent than an attraction; and here in a new sense it might almost be said of Noyes . . . that he was making omni-science his foible, so varied were the fields which he had to explore before he could present his greatly conceived story in its tripartite fulness. How thoroughly he carried out that exploration, with what astonishing sureness he fixed on the particular "moments" best suited to his poetic treatment can only be appreciated by a reading of the three volumes; how effectively he rendered those moments and linked them with something like epic unity even the least scientifically minded of us can realise with delight.

Although *The Torch-Bearers* is in three parts, published at intervals of some years, the unity of design is preserved, and far from there being any diminishing of the power recognised in the first portion, the impressive fervour of the story has been maintained in continuity, while the sure touch of the poet has if anything but strengthened as he neared the close where the affirmations of science neighbour the beliefs of religion—and that reuniting of truth and beauty which he adumbrated at setting out is achieved. Truth and beauty are, indeed, to be found all through the successive stages of the presentation of those moments by which knowledge grew from more to more, his rendering of which affords splendid justification of the poet's confidence. This may be taken as providing further evidence that poetry is a more effective and a more concise medium than prose. . . . No prose work of like length could indeed make real for us the story of science as does *The Torch-Bearers;* it might set forth certain outlines, facts in the annals of astronomy, geology, botony, and other of the many sciences illuminated, and even do that more briefly, but the spirit, the significance, the impressiveness, even the essential reality of which the mere facts are but part, would be lacking. (pp. 27-30)

The poet who could so happily apply a figure taken from science has imagined the successive workers on the problems of the universe as torch-bearers, each enabled to throw light on some new patch of knowledge during his short life, and then consciously or unconsciously passing on the torch to another who should, in his turn, throw the light a little further before he, too, passed it on to a successor. Here was an epic subject; not one with any individual dominating hero as in the conventional idea of an epic, but one of which Man comprehensively may be said to be the hero. (p. 31)

Those who elect to say what Noyes might have essayed would be better engaged in appraising what he has actually achieved; he elected to illustrate the march of human knowledge by rendering in verse certain "great moments" of scientific progress, and he has done so in a way that is at once strikingly effective, deeply impressive, and rich in beauty.

The first portion of the work, dealing with the astronomers and all that they have discovered was itself hailed as an achievement. . . . (pp. 33-4)

In strong blank verse, varied by the occasional introduction of lyrics, the author presents the succession of moments which he has selected for illustrating his central idea—the way in which Science in its patient ascertainment of the laws governing the planet on which we live and the universe to which it belongs, leads "to vision of that one Power which guides the world." (pp. 35-6)

Each of the great watchers of the skies . . . is shown as the central figure of an episode, now romantic, now dramatic, but always significant as marking a stage in the great human effort to blaze the way of knowledge into the depths of the universe and the Infinite. (pp. 37-8)

From Pythagoras, with his belief in the transmigration of souls, we pass to Aristotle, and the true beginning of the central subject of the "**Book of Earth**," the growth of that new knowledge concerning the transformation of bodies which was to take final shape in the nineteenth century over two thousand years later as the theory of evolution. . . . Each successive stage is realised both philosophically and visually by the poet so thoroughly that he is able to place it convincingly and vividly before the reader, and with different climes, different ages, different men, all working with the one great object of making the bounds of knowledge wider yet, there is never monotony of theme or treatment, the author's mastery of his blank verse medium imparting to it a flexibility makes it serve alike for bright description, for quick dialogue, or philosophical monologue. (pp. 47-8)

The largest single section of this second part of the trilogy of *The Torch-Bearers* is that which deals with the latest great advance in the reading by Science of the Book of Earth—the enunciation of the theory of evolution, as established by Charles Darwin. Here, dealing with recent events, instead of those which have over them something of the glamorous atmosphere of the more distant past the poet has, it seems to me, been peculiarly successful where something short of success might have been predicated. (p. 51)

In the second portion of *The Torch-Bearers,* the author showed no falling off in his treatment of his great theme, and with the concluding volume of the trilogy, after an interval of nearly five years, he rises once more to the height of his great argument in dealing with the deeper question—to what end is this scientific unification of the world, with its annihilation of Time and Space, and its linking of mankind in an organic interdependence leading us? (p. 59)

Through the whole series of theme-linked poems that make up the epical story of *The Torch-Bearers* there is an emphasising of the idea of the beauty of all-penetrating law. To this the poet again and again gives new and impressive expression. Carry the search for knowledge as far as we may we come ever at last to that sense of the Great Unknowable where the most penetrating searcher and discoverer can do no more than share the candlelight of the simplest possessor of faith. . . . (pp. 60-1)

[*Drake*] stands as a vivid and forceful poetic presentation of the story of the rise of England's sea-power with Drake as the central figure, the dominating one of the earlier part, before the narrative has swept towards that splendid close where the poet with impressive passages of great descriptive power brings on Spain's "Invincible" Armada and follows it to its disastrous fate. . . . It is a great story, greatly told. The author's opulent powers of description find fitting material on which to lavish themselves. . . . (pp. 69-70)

Noyes had the courage to take a subject of almost recent modernity. Drake is a national hero, and the poet has seen him as the central figure in a period of momentous action. . . . It is easy to say that the theme of those great years of that latter part of the 16th century is an epic one, but Noyes, accepting the fact, has emphasized it by achievement. Even those who took up the new work with some misgivings readily acknowledged those misgivings as in part if not entirely agreeably disappointed. (p. 71)

Whatever may be the details to which one or other critic may take exception, the whole is a finely impressive performance, and it may be claimed that—widely as they differ—Alfred Noyes's *Drake* worthily companions Thomas Hardy's *The Dynasts*, a modern achievement in such an imaginatively realised presentation of history as can never be attained by a prose historian.

In this comment on the poem as a whole, nothing has yet been said of the way in which Noyes broke away from conventional epic regularity by interspersing the narrative with lyrics, some of them of very sweet note and haunting beauty, and on occasions by passing into rhymed verse. Thus in following the account of the Spanish Armada's sweeping up the Channel, almost imperceptibly we find that we have passed from blank verse to rhyme. . . . (p. 78)

It is only towards the close of his poem that the poet . . . passes to the using of rhyme in his narrative; in the earlier part, lyrical "swallow-flights" are employed to vary the continuity of the blank verse, and as it is recorded that Drake took "skilled musicians" with him on the voyage to the West the interpolating of those lyrics may be regarded as historically appropriate. Tennyson had thus used the lyric to vary a blank verse narrative, but Noyes more daringly challenged convention in turning to rhyme in accordance with the changing mood of the story he was unfolding, as it passed from the time of individual dogged determination to the supreme realisation of national achievement. The whole poem moves with so much vigour, is lit by so much vision, is remarkable for so many beautiful passages of impressive poetry, and so many vividly picturesque scenes, that it is something like quibbling over an unimportant detail to concentrate on discussion as to whether it is or is not to be described as being technically an epic. It is at least a magnificently moving and memorable narrative poem, the reading of which is productive of present delight and an enriching of the memory. (pp. 82-3)

It is to no small extent the lyrical quality pervading his narrative work that gives it much of its charm; and perhaps it is the lyrical spontaneity of the poet that has made some of his critics reproach him with being over-facile—a reproach which might as well be addressed by the tongue-tied to the gifted orator. Combined with this gift—"sweet-silvery, sheer lyrical"—are three qualities all of which adapt themselves happily to the purposes of the lyrist: sensuous joy of beauty, love of country and firmness of faith; three qualities which one of the earliest of his American critics emphasised as being characteristic of Noyes's work. (p. 88)

[It] was the charm of lyric spontaneity in Alfred Noyes that first won for him the delighted attention of many of us. It was to the lyric impulse of *The Flower of Old Japan* and *The Forest of Wild Thyme*, wedded to the weird, fanciful, tender adventurings in a world of the imagination, that we responded, "children and grown-ups too." The lyric impulse is observable in the poet's work even when it might well have been subordinated

to the severity of the form, as in blank verse and sonnets. I have heard it objected that his blank verse suffers from the singing note, and his warmest admirers would not I think claim a high place for his sonnets. (p. 89)

Alfred Noyes gives us many . . . glimpses "across the fringes of the fern," both in his lyrics, and his ballads, which are lyric-narratives. Love and beauty, colour and life, these are the themes infinite in their variety, that move him to music again and again—and all may be said to be combined in that delightful lyrical symphony, *The Progress of Love*, which in its varied measures, its tenderness and sadness, hints at the fuller, more direct, beauties of *The Forest of Wild Thyme*. (p. 91)

The lyric ease of Alfred Noyes lends itself especially to part wistful, part fanciful excursions about the border land of the fantastic. . . . This same lyric ease is well employed also in pieces that approach the ballad in theme yet possess greater elasticity of presentation than is afforded by the ordinary ballad metre. (pp. 92-3)

Noyes lavishes in his lines something of sunlit water colour. He might, indeed, if regarded only from these colourful lyrical pieces of his, be termed the Turner of poets—imparting to the reader something of that uplifting feeling of delight which we get when looking upon the joyous colour sketches of the prime master of joy in painting. It is joy in life—in being one with the sun and the wind, the birds and the flowers; in belonging to a great nation and a great race—that we find the poet expressing again and again; although it should be added that he is far removed from the idle optimistic insistence upon joy where joy is not. It would be quite easy to cite poem after poem informed with high purpose, with intense patriotism, with fervent belief in the faith that the ways of God may be justified to man—to stress, in a word, the poet's consciousness of poetic responsibility in so far as that is made manifest in work the high aim of which is obvious; but merely to do so would be to do scant justice to that permeating characteristic which I have sought to summarise in the single word joy. In his faith, in his patriotism, in his excursions into philosophy, there is to be realised this sense of joy, latent if not finding its way to explicit utterance; and this is itself, consciously or unconsciously, the very expression of that sense of poetic responsibility inherent in the true poet. (pp. 97-8)

[It] may be admitted that some of us find the exuberance of the poet's expression, speaking broadly, least satisfactory when it is expended on those classical themes which make perennial appeal to successive generations of writers endowed with the gift of poetry. It is true that Noyes has a way of linking those themes with the living present in a manner that emphasises their immortality as expressions of Man's beliefs or aspirations; but the romantic method does not lend itself, or but rarely lends itself, to impressive presentation of classical subjects. (pp. 101-02)

Any division of the work of a poet possessed of the unity in diversity that is discoverable in Alfred Noyes must be more or less arbitrary. Though here it is some of the individual lyrics that are being indicated, the lyric note rings throughout his work, is as the instinctive impulse in which his poetry finds its way to expression, even when the poet has sought to shape his ideas within the more formal measures. In any of the broad divisions of his work that we may pause over, the lyrical will always be found contributing to the total effect—in the rollicking rhythms of such pieces as *The Barrel-Organ, Forty*

Singing Seamen, and many others; in the varied measures of the narratives; even in the blank verse of the epics, where the lyric impulse now and again seems to overmaster the poet and the statelier measure gives way to an outburst of song. (p. 117)

The Highwayman has not only made the most popular appeal of all his ballads, but has been described by a competent critic as being the best narrative poem in existence for oral delivery— it even "gets across" through the lips of an indifferent reciter. In it the poet invented or discovered one of those intensely moving tragical incidents that best lend themselves to ballad treatment, and has presented it as a sweeping, vigorously-told story in which the tender romance passes into terrible tragedy with something of inevitable swiftness. It has been objected by some readers that the poet has presented the story over pictorially, with an over-stressing of what may be termed the "local colour" of the period to which it belongs. The objection is of course but an individual one; if to the action of the story which he is telling the ballad writer adds that colour which it is one of his characteristics to visualise in seemingly sponta- neous fashion, his work should surely be regarded as enriched rather than marred thereby, in so far as the dramatic intensity of the story is not lessened by the decoration, as it certainly is not lessened in the instance of *The Highwayman* from which we get that thrill that comes on reading a fine rendering of something finely done. (pp. 119-20)

The song of England has been captured by Alfred Noyes with a fulness of note, a sweetness of tone, a fervour of love and a depth of understanding that combine to make it one of the most notable contributions to the poetic expression of his gen- eration, and it is on some of the diversified renderings of this song that I propose to touch. . . . The portion of his work which may thus be singled out as peculiarly English alike in theme and treatment, in its healthy robustness and its joyous note is by no means inconsiderable. (p. 132)

Here we have a writer—a score of his poems bear witness to it—who has seen that in the past of England there is a plenitude of things requiring but the touch of poetry to make them live again; things not only in the outstanding events of history— though many of them want resurrecting by vivifying imagi- nation from amid the cere-cloths of the school history books— but in the life of the people, in their traditions and in the lilt of old-time snatches of their song. With something of the free- dom of the great Elizabethans themselves he can take an old theme, or it may be a lyric scrap, or a phrase, and evoke from that seed a new and vital growth. (pp. 134-35)

It would not be easy to pick out any other single book that appears to have recaptured so well the life, the colour, the very spirit of the time as has this combination of lyric and narrative *Tales of the Mermaid Tavern.* The poet has not set out in any laboured attempt at archaism; he begins by describing a walk in one of those wonderful sunset hours with which London is occasionally set aglow, and, telling how he passes along Fleet Street towards St Paul's, greatly daring, does not hesitate to emphasise the modernity of things. . . . (p. 136)

Then from the present, and from that prophetic glance at the future, he seems to suggest the romantic relativity of all time by switching us with metrical magic into a past of more than three centuries ago. Future and the present that we know are blotted out as if by the passing of a hand across the eyes, and we are in a past that has become the present. (p. 137)

The *Tales of the Mermaid Tavern* make up a volume which must naturally stand in the forefront of any consideration of

its author's peculiarly English poems, breathing as it does the spirit of a great national period. Never, perhaps, at any other time was England so much England, lusty, self-conscious, self- contained and self-sufficing as in the days of Queen Elizabeth. (p. 139)

[In] introducing us to some of the great ones of the time in his assumed character of a "drawer," . . . Alfred Noyes does not seek to compel us to see them by any over-elaborate presen- tation, defeating his end of bringing the dead to life by sheer accentuation of detail, such as a novelist would feel impelled to employ. The poet does it rather in a flash of happy descrip- tion, by which he makes the reader realise the people whom he himself sees as real. (p. 141)

All through [the] tales told by members of the great company that gathered at the Mermaid Tavern we have the English spirit of the great time of Elizabeth rendered afresh in what may be described as terms of imaginative truth rather than in any self- conscious and painstaking effort after absolute accuracy of descriptive details. There is . . . a spiritual and mental real- isation, though the author does not hesitate to adopt and in- corporate some phrase or lyric snatch, in a manner clear to those acquainted with the literature of the period. . . . In these we have an imaginative re-living in a period rather than any attempt to depict it, and the success of the method as he applies it in poetry is perhaps most closely akin to that of Scott in prose fiction. (pp. 150-51)

Those readers who would sum up Alfred Noyes as rhetorician ignore one of the most beautiful, and to some of us one of the most fascinating of the broad divisions of his work—his ex- plorations of that land of faery which is remote as can be from the rostrum of rhetoric. Many of us who warmly welcomed the "new poet" of more than a quarter of a century ago were especially moved to admiration of excursions into those un- mapped territories . . .—vague wonderful places into which the poets alone, or those possessed of some share of the poetic spirit, can penetrate. (p. 166)

In *The Forest of Wild Thyme* we are taken to . . . that fairyland of here and now on which the poet insists again and again— fairyland, heaven, call it what you will. At setting out as though desirous of placating such critics as ask *cui bono?* about things of mere charm and beauty the young writer begged to be al- lowed to take one more hour in which to "hunt the fairy dream," after which, he said, "I'll light the lamp. I'll close the door." If by those words, he meant that he would devote himself to study and permit his fancy to go no more a-roaming in the fairyland of dream and imagination, we may feel thankful that the youthful resolve was not too closely adhered to. (p. 175)

Beauty of colour, of music, of fancy and a triumphant blending of the imaginative and the real have helped to create something that should long occupy a place among the classics in which children delight; while the underlying thought, the brave ex- pression of faith, the simple tenderness, add to the "fairy tale" something likely long to continue deeply moving to older read- ers. (p. 177)

In this tale . . . Noyes gave evidence of his mastery of varied rhythms, his happy instinct for bringing new music out of the matching of words in fresh metrical combinations. What is more, these two tales, so far as I can recall, stand alone as poems of some length that while designed for young readers (or listeners) remain poetry; and, though including much which is beyond the child's comprehension, do not fail to hold the child's attention. Many poets have written poetry that has been acceptable to, and dwelt in the memory of, childhood, but none other I think has made so sustainedly successful an effort as has the author of *The Flower of Old Japan* and *The Forest Wild Thyme.* (p. 183)

Examination of Alfred Noyes's work, in prose as well as in verse, reveals a fact which those who accept the conventional view of "Revolt" and "Tradition" have failed to observe,—namely, that he has been a consistent thinker in consistent "revolt" against that merely conventional view, and especially against that fundamental error of Victorian science and philosophy which insisted that the truth about the Universe must be reached along what he calls, in one of his essays, "The Diminishing Road," and through the explanation of the greater by the less. He goes back to the saying of the Greek philosopher that the order nature is the reverse of the order of thought, and that we must look for explanations, not in the first term of a series, but in the last. (pp. 232-33)

> *Walter Jerrold, in his* Alfred Noyes, *Harold Shaylor, 1930, 251 p.*

RICA BRENNER (essay date 1930)

"Alfred Noyes, ambassador," is what the poet might very aptly be called. . . . For he has been an ambassador of poetry to a people scornful or suspicious of the art; he has made poetry popular. But, more than that, to those grown old he has been ambassador of myth, of fairyland, and of childhood. . . . And at the same time, he has been an ambassador of simple truth and faith to those bewildered by the complexities of life. (p. 255)

It is with a fairy-like directness, a childlike optimism and faith that he reaches his conception of reality, his belief in a God who created the universe as a harmonious whole, whose laws—however unfathomable to man—exist and govern logically. (p. 256)

[Alfred Noyes] had a rich conception of poetry as a force that analyzes mankind's various activities, evaluates them, and, binding them together again, presents them as reflections of the soul of the universe. (p. 258)

Poetry for Noyes "is the revelation of the abiding beauty behind the transient." It must have the rhythm and the beat of music; it must be something that can be remembered. Furthermore, it is based on the past; and it is based on law. (p. 264)

This theory put into practice results in poetry that is simple and straightforward. It contains no very great subtleties; it is never unduly intellectualized. In method it carries on the tradition of the English poets of the past. Noyes is unalterably opposed to radicalism, and particularly to radicalism in verse, which he sees as an effort to upset necessary and logical laws. . . .

But if Noyes did not ally himself with the "new poetry," which he felt was formless, he did experiment with the old poetic forms, and succeeded in creating new rhythms and effects. (p. 265)

Noticeable in Noyes's verse is a spondaic effect, an effect which gives weight and emphasis to a line. This he achieves by the actual introduction of a spondee, a foot made up of two long syllables, as in the second foot of the line: "On the broad black breast of a midnight lake." Or, as is much more frequent, he achieves it by omitting the unaccented syllable from one or more of the feet in a line. (p. 266)

Even in so formalized a meter as blank verse, Noyes introduces modifications. His long blank-verse narratives are interspersed with delicate lyrics in totally different meters; and even the narrative itself may be punctuated with lines that vary from the required iambic pentameter. . . . In Book XI of *Drake*, the verse alternates between blank verse and a rhymed stanza, now one, now the other, to suggest the opposing movements of the English and the Spanish squadrons.

Perhaps nowhere is this flexibility of rhythm better expressed than in "The Barrel-Organ." Quotations of isolated lines will illustrate nothing. The poem should be read in its entirety to see how the meter changes to suggest the various songs the organ plays and the thoughts of the London people who hear its songs. (pp. 266-67)

In rhyme, Noyes shows an equal dexterity. Nimbly he uses double rhyme and internal rhyme. Rhymes seem to come spontaneously. (p. 267)

The subjects which lend themselves to Noyes as material for poetry are not necessarily the conventionalized subjects of the older poets—busses, coffee stands, tramps, did not appear with any frequency in their lines. But the treatment which he gives to them is traditional poetic treatment; they are made to shine with the glamor of fancy and romance. (p. 272)

Whether it be with humor or pathos, with wistfulness or direct energy, that Noyes presents his material, the variety of his moods is outnumbered by the variety of his subjects. Classical mythology, history, science, nature, philosophy—these all become the material for poems. Frequently, they are given a lyric treatment, as the love song of "The Return," or the country song of "A Devonshire Ditty," or the fancy of "Our Lady of the Twilight."

But however charming Noyes may be when singing his lyrics, he is happiest when telling a tale and creating the atmosphere for a story. "The Highwayman" is an example of compression and of rapid movement of incident; "The Admiral's Ghost," of the mystery and supernatural to be found in a folk ballad.

This narrative skill leads frequently to an epic and dramatic handling of the material of the past. This past, for Noyes, may be either the past of an individual—his childhood and his childhood fancies, as in "The Flower of Old Japan" and "The Forest of Wild Thyme"—or the past of a race, the tapestry of English history, as in "Sherwood." (pp. 273-74)

England's historical, as well as legendary, past gives Noyes inspiration for many poems. Particularly successful are the nine making up the *Tales of the Mermaid Tavern*. Whether or not these are historically accurate pictures is a matter of indifference; at all events, they possess poetic verity and satisfactorily re-create the Elizabethan spirit and the spirit of the group of frequenters at the Mermaid Tavern that numbered among its members Marlowe and Jonson, and Shakespeare. These do more than create atmosphere; they tell good stories, whether it be the whole-hearted, humorous tale of "Black Bill's Honeymoon," or the gentle one of "The Companion of a Mile," the familiar story of Dick Whittington in "Flos Mercatorum," the tragic death of Marlowe in "The Sign of the Golden Shoe," or the supernaturally moving one of "The Burial of a Queen."

Underlying these tales is the implication that the characters are more than people passing through adventures. They are, for Noyes, manifestations of England's greatness, forces contributing to the working out of England's destiny. This belief in England, this passionate devotion, colors almost all of Noyes's poetry. There are poems, like "Nelson's Year," "The Peacemaker," "To the Memory of Cecil Spring-Rice," "The Union," that were inspired by specific events and that prompted the suggestion in 1913, after the death of Alfred Austin, that Noyes be made Poet Laureate. There are poems that sing the love of the English country, poems like "A Devonshire Ditty," "The White Cliffs," "On the South Coast," "The World's May Queen." . . . (pp. 274-75)

These poems are made up of the flowers, and birds, the lanes, and the hedgerows of England. But most important as a symbol of England's position and of England's purpose is the sea; and the most important poem of England's greatness is *Drake*, the epic of the sea. However *Drake* may be criticized because of its structure, its loosely organized plot, its introduction of a personal love motif into the story of a nation, it nevertheless remains a sweeping tale of grandeur, with moving, thrilling incidents. The story of *Drake* is more than the tale of a conquering buccaneer; it is a panegyric of England as the champion of righteousness. Yet it is no confining patriotism that motivates Noyes. England is to be a liberating force, and her ideals are to embrace the world. (pp. 275-76)

It might seem unwise to place too heavy a burden of philosophy upon the poems of Alfred Noyes. When Noyes is most concerned with the logical, reasoned exposition of his philosophy, he is least successful as a poet. He is most successful when his poems are touched by his imagination and carry only an implied message. It is not for his philosophy that one returns to Noyes, but for his moving narratives, light with rhyme and rhythm. (p. 276)

In *The Torch-Bearers* he is creating a work that in plan and in method throws light upon and epitomizes his previous writing. . . .

The theme was long in the poet's mind. But the first volume, *Watchers of the Sky,* began to take definite shape when Noyes saw the first trial of the one-hundred-inch telescope at the Mt. Wilson Observatory in California. This volume tells the story of astronomy; the second, *The Book of Earth,* tells the story of the evolutionary interpretation of creation, the story of geology and biology; the third, not yet completed, is to tell the story of discovery in physics. (p. 277)

These stories have an essential unity. All the characters are on the same quest that Drake was on, that the children in "The Forest of Wild Thyme" pursued. And in their quest for truth, each realizes the dependence of his work upon the work of his predecessor and its importance for those who are to come after him. Each holds the torch of knowledge and hands it on. . . .

The truth which these torch-bearers find is not the truth of disillusionment, of negation, or of blind chance. It is the truth of faith, faith in a universe of harmonious law, in a law of love, in God. . . .

Fairyland, heaven—call it what you will—lies about us. This is the message of Noyes, the ambassador of poetry. Beauty and song he brings to those who will listen, and to those who will believe, love and an abiding faith. (p. 278)

Rica Brenner, "Alfred Noyes," in her Ten Modern Poets *(copyright 1930 by Harcourt Brace Jovanovich, Inc.; copyright 1958 by Rica Brenner; reprinted by permission of the publisher), Harcourt, 1930, pp. 253-79.*

PATRICK BRAYBROOKE   (essay date 1932)

In the title of this essay I have suggested that Alfred Noyes is a romantic poet. And I wrote this because I feel that Noyes unlike so many modern poets, is in a limited sense merry. I suggest that he is romantic because some of his best poetry has to do with *popular* romance. One of his most famous poems is deservedly known as a fine romantic poem. And that is "The Highwayman." There is true romance in this, getting back to the days when the roads were romantically dangerous because of highwaymen and not sordidly dangerous because of bad motor-drivers. There is even in his melancholy some keen degree of romance. For underlying all the poetry of Noyes we find a thrust after bravery, purity, hope. Life is for the poet worth living. He has none of the despair of Byron, the bitterness of some of the modern novelists, the hopeless paganism of so many of the writers of our own age. (pp. 174-75)

Alfred Noyes rightly is considered by many as a national poet. He has a great sense of English prestige. He has the further good sense to realise that a poet can express national emotions in a peculiarly perfect way. The national poet can express political opinions and yet be free from the suggestion of being a political poet. The national poet is the servant of his people. He has to attempt to express in words what they can only express in gestures patriotic and possibly vulgar. He has to interpret the collective emotions of a people for a country and treat of that country as though he were treating of a loved individual. Now Noyes is eminently fitted to fulfil these requirements. He is free from any suggestion of being a political poet. (pp. 176-77)

[Noyes] loves England because she is the very symbol and actual presentation of beauty. She is a certain bulwark, her way of life is sure, she will respond to the mood of the poet. In fact she is a very willing collaborator with him. She is broadminded in her affections and can show forth her charm both in rest and in movement. And she can call forth to her sons so that their blood thrills and finally she has a song that must be heard in heaven. The poet allows his imagination to soar, possibly a little dangerously, possibly savouring of an Imperialism slightly offensive. That is a danger I believe patriotic poets have to guard against. Believing rightly in the sanctity of their country, they are inclined to place her in a position specially near to Heaven, and there is thereby created a sense of exclusiveness that may blind to faults and lead to an intolerant attitude to others. I do not say that the verse I quote does this, but I do say that it leads in a direction that should keep the poet in a state of watchfulness to see that he does not go too far and turn patriotism into a suggestion that his country is particularly under Divine guidance. (pp. 178-79)

Noyes is fond of letting his verse tell a story. He falls pretty often into narrative verse of a considerable length. His "Drake" is the most outstanding example of this. The critics who object to narrative verse do so partly on the ground that a story "humanises" verse too much and partly on the ground that a poet may give too much attention to the story part of his poetry and too little to the technique. In the case of Noyes I cannot see that this criticism really applies at all. He keeps to a story and keeps to a high and elegant technique. Let us take just a few examples from his fine poem "Drake." The subject is obviously well chosen and is naturally acceptable to a poet who would write of England. . . . He tells us at the very outset that he has a simple tale to tell and his prayer goes to England that she will be his auxiliary in the task. And, indeed, she ought to help, for what indeed has Drake been to England? (pp. 180-81)

The art of Noyes does not in the least fail when the story of Drake reaches to high drama. Drake has to execute Doughty and the scene is exquisitely shown. Drake will not fail even in a duty the most unpleasant possible. And as if in sympathy with the grim solemnity of the occasion, the sun bows her head and all the world is dark. The scene leads swiftly to its deplorable climax—the perishing of a traitor. (p. 183)

And so we proceed to a picture of the great fleet smashed by Drake. The climax is sure and it is steady. Drake realises that he is but an instrument in the victory. Pure simple narrative marks the close of the great epic. . . .

The story has been told, there is no "poetic" polish and nothing exaggerated or underestimated. It is just the end to a big nautical adventure related in a very notable poem. (p. 184)

"**Drake**" proves, I think, that in the hands of a master craftsman narrative verse does not lose anything of the essential technique of poetry. It is true that there is not the same scope for "brilliance" as there is in other forms. It may be that this kind of verse does not allow as much "licence" as other kinds, that the proper word for this "licence" should be liberty. These two contentions may be true. And if they *are* true are they detrimental to true poetry? They are not directly, we admit that poetry is something very much more than form. And in a great poem like "**Drake**" the poet is only his own poetic master in so far as he does not let his story suffer. If we get a perfect blending of the story with the language in which it is told, we obtain narrative verse in perfection. And if we have this I see no good reason why this kind of perfection (if I can use perfection in a relative sense) should be alleged to be of an inferior nature. Alfred Noyes imparts a sense of dignity to his narrative verse. He proves what the modern man so often denies, that poetry is a practical art, that it can recreate the past as easily as prose, that it can be as dramatic as the prose of a dramatist. . . . (pp. 185-86)

For many people the most notable romantic poem written by Alfred Noyes is undoubtedly "**The Highwayman**." The whole poem is an absolute model of careful and skilled romanticism. There is not a line that the poem could have done without. Consider for a moment the background of the first verse. There is an old inn, and up to this old inn there's a highwayman riding. Heigh-ho and what cares he for the weather! What cares he that the wind is a torrent, what matters it to him that the moon sails along like a ghostly ship—what does he trouble that the road before him is like a bit of moonlight? The whole atmosphere of the first verse is magificent and magnificently real. Listen to the verse and then take a peep through the shutters for surely in the distance there has been the sound of a man riding fast, and he must ride fast if he wishes to get to the old inn before the doors are closed for the night. (pp. 187-88)

There is in this verse not only the accuracy of the background but there is the feeling of someone not only riding, but riding in haste and riding from far. And why does the highwayman ride so fast and so far? Because, oh it is so simple, he loved the landlord's daughter, and what is even more absurdly simple, she loves him and is loved by the ostler. So a trap is laid for the bold highwayman when next he comes up to the inn. We find the inn guarded by those who will shoot and kill the highwayman. And as they watch there rings out the clear sound

of the hoofs of a horse. Noyes makes the whole dramatic scene live as though we too watched from the old inn. (pp. 188-89)

This delightful poem, a bit of the real old romance of a bygone age, is deservedly popular. For there is about it a wonderful suggestion of movement, with the ever recurring sounds of the highwayman, riding, riding, riding. (pp. 189-90)

If we compare "**Drake**" with "**The Highwayman**" it will be seen that in two very different forms of the poetic art Noyes is a "true" poet. That is I mean that he does not expect his art to perform miracles for him. He gives it almost human qualties and allows it to express its different technique in a way that will not strain or hurt it. I am not at all sure that it would be critical to observe that Noyes is a poet who can transcend beauty and produce poetry of a "terrific" nature. I feel that in a way he is a very "sane" poet. He seems to me to know the limits of his craft and these limits are clearly defined. Noyes does not go in for mere beauty of language as did Shelley. His beauty in language is more or less accidental. I do not find in his work traces of a deep classical dependence that I discover in so many poets. I find rather an acute observation of contemporary life, a fine understanding of history and a tremendous sense, as I have emphasised, of the romantic. (pp. 190-91)

Patrick Braybrooke, "Alfred Noyes: Poet and Romantic," in his Some Victorian and Georgian Catholics: Their Art and Outlook, *Burns Oates & Washbourne Ltd., 1932 (and reprinted by Books for Libraries Press, Inc., 1966; distributed by Arno Press, Inc.), pp. 171-202.*

OSBERT SITWELL   (essay date 1935)

A very active man is Mr Noyes. A dozen or so books of verse stand to his credit; it would not, therefore, be fair . . . to expect every poem in every book to be a good one.

But these verses are tiring to read, and must have been more so, surely, to write? No posture is so fatiguing as that of defence, when no enemy is attacking; no attitude more undignified than that of assault, when there is no enemy to attack. Mr Noyes believes in vigorous hitting; but the wooden antagonists which he himself has constructed fall down directly he hits them, and in falling, invariably injure their maker. Two things, it is evident, Mr Noyes cannot abide—the progressive in politics, the Bolshevik in poetry.

As we know, a properly brought-up bull, sharing Mr Noyes's antipathy to Bolshevism, will charge anyone or anything, however faintly tinged with red. But even a bull, an animal perhaps with greater reputation for courage than for intelligence, chooses his colour carefully, whereas Mr Noyes go further: he sees red first, and then charges! If he charges, the object of his assault must be red.

In the intervals of his many books, between an epic on science, a whirlwind tour of the American universities or a masterly raid on the tomb of Drake, our active hero spends much time in defending Tennyson and other Victorian idols, clearing their characters for ever of crimes of which they have never been accused. But, though privileged to hear Mr Noyes's opinion of the late Lord Tennyson, never—except in our own hearts—shall we be privileged to know Alfred Lord Tennyson's view of Mr Alfred Noyes. It is, however, our own conviction that there would have been trouble between the two Alfreds had they been contemporary; that His Lordship might even have risen from his seat as hereditary legislator to demand the impeachment of the younger Alf.

Mr Noyes's verse, we take it, is intended to follow up and justify his defence of the great who have preceded him. The quality, we are given to understand, shared by Swinburne, Tennyson, Keats and Noyes is that of "singing". . . . But to sing is not really sufficient. No one has ever accused Mr Noyes of not "singing". "Come down to Kew in lilac time" should have been—and perhaps was—whistled by every errand boy in town. **"Pagan Marjorie"** and **"Fey Joan"** . . . manifest the same quality. Alas! the effect of all this "singing" is but to make us prefer quiet. If Mr Noyes *must* "sing," it would be easier to bear if he would even sing flat occasionally, or do something unexpected.

But the process of his ratiocination, even more that his singing, is at fault. Mr Noyes argues, in effect, but with much force: "Tennyson was a great poet. He was also, occasionally a great bore. I am sometimes a bore. . . . Therefore I am a great poet." (pp. 335-37)

> *Osbert Sitwell, "Ta-ra-ra-boom-de-ay!: The Muse of Alfred Noyes," in his* Penny Foolish: A Book of Tirades & Panegyrics *(reprinted by permission of David Higham Associates Limited, as agents for the Literary Estate of Osbert Sitwell), Macmillan, London and Basingstoke, 1935 (and reprinted by Books for Libraries Press, 1967; distributed by Arno Press, Inc.), pp. 334-38.*

DEREK STANFORD   (essay date 1958)

[In Alfred Noyes] there existed two strains of mind seldom discoverable together. The first was a vein of popular imagination, reponsible for such justly famous lyrics as *The Barrel-Organ, A Highwayman, Dick Turpin's Ride,* and *A Song of Sherwood,* as well as for less felicitous but none the less rousing narrative compositions in the manner of [*Drake* and *Tales of the Mermaid Tavern*]. . . . The second strain was one of scientific curiosity, and led to the three-volume 'epic' *The Torch-bearers* . . . , in which the poet celebrated the great figures of European Science: Copernicus, Galileo, and others. It was also, in part, from this vein that he wrote, after entering the Roman Church, two works of unusual apologetic: [*The Unkown God* and *Voltaire*]. . . . Here, with a deal of originality, he tried to show that the scientific spirit had reached certain conclusions consonant with the Nicene Creed. Science, he suggested, was opposed to religion only in so far as it adopted a positivist temper foreign to its true workings. The agnosticism proper to the scientific spirit was essentially one of openness and wonder. . . . Chief of [his] pitfalls was the poet's proneness to a kind of romantic over-simplification. With a limited theme, as in *The Highwayman,* this could result in conservation of strength—in stark, rapid, and graphic narration—but where the canvas and cast were larger, as in the blank-verse 'epic' *Drake,* the complexity of historical conflict was reduced to that of a boy's tale. . . . Even more is the lack of psychological subtlety apparent in the *Tales of the Mermaid Tavern,* where Elizabethan literary low-life is given an idealistic silver lining. Noyes's treatment of Marlowe's death is an instance of this unrealistic approach. (p. 86)

In pin-pointing Noyes's strength as a poet, we are driven back to his use of rhythm as the means by which he secured his best effects. . . . Half of the attraction of Noyes's rhythm is allied to that of the music-hall in its palmy days before the Great War killed it. The rhythms of English poetry since 1918 have been esoteric. Their beat is that of a lonely pulse, of an occult school, not a vast community. (pp. 86-7)

Noyes's most ambitious work is undoubtedly *The Torch-bearers,* but few contemporary critics would consider it his best. The medium he chose for this long celebration of scientific research was blank verse, a measure he never handled so well as rhymed verse with a lilting lyric metre. Sometimes his employment of it is rough, sometimes flat, and sometimes diffuse, and seldom did he achieve more than competent expression in it. . . . Most of us nowadays acquaint ourselves with science through its literature of popularization; and we can, if we choose, regard *The Torch-bearers* as an impressive feat of such wonder-baiting journalism in verse. Wordsworth certainly envisaged a time when science, familiarized by usage and reference, should—in the transfiguration of the poet—become 'a dear and genuine inmate of the household of man'. . . . But however we may look upon the general problem of poetry and science, Noyes's poem stands as a large-scale venture in familiarizing the second in terms of the first. Those who do not think it comes off can at least point to no superior endeavour.

In his last volume, *A Letter to Lucian, and other poems,* all Noyes's lifelong interests came together between two covers. The title-piece can perhaps be taken as a light-hearted critique of early Greek sceptical science. Other pieces hymned the Christian theme, while others spoke of his first love, the sea. **'Four Poems for Children'** and some further lyrics recall his nice attunement to the juvenile ear, and a group of four ballades at the book's end point to the satirist still much alive in him. (pp. 87-8)

> *Derek Stanford, "The Poetic Achievement of Alfred Noyes," in* English, *Vol. XII, No. 69, Autumn, 1958, pp. 86-8.*

H[ENRY] N[OYES]   (essay date 1963)

The present edition of my father's poems [*Collected Poems*] is the most complete collection yet to have been published in one volume in England. . . . These include one or two poems which I feel are among his finest work, particularly **"Night Journey"**, written shortly after an unsuccessful eye operation when he knew that he would soon be blind. (p. 7)

Two of them, **"Dobbin"**, and **"The Man who Discovered the Use of a Chair"**, I have included because although not great poems, I remember them with affection from my childhood and also because I feel that their inclusion helps to illustrate the great range of my father's writing which could provide entertainment and interest for the smallest child as well as for the most learned scholar.

The third poem of this group, **"The Old Fool in the Wood"**, is a particularly good example of his belief in the ultimate nature of things, and as he says in *The Unknown God,* in the universe, or "Nature", as an expression of the thought of God. It was this faith that enabled him to write a poem such as **"Night Journey"** at a time when he realized that he was soon to lose his sight which to him, whose whole life revolved around reading and writing, was so indescribably precious.

Throughout his life, his writings centred on the belief that the function of all great art was to establish a right relationship between things temporal and things eternal. . . . He saw beauty and truth as aspects of the divine perfection. Never, by eccentricity of expression, nor by the help of needless gimmicks, did he attempt to attract attention to his writings. (pp. 7-8)

> H[enry] N[oyes], *in his preface to* Collected Poems in One Volume *by Alfred Noyes, second edition, John Murray, 1963 (and reprinted by John Murray, 1966), pp. 7-8.*

ADDITIONAL BIBLIOGRAPHY

Adcock, Arthur St. John. "Alfred Noyes." In his *Gods of Modern Grub Street: Impressions of Contemporary Authors,* pp. 253-59. New York: Frederick A. Stokes Co., 1923.
    Dismisses criticism of Noyes's popularity and style.

Benét, William Rose. "Round About Parnassus." *The Saturday Review of Literature* VII, No. 20 (6 December 1930): 420.
    Review of *The Last Voyage* and *The Forty Singing Seamen and Other Poems.* Benét discusses why he prefers Noyes's lyric poems to the epics.

Bennett, Arnold. "Sea and Slaughter." In his *Books and Persons: Being Comments On a Past Epoch—1908-1911,* pp. 325-27. New York: George H. Doran Co., 1917.
    Attacks Noyes as a "patriotic versifier."

Boyd, Ernest. "Voltairianism without Tears." *The Saturday Review of Literature* XIV, No. 20 (12 September 1936): 7.
    Claims that Noyes misconstrues or alters Voltaire's beliefs for his own ends.

Fairchild, Hoxie Neale. "Nothing Very New." In his *Religious Trends in English Poetry: 1880-1920, Gods of a Changing Poetry,* Vol. V, pp. 195-221. New York: Columbia University Press, 1962.*
    Discussion of Noyes's changing religious convictions.

Scott, W. T. "An Old Pro Speaks Out." *Saturday Review* XXXVI, No. 25 (20 June 1953): 22-3.
    Review of *Two Worlds for Memory,* which mentions Noyes's acquaintances and accomplishments.

Sencourt, Robert. "Alfred Noyes." *The Contemporary Review* 194 (September 1958): 118-20.
    Respectful homage paid to late poet.

Stanford, Derek. "Alfred Noyes: 1880-1958." *The Catholic World* 188, No. 1126 (January 1959): 297-301.
    Review of Noyes's most popular and most ambitious poems.

Tobin, James Edward. "Alfred Noyes: A Corrected Bibliography." *Catholic Library World* XV, No. 6 (March 1944): 181-84, 189.
    Revised and expanded bibliography, first published in October 1941, of works by Noyes and criticism about him.

Marcel Proust

1871-1922

French novelist, critic, essayist, translator, short story writer, and poet.

Proust's multivolume novel *À la recherche du temps perdu (Remembrance of Things Past)* is among literature's works of highest genius, a work whose nature extends substantially beyond literature itself while also embodying one of its quintessential achievements. Renowned for its artistic construction, this masterpiece is as often appreciated for presenting an historian's chronicle of turn-of-the-century Paris society, a philosopher's reflections on the nature of time and consciousness, and a psychologist's insight into a tangled network of personalities. Unlike his novelistic predecessors, such as Balzac, who populated their books with characters from all social classes, Proust drew almost exclusively upon the upper classes for his novel, filling it in large part with snobs, neurotics, and homosexuals. The fact that his work is praised by readers and critics for conveying a profound view of human existence, despite its narrow range of characters, testifies to the success of Proust's narrator, protagonist, and guiding conscience, Marcel.

Proust was born at Auteuil, which in part served as a model for Combray in *Remembrance of Things Past*. His childhood was a sheltered but for the most part comfortably idyllic one. In 1880, however, he suffered his first attack of asthma, and the condition became chronic. Asthma was only one among a cluster of maladies suffered by the acutely sensitive Proust. But his uncertain health did not interrupt his formal education at the Lycée Condorcet, where he was a major contributor to the class magazine, or his attendance at the École des Sciences Politiques, where he studied under Henri Bergson. Neither did his condition keep him from a year of military service, which he recalled as one of the happiest periods of his life. Some of Proust's commentators suggest that although he genuinely suffered from ill health, he sometimes exaggerated it to diminish others' expectations of him. As a young man he moved in the complex society of salon matrons, aristocrats, and the literati, distinguishing himself as an entertaining wit with a talent for mimicking people's conversation and mannerisms. Particularly applauded were his imitations of Count Robert de Montesquiou, whose flamboyant personality provided some of the character traits for the pederast Baron de Charlus in *Remembrance of Things Past*.

In the mid-1890s Proust was chiefly known as a contributor of short prose works to various Paris reviews. These pieces, collected in *Les plaisirs et les jours (Pleasures and Days, and Other Writings)*, are often described as precious, though in retrospect they have gained value as examples of Proust's earliest experiments with the themes and techniques of his major work. Likewise *Jean Santeuil*, Proust's first attempt at extended fiction, served as a rehearsal for many of the characters and scenes in *Remembrance of Things Past* while lacking, in Martin Turnell's phrase, the "richness and complexity" of the later novel. A number of critics note that in *Jean Santeuil* Proust does not utilize the perspective of a first person narrator, which in *Remembrance of Things Past* becomes a unifying device for a vast and complicated scenario.

Culver Pictures

Proust's most important early work is to be found in the critical writings of *Contre Sainte-Beuve (By Way of Sainte-Beuve)*, where he puts forth his personal view of literature in opposition to the doctrines of the nineteenth-century critic. While Sainte-Beuve failed to make a distinction between the writer's life and his work, Proust contended that a work of literature offers a perspective unique to itself, independent of its author's biography. Walter A. Straus explains that Proust was a critic who looked "deeply into the writer's creative personality, discerning the writer's special vision and his method of re-creating this vision in terms of literature." This concern with a special vision achieved through art became one of the basic precepts of the work that occupied Proust for the remainder of his life.

The title of *À la recherche du temps perdu* is often rendered more literally as *In Search of Lost Time* to emphasize the conscious pursuit of the narrator for past selves which have been altered over the years, and for the original qualities of experiences which have been effaced in normal memory. For the narrator there are two means of recapturing a former stage of one's life: either through the consciously willed effort of "voluntary memory," or through the unwilled and unexpected outpouring of "involuntary memory." The first yields only limited and deceptive impressions of the past, while the second creates a vivid and faithful recollection. In the absence of religion, memory becomes a vehicle of transcendence beyond the annihilation by change and death of all things known in one's life. Another source of triumph over the frustrations of human existence is that of art, which allows viewpoints not possible in lived experience. Among life's major frustrations presented in Proust's novel are the unstable nature of personal identity and the deceptive quality of private truths subsequently revealed as illusion. These are symptomatic of what Proust calls the "intermittences of the heart," which transform seemingly durable emotions such as romantic love into occasional phenomena without continuity.

The world of *Remembrance of Things Past* is based upon two paths of life set forth by the narrator in the first volume: "Swann's Way," which leads to deceptions, complications, and agony in the domain of romance; and "Guermantes Way," which leads to much the same experience in the domain of society. Many of the main characters, excluding the narrator himself, are also revealed as homosexuals, as in the case of Baron de Charlus, or suspected of sexual inversion, as is Marcel's beloved Albertine. Though Proust himself was homosexual, he used this trait, some critics say overused, to unveil only the most degraded aspects in a character. In general Proust is seen as portraying the human condition primarily in its more sordid and desolate phases. Edmund Wilson calls *Remembrance of Things Past* "one of the gloomiest books ever written." François Maurois and Roger Shattuck, on the other hand, make a point of discussing the sense of humor that pervades the novel.

One of the most important issues in Proust criticism is the role of Marcel as protagonist and narrator of *Remembrance of Things Past*, and his relationship to Proust himself. Briefly, there is strong evidence for both identifying Proust with Marcel and for isolating them, and some critics' readings of the novel are more autobiographical than those of others. Perhaps the firmest ground for likening Proust with Marcel is their mutual struggle to realize themselves as artists, with each making art the highest value in their lives. The search for lost time ends in the disillusioned abandonment of life and in its recreation as a work of art. As Proust wrote: "The pleasure that an artist gives us is to make us know one universe more."

PRINCIPAL WORKS

Les plaisirs et les jours (short stories, sketches, poetry, and criticism) 1896
  [*Pleasures and Days, and Other Writings*, 1957]
Portraits de peintres (poetry) 1896
*Du côté de chez Swann (novel) 1913
  [*Swann's Way*, 1922]
*A l'ombre des jeunes filles en fleurs (novel) 1919
  [*Within a Budding Grove*, 1924]
Pastiches et mélanges (parodies and essays) 1919
*Le côté de Guermantes (novel) 1920
  [*The Guermantes Way*, 1924]
*Sodome et Gommorrhe (novel) 1922
  [*Cities of the Plain*, 1927]
*La prisonnière (novel) 1923
  [*The Captive*, 1929]
*La fugitive (novel) 1925
  [*The Sweet Cheat Gone*, 1930]
*Le temps retrouvé (novel) 1927
  [*Time Regained*, 1931]

Oeuvres complètes de Marcel Proust (novels, criticism, short stories, sketches, poetry, parodies, and essays) 1929-36
Jean Santeuil (novel) 1952
  [*Jean Santeuil*, 1955]
Contre Sainte-Beuve (criticism) 1954
  [*By Way of Sainte-Beuve*, 1958]

*These works were published as *À la recherche du temps perdu* in *Oeuvres complètes de Marcel Proust* in 1929-36.

ANATOLE FRANCE (essay date 1896)

Why did [Marcel Proust] ask me to stand sponsor to his book, and why did I promise to undertake that very pleasant but quite superfluous task? His book is like a young poet, full of rare and delicate charm. It bears with it its own commendation; it pleads its own cause and offers itself in its own despite.

Of course it is young. It is young with the author's own youthfulness. But it is old too, as old as the world. It is the leafage of springtime on the ancient branches of the age-old forest; yet it might be said that the fresh shoots sadden over the immemorial past of the woods and robe themselves in sorrow for so many dead springs.

To the goatherds of Helicon, the grave Hesiod sang the *Works and Days*. It would be a sadder task to sing *The Pleasures and Days* to the fashionable men and women of our times, if there be any truth in the saying of that English statesman who averred that "life would be tolerable were it not for its pleasures." And so our young friend's book shows smiles tinged with languor, attitudes of fatigue which are not devoid of beauty or nobility.

In its sadness it will touch many soft and divers chords, sustained as it is by a marvellous spirit of observation, by a penetrating and truly subtle intelligence. This calendar of the *Pleasures and Days* portrays alike the moods of nature by harmonious pictures of sky and sea and forest, and depicts the moods of man by faithful portraits and by *genre* paintings of wonderful minuteness.

Marcel Proust takes equal pleasure in describing the lonely splendours of the setting sun and the restless vanities of a worldly heart. He excels in the telling of exquisite sorrows, of artificial sufferings, which are at least as cruel as those which Nature lavishes upon us with maternal generosity. I confess that these far sought sufferings, these sorrows discovered by human ingenuity, these factitious griefs, strike me as wonderfully interesting and valuable, and I am grateful to Marcel Proust for having studied them and furnished a few choice examples.

He attracts us and holds us in an exotic atmosphere amid cultivated orchids whose strange and morbid beauty is nourished on no earthly soil. Suddenly through the heavy-scented air, there strikes a shaft of light, a flash which, like the ray of the German scientist, traverses the body. In an instant, with a single stroke, the poet has probed the hidden thought, the longing unavowed.

Such is his manner, his art. He displays in it a sureness of aim surprising in so young an archer. He is not in the least innocent. But so sincere is he, and so true, that he takes on a character of *naïveté*, and that in itself conveys a charm. In him there is something of a depraved Bernardin de Saint-Pierre and an ingenuous Petronius. (pp. 223-25)

> *Anatole France, in his preface to* Les plaisirs et les jours *by Marcel Proust, Calman Lévy, 1896 (and reprinted as a chapter in his* Prefaces, Introductions and Other Uncollected Papers, *translated by J. Lewis May, Dodd, Mead & Company, 1928, pp. 223-28).*

THE SPECTATOR   (essay date 1922)

It is a singular chance that has given popular success to the works of M. Marcel Proust. . . . The award of the Prix Goncourt, instituted to encourage, both morally and financially, young and unknown authors, recommended to the public in 1920 the curious work of this mysterious writer, of whom all that was known was that he was over forty, that he drew out a delicate existence amid considerable but tasteful luxury, and that heart disease condemned him to endless leisure. Those who sought quick or easy reading shrank back from the two closely printed volumes of the successful work, in spite of the enticingly enigmatic title, *A l'Ombre des Jeunes Filles en Fleur*. They discovered, to their confusion, that these volumes were in truth only a single chapter of an enormous sequence called *A la Recherche du Temps Perdu*. . . . (p. 298)

What, then, is this colossal work? On what was all this time lost? In living simply—and in living neither particularly excitingly nor yet monotonously enough, one would have said, to form a subject for modern literature. We are shown the thread of an existence passing before backgrounds more often imposed by chance than chosen of free will—an existence which with singular tact the author lets us imagine may well be his own, without ever imposing on us the certainty and without disenchanting us by plain statement.

This expedient so deliciously tantalizing, this mixture of real incident and creative fantasy, makes any definite classification of these books impossible. (For example, M. Proust will conjure up in the *salon* of some fictitious Princess of his creation the shade of the late M. Detaille, the painter of battle-pieces, or of one or other of the present Academicians.)

The interminable narrative is interrupted sometimes by the delightful archaism of an aside to the reader, more often by some minute analysis, exhaustive to excess, that gives us brilliant glimpses of the most unexpected subjects. The volumes can be called neither a novel nor a "Journal Intime." They lie somewhere between the two. . . . It was *Du Côté de Chez Swann* that the tiny events of the narrator's childhood flowed by. They were set in the frame of the green country of L'Ile-de-France, geographically indefinite, yet more vivid to the reader than his own native countryside; or among the thousand trivial agitations of the life of a little country town, on which the author has thrown so penetrating a vision that he has revealed to us a universe. There he heard, later to retail it to us, the story of the melancholy and ill-starred love affairs of a friend of his family—this Charles Swann, a Jew, rich, gifted with every charm of mind, with every delicacy of feeling, and with all the refinements of an immense culture. One might have imagined that one saw in this character, at once passionate and detached, the portrait of the author himself, even though Swann was a typical representative of the society of the end of the last century, and though the author is shown by his side as his younger admirer and the boy lover of his daughter. Six volumes later M. Proust releases us from our error and rec-

ognizes with us the immense influence which the fiery but delicate spirit of his older friend had exercised on his youth. With his years of adolescence M. Proust takes us to Paris, where outside the circles of "high-official" society, which are those of his family, the young man is a social success—his modesty attributes this to chance—in the most aristocratic *salons* of the Faubourg St. Germain.

Just as he was able to see a whole world in his provincial gardens, so here he presents with implacable detail three or four different "soirées," where meet his characters in more or less familiar frames. Yet he reconstructs each of these evenings with such extreme delicacy of nuance that they seem suddenly to stand out distinct, individual, before our eyes.

It is a study, torturedly subtle, of every scale of values, every *mondaine* quotation in the whole gamut of snobbery, and it is pursued—beyond this holy ground of the Faubourg St. Germain—into each one of the lower strata of "the world," to the kitchens and the pantries themselves, whose uttermost niceties of etiquette M. Proust knows to the bottom. Indeed, the souls of butlers, of waiters, and of pantry boys, thus dissected, thus flayed alive for us, expose but the same springs of action as their masters. But they cannot compete in savagery, in violence, in bitter cruelty, with those of the "intellectuals" who keep or are kept in those "Salons Littéraires" where are manufactured the academic glories of to-morrow.

Here the vast indulgence, the infinite comprehension of the human heart which usually tempers his irony, contrives his excuse and sweetens his satire, deserts M. Proust, and it is with a Swiftian bitterness that he exposes the terrifying, the odious, the nightmarish figure of Madame Verdurin. It is she who rules her managerie of sabre-toothed wild beasts with a ferocity now veiled, now insolent. It is she who fabricates great men from the *habitués* of her *petit-clan* because she must rule over a *petit-clan* of great men. Before her we feel ourselves at the monstrous summit of human vanities. And so in all these pages, where nothing happens but errors of etiquette or faults of good breeding, contests of vanity or the catastrophes of *amour-propre*, is there anything but an interminable commentary on the words of Ecclesiasticus? But somehow the book enthrals us. But is it a book? If so, only in so subtle a way that it seems to be life itself—nay more, that it pales, it eclipses, the life around us. By a *tour de force* of delicacy and of tact, the personality of the author (when he is not himself one of the players on his stage) does not interpose a useless commentary between the characters and ourselves. It seems as if (and it is only what we might expect from so perfectly delicate a spirit) M. Proust simply introduces us to those houses into which he wants to take us. On the doorsteps he whispers a few enlightening words which will help us to avoid mistakes. He tells us all he knows of our hosts, but he cannot know everything. Sometimes his information is incorrect, sometimes both he and we get on a wrong track. With us he makes discoveries, with us he discusses them, with us he is deceived. With us he carries on his visits and his walks, mixing us in his life to such a point that he peoples our days and our thoughts with a new set of friends, so much alive that they make us forget our own.

Shall we not, then, excuse these vanities that so deliciously excite our own, this snobbery on which we smile in irony—and in pleasure? But it would be to under-estimate the quality of the work of M. Proust if we found in it nothing beyond this. For if he takes us with him to the party, he requires us also to share in his reflections on it, to learn the lesson that it has taught him.

One likes to think that, like a new Pascal, M. Proust, after consecrating the years of a brilliant youth to taking his place in the life, the vanities, of his century, is now, in his solitude, reconstructing, in incredible minuteness and almost morbid precision, with the million grains of sand that are his memories the vast panorama which has rolled out before his eyes. In it he himself is one of the figures, and in his revelation he is uncovering the meaning of a life and the lore of a philosophy. For even the study of the vanities is ennobled when it is undertaken with so scrupulous, so visionary, so passionate, a sincerity. And when, in the most striking and the most attractive of the characters, who are alone worthy to contain them, are discovered traces of the great moral forces—love of man for woman, of mother for son, of daughter for mother—the story plumbs the very depths of truth with a pathos the most poignant and the most Christian, and gives us that miracle of reconstruction the real man, neither angel nor beast, who has been realized by the great thinkers alone. (pp. 298-99)

[M. Proust] is something of a sage, at once in a most true and a most unorthodox sense of the word. He is as far from the contemptuous coldness of M. de Regnier as from the gay Alexandrianism of M. Anatole France or the dogmatic perversity of M. Gide. To disciples, or indeed to anyone who will inquire, he will tell his wonderful secret, which lies neither in a facile epicureanism nor a still easier asceticism but in the very synthesis, the fusion, of the activity of exterior life with the intensity of inner spiritual life—in his own phrase, *La Recherche du Temps Perdu.* (p. 299)

"The Phenomenon of M. Proust," in The Spectator *(© 1922 by* The Spectator; *reprinted by permission of* The Spectator*), Vol. 129, No. 4914, September 2, 1922, pp. 298-99.*

AFFABLE HAWK [J. C. Squire]   (essay date 1922)

I do not see the affinity between Proust and Balzac. Proust's methods are those of the miniaturist, though they are devoted to a picture on the scale of a fresco, and such an analogy does not hold good of Balzac's work, whose thoroughness is of another description. Proust, too, is profoundly æsthetic in his response to experience, and this implies so fundamental a difference between any writer of whom that can be said and any other of whom it cannot, that it makes superficial resemblances, due to both reflecting in their work a whole environment, uninteresting. On the other hand, I do see an analogy between Proust and Petronius; Proust, too, is an *arbiter elegantiae,* and no one who is not amused by, or who is out of sympathy with, the application of such standards to life, will find much of Proust's writings trivial and unreadable. . . . "The mind longs for what it has lost, and is wholly occupied in conjuring up the past." That quotation from the *Satyricon* would have made a perfect motto for Proust's book. It is an odd coincidence. . . .

Proust was a great admirer of Ruskin.

The qualities which appealed to him in Ruskin were a capacity for rapture and this intense analytical faculty dedicated to impressions made upon him by material objects. Proust possessed both himself, otherwise two men could hardly be more different. His analysis of his impressions is more patient and minute than Ruskin's; the impetus, in his case, is never moral fervour, but the resemblance is there; both make an extraordinary intellectual effort to discover what is behind the impressions which have excited them. Proust traces to the last tiny filament root the sources of his impressions of joy, beauty or disgust. He never rests until the confused ideas which have exalted him have been dragged up into daylight. (pp. 239)

Affable Hawk [pseudonym of J. C. Squire], "Books in General," in New Statesman *(© 1922 The Statesman & Nation Publishing Co. Ltd.), Vol. XX, No. 502, November 25, 1922, p. 239.*

JOSEPH CONRAD   (essay date 1923)

As to Marcel Proust, *créateur,* I don't think he has been written about much in English, and what I have seen of it was rather superficial. I have seen him praised for his "wonderful" pictures of Paris life and provincial life. But that has been done admirably before, for us, either in love, or in hatred, or in mere irony. One critic goes so far as to say that Proust's great art reaches the universal, and that in depicting his own past he reproduces for us the general experience of mankind. But I doubt it. I admire him rather for disclosing a past like nobody else's, for enlarging, as it were, the general experience of mankind by bringing to it something that has not been recorded before. However, all that is not of much importance. The important thing is that whereas before we had analysis allied to creative art, great in poetic conception, in observation, or in style, his is a creative art absolutely based on analysis. It is really more than that. He is a writer who has pushed analysis to the point when it becomes creative. All that crowd of personages in their infinite variety through all the gradations of the social scale are rendered visible to us by the force of analysis alone. I don't say Proust has no gift of description or characterisation; but, to take an example from each end of the scale: Françoise, the devoted servant, and the Baron de Charlus, a consummate portrait—how many descriptive lines have they got to themselves in the whole body of that immense work? Perhaps, counting the lines, half a page each. And yet no intelligent person can doubt for a moment their plastic and coloured existence. One would think that this method (and Proust has no other, because his method is the expression of his temperament) may be carried too far, but as a matter of fact it is never wearisome. There may be here and there amongst those thousands of pages a paragraph that one might think oversubtle, a bit of analysis pushed so far as to vanish into nothingness. But those are very few, and all minor instances. The intellectual pleasure never flags, because one has the feeling that the last word is being said upon a subject much studied, much written about, and of human interest—the last word of its time. Those that have found beauty in Proust's work are perfectly right. It is there. What amazes one is its inexplicable character. In that prose so full of life there is no reverie, no emotion, no marked irony, no warmth of conviction, not even a marked rhythm to charm our ear. It appeals to our sense of wonder and gains our homage by its veiled greatness. I don't think there ever has been in the whole of literature such an example of the power of analysis, and I feel pretty safe in saying that there will never be another. (pp. 126-28)

Joseph Conrad, in his letter to C. K. Moncrieff in 1923 (reprinted by permission of the Literary Estate of Joseph Conrad), in Marcel Proust: An English Tribute, *edited by C. K. Moncrieff, Thomas Seltzer, 1923, pp. 126-28.*

EDITH WHARTON   (essay date 1925)

The more one reads of Proust the more one sees that his strength is the strength of tradition. All his newest and most arresting effects have been arrived at through the old way of selection and design. In the construction of these vast, leisurely, and purposeful compositions nothing is really wasted, or brought in at random. If at first Proust seemed so revolutionary it was partly because of his desultory manner and parenthetical syntax, and chiefly because of the shifting of emphasis resulting from his extremely personal sense of values. (pp. 154-55)

It was one of the distinctive characters of Proust's genius that he combined with his great sweep of vision an exquisite delicacy of touch, a solicitous passion for detail. Many of his pages recall those mediaeval manuscripts where the roving fancy of the scribe has framed some solemn gospel or epistle in episodes drawn from the life of towns and fields, or the pagan extravagances of the Bestiary. Jane Austen never surpassed in conciseness of irony some of the conversations between Marcel's maiden aunts, or the description of Madame de Cambremer and Madame de Franquetot listening to music. . . . (pp. 166-67)

But just as the reader is sinking delectably into the feather-bed of the small town, Proust snatches him up in eagle's talons and swings him over the darkest abysses of passion and intrigue—showing him, in the slow tortures of Swann's love for Odette, and of Saint-Loup's for Rachel, the last depths and involutions of moral anguish, or setting the frivolous careers of the two great Guermantes ladies, the Duchess and the Princess, on a stage vaster than any since Balzac's, and packed with a human comedy as multifarious. (pp. 167-68)

Every reader enamoured of the art must brood in amazement over the way in which Proust maintains the balance between these two manners—the broad and the minute. His endowment as a novelist—his range of presentation combined with mastery of his instruments—has probably never been surpassed.

Fascinating as it is to the professional to dwell on this amazing virtuosity, yet the lover of Proust soon comes to feel that his rarest quality lies beyond and above it—lies in the power to reveal, by a single allusion, a word, an image, those depths of soul beyond the soul's own guessing. . . . [The] man who could find words in which to express the inexpressible emotion with which one comes suddenly, in some apparently unknown landscape, upon a scene long known to the soul (like that mysterious group of trees encountered by Marcel in the course of a drive with Madame de Villeparisis)—the man who could touch with so sure and compassionate a hand on the central mysteries of love and death, deserves at such moments to be ranked with Tolstoy when he describes the death of Prince Andrew, with Shakespeare when he makes Lear say: "Pray you, undo this button. . . ." (pp. 169-71)

In writing of a great creative artist, and especially of one whose work is over, it is always better worth while to dwell on the beauties than to hunt down the blemishes. Where the qualities outweigh the defects the latter lose much of their importance, even when, as sometimes in Proust's case, they are defects in the moral sensibility, that tuning-fork of the novelist's art.

It is vain to deny, or to try to explain away, this particular blemish—deficiency, it should be rather called—in Proust's work. Undoubtedly there are blind spots in his books, as there are in Balzac's, in Stendhal's, in Flaubert's; but Proust's blind spots are peculiarly disconcerting because they are intermittent. One cannot dismiss the matter by saying that a whole category of human emotions is invisible to him, since at certain times his vision is acutest at the precise angle where the blindness had previously occurred.

A well-known English critic, confusing the scenes in which Proust's moral sense has failed him with those (far more numerous) in which he deliberately portrays the viler aspects of the human medley, suggests that timorous readers might find unmingled enjoyment in the perusal of **"A la Recherche du Temps Perdu"** by the simple expedient of "thinking away" M. de Charlus—as who should propose "thinking away" Falstaff from the plays in which he figures! It would, in fact, be almost as difficult to dismiss M. de Charlus with an "I know thee not, old man," as Falstaff; and quite as unnecessary. It is not by daring to do "in the round" a mean or corrupt character—an Iago, a Lord Steyne, a Philippe Bridau, or a Valérie Marneffe—that a novelist diminishes the value of his work. On the contrary, he increases it. Only when the vileness and the cruelty escape him, when he fails to see the blackness of the shadow they project, and thus unconsciously flattens his modelling, does he correspondingly empoverish the picture; and this Proust too often did—but never in drawing M. de Charlus, whose ignominy was always as vividly present to him as Iago's or Goneril's to their creator.

There is one deplorable page where the hero and narrator, with whose hyper-sensitiveness a hundred copious and exquisite passages have acquainted us, describes with complacency how he has deliberately hidden himself to spy on an unedifying scene. This episode—and several others marked by the same abrupt lapse of sensibility—might be "thought away" with all the less detriment that, at such moments, Proust's characters invariably lose their *probableness* and begin to stumble through their parts like good actors vainly trying to galvanize a poor play. All through his work there are pages literally trembling with emotion; but wherever the moral sensibility fails, the tremor, the vibration, ceases. When he is unaware of the meanness of an act committed by one of his characters, that character loses by so much of its life-likeness, and, reversing Pygmalion's gesture, the author turns living beings back to stone. (pp. 171-74)

[Proust] could conceive of human beings as good, as pitiful, as self-sacrificing, as guided by the most delicate moral scruples; but never, apparently, as brave, either by instinct or through conscious effort.

Fear ruled his moral world: fear of death, fear of love, fear of responsibility, fear of sickness, fear of draughts, fear of fear. It formed the inexorable horizon of his universe and the hard delimitation of his artist's temperament.

In saying so one touches on the narrow margin between the man's genius and his physical disabilities, and at this point criticism must draw back, or linger only in reverent admiration of the great work achieved, the vast register covered, in spite of that limitation, in conflict with those disabilities.

Nietzsche's great saying, "Everything worth while is accomplished notwithstanding" [*trotzdem*], might serve as the epitaph of Proust. (pp. 177-78)

Edith Wharton, "Marcel Proust," in her The Writing of Fiction *(copyright © 1924, 1925 by Charles Scribner's Sons; 1925 by The Yale Publishing Association, Inc.; renewal copyright 1953 by Fredric R. King: reprinted with the permission of Charles Scribner's Sons), Charles Scribner's Sons, 1925 (and reprinted by Octagon Books, 1966), pp. 149-78.*

CLIVE BELL (essay date 1928)

I began reading [*Du Côté de chez Swann*] in a hypercritical, not to say cantankerous, frame of mind; and, as things have turned out, that was no bad beginning. Soon enough I was seduced. In my turn I fell, duly swept off my feet by that current which has floated so many of the more intelligent and sensitive of my contemporaries into oceans of uncritical enthusiasm. I went down before the revelation and wallowed. By 1925 Proust meant for me what seventy-five years earlier I suppose Balzac must have meant for people of my sort. Here was a contemporary possessing imaginatively and giving form to the vague, half-conscious experience of two generations; here was a path cut into an unexplored shrubbery of that backgarden men call life; and here were the memoirs of my age. Also, it will be, I surmise, with Proust's contribution to experience as it has been with Balzac's: something will remain, something will be discarded, much will be lost. To-day only the historically minded appreciate the shades by which Balzac differentiates "restauration" from "Louis-Philippe", and our grandchildren will hardly feel as we feel the delicate touches by which Odette is made to represent one epoch and Albertine to announce another. The most variegated periods tend, at a distance, to appear monochrome; wherefore one of Proust's most delicious gifts for us, his gift of rendering temporal colour, inevitably will cease to charm as the age of which he is the memorialist loses its bloom. . . . I can see that, though *A la recherche du temps perdu* will always mean to me more than any other long novel, that does not prove that it is more. *Clarissa, Tristram Shandy,* even *Jean Christophe*—which the French have put in the corner quite as much because it was written by a Protestant and a pacificist as because it is written in a woefully undistinguished manner—may each in its way be a match, and more than a match, for *La Recherche:* but none of them can be for us our masterpiece, our *temps retrouvé.* (pp. 6-8)

When I began to read *Swann* the first fault on which I pounced was that of which anyone, however unpouncingly disposed, is sure to complain at first. I complained that Proust was tedious. Tedious he is, but his tediousness becomes excusable once its cause is perceived. Proust tries our patience so long as we expect his story to move forward: that not being the direction in which it is intended to move. Novelists, as a rule, are concerned, to some extent at any rate, with getting on with their tale; Proust cares hardly more what becomes of his than did Sterne. It is in states, not action, he deals. The movement is as that of an expanding flower or insect. He exhibits a fact: we expect another to succeed it, effect following cause. Not at all: the fact remains suspended while we watch it gradually changing its shape, its colour, its consistency. For fifty pages we watch the process; after which Proust proposes another fact, new and seemingly irrelevant. Because very often there is no progressive relation we have a sense of being thwarted. We are annoyed. Proust does not get forward, we complain. Why should he? Is there no other line of development in the universe?

This sense of weariness, born of continual checking and marking time, is aggravated by the fact that, at first reading, Proust's sentences seem unconscionably and unnecessarily long. . . . His object was to tell the truth about life as he saw it; wherefore he intended originally to write a book without a single paragraph or chapter, so unlifelike—so unreal—did these arbitrary and convenient divisions appear. For the same reason he may have had a horror of full stops. He was to render his sense of life—of something which has relations in space, and is also, as he saw it, a mode of time. But time, he may have argued, is what the hymn says it is—an ever-flowing stream, not a ball of string cut into neat lengths. Time overflows punctuation. Also, how is a style to be anything but complicated and prolix

when an artist is trying to say four things at once—to give a bird's-eye view and "a close up" at once in time and space? (pp. 11-13)

It is customary to compare Proust, stylist and memorialist of his age, or at least to say that one will not compare him, with St. Simon. Certainly his style may be compared profitably with that of the seventeenth-century writers of whom St. Simon, for all that he wrote every word of his memoirs in the eighteenth and died in 1755, was one. Proust is comparable with the seventeenth-century writers in that his style may be considered periodic; and this is worth noting because it may help us to understand the workings of Proust's mind when he sat down to express the truth that was in him. . . . The sign of a perfect period is the impossibility of placing a full stop, without making nonsense of the grammar, anywhere in the sentence before the close: "On being contradicted, to shout and scream, to beat on table with the butt-end of a beer bottle, menacing a blow with the hand disengaged, to kick under the cloth and spit in your neighbour's face, is the conduct neither of a gentleman nor a philosopher". This is perfect: the reader is kept in doubt as to the exact purport of the statement to the very last word, and at no point before the last is it possible grammatically to close the sentence. . . . Proust, like the seventeenth-century masters, is periodic: only, whereas the great prose writers of that age deal generally in general ideas, Proust is plaiting very particular strands of emotion and sensation experienced by a very definite individual, and experienced simultaneously. That is why the interminable dependent clauses, instead of following one another duckwise, go side by side, like horses driven abreast, and sometimes higgledy-piggledy like a flock of feeding starlings. A critic with sharper eyes than mine (could I remember who it was I would cite him by name) has pointed out that the recurring *que* of the seventeenth century becoming *soit que* in Proust (*that* becoming *whether* or *albeit*) is the symbol of a mind which tends to move to one side or even to take a half step back rather than go straight ahead. Proust composed in the periodic manner in that his meaning is often not revealed till the close, or near the close, of the sentence. Often a careless or sleepy reader will find himself at the end of the sentence with a principal verb on his hands which he hardly knows what to do with. This shows that the period has been well sustained and that the periodic structure has served its purpose. He who would understand Proust must attend to every word he utters. This means stiff reading. Hence fatigue: hence also the revelation. I see no reason for supposing that Proust acquired his style by the study or imitation of other writers. Like all styles worthy the name it was an instrument developed gradually to serve the single purpose of self-expression; it is the nearest Proust can get in words to an equivalent for what Proust felt and thought and Proust's way of thinking and feeling. (pp. 15-18)

Proust wanted to tell the truth as he knew it. He had a passion for the fact. And this pursuit of truth, of reality I had rather say, is the only begetter and conditioner of his style. It was the contemplation, the realisation, of facts which provoked the poet that was in him. He kept his eye on the object much as the great impressionists had done, he observed, he analysed, he rendered; but what he saw was not what the writers of his generation saw, but the object, the fact, in its emotional significance. And, like the impressionists, he has taught the more sensitive of a new generation to see with him. (p. 21)

What Proust knew, if he knew anything at all, about the nature of the universe is unimportant; it is what he knew and still more what he could tell about that microcosm which is man, which is the marvel of our age. From the unsurveyed mines of sub-conscious memory he dragged up experience vital yet stingless and made the past live sterilised in the present. Then, on a pin's point, he held his living captive till he had described it, and describing created a world. He was a creator whose philosophy served him to keep ever in the forefront of his mind that critical spirit, that respect for truth, which alone, it seems, can preserve a creator from nauseous egotism or sprawling optimism. From exaggeration he was not saved; but he is never vulgar, never sentimental. And if, some unlucky divagations notwithstanding, he avoided those messy pits into which most modern creators—Dickens, Hugo, Balzac, Dostoievsky—have fallen, that may have been because a philosopher was ever at hand to remind him, that the one wholly good gift the gods have given man is death. (pp. 88-9)

> *Clive Bell, in his* Proust *(reprinted by permission of the Author's Literary Estate and The Hogarth Press Ltd), Leonard and Virginia Woolf at the Hogarth Press, 1928, 89 p.*

GEORGE SANTAYANA   (essay date 1929)

"No novelist," writes Mr. Desmond MacCarthy, "has ever done such complete justice (as has Proust) to the great fact that all things pass and change." Yet this complete absorption in the flux of sensations, and abstention from all judgments about their causes or their relative values, leads Proust in the end to a very remarkable perception: that the flux of phenomena is after all accidental to them, and that the positive reality in each is not the fact that it appears or disappears, but rather the intrinsic quality which it manifests, an eternal essence which may appear and disappear a thousand times. Such an essence, when it is talked about, may seem mysterious and needlessly invented, but when noticed it is the clearest and least doubtful of things—the only sort of thing, indeed, that can ever be observed with direct and exhaustive clearness. An essence is simply the recognizable character of any object or feeling, all of it that can actually be possessed in sensation or recovered in memory, or transcribed in art, or conveyed to another mind. All that was intrinsically real in past time is accordingly recoverable. The hopeless flux and the temporal order of things are not ultimately interesting; they belong merely to the material occasions on which essences recur, or to the flutterings of attention, hovering like a moth about lights which are eternal. (pp. 273-74)

No wonder that a sensibility so exquisite and so voluminous as that of Proust, filled with endless images and their distant reverberations, could be rescued from distraction only by finding certain repetitions or rhymes in this experience. He was a tireless husbandman of memory, gathering perhaps more poppies than corn; and the very fragility and worthlessness of the weeds collected may have led him to appreciate their presence only when lost, and their harsh scent only when recovered. Thus he required two phenomena to reveal to him one essence, as if essences needed to appear a second time in order to appear at all. A mind less volatile and less retentive, but more concentrated and loyal, might easily have discerned the eternal essence in any single momentary fact. It might also have felt the scale of values imposed on things by human nature, and might have been carried towards some by an innate love and away from others by a quick repulsion: something which in Proust is remarkably rare. Yet this very inhumanity and innocent openness, this inclination to be led on by endlessly rambling perception, makes his testimony to the reality of essences all the more remarkable. We could not have asked for a more competent or a more unexpected witness to the fact that life as it flows is so much time wasted, and that nothing can ever be recovered or truly possessed save under the form of eternity which is also, as he tells us, the form of art. (pp. 276-77)

> *George Santayana, "Proust on Essences" (originally published in* Life and Letters, *Vol. II, No. 13, June, 1929), in his* Obiter Scripta: Lectures, Essays and Reviews, *edited by Justus Buchler and Benjamin Schwartz (reprinted with the permission of Charles Scribner's Sons), Charles Scribner's Sons, 1936, pp. 273-79).*

E. M. FORSTER   (essay date 1929)

Mr. Scott Moncrieff's monumental translation of Proust's *A la Recherche du Temps perdu* is both sensitive and accurate; it has been unreservedly praised by the best judges, and if I do not altogether concur it is because I was hoping to find Proust easier in English than in French, and do not. All the difficulties of the original are here faithfully reproduced. A sentence begins quite simply, then it undulates and expands, parentheses intervene like quick-set hedges, the flowers of comparison bloom, and three fields off, like a wounded partridge, crouches the principal verb, making one wonder as one picks it up, poor little thing, whether after all it was worth such a tramp, so many guns, and such expensive dogs, and what, after all, is its relation to the main subject, potted so gaily half a page back, and proving finally to have been in the accusative case. These, however, are the disciplines of Proust. (p. 96)

The work as a whole! Ten times as long as an ordinary novel! And as baffling as life itself—life when apprehended by the modern cultivated man. "Life" and "Proust" are not identical, it is true; as we shall see, there are notable differences between them, all in life's favour. But the main features correspond, and it is possible to say that the work, more than any other, expresses the spirit of our age. As a contemporary document, it is invaluable. Just as the historian of the early Roman Empire turns to Virgil and finds in his sensitive verse not the exploits of Aeneas but the semi-content and the half-expressed regrets of a generation that had escaped the republican storms and abandoned the risks of liberty: just as the historian of the late Middle Ages turns to Dante and finds there described not a personal fantasy but the last and the greatest of the crusades that were supposed to end in heaven; so, reading Proust, the historian of the early twentieth century will see not the dallyings of the insignificant hero, not the local snobberies of the Faubourg Saint Germain, but—you and me! He will say, "This work, whatever its qualities as art, is an epic, for it expresses the spirit of its age." And he will add (perhaps rather to our surprise if we still take notice of the remarks of wise men): "It was pre-eminently an age of adventure."

There is, of course, nothing of the swashbuckler about Proust, me, or you. There is no question of adventure of that sort; the laurels of the House of Guermantes have faded long before the action starts; the martial ardours of Saint Loup are slightly démodé and absurd, like the caperings of a heraldic lion; there is no true summons to battle when the bugles of Doncières blow and its fortifications take shape in the mists. And when the Great War does come it is a monster, indecent and imbecile, shaggy with dispatches, in whose foetid darkness M. de Charlus waddles about seeking pleasure and Madame Verdurin personates Joan of Arc. Of adventure in the chivalrous or romantic sense there is nothing, nothing. But the characters want to live, the author wants to write about them, and when we ask why, in a world so obviously unsatisfactory, we get an answer which will be echoed in our own private diary, namely, "We want to know what will happen tomorrow." Tomorrow may not be better than today, and may well be worse, but it has one unique attraction: it has not yet come. Proust, though introspective, and unhappy, was full of vitality—he could not have written a million words if he was not—he was inquisitive about tomorrow, he and his characters cling to existence though logic indicates suicide, and though disease drags them down still keep one eye open, half an eye, and scan the bitter unremunerative levels of the sea. *A la Recherche du Temps perdu* is an epic of curiosity and of despair. It is an adventure in the modern mode where the nerves and brain as well as the blood take part, and the whole man moves forward to encounter he does not know what; certainly not to any goal.

His despair is fundamental. It is not a theory in him, but an assumption, so that the wreckage of his creation evolves as naturally as the music of the spheres. Consider his insistence on illness. Disease and death await every individual, but it is only when we are ill ourselves, or are nursing a friend or passing through a hospital ward that we realize this vividly. To Proust it was always vivid, at garden parties and dinners the germs continue to work and disintegrate the bodies of the guests, Swann trails about with dotlets of prussian blue on his face, a cuirass of diamonds heaves above Princesse d'Orvillers's cancer, the grandmother poses coquettishly for her photograph after a stroke. The cumulative effect (and this is an important point) is *not* macabre. He was too great an artist to indulge in the facile jiggle of a Dance of Death. They are living beings, not masked skeletons or physiological transparencies who climb the height of La Raspelière or talk against the music of Vinteuil. But they are doomed more obviously than ourselves to decay. Avoiding tragic horror, which perhaps he mistrusted, and pity, which he could seldom supply, he has achieved a new view of the impermanence of the human race. . . . (pp. 97-9)

> *E. M. Forster, "Proust" (1929), in his* Abinger Harvest *(copyright 1936, 1964 by E. M. Forster; reprinted by permission of Harcourt Brace Jovanovich, Inc.; in Canada by Edward Arnold (Publishers) Ltd.), Harcourt, 1936, pp. 96-101.*

EDMUND WILSON (essay date 1931)

"A la Recherche du Temps Perdu," in spite of all its humor and beauty, is one of the gloomiest books ever written. Proust tells us that the idea of death has "kept him company as incessantly as the idea of his own identity''; and even the water-lilies of the little river at Combray, continually straining to follow the current and continually jerked back by their stems, are likened to the futile attempts of the neurasthenic to break the habits which are eating his life. Proust's lovers are always suffering: we scarcely ever see them in any of those moments of ecstasy or contentment which, after all, not seldom occur even in the case of an unfortunate love affair—and on the rare occasions when they *are* supposed to be enjoying themselves, the whole atmosphere is shadowed by the sadness and corrupted by the odor of the putrescence which are immediately to set in. And Proust's artists are unhappy, too: they have only the consolations of art. Proust's interminable, relentlessly repetitious and finally almost intolerable disquisitions on these themes

end by goading us to the same sort of rebellion that we make against those dialogues of Leopardi in which, in a similar insistent way, Leopardi rings the changes on a similar theme: that man is never happy, that there is no such thing as satisfaction in the present. We have finally to accept with dismay the fact that Leopardi is a sick man and that, in spite of the strength of his intellect, in spite of his exact, close, sober classical style, all his thinking is sick. And so with Proust we are forced to recognize that his ideas and imagination are more seriously affected by his physical and psychological ailments than we had at first been willing to suppose. His characters, we begin to observe, are always becoming ill like the hero—an immense number of them turn out homosexual, and homosexuality is "an incurable disease." Finally, they all suddenly grow old in a thunderclap—more hideously and humiliatingly old than we have ever known any real group of people to be. And we find that we are made more and more uncomfortable by Proust's incessant rubbing in of all these ignominies and disabilities. We begin to feel less the pathos of the characters than the author's appetite for making them miserable. And we realize that the atrocious cruelty which dominates Proust's world, in the behavior of the people in the social scenes no less than in the relations of the lovers, is the hysterical sadistic complement to the hero's hysterical masochistic passivity. (pp. 164-66)

Like all the graduates of the Symbolist school, Proust was a determined opponent of Naturalism: in the last part of "A la Recherche du Temps Perdu," when he explains the plan of his novel, he expresses himself emphatically and at great length on the futility of trying to represent reality by collecting and organizing the data of the external world, and he handles with what is evidently deliberate carelessness all those facts which a Naturalistic novelist would have been scrupulous to have consistent and precise. What is more, there is no explicit logical connection between the different elements of "A la Recherche du Temps Perdu." There is a story, the story of the narrator, his illusions and disillusions in connection with the world of snobbery and his attachments for Gilberte and Albertine; yet what must have been, what would by any other novelist be presented as having been, some of the most important relations and experiences of his life are scarcely touched upon at all. We hear much about the narrator's grandmother, but almost nothing about his father and are never told precisely what his father does; we hear much about his holidays at the seashore, but nothing about his education; we are told at length about his visit to Saint-Loup when the latter is doing his year of military service, but nothing save through casual allusion about his own term in barracks. On the other hand, certain of the characters that figure most prominently in the novel have almost no relation to the hero at all—at least no relation which the story accounts for: Swann is merely a friend of the family whom the narrator has occasionally seen in his youth, Charlus a person he sometimes meets later on. Yet these two characters almost dominate, respectively, the earlier and the later parts of the book—and as we read, we never question their significance: it is only when we think to examine Proust's novel from the point of view of ordinary fiction that we become aware of their irrelevance to the main narrative. Then we perceive that "A la Recherche du Temps Perdu," which begins in the darkened room of sleep, stands alone as a true dream-novel among works of social observation. It has its harmony, development and logic, but they are the harmony, development and logic of the unconscious. (pp. 177-79)

[It] may be that Proust's strange poetry and brilliance are the last fires of a setting sun—the last flare of the aesthetic idealism of the educated classes of the nineteenth century. If Proust is more dramatic, more complete and more intense than Thackeray or Chekov or Edith Wharton or Anatole France, it may be because he comes at the close of an era and sums up the whole situation. Surely the lament over the impossibility of ideal romantic love which Proust is always chanting on a note which wavers between the tragic and the maudlin announces by its very falling into absurdity the break-up of a whole emotional idealism and its ultimate analysis and readjustment along lines which Proust's own researches, running curiously close to Freud, have been among the first to suggest. **"A la Recherche du Temps Perdu"** subsumes, in this respect, "The Great Gatsby," "The Sun Also Rises," "The Bridge of San Luis Rey," the sketches of Dorothy Parker, and how many contemporary European novels! Proust is perhaps the last great historian of the loves, the society, the intelligence, the diplomacy, the literature and the art of the Heartbreak House of capitalist culture. . . . (pp. 189-90)

> *Edmund Wilson, "Marcel Proust," in his* Axel's Castle: A Study in the Imaginative Literature of 1870-1930 *(copyright 1931 by Charles Scribner's Sons; renewal copyright © 1959 by Edmund Wilson; reprinted with the permission of Charles Scribner's Sons), Charles Scribner's Sons, 1931 (and reprinted by Scribner's, 1953), pp. 132-90.*

SAMUEL BECKETT (essay date 1931)

[If] love, for Proust, is a function of man's sadness, friendship is a function of his cowardice; and, if neither can be realised because of the impenetrability (isolation) of all that is not 'cosa mentale,' at least the failure to possess may have the nobility of that which is tragic, whereas the attempt to communicate where no communication is possible is merely a simian vulgarity, or horribly comic, like the madness that holds a conversation with the furniture. Friendship, according to Proust, is the negation of that irremediable solitude to which every human being is condemned. Friendship implies an almost piteous acceptance of face values. Friendship is a social expedient, like upholstery or the distribution of garbage buckets. It has no spiritual significance. For the artist, who does not deal in surfaces, the rejection of friendship is not only reasonable, but a necessity. Because the only possible spiritual development is in the sense of depth. The artistic tendency is not expansive, but a contraction. And art is the apotheosis of solitude. (pp. 46-7)

Proust situates friendship somewhere between fatigue and ennui. He does not agree with the Nietzschean conception that friendship must be based on intellectual sympathy, because he does not see friendship as having the least intellectual significance. 'We agree with those whose ideas (non-Platonic) are at the same degree of confusion as our own.' For him the exercise of friendship is tantamount to a sacrifice of that only real and incommunicable essence of oneself to the exigencies of a frightened habit whose confidence requires to be restored by a dose of attention. It represents a false movement of the spirit—from within to without, from the spiritual assimilation of the immaterial as provided by the artist, as extracted by him from life, to the abject and indigestible husks of direct contact with the material and concrete, with what we call the material and the concrete. Thus he visits Balbec and Venice, meets Gilberte and the Duchesse de Guermantes and Albertine, attracted not by what they are but impelled by their arbitrary and ideal equivalents. The only fertile research is excavatory, immersive, a contraction of the spirit, a descent. The artist is active, but negatively, shrinking from the nullity of extracircumferential phenomena, drawn in to the core of the eddy. He cannot practise friendship, because friendship is the centrifugal force of self-fear, self-negation. Saint-Loup must be considered as more general than himself, as a product of the oldest French nobility, and the beauty and ease of his tenderness for the narrator—as when, for example, he accomplishes the most delicate and graceful gymnastics in a Paris restaurant so that his friend shall not be disturbed—are appreciated, not as the manifestations of a special and charming personality, but as the inevitable adjuncts of excessively good birth and breeding. 'Man,' writes Proust, 'is not a building that can receive additions to its superficies, but a tree whose stem and leafage are an expression of inward sap.' We are alone. We cannot know and we cannot be known. 'Man is the creature that cannot come forth from himself, who knows others only in himself, and who, if he asserts the contrary, lies.'

Here, as always, Proust is completely detached from all moral considerations. There is no right and wrong in Proust nor in his world. (Except possibly in those passages dealing with the war, when for a space he ceases to be an artist and raises his voice with the plebs, mob, rabble, canaille). Tragedy is not concerned with human justice. Tragedy is the statement of an expiation, but not the miserable expiation of a codified breach of a local arrangement, organised by the knaves for the fools. The tragic figure represents the expiation of original sin, of the original and eternal sin of him and all his 'soci malorum,' the sin of having been born. (pp. 47-9)

> *Samuel Beckett, in his* Proust *(reprinted by permission of Grove Press, Inc.), Chatto & Windus, 1931 (and reprinted by Grove Press, 1957), 72 p.*

ANDRÉ GIDE (essay date 1938)

[Finished *Les Jeunes Filles en fleurs*] with an uncertain mixture of admiration and irritation. Though a few sentences (and, in spots, very numerous ones) are insufferably badly written, Proust always says precisely what he wants to say. And it is because he succeeds so well in doing so that he delights in it. So much subtlety is, at times, utterly useless; he merely yields to a finicky need of analysis. But often that analysis leads him to extraordinary discoveries. Then I read him with rapture. I even like the fact that the point of his scalpel attacks everything that offers itself to his mind, to his memory; to everything and to anything whatever. If there is waste here, it's just too bad! What matters is not so much the result of the analysis as the method. Often one follows attentively, not so much the matter on which he is operating, as the minute work of the instrument and the slow patience of his operation. But it constantly appears to me that if the true work of art cannot do without that preliminary operation, it really begins only with that accomplished. The work of art presupposes it, to be sure, but rises up only after that original operation has ended. The architecture in Proust is very beautiful; but it often happens, since he removes none of the scaffolding, that the latter assumes more importance than the monument itself, in which one's glance, constantly distracted by the detail, does not succeed in grasping the whole. Proust knew this, and this is what made him, in his letters and in his conversation, insist so much on the general composition of his work: he was well aware that it would not be obvious. (pp. 404-05)

André Gide, in a journal entry in 1938, in his The Journals of André Gide: 1928-1939, Vol. III, *edited and translated by Justin O'Brien (reprinted by permission of Alfred A. Knopf, Inc.), Knopf, 1949, Secker & Warburg, 1949, pp. 381-411.*

HENRY MILLER   (essay date 1938)

[We see in Proust] the full flower of psychologism—confession, self-analysis, arrest of living, making of art the final justification, but thereby divorcing art from life. An intestinal conflict in which the artist is immolated. The great retrospective curve back towards the womb: suspension in death, living death, for the purposes of dissection. Pause to question, but no questions forthcoming, the faculty having atrophied. A worship of art for its own sake—not for man. Art, in other words, regarded as a means of salvation, as a redemption from suffering, as a compensation for the terror of living. *Art a substitute for life.* The literature of flight, of escape, of a neurosis so brilliant that it almost makes one doubt the efficacy of health. *Until* one casts a glance at that "neurosis of health" of which Nietzsche sings in *The Birth of Tragedy.* (pp. 109-10)

[If] Proust may be said to have provided the tomb of art, in Joyce we can witness the full process of decomposition. (p. 110)

In Joyce we see the incapacity of the modern man even to doubt: it is the simulacrum of doubt, not its substance, that he gives us. With Proust there is a higher appreciation of doubt, of the inability to act. Proust is more capable of presenting the metaphysical aspect of things, partly because of a tradition so firmly anchored in the Mediterranean culture, and partly because his own schizoid temperament enabled him to examine objectively the evolution of a vital problem from its metaphysical to its psychological aspect. The progression from nerves to insanity, from a tragic confrontation of the duality in man to a pathologic split in the personality, is mirrored in the transition from Proust to Joyce. Where Proust held himself suspended over life in a cataleptic trance, weighing, dissecting, and eventually corroded by the very scepticism he had employed, Joyce had already plunged into the abyss. In Proust there is still a questioning of values; with Joyce there is a denial of all values. With Proust the schizophrenic aspect of his work is not so much the cause as the result of his world-view. With Joyce there is no world-view. (p. 111)

Proust, in his classic retreat from life, is the very symbol of the modern artist—the sick giant who locks himself up in a cork-lined cell to take his brains apart. He is the incarnation of that last and fatal disease: *the disease of the mind....* [In] the works of Proust and Joyce the same qualities manifest themselves. A perpetual stretching of time and space, an obedience to the law of inertia, as if to atone, or compensate, for the lack of a higher urge. Joyce takes Dublin with its worn-out types; Proust takes the microscopic world of the Faubourg St. Germain, symbol of a dead past. The one wears us out because he spreads himself over such an enormous artificial canvas; the other wears us out by magnifying his thumb-nail fossil beyond all sensory recognition. The one uses the city as a universe, the other as an atom. The curtain never falls. Meanwhile the world of living men and women is huddling in the wings clamoring for the stage.

In these epics everything is of equal prominence, equal value, whether spiritual or material, organic or inorganic, live or abstract. The array and content of these works suggest to the

mind the interior of a junk-shop. The effort to parallel space, to devour it, to install oneself in the time process—the very nature of the task is foreboding. The mind runs wild. We have sterility, onanism, logomachy. *And*—the more colossal the scope of the work the more monstrous the failure! (pp. 111-12)

It is interesting to observe in the works of Proust and Joyce . . . how the milieu from which they sprang determined the choice of the protagonist as well as the nature of the disease against which they fought. Joyce, springing from the priest class, makes Bloom, his "average" man or double, the supreme object of ridicule. Proust, springing from the cultured middle-class, though himself living only on the fringe of society, *tolerated,* as it were, makes Charlus, his king figure, a bitter object of ridicule. (p. 115)

[Charlus] is a colossal figure, and Proust has handled him in colossal fashion. As symbol of the dying world of caste, ideals, manners, etc., Charlus was selected, whether with thought or not, from the forefront of the enemy's ranks. Proust, we know, was outside that world which he has so minutely described. As a pushing little Jew, he fought or wormed his way inside— and with disastrous results. Always shy, timid, awkward, embarrassed. Always a bit ridiculous. A sort of cultivated Chaplin! And, characteristically, this world which he so ardently desired to join he ended by despising. It is a repetition of the Jew's eternal fight with an alien world. A perpetual effort to become part of this hostile world and then, because of inability to become assimilated, rejecting it or destroying it. But if it is typical of the mechanism of the Jew, it is no less typical of the artist. And, true artist that he was, thoroughly sincere, Proust chose the best example of that alien world for his hero, Charlus. Did he not, in part, become like that hero himself later on, in his unnatural effort to become assimilated? For Charlus, though he had his counterpart in reality, quite as famous as the fictive creation, Charlus is, nevertheless, the image of the later Proust. He is, indeed, the image of a whole world of aesthetes who have now incorporated under the banner of homosexualism. (pp. 116-17)

[We] have in Proust the austere atmosphere of the Jewish home contaminated by a hostile culture, the most strongly rooted culture left in the Western world—French Hellenism. We have an uneasiness, a maladjustment, a war in the spiritual realm which, projected in the novel, continued throughout his life. Proust was touched only superficially by French culture. His art is eminently un-French. We have only to think of his devout admiration for Ruskin. Ruskin! of all men!

And so, in describing the decay of his little world, this microcosm which was for him *the* world, in depicting the disintegration of his hero, Charlus, Proust sets before us the collapse of the outer and the inner world. The battleground of love, which began normally enough with Gilberte, becomes transferred, as in the world to-day, to that plane of depolarized love wherein the sexes fuse, the world where doubt and jealousy, thrown out of their normal axes, play diabolical roles. Where in Joyce's world a thoroughly normal obscenity slops over into a slimy, glaucous fluid in which life sticks, in Proust's world vice, perversion, loss of sex breaks out like a pox and corrodes everything.

In their analysis and portrayal of disintegration both Proust and Joyce are unequalled, excepting perhaps by Dostoievski and Petronius. They are both *objective* in their treatment—technically classic, though romantic at heart. They are naturalists who present the world as they find it, and say nothing about the causes, nor derive from their findings any conclusions. They are defeatists, men who escape from a cruel, hideous, loathsome reality into ART. After writing the last volume, with its memorable treatise on art, Proust goes back to his death-bed to revise the pages on Albertine. This episode is the core and climax of his great work. It forms the arch of that Inferno into which the mature Proust descended. For if, retiring ever deeper into the labyrinth, Proust had cast a glance back at that which he left behind, he must have seen there in the figure of women that image of himself in which all life was mirrored. It was an image which tantalized him, an image which lied to him from every reflection, because he had penetrated to an underworld in which there were nothing but shadows and distortions. The world he had walked out on was the masculine world in process of dissolution. With Albertine as the clue, with this single thread in his hand which, despite all the anguish and sorrow of knowledge he refuses to let slip, he feels his way along the hollows of the nerves, through a vast, subterranean world of remembered sensations in which he hears the pumping of the heart but knows not whence it comes, or what it is. (pp. 117-18)

Weary of realism and naturalism, as were the painters, or rather finding the existent picture of reality unsatisfying, *unreal,* owing to the explorations of the physicists, Proust strove, through the elaborate diffraction of incident and character, to displace the psychologic realism of the day. His attitude is coincident with the emergence of the new analytical psychology. Throughout those veritably ecstatic passages in the last volume of his work—the passages on the function of art and the role of the artist—Proust finally achieves a clarity of vision which presages the finish of his own method and the birth of a wholly new kind of artist. Just as the physicists, in their exploration of the material nature of the universe, arrived at the brink of a new and mysterious realm, so Proust, pushing his powers of analysis to the utmost limits, arrived at that frontier between dream and reality which henceforth will be the domain of the truly creative artists. (p. 127)

> *Henry Miller, "The Universe of Death" (originally published in his* Max and the White Phagocytes, *Obelisk Press, 1938), in his* The Cosmological Eye *(copyright 1939 by New Directions Publishing Corporation; reprinted by permission of New Directions), New Directions, 1939, pp. 107-34.*

DERRICK LEON   (essay date 1940)

[*À la Recherche du Temps Perdu*] is by no means a faultless book. Undoubtedly it is too long: not only hundreds of words but hundreds of pages too long. It is true that the various circumstances which made impossible publication in the manner that the author at first desired, permitted him later to make considerable amplifications to his work; but it is also true that all such elaborations were not equally necessary. . . .

The fact that he died before he was able to correct and revise the last three parts of his novel was as great a tragedy for his work as it was for the author. *Albertine Disparue* and *Le Temps Retrouvé,* in particular, are marred by an occasional sketchiness and uncertainty that is far less apparent in any of the previous volumes. . . . (p. 297)

In *Albertine Disparue,* for example, there is a passage stating that Saint-Loup is to keep his wife continuously supplied with offspring, when in the succeeding volume he leaves but one daughter; just as it is stated that Gilberte is eventually to become the Duchesse de Guermantes, an event which certainly never happens during the course of our acquaintance with her, and is, presumably, some error left from the original version, in which, of course, her husband could not have been killed in the War. (p. 298)

[In *À la Recherche du Temps Perdu*] there are to be found long and redundant passages which could add little of value to any novel. The famous introduction to *Sodome et Gomorrhe,* is, although a remarkable innovation, indispensable to the development of the work, and a treatise of great power and understanding. But it is difficult to find any adequate justification for the lengthy expositions of military tactics, or Brichot's endless dissertations upon the meaning of the place-names about Balbec. The sum of many such digressions, when it does little to advance the portrayal of character or the development of the action, merely serves to weaken the cumulative effect of a work which was composed with the most detailed and passionate care. Yet despite all its diffuseness, it is amazing how the subtle and persistent interlocking of episodes never weakens. Not only is the moment when Albertine announces to Marcel her knowledge of Mlle Vinteuil prepared for thousands of pages before, when as a child, he looks through the window of Montjouvain; and the climax in *Albertine Disparue,* when he receives Gilberte's telegram and imagines that it comes from Albertine, anticipated already in the early days of *À l'Ombre des Jeunes Filles en Fleur,* when Gilberte writes to him for the first time, and, owing to her ornate and pretentious calligraphy, he finds the utmost difficulty in deciphering her signature; but nearly every fresh episode in the book at once develops some past theme, and simultaneously introduces a new one. With what ingenious skill the introduction to *Sodome et Gomorrhe* is foreshadowed in the conversation about the fertilization of her plant at Mme de Guermantes' dinner party, or M. de Vagoubert is first discussed by M. de Norpois, and the full significance of certain implications demonstrated only much later, when he is shown at the Princesse de Guermantes' in conversation with M. de Charlus. (pp. 299-300)

[The] greatest weaknesses of the book are the expression of precisely the same qualities that contrived to produce its extraordinary power, and are consequently inseparable from it. For Proust was so determined to give everything that he possessed, so determined to express himself with ultimate freedom and completeness, so determined that nothing that might add to the value of his work should be omitted, that he could not restrain himself from saying everything too frequently, too persistently and too much. Every idea, every psychological law, every theme that he utilized to express the truths he desired to illustrate, is repeated again and again; applied now to this character and now to that, stressed and overstressed with so consistent an emphasis that the result appears, sometimes, one of such deadly and hopeless monotony that it becomes almost unbearable. Every painful throb of jealousy and desire that is experienced by Swann for Odette is felt again by Marcel for Gilberte, and then superlatively and for the third time, by Marcel for Albertine. While this skilfully illustrates the fact that we learn never through our knowledge of the suffering of others but only, ultimately, through our own; and that the path by which we come to understand the truth of ideas which hitherto we have admitted only theoretically, and as platitudes, is essentially the same for each one of us: nevertheless, by lack of contrast, it tends ultimately to diffuse its force by reason of its very persistence. (pp. 300-01)

It is frequently observed of Proust that he is the supreme example of a novelist without discrimination. In reality it would be far more accurate to say that his work suffers from an embarrassment of riches. Certainly there are some long digressions that might well have been deleted; but lack of discrimination in this sense is but a minor technical weakness. Evidently it is not a psychological one. For it is almost wholly in his quite extraordinarily sensitive intellectual and emotional sense of discrimination that the whole value and significance of his work resides. But this discrimination is manifest not in the actual choice of his material, but in the persistent contrast between spurious, relative and ultimate values, and the sources and intensity of various impressions. The princely parties of the Guermantes are described in such punctilious detail, not because Proust considers them as important as the vivid and joyful impressions of his childhood, but because this is the supreme method by which he can show the ignorance, arrogance, complacence and stupidity which are the greatest barriers to our true life, and demonstrate his final proposition that the depth, validity and power of our most valuable impressions are quite independent of any worldly grandeur. (p. 303)

In conclusion, it must be emphasized how inconspicuous, almost irrelevant indeed, Proust's faults become in comparison with the superb success and ingenuity with which so many supplementary themes are continually interwoven and continuously developed until they are combined at last in the incomparable final chapter. This alone would make it impossible to deny Proust's right to claim his place amongst the greatest novelists of the world. Essentially different from those others from whom, nevertheless, he has derived those qualities of depth and solidity which place him, despite his various innovations, in the direct line of the great tradition, his subtlety and power so far exceed his obvious deficiencies that he can well stand with Tolstoy, Dostoievsky, Balzac, Stendhal and Thackeray, with all of whom he has so much in common. (p. 308)

[Proust] has lifted the novel out of the realm of fiction altogether. His book is no arbitrary portrayal of life, but the lives of himself and of his circle, penetrated to the most obscure and inaccessible depths that he could reach. No other novelist has ever been so little concerned with entertainment or distraction. His work contains humour, poetry, drama, passion and tragedy: all the irony, the triviality, the beauty and the disillusion of human life. (p. 309)

> *Derrick Leon, in his* Introduction to Proust: His Life, His Circle, and His Work *(reprinted by permission of the Estate of Derrick Leon), Kegan Paul, Trench, Trubner & Co., Ltd., 1940, 319 p.*

JUSTIN O'BRIEN (essay date 1947)

Supposedly the unfinished life story of a famous writer, *Jean Santeuil* relates in the third person (though later Proust was to be more at home in the first person) his childhood and young manhood in Paris society and at various attractive vacation spots. The more delightful chapters—pleasing partly because we see in them the first draft of [*Rembrance of Things Past*]—recount his loves and social encounters, while the duller ones, without counterpart in the definitive work, trace the Dreyfus affair and government scandals. The whole is so disjointed that, despite the descriptive chapter headings supplied by the editor, one occasionally wonders if the same hero is concerned throughout.

Hardly a novel in itself, *Jean Santeuil* interests by the light it throws on Proust's later work, affording us that special pleasure

we take in comparing an original piano score with its full orchestration that we know and love. Again and again the reader feels enveloped in the familiar atmospheres of the Proustian world, whether in the haughty Faubourg Saint-Germain peopled with duchesses or in the quiet provincial town with its Gothic steeple beckoning over the trees by the river. And many of the later themes—from the glamor of nobility to the mysterious resurrection of the past—are already sounded somewhat timidly.

The best of the incidents that we excitedly recognize throughout the book—the mother's good-night kiss, the childish love for a playmate in the Champs-Elysées, the rapture caused by remembered scenes, the mingled joy and anguish at hearing the mother's voice over a long-distance telephone, the thwarted kiss, and the jealous peeking through the shutters of the mistress' window—seem crude here only because they have not been fully integrated with those themes. A word-by-word comparison of parallel passages often separated by a fifteen-year interval is not always to the disadvantage of the earlier one.

For instance, various loves of the hero emerge in some detail, delighting us with episodes and reflections that Proust was later to embody in the love of "Marcel" for Gilberte and Albertine and in Swann's love for Odette. But here we do not feel any particular relationship or progression among those affairs, nor have they any necessary bond with the rest of the hero's life as we are told it. After these first notes were finished and put aside, it occurred to Proust to split up his own personality into three memorable characters: Marcel the narrator, the somber Baron de Charlus, and the urbane Swann. Charlus could stand for Sodom, which only once and discreetly peeks out of this early narrative; whereas Swann, as a rich and cultured commoner who had already penetrated the charmed circle of the Guermantes and lived among the Verdurins, could prefigure the narrator's ascent in society and offer a foretaste of that youth's pathologically jealous loves.

Rarely, if ever, has a great writer been so obviously the author of a single book. Everything in Marcel Proust's life, from his wealth and snobbery to his sexual orientation and providential asthma, served to prepare him for the writing of the particular novel he eventually wrote. His early precious essays, the society chronicles for the *Figaro,* and the clever parodies he made of such classics as Balzac, Saint-Simon, and Flaubert all represent obscure gropings in the direction of his single masterwork.

In *Jean Santeuil* we now have the first nearly complete "dry run" of *Remembrance of Things Past.* Obviously it was too early—these pages were written before he reached thirty—for him to create a system out of his own susceptibility to the involuntary memory. Doubtless he had to reach middle life before seeing that his true purpose, as he tells us in *The Past Recaptured,* was to relive the past in the present and thus to cancel the effects of time through his art. It is chiefly this, however, that makes Proust's finished classic universal.

Yet, in *Jean Santeuil* he is already recording the story of another writer inordinately sensitive to that particular affective memory—in the Paris bells, in the scent of white lilacs and the sight of pink hawthorn, in a sea breeze or the smell of a wooden cottage by the shore, in the buzzing of summer flies or a combination of notes from the piano. Already he can prophetically say, surely without sensing how accurately he was foretelling a part of his mature credo: "I write nothing of what I see, nothing at which I arrive by a process of reasoning, or of what I have remembered in the ordinary sense of remembering, but only of what the past brings suddenly to life in a smell, in a sight, in what has, as it were, exploded within me and set the imagination quivering, so that the accompanying joy stirs me to inspiration.''

Undeniably the germ of Proust's later, famous work is here, although he has not yet learned to orchestrate his themes. The greatest value of this volume, in no sense a substitute for *Remembrance of Things Past,* is to make the world appreciate at last the ingenious composition of his more familiar definitive work—the very quality upon which, as it was least apparent at first, he himself most insisted. (pp. 30-2)

> *Justin O'Brien, " 'Jean Santeuil',"* in The New York Times (© *1947 by The New York Times Company; reprinted by permission), December 28, 1947 (and reprinted in his* The French Literary Horizon, *Rutgers University Press, 1967, pp. 29-32).*

GERMAINE BRÉE   (essay date 1950)

A la Recherche du Temps perdu is the story of the narrator's life, told in retrospect. Though it seems almost an apologia, his life is, in fact, a veritable triumph. As a child he dreams of certain very definite future accomplishments: he wants to go to Balbec, to Venice; to know the Swanns, the Guermantes; to be loved by a woman, several women, in some romantic setting; and, finally, he cherishes the vague but ambitious dream of becoming a great writer. His life is like a game of solitaire in which the cards, falling one by one, end by forming the one combination that makes the game come out successfully. As the years pass, one by one all these childhood dreams come true. He becomes intimate with the Swanns; at Balbec he meets a group of young girls all of whom later grant him passing favors in this exceedingly romantic setting. He enters the world of the Guermantes, and possesses one of the Balbec girls to the point of keeping her a virtual prisoner for a certain length of time in his apartment. Eventually, he goes to Venice. Then, as his last card and final triumph, he even attains his most problematical goal: he discovers he has a real vocation as a writer.

And all around him other successes accumulate: the social successes of Odette, of Gilberte, of Mme Verdurin, of Legrandin, of Bloch and many others; the professional successes of Brichot, Cottard, Rachel; the artistic successes of Vinteuil, Bergotte, Elstir. In this respect *A la Recherche du Temps perdu* differs markedly from Flaubert's *L'Education Sentimentale.* The world of *A la Recherche du Temps perdu* is not ostensibly peopled with failures, mediocrities, or disabled characters; quite the contrary. Nor does the narrator belong to the rebellious line of the Werthers, Renés, Childe Harolds and other misfits in a life which they denounce as inadequate.

The narrator recounts the life of a wealthy and sensitive young man who, with a great deal of curiosity and, at first, pleasure, moves in the social circles of Paris—that particularly brilliant and elegant Paris which flourished during the quarter of a century preceding the First World War. (pp. 14-15)

The narrator distinguishes two stages in the life he has lived. The first is a long one during which all his dreams, except one, come true, but without bringing him any satisfaction, for the real world never fulfills his desires. The exception is his failure to become a writer. His life becomes more and more arid as we follow him from the world of Combray to his final return to Paris after the war. This long first period is followed by a second stage, contained in its entirety in the third chapter of *Le Temps retrouvé,* which lasts only a few hours to end in a sudden revelation, brief and awesome, a revelation which completely alters everything that has preceded it. Without this revelation the ground covered in the first stage of his life leads nowhere. Though extremely brief in comparison with the first period, it nevertheless imparts meaning to the road already travelled, the road which, at that moment, leads him to his destination. Yet the long first part of the novel is told by the man for whom the road as yet has no destination, the man without a recognized destiny, who does not know what awaits him. The further he goes, the more he despairs. Between this and the second stage stretches a long period of silence, those "sixteen years" of which the narrator speaks. Then, in a few brief moments the discovery of the meaning of his long journey totally transforms his point of view and forces him to re-evaluate everything that went on during its progress. (p. 16)

The point at which the narrator arrives at the end of the novel cannot possibly be superimposed upon the point of his departure, for this would bring the esthetic validity of the novel's composition into question. The title of the book indicates a quest in which the narrator is engaged. How could he tell of his hopeless "search" if he already knew its successful outcome? The "revelation" at the end would then be faked; the climax of the novel would lose all its value. Only at that point are the narrator's eyes opened, and only then does he reach the end of his long despair. If the narrator had known at the very outset of his story what the end was going to be and had capriciously held in reserve the "revelation" as a surprise for the reader alone, his experience and the emotions it entails would take on the appearance of a cheap mystification for the reader. As a matter of fact, at no point before the last chapter of *Le Temps retrouvé* does the narrator expect, or even suspect, the end of his story which, as it proceeds, appears to him to be leading nowhere. (pp. 19-20)

[Proust had] to construct his world on three superimposed levels: first as the narrator thought he was living it at the time (an experience he can describe in detail through the device of the madeleine); second as he judges it when he recalls it a long time later; and third as he discovers it at the end. On the first level the child, adolescent, or young man advances toward the future and his conception of life slowly changes. As he grows older his point of view gradually comes to coincide with that of the elderly narrator who looks backward at events and sees them only in the light of what he has become. The movement which carries the child toward the future is stopped, immobilized, neutralized by the retrospective meditation of the man. The narrator meditates upon the disillusioning changes in his life, not on that life itself. The child's progress toward the future is thwarted, destroyed by the very fact that the narrator's thought is oriented so entirely toward the past, for this past was the future the child so eagerly anticipated. This delicate equilibrium is shattered at the end when the narrator's revelation totally reverses his values. It is only then that the Proustian world takes on its real dimensions. Between the void of the past and that of the future the narrator catches a glimpse of the edifice of his own life, fashioned by time. This life is a joyous denial of that double void; it exists, it asserts its own existence, it is itself beautiful.

Proust's world is deliberately ambivalent. His narrator's life has two facets: it is totally without value when he examines it before the revelation of the Guermantes reception; it is infinitely precious yet exactly the same when he considers it after the revelation. The whole Proustian world reflects the same ambivalence. The lives of Swann, Odette, Charlus, which first appear to be wasted, become infinitely precious and valuable when the narrator sees them in their full mystery as Proust created them. For from the start Proust had to introduce into his universe that value which the narrator would eventually discover. He had to give it a quality which would contradict the increasingly pessimistic conclusions of the "I." As the narrator sees his life according to the perspective of "time lost" or of "time regained" its whole significance changes for him. The same holds true for the reader who, spellbound by the use of the first person, embraces the narrator's point of view to the end; but the journey is long, and the reader does not always take the last step which qualifies—without transforming—the vision inherent in the lengthy "time lost" section of the novel. The very existence of Combray, of Balbec, of the Verdurins, or of the Baron de Charlus is enough to counterbalance all the pessimistic judgments of the world formed by the narrator—perhaps also by the reader and by Marcel Proust himself. The overall architecture of *A la Recherche du Temps perdu* enables Proust to describe both the joyous reality of life and the manner in which it eludes the narrator. He then goes on to show that once the narrator has grasped the nature of reality it immediately transforms those things it touches, placing upon them the magic stamp of beauty and happiness.

A la Recherche du Temps perdu is a success story, but it is not concerned with ordinary, tangible success. The narrator attains his goal and his life becomes a success in Proust's sense when he passes from the inner perspective of "time lost" to the inner perspective of "time regained." The entire novel is constructed with this revelatory passage in view. The two great stages of his narrator's life are necessarily assymetrical, for the very essence of the second stage is that it is a revelation about the first. A short transition in the introductory passages of *Le Temps retrouvé* marks the passage from one to the other. It is a "return" to life by a quick succession of steps recalling in a few pages the slow movement of the narrator's life as it has gradually lost all meaning. In brief, what Proust has done is to describe the narrator's long, slow progress toward a goal which he perceives only intermittently, and often forgets altogether. Failure to reach this goal would destroy all the significance of his life; its attainment gives meaning to the very discouragements which have marked his road. The narrator passes from failure to success, but a success made possible only by his failure: the "time lost" during the first long stage of his journey becomes "time regained."

There is no question in *A la Recherche du Temps perdu* of a return to the past, nor is the novel composed "in a circle," that is with no beginning or end. It is concerned with the problems of destination, of attainment. The narrator's last long meditation upon his past allows him to sum up all the various stages of his journey. But it is itself a stage, the next to the last one that the narrator must cover before reaching his destination, a stage at which he almost stops. He draws up the balance sheet of his life, a balance sheet which life itself will undertake to rectify. But it has to be drawn up before it can be rectified. In the process the narrator evaluates life as he never has before. This evaluation makes of his meditation something more than a long and pointless journey into the past, even though he finally passes a judgment of sterility upon that past. For because of this judgment, the narrator takes one more step toward his goal. Even this step would be useless, however, were it not followed by another more important one. Proust, who constructed his work with the dual possibility of success

or failure in mind, was well aware of this. A great many commentaries on *A la Recherche du Temps perdu* forget that, in the long run, it is not this lengthy meditation that contains the significance of the novel; it is contained in the real joy of the revelation of *Le Temps retrouvé,* a joy which encompasses the whole of Proust's work and illuminates it. This joy alone assigns their true value to the themes of the narrator's meditation because it makes clear that they are limited, that they refer only to a partial vision of life. When the narrator judges his life, his judgment must be subordinated to the fact that he is alive, a fact without which such an evaluation could never exist. The narrator's meditations can only inadequately translate his actual experience. They almost succeed in stopping him on the road to realization because they leave in shadow what is essential: the very joy of being alive. (pp. 22-5)

Germaine Brée, in her Marcel Proust and Deliverance from Time, *translated by C. J. Richards and A. D. Truitt (translation copyright © 1969 by Rutgers University, The State University of New Jersey; reprinted by permission of Rutgers University Press; originally published as* Du temps perdu au temps retrouvé, *Belles Lettres, 1950), Rutgers University Press, 1969, 252 p.*

ANDRÉ MAUROIS   (essay date 1950)

Stendhal said that the novelist, having constructed his novel, must add to it an element of the ridiculous. Proust uses an even stronger word. It was his opinion that there must, in every great work of art, be something of the grotesque. A short book, whether prose narrative or stage play, can be uniformly emotional and moving—though on this point Shakespeare would not have agreed with him. But in a long novel, as in life itself, there must be comic moments, the purpose of which is to restore the balance of the whole and to relieve the tension. . . . Proust, although, and perhaps because, he was one of the great analysts of misery, could note the oddities and futilities of mankind. The human comedy fascinated and amused him. (p. 225)

Proust's comic themes are of two kinds: those that are a permanent part of human nature, that have frightened and consequently amused mankind from the beginning of recorded history, and those that were peculiar to his period, his world, and his temperament.

First and foremost among the permanent themes is what we may call *"La Danse Macabre."* From time immemorial the comic writer has always exploited the contrast between the panic engendered by the idea of death, and the mechanical routine of living which compels us, when faced by the most terrifying of all dramas, to continue acting and talking as we have always done. (p. 228)

In one of the saddest passages of [*Remembrance of Things Past*], the scene in which the grandmother dies, Proust, the humorist with the implacable eye, gives a subtle, balanced, but profoundly comic sketch of Professor Dieulafoy, the usher of Death and master of the funeral ceremonies. (pp. 229-30)

From the days of Molière to those of Jules Romains, doctors have been among the favorite butts of comic writers, because their power and their learning inspire all mankind with a secret terror. Proust, the son and the brother of doctors, is, at one moment, full of respect for medicine, at another, severe in his criticism of medical men. He created in Dr. Cottard a man who was almost half-witted, and yet, at the same time, a great practitioner. He wrote that "medicine knows nothing of the secret of curing, but has mastered the art of prolonging illness''; that ''medicine is a compendium of the successive and contradictory mistakes of doctors.'' But he could also give it as his opinion that ''to believe in medicine would be the greatest folly, were it not that refusal to believe in it would be a greater.'' (p. 231)

Proust becomes harsher when he touches on his favorite theme of snobbery. That Proust himself, in the days of his youth, manifested certain symptoms of snobbery is of small importance. Not only is the perfect lucidity of the comic writer not incompatible with personal experience, but actually presupposes it. The ''sense of humor'' consists of mocking in oneself what deserves mockery. (pp. 231-32)

Snobbery, in Proust's novel, appears in many different forms. There is the snobbery of the man (or the woman) who, wishing to belong to a certain coterie, and having succeeded in getting a foot over the threshold, feels so little sure of himself that, rather than run the risk of compromising himself in the eyes of his new friends he is prepared to deny his old ones. This is the case of Legrandin, who, with his flowing, spotted tie, his candid glance, and his charming utterances, has the appearance of a poet though, in fact, he is obsessed by a violent and unsatisfied desire to be on terms of intimacy with the Duchesse de Guermantes and the local bigwigs. So long as no countess or marchioness is in sight, he is extremely affable to the Narrator's grandfather, but when walking with one of the neighboring great ladies, he pretends not to know his Commoner friend. (p. 232)

Second specimen: the snobbery of genuine aristocrats, belonging to a noble family, but to a junior branch of it, who, as the result of constant snubs, are like ''trees which, springing from a bad position on the edge of a precipice, are compelled to grow with a backward slant in order to maintain their equilibrium.'' Of this type is Madame Gallardon. . . . (pp. 233-34)

Third specimen: the snobbery of the Guermantes themselves, who are so sure of their own social superiority that they regard the whole of humanity with an undiscriminating good will born of an undiscriminating contempt. They attach very little importance to having aristocratic relations, because all their relations are aristocratic: they are severe in their judgment on those who want to move in high society, but, at the same time, find an odd sort of pleasure in entertaining a ''Highness,'' of speaking of their royal connections, and also, or at least this was so in the case of the Duchess, of appraising intellectual achievements with an air of knowledgeable authority which had no real justification. The Guermantes, who had once been, for the Narrator, figures in a fairy tale, quickly become a group of comic characters as a result of that artless self-assurance which led the Duke to quote and to provoke his Duchess's ''witticisms,'' and her to live up to the part for which she had thus been cast.

Finally, at the very top of the social ladder are perched those Royal Highnesses—such as the Princesse de Parme and the Princesse de Luxembourg—who want to be kindly, but behave in so remote and condescending a fashion that they give the impression of being barely able to distinguish a human being from an animal, as when one of them offers a cake to the Narrator's grandmother much in the same way as a visitor to the zoo might feed one of the exhibits. (pp. 234-35)

The culminating point of Proust's satirical treatment of snobbery is to be found in the ''Marquise'' episode. ''Marquise'' was the nickname given by the Narrator's grandmother to the lessee of the small shabby pavilion, masked by a green trellis, which did duty in the Champs-Elysées for a public lavatory. The ''Marquise'' was the possessor of an enormous face, smothered in a sort of rough cast of powder, and wore, on her red wig, a small black lace bonnet. She was of a friendly disposition, but inclined to be haughty, and was ruthless in the contempt with which she refused admission to such visitors as she happened to dislike. ''I choose my customers,'' she said; ''I don't let just anybody into what I call my parlors. Don't they just look like parlors with all them flowers? Some of my customers are very nice people, and not a day passes but one or another of them brings me some lilac or jasmine or roses— the which is my favorite blooms. . . .'' The Narrator's grandmother, who has overheard the conversation, makes the following comment: ''No one could be more Guermantes or more Verdurin-little-nucleus.''

That single short phrase pricks the bubble of snobbery more effectively than any diatribe by a moralist could do, because it shows that vanity and disdain are universal sentiments, and that there exists no man or woman so completely disinherited but can find someone to exclude from his or her own particular circle.

The comic writer's favorite method is imitation. Dickens, when he wants to hold the barristers of his day up to ridicule, introduces into *Pickwick* a prosecuting counsel's speech which is *almost* genuine, but sufficiently distorted to underline the point of the mockery. Proust was a perfect imitator. Imitation is a difficult art, because it demands not only that the imitator should be able to reproduce the very voice, the very gestures of his victim, but also that he should have mastered his tricks of speech and ways of thinking. To be able to talk like Charlus or Norpois is nothing if one cannot think, and arrange one's thoughts, like Charlus or Norpois. Therein lay Proust's supreme gift. Not content with analyzing a character in abstract phrases, he delighted in bringing him on to the stage and letting him speak for himself.

Take, for instance, the astonishing figure of the old diplomat. Proust never just says, ''This was what Monsieur de Norpois was thinking''; but the long speeches which he puts into his mouth enable us to grasp the mechanism of his thought. The essence, the mainspring, of the Norpois style is this, that the diplomat will never allow himself to say anything that might possibly commit him irrevocably to any statement whatever. So precisely does he balance his sentences that they cancel one another out. At the end of any of his speeches we discover that he has said precisely nothing at all which could possibly be interpreted as a definite expression of opinion. Add to this his use of a number of professional formulas, his habit of referring to the Great Powers in terms of the buildings associated with the practice of diplomacy—the Quai d'Orsay, Downing Street, the Wilhelmstrasse, the Pont aux Chantres— or reveling in subtleties and discovering in the use of an adjective the key to a national policy, and we are in a position to establish the true Norpois ''tone.'' This particular character who, on his first appearance, may deceive the reader just as he deceived the Narrator, is comic because, behind the imposing façade, there is nothing but utter emptiness, a sham subtlety, and a few elementary emotions—an ambition that does not lessen with increasing age, and a rather touching desire to please Madame de Villeparisis. (pp. 235-37)

Another method common to Proust and Dickens, which partially confirms Bergson's theory of the significance of the comic, is that by which amusing effects are produced from the mechanical aspects of the human creature, or from his occasional resemblance to members of the animal, vegetable, or mineral worlds. The passage in which Proust describes the auditorium of the Opera as being an immense aquarium, a sort of marine cave, where white Nereids float in the recesses of their boxes, is followed by this:

> The Marquis de Palancy, his face bent downwards at the end of his long neck, his round, bulging eye glued to the glass of his monocle, was moving with a leisurely displacement through the transparent shade and appeared no more to see the public in the stalls than a fish that drifts past, unconscious of the press of curious gazers, behind the glass walls of an aquarium.

(p. 242)

This transformation of man into fish is as productive of laughter as might be the successful completion of a conjuring trick.

For a third method he was indebted to [Anatole] France, rather than to Dickens—for the method, that is—which consists in achieving a comic contrast between the nature of the thing described and the solemn tone of a description conceived in terms of Homer or of Bossuet. To write with gravity about frivolous subjects, or with magnificence about trivial objects or mediocre people, produces just that sense of shocked surprise which is the very essence of the comic. Proust (like Aristophanes) loves to spin out a long lyric line, and then end it by a sudden drop into bathos. (pp. 242-43)

If we are fully to explore this whole great subject, it is important to note how ill-defined is the dividing line between the comic and the monstrous. I have already pointed out that men laugh whenever the shock of surprise, provoked by extraordinary actions or words, is followed by a feeling of safety, born of the fact either that the oddities to which their attention has been drawn are harmless, or that they decide, as a result of their amused scrutiny, that such things are only a part of that same human nature which can be seen at work in ourselves. This feeling of safety ceases to exist when the actions (or the words) in question overstep the normal limits of human fatuity, and we find ourselves in the presence of a strange and antisocial phenomenon which, by its very nature, produces a sense of terror. This overstepping is what happens in the case of Monsieur de Charlus who, when he first appears upon the scene, merely provokes us to laugh at his inordinate pride, but who, later in the book, turns into a monster.

It is a fact of importance that in all the greatest works of fiction, there is almost always a monster, and sometimes more than one. The characters thus designated are at once superhuman and inhuman, and they dominate the works in which they appear, giving them unity in a way that nothing else could do. This is true of Balzac's Vautrin, and it is true of Proust's Charlus. The monster opens windows on to mysterious depths just because it is beyond our power to understand him completely. He passes beyond our range of vision, if only by the horror he inspires; but he does, nevertheless, contain elements of a kind that are in us as well. Had the circumstances been different, we might have become what he is, and this thought at once terrifies and fascinates us. Monsters provide the story with unexplored and secret depths which reveal the sublime.

Before Proust, Shakespeare alone had succeeded in orchestrating the magic dissonances amidst which these monsters move. The humor which expresses itself in lovely lines, the

earthbound bodies which can loose spirits on the world, the allegories and the ravishing images which end in horseplay, the flicker of fairy lights, all these things bring the world of Shakespeare to our minds. Proust, like Shakespeare, had plumbed the extremes of human misery, but, like Shakespeare, found in humor a saving grace, and again like Shakespeare, serenity in Time Regained. The end of *A la Recherche du temps perdu* is not unlike the end of Shakespeare's *Tempest*. The play is ended; the Enchanter has surrendered his secret. Back into their box he has put the marionnettes whom he has shown us for the last time, touched with hoarfrost, at the Prince de Guermantes' great reception. Now he says, like Prospero: "We are such stuff as dreams are made on, and our little life is rounded with a sleep. . . ." The Guermantes and the Verdurins vanish in smoke: Swann's bell tinkles for the last time at the garden gate and, while the final cadences on the nature of Time are drawing to a close, we seem to hear, in the moon-drenched trees, far away and barely audible, Marcel's laughter, the laughter of a schoolboy spluttering behind his hand, but softened now, and become the laughter of a very old child to whom life has taught the lesson not only of pain but of pity. (pp. 245-47)

André Maurois, in his Proust: Portrait of a Genius, *translated by Gerard Hopkins (translation copyright ©1950 by André Maurois; copyright renewed © 1978 by Gerard Maurois; reprinted by permission of the author and the author's agents, Scott Meredith Literary Agency, Inc., 845 Third Avenue, New York, New York 10022; originally published as* A la recherche de Marcel Proust, Hachette, 1949), Harper & Brothers, 1950, 332 p.*

ALFRED KAZIN (essay date 1955)

[Proust's] letters are really a handbook to the novel; they do not have the independent interest of D. H. Lawrence's letters or the journals of André Gide. In fact, unless one goes to the letters with a very keen sense of how great the novel is, how much, in Proust's mind, it was the grand justification of a life that up to the time he began the book had been largely "wasted"—on just the social career that these elaborately deferential letters to all and sundry had to feed—it is easy to misjudge the man who wrote them. They are full of his intellectual radiance, often winning—almost too winning—with the gifted neurotic's special need and knowledge of how to please, but they purr so evenly that they often become in the reader's mind indistinguishable expressions of the same social manner. (pp. 23-4)

[Proust] might flatter "society," but, as he was later to write about his novel, "In spite of my desire to be extremely fair and impersonal, it happens, things being what they are, that in *Temps Perdu* the class that is slandered, that is always wrong, talks only nonsense, the vulgar and hateful class, is '*le monde*.'" For he was slowly finding his way to his vocation, outside the society that had always been so important to him, superior even to friendships (and these were peculiarly necessary to him, for he was often anxious and usually ill), which, as he was to confess in a summary passage of the novel apropos of his beloved Robert de Saint-Loup, diminished loneliness but could not involve a man's essential self. (p. 25)

[The] separation from "*le monde*" was final, and if he retired to his cork-lined room, it was certainly not to find safety or tranquillity but to fit the skin of language over the whole world he had once known. (p. 26)

The letters from the cork-lined room bring us near the Proust of the novel—not the "I" who tells the story, since he is a personification of human consciousness, but the heroic invalid who detached himself from his narrator to write the book— the Proust who was interested *not* in doing a self-portrait but in "general laws." And it is only in this period, as we watch him forced to communicate with the outside world largely by letters, yet—through all his pain and desperate fatigue, his appeals to friends to understand how very ill he is, his instinctive demands for sympathy—slowly building his novel up through the years, that we grasp how much its grand style had been formed by his long uneasiness in *"le monde,"* out of the effusiveness that had always hidden his deepest feelings. He would have liked to be "concise" in the manner of certain admired friends, but he knew that for him there was only one way of writing. "I must perforce weave these long silken threads as I spin them, and if I shortened my sentences, the results would be fragments, not whole sentences. So I continue like a silkworm, and live in the same temperature." His indirectness had been one way of withholding himself from a society to which he had been forced to pay tribute, in which he had always felt his position to be slightly false. Now, as he converted his social manner into an instrument of vision, still formal, still polite, he was dazzled by his own abundance. The sentences rose up like cathedrals, infinitely and secretly joined by a continuous rapture at how much could be seized by his consciousness. (p. 27)

> Alfred Kazin, *"Proust in His Letters,"* in his The Inmost Leaf: A Selection of Essays *(copyright 1949, 1977 by Alfred Kazin; reprinted by permission of Harcourt Brace Jovanovich, Inc.), Harcourt, 1955, pp. 21-8.*

WALTER A. STRAUSS (essay date 1957)

Proust was a literary critic of remarkable sensitivity—which is to say that he brought the sensibility of the novelist to bear upon his critical judgment; and the result is a kind of criticism that is not only illuminating with respect to his practice as a novelist but also perceptive in itself, filled with numerous *aperçus* and discoveries that alter the reader's conceptions of the work discussed and enables him to read it with more sharply focused eyes. (pp. 3-4)

Proust's criticism has a tendency to be sporadic and unsystematic, since it arises spontaneously in relation to certain literary and other experiences. . . .

The various essays are loosely built, and tend to undulate; the digressions often become more important than the thread, but the thread is never lost. This is altogether what one would expect, in view of Proust's literary style and his artistic personality in general. Since Proust never compartmentalized any datum of experience, one is not surprised at the digressions; moreover, this method is seasoned with a particular Proustian flavor, consisting of the author's special interests, which inevitably point to *A la recherche.* (p. 4)

Proust's high regard for the function of the critic is attested in the preface to his translation of Ruskin's *Bible of Amiens,* in which he sees the critic playing the part of an "optician," not unlike the novelist. . . . [The] great critic, in Proust's opinion, looks . . . deeply into the writer's creative personality, discerning the writer's special vision and his method of re-creating this vision in terms of literature. Just as the novelist is not merely a technician but above all a "seer" presenting his par-

ticular vision to the reader, so the critic's task too is to help the reader to see. Proust consistently uses optical imagery to emphasize this point: in one case the novelist is an optician, in another, the style is a "reflet insaisissable"; here the critic's duty is to define the "vision durable et claire." . . . In his best critical essays—and this includes his pastiches—he fulfills this dual aim of the critic. In many other pieces of criticism he at least reveals the "artist's unique characteristics," with exciting results.

Proust's practice of literary criticism may be divided into three categories, all of them serving the growing or matured author in one way or another. For it must never be forgotten that Proust's criticism derives from a deeply felt response to an author or a text and cannot be treated as methodical in any sense. The Sainte-Beuve novel-essay [*Contre Sainte-Beuve*] is an excellent case in point. The two principal methods Proust employed were the critical essay—the direct, analytical method, which may also be called "the approach from without"—and the pastiche, an indirect, synthetic form of criticism, but a more subtle one, enabling the critic to work from within. The interests voiced in the critical essays are to some extent reflected in the pastiches. Here again the author's preoccupation with styles is made manifest: pastiches of Balzac, Flaubert, Sainte-Beuve; and the masterful pastiche of Saint-Simon, the most ambitious of them all. (pp. 22-4)

The third method which Proust uses makes literary criticism a facet in character analysis. It is a device frequently used in *A la recherche du temps perdu* whereby a criticism of a certain author is produced in terms of a character of the novel, and conversely, where a character may be criticized in terms of his response to literature. This method is exceedingly complicated and makes no claim to thoroughness, serving frequently to broaden the study of a certain character (rather than to offer highly refined literary analysis)—a practice differing widely from that used in a number of modern novels in which characters tend to become embodiments of ideas and conversations, tend to become forensic exercises on some given subject (the novels of Huxley, Sartre, and Koestler, for instance). Proust knew that the appreciation of certain books by a fictitious person may illustrate a certain aspect of this person's character as well as certain actions or gestures would. He accordingly makes use of this method in order to view certain authors from another point of view, so to speak, or to criticize an author by criticizing a character of his novel. . . . In most cases, however, such criticisms must be amplified by the opinions of the Narrator. The method had already been used with considerable skill in *Jean Santeuil*. In *A la recherche,* Marcel modifies and corrects the fragmentary canvas of literary judgments left by the other characters. Here the reader is always in the presence of Proust's own literary opinions at a certain stage of his development, as can be shown, wherever possible, by reference to Proust's correspondence and to his critical writings. This unorthodoxy led an English critic to remark: "Actually his books are filled from end to end with criticisms of music, of painting, of literature, not in the way that is unfortunately familiar in this country, as unassimilated chunks in the main stream of the narrative, but as expressions of the opinions of different characters." Since this assimilation is usually so successful, it is often dangerous to draw rash conclusions with regard to Proust's own critical opinions. . . . Generally speaking, Proust and Marcel coincide on intellectual matters, though not on biographical ones; a congruence between the Narrator and Proust does not occur until the latter portions of *A la recherche* are reached. In other words, Marcel has been delegated to help Proust conquer Time: he serves as an intermediary between the author and his subject matter. (pp. 27-8)

"**Contre l'obscurité**" sounds like a preliminary draft of Proust's aesthetics and actually marks the first stage in his search for criteria of literary excellence. It is also an indication of his progress in overcoming the *préciosité* of *Les Plaisirs et les jours* and looks forward to (or possibly coincides with, at least in its initial stages) the reflections on literature in *Jean Santeuil*, and the more concise and better consolidated remarks on literary art inspired by Ruskin. Proust's method here is not to condemn symbolism wholesale, but merely the affectations and obfuscations that came to characterize the Symbolist movement. To deny the lasting influence of symbolism on Proust would be incorrect; many of the passages of *Jean Santeuil*, especially nature descriptions, even certain passages in *A la recherche,* are in the best symbolist ("superimpressionist," as [Benjamin] Crémieux put it) manner, but Proust went far beyond symbolism. Nevertheless, it was evident to Proust as early as 1896 that the business of the writer was to be as clear and precise as possible, even if the effort required a recourse to certain new techniques that might at first *seem* obscure to his readers. It is this dilemma whose nature he is trying to define in "**Contre l'obscurité.**" (p. 80)

Obscurity, Proust maintains in "**Contre l'obscurité,**" must not be pursued as a result of private interests—since it is the poet's function to make obscure sensations clear; nor out of a desire to safeguard one's work from the "*profanum vulgus*"—which does not tamper with works of art anyway. ("If the mob could touch it, it would not be the mob.") Instead, it is the poet's function to use the language as he finds it. This does not prevent the symbolists from exploiting the hidden resources of their language, but it should discourage esoteric language and neologisms.

> The symbolists will be the first to grant us that [however] much magic each word, taken by itself or in its harmony with other words, retains from its origins or from the grandeur of its past, it has on our imagination and sensibility a power of evocation which is at least as great as its power of strict denotation.
>
> (pp. 82-3)

This poetic creed of Proust is basic to his entire criticism of the poetry of the nineteenth century—and by extension to all literature, since for Proust poetry and prose are but diverse aspects of literary art, and since every century has its own classics. In the great poets of the nineteenth century he appreciates the ability to treat their language with love and insight, drawing new effects from its endless resources; an ability to render experience in terms of well-conceived poetic images; a classical sense of form in which the framework serves to hold in check the brimming content; and an awareness of the mystery that resides behind each discovery in nature or in the sphere of intellectual activity—a mystery that must be preserved or deepened because it is the very essence of life. (p. 83)

[Sainte-Beuve's] name had a way of obtruding itself whenever Proust's favorite authors of the nineteenth century were under consideration, with Proust reiterating the idea that Sainte-Beuve, whose business it was to appreciate these writers, failed to understand them. Yet his grievances with the nineteenth-century critic are more deeply rooted, for Sainte-Beuve's entire critical method comes under attack; and we find ourselves, in the last analysis, in the presence of a deep-seated antagonism

between two attitudes toward the psychology of the artist and the nature of literary art itself. (pp. 141-42)

Sainte-Beuve is wrong, says Proust, in his method of judging literature; he misunderstands the entire process of literary creation; and even though he is in some ways a fine critic, especially of the classics, and even though he is a good stylist, he must be rejected by the serious writer. The importance for Proust's career of the casting out of Sainte-Beuve must not be underestimated. Before *Contre Sainte-Beuve* we have Proust, very much like the Narrator in his great work, "à la recherche d'une vocation"; with *Contre Sainte-Beuve,* and particularly right after it, we have "la vocation trouvée" (or *retrouvée*).

Another factor influencing Proust's need to come to grips with Sainte-Beuve (or, for that matter, with any rationalistically oriented critic of the nineteenth century, such as Taine) lies in his growing conviction around 1908 that the intelligence is inadequate when used as the sole instrument of literary analysis—and, by implication, of literary creation. He had felt for a long time that impressions were nearer artistic truth than were intellectualizations. The content of *Jean Santeuil* is, accordingly, strongly impressionistic. But the work was abandoned. What Proust needed was a conception of his work in which the impression would be preserved in a pure state, without being clouded by excessive subjectivity, and in which the intelligence would find its proper place, albeit a subsidiary one. Feeling must precede analysis, without creating discontinuities and imbalances. After all, Proust is as much an heir of the "dreaming" romantics (Nerval, for instance) as of the realists (Balzac and, to a lesser degree, Flaubert). *A la recherche* is a monumental synthesis of the two traditions. Here again *Contre Sainte-Beuve* stands midway between the aspiration (*Jean Santeuil*) and the fulfillment (*A la recherche*). But the work already looks toward the great novel to be created. (pp. 142-43)

Sainte-Beuve becomes the subject of a lengthy investigation to illustrate by concrete examples the shortcomings of the "intelligent" critic confronted by great literary works. (p. 143)

Whereas Sainte-Beuve makes no real distinction between the writer and his work, Proust asserts that there is a sharp cleavage between the social or habitual self of the writer and the creative self. The case of Stendhal illustrates Sainte-Beuve's error clearly enough . . . ; but, as a matter of fact, he claims that the same error of judgment lies at the base of all of Sainte-Beuve's criticisms of the great ones among his literary contemporaries. For the critic did not really understand that the poet works in solitude; and that the true appreciation of literature lies in the critic's ability to listen to the poet's solitude, as it were, rather than to his conversation. "The writer's *moi* shows itself only in his books; he does not show his *moi* to society." Conversation is therefore not the right method of approach; and just as reading is not a substitute for conversation, or a higher form of it, as Proust had been at pains to point out in his preface to *Sésame et les lys,* criticism or literary analysis is not a way of holding converse with an author. There is something incomplete and misleading in this method of analyzing a work of art by consulting the artist's social or everyday personality. Proust finds this inadequacy exemplified in the very nature of Sainte-Beuve's *Lundis:* the critic's thought is incomplete, it takes pleasure in this very fact, since thereby he establishes a sort of conversational contact with his readers, who are expected to complete the idea. He compares it to an arch which takes its origin in Sainte-Beuve's mind and which completes its curve and receives its coloring from the admiring reader. For Sainte-Beuve, he concludes, all literature is like that: it is a series of

Monday chats, pleasing to the Monday audiences, unmindful of the judgment of posterity. This is the real crux of Proust's objection to Sainte-Beuve: the author of the *Lundis* saw literature *sub specie temporis* and literature for him was time-bound, its worth was equivalent to the worth of the person producing it. In Sainte-Beuve the attitude is aggravated by a parallel impulse to preserve his freedom, with the result that if a man wishes to please and yet remain independent, he will find himself writing contradictory articles, such as Sainte-Beuve's on Chateaubriand, or Hugo or Lamartine or Lamennais or even Béranger.

All this is a consequence of Sainte-Beuve's personality and his critical method—to misunderstand the nature of artistic creation, to judge the artist in terms of his social self, to evaluate art in terms of an epoch rather than of eternity: it all adds up to a critical method which is not only conditioned by time but also operates materially (Taine was to go so far as to say "scientifically") on the epoch under consideration. "This ill will which refuses to look into the depths of oneself . . . is my main objection to Sainte-Beuve; it is a material criticism (even though the author speaks only of Ideas, etc.)." (pp. 144-46)

To be sure, Proust is extremely harsh on Sainte-Beuve, forgetting perhaps too readily that Sainte-Beuve often made perspicacious and relevant remarks on a few first-rate authors of his day, including Chateaubriand and Flaubert. Nor is he interested in paying tribute to Sainte-Beuve for his fine perceptions on the "classics." He does not give Sainte-Beuve credit for having made literary criticism into a craft, even into a genre. Proust, after all, is not concerned with matters of literary history. His position is as follows: Sainte-Beuve's final rating as a judge of the nineteenth century is not high. He aptly points out that Sainte-Beuve has a way of spoiling his praises by condescension and patronizing airs. Proust is certain that Sainte-Beuve, by adopting for himself the perspective of history rather than of art, aggravates his blunders of taste. . . . (p. 147)

Ruskin was probably the only [foreign] author whom Proust read, at least to some extent, in the original. . . . (p. 160)

The problem of Ruskin's influence on Proust's style and ideas is of considerable importance to anyone who wishes to form a comprehensive idea of Proust's development as a writer and a thinker. (pp. 177-78)

Most important of all, Proust enriched both his translations [of Ruskin] with copious commentary, full of fascinating criticisms, revealing at the same time the preoccupations that were to come to fruition in *A la recherche.* Moreover, the two long prefaces to the translations provide a comprehensive summary of his appreciation and criticism of Ruskin (in *La Bible d'Amiens,* reprinted in *Pastiches et mélanges*), as well as evidence that Ruskin had by that time been left behind and that Proust had found his own way. . . . (p. 178)

Ruskin can be classed with what Proust liked to call the "self-contemplating" artists of the nineteenth century, such as Wagner and Balzac, who retroactively gave their work a unity and a beauty which it had not originally possessed but which had been latent in it. In Ruskin, Proust admires the skilfully manipulated images or symbols which Ruskin has found in the course of a lecture. As an example, Proust points out the final sentence of the first lecture, entitled "Of Kings' Treasuries," of *Sesame and Lilies,* in which Proust notes the adroit interweaving of images:

That is the way he works. He moves from one idea to the next without any apparent order. But in reality the train of the imagination leading him forward follows its profound affinities which, in spite of himself, impose a superior logic on his writings. So that in the long run he finds that he has followed some sort of secret plan, that, unveiled at the end, retrospectively imposes on the whole a sort of order and causes it to appear wonderfully working up to that final apotheosis.

The reader of this sentence cannot help but think of Proust's own final volume, even the final sentence, of *A la recherche.* However, if Proust admires the over-all pattern of Ruskin's thought as it expresses itself in his books, he has certain reservations about the more detailed procedures of Ruskin the stylist. For instance, he finds in Ruskin's sentences a balance imposed from without—that is, imposed by Ruskin's will, not by an inner compulsion on his part (". . . the pleasure . . . which Ruskin takes in giving to his phrases a balance which has the appearance of imposing *on* his thought, rather than deriving from it, a symmetrical pattern"). An even more serious flaw in Ruskin's style is his tendency to play eruditely with words; Proust points out the uselessness of this practice in one of his notes to *La Bible d'Amiens,* explaining that Ruskin (as he stated in *Sesame and Lilies*) believed that an educated man should know the etymologies and the genealogies of words. . . . Veneration for words is, for Proust, but another aspect of John Ruskin's idolatry, which is his principal weakness, the shortcoming for which Proust reproached him most. "It is the favorite sin of artists, and there are few who have not succumbed to it." Proust knew the temptation of the idolatry of things; his own alter ego, Swann, is guilty of that intellectual sin; and the idolatry of books is one of the dangers of reading against which he inveighs in **"Journées de lecture."** (pp. 178-80)

This struggle between idolatry and sincerity, according to Proust, went on during Ruskin's entire lifetime; and Ruskin, by a self-imposed compromise with his conscience, gradually succumbed to insincerity. . . . This is the real point of dissension between Proust and Ruskin, one of particular importance to the Proust who was trying to find himself. The problem which is raised here is enormous, inasmuch as it involves the entire relationship between art and morality. This explains perhaps why Proust decided to be so blunt in his condemnation of Ruskin's presumed "sincerity." He is primarily rejecting the implication in Ruskin's writings that morality and art are closely interwoven, and that morality (fortified by the Scriptures) takes the precedence. . . . Yet it is doubtful whether the charge of insincerity is to be taken at its face value. Proust certainly did not mean to equate it with hypocrisy. As usual, he tries to detect in writers the inner motivations of their creative personalities, and he finds that in Ruskin a certain insincerity was at work, more or less unconsciously, which found its expression in terms of a certain idolatry or a misplaced reverence.

Proust is aware of his harshness: "I have here, in my effort to push intellectual sincerity to its furthest, its cruellest limits, to wrestle with my most cherished aesthetic impressions." He realizes, and admits, that the criticism he has just made does not detract from the beauty of Ruskin's works and from his excellence as a literary artist. (pp. 181-82)

Ruskin was for Proust a good guide—a fact which Proust never denied in spite of all his criticisms of Ruskin—as contrasted with Sainte-Beuve, who was his idea of a bad guide. For in the long run, Proust insisted in **"Journées de lecture"** and again in *Le Temps retrouvé,* books exist in order to enable the reader to read *himself;* they are like so many optical instruments trained upon the reader's undiscovered self. (p. 185)

Criticism for Proust was a means to an end. . . . He found it to his advantage to use an author's text in the same way in which he intended his own novel to be read—as a sort of optical device whereby the reader can read himself. This process of making a text one's own necessarily implies an intermediate analytical and critical stage, in which the Proustian reader attempts to seize the essence behind an author's "vision." For the author's vision is not necessarily one which he can analyze consciously; the very texture of his writings is the result of a more or less mysterious process, in which the artist's inner organization imposes a secret and profound order upon his materials. (pp. 209-10)

Thus, criticism and analysis were a method of self-discovery for Proust. (pp. 213-14)

To be sure, as we look back to *Jean Santeuil,* we can see that the germ of Proust's idealistic aesthetics was already there. In that novel Jean Santeuil muses at length about the relation of art to life, and about the nature of artistic creation. Proust's most cherished ideas are already sketched out there. The value of literature does not lie in a (naturalistic) use of materials but in the way in which the writer "operates" on his materials. The ironic relationship of life to art is compared—with Platonic overtones—to the difference between shadow and prey; and those who seek reality by embracing life and leaving behind the realm of art are substituting the illusion of material possession for the reality of spiritual possession. . . . The artist's rendering of the reality as he perceives it takes the form of impressions, and the way in which these impressions are organized in the artist's consciousness remains mysterious to him, so that he can never explain to others how the amalgamation took place. Proust's great achievement as a literary critic lies in the fact that he attempted to elucidate the mystery, without dispelling it—because for him art, like religion, needs its mysteries. (pp. 214-15)

> *Walter A. Strauss, in his* Proust and Literature: The Novelist As Critic *(copyright © 1957 by the President and Fellows of Harvard College; excerpted by permission), Cambridge, Mass.: Harvard University Press, 1957, 263 p.*

JOSÉ ORTEGA y GASSET   (essay date 1958-59)

In the midst of contemporary production, which is so capricious, so lacking in necessity, [Proust's] work presents itself with the stamp of something ordained. If it had never come into being, there would have remained, in the literary evolution of the nineteenth century, a specific gap with a clearly defined outline. One might even say, in order to point up its inevitability, that it was created a little late, that analysis would disclose a slight anachronism in its physiognomy. (pp. 504-05)

The narrative themes that come and go on the surface of [Proust's] work have only a tangential and secondary interest; they are like buoys adrift on the bottomless flood of his memories. Before Proust, writers had commonly taken memory as the material with which to reconstruct the past. Since the data of memory are incomplete and retain of the prior reality only an arbitrary extract, the traditional novelist fills them out with

observations drawn from the present, together with chance hypotheses and conventional ideas. In other words, he unites fraudulent elements with the authentic materials of memory.

This method makes sense as long as the intention is, as it formerly was, to *restore* things of the past, i.e. to feign a new presence and actuality for them. The intention of Proust is the very opposite. He does not wish to use his memories as materials for reconstructing former realities; on the contrary, by using all conceivable methods—observations of the present, introspective analyses, psychological generalizations—he wants literally to reconstruct the very memories themselves. Thus, it is not things that are remembered, but the memory of things, which is the central theme of Proust. Here for the first time memory ceases to be treated as the means of describing other things and becomes itself the very thing described. For this reason Proust does not generally add to what is remembered those parts of reality which have eluded memory. Instead, he leaves memory intact, just as he finds it, objectively incomplete, occasionally mutilated and agitating in its spectral remoteness the truncated stumps that still remain to it. There is a very suggestive page in which Proust speaks of three trees on a ridge. He remembers that behind them there was something of great importance, something which has been effaced by time, abolished from memory. In vain the author struggles to recapture what has escaped him, to integrate it with that bit of decimated landscape—those three trees, sole survivors of the mental catastrophe which is forgetting.

The narrative themes in Proust are, then, mere pretexts and, as it were, *spiracula,* air-holes, tiny portals of the hive through which the winged and shuddering swarm of reminiscences succeed in liberating themselves. It is not for nothing that Proust gave his work the general title of *A la recherche du temps perdu.* Proust is an investigator of lost time as such. With utter scrupulousness he refuses to impose upon the past the anatomy of the present; he practices a rigorous non-intervention guided by an unshakable will to avoid reconstruction of any sort. From the nocturnal depths of the soul a memory surges upwards, excitingly, like a constellation in the night which ascends above the horizon. Proust represses all interest in restoration and limits himself to describing what he sees as it arises out of his memory. Instead of reconstructing lost time, he contents himself with making an edifice of its ruins. You might say that in Proust the genre of Memoirs attains the distinction of a pure literary method.

So much for his treatment of time. But even more elemental and stupefying is the nature of his invention with regard to space.

Various people have counted the number of pages that Proust employs in telling us that his grandmother is taking her temperature. Indeed, one cannot talk about Proust without noting his prolixity and concern for minutiae. In his case, prolixity and minute analysis cease to be literary vices and become two sources of inspiration, two muses that might well be added to the other nine. It is necessary for Proust to be prolix and minute for the simple reason that he gets much closer to objects than people are accustomed to. He is the inventor of a new distance between us and things. This fundamental revolution has had such tremendous consequences—as I have said—that almost all previous literature appears to be grossly panoramic, written from a bird's-eye point of view, as compared with the work of this delectably myopic genius. (pp. 505-07)

The monograph on Swann's love is an example of psychological pointillism. For the medieval author of *Tristan and Iseult* love is a sentiment that possesses a clear and definite outline of its own: for him, a primitive psychological novelist, love is love and nothing other than love. As opposed to this, Proust describes Swann's love as something that has nothing like the form of love. All kinds of things can be found in it: touches of flaming sensuality, purple pigments of distrust, browns of habitual life, grays of vital fatigue. The only thing *not* to be found is love. It comes out just as the figure in a tapestry does, by the intersection of various threads, no one of which contains the form of the figure. Without Proust there would have remained unwritten a literature that must be read in the way that the paintings of Monet are looked at, with the eyes half-shut.

It is for this reason that when Proust is compared to Stendhal one must proceed with caution. In many respects they represent two opposite poles, and are antagonistic one toward the other. Above all else, Stendhal is a man of imagination: he imagines the plots, the situations, and the characters. He copies nothing: everything in him resolves to fantasy, into clear and concentrated fantasy. His characters are as much "designed" as are the features of a madonna in the paintings of Raphael. Stendhal believes firmly in the reality of his characters and makes every effort to draw a sharp and unequivocal outline of them. The characters of Proust, on the other hand, have no silhouette; rather, they are changeable atmospheric condensations, spiritual cloud-formations that varying wind and light transform from one hour to the next. Certainly Proust belongs in the company of Stendhal, "investigator of the human heart." But while Stendhal takes the human heart as a solid with a definite though plastic shape, it is for Proust a diffuse and gaseous volume that varies from moment to moment with a kind of meteorological versatility. (p. 509)

[In the volumes of Proust], nothing happens, there is no dramatic action, there is no process. They are composed of a series of pictures extremely rich in content, but static. We mortals, however, by our very nature, are dynamic; we are interested in nothing but movement.

When Proust tells us that the little bell jangles in the gateway of the garden in Combray and that one can hear the voice of Swann who has just arrived, our attention lights upon this event and gathering up its forces prepares to leap to another event which doubtless is going to follow and for which the first one is preparatory. We do not inertly install ourselves in the first event; once we have summarily understood it, we feel ourselves dispatched towards another one still to come. In life, we believe, each event announces its successor and is the point of transition towards it, and so on until a trajectory has been traced, just as one mathematical point succeeds another until a line has been formed. Proust ruthlessly ignores our dynamic nature. He constantly forces it to remain in the first event, sometimes for a hundred pages and more. Nothing follows the arrival of Swann; no other point links up with this one. On the contrary, the arrival of Swann in the garden, that simple momentary event, that point of reality, expands without progressing, stretches without changing into another, increases in volume and for page after page we do not depart from it: we only see it grow elastically, swell up with new details and new significance, enlarge like a soap-bubble embroidering itself with rainbows and images.

We experience, thus, a kind of torture in reading Proust. His art works upon our hunger for action, movement, progression as a continual restraint that holds us back; we suffer like the quail that, taking flight within its cage, strikes against the wire vault in which its prison terminates. The muse of Proust could

well be called "Morosidad" (Sloth), his style consisting in the literary exploitation of that *delectatio morosa* which the Councils of the Church punished so severely. (pp. 511-12)

José Ortega y Gasset, "Time, Distance, and Form in Proust," in The Hudson Review *(copyright © 1959 by The Hudson Review, Inc.; reprinted by permission), Vol. XI, No. 4, Winter, 1958-59, pp. 504-13.*

GEORGE D. PAINTER   (essay date 1959)

It has become one of the dogmas of Proustian criticism that his novel can and must be treated as a closed system, containing in itself all the elements necessary for its understanding. To take two examples from many dozens, Monsieur X is praised for having 'emptied his mind'—did he have to empty it of so very much?—'of all Proustian matter extraneous to the novel which he has set himself to examine'; "I do not propose," says Professor Y, "in this study, which is an attempt to interpret Proust's great novel, to discuss the external facts of his life." . . . In general, however, there is no aspect of Proust or his work—his style, philosophy, character, morality, his attitude to music, painting, Ruskin, snobism and so on—which can be studied without an accurate and detailed knowledge of his life, or which has so far escaped distortion for lack of such knowledge. (pp. xi-xii)

[It] is possible to identify and reconstruct from ample evidence the sources in Proust's real life for all major, and many minor characters, events and places in his novel. By discovering which aspects of his originals he chose or rejected, how he combined many models into each new figure, and most of all how he altered material reality to make it conform more closely to symbolic reality, we can observe the workings of his imagination at the very moment of creation. The 'closed system' Proustians have been egoistically contented to know of Proust's novel only what it means to themselves. It is surely relevant to learn what the novel meant to the author, to understand the special significance which, because they were part of his life and being, every character and episode had for Proust and still retains in its substance. What do they know of *A la Recherche* who only *A la Recherche* know?

A still more important consequence follows from the study of Proust's novel in the light of his biography. *A la Recherche* turns out to be not only based entirely on his own experiences: it is intended to be the symbolic story of his life, and occupies a place unique among great novels in that it is not, properly speaking, a fiction, but a creative autobiography. Proust believed, justifiably, that his life had the shape and meaning of a great work of art: it was his task to select, telescope and transmute the facts so that their universal significance should be revealed; and this revelation of the relationship between his own life and his unborn novel is one of the chief meanings of Time Regained. But though he invented nothing, he altered everything. His places and people are composite in space and time, constructed from various sources and from widely separate periods of his life. His purpose in so doing was not to falsify reality, but, on the contrary, to induce it to reveal the truths it so successfully hides in this world. Behind the diversity of the originals is an underlying unity, the quality which, he felt, they had in common, the Platonic ideal of which they were the obscure earthly symbols. He fused each group of particular cases into a complex, universal whole, and so disengaged the truth about the poetry of places, or love and jealousy, or the nature of duchesses, and, most of all, the meaning of the mystery of his own life. . . . "A man's life of any worth is a continual allegory," said Keats: *A la Recherche* is the allegory of Proust's life, a work not of fiction but of imagination interpreting reality.

It would be absurd to suppose that Proust's greatness is in any degree lessened by his reliance on reality. His work is an illustration of Wordsworth's distinction between Fancy and Imagination—between the art which invents what has never existed and the art which discovers the inner meanings of what exists. We may or may not feel that Imagination is superior to Fancy; but we cannot possibly maintain that it is inferior. Proust was perhaps deficient in or indifferent to Fancy; but he was among the greatest masters of Imagination. It would be equally absurd to pretend that *A la Recherche* is a mere *roman à clef*—a novel, that is, which is a literal narrative of real events in which only the names are changed. As Proust himself explained to a friend, "there are no keys to the people in my novel; or rather, there are eight or ten keys to each character". (pp. xii-xiv)

> *George D. Painter, in his* Marcel Proust: A Biography, Vol. 1 *(copyright © 1959 by George D. Painter; reprinted by permission of Random House, Inc.; in Canada by Chatto and Windus Ltd.), Chatto and Windus Ltd., 1959 (and reprinted by Vintage Books, 1978, 351 p.).*

WALTER BENJAMIN (essay date 1961)

The thirteen volumes of Marcel Proust's *À la Recherche du temps perdu* are the result of an unconstruable synthesis in which the absorption of a mystic, the art of a prose writer, the verve of a satirist, the erudition of a scholar, and the self-consciousness of a monomaniac have combined in an autobiographical work. It has rightly been said that all great works of literature found a genre or dissolve one—that they are, in other words, special cases. Among these cases this is one of the most unfathomable. From its structure, which is fiction, autobiography, and commentary in one, to the syntax of endless sentences (the Nile of language, which here overflows and fructifies the regions of truth), everything transcends the norm. The first revealing observation that strikes one is that this great special case of literature at the same time constitutes its greatest achievement of recent decades. The conditions under which it was created were extremely unhealthy: an unusual malady, extraordinary wealth, and an abnormal disposition. This is not a model life in every respect, but everything about it is exemplary. The outstanding literary achievement of our time is assigned a place in the heart of the impossible, at the center—and also at the point of indifference—of all dangers, and it marks this great realization of a "lifework" as the last for a long time. The image of Proust is the highest physiognomic expression which the irresistibly growing discrepancy between literature and life was able to assume. (pp. 203-04)

> *Walter Benjamin, "The Image of Proust," in his* Illuminations, *edited by Hannah Arendt, translated by Harry Zohn (translation copyright © 1968 by Harcourt Brace Jovanovich, Inc.; reprinted by permission of the publisher; originally published as* Illuminationen; ausgewählte Schriften, *Suhrkamp Verlag, 1961), Harcourt, 1968, pp. 203-18.*

W. L. HODSON (essay date 1962)

Five characters came from Proust's pen in the tales collected in *Les Plaisirs et les Jours*. The tales—*La Mort de Baldassare Silvande, Violante, ou la Mondanité, Mélancolique Villégiature de Mme de Breyves, La Confession d'une Jeune Fille* and *La Fin de la Jalousie*—have all an atmosphere of regret, melancholy and death. All five people are marred by some flaw, physical or mental. Baldassare is suffering from incurable paralysis and has only a few years to live; Violante, an orphan at an early age, grows up without the guidance of parents and also without willpower; Mme de Breyves, a young widow who has conceived a passion for a man of inferior quality allows the fact that they can never meet to prey on her; the anonymous heroine of *La Confession d'une Jeune Fille* has tried to shoot herself in the belief that her mother from a balcony window saw her in the arms of her lover; and, finally, Honoré, in *La Fin de la Jalousie,* is tormented by jealousy because of reports (quite unproven) about his mistress's behaviour.

But are these people? The reader never comes to know Baldassare in the round. The main interest of the story falls on Baldassare's apparent recovery and subsequent relapse, most of all upon his death. How can one believe in Violante? As she grows up a young man tries to stimulate her feelings of love but she ignores him because she is not ready; later she turns her attention to a young Englishman who is not interested and ignores her. She decides to leave her own country for a foreign court where she becomes a successful leader of fashion and marries a rich duke. She stays on at court and spends her life there to the end in boredom. Violante is not a living person but a peg on which Proust has hung certain reflexions about the awakening of love and the invasion of the soul by boredom and routine. The story, one can say, is about *mondanité* and not Violante just as *La Mort de Baldassare Silvande* is about 'dying' and not about Baldassare. In its turn *La Mélancolique Villégiature* provides the reader with an analysis of the amorous feelings of Mme de Breyves for M. de Laléande: love is no more for her than the memories stimulated by music or by natural sights and sounds of the time when she has seen M. de Laléande. In fact, they are, neither of them, people but mere terms of reference. And the Girl in *La Confession,* how improbable she is! The treatment of her character is much like that of Henri van Blarenberghe's in a later story of Proust's called *Sentiments Filiaux d'un Parricide.* Henri, who kills his mother, is equally improbable because the author does not succeed in bringing him to life but uses him as a means of commenting on the relationship of mother to son. So it is in this story of a confession when the Girl and a former lover revert behind closed doors to their old habits; the Girl, as her lover is kissing her, is overwhelmed with sadness at the thought of her mother. The idea of mother-desecration is more important to the author than his story so that his 'protagonists', mother and daughter, remain shadowy and unreal. Lastly, Honoré of *La Fin de la Jalousie* is an excuse for observations on jealousy. As he lies ill after being thrown from his horse, the torment of not being sure that his mistress has received attentions from someone else, even though she asserts her innocence, pursues him right up to his death. He too remains unreal. However true Proust's observations may be about death, jealousy or love, the reader is still unconvinced by these people into whose lives he is supposed to have been introduced.

This conclusion modifies the view of the kind of character Proust is able to create. The sample in *Les Plaisirs et les Jours* indicates an interest in drawing characters which are not of the dramatic type nor of the portrait type as seen from the outside. Proust's approach is subjective even though these tales are all, except in one instance, told in the third person and his method of presenting his characters is to get inside them and tell us their thoughts. Actions are not recounted nor are they important; what matters are reactions to certain situations and experiences. Freed in this way from having to give his character any dramatic cogency Proust practises even here in *Les Plaisirs et les Jours* the technique of developing his characters in Time. In *La Recherche,* for instance, he shows the reader Swann as he appears to the family at Combray, as he appears in his affair with Odette, as father of Gilberte, as friend of the Guermantes. . . . In *Les Plaisirs et les Jours* Proust has not yet secured our interest so well but the method is sure and put to good use. (pp. 41-2)

Related to this method of letting his characters evolve in Time is Proust's predilection for giving the reader a sudden and unexpected revelation about parts of their nature that have been either taken for granted or have gone completely unsuspected. Appearances or first impressions lead us astray. People are not what they seem; subsequent observations or accidental meetings or chance remarks yield us a second impression about them which is to be added to the first, so modifying it. *La Recherche* offers many examples of this, notably Marcel's observations of Charlus and Jupien.

This feature of Proust's method of presenting his characters makes its appearance in the very first attempts at character drawing in *Les Plaisirs et les Jours.* There is even an example of the 'hidden observer' in the mother in *La Confession . . .* , reminiscent of Marcel at the *oeil de boeuf* at Jupien's hotel. She finds that her daughter is not as pure as she had believed when by chance she looks through the balcony window just as her daughter is yielding herself avidly to the embraces of her lover. This accidental discovery of a new side to her daughter's character, bringing with it the revelation of what she is really like, kills her. Furthermore, Honoré in *La Fin de la Jalousie . . .* approaches the technique of the *voyeur* when he considers hiding in a bedroom to see what his mistress is up to!

Proust's technique, therefore, is to show his characters evolving in Time or to give the reader some insight into their natures by revealing unsuspected features. It may be objected that he shares these methods with other novelists. This is so, but these methods seem to have a particular value for him because of the primary importance he attaches to the flow of Time and the pleasure he takes in revealing what is hidden in the time-lag between first and subsequent impressions.

Necessarily this treatment of his characters is very restricted in a short tale so that, to show up his method to the best advantage, he needs a broader canvas. The fullest expression of his method is revealed in *La Recherche.* There he uses, first, the simple type of character-evolution in Time as in *Le Plaisirs et les Jours;* secondly, an extension of this method, whereby the reader gains a picture of a character built up from the contrasting of different moments in the career of that character, a method that may be called the multilateral presentation of characters; and, finally, the revelation of facts or behavior previously unsuspected, executed, however, with far greater boldness and dramatic effectiveness than in *Les Plaisirs et les Jours.* (p. 43)

In *Jean Santeuil,* though the technique is the same (as would be expected), the methods are so well applied that the book must be placed for its quality in character presentation nearer the mature writing of *La Recherche.*

The process has become more complex than that used in *Les Plaisirs et les Jours;* the area of work is no longer a tale but a novel. Though Proust has mastered the technique in *Jean San-*

teuil the one feature that binds *La Recherche* into a satisfying whole, the need for characters to throw out tentacles, to cross their fates with those of others, all surveyed by the central observer, Marcel, is here only partly developed. (p. 44)

What *Jean Santeuil* lacks is the exploitation of these methods to the full in order to create a network of cross-references, though there is a suggestion of the growth of these cross-references even here. It is with the emergence of these tentacles that Proust shows he has grasped the essential element that gives meaning to the treatment of characters in Time and their presentation from different angles. In *Les Plaisirs et les Jours* the method appears vaguely, in *Jean Santeuil* it is almost made to work, the tentacles providing the necessary contact where none would seem possible. (pp. 44-5)

From Balzac's novels Proust learned the value of the multiplicity of characters that go to make up a world. With *Jean Santeuil* he had produced the multiplicity of characters and had made headway with the evolution of his characters in Time. Yet, coming so near the method used in his mature work, he stopped short at the promise of what he could achieve.

As far as character presentation was concerned Balzac was to lead the way by showing the attraction of the large-scale work with its broad canvas and its coverage of the passing of Time. What finally made the change between *Jean Santeuil* and *La Recherche* was the second discovery contained in *Contre Sainte-Beuve:* the use of the first-person narrator. The techniques of character presentation suggested in *Les Plaisirs et les Jours* and worked out in *Jean Santeuil* in preparation for the elaborate and confident method used in *La Recherche* are unsatisfactory until given a central point from which to radiate. That centre in *La Recherche* is Marcel who is a fixed point for all observations. Behind Marcel, we know, is the real Marcel Proust. In *Jean Santeuil* the situation is more complex. The real creator of Jean is Marcel Proust who adopts for the purpose the *persona* of a novelist, C. . . . In his turn C. . . is presented by another narrator, the First of the Two Friends who meet C. . . in Kerengrimen and publish his book for him. The character Jean in C. . .'s novel is undoubtedly Proust himself, and so is the First Friend, and so in part is C. . . . For all the external disguises Proust is speaking in his own voice. In fact, *Jean Santeuil,* in spite of appearances, is not a novel written in the third person. The desire to disguise is as one was the first step towards its failure; this Proust realized, and it was probably one of the reasons why he put it aside. The use of the third person was always a pretence and an encumbrance. The apparent third person narration was Proust's method in *Les Plaisirs et les Jours* for into the characters in that work he has put his own experiences. The only earlier first person narration is *La Confession d'une Jeune Fille* and that is a transposition of his own feelings towards his mother. The tales in this book are not quite successful because Proust has not discovered the right standpoint from which to write; *Jean Santeuil* is in the same stream of development. The natural standpoint for a Proust in relation to his characters is the first person. For a moment in *Jean Santeuil* the third person mask is dropped. In a chapter which develops into an essay on Balzac the novelist C. . . speaks out in his own voice on the problem of art and life. The use of 'I' (obviously Proust himself) came naturally in these pages of speculation. . . . He sensed the need to break away from the restriction of putting his thoughts on this problem into the mind of Jean. In *La Recherche* the only survival of the old third person technique is *Un amour de Swann.* In *Contre Sainte-Beuve* he discovered the right tone and approach and retained them for his subsequent work. (pp. 45-6)

W. L. Hodson, "Proust's Methods of Character Presentation in 'Les plaisirs et les jours' and 'Jean Santeuil'," in The Modern Language Review (© Modern Humanities Research Association 1962), Vol. LVII, No. 1, January, 1962, pp. 41-6.

HARRY LEVIN (essay date 1963)

The cherished sonata by Vinteuil, which furnishes a musical theme for the love of Swann and Odette, suggests a paradigm for the temporal structure of *A la recherche du temps perdu*. Proust was so little concerned with the articulation of his seven subnovels, which came out in two or three volumes apiece, that—for ulterior reasons—he printed the first part of *Sodome et Gomorrhe* with the last part of *Le Côté des Guermantes*. But he was deeply concerned with locales and seasons, and with the flow of associations that bound them together in the mind. His first and second subtitles seem to indicate two themes, which are being singly introduced, to be intermingled by further development. The second continues the first: *Du côté de chez Swann* moves from Combray to Paris, *A l'ombre des jeunes filles en fleurs* from Paris to Balbec. Emphasis falls on the countryside in the one, and upon the seaside in the other, as contrasted with the bustling and disillusioning city, which we mainly glimpse through parks and drawing-rooms or dining-rooms, where hints are dropped about the best shops for comestibles and luxury articles. Vacations seem to last indefinitely. Except for the servants, few of the characters ever seem to work. The basis of human relation, which is exchange with Balzac and production with Zola, is leisure with Proust.

Through the enamored eyes of Marcel, as infant and adolescent, we visualize the awakening idyll. Landscapes—those dreamy walks at Combray, the family, the figure of Swann, the romantic aura of Guermantes in the background. And seascapes—the Grand Hotel at Balbec, the grandmother, Albertine and those blooming girls on the beach, new acquaintances vaguely related to others that we have already met or shall soon be meeting. These first encounters, with their special enchantment and indelible imprint, are presented through a pair of subnovels, poetic in tone and philosophic in mood. A certain amount of Bergsonian exposition makes it explicit that this will be a novelistic experiment. There is more description than narration, and much less illustration than commentary. We seem to be confronting a sequence of essays and memoirs, rather than the usual sort of story. It is as if we were engaged in playing chess by mail, and going through correspondence after each move. Though Proust's ultimate concern is with recollection, here he is creating expectation, looking back at the budding consciousness that is looking forward; and, of course, the spells that are woven here will be exorcised by disenchantments. Later on, he would conceive his work as a conflation of *The Thousand and One Nights* and *The Memoirs of Saint-Simon*. To be growing up was to be moving from the arabesque of the former toward the acumen of the latter. (pp. 396-97)

As we advance through Proust's novel, the rarefied becomes familiar and the remote comes under close scrutiny, under the kind of analysis that can only be described as microscopic— and he does not altogether avoid the comparison. The outlook shifts from the psychological to the sociological; the mode is not so lyrical or impressionistic as it is satirical and increasingly dramatic; the monologue branches out into dialogue. In contrast to Marcel's youthful reveries and reflections, we have an increasing number of conversations and drawing-room scenes

designed to bring out personality. "The more we read of Proust," said Edith Wharton [see excerpt above], "the more we see that his strength is the strength of tradition." He pokes fun at the self-appointed society novelist, who stands in the corner at a reception, squints through his monocle, and murmurs fiercely: "I am observing." So much for Paul Bourget! But what of Balzac? It was not for nothing that the *Comédie humaine* had formed the foundation of Jean Santeuil's avid reading, or the means by which Proust, in counter-attacking Sainte-Beuve, had found his way back from criticism to fiction. It is in *Contre Sainte-Beuve* that a Monsieur de Guermantes makes his first appearance, extolling Balzac; in *A la recherche du temps perdu* that enthusiasm is transferred to the Duke's brother, the Baron de Charlus; and when the Baron admires "such grand frescoes as the series of *Illusions perdues*" and *Splendeurs et misères des courtisanes*, his very words are the almost literal echoes of Proust's own in his correspondence. (pp. 398-99)

A la recherche du temps perdu is a work which changed with its ever-changing subject, grew with the growing awareness and skill of its author, and expanded like those metaphorical Japanese pellets which open up into flowers. Proust's undulating conception of human nature, which inspired him to present his characters under such diverse aspects, was mirrored in the growth and development through which he composed his novel. (p. 431)

Except for Walt Whitman and his *Leaves of Grass,* it would be hard to think of another writer living from day to day and year to year in such an organic relation to his writing; even Goethe had many other concerns than *Faust;* and it would be even harder to think of Proust completing *A la recherche du temps perdu* and going on to write something else. "Who touches this, touches a man." Whoever writes such a book must be, by his own definition, *homo unius libri*. (p. 432)

Art, Proust tells us, again religiously, is the true Last Judgment. It is our one chance for a conquest over time, as André Malraux would more belligerently put it, the single triumph of man, the time-binding animal, over circumstances highly unfavorable to the survival of anything. Survival does not promise immortality for books, any more than for authors, Proust concedes in one of his last marginalia. Yet art is a path for man's escape from history, the fulfillment of his yearning for timelessness, or eternal return, which Mircea Eliade has shown to be at the base of so many fundamental mythologies. In the endless issue between the schools of Heraclitus and Parmenides, exponents of the Many and of the One, which has been joined by innumerable moderns, poetized by Valéry in *Le Cimetière marin* and by T. S. Eliot in *Burnt Norton,* Proust seems to gravitate from the pole of change toward that of permanence. Joyce, in one of his notebooks under the heading of "Proust," jotted down the formulation "analytic still life." It was the tribute of stasis to kinesis; for *Ulysses* is ultimately spatial, even as *A la recherche du temps perdu* is temporal in its element. But the adjectival focus is thoroughly warranted because, as Joseph Conrad noted [see excerpt above], Proust had pushed analysis to the point where it became creative. He could only have reached that point through self-analysis, which he termed *autocontemplation,* and through the most intimate sort of transference to those other selves, his readers.

In his youthful manifesto, *Contre l'obscurité,* he had praised the characters of *War and Peace* and *The Mill on the Floss* for achieving universality by way of individuality. *A la recherche du temps perdu,* as an achievement of that kind, is even more surprising, because its premises are so idiosyncratic, so far-fetched and special. Yet it bridges, as every great novel must do in its own way, the vast distance between the *moi* and the *nous*. Marcel retells his dreams and fantasies, but he reamins essentially an insomniac, who stays wide awake while others sleep. Among the various optical instruments with which he metaphorically supplements the naked eye, he suggests that his book could be used as a sort of magnifying glass for studying ourselves—scanning the fine print, no doubt, and reading between the lines. Elsewhere, apropos of [John Ruskin's] *Sesame and Lilies,* he remarks of books in general what seems to be particularly true of *A la recherche du temps perdu:* "reading is our guide whose magic keys open the door of dwellings we could not have entered within the depths of ourselves." Not so much for the modelling of his characters as for the training of our perceptions, for our enhanced awareness of the way things happen to happen, of how human beings respond or do not respond to one another, we may talk of keys in connection with Proust. That is why the serious reader, completing the final page of the many-volumed novel, is not the same person who opened the first volume some time ago. (pp. 443-44)

> *Harry Levin, "Proust," in his* The Gates of Horn: A Study of Five French Realists *(copyright © 1963 by Harry Levin; reprinted by permission of Oxford University Press, Inc.), Oxford University Press, New York, 1963, pp. 372-444.*

GEORGES POULET　(essay date 1963)

"We juxtapose," says Bergson, "our states of consciousness in such a way as to perceive them simultaneously: Not one following the other, but one alongside the other; in brief, we project time into space."

This is perhaps the most serious piece of criticism addressed by Bergsonism to the intellect. Intellect would tend to annihilate the true continuity of our being, by substituting for it a sort of mental space in which the moments would align themselves without ever interpenetrating themselves. Hence, there is for Bergson the necessity of destroying this "space" in order to come back by intuition to pure duration, to the modulated murmur by which existence reveals its inexhaustibly changing nature to the mind. It is singular that one who had so often been taken for a disciple of Bergson should have assumed, probably without knowing it, a position diametrically opposite. If the thought of Bergson denounces and rejects the metamorphosis of time into space, Proust not only accommodates himself to it, but installs himself in it, carries it to extremes, and makes of it finally one of the principles of his art. . . . To the bad juxtaposition, to the intellectual space condemned by Bergson, there is opposed a good juxtaposition, an aesthetic space, where, in ordering themselves, moments and places form the work of art, altogether memorable and admirable. (pp. 3-4)

In terms of the title it bears, one knows that the Proustian novel is very exactly a "search for lost time." A being sets out in quest of his past, makes every effort to rediscover his preceding existence. Thus one sees the hero awakening in the middle of the night and asking himself to what epoch of his life there is attached this moment in which he recovers consciousness. This is a moment totally deprived of any connection with the rest of duration, a moment suspended in itself, and profoundly anguished, because the one who lives it does not literally know *when* he lives. Lost in time, he is reduced to an entirely momentary life.

But the ignorance of this awakened sleeper is much graver than it seems. If he does not know *when* he lives, he no longer knows *where* he lives. His ignorance is no less important as to his position in space than as to his position in duration: "And when I awakened in the middle of the night, as I was *ignorant as to where I found myself,* I did not know in the first instant who I was." (pp. 7-8)

[With] Proust, there is a diversity of places, unmingled with others, which seem to live within their frontiers an absolutely independent life. Such is their essential characteristic. From the external world to themselves, there is not this natural topographical continuity that is found everywhere between one place and other places. From the moment one perceives them, on the contrary, one gets the clear idea that they do not extend into the surrounding universe, that they are separate from it. There is, for example, not far from Raspelière a certain landscape of forest and shingles: "One instant, the denuded rocks by which I was surrounded, the sea, which one perceived through their clefts, *floated before my eyes like the fragments of another universe.*" (pp. 19-20)

[There is nothing less objective] than genuine Proustian places; genuine places, those which are invariably connected with certain human presences. There is never, in fact, with Proust, a place described without in the foreground, the profile of such or such a figure; in the same way that there never appears in Proust a figure without the presence of a framework ready to insert and support it. Invariably it is in a landscape minutely circumscribed that the Proustian personage shows itself for the first time.

From the moment it appears, this place, associating itself with him, gives him a note as distinct and recognizable as a Wagnerian *leitmotiv.* Yes, no doubt, in what follows the personage will reappear elsewhere. But he will not cease to be bound to the primitive site in our memory. It is of this that we are reminded from the very first moment; it is this that we see unfold, unfold promptly, in whatever spot the personage finds himself; as if he had been fixed in a painting more revealing than anything else, where he will always be showing up against the same background.

It is thus with all Proustian personages. How to recall, for example, Gilberte, or rather the image the hero has formed of her, if not under the aspect of a little girl, accompanied by an old gentleman, and silhouetting herself with him against the background of the cathedrals they visit by turn. (pp. 23-4)

Thus, for Proust, human beings appear located in certain places that give them support and outline, and that determine the perspective according to which one is allowed to see them. A singular thing, this novelist of interiority invariably obliges himself to present his personages (except for one central consciousness) under the aspect of exteriority. (p. 25)

Infallibly, then, with Proust, in reality as in dream, persons and places are united. The Proustian imagination would not know how to conceive beings otherwise than in placing them against a local background that plays for them the part of foil and mirror. To evoke a human being, this act so simple, which is the first act of the novelist composing his work, is tantamount with Proust to rendering a form visible and putting it in a framework. It is a trick of mind veritably essential, and which, with Proust, can be noticed not only in his novels, but in his critical writings and ideological essays, and even in his correspondence. (pp. 27-8)

Like works by the same painter on display at different museums of Europe, a whole series of Proustian sites seem . . . to proclaim their belonging to a single universe. But these sites or pictures have been spearated, the ones from the others, by great neutral distances, in such a way that the first aspect suggested by the work of Proust is that of a very incomplete ensemble, where the number of subsisting traces is largely surpassed by the number of gaps. Rarely does the representation of things there appear total or panoramic. It is nearly always fragmentary, now larger, now narrower, but most often reduced, whether it be by some obstruction, or more often, by some ''fracture'' in the field of vision—to a section of the real, strictly limited, beyond which it is hopeless to try to see anything. In brief, the most exact image of the Proustian universe is no different from that image of Combray which appears at the beginning of Proust's tale: *''a sort of luminous wall looming up on the midst of indistinct shadows* like those that the flaming up of a Bengal light or some electrical projection brightens up and *divides into sections* in an edifice of which all other parts remain immersed in night.'' (pp. 37-8)

But what is it, to juxtapose?

It is to place one thing *beside* another.

Beside, and not above! In fact it is necessary carefully to distinguish juxtaposition from its analogue, superposition. (p. 91)

The experience of Proust is not at all the burial of the past under the present; quite the contrary, it is a resurrection of the past in spite of the present. Proust dreams of a kind of superposition periodically or irregularly broken by an inverse phenomenon of upheaval. He conceives of a superposition of a geological and Plutonian type, a sort of unstable stratification, where, from time to time, ''the upheavals bring to the level of the surface old strata.'' Or he imagines an arrangement similar to that of the magic lantern. Of course, as to what concerns its internal functioning, the magic lantern offers a process that one should not confound with superposition. It does not conceal; it supersedes. To the previous moment, through a mixed movement, interrupted and abrupt, which, besides, is bound to please Proust more than the fluid and uninterrupted gliding of cinematographic images, it substitutes a subsequent moment that involves the total annihilation of the one preceding it. The Proustian universe is not, therefore, that of the magic lantern; or, if one wishes, it is just that, but on the condition of imagining the painted plates not in the motion that projects the ones *after* the others, but arranged, the ones *beside* the others, in a simultaneous order. (pp. 92-3)

Do not let us be deceived then by the declaration so often reported of Proust, according to which, in his novel, he had wanted to render palpable a fourth dimension, the dimension of time. For the dimension of time is, in his mind, only a dimension entirely similar to all three others, a dimension, itself also, purely spatial. *''Time for him is like space,''* he writes of one of his characters, Jean Santeuil. And in the same way, one can say of his novel what he himself said of a certain place called Guermantes, which like the church of Combray, was full of memories: *''Time has taken there the form of space.''*

Now if Proustian time *always* takes the form of space, it is because it is of a nature that is directly opposed to Bergsonian time. Nothing resembles less the melodic continuity of pure duration; but nothing, in return, more resembles what Bergson denounced as being a false duration, a duration the elements of which would be exteriorized, the ones relatively to the oth-

ers, and aligned, the ones beside the others. Proustian time is time spatialized, juxtaposed. . . .

It could not happen differently, from the moment when Proust had conceived the temporality of his universe under the form of a series of pictures, which, successively presented in the course of the work, would finally reappear all together, simultaneously, to be sure, outside of time, but not outside of space. Proustian space is this final space, made of the order in which there are distributed, the ones in harmony with the others, the different episodes of the Proustian novel. The order is not different from that which binds between them the predellas, and the predellas to the reredos. A plurality of episodes makes way for and constructs its own space, which is the space of the work of art. (pp. 105-06)

Georges Poulet, in his Proustian Space, *translated by Elliott Coleman (translation copyright © 1977 by The Johns Hopkins University Press; originally published as* L'espace Proustien, *Editions Gallimard, 1963),* The Johns Hopkins University Press, 1977, 113 p.

ROGER SHATTUCK   (essay date 1963)

The variety and power and significance of Proust's images have often been studied, yet very few of them have been tracked to their source and revealed in their full significance. The two portions of the world he invoked most frequently to yield comparisons are the realm of art and the realm of science. The two great illusory values in the book, the sentiment of love and the prestige of nobility, crystallize and dissolve in a solution of images based on music and painting; the great transformations of social upheaval and old age at the end are set before us in terms of zoology. And like Homer, Proust is full of images of eating and culinary enjoyment, as if the surest way of knowing a thing is to eat it, or at least to pick it up and smell it. Yet there is a further class of images, partaking of both art and science, which gradually reveals itself as significant in a particular manner.

The first objects distinct from the *I* mentioned in *A la recherche* appear in the second sentence: Marcel's candle and his eyes. On the following page his lengthy reveries on the verge of sleep are condensed into the image of ''the kaleidoscope of darkness''; six pages later the first familiar object seized and described out of his childhood world of Combray turns out to be a magic lantern; it entertains Marcel by transforming his bedroom into a series of legendary and historical scenes. This strand of imagery, linking not so much things seen as particular circumstances or modes of vision, never slackens through three thousand pages of text. Thus we should reach the final figure in the book prepared to understand its composite meaning. The ''stilts'' on which a man sways dizzily in old age represent not only the precariousness of his life and the awkwardness of his movements but also the perspective of his mind, the lofty vantage point from which he views the world. The point is worth belaboring. Proust drew on an incredibly rich repertory of metaphors. But it is principally through the science and the art of *optics* that he beholds and depicts the world. Truth— and Proust believed in it—is a miracle of vision. (pp. 5-6)

It is not merely the number and vividness of these optical images that indicate their importance in Proust's work. They occur at the most strategic places and illuminate values central to the development of the action. The social ordering of the novel will bring this out most readily. At first the social classes appear to Marcel and to the reader as clearly defined layers; and, of necessity, perception from one level to the next, or to a level several times removed, entails severe refraction and distortion. Marcel, looking up toward the higher circles, misjudges everyone in the beginning. This distortion in social depth perception is described occurring in the opposite direction in the scene where the Princesse de Luxembourg, from the altitude of her nobility, tries to be gracious on meeting Marcel and his grandmother. "And, even, in her desire not to appear to hold forth from a sphere superior to ours, she had miscalculated the distance, for, by an error in adjustment, her looks were filled with so great a kindness I foresaw the moment when she would pet us like two lovable animals who had stretched out our necks toward her through the grillwork at the Jardin d'Acclimatation". . . . This miscalculation of station is brief and trivial compared to the complex stages of Marcel's attitude toward the Guermantes. Out of his youthful admiration for the Duchesse de Guermantes—a sentiment copied in him like a "magic-lantern slide and a stained-glass window" . . . —grows the "artificial enlargement" . . . of his image of that whole clan. It engulfs him. Gradually these simple images of distorted perception yield to figures which contain an expression of social mobility—above all the famous "social kaleidoscope". . . . The social levels lose their hierarchy, and by the end we lose sight even of the two *côtés* whose originally opposed perspectives are fragmented and crossed in both social and subjective upheaval. (pp. 10-11)

Error establishes itself as one persistent principle of Proust's universe, error in both social and the subjective domains. Within this skewed world Marcel erects and clings to three structures that offer temporary habitation to the questing mind. There is the refuge of habit, which allows us to adjust to new surroundings and people by becoming blind to all but the parts we can put to our own personal use; the refuge of laws, which define and explain the mystery of human behavior without penetrating it; and the refuge of the comic, which perceives the ridiculousness of both the above procedures and enjoys it without surpassing it. Marcel's comedy of errors continues until he and we begin to understand that art itself is an optic, but a superior optic which will finally transform error into truth for our mortal eyes. " . . . The original painter or the original writer proceeds like an oculist. The treatment he prescribes—by his painting or his writing—is not always agreeable. When he has finished, he tells us: 'Now have a look.' And all at once the world, which was not created only once, but it is created as often as a new artist comes along, appears to us perfectly clear—so different from the former world.". . . Not only are all the principal "orders"—social, individual, and subjective—of Proust's novel continually cast in optical terms, the ultimate transformation of all experience by art also finds expression in figures of vision and illusion. (pp. 18-19)

Optics furnishes a vocabulary that implies fixed units of observation and retention. When the testimony of our senses reaches the mind, it becomes image. But—and here's both the rub and the way out—never one only: *many images,* in rapid and delayed and intermittent succession, and for the most part contradictory. (p. 22)

A succession of contradictory images going under one name and "passing" by convention as a single person or sentiment or social entity—this is probably the most striking aspect of Proust's universe to the unprepared reader. In this respect he reveals himself a creature of his age, a fact which by no means strips him of originality in his literary work. His vision was

not of a unified, comprehensible, and essentially motionless world like that of Renaissance art, Albertian perspective, and the psychology of types and temperaments. The character Saint-Loup, for example, first appears as an insolent, unapproachable, exceedingly chic young aristocrat who will not deign to look at Marcel, and then within two pages he turns out to be the most loyal and considerate of friends. One paragraph later, he reveals himself as not merely a republican suspicious of the aristocratic principles he first seemed to incarnate, but a socialist who has steeped himself in Nietzsche and Proudhon. Three hundred pages later we watch him in the role of the headstrong, jealous lover of the actress Rachel, and blind to the extravagance of his own behavior. In his next transformation, after an equal interval, he has become simultaneously a selfish and cruel husband and a philandering homosexual keeping mistresses in order to cover up his carryings-on with young men. And yet Saint-Loup turns out in the end to be the only character in the novel who is killed in combat, a patriot and a true hero.

A similar series of mutations is followed in practically every development of character and action. . . . Not one image, but a multitude. The action of the first twenty-eight hundred pages out of three thousand can be seen as consisting in Marcel's gradual discovery and acceptance of the truth that no person, no action, no sentiment, no social phenomenon is ever simple or consistent. Most of the way through, *A la recherche* remains a book of disenchantments. Things are never what they seem. (pp. 23-5)

Roger Shattuck, in his Proust's Binoculars: A Study of Memory, Time, and Recognition in 'A la recherche du temps perdu' *(copyright © 1963 by Roger Shattuck; reprinted by permission of Joan Daves), Random House, 1963, 153 p.*

WALLACE FOWLIE   (essay date 1964)

The first of the seven parts of Proust's novel, *Du Côté de chez Swann* [(*Swann's Way*)], serves as an introduction to the long work, but it is far more than that. It is itself a novel, with a beginning, a middle, and an end. It is true that these three demarcations, as they occur in *Du Côté de chez Swann,* are not typical of the usual novel. The beginning of the book, *Combray,* is the introduction to characters and the announcement of themes to be continued throughout the entire work. The themes of *Combray* will be explored with the ever-deepening sensibility of the protagonist, and the characters will evolve and change with the passing of time. The ending of *Du Côté de chez Swann,* which is given the special title: *Noms de Pays: le Nom (Place Names),* is both an end and a rebeginning, a recapitulation of *Combray,* the child's world which constantly returns in that circular movement we call memory with no absolute beginning and no absolute ending. The middle section, *Un Amour de Swann (Swann in love),* is a flashback, but so elaborate and so unified a flashback, that it is a novel in itself, a love story, the first of a series of love stories. But it is also quite literally the middle of *Du Côté de chez Swann,* because it initiates the boy of *Combray* to the world. It is Marcel's introduction to the world in a general sense, that is, to everything that is not his parents' home, as well as to the three specific worlds or experiences that form the substance of *A la recherche du temps perdu:* the world of passion, the world of society, and the world of art.

With the very first word of the novel, *Longtemps* (which will reappear capitalized, as if it had become one of the characters, as the very last word of the novel: *dans le Temps*), Proust offers the key to his work. It is the phenomenon of the time during which the novel was written, because of which the novel was conceived, and which the novelist hopes to defeat in the successful completion of the novel.

A preoccupation with time and its irrevocability is a familiar human experience. With Marcel Proust it became a veritable obsession. The changes brought about in nature, in human beings, in society, by the passing of time are sung by him almost as a lament. Time is the relentless force that attacks the beauty of the human body, the stability of human personality, the freshness and the completeness of works of art—a painting, for example, or a cathedral. Proust grew to look upon life itself as a constant struggle against time. Much of the so-called pessimism of his book comes from the hopelessness of this struggle, from the inevitable failure of life to preserve itself intact from the encroachments of time.

He analyzes one after the other those major experiences of life that are the most hallowed efforts of man to reach some absolute within time, some stable value that will oppose the flow of time: the loyalty of friendship, for example, the passions of love, the steadfastness of convictions, either theological or philosophical or political. Proust the novelist discovers that even such experiences, which, when they are real, seem absolute, are, in time, subjected to change and even oblivion. The human self, immersed in time, is never exactly the same two days in succession. All the elements of personality are constantly being affected by time: they are either being weakened or strengthened. They are receding or in the ascendant. Even the self which is in love, deeply, jealously and passionately, will change, according to Proust, and become disillusioned.

The self is never one but a succession of selves. If this is true—and the substance of the book as well as the method of writing are based upon this Bergsonian assumption—what happens to the selves we once were? Do these selves, which were once real, sink into oblivion? Proust answers this question with a vigorous no! They are not lost. They do not disappear. They are in us, in that part of us that is often called the subconscious. They live in our dreams and indeed at times in our states of consciousness. The opening theme of Proust's novel is the protagonist's literal awakening. This is a familiar experience for everyone every morning when we leave the state of sleep for the state of consciousness. Proust looks upon this emergence as an effort to recover our identity, to find out who we are, where we are, and what particular self we are inhabiting. (pp. 51-3)

Proust explains early in his novel that there are for him two ways in particular by which the past can be recalled. The first, on which he will rely a great deal, and which he acknowledges to be, of the two, less sure and less sound, is the willful memory of the intelligence. *La Mémoire volontaire*, as he calls it, seems to be the rationalistic, the deductive method which is based on documents, testimonials, and ratiocination. When Marcel evokes a typical summer evening at Combray, when the family spends the last hours of daylight in the garden, we have a good example of willful memory. (p. 55)

[The narrator] indicates the limitations of *la mémoire volontaire*. He realizes that this kind of memory is able to recall only a small part of his past, and he asks whether all the rest of Combray has been forgotten. The answer again is no. Another kind of memory—involuntary—*la mémoire involontaire*

is able to evoke the real past. But the operation of this kind of memory depends on chance. To illustrate, the narrator now relates the episode of the madeleine cake, *la petite madeleine*. Once when dipping a madeleine into a cup of tea, he remembers his tante Léonie at Combray who used to give him a madeleine and a cup of linden tea (*tilleul*). Through the sensation of taste, he recalls, without effort, a similar experience (of *déjà vu*), and the complete picture of the past returns to him: his aunt, his room in her house, the garden, the town, the square where the church is, the streets and the paths. All of Combray, in fact, as if by magic, came out of his cup of tea. (p. 56)

After the announcement of the two principles of voluntary and involuntary memory, the narrator describes the past he associates with Combray. (p. 57)

Marcel's life in Combray was very much related to two walks he describes. . . . After the brief analysis of past time, and the possibilities of bringing it back, he reconstructs the past by means of another dimension: space. Swann's Way (*le côté de chez Swann*), or, as it is sometimes called, Méséglise, is a long walk that leads past the park of Tansonville, the estate of M. Swann. Guermantes' Way (*le côté de Guermantes*) is an even longer walk which leads in the direction of the Guermantes', the aristocratic family that resides at least part of the year at Combray. (p. 58)

To Marcel, both Swann's Way and Guermantes', are remote. Both represent a vague geographical distance. Swann's Way is far off, a point somewhere on the horizon. Guermantes' Way is even farther off, and more removed from reality. It has the remote unreality of the equator, or the North Pole, or the Orient. Each "way" is related to an aspect of Marcel's initiation to life. Méséglise (or Swann's Way) is the hawthorn-lined park of Tansonville where he first sees Gilberte and hears someone call her name. It is also the way to Montjouvain where he observes the scandalous scene of sexuality. Swann's Way is Marcel's introduction to pure and impure love. Guermantes' Way, from which he can see the water lilies of the Vivonne and the steeples of Martinville, is associated not only with all the Guermantes' prestige, but also with Marcel's concern with his own literary talent and his vocation.

The two ways lead Marcel away from his family and initiate him into the three orders of experience which are to dominate his life: love, society and art. At Combray the two ways seemed to the boy to lead in opposite directions, toward opposite goals, totally cut off one from the other. But one of the principal actions of the entire novel is to demonstrate that time, in its fluidity and its power to effect metamorphosis, will join the two ways and fuse them in an extraordinary fashion. (pp. 59-60)

Un Amour de Swann, the second section of **Du Côté de chez Swann,** has been often looked upon as a separate novel that interrupts the life story of the protagonist. In reality, this episode has innumerable bonds with all parts of the work, and the significance of Swann's role becomes more evident the closer we read the novel.

The importance of Charles Swann, at least in the three divisions of **Du Côté de chez Swann,** is clear. In *Combray* he is the refined and rather mysterious friend who visits the boy's parents. We are made aware of his intelligence, his erudition, his elegance of manner and dress. We even learn some things about him that Marcel's family does not know: his cordial relations with the highest society, with the aristocratic Guermantes, even with the Prince of Wales. For the boy Marcel, M. Swann is a gentleman of sympathetic kindness, endowed with great prestige, who stands out as an almost godlike figure in Combray. In the second division, *Un Amour de Swann,* Swann is the protagonist and the story is centered on his love for Odette: the origin of his love, the experience of suffering and jealousy, and love's end. In the third division, *Noms de Pays: le Nom,* Swann plays a more effaced, a more subtle role. Marcel's dreams about Balbec and Italy have been somewhat induced by Swann's conversations and allusions. The boy's dreams about Gilberte, and his love for her in the Champs-Elysées scenes, are also dreams about the name of Swann and the strong attraction the boy feels for the glamorous Mme Swann. One always feels behind the sentimental boyish love of Marcel for Gilberte, the stronger, more violent and more deeply analyzed love of Swann for Odette.

Un Amour de Swann is far more than a separate monograph on passion. Swann, as Marcel's precursor, is related to the two "ways"; his own way, first, which leads us to Odette, and the Verdurin clan where Swann sees Odette, and to Elstir (or rather, M. Biche), the painter, and the work of the composer Vinteuil. But Swann is also a close friend of Oriane, duchesse de Guermantes, and of the baron de Charlus, both of whom represent Guermantes' Way. Swann's daughter, Gilberte, will finally marry a Guermantes, Robert de Saint-Loup. With this marriage, at the end of the novel, in Mlle de Saint-Loup, the two ways are joined. Thus, *Un Amour de Swann* is the indirect but indispensable prelude to the great social upheaval which will be described in *Le Temps retrouvé.* (pp. 67-8)

Swann's liaison with Odette before their marriage is the first full illustration in the novel—prelude to the rest—of the dual experience with which man is involved every moment of life, consciously or unconsciously: the duality of destruction and preservation. Time is the force that slowly and inexorably destroys everything. But memory is time's only deterrent, the one staying factor, the one force for permanence. The scene where by chance Swann hears again Vinteuil's sonata at Mme de Saint-Euverte's concert is Swann's most exalted moment. At this point in the liaison, he senses that Odette is unfaithful and has become Forcheville's mistress. But before the scene closes, he relives the past: he recaptures what is lost to time. The musical phrase of the sonata, which his sentimentality identified with Odette, forces him, without his willing it, to feel once again the sensations and the gestures and the loving kindnesses that he shared with Odette. These memories are so precisely real as to be almost intolerable. This moment of total recall transcends the mere story of the liaison: its slow beginning, its passion, and its decline. (p. 72)

In the third section of *Du Côté de chez Swann, Noms de Pays: le Nom,* we leave Swann's world of passion and disillusionment, and return to Marcel and a boy's world of mystery. It is not Combray now but Paris. And throughout the meditations on names (Balbec, Venice, Florence especially, and the towns through which the train passes: Bayeux, Coutances, Vitré, Lannion, Lamballe, Pont-Aven), and on the afternoons spent in the Champs-Elysées where Gilberte, known at first only as a cipher, comes to life, and in the Bois de Boulogne, where Mme Swann passes in her carriage along the Avenue des Acacias, the theme of love is never lost: it is only momentarily subdued in Marcel's thoughts of Balbec and La Berma. (p. 75)

This section of the novel, which completes *Du Côte de chez Swann,* returns to Marcel's principal narrative by its allusion to the moment back at Combray when he had first heard the name of Gilberte in the garden of Tansonville. The first elab-

oration of the major philosophical theme of the disparity between the imagination and reality, the section is also an analysis of an initial phase in Proustian love, which will be more lengthily treated in the case of Marcel than in the case of Swann.

Marcel's love for Gilberte has little or nothing to do with the satisfaction of the senses (which was of vital importance in Swann's love for Odette). It is predominantly the proliferation of the lover's imagination. Marcel forms an elaborate mental world in which Gilberte is the center. Exalted by the slightest attention she manifests, he is equally depressed by her slightest indifference. The fits of despondency are forms of suffering which have the strange perverse power of attaching Marcel to Gilberte even more firmly than in moments of happiness. (p. 79)

The third section of Proust's novel, *Le Côté de Guermantes,* [*Guermantes' Way*], is divided into two parts, both dominated by a vast social fresco, the setting of French society: the first at the Paris home of Mme de Villeparisis, and the second a dinner party at the Paris residence of Mme de Guermantes. (p. 114)

The prevailing emphasis in *Le Côté de Guermantes* is on society's forms and the false perceptions we constantly cultivate because of our limited knowledge and our misconceptions of human relationships. We are led to these scenes by individuals whom Marcel knows. There is, in reality, only one character— Marcel—in *A la recherche du temps perdu* in the triple role of protagonist, narrator, and novelist, but he succeeds, despite the staggering subjectivity of the work, in bringing countless characters to life outside himself, yet formed by his perceptions and seen through his rich and tolerant sensitivity.

One of the most fully developed of these Proustian characters is the duchesse de Guermantes, Oriane, who presides over the beginning and the ending of *Le Côté de Guermantes* and who introduces us, more dramatically than any other character, to the complexities and the cruelties of society. (p. 115)

The originality of Proust's art as novelist lies in the extraordinary skill with which he is able to present so many themes simultaneously: the personal dramas of individual characters (the adaptation of Françoise to a new house, Marcel's infatuation with Mme de Guermantes, Saint-Loup's stormy liaison with his actress-mistress); the large social settings, the tableaux of characters involved in a comedy of manners and class distinctions (the Opéra where the *baignoire* of the princesse de Guermantes is the center of attention, the descriptions of the life in a garrison town, the matinée at Mme de Villeparisis', the first very detailed social fresco in *A la recherche du temps perdu*). Other novelists, Stendhal, for example, emphasize either society or the individual. At no point in the closely woven texture of Proust's writing is any demarcation visible between society and the individuals interacting within the society.

In accordance with the usual preoccupation of the novelist, Proust shows us what is actually seen in such a town as Doncières: streets, shops, hotel rooms, military men. But he is constantly adding to what can be seen by everyone, an artist's personal subjective vision. In other words, he is interested in telling us in what way he was led to see what he does see. For example, in describing a tawdry secondhand novelty shop in Doncières (*un petit magasin de bric-à-brac . . .*), the light of a candle and the light of a lamp fall in such a way on various odd objects that, for Marcel, the drabness of the scene is momentarily transformed into a Rembrandt painting.

In addition to these two kinds of writing—the description of what can be seen and the peculiarly subjective way in which

Marcel Proust sees it—there is a theoretical kind of writing far more occasional than the other two, in which the writer tells his reader why he has chosen to describe his society and the customs of his time. This is the function of the memorialist who, more than the historian, seeks to understand the meaning of individual and social behavior, to derive general theories concerning the relationship between man and man, and man and society. The writing of a novel would never be sufficient for Marcel Proust. Consciously, and at times unconsciously, he makes the novel a justification for writing, and, more than that, a justification for his own life. The protagonist in *A la recherche du temps perdu* is never seen alone: he is portrayed in conjunction with some object (such as the porch of a church), or with some human being, or with some social group. In the same way, Marcel Proust is never solely the novelist. He is the novelist who is at the same time aesthetician and memorialist. (p. 120)

By instinct and by habit, Proust is an observer never satisfied until he has divided any phenomenon he is studying into as many elements as possible. The worlds he knows and observes are the worlds in his novel. A futile criticism often levelled against Marcel Proust is the narrowness of the world he chose to depict. This criticism is not accurate because, in the first place, Proust did not limit himself to one world in Paris. Several different, interacting classes are present in his novel. But wisely, in keeping with the most permanent tradition of art, he focused his attention on those worlds he knew the most intimately: the aristocracy, the upper bourgeoisie, and the servant class. The universality of genius lies in the profundity of its understanding, and not in the mere multiplicity of its themes. The major novelists have quite consistently sought that historical moment and that social world most favorable to their talent. Dickens, Balzac, Henry James carefully chose a world they knew or could easily document: they recreated these worlds into what is recognizable today as a Dickensian, a Balzacian, a Jamesian world. Proust belongs to this category of novelists whose power of observation is coupled with an imaginative visionary power which exaggerates and deepens and clarifies the observable and the documented elements of their writing. (pp. 122-23)

Most of the observations Marcel makes on the Guermantes and their *esprit* are fairly objective analyses, but in a few very important instances in the narrative of the dinner, he relates this study to himself and thus attaches it firmly to the leading theme of the novel—Marcel's initiation to the great concepts of time and eternity. In his description of the attractive suppleness in the ceremonial physical movements of the Guermantes, we are led to feel that this is a special attribute which separates them from Marcel whose own physical movements are somewhat bourgeois. He realizes that Oriane's mind was formed long before his own and he realizes in particular that Oriane, being a Guermantes, possibly the highest representative of her family, cannot understand what he had first looked for in her, in Combray, when he was a boy, and what he is now looking for in Paris: the magical spell (*le charme*) of the Guermantes name. In a sense, their relationship is between a highly imaginative young man and a highly sophisticated lady of the world. Oriane de Guermantes creates for Marcel a magic spell that exerts a strong attraction over him. She incarnates it every day so naturally, so unthinkingly, that she could not possibly understand what it is to be someone else.

Marcel sees in the Guermantes the persistence of the past. Geography, history, trees, and Gothic spires are in their name.

All of these elements, and many others, have shaped their faces, the characteristics of their minds and attitudes, their prejudices. Their history is of far more interest to Marcel than to the Guermantes (despite their endless discussion of genealogies). Marcel, in this regard, compares himself to an anticlerical archaeologist who knows far more about the history of a church than the curé who celebrates his daily mass in the church. . . . (pp. 140-41)

The title of the fourth section of *A la recherche du temps perdu* [*Sodome et Gomorrhe* (**Cities of the Plain**)] calls attention to a new theme which the section is to be concerned with—a theme only briefly and intermittently referred to previously in the novel. By using the biblical title, with its implicit disapproval of sexual inversion, Proust announces an attitude that would seem moralistic. And yet he is hostile to the moralizing novelist. The drama of inversion is an important part of his novel. By "drama" is meant the suffering and the social ostracism inversion entails. All the vices exist to some degree in Proust's work, but they are not condemned as vices. Proust affirms them, and he studies in particular the subconscious role they play in the moral and spiritual and social make-up of his characters. Proust is far more fully conscious of the vice of inversion in Charlus than Charlus himself. According to Proust's canon, only the artist, when functioning as artist, is fully conscious.

Inversion is only one reflection, however strong and dramatic, of the entire moral problem of the protagonist, and hence of the entire novel. Almost as if he were the protagonist of a mediaeval morality play, Marcel faces two sets of alternatives throughout the history of his life: the virtues of Combray, on the one hand, and the vices of society, on the other. The novel asks the question: Which will win Marcel's heart? The answer to this leading question is saved for the very end of the work. (p. 147)

Charlus will be the major representative of Sodom in the novel, but he is also one of the major representatives of the Guermantes, and his personal anomaly will designate metaphorically the decadence of the French aristocracy and, beyond that, a point in the cyclical movement of history when the weaknesses and defects of man suddenly show themselves under the hard carapace of continuous tradition. In fact, it would be difficult to find a major theme in Proust's novel that Charlus does not incarnate.

Everything Proust says about personality is exemplified in Charlus. He is both changeable and unchanging. He is one man, and he is all men. This dual aspect of human character, in one man, Charlus, means that everything that can be said about personality is true. Truth is, for Proust, the container of contradictions. And this is one aspect of Proust's concept of the absolute. Charlus' impeccable good taste, his knowledge and love of the arts, his magnanimity and kindness, revealed on many occasions, his understanding of history and politics and the ways of man, have been acquired during his conscious life as a highly privileged French aristocrat. When sexual desire transforms him into a reprobate, he is the same man, responding to a bestial trait inherited from some distant ancestor. No part of past human conduct is ever completely lost. Our instincts and our feelings are predetermined, even if our will is free to carry out or repress these instincts, to submerge or express these feelings. The love Charlus has doubtless already felt for Marcel in the first part of the novel—not exactly the same attraction he demonstrates for Jupien in the courtyard scene—is the adventure of a stranger alienated from himself. This is the persistent Proustian formula for the experience of love. Its full analysis comes in time, with Marcel himself, in his love for Albertine. But in Charlus, more than in Marcel, we are able to follow a conscience, actually a consciousness in perpetual motion, traversing all the levels of an awareness of the past, an awareness implicit in the living conscience, and able, under certain conditions, to take hold and direct the present. (pp. 150-51)

In the classical sense of the tragic hero, Charlus qualifies far more easily than Marcel Proust.

At this stage in the novel, the opening of *Sodome et Gomorrhe,* the Guermantes, including not only Charlus but the others as well, have triumphed over time. They have resisted its power of change more successfully than others. They form a bastion of prestige and strength and invincibility. But the revelation of Charlus' character, made to Marcel as he watches the courtyard and the fertilization of the flower, marks the beginning of change, the first crack in the bastion wall. The depiction of Charlus' moral defect is the sinister sign of change and evil which will spread, in similar and other manifestations, to an entire family, a caste, and even, it can be argued, a civilization. With the Charlus-Jupien pantomime scene, a new epoch begins; one characterized by disenchantment, decadence, and vanity.

After the incisiveness, the glaring crudity of the action, the sinister quasi-comic, quasi-tragic quality of the prelude comes the opening chapter of *Sodome et Gomorrhe,* one of the most elaborate in the novel: the reception at the princesse de Guermantes' which Proust sees as dominated by the position of M. Charlus in society. There are so many characters, so many dramas—trivial and significant—that begin or continue during the soirée, so much falseness and wit are exhibited and so much humor at the expense of human feelings, that no theme, no character is given the stage for long. (p. 154)

Following the reception at the princesse de Guermantes', there is a brief preparatory passage for Marcel's return to Balbec (his second and last visit to the beach resort), and before the narrative in *Sodome et Gomorrhe* is devoted to a spring-summer visit in Balbec and the environs. The figure of Marcel becomes more important in the narrative. Now definitely the protagonist, he is extremely concerned with his fluctuating erotic thoughts. (p. 163)

Sodome et Gomorrhe, after the prelude with Charlus and Jupien and the reception chez la princesse de Guermantes, is Balbec, seen now not as the romantic setting for a youth's reverie, where Marcel was awed and even terrified by much that he saw, but seen as a kind of hell, a city of the plain. The revelation of Balbec as Sodom and Gomorrah is gradual.

However, in contrast to the preoccupation in the first part with inversion, Balbec is reintroduced by a remarkable prelude that has nothing to do with inversion. The prelude has a title: *Les Intermittences du Coeur.* This passage on "the intermittences of the heart" (a title Proust once thought of giving to the entire novel) contains an episode of involuntary memory which is as important for the second half of the novel, as the madeleine-tea episode is for the first half. It is one of Marcel's sobering and deeply felt experiences, and one not to be recaptured throughout the rest of *Sodome et Gomorrhe.* Its poignancy, despite its brevity, is strong enough to counteract the continual erotic preoccupations which occupy so much of this section of the novel. (pp. 163-64)

The intermittences of the heart, with which the novel henceforth is going to be increasingly concerned, are what controls the accumulation of our memories. Proust believes that this accumulation is at all times present within us, but not always accessible to our conscious mind. As he lives in the present, Marcel is going to testify over and over again to the disappearance of strong sentiments in him, to the cessation of loves that at one time dominated his existence. Even those individuals whom he loved dearly, such as his grandmother, are destined to die a second time. There is first the physical death, and then there is the death in the conscious mind of the one who lives. But the experience of deep love or strong sentiment never dies in the subconscious memory of a man. Although it is, of course, possible that no sensation in the present will ever bring back the love that once existed.

In the prelude scene to the new Balbec, we reach a high level of meditation on Marcel's meaning of the word *real.* It is true that he is held only briefly by this overwhelming experience of recall, and soon plunges into the "unreal" world of Balbec society. But the long narrative rests on these rare intuitions of time and the reality of the objective world. We have just learned once again, with Marcel, that things are not what they are. They are what we make them, they are the record of our subjective memory and totally present within us, although removed from the dangerous contingencies of the present. In other words, time is a form that beings and objects take within us. It is not, therefore, solely the chronological force that destroys sentiments and beings and things. (pp. 165-66)

Wallace Fowlie, in his A Reading of Proust *(copyright © 1963, 1964 by Wallace Fowlie; reprinted by permission of Doubleday & Company, Inc.), Anchor Books, 1964, 307 p.*

PHILIP KOLB (essay date 1965)

There are five characters in *A la recherche du temps perdu* whom Proust seems to place in a favored category and to view in a somewhat different light from the others. (p. 38)

The one about whom the least has been written, although the most problematical, is the protagonist. The first problem that he presents is the question of establishing his identity. According to the Webster-Merriam unabridged international dictionary, third edition, a protagonist is "the chief character of a novel or story in or around whom the action centers." By such a definition, the protagonist of Proust's novel would seem to be his narrator, since the plot of *Le Temps perdu* centers on the narrator's experiences in a quest that leads ultimately to the discovery of his true vocation.

Objections might, however, be raised. The narrator of this novel is so modest and unobtrusive that he seems at times to disappear from the scene altogether. That is precisely what he does during the episode of the first part entitled *Un Amour de Swann,* where events are recounted that occur before the narrator's birth. The novel does, of course, embrace his own story. And yet, in the course of thousands of pages, so few hints are interspersed about his physical appearance that it is impossible to imagine what sort of man he is, at least physically. We learn that he is frail and suffers from asthma and insomnia, but little else about him except his attitudes toward love and literature.

While he observes many people, he himself takes little part in their activities. Proust's reputation is based in part on the splendid portrait gallery with which he has endowed French literature. His gifts for characterisation have earned him a place alongside Saint-Simon, the great memorialist of Louis XIVth's court. Proust's characters, like Dicken's, have entered, during the past fifty years, the vocabulary of the reading public. People are wont to refer familiarly to the domineering Mme Verdurin, eccentric of old Aunt Léonie, the ambiguous Baron de Charlus, and many others. But it would hardly occur to us to characterize someone by comparing him to Proust's narrator. Alongside of his other characters, the narrator seems pale and elusive, scarcely a character at all. (pp. 38-9)

If then we agree to designate the narrator as the key character, the question arises why he is so much less vividly portrayed than the others. Several reasons might explain this apparent anomaly. In the first place, when we look about us, unless we use a mirror, the visual impression we receive will necessarily exclude our own image. Then, too, the narrator's lack of participation in the actions he describes is due at least in part to his resemblance to the author, a semi-invalid who led a sedentary life. As we know, Proust was almost completely bedridden during the period of his novel's composition. There is, however, another reason which is, in my opinion, all the more plausible because it is based on aesthetics. If such a master of portraiture presents his narrator with such vague and imprecise traits, we can be assured that he does so with a purpose. The vast accumulation of notebooks Proust used in planning the novel show conclusively that he left nothing to improvisation. His purpose in this instance was in all probability to allow his reader to identify himself more readily with the narrator. It is evident that the less we know of his physical characteristics, the easier it is for us to imagine ourselves in his place. (p. 40)

If now we direct our attention to the Proustian portrait gallery mentioned earlier, I believe it possible to discern a difference in Proust's attitude toward two sets of characters. There is, on the one hand, the majority of characters, and, on the other, a separate little group seeming to belong to a favored category. In the first, larger group, we find a variety of persons whom the narrator observes with a relentless, penetrating gaze, subjecting them sooner or later to the subtly desintegrating effects of his satire. His treatment of the more select group, however, shows little of this tendency, and appears marked by restraint. This is particularly true of the four full-length portraits of Vinteuil, La Berma, Elstir and Bergotte. These four seem to stand apart and above the rest.

If such is the case, there must be a reason. Proust's intention, as I see it, is to present idealized portraits of these four artists. Let us review the elements of each character that conform to such a purpose.

Vinteuil is at first seen through the eyes of indifferent townspeople, who think him to be a sad, timid, insignificant piano teacher, exceedingly prudish although obliged to close his eyes to the scandalous conduct of his daughter. Only after his death is his full stature as a composer recognized. His music finally reveals his true nature to have been the very opposite of what it had seemed in the eyes of his neighbors. His true character is marked not by sadness, shyness and timidity, but is, on the contrary, infused with vigor, boldness and the joy of creative endeavor. . . . He exemplifies what Proust designated as his "prepared" characters, that is, characters who, according to plan, turn out to be quite different from what we had been led to suppose. Vinteuil's music is associated, at first anonymously, with the themes of love and memory, playing the role of catalyst in connection with Swann's love for Odette. But later in the novel, his music has a much greater importance. For it causes the narrator to meditate on the true nature of art, and to realize that through it alone can an artist achieve a sort

of immortality. He feels that all the joys he has known are as nothing compared to the joy Vinteuil expressed in his music. In such a manner, Vinteuil's music inspires the narrator to dedicate himself to his art, and prepares the novel's *dénouement*.

Elstir represents Proust's ideal of a modern painter. His originality consists in his ability to reveal a special universe, or to enable us to see through his eyes, just as the oculist gives vision by means of his lenses. Vinteuil did the same by revealing an unknown universe of the audible world. Bergotte does the same in the realm of literature. And La Berma helps the narrator to understand the essence and nature of dramatic art in its highest manifestations. These four artists represent pre-eminence in their respective artistic domains. (pp. 43-4)

The heroes of *Le Temps perdu* had of necessity to be artists. The sacrifice of the others was required for esthetic reasons bearing on the unity and artistic economy of the novel. . . . [Proust] has rejected the idealized portraits of men who were not artists in order to show that art alone can lead the narrator to the goal of his quest. Only the "beacons" can light his path and show the way to a greater happiness. At first he had failed to see or understand their message. He had sought happiness in his love for Gilberte, in his friendship for Saint-Loup, in his infatuation for the Duchess de Guermantes, in his deeper but jealous love for Albertine. Each time he had found disillusionment; neither love nor friendship gave him lasting satisfaction. But a higher, more exhilarating joy than these could give him he found in the art of the masters. This joy then he would seek, by creating his own work of art, after the example of his beacons, Elstir, Vinteuil and the others. Thanks to them, he finds his true vocation.

The novel's conclusion has a deep mystical tonality. The novelist setting out to recapture his past is almost a modern transposition of the mediaeval knight in quest of the holy grail. Such passages are marked by an unmistakable religious sentiment, in which Proust consciously and consistently uses terms borrowed from the vocabulary of Catholicism. He manages to convey, in such instances, a profound, reverent sense of the beauty and mystery of the universe, as in the descriptions of the hawthorn bushes, the apple trees in blossom, the scent of lilacs after a storm, the many seascapes and effects of sunlight on land and water.

The narrator, at the end of the novel, achieves a new dimension in his relationship with the four artists he admires. Until then, they have towered above him and all the other characters of the novel. But once their example has illuminated him and guided him, and he finds his true vocation, he is transformed, and assumes a new role. The *dénouement* suggests that he will take his place alongside these beacons, these creative artists. Thus he is worthy of being the novel's protagonist. For he himself becomes a beacon who will guide others, and shine, like a new star, in the night. (pp. 46-7)

Philip Kolb, "Proust's Protagonist As a 'Beacon'," in L'Esprit Créateur *(copyright © 1965 by L'Esprit Créateur), Vol. V, No. 1, Spring, 1965, pp. 38-47.*

HENRI PEYRE (essay date 1970)

If there is substantial agreement on Proust's greatness, there is much less concerning the fields where that greatness chiefly lies. No work of art once completed remains steadfast like a lodestar. The syntax, the imagery, the cadences, and the style of Proust, which had aroused the ire of purists in the 1920s, may well appear in the future as the most cherished side of his work. His philosophy and the psychological truths which he wanted to establish may on the contrary fade into near banality as we have assimilated their content. Tolstoy, Dostoevsky, Balzac, and Flaubert are not, after all, great to us on account of their "philosophy" or their theoretical views. Proust was the first to proclaim this in the last volume of his work, where he belittles the value of theories in a work of fiction. Conventional labels hardly apply to him. It has been questioned (he wondered himself) whether the name of novel suited that long, sprawling volume of imaginary and real memories, of fictional episodes, of analysis of the self of the narrator, and of apparent digressions on literature, architecture, painting, and music which make, however, the very skeleton of the work. (pp. 16-17)

Still Proust's achievement remains that of a novelist. Like half a dozen other important novels of our age, those of Joyce, of Mann, of Hesse, of Broch, *A la Recherche du Temps perdu* was Proust's audacious endeavor to write a work of fiction which would ring the knell of all other novels. (pp. 17-18)

Recent scholars have driven the notion of the perfect architecture (symmetrical or circular) of the Proustian saga to an excess which showed their naïveté, just as they had for Baudelaire's book of poems or for essays by Montaigne and Diderot whose very originality lay in their digressiveness and desultory tone. Proust protested too much that every section of his book had been lucidly calculated and that every theme would be integrated further on into a secret harmony for him not to have wanted us to admit his contention because he realized how paradoxical it was. The very first section of *Du Côté de chez Swann* and the last one of *Le Temps retrouvé* are indeed symmetrical. The conclusion of the whole work was perhaps written, as the author maintained, or in any case probably planned, while the first volumes were composed. Such an endeavor to descry a geometrical structure in *A la Recherche* proves chiefly the ingeniosity of the scholars who attempt it and does not accrue to the novelist's greatness. Unpredictability and even the "fine disorder" naïvely praised by Boileau in Pindaric odes and less naïvely by Herrick as an elegance in a lady's dress may well be qualities far more attractive than composition, structure, and planning. Strictness in an almost geometric and often artificial arrangement of the several moments in a symphony or parts of a long literary composition can be a merit very secondary to the irruption of the unpredictable which supreme masters have often preferred when they had given free rein to the demon inhabiting them. Proust himself remarked that an author might well, if he aims at the virtue of solidity, plan his book as a builder plans a church; however, there are parts thus planned which are merely sketched and never are completed. "How many great cathedrals remained unfinished!" And inversely, additions which are afterthoughts come to be incorporated in a work to which they were not destined and are then inseparable from it. Wagner's "Good Friday Spell" had been composed before the musician had thought of *Parsifal,* Proust remarked; but it found its place in the opera harmoniously.

The general outline of the work, moving in a meandering way from time past and lost toward time recaptured, traces the passing from the level of life to the level of artistic creation. Elstir and Vinteuil succeeded in effecting that ascent; Swann and Charlus did not. Marcel, the protagonist, observes the experience of those who have failed to effect the maturing metamorphosis, yields to the same temptations (mundane life,

snobbery, dispersion of the self through friendship, love affairs), learns through suffering and anguish. From the melancholy wear and tear of an existence abandoned to the flux of temporality, he rises to a victory over time and to an ascent into the intemporal. That triumph is not achieved without the loss of many illusions and without the disenchantment brought about by the piercing eye of the narrator who sees through the glamor of all the characters who had at first dazzled him: the actress La Berma, the radiant young Gilberte, Odette, Oriane de Guermantes, dashing Saint Loup. None of them, except the painter and the musician (both disappear long before the novel reaches its middle section), are spared. Gradually, painfully, the two "I's" or even the three "I's" come to coincide in the last volume: the child or the adolescent of the beginning, enraptured by the magic lantern of life as he transfigures it with wonderment, the disabused and solitary man at the end, the author commenting upon the hero's experiences and judging them. Likewise, the several worlds at first separated by social barriers and class prejudices come to be merged: that of Combray and its stable, self-contented, monotonous existence, that of the Paris aristocracy, that of the comic and pompous middle class (Legrandin, Cambremer), that of servants, pimps, and procurers. The boy or the adolescent of the early sections, whose sense of wonder, similar to that of the Symbolists and of romantic poets, transfigured the meanest and most derelict objects into effulgent and meaningful things of beauty, withdraws from a life of woe and of self-torture. In a revealing passage of *La Prisonnière* (in several respects the richest and the highest volumes of the whole saga), Proust, alluding to Balzac and Wagner, but also to himself, voices his admiration for those artists of the last century who, "watching themselves work as if they were both the workman and the judge, have derived from that contemplation of themselves a new beauty, exterior and superior to the work and which retroactively imposes upon it a unity, a greatness which it does not have." The centrifugal movements of the middle of the long novel (in *Le Côté de Guermantes* and *Sodome et Gomorrhe*), with the multiplicity of their digressions, correspond to a painful season in hell, during which the hero, like Ulysses and Aeneas, long forgets the vocation or the mission which had been proposed to him. He failed to heed the signs given him by the spires of Martinville, by the three trees, by those (the diplomat Norpois, the novelist Bergotte, his own somewhat conventional father) whom he desperately wanted not to resemble. At last, the suffering caused by love and jealousy, the realization of the utter emptiness of worldly pursuits in society, and the degradation into which vice may have plunged him have brought the narrator back to the deeper and purer springs from which his creation may emerge. Love had at first appeared linked with art. But love tended to devour what should nourish art. It is, in the end, transcended or bypassed. (pp. 20-3)

Henri Peyre, in his Marcel Proust *(Columbia Essays on Modern Writers Pamphlet No. 48; copyright © 1970 Columbia University Press; reprinted by permission of the publisher), Columbia University Press, 1970, 48 p.*

WILLIAM H. GASS (essay date 1971)

Remembrance of Things Past is, like most great examples of the novelist's art, an act of love, of hate and revenge, and finally, of reparation. Proust lives in it as he failed to live in life, and it would be more appropriate to celebrate the hours in which he began it, were there such moments, than the confused and frightened days of his confinement. But before he could embark upon its composition, Proust had to devise a fictional strategy that would radically single his mind, slow the drain of neurasthenia on his spirit, and by indulging his deepest nature find employment for all his vagrant energies; in this way permitting, for example, his morbid suspicion and excessive possessiveness, his inclination to symbolic cruelty and ritual desecration, to have a constructive outlet; and allowing him to exercise exactly the painstaking and painful reappraisal of every occasion which was his constant bedtime occupation.

For then his mind was not one wolf but twenty, it could bring down anything; there his jealous instability was a law of love; and in the scheme he finally settled on, his obsessive concerns (homosexuality, snobbery and the break-up of classes, the pleasures and anxieties of being "in society," the religion of art) became recurrent themes in an enormous Mahleresque composition in which these subjects, themselves, were entered, overcome, and evetually replaced by the style of their own depiction. Remember that description of Madame Swann's gowns which is more laced and bowed and ruffled, more exquisitely daring, more utterly elaborated, than they are, and beneath which she sinks from sight as a thread of grass does in a bouquet of daisies?

Proust was always ready to have his friends defend the organization of *Remembrance of Things Past,* and there can be no doubt his tapestry is intricate and cunningly worked; yet much of the so-called form in Proust is meaningless—an excuse. Like the elaborate Homeric correspondence in *Ulysses,* it is meant only for the mind. It placates critics who chase relations like lawyers trying to settle rich estates. An unfeelable form is a failure. Furthermore, it is hard to imagine what the architecture of this novel would have excluded, since forms, like fences, are meant to keep the cows out as well as the corn in. No, it is largely a wonderful wallow; it can accommodate anything, including little essays on art, love, literature, and life. Nor should we too readily accept the idea that the fuses of those involuntary memories (the madeleine, the shoe button, the paving stone, etc.) really set off the rest of the text; otherwise we should have to believe that, when those little powdered strings are lit, a miracle of physics occurs—one in which the boom blows up the bomb.

Proust despised the esthete with all the hate hog has for hog, and believed that his novel would uncover, in a way no other method could manage, the essential truth of his life; but he was a liar like all the others, a master of dissimulation and subterfuge; there is no special truth in him; he would capture our consciousness if he could and give us a case of his nerves. Still—no danger. When the fuss over Proust's theories about memory and time has faded; when we have taken what we can for psychology from his own reflections on his characters; when we have faithfully observed, as Proust did, the intrusion, like a second row of teeth, of the middle into the upper classes; when we have ceased to be shocked by inversion or amused by period dress and manners (and it's been well past "when" now for many years); then it is only Proust's style that will carry this enormous book: the style of his mind, his sight and hearing, touch and feeling, and above all, the unique character of his language and its extraordinary composition—a style where image and object, like Jack and Jill, go up and down together.

Carry it? The standard French edition is in 15 volumes; the Random House is a pair comprising 2,265 pages; and each page should be sounded, each sentence thought slowly over as a mind on a walk for pleasure. So taken, the pace of every one of them is slow, the path of every one of them is lengthy. When reading, one wonders first if the book will ever end, and then, in despair, if it will ever begin. In comparision, the Russian steppes—were they so vast? Or winters in upper Michigan prolonged? Lawrence said it was like tilling a field with knitting needles, and James, reading *Swann's Way,* confessed to an inconceivable boredom.

Well, we are safe from it, since it is difficult to imagine a work more out of step with modern consciousness, not simply because its sexual revelations are tame, its social preoccupations fairly innocent and out of date, its politics impossibly square, but because the rich and thoughtful musical approach Proust takes, the deep analytical poetry he writes, is both duller and quieter than silence is among the loud impatient honks and heartfelt belches which these days pass for books. "Inconceivable boredom," James said, "associated with the most extreme ecstasy which it is possible to imagine."

Carry it? This style? How? Proust writes a careless self-indulgent prose, doesn't he? Developing trivialities endlessly, as if he were in terror that anything should be thought trivial. Oh, he would sanctify if he could, his every wink, pang, or sniffle. My god, how he fawns over the asparagus, "stippled in mauve and azure." Does he plan to make a mayonnaise with his effusions? And note how he flatters the lilacs. Epithet follows epithet like tea cakes in flutes of paper. You'd suppose every bloom were a baron. Indeed, botanical metaphors are plentiful as plants, and the growth of the action is like theirs—imperceptible, steady, continuous—yes, and it's the same for the revelation of character; it's the same for the course of his thought; thus he slows things to permit the fullest flight of his fancy, the tireless play of his sensibilities, the utmost smother of his love. He slows, then stops; and then his scenes are like those cell cross-sections cut by the microtome and stained till they glow like glass.

It is a style that endangers the identity of the self in its reckless expression of it.

Proust has always had his Proustians, which seems inevitable, though a pity, for they have tended to admire everything in him but his art; they fatten on content; but this work, like all truly great ones, spits life out of time like the pit from a fruit. Out of the architecture of the word, the great work rises, but its reading requires a similar commitment, a similar elevation of the soul above mere living, mere mortal concerns. One hundred years—and we remember him. (pp. 154-57)

William H. Gass, "Marcel Proust at 100," in The New York Times Book Review *(© 1971 by The New York Times Company; reprinted by permission), July 11, 1971 (and reprinted as "Proust at 100," in his* The World within the Word, *Alfred A. Knopf, 1978, pp. 147-57).*

GÉRARD GENETTE (essay date 1972)

It seems to me impossible to treat the *Recherche du temps perdu* as a mere example of what is supposedly narrative in general, or novelistic narrative, or narrative in autobiographical form, or narrative of God knows what other class, species, or variety. The specificity of Proustian narrative taken as a whole is *irreducible,* and any extrapolation would be a mistake in method; the *Recherche* illustrates only itself. But, on the other hand, that specificity is not *undecomposable,* and each of its analyzable features lends itself to some connection, comparison, or putting into perspective. Like every work, like every organism, the *Recherche* is made up of elements that are universal, or at least transindividual, which it assembles into a specific synthesis, into a particular totality. (pp. 22-3)

We know that Proust spent more than ten years writing his novel, but Marcel's act of narrating bears no mark of duration, or of division: it is instantaneous. The narrator's present, which on almost every page we find mingled with the hero's various pasts, is a single moment without progression. . . . Proust was anxious to tune the narrator's discourse to the hero's "errors," and thus to impute to the narrator a belief not his own, in order to avoid disclosing his own mind too early. Even the narrative Marcel produces after the Guermantes soirée, the narrative of his beginnings as a writer (seclusion, rough drafts, first reactions of readers), which necessarily takes into account the length of writing ("like him too, . . . I had something to write. But my task was longer than his, my words had to reach more than a single person. My task was long. By day, the most I could hope for was to try to sleep. If I worked, it would be only at night. But I should need many nights, a hundred perhaps, or even a thousand") and the interrupting fear of death—even this narrative does not gainsay the fictive instantaneousness of its narrating: for the book Marcel then begins to write *in the story* cannot legitimately be identified with the one Marcel has then almost finished writing *as narrative*—and which is the *Recherche* itself. Writing the fictive book, which is the subject of the narrative, is, like writing every book, a "task [that] was long." But the actual book, the narrative-book, does not have knowledge of its own "length": it does away with its own duration.

The present of Proustian narrating—from 1909 to 1922—corresponds to many of the "presents" of the writing, and we know that almost a third of the book—including, as it happens, the final pages—was written by 1913. The fictive moment of narrating has thus *in fact* shifted in the course of the real writing; today it is no longer what it was in 1913, at the moment when Proust thought his work concluded. . . . Therefore, the temporal intervals he had in mind—and wanted to signify—when he wrote, for example apropos of the bedtime scene, "Many years have passed since that night," or apropos of the resurrection of Combray by the madeleine, "I can measure the resistance, I can hear the echo of great spaces traversed"—these spaces have increased by more than ten years simply because the story's time has lengthened: the signified of these sentences is no longer the same. Whence certain irreducible contradictions like this one: the narrator's *today* is obviously, for us, later than the war, but the "Paris today" of the last pages of *Swann* remains in its historical determinations (its referential content) a prewar Paris, as it was seen and described in its better days. The novelistic *signified* (the moment of the narrating) has become something like 1925, but the historical *referent*, which corresponds to the moment of the writing, did not keep pace and continues to say: 1913. Narrative analysis must register these shifts—and the resulting discordances—as effects of the actual genesis of the work; but in the end analysis can look at the narrating instance only as it is given in the final state of the text, as a single moment without duration, necessarily placed several years after the last "scene," therefore after the war, and even . . . after the death of Marcel Proust. This paradox, let us remember, is not one: Marcel is not Proust, and nothing requires him to die with Proust. What is required, on the other hand, is that Marcel spend "many years" after 1916 in a clinic, which necessarily puts his return to Paris and the Guermantes matinée in 1921 at the earliest, and the meeting

with an Odette "showing signs of senility" in 1923. That consequence is a must.

Between this single narrating instant and the different moments of the story, the interval is necessarily variable. If "many years" have elapsed since the bedtime scene in Combray, it is only "of late" that the narrator has again begun to hear his childhood sobs, and the interval separating the narrating instant from the Guermantes matinée is obviously smaller than the interval separating narrating instant and the hero's first arrival in Balbec. The system of language, the uniform use of the past tense, does not allow this gradual shrinking to be imprinted in the very texture of the narrative discourse, but . . . to a certain extent Proust had succeeded in making it felt, by modifications in the temporal pacing of the narrative: gradual disappearance of the iterative [narrating once what happened more than once], lengthening of the singulative [narrating once what happened once] scenes, increasing discontinuity, accentuation of the rhythm—as if the story time were tending to dilate and make itself more and more conspicuous while drawing near its end, *which is also its origin*.

According to . . . the common practice of "autobiographical" narrating, we could expect to see the narrative bring its hero to the point where the narrator awaits him, in order that these two hypostases might meet and finally merge. People have sometimes, a little quickly, claimed that this is what happens. In fact, as Marcel Muller well notes [in *Les Voix narratives dans A.L.R.T.P.*] "between the day of the reception at the Princess's and the day when the Narrator recounts that reception there extends a whole era which maintains a gap between the Hero [Marcel as protagonist] and the Narrator [Marcel as author], a gap that cannot be bridged: the verbal forms in the conclusion of the *Temps retrouvé* are all in the past tense." The narrator brings his hero's story—his own story—precisely to the point when, as Jean Rousset says, "the hero is about to become the narrator"; I would say rather, *is beginning to become* the narrator, since he actually starts in on his writing. Muller writes that "if the Hero overtakes the Narrator, it is like an asymptote: the interval separating them approaches zero, but will never reach it," but his image connotes a Sterneian play on the two durations that does not in fact exist in Proust. There is simply the narrative's halt at the point when the hero has discovered the truth and meaning of his life: at the point, therefore, when this "story of a vocation"—which, let us remember, is the avowed subject of Proustian narrative—comes to an end. The rest, whose outcome is already known to us by the very novel that concludes here, no longer belongs to the "vocation" but to the effort that follows it up, and must therefore be only sketched in. The subject of the *Recherche* is indeed "Marcel becomes a writer," not "Marcel the writer": the *Recherche* remains a novel of development, and to see it as a "novel about the novelist," like [André Gide's] *Faux Monnayeurs* [*The Counterfeiters*], would be to distort its intentions and above all to violate its meaning; it is a novel about the future novelist. "The continuation," Hegel said, precisely apropos of the Bildungsroman, "no longer has anything novelistic about it." Proust probably would have been glad to apply that formulation to his own narrative: what is novelistic is the quest, the *search* [*recherche*], which ends at the discovery (the revelation), not at the use to which that discovery will afterward be put. The final discovery of the truth, the late encounter with the vocation, like the happiness of lovers reunited, can be only a denouement, not an interim stopping place; and in this sense, the subject of the *Recherche* is indeed a traditional subject. So it is necessary that the narrative be interrupted before the hero overtakes the narrator; it is inconceivable for them both together to write: The End. The narrator's last sentence is when—is *that*—the hero finally reaches his first. The interval between the end of the story and the moment of the narrating is therefore the time it takes the hero to write this book, which is and is not the book the narrator, in his turn, reveals to us in a moment brief as a flash of lightning. (pp. 223-27)

I cannot deny that the purpose of my work is defined almost exactly by the opposite view to what is expressed in the preliminary statement of a recent, excellent study on the art of the novel in Proust [Jean-Yves Tadié's *Proust et le roman*], a statement which no doubt meets immediately with the unanimous acceptance of well-thinking people:

> We did not want to impose on Proust's work categories external to it, or a general idea of the novel or of the way in which one should study a novel; we did not want a treatise on the novel, with illustrations taken from the *Recherche,* but concepts arising from the work, and allowing us to read Proust as he read Balzac and Flaubert. The only theory of literature is in criticism of the particular.

We can certainly not maintain that here we are using concepts exclusively "arising from the work," and the description here of Proustian narrative can hardly be considered to conform to Proust's own idea of it. Such a gap between *indigenous theory* and critical method might seem inappropriate, like all anachronisms. It seems to me, however, that one should not rely blindly on the explicit aesthetics of a writer, even if he is a critic as inspired as the author of the *Contre Sainte-Beuve.* The aesthetic consciousness of an artist, when he is major, is so to speak never at the level of his practice, and this is only one manifestation of what Hegel symbolized by the late flight of Minerva's owl. We do not have at our disposal one hundredth of Proust's genius, but we do have the advantage over him (which is a little like the live donkey's advantage over the dead lion) of reading him precisely from the vantage point of what he contributed to fathering (fathering that modern literature which owes him so much) and thus the advantage of perceiving clearly in his work what was there only in its nascent state— all the more nascent because with him the transgression of norms, the aesthetic invention, are most often, as we have seen, involuntary and sometimes unconscious. His goal was otherwise, and this scorner of the avant-garde is almost always a revolutionary despite himself. . . . To repeat it once more and following so many others, we read the past by the light of the present, and is not that how Proust himself read Balzac and Flaubert, and does one really believe that his were critical concepts "arising from" the *Comédie humaine* or the *Education sentimentale?* (pp. 264-65)

> *Gérard Genette, in his* Narrative Discourse: An Essay in Method, *translated by Jane E. Lewin (copyright ©1980 by Cornell University; used by permission of the publisher, Cornell University Press; originally published as "Discours du récit," in his* Figures III, *Editions du Sevil, 1972), Cornell University Press, 1980, 285 p.**

VLADIMIR NABOKOV (essay date 1980)

The whole is a treasure hunt where the treasure is time and the hiding place the past: this is the inner meaning of the title *In Search of Lost Time*. The transmutation of sensation into sentiment, the ebb and tide of memory, waves of emotions such as desire, jealousy, and artistic euphoria—this is the material of the enormous and yet singularly light and translucid work.

In his youth Proust had studied the philosophy of Henri Bergson. Proust's fundamental ideas regarding the flow of time concern the constant evolution of personality in terms of duration, the unsuspected riches of our subliminal minds which we can retrieve only by an act of intuition, of memory, of involuntary associations; also the subordination of mere reason to the genius of inner inspiration and the consideration of art as the only reality in the world; these Proustian ideas are colored editions of the Bergsonian thought. (pp. 207-08)

One thing should be firmly impressed upon your minds: the work is not an autobiography; the narrator is not Proust the person, and the characters never existed except in the author's mind. Let us not, therefore, go into the author's life. It is of no importance in the present case and would only cloud the issue, especially as the narrator and the author do resemble each other in various ways and move in much the same environment.

Proust is a prism. His, or its, sole object is to refract, and by refracting to recreate a world in retrospect. The world itself, the inhabitants of that world, are of no social or historical importance whatever. They happen to be what the gazettes call society people, men and ladies of leisure, the wealthy unemployed. The only professions we are shown in action, or in result, are artistic and scholarly ones. Proust's prismatic people have no jobs: their job is to amuse the author. They are as free to indulge in conversation and pleasure as those legendary ancients that we see so clearly reclining around fruit-laden tables or walking in high discourse over painted floors, but whom we never see in the countinghouse or the shipyard.

In Search of Lost Time is an evocation, not a description of the past, as Arnaud Dandieu, a French critic, has remarked. This evocation of the past, he continues, is made possible by bringing to light a number of exquisitely chosen moments which are a sequence of illustrations, of images. Indeed, the whole enormous work, he concludes, is but an extended comparison revolving on the words *as if—*. The key to the problem of reestablishing the past turns out to be the key of art. The treasure hunt comes to a happy end in a cave full of music, in a temple rich with stained glass. The gods of standard religions are absent, or, perhaps more correctly, they are dissolved in art.

To a superficial reader of Proust's work—rather a contradiction in terms since a superficial reader will get so bored, so engulfed in his own yawns, that he will never finish the book—to an inexperienced reader, let us say, it might seem that one of the narrator's main concerns is to explore the ramifications and alliances which link together various houses of the nobility, and that he finds a strange delight when he discovers that a person whom he has been considering as a modest businessman revolves in the *grand monde*, or when he discovers some important marriage that has connected two families in a manner such as he had never dreamed possible. The matter-of-fact reader will probably conclude that the main action of the book consists of a series of parties; for example, a dinner occupies a hundred and fifty pages, a soirée half a volume. In the first part of the work, one encounters Mme. Verdurin's philistine salon in the days when it was frequented by Swann and the evening party at Mme. de Saint-Euverte's when Swann first realizes the hopelessness of his passion of Odette; then in the next books there are other drawing rooms, other receptions, a dinner party at Mme. de Guermantes', a concert at Mme. Verdurin's, and the final afternoon party at the same house of the same lady who has now become a Princesse de Guermantes by marriage—that final party in the last volume, **Time Found Again,** during which the narrator becomes aware of the changes that time has wrought upon all his friends and he receives a shock of inspiration—or rather a series of shocks—causing him to decide to set to work without delay upon his book, the reconstruction of the past.

At this late point, then, one might be tempted to say that Proust *is* the narrator, that he *is* the eyes and ears of the book. But the answer is still no. The book that the narrator in Proust's book is supposed to write is still a book-within-the-book and is not quite *In Search of Lost Time*—just as the narrator is not quite Proust. There is a focal shift here which produces a rainbow edge: this is the special Proustian crystal through which we read the book. It is not a mirror of manners, not an auto-biography, not a historical account. It is pure fantasy on Proust's part, just as *Anna Karenin* is a fantasy, just as Kafka's "The Metamorphosis" is fantasy—just as Cornell University will be a fantasy if I ever happen to write about it some day in ret-rospect. The narrator in the work is one of its characters, who is called Marcel. In other words, there is Marcel the eaves-dropper and there is Proust the author. Within the novel the narrator Marcel contemplates, in the last volume, the ideal novel he will write. Proust's work is only a copy of that ideal novel—but what a copy! (pp. 208, 210-11)

> *Vladimir Nabokov, "Marcel Proust: 'The Walk by Swann's Place'" (1913), in his* Lectures on Litera-ture, *edited by Fredson Bowers (copyright © 1980 by the Estate of Vladimir Nabokov; reprinted by per-mission of Harcourt Brace Jovanovich, Inc.), Har-court, 1980, pp. 207-50.*

ADDITIONAL BIBLIOGRAPHY

Albaret, Céleste. *Monsieur Proust*. Edited by Georges Belmont. Trans-lated by Barbara Bray. New York: McGraw-Hill Book Co., 1976, 387 p.
> Memoirs of the woman who handled Proust's domestic affairs and shared his daily life during his last eight years.

Alden, Douglas W. *Marcel Proust and His French Critics*. New York: Russell & Russell, 1973, 259 p.
> Chronicle of Proust's critical reputation in France to 1940, with a bibliography of French language criticism arranged by country of origin.

Alley, John N. "Proust and Art: The Anglo-American Critical View." *Revue de littérature comparée* XXXVII, No. 3 (July-September): 410-30.
> Survey of critical commentaries on Proust's use of painting, mu-sic, and literature in *Remembrance of Things Past*.

Ames, Van Meter. *Proust and Santayana: The Aesthetic Way of Life*. New York: Russell & Russell, 1964, 176 p.*
> Study of Proust's philosophy of art.

Barker, Richard H. *Marcel Proust: A Biography*. New York: Criterion Books, 1958, 373 p.
> Includes descriptive critical sections.

Bell, William Stewart. *Proust's Nocturnal Muse*. New York, London: Columbia University Press, 1962, 288 p.

Analyzes Proust's use of dream states from his early works through *Remembrance of Things Past*.

Brady, Patrick. *Marcel Proust*. Boston: Twayne Publishers, 1977, 168 p.
> Introductory critical study.

Butor, Michel. "The Imaginary Works of Art in Proust." In his *In-ventory: Essays*, pp. 146-84. London: Jonathan Cape, 1970.
> Examines the function of the writer Bergotte, the painter Elstir, and the composer Vinteuil in *Remembrance of Things Past,* and the way Proust used their imaginary works in structuring his novel.

Coleman, Elliott. *The Golden Angel: Papers on Proust*. New York: Coley Taylor, 1954, 128 p.
> Essays on various themes and subjects in *Remembrance of Things Past,* including humor, dreams, morality, and death.

Croce, Benedetto. "Proust: An Example of Decadent Historical Method." In his *My Philosophy and Other Essays on the Moral and Political Problems of Our Time*, pp. 208-13. London: George Allen & Unwin, 1949.
> States that Proust's consciousness of the past lacks moral and religious dimensions, and that he treats the "noble matron of history . . . as if she were a shameless hussy to provide exquisite titillations."

Girard, René, ed. *Proust: A Collection of Critical Essays*. Englewood Cliffs, N.J.: Prentice-Hall, 1962, 182 p.
> Includes essays by Henri Peyre, Jacques Rivière, Albert Thibau-det, Leo Spitzer, Charles Du Bos, and Georges Poulet. The essays cover various aspects of Proust's writings, including imagery, style, and the meaning of time in *Remembrance of Things Past*.

Graham, Victor. *The Imagery of Proust*. Oxford: Basil Blackwell, 1966, 274 p.
> Regards motifs of imagery in *Remembrance of Things Past* as a unifying technique.

Green, F.C. *The Mind of Proust: A Detailed Interpretation of "A la recherche du temps perdu."* Cambridge: Cambridge University Press, 1949, 546 p.
> Discusses Proust's novel without reference to his life.

Haldane, Charlotte. *Marcel Proust*. London: Arthur Baker, 1951, 140 p.
> Critical study including a section of plot outlines for each volume of *Remembrance of Things Past*.

Kopp, Richard L. *Marcel Proust As a Social Critic*. Rutherford, N.J.: Fairleigh Dickinson University Press, 1971, 230 p.
> Examines Proust's "impressions of society," discussing "not the man as revealed by his impression but the impressions themselves."

Lemaitre, Georges. "Marcel Proust." In his *Four French Novelists: Marcel Proust, Andre Gide, Jean Giraudoux, Paul Morand*, pp. 3-111. 1938. Reprint. Port Washington, N.Y.: Kennikat Press, 1969.
> Biocritical study.

Lesage, Laurent. *Marcel Proust and His Literary Friends*. Urbana: The University of Illinois Press, 1958, 113 p.
> Examines Proust's relationships with such nineteenth-century lit-erary figures as Robert de Montesquiou and Henri de Régnier.

Linder, Gladys Dudley, ed. *Marcel Proust: Reviews and Estimates*. Stanford: Stanford University Press, 1942, 314 p.
> Essays and appreciations by prominent English critics and authors, including J. Middleton Murry, Clive Bell, Arnold Bennett, Edith Wharton, Wyndham Lewis, and John Cowper Powys.

March, Harold. *The Two Worlds of Marcel Proust*. Philadelphia: Uni-versity of Pennsylvania Press, 1948, 276 p.
> Biocritical study.

Miller, Milton L. *Nostalgia: A Psychoanalytic Study of Marcel Proust*. Boston: Houghton Mifflin Co., 1956, 306 p.

Psychological analysis of Proust's "aesthetic approach to the un-conscious," with chapters on Proust and Freud, Proust's homo-sexuality, and the use of dreams in *Remembrance of Things Past*.

Moss, Howard. *The Magic Lantern of Marcel Proust*. New York: The Macmillan Co., 1962, 111 p.
    Study of various themes and symbols in *Remembrance of Things Past*.

Pound, Ezra. "Paris Letter." *The Dial* LXXI, No. 2 (October 1921): 458-61.
    Compares Proust to Henry James as an author of "precise nuance."

Price, Larkin B., ed. *Marcel Proust: A Critical Panorama*. Urbana: University of Illinois Press, 1973, 288 p.
    Essays in French and English on various aspects of Proust's work.

Rivers, J. E. *Proust and the Art of Love: The Aesthetics of Sexuality in the Life, Times, and Art of Marcel Proust*. New York: Columbia University, 1980, 327 p.
    Designed as an extended explication of the first part of *Sodome et Gommorrhe*.

Roche, A. J. "Proust As Translator of Ruskin." *PMLA* XLV, No. 4 (December 1930): 1214-17.
    Shows that although Proust's rendering of Ruskin's lectures is occasionally well done, "on the whole he translated poorly."

Shattuck, Roger. "Kilmartin's Way." *The New York Review of Books* XXVIII, No. 11 (June 25, 1981): 16, 18-20.
    Critique of Terence Kilmartin's translation of *À la recherche du temps perdu*.

Turnell, Martin. "Proust's Early Novel." *The Commonweal* LXIII, No. 13 (December 30, 1955): 333-35.
    Study which concludes that *Jean Santeuil* "does not possess the richness and complexity of *Remembrance of Things Past*."

Marina (Ivanovna) Tsvetaeva (Éfron)

1892-1941

(Also transliterated as Maryna and Mariny; also Tsvetayeva, Cvetaeva, Zvétaieva, Zwetajewa, Cvětajevová, Cweitajewa, Ťsvetaevoǐ, Tzvetayeva, and Tzvetaéva) Russian poet, essayist, critic, translator, autobiographer, and dramatist.

Tsvetaeva is recognized as one of modern Russia's "poetic quartet," along with Anna Akhmatova, Boris Pasternak, and Osip Mandelstam, who acted as poet-witnesses of the country's changing values in a difficult period. Their lives and art were influenced by one another and by the cataclysmic political and social upheavals occurring in Russia during the early decades of the twentieth century. Tsvetaeva is often likened to her three contemporaries—to Pasternak for an intense love of Moscow, to Akhmatova for shared feminist concerns, and to Mandelstam for tumultuous emotions. Her central interest was language, and she used a terse, often verbless construction, with an energy described as taut and virile. Her experiments with syntax and rhythm are considered a unique contribution to Russian literature. *Remeslo*, Tsvetaeva's last volume of poetry completed before her emigration, is praised for its metrical experiments and effective use of folk language, archaisms, and Biblical idioms, while *Posle Rossii*, written after emigration, is highly acclaimed for its technical experimentation, strong themes, and emotional depth.

Tsvetaeva grew up in Moscow, a member of an artistic, scholarly, upper-middle-class family. She privately published her first volume of verse, *Vechernii al'bom*, in 1910. Critic Max Voloshin and poets Nikolay Gumilyov and Valery Bryusov reviewed the volume favorably, responding to the poet's romantic, emotional evocation of her childhood experiences. Tsvetaeva's second collection, *Volshebnyǐ fonar'*, published in 1912, was in the same lyrical, romantic style. For the next ten years, years which spanned the Russian Revolution, the poet wrote prodigiously—poetry, essays, memoirs, and dramas—though she did not publish her works. Motifs of Russia, love, death, art, and woman's roles shaped her work. In 1922 Tsvetaeva emigrated with her young daughter to western Europe to join her husband, Sergei Efron, a former White Army officer who had left Russia after the Bolsheviks took power. While the Éfrons lived in Berlin and Prague, Tsvetaeva began publishing the products of her previous decade's labor; these found critical favor with émigré writers and publishers. Moving to Paris, Tsvetaeva continued her poetic writing in times marked by physical and emotional hardship. She was unable to sustain her early acceptance by other émigré writers because of her marked independence, her emotional intensity, and because of her own and her husband's suspected political sympathies. Sergei Efron had become involved in the Communist party. Tsvetaeva refused to adopt the militant anti-Soviet posture of many émigrés. She praised Soviet poets Pasternak and Vladimir Mayakovsky, persisted in championing lost causes, and aided victims of social injustice. In the late 1930s Tsvetaeva's son entreated her to follow her husband and daughter who had already returned to Russia. The poet and her son arrived in Moscow in 1939 to an extreme political situation of totalitarian dictatorship. Artists and intellectuals were automatically suspect and Tsvetaeva was especially endangered by

the political activities of her husband, who had been arrested and executed. When German troops attacked Moscow in 1941 Tsvetaeva and her son were evacuated to the village of Elabuga in the Tartar Republic. Tsvetaeva, denied the right to publish, was unable to find acceptable work there or in nearby Christopol where a colony of writers had gathered. Three weeks after her evacuation, she took her life.

Departing sharply from her earlier romantic style, Tsvetaeva began her mature poetry with her poetic diary of 1916, *Versty I*. In this work centered around life in Moscow, the poet shows a development in rhythmic control and restraint. While not a follower of any particular poetic school, Tsvetaeva shared the acmeists's passion for precision and hard, factual detail and the symbolists's refinement of poetic craftsmanship. She excelled at fast, sharp rhythms, and uncovered the power of words by cutting to their roots, omitting prefixes. By the mid 1920s Tsvetaeva's emphasis had shifted from lyric poetry to narrative verse. She adapted traditional Russian folktales in her narratives *Tsar'-devitsa* and *Molodetš*. This fusion of metrical ingenuity and popular motifs met with mixed reviews. Also criticized was her political cycle *Lebedinyǐ stan (The Demesne of the Swans)*, a eulogy to the defeated White cause, which some critics viewed as too outspoken and ideologically militant.

As the 1930s progressed Tsvetaeva devoted more energy to prose than to poetry. In her literary and personal memoirs her thoughts turned more and more to her past. "Captive Spirit," a memoir of the poet Andrey Bely, expresses Tsvetaeva's subjective impressions about her friend. In the essay "My Pushkin" she recreates her childhood, remembering with youthful fervor her lifelong idol. Tsvetaeva sets forth her views on art and the artist's social role in her major prose piece, "Art in the Light of Conscience."

The unpopularity of Tsvetaeva's experimental style along with her status as a political suspect led to her neglect by émigré publishers. However, scholarly interest in Tsvetaeva during the 1950s and 60s has led to new biographies and translations in the last decade bringing her work new Russian and English audiences. Tsvetaeva's technical innovativeness, emotional power, thematic range, and proficiency in a number of literary genres set a precedent for succeeding Russian writers.

PRINCIPAL WORKS

Vecherniĭ al'bom (poetry) 1910
Volshebnyĭ fonar' (poetry) 1912
 Tsar'-devista (poetry) 1922
Versty I (poetry) 1922
Remeslo (poetry) 1923
Molodets (poetry) 1924
Posle Rossii (poetry) 1928
Proza (letters and reminiscences) 1953
Lebedinyĭ stan (poetry) 1957
  [*The Demesne of the Swans,* 1980]
Izbrannye proizvedeniĭa (drama and poetry) 1965
Pis'ma k A. Teskovoĭ (letters) 1969
Selected Poems (poetry) 1971
"Art in the Light of Conscience" (essay) 1976;
   published in *Modern Russian Poets on Poetry*
"A Poet on Criticism" (essay) 1977; published in *The Bitter Air of Exile*
A Captive Spirit: Selected Prose (essays, criticism, literary portraits, and autobiographical sketches) 1980

D. S. MIRSKY (essay date 1926)

The great event in Russian literature within these last two or three years is the extraordinary, one has to say unexpected, growth of the poetic genius of Marina Tsvetayeva. Ever since 1922, when her lyrical poetry written in Moscow in 1916-1922 was first revealed to the public, she has been one of the major lights of our poetical firmament. But there was in those wonderfully spontaneous and always fresh lyrics a certain excess of fluency, a certain lack of fixity which made one fear that she would not be able to master her inspiration, and would succumb to her own excessive productiveness. Her latest work, beginning with the poem quoted in the heading [*Mólodets*], belies those fears. To her inimitable spontaneousness, Marina Tsvetayeva has added now a mastery and a discipline of form that make her possibilities unlimited. *Mólodets* is only the first in a series of poems that display her genius in a new aspect, enormously strengthened by conscious workmanship and discipline.

The two long poems she has published since, and which have not yet appeared in book form, ["The Poem of the End" and "The Ratcatcher"] . . . , are still further achievements in the same directions. Without hesitation they must be qualified as great poetry, of an entirely new kind. There can be no doubt that, with the exception of Boris Pasternak, Marina Tsvetayeva has no rivals among the Russian poets of the generation under thirty-five. (p. 775)

*D. S. Mirsky, "Reviews: 'Mólodets: A Fairy Tale',"
in* The Slavonic Review *(reprinted by permission of the University of London), Vol. IV, No. 12, March, 1926, pp. 775-76.*

D. S. MIRSKY (essay date 1926)

Marina Tsvetaeva must be considered a poet of the postrevolutionary period.

And she is entitled to first place among postrevolutionary poets—or to one of the first two places; her only possible rival, Boris Pasternak, is a poet of a totally different stamp. Considering the unlikeness of the two, it is interesting to note the characteristics they have in common. Besides a clear, evident, unquestionable newness (I use this word in the strictest Bergsonian sense), a trait that seems inevitable and inescapable in a truly great contemporary poet, and besides an elevation common to both which really cannot be considered an individual trait in a lyric poet, the one thing we find in both Tsvetaeva and Pasternak is their major key: a buoyant vitality, an acceptance of life and the world. . . . The fact is significant: all Russian literature of the preceding generation (with the exception of [Nikolai] Gumilyov) was united by exactly the opposite qualities—hatred, rejection, and fear of life. (pp. 88-9)

But, I repeat, with the exception of these qualities, Pasternak and Marina Tsvetaeva are unlike, almost opposites. Pasternak is visual and material. His poetry is a mastering of the world by means of words. His words strive to depict, to transmit, to embrace the world of things. In this embrace and this mastery of real things lies all Pasternak's strength. He is a "naive realist." Marina Tsvetaeva is an idealist. . . . The material world is for her only an emanation of essence. Things live only in words; not *sunt,* but *percipiuntur.* Only their essences *sunt.* Her very perception, so sharp and persuasive, especially in her prose, seems practically disembodied. The people in her reminiscences, so alive and inimitable, are not so much everyday, three-dimensional people as they are reductions of individuality and of inimitability almost to a point. The ability to see past and through the "visual tegument" to the nucleus of identity and, despite the boundlessness of personality, to convey the singleness and the inimitability of that nucleus—this is the incomparable enchantment of Marina Tsvetaeva's prose. (pp. 89-90)

In poetry, the difference is revealed thus: for Pasternak the word is the sign of a thing. His language is neutral, international, fully translatable. For Tsvetaeva the word cannot be the sign of a thing, for the thing itself is only a sign. Words for her are more ontological than things; they bypass things and are directly connected with essences: absolute, self-contained, irreplaceable, untranslatable. Her poems are indissolubly Russian, the most indissolubly Russian in all contemporary poetry. And rhythm, for Pasternak only a grid of length and breadth . . . , is for Marina Tsvetaeva the essence of the poem; it is the poem itself, its soul, its source of life. Time in Pasternak's rhythm is Kantian; in Tsvetaeva's rhythm it is Bergsonian. (p. 90)

In poems she wrote before 1919-1920 there was an excessive lightness, a want of restraint, that made it possible to speak of lack of control. The discipline of style was not in these poems. Beginning about 1920, she unswervingly and victoriously overcame her illimitability—and, like every master, she *zeigt sich erst in die Beschräkung* [shows her talents only when limiting herself]. (Let me add that in her prose this process began later, and had not yet reached the same level.) In the poems she wrote between 1916 and 1920 she achieves amazing, solitary, short-lived epiphanies, the God-given, unique "personal expresion" that totally rescues even the worst lapses of taste (not infrequent in those years). But she had not yet fully mastered her demon. In her most recent work—**"The Swain," "Poem of the End," "The Pied Piper," "Poem of the Hill," "Theseus"**—it is precisely this full mastery, this complete technical success, that is so striking.

For a poet so romantic by nature (that is, so subjective and spontaneous) as Marina Tsvetaeva was, such a path is a rarity. The main role in overcoming her illimitability was played by her "verbality"—that is, her sensitivity (and for this reason her integrity) toward the word. A large role was played also by her involvement with folklore (beginning with **"The Tsar-Maiden"**) and especially (beginning also with the same poem) by the discipline of a longer form, narrative and impersonal. It was thus she was able to overcome the empirical subjectivity of her early lyrics—that is, to change her poetry from a means for emotional outpouring into a tool of poetic construction. **"The Tsar-Maiden"** and **"The Swain"** are written upon themes imposed from without and are free from psychological information. But even as a lyric poet Marina Tsvetaeva has come forth transfigured from this school. Her most recent long lyric poems, **"Poem of the Hill"** and **"Poem of the End"** are completely non-"phonographic"; they are fully constructivist. These are not the lyrical jottings of experience, but poetic (*poetikos* means creator-ly, constructivist) constructions out of the material of experience.

The main thing that is new and unusual in the most recent work of Marina Tsvetaeva—and unexpected after her first poems—is the presence of style. Not stylization, but a real, personal, freely born style. In our time she is the only poet to have achieved style. Its presence assures the reader that he will be neither deceived nor offended by a false note. This judgment of mine probably surprises those readers who, to the contrary, find in Tsvetaeva's poems an insolent violation of all *their* canons of taste, and an unjustifiable (and incomprehensible) diversity. But her style must be understood from within, and for that, what Turgenev called "a sympathetic humor" is needed (and without it there seems no point in reading poetry at all).

"The Swain" is the first poem in which Marina Tsvetaeva attained her style. It is distinct from **"The Tsar-Maiden"** and from **"Sidestreets"** in this: there is no stylization in it. It is no longer an imitation of folk poetry, it does not resemble folk poetry, and yet it is as closely connected with folk poetry as a tree with the soil—not by likeness, but by root kinship. Tsvetaeva has long worked at freeing the Russian language from the fetters of Graeco-Latin and Romano-Germanic grammar and returning it to its natural freedom and natural forms of connection. (In this she is a brother-in-arms with Remizov.) In **"The Swain"** she has accomplished the task. Russian "verbless" syntax reigns totally in the poem. . . . And the direct consequence of this is the "broken" quality of her rhythm. . . .

Marina Tsvetaeva is extraordinarily skillful in her ability to use monosyllabic words and contiguous stresses. The word, even the syllable, in her work receives a new freedom and importance, and intonation becomes a major grammatical force. (pp. 90-2)

D. S. Mirsky, "Marina Tsvetaeva, translated by Paul Schmidt (1926)," in TriQuarterly 27 *(© 1973 by TriQuarterly), No. 27, Spring, 1973 (and reprinted in* The Bitter Air of Exile: Russian Writers in the West, 1922-1972, *edited by Simon Karlinsky and Alfred Appel, Jr., University of California Press, 1977), pp. 88-93.*

MARC SLONIM (essay date 1953)

Impetuous, passionate, dynamic, Tsvetayeva was a typical romantic, with certain mystical overtones. She underwent pain and suffering 'down here, in the prison of existence,' and always dreamed of overcoming 'the law of gravitation—in nature and in emotions.' 'What can I do in this world of measures, numbers, and weights—I, a poet?' she asked in one of her most revealing stanzas.

Tsvetayeva wrote lyrics, epic poems, and drama in verse, as well as remarkable prose recollections of Briussov, Blok, Rilke, and other poets whom she had known well. Only a part of her writing has been published outside Russia: [**Verstes, The Czar-Maiden, Parting, Poems to Blok, A Bold Fellow, Craft, After Russia**]. . . . Most of her poetry and prose is scattered in various *émigré* publications; many of her manuscripts have been lost but some were preserved by her friends.

Tsvetayeva wrote in short, abrupt lines that revealed her interest in semantics as well as in tonal problems. Some of her narratives in verse, such as the fairy tale of *The Czar-Maiden* (reprinted by the Moscow Gosidzat from an *émigré* edition) and *A Bold Fellow*, a Gothic tale of magic and witchcraft, are successful imitations of early Russian folklore. Her other poems are also often in a folklore key and maintain the meters and beats of peasant songs. In her purely lyrical pieces, of which only comparatively few deal with love, Tsvetayeva dug at the very roots of words and, by cutting prefixes, changing endings, or resorting to verbal twists, succeeded in laying bare their original meaning, thus conveying a surprising sense of freshness and discovery. This linguistic quest, only slightly similar to that of Gertrude Stein, frequently bordered on extravagance and earned Tsvetayeva a reputation for obscurity and madness. Some of her poems were written in a 'telegraphic' style, in which snipped sentences, short lines, and isolated words served simply as signposts along a road the poet was traversing at an accelerated pace.

Her exclamatory poetry, with its whirlwind of alliterations, extraordinary rhymes, and intricate sound play, bore some resemblance to [Vladimir] Mayakovsky's work—especially in its highly accented diction, dynamic flow, and sharp expressiveness. But where Mayakovsky used the vernacular for the 'de-poetization' of verse and put the stress on single words, working in flashes and shouts, Tsvetayeva aimed at the effect of a torrential stream, of a unity that made her poems sound like one long sentence uttered in a single breath. Another aspect of her poetry is the sense of movement, expressed by the fast tempo of her 'windy and winged' rhythms. Idealism, which made her akin to the German poets of the 1820's and, among her Russian predecessors, to Karolina Pavlova, was her hallmark. But it was shot with the lightning of rebellion, and her meditations were often interrupted by violent outbursts.

What gave a special flavor to her romantic flights was the dynamic sweep of her stormy lines and their unique combination of sensitivity and strength. The very sonorousness of her full rhymes and astonishing alliterations, which no translation can convey, had a virile quality. This exclamatory, impetuous, almost aggressive poetess had, however, a distinct femininity, which never lapsed into softness or weakness; in the midst of her emotional turmoil, she always preserved a keen mind and a forceful philosophical insight. The day will come when her work will be rediscovered, reappraised, and given the place it deserves as one of the most interesting poetic documents of the post-Revolutionary era. (pp. 339-40)

> *Marc Slonim, "The Last Romantics," in his* Modern Russian Literature: From Chekhov to the Present *(copyright 1953 by Oxford University Press, Inc.; renewed 1981 by Tatiana Slonim; reprinted by permission of Oxford University Press, Inc.), Oxford University Press, New York, 1953, pp. 319-46.**

BORIS PASTERNAK (essay date 1959)

[Ilya] Ehrenburg spoke to me in high terms of Marina Tsvetayeva and showed me her poems. I was present at a literary meeting at the beginning of the Revolution at which she, among other writers, read her verses. During one of the winters of the Civil War I went to see her with some kind of message. I talked about all sorts of unimportant things and listened to all sorts of trivialities in turn. Marina Tsvetayeva made no impression on me.

My ear was at the time perverted by the pretentious extravagances and the break from everything natural that were in vogue in those days. Everything spoken in a normal way rebounded from me. I forgot that words by themselves can mean and contain something apart from the cheap toys with which they are strung.

It was just the harmony of Marina Tsvetayeva's verses, the clarity of their meaning, the presence of fine qualities and absence of defects that interfered with and barred the way to my understanding of their true nature. It was not the essential I looked for in everything, but some nicety which had nothing to do with it.

For a long time I underestimated Marina Tsvetayeva as in different ways I had underestimated [Eduard Bagritsky, Velemir Khlebnikov, Osip Mandelstam, and Nikolai Gumilyov].

I have already said that among the young people who could not express themselves intelligibly and who raised their tongue-tied babblings into a virtue and tried to be original at all costs, only two, [Nikolay] Aseyev and Marina Tsvetayeva, expressed themselves in human language and wrote in a classical style and language.

And suddenly both of them renounced their skill. Aseyev was tempted by Khlebnikov's example. Marina Tsvetayeva had undergone some inward changes of her own. But it was the original, the traditional Marina Tsvetayeva who in the end prevailed over me long before she suffered a rebirth.

One had to read oneself into her. When I had done so, I was amazed to discover such an abyss of purity and power. Nothing at all comparable existed anywhere else. Let me be brief. I don't think I shall go far wrong if I say that with the exception of [Innokenty Annensky and Aleksandr Blok] and, with certain reservations, Andrey Bely, the early Marina Tsvetayeva was what all the rest of the symbolists taken together wanted to be but were not. Where their literary efforts floundered helplessly in a world of artificial contrivances and lifeless archaisms, Marina Tsvetayeva skimmed with the greatest of ease over the difficulties of true creative art, solving its problems with remarkable facility and with incomparable technical brilliance.

In the spring of 1922, when she was already abroad, I bought in Moscow her little volume *Versts*. I was instantly won over by the great lyrical power of the form of her poetry, which stemmed from personal experience, which was not weak-chested but wonderfully compact and condensed, which did not get out of breath at the end of each separate line, but which by the development of its periods without interruption of rhythm sustained itself for a whole succession of strophes.

These peculiarities seemed to conceal a sort of closeness or, perhaps, a community of experienced influences, or a similarity of stimuli in the formation of character, a resemblance in the part played by family and music, a homogeneity of points of departure, aims, and preferences.

I wrote a letter to Marina Tsvetayeva in Prague full of expressions of my enthusiasm and my surprise that I had failed to recognize her genius for so long and had made myself familiar with her work so late. She replied to my letter. We began a correspondence which grew particularly frequent in the middle of the twenties after the appearance of her *Craftsmanship*. In Moscow her other poems became known in manuscript, poems that were outstanding for the sweep of their ideas and brilliant and quite extraordinary for their novelty, such as *The Poem of the End, The Poem of the Mountain,* and *The Ratcatcher*. (pp. 105-08)

Marina Tsvetayeva was a woman with the soul of an active man, determined, militant, indomitable. In her life and in her work she rushed impetuously, eagerly, and almost rapaciously toward the achievement of finality and definitiveness, in the pursuit of which she had gone far and was ahead of everybody else.

In addition to the small number of her known poems, she wrote a great number of things that are not generally known, immense, violent works, some in the style of Russian fairy tales, others on subjects of well-known historical legends and myths.

Their publication would be a great triumph and a great find for Russian poetry. It would be a belated gift that would enrich it all at once.

I think that a thorough re-examination of her work and the fullest possible recognition of her genius await Marina Tsvetayeva. (pp. 109-10)

> *Boris Pasternak, "Three Shadows," in his* I Remember: Sketch for an Autobiography, *translated by David Magarshack (translation copyright © 1959 by Pantheon Books, Inc.; reprinted by permission of Pantheon Books, a Division of Random House, Inc.; in Canada by William Collins Sons & Co. Ltd.), Pantheon Books, 1959, pp. 103-18.**

RENATO POGGIOLI (essay date 1960)

Marina Tsvetayeva learned her *métier* (we have seen that she took a Russian synonym of this term as the title of one of her books) from two very different sources. One was the "grand style'' of the eighteenth century, as exemplified by [Gavrila] Derzhavin, with his lofty rhetorics and weighty archaisms. The other was the popular tradition of the heroic or lyric folk song. Yet she learned also from her contemporaries, for instance Khlebnikov, whose example perhaps she followed when she freely reinterpreted in *King-Maiden* ancient Russian myths and old folk motifs. But the poet of her time who taught her most was the early Pasternak, whom Tsvetaeva resembles in her romantic temper, as well as in her expressionistic technique. As in Pasternak's case, the marks of her style are a tight syntaxis and an elliptic imagery, a discordant sound pattern and a rigid metrical design.

Tsvetaeva's poetry is deeply feminine, but of a femininity which is neither soft nor weak. Unlike Akhmatova, who cannot express her experience except personally and directly, by means of poems which read like fragments from a private diary, Tsvetaeva is often able to convey her vision of life through historical or legendary ''masks.'' It is from the Biblical and the Christian tradition, as well as from mythological and literary lore, that she takes all the exalted figures of saints and knights, lovers and poets, heroes and heroines whom she turns into objects of praise: David and Saint George, Phaedra and Hippolytus, Don Juan and *Manon Lescaut's* Chevalier de Grieux, Pushkin and Byron, Napoleon and Marina Mniszek, the Polish princess who married the Pseudo-Dmitrij to seize with him the Russian crown. Tsvetaeva does not hesitate, however, to seek her idols or *personae* even among the women and men of her circle, paying her homage in verse to Anna Akhmatova or Aleksandr Blok. To the latter she consecrated a lyrical cycle full of loving admiration and of lucid psychological insight.

If Akhmatova speaks only with the voice of a fiancée, bride, or mistress, Tsvetaeva speaks also with the voice of wife, mother, and sister. Woman is in her poetry the equal of man, not in a modern, but in a primitive, almost heroic sense. So it is only natural that in *The Swans' Camp,* when re-evoking her ordeal as the wife of a man fighting faraway for a lost cause, she chose to echo the most famous passage in the *Lay of the Host of Igor'*, the complaint of Jaroslavna, waiting with trembling and fear for her princely husband, threatened by all the curses of war. Yet even in her less subjective and more elegant pieces, often written on ancient Greek themes, Tsvetaeva looks at life with primordial and barbaric simplicity, with a kind of rebellious fatalism. Like a tribal mourner, she both laments destiny and condemns it. She expresses the ferocious absurdity of the human condition, especially in times of storm and stress, with an almost stuttering diction, with sobbing, often monosyllabic words, with sharp masculine rhymes that rend the ear and tear the heart.

Sometimes Tsvetaeva conveys all the cruelty of life with the eloquence of an accusing finger, of a wordless and tearless grief. Nothing proves better the poignant power of her art than the closing stanza of a poem inspired by the Civil War, where, despite her partisan sympathies, she looks with equal terror and pity at the youths who fell on either side of the barricade. There the poetess produces a sense of tragic irony with a conjuring trick and with a verbal conceit: by inverting the emblematic colors of the two party flags and converting them into the all-too-real hues of blood and death. In those haunting lines the poetess projects a single horror within a double vision of the same lethal metamorphosis, reflecting and reversing itself into two parallel metaphors: ''he from white turned red, blood coloring him; he from red turned white, death discoloring him.'' Unlike the Whites and Reds who fell in open battle or before

an execution squad, Marina Tsvetaeva died by her own hand: yet even so, she perished as a belated victim of the same hecatomb. (pp. 314-15)

> Renato Poggioli, ''The Poets of Yesterday,'' in his
> The Poets of Russia: 1890-1930 *(copyright © 1960
> by the President and Fellows of Harvard College;
> excerpted by permission), Cambridge, Mass.: Harvard University Press, 1960, pp. 276-315.**

SIMON KARLINSKY   (essay date 1966)

The first two volumes of Cvetaeva's work [*Večernij al' bom (Evening Album)* and *Volšebnyj fonar' (Magic Lantern)*] can best be considered as a unit, not only thematically and stylistically, but chronologically as well. (pp. 171-72)

The early Cvetaeva is a poet of a definite historical and even philosophical orientation. . . . In her poetic culture, the young Cvetaeva was rooted in the traditions of the second half of the nineteenth century, while at the same time being clearly aware of the magnificent flowering of new Russian poetry in the midst of which she was living. Her emotional and intellectual outlook, however, can best be explained in terms of the idealistic and romantic revival among certain lesser French writers at the end of the nineteenth century. (p. 172)

These romantic and idealistic views lead the poet to expect from life more than it can possibly give; a concomitant tendency is to admire everything that is exceptional and heroic and to reject the average, the everyday, the prosaic. (pp. 172-73)

The books faithfully reflect Cvetaeva's travels to France and to the Black Forest, the details of her schooling and everyday life, her relations with her relatives and friends. This is the ''Acmeist'' side of the early Cvetaeva. Her preoccupation with everyday detail . . . may at first glance appear incongruous in a poet of her idealistic outlook. But she justifies this preoccupation with great passion in the poem **''Literaturnym prokuroram'' (''To Literary Prosecutors''),** which concludes the second collection, as her only way to preserve her evanescent youth from oblivion. (p. 177)

The early period ends with Cvetaeva's marriage. The next stage in her poetic development is represented by the poems written between 1913 and 1915. . . . The preoccupation with the subject of death, manifest in Cvetaeva's early poetry, is now even more marked, but the basic attitude to death is quite different; the desire for an early and glorious end is replaced by a calm acceptance of death as an inevitable fact. (pp. 179-80)

[The collection *Versty I (Versts I)*] is the book in which the poet Cvetaeva rises to her full stature. She went on maturing and developing in her later poetry, but *Versty I* is the first book in which her magnitude as a poet becomes apparent. (p. 181)

Versty I adds up to a lyrical diary of Cvetaeva's personal and literary life during the year 1916. For all its technical and thematic variety, the collection has a central unifying leitmotif: the city of Moscow. Cvetaeva wrote of the Moscow Kremlin in one of the poems in *Večernij al'bom,* using an exalted, almost melodramatic diction. In *Versty I* she is conscious of Moscow as her home, as her rightful dwelling place, almost as her personal property. (p. 182)

To express the personal drama which is the subject of much of *Versty I,* Cvetaeva makes a wide use of stylistic masks or *personae.* . . . [For] the most part, Cvetaeva speaks through the *persona* of a Moscow woman of the lower classes, sinful, proud, passionate, occasionally a criminal, occasionally dabbling in magic. This enables Cvetaeva to make use of a wide range of colloquial diction, which becomes a prominent feature of her poetry from this point on. Stylistically and technically, this is the most daringly experimental of Cvetaeva's collections, yet for all the variety of its versification and for all its stylistic range, *Versty I* possesses a unity and produces a more definite total effect than the first two published collections. (pp. 183-84)

[The poetry of *Lebedinyj stan (The Demesne of the Swans)*] is primarily political, which in relation to Cvetaeva's earlier work represents an entirely new departure. Specifically, the volume is a record of Cvetaeva's reactions to the events of the February and October revolutions and of the ensuing Civil War. The poems are full of topical political and military references. . . . The personal preoccupations of the poet which are the subject of certain poems (the death of Staxovič, the friendship with Bal'mont, the impact of the last poems of Blok) are all treated against the strongly suggested background of the Civil War and the hungry epoch of early Communism. Historical themes are also selected for their pertinence to the current situation. . . . [The] likening of the Civil War situation to the destruction of cultural values and the general chaotic conditions during the medieval Mongol invasions, which is continued and developed by Cvetaeva in [*Craft (Remeslo)*], enables her to draw on the imagery and themes of the famous medieval Russian epic, the *Igor Tale,* which she does with great effect in several of the poems of *Lebedinyj stan.* (p. 185)

The poems of *Lebedinyj stan* have their counterpart in certain of Cvetaeva's prose memoirs dealing with the same period. . . . The poetry of *Lebedinyj stan,* subdued and simple in comparison to Cvetaeva's preceding and following collections, reveals its fine texture and great verbal subtlety only on repeated and attentive reading. (p. 186)

Remeslo, which Cvetaeva began . . . with a cycle of poems "Učenik" ("The Disciple") addressed to Sergei Volkonsky, is a collection that again represents a radical new departure. The romantic manner is suddenly abandoned for good. The impact of Russian Futurism, mildly felt in *Versty I* and very strongly in the *poèma* ["Na krasnom kone" ("On a Red Steed")] . . . , now becomes organically blended with a newly evolved style that may be described as classical and odic. The choriambic meters, tried out in *Versty I,* are now extremely important and so is the new persistent use of archaisms. The poems are grouped into cycles according to their subject matter, but at the same time *Remeslo* repeats the precedent of *Versty I* in being an uninterrupted poetic diary of a single year: April 1921 to April 1922. (p. 189)

Remeslo does not have a unifying theme or leitmotif, as did *Versty I* and *Lebedinyj stan.* Its essential unity is due to the great energy and expressiveness of its verse. The combination of a passionate tone with the wide use of syntactic ellipsis in this collection has led some hostile critics to speak of obscurity and hysteria—the two charges that have been repeatedly made against Cvetaeva's poetry from *Remeslo* onward. Thematically, much of *Remeslo* is a continuation of *Lebedinyj stan.* The Civil War is still a major preoccupation in the cycles. . . . (p. 190)

The new classicist strain is most noticeable in the cycle about the destructive power of erotic love, "Xvala Afrodite" ("Eulogy of Aphrodite"), which introduces some of the principal themes of [*Posle Rossii (After Russia)*]. Such "classical" poems form one pole of *Remeslo,* while at the opposite pole we find

the veritable explosion of magic chants and incantations. . . . The incantatory poems explore to the full Cvetaeva's gift for verbal creativity and colloquial diction. (p. 191)

[If] we were to select the verse collection by Cvetaeva in which her poetic craft reaches its highest peak, and her human and poetic stature its most awesome dimensions and sweep, we would have to choose *Posle Rossii.* . . . (pp. 193-94)

[Cvetaeva] attempts and achieves in *Posle Rossii* something she had never tried before—she writes philosophical poetry. The meditations on the nature of time in "Minuta," of space in "Zaočnost'," and of human speech and communication in "Emče organa" . . . take their place next to the best poems in the Russian tradition of philosophical poetry. . . . The point of view in these poems is Cvetaeva's intensely personal one, but the conclusions she reaches have a general and universal significance. (pp. 195-96)

One aspect of the universality of *Posle Rossii* is Cvetaeva's use of traditional myths as subject matter in the poems derived from literary sources. . . . [The] heroes and heroines of Cvetaeva's poems come from the *Iliad* . . . , from Greek mythology . . . , and from Shakespeare. . . .

A significant portion of *Posle Rossii* is devoted to the poems with pointedly realistic settings. . . . [The] frequent settings of the industrial suburbs of Prague, its railroad yards, its barrack-like housing projects provide the poet with an appropriately drab contrast to the powerful and colorful world of poetry and mythology. Several striking symbols, associated with such settings, reappear throughout the whole volume: railroad tracks, trains, telegraph wires. Railroad imagery in particular is put to a variety of uses, both concrete and symbolic, and it is also connected to the theme of homesickness for Russia, which despite the title of the collection finds its expression in only two of the poems. The theme of a poet's loneliness, which is deliberately sought in order to survive in a world where love is either slavery or pain, is very important in *Posle Rossii* and is eloquently expressed in several poems. . . . (pp. 196-97)

In terms of language and versification, the poetry of *Posle Rossii* is a staggering accomplishment—a synthesis of meaning, word, and verbal music which the Russian Futurist poetry strove for and so rarely achieved to such a degree. The fusion of sense and language expressed in unique sequences of internal rhymes is so organic that for once it seems irrelevant to discuss sound instrumentation, the clashing consonants, or the alliterative vowels. (p. 197)

The idealistic romantic outlook of Cvetaeva's first two collections is also present in *Posle Rossii:* the poet still expects and demands from life more than she knows it can possibly give. But the most important thing about *Posle Rossii* is that in this book, as nowhere else, Marina Cvetaeva found a completely new and original way of looking at life, evolved a successful personal idiom in which to express this view, and did so in a poetry of unique metrical freshness and verbal beauty. (p. 199)

The body of lyric poetry written by Cvetaeva is vast and varied. It has become customary in criticism, when mentioning this fact, to comment on the uneven artistic worth of this body of poetry. This is probably the place to take issue with this majority opinion. The interpretation of Cvetaeva's poetry presents difficulties; one of these, perhaps the greatest, stems from her tremendous versatility and variety within what may at first appear as a unified manner. Her specific "poetic voice," the individual and unmistakable timbre that is so entirely her own, is apparent in everything she wrote from *Versty I* on. But her constant evolution continually added new dimensions to her basic manner. This accounts for the recurrent phenomenon of the critics' enthusiasm for one work and their violent rejection of some later one that is of equal and often superior artistic value. Appreciation of *Remeslo,* for example, in no way prepared one for a grasp of *Posle Rossii,* while a familiarity with Cvetaeva's later poetry could at times prevent one from realizing the poetic value of *Lebedinyj stan.* The critics often looked for the qualities that had charmed them in a previous poem or collection of Cvetaeva's, and, not finding them in a later work under examination, they pronounced it poor. (pp. 205-06)

The narrative poetry of Cvetaeva can be classified in two basic categories: the *poèmy* which follow the Symbolist tradition in narrating episodes from the poet's life and describe her subjective experiences; and the group of epic and satirical poems which are based on plots borrowed from literary sources. For all her tremendous talent as a poet and prose writer, the one thing Marina Cvetaeva (like Shakespeare) never attempted to do was to invent a plot. This did not prevent her from creating works of undoubted originality, whether based on folk motifs, diaries of others, or her personal life. . . . The lyrical-autobiographical *poèmy* are closer in subject and form to Cvetaeva's lyric poetry. . . .

["**Na krasnom kone**"] is basically a personal and lyrical work, although, alone among Cvetaeva's lyrical *poèmy,* it shows marked features of epic poetry and folk tradition. The violent and turbulent poem falls into three principal sections with an introduction and an epilogue. Against the background of some natural calamity, the heroine, who is the poet, is exposed to three temptations and is rescued each time by a symbolic figure of a winged knight riding a red steed, who, as the epilogue first makes clear, represents her poetic genius. (p. 208)

Stylistically, "**Na krasnom kone**" is related to the lyric poetry of *Remeslo.* In this poem, the subjective experiences of the poet have found an adequate symbolic representation, and the narrative elements derived from Slavic folklore (the triple temptation, the introductory trope) are organically blended with elements of personal and emotional biography to result in a work of art that is both clear and sophisticated. (p. 211)

"**Poèma gory**" ("**Poem of the Hill**") and "**Poèma konca**" ("**Poem of the End**") were both written in Prague in 1924, and they both deal with the same emotional event in Cvetaeva's life: the end of her love affair with the former White army officer she had met in Prague. There is very little narration in "**Poèma gory**." It is simply a series of ten interconnected lyric poems followed by an epilogue, of the Prague hill on which the lovers met in the days of their happiness. . . . The poem ends in complete bitterness, directed both at the world and at the former lover. . . . There is great pain in this poem, and its hatred and destructive urge produce a frightening impression. One wonders whether it was Cvetaeva's dissatisfaction with such an epitaph to her love affair that made her treat the same subject all over in "**Poèma konca**" only a few months later.

"**Poèma konca**" is considerably longer than its predecessor. It describes the last evening the lovers spent together. . . . The events of the evening are told in minute detail, with the lovers' conversations alternating with descriptions of heroine's emotions. The method is that of a stream of consciousness, and "**Poèma konca**" is one of the great psychological poems in the Russian language. Every word, glance, and action of her

departing lover is analyzed by the desperate heroine, with the constant conflict between her imagination and what her reason and senses tell her to be facts. The imagery is bold and varied, and there are numerous digressions, such as the antiphilistine diatribe during the visit to the café and the meditation on the similarity between poets and Jews when the lovers walk past the Jewish quarter of Prague. Brief recollections of past happiness occasionally change the gloomy and desperate tone of the work into a sunny or gently humorous one. (pp. 211-12)

Metrically, the poem shows great variety and imagination in its selection of appropriate meters to express the shifts of the heroine's mood. . . . "**Poèma konca**" is one of Cvetaeva's finest accomplishments. This poem and "**Poèma gory**" (which is somewhat marred by the excessive self-pity and the blind hatred of its tone) show us the poet at the peak of her originality and poetic stature. The advanced and even revolutionary means of expression used in these two poems explain the derision and incomprehension with which they were met by such important older writers as [Ivan Bunin, Maxim Gor'kij, and Zinaida Gippius]. (p. 214)

The lyrical *poèmy* of Cvetaeva are subjective and introspective poems, in which the author at all times has the center of the stage. This is their main difference from another set of *poèmy* which we have chosen to call epic for the sake of convenience. The earliest of these chronologically is *Car'-devica (The Tsar-Maiden).* . . . Cvetaeva's basic source for her long narrative tale is Afanas'ev's collection of popular Russian magic tales. She combined the elements of the two tales on the subject of the Tsar-Maiden found in Afanas'ev's collection to form her own plot and added to it a situation from the Greek myth that fascinated her most of all—that of Phaedra and Hippolytos. (pp. 222-23)

The style and language of *Car'-devica* merit a special study. The authentic folklore tone of this tale is a marvel of its kind. By turning to the genuine Russian folklore tradition, Cvetaeva puzzled her Russian readers, accustomed to nineteenth-century stylizations of folktales, stylizations which were frequently based on Western European models. (pp. 223-24)

Her "lyrical satire" (as she called it), "**Krysolov**," is of course based on the medieval German legend of the Pied Piper of Hameln. . . . While most of the adaptations of this legend are romantic in style, Cvetaeva uses it for a devastating social and political satire. . . .

"**Krysolov**" is in six cantos. The first canto is a description, both bitter and humorous, of a provincial German town. Cvetaeva, who loved Germany deeply and in her earlier poetry saw it as a country of poets and philosophers, here found biting and sarcastic words for German philistinism. . . . (p. 230)

The second canto reinforces the impression left by the first in describing the prosaic and materialistic dreams of the burghers. The third canto opens with a description of the food market. . . . In "**Krysolov**," the monstrous abundance of food is equated with moral decay and is seen as the direct cause of the rat plague. . . . In the fourth canto, a flutist garbed in green, whose "only Mistress is Music," enters Hameln. Learning that the mayor has promised to give his adolescent daughter Greta in marriage to the person who delivers the city from the rat plague, he uses his flute to lure the rats into a swamp, where they drown. . . . When the flutist tries to claim his prize in the fifth canto, the entire city council lectures him on the impossibility of a marriage between the mayor's daughter and the impoverished artist. In the slighting and contemptuous speeches of the city officials about the nature and uses of art, Cvetaeva's satirical war on philistinism achieves its most vivid expression. (pp. 231-32)

The real revenge of the Pied Piper is luring the children into an anarchy of freedom and opening to them a world of the spirit and of the imagination, which their parents are unable to perceive. (p. 232)

[The] finale of **"Krysolov"** is another of Cvetaeva's apotheoses—the children escape into an eternal childhood like the heroine of Cvetaeva's first two books of verse, into the life of the spirit like Rilke and the heroine of **"Na krasnom kone,"** into their own private paradise like Marusja in **Mólodec.** (p. 233)

The prose of Marina Cvetaeva belongs entirely to the period after her emigration. . . . [Cvetaeva's prose work] is all in the form of memoirs, literary criticism, and philosophical-ethical meditations. Cvetaeva continued to write prose throughout her residence abroad and, during the nineteen-thirties . . . her prose works became the major portion of her literary output. Although some of her later prose works are referred to in criticism and bibliographies as short stories or novellas, she actually wrote no fiction. (pp. 266-67)

The stylistic peculiarities of Cvetaeva's prose are all manifest in her earliest prose works of the nineteen-twenties. In them we already observe her personalized and varied use of syntax—from staccato one-word phrases to long developed periods, with a frequent tendency to terse, aphoristic formulations and asides. . . . In poetry, Cvetaeva was always a mistress of balanced and clearly organized verse structure, but in her early prose the architecture of the whole tends toward the amorphous. . . . (p. 272)

In her prose, Cvetaeva retained the viewpoint of a lyrical poet. She could only write about herself, about life as *she* saw it, about the people she knew, and about literature. This did not necessarily lead to narrowness of vision, because Cvetaeva was enough of a creator to conjure a convincing universe of her own. (p. 273)

The single most successful and valuable piece among Cvetaeva's prose writings of the twenties is in all probability her essay on the art of criticism, **"Poèt o kritike"** (**"A Poet on Criticism"**). The essay is remarkable not only for its fresh and well-argued views, its obvious and passionate sincerity, and its witty use of unexpected parallels and comparisons, but also for its striking and enormously original prose style in which Cvetaeva managed to transpose the syntactic and lexical innovations of her poetry of the nineteen-twenties into adequate prose equivalents. **"Poèt o kritike"** is not only a work of literary criticism; it also is concerned with the problems of personal and literary ethics and thus belongs in a sense together with such later essays on ethical problems as **"Iskusstvo pri svete sovesti."** In **"Poèt o kritike,"** as she often does, Cvetaeva uses a multiple vantage point, in this case that of an innovating creative artist and that of an intelligent and inquisitive reader. The alternation and occasional combination of these vantage points makes Cvetaeva's statements on criticism forceful and convincing.

The meditations on the nature of art and of the creative process that began in **"Poèt o kritike"** are continued in her articles of the early nineteen-thirties. If Cvetaeva's longer prose works had been published in book form, as she originally planned, Cvetaeva's third book of prose would have been called "Isskustvo pri svete sovesti." This plan was never realized, and we have only a few fragments that were published in *Sovre-*

mennye Zapiski under that title with the numerous editorial deletions of Vadim Rudnev and with the note that they are part of a book. In these fragments, as in **"Poèt o kritike"** and in the subsequent **"Poèt i vremja,"** Cvetaeva elaborates her theory of literature and art. Art, according to Cvetaeva, is a natural organic process like life itself. As such, it is completely amoral in essence. The illusion of the basic moral quality of art and of beauty is based on a misunderstanding: people mistake strength for truth and magic for saintliness. (pp. 274-75)

Cvetaeva is one of the most interesting Russian letter writers of the twentieth century. Only a portion of her correspondence has been published so far, yet the letters that are available are an invaluable aid in understanding her personality and her literary production. Many of these letters open up aspects of Cvetaeva which we could not know from her poetry and published prose. Not necessarily written for subsequent publication, many of those letters are, nevertheless, works of art. Cvetaeva was too much of a literary artist for her skill not to have been reflected in her private correspondence. . . . Heightened emotion was inevitably connected with literary creativity for Cvetaeva, and the most imaginative letters of the ones we know are addressed to persons with whom she was emotionally involved. . . . (pp. 280-81)

Cvetaeva's memoirs, literary criticism, and letters, are an essential part of her total work. As [Vladislav] Xodasevič has pointed out, she really found herself as a prose writer only during the last decade of her life. Her best prose pieces— **"Plennyj dux"** or **"Moj Puškin,"** for instance—can compare in sheer originality of conception and execution with anything produced in Russian prose during the present century. (p. 282)

Twenty years after her death, the poet Marina Cvetaeva became a legend—a legend potentially as rich as the personal legends of a Rimbaud, of an André Chénier, of a Lermontov. Considered at the distance of almost a quarter of a century, she appears as an archetype of a struggling artist, eternally and tragically at odds with society and her environment, extracting from her very isolation the substance of a unique and revolutionary artistic creation. This widespread nineteenth-century cliché is applicable to Marina Cvetaeva's life and art to an uncanny extent, but there are significant aspects in which it is inapplicable or at least insufficient.

Cvetaeva knew and understood the darker sides of existence as well as any of the French *poètes maudits* or the Russian turn-of-the-century Symbolists. But through both her life and her work there runs a strong current of vitality and affirmation. . . . Through all the tragedy that is the substance of much of her work, through all the pain that throbs in some of her personal correspondence, there is this thread of refusal to yield to darkness, to tragedy, to death.

Another basic difference between Cvetaeva and the poet-pariah as conceived in the nineteenth century is her absence of destructive attitudes, her constant strain of pity and compassion. . . . From this, there follows logically Cvetaeva's refusal to align herself with any specific literary program or political creed—a refusal that brought her the hostility of many adversaries. (pp. 283-84)

Cvetaeva had the fortune to live in one of the most brilliant and significant periods that Russian or any other poetry has ever known. Her tragedy and that of poetry was that it was also a period when the lot of all significant poets was isolation, persecution, and violent physical annihilation. The additional tragic aspect of Cvetaeva's poetic fate was the apparent (but only apparent) dichotomy between the substance and the manner of her poetry. If the content of her poetry often took her to the poetic vicinity of such important but non-innovating poets as Axmatova or Xodasevič, the form of her poetry, her language, and her subject matter often lead us to place her into an entirely different literary configuration. Cvetaeva never took part in the Futurist movement in Russian poetry, but if we go beyond the limitations of literary politics and apply to this movement the term "verbalism" (*verbizm*), as Remizov and certain émigré critics have done to describe the whole phenomenon of the verbal-phonetic preoccupations in the Russian poetry of the twentieth century, we can recognize Cvetaeva as one of the four great verbal innovators in that poetry, alongside Xlebnikov, Majakovskij, and Pasternak. (pp. 286-87)

There are other literary configurations into which one could place Cvetaeva in one's effort to understand her poetry and to assess its value. Going outside of Russian literature, one could bring up Virginia Woolf, who was also interested in new ways of putting words together to convey new meanings and who also died by her own hand at approximately the same time. Future scholars may find thematic affinities with the poetry of Emily Dickinson and stylistic and personal parallels with Arthur Rimbaud. Cvetaeva's otherworldly orientation (to use Lovejoy's terminology), which persists in her writing throughout, betrays her lasting affinity with the Russian Symbolist poets, under whose impact her own poetic language first began to evolve. However, both the analytical and the comparative methods can take us only so far. After examining the obvious connections between the poetry of Marina Cvetaeva and the work of Remizov or Majakovskij, or analyzing the more remote, yet subtle ties that unite her to Rilke, after describing her vocabulary or her versification, we are obliged to put all the pieces back where we found them so as not to blur the initial and the final picture of what Marina Cvetaeva is first and foremost.

The moral strength implicit in Marina Cvetaeva's life is impressive and exhilarating. The story of this life and her role in the history of Russian literature is absorbing. What ultimately remains after all is said and done, however, is her poetry, which she herself called "my transfigured, my real life." As is the case with most poets, the comprehension of Cvetaeva's poetry is enhanced by what we know of her life, and Cvetaeva is right in saying that "chronology is a key to understanding." The poetry of Cvetaeva is not easy, it requires "imagination and good will." When read with attention and sympathy, it reveals itself as a very great poetry indeed. (pp. 287-88)

> *Simon Karlinsky, in his* Marina Cvetaeva: Her Life and Art *(copyright © 1966 by The Regents of the University of California; reprinted by permission of the author), University of California Press, 1966, 317 p. (revised by the author for this publication).*

ANGELA LIVINGSTONE (essay date 1971)

[Where] does Marina Tsvetaeva belong in Russian poetry? She never joined any school or movement, nor did she consider herself to be a member of either. . . . She lived and wrote in Russia during the emergence of two very vocal new schools of thought about the nature of poetry—Acmeism and Futurism, both of which came into being in 1909. They introduced poetic methods and philosophies which they saw as overcoming Symbolism. (pp. 178-79)

The programme and the paraphernalia of Symbolism are utterly lacking in her work. But when we see in the Russian Symbolists' poetry and in their statements about poetry that they communicate, through a careful verbal 'music' and deliberate beauty, finely perceived states of mind, and, more, an elusive something else which is often expressed as the presence of the divine in, or seen through the earthly, then we shall find something of this in Tsvetaeva's earlier verse. There are the simple radiant cosmic images of Romantic and Symbolist poetry—sun, moon, snowstorm, angel, hell, or there is the selecting of the beautiful as subject-matter—the burning domes of Moscow churches, the eyelashes of a charming minstrel. There is, too, the mainly smooth-flowing melodious line and lulling repetition of stressed vowels in a verse that is made (unlike much of her later, more rugged verse) of entire sentences in which the syntax is relatively inconspicuous so that sounds, feelings, hints and evocations may dominate. . . . Many of her *Poems about Moscow,* the cycle *Insomnia,* poems addressed to Mandel'štam, and a cycle of *Poems to Blok* are melodious and evocative in these ways.

A typically Symbolist feature, moreover, is the adoption of an attitude of adoration. This is found in many of Tsvetaeva's poems of the early period. She adores particularly persons rather than the world, or the other world, or God. She expresses her love or admiration as worship and deifies the person. 'Divine boy' she calls Mandel'štam in one poem and is never afraid of being as outspoken as this. She uses the language of prayer—'Zaxodi—grjadi . . .' (Drop in—be manifest . . .). This is not just a hyperbolic trick; nor is it an exaggerated piece of flattery which would suggest no more than itself and make one think at most about the strength of the poet's emotions. Throughout the *Poems to Blok*—whom she often deifies, or sees as a priest, the ecclesiastical language is used with a rigour and firmness that prune it of excess, and make one think rather of the nature of admiration and the nature of genius. In writing of her admiration for men who were poets she is writing about poetry itself, about the inhering of that other, 'divine', element in human beings. These poems always centre upon a person. They are not philosophical, but express rather the "divinity" in terms of how Tsvetaeva feels about it. They are, however, just as much the assertion of something 'more', but perhaps expressed with a deliberate bluntness and vigour, neglecting the delicate but worn-out effects of Symbolism. They move away from the earth, not because of any spiritual longing, but rather as if they were leaping away from it with both feet. (pp. 180-81)

Most theories of poetry speak of getting back to what is real and genuine. The Symbolist too wanted to lift the veil of familiarity and ordinariness from the world and reveal its pristine strangeness or divinity (similarly, the Futurist wanted to tear all the masks and pretences from everyone). . . . Perhaps the special quality of Tsvetaeva's poetry derives from the way she does this instinctively and unprogrammatically, and as if there never *were* a veil or mask. Characteristic of all her work is this: the declaring and exhibiting of immediate feeling in all its undisguised detail. The unleashed, point-blank, absolutely unintimidated quality of her poetry is perhaps what makes it her own and unlike either of those schools through which she marches like a walker with rucksack and climbing stick who, though he breathes the air and climate of the lands he is tramping through, keeps his eyes fixed on his road. (p. 182)

The attitude of worship is far from being typical of Futurist writing, and it is by no means Tsvetaeva's only attitude. Just as she readily, wholeheartedly, glorifies, so she readily attacks and vilifies—especially the bourgeois philistine, that complacent 'reader of newspapers' in the Paris train, or the stuporous suburb-dweller on the hills of Prague. Her friend and critic, Ivask summed her up as the 'poet of eulogy and slander.' . . . And just as clearly she expresses her complete certainty about her own knowledge and gift. Is she arrogant, over self-assured? Among the miseries and disasters of her life, the lack of recognition and her being repudiated by so many people, the poet's inner certainty of rightness stands up—strangely like a column in a falling building. Every poet must have this certainty, which becomes a theme instead of an impulse or implication felt only in particular circumstances, for example, in the poetically permissive atmosphere of Futurism, in an epoch of violence and noise where one has to shout to be heard, in an age where the poet is misunderstood, even rejected by most people. Her *speaking* of the assurance of genius shows the influence of the age, while her *feeling* it is something ageless. . . . From the early Tsvetaeva one hears the shout: 'I know the truth—give up all other truths!' In her later work we find both the repeated declaration that she is not writing for those who cannot understand and the brilliant analysis of 'rightness' as the poet's central experience. (p. 183)

Rhythm is the most assertive and noticeable element in Tsvetaeva's poetry altogether, and she is particularly original and skilful in finding ways of basing poems upon the rhythms of physical or emotional 'reality' (or in precisely evoking those realities through the invention of suggestive rhythms). This she does with more realistic exactness and consistency than Mayakovsky, despite his theory about it. In the essay *How to Make Verse* (1926) Mayakovsky demanded that the rhythms of poetry should be produced by the actual rhythms of life, and, describing the sources of one of his long poems (*To Sergej Esenin*) he mentioned the rhythms of walking along streets and of riding on trams, getting on and off them. Yet the relation between those 'real' rhythms and the rhythms of that poem has to be expounded and is nothing like so direct as that between some of Tsvetaeva's poetic metres and the rhythms of the movement or feeling that is her poem's subject.

Much of Tsvetaeva's originality lies in this combining of something undisguisedly, extraordinarily simple and basic—the shouting or sobbing throat itself, the very stamping feet of her life—with an intellectual sharpness, with poetic conceits, with literary-technical complexity. She has in common with Futurism the element of violence, the shout about herself, self-assurance as a theme and an attitude—hatred of the conservative and philistine mass.

In all this, she is especially like Mayakovsky; but she is unlike him in that she did not 'tread upon the throat of her song' and her emotional range is far wider than his. She remains lyrical, personal, sensitive, private and scornful of those who limit their sensibility to what they conceive to be 'modern' (she says, in another context 'He is of the twentieth century, but I am before all centuries').

Between Tsvetaeva's poetic techniques and those of Futurism there are many more affinities. Karlinsky says that after 1916 she 'entered the language-conscious area of the Russian literary tradition'. Now Tsvetaeva differs from the Futurist experimenters in that, like Pasternak, she preserves strict traditional stanza forms (generally quatrains) and rhyme schemes. Her metres are often highly original and complex, but they are almost always contained in a very regular pattern. Indeed, the

regularity or rigidity of the pattern, contrasting with the oddness of the metres, becomes so conspicuous as to seem a novelty.

Another new device, belonging more to the category of rhythmic than of verbal inventiveness, but having the same effect of novelty and strength and of focus upon both the physicality of the word and the inalienability of its meaning, is the emphatic isolation of the monosyllable. Russian is given to polysyllabic words while English abounds in monosyllables—the bane of English translators from a complexly inflected language. But the English monosyllables are, in the main, articles, prepositions, conjunctions and various particles, which in Russian tend to be either represented by longer words or, more often, omitted altogether. Where Russian does have one-syllable words, these are more usually nouns or parts of verbs, which seem to gain a quite inimitable strength from being in a naturally polysyllabic context and *not* being drained of their originality by a surrounding of unemphasised grammatical monosyllables. (pp. 184-85)

There are several ways in which monosyllables are highlighted in Tsvetaeva's verse; the exploiting of this natural feature of Russian is one of them. Another is the repetitive placing of such words at the beginning and end of lines. . . .

One more device used by Tsvetaeva for the isolating of the monosyllable is the use of an extraordinary hyphen to divide a word into its component syllables—each of them stressed. (p. 186)

Two devices remain to be discussed: ellipsis and the basing of a poem upon one dominant syntactic pattern. In her later poems Tsvetaeva uses an elliptical style more and more frequently. . . .

[When] Tsvetaeva omits verbs almost altogether, or, as very often, she omits the small auxiliary words, she makes their omission as perceptible as possible. Their absence jolts and increases the oddness and vigour of the rhythm. . . .

The pruning away of particles from the imagery is accompanied by the parallel device of a sharp reduction of environment. . . . The 'furniture' of the poem is existential; emotions are as fiercely laid bare among the sharply selected *words*, as rhythmic stresses are. (p. 187)

Tsvetaeva is most original of all in her syntax. Sometimes, in the fundamentally elliptical poems . . . , verbs are omitted, so that there is no clear syntax at all. More often, syntactic forms are not only fully present, but there is an intensification of the normal, if poetically compressed, syntactic unit intensified by an extravagantly unvarying repetition of it. Very often this is done in phrases dominated by the instrumental case (a noun case in Russian—rendered not only by 'through' or 'by' or 'by means of' but also, or alternatively, by 'like' or 'as'). (pp. 187-88)

Tsvetaeva shares with all the major poets of her time an intense concern with the origin of poetry, or with the nature of inspiration. Many poets have made this, implicitly or explicitly, the subject of their poems. Tsvetaeva wrote about it mainly in her works of prose, the remarkable essays on her own life, on literature, and on poets she knew, written in the years of her emigration. (p. 189)

What seems the essential distinction here is this : where for the Romantic or Symbolist, poetry comes from 'outside', and is *received* by the poet, the Acmeist and the Futurist, in their different ways, both denied any 'outside', any other reality than 'this' one and insisted that poetry is *made* by us, *inside* the world and *of* the world.

To some extent Tsvetaeva shares the Symbolist experience. The thing that makes poetry, happens, for her, outside the poet. Yet, her formulation of this experience is quite un-symbolist, and, in fact, very much in the language and tone of the Futurist. The loudness and violence with which the latter affirms this world and himself in it is, in the case of Tsvetaeva, joined to a quasi-religious conception of inspiration, in a way that may be unique. (pp. 190-91)

Tsvetaeva, now, says something like this: inspiration comes from 'outside' but the poet *resists* it. (p. 191)

If the Symbolist waits for revelation, accepts the vision when it comes, falls back into the boredom of the everyday when it passes, while the Futurist, far from waiting for, or passively recognising anything, actively asserts *himself* in the labour of *making* verse, then Tsvetaeva is like both in her combination of revelation and self-assertion, of overwhelming vision and the ego's resistance to it.

The interesting thing is that, again unlike those poets with whom in some ways she has so much in common, Tsvetaeva is not concerned to make any metaphysical statement about reality. . . . [Tsvetaeva] does not resort to philosophy. By sticking to the *experience* she indubitably knows, she is able to describe to the full the inner dynamic of her inspiration. She does not decide what is real, what is unreal or what is more real. By the same token, she is unlike those Futurists who decided that 'this world', or the social world, is real, while somehow what is subjective is not, or is less so. (p. 192)

A final comment: both Symbolist and Futurist rejected the idea of poetry as an individual activity: the Symbolist believed he escaped the bonds of individuality and communed with the universal consciousness, the world-soul. The Futurist, or at least Mayakovsky, wanted to see his poems as written not by himself alone, but by the whole mass of the people (the title of his poem, *150 Million,* purports to be the number of its authors, and the poem was left unfinished for everyone else to continue). But Tsvetaeva, despite her idea about annihilation, constantly stresses that her art is individual and personal, that it is her own, and is herself. (pp. 192-93)

> *Angela Livingstone, "Marina Tsvetaeva and Russian Poetry," in* Melbourne Slavonic Studies, *Nos. 5 & 6, 1971, pp. 178-93.*

MAX HAYWARD   (essay date 1971)

The best way to define Marina Tsvetayeva's place in modern Russian poetry is to say that she had none—this was her personal tragedy and her lonely distinction as an artist. (p. vii)

Her first volume of poetry appeared in 1910, when she was only sixteen, and was noticed and praised by Gumilev and others—they were impressed by the stark, down-to-earth quality, the 'common-labourer' side of her which always appealingly corrects her romantic tendencies—a very Russian trait. . . .

The misery of [her emigrè existence], as well as her haughty isolation from all possible worlds, is well conveyed in '**Homesickness**'. . . . Yet much of her finest work was written in these years: '**Poem of the Mountain**' and '**Poem of the End**'— two lyrical sequels to characteristically impossible loves—and her epic adaptation of the German story of the Pied Piper and other long poems based on Russian folklore, as well as her

verse dramas on classical themes ('**Theseus**', '**Phaedra**' and '**Ariadne**'), and many cycles of shorter poems, of which those on Czechoslovakia translated here are outstanding examples. (p. viii)

Poets, more than other people, shape their own lives, and [Tsvetayeva] would have found tragedy even if she had not lived at a time and in circumstances where tragedy so readily found her. (p. ix)

However, if one tries to define her fate and her art in terms of her affinities to others, it is Vladimir Mayakovsky who, paradoxically, first comes to mind. . . . It is only a seeming paradox that the self-appointed troubadour of the Revolution should have been so akin to one who devoted her poetic gift, with equal passion, to the cause of the Revolution's mortal enemies: her cycle entitled *Swans' camp,* written between 1917 and 1921, but published in full only long after her death, is perhaps the finest poetry to which the White movement can legitimately lay claim. The bond between her and Mayakovsky was, of course, in the astonishing similarity of their poetic and human temperaments, which forced both of them to seek in public causes the abnegation of self demanded by their unfulfillable natures; that they did so in opposite political camps was fortuitous. In both cases this search led them into a dead-end and then inexorably to suicide. It is not surprising, therefore, that the *accent* of their verse is so much alike in its general effect, even if not in its actual devices. Hammering, as it were, against the outer limits of their own being, they did what one can only call violence to the language, twisting and wrenching and pounding it, as a sculptor might wrestle with some tough, barely pliant material. This artistically controlled violence to language was their therapy and it gave rise to a peculiar, taut energy in their verse. . . . [Tsvetayeva] can always be recognized by the thud, like a heartbeat, of her monosyllabic masculine rhymes (more Anglo-Saxon than Russian in quality), and pauses in odd places.

But there was a great difference between Tsvetayeva and Mayakovsky. Whatever they may have had in common by way of their *goût de l'absolu,* vulnerability and treatment of language, she nevertheless belonged to a more select company. This was not only by virtue of her incomparably greater culture and taste, but also because she possessed a moral power which Mayakovsky either never had or dissipated in hollow public posturings. Marina Tsvetayeva's unflinching integrity in the employment of her genius puts her among the small band of Russian poet-witnesses who felt themselves to be, and recognized in each other the voices of the country and the keepers of its values during what Blok called the 'terrible years'. There were only four of them—besides Tsvetayeva: Pasternak, Akhmatova and Mandelstam. The last of them to die was Akhmatova who, towards the end of her life, in 1961, wrote about them all in a remarkable poem entitled quite simply: 'There are four of us'. By numbering Marina Tsvetayeva—the only one mentioned by name—among this chosen few, Akhmatova at last gave her the place she was never able to find in her life. (pp. ix-xi)

> *Max Hayward, in his foreword to* Marina Tsvetayeva: Selected Poems *by Marina Tsvetayeva, translated by Elaine Feinstein (© Oxford University Press 1971; reprinted by permission of Oxford University Press), Oxford University Press, London, 1971, pp. vii-xi.*

JANE ANDELMAN TAUBMAN (essay date 1972)

As she did with many of her other friends, Tsvetaeva made Pasternak the central figure of a private myth, which her poems to him project. She and he are two poetic giants, each the other's only equal in the contemporary world. Circumstances have kept them apart and seem likely to do so as long as they remain on "this earth." But she is determined to maintain communication, despite the barriers erected by the tangible world of reality, through the language of another spiritual world—through poetry.

Underlying this myth are two important motifs which recur throughout Tsvetaeva's work. The first is her division of the world into two realms, that of *byt* or everyday reality (where she and Pasternak, according to the myth, are aliens), and that of *bytie,* spiritual being (where they are at home). The other factor is her often expressed preference for the soul over the flesh. This friendship of poetic giants, says her myth, is a spiritual one which will not be impeded (and in fact may be strengthened) by physical separation.

But the poems themselves, and some of the other evidence, reveal strong hints of a more human, feminine passion which she continually, though unsuccessfully, tried to ignore or suppress. The history of the friendship reflects a constant tension between myth and reality, a tension which Tsvetaeva never managed to resolve.

1922: The correspondence began more cautiously than some of Tsvetaeva's other epistolary friendships. At first, its tenor was almost entirely literary, two colleagues engaged in admiration and criticism of each other's work. (pp. 308-09)

Tsvetaeva obviously restrained herself in the first months of their correspondence, trying not to frighten Pasternak away, as she had many others, with the intensity of her involvement. It is almost certain that these first poems [to him] were written for her eyes alone and not sent to their addressee until the friendship had ripened considerably. Yet at the same time it seems that the very fact of Pasternak's departure for Russia, where he would be safely unreachable for the foreseeable future, was the step which triggered Tsvetaeva's final idealization and mythification of him—with its hero off stage, Tsvetaeva could construct her myth as she liked. (pp. 310-11)

1924: Tsvetaeva's long poem *The Swain* was published in Prague, with a dedication to Boris Pasternak: "for your majestic play / for your tender consolation . . .''. It was the only work to appear during his lifetime with an explicit dedication to him. The work, one of her favorites, was finished in December 1922, soon after their correspondence began, but the dedication probably belongs to a later stage of the friendship, closer to the date of publication.

In the privacy of the notebook, she dedicated the cycle **"Dvoe"** **(The Two of Us)**, dated June 30-July 3, 1924, to "my brother in the fifth season of the year, the sixth sense and the fourth dimension, Boris Pasternak." Developing her myth of their friendship, she declares to him: "It is not fated that the strong / Be united with the strong in this world''. . . . She has only one equal in a world where all others are spiritual cripples and weaklings. That one is Pasternak. (pp. 311-12)

In May 1926, while at a French seaside resort, Tsvetaeva composed the . . . cryptic long poem **"For the Sea."** It is a "dream-letter'' to Pasternak: impatient with postal communication, Tsvetaeva has "jumped out of her own dream into his,'' a far more successful mode of communication, she implies, for poets.

She will come through, "Without censorship, without even a postage stamp!'' This much is clear from the first, rather bantering section of the poem. But in the second half, her meaning becomes obscure, couched in a dream-language known only to the two poets, for their meaning is not clear from the context of the poem. (p. 313)

1928-1929: Pasternak's statement that the correspondence was "particularly frequent in the mid-twenties, after the publication of Tsvetaeva's *Craft,*'' implies that it was less frequent in other periods. This seems to be true for the late twenties. In April 1929 the oaks standing silent in her yard reminded Tsvetaeva of the equally silent Pasternak: "He doesn't write either.'' (p. 314)

[Tsvetaeva's letter to Anna Teskova,] the same one in which she revealed Pasternak's "mad longing'' to see her in 1926, is fascinating and unique among the published sources. Nowhere else does Tsvetaeva admit a potential "earthly'' side to their spiritual friendship; nowhere else does she compare her role to that of other women in Pasternak's life. Events were beginning to undermine her myth of a "fated, but separated pair.'' The facts supporting this myth were Tsvetaeva's enigmatic relationship with her husband and Pasternak's increasing unhappiness with his first wife, a lady with a reputation for "bourgeois'' tastes. As long as they remained separated and committed to marriages which were, perhaps, confined to the world of *byt,* Tsvetaeva could indeed have Pasternak "completely alone'' in the world of *bytie.* But Pasternak had found a new love—a woman who was filling his life on the level not only of physical presence, but of spiritual companionship as well; Zinaida served as the major inspiration for his collection *Second Birth* (1932). As far as we know, all the poems which Pasternak dedicated to Tsvetaeva during her lifetime date from the late 1920s—none are from this later period. She had good cause to feel that her "place had been supplanted.'' (p. 315)

1932-1933: Though the friendship continued, Tsvetaeva's confidence in Pasternak seemed badly shaken. The next two years saw the writing of her two long essays on Pasternak. In contrast to her private poems to him in the 1920s, these are "public'' works meant for the general (or at least the appreciative) reader. Though they show a thorough—unique—understanding of it, their approach is from the works rather than from the man; they speak about him rather than *to* him. In fact, though she must have expected he would read them sooner or later, we never have the feeling that she was writing for his eyes. (p. 316)

Jane Andelman Taubman, "Marina Tsvetaeva and Boris Pasternak: Toward the History of a Friendship," in Russian Literature Triquarterly (© 1972 by Ardis Publishers), Vol. V, No. 3, May, 1972, pp. 304-21.*

MARC SLONIM (essay date 1977)

Tsvetayeva arrived in Europe at the height of her creative development and during seventeen years of exile produced her best poetry and prose. The years of her sojourn in Czechoslovakia were particularly fruitful and affirmed the originality of her genius. The two long poems, *Poem of the Mount* and *Poem of the End,* both on love, its intricacies, emotional contrasts, and the anguish of tormented separation, written with fiery intensity, deep feeling, and extraordinary verbal brilliance, and the seventy-five-page tale in verse *The Pied Piper* belong indubitably to the most remarkable works of Russian twentieth-century poetry. *The Pied Piper,* based on a medieval legend, is partly a ferocious exposé of pettiness, banality, mediocrity, and meanness of the bourgeois of Hameln, a small town in Germany, plagued by an invasion of rats, and partly a romantic yarn on a mysterious young flute player, a symbol of poetry and magic. The rats abandon the town, following the sound of the Piper's flute, and in recompense he demands to marry Greta, the mayor's beautiful daughter. Snubbed, cheated, and vilified, he takes his revenge by abducting the town's children bewitched by his appealing tune. The Piper brings them to an imaginary paradise and they happily drown in an enchanted lake.

The form of this "lyrical satire," as Tsvetayeva called it, is completely its own. It has a succession of nervous rapid meters, of aphoristic lines, often reduced to one word, displays linguistic virtuosity united with the art of epigrammatic definitions and sharp maxims. (p. 261)

Like all true poets, she was bent on sublimating reality, on transforming the tiniest occurrence into an emotional event, into something elevated, often mythical. She magnified objects, feelings, and ideas: whatever occupied her mind and heart at the moment was rendered—in verse or even in simple conversation—with such intensity as to leave her readers and listeners breathless. (p. 264)

She cut a strange and solitary figure in *émigré* literary circles, where the predominant mood was either conservative or in the tradition of symbolism and acmeism. Tsvetayeva occasionally used symbolist metaphors and she loved Blok and Bely but did not belong to their or any other school. The whole tenor of her work and the daring of her linguistic experimentation place her close to Khlebnikov, Pasternak, and sometimes to Mayakovsky, and in general in the avant-garde of the 'twenties. Her style is precise, articulate, clear-cut, she prefers brass to flutes, her muse is violent, brisk, dynamic, the rhythm of her verse is a rapid vehement staccato, her diction is strongly accented, separate words and tone-syllables are scanned, and carried from one line or couplet to another (enjambement). The emphasis is definitely on expressiveness, on verbal stress, not on melody. She does not shout like Mayakovsky, her poetry is exclamatory rather than declamatory, she prefers to play percussion instruments instead of trumpets, and there is often harshness, almost shrillness, in her voice.

This poetic Amazon, as literary foes called her, was as exacting with herself as she was with others: she abhorred half-baked amateurs, empty redundance, and took time to find the right word and a fitting intonation. There was something ascetic in this sacrificial concentration on her work. (p. 265)

Tsvetayeva's poetry may seem difficult and obscure at first glance, but this superficial impression is caused mainly by her concise, almost telegraphic style, so different from the verbosity, elusiveness, and tongue-tied babblings of mediocre rhymesters. Her clipped sentences resemble sparkling flashes and pass through one like an electric current. Grammatical links between phrases are often omitted and the verbal chain is constantly interrupted, while isolated words serve as signposts along the road the poet travels at an accelerated pace. With the exception of her forlklore tales of the early 'twenties (**"The Czar Maiden"** and **"The Lad"**), the vernacular becomes but a part of her extremely vast vocabulary and blends with her refined metrics and language innovations.

Her favorite method was to dig into the very root of words. By cutting prefixes, by changing endings, one or two vowels or consonants (not unlike the French surrealists), she succeeds in baring the original meaning of various vocables. Playing on phonetics, she derives a new significance of words from the closeness of sound. For example, her long *Poem of the Mount* is structured on the parallelism of the words "mount" and "grief" in Russian (*gorà-gòre*) with an amazingly rich display of all the derivatives from the master word. This "game of phonemes" did not degenerate into mannerism and linguistic tricks. The search for the "core," the "truth" of words not only made them shine anew, but also gave them a deeper meaning, brought forth their emotional substance and ideational value, thus achieving a rare unity of form and spirit. The thrust of her short lines, the stormy and winged rhythms of her meters and alliterations, the high voltage of her exclamations express the poet's indomitable, rebellious nature. (pp. 265-66)

Marc Slonim, "The Fate of Poets: Mandelstam, Akhmatova, Tsvetayeva," in his Soviet Russian Literature: Writers and Problems 1917-1977 *(copyright © 1964, 1967, 1977 by Oxford University Press, Inc.; reprinted by permission), second revised edition, Oxford University Press, New York, 1977, pp. 248-67.**

ANYA M. KROTH　(essay date 1979)

The peculiar treatment of sex in Marina Tsvetaeva's poetry has been noted by a number of literary critics. . . .

The purpose of my essay is to establish a link between the androgynous make-up of Tsvetaeva's characters and the dichotomous nature of her vision. (p. 563)

Androgyny for Tsvetaeva was not so much a reaction to the social, political, and cultural context of her time (she liked to stress that her poetry was beyond contemporary literary and cultural currents) as an intrinsic quality of her artistic method. In other words, androgyny would have been manifest in Tsvetaeva's work regardless of her milieu. (p. 564)

[The] very existence of and penchant for androgynous characters in Tsvetaeva's work is intrinsic to and determined by her poetic vision. This vision, intimately connected with the poet's artistic method and temperament, is dichotomous and leads the artist to rest her creation upon a series of dichotomous antitheses. It also leads Tsvetaeva to search for means, of which androgyny may be one, of generating dichotomous pairs.

An examination of androgyny in Tsvetaeva's work presupposes some agreement over the meaning of the term. . . . In this essay, the term "androgynous" will be used in reference to a condition which suggests "a spirit of reconciliation between the sexes," or a condition wherein two opposite elements (masculine and feminine) lie in the matrix of one. (p. 565)

Androgynous representation of a character can be achieved through the depiction of pronounced attributes of the opposite sex in that character, or it can be established by playing down or removing altogether the telltale properties of a character's stated sex. A male character, for example, can be portrayed with explicitly feminine features, or his masculine traits can be minimized. The cycle of poems entitled **"Sergeiu Efron-Durnovo"** (**"To Serge Efron-Durnovo"**) provides an illustration. . . . The fair, frail, gentle, relaxed humanity of the portrayed person focuses the reader's attention on features kindred to men and women, and the character's dissolved masculinity accounts for this impression.

A similar method of androgynous characterization is employed by Tsvetaeva in the seven-poem cycle **"Georgii"** (**"George"**).

The effeminate nature of the main character is revealed clearly in the characterization of Saint George the Dragon Slayer. . . . Association with a nonmasculine figure, created by metaphorically comparing Saint George to a beautiful maiden, is reinforced by the verbs *plachesh'* and *bledneesh'*, descriptions characteristic of nonmasculine manifestations of feelings rather than the triumphant composure of a victorious warrior. In the cycle as a whole, a similar impression is conveyed by a string of diminutives. . . . (pp. 566-67)

The intensely expressive and polysemous nature of poetic language can cause a simple item of attire to become a powerful means of androgynous characterization, as illustrated in the poem "Ale" ("To Alia"). One of the greatest Greek heroes, depicted here as a young boy, is dressed in feminine attire. . . .

By admixing feminine or nonmasculine characteristics—such as emotional sensitivity, physical delicacy, states of physical and psychological repose, and so forth—in her male personae, Tsvetaeva elicits recognition of them as androgynous.

Female androgynous characters, however, are more prevalent and conspicuous than males in Tsvetaeva's poetic world. Tsvetaeva also uses more numerous and diversified means in the depiction of androgyny in her female characters. A striking example of a female androgyne, depicted in a fashion similar to her treatment of male androgynes, can be found in the short play *Prikliuchenie (An Adventure)*. The play is based on an episode from Casanova's memoirs and features the female character, Henry-Henriette, in whom feminine and masculine elements coexist conspicuously. The play opens with Henry-Henriette appearing in Casanova's room late at night dressed as a hussar. When questioned by Casanova as to the reasons for her late visit, Henry-Henriette, in no haste to disclose her real identity, responds ambiguously, using terms equally descriptive of both a man and a woman. . . . (p. 567)

[Tsvetaeva] achieves an androgynous depiction of Henriette by an admixture of the masculine element in the description of her attire and speech, past and present actions, and in her dramatic characterization.

Besides combining masculine and feminine traits, Tsvetaeva employs a number of other techniques to depict her female personae as androgynous. One of the most common devices is direct references to mythological or folkloric androgynous figures, such as Artemis or Antiope (both figure in *Fedra*), Brunhilde (in the cycle "Dvoe" ["A Pair"]), an amazon or a tsar-maiden, and so forth. Frequent references or allusions to amazons or horse-women, for example, are found in poems sympathetically portraying various female personae. . . . Such portrayals of lyrical personae account for the impression that an amazon, or perhaps a horse-woman, represents a desirable ideal and is compatible with the lyrical persona most often identified as the poet herself. . . . (pp. 568-69)

Images of a tsar-maiden, a folk androgyne frequently found in Russian *byliny* and fairy tales, are more recurrent in Tsvetaeva's lyric poems. . . . Here the conventional female roles of wife, widow, and bride are questioned and rejected in favor of the already existing androgynous image of the tsar-maiden. (p. 569)

Gender can be considered a stylistic device if the reader, consciously or subconsciously, transfers male or female characteristics to an object as a result of its grammatical gender. . . . Tsvetaeva consciously employs masculine grammatical forms

to describe a female figure and thereby communicates the figure's androgyny at the morphological level. (p. 570)

Finally, another device favored by the poet to establish an androgynous characterization of her female characters is closely related to the principle by which relationships among characters are formed. Specifically, whenever alliances are established between Tsvetaeva's female androgynes and other characters, the latter are usually either of the supernatural order or are distinctly masculine, or both. In both the prologue and the conclusion to the *poema*, **Na krasnom kone (On the Red Steed),** for example, the poetic persona insists that she is guided by the divine power of inspiration, which is not that of the Muse, traditionally a feminine figure, but that of the red steed rider. . . . (p. 571)

The predominance of female androgynous characters in Tsvetaeva's work can lead to the conclusion that female characters are more significant and, in a sense, superior to her male characters. It is also possible to transfer to her female characters the rare and outstanding qualities of the poet herself. Before such inferences are made, however, it is useful to examine a major work by Tsvetaeva in which male and female androgynous characters exist side by side. The fairy tale *Tsar'-Devitsa* demonstrates that, in Tsvetaeva's poetic universe not only are male and female forms of androgyny complementary, but that they can exist in perfect harmony, only if each character is a truly whole—androgynous—being, however, (p. 572)

[The] subject matter of *Tsar'-Devitsa* was borrowed, by Tsvetaeva's own admission, from a Russian fairy tale recorded by Afanas'ev. Other treatments of the same motif existed, some of which, if not all, were available to the poet, but Afanas'ev's tale was Tsvetaeva's point of departure. A comparison of Tsvetaeva's *poema* and the folk tale reveals not only Tsvetaeva's view of the essence of the folk tale, but the very core of her poetic vision as well.

The feature which most strikingly distinguishes Tsvetaeva's main characters from those of the folk tale is their androgyny. The poet makes this clear at the very outset of the *poema*. The main male character is introduced in the second stanza as one who is *not* like anything a main hero of a fairy tale is expected to be: he is neither a robber, a rider, an archer, nor a superman. . . . [The] masculinity of the tsarevich, in terms of his physical appearance and the absence of manly vocational and amorous interests, is undermined in the very beginning of the *poema*.

There is nothing in the Afanas'ev tale to suggest the effeminate nature of the tsarevich. On the contrary, the folk tale (and all other sources which treat this motif) depicts him in the traditional manner as a superman. . . . But in Tsvetaeva's *poema* he is transformed into a weak, effeminate, diminutive young man, interested in neither making war nor in women. . . . (pp. 572-74)

In contrast to the tsarevich who cannot conceive of mounting a horse (or a woman), Tsvetaeva's tsar-maiden is inseparable from her steed. Her place is in front of an army of warriors. . . . In the Afanas'ev tale (number 232), the tsar-maiden first appears on a ship surrounded by thirty maidens. Nothing suggests her masculinity except the title of the fairy tale, "Tsar'-Devitsa," and perhaps her initiative in courtship. . . . In Tsvetaeva's *poema* expectations evoked by the title, *Tsar'-Devitsa*, are fulfilled. Indeed, Tsvetaeva's maiden is a hero, not a heroine. She appears first in the story as a warrior, with almost every appellative in the masculine gender. . . . The reversal of features traditionally associated with men and women is particularly prominent in the scene when the tsar-maiden, looking at the sleeping tsarevich, compares him to herself: his hands are small and soft, hers are big and strong; his hair is thin and silky, hers is thick and coarse. The tsar-maiden in Tsvetaeva's fairy tale has all the attributes of a traditional folk male hero. If she is the tsar-maiden, he is a maiden-tsar. . . . (pp. 574-75)

Tsvetaeva's portrayal of the maid as an androgyne is not her only point of departure from the Afanas'ev tale. She goes still further in breaking with the oral tradition. The description of the tsar-maiden in the *poema* is perhaps not out of tune with images of such women existing in Russian *byliny*. However, the depiction of the male counterpart to the warrior-woman as a weakling is unprecedented. The poet's departure from the specific tale and the oral tradition overall prompts one to imbue the androgynous representation of the male character of the *poema* with still greater significance. This significance becomes fully apparent only when the androgynous natures of the tsar-maiden and the tsarevich, albeit so different, are juxtaposed.

The poet emphatically states that the weak tsarevich and the strong tsar-maiden make a perfect pair. Being so different, the tsar-maiden and the tsarevich nevertheless have so much in common that it is difficult to tell them apart. . . . The tsarevich transported into the domain of the feminine and the tsar-maiden into that of the masculine are perfectly compatible. Either has enough of the opposite element, masculine or feminine, to make a congenial pair on *either* side of the sexual barrier. (pp. 575-76)

The tsar-maiden and the tsarevich, Tsvetaeva suggests, are the two angels, the seraph and the cherub.

The suggestion that the tsar-maiden and the tsarevich are perhaps both angels is intrinsically significant, more significant than the hierarchical difference between cherubim and seraphim. Both are angels of a higher order. To see the main characters of the *poema* as two angels is to render the issue of their sexual identity irrelevant. One is not usually puzzled over an angel's sex. One should, therefore, not be overly concerned with the sexual identity of either of the main characters, for they are also the two angels, or two kindred souls. In this lies the key to Tsvetaeva's predilection for androgynous characters.

The unbroken unity of the tsarevich and the tsar-maiden as a pair . . . is of ultimate importance to the poet. In deference to the reader, Tsvetaeva willingly moves them from one sexual domain to the other, but constantly preserves their kindred unity. Both versions of the fairy tale state that the tsar-maiden and the tsarevich were destined for each other. The poet underlines their betrothal and their kinship by marking them off with a sign of androgyny. By portraying them both as androgynes, Tsvetaeva explicitly states their kindred nature and distinguishes them from the rest of the world. No matter what their differences, the rest of the world (that is, the reader) is made to see them, at the moment of their union, as a kindred pair. Thus, in this fairy tale, one of the functions of androgyny is to serve as an external sign, an indication of the profound kinship between the tsarevich and the tsar-maiden.

There is, however, another less obvious reason for the androgyny of this particular pair and of other of Tsvetaeva's poetic personae. An analogy can facilitate understanding of the second function of androgyny in Tsvetaeva's poetic world. Tsvetaeva's ultimate goal in writing is to uncover the essence—also referred

to as the "soul" by Tsvetaeva—of things. In her poetry, the soul is perceived as immortal, invisible, weightless, and so forth, and defies what can be called, using Tsvetaeva's language, "terrestrial" categories of matter, measure, weight, and so forth. To express the soul is to weigh it down. Writing for Tsvetaeva is descending into matter. To make, for example, the invisible soul visible, she must resort to "terrestrial" language. . . . To express the weightless soul in "terrestrial" language, it is necessary, therefore, to use a certain measure of weight already familiar to earthlings. Similarly, to express the asexuality of the soul, Tsvetaeva is compelled to resort to a certain terrestrial measure of "sex," and in choosing this, the poet is guided by her poetic vision and temperament.

One of the most conspicuous characteristics of Tsvetaeva's poetic and personal temperament is defiance and revolt against the existing order of things. Tsvetaeva used to say that her instinct always sought and created barriers in life and poetry. (pp. 577-79)

Tsvetaeva's world view is generally described by her critics as dualistic. (p. 579)

Without denying the existence of various conceptual antitheses in Tsvetaeva's world view, it is essential to refer to these antitheses as "dichotomous" rather than "dualistic." It can be argued that the distinction between these two terms and the ensuing implications are crucial for understanding the artistic function of androgyny in Tsvetaeva's work and its central place in Tsvetaeva's poetic world. . . .

Even though Tsvetaeva's poetic model of the world may be described by a series of antitheses, the relationship between the conceptual poles of each antithesis is not that of radical independence but rather that of mutual interconnection. In other words, Tsvetaeva's various antithetical notions do not pertain to distinct realms, hermetically sealed and mutually exclusive, but, on the contrary, are related and represent opposite sides of one and the same phenomenon. (p. 580)

Juxtaposing the earthly and the heavenly, Tsvetaeva draws correspondences between them and establishes their interdependence. . . . Various "dualistic" manifestations of Tsvetaeva's poetic vision are not so much twofold representations of externally conflicting principles as they are integral, though antithetical, parts of a whole, of a one. (pp. 580-81)

Just as the duality of Tsvetaeva's world view was noted by her critics, either implicitly or directly, the interrelation and correspondence between the poles of various antitheses were ignored by all but a few of Tsvetaeva's critics. . . . Ariadna Efron, Tsvetaeva's daughter and the author of very interesting memoirs, is not deluded by the contradictions intrinsic to Tsvetaeva's outlook. She emphatically states that dualism was alien to Tsvetaeva's nature: . . . ("The integrity of her character, the wholeness of her personality was based on contradictions; *dichotomy* [but *not* at all *duality*] was inherent in her perception and self-expression"). Consequently, recognition of the dichotomous, rather than dualistic, origins of Tsvetaeva's antithetical pairs is essential for an understanding of certain aspects of her poetry and, what is more pertinent to our discussion, it is instrumental in the interpretation of the phenomenon of androgyny.

Androgyny and Tsvetaeva's dichotomous vision are interrelated and mutually supportive. As previously suggested, to express the sexlessness of the soul, Tsvetaeva must resort to a certain measure of "sex." The terrestrial world offers two choices for sexually identifying characters. Tsvetaeva could have chosen one sex over the other, for example masculine over feminine or vice versa. To have done so, however, would have meant acceptance of the division and duality of sex and would have been inconsistent with the poet's world view. Moreover, one should not forget that Tsvetaeva felt compelled to use an earthly measure to make the heavenly soul terrestrially palpable. To "prefer" one sex over the other (the "choice" itself being forced upon the poet) would have been contrary to her defiant nature. On the other hand, combining both characteristics of divided sexual domain and reconciling them in one being, the result being the androgynous natures of her poetic personae, captures the dichotomous nature of Tsvetaeva's perception and self-expression, as well as the defiant aspect of her personality. Consequently, Tsvetaeva's androgynous characters are imprinted with the poet's temperament, vision, and artistic method. It would be difficult to find another concept possessed of the same power to capture simultaneously several substantive peculiarities of Tsvetaeva's art. The poet's dichotomous vision, artistic method, and poetic temperament all find full expression in the phenomenon of androgyny. (pp. 581-82)

Anya M. Kroth, "Androgyny As an Exemplary Feature of Marina Tsvetaeva's Dichotomous Poetic Vision," in Slavic Review *(copyright © 1979 by the American Association for the Advancement of Slavic Studies, Inc.), Vol. 38, No. 4, December, 1979, pp. 563-82.*

J. MARIN KING (essay date 1980)

Tsvetaeva's prose has sometimes been considered "difficult" even among Russian-speaking readers and still more so among readers who learned Russian as a second or third language. Tsvetaeva herself knew about her reputation, and she countered by insisting that her prose was absolutely clear, simple enough for one-year-old children. There is evidence to favor both sides of the question. Readers brought up on Turgenev and Tolstoi will not feel at home with Tsvetaeva's prose: there is no sense of leisure here, no feeling of a comfortable armchair from which this set of memoirs might have originated, not even the sense—oddly enough—of a comforting familiarity with the past. Instead we have an overwhelming sense of haste, of the urgency and even anxiety of someone who writes to *discover* the essential truths hidden in the past and only those hidden truths—"All other truths make way!" Year-old children, on the other hand, respond wonderfully well to the sound and rhythm of a human voice, and an adult reader who gives Tsvetaeva's written text time to return to what it originally was, a speaking voice, will have no difficulty after the first few pages.

For Tsvetaeva wants us to rush headlong into the world of her voice with all its variety, perplexity, and delight: the heightened emotions that subdue and exalt us by turns, the sudden paradoxes that make us halt and turn mental somersaults, the questions and exclamations that hurry us on again over dizzying intonational peaks and drops. Tsvetaeva wrote her prose to read aloud—and certainly her works display the full range of rhetorical device. Among them, two characteristic features of Tsvetaeva's prose style can be mentioned so as to smooth out any remaining "difficulty." Tsvetaeva's favorite way of heightening the impression that we are listening rather than reading is to shift the word order of her sentences, to withhold the main point, the key image, until the final, climactic moment. Her prose pieces, moreover, frequently open on the sound of some other speaker's voice with no preliminary background, or introduction. Tsvetaeva loved the *in medias res* technique of the romantic ballad. All at once she presents someone talking about something absolutely vital. Her own voice enters with a series of images which remain unexplained for the time but which later prove to be the very heart of the work, for the logic of Tsvetaeva's prose rests primarily in her images and even the most conventional narratives in her prose depend on them.

The importance of images, in turn, goes far to explain Tsvetaeva's individualistic punctuation. Tsvetaeva's dashes are even more frequent in the Russian original than in these translations, and they serve to reinforce the importance of images and of intonation by dividing sentences into segments. The pauses signalled by the dashes, like the "rests" in music, have a specific rhythmic and semantic function. At times Tsvetaeva uses dashes not to separate, but to bring ideas and images together. Russian allows the omission of the verb "to be" in the present tense, but Tsvetaeva carries this particular resource of the language very far. She bridges antithetical notions with her dashes and allows us to play with them and to reconsider their relation without the interference of any intervening words, even in cases where whole sentences seem to have dropped out and disappeared. Hence the elliptical quality of Tsvetaeva's prose which will be familiar to readers of her poetry. And the use of dashes to reinforce sound has its own antithesis—the use of the dash to suggest that words have passed into silence; the silences indicated by the dashes must suggest what cannot adequately be said in words.

Tsvetaeva was among the most generous and responsive of writers. As she turned during the thirties more and more to the writing of prose, she found inspiration in the writers of the preceding generation. Thus she praised Maximilian Voloshin as a mythmaker, and declared her allegiance to the purifying power of a mythological vision which searches out and illuminates only the essential, the enduring. (pp. 7-8)

Roughly speaking, and apart from her letters, Tsvetaeva's prose can be divided into three periods. The first period extends from 1917 to about 1920-21. This is the period of diaries and prose sketches. During these years Tsvetaeva kept a journal, parts of which she later gathered into a book titled *Signs of Earth (Zemnye primety)*. The history of these journals and sketches and of Tsvetaeva's unsuccessful efforts to publish them as one book is well documented in Tsvetaeva's letters to Roman Gul from December 12, 1922 to March 11, 1923. (p. 15)

[The] book was never published as a whole, only in excerpts: nine different publications over a period of three years.

The subjects of these early prose excerpts vary, but they all share a reliance on chronology and a terse, aphoristic, extremely elliptical style. Paragraphs are often short, even one sentence in length. (p. 16)

If Tsvetaeva's early pieces can all be traced to her diaries (however individualistic any diary or journal kept by Tsvetaeva was sure to be), the second prose period produces several different genres. The period opens with "**A Cloudburst of Light**" . . . and closes with "**Epic and Lyric in Contemporary Russia**". . . . Both are essays in literary criticism and history, and both deal with the work of Boris Pasternak. Literature, writing and writers now become the main material of Tsvetaeva's prose. Tsvetaeva also evolved her own philosophy and ethics of writing, an effort that produced "**Art in the Light of Conscience**," "**The Poet and Time**," and a third essay "**A Poet on Criticism**." Tsvetaeva very likely would have combined all three titles into a single book of essays and meditations on art. But her experience with *Signs of Earth* was repeated; the book was never published as a whole, and we still have apparently only excerpts from the projected volume.

The second prose period produced yet another genre which Tsvetaeva developed and immensely altered in the Thirties—the literary portrait. The textual history of Tsvetaeva's piece on the Symbolist poet [Konstantin] Balmont (**"For Balmont"**) shows that the literary portrait grew out of Tsvetaeva's journals and diaries. (pp. 16-17)

Tsvetaeva's **"The History of a Dedication"** can be considered a transition to the prose of the third period, even though the date of writing, April-May 1931, very likely preceeds the writing of the philosophical essays of **"Art in the Light of Conscience."** The memoir opens with a scene from the present in which Tsvetaeva is helping a friend sort old papers and manuscripts and proceeds from ruminations on the importance to the poet of blank paper to scenes from Tsvetaeva's childhood, and eventually to the years of her friendship with the poet Osip Mandelstam. The use of several overlapping or concentric time frames allows the narrator's voice to move easily from the present to the past—a device that becomes an important characteristic of her late prose. (p. 17)

[In her last prose period, 1932 to 1937,] Tsvetaeva continues to rely heavily on autobiographical material. But the late works are very different from the diaristic prose of the teens. The difference becomes vividly evident in **"A Living Word about a Living Man,"** finished in February 1933. In the piece on Voloshin the raw biographical and autobiographical data are shaped into a story, a story propelled not by any sort of plot, but by the linking and variation of several key images. And at the center of the piece stands not so much Voloshin as he really was (a feature noted immediately by the poet Khodasevich) as Tsvetaeva's images for Voloshin: the sphere filled with fire, both sun and earth; the mountain creature, the goat-man who climbs the mountain; and Voloshin's profile embedded in the rock face. Tsvetaeva recorded a myth of the poet Voloshin. She did not, however, consider her record a "personal" myth. Rather, she was the person through whose memory Myth itself dispelled the trivia and enhanced the grandeur of its chosen hero, the man-become-hero as his life passes from mere history into the magnitude of the mythic story. Tsvetaeva explains it all right in the pages of **"A Living Word about a Living Man."** The role that Tsvetaeva ascribes to Voloshin in his relationship to people—the myth-maker, the world-maker—is also and equally Tsvetaeva's role as a prose writer. The prose piece on Voloshin, then, is an autothematic work, and the approach to life which Tsvetaeva expounds in it can serve as the approach and introduction to all of the late works in [*A Captive Spirit: Selected Prose*].

Paradoxically—for Tsvetaeva was always the master of paradox—the other key to Tsvetaeva's prose during the third period is history. Tsvetaeva insists on fidelity to historical facts whenever such facts can be ascertained. (pp. 17-18)

Fidelity to historical fact is the key to Tsvetaeva's use of autobiographical episodes in the literary portraits, and these portraits must not be considered as just so many more chapters of autobiography. Although Tsvetaeva's portraits of Voloshin and Bely do contain autobiographical material, it is clear that Tsvetaeva intended that material mainly as documentation and authentification of the picture she presents of the two poets. Her veracity as an *eyewitness* was uppermost in her mind.

In the case of Voloshin, Tsvetaeva read and indignantly rejected as a degrading half-truth the small vignette of her friend that she quotes in the final pages of **"A Living Word about a Living Man."** Her detailed account of her personal experience of Voloshin was not designed to shift the focus to her own past, but planned as living evidence in support of her nobler view of the man. And when Tsvetaeva set to work on her long portrait of Bely, she had already heard Vladislav Khodasevich read his own piece on the poet and novelist. Tsvetaeva praised Khodasevich's prose, but she also wanted to praise Bely in her own right. She turned, therefore, to her days with Bely in Berlin, a unique, personal picture that revealed the true Bely but did not duplicate what had already been said and written, even though other voices and pens had served Bely well.

In the portraits of both Voloshin and Bely, Tsvetaeva succeeds extraordinarily well in combining the mythic with the historico-biographical. The images and associations linked with each poet seem to grow of themselves out of the details of memory as well as to encompass the picture as a whole. No doubt the physique and personality of each man—the curly-haired, round-bellied Voloshin with his nimble feet; the wraith-like, quick-silver Bely spinning dervishly among cafe tables—and the very eccentricities of their demeanor seemed to bring the legendary into the workaday world. Tsvetaeva, however, used her images for each poet not to embellish what was odd and unusual, but to seek out what eternally recurred. What for others remained analogy, simile, metaphor, was for Tsvetaeva the actual fact, the deep truth of each poet's inner being, and both writers are deftly poised between fact and legend—Voloshin on his outcropping of mountain rock, Bely perched on a chair in the Pragerdiele ready for flight.

If Tsvetaeva's literary portraits seem a relatively well-defined genre with a largely uncomplicated career in print, the opposite is the case with the [autobiographical] pieces. . . . It seems very likely, first of all, that these pieces did not appear in print in the final form Tsvetaeva hoped for. The evidence of the actual published texts, therefore, is rather misleading. We have a set of medium-length pieces—**"The House at Old Pimen," "Mother and Music," "The Devil,"** and **"My Pushkin"**—while the remaining pieces, very short and quite spirited, could accurately be called *feuilletons*. During the years when all these works were being written, Tsvetaeva's correspondence with her friend Vera Nikolaevna Bunina (the wife of Ivan Bunin) and with Anna Tesková makes it clear that Tsvetaeva transferred from poetry to prose her drive to work on longer pieces, lengthy narratives or narrative cycles, and to see them in print. Beginning with the portrait of Voloshin, Tsvetaeva alternately demanded and begged (even tears had to fall) that her longer prose works be printed without cuts. Publishers went on slashing whole passages. At times, as was the case with "Grandfather Iloviasky," the first section of **"The House at Old Pimen,"** it seemed as if no one would print her prose at all. Despite the discouraging final outcome, Tsvetaeva's experience with the journal sketches of 1917-1919 may have suggested a necessary compromise. Shorter pieces had a better chance of getting into print. Therefore, long works might best be subdivided into shorter sections from the outset. (pp. 18-19)

Perhaps the most important key to the relationship among [**"The House at Old Pimen," "Mother and Music," "The Devil,"** and **"My Pushkin"**] is Tsvetaeva's use of imagery and myth. Indeed, the mythic symbolism of the prose is so consistent and coherent, and goes so far beyond so-called classical allusions, that the term mythobiography would be more appropriate for these four pieces than would the word autobiography. Myth is the real framework of the story, and it by no means contradicts a faithful account of historical events. In Tsvetaeva's world-view, myth and history were not contradictory but dynamically interrelated, and her prose demonstrates in myriad ways that myth will always emerge from history, that myth will, so to speak, "use" history to sustain itself. When Tsvetaeva refers in her letters to her work on the prose, she constantly uses the word "duty," for it is the poet who can and must bear witness to this double truth.

The final section of [*A Captive Spirit: Selected Prose*] juxtaposes two works of literary criticism. Together they show the impressive range of Tsvetaeva's resources as a critic and the excellence of her critical and analytical intelligence. **"Two Forest Kings"** compares Goethe's "Erlkönig" with [Vasily] Zhukovsky's "Lesnoi Tsar'," using succinct, highly professional philological methods. **"Pushkin and Pugachev,"** on the other hand, boldly takes literary criticism beyond analysis and ventures into a prose that combines autobiography, biography, criticism, philosophy, and ethics. In this work Tsvetaeva draws upon all her discoveries and achievements of the preceeding years. Her letters reveal what hard years they were. But we can all be grateful for the prose which came out of those years, and for the poems too that Tsvetaeva never abandoned. We cannot forget how much Tsvetaeva endured in the final years, but above all it is the greatness of her endurance and achievement that we remember. Tsvetaeva resisted prose, but prose overcame her resistance because she felt that her duty was to resurrect the past, to make her own life and the lives of others go on living in art. (pp. 21-2)

> *J. Marin King, in his translator's note and introduction to* A Captive Spirit: Selected Prose *by Marina Tsvetaeva, edited and translated by J. Marin King (© 1980 by Ardis Publishers), Ardis, 1980, pp. 7-8, 11-22.*

ADDITIONAL BIBLIOGRAPHY

Brodsky, Joseph. "A Poet and Prose." *Parnassus: Poetry in Review* 9, No. 1 (Spring/Summer 1981): 4-16.
    Exposition of the methodology of Tsvetaeva's prose. Brodsky discusses how in her philosophy and in her linguistic style Tsvetaeva projects the tragic.

Carlisle, Olga Andreyev. *Voices in the Snow: Encounters with Russian Writers.* New York: Random House, 1962, 224 p.*
    Reminiscences of a Russian émigré. Carlisle describes her childhood in Paris, a trip to Moscow, and remembers Tsvetaeva, Ehrenburg, Evtushenko, and Pasternak.

Gove, Antonia Filonov. "The Feminine Stereotype and Beyond: Role Conflict and Resolution in the Poetics of Marina Tsvetaeva." *Slavic Review* 36, No. 2 (June 1977): 231-55.
    Examines Tsvetaeva's rejection of conventional sexual roles and stereotypes and identifies androgynous qualities of characters in her work.

Hingley, Ronald. *Nightingale Fever: Russian Poets in Revolution.* New York: Alfred A. Knopf, 1981, 269 p.*
    Biocritical examination of Anna Akhmatova, Osip Mandelstam, Boris Pasternak, and Marina Tsvetaeva, which interweaves the lives and works of the four.

Karlinsky, Simon. "Cvetaeva in English: A Review Article." *The Slavic and East European Journal* X, No. 2 (1966): 191-96.
    Translation and study of the poem "Pis'mo."

Livingstone, Angela. "Tsvetaeva's 'Art in the Light of Conscience'." *Russian Literature Triquarterly* V, No. 11 (1975): 363-78.
    Explores Tsvetaeva's contention that "art is non-moral" in her major essay on the function of art and the artist in society.

Muchnic, Helen. "Chosen and Used by Art." *The New York Times Book Review* (12 October 1980): 7, 32.
    Biographical sketch with general critical remarks.

Proffer, Ellendea, ed. *Tsvetaeva: A Pictorial Biography.* Ann Arbor, Mich.: Ardis Publishers, 1980, 143 p.
    Bilingual text of letters, poems, and prose along with black and white photo reproductions of Tsvetaeva, her family, and her contemporaries.

Schweitzer, Viktoria. "Journey to Elabuga." *Russian Literature Triquarterly* 16 (1979): 269-77.
    Account of the writer's journey to Elabuga and Christopol in her attempt to relive Tsvetaeva's final days. Schweitzer also includes interesting information from an interview she had with the residents of the house where Tsvetaeva spent her last days.

Smith, G. S. "Versification and Composition in Marina Cvetaeva's 'Pereuločki'." *International Journal of Slavic Linguistics and Poetics* XX, No. 3 (1975): 61-92.
    Detailed structural analysis of the epic poem "Pereuločki."

Smith, G. S. "Characters and Narrative Modes in Marina Tsvetaeva's *Tsaŕ Devitsa*." *Oxford Slavonic Papers* n.s. XII (1979): 117-34.
    Detailed narrative of Tsvetaeva's most famous epic poem.

Taubman, Jane Andelman. "Tsvetaeva and Akhmatova: Two Female Voices in a Poetic Quartet." *Russian Literature Triquarterly* V, No. 9 (Spring 1974): 355-69.*
    Considers Tsvetaeva's correspondence with and poetry dedicated to Anna Akhmatova. Taubman emphasizes marked stylistic and emotional differences between the two women.

Vitins, Ieva. "Escape from Earth: A Study of Tsvetaeva's Elsewheres." *Slavic Review* 36, No. 4 (December 1977): 644-57.
    Traces Tsvetaeva's theme of escape from earthly reality through her works and correspondence from 1917 to the late 1930s.

Žekulin, Gleb. "Marina Tsvetaeva's Cycle 'Poems for Bohemia'." *Melbourne Slavonic Studies* Nos. 9-10 (1975): 30-8.
    Structural analysis of "Poems for Bohemia." Žekulin intersperses his remarks with biographical material.

(Benjamin) Frank(lin) Wedekind

1864-1918

(Also wrote under pseudonym of Cornelius Minehaha) German dramatist, essayist, short story writer, novelist, and poet.

Wedekind's dramas were primarily concerned with attacking the hypocrisies of society, particularly the prohibitions against discussing sexuality. Though Wedekind avoided identification with any literary movement, his attacks on naturalism and his theatrical innovations made him a forerunner of both expressionism and the theater of the absurd. Wedekind's works introduced many of the techniques of modern dramaturgy to the German stage, including stylized, nonrealistic dialogue, an episodic format, grotesque characters, and bizarre plots.

The son of a physician and an actress, Wedekind was born in Hanover, Germany. In 1872 the Wedekinds moved to Switzerland to escape Germany's instability and social repression. As a young man Wedekind reluctantly obeyed his father's request to attend classes at the University of Zurich's law school, foregoing his literary interests, but his father's unexpected death freed Wedekind from his studies and his inheritance allowed him to enjoy life in Paris and London for some time. Whether abroad or back home in Germany, Wedekind chose the bohemian life, expressing his contempt for what he considered the repressed, hypocritical members of the respectable middle class.

Wedekind's first produced play, *Frühlings Erwachen (Spring's Awakening)*, shocked its audience, for it dealt graphically with adolescent sexuality. Critics commended the work for shedding light on a taboo subject; enraged citizens, however, attacked Wedekind's portrayal of parents and teachers as repressive for keeping children ignorant of basic biological facts. The theme of sex and its power recurs in all of Wedekind's works. In the "Lulu" plays, *Erdgeist (Earth Spirit)* and *Die Buchse der Pandora (Pandora's Box)*, Lulu, the sensual, predatory female, attracts and destroys men through their own passions until she meets a grisly death at the hands of Jack the Ripper. Though Lulu is sexually adept, she is portrayed by Wedekind as a primitive individual in constant conflict with a hypocritical society. Such characters are found throughout Wedekind's works. Because his aim was to force his audience to recognize how distorted conventional views of life were, Wedekind's characters are not fully realized portraits but exaggerated caricatures that embody specific ideas. They speak not *to* each other, but *at* each other, suggesting the alienation of modern life. The plays themselves are often disjointed and loosely connected and invariably concern the confrontation between society and the social outcast. Because Wedekind considered antisocial behavior heroic, criminals and prostitutes are usually the most admirable characters in his dramas. For example, in *Der Marquis von Keith (The Marquis of Keith)* the protagonist is a clever con-man who almost succeeds in duping society by preying upon its weaknesses.

The audience of Wedekind's day regarded his plays as pornographic and his work was repeatedly banned by the German censor. In addition, he received a prison term in 1899 for writing a poem satirizing Kaiser Wilhelm. Although his professed aim was usually to shock, Wedekind did so with the

The Granger Collection

hope of enlightening and reeducating the public; for this reason he became very outspoken in defense of his work. After the turn of the century his plays became more autobiographical, often portraying a misunderstood artist in revolt against society. He acted major roles in these plays, and often entertained in cabarets by performing his ballads. The public eventually grew used to him and his later dramas were met with a modest level of acclaim.

Wedekind's work exerted a strong influence on twentieth-century German drama, particularly on the plays and aesthetic theories of Bertolt Brecht, who called Wedekind "one of the great educators of the new Europe." His work forms a solid bridge between naturalistic realism and modern German drama. Though banned by the Nazis and neglected after World War II, his plays were frequently revived throughout the 1960s, when the shock value of his work had been dissipated and more serious attention could be paid to his ideas. According to Martin Esslin, Wedekind was "a pioneer of sexual freedom, for men as well as for women, and played in Germany in the first two decades of this century the part which D. H. Lawrence assumed in Britain."

PRINCIPAL WORKS

*Der Schnellmaler; oder, Kunst und Mammon (drama)
1889

*Frühlings Erwachen (drama) 1891
  [*The Awakening of Spring*, 1909; also published as
    Spring's Awakening in *Tragedies of Sex*, 1923]

* **Erdgeist (drama) 1895
  [*Erdgeist: Earth Spirit*, 1914]

Fürstin Russalka (essays, short stories, poetry, and
    dramas) 1897
  [*Princess Russalka*, 1919]

Der Kammersänger (drama) 1899
  [*The Tenor* published in *Angles of Vision*, 1962]

Der Marquis von Keith (drama) 1901
  [*The Marquis of Keith* published in *From the Modern
    Repertoire*, 1952]

Mine-Haha (novel) 1901

König Nicolo; oder, So ist das Leben (drama) 1902
  [*Such is Life* published in *Modern Continental Plays*,
    1929; also published as *King Nicolo; or, Such is Life* in
    The Genius of the German Theater, 1968]

**Die Büchse der Pandora (drama) 1904
  [*Pandora's Box*, 1918]

*Hidalla; oder, Sein und haben (drama) 1904

*Tod und Teufel (drama) 1905
  [*Damnation!* published in *Tragedies of Sex*, 1923; also
    published as *Death and the Devil* in *Five Tragedies of
    Sex*, 1952]

Die vier Jahreszeiten (poetry) 1905

Feuerwerk (short stories) 1906

Musik (drama) 1908

Die Zensur (drama) 1909

Franziska (drama) 1912

*Schloss Wetterstein (drama) 1912
  [*Castle Wetterstein* published in *Five Tragedies of Sex*,
    1952]

*Bismarck (drama) 1916

Herakles (drama) 1919

*Der vermummte Herr: Briefe Frank Wedekinds aus den
    Jahren 1881-1917* (letters) 1967

Griefe wacker nach der Sunde (poetry) 1973

*These are the dates of first publication rather than first performance.

**These works were performed together as *Lulu* in 1905.

PERCIVAL POLLARD (essay date 1911)

Wedekind chiefly represents complete divorce from all the old man-made moralities. He and his characters are not so much above those moralities, as outside of them. He treats humanity diabolically; there is never any trace of divine pity in him. The music-hall's complete freedom from society's ordinary restraints; its sheerly physiologic interpretation of life; its entire forgetfulness of ethical or moral reasonableness; are all typified in Wedekind's art. All life is for him a music-hall performance. The effects of things move him; causes, morals, old labels like "good and evil," or "the wages of sin," do not move him at all. He is the essential modern expression, through art, of that savage doctrine in nature which orders that the stronger reptile devour the weaker. Doctrine, however, is the wrong word to apply to Wedekind; he is as above doctrines as he is outside of the old humanities. He has in him something of Machiavelli, something of Casanova, and the more satanic egoisms of Nietzsche; he remains a strange, uncanny, isolated, abnormal figure, and is yet, in his very remoteness from all normalities and all moralities, typical of modern Germany's throwing away from old, too long accepted things. (pp. 231-32)

An abnormal, an eccentric, Wedekind has always been. . . . Little that was abnormal in pathology of sex, or nerves, or sanity, escaped his treatment as material for plays. He was eccentric, outside of all the elder moral, or critical, or artistic scruples, or even scruples about the public or his own profit. He did not merely satirize his public, as Shaw did; he insulted it, both as playwright and as performer. Neither censors nor jailors lessened the fury with which he imposed his eccentric ego upon his time in Germany. . . . He cared as little for style or form in his plays as he cared for morals. For him, as for Meredith, the "chaos illumined by lightning" of Wilde applies; his dramatic work is more chaotic than any other in our time, and yet has flashes, moments, of genius, that irritate by their very impertinence. He treats humanity as an aggregation of atoms; it amuses him to galvanize those atoms into this or that attitude. He has no cowardices of texts and teachings, no hymns to sing to humanity. We are marionettes for his amusement; that is all. (pp. 234-35)

What has always been to the fore in his preoccupation with the sexual relation between the sexes is the brutal, the diabolic, in them. His bitter, cynic irony has played about every normal and abnormal gesture of human passion that experience or imagination can conceive. He is the great Denier of our time. He denies morals, denies custom, denies the laws and scruples of society and art. Whether the barriers of nicety and decency— to use words intelligible to the polite!—which Wedekind has kicked down can ever again be put up as permanently as before in art, is a fine question. He denies the ideal, denies even what is. (p. 238)

Wedekind stopped for no realities; his characters were as chaotic as the dialogue; all was on the abnormal and screaming note of the *affiche* larger than life. The voice was the same in a hundred of his characters, the voice of Wedekind. His caricatures sketched the living, but never filled them with breath. As he has no concern for methods in art, so, too, he never moves you more than some chaotic monstrosity might move you. Yet, like chaos, like all monstrous things, there is something so vast, so inhuman in him, that the world must eventually take note of him.

It is in the volume **"Countess Russalka"** . . . that one should look for the first signs of Wedekind's artistic temper. This volume held stories, poems, and pantomimes. It gave some of his earliest, and also some of his most characteristic work.

"Spring's Awakening" will probably live longer than any other Wedekind play. Brutal as it is, it still has a vestige of idealism, of which the later Wedekind retains no trace. It was a children's tragedy of the most awful, this play, and no greater indictment of the folly of letting hypocrisy and shamefulness keep the young of both sexes blind to what sex means has ever been written. (pp. 239-40)

Almost every hypocrisy common in every modern country's attitude toward children is flayed bitterly by Wedekind. (p. 241)

If in **"Spring's Awakening"** our modern world first came to realize Wedekind's concentration upon sex, that concentration was to be expressed even more forcibly afterwards. There was, in the children's tragedy referred to, still much of the unquenched idealist in Wedekind; indeed, it was what gleamed through the lines suggesting the bitter way in which the great world of experience had brutally upset the ideal in Wedekind's own youth that gave this play much of its power. The play was applicable wherever old hypocrisies between parent and child still linger; but the most tremendously international creation of Wedekind was to come later, in the character of Lulu, the heroine of **"Earth Spirit"** and its sequel, **"The Box of Pandora."**

Lulu is of all time, of all climes. She is the Eternal Woman, in whose body the world, the flesh and the devil reign supreme. In the apparent chaos of her contradictory passions are all those eternal femininities that defy the classifications of society or of science. She would give her body to the most brutal ruffian, the while her spirit soared to strange heights of sensuous finesse. She is the elemental female, the essence of her sex. (pp. 243-44)

The most individual talent of the theatre in our time, perhaps, is this Frank Wedekind, and yet as full of faults as of strength. All his characters talk his own tongue; all utter monologues; there is never dialogue. Everything is sacrificed for a biting cynicism, for a mordant caricature; completeness or balance are never achieved; everywhere the jagged and raw edges of chaotic whims and passions obtrude in his work. In the moment of the deepest tragedy he grins like the most insensate clown; and into his absurdest clowning he infuses the bitterest irony. (pp. 249-50)

[But a curious preoccupation] runs through everything he ever wrote. Preoccupation, namely, with the human body, especially the human body's gait and gestures.

Wedekind's intense joy in the body is as pagan as that of the Greeks, but expressed far more in terms of literal physics. For him there is no veiling the essential thing itself by phrases about a "human form divine." . . . He goes straight to the rude core of man's delight in woman's body. If he himself declared once that "life is a toboggan-slide," we must, as we examine his paramount obsession, declare that in him the cult of the human body is chiefly expressed in intense devotion to woman's every gesture, every motion of her gait. (pp. 252-53)

Through the most grotesque situations that occur between the extraordinary people in his plays . . . the idea that only in a perfect body can the perfect spirit dwell rings out. . . . The case of *Hidalla* is nothing but a girl's education in worship of her own body. The gradual dawning in her of appreciation for the suavity of her limbs, of "that joy which came to her as the consciousness of her own body came to her, and which found vent again in every slightest gesture," is typical of this trait in Wedekind's art. (pp. 253-54)

As we remember the emphasis on these qualities in body and gait that runs through all Wedekind writes, those early "Pantomime Dances" in the [**"Countess Russalka"**] volume come more and more to express Wedekind's real attitude toward life. That attitude is one of inhuman disdain. Before his cynically distorting mirror he lets all life pass; all are equal before that ironic reflector. His relentless determination to fling his figures about into frightful and abnormal postures, detracts from our ability to feel anything of his as a complete work of art. Wedekind is as chaotic as Nature herself; there is no notion absurder than that Nature is logical or artistic in the petty sense.

The sheerly profane expression of Nietzsche's most inhuman egoism is Wedekind. Humanity has moved his pity as much as it has moved Vesuvius when that volcano was in eruption. (p. 255)

[Wedekind] has laid bare all the brute in normal, as well as in abnormal mankind. If he has gone to the other extreme—has refused to see that in us human creatures there is also something beside the brute—he has none the less perfectly fulfilled the old artistic law that you must always, to bring your point home, tell not only the truth but more than the truth: you must exaggerate. Wedekind has exaggerated the brutal qualities in us, until he has made us shudder. He is eccentric and perverse; the tragic comedian of the abnormal; whether he is genius of psychology or only genius of chaos, he has gashed the irremediable savagery of our time, surviving through centuries of so-called civilization, so deeply upon the theatre and upon literature that he may survive when time-serving photographers, or complaining idealists, are forgotten. (p. 256)

> *Percival Pollard, "Drama and Frank Wedekind,"*
> *in his* Masks and Minstrels of New Germany, *John*
> *W. Luce and Company, 1911, pp. 227-56.*

ASHLEY DUKES   (essay date 1911)

In his "Playboy of the Western World" Mr. J. M. Synge satirised bitterly the effect of even a self-styled giant upon a race of pigmies. His Christopher comes to a remote village in the West of Ireland with the tale that he has killed his father, and the decadent peasants, drained of their best blood by emigration and reduced to a group of women, old men and weaklings, make a hero of him. The story of his crime fascinates them. He has at least done something notable, something powerful, something that stands for will and firm resolve in this land of dreams and despair. The women worship him and bring him presents; the loafers of the village inn regard him with awe. Christy finds himself famous.

Even so Frank Wedekind came, a few years ago, to the German Theatre, with the reputation of having slain, not his father, but morality. His plays were the last word in unconventionality and daring. Where other dramatists touched delicately, for fear of over-boldness, upon the woman with a past or the life of the *demimonde*, he dragged pathology, sex perversion and insanity relentlessly upon the stage. He thrived upon prohibitions, prosecutions, newspaper outcry and notoriety in general. He proclaimed openly his contempt for the public, and no critical attacks could penetrate his monstrous egoism. Beside the other playwrights of the period—[Hermann] Sudermann the trimmer and Gerhart Hauptmann the sensitive idealist—he seemed a giant individuality, like a Bismarck or a Nietzsche. A self-styled giant, perhaps; but that only made him the more attractive to the weaklings. He insulted them, and they rushed to see his plays. (pp. 95-6)

Mr. Synge's Christy, of course, had not really killed his father, and neither had Wedekind really killed morality. Like most alleged immoralists, he had a stern gospel of his own to preach. Behind the brutality of his plays there is the force of conviction that no mere sensationalist or commercial playwright can ever show. Wedekind's contempt for "das Publikum" is real. He despises the theatre-going mob so sincerely that he refuses even to make use of it as a speculative investment. He may be a fanatic, but he is never a charlatan. (p. 97)

Wedekind as dramatist is something more than an eccentric, but something less than a creative genius. Flashes of genius he has, emerging fitfully from clouds of eccentricity. He is an author who cannot readily be "placed." To the critic bent upon classification, who would label him as naturalist or symbolist, realist or idealist or mystic, he must remain an enigma. He belongs to no school, and hitherto he has had no followers. His plays are the most aggressively individual of our time. Some of them, like **"Oaha"** and **"Hidalla,"** are not only frankly autobiographical, but appear to exploit a personal grievance. The individuality behind them is crude and obtrusive. It is almost devoid of taste or sense of form. But it is valuable because of its power. It offers us a rare criticism of modern life by presenting it from a new angle. Wedekind is no hawker of a cheap optimistic philosophy, like Sudermann. He has none of Hauptmann's sympathy with the common man. (pp. 98-9)

His practice of the playwright's craft is just as individual. In the construction of his plays he obeys no law but his own convenience. He has revived the monologue, which was said to have been destroyed by Ibsen twenty years ago. He writes speeches as long as those in the hell scene of "Man and Superman." His "curtains" are no more than chance interruptions of an otherwise interminable dialogue. He never leads up to a scene; it simply occurs casually and passes. . . . Of many of Wedekind's plays it may be said that they represent life neither as it is, nor as it ought to be, but as we see it in our nightmares. They create the same effect of vague oppression, of meaningless effort, of vast heights and depths, of tremblings upon the precipice of insanity. (pp. 99-101)

> *Ashley Dukes, "Frank Wedekind," in his* Modern Dramatists *(reprinted by permission of the Estate of Ashley Dukes), Frank Palmer, 1911, Charles H. Sergel and Company, 1911, pp. 95-113.*

THOMAS MANN (essay date 1913)

It is an unusually responsible task to have to pass judgment on this play [*Lulu*] as literary adviser of the censorship board. But I would nevertheless rather assume responsibility for advocating release of the play than advise that public performance be forbidden. I urgently request you to consider that it is not a worthless piece of hackwork aimed at sensationalism, sensual titillation, and glorification of vice, but a modern work of art whose importance, profundity, seriousness, and value have long been acknowledged among literary experts. It will always hold an honorable place in the history of the German drama, in spite of all the grotesque and dubious elements it contains. I have attended both private performances of the second part (*Pandora's Box*). In 1904 the audience was thoroughly outraged, repelled, and inclined to angry protests, and the evening ended with an out-and-out theatrical scandal. In 1910, at the Artists' Theater, the same play enjoyed a serious and unqualified triumph. This shows that superior public opinion has changed greatly in favor of Wedekind the artist in the last decade; in fact, this change is not confined to "superior" audiences, as was demonstrated by the surprising success with the wider middle-class public of his *Franziska*, which to my mind is artistically weaker. There is no longer any need to fear that public performances of Wedekind will scandalize audiences; and anyone who desires that the actions of the board will not unnecessarily infringe on the best interests of culture must in this case recommend prudent broad-mindedness.

I have already said that the proposed cuts are equivalent to substantial alterations. The boldest dialogue has actually been eliminated. And as for the last act, which you have called "brutal"—undoubtedly with some justice—it nevertheless carries such somber ethical weight that to my mind there can be no moral objection to it, quite aside from its dramatic indispensability.

I have not the slightest personal reason for advocating Herr Wedekind's cause. Ever since I joined the censorship advisory board he has behaved with extreme hostility and has irresponsibly and indeed insanely picked quarrels with me. I completely agree with you in your opinion of his dubious character. But as history teaches, dubious characters can make significant cultural contributions. I, and many other people, believe that this is such a case. And I believe, finally, that one should not feed Herr Wedekind's delusions of martyrdom by a new act of "suppression." (pp. 64-5)

> *Thomas Mann, in his letter to the Royal Bavarian Commissioner of Police, Munich on April 30, 1913, in his* Letters of Thomas Mann: 1889-1955, *edited and translated by Richard Winston and Clara Winston (copyright © 1970 by Alfred A. Knopf, Inc.; reprinted by permission of Alfred A. Knopf, Inc.), Knopf, 1971, pp. 64-5.*

O. F. THEIS (essay date 1913)

Frank Wedekind, a number of whose works have recently appeared in English translation, is one of the most perplexing figures in modern European literature. Any attempt to classify him with one or the other of the groups of naturalists, realists, romanticists, symbolists, decadents, or whatever they may be called, is sure to fail, for traces of all these movements are found in his work, but they are so jumbled, the one with the other, that he has evolved a style and method entirely his own, in which cynicism, scepticism, satire, grotesqueness of metaphor and capricious paradox play a large part. Nuances, delicacies, and subtilties of thought or treatment, the reader will rarely find in Wedekind.

The nearest analogue among English writers is probably George Bernard Shaw. Both take the same keen delight in 'having a shy' at every conceivable accepted opinion and belief; both are clever in building up preposterous theses with artificial logic; both fundamentally are very much in earnest in their *clownerie*. Shaw's boldest situations and most daring fantasies are always dominated by a purely intellectual element and contain traces of unadulterated puritanism, which are totally lacking in Wedekind, who is more emotional and tends toward sentimentality. Perhaps it is in the latter that the root of his cynicism lies. He calls a spade a spade, always with extravagant emphasis, and dealing so much in hardware is sure to cause considerable clatter. Whether writers like Shaw and Wedekind are a symptom or a disease in modern literature is immaterial; for the present, at least, they are a force that cannot be ignored, and their genuine abilities have been recognized by friend and foe alike.

Wedekind's admirers consider him as the forerunner of a new form of drama, and compare him to pre-Shakespearean writers, like Christopher Marlowe, whose work was also full of violence and extravagance, and yet contained the kernel of what later developed into the greatest dramatic movement which the world has known. Many of his disciples with the enthusiasm of recent converts, hail him in addition as the prophet of a new morality. His opponents, leaving out those who always attack everything that does not follow prescribed rules, speak of Wedekind as the 'clown of German literature'—there is not a little in his work to support their contention. They claim that he is an aesthetic sensualist, and that his valuations are unimportant; that he has taken the sex problem and turned it into vaudeville, and genuine satire into coarse burlesque, and that in his hands the beautiful form of tragedy becomes an ugly changeling of caricature and tragi-comedy; technique, mere virtuosity; and art, tricky cleverness. (pp. 237-38)

[The] majority of Wedekind's characters are outside of the pale of conventional society and current morality. It is a gallery of motley portraits which he has drawn: artists, actors, actresses, musicians, circus performers, adolescents in the ferment of puberty, neurasthenes, pseudosupermen, degenerates and perverts, visionaries, cosmopolitans, promoters of shady enterprises, fashionable swindlers. (p. 238)

In his poetry, prose and dramas, sex and morals are always in the forefront. Wedekind's sex has little of the spiritual in it. It is frequently brutal and portrayed in its most physical aspects, for he does not hesitate to follow it into the dark alleys where the extremes of abnormality dwell. Love is war between the sexes, war to death. . . .

Wedekind's emphasis upon sex has not a few points of contact with the Freudian psychology, which is at present creating so much discussion. According to it, actions are principally determined by sexual complexes, repression of which leads to abnormality, hysteria, and discontent. This thought is not infrequent in Wedekind, and, like the Freudians, he seems to enjoy rooting about in the unconscious for suppressed sexual moments. (p. 239)

[Clarity] and simplicity are the very elements that are most lacking in Wedekind. Of the cheaply theatrical there is perhaps not so much. Long speeches abound. The dialogue is often nothing but a monologue in which the interjections or questions of the second speakers are hardly more than breathing spaces.

When a thought comes to his mind his characters fly off and are as difficult to stop as John Tanner in Shaw's 'Man and Superman.' These frequent digressions make for diffuseness and are for the most part purposeless, differing in that, for example, from the digressions in Tchekhoff's plays which are intended to convey atmosphere and to show group emotions.

The ideas often are brilliant enough and betray a remarkable intellectual energy, but the effect of such speeches is irritating when it is apparent that their only purpose is the making of a point. A pompous rhetoric, filled in the manner of the old-fashioned drama with high-sounding words, and a turbid style are even worse defects. When read in succession Wedekind's dramas do not leave any clear artistic impression; at most one or two scenes stand out.

Few other dramatists have been less objective. It is almost always Wedekind who speaks. Among all his characters there is hardly a living human being, if a few of the children in the **'Awakening of Spring'** are excepted. When his characters die or commit suicide it is words that kill them, not any inherent tragic necessity. They are ideas, brains, intelligences, instincts, seldom beings of flesh and blood. The true creative artist must be father and mother to his creatures; Wedekind is only father. (pp. 244-45)

O. F. Theis, "Frank Wedekind," in Poet Lore, Vol. 24, No. IV, Vacation, 1913, pp. 237-47.

ARTHUR ELOESSER　(essay date 1931)

When Frank Wedekind made his début in 1891 with *Frühlings Erwachen (The Awakening of Spring),* which at once alarmed and attracted the public, it was hard to classify him in any recognized literary school. The piece seemed naturalistic, for it was drawn direct from life and used an exaggerated realism in dealing with the physical side of human nature; but on the other hand it was romantic at the end. . . . Wedekind's picture was drawn with too hard a line, with a ruthlessness upon which no naturalist would have ventured, so that his fantastic caricature quite overshot the mark. Yet the piece had a soul, born of the melancholy pleasure of spring, whose sweet, yet dangerous awakening was the leading motive in the play, dominating this loose succession of tragedies in miniature, schoolboy burlesques, the perversions of the house of correction, schoolgirl chatter, middle-class interiors, the magic of gardens, and the atmosphere of the forest. (p. 126)

In spite of all its audacities and over-realistic distortions, verging on caricature, *Frühlings Erwachen* had the touching insight of a first work, the profound note of a lament over a lost paradise; its various tableaux, whether cynical or tender, provocative or ecstatic, do not clash with one another, because they have as their background a spiritual atmosphere and are borne gently along on an undercurrent of lyricism, which the author introduced into his work on the model of *Wozzek,* for he was a great admirer of [Georg] Büchner. (p. 127)

Wedekind was fanatically possessed by a single idea—that of complete sexual emancipation, which could not but lead, he thought, to a new order of society and bring about its salvation. In the Middle Ages, to which, with his inhibitions, repressions, and torments of conscience, he still in some sort belonged, an experienced priest would probably have been found to exorcize his evil spirit; but as things were, he performed this office for himself, his dramatic work being a stern process of exorcism carried out upon himself. At first people would almost cross themselves at his works, as though he were Satan incarnate, but posterity may prefer to recognize him rather as a priest listening to humanity's confession of its perturbing and shameful secrets. His creed had its answers and remedies in readiness: his confessions of his faith were inspired by a purpose, essentially opposed to that of Nature, which made him the father of expressionism and activism in Germany. (pp. 132-33)

From the very first Wedekind had not been a naturalist, but had pushed realism beyond the point up to which it had existed for its own sake only, in order that he might hold the stage himself. If we consider his work as a whole, he always appears as the organizer of a world of infernal visions, a circus director who sends his mask-like figures, with their purposely exaggerated make-up, jumping through the hoops that he holds up for them, till they fall and crush one another to death. This was accepted as a conventional device, which, if not a mere piece of fantasy, was a parable whose terrible warnings ended with a moral that people could carry away with them. (p. 133)

Arthur Eloesser, "The Literary Revolution," in his Modern German Literature, *translated by Catherine Alison Phillips (copyright 1933 by Alfred A. Knopf, Inc.; reprinted by permission of Alfred A. Knopf, Inc.; originally published as* Die Deutsche Literatur vom Barock bis zur Gegenwart, *Bruno Cassirer, 1931), Knopf, 1933, pp. 57-155.**

ERIC BENTLEY   (essay date 1946)

If Ibsen and Strindberg represent the decline of the burgher and his morality, Wedekind invents a world in which there are no burghers and no morality. (p. 42)

Wedekind has a satirist's draughtsmanship. But his standpoint is not reason, or common sense, the often rather stolid pragmatism of the comic writers from Aristophanes to Molière. It is religious. But like Baudelaire, Wedekind is only negatively religious. He is not a believer, and his vision is solely of evil. Those who are unacquainted with this cultural phenomenon simply have to take Wedekind's word for it that his aim was to unite holiness with beauty. (pp. 42-3)

The distortions and involutions of Wedekind's moral symbols are an early objectification of the same spiritual sickness which later showed itself in surrealism after one fashion, in D. H. Lawrence and Henry Miller, and after a different fashion in Franz Kafka. In all these diverse figures there is a deep consciousness of chaos, a longing for the numinous, for that mystic and mysterious part of experience which the modern imagination has so often overlooked. Wedekind is surrealist in his shock technique, his atmosphere of nightmare, his mastery of the sexual-grotesque. In his moral stand he is Lawrentian. Unlike all these men, his imagination functioned in theatrical terms, and occasionally in tragic, or, perhaps we should say, pseudo-tragic terms. His most celebrated pseudo tragedy is *Lulu,* as the double drama of *Erdgeist* and *Die Büchse der Pandora* is generally known. The first part of the play, of which Wedekind wrote: "I wanted to exclude all ideas which are logically untenable, such as love, loyalty, gratitude," ends when Lulu shoots her man. In the second part, where Wedekind attempts to bring the piece to a tragic culmination, the Countess Geschwitz, till now a ridiculous Lesbian lover of Lulu's, is slowly transformed until—without many of the critics' noticing it—she attains a sort of tragic grandeur by expressing love, loyalty, and gratitude. Lesbianism is not sentimentalized. The Countess is made Lesbian to give her virtue the most abnormal origin. In our world only a twisted virtue can triumph. Such is Wedekind's version of poetic justice. *Lulu* is the epitaph of bourgeois tragedy. (pp. 43-4)

> *Eric Bentley, "Tragedy in Modern Dress," in his* The Playwright As Thinker: A Study of Drama in Modern Times *(copyright 1946, 1974 by Eric Bentley; reprinted by permission of Harcourt Brace Jovanovich, Inc.), Reynal & Hitchcock, 1946 (and reprinted by Harcourt, 1967, pp. 23-47).**

LION FEUCHTWANGER   (essay date 1952)

The basic element in Frank Wedekind's work is contradiction, the antithesis which lies at the very core of things. The false bottom, Janus with his two faces, these form the vital stuff of his writings for the stage.

Wedekind tries to take up a position outside the world he has created, and from this Archimedean point of vantage to demonstrate as a detached observer the tragic absurdity of his world and ours.

But his cold detachment is assumed. In reality he feels to the very marrow the searing tragedy of his characters and situations. His sympathy is merely concealed behind ironic laughter and clownish posturings.

No other writer has his way of expressing the most daring truths with such icy correctitude. His plays and ballads proclaim their seditious messages with properly respectable gestures and in precise, often sententious and aphoristic phrases.

Horror and laughter are perpetually mingled in his work. (p. 7)

As an artist and thinker Wedekind has much in common with Jean-Jacques Rousseau. Just as the latter rebelled against the rationalistic hedonism of his time and sought to penetrate to what is essential, to Nature, so Wedekind sought to escape from the hypocrisy and artificiality of bourgeois society, back to a natural way of life.

He regarded unfeigned sensual pleasure as the highest aim of every spiritually and physically well-rounded human being. He attributed the tragi-comic situation of bourgeois society to the fact that its hypocrisy forces people to maim and conceal their natural instincts. Anyone acknowledging the truth either by words or actions is repudiated by society. The only man who can live a natural life is he who puts himself beyond the range of this society and its laws and who robs and betrays it with every means that comes to hand. According to which the true hero of this society is the unscrupulous thief and swindler, the industrial brigand in the grand style. His female counterpart is the magnificent, heartless whore, born for pleasure. Wedekind does not seek merely, like the naturalistic school, to render photographically the surface of society, but to penetrate to its interior, to present it in all its complexities and contradictions. In order to view it thus comprehensively he must find a point of vantage outside it. He finds that Archimedean point and from it turns his world this way and that, ever and again exposing its tragic and ridiculous aspects in abrupt alternation, letting them in abrupt alternation explode against and mingle with each other. With the result that in his big scenes he achieves a parallelism of situation which makes the tragic and the comic apparent simultaneously to all who have eyes to see.

Like Jean-Jacques Rousseau he has an irresistible urge to put the ultimate, the most daring, into words, everything that others carefully suppress, the simple truths. He fights dishonesty with all the weapons at his disposal. (pp. 13-14)

He finds the aesthetic theories of the time as false as its morality, and the way in which contemporary art so faithfully reproduces the outer shell of things is to him the summit of hypocrisy. He is not interested in this sad, sterile exterior. He wants to thrust his way through to the tragic interior of life. Like Nietzsche he feels compelled to present the tragedy which springs from Nature itself, the elemental force, not the melancholy insipidity of everyday things which the naturalistic dramatists, "Gerhart Hauptmann and Co.", reproduce with such painstaking attention to detail. To counteract the dull, discreet, prosaic method of presentation in favour with his colleagues of the naturalistic school, he makes use of a romantic realism consistent with his nature and temperament: he makes use of effect, sensational effect as he learnt it from the circus, from the Parisian stage, from the Grand Guignol above all. He hates and despises true-to-life dialogue, the unobtrusive transitions, the bad language borrowed from "real life", the creation of "atmosphere".

He himself does not shrink from the harsh contraposition of black and white, God and the Devil, nor from abrupt leaps into the wildest antitheses.

The stuff of his creation is the poetry of the people, the vernacular, ballad and *moritat,* the wealth of imagery to be found in proverbs and the coarsest of slang alike.

His whole poetry springs from the urge to make available and comprehensible to everyone the knowledge which he has acquired through so much suffering and acute reflection. . . . [He] does not hesitate to compress his scenes, is indifferent to the crudity of his plots, wastes almost no time on establishing motivation. What matters to him is that the symbolism of his situations should be obvious, that they should hammer his doctrines home to the public, doctrines which go against the public grain. So that with their forceful, frenzied melodramatic situations, their provocative blasphemies, their garish colours, their unstudied effects and over-emphatic, sententious language, his plays are a mixture of mystery-play, Shakespeare, puppet-show, Grand Guignol and demagogy. (pp. 14-15)

[Wedekind] invented the modern morality play. All his characters distil their impressions and experiences into definite precepts. He demonstrates how praiseworthy is the man who seeks to alter our false society and at the same time how ridiculous he is and how ill he fares. All this he demonstrates in a childlike way with the childlike simplicity of genius which sees everything, and in the midst of the most tragic events is not afraid to roar with laughter at the absurdities of the attendant circumstances. (p. 15)

Like the works of Jean-Jacques Rousseau, the plays of Wedekind are one long confession. He is forever laying bare his bosom, forever shouting to make himself understood and it is this desperate emotional tinge to his objectivity which gives his plays their chief charm. For all their artificial dryness, they shimmer all over. His way of swinging from one mood to the other is emphasised by the fact that for all his hatred of bourgeois existence Wedekind cannot resist the temptations which this existence has to offer. When he wages his war against bourgeois society with bourgeois manners, speech and mode of dress, this is more than an effective piece of technique; it is also the expression of one of his personalities. (p. 16)

> *Lion Feuchtwanger, in his introduction to* Five Tragedies of Sex *by Frank Wedekind, translated by Frances Fawcett and Stephen Spender (copyright by Vision Press Ltd), Vision Press, 1952, pp. 7-21.*

WALTER H. SOKEL (essay date 1959)

Wedekind wrote his first and most important dramas in the eighteen-nineties, a period when Ibsen's and Hauptmann's Naturalism had barely been accepted on the German stage. What distinguished Wedekind's plays from Naturalism, despite their highly modern, semi-Naturalistic subject matter, was the grotesqueness of situations depicted in them and the quality of the dialogue. Wedekind applied the identical idiom of stilted phrases and caustic epigrams to all his characters from newspaper publisher to ragpicker. From the point of view of Naturalism, this was outrageous ineptitude. But Wedekind's purpose was not to present actual society on the stage. By his peculiar idiom he created a closed world similar to the autonomous space of the Cubist or the closed universe of [Franz] Kafka and [Georg] Trakl. In contrast to Kafka, Trakl, and the Strindbergian drama, however, Wedekind built his closed world not for the purpose of visualizing existential situations, but for the purpose of exaggerating and distorting social reality. Like the figures of the Cubist, Wedekind's characters correspond to objectively existing reality, but they are seen and presented in their essential structure rather than in their empirical surface appearance. Wedekind sees sex and drive for power and prestige as the basic conflicting forces dominating life. He distills these forces from actual society in which they are hidden in layers of hypocritical convention and, with provocative glee, exhibits their "pure essence" embodied in empirically impossible specimens. Lulu, his "earth spirit," is nothing but the tyranny of sex become flesh and blood, and his incredibly domineering and successful newspaper publisher Schön is the embodiment of the relentless drive for power that rules modern society. Wedekind demonstrates the basic conflict between the two in the "test tube" of his drama which his artificial but ruthlessly expressive dialogue creates. In the prologue to his drama **Earth Spirit,** he compares himself to an animal tamer in a circus. Here, as in all other Expressionist works, distortion reveals essence. But in the drama of Wedekind, and that of his successors [Carl] Sternheim and [Georg] Kaiser, essence lies less in visionary fantasy than in the uniformly exaggerated, epigrammatically concentrated quality of speech. (pp. 61-2)

> *Walter H. Sokel, "Poeta Dolorosus," in his* The Writer in Extremis: Expressionism in Twentieth-Century German Literature *(© 1959 by the Board of Trustees of the Leland Stanford Junior University; with the permission of the publishers, Stanford University Press), Stanford University Press, 1959 (and reprinted by Stanford University Press, 1968), pp. 55-82.*

CLAUDE HILL (essay date 1960)

With the exception of several ballads, some lyrical poems and a few short stories, Wedekind's work is devoted to the stage. His eternal theme is a new philosophy of beauty and sex, freed from the taboos and prejudices of middle class society. Wedekind is the eroticist *par excellence* to whom aesthetics and ethics are but two sides of the same thing. The physical, if healthy and strong, is basically good. Immorality is caused by repressions and inhibitions. "The flesh has its own soul," he has one of his characters say. The development of physical beauty is a moral obligation, and the sex urge is the most powerful impulse of human motivation. Consequently, proper sex education and a new morale, opposed to bourgeois conventionality, are needed. The prostitute becomes the idealized practitioner of a recognized profession; the traditional institution of monogamous marriage is looked upon not only as hypocritical but actually wicked because it runs counter to "the soul of the flesh." The man who is not afraid of his instincts, desires and emotions, the adventurer or even the criminal, becomes the new hero. (p. 83)

Wedekind was so exclusively a dramatic author at heart, that his lyrical output and his prose also show typical dramatic characteristics: antithetic structure, speed, dialogism, surprise endings, and constant vibration. He was no genuine lyrical poet, but rather a chansoneur of songs and ballads which he, incidentally, often recited at cabaret appearances while accompanying himself on the guitar. He was a master of political satire and contributed, under different pen names, many pieces to the famous Munich weekly, *Simplicissimus*. Better known, however, are his slightly frivolous, mocking and flirtatious love songs and ballads which reveal him as a post-romantic follower of Heine, even using the same technique of the slap in the face of the listener, thereby destroying the originally established poetic mood through a trivial twist in the closing strophe.

As to Wedekind's prose, it is significant that he never attempted a novel, that he was exclusively a master of the short pointed tale and some very subjectively colored essayistic pieces. The theme here is again, of course, love, eros, sex. His prose style is lucid and sophisticated. . . . (p. 87)

This writer holds no brief for the sniper technique of the psychoanalyst who aims at literary victims, and there is no question that the Freudian approach to contemporary criticism has done much harm, but in the case of Wedekind one is almost tempted to say that his personality and work can only be interpreted psychoanalytically. In the absence of any available material on this question, it can only be stated that Wedekind seemed to have anticipated many of the later insights of modern depth-psychology in several of his characters and plots. His mistake was the one-track-mindedness of his obsession with the physical, and the physical only. He was right in the complaint that modern literature had become a life-removed affair among and about literary and literate practitioners, but he was wrong in the belief that the remedy was to go back to people who had never read a book. He ignored the mind and it took him considerable time until he realized that instinct and lust could also turn out to be negative forces. That is why Wedekind was fond of the world of the circus and its people, of muscle-men, of the demi-monde, and prostitutes and their like, because all these anti-literate characters lived closest to what was for him life and possessed most of what he thought was the soul of the flesh. And that is why he became defensive and apologetic when he modified his belief in his second creative phase.

Wedekind might best be classified as a Post-Romanticist with a mania for sex. He prophetically foresaw a revolt of the body against the inhibitions of a hypocritical pseudo-morality of the bourgeois grown fat and lazy. He was one of the first to express what the Germans call "Körpergefühl" (a feeling for bodily harmony), and during his lifetime he was almost the only one to tackle the ticklish topics of nudity, physical education of women, healthier and more becoming fashions, sex education in school, etc. He was a moralist par excellence. His was not a great mind. He was the typical bohemian who always singles out one object for unrelenting attack and in his occupation with single trees loses sight of the forest. He was a lonely, provocative often grotesque and always interesting enemy of bourgeois morality. He is Germany's less profound and less sophisticated substitute for Bernard Shaw.

As a literary craftsman, Wedekind reveals the ambiguity of his mental make-up and the bohemian's inability to achieve true measure and carefully worked-out proportion. For that reason only very few of his creations are completely satisfying from an aesthetic point of view: of the plays, *Awakening of Spring,* and *Earth Spirit* perhaps, and of his prose *The Fire of Egliswyl.* Artistically, there are many faults in his dramas: accidents play an undue part, improbabilities occur, plots tumble, curtain lines and exits are often weak, characters remain mostly caricatures, and the language shifts between verse and prose for no apparent reason within the same drama, sometimes even within one act. Of course, some of these critical objections would seem to be petty to the author, who obviously was aware of them. They prove that Wedekind always aimed at stylization (in order to drive home a point more effectively), and that he was at no time a realistic or naturalistic writer. . . . (pp. 89-90)

Furthermore, outside of the theater one hardly ever hears a dialogue like Wedekind's. It is a queer mixture of odd clichés, newspaper style, legal idioms, preaching editorials, violent outbursts, strong invectiveness, purple phrases, mediocre verses, tasteless images, genuine poetry and, occasionally, normal everyday speech. There has never been anything like it in the history of modern German drama. Since his heroes are just as

obsessed with some central idea or quality as their creator was when he conceived them, Wedekind's characters are incapable of the art of conversation; they are constantly at cross purposes; they monologize when they talk to each other; they hardly ever listen; they are too busy explaining themselves. The dialogue becomes a concentration of simultaneous monologues. This psychological exhibitionism of tearing one's inside out (so characteristic of German conversation) is probably one of the reasons why Wedekind is little suited to the Anglo-Saxon stage where underplaying is the desired style of acting. No Wedekind part can be underplayed, and even the German actors of the naturalistic era were unable to do full justice to the intentions of the author. He constantly feuded with them, made them responsible for some of his critical failures and finally, although neither trained nor gifted as an actor, he appeared (often together with his actress wife) in many of his own plays and, indeed, scored great triumphs with audiences all over Germany. Although he was too often bent on shocking his public at any price, and allowed himself many lapses into distastefulness and grotesque exaggeration, the fact remains that he—and he almost alone—saw through the inadequacy of traditional realistic psychology at a time when Europe's stages were filled with weakly pseudo-intellectuals à la Ibsen and Hauptmann. He aimed at a dialogue which would break through conventional patterns and bare the deeper layers where the real decisions are made in the human sphere: the subconscious. He tried to follow the hidden logic of the instinct. In *Earth Spirit* and *Marquis von Keith* he came close to the ideal; and these plays might conceivably be studied by future dramatists or be revived in times tired of the realistic theater of today. On the other hand, Wedekind's dialogue is at the same time his doom and the chief reason why many of his dramas seem beyond rescue on account of linguistic stiltedness and exasperating clichés. Wedekind often lacks the proper word or the fitting phrase and, similar to Eugene O'Neill, generally damages his writing through an apparent deficiency in artistic intelligence. (pp. 90-1)

It is customary to link Wedekind with the Expressionistic Movement. However, it should be pointed out that he remained indifferent to their young leaders. . . . However, he influenced the expressionists more than any other German dramatist of the older generation, and since they dominated Germany's stages after 1918, they carried him to general acclaim. . . . Thus, he must be considered a lonely forerunner of the expressionist movement in the twentieth century. His influence upon writers like Heinrich Mann, Bert Brecht and Friedrich Dürrenmatt is manifest, and since the latter two are Germany's outstanding contemporary dramatists, Wedekind represents an important link in the development of modern drama. Should the theater ever outgrow its current phase of deadening timidity all over the world, Frank Wedekind's undervalued stock is bound to rise again. (p. 92)

> *Claude Hill, "Wedekind in Retrospect," in* Modern Drama *(copyright* Modern Drama, *University of Toronto), Vol. 3, No. 1, May, 1960, pp. 82-92.*

ALEX NATAN   (essay date 1963)

Since the death of [Christian Friedrick] Hebbel and [Franz] Grillparzer German drama had only been a pale reflection of its great past. At about 1890, however, a spirit of fertile, if not revolutionary unrest began to make itself felt in Germany. A period of creative activity set in such as the German stage had rarely experienced before or ever since. A new "Sturm und Drang" burst forth using multiple forms of poetic expression and aiming often at diverse goals. Gerhart Hauptmann wrote his naturalistic plays and Hermann Sudermann dramatically chronicled the "juste milieu" of Wilhelminian Germany. At the same time the first poems of Stefan George displayed a tendency towards a Neo-Romanticism while the young prodigy, Hugo von Hofmannsthal, confessed to a new Symbolism in his remarkable verses. To this vanguard Frank Wedekind belonged but did not acknowledge any aesthetic doctrine, even though his first major play *Frühlings Erwachen* (**Spring's Awakening**) . . . showed distinct naturalistic descriptions and confessed to a romantic mood. In the last act of his drama Wedekind undertook the breakthrough to a grotesque symbolism, which was desinted to pave the way to German Expressionism and Surrealism, and which Friedrich Dürrenmatt's plays still re-echo seventy years later.

Frühlings Erwachen is the first German "Erziehungsdrama" and was followed by a number of similar plays. Wedekind has set his *Kindertragödie* among adolescents standing on the threshold of their so ambivalent puberty. Novalis had already observed that "We are too fond of calling children blessed, and are apt to forget that though they may in truth more lightly rejoice they suffer immeasurably more deeply than adults". The sufferings of awakening children is the theme of Wedekind's tragedy. . . . He confronts his juvenile characters with somewhat unrealistic persons who, through their grotesque distortion, are unable to act as real antagonists. More than once in his plays Wedekind is carried away into dramatically dubious situations by his hatred for middle-class prudery and by his wrath against the mustiness of a mendacious bourgeois morality. But there can be little doubt that this tragedy belongs to the great plays of lasting importance because it admirably invokes the troubled spirit of young people worried by their stirring sexuality which they cannot master physically or emotionally. This drama displays such a deep comprehension of the adolescent psyche as Wedekind never again was able to show. Those who see in *Frühlings Erwachen* no more than a call to sexual licentiousness must surely consider the subject matter trivial and dull, and its text insufferably old-fashioned. But this tragedy, echoing the tormenting experience of the poet himself, embraces something imperishable, something which has remained dramatically unparalleled because it stands in tragic contrast to a perishable convention. One must see through the text, the scenes and characters, which were very likely conceived transparent on purpose, in order to understand Wedekind's genius and his contorted intentions. To grope for the hidden meaning, disguised under dramatic artifices, is the only possible approach to an appreciation of Wedekind's works in our times. "The primitive, eternal moral that the most miserable life is preferable to death is proclaimed in an entirely new way."

The lack of a unified style is already noticeable in this early masterpiece. Moods prevail which create their own, permanently changing style. In the sequence of scenes, which are really only dialogues, a secret unity, a dramatic urgency are clearly dominant. Actions and moods end together in this vernal storm of youthful awakening. Wedekind's tragedy of childhood has remained his only play which shows an intimate awareness of Nature. This mood for landscape, his delicate reaction to the seasons present an essential element in this drama of awakening eroticism, which shows the poet a worthy descendant of [Georg] Büchner's *Wozzeck* and brings to mind his tremendous influence on the expressionistic plays of a later period. . . . *Frühlings Erwachen* is Wedekind's first, timid attempt to preach the revolt of the male slaves against the ["Feudalism of Love".]

The poet does not yet crack his whip but lets the tormented creature speak up for himself. But the last scene already contains Wedekind's philosophy: only he who is willing to jump over open graves will find life interesting and rewarding.

Melchior Gabor is already such an apprentice of the fine art of living. . . . Eternal youth breathes in Melchior Gabor, in his love for Wendla Bergmann, in their mutual melancholic friend, Moritz Stiefel, and, above all, in Hänschen Rilow, the valiant knight of romantic illusions, who becomes the captive of his own sensuality so willingly. The boys linger and loiter in the school playground or stand at street corners then as now. The girls are still widely ignorant and cast uninhibited glances across to the boys. But their smile is already seductive, accompanied by an occasional innocent but telling gesture. . . . The time comes when the boys stand apart wrapped up in secret speculations. The gust of spring has shaken them. They do not sense whence it blows into their blood. Moritz Stiefel gropes about like a blind man and suffers already "Lebensangst" ["Fear of Life"] which will become such a significant feature in German Literature. His friend Melchior is already worldly-wise by instinct, for he has observed a lot and drawn his own conclusions. He is quite prepared to take Moritz Stiefel in tow and provide the rudiments of sexual enlightenment. But his friend shows all the timidity of children in face of a sterling reality. He rather prefers to fathom the mystery of Nature from readings of forbidden books. Melchior provides him with the book of knowledge which turns out a fatal promissory note and will prove his doom. But nobody enlightens the girls. . . . The impotence and hypocrisy of the respectable middle classes stand revealed as a telling accusation against a doomed society. The play is, however, also filled with pure, elemental poetry responsible for the delicate shades and rare moods of tenderness and budding love. When Melchior meets Wendla in the woods, the dark impulses of their blood interfere with their childlike stammerings. Melchior beats her with cruelty and passion, as he has not yet learnt the message of tender caress. In this and in other scenes the absurdity of expecting a logical behaviour of adolescents is underlined but also the disturbing oscillation between the Ego and the Thou proved. The unforgettable conversation between Hänschen Rilow and his friend Ernst Röbel in the vineyard, high above the river, when both boys drink the juice of ripe grapes and dream of the happiness of maturity, belongs to one of the outstanding confessions of modern German drama. . . . (pp. 104-07)

Never again has Wedekind written anything so tender as this dialogue. Wherever the blind Eros will shoot his arrows like lightning out of the blue he will cause unfathomable havoc. This central problem of the *Kindertragödie* explains sufficiently why *Frühlings Erwachen* will stay alive when the rest of Wedekind's work might only interest the literary historian. It is the gift of the poet to convey the deeper meaning of groping conversations of adolescents which is so revealing. There is the brief scene when Wendla looks for Melchior in the hayloft and surrenders to his bewildered lust without resistance. Truthfulness cannot be uttered more heart-wrenchingly. (p. 108)

Wedekind attempted in *Frühlings Erwachen* to show the sexual instinct as an archetypal force of life, a theme which he consequently treated and varied in all his other works. In their centre stand men of impulse and instinct, unspoilt by the shallow conventions of morality of doubtful value. Melchior Gabor is wholly given over to his desires and enjoys instinctively the sport of jumping over open graves. Moritz Stiefel represents the helpless victim of life, whom his stunted instincts drive to his early death. Wedekind, the missionary of a new morality, is therefore not afraid to appear as Life and later, in the disguise of the sexual maniac Jack the Ripper, as Death (*Pandora's Box*). The somewhat shadowy character of Ilse will soon ripen into Lulu, into Klara Hühnerwadel (*Musik*), into Effi (*Castle Wetterstein*) and finally into Franziska. The grotesque popinjays of the school staff will recur. . . . They provide the sounding-board in almost every play of Wedekind, since he was not concerned with their moral or social significance but only with their appearance of serving as intellectual inventions. Wedekind always drew his effects from radical contrasts, even if the antagonists will not come convincingly to life. What mattered for him were the protagonists. . . . (pp. 109-10)

Wedekind's fame in Germany is based on his play *Lulu*. . . . In order to circumvent the rigid censorship against which the playwright fought a running battle throughout his life, he divided it into separate parts: [*Erdgeist (Earth Spirit)* and *(Die Büchse der Pandora (Pandora's Box)*)]. . . .

Wedekind, like D. H. Lawrence, was obsessed and possessed with the destructive power that sex so often exerts in a society which represses and abuses it. Wedekind wanted to be looked upon as the prophet of a new society. When the very society, however, whose shallow moral he pilloried, regarded him as a clown, he donned . . . the fool's cap to draw compelling attention to his message. This was not a voluntary disguise but forced upon him by his contemporaries, an act which made him suffer throughout his life. In *Lulu* he put the dregs of society on the stage, those confidence tricksters, sexual murderers, thieves, whores, white-slave traffickers and athletes, of whom Wedekind was convinced they alone still displayed natural, naked and genuine desires. They all move like puppets, manipulated by a fanatic seeker of truth, around Lulu, the woman identical with the elemental principle of destruction. (p. 110)

Wedekind sets out to show the archetypal character of Woman whose name may be Eva, Lilith, Lulu: "The principle remains always the same." To outline the contents of the tragedy to an unprepared listener would invite today his protest, for they must appear to him as mere colportage from the back stairs. . . . Wedekind conjures up the grotesque world of a penny dreadful. It is the deliberate purpose of the playwright to blow up the action to gigantic proportions, in order to justify the reduction of the consequences to their utmost logical conclusions. Wedekind coarsens his characters to such an extent that they become puppets out of all dimensions, so that their shadows fall pointedly on the reality. Lulu breaks into the world of bourgeois respectability and this world turns into a macabre Punch and Judy show. Once more it will not do to judge this play from its external events. One must try to fathom the poet's intentions by analysing the meaning behind the action. The play is indeed called *Lulu,* but Lulu is no longer an acting part of importance, once the surfeit of eroticism has become simply pathetic, if not downright funny, as it must appear to an audience in our own times. . . . The tragedy does not turn around Lulu but draws its profound meaning through her. All Lulu does, is the result of her dynamic originality, the emanation of a blind force of Nature. The biblical story of the alliance between Woman and Serpent assumes a new significance: both possess the irresistible charm of seduction and loquacity to deliver Man to his perdition, without desiring anything else but his virility. Both have possessed him completely when they succeed in destroying him. Their counterpart is therefore the man who is able, out of sheer impotence, to murder a woman, in order to

possess her only in this dreadful moment. If man and wife act as destructive forces, both remain beautiful and terrible like real forces of Nature. . . . Because Lulu has challenged and flaunted all conventions of a bourgeois society she is doomed to finish her life in filth and in indescribable horror. It is the revenge of this society that Jack the Ripper, a sinister symbol of human depravity, becomes her butcher.

Lulu, a "somnambulist of love", means the naked manifestation of the everlasting sexual urge, always creating anew, always destroying afresh, always remaining the same. Therefore Man executes his obtrusive dance around this golden calf: the nakedness of Lulu. (pp. 111-13)

Between the two parts of the *Lulu* tragedy Wedekind wrote a comedy in praise of a confidence trickster [*Marquis von Keith*]. His character is a cynical mountebank who wages war against the stupidity of the "juste milieu". But the deceiver finds himself ultimately cheated. This conclusion only underlines the moral and social process of corrosion, clearly noticeable in Wilhelminian Germany. All traditional values become depreciated. (p. 115)

The daring spirit of the Marquis shows itself in his magnificent schemes and designs. This bold adventurer aims so high that he loses sight of the nearest hurdles. He leaps blindly across abysses where other people would fall in. But he comes to grief at the slightest obstacle which the average man knows very well how to circumvent. An opportunist like the Marquis . . . will always lose to the stolid and consistent prudence of the "juste milieu". . . . The Marquis is confronted with a counterpart, another modern Don Quixote, a nobleman of fluid circumstances: Ernst Scholz, alias Graf Trautenau. He wants the Marquis to teach him complete enjoyment of life, and he does so. . . . The Marquis, accustomed to living on credit, welcomes the fortune of his friend which he intends to use for a new fraudulent coup in Munich, involving millions of marks. For he possesses the gift of creating scintillating illusions out of nothing. The world will always admire confidence tricksters as long as they do not commit any mistakes. It will never pardon stupidity, even if it understands it. For the cleverness of genius is the only justification for a criminal's existence. (p. 116)

Even today the *Marquis von Keith* will exercise a considerable effect when staged with a superb actor. Life has become a tremendous switchback since the death of the playwright, though our society still possesses sufficient moral discrimination to brand a confidence trickster as a permanent outsider of society. But as long as our form of society remains an unstable economic entity, a clever man will go on trying to outwit his fellow-man by means which the very society will supply him with. Far more than *Lulu* this play may prove in the hands of an imaginative producer to be one of the most essential and significant dramas of our times. (pp. 117-18)

Wedekind's poetry has been collected under the title *Die Vier Jahreszeiten*. . . . Torment, lust and sensuality are usually their central theme. Some sound like French frivolities, others like laments for a world from which the gods have departed. In these poems one senses [Heinrich] Heine's wit and derision. It is again youth and its impudence which now leaps across the fallen and broken statues of the expelled gods. One is never quite sure whether it is mocking laughter or a veiled weeping which echoes from this poetry. Satyros is the final conquering hero and Wedekind his devotee. Even if the alluring tones of the lute in the evening or the note of pensive reflection are sometimes heard, Wedekind never displays the pure innocence of a real lyrist. . . . (p. 121)

Wedekind did not possess the love of the creator but only the dubious obsession of the destroyer. He showed little compassion for human nature. His almost pathological occupation of "épater le bourgeois" [shocking the bourgeois] has brought him only the thorny crown of a clown. His "idée fixe" began early to bore people by its repetition. Here lies the fundamental difference from D. H. Lawrence, with whom Wedekind is often compared in Germany. Making up one's mind about Lawrence is a task nobody has been able to avoid since his death. As one reads Lawrence, one is made increasingly aware of how he changed the lives of subsequent generations. It is impossible to pass the same verdict on Wedekind. Lawrence perceived life as a human struggle for a better, healthier future, while Wedekind remained a grotesque reflection of his own generation. While Lawrence loved life in all its manifestations and assigned to sex its rightful place, Wedekind distorted it by his flirtation with death, which is the destruction of life. The discovery of Lawrence is still a tremendous experience for young people today, because they sense kindred moods and attitudes in his novels. Wedekind's real and often tragic intentions remain incomprehensible to any young German reader if he finds his way to Wedekind at all. Frank Wedekind, despite his importance as a pioneer of modern German literature, shares only the fate of those many German poets and playwrights, eager to set loose a new "Sturm und Drang": occasionally mentioned, insufficiently known and hardly appreciated. (pp. 122-23)

> Alex Natan, "Frank Wedekind," in German Men of Letters: Twelve Literary Essays, Vol. II, edited by Alex Natan (©1963 Oswald Wolff (Publishers) Limited, London), Wolff, 1963, pp. 101-30.

SOL GITTLEMAN   (essay date 1969)

Given the nature of Frank Wedekind's argument with civilization, it is not surprising that he became one of the most controversial figures in the history of German literature. He was a most "unpleasant" writer. Wedekind was the first German writer, indeed, almost the first western writer, to use Freud's thesis that "civilization is based on the permanent subjugation of the human instincts." Now, no society likes to think of itself as subjugating its instincts, and the society of Wedekind's time took his insinuation as a direct attack—just as it was intended. But Wedekind was always an "engaged" writer, and his conflict with the world around him was clearly brought on by him quite intentionally. Like his spiritual mentor Friedrich Nietzsche, Wedekind wanted a changed order, a liberated society free from the limitations of a traditional, repressive culture, one uninhibited by taboos. He rejected a world order which, he felt, had for centuries cultivated man the worker, not man the pleasure-seeker.

Wedekind sought for a new kind of relationship between the human being and his biological instincts, which, he insisted, had become incompatible with one another, in the light of civilized society. He hoped to show that mankind's energies needed redirection, back to a more primitive, instinctive form which would allow for a freer, more natural, fundamentally more honest life. (p. 1)

Wedekind was first and foremost a dramatist. . . . His great passion was the theater, and he found his first model in the German dramatist Georg Büchner. . . . Through all of Büchner

runs the bleak fatalism of a visionary playwright who sees society as depraved and incorrigible. Büchner also created a technical corollary to this philosophical nihilism by dislocating and disrupting the structure of his plays in a fashion which found its ultimate echo in the German Expressionists a hundred years later. Scene rushes in upon scene, phrase vies with phrase. Büchner drew from a linguistic heritage rooted in Shakespeare, the commedia dell' arte, and the gutter. Allied to this violent world of negation is a black humor which makes Büchner's few dramatic writings among the most grotesque in all of dramatic literature.

From the very outset Büchner's dramatic inventiveness had a major influence on Wedekind's writings for the stage. The hilarious is never far from the universally serious. The concept was more important than the characterization, and as a result, characterization was often replaced by caricature. Actually, almost half of Wedekind's plays are labeled as comedies, and, like Anton Chekhov, he had the unique ability to create in his dramatic works a tragicomic sense that marks his plays as being beyond the normal pale of dramatic convention.

Wedekind's first serious effort at dramatic writing served as a prelude for what came later to be known as "the Wedekind style." *Der Schnellmaler oder Kunst und Mammon* . . . gave Wedekind an opportunity to try out the ideas which would mature eventually in the later works. In the best tradition of the Viennese popular "Volksstück," Wedekind employs every trick of dramatic gamesmanship so well-known on the Austrian and German stage: disguises, eavesdropping, an endless flow of letters, farcical entrances and exits demonstrate that Wedekind knew the popular stage of his time. . . . (pp. 32-3)

No doubt, *Der Schnellmaler* is little more than a trivial situation comedy with distinctly farcical overtones, but one notices particular qualities and concepts which Wedekind never abandoned. Already at this stage, Wedekind demonstrates a thorough dislike for the "homo economicus," the business man whose primary instinct is the making of money. (p. 33)

Even in this first dramatic work, with its traditional elements of folk burlesque, Wedekind's sense of the comic stands out as something quite distinctive. Fridolin's urge for self-destruction, for all its farcical qualities, still gives the entire play an an aura of death, which is never far from the comic. . . . The good humor of the work is constantly undercut by this proximity of death, and the reader suspects that Fridolin may ultimately succeed in his suicide attempts and plunge the story into some unexpected tragic sphere. But Wedekind is careful never to delineate his characters so well as to involve the audience with their actions. . . . When the satire bites, it is directed inevitably against the businessmen. But fundamentally Wedekind's humor in *Der Schnellmaler* is benign, and the caricatures are never really destructive. Furthermore, no consideration is given to the theme of sexuality. Thus it is convenient for those critics who would concentrate on the erotic aspects of Wedekind's art to dismiss this work as a false start. Yet, clearly, *Der Schnellmaler* is the obvious first step, when viewed in respect to all of Wedekind's subsequent plays. Even the dialogue is singularly his own. He abandons any sense of psychological motivation and verisimilitude and creates a language and tension which, even for the 1880's, was strikingly his own. The characters do not communicate with one another, talk past each other, and in effect exist in total isolation from the action of the play. . . . Through these devices Wedekind retains the responsibility for his characters and never permits them to develop along naturalistic lines. Behind the burlesque aspects of the play one can see a more significant development for the later more serious plays, when this style would create a sense of complete alienation. But even in *Der Schnellmaler* there are clear hints of things to come. (pp. 34-5)

Wedekind very early sensed a link between the "homo economicus" and the fundamental antipathy to a free, unrestricted eroticism. Throughout his plays, he parades a long line of social, economic, and sexual predatory types, robber barons of sex and society, who demonstrate a lust for power both financial and physical. Dedicated to the accumulation of wealth, these men inevitably come into conflict with an either sexually or morally emancipated representative of Wedekind's "positive" forces and ruthlessly go about destroying all efforts to accomplish a transformation of mankind's ethics. These "Raubtiere" [beast of prey] are the surrogates of the economically oriented, rational, and civilization-conditioned society which Wedekind persistently attacks, but which inevitably win out. These individuals are consistently power hungry . . . and extend this insatiable lust for power to the physical sphere, a "body and soul" domination of others. (p. 37)

[In *Frühlings Erwachen*,] as in no other of his works [is] Wedekind . . . so clearly the zealot, deliberately distorting his vision of the human condition to present the allegory of good and evil. When Eric Bentley states that Wedekind's world is totally devoid of any morality, one might suspect that he is missing the essential point of *Frühlings Erwachen* [see excerpt above]. In this bitter, often cynical diatribe against inhumanity, Wedekind collides with the accepted puritanical morality of his age and advocates a new standard of education, for adult and adolescent alike. But the traditional criticism for *Frühlings Erwachen* from the first was based on the assumption that the play was pornographic and obscene, and that its author nihilistically smashed the existing social order without supplying a substitute. (pp. 51-2)

What Wedekind had to say was closely related to the manner in which he said it, and for that he needed "The Wedekind style," which for the first time came to complete fruition in *Frühlings Erwachen.* Deeply tragic scenes mingle with moments of hilarious farce; endless speeches mouthed by dehumanized marionettes are followed by the staccato dialogue of children-poets. Psychological and dramatic motivation disappears, as scene after scene races by in a whirling of dynamic tension. The stage is estranged from reality. . . . (p. 52)

Wedekind's flexibility deserves mention at this point. He completely abandoned the poetic seriousness of his theme in *Frühlings Erwachen* to write what is his most enduring comic work. *Fritz Schwigerling,* later renamed *Der Liebestrank,* was admittedly inspired by his fascination with the circus, and Wedekind poured into this farce all the gaiety which he could muster. He immortalized his friend Rudinoff in the character of Schwigerling, who embodies all the attractive qualities of the strong-man, bareback rider, ringmaster, and above all, the educator which Wedekind saw as the ultimate function of this exuberant figure. The hero demonstrates a tremendous vitality and elasticity which places him far above the maddening crowd of little people who dash about him. He is the doer, the activist. . . . (p. 53)

Schwigerling is the first fully developed "Kraftsmensch" [strong man] created by Wedekind, the author's conscious emissary on stage and the embodiment of the "Übermensch" [superman] as Wedekind saw him. He always is the ringmaster, and with a magnificent flair, even in the grimmest situations, is quite

in control of matters. Schwigerling's interest in the whole business is a passing one, an entr'acte, a sort of one-night stand between his endless engagements. He is not governed by the petty laws which rule other men, and as a result he is capable of performing some incredible feats. . . . He is also a serious educational theoretician, and his esthetic principles are constantly serving as the foil to Rogoschin's alcoholic ravings. (pp. 56-7)

In spite of the burlesque nature of the play, *Der Liebestrank* represents a significant aspect of Wedekind's art. There is a clear moral intent, an extension of the "Fleischmoral" [the body's law] of *Frühlings Erwachen* with its plea for sexual enlightenment. In *Der Liebestrank* Wedekind offers a companion esthetic to that of freedom from sexual oppression, as he argues for full appreciation of "the body's soul," as well as for the acceptance of physical spirituality as fundamentally more honest than the traditional sort. As in his earlier plays, the implication is obvious: civilization denies man his instincts.

It was merely a short step from the esthetics of motion of *Der Liebestrank* to a more complete expression of physical perfection and grace. Wedekind's interest in the ballet was a natural outcome of . . . the revived interest in this art form which Nietzsche initiated. It was in Nietzsche most likely that Wedekind found the spiritual connection between his own innate theories of physical beauty and the rejection of civilization as a positive force. His four pantomimes represent the absolute abandonment of the limitations imposed by theatrical necessity in favor of a Dyonisian primitivism of pure theater. Wedekind leaped over two thousand years back to the original nature of the dance as a religious experience of erotic conception and fantasy. These works are totally physical as well as imaginative. It appears that Wedekind, in his contempt for the language of civilization, adopted a form which freed him from the necessities of any sort of intellectual articulation. Gesture and the physical motion of the dance were his only tools here, and the intent was to employ these to revive the mythic, sensual nature of the ancient dance form as it was recognized in pagan times. It should come as no surprise that, of all of Wedekind's works, his pantomimes are by far the most erotic and overtly sexual. (pp. 57-8)

In his ballets as nowhere else Wedekind approached the doctrine of "Art for Art's Sake"; and, certainly [*Die Flöhe, oder Der Schmerzentanz* (The Fleas, or the Dance of Pain)] is a break in Wedekind's moralizing posture. It is light and frivolous, and yet one detects certain hallmarks of the Wedekind stagecraft. . . . Since he was unable *to speak* of animals, Wedekind simply filled the stage with them, and the chorus of fleas gives the work the flavor of a romantic bestiary, much like the menageries encountered in the preceding plays. But, above all, there is the emphasis on motion. Wedekind's directions for the technical aspects of the ballet are surprisingly professional and specific, and the pantomime is constantly punctuated by a wide variety of classical ballet dances, as well as those more often found in the music halls of Paris. (pp. 58-9)

Wedekind's use of pantomime represents an important step for him and for the development of the art form itself. Initially, it is the culmination of his efforts to escape the drab, sociologically based theater of his generation. By withdrawing completely from the necessities of verbal expression he was able to minimize the importance of language. (p. 62)

Up to this point in his development, Wedekind had concentrated on male characters in employing either spokesmen or ideal types to represent his moral and philosophical position. (p. 64)

Wedekind now turned all of his attention to his image of the woman's role in society. [It] was evident that, typically, he was running counter to the mainstream of the women's emancipation movement and the efforts of the female to "defeminize" herself. The only other contemporary writer to deal with the problem of the "Eternal Feminine" was August Strindberg, but ultimately Strindberg's combativeness in such matters led him to assume his legendary negative attitude. For him the power of the female over the male was a destructive force, violently undermining the survival of humanity. In his plays and novels, a similar status is given to the woman; she has been elevated to a role of mythic proportions. As in Wedekind's works, Strindberg's mythical treatment takes on the nature of a sexual struggle, with the resulting victory of the female's sexual drive destroying a helplessly struggling male victim. But Strindberg laments this situation, whereas Wedekind glorifies it. It is the instinctive power of Eros which, for Wedekind, could rid civilization of its repressiveness. [He] particularly deplores and ridicules those women who would attain equality with men by voluntarily denying their womanhood. . . . Wedekind created his Lulu as the personification of the eternal struggle between sex and society. (pp. 64-5)

Lulu was Wedekind's single most imposing symbol of his fight against civilization. She represents the antithesis of a civilized society, someone totally alien to the everyday world of reality. Lulu represents for Wedekind mankind in his precivilized state, innocent and unpsychological, instinctive and supercharged with a strength which has become sublimated in modern society. In its present form, society has progressed to the stage where the likes of Lulu have been purged. Civilization had bypassed the instincts, Wedekind felt. In creating her and by placing her once again into the mainstream of a civilization which had progressed beyond her, Wedekind was hoping to establish a conflict.

The result is a brutal collision of intelligence and primal instinct, with no holds barred. For a time, anarchy runs loose on the stage. In this struggle between the unknown and the known, psychological meaning, accepted realities, and discursive thought are condemned, as Wedekind weaves the fabric of his theater of cruelty. (pp. 65-7)

Wedekind represents two sides of the artist's mentality in the first of his confessional dramas, *Der Kammersänger (The Tenor . . .),* a one-act play which ultimately became the most performed of his dramatic works as well as a standard anthology piece. One aspect of the artist is depicted by Gerardo. . . . Wedekind himself described Gerardo as "a brutal intelligence, a blown-up Philistine soul," but one who is trapped and controlled by an adoring public. Yet he considers himself the epitome of artistic success, the object of nightly applause. (pp. 80-1)

[Professor Dühring] has spent his entire life in devotion to his art, but has never had one single work performed or published. At seventy, Dühring remains in every fiber of his being the artist who will not bend to the public's desires. A proud, lonely man, he comes now to Gerardo to beg. . . . (p. 81)

Wedekind's sense of irony is too highly developed to make the Gerardo-Dühring conflict a black-and-white confrontation of artless cynicism and artistic idealism. His self-pity does not go so far as make the ancient professor his symbol of righteous defiance, the truly great artist scorned by society. For Dühring

is *not* a genius, or at least Wedekind prefers not to take him too seriously. . . . Wedekind's reference to his own artistic merit is not the only instance of sardonic irony which we encounter in this group of plays which are intended to define the cleavage between artist and audience.

In *Der Kammersänger* Wedekind explored the relationship of the artist to his public by contrasting the values of two men. Having found the formula, he plays with variations of it in *Der Marquis von Keith.* . . . In *Keith* Wedekind goes in for some fairly extensive self-analysis in exploring what he considered the two souls within himself: the amoral, detached artist living outside of society, and the committed moralist who wants to improve it. From all indications, Wedekind, at this time of his life, saw himself in the role of the amoralist, but there always gnawed deep inside him the thoughts that he would be happiest living within a society that could accept him. (pp. 83-4)

The problem which Wedekind solved for himself in *Keith* is that of the choice between alternatives: renunciation in the face of defeat or continuation of the struggle, although the world considers you an outsider. Keith, with "his coarse red hands of a clown" and his limp, mocked by society and scorned as a rogue, laughs and goes on. His decision *to continue* the struggle was also Wedekind's.

Between the writing of *Keith* and his next play, *König Nicolo,* Wedekind served his jail sentence for "Majestätsbeleidigung" [offending the Kaiser]. The impact of that experience was most significant for him; given the particular autobiographical bent of the two previous plays, Wedekind's reaction to what he considered a monumental travesty of justice was naturally channeled into *König Nicolo.* The energetic tone of *Der Kammersänger* and *Keith* gives way to an uncharacteristically elegiac mood, one that borders on self-pity, as Wedekind moves closer and closer to a more complete identification with the protagonist. (pp. 87-8)

[During the years between 1897 and 1905 Wedekind] shifted the focus of his artistic vision from the universal problems of man and his society to the specific problem of *a* man and his relationship to the world around him. The man was Frank Wedekind, and society was declared guilty as charged of the heinous crime of ridiculing or ignoring the true artist.

But Wedekind did not spare himself in his accusations. Dühring [and Nicolo] are also guilty of a serious crime, ironically: they take themselves too seriously, and their inflexibility causes their destruction. Keith almost succumbs at the end, but manages to ward off the temptation. The often exaggerated pathos of the fallen heroes of Wedekind's confessional plays is what saves them from becoming morbid expressions of a self-pitying artist, for one sees Wedekind viewing Wedekind with some misgivings. Yet, there can be little question that these . . . plays constitute one of the most complete autobiographical statements to be found in all of German literature. . . . (pp. 95-6)

[The] plays of the last decade of Wedekind's life develop no new thematic material, but return again and again to the successful formulas of the earlier works. . . . (p. 103)

Franziska is one of the most successful of his late plays, for Wedekind forced himself away from the themes he had been dealing with over the years; and the new material breathed a freshness into an airy mixture of prose and verse which forms the body of this "modern mysterium." From Goethe Wedekind took the free theatrical inventiveness of *Faust;* and for the first time since *Frühlings Erwachen* he moved out of a fourth-wall conventional set into the free air.

Yet there is much vintage Wedekind. Who else but Wedekind would have created a female Faust? . . .

Wedekind stays remarkably close to the action in Goethe's play, and the parallels are obvious throughout. . . . For the first time in years, Wedekind's language takes on the hypnotic quality which is so typical of the earlier plays. Lofty artistic insights alternate with obscenities and a seemingly uncontrolled stream-of-consciousness. The hackneyed and the esoteric blend in this most interesting scene; and for a moment, Wedekind is at his very best. (p. 114)

It is almost inconceivable that Wedekind should have written a play in justification of conventional marriage and motherhood, two institutions which he battled for most of his adult life. But when we consider the extent to which his personal experiences find their way into his literary works, it makes somewhat more sense. (pp. 115-16)

Wedekind's "Freudenmädchen" has run the full cycle. She has come home to roost, after a tempestuous history of freedom from society, a confrontation which resulted in society's destruction, and finally society's revenge. What had been an instinctive, primal urge for gratification of the life-instinct settles down to a placid acceptance of the social responsibilities within the framework of a civilized, mature culture. Lulu has finally been domesticated. Franziska's renunciation of dissatisfaction represents the taming of "das wilde, schöne Tier" [the wild, beautiful animal], which was her essential nature at the beginning of her search for happiness. Wedekind has abandoned Eros in favor of civilization. (p. 116)

As a lyric poet, Wedekind demonstrated that he had little sympathy with the traditional meaning of the word "lyric." His poems reflect a brutality and a clinical cynicism which often go beyond the scope of what his plays reflected. In spite of this dark vision, Wedekind considered himself a folk-singer, because his material had popular roots. The poet found his particular muse in the back streets of Munich. He was one of the first German lyricists to find inspiration in city life, in the sordid realities of death, murder, and prostitution. With his guitar in hand, Wedekind sang, like a twentieth-century minstrel, of the wretchedness of his time.

Wedekind's poetry does not need "rediscovery," having inspired a whole generation of poets, beginning with Brecht whose own genius transcended the lyrical artistry of Wedekind while securing his place as a major influence. But in the case of the considerable body of Wedekind's narrative prose, there is no such influence, and as a result, the perhaps overzealous Wedekind scholar is tempted to "rediscover," to search for a significance where others have found none. For Wedekind's prose writings have elicited hardly any critical attention. These dozen short stories are rarely anthologized; and unlike his impact as a dramatist and lyricist, Wedekind's force as a writer of prose fiction has made no appreciable contribution to German or European letters. This fact is all the more astonishing, for even the most cautious critic would have to admit that a few stories merit considerable attention, and one rivals almost any short story in the German language. (p. 120)

Throughout the entire *Fürstin Russalka* collection, Wedekind consistently demonstrates his inclination for the flashback story which frames his stories. Almost invariably, the flashback takes the form of a first-person narrative, as Wedekind instinctively moves closer to a sort of dramatic monologue in the telling of his stories, until in *Rabbi Esra* he abandons narrative exterior almost completely and creates what in effect is a play with one character. (p. 125)

In *Rabbi Esra* Wedekind has set himself a difficult task: to explore the problem of sex in the life of an elderly Jew. In spite of what seems an unlikely subject, *Rabbi Esra* is one of the most moving of Wedekind's prose pieces. (p. 126)

Personally Wedekind always felt that *Rabbi Esra* was one of his most satisfying works. . . . It is one of the few expressions of his belief in the union of flesh and spirit that is in no way marred by irony or skepticism. (pp. 126-27)

By far the most significant of Wedekind's prose works is *Der Brand von Egliswyl (The Fire at Egliswyl)*, the latest and most mature of the shorter pieces. Still another first-person story, it is clearly autobiographical, and Wedekind makes no effort to hide this fact. (p. 127)

[There] is a remarkable shift in mood and temper from the outer framework story to the tale itself. Even Wedekind's prose, which is untypically realistic and discursive, and never approaches the eccentric virtuosity of much of his dramatic language, shifts in intensity. Once again the dark power of the narrative is associated with the sexual drive. (p. 218)

In this story, Wedekind comes closest to paralleling Strindberg's particular attitude toward the female. In general, it would be safe to state that whereas Strindberg was a confirmed denigrator, Wedekind was just as firm an admirer of women. But in this single narrative Wedekind demonstrates a Strindbergian misogyny. Maria systematically attempts psychologically to emasculate the otherwise uncomplicated and contented young farm lad. She is diabolical, and the contest is unequal from the start. Wedekind's conception of her is that of a representative of society's unhealthy repressions, since she controls and contains Hans's instincts until he is driven wild. But in spite of this suggested bias, Wedekind is careful enough not to allow it to intrude too overtly into the telling of the story. He allows Hans's naïvete and Maria's destructive teasing to speak for themselves; and in a coolly ironical manner, aided by the framework, the author remains detached from the action. The arsonist tells his story in his own words; and Hans's simple language, like that of Büchner's *Wozzeck,* mirrors his true nature, while the language of the frame is much more elevated and stylized. (p. 129)

Wedekind's only novel remained a fragment. . . . *Mine-Haha* is a novel of education, Wedekind's personal statement of how to bring up young women. It is a Utopian, purely theoretical novel, and Wedekind admitted that he considered it "a daydream, not concerned with the question of feasibility." (p. 130)

For all its apparent idiosyncrasies, this strange paean to physical fitness is one of Wedekind's most sincere statements. . . . [Wedekind] conceived of *Mine-Haha* as the most reasoned argument against the charges of obscenity which were still being leveled against him. His children's world is, for the most part, wholesome, if one will forgive the erotic ballet, which is, after all, meant for the jaded and genuinely obscene outside world. Wedekind tried to show innocence in its most delightful form and felt pride in bodily beauty. If this was eroticism, concluded Wedekind, it was not bad, for it was not obscene. . . . In *Mine-Haha,* Wedekind attempts to demonstrate the innocence of bodily pleasure and sexuality, which is naturally implied as the group of young people walks through the town displaying the perfection of their physical existence. He reminds his audience of an old saying by suggesting that it might apply to it: filth is in the mind of the beholder. For Wedekind, as far as his novel is concerned, the utopian world of the children is blissfully wholesome. (pp. 131-32)

Sol Gittleman, in his Frank Wedekind *(copyright ©1969 by Twayne Publishers, Inc.; reprinted with the permission of Twayne Publishers, a Division of G. K. Hall & Co., Boston), Twayne, 1969, 151 p.*

ROBERT A. JONES (essay date 1970)

While it is almost common nowadays to find Frank Wedekind numbered among the predecessors of the Theater of the Absurd, it is equally common to have the matter summarily dismissed with a few lines to the effect that Wedekind "has always been acclaimed" as a principal forerunner to the modern avant-garde (Absurd) theater, and that that theater's "debt" to him cannot be denied. . . . Now in the first place it is debatable whether Wedekind's importance for the modern theater has ever been "acclaimed" or "overestimated." . . . Wedekind's admirers have concentrated principally—and quite legitimately—on his role as a forerunner to much that took place in the theater during the Expressionist movement, and subsequently in the theater of Bertolt Brecht. But with the greater attention paid to his successors, Wedekind's position has become almost entirely an historical one, and in that quarter his significance has become very generalized. Secondly, such claims all but imply that Wedekind exerted a genuine "influence" on the much later Absurdists, although the evidence now available would not justify our assuming that they paid Wedekind's works any significant attention; at least none have acknowledged even the slightest debt to him. (p. 283)

Possibly the most strategic factor in a comparison of Wedekind and the dramatists of the Absurd, and likely the root of many of the original claims, is their common desire to make the theater more theatrical and the innovative way in which they sought to put this into practice. In Wedekind's case the majority of his innovations stemmed from a reaction against the naturalistic theater of his day, a theater that, in his opinion, was too intellectual, too wordy, and too superficial because it overlooked the real governing forces of life. He objected to the emphasis on purely social aspects, and the naturalist's attitude of reform which paid virtually no attention to the bourgeois values. (p. 284)

By contemporary standards, Wedekind's ideas of a non-intellectual theater are not remarkable, but they are indeed impressive when one considers how similar they were to what the "revolutionary" Absurdists proposed several decades later. We may immediately note that the Absurdists likewise found a source for many of the "dramatic" elements in their plays in the same unsophisticated world of the circus, varieté, and music-hall. Many of their character types (tramps, clowns, fools) and much of the stage action (the acrobatics, use of mime, and exaggerated gestures) can be traced back to these popular forms. Furthermore, in their attempts to develop an "anti-literary" theatrical style, a significant aspect of the Absurdists' experimentation was the devaluation of language as the primary medium of expression. (p. 285)

Like the Absurdists, Wedekind also achieved a certain dramatic freedom by using "language" as only one of several components. Although he became somewhat disenchanted with pure pantomime as a dramatic medium—his own pantomimes at-

tracted little attention and brought him none of the fame he hoped would come his way—he nevertheless continued to incorporate a strong mimic (visual) element in his other works. (p. 286)

[The] intrusion into the auditory plane by the visual was a device Wedekind used, not necessarily to break up the audile continuity, but to provide a separate and contrasting element in form and theme, whereby the significance of the action in the foreground is either accentuated or minimized. (p. 287)

The visual plane in Wedekind's plays less often reaches the level of metaphor, and his depictions are relatively less grotesque and less absurd than one finds in Absurdist works. This variance here in "form" can of course be explained in terms of the radical existential changes that took shape during the critical decades separating Wedekind from the Absurdists; Wedekind's attitude or "philosophy" of absurdity and despair obviously could not be as encompassing, as cosmically-proportioned as theirs: If there are implications in Wedekind's works that man's condition, unless it is changed, is unfortunate, even tragic, that possibility of change is there, and man's state is never viewed as "hopeless" by virtue of his very nature. If in the Theater of the Absurd we are confronted on stage with *the* irrationality of the human condition, Wedekind depicts, on a smaller scale, *an* irrationality of life, showing man suffering within a situation in which his true self rebels against an imposed morality, in which his experiences and desires are contrary to the demands of that morality. If the Absurdists characterize life as absurd in its lack of a goal, in its inherent purposelessness . . . , Wedekind finds it absurd only in its onesidedness. Thus despite the common grotesque element, there are basic differences in the philosophical positions from which it arises, and these differences result in distinct variances in the respective theaters.

With such differences accepted, it is nevertheless valid to recognize the similarity in the function of Wedekind's and the Absurdists' grotesquerie, i.e. to equate the sense behind it. It can be argued that a grotesque portrayal on the part of a dramatist arises from a conviction that the world of the audience was moving, or had moved, toward an extreme—conceived by the playwright as absurd and negative—and that expression in terms of an opposite extreme represents a constructive intent. Employing the grotesque to increase and underline the dissonance between the real world and the stage world, so that the spectator is confronted with a distortion that directs and forces a comparison, in other words as technique (form) to scenically express his disenchantment and disillusionment with the absurdity of that existence, the playwright is really attempting to counteract the negativity of reality. . . . If the playwrights conceive of their respective worlds in terms of despair, if these worlds appear to be absurd, chaotic, out-of-focus, wrongly oriented, and undesirable, then their treatment and formulation of it by means of the grotesque is their way of disarming it, their method, as it were, of immunization.

Another aspect common to Wedekind's and the Absurdists' dramatic method that should be evaluated is the frequent use of the tragicomic. It is often difficult to distinguish this aspect from the grotesque, since both are two-sided in nature and depend on the juxtaposition of opposite poles—the tragic and the comic, the sad and the ludicrous. Basically what distinguishes them, however, is a shift in emphasis. . . . We are dealing here simply with dramatic formulations that are less concerned with the uncanny, the demonic, with creating worried bafflement, or fright, than with logically delineating a disorientation over which one can both laugh and cry. From this standpoint, Wedekind's and the Absurdists' tragicomedy are again functionally similar and designed to achieve, consciously or unconsciously, the same results. (pp. 289-90)

[Functionally,] tragicomic formulations are in essence attempts to overcome despair by recognizing it, outlive it by living it, triumph over it by analyzing it, in other words, an artistic method of handling a problem. And this is true for Wedekind as well as for the Absurdists; but relative to the Absurdists one again has to acknowledge that Wedekind's reasons and concerns are more personal and limited in scope, less drastic, as it were. (p. 292)

Neither Wedekind nor the Absurdist succumbs to tragedy nor triumphs completely through comedy; both rather, manage to co-exist with the lamentable conditions they face. But Wedekind's can never be viewed in terms of the almost cosmic proportions which the absurdity of life itself lends to the works of the Absurdists. For both, the comedy of life and the tragedy of life point each other up, each throws the other strongly into relief. But for Wedekind, the combination and balance of the two is directed toward enabling specific man, never man in general, to bear it all.

With this closer look at the situation then, we are better able to decide whether claims of Wedekind's ''predecessor'' status are justified. On the basis of the evidence, it should be clear that, as always, generalizations can be misleading, and that Wedekind's position in this question cannot be stated so unequivocally. Once the question of direct influence has been eliminated, the terms of the Wedekind-Theater of the Absurd connection might be stated as follows: On the level of theatrical technique and method, the reduction of language and subsequent elevation of mimic action so frequent in the Theater of the Absurd had been tried and executed much earlier by Wedekind—and in much the same spirit: from a strikingly similar belief in the theatricality of the stage, both Wedekind and the later Absurdists sought to overcome the inadequacies of the conventional theater of their respective eras. Wedekind's four pantomimes, representing the most radical form of the mimic element in general, attest to his efforts toward the incorporation of that element in the theater, and are doubtless the origin of the attention he paid to the mimic element throughout his career. Perhaps more than any other playwright before him, Wedekind's attention to, and concern with, this element give his plays their peculiarly visual character, and point to the similarity between his dramatic philosophy and that of more contemporary figures. (pp. 292-93)

> Robert A. Jones, ''Frank Wedekind: A German Dramatist of the Absurd?'' in Comparative Drama (© copyright 1970, by the Editors of Comparative Drama), Vol. 4, No. 2, Summer, 1970, pp. 283-95.

MARTIN ESSLIN   (essay date 1974)

Wedekind's rejection of naturalism was based on his contempt for the small-mindedness of the naturalists, the narrowness of their political and social aims and the pettiness of their concern with the reproduction of external detail. . . . Wedekind despised the respectable, social-democratic reformism of a man like Gerhart Hauptmann who tried to improve society without attacking its true basis, bourgeois morality. He saw himself as far more destructive, far less healthy and wholesome, but for that very reason far more *modern*, than Hauptmann. . . . (pp. 527-28)

The significance of naturalism in the development of Modernism in drama lay with its adoption of the scientific attitude by postulating that, ultimately, *truth* was the highest value, and that beauty without truth was a contradiction in terms. The description of external surfaces *could* however, only be the first phase, for it soon became obvious that outward appearances could never be the whole truth. In the novel this led to the introspective method of the internal monologue, to Henry James's subjective narrator. In drama the consequences were Ibsen's use of symbols, Strindberg's dream plays, Chekhov's use of surface dialogue to point towards the hidden reality of the unspoken sub-text behind it—and Wedekind's resort to the heightened realism of grotesquely caricatured characters and situations. *Realism* remained the objective of all these efforts and experiments, but a realism *more* real, more profoundly *true* than that of merely external reality.

In Wedekind's case, his determination to reach a deeper layer of truth by grotesque caricature and black humour went hand in hand with the opening up of hitherto taboo subject matter. (pp. 529-30)

Because he despised the meticulous pedantry of naturalism and because he was essentially an ideologue, a fighter for his ideas, and because he used the methods of a satirist, a cartoonist, Wedekind was one of the main influences which moved dramatic writing away from the *Impressionism* of naturalistic drama which built up its effects from a multitude of minute details, a veritable *pointillisme* of theatrical technique. The mainstream continuation of naturalism, the symbolism of [Maurice] Maeterlinck, the late Ibsen; or the neo-romanticism of the later [Gerhart] Hauptmann and [Hugo von] Hofmannsthal also relied on subtle atmospheric effects; in Britain this tendency was represented by the drawings of Beardsley or plays like Wilde's *Salome*. Wedekind rejected the subtle half-tones of this *art nouveau* of atmospheres and moods. He opted for bold, direct effects. It is no coincidence that it is Wedekind who forms the first link between the tradition of German cabaret and the legitimate stage. (pp. 531-32)

The cabaretistic element—the short sketch in bold strokes which aims at producing a heightened, compressed form of comment on social reality—is an important stylistic component of Wedekind's plays. Here impressionism gives way to the primacy of the *ideas* to be expressed—*expressionism*. It is, however, interesting that Wedekind refrained from using cabaretistic songs in his plays; it was Brecht who—very much under the influence of Wedekind—took that logical next step. On the other hand Wedekind liked using the imagery of the *circus* in his drama: the prologue to the Lulu plays, for example, is spoken by a trainer of wild animals who introduces Lulu as a dangerous, snake.

All these endeavours must be seen as attempts to realize the original programme of the naturalists in a more far-reaching, more radical, more revolutionary manner. If the naturalists wanted truth, reality unvarnished and unadorned, then clearly the mere representation of surface detail would not do. The playwright had to get *behind* the mere surface of outward appearances, behind the polite small talk over coffee-cups which naturalism inevitably produced. On the other hand, the impulse to portray life as it really is led to a number of important discoveries which made stage dialogue more naturalistic than Ibsen, Zola or the early Hauptmann had ever thought of. It was Chekhov who realized that in dialogue what is not said explicitly, and hardly even hinted at by implication, very often is the decisive dramatic ingredient: in the last act of *The Cherry*

Orchard Lopakhin's failure to declare his love for Varya is expressed indirectly under a surface of trivial dialogue about galoshes which have been mislaid. Wedekind on the other hand made another discovery which has had equally far-reaching consequences: he saw that people very often do not listen to each other, and that therefore in real life there is often no dialogue at all—merely monologues running on parallel lines. Again and again, in Wedekind's plays, we find such cross-cut monologues often with highly dramatic effect: for the audience the tension in seeing two characters talk to each other who are not communicating becomes almost unbearable: for they, the audience, realize what the characters are unable to see, namely that opportunities of establishing a relationship, of solving a problem are being tragically missed. (pp. 532-33)

Wedekind himself must be seen in the context of an older tradition: the wild, revolutionary radicals of the *Sturm und Drang* (Storm and Stress) movement of the last quarter of the eighteenth century; the proto-realists of the early nineteenth century, notably Georg Büchner (1813-37) whose three astonishingly modern plays only reached the stage at the turn of the twentieth century; and Christian Dietrich Grabbe (1801-36) another wild and unhappy genius; and above all the revolutionary influence of the writings of Friedrich Nietzsche, whose attack on bourgeois morality and its Christian basis formed the starting point for Wedekind's attempts to formulate a new sexual morality. There can be no doubt that, quite apart from Wedekind's own influence, these were some of the basic sources of the movement which has become known as German Expressionism, although to this day there is still considerable doubt whether such a movement can actually be said to have existed. (p. 533)

> *Martin Esslin, "Modern Drama: Wedekind to Brecht," in* Modernism: 1890-1930, *edited by Malcolm Bradbury and James McFarlane (copyright © Penguin Books, 1976, 1978; reprinted by permission of Penguin Books Ltd), Penguin Books, 1974 (and reprinted by Humanities Press Inc., 1978, pp. 527-60).**

LEON TROTSKY   (essay date 1975)

[Wedekind offers] a combination of social nihilism—this disdainful skepticism about man as a collective being—and erotic esthetics. . . .

Yet Wedekind, the cynic and skeptic, also has his god. Not a social one, to be sure, nor even an ethical one, but an esthetic one. He worships beautiful human bodies—or, to be more precise, female bodies—a noble bearing, a smooth execution of movements A worship of perfection in the human body inevitably permeates everything Wedekind ever wrote—inevitably and almost monotonously. Nothing is vague for him in this field. He has carefully studied his thoughts down to the last detail. . . .

Out of his esthetic ideal, Wedekind constructs a system of education. This, by the way, is an overstatement: Mine-Haha is something that lies somewhere between an "education of young girls" and body-building. (p. 42)

Mine-Haha is the "physical education of young girls." This is the way Wedekind himself refers to his system. But what about spiritual education? Nothing is said about this. What is more, not even the slightest room is left for it. The whole time is taken up with physical exercises and music. There are no

books, no paper, and no ink! It is no accident that, for Wedekind, a woman's entire education consists of an esthetic cultivation of the body. Whenever he speaks of perfect woman, of a "thoroughbred" woman who "in the best sense of the word represents a work of art," what he has in mind is always only the perfect incarnation of the sex concept. "The woman who earns her livelihood through love always stands higher in my esteem than one who has so degraded herself that she writes feuilletons or even books." With these words, Hidalla is only expressing the basic ideas behind the entire system of Mine-Haha.

The woman who degrades herself through intellectual work is inferior to one who sells her hips. What audacity! But is it really audacity? Actually, of course, here, as with many other questions, Wedekind is only expressing openly, and with the moral cynicism of the esthete for whom everything is permitted, what just about every philistine thinks to himself. (p. 43)

> *Leon Trotsky, "Frank Wedekind: Esthetics and Eroticism," in* The Boston University Journal *(copyright 1975 by the Trustees of Boston University), Vol. XXIII, No. 2, 1975, pp. 40-7.*

ALAN BEST   (essay date 1975)

In the sultry atmosphere of Wedekind's plays the artistic pursuit and its equivalent prevarications are demonstrably sterile, self-indulgent and socially objectionable; the adherents of such a way of life are invariably shown on the path to self-destruction. For this reason Walter Sokel's assessment of Wedekind in *The Writer in Extremis* [see excerpt above] misses the real issue, for Sokel's thesis requires Wedekind to be presented as a writer of confessional documents on the plight of the artist misunderstood and neglected by a hostile and uncomprehending public. Such an approach ignores the satirical element of Wedekind's technique, for the plain fact is, that where his artists are failures, it is because they deserve to fail, and the much-maligned public is shown to have more sense than might at first sight be apparent. (p. 24)

Since it is society itself which regards the artistic world as a world apart Wedekind may be quite ruthless in his criticisms of the artistic community without appearing to attack society. He sees the artistic world as a microcosm of society and it is society at large with its taboos, hypocrisies and conventions that is Wedekind's real target. Within the framework of the artistic world Wedekind can better isolate the effect of these factors and present them more graphically to his respectable bourgeois audiences. (p. 25)

Wedekind's artists fail, not because they fall foul of the practices of bourgeois society, but because they carry them out to the letter in an environment where the inhuman and unfeeling basis of these practices is all too apparent. The artist-figure and his parallel manifestations are the means to an end in Wedekind's work. They are searching for happiness and a sense of personal freedom in which they may fully express their own personalities and 'be themselves'. Unfortunately, however, society has so distorted the standards of the individual that self-expression assumes the guise of self-assertion at the expense of someone else. Twisted and deformed by the society which surrounds them and which Wedekind holds accountable, his characters lack an understanding of real happiness and equate it with an outward show of superiority or the ability to impose one's will on others. This is an all-pervasive attitude, Wedekind believes, but is particularly clear-cut in society's ambivalent, hypocritical and degrading attitude to sexual matters. (pp. 25-6)

There is no warmth in Wedekind's work because very few characters have the capacity to show or feel it. His characters, unable to achieve a harmonious human relationship with its demands of give and take, confront each other in more or less open conflict. Yet it would be misleading to define these relationships as the law of the jungle, for that presupposes a conflict between wild, free, powerful animals; rather we should turn to the convention and routine of the circus for the paradigm. Here the participants are shadows of their natural potential, a mockery of their true selves and it is society which has so reduced them. (p. 28)

For the most part Wedekind's characters are like the trapeze artist; they have discovered some protective illusion or fixed point that sustains them and encourages them in delusions of grandeur and a misplaced sense of well-being. They do not see the weakness of their position, or choose to ignore it. They are so taken up with their illusions that even when they fall there is a safety-net beneath them and they bounce back to start again. They manufacture a scenario for themselves that will survive for as long as they are able to maintain the arbitrary fixed points of reference which protect them, and they bounce back not through fortitude but in desperation. Wedekind's characters cannot admit failure to themselves and they constantly find themselves forced to adapt to new circumstances in order to conceal their inadequacy from themselves and others. (p. 31)

The question insistently posed throughout Wedekind's work is: how is it possible to pass through adolescence in such a society and yet emerge a normal balanced personality? While he offers no clear answer either way, the characters of *Frühlings Erwachen* share childhood experiences that are very similar to those which the characters in such plays as *Lulu, Franziska* and *Der Marquis von Keith* reveal that they have suffered too. The detailed analysis of adolescence in *Frühlings Erwachen* provides an insight into the adult world of Wedekind's social circus. *Frühlings Erwachen* is a tragedy of adolescence, but the tragic flaw in all Wedekind's characters is that they never grow up. Their emotional development is checked by their childhood experiences and bourgeois upbringing. (p. 81)

Wedekind's plays are set on the fringe of the respectable and bourgeois society from which the bulk of his audience, both in his lifetime and since, is drawn. Though the artist, the speculator and the confidence-trickster occupy the foreground of his works, Wedekind's real concern is to question the social morality that tolerates, and indeed spawns, such figures and to expose the rootless nature of the society in which his audience moves.

The smug complacency with which Wedekind's audiences watch him expose and ridicule the positions taken up by characters like Dr. Schön, Gerardo, the Marquis von Keith and King Nicolo is rudely shattered when the close similarity of the world on the stage and that of the audience is made clear. Much of the hostility that Wedekind aroused may reflect the general public's indignation at being made to wear a cap which they know fits all too well. Wedekind not only illustrates the faults in society, he refuses to let its members unload their complicity on to a scapegoat on the stage and requires his audience to live with the truth of the social conditions they have just seen in exaggerated form. This is the justification for art; it should make an audience think, and jolt it out of its complacency, but society depends on complacency and an acceptance of the *status*

quo for its survival and is quick to forestall attempts to introduce change. (p. 115)

Wedekind's intention is to guide his audience and help them keep an open mind as to the relative motives of his characters. His use of scenic montage, of anticipation, variation and repetition in situation and character is extended and reflected in the register of vocabulary which his characters employ. There is a complex undercurrent of verbal implications in Wedekind's dialogue which it is impossible to render in translation because it is ingrained in the idiom and implications of the German language, but its effect is to tar all Wedekind's characters with the same brush. They may adopt different social masks, but they use the same terminology and unwittingly reveal the same fears and illusions.

The irony is that the characters on stage speak the language and think the thoughts that come naturally to the audience that is watching them. The 'unsuspecting member of the public' is thus presented with a caricature of his own situation which, Wedekind hopes, will cause him to reassess his position or at the least recognise it for a façade. It must be said, however, that the society to which Wedekind addressed himself in his lifetime had little to learn in the art of wilful myopia and deafness from the characters they saw, and today's audiences may conveniently hide behind the fiction that Wedekind's true significance is as an interesting eccentric in the history of theatre. (p. 116)

> *Alan Best, in his* Frank Wedekind *(© 1975 Oswald Wolff (Publishers) Limited), Wolff, 1975, 125 p.*

J. L. HIBBERD   (essay date 1979)

Unter Moral verstehe ich das reelle Produkt zweier imaginärer Größen. Die imaginären Größen sind *Sollen* und *Wollen*. Das Produkt heißt Moral und läßt sich in seiner Realität nicht leugnen.

These three short but somewhat enigmatic sentences spoken in the last scene of *Frühlings Erwachen* purport to define morality and promise to be of considerable importance for our understanding of Wedekind's first dramatic masterpiece. The assumption that he called for the abandonment of all sexual restraint caused him to be branded an advocate of immorality. That is not an unusual reaction to suggestions for radical moral reform; yet even now, when more liberal attitudes are fashionable, his new morality must seem either to amount to a formula for the abdication of moral responsibility or to be so sketchily intimated in the drama as to offer no alternative to more conventional codes. The serious satirical purpose of the play suffices to belie charges of gratuitous obscenity. But the accusation of naive moral anarchism is not so easily countered. For the supreme scorn with which Wedekind rejected the sexual morality of his time as it affected adolescents does appear to rest on a simple-minded faith in the free play of natural impulse. The epigrammatic definition of morality does not, however, suggest an obviously naive mind. (p. 633)

A new morality that should replace the old is not described in *Frühlings Erwachen*. We may conclude that it ought to be realistic, to acknowledge the power of sexual instincts, to accept the differences between individuals, and to recognize that men are motivated by selfishness, but also that in seeking self-gratification they must try not to hurt others. To what extent or in what way instincts might need to be limited to avoid hurting others, or in the interests of social harmony, is not clear. It is doubtful whether Wedekind, who observed that nature is not always beautiful or even pleasurable . . . , could conceive of a utopian solution to social problems, though he believed that greater realism would reduce unnecessary suffering. Certainly he did not think that sex education by itself (without a transformation of moral values) would solve anything . . .). Equally clearly his play shows that sex and attitudes to sex cannot be isolated, rather they impinge on questions about the worth or worthlessness of living. . . . The moral problem is thus linked with an existential one (so that the allusions in the text to Goethe's *Faust* and the reference to the philosophy of Nietzsche are not out of place).

The definition of morality is indeed a witty firework, impressive in its brilliance, but with no power to illumine our darkness for long. It makes sense when applied simply to the morality that Wedekind attacks, in which case 'imaginäre Größen' may be understood as unreal factors. In this restricted application its meaning is clear; the insistence on the relativity of morality and the dubiousness of duty and volition has a clear function within the drama. . . . Because the definition invites misunderstanding, it allows Wedekind to seem to deny duty and will without doing anything of the kind—his denunciation of the adults in the play presupposes, after all, that they are free to act differently and have a duty to do so. Perhaps the real joke, however, is not that the definition has a double meaning, but lies in the irony of its presentation; the pronouncement on imaginary numbers is made by an 'imaginary number' posturing as a human being. . . . The disconcerting mixture of moving pathos and sobering paradox, of tragedy and farce, is a product of his 'Humor'. Its moral, 'Alles ist eitel', applies here to intellectualizations, to generalizations, rather than the particulars of concrete experience. Wedekind is not cynical about life, but chary of speculations about its meaning.

As a conceit the definition of morality does not invite us to look beyond the immediate point of resemblance between mathematics and morals; *Frühlings Erwachen* is similarly restricted as a bearer of meaning. Wedekind asks us to accept the justness of his comment on unreal notions of innocence and their effect on real people, but in inviting us to make different assumptions and search for a different code of behaviour, perhaps to institute a series of moral experiments, he does no more than point in a certain direction. That he goes no further reflects his individualist dislike of norms or precepts as well as his suspicion of generalizations; it suggests that he had few gifts as a moral philosopher. But it does not detract from his courage and incisiveness as a critic of society. Nor does it diminish the theatrical impact of his play. (pp. 646-47)

> *J. L. Hibberd, "Imaginary Numbers and 'Humor': On Wedekind's 'Frühlings erwachen'," in* The Modern Language Review *(© Modern Humanities Research Association 1979), Vol. 74, Part 3, July, 1979, pp. 631-47.*

ADDITIONAL BIBLIOGRAPHY

Fay, Frances C. "Frank Wedekind." *Drama,* No. 19 (August 1913): 479-94.
> Finds that "Wedekind has no positive goal, he is not sure of himself, and furthermore, he treats his medium of expression altogether too negligently." For this reason Fay believes that Wedekind is not a great artist and that his arguments do not always carry conviction.

Garten, H. F. "Frank Wedekind." In his *Modern German Drama,* pp. 87-96. London: Methuen & Co, 1964.
> Considers "the elemental force of sex and its antagonism to a society hemmed in by hypocritical conventions" the central theme of all Wedekind's plays.

Huneker, James. "Frank Wedekind." In his *Ivory, Apes, and Peacocks,* pp. 121-40. New York: Charles Scribner's Sons, 1915.
> Refers to Wedekind as "the naughty boy of the modern German drama," and "the clown of the German stage." Huneker views Wedekind as both humorist and moralist.

Jelavich, Peter. "Art and Mammon in Wilhemine Germany: The Case of Frank Wedekind." *Central European History* XII, No. 3 (September 1979): 203-36.
> Examines "the clash of the real and the ideal in Wedekind's life."

Lange, Victor. "Irony and Resolution." In his *Modern German Literature: 1870-1940,* pp. 57-75. Ithaca: Cornell University Press, 1945.
> Describes literary trends and figures important during Wedekind's lifetime.

MacCarthy, Desmond. "In Germany." In his *Experience,* pp. 179-82. 1935. Reprint. Freeport, N.Y.: Books for Libraries Press, 1968.
> Recalls his student days in Germany and a production of *Erdgeist.*

Maclean, Hector. "Wedekind's *Der Marquis von Keith:* An Interpretation Based on the *Faust* and Circus Motifs." *The Germanic Review* XLIII (1968): 163-87.
> Examines Wedekind's "very personal use of *Faust.*" Includes untranslated German passages.

Maclean, Hector. "The King and the Fool in Wedekind's *König Nicolo.*" *Seminar* V, No. 1 (Spring 1969): 21-35.
> Views the play as Wedekind's "voyage of self-discovery." Includes untranslated German passages.

Osborne, John. "Anti-Aristotelian Drama from Lenz to Wedekind." In *The German Theatre: A Symposium,* edited by Ronald Hayman, pp. 87-105. London: Oswald Wolff, 1975.*
> Survey of two centuries of German drama. Osborne examines the ways Wedekind upheld naturalistic traditions in his early plays, and the ways he countered the traditional concerns of German tragedy in his later works.

Shaw, Leroy R. "The Strategy of Reformulation: Frank Wedekind's *Frühlingserwachen.*" In his *The Playwright and Historical Change: Dramatic Strategies in Brecht, Hauptmann, Kaiser and Wedekind,* pp. 49-65. Madison: University of Wisconsin, 1970.
> Analysis of puberty as symbol in *Frühlings Erwachen.*

Willett, John. "Frank Wedekind." In *Brecht on Theatre: The Development of an Aesthetic,* by Bertolt Brecht, translated and edited by John Willett, pp. 3-4. London: Methuen & Co, 1964.
> Brecht's character sketch of Wedekind.

Appendix

THE EXCERPTS IN TCLC, VOLUME 7, WERE REPRINTED FROM THE FOLLOWING PERIODICALS:

The Academy
The Academy and Literature
American Literature
The American Mercury
The American Poetry Review
American Quarterly
The American Review
The American Review of Reviews
The American Scholar
The Arena
The Athenaeum
The Atlantic Monthly
Best Sellers
The Bookman, London
The Bookman, New York
Book World—The Washington Post
Books Abroad
The Boston University Journal
The Canadian Forum
Canadian Literature
The Century
The Charioteer
The Chesterton Review
Children's Literature
CLA Journal
Comparative Drama
Comparative Literature
The Cosmopolitan
The Crisis
The Criterion
The Critic
Critical Quarterly
Daily News, London
The Dalhousie Review
The Dial
Drama
Drama Review
English
Forum
The French Review
The Georgia Review
Harper's
Harper's Monthly Magazine

Harper's Weekly
Harvard Library Bulletin
Horizon
The Hudson Review
Irish Renaissance Annual I
The Journal of Aesthetics and Art Criticism
Journal of English and German Philology
Journal of Narrative Technique
The Kenyon Review
L'Esprit Créateur
Life and Letters
The Listener
The London Mercury
Melbourne Slavonic Studies
Merry England
The Mississippi Quarterly
Modern Drama
Modern Fiction Studies
The Modern Language Journal
Modern Language Quarterly
Modern Language Review
The Nation
The Nation and The Athenaeum
The New Age
The New Colophon
The New England Quarterly
The New Republic
The New Statesman
The New Statesman & Nation
New York Herald Tribune Books
New York Herald Tribune Weekly Book
  Review
The New York Review of Books
The New York Times
The New York Times Book Review
The New York Times Saturday Review
The New York Times Saturday Review of
  Books
The New York Tribune
The North American Review
Northern Review
Nyctalops
The Overland Monthly

Papers on Language and Literature
Parnassus: Poetry in Review
Partisan Review
PHYLON
PMLA
Poet Lore
Poetry
Prairie Schooner
Queen's Quarterly
Romance Notes
Russian Literature Triquarterly
Satire Newsletter
The Saturday Evening Post
The Saturday Review, London
The Saturday Review of Literature
Scandinavian Studies
Scandinavica
Scando-Slavica
Scribner's Magazine
The Sewanee Review
The Shaw Review
Slavic Review
The Slavonic Review
The Smart Set
Southerly
The Southern Review
Stanford French Review
The Spectator
Studies in Contemporary Satire
Temple Bar
Texas Studies in Literature and
  Language
Time & Tide
The Times Literary Supplement
TriQuarterly
Tulane Drama Review
University of Toronto Quarterly
Vanity Fair
The Virginia Quarterly Review
Weekly Critical Review
The Western Review
Writer's Digest
The Yale Review

THE EXCERPTS IN TCLC, VOLUME 7, WERE REPRINTED FROM THE FOLLOWING BOOKS:

Aldington, Richard. Literary Studies and Reviews. *Dial Press, 1924.*

Anthony, Edward. O Rare Don Marquis. *Doubleday, 1962.*

Aragon, Louis. Introduction to Selected Writings, *by Paul Eluard. Edited and translated by Lloyd Alexander. New Directions, 1951.*

Archer, William. Poets of the Younger Generation. *John Lane, 1902, Scholarly Press, 1969.*

Atterbury, Brian. The Fantasy Tradition in American Literature: From Irving to Le Guin. *Indiana University Press, 1980.*

Balakian, Anna. Surrealism: The Road to the Absolute. *Rev. ed. Dutton, 1970.*

Balmforth, Ramsden. The Problem-Play and Its Influence on Modern Thought and Life. *Allen & Unwin, 1928.*

Baring, Maurice. Punch and Judy and Other Essays. *Doubleday, 1924.*

Barnard, Marjorie. Miles Franklin. *Twayne, 1967.*

Baum, L. Frank. Introduction to The Wonderful World of Oz, by L. Frank Baum. George M. Hill, 1900.

Beckett, Samuel. Proust. *Chatto & Windus, 1931, Grove Press, 1957.*

Beerbohm, Max. Around Theatres. *Rev. ed. Rupert Hart-Davis, 1953.*

Beier, Ulli, ed. African Literature: An Anthology of Critical Writing from ''Black Orpheus.'' *Longmans, 1967, Northwestern University Press, 1970.*

Bell, Clive. Proust. *Hogarth Press, 1928.*

Benjamin, Walter. Illuminations. *Edited by Hannah Arendt. Translated by Harry Zohn. Schocken Books, 1969.*

Bensen, Alice R. Rose Macauley. *Twayne, 1969.*

Bentley, Eric. The Playwright As Thinker: A Study of Drama in Modern Times. *Reynal & Hitchcock, 1946, Harcourt, 1967.*

Bergonzi, Bernard. Heroes' Twilight: A Study of the Literature of the Great War. *Constable, 1965.*

Bergonzi, Bernard. The Turn of a Century: Essays on Victorian and Modern English Literature. *Barnes & Noble, 1973.*

Bernstein, Melvin H. John Jay Chapman. *Twayne, 1964.*

Best, Alan. Frank Wedekind. *Wolff, 1975.*

Beyer, Harald. A History of Norwegian Literature. *Edited and translated by Einar Huagen. New York University Press, 1956.*

Bierce, Ambrose. The Letters of Ambrose Bierce. *Book Club of California, 1922, Gordian Press, 1967.*

Bierce, Ambrose. Twenty-One Letters of Ambrose Bierce. *George Kirk, 1922.*

Bishop, John Peale. The Collected Essays of John Peale Bishop. *Edited by Edmund Wilson. Scribner's, 1948.*

Bleiler, E. F. Introduction to The Best Supernatural Tales of Arthur Conan Doyle, *by Arthur Conan Doyle. Edited by E. F. Bleiler. Dover Publications, 1979.*

Bogan, Louise. Selected Criticism: Prose, Poetry. *Noonday Press, 1955.*

Bone, Robert. The Negro Novel in America. *Yale University Press, 1958.*

Bowen, Elizabeth. Collected Impressions. *Knopf, 1950.*

Brandes, Georg. Eminent Authors of the Nineteenth Century. *Translated by Rasmus B. Anderson. Crowell, 1886.*

Brandes, Georg. Creative Spirits of the Nineteenth Century. *Translated by Rasmus B. Anderson. Crowell, 1923.*

Brawley, Benjamin. The Negro Genius: A New Appraisal of the Achievement of the American Negro in Literature and the Fine Arts. *Dodd, Mead, 1937, Biblo and Tannen, 1966.*

Braybrooke, Patrick. Some Victorian and Georgian Catholics: Their Art and Outlook. *Burns Oates & Washbourne, 1932, Books for Libraries Press, 1966.*

Brée, Germaine. Marcel Proust and Deliverance from Time. *Translated by C. J. Richards and A. D. Truitt. Rutgers University Press, 1969.*

Brenner, Rica. Ten Modern Poets. *Harcourt, 1930.*

Brown, E. K. On Canadian Poetry. *Rev. ed. Ryerson Press, 1944, Tecumseh Press, 1973.*

Brown, Malcolm. George Moore: A Reconsideration. *University of Washington Press, 1955.*

Bruccoli, Matthew J., ed. Chandler before Marlowe: Raymond Chandler's Early Prose and Poetry, 1908-1912. *University of South Carolina Press, 1973.*

Budd, Louis J.; Cady, Edwin H.; and Anderson, Carl L., eds. Toward a New American Literary History: Essays in Honor of Arlin Turner. *Duke University Press, 1980.*

Burnshaw, Stanley, ed. The Poem Itself, 45 Modern Poets in a New Presentation: The French, German, Spanish, Portuguese, Italian Poems, Each Rendered Literally in an Interpretative Discussion. *Holt, 1960, Schocken Books, 1967.*

Cabell, James Branch. Let Me Lie: Being in the Main an Ethnological Account of the Remarkable Commonwealth of Virginia and the Making of Its History. *Farrar, Straus and Giroux, 1947.*

Cady, Edwin H. The Road to Realism: The Early Years 1837-1885 of William Dean Howells. *Syracuse University Press, 1956.*

Cammell, Charles Richard. Aleister Crowley: The Man, the Image, the Poet. *Richards Press, 1951, University Books, 1962.*

Cappon, James. Bliss Carman and the Literary Currents and Influences of His Time. *Ryerson Press, 1930.*

Cardinal, Roger, ed. Sensibility and Creation: Studies in Twentieth Century French Poetry. *Barnes & Noble, 1977.*

Cargill, Oscar. Intellectual America: Ideas on the March. *Macmillan, 1941.*

Carner, Mosco. Puccini: A Literary Biography. *Duckworth, 1974.*

Cavafy, C. P. Poems. *Translated by John Mavrogordato. Hogarth Press, 1951, Chatto & Windus, 1971.*

Caws, Mary Ann. The Poetry of Dada and Surrealism: Aragon, Breton, Tzara, Eluard and Desnos. *Princeton University Press, 1970.*

Chandler, Frank W. Modern Continental Playwrights. *Harper, 1931.*

Chandler, Raymond. Raymond Chandler Speaking. *Edited by Dorothy Gardiner and Katherine Sorley Walker. Four Square Books, 1962.*

Chapman, John Jay. The Selected Writings of John Jay Chapman. *Edited by Jacques Barzun. Farrar, Straus and Cudahy, 1957.*

Chesterton, G. K. Mr. Crowley and the Creeds and the Creed of Mr. Chesterton. *Privately printed, 1904.*

Chesterton, G. K. Heretics. *John Lane, 1905.*

Chesterton, G. K. The Autobiography of G. K. Chesterton. *Sheed and Ward, 1936.*

Chesterton, G. K. A Handful of Authors: Essays on Books and Writers. *Edited by Dorothy Collins. Sheed and Ward, 1953.*

Chiari, Joseph. Contemporary French Poetry. *Philosophical Library, 1952*.

Cioran, Samuel D. The Apocalyptic Symbolism of Andrej Belyi. *Mouton, 1973*.

Clark, Barrett H., and Freedley, George, eds. A History of Modern Drama. *Appleton-Century-Crofts, 1947*.

Craige, Betty Jean. Lorca's "Poet in New York": The Fall into Consciousness. *University Press of Kentucky, 1977*.

Crawford, Virginia M. Studies in Foreign Literature. *Duckworth, 1899, Kennikat Press, 1970*.

Crowley, Aleister. The Confessions of Aleister Crowley: An Autohagiography. *Edited by John Symonds and Kenneth Grant. Hill & Wang, 1970, Bantam, 1971*.

Davison, Edward. Some Modern Poets and Other Critical Essays. *Harper, 1928*.

Dean, James L. Howells' Travels toward Art. *University of New Mexico Press, 1970*.

De Graffenreid, Thomas P. The de Graffenreid Family Scrapbook. *The University of Virginia Press, 1945*.

Derleth, August. Still Small Voice: The Biography of Zona Gale. *D. Appleton-Century, 1940*.

De Voto, Bernard. The Easy Chair. *Houghton Mifflin, 1955*.

Dick, Susan. Introduction to Confessions of a Young Man, *by George Moore. Edited by Susan Dick. McGill-Queen's University Press, 1972*.

Downs, Brian W. Modern Norwegian Literature: 1860-1918. *Cambridge University Press, 1966*.

Drinkwater, John. Prose Papers. *Elkin Mathews, 1918*.

Dukes, Ashley. Modern Dramatists. *Frank Palmer, 1911, Charles H. Sergel and Co., 1911*.

Dunleavy, Janet Egleson. George Moore: The Artist's Vision, the Storyteller's Art. *Bucknell University Press, 1973*.

Duran, Manuel, ed. Lorca: A Collection of Critical Essays. *Prentice-Hall, 1962*.

Dutton, Geoffrey, ed. The Literature of Australia. *Penguin Books Australia, 1976*.

Eble, Kenneth E., ed. Howells: A Century of Criticism. *Southern Methodist University Press, 1962*.

Edwards, Gwynne. Lorca: The Theatre beneath the Sand. *Marion Boyars, 1980*.

Egoff, Sheila; Stubbs, G. T.; and Ashley, L. F., eds. Only Connect: Readings on Children's Literature. *Oxford University Press, 1969*.

Ellis, Havelock. Affirmations. *2d ed. Houghton Mifflin, 1922*.

Eloesser, Arthur. Modern German Literature. *Translated by Catherine Alison Phillips. Knopf, 1933*.

Elsworth, John. Studies in Twentieth Century Russian Literature. *Edited by Christopher J. Barnes. Barnes & Noble, 1976*.

Enright, D. J. Man Is an Onion: Reviews and Essays. *Open Court, 1972*.

Enright, D. J. The Modern Age: Volume 7 of the Pelican Guide to English Literature. *Edited by Boris Ford. Penguin, 1973*.

Eschholz, Paul A., ed. Critics on William Dean Howells. *University of Miami Press, 1975*.

Esslin, Martin. Modernism: 1890-1930. *Edited by Malcolm Bradbury and James McFarlane. Penguin, 1974, Humanities Press, 1978*.

Ewers, John K. Creative Writing in Australia: A Selective Survey. *Rev. ed. Georgian House, 1959*.

Farrow, Anthony. George Moore. *Twayne, 1978*.

Festa-McCormick, Diana. The City As a Catalyst: A Study of Ten Novels. *Associated University Press, 1979*.

Feuchtwanger, Lion. Introduction to Five Tragedies of Sex, *by Frank Wedekind. Translated by Frances Fawcett and Stephen Spender. Vision Press, 1952.*

Firkins, Oscar W. William Dean Howells: A Study. *Harvard University Press, 1924.*

Forster, E. M. Abinger Harvest. *Harcourt, 1936.*

Forster, E. M. Two Cheers for Democracy. *Harcourt, 1951.*

Fowlie, Wallace. Age of Surrealism. *The Swallow Press, 1950, Indiana University Press, 1960.*

Fowlie, Wallace. A Reading of Proust. *2d ed. University of Chicago Press, 1975.*

France, Anatole. Prefaces, Introductions and Other Uncollected Papers. *Translated by J. Lewis May. Dodd, Mead, 1928.*

Freeman, John. A Portrait of George Moore in a Study of His Work. *T. Werner Laurie, 1922, Scholarly Press, 1971.*

French, Warren, ed. The Twenties: Fiction, Poetry, Drama. *Everett/Edwards, 1975.*

Frierson, William C. The English Novel in Transition, 1885-1940. *University of Oklahoma Press, 1942, Cooper Square Publishers, 1965.*

Frye, Northrop. The Bush Garden: Essays on the Canadian Imagination. *Anansi, 1971.*

Gardner, Martin, and Nye, Russel B. The Wizard of Oz and Who He Was. *Michigan State University Press, 1957.*

Garland, Hamlin. My Friendly Contemporaries: A Literary Log. *Macmillan, 1932.*

Gass, William H. The World within the Word. *Knopf, 1978.*

Gassner, John. The Theatre in Our Times: A Survey of Men, Materials and Movements in the Modern Theatre. *Crown, 1954.*

Genette, Gérard. Narrative Discourse: An Essay in Method. *Translated by Jane E. Lewin. Cornell University Press, 1980.*

Gibson, William M. William D. Howells. *University of Minnesota Press, 1967.*

Gide, André. The Journals of André Gide: 1914-1927, Vol. II. *Edited and translated by Justin O'Brien. Knopf, 1948, Secker & Warburg, 1948.*

Gide, André. The Journals of André Gide: 1928-1939, Vol. III. *Edited and translated by Justin O'Brien. Knopf, 1949, Secker & Warburg, 1949.*

Giles, James R. Claude McKay. *Twayne, 1976.*

Gittleman, Sol. Frank Wedekind. *Twayne, 1969.*

Glasgow, Ellen. A Certain Measure: An Interpretation of Prose Fiction. *Harcourt, 1943.*

Goist, Park Dixon. From Main Street to State Street: Town, City, and Community in America. *Kennikat, 1970.*

Gosse, Edmund. Introduction to The Novels of Bjornstjerne Bjornson: Synnove Solbakken, Vol. I, *by Bjornstjerne Bjornson. Edited by Edmund Gosse. Translated by Julie Sutter. Macmillan, 1894, Heinemann, 1909.*

Gosse, Edmund. More Books on the Table. *Scribner's, 1923.*

Gourmont, Remy de. The Book of Masks. *Translated by Jack Lewis. J. W. Luce, 1921, Books for Libraries Press, 1967.*

Granville-Barker, H. Preface to Little Plays of St. Francis: A Dramatic Cycle from the Life and Legend of St. Francis of Assisi, *by Laurence Housman. Rev. ed. Sidgwick & Jackson, 1926.*

Greene, Ellin. Afterword to The Rat-Catcher's Daughter, *by Laurence Housman. Atheneum, 1974.*

Gross, Miriam, ed. The World of Raymond Chandler. *A & W Publishers, 1978.*

Gumilev, Nikolai. Nikolai Gumilev on Russian Poetry. *Edited and translated by David Lapeza. Ardis Publishers, 1977.*

Hadgraft, Cecil. Australian Literature: A Critical Account to 1955. *Heinemann, 1960.*

Hall, Trevor H. Sherlock Holmes: Ten Literary Studies. *St. Martin's Press, 1970.*

Hall, Wayne E. Shadowy Heroes: Irish Literature of the 1890s. *Syracuse University Press, 1980.*

Harris, William J. A Question of Quality: Popularity and Value in Modern Creative Writing. *Bowling Green University Popular Press, 1976.*

Harrison, Michael D., ed. Beyond Baker Street: A Sherlockian Anthology. *Bobbs-Merrill, 1976.*

Hassall, Christopher. Introduction to The Prose of Rupert Brooke, *by Rupert Brooke. Sidgewick and Jackson, 1956.*

Hastings, Michael. The Handsomest Young Man in England: Rupert Brooke. *Michael Joseph, 1967.*

Hathaway, R. H. "Bliss Carman: An Appreciation" in Later Poems, *by Bliss Carman. Small, Maynard & Co., 1922.*

Haynes, Renée. Hilaire Belloc. *Longmans, 1953.*

Hayward, Max. Foreword to Marina Tsvetayeva: Selected Poems, *by Marina Tsvetayeva. Translated by Elaine Feinstein. Oxford University Press, 1971.*

Hearn, Lafcadio. Interpretations of Literature. *Dodd, Mead, 1926.*

Herron, Ima Honaker. The Small Town in American Literature. *Duke University Press, 1939.*

Hicks, Granville. The Great Tradition: An Interpretation of American Literature since the Civil War. *Rev. ed. Macmillan, 1935.*

Hicks, Granville. The Man of Wax: Critical Essays on George Moore. *Edited by Douglas A. Hughes. New York University Press, 1971.*

Higginbotham, Virginia. The Comic Spirit of Federico García Lorca. *University of Texas Press, 1976.*

Hilfer, Anthony Channell. The Revolt from the Village: 1915-1930. *University of North Carolina Press, 1969.*

Hind, Charles Lewis. Authors and I. *John Lane, 1921.*

Hovey, Richard Bennett. John Jay Chapman—An American Mind. *Columbia University Press, 1959.*

Howe, M. A. DeWolfe. John Jay Chapman and His Letters. *Houghton Mifflin, 1937.*

Howells, William Dean. Life in Letters of William Dean Howells, Vol. II. *Edited by Mildred Howells. Doubleday, 1928.*

Hoyt, Charles Alva, ed. Minor British Novelists. *Southern Illinois University Press, 1967.*

Huggins, Nathan Irvin. Harlem Renaissance. *Oxford University Press, 1971.*

Huneker, James. Egoists, a Book of Supermen: Stendahl, Baudelaire, Flaubert, Anatole France, Huysmans, Barres, Nietzsche, Blake, Ibsen, Stirner, and Ernest Hello. *Scribner's, 1920.*

Huysmans, J. K. Preface to Against the Grain (Á Rebours), *by J. K. Huysmans. Translated by John Howard. Three Sirens Press, 1931, Dover Publications, 1969.*

Isherwood, Christopher. Exhumations: Stories, Articles, Verses. *Methuen, 1966.*

James, Henry. The Letters of Henry James, Vol. II. *Edited by Percy Lubbock. Scribner's, 1920.*

Jerrold, Walter. Alfred Noyes. *Harold Shaylor, 1930.*

Johnson, James Weldon, ed. The Book of American Negro Poetry. *Harcourt, 1931.*

Johnson, R. Brimley. Some Contemporary Novelists (Women). *Leonard Parsons, 1920, Books for Libraries Press, 1967.*

Jones, D. G. Butterfly on Rock: A Study of Themes and Images in Canadian Literature. *University of Toronto Press, 1970.*

Kallet, Marilyn. Introduction to Last Love Poems of Paul Eluard, *by Paul Eluard. Translated by Marilyn Kallet. Louisiana State University Press, 1980.*

Karlinsky, Simon. Marina Cvetaeva: Her Life and Art. *University of California Press, 1966.*

Kazin, Alfred. On Native Grounds: An Interpretation of Modern American Prose Literature. *Reynal & Hitchcock, 1942.*

Kazin, Alfred. The Inmost Leaf: A Selection of Essays. *Harcourt, 1955.*

Kazin, Alfred. Contemporaries. *Atlantic-Little, Brown, 1962.*

Kennelly, Brendan. George Moore's Mind and Art. *Edited by Graham Owens. Oliver and Boyd, 1968, Barnes & Noble, 1970.*

Kent, George E. Blackness and the Adventure of Western Culture. *Third World Press, 1972.*

King, J. Marin. Translator's note and introduction to A Captive Spirit: Selected Prose, *by Marina Tsvetaeva. Edited and translated by J. Marin King. Ardis, 1980.*

Knaust, Rebecca. The Complete Guide to "La Bohème." *McAfee Books, 1978.*

Larson, Harold. Bjornstjerne Bjornson: A Study in Norwegian Nationalism. *King's Crown Press, 1944.*

Lavrin, Janko. An Introduction to the Russian Novel. *Whittlesey House, 1947.*

Lawrence, Margaret. The School of Femininity: A Book for and about Women as They Are Interpreted through Feminine Writers of Yesterday and Today. *Frederick A. Stokes, 1936, Kennikat Press, 1966.*

Lee, Lynn. Don Marquis. *Twayne, 1981.*

Lehmann, John. Rupert Brooke: His Life and His Legend. *Weidenfeld & Nicholson, 1980.*

Leon, Derrick. Introduction to Proust: His Life, His Circle, and His Work. *Kegan Paul, Trench, Trubner, 1940.*

Levin, Harry. The Gates of Horn: A Study of Five French Realists. *Oxford University Press, 1963.*

Lewis, Allen. The Contemporary Theatre: The Significant Playwrights of Our Time. *Rev. ed. Crown, 1971.*

Lewis, Sinclair. The Man from Main Street: Selected Essays and Other Writings 1904-1950. *Edited by Harry E. Maule and Melville H. Cane. Random House, 1953.*

Lewisohn, Ludwig. Expression in America. *Harper & Row, 1932.*

Longford, Elizabeth. Introduction to Adventures of Gerard, *by Sir Arthur Conan Doyle. Jonathan Cape, 1976, Pan Books, 1977.*

Lucas, F. L. Introduction to The Complete Works of John Webster, *by John Webster. Edited by F. L. Lucas. Houghton Mifflin, 1928.*

Luciani, Vincent. Introduction to Come le foglie, *by Giuseppe Giacosa. Edited by Vincent Luciani. S. F. Vanni, 1961.*

MacClintock, Lander. The Contemporary Drama of Italy. *Little, Brown, 1920.*

MacShane, Frank. The Life of Raymond Chandler. *Dutton, 1976.*

Maguire, Robert A., and Malmstad, John E. Introduction to Petersburg, *by Andrei Bely. Edited and translated by Robert A. Maguire and John E. Malmstad. Indiana University Press, 1978.*

Manganiello, Dominic. Myth and Reality in Irish Literature. *Edited by Joseph Ronsley. Wilfred Laurier University Press, 1977.*

Mann, Thomas. Letters of Thomas Mann: 1889-1955. *Edited and translated by Richard Winston and Clara Winston. Knopf, 1971.*

Mansfield, Katherine. Novels and Novelists. *Edited by J. Middleton Murry. Knopf, 1930.*

Maslenikov, Oleg A. The Frenzied Poets: Andrey Biely and the Russian Symbolists. *University of California Press, 1952.*

Mathew, Ray. Miles Franklin. *Lansdowne Press, 1963.*

Matthews, J. H. Surrealist Poetry in France. *Syracuse University Press, 1969.*

Maugham, W. Somerset. The Magician. *Rev. ed. William Heinemann Ltd, 1956.*

Mauriac, Francois. Second Thoughts: Reflections on Literature and on Life. *Translated by Adrienne Foulke. World, 1961.*

Maurois, Andre. Proust: Portrait of a Genius. *Harper, 1950.*

McFarlane, James Walter. Ibsen and the Temper of Norwegian Literature. *Oxford University Press, 1960.*

McLeod, Addison. Plays and Players in Modern Italy; Being a Study of the Italian Stage as Affected by the Political and Social Life, Manners and Character of To-day. *Smith, Elder & Co., 1912, Kennikat Press, 1970.*

McMurray, William. The Literary Realism of William Dean Howells. *Southern Illinois University Press, 1967.*

Meeker, Richard K. Introduction to The Collected Stories of Ellen Glasgow, *by Ellen Glasgow. Edited by Richard K. Meeker. Louisiana State University Press, 1963.*

Mencken, H. L. Prejudices, first series. *Knopf, 1919.*

Mencken, H. L. Prejudices, sixth series. *Octagon Books, 1927, Alfred A. Knopf, 1977.*

Meserve, Walter J. Introduction to The Complete Plays of W. D. Howells, *by W. D. Howells. Edited by William M. Gibson and George Arms. New York University Press, 1960.*

Miller, Henry. Max and the White Phagocytes. *Obelisk Press, 1938.*

Miller, Henry. The Cosmological Eye. *New Directions, 1961.*

Mirsky, D. S. Contemporary Russian Literature: 1881-1925. *Knopf, 1926, Routledge, 1926.*

Mochulsky, Konstantin. Andrei Bely: His Life and Works. *Translated by Nora Szalavitz. Ardis, 1977.*

Moncrieff, C. K., ed. Marcel Proust: An English Tribute. *Thomas Seltzer, 1923.*

Moore, Raylyn. Wonderful Wizard, Marvelous Land. *Bowling Green University Popular Press, 1974.*

Morgan, Charles. Epitaph on George Moore. *Macmillan, 1935.*

Morley, Christopher. Shandygaff: A Number of Most Agreeable Inquirendoes upon Life and Letters, Interspersed with Short Stories and Skitts, the Whole Most Diverting to the Reader. *Doubleday, 1918, Scholarly Press, 1971.*

Morley, Christopher. Internal Revenue. *Doubleday, 1933.*

Morley, Christopher. Letters of Askance. *Lippincott, 1939.*

Morley, Christopher. Introduction to The Best of Don Marquis, *by Don Marquis. Doubleday, 1946.*

Morton, J. B. Introduction to Selected Essays of Hilaire Belloc, *by Hilaire Belloc. Edited by J. B. Morton. Methuen, 1948.*

Nabokov, Vladimir. Strong Opinions. *McGraw-Hill, 1973.*

Nabokov, Vladimir. Lectures on Literature. *Edited by Fredson Bowers. Harcourt, 1980.*

Natan, Alex, ed. German Men of Letters: Twelve Literary Essays, Vol. II. *Wolff, 1963.*

Nejdefors-Frisk, Sonya. George Moore's Naturalistic Prose. *Harvard University Press, 1952.*

Nordon, Pierre. Conan Doyle. *Translated by Frances Partridge. John Murray, 1966.*

Noyes, Henry. Preface to Collected Poems in One Volume, *by Alfred Noyes. John Murray, 1963, 1966.*

Nugent, Robert. Paul Eluard. *Twayne, 1974.*

O'Brien, Justin. The French Literary Horizon. *Rutgers University Press, 1967.*

Painter, George D. Marcel Proust: A Biography, Vol. I. *Chatto and Windus, 1959, Vintage Books, 1978.*

Pasternak, Boris. I Remember: Sketch for an Autobiography. *Translated by David Magarshack. Pantheon Books, 1959.*

Payne, William Morton. Introduction to Arnljot Gelline, *by Bjornstjerne Bjornson. American Scandinavian Foundation, 1917.*

Pearsall, Ronald. Conan Doyle: A Biographical Solution. *St. Martin's Press, 1977.*

Pearson, Hesketh. Conan Doyle: His Life and Art. *2d ed. Methuen, 1943.*

Peary, Gerald, and Shatzkin, Roger, eds. The Classic American Novel and the Movies. *Ungar, 1977.*

Peck, Harry Thurston. The Personal Equation. *Harper, 1898.*

Pendo, Stephen. Raymond Chandler on Screen: His Novels into Film. *Scarecrow Press, 1976.*

Percival, W. P., ed. Leading Canadian Poets. *Ryerson Press, 1948.*

Phelps, William Lyon. The Advance of English Poetry in the Twentieth Century. *Dodd, Mead, 1918, 1925.*

Phelps, William Lyon. As I Like It. *Scribner's, 1923.*

Phelps, William Lyon. Essays on Modern Novelists. *Macmillan, 1924.*

Phelps, William Lyon. Howells, James, Bryant and Other Essays. *Macmillan, 1924.*

Poggioli, Renato. The Poets of Russia: 1890-1930. *Harvard University Press, 1960.*

Pollard, Percival. Masks and Minstrels of New Germany. *John W. Luce, 1911.*

Poulet, Georges. Proustian Space. *Translated by Elliott Coleman. Johns Hopkins University Press, 1977.*

Punter, David. The Literature of Terror: A History of Gothic Fiction from 1765 to the Present Day. *Longman, 1980.*

Quiller-Couch, Arthur. Adventures in Criticism. *Scribner's, 1896, Putnam, 1925.*

Ramchand, Kenneth. The West Indian Novel and Its Background. *Barnes & Noble, 1970.*

Raper, Julius Rowan. From the Sunken Garden: The Fiction of Ellen Glasgow, 1916-1945. *Louisiana State University Press, 1980.*

Read, Herbert. Reason and Romanticism: Essays in Literary Criticism. *Faber and Gwyer, 1926, Russell and Russell, 1963.*

Reilly, John H. Jean Giraudoux. *Twayne, 1978.*

Rexroth, Kenneth. The Elastic Retort: Essays in Literature and Ideas. *Continuum, 1973.*

Richards, I. A. Complimentaries: Uncollected Essays. *Edited by John Paul Russo. Harvard University Press, 1976.*

Ridge, George Ross. The Hero in French Decadent Literature. *University of Georgia Press, 1961.*

Roberts, C.G.D. Introduction to Sappho: One Hundred Lyrics, *by Bliss Carman. L. C. Page, 1904, Chatto and Windus, 1930.*

Roberts, S. C. Holmes and Watson: A Miscellany. *Oxford University Press, 1953.*

Rosenburg, Samuel. Naked Is the Best Disguise: The Death and Resurrection of Sherlock Holmes. *Bobbs-Merrill, 1974.*

Rosten, Norman. *Foreword to* We Stand United, *by Stephen Vincent Benét. Farrar and Rinehart, 1945.*

Rouse, Blair. Ellen Glasgow. *Twayne Books, 1962.*

Sale, Roger. Fairy Tales and After: From Snow White to E. B. White. *Harvard University Press, 1978.*

Sandburg, Carl. Home Front Memo. *Harcourt, 1943.*

Santayana, George. Obiter Scripta: Lectures, Essays and Reviews. *Edited by Justus Buchler and Benjamin Schwartz. Scribner's, 1936.*

Sartre, Jean-Paul. Literary and Philosophical Essays. *Translated by Annette Michelson. Rider and Co., 1955.*

Sayers, Dorothy L. *Introduction to* The Omnibus of Crime. *Edited by Dorothy L. Sayers. Payson and Clark, 1929.*

Seferis, George. On the Greek Style: Selected Essays in Poetry and Hellenism. *Translated by Rex Warner and Th. D. Frangopoulos, Bodley Head, 1966.*

Shanks, Edward. *Epilogue to* The Works of M. P. Shiel: A Study in Bibliography, *by A. Reynolds Morse. Fantasy Publishing Co., 1948.*

Shattuck, Roger. Proust's Binoculars: A Study of Memory, Time and Recognition in "A la recherche du temps perdu." *Random House, 1963.*

Shaw, Bernard. Dramatic Opinions and Essays with an Apology, Vol. 1. *Brentano's, 1907.*

Shaw, Bernard. Pen Portraits and Reviews. *Rev. ed. Constable, 1932.*

Shepard, Odell. Bliss Carman. *McClelland and Stewart, 1923.*

Sherrard, Philip. The Marble Threshing Floor: Studies in Modern Greek Poetry. *Vallentine, Mitchell, 1956.*

Shumaker, Wayne. The Man of Wax: Critical Essays of George Moore. *Edited by Douglas A. Hughes. New York University Press, 1971.*

Sidney-Fryer, Donald. A Vision of Doom: Poems by Ambrose Bierce. *Donald M. Grant, 1980.*

Simonson, Harold P. Zona Gale. *Twayne, 1962.*

Sitwell, Osbert. Penny Foolish: A Book of Tirades and Panegyrics. *Macmillan, London and Basingstroke, 1935, Books for Libraries Press, 1967.*

Slonim, Marc. Modern Russian Literature: From Chekhov to the Present. *Oxford University Press, 1953.*

Slonim, Marc. Soviet Russian Literature: Writers and Problems 1917-1977. *Rev. ed. Oxford University Press, 1977.*

Smith, Stanley Astredo. *Introduction to* Tristi amori, *by Giuseppe Giacosa. Edited by Rudolph Altrocchi and Benjamin Mather Woodbridge. University of Chicago Press, 1920.*

Sochen, June. Movers and Shakers: American Women Thinkers and Activists, 1900-1970. *Quadrangle, 1973.*

Sokel, Walter H. The Writer in Extremis: Expressionism in Twentieth Century German Literature. *Stanford University Press, 1968.*

Sorley, Charles Hamilton. The Poems and Selected Letters of Charles Hamilton Sorley. *Edited by Hilda D. Spear. Blackness Press, 1978.*

Speir, Jerry. Raymond Chandler. *Ungar, 1981.*

Stanton, Edward F. The Magic Myth: Lorca and "Cante Jondo." *University Press of Kentucky, 1978.*

Starrett, Vincent. Buried Caesars: Essays in Literary Appreciation. *Covici-McGee, 1923.*

Starrett, Vincent. Books Alive: A Profane Chronicle of Literary Endeavor and Literary Misdemeanor. *Random House, 1940.*

Stephensen, P. R. The Legend of Aleister Crowley: Being a Study of the Documentary Evidence Relating to a Campaign of Personal Vilification Unparalleled in Literary History. *Llewellyn Publications, 1970.*

Sterling, George. *Introduction to* An Invocation, *by Ambrose Bierce. J. H. Nash, 1928.*

Strauss, Walter A. Proust and Literature: The Novelist As Critic. *Harvard University Press, 1957.*

Stroud, Parry. Stephen Vincent Benet. *Twayne, 1962.*

Swinnerton, Frank. The Georgian Literary Scene, 1910-1935. *Rev. ed. Hutchinson, 1969.*

Symonds, John. *Introduction to* White Stains, *by Aleister Crowley. Edited by John Symonds. Duckworth, 1973.*

Symons, Arthur. The Symbolist Movement in Literature. *Rev. ed. Dutton, 1908.*

Symons, Julian. Portrait of an Artist: Conan Doyle. *Whizzard Press, 1979.*

Thompson, Francis. Literary Criticism. *Edited by Terrence L. Connolly, S.J. Dutton, 1948.*

Trotsky, Leon. Literature and Revolution. *Translated by Rose Strunsky. Russell & Russell, 1925.*

Twain, Mark. What Is Man? and Other Essays. *Harper, 1917.*

Valency, Maurice. The End of the World: An Introduction to Contemporary Drama. *Oxford University Press, 1980.*

Van Doren, Carl. Contemporary American Novelists: 1900-1920. *Macmillan, 1922.*

Wagenknecht, Edward. Utopia Americana. *University of Washington Book Store, 1929.*

Wagner, Jean. Black Poets of the United States: From Paul Laurence Dunbar to Langston Hughes. *University of Illinois Press, 1973.*

Ward, A. C. Twentieth-Century Literature: 1901-1950. *3d ed. Methuen, 1956.*

Weales, Gerald. Religion in Modern English Drama. *University of Pennsylvania Press, 1962.*

Wellek, René. A History of Modern Criticism: 1750-1950, the Later Nineteenth Century. *Yale University Press, 1965.*

Wells, H. G. Mr. Belloc Objects to ''The Outline of History.'' *Watts & Co., 1926.*

Wells, Henry W. The American Way of Poetry. *Columbia University Press, 1943, Russell & Russell, 1964.*

Weygandt, Cornelius. Irish Plays and Playwrights. *Houghton Mifflin, 1913, Kennikat Press, 1966.*

Wharton, Edith. The Writing of Fiction. *Scribner's, 1925, Octagon Books, 1966.*

White, E. B. *Introduction to* The Lives and Times of Archy and Mehitabel, *by Don Marquis. Doubleday, 1950.*

Williams, Harold. Modern English Writers: Being a Study of Imaginative Literature, 1890-1914. *Sidgwick & Jackson, 1918.*

Williams, William Carlos. Selected Essays of William Carlos Williams. *Random House, 1954.*

Wilson, Edmund. The Triple Thinkers: Twelve Essays on Literary Subjects. *Oxford University Press, 1948.*

Wilson, Edmund. Classics and Commercials: A Literary Chronicle of the Forties. *Noonday Press, 1950.*

Wilson, Edmund. Axel's Castle: A Study in the Imaginative Literature of 1870-1930. *Scribner's, 1953.*

Woolf, Virginia. The Death of the Moth and Other Essays. *Harcourt, 1942.*

Woolf, Virginia. The Common Reader, first and second series. *Harcourt, 1948.*

Woolf, Virginia. Granite and Rainbow. *Harcourt, 1958.*

Yates, Norris W. The American Humorist: Conscience of the Twentieth Century. *Iowa State University Press, 1964.*

Yeats, W. B. Autobiographies. *Macmillan, 1955.*

Zamyatin, Yevgeny. A Soviet Heretic: Essays. *Edited and translated by Mirra Ginsburg. University of Chicago Press, 1970.*

Ziff, Larzer. The American 1890s: Life and Times of a Lost Generation. *Viking Penguin, 1966.*

Zola, Emile. The Experimental Novel and Other Essays. *Translated by Belle M. Sherman. Cassell Publishing Co., 1893.*

Cumulative Index to Authors

A. E. 3
Abhavananda
  See Crowley, Aleister
Adams, Henry (Brooks) 4
Agee, James 1
Akers, Floyd
  See Baum, L(yman) Frank
Alain-Fournier 6
Alain Fournier, Henri
  See Alain-Fournier
Alcayaga, Lucila Godoy
  See Mistral, Gabriela
Aleichem, Sholom 1
Amo, Tauraatua i
  See Adams, Henry (Brooks)
Anderson, Maxwell 2
Anderson, Sherwood 1
Andouard
  See Giraudoux, (Hippolyte)
  Jean
Andreyev, Leonid
  (Nikolaevich) 3
Apollinaire, Guillaume 3
Artaud, Antonin 3
Asch, Sholem 3
Atherton, Gertrude (Franklin
  Horn) 2
Atherton, Lucius
  See Masters, Edgar Lee
Azuela, Mariano 3
"Bab"
  See Gilbert, (Sir) W(illiam)
  S(chwenk)
Babel, Isaak (Emmanuilovich) 2
Bancroft, Laura
  See Baum, L(yman) Frank
Barbusse, Henri 5
Barrie, (Sir) J(ames)
  M(atthew) 2
Bassetto, Corno di
  See Shaw, George Bernard
Baum Louis F.
  See Baum, L(yman) Frank
Baum, L(yman) Frank 7

Beauchamp, Kathleen Mansfield
  See Mansfield, Katherine
Bean, Normal
  See Burroughs, Edgar Rice
Beerbohm, (Sir Henry)
  Max(imilian) 1
Belasco, David 3
Beleño
  See Azuela, Mariano
Belloc, (Joseph) Hilaire
  (Pierre) 7
Benavente (y Martinez),
  Jacinto 3
Benchley, Robert 1
Benét, Stephen Vincent 7
Benn, Gottfried 3
Bennett, (Enoch) Arnold 5
Bernanos, (Paul Louis)
  Georges 3
Betti, Ugo 5
Bierce, Ambrose (Gwinett) 1, 7
Bishop, George Archibald
  See Crowley, Aleister
Bjarme, Brynjolf
  See Ibsen, (Johan) Henrik
Bjørnson, Bjørnstjerne
  (Martinius) 7
Blackwood, Algernon (Henry) 5
Blair, Eric Arthur
  See Orwell, George
Bliss, Reginald
  See Wells, H(erbert) G(eorge)
Blok, Aleksandr
  (Aleksandrovich) 5
Borchert, Wolfgang 5
Boyd, Nancy
  See Millay, Edna St. Vincent
Brecht, (Eugen) Bertolt
  (Friedrich) 1, 6
Brent of Bin Bin
  See Franklin, (Stella Maria
  Sarah) Miles
Bridges, Robert 1
Bridie, James 3
Brooke, Rupert (Chawner) 2, 7

Bugaev, Boris Nikolayevich
  See Bely, Andrey
Bulgakov, Mikhail
  (Afanas'evich) 2
Bunin, Ivan (Alexeyevich) 6
Burroughs, Edgar Rice 2
Butler, Samuel 1
Caballera
  See Machado, (y Ruiz),
  Antonio
Cabell, James Branch 6
Cable, George Washington 4
Campbell, (Ignatius) Roy
  (Dunnachie) 5
Čapek, Karl 6
Carman, (William) Bliss 7
Carr, H. D.
  See Crowley, Aleister
Cary, (Arthur) Joyce 1
Casey, Patrick
  See Thurman, Wallace
Cather, Willa (Sibert) 1
Cavafy, C(onstantine) P(eter) 2,
  7
Chandler, Raymond 1, 7
Chapman, John Jay 7
Chekhonte, Antosha
  See Chekhov, Anton
  (Pavlovich)
Chekhov, Anton (Pavlovich) 3
Chesnutt, Charles Waddell 5
Chesterton, G(ilbert) K(eith) 1,
  6
Chopin, Kate (O'Flaherty) 5
Chou Ch'o
  See Lu Hsün
Chou Shu-jen
  See Lu Hsün
Chubb, Elmer
  See Masters, Edgar Lee
Claudel, Paul (Louis Charles
  Marie) 2
Clemens, Samuel Langhorne
  See Twain, Mark

Clive, Arthur
  See O'Grady, Standish (James)
Colette (Sidonie-Gabrielle) 1, 5
Conrad, Joseph 1, 6
Conte, Sieur Louis de
  See Twain, Mark
Cooke, John Estes
  See Baum, L(yman) Frank
Coppard, A(lfred) E(dgar) 5
Cordelier, Jean
  See Giraudoux, (Hippolyte)
  Jean
Cordelier, Maurice
  See Giraudoux, (Hippolyte)
  Jean
Crane, (Harold) Hart 2, 5
Crowley, Aleister 7
Crowley, Edward Alexander
  See Crowley, Aleister
Cullen, Countee 4
D'Annunzio, Gabriele 6
Darío, Rubén 4
David, Leon
  See Jacob, (Cyprien) Max
Davies, W(illiam) H(enry) 5
Davis, Rebecca (Blaine)
  Harding 6
De la Mare, Walter (John) 4
Dowson, Ernest (Christopher) 4
Doyle, (Sir) Arthur Conan 7
Drop Shot
  See Cable, George Washington
du Hault, Jean
  See Eluard, Paul
Dunbar, Paul Laurence 2
Dunsany, Lord (Edward John
  Moreton Drax Plunkett) 2
Echegaray (y Eizaguirre), José
  (María Waldo) 4
Edwards, Eli
  See McKay, Claude
Éluard, Paul 7
Esenin, Sergei
  (Aleksandrovich) 4
Feuchtwanger, Lion 3

AUTHOR INDEX

Firbank, (Arthur Annesley)
Ronald **1**
Fitzgerald, Captain Hugh
See Baum, L(yman) Frank
Fitzgerald, F(rancis) Scott
(Key) **1, 6**
Ford, Ford Madox **1**
Ford, Webster
See Masters, Edgar Lee
Franklin, Benjamin
See Hašek, Jaroslav (Matej
Frantisek)
Franklin, (Stella Maria Sarah)
Miles **7**
Gaelique, Morven le
See Jacob, (Cyprien) Max
Gale, Zona **7**
Galsworthy, John **1**
García Lorca, Federico **1, 7**
Garland, (Hannibal) Hamlin **3**
A Gentleman of the University of
Cambridge
See Crowley, Aleister
George, Stefan (Anton) **2**
Gerden, Friedrich Carl
See Grove, Frederick Philip
Giacosa, Giuseppe **7**
Gibbon, Lewis Grassic **4**
Gibran, Kahlil **1**
Gide, André (Paul Guillaume) **5**
Gilbert, (Sir) W(illiam)
S(chwenck) **3**
Giraudoux, (Hippolyte) Jean **2,
7**
Gissing, George (Robert) **3**
Glasgow, Ellen (Anderson
Gholson) **2, 7**
Glockenhammer, Walter
See Wells, H(erbert) G(eorge)
Grafe, Felix
See Grove, Frederick Philip
Graham, Tom
See Lewis, (Harry) Sinclair
Granville-Barker, Harley **2**
Gregory, Lady (Isabella Augusta
Persse) **1**
Greve, Elsa
See Grove, Frederick Philip
Greve, Felix Paul Berthold
Friedrich
See Grove, Frederick Philip
Grey, (Pearl) Zane **6**
Grile, Dod
See Bierce, Ambrose (Gwinett)
Grindel, Eugène
See Eluard, Paul
Grove, Frederick Philip **4**
Grumbler
See Twain, Mark
Gudabutsu
See Natsume, Sōseki
Hamsun, Knut **2**
Hardy, Thomas **4**
Harris, Joel Chandler **2**
Harte, (Francis) Bret(t) **1**
Haruki, Shimazaki
See Shimazaki, Tōson
Hašek, Jaroslav (Matej
Frantisek) **4**
Hauptmann, Gerhart (Johann
Robert) **4**

Hayaseca y Eizaguirre, Jorge
See Echegaray (y Eizaguirre),
José (María Waldo)
Heidenstam, (Karl Gustaf) Verner
von **5**
Hellenhofferu, Vojtech Kapristían
z
See Hašek, Jaroslav (Matej
Frantisek)
Henderson, Mary
See Bridie, James
Henry, O. **1**
Herman, William
See Bierce, Ambrose (Gwinett)
Hervent, Maurice
See Eluard, Paul
Housman, A(lfred) E(dward) **1**
Housman, Laurence **7**
Howells, William Dean **7**
Hueffer, Ford Madox
See Ford, Ford Madox
Huysmans, Charles-Marie-George
See Huysmans, Joris-Karl
Huysmans, Joris-Karl **7**
Ibsen, Henrik (Johan) **2**
Jacob, (Cyprien) Max **6**
James, Henry **2**
James, M(ontague) R(hodes) **6**
Jarry, Alfred **2**
Jewett, Sarah Orne **1**
Jiménez (Mantecón), Juan
Ramón **4**
Johnson, James Weldon **3**
Josh
See Twain, Mark
Joyce, James (Augustine
Aloysius) **3**
Kafka, Franz **2, 6**
Kazantzakis, Nikos **2, 5**
Kellock, Archibald P.
See Bridie, James
Kielland, Alexander (Lange) **5**
Korzeniowski, Teodor Jozef
Konrad
See Conrad, Joseph
Kostrowitzki, Wilhelm
Apollinaris de
See Apollinaire, Guillaume
Kraus, Karl **5**
Kuprin, Aleksandr (Ivanovich) **5**
Lagerlöf, Selma (Ottiliana
Lovisa) **4**
Lardner, Ring(gold Wilmer) **2**
Lawrence, D(avid) H(erbert) **2**
Lazarus, Felix
See Cable, George Washington
Leacock, Stephen (Butler) **2**
Lee, Vernon **5**
Leigh, Johanna
See Sayers, Dorothy L.
Lewis, Alun **3**
Lewis, (Harry) Sinclair **4**
Lewis, (Percy) Wyndham **2**
Lie, Jonas (Lauritz Idemil) **5**
Lin, Frank
See Atherton, Gertrude
(Franklin Horn)
Littlewit, Gent., Humphrey
See Lovecraft, H(oward)
P(hillips)
Litwos
See Sienkiewicz, Henryk
(Adam Aleksandr Pius)

Lovecraft, H(oward) P(hillips) **4**
Lowell, Amy **1**
Lowry, (Clarence) Malcolm **6**
Lu Hsün **3**
Lynch, James
See Andreyev, Leonid
(Nikolaevich)
Macaulay, (Dame Emile)
Rose **7**
Machado (y Ruiz), Antonio **3**
Machen, Arthur (Llewellyn
Jones) **4**
Maeterlinck, Maurice **3**
A Man without a Spleen
See Chekhov, Anton
(Pavlovich)
Mandelstam, Osip
(Emilievich) **2, 6**
Mandrake, Ethel Belle
See Thurman, Wallace
Manière, J.-E.
See Giraudoux, (Hippolyte)
Jean
Mann, Thomas **2**
Mansfield, Katherine **2**
Marquis, Don(ald Robert
Perry) **7**
Martínez Sierra, Gregorio and
Martínez Sierra, María (de la
O'LeJárraga) **6**
Masters, Edgar Lee **2**
Mavor, Osborne Henry
See Bridie, James
Mayakovsky, Vladimir
(Vladimirovich) **4**
McKay, Claude **7**
McKay, Festus Claudius
See McKay, Claude
Metcalf, Suzanne
See Baum, L(yman) Frank
Meynell, Alice (Christiana
Gertrude Thompson) **6**
Millay, Edna St. Vincent **4**
Milne, A(lan) A(lexander) **6**
Minehaha, Cornelius
See Wedekind, (Benjamin)
Frank(lin)
Miró (Ferrer), Gabriel (Francisco
Víctor) **5**
Mistral, Gabriela **2**
Mitchell, James Leslie
See Gibbon, Lewis Grassic
Moore, Edward
See Muir, Edwin
Moore, George (Augustus) **7**
Muggins
See Twain, Mark
Muir, Edwin **2**
Munro, H[ector] H[ugh]
See Saki
My Brother's Brother
See Chekhov, Anton
(Pavlovich)
Natsume, Kinnosuke
See Natsume, Sōseki
Natsume, Sōseki **2**
Netterville, Luke
See O'Grady, Standish (James)
Norman, Louis
See Carman, (William) Bliss
Noyes, Alfred **7**
O'Grady, Standish (James) **5**

Oldcastle, Alice
See Meynell, Alice (Christiana
Gertrude Thompson)
O'Neill, Eugene (Gladstone) **1,
6**
Orwell, George **2, 6**
Owen, Wilfred (Edward
Salter) **5**
Paget, Violet
See Lee, Vernon
Palamas, Kostes **5**
Pavese, Cesare **3**
Pedersen, Knut
See Hamsun, Knut
Perderabo, Frater
See Crowley, Aleister
Perry, Brighton
See Sherwood, Robert E(mmet)
Phillimore, Francis
See Meynell, Alice (Christiana
Gertrude Thompson)
Phillips, Ward
See Lovecraft, H(oward)
P(hillips)
Pirandello, Luigi **4**
Porter, William Sydney
See Henry, O.
Proust, Marcel **7**
Prowler, Harley
See Masters, Edgar Lee
Puckett, Lute
See Masters, Edgar Lee
Rabinowitz, Solomon
See Aleichem, Sholom
Raleigh, Richard
See Lovecraft, H(oward)
P(hillips)
Ramal, Walter
See De la Mare, Walter (John)
Rawlings, Marjorie Kinnan **4**
Révélé, Le
See Artaud, Antonin
Reymont, Władysław
Stanisław **5**
Richardson, Dorothy (Miller) **3**
Richardson, Henry Handel **4**
Rilke, Rainer Maria **1, 6**
Robertson, Ethel Florence
Lindesay Richardson
See Richardson, Henry Handel
Robinson, Edwin Arlington **5**
Rostand, Edmond (Eugène
Alexis) **6**
Ruffian, M.
See Hašek, Jaroslav (Matej
Frantisek)
Russell, George William
See A. E.
St. E. A. of M. and S.
See Crowley, Aleister
Saint-Exupéry, Antoine (Jean
Baptiste Marie Roger) de **2**
Saki **3**
Sarmiento, Félix Rubén García
See Darío, Rubén
Sayers, Dorothy L(eigh) **2**
Schmitz, Ettore
See Svevo, Italo
Schnitzler, Arthur **4**
Schulz, Bruno **5**
Scott, Duncan Campbell **6**
Shaw, George Bernard **3**
Sherwood, Robert E(mmet) **3**

Shimazaki, Tōson **5**
Sienkiewicz, Henryk (Adam
    Aleksander Pius) **3**
Siluriensis, Leolinus
    See Machen, Arthur (Llewellyn
    Jones)
Sinclair, Julian
    See Sinclair, May
Sinclair, May **3**
Smith, Sosthenes
    See Wells, H(erbert) G(eorge)
Snodgrass, Thomas Jefferson
    See Twain, Mark
Snow, Frances Compton
    See Adams, Henry (Brooks)
Softly, Edgar
    See Lovecraft, H(oward)
    P(hillips)
Staunton, Schuyler
    See Baum, L(yman) Frank
Stein, Gertrude **1, 6**
Stephens, James **4**
Stevens, Wallace **3**
Storni, Alfonsina **5**
Strindberg, (Johan) August **1**
Sutro, Alfred **6**

Svarev, Count Vladimir
    See Crowley, Aleister
Svevo, Italo **2**
Swift, Augustus T.
    See Lovecraft, H(oward)
    P(hillips)
Synge, (Edmund) John
    Millington **6**
Tagore, (Sir) Rabindranath **3**
Teasdale, Sara **4**
Thākura, Sir Ravīndranāth
    See Tagore, (Sir) Rabindranath
Theobald, Jr., Lewis
    See Lovecraft, H(oward)
    P(hillips)
Therion, Master
    See Crowley, Aleister
Thomas, Dylan **1**
Thompson, A. C.
    See Meynell, Alice (Christiana
    Gertrude Thompson)
Thompson, Francis (Joseph) **4**
Thorer, Konrad
    See Grove, Frederick Philip
Thorne, Edouard
    See Grove, Frederick Philip
Thurman, Wallace **6**

Tolstoy, (Count) Leo (Lev
    Nikolaevich) **4**
Tonson, Jacob
    See Bennett, (Enoch) Arnold
Trakl, Georg **5**
Twain, Mark **6**
Tynan (Hinkson), Katharine **3**
Unamuno (y Jugo), Miguel de **2**
Undset, Sigrid **3**
Valéry, Paul (Ambroise Toussaint
    Jules) **4**
Valle-Inclán (y Montenegro),
    Ramón (María) del **5**
Valle y Peña, Ramón José Simón
    See Valle-Inclán (y
    Montenegro), Ramón (María)
    del
Vallejo, César (Abraham) **3**
Van Druten, John (William) **2**
Van Dyne, Edith
    See Baum, L(yman) Frank
Verey, Rev. C.
    See Crowley, Aleister
Verga, Giovanni **3**
Verne, Jules (Gabriel) **6**
Wallace, Dexter
    See Masters, Edgar Lee

Walpole, (Sir) Hugh
    (Seymour) **5**
Wassermann, Jakob **6**
Wedekind, (Benjamin)
    Frank(lin) **7**
Weinstein, Nathan Wallenstein
    See West, Nathanael
Wells, H(erbert) G(eorge) **6**
West, Nathanael **1**
Wetcheek, J. L.
    See Feuchtwanger, Lion
Wharton, Edith (Newbold
    Jones) **3**
Wilde, Oscar (Fingal O'Flahertie
    Wills) **1**
Williams, Charles **1**
Willie, Albert Frederick
    See Lovecraft, H(oward)
    P(hillips)
Wolfe, Thomas (Clayton) **4**
Woolf, (Adeline) Virginia **1, 5**
Woollcott, Alexander
    (Humphreys) **5**
Yeats, William Butler **1**
Zola, Émile **1, 6**

AUTHOR INDEX

Cumulative Index to Nationalities

AMERICAN

Adams, Henry **4**
Agee, James **1**
Anderson, Maxwell **2**
Anderson, Sherwood **1**
Atherton, Gertrude **2**
Baum, L. Frank **7**
Belasco, David **3**
Benchley, Robert **1**
Benét, Stephen Vincent **7**
Bierce, Ambrose **1, 7**
Burroughs, Edgar Rice **2**
Cabell, James Branch **6**
Cable, George Washington **4**
Cather, Willa **1**
Chandler, Raymond **1, 7**
Chapman, John Jay **7**
Chesnutt, Charles Waddell **5**
Chopin, Kate **5**
Crane, Hart **2, 5**
Cullen, Countee **4**
Davis, Rebecca Harding **6**
Dunbar, Paul Laurence **2**
Fitzgerald, F. Scott **1, 6**
Gale, Zona **7**
Garland, Hamlin **3**
Glasgow, Ellen **2, 7**
Grey, Zane **6**
Harris, Joel Chandler **2**
Harte, Bret **1**
Henry, O. **1**
Howells, William Dean **7**
James, Henry **2**
Jewett, Sarah Orne **1**
Johnson, James Weldon **3**
Lardner, Ring **2**
Lewis, Sinclair **4**
Lovecraft, H. P. **4**
Lowell, Amy **1**

Marquis, Don **7**
Masters, Edgar Lee **2**
McKay, Claude **7**
Millay, Edna St. Vincent **4**
O'Neill, Eugene **1, 6**
Rawlings, Majorie Kinnan **4**
Robinson, Edwin Arlington **5**
Sherwood, Robert E. **3**
Stein, Gertrude **1, 6**
Stevens, Wallace **3**
Teasdale, Sara **4**
Thurman, Wallace **6**
Twain, Mark **6**
West, Nathanael **1**
Wharton, Edith **3**
Wolfe, Thomas **4**
Woollcott, Alexander **5**

ARGENTINIAN

Storni, Alfonsina **5**

AUSTRALIAN

Franklin, Miles **7**
Richardson, Henry Handel **4**

AUSTRIAN

Kafka, Franz **2, 6**
Kraus, Karl **5**
Schnitzler, Arthur **4**
Trakl, Georg **5**

BELGIAN

Maeterlinck, Maurice **3**

CANADIAN

Carman, Bliss **7**
Grove, Frederick Philip **4**
Leacock, Stephen **2**
Scott, Duncan Campbell **6**

CHILEAN

Mistral, Gabriela **2**

CHINESE

Lu Hsün **3**

CZECHOSLOVAKIAN

Capek, Karel **6**
Hašek, Jaroslav **4**

ENGLISH

Beerbohm, Max **1**
Belloc, Hilaire **7**
Bennett, Arnold **5**
Blackwood, Algernon **5**
Bridges, Robert **1**
Brooke, Rupert **2, 7**
Butler, Samuel **1**
Chesterton, G. K. **1, 6**
Conrad, Joseph **1, 6**
Coppard, A. E. **5**
Crowley, Aleister **7**
de la Mare, Walter **4**
Dowson, Ernest **4**
Doyle, Arthur Conan **7**
Firbank, Ronald **1**
Ford, Ford Madox **1**
Galsworthy, John **1**
Gilbert, W. S. **3**
Gissing, George **3**
Granville-Barker, Harley **2**
Hardy, Thomas **4**
Housman, A. E. **1**
Housman, Laurence **7**
James, M. R. **6**
Lawrence, D. H. **2**
Lee, Vernon **5**
Lewis, Wyndham **2**
Lowry, Malcolm **6**

Macaulay, Rose **7**
Meynell, Alice **6**
Milne, A. A. **6**
Noyes, Alfred **7**
Orwell, George **2, 6**
Owen, Wilfred **5**
Richardson, Dorothy **3**
Saki **3**
Sayers, Dorothy L. **2**
Sinclair, May **3**
Sutro, Alfred **6**
Thompson, Francis **4**
Van Druten, John **2**
Walpole, Hugh **5**
Wells, H. G. **6**
Williams, Charles **1**
Woolf, Virginia **1, 5**

FRENCH

Alain-Fournier **6**
Apollinaire, Guillaume **3**
Artaud, Antonin **3**
Barbusse, Henri **5**
Bernanos, Georges **3**
Claudel, Paul **2**
Colette **1, 5**
Éluard, Paul **7**
Gide, André **5**
Giraudoux, Jean **2, 7**
Huysmans, Joris-Karl **7**
Jacob, Max **6**
Jarry, Alfred **2**
Proust, Marcel **7**
Rostand, Edmond **6**
Saint-Exupéry, Antoine de **2**
Valéry, Paul **4**
Verne, Jules **6**
Zola, Émile **1, 6**

GERMAN
Benn, Gottfried   3
Borchert, Wolfgang   5
Brecht, Bertolt   1, 6
Feuchtwanger, Lion   3
George, Stefan   2
Hauptmann, Gerhart   4
Mann, Thomas   2
Rilke, Rainer Maria   1, 6
Wassermann, Jakob   6
Wedekind, Frank   7

GREEK
Cafavy, C. P.   2, 7
Kazantzakis, Nikos   2, 5
Palamas, Kostes   5

INDIAN
Tagore, Rabindranath   3

IRISH
A. E.   3
Cary, Joyce   1
Dunsany, Lord   2
Gregory, Lady   1
Joyce, James   3
Moore, George   7
O'Grady, Standish   5
Shaw, George Bernard   3
Stephens, James   4
Synge, J. M.   6
Tynan, Katharine   3

Wilde, Oscar   1
Yeats, William Butler   1

ITALIAN
Betti, Ugo   5
D'Annunzio, Gabriel   6
Giacosa, Giuseppe   7
Pavese, Cesare   3
Pirandello, Luigi   4
Svevo, Italo   2
Verga, Giovanni   3

JAPANESE
Natsume, Sōseki   2
Shimazaki, Tōson   5

LEBANESE
Gibran, Kahlil   1

MEXICAN
Azuela, Mariano   3

NEW ZEALAND
Mansfield, Katherine   2

NICARAGUAN
Darío, Rubén   4

NORWEGIAN
Bjørnson, Bjørnstjerne   7
Hamsun, Knut   2

Ibsen, Henrik   2
Kielland, Alexander   5
Lie, Jonas   5
Undset, Sigrid   3

PERUVIAN
Vallejo, César   3

POLISH
Reymont, Wladyslaw
   Stanislaw   5
Schulz, Bruno   5
Sienkiewitz, Henryk   3

RUSSIAN
Andreyev, Leonid   3
Babel, Isaak   2
Bely, Andrey   7
Blok, Aleksandr   5
Bulgakov, Mikhail   2
Bunin, Ivan   6
Chekhov, Anton   3
Esenin, Sergei   4
Kuprin, Aleksandr   5
Mandelstam, Osip   2, 6
Mayakovsky, Vladimir   4
Tolstoy, Leo   4
Tsvetaeva, Marina   7

SCOTTISH
Barrie, J. M.   2
Bridie, James   3

Gibbon, Lewis Grassic   4
Muir, Edwin   2

SOUTH AFRICAN
Campbell, Roy   5

SPANISH
Benavente, Jacinto   3
Echegaray, José   4
García Lorca, Federico   1, 7
Jiménez, Juan Ramón   4
Machado, Antonio   3
Martínez Sierra, Gregorio   6
Miró, Gabriel   5
Unamuno, Miguel de   2
Valle-Inclán, Ramón del   5

SWEDISH
Heidenstam, Verner von   5
Lagerlöf, Selma   4
Strindberg, August   1

WELSH
Davies, W. H.   5
Lewis, Alun   3
Machen, Arthur   4
Thomas, Dylan   1

YIDDISH
Aleichem, Sholom   1
Asch, Sholem   3

Cumulative Index to Critics

Aaron, Daniel
Nathanael West **1**:485

Abcarian, Richard
Sherwood Anderson **1**:59

Abel, Lionel
Bertolt Brecht **1**:109
Henrik Ibsen **2**:232

Abercrombie, Lascelles
Thomas Hardy **4**:153

Abrams, Ivan B.
Sholom Aleichem **1**:24

Abramson, Doris E.
Wallace Thurman **6**:449

Abril, Xavier
Cesar Vallejo **3**:526

Adams, Henry
William Dean Howells **7**:363

Adams, J. Donald
F. Scott Fitzgerald **1**:239

Adams, Marion
Gottfried Benn **3**:111

Adams, Phoebe-Lou
Malcolm Lowry **6**:237

Adams, Robert M.
Gabriele D'Annunzio **6**:140

Adams, Robert Martin
James Joyce **3**:273

Adams, Samuel Hopkins
Alexander Woollcott **5**:524

Adams, Walter S.
Thomas Wolfe **4**:506

Adcock, A. St. John
O. Henry **1**:347
George Bernard Shaw **3**:386

Adell, Alberto
Ramón del Valle-Inclán **5**:484

Aguirre, Ángel Manuel
Juan Ramón Jiménez **4**:223

Aguinaga, Carlos Blanco
Miguel de Unamuno **2**:561

Aiken, Conrad
Sherwood Anderson **1**:37
Robert Bridges **1**:127
James Branch Cabell **6**:62
Walter de la Mare **4**:71
F. Scott Fitzgerald **1**:237
John Galsworthy **1**:296
Federico García Lorca **1**:308
Thomas Hardy **4**:155
D. H. Lawrence **2**:344
Edgar Lee Masters **2**:460
Eugene O'Neill **1**:383
Dorothy Richardson **3**:349
Rainer Maria Rilke **1**:414
Edwin Arlington Robinson
5:403
Gertrude Stein **6**:406
Dylan Thomas **1**:466
Virginia Woolf **1**:529

Akhsharumov, N. D.
Leo Tolstoy **4**:446

Alcott, Louisa May
Rebecca Harding Davis **6**:148

Aldington, Richard
Oscar Wilde **1**:499

Aldiss, Brian W.
Jules Verne **6**:497

Aldridge, John
F. Scott Fitzgerald **1**:246

Alexandrova, Vera
Sergei Esenin **4**:113

Allen, Paul M.
Jakob Wassermann **6**:520

Allen, Walter
Arnold Bennett **5**:40
Wyndham Lewis **2**:394
Dorothy Richardson **3**:358

Alpert, Hollis
O. Henry **1**:350

Alsen, Eberhard
Hamlin Garland **3**:200

Altrocchi, Rudolph
Gabriele D'Annunzio **6**:135

Alvarez, A.
Hart Crane **2**:118
D. H. Lawrence **2**:364
Wallace Stevens **3**:454
William Butler Yeats **1**:564

Amann, Clarence A.
James Weldon Johnson **3**:247

Amis, Kingsley
G. K. Chesterton **1**:185
Jules Verne **6**:493

Amoia, Alba della Fazia
Edmond Rostand **6**:381

Anders, Gunther
Franz Kafka **2**:302

Anderson, David D.
Sherwood Anderson **1**:52

Anderson, Isaac
Raymond Chandler **7**:167

Anderson, Maxwell
Edna St. Vincent Millay **4**:306

Anderson, Quentin
Willa Cather **1**:163

Anderson, Sherwood
Gertrude Stein **6**:407
Mark Twain **6**:459

Andrews, William L.
Charles Waddel Chesnutt **5**:136

Angenot, Marc
Jules Verne **6**:501

Annenkov, P. V.
Leo Tolstoy **4**:444

Anouilh, Jean
Jean Giraudoux **7**:320

Anthony, Edward
Don Marquis **7**:443

Antoninus, Brother
Hart Crane **2**:119

Aquilar, Helene J.F. de
Federico García Lorca **7**:302

Aragon, Louis
Paul Éluard **7**:249

Aratari, Anthony
Federico García Lorca **1**:316

Arce de Vazquez, Margot
Gabriela Mistral **2**:477

Archer, William
Bliss Carman **7**:135
W. S. Gilbert **3**:207
Laurence Housman **7**:352
Henrik Ibsen **2**:224
Selma Lagerlöf **4**:229
Alice Meynell **6**:294
Duncan Campbell Scott **6**:385
Francis Thompson **4**:434

Arendt, Hannah
Bertolt Brecht **1**:114
Franz Kafka **2**:301

Arms, George
Kate Chopin 5:149

Armstrong, Martin
Katherine Mansfield 2:446

Arner, Robert D.
Kate Chopin 5:155

Aron, Albert W.
Jakob Wassermann 6:509

Arrowsmith, William
Cesare Pavese 3:334
Dylan Thomas 1:468

Arvin, Newton
Henry Adams 4:12

Ashbery, John
Gertrude Stein 1:442

Ashworth, Arthur
Miles Franklin 7:264

Aswell, Edward C.
Thomas Wolfe 4:515

Atherton, Gertrude
Ambrose Bierce 7:88
May Sinclair 3:434

Atkins, Elizabeth
Edna St. Vincent Millay 4:311

Atkins, John
Walter de la Mare 4:75
George Orwell 6:341

Atlas, James
Gertrude Stein 1:442
Thomas Wolfe 4:538

Attebery, Brian
L. Frank Baum 7:25

Auchincloss, Louis
Willa Cather 1:164
Ellen Glasgow 2:188
Henry James 2:275
Sarah Orne Jewett 1:367
Edith Wharton 3:570

Auden, W. H.
Max Beerbohm 1:72
Hilaire Belloc 7:41
C. P. Cavafy 2:90
Raymond Chandler 7:168
G. K. Chesterton 1:184, 186
Walter de la Mare 4:81
A. E. Housman 1:358
George Orwell 2:512
Rainer Maria Rilke 6:359
George Bernard Shaw 3:389
Paul Valéry 4:499
Nathanael West 1:480
Oscar Wilde 1:504, 507
Charles Williams 1:516
Virginia Woolf 1:546
William Butler Yeats 1:562

Austin, James C.
Rebecca Harding Davis 6:151

Avseenko, V. G.
Leo Tolstoy 4:446

Azorín
Ramón del Valle-Inclán 5:479

B., M.
W. S. Gilbert 3:207

Bacon, Leonard
Alexander Woollcott 5:522

Bailey, Joseph W.
Arthur Schnitzler 4:391

Bailey, Mabel Driscoll
Maxwell Anderson 2:7

Baird, James
Wallace Stevens 3:471

Baker, Carlos
Sherwood Anderson 1:64
Edwin Muir 2:483

Baker, Houston A., Jr.
Countee Cullen 4:52

Balakian, Anna
Paul Éluard 7:257

Baldwin, Richard E.
Charles Waddell Chesnutt
5:135

Ball, Robert Hamilton
David Belasco 3:88

Balmforth, Ramsden
Laurence Housman 7:355

Bander, Elaine
Dorothy L. Sayers 2:537

Banks, Nancy Huston
Charles Waddell Chesnutt
5:130

Bannister, Winifred
James Bridie 3:134

Barbusse, Henri
Henri Barbusse 5:14

Barclay, Glen St John
H. P. Lovecraft 4:273

Barea, Arturo
Miguel de Unamuno 2:559

Barea, Ilsa
Miguel de Unamuno 2:559

Bareham, Terence
Malcolm Lowry 6:251

Baring, Maurice
Hilaire Belloc 7:32
Anton Chekhov 3:145
W. S. Gilbert 3:211
Saki 3:363

Barker, Dudley
G. K. Chesterton 6:101

Barker, Frank Granville
Joseph Conrad 1:219

Barksdale, Richard K.
Claude McKay 7:466

Barnard, Ellsworth
Edwin Arlington Robinson
5:411

Barnard, Marjorie
Miles Franklin 7:270

Barnstone, Willis
C. P. Cavafy 7:163
Edgar Lee Masters 2:472

Barrett, Francis X.
Wallace Thurman 6:450

Barrett, William
F. Scott Fitzgerald 1:246

Barthes, Roland
Bertolt Brecht 1:102
Jules Verne 6:491

Barzun, Jacques
Raymond Chandler 7:171, 176
John Jay Chapman 7:195
Malcolm Lowry 6:236
George Bernard Shaw 3:398

Basdekis, Demetrios
Miguel de Unamuno 2:566

Baskervill, William Malone
George Washington Cable 4:24
Joel Chandler Harris 2:209

Bates, H. E.
A. E. Coppard 5:179
Thomas Hardy 4:161

Bates, Scott
Guillaume Apollinaire 3:37

Bauland, Peter
Gerhart Hauptmann 4:209

Baum, L. Frank
L. Frank Baum 7:12, 15

Baxandall, Lee
Bertolt Brecht 1:119

Bayerschmidt, Carl F.
Sigrid Undset 3:525

Bayley, John
Thomas Hardy 4:177
Bruno Schulz 5:427
Virginia Woolf 1:550

Beach, Joseph Warren
Joseph Conrad 1:199
Thomas Hardy 4:154
James Joyce 3:257
D. H. Lawrence 2:350
Hugh Walpole 5:498
Edith Wharton 3:562
Émile Zola 1:588

Beals, Carleton
Mariano Azuela 3:74

Beckelman, June
Paul Claudel 2:104

Beckett, Samuel
James Joyce 3:255
Marcel Proust 7:525

Bédé, Jean-Albert
Émile Zola 1:596

Bedient, Calvin
D. H. Lawrence 2:370

Beerbohm, Max
J. M. Barrie 2:39
Joseph Conrad 1:195
Arthur Conan Doyle 7:217
José Echegaray 4:98
John Galsworthy 1:301
W. S. Gilbert 3:209
Harley Granville-Barker 2:192
Laurence Housman 7:353
Edmond Rostand 6:372, 376
George Bernard Shaw 3:378
Alfred Sutro 6:419, 420
John Millington Synge 6:425

Beharriell, S. Ross
Stephen Leacock 2:382

Behrman, S. N.
Robert E. Sherwood 3:414

Beicken, Peter U.
Franz Kafka 2:309

Bell, Aubrey F. G.
Juan Ramón Jiménez 4:212
Gregorio Martinez Sierra and
Maria Martinez Sierra 6:278

Bell, Clive
Marcel Proust 7:521

Bell, David F.
Alfred Jarry 2:286

Bellman, Samuel I.
Marjorie Kinnan Rawlings
4:365

Belloc, Hilaire
G. K. Chesterton 1:178
H. G. Wells 6:530

Bellow, Saul
Sholom Aleichem 1:23

Benamou, Michel
Wallace Stevens 3:457

Benavente, Jacinto
Ramón del Valle-Inclán 5:479

Bender, Bert
Kate Chopin 5:157

Benet, Mary Kathleen
Colette 5:171

Benét, Stephen Vincent
Stephen Vincent Benét 7:69

Benét, William Rose
Hart Crane 5:185
F. Scott Fitzgerald 1:236
Alfred Noyes 7:505

Benjamin, Walter
Marcel Proust 7:538

Bennett, Arnold
Joseph Conrad 1:196
John Galsworthy 1:292
George Gissing 3:223
Joris-Karl Huysmans 7:408

Bennett, Charles A.
John Millington Synge 6:427

Benoit, Leroy J.
Paul Éluard 7:247

Bensen, Alice R.
Rose Macaulay 7:430

Benson, Eugene
Gabriele D'Annunzio 6:127

Benson, Ruth Crego
Leo Tolstoy 4:481

Bentley, D.M.R.
Bliss Carman 7:149

Bentley, Eric
Stephen Vincent Benét 7:78
Bertolt Brecht 1:98, 99; 6:40
James Bridie 3:134
Anton Chekhov 3:156
Federico García Lorca 1:310
Henrik Ibsen 2:225
Eugene O'Neill 1:392
Luigi Pirandello 4:337, 340
August Strindberg 1:446
Frank Wedekind 7:578
Oscar Wilde 1:499
William Butler Yeats 1:562

Berendsohn, Walter A.
Selma Lagerlöf 4:231

Beresford, J. D.
Dorothy Richardson 3:349

Bereza, Henryk
Bruno Schulz 5:421

Bergin, Thomas Goddard
Giovanni Verga 3:540

Bergonzi, Bernard
Hilaire Belloc 7:39
Rupert Brooke 7:127
G. K. Chesterton 1:180
Ford Madox Ford 1:289
John Galsworthy 1:302
Wilfred Owen 5:371
H. G. Wells 6:541

Berkman, Sylvia
Katherine Mansfield 2:452

Berlin, Isaiah
Osip Mandelstam 6:259
Leo Tolstoy 4:463

Bermel, Albert
Antonin Artaud 3:61

Bernhard, Svea
Verner von Heidenstam 5:250

Bernstein, Melvin H.
John Jay Chapman 7:198

Berryman, John
Isaak Babel 2:36
F. Scott Fitzgerald 1:240
Ring Lardner 2:334

Bersani, Leo
D. H. Lawrence 2:374

Bertaux, Felix
Jakob Wassermann 6:512

Berthoff, Warner
Ambrose Bierce 1:94
Willa Cather 1:165
Gertrude Stein 1:434

Best, Alan
Frank Wedekind 7:590

Bettany, F. G.
Arnold Bennett 5:22

Bettinson, Christopher
André Gide 5:244

Bevington, Helen
Laurence Housman 7:360

Bewley, Marius
F. Scott Fitzgerald 1:260
Wallace Stevens 3:450

Beyer, Harald
Bjørnstjerne, Bjørnson 7:112
Alexander Kielland 5:279

Bhattacharya, Bhabani
Rabindranath Tagore 3:494

Bien, Peter
C. P. Cavafy 2:91
Nikos Kazantzakis 2:315, 321,
5:268

Bier, Jesse
Ambrose Bierce 1:96

Bierce, Ambrose
William Dean Howells 7:367

Bierstadt, Edward Hale
Lord Dunsany 2:138

Bigelow, Gordon E.
Marjorie Kinnan Rawlings
4:362

Bilton, Peter
Saki 3:372

Binion, Rudolph
Franz Kafka 6:221

Birmingham, George A.
John Millington Synge 6:425

Birnbaum, Martin
Arthur Schnitzler 4:385

Birrell, Francis
Alfred Sutro 6:422

Bishop, Ferman
Sarah Orne Jewett 1:365

Bishop, John Peale
Stephen Vincent Benét 7:69
F. Scott Fitzgerald 6:160
Thomas Wolfe 4:511

Bjorkman, Edwin
Selma Lagerlöf 4:229
Maurice Maeterlinck 3:323
Wladyslaw Stanislaw Reymont
5:391
Arthur Schnitzler 4:388
Sigrid Undset 3:510
Edith Wharton 3:556

Björnson, Björnstjerne
Jonas Lie 5:325

Blackmur, R. P.
Henry Adams 4:9
Samuel Butler 1:135
Hart Crane 2:113
Thomas Hardy 4:165
Henry James 2:252, 258, 263
D. H. Lawrence 2:351
Thomas Mann 2:421
Edwin Muir 2:484
Wallace Stevens 3:445
Leo Tolstoy 4:471
William Butler Yeats 1:565

Blair, Walter
Robert Benchley 1:77, 79
Mark Twain 6:463

Blake, Caesar R.
Dorothy Richardson 3:355

Blake, George
J. M. Barrie 2:46

Blake, Patricia
Vladimir Mayakovsky 4:298

Blankenagel, John C.
Jakob Wassermann 6:513, 517

Blankner, Frederick V.
Luigi Pirandello 4:330

Bleiler, E. F.
Algernon Blackwood 5:77
Arthur Conan Doyle 7:237
M. R. James 6:211
H. P. Lovecraft 4:271

Blissett, William
Thomas Mann 2:428

Bloch, Adèle
Nikos Kazantzakis 2:319

Bloom, Harold
Wallace Stevens 3:476

Bloom, Robert
H. G. Wells 6:548

Blunden, Edmund
Robert Bridges 1:128
W. H. Davies 5:202
Wilfred Owen 5:360

Bodenheim, Maxwell
Eugene O'Neill 1:382

Bogan, Louise
Colette 1:190
Paul Éluard 7:244
Federico García Lorca 1:308
James Joyce 3:261
Edwin Arlingtn Robinson 5:410
Sara Teasdale 4:427

Bogard, Carley Rees
Kate Chopin 5:158

Bold, Alan
Wyndham Lewis 2:397

Boll, Theophilus E. M.
May Sinclair 3:440

Bond, Tonette L.
Ellen Glasgow 7:344

Bondanella, Peter E.
Italo Svevo 2:553

Bone, Robert A.
Charles Waddell Chesnutt
5:133
Countee Cullen 4:49
Paul Laurence Dunbar 2:131
James Weldon Johnson 3:242
Claude McKay 7:458
Wallace Thurman 6:449

Bonheim, Helmut
James Joyce 3:277

Bonnell, Peter H.
Aleksandr Kuprin 5:301

Bonwit, Marianne
Wolfgang Borchert 5:102

Böök, Fredrik
Verner von Heidenstam 5:251

Booker, John Manning
Henri Barbusse 5:13

Borelli, Mary
Ramón del Valle-Inclán 5:476

Borges, Jorge Luis
G. K. Chesterton 1:181
H. G. Wells 6:545
Oscar Wilde 1:498

Borrello, Alfred
H. G. Wells 6:545

Bose, Buddhadeva
Rabindranath Tagore 3:495

Bouraoui, H. A.
Georges Bernanos 3:128

Bourget, Paul
Joris-Karl Huysmans 7:403

Bourne, Randolph
George Washington Cable 4:25
Dorothy Richardson 3:346

Bovary, Claude
Willa Cather 1:151

Bowen, Elizabeth
Rose Macaulay 7:424
Henry Handel Richardson 4:374

Bowie, Malcolm
Paul Éluard 7:258

Bowra, C. M.
Guillaume Apollinaire 3:34
Aleksandr Blok 5:85
C. P. Cavafy 2:87
Federico García Lorca 1:309
Stefan George 2:150
Vladimir Mayakovsky 4:293
Rainer Maria Rilke 1:409, 414
Paul Valéry 4:490
William Butler Yeats 1:560

Boyd, Ernest A.
A. E. 3:3
Lord Dunsany 2:136
Standish O'Grady 5:349
Wladysław Stanisław Reymont
5:392
Gregorio Martínez Sierra and
María Martínez Sierra 6:278
Katharine Tynan 3:504

Boyd, Ian
G. K. Chesterton 6:103

Boyesen, Hjalmar Hjorth
Bjørnstjerne Bjørnson 7:100
George Washington Cable 4:23
Alexander Kielland 5:275
Jonas Lie 5:324

Boynton, H. W.
Don Marquis 7:434

Boynton, Percy H.
Sherwood Anderson 1:38
Ambrose Bierce 1:84
Sinclair Lewis 4:247

Brachfeld, Georges I.
André Gide 5:234

Bradbrook, M. C.
Henrik Ibsen 2:238

Bradbury, Malcolm
Malcolm Lowry 6:249
Virginia Woolf 1:546

Bradbury, Ray
L. Frank Baum 7:20
Edgar Rice Burroughs 2:86

Bragdon, Claude
Kahlil Gibran 1:326

Braithwaite, William Stanley
Countee Cullen 4:44
Claude McKay 7:455
Sara Teasdale 4:424

Branch, Douglas
Zane Grey 6:179

Brandes, George
Bjørnstjerne Bjørnson 7:101
Henrik Ibsen 2:218

Braun, Lucille V.
Miguel de Unamuno 2:570

Brawley, Benjamin
Countee Cullen 4:41
Claude McKay 7:457

Braybrooke, Neville
George Orwell 2:498

Braybrooke, Patrick
J. M. Barrie 2:43
Alfred Noyes 7:513
Katharine Tynan 3:505
Hugh Walpole 5:497
H. G. Wells 6:531

Brée, Germaine
Georges Bernanos 3:119
André Gide 5:221
Jean Giraudoux 2:162
Marcel Proust 7:529

Brégy, Katharine
Ernest Dowson 4:87
Katharine Tynan 3:503

Brenan, Gerald
Juan Ramón Jiménez 4:213

Brennan, Joseph Payne
H. P. Lovecraft 4:270

Brennan, Joseph X.
Edith Wharton 3:568

Brenner, Rica
Alfred Noyes 7:512

Breunig, Leroy C.
Guillaume Apollinaire 3:42

Brewster, Dorothy
Virginia Woolf 1:531

Briggs, A.D.P.
Leo Tolstoy 4:482

Briggs, Julia
Algernon Blackwood 5:78
M. R. James 6:211
Vernon Lee 5:320

Brinnin, John Malcolm
Gertrude Stein 1:431
Dylan Thomas 1:473

Britten, Florence Haxton
Stephen Vincent Benét 7:73

Brittin, Norman A.
Edna St. Vincent Millay 4:318

Broadus, Edmund Kemper
Robert Bridges 1:125

Brockway, James
O. Henry 1:352

Brod, Max
Franz Kafka 2:304

Brooks, Cleanth
Ivan Bunin 6:47
F. Scott Fitzgerald 6:163
A. E. Housman 1:355
William Butler Yeats 1:571

Brooks, Van Wyck
Ambrose Bierce 1:89
Willa Cather 1:160
Bret Harte 1:342
O. Henry 1:350
Vernon Lee 5:311
Gertrude Stein 1:430
Mark Twain 6:461

Brophy, Brigid
Colette 1:192
Ronald Firbank 1:229
Francis Thompson 4:441

Brosman, Catherine Savage
Alain-Fournier 6:22

Brotherston, Gordon
Rubén Darío 4:68

Brouta, Julius
Jacinto Benavente 3:93

Brown, Clarence
Osip Mandelstam 2:401; 6:260, 262

Brown, Daniel R.
Sinclair Lewis 4:261
Nathanael West 1:491

Brown, E. K.
Duncan Campbell Scott 6:389
Bliss Carman 7:144
Thomas Wolfe 4:514

Brown, G. G.
Gabriel Miró 5:339

Brown, Ivor
Lewis Grassic Gibbon 4:122
Alfred Sutro 6:422

Brown, J. F.
Aleister Crowley 7:211

Brown, John Mason
Eugene O'Neill 1:394
Robert E. Sherwood 3:416
John Van Druten 2:573, 575
Alexander Woollcott 5:525

Brown, Malcolm
George Moore 7:486

Brown, Sterling
Charles Waddell Chesnutt 5:132
James Weldon Johnson 3:241
Wallace Thurman 6:447

Brown, Stuart Gerry
John Jay Chapman 7:192

Brownstein, Michael
Max Jacob 6:203

Broyde, Steven
Osip Mandelstam 6:267

Bruehl, Charles P.
Georges Bernanos 3:117

Brustein, Robert
Antonin Artaud 3:50
Bertolt Brecht 1:111
Eugene O'Neill 1:400
Luigi Pirandello 4:345
George Bernard Shaw 3:404
August Strindberg 1:451

Buber, Martin
Franz Kafka 2:295

Buchan, A. M.
Sarah Orne Jewett 1:363

Buck, Philo M., Jr.
Henrik Ibsen 2:224
Eugene O'Neill 1:388
Émile Zola 1:588

Buckley, Vincent
Henry Handel Richardson 4:377

Budd, Louis J.
William Dean Howells 7:380
Mark Twain 6:473
Thomas Wolfe 4:525

Büdel, Oscar
Luigi Pirandello 4:351

Bunin, Ivan
Ivan Bunin 6:44
Aleksandr Kuprin 5:298

Burbank, Rex
Sherwood Anderson 1:55

Burdett, Osbert
Alice Meynell 6:300

Burgess, Anthony
C. P. Cavafy 7:162
John Galsworthy 1:305

Burke, Kenneth
Gertrude Stein 1:425

Burkhart, Charles
George Moore 7:493

Burnshaw, Stanley
Rainer Maria Rilke 1:418

Bush, Douglas
Robert Bridges 1:130

Bush, William
Georges Bernanos 3:127

Butcher, Philip
George Washington Cable 4:29

Butler, E. M.
Rainer Maria Rilke 6:360

Butor, Michel
Guillaume Apollinaire 3:37

Butter, P. H.
Edwin Muir 2:486

Butter, Peter
Francis Thompson 4:439

Butts, Mary
M. R. James 6:206

Cabell, James Branch
James Branch Cabell 6:61
Ellen Glasgow 7:337

Cady, Edwin H.
William Dean Howells 7:381

Cahan, Abraham
Sholem Asch 3:65

Cairns, Christopher
Ugo Betti 5:66

Calder, Jenni
George Orwell 2:509

Calder-Marshall, Arthur
Wyndham Lewis 2:384

Calisher, Hortense
Henry James 2:274

Calvin, Judith S.
Jean Giraudoux 7:321

Cambon, Glauco
Hart Crane 2:121
Gabriele D'Annunzio 6:139

Cammell, Charles Richard
Aleister Crowley 7:205

Campbell, Ian
Lewis Grassic Gibbon 4:129, 130

Campbell, Joseph
James Joyce 3:261

Campbell, Roy
Federico García Lorca 1:311

Campbell, T. M.
Gerhart Hauptmann 4:198

Camus, Albert
Franz Kafka 2:297

Canby, Henry Seidel
Gertrude Atherton 2:15
Stephen Vincent Benét 7:71
F. Scott Fitzgerald 1:235
John Millington Synge 6:430
Mark Twain 6:470

Cancalon, Elaine D.
Alain-Fournier 6:24

Canetti, Elias
Franz Kafka 6:222

Cantwell, Robert
Kate Chopin 5:147

Capetanakis, Demetrios
Stefan George 2:148

Cappon, James
Bliss Carman 7:141

Carden, Patricia:141
Isaak Babel 2:23, 25

Cargill, Oscar
Sherwood Anderson 1:41
Sholem Asch 3:68
James Branch Cabell 6:69
F. Scott Fitzgerald 1:239
Henry James 2:269
George Moore 7:483
Eugene O'Neill 1:387
George Bernard Shaw 3:388
Gertrude Stein 1:427
August Strindberg 1:445
Sara Teasdale 4:428
Émile Zola 1:589

Carner, Mosco
Guiseppe Giacosa 7:313

Carpenter, Margaret Haley
Sara Teasdale 4:429

Carpenter, William H.
Alexander Kielland 5:277

Carr, John Dickson
Raymond Chandler 1:169

Carruth, Hayden
Edwin Muir 2:484
William Butler Yeats 1:575

Carter, Eunice Hunton
Wallace Thurman 6:446

Carter, Lawson A.
Émile Zola 6:567

Cary, Richard
Sarah Orne Jewett 1:365
Vernon Lee 5:313

Casey, T. J.
Georg Trakl 5:460

Cassity, Turner
James Agee 1:12

Cather, Willa
Kate Chopin 5:142
Sarah Orne Jewett 1:361
Thomas Mann 2:417
Katherine Mansfield 2:450

Caws, Mary Ann
Paul Éluard 7:255

Cecchetti, Giovanni
Giovanni Verga 3:546

Cecil, David
Max Beerbohm 1:71
W. S. Gilbert 3:213
Virginia Woolf 5:508

Cell, David
Walter de la Mare 4:80

Cerf, Bennett
O. Henry 1:350

Cevasco, G. A.
Joris-Karl Huysmans 7:416

Chakravarty, Amiya
Thomas Hardy **4**:163

Chamberlain, John
Charles Waddell Chesnutt
5:131
Claude McKay **7**:456
Thomas Wolfe **4**:506

Chambers, Edmund K.
Alice Meynell **6**:293

Champigny, Robert
Alain-Fournier **6**:14

Chandler, Frank W.
José Echegaray **4**:102
Guiseppe Giacosa **7**:312

Chandler, Raymond
Raymond Chandler **7**:167, 168
A. A. Milne **6**:311

Chapman, C. A.
Jaroslav Hasek **4**:181

Chapman, Edward M.
Sarah Orne Jewett **1**:360

Chapman, John Jay
G. K. Chesterton **1**:177

Chapman, Raymond
Samuel Butler **1**:138

Chase, Richard
George Washington Cable **4**:27

Chatterton, Wayne
Alexander Woollcott **5**:526

Chekhov, A. P.
Leo Tolstoy **4**:449

Chernyshevsky, N. G.
Leo Tolstoy **4**:444

Chesterton, Cecil
Hilaire Belloc **7**:31

Chesterton, G. K.
Hilaire Belloc **7**:37
Aleister Crowley **7**:203, 204
Walter de la Mare **4**:75
Arthur Conan Doyle **7**:217
Henrik Ibsen **2**:221
Bret Harte **1**:339
Alice Meynell **6**:295
George Moore **7**:475
George Bernard Shaw **3**:380
Francis Thompson **4**:439
Leo Tolstoy **4**:452
H. G. Wells **6**:524

Chevalley, Abel
May Sinclair **3**:439

Chiari, Joseph
Paul Claudel **2**:103
Paul Éluard **7**:250
Edmond Rostand **6**:380

Chiaromonte, Nicola
Luigi Pirandello **4**:353

Childs, Herbert Ellsworth
Edgar Lee Masters **2**:466

Chisolm, Lawrence W.
Lu Hsün **3**:298

Christian, R. F.
Leo Tolstoy **4**:470

Chukovsky, Korney
Vladimir Mayakovsky **4**:288

Church, Dan M.
Alfred Jarry **2**:281

Church, Richard
Laurence Housman **7**:357

Ciancio, Ralph
Sherwood Anderson **1**:64

Ciardi, John
Roy Campbell **5**:122
Edna St. Vincent Millay **4**:316

Ciholas, Karin Nordenhaug
André Gide **5**:241

Cioran, E. M.
Paul Valéry **4**:500

Cioran, Samuel D.
Andrey Bely **7**:57

Clark, Barrett H.
Maxwell Anderson **2**:1

Clark, Earl John
James Joyce **3**:278

Clarke, Arthur C.
Jules Verne **6**:492

Clarke, Helen A.
Bliss Carman **7**:134

Cleman, John
George Washington Cable **4**:36

Clemens, S. L.
Mark Twain **6**:454

Clements, Clyde C., Jr.
Thomas Wolfe **4**:533

Clever, Glenn
Duncan Campbell Scott **6**:398,
400

Closs, August
Stefan George **2**:149

Clurman, Harold
Bertolt Brecht **1**:108, 109, 115,
122
Eugene O'Neill **1**:395

Cobb, Carl W.
Antonio Machado **3**:311

Coblentz, Stanton A.
Sinclair Lewis **4**:246

Cock, Albert A.
Francis Thompson **4**:436

Cocteau, Jean
Colette **5**:163
Paul Valéry **4**:493

Coffman, Stanley K., Jr.
Hart Crane **5**:187

Cogswell, Fred
Duncan Campbell Scott **6**:399

Cohen, Arthur A.
Osip Mandelstam **2**:406

Cohen, J. M.
Georg Trakl **5**:460

Cohen, Robert
Jean Giraudoux **2**:167

Cohn, Ruby
Bertolt Brecht **1**:116

Colbron, Grace Isabel
Algernon Blackwood **5**:70

Colby, Frank Moore
Gabriele D'Annunzio **6**:130

Colby, Vineta
Vernon Lee **5**:316

Cole, Leo R.
Juan Ramón Jiménez **4**:220

Collier, Eugenia W.
James Weldon Johnson **3**:242

Collier, S. J.
Max Jacob **6**:191

Collins, Joseph
Edna St. Vincent Millay **4**:309

Colombo, J. R.
Malcolm Lowry **6**:237

Colum, Padraic
A. E. **3**:6
Lord Dunsany **2**:142
Kahlil Gibran **1**:328
Lady Gregory **1**:333
George Moore **7**:478
Edna St. Vincent Millay **4**:306
James Stephens **4**:414

Combs, Robert
Hart Crane **2**:125

Comerchero, Victor
Nathanael West **1**:482

Commager, Henry Steele
Henry Adams **4**:6
Stephen Vincent Benét **7**:75
Willa Cather **1**:155
F. Scott Fitzgerald **1**:245

Connolly, Cyril
A. E. Housman **1**:354
James Joyce **3**:276
D. H. Lawrence **2**:369
Gertrude Stein **1**:434

Connolly, Francis X.
Willa Cather **1**:156

Connolly, Julian W.
Ivan Bunin **6**:58

Conrad, Joseph
Joseph Conrad **6**:112
Henry James **2**:245
Marcel Proust **7**:520
Hugh Walpole **5**:495
H. G Wells **6**:523

Cook, Bruce
Raymond Chandler **1**:175

Cooper, Frederic Taber
Gertrude Atherton **2**:13
Arnold Bennett **5**:23
Zona Gale **7**:277
Ellen Glasgow **2**:175; **7**:332
Zane Grey **6**:176

Cordle, Thomas
André Gide **5**:222

Corkery, Daniel
John Millington Synge **6**:432

Corn, Alfred
Andrey Bely **7**:66

Cornford, Frances
Rupert Brooke **7**:123

Correa, Gustavo
Federico García Lorca **7**:294

Corrigan, Matthew
Malcolm Lowry **6**:244

Corrigan, Robert W.
Bertolt Brecht **1**:119
Federico García Lorca **1**:324
Henrik Ibsen **2**:239
Gregorio Martinez
Sierra and Maria Martinez
Sierra **6**:284

Cortissoz, Royal
Hamlin Garland **3**:190

Cosman, Max
Joyce Cary **1**:141

Costa, Richard Haver
Malcolm Lowry **6**:246

Costello, Peter
Jules Verne **6**:499

Costich, Julia F.
Antonin Artaud **3**:62

Coustillas, Pierre
George Gissing **3**:236

Coward, Noël
Saki **3**:373

Cowley, Malcolm
Sherwood Anderson **1**:51
Guillaume Apollinaire **3**:33
Henri Barbusse **5**:13
A. E. Coppard **5**:176
Hart Crane **2**:117
F. Scott Fitzgerald **1**:238, 272;
6:166
Amy Lowell **1**:371, 378
Katherine Mansfield **2**:445
Arthur Schnitzler **4**:392
Virginia Woolf **1**:533

Cox, C. B.
Joseph Conrad **1**:218

Cox, James Trammell
Ford Madox Ford **1**:286

Coxe, Louis O.
Edith Wharton **3**:567

Coxhead, Elizabeth
Lady Gregory **1**:335

Craig, G. Dundas
Rubén Darío **4**:63

Craige, Betty Jean
Federico García Lorca **7**:297

Crane, Hart
Hart Crane **5**:184

Crankshaw, Edward
Jakob Wassermann **6**:511

Crawford, Virginia M.
Joris-Karl Huysmans **7**:407
Edmond Rostand **6**:373

Crews, Frederick
Joseph Conrad **1**:216

Croce, Arlene
Eugene O'Neill **1**:404

Croce, Benedetto
Émile Zola **1**:588

Cross, Richard K.
Malcolm Lowry **6**:253

Cross, Wilbur
Arnold Bennett **5**:33
John Galsworthy **1**:297

Crowley, Aleister
James Branch Cabell **6**:65
Aleister Crowley **7**:205, 208

Cruse, Harold
James Weldon Johnson 3:246

Cullen, Countee
James Weldon Johnson 3:240

Cunliffe, John W.
A. E. Housman 1:354

Cunningham, J. V.
Wallace Stevens 3:454

Cuppy, Will
Raymond Chandler 7:167

Currey, R. N.
Alun Lewis 3:289

Curtis, Penelope
Anton Chekhov 3:170

Cushman, Keith
Ernest Dowson 4:93

D., B.
Kahlil Gibran 1:327

Dabney, Virginius
Ellen Glasgow 7:337

Daemmrich, Horst S.
Thomas Mann 2:441

Dahlberg, Edward
Sherwood Anderson 1:56
F. Scott Fitzgerald 1:256

Daiches, David
Willa Cather 1:157
Joseph Conrad 1:211
A. E. Housman 1:355
James Joyce 3:258
Katherine Mansfield 2:449
Wilfred Owen 5:362
Dylan Thomas 1:469
Virginia Woolf 1:539
William Butler Yeats 1:558

Daleski, H. M.
Joseph Conrad 1:220

Dalphin, Marcia
A. A. Milne 6:309

Damon, S. Foster
Amy Lowell 1:374

Dane, Clemence
Hugh Walpole 5:497

Daniel, John
Henri Barbusse 5:16

Daniels, Jonathan
Marjorie Kinnan Rawlings
4:359

Danielson, Larry W.
Selma Lagerlöf 4:242

Damon, S. Foster
Amy Lowell 1:374

Darton, F. J. Harvey
Arnold Bennett 5:25

Dauner, Louise
Joel Chandler Harris 2:212

Davenport, Basil
Lewis Grassic Gibbon 4:120,
121

Daviau, Donald G.
Karl Kraus 5:282

Davidson, Donald
Joseph Conrad 6:114

Davie, Donald
D. H. Lawrence 2:373
Wallace Stevens 3:449

Davies, A. Emil
Laurence Housman 7:354

Davies, J. C.
André Gide 5:237

Davies, John
Alun Lewis 3:289

Davies, Margaret
Colette 5:165

Davies, Robertson
Stephen Leacock 2:381

Davies, Ruth
Leonid Andreyev 3:27
Anton Chekhov 3:168

Davis, Arthur P.
Countee Cullen 4:44
Wallace Thurman 6:450

Davis, Beatrice
Miles Franklin 7:267

Davis, Cynthia
Dylan Thomas 1:475

Davis, Robert Murray
F. Scott Fitzgerald 6:167

Davis, Oswald H.
Arnold Bennett 5:45

Davison, Edward
Robert Bridges 1:125
Walter de la Mare 4:74
Alfred Noyes 7:507
Saki 3:365

Day, Douglas
Malcolm Lowry 6:241, 247

Dean, James L.
William Dean Howells 7:394

Debicki, Andrew P.
César Vallejo 3:530

de Bosschere, Jean
May Sinclair 3:437

De Castris, A. L.
Luigi Pirandello 4:342

Decavalles, A.
C. P. Cavafy 7:162

De Fornaro, Sofia
Giuseppe Giacosa 7:305

DeKoven, Marianne
Gertrude Stein 6:415

de la Mare, Walter
Rupert Brooke 2:53

de la Selva, Salomón
Rubén Darío 4:55

Dennis, Scott A.
William Dean Howells 7:397

de Ónis, Harriet
Mariano Azuela 3:80

Derleth, August
Zona Gale 7:282
H. P. Lovecraft 4:266

De Selincourt, E.
Robert Bridges 1:129

Desmond, Shaw
Lord Dunsany 2:143

Des Pres, Terrence
Bertolt Brecht 6:38

Deutsch, Babette
Stephen Vincent Benét 7:69
A. E. Coppard 5:177
Hart Crane 5:186
Countee Cullen 4:40
Edna St. Vincent Millay 4:311
Wilfred Owen 5:365
Edwin Arlington Robinson
5:413
Sara Teasdale 4:426, 427

Deutscher, Isaac
George Orwell 2:500

DeVoto, Bernard
Don Marquis 7:440
Eugene O'Neill 6:328
Mark Twain 6:465
Thomas Wolfe 4:509

Dick, Kay
Colette 1:192

Dick, Susan
George Moore 7:495

Dickey, James
Edwin Arlington Robinson
5:414

Dickman, Adolphe-Jacques
André Gide 5:213

Didier, Pierre
Georges Bernanos 3:117

Dimock, Edward C., Jr.
Rabindranath Tagore 3:493

Disch, Thomas M.
Rose Macaulay 7:432

Dobie, Ann B.
Gerhart Hauptmann 4:207

Dobrée Bonamy
D. H. Lawrence 2:345

Dobson, A.
Miguel de Unamuno 2:569

Doggett, Frank
Wallace Stevens 3:469

Donnelly, Mabel Collins
George Gissing 3:233

Donoghue, Denis
Malcolm Lowry 6:239
Eugene O'Neill 1:404
Dorothy L. Sayers 2:533
Wallace Stevens 3:473
William Butler Yeats 1:580

Dorosz, Kristofer
Malcolm Lowry 6:251

Dos Passos, John
Jacinto Benavente 3:96
F. Scott Fitzgerald 1:240

Dostoievsky, F. M.
Leo Tolstoy 4:447

Douglas, Frances
Gabriel Miró 5:337
Gregorio Martinez Sierra and
Maria Martinez Sierra 6:276

Downer, Alan S.
Harley Granville-Barker 2:195
Eugene O'Neill 1:393

Downey, Fairfax
Rebecca Harding Davis 6:150

Downs, Brian W.
Bjørnstjerne Bjørnson 7:115

Drake, Robert
Saki 3:367, 368

Drake, William A.
Karel Čapek 6:38
Ramón del Valle-Inclán 5:474
Jakob Wassermann 6:509

Drayton, Arthur D.
Claude McKay 7:463

Drew, Elizabeth
Arnold Bennett 5:31
Joseph Conrad 1:212
James Joyce 3:276
D. H. Lawrence 2:368
Saki 3:366

Drinkwater, John
Rupert Brooke 7:121
Alice Meynell 6:298

Driver, Tom F.
Eugene O'Neill 1:397

DuBois, W. E. Burghardt
Claude McKay 7:455
Wallace Thurman 6:446

Duffey, Bernard
Sherwood Anderson 1:46

Duffin, Henry Charles
Walter de la Mare 4:78

Duke, Maurice
James Branch Cabell 6:78

Dukes, Ashley
Karel Čapek 6:81
Anton Chekhov 3:147
Gerhart Hauptmann 4:195
A. A. Milne 6:307
Arthur Schnitzler 4:390
Leo Tolstoy 4:453
George Bernard Shaw 3:381
Frank Wedekind 7:575

Dunbar, Olivia Howard
Alice Meynell 6:296

Dunleavy, Janet Egleston
George Moore 7:497

Dupee, F. W.
Henry James 2:274

Dusenbury, Winifred L.
Robert E. Sherwood 3:414

Duus, Louise
Rebecca Harding Davis 6:155

Dyboski, Roman
Wladyslaw Stanislaw Reymont
5:392
Henryk Sienkiewicz 3:425

Dyson, A. E.
F. Scott Fitzgerald 1:252
Oscar Wilde 1:504

E., A.
Standish O'Grady 5:348, 349
James Stephens 4:407
Leo Tolstoy 4:459
Katharine Tynan 3:505
See also **Russell, George
William**

Eagleson, Harvey
Dorothy Richardson 3:352

Eaker, J. Gordon
John Galsworthy **1**:300

Eakin, Paul John
Sarah Orne Jewett **1**:368

Eastman, Max
Stephen Vincent Benét **7**:72

Eaton, Walter Prichard
David Belasco **3**:87

Eberhart, Richard
Edwin Muir **2**:481
Wallace Stevens **3**:475

Eble, Kenneth
Kate Chopin **5**:147

Echegaray, José
José Echegaray **4**:97

Economou, George
C. P. Cavafy **7**:164

Edel, Leon
Willa Cather **1**:161
Ford Madox Ford **1**:287
Henry James **2**:271, 274
Dorothy Richardson **3**:354
Dylan Thomas **1**:473
Virginia Woolf **1**:540

Edgar, Pelham
Sherwood Anderson **1**:40
Bliss Carman **7**:145
Duncan Campbell Scott **6**:386
Virginia Woolf **1**:530

Edman, Irwin
A. E. **3**:5

Edmonds, Dale
Malcolm Lowry **6**:240

Edwards, Gwynne
Federico García Lorca **7**:300

Eggleston, Wilfrid
Frederick Philip Grove **4**:137

Eglinton, John
A. E. **3**:6

Eikenbaum, Boris
Leo Tolstoy **4**:456

Ekström, Kjell
George Washington Cable **4**:27

Elder, Donald
Ring Lardner **2**:335

Eldershaw, M. Barnard
Henry Handel Richardson **4**:373

Eliot, T. S.
Henry Adams **4**:5
Gottfried Benn **3**:105
Arthur Conan Doyle **7**:218
Thomas Hardy **4**:161
Henry James **2**:250
James Joyce **3**:252
Edwin Muir **2**:487
Edmond Rostand **6**:378
Mark Twain **6**:468
Paul Valéry **4**:495
William Butler Yeats **1**:557

Elliot, Walter
James Bridie **3**:134

Elliott, George P.
Edgar Rice Burroughs **2**:76
Raymond Chandler **1**:169
George Orwell **6**:346

Ellis, Havelock
Alain-Fournier **6**:12
Miles Franklin **7**:264
Thomas Hardy **4**:147
Joris-Karl Huysmans **7**:404
Émile Zola **6**:560

Ellis-Fermor, Una
John Millington Synge **6**:438

Ellmann, Mary
Colette **1**:193

Ellmann, Richard
James Joyce **3**:267
Italo Svevo **2**:550
Oscar Wilde **1**:506
William Butler Yeats **1**:572

Eloesser, Arthur
Jakob Wassermann **6**:510
Frank Wedekind **7**:577

Elsworth, John
Andrey Bely **7**:58

Emrich, Wilhelm
Franz Kafka **2**:309

Engel, Edwin A.
Eugene O'Neill **1**:399

Engle, Paul
Stephen Vincent Benét **7**:75

Englekirk, John E.
Mariano Azuela **3**:75, 79

Enright, D. J.
Bertolt Brecht **1**:121
Rupert Brooke **7**:129
Aleister Crowley **7**:207
Knut Hamsun **2**:208
D. H. Lawrence **2**:371
Thomas Mann **2**:427
Georg Trakl **5**:461

Epstein, Perle S.
Malcolm Lowry **6**:242

Erickson, John D.
Joris-Karl Huysmans **7**:414

Ericson, Edward E., Jr.
Mikhail Bulgakov **2**:69

Erlich, Victor
Aleksandr Blok **5**:94

Ervine, St. John G.
G. K. Chesterton **1**:178
John Galsworthy **1**:293
George Bernard Shaw **3**:385
William Butler Yeats **1**:552

Erwin, John F., Jr.
Paul Claudel **2**:108

Eshleman, Clayton
César Vallejo **3**:527

Esslin, Martin
Antonin Artaud **3**:59
Bertolt Brecht **1**:102, 117
Henrik Ibsen **2**:237
Alfred Jarry **2**:285
Luigi Pirandello **4**:352
Arthur Schnitzler **4**:401
Frank Wedekind **7**:588

Eto, Jun
Soseki Natsume **2**:492

Etulain, Richard W.
Zane Grey **6**:182

Evans, Calvin
Maurice Maeterlinck **3**:330

Evans, I. O.
Jules Verne **6**:494

Ewers, John K.
Miles Franklin **7**:267

Fackler, Herbert V.
A. E. **3**:12

Fadiman, Clifton
Ambrose Bierce **1**:87
Ring Lardner **2**:328
Leo Tolstoy **4**:466
Thomas Wolfe **4**:513

Fagin, N. Bryllion
Anton Chekhov **3**:151

Fairchild, Hoxie Neale
Alice Meynell **6**:302
Charles Williams **1**:521

Falen, James E.
Isaak Babel **2**:32

Falk, Doris V.
Eugene O'Neill **6**:332

Fallis, Richard
Standish O'Grady **5**:357

Fanger, Donald
Mikhail Bulgakov **2**:64

Farber, Manny
James Agee **1**:6

Farnsworth, Robert M.
Charles Waddell Chesnutt **5**:134

Farrar, John
Robert Benchley **1**:77

Farrell, James T.
Sherwood Anderson **1**:45
Leo Tolstoy **4**:461

Farren, Robert
John Millington Synge **6**:435

Farrow, Anthony
George Moore **7**:498

Farwell, Marilyn R.
Virginia Woolf **1**:549

Faulhaber, Uwe Karl
Lion Feuchtwanger **3**:184

Faulkner, William
Sherwood Anderson **1**:45
Mark Twain **6**:471
Thomas Wolfe **4**:521

Fauset, Jessie
Countee Cullen **4**:40

Feder, Lillian
William Butler Yeats **1**:583

Fender, Stephen
Eugene O'Neill **6**:337

Fergusson, Francis
Anton Chekhov **3**:158
Federico García Lorca **1**:315
James Joyce **3**:262
D. H. Lawrence **2**:351
Robert E. Sherwood **3**:413
Paul Valéry **4**:496

Festa-McCormick, Diana
Andrey Bely **7**:65

Feuchtwanger, Lion
Lion Feuchtwanger **3**:178, 180
Frank Wedekind **7**:578

Fickert, Kurt J.
Wolfgang Borchert **5**:110

Ficowski, Jerzy
Bruno Schulz **5**:425

Fiedler, Leslie A.
James Agee **1**:1
Ronald Firbank **1**:228
F. Scott Fitzgerald **1**:249, 263
Jaroslav Hasek **4**:181
Nikos Kazantzakis **5**:260
Cesare Pavese **3**:335
Mark Twain **6**:467
Nathanael West **1**:485

Field, Frank
Henri Barbusse **5**:17

Field, Louise Maunsell
Algernon Blackwood **5**:71
F. Scott Fitzgerald **1**:235

Figgis, Darrell
A. E. **3**:4

Figh, Margaret Gillis
Marjorie Kinnan Rawlings **4**:362

Firkins, Oscar W.
William Dean Howells **7**:372
Edgar Lee Masters **2**:463
Sara Teasdale **4**:425

Fitzgerald, F. Scott
Ring Lardner **2**:330

Fitzgibbon, Constantine
Dylan Thomas **1**:474

Flanagan, John T.
Edgar Lee Masters **2**:468

Flanner, Hildegarde
Edna St. Vincent Millay **4**:313

Flanner, Janet
Colette **1**:192

Flatin, Kjetil A.
Alexander Kielland **5**:279

Flaubert, Gustave
Leo Tolstoy **4**:448

Flautz, John T.
Edgar Rice Burroughs **2**:81

Flay, Joseph C.
Nikos Kazantzakis **2**:319

Fleming, Robert E.
James Weldon Johnson **3**:247

Fletcher, John Gould
Amy Lowell **1**:370

Flexner, Eleanor
Robert E. Sherwood **3**:410

Flint, F. Cudworth
Amy Lowell **1**:379

Flint, R. W.
James Agee **1**:7
Cesare Pavese **3**:340

Fogelquist, Donald F.
Juan Ramón Jiménez **4**:224

Folsom, James K.
Hamlin Garland **3**:199
Zane Grey **6**:180

Foltin, Lore B.
Arthur Schnitzler **4**:401

Forbes, Helen Cady
A. A. Milne **6**:307, 309

Ford, Ford Madox
Joseph Conrad **1**:202
John Galsworthy **1**:299
Henry James **2**:245
H. G. Wells **6**:532

Ford, Julia Ellsworth
A. E. **3**:1

Forman, Henry James
Kahlil Gibran **1**:327
O. Henry **1**:347

Forster, E. M.
Samuel Butler **1**:136
C. P. Cavafy **2**:87; **7**:154
Joseph Conrad **1**:196
Gabriele D'Annunzio **6**:134
Ronald Firbank **1**:225
Thomas Hardy **4**:156
Henrik Ibsen **2**:221
Henry James **2**:252
George Orwell **6**:340
Marcel Proust **7**:523
Rabindranath Tagore **3**:484
Leo Tolstoy **4**:457
Virginia Woolf **1**:527, 533,
  5:506

Fortebus, Thos.
Maurice Maeterlinck **3**:318

Foster, Richard
F. Scott Fitzgerald **1**:264, 267
William Dean Howells **7**:384

Fowlie, Wallace
Guillaume Apollinaire **3**:35
Antonin Artaud **3**:47
Paul Claudel **2**:103
Paul Éluard **7**:246
André Gide **5**:233
Jean Giraudoux **2**:159
Max Jacob **6**:193
Marcel Proust **7**:543
Paul Valéry **4**:492

Fraiberg, Selma
Franz Kafka **2**:299

France, Anatole
Marcel Proust **7**:518

Franco, Jean
Ramón del Valle-Inclán **5**:477
César Vallejo **3**:534

Frank, Waldo
Mariano Azuela **3**:75
Hart Crane **2**:112

Frankenberg, Lloyd
James Stephens **4**:414

Franklin, Miles
Miles Franklin **7**:266

Franz, Thomas R.
Ramón del Valle-Inclán **5**:489

Fraser, G. S.
Roy Campbell **5**:118, 121
Wallace Stevens **3**:451
Dylan Thomas **1**:472
Oscar Wilde **1**:505
William Butler Yeats **1**:563

Fraser, Howard M.
Rubén Darío **4**:67

Freccero, John
Italo Svevo **2**:543

Freedley, George
Lady Gregory **1**:335

Freedman, Morris
Federico García Lorca **1**:324
Luigi Pirandello **4**:344

Freeman, John
Robert Bridges **1**:124
Joseph Conrad **1**:196
Maurice Maeterlinck **3**:326
George Moore **7**:477
George Bernard Shaw **3**:384

Freeman, Kathleen
Katherine Mansfield **2**:447

Freeman, Mary
D. H. Lawrence **2**:358

French, Warren
Hamlin Garland **3**:203

Freud, Sigmund
Arthur Schnitzler **4**:391

Friar, Kimon
C. P. Cavafy **7**:155
Nikos Kazantzakis **2**:311

Friedman, Alan
Joseph Conrad **1**:215

Friedrich, Otto
Ring Lardner **2**:340

Frierson, William C.
Rose Macaulay **7**:424
George Moore **7**:484

Frohock, W. M.
James Agee **1**:2
F. Scott Fitzgerald **1**:253
Thomas Wolfe **4**:522

Frost, Robert
Edwin Arlington Robinson
  5:406

Frye, Northrop
Bliss Carman **7**:147
Frederick Philip Grove **4**:135
Wallace Stevens **3**:452

Frynta, Emanuel
Jaroslav Hašek **4**:183

Fuchs, Daniel
Wallace Stevens **3**:462

Fuller, Edmund
Sholem Asch **3**:68
James Joyce **3**:271
Nikos Kazantzakis **5**:259
Charles Williams **1**:522

Fuller, Henry Blake
William Dean Howells **7**:364

Fuller, Roy
Thomas Hardy **4**:176

Furbank, P. N.
G. K. Chesterton **1**:186
Italo Svevo **2**:547

Furness, Edna Lue
Alfonsina Storni **5**:446

Fussell, Edwin
Sherwood Anderson **1**:51
F. Scott Fitzgerald **1**:248

Gagey, Edmond M.
Eugene O'Neill **6**:329

Gaines, Francis Pendleton
Joel Chandler Harris **2**:210

Gale, Zona
Zona Gale **7**:278

Galloway, David D.
Nathanael West **1**:481

Galsworthy, John
Joseph Conrad **1**:199
Leo Tolstoy **4**:457

Ganz, Arthur
Jean Giraudoux **2**:173

García Lorca, Federico
Rubén Darío **4**:63

Gardner, Martin
L. Frank Baum **7**:19

Gardner, May
Gregorio Martinez Sierra and
  Maria Martinez Sierra **6**:279

Gardner, Monica M.
Henryk Sienkiewicz **3**:425

Garland, Hamlin
Zona Gale **7**:281
Zane Grey **6**:180

Garnett, Constance
Leo Tolstoy **4**:450

Garnett, David
Virginia Woolf **1**:526

Garnett, Edward
Roy Campbell **5**:115
Anton Chekhov **3**:152
Joseph Conrad **1**:198
Sarah Orne Jewett **1**:359
D. H. Lawrence **2**:343
Leo Tolstoy **4**:450

Garrigue, Jean
Dylan Thomas **1**:471

Garten, F.
Gerhart Hauptmann **4**:203, 205

Gascoigne, Bamber
Eugene O'Neill **1**:403

Gass, William H.
Bertolt Brecht **6**:33
Colette **5**:172
Malcolm Lowry **6**:244
Marcel Proust **7**:549
Gertrude Stein **1**:438
Paul Valéry **4**:502

Gasset, José Ortega y
Marcel Proust **7**:536

Gassner, John
Maxwell Anderson **2**:3
Bertolt Brecht **1**:100
Anton Chekhov **3**:167
Jean Giraudoux **2**:160
Lady Gregory **1**:334
Federico García Lorca **7**:294
Eugene O'Neill **1**:389
August Strindberg **1**:460
John Van Druten **2**:576
Oscar Wilde **1**:498

Geddes, Gary
Duncan Campbell Scott **6**:395

Geduld, Harry M.
J. M. Barrie **2**:47

Geismar, Maxwell
Sherwood Anderson **1**:50
Willa Cather **1**:153
F. Scott Fitzgerald **1**:244
Ellen Glasgow **2**:179
Ring Lardner **2**:330, 339
Sinclair Lewis **4**:253

Gekle, William Francis
Arthur Machen **4**:280

Genette, Gerard
Marcel Proust **7**:550

George, Ralph W.
Sholem Asch **3**:69

Gerber, Helmut E.
George Moore **7**:489

Gerhardi, William
Anton Chekhov **3**:153

Gershman, Herbert S.
Paul Éluard **7**:254

Getsi, Lucia
Georg Trakl **5**:464

Ghiselin, Brewster
James Joyce **3**:266

Ghose, Sisirkumar
Rabindranath Tagore **3**:486

Gibbon, Monk
A. E. **3**:7

Gibbs, Wolcott
Robert Benchley **1**:78
John Van Druten **2**:574

Gibson, Robert
Alain-Fournier **6**:25

Gibson, William M.
William Dean Howells **7**:391

Gide, André
Jean Giraudoux **7**:317
Marcel Proust **7**:525
Antoine de Saint-Exupéry **2**:515
Oscar Wilde **1**:501

Giergielewicz, Mieczyslaw
Henryk Sienkiewicz **3**:430

Gifford, Henry
Osip Mandelstam **2**:409; **6**:269

Gilbert, Stuart
Algernon Blackwood **5**:73
James Joyce **3**:265

Giles, James R.
Claude McKay **7**:470

Gill, Brendan
Eugene O'Neill **1**:407

Gillen, Charles H.
Saki **3**:373

Gilman, Richard
Sholom Aleichem **1**:26
Bertolt Brecht **1**:121
Anton Chekhov **3**:173
Henrik Ibsen **2**:233
Eugene O'Neill **1**:399
George Bernard Shaw **3**:402
August Strindberg **1**:461
Italo Svevo **2**:546

Gindin, James
F. Scott Fitzgerald **1**:265
Virginia Woolf **1**:544

Gingrich, Arnold
F. Scott Fitzgerald **1**:238

Ginzburg, Lidija
Osip Mandelstam 2:407

Ginzburg, Natalia
Cesare Pavese 3:337

Gittleman, Sol
Frank Wedekind 7:583

Glasgow, Ellen
Ellen Glasgow 7:336

Gloster, Hugh M.
James Weldon Johnson 3:242
Wallace Thurman 6:448

Goble, Danney
Zane Grey 6:184

Godwin, A. H.
W. S. Gilbert 3:211

Gogarty, Oliver St. John
Lord Dunsany 2:144
Oscar Wilde 1:501

Goist, Park Dixon
Zona Gale 7:287

Gold, Herbert
Sherwood Anderson 1:49

Goldberg, Isaac
Sholem Asch 3:65
Jacinto Benavente 3:97
Rubén Darío 4:59

Golden, Bruce
Ford Madox Ford 1:285

Golding, William
Jules Verne 6:492

Goldsmith, Ulrich K.
Stefan George 2:154

Golffing, Francis
Gottfried Benn 3:104
C. P. Cavafy 7:155

Gordon, Ambrose, Jr.
Ford Madox Ford 1:280, 286

Gordon, Caroline
James Joyce 3:266

Gordon, Ian A.
Katherine Mansfield 2:456

Gorky, Maxim
Leonid Andreyev 3:25
Anton Chekhov 3:145
Sergei Esenin 4:107

Gorman, Herbert S.
Sholem Asch 3:66
Katharine Tynan 3:504

Gosse, Edmund
Bjørnstjerne Bjørnson 7:105
André Gide 5:213
Thomas Hardy 4:149
Jonas Lie 5:323
George Moore 7:478
Henryk Sienkiewicz 3:421
Émile Zola 1:585

Gould, Gerald
May Sinclair 3:438

Gourmont, Remy de
Joris-Karl Huysmans 7:412

Graham, Eleanor
A. A. Milne 6:313

Graham, Stephen
Aleksandr Kuprin 5:296

Gramont, Sanche de
Antonin Artaud 3:54

Grandgent, Charles Hall
John Jay Chapman 7:187

Granville-Barker, Harley
Laurence Housman 7:355

Granville-Barker, Helen
Gregorio Martinez Sierra and
Maria Martinez Sierra 6:275

Grattan, C. Hartley
Ambrose Bierce 1:85

Graver, Lawrence
Ronald Firbank 1:232

Graves, Robert
Samuel Butler 1:134
Alun Lewis 3:284
George Moore 7:488

Gray, James
Edna St. Vincent Millay 4:318

Gray, Ronald
Franz Kafka 6:222

Gray, Ronald D.
Bertolt Brecht 6:35

Grayburn, William Frazer
Rebecca Harding Davis 6:152

Grebstein, Sheldon Norman
Sinclair Lewis 4:256

Green, Dorothy
Henry Handel Richardson 4:380

Green, Ellin
Laurence Housman 7:360

Green, Martin
Dorothy L. Sayers 2:532

Greenberg, Clement
Bertolt Brecht 1:97

Greene, Anne
James Bridie 3:139

Greene, Graham
George Bernanos 3:126
Samuel Butler 1:135
Ford Madox Ford 1:282
Henry James 2:256
Dorothy Richardson 3:353
Saki 3:366
Hugh Walpole 5:501

Greene, Naomi
Antonin Artaud 3:54

Greenslet, Ferris
Ernest Dowson 4:85

Gregor, Ian
Thomas Hardy 4:170
Oscar Wilde 1:505

Gregory, Alyse
Sherwood Anderson 1:36
Paul Valéry 4:487

Gregory, Horace
Vernon Lee 5:318
Amy Lowell 1:378

Grey, Zane
Zane Grey 6:177

Griffith, John
Stephen Vincent Benét 7:82

Griffith, Marlene
Ford Madox Ford 1:284

Griffiths, Richard
Paul Claudel 2:105

Grigson, Geoffrey
Wyndham Lewis 2:386
A. A. Milne 6:319
Dylan Thomas 1:467

Gross, Seymour L.
Ivan Bunin 6:52

Gross, Theodore L.
F. Scott Fitzgerald 1:269

Grosshut, F. S.
Lion Feuchtwanger 3:178

Grossman, Manual L.
Alfred Jarry 2:284

Grossvogel, David I.
Bertolt Brecht 1:106

Grubbs, Henry A.
Alfred Jarry 2:278

Gruening, Martha
Wallace Thurman 6:447

Grummann, Paul H.
Gerhart Hauptmann 4:197

Guerard, Albert J.
Joseph Conrad 6:115
André Gide 5:224
Thomas Hardy 4:171

Guha-Thakurta, P.
Rabindranath Tagore 3:485

Guicharnaud, Jacques
Paul Claudel 2:104

Guillen, Claudio
Juan Ramón Jiménez 4:214

Guiton, Margaret
Georges Bernanos 3:119

Gullace, Giovanni
Gabrielle D'Annunzio 6:136

Gullón, Ricardo
Ramón del Valle-Inclán 5:482

Gumilev, Nikolai
Andrey Bely 7:46

Gunn, Peter
Vernon Lee 5:313

Gunther, John
Arthur Machen 4:279

Gurko, Leo
Sinclair Lewis 4:251

Gurko, Miriam
Sinclair Lewis 4:251

Gustafson, Alrik
Bjørnstjerne Bjørnson 7:111
Knut Hamsun 2:205
Verner von Heidenstam 5:253
Selma Lagerlöf 4:236
Jonas Lie 5:325
August Strindberg 1:448
Sigrid Undset 3:516

Guthrie, William Norman
Gerhart Hauptmann 4:192

Gwynn, Stephen
Henri Barbusse 5:11
W. H. Davies 5:198

Haber, Edythe C.
Mikhail Bulgakov 2:71

Hackett, Francis
Henri Barbusse 5:12
O. Henry 1:349

Hadfield, Alice Mary
Charles Williams 1:516

Hadgraft, Cecil
Miles Franklin 7:268

Hale, Jr., Edward Everett
John Jay Chapman 7:186
Edmond Rostand 6:376

Hall, J. C.
Edwin Muir 2:483

Hall, James
Joyce Cary 1:142

Hall, Robert A., Jr.
W. S. Gilbert 3:213

Hall, Trevor H.
Arthur Conan Doyle 7:228

Hall, Wayne F.
George Moore 7:499

Halline, Allan G.
Maxwell Anderson 2:5

Halls, W. D.
Maurice Maeterlinck 3:328

Halpern, Joseph
Joris-Karl Huysmans 7:417

Haman, Aleš
Karel Čapek 6:90

Hamburger, Michael
Gottfried Benn 3:105
Georg Trakl 5:457

Hamilton, Clayton
Alfred Sutro 6:420
Leo Tolstoy 4:453
Alexander Woollcott 5:520

Hamilton, G. Rostrevor
Alice Meynell 6:302

Hammond, Josephine
Lord Dunsany 2:142

Hanan, Patrick
Lu Hsün 3:300

Hankin, Cherry
Katherine Mansfield 2:458

Hankin, St. John
Oscar Wilde 1:495

Hannum, Hunter G.
Arthur Schnitzler 4:398

Hansen, Harry
Sherwood Anderson 1:37

Hanser, Richard
Karl Kraus 5:287

Hardison, Felicia
Ramón del Valle-Inclán 5:480

Hardwick, Elizabeth
Henrik Ibsen 2:240
Leo Tolstoy 4:480

Hardy, Thomas
Thomas Hardy 4:152

Harkins, William E.
Karel Čapek 6:87, 88

Harman, H. E.
Joel Chandler Harris 2:210

Harris, Austin
Francis Thompson 4:437

Harris, Frank
Lord Dunsany 2:142
Oscar Wilde 1:508

Harris, William J.
Stephen Vincent Benét 7:84

Harrison, Barbara Grizzuti
Dorothy L. Sayers 2:536

Harrison, Stanley R.
Hamlin Garland 3:202

Hart, Jeffrey
F. Scott Fitzgerald 1:274

Hart, Pierre
Andrey Bely 7:55

Hart, Pierre R.
Mikhail Bulgakov 2:67

Harte, Bret
Mark Twain 6:453

Hartley, L. P.
Saki 3:364

Hartnett, Edith
Joris-Karl Huysmans 7:417

Hasley, Louis
Don Marquis 7:446

Hassall, Christopher
Rupert Brooke 2:56; 7:124

Hassan, Ihab
Franz Kafka 2:306
Edwin Muir 2:485

Hastings, Michael
Rupert Brooke 7:128

Hastings, R.
Gabriele D'Annunzio 6:141

Hatfield, Henry
Thomas Mann 2:435

Hathaway, R. H.
Bliss Carman 7:136

Hatvary, George Egon
James Stephens 4:412

Hatzantonis, Emmanuel
Nikos Kazantzakis 5:260

Hawk, Affable
Marcel Proust 7:520

Haycraft, Howard
Dorothy L. Sayers 2:529

Hayes, Richard
James Agee 1:4
Colette 5:163

Haynes, Reneé
Hilaire Belloc 7:38

Haynes, Roslynn D.
H. G. Wells 6:553

Hayward, Max
Marina Tsvetaeva 7:565

Hazo, Samuel
Hart Crane 2:119
Wilfred Owen 5:366

Heard, Gerald
Kahlil Gibran 1:328

Hearn, Lafcadio
Bjørnsterne Bjørnson 7:108
Leo Tolstoy 4:455
Émile Zola 6:559

Hebblethwaite, Peter, S.J.
Georges Bernanos 3:122

Hecht, Ben
Sholom Aleichem 1:22

Heermance, J. Noel
Charles Waddell Chesnutt
5:137

Heidegger, Martin
Georg Trakl 5:459

Heilburn, Carolyn
Dorothy L. Sayers 2:535

Heiney, Donald
Cesare Pavese 3:341

Heller, Erich
Franz Kafka 6:225
Karl Kraus 5:288
Thomas Mann 2:442
Rainer Maria Rilke 1:419

Heller, Otto
Gerhart Hauptmann 4:193
August Strindberg 1:443

Hemmings, F.W.J.
Émile Zola 6:561, 570

Hemmingway, Ernest
Joseph Conrad 6:113
Mark Twain 6:463

Henderson, Alice Corbin
Edgar Lee Masters 2:460

Henderson, Archibald
John Galsworthy 1:295
Harley Granville-Barker 2:193
Maurice Maeterlinck 3:322
George Bernard Shaw 3:382
August Strindberg 1:444
Mark Twain 6:458
Oscar Wilde 1:496

Hendricks, Frances Kellam
Mariano Azuela 3:79

Henighan, Tom
Edgar Rice Burroughs 2:83

Henshaw, N. W.
W. S. Gilbert 3:216

Heppenstall, Rayner
Paul Claudel 2:99

Hergesheimer, Joseph
Gabriele D'Annunzio 6:131
Hugh Walpole 5:494

Herrick, Robert
Henri Barbusse 5:12

Herron, Ima Honaker
Zona Gale 7:281

Heseltine, Harry
Miles Franklin 7:273

Hesford, Walter
Rebecca Harding Davis 6:156

Hesse, Hermann
Rainer Maria Rilke 1:409
Rabindranath Tagore 3:493

Hewett-Thayer, Harvey W.
Gerhart Hauptmann 4:199

Hewitt, Douglas
Joseph Conrad 6:122

Hibberd, Dominic
Wilfred Owen 5:372

Hibberd, J. L.
Frank Wedekind 7:590

Hicks, Granville
Henry Adams 4:6
George Washington Cable 4:26
Ford Madox Ford 1:275
George Gissing 3:230
William Dean Howells 7:375
Henry James 2:255
Sarah Orne Jewett 1:362
George Moore 7:495
Eugene O'Neill 1:385
Oscar Wilde 1:497

Higginbotham, Virginia
Federico García Lorca 7:296

Higgins, F. R.
William Butler Yeats 1:556

Higgins, James
César Vallejo 3:531

Highet, Gilbert
A. E. Housman 1:357
James Joyce 3:264

Highsmith, James Milton
Ambrose Bierce 7:92

Hilfer, Anthony Channell
Zona Gale 7:286

Hill, Claude
Arthur Schnitzler 4:397
Frank Wedekind 7:579

Hill, Hamlin L.
Don Marquis 7:442

Hillyer, Robert
Kahlil Gibran 1:327

Hilton, Ian
Gottfried Benn 3:109

Hind, Charles Lewis
G. K. Chesterton 1:177
Laurence Housman 7:353

Hindus, Milton
F. Scott Fitzgerald 1:243

Hingley, Ronald
Anton Chekhov 3:165

Hinton, Norman D.
Hart Crane 5:194

Hochfield, George
Henry Adams 4:16

Hockey, Lawrence
W. H. Davies 5:208

Hodson, W. L.
Marcel Proust 7:538

Hoffman, Charles G.
Joyce Cary 1:143

Hoffman, Daniel
Edwin Muir 2:488

Hoffman, Frederick J.
Sherwood Anderson 1:48, 53
Willa Cather 1:159, 161
Hart Crane 2:117
F. Scott Fitzgerald 1:255, 256
James Joyce 3:263
Franz Kafka 2:293
D. H. Lawrence 2:354
Thomas Mann 2:420
Gertrude Stein 1:432

Hofmannsthal, Hugo von
Eugene O'Neill 6:325

Hoggart, Richard
George Orwell 2:506

Holdheim, William W.
André Gide 5:230

Holl, Karl
Gerhart Hauptmann 4:196

Hollis, Christopher
George Orwell 2:502

Holloway, John
Wyndham Lewis 2:393

Holman, C. Hugh
Ellen Glasgow 7:348
Thomas Wolfe 4:526, 528

Holroyd, Stuart
Rainer Maria Rilke 1:416
Dylan Thomas 1:470
William Butler Yeats 1:564

Honig, Edwin
Federico García Lorca 1:318

Hope, A. D.
Henry Handel Richardson 4:376

Hopkins, Kenneth
Walter de la Mare 4:81

Hough, Graham
Wallace Stevens 3:457

Houston, Ralph
Alun Lewis 3:287

Hovey, Richard B.
John Jay Chapman 7:196, 200

Howarth, Herbert
A. E. 3:8
Ford Madox Ford 1:291
James Joyce 3:270

Howe, Irving
Sholom Aleichem 1:23, 26
Sherwood Anderson 1:43
George Gissing 3:235
Sarah Orne Jewett 1:364
Sinclair Lewis 4:256
George Orwell 2:512
Luigi Pirandello 4:341
Wallace Stevens 3:464
Leo Tolstoy 4:472
Edith Wharton 3:574
Émile Zola 1:595

Howe, M. A. DeWolfe
John Jay Chapman 7:189

Howe, P. P.
John Millington Synge 6:428

Howell, Elmo
George Washington Cable 4:34

Howells, Bernard
Paul Claudel 2:106

Howells, William Dean
Bjørnsterne Bjørnson 7:105
George Washington Cable 4:25
Charles Waddell Chesnutt
5:130
Paul Laurence Dunbar 2:127
Hamlin Garland 3:190
Thomas Hardy 4:150
William Dean Howells 7:368
Henrik Ibsen 2:218
Leo Tolstoy 4:450
Mark Twain 6:456
Giovanni Verga 3:538
Émile Zola 1:586

Hsia, T. A.
Lu Hsün 3:296

Hsueh-Feng, Feng
Lu Hsün 3:295

Hubben, William
Franz Kafka 2:296

Hueffer, Ford Madox
See **Ford, Ford Madox**

Huggins, Nathan Irvin
Claude McKay 7:465

Hughes, Glenn
David Belasco 3:88

Hughes, Helen Sard
May Sinclair 3:440

Hughes, Langston
Wallace Thurman 6:447
Mark Twain 6:474

Hughes, Merritt Y.
Luigi Pirandello 4:329

Hughes, Riley
F. Scott Fitzgerald 1:247

Hughes, Ted
Wilfred Owen 5:370

Hulbert, Ann
W. H. Davies 5:210

Hume, Robert A.
Henry Adams 4:10

Humphries, Rolfe
Federico García Lorca 1:309
Lady Gregory 1:334

Huneker, James
Joris-Karl Huysmans 7:411
Henrik Ibsen 2:222
Maurice Maeterlinck 3:319
George Bernard Shaw 3:381
Leo Tolstoy 4:453

Hunt, Elizabeth R.
José Echegaray 4:99

Hunt, Peter R.
G. K. Chesterton 6:107

Hutchison, Percy
Marjorie Kinnan Rawlings
4:360

Hutchinson, Percy A.
Alfred Noyes 7:506

Hutman, Norma Louise
Antonio Machado 3:311

Hutton, Richard Holt
H. G. Wells 6:523

Huxley, Aldous
Ernest Dowson 4:86
D. H. Lawrence 2:352
Katherine Mansfield 2:447

Huysmans, J. K.
Joris-Karl Huysmans 7:409

Hyde, Fillmore
Kahlil Gibran 1:325

Hyde, Lawrence
Dorothy Richardson 3:348

Hyman, Stanley Edgar
F. Scott Fitzgrald 1:263

Hynes, Samuel
G. K. Chesterton 1:183
Joseph Conrad 1:213
Ford Madox Ford 1:278
Thomas Hardy 4:168

Hytier, Jean
André Gide 5:214

Iggers, Wilma Abeles
Karl Kraus 5:285

Ilie, Paul
Miguel de Unamuno 2:565

Illiano, Antonio
Ugo Betti 5:65

Irvine, William
George Bernard Shaw 3:394

Irwin, W. R.
Rose Macaulay 7:425
Charles Williams 1:523

Isaacs, Edith J. R.
Robert E. Sherwood 3:411

Isherwood, Christopher
Arthur Conan Doyle 7:228

Isola, Pietro
Gabriele D'Annunzio 6:130

Jack, Peter Monro
Federico García Lorca 1:307
Lewis Grassic Gibbon 4:121

Jackson, Blyden
Countee Cullen 4:51

Jackson, David
James Agee 1:16

Jackson, Holbrook
Maurice Maeterlinck 3:322

Jackson, Robert Louis
Aleksandr Kuprin 5:298

Jacob, Max
Max Jacob 6:190

Jaffe, Don
Don Marquis 7:450

Jahn, Werner
Lion Feuchtwanger 3:183

Jakobson, Roman
Vladimir Mayakovsky 4:291

James, Clive
Arthur Conan Doyle 7:232

James, Henry
Rupert Brooke 2:51; 7:120, 121
John Jay Chapman 7:185
Joseph Conrad 6:113
George Gissing 3:221
Thomas Hardy 4:156
William Dean Howells 7:365
Henrik Ibsen 2:218
Henry James 2:244
Edmond Rostand 6:375
Hugh Walpole 5:492
H. G. Wells 6:525, 526
Edith Wharton 3:555, 557
Émile Zola 1:586

James, M. R.
M. R. James 6:206

Jameson, Fredric
Raymond Chandler 7:170

Jameson, Storm
Jacinto Benavente 3:95
Walter de la Mare 4:71
José Echegaray 4:100

Janeway, Elizabeth
Joyce Cary 1:140

Janson, Kristofer
Bjørnstjerne, Bjørnson 7:101

Jarrell, Randall
Ellen Glasgow 7:334
Walter de la Mare 4:79
Wallace Stevens 3:449

Jean-Aubry, G.
Edmond Rostand 6:377

Jennings, Elizabeth
Wallace Stevens 3:459

Jerrold, Walter
Alfred Noyes 7:508

Jiménez, Juan Ramón
Antonio Machado 3:306

Joad, C.E.M.
Samuel Butler 1:134

Johannesson, Eric O.
Selma Lagerlöf 4:241

John, Alun
Alun Lewis 3:291

Johnson, Diane
Colette 5:173

Johnson, James Weldon
Countee Cullen 4:41
Claude McKay 7:456

Johnson, R. Brimley
Rose Macaulay 7:421
May Sinclair 3:435

Johnson, Robert Underwood
George Washington Cable 4:26

Johnson, Roberta
Gabriel Miró 5:342

Jones, D. G.
Bliss Carman 7:149

Jones, Ernest
Ronald Firbank 1:225

Jones, Frank
Stephen Vincent Benét 7:75

Jones, John Bush
W. S. Gilbert 3:215

Jones, Robert A.
Frank Wedekind 7:587

Jones, Sonia
Alfonsina Storni 5:451

Jong, Erica
Colette 1:193, 194

Jordy, William H.
Henry Adams 4:13

Josipovici, Gabriel
Bruno Schulz 5:427

Joyce, James
Henrik Ibsen 2:219
George Bernard Shaw 3:381
Oscar Wilde 1:494

Juhnke, Janet
L. Frank Baum 7:23

Jullian, Philipe
Gabriele D'Annunzio 6:143

Jung, C. G.
James Joyce 3:257

Justice, Donald
A. E. Housman 1:357

Kafka, Franz
Franz Kafka 6:219

Kahn, Coppélia
Rebecca Harding Davis 6:155

Kahn, Lothar
Lion Feuchtwanger 3:183, 187

Kallet, Marilyn
Paul Éluard 7:260

Kam, Rose Salberg
Joseph Conrad 1:220

Kanfer, Stefan
Kahlil Gibran 1:329

Kaplan, Sydney Janet
Dorothy Richardson 3:359

Karl, Frederick R.
Joyce Cary 1:146
Joseph Conrad 6:117
George Orwell 6:349

Karlinsky, Simon
Marina Tsvetaeva 7:559

Kauffman, Stanley
James Agee 1:5

Kaufmann, R. J.
August Strindberg 1:454

Kaun, Alexander
Leonid Andreyev 3:21
Sergei Esenin 4:110

Kayden, Eugene M.
Leonid Andreyev 3:20

Kazin, Alfred
James Agee 1:4
Sholom Aleichem 1:25
Sherwood Anderson 1:47
James Branch Cabell 6:69
John Jay Chapman 7:194
F. Scott Fitzgerald 1:250
Hamlin Garland 3:195
Ellen Glasgow 2:176
William Dean Howells 7:378
James Joyce 3:259
Franz Kafka 2:296
D. H. Lawrence 2:365
Sinclair Lewis 4:250
Rose Macaulay 7:423
Marcel Proust 7:532
Gertrude Stein 1:431
Edith Wharton 3:565
Thomas Wolfe 4:516

Keefer, L. B.
Gerhart Hauptmann 4:199

Keeley, Edmund
C. P. Cavafy 2:93, 94

Keene, Donald
Tōson Shimazaki 5:433

Kelly, Robert Glynn
Dorothy Richardson 3:353

Kemelman, H. G.
Eugene O'Neill 6:326

Kennedy, Andrew K.
George Bernard Shaw 3:406

Kennedy, Edwin J. Jr.
Virginia Woolf 5:517

Kennedy, Eileen 7:274

Kennedy, P. C.
Virginia Woolf 5:506

Kennedy, Ruth Lee
José Echegaray 4:100

Kennelly, Brendan
George Moore 7:491

Kent, George E.
Claude McKay 7:467

Kenner, Hugh
Roy Campbell 5:120
F. Scott Fitzgerald 1:273
Ford Madox Ford 1:278
James Joyce 3:268
Wyndham Lewis 2:388, 389
Wallace Stevens 3:474
William Butler Yeats 1:566

Kercheville, F. M.
Rubén Darío 4:62

Kermode, Frank
Ernest Dowson 4:90
D. H. Lawrence 2:372
Wallace Stevens 3:458

Kerrigan, Anthony
Miguel de Unamuno 2:568

Kestner, Joseph
Antoine de Saint-Exupéry 2:523

Kettle, Arnold
Arnold Bennett 5:48
Joyce Cary 1:141
Joseph Conrad 1:206
John Galsworthy 1:301
Henry James 2:264

Kiddle, Lawrence B.
Mariano Azuela 3:75

Kilmer, Joyce
Don Marquis 7:434
Rabindranath Tagore 3:482
Sara Teasdale 4:424

Kimball, Sidney Fiske
Henry Adams 4:4

Kinahan, Frank
F. Scott Fitzgerald 1:267

Kindilien, Carlin T.
Hamlin Garland 3:197

King, Edmund L.
Gabriel Miró 5:345

King, J. Marin
Marina Tsvetaeva 7:570

King, Jonathan
Henri Barbusse 5:18

Klarmann, Adolf D.
Wolfgang Borchert 5:103

Klotz, Martin B.
Isaak Babel 2:31

Knapp, Bettina L.
Antonin Artaud 3:52
Maurice Maeterlinck 3:331

Knaust, Rebecca
Guiseppe Giacosa 7:315

Knickerbocker, Conrad
Malcolm Lowry 6:238

Knight, G. Wilson
Oscar Wilde 1:503

Knister, Raymond
Duncan Campbell Scott 6:385

Knox, Ronald
G. K. Chesterton 6:99

Koch, Stephen
Antonin Artaud 3:51

Koestler, Arthur
George Orwell 2:498

Kolb, Philip
Marcel Proust 7:547

Königsberg, I.
Alfred Jarry 2:283

Korg, Jacob
George Gissing 3:235

Kosove, Joan Pataky
Maurice Maeterlinck 3:330

Kostelanetz, Richard
Gertrude Stein 6:414

Kramer, Leonie
Henry Handel Richardson 4:380

Kramer, Victor A.
James Agee 1:16

Kreuter, Gretchen
F. Scott Fitzgerald 1:252

Kreuter Kent
F. Scott Fitzgerald 1:252

Kreymborg, Alfred
Edgar Lee Masters 2:465
Thomas Wolfe 4:518

Kridl, Manfred
Władysław Stanisław Reymont 5:393
Henryk Sienkiewicz 3:429

Kronenberger, Louis
Henry Adams 4:6
Max Beerbohm 1:67
W. H. Davies 5:204
Ronald Firbank 1:225
Jean Giraudoux 7:317
Virginia Woolf 5:507
Alexander Woollcott 5:523

Krook, Dorothea
Henry James 2:272

Kroth, Anya M.
Marina Tsvetaeva 7:567

Krutch, Joseph Wood
Maxwell Anderson 2:6
Ivan Bunin 6:44
Colette 1:192
Zona Gale 7:280
Ellen Glasgow 7:335
Henrik Ibsen 2:230
Sinclair Lewis 4:255
Rose Macaulay 7:423
Arthur Machen 4:277
Eugene O'Neill 1:396
Władysław Stanisław Reymont 5:390
George Bernard Shaw 3:397
Robert E. Sherwood 3:412
May Sinclair 3:438
August Strindberg 1:450
Oscar Wilde 1:502
Jakob Wassermann 6:508
Alexander Woollcott 5:521

Krzyzanowski, Jerzy R.
Władysław Stanisław Reymont 5:395

Kurrick, Maire Jaanus
Georg Trakl 5:466

Kustow, Michael
Bertolt Brecht 1:122

Lafourcade, Georges
Arnold Bennett 5:38

Lagerkvist, Pär
August Strindberg 1:456

Lagerroth, Erland
Selma Lagerlöf 4:241

Lago, Mary M.
Rabindranath Tagore 3:498, 499

Lakshin, Vladimir
Mikhail Bulgakov 2:73

Lambert, J. W.
John Galsworthy 1:304
Saki 3:369

Lamm, Martin
Federico García Lorca 1:314
August Strindberg 1:444

Landis, Joseph C.
Sholem Asch 3:70

Lang, A.
Émile Zola 6:559

Lapp, John C.
Émile Zola 6:568

Larsen, Erling
James Agee 1:16

Larsen, Hanna Astrup
Knut Hamsun 2:202
Selma Lagerlöf 4:234
Sigrid Undset 3:511

Larson, Harold
Bjørnstjerne Bjørnson 7:109

Lauterbach, Charles E.
W. S. Gilbert 3:212

Lavrin, Janko
Leonid Andreyev 3:26
Andrey Bely 7:49
Aleksandr Blok 5:98
Sergei Esenin 4:110
Knut Hamsun 2:203

Lawler, James R.
Paul Claudel 2:109

Lawrence, D. H.
Thomas Hardy 4:162
Giovanni Verga 3:539, 543
H. G. Wells 6:529

Lawrence, Margaret
Rose Macaulay 7:423

Lawson, Henry
Miles Franklin 7:264

Lawson, John Howard
Robert E. Sherwood 3:410

Lawson, Richard H.
Edith Wharton 3:579

Lawson, Robb
Algernon Blackwood 5:70

Leach, Henry Goddard
Selma Lagerlöf 4:230

Leacock, Stephen
O. Henry 1:346

Leal, Luis
Mariano Azuela 3:80

Leary, Lewis
Kate Chopin 5:150
Mark Twain 6:475

Leaska, Mitchell A.
Virginia Woolf 5:512

Leavis, F. R.
Joseph Conrad 1:204
Thomas Hardy 4:164
Henry James 2:262
D. H. Lawrence 2:360

Leavis, Q. D.
Dorothy L. Sayers 2:528
Edith Wharton 3:564

Leblanc-Maeterlinck, Georgette
Maurice Maeterlinck 3:320

Lebowitz, Naomi
Italo Svevo 2:554

Lederman, Marie Jean
Katherine Mansfield 2:456

Lednicki, Waclaw
Henryk Sienkiewicz 3:427

Lee, Alice
Isaak Babel 2:23

Lee, Lynn
Don Marquis 7:450

Le Gallienne, Richard
Don Marquis 7:435
Alfred Noyes 7:504

Legh-Jones, J.
Guillaume Apollinaire 3:40

Lehan, Richard
F. Scott Fitzgerald 1:267
Ford Madox Ford 1:287

Lehmann, John
Rupert Brooke 7:129
Lewis Grassic Gibbon 4:121
Alun Lewis 3:287
Virginia Woolf 1:538

Leiber, Fritz, Jr.
H. P. Lovecraft 4:267

Leibowitz, Herbert A.
Hart Crane 2:122

Lemaitre, Georges
André Gide 5:216
Jean Giraudoux 2:169

Lenin, Nikolai
Vladimir Mayakovsky 4:289

Lenin, V. I.
Leo Tolstoy 4:452

Leon, Derrick
Marcel Proust 7:527

LeSage, Laurent
Jean Giraudoux 2:163

Lessing, Doris
A. E. Coppard 5:181

Levey, Michael
Francis Thompson 4:441

Levin, Harry
James Joyce 3:272
Marcel Proust 7:540
Émile Zola 6:566

Levine, Robert T.
Franz Kafka 6:229

Levitt, Morton P.
Nikos Kazantzakis 2:318

Levy, Karen D.
Alain-Fournier 6:28

Levy, Kurt L.
Mariano Azuela 3:82

Lewis, Allan
Federico García Lorca 7:296

Lewis, C. Day
Wilfred Owen 5:368

Lewis, C. S.
G. K. Chesterton 6:99
George Orwell 2:501
Charles Williams 1:511

Lewis, Charlton M.
Francis Thompson 4:437

Lewis, R. W. B.
Joseph Conrad 1:210
Hart Crane 5:191
F. Scott Fitzgerald 1:245
Henry James 2:267
Edith Wharton 3:575

Lewis, Sinclair
Willa Cather 1:151
Hamlin Garland 3:194
William Dean Howells 7:374

Lewis, Theophilus
Wallace Thurman 6:445

Lewis, Wyndham
James Joyce 3:253

Lewisohn, Ludwig
A. E. Coppard 5:176
Zona Gale 7:278
John Galsworthy 1:295
Gerhart Hauptmann 4:197
William Dean Howells 7:374
Luigi Pirandello 4:327
Rainer Maria Rilke 1:408

Lid, R. W.
Raymond Chandler 7:168

Liddell, Robert
C. P. Cavafy 7:152

Light, James F.
Nathanael West 1:486

Lima, Robert
Federico García Lorca 1:321
Ramón del Valle-Inclán 5:485

Lindenberger, Herbert
Georg Trakl 5:462

Lindbergh, Anne Morrow
Antoine de Saint-Exupéry 2:516

Linklater, Eric
James Bridie 3:131

Liptzin, Sol
Arthur Schnitzler 4:393

Littell, Robert
Ambrose Bierce 1:83

Little, Roger
Guillaume Apollinaire 3:45

Littlefield, Hazel
Lord Dunsany 2:145

Littlefield, Henry M.
L. Frank Baum 7:17

Littlejohn, David
F. Scott Fitzgerald 1:254

Livingstone, Angela
Marina Tsvetaeva 7:563

Livingstone, L.
Miguel de Unamuno 2:558

Locke, Frederick W.
Alain-Fournier 6:17

Lockerbie, S. I.
Max Jacob 6:197

Lockert, Lacy
Henryk Sienkiewicz 3:423

Locklin, Gerald
Nathanael West 1:489

Lockwood, William J.
Rose Macaulay 7:428

Lodge, David
G. K. Chesterton 1:181
Gertrude Stein 1:442

Lodge, Oliver
Alfred Noyes 7:506

Loftus, Richard J.
A. E. 3:9
James Stephens 4:415

Loggins, Vernon
Amy Lowell 1:378
Gertrude Stein 1:427

Lohner, Edgar
Gottfried Benn 3:104

Longaker, Mark
Ernest Dowson 4:89

Longford, Elizabeth
Arthur Conan Doyle 7:232

Loomis, Emerson Robert
Bertolt Brecht 6:30

Lovecraft, H. P.
Ambrose Bierce 7:90
Algernon Blackwood 5:72
M. R. James 6:206

Loveman, Samuel
Ambrose Bierce 7:89

Lovett, Robert Morss
Sherwood Anderson 1:35, 37, 41
May Sinclair 3:435, 440
Edith Wharton 3:559

Lowell, Amy
Edgar Lee Masters 2:462
Edwin Arlington Robinson 5:401

Lowell, James Russell
William Dean Howells 7:363

Lowell, Robert
Wallace Stevens 3:448

Lowry, Malcolm
Malcolm Lowry 6:235

Lubbock, Percy
Leo Tolstoy 4:454
Edith Wharton 3:557

Lucas, F. L.
Rupert Brooke 7:123
Roy Campbell 5:116

Lucas, Frank
W. H. Davies 5:202

Lucas, John
Arnold Bennett 5:50

Luciani, Vincent
Guiseppe Giacosa 7:313

Lucie-Smith, Edward
Paul Claudel 2:107

Lukacs, Georg
Lion Feuchtwanger 3:179
Thomas Mann 2:419
Leo Tolstoy 4:462

Lukashevich, Olga
Bruno Schulz 5:422

Luker, Nicholas
Aleksandr Kuprin 5:303

Lumley, Frederick
James Bridie 3:137
Jean Giraudoux 2:157

Lundquist, James
Sinclair Lewis 4:261

Lupoff, Richard A.
Edgar Rice Burroughs 2:77

Luquiens, Frederick Bliss
Henry Adams 4:5

Lurie, Alison
A. A. Milne 6:320

Luyben, Helen L.
James Bridie 3:140

Lyell, William, Jr.
Lu Hsün 3:302

Lynd, Robert
John Millington Synge 6:431

Lyngstad, Sverre
Jonas Lie 5:330

Lynn, Kenneth S.
Mark Twain 6:482

Lyon, Melvin
Henry Adams 4:19

Mabbott, T. O.
H. P. Lovecraft 4:265

MacAndrew, Andrew R.
Aleksandr Kuprin 5:299

Macaree, David
Lewis Grassic Gibbon 4:124

MacCarthy, Desmond
Vernon Lee 5:312
Gregorio Martínez Sierra and
María Martínez Sierra 6:281
Gertrude Stein 6:403

MacClintock, Lander
Guiseppe Giacosa 7:308
Luigi Pirandello 4:338

MacDiarmid, Hugh
Lewis Grassic Gibbon 4:122

Macdonald, Dwight
James Agee 1:7
George Orwell 2:505

Macdonald, Ian R.
Gabriel Miró 5:342

Mackail, J. W.
Maurice Maeterlinck 3:317

MacKay, L. A.
Bliss Carman 7:144

Mackenzie, Compton
Joseph Conrad 1:201
John Galsworthy 1:298

Mackridge, Peter
Nikos Kazantzakis 5:272

Maclaren, Hamish
A. E. Coppard 5:177

MacLean, Hugh N.
John Millington Synge 6:437

MacLeish, Archibald
Amy Lowell 1:373
William Butler Yeats 1:560

MacShane, Frank
Raymond Chandler 7:172

Madariaga, Salvador de
Gabriel Miró 5:334
Ramón del Valle-Inclán 5:471

Madeleva, Sister M.
Edna St. Vincent Millay 4:309

Madison, Charles A.
Sholom Aleichem 1:28
Sholem Asch 3:70

Magalaner, Marvin
Katherine Mansfield 2:454

Magarshack, David
Anton Chekhov 3:161

Magny, Claude-Edmonde
Franz Kafka 2:292

Maguire, Robert A.
Andrey Bely 7:62

Mahony, Patrick
Maurice Maeterlinck 3:328

Mallarmé, Stéphane
Émile Zola 6:558

Malmstad, John E.
Andrey Bely 7:62

Malone, Andrew W.
Lord Dunsany 2:143

Mandelstam, Nadezhda
Osip Mandelstam 2:403; 6:265

Manganiello, Dominic
Guiseppe Giacosa 7:314

Mankin, Paul A.
Ugo Betti 5:57
Jean Giraudoux 2:172

Mann, Thomas
Anton Chekhov 3:160
Joseph Conrad 1:200
Franz Kafka 2:291
George Bernard Shaw 3:396
Leo Tolstoy 4:459
Frank Wedekind 7:576
Oscar Wilde 1:503

Manning, Clarence Augustus
Sergei Esenin 4:108

Mansfield, Katherine
John Galsworthy 1:293
Rose Macaulay 7:421
George Moore 7:476
Dorothy Richardson 3:347
Hugh Walpole 5:492
Edith Wharton 3:558

Marble, Annie Russell
Verner von Heidenstam 5:253
Władysław Stanisław Reymont 5:391

March, George
Thomas Mann 2:412

Marcus, Phillip L.
Standish O'Grady 5:354

Marcus, Steven
O. Henry 1:351

Marder, Herbert
Isaak Babel 2:30

Marias, Julian
Miguel de Unamuno 2:563

Marker, Lise-Lone
David Belasco 3:90

Marks, Elaine
Colette 5:164

Marquerie, Alfredo
Jacinto Benavente 3:101

Marquis, Don
Don Marquis 7:438

Marsh, E.
Rupert Brooke 2:50

Marshall, Margaret
James Bridie 3:132

Martin, Edward A.
Don Marquis 7:448

Martin, Jay
Hamlin Garland 3:200

Marx, Leo
F. Scott Fitzgerald 6:172

Maskaleris, Thanasis
Kostes Palamas 5:382

Maslenikov, Oleg A.
Hilaire Belloc 7:49

Mason, Eudo C.
Rainer Maria Rilke 6:364

Mason, Lawrence
Robert Benchley 1:76

Mathew, Ray
Miles Franklin 7:269

Mathews, Jackson
Paul Valéry 4:492

Mathewson, Ruth
Raymond Chandler 1:176

Matthews, Brander
James Weldon Johnson 3:239
Mark Twain 6:454

Matthews, J. H.
Paul Éluard 7:253

Matthews, John F.
George Bernard Shaw 3:405

Matthews, T. S.
James Agee 1:9

Matthiessen, Francis Otto
Henry James 2:259
Sarah Orne Jewett 1:362

Maude, Aylmer
Leo Tolstoy 4:458

Maugham, W. Somerset
Arnold Bennett 5:34
Aleister Crowley 7:207

Mauriac, François
Jean Giraudoux 7:321

Maurice, Arthur Bartlett
Arthur Conan Doyle 7:216

Maurois, André
Antoine de Saint-Exupéry 2:516
Marcel Proust 7:530

Mautner, Franz H.
Karl Kraus 5:292

Maxwell, William
Samuel Butler 1:138

May, Frederick
Luigi Pirandello 4:349

May, Georges
Jean Giraudoux 2:156

Mayne, Richard
Wyndham Lewis 2:398

McArthur, Peter
Stephen Leacock 2:377

McCarthy, Mary
Henrik Ibsen 2:230
Eugene O'Neill 1:389, 393
John Van Druten 2:575

McCarthy, Patrick
Alice Meynell 6:303

McClellan, Edwin
Sōseki Natsume 2:490
Tōson Shimazaki 5:434

McCormick, John
Sherwood Anderson 1:62
F. Scott Fitzgerald 1:270

McCourt, Edward A.
Rupert Brooke 2:55

McDowell, Frederick P. W.
Ellen Glasgow 2:185

McDowell, Margaret B.
Edith Wharton 3:578

McElderry, Bruce R., Jr.
Max Beerbohm 1:73
Thomas Wolfe 4:522

McFarlane, Brian
Henry Handel Richardson 4:381

McFarlane, James Walter
Bjørnstjerne, Bjørnson 7:113
Knut Hamsun 2:206
Jonas Lie 5:330
Sigrid Undset 3:525

McFate, Patricia
Ford Madox Ford 1:285
James Stephens 4:418

McGreivey, John C.
Hamlin Garland 3:204

McKay, D. F.
Dylan Thomas 1:475

McKee, Mary J.
Edna St. Vincent Millay 4:317

McKeon, Joseph T.
Antone de Saint-Exupéry 2:526

McLaughlin, Ann L.
Katherine Mansfield 2:456

McLean, Robert C.
Ambrose Bierce 7:94

McLeod, Addison
Guiseppe, Giacosa 7:305

McLuhan, Herbert Marshall
Wyndham Lewis 2:387
G. K. Chesterton 6:107

McMillin, A. B.
Aleksandr Kuprin 5:300

McMurray, William
William Dean Howells 7:390

McVay, Gordon
Sergei Esenin 4:117

McWilliam, G. H.
Ugo Betti 5:55, 59, 61

Mechem, Rose Mary
Bertolt Brecht 1:121

Meeker, Richard K.
Ellen Glasgow 7:342

Meixner, John A.
Ford Madox Ford 1:283

Mencken, H. L.
Ambrose Bierce 1:85; 7:90
James Branch Cabell 6:66
Joseph Conrad 1:197
F. Scott Fitzgerald 6:159
Hamlin Garland 3:191
Ellen Glasgow 7:333
William Dean Howells 7:369
Henry James 2:151
Ring Lardner 2:328
Sinclair Lewis 4:246
George Bernard Shaw 3:378
Mark Twain 6:459
H. G. Wells 6:528

Menes, Bonnie
Arthur Conan Doyle 7:240

Merchant, W. Moelwyn
Bertolt Brecht 1:113

Mercier, Vivian
Standish O'Grady 5:353
James Stephens 4:411

Merrill, James
C. P. Cavafy 7:162

Meredith, George
Alice Meynell 6:293

Merwin, W. S.
Edwin Muir 2:482

Meserve, Walter J.
William Dean Howells 7:386
Robert E. Sherwood 3:417

Meyers, Jeffrey
George Orwell 6:350

Michael, D.P.M.
Arthur Machen 4:285

Michaels, Leonard
Raymond Chandler 1:175

Michaud, Regis
Max Jacob 6:191

Michelson, Bruce
Mark Twain 6:485

Michie, James A.
James Bridie 3:142

Mickelson, Anne Z.
Thomas Hardy 4:176

Mikes, George
Stephen Leacock 2:379

Miles, Hamish
Arthur Machen 4:278

Miller, Arthur M.
Ambrose Bierce 7:91

Miller, Henry
James Joyce 3:272
D. H. Lawrence 2:366
Marcel Proust 7:526
Jakob Wassermann 6:519

Miller, J. Hillis
Joseph Conrad 1:213
Thomas Hardy 4:174
Wallace Stevens 3:468
Dylan Thomas 1:474
William Butler Yeats 1:575

Miller, James E., Jr.
Willa Cather 1:167
F. Scott Fitzgerald 1:257

Miller, Richard F.
Henry Adams 4:11

Miller, Walter James
Jules Verne 6:498

Miller, William Lee
Robert Benchley 1:79

Milligan, E. E.
Antoine de Saint-Exupéry 2:519

Mills, Ralph J., Jr.
W. H. Davies 5:207

Milne, A. A.
A. A. Milne 6:311
Saki 3:363

Miłosz, Czesław
Joseph Conrad 1:207

Mirsky, D. S.
Leonid Andreyev 3:27
Andrey Bely 7:47
Aleksandr Blok 5:83
Anton Chekhov 3:154
Sergei Esenin 4:111
Aleksandr Kuprin 5:298
Marina Tsvetaeva 7:556

Mitchell, Bonner
Antoine de Saint-Exupéry 2:521

Mitchell, Julian
Aleister Crowley 7:207

Miyoshi, Masao
Sōseki Natsume 2:494

Mizener, Arthur
F. Scott Fitzgerald 1:241, 261

Mochulsky, Konstantin
Andrey Bely 7:53

Moers, Ellen
F. Scott Fitzgerald 1:254

Moestrup, Jørn
Luigi Pirandello 4:353

Molnar, Thomas
Georges Bernanos 3:118

Monahan, Michael
Gabriele D'Annunzio 6:132

Monas, Sidney
Andrey Bely 7:53
Osip Mandelstam 2:404; 6:267

Monkhouse, Cosmo
Vernon Lee 5:309

Monroe, Harriet
Stephen Vincent Benét 7:73
Robert Bridges 1:127
Hart Crane 5:184
Thomas Hardy 4:157
Edgar Lee Masters 2:462
Edna St. Vincent Millay 4:307
Edwin Arlington Robinson
5:405
Sara Teasdale 4:427

Monroe, N. Elizabeth
Selma Lagerlöf **4**:239
Sigrid Undset **3**:520

Montague, C. E.
John Millington Synge **6**:426

Moody, A. D.
Virginia Woolf **5**:509

Mooney, Harry J., Jr.
Leo Tolstoy **4**:477

Moore, Marianne
Laurence Housman **7**:355
Wallace Stevens **3**:446

Moore, Raylyn
L. Frank Baum **7**:21

Moore, Virginia
Alice Meynell **6**:301

Moorman, Charles
Charles Williams **1**:519

Mora, José Ferrater
Miguel de Unamuno **2**:560

Moran, Carlos Alberto
Raymond Chandler **1**:174

More, Paul Elmer
James Branch Cabell **6**:66

Morgan, A. E.
Harley Granville-Barker **2**:194

Morgan, Bayard Quincy
Arthur Schnitzler **4**:386

Morgan, Charles
George Moore **7**:481

Morgan, Edwin
Edwin Muir **2**:489

Morgan, Florence A. H.
Charles Waddell Chesnutt **5**:129

Morgan, H. Wayne
Hart Crane **2**:122
Hamlin Garland **3**:198

Morita, James R.
Tōson Shimazaki **5**:438

Morley, Christopher
Arthur Conan Doyle **7**:219
Don Marquis **7**:434, 439
Saki **3**:365

Morley, S. Griswold
Rubén Darío **4**:57

Morris, Irene
Georg Trakl **5**:456

Morris, Lloyd
Sherwood Anderson **1**:42
Willa Cather **1**:12
F. Scott Fitzgerald **1**:244
O. Henry **1**:349
Eugene O'Neill **1**:391
Marjorie Kinnan Rawlings **4**:361
Edwin Arlington Robinson **5**:405

Morris, Wright
F. Scott Fitzgerald **1**:251

Morrow, Carolyn
Antonio Machado **3**:306

Morsberger, Robert E.
Edgar Rice Burroughs **2**:85

Morse, J. Mitchell
James Joyce **3**:272

Morse, Samuel French
Wallace Steen **3**:477

Morton, J. B.
Hilaire Belloc **7**:37

Moseley, Edwin M.
F. Scott Fitzgerald **1**:264

Moser, Thomas
Joseph Conrad **1**:208

Moses, Montrose J.
David Belasco **3**:85

Mosig, Dirk
H. P. Lovecraft **4**:272

Moskowitz, Sam
Arthur Conan Doyle **7**:224

Moss, Howard
Anton Chekhov **3**:175

Mott, Frank Luther
Zane Grey **6**:180

Muchnic, Helen
Andrey Bely **7**:61
Aleksandr Blok **5**:93
Mikhail Bulgakov **2**:65
Vladimir Mayakovsky **4**:296

Muddiman, Bernard
Duncan Campbell Scott **6**:396

Mudrick, Marvin
D. H. Lawrence **2**:366
Wyndham Lewis **2**:386
George Bernard Shaw **3**:402

Mueller, Dennis
Lion Feuchtwanger **3**:185

Muir, Edwin
Joseph Conrad **1**:198
Thomas Hardy **4**:173
Franz Kafka **6**:219
Virginia Woolf **1**:527, **5**:507

Muller, Herbert J.
Thomas Wolfe **4**:519

Munro, Ian S.
Lewis Grassic Gibbon **4**:126

Munson, Gorham B.
Hart Crane **2**:111
Wallace Stevens **3**:445
Émile Zola **1**:590

Murch, A. E.
Cesare Pavese **3**:340
Dorothy L. Sayers **2**:531

Murray, Edward
F. Scott Fitzgerald **1**:272

Murry, John Middleton
Ivan Bunin **6**:43
Anton Chekhov **3**:150
George Gissing **3**:233
Aleksandr Kuprin **5**:296
D. H. Lawrence **2**:346
Katherine Mansfield **2**:451
Wilfred Owen **5**:359
Hugh Walpole **5**:493

Nabokov, Vladimir
Andrey Bely **7**:55
Franz Kafka **6**:230
Marcel Proust **7**:552

Naff, William E.
Tōson Shimazaki **5**:441

Nagy, Moses M.
Paul Claudel **2**:109

Naipaul, V. S.
Joyce Cary **1**:142

Naremore, James
Virginia Woolf **5**:514

Nash, Berta
Arthur Machen **4**:284

Natan, Alex
Frank Wedekind **7**:580

Nathan, George Jean
David Belasco **3**:87
Jacinto Benavente **3**:96
Ugo Betti **5**:54
Ambrose Bierce **1**:87
James Bridie **3**:132
Karel Čapek **6**:87
A. A. Milne **6**:306
Eugene O'Neill **1**:386
Luigi Pirandello **4**:331
George Bernard Shaw **3**:387
John Van Druten **2**:573
Oscar Wilde **1**:500
Alexander Woolcott **5**:520

Neale-Silva, Eduardo
César Vallejo **3**:529

Nejdefors-Frisk, Sonya
George Moore **7**:486

Nelson, Donald F.
Wolfgang Borchert **5**:112

Nelson, Lowry, Jr.
Italo Svevo **2**:539

Nemerov, Howard
James Joyce **3**:280
Thomas Mann **2**:431
Wallace Stevens **3**:453

Nemes, Graciela P.
Juan Ramón Jiménez **4**:215

Neruda, Pablo
Rubén Darío **4**:63

Nettelbeck, C. W.
Georges Bernanos **3**:124

Nevius, Blake
Edith Wharton **3**:566

Newberry, Wilma
José Echegaray **4**:104

Newcombe, Josephine M.
Leonid Andreyev **3**:29

Newton, Nancy A.
Antonio Machado **3**:314

Nevins, Allan
Ring Lardner **2**:327

Nichols, Wallace B.
Alfred Noyes **7**:508

Nicoll, Allardyce
Henrik Ibsen **2**:228
Eugene O'Neill **1**:391
George Bernard Shaw **3**:395
August Strindberg **1**:450

Niger, Shmuel
Sholom Aleichem **1**:20

Nilsson, Nils Ake
Osip Mandelstam **6**:257

Nin, Anaïs
D. H. Lawrence **2**:348

Nissenson, Hugh
Ivan Bunin **6**:54

Noble, David W.
F. Scott Fitzgerald **1**:264

Nock, Albert J.
Bret Harte **1**:341

Nordon, Pierre
Arthur Conan Doyle **7**:226

Noreng, Harald
Bjørnstjerne Bjørnson **7**:114

Normand, Guessler
Henri Barbusse **5**:19

Norris, Margot
James Joyce **3**:281

Novak, Barbara
A. A. Milne **6**:313

Noyes, Henry
Alfred Noyes **7**:515

Nozick, Martin
Miguel de Unamuno **2**:568

Nugent, Robert
Paul Eluard **7**:257

Nye, Russel
L. Frank Baum **7**:15
Zane Grey **6**:182

Oates, Joyce Carol
Thomas Mann **2**:441
Virginia Woolf **1**:540
William Butler Yeats **1**:582

O'Brien, Justin
Marcel Proust **7**:528

O'Casey, Sean
George Bernard Shaw **3**:399

O'Connor, Frank
A. E. **3**:8
Anton Chekhov **3**:161
A. E. Coppard **5**:180
Lady Gregory **1**:336
Thomas Hardy **4**:168
James Stephens **4**:416

O'Connor, Patricia Walker
Gregorio Martínez Sierra and
María Martínez Sierra **6**:282, 284

O'Connor, William Van
Joyce Cary **1**:145
Wallace Stevens **3**:464

O'Conor, Norreys Jepson
Standish O'Grady **5**:353

O'Donnell, J. P.
Bertolt Brecht **1**:116

O'Faolain, Sean
A. E. **3**:8
George Moore **7**:482
Leo Tolstoy **4**:461

O'Hagan, Thomas
John Millington Synge **6**:431

O'Hara, John
Robert Benchley **1**:78

Ohlin, Peter H.
James Agee **1**:10

Olgin, Moissaye J.
Leonid Andreyev **3**:21
Aleksandr Kuprin **5**:297

Oliphant, Margaret
Thomas Hardy 4:150

Olsen, Tillie
Rebecca Harding Davis 6:153

Olson, Elder
Dylan Thomas 1:470

Olson, Paul R.
Juan Ramón Jiménez 4:218

Orage, A. R.
Ernest Dowson 4:87

Ornstein, Robert
F. Scott Fitzgerald 1:250

Ortega y Gasset, José
Ramón del Valle-Inclán 5:479

Ortiz-Vargas, A.
Gabriela Mistral 2:475

Orwell, George
D. H. Lawrence 2:354
Jules Verne 6:491
H. G. Wells 6:533

Osborne, Charles
Francis Thompson 4:411

O'Sheel, Shaemas
Lady Gregory 1:333

O'Sullivan, Susan
Gabriel Miró 5:337

Overmyer, Janet
Saki 3:371

Ozick, Cynthia
Bruno Schulz 5:424

Pacey, Desmond
Bliss Carman 7:145
Frederick Philip Grove 4:140
Duncan Campbell Scott 6:393

Pack, Robert
Wallace Stevens 3:455

Pacifici, Sergio
Giovanni Verga 3:545

Painter, George D.
Marcel Proust 7:537

Palamari, Demetra
Émile Zola 6:569

Palamas, Kostes
Kostes Palamas 5:377

Palmer, Nettie
Henry Handel Richardson 4:375

Paolucci, Anne
Luigi Pirandello 4:356

Parker, Alexander A.
Miguel de Unamuno 2:565

Parker, H. T.
Karl Čapek 6:82

Parks, Edd Winfield
Edna St. Vincent Millay 4:310

Parrington, Vernon Louis
James Branch Cabell 6:63
Hamlin Garland 3:193

Parrot, Louis
Paul Éluard 7:249

Parrott, Cecil
Jaroslav Hašek 4:189

Parry, Idris
Rainer Maria Rilke 1:422

Parry, M.
Antoine de Saint-Exupéry 2:524

Pasternak, Boris
Vladimir Mayakovsky 4:298
Marina Tsvetaeva 7:558

Pater, Walter
Oscar Wilde 1:495

Patmore, Coventry
Alice Meynell 6:290
Francis Thompson 4:433

Patrick, Walton R.
Ring Lardner 2:338

Pattee, Fred Lewis
Gertrude Atherton 2:17
Kate Chopin 5:144
Rebecca Harding Davis 6:150
Bret Harte 1:340
O. Henry 1:348
Edith Wharton 3:560

Pattison, Walter T.
Juan Ramón Jiménez 4:212

Paul, David
Alain-Fournier 6:12

Paul, Sherman
John Jay Chapman 7:197

Pavese, Cesare
Edgar Lee Masters 2:473

Payne, William Morton
Arnold Bennett 5:22
Bjørnstjerne Bjørnson 7:109
Arthur Conan Doyle 7:216
Ellen Glasgow 7:332
Zane Grey 6:177
Selma Lagerlöf 4:229
Duncan Campbell Scott 6:385
Leo Tolstoy 4:449
Edith Wharton 3:551

Paz, Octavio
Guillaume Apollinaire 3:44
Rubén Darío 4:64

Peacock, Ronald
Henrik Ibsen 2:227
George Bernard Shaw 3:389
William Butler Yeats 1:561

Pearsall, Robert Brainard
Rupert Brooke 2:58

Pearsall, Ronald
Arthur Conan Doyle 7:236

Pearson, Hesketh
Arthur Conan Doyle 7:221
George Bernard Shaw 3:395

Pearson, Norman Holmes
Sherwood Anderson 1:42

Peck, Harry Thurston
William Dean Howells 7:367
Joris-Karl Huysmans 7:407
Edith Wharton 3:551

Peers, E. Allison
Rubén Darío 4:64
José Echegaray 4:103

Pehrson, Elsa
Selma Lagerlöf 4:240

Pellizzi, Camillo
Eugene O'Neill 6:327

Pendo, Stephen
Raymond Chandler 7:174

Penzoldt, Peter
Algernon Blackwood 5:74
M. R. James 6:208
H. P. Lovecraft 4:269

Perkins, George
William Dean Howells 7:395

Perkins, Maxwell E.
F. Scott Fitzgerald 6:159
Thomas Wolfe 4:518

Perlmutter, Elizabeth P.
Edna St. Vincent Millay 4:321

Perry, Henry Ten Eyck
W. S. Gilbert 3:212

Persky, Serge
Leonid Andreyev 3:17

Person, Leland S., Jr.
F. Scott Fitzgerald 6:164

Peters, H. F.
Rainer Maria Rilke 6:363

Peterson, Dale E.
Vladimir Mayakovsky 4:300

Peyre, Henri
Paul Claudell 2:100
Colette 5:170
Paul Éluard 7:252
André Gide 5:219, 227
Marcel Proust 7:548

Pfohl, Russell
Italo Svevo 2:542

Phelan, Kappo
Federico García Lorca 1:309

Phelps, Arthur L.
Frederick Philip Grove 4:132

Phelps, William Lyon
Leonid Andreyev 3:16
J. M. Barrie 2:40
Bjørnstjerne Bjørnson 7:107
Rupert Brooke 7:122
Anton Chekhov 3:146
Zona Gale 7:280
O. Henry 1:346
William Dean Howells 7:371
Aleksandr Kuprin 5:296
Alfred Noyes 7:502
George Bernard Shaw 3:384
Henryk Sienkiewicz 3:422
May Sinclair 3:433
Edith Wharton 3:557

Phillips, Klaus
Rainer Maria Rilke 6:369

Phillips, Rachel
Alfonsina Storni 5:447

Phoutrides, Aristides E.
Kostes Palamas 5:378

Pickford, John
Wolfgang Borchert 5:112

Pickman, Hester
Rainer Maria Rilke 6:357

Picon, Gaëtan
André Gide 5:218

Pierce, Lorne
Frederick Philip Grove 4:136

Pikoulis, John
Alun Lewis 3:291

Pinchin, Jane Lagoudis
C. P. Cavafy 2:98

Pinkerton, Jan
Wallace Stevens 3:474

Pinsker, Sanford
Sholom Aleichem 1:30

Pinto, Vivian De Sola
A. E. Housman 1:358
D. H. Lawrence 2:367

Pirandello, Luigi
Giovanni Verga 3:542

Pisarev, Dmitri
Leo Tolstoy 4:466

Pitcher, Harvey
Anton Chekhov 3:172

Pizer, Donald
Hamlin Garland 3:197, 198
William Dean Howells 7:385

Plant, Richard
Arthur Schnitzler 4:395

Plomer, William
Lewis Grassic Gibbon 4:120
George Gissing 3:231

Podhoretz, Norman
Sholom Aleichem 1:23
John Millington Synge 6:436
Nathanael West 1:478

Poggioli, Renato
Isaak Babel 2:20
Aleksandr Blok 5:90
Ivan Bunin 6:49
C. P. Cavafy 7:158
Sergei Esenin 4:112
Osip Mandelstam 2:400
Vladimir Mayakovsky 4:299
Marina Tsvetaeva 7:558

Politis, Linos
Kostes Palamas 5:384

Politzer, Heinz
Bertolt Brecht 6:31
Arthur Schnitzler 4:400

Pollard, Percival
Kate Chopin 5:143
Rainer Maria Rilke 6:357
Arthur Schnitzler 4:385
Frank Wedekind 7:574

Pollock, John
A. A. Milne 6:306

Ponomareff, Constantin V.
Sergei Esenin 4:116

Popper, Hans
Wolfgang Borchert 5:108

Porter, Katherine Anne
Max Beerbohm 1:69
Willa Cather 1:160
Colette 1:191
Ford Madox Ford 1:277
D. H. Lawrence 2:367
Katherine Mansfield 2:450
Gertrude Stein 1:428
Virginia Woolf 1:534

Porter, Richard N.
Ivan Bunin 6:55

Porter, Thomas E.
Eugene O'Neill 1:404

Poster, William
H. P. Lovecraft 4:265

Potoker, Edward Martin
Ronald Firbank 1:230

Poulakidas, Andreas K.
Nikos Kazantzakis 2:320

Poulet, George
Marcel Proust 7:541

Pound, Ezra
W. H. Davies 5:199
Thomas Hardy 4:174
Henry James 2:249
James Joyce 3:252
Wyndham Lewis 2:386
Rabindranath Tagore 3:481

Povey, John
Roy Campbell 5:126

Powell, Anthony
George Orwell 2513

Powell, Lawrence Clark
Gertrude Atherton 2:18
Raymond Chandler 1:172

Powys, John Cowper
Edgar Lee Masters 2:464
Dorothy Richardson 3:350

Praz, Mario
Luigi Pirandello 4:326

Predmore, Michael P.
Juan Ramón Jiménez 4:221,
225

Prescott, Orville
Joyce Cary 1:141

Preston, Harriet Waters
Vernon Lee 5:309

Prevelakis, Pandelis
Nikos Kazantzakis 2:313

Price, Lucien
John Jay Chapman 7:188

Price, Martin
Joyce Cary 1:141

Price, Nancy
Lord Dunsany 2:144

Priestley, J. B.
J. M. Barrie 2:45
Arnold Bennett 5:29
James Bridie 3:137
Walter de la Mare 4:72
Henrik Ibsen 2:231
Stephen Leacock 2:380
Sinclair Lewis 4:255
August Strindberg 1:451
Hugh Walpole 5:495
William Butler Yeats 1:567
Émile Zola 1:594

Primeau, Ronald
Countee Cullen 4:52

Pritchard, William H.
Edwin Arlington Robinson
5:417

Pritchett, V. S.
Arnold Bennett 5:44
Samuel Butler 1:136, 137
Karel Čapek 6:86
Anton Chekhov 3:155
Joseph Conrad 1:203, 206
Ronald Firbank 1:229
George Gissing 3:232

Thomas Hardy 4:165
D. H. Lawrence 2:355
Wyndham Lewis 2:387
Katherine Mansfield 2:451
George Orwell 2:497
Dorothy Richardson 3:358
Saki 3:366
Bruno Schulz 5:425
John Millington Synge 6:434
Giovanni Verga 3:545
H. G. Wells 6:534
Émile Zola 1:594

Proffer, Carl R.
Aleksandr Kuprin 5:301

Proust, Marcel
Leo Tolstoy 4:466

Prusek, Jaroslav
Lu Hsün 3:299

Pryce-Jones, Alan
Alain-Fournier 6:18
Bertolt Brecht 1:107

Punter, David
Ambrose Bierce 7:98

Purdom, C. B.
Harley Granville-Barker 2:196

Purser, John Thibaut
Ivan Bunin 6:47

Pyatkovsky, A. Ya.
Leo Tolstoy 4:445

Pyne-Timothy, Helen
Claude McKay 7:468

Quiller-Couch, Arthur
George Moore 7:474

Quinn, Arthur Hobson
James Branch Cabell 6:67
Rebecca Harding Davis 6:150
Joel Chandler Harris 2:210
Bret Harte 1:342

Quinn, Vincent
Hart Crane 5:188

Rabinovich, Isaiah
Sholom Aleichem 1:29

Rabinowitz, Peter J.
Raymond Chandler 7:177

Ragussis, Michael
D. H. Lawrence 2:373

Rahv, Philip
Franz Kafka 2:289
George Orwell 6:340
Virginia Woolf 5:509

Raknes, Ola
Jonas Lie 5:325

Raleigh, John Henry
F. Scott Fitzgerald 1:251
Eugene O'Neill 6:335

Ralston, W.R.S.
Leo Tolstoy 4:447

Ramchand, Kenneth
Claude McKay 7:464

Ramsey, Warren
Guillaume Apollinaire 3:36
Paul Valéry 4:493

Rankin, Daniel S.
Kate Chopin 5:144

Ransom, John Crowe
Thomas Hardy 4:164
Edna St. Vincent Millay 4:314
Edith Wharton 3:563

Raper, J. R.
Ellen Glasgow 2:189; 7:345

Rascoe, Burton
Zane Grey 6:180
Don Marquis 7:455

Raven, Simon
Joyce Cary 1:142

Ray, Gordon N.
H. G. Wells 6:540

Ray, Robert J.
Ford Madox Ford 1:285

Rayfield, Donald
Osip Mandelstam 6:266

Read, Herbert
Robert Bridges 1:126
George Moore 7:479

Reck, Rima Drell
Georges Bernanos 3:121

Redding J. Saunders
Charles Waddell Chesnutt
5:132
Countee Cullen 4:42
Paul Laurence Dunbar 2:128
James Weldon Johnson 3:241

Redman, Ben Ray
Georges Bernanos 3:116

Reed, F. A.
Nikos Kazantzakis 5:267

Reed, John R.
H. G. Wells 6:551

Reeve, F. D.
Aleksandr Blok 5:88

Rehder, R. M.
Thomas Hardy 4:177

Reilly, John H.
Jean Giraudoux 7:324

Reilly, Joseph J.
Kate Chopin 5:146
Alice Meynell 6:300

Reinert, Otto
August Strindberg 1:458

Reiss, H. S.
Arthur Schnitzler 4:394

Repplier, Agnes
Laurence Housman 7:358
Alice Meynell 6:295

Revitt, Paul J.
W. S. Gilbert 3:215

Rexroth, Kenneth
Roy Campbell 5:124
Arthur Conan Doyle 7:229
Ford Madox Ford 1:290
Wallace Stevens 3:459

Rhodes, Anthony
Gabriele D'Annunzio 6:137

Rhys, Brian
Henri Barbusse 5:14

Rhys, Ernest
Rabindranath Tagore 3:483

Ribbans, Geoffrey
Miguel de Unamuno 2:564

Rich, Amy C.
Zona Gale 7:277

Richards, I. A.
George Moore 7:494

Richardson, Jack
Eugene O'Neill 1:406

Richardson, Maurice
M. R. James 6:209

Richey, Elinor
Gertrude Atherton 2:18

Riddel, Joseph N.
Wallace Stevens 3:466

Rideout, Walter B.
Sherwood Anderson 1:54

Ridge, George Ross
Joris-Karl Huysmans 7:413
Émile Zola 6:565

Ridge, Lola
Henri Barbusse 5:13

Riewald, J. G.
Max Beerbohm 1:69

Riley, Anthony W.
Frederick Philip Grove 4:142,
144

Rimanelli, Giose
Cesare Pavese 3:339

Ringe, Donald A.
George Washington Cable 4:35

Río, Angel del
Federico García Lorca 7:291

Ritchie, J. M.
Gottfried Benn 3:113

Rittenhouse, Jessie B.
Edna St. Vincent Millay 4:305
Sara Teasdale 4:425

Rizzo, Gino
Ugo Betti 5:57, 62

Roback, A. A.
Sholem Asch 3:67

Roberts, C.G.D.
Bliss Carman 7:136

Roberts, S. C.
Arthur Conan Doyle 7:223

Robertson, J. G.
Henry Handel Richardson 4:371

Robinson, Christopher
Kostes Palamas 5:385

Robinson, Henry Morton
James Joyce 3:261

Robinson, Lennox
Lady Gregory 1:333

Robinson, W. R.
Edwin Arlington Robinson
5:416

Robson, W. W.
G. K. Chesterton 1:188

Rodgers, Lise
Hart Crane 5:194

Roditi, Edouard
Oscar Wilde 1:500

Rogers, Timothy
Rupert Brooke 2:57

CRITIC INDEX

Rogers, W. G.
Gertrude Stein 1:429

Roggendorf, Joseph
Toson Shimazaki 5:430

Ronald, Ann
Zane Grey 6:185

Rose, Marilyn Gaddis
Katharine Tynan 3:506

Rose, Mark
Jules Verne 6:504

Rose, Shirley
Dorothy Richardson 3:358

Rosen, Norma
Rebecca Harding Davis 6:154

Rosenbaum, Sidonia Carmen
Gabriela Mistral 2:476
Alfonsina Stroni 5:444

Rosenberg, Harold
James Weldon Johnson 3:241

Rosenberg, Samuel
Arthur Conan Doyle 7:230

Rosenblatt, Roger
John Millington Synge 6:442

Rosenfeld, Paul
Sherwood Anderson 1:34

Rosenthal, M. L.
César Vallejo 3:529
William Butler Yeats 1:567

Rosenthal, Michael
Joyce Cary 1:147

Rosenthal, Raymond
Leo Tolstoy 4:469
Giovanni Verga 3:544

Ross, Alan
Nathanael West 1:478

Ross, Stephen M.
James Weldon Johnson 3:249

Rosten, Norman
Stephen Vincent Benét 7:77

Rostropowicz, Joanna
Bruno Schulz 5:424

Rourke, Constance Mayfield
Zona Gale 7:277

Rouse, Blair
Ellen Glasgow 7:339

Rowse, A. L.
Alun Lewis 3:285

Rozhdestvensky, Vsevolod
Sergei Esenin 4:113

Rubens, Philip M.
Ambrose Bierce 7:95

Rubin, Louis D., Jr.
George Washington Cable 4:32
Countee Cullen 4:51
Ellen Glasgow 2:184
Thomas Wolfe 4:536

Ruehlen, Petroula Kephala
C. P. Cavafy 2:92

Ruhm, Herbert
Raymond Chandler 1:171

Rule, Jane
Gertrude Stein 6:413

Rumbold, Richard
Antoine de Saint-Exupéry 2:518

Russell, Bertrand
Joseph Conrad 1:207
Henrik Ibsen 2:231
George Bernard Shaw 3:400
May Sinclair 3:436
H. G. Wells 6:538

Russell, D. C.
Raymond Chandler 1:168

Russell, Frances Theresa
Edith Wharton 3:561

Russell, Francis
Gertrude Stein 6:410

Russell, George William
Kahlil Gibran 1:327
See also E., A.

Ryf, Robert S.
Joseph Conrad 1:218

Sackville-West, Edward
Joseph Conrad 1:204
Stefan George 2:147
Henry James 2:261
Émile Zola 1:589

Sackville-West, V.
Hilaire Belloc 7:36
Selma Lagerlöf 4:230

Sandemyer, Ann
Lady Gregory 1:336

Sagar, Keith
D. H. Lawrence 2:371

St. Martin, Hardie
Antonio Machado 3:307

Saintsbury, George
Émile Zola 6:560

Sale, Roger
L. Frank Baum 7:24
Ford Madox Ford 1:288
A. A. Milne 6:321

Salinas, Pedro
Ramón del Valle-Inclán 5:476

Salmon, Eric
Ugo Betti 5:63

Sampley, Arthur M.
Maxwell Anderson 2:6

Samuel, Maurice
Sholom Aleichem 1:21

Samuels, Ernest
Henry Adams 4:15

Sanchez, Roberto G.
Jacinto Benavente 3:100

Sandburg, Carl
Stephen Vincent Benét 7:77
Robert E. Sherwood 3:412

San Juan, E., Jr.
André Gide 5:232

Sandwell, B. K.
Frederick Philip Grove 4:135

Santas, Joan Foster
Ellen Glasgow 2:186

Santayana, George
Marcel Proust 7:523

Sapir, Edward
A. E. Housman 1:353

Sartre, Jean-Paul
Jean Giraudoux 7:318

Sassoon, Siegfried
Wilfred Owen 5:358

Saul, George Brandon
A. E. Coppard 5:178, 181
Lord Dunsany 2:145
James Stephens 4:416
Sara Teasdale 4:428

Saunders, Thomas
Frederick Philip Grove 4:137

Savage, D. S.
F. Scott Fitzgerald 1:248

Savage, George
David Belasco 3:88

Saveth, Edward N.
Henry Adams 4:14

Sayers, Dorothy L.
Arthur Conan Doyle 7:219

Scarborough, Dorothy
Arthur Machen 4:277

Scarfe, Francis
Dylan Thomas 1:465

Schevill, James
Eugene O'Neill 1:405

Schickel, Richard
Raymond Chandler 1:170

Schier, Donald
Alain-Fournier 6:14

Schlegel, Dorothy B.
James Branch Cabell 6:72

Schlesinger, Arthur M., Jr.
George Orwell 2:497

Schlochower, Harry
Thomas Mann 2:413

Schlueter, Paul
Arthur Schnitzler 4:403

Schmidt, Michael
Walter de la Mare 4:82

Schneider, Judith Morganroth
Max Jacob 6:201

Schneider, Sister Lucy
Willa Cather 1:165

Schorer, Mark
Sherwood Anderson 1:60
F. Scott Fitzgerald 1:239
Ford Madox Ford 1:277
Sinclair Lewis 4:259
Malcolm Lowry 6:236
Gertrude Stein 1:437
H. G. Wells 6:535
Thomas Wolfe 4:521

Schubert, P. Z.
Jaroslav Hasek 4:189

Schultz, Robert
Joseph Conrad 6:123

Schwartz, Delmore
Ring Lardner 2:334
Edna St. Vincent Millay 4:314
Wallace Stevens 3:451
William Butler Yeats 1:556

Schwartz, Kessel
Antonio Machado 3:309

Schweitzer, Darrell
H. P. Lovecraft 4:274

Scott, Dixon
George Bernard Shaw 3:382

Scott, J. A.
Ugo Betti 5:54

Scott, J. D.
André Gide 5:217

Scott, Kenneth W.
Zane Grey 6:181

Scott, Nathan A., Jr.
D. H. Lawrence 2:357

Scott, Winfield Townley
H. P. Lovecraft 4:265
Edna St. Vincent Millay 4:315

Scrimgeour, Gary J.
F. Scott Fitzgerald 1:262
John Galsworthy 1:303

Seaton, Jerome F.
Lu Hsün 3:300

Seccombe, Thomas
George Gissing 3:223

Sedgewick, G. G.
Stephen Leacock 2:378

Sedgewick, Henry Dwight
Edith Wharton 3:551

Sedgwick, Jr., H. D.
Gabriele D'Annunzio 6:129

Seeley, Carol
Paul Éluard 7:245

Seferis, George
C. P. Cavafy 7:159

Segall, Brenda
Rubén Darío 4:66

Segel, Harold B.
Leonid Andreyev 3:29
Aleksandr Blok 5:99
Vladimir Mayakovsky 4:301

Sehmsdorf, Henning K.
Bjørnstjerne Bjørnson 7:117

Seib, Kenneth
James Agee 1:12

Seidlin, Oskar
Gerhart Hauptmann 4:201
Thomas Mann 2:423

Seldes, Gilbert
Max Beerbohm 1:66
F. Scott Fitzgerald 1:237
Ring Lardner 2:333
Eugene O'Neill 1:383

Seltzer, Alvin J.
Joyce Cary 1:149
Joseph Conrad 1:219
Franz Kafka 6:224
Virginia Woolf 1:548

Seltzer, Thomas
Leonid Andreyev 3:18

Sender, Ramon
Federico García Lorca 1:317

Sergeant, Howard
Roy Campbell 5:122
Wilfred Owen 5:365

Sewell, Elizabeth
Paul Valéry 4:494

Seyersted, Per
Kate Chopin 5:150

Seymour, Alan
Antonin Artaud 3:49

Seymour-Smith, Martin
Wyndham Lewis 2:396

Shafer, Robert
James Stephens 4:408

Shain, Charles E.
F. Scott Fitzgerald 1:259; 6:161

Shapiro, Karl
Dylan Thomas 1:476
William Butler Yeats 1:568

Sharp, William
Bliss Carman 7:133

Shattuck, Roger
Guillaume Apollinaire 3:33
Antonin Artaud 3:59
Alfred Jarry 2:278, 283
Marcel Proust 7:542
Paul Valéry 4:501

Shaw, Donald L.
José Echegaray 4:105

Shaw, George Bernard
David Belasco 3:84
Hilaire Belloc 7:36
Samuel Butler 1:136
G. K. Chesterton 6:97
W. H. Davies 5:198
José Echegaray 4:96
William Dean Howells 7:367
Henrik Ibsen 2:220
Edmond Rostand 6:372

Shaw, Priscilla Washburn
Paul Valéry 4:498

Shaw, Vivian
F. Scott Fitzgerald 1:236

Sheean, Vincent
Sinclair Lewis 4:252

Sheed, Wilfrid
G. K. Chesterton 1:182

Shepard, Odell
Bliss Carman 7:137
Alexander Woollcott 5:523

Sherman, Stuart P.
Arnold Bennett 5:27
Don Marquis 7:437

Sherrard, Philip
C. P. Cavafy 7:155

Sherwood, Robert Emmet
Robert Sherwood 3:409

Shestov, Lev
Anton Chekhov 3:147
Leo Tolstoy 4:478

Shivers, Albert S.
Maxwell Anderson 2:9

Short, Clarice
James Stephens 4:413

Showalter, Elaine
Dorothy Richardson 3:360

Shreffler, Philip A.
H. P. Lovecraft 4:272

Shumaker, Wayne
George Moore 7:495

Shuman, R. Baird
Robert E. Sherwood 3:414

Shuttleworth, Martin
Henri Barbusse 5:16

Sichel, Walter
W. S. Gilbert 3:209

Sidney-Fryer, Donald
Ambrose Bierce 7:96

Simmons, Ernest J.
Leo Tolstoy 4:473

Simon, John
Henrik Ibsen 2:232
George Bernard Shaw 3:405

Simonson, Harold P.
Zona Gale 7:284

Simpson, Lesley Byrd
Mariano Azuela 3:79

Sinclair, May
Dorothy Richardson 3:345
Edwin Arlington Robinson 5:400

Sinden, Margaret
Gerhart Hauptmann 4:201

Singer, Isaac B.
Bruno Schulz 5:420, 426

Singh, Amritjit
Wallace Thurman 6:450

Sirin, Vladimir
Rupert Brooke 2:54

Sitwell, Edith
W. H. Davies 5:203
D. H. Lawrence 2:369
Gertrude Stein 6:403
William Butler Yeats 1:555

Sitwell, Sir Osbert
Ronald Firbank 1:227
Alfred Noyes 7:514

Sizemore, Christine W.
Franz Kafka 6:227

Skelton, Isabel
Frederick Philip Grove 4:133

Skelton, Robin
John Millington Synge 6:439

Skinner, B. F.
Gertrude Stein 6:404

Skinner, Richard Dana
Wallace Thurman 6:445
Alexander Woollcott 5:522

Slate, Tom
Edgar Rice Burroughs 2:82

Slater, Candace
César Vallejo 3:534

Slochower, Harry
Sholem Asch 3:67
Arthur Schnitzler 4:393
Sigrid Undset 3:515

Slonim, Marc
Isaak Babel 2:37
Andrey Bely 7:52
Aleksandr Blok 5:87
Ivan Bunin 6:51
Marina Tsvetaeva 7:557, 566

Smertinko, Johan J.
Sholem Asch 3:65

Smith, A.J.M.
Duncan Campbell Scott 6:390

Smith, Grover
Ford Madox Ford 1:288

Smith, Harrison
Joyce Cary 1:141

Smith, Hazel Littlefield
See **Littlefield, Hazel**

Smith, Henry James
O. Henry 1:345

Smith, Henry Nash
Mark Twain 6:478

Smith, Hugh Allison
Edmond Rostand 6:379

Smith, Maxwell A.
Antoine de Saint-Exupéry 2:520

Smith, Nora Archibald
José Echegaray 4:98

Smith, Robert A.
Claude McKay 7:457

Smith, Rowland
Roy Campbell 5:125
Wyndham Lewis 2:399

Smith, Stanley Astredo
Guiseppe Giacosa 7:306, 312

Smith, Verity
Ramón del Valle-Inclán 5:487

Smith, Winifred
Arthur Schnitzler 4:387

Snell, George
Ambrose Bierce 1:88

Snider, Clifton
Virginia Woolf 5:516

Snodgrass, Chris
Oscar Wilde 1:509

Snodgrass, W. D.
Gottfried Benn 3:108

Snow, C. P.
Ronald Firbank 1:227

Sochen, June
Zona Gale 7:286

Sokel, Walter H.
Gottfried Benn 3:107
Franz Kafka 2:305
Frank Wedekind 7:579

Sonnerfeld, Albert
Georges Bernanos 3:120, 123

Sontag, Susan
Antonin Artaud 3:56
Cesare Pavese 3:338

Sorley, Charles Hamilton
Rupert Brooke 7:120

Soskin, William
Marjorie Kinnan Rawlings 4:360

Southworth, James Granville
Hart Crane 2:117
Thomas Hardy 4:166

Spacks, Patricia Meyer
Charles Williams 1:524

Spalter, Max
Karl Kraus 5:283

Spangler, George M.
Kate Chopin 5:154

Spanos, William V.
Dorothy L. Sayers 2:534

Spear, Allan H.
James Weldon Johnson 3:246

Spears, Monroe K.
Hart Crane 2:119

Spector, Ivar
Leonid Andreyev 3:25

Speir, Jerry
Raymond Chandler 7:179

Spell, Jefferson Rea
Mariano Azuela 3:76

Spencer, Benjamin T.
Sherwood Anderson 1:61

Spencer, Theodore
William Butler Yeats 1:554

Spender, Natasha
Raymond Chandler 1:176

Spender, Stephen
Wolfgang Borchert 5:106
Robert Bridges 1:131
C. P. Cavafy 2:93
Henry James 2:253
James Joyce 3:277
D. H. Lawrence 2:369
Wyndham Lewis 2:385
Malcolm Lowry 6:238
Wilfred Owen 5:361
George Bernard Shaw 3:393
William Butler Yeats 1:555

Sperber, Murray
George Orwell 6:353

Spettigue, Douglas O.
Frederick Philip Grove 4:138, 143, 144

Spiller, Robert E.
Henry Adams 4:11
Hamlin Garland 3:195

Sprague, Claire
Virginia Woolf 1:545

Sprague, Rosemary
Sara Teasdale 4:431

Squire, J. C.
Robert Bridges 1:125
G. K. Chesterton 6:97
W. H. Davies 5:201
Walter de la Mare 4:72
A. E. Housman 1:353
Alice Meynell 6:297
George Bernard Shaw 3:385
William Butler Yeats 1:553

Stafford, John
Joel Chandler Harris 2:211

Stahl, E. L.
Rainer Maria Rilke 1:411

Stamm, Rudolf
Eugene O'Neill 1:390

Stanford, Derek
Alfred Noyes 7:515

Stanford, W. B.
Nikos Kazantzakis 2:314

Stansbury, Milton H.
Jean Giraudoux 2:155

Stanton, Edward F.
Federico García Lorca 7:298

Starkie, Walter
Jacinto Benavente 3:97
Federico García Lorca 1:317
Gregorio Martinez Sierra and Maria Martinez Sierra 6:277

Starrett, Vincent
Ambrose Bierce 7:89
Arthur Conan Doyle 7:220
Arthur Machen 4:278

Stavrou, C. N.
Nikos Kazantzakis 5:261

Steele, Elizabeth
Hugh Walpole 5:502

Steen, Marguerite
Hugh Walpole 5:499

Stegner, Wallace
Willa Cather 1:167
Bret Harte 1:343

Stein, Allen F.
Ring Lardner 2:340

Stein, Gertrude
Henry James 2:261

Steiner, George
Ford Madox Ford 1:288
Leo Tolstoy 4:467

Stender-Petersen, Adolph
Władysław Stanisław Reymont
5:390

Stephens, Donald
Bliss Carman 7:147

Stephensen, P. R.
Aleister Crowley 7:210

Sterling, George
Ambrose Bierce 7:88, 91

Stern, J. P.
Jaroslav Hašek 4:186
Thomas Mann 2:438
Rainer Maria Rilke 1:424

Stern, Philip Van Doren
Arthur Machen 4:279

Stevens, Wallace
Paul Valéry 4:494

Stevenson, Lionel
Gertrude Atherton 2:16

Stewart, Allegra
Gertrude Stein 1:434

Stewart, Donald Ogden
Robert Benchley 1:78

Stewart, J.I.M.
James Joyce 3:274
D. H. Lawrence 2:368
William Butler Yeats 1:569

Stewart, Lady Margaret
Antoine de Saint-Exupéry 2:518

Stine, Peter
Franz Kafka 6:232

Stirling, Monica
Colette 1:191

Stone, Jr., Albert E.
Mark Twain 6:471

Stone, Geoffrey
Roy Campbell 5:117

Stonesifer, Richard J.
W. H. Davies 5:205

Storer, Edward
Luigi Pirandello 4:325

Stork, Charles Wharton
Sigrid Undset 3:511
Verner von Heidenstam 5:248,
249, 256

Stouck, David
Sarah Orne Jewett 1:369

Strachey, John
George Orwell 2:505

Strachey, Lytton
Thomas Hardy 4:154

Strakhov, Nikolai N.
Leo Tolstoy 4:449

Strakhovsky, Leonid I.
Osip Mandelstam 6:257

Strauss, Harold
Jakob Wassermann 6:512

Strauss, Walter A.
Marcel Proust 7:533

Stream, George G.
Ugo Betti 5:63

Strier, Richard
Hart Crane 2:125

Strong, Kenneth
Toson Shimazaki 5:440

Strong, L.A.G.
Lewis Grassic Gibbon 4:120
Hugh Walpole 5:501

Stroud, Parry
Stephen Vincent Benét 7:78

Struve, Gleb
Mikhail Bulgakov 2:63, 65
Ivan Bunin 6:44

Stubbs, Marcia C.
Alain-Fournier 6:15

Stuckey, W. J.
Marjorie Kinnan Rawlings
4:365

Sturgeon, Mary C.
James Stephens 4:409

Sturtevant, Albert Morey
Alexander Kielland 5:278

Styron, William
Thomas Wolfe 4:535

Sullivan, Jack
Algernon Blackwood 5:78
M. R. James 6:214

Sullivan, Kevin
Lady Gregory 1:335
Oscar Wilde 1:507

Sutherland, Donald
Gertrude Stein 6:407

Sutherland, Ronald
Frederick Philip Grove 4:140

Sutton, Graham
Harley Granville-Barker 2:195
A. A. Milne 6:308
Alfred Sutro 6:421

Sutton, Max Keith
W. S. Gilbert 3:217

Suvin, Darko
Karel Čapek 6:930

Swales, Martin
Arthur Schnitzler 4:402

Swallow, Alan
Hart Crane 2:116

Swan, Michael
Max Beerbohm 1:71

Swann, Thomas Burnett
Ernest Dowson 4:90
A. A. Milne 6:315

Swanson, Roy Arthur
Kostes Palamas 5:382

Sweetser, Wesley D.
Arthur Machen 4:282

Swinnerton, Frank
Hilaire Belloc 7:40
Arnold Bennett 5:43
Robert Bridges 1:130
Joseph Conrad 1:201
Ford Madox Ford 1:277
John Galsworthy 1:298
George Gissing 3:226
Rose Macaulay 7:426
A. A. Milne 6:310
George Moore 7:480
Wilfred Owen 5:360
Dorothy Richardson 3:352
Dorothy L. Sayers 2:527
James Stephens 4:411
George Bernard Shaw 3:388
H. G. Wells 6:536
Virginia Woolf 1:532

Sykes, W. J.
Duncan Campbell Scott 6:387

Symes, Gordon
Alun Lewis 3:286

Symonds, John
Aleister Crowley 7:211

Symonds, John Addington
Vernon Lee 5:309

Symons, Arthur
Gabriele D'Annunzio 6:128
Ernest Dowson 4:85
Thomas Hardy 4:154
Joris-Karl Huysmans 7:410
Alfred Jarry 2:277
Maurice Maeterlinck 3:327
George Moore 7:474
Sara Teasdale 4:423

Symons, Julian
Raymond Chandler 1:173;
7:175
Arthur Conan Doyle 7:238

Szczesny, Gerhard
Bertolt Brecht 6:32

T., C.
Lady Gregory 1:332

Talamantes, Florence
Alfonsina Storni 5:446

Tarrant, Desmond
James Branch Cabell 6:76

Tate, Allen
Stephen Vincent Benét 7:70
Roy Campbell 5:117
Hart Crane 2:114, 117
Edwin Muir 2:481
Edwin Arlington Robinson
5:405

Taubman, Jane Adelman
Marina Tsvetaeva 7:566

Taylor, Colleen M.
Bruno Schulz 5:423

Taylor, Desmond Shaw
Lady Gregory 1:338

Taylor, Martin C.
Gabriela Mistral 2:480

Taylor, Una
Maurice Maeterlinck 3:324

Tenenbaum, Louis
Cesare Pavese 3:337

Terras, V.
Osip Mandelstam 2:402

Terras, Victor
Isaak Babel 2:21
Osip Mandelstam 6:262

Test, George A.
Karel Čapek 6:92

Thau, Annette
Max Jacob 6:195, 199

Theis, O. F.
Frank Wedekind 7:576

Thomas, Dylan
Wilfred Owen 5:363

Thomas, Lawrence
André Gide 5:219

Thompson, Edward J.
Rabindranath Tagore 3:484,
490

Thompson, Ewa M.
Aleksandr Blok 5:97

Thompson, Francis
Bliss Carman 7:133
Gabriele D'Annunzio 6:128
Ernest Dowson 4:90
Alice Meynell 6:291

Thompson, William Irwin
A. E. 3:12

Thomson, Paul van Kuykendall
Francis Thompson 4:440

Thorp, Willard
Sherwood Anderson 1:52

Thurber, James
L. Frank Baum 7:14
Robert Benchley 1:80

Thurley, Geoffrey
Sergei Esenin 4:114

Thurman, Wallace
Countee Cullen 4:41

Thurman, Wallace
Claude McKay 7:456

Thurston, Henry W.
Henry Adams 4:4

Tikhonov, Nikolay
Sergei Esenin 4:113

Tilles, Solomon H.
Rubén Darío 4:65

Tillotson, Geoffrey
Ernest Dowson 4:88

Tillyard, E.M.W.
Joseph Conrad 1:209
James Joyce 3:269

Timberlake Craig
David Belasco 3:89

Timms, Edward
Karl Kraus 5:291

Tindall, Gillian
George Gissing 3:237

Tindall, William York
D. H. Lawrence 2:356
Wallace Stevens 3:460
William Butler Yeats 1:578

Titiev, Janice Geasler
Alfonsina Storni 5:450

Tobin, Patricia
James Joyce 3:278

Toksvig, Signe
Sigrid Undset 3:510

Tolstoy, Leo
Leonid Andreyev 3:16

Tolton, C.D.E.
André Gide 5:243

Tomlin, E.W.F.
Wyndham Lewis 2:391

Topping, Gary
Zane Grey 6:183, 186

Toumanova, Nina Andronikova
Anton Chekhov 3:155

Towson, M. R.
Gottfried Benn 3:110

Toynbee, Philip
André Gide 5:228
James Joyce 3:264

Traschen, Isadore
Thomas Mann 2:436

Treece, Henry
Dylan Thomas 1:467

Tremper, Ellen
A. A. Milne 6:320

Trend, J. B.
Antonio Machado 3:305

Trensky, Paul I.
Karel Čapek 6:90

Trent, William P.
Edwin Arlington Robinson
5:400

Trickett, Rachel
Dorothy Richardson 3:355

Trilling, Lionel
Willa Cather 1:162
Eugene O'Neill 1:402
George Orwell 2:499

Trombly, Albert Edmund
W. H. Davies 5:200

Trotsky, Leon
Andrey Bely 7:46
Aleksandr Blok 5:83
Vladimir Mayakovsky 4:289
Frank Wedekind 7:589

Troy, William
James Joyce 3:259
Virginia Woolf 1:534

Trueblood, Charles K.
John Galsworthy 1:296

Tucker, Carll
Eugene O'Neill 1:407

Tuell, Anne Kimball
Alice Meynell 6:297

Turgenev, Ivan
Leo Tolstoy 4:448, 460

Turnell, Martin
Alain-Fournier 6:19
Guillaume Apollinaire 3:40

Turner, Arlin
George Washington Cable 4:28

Turner, Darwin T.
Countee Cullen 4:49
Paul Laurence Dunbar 2:129
Joel Chandler Harris 2:216

Turner, Sheila
Kahlil Gibran 1:328

Turquet-Milnes, G.
Paul Valéry 4:490

Turrell, Charles Alfred
Gregorio Martinez Sierra and
Maria Martinez Sierra 6:273

Twain, Mark
William Dean Howells 7:368

Tyler, Robert L.
Arthur Machen 4:281

Tynan, Katherine
Rose Macaulay 7:421

Tynan, Kenneth
Bertolt Brecht 1:102

Ueda, Makoto
Soseki Natsume 2:495

Ullmann, Stephen
Alain-Fournier 6:19

Umphrey, George W.
Rubén Darío 4:58

Underhill, John Garrett
Jacinto Benavente 3:93, 95
Gregorio Martinez Sierra and
Maria Martinez Sierra 6:273

Undset, Sigrid
D. H. Lawrence 2:353

Unterecker, John
Hart Crane 2:123

Untermeyer, Louis
W. H. Davies 5:205
Lion Feuchtwanger 3:178
F. Scott Fitzgerald 1:250
Amy Lowell 1:371
Edna St. Vincent Millay 4:307
Sara Teasdale 4:425, 426

Updike, John
James Agee 1:6
Max Beerbohm 1:71, 72
Bruno Schulz 5:428

Urban, G. R.
Stefan George 2:152

Ureña, Pedro Henriquez
Rubén Darío 4:56

Uroff, M. D.
Hart Crane 2:124

Usmiani, Renate
Gerhart Hauptmann 4:208

Valency, Maurice
Anton Chekhov 3:163
Jean Giraudoux 7:327

Van Doren, Carl
James Branch Cabell 6:64
Willa Cather 1:150
F. Scott Fitzgerald 1:236
Zona Gale 7:279
John Galsworthy 1:300
Hamlin Garland 3:192
Ring Lardner 2:326
Don Marquis 7:436
Edgar Lee Masters 2:461
Edna St. Vincent Millay 4:308
Gertrude Stein 1:427

Van Doren, Mark
John Galsworthy 1:300
Thomas Hardy 4:167
Thomas Mann 2:425
Luigi Pirandello 4:333
Sara Teasdale 4:425

Van Horne, John
Jacinto Benavente 3:94

Van Kranendonk, A. G.
Katherine Mansfield 2:448

Van Vechten, Carl
Gertrude Atherton 2:15
Countee Cullen 4:39
Ronald Firbank 1:224
James Weldon Johnson 3:240

Vedder, Henry C.
George Washington Cable 4:24

Vendler, Helen Hennessy
William Butler Yeats 1:570

Ventura, L. D.
Guiseppe Giacosa 7:305

Verne, Jules
Jules Verne 6:490
H. G. Wells 6:524

Verschoyle, Derek
Malcolm Lowry 6:235

Vessey, David
Arthur Machen 4:286

Vial, Fernand
Paul Claudel 2:102

Vidal, Gore
L. Frank Baum 7:21
Edgar Rice Burroughs 2:76
F. Scott Fitzgerald 6:167

Vigar, Penelope
Thomas Hardy 4:174

Vinde, Victor
Sigrid Undset 3:513

Vittorini, Domenico
Gabriele D'Annunzio 6:132
Luigi Pirandello 4:331, 333

Vlach, Robert
Jaroslav Hăsek 4:181

Vogt Gapp, Samuel
George Gissing 3:229

Völker, Klaus
Bertolt Brecht 6:34

Volpe, Edmond L.
Nathanael West 1:479

von Hofmannsthal, Hugo
Arthur Schnitzler 4:392

Vonnegut, Kurt, Jr
Mark Twain 6:482

Voss, Arthur
Bret Harte 1:344
O. Henry 1:351

Wadlington, Warwick
Nathanael West 1:489

Wadsworth, Frank W.
Ugo Betti 5:56

Wadsworth, Philip A.
Antoine de Saint-Exupéry 2:516

Wagenknecht, Edward
L. Frank Baum 7:13
Walter de la Mare 4:77
Ellen Glasgow 2:178
Katherine Mansfield 2:447

Waggoner, Hyatt Howe
Edwin Arlington Robinson
5:409

Wagner, Geoffrey
Lewis Grassic Gibbon 4:123
Wyndham Lewis 2:391

Wagner, Jean
Countee Cullen 4:46
James Weldon Johnson 3:243
Claude McKay 7:459

Wahr, F. B.
Gerhart Hauptmann 4:200

Wain, John
Arnold Bennett 5:47
George Orwell 6:343
Dylan Thomas 1:471

Walbrook, H. M.
J. M. Barrie 2:42

Walcutt, Charles Child
Sherwood Anderson 1:48
Hamlin Garland 3:196

Walkley, A. B.
Harley Granville-Barker 2:192

Wallace, William
George Moore 7:473

Walpole, Hugh
James Branch Cabell 6:63

Walser, Richard
Thomas Wolfe 4:530

Walsh, William
Katherine Mansfield 2:453

Ward, A. C.
Rupert Brooke 7:125
George Gissing 3:233

Wardropper, Bruce W.
Antonio Macado 3:309

Ware, Martin
Duncan Campbell Scott 6:399

Warncke, Wayne
George Orwell 6:346

Warner, Rex
C. P. Cavafy 7:153

Warren, Austin
Henry Adams 4:19
M. R. James 6:210
Franz Kafka 2:295

Warren, L. A.
Jacinto Benavente 3:99
Gregorio Martinez Sierra and
Maria Martinez Sierra 6:280
Ramón del Valle-Inclán 5:476

Warren, Robert Penn
Ivan Bunin **6**:47
Joseph Conrad **1**:205
Mark Twain **6**:480
Thomas Wolfe **4**:507

Waters, Brian
W. H. Davies **5**:205

Watkins, Floyd C.
Thomas Wolfe **4**:524

Watson, Barbara Bellow
George Bernard Shaw **3**:402

Watson, E. H. Lacon
Edgar Rice Burroughs **2**:75

Watson, George
Alice Meynell **6**:303

Watson, Harold
Paul Claudel **2**:108

Watters, R. E.
Stephen Leacock **2**:381

Watts, Harold H.
Maxwell Anderson **2**:4
Ugo Betti **5**:65

Waugh, Arthur
Robert Bridges **1**:128
Rupert Brooke **2**:54
Samuel Butler **1**:133
D. H. Lawrence **2**:344

Way, Brian
F. Scott Fitzgerald **6**:168

Weales, Gerald
James Bridie **3**:138
Harley Granville-Barker **2**:199
Laurence Housman **7**:358
Dorothy L. Sayers **2**:531
Charles Williams **1**:521

Webb, Charles Henry
Mark Twain **6**:453

Webb, Howard W., Jr.
Ring Lardner **2**:336

Weber, Brom
Sherwood Anderson **1**:56
Hart Crane **2**:115

Webster, Harvey Curtis
Countee Cullen **4**:43
Thomas Hardy **4**:166

Webster, Wentworth
José Echegaray **4**:97

Weigand, Hermann J.
Gerhart Hauptmann **4**:202
Thomas Mann **2**:414

Weightman, John
Colette **5**:170

Weimar, Karl S.
Wolfgang Borchert **5**:106

Weinstein, Arnold L.
Joseph Conrad **1**:219
Ford Madox Ford **1**:290
James Joyce **3**:279
Franz Kafka **2**:308

Weinstein, Norman
Gertrude Stein **1**:439

Weintraub, Stanley
George Bernard Shaw **3**:400

Weir, Charles, Jr.
F. Scott Fitzgerald **1**:239

Weiss, Beno
Italo Svevo **2**:552

Welland, Dennis
Wilfred Owen **5**:373

Wellek, René
Karel Čapek **6**:84
William Dean Howells **7**:388
Henry James **2**:268

Wells, Arvin B.
James Branch Cabell **6**:73

Wells, H. G.
Hilaire Belloc **7**:34
Arnold Bennett **5**:23
George Gissing **3**:222
Henry James **2**:247
James Joyce **3**:252
Dorothy Richardson **3**:345
Jules Verne **6**:491
H. G. Wells **6**:531

Wells, Henry W.
Stephen Vincent Benét **7**:76

Wellwarth, G. E.
Antonin Artaud **3**:48
Alfred Jarry **2**:280

Wescott, Glenway
F. Scott Fitzgerald **6**:160

West, Anthony
Joyce Cary **1**:142
Nikos Kazantzakis **5**:259
George Orwell **2**:504
H. G. Wells **6**:538

West, Geoffrey
Arnold Bennett **5**:35

West, Rebecca
Sherwood Anderson **1**:39
Arnold Bennett **5**:32
Willa Cather **1**:153
Colette **1**:191
Ford Madox Ford **1**:275
Henry James **2**:248
Franz Kafka **2**:298
Wyndham Lewis **2**:397
May Sinclair **3**:436
H. G. Wells **6**:525
Virginia Woolf **1**:530

Weygandt, Cornelius
A. E. **3**:2
George Moore **7**:476
James Stephens **4**:410

Wharton, Edith
F. Scott Fitzgerald **6**:160
Marcel Proust **7**:520

Wheatley, Elizabeth D.
Arnold Bennett **5**:36

Wheelwright, John
Federico García Lorca **1**:307

Whipple, T. K.
Sherwood Anderson **1**:39
Willa Cather **1**:151
Zane Grey **6**:178
Sinclair Lewis **4**:248
Eugene O'Neill **1**:384

White, E. B.
Don Marquis **7**:441

White, Gertrude M.
Hilaire Belloc **7**:42

White, Greenough
Bliss Carman **7**:134
Francis Thompson **4**:434

White, Ray Lewis
Sherwood Anderson **1**:58

Whittemore, Reed
Joseph Conrad **1**:212
George Bernard Shaw **3**:401

Wiggins, Robert A.
Ambrose Bierce **1**:90

Wilden, Anthony
Italo Svevo **2**:550

Wilkins, Ernest Hatch
Gabriele D'Annunzio **6**:136

Will, Frederic
Nikos Kazantzakis **5**:264
Kostes Palamas **5**:381-82

Willard, Nancy
Rainer Maria Rilke **1**:421

Williams, Cratis D.
Sherwood Anderson **1**:55

Williams, Harold
W. H. Davies **5**:200
Harley Granville-Barker **2**:193
Laurence Housman **7**:353
Katharine Tynan **3**:504

Williams, John Stuart
Alun Lewis **3**:288

Williams, Orlo
Luigi Pirandello **4**:327

Williams, Raymond
Bertolt Brecht **1**:105
George Orwell **6**:348
August Strindberg **1**:457

Williams, William Carlos
Federico García Lorca **7**:290
Wallace Stevens **3**:451

Williamson, Audrey
James Bridie **3**:133

Williamson, Hugh Ross
Alfred Sutro **6**:423

Willson, A. Leslie
Wolfgang Borchert **5**:110

Wilson, Angus
Arnold Bennett **5**:43
Samuel Butler **1**:137
George Bernard Shaw **3**:398
Émile Zola **1**:591

Wilson, Colin
Henri Barbusse **5**:14
Arthur Conan Doyle **7**:233
F. Scott Fitzgerald **1**:251
M. R. James **6**:210
Nikos Kazantzakis **2**:317
H. P. Lovecraft **4**:270
Rainer Maria Rilke **1**:417
George Bernard Shaw **3**:400

Wilson, Daniel J.
Zane Grey **6**:186

Wilson, Donald
André Gide **5**:240

Wilson, Edmund
Henry Adams **4**:13
Maxwell Anderson **2**:3
Sherwood Anderson **1**:35, 50
Max Beerbohm **1**:68, 73
Robert Benchley **1**:76
Ambrose Bierce **1**:89
Samuel Butler **1**:134
James Branch Cabell **6**:70
George Washington Cable **4**:29
Willa Cather **1**:152
John Jay Chapman **7**:187, 190
Anton Chekhov **3**:159
Kate Chopin **5**:148
Hart Crane **5**:185
Arthur Conan Doyle **7**:222
Ronald Firbank **1**:226, 228
F. Scott Fitzgerald **1**:233; **6**:159
James Weldon Johnson **3**:240
James Joyce **3**:256, 260
Franz Kafka **2**:294
Ring Lardner **2**:325
D. H. Lawrence **2**:345
H. P. Lovecraft **4**:268
Edna St. Vincent Millay **4**:317
Marcel Proust **7**:524
Dorothy L. Sayers **2**:530
George Bernard Shaw **3**:391, 396
Gertrude Stein **1**:426; **6**:404
Wallace Stevens **3**:444
Leo Tolstoy **4**:480
Paul Valéry **4**:487
Edith Wharton **3**:558, 579
William Butler Yeats **1**:554

Wilson, H. Schütz
Émile Zola **6**:558

Wing, George Gordon
César Vallejo **3**:527

Winkler, R.O.C.
Franz Kafka **2**:288

Winner, Anthony
Joris-Karl Huysmans **7**:415

Winship, George P., Jr.
Charles Williams **1**:523

Winsnes, A. H.
Sigrid Undset **3**:521

Winter, Calvin
Edith Wharton **3**:553

Winter, William
David Belasco **3**:86

Winters, Yvor
Henry Adams **4**:8
Hart Crane **2**:112
Robert Bridges **1**:131
Henry James **2**:257
Edwin Arlington Robinson **5**:407
Wallace Stevens **3**:447

Wisse, Ruth R.
Sholom Aleichem **1**:32

Wister, Owen
John Jay Chapman **7**:189

Wittig, Kurt
Lewis Grassic Gibbon

Wolfe, Bernard
Joel Chandler Harris **2**:214

Wolfe, Thomas
Thomas Wolfe **4**:510

Wolff, Cynthia Griffin
Kate Chopin **5**:156

Wood, Clement
Edgar Lee Masters **2**:464

Woodburn, John
Thomas Wolfe **4**:521

Woodcock, George
Alain-Fournier **6**:23
Wyndham Lewis **2**:395
Malcolm Lowry **6**:236
George Orwell **2**:508
Oscar Wilde **1**:502

Woodring, Carl
Virginia Woolf **1**:542

Woodruff, Bertram L.
Countee Cullen **4**:42

Woodruff, Stuart C.
Ambrose Bierce **1**:92

Woodward, James B.
Leonid Andreyev **3**:27
Aleksandr Blok **5**:96
Ivan Bunin **6**:56

Woolf, D.
Giovanni Verga **3**:546

Woolf, Leonard S.
Hilaire Belloc **7**:33
Anton Chekhov **3**:149
Mark Twain **6**:460

Woolf, Virginia
Hilaire Belloc **7**:34
Arnold Bennett **5**:28
Rupert Brooke **2**:53
Joseph Conrad **1**:198
George Gissing **3**:228
Thomas Hardy **4**:160

Henry James **2**:251
Ring Lardner **2**:326
Sinclair Lewis **4**:247
George Moore **7**:483
Dorothy Richardson **3**:347
Leo Tolstoy **4**:456
H. G. Wells **6**:527

Woollcott, Alexander
Zona Gale **7**:278
Eugene O'Neill **1**:381
George Bernard Shaw **3**:387

Worsley, T. C.
James Bridie **3**:133

Worster, W. W.
Knut Hamsun **2**:201

Wright, Walter F.
Arnold Bennett **5**:49

Wycherley, H. Alan
F. Scott Fitzgerald **1**:261

Yates, May
George Gissing **3**:224

Yates, Norris W.
Robert Benchley **1**:80
Don Marquis **7**:443

Yatron, Michael
Edgar Lee Masters **2**:470

Yeats, William Butler
A. E. **3**:5
Robert Bridges **1**:123
Ernest Dowson **4**:87
Lord Dunsany **2**:135
Lady Gregory **1**:331
George Moore **7**:482

Standish O'Grady **5**:347
Wilfred Owen **5**:362
John Millington Synge **6**:425
Rabindranath Tagore **3**:501
Katharine Tynan **3**:502

York, Lamar
Marjorie Kinnan Rawlings
4:367

Young, Douglas F.
Lewis Grassic Gibbon **4**:126

Young, Howard T.
Federico García Lorca **1**:321
Juan Ramón Jiménez **4**:216
Antonio Machado **3**:307
Miguel de Unamuno **2**:562

Young, Kenneth
H. G. Wells **6**:547

Young, Stark
David Belasco **3**:89
Federico García Lorca **7**:290
Eugene O'Neill **1**:385; **6**:324
Luigi Pirandello **4**:327
George Bernard Shaw **3**:390
Robert E. Sherwood **3**:410
Gregorio Martinez Sierra and
Maria Martinez Sierra **6**:281

Youngberg, Karin
G. K. Chesterton **6**:105

Yourcenar, Marguerite
Thomas Mann **2**:433

Yu, Beongcheon
Soseki Natsume **2**:493

Yuill, W. E.
Lion Fewuchtwanger **3**:181,
186

Yutang, Lin
Lu Hsün **3**:294

Zabel, Morton Dauwen
Stephen Vincent Benét **7**:74
Joseph Conrad **1**:202
A. E. Coppard **5**:177
James Joyce **3**:255

Zamyatin, Yevgeny
Andrey Bely **7**:48

Zaturenska, Marya
Amy Lowell **1**:378
Sara Teasdale **4**:430

Zavalishin, Vyacheslav
Mikhail Bulgakov **2**:64

Zegger, Hrisey Dimitrakis
May Sinclair **3**:441

Ziff, Larzer
Ambrose Bierce **1**:94
John Jay Chapman **7**:199
Kate Chopin **5**:148
Hamlin Garland **3**:199
Sarah Orne Jewett **1**:368

Zimmerman, Dorothy
Virginia Woolf **1**:543

Zinman, Toby Silverman
Katherine, Mansfield **2**:457

Ziolkowski, Theodore
Rainer Maria Rilke **6**:366

Zohn, Harry
Karl Kraus **5**:290

Zola, Émile
Joris-Karl Huysmans **7**:403

Zweig, Stefan
Thomas Mann **2**:418
Leo Tolstoy **4**:458

CRITIC INDEX